D0712984

Statistical Abstract of the United States

120th edition

2000

The National Data Book

Issued December 2000

U.S. Department of Commerce
Norman Y. Mineta,
Secretary

Economics and Statistics
Administration
Robert J. Shapiro,
Under Secretary for Economic Affairs

BUSINESS PRESS

ECONOMICS
AND STATISTICS
ADMINISTRATION

Economics and Statistics Administration

Robert J. Shapiro, Under Secretary
for Economic Affairs

U.S. CENSUS BUREAU

Kenneth Prewitt, Director
William G. Barron, Deputy Director
Nancy A. Potok, Principal Associate
Director and Chief Financial Officer
Michael S. McKay, Associate Director
for Finance and Administration

**ADMINISTRATIVE AND
CUSTOMER SERVICES DIVISION**

Walter C. Odom, Chief

Acknowledgments

Lars B. Johanson was responsible for the technical supervision and coordination of this volume under the general direction of **Glenn W. King**, Chief, Statistical Compendia Branch. Assisting in the research and analytical phases of assigned sections and in the developmental aspects of new tables were **Rosemary E. Clark**, **Edward C. Jagers**, and **David J. Fleck**. **Geraldine W. Blackburn** provided primary editorial assistance. Other editorial assistance was rendered by **Patricia S. Lancaster**, **Catherine Lavender**, **Joyce Mori**, and **Barbara Shugart**.

Benjamin D. Cromer, Penny Heiston, Gloria Davis, Kevin Proctor, and **Arlene C. Butler** of the Administrative and Customer Services Division, **Walter C. Odom**, Chief, provided publications and printing management, graphics design and composition, and editorial review for print and electronic media. General direction and production management were provided by **Michael G. Garland**, Assistant Chief, and **Gary J. Lauffer**, Chief, Publications Services Branch.

The cooperation of many contributors to this volume is gratefully acknowledged. The source note below each table credits the various government and private agencies that have collaborated in furnishing information for the *Statistical Abstract*. In a few instances, contributors have requested that their data be designated as subject to copyright restrictions, as indicated in the source notes to the tables affected. Permission to use copyright material should be obtained directly from the copyright owner.

Library of Congress Card No. 4-18089

Suggested Citation

U.S. Census Bureau, *Statistical Abstract of the United States: 2000*
(120th edition) Washington, DC, 2000

For sale by Hoover's Business Press for $35.95
1033 La Posada Drive, Suite 250, Austin, Texas 78752
Phone: 800-486-8666 (orders only) or 512-374-4500

Features

Visit us on the web at
http://www.census.gov/statab/www/

Introduction to Hoover's Edition of
the *Statistical Abstract of the United States 2000*

The *Statistical Abstract of the United States* is the single most useful reference book available to anyone interested in knowing about the vital statistics of our country. It is compiled by the Bureau of the Census and has been published annually for 120 years by the Government Printing Office.

This hardcover edition of the *Statistical Abstract of the United States 2000* was prepared by Hoover's Business Press to provide an affordable, accessible edition of this great reference book. Except for this introduction and the addition of some information on our company's other reference products in the back of this book, Hoover's edition is the same as the version published by the GPO. For the convenience of libraries, we have also added an ISBN designation.

Hoover's is dedicated to providing reasonably priced reference books to the public through mass distribution channels. If there are reference books you want but haven't seen at your library or bookstore, let us know.

We would like to thank Glenn W. King and Lars B. Johanson at the Bureau of the Census and George O'Donnoghue at the Government Printing Office for their cooperation and assistance with this project. These dedicated public servants were instrumental in inspiring us and helping us complete this book.

—The Editors
January 2001

This Hoover's edition was published in 2001 by Hoover's Business Press, Austin, Texas. No copyright of this work is claimed by Hoover's, Inc. Manufactured in the United States of America.

10 9 8 7 6 5 4 3 2 1

Publisher Cataloging-in-Publication Data

Statistical Abstract of the United States. U.S. Department of Commerce, Bureau of the Census

Various pagings chiefly tables. Includes bibliographic references and index.
1. U.S. — Statistics. 2. Statistics — U.S.
HA202 S797
L/C Dewey 317.73 S79

ISBN 1-57311-063-9 clothbound $35.95 list price

The Hoover's edition of the *Statistical Abstract of the United States 2000* is available through all major U.S. book distributors and directly from Hoover's. The following companies are authorized distributors:

DIRECT SALES: US and World
Hoover's, Inc.
1033 La Posada Drive, Suite 250
Austin, Texas 78752
Phone: 512-374-4500
Fax: 512-374-4501
e-mail: orders@hoovers.com

Europe
William Snyder Publishing Associates
5 Five Mile Drive
Oxford OX2 8HT
England
Phone and Fax: +44-186-551-3186
e-mail: snyderpub@cs.com

Preface

The *Statistical Abstract of the United States,* published since 1878, is the standard summary of statistics on the social, political, and economic organization of the United States. It is designed to serve as a convenient volume for statistical reference and as a guide to other statistical publications and sources. The latter function is served by the introductory text to each section, the source note appearing below each table, and Appendix I, which comprises the Guide to Sources of Statistics, the Guide to State Statistical Abstracts, and the Guide to Foreign Statistical Abstracts.

This volume includes a selection of data from many statistical publications, both government and private. Publications cited as sources usually contain additional statistical detail and more comprehensive discussions of definitions and concepts than can be presented here. Data not available in publications issued by the contributing agency but obtained from unpublished records are identified in the source notes as "unpublished data." More information on the subjects covered in the tables so noted may generally be obtained from the source.

Except as indicated, figures are for the United States as presently constituted. Although emphasis in the *Statistical Abstract* is primarily given to national data, many tables present data for regions and individual states and a smaller number for metropolitan areas and cities. Appendix II, Metropolitan Area Concepts and Components, presents explanatory text, a complete current listing and population data for metropolitan statistical areas (MSAs), the primary metropolitan statistical areas (PMSAs), and the consolidated metropolitan statistical areas (CMSAs) defined as of June 30, 1999. Table 34 in Section 1 presents selected population characteristics for MSAs with population of 250,000 or more. Statistics for the Commonwealth of Puerto Rico and for outlying areas of the United States are included in many state tables and are supplemented by information in Section 29. Additional information for states, cities, counties, metropolitan areas, and other small units, as well as more historical data are available in various supplements to the *Abstract* (see inside back cover).

Statistics in this edition are generally for the most recent year or period available by spring 2000. Each year almost 1,500 tables and charts are reviewed and evaluated; new tables and charts of current interest are added, continuing series are updated, and less timely data are condensed or eliminated. Text notes and appendices are revised as appropriate.

USA Statistics in Brief, a pocket-size pamphlet highlighting many statistical series in the *Abstract,* is available separately. Single copies can be obtained free from U.S. Census Bureau, Customer Services, Washington, DC 20233 (telephone 301-457-4100). We attempt to update the pamphlet several times during the year. The latest data can be found on our Web site: <http://www.census.gov/statab/www/brief.html>

Changes in this edition—This year we have reinstated a smaller version of the Industrial Outlook Section with tables updated to 1998 and have included a separate section (32) with 21 tables from the 1997 Economic Census, based on the NAICS. In order to make space available for these sections, we have not included the 20th Century Statistics, although these tables will be available on our Web site and on the CD-ROM. In addition to the above, we have introduced 78 new tables throughout our core sections. These cover a variety of topics including prescription drug sales, public school building conditions, charter schools, distance education, HMOs, income-tested benefits, employment projections, household debt, mutual fund ownership, commercial industry space revenue, hazardous material shipments, bridge conditions, home remodeling, firearms manufactures, and e-commerce sales. For a complete list of new tables, see Appendix VI, p. 941.

V

Statistical Abstract on other media— The Abstract is available in its entirety on the Internet and, an enhanced version, on CD-ROM (except for a few copyrighted tables deleted by the request of source organizations). Our Internet site, <http://www.census.gov/statab/www>, contains this 2000 edition and earlier editions of the book, as well as summary items—Statistics in Brief, Frequently Requested Tables, and State Rankings, which will be updated as time allows. State and County Profiles is also on the site.

The CD-ROM version of the *Abstract* is enriched with links from tables to the Internet sites of appropriate government agencies. In addition, links are provided to the underlying spreadsheets (both .WK1 and .XLS) from which the data in the tables are based. Ordering information for the CD-ROM is located in the inside back cover.

Statistics for states and metropolitan areas—Extensive data for the states and metropolitan areas of the United States can be found in the *State and Metropolitan Area Data Book: 1997-98*. It features 859 data items covering everything from age and agriculture to wages and welfare for the 50 states and the District of Columbia with United States totals for comparison. Also included are over 150 data items for metropolitan areas (MAs), 43 items for component counties of MAs, and 3 population items for central cities of MAs.

This publication, as well as selected rankings of the states and metropolitan areas, is available on our Internet site at <http://www.census.gov/statab/www/smadb.html>. Some data items that appear in the book from private sources are not available on the Internet or CD-ROM versions because we did not receive copyright permission to release the data items in these formats. The CD-ROM version also includes links from the data tables to spreadsheets (both .WK1 and .XLS) with the data and pertinent geographic information, to contributing government agency Internet sites, and to related source notes and explanations. See the inside back cover for ordering information.

Limitations of the data—The contents of this volume were taken from many sources. All data from either censuses and surveys or from administrative records are subject to error arising from a number of factors: Sampling variability (for statistics based on samples), reporting errors in the data for individual units, incomplete coverage, nonresponse, imputations, and processing error. (See also Appendix III, pp. 918-936.) The Census Bureau cannot accept the responsibility for the accuracy or limitations of the data presented here, other than those for which it collects. The responsibility for selection of the material and for proper presentation, however, rests with the Census Bureau.

For additional information on data presented—Please consult the source publications available in local libraries or write to the agency indicated in the source notes. Write to the Census Bureau only if it is cited as the source.

Suggestions and comments—Users of the *Statistical Abstract* and its supplements (see inside back cover) are urged to make their data needs known for consideration in planning future editions. Suggestions and comments for improving coverage and presentation of data should be sent to the Director, U.S. Census Bureau, Washington, DC 20233.

Statistical Abstract User Survey—We would like to thank everyone who filled out the questionnaire inserted in last year's *Abstract*. By the end of September, 465 questionnaires had been returned and processed. Brief highlights include the following: 41% of respondents were librarians, and 34% were researchers or analysts; three most frequently used sections are Population (79%), Vital Statistics (67%), Income (66%); 81% of respondents reported using the *Abstract* at least once a month. Those who took the time to complete the survey help us to adapt the *Statistical Abstract* and related products to the needs of our customers.

Contents

[Numbers following subjects are page numbers]

U.S. Census Bureau, Statistical Abstract of the United States: 2000

Example of Table Structure

No. 1090. Private Shipyards—Summary: 1980 to 2000

[For calendar year, unless noted. (178.0 represents 178,000)]

Item	Unit	1980	1985	1990	1995	1996	1997	1998	1999	2000 [1]
Employment [2]	1,000. . .	178.0	138.3	130.8	105.0	100.4	98.6	104.4	99.1	98.1
Production workers	1,000. . .	138.8	101.2	93.6	77.8	73.5	70.8	74.9	67.7	67.6
Building activity:										
Merchant vessels: [3]										
Under construction [4] . . .	Number .	69	10	-	3	10	14	12	5	9
Ordered.	Number .	7	-	3	8	5	6	1	6	-
Delivered	Number .	23	3	-	1	1	4	5	2	-
Cancelled.	Number .	4	-	-	-	-	4	3	-	-
Under contract [5]	Number .	49	7	3	10	14	12	5	9	9
Naval vessels: [3]										
Under construction [4] . . .	Number .	99	100	95	57	46	46	42	50	44
Ordered.	Number .	11	11	7	6	11	4	20	-	2
Delivered	Number .	19	26	15	17	11	8	12	6	-
Under contract [5]	Number .	91	85	87	46	46	42	50	44	46
Unfinished work: [4]										
Commercial ships	Mil. dol. .	2,070	450	-	93.4	365.4	572.1	746.5	594.6	1917.0
Naval ships	Mil. dol. .	7,107	12,091	24,495	20,768	17,734	20,116	19,097	22,385.6	21,589.5

- Represents zero.   [1] As of June 1.   [2] Annual average of monthly data.   [3] Vessels of 1,000 tons or larger.   [4] As of Jan. 1.
[5] As of Dec. 31.
Source: 1980 and 1985, Shipbuilders Council of America, Arlington, VA., unpublished data; beginning 1990, U.S. Maritime Administration, unpublished data.

Headnotes immediately below table titles provide information important for correct interpretation or evaluation of the table as a whole or for a major segment of it.

Footnotes below the bottom rule of tables give information relating to specific items or figures within the table.

Unit indicators show the *specified quantities* in which data items are presented. They are used for two primary reasons. Sometimes data are not available in absolute form and are estimates (as in the case of many surveys). In other cases we round the numbers in order to save space to show more data, as in the case above.

EXAMPLES OF UNIT INDICATOR INTERPRETATION FROM TABLE

Year	Item	Unit Indicator	Number shown	Multiplier
1980.	Employment	Thousands.	178.0	1,000
1980.	Unfinished work	$ Millions.	2,070	1,000,000

**To Determine the Figure It Is Necessary to Multiply the
Number Shown by the Unit Indicator:**
Employment - 178.0 x 1,000 = 178,000 (Almost 180 thousand)
Unfinished work - 2,070 x 1,000,000 - $2,070,000,000 (over $2 billion).

When a table presents data with more than one unit indicator, they are found in the headnotes and column headings (Tables 2 and 4), spanner (Table 42), stub (Table 30), or unit column (shown above). When the data in a table are shown in the same unit indicator, it is shown in boldface as the first part of the headnote (Table 2). If no unit indicator is shown, data presented are in absolute form (Table 1).

Vertical rules are used to separate independent sections of a table, (Table 1), or in tables where the stub is continued into one or more additional columns (Table 2).

Averages—An average is a single number or value that is often used to represent the "typical value" of a group of numbers. It is regarded as a measure of "location" or "central tendency" of a group of numbers.

The *arithmetic mean* is the type of average used most frequently. It is derived by summing the individual item values of a particular group and dividing the total by the number of items. The arithmetic mean is often referred to as simply the "mean" or "average."

The *median* of a group of numbers is the middle number or value when each item in the group is arranged according to size (lowest to highest or visa versa); it generally has the same number of items above it as well as below it. If there is an even number if items in the group, the median is taken to be the average of the two middle numbers.

Per capita (or per person) quantities. A per capita figure represents an average computed for every person in a specified group (or population). It is derived by taking the total for an item (such as income, taxes, or retail sales) and dividing it by the number of persons in the specified population.

Guide to Tabular Presentation   ix

Index numbers—An index number is the measure of difference or change, usually expressed as a percent, relating one quantity (the variable) of a specified kind to another quantity of the same kind. Index numbers are widely used to express changes in prices over periods of time but may also be used to express differences between related subjects for a single point in time.

To compute a price index, a base year or period is selected. The base year price (of the commodity or service) is then designated as the base or reference price to which the prices for other years or periods are related. Many price indexes use the year 1982 as the base year; in tables this is shown as "1982=100." A method of expressing the price relationship is: The price of a set of one or more items for a related year (e.g. 1990) **divided by** the price of the same set of items for the base year (e.g. 1982). The result multiplied by 100 provides the index number. When 100 is subtracted from the index number, the result equals the percent change in price from the base year.

Average annual percent change—
Unless otherwise stated in the *Abstract* (as in Section 1, Population), average annual percent change is computed by use of a *compound interest formula*. This formula assumes that the rate of change is constant throughout a specified compounding period (1 year for average annual rates of change). The formula is similar to that used to compute the balance of a savings account which receives compound interest. According to this formula, at the end of a compounding period the amount of accrued change (e.g. school enrollment or bank interest) is added to the amount which existed at the beginning the period. As a result, over time (e.g., with each year or quarter), the same rate of change is applied to a larger and larger figure.

The *exponential formula*, which is based on continuous compounding, is often used to measure population change. It is preferred by population experts because they view population and population-related subjects as changing without interruption, ever ongoing. Both exponential and compound interest formulas assume a constant rate of change. The former, however, applies the amount of change continuously to the base rather than at the end of each compounding period. When the average annual rates are small (e.g., less than 5 percent) both formulas give virtually the same results. For an explanation of these two formulas as

they relate to population, see U.S. Census Bureau, *The Methods and Materials of Demography,* Vol. 2, 3d printing (rev.), 1975, pp. 372-381.

Current and constant dollars—
Statistics in some tables in a number of sections are expressed in both current and constant dollars (see, for example, Table 727 in Section 14, Income). Current dollar figures reflect actual prices or costs prevailing during the specified year(s). Constant dollar figures are estimates representing an effort to remove the effects of price changes from statistical series reported in dollar terms. In general, constant dollar series are derived by dividing current dollar estimates by the appropriate price index for the appropriate period (for example, the Consumer Price Index). The result is a series as it would presumably exist if prices were the same throughout, as in the base year—in other words as if the dollar had constant purchasing power. Any changes in this constant dollar series would reflect only changes in real volume of output, income, expenditures, or other measure.

Explanation of Symbols

The following symbols, used in the tables throughout this book, are explained in condensed form in footnotes to the tables where they appear:

- Represents zero or rounds to less than half the unit of measurement shown.

B Base figure too small to meet statistical standards for reliability of a derived figure.

D Figure withheld to avoid disclosure pertaining to a specific organization or individual.

NA Data not enumerated, tabulated, or otherwise available separately.

NS Percent change irrelevant or insignificant.

S Figure does not meet publication standards for reasons other than that covered by symbol B, above.

X Figure not applicable because column heading and stub line make entry impossible, absurd, or meaningless.

Z Entry would amount to less than half the unit of measurement shown.

In many tables, details will not add to the totals shown because of rounding.

Telephone and Internet Contacts

To help *Abstract* users find more data and information about statistical publications, we are issuing this list of contacts for Federal agencies with major statistical programs. The intent is to give a single, first-contact point-of-entry for users of statistics. These agencies will provide general information on their statistical programs and publications, as well as specific information on how to order their publications. We are also including the Internet (World Wide Web) addresses for many of these agencies. These URLs were current in October 2000.

Executive Office of the President
Office of Management and Budget
Administrator
Office of Information and Regulatory Affairs
Office of Management and Budget
Washington, DC 20503
Information: 202-395-3080
Internet address: <http://www. whitehouse.gov/omb>

Department of Agriculture
Economic Research Service
Information Center
U.S. Department of Agriculture
1800 M St. NW, Room 3100
Washington, DC 20036-5831
Information and Publications:
202-694-5050
Internet address: <http://www. ers.usda.gov/>
National Agricultural Statistics Service
National Agricultural Statistics Service
U.S. Department of Agriculture
1400 Independence Ave., SW, Room 5829
Washington, DC 20250
Information hotline: 1-800-727-9540
Internet address: <http://www. usda.gov/nass/>

Department of Commerce
U.S. Census Bureau
Customer Services Branch
U.S. Census Bureau
U.S. Department of Commerce
Washington, DC 20233
Information and Publications:
301-457-4100
Internet address: <http://www. census.gov/>
Bureau of Economic Analysis
Current Business Analysis Division, BE-53
Bureau of Economic Analysis
U.S. Department of Commerce
Washington, DC 20230
Information and Publications:
202-606-9900
Internet address: <http://www.bea. doc.gov/>

International Trade Administration
Trade Statistics Division
Office of Trade and Economic Analysis
International Trade Administration
Room 2814 B
U.S. Department of Commerce
Washington, DC 20230
Information and Publications:
202-482-2185
Internet address: <http://www.ita. doc.gov/tradestats/>
National Oceanic and Atmospheric Administration
National Oceanic and Atmospheric Administration Central Library
U.S. Department of Commerce
1315 East-West Highway
2nd Floor
Silver Spring MD 20910
Library: 301-713-2600
Internet address: <http://www.lib. noaa.gov/>

Department of Defense
Department of Defense
Office of the Assistant Secretary of Defense (Public Affairs)
Room 1E757
Attention: Directorate for Public Communications
1400 Defense Pentagon
Washington, DC 20301-1400
Information: 703-697-5737
Internet address: <http://web1.whs. osd.mil/diorhome.htm>

Department of Education
National Library of Education
U.S. Department of Education
400 Maryland Avenue, SW
Washington, DC 20202-5621
Education Information and Statistics
1-800-424-1616
Education Publications 1-877-433-7827
Internet address: <http://www.ed.gov/>

Department of Energy

Energy Information Administration

National Energy Information Center
U.S. Department of Energy
1000 Independence Ave., SW
1E248-EI-30
Washington, DC 20585
Information and Publications:
202-586-8800
Internet address: <http://www.eia. doe.gov/>

Department of Health and Human Services

Health Resources and Services Administration

HRSA Office of Communications
5600 Fishers Lane, Room 14-45
Rockville, MD 20857
Information Center: 301-443-3376
Internet address: <http://www.hrsa. gov/>

Substance Abuse Mental Health Services Administration

U.S. Department of Health and Human Services
5600 Fishers Lane, Room 12-105
Rockville, MD 20857
Information: 301-443-4795
Publications: 1-800-729-6686
Internet address: <http://www.samhsa. gov/>

Centers for Disease Control and Prevention

Office of Public Affairs
1600 Clifton Road, NE
Atlanta, GA 30333
Public Inquiries: 1-800-311-3435
Internet address: <http://www.cdc.gov/>

Health Care Financing Administration

Office of Public Affairs
Health Care Financing Administration
U.S. Department of Health and Human Services
Room 303D, Humphrey Building
200 Independence Ave., SW
Washington, DC 20201
Media Relations: 202-690-6145
Internet address: <http://www.hcfa. gov/>

National Center for Health Statistics

U.S. Department of Health and Human Services - Centers for Disease Control and Prevention
National Center for Health Statistics
Data Dissemination Branch
6525 Belcrest Rd., Rm. 1064
Hyattsville, MD 20782 301-458-INFO
Internet address: <http://www.cdc. gov/nchs>

U.S. Department of Housing and Urban Development

Office of the Assistant Secretary for Community Planning and Development

451 7th St., SW
Washington, DC 20410-0555
Information: 202-708-2690
Publications: 1-800-998-9999
Internet address: <http://www.hud.gov/>

Department of the Interior

Geological Survey

Earth Science Information Center
Geological Survey
U.S. Department of the Interior
507 National Center
Reston, VA 20192
Information and Publications:
703-648-5953
Internet address for minerals:
<http://minerals.usgs.gov/>
Internet address for other materials:
<http://ask.usgs.gov/>

Department of Justice

Bureau of Justice Statistics

Statistics Division
810 7th St., NW 2nd Floor
Washington, DC 20531
Information and Publications:
202-307-0765
Internet address: <http://www.ojp. usdoj.gov/bjs/>

National Criminal Justice Reference Service

Box 6000
Rockville, MD 20849-6000
Information and Publications:
301-519-5500
Publications: 1-800-732-3277
Internet address: <http://www.ncjrs. org/>

Federal Bureau of Investigation

U.S. Department of Justice
J. Edgar Hoover FBI Building
935 Pennsylvania Ave., NW
Washington, DC 20535
202-324-7222
Information and Publications:
202-324-3691
Research and Communications Unit: 202-324-5611
Internet address: <http://www.fbi.gov/>

Immigration and Naturalization Service

Statistics Branch
Immigration and Naturalization Service
U.S. Department of Justice
425 I St., NW, Room 4034
Washington, DC 20536
Information and Publications:
202-305-1613
Internet address: <http://www.ins.usdoj. gov/graphics/ index.htm>

Department of Labor

Bureau of Labor Statistics
Office of Publications and Special Studies
Services
Division of Information
Bureau of Labor Statistics
U.S. Department of Labor
2 Mass. Ave., NE, Room 2850
Washington, DC 20212
Information and Publications:
202-691-5200
Internet address: <http://stats.bls.gov/>
Employment and Training Administration
Office of Public Affairs
Employment and Training Administration
U.S. Department of Labor
200 Constitution Ave., NW, Room S4206
Washington, DC 20210
Information and Publications:
202-219-6871
Internet address: <http://www.doleta.gov/>

Department of Transportation

Federal Aviation Administration
U.S. Department of Transportation
800 Independence Ave., SW
Washington, DC 20591
Information and Publications:
202-267-3484
Internet address: <http://www.faa.gov/>
Bureau of Transportation Statistics
400 7th Street, SW
Washington, DC 20590
Products: 703-848-7335
Statistical Information: 800-853-1351
Internet address: <http://www.bts.gov/>
Federal Highway Administration
Office of Public Affairs
Federal Highway Administration
U.S. Department of Transportation
400 7th Street, SW
Washington, DC 20590
Information: 202-366-0660
Internet address: <http://www.fhwa.dot.gov/>
National Highway Traffic Safety Administration
Office of Public & Consumer Affairs
National Highway Traffic Safety
Administration
U.S. Department of Transportation
400 7th Street, SW
Washington, DC 20590
Information: 202-366-1503
Publications: 202-366-8892
Internet address: <http://www.nhtsa.dot.gov/>

Department of the Treasury

Internal Revenue Service
Statistics of Income Division
Internal Revenue Service
P.O. Box 2608
Washington, DC 20013-2608
Information and Publications:
202-874-0410
Internet address: <http://www.irs.ustreas.gov/cover.html>

Department of Veterans Affairs

Office of Public Affairs
Department of Veterans Affairs
810 Vermont Ave., NW
Washington, DC 20420
Information: 202-273-5400
Internet address: <http://www.va.gov/>

Independent Agencies

Administrative Office of the U.S. Courts
Statistics Division
1 Columbus Circle, NE
Washington, DC 20544
Information: 202-502-1455
Internet address: <http://www.uscourts.gov/>
Environmental Protection Agency
Information Resource Center, Rm. M2904
Environmental Protection Agency
1200 Pennsylvania. Ave., NW, MC 3201
Washington, DC 20460
Information: 202-260-9152
Internet address: <http://www.epa.gov/>
Federal Reserve Board
Division of Research and Statistics
Federal Reserve Board
Washington, DC 20551
Information: 202-452-3301
Publications: 202-452-3245
Internet address: <http://www.federalreserve.gov/>
National Science Foundation
Office of Legislation and Public Affairs
National Science Foundation
4201 Wilson Boulevard
Arlington, Virginia 22230
Information: 703-306-1234
Publications: 301-947-2722
Internet address: <http://www.nsf.gov/>
Securities and Exchange Commission
Office of Public Affairs
Securities and Exchange Commission
450 5th Street, NW, Mail Stop 7-11
Washington, DC 20549
Information: 202-942-0020
Publications: 202-942-4040
Internet address: <http://www.sec.gov/>
Social Security Administration
6400 Security Blvd.
Baltimore, MD 21235
Information and Publications:
1-800-772-1213
Internet Address: <http://www.ssa.gov/>

U.S. Census Bureau, Statistical Abstract of the United States: 2000

Section 1

Population

This section presents statistics on the growth, distribution, and characteristics of the U.S. population. The principal source of these data is the Bureau of the Census, which conducts a decennial census of population, a monthly population survey, a program of population estimates and projections, and a number of other periodic surveys relating to population characteristics. For a list of relevant publications, see the Guide to Sources of Statistics in Appendix I.

Decennial censuses—The U.S. Constitution provides for a census of the population every 10 years, primarily to establish a basis for apportionment of members of the House of Representatives among the states. For over a century after the first census in 1790, the census organization was a temporary one, created only for each decennial census. In 1902, the Bureau of the Census was established as a permanent Federal agency, responsible for enumerating the population and also for compiling statistics on other subjects.

Historically the census of population has been a complete count. That is, an attempt is made to account for every person, for each person's residence, and for other characteristics (sex, age, family relationships, etc.). Since the 1940 census, in addition to the complete count information, some data have been obtained from representative samples of the population. In the 1990 census, variable sampling rates were employed. For most of the country, 1 in every 6 households (about 17 percent) received the long form or sample questionnaire; in governmental units estimated to have fewer than 2,500 inhabitants, every other household (50 percent) received the sample questionnaire to enhance the reliability of sample data for small areas. Exact agreement is not to be expected between sample data and the complete census

count. Sample data may be used with confidence where large numbers are involved and assumed to indicate trends and relationships where small numbers are involved.

Census data presented here have not been adjusted for underenumeration. Results from the evaluation program for the 1990 census indicate that the overall national undercount was between 1 and 2 percent. The estimate from the Post Enumeration Survey (PES) was 1.6 percent, and the estimate from Demographic Analysis (DA) was 1.8 percent. Both the PES and DA estimates show disproportionately high undercounts for some demographic groups. For example, the PES estimates of percent net undercount for Blacks (4.4 percent), Hispanics (5.0 percent), and American Indians (4.5 percent) were higher than the estimated undercount of non-Hispanic Whites (0.7 percent). Historical DA estimates demonstrate that the overall undercount rate in the census has declined significantly over the past 50 years (from an estimated 5.4 percent in 1940 to 1.8 percent in 1990), yet the undercount of Blacks has remained disproportionately high.

Current Population Survey (CPS)—This is a monthly nationwide survey of a scientifically selected sample representing the noninstitutional civilian population. The sample is located in 754 areas comprising 2,121 counties, independent cities, and minor civil divisions with coverage in every state and the District of Columbia and is subject to sampling error. At the present time, about 50,000 occupied households are eligible for interview every month; of these between 4 and 5 percent are, for various reasons, unavailable for interview.

While the primary purpose of the CPS is to obtain monthly statistics on the labor force, it also serves as a vehicle for inquiries on other subjects. Using CPS data, the

Population   1

Bureau issues a series of publications under the general title of *Current Population Reports*, which cover population characteristics (P20), consumer income (P60), special studies (P23), and other topics.

Estimates of population characteristics based on the CPS will not agree with the counts from the census because the CPS and the census use different procedures for collecting and processing the data for racial groups, the Hispanic population, and other topics. Caution should also be used when comparing estimates for various years because of the periodic introduction of changes into the CPS. Beginning in January 1994, a number of changes were introduced into the CPS that effect all data comparisons with prior years. These changes include the results of a major redesign of the survey questionnaire and collection methodology and the introduction of 1990 census population controls, adjusted for the estimated undercount. This change in population controls had relatively little impact on derived measures such as means, medians, and percent distribution, but did have a significant impact on levels.

Population estimates and projections— National population estimates start with decennial census data as benchmarks and add annual population component of change data. Component of change data comes from various agencies, as follows: National Center for Health Statistics (births and deaths), Immigration and Naturalization Service (legal immigrants), Office of Refugee Resettlement (refugees), U.S. Census Bureau's International Programs Center (net movement between Puerto Rico and the U.S. mainland), Armed Forces, Department of Defense, and Office of Personnel Management (movement of military and civilian citizens abroad). Emigration and net undocumented immigration are projected based on research using census data. Estimates for states, counties, and smaller areas are based on the same component of change data, and sources as the national estimates. School statistics from state departments of education and parochial school systems, Federal income tax returns from the Internal Revenue Service,

group quarters from the Federal-State Cooperative program and the Veterans Administration, and medicare data from the Health Care Financing Administration are also included.

Data for the population by age for April 1, 1990, (shown in Tables 14, 21, and 23) are modified counts. The review of detailed 1990 information indicated that respondents tended to provide their age as of the date of completion of the questionnaire, not their age as of April 1, 1990. In addition, there may have been a tendency for respondents to round up their age if they were close to having a birthday. A detailed explanation of the age modification procedure appears in 1990 Census of Population and Housing Data Paper Listing (CPH-L-74).

Population estimates and projections are published in the P25 series of *Current Population Reports* and as *Population Paper Listings* (PPLs). These estimates and projections are generally consistent with official decennial census figures and do not reflect the amount of estimated census underenumeration. However, these estimates and projections by race have been modified and are not comparable to the census race categories (see section below under "race"). For details on methodology, see the sources cited below the individual tables.

The state population projections, by single year of age, sex, race, and Hispanic origin, prepared for 1995 to 2025 use a cohort-component methodology to generate the projected populations. This method requires separate assumptions for each population component of change: births, deaths, internal migration, and international migration. Data for population components of change derive from various governmental administrative records and census distributions. The 1994 state population estimates serve as the starting point for these projections, which are consistent with the national population projections listed in *Current Population Reports*, Series P25-1130. The two series of projections (see Table 35) are based on different internal

2 Population

migration assumptions: Series A, the preferred series model, which uses state-to-state migration observed from 1975-76 through 1993-94; and Series B, the economic model, which uses the Bureau of Economic Analysis employment projections.

Immigration—The principal source of immigration data is the *Statistical Yearbook of the Immigration and Naturalization Service*, published annually by the Immigration and Naturalization Service (INS), a unit of the Department of Justice. Immigration statistics are prepared from entry visas and change of immigration status forms. Immigrants are aliens admitted for legal permanent residence in the United States. The procedures for admission depend on whether the alien is residing inside or outside the United States at the time of application for permanent residence. Eligible aliens residing outside the United States are issued immigrant visas by the U.S. Department of State. Eligible aliens residing in the United States are allowed to change their status from temporary to permanent residence at INS district offices. The category, immigrant, includes persons who may have entered the United States as nonimmigrants or refugees, but who subsequently changed their status to that of a permanent resident. Nonresident aliens admitted to the United States for a temporary period are nonimmigrants (Tables 7 and 461). Refugees are considered nonimmigrants when initially admitted into the United States but are not included in nonimmigrant admission data. A refugee is any person who is outside his or her country of nationality who is unable or unwilling to return to that country because of persecution or a well-founded fear of persecution.

U.S. immigration law gives preferential immigration status to aliens who are related to certain U.S. citizens or legal permanent residents, aliens with needed job skills, or aliens who qualify as refugees. Immigration to the United States can be divided into two general categories: (1) those subject to the annual worldwide limitation, and (2) those exempt from it. The Immigration Act of 1990 established major revisions in the numerical limits and preference system regulating legal immigration. The numerical limits are imposed on visas issued and not on admissions. The maximum number of visas allowed to be issued under the preference categories in 1997 was 366,000 — 226,000 for family-sponsored immigrants and 140,000 for employment-based immigrants. There are nine categories among which the family-sponsored and employment-based immigrant visas are distributed, beginning in fiscal year 1992. The family-sponsored preferences are based on the alien's relationship with a U.S. citizen or legal permanent resident (see Table 6). The employment-based preferences are 1) priority workers (persons of extraordinary ability, outstanding professors and researchers, and certain multinational executives and managers); 2) professionals with advanced degrees or aliens with exceptional ability; 3) skilled workers, professionals without advanced degrees, and needed unskilled workers; 4) special immigrants; and 5) employment creation immigrants (investors). Within the overall limitations the per-country limit for independent countries is set to 7 percent of the total family-sponsored and employment-based limits, while dependent areas are limited to 2 percent of the total. The 1997 limit allowed no more than 25,620 preference visas for any independent country and 7,320 for any dependency. Those exempt from the worldwide limitation include immediate relatives of U.S. citizens, refugees and asylees adjusting to permanent residence, and other various classes of special immigrants (see Table 6).

The Refugee Act of 1980, effective April 1, 1980, provides for a uniform admission procedure for refugees of all countries, based on the United Nations' definition of refugees. Authorized admission ceilings are set annually by the President in consultation with Congress. After 1 year of residence in the United States, refugees are eligible for immigrant status.

The Immigration Reform and Control Act of 1986 (IRCA) allows two groups of illegal aliens to become temporary and then permanent residents of the United States:

Population   3

aliens who have been in the United States unlawfully since January 1, 1982 (legalization applicants), and aliens who were employed in seasonal agricultural work for a minimum period of time (Special Agricultural Worker (SAW) applicants). The application period for temporary residency for legalization applicants began on May 5, 1987, and ended on May 4, 1988, while the application period for SAW applicants began on June 1, 1987, and ended on November 30, 1988. Legalization applicants became eligible for permanent residence beginning in fiscal year 1989. Beginning 1989 immigrant data include temporary residents who were granted permanent residence under the legalization program of IRCA.

Metropolitan Areas (MAs)—The general concept of a metropolitan area is one of a core area containing a large population nucleus, together with adjacent communities that have a high degree of social and economic integration with that core. Metropolitan statistical areas (MSAs), consolidated metropolitan statistical areas (CMSAs), and primary metropolitan statistical areas (PMSAs) are defined by the Office of Management and Budget (OMB) as a standard for Federal agencies in the preparation and publication of statistics relating to metropolitan areas. The entire territory of the United States is classified as metropolitan (inside MSAs or CMSAs—PMSAs are components of CMSAs) or nonmetropolitan (outside MSAs or CMSAs). MSAs, CMSAs, and PMSAs are defined in terms of entire counties except in New England, where the definitions are in terms of cities and towns. The OMB also defines New England County Metropolitan Areas (NECMAs) which are county-based alternatives to the MSAs and CMSAs in the six New England states. Over time, new MAs are created and the boundaries of others change. The analysis of historical trends, therefore, must be made cautiously. For descriptive details and a listing of titles and components of MAs, see Appendix II.

Urban and rural—According to the 1990 census definition, the urban population comprises all persons living in (a) places of 2,500 or more inhabitants incorporated as cities, villages, boroughs (except in Alaska and New York), and towns (except in the New England states, New York, and Wisconsin), but excluding those persons living in the rural portions of extended cities (places with low population density in one or more large parts of their area); (b) census designated places (previously termed unincorporated) of 2,500 or more inhabitants; and (c) other territory, incorporated or unincorporated, included in urbanized areas. An urbanized area comprises one or more places and the adjacent densely settled surrounding territory that together have a minimum population of 50,000 persons. In all definitions, the population not classified as urban constitutes the rural population.

Residence—In determining residence, the Bureau of the Census counts each person as an inhabitant of a usual place of residence (i.e., the place where one usually lives and sleeps). While this place is not necessarily a person's legal residence or voting residence, the use of these different bases of classification would produce the same results in the vast majority of cases.

Race—The Bureau of the Census collects and publishes racial statistics as outlined in Statistical Policy Directive No. 15 issued by the U.S. Office of Management and Budget. This directive provides standards on ethnic and racial categories for statistical reporting to be used by all Federal agencies. According to the directive, the basic racial categories are American Indian or Alaska Native, Asian or Pacific Islander, Black, and White. (The directive identifies Hispanic origin as an ethnicity.) The concept of race the Bureau of the Census uses reflects self-identification by respondents; that is the individual's perception of his/her racial identity. The concept is not intended to reflect any biological or anthropological definition. Although the Bureau of the Census adheres to the overall guidelines of Directive No. 15, it recognizes that there are persons who do not identify with a specific racial group. The 1990 census race question included an "Other race" category with provisions for a write-in entry.

Furthermore, the Bureau of the Census recognizes that the categories of the race item include both racial and national origin or socio-cultural groups.

Differences between the 1990 census and earlier censuses affect the comparability of data for certain racial groups and American Indian tribes. The lack of comparability is due to changes in the way some respondents reported their race as well as changes in 1990 census procedures related to the racial classification. (For a fuller explanation, see *1990 Census of Population, Volume I, General Population Characteristics* (1990 CP-1).)

Data for the population by race for April 1, 1990 (shown in Tables 12, 13, 18, 19, 21, and 23) are modified counts and are not comparable to the 1990 census race categories. These numbers were computed using 1990 census data by race which had been modified to be consistent with the guidelines in Federal Statistical Policy Directive No. 15 issued by the Office of Management and Budget. A detailed explanation of the race modification procedure appears in 1990 Census of Population and Housing Data Paper Listing (CPH-L-74).

In the CPS and other household sample surveys in which data are obtained through personal interview, respondents are asked to classify their race as: (1) White; (2) Black; (3) American Indian, Aleut, or Eskimo; or (4) Asian or Pacific Islander. The procedures for classifying persons of mixed races who could not provide a single response to the race question are generally similar to those used in the census.

Hispanic population—In the 1990 census, the Bureau of the Census collected data on the Hispanic origin population in the United States by using a self-identification question. Persons of Spanish/Hispanic origin are those who classified themselves in one of the specific Hispanic origin categories listed on the questionnaire—Mexican, Puerto Rican, Cuban, as well as those who indicated that they were of Other Spanish/Hispanic origin. Persons of "Other Spanish/Hispanic" origin are those whose origins are from Spain, the Spanish-speaking countries of Central or South America, or the Dominican Republic. Both in 1980 and 1990, the Hispanic origin question contained prelisted categories for the largest Hispanic-origin groups—Mexican, Puerto Rican, Cuban, and Other Spanish/Hispanic. The 1990 Hispanic origin question differed from the 1980 question in that in 1990, unlike in 1980, the question contained a write-in line for the Other Spanish/Hispanic category which were coded only for sample data. Another difference between the 1980 and 1990 Hispanic-origin question is that in 1980 the wording of the Hispanic origin question read: "Is this person of Spanish/Hispanic origin or descent?" while in 1990 the word "descent" was dropped from the question. Persons of Hispanic-origin may be of any race.

In the CPS information on Hispanic persons is gathered by using a self-identification question. Persons classify themselves in one of the Hispanic categories in response to the question: "What is the origin or descent of each person in this household?" Hispanic persons in the CPS are persons who report themselves as Mexican-American, Chicano, Mexican, Puerto Rican, Cuban, Central or South American (Spanish countries), or other Hispanic origin.

Nativity—The native population consists of all persons born in the United States, Puerto Rico, or an outlying area of the United States. It also includes persons born in a foreign country who had at least one parent who was a U.S. citizen. All other persons are classified as "foreign born."

Mobility status—The U.S. population is classified according to mobility status on the basis of a comparison between the place of residence of each individual at the time of the survey or census and the place of residence at a specified earlier date. Nonmovers are all persons who were living in the same house or apartment at the end of the period as at the beginning of the period. Movers are all persons who were living in a different house or apartment at the end of the period than at the beginning of

U.S. Census Bureau, Statistical Abstract of the United States: 1999

the period. Movers are further classified as to whether they were living in the same or different county, state, or region or were movers from abroad. Movers from abroad include all persons, either U.S. citizens or noncitizens, whose place of residence was outside the United States at the beginning of the period; that is, in Puerto Rico, an outlying area under the jurisdiction of the United States, or a foreign country.

Living arrangements—Living arrangements refer to residency in households or in group quarters. A "household" comprises all persons who occupy a "housing unit," that is, a house, an apartment or other group of rooms, or a single room that constitutes "separate living quarters." A household includes the related family members and all the unrelated persons, if any, such as lodgers, foster children, wards, or employees who share the housing unit. A person living alone or a group of unrelated persons sharing the same housing unit is also counted as a household. See text, Section 25, Construction and Housing, for definition of housing unit.

All persons not living in housing units are classified as living in group quarters. These individuals may be institutionalized, e.g., under care or custody in juvenile facilities, jails, correctional centers, hospitals, or nursing homes; or they may be residents in noninstitutional group quarters such as college dormitories, group homes, or military barracks.

Householder—The householder is the first adult household member listed on the questionnaire. The instructions call for listing first the person (or one of the persons) in whose name the home is owned or rented. If a home is owned or rented jointly by a married couple, either the husband or the wife may be listed first. Prior to 1980, the husband was always considered the household head (householder) in married-couple households.

Family—The term "family" refers to a group of two or more persons related by birth, marriage, or adoption and residing together in a household. A family includes among its members the householder.

Subfamily—A subfamily consists of a married couple and their children, if any, or one parent with one or more never-married children under 18 years old living in a household. Subfamilies are divided into "related" and "unrelated" subfamilies. A related subfamily is related to, but does not include, the householder. Members of a related subfamily are also members of the family with whom they live. The number of related subfamilies, therefore, is not included in the count of families. An unrelated subfamily may include persons such as guests, lodgers, or resident employees and their spouses and/or children; none of whom is related to the householder.

Married couple—A "married couple" is defined as a husband and wife living together in the same household, with or without children and other relatives.

Statistical reliability—For a discussion of statistical collection and estimation, sampling procedures, and measures of statistical reliability applicable to Census Bureau data, see Appendix III.

No. 1. Population and Area: 1790 to 1990

[Area figures represent area on indicated date including in some cases considerable areas not then organized or settled, and not covered by the census. Total area figures for 1790 to 1970 have been recalculated on the basis of the remeasurement of states and counties for the 1980 census, but not on the basis of the 1990 census. The land and water area figures for past censuses have not been adjusted and are not strictly comparable with the total area data for comparable dates because the land areas were derived from different base data, and these values are known to have changed with the construction of reservoirs, draining of lakes, etc. Density figures are based on land area measurements as reported in earlier censuses]

	Resident population				Area (square miles)		
Census date	Number	Per square mile of land area	Increase over preceding census Number	Percent	Total	Land	Water
CONTERMINOUS U.S. [1]							
1790 (Aug. 2)	3,929,214	4.5	(X)	(X)	891,364	864,746	24,065
1800 (Aug. 4)	5,308,483	6.1	1,379,269	35.1	891,364	864,746	24,065
1810 (Aug. 6)	7,239,881	4.3	1,931,398	36.4	1,722,685	1,681,828	34,175
1820 (Aug. 7)	9,638,453	5.5	2,398,572	33.1	1,792,552	1,749,462	38,544
1830 (June 1)	12,866,020	7.4	3,227,567	33.5	1,792,552	1,749,462	38,544
1840 (June 1)	17,069,453	9.8	4,203,433	32.7	1,792,552	1,749,462	38,544
1850 (June 1)	23,191,876	7.9	6,122,423	35.9	2,991,655	2,940,042	52,705
1860 (June 1)	31,443,321	10.6	8,251,445	35.6	3,021,295	2,969,640	52,747
1870 (June 1)	[2]39,818,449	[2]13.4	8,375,128	26.6	3,021,295	2,969,640	52,747
1880 (June 1)	50,155,783	16.9	10,337,334	26.0	3,021,295	2,969,640	52,747
1890 (June 1)	62,947,714	21.2	12,791,931	25.5	3,021,295	2,969,640	52,747
1900 (June 1)	75,994,575	25.6	13,046,861	20.7	3,021,295	2,969,834	52,553
1910 (Apr. 15)	91,972,266	31.0	15,977,691	21.0	3,021,295	2,969,565	52,822
1920 (Jan. 1)	105,710,620	35.6	13,738,354	14.9	3,021,295	2,969,451	52,936
1930 (Apr. 1)	122,775,046	41.2	17,064,426	16.1	3,021,295	2,977,128	45,259
1940 (Apr. 1)	131,669,275	44.2	8,894,229	7.2	3,021,295	2,977,128	45,259
1950 (Apr. 1)	150,697,361	50.7	19,028,086	14.5	3,021,295	2,974,726	47,661
1960 (Apr. 1)	178,464,236	60.1	27,766,875	18.4	3,021,295	2,968,054	54,207
UNITED STATES							
1950 (Apr. 1)	151,325,798	42.6	19,161,229	14.5	3,618,770	3,552,206	63,005
1960 (Apr. 1)	179,323,175	50.6	27,997,377	18.5	3,618,770	3,540,911	74,212
1970 (Apr. 1)	[3]203,302,031	[3]57.4	23,978,856	13.4	3,618,770	[3]3,540,023	[3]78,444
1980 (Apr. 1)	[4]226,542,199	64.0	23,240,168	11.4	3,618,770	3,539,289	79,481
1990 (Apr. 1)	[5]248,718,301	70.3	22,176,102	9.8	[6]3,717,796	[6]3,536,278	[6][7]181,518

X Not applicable.   [1] Excludes Alaska and Hawaii.   [2] Revised to include adjustments for underenumeration in southern states; unrevised number is 38,558,371 (13.0 per square mile).   [3] Figures corrected after 1970 final reports were issued.   [4] Total population count has been revised since the 1980 census publications. Numbers by age, race, Hispanic origin, and sex have not been corrected.   [5] The April 1, 1990, census count includes count question resolution corrections processed through December 1997, and does not include adjustments for census coverage errors.   [6] Data reflect corrections made after publication of the results.   [7] Comprises Great Lakes, inland, and coastal water. Data for prior years cover inland water only. For further explanation, see Table 380.

Source: U.S. Census Bureau, *1990 Census of Population and Housing, Population and Housing Unit Counts* (CPH-2); 1990 Census of Population and Housing Listing (1990 CPH-L-157); and unpublished data.

No. 2. Population: 1960 to 1999

[**In thousands, except percent (180,671 represents 180,671,000)**. Estimates as of **July 1**. Total population includes Armed Forces abroad; civilian population excludes Armed Forces. For basis of estimates, see text of this section]

Year	Total Population	Percent change [1]	Resident population	Civilian population	Year	Total Population	Percent change [1]	Resident population	Civilian population
1960	180,671	1.60	179,979	178,140	1980	227,726	1.19	227,225	225,621
1961	183,691	1.67	182,992	181,143	1981	229,966	0.98	229,466	227,818
1962	186,538	1.55	185,771	183,677	1982	232,188	0.97	231,664	229,995
1963	189,242	1.45	188,483	186,493	1983	234,307	0.91	233,792	232,097
1964	191,889	1.40	191,141	189,141	1984	236,348	0.87	235,825	234,110
1965	194,303	1.26	193,526	191,605	1985	238,466	0.90	237,924	236,219
1966	196,560	1.16	195,576	193,420	1986	240,651	0.92	240,133	238,412
1967	198,712	1.09	197,457	195,264	1987	242,804	0.89	242,289	240,550
1968	200,706	1.00	199,399	197,113	1988	245,021	0.91	244,499	242,817
1969	202,677	0.98	201,385	199,145	1989	247,342	0.95	246,819	245,131
1970	205,052	1.17	203,984	201,895	1990	249,973	1.06	249,464	247,824
1971	207,661	1.27	206,827	204,866	1991	252,665	1.08	252,153	250,542
1972	209,896	1.08	209,284	207,511	1992	255,410	1.09	255,030	253,445
1973	211,909	0.96	211,357	209,600	1993	258,119	1.06	257,783	256,310
1974	213,854	0.92	213,342	211,636	1994	260,637	0.98	260,327	258,915
1975	215,973	0.99	215,465	213,789	1995	263,082	0.94	262,803	261,452
1976	218,035	0.95	217,563	215,894	1996	265,502	0.92	265,229	263,943
1977	220,239	1.01	219,760	218,106	1997	268,048	0.96	267,784	266,531
1978	222,585	1.06	222,095	220,467	1998	270,509	0.92	270,248	269,027
1979	225,055	1.11	224,567	222,969	1999	272,945	0.90	272,691	271,491

[1] Percent change from immediate preceding year.

Source: U.S. Census Bureau, *Current Population Reports*, P25-802 and P25-1095; and "Monthly estimates of the United States population: April 1, 1980, to July 1, 1999; with short-term projections to April 1, 2000"; published: 24 May 2000; <http://www.census.gov/population/estimates/nation/intfile1-1.txt>.

Population   7

No. 3. Resident Population Projections: 2000 to 2100

[In thousands (275,306 represents 275,306,000). As of July 1. The projections are based on assumptions about future childbearing, mortality, and migration. The level of childbearing among women for the middle series is assumed to remain close to present levels, with differences by race and Hispanic origin diminishing over time. Mortality is assumed to decline gradually with less variation by race and Hispanic origin than at present. International migration is assumed to vary over time and decrease generally relative to the size of the population. Assumptions for the lowest and highest series are summarized in "Methodology and Assumptions for the Population Projections of the United States: 1999 to 2100, Working Paper #38"]

Year	Middle series [1]	Lowest series [2]	Highest series [3]	Zero international migration series [4]	Year	Middle series [1]	Lowest series [2]	Highest series [3]	Zero international migration series [4]
2000	275,306	274,853	275,816	273,818	2010	299,862	291,413	310,910	287,710
2001	277,803	276,879	278,869	275,279	2015	312,268	297,977	331,636	294,741
2002	280,306	278,801	282,087	276,709	2020	324,927	303,664	354,642	301,636
2003	282,798	280,624	285,422	278,112	2025	337,815	308,229	380,397	307,923
2004	285,266	282,352	288,841	279,493	2030	351,070	311,656	409,604	313,219
2005	287,716	284,000	292,339	280,859	2035	364,319	313,819	441,618	317,534
2006	290,153	285,581	295,911	282,219	2040	377,350	314,673	475,949	321,167
2007	292,583	287,106	299,557	283,579	2050	403,687	313,546	552,757	327,641
2008	295,009	288,583	303,274	284,945	2075	480,504	303,970	809,243	349,032
2009	297,436	290,018	307,060	286,322	2100	570,954	282,706	1,182,390	377,444

[1] Total fertility rate in 2050 = 2,219; life expectancy in 2050 = 83.9 years; and annual net immigration in 2050 = 984,000. These are middle level assumptions. For explanation of total fertility rate; see headnote, Table 82. [2] Total fertility rate in 2050 = 1,800; life expectancy in 2050 = 82.2 years; and annual net immigration in 2050 = 169,000. These are lowest level assumptions. [3] Total fertility rate in 2050 = 2,647; life expectancy in 2050 = 86.1 years; and annual net immigration in 2050 = 2,812,000. These are highest level assumptions. [4] Middle level assumptions for fertility and mortality; zero level assumption for international migration.

Source: U.S. Census Bureau, "Annual Projections of the Total Resident Population as of July 1: Middle, Lowest, Highest, and Zero International Migration Series, 2000 to 2100"; published: 14 February 2000; <http://www.census.gov/population/projections/nation/summary/np-t1.txt>.

No. 4. Components of Population Change, 1980 to 1999, and Projections, 2000 to 2050

[226,546 represents 226,546,000. Resident population. The estimates prior to 1990 are consistent with the original 1990 census count of 248,709,873. Starting with 1990, estimates reflect the revised April 1, 1990, estimates base count of 248,790,925 which includes count resolution corrections processed through August 1997. It generally does not include adjustments for census coverage errors. However, it includes adjustments estimated for the 1995 Test Census in various localities in California, New Jersey, and Louisiana, and the 1998 census dress rehearsals in localities in California and Wisconsin. These adjustments amounted to a total of 81,052 persons]

Year	Population as of Jan. 1 (1,000)	Net increase [1] Total (1,000)	Net increase [1] Per-cent [2]	Births (1,000)	Deaths (1,000)	Net migration [3] (1,000)	Net growth rate [1]	Birth rate	Death rate	Net migration rate [3]
1980 [4]	226,546	1,900	0.8	2,743	1,463	724	11.1	16.0	8.6	4.2
1981	228,446	2,200	1.0	3,629	1,978	690	9.6	15.8	8.6	3.0
1982	230,645	2,157	0.9	3,681	1,975	595	9.3	15.9	8.5	2.6
1983	232,803	2,066	0.9	3,639	2,019	592	8.8	15.6	8.6	2.5
1984	234,868	2,070	0.9	3,669	2,039	589	8.8	15.6	8.6	2.5
1985	236,938	2,171	0.9	3,761	2,086	649	9.1	15.8	8.8	2.7
1986	239,109	2,158	0.9	3,757	2,105	661	9.0	15.6	8.8	2.8
1987	241,267	2,195	0.9	3,809	2,123	666	9.1	15.7	8.8	2.7
1988	243,462	2,243	0.9	3,910	2,168	662	9.2	16.0	8.9	2.7
1989	245,705	2,438	1.0	4,041	2,150	712	9.9	16.4	8.7	2.9
1990 [5]	248,143	2,535	1.0	4,148	2,155	[6]542	10.2	16.6	8.6	[6]2.2
1991	250,718	2,901	1.2	4,111	2,170	[6]960	11.5	16.3	8.6	[6]3.8
1992	253,620	2,896	1.1	4,065	2,176	1,007	11.4	15.9	8.5	3.9
1993	256,516	2,614	1.0	4,000	2,269	883	10.1	15.5	8.8	3.4
1994	259,131	2,485	1.0	3,953	2,279	811	9.5	15.2	8.8	3.1
1995	261,615	2,446	0.9	3,900	2,312	858	9.3	14.8	8.8	3.3
1996	264,061	2,513	1.0	3,891	2,315	937	9.5	14.7	8.7	3.5
1997	266,574	2,544	1.0	3,881	2,314	977	9.5	14.5	8.6	3.6
1998	269,118	2,466	0.9	3,944	2,338	860	9.1	14.6	8.7	3.2
1999	271,584	2,440	0.9	3,934	2,350	856	8.9	14.4	8.6	3.1
PROJECTIONS [7]										
2000	274,110	2,492	0.9	3,914	2,393	970	9.1	14.2	8.7	3.5
2005	286,549	2,443	0.9	4,045	2,480	878	8.5	14.1	8.6	3.1
2010	298,710	2,425	0.8	4,283	2,578	720	8.1	14.3	8.6	2.4
2015	311,069	2,521	0.8	4,476	2,695	740	8.1	14.3	8.6	2.4
2020	323,724	2,530	0.8	4,613	2,840	757	7.8	14.2	8.7	2.3
2025	336,566	2,621	0.8	4,736	3,033	918	7.8	14.0	9.0	2.7
2030	349,789	2,688	0.8	4,878	3,257	1,067	7.7	13.9	9.3	3.0
2040	376,123	2,601	0.7	5,286	3,702	1,018	6.9	14.0	9.8	2.7
2050	402,420	2,699	0.7	5,661	3,952	990	6.7	14.0	9.8	2.5

[1] Prior to April 1, 1990, includes "error of closure" (the amount necessary to make the components of change add to the net change between censuses), for which figures are not shown separately. [2] Percent of population at beginning of period. [3] Covers net international migration and movement of Armed Forces, federally affiliated civilian citizens, and their dependents. [4] Data are for period April 1 to December 31. [5] Net change for 1990 excludes "error of closure" for the 3 months prior to the April 1 census date. Therefore, it may not equal the difference between the populations at the beginning of 1990 and 1991. [6] Data reflect movement of Armed Forces due to the Gulf War. [7] Based on middle series of assumptions. See footnote 1, Table 3.

Source: U.S. Census Bureau, Current Population Reports, P25-1095 and unpublished data; and "Population Projections of the Total Resident Population by Quarter: Middle Series, April 1, 1999, to January 1, 2101"; published 13 January 2000; <http://www.census.gov/population/projections/nation/summary/np-t2.txt>; and "Components of Change for the Total Resident Population: Middle Series, 1999 to 2100;" published 13 January 2000; <http://www.census.gov/population/projections/nation/summary/np-t6-a.txt> and <http://www.census.gov/population/projections/nation/summary/np-t6-b.txt>.

No. 5. Immigration: 1901 to 1998

[In thousands, except rate (8,795 represents 8,795,000). For fiscal years ending in year shown; see text, Section 9, State and Local Government. For definition of immigrants, see text of this section. Data represent immigrants admitted. Rates based on Census Bureau estimates as of July 1 for resident population through 1929 and for total population thereafter (excluding Alaska and Hawaii prior to 1959)]

Period	Number	Rate [1]	Year	Number	Rate [1]
1901 to 1910	8,795	10.4	1980	531	2.3
1911 to 1920	5,736	5.7	1990	1,536	6.1
1921 to 1930	4,107	3.5	1991	1,827	7.2
1931 to 1940	528	0.4	1992	974	3.8
1941 to 1950	1,035	0.7	1993	904	3.5
1951 to 1960	2,515	1.5	1994	804	3.1
1961 to 1970	3,322	1.7	1995	720	2.7
1971 to 1980	4,493	2.1	1996	916	3.4
1981 to 1990	7,338	3.1	1997	798	3.0
1991 to 1998	7,605	3.6	1998	660	2.4

[1] Annual rate per 1,000 U.S. population. Rate computed by dividing sum of annual immigration totals by sum of annual U.S. population totals for same number of years.

Source: U.S. Immigration and Naturalization Service, *Statistical Yearbook*, annual.

No. 6. Immigrants Admitted by Class of Admission: 1990 to 1998

[For fiscal year ending September 30. For definition of immigrants, see text of this section]

Class of admission	1990	1994	1995	1996	1997	1998
Immigrants, total.	**1,536,483**	**804,416**	**720,461**	**915,900**	**798,378**	**660,477**
New arrivals	435,729	490,429	380,291	421,405	380,719	357,037
Adjustments	1,100,754	313,987	340,170	494,495	417,659	303,440
Preference immigrants, total	272,742	335,252	323,458	411,673	303,938	268,997
Family-sponsored immigrants, total.	214,550	211,961	238,122	294,174	213,331	191,480
Unmarried sons/daughters of U.S. citizens and their children.	15,861	13,181	15,182	20,909	22,536	17,717
Spouses, unmarried sons/daughters of alien residents, and their children	107,686	115,000	144,535	182,834	113,681	88,488
Married sons/daughters of U.S. citizens [1]	26,751	22,191	20,876	25,452	21,943	22,257
Brothers or sisters of U.S. citizens [1]	64,252	61,589	57,529	64,979	55,171	63,018
Employment-based immigrants, total.	58,192	123,291	85,336	117,499	90,607	77,517
Priority workers [1]	(X)	21,053	17,339	27,501	21,810	21,408
Professionals with advanced degrees [1]	(X)	14,432	10,475	18,462	17,059	14,384
Skilled workers, professionals, unskilled workers [1]	(X)	76,956	50,245	62,756	42,596	34,317
Special immigrants [1]	4,463	10,406	6,737	7,844	7,781	6,584
Employment creation [1]	(X)	444	540	936	1,361	824
Professional or highly skilled immigrants [1][2]	26,546	(X)	(X)	(X)	(X)	(X)
Needed skilled or unskilled workers [1][2]	27,183	(X)	(X)	(X)	(X)	(X)
Immediate relatives	234,090	251,647	222,254	302,090	322,440	284,270
Spouses of U.S. citizens	125,426	145,247	123,238	169,760	170,263	151,172
Children of U.S. citizens	46,065	48,147	48,740	63,971	76,631	70,472
Orphans	7,088	8,200	9,384	11,316	12,596	14,867
Parents of U.S. citizens	60,189	56,370	48,382	66,699	74,114	61,724
Children born abroad to alien residents	2,410	1,883	1,894	1,660	1,432	902
Refugees and asylees	97,364	121,434	114,664	128,565	112,158	54,645
Refugee adjustments	92,427	115,451	106,827	118,528	102,052	44,645
Asylee adjustments	4,937	5,983	7,837	10,037	10,106	10,000
Other immigrants [3]	932,287	96,083	60,085	73,572	59,842	52,565
Diversity Programs [3]	29,161	41,056	47,245	58,790	49,374	45,499
Amerasians (P.L. 100-202) [4]	13,059	2,822	939	956	738	346
Immigration Reform and Control Act of 1986 legalization adjustments	880,372	6,022	4,267	4,635	2,548	955
Legalization dependents [5]	(X)	34,074	277	184	64	21
Other	9,695	12,109	7,357	9,007	7,118	5,744

X Not applicable. [1] Includes spouses and children. [2] Category was eliminated in 1992 by the Immigration Act of 1990. [3] Includes categories of immigrants admitted under three laws intended to diversify immigration: P.L. 99-603, P.L. 100-658, and P.L. 101-649. [4] Under Public Law 100-202, Amerasians are aliens born in Vietnam between January 1, 1962, and January 1, 1976, who were fathered by U.S. citizens. [5] Spouses and children of persons granted permanent resident status under provisions of the Immigration Reform and Control Act of 1986.

Source: U.S. Immigration and Naturalization Service, *Statistical Yearbook*, annual.

No. 7. Immigrants by Country of Birth: 1981 to 1998

[In thousands (7,338.1 represents 7,338,100). For fiscal years ending Sept. 30. For definition of immigrants, see text of this section]

Country of birth	1981-90, total	1991-96, total	1997	1998	Country of birth	1981-90, total	1991-96, total	1997	1998
All countries	7,338.1	6,146.2	798.4	660.5	Taiwan	([4])	76.8	6.7	7.1
Europe [1]	705.6	875.6	119.9	90.8	Thailand	64.4	36.1	3.1	3.1
France	23.1	16.9	2.6	2.4	Turkey	20.9	15.7	3.1	2.7
Germany	70.1	43.7	5.7	5.5	Vietnam	401.4	317.8	38.5	17.6
Greece	29.1	10.0	1.0	0.9	North America [1]	3,125.0	2,740.7	307.5	253.0
Ireland	32.8	54.9	1.0	0.9	Canada	119.2	90.7	11.6	10.2
Italy	32.9	14.7	2.0	1.8	Mexico	1,653.3	1,651.4	146.9	131.6
Poland	97.4	130.2	12.0	8.5	Caribbean [1]	892.7	655.4	105.3	75.5
Portugal	40.0	17.1	1.7	1.5	Cuba	159.2	94.9	33.6	17.4
Romania	38.9	34.3	5.5	5.1	Dominican				
Soviet Union, former [2] .	84.0	339.9	49.1	30.2	Republic	251.8	258.1	27.1	20.4
Armenia	(NA)	[3]20.8	2.1	1.1	Haiti	140.2	114.4	15.1	13.4
Azerbaijan	(NA)	[3]12.3	1.5	0.5	Jamaica	213.8	109.8	17.8	15.1
Belarus	(NA)	[3]21.4	3.1	1.0	Trinidad and				
Russia	(NA)	[3]70.4	16.6	11.5	Tobago	39.5	41.1	6.4	4.9
Ukraine	(NA)	[3]92.2	15.7	7.4	Central America [1]	458.7	342.8	43.7	35.7
Uzbekistan	(NA)	[3]16.1	3.3	0.6	El Salvador	214.6	147.7	18.0	14.6
United Kingdom	142.1	95.0	10.7	9.0	Guatemala	87.9	70.3	7.8	7.8
Yugoslavia	19.2	31.7	10.8	8.0	Honduras	49.5	41.9	7.6	6.5
Asia [1]	2,817.4	1,941.9	265.8	219.7	Nicaragua	44.1	50.4	6.3	3.5
Afghanistan	26.6	13.6	1.1	0.8	Panama	29.0	16.9	2.0	1.6
Bangladesh	15.2	35.4	8.7	8.6	South America [1]	455.9	344.0	52.9	45.4
Cambodia	116.6	11.9	1.6	1.4	Argentina	25.7	17.1	2.0	1.5
China	[4]388.8	268.7	41.1	36.9	Brazil	23.7	32.4	4.6	4.4
Hong Kong	63.0	52.9	5.6	5.3	Chile	23.4	11.4	1.4	1.2
India	261.9	236.5	38.1	36.5	Colombia	124.4	81.7	13.0	11.8
Iran	154.8	79.4	9.6	7.9	Ecuador	56.0	45.2	7.8	6.9
Iraq	19.6	26.8	3.2	2.2	Guyana	95.4	53.6	7.3	4.0
Israel	36.3	22.9	2.4	2.0	Peru	64.4	66.7	10.9	10.2
Japan	43.2	39.9	5.1	5.1	Venezuela	17.9	16.2	3.3	3.1
Jordan	32.6	25.1	4.2	3.3	Africa [1]	192.3	213.1	47.8	40.7
Korea	338.8	114.1	14.2	14.3	Egypt	31.4	28.0	5.0	4.8
Laos	145.6	37.8	1.9	1.6	Ethiopia	27.2	30.9	5.9	4.2
Lebanon	41.6	29.9	3.6	3.3	Ghana	14.9	18.0	5.1	4.5
Pakistan	61.3	70.5	13.0	13.1	Nigeria	35.3	37.9	7.0	7.7
Philippines	495.3	348.5	49.1	34.5	South Africa	15.7	14.2	2.1	1.9
Syria	20.6	16.6	2.3	2.8	Other countries [5]	41.9	31.0	4.5	10.9

NA Not available. [1] Includes countries not shown separately. [2] Includes other republics and unknown republics, not shown separately. [3] Covers years 1992-1996. [4] Data for Taiwan included with China. [5] Includes unknown countries.

Source: U.S. Immigration and Naturalization Service, *Statistical Yearbook,* annual; and releases.

No. 8. Immigrants Admitted as Permanent Residents Under Refugee Acts by Country of Birth: 1981 to 1998

[For fiscal years ending September 30]

Country of birth	1981-90, total	1991-96, total	1997	1998	Country of birth	1981-90, total	1991-96, total	1997	1998
Total	1,013,620	748,122	112,158	54,645	Cambodia	114,064	6,088	163	62
Europe [1]	155,512	312,815	39,795	19,048	China	[4]7,928	5,079	692	898
Czechoslovakia,					India	(NA)	1,125	462	373
former	8,204	1,201	40	15	Iran	46,773	20,126	1,447	754
Hungary	4,942	1,231	24	14	Iraq	7,540	14,464	1,774	999
Poland	33,889	7,210	143	54	Laos	142,964	33,701	1,363	1,110
Romania	29,798	15,139	322	116	Thailand	30,259	19,323	1,112	1,134
Soviet Union,					Vietnam	324,453	169,560	22,297	4,921
former [2]	72,306	264,187	30,880	13,200	North America [1] . .	121,840	111,744	32,898	16,372
Armenia	(NA)	[3]1,546	213	158	Cuba	113,367	76,370	30,377	14,915
Azerbaijan . . .	(NA)	[3]10,049	1,000	196	El Salvador	1,383	3,623	198	129
Belarus	(NA)	[3]19,545	2,486	557	Haiti	(NA)	7,309	1,074	537
Georgia	(NA)	[3]1,834	425	100	Nicaragua	5,590	21,252	666	316
Kazakhstan . . .	(NA)	[3]2,823	612	152	South America [1] . .	1,976	3,025	890	712
Moldova	(NA)	[3]9,300	1,043	272	Peru	(NA)	1,285	489	338
Russia	(NA)	[3]44,367	6,985	2,225	Africa [1]	22,149	34,224	7,651	4,225
Tajikistan	(NA)	[3]2,191	239	24	Ethiopia	18,542	15,849	1,056	507
Ukraine	(NA)	[3]81,263	12,137	3,641	Liberia	(NA)	2,712	505	225
Uzbekistan . . .	(NA)	[3]14,638	2,885	292	Somalia	(NA)	7,864	3,607	2,270
Yugoslavia	324	[3]13,271	7,597	5,312	Sudan	(NA)	3,422	1,119	287
Asia [1]	712,092	286,125	30,835	11,743	Other	51	189	89	2,545
Afghanistan . . .	22,946	9,065	356	137					

NA Not available. [1] Includes other countries, not shown separately. [2] Includes other republics and unknown republics, not shown separately. [3] Covers years 1992-1996. [4] Includes Taiwan.

Source: U.S. Immigration and Naturalization Service, *Statistical Yearbook,* annual; and releases.

No. 9. Immigrants Admitted by State and Leading Country of Birth: 1998

[**For year ending September 30.** For definition of immigrants, see text of this section]

State and other area	Total [1]	Mexico	China	India	Philippines	Dominican Republic	Vietnam	Cuba	Jamaica
Total	660,477	131,575	36,884	36,482	34,466	20,387	17,649	17,375	15,146
Alabama...........	1,608	178	117	165	85	2	51	29	15
Alaska	1,008	105	56	14	254	32	13	1	1
Arizona...........	6,211	3,209	253	230	220	7	96	7	7
Arkansas	914	305	46	59	42	2	38	3	-
California	170,126	62,113	12,582	7,177	16,202	72	6,519	289	186
Colorado...........	6,513	2,293	317	218	143	10	287	27	6
Connecticut.........	7,780	272	304	478	181	186	145	43	856
Delaware	1,063	135	79	141	26	11	23	8	28
District of Columbia	2,377	42	112	36	80	46	111	4	83
Florida	59,965	2,788	628	1,079	837	1,483	437	14,265	4,795
Georgia	10,445	1,630	435	882	163	44	592	110	211
Hawaii	5,465	75	482	16	3,140	2	101	-	3
Idaho.............	1,504	984	63	29	25	4	37	1	-
Illinois	33,163	10,127	1,357	3,446	1,350	67	306	98	131
Indiana............	3,981	904	208	375	117	9	78	20	25
Iowa	1,655	366	78	129	56	4	218	1	1
Kansas............	3,184	1,357	91	184	78	4	279	8	6
Kentucky	2,017	141	72	119	50	5	195	243	7
Louisiana	2,193	132	94	129	70	32	201	83	4
Maine.............	709	9	80	41	9	5	23	8	9
Maryland	15,561	364	697	1,108	625	137	251	44	545
Massachusetts........	15,869	105	1,355	958	179	1,138	443	40	340
Michigan...........	13,943	1,055	557	1,484	330	72	206	124	93
Minnesota..........	6,981	536	270	455	156	10	328	14	34
Mississippi	701	56	69	94	64	1	31	27	4
Missouri	3,588	491	197	271	139	7	184	23	16
Montana	299	21	42	8	17	-	6	-	-
Nebraska	1,267	542	52	88	36	2	71	3	1
Nevada	6,106	2,881	231	145	712	14	95	195	9
New Hampshire.......	1,010	28	73	91	56	28	39	3	8
New Jersey.........	35,091	772	1,318	4,284	1,648	2,478	271	437	1,037
New Mexico	2,199	1,359	76	116	32	1	43	59	4
New York	96,559	1,616	8,850	4,017	1,490	10,719	646	322	5,874
North Carolina........	6,415	880	318	618	151	33	310	78	40
North Dakota.........	472	12	9	41	9	2	16	18	-
Ohio	7,697	311	493	900	221	32	263	18	51
Oklahoma...........	2,273	812	96	204	60	2	131	3	5
Oregon............	5,909	1,879	411	239	165	1	365	81	8
Pennsylvania........	11,942	625	938	1,127	265	245	586	78	349
Rhode Island........	1,976	27	73	62	38	284	15	1	6
South Carolina.......	2,125	259	96	182	96	2	63	4	11
South Dakota	356	36	13	8	19	-	6	13	1
Tennessee	2,806	300	148	291	60	9	118	43	19
Texas.............	44,428	22,956	1,159	2,663	851	97	1,576	218	108
Utah	3,360	1,035	120	101	72	5	133	17	6
Vermont	513	9	30	53	6	4	13	1	2
Virginia............	15,686	541	523	910	921	31	686	60	117
Washington.........	16,920	4,129	843	599	1,159	5	940	47	27
West Virginia........	375	10	23	65	20	-	2	5	4
Wisconsin	3,724	680	234	314	106	5	50	4	44
Wyoming	159	42	10	15	7	-	2	-	-
Guam	1,835	1	54	10	1,507	-	9	-	-
Northern Mariana Islands	103	-	10	1	76	-	-	-	-
Puerto Rico..........	3,251	39	36	1	1	2,647	1	147	-
Virgin Islands........	979	-	5	12	6	349	-	-	9
Armed Services posts ...	88	1	-	-	38	-	-	-	-
Other.............	6,030	-	1	-	-	-	-	-	-

- Represents zero.   [1] Includes other countries, not shown separately.

Source: U.S. Immigration and Naturalization Service, *Statistical Yearbook,* annual.

Population 11

No. 10. Resident Population—Selected Characteristics, 1790 to 1999, and Projections, 2000 to 2050

[In thousands (3,172 represents 3,172,000)]

Date	Sex		Race					
					Other			
						American Indian, Eskimo, Aleut	Asian, Pacific Islander	Hispanic origin [1]
	Male	Female	White	Black	Total			
1790 (Aug. 2) [2]	(NA)	(NA)	3,172	757	(NA)	(NA)	(NA)	(NA)
1800 (Aug. 4) [2]	(NA)	(NA)	4,306	1,002	(NA)	(NA)	(NA)	(NA)
1850 (June 1) [2]	11,838	11,354	19,553	3,639	(NA)	(NA)	(NA)	(NA)
1900 (June 1) [2]	38,816	37,178	66,809	8,834	351	(NA)	(NA)	(NA)
1910 (Apr. 15) [2]	47,332	44,640	81,732	9,828	413	(NA)	(NA)	(NA)
1920 (Jan. 1) [2]	53,900	51,810	94,821	10,463	427	(NA)	(NA)	(NA)
1930 (Apr. 1) [2]	62,137	60,638	110,287	11,891	597	(NA)	(NA)	(NA)
1940 (Apr. 1) [2]	66,062	65,608	118,215	12,866	589	(NA)	(NA)	(NA)
1950 (Apr. 1) [2] .	74,833	75,864	134,942	15,042	713	(NA)	(NA)	(NA)
1950 (Apr. 1)	75,187	76,139	135,150	15,045	1,131	(NA)	(NA)	(NA)
1960 (Apr. 1)	88,331	90,992	158,832	18,872	1,620	(NA)	(NA)	(NA)
1970 (Apr. 1) [3]	98,926	104,309	178,098	22,581	2,557	(NA)	(NA)	(NA)
1980 (Apr. 1) [4 5]	110,053	116,493	194,713	26,683	5,150	1,420	3,729	14,609
1990 (Apr. 1) [4 6]	121,284	127,507	208,741	30,517	9,534	2,067	7,467	22,379
1991 (July 1) [7]	122,956	129,197	210,975	31,137	10,041	2,112	7,929	23,391
1992 (July 1) [7]	124,424	130,606	212,874	31,683	10,473	2,149	8,324	24,283
1993 (July 1) [7]	125,788	131,995	214,691	32,195	10,897	2,187	8,710	25,222
1994 (July 1) [7]	127,049	133,278	216,379	32,672	11,276	2,222	9,054	26,160
1995 (July 1) [7]	128,294	134,510	218,023	33,116	11,664	2,256	9,408	27,107
1996 (July 1) [7]	129,504	135,724	219,636	33,537	12,055	2,290	9,765	28,099
1997 (July 1) [7]	130,783	137,001	221,333	33,989	12,461	2,326	10,135	29,182
1998 (July 1) [7]	132,030	138,218	222,980	34,427	12,840	2,361	10,479	30,252
1999 (July 1) [7]	133,277	139,414	224,611	34,862	13,217	2,397	10,820	31,337
2000 (July 1) [8]	134,554	140,752	226,266	35,332	13,708	2,433	11,275	32,479
2005 (July 1) [8]	140,698	147,018	234,221	37,619	15,874	2,625	13,251	38,189
2010 (July 1) [8]	146,679	153,183	241,770	39,982	18,109	2,821	15,289	43,688
2015 (July 1) [8]	152,744	159,524	249,468	42,385	20,415	3,016	17,399	49,255
2020 (July 1) [8]	158,856	166,071	257,394	44,736	22,796	3,207	19,589	55,156
2025 (July 1) [8]	165,009	172,806	265,306	47,089	25,419	3,399	22,020	61,433
2050 (July 1) [8]	197,047	206,640	302,453	59,239	41,994	4,405	37,589	98,229

NA Not available. [1] Persons of Hispanic origin may be of any race. [2] Excludes Alaska and Hawaii. [3] The revised 1970 resident population count is 203,302,031; which incorporates changes due to errors found after tabulations were completed. The race and sex data shown here reflect the official 1970 census count. [4] The race data shown have been modified; see text of this section for explanation. [5] See footnote 4, Table 1. [6] The April 1, 1990, estimates base (248,790,925) includes count resolution corrections processed through August 1997. It generally does not include adjustments for census coverage errors. However, it includes adjustments estimated for the 1995 Test Census in various localities in California, New Jersey, and Louisiana; and the 1999 census dress rehearsals in localities in California and Wisconsin. These adjustments amounted to a total of 81,052 persons. [7] Estimated. [8] Middle series projection; for assumptions, see Table 3.

No. 11. Resident Population Characteristics—Percent Distribution and Median Age, 1850 to 1999, and Projections, 2000 to 2050

[In percent, except as indicated. For definition of median, see Guide to Tabular Presentation]

Date	Sex		Race					Median age (years)
	Male	Female	White	Black	American Indian, Eskimo, Aleut	Asian and Pacific Islander	Hispanic origin [1]	
1850 (June 1) [2]	51.0	49.0	84.3	15.7	(NA)	(NA)	(NA)	18.9
1900 (June 1) [2]	51.1	48.9	87.9	11.6	(NA)	(NA)	(NA)	22.9
1910 (Apr. 15) [2]	51.5	48.5	88.9	10.7	(NA)	(NA)	(NA)	24.1
1920 (Jan. 1) [2]	51.0	49.0	89.7	9.9	(NA)	(NA)	(NA)	25.3
1930 (Apr. 1) [2]	50.6	49.4	89.8	9.7	(NA)	(NA)	(NA)	26.4
1940 (Apr. 1) [2]	50.2	49.8	89.8	9.8	(NA)	(NA)	(NA)	29.0
1950 (Apr. 1)	49.7	50.3	89.3	9.9	(NA)	(NA)	(NA)	30.2
1960 (Apr. 1)	49.3	50.7	88.6	10.5	(NA)	(NA)	(NA)	29.5
1970 (Apr. 1)	48.7	51.3	87.6	11.1	(NA)	(NA)	(NA)	28.0
1980 (Apr. 1) [3 4]	48.6	51.4	85.9	11.8	0.6	1.6	6.4	30.0
1990 (Apr. 1) [3 5]	48.7	51.3	83.9	12.3	0.8	3.0	9.0	32.8
1995 (July 1) [6]	48.8	51.2	83.0	12.6	0.9	3.6	10.3	34.3
1999 (July 1) [6]	48.9	51.1	82.4	12.8	0.9	4.0	11.5	35.5
2000 (July 1) [7]	48.9	51.1	82.2	12.8	0.9	4.1	11.8	35.8
2025 (July 1) [7]	48.8	51.2	78.5	13.9	1.0	6.5	18.2	38.5
2050 (July 1) [7]	48.8	51.2	74.9	14.7	1.1	9.3	24.3	38.8

NA Not available. [1] Persons of Hispanic origin may be of any race. [2] Excludes Alaska and Hawaii. [3] The race data shown have been modified; see text of this section for explanation. [4] See footnote 4, Table 1. [5] See footnote 6, Table 10. [6] Estimated. [7] Middle series projection; for assumptions, see Table 3.

Source of Tables 10 and 11: U.S. Census Bureau, U.S. Census of Population: 1940, Vol. II, Part 1, and Vol. IV, Part 1; 1950, Vol. II, Part 1; 1960, Vol. I, Part 1; 1970, Vol. I, Part B; Current Population Reports, P25-1095; "Resident Population Estimates of the United States by Sex, Race, and Hispanic Origin: April 1, 1990, to July 1, 1999"; published 24 May 2000; <http://www.census.gov/population/estimates/nation/intfile3-1.txt>; and "National Population Projections-Summary Tables"; published 13 January 2000; <http://www.census.gov/population/www/projections/natsum-T3.html>.

12 Population

No. 12. Resident Population by Age and Sex: 1980 to 1999

[In thousands, except as indicated (226,546 represents 226,546,000). 1980 and 1990 data are enumerated population as of April 1; data for other years are estimated population as of July 1. Excludes Armed Forces overseas. For definition of median, see Guide to Tabular Presentation]

Year and sex	Total, all years	Under 5 years	5-9 years	10-14 years	15-19 years	20-24 years	25-29 years	30-34 years	35-39 years	40-44 years	45-49 years	50-54 years	55-59 years	60-64 years	65-74 years	75-84 years	85 years and over	5-13 years	14-17 years	18-24 years	Median age (yr.)
1980, total [1]	**226,546**	**16,348**	**16,700**	**18,242**	**21,168**	**21,319**	**19,521**	**17,561**	**13,965**	**11,669**	**11,090**	**11,710**	**11,615**	**10,088**	**15,581**	**7,729**	**2,240**	**31,159**	**16,247**	**30,022**	**30.0**
Male	110,053	8,362	8,539	9,316	10,755	10,663	9,705	8,677	6,862	5,708	5,388	5,621	5,482	4,670	6,757	2,867	682	15,923	8,298	15,054	28.8
Female	116,493	7,986	8,161	8,926	10,413	10,655	9,816	8,884	7,104	5,961	5,702	6,089	6,133	5,418	8,824	4,862	1,559	15,237	7,950	14,969	31.3
1981, total	229,466	16,893	16,060	18,300	20,541	21,663	20,169	18,731	14,366	12,028	10,985	11,595	11,554	10,359	15,890	7,982	2,349	30,711	15,609	30,245	30.3
1982, total	231,664	17,228	15,958	18,145	19,962	21,682	20,704	18,714	15,566	12,464	11,011	11,414	11,463	10,567	16,147	8,203	2,437	30,528	15,507	30,162	30.5
1983, total	233,792	17,547	16,053	17,869	19,388	21,632	21,141	19,067	16,117	13,150	11,201	11,155	11,457	10,655	16,414	8,429	2,518	30,279	14,740	29,922	30.8
1984, total	235,825	17,695	16,053	17,450	18,931	21,529	21,459	19,503	16,867	13,636	11,606	10,957	11,352	10,803	16,626	8,656	2,595	30,062	14,725	29,492	31.1
1985, total	237,924	17,842	16,665	17,027	18,727	21,265	21,671	20,025	17,604	14,087	11,878	10,781	11,229	10,906	16,858	8,890	2,667	29,893	14,888	28,902	31.4
1986, total	240,133	17,963	17,098	16,474	18,813	20,744	21,893	20,479	18,611	14,398	12,294	10,854	11,135	10,859	17,137	9,129	2,742	30,078	14,824	28,227	31.7
1987, total	242,289	18,052	17,430	16,377	18,698	20,192	21,857	20,984	18,619	15,608	12,954	10,802	10,968	10,783	17,426	9,376	2,823	30,502	14,502	27,694	32.0
1988, total	244,499	18,195	17,759	16,496	18,496	19,655	21,739	21,391	18,993	16,188	13,421	10,995	10,722	10,791	17,626	9,612	2,885	31,028	14,023	27,356	32.2
1989, total	246,819	18,508	17,917	16,797	18,133	19,258	21,560	21,676	19,455	16,960	13,611	11,212	10,534	10,707	17,864	9,850	2,968	31,413	13,536	27,156	32.6
1990, total [2]	**248,791**	**18,765**	**18,042**	**17,067**	**17,893**	**19,143**	**21,336**	**21,838**	**19,851**	**17,593**	**13,747**	**11,315**	**10,489**	**10,627**	**18,048**	**10,014**	**3,022**	**31,839**	**13,345**	**26,961**	**32.8**
Male	121,284	9,603	9,236	8,742	9,178	9,749	10,708	10,866	9,837	8,679	6,741	5,494	5,009	4,947	7,908	3,745	842	16,301	6,860	13,744	31.6
Female	127,507	9,162	8,806	8,325	8,714	9,394	10,629	10,973	10,014	8,914	7,006	5,821	5,480	5,679	10,140	6,268	2,180	15,538	6,485	13,217	34.0
1991, total	252,153	19,189	18,205	17,679	17,235	19,156	20,713	22,157	20,530	18,761	14,099	11,648	10,422	10,581	18,271	10,319	3,189	32,470	13,452	26,352	33.1
1992, total	255,030	19,492	18,293	18,102	17,180	19,047	20,140	22,240	21,098	18,807	15,359	12,055	10,483	10,438	18,442	10,538	3,315	32,943	13,703	25,976	33.4
1993, total	257,783	19,674	18,442	18,508	17,375	18,785	19,570	22,227	21,605	19,209	15,931	12,728	10,678	10,236	18,629	10,738	3,446	33,382	13,989	25,740	33.7
1994, total	260,327	19,700	18,752	18,716	17,743	18,389	19,107	22,133	21,978	19,716	16,678	13,195	10,931	10,077	18,703	10,946	3,562	33,713	14,492	25,397	34.1
1995, total	262,803	19,532	19,096	18,853	18,203	17,982	18,905	21,825	22,296	20,259	17,458	13,642	11,086	10,046	18,757	11,178	3,685	34,195	14,828	25,112	34.3
1996, total	265,229	19,292	19,439	19,004	18,708	17,508	18,933	21,313	22,553	20,812	18,430	13,928	11,356	9,997	18,690	11,466	3,800	34,604	15,213	24,843	34.7
1997, total	267,784	19,099	19,754	19,097	19,146	17,488	18,820	20,739	22,636	21,378	18,467	15,158	11,755	10,061	18,528	11,744	3,913	35,005	15,499	24,980	34.9
1998, total	270,248	18,989	19,929	19,242	19,542	17,678	18,575	20,168	22,615	21,883	18,853	15,722	12,403	10,263	18,390	11,947	4,050	35,396	15,518	25,476	35.2
1999, total	**272,691**	**18,942**	**19,947**	**19,548**	**19,748**	**18,026**	**18,209**	**19,727**	**22,545**	**22,268**	**19,356**	**16,446**	**12,875**	**10,514**	**18,218**	**12,147**	**4,175**	**35,603**	**15,654**	**26,011**	**35.5**
Male	133,277	9,683	10,208	10,012	10,151	9,183	9,055	9,771	11,216	11,039	9,501	7,998	6,183	4,968	8,199	4,871	1,241	18,223	8,055	13,276	34.3
Female	139,414	9,259	9,739	9,537	9,597	8,843	9,154	9,956	11,329	11,229	9,856	8,448	6,693	5,546	10,020	7,275	2,936	17,379	7,600	12,736	36.6
Percent:																					
1980 [1]	100.0	7.2	7.4	8.1	9.3	9.4	8.6	7.8	6.2	5.2	4.9	5.2	5.1	4.5	6.9	3.4	1.0	13.8	7.2	13.3	(X)
1990 [2]	100.0	7.5	7.3	6.9	7.2	7.7	8.6	8.8	8.0	7.1	5.5	4.5	4.2	4.3	7.3	4.0	1.2	12.8	5.4	10.8	(X)
1999	100.0	6.9	7.3	7.2	7.2	6.6	6.7	7.2	8.3	8.2	7.1	6.0	4.7	3.9	6.7	4.5	1.5	13.1	5.7	9.5	(X)
Male	100.0	7.3	7.7	7.5	7.6	6.9	6.8	7.3	8.4	8.3	7.1	6.0	4.6	3.7	6.2	3.7	0.9	13.7	6.0	10.0	(X)
Female	100.0	6.6	7.0	6.8	6.9	6.3	6.6	7.1	8.1	8.1	7.1	6.1	4.8	4.0	7.2	5.2	2.1	12.5	5.5	9.1	(X)

X Not applicable. [1] Total population count has been revised since the 1980 census counts. See text of this section for explanation. The April 1, 1990, estimates base (248,790,925) includes count resolution corrections processed through August 1997. It generally does not include adjustments for census coverage errors. However, it includes adjustments estimated for the 1995 Test Census in various localities in California, New Jersey, and Louisiana; and the 1998 census dress rehearsals in localities in California and Wisconsin. These adjustments amounted to a total of 81,052 persons. [2] The data shown have been modified from the official 1990 census counts.

Source: U.S. Census Bureau, Current Population Reports, P25-1095; and "Resident Population Estimates of the United States by Age and Sex: April 1, 1990, to July 1, 1999; with short-term projections to April 1, 2000"; published 24 May 2000; <http://www.census.gov/population/estimates/nation/intfile2-1.txt>.

No. 13. Resident Population by Sex and Age: 1999

[In thousands, except as indicated (272,691 represents 272,691,000). As of **July 1**. For derivation of estimates, see text of this section]

Age	Total	Male	Female	Age	Total	Male	Female
Total	**272,691**	**133,277**	**139,414**	50 to 54 yrs. old	16,446	7,998	8,448
				50 yrs. old	3,649	1,781	1,868
Under 5 yrs. old	18,942	9,683	9,259	51 yrs. old	3,502	1,707	1,795
Under 1 yr. old	3,820	1,952	1,868	52 yrs. old	3,728	1,818	1,910
1 yr. old	3,757	1,920	1,837	53 yrs. old	2,732	1,322	1,410
2 yrs. old	3,758	1,921	1,837	54 yrs. old	2,835	1,371	1,464
3 yrs. old	3,755	1,920	1,835	55 to 59 yrs. old	12,875	6,183	6,693
4 yrs. old	3,853	1,970	1,882	55 yrs. old	2,750	1,323	1,427
5 to 9 yrs. old	19,947	10,208	9,739	56 yrs. old	2,935	1,413	1,522
5 yrs. old	3,895	1,994	1,901	57 yrs. old	2,581	1,238	1,343
6 yrs. old	3,944	2,020	1,924	58 yrs. old	2,285	1,094	1,191
7 yrs. old	4,030	2,059	1,972	59 yrs. old	2,325	1,115	1,210
8 yrs. old	3,909	1,999	1,910	60 to 64 yrs. old	10,514	4,968	5,546
9 yrs. old	4,170	2,137	2,033	60 yrs. old	2,232	1,054	1,177
10 to 14 yrs. old	19,548	10,012	9,537	61 yrs. old	2,147	1,020	1,127
10 yrs. old	4,036	2,070	1,966	62 yrs. old	2,029	958	1,071
11 yrs. old	3,896	1,994	1,902	63 yrs. old	2,022	958	1,065
12 yrs. old	3,846	1,967	1,879	64 yrs. old	2,084	977	1,106
13 yrs. old	3,878	1,985	1,893	65 to 69 yrs. old	9,447	4,337	5,111
14 yrs. old	3,892	1,996	1,896	65 yrs. old	1,909	889	1,021
15 to 19 yrs. old	19,748	10,151	9,597	66 yrs. old	1,879	869	1,010
15 yrs. old	3,820	1,962	1,858	67 yrs. old	1,877	861	1,015
16 yrs. old	3,924	2,022	1,902	68 yrs. old	1,880	856	1,025
17 yrs. old	4,017	2,074	1,943	69 yrs. old	1,902	862	1,040
18 yrs. old	3,875	1,989	1,886	70 to 74 yrs. old	8,771	3,862	4,909
19 yrs. old	4,111	2,104	2,007	70 yrs. old	1,841	828	1,014
				71 yrs. old	1,843	822	1,021
20 to 24 yrs. old	18,026	9,183	8,843	72 yrs. old	1,771	783	988
20 yrs. old	3,898	1,999	1,900	73 yrs. old	1,661	719	942
21 yrs. old	3,705	1,897	1,808	74 yrs. old	1,656	710	945
22 yrs. old	3,564	1,817	1,746	75 to 79 yrs. old	7,329	3,057	4,272
23 yrs. old	3,378	1,714	1,664	75 yrs. old	1,600	681	919
24 yrs. old	3,481	1,756	1,724	76 yrs. old	1,510	639	871
25 to 29 yrs. old	18,209	9,055	9,154	77 yrs. old	1,488	622	866
25 yrs. old	3,369	1,690	1,679	78 yrs. old	1,441	593	848
26 yrs. old	3,424	1,704	1,720	79 yrs. old	1,291	522	769
27 yrs. old	3,645	1,813	1,832	80 to 84 yrs. old	4,817	1,814	3,003
28 yrs. old	3,698	1,829	1,869	80 yrs. old	1,142	449	693
29 yrs. old	4,074	2,021	2,053	81 yrs. old	1,038	398	640
30 to 34 yrs. old	19,727	9,771	9,956	82 yrs. old	949	358	591
30 yrs. old	3,879	1,921	1,959	83 yrs. old	883	323	560
31 yrs. old	3,748	1,856	1,893	84 yrs. old	804	285	519
32 yrs. old	3,844	1,902	1,943				
33 yrs. old	3,936	1,943	1,993	85 to 89 yrs. old	2,625	847	1,778
34 yrs. old	4,320	2,150	2,169	85 yrs. old	675	232	443
35 to 39 yrs. old	22,545	11,216	11,329	86 yrs. old	603	199	404
35 yrs. old	4,441	2,208	2,233	87 yrs. old	516	166	350
36 yrs. old	4,420	2,196	2,224	88 yrs. old	448	137	311
37 yrs. old	4,554	2,265	2,289	89 yrs. old	384	113	270
38 yrs. old	4,307	2,137	2,170	90 to 94 yrs. old	1,148	307	841
39 yrs. old	4,823	2,410	2,413	90 yrs. old	325	93	232
				91 yrs. old	274	75	199
40 to 44 yrs. old	22,268	11,039	11,229	92 yrs. old	221	58	163
40 yrs. old	4,612	2,291	2,322	93 yrs. old	179	45	134
41 yrs. old	4,516	2,239	2,278	94 yrs. old	149	36	113
42 yrs. old	4,486	2,225	2,261				
43 yrs. old	4,270	2,103	2,166	95 to 99 yrs. old	343	76	268
44 yrs. old	4,383	2,181	2,202	95 yrs. old	114	27	88
45 to 49 yrs. old	19,356	9,501	9,856	96 yrs. old	86	19	67
45 yrs. old	4,165	2,055	2,110	97 yrs. old	61	13	48
46 yrs. old	3,931	1,931	1,999	98 yrs. old	49	10	39
47 yrs. old	3,887	1,904	1,984	99 yrs. old	33	6	26
48 yrs. old	3,532	1,724	1,808	100 yrs. old and over. . .	59	11	49
49 yrs. old	3,841	1,887	1,955	Median age (yr.)	35.5	34.3	36.6

Source: U.S. Census Bureau, "Monthly Postcensal Resident Population, by single year of age, sex, race, and Hispanic origin"; published June 2000; <http://www.census.gov/population/www/estimates/nat90s1.html>.

No. 14. Resident Population Projections by Sex and Age: 2000 to 2050

[In thousands, except as indicated (275,306 represents 275,306,000). As of July. Data shown are for middle series; for assumptions, see Table 3]

Age	2000			2005			2010			2015	2020	2025	2030	2035	2040	2045	2050	Percent distribution		
	Total	Male	Female	Total	Male	Female	Total	Male	Female									2000	2005	2010
Total	275,306	134,554	140,752	287,716	140,698	147,018	299,862	146,679	153,183	312,268	324,927	337,815	351,070	364,319	377,350	390,398	403,687	100.0	100.0	100.0
Under 5 years	18,865	9,639	9,227	19,212	9,815	9,397	20,099	10,272	9,827	21,179	21,951	22,551	23,183	24,016	25,014	26,013	26,914	6.9	6.7	6.7
5 to 9 years	19,781	10,122	9,659	19,122	9,774	9,348	19,438	9,936	9,502	20,321	21,403	22,197	22,845	23,509	24,358	25,364	26,366	7.2	6.6	6.6
10 to 14 years	19,908	10,196	9,712	20,634	10,564	10,069	19,908	10,183	9,724	20,229	21,146	22,289	23,166	23,870	24,571	25,459	26,503	7.2	7.2	6.6
15 to 19 years	19,897	10,227	9,670	20,990	10,788	10,202	21,668	11,132	10,536	20,892	21,224	22,203	23,449	24,380	25,100	25,813	26,715	7.2	7.3	7.2
20 to 24 years	18,518	9,433	9,085	20,159	10,269	9,889	21,151	10,776	10,375	21,748	21,224	21,411	22,481	23,748	24,660	25,360	26,054	6.7	7.0	7.0
25 to 29 years	17,861	8,876	8,984	18,351	9,144	9,207	19,849	9,901	9,948	20,765	21,384	21,020	21,257	22,333	23,552	24,430	25,104	6.5	6.4	6.3
30 to 34 years	19,580	9,682	9,898	18,582	9,146	9,436	19,002	9,385	9,617	20,484	21,410	20,761	21,615	22,481	23,660	24,475	25,354	7.1	6.5	6.3
35 to 39 years	22,276	11,071	11,205	20,082	9,927	10,155	19,039	9,380	9,659	19,442	20,938	21,926	21,308	22,281	22,845	23,928	25,152	8.1	7.0	6.5
40 to 44 years	22,618	11,218	11,400	22,634	11,222	11,412	20,404	10,069	10,334	19,346	19,804	21,308	22,728	22,112	22,953	23,349	24,436	8.2	7.9	6.3
45 to 49 years	19,901	9,776	10,125	22,230	10,965	11,264	22,227	10,967	11,260	20,057	19,034	19,473	22,374	22,112	22,522	22,522	23,072	7.2	7.7	5.8
50 to 54 years	17,265	8,398	8,867	19,661	9,578	10,082	21,934	10,739	11,195	21,929	19,717	18,818	21,031	20,884	21,966	22,798	22,373	6.3	6.8	5.7
55 to 59 years	13,324	6,397	6,927	16,842	8,101	8,741	19,177	9,248	9,929	21,400	21,412	19,366	18,853	18,027	20,543	21,622	22,445	4.8	5.9	5.7
60 to 64 years	10,677	5,046	5,631	12,848	6,086	6,762	16,252	7,725	8,528	18,519	20,696	20,759	18,452	18,104	18,575	20,123	21,199	3.9	4.5	6.1
65 to 69 years	9,436	4,334	5,102	10,086	4,661	5,425	12,159	5,640	6,520	15,410	17,598	19,717	19,844	18,068	17,349	17,962	19,477	3.4	3.5	5.8
70 to 74 years	8,753	3,876	4,877	8,375	3,757	4,618	8,995	4,066	4,929	10,897	13,864	15,886	17,878	15,895	16,555	15,912	16,537	3.2	2.9	4.7
75 to 79 years	7,422	3,103	4,319	7,429	3,172	4,257	7,175	3,110	4,065	7,772	9,484	12,159	14,029	11,220	16,170	14,908	14,407	2.7	2.6	3.6
80 to 84 years	4,913	1,866	3,047	5,514	2,157	3,356	5,600	2,247	3,353	5,484	6,024	7,439	9,638	6,678	12,820	13,140	12,225	1.8	1.9	2.2
85 to 89 years	2,705	883	1,821	3,028	1,046	1,982	3,476	1,242	2,234	3,612	3,611	4,045	5,077	3,155	7,884	8,766	9,463	1.0	1.1	1.2
90 to 94 years	1,179	319	861	1,402	404	998	1,625	497	1,128	1,930	2,074	2,135	2,457	1,213	4,243	5,115	6,030	0.4	0.5	0.6
95 to 99 years	364	81	283	442	104	338	556	139	417	678	844	948	1,015	441	1,606	2,226	2,764	0.1	0.2	0.3
100 years and over	65	12	53	96	18	77	129	26	103	177	235	313	381	441	551	757	1,095	(Z)	(Z)	0.1
5 to 13 years	35,775	18,309	17,465	35,475	18,144	17,331	35,321	18,056	17,265	36,497	38,361	40,054	41,377	42,592	44,004	45,740	47,582	13.0	12.3	11.9
14 to 17 years	15,734	8,096	7,637	16,931	8,709	8,222	16,681	8,583	8,098	16,437	16,839	17,741	18,653	19,325	19,881	20,477	21,252	5.7	5.9	5.3
18 to 24 years	26,596	13,572	13,023	28,498	14,543	13,956	30,163	15,388	14,774	30,254	29,593	30,305	31,910	33,590	34,803	35,779	36,804	9.7	9.9	9.0
16 years and over	212,810	102,573	110,237	224,447	108,336	116,111	236,301	114,175	122,126	246,455	256,200	266,342	277,857	288,108	298,450	308,456	318,601	77.3	78.0	78.8
18 years and over	204,932	98,509	106,423	216,098	104,030	112,068	227,761	109,768	117,993	238,155	247,776	257,469	267,857	278,386	288,450	298,168	307,938	74.4	75.1	76.2
10 to 49 years	160,558	80,479	80,079	163,661	82,026	81,635	163,247	81,794	81,453	162,961	165,929	171,482	178,100	184,120	189,717	195,335	202,390	58.3	56.9	50.8
16 to 64 years	177,974	88,100	89,874	188,100	93,017	95,059	196,586	97,208	99,377	200,496	202,498	203,701	206,903	213,334	221,276	229,314	236,602	64.6	65.4	60.3
55 years and over	58,836	25,916	32,920	66,060	29,505	36,555	75,145	33,939	41,206	85,878	95,841	102,766	107,624	111,790	116,295	120,888	125,643	21.4	23.0	30.4
65 years and over	34,835	14,473	20,362	36,370	15,318	21,052	39,715	16,966	22,749	45,959	53,733	62,641	70,319	74,774	77,177	79,142	81,999	12.7	12.6	18.5
85 years and over	4,312	1,294	3,018	4,968	1,572	3,396	5,786	1,904	3,882	6,396	6,763	7,441	8,931	11,486	14,284	17,220	19,352	1.6	1.7	2.2
Median age (years)	35.8	34.6	36.9	36.7	35.4	37.9	37.4	36.0	38.8	37.6	38.1	38.5	38.9	39.1	39.0	38.8	38.8	(X)	(X)	(X)

X Not applicable.   Z Less than 0.05 percent.

Source: U.S. Census Bureau, "National Population Projections-Summary Tables"; published 13 January 2000; <http://www.census.gov/population/www/projections/natsum-T3.html>.

Population   15

No. 15. Resident Population by Race, 1980 to 1999, and Projections, 2000 to 2050

[In thousands, except as indicated (226,546 represents 226,546,000). As of July, except as indicated. These data are consistent with the 1980 and 1990 decennial enumerations and have been modified from the official census counts; see text of this section for explanation]

Year	Total	White	Black	American Indian, Eskimo, Aleut	Asian, Pacific Islander
1980 (April) [1]	226,546	194,713	26,683	1,420	3,729
1981	229,466	196,635	27,133	1,483	4,214
1982	231,664	198,037	27,508	1,537	4,581
1983	233,792	199,420	27,867	1,596	4,909
1984	235,825	200,708	28,212	1,656	5,249
1985	237,924	202,031	28,569	1,718	5,606
1986	240,133	203,430	28,942	1,783	5,978
1987	242,289	204,770	29,325	1,851	6,343
1988	244,499	206,129	29,723	1,923	6,724
1989	246,819	207,540	30,143	2,001	7,134
1990 (April) [2]	248,791	208,741	30,517	2,067	7,467
1991	252,153	210,975	31,137	2,112	7,929
1992	255,030	212,874	31,683	2,149	8,324
1993	257,783	214,691	32,195	2,187	8,710
1994	260,327	216,379	32,672	2,222	9,054
1995	262,803	218,023	33,116	2,256	9,408
1996	265,229	219,636	33,537	2,290	9,765
1997	267,784	221,333	33,989	2,326	10,135
1998	270,248	222,980	34,427	2,361	10,479
1999	272,691	224,611	34,862	2,397	10,820
PROJECTIONS [3]					
2000	275,306	226,266	35,332	2,433	11,275
2005	287,716	234,221	37,619	2,625	13,251
2010	299,862	241,770	39,982	2,821	15,289
2015	312,268	249,468	42,385	3,016	17,399
2020	324,927	257,394	44,736	3,207	19,589
2025	337,815	265,306	47,089	3,399	22,020
2030	351,070	273,079	49,535	3,599	24,858
2040	377,350	287,787	54,462	4,006	31,095
2050	403,687	302,453	59,239	4,405	37,589
Percent distribution:					
2000	100.0	82.2	12.8	0.9	4.1
2005	100.0	81.4	13.1	0.9	4.6
2010	100.0	80.6	13.3	0.9	5.1
2015	100.0	79.9	13.6	1.0	5.6
2020	100.0	79.2	13.8	1.0	6.0
2025	100.0	78.5	13.9	1.0	6.5
2030	100.0	77.8	14.1	1.0	7.1
2040	100.0	76.3	14.4	1.1	8.2
2050	100.0	74.9	14.7	1.1	9.3
Percent change:					
2000-2010	8.9	6.9	13.2	16.0	35.6
2010-2020	8.5	6.5	12.7	14.9	31.3
2020-2030	8.4	6.5	11.9	13.7	28.1
2030-2040	8.2	6.3	11.1	12.7	26.6
2040-2050	8.0	6.1	10.7	12.2	26.9

[1] See footnote 4, Table 1.   [2] The April 1, 1990, estimates base (248,790,925) includes count resolution corrections processed through August 1997. It generally does not include adjustments for census coverage errors. However, it includes adjustments estimated for the 1995 Test Census in various localities in California, New Jersey, and Louisiana; and the 1999 census dress rehearsals in localities in California and Wisconsin. These adjustments amounted to a total of 81,052 persons.   [3] Based on middle series of assumptions. See footnote 1, Table 3.

Source: U.S. Census Bureau, *Current Population Reports*, P25-1095; "Annual Population Estimates by Sex, Race, and Hispanic Origin, selected years from 1990 to 2000"; published 26 May 2000; <http://www.census.gov/population/www/estimates/nation3.html>; and "(NP-T4) Projections of the Total Resident Population by 5-year Age Groups, Race, and Hispanic Origin with Special Age Categories: Middle Series, 1999 to 2100"; published 13 January 2000; <http://www.census.gov/population/www/projections/natsum-T3.html>.

No. 16. Resident Population by Hispanic-Origin Status, 1980 to 1999, and Projections, 2000 to 2050

[In thousands, except as indicated (226,546 represents 226,546,000). As of July, except as indicated. These data are consistent with the 1980 and 1990 decennial enumerations and have been modified from the official census counts; see text of this section for explanation]

Year	Total	Hispanic origin [1]	Not of Hispanic origin			
			White	Black	American Indian, Eskimo, Aleut	Asian, Pacific Islander
1980 (April) [2]	226,546	14,609	180,906	26,142	1,326	3,563
1981	229,466	15,560	181,974	26,532	1,377	4,022
1982	231,664	16,240	182,782	26,856	1,420	4,367
1983	233,792	16,935	183,561	27,159	1,466	4,671
1984	235,825	17,640	184,243	27,444	1,512	4,986
1985	237,924	18,368	184,945	27,738	1,558	5,315
1986	240,133	19,154	185,678	28,040	1,606	5,655
1987	242,289	19,946	186,353	28,351	1,654	5,985
1988	244,499	20,786	187,012	28,669	1,703	6,329
1989	246,819	21,648	187,713	29,005	1,755	6,698
1990 (April) [3]	248,791	22,379	188,315	29,304	1,797	6,996
1991	252,153	23,391	189,634	29,858	1,831	7,439
1992	255,030	24,283	190,726	30,346	1,858	7,817
1993	257,783	25,222	191,697	30,795	1,884	8,184
1994	260,327	26,160	192,538	31,210	1,909	8,511
1995	262,803	27,107	193,328	31,590	1,932	8,846
1996	265,229	28,099	194,037	31,951	1,956	9,186
1997	267,784	29,182	194,746	32,339	1,979	9,537
1998	270,248	30,252	195,414	32,718	2,002	9,863
1999	272,691	31,337	196,049	33,092	2,026	10,186
PROJECTIONS [4]						
2000	275,306	32,479	196,670	33,490	2,048	10,620
2005	287,716	38,189	199,414	35,446	2,171	12,497
2010	299,862	43,688	201,956	37,483	2,300	14,436
2015	312,268	49,255	204,590	39,551	2,428	16,444
2020	324,927	55,156	207,145	41,549	2,550	18,527
2025	337,815	61,433	209,340	43,528	2,668	20,846
2030	351,070	68,168	210,984	45,567	2,787	23,564
2040	377,350	82,692	212,475	49,618	3,023	29,543
2050	403,687	98,229	212,991	53,466	3,241	35,760
Percent distribution:						
2000	100.0	11.8	71.4	12.2	0.7	3.9
2005	100.0	13.3	69.3	12.3	0.8	4.3
2010	100.0	14.6	67.3	12.5	0.8	4.8
2015	100.0	15.8	65.5	12.7	0.8	5.3
2020	100.0	17.0	63.8	12.8	0.8	5.7
2025	100.0	18.2	62.0	12.9	0.8	6.2
2030	100.0	19.4	60.1	13.0	0.8	6.7
2040	100.0	21.9	56.3	13.1	0.8	7.8
2050	100.0	24.3	52.8	13.2	0.8	8.9
Percent change:						
2000-2010	8.9	34.5	2.7	11.9	12.3	35.9
2010-2020	8.5	29.0	2.6	11.6	11.8	31.6
2020-2030	8.4	26.3	2.6	10.8	10.9	28.3
2030-2040	8.2	24.7	2.3	10.1	9.9	26.8
2040-2050	8.0	23.6	1.9	9.7	9.3	27.2

[1] Persons of Hispanic origin may be of any race.   [2] See footnote 4, Table 1.   [3] The April 1, 1990, estimates base (248,790,925) includes count resolution corrections processed through August 1997. It generally does not include adjustments for census coverage errors. However, it includes adjustments estimated for the 1995 Test Census in various localities in California, New Jersey, and Louisiana; and the 1999 census dress rehearsals in localities in California and Wisconsin. These adjustments amounted to a total of 81,052 persons.   [4] Based on middle series of assumptions. See footnote 1, Table 3.

Source: U.S. Census Bureau, Current Population Reports, P25-1095; "Annual Population Estimates by Sex, Race, and Hispanic Origin, selected years from 1990 to 2000"; published 26 May 2000; <http://www.census.gov/population/www/estimates/nation3.html>; and "(NP-T4) Projections of the Total Resident Population by 5-year Age Groups, Race, and Hispanic Origin with Special Age Categories: Middle Series, 1999 to 2100"; published 13 January 2000; <http://www.census.gov/population/www/projections/natsum-T3.html>.

Population   17

No. 17. Resident Population by Race and Age, 1990 to 1999, and Projections, 2000 and 2010

[In thousands (208,741 represents 208,741,000), except as indicated. As of July 1, except 1990 as of April 1. For definition of median, see Guide to Tabular Presentation. Projections are based on middle series of assumptions; see footnote 1, Table 3]

Age group	White					Black					American Indian, Eskimo, Aleut					Asian, Pacific Islander				
	1990	1995	1999	2000, proj.	2010, proj.	1990	1995	1999	2000, proj.	2010, proj.	1990	1995	1999	2000, proj.	2010, proj.	1990	1995	1999	2000, proj.	2010, proj.
Total	208,741	218,023	224,611	226,266	241,770	30,517	33,116	34,862	35,332	39,982	2,067	2,256	2,397	2,433	2,821	7,467	9,408	10,820	11,275	15,289
Under 5 years	14,963	15,452	15,043	14,948	15,609	2,943	3,039	2,796	2,784	3,103	221	204	202	203	240	639	837	902	930	1,147
5 to 9 years	14,505	15,137	15,706	15,575	15,127	2,715	3,017	3,146	3,087	2,953	210	228	219	212	232	613	715	875	908	1,126
10 to 14 years	13,672	14,993	15,389	15,626	15,506	2,633	2,872	3,087	3,173	2,977	197	234	249	254	237	565	753	824	855	1,187
15 to 19 years	14,357	14,481	15,648	15,755	16,804	2,718	2,831	3,044	3,056	3,444	191	204	235	238	242	627	688	822	848	1,178
20 to 24 years	15,644	14,369	14,367	14,732	16,524	2,658	2,654	2,697	2,787	3,303	179	189	193	202	240	662	823	768	797	1,068
25 to 29 years	17,643	15,302	14,505	14,166	16,586	2,783	2,596	2,611	2,592	2,915	188	182	181	192	255	745	875	900	909	1,109
30 to 34 years	18,192	17,939	15,927	15,749	14,891	2,720	2,825	2,675	2,659	2,775	181	187	186	184	208	678	850	944	988	1,127
35 to 39 years	16,654	18,476	18,504	18,209	14,894	2,362	2,791	2,902	2,900	2,744	157	179	173	185	193	575	764	953	983	1,207
40 to 44 years	15,003	16,945	18,443	18,691	16,247	1,884	2,393	2,751	2,816	2,775	132	157	177	177	182	405	622	902	934	1,199
45 to 49 years	11,828	14,855	16,206	16,625	18,095	1,415	1,855	2,240	2,326	2,855	100	126	143	148	175	312	442	767	802	1,102
50 to 54 years	9,746	11,724	16,044	14,689	18,119	1,178	1,382	1,689	1,810	2,676	79	94	113	118	159	252	341	601	648	980
55 to 59 years	9,381	9,534	11,077	11,450	16,041	1,042	1,139	1,289	1,331	2,194	64	72	84	86	130	220	281	425	457	813
60 to 64 years	9,132	8,718	9,056	9,163	13,824	972	990	1,056	1,086	1,676	53	58	65	66	101	179	237	337	362	652
65 to 69 years	8,985	8,720	8,189	8,156	10,393	860	922	935	940	1,230	43	47	50	51	71	121	183	273	289	465
70 to 74 years	7,192	7,912	7,770	7,723	7,724	639	698	743	758	872	30	38	40	41	52	80	115	217	231	346
75 to 79 years	5,519	6,047	6,585	6,658	6,237	484	513	558	564	648	22	25	31	33	39	42	66	156	166	251
80 to 84 years	3,567	4,076	4,381	4,458	4,976	288	320	331	342	428	12	17	19	20	28	20	30	86	93	168
85 to 89 years	1,858	2,148	2,389	2,461	3,131	150	165	181	185	230	6	9	11	12	18	6	13	43	47	96
90 to 94 years	690	916	1,034	1,061	1,453	50	83	89	92	118	2	4	6	6	10	2	3	18	20	44
95 to 99 years	184	239	300	317	485	17	24	35	37	49	1	1	1	3	5	1	1	6	7	16
100 years and over	29	41	50	54	105	6	6	7	9	17	-	-	1	1	3	-	-	1	1	4
5 to 13 years	25,561	27,150	28,019	28,116	27,494	4,844	5,315	5,635	5,653	5,334	369	415	418	415	421	1,065	1,314	1,531	1,590	2,072
14 to 17 years	10,665	11,770	12,380	12,424	12,940	2,059	2,306	2,406	2,423	2,593	151	176	195	198	194	470	575	673	689	955
18 to 24 years	21,951	20,060	20,710	21,148	23,527	3,821	3,754	3,933	4,026	4,750	257	263	283	293	351	932	1,036	1,085	1,129	1,534
16 years and over	162,943	169,436	175,463	177,010	192,336	21,717	23,586	25,242	25,676	30,313	1,401	1,543	1,678	1,714	2,065	5,533	6,955	8,050	8,409	11,587
18 years and over	157,552	163,651	169,169	170,778	185,727	20,671	22,456	24,026	24,472	28,952	1,326	1,460	1,582	1,616	1,967	5,293	6,681	7,715	8,066	11,115
16 to 64 years	134,920	139,337	144,766	146,122	157,833	19,223	20,855	22,361	22,749	26,720	1,285	1,402	1,517	1,547	1,837	5,083	6,307	7,250	7,556	10,196
55 years and over	46,536	48,350	50,831	51,501	64,369	4,508	4,859	5,226	5,343	7,462	233	272	310	320	459	923	1,269	1,563	1,672	2,855
65 years and over	28,023	30,099	30,698	30,888	34,504	2,494	2,731	2,881	2,927	3,592	116	142	161	167	228	450	648	800	853	1,391
85 years and over	2,761	3,344	3,773	3,893	5,174	223	278	313	322	414	9	15	20	22	37	29	48	68	75	161
Median age (yrs)	33.7	35.4	36.6	36.9	38.8	27.9	29.2	30.1	30.3	32.3	26.0	26.8	27.6	27.8	29.3	29.4	30.7	31.7	32.0	33.7

- Represents or rounds to zero.

Source: U.S. Census Bureau, "Monthly Postcensal Resident Population, by single year of age, sex, race and Hispanic origin," published June 2000; <http://www.census.gov/population/www/estimates/nat9061.html>; "Annual Population Estimates by Sex, Race, and Hispanic origin, selected years from 1990 to 2000": published 26 May 2000; <http://www.census.gov/population/www/estimates/nation3.html>; and "Projections of the Total Resident Population by 5-year Age Groups, Race, and Hispanic Origin with Special Age Categories: Middle Series, 1999 to 2100": published 13 January 2000; <http://www.census.gov/population/www/projections/natsum-T3.html>.

No. 18. Resident Population by Hispanic-Origin Status and Age, 1990 to 1999, and Projections, 2000

[In thousands (22,379 represents 22,379,000), except as indicated. As of July 1, except 1990 as of April 1. For definition of median, see Guide to Tabular Presentation. Projections are based on middle series of assumptions; see footnote 1, Table 3]

Note: The White, Black, American Indian/Eskimo/Aleut, and Asian/Pacific Islander groups are all "Not of Hispanic origin."

Age group	Hispanic origin				White				Black				American Indian, Eskimo, Aleut				Asian, Pacific Islander			
	1990	1995	1999	2000 proj.	1990	1995	1999	2000 proj.	1990	1995	1999	2000 proj.	1990	1995	1999	2000 proj.	1990	1995	1999	2000 proj.
Total	22,379	27,107	31,337	32,479	188,315	193,328	196,049	196,670	29,304	31,590	33,092	33,490	1,797	1,932	2,026	2,048	6,996	8,846	10,186	10,620
Under 5 years	2,469	3,206	3,467	3,549	12,722	12,523	11,871	11,699	2,802	2,859	2,603	2,588	186	171	165	165	587	773	836	865
5 to 9 years	2,180	2,609	3,243	3,347	12,516	12,774	12,749	12,520	2,600	2,863	2,961	2,897	179	191	184	177	567	659	810	840
10 to 14 years	1,991	2,417	2,739	2,874	11,855	12,801	12,913	13,030	2,528	2,737	2,926	3,002	170	198	207	211	523	699	763	791
15 to 19 years	2,087	2,401	2,780	2,848	12,451	12,290	13,117	13,165	2,608	2,700	2,891	2,897	165	172	195	198	582	640	765	789
20 to 24 years	2,324	2,394	2,690	2,801	13,525	12,179	11,903	11,769	2,531	2,529	2,556	2,638	151	159	160	166	612	722	717	744
25 to 29 years	2,341	2,447	2,570	2,624	15,509	13,078	12,159	11,769	2,652	2,459	2,475	2,454	161	151	160	158	674	770	846	856
30 to 34 years	2,047	2,519	2,660	2,692	16,332	15,648	13,508	13,304	2,603	2,679	2,522	2,504	156	158	156	154	701	822	888	931
35 to 39 years	1,643	2,177	2,583	2,668	15,162	16,503	16,157	15,786	2,267	2,661	2,748	2,739	138	153	156	149	641	803	900	928
40 to 44 years	1,278	1,740	2,165	2,274	13,660	15,369	16,482	16,030	1,813	2,290	2,619	2,677	117	136	147	150	546	726	856	886
45 to 49 years	937	1,314	1,658	1,760	10,971	13,660	14,702	15,030	1,364	1,779	2,140	2,220	90	111	124	128	385	593	731	764
50 to 54 years	750	964	1,257	1,344	9,058	10,844	13,660	13,466	1,138	1,328	1,617	1,731	72	84	99	104	297	421	575	620
55 to 59 years	634	762	932	985	8,548	8,836	10,226	10,551	1,009	1,096	1,236	1,274	58	65	75	77	240	326	407	437
60 to 64 years	550	634	747	775	8,872	8,136	8,372	8,455	946	955	1,014	1,041	48	53	58	59	210	269	323	347
65 to 69 years	431	542	612	635	8,584	8,221	7,628	7,574	840	893	900	903	40	43	45	46	172	228	262	278
70 to 74 years	284	406	490	513	6,928	7,535	7,317	7,250	625	679	718	731	28	35	37	37	116	176	209	222
75 to 79 years	212	260	351	372	5,321	5,806	6,259	6,313	475	500	541	546	20	24	29	30	76	111	150	160
80 to 84 years	128	174	203	216	3,446	3,913	4,192	4,257	284	312	322	332	11	16	18	18	40	63	83	90
85 to 89 years	65	90	117	124	1,797	2,063	2,279	2,345	148	162	177	180	6	8	11	11	19	29	41	45
90 to 94 years	19	40	53	56	672	879	984	1,008	49	82	87	90	2	4	6	6	6	13	17	19
95 to 99 years	6	9	17	19	178	231	284	299	17	23	34	36	1	—	2	3	2	3	6	7
100 years and over	2	2	3	3	28	39	48	51	6	6	7	8	—	—	1	1	—	1	1	1
5 to 13 years	3,786	4,539	5,451	5,667	22,107	23,038	23,067	22,965	4,644	5,053	5,319	5,325	316	349	349	346	985	1,216	1,416	1,471
14 to 17 years	1,576	1,922	2,167	2,225	9,224	10,022	10,414	10,407	1,978	2,200	2,285	2,297	131	149	163	165	436	535	626	640
18 to 24 years	3,219	3,361	3,835	3,978	17,511	16,984	17,200	17,200	3,645	3,576	3,730	3,813	218	222	234	241	863	970	1,012	1,053
16 years and over	15,349	18,391	21,359	22,160	148,919	152,663	155,985	156,811	20,885	22,556	24,040	24,421	1,230	1,334	1,429	1,454	5,211	6,577	7,620	7,963
18 years and over	14,547	17,440	20,252	21,037	144,263	147,744	150,697	151,599	19,880	21,478	22,886	23,280	1,164	1,263	1,349	1,372	4,988	6,323	7,308	7,644
16 to 64 years	14,202	16,869	19,514	20,223	121,965	123,976	126,994	127,713	18,441	19,899	21,254	21,594	1,122	1,203	1,282	1,302	4,780	5,954	6,850	7,142
55 years and over	2,331	2,918	3,524	3,697	44,374	45,659	47,589	48,103	4,398	4,708	5,035	5,142	214	249	280	288	882	1,218	1,500	1,606
65 years and over	1,147	1,522	1,845	1,938	26,954	28,687	28,991	29,097	2,443	2,657	2,786	2,827	108	130	147	152	432	623	770	822
85 years and over	91	141	189	202	2,675	3,211	3,595	3,704	219	273	306	314	9	14	19	20	27	45	66	72
Median age (yrs)	25.3	26.1	26.5	26.6	34.8	36.6	38.1	38.5	28.0	29.4	30.3	30.5	26.5	27.4	28.2	28.5	29.7	31.0	32.0	32.3

- Represents or rounds to zero.

Source: U.S. Census Bureau, "Monthly Postcensal Resident Population, by single year of age, sex, race and Hispanic origin"; published June 2000; <http://www.census.gov/population/www/estimates/nat90s1.html>; "Annual Population Estimates by Sex, Race, and Hispanic origin, selected years from 1990 to 2000"; published 26 May 2000; <http://www.census.gov/population/www/estimates/nation3.html>; and "Projections of the Total Resident Population by 5-year Age Groups, Race, and Hispanic Origin with Special Age Categories: Middle Series, 1999 to 2100"; published 13 January 2000; <http://www.census.gov/population/www/projections/natsum-T3.html>.

No. 19. Resident Population by Race, Hispanic Origin, and Single Years of Age: 1999

[In thousands, except as indicated (272,691 represents 272,691,000). As of **July 1**. Resident population. For derivation of estimates, see text of this section]

Age	Race						Not of Hispanic origin			
	Total	White	Black	American Indian, Eskimo, Aleut	Asian, Pacific Islander	Hispanic origin [1]	White	Black	American Indian, Eskimo, Aleut	Asian, Pacific Islander
Total	**272,691**	**224,611**	**34,862**	**2,397**	**10,820**	**31,337**	**196,049**	**33,092**	**2,026**	**10,186**
Under 5 yrs. old	18,942	15,043	2,796	202	902	3,467	11,871	2,603	165	836
Under 1 yr. old	3,820	3,027	569	43	181	722	2,367	529	35	168
1 yr. old	3,757	2,984	554	40	179	703	2,340	515	33	166
2 yrs. old	3,758	2,987	550	40	181	693	2,353	512	32	169
3 yrs. old	3,755	2,993	541	40	182	669	2,381	504	33	169
4 yrs. old	3,853	3,052	582	40	179	680	2,431	544	33	165
5-9 yrs. old	19,947	15,706	3,146	219	875	3,243	12,749	2,961	184	810
5 yrs. old	3,895	3,068	605	42	180	674	2,453	566	35	166
6 yrs. old	3,944	3,108	619	42	175	667	2,498	581	35	162
7 yrs. old	4,030	3,174	634	43	179	669	2,562	597	36	166
8 yrs. old	3,909	3,079	615	42	173	616	2,516	581	36	161
9 yrs. old	4,170	3,278	673	50	168	617	2,719	636	42	155
10-14 yrs. old	19,548	15,389	3,087	249	824	2,739	12,913	2,926	207	763
10 yrs. old	4,036	3,158	662	51	165	577	2,637	627	42	152
11 yrs. old	3,896	3,064	621	49	162	557	2,561	588	41	150
12 yrs. old	3,846	3,024	611	49	161	535	2,542	579	41	149
13 yrs. old	3,878	3,066	594	50	168	539	2,578	563	42	155
14 yrs. old	3,892	3,076	598	50	168	531	2,595	568	42	156
15-19 yrs. old	19,748	15,648	3,044	235	822	2,780	13,117	2,891	195	765
15 yrs. old	3,820	3,010	592	49	169	529	2,532	562	41	157
16 yrs. old	3,924	3,108	599	49	168	547	2,611	569	41	156
17 yrs. old	4,017	3,186	617	48	167	559	2,677	586	40	156
18 yrs. old	3,875	3,083	593	44	155	558	2,573	563	36	144
19 yrs. old	4,111	3,261	643	45	162	587	2,725	611	37	151
20-24 yrs. old	18,026	14,367	2,697	194	768	2,690	11,903	2,556	160	717
20 yrs. old	3,898	3,098	602	42	157	569	2,578	571	34	146
21 yrs. old	3,705	2,949	561	40	155	552	2,444	532	33	144
22 yrs. old	3,564	2,845	531	38	149	531	2,358	504	31	139
23 yrs. old	3,378	2,694	498	37	150	516	2,221	471	30	140
24 yrs. old	3,481	2,781	505	38	157	522	2,302	478	31	147
25-29 yrs. old	18,209	14,505	2,611	193	900	2,570	12,159	2,475	160	846
25 yrs. old	3,369	2,676	493	38	163	504	2,214	467	31	152
26 yrs. old	3,424	2,709	506	38	171	511	2,242	480	31	161
27 yrs. old	3,645	2,894	528	39	184	510	2,428	501	32	173
28 yrs. old	3,698	2,965	516	38	180	501	2,507	489	31	169
29 yrs. old	4,074	3,261	569	41	203	544	2,768	537	34	190
30-34 yrs. old	19,727	15,927	2,675	181	944	2,660	13,508	2,522	148	888
30 yrs. old	3,879	3,134	518	37	190	530	2,651	488	30	179
31 yrs. old	3,748	3,014	513	35	186	517	2,544	484	29	175
32 yrs. old	3,844	3,105	519	36	185	526	2,627	489	29	174
33 yrs. old	3,936	3,178	538	35	185	533	2,693	507	29	174
34 yrs. old	4,320	3,496	588	38	198	554	2,994	555	31	186
35-39 yrs. old	22,545	18,504	2,902	186	953	2,583	16,157	2,748	156	900
35 yrs. old	4,441	3,620	586	38	197	545	3,125	554	32	186
36 yrs. old	4,420	3,626	567	37	191	531	3,143	536	31	180
37 yrs. old	4,554	3,741	587	37	188	509	3,279	556	31	177
38 yrs. old	4,307	3,558	536	35	178	485	3,116	508	29	169
39 yrs. old	4,823	3,959	626	39	199	513	3,494	595	33	188
40-44 yrs. old	22,268	18,443	2,751	173	902	2,165	16,482	2,619	147	856
40 yrs. old	4,612	3,805	582	37	189	470	3,378	553	31	179
41 yrs. old	4,516	3,742	554	36	184	450	3,335	527	30	175
42 yrs. old	4,486	3,723	552	34	177	427	3,336	526	29	168
43 yrs. old	4,270	3,524	527	35	185	411	3,152	501	29	175
44 yrs. old	4,383	3,649	536	31	166	407	3,280	511	27	158

See footnotes at end of table.

U.S. Census Bureau, Statistical Abstract of the United States: 2000

No. 19. Resident Population by Race, Hispanic Origin, and Single Years of Age: 1999—Continued

[See headnote, page 20]

Age	Race						Not of Hispanic origin			
	Total	White	Black	American Indian, Eskimo, Aleut	Asian, Pacific Islander	Hispanic origin [1]	White	Black	American Indian, Eskimo, Aleut	Asian, Pacific Islander
45-49 yrs. old	19,356	16,206	2,240	143	767	1,658	14,702	2,140	124	731
45 yrs. old	4,165	3,480	492	31	162	369	3,145	470	27	154
46 yrs. old	3,931	3,303	444	29	155	346	2,988	423	25	148
47 yrs. old	3,887	3,248	455	30	154	325	2,955	436	26	147
48 yrs. old	3,532	2,973	394	25	140	304	2,696	376	22	133
49 yrs. old	3,841	3,202	454	28	157	313	2,919	435	25	150
50-54 yrs. old	16,446	14,044	1,689	113	601	1,257	12,898	1,617	99	575
50 yrs. old	3,649	3,081	400	26	142	286	2,821	383	23	136
51 yrs. old	3,502	2,987	363	24	129	264	2,747	347	21	123
52 yrs. old	3,728	3,240	346	23	119	259	3,003	332	20	114
53 yrs. old	2,732	2,325	281	20	105	227	2,118	268	18	101
54 yrs. old	2,835	2,411	299	20	106	220	2,210	286	17	101
55-59 yrs. old	12,875	11,077	1,289	84	425	932	10,226	1,236	75	407
55 yrs. old	2,750	2,346	289	19	96	202	2,163	277	17	92
56 yrs. old	2,935	2,554	275	18	88	204	2,367	263	16	84
57 yrs. old	2,581	2,210	269	17	85	185	2,042	257	15	81
58 yrs. old	2,285	1,977	218	14	75	170	1,822	209	13	72
59 yrs. old	2,325	1,989	239	16	81	172	1,833	229	14	78
60-64 yrs. old	10,514	9,056	1,056	65	337	747	8,372	1,014	58	323
60 yrs. old	2,232	1,917	226	14	74	162	1,770	217	13	70
61 yrs. old	2,147	1,850	215	13	69	152	1,710	207	12	66
62 yrs. old	2,029	1,742	207	13	68	144	1,610	199	11	65
63 yrs. old	2,022	1,749	198	12	63	144	1,616	191	11	61
64 yrs. old	2,084	1,799	209	12	64	145	1,666	201	11	61
65-69 yrs. old	9,447	8,189	935	50	273	612	7,628	900	45	262
65 yrs. old	1,909	1,637	201	11	60	130	1,519	193	10	58
66 yrs. old	1,879	1,618	194	10	56	125	1,504	187	9	54
67 yrs. old	1,877	1,626	189	10	53	120	1,516	181	9	51
68 yrs. old	1,880	1,641	177	9	52	120	1,531	171	8	50
69 yrs. old	1,902	1,667	174	9	52	118	1,558	168	8	50
70-74 yrs. old	8,771	7,770	743	40	217	490	7,317	718	37	209
70 yrs. old	1,841	1,614	169	9	49	110	1,513	163	8	47
71 yrs. old	1,843	1,630	159	8	45	105	1,532	154	8	44
72 yrs. old	1,771	1,570	147	8	45	97	1,480	142	8	43
73 yrs. old	1,661	1,476	137	7	40	90	1,392	133	7	39
74 yrs. old	1,656	1,480	131	7	38	86	1,400	126	7	37
75-79 yrs. old	7,329	6,585	558	31	156	351	6,259	541	29	150
75 yrs. old	1,600	1,435	123	7	36	81	1,359	119	6	34
76 yrs. old	1,510	1,357	113	7	33	75	1,287	109	6	32
77 yrs. old	1,488	1,341	110	6	31	70	1,276	107	6	30
78 yrs. old	1,441	1,299	107	6	29	67	1,237	104	6	28
79 yrs. old	1,291	1,153	105	5	27	58	1,099	102	5	26
80-84 yrs. old	4,817	4,381	331	19	86	203	4,192	322	18	83
80 yrs. old	1,142	1,035	82	5	21	49	989	79	4	20
81 yrs. old	1,038	946	71	4	18	44	905	69	4	17
82 yrs. old	949	866	64	4	16	39	830	62	3	16
83 yrs. old	883	807	57	4	16	37	772	56	3	15
84 yrs. old	804	728	57	3	15	34	696	56	3	14
85-89 yrs. old	2,625	2,389	181	11	43	117	2,279	177	11	41
90-94 yrs. old	1,148	1,034	89	6	18	53	984	87	6	17
95-99 yrs. old	343	300	35	2	6	17	284	34	2	6
100 yrs. old and over	59	50	7	1	1	3	48	7	1	1
Median age (yr.) . .	35.5	36.6	30.1	27.6	31.7	26.5	38.1	30.3	28.2	32.0

[1] Persons of Hispanic origin may be of any race.

Source: U.S. Census Bureau, "National Population Estimates for the 1990s. Postcensal Resident Population, by single year of age, sex, race and Hispanic Origin"; published 26 May 2000; <http://www.census.gov/population/www/estimates/nat90s1.html>.

Figure 1.1
Center of Population: 1790 to 1990

[Prior to 1960, excludes Alaska and Hawaii. The median center is located at the intersection of two median lines, a north-south line constructed so that half of the Nation's population lives east and half lives west of it, and an east-west line selected so that half of the Nation's population lives north and half lives south of it. The mean center of population is that point at which an imaginary, flat, weightless, and rigid map of the United States would balance if weights of identical value were placed on it so that each weight represented the location of one person on the date of the census]

Year	Median center		Mean center		
	Latitude-N	Longitude	Latitude-N	Longitude-W	Approximate location
1790 (August 2)	(NA)	(NA)	39 16 30	76 11 12	In Kent County, MD, 23 miles E of Baltimore MD
1850 (June 1)..	(NA)	(NA)	38 59 00	81 19 00	In Wirt County, WV, 23 miles SE of Parkersburg, WV[1]
1900 (June 1)..	40 03 32	84 49 01	39 09 36	85 48 54	In Bartholomew County, IN, 6 miles SE of Columbus, IN
1950 (April 1)..	40 00 12	84 56 51	38 50 21	88 09 33	In Richland County, IL, 8 miles NNW of Olney, IL
1960 (April 1)..	39 56 25	85 16 60	38 35 58	89 12 35	In Clinton County, IL, 6.5 miles NW of Centralia, IL
1970 (April 1) .	39 47 43	85 31 43	38 27 47	89 42 22	In St. Clair County, IL, 5.3 miles ESE of Mascoutah, IL
1980 (April 1)..	39 18 60	86 08 15	38 08 13	90 34 26	In Jefferson County, MO, .25 mile W of DeSoto, MO
1990 (April 1)..	38 57 55	86 31 53	37 52 20	91 12 55	In Crawford County, MO, 10 miles SE of Steelville, MO

NA Not available.   [1]West Virginia was set off from Virginia, Dec. 31, 1862, and admitted as a state, June 19, 1863.

▲ Median Center of Population

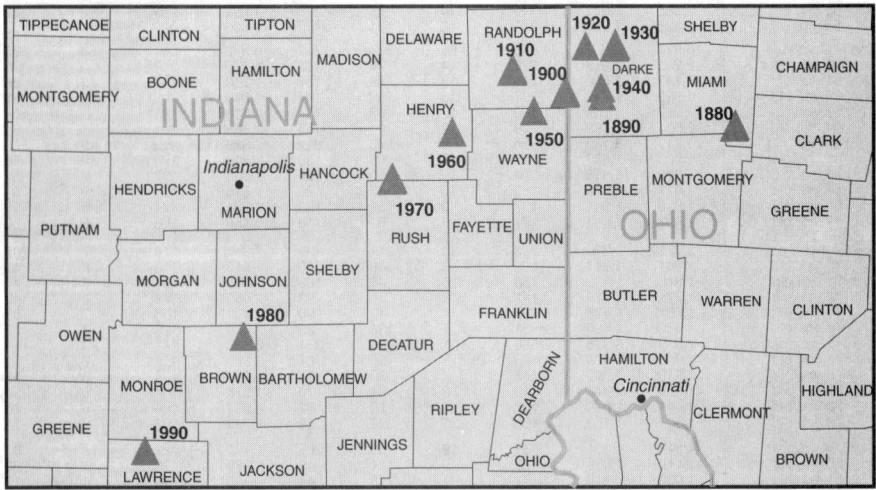

▲ Mean Center of Population

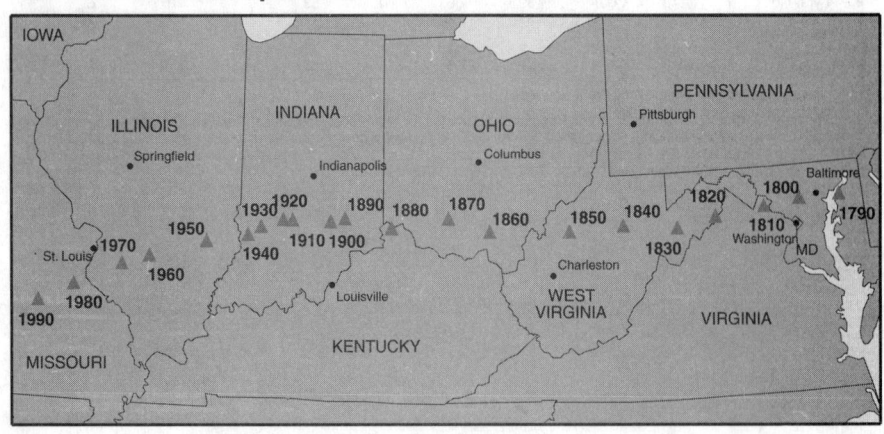

Source: Chart prepared by U.S. Census Bureau.

22 Population

No. 20. Resident Population by State: 1980 to 1999

[In thousands (226,546 represents 226,546,000). As of July 1; except 1980 and 1990, as of April 1. Insofar as possible, population shown for all years is that of present area of state]

State	1980 [1]	1990 [2]	1991	1992	1993	1994	1995	1996	1997	1998	1999
United States. .	226,546	248,791	252,153	255,030	257,783	260,327	262,803	265,229	267,784	270,248	272,691
Alabama	3,894	4,040	4,091	4,139	4,193	4,233	4,263	4,290	4,320	4,351	4,370
Alaska	402	550	569	587	597	601	601	605	609	615	620
Arizona	2,718	3,665	3,762	3,867	3,993	4,148	4,307	4,432	4,552	4,667	4,778
Arkansas.	2,286	2,351	2,371	2,394	2,424	2,451	2,480	2,505	2,524	2,538	2,551
California.	23,668	29,811	30,414	30,876	31,147	31,317	31,494	31,781	32,218	32,683	33,145
Colorado	2,890	3,294	3,368	3,460	3,561	3,654	3,738	3,813	3,891	3,969	4,056
Connecticut	3,108	3,287	3,289	3,275	3,272	3,268	3,265	3,267	3,269	3,273	3,282
Delaware.	594	666	680	690	699	708	718	727	735	744	754
District of Columbia.	638	607	593	584	576	565	551	538	529	521	519
Florida	9,746	12,938	13,289	13,505	13,714	13,962	14,185	14,427	14,683	14,908	15,111
Georgia	5,463	6,478	6,621	6,759	6,894	7,046	7,189	7,332	7,486	7,637	7,788
Hawaii	965	1,108	1,131	1,150	1,162	1,174	1,180	1,184	1,189	1,190	1,185
Idaho	944	1,007	1,039	1,066	1,101	1,135	1,165	1,188	1,211	1,231	1,252
Illinois.	11,427	11,431	11,536	11,635	11,726	11,805	11,885	11,953	12,012	12,070	12,128
Indiana	5,490	5,544	5,602	5,649	5,702	5,746	5,792	5,835	5,872	5,908	5,943
Iowa	2,914	2,777	2,791	2,807	2,821	2,829	2,841	2,848	2,854	2,861	2,869
Kansas	2,364	2,478	2,495	2,526	2,548	2,569	2,587	2,598	2,616	2,639	2,654
Kentucky.	3,661	3,687	3,715	3,756	3,792	3,823	3,855	3,881	3,908	3,934	3,961
Louisiana	4,206	4,222	4,241	4,271	4,285	4,307	4,328	4,339	4,351	4,363	4,372
Maine.	1,125	1,228	1,235	1,236	1,238	1,238	1,237	1,241	1,245	1,248	1,253
Maryland.	4,217	4,781	4,856	4,903	4,943	4,985	5,024	5,057	5,093	5,130	5,172
Massachusetts . . .	5,737	6,016	5,999	5,993	6,011	6,031	6,062	6,085	6,115	6,144	6,175
Michigan	9,262	9,295	9,395	9,470	9,529	9,584	9,660	9,739	9,785	9,820	9,864
Minnesota	4,076	4,376	4,427	4,472	4,522	4,566	4,605	4,648	4,688	4,726	4,776
Mississippi.	2,521	2,575	2,591	2,610	2,636	2,663	2,691	2,710	2,732	2,751	2,769
Missouri	4,917	5,117	5,158	5,194	5,238	5,281	5,325	5,368	5,407	5,438	5,468
Montana	787	799	808	822	840	855	869	877	879	880	883
Nebraska	1,570	1,578	1,591	1,602	1,612	1,622	1,635	1,648	1,656	1,661	1,666
Nevada.	800	1,202	1,285	1,331	1,380	1,456	1,526	1,596	1,676	1,744	1,809
New Hampshire . .	921	1,109	1,107	1,113	1,122	1,133	1,146	1,161	1,173	1,186	1,201
New Jersey	7,365	7,748	7,784	7,828	7,875	7,919	7,966	8,010	8,054	8,096	8,143
New Mexico.	1,303	1,515	1,547	1,581	1,615	1,653	1,682	1,706	1,723	1,734	1,740
New York	17,558	17,991	18,030	18,082	18,141	18,157	18,151	18,144	18,143	18,159	18,197
North Carolina . . .	5,882	6,632	6,748	6,832	6,947	7,061	7,185	7,308	7,429	7,546	7,651
North Dakota	653	639	634	635	637	640	642	643	641	638	634
Ohio.	10,798	10,847	10,934	11,008	11,070	11,111	11,155	11,187	11,212	11,238	11,257
Oklahoma	3,025	3,146	3,166	3,204	3,229	3,246	3,266	3,290	3,314	3,339	3,358
Oregon	2,633	2,842	2,919	2,974	3,034	3,087	3,141	3,195	3,243	3,282	3,316
Pennsylvania	11,864	11,883	11,943	11,981	12,022	12,043	12,045	12,038	12,016	12,002	11,994
Rhode Island	947	1,003	1,004	1,001	998	993	989	988	987	988	991
South Carolina . . .	3,122	3,486	3,559	3,601	3,635	3,666	3,700	3,739	3,790	3,840	3,886
South Dakota. . . .	691	696	701	709	716	723	728	731	731	731	733
Tennessee.	4,591	4,877	4,947	5,014	5,086	5,163	5,241	5,314	5,378	5,433	5,484
Texas	14,229	16,986	17,340	17,650	17,997	18,338	18,680	19,006	19,355	19,712	20,044
Utah.	1,461	1,723	1,772	1,821	1,876	1,930	1,977	2,022	2,065	2,101	2,130
Vermont	511	563	567	570	574	579	583	586	589	591	594
Virginia	5,347	6,189	6,284	6,383	6,465	6,537	6,601	6,665	6,733	6,789	6,873
Washington	4,132	4,867	5,013	5,139	5,248	5,335	5,431	5,510	5,604	5,688	5,756
West Virginia	1,950	1,793	1,798	1,805	1,816	1,818	1,821	1,819	1,816	1,812	1,807
Wisconsin	4,706	4,892	4,953	5,005	5,055	5,096	5,137	5,174	5,200	5,222	5,250
Wyoming	470	454	458	463	469	475	478	480	480	480	480

[1] See footnote 4, Table 1.   [2] The April 1, 1990, census counts include corrections processed through August 1997, results of special censuses and test censuses, and do not include adjustments for census coverage errors.

Source: U.S. Census Bureau, *1990 Census of Population and Housing, Population and Housing Unit Counts* (CPH-2); and "ST-99-3 State Population Estimates: Annual Time Series, July 1, 1990, to July 1, 1999"; published 29 December 1999; <http://www.census.gov/population/estimates/state/st-99-3.txt>.

Population   23

No. 21. State Population by Rank, Percent Change, and Population Density: 1980 to 1999

[As of **April 1**, except **1999**, as of **July 1**. For area figures of states, see Table 380. Minus sign (-) indicates decrease]

State	Rank			Percent change			Population per sq. mile of land area [1]		
	1980	1990	1999	1980-90	1990-95	1995-99	1980	1990	1999
United States	(X)	(X)	(X)	9.8	5.6	3.8	64.1	70.4	77.1
Alabama.	22	22	23	3.8	5.5	2.5	76.7	79.6	86.1
Alaska	50	49	48	36.9	9.3	3.0	0.7	1.0	1.1
Arizona.	29	24	20	34.9	17.5	10.9	23.9	32.3	42.0
Arkansas	33	33	33	2.8	5.5	2.9	43.9	45.1	49.0
California	1	1	1	26.0	5.6	5.2	151.7	191.1	212.5
Colorado.	28	26	24	14.0	13.5	8.5	27.9	31.8	39.1
Connecticut.	25	27	29	5.8	-0.7	0.5	641.4	678.5	677.4
Delaware	47	46	45	12.1	7.8	4.9	304.0	340.8	385.4
District of Columbia	(X)	(X)	(X)	-4.9	-9.2	-5.9	10,397.9	9,884.4	8,452.8
Florida	7	4	4	32.7	9.6	6.5	180.7	239.9	280.2
Georgia	13	11	10	18.6	11.0	8.3	94.3	111.8	134.5
Hawaii	39	41	42	14.9	6.5	0.4	150.2	172.5	184.6
Idaho.	41	42	40	6.6	15.7	7.4	11.4	12.2	15.1
Illinois	5	6	5	(Z)	4.0	2.0	205.6	205.6	218.2
Indiana.	12	14	14	1.0	4.5	2.6	153.1	154.6	165.7
Iowa	27	30	30	-4.7	2.3	1.0	52.1	49.7	51.4
Kansas.	32	32	32	4.8	4.4	2.6	28.9	30.3	32.4
Kentucky	23	23	25	0.7	4.6	2.7	92.1	92.8	99.7
Louisiana	19	21	22	0.4	2.5	1.0	96.5	96.9	100.4
Maine.	38	38	39	9.1	0.8	1.3	36.5	39.8	40.6
Maryland	18	19	19	13.4	5.1	2.9	431.4	489.1	529.1
Massachusetts.	11	13	13	4.9	0.8	1.9	732.0	767.6	787.9
Michigan.	8	8	8	0.4	3.9	2.1	163.0	163.6	173.6
Minnesota.	21	20	21	7.4	5.3	3.7	51.2	55.0	60.0
Mississippi	31	31	31	2.2	4.5	2.9	53.7	54.9	59.0
Missouri	15	15	17	4.1	4.1	2.7	71.4	74.3	79.4
Montana.	44	44	44	1.6	8.7	1.6	5.4	5.5	6.1
Nebraska	35	36	38	0.5	3.6	1.9	20.4	20.5	21.7
Nevada	43	39	35	50.1	27.0	18.6	7.3	10.9	16.5
New Hampshire	42	40	41	20.5	3.3	4.8	102.6	123.7	133.9
New Jersey.	9	9	9	5.2	2.8	2.2	992.7	1,044.3	1,097.6
New Mexico	37	37	37	16.2	11.0	3.4	10.7	12.5	14.3
New York	2	2	3	2.5	0.9	0.3	371.8	381.0	385.3
North Carolina	10	10	11	12.8	8.3	6.5	120.7	136.1	157.0
North Dakota.	46	47	47	-2.1	0.4	-1.2	9.5	9.3	9.2
Ohio	6	7	7	0.5	2.8	0.9	263.7	264.9	274.9
Oklahoma.	26	28	27	4.0	3.8	2.8	44.1	45.8	48.9
Oregon.	30	29	28	7.9	10.5	5.6	27.4	29.6	34.5
Pennsylvania.	4	5	6	0.2	1.4	-0.4	264.7	265.1	267.6
Rhode Island.	40	43	43	5.9	-1.4	0.2	906.4	960.3	948.2
South Carolina.	24	25	26	11.7	6.1	5.0	103.6	115.8	129.0
South Dakota.	45	45	46	0.8	4.6	0.7	9.1	9.2	9.7
Tennessee	17	17	16	6.2	7.5	4.6	111.4	118.3	133.0
Texas.	3	3	2	19.4	10.0	7.3	54.3	64.9	76.5
Utah	36	35	34	17.9	14.7	7.7	17.8	21.0	25.9
Vermont	48	48	49	10.0	3.6	1.9	55.3	60.8	64.2
Virginia.	14	12	12	15.8	6.7	4.1	135.0	156.3	173.6
Washington	20	18	15	17.8	11.6	6.0	62.1	73.1	86.5
West Virginia.	34	34	36	-8.0	1.5	-0.7	81.0	74.5	75.0
Wisconsin.	16	16	18	4.0	5.0	2.2	86.6	90.1	96.7
Wyoming	49	50	50	-3.4	5.5	0.2	4.8	4.7	4.9

X Not applicable.   Z Less than 0.05 percent.   [1] Persons per square mile were calculated on the basis of land area data from the 1990 census.

Source: U.S. Census Bureau, *1990 Census of Population and Housing, Population and Housing Unit Counts* (CPH-2); and "ST-99-3 State Population Estimates: Annual Time Series, July 1, 1990, to July 1, 1999"; published 29 December 1999; <http://www.census.gov/population/estimates/state/st-99-3.txt>.

No. 22. Components of Population Change by State: 1990 to 1999

[In thousands, except percent (23,900 represents 23,900,000). Covers period April 1, 1990, to July 1,1999]

State	Net change [1]		Births	Deaths	Net movement from abroad		Net domestic migration
	Number	Percent			International migration	Net federal movement	
United States	23,900	9.6	36,820	20,934	7,478	536	-
Alabama	329	8.2	569	387	14	7	112
Alaska	69	12.6	99	22	9	9	-24
Arizona	1,113	30.4	671	317	106	8	577
Arkansas	201	8.5	330	244	10	2	111
California	3,334	11.2	5,227	2,039	2,280	88	-2,171
Colorado	762	23.1	514	226	65	14	403
Connecticut	-5	-0.2	424	269	73	4	-226
Delaware	87	13.1	98	58	9	2	35
District of Columbia	-88	-14.5	87	60	30	3	-147
Florida	2,173	16.8	1,782	1,370	640	33	1,109
Georgia	1,310	20.2	1,053	526	106	25	665
Hawaii	77	7.0	173	68	54	19	-99
Idaho	245	24.3	166	78	18	2	136
Illinois	698	6.1	1,735	972	384	10	-560
Indiana	399	7.2	779	483	29	1	83
Iowa	93	3.3	349	257	21	(Z)	-16
Kansas	176	7.1	348	216	28	8	-16
Kentucky	274	7.4	495	341	16	10	97
Louisiana	150	3.6	629	362	26	9	-140
Maine	25	2.0	138	108	4	2	-7
Maryland	391	8.2	687	375	132	15	-55
Massachusetts	159	2.6	779	507	148	3	-244
Michigan	568	6.1	1,288	763	100	2	-199
Minnesota	400	9.1	603	338	55	1	87
Mississippi	193	7.5	389	246	7	6	45
Missouri	351	6.9	697	492	38	5	101
Montana	84	10.5	103	69	3	2	48
Nebraska	88	5.6	218	140	15	4	-4
Nevada	608	50.6	228	110	56	3	433
New Hampshire	92	8.3	142	84	7	(Z)	30
New Jersey	396	5.1	1,079	667	378	5	-378
New Mexico	225	14.8	255	112	38	6	42
New York	206	1.1	2,539	1,520	1,108	11	-1,889
North Carolina	1,018	15.4	967	586	58	38	554
North Dakota	-5	-0.8	79	54	5	3	-37
Ohio	410	3.8	1,455	957	53	4	-166
Oklahoma	212	6.8	437	298	29	10	43
Oregon	474	16.7	399	255	66	1	271
Pennsylvania	111	0.9	1,439	1,163	115	3	-251
Rhode Island	-13	-1.3	125	89	16	2	-63
South Carolina	399	11.5	498	301	19	17	143
South Dakota	37	5.3	98	63	5	2	-3
Tennessee	606	12.4	688	464	30	7	357
Texas	3,058	18.0	3,026	1,254	715	44	570
Utah	407	23.6	369	98	30	2	73
Vermont	31	5.5	67	45	5	(Z)	6
Virginia	684	11.0	873	477	146	62	97
Washington	890	18.3	729	373	147	20	382
West Virginia	13	0.7	198	185	3	(Z)	2
Wisconsin	358	7.3	638	412	25	(Z)	90
Wyoming	26	5.7	60	33	2	1	-4

- Represents zero.   Z Less than 500.   [1] Includes residual change, not shown separately. The residual is the effect of national controls on subnational estimates. It is the difference between the implementation of the national estimates model and the county/state estimates model.

Source: U.S. Census Bureau, "ST-99-7 State Population Estimates and Demographic Components of Population Change; published 29 December 1999"; <http://www.census.gov/population/estimates/state/st-99-7.txt>.

Population   25

No. 23. State Population Projections: 2000 to 2025

[In thousands (274,634 represents 274,634,000). As of **July 1**. The two series of projections are based on different internal migration assumptions: (1) Series A is the preferred series model and uses state-to-state migration observed from 1975-76 through 1993-94; and (2) Series B, the economic model, uses the Bureau of Economic Analysis employment projections. For explanation of methodology, see text of this section]

State	Series A						Series B					
	2000	2005	2010	2015	2020	2025	2000	2005	2010	2015	2020	2025
U.S	274,634	285,981	297,716	310,133	322,742	335,050	274,634	285,981	297,716	310,134	322,742	335,050
AL.......	4,451	4,631	4,798	4,956	5,100	5,224	4,436	4,617	4,802	4,986	5,162	5,319
AK.......	653	700	745	791	838	885	632	659	690	728	773	825
AZ.......	4,798	5,230	5,522	5,808	6,111	6,412	4,838	5,432	6,025	6,620	7,193	7,729
AR.......	2,631	2,750	2,840	2,922	2,997	3,055	2,623	2,757	2,887	3,008	3,109	3,184
CA.......	32,521	34,441	37,644	41,373	45,278	49,285	32,423	33,511	34,968	36,838	39,034	41,480
CO.......	4,168	4,468	4,658	4,833	5,012	5,188	4,154	4,510	4,837	5,152	5,454	5,743
CT.......	3,284	3,317	3,400	3,506	3,621	3,739	3,286	3,291	3,303	3,332	3,376	3,428
DE.......	768	800	817	832	847	861	758	793	823	851	877	899
DC.......	523	529	560	594	625	655	530	542	572	611	654	702
FL.......	15,233	16,279	17,363	18,497	19,634	20,710	15,250	16,273	17,299	18,318	19,262	20,066
GA	7,875	8,413	8,824	9,200	9,552	9,869	7,893	8,540	9,167	9,785	10,386	10,962
HI.......	1,257	1,342	1,440	1,553	1,677	1,812	1,238	1,297	1,367	1,447	1,537	1,634
ID.......	1,347	1,480	1,557	1,622	1,683	1,739	1,332	1,489	1,637	1,775	1,900	2,008
IL	12,051	12,266	12,515	12,808	13,121	13,440	12,069	12,314	12,601	12,945	13,323	13,717
IN	6,045	6,215	6,318	6,404	6,481	6,546	6,060	6,301	6,532	6,758	6,969	7,158
IA	2,900	2,941	2,968	2,994	3,019	3,040	2,891	2,939	2,992	3,047	3,095	3,133
KS.......	2,668	2,761	2,849	2,939	3,026	3,108	2,675	2,788	2,908	3,034	3,158	3,273
KY.......	3,995	4,098	4,170	4,231	4,281	4,314	3,990	4,109	4,220	4,322	4,411	4,480
LA.......	4,425	4,535	4,683	4,840	4,991	5,133	4,445	4,558	4,687	4,828	4,972	5,111
ME	1,259	1,285	1,323	1,362	1,396	1,423	1,250	1,259	1,268	1,276	1,282	1,282
MD	5,275	5,467	5,657	5,862	6,071	6,274	5,261	5,426	5,577	5,736	5,904	6,072
MA	6,199	6,310	6,431	6,574	6,734	6,902	6,224	6,361	6,498	6,653	6,824	7,001
MI	9,679	9,763	9,836	9,917	10,002	10,078	9,711	9,835	9,966	10,115	10,272	10,423
MN	4,830	5,005	5,147	5,283	5,406	5,510	4,822	5,014	5,212	5,414	5,606	5,778
MS	2,816	2,908	2,974	3,035	3,093	3,142	2,826	2,949	3,072	3,195	3,310	3,413
MO	5,540	5,718	5,864	6,005	6,137	6,250	5,547	5,750	5,953	6,153	6,336	6,492
MT.......	950	1,006	1,040	1,069	1,097	1,121	937	998	1,056	1,108	1,152	1,187
NE.......	1,705	1,761	1,806	1,850	1,892	1,930	1,700	1,766	1,837	1,912	1,984	2,050
NV.......	1,871	2,070	2,131	2,179	2,241	2,312	1,863	2,130	2,355	2,547	2,712	2,854
NH	1,224	1,281	1,329	1,372	1,410	1,439	1,217	1,267	1,307	1,344	1,377	1,402
NJ.......	8,178	8,392	8,638	8,924	9,238	9,558	8,185	8,387	8,594	8,832	9,096	9,369
NM	1,860	2,016	2,155	2,300	2,454	2,612	1,858	2,035	2,223	2,425	2,636	2,850
NY.......	18,146	18,250	18,530	18,916	19,359	19,830	18,174	18,227	18,363	18,616	18,969	19,396
NC	7,777	8,227	8,552	8,840	9,111	9,349	7,789	8,312	8,780	9,206	9,588	9,916
ND	662	677	690	704	717	729	657	677	701	727	754	778
OH	11,319	11,428	11,505	11,588	11,671	11,744	11,352	11,534	11,726	11,937	12,148	12,343
OK	3,373	3,491	3,639	3,789	3,930	4,057	3,370	3,471	3,578	3,684	3,784	3,871
OR	3,397	3,613	3,803	3,992	4,177	4,349	3,397	3,625	3,837	4,036	4,213	4,361
PA.......	12,202	12,281	12,352	12,449	12,567	12,683	12,220	12,329	12,443	12,580	12,727	12,854
RI	998	1,012	1,038	1,070	1,105	1,141	989	986	986	989	998	1,007
SC.......	3,858	4,033	4,205	4,369	4,517	4,645	3,852	4,015	4,169	4,318	4,455	4,574
SD.......	777	810	826	840	853	866	770	811	853	893	930	962
TN.......	5,657	5,966	6,180	6,365	6,529	6,665	5,668	6,039	6,385	6,707	6,998	7,249
TX.......	20,119	21,487	22,857	24,280	25,729	27,183	20,178	21,635	23,158	24,775	26,453	28,170
UT.......	2,207	2,411	2,551	2,670	2,781	2,883	2,216	2,477	2,738	2,995	3,246	3,487
VT.......	617	638	651	662	671	678	607	623	636	646	655	661
VA.......	6,997	7,324	7,627	7,921	8,204	8,466	6,965	7,234	7,474	7,708	7,939	8,165
WA	5,858	6,258	6,658	7,058	7,446	7,808	5,829	6,184	6,524	6,857	7,179	7,480
WV	1,841	1,849	1,851	1,851	1,850	1,845	1,833	1,842	1,852	1,861	1,866	1,864
WI	5,326	5,479	5,590	5,693	5,788	5,867	5,324	5,502	5,682	5,864	6,035	6,185
WY	525	568	607	641	670	694	519	559	598	636	671	702

Source: U.S. Census Bureau, Population Paper Listings PPL-47.

U.S. Census Bureau, Statistical Abstract of the United States: 2000

No. 24. Resident Population by Age and State: 1999

[In thousands, except percent (272,691 represents 272,691,000). As of July 1. Includes Armed Forces stationed in area. See text of this section for basis of estimates]

State	Total	Under 5 years	5 to 17 years	18 to 24 years	25 to 34 years	35 to 44 years	45 to 54 years	55 to 64 years	65 to 74 years	75 to 84 years	85 years and over	Percent 65 years and over
U.S.	272,691	18,942	51,257	26,011	37,936	44,813	35,802	23,389	18,218	12,147	4,175	12.7
AL.	4,370	291	775	440	615	693	582	407	311	192	65	13.0
AK.	620	50	147	71	72	106	91	47	22	10	2	5.6
AZ.	4,778	386	949	460	629	736	588	402	341	222	66	13.2
AR.	2,551	178	483	251	328	379	326	246	191	126	44	14.2
CA.	33,145	2,499	6,424	3,319	5,115	5,592	4,107	2,441	1,931	1,293	424	11.0
CO	4,056	288	777	393	524	699	608	360	222	138	48	10.1
CT.	3,282	218	610	256	446	564	436	283	232	173	63	14.3
DE.	754	50	132	69	113	130	97	63	54	34	10	13.0
DC	519	27	68	46	95	89	73	49	38	25	9	13.9
FL.	15,111	952	2,618	1,236	1,881	2,357	1,891	1,434	1,430	991	321	18.1
GA	7,788	580	1,477	774	1,205	1,338	1,023	630	419	257	85	9.8
HI	1,185	80	209	120	147	198	166	104	88	57	17	13.7
ID	1,252	93	258	144	154	187	163	111	74	51	18	11.3
IL	12,128	878	2,304	1,143	1,702	2,003	1,570	1,033	771	533	192	12.3
IN	5,943	414	1,115	576	824	963	785	523	391	261	90	12.5
IA	2,869	183	537	282	357	441	380	262	208	156	65	14.9
KS.	2,654	184	515	271	340	427	343	220	175	127	52	13.3
KY.	3,961	259	706	405	543	641	542	373	268	168	57	12.5
LA.	4,372	314	876	481	572	675	568	384	277	168	56	11.5
ME	1,253	67	223	111	166	218	181	111	93	61	22	14.0
MD	5,172	347	963	442	760	938	699	426	322	209	66	11.5
MA	6,175	392	1,076	513	939	1,056	825	513	430	314	115	13.9
MI	9,864	655	1,906	928	1,362	1,632	1,315	841	645	434	144	12.4
MN	4,776	322	950	454	630	813	627	394	291	210	84	12.3
MS	2,769	202	550	302	378	417	342	240	182	112	41	12.1
MO	5,468	363	1,036	520	721	890	704	488	388	260	98	13.6
MT	883	53	171	89	94	137	132	89	60	42	15	13.3
NE.	1,666	115	329	170	206	261	215	141	114	80	34	13.7
NV.	1,809	143	348	156	248	297	242	168	124	67	16	11.5
NH	1,201	74	231	98	178	223	161	92	77	50	18	12.0
NJ.	8,143	543	1,460	673	1,107	1,426	1,101	726	577	397	133	13.6
NM	1,740	131	364	176	211	278	229	150	111	67	22	11.5
NY.	18,197	1,214	3,227	1,619	2,622	3,022	2,432	1,631	1,275	845	310	13.4
NC	7,651	534	1,407	709	1,111	1,241	1,008	685	525	325	105	12.5
ND	634	39	121	69	78	97	82	55	45	33	15	14.6
OH	11,257	740	2,104	1,065	1,532	1,827	1,494	993	789	536	176	13.3
OK	3,358	233	649	343	417	508	439	319	238	153	57	13.4
OR	3,316	220	608	312	425	527	488	302	218	160	56	13.1
PA.	11,994	712	2,140	1,025	1,570	1,945	1,615	1,087	972	695	232	15.8
RI	991	62	179	84	144	164	125	78	75	58	21	15.6
SC.	3,886	253	702	393	560	629	525	349	268	159	47	12.2
SD.	733	50	148	78	86	112	92	61	52	38	16	14.4
TN.	5,484	367	974	520	776	897	754	515	370	232	79	12.4
TX.	20,044	1,640	4,080	2,100	2,772	3,262	2,555	1,620	1,109	674	234	10.1
UT.	2,130	210	497	301	293	280	222	141	99	65	21	8.7
VT.	594	32	107	53	83	105	89	51	38	25	10	12.3
VA.	6,873	451	1,214	673	1,048	1,194	931	588	428	263	84	11.3
WA	5,756	390	1,096	558	789	986	804	476	335	240	83	11.4
WV	1,807	101	303	179	226	270	266	189	146	95	32	15.1
WI.	5,250	332	1,016	508	688	868	696	450	349	248	95	13.2
WY	480	30	96	54	53	74	71	45	30	19	6	11.6

Source: U.S. Census Bureau, "Population Estimates for the U.S., Regions, Divisions, and States by 5-Year Age Groups and Sex: Annual Time Series Estimates, July 1, 1990, to July 1, 1999, and April 1, 1990, Census Population Counts"; published 9 March 2000; <http://www.census.gov/population/estimates/state/st-99-08.txt>; and "Population Estimates for the U.S., Regions, and States by Selected Age Groups and Sex: Annual Time Series, July 1, 1990, to July 1, 1999, (includes revised April 1, 1990, population counts)"; published 9 March 2000; <http://www.census.gov/population/estimates/state/st-99-09.txt>.

Population 27

No. 25. Resident Population by Race, Hispanic Origin, and State: 1999

[In thousands (272,691 represents 272,691,000). As of July 1. These estimates are developed using a cohort-component method whereby each component of population change - births, deaths, domestic migration, and international migration is estimated separately for each birth cohort by sex and race]

State		Race						
	Total	White			Black	American Indian, Eskimo, Aleut	Asian, Pacific Islander	Hispanic origin [1]
		Total	Hispanic	Non-Hispanic				
U.S.	272,691	224,611	28,561	196,049	34,862	2,397	10,820	31,337
AL.	4,370	3,188	39	3,149	1,139	15	28	45
AK.	620	466	20	446	24	101	28	25
AZ.	4,778	4,239	1,010	3,229	176	261	103	1,084
AR.	2,551	2,108	48	2,060	411	14	19	54
CA.	33,145	26,306	9,780	16,526	2,487	314	4,038	10,460
CO	4,056	3,742	565	3,177	176	38	100	604
CT.	3,282	2,881	247	2,633	309	8	84	279
DE.	754	586	24	562	149	2	16	28
DC	519	182	32	151	319	2	16	38
FL.	15,111	12,436	2,161	10,275	2,333	60	281	2,334
GA	7,788	5,373	211	5,162	2,236	19	161	240
HI	1,185	391	51	340	34	7	754	95
ID	1,252	1,213	86	1,127	8	17	14	93
IL	12,128	9,830	1,193	8,637	1,854	28	416	1,276
IN	5,943	5,371	140	5,231	498	15	59	154
IA	2,869	2,766	56	2,710	58	9	37	62
KS.	2,654	2,426	135	2,291	157	24	48	148
KY.	3,961	3,639	31	3,608	288	6	28	35
LA	4,372	2,883	103	2,780	1,415	19	55	119
ME	1,253	1,232	8	1,223	6	6	9	9
MD	5,172	3,492	168	3,324	1,454	16	209	199
MA	6,175	5,522	309	5,213	405	15	233	391
MI	9,864	8,222	245	7,977	1,415	60	166	276
MN	4,776	4,438	81	4,357	149	59	131	93
MS	2,769	1,729	20	1,709	1,010	10	20	24
MO	5,468	4,769	81	4,688	617	21	61	91
MT	883	817	14	803	3	57	5	16
NE.	1,666	1,560	70	1,490	68	15	23	77
NV.	1,809	1,548	277	1,271	140	33	88	304
NH	1,201	1,175	18	1,157	9	3	15	20
NJ.	8,143	6,454	886	5,568	1,197	23	469	1,027
NM	1,740	1,502	676	826	46	166	26	708
NY.	18,197	13,873	2,021	11,851	3,222	77	1,025	2,661
NC	7,651	5,760	152	5,607	1,686	99	106	176
ND	634	594	6	588	4	31	5	7
OH	11,257	9,797	164	9,633	1,304	23	133	185
OK	3,358	2,788	115	2,673	262	263	45	137
OR	3,316	3,098	195	2,904	62	46	110	213
PA.	11,994	10,603	275	10,328	1,170	18	203	326
RI	991	912	55	857	50	5	23	69
SC.	3,886	2,684	46	2,638	1,157	10	36	54
SD.	733	663	7	655	5	60	5	9
TN.	5,484	4,505	58	4,447	913	12	54	67
TX.	20,044	16,899	5,811	11,088	2,470	97	577	6,045
UT.	2,130	2,026	139	1,886	19	30	55	151
VT.	594	584	5	579	3	1	5	5
VA.	6,873	5,210	233	4,977	1,385	19	258	266
WA	5,756	5,104	335	4,769	204	105	344	377
WV	1,807	1,740	9	1,730	56	2	9	10
WI	5,250	4,827	126	4,701	293	47	83	140
WY	480	460	27	434	4	11	4	29

[1] Persons of Hispanic origin may be of any race.

Source: U.S. Census Bureau, "Population estimates for States by Race and Hispanic Origin: July 1, 1999"; published 30 August 2000; <http://www.census.gov/population/estimates/state/srh/srhus99.txt>.

No. 26. Resident Population by Region, Race, and Hispanic Origin: 1990

[As of **April 1 (248,710 represents 248,710,000)**. For composition of regions, see map, inside front cover]

Race and Hispanic origin	Population (1,000)					Percent distribution				
	United States	North-east	Midwest	South	West	United States	North-east	Midwest	South	West
Total.	248,710	50,809	59,669	85,446	52,786	100.0	20.4	24.0	34.4	21.2
White.	199,686	42,069	52,018	65,582	40,017	100.0	21.1	26.0	32.8	20.0
Black.	29,986	5,613	5,716	15,829	2,828	100.0	18.7	19.1	52.8	9.4
American Indian, Eskimo, Aleut	1,959	125	338	563	933	100.0	6.4	17.2	28.7	47.6
American Indian	1,878	122	334	557	866	100.0	6.5	17.8	29.7	46.1
Eskimo.	57	2	2	3	51	100.0	2.9	3.5	4.9	88.8
Aleut	24	2	2	3	17	100.0	8.1	8.1	11.5	72.3
Asian and Pacific Islander .	7,274	1,335	768	1,122	4,048	100.0	18.4	10.6	15.4	55.7
Chinese	1,645	445	133	204	863	100.0	27.0	8.1	12.4	52.4
Filipino	1,407	143	113	159	991	100.0	10.2	8.1	11.3	70.5
Japanese	848	74	63	67	643	100.0	8.8	7.5	7.9	75.9
Asian Indian	815	285	146	196	189	100.0	35.0	17.9	24.0	23.1
Korean.	799	182	109	153	355	100.0	22.8	13.7	19.2	44.4
Vietnamese	615	61	52	169	334	100.0	9.8	8.5	27.4	54.3
Laotian.	149	16	28	29	76	100.0	10.7	18.6	19.6	51.0
Cambodian	147	30	13	19	85	100.0	20.5	8.8	13.1	57.7
Thai.	91	12	13	24	43	100.0	12.9	14.2	26.0	46.8
Hmong	90	2	37	2	50	100.0	1.9	41.3	1.8	55.0
Pakistani.	81	28	15	22	17	100.0	34.3	18.9	26.5	20.4
Hawaiian.	211	4	6	12	189	100.0	2.0	2.6	5.8	89.6
Samoan	63	2	2	4	55	100.0	2.4	3.6	6.4	87.6
Guamanian	49	4	3	8	34	100.0	7.3	6.4	16.8	69.5
Other Asian or Pacific Islander	263	49	34	54	126	100.0	18.5	12.9	20.6	48.0
Other races	9,805	1,667	829	2,350	4,960	100.0	17.0	8.5	24.0	50.6
Hispanic origin [1]	22,354	3,754	1,727	6,767	10,106	100.0	16.8	7.7	30.3	45.2
Mexican	13,496	175	1,153	4,344	7,824	100.0	1.3	8.5	32.2	58.0
Puerto Rican	2,728	1,872	258	406	192	100.0	68.6	9.4	14.9	7.0
Cuban	1,044	184	37	735	88	100.0	17.6	3.5	70.5	8.5
Other Hispanic.	5,086	1,524	279	1,282	2,002	100.0	30.0	5.5	25.2	39.4
Not of Hispanic origin . . .	226,356	47,055	57,942	78,679	42,680	100.0	20.8	25.6	34.8	18.9

[1] Persons of Hispanic origin may be of any race.

Source: U.S. Census Bureau, *1990 Census of Population, General Population Characteristics, United States* (CP-1-1).

No. 27. Annual Inmigration, Outmigration, and Net Migration for Regions: 1980 to 1999

[In thousands (464 represents 464,000). As of **March. For persons 1 year old and over.** Excludes members of the Armed Forces except those living off post or with their families on post. Based on Current Population Survey; see text of this section and Appendix III. For composition of regions, see map, inside front cover. Minus sign (-) indicates net outmigration]

Period	North-east	Mid-west	South	West	Period	North-east	Mid-west	South	West
1980-81:					**1996-97:**				
Inmigrants.	464	650	1,377	871	Inmigrants.	481	661	1,338	688
Outmigrants	706	1,056	890	710	Outmigrants	600	814	947	806
Net internal migration . .	-242	-406	487	161	Net internal migration . .	-119	-154	391	-118
Movers from abroad	207	180	412	514	Movers from abroad	239	169	445	450
Net migration	-35	-226	899	675	Net migration	120	15	836	332
1985-86:					**1997-98:**				
Inmigrants.	502	1,011	1,355	910	Inmigrants.	504	873	1,335	660
Outmigrants	752	996	1,320	710	Outmigrants	708	753	1,105	806
Net internal migration . .	-250	15	35	200	Net internal migration . .	-203	120	230	-146
Movers from abroad	198	158	342	502	Movers from abroad	247	170	416	370
Net migration	-52	173	377	702	Net migration	44	290	646	224
1990-91:					**1998-99:**				
Inmigrants.	346	782	1,421	835	Total inmigrants	461	736	1,339	743
Outmigrants	932	797	987	668	From Northeast	(X)	94	383	146
Net internal migration . .	-585	-15	433	167	From Midwest	98	(X)	556	253
Movers from abroad	209	208	351	617	From South	262	463	(X)	344
Net migration	-376	193	784	784	From West	101	178	400	(X)
1995-96:					Total outmigrants	624	906	1,068	679
Inmigrants.	441	842	1,284	792	To Northeast	(X)	98	262	101
Outmigrants	675	775	1,134	775	To Midwest	94	(X)	463	178
Net internal migration . .	-234	68	150	16	To South	262	463	(X)	344
Movers from abroad	285	130	470	476	To West	146	253	344	(X)
Net migration	51	198	620	492	Net internal migration . .	-163	-171	270	63
					Movers from abroad	198	221	544	466
					Net migration	35	50	814	529

X Not applicable.

Source: U.S. Census Bureau, *Current Population Reports*, P20-531, and earlier reports.

Population   29

No. 28. Mobility Status of the Population by Selected Characteristic: 1980 to 1999

[As of **March (221,641 represents 221,641,000). For persons 1 year old and over.** Excludes members of the Armed Forces except those living off post or with their families on post. Based on Current Population Survey; see text of this section and Appendix III. For composition of regions, see map, inside front cover]

Mobility period and characteristic	Total (1,000)	Non-movers	Percent distribution					
			Movers (different house in United States)					Movers from abroad
			Total	Same county	Different county			
					Total	Same state	Different state	
1980-81.	221,641	83	17	10	6	3	3	1
1985-86.	232,998	82	18	11	7	4	3	1
1990-91.	244,884	83	16	10	6	3	3	1
1995-96.	260,406	84	16	10	6	3	3	1
1998-99, total	**267,933**	**84**	**15**	**9**	**6**	**3**	**3**	**1**
1 to 4 years old.	15,792	76	23	16	8	4	4	1
5 to 9 years old.	20,557	81	18	13	6	3	3	1
10 to 14 years old.	19,909	86	13	8	5	2	2	(Z)
15 to 19 years old.	19,864	84	15	9	6	3	3	1
20 to 24 years old.	18,058	67	32	19	13	7	6	1
25 to 29 years old.	18,639	68	31	18	13	7	6	1
30 to 44 years old.	64,579	83	16	10	6	3	3	1
45 to 64 years old.	58,141	92	8	5	4	2	2	(Z)
65 to 74 years old.	17,844	95	5	3	2	1	1	(Z)
75 to 84 years old.	11,497	96	4	2	1	1	1	(Z)
85 years old and over	3,054	96	4	2	2	1	1	(Z)
Northeast.	51,253	88	11	7	4	2	2	(Z)
Midwest.	62,363	85	15	9	6	3	3	(Z)
South	93,489	83	17	10	7	4	3	1
West.	60,828	81	18	12	6	3	3	1
Persons 16 years and over	**207,777**	**85**	**15**	**9**	**6**	**3**	**3**	**1**
Civilian labor force.	138,120	83	17	10	7	4	3	1
Employed.	131,806	83	16	10	6	4	3	(Z)
Unemployed.	6,314	72	26	15	11	6	5	1
Armed Forces.	739	60	35	12	23	4	20	4
Not in labor force	68,918	89	10	6	4	2	2	1
Persons 15 years and over	**211,676**	**85**	**15**	**9**	**6**	**3**	**3**	**1**
Without income.	18,034	83	15	10	6	3	3	2
With income.	193,642	85	15	9	6	3	3	(Z)
Less than $5,000	26,507	84	15	9	6	3	3	1
$5,000 to $9,999	27,605	85	15	10	5	3	3	(Z)
$10,000 to $14,999	23,661	84	16	9	6	3	3	(Z)
$15,000 to $24,999	36,637	83	16	10	7	3	3	(Z)
$25,000 to $34,999	27,222	85	15	9	6	3	3	(Z)
$35,000 to $49,999	24,383	86	14	8	6	3	2	(Z)
$50,000 to $74,999	16,857	88	12	6	6	3	3	(Z)
$75,000 and over.	10,770	89	11	6	5	2	3	(Z)
Tenure:								
Owner-occupied units.	186,416	92	8	5	3	2	1	(Z)
Renter-occupied units.	81,517	67	32	20	12	6	6	1

Z Less than 0.5 percent.

Source: U.S. Census Bureau, *Current Population Reports*, P20-531.

No. 29. Mobility Status of Households by Household Income: 1998-99

[As of **March (103,890 represents 103,890,000).** See headnote, Table 28]

Household income	Total (1,000)	Non-movers	Percent distribution					
			Movers (different house in United States)					Movers from abroad
			Total	Same county	Different county			
					Total	Same state	Different state	
Householders, 15 years and over. . .	**103,890**	**85**	**15**	**9**	**6**	**3**	**3**	**(Z)**
Less than $5,000	3,376	74	23	14	9	4	4	3
$5,000 to $9,999.	7,332	82	18	13	5	3	3	1
$10,000 to $14,999	8,093	82	18	11	6	3	3	(Z)
$15,000 to $24,999	14,592	82	18	11	6	4	3	(Z)
$25,000 to $34,999	13,699	83	16	10	6	3	3	(Z)
$35,000 to $49,999	16,663	85	15	9	6	3	3	(Z)
$50,000 to $69,999	16,204	86	13	8	6	3	2	(Z)
$70,000 and over	23,931	89	11	6	5	2	2	(Z)

Z Less than 0.5 percent.

Source: U.S. Census Bureau, *Current Population Reports*, P20-531.

No. 30. Population in Coastal Counties: 1970 to 1999

[Enumerated population as of **April 1, except as indicated (3,536 represents 3,536,000)**. Areas as defined by U.S. National Oceanic and Atmospheric Agency, 1992. Covers 673 counties and equivalent areas with at least 15 percent of their land area either in a coastal watershed (drainage area) or in a coastal cataloging unit (a coastal area between watersheds)]

Year	Counties in coastal regions						Balance of United States
	Total	Total	Atlantic	Gulf of Mexico	Great Lakes	Pacific	
Land area, 1990 (1,000 sq. mi.)	3,536	888	148	114	115	510	2,649
POPULATION							
1970 (mil.).	203.3	110.0	51.1	10.0	26.0	22.8	93.3
1980 (mil.).	226.5	119.8	53.7	13.1	26.0	27.0	106.7
1990 (mil.).	248.7	133.4	59.0	15.2	25.9	33.2	115.3
1995 (July 1) (mil.)	262.8	139.4	61.0	16.5	26.6	35.2	123.4
1999 (July 1) (mil.)	272.7	143.9	62.7	17.3	26.8	37.0	128.8
1970 (percent)	100	54	25	5	13	11	46
1980 (percent)	100	53	24	6	11	12	47
1990 (percent)	100	54	24	6	10	13	46
1995 (July 1) (percent)	100	53	23	6	10	13	47
1999 (July 1) (percent)	100	53	23	6	10	14	47

Source: U.S. Census Bureau, *U.S. Census of Population: 1970; 1980 Census of Population*, Vol. 1, Chapter A (PC80-1-A-1), *U.S. Summary; 1990 Census of Population and Housing* (CPH1); and unpublished data.

No. 31. Metropolitan and Nonmetropolitan Area Population: 1970 to 1998

[As of **April 1, except 1998**, as of **July 1 (139,480 represents 139,480,000)**. Data exclude Puerto Rico. Metropolitan areas are defined by U.S. Office of Management and Budget as of year shown, except as noted]

Item	1970	1980 [1] (SMSAs)	MSAs and CMSAs [2]		
			1980	1990	1998
Metropolitan areas:					
Number of areas	243	318	276	276	276
Population (1,000)	139,480	169,431	177,505	198,407	216,478
Percent change over previous year shown . .	[3]23.6	21.5	(X)	11.8	9.1
Percent of total U.S. population	68.6	74.8	78.4	79.8	80.1
Land area, percent of U.S. land area	10.9	16.0	20.0	20.0	20.0
Nonmetropolitan areas, population (1,000)	63,822	57,115	49,037	50,311	53,820

X Not applicable.   [1] SMSA=standard metropolitan statistical area. Areas are as defined June 30, 1981.   [2] Areas are as defined June 30, 1999.   [3] Percent change from 1960.

Source: U.S. Census Bureau, *U.S. Census of Population: 1970*; "MA-98-3a Population Estimates for Metropolitan Areas and Components, Annual Time Series April 1, 1990, to July 1, 1998"; published 17 December 1999; <http://www.census.gov/population/estimates/metro-city/ma98-03a.txt>; and unpublished data.

No. 32. Number and Population of Metropolitan Areas by Population Size of Area in 1998: 1990 and 1998

[As of **April 1** for **1990** and as of **July** for **1998 (198.5 represents 198,500,000)**. Data exclude Puerto Rico. CMSA=consolidated metropolitan statistical area. MSA=metropolitan statistical area. PMSA=primary metropolitan statistical area. Areas are as defined by U.S. Office of Management and Budget, June 30, 1999. For area definitions, see Appendix II]

Population size of metropolitan area in 1998	CMSAs and MSAs				MSAs and PMSAs		
	Number	Popu- lation, 1990 (mil.)	Population, 1998		Number	Population, 1998	
			Total (mil.)	Percent in each class		Total (mil.)	Percent in each class
Total, all metropolitan areas . . .	**276**	**198.5**	**216.5**	**100**	**331**	**216.5**	**100**
1,000,000 or more	48	140.2	153.2	71	60	139.0	64
2,500,000 or more	18	101.4	110.0	51	17	73.7	34
1,000,000 to 2,499,999	30	38.8	43.2	20	43	65.2	30
250,000 to 999,999	91	39.8	43.4	20	115	54.1	25
500,000 to 999,999	31	19.9	21.5	10	39	26.4	12
250,000 to 499,999	60	19.9	21.9	10	76	27.7	13
100,000 to 249,999	115	16.7	18.0	8	134	21.6	10
Less than 100,000	22	1.8	1.9	1	22	1.9	1

Source: U.S. Census Bureau, "(MA-98-1) Metropolitan Area Population Estimates for July 1, 1998 and Population Change for April 1, 1990 to July 1, 1998 (includes revised April 1, 1990 census population counts)"; published 17 December 1999; <http://www.census.gov/population/estimates/metro-city/ma98-01.txt>.

[As of **April 1, except 1998**, as of **July (177,505 represents 177,505,000)**. Metropolitan refers to 258 metropolitan statistical areas and 18 consolidated metropolitan statistical areas as defined by U.S. Office of Management and Budget, June 30, 1999; nonmetropolitan is the area outside metropolitan areas; see Appendix II. Minus sign (-) indicates decrease]

State	Metropolitan population						Nonmetropolitan population					
	Total (1,000)			Percent change,	Percent of state		Total (1,000)			Percent change,	Percent of state	
	1980	1990	1998	1990-98	1990	1998	1980	1990	1998	1990-98	1990	1998
U.S. ...	177,505	198,407	216,478	9.1	79.8	80.1	49,037	50,311	53,820	7.0	20.2	19.9
AL	2,636	2,797	3,050	9.1	69.2	70.1	1,258	1,244	1,302	4.7	30.8	29.9
AK	174	226	255	12.7	41.1	41.5	227	324	359	10.9	58.9	58.5
AZ	2,339	3,202	4,099	28.0	87.4	87.8	378	463	570	23.1	12.6	12.2
AR	1,026	1,109	1,234	11.3	47.2	48.6	1,260	1,242	1,304	5.0	52.8	51.4
CA	22,907	28,797	31,581	9.7	96.8	96.7	760	961	1,086	12.9	3.2	3.3
CO	2,408	2,779	3,335	20.0	84.4	84.0	482	515	636	23.6	15.6	16.0
CT	2,982	3,148	3,129	-0.6	95.8	95.6	126	140	145	3.7	4.2	4.4
DE	496	553	607	9.8	83.0	81.6	98	113	137	20.7	17.0	18.4
DC	638	607	523	-13.8	100.0	100.0	(X)	(X)	(X)	(X)	(X)	(X)
FL	9,039	12,024	13,866	15.3	92.9	93.0	708	915	1,050	14.8	7.1	7.0
GA	3,507	4,351	5,262	20.9	67.2	68.9	1,956	2,127	2,380	11.9	32.8	31.1
HI	763	836	872	4.3	75.5	73.1	202	272	321	17.8	24.5	26.9
ID	322	362	471	30.1	35.9	38.3	622	645	758	17.5	64.1	61.7
IL	9,461	9,574	10,175	6.3	83.8	84.5	1,967	1,857	1,870	0.7	16.2	15.5
IN	3,885	3,962	4,230	6.8	71.5	71.7	1,605	1,582	1,669	5.5	28.5	28.3
IA	1,198	1,200	1,278	6.5	43.2	44.6	1,716	1,577	1,585	0.5	56.8	55.4
KS	1,184	1,333	1,483	11.2	53.8	56.4	1,180	1,145	1,146	0.2	46.2	43.6
KY	1,735	1,780	1,902	6.8	48.3	48.3	1,925	1,907	2,035	6.7	51.7	51.7
LA	3,125	3,160	3,287	4.0	74.9	75.2	1,082	1,061	1,082	2.0	25.1	24.8
ME	405	443	446	0.7	36.1	35.8	721	785	798	1.7	63.9	64.2
MD	3,920	4,438	4,760	7.3	92.8	92.7	297	343	374	9.3	7.2	7.3
MA	5,530	5,788	5,908	2.1	96.2	96.1	207	229	239	4.6	3.8	3.9
MI	7,719	7,698	8,110	5.4	82.8	82.6	1,543	1,598	1,707	6.9	17.2	17.4
MN	2,674	3,011	3,311	9.9	68.8	70.1	1,402	1,364	1,415	3.7	31.2	29.9
MS	806	874	987	12.9	34.0	35.9	1,715	1,701	1,765	3.8	66.0	64.1
MO	3,314	3,491	3,696	5.9	68.2	68.0	1,603	1,626	1,742	7.1	31.8	32.0
MT	265	270	294	9.0	33.8	33.4	522	529	586	10.8	66.2	66.6
NE	728	787	862	9.5	49.9	51.8	842	791	801	1.2	50.1	48.2
NV	666	1,014	1,505	48.4	84.4	86.1	135	188	242	29.0	15.6	13.9
NH	535	659	713	8.2	59.4	60.2	386	450	472	4.8	40.6	39.8
NJ	7,365	7,730	8,115	5.0	100.0	100.0	(X)	(X)	(X)	(X)	(X)	(X)
NM	675	842	990	17.6	55.6	57.0	628	673	747	11.0	44.4	43.0
NY	16,144	16,516	16,697	1.1	91.8	91.9	1,414	1,475	1,478	0.2	8.2	8.1
NC	3,749	4,380	5,061	15.5	66.0	67.1	2,131	2,253	2,486	10.3	34.0	32.9
ND	234	257	275	6.9	40.3	43.1	418	381	363	-4.8	59.7	56.9
OH	8,791	8,826	9,075	2.8	81.4	81.0	2,007	2,021	2,135	5.6	18.6	19.0
OK	1,724	1,870	2,024	8.2	59.4	60.5	1,301	1,276	1,323	3.7	40.6	39.5
OR	1,867	2,056	2,387	16.1	72.3	72.7	766	787	895	13.7	27.7	27.3
PA	10,067	10,084	10,144	0.6	84.9	84.5	1,798	1,799	1,858	3.3	15.1	15.5
RI	886	938	927	-1.2	93.5	93.8	61	65	61	-6.4	6.5	6.2
SC	2,114	2,422	2,687	10.9	69.5	70.0	1,006	1,064	1,149	7.9	30.5	30.0
SD	194	221	251	13.8	31.7	34.0	497	475	487	2.4	68.3	66.0
TN	3,058	3,311	3,685	11.3	67.9	67.8	1,533	1,567	1,746	11.5	32.1	32.2
TX	11,539	14,166	16,688	17.8	83.4	84.5	2,686	2,821	3,072	8.9	16.6	15.5
UT	1,132	1,341	1,610	20.0	77.8	76.7	329	382	490	28.4	22.2	23.3
VT	133	152	165	8.6	26.9	27.9	378	411	426	3.7	73.1	72.1
VA	3,966	4,775	5,307	11.1	77.2	78.1	1,381	1,414	1,484	5.0	22.8	21.9
WA	3,366	4,036	4,718	16.9	82.9	82.9	766	830	972	17.0	17.1	17.1
WV	796	748	759	1.4	41.7	41.9	1,155	1,045	1,052	0.7	58.3	58.1
WI	3,176	3,331	3,543	6.4	68.1	67.8	1,530	1,561	1,681	7.7	31.9	32.2
WY	141	134	142	5.8	29.6	29.6	329	319	339	6.1	70.4	70.4

X Not applicable.

Source: U.S. Census Bureau, *1990 Census of Population and Housing, Population and Housing Unit Counts* (CPH-2-1); "MA-98-3a Population Estimates for Metropolitan Areas and Components, Annual Time Series April 1, 1990, to July 1, 1998"; published 17 December 1999; <http://www.census.gov/population/estimates/metro-city/ma98-03a.txt>; and unpublished data.

No. 34. Large Metropolitan Areas—Population: 1980 to 1998

[In thousands, except percent (825 represents 825,000). As of **April 1**, except as noted. Covers 18 consolidated metropolitan statistical areas (CMSAs), their 73 component primary metropolitan statistical areas (PMSAs), and the remaining 121 MSAs with 250,000 and over population in 1998 as defined by the U.S. Office of Management and Budget as of June 30, 1999. For definitions and components of all metropolitan areas and population of NECMAs (New England County Metropolitan Areas), see Appendix II. Minus sign (-) indicates decrease]

Metropolitan area	Number (1,000)					Rank, 1998	Percent change	
	1980	1990 [1]	1995 (July)	1997 (July)	1998 (July)		1980-90	1990-98
Albany-Schenectady-Troy, NY MSA............	825	862	881	874	872	55	4.5	1.2
Albuquerque, NM MSA....................	485	589	660	674	679	62	21.4	15.2
Allentown-Bethlehem-Easton, PA MSA..........	551	595	611	615	617	65	8.0	3.7
Anchorage, AK MSA....................	174	226	251	251	255	138	29.8	12.7
Appleton-Oshkosh-Neenah, WI MSA..........	291	315	336	342	344	115	8.2	9.3
Atlanta, GA MSA.....................	2,233	2,960	3,430	3,634	3,746	11	32.5	26.6
Augusta-Aiken, GA-SC MSA...............	363	415	452	455	458	85	14.2	10.4
Austin-San Marcos, TX MSA..............	585	846	1,002	1,070	1,106	41	44.6	30.7
Bakersfield, CA MSA...................	403	545	613	625	631	64	35.2	15.9
Baton Rouge, LA MSA..................	494	528	562	571	575	70	6.9	8.9
Beaumont-Port Arthur, TX MSA............	373	361	375	374	376	106	-3.2	4.0
Biloxi-Gulfport-Pascagoula, MS MSA..........	300	312	341	344	349	113	4.1	11.8
Birmingham, AL MSA...................	815	840	895	901	909	53	3.0	8.2
Boise City, ID MSA....................	257	296	361	384	396	100	15.2	33.8
Boston-Worcester-Lawrence, MA-NH-ME-CT CMSA .	5,122	5,455	5,521	5,593	5,633	7	6.5	3.3
Boston, MA-NH PMSA..................	3,149	3,228	3,244	3,273	3,289	(X)	2.5	1.9
Brockton, MA PMSA...................	225	236	244	248	251	(X)	5.1	6.2
Fitchburg-Leominster, MA PMSA...........	125	138	139	141	142	(X)	10.5	2.4
Lawrence, MA-NH PMSA...............	298	353	367	377	382	(X)	18.4	8.2
Lowell, MA-NH PMSA.................	249	281	287	293	295	(X)	12.5	5.3
Manchester, NH PMSA................	146	174	180	184	187	(X)	18.9	7.9
Nashua, NH PMSA..................	134	168	176	180	182	(X)	25.4	8.5
New Bedford, MA PMSA...............	167	176	175	175	176	(X)	5.4	0.1
Portsmouth-Rochester, NH-ME PMSA.......	189	223	228	233	236	(X)	18.0	5.5
Worcester, MA-CT PMSA..............	439	478	483	488	492	(X)	8.9	2.9
Brownsville-Harlingen-San Benito, TX MSA	210	260	304	319	326	118	24.0	25.5
Buffalo-Niagara Falls, NY MSA.............	1,243	1,189	1,181	1,163	1,153	38	-4.3	-3.1
Canton-Massillon, OH MSA...............	404	394	402	403	402	97	-2.6	2.1
Charleston-North Charleston, SC MSA.........	430	507	526	534	541	76	17.8	6.8
Charleston, WV MSA...................	270	250	254	253	253	139	-7.1	1.1
Charlotte-Gastonia-Rock Hill, NC-SC MSA.......	971	1,162	1,287	1,352	1,383	32	19.6	19.0
Chattanooga, TN-GA MSA................	418	424	442	448	450	88	1.6	6.1
Chicago-Gary-Kenosha, IL-IN-WI CMSA........	8,115	8,240	8,629	8,751	8,810	3	1.5	6.9
Chicago, IL PMSA..................	7,246	7,411	7,769	7,883	7,939	(X)	2.3	7.1
Gary, IN PMSA....................	643	605	620	623	624	(X)	-5.9	3.2
Kankakee, IL PMSA.................	103	96	101	102	102	(X)	-6.5	6.1
Kenosha, WI PMSA.................	123	128	139	143	144	(X)	4.1	12.6
Cincinnati-Hamilton, OH-KY-IN CMSA	1,726	1,818	1,906	1,934	1,948	23	5.3	7.2
Cincinnati, OH-KY-IN PMSA.............	1,468	1,526	1,587	1,607	1,618	(X)	4.0	6.0
Hamilton-Middletown, OH PMSA..........	259	291	320	327	330	(X)	12.6	13.4
Cleveland-Akron, OH CMSA..............	2,938	2,860	2,911	2,915	2,912	15	-2.7	1.8
Akron, OH PMSA...................	660	658	681	687	689	(X)	-0.4	4.8
Cleveland-Lorain-Elyria, OH PMSA	2,278	2,202	2,231	2,227	2,223	(X)	-3.3	0.9
Colorado Springs, CO MSA..............	309	397	465	480	490	80	28.3	23.5
Columbia, SC MSA...................	410	454	491	504	512	79	10.7	12.9
Columbus, GA-AL MSA.................	255	261	272	272	272	135	2.4	4.3
Columbus, OH MSA...................	1,214	1,345	1,430	1,456	1,470	31	10.8	9.2
Corpus Christi, TX MSA................	326	350	378	386	388	103	7.3	10.8
Dallas-Fort Worth, TX CMSA.............	3,046	4,037	4,447	4,678	4,802	9	32.5	19.0
Dallas, TX PMSA...................	2,055	2,676	2,960	3,123	3,210	(X)	30.2	19.9
Fort Worth-Arlington, TX PMSA..........	991	1,361	1,487	1,555	1,593	(X)	37.4	17.0
Davenport-Moline-Rock Island, IA-IL MSA......	385	351	357	357	358	109	-8.8	2.0
Dayton-Springfield, OH MSA.............	942	951	958	952	949	51	1.0	-0.3
Daytona Beach, FL MSA................	270	399	449	463	471	82	48.1	17.9
Denver-Boulder-Greeley, CO CMSA.........	1,742	1,980	2,227	2,319	2,365	19	13.7	19.5
Boulder-Longmont, CO PMSA............	190	225	253	262	267	(X)	18.8	18.6
Denver, CO PMSA..................	1,429	1,623	1,826	1,902	1,939	(X)	13.6	19.4
Greeley, CO PMSA..................	123	132	148	156	159	(X)	6.8	20.9
Des Moines, IA MSA..................	368	393	423	432	437	92	6.9	11.2
Detroit-Ann Arbor-Flint, MI CMSA..........	5,293	5,187	5,380	5,443	5,458	8	-2.0	5.2
Ann Arbor, MI PMSA................	455	490	521	539	548	(X)	7.7	11.8
Detroit, MI PMSA..................	4,388	4,267	4,425	4,469	4,474	(X)	-2.8	4.9
Flint, MI PMSA...................	450	430	434	435	436	(X)	-4.4	1.3
El Paso, TX MSA....................	480	592	672	690	703	60	23.3	18.8
Erie, PA MSA......................	280	276	279	278	276	133	-1.5	0.3
Eugene-Springfield, OR MSA.............	275	283	303	311	314	122	2.8	11.0
Evansville-Henderson, IN-KY MSA..........	276	279	287	289	291	129	1.0	4.2
Fayetteville, NC MSA..................	247	275	284	284	285	131	11.1	3.6
Fayetteville-Springdale-Rogers, AR MSA........	179	211	254	268	273	134	18.1	29.3
Fort Myers-Cape Coral, FL MSA............	205	335	374	386	393	101	63.3	17.2
Fort Pierce-Port St. Lucie, FL MSA..........	151	251	281	291	295	127	66.1	17.5
Fort Wayne, IN MSA..................	445	456	471	478	481	81	2.6	5.5
Fresno, CA MSA.....................	578	756	841	863	870	56	30.8	15.2

See footnotes at end of table.

Population   33

[See headnote, page 33]

Metropolitan area	Number (1,000)					Percent change	
	1980	1990 [1]	1995 (July)	1997 (July)	1998 (July)	Rank, 1998	1980-90	1990-98
Grand Rapids-Muskegon-Holland, MI MSA........	841	938	1,002	1,028	1,038	47	11.5	10.7
Greensboro—Winston-Salem—High Point, NC MSA .	951	1,050	1,123	1,153	1,168	36	10.5	11.2
Greenville-Spartanburg-Anderson, SC MSA	744	831	882	907	918	52	11.6	10.6
Harrisburg-Lebanon-Carlisle, PA MSA	556	588	611	615	616	66	5.7	4.8
Hartford, CT MSA	1,081	1,158	1,142	1,141	1,144	39	7.1	-1.2
Hickory-Morganton, NC MSA..................	270	292	310	318	323	119	8.1	10.3
Honolulu, HI MSA	763	836	873	874	872	54	9.7	4.3
Houston-Galveston-Brazoria, TX CMSA..........	3,118	3,731	4,153	4,314	4,408	10	19.6	18.1
Brazoria, TX PMSA........................	170	192	215	225	230	(X)	13.0	20.1
Galveston-Texas City, TX PMSA.............	196	217	237	242	246	(X)	11.1	13.0
Houston, TX PMSA........................	2,753	3,322	3,701	3,847	3,932	(X)	20.7	18.4
Huntington-Ashland, WV-KY-OH MSA............	336	313	316	315	314	123	-7.1	0.4
Huntsville, AL MSA	243	293	328	334	340	116	20.6	16.2
Indianapolis, IN MSA	1,306	1,380	1,474	1,504	1,519	29	5.7	10.0
Jackson, MS MSA	362	395	415	425	430	93	9.2	8.7
Jacksonville, FL MSA	722	907	980	1,029	1,045	45	25.5	15.2
Johnson City-Kingsport-Bristol, TN-VA MSA	434	436	453	460	462	84	0.6	6.0
Kalamazoo-Battle Creek, MI MSA..............	421	429	442	445	446	91	2.1	3.9
Kansas City, MO-KS MSA.....................	1,449	1,583	1,686	1,717	1,737	24	9.2	9.7
Killeen-Temple, TX MSA	215	255	291	299	301	126	19.0	18.1
Knoxville, TN MSA...........................	546	586	639	655	659	63	7.2	12.5
Lafayette, LA MSA...........................	331	345	364	372	376	105	4.3	8.9
Lakeland-Winter Haven, FL MSA	322	405	435	446	453	87	26.0	11.6
Lancaster, PA MSA	362	423	447	454	456	86	16.7	7.9
Lansing-East Lansing, MI MSA.................	420	433	454	450	450	89	3.1	3.9
Las Vegas, NV-AZ MSA	528	853	1,138	1,262	1,322	33	61.5	55.0
Lexington, KY MSA	371	406	434	444	450	90	9.4	10.8
Little Rock-North Little Rock, AR MSA	474	513	542	552	556	72	8.1	8.4
Los Angeles-Riverside-Orange County, CA CMSA .	11,498	14,532	15,259	15,550	15,781	2	26.4	8.6
Los Angeles-Long Beach, CA PMSA	7,477	8,863	9,029	9,117	9,214	(X)	18.5	4.0
Orange County, CA PMSA	1,933	2,411	2,572	2,664	2,722	(X)	24.7	12.9
Riverside-San Bernardino, CA PMSA.........	1,558	2,589	2,954	3,048	3,114	(X)	66.1	20.3
Ventura, CA MSA..........................	529	669	704	722	732	(X)	26.4	9.4
Louisville, KY-IN MSA........................	954	949	984	995	999	49	-0.5	5.3
Macon, GA MSA	273	291	309	316	320	121	6.6	9.8
Madison, WI MSA	324	367	409	422	425	95	13.5	15.7
McAllen-Edinburg-Mission, TX MSA	283	384	477	505	522	78	35.4	36.2
Melbourne-Titusville-Palm Bay, FL MSA.........	273	399	450	460	466	83	46.2	16.8
Memphis, TN-AR-MS MSA	939	1,007	1,064	1,083	1,093	42	7.3	8.5
Miami-Fort Lauderdale, FL CMSA..............	2,644	3,193	3,478	3,602	3,656	12	20.8	14.5
Fort Lauderdale, FL PMSA..................	1,018	1,256	1,413	1,473	1,503	(X)	23.3	19.7
Miami, FL PMSA..........................	1,626	1,937	2,064	2,129	2,152	(X)	19.2	11.1
Milwaukee-Racine, WI CMSA..................	1,570	1,607	1,644	1,645	1,646	26	2.4	2.4
Milwaukee-Waukesha, WI PMSA.............	1,397	1,432	1,461	1,460	1,460	(X)	2.5	1.9
Racine, WI PMSA.........................	173	175	184	185	186	(X)	1.1	6.3
Minneapolis-St. Paul, MN-WI MSA	2,198	2,539	2,726	2,795	2,831	16	15.5	11.5
Mobile, AL MSA.............................	444	477	516	527	532	77	7.5	11.6
Modesto, CA MSA...........................	266	371	409	419	426	94	39.3	15.1
Montgomery, AL MSA........................	273	293	314	319	322	120	7.3	10.0
Nashville, TN MSA...........................	851	985	1,092	1,137	1,156	37	15.8	17.4
New London-Norwich, CT-RI MSA..............	273	291	285	285	282	132	6.5	-2.9
New Orleans, LA MSA	1,304	1,285	1,311	1,308	1,309	34	-1.5	1.9
New York-Northern New Jersey-Long Island, NY-NJ-CT-PA CMSA........................	18,906	19,565	19,844	20,006	20,124	1	3.5	2.9
Bergen-Passaic, NJ PMSA..................	1,293	1,296	1,321	1,336	1,344	(X)	0.3	3.7
Bridgeport, CT PMSA	439	442	440	442	443	(X)	0.8	0.3
Danbury, CT PMSA	175	194	197	200	202	(X)	10.3	4.3
Dutchess County, NY PMSA................	245	259	261	264	265	(X)	5.9	2.3
Jersey City, NJ PMSA.....................	557	553	551	555	557	(X)	-0.7	0.7
Middlesex-Somerset-Hunterdon, NJ PMSA ...	886	1,020	1,077	1,106	1,122	(X)	15.1	10.0
Monmouth-Ocean, NJ PMSA	849	986	1,051	1,079	1,093	(X)	16.1	10.8
Nassau-Suffolk, NY PMSA..................	2,606	2,609	2,648	2,661	2,673	(X)	0.1	2.5
New Haven-Meriden, CT PMSA	500	530	523	522	523	(X)	5.9	-1.4
New York, NY PMSA......................	8,275	8,547	8,602	8,650	8,693	(X)	3.3	1.7
Newark, NJ PMSA	1,964	1,916	1,934	1,943	1,952	(X)	-2.4	1.9
Newburgh, NY-PA PMSA...................	278	336	358	365	369	(X)	20.8	10.1
Stamford-Norwalk, CT PMSA...............	326	330	330	332	333	(X)	1.3	0.9
Trenton, NJ PMSA	308	326	329	330	332	(X)	5.8	1.8
Waterbury, CT PMSA	205	222	221	222	222	(X)	8.1	0.2
Norfolk-Virginia Beach-Newport News, VA-NC MSA ..	1,201	1,445	1,532	1,545	1,542	27	20.3	6.7
Oklahoma City, OK MSA......................	861	959	1,013	1,031	1,039	46	11.4	8.4
Omaha, NE-IA MSA..........................	605	640	670	687	694	61	5.6	8.5
Orlando, FL MSA............................	805	1,225	1,389	1,463	1,505	30	52.2	22.8
Pensacola, FL MSA..........................	290	344	377	395	400	99	18.9	16.0
Peoria-Pekin, IL MSA	366	339	345	345	345	114	-7.3	1.7

See footnotes at end of table.

U.S. Census Bureau, Statistical Abstract of the United States: 2000

[See headnote, page 33]

Metropolitan area	Number (1,000)					Rank, 1998	Percent change	
	1980	1990 [1]	1995 (July)	1997 (July)	1998 (July)		1980-90	1990-98
Philadelphia-Wilmington-Atlantic City, PA-NJ-DE-MD CMSA	5,649	5,893	5,973	5,975	5,988	6	4.3	1.6
Atlantic-Cape May, NJ PMSA	276	319	331	334	336	(X)	15.6	5.2
Philadelphia, PA-NJ PMSA.	4,781	4,922	4,953	4,940	4,947	(X)	2.9	0.5
Vineland-Millville-Bridgeton, NJ PMSA	133	138	141	141	140	(X)	3.9	1.7
Wilmington-Newark, DE-MD PMSA	459	513	548	560	565	(X)	11.9	10.1
Phoenix-Mesa, AZ MSA	1,600	2,238	2,661	2,842	2,931	14	39.9	30.9
Pittsburgh, PA MSA	2,571	2,395	2,386	2,360	2,346	20	-6.9	-2.0
Portland-Salem, OR-WA CMSA	1,584	1,793	2,025	2,115	2,149	22	13.3	19.8
Portland-Vancouver, OR-WA PMSA	1,334	1,515	1,712	1,790	1,819	(X)	13.6	20.0
Salem, OR PMSA.	250	278	313	325	330	(X)	11.3	18.7
Providence-Fall River-Warwick, RI-MA MSA	1,077	1,134	1,123	1,121	1,123	40	5.4	-1.0
Provo-Orem, UT MSA.	218	264	320	329	336	117	20.9	27.3
Raleigh-Durham-Chapel Hill, NC MSA	665	858	993	1,050	1,080	44	29.1	25.8
Reading, PA MSA	313	337	350	354	356	111	7.7	5.8
Reno, NV MSA	194	255	290	307	314	124	31.5	23.2
Richmond-Petersburg, VA MSA	761	866	927	947	957	50	13.7	10.6
Rochester, NY MSA.	1,031	1,062	1,085	1,084	1,082	43	3.1	1.8
Rockford, IL MSA	326	330	349	355	357	110	1.2	8.3
Sacramento-Yolo, CA CMSA	1,100	1,481	1,605	1,656	1,686	25	34.7	13.8
Sacramento, CA PMSA.	986	1,340	1,458	1,504	1,532	(X)	35.8	14.3
Yolo, CA PMSA.	113	141	148	152	154	(X)	24.6	9.0
Saginaw-Bay City-Midland, MI MSA	422	399	402	402	402	98	-5.3	0.7
St. Louis, MO-IL MSA.	2,414	2,492	2,542	2,559	2,564	18	3.2	2.9
Salinas, CA MSA	290	356	343	358	366	108	22.5	2.8
Salt Lake City-Ogden, UT MSA	910	1,072	1,213	1,251	1,268	35	17.8	18.2
San Antonio, TX MSA.	1,089	1,325	1,455	1,507	1,538	28	21.7	16.1
San Diego, CA MSA.	1,862	2,498	2,641	2,724	2,781	17	34.2	11.3
San Francisco-Oakland-San Jose, CA CMSA	5,368	6,278	6,552	6,718	6,816	5	16.9	8.6
Oakland, CA PMSA	1,762	2,108	2,214	2,274	2,319	(X)	19.7	10.0
San Francisco, CA PMSA	1,489	1,604	1,642	1,670	1,683	(X)	7.7	5.0
San Jose, CA PMSA	1,295	1,498	1,567	1,620	1,641	(X)	15.6	9.6
Santa Cruz-Watsonville, CA PMSA	188	230	235	238	243	(X)	22.1	5.8
Santa Rosa, CA PMSA	300	388	415	426	433	(X)	29.5	11.6
Vallejo-Fairfield-Napa, CA PMSA.	334	450	480	489	497	(X)	34.6	10.3
Santa Barbara-Santa Maria-Lompoc, CA MSA	299	370	381	387	390	102	23.7	5.4
Sarasota-Bradenton, FL MSA.	351	489	523	535	543	75	39.6	11.0
Savannah, GA MSA	231	258	279	284	286	130	11.8	10.7
Scranton—Wilkes-Barre—Hazleton, PA MSA	659	639	631	621	615	67	-3.2	-3.6
Seattle-Tacoma-Bremerton, WA CMSA	2,409	2,970	3,264	3,378	3,424	13	23.3	15.3
Bremerton, WA PMSA.	147	190	226	234	233	(X)	28.9	22.6
Olympia, WA PMSA	124	161	192	200	202	(X)	29.8	25.4
Seattle-Bellevue-Everett, WA PMSA.	1,652	2,033	2,199	2,279	2,313	(X)	23.1	13.8
Tacoma, WA PMSA	486	586	647	665	677	(X)	20.7	15.4
Shreveport-Bossier City, LA MSA	377	376	379	379	379	104	-0.1	0.6
South Bend, IN MSA	242	247	256	258	258	137	2.2	4.5
Spokane, WA MSA	342	361	401	405	409	96	5.7	13.1
Springfield, MO MSA	228	264	294	301	305	125	15.9	15.3
Springfield, MA MSA	570	588	577	575	574	71	3.2	-2.4
Stockton-Lodi, CA MSA.	347	481	524	540	550	73	38.4	14.5
Syracuse, NY MSA	723	742	748	738	735	59	2.7	-1.0
Tallahassee, FL MSA	190	234	257	260	261	136	22.7	11.7
Tampa-St. Petersburg-Clearwater, FL MSA.	1,614	2,068	2,175	2,225	2,257	21	28.2	9.1
Toledo, OH MSA	617	614	611	611	610	68	-0.4	-0.7
Tucson, AZ MSA	531	667	754	779	791	57	25.5	18.6
Tulsa, OK MSA	657	709	745	765	777	58	7.9	9.6
Utica-Rome, NY MSA	320	317	308	298	295	128	-1.1	-6.9
Visalia-Tulare-Porterville, CA MSA	246	312	345	350	355	112	26.9	13.9
Washington-Baltimore, DC-MD-VA-WV CMSA.	5,791	6,726	7,085	7,213	7,285	4	16.2	8.3
Baltimore, MD PMSA	2,199	2,382	2,462	2,476	2,484	(X)	8.3	4.3
Hagerstown, MD PMSA	113	121	127	128	127	(X)	7.3	4.9
Washington, DC-MD-VA-WV PMSA.	3,478	4,223	4,495	4,609	4,674	(X)	21.4	10.7
West Palm Beach-Boca Raton, FL MSA.	577	864	974	1,013	1,033	48	49.7	19.6
Wichita, KS MSA.	442	485	520	533	544	74	9.7	12.2
York, PA MSA	313	340	365	371	373	107	8.5	9.9
Youngstown-Warren, OH MSA	645	601	600	595	592	69	-6.8	-1.5

X Not applicable. [1] The April 1, 1990, census count includes resolution corrections processed through December 1996 and does not include adjustments for census coverage errors.

Source: U.S. Census Bureau, *1990 Census of Population and Housing, Supplementary Reports, Metropolitan Areas as Defined by the Office of Management and Budget, June 30, 1993* (CPH-S-1-1); *1990 Census of Population and Housing, Population and Housing Unit Counts* (CPH-2-1); "MA-98-3b Population Estimates for Metropolitan Areas and Components, Annual Time Series April 1, 1990, to July 1, 1998"; published: 17 December 1999; <http://www.census.gov/population/estimates/metro-city/ma98-03b.txt>; and unpublished data.

Population 35

[As of **July 1 (20,033 represents 20,033,000)**. Areas as defined by U.S. Office of Management and Budget, June 30, 1996. Covers 273 metropolitan areas: 17 consolidated metropolitan statistical area (CMSAs) and 245 metropolitan statistical areas (MSAs) located outside of New England as well as 11 New England county metropolitan areas (NECMAs) in New England. For area definitions, see Appendix II]

Metropolitan area [1]	Total population (1,000)	Black	American Indian, Eskimo, Aleut	Asian and Pacific Islander	Hispanic origin [2]
		Percent of total metropolitan population			
New York-Northern New Jersey-Long Island, NY-NJ-CT-PA CMSA/NECMA [3]	20,033	19.4	0.3	6.7	17.4
Los Angeles-Riverside-Orange County, CA CMSA	15,781	8.4	0.7	11.4	38.5
Chicago-Gary-Kenosha, IL-IN-WI CMSA	8,810	19.2	0.2	4.2	13.8
Washington-Baltimore, DC-MD-VA-WV CMSA	7,285	25.9	0.3	5.1	5.3
San Francisco-Oakland-San Jose, CA CMSA	6,816	8.9	0.7	18.8	19.3
Philadelphia-Wilmington-Atlantic City, PA-NJ-DE-MD CMSA	5,988	19.5	0.2	3.0	5.0
Boston-Worcester-Lawrence-Lowell-Brockton, MA-NH NECMA	5,867	5.9	0.2	3.7	5.5
Detroit-Ann Arbor-Flint, MI CMSA	5,458	20.9	0.4	2.0	2.5
Dallas-Fort Worth, TX CMSA	4,802	14.2	0.6	3.7	15.8
Houston-Galveston-Brazoria, TX CMSA	4,408	18.3	0.4	5.2	24.6
Atlanta, GA MSA	3,746	25.9	0.2	2.8	3.4
Miami-Fort Lauderdale, FL CMSA	3,656	19.5	0.3	1.9	38.5
Seattle-Tacoma-Bremerton, WA CMSA	3,424	5.0	1.4	8.2	4.3
Phoenix-Mesa, AZ MSA	2,931	4.2	2.4	2.3	20.5
Cleveland-Akron, OH CMSA	2,912	16.8	0.2	1.4	2.4
Minneapolis-St. Paul, MN-WI MSA	2,831	4.7	1.0	3.7	2.2
San Diego, CA MSA	2,781	6.4	0.9	10.7	25.9
St. Louis, MO-IL MSA	2,564	17.6	0.2	1.3	1.4
Denver-Boulder-Greeley, CO CMSA	2,365	5.3	0.8	2.9	14.6
Pittsburgh, PA MSA	2,346	8.5	0.1	1.0	0.8
Tampa-St. Petersburg-Clearwater, FL MSA	2,257	10.4	0.4	1.7	9.6
Portland-Salem, OR-WA CMSA	2,149	2.7	1.1	4.2	6.1
Cincinnati-Hamilton, OH-KY-IN CMSA	1,948	11.6	0.1	1.1	0.7
Kansas City, MO-KS MSA	1,737	13.3	0.5	1.6	3.8
Sacramento-Yolo, CA CMSA	1,686	7.1	1.3	10.1	15.0
Milwaukee-Racine, WI CMSA	1,646	15.0	0.6	1.7	5.0
Norfolk-Virginia Beach-Newport News, VA-NC MSA	1,542	30.3	0.4	3.5	3.1
San Antonio, TX MSA	1,538	6.6	0.4	1.7	53.5
Indianapolis, IN MSA	1,519	13.7	0.2	1.1	1.3
Orlando, FL MSA	1,505	13.9	0.4	2.7	11.6
Columbus, OH MSA	1,470	13.3	0.2	2.1	1.1
Charlotte-Gastonia-Rock Hill, NC-SC MSA	1,383	20.4	0.4	1.6	1.8
Las Vegas, NV-AZ MSA	1,322	9.3	1.2	4.6	15.9
New Orleans, LA MSA	1,309	34.8	0.3	2.2	5.1
Salt Lake City-Ogden, UT MSA	1,268	1.3	0.8	3.2	8.1
Greensboro—Winston-Salem—High Point, NC MSA	1,168	19.5	0.4	1.1	1.5
Nashville, TN MSA	1,156	15.7	0.2	1.5	1.3
Buffalo-Niagara Falls, NY MSA	1,153	11.6	0.7	1.4	2.7
Hartford, CT NECMA	1,110	9.5	0.2	2.5	8.5
Austin-San Marcos, TX MSA	1,106	10.0	0.5	3.2	25.6
Memphis, TN-AR-MS MSA	1,093	42.2	0.2	1.2	1.3
Rochester, NY MSA	1,082	10.1	0.4	2.0	3.9
Raleigh-Durham-Chapel Hill, NC MSA	1,080	24.0	0.3	2.7	2.4
Jacksonville, FL MSA	1,045	22.3	0.4	2.7	3.6
Oklahoma City, OK MSA	1,039	10.9	4.7	2.3	5.1
Grand Rapids-Muskegon-Holland, MI MSA	1,038	7.4	0.6	1.4	3.9
West Palm Beach-Boca Raton, FL MSA	1,033	14.5	0.2	1.6	10.7
Louisville, KY-IN MSA	999	13.0	0.2	0.8	0.9
Richmond-Petersburg, VA MSA	957	30.2	0.3	1.9	1.6
Dayton-Springfield, OH MSA	949	14.6	0.2	1.3	1.0
Greenville-Spartanburg-Anderson, SC MSA	918	17.9	0.2	0.9	1.1
Birmingham, AL MSA	909	28.9	0.2	0.6	0.7
Providence-Warwick-Pawtucket, RI NECMA	906	5.1	0.5	2.4	7.0
Honolulu, HI MSA	872	3.7	0.5	64.9	7.4
Albany-Schenectady-Troy, NY MSA	872	5.2	0.2	1.8	2.2
Fresno, CA MSA	870	5.0	1.4	9.5	42.4
Tucson, AZ MSA	791	3.9	3.4	2.4	28.9
Tulsa, OK MSA	777	8.7	6.6	1.1	3.0
Syracuse, NY MSA	735	6.3	0.6	1.6	1.8
El Paso, TX MSA	703	3.5	0.5	1.5	74.5
Omaha, NE-IA MSA	694	8.6	0.6	1.6	4.9
Albuquerque, NM MSA	679	3.4	6.0	2.2	39.2
Knoxville, TN MSA	659	6.5	0.3	1.1	1.0
Bakersfield, CA MSA	631	6.5	1.8	4.6	35.1
Allentown-Bethlehem-Easton, PA MSA	617	2.6	0.1	1.6	6.2
Harrisburg-Lebanon-Carlisle, PA MSA	616	7.8	0.2	1.6	2.4
Scranton—Wilkes-Barre—Hazleton, PA MSA	615	1.1	0.1	0.7	0.8
Toledo, OH MSA	610	12.5	0.3	1.3	4.2
Youngstown-Warren, OH MSA	592	10.4	0.2	0.5	1.6
Springfield, MA NECMA	589	8.0	0.2	2.1	10.5
Baton Rouge, LA MSA	575	31.1	0.2	1.4	1.7
Little Rock-North Little Rock, AR MSA	556	20.9	0.3	0.9	1.8
Stockton-Lodi, CA MSA	550	5.8	1.1	15.8	28.8
Wichita, KS MSA	544	8.1	1.1	2.5	5.9
Sarasota-Bradenton, FL MSA	543	7.0	0.3	0.9	4.6

[1] Metropolitan areas are shown in rank order of total population. [2] Persons of Hispanic origin may be of any race.
[3] Includes data for New Haven-Bridgeport-Stamford-Waterbury-Danbury, CT NECMA.
Source: U.S. Census Bureau, unpublished data.

No. 36. Metropolitan Areas With Large Numbers of Selected Racial Groups and of Hispanic-Origin Population: 1998

[As of July 1 (3,887 represents 3,887,000). For Black, Hispanic origin, and Asian and Pacific Islander populations, areas selected had more than 110,000 of specified group; for American Indian, Eskimo, and Aleut population, areas selected had 50,000 or more of specified group. See headnote, Table 35]

Metropolitan area	Number of specified group (1,000)	Percent of total metro. area
BLACK		
New York-Northern New Jersey-Long Island, NY-NJ-CT-PA CMSA/NECMA [2]	3,887	19.4
Washington-Baltimore, DC-MD-VA-WV CMSA	1,884	25.9
Chicago-Gary-Kenosha, IL-IN-WI CMSA	1,687	19.2
Los Angeles-Riverside-Orange County, CA CMSA	1,330	8.4
Philadelphia-Wilmington-Atlantic City, PA-NJ-DE-MD CMSA	1,169	19.5
Detroit-Ann Arbor-Flint, MI CMSA	1,142	20.9
Atlanta, GA MSA	970	25.9
Houston-Galveston-Brazoria, TX CMSA	806	18.3
Miami-Fort Lauderdale, FL CMSA	713	19.5
Dallas-Fort Worth, TX CMSA	682	14.2
San Francisco-Oakland-San Jose, CA CMSA	609	8.9
Cleveland-Akron, OH CMSA	488	16.8
Norfolk-Virginia Beach-Newport News, VA-NC MSA	467	30.3
Memphis, TN-AR-MS MSA	462	42.2
New Orleans, LA MSA	456	34.8
St. Louis, MO-IL MSA	452	17.6
Boston-Worcester-Lawrence-Lowell-Brockton, MA-NH NECMA	346	5.9
Richmond-Petersburg, VA MSA	289	30.2
Charlotte-Gastonia-Rock Hill, NC-SC MSA	283	20.4
Birmingham, AL MSA	263	28.9
Raleigh-Durham-Chapel Hill, NC MSA	259	24.0
Milwaukee-Racine, WI CMSA	247	15.0
Tampa-St. Petersburg-Clearwater, FL MSA	236	10.4
Jacksonville, FL MSA	233	22.3
Kansas City, MO-KS MSA	232	13.3
Greensboro—Winston-Salem—High Point, NC MSA	228	19.5
Cincinnati-Hamilton, OH-KY-IN CMSA	226	11.6
Orlando, FL MSA	210	13.9
Indianapolis, IN MSA	208	13.7
Pittsburgh, PA MSA	199	8.5
Columbus, OH MSA	196	13.3
Jackson, MS MSA	186	43.3
Nashville, TN MSA	182	15.7
Baton Rouge, LA MSA	179	31.1
San Diego, CA MSA	179	6.4
Seattle-Tacoma-Bremerton, WA CMSA	173	5.0
Charleston-North Charleston, SC MSA	169	31.2
Greenville-Spartanburg-Anderson, SC MSA	164	17.9
Columbia, SC MSA	152	29.7
Augusta-Aiken, GA-SC MSA	152	33.2
West Palm Beach-Boca Raton, FL MSA	150	14.5
Mobile, AL MSA	150	28.1
Shreveport-Bossier City, LA MSA	139	36.6
Dayton-Springfield, OH MSA	138	14.6
Buffalo-Niagara Falls, NY MSA	134	11.6
Minneapolis-St. Paul, MN-WI MSA	133	4.7
Louisville, KY-IN MSA	130	13.0
Macon, GA MSA	124	38.9
Denver-Boulder-Greeley, CO CMSA	124	5.3
Las Vegas, NV-AZ MSA	122	9.3
Phoenix-Mesa, AZ MSA	122	4.2
Sacramento-Yolo, CA CMSA	119	7.1
Montgomery, AL MSA	119	36.9
Little Rock-North Little Rock, AR MSA	116	20.9
Oklahoma City, OK MSA	113	10.9
Austin-San Marcos, TX MSA	111	10.0
Lafayette, LA MSA	111	29.5

Metropolitan area	Number of specified group (1,000)	Percent of total metro. area
HISPANIC ORIGIN [1]		
Los Angeles-Riverside-Orange County, CA CMSA	6,081	38.5
New York-Northern New Jersey-Long Island, NY-NJ-CT-PA CMSA/NECMA [2]	3,490	17.4
Miami-Fort Lauderdale, FL CMSA	1,407	38.5
San Francisco-Oakland-San Jose, CA CMSA	1,314	19.3
Chicago-Gary-Kenosha, IL-IN-WI CMSA	1,213	13.8
Houston-Galveston-Brazoria, TX CMSA	1,084	24.6
San Antonio, TX MSA	823	53.5
Dallas-Fort Worth, TX CMSA	757	15.8
San Diego, CA MSA	722	25.9
Phoenix-Mesa, AZ MSA	601	20.5
El Paso, TX MSA	524	74.5
McAllen-Edinburg-Mission, TX MSA	460	88.1
Washington-Baltimore, DC-MD-VA-WV CMSA	387	5.3
Fresno, CA MSA	369	42.4
Denver-Boulder-Greeley, CO CMSA	344	14.6
Boston-Worcester-Lawrence-Lowell-Brockton, MA-NH NECMA	323	5.5
Philadelphia-Wilmington-Atlantic City, PA-NJ-DE-MD CMSA	300	5.0
Austin-San Marcos, TX MSA	283	25.6
Brownsville-Harlingen-San Benito, TX MSA	278	85.2
Albuquerque, NM MSA	266	39.2
Sacramento-Yolo, CA CMSA	252	15.0
Tucson, AZ MSA	229	28.9
Corpus Christi, TX MSA	225	58.2
Bakersfield, CA MSA	222	35.1
Tampa-St. Petersburg-Clearwater, FL MSA	216	9.6
Las Vegas, NV-AZ MSA	210	15.9
Laredo, TX MSA	179	95.2
Orlando, FL MSA	174	11.6
Visalia-Tulare-Porterville, CA MSA	165	46.4
Stockton-Lodi, CA MSA	158	28.8
Salinas, CA MSA	149	40.6
Seattle-Tacoma-Bremerton, WA CMSA	148	4.3
Detroit-Ann Arbor-Flint, MI CMSA	136	2.5
Portland-Salem, OR-WA CMSA	131	6.1
Santa Barbara-Santa Maria-Lompoc, CA MSA	128	32.9
Atlanta, GA MSA	126	3.4
Modesto, CA MSA	119	27.9
West Palm Beach-Boca Raton, FL MSA	110	10.7
ASIAN AND PACIFIC ISLANDER		
Los Angeles-Riverside-Orange County, CA CMSA	1,799	11.4
New York-Northern New Jersey-Long Island, NY-NJ-CT-PA CMSA [2]	1,343	6.7
San Francisco-Oakland-San Jose, CA CMSA	1,279	18.8
Honolulu, HI MSA	566	64.9
Washington-Baltimore, DC-MD-VA-WV CMSA	373	5.1
Chicago-Gary-Kenosha, IL-IN-WI CMSA	367	4.2
San Diego, CA MSA	297	10.7
Seattle-Tacoma-Bremerton, WA CMSA	280	8.2
Houston-Galveston-Brazoria, TX CMSA	229	5.2
Boston-Worcester-Lawrence-Lowell-Brockton, MA-NH NECMA	217	3.7
Philadelphia-Wilmington-Atlantic City, PA-NJ-DE-MD CMSA	179	3.0
Dallas-Fort Worth, TX CMSA	175	3.7
Sacramento-Yolo, CA CMSA	171	10.1
Detroit-Ann Arbor-Flint, MI CMSA	110	2.0
AMERICAN INDIAN, ESKIMO, ALEUT		
Los Angeles-Riverside-Orange County, CA CMSA	114	0.7
Phoenix-Mesa, AZ MSA	69	2.4
New York-Northern New Jersey-Long Island, NY-NJ-CT-PA CMSA/NECMA [2]	64	0.3
Tulsa, OK MSA	51	6.6
San Francisco-Oakland-San Jose, CA CMSA	50	0.7

[1] Persons of Hispanic origin may be of any race. [2] Includes data for New Haven-Bridgeport-Stamford-Waterbury-Danbury, CT NECMA.

Source: U.S. Census Bureau, unpublished data.

U.S. Census Bureau, Statistical Abstract of the United States: 2000

No. 37. Urban and Rural Population, 1960 to 1990, and by State, 1990

[In thousands, except percent (179,323 represents 179,323,000). As of **April 1**. Resident population]

State	Total	Urban Number	Urban Percent	Rural	State	Total	Urban Number	Urban Percent	Rural
1960	179,323	125,269	69.9	54,054	MN	4,375	3,056	69.9	1,319
1970	¹203,212	149,647	73.6	53,565	MS	2,573	1,211	47.1	1,362
1980	²226,546	167,051	73.7	59,495					
1990, total	**²248,710**	**187,053**	**75.2**	**61,656**	MO	5,117	3,516	68.7	1,601
					MT	799	420	52.5	379
AL	4,041	2,440	60.4	1,601	NE	1,578	1,044	66.1	534
AK	550	371	67.5	179	NV	1,202	1,061	88.3	140
AZ	3,665	3,207	87.5	458	NH	1,109	566	51.0	544
AR	2,351	1,258	53.5	1,093					
CA	29,760	27,571	92.6	2,189	NJ	7,730	6,910	89.4	820
					NM	1,515	1,106	73.0	409
CO	3,294	2,716	82.4	579	NY	17,990	15,164	84.3	2,826
CT	3,287	2,602	79.1	686	NC	6,629	3,338	50.4	3,291
DE	666	487	73.0	180	ND	639	340	53.3	298
DC	607	607	100.0	-					
FL	12,938	10,967	84.8	1,971	OH	10,847	8,039	74.1	2,808
					OK	3,146	2,130	67.7	1,015
GA	6,478	4,097	63.2	2,381	OR	2,842	2,003	70.5	839
HI	1,108	986	89.0	122	PA	11,882	8,188	68.9	3,693
ID	1,007	578	57.4	429	RI	1,003	863	86.0	140
IL	11,431	9,669	84.6	1,762					
IN	5,544	3,598	64.9	1,946	SC	3,487	1,905	54.6	1,581
					SD	696	348	50.0	348
IA	2,777	1,683	60.6	1,094	TN	4,877	2,970	60.9	1,907
KS	2,478	1,713	69.1	765	TX	16,987	13,635	80.3	3,352
KY	3,685	1,910	51.8	1,775	UT	1,723	1,499	87.0	224
LA	4,220	2,872	68.1	1,348					
ME	1,228	548	44.6	680	VT	563	181	32.2	382
					VA	6,187	4,293	69.4	1,894
					WA	4,867	3,718	76.4	1,149
MD	4,781	3,888	81.3	893	WV	1,793	648	36.1	1,145
MA	6,016	5,070	84.3	947	WI	4,892	3,212	65.7	1,680
MI	9,295	6,556	70.5	2,739	WY	454	295	65.0	159

- Represents zero. [1] The revised 1970 resident population count is 203,302,031, which incorporates changes due to errors found after tabulations were completed. [2] Total population count has been revised since the 1980 and 1990 census publications to 226,542,199 and 248,718,301, respectively.

Source: U.S. Census Bureau, *1990 Census of Population and Housing, Population and Housing Unit Counts* (1990 CPH-2).

No. 38. Incorporated Places by Population Size: 1970 to 1998

[131.9 represents 131,900,000]

Population size	Number of incorporated places				Population (mil.)				Percent of total			
	1970	1980	1990	1998	1970	1980	1990	1998	1970	1980	1990	1998
Total	18,666	19,097	19,262	19,362	131.9	140.3	152.9	165.7	100.0	100.0	100.0	100.0
1,000,000 or more	6	6	8	9	18.8	17.5	20.0	21.7	14.2	12.5	13.0	13.1
500,000 to 999,999	20	16	15	17	13.0	10.9	10.1	10.8	9.8	7.8	6.6	6.5
250,000 to 499,999	30	33	41	41	10.5	11.8	14.2	14.7	7.9	8.4	9.3	8.8
100,000 to 249,999	97	114	131	151	13.9	16.6	19.1	22.3	10.5	11.8	12.5	13.5
50,000 to 99,999	232	250	309	354	16.2	17.6	21.2	24.3	12.2	12.3	13.9	14.7
25,000 to 49,999	455	526	567	622	15.7	18.4	20.0	21.7	11.9	13.1	13.0	13.1
10,000 to 24,999	1,127	1,260	1,290	1,384	17.6	19.8	20.3	21.6	13.3	14.1	13.3	13.1
Under 10,000	16,699	16,892	16,901	16,784	26.4	28.0	28.2	28.5	20.0	20.0	18.4	17.2

Source: U.S. Census Bureau, *Census of Population: 1970* and *1980*, Vol. I; *1990 Census of Population and Housing, Population and Housing Unit Counts* (CPH-2-1); and "SU-98-9 Population Estimates for States, Counties, Places, and Minor Civil Divisions: Annual Time Series, July 1, 1990, to July 1, 1998"; published: 30 June 1999; <http://www.census.gov/population/estimates/metro-city/scful/SC98FUL-DR.txt>.

No. 39. Cities With 100,000 or More Inhabitants in 1998—Population, 1980 to 1998, and Land Area, 1990

[**Population**: As of **April 1; except 1998**, as of **July 1 (98 represents 98,000)**. Data refer to boundaries in effect December 1994. Minus sign (-) indicates decrease]

City	1980, total (1,000)	1990 Total (1,000)	1990 Black	1990 American Indian, Eskimo, Aleut	1990 Asian, Pacific Islander	1990 His-panic [1]	1998 Total (1,000)	1998 Rank	1998 Percent change 1990-98	Land area, 1990 (square miles)
Abilene, TX	98	107	7.0	0.4	1.3	15.5	108	203	1.5	103.1
Akron, OH	237	223	24.5	0.3	1.2	0.7	216	74	-3.3	62.2
Albuquerque, NM	332	385	3.0	3.0	1.7	34.5	419	36	8.9	132.2
Alexandria, VA	103	111	21.9	0.3	4.2	9.7	118	173	6.4	15.3
Allentown, PA	104	105	5.0	0.2	1.3	11.7	101	215	-4.3	17.7
Amarillo, TX	149	158	6.0	0.8	1.9	14.7	171	113	8.7	87.9
Anaheim, CA	219	266	2.5	0.5	9.4	31.4	295	57	10.8	44.3
Anchorage, AK	174	226	6.4	6.4	4.8	4.1	255	65	12.7	1,697.6
Ann Arbor, MI	108	110	9.0	0.4	7.7	2.6	110	197	0.3	25.9
Arlington, TX	160	262	8.4	0.5	3.9	8.9	306	54	17.1	93.0
Arlington, VA [2]	153	171	10.5	0.3	6.8	13.5	177	108	3.7	25.9
Atlanta, GA	425	394	67.1	0.1	0.9	1.9	404	39	2.5	131.8
Augusta-Richmond County, GA [3]	(NA)	187	(NA)	(NA)	(NA)	(NA)	188	96	0.6	(NA)
Aurora, CO	159	222	11.4	0.6	3.8	6.6	251	67	12.8	132.5
Aurora, IL	81	100	11.9	0.2	1.3	23.0	125	162	25.1	33.5
Austin, TX	346	472	12.4	0.4	3.0	23.0	552	21	17.0	217.8
Bakersfield, CA	106	176	9.4	1.1	3.6	20.5	210	79	19.3	91.8
Baltimore, MD	787	736	59.2	0.3	1.1	1.0	646	16	-12.3	80.8
Baton Rouge, LA	220	220	43.9	0.1	1.7	1.6	212	77	-3.6	73.9
Beaumont, TX	118	114	41.3	0.2	1.7	4.3	110	198	-3.9	80.1
Bellevue, WA	(NA)	95	(NA)	(NA)	(NA)	(NA)	104	208	9.3	(NA)
Berkeley, CA	103	103	18.8	0.6	14.8	8.4	108	204	5.2	10.5
Birmingham, AL	284	265	63.3	0.1	0.6	(Z)	253	66	-4.7	148.5
Boise City, ID	102	127	0.6	0.6	1.6	2.7	157	122	24.3	46.1
Boston, MA	563	574	25.6	0.3	5.3	10.8	555	20	-3.3	48.4
Bridgeport, CT	143	142	26.6	0.3	2.3	26.5	137	143	-3.0	16.0
Brownsville, TX	85	107	0.2	0.1	0.3	90.1	138	141	28.8	27.9
Buffalo, NY	358	328	30.7	0.8	1.0	4.9	301	56	-8.4	40.6
Carrollton, TX	41	82	4.9	0.4	6.8	10.2	100	216	22.3	34.8
Cedar Rapids, IA	110	109	2.9	0.2	1.0	1.1	115	182	5.3	53.5
Chandler, AZ	30	90	2.6	1.2	2.4	17.3	160	121	78.4	47.6
Charlotte, NC	315	420	31.8	0.4	1.8	1.4	505	25	20.3	174.3
Chattanooga, TN	170	152	33.7	0.2	1.0	0.6	148	133	-3.0	118.4
Chesapeake, VA	114	152	27.4	0.3	1.2	1.3	200	83	31.3	340.7
Chicago, IL	3,005	2,784	39.1	0.3	3.7	19.6	2,802	3	0.7	227.2
Chula Vista, CA	84	135	4.6	0.6	8.9	37.3	161	120	18.8	29.0
Cincinnati, OH	385	364	37.9	0.2	1.1	0.7	336	51	-7.6	77.2
Clearwater, FL	85	99	9.0	0.2	1.0	2.9	101	212	2.8	24.9
Cleveland, OH	574	506	46.6	0.3	1.0	4.6	496	28	-1.9	77.0
Colorado Springs, CO	215	280	7.0	0.8	2.4	9.1	345	48	23.0	183.2
Columbia, SC [3]	101	111	43.7	0.3	1.4	2.0	111	192	0.1	117.1
Columbus, GA [3]	169	179	38.1	0.3	1.4	3.0	182	102	2.0	216.1
Columbus, OH	565	633	22.6	0.2	2.4	1.1	670	15	5.9	190.9
Concord, CA	104	111	2.4	0.7	8.7	11.5	118	174	5.7	29.5
Coral Springs, FL	37	79	3.5	0.2	2.1	7.1	112	187	41.7	23.5
Corona, CA	38	76	2.8	0.8	7.1	30.4	113	186	48.6	28.5
Corpus Christi, TX	232	257	4.8	0.4	0.9	50.4	281	59	9.3	135.0
Costa Mesa, CA	83	96	1.3	0.5	6.6	20.0	102	211	6.2	15.6
Dallas, TX	905	1,008	29.5	0.5	2.2	20.9	1,076	9	6.8	342.4
Dayton, OH	194	182	40.4	0.2	0.6	0.7	167	115	-8.0	55.0
Denver, CO	493	468	12.8	1.2	2.4	23.0	499	27	6.7	153.3
Des Moines, IA	191	193	7.1	0.4	2.4	2.4	191	91	-1.0	75.3
Detroit, MI	1,203	1,028	75.7	0.4	0.8	2.8	970	10	-5.6	138.7
Durham, NC	101	139	45.7	0.2	2.0	1.2	154	125	10.5	69.3
Elizabeth, NJ	106	110	19.8	0.3	2.7	39.1	111	194	0.6	12.3
El Monte, CA	79	106	1.0	0.6	11.8	72.5	112	188	5.2	9.5
El Paso, TX	425	515	3.4	0.4	1.2	69.0	615	17	19.3	245.4
Erie, PA	119	109	12.0	0.2	0.5	2.4	103	209	-5.6	22.0
Escondido, CA	64	109	1.5	0.8	3.7	23.4	121	169	11.0	35.6
Eugene, OR	106	113	1.3	0.9	3.5	2.7	128	156	13.8	38.0
Evansville, IN	130	126	9.5	0.2	0.6	0.6	123	166	-2.8	40.7
Flint, MI	160	141	47.9	0.7	0.5	2.9	132	152	-6.6	33.8
Fontana, CA	37	88	8.7	0.9	4.5	36.1	110	199	25.4	35.6
Fort Collins, CO	65	87	1.0	0.5	2.4	7.1	109	200	24.5	41.2
Fort Lauderdale, FL	153	149	28.1	0.2	0.9	7.2	154	124	3.0	31.4
Fort Wayne, IN	172	196	16.7	0.3	1.0	2.7	186	98	-5.1	62.7
Fort Worth, TX	385	448	22.0	0.4	2 0	19.5	492	29	9.9	281.1
Fremont, CA	132	173	3.8	0.7	19.4	13.3	204	81	17.9	77.0
Fresno, CA	217	354	8.3	1.1	12.5	29.9	398	40	12.4	99.1
Fullerton, CA	102	114	2.2	0.5	12.2	21.3	122	167	6.8	22.1
Garden Grove, CA	123	143	1.5	0.6	20.5	23.5	151	129	5.8	17.9
Garland, TX	139	181	8.9	0.5	4.5	11.6	193	90	7.1	57.3
Gary, IN	152	117	80.6	0.2	0.2	5.7	108	201	-7.0	50.2
Glendale, AZ	97	147	3.0	0.9	2.1	15.5	193	89	31.6	52.2
Glendale, CA	139	180	1.3	0.3	14.1	21.0	185	100	2.8	30.6
Grand Prairie, TX	71	100	9.7	0.8	3.0	20.5	113	185	13.8	68.5
Grand Rapids, MI	182	189	18.5	0.8	1.1	5.0	185	99	-2.0	44.3

See footnotes at end of table.

U.S. Census Bureau, Statistical Abstract of the United States: 2000

No. 39. Cities With 100,000 or More Inhabitants in 1998—Population, 1980 to 1998, and Land Area, 1990—Continued

[See headnote, p. 39]

City	Population									Land area, 1990 (square miles)
	1990						1998			
			Percent—							
	1980, total (1,000)	Total (1,000)	Black	American Indian, Eskimo, Aleut	Asian, Pacific Islander	His-panic[1]	Total (1,000)	Rank	Percent change, 1990-98	
Greensboro, NC	156	184	33.9	0.5	1.4	1.0	198	84	7.6	79.8
Hampton, VA	123	134	38.9	0.3	1.7	2.0	137	144	2.4	51.8
Hartford, CT	136	140	38.9	0.3	1.4	31.6	132	153	-5.9	17.3
Hayward, CA	94	115	9.8	1.0	15.5	23.9	129	155	12.4	43.5
Henderson, NV	24	65	2.7	1.0	2.0	8.1	153	126	135.1	71.5
Hialeah, FL	145	188	1.9	0.1	0.5	87.6	211	78	12.4	19.2
Hollywood, FL	121	122	8.5	0.2	1.3	11.9	130	154	6.8	27.3
Honolulu, HI [4]	365	377	1.3	0.3	70.5	4.6	396	41	5.0	85.7
Houston, TX	1,595	1,638	28.1	0.3	4.1	27.6	1,787	4	9.1	539.9
Huntington Beach, CA	171	182	0.9	0.6	8.3	11.2	195	87	7.6	26.4
Huntsville, AL	143	160	24.4	0.5	2.1	1.2	176	109	10.1	164.4
Independence, MO	112	112	1.4	0.6	1.0	2.0	117	178	4.0	78.2
Indianapolis, IN [3]	701	731	22.6	0.2	0.9	1.1	741	13	1.4	361.7
Inglewood, CA	94	110	51.9	0.4	2.5	38.5	112	189	1.8	9.2
Irvine, CA	62	110	1.8	0.2	18.1	6.3	136	147	23.7	42.3
Irving, TX	110	155	7.5	0.6	4.6	16.3	178	107	15.0	67.6
Jackson, MS	203	202	55.7	0.1	0.5	0.4	188	94	-6.8	109.0
Jacksonville, FL [3]	541	635	25.2	0.3	1.9	2.6	694	14	9.2	758.7
Jersey City, NJ	224	229	29.7	0.3	11.4	24.2	232	71	1.7	14.9
Kansas City, KS	161	152	29.3	0.7	1.2	7.1	141	139	-6.7	107.8
Kansas City, MO	448	435	29.6	0.5	1.2	3.9	442	33	1.6	311.5
Knoxville, TN	175	170	15.8	0.2	1.0	0.7	166	117	-2.5	77.2
Lafayette, LA	81	102	27.2	0.2	1.3	1.7	114	184	11.5	40.9
Lakewood, CO	114	126	1.0	0.7	1.9	9.1	137	145	8.2	40.8
Lancaster, CA	48	97	7.4	0.9	3.7	15.2	119	172	21.8	88.8
Lansing, MI	130	127	18.6	1.0	1.8	7.9	128	157	0.4	33.9
Laredo, TX	91	123	0.1	0.2	0.4	93.9	176	110	43.0	32.9
Las Vegas, NV	165	258	11.4	0.9	3.6	12.5	404	37	56.6	83.3
Lexington-Fayette, KY	204	225	13.4	0.2	1.6	1.1	242	68	7.3	284.5
Lincoln, NE	172	192	2.4	0.6	1.7	2.0	213	76	11.0	63.3
Little Rock, AR	159	176	34.0	0.3	0.9	0.8	175	111	-0.2	102.9
Livonia, MI	105	101	0.3	0.2	1.3	1.3	101	213	0.5	35.7
Long Beach, CA	361	429	13.7	0.6	13.6	23.6	431	35	0.4	50.0
Los Angeles, CA	2,969	3,486	14.0	0.5	9.8	39.9	3,598	2	3.2	469.3
Louisville, KY	299	270	29.7	0.2	0.7	0.7	255	64	-5.4	62.1
Lowell, MA	92	103	2.4	0.2	11.1	10.1	101	214	-2.3	13.8
Lubbock, TX	174	186	8.6	0.3	1.4	22.5	191	92	2.6	104.1
Macon, GA	117	107	52.2	0.1	0.4	0.6	114	183	6.5	47.9
Madison, WI	171	191	4.2	0.4	3.9	2.0	209	80	9.7	57.8
Manchester, NH	91	99	1.0	0.2	1.1	2.1	103	210	3.2	33.0
McAllen, TX	66	84	0.3	0.2	0.7	77.0	107	206	27.1	32.4
Memphis, TN	646	619	54.8	0.2	0.8	0.7	604	18	-2.4	256.0
Mesa, AZ	152	289	1.9	1.0	1.5	10.9	360	46	24.5	108.6
Mesquite, TX	67	101	5.8	0.5	2.6	8.8	115	181	13.0	42.8
Miami, FL	347	359	27.4	0.2	0.6	62.5	369	44	2.8	35.6
Milwaukee, WI	636	628	30.5	0.9	1.9	6.3	578	19	-7.9	96.1
Minneapolis, MN	371	368	13.0	3.3	4.3	2.1	352	47	-4.5	54.9
Mobile, AL	200	196	38.9	0.2	1.0	1.0	202	82	3.0	118.0
Modesto, CA	107	165	2.7	1.0	7.9	16.3	182	103	10.5	30.2
Montgomery, AL	178	190	42.3	0.2	0.7	0.8	197	85	3.5	135.0
Moreno Valley, CA	([5])	119	13.8	0.7	6.6	22.9	145	135	21.7	49.1
Naperville, IL	43	86	2.1	0.1	4.8	1.8	117	177	36.5	27.9
Nashville-Davidson, TN [3]	456	488	24.3	0.2	1.4	0.9	510	24	4.5	473.3
Newark, NJ	329	275	58.5	0.2	1.2	26.1	268	60	-2.7	23.8
New Haven, CT	126	130	36.1	0.3	2.4	13.2	123	165	-5.6	18.9
New Orleans, LA	558	497	61.9	0.2	1.9	3.5	466	31	-6.3	180.6
Newport News, VA	145	171	33.6	0.3	2.3	2.8	179	106	4.2	68.3
New York, NY	7,072	7,323	28.7	0.4	7.0	24.4	7,420	1	1.3	308.9
Norfolk, VA	267	261	39.1	0.4	2.6	2.9	215	75	-17.6	53.8
Oakland, CA	339	372	43.9	0.6	14.8	13.9	366	45	-1.7	56.1
Oceanside, CA	77	128	7.9	0.7	6.1	22.6	152	127	19.0	40.7
Oklahoma City, OK	404	445	16.0	4.2	2.4	5.0	472	30	6.2	608.2
Omaha, NE	314	343	13.1	0.7	1.0	3.1	371	43	8.3	100.6
Ontario, CA	89	133	7.3	0.7	3.9	41.7	147	134	10.5	36.7
Orange, CA	91	111	1.4	0.5	7.9	22.8	124	164	11.9	23.3
Orlando, FL	128	165	26.9	0.3	1.6	8.7	181	104	10.0	67.3
Overland Park, KS	82	112	1.8	0.3	1.9	2.0	140	140	25.0	55.7
Oxnard, CA	108	143	5.2	0.8	8.6	54.4	155	123	8.5	24.4
Palmdale, CA	12	70	6.4	0.9	4.4	22.0	100	218	42.5	77.6
Pasadena, CA	118	132	19.0	0.4	8.1	27.3	135	149	2.3	23.0
Pasadena, TX	113	120	1.0	0.5	1.6	28.8	134	150	12.0	43.8
Paterson, NJ	138	141	36.0	0.3	1.4	41.0	148	131	5.2	8.4
Pembroke Pines, FL	36	66	5.3	0.2	2.0	11.5	115	180	75.9	31.9
Peoria, IL	124	114	20.9	0.2	1.7	1.6	111	191	-2.1	40.9
Philadelphia, PA	1,688	1,586	39.9	0.2	2.7	5.6	1,436	5	-9.4	135.1
Phoenix, AZ	790	984	5.2	1.9	1.7	20.0	1,198	7	21.7	419.9
Pittsburgh, PA	424	370	25.8	0.2	1.6	0.9	341	49	-7.9	55.6

See footnotes at end of table.

U.S. Census Bureau, Statistical Abstract of the United States: 2000

No. 39. Cities With 100,000 or More Inhabitants in 1998—Population, 1980 to 1998, and Land Area, 1990—Continued

[See headnote, p. 39]

		Population								Land area, 1990 (square miles)
		1990					1998			
City			Percent—							
	1980, total (1,000)	Total (1,000)	Black	American Indian, Eskimo, Aleut	Asian, Pacific Islander	His- panic [1]	Total (1,000)	Rank	Percent change, 1990-98	
Plano, TX	72	128	4.1	0.3	4.0	6.2	219	72	71.6	66.2
Pomona, CA	93	132	14.4	0.6	6.7	51.3	136	148	3.0	22.8
Portland, OR	368	464	7.7	1.2	5.3	3.2	504	26	8.7	124.7
Providence, RI	157	161	14.8	0.9	5.9	15.5	151	130	-6.1	18.5
Provo, UT	74	87	0.3	1.1	2.7	4.2	110	196	27.2	38.6
Pueblo, CO	102	99	2.2	0.8	0.6	39.5	107	205	8.8	35.9
Raleigh, NC	150	212	27.6	0.3	2.5	1.4	259	62	22.3	88.1
Rancho Cucamonga, CA	55	101	5.9	0.6	5.4	20.0	120	170	18.4	37.8
Reno, NV	101	134	2.9	1.4	4.9	11.1	163	119	22.0	57.5
Richmond, VA	219	203	55.2	0.2	0.9	0.9	194	88	-4.3	60.1
Riverside, CA	171	227	7.4	0.8	5.2	26.0	262	61	15.7	77.7
Rochester, NY	242	230	31.5	0.5	1.8	8.7	217	73	-5.8	35.8
Rockford, IL	140	142	15.0	0.3	1.5	4.2	144	136	1.3	45.0
Sacramento, CA	276	369	15.3	1.2	15.0	16.2	404	38	9.4	96.3
St. Louis, MO	453	397	47.5	0.2	0.9	1.3	339	50	-14.5	61.9
St. Paul, MN	270	272	7.4	1.4	7.1	4.2	257	63	-5.5	52.8
St. Petersburg, FL	239	240	19.6	0.2	1.7	2.6	236	70	-1.8	59.2
Salem, OR	89	108	1.5	1.6	2.4	6.1	127	161	17.5	41.5
Salinas, CA	80	109	3.0	0.9	8.1	50.6	121	168	11.7	18.6
Salt Lake City, UT	163	160	1.7	1.6	4.7	9.7	174	112	9.0	109.0
San Antonio, TX	786	959	7.0	0.4	1.1	55.6	1,114	8	16.1	333.0
San Bernardino, CA	119	164	16.0	1.0	4.0	34.6	186	97	9.6	55.1
San Diego, CA	876	1,111	9.4	0.6	11.8	20.7	1,221	6	9.9	324.0
San Francisco, CA	679	724	10.9	0.5	29.1	13.9	746	12	3.0	46.7
San Jose, CA	629	782	4.7	0.7	19.5	26.6	861	11	10.1	171.3
Santa Ana, CA	204	294	2.6	0.5	9.7	65.2	306	55	4.1	27.1
Santa Clara, CA	88	94	2.6	0.5	18.6	15.2	100	217	7.2	18.3
Santa Clarita, CA	(5)	120	1.5	0.6	4.2	13.4	127	159	5.8	40.5
Santa Rosa, CA	83	113	1.8	1.2	3.4	9.5	127	160	12.0	33.7
Savannah, GA	142	138	51.3	0.2	1.1	1.4	132	151	-4.5	62.6
Scottsdale, AZ	89	130	0.8	0.6	1.2	4.8	195	86	50.2	184.4
Seattle, WA	494	516	10.1	1.4	11.8	3.6	537	22	4.0	83.9
Shreveport, LA	206	199	44.8	0.2	0.5	1.1	188	95	-5.1	98.6
Simi Valley, CA	78	100	1.5	0.6	5.5	12.7	110	195	10.2	33.0
Sioux Falls, SD	81	101	0.7	1.6	0.7	0.6	117	179	15.8	45.1
Spokane, WA	171	177	1.9	2.0	2.1	2.1	184	101	3.9	55.9
Springfield, IL	100	105	13.0	0.2	1.0	0.8	117	176	11.1	42.5
Springfield, MA	152	157	19.2	0.2	1.0	16.9	148	132	-5.6	32.1
Springfield, MO	133	140	2.5	0.7	0.9	1.0	143	137	1.7	68.0
Stamford, CT	102	108	17.8	0.1	2.6	9.8	111	193	2.4	37.7
Sterling Heights, MI	109	118	0.4	0.2	2.9	1.1	124	163	5.5	36.6
Stockton, CA	150	211	9.6	1.0	22.8	25.0	240	69	13.8	52.6
Sunnyvale, CA	107	117	3.4	0.5	19.3	13.2	127	158	8.6	21.9
Syracuse, NY	170	164	20.3	1.3	2.2	2.9	152	128	-7.1	25.1
Tacoma, WA	159	177	11.4	2.0	6.9	3.8	180	105	1.8	48.0
Tallahassee, FL	82	125	29.1	0.2	1.8	3.0	137	146	9.5	63.3
Tampa, FL	272	280	25.0	0.3	1.4	15.0	289	58	3.3	108.7
Tempe, AZ	107	142	3.2	1.3	4.1	10.9	168	114	18.0	39.5
Thousand Oaks, CA	77	104	1.2	0.4	4.8	9.6	117	175	12.3	49.6
Toledo, OH	355	333	19.7	0.3	1.0	4.0	312	53	-6.2	80.6
Topeka, KS	119	120	10.6	1.3	0.8	5.8	119	171	-0.8	55.2
Torrance, CA	130	133	1.5	0.4	21.9	10.1	138	142	3.3	20.5
Tucson, AZ	331	411	4.3	1.6	2.2	29.3	460	32	11.9	156.3
Tulsa, OK	361	367	13.6	4.7	1.4	2.6	381	42	3.8	183.5
Vallejo, CA	80	109	21.2	0.7	23.0	10.8	112	190	2.1	30.2
Virginia Beach, VA	262	393	13.9	0.4	4.3	3.1	432	34	10.0	248.3
Waco, TX	101	104	23.1	0.3	0.9	16.3	108	202	4.5	75.8
Warren, MI	161	145	0.7	0.5	1.3	1.1	142	138	-1.7	34.3
Washington, DC	638	607	65.8	0.2	1.8	5.4	523	23	-13.8	61.4
Waterbury, CT	103	109	13.0	0.3	0.7	13.4	105	207	-3.3	28.6
Wichita, KS	280	304	11.3	1.2	2.6	5.0	329	52	8.3	115.1
Winston-Salem, NC	132	151	39.3	0.2	0.8	0.9	164	118	8.8	71.1
Worcester, MA	162	170	4.5	0.3	2.8	9.6	167	116	-1.9	37.6
Yonkers, NY	195	188	14.1	0.2	3.0	16.7	190	93	1.1	18.1

NA Not available. Z Less than .05 percent. [1] Hispanic persons may be of any race. [2] Data are for Arlington CDP (census designated place) which is not incorporated as a city but is recognized for census purposes as a large urban place. Arlington CDP is coextensive with Arlington County. [3] Represents the portion of a consolidated city that is not within one or more separately incorporated places. [4] The population shown in this table is for the CDP; the 1990 census population for the city and county of Honolulu is 836,231. [5] Not incorporated.

Source: U.S. Census Bureau, *1980 Census of Population*, Vol. 1, Chapters A and B; *1990 Census of Population and Housing, Population and Housing Unit Counts*, (CPH-2) and *General Population Characteristics*, (CP-1); and "Population Estimates for Places: Annual Time Series, July 1, 1990, to July 1, 1998"; published 30 June 1999; <http://www.census.gov/population/estimates/metro-city/scts/SC98TS-DR.txt>.

No. 40. Persons 65 Years Old and Over—Characteristics by Sex: 1980 to 1999

[As of **March, except as noted (24.2 represents 24,200,000).** Covers civilian noninstitutional population. Excludes members of Armed Forces except those living off post or with their families on post. Data for 1980 and 1990 are based on 1980 census population controls; 1995 and 1999 data based on 1990 census population controls. Based on Current Population Survey; see text, this section, and Appendix III]

Characteristic	Total				Male				Female			
	1980	1990	1995	1999	1980	1990	1995	1999	1980	1990	1995	1999
Total (million)	**24.2**	**29.6**	**31.7**	**32.4**	**9.9**	**12.3**	**13.2**	**13.7**	**14.2**	**17.2**	**18.5**	**18.7**
PERCENT DISTRIBUTION												
Marital status:												
Never married	5.5	4.6	4.2	3.8	4.9	4.2	4.2	3.6	5.9	4.9	4.2	4.0
Married	55.4	56.1	56.9	57.7	78.0	76.5	77.0	75.9	39.5	41.4	42.5	44.3
Spouse present	53.6	54.1	54.7	55.3	76.1	74.2	74.5	73.6	37.9	39.7	40.6	41.8
Spouse absent	1.8	2.0	2.2	2.4	1.9	2.3	2.5	2.3	1.7	1.7	1.9	2.5
Widowed	35.7	34.2	33.2	31.8	13.5	14.2	13.5	14.0	51.2	48.6	47.3	44.9
Divorced	3.5	5.0	5.7	6.7	3.6	5.0	5.2	6.5	3.4	5.1	6.0	6.8
Family status:												
In families [1]	67.6	66.7	66.6	67.3	83.0	81.9	80.6	80.4	56.8	55.8	56.7	57.7
Nonfamily householders	31.2	31.9	32.4	31.2	15.7	16.6	18.4	17.5	42.0	42.8	42.4	41.2
Secondary individuals	1.2	1.4	1.0	1.5	1.3	1.5	1.0	2.0	1.1	1.4	0.9	1.0
Living arrangements:												
Living in household	99.8	99.7	99.9	100.0	99.9	99.9	100.0	100.0	99.7	99.5	99.9	100.0
Living alone	30.3	31.0	31.5	30.0	14.9	15.7	17.3	16.4	41.0	42.0	41.7	40.1
Spouse present	53.6	54.1	54.7	55.3	76.1	74.3	74.5	73.6	37.9	39.7	40.6	41.8
Living with someone else	15.9	14.6	13.7	14.7	8.9	9.9	8.1	10.0	20.8	17.8	17.6	18.1
Not in household [2]	0.2	0.3	0.1	-	0.1	0.1	-	-	0.3	0.5	0.1	-
Years of school completed:												
8 years or less	43.1	28.5	21.0	17.6	45.3	30.0	22.0	18.3	41.6	27.5	20.3	17.1
1 to 3 years of high school	16.2	16.1	[3]15.2	[3]14.3	15.5	15.7	[3]14.5	[3]12.9	16.7	16.4	[3]15.6	[3]15.4
4 years of high school	24.0	32.9	[4]33.8	[4]34.9	21.4	29.0	[4]29.2	[4]29.9	25.8	35.6	[4]37.1	[4]38.5
1 to 3 years of college	8.2	10.9	[5]17.1	[5]17.8	7.5	10.8	[5]17.1	[5]18.1	8.6	11.0	[5]17.0	[5]17.7
4 years or more of college	8.6	11.6	[6]13.0	[6]15.3	10.3	14.5	[6]17.2	[6]20.9	7.4	9.5	[6]9.9	[6]11.3
Labor force participation: [7]												
Employed	12.2	11.5	11.7	12.0	18.4	15.9	16.1	16.4	7.8	8.4	8.5	8.7
Unemployed	0.4	0.4	0.5	0.4	0.6	0.5	0.7	0.5	0.3	0.3	0.3	0.3
Not in labor force	87.5	88.1	87.9	87.7	81.0	83.6	83.2	83.1	91.9	91.3	91.2	91.1
Percent below poverty level [8]	15.2	11.4	11.7	10.5	11.1	7.8	7.2	7.2	17.9	13.9	14.9	12.8

- Represents zero. [1] Excludes those living in unrelated subfamilies. [2] In group quarters other than institutions. [3] Represents those who completed 9th to 12th grade, but have no high school diploma. [4] High school graduate. [5] Some college or associate degree. [6] Bachelor's or advanced degree. [7] Annual averages of monthly figures. Source: U.S. Bureau of Labor Statistics, *Employment and Earnings*, January issues. See footnote 2, Table 643. [8] Poverty status based on income in preceding year.

Source: Except as noted, U.S. Census Bureau, *Current Population Reports*, P20-514, and earlier reports; P60-207; and unpublished data.

No. 41. Social and Economic Characteristics of the White and Black Populations: 1990 to 1999

[As of **March, except labor force status, annual average (206,983 represents 206,983,000).** Excludes members of Armed Forces except those living off post or with their families on post. Data for 1990 are based on 1980 census population controls; 1995 and 1999 data based on 1990 census population controls. Based on Current Population Survey; see text, this section, and Appendix III]

Characteristic	Number (1,000)						Percent distribution			
	White			Black			White		Black	
	1990	1995	1999	1990	1995	1999	1990	1999	1990	1999
Total persons	206,983	216,751	223,294	30,392	33,531	35,070	100.0	100.0	100.0	100.0
Under 5 years old	15,161	15,915	15,429	2,932	3,342	3,025	7.3	6.9	9.6	8.6
5 to 14 years old	28,405	30,786	31,652	5,546	6,268	6,599	13.7	14.2	18.2	18.8
15 to 44 years old	96,656	97,876	97,975	14,660	16,101	16,584	46.6	43.9	48.2	47.3
45 to 64 years old	40,282	44,189	49,478	4,766	5,264	6,139	19.5	22.2	15.7	17.5
65 years old and over.	26,479	27,985	28,759	2,487	2,557	2,723	12.8	12.9	8.2	7.8
EDUCATIONAL ATTAINMENT										
Persons 25 years old and over	134,687	141,113	146,080	16,751	18,457	19,732	100.0	100.0	100.0	100.0
Elementary:										
0 to 8 years.	14,131	11,101	10,206	2,701	1,800	1,544	10.5	7.0	16.1	7.8
High school:										
1 to 3 years.	14,080	[1]12,882	[1]12,743	2,969	[1]3,041	[1]3,000	10.5	[1]8.7	17.7	[1]15.2
4 years.	52,449	[2]47,986	[2]48,970	6,239	[2]6,686	[2]7,042	38.9	[2]33.5	37.2	[2]35.7
College:										
1 to 3 years.	24,350	[3]35,321	[3]36,367	2,952	[3]4,486	[3]5,103	18.1	[3]24.9	17.6	[3]25.9
4 years or more	29,677	[4]33,824	[4]37,793	1,890	[4]2,444	[4]3,043	22.0	[4]25.9	11.3	[4]15.5
LABOR FORCE STATUS [5]										
Civilians 16 years old and over	160,625	166,914	173,085	21,477	23,246	24,855	100.0	100.0	100.0	100.0
Civilian labor force	107,447	111,950	116,509	13,740	14,817	16,365	66.9	67.3	64.0	65.8
Employed	102,261	106,490	112,235	12,175	13,279	15,056	63.7	64.8	56.7	60.6
Unemployed	5,186	5,459	4,273	1,565	1,538	1,309	3.2	2.5	7.3	5.3
Unemployment rate [6]	4.8	4.9	3.7	11.4	10.4	8.0	(X)	(X)	(X)	(X)
Not in labor force.	53,178	54,965	56,577	7,737	8,429	8,490	33.1	32.7	36.0	34.2
FAMILY TYPE										
Total families . . . . ., . . .	56,590	58,437	60,068	7,470	8,093	8,444	100.0	100.0	100.0	100.0
With own children [7] . . .	26,718	27,951	28,240	4,378	4,682	4,714	47.2	47.0	58.6	55.8
Married couple . . . ., ...	46,981	47,899	48,456	3,750	3,842	3,975	83.0	80.7	50.2	47.1
With own children [7].	21,579	22,005	21,759	1,972	1,926	1,971	38.1	36.2	26.4	23.3
Female householder,										
no spouse present ., ...	7,306	8,031	8,526	3,275	3,716	3,809	12.9	14.2	43.8	45.1
With own children [7].	4,199	4,841	5,110	2,232	2,489	2,477	7.4	8.5	29.9	29.3
Male householder, no										
spouse present . . ., ...	2,303	2,507	3,086	446	536	660	4.1	5.1	6.0	7.8
With own children [7].	939	1,105	1,371	173	267	266	1.7	2.3	2.3	3.2
FAMILY INCOME IN PREVIOUS YEAR IN CONSTANT (1998) DOLLARS										
Total families [8]	56,590	58,444	60,077	7,470	8,093	8,452	100.0	100.0	100.0	100.0
Less than $5,000.	(NA)	(NA)	1,225	(NA)	(NA)	545	1.8	2.0	7.4	6.5
$5,000 to $9,999	(NA)	(NA)	1,768	(NA)	(NA)	806	3.2	2.9	12.1	9.5
$10,000 to $14,999	(NA)	(NA)	2,844	(NA)	(NA)	1,618	4.7	4.7	9.7	9.5
$15,000 to $24,999	(NA)	(NA)	6,995	(NA)	(NA)	697	12.2	11.6	18.4	17.9
$25,000 to $34,999	(NA)	(NA)	7,570	(NA)	(NA)	1,145	12.9	12.6	13.2	13.6
$35,000 to $49,999	(NA)	(NA)	10,268	(NA)	(NA)	1,245	18.7	17.1	15.5	14.7
$50,000 or more	(NA)	(NA)	29,404	(NA)	(NA)	2,395	46.5	48.9	23.6	28.4
Median income (dol.) [9]	47,290	44,967	49,023	26,565	27,164	29,404	(X)	(X)	(X)	(X)
POVERTY										
Families below poverty level [10].	4,409	5,312	4,829	2,077	2,212	1,981	7.8	8.0	27.8	23.4
Persons below poverty level [10].	20,785	25,379	23,454	9,302	10,196	9,091	10.0	10.5	30.7	26.1
HOUSING TENURE										
Total occupied units	80,163	83,737	87,212	10,486	11,655	12,579	100.0	100.0	100.0	100.0
Owner-occupied	54,094	57,449	61,350	4,445	4,888	5,723	67.5	70.3	42.4	45.5
Renter-occupied	24,685	24,793	24,526	5,862	6,547	6,664	30.8	28.1	55.9	53.0
No cash rent.	1,384	1,494	1,337	178	220	192	1.7	1.5	1.7	1.5

NA Not available.   X Not applicable.   [1] Represents those who completed 9th to 12th grade, but have no high school diploma.   [2] High school graduate.   [3] Some college or associate degree.   [4] Bachelor's or advanced degree.   [5] Source: U.S. Bureau of Labor Statistics, *Employment and Earnings,* January issues. See footnote 2, Table 643.   [6] Total unemployment as percent of civilian labor force.   [7] Children under 18 years old.   [8] Includes families in group quarters.   [9] For definition of median, see Guide to Tabular Presentation.   [10] For explanation of poverty level, see text, Section 14, Income.

Source: Except as noted, U.S. Census Bureau, *Current Population Reports,* P20-530, and earlier reports; P60-206; P60-207; and unpublished data.

Population   43

No. 42. Social and Economic Characteristics of the Asian and Pacific Islander Population: 1990 and 1999

[As of **March (6,679 represents 6,679,000)**. Excludes members of Armed Forces except those living off post or with their families on post. Data for 1990 are based on 1980 census population controls; 1999 data are based on 1990 census population controls. Based on Current Population Survey; see text, this section, and Appendix III]

Characteristic	Number (1,000)		Percent distribution	
	1990	1999	1990	1999
Total persons	**6,679**	**10,897**	**100.0**	**100.0**
Under 5 years old	602	950	9.0	8.7
5 to 14 years old	1,112	1,648	16.6	15.1
15 to 44 years old	3,345	5,474	50.1	50.2
45 to 64 years old	1,155	2,040	17.3	18.7
65 years old and over.	465	785	7.0	7.2
EDUCATIONAL ATTAINMENT				
Persons 25 years old and over	**3,961**	**6,594**	**100.0**	**100.0**
Elementary:				
0 to 8 years.	543	539	13.7	8.2
High school:				
1 to 3 years.	234	[1]478	5.9	[1]7.3
4 years	1,038	[2]1,478	26.2	[2]22.4
College:				
1 to 3 years.	568	[3]1,326	14.3	[3]20.1
4 years or more	1,578	[4]2,772	39.9	[4]42.0
LABOR FORCE STATUS [5]				
Civilians 16 years old and over	**4,849**	**8,103**	**100.0**	**100.0**
Civilian labor force	3,216	5,383	66.3	66.4
Employed	3,079	5,156	63.5	63.6
Unemployed	136	227	2.8	2.8
Unemployment rate [6].	4.2	4.2	(X)	(X)
Not in labor force.	1,634	2,720	33.7	33.6
FAMILY TYPE				
Total families	**1,531**	**2,459**	**100.0**	**100.0**
Married couple	1,256	1,966	82.1	79.9
Female householder, no spouse present	188	318	12.3	12.9
Male householder, no spouse present	86	176	5.6	7.2
FAMILY INCOME IN PREVIOUS YEAR IN CONSTANT (1998) DOLLARS				
Total families	**1,531**	**2,459**	**100.0**	**100.0**
Less than $5,000.	(NA)	95	2.4	3.9
$5,000 to $9,999	(NA)	86	3.6	3.5
$10,000 to $14,999	(NA)	101	5.6	4.1
$15,000 to $24,999	(NA)	234	10.1	9.5
$25,000 to $34,999	(NA)	260	10.2	10.6
$35,000 to $49,999	(NA)	388	15.0	15.8
$50,000 or more	(NA)	1,297	53.1	52.8
Median income [7]	$53,042	$52,826	(X)	(X)
POVERTY				
Families below poverty level [8]	182	270	11.9	11.0
Persons below poverty level [8]	938	1,360	14.1	12.5
HOUSING TENURE				
Total occupied units	**1,988**	**3,308**	**100.0**	**100.0**
Owner-occupied	977	1,723	49.1	52.1
Renter-occupied	982	1,537	49.4	46.5
No cash rent.	30	49	1.5	1.5

NA Not available. X Not applicable. [1] Represents those who completed 9th to 12th grade but have no high school diploma. [2] High school graduate. [3] Some college or associate degree. [4] Bachelor's or advanced degree. [5] Data beginning 1994 not directly comparable with earlier years. See text, Section 13, Labor Force. [6] Total unemployment as percent of civilian labor force. [7] For definition of median, see Guide to Tabular Presentation. [8] For explanation of poverty level, see text, Section 14, Income.

Source: U.S. Census Bureau, Current Population Reports, P20-459, and "The Asian and Pacific Islander Population in the United States: March 2000 (Update)" (PPL-131).

No. 43. Population Living on Selected Reservations and Trust Lands and American Indian Tribes With 10,000 or More American Indians: 1990

[As of **April**]

Reservation and trust lands with 5,000 or more American Indians, Eskimos, and Aleuts	American Indians, Eskimos, Aleuts			American Indian tribe		
	Total population	Number	Percent of total		Number	Percent distribution
All reservation and trust lands	**808,163**	**437,431**	**54.1**	**American Indian population, total** [2]	**1,878,285**	**100.0**
Navajo and Trust Lands, AZ-NM-UT.	148,451	143,405	96.6	Cherokee	308,132	16.4
Pine Ridge and Trust Lands, NE-SD	12,215	11,182	91.5	Navajo	219,198	11.7
				Chippewa	103,826	5.5
Fort Apache, AZ	10,394	9,825	94.5	Sioux [3]	103,255	5.5
Gila River, AZ	9,540	9,116	95.6	Choctaw	82,299	4.4
Papago, AZ.	8,730	8,480	97.1	Pueblo	52,939	2.8
Rosebud and Trust Lands, SD.	9,696	8,043	83.0	Apache	50,051	2.7
				Iroquois [4]	49,038	2.6
San Carlos, AZ	7,294	7,110	97.5	Lumbee	48,444	2.6
				Creek.	43,550	2.3
Zuni Pueblo, AZ-NM	7,412	7,073	95.4	Blackfoot	32,234	1.7
Hopi and Trust Lands, AZ . . .	7,360	7,061	95.9	Canadian and Latin American. .	22,379	1.2
Blackfeet, MT	8,549	7,025	82.2	Chickasaw	20,631	1.1
Turtle Mountain and Trust Lands, ND-SD	7,106	6,772	95.3	Potawatomi [4]	16,763	0.9
				Tohono O'Odham	16,041	0.9
Yakima and Trust Lands, WA .	27,668	6,307	22.8	Pima	14,431	0.8
				Tlingit.	13,925	0.7
Osage, OK [1]	41,645	6,161	14.8	Seminole	13,797	0.7
Fort Peck, MT	10,595	5,782	54.6	Alaskan Athabaskans	13,738	0.7
Wind River, WY	21,851	5,676	26.0	Cheyenne	11,456	0.6
Eastern Cherokee, NC	6,527	5,388	82.5	Comanche	11,322	0.6
Flathead, MT.	21,259	5,130	24.1	Paiute	11,142	0.6
Cheyenne River, SD	7,743	5,100	65.9	Puget Sound Salish	10,246	0.5

[1] The Osage Reservation is coextensive with Osage County. Data shown for the reservation are for the entire reservation.
[2] Includes other American Indian tribes, not shown separately.   [3] Any entry with the spelling "Siouan" was miscoded to Sioux in North Carolina.   [4] Reporting and/or processing problems have affected the data for this tribe.

Source: U.S. Census Bureau, *1990 Census of Population, General Population Characteristics, American Indian and Alaska Native Areas* (CP-1-1A); and press releases CB91-232 and CB92-244.

No. 44. Social and Economic Characteristics of the American Indian Population: 1990

[As of **April**. Based on a sample and subject to sampling variability]

Characteristic	American Indian, total [1]	Cherokee	Navajo	Sioux [2]	Chippewa	Choctaw	Pueblo	Apache	Iroquois [3]	Lumbee
Total persons.	**1,937,391**	**369,035**	**225,298**	**107,321**	**105,988**	**86,231**	**55,330**	**53,330**	**52,557**	**50,888**
Percent under 5 yrs. old.	9.7	6.3	13.6	12.3	10.3	8.2	10.3	10.2	8.1	8.3
Percent 18 yrs. old and over. .	65.8	73.3	57.7	60.0	64.0	68.8	64.2	64.7	71.1	66.2
Percent 65 yrs. old and over. .	5.9	7.2	4.6	4.4	4.7	8.0	5.8	3.4	6.7	5.6
EDUCATIONAL ATTAINMENT										
Persons 25 years old and over.	1,040,955	229,231	100,594	51,014	54,804	49,128	28,597	27,717	30,882	27,343
Percent high school graduates or higher.	65.6	68.2	51.0	69.7	69.7	70.3	71.5	63.8	71.9	51.6
Percent bachelor's degree or higher.	9.4	11.1	4.5	8.9	8.2	13.3	7.3	6.9	11.3	9.4
FAMILY TYPE										
Total families	449,281	98,610	44,845	22,669	25,077	21,856	11,825	12,314	12,988	12,650
Percent distribution:										
Married couple	65.8	73.1	61.1	54.2	58.4	75.2	61.2	66.9	67.5	68.5
Female householder, no spouse present	26.2	20.8	28.6	36.0	33.1	20.0	29.2	24.7	25.5	23.9
Male householder, no spouse present	8.0	6.1	10.3	9.8	8.5	4.8	9.6	8.4	7.0	7.6
INCOME IN 1989										
Median family (dol.) [4]	21,619	24,907	13,940	16,525	20,249	24,467	19,845	19,690	27,025	23,934
Median household (dol.) [4] . . .	19,900	21,922	12,817	15,611	18,801	21,640	19,097	18,484	23,460	21,708
Per capita (dol.)	8,284	10,469	4,788	6,508	7,777	9,463	6,679	7,271	10,568	8,625
Families below poverty level [5]	122,237	19,100	21,204	8,939	7,814	4,347	3,691	3,913	2,249	2,554
Percent below poverty level.	27.2	19.4	47.3	39.4	31.2	19.9	31.2	31.8	17.3	20.2
Persons below poverty level [5]	585,273	79,271	107,526	45,658	35,231	19,453	17,981	19,246	10,253	10,966
Percent below poverty level.	31.2	22.0	48.8	44.4	34.3	23.0	33.2	37.5	20.1	22.1

[1] Includes other American Indian tribes not shown separately.   [2] Any entry with the spelling "Siouan" was miscoded to Sioux in North Carolina.   [3] Reporting and/or processing problems have affected the data for this tribe.   [4] For definition of median, see Guide to Tabular Presentation.   [5] For explanation of poverty level, see text, Section 14, Income.

Source: U.S. Census Bureau, *1990 Census of Population, Characteristics of American Indians by Tribe and Language*, 1990 CP-3-7.

Population   45

No. 45. Social and Economic Characteristics of the Hispanic Population: 1999

[As of **March, except labor force status, annual average (31,689 represents 31,689,000).** Excludes members of the Armed Forces except those living off post or with their families on post. Based on Current Population Survey; see text of this section and Appendix III]

Characteristic	Number (1,000)						Percent distribution					
	His-panic, total	Mexi-can	Puerto Rican	Cuban	Central and South Ameri-can	Other His-panic	His-panic, total	Mexi-can	Puerto Rican	Cuban	Central and South Ameri-can	Other His-panic
Total persons........	31,689	20,652	3,039	1,370	4,536	2,091	100.0	100.0	100.0	100.0	100.0	100.0
Under 5 years old........	3,548	2,522	314	76	428	208	11.2	12.2	10.3	5.5	9.4	10.0
5 to 14 years old........	6,146	4,261	563	147	760	415	19.4	20.6	18.5	10.7	16.7	19.9
15 to 44 years old........	15,731	10,371	1,450	538	2,435	937	49.6	50.2	47.7	39.2	53.7	44.8
45 to 64 years old........	4,569	2,592	515	368	722	372	14.4	12.6	16.9	26.8	15.9	17.8
65 years old and over	1,696	905	197	243	192	159	5.4	4.4	6.5	17.7	4.2	7.6
EDUCATIONAL ATTAINMENT												
Persons 25 years old and over........	16,425	10,020	1,636	1,008	2,634	1,127	100.0	100.0	100.0	100.0	100.0	100.0
High school graduate or higher..............	9,220	4,981	1,044	709	1,685	801	56.1	49.7	63.9	70.3	64.0	71.1
Bachelor's degree or higher ..	1,786	711	182	250	474	169	10.9	7.1	11.1	24.8	18.0	15.0
LABOR FORCE STATUS [1]												
Civilians 16 years old and over........	21,650	13,582	2,058	1,141	3,390	1,479	100.0	100.0	100.0	100.0	100.0	100.0
Civilian labor force	14,665	9,267	1,269	714	2,426	989	67.7	68.2	61.7	62.6	71.6	66.9
Employed	13,720	8,656	1,165	681	2,288	930	63.4	63.7	56.6	59.7	67.5	62.9
Unemployed............	945	611	104	33	138	59	4.4	4.5	5.1	2.9	4.1	4.0
Unemployment rate [2] ...	6.4	6.6	8.2	4.6	5.7	6.0	(X)	(X)	(X)	(X)	(X)	(X)
Male.............	5.6	5.8	7.6	4.4	4.6	5.2	(X)	(X)	(X)	(X)	(X)	(X)
Female...........	7.6	7.9	8.8	4.8	7.0	7.0	(X)	(X)	(X)	(X)	(X)	(X)
Not in labor force	6,985	4,315	789	427	963	491	32.3	31.8	38.3	37.4	28.4	33.2
FAMILY TYPE												
Total families........	7,270	4,608	765	402	1,002	492	100.0	100.0	100.0	100.0	100.0	100.0
Married couple........	4,945	3,222	434	319	667	304	68.0	69.9	56.7	79.2	66.6	61.7
Female householder, no spouse present	1,725	984	285	68	238	150	23.7	21.3	37.2	17.0	23.7	30.6
Male householder, no spouse present	600	403	47	15	97	38	8.2	8.7	6.1	3.7	9.7	7.8
FAMILY INCOME IN 1998												
Total families [3]......	7,273	4,612	765	402	1,002	492	100.0	100.0	100.0	100.0	100.0	100.0
Less than $5,000	351	209	52	15	43	33	4.8	4.5	6.8	3.6	4.3	6.6
$5,000 to $9,999	515	340	80	18	46	32	7.1	7.4	10.4	4.4	4.6	6.4
$10,000 to $14,999........	758	491	79	47	94	46	10.4	10.7	10.4	11.8	9.3	9.3
$15,000 to $24,999........	1,371	947	116	57	184	67	18.9	20.5	15.2	14.2	18.4	13.5
$25,000 to $34,999........	1,247	848	129	42	160	68	17.1	18.4	16.9	10.4	16.0	13.7
$35,000 to $49,999........	1,168	726	114	52	181	94	16.1	15.8	14.8	13.0	18.1	19.1
$50,000 or more...........	1,864	1,049	196	171	294	154	25.6	22.8	25.6	42.6	29.4	31.2
Median income (dol.) [4]......	29,608	27,883	28,953	39,530	32,676	35,264	(X)	(X)	(X)	(X)	(X)	(X)
Families below poverty level [5].	1,648	1,125	204	44	185	90	22.7	24.4	26.7	11.0	18.5	18.2
Persons below poverty level [5].	8,070	5,566	929	186	896	493	25.6	27.1	30.9	13.6	19.9	23.6
HOUSING TENURE												
Total occupied units ...	9,060	5,525	1,025	539	1,287	685	100.0	100.0	100.0	100.0	100.0	100.0
Owner-occupied...........	4,096	2,689	336	310	446	314	45.2	48.7	32.8	57.6	34.7	45.9
Renter-occupied [6]........	4,964	2,836	688	228	841	371	54.8	51.3	67.2	42.4	65.3	54.1

X Not applicable.   [1] Source: U.S. Bureau of Labor Statistics, *Employment and Earnings*, January 2000.   [2] Total unemployment as percent of civilian labor force.   [3] Includes families in group quarters.   [4] For definition of median, see Guide to Tabular Presentation.   [5] For explanation of poverty level, see text, Section 14, Income.   [6] Includes no cash rent.

Source: Except as noted, U.S. Census Bureau, *Current Population Reports*, P20-527.

No. 46. Native and Foreign-Born Populations by Place of Birth: 1950 to 1990

[In thousands, except percent (150,216 represents 150,216,000). Data are based on a sample from the census; for details, see text, this section. See source for sampling variability]

Year	Total population	Native population Total	Born in state of residence	Born in other states	State of birth not reported	Born in outlying areas [1]	Born abroad or at sea of American parents	Foreign born Number	Percent of total population
1950	150,216	139,869	102,788	35,284	1,370	330	96	10,347	6.9
1960	178,467	168,806	118,802	44,264	4,526	817	397	9,661	5.4
1970	203,194	193,454	131,296	51,659	8,882	873	744	9,740	4.8
1980	226,546	212,466	144,871	65,452	(NA)	1,088	1,055	14,080	6.2
1990	248,710	228,943	153,685	72,011	(NA)	1,382	1,864	19,767	7.9

NA Not available.   [1] 1950, includes Alaska and Hawaii. Includes Puerto Rico.

Source: U.S. Census Bureau, *1970 Census of Population*, Vol. II, PC(2)-2A; and *1990 Census of Population Listing* (1990CPH-L-121).

No. 47. Native and Foreign-Born Populations by Age, Sex, Race, and Hispanic Origin: 1990 to 1999

[In thousands (228,945 represents 228,945,000), except as indicated. As of July, except 1990 as of April. Foreign-born residents are those people born outside the United States to noncitizen parents, while native residents are those people born inside the United States or born abroad to United States citizen parents. One notable difference between the two populations concern children. Any child born to foreign-born parents after entering the United States, by definition, becomes part of the native population. The foreign-born child population, therefore, is quite small, while the native child population (and the overall native population) are inflated by births to foreign-born parents after migrating to the United States. Data are consistent with the 1990 population estimates base]

Characteristic	Native population 1990	Native population 1995	Native population 1999	Foreign-born population 1990	Foreign-born population 1995	Foreign-born population 1999	Percent distribution, 1999 Native	Percent distribution, 1999 Foreign born
Total	228,945	239,826	246,859	19,846	22,978	25,831	100.0	100.0
Under 5 years old	18,495	19,372	18,766	270	160	176	7.6	1.4
5 to 9 years old	17,555	18,580	19,481	488	517	466	7.9	2.5
10 to 14 years old	16,334	18,001	18,645	733	852	904	7.6	3.7
15 to 19 years old	16,687	16,886	18,317	1,206	1,317	1,431	7.4	6.1
20 to 24 years old	17,260	16,146	16,077	1,883	1,837	1,949	6.5	9.5
25 to 29 years old	19,077	16,566	15,827	2,259	2,338	2,382	6.4	11.4
30 to 34 years old	19,583	19,103	16,832	2,255	2,723	2,895	6.8	11.4
35 to 39 years old	17,862	19,719	19,524	1,989	2,577	3,021	7.9	10.0
40 to 44 years old	15,865	18,031	19,554	1,729	2,229	2,714	7.9	8.7
45 to 49 years old	12,400	15,607	17,117	1,347	1,851	2,239	6.9	6.8
50 to 54 years old	10,166	12,207	14,614	1,150	1,435	1,832	5.9	5.8
55 to 59 years old	9,547	9,877	11,452	942	1,209	1,423	4.6	4.7
60 to 64 years old	9,763	9,059	9,320	864	988	1,194	3.8	4.4
65 to 69 years old	9,278	9,050	8,483	789	876	964	3.4	4.0
70 to 74 years old	7,452	8,095	7,975	529	736	796	3.2	2.7
75 to 79 years old	5,577	6,226	6,700	527	474	629	2.7	2.7
80 to 84 years old	3,479	4,082	4,463	431	396	354	1.8	2.2
85 to 89 years old	1,740	2,088	2,367	296	264	258	1.0	1.5
90 to 94 years old	628	869	1,007	121	148	140	0.4	0.6
95 to 99 years old	168	224	289	35	44	54	0.1	0.2
100 years old and over	30	39	48	6	9	11	-	-
65 years old and over	28,351	30,672	31,334	2,733	2,947	3,206	12.7	13.8
85 years old and over	2,565	3,220	3,712	457	465	463	1.5	2.3
Female	117,398	122,705	126,055	10,109	11,805	13,360	51.1	50.9
Male	111,547	117,121	120,805	9,737	11,173	12,472	48.9	49.1
White	195,313	203,093	208,035	13,428	14,930	16,575	84.3	67.7
Black	28,812	30,999	32,346	1,705	2,117	2,517	13.1	8.6
American Indian, Eskimo, and Aleut	1,981	2,136	2,247	86	120	150	0.9	0.4
Asian and Pacific Islander	2,840	3,597	4,231	4,627	5,811	6,589	1.7	23.3
Hispanic origin	14,381	17,575	20,234	7,997	9,532	11,103	8.2	40.3
White, not Hispanic	182,131	186,993	189,502	6,184	6,335	6,547	76.8	31.2
Black, not Hispanic	28,096	30,096	31,288	1,208	1,494	1,805	12.7	6.1
American Indian, Eskimo, and Aleut, not Hispanic	1,771	1,897	1,982	26	35	43	0.8	0.1
Asian and Pacific Islander, not Hispanic .	2,565	3,264	3,853	4,431	5,582	6,333	1.6	22.3

- Represents or rounds to zero.

Source: U.S. Census Bureau, "National Population Estimates by Nativity"; published 25 April 2000; <http://148.129.129.31:80/population/www/estimates/us_nativity.html>.

Population   47

No. 48. Native and Foreign-Born Populations by Selected Characteristics: 1999

[In thousands (245,295 represents 245,295,000). As of **March**. The foreign-born population includes some undocumented immigrants, refugees, and temporary residents such as students and temporary workers as well as legally-admitted immigrants. Based on Current Population Survey; see text, this section, and Appendix III]

Characteristic	Native population	Foreign-born population				
		Total	Year of entry			
			Before 1970	1970 to 1979	1980 to 1989	1990 to 1999
Total	245,295	26,448	4,629	4,600	7,928	9,290
Under 5 years old	19,335	266	(X)	(X)	(X)	266
5 to 17 years old	50,315	2,106	(X)	(X)	571	1,535
18 to 24 years old	23,085	2,883	(X)	204	954	1,725
25 to 29 years old	15,783	2,856	4	366	839	1,647
30 to 34 years old	16,631	3,204	129	457	1,308	1,309
35 to 44 years old	39,031	5,713	627	1,377	2,312	1,397
45 to 64 years old	51,728	6,413	2,002	1,862	1,502	1,046
65 years old and over	29,387	3,008	1,867	334	441	365
Male	119,656	13,108	2,071	2,272	4,001	4,764
Female	125,640	13,339	2,558	2,328	3,927	4,526
White	205,451	17,842	3,968	3,011	4,875	5,989
Black	33,034	2,036	218	362	706	750
American Indian/Eskimo/Aleut	2,328	154	18	41	44	52
Asian or Pacific Islander	4,482	6,415	425	1,187	2,303	2,499
Hispanic origin [1]	19,906	11,783	1,542	2,122	3,874	4,246
EDUCATIONAL ATTAINMENT						
Persons 25 years old and over	152,560	21,193	4,629	4,397	6,403	5,765
Not high school graduate	21,571	7,269	1,466	1,484	2,441	1,879
High school grad/some college	92,579	8,531	2,118	1,815	2,485	2,114
Bachelor's degree	26,143	3,352	598	738	904	1,112
Graduate or professional degree	12,267	2,042	448	361	573	660
INCOME IN 1998						
Persons 16 years old and over	186,862	24,814	4,629	4,600	7,674	7,910
Without income	14,389	3,645	251	376	1,144	1,874
With income	172,473	21,168	4,378	4,224	6,530	6,036
$1 to $9,999 or loss	47,549	6,562	1,417	1,045	1,969	2,130
$10,000 to $19,999	36,950	5,917	1,072	1,078	1,878	1,889
$20,000 to $34,999	40,318	4,336	773	1,000	1,457	1,106
$35,000 to $49,999	22,494	1,889	444	466	564	415
$50,000 or more	25,162	2,465	672	634	663	496
POVERTY STATUS [2]						
In poverty	29,709	4,769	482	627	1,371	2,289
Not in poverty	214,927	21,655	4,147	3,973	6,557	6,978
HOMEOWNERSHIP						
In owner-occupied unit	175,481	13,093	3,586	2,918	3,799	2,791
In renter-occupied unit	69,814	13,354	1,043	1,682	4,129	6,499

X Not applicable.   [1] Persons of Hispanic origin may be of any race.   [2] Persons for whom poverty status is determined.
Source: U.S. Census Bureau, *Current Population Reports*, P20-519.

No. 49. Foreign-Born Population by Country of Origin and Citizenship Status: 1999

[In thousands, except percent (26,448 represents 26,448,000). See headnote, Table 48]

Country of origin	Foreign born, total		Naturalized citizen		Not U.S. citizen	
	Number	Percent	Number	Percent	Number	Percent
All countries	**26,448**	**100.0**	**9,868**	**100.0**	**16,579**	**100.0**
Mexico	7,197	27.2	1,452	14.7	5,746	34.7
Cuba	943	3.6	540	5.5	403	2.4
Dominican Republic	679	2.6	221	2.2	458	2.8
El Salvador	761	2.9	136	1.4	625	3.8
Great Britain	655	2.5	252	2.6	403	2.4
China and Hong Kong	985	3.7	422	4.3	563	3.4
India	839	3.2	307	3.1	532	3.2
Korea	611	2.3	252	2.6	359	2.2
Philippines	1,455	5.5	893	9.1	562	3.4
Vietnam	966	3.7	464	4.7	502	3.0
Elsewhere	11,357	42.9	4,930	50.0	6,427	38.8

Source: U.S. Census Bureau, *Current Population Reports*, P20-519.

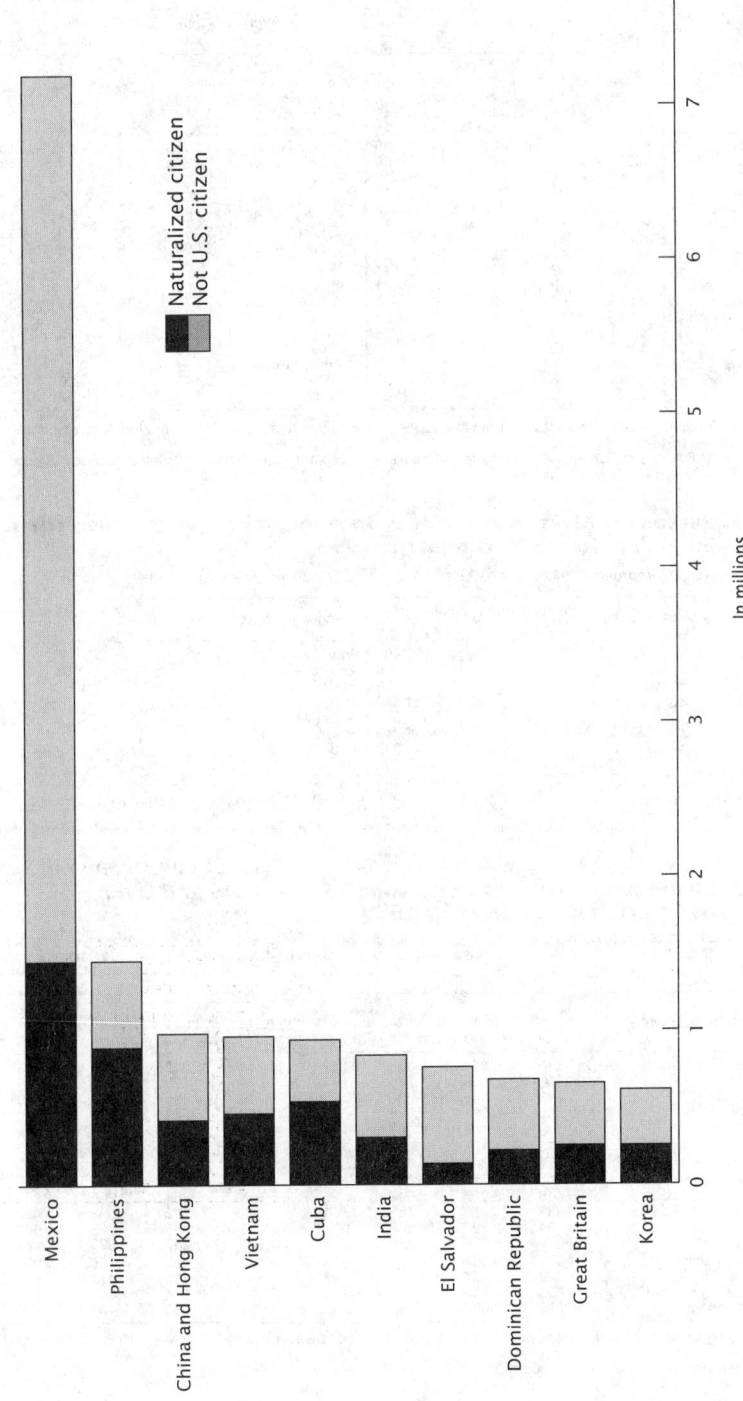

Figure 1.2
Foreign-Born Population by Country of Origin and Citizenship Status: 1999

■ Naturalized citizen
▨ Not U.S. citizen

In millions

Mexico
Philippines
China and Hong Kong
Vietnam
Cuba
India
El Salvador
Dominican Republic
Great Britain
Korea

Source: Chart prepared by U.S. Census Bureau. For data, see Table 49.

No. 50. Population by Selected Ancestry Group and Region: 1990

[As of **April 1 (1,119 represents 1,119,000).** Covers persons who reported single and multiple ancestry groups. Persons who reported a multiple ancestry group may be included in more than one category. Major classifications of ancestry groups do not represent strict geographic or cultural definitions. Based on a sample and subject to sampling variability; see text, this section. For composition of regions, see map, inside front cover]

Ancestry group	Total (1,000)	Percent distribution, by region				Ancestry group	Total (1,000)	Percent distribution, by region			
		North-east	Mid-west	South	West			North-east	Mid-west	South	West
European: [1]						Central & South America [3]					
British......	1,119	17	18	39	26	and Spain:					
Czech	1,296	10	52	22	16	Hispanic [4]....	1,113	13	6	31	50
Danish	1,635	9	34	12	45	Mexican	11,587	1	9	33	57
Dutch......	6,227	16	34	29	21	Puerto Rican ..	1,955	66	11	15	8
English.....	32,652	18	22	35	25	Spanish	2,024	16	8	30	45
French [2]	10,321	26	26	29	20						
German	57,947	17	39	25	19	Asia:					
Greek......	1,110	37	23	21	19	Chinese	1,505	25	8	12	55
Hungarian....	1,582	36	32	17	16	Filipino	1,451	10	9	13	68
Irish.......	38,736	24	25	33	17	Japanese	1,005	9	8	11	72
Italian......	14,665	51	17	17	15						
Norwegian....	3,869	6	52	10	33	North America:					
Polish......	9,366	37	37	15	11	Afro-American .	23,777	15	21	54	10
Portuguese ...	1,153	49	3	8	41	American					
Russian.....	2,953	44	16	18	22	Indian......	8,708	9	22	47	23
Scotch-Irish...	5,618	14	19	47	20	American	12,396	10	18	61	11
Scottish	5,394	20	21	33	26	French Cana-					
Slovak	1,883	40	34	14	11	dian........	2,167	45	20	20	15
Swedish	4,681	14	40	14	32	White.......	1,800	7	13	53	28
Swiss......	1,045	16	36	17	30						
Welsh......	2,034	22	24	27	27						

[1] Non-Hispanic groups. [2] Excludes French Basque. [3] Hispanic groups. [4] A general type of response which may encompass several ancestry groups.

Source: U.S. Census Bureau, *1990 Census of Population, Supplementary Reports, Detailed Ancestry Groups for States* (1990 CP-S-1-2).

No. 51. Persons 5 Years Old and Over Speaking a Language Other Than English at Home by Language: 1990

[As of **April (198,601 represent 198,601,000).** Based on a sample and subject to sampling variability]

Language spoken at home	Persons who speak language (1,000)	Language spoken at home	Persons who speak language (1,000)
Speak only English	198,601	Portuguese	430
Spanish	17,339	Japanese	428
French	1,702	Greek................	388
German	1,547	Arabic...............	355
Italian...............	1,309	Hindi (Urdu)...........	331
Chinese	1,249	Russian	242
Tagalog..............	843	Yiddish	213
Polish...............	723	Thai (Laotian).........	206
Korean	626	Persian..............	202
Vietnamese...........	507	French Creole	188

Source: U.S. Census Bureau, *1990 Census of Population and Housing Data Paper Listing* (CPH-L-133); and Summary Tape File 3C.

No. 52. Living Arrangements of Persons 15 Years Old and Over by Selected Characteristic: 1999

[In thousands (211,676 represents 211,676,000). As of **March.** Based on Current Population Survey which includes members of Armed Forces living off post or with families on post but excludes other Armed Forces; see text, this section, and Appendix III]

Living arrangement	Total	15 to 19 years old	20 to 24 years old	25 to 34 years old	35 to 44 years old	45 to 54 years old	55 to 64 years old	65 to 74 years old	75 years old and over
Total [1]	211,676	19,864	18,058	38,474	44,744	35,232	22,909	17,843	14,551
Alone	26,606	138	1,175	3,714	4,074	4,208	3,549	4,125	5,622
With spouse.	111,715	345	3,358	20,350	29,210	24,495	16,047	11,428	6,479
With other persons	73,355	19,381	13,525	14,410	11,460	6,529	3,313	2,290	2,450
White	176,213	15,736	14,397	30,897	36,946	29,754	19,725	15,642	13,118
Alone	22,176	122	908	2,910	3,245	3,372	2,885	3,577	5,158
With spouse.	98,374	304	3,028	17,518	25,303	21,402	14,383	10,405	6,032
With other persons	55,663	15,310	10,461	10,469	8,398	4,980	2,457	1,660	1,928
Black	25,446	3,067	2,647	5,257	5,613	3,854	2,285	1,603	1,120
Alone	3,633	10	183	569	692	722	593	455	409
With spouse.	8,134	21	198	1,717	2,379	1,865	993	667	295
With other persons	13,679	3,036	2,266	2,971	2,542	1,267	699	481	416
Hispanic origin [2]	21,995	2,837	2,734	5,531	4,630	2,864	1,705	1,092	604
Alone	1,329	27	98	261	211	197	177	212	145
With spouse.	10,606	113	744	3,121	2,898	1,844	1,041	590	254
With other persons	10,060	2,697	1,892	2,149	1,521	823	487	290	205

[1] Includes other races and persons not of Hispanic origin, not shown separately. [2] Persons of Hispanic origin may be of any race.

Source: U.S. Census Bureau, unpublished data.

50 Population

No. 53. Marital Status of the Population by Sex, Race, and Hispanic Origin: 1980 to 1999

[In millions, except percent (159.5 represents 159,500,000). As of **March. Persons 18 years old and over.** Excludes members of Armed Forces except those living off post or with their families on post. Based on Current Population Survey, see text, this section, and Appendix III]

Marital status, race, and Hispanic origin	Total				Male				Female			
	1980	1990	1995	1999	1980	1990	1995	1999	1980	1990	1995	1999
Total [1]	**159.5**	**181.8**	**191.6**	**199.7**	**75.7**	**86.9**	**92.0**	**95.9**	**83.8**	**95.0**	**99.6**	**103.9**
Never married	32.3	40.4	43.9	47.6	18.0	22.4	24.6	25.8	14.3	17.9	19.3	21.9
Married	104.6	112.6	116.7	118.9	51.8	55.8	57.7	59.0	52.8	56.7	58.9	59.9
Widowed	12.7	13.8	13.4	13.5	2.0	2.3	2.3	2.5	10.8	11.5	11.1	10.9
Divorced	9.9	15.1	17.6	19.7	3.9	6.3	7.4	8.5	6.0	8.8	10.3	11.1
Percent of total	100.0	100.0	100.0	100.0	100.0	100.0	100.0	100.0	100.0	100.0	100.0	100.0
Never married	20.3	22.2	22.9	23.9	23.8	25.8	26.8	26.9	17.1	18.9	19.4	21.0
Married	65.5	61.9	60.9	59.5	68.4	64.3	62.7	61.5	63.0	59.7	59.2	57.7
Widowed	8.0	7.6	7.0	6.7	2.6	2.7	2.5	2.7	12.8	12.1	11.1	10.5
Divorced	6.2	8.3	9.2	9.9	5.2	7.2	8.0	8.9	7.1	9.3	10.3	10.7
White, total	**139.5**	**155.5**	**161.3**	**166.8**	**66.7**	**74.8**	**78.1**	**80.9**	**72.8**	**80.6**	**83.2**	**85.9**
Never married	26.4	31.6	33.2	35.7	15.0	18.0	19.2	20.0	11.4	13.6	14.0	15.6
Married	93.8	99.5	102.0	103.5	46.7	49.5	50.6	51.6	47.1	49.9	51.3	51.9
Widowed	10.9	11.7	11.3	11.3	1.6	1.9	1.9	2.1	9.3	9.8	9.4	9.2
Divorced	8.3	12.6	14.8	16.3	3.4	5.4	6.3	7.1	5.0	7.3	8.4	9.1
Percent of total	100.0	100.0	100.0	100.0	100.0	100.0	100.0	100.0	100.0	100.0	100.0	100.0
Never married	18.9	20.3	20.6	21.4	22.5	24.1	24.6	24.7	15.7	16.9	16.9	18.2
Married	67.2	64.0	63.2	62.0	70.0	66.2	64.9	63.8	64.7	61.9	61.7	60.4
Widowed	7.8	7.5	7.0	6.8	2.5	2.6	2.5	2.6	12.8	12.2	11.3	10.8
Divorced	6.0	8.1	9.1	9.8	5.0	7.2	8.1	8.9	6.8	9.0	10.1	10.6
Black, total	**16.6**	**20.3**	**22.1**	**23.6**	**7.4**	**9.1**	**9.9**	**10.5**	**9.2**	**11.2**	**12.2**	**13.0**
Never married	5.1	7.1	8.5	9.2	2.5	3.5	4.1	4.3	2.5	3.6	4.4	5.0
Married	8.5	9.3	9.6	9.8	4.1	4.5	4.6	4.7	4.5	4.8	4.9	5.0
Widowed	1.6	1.7	1.7	1.8	0.3	0.3	0.3	0.4	1.3	1.4	1.4	1.4
Divorced	1.4	2.1	2.4	2.8	0.5	0.8	0.8	1.1	0.9	1.3	1.5	1.7
Percent of total	100.0	100.0	100.0	100.0	100.0	100.0	100.0	100.0	100.0	100.0	100.0	100.0
Never married	30.5	35.1	38.4	39.2	34.3	38.4	41.7	40.7	27.4	32.5	35.8	37.9
Married	51.4	45.8	43.2	41.4	54.6	49.2	46.7	44.8	48.7	43.0	40.4	38.6
Widowed	9.8	8.5	7.6	7.6	4.2	3.7	3.1	3.7	14.3	12.4	11.3	10.7
Divorced	8.4	10.6	10.7	11.9	7.0	8.8	8.5	10.8	9.5	12.0	12.5	12.8
Hispanic, [2] total	**7.9**	**13.6**	**17.6**	**20.3**	**3.8**	**6.7**	**8.8**	**10.1**	**4.1**	**6.8**	**8.8**	**10.3**
Never married	1.9	3.7	5.0	5.9	1.0	2.2	3.0	3.3	0.9	1.5	2.1	2.6
Married	5.2	8.4	10.4	12.1	2.5	4.1	5.1	6.0	2.6	4.3	5.3	6.1
Widowed	0.4	0.5	0.7	0.8	0.1	0.1	0.2	0.1	0.3	0.4	0.6	0.7
Divorced	0.5	1.0	1.4	1.5	0.2	0.4	0.6	0.6	0.3	0.6	0.8	0.9
Percent of total	100.0	100.0	100.0	100.0	100.0	100.0	100.0	100.0	100.0	100.0	100.0	100.0
Never married	24.1	27.2	28.6	29.0	27.3	32.1	33.8	32.7	21.1	22.5	23.5	25.3
Married	65.6	61.7	59.3	59.4	67.1	60.9	57.9	59.6	64.3	62.4	60.7	59.3
Widowed	4.4	4.0	4.2	4.0	1.6	1.5	1.8	1.5	7.1	6.5	6.6	6.5
Divorced	5.8	7.0	7.9	7.6	4.0	5.5	6.6	6.3	7.6	8.5	9.2	8.8

[1] Includes persons of other races, not shown separately.   [2] Hispanic persons may be of any race.

Source: U.S. Census Bureau, *Current Population Reports*, P20-491, and earlier reports; and unpublished data.

No. 54. Married Couples of Same or Mixed Races and Origins: 1980 to 1999

[In thousands (49,714 represents 49,714,000). As of **March. Persons 15 years old and over.** Persons of Hispanic origin may be of any race. Except as noted, based on Current Population Survey; see headnote, Table 60]

Race and origin of spouse	1980	1990	1995	1998	1999 [1]
Married couples, total	**49,714**	**53,256**	**54,937**	**55,305**	**55,849**
RACE					
White/White	44,910	47,202	48,030	48,050	42,669
Black/Black	3,354	3,687	3,703	3,839	3,765
Black/White	167	211	328	330	307
Black husband/White wife	122	150	206	210	215
White husband/Black wife	45	61	122	120	92
White/other race [2]	450	720	988	975	983
Black/other race [2]	34	33	76	43	27
All other couples [2]	799	1,401	1,811	2,068	1,972
HISPANIC ORIGIN					
Hispanic/Hispanic	1,906	3,085	3,857	4,279	4,480
Hispanic/other origin (not Hispanic)	891	1,193	1,434	1,662	1,647
All other couples (not of Hispanic origin)	46,917	48,979	49,646	49,363	49,722

[1] Race categories exclude persons of Hispanic origin.   [2] Excluding White and Black.

Source: U.S. Census Bureau, *Current Population Reports*, P20-488, and earlier reports; and unpublished data.

Population   51

No. 55. Marital Status of the Population by Sex and Age: 1999

[As of **March (95,853 represents 95,853,000). Persons 18 years old and over.** Excludes members of Armed Forces except those living off post or with their families on post. Based on Current Population Survey; see text, this section, and Appendix III]

Sex and age	Number of persons (1,000)					Percent distribution				
	Total	Never married	Married	Wid-owed	Divorced	Total	Never married	Married	Wid-owed	Divorced
Male	**95,853**	**25,782**	**58,986**	**2,542**	**8,543**	**100.0**	**26.9**	**61.5**	**2.7**	**8.9**
18 to 19 years old	3,999	3,921	75	-	4	100.0	98.0	1.9	-	0.1
20 to 24 years old	8,937	7,434	1,419	-	83	100.0	83.2	15.9	-	0.9
25 to 29 years old	9,157	4,776	3,966	4	411	100.0	52.1	43.3	-	4.5
30 to 34 years old	9,767	2,997	6,062	11	696	100.0	30.7	62.0	0.1	7.1
35 to 39 years old	11,189	2,357	7,528	46	1,258	100.0	21.1	67.3	0.4	11.2
40 to 44 years old	10,967	1,738	7,658	61	1,511	100.0	15.8	69.8	0.6	13.8
45 to 54 years old	17,144	1,474	13,089	182	2,399	100.0	8.6	76.3	1.1	13.9
55 to 64 years old	10,967	596	8,770	310	1,289	100.0	5.4	80.0	2.8	11.7
65 to 74 years old	8,027	277	6,389	705	656	100.0	3.4	79.6	8.7	8.1
75 years old and over . . .	5,700	212	4,029	1,222	237	100.0	3.7	70.7	21.4	4.1
Female	**103,867**	**21,865**	**59,918**	**10,944**	**11,141**	**100.0**	**21.0**	**57.7**	**10.5**	**10.7**
18 to 19 years old	3,910	3,655	248	-	6	100.0	93.5	6.3	-	0.1
20 to 24 years old	9,121	6,585	2,350	9	178	100.0	72.3	25.8	0.1	1.9
25 to 29 years old	9,482	3,690	5,244	27	520	100.0	38.9	55.3	0.3	5.5
30 to 34 years old	10,069	2,223	6,801	46	1,000	100.0	22.1	67.5	0.5	9.9
35 to 39 years old	11,340	1,727	8,084	120	1,410	100.0	15.2	71.3	1.1	12.4
40 to 44 years old	11,248	1,233	8,007	180	1,827	100.0	10.9	71.2	1.6	16.2
45 to 54 years old	18,088	1,408	12,873	689	3,118	100.0	7.8	71.2	3.8	17.2
55 to 64 years old	11,942	593	8,043	1,488	1,819	100.0	4.9	67.4	12.5	15.2
65 to 74 years old	9,816	385	5,503	3,074	856	100.0	3.9	56.0	31.3	8.7
75 years old and over . . .	8,851	366	2,767	5,311	407	100.0	4.1	31.3	60.0	4.6

- Represents or rounds to zero.

Source: U.S. Census Bureau, unpublished data.

No. 56. Married Couples by Differences in Ages Between Husband and Wife: 1999

[In thousands **(55,849 represents 55,849,000).** As of **March. Persons 15 years old and over.** Excludes members of Armed Forces except those living off post or with their families on post. Based on Current Population Survey; see text, this section, and Appendix III]

Age difference	All married couples		Without own children under 18 years old		With own children under 18 years old	
	Number	Percent distribution	Number	Percent distribution	Number	Percent distribution
Total	**55,849**	**100.0**	**30,311**	**100.0**	**25,538**	**100.0**
Husband 20 or more years older than wife	447	0.8	290	1.0	157	0.6
Husband 15 to 19 years older than wife	830	1.5	489	1.6	341	1.3
Husband 10 to 14 years older than wife	2,735	4.9	1,550	5.1	1,185	4.6
Husband 6 to 9 years older than wife	6,891	12.3	3,856	12.7	3,034	11.9
Husband 4 to 5 years older than wife	7,687	13.8	4,322	14.3	3,364	13.2
Husband 2 to 3 years older than wife	12,321	22.1	6,640	21.9	5,681	22.2
Husband and wife within one year	18,096	32.4	9,437	31.1	8,659	33.9
Wife 2 to 3 years older than husband	3,320	5.9	1,677	5.5	1,643	6.4
Wife 4 to 5 years older than husband	1,622	2.9	888	2.9	734	2.9
Wife 6 to 9 years older than husband	1,222	2.2	688	2.3	534	2.1
Wife 10 to 14 years older than husband	480	0.9	328	1.1	152	0.6
Wife 15 to 19 years older than husband	112	0.2	90	0.3	21	0.1
Wife 20 or more years older than husband	87	0.2	56	0.2	31	0.1

Source: U.S. Census Bureau, unpublished data.

No. 57. Unmarried Couples by Selected Characteristic: 1980 to 1999

[In thousands **(1,589 represents 1,589,000).** As of **March.** An "unmarried couple" is two unrelated adults of the opposite sex sharing the same household. See headnote, Table 60]

Presence of children and age of householder	1980	1985	1990	1995	1999
Unmarried couples, total.	**1,589**	**1,983**	**2,856**	**3,668**	**4,486**
No children under 15 years old	1,159	1,380	1,966	2,349	2,981
Some children under 15 years old	431	603	891	1,319	1,505
Under 25 years old	411	425	596	742	824
25 to 44 years old	837	1,203	1,775	2,188	2,554
45 to 64 years old	221	239	358	558	888
65 years old and over	119	116	127	180	220

Source: U.S. Census Bureau, *Current Population Reports*, P20-491, and earlier reports; and unpublished data.

No. 58. Marriage and Cohabitation Experience of Women 15 to 44 Years of Age by Selected Characteristic: 1995

[In percent, except as indicated (60,201 represents 60,201,000). Based on the National Survey of Family Growth, a sample survey of women 15 to 44 years of age in the civilian noninstitutionalized population; for details, see source]

Characteristic	Number (1,000)	Ever married or co-habited	Ever married	Ever cohabited Total	Ever cohabited Never married	Ever cohabited Before first marriage	Ever cohabited After first marriage	Never cohab-ited	Currently cohabiting
Total women	**60,201**	**72.5**	**62.3**	**41.1**	**10.2**	**23.6**	**7.3**	**58.9**	**7.0**
15 to 19 years old	8,961	11.4	4.5	8.9	7.0	1.8	0.1	91.1	4.1
20 to 24 years old	9,041	54.5	34.3	38.4	20.2	17.2	0.9	61.6	11.2
25 to 29 years old	9,693	79.7	64.3	49.3	15.4	30.1	3.8	50.7	9.8
30 to 34 years old	11,065	89.2	79.9	51.4	9.3	33.8	8.3	48.6	7.5
35 to 39 years old	11,211	92.9	86.5	50.0	6.4	31.0	12.6	50.0	5.2
40 to 44 years old	10,230	94.5	90.4	43.0	4.1	23.0	15.9	57.0	4.4
Hispanic	6,702	71.8	61.4	36.7	10.4	19.2	7.1	63.3	8.2
Non-Hispanic White	42,522	75.3	66.4	42.6	8.9	25.6	8.1	57.4	7.0
Non-Hispanic Black	8,210	60.3	43.1	40.1	17.3	17.9	5.0	59.9	6.9
Non-Hispanic other	2,767	66.8	58.5	31.7	8.3	19.8	3.6	68.3	4.6
Never married	22,679	27.0	(X)	27.0	27.0	(X)	(X)	73.0	11.4
Currently married	29,673	100.0	100.0	45.4	(X)	36.8	8.6	54.6	(X)
Formerly married	7,849	100.0	100.0	65.4	(X)	41.8	23.7	34.6	20.7
Education: [1] No high school diploma or GED [2]	5,424	91.4	76.8	60.1	14.6	31.1	14.5	39.9	11.6
High school diploma or GED [2]	18,169	91.3	81.9	52.0	9.4	30.1	12.5	48.0	8.0
Some college, no bachelor's degree	12,399	82.9	72.8	46.3	10.1	28.7	7.5	53.7	6.8
Bachelor's degree or higher	11,748	79.8	70.5	37.8	9.2	25.1	3.5	62.2	5.1

X Not applicable.   [1] Covers only women 22 to 44 years old at time of interview.   [2] GED is general equivalency diploma.

Source: U.S. National Center for Health Statistics, *"Fertility, Family Planning, and Women's Health: New data from the 1995 National Survey of Family Growth,"* Vital and Health Statistics, Series 23, No. 19, 1997.

No. 59. Percent Distribution of Women 15 to 44 Years of Age by Number of Husbands or Cohabiting Partners: 1995

[In percent, except as indicated (60,201 represents 60,201,000). Based on the National Survey of Family Growth, a sample survey of women 15 to 44 years of age in the civilian noninstitutionalized population; for details, see source]

Characteristic	Number (1,000)	Total	Never married and never cohabited	Number of husbands or cohabiting partners [1] One	Two	Three	Four or more
Total women	**60,201**	**100.0**	**27.5**	**49.8**	**16.0**	**4.8**	**1.9**
15 to 19 years old	8,961	100.0	88.6	10.8	0.4	0.2	0.1
20 to 24 years old	9,041	100.0	45.5	46.1	6.9	1.3	0.2
25 to 29 years old	9,693	100.0	20.3	60.2	16.0	2.8	0.7
30 to 34 years old	11,065	100.0	10.8	59.0	21.6	6.0	2.6
35 to 39 years old	11,211	100.0	7.1	59.1	21.6	8.6	3.6
40 to 44 years old	10,230	100.0	5.5	57.5	25.2	8.3	3.5
Hispanic	6,702	100.0	28.2	51.8	16.0	3.1	0.9
Non-Hispanic White	42,522	100.0	24.7	50.9	16.7	5.4	2.2
Non-Hispanic Black	8,210	100.0	39.7	42.3	13.1	3.6	1.3
Non-Hispanic other	2,767	100.0	33.2	51.7	12.1	2.3	0.7
Never married	22,679	100.0	73.0	19.4	5.5	1.5	0.5
Currently married	29,673	100.0	(X)	74.2	19.4	5.0	1.5
Formerly married	7,849	100.0	(X)	45.7	33.5	13.5	7.3
Education: [2] No high school diploma or GED [3]	5,424	100.0	8.6	52.8	25.9	8.9	3.8
High school diploma or GED [3]	18,169	100.0	8.7	58.4	22.7	7.1	3.0
Some college, no bachelor's degree	12,399	100.0	17.1	56.8	18.2	5.9	2.0
Bachelor's degree or higher	11,748	100.0	20.2	61.9	14.0	2.9	1.0

X Not applicable.   [1] Husbands with whom a woman also cohabited (outside of marriage) are counted only once.   [2] Limited to women 22 to 44 years old at time of interview.   [3] GED is general equivalency diploma.

Source: U.S. National Center for Health Statistics, *"Fertility, Family Planning, and Women's Health: New data from the 1995 National Survey of Family Growth,"* Vital and Health Statistics, Series 23, No. 19, 1997.

Population   53

No. 60. Households, Families, Subfamilies, and Married Couples: 1970 to 1999

[In thousands, except as indicated (63,401 represents 63,401,000). As of March. Based on Current Population Survey; includes members of Armed Forces living off post or with their families on post, but excludes all other members of Armed Forces; see text, this section, and Appendix III. For definition of terms, see text, this section. Minus sign (-) indicates decrease]

Type of unit	1970	1980	1985	1990	1995	1998	1999	Percent change		
								1970-80	1980-90	1990-99
Households	**63,401**	**80,776**	**86,789**	**93,347**	**98,990**	**102,528**	**103,874**	27	16	11
Average size	3.14	2.76	2.69	2.63	2.65	2.62	2.61	(X)	(X)	(X)
Family households	51,456	59,550	62,706	66,090	69,305	70,880	71,535	16	11	8
Married couple	44,728	49,112	50,350	52,317	53,858	54,317	54,770	10	7	5
Male householder[1]	1,228	1,733	2,228	2,884	3,226	3,911	3,976	41	66	38
Female householder[1]	5,500	8,705	10,129	10,890	12,220	12,652	12,789	58	25	17
Nonfamily households	11,945	21,226	24,082	27,257	29,686	31,648	32,339	78	28	19
Male householder	4,063	8,807	10,114	11,606	13,190	14,133	14,368	117	32	24
Female householder	7,882	12,419	13,968	15,651	16,496	17,516	17,971	58	26	15
One person	10,851	18,296	20,602	22,999	24,732	26,327	26,606	69	26	16
Families	**51,586**	**59,550**	**62,706**	**66,090**	**69,305**	**70,880**	**71,535**	15	11	8
Average size	3.58	3.29	3.23	3.17	3.19	3.18	3.18	(X)	(X)	(X)
With own children[2]	28,812	31,022	31,112	32,289	34,296	34,760	34,613	8	4	7
Without own children[2]	22,774	28,528	31,594	33,801	35,009	36,120	36,922	25	18	9
Married couple	44,755	49,112	50,350	52,317	53,858	54,317	54,770	10	7	5
With own children[2]	25,541	24,961	24,210	24,537	25,241	25,269	25,066	-2	-2	2
Without own children[2]	19,214	24,151	26,140	27,780	28,617	29,048	29,703	26	15	7
Male householder[1]	1,239	1,733	2,228	2,884	3,226	3,911	3,976	40	66	38
With own children[2]	345	616	896	1,153	1,440	1,798	1,706	79	87	48
Without own children[2]	894	1,117	1,332	1,731	1,786	2,113	2,270	25	55	31
Female householder[1]	5,591	8,705	10,129	10,890	12,220	12,652	12,789	56	25	17
With own children[2]	2,971	5,445	6,006	6,599	7,615	7,693	7,841	83	21	19
Without own children[2]	2,620	3,261	4,123	4,290	4,606	4,960	4,948	24	32	15
Unrelated subfamilies	130	360	526	534	674	575	522	177	48	-2
Married couple	27	20	46	68	64	41	50	(B)	(B)	(B)
Male reference persons[1]	11	36	85	45	59	72	64	(B)	(B)	(B)
Female reference persons[1]	91	304	395	421	550	463	408	234	39	-3
Related subfamilies	1,150	1,150	2,228	2,403	2,878	2,870	2,901	-	109	21
Married couple	617	582	719	871	1,015	947	1,029	-6	50	18
Father-child[1]	48	54	116	153	195	250	281	(B)	(B)	84
Mother-child[1]	484	512	1,392	1,378	1,668	1,673	1,591	6	169	15
Married couples	**45,373**	**49,714**	**51,114**	**53,256**	**54,937**	**55,305**	**55,849**	10	7	5
With own household	44,728	49,112	50,350	52,317	53,858	54,317	54,770	10	7	5
Without own household	645	602	764	939	1,079	988	1,079	-7	56	15
Percent without	1.4	1.2	1.5	1.8	2.0	1.8	1.9	(X)	(X)	(X)

- Represents or rounds to zero.   B Not shown; base less than 75,000.   X Not applicable.   [1] No spouse present.   [2] Under 18 years old.

Source: U.S. Census Bureau, Current Population Reports, P20-515, and unpublished data.

No. 61. Households by Age of Householder and Size of Household: 1980 to 1999

[In millions (80.8 represents 80,800,000). As of March. Based on Current Population Survey; see headnote, Table 60]

Age of householder and size of household	1980	1985	1990	1995	1998	1999			
						Total[1]	White	Black	Hispanic[2]
Total	**80.8**	**86.8**	**93.3**	**99.0**	**102.5**	**103.9**	**87.2**	**12.6**	**9.1**
Age of householder:									
15 to 24 years old	6.6	5.4	5.1	5.4	5.4	5.9	4.6	0.9	0.9
25 to 29 years old	9.3	9.6	9.4	8.4	8.5	8.5	6.8	1.3	1.1
30 to 34 years old	9.3	10.4	11.0	11.1	10.6	10.3	8.3	1.5	1.3
35 to 44 years old	14.0	17.5	20.6	22.9	23.9	24.0	19.8	3.1	2.4
45 to 54 years old	12.7	12.6	14.5	17.6	19.5	20.2	16.9	2.4	1.4
55 to 64 years old	12.5	13.1	12.5	12.2	13.1	13.6	11.6	1.5	0.9
65 to 74 years old	10.1	10.9	11.7	11.8	11.3	11.4	10.0	1.1	0.6
75 years old and over	6.4	7.3	8.4	9.6	10.2	10.2	9.3	0.8	0.3
One person	18.3	20.6	23.0	24.7	26.3	26.6	22.2	3.6	1.3
Male	7.0	7.9	9.0	10.1	11.0	11.0	9.0	1.5	0.6
Female	11.3	12.7	14.0	14.6	15.3	15.6	13.1	2.1	0.7
Two persons	25.3	27.4	30.1	31.8	33.0	34.3	29.9	3.3	2.0
Three persons	14.1	15.5	16.1	16.8	17.3	17.4	14.2	2.3	1.8
Four persons	12.7	13.6	14.5	15.3	15.4	15.0	12.5	1.8	1.8
Five persons	6.1	6.1	6.2	6.6	7.0	7.0	5.7	0.9	1.3
Six persons	2.5	2.3	2.1	2.3	2.2	2.4	1.8	0.3	0.5
Seven persons or more	1.8	1.3	1.3	1.4	1.3	1.3	0.9	0.2	0.4

[1] Includes other races, not shown separately.   [2] Hispanic persons may be of any race.

Source: U.S. Census Bureau, Current Population Reports, P20-515, and earlier reports; and unpublished data.

No. 62. Households, 1980 to 1999, and Persons in Households, 1999 by Type of Household

[As of **March (80,776 represents 80,776,000).** Based on Current Population Survey; see headnote, Table 60]

Type of household	Households					Persons in households, 1999		Persons per house- hold, 1999
	Number (1,000)			Percent distribution		Number (1,000)	Percent distribu- tion	
	1980	1990	1999	1990	1999			
Total households	80,776	93,347	103,874	100	100	271,545	100	**2.61**
Family households	59,550	66,090	71,535	71	69	231,226	85	3.23
Married couple family..............	49,112	52,317	54,770	56	53	177,952	66	3.25
Male householder, no spouse present. . .	1,733	2,884	3,976	3	4	12,514	5	3.15
Female householder, no spouse present .	8,705	10,890	12,789	12	12	40,760	15	3.19
Nonfamily households...............	21,226	27,257	32,339	29	31	40,319	15	1.25
Living alone	18,296	22,999	26,606	25	26	26,606	10	1.00
Male householder	8,807	11,606	14,368	12	14	19,351	7	1.35
Living alone	6,966	9,049	10,966	10	11	10,966	4	1.00
Female householder	12,419	15,651	17,971	17	17	20,969	8	1.17
Living alone	11,330	13,950	15,640	15	15	15,640	6	1.00

Source: U.S. Census Bureau, *Current Population Reports*, P20-447, and earlier reports; and unpublished data.

No. 63. Households by State: 1990 and 1998

[**1990**, as of **April 1**; **1998**, as of **July 1 (91,946 represents 91,946,000).** Minus sign (-) indicates decrease]

State	Number (1,000)		Percent change, 1990-98	Persons per house- hold, 1998	State	Number (1,000)		Percent change, 1990-98	Persons per house- hold, 1998
	1990	1998				1990	1998		
U.S......	**91,946**	**101,041**	**9.9**	**2.61**	MO	1,961	2,089	6.5	2.53
					MT	306	346	13.0	2.47
AL	1,507	1,663	10.4	2.56	NE	602	636	5.5	2.54
AK	189	215	13.7	2.78	NV	466	676	45.0	2.54
AZ	1,369	1,762	28.7	2.60	NH	411	450	9.5	2.56
AR	891	970	8.9	2.56					
CA	10,381	11,446	10.3	2.79	NJ........	2,795	2,957	5.8	2.69
					NM	543	632	16.5	2.70
CO	1,282	1,561	21.7	2.49	NY	6,639	6,766	1.9	2.61
CT	1,230	1,238	0.6	2.57	NC	2,517	2,883	14.5	2.54
DE	247	284	14.7	2.54	ND	241	247	2.5	2.48
DC	250	225	-10.0	2.15					
FL........	5,135	5,881	14.5	2.48	OH	4,088	4,285	4.8	2.55
					OK	1,206	1,288	6.8	2.52
GA	2,366	2,843	20.1	2.63	OR	1,103	1,286	16.5	2.50
HI........	356	401	12.5	2.87	PA	4,496	4,593	2.2	2.54
ID........	361	448	24.3	2.69	RI	378	376	-0.5	2.53
IL........	4,202	4,438	5.6	2.65					
IN........	2,065	2,231	8.0	2.57	SC	1,258	1,441	14.6	2.58
					SD	259	277	6.8	2.55
IA........	1,064	1,103	3.7	2.50	TN	1,854	2,100	13.3	2.52
KS	945	999	5.8	2.55	TX	6,071	7,113	17.2	2.71
KY	1,380	1,497	8.5	2.56	UT	537	677	26.0	3.06
LA	1,499	1,599	6.6	2.66					
ME	465	490	5.3	2.48	VT	211	231	9.8	2.46
					VA	2,292	2,579	12.5	2.55
MD	1,749	1,906	9.0	2.63	WA	1,872	2,211	18.1	2.52
MA	2,247	2,349	4.5	2.52	WV	689	716	4.0	2.48
MI........	3,419	3,693	8.0	2.60	WI........	1,822	1,973	8.3	2.58
MN	1,648	1,791	8.7	2.58	WY	169	185	9.6	2.54
MS	911	997	9.4	2.68					

Source: U.S. Census Bureau, "ST-98-51 Estimates of Housing Units, Households, Households by Age of Householder, and Persons Per Household of States: Annual Time Series, July 1, 1991, to July 1, 1998"; published: 8 December 1999; <http://www.census.gov/population/estimates/housing/sthuhh6.txt>.

Population 55

No. 64. Family Groups With Children Under 18 Years Old by Race and Hispanic Origin: 1980 to 1999

[In thousands. As of March (32,150 represents 32,150,000). Family groups comprise family households, related subfamilies, and unrelated subfamilies. Excludes members of Armed Forces except those living off post or with their families on post. Based on Current Population Survey; see text, this section, and Appendix III]

Race and Hispanic origin of householder or reference person	1980	1990	1995	1999 Total	1999 Family house-holds	1999 Subfamilies Total	1999 Subfamilies Related	1999 Subfamilies Unrelated
All races, total [1]	32,150	34,670	37,168	37,430	34,613	2,816	2,328	488
Two-parent family groups	25,231	24,921	25,640	25,538	25,066	472	456	16
One-parent family groups	6,920	9,749	11,528	11,892	9,547	2,344	1,872	472
Maintained by mother	6,230	8,398	9,834	9,841	7,841	1,999	1,591	408
Maintained by father	690	1,351	1,694	2,051	1,706	345	281	64
White, total	27,294	28,294	29,846	30,132	28,240	1,892	1,475	417
Two-parent family groups	22,628	21,905	22,320	22,139	21,759	379	364	15
One-parent family groups	4,664	6,389	7,525	7,993	6,481	1,512	1,111	401
Maintained by mother	4,122	5,310	6,239	6,368	5,110	1,258	918	340
Maintained by father	542	1,079	1,286	1,625	1,371	254	193	61
Black, total	4,074	5,087	5,491	5,480	4,715	768	713	55
Two-parent family groups	1,961	2,006	1,962	2,017	1,971	46	46	-
One-parent family groups	2,114	3,081	3,529	3,463	2,744	721	666	55
Maintained by mother	1,984	2,860	3,197	3,139	2,477	663	611	52
Maintained by father	129	221	332	324	267	58	55	3
Hispanic, total [2]	2,194	3,429	4,527	5,193	4,614	579	497	82
Two-parent family groups	1,626	2,289	2,879	3,354	3,218	136	129	7
One-parent family groups	568	1,140	1,647	1,839	1,396	443	368	75
Maintained by mother	526	1,003	1,404	1,560	1,174	386	319	67
Maintained by father	42	138	243	279	222	57	49	8

- Represents or rounds to zero.   [1] Includes other races, not shown separately.   [2] Hispanic persons may be of any race.

Source: U.S. Census Bureau, *Current Population Reports*, P20-515, and earlier reports; and unpublished data.

No. 65. Families by Number of Own Children Under 18 Years Old: 1980 to 1999

[As of March (59,550 represents 59,550,000) and based on Current Population Survey; see headnote, Table 66]

Race, Hispanic origin, and year	Number of families (1,000) Total	No children	One child	Two children	Three or more children	Percent distribution Total	No children	One child	Two children	Three or more children
ALL FAMILIES [1]										
1980	59,550	28,528	12,443	11,470	7,109	100	48	21	19	12
1985	62,706	31,594	13,108	11,645	6,359	100	50	21	19	10
1990	66,090	33,801	13,530	12,263	6,496	100	51	20	19	10
1995	69,305	35,009	14,088	13,213	6,995	100	51	20	19	10
1998	70,880	36,120	14,363	13,122	7,275	100	51	20	19	10
1999	71,535	36,922	14,331	13,070	7,212	100	52	20	18	10
Married couple	54,770	29,703	9,545	10,040	5,481	100	54	17	18	10
Male householder [2]	3,976	2,270	1,023	480	202	100	57	26	12	5
Female householder [2] . . .	12,789	4,948	3,763	2,549	1,529	100	39	29	20	12
WHITE FAMILIES										
1980	52,243	25,769	10,727	9,977	5,769	100	49	21	19	11
1985	54,400	28,169	11,174	9,937	5,120	100	52	21	18	9
1990	56,590	29,872	11,186	10,342	5,191	100	53	20	18	9
1995	58,437	30,486	11,491	10,983	5,478	100	52	20	19	9
1998	59,511	31,175	11,716	10,796	5,824	100	52	20	18	10
1999	60,068	31,828	11,636	10,777	5,828	100	53	19	18	10
BLACK FAMILIES										
1980	6,184	2,364	1,449	1,235	1,136	100	38	23	20	18
1985	6,778	2,887	1,579	1,330	982	100	43	23	20	15
1990	7,470	3,093	1,894	1,433	1,049	100	41	25	19	14
1995	8,093	3,411	1,971	1,593	1,117	100	42	24	20	14
1998	8,408	3,561	1,961	1,749	1,138	100	42	23	21	14
1999	8,444	3,730	1,985	1,642	1,088	100	44	24	19	13
HISPANIC FAMILIES [3]										
1980	3,029	946	680	698	706	100	31	22	23	23
1985	3,939	1,337	904	865	833	100	34	23	22	21
1990	4,840	1,790	1,095	1,036	919	100	37	23	21	19
1995	6,200	2,216	1,408	1,406	1,171	100	36	23	23	19
1998	6,961	2,486	1,585	1,616	1,273	100	36	23	23	18
1999	7,270	2,656	1,673	1,614	1,328	100	37	23	22	18

[1] Includes other races, not shown separately.   [2] No spouse present.   [3] Hispanic persons may be of any race.

Source: U.S. Census Bureau, *Current Population Reports*, P20-515, and earlier reports; and unpublished data.

No. 66. Families by Size and Presence of Children: 1980 to 1999

[In thousands, except as indicated (59,550 represents 59,550,000). As of March. Excludes members of Armed Forces except those living off post or with their families on post. Based on Current Population Survey; see text, this section, and Appendix III. For definition of families, see text, this section]

Characteristic	Number					Percent distribution				
	1980	1985	1990	1995	1999	1980	1985	1990	1995	1999
Total.............	**59,550**	**62,706**	**66,090**	**69,305**	**71,535**	**100**	**100**	**100**	**100**	**100**
Size of family:										
Two persons	23,461	25,349	27,606	29,176	31,100	39	40	42	42	43
Three persons	13,603	14,804	15,353	15,903	16,219	23	24	23	23	23
Four persons.........	12,372	13,259	14,026	14,624	14,386	21	21	21	21	20
Five persons	5,930	5,894	5,938	6,283	6,570	10	9	9	9	9
Six persons	2,461	2,175	1,997	2,106	2,135	4	4	3	3	3
Seven or more persons ..	1,723	1,225	1,170	1,213	1,124	3	2	2	2	2
Average per family	3.29	3.23	3.17	3.19	3.18	(X)	(X)	(X)	(X)	(X)
Own children under age 18:										
None	28,528	31,594	33,801	35,009	36,922	48	50	51	51	52
One................	12,443	13,108	13,530	14,088	14,331	21	21	20	20	20
Two	11,470	11,645	12,263	13,213	13,070	19	19	19	19	18
Three	4,674	4,486	4,650	5,044	5,242	8	7	7	7	7
Four or more	2,435	1,873	1,846	1,951	1,970	4	3	3	3	3
Own children under age 6:										
None	46,063	48,505	50,905	53,695	56,303	77	77	77	77	79
One	9,441	9,677	10,304	10,733	10,708	16	15	16	15	15
Two or more	4,047	4,525	4,882	4,876	4,524	7	7	7	7	6

X Not applicable.

Source: U.S. Census Bureau, *Current Population Reports*, P20-488, and earlier reports; and unpublished data.

No. 67. Families by Type, Race, and Hispanic Origin: 1999

[In thousands, except as indicated (71,535 represents 71,535,000). As of March. Excludes members of Armed Forces except those living off post or with their families on post. Based on Current Population Survey; see text of this section and Appendix III. For definition of families, see text of this section]

Characteristic	All families	Married couple families				Female family householder [3]				Male family householder, [3] all races
		All races [1]	White	Black	Hispanic [2]	All races [1]	White	Black	Hispanic [2]	
All families...........	**71,535**	**54,770**	**48,456**	**3,975**	**4,945**	**12,789**	**8,526**	**3,809**	**1,725**	**3,976**
Age of householder:										
Under 25 years old.	3,242	1,483	1,355	81	332	1,228	765	406	214	530
25 to 34 years old	13,219	9,376	8,074	818	1,366	2,912	1,758	1,063	438	932
35 to 44 years old	18,819	14,141	12,304	1,110	1,443	3,683	2,499	1,061	555	995
45 to 54 years old	15,122	12,152	10,708	921	858	2,251	1,557	601	269	720
55 to 64 years old	9,634	8,091	7,249	521	499	1,122	773	307	148	421
65 to 74 years old	7,051	5,975	5,468	353	310	868	616	220	73	208
75 years old and over......	4,447	3,552	3,297	173	136	725	558	151	29	170
Without own children under 18. .	36,922	29,703	26,697	2,005	1,727	4,948	3,416	1,332	551	2,270
With own children under 18....	34,613	25,066	21,759	1,971	3,218	7,841	5,110	2,477	1,174	1,706
One own child under 18	14,331	9,545	8,208	774	1,064	3,763	2,643	1,019	498	1,023
Two own children under 18 ..	13,070	10,040	8,760	731	1,193	2,549	1,605	862	349	480
Three or more own children under 18.	7,212	5,481	4,791	466	961	1,529	862	596	327	202
Average per family with own children under 18.	1.86	1.91	1.90	1.93	2.17	1.78	1.70	1.91	2.09	1.54
Marital status of householder:										
Married, spouse present	54,770	54,770	48,456	3,975	4,945	(X)	(X)	(X)	(X)	(X)
Married, spouse absent.....	2,521	(X)	(X)	(X)	(X)	1,966	1,276	609	409	555
Widowed	2,648	(X)	(X)	(X)	(X)	2,209	1,657	480	205	439
Divorced..............	6,008	(X)	(X)	(X)	(X)	4,620	3,602	874	469	1,387
Never married	5,589	(X)	(X)	(X)	(X)	3,994	1,991	1,846	643	1,595

X Not applicable.   [1] Includes other races now shown separately.   [2] Persons of Hispanic origin may be of any race.   [3] No spouse present.

Source: U.S. Census Bureau, unpublished data.

U.S. Census Bureau, Statistical Abstract of the United States: 2000

No. 68. Family Households With Own Children Under Age 18 by Type of Family, 1980 to 1999, and by Age of Householder, 1999

[As of **March (31,022 represents 31,022,000).** Excludes members of Armed Forces except those living off post or with their families on post. Based on Current Population Survey; see text, this section, and Appendix III]

Family type	1980	1990	1999						
			Total	15 to 24 years old	25 to 34 years old	35 to 44 years old	45 to 54 years old	55 to 64 years old	65 years old and over
NUMBER (1,000)									
Family households with children...	31,022	32,289	34,613	1,995	10,075	15,185	6,336	892	132
Married couple...	24,961	24,537	25,066	889	6,865	11,416	5,104	700	93
Male householder [1]...	616	1,153	1,706	119	520	663	315	75	13
Female householder [1]...	5,445	6,599	7,841	987	2,690	3,106	917	117	25
PERCENT DISTRIBUTION									
Family households with children...	100	100	100	100	100	100	100	100	100
Married couple...	81	76	72	45	68	75	81	78	70
Male householder [1]...	2	4	5	6	5	4	5	8	10
Female householder [1]...	18	20	23	49	27	20	14	13	19
HOUSEHOLDS WITH CHILDREN, AS A PERCENT OF ALL FAMILY HOUSEHOLDS, BY TYPE									
Family households with children, total...	52	49	48	62	76	81	42	9	1
Married couple...	51	47	46	60	73	81	42	9	1
Male householder [1]...	36	40	43	22	56	67	44	18	3
Female householder [1]...	63	61	61	80	92	84	41	10	2

[1] No spouse present.

Source: U.S. Census Bureau, *Current Population Reports*, P20-447, and earlier reports; and unpublished data.

No. 69. Children Under 18 Years Old by Presence of Parents: 1980 to 1998

[As of **March (63,427 represents 63,427,000).** Excludes persons under 18 years old who maintained households or family groups. Based on Current Population Survey; see headnote, Table 66]

Race, Hispanic origin, and year	Percent living with—								
	Number (1,000)	Both parents	Mother only					Father only	Neither parent
			Total	Divorced	Married, spouse absent	Never married	Widowed		
ALL RACES [1]									
1980...	63,427	77	18	8	6	3	2	2	4
1985...	62,475	74	21	9	5	6	2	3	3
1990...	64,137	73	22	8	5	7	2	3	3
1995...	70,254	69	23	9	6	8	1	4	4
1998...	71,377	68	23	8	5	9	1	4	4
WHITE									
1980...	52,242	83	14	7	4	1	2	2	2
1985...	50,836	80	16	8	4	2	1	2	2
1990...	51,390	79	16	8	4	3	1	3	2
1995...	55,327	76	18	8	5	4	1	3	3
1998...	56,124	74	18	8	4	5	1	5	3
BLACK									
1980...	9,375	42	44	11	16	13	4	2	12
1985...	9,479	40	51	11	12	25	3	3	7
1990...	10,018	38	51	10	12	27	2	4	8
1995...	11,301	33	52	11	11	29	2	4	11
1998...	11,414	36	51	9	9	32	1	4	9
HISPANIC [2]									
1980...	5,459	75	20	6	8	4	2	2	4
1985...	6,057	68	27	7	11	7	2	2	3
1990...	7,174	67	27	7	10	8	2	3	3
1995...	9,843	63	28	8	9	10	1	4	4
1998...	10,863	64	27	6	8	12	1	4	5

[1] Includes other races not shown separately.   [2] Hispanic persons may be of any race.

Source: U.S. Census Bureau, *Current Population Reports*, P20-514, and earlier reports; and unpublished data.

No. 70. Living Arrangements of Children Under 18 Years Old Living With One or Both Parents: 1998

[In thousands (68,418 represents 68,418,000). As of March. Covers only those persons under 18 years old who are living with one or both parents. Characteristics are shown for the householder or reference person in married-couple situations. See also headnote, Table 66]

Characteristic of parent	All races[1] Total	Both parents	Mother only	Father only	White Total	Both parents	Mother only	Father only	Black Total	Both parents	Mother only	Father only	Hispanic[2] Total	Both parents	Mother only	Father only
Children under 18 years old	68,418	48,642	16,634	3,143	54,319	41,547	10,210	2,562	10,392	4,137	5,830	424	10,306	6,909	2,915	482
Age:																
15 to 24 years old	3,869	1,309	2,250	310	2,588	1,142	1,220	226	1,155	128	968	59	977	387	512	77
25 to 29 years old	7,871	4,694	2,746	432	5,878	3,962	1,552	364	1,699	549	1,098	52	1,553	939	511	103
30 to 34 years old	13,978	9,653	3,861	464	10,817	8,178	2,275	363	2,464	935	1,464	64	2,453	1,651	709	93
35 to 39 years old	17,035	12,721	3,656	658	13,823	11,011	2,278	533	2,352	1,005	1,275	72	2,275	1,635	574	66
40 to 44 years old	14,189	11,093	2,452	644	11,941	9,622	1,755	564	1,421	762	587	72	1,731	1,307	346	78
45 to 54 years old	10,247	8,209	1,498	540	8,336	6,863	1,030	444	1,108	656	374	79	1,127	834	237	56
55 to 64 years old	1,019	811	136	74	811	663	87	60	120	64	44	13	172	136	27	8
65 years old and over	208	152	33	23	127	107	12	8	72	38	21	13	20	19	-	2
Educational attainment:																
Less than 9th grade	4,061	2,719	1,180	162	3,428	2,415	868	144	323	110	200	13	2,790	1,937	764	89
9th to 12th grade, no diploma	7,527	3,999	2,980	547	5,345	3,332	1,581	433	1,829	449	1,300	80	2,207	1,306	770	132
High school graduate[3]	22,101	14,693	6,079	1,329	17,126	12,454	3,589	1,083	4,041	1,508	2,314	220	2,701	1,848	678	175
Some college, no degree or associate degree	18,901	13,265	4,881	755	14,938	11,280	3,067	591	3,092	1,322	1,669	101	1,827	1,212	554	61
Bachelor's degree	10,489	9,125	1,126	237	8,966	7,947	810	208	846	567	269	10	591	456	118	17
Graduate or professional degree	5,340	4,840	388	112	4,517	4,118	295	104	261	182	79	-	189	150	31	8
Employment status:[4]																
In the civilian labor force	57,277	42,160	12,282	2,835	46,045	36,076	7,634	2,335	8,190	3,542	4,289	360	8,111	5,806	1,876	429
Employed	54,220	40,706	10,888	2,626	44,088	34,948	6,967	2,174	7,264	3,358	3,584	322	7,539	5,502	1,641	396
Both parents employed	28,961	28,961	(X)	(X)	24,784	24,784	(X)	(X)	2,617	2,617	(X)	(X)	3,174	3,174	(X)	(X)
Unemployed	3,058	1,454	1,395	210	1,957	1,128	668	162	927	183	705	38	572	304	235	33
Not in the labor force	10,386	5,761	4,345	280	7,637	4,858	2,569	211	2,113	517	1,541	54	2,144	1,052	1,039	53
Family income:																
Under $5,000	3,030	562	2,267	201	1,771	415	1,194	162	1,067	72	965	30	637	175	421	40
$5,000 to $9,999	3,987	692	3,113	182	2,423	520	1,771	132	1,374	89	1,243	41	1,112	314	755	44
$10,000 to $14,999	4,394	1,698	2,419	278	3,037	1,405	1,389	244	1,053	123	902	27	1,226	690	454	82
$15,000 to $24,999	8,433	4,372	3,465	596	6,245	3,574	2,185	485	1,853	552	1,202	99	2,199	1,477	632	90
$25,000 to $29,999	4,203	2,670	1,183	350	3,275	2,229	771	275	697	283	352	62	867	679	133	54
$30,000 to $39,999	8,041	5,971	1,583	487	6,547	5,159	1,008	380	1,100	483	545	73	1,397	1,112	210	75
$40,000 to $49,999	7,678	6,444	915	319	6,318	5,388	657	272	977	713	237	26	997	836	125	36
$50,000 and over	28,653	26,233	1,690	730	24,704	22,857	1,234	613	2,270	1,821	384	65	1,871	1,626	184	61
Tenure:[5]																
Owned	44,750	36,875	6,216	1,658	38,292	32,401	4,503	1,388	4,211	2,534	1,502	175	4,564	3,672	733	159
Rented	23,669	11,766	10,418	1,485	16,028	9,146	5,707	1,175	6,181	1,603	4,329	250	5,742	3,237	2,182	323

- Represents or rounds to zero. X Not applicable. [1] Includes other races, not shown separately. [2] Persons of Hispanic origin may be of any race. [3] Includes equivalency. [4] Excludes children whose parent is in the Armed Forces. [5] Refers to the tenure of the householder (who may or may not be the child's parent).

Source: U.S. Census Bureau, Current Population Reports, P20-514; and unpublished data.

No. 71. Grandchildren Living in the Home of Their Grandparents: 1980 to 1998

[In thousands (63,369 represents 63,369,000). Except as noted, based on Current Population Survey; see headnote, Table 66]

Living arrangements	1980 [1]	1990	1993	1994	1995	1996	1997	1998
Total children under 18 years old...	63,369	64,137	66,893	69,508	70,254	70,908	70,983	71,377
Children living in home of grandparents	**2,306**	**3,155**	**3,368**	**3,735**	**3,965**	**4,060**	**3,894**	**3,989**
With parent(s) present	1,318	2,221	2,351	2,375	2,498	2,629	2,585	2,571
Both parents present	310	467	475	436	427	467	554	503
Mother only present	922	1,563	1,647	1,764	1,876	1,943	1,785	1,827
Father only present	86	191	229	175	195	220	247	241
Without parent(s) present	988	935	1,017	1,359	1,466	1,431	1,309	1,417

[1] Based on census of population.

Source: U.S. Census Bureau, *1980 Census of Population*, PC80-2-4B, *Living Arrangements of Children and Adults*, and *Current Population Reports*, P20-514, and earlier reports.

No. 72. Nonfamily Households by Sex and Age of Householder: 1990 and 1999

[In thousands (11,606 represents 11,606,000). As of **March**. See headnote, Table 66]

Item	Male householder					Female householder				
	Total	15 to 24 yr. old	25 to 44 yr. old	45 to 64 yr. old	65 yr. old and over	Total	15 to 24 yr. old	25 to 44 yr. old	45 to 64 yr. old	65 yr. old and over
1990, total	**11,606**	**1,236**	**5,780**	**2,536**	**2,053**	**15,651**	**1,032**	**3,697**	**3,545**	**7,377**
One person (living alone)	9,049	674	4,231	2,203	1,943	13,950	536	2,881	3,300	7,233
Nonrelatives present	2,557	560	1,551	334	112	1,701	497	817	245	143
Never married	5,844	1,175	3,689	696	285	4,382	976	2,406	510	491
Married [1]	1,117	28	513	391	187	794	15	261	320	198
Widowed	1,417	-	29	221	1,166	7,428	4	52	1,333	6,038
Divorced	3,228	33	1,550	1,229	416	3,046	37	977	1,382	649
1999, total	**14,368**	**1,363**	**6,572**	**4,033**	**2,399**	**17,971**	**1,164**	**4,175**	**4,939**	**7,692**
One person (living alone)	10,966	644	4,687	3,380	2,254	15,640	668	3,102	4,377	7,493
Nonrelatives present	3,402	718	1,886	653	144	2,331	497	1,074	561	199
Never married	7,180	1,315	4,368	1,181	317	5,464	1,105	2,806	1,016	538
Married [1]	1,286	22	596	486	183	1,123	33	324	470	296
Widowed	1,551	-	26	228	1,297	7,128	-	66	1,097	5,967
Divorced	4,351	26	1,582	2,141	603	4,256	27	982	2,357	891

- Represents or rounds to zero.   [1] No spouse present.

Source: U.S. Census Bureau, *Current Population Reports*, P20-515, and unpublished data.

No. 73. Persons Living Alone by Sex and Age: 1980 to 1999

[As of **March** (18,296 represents 18,296,000). Based on Current Population Survey; see headnote, Table 66]

Sex and age	Number of persons (1,000)					Percent distribution				
	1980	1985	1990	1995	1999	1980	1985	1990	1995	1999
Both sexes	**18,296**	**20,602**	**22,999**	**24,732**	**26,606**	**100**	**100**	**100**	**100**	**100**
15 to 24 years old	1,726	1,324	1,210	1,196	1,313	9	6	5	5	5
25 to 34 years old	[1]4,729	3,905	3,972	3,653	3,714	[1]26	19	17	15	14
35 to 44 years old	(1)	2,322	3,138	3,663	4,074	(1)	11	14	15	15
45 to 64 years old	4,514	4,939	5,502	6,377	7,757	25	24	24	26	29
65 to 74 years old	3,851	4,130	4,350	4,374	4,125	21	20	19	18	16
75 years old and over	3,477	3,982	4,825	5,470	5,622	19	19	21	22	21
Male	**6,966**	**7,922**	**9,049**	**10,140**	**10,966**	**38**	**39**	**39**	**41**	**41**
15 to 24 years old	947	750	674	623	644	5	4	3	3	2
25 to 34 years old	[1]2,920	2,307	2,395	2,213	2,166	[1]16	11	10	9	8
35 to 44 years old	(1)	1,406	1,836	2,263	2,521	(1)	7	8	9	9
45 to 64 years old	1,613	1,845	2,203	2,787	3,380	9	9	10	11	13
65 to 74 years old	775	868	1,042	1,134	1,127	4	4	5	5	4
75 years old and over	711	746	901	1,120	1,127	4	4	4	5	4
Female	**11,330**	**12,680**	**13,950**	**14,592**	**15,640**	**62**	**62**	**61**	**59**	**59**
15 to 24 years old	779	573	536	572	668	4	3	2	2	3
25 to 34 years old	[1]1,809	1,598	1,578	1,440	1,549	[1]10	8	7	6	6
35 to 44 years old	(1)	916	1,303	1,399	1,553	(1)	4	6	6	6
45 to 64 years old	2,901	3,095	3,300	3,589	4,377	16	15	14	15	16
65 to 74 years old	3,076	3,262	3,309	3,240	2,998	17	16	14	13	11
75 years old and over	2,766	3,236	3,924	4,351	4,495	15	16	17	18	17

[1] Data for persons 35 to 44 years old included with persons 25 to 34 years old.

Source: U.S. Census Bureau, *Current Population Reports*, P20-491, and earlier reports; and unpublished data.

No. 74. Religious Bodies—Selected Data

[**Membership data: (2,500 represents 2,500,000).** Includes the self-reported membership of religious bodies with 60,000 or more as reported to the *Yearbook of American and Canadian Churches*. Groups may be excluded if they do not supply information. The data are not standardized so comparisons between groups are difficult. The definition of "church member" is determined by the religious body]

Religious body	Year reported	Churches reported	Membership (1,000)	Pastors serving parishes [1]
African Methodist Episcopal Church.	1999	6,200	2,500	(NA)
African Methodist Episcopal Zion Church	1998	3,098	1,252	2,571
American Baptist Association	1998	1,760	275	1,740
American Baptist Churches in the U.S.A.	1998	3,800	1,507	4,145
Antiochian Orthodox Christian Diocese of North America.	1998	220	65	263
Armenian Apostolic Church of America.	1998	28	200	25
Assemblies of God.	1998	11,937	2,526	18,148
Baptist Bible Fellowship International	1997	4,500	1,200	(NA)
Baptist General Conference	1998	876	141	(NA)
Baptist Missionary Association of America.	1999	1,334	235	1,525
Buddhist [2]	1990	(NA)	401	(NA)
Christian and Missionary Alliance, The.	1998	1,964	346	1,629
Christian Brethren (Plymouth Brethren)	1997	1,150	100	(NA)
Christian Church (Disciples of Christ).	1997	3,818	879	3,419
Christian Churches and Churches of Christ.	1998	5,579	1,072	5,525
Christian Congregation, Inc., The	1998	1,438	117	1,436
Christian Methodist Episcopal Church	1983	2,340	719	(NA)
Christian Reformed Church in North America.	1998	733	199	655
Church of God in Christ.	1991	15,300	5,500	28,988
Church of God of Prophecy.	1997	1,908	77	2,000
Church of God (Anderson, IN)	1998	2,353	234	3,034
Church of God (Cleveland, TN).	1995	6,060	753	3,121
Church of Jesus Christ of Latter-day Saints, The	1997	10,811	4,923	32,433
Church of the Brethren	1997	1,095	141	827
Church of the Nazarene	1998	5,101	627	4,598
Churches of Christ	1999	15,000	1,500	14,500
Conservative Baptist Association of America	1998	1,200	200	(NA)
Coptic Orthodox Church	1992	85	180	65
Cumberland Presbyterian Church	1998	774	87	634
Episcopal Church.	1996	7,390	2,365	8,131
Evangelical Covenant Church, The	1998	628	97	607
Evangelical Free Church of America, The.	1995	1,224	243	1,936
Evangelical Lutheran Church in America.	1998	10,862	5,178	9,646
Evangelical Presbyterian Church.	1998	187	61	262
Free Methodist Church of North America	1998	990	73	(NA)
Full Gospel Fellowship of Churches and Ministers International	1999	896	275	2,070
General Association of General Baptists.	1997	790	72	1,085
General Association of Regular Baptist Churches.	1998	1,415	102	(NA)
General Conference Mennonite Brethren Churches	1996	368	82	590
Grace Gospel Fellowship.	1992	128	60	160
Greek Orthodox Archdiocese of America	1998	523	1,955	596
Hindu [2].	1990	(NA)	227	(NA)
Independent Fundamental Churches of America	1999	659	62	(NA)
International Church of the Foursquare Gospel	1998	1,851	238	4,900
International Council of Community Churches	1998	150	250	182
International Pentecostal Holiness Church	1998	1,716	177	1,507
Jehovah's Witnesses	1999	11,064	1,040	(NA)
Jewish [3]	1998	(NA)	6,041	(NA)
Lutheran Church—Missouri Synod, The	1998	6,218	2,594	5,227
Mennonite Church	1998	926	92	(NA)
Muslim/Islamic [2].	1990	(NA)	527	(NA)
National Association of Congregational Christian Churches	1998	416	67	534
National Association of Free Will Baptists	1998	2,297	210	2,800
National Baptist Convention of America, Inc.	1987	2,500	3,500	8,000
National Baptist Convention, USA, Inc.	1992	33,000	8,200	32,832
National Missionary Baptist Convention of America.	1992	(NA)	2,500	(NA)
Old Order Amish Church	1993	898	81	3,592
Orthodox Church in America.	1998	625	1,000	700
Pentecostal Assemblies of the World, Inc..	1998	1,750	1,500	4,500
Pentecostal Church of God	1998	1,237	104	(NA)
Presbyterian Church in America	1997	1,340	280	1,642
Presbyterian Church (U.S.A.)	1998	11,260	3,575	9,390
Progressive National Baptist Convention, Inc.	1995	2,000	2,500	(NA)
Reformed Church in America	1998	902	296	915
Religious Society of Friends (Conservative).	1994	1,200	104	(NA)
Reorganized Church of Jesus Christ of Latter Day Saints	1998	1,236	140	19,319
Roman Catholic Church, The	1998	19,584	62,018	(NA)
Romanian Orthodox Episcopate of America, The	1996	37	65	37
Salvation Army, The	1998	1,388	471	2,920
Serbian Orthodox Church in the U.S.A. and Canada.	1986	68	67	60
Seventh-day Adventist Church	1998	4,405	840	2,454
Southern Baptist Convention	1998	40,870	15,729	71,520
Unitarian Universalist [2]	1990	(NA)	502	(NA)
United Church of Christ.	1998	6,017	1,421	4,317
United Methodist Church, The	1998	36,170	8,400	(NA)
Wesleyan Church, The	1998	1,590	120	1,806
Wisconsin Evangelical Lutheran Synod	1997	1,240	411	1,222

NA Not available. [1] Does not include retired clergy or clergy not working with congregations. [2] Figures obtained from the National Survey of Religious Identification, a survey conducted by the City University of New York in 1990 and published in *One Nation Under God: Religion in Contemporary American Society*, by Barry Kosmin and Seymour Lachman (1993). [3] Source: American Jewish Committee, New York, NY, *American Jewish Year Book* (copyright). See Table 76.

Source: Except as noted, National Council of the Churches of Christ in the USA, New York, NY, *1999 Yearbook of American and Canadian Churches*, annual (copyright). (For more info visit www.ncccusa.org).

Population 61

No. 75. Religious Preference, Church Membership, and Attendance: 1980 to 1999

[In percent. Covers civilian noninstitutional population, 18 years old and over. Data represent averages of the combined results of several surveys during year or period indicated. Data are subject to sampling variability, see source]

Year	Religious preference					Church/ synagogue members	Persons attending church/ synagogue [1]	Age and region	Church/ synagogue members, 1999
	Protes- tant	Catholic	Jewish	Other	None				
1980	61	28	2	2	7	69	40	18-29 years old....	68
1985	57	28	2	4	9	71	42	30-49 years old....	64
1990	56	25	2	6	11	65	40	50-64 years old....	72
1995	58	25	2	(NA)	(NA)	69	43	65 years and over..	82
1996	58	25	3	5	[2]9	65	38	East [3]	67
1997	58	26	2	6	[2]8	67	40	Midwest [4]	72
1998	59	27	2	5	[2]7	70	40	South [5]	75
1999	55	28	2	6	[2]8	70	43	West [6]	60

NA Not available. [1] Persons who attended a church or synagogue in the last 7 days. [2] Includes those respondents who did not designate. [3] ME, NH, RI, NY, CT, VT, MA, NJ, PA, WV, DE, MD, and DC. [4] OH, IN, IL, MI, MN, WI, IA, ND, SD, KS, NE, and MO. [5] KY, TN, VA, NC, SC, GA, FL, AL, MS, TX, AR, OK, and LA. [6] AZ, NM, CO, NV, MT, ID, WY, UT, CA, WA, OR, AK, and HI.

Source: Princeton Religion Research Center, Princeton, NJ, *Religion in America*, annual. Based on surveys conducted by The Gallup Organization, Inc.

No. 76. Christian Church Adherents, 1990, and Jewish Population, 1998—State

[Christian church adherents were defined as "all members, including full members, their children and the estimated number of other regular participants who are not considered as communicant, confirmed or full members." Data on Christian church adherents are based on reports of 133 church groupings and exclude 34 church bodies that reported more than 100,000 members to the *Yearbook of American and Canadian Churches*. The Jewish population includes Jews who define themselves as Jewish by religion as well as those who define themselves as Jewish in cultural terms. Data on Jewish population are based primarily on a compilation of individual estimates made by local Jewish federations. Additionally, most large communities have completed Jewish demographic surveys from which the Jewish population can be determined]

State	Christian adherents, 1990		Jewish population, 1998		State	Christian adherents, 1990		Jewish population, 1998	
	Number (1,000)	Percent of population [1]	Number (1,000)	Percent of population [1]		Number (1,000)	Percent of population [1]	Number (1,000)	Percent of population [1]
U.S.	131,084	52.7	6,041	2.3	MO	2,892	56.6	62	1.2
AL	2,858	70.7	9	0.2	MT	341	42.7	1	0.1
AK	175	31.8	4	0.6	NE......	1,000	63.4	7	0.4
AZ	1,505	41.1	82	1.8	NV......	366	29.6	58	3.4
AR	1,423	60.5	2	0.1	NH.....	431	38.9	10	0.8
CA	11,665	39.2	967	3.0	NJ	4,305	55.7	465	5.8
CO.....	1,244	37.8	68	1.8	NM.....	883	58.3	10	0.6
CT	1,933	58.9	101	3.1	NY.....	9,970	55.5	1,652	9.1
DE	297	44.6	14	1.8	NC.....	3,949	59.6	25	0.3
DC.....	349	57.5	25	4.8	ND.....	485	75.9	1	0.1
FL	5,106	39.5	628	4.3	OH.....	5,313	48.9	145	1.3
GA	3,659	56.5	87	1.1	OK.....	2,097	66.5	5	0.2
HI	391	35.3	7	0.6	OR.....	904	31.8	23	0.7
ID	507	50.4	1	0.1	PA	6,960	58.6	282	2.3
IL......	6,579	57.5	269	2.3	RI	754	75.1	16	1.6
IN	2,615	47.1	18	0.3	SC.....	2,149	61.7	10	0.3
IA	1,674	60.3	6	0.2	SD.....	474	68.1	(Z)	0.1
KS	1,346	54.3	14	0.6	TN.....	2,968	60.8	18	0.3
KY	2,213	60.1	11	0.3	TX.....	10,788	63.5	124	0.6
LA	2,959	70.1	16	0.4	UT.....	1,371	79.6	4	0.2
ME	439	36.1	8	0.6	VT......	233	40.4	6	1.0
MD.....	2,101	43.9	214	4.2	VA.....	2,898	46.8	76	1.1
MA.....	3,666	60.9	274	4.5	WA	1,579	32.4	35	0.6
MI	4,580	49.2	107	1.1	WV.....	740	41.3	2	0.1
MN.....	2,807	64.2	42	0.9	WI	3,125	63.9	28	0.5
MS.....	1,804	70.1	1	0.1	WY	216	47.6	(Z)	0.1

Z Fewer than 500. [1] Based on U.S. Census Bureau data for resident population enumerated as of April 1, 1990, and estimated as of July 1, 1998.

Source: Christian church adherents—M. Bradley; N. Green, Jr.; D. Jones; M. Lynn; and L. McNeil; *Churches and Church Membership in the United States 1990*, Glenmary Research Center, Atlanta, GA, 1992 (copyright); Jewish population—American Jewish Committee, New York, NY, *American Jewish Year Book* (copyright).

Section 2

Vital Statistics

This section presents vital statistics data on births, deaths, abortions, fetal deaths, fertility, life expectancy, marriages, and divorces. Vital statistics are compiled for the country as a whole by the National Center for Health Statistics (NCHS) and published in its annual report, *Vital Statistics of the United States*, in certain reports of the *Vital and Health Statistics* series, and in the *National Vital Statistics Reports* (formerly *Monthly Vital Statistics Report*). Reports in this field are also issued by the various state bureaus of vital statistics. Data on fertility, on age of persons at first marriage, and on marital status and marital history are compiled by the U.S. Census Bureau from its Current Population Survey (CPS; see text, Section 1) and published in *Current Population Reports*, P20 Series. Data on abortions are published by the Alan Guttmacher Institute, New York, NY, in selected issues of *Family Planning Perspectives*.

Registration of vital events—The registration of births, deaths, fetal deaths, and other vital events in the United States is primarily a state and local function. The civil laws of every state provide for a continuous and permanent birth- and death-registration system. Many states also provide for marriage- and divorce-registration systems. Vital events occurring to U.S. residents outside the United States are not included in the data.

Births and deaths—The live-birth, death, and fetal-death statistics prepared by NCHS are based on vital records filed in the registration offices of all states, of New York City, and of the District of Columbia. The annual collection of death statistics on a national basis began in 1900 with a national death-registration area of 10 states and the District of Columbia; a similar annual collection of birth statistics for a national birth-registration area began in

1915, also with 10 reporting states and the District of Columbia. Since 1933, the birth- and death-registration areas have comprised the entire United States, including Alaska (beginning 1959) and Hawaii (beginning 1960). National statistics on fetal deaths were first compiled for 1918 and annually since 1922.

Prior to 1951, birth statistics came from a complete count of records received in the Public Health Service (now received in NCHS). From 1951 through 1971, they were based on a 50-percent sample of all registered births (except for a complete count in 1955 and a 20- to 50-percent sample in 1967). Beginning in 1972, they have been based on a complete count for states participating in the Vital Statistics Cooperative Program (VSCP) (for details, see the technical appendix in *Vital Statistics of the United States*) and on a 50-percent sample of all other areas. Beginning 1986, all reporting areas participated in the VSCP. Mortality data have been based on a complete count of records for each area (except for a 50-percent sample in 1972). Beginning in 1970, births to and deaths of nonresident aliens of the United States and U.S. citizens outside the United States have been excluded from the data. Fetal deaths and deaths among Armed Forces abroad are excluded. Data based on samples are subject to sampling error; for details, see annual issues of *Vital Statistics of the United States*.

Mortality statistics by cause of death are compiled in accordance with World Health Organization regulations according to the *International Classification of Diseases* (ICD). The ICD is revised approximately every 10 years. The ninth revision of the ICD was employed beginning in 1979. Deaths for prior years were classified according to the revision of the ICD in use at the time. Each revision of the ICD

U.S. Census Bureau, Statistical Abstract of the United States: 2000

introduces a number of discontinuities in mortality statistics; for a discussion of those between the eighth and ninth revisions of the ICD, see *Monthly Vital Statistics Report* (renamed, *National Vital Statistics Report*), Vol. 28, No. 11, supplement.

Some of the tables present age-adjusted death rates in addition to crude death rates. Age adjusted death rates shown in this section were prepared using the direct method, in which age-specific death rates for a population of interest are applied to a standard population distributed by age. Age adjustment eliminates the differences in observed rates between points in time or among compared population groups that result from age differences in population composition.

Fertility and life expectancy—The total fertility rate, defined as the number of births that 1,000 women would have in their lifetime if, at each year of age, they experienced the birth rates occurring in the specified year, is compiled and published by NCHS. Other data relating to social and medical factors which affect fertility rates, such as contraceptive use and birth expectations, are collected and made available by both NCHS and the Census Bureau. NCHS figures are based on information in birth and fetal death certificates and on the periodic National Surveys of Family Growth; Census Bureau data are based on decennial censuses and the CPS.

Data on life expectancy, the average remaining lifetime in years for persons who attain a given age, are computed and published by NCHS. For details, see the technical appendix in *Vital Statistics of the United States*.

Marriage and divorce—The compilation of nationwide statistics on marriages and divorces in the United States began in 1887-88 when the National Office of Vital Statistics prepared estimates for the years 1867-86. Although periodic updates took place after 1888, marriage and divorce statistics were not collected and published annually until 1944 by that office. In 1957 and 1958, respectively, the same office established marriage- and divorce-registration areas. Beginning in 1957, the marriage-registration area comprised 30 states, plus Alaska, Hawaii, Puerto Rico, and the Virgin Islands; it currently includes 42 states and the District of Columbia. The divorce-registration area, starting in 1958 with 14 states, Alaska, Hawaii, and the Virgin Islands, it currently includes a total of 31 states and the Virgin Islands. Procedures for estimating the number of marriages and divorces in the registration states are discussed in *Vital Statistics of the United States*, Vol. III—Marriage and Divorce. Total counts of events for registration and nonregistration states are gathered by collecting already summarized data on marriages and divorces reported by state offices of vital statistics and by county offices of registration.

Vital statistics rates—Except as noted, vital statistics rates computed by NCHS are based on decennial census population figures as of April 1 for 1940, 1950, 1960, 1970, 1980, and 1990; and on midyear population figures for other years, as estimated by the Census Bureau (see text, Section 1).

Race—Data by race for births, deaths, marriages, and divorces from NCHS are based on information contained in the certificates of registration. The Census Bureau's Current Population Survey obtains information on race by asking respondents to classify their race as (1) White, (2) Black, (3) American Indian, Eskimo, or Aleut, or (4) Asian or Pacific Islander.

Beginning with the 1989 data year, NCHS is tabulating its birth data primarily by race of the mother. In 1988 and prior years, births were tabulated by race of the child, which was determined from the race of the parents as entered on the birth certificate.

Trend data by race shown in this section are by race of mother beginning with the 1980 data. Hispanic origin of the mother is reported and tabulated independently of race. Thus persons of Hispanic origin maybe of any race. In 1994, 91 percent of women of Hispanic origin were reported as White.

No. 77. Live Births, Deaths, Marriages, and Divorces: 1950 to 1998

[**3,632 represents 3,632,000.** Prior to 1960, excludes Alaska and Hawaii. Beginning 1970, excludes births to, and deaths of nonresidents of the United States. See Appendix III]

Year	Number (1,000)					Rate per 1,000 population				
		Deaths		Mar-riages [3]	Div-orces [4]		Deaths		Mar-riages [3]	Div-orces [4]
	Births [1]	Total	Infant [2]			Births [1]	Total	Infant [2]		
1950	3,632	1,452	104	1,667	385	24.1	9.6	29.2	11.1	2.6
1955	4,097	1,529	107	1,531	377	25.0	9.3	26.4	9.3	2.3
1957	4,300	1,633	112	1,518	381	25.3	9.6	26.3	8.9	2.2
1960	4,258	1,712	111	1,523	393	23.7	9.5	26.0	8.5	2.2
1965	3,760	1,828	93	1,800	479	19.4	9.4	24.7	9.3	2.5
1970	3,731	1,921	75	2,159	708	18.4	9.5	20.0	10.6	3.5
1971	3,556	1,928	68	2,190	773	17.2	9.3	19.1	10.6	3.7
1972	3,258	1,964	60	2,282	845	15.6	9.4	18.5	10.9	4.0
1973	3,137	1,973	56	2,284	915	14.8	9.3	17.7	10.8	4.3
1974	3,160	1,934	53	2,230	977	14.8	9.1	16.7	10.5	4.6
1975	3,144	1,893	51	2,153	1,036	14.6	8.8	16.1	10.0	4.8
1976	3,168	1,909	48	2,155	1,083	14.6	8.8	15.2	9.9	5.0
1977	3,327	1,900	47	2,178	1,091	15.1	8.6	14.1	9.9	5.0
1978	3,333	1,928	46	2,282	1,130	15.0	8.7	13.8	10.3	5.1
1979	3,494	1,914	46	2,331	1,181	15.6	8.5	13.1	10.4	5.3
1980	3,612	1,990	46	2,390	1,189	15.9	8.8	12.6	10.6	5.2
1981	3,629	1,978	43	2,422	1,213	15.8	8.6	11.9	10.6	5.3
1982	3,681	1,975	42	2,456	1,170	15.9	8.5	11.5	10.6	5.1
1983	3,639	2,019	41	2,446	1,158	15.6	8.6	11.2	10.5	5.0
1984	3,669	2,039	40	2,477	1,169	15.6	8.6	10.8	10.5	5.0
1985	3,761	2,086	40	2,413	1,190	15.8	8.8	10.6	10.1	5.0
1986	3,757	2,105	39	2,407	1,178	15.6	8.8	10.4	10.0	4.9
1987	3,809	2,123	38	2,403	1,166	15.7	8.8	10.1	9.9	4.8
1988	3,910	2,168	39	2,396	1,167	16.0	8.9	10.0	9.8	4.8
1989	4,041	2,150	40	2,403	1,157	16.4	8.7	9.8	9.7	4.7
1990	4,158	2,148	38	2,443	1,182	16.7	8.6	9.2	9.8	4.7
1991	4,111	2,170	37	2,371	1,187	16.3	8.6	8.9	9.4	4.7
1992	4,065	2,176	35	2,362	1,215	15.9	8.5	8.5	9.3	4.8
1993	4,000	2,269	33	2,334	1,187	15.5	8.8	8.4	9.0	4.6
1994	3,979	2,279	31	2,362	1,191	15.0	8.8	8.0	9.1	4.6
1995	3,900	2,312	30	1,954	973	14.8	8.8	7.6	7.6	4.1
1996	3,891	2,315	28	2,344	1,150	14.7	8.7	7.3	8.8	4.3
1997	3,881	2,314	28	(NA)	(NA)	14.5	8.6	7.2	(NA)	(NA)
1998 prel.	3,942	2,338	28	(NA)	(NA)	14.6	8.7	7.2	(NA)	(NA)

NA Not available.   [1] Prior to 1960, data adjusted for underregistration.   [2] Infants under 1 year, excluding fetal deaths; rates per 1,000 registered live births.   [3] Includes estimates for some States through 1965 and also for 1976 and 1977 and marriage licenses for some States for all years except 1973 and 1975. Beginning 1978, includes nonlicensed marriages in California. [4] Includes reported annulments and some estimated state figures for all years.

Source: U.S. National Center for Health Statistics, *Vital Statistics of the United States*, annual; and *National Vital Statistics Reports (NVSR)* (formerly *Monthly Vital Statistics Report*); and unpublished data.

No. 78. Live Births by Race and Type of Hispanic Origin—Selected Characteristics: 1990 and 1998

[**4,158 represents 4,158,000.** Represents registered births. Excludes births to nonresidents of the United States. Data are based on Hispanic origin of mother and race of mother. Hispanic origin data are available from only 48 States and the District of Columbia in 1990]

Race and Hispanic origin	Number of births (1,000)		Births to teen-age mothers, percent of total		Births to unmarried mothers, per-cent of total		Prenatal care beginning first trimester		Late or no prenatal care		Percent of births with low birth weight [1]	
	1990	1998	1990	1998	1990	1998	1990	1998	1990	1998	1990	1998
Total	4,158	3,942	12.8	12.5	26.6	32.8	74.2	82.8	6.0	3.9	7.0	7.6
White	3,290	3,119	10.9	11.1	16.9	26.3	77.7	84.8	4.9	3.3	5.7	6.5
Black	684	610	23.1	21.5	66.7	69.1	60.7	73.3	10.9	7.0	13.3	13.0
American Indian, Eskimo, Aleut	39	40	19.5	20.9	53.6	59.3	57.9	68.8	12.9	8.5	6.1	6.8
Asian and Pacific Islander [2]	142	173	5.7	5.4	(NA)	15.6	(NA)	83.1	(NA)	3.6	(NA)	7.4
Filipino	26	31	6.1	6.2	15.9	19.7	77.1	84.2	4.5	3.1	7.3	8.2
Chinese	23	28	1.2	0.9	5.0	6.4	81.3	88.5	3.4	2.2	4.7	5.3
Japanese	9	9	2.9	2.4	9.6	9.7	87.0	90.2	2.9	2.1	6.2	7.5
Hawaiian [3]	6	6	18.4	18.8	45.0	51.1	65.8	78.8	8.7	4.7	7.2	7.2
Hispanic origin [3]	595	735	16.8	16.9	36.7	41.6	60.2	74.3	12.0	6.3	6.1	6.4
Mexican	386	516	17.7	17.5	33.3	39.6	57.8	72.8	13.2	6.8	5.5	6.0
Puerto Rico	59	57	21.7	21.9	55.9	59.5	63.5	76.9	10.6	5.1	9.0	9.7
Cuban	11	13	7.7	6.9	18.2	24.8	84.8	91.8	2.8	1.2	5.7	6.5
Central and South American	83	98	9.0	10.3	41.2	42.0	61.5	78.0	10.9	4.9	5.8	6.5
Other and unknown Hispanic	56	50	(NA)	20.2	(NA)	45.3	(NA)	74.8	(NA)	6.0	(NA)	7.6

NA Not available.   [1] Births less than 2,500 grams (5 lb.-8 oz.).   [2] Includes other races not shown separately.   [3] Hispanic persons may be of any race. Includes other types, not shown separately.

Source: U.S. National Center for Health Statistics; *Vital Statistics of the United States*, annual; *National Vital Statistics Report (NVSR)* (formerly *Monthly Vital Statistics Report*); and unpublished data.

Vital Statistics   65

No. 79. Births and Birth Rates by Race, Sex, and Age: 1980 to 1998

[Births in thousands. (3,612 represents 3,612,000). Births by race of mother. Excludes births to nonresidents of the United States. For population bases used to derive these data, see text this section, and Appendix III]

Item	1980	1985	1990	1991	1992	1993	1994	1995	1996	1997	1998
Live births [1]	3,612	3,761	4,158	4,111	4,065	4,000	3,953	3,900	3,891	3,895	3,942
White	2,936	3,038	3,290	3,241	3,202	3,126	3,121	2,753	3,093	3,085	3,119
Black	568	582	684	683	674	695	636	394	595	601	610
American Indian	29	34	39	39	39	39	38	26	38	38	40
Asian or Pacific Islander	74	105	142	145	150	153	158	135	166	170	173
Male	1,853	1,928	2,129	2,102	2,082	2,049	2,023	1,996	1,990	(NA)	(NA)
Female	1,760	1,833	2,029	2,009	1,983	1,951	1,930	1,903	1,901	(NA)	(NA)
Males per 100 females	105	105	105	105	105	105	105	105	105	(NA)	(NA)
Age of mother:	-25	-31	-50	-53	-58	-61	-67	-70	-74	-78	-10
Under 20 years old	562	478	533	532	518	514	518	512	503	500	485
20 to 24 years old	1,226	1,141	1,094	1,090	1,070	1,038	1,001	966	945	946	965
25 to 29 years old	1,108	1,201	1,277	1,220	1,179	1,129	1,089	1,064	1,071	1,075	1,083
30 to 34 years old	550	696	886	885	895	901	906	905	898	888	889
35 to 39 years old	141	214	318	331	345	357	372	384	400	408	425
40 to 44 years old	(NA)	(NA)	(NA)	(NA)	(NA)	(NA)	(NA)	(NA)	(NA)	(NA)	81
45 to 49 years old	(NA)	(NA)	(NA)	(NA)	(NA)	(NA)	(NA)	(NA)	(NA)	(NA)	4
Birth rate per 1,000 population	15.9	15.8	16.7	16.3	15.9	15.5	15.2	14.8	14.7	14.5	14.6
White	15.1	15.0	15.8	15.4	15.0	14.7	14.4	14.2	14.1	13.9	14.0
Black	21.3	20.4	22.4	21.9	21.3	20.5	19.5	18.2	17.8	17.7	17.7
American Indian	20.7	19.8	18.9	18.3	18.4	17.8	17.1	16.6	16.6	16.6	17.1
Asian or Pacific Islander	19.9	18.7	19.0	18.2	18.0	17.7	17.5	17.3	17.0	16.9	16.4
Male	16.8	16.7	17.6	17.1	16.7	(NA)	(NA)	(NA)	(NA)	(NA)	(NA)
Female	15.1	15.0	15.9	15.6	15.2	(NA)	(NA)	(NA)	(NA)	(NA)	(NA)
Plural birth ratio [2]	19.3	21.0	23.3	23.9	24.4	25.2	25.7	26.1	27.4	28.6	30.0
White	18.5	20.4	22.9	23.4	24.0	24.9	25.5	26.0	27.5	28.7	30.2
Black	24.1	25.3	27.0	27.8	28.2	28.7	29.4	28.8	29.8	30.9	32.0
Fertility rate per 1,000 women [3]	68.4	66.2	70.9	69.6	68.9	67.6	66.7	65.6	65.3	65.3	65.6
White [3]	64.8	64.1	68.3	67.0	66.5	65.4	64.9	64.4	64.3	64.2	64.6
Black [3]	84.7	78.8	86.8	85.2	83.2	80.5	76.9	72.3	70.7	70.8	71.0
American Indian [3]	82.7	78.6	76.2	75.1	75.4	73.4	70.9	69.1	68.7	68.9	70.7
Asian or Pacific Islander [3]	73.2	68.4	69.6	67.6	67.2	66.7	66.8	66.4	65.9	66.5	64.0
Age of mother:											
10 to 14 years old	1.1	1.2	1.4	1.4	1.4	1.4	1.4	1.3	1.2	1.1	1.0
15 to 19 years old	53.0	51.0	59.9	62.1	60.7	59.6	58.9	56.8	54.4	52.3	51.1
20 to 24 years old	115.1	108.3	116.5	115.7	114.6	112.6	111.1	109.8	110.4	110.4	111.2
25 to 29 years old	112.9	111.0	120.2	118.2	117.4	115.5	113.9	111.2	113.1	113.8	115.9
30 to 34 years old	61.9	69.1	80.8	79.5	80.2	80.8	81.5	82.5	83.9	85.3	87.4
35 to 39 years old	19.8	24.0	31.7	32.0	32.5	32.9	33.7	34.3	35.3	36.1	37.4
40 to 44 years old	3.9	4.0	5.5	5.5	5.9	6.1	6.4	6.6	6.8	7.1	7.3
45 to 49 years old	0.2	0.2	0.2	0.2	0.3	0.3	0.3	0.3	0.3	0.4	0.4

NA Not available. [1] Includes other races not shown separately. [2] Number of multiple births per 1,000 live births. [3] Per 1,000 women, 15 to 44 years old in specified group. The rate for *age of mother 45 to 49 years old* computed by relating births to mothers 45 years old and over to women 45 to 49 years old.

Source: U.S. National Center for Health Statistics, *Vital Statistics of the United States,* annual; *National Vital Statistics Report (NVSR)* (formerly *Monthly Vital Statistics Report*); and unpublished data.

No. 80. Teenagers—Births and Birth Rates by Race and Sex: 1990 to 1998

[Birth rates per 1,000 women in specified group, see text, this section]

Item	1990	1991	1992	1993	1994	1995	1996	1997	1998
NUMBER OF BIRTHS									
All races, total [1]	521,826	519,577	505,415	501,093	505,488	499,873	494,272	489,211	484,975
15-17 years	183,327	188,226	187,549	190,535	195,169	192,508	186,762	183,324	173,252
18-19 years	338,499	331,351	317,866	310,558	310,319	307,365	307,509	305,886	311,724
White	354,482	352,359	342,739	341,817	348,081	346,509	346,635	342,029	340,894
15-17 years	114,934	118,809	118,786	121,309	126,388	127,165	124,031	121,864	116,699
18-19 years	239,548	233,550	223,953	220,508	221,693	222,470	222,477	220,164	224,195
Black	151,613	150,956	146,800	143,153	140,968	133,694	131,059	130,401	126,865
15-17 years	62,881	63,571	63,002	63,156	62,563	59,112	56,218	54,883	50,062
18-19 years	88,732	87,385	83,798	79,997	78,405	74,582	74,841	75,518	76,803
BIRTH RATE									
All races, total [1]	59.9	62.1	60.7	59.6	58.9	56.8	54.7	52.3	51.1
15-17 years	37.5	38.7	37.8	37.8	37.6	36.0	34.0	32.1	30.4
18-19 years	88.6	94.4	94.5	92.1	91.5	89.1	86.5	83.6	82.0
White	50.8	52.8	51.8	51.1	51.1	50.1	48.4	46.3	45.4
15-17 years	29.5	30.7	30.1	30.3	30.7	30.0	28.6	27.1	25.9
18-19 years	78.0	83.5	83.8	82.1	82.1	81.2	78.8	75.9	74.7
Black	112.8	115.5	112.4	108.6	104.5	96.1	91.7	88.2	85.3
15-17 years	82.3	84.1	81.3	79.8	76.3	69.7	64.9	60.8	56.8
18-19 years	152.9	158.6	157.9	151.9	148.3	137.1	133.0	130.1	126.8

[1] Includes races other than White and Black.

Source: U.S. National Center for Health Statistics, *Monthly Vital Statistics Report*, Vol. 47, No. 6, Supplement.

66   Vital Statistics

No. 81. Live Births by State: 1998

[Number of births, except rate. Registered births. Excludes births to nonresidents of the United States. By race of mother. See Appendix III]

State	All races [1]	White		Black		Hispanic [2]	Birth rate [3]	Fertility rate [4]
		Total	Non-Hispanic	Total	Non-Hispanic			
United States..	**3,941,553**	**3,118,727**	**2,361,462**	**609,902**	**593,127**	**734,661**	**14.6**	**65.6**
Alabama.........	62,074	41,522	40,203	20,033	20,021	1,345	14.3	63.2
Alaska..........	9,926	6,628	6,148	401	386	593	16.2	73.1
Arizona..........	78,243	68,265	38,621	2,653	2,465	29,682	16.8	78.2
Arkansas	36,865	28,296	26,545	7,979	7,970	1,724	14.5	67.5
California	521,661	424,659	176,886	36,745	35,282	247,854	16.0	70.7
Colorado.........	59,577	54,323	39,936	2,870	2,761	14,654	15.0	67.2
Connecticut.......	43,820	36,837	28,845	5,461	4,990	6,224	13.4	61.3
Delaware	10,578	7,700	6,937	2,621	2,604	753	14.2	61.2
Dist of Columbia ...	7,686	2,043	1,314	5,469	5,435	730	14.7	60.8
Florida	195,637	146,219	107,754	44,387	43,483	39,540	13.1	65.1
Georgia	122,368	78,195	69,495	41,247	40,913	8,239	16.0	67.2
Hawaii	17,583	4,176	3,529	560	524	2,240	14.7	69.6
Idaho...........	19,391	18,773	16,091	82	80	2,428	15.8	72.3
Illinois	182,588	140,002	105,367	35,699	35,481	34,780	15.2	68.3
Indiana..........	85,122	74,646	70,642	9,262	9,222	3,770	14.4	64.3
Iowa	37,282	35,229	33,188	1,094	1,034	1,739	13.0	61.4
Kansas	38,422	34,296	30,013	2,789	2,759	3,968	14.6	67.1
Kentucky	54,329	48,840	48,095	4,862	4,845	751	13.8	61.6
Louisiana	66,888	38,128	36,756	27,452	27,385	1,327	15.3	66.7
Maine..........	13,733	13,368	12,674	91	78	131	11.0	49.7
'Maryland	71,972	44,565	40,893	24,040	23,741	3,580	14.0	60.1
Massachusetts.....	81,411	69,494	62,073	7,872	6,322	8,684	13.2	58.5
Michigan.........	133,666	105,599	92,972	24,264	24,007	5,945	13.6	60.4
Minnesota........	65,202	57,291	51,089	3,664	3,594	2,967	13.8	61.8
Mississippi	42,939	22,972	22,523	19,351	19,343	403	15.6	68.3
Missouri	75,358	62,510	60,554	11,399	11,367	1,970	13.9	62.9
Montana	10,795	9,467	8,951	44	38	336	12.3	59.0
Nebraska	23,534	21,443	18,753	1,236	1,227	2,192	14.2	65.2
Nevada	28,699	24,359	15,603	2,248	2,182	8,727	16.4	77.9
New Hampshire....	14,429	14,073	13,332	134	116	256	12.2	52.3
New Jersey.......	114,550	85,029	66,244	21,463	19,424	20,493	14.1	64.3
New Mexico	27,318	23,004	9,453	509	468	13,714	15.7	72.2
New York	258,207	186,251	124,220	54,463	48,533	52,259	14.2	63.9
North Carolina.....	111,688	79,335	71,294	28,242	28,153	8,104	14.8	66.6
North Dakota......	7,932	7,035	6,707	87	82	152	12.4	58.3
Ohio	152,794	127,289	123,800	22,796	22,286	3,470	13.6	61.2
Oklahoma........	49,461	38,917	35,059	4,803	4,688	3,616	14.8	69.0
Oregon..........	45,273	41,610	35,138	966	949	6,501	13.8	64.7
Pennsylvania.....	145,899	121,436	114,265	20,760	20,272	6,897	12.2	56.9
Rhode Island......	12,599	11,029	7,743	967	828	1,865	12.7	57.5
South Carolina.....	53,877	34,169	32,885	18,868	18,840	1,307	14.0	61.3
South Dakota	10,288	8,392	8,252	85	82	153	13.9	65.1
Tennessee	77,396	59,308	57,345	16,884	16,853	1,997	14.3	63.1
Texas...........	342,283	291,817	139,980	40,212	39,631	151,487	17.3	76.2
Utah	45,165	42,937	37,982	282	263	4,879	21.5	91.4
Vermont	6,582	6,497	6,297	24	20	37	11.1	49.1
Virginia.........	94,351	67,815	62,119	22,016	21,913	5,806	13.9	59.1
Washington.......	79,663	69,024	57,214	3,111	2,888	10,074	14.0	62.3
West Virginia......	20,747	19,850	19,728	760	757	93	11.5	53.7
Wisconsin.......	67,450	58,184	54,636	6,541	6,490	3,641	12.9	58.5
Wyoming	6,252	5,881	5,319	54	52	584	13.0	60.9

[1] Includes other races not shown separately. [2] Persons of Hispanic origin may be of any race. Births by Hispanic origin of mother. [3] Per 1,000 estimated population. [4] Per 1,000 women aged 15-44 years estimated.

Source: U.S. National Center for Health Statistics, *Vital Statistics of the United States*, annual; and *National Vital Statistics Reports (NVSR)* (formerly *Monthly Vital Statistics Report*, Vol. 48, No. 3).

Vital Statistics   67

No. 82. Total Fertility Rate and Intrinsic Rate of Natural Increase: 1960 to 1998

[Based on race of child and registered births only, thru 1979. Beginning 1980, based on race of mother. Beginning 1970, excludes births to nonresidents of United States. The *total fertility rate* is the number of births that 1,000 women would have in their lifetime if, at each year of age, they experienced the birth rates occurring in the specified year. A total fertility rate of 2,110 represents "replacement level" fertility for the total population under current mortality conditions (assuming no net immigration). The *intrinsic rate of natural increase* is the rate that would eventually prevail if a population were to experience, at each year of age, the birth rates and death rates occurring in the specified year and if those rates remained unchanged over a long period of time. Minus sign (-) indicates decrease. See also Appendix III]

Annual average and year	Total fertility rate			Intrinsic rate of natural increase			Annual average and year	Total fertility rate			Intrinsic rate of natural increase		
	Total	White	Black [1]	Total	White	Black [1]		Total	White	Black [1]	Total	White	Black [1]
1960-64 ..	3,449	3,326	4,326	18.6	17.1	27.7	1981	1,812	1,748	2,118	-5.6	-7.4	3.0
1965-69 ..	2,622	2,512	3,362	8.2	6.4	18.6	1982	1,828	1,767	2,107	-5.2	-7.0	3.0
1970-74 ..	2,094	1,997	2,680	-0.7	-2.5	9.1	1983	1,799	1,741	2,066	-5.8	-7.5	2.2
1975-79 ..	1,774	1,685	2,270	-6.6	-8.5	3.0	1984	1,807	1,749	2,071	-5.6	-7.3	2.1
1980-84 ..	1,819	1,731	2,262	-5.4	-7.3	3.0	1985	1,844	1,787	2,109	-4.8	-6.5	2.7
1985-88 ..	1,870	1,769	2,339	-4.2	-6.3	4.3	1986	1,838	1,776	2,136	-4.9	-6.7	2.8
							1987	1,872	1,805	2,198	-4.1	-6.1	4.0
1970	2,480	2,385	3,067	6.0	4.5	14.4	1988	1,934	1,857	2,298	-2.9	-5.1	5.7
1971	2,267	2,161	2,920	2.6	0.8	12.6	1989	2,014	1,931	2,433	-1.4	-3.6	7.4
1972	2,010	1,907	2,628	-2.0	-3.9	8.6	1990	2,081	2,003	2,480	-0.1	-2.3	8.3
1973	1,879	1,783	2,443	-4.5	-6.5	5.7	1991	2,073	1,996	2,480	-0.2	-2.4	8.2
1974	1,835	1,749	2,339	-5.4	-7.2	4.0	1992	2,065	1,994	2,442	-0.4	-2.5	7.5
1975	1,774	1,686	2,276	-6.7	-8.6	3.0	1993	2,046	1,982	2,385	-0.7	-1.9	3.7
1976	1,738	1,652	2,223	-7.4	-9.3	2.1	1994	2,036	1,985	2,300	(NA)	(NA)	(NA)
1977	1,790	1,703	2,279	-6.2	-8.1	3.2	1995	2,019	1,989	2,175	(NA)	(NA)	(NA)
1978	1,760	1,668	2,265	-6.8	-8.8	2.9	1996	2,040	2,019	2,149	(NA)	(NA)	(NA)
1979	1,808	1,716	2,310	-5.7	-7.7	3.8	1997	2,040	2,017	2,158	(NA)	(NA)	(NA)
1980	1,840	1,773	2,177	-5.1	-7.0	4.0	1998	2,058	2,041	2,171	(NA)	(NA)	(NA)

NA Not available.   [1] Data for 1984 and earlier includes races other than Black.

Source: U.S. National Center for Health Statistics, *Vital Statistics of the United States*, annual; and unpublished data.

No. 83. Projected Fertility Rates by Race, Origin, and Age Group: 1999 and 2010

[For definition of total fertility rate, see headnote, Table 82. Birth rates represent live births per 1,000 women in age group indicated. Projections are based on middle fertility assumptions. For explanations of methodology, see text, Section 1, Population]

Age group	All races [1]		White		Black		American Indian, Eskimo, Aleut		Asian and Pacific Islander		Hispanic [2]	
	1999	2010	1999	2010	1999	2010	1999	2010	1999	2010	1999	2010
Total fertility rate ..	2,048	2,123	2,010	2,098	2,122	2,140	2,507	2,451	2,277	2,252	2,921	2,818
Birth rates:												
10 to 14 years old....	1.2	1.3	0.8	0.9	3.4	3.5	2.0	2.0	0.7	0.7	2.4	2.3
15 to 19 years old....	56.4	60.2	49.7	54.3	93.8	95.6	93.9	93.6	29.8	29.6	99.6	95.7
20 to 24 years old....	112.1	115.8	108.1	112.6	136.0	137.1	163.7	159.6	84.8	83.7	181.7	175.2
25 to 29 years old....	112.2	115.7	114.2	118.5	94.1	95.5	120.7	118.6	134.5	134.5	152.0	146.7
30 to 34 years old....	84.3	87.8	86.0	90.0	62.0	63.4	77.9	77.3	129.7	128.2	94.4	91.6
35 to 39 years old....	35.4	36.7	35.4	36.6	28.9	28.9	34.2	33.7	60.3	59.0	43.7	41.9
40 to 44 years old....	6.9	7.3	6.7	7.1	6.1	6.0	7.4	7.4	13.9	13.8	10.5	9.9
45 to 49 years old....	0.3	0.3	0.3	0.3	0.3	0.3	0.3	0.3	0.9	0.9	0.6	0.6

[1] Includes other races not shown separately.   [2] Persons of Hispanic origin may be of any race.

Source: U.S. Census Bureau, Population Division Working Paper No. 38.

No. 84. Birth Rates by Live-Birth Order and Race: 1980 to 1998

[**Births per 1,000 women 15 to 44 years old in specified racial group.** Live-birth order refers to number of children born alive. Figures for births of order not stated are distributed. See also headnote, Table 79]

Live-birth order	All races [1]					White					Black				
	1980	1990	1995	1997	1998	1980	1990	1995	1997	1998	1980	1990	1995	1997	1998
Total...........	68.4	70.9	65.6	65.3	65.6	65.6	68.3	64.4	64.2	64.6	84.9	86.8	72.3	70.8	71.0
First birth	29.5	29.0	27.3	26.5	26.4	28.8	28.4	26.9	26.2	26.1	33.7	32.4	28.7	27.3	27.0
Second birth	21.8	22.8	21.1	21.1	21.4	21.3	22.4	21.1	21.2	21.5	24.7	25.6	20.7	20.7	21.1
Third birth	10.3	11.7	10.5	10.6	10.8	9.6	11.1	10.3	10.4	10.7	14.0	15.6	12.0	12.1	12.3
Fourth birth [2]	3.9	4.5	4.0	4.1	4.2	3.4	4.0	3.8	3.8	3.9	6.5	7.4	5.7	5.7	5.7
Fifth birth	1.5	1.7	1.5	1.5	1.5	1.3	1.4	1.3	1.3	1.3	2.9	3.2	2.6	2.5	2.6
Sixth and seventh ...	1.0	1.0	0.9	0.9	0.9	0.8	0.8	0.7	0.8	0.8	2.1	2.0	1.8	1.8	1.7
Eighth and over	0.4	0.3	0.3	0.3	0.3	0.3	0.2	0.2	0.2	0.2	0.9	0.5	0.6	0.6	0.6

NA Not available.   [1] Includes other races not shown separately.   [2] 1996 data represents 'fourth child and over'.

Source: U.S. National Center for Health Statistics, *Vital Statistics of the United States*, annual; and *National Vital Statistics Reports (NVSR)* (formerly *Monthly Vital Statistics Report*).

No. 85. Births to Teens, Unmarried Mothers, and Prenatal Care: 1990 to 1998

[In percent. Represents registered births. See headnote, Table 78]

Characteristics	1990	1993	1994	1995	1996	1997	1998
Percent of births to teenage mothers...	**12.8**	**12.8**	**13.1**	**13.1**	**12.9**	**12.7**	**12.5**
White............................	10.9	11.0	11.3	11.5	11.3	11.2	11.1
Black............................	23.1	22.7	23.2	23.1	22.8	22.2	21.5
American Indian, Eskimo, Aleut............	19.5	20.3	21.0	21.4	20.9	20.8	20.9
Asian and Pacific Islander [1].............	5.7	5.7	5.7	5.6	5.3	5.2	5.4
Filipino	6.1	5.8	6.0	6.2	6.1	5.9	6.2
Chinese	1.2	1.0	1.0	0.9	0.9	0.9	0.9
Japanese	2.9	2.7	2.8	2.5	2.5	2.2	2.4
Hawaiian.....................	18.4	18.5	19.6	19.1	18.4	18.6	18.8
Other	(NA)	6.5	6.4	6.3	5.8	5.7	5.8
Hispanic origin [2].................	16.8	17.4	17.8	17.9	17.4	17.0	16.9
Mexican	17.7	18.2	18.6	18.8	18.1	17.7	17.5
Puerto Rican	21.7	22.3	23.2	23.5	23.1	22.3	21.9
Cuban	7.7	6.8	7.3	7.7	7.6	7.4	6.9
Central and South American	9.0	9.9	10.4	10.6	10.5	10.5	10.3
Other and unknown Hispanic	(NA)	21.0	20.8	20.1	19.8	19.8	20.2
Percent births to unmarried mothers...	**26.6**	**31.0**	**32.6**	**32.2**	**32.4**	**32.4**	**32.8**
White............................	16.9	23.6	25.4	25.3	25.7	25.8	26.3
Black............................	66.7	68.7	70.4	69.9	69.8	69.2	69.1
American Indian, Eskimo, Aleut............	53.6	55.8	57.0	57.2	58.0	58.7	59.3
Asian and Pacific Islander [1].............	(NA)	15.7	16.2	16.3	16.7	15.6	15.6
Filipino	15.9	17.7	18.5	19.5	19.4	19.5	19.7
Chinese	5.0	6.7	7.2	7.9	9.2	6.5	6.4
Japanese	9.6	10.0	11.2	10.8	11.4	10.1	9.7
Hawaiian.....................	45.0	47.8	48.6	49.0	49.9	49.1	51.1
Hispanic origin [2].................	36.7	40.0	43.1	40.8	40.7	40.9	41.6
Mexican	33.3	37.0	40.8	38.1	37.9	38.9	39.6
Puerto Rican	55.9	59.4	60.2	60.0	60.7	59.4	59.5
Cuban	18.2	21.0	22.9	23.8	24.7	24.4	24.8
Central and South American	41.2	45.2	45.9	44.1	44.7	41.8	42.0
Percent of mothers beginning prenatal care 1st trimester..........	**74.2**	**78.9**	**80.2**	**81.3**	**81.9**	**82.5**	**82.8**
White............................	77.7	81.8	82.8	83.6	84.0	84.7	84.8
Black............................	60.7	66.0	68.3	70.4	71.4	72.3	73.3
American Indian, Eskimo, Aleut............	57.9	63.4	65.2	66.7	67.7	68.1	68.8
Asian and Pacific Islander [1].............	(NA)	77.6	79.7	79.9	81.2	82.1	83.1
Filipino	77.1	79.3	81.3	80.9	82.5	83.3	84.2
Chinese	81.3	84.6	86.2	85.7	86.8	87.4	88.5
Japanese	87.0	87.2	89.2	89.7	89.3	89.3	90.2
Hawaiian.....................	65.8	70.6	77.0	75.9	78.5	78.0	78.8
Hispanic origin [2].................	60.2	66.6	68.9	70.8	72.2	73.7	74.3
Mexican	57.8	64.8	67.3	69.1	70.7	72.1	72.8
Puerto Rican	63.5	70.0	71.7	74.0	75.0	76.5	76.9
Cuban	84.8	88.9	90.1	89.2	89.2	90.4	91.8
Central and South American	61.5	68.7	71.2	73.2	75.0	76.9	78.0
Percent of mothers beginning prenatal care 3d trimester or no care...	**6.0**	**4.8**	**4.4**	**4.2**	**4.0**	**3.9**	**3.9**
White............................	4.9	3.9	3.6	3.5	3.3	3.2	3.3
Black............................	10.9	9.0	8.2	7.6	7.3	7.3	7.0
American Indian, Eskimo, Aleut............	12.9	10.3	9.8	9.5	8.6	8.6	8.5
Asian and Pacific Islander [1].............	(NA)	4.6	4.1	4.3	3.9	3.8	3.6
Filipino	4.5	4.0	3.6	4.1	3.3	3.3	3.1
Chinese	3.4	2.9	2.7	3.0	2.5	2.4	2.2
Japanese	2.9	2.8	1.9	2.3	2.2	2.7	2.1
Hawaiian.....................	8.7	6.7	4.7	5.1	5.0	5.4	4.7
Hispanic origin [2].................	12.0	8.8	7.6	7.4	6.7	6.2	6.3
Mexican	13.2	9.7	8.3	8.1	7.2	6.7	6.8
Puerto Rican	10.6	7.1	6.5	5.5	5.7	5.4	5.1
Cuban	2.8	1.8	1.6	2.1	1.6	1.5	1.2
Central and South American	10.9	7.3	6.5	6.1	5.5	5.0	4.9
Percent of births with low birth weight [3].	**7.0**	**7.2**	**7.3**	**7.3**	**7.4**	**7.5**	**7.6**
White............................	5.7	6.0	6.1	6.2	6.3	6.5	6.5
Black............................	13.3	13.3	13.2	13.1	13.0	13.0	13.0
American Indian, Eskimo, Aleut............	6.1	6.4	6.4	6.6	6.5	6.8	6.8
Asian and Pacific Islander [1].............	(NA)	6.6	6.8	6.9	7.1	7.2	7.4
Filipino	7.3	7.0	7.8	7.8	7.9	8.3	8.2
Chinese	4.7	4.9	4.8	5.3	5.0	5.1	5.3
Japanese	6.2	6.5	6.9	7.3	7.3	6.8	7.5
Hawaiian.....................	7.2	6.8	7.2	6.8	6.8	7.2	7.2
Hispanic origin [2].................	6.1	6.2	6.2	6.3	7.4	6.4	6.4
Mexican	5.5	5.8	5.8	5.8	5.9	6.0	6.0
Puerto Rican	9.0	9.2	9.1	9.4	9.2	9.4	9.7
Cuban	5.7	6.2	6.3	6.5	6.5	6.8	6.5
Central and South American	5.8	5.9	6.0	6.2	6.0	6.3	6.5

NA Not available.　　[1] Includes other races not shown separately.　　[2] Hispanic persons may be of any race. Includes other types, not shown separately.　　[3] Births less than 2,500 grams (5 lb.-8 oz.).

Source: U.S. National Center for Health Statistics, *Vital Statistics of the United States*, annual; and *National Vital Statistics Reports (NVSR)* (formerly *Monthly Vital Statistics Report*).

Vital Statistics　69

No. 86. Births to Unmarried Women by Race of Child and Age of Mother: 1990 to 1998

[Excludes births to nonresidents of United States. Marital status is inferred from a comparison of the child's and parents' surnames on the birth certificate for those States that do not report on marital status. No estimates included for misstatements on birth records or failures to register births. See also Appendix III]

Race of child and age of mother	1990	1995	1996	1997	1998
NUMBER (1,000)					
Total live births [1]	1,165	1,254	1,260	1,257	1,294
White	647	785	965	793	821
Black	473	421	415	415	421
Under 15 years	11	11	10	10	9
15 to 19 years	350	376	373	376	381
20 to 24 years	404	432	431	439	460
25 to 29 years	230	229	235	235	243
30 to 34 years	118	133	133	125	125
35 to 39 years	(NA)	(NA)	(NA)	60	61
40 years and over	(NA)	(NA)	(NA)	14	14
PERCENT DISTRIBUTION					
Total [1]	100.0	100.0	100.0	100.0	100.0
White	55.6	62.6	76.6	63.1	63.5
Black	40.6	33.6	32.9	33.0	32.6
Under 15 years	0.9	0.9	0.8	0.8	0.7
15 to 19 years	30.0	30.0	29.6	29.9	29.4
20 to 24 years	34.7	34.4	34.2	34.9	35.6
25 to 29 years	19.7	18.3	18.7	18.7	18.8

Race of child and age of mother	1990	1995	1996	1997	1998
30 to 34 years	10.1	10.6	10.6	9.9	9.6
35 to 39 years	(NA)	(NA)	(NA)	4.8	4.7
40 years and over	(NA)	(NA)	(NA)	1.1	1.1
AS PERCENT OF ALL BIRTHS IN RACIAL GROUPS					
Total [1]	28.0	32.2	32.4	32.4	32.8
White	20.1	25.3	25.7	25.8	26.3
Black	65.2	69.9	69.8	69.2	69.1
BIRTH RATE [2]					
Total [1][3]	43.8	45.1	44.8	44.0	44.3
White [3]	31.8	37.5	37.6	37.0	37.5
Black [3]	93.9	75.9	74.4	73.4	73.3
15 to 19 years	42.5	44.4	42.9	42.2	41.5
20 to 24 years	65.1	70.3	70.7	71.0	72.3
25 to 29 years	56.0	56.1	56.8	56.2	58.4
30 to 34 years	37.6	39.6	41.1	39.0	39.1
35 to 39 years	(NA)	(NA)	(NA)	19.0	19.0
40 to 44 years	(NA)	(NA)	(NA)	4.6	4.6

NA Not Available. [1] Includes other races not shown separately. [2] Rate per 1,000 unmarried women (never-married, widowed, and divorced) estimated as of July 1. [3] Covers women aged 15 to 44 years.

Source: U.S. National Center for Health Statistics, Vital Statistics of the United States, annual; and National Vital Statistics Reports (NVSR) (formerly Monthly Vital Statistics Report).

No. 87. Live Births by Plurality of Birth and Ratios and Race of Mother: 1994 to 1998

Plurality and race of mother	1994	1995	1996	1997	1998
NUMBER					
Live births, total [1]	3,952,767	3,899,589	3,891,494	3,880,894	3,941,553
White	3,121,004	3,098,885	3,093,057	3,072,640	3,118,727
Black	636,391	603,139	594,781	599,913	609,902
Live births in single deliveries [1]	3,851,109	3,797,880	3,784,805	3,770,020	3,823,258
White	3,041,559	3,018,184	3,007,997	2,984,532	3,024,693
Black	617,689	585,787	577,057	581,394	590,372
Live births in twin deliveries [1]	97,064	96,736	100,750	104,137	110,670
White	75,318	76,196	79,677	82,090	87,163
Black	18,344	17,000	17,285	17,989	19,001
Live births in higher-order multiple deliveries [1]	4,594	4,973	5,939	6,737	7,625
White	4,127	4,505	5,383	6,018	6,871
Black	358	352	439	530	529
RATIO PER 1,000 LIVE BIRTHS					
All multiple births [1]	25.7	26.1	27.4	28.6	30.0
White	25.5	26.0	27.5	28.7	30.2
Black	29.4	28.8	29.8	30.9	32.0
Twin births [1]	24.6	24.8	25.9	26.8	28.1
White	24.1	24.6	25.8	26.7	27.9
Black	28.8	28.2	29.1	30.0	31.2
RATIO PER 100,000 LIVE BIRTHS					
Higher-order multiple births [1]	116.2	127.5	152.6	173.6	193.5
White	132.2	145.4	174.0	195.9	220.3
Black	56.3	58.4	73.8	88.3	86.7

[1] Includes races other than White and Black.

Source: U.S. National Center for Health Statistics, Advance report of Final Natality Statistics, and National Vital Statistics Reports (NVSR) (formerly Monthly Vital Statistics Report).

No. 88. Low Birth Weight and Births to Teenage Mothers and to Unmarried Women by State: 1990 to 1998

[Represents registered births. Excludes births to nonresidents of the United States. Based on 100 percent of births in all states and the District of Columbia. See Appendix III]

State	Percent of births with low birth weight [1]			Births to teenage mothers percent of total			Births to unmarried women percent of total		
	1990	1995	1998	1990	1995	1998	1990	1995	1998
U.S.	7.0	7.3	7.6	12.8	13.1	14.6	28.0	32.2	32.8
AL.	8.4	9.0	9.3	18.2	18.5	14.3	30.1	34.5	34.1
AK.	4.8	5.3	6.0	9.7	11.2	16.2	26.2	29.9	31.1
AZ.	6.4	6.8	6.8	14.2	15.1	16.8	32.7	38.2	38.4
AR.	8.2	8.2	8.9	19.7	19.6	14.5	29.4	32.9	35.0
CA.	5.8	6.1	6.2	11.6	12.4	16.0	[2]31.6	32.1	32.8
CO	8.0	8.4	8.6	11.3	12.1	15.0	21.2	24.9	25.6
CT.	6.6	7.1	7.8	8.2	8.6	13.4	[2]26.6	30.6	31.2
DE.	7.6	8.4	8.4	11.9	13.2	14.2	29.0	34.9	37.1
DC	15.1	13.4	13.1	17.8	16.3	14.7	64.9	65.8	62.9
FL.	7.4	7.7	8.1	13.9	13.7	13.1	31.7	35.8	36.6
GA	8.7	8.8	8.5	16.7	16.3	16.0	32.8	35.2	36.2
HI	7.1	7.0	7.5	10.5	10.1	14.7	24.8	29.2	31.5
ID	5.7	5.9	6.0	12.3	14.0	15.8	16.7	19.9	22.0
IL	7.6	7.9	8.0	13.1	12.9	15.2	31.7	33.8	34.1
IN	6.6	7.5	7.9	14.5	14.7	14.4	26.2	31.9	33.5
IA	5.4	6.0	6.4	10.2	11.0	13.0	21.0	25.2	27.2
KS.	6.2	6.4	7.0	12.3	13.1	14.6	21.5	25.9	27.8
KY.	7.1	7.6	8.1	17.5	17.2	13.8	23.6	28.5	30.1
LA.	9.2	9.7	10.1	17.6	19.1	15.3	36.8	42.4	44.9
ME	5.1	6.1	5.8	10.8	10.3	11.0	22.6	27.8	30.6
MD	7.8	8.5	8.7	10.5	10.3	14.0	[2]29.6	33.3	34.4
MA	5.9	6.3	6.9	8.0	7.5	13.2	24.7	25.6	26.1
MI	7.6	7.7	7.8	13.5	12.5	13.6	[2]26.2	34.3	33.9
MN	5.1	5.9	5.8	8.0	8.4	13.8	20.9	23.9	25.6
MS	9.6	9.8	10.1	21.3	22.2	15.6	40.5	45.3	45.4
MO	7.1	7.6	7.8	14.4	14.4	13.9	28.6	32.1	34.1
MT.	6.2	5.8	7.0	11.5	12.6	12.3	[2]23.7	26.5	29.9
NE.	5.3	6.3	6.5	9.8	10.0	14.2	20.7	24.3	26.2
NV.	7.2	7.4	7.6	12.6	13.7	16.4	[2]25.4	42.0	35.0
NH	4.9	5.5	5.7	7.2	7.6	12.2	16.9	22.2	24.1
NJ.	7.0	7.6	8.0	8.4	8.2	14.1	24.3	27.6	28.3
NM	7.4	7.5	7.6	16.3	18.4	15.7	35.4	42.6	44.0
NY.	7.6	7.6	7.8	9.1	9.3	14.2	[2]33.0	37.9	34.9
NC	8.0	8.7	8.8	16.2	15.2	14.8	29.4	31.4	32.8
ND	5.5	5.3	6.5	8.6	9.6	12.4	18.4	23.5	27.0
OH	7.1	7.6	7.7	13.8	13.7	13.6	[2]28.9	33.0	34.0
OK	6.6	7.0	7.2	16.2	17.1	14.8	25.2	30.5	33.2
OR	5.0	5.5	5.4	12.0	13.0	13.8	25.7	28.9	29.7
PA.	7.1	7.4	7.6	10.9	10.8	12.2	28.6	32.4	32.8
RI	6.2	6.8	7.6	10.5	10.1	12.7	26.3	31.1	33.9
SC.	8.7	9.3	9.5	17.1	17.3	14.0	32.7	37.4	38.8
SD.	5.1	5.6	5.8	10.8	11.4	13.9	22.9	28.0	32.0
TN.	8.2	8.7	9.1	17.6	16.9	14.3	30.2	33.1	34.9
TX.	6.9	7.1	7.4	15.6	16.6	17.3	[2]17.5	30.0	31.5
UT.	5.7	6.3	6.7	10.3	10.8	21.5	13.5	15.7	17.1
VT.	5.3	5.4	6.5	8.5	8.2	11.1	20.1	24.9	28.0
VA.	7.2	7.7	7.9	11.7	11.4	13.9	26.0	29.3	29.8
WA	5.3	5.5	5.7	10.8	11.5	14.0	23.7	26.7	27.9
WV	7.1	7.9	8.0	17.8	17.2	11.5	25.4	30.5	32.4
WI	5.9	6.0	6.5	10.2	10.5	12.9	24.2	27.4	28.5
WY	7.4	7.4	8.9	13.6	15.2	13.0	19.8	26.4	29.6
Puerto Rico.	(NA)	(NA)	10.9	(NA)	(NA)	15.7	(NA)	(NA)	47.0
Virgin Islands.	(NA)	(NA)	9.2	(NA)	(NA)	15.2	(NA)	(NA)	69.6
Guam	(NA)	(NA)	7.6	(NA)	(NA)	29.0	(NA)	(NA)	54.2
American Samoa	(NA)	(NA)	3.0	(NA)	(NA)	27.2	(NA)	(NA)	34.2
Northern Marianas	(NA)	(NA)	8.6	(NA)	(NA)	21.9	(NA)	(NA)	45.6

NA Not available.   [1] Less than 2,500 grams (5 pounds-8 ounces).   [2] Marital status of mother is inferred.

Source: U.S. National Center for Health Statistics, *Vital Statistics of the United States*, annual; and *National Vital Statistics Reports (NVSR)* (formerly *Monthly Vital Statistics Report*).

Vital Statistics   71

No. 89. Live Births by Place of Delivery, Median and Low Birth Weight, and Prenatal Care: 1990 to 1997

[Represents registered births. Excludes births to nonresidents of the United States. For total number of births, see Table 79. See Appendix III]

Item	1990	1992	1993	1994	1995	1996	1997
Births attended (1,000):							
In hospital [1]	4,110	4,022	3,959	3,912	3,861	3,891	3,881
By physician, not in hospital	14	10	8	7	6	6	5
By midwife and other, not in hospital [2]	21	21	20	21	21	20	20
Median birth weight [3]	7 lb.-7 oz.	7 lb.-7 oz.	7 lb.-7 oz.	(NA)	(NA)	7 lb.-7 oz.	7 lb.-7 oz.
Percent of births with low birth weight	7.0	7.1	7.2	7.3	7.3	7.4	7.5
White	5.7	5.8	6.0	6.1	6.2	6.3	6.5
Black	13.3	13.3	13.3	13.2	13.1	13.0	13.0
Percent of births by period in which prenatal care began:							
1st trimester	74.2	77.7	78.9	80.2	81.3	81.9	82.5
3d trimester or no prenatal care	6.0	5.2	4.8	4.4	4.2	4.0	3.9

NA Not available. [1] Includes all births in hospitals or institutions and in clinics. [2] Includes births with attendant not specified. [3] Median birth weight based on race of mother; prior to 1990, based on race of child.

No. 90. Cesarean Section Deliveries by Age of Mother: 1990 to 1997

[In thousands (4,111 represents 4,111,000), except rate. 1990 excludes data for Oklahoma, which did not report method of delivery on the birth certificate]

Age of mother	1990	1995	1997	Age of mother	1990	1995	1997
Births by method of delivery	4,111	3,900	3,881	Cesarean deliveries	733	640	631
Vaginal	3,111	3,064	3,047	Black births by method of			
After previous cesarean	84	112	112	delivery	679	603	600
Cesarean deliveries	914	807	799	Vaginal	517	469	466
Primary	575	510	503	Cesarean deliveries	146	130	130
Repeat	339	297	297	Cesarean delivery rate [1]	22.7	21.0	20.8
White births by method of				Primary [2]	16.0	15.0	14.6
delivery	3,252	3,099	3,073	Rate of vaginal cesarean birth			
Vaginal	2,215	2,435	2,415	after previous cesarean [3]	19.0	28.0	27.4

[1] Percent of all live births by cesarean delivery. [2] Number of primary cesareans per 100 live births to women who have not had a previous cesarean. [3] Number of vaginal births after previous cesarean delivery per 100 live births to women with a previous cesarean delivery.

No. 91. Live Births and Births to Teen Mothers—20 Largest Metropolitan Areas: 1993

[Excludes births to nonresidents of the United States. Data are by place of residence. Metropolitan statistical areas (MSAs), consolidated metropolitan statistical areas (CMSAs), and New England County Metropolitan Areas (NECMAs) are defined by the U.S. Office of Management and Budget as of June 30,1990. See Appendix II for definitions and components]

Metropolitan area	All births		Births to teens	
	Number	Rate per 1,000 population	Number of teen births	Percent of total births
New York-Northern New Jersey-Long Island, NY-NJ-CT-PA CMSA/NECMA	290,532	16	22,950	8
Los Angeles-Anaheim-Riverside, CA CMSA	310,792	20	36,390	12
Chicago-Gary-Lake County, IL-IN-WI CMSA	146,678	18	17,688	12
Washington, DC-MD-VA MSA	66,625	16	5,262	8
San Francisco-Oakland-San Jose, CA CMSA	101,011	16	8,753	9
Philadelphia-Wilmington-Trenton, PA-NJ-DE-MD CMSA	89,732	15	9,609	11
Boston-Lawrence-Salem-Lowell-Brockton, MA NECMA	54,291	14	3,402	6
Detroit-Ann Arbor, MI CMSA	72,354	15	8,347	12
Dallas-Fort Worth, TX CMSA	73,645	18	9,788	13
Houston-Galveston-Brazoria, TX CMSA	74,277	19	10,226	14
Miami-Fort Lauderdale, FL CMSA	52,393	16	5,476	10
Seattle-Tacoma, WA CMSA	40,565	15	3,458	9
Atlanta, GA MSA	51,280	17	5,955	12
Cleveland-Akron-Lorain, OH CMSA	40,822	15	4,891	12
Minneapolis-St.Paul, MN-WI MSA	40,314	16	2,972	7
San Diego, CA MSA	48,935	19	5,207	11
St. Louis, MO-IL MSA	38,042	15	4,953	13
Pittsburgh-Beaver Valley, PA CMSA	27,177	12	2,548	9
Phoenix, AZ MSA	40,406	18	5,643	14
Tampa-St. Petersburg-Clearwater, FL MSA	27,658	13	3,653	13
Baltimore, MD MSA	36,237	15	4,028	11
Denver-Boulder, CO CMSA	31,139	16	3,330	11
Cincinnati-Hamilton, OH-KY-IN CMSA	27,104	15	3,611	13
Milwaukee-Racine, WI CMSA	25,099	15	3,235	13
Kansas City, MO-KS MSA	24,787	15	3,011	12

Source of Tables 89-91: U.S. National Center for Health Statistics, Vital Statistics of the United States, annual; and unpublished data.

72 Vital Statistics

No. 92. Women Who Have Had a Child in the Last Year by Age: 1980 to 1998

[**3,247 represents 3,247,000.** See headnote, Table 91]

Age of mother	Women who had a child in last year (1,000)			Total births per 1,000 women			First births per 1,000 women		
	1980	1990	1998	1980	1990	1998	1980	1990	1998
Total	**3,247**	**3,913**	**3,671**	**71.1**	**67.0**	**60.7**	**28.5**	**26.4**	**24.6**
15 to 29 years old [1] . .	2,476	2,568	2,274	103.7	90.8	81.7	48.6	43.2	40.2
15 to 19 years old . .	(NA)	338	460	(NA)	39.8	48.0	(NA)	30.1	29.3
20 to 24 years old . .	1,396	1,038	864	96.6	113.4	98.2	(NA)	51.8	50.4
25 to 29 years old . .	1,081	1,192	950	114.8	112.1	100.5	(NA)	46.2	41.8
30 to 44 years old	770	1,346	1,397	35.4	44.7	42.7	6.3	10.6	11.3
30 to 34 years old	519	892	843	60.0	80.4	82.4	(NA)	21.9	23.8
35 to 39 years old	192	377	437	26.9	37.3	38.5	(NA)	6.5	8.7
40 to 44 years old	59	77	117	9.9	8.6	10.5	(NA)	1.2	2.6

NA Not available.   [1] For 1980-88, 18 to 29 years old.

Source: U.S. Census Bureau, *Current Population Reports*, P20-375, P20-454, P20-470, and P20-499.

No. 93. Characteristics of Women Who Have Had a Child in the Last Year: 1995 and 1998

[**As of June. Covers civilian noninstitutional population.** Since the number of women who had a birth during the 12-month period was tabulated and not the actual numbers of births, some small underestimation of fertility for this period may exist due to the omission of: (1) Multiple births, (2) Two or more live births spaced within the 12-month period (the woman is counted only once), (3) Women who had births in the period and who did not survive to the survey date, (4) Women who were in institutions and therefore not in the survey universe. These losses may be somewhat offset by the inclusion in the CPS of births to immigrants who did not have their children born in the United States and births to nonresident women. These births would not have been recorded in the vital registration system. Based on Current Population Survey (CPS); see text, Section 1 and Appendix III]

Characteristic	1995			1998		
	Women who have had a child in the last year			Women who have had a child in the last year		
	Number of women (1,000)	Total births per 1,000 women	First births per 1,000 women	Number of women (1,000)	Total births per 1,000 women	First births per 1,000 women
Total [1].	**60,225**	**61.4**	**23.2**	**60,519**	**60.7**	**24.6**
White	48,603	59.2	22.6	48,487	60.8	24.2
Black	8,617	70.6	26.4	8,809	62.9	27.8
Hispanic [2]	6,632	79.6	25.0	7,359	84.0	36.1
Currently married	31,616	85.5	30.3	30,903	81.8	29.7
Married, spouse present	29,202	87.2	31.4	28,344	85.5	31.4
Married, spouse absent [3]	2,414	64.5	17.4	2,559	40.7	11.8
Widowed or divorced	5,762	28.4	4.1	5,430	26.4	6.4
Never married	22,846	36.3	18.0	24,185	41.3	22.1
Educational attainment:						
Less than high school	12,629	57.3	19.6	13,048	60.8	23.5
High school, 4 years	18,404	67.4	25.5	17,536	59.0	21.9
College: 1 or more years	29,192	59.3	23.2	29,935	61.6	26.7
No degree	12,724	56.1	21.2	12,626	54.6	21.7
Associate degree.	4,663	56.9	19.2	4,413	65.3	28.6
Bachelor's degree	8,884	65.3	27.0	9,762	64.2	29.1
Graduate or professional degree .	2,921	59.2	26.8	3,134	76.2	36.6
Labor force status:						
Employed	39,989	46.5	20.9	40,957	47.6	19.8
Unemployed	3,287	53.5	22.8	2,808	73.6	33.5
Not in labor force	16,949	98.1	28.5	16,754	90.5	34.8
Occupation of employed women:						
Managerial-professional	11,059	46.2	22.3	12,044	55.3	23.2
Technical, sales, admin. support . . .	16,997	48.6	21.5	16,801	45.9	21.7
Service workers	7,612	44.0	16.6	7,796	42.0	14.5
Farming, forestry, and fishing	501	41.0	27.9	467	30.1	4.0
Precision prod., craft, repair.	813	56.6	37.5	784	36.9	15.6
Operators, fabricators, laborers	3,007	39.5	17.8	3,064	46.0	13.4
Family income:						
Under $10,000	6,957	91.0	32.8	5,631	73.3	29.5
$10,000 to $19,999	8,159	64.3	25.8	6,917	74.3	30.6
$20,000 to $24,999	4,542	60.6	20.3	3,902	77.3	36.4
$25,000 to $29,999	4,364	57.0	18.9	3,848	61.4	20.8
$30,000 to $34,999	4,076	60.6	24.3	3,928	58.6	21.6
$35,000 to $49,999	9,949	59.1	20.8	9,478	55.1	21.9
$50,000 to $74,999	9,720	52.5	23.3	11,003	60.3	24.1
$75,000 and over	7,088	53.1	19.2	9,627	50.2	21.7

[1] Includes women of other races and women with family income not reported, not shown separately.   [2] Persons of Hispanic origin may be of any race.   [3] Includes separated women.

Source: U.S. Census Bureau, *Current Population Reports*, P20-375, P20-499; and unpublished data.

Vital Statistics   73

No. 94. Women Who Have Had a Child in the Last Year by Age and Labor Force Status: 1980 to 1998

[3,247 represents 3,247,000. See headnote, Table 93]

Year	Total, 18 to 44 years old			18 to 29 years old			30 to 44 years old		
		In the labor force			In the labor force			In the labor force	
	Number (1,000)	Number (1,000)	Percent	Number (1,000)	Number (1,000)	Percent	Number (1,000)	Number (1,000)	Percent
1980	3,247	1,233	38	2,476	947	38	770	287	37
1981	3,381	1,411	42	2,499	1,004	40	881	407	46
1982	3,433	1,508	44	2,445	1,040	43	988	469	48
1983	3,625	1,563	43	2,682	1,138	42	942	425	45
1984	3,311	1,547	47	2,375	1,058	45	936	489	52
1985	3,497	1,691	48	2,512	1,204	48	984	488	50
1986	3,625	1,805	50	2,452	1,185	48	1,174	620	53
1987	3,701	1,881	51	2,521	1,258	50	1,180	623	53
1988	3,667	1,866	51	2,384	1,177	49	1,283	688	54
1990 [1]	3,913	2,068	53	2,568	1,275	50	1,346	793	59
1992 [1]	3,688	1,985	54	2,346	1,182	50	1,342	802	60
1994 [1]	3,890	2,066	53	2,389	1,209	51	1,501	857	57
1995 [1]	3,696	2,034	55	2,252	1,150	51	1,444	884	61
1998 [1]	3,671	2,155	59	(NA)	(NA)	(NA)	(NA)	(NA)	(NA)

NA Not available.   [1] Lower age limit is 15 years old.

Source: U.S. Census Bureau, Current Population Reports, P20-482; and unpublished data.

No. 95. Childless Women and Children Ever Born by Race, Age, and Marital Status: 1998

[See headnote, Table 93]

Characteristics	Total number of women (1,000)	Women by number of children ever born (percent)				Children ever born	
		Total	None	One	Two or more	Total number (1,000)	Per 1,000 women
ALL RACES [1]							
Women ever married	36,334	100	18.7	21.7	59.7	64,305	1,770
15 to 19 years old.	372	100	49.8	32.2	18.1	254	683
20 to 24 years old.	2,485	100	34.3	36.3	29.4	2,576	1,037
25 to 29 years old.	5,846	100	29.6	28.5	42.0	7,728	1,322
30 to 34 years old.	7,952	100	18.0	21.7	60.3	13,879	1,745
35 to 39 years old.	9,685	100	12.8	17.1	70.0	19,858	2,050
40 to 44 years old.	9,995	100	13.7	18.1	68.3	20,011	2,002
Women never married.	24,185	100	77.5	11.6	11.0	9,926	410
15 to 19 years old.	9,204	100	91.8	5.7	2.6	1,071	116
20 to 24 years old.	6,315	100	75.7	15.6	8.8	2,311	366
25 to 29 years old.	3,606	100	66.1	15.4	18.5	2,315	642
30 to 34 years old.	2,277	100	60.2	16.3	23.6	1,931	848
35 to 39 years old.	1,666	100	60.5	15.2	24.4	1,451	871
40 to 44 years old.	1,118	100	66.8	10.9	22.3	847	758
WHITE							
Women ever married	30,664	100	19.3	21.9	58.8	53,274	1,737
15 to 19 years old.	324	100	48.7	35.0	16.3	219	676
20 to 24 years old.	2,190	100	34.0	37.4	28.7	2,249	1,027
25 to 29 years old.	4,978	100	30.7	28.8	40.5	6,356	1,277
30 to 34 years old.	6,668	100	18.6	21.9	59.4	11,444	1,716
35 to 39 years old.	8,184	100	13.0	17.0	70.1	16,662	2,036
40 to 44 years old.	8,320	100	14.0	18.1	68.0	16,344	1,964
Women never married.	17,823	100	84.1	9.2	6.7	4,738	266
15 to 19 years old.	7,233	100	93.5	4.3	2.2	713	99
20 to 24 years old.	4,772	100	81.1	12.8	6.1	1,320	277
25 to 29 years old.	2,534	100	74.8	13.6	11.7	1,078	425
30 to 34 years old.	1,484	100	71.4	12.2	16.3	859	579
35 to 39 years old.	1,066	100	75.9	12.4	11.7	465	436
40 to 44 years old.	735	100	80.9	7.5	11.6	303	412
BLACK							
Women ever married	3,710	100	13.6	19.9	66.4	7,600	2,049
15 to 19 years old.	29	(B)	(B)	(B)	(B)	30	(B)
20 to 24 years old.	199	100	36.2	24.9	38.9	233	1,172
25 to 29 years old.	573	100	17.5	25.6	56.8	1,023	1,778
30 to 34 years old.	801	100	10.9	19.1	70.0	1,634	2,040
35 to 39 years old.	1,002	100	10.5	17.6	72.0	2,253	2,248
40 to 44 years old.	1,107	100	11.7	19.0	69.2	2,427	2,193
Women never married.	5,099	100	52.4	21.1	26.6	4,835	948
15 to 19 years old.	1,525	100	83.2	13.1	3.7	312	205
20 to 24 years old.	1,178	100	49.7	29.2	21.0	920	782
25 to 29 years old.	849	100	37.4	21.2	30.5	1,153	1,358
30 to 34 years old.	666	100	33.1	26.4	40.4	989	1,485
35 to 39 years old.	545	100	29.5	20.8	49.6	941	1,728
40 to 44 years old.	336	100	34.4	18.1	47.4	519	1,545

B Base figure too small to meet statistical standards for reliability.   [1] Includes other races, not shown separately.

Source: U.S. Census Bureau, Current Population Reports, Series P20-526.

No. 96. Number of Partners in Lifetime by Selected Characteristics and by Distribution: 1995

[60,201 represents 60,201,000. Based on responses from the National Survey of Family Growth (NSFG) sponsored by National Center for Health Statistics. Based on interview conducted in person in homes of 10,847 women between January and October 1995, using computer-assisted personal interviewing. A small part of the NSFG, including the questions on which this table is based, was conducted with self-administered technique called Audio-Assisted Self Interviewing. See source for details]

Women 15-44 years of age	Number (1,000)	Number of partners in lifetime by percent distribution							
		0 [1]	1	2	3	4	5	6-9	10 or more
All women.	60,201	10.5	23.5	12.3	9.6	8.4	8.1	12.1	15.5
Age:									
15-19 years old.	8,961	45.8	19.4	11.0	7.9	3.6	2.9	5.7	3.7
20-24 years old.	9,041	11.0	21.6	13.4	11.5	9.0	7.7	11.9	13.9
25-29 years old.	9,693	4.3	22.0	13.5	10.1	9.2	10.1	13.8	16.9
30-34 years old.	11,065	2.8	23.4	11.8	9.1	11.5	9.7	13.7	18.0
35-39 years old.	11,211	1.8	24.3	11.7	9.4	8.5	9.3	14.5	20.5
40-44 years old.	10,230	2.4	29.4	12.6	9.7	8.0	8.4	11.7	17.7
Married.	29,673	0.5	34.5	13.8	9.9	8.9	8.0	11.2	13.2
Unmarried.	30,528	20.2	12.8	10.9	9.4	7.9	8.2	12.8	17.7
First intercourse:									
Under 16 years old	13,944	(X)	11.3	11.2	10.2	8.6	10.6	18.5	29.0
16 years old	8,750	(X)	18.6	12.6	12.9	10.9	9.4	16.5	18.8
17 years old	8,754	(X)	17.3	14.4	11.4	12.3	12.5	13.1	18.8
18 years old	6,941	(X)	26.0	14.3	11.0	11.0	9.0	13.1	14.9
19 years old	4,759	(X)	37.6	14.7	11.6	8.0	7.2	11.0	9.2
20 years old and over	10,653	(X)	52.2	16.5	8.6	6.3	4.7	5.9	4.6
Education: [2]									
No high school diploma or GED [3] . .	5,424	1.3	27.7	15.8	10.1	7.6	10.1	11.7	15.8
High school diploma or GED	18,169	2.5	23.5	13.0	10.8	9.8	9.6	13.7	17.1
Some college, no bachelor's degree.	12,399	4.6	22.3	10.3	9.6	9.1	10.2	14.1	19.9
Bachelor's degree or higher.	11,748	4.7	26.1	11.7	8.6	9.5	7.1	13.5	18.9
Poverty level income: [2]									
0-149 percent	10,072	3.8	21.8	13.7	9.9	9.4	10.1	13.6	17.7
Race and Hispanic origin:									
Hispanic	6,702	12.1	37.1	15.8	8.9	5.1	5.7	6.9	8.5

X Not applicable. [1] Never had intercourse, or never had voluntary intercourse if first intercourse was not voluntary. [2] Limited to women 22-44 years of age at time of interview. [3] GED = general equivalency diploma.

No. 97. Unmarried Women Who Have Had Intercourse in the 12 Months Prior to Interview: 1995

[12,708 represents 12,708,000. See headnote, Table 96]

Women 15-44 years of age	Number (1,000)	Partners used condoms for disease prevention— percent distribution				
		Every time	More than half the time	Half the time	Less than half the time	Not at all
Total [1]	12,708	31.3	13.9	8.4	13.9	32.5
Age and number of partners: [2]						
1 partner	8,197	31.6	9.0	6.1	10.9	42.3
2 or more partners.	4,504	30.9	22.7	12.6	19.4	14.5
15-29 years old.	8,570	32.2	15.1	9.6	13.8	29.3
1 partner	5,315	32.7	10.1	7.3	10.4	39.5
2 or more partners	3,252	31.4	23.2	13.4	19.4	12.5
30-44 years old.	4,139	29.5	11.4	5.9	14.1	39.2
1 partner	2,882	29.6	7.0	3.9	11.8	47.6
2 or more partners	1,251	29.5	21.4	10.4	19.4	19.4
Race and Hispanic origin of partners: [2]						
Hispanic	1,077	30.9	15.4	11.3	13.7	28.7
1 partner	707	29.8	12.5	9.4	11.5	36.8
2 or more partners	370	33.1	21.0	14.9	17.8	13.2
Non-Hispanic White.	8,202	27.7	13.0	8.1	14.7	36.5
1 partner	5,341	28.6	7.7	5.9	10.5	47.4
2 or more partners	2,861	26.2	23.0	12.1	22.5	16.3
Non-Hispanic Black.	3,042	39.2	15.4	9.2	12.8	23.4
1 partner	1,890	38.4	12.0	6.4	12.3	30.8
2 or more partners	1,153	40.5	21.0	13.8	13.6	11.2
Education: [3]						
No high school diploma or GED [4]	2,128	26.6	13.9	7.6	10.8	41.1
High school diploma or GED	5,247	26.2	12.5	7.6	14.5	39.1
Some college, no bachelor's degree	3,779	29.7	10.6	6.1	13.9	39.7
Bachelor's degree or higher	3,111	32.4	13.6	7.0	12.0	35.1

[1] Includes women with missing information on number of partners in the 12 months prior to interview. [2] Number of male partners in the 12 months prior to interview. [3] Limited to women 22-44 years of age at time of interview. [4] GED is general equivalency diploma.

Source of Tables 96 and 97: U.S. National Center for Health Statistics, *Fertility, Family Planning, and Women's Health: New data from the 1995 National Survey of Family Growth, Vital and Health Statistics*, Series 23, No. 19, 1997.

No. 98. Measures of Teenage Sexual Activity and Pregnancy for Women 15-19 Years of Age by Race and Hispanic Origin: 1995

Measure	Total [1]	White, non-Hispanic	Black, non-Hispanic	Hispanic [2]
Women 15-19 years of age in the sample.	1,396	842	289	210
Weighted number [3] (mil.).	8.9	5.9	1.4	1.1
Pregnancy rate (per 1,000 women)	102.7	71.6	184.4	162.8
Percent who ever had intercourse	51.3	50.4	60.5	56.0
Pregnancy rate for those who have ever had intercourse	200	142	305	291
Percent who had sex in the last 12 months. . . .	46.9	46.0	56.6	51.8
Pregnancy rate for those who had intercourse in the last 12 months.	219	156	326	314

[1] Includes races other than White and Black.   [2] Includes all persons of Hispanic origin of any race.   [3] Estimated from the National Survey of Family Growth.

No. 99. Women 15-19 Years of Age and Measures of Sexual Activity, Pregnancy, and Births for Women 15-19 Years: 1982 to 1995

Measure	1982	1988	1990	1995
Women 15-19 years of age (mil.) [1]	9.8	9.0	8.7	8.8
Births to women 15-19 years of age	513,758	478,353	521,826	499,873
Births to unmarried women 15-19 years of age	260,626	312,499	349,970	375,738
Percent ever had sexual intercourse	46.9	52.6	54.7	51.3
Sexually experienced women 15-19 years of age (mil.) . .	4.6	4.7	4.8	4.5
Pregnancy rate, all teens	107.8	109.9	116.3	102.7
Number of pregnancies	1,058,000	993,000	1,013,000	904,000
Number of abortions	419,000	393,000	351,000	264,000
Pregnancies to women 15-19 years of age that ended in abortion (percent)	40	40	35	29
Pregnancies to women 15-19 years of age that ended in nonmarital births (percent)	25	31	35	42

[1] U.S. Census Bureau, various reports.

No. 100. Never Married Males and Females 15-19 Years of Age Who Have Had Sexual Intercourse by Selected Age Groups and Sociodemographic Characteristics: 1988 and 1995

Characteristic	Females 1988	Females 1995	Males 1988	Males 1995
All teenagers 15-19 years old [1].	**51.1**	**49.3**	**60.4**	**55.2**
AGE				
15 years old	27.9	24.3	32.6	27.1
16 years old	34.1	38.3	49.9	44.6
17 years old	47.6	50.8	65.6	58.4
18 years old	65.5	62.3	71.6	67.0
19 years old	79.7	74.0	85.7	84.0
15-17 years old	37.2	38.0	50.0	43.1
18-19 years old	72.6	68.0	77.3	75.4
AGE, RACE, AND HISPANIC ORIGIN				
White non-Hispanic	50.4	48.5	56.8	49.5
15-17 years old	34.7	35.6	44.4	34.8
18-19 years old	72.7	68.0	76.8	74.7
Black non-Hispanic.	60.4	59.3	80.6	80.4
15-17 years old	50.2	48.9	76.6	75.4
18-19 years old	77.5	77.1	87.7	89.0
Hispanic [2].	45.8	52.7	59.7	60.9
15-17 years old	35.2	49.0	57.1	49.7
18-19 years old	67.5	59.0	63.6	78.6
MOTHER'S EDUCATION				
0-11 years	55.4	60.2	67.3	59.8
12 years	49.4	47.2	65.3	58.0
13-15 years	51.2	55.2	53.9	57.5
16 years or more.	48.5	37.2	50.9	45.5
FAMILY STRUCTURE AT AGE 14				
Both biological/adoptive parents	44.9	42.5	57.0	50.4
Single parent [3]	58.7	58.9	71.1	67.6
Parent and stepparent	66.2	55.3	56.5	54.0
Nonparental/other	72.8	64.2	91.0	80.3

[1] Includes races other than White and Black.   [2] Includes all persons of Hispanic origin of any race.   [3] Includes parent and girl/boyfriend; also includes parent and other adults.

Sources of Tables 98-100: U.S. National Center for Health Statistics, *Vital and Health Statistics, Trends in Pregnancies and Pregnancy Rates by Outcome: Estimates for the United States, 1976-96;* Series 21 No. 56.

No. 101. Receipt of Any Infertility Services, by Women 15-44 Years of Age by Selected Characteristics: 1995

[Represents characteristics at time of interview, unless otherwise stated. (60,201 represents 60,201,000). In percents, except as indicated]

Characteristics	Number (1,000)	Any services [1]	Advice	Tests on woman or man	Ovulation drugs	Surgery or treatment for blocked tubes	Assisted reproductive technology [2]
Total.....................	60,201	15.4	6.4	4.2	3.0	1.5	1.0
AGE							
15-24 years old	18,002	4.4	1.1	0.2	0.3	0.1	(Z)
25-34 years old	20,758	17.1	6.3	3.7	3.1	1.2	0.8
35-44 years old	21,440	22.9	10.9	8.1	5.2	2.9	2.1
PARITY, AGE, AND MARITAL STATUS							
One or more births..............	34,958	21.8	7.7	4.6	3.6	1.8	0.9
15-24 years old	3,889	16.1	3.3	0.3	0.6	0.5	-
25-34 years old	13,620	21.5	6.2	3.1	3.1	1.3	0.6
35-44 years old	17,449	23.4	9.8	6.7	4.6	2.4	1.4
Married....................	23,988	24.1	9.2	6.0	4.6	2.1	1.1
Unmarried..................	10,970	16.8	4.3	1.6	1.3	0.9	0.5
EDUCATION [3]							
No high school diploma or GED [4]	5,424	14.9	3.3	2.0	1.2	0.7	0.2
High school diploma or GED	18,169	20.0	7.8	4.9	3.9	2.0	1.1
Some college, no bachelor's degree ...	12,399	19.4	7.8	5.6	3.3	2.0	1.2
Bachelor's degree or higher	11,748	18.0	10.3	7.1	5.3	1.9	2.2
POVERTY LEVEL INCOME [3]							
0-149 percent	10,072	16.6	4.8	2.1	1.5	0.9	0.2

- Represents zero. Z Less than 0.5 percent. [1] Includes services to help get pregnant as well as to help prevent miscarriage. [2] Includes artificial insemination, in vitro fertilization (IVF), gamete intrafallopian transfer (GIFT), and other techniques not shown separately. [3] Limited to women 22-44 years of age at time of interview. The poverty index ratio was calculated by dividing the total family income by the weighted average threshold income of families whose head of household was under 65 years of age, based on the 1994 poverty levels defined by the U.S. Census Bureau. [4] GED = general equivalency diploma.

Source: U.S. National Center for Health Statistics, *Fertility, Family Planning, and Women's Health: New data from the 1995 National Survey of Family Growth, Vital and Health Statistics,* Series 23, No. 19, 1997.

No. 102. Pregnancies Ending in Live Birth to Women 15-44 Years Old and Months Pregnant When Prenatal Care Began: 1991-95

Characteristic		Percent distribution			
			Months pregnant when prenatal care began		
	Number (1,000)	Total	Less than 3 months	3-4 months	5 months or more or no prenatal care
All pregnancies [1]	17,052	100.0	88.1	5.4	6.6
AGE AT TIME OF BIRTH					
Under 20 years old.........................	2,023	100.0	75.3	10.7	14.0
20-24 years old	4,388	100.0	84.5	7.3	8.2
25-29 years old	5,088	100.0	91.3	4.0	4.7
30-44 years old	5,553	100.0	92.5	3.1	4.3
MARITAL STATUS AT TIME OF BIRTH					
Never married	3,940	100.0	77.3	9.6	13.1
Married.............................	12,171	100.0	91.5	4.0	4.5
Formerly married	942	100.0	88.6	5.3	6.1
WANTEDNESS STATUS AT CONCEPTION [2]					
Intended.............................	11,833	100.0	91.2	3.9	4.9
Mistimed.............................	3,715	100.0	82.2	9.1	8.7
Unwanted.............................	1,485	100.0	78.0	8.2	13.8
EDUCATION [3]					
No high school diploma or GED [4]	2,368	100.0	78.9	6.9	14.3
High school diploma or GED	6,076	100.0	88.5	6.3	5.2
Some college, no bachelor's degree	3,582	100.0	94.5	3.0	2.5
Bachelor's degree or higher.................	3,144	100.0	93.8	2.3	3.9

[1] Includes pregnancies with missing information on prenatal care or wantedness status. [2] Based on new questions in Cycle 5. See source "Definitions of Terms." [3] Limited to women 22-44 years of age at time of interview. [4] GED = general equivalency diploma.

Source: U.S. National Center for Health Statistics, *Fertility, Family Planning, and Women's Health: New data from the 1995 National Survey of Family Growth, Vital and Health Statistics,* Series 23, No. 19, 1997.

Vital Statistics 77

No. 103. Number of Pregnancies, Live Births, and Induced Abortions by Age and Race of Woman: 1980 to 1996

[Due to rounding, figures may not add to totals]

Age and race of woman	1980	1985	1990	1991	1992	1993	1994	1995	1996
ALL PREGNANCIES									
Total [1]	5,912	6,144	6,778	6,674	6,596	6,494	6,373	6,245	6,240
Under 15 years	29	30	29	29	30	30	30	28	26
15 to 19 years	1,146	981	1,013	975	939	928	923	904	893
20 to 24 years	1,956	1,891	1,847	1,843	1,813	1,762	1,682	1,602	1,570
25 to 29 years	1,626	1,764	1,908	1,827	1,771	1,701	1,637	1,598	1,617
30 to 34 years	844	1,045	1,319	1,313	1,326	1,332	1,333	1,322	1,312
35 to 39 years	258	373	562	581	603	622	642	659	683
40 years and over	54	60	100	106	113	119	127	132	140
Race:									
White	4,585	4,733	5,117	5,006	4,924	4,834	4,755	4,692	(NA)
All other	1,328	1,411	1,660	1,668	1,671	1,660	1,618	1,553	(NA)
LIVE BIRTHS									
Total	3,612	3,761	4,158	4,111	4,065	4,000	3,953	3,900	3,891
Race:									
White	2,936	3,038	3,290	3,241	3,202	3,150	3,121	3,099	3,093
All other	676	723	868	870	863	850	832	801	798
INDUCED ABORTIONS									
Total	1,554	1,589	1,609	1,557	1,529	1,500	1,431	1,364	1,366
Under 15 years	15	17	13	12	13	12	12	11	10
15 to 19 years	445	399	351	314	295	289	276	264	264
20 to 24 years	549	548	532	533	526	514	478	442	434
25 to 29 years	304	336	360	348	341	332	316	308	318
30 to 34 years	153	181	216	213	213	211	205	196	195
35 to 39 years	67	87	108	107	110	111	111	110	112
40 years and over	21	21	29	29	31	31	32	32	33
Race:									
White	1,094	1076	1,039	982	944	911	861	820	(NA)
All other	460	513	570	574	585	589	570	544	(NA)

NA Not available. [1] Includes fetal losses not shown.
Source: U.S. National Center for Health Statistics, *Vital and Health Statistics, Trends in Pregnancies and Pregnancy Rates by Outcome: 1976-96*, Series 21 No. 56.

No. 104. Numbers and Rates of Pregnancies, Live Births, Induced Abortions, and Fetal Losses for Teenagers by Age, Race, and Hispanic Origin: 1996

Pregnancy outcome and race and Hispanic origin	Number (1,000)				Rate per 1,000 women			
	10-14 years old	15-19 years old			10-14 years old	15-19 years old		
		Total	15-17 years old	18-19 years old		Total	15-17 years old	18-19 years old
ALL RACES [1]								
All pregnancies	26	893	372	521	2.8	98.7	67.8	146.4
Live births	11	492	186	306	1.2	54.4	33.8	86.0
Induced abortions	10	264	104	160	1.1	29.2	19.0	44.9
Fetal losses [2]	4	137	82	55	0.5	15.2	15.0	15.5
NON-HISPANIC								
White:								
All pregnancies	7	416	163	253	1.1	68.1	43.9	105.6
Live births	3	229	76	153	0.4	37.6	20.6	63.7
Induced abortions	3	117	46	71	0.5	19.1	12.5	29.4
Fetal losses [2]	1	70	40	30	0.2	11.4	10.8	12.4
Black:								
All pregnancies	12	242	106	136	8.7	177.8	128.1	254.4
Live births	5	128	55	73	3.8	94.2	66.6	136.6
Induced abortions	5	90	36	54	3.9	65.9	43.7	100.1
Fetal losses [2]	1	24	15	9	1.0	17.7	17.7	17.7
HISPANIC [3]								
All pregnancies	5	183	74	110	4.3	157.1	105.0	235.4
Live births	3	119	48	71	2.6	101.8	69.0	151.1
Induced abortions	2	45	17	28	1.3	38.6	24.7	59.5
Fetal losses [2]	1	20	8	12	0.4	16.7	11.3	24.8

[1] Includes races other than White and Black. [2] Spontaneous fetal losses from recognized pregnancies of all gestational periods as reported by women in the 1995 National Survey of Family Growth charted by the National Center for Health Statistics. The rate of pregnancy loss depends on the degree to which losses at very early gestations are detected. [3] Includes all persons of Hispanic origin of any race.
Source: U.S. National Center for Health Statistics, *Trends in Pregnancies and Pregnancy Rates by Outcome: Estimates for the United States, 1976-96*, Series 21, No. 56.

No. 105. Mistimed or Unwanted First Unintended Births to Women 15-44 Years of Age: 1995

[See headnote, Table 96]

Characteristic	Number of women, total (1,000)	Women who had an unintended birth [1]		
		First unintended birth		
		Number (1,000)	Percent mistimed	Percent unwanted
Total.	**60,201**	**17,077**	**80.4**	**19.6**
AGE AT BIRTH				
Under 20 years	8,961	7,666	83.4	16.6
20-24 years	9,041	5,674	84.7	15.3
25-29 years	9,693	2,440	73.6	26.4
30-44 years	11,065	1,292	56.8	43.2
BIRTH ORDER				
First birth	(NA)	12,540	84.9	15.1
Second birth	(NA)	2,926	77.5	22.5
Third or higher birth	(NA)	1,611	51.1	48.9
POVERTY LEVEL [2]				
0-149 percent	10,072	5,386	75.5	24.5
0-99 percent	5,992	3,417	73.2	26.8
RACE, HISPANIC ORIGIN, AND AGE AT BIRTH				
Hispanic	6,702	2,293	74.8	25.2
Non-Hispanic White	45,522	10,641	84.4	15.6
Non-Hispanic Black	8,210	3,469	72.9	27.1
Non-Hispanic other	2,767	674	74.8	25.2

NA Not available.   [1] Based on "traditional" version (comparable to Cycle 4 and previous cycles) of wantedness status. See source "Definition of Terms."   [2] Limited to women 22-44 years of age at time of interview.

Source: U.S. National Center for Health Statistics, *Fertility, Family Planning, and Women's Health: New data from the 1995 National Survey of Family Growth, Vital and Health Statistics,* Series 23, No. 19, 1997.

No. 106. Single Babies Born in 1990-93 Who Were Ever Breastfed, Duration, and Mean Duration of Breastfeeding in Weeks by Selected Characteristics: 1995

Characteristic	Percent breastfed at all	Percent distribution				Mean duration in weeks
			Duration of breastfeeding			
		Total	0-2 months	3-4 months	5 or more months	
All babies [1]	**55.2**	**100.0**	**40.3**	**8.6**	**51.1**	**28.7**
Under 20 years	36.0	100.0	69.7	4.5	25.8	17.5
20-24 years	46.4	100.0	46.6	12.4	41.0	24.1
25 years and over	63.0	100.0	35.0	7.8	57.3	31.5
25-29 years	56.4	100.0	39.8	8.7	51.5	28.2
30-44 years	69.1	100.0	31.3	7.1	61.6	34.0
MARITAL STATUS AT TIME OF BIRTH						
Never married	31.4	100.0	54.8	8.3	36.8	20.8
Married	63.4	100.0	37.7	8.5	53.8	30.1
Formerly married	50.2	100.0	45.3	11.3	43.4	26.4
WANTEDNESS STATUS AT CONCEPTION						
Intended	60.4	100.0	38.1	9.4	52.6	29.7
Mistimed	46.3	100.0	50.7	6.7	42.6	23.3
Unwanted	36.9	100.0	38.1	4.7	57.3	31.6
EDUCATION [2]						
No high school diploma or GED [3]	38.9	100.0	44.9	8.8	46.4	26.8
High school diploma or GED	49.0	100.0	44.0	9.8	46.2	27.2
Some college, no bachelor's degree	63.0	100.0	43.9	7.1	49.1	26.5
Bachelor's degree or higher	81.1	100.0	28.7	8.5	62.8	35.2
POVERTY LEVEL INCOME [2]						
0-149 percent	42.6	100.0	42.4	8.3	49.2	30.2
150-299 percent	58.1	100.0	39.5	9.6	50.8	29.4
300 percent or higher	68.2	100.0	38.8	8.1	53.1	28.3
RACE AND HISPANIC ORIGIN						
Hispanic	62.2	100.0	42.7	7.1	50.2	26.7
Non-Hispanic White	59.1	100.0	38.5	8.1	53.3	29.8
Non-Hispanic Black	25.1	100.0	45.0	14.0	40.9	22.9

[1] Includes babies born to women of other race and origin groups not shown separately.   [2] The poverty index ratio was calculated by dividing the total family income by the weighted average threshold income of families whose head of household was under 65 years of age, based on the U.S. Census Bureau. Limited to women 22-44 years of age at time of interview.   [3] GED = general equivalency diploma.

Source: U.S. National Center for Health Statistics, *Fertility, Family Planning, and Women's Health: New data from the 1995 National Survey of Family Growth, Vital and Health Statistics,* Series 23, No. 19, 1997.

Vital Statistics   79

No. 107. Contraceptive Use by Women, 15 to 44 Years of Age: 1995

[60,201 represents 60,201,000. Based on samples of the female population of the United States; see source for details. See Appendix III]

Contraceptive status and method	All women[1]	Age 15-24 years	Age 25-34 years	Age 35-44 years	Non-Hispanic White	Non-Hispanic Black	Hispanic	Never married	Currently married	Formerly married
All women (1,000)	60,201	18,002	20,758	21,440	42,522	8,210	6,702	22,679	29,673	7,849
PERCENT DISTRIBUTION										
Sterile[2]	29.7	2.6	25.0	57.0	30.2	31.5	28.4	6.9	43.2	45.1
Surgically sterile	27.9	1.8	23.6	54.0	28.5	29.7	26.3	5.7	41.1	42.5
Noncontraceptively sterile[3]	3.1	0.1	1.2	7.4	3.2	3.7	2.3	0.9	4.1	5.8
Contraceptively sterile[4]	24.8	1.7	22.4	46.6	25.3	26.0	24.0	4.8	37.0	36.7
Nonsurgically sterile[5]	1.7	0.7	1.3	2.8	1.6	1.8	2.0	1.1	2.0	2.2
Pregnant, postpartum	4.6	5.9	6.9	1.3	4.3	4.5	6.3	3.1	6.4	1.9
Seeking pregnancy	4.0	2.1	6.2	3.5	3.7	4.6	4.0	1.5	6.4	2.1
Other nonusers	22.3	44.4	13.3	12.6	21.1	23.1	26.3	46.8	4.7	18.4
Never had intercourse	10.9	30.8	3.4	1.4	10.4	8.9	12.1	28.9	-	-
No intercourse in last month[6]	6.2	7.0	5.3	6.5	5.7	7.2	8.6	11.5	0.5	12.7
Had intercourse in last month[6]	5.2	6.6	4.6	4.7	5.0	7.0	5.6	6.4	4.2	5.7
Nonsurgical contraceptors	39.7	45.0	49.1	26.1	41.2	36.1	35.1	41.8	39.7	32.4
Pill	17.3	23.1	23.7	6.3	18.8	14.8	13.6	20.4	15.6	14.6
IUD	0.5	0.1	0.6	0.8	0.5	0.5	0.9	0.3	0.7	0.4
Diaphragm	1.2	0.2	1.2	2.0	1.5	0.5	0.4	0.5	1.8	0.9
Condom	13.1	13.9	15.0	10.7	13.0	12.5	12.1	13.9	13.3	10.1
Periodic abstinence	1.5	0.5	1.8	2.0	1.6	0.7	1.3	0.6	2.3	0.7
Natural family planning	0.2	-	0.3	0.3	0.3	-	0.1	-	0.4	-
Withdrawal	2.0	1.6	2.3	1.9	2.1	0.9	2.0	1.5	2.3	1.8
Other methods[7]	3.9	5.6	4.2	2.1	3.4	6.2	4.7	4.6	3.3	3.9

- Represents or rounds to zero. [1] Includes other races, not shown separately. [2] Total sterile includes male sterile for unknown reasons. [3] Persons who had sterilizing operation and who gave as one reason that they had medical problems with their female organs. [4] Includes all other sterilization operations, and sterilization of the husband or current partner. [5] Persons sterile from illness, accident, or congenital conditions. [6] Data refer to no intercourse in the 3 months prior to interview. [7] Includes implants, injectables, morning-after-pill, suppository, Today™ sponge and less frequently used methods.
Source: U.S. National Center for Health Statistics, special tabulations from the 1995 National Survey of Family Growth.

No. 108. Women 15-44 Years of Age Who Have Ever Had a Live Birth and Use of Maternity Leave for the Most Recent Birth: 1995

Characteristics of the mother	Number (1,000)	Total	Not employed	Employed	Took maternity leave	Did not take leave[1] Not needed	Did not take leave[1] Not offered	Did not take leave[1] Other reasons
All women	34,958	100.0	48.0	52.0	37.3	2.3	0.9	11.6
AGE AT TIME OF BIRTH								
15-19 years old	3,436	100.0	71.9	28.1	14.8	0.7	0.1	12.5
20-24 years old	10,094	100.0	52.8	47.2	29.8	1.3	1.3	14.9
25-29 years old	11,629	100.0	44.8	55.2	41.1	2.7	0.8	10.5
30-44 years old	9,799	100.0	38.3	61.7	48.3	3.5	0.8	9.1
YEAR OF CHILD's BIRTH								
1991-95	13,999	100.0	43.2	56.8	43.5	2.2	0.9	10.3
1981-90	15,344	100.0	47.4	52.6	37.2	2.7	0.8	11.8
1980 and before	5,616	100.0	61.5	38.5	22.0	1.6	0.9	14.0
MARITAL STATUS AT TIME OF BIRTH								
Never married	6,379	100.0	58.4	41.6	26.8	0.8	1.0	13.0
Married	26,439	100.0	44.9	55.1	40.3	2.8	0.8	11.1
Formerly married	2,140	100.0	54.3	45.7	31.1	0.8	1.3	12.5
BIRTH ORDER OF CHILD								
First	10,901	100.0	35.8	64.2	46.9	1.8	1.1	14.4
Second	13,965	100.0	47.7	52.3	38.1	2.6	1.0	10.7
Third or higher	10,092	100.0	61.5	38.5	25.8	2.5	0.4	9.7
EDUCATION AT INTERVIEW[2]								
No high school diploma or GED[3]	4,961	100.0	69.6	30.4	16.5	0.7	0.4	12.8
High school diploma or GED	14,295	100.0	48.8	51.2	36.2	1.6	1.0	12.4
Some college, no bachelor's degree	7,967	100.0	40.1	59.9	44.4	2.6	1.1	11.8
Bachelor's degree or higher	5,929	100.0	32.8	67.2	52.8	5.6	0.9	7.9
RACE AND HISPANIC ORIGIN								
Hispanic	4,372	100.0	57.8	42.2	28.9	1.1	0.8	11.4

[1] The group labeled "not needed" includes women who did not need to take maternity leave: (1) Due to the timing of their birth relative to their job schedule (for example, teachers who delivered during summer break. (2) Due to the nature of their jobs (for example, worked out of their homes, self-employed). (3) Because they decided to quit their jobs after delivery. The group labeled "not offered" includes: (1) Woman whose employers did not offer (or denied) maternity leave at all (for example, woman would be fired if she took leave. (2) woman whose job benefits did not include maternity leave. The final group labeled "other reasons" includes women who decided to quit their jobs before delivery, who could not afford to take maternity leave for personal or financial reasons, and who continued to work right after delivery. [2] Women 22-44 years of age at time of interview. [3] GED is general equivalency diploma.
Source: U.S. National Center for Health Statistics, Fertility, Family Planning, and Women's Health: New data from the 1995 National Survey of Family Growth, Vital and Health Statistics, Series 23, No. 19, 1997.

No. 109. Live Births—Mothers Who Smoked During Pregnancy: 1997

[Excludes California, Indiana, New York, and South Dakota, which did not require reporting of tobacco use during pregnancy]

Smoking measure and race of mother	Total	Years of school completed by mother					
		0-8 years	9-11 years	12 years	13-15 years	16 years or more	Not stated
All races [1]	**3,124,110**	**148,048**	**493,433**	**1,030,964**	**690,118**	**714,838**	**46,709**
White	2,444,987	124,740	342,637	782,868	544,288	618,550	31,904
Black	539,157	16,338	132,643	205,543	118,926	55,076	10,631
PERCENT DISTRIBUTION							
All races smoker	100.0	100.0	100.0	100.0	100.0	100.0	100.0
10 cigarettes or less	67.9	62.6	67.5	67.3	69.8	74.8	68.5
11-20 cigarettes	28.1	30.9	28.1	28.9	26.9	22.7	27.1
21 cigarettes or more.	4.0	6.5	4.4	3.8	3.3	2.5	4.4
White smoker	100.0	100.0	100.0	100.0	100.0	100.0	100.0
10 cigarettes or less	65.4	60.3	64.1	65.1	67.9	73.9	65.3
11-20 cigarettes	30.3	32.7	31.1	30.9	28.6	23.5	29.7
21 cigarettes or more.	4.3	7.0	4.9	4.0	3.5	2.6	5.0
Black smoker.	100.0	100.0	100.0	100.0	100.0	100.0	100.0
10 cigarettes or less	82.2	78.8	82.0	82.6	83.3	83.9	77.8
11-20 cigarettes	15.6	17.6	15.7	15.3	15.4	14.5	19.7
21 cigarettes or more.	2.1	3.5	2.3	2.1	1.3	(B)	2.5

B Base data too small to meet statistical standards for reliability of a derived figure.   [1] Includes races other than White and Black.

No. 110. Percent Low Birthweight by Smoking Status, Age, and Race of Mother: 1997

[Low birthweight is defined as weight of less than 2,500 grams (5 lb. 8 oz.). Excludes California, Indiana, New York, and South Dakota, which did not require reporting of tobacco use during pregnancy]

Smoking status and race of mother	Age of mother									
	All ages	Under 15 years	15-19 years			20-24 years	25-29 years	30-34 years	35-39 years
			Total	15-17 years	18-19 years				
All races [1]	**7.8**	**14.2**	**9.9**	**10.7**	**9.4**	**7.7**	**6.8**	**7.1**	**8.6**
Smoker	12.1	15.7	11.4	12.1	11.1	10.4	11.4	13.6	16.8
Nonsmoker	7.1	13.9	9.5	10.5	9.0	7.1	6.2	6.4	7.5
White.	6.6	12.1	8.4	9.1	8.1	6.5	5.9	6.2	7.4
Smoker.	10.7	17.2	10.9	11.5	10.6	9.7	10.0	11.4	14.2
Nonsmoker	5.9	10.9	7.7	8.4	7.3	5.7	5.2	5.5	6.6
Black	13.1	16.3	13.4	14.0	12.9	12.0	12.4	13.8	16.2
Smoker.	21.3	(B)	16.4	16.9	16.1	16.2	21.7	26.1	28.8
Nonsmoker	12.2	16.3	13.1	13.8	12.6	11.5	11.3	11.9	13.7

B Base data too small to meet statistical standards of reliability.   [1] Includes races other than White and Black.

No. 111. Live Births—Drinking Status of Mother: 1997

[Excludes California, New York, and South Dakota, which did not require reporting of alcohol use during pregnancy]

Drinking status, drinking measure, and race of mother	Age of mother									
	All ages	Under 15 years	15-19 years	20-24 years	25-29 years	30-34 years	35-39 years	40-44 years	45-49 years	50-54 years
All races [1]	**3,880,894**	**10,121**	**483,220**	**942,048**	**1,069,436**	**886,798**	**409,710**	**76,084**	**3,333**	**144**
Nondrinker	3,259,763	8,660	412,852	797,272	902,990	741,220	334,044	60,128	2,506	91
Drinker.	27,498	18	1,856	4,556	6,557	8,001	5,183	991	36	-
White.	3,072,640	5,021	338,272	720,546	871,636	735,571	337,423	61,417	2,633	121
Nondrinker.	2,572,079	3,934	281,028	600,324	737,421	620,554	277,842	48,881	2,013	82
Drinker	20,064	7	1,348	3,511	4,556	5,884	3,956	772	30	-
Black	599,913	4,712	128,539	182,600	135,529	94,123	45,069	8,981	357	3
Nondrinker.	547,268	4,452	120,021	169,033	122,777	83,382	39,432	7,856	314	1
Drinker	6,553	10	393	1,131	1,758	1,921	1,125	209	6	-
American Indian. . . .	38,572	202	7,810	12,316	9,168	5,812	2,694	542	28	-
Nondrinker.	31,290	163	6,299	10,094	7,398	4,725	2,147	442	22	-
Drinker	647	1	97	168	181	132	63	5	-	-
Asian/Pacific Islander	169,769	186	8,599	26,586	53,103	51,292	24,524	5,144	315	20
Nondrinker.	109,126	111	5,504	17,821	35,394	32,559	14,623	2,949	157	8
Drinker	234	-	18	46	62	64	39	5	-	-

- Represents zero.   [1] Includes races other than White or Black. Includes unknown or not stated.

Source of Tables 109-111: U.S. National Center for Health Statistics, *National Vital Statistics Reports (NVSR)* (formerly *Monthly Vital Statistics Reports*).

Vital Statistics 81

No. 112. Abortions—Number, Rate, and Ratio by Race: 1975 to 1996

Year	All races — Women 15-44 years old (1,000)	Abortions Number (1,000)	Rate per 1,000 women	Ratio per 1,000 live births [1]	White — Women 15-44 years old (1,000)	Abortions Number (1,000)	Rate per 1,000 women	Ratio per 1,000 live births [1]	Black and other — Women 15-44 years old (1,000)	Abortions Number (1,000)	Rate per 1,000 women	Ratio per 1,000 live births [1]
1975 ..	47,606	1,034	21.7	331	40,857	701	17.2	276	6,749	333	49.3	565
1979 ..	52,016	1,498	28.8	420	44,266	1,062	24.0	373	7,750	435	56.2	625
1980 ..	53,048	1,554	29.3	428	44,942	1,094	24.3	376	8,106	460	56.5	642
1981 ..	53,901	1,577	29.3	430	45,494	1,108	24.3	377	8,407	470	55.9	645
1982 [2] .	54,679	1,574	28.8	428	46,049	1,095	23.8	373	8,630	479	55.5	646
1983 [2] .	55,340	1,575	28.5	436	46,506	1,084	23.3	376	8,834	491	55.5	670
1984 ..	56,061	1,577	28.1	423	47,023	1,087	23.1	366	9,038	491	54.3	646
1985 [2] .	56,754	1,589	28.0	422	47,512	1,076	22.6	360	9,242	513	55.5	659
1986 [2] .	57,483	1,574	27.4	416	48,010	1,045	21.8	350	9,473	529	55.9	661
1987 ..	57,964	1,559	27.1	405	48,288	1,017	21.1	338	9,676	542	56.0	648
1988 ..	58,192	1,591	27.3	401	48,325	1,026	21.2	333	9,867	565	57.3	638
1989 [2] .	58,365	1,567	26.8	380	48,104	1,006	20.9	309	10,261	561	54.7	650
1990 [2] .	58,700	1,609	27.4	389	48,224	1,039	21.5	318	10,476	570	54.4	655
1991 ..	59,080	1,557	26.3	379	48,406	982	20.3	303	10,674	574	53.8	661
1992 [2] .	59,020	1,529	25.9	380	48,161	943	19.6	298	10859	585	53.9	681
1993 [2] .	59,143	1,500	25.4	378	48,137	911	18.9	291	11,007	589	53.5	700
1994 [2] .	59,284	1,431	24.1	364	48,121	861	17.9	277	11,163	570	51.1	699
1995 ..	59,442	1,364	22.9	351	48,140	820	17.0	265	11,302	544	48.1	686
1996 ..	59,606	1,366	22.9	351	48,120	800	16.6	259	11,486	566	49.2	701

[1] Live births are those which occurred from July 1 of year shown through June 30 of the following year (to match time of conception with abortions). Births are classified by race of child 1972-1988, and by race of mother after 1988. [2] Total numbers of abortions in 1983 and 1986 have been estimated by interpolation; 1989, 1990, 1993, and 1994 have been estimated using trends in CDC data.

Source:1975-1988, S.K. Henshaw and J. Van Vort, eds., Abortion Factbook, 1992 Edition: Readings, Trends, and State and Local Data to 1988, The Alan Guttmacher Institute, New York, NY, 1992 (copyright); 1989-1992, S.K. Henshaw and J. Van Vort, "Abortion Services in the United States, 1991 and 1992, "Family Planning Perspectives, 26:100, 1994-95, unpublished data.

No. 113. Abortions by Selected Characteristics: 1990 to 1996

[Number of abortions from surveys conducted by source; characteristics from the U.S. Centers for Disease Control's (CDC) annual abortion surveillance summaries, with adjustments for changes in states reporting data to the CDC each year. Total number of abortions in 1990 have been estimated using trends in CDC data]

Characteristic	Number (1,000) 1990	1995	1996	Percent distribution 1990	1995	1996	Abortion ratio [1] 1990	1995	1996
Total abortions	1,609	1,364	1,366	100	100	100	280	260	260
Age of woman:									
Less than 15 years old	13	11	10	1	1	1	515	480	494
15 to 19 years old	351	264	264	22	19	19	403	348	351
20 to 24 years old	532	442	434	33	32	32	328	317	315
25 to 29 years old	360	308	318	22	23	23	224	225	228
30 to 34 years old	216	196	195	13	14	14	196	179	179
35 to 39 years old	108	110	112	7	8	8	249	220	216
40 years old and over.	29	32	33	2	2	2	354	310	301
Race of woman:									
White.	1,039	820	800	65	60	59	241	210	206
Black and other.	570	544	566	35	40	41	396	409	412
Marital status of woman: [2]									
Married	341	269	272	21	20	20	102	93	94
Unmarried	1,268	1,095	1,094	79	80	80	521	466	466
Number of prior live births:									
None.	780	614	599	49	45	44	316	277	273
One.	396	359	369	25	26	27	230	223	226
Two.	280	248	250	17	18	18	292	285	284
Three	102	95	96	6	7	7	279	284	284
Four or more.	50	48	50	3	4	4	223	228	236
Number of prior induced abortions:									
None.	891	721	715	55	53	52	(NA)	(NA)	(NA)
One.	443	383	382	28	28	28	(NA)	(NA)	(NA)
Two or more	275	260	268	17	19	20	(NA)	(NA)	(NA)
Weeks of gestation: [3]									
Less than 9 weeks.	817	728	739	51	53	54	(NA)	(NA)	(NA)
9 to 10 weeks.	418	317	310	26	23	23	(NA)	(NA)	(NA)
11 to 12 weeks	199	153	154	12	11	11	(NA)	(NA)	(NA)
13 weeks or more	175	166	163	11	12	12	(NA)	(NA)	(NA)

NA Not available. [1] Number of abortions per 1,000 abortions and live births. Live births are those which occurred from July 1 of year shown through June 30 of the following year (to match time of conception with abortions). [2] Separated women included with unmarried. [3] Data not exactly comparable with prior years because of a change in the method of calculation.

Source of Tables 112 and 113: 1975 1988, S.K. Henshaw and J. Van Vort, eds., Abortion Factbook, 1992 Edition: Readings, Trends, and State and Local Data to 1988, The Alan Guttmacher Institute, New York, NY, 1992 (copyright); S.K. Henshaw and J. Van Vort, Abortion Services in the United States, 1991 and 1992; Family Perspectives, 26:100, 1994; and unpublished data.

No. 114. Abortions—Number and Rate by State: 1992 and 1996

[Number of abortions from surveys of hospitals, clinics, and physicians identified as providers of abortion services conducted by The Alan Guttmacher Institute. Abortion rates are computed per 1,000 women 15 to 44 years of age on **July** 1 of specified year]

State	Number (1,000) 1992	1996	Rate [1] 1992	1996	State	Number (1,000) 1992	1996	Rate [1] 1992	1996
U.S.	**1,529**	**1,366**	**25.9**	**22.9**	MO	14	11	11.6	9.1
AL	17	15	18.2	15.6	MT	3	3	18.2	15.6
AK	2	2	16.5	14.6	NE	6	4	15.7	12.3
AZ	21	19	24.1	19.8	NV	13	15	44.2	44.6
AR	7	6	13.5	11.4	NH	4	3	14.6	12.7
CA	304	238	42.1	33.0	NJ	55	63	31.0	35.8
CO	20	18	23.6	20.9	NM	6	5	17.7	14.4
CT	20	16	26.2	22.5	NY	195	168	46.2	41.1
DE	6	4	35.2	24.1	NC	36	34	22.4	20.2
DC	21	21	138.4	154.5	ND	1	1	10.7	9.4
FL	85	94	30.0	32.0	OH	50	43	19.5	17.0
GA	40	37	24.0	21.1	OK	9	8	12.5	11.8
HI	12	7	46.0	27.3	OR	16	15	23.9	21.6
ID	2	2	7.2	6.1	PA	50	40	18.6	15.2
IL	68	69	25.4	26.1	RI	7	5	30.0	24.4
IN	16	15	12.0	11.2	SC	12	10	14.2	11.6
IA	7	6	11.4	9.4	SD	1	1	6.8	6.5
KS	13	11	22.4	18.9	TN	19	18	16.2	14.8
KY	10	8	11.4	9.6	TX	97	91	23.1	20.7
LA	14	15	13.4	14.7	UT	4	4	9.3	7.8
ME	4	3	14.7	9.7	VT	3	2	21.2	17.1
MD	31	31	26.4	26.3	VA	35	30	22.7	18.9
MA	41	41	28.4	29.3	WA	33	26	27.7	20.9
MI	56	49	25.2	22.3	WV	3	3	7.7	6.6
MN	16	15	15.6	13.9	WI	15	14	13.6	12.3
MS	8	4	12.4	7.2	WY	-	-	4.3	2.7

- Represents or rounds to zero.   [1] Rate per 1,000 women, 15 to 44 years old.

Source: S.K. Henshaw and J. Van Vort, *Abortion Services in the United States, 1991 and 1992, Family Planning Perspectives*, 26:100, 1994; and unpublished data.

No. 115. Average Lifetime in Years by Race by State: 1989-91

State	Total	White	Black	State	Total	White	Black
U.S.	**75.37**	**76.13**	**69.16**	MT	76.23	76.72	(S)
AL	73.64	75.01	69.23	NE	76.92	77.21	(S)
AZ	76.10	76.42	70.84	NV	74.18	74.44	(S)
AR	74.33	75.20	68.93	NH	76.72	76.68	(S)
CA	75.86	75.92	69.65	NJ	75.42	76.46	68.47
CO	76.96	77.06	72.41				
				NM	75.74	76.08	(S)
CT	76.91	77.44	70.84	NY	74.68	75.61	69.33
DE	74.76	75.76	69.26	NC	74.48	75.89	69.38
DC	67.99	76.09	64.44	ND	77.62	77.99	(S)
FL	75.84	76.82	68.77	OH	75.32	75.93	70.15
GA	73.61	75.24	68.79				
				OK	75.10	75.21	70.85
HI	78.21	77.92	(S)	OR	76.44	76.51	(S)
ID	76.88	76.89	(S)	PA	75.38	76.15	68.27
IL	74.90	76.16	67.46	RI	76.54	76.80	(S)
IN	75.39	75.82	69.80	SC	73.51	75.33	68.82
IA	77.29	77.38	(S)				
				SD	76.91	77.91	(S)
KS	76.76	77.06	71.22	TN	74.32	75.27	68.97
KY	74.37	74.65	70.16	TX	75.14	75.75	69.79
LA	73.05	74.87	68.62	UT	77.70	77.77	(S)
ME	76.35	76.35	(S)	VT	76.54	76.50	(S)
MD	74.79	76.30	69.69				
				VA	75.22	76.34	70.05
MA	76.72	76.90	72.45	WA	76.82	76.92	71.34
MI	75.04	76.18	68.49	WV	74.26	74.37	69.75
MN	77.76	77.97	(S)	WI	76.87	77.18	70.96
MS	73.03	74.78	69.41	WY	76.21	76.34	(S)
MO	75.25	76.02	68.81				

S Does not meet standards of reliability and precision.

Source: U.S. National Center for Health Statistics, *U.S. Decennial Life Tables for 1989-91*, Volume II.

U.S. Census Bureau, Statistical Abstract of the United States: 2000

No. 116. Expectation of Life at Birth, 1970 to 1998, and Projections, 1999 to 2010

[**In years.** Excludes deaths of nonresidents of the United States]

Year	Total			White			Black and other			Black		
	Total	Male	Female	Total	Male	Female	Total	Male	Female	Total	Male	Female
1970	70.8	67.1	74.7	71.7	68.0	75.6	65.3	61.3	69.4	64.1	60.0	68.3
1975	72.6	68.8	76.6	73.4	69.5	77.3	68.0	63.7	72.4	66.8	62.4	71.3
1980	73.7	70.0	77.4	74.4	70.7	78.1	69.5	65.3	73.6	68.1	63.8	72.5
1982	74.5	70.8	78.1	75.1	71.5	78.7	70.9	66.8	74.9	69.4	65.1	73.6
1983	74.6	71.0	78.1	75.2	71.6	78.7	70.9	67.0	74.7	69.4	65.2	73.5
1984	74.7	71.1	78.2	75.3	71.8	78.7	71.1	67.2	74.9	69.5	65.3	73.6
1985	74.7	71.1	78.2	75.3	71.8	78.7	71.0	67.0	74.8	69.3	65.0	73.4
1986	74.7	71.2	78.2	75.4	71.9	78.8	70.9	66.8	74.9	69.1	64.8	73.4
1987	74.9	71.4	78.3	75.6	72.1	78.9	71.0	66.9	75.0	69.1	64.7	73.4
1988	74.9	71.4	78.3	75.6	72.2	78.9	70.8	66.7	74.8	68.9	64.4	73.2
1989	75.1	71.7	78.5	75.9	72.5	79.2	70.9	66.7	74.9	68.8	64.3	73.3
1990	75.4	71.8	78.8	76.1	72.7	79.4	71.2	67.0	75.2	69.1	64.5	73.6
1991	75.5	72.0	78.9	76.3	72.9	79.6	71.5	67.3	75.5	69.3	64.6	73.8
1992	75.8	72.3	79.1	76.5	73.2	79.8	71.8	67.7	75.7	69.6	65.0	73.9
1993	75.5	72.2	78.8	76.3	73.1	79.5	71.5	67.3	75.5	69.2	64.6	73.7
1994	75.7	72.3	79.0	76.4	73.2	79.6	71.7	67.5	75.8	69.6	64.9	74.1
1995	75.8	72.5	78.9	76.5	73.4	79.6	71.9	67.9	75.7	69.6	65.2	73.9
1996	76.1	73.0	79.0	76.8	73.8	79.6	72.6	68.9	76.1	70.3	66.1	74.2
1997	76.5	73.6	79.4	77.1	74.3	79.9	(NA)	(NA)	(NA)	71.1	67.2	74.7
1998, prel [1]	76.7	73.9	79.4	77.3	74.6	79.9	(NA)	(NA)	(NA)	71.5	67.8	75.0
Projections: [2]												
1999	77.0	74.1	79.7	77.5	74.7	80.2	(NA)	(NA)	(NA)	72.2	68.7	75.4
2000	77.1	74.2	79.9	77.7	74.8	80.4	(NA)	(NA)	(NA)	72.4	68.9	75.6
2005	77.8	74.9	80.7	78.3	75.4	81.1	(NA)	(NA)	(NA)	73.5	69.9	76.8
2010	78.5	75.6	81.4	79.0	76.1	81.8	(NA)	(NA)	(NA)	74.5	70.9	77.8

NA Not available.   [1] The 1998 life table values are based upon an 85 percent sample of deaths.   [2] Based on middle mortality assumptions; for details, see source. Source: U.S. Census Bureau, Population Division Working Paper No. 38.

Source: Except as noted, U.S. National Center for Health Statistics, *Vital Statistics of the United States*, annual, and *National Vital Statistics Reports (NVSR)* (formerly *Monthly Vital Statistics Reports*).

No. 117. Selected Life Table Values: 1979 to 1998

Age and sex	Total [1]			White			Black		
	1979-1981	1990	1998	1979-1981	1990	1998	1979-1981	1990	1998
AVERAGE EXPECTATION OF LIFE IN YEARS									
At birth: Male	70.1	71.8	73.9	70.8	72.7	74.6	64.1	64.5	67.8
Female	77.6	78.8	79.4	78.2	79.4	79.9	72.9	73.6	75.0
Age 20: Male	51.9	53.3	55.0	52.5	54.0	55.5	46.4	46.7	49.6
Female	59.0	59.8	60.3	59.4	60.3	60.7	54.9	55.3	56.3
Age 40: Male	33.6	35.1	36.5	34.0	35.6	36.8	29.5	30.1	32.0
Female	39.8	40.6	41.0	40.2	41.0	41.3	36.3	36.8	37.6
Age 50: Male	25.0	26.4	27.6	25.3	26.7	27.9	22.0	22.5	24.1
Female	30.7	31.3	31.7	31.0	31.6	32.0	27.8	28.2	28.9
Age 65: Male	14.2	15.1	16.0	14.3	15.2	16.1	13.3	13.2	14.4
Female	18.4	18.9	19.1	18.6	19.1	19.2	17.1	17.2	17.5
EXPECTED DEATHS PER 1,000 ALIVE AT SPECIFIED AGE [2]									
At birth: Male	13.9	10.3	(NA)	12.3	8.6	(NA)	23.0	19.7	(NA)
Female	11.2	8.2	(NA)	9.7	6.6	(NA)	19.3	16.3	(NA)
Age 20: Male	1.8	1.6	(NA)	1.8	1.4	(NA)	2.2	2.7	(NA)
Female	0.6	0.5	(NA)	0.6	0.5	(NA)	0.7	0.7	(NA)
Age 40: Male	3.0	3.1	(NA)	2.6	2.7	(NA)	6.9	7.1	(NA)
Female	1.6	1.4	(NA)	1.4	1.2	(NA)	3.2	3.1	(NA)
Age 50: Male	7.8	6.2	(NA)	7.1	5.6	(NA)	14.9	12.8	(NA)
Female	4.2	3.5	(NA)	3.8	3.2	(NA)	7.7	6.6	(NA)
Age 65: Male	28.2	12.9	(NA)	27.4	23.0	(NA)	38.5	36.8	(NA)
Female	14.3	13.5	(NA)	13.6	12.8	(NA)	21.6	21.4	(NA)
NUMBER SURVIVING TO SPECIFIED AGE PER 1,000 BORN ALIVE									
Age 20: Male	973	979	(NA)	975	981	(NA)	961	963	(NA)
Female	982	986	(NA)	984	988	(NA)	972	976	(NA)
Age 40: Male	933	938	(NA)	940	946	(NA)	885	880	(NA)
Female	965	971	(NA)	969	975	(NA)	941	944	(NA)
Age 50: Male	890	899	(NA)	901	912	(NA)	801	801	(NA)
Female	941	950	(NA)	947	957	(NA)	896	904	(NA)
Age 65: Male	706	741	(NA)	724	760	(NA)	551	571	(NA)
Female	835	851	(NA)	848	864	(NA)	733	751	(NA)

NA Not available.   [1] Includes other races not shown separately. [2] See footnote 1, Table 118.

Source: U.S. National Center for Health Statistics, *U.S. Life Tables and Actuarial Tables, 1959-61, 1969-71, and 1979-81; Vital Statistics of the United States*, annual; and unpublished data.

84   Vital Statistics

No. 118. Expectation of Life and Expected Deaths by Race, Sex, and Age: 1997

Age (years)	Expectation of life in years					Expected deaths per 1,000 alive at specified age [1]				
		White		Black			White		Black	
	Total	Male	Female	Male	Female	Total	Male	Female	Male	Female
At birth	76.5	74.3	79.9	67.2	74.7	7.23	6.67	5.36	15.49	12.83
1	76.1	73.8	79.3	67.2	74.7	0.55	0.53	0.45	1.05	0.80
2	75.1	72.8	78.4	66.3	73.8	0.36	0.36	0.27	0.69	0.55
3	74.1	71.9	77.4	65.3	72.8	0.29	0.29	0.23	0.58	0.39
4	73.2	70.9	76.4	64.4	71.8	0.23	0.23	0.17	0.39	0.32
5	72.2	69.9	75.4	63.4	70.9	0.21	0.20	0.16	0.38	0.33
6	71.2	68.9	74.4	62.4	69.9	0.20	0.19	0.15	0.35	0.31
7	70.2	67.9	73.4	61.4	68.9	0.19	0.19	0.14	0.32	0.29
8	69.2	66.9	72.4	60.5	67.9	0.17	0.17	0.13	0.28	0.26
9	68.2	66.0	71.4	59.5	66.9	0.15	0.15	0.12	0.23	0.24
10	67.2	65.0	70.5	58.5	66.0	0.14	0.13	0.12	0.18	0.23
11	66.2	64.0	69.5	57.5	65.0	0.14	0.14	0.12	0.18	0.22
12	65.3	63.0	68.5	56.5	64.0	0.19	0.20	0.15	0.28	0.23
13	64.3	62.0	67.5	55.5	63.0	0.28	0.33	0.20	0.49	0.27
14	63.3	61.0	66.5	54.5	62.0	0.41	0.50	0.26	0.79	0.32
15	62.3	60.0	65.5	53.6	61.0	0.55	0.68	0.34	1.11	0.38
16	61.3	59.1	64.5	52.6	60.1	0.68	0.85	0.41	1.40	0.44
17	60.4	58.1	63.6	51.7	59.1	0.78	0.99	0.46	1.67	0.50
18	59.4	57.2	62.6	50.8	58.1	0.85	1.07	0.47	1.92	0.54
19	58.5	56.3	61.6	49.9	57.1	0.89	1.13	0.46	2.15	0.59
20	57.5	55.3	60.7	49.0	56.2	0.93	1.18	0.45	2.41	0.64
21	56.6	54.4	59.7	48.1	55.2	0.98	1.24	0.45	2.68	0.70
22	55.6	53.4	58.7	47.3	54.3	1.01	1.28	0.44	2.87	0.76
23	54.7	52.5	57.7	46.4	53.3	1.01	1.28	0.45	2.94	0.83
24	53.8	51.6	56.8	45.5	52.3	1.01	1.26	0.46	2.92	0.89
25	52.8	50.6	55.8	44.7	51.4	1.00	1.24	0.47	2.85	0.96
26	51.9	49.7	54.8	43.8	50.4	0.99	1.22	0.48	2.81	1.04
27	50.9	48.8	53.8	42.9	49.5	1.00	1.22	0.50	2.81	1.11
28	50.0	47.8	52.9	42.0	48.5	1.03	1.26	0.52	2.85	1.18
29	49.0	46.9	51.9	41.1	47.6	1.08	1.32	0.56	2.94	1.26
30	48.1	45.9	50.9	40.3	46.7	1.14	1.39	0.59	3.04	1.33
31	47.1	45.0	49.9	39.4	45.7	1.19	1.46	0.63	3.14	1.41
32	46.2	44.1	49.0	38.5	44.8	1.26	1.53	0.68	3.27	1.53
33	45.2	43.1	48.0	37.6	43.8	1.33	1.60	0.73	3.43	1.68
34	44.3	42.2	47.0	36.8	42.9	1.40	1.68	0.78	3.62	1.85
35	43.4	41.3	46.1	35.9	42.0	1.49	1.75	0.84	3.83	2.04
36	42.4	40.4	45.1	35.0	41.1	1.57	1.83	0.90	4.06	2.22
37	41.5	39.4	44.2	34.2	40.2	1.67	1.94	0.97	4.31	2.40
38	40.5	38.5	43.2	33.3	39.3	1.78	2.06	1.04	4.60	2.57
39	39.6	37.6	42.2	32.5	38.4	1.92	2.21	1.13	4.94	2.75
40	38.7	36.7	41.3	31.6	37.5	2.06	2.38	1.23	5.29	2.93
41	37.8	35.8	40.3	30.8	36.6	2.22	2.56	1.34	5.68	3.14
42	36.9	34.8	39.4	30.0	35.7	2.39	2.76	1.45	6.15	3.37
43	35.9	33.9	38.5	29.1	34.8	2.57	2.97	1.57	6.72	3.64
44	35.0	33.0	37.5	28.3	33.9	2.78	3.19	1.69	7.38	3.94
45	34.1	32.1	36.6	27.5	33.1	3.00	3.44	1.83	8.15	4.29
46	33.2	31.2	35.6	26.8	32.2	3.25	3.72	2.00	8.97	4.65
47	32.3	30.4	34.7	26.0	31.4	3.52	4.02	2.19	9.74	5.02
48	31.5	29.5	33.8	25.3	30.5	3.80	4.35	2.41	10.40	5.37
49	30.6	28.6	32.9	24.5	29.7	4.11	4.71	2.67	10.98	5.73
50	29.7	27.7	32.0	23.8	28.8	4.44	5.12	2.96	11.61	6.13
51	28.8	26.9	31.0	23.1	28.0	4.82	5.57	3.27	12.38	6.61
52	28.0	26.0	30.1	22.3	27.2	5.24	6.05	3.61	13.25	7.15
53	27.1	25.2	29.3	21.6	26.4	5.71	6.59	3.96	14.22	7.73
54	26.3	24.4	28.4	20.9	25.6	6.23	7.19	4.36	15.26	8.34
55	25.4	23.5	27.5	20.3	24.8	6.85	7.90	4.82	16.30	8.96
56	24.6	22.7	26.6	19.6	24.0	7.55	8.74	5.36	17.40	9.63
57	23.8	21.9	25.8	18.9	23.3	8.33	9.68	5.95	18.72	10.42
58	23.0	21.1	24.9	18.3	22.5	9.16	10.68	6.56	20.34	11.36
59	22.2	20.3	24.1	17.6	21.8	10.05	11.76	7.20	22.25	12.46
60	21.4	19.6	23.2	17.0	21.0	11.01	12.91	7.91	24.43	13.71
61	20.6	18.8	22.4	16.4	20.3	12.08	14.20	8.71	26.64	15.00
62	19.9	18.1	21.6	15.9	19.6	13.21	15.65	9.56	28.53	16.18
63	19.1	17.4	20.8	15.3	18.9	14.39	17.24	10.45	29.81	17.10
64	18.4	16.7	20.0	14.8	18.2	15.60	18.94	11.37	30.63	17.85
65	17.7	16.0	19.3	14.2	17.6	16.79	20.63	12.29	31.09	18.42
70	14.3	12.7	15.5	11.5	14.3	25.65	32.00	19.24	44.61	28.83
75	11.2	9.9	12.1	9.3	11.5	38.43	47.96	30.21	62.78	40.68
80	8.5	7.4	9.1	7.3	8.9	59.38	74.08	49.39	85.45	58.43
85 and over . .	6.3	5.4	6.6	5.7	6.7	1,000.00	1,000.00	1,000.00	1,000.00	1,000.00

[1] Based on the proportion of the cohort who are alive at the beginning of an indicated age interval who will die before reaching the end of that interval. For example, out of every 1,000 people alive and exactly 50 years old at the beginning of the period, between 4 and 5 (4.44) will die before reaching their 51st birthdays.

Source: U.S. National Center for Health Statistics, *Vital Statistics of the United States*, annual; and *National Vital Statistics Report*, Vol. 47, No. 28; and unpublished data.

Vital Statistics   85

No. 119. Deaths and Death Rates by Sex and Race: 1980 to 1998

[1,990 represents 1,990,000. **Rates are per 1,000 population for specified groups.** Excludes deaths of nonresidents of the United States and fetal deaths. For explanation of age-adjustment, see text, this section. The standard population for this table is the total population of the United States enumerated in 1940. See Appendix III]

Sex and race	1980	1985	1989	1990	1991	1992	1993	1994	1995	1996	1997	1998
Deaths [1] (1,000)	**1,990**	**2,086**	**2,150**	**2,148**	**2,170**	**2,176**	**2,269**	**2,286**	**2,312**	**2,315**	**2,314**	**2,338**
Male [1] (1,000)	1,075	1,098	1,114	1,113	1,122	1,122	1,162	1,163	1,173	1,164	1,154	1,156
Female [1] (1,000)	915	989	1,036	1,035	1,048	1,053	1,107	1,116	1,139	1,151	1,160	1,182
White (1,000)	1,739	1,819	1,854	1,853	1,869	1,874	1,951	1,960	1,987	1,993	1,996	2,020
Male (1,000)	934	950	951	951	956	957	988	989	997	992	987	991
Female (1,000)	805	869	903	902	912	917	963	971	990	1,001	1,010	1,029
Black (1,000)	233	244	268	266	270	269	282	282	286	282	277	275
Male (1,000)	130	134	146	145	147	147	154	153	154	149	144	142
Female (1,000)	103	111	121	120	122	123	129	129	132	133	132	134
Death rates [1]	**8.8**	**8.8**	**8.7**	**8.6**	**8.6**	**8.5**	**8.8**	**8.8**	**8.8**	**8.7**	**8.6**	**8.7**
Male [1]	9.8	9.5	9.3	9.2	9.1	9.0	9.2	9.2	9.1	9.0	8.8	8.8
Female [1]	7.9	8.1	8.2	8.1	8.1	8.1	8.4	8.4	8.5	8.5	8.5	8.6
White	8.9	9.0	8.9	8.9	8.9	8.8	9.1	9.1	9.1	9.1	9.0	9.1
Male	9.8	9.6	9.4	9.3	9.3	9.2	9.4	9.3	9.3	9.2	9.1	9.0
Female	8.1	8.4	8.5	8.5	8.5	8.4	8.8	8.8	8.9	9.0	9.0	9.1
Black	8.8	8.5	8.9	8.8	8.6	8.5	8.8	8.8	8.6	8.4	8.1	8.0
Male	10.3	9.9	10.3	10.1	10.0	9.8	10.1	9.9	9.8	9.4	8.9	8.7
Female	7.3	7.3	7.6	7.5	7.4	7.4	7.6	7.5	7.6	7.5	7.4	7.4
Age-adjusted death rates [1]	**5.9**	**5.5**	**5.3**	**5.2**	**5.1**	**5.0**	**5.1**	**5.1**	**5.0**	**4.9**	**4.8**	**4.7**
Male [1]	7.8	7.2	6.9	6.8	6.7	6.6	6.6	6.5	6.5	6.2	6.0	5.9
Female [1]	4.3	4.1	4.0	3.9	3.9	3.8	3.9	3.9	3.9	3.8	3.8	3.7
White	5.6	5.2	5.0	4.9	4.9	4.8	4.9	4.8	4.8	4.7	4.6	4.5
Male	7.5	6.9	6.5	6.4	6.3	6.2	6.3	6.2	6.1	5.9	5.7	5.6
Female	4.1	3.9	3.8	3.7	3.7	3.6	3.7	3.6	3.6	3.6	3.6	3.6
Black	8.4	7.9	8.1	7.9	7.8	7.7	7.9	7.7	7.7	7.4	7.1	6.8
Male	11.1	10.5	10.8	10.6	10.5	10.3	10.5	10.3	10.2	9.7	9.1	8.7
Female	6.3	5.9	5.9	5.8	5.8	5.7	5.8	5.7	5.7	5.6	5.5	5.4

[1] Includes other races, not shown separately.

Source: U.S. National Center for Health Statistics, *Vital Statistics of the United States,* annual; and *National Vital Statistics Reports (NVSR)* (formerly *Monthly Vital Statistics Report*).

No. 120. Death Rates by Age, Sex, and Race: 1980 to 1998

[**Number of deaths per 100,000 population in specified group.** See headnote, Table 119]

Sex, year, and race	All ages [1]	Under 1 yr. old	1-4 yr. old	5-14 yr. old	15-24 yr. old	25-34 yr. old	35-44 yr. old	45-54 yr. old	55-64 yr. old	65-74 yr. old	75-84 yr. old	85 yr. old and over
MALE [2]												
1980	977	1,429	73	37	172	196	299	767	1,815	4,105	8,817	18,801
1990	918	1,083	52	29	147	204	310	610	1,553	3,492	7,889	18,057
1995	914	844	45	27	141	205	333	599	1,417	3,285	7,377	17,979
1997	881	813	40	24	124	160	266	551	1,337	3,191	7,116	17,462
1998	876	822	38	23	118	150	256	539	1,293	3,138	7,038	16,827
White:												
1980	983	1,230	66	35	167	171	257	699	1,729	4,036	8,830	19,097
1990	931	896	46	26	131	176	268	549	1,467	3,398	7,845	18,268
1995	932	718	39	25	122	178	288	535	1,331	3,199	7,321	18,153
1997	906	678	35	22	109	140	235	496	1,252	3,123	7,086	17,767
1998	905	682	32	21	106	133	231	486	1,216	3,082	7,012	17,122
Black:												
1980	1,034	2,587	111	47	209	407	690	1,480	2,873	5,131	9,232	16,099
1990	1,008	2,112	86	41	252	431	700	1,261	2,618	4,946	9,130	16,955
1995	981	1,591	78	40	249	417	721	1,273	2,438	4,611	8,779	16,729
1997	894	1,672	67	35	216	309	524	1,114	2,320	4,298	8,297	16,084
1998	868	1,693	69	35	194	277	475	1,074	2,238	4,136	8,259	15,442
FEMALE [2]												
1980	785	1,142	55	24	58	76	159	413	934	2,145	5,440	14,747
1990	812	856	41	19	49	74	138	343	879	1,991	4,883	14,274
1995	847	690	36	18	48	78	150	328	841	1,986	4,883	14,492
1997	849	661	32	17	46	70	141	316	815	1,959	4,821	14,492
1998	855	684	31	16	43	68	140	307	787	1,970	4,846	14,494
White:												
1980	806	963	49	23	56	65	138	373	876	2,067	5,402	14,980
1990	847	690	36	18	46	62	117	309	823	1,924	4,839	14,401
1995	891	572	31	17	44	64	126	294	788	1,925	4,831	14,639
1997	898	546	28	16	44	60	121	285	766	1,901	4,786	14,681
1998	907	571	27	15	41	58	121	277	740	1,918	4,816	14,705
Black:												
1980	733	2,124	84	31	71	150	324	768	1,561	3,057	6,212	12,367
1990	748	1,736	68	28	69	160	299	639	1,453	2,866	5,688	13,310
1995	759	1,342	63	27	70	167	328	619	1,350	2,824	5,840	13,472
1997	743	1,384	51	27	62	135	287	590	1,307	2,740	5,669	13,702
1998	738	1,363	54	23	57	128	280	574	1,262	2,702	5,748	13,450

[1] Includes unknown age. [2] Includes other races not shown separately.

Source: U.S. National Center for Health Statistics, *Vital Statistics of the United States,* annual; *National Vital Statistics Reports (NVSR)* (formerly *Monthly Vital Statistics Report*); and unpublished data.

No. 121. Deaths and Death Rates by State: 1990 to 1998

[By state of residence. Excludes deaths of nonresidents of the United States, except as noted. Caution should be used in comparing death rates by state; rates are affected by the population composition of the area. See also Appendix III]

State	Number of deaths (1,000)							Rate per 1,000 population [1]						
	1990	1993	1994	1995	1996	1997	1998	1990	1993	1994	1995	1996	1997	1998
United States..	2,148	2,269	2,279	2,312	2,315	2,314	2,338	8.6	8.8	8.8	8.8	8.7	8.6	8.7
Alabama.........	39	41	42	42	43	43	44	9.7	9.9	9.9	10.0	10.0	10.0	10.1
Alaska	2	2	2	3	3	3	3	4.0	3.8	4.0	4.2	4.3	4.2	4.2
Arizona.........	29	33	34	35	37	37	38	7.9	8.2	8.4	8.4	8.3	8.1	8.2
Arkansas	25	27	26	27	27	28	28	10.5	10.9	10.7	10.8	10.6	11.0	10.8
California	214	222	224	224	223	225	227	7.2	7.0	7.1	7.1	7.0	7.0	6.9
Colorado........	22	24	24	25	26	26	27	6.6	6.7	6.6	6.7	6.7	6.6	6.7
Connecticut......	28	29	29	29	30	29	30	8.4	8.9	8.9	9.0	9.0	9.0	9.1
Delaware	6	6	6	6	7	7	7	8.7	8.7	9.0	8.8	9.0	8.9	8.9
Dist. of Columbia ...	7	7	7	7	7	6	6	12.0	11.6	12.6	12.4	12.2	11.6	11.4
Florida	134	147	149	153	153	155	158	10.4	10.7	10.7	10.8	10.7	10.5	10.6
Georgia	52	56	57	58	59	59	60	8.0	8.1	8.0	8.1	8.0	7.9	7.9
Hawaii	7	7	7	8	8	8	8	6.1	6.2	6.2	6.4	6.7	6.7	6.8
Idaho...........	7	8	8	9	9	9	9	7.4	7.6	7.5	7.3	7.3	7.4	7.5
Illinois	103	107	107	108	106	103	105	9.0	9.2	9.1	9.2	9.0	8.7	8.7
Indiana.........	50	52	52	53	53	53	53	8.9	9.1	9.1	9.2	9.1	9.1	8.9
Iowa	27	28	28	28	28	28	28	9.7	9.9	9.8	9.9	9.8	9.7	9.9
Kentucky	35	37	37	37	37	38	38	9.5	9.7	9.7	9.6	9.6	9.7	9.6
Louisiana	38	40	39	40	40	40	40	8.9	9.3	9.0	9.1	9.1	9.2	9.2
Maine...........	11	12	12	12	11	12	12	9.0	9.3	9.4	9.5	9.4	9.7	9.8
Maryland	38	40	41	42	42	42	42	8.0	8.7	8.2	8.3	8.3	8.2	8.2
Massachusetts.....	53	56	55	55	55	55	55	8.8	9.4	9.1	9.1	9.1	8.9	9.0
Michigan........	79	83	83	84	84	83	85	8.5	8.7	8.7	8.8	8.7	8.5	8.7
Minnesota.......	35	36	37	38	37	37	37	7.9	8.0	8.0	8.1	8.0	7.9	7.9
Mississippi	25	26	27	27	27	28	28	9.8	10.1	10.0	10.0	9.8	10.1	10.1
Missouri	50	54	54	54	54	54	55	9.8	10.8	10.2	10.2	10.1	10.1	10.1
Montana........	7	7	7	8	8	8	8	8.6	8.9	8.6	8.8	8.8	8.8	9.0
Nebraska	15	15	15	15	15	15	15	9.4	9.6	9.3	9.3	9.4	9.2	9.1
Nevada	9	11	12	13	13	13	14	7.8	7.8	8.2	8.2	8.2	8.0	8.3
New Hampshire	8	9	9	9	9	9	10	7.7	7.9	7.8	8.0	8.1	8.1	8.1
New Jersey.......	70	73	72	74	73	72	71	9.1	9.2	9.1	9.3	9.2	9.0	8.8
New Mexico	11	12	12	13	12	13	13	7.0	7.3	7.3	7.4	7.3	7.3	7.7
New York	169	171	169	168	164	159	157	9.4	9.4	9.3	9.3	9.0	8.7	8.6
North Carolina.....	57	62	63	65	66	66	68	8.6	9.0	8.9	9.0	9.1	8.9	9.0
North Dakota......	6	6	6	6	6	6	6	8.9	9.3	9.2	9.3	9.3	9.2	9.3
Ohio	99	103	103	106	105	105	106	9.1	9.1	9.3	9.5	9.4	9.4	9.5
Oklahoma........	30	32	32	33	33	34	34	9.7	10.1	9.9	10.0	10.0	10.2	10.2
Oregon..........	25	28	27	28	29	29	29	8.8	9.0	8.9	9.0	9.0	8.9	9.0
Pennsylvania.....	122	126	128	128	129	128	127	10.3	10.5	10.6	10.6	10.7	10.6	10.6
Rhode Island......	10	10	9	10	10	10	10	9.5	9.7	9.4	9.8	9.6	9.9	9.7
South Carolina.....	30	32	32	34	34	34	35	8.5	8.6	8.8	9.1	9.2	9.0	9.1
South Dakota	6	7	7	7	7	7	7	9.1	9.6	9.4	9.5	9.3	9.3	9.3
Tennessee	46	49	51	51	51	53	54	9.5	9.7	9.8	9.8	9.7	9.8	10.0
Texas...........	125	135	136	138	140	143	142	7.4	7.5	7.4	7.4	7.3	7.3	7.2
Utah	9	10	10	11	11	12	12	5.3	5.5	5.5	5.6	5.6	5.6	5.6
Vermont	5	5	5	5	5	5	5	8.2	8.5	8.2	8.5	8.3	8.6	8.4
Virginia.........	48	52	52	53	54	54	55	7.8	8.0	8.0	8.0	8.0	8.0	8.0
Washington......	37	40	40	41	42	41	43	7.6	8.0	7.5	7.5	7.6	7.4	7.5
West Virginia......	19	20	20	20	20	21	21	10.8	11.0	11.1	11.1	11.2	11.5	11.5
Wisconsin........	43	45	44	45	45	45	46	8.7	8.7	8.7	8.8	8.7	8.7	8.8
Wyoming	3	3	3	4	4	4	4	7.1	7.5	7.3	7.7	7.5	7.8	8.0
Puerto Rico.......	(NA)	(NA)	(NA)	(NA)	(NA)	29	29	(NA)	(NA)	(NA)	(NA)	(NA)	7.6	7.5
Virgin Islands......	(NA)	(NA)	(NA)	(NA)	(NA)	1	1	(NA)	(NA)	(NA)	(NA)	(NA)	5.4	5.3
Guam	(NA)	(NA)	(NA)	(NA)	(NA)	1	1	(NA)	(NA)	(NA)	(NA)	(NA)	4.2	4.2

NA Not available. [1] Rates based on enumerated resident population as of April 1 for 1990; estimated resident population as of July 1 for all other years.

Source: U.S. National Center for Health Statistics, *Vital Statistics of the United States*, annual; *National Vital Statistics Reports (NVSR)* (formerly *Monthly Vital Statistics Report*).

Vital Statistics 87

No. 122. Infant, Maternal, and Neonatal Mortality Rates and Fetal Mortality Ratios by Race: 1980 to 1998

[Deaths per 1,000 live births, except as noted. Excludes deaths of nonresidents of U.S. Race for live births tabulated according to race of mother, for infant and neonatal mortality rates. Beginning 1989, race for live births tabulated according to race of mother, for maternal mortality rates and mortality rates. See also Appendix III]

Item	1980	1990	1993	1994	1995	1996	1997	1998
Infant deaths [1]...............	12.6	9.2	8.4	8.0	7.6	7.3	7.2	7.2
White......................	10.9	7.6	6.8	6.6	6.3	6.0	6.0	6.0
Black and other..............	20.2	15.5	14.1	13.5	(NA)	(NA)	(NA)	(NA)
Black	22.2	18.0	16.5	15.8	15.1	14.2	13.7	14.1
Maternal deaths [2]	9.2	8.2	7.5	8.3	7.1	7.6	8.4	(NA)
White......................	6.7	5.4	4.8	6.2	4.2	5.1	5.8	(NA)
Black and other..............	19.8	19.1	17.6	16.2	18.5	16.9	18.3	(NA)
Black	21.5	22.4	20.5	18.5	22.1	20.3	20.8	(NA)
Fetal deaths [3]	9.2	7.5	(NA)	(NA)	(NA)	(NA)	(NA)	(NA)
White......................	8.2	6.4	(NA)	(NA)	(NA)	(NA)	(NA)	(NA)
Black and other..............	13.4	11.9	(NA)	(NA)	(NA)	(NA)	(NA)	(NA)
Neonatal deaths [4]	8.5	5.8	5.3	5.1	4.9	4.7	4.7	(NA)
White......................	7.4	4.8	4.3	4.2	4.1	3.9	3.9	(NA)
Black and other..............	13.2	9.9	9.0	8.6	(NA)	(NA)	(NA)	(NA)
Black	14.6	11.6	10.7	10.2	9.8	9.2	9.0	(NA)

NA Not available. [1] Represents deaths of infants under 1 year old, exclusive of fetal deaths. [2] Per 100,000 live births from deliveries and complications of pregnancy, childbirth, and the puerperium. Deaths are classified according to the ninth revision of the *International Classification of Diseases*; earlier years classified according to the revision in use at the time; see text, Section 2. [3] Includes only those deaths with stated or presumed period of gestation of 20 weeks or more. [4] Represents deaths of infants under 28 days old, exclusive of fetal deaths.

No. 123. Fetal and Infant Deaths—Number and Percent Distribution: 1980 to 1993

[State requirements for reporting of fetal deaths vary. Most states require reporting of fetal deaths of gestations of 20 weeks or more. There is substantial evidence that not all fetal deaths for which reporting is required are reported. For details of methodology, see Appendix III and source]

Year	Number					Percent distribution				
	Fetal deaths		Infant deaths			Fetal deaths		Infant deaths		
			Neonatal		Post-neo-natal [5]			Neonatal		Post-neo-natal [5]
	Total	Early [1]	Late [2]	Early [3]	Late [4]	Total	Early [1]	Late [2]	Early [3]	Late [4]
1980	78,879	10,754	22,599	25,492	5,126	14,908	100.0	13.6	28.7	32.3	6.5	18.9
1985	69,691	10,958	18,703	21,865	4,314	13,851	100.0	15.7	26.8	31.4	6.2	19.9
1986	67,863	11,100	17,872	21,053	4,159	13,679	100.0	16.4	26.3	31.0	6.1	20.2
1987	67,757	11,656	17,693	20,471	4,156	13,781	100.0	17.2	26.1	30.2	6.1	20.3
1988	68,352	11,833	17,609	20,471	4,219	14,220	100.0	17.3	25.8	29.9	6.2	20.8
1989	70,124	12,397	18,072	20,796	4,372	14,487	100.0	17.7	25.8	29.7	6.2	20.7
1990	67,696	12,554	16,791	20,020	4,289	14,042	100.0	18.5	24.8	29.6	6.3	20.7
1991	65,000	12,310	15,924	18,916	4,062	13,788	100.0	18.9	24.5	29.1	6.2	21.2
1992	63,153	12,704	15,821	17,798	4,051	12,779	100.0	20.1	25.1	28.2	6.4	21.8
1993	55,387	12,588	14,243	(NA)	(NA)	(NA)	100.0	22.7	25.7	(NA)	(NA)	(NA)

NA Not available. [1] 20-27 weeks gestation. [2] 28 weeks or more gestation. [3] Less than 7 days. [4] 7-27 days. [5] 28 days-11 months.

No. 124. Infant Deaths and Infant Mortality Rates by Cause of Death: 1990 to 1998

[Excludes deaths of nonresidents of the United States. Deaths classified according to ninth revision of *International Classification of Diseases*. See also Appendix III]

Cause of death	Number			Percent distribution			Infant mortality rate [1]		
	1990	1995	1998	1990	1995	1998	1990	1995	1998
Total......................	38,351	29,583	28,488	100	100	100	9.2	7.6	7.2
Congenital anomalies	8,239	6,554	6,266	21	22	22	2.0	1.7	1.6
Disorders relating to short gestation and unspecified low birth weight	4,013	3,933	4,011	10	13	14	1.0	1.0	1.0
Sudden infant death syndrome	5,417	3,397	2,529	14	11	9	1.3	0.9	0.6
Respiratory distress syndrome	2,850	1,454	1,328	7	5	5	0.7	0.4	0.3
Newborn affected by maternal complications of pregnancy	1,655	1,309	1,328	4	4	5	0.4	0.3	0.3
Newborn affected by complications of placenta, cord, and membranes	975	962	932	3	3	3	0.2	(NA)	0.2
Accidents and adverse effects	930	787	726	2	3	3	0.2	(NA)	0.2
Infections specific to the perinatal period ..	875	788	815	2	3	3	0.2	(NA)	0.2
Pneumonia and influenza	634	492	400	2	2	1	0.2	(NA)	0.1
Intrauterine hypoxia and birth asphyxia ...	762	475	459	2	2	2	0.2	(NA)	0.1
All other causes..................	12,001	9,432	9,694	31	32	34	2.9	(NA)	2.5

NA Not available. [1] Deaths of infants under 1 year old per 1,000 live births.

Source of Tables 122-124: U.S. National Center for Health Statistics, *Vital Statistics of the United States*, annual; *National Vital Statistics Reports (NVSR)* (formerly *Monthly Vital Statistics Report);* and unpublished data.

No. 125. Infant Mortality Rates by Race and State: 1980 to 1997

[**Deaths per 1,000 live births, by place of residence.** Represents deaths of infants under 1 year old, exclusive of fetal deaths. Excludes deaths of nonresidents of the United States. See Appendix III]

State	Total [1]				White				Black			
	1980	1990	1995	1997	1980	1990	1995	1997	1980	1990	1995	1997
U.S	**12.6**	**9.2**	**7.6**	**7.2**	**11.0**	**7.3**	**6.3**	**6.0**	**21.4**	**18.0**	**15.1**	**14.2**
Alabama	15.1	10.8	9.8	9.5	11.6	8.1	7.1	7.5	21.6	16.0	15.2	13.9
Alaska	12.3	10.5	7.7	7.5	9.4	7.6	6.1	6.8	19.5	(B)	(B)	(B)
Arizona	12.4	8.8	7.5	7.1	11.8	7.8	7.2	6.8	18.4	20.6	17.0	14.4
Arkansas	12.7	9.2	8.8	8.7	10.3	8.4	7.2	7.4	20.0	13.9	14.3	13.8
California	11.1	7.9	6.3	5.9	10.6	7.0	5.8	5.6	18.0	16.8	14.4	13.1
Colorado	10.1	8.8	6.5	7.0	9.8	7.8	6.0	6.7	19.1	19.4	16.8	16.3
Connecticut	11.2	7.9	7.2	7.2	10.2	6.3	6.5	6.3	19.1	17.6	12.6	14.3
Delaware	13.9	10.1	7.5	7.8	9.8	9.7	6.0	5.7	27.9	20.1	13.1	14.5
District of Columbia	25.0	20.7	16.2	13.2	17.8	-	(B)	(B)	26.7	24.6	19.6	16.7
Florida	14.6	9.6	7.5	7.1	11.8	6.7	6.0	5.7	22.8	16.8	13.0	12.3
Georgia	14.5	12.4	9.4	8.6	10.8	7.4	6.5	6.1	21.0	18.3	15.1	13.8
Hawaii	10.3	6.7	5.8	6.6	11.6	6.1	(B)	(B)	11.8	(B)	(B)	(B)
Idaho	10.7	8.7	6.1	6.8	10.7	8.6	5.8	6.9	(NA)	(B)	(B)	(B)
Illinois	14.8	10.7	9.4	8.4	11.7	7.9	7.2	6.4	26.3	22.4	18.7	17.1
Indiana	11.9	9.6	8.4	8.2	10.5	7.9	7.3	7.3	23.4	17.4	17.5	15.8
Iowa	11.8	8.1	8.2	6.2	11.5	7.9	7.8	5.9	27.2	21.9	21.2	18.2
Kansas	10.4	8.4	7.0	7.4	9.5	8.0	6.2	6.6	20.6	17.7	17.6	17.1
Kentucky	12.9	8.5	7.6	7.3	12.0	8.2	7.4	7.0	22.0	14.3	10.7	11.0
Louisiana	14.3	11.1	9.8	9.5	10.5	8.1	6.2	6.6	20.6	16.7	15.3	13.8
Maine	9.2	6.2	6.5	5.1	9.4	6.7	6.3	5.3	(B)	(B)	(B)	(B)
Maryland	14.0	9.5	8.9	8.8	11.6	6.8	6.0	5.1	20.4	17.1	15.3	16.2
Massachusetts	10.5	7.0	5.2	5.2	10.1	6.1	4.7	5.0	16.8	11.9	9.0	8.8
Michigan	12.8	10.7	8.3	8.2	10.6	7.4	6.2	6.1	24.2	21.6	17.3	17.5
Minnesota	10.0	7.3	6.7	5.9	9.6	6.7	6.0	5.1	20.0	23.7	17.6	16.5
Mississippi	17.0	12.1	10.5	10.6	11.1	7.4	7.0	7.1	23.7	16.2	14.7	14.9
Missouri	12.4	9.4	7.4	7.6	11.1	7.9	6.4	6.1	20.7	18.2	13.8	16.3
Montana	12.4	9.0	7.0	6.9	11.8	6.0	7.0	6.0	(NA)	(B)	(B)	(B)
Nebraska	11.5	8.3	7.4	7.4	10.7	6.9	7.3	6.8	25.2	18.9	(B)	19.2
Nevada	10.7	8.4	5.7	6.5	10.0	8.2	5.5	6.2	20.6	14.2	(B)	13.6
New Hampshire	9.9	7.1	5.5	4.3	9.9	6.0	5.5	4.3	22.5	(B)	(B)	(B)
New Jersey	12.5	9.0	6.6	6.3	10.3	6.4	5.3	4.9	21.9	18.4	13.3	13.4
New Mexico	11.5	9.0	6.2	6.1	11.3	7.6	6.1	5.6	23.1	(B)	(B)	(B)
New York	12.5	9.6	7.7	6.7	10.8	7.4	6.2	5.7	20.0	18.1	13.9	10.9
North Carolina	14.5	10.6	9.2	9.2	12.1	8.0	6.7	6.9	20.0	16.5	15.9	15.7
North Dakota	12.1	8.0	7.2	6.2	11.7	7.2	6.7	5.9	27.5	(B)	(B)	(B)
Ohio	12.8	9.8	8.7	7.8	11.2	7.8	7.3	6.5	23.0	19.5	17.5	15.6
Oklahoma	12.7	9.2	8.3	7.5	12.1	9.1	8.0	6.7	21.8	14.3	15.1	15.0
Oregon	12.2	8.3	6.1	5.8	12.2	7.0	5.9	5.7	15.9	(B)	(B)	(B)
Pennsylvania	13.2	9.6	7.8	7.6	11.9	7.4	6.2	6.0	23.1	20.5	17.6	17.6
Rhode Island	11.0	8.1	7.2	7.0	10.9	7.0	7.0	7.0	(B)	(B)	(B)	(B)
South Carolina	15.6	11.7	9.6	9.6	10.8	8.1	6.7	6.4	22.9	17.3	14.6	15.4
South Dakota	10.9	10.1	9.5	7.7	9.0	8.0	7.9	5.3	(NA)	(B)	(B)	(B)
Tennessee	13.5	10.3	9.3	8.6	11.9	7.3	6.8	6.5	19.3	17.9	17.9	16.3
Texas	12.2	8.1	6.5	6.4	11.2	6.7	5.9	5.9	18.8	14.7	11.7	10.9
Utah	10.4	7.5	5.4	5.8	10.5	6.0	5.3	5.8	27.3	(B)	(B)	(B)
Vermont	10.7	6.4	6.0	6.1	10.7	5.9	6.2	6.1	(B)	(B)	(B)	(B)
Virginia	13.6	10.2	7.8	7.8	11.9	7.4	5.7	6.0	19.8	19.5	15.3	14.2
Washington	11.8	7.8	5.9	5.6	11.5	7.3	5.6	5.3	16.4	20.6	16.2	15.4
West Virginia	11.8	9.9	7.9	9.6	11.4	8.1	7.6	9.1	21.5	(B)	(B)	(B)
Wisconsin	10.3	8.2	7.3	6.5	9.7	7.7	6.3	5.7	18.5	19.0	18.6	13.9
Wyoming	9.8	8.6	7.7	5.8	9.3	7.5	6.8	5.6	25.9	(S)	(B)	(B)

- Represents zero.   B Base figure too small to meet statistical standards for reliability.   NA Not available.   S Figure does not meet publication standards.   [1] Includes other races, not shown separately.

Source: U.S. National Center for Health Statistics, *Vital Statistics of the United States*, annual; and unpublished data.

Vital Statistics   89

No. 126. Deaths and Death Rates by Selected Causes: 1990 to 1998

[2,148.5 represents 2,148,500. Excludes deaths of nonresidents of the United States, except as noted. Beginning 1980, deaths classified according to ninth revision of *International Classification of Diseases;* for earlier years, classified according to revision in use at that time. See also Appendix III]

Cause of death	Deaths (1,000)				Crude death rate per 100,000 population [1]			
	1990	1995	1997	1998	1990	1995	1997	1998
All causes	**2,148.5**	**2,312.1**	**2,314.2**	**2,338.1**	**863.8**	**880.0**	**864.7**	**865.0**
Major cardiovascular diseases	916.0	951.4	944.1	939.6	368.3	362.1	352.8	347.6
Diseases of heart	720.1	737.6	727.0	724.3	289.5	280.7	271.6	268.0
Percent of total	33.5	31.9	31.4	31.0	33.5	31.9	31.4	31.0
Rheumatic fever and rheumatic heart disease	6.0	5.1	5.0	4.8	2.4	2.0	1.9	1.8
Hypertensive heart disease [2]	23.4	25.0	26.6	27.3	9.5	9.5	9.9	10.1
Ischemic heart disease	489.2	481.3	466.1	460.4	196.7	183.2	174.2	170.3
Other diseases of endocardium ...	13.0	16.2	17.7	18.5	5.2	6.2	6.6	6.9
All other forms of heart disease ...	188.4	207.4	209.2	210.8	75.8	78.9	78.2	78.0
Hypertension [2]	9.2	12.5	13.5	14.2	3.7	4.8	5.1	5.3
Cerebrovascular diseases	144.1	158.0	159.8	158.1	57.9	60.1	59.7	58.5
Atherosclerosis	18.0	16.7	16.1	15.4	7.3	6.4	6.0	5.7
Other	24.6	26.6	27.8	27.6	9.9	10.1	10.4	10.2
Malignancies [3]	505.3	538.5	539.6	538.9	203.2	204.9	201.6	199.4
Percent of total	23.5	23.3	23.3	23.1	23.5	23.3	23.3	23.1
Of respiratory and intrathoracic organs	146.4	156.4	158.5	159.2	58.9	59.5	59.2	58.9
Of digestive organs and peritoneum	120.8	126.6	127.1	127.7	48.6	48.2	47.5	47.2
Of genital organs	57.5	60.5	59.0	58.1	23.1	23.0	22.0	21.5
Of breast	43.7	44.2	42.3	41.9	17.6	16.8	15.8	15.5
Of urinary organs	20.7	22.6	23.4	23.7	8.3	8.6	8.7	8.8
Leukemia	18.6	20.1	20.3	20.2	7.5	7.7	7.6	7.5
Accidents and adverse effects	92.0	93.3	95.6	93.2	37.0	35.5	35.7	34.5
Motor vehicle.................	46.8	43.4	43.5	41.8	18.8	16.5	16.2	15.5
All other	45.2	50.0	52.2	51.4	18.2	19.0	19.5	19.0
Chronic obstructive pulmonary diseases and allied conditions	86.7	102.9	109.0	114.4	34.9	39.2	40.7	42.3
Bronchitis, chronic and unspecified ..	3.6	3.3	3.1	3.1	1.4	1.3	1.1	1.2
Emphysema	15.7	16.9	17.5	17.9	6.3	6.4	6.5	6.6
Asthma....................	4.8	5.6	5.4	5.3	1.9	2.1	2.0	2.0
Other......................	62.6	77.0	83.0	88.0	25.2	29.3	31.0	32.6
Pneumonia and influenza	79.5	82.9	86.4	94.8	32.0	31.6	32.3	35.1
Pneumonia	77.4	82.3	85.7	92.7	31.1	31.3	32.0	34.3
Influenza...................	2.1	0.6	0.7	2.1	0.8	0.2	0.3	0.8
Diabetes mellitus...............	47.7	59.3	62.6	64.6	19.2	22.6	23.4	23.9
Suicide	30.9	31.3	30.5	29.3	12.4	11.9	11.4	10.8
Chronic liver disease and cirrhosis	25.8	25.2	25.2	24.9	10.4	9.6	9.4	9.2
Other infectious and parasitic diseases .	32.2	50.3	23.3	20.0	13.0	19.1	8.7	7.4
Homicide and legal intervention	24.9	22.9	19.8	17.4	10.0	8.7	7.4	6.4
Nephritis, nephrotic syndrome, and nephrosis	20.8	23.7	25.3	26.3	8.3	9.0	9.5	9.7
Septicemia...................	19.2	21.0	22.4	23.6	7.7	8.0	8.4	8.7
Certain conditions originating in the perinatal period	17.7	13.5	13.1	13.3	7.1	5.1	4.9	4.9
Congenital anomalies	13.1	11.9	11.9	11.9	5.3	4.5	4.5	4.4
Benign neoplasms [4]	6.8	7.8	7.7	7.9	2.7	3.0	2.9	2.9
Ulcer of stomach and duodenum	6.2	5.5	5.1	4.7	2.5	2.1	1.9	1.7
Hernia of abdominal cavity and intestinal obstruction [5]	5.8	6.2	6.5	6.6	2.3	2.4	2.4	2.4
Anemias....................	4.1	4.6	4.5	4.5	1.6	1.7	1.7	1.7
Cholelithiasis and other disorders of gall bladder.................	3.0	2.8	2.8	2.7	1.2	1.0	1.0	1.0
Nutritional deficiencies	3.0	3.6	3.9	4.1	1.2	1.4	1.5	1.5
Tuberculosis	1.8	1.3	1.2	1.1	0.7	0.5	0.4	0.4
Infections of kidney	1.3	0.9	0.8	0.8	0.5	0.3	0.3	0.3
Viral hepatitis	1.6	3.4	4.1	4.7	0.6	1.3	1.5	1.7
Meningitis...................	1.0	0.8	0.8	0.8	0.4	0.3	0.3	0.3
Acute bronchitis and bronchiolitis	0.6	0.5	0.5	0.4	0.3	0.2	0.2	0.2
Hyperplasia of prostate...........	0.5	0.4	0.4	0.4	0.2	0.2	0.2	0.2
Symptoms, signs, and ill-defined conditions...................	24.1	27.3	25.8	35.5	9.7	10.4	9.6	13.1
All other causes...............	172.9	214.1	235.4	246.1	69.5	81.5	88.0	91.0

[1] 1990 based on resident population enumerated as of April 1. Other years based on resident population estimated as of July 1. [2] With or without renal disease. [3] Includes other types of malignancies not shown separately. [4] Includes neoplasms of unspecified nature; beginning 1980 also includes carcinoma in situ. [5] Without mention of hernia.

Source: U.S. National Center for Health Statistics, *Vital Statistics of the United States*, annual; and *National Vital Statistics Report (NVSR)* (formerly *Monthly Vital Statistics Report*); and unpublished data.

No. 127. Age-Adjusted Death Rates by Selected Causes: 1990 to 1998

[Rates per 100,000 population. For explanation of age-adjustment, see text, this section. The standard population for this table is the total population of the United States enumerated in 1940. See also headnote, Table 126]

Cause of death	1990	1993	1994	1995	1996	1997	1998
All causes	**520.2**	**513.3**	**507.4**	**503.9**	**491.6**	**479.1**	**470.7**
Major cardiovascular diseases	189.8	181.8	176.8	174.9	170.7	166.1	160.4
Diseases of heart	152.0	145.3	140.4	138.3	134.5	130.5	126.0
Rheumatic fever and rheumatic							
heart disease	1.5	1.3	1.2	1.1	1.1	1.0	1.0
Hypertensive heart disease [1]	4.8	4.9	5.0	5.1	5.2	5.2	5.2
Ischemic heart disease	102.6	94.9	91.4	89.5	86.7	82.9	79.4
Acute mycocardial infraction	53.7	47.5	45.6	43.8	42.0	39.7	38.0
Other diseases of endocardium	2.5	2.6	2.6	2.6	2.7	2.7	2.7
Old mycocardial infraction and other . . .	47.8	46.5	45.0	44.9	44.0	42.5	40.8
Hypertension [1]	1.9	2.2	2.2	2.3	2.3	2.3	2.4
Cerebrovascular diseases.	27.7	26.5	26.5	26.7	26.4	25.9	25.0
Atherosclerosis	2.7	2.4	2.3	2.3	2.2	2.1	1.9
Intracerebral/intracranial hemorrage	5.2	5.1	5.0	5.1	5.2	5.6	5.4
Cerebral thrombosis	3.3	2.5	2.4	2.2	2.0	1.8	1.6
Cerebral embolism	0.1	0.1	0.1	0.1	0.1	0.1	0.1
Malignancies [2]	135.0	132.6	131.5	129.9	127.9	125.6	122.9
Of respiratory and intrathoracic organs . . .	41.4	40.8	40.1	39.7	39.3	38.7	38.2
Of digestive organs and peritoneum	30.2	29.5	29.3	29.1	28.5	28.2	27.9
Of genital organs	13.6	13.2	13.2	12.8	12.5	12.0	11.6
Of breast	12.7	11.8	11.6	11.5	11.0	10.5	10.2
Of urinary organs	5.1	5.0	5.1	5.1	5.1	5.0	5.0
Leukemia.	5.0	4.9	4.9	4.8	4.8	4.7	4.6
Of lip, oral cavity, and pharynx.	2.4	2.3	2.1	2.1	2.1	2.0	2.0
Accidents and adverse effects	32.5	30.3	30.3	30.5	30.4	30.1	28.5
Motor vehicle	18.5	16.0	16.1	16.3	16.2	15.9	15.0
All other	14.0	14.4	14.2	14.2	14.2	14.2	13.5
Chronic obstructive pulmonary diseases							
and allied conditions [3]	19.7	21.4	21.0	20.8	21.0	21.1	21.6
Bronchitis, chronic and unspecified.	0.8	0.8	0.7	0.6	0.6	0.6	0.6
Emphysema	3.7	3.9	3.7	3.6	3.6	3.6	3.6
Asthma	1.4	1.4	1.5	1.5	1.5	1.4	1.3
Other	13.7	15.2	15.1	15.0	15.2	15.5	16.0
Pneumonia and influenza.	14.0	13.5	13.0	12.9	12.8	12.9	13.5
Pneumonia	13.7	13.3	12.8	12.8	12.7	12.8	13.2
Influenza	0.3	0.2	0.2	0.1	0.1	0.1	0.3
Diabetes mellitus	11.7	12.4	12.9	13.3	13.6	13.5	13.6
Suicide	11.5	11.3	11.2	11.2	10.8	10.6	10.0
Chronic liver disease and cirrhosis.	8.6	7.9	7.9	7.6	7.5	7.4	7.1
Homicide and legal intervention.	10.2	10.7	10.3	9.4	8.5	8.0	6.9
Nephritis, nephrotic syndrome, and							
renal failure	3.9	4.1	3.9	4.0	3.9	4.1	4.1
Acute glomerulonephritis/nephrotic							
syndrome	0.1	(NA)	0.1	-	-	-	-
Septicemia	4.1	4.1	4.0	4.1	4.1	4.2	4.4
Other infectious and parasitic diseases.	12.0	15.9	17.5	17.6	13.0	7.6	6.3
Benign neoplasms [4]	1.7	1.7	1.7	1.7	1.7	1.6	1.6
Ulcer of stomach and duodenum.	1.3	1.2	1.2	1.0	0.9	0.9	0.8
Hernia of abdominal cavity and							
intestinal obstruction [5]	1.1	1.0	1.1	1.0	1.0	1.0	1.0
Anemias	0.9	0.9	0.9	0.9	0.8	0.8	0.8
Cholelithiasis and other disorders of							
gallbladder.	0.6	0.5	0.5	0.5	0.5	0.5	0.5
Nutritional deficiencies.	0.5	0.5	0.5	0.5	0.5	0.5	0.5
Tuberculosis	0.5	0.4	0.4	0.3	0.3	0.3	0.2
Tuberculosis of respiratory system	0.4	0.3	0.3	0.2	0.2	0.2	0.2
Other tuberculosis	0.1	0.1	0.1	0.1	0.1	0.1	0.1
Infections of kidney	0.2	0.2	0.2	0.2	0.2	0.1	0.1
Viral hepatitis.	0.5	0.8	0.9	1.0	1.1	1.2	1.4
Meningitis	0.3	0.3	0.3	0.2	0.3	0.3	0.3
Acute bronchitis and bronchiolitis.	0.1	0.1	0.1	0.1	0.1	0.1	0.1
Hyperplasia of prostate	0.1	0.1	0.1	0.1	0.1	0.1	0.1
Symptoms, signs, and ill-defined conditions. .	7.3	7.4	6.8	7.2	6.6	6.4	9.4
Meningococcal infection.	0.1	0.1	0.1	0.1	0.1	0.1	0.1
Angina pectoris	0.2	0.2	0.2	0.1	0.1	0.1	0.1
Appendicitis.	0.1	0.1	0.1	0.1	0.1	0.1	0.1
Complications of pregnancy, childbirth	0.1	0.1	0.1	0.1	0.1	0.1	0.1
Congenital anomalies	5.0	4.6	4.5	4.4	4.3	4.2	4.2
Perinatal period conditions	6.9	5.9	4.8	5.4	5.3	5.3	5.4
Birth trauma, intrauterine hypoxia, etc.	1.5	1.0	0.9	0.9	0.8	0.8	0.8

- Represents or rounds to zero.   NA Not available.   [1] With or without renal disease.   [2] Includes other types of malignancies not shown separately.   [3] Prior to 1980, data are shown for bronchitis, emphysema, and asthma.   [4] Includes neoplasms of unspecified nature; also includes carcinoma in situ.   [5] Without mention of hernia.

Source: U.S. National Center for Health Statistics, *Vital Statistics of the United States*, annual; and *National Vital Statistics Report (NVSR)* (formerly *Monthly Vital Statistics Report*); and unpublished data.

No. 128. Deaths by Selected Causes and Selected Characteristics: 1997

[In thousands (2,314.2 represents 2,314,200). Excludes deaths of nonresidents of the United States. Deaths classified according to ninth revision of *International Classification of Diseases*. See also Appendix III]

Age, sex, and race	Total [1]	Heart disease	Cancer	Accidents and adverse effects	Cerebrovascular diseases	Chronic obstructive pulmonary diseases [2]	Pneumonia	Suicide	Chronic liver disease, cirrhosis	Diabetes mellitus	Homicide and legal intervention
ALL RACES[3]											
Both sexes, total [4]	**2,314.2**	**727.0**	**539.6**	**95.6**	**159.8**	**109.0**	**85.7**	**30.5**	**25.2**	**62.6**	**19.8**
Under 1 years old	28.0	0.6	0.1	0.8	0.3	0.1	0.4	-	-	-	0.3
1 to 4 years old	5.5	0.2	0.4	2.0	0.1	-	0.2	-	-	-	0.4
5 to 14 years old	8.1	0.3	1.0	3.4	0.1	0.1	0.1	0.3	-	-	0.5
15 to 19 years old	31.5	1.1	1.6	13.4	0.2	0.2	0.2	4.2	-	0.1	6.1
25 to 34 years old	45.5	3.3	4.6	12.6	0.7	0.4	0.5	5.7	0.5	0.6	5.1
35 to 44 years old	89.4	13.2	17.1	14.5	2.8	0.9	1.4	6.7	3.5	1.9	3.7
45 to 54 years old	144.9	35.3	45.4	10.4	5.7	2.8	2.2	4.9	5.6	4.3	1.9
55 to 64 years old	232.0	66.0	86.3	7.1	9.7	10.1	3.7	2.9	5.3	8.4	0.9
65 to 74 years old	464.3	139.4	156.7	8.6	24.9	30.6	10.5	2.7	5.8	16.3	0.5
75 to 84 years old	670.5	227.5	156.3	12.1	54.1	42.1	27.2	2.3	3.5	19.6	0.3
85 years old and over . . .	594.1	240.0	69.9	10.7	61.3	21.8	39.3	0.8	0.9	11.4	0.1
WHITE											
Both sexes, total [4] . . .	**1,996.4**	**639.2**	**468.5**	**79.9**	**138.3**	**100.8**	**76.2**	**27.5**	**21.7**	**49.9**	**9.9**
Under 1 years old	18.5	0.4	0.1	0.5	0.2	-	0.3	-	-	-	0.2
1 to 4 years old	3.8	0.1	0.3	1.4	-	-	0.1	-	-	-	0.2
5 to 9 years old	2.5	0.1	0.4	1.0	-	-	0.1	-	-	-	0.1
10 to 14 years old	3.3	0.1	0.4	1.4	-	-	-	0.3	-	-	0.1
15 to 19 years old	10.5	0.3	0.5	5.6	0.1	0.1	0.1	1.5	-	-	1.1
20 to 24 years old	12.0	0.4	0.7	5.6	0.1	0.1	0.1	1.9	-	0.1	1.3
25 to 29 years old	13.4	0.7	1.2	4.9	0.1	0.1	0.1	2.3	0.1	0.1	1.2
30 to 34 years old	18.8	1.6	2.4	5.3	0.3	0.1	0.2	2.6	0.3	0.3	1.2
35 to 39 years old	27.6	3.3	4.7	6.0	0.6	0.2	0.4	3.1	1.0	0.5	1.1
40 to 44 years old	37.6	6.2	8.6	5.7	1.1	0.4	0.6	3.0	1.9	0.8	0.9
45 to 49 years old	48.5	10.8	14.3	4.7	1.5	0.7	0.7	2.6	2.3	1.2	0.7
50 to 54 years old	62.9	16.2	22.5	3.6	2.2	1.6	0.9	2.0	2.3	1.8	0.4
55 to 59 years old	78.4	21.6	30.2	3.0	2.8	3.0	1.1	1.6	2.1	2.5	0.3
60 to 64 years old	109.5	31.4	42.0	2.8	4.2	6.0	1.8	1.2	2.3	3.5	0.2
65 to 69 years old	165.6	48.3	60.7	3.3	7.3	11.2	3.1	1.2	2.6	5.3	0.2
70 to 74 years old	234.2	71.2	76.1	4.1	13.1	17.1	5.8	1.3	2.6	7.5	0.2
75 to 79 years old	290.6	94.8	77.1	5.2	20.7	20.5	9.9	1.3	2.0	8.4	0.2
80 to 84 years old	313.0	110.3	63.4	5.8	27.5	19.2	14.6	0.9	1.3	8.0	0.1
85 years old and over . . .	545.3	221.2	62.9	10.0	56.5	20.5	36.4	0.8	0.8	9.7	0.1
BLACK											
Both sexes, total [4] . . .	**276.5**	**77.2**	**61.3**	**12.7**	**18.1**	**6.9**	**7.9**	**2.1**	**2.8**	**11.1**	**9.3**
Under 1 years old	8.5	0.2	-	0.2	0.1	-	0.1	-	-	-	0.1
1 to 4 years old	1.4	0.1	0.1	0.5	-	-	-	-	-	-	0.1
5 to 9 years old	0.9	-	0.1	0.4	-	-	-	-	-	-	0.1
10 to 14 years old	0.9	-	0.1	0.3	-	-	-	-	-	-	0.1
15 to 19 years old	3.2	0.1	0.1	0.8	-	-	-	0.2	-	-	1.4
20 to 24 years old	4.6	0.2	0.2	0.9	-	-	-	0.3	-	-	2.1
25 to 29 years old	5.1	0.4	0.3	1.0	-	0.1	0.1	0.3	-	0.1	1.5
30 to 34 years old	6.6	0.6	0.5	0.9	0.1	0.1	0.1	0.3	0.1	0.1	1.1
35 to 39 years old	9.5	1.2	1.2	1.2	0.3	0.1	0.2	0.2	0.2	0.2	0.9
40 to 44 years old	12.2	2.1	2.0	1.2	0.6	0.2	0.2	0.2	0.3	0.3	0.7
45 to 49 years old	14.7	3.3	3.2	1.0	0.8	0.2	0.3	0.1	0.5	0.5	0.4
50 to 54 years old	14.9	4.1	4.2	0.7	0.9	0.3	0.2	0.1	0.4	0.7	0.2
55 to 59 years old	17.3	5.1	5.4	0.6	1.0	0.4	0.3	0.1	0.4	0.9	0.1
60 to 64 years old	21.4	6.5	6.9	0.5	1.3	0.6	0.4	0.1	0.3	1.2	0.1
65 to 69 years old	25.3	7.8	8.1	0.5	1.6	0.9	0.5	0.1	0.3	1.4	0.1
70 to 74 years old	30.6	9.8	9.2	0.5	2.2	1.1	0.8	0.1	0.2	1.6	0.1
75 to 79 years old	30.2	10.0	7.9	0.5	2.4	1.1	1.0	-	0.1	1.5	-
80 to 84 years old	27.1	9.5	5.7	0.4	2.4	0.9	1.1	-	0.1	1.2	-
85 years old and over . . .	42.1	16.2	6.1	0.6	4.1	1.0	2.3	-	-	1.5	-

- Represents zero. [1] Includes other causes, not shown separately. [2] Includes allied conditions. [3] Includes other races, not shown separately. [4] Includes those deaths with age not stated.

Source: U.S. National Center for Health Statistics, *Vital Statistics of the United States,* annual.

No. 129. Deaths by Age and Leading Cause: 1997

[Excludes deaths of nonresidents of the United States. Deaths classified according to ninth revision of *International Classification of Diseases*. See also Appendix III]

Age and leading cause of death	Number of deaths			Death rate per 100,000 population		
	Total	Male	Female	Total	Male	Female
All ages [1]	**2,314,245**	**1,154,039**	**1,160,206**	**864.7**	**880.8**	**849.2**
1 to 4 yrs. old, total	**5,501**	**3,121**	**2,380**	**35.8**	**39.7**	**31.8**
Leading causes of death:						
Accidents	2,005	1,192	813	13.1	15.2	10.8
Congenital anomalies	589	317	272	3.8	4.0	3.6
Malignant neoplasms (cancer)........	438	240	198	2.9	3.1	2.6
Homicide and legal intervention......	375	209	166	2.4	2.7	2.2
Heart disease.................	212	119	93	1.4	1.5	1.2
HIV infection [2]	(NA)	(NA)	29	(NA)	(NA)	0.4
Pneumonia and influenza...........	(NA)	(NA)	91	1.2	1.1	1.2
Certain conditions originating in the perinatal period	75	46	29	0.5	0.6	0.4
Septicemia	73	38	35	0.5	0.5	0.5
Cerebrovascular diseases	56	36	(NA)	0.4	0.5	(NA)
5 to 14 yrs. old, total.	**8,061**	**4,763**	**3,298**	**20.8**	**24.0**	**17.4**
Leading causes of death:						
Accidents	3,371	2,110	1,261	8.7	10.6	6.7
Malignant neoplasms (cancer)........	1,030	560	470	2.7	2.8	2.5
Homicide and legal intervention......	457	295	162	1.2	1.5	0.9
Congenital anomalies	447	232	215	1.2	1.2	1.1
Suicide	307	233	74	0.8	1.2	0.4
Heart disease...............	313	180	133	0.8	0.9	0.7
HIV infections [2]	102	63	39	0.3	0.3	0.2
Chronic obstructive pulmonary diseases .	129	71	58	0.3	0.4	0.3
Pneumonia and influenza..........	141	71	70	0.4	0.4	0.4
Benign neoplasms & carcinoma in situ ..	76	(NA)	46	0.2	(NA)	0.2
15 to 24 yrs. old, total.	**31,544**	**23,312**	**8,232**	**86.2**	**124.0**	**46.3**
Leading causes of death:						
Accidents	13,367	9,791	3,576	36.5	52.1	20.1
Homicide and legal intervention......	6,146	5,302	844	16.8	28.2	4.7
Suicide	4,186	3,559	627	11.4	18.9	3.5
Malignant neoplasms (cancer)........	1,645	981	664	4.5	5.2	3.7
Heart disease...............	1,098	674	424	3.0	3.6	2.4
HIV infection [2]	276	145	131	0.8	0.8	0.7
Congenital anomalies	420	241	179	1.1	1.3	1
Chronic obstructive pulmonary disease ..	201	135	(NA)	0.5	0.7	(NA)
Pneumonia and influenza..........	220	119	101	0.6	0.6	0.6
Cerebrovascular diseases	188	106	82	0.5	0.6	0.5
25 to 44 yrs. old, total.	**134,946**	**89,848**	**45,098**	**161.4**	**215.5**	**107.6**
Leading causes of death:						
HIV infection [2]	11,066	8,569	2,497	13.2	20.6	6.0
Accidents	27,129	20,412	6,717	32.4	49.0	16.0
Malignant neoplasms (cancer)........	21,706	9,841	11,865	26.0	23.6	28.3
Heart disease................	16,513	11,714	4,799	19.8	28.1	11.4
Suicide	12,402	9,907	2,495	14.8	23.8	6.0
Homicide and legal intervention......	8,752	6,803	1,949	10.5	16.3	4.6
Chronic liver disease and cirrhosis.....	4,024	2,800	1,224	4.8	6.7	2.9
Cerebrovascular diseases	3,465	1,754	1,711	4.1	4.2	4.1
Diabetes mellitus	2,478	1,483	995	3.0	3.6	2.4
Pneumonia and influenza..........	1,928	1,164	764	2.3	2.8	1.8
45 to 64 yrs. old, total.	**376,875**	**229,463**	**147,412**	**679.7**	**854.7**	**515.5**
Leading causes of death:						
Malignant neoplasms (cancer)........	131,743	69,819	61,924	237.6	260.1	216.5
Heart disease................	101,235	71,112	30,123	182.6	264.9	105.3
Accidents	17,521	12,411	5,110	31.6	46.2	17.9
Cerebrovascular diseases	15,371	8,502	6,869	27.7	31.7	24.0
Chronic obstructive pulmonary diseases .	12,947	6,690	6,257	23.4	24.9	21.9
Diabetes mellitus	12,705	6,655	6,050	22.9	24.8	21.2
Chronic liver disease and cirrhosis.....	10,875	7,852	3,023	19.6	29.2	10.6
HIV infection [2]	4,578	3,744	(NA)	8.3	13.9	(NA)
Suicide	7,894	6,028	1,866	14.2	22.5	6.5
Pneumonia and influenza..........	5,992	3,569	2,423	10.8	13.3	8.5
65 yrs. old and over, total	**1,728,872**	**787,427**	**941,445**	**5,073.6**	**5,620.6**	**4,691.7**
Leading causes of death:						
Heart disease................	606,913	272,401	334,512	1,781.1	1,944.4	1,667.1
Malignant neoplasms (cancer)........	382,913	199,617	183,296	1,123.7	1,424.9	913.5
Cerebrovascular diseases	140,366	51,972	88,394	411.9	371.0	440.5
Chronic obstructive pulmonary diseases .	94,411	48,419	45,992	277.1	345.6	229.2
Pneumonia and influenza..........	77,561	34,011	43,550	227.6	242.8	217.0
Diabetes mellitus	47,289	19,966	27,323	138.8	142.5	136.2
Accidents	31,386	15,526	15,860	92.1	110.8	79.0
Alzheimer's disease.............	22,154	6,885	15,269	65.0	49.1	76.1
Nephritis, nephrotic syndrome, and nephrosis.................	21,787	10,156	11,631	63.9	72.5	58.0
Septicemia	18,079	7,372	10,707	53.1	52.6	53.4

NA Not available.   [1] Includes those deaths with age not stated.   [2] Human immunodeficiency virus.

Source: U.S. National Center for Health Statistics, *Vital Statistics of the United States,* annual; and unpublished data.

U.S. Census Bureau, Statistical Abstract of the United States: 2000

No. 130. Death Rates by Leading Cause and State: 1997

[**Deaths per 100,000 resident population enumerated as of April 1.** By place of residence. Excludes nonresidents of the United States. Causes of death classified according to ninth revisions of International Classification of Diseases]

State	Total [1]	Heart disease	Cancer	Cerebro- vascular diseas- es [2]	Acci- dents and adverse effects	Motor vehicle acci- dents	Chronic obstruc- tive pulmo- nary diseas- es [2]	Diabetes mellitus	HIV [3]	Suicide	Homicide
U.S. ..	**864.7**	**271.6**	**201.6**	**59.7**	**35.7**	**16.2**	**40.7**	**23.4**	**6.2**	**11.4**	**7.4**
AL	1,001.5	314.2	221.7	66.8	53.2	28.8	42.9	27.2	4.5	11.9	12.0
AK	422.6	91.4	102.1	21.7	44.1	13.8	19.5	13.3	(NA)	21.0	9.0
AZ	813.7	223.4	185.5	54.5	47.1	20.9	52.2	20.8	3.6	16.6	9.5
AR	1,103.7	335.5	240.3	97.5	53.3	28.9	49.7	25.3	2.6	14.1	11.8
CA	696.0	212.8	161.1	51.8	28.0	11.9	36.5	17.4	5.8	10.6	8.8
CO	658.3	166.6	145.1	43.9	36.8	16.2	42.6	13.4	3.2	15.7	4.7
CT	899.6	297.8	218.3	58.2	30.9	11.2	38.7	19.0	6.1	7.9	3.9
DE	889.9	272.3	228.1	47.4	39.6	18.9	40.5	27.9	8.2	11.9	4.4
DC	1,158.7	305.5	254.8	63.5	33.5	10.0	30.4	38.9	51.2	6.6	48.2
FL	1,054.3	339.8	260.0	68.4	37.9	18.9	55.2	26.2	12.8	14.3	7.7
GA	792.8	236.0	174.0	57.0	41.2	21.5	33.5	17.0	9.9	12.1	8.7
HI.	665.1	200.6	155.6	59.8	29.9	11.9	21.6	17.0	3.0	11.6	4.0
ID.	741.7	208.1	160.9	58.7	45.1	20.6	43.2	20.0	(NA)	17.3	3.6
IL.	865.1	274.3	205.8	60.7	29.2	12.1	35.8	23.0	4.3	7.6	9.8
IN.	906.0	284.1	210.3	65.3	35.7	16.7	45.6	25.3	2.6	12.4	7.4
IA.	970.9	319.4	222.0	75.7	38.1	17.2	45.2	23.7	0.9	12.1	2.5
KS	915.3	280.4	201.1	66.2	39.0	20.2	49.0	22.3	1.7	12.3	6.1
KY	972.3	318.8	229.5	64.0	46.1	21.8	49.8	25.9	1.9	12.5	6.6
LA	919.3	272.7	214.9	58.1	43.8	21.3	33.9	38.7	9.2	12.1	16.1
ME	965.6	292.8	239.9	63.5	34.5	15.2	56.0	24.4	2.2	11.0	1.8
MD	820.4	235.7	198.8	51.2	26.9	12.7	35.6	27.4	11.6	10.2	10.9
MA	893.9	269.8	223.7	55.7	21.0	8.2	39.8	22.2	4.0	8.0	2.3
MI	852.3	278.8	200.6	58.9	32.4	15.8	37.2	24.9	3.2	10.3	8.1
MN	787.8	205.1	187.3	64.0	36.4	12.8	34.8	22.4	1.5	10.1	2.8
MS	1,007.3	355.3	214.2	68.0	58.2	32.0	40.7	20.9	5.7	12.4	14.2
MO	1,005.6	341.7	221.4	68.6	44.1	21.7	47.7	24.1	2.7	13.1	8.0
MT	884.0	239.9	203.5	61.9	51.2	26.6	60.8	19.2	(NA)	20.8	4.2
NE	922.3	298.0	195.4	66.5	40.2	18.5	47.8	19.0	1.9	10.6	3.9
NV	797.9	232.4	189.6	47.6	39.5	21.4	51.8	14.5	5.2	24.5	10.5
NH	806.5	238.9	205.8	58.8	27.4	11.3	46.7	23.6	(NA)	11.6	2.2
NJ	895.8	290.5	225.5	51.3	29.5	10.4	35.4	29.1	12.5	7.3	4.5
NM	731.5	189.3	159.9	44.4	57.9	24.7	42.7	23.1	2.5	17.3	9.5
NY	874.7	335.9	206.0	44.2	27.3	10.1	33.6	20.1	16.0	7.6	6.3
NC	889.2	260.0	204.3	70.4	41.2	21.0	43.0	24.7	6.6	12.2	9.2
ND	919.5	285.1	206.3	75.2	38.2	16.5	36.7	28.6	(NA)	12.5	(NA)
OH	941.7	306.8	220.7	61.5	30.8	12.9	46.3	29.9	2.6	10.1	4.4
OK	1,023.3	339.8	218.1	72.1	48.4	25.8	52.1	28.1	3.3	15.0	8.7
OR	887.0	231.8	208.7	79.2	40.2	16.9	50.5	25.0	2.5	16.5	4.1
PA	1,064.3	350.5	251.1	69.6	39.8	13.8	44.3	29.5	4.8	11.7	6.5
RI.	994.5	330.7	249.7	69.3	24.5	10.1	43.6	27.7	4.2	7.3	2.8
SC	896.0	263.2	203.2	75.7	45.6	24.0	39.8	27.4	8.4	11.5	9.5
SD	930.3	288.6	209.8	77.4	41.5	20.5	45.5	26.6	(NA)	17.2	3.0
TN	981.1	310.3	220.9	74.9	47.0	23.4	46.0	24.5	5.2	13.6	10.4
TX	734.5	224.4	165.6	52.2	36.9	19.3	34.5	24.5	6.2	11.0	7.6
UT	562.3	146.0	103.6	42.5	33.3	18.3	21.5	21.0	1.2	14.6	3.1
VT	857.9	255.7	208.8	58.9	34.1	13.1	48.7	24.3	(NA)	12.4	(NA)
VA	799.7	232.1	192.0	60.0	34.3	14.3	35.8	18.5	4.9	11.3	7.6
WA	739.0	198.1	178.9	60.0	34.2	13.6	41.8	19.5	3.1	13.0	4.7
WV	1,150.0	381.3	262.0	68.1	44.2	21.3	62.7	37.6	1.7	14.4	5.3
WI	868.4	264.9	204.6	71.2	35.6	14.5	39.0	22.7	1.5	11.1	4.1
WY	780.6	216.8	175.9	48.6	51.3	25.0	56.3	16.7	(NA)	19.8	4.4

NA Not available. [1] Includes other causes not shown separately. [2] Includes allied conditions. [3] Human immunodeficiency virus.

Source: U.S. National Center for Health Statistics, *National Vital Statistics Report (NVSR)*.

No. 131. Estimated Persons Living With Acquired Immunodeficiency Syndrome (AIDS) by Selected Characteristics: 1993 to 1998

[These numbers do not represent actual cases of persons living with AIDS. Rather, these numbers are point estimates of persons living with AIDS derived by subtracting the estimated cumulative number of deaths in persons with AIDS from the estimated cumulative number of persons with AIDS. Estimated AIDS cases and estimated deaths are adjusted for reporting delays and for redistribution of cases initially reported with no identified risk, but not for incomplete reporting. See source, "Technical Notes"]

Characteristic	1993	1994	1995	1996	1997	1998
Total	174,369	197,394	216,812	240,189	268,353	294,425
RACE/ETHNICITY						
White, not Hispanic.	80,445	86,678	91,737	98,544	107,110	114,846
Black, not Hispanic	60,649	71,847	81,317	92,319	105,464	117,890
Hispanic	31,209	36,485	41,071	46,216	52,215	57,722
Asian/Pacific Islander	1,288	1,451	1,613	1,856	2,093	2,324
American Indian/Alaska Native	566	664	718	804	893	978
MALE ADULT/ADOLESCENT EXPOSURE CATEGORY						
Male total.	144,467	161,463	175,151	192,239	213,378	232,913
Men who have sex with men	86,720	95,171	101,717	111,076	122,874	133,840
Injecting drug use	34,465	40,153	44,589	49,074	54,249	58,643
Men who have sex with men and inject drugs . . .	13,645	14,635	15,369	16,034	17,203	16,181
Hemophilia/coagulation disorder	1,618	1,698	1,728	1,742	1,788	1,838
Heterosexual contact.	6,086	7,890	9,771	12,219	15,011	17,765
Receipt of blood transfusion, blood components, or tissue	918	947	1,008	1,083	1,189	1,313
Risk not reported or identified	1,015	969	969	1,011	1,064	1,133
FEMALE ADULT/ADOLESCENT EXPOSURE CATEGORY						
Female total.	26,862	32,667	38,255	44,475	51,407	57,838
Injecting drug use	13,793	16,175	18,294	20,285	22,586	24,500
Hemophilia/coagulation disorder	91	108	137	167	207	240
Heterosexual contact.	11,829	15,140	18,524	22,588	27,017	31,336
Receipt of blood transfusion, blood components, or tissue	766	854	908	1,006	1,120	1,243
Risk not reported or identified	383	390	392	429	477	519
Pediatric [1] exposure category	3,039	3,267	3,404	3,475	3,569	3,673

[1] Less than 13 years old.
Source: Centers for Disease Control and Prevention, HIV/AIDS Surveillance Report, annual.

No. 132. Death Rates From Heart Disease by Sex and Age: 1980 to 1998

[**Deaths per 100,000 population in specified age groups**. Beginning 1970, excludes deaths of nonresidents of the United States. Beginning 1980, deaths classified according to the ninth revision of the International Classification of Diseases. For earlier years, classified according to the revision in use at the time; see text, this section. See Appendix III]

Age at death and selected type of heart disease	Male					Female				
	1980	1990	1995	1997	1998	1980	1990	1995	1997	1998
Total U.S. rate [1]	369	298	283	272	267	305	282	279	271	268
25 to 34 years	11	10	11	11	10	5	5	6	6	6
35 to 44 years old.	69	48	47	44	42	21	15	17	17	16
45 to 54 years old.	283	183	169	158	149	85	61	56	54	52
55 to 64 years old.	747	537	465	435	405	272	216	194	182	173
65 to 74 years old.	1,728	1,250	1,102	1,031	996	829	617	558	529	524
75 to 84 years old.	3,834	2,968	2,615	2,444	2,382	2,497	1,894	1,715	1,617	1,587
85 years old and over	8,753	7,418	7,040	6,659	6,354	7,351	6,478	6,268	6,014	5,898
Persons 45 to 54 years old:										
Ischemic heart.	217.3	123.8	107.5	98.0	90.9	52.2	33.6	29.4	27.8	25.3
Rheumatic heart	3.1	1.1	0.7	0.8	0.9	4.3	1.9	1.3	1.3	1.1
Hypertensive heart [2].	8.3	7.6	8.8	9.4	8.9	5.5	4.3	3.9	4.2	4.0
Persons 55 to 64 years old:										
Ischemic heart.	581.1	375.4	312.6	286.0	264.7	189.0	135.4	116.8	108.2	101.3
Rheumatic heart	6.2	3.4	2.2	2.0	1.8	9.2	4.7	3.4	2.9	3.1
Hypertensive heart [2].	21.8	18.1	18.2	18.2	19.1	13.3	10.9	9.3	9.6	9.6
Persons 65 to 74 years old:										
Ischemic heart.	1,355.5	898.5	770.5	712.1	684.1	605.3	415.2	362.8	336.5	329.3
Rheumatic heart	11.8	7.1	4.5	4.3	4.0	18.6	10.5	8.3	7.5	7.5
Hypertensive heart [2].	44.3	33.2	30.9	31.6	31.4	36.2	25.9	22.1	21.7	22.4
Persons 75 to 84 years old:										
Ischemic heart.	2,953.7	2,129.6	1,824.0	1,688.0	1,636.6	1,842.7	1,287.6	1,116.3	1,032.3	1,007.8
Rheumatic heart	16.7	12.3	10.7	10.3	9.1	25.4	22.5	17.9	15.9	15.2
Hypertensive heart [2].	90.7	67.9	59.7	58.5	59.3	101.1	69.7	62.4	61.4	61.6
Persons 85 years old and over:										
Ischemic heart.	6,501.6	5,120.7	4,674.4	4,370.7	4,145.7	5,280.6	4,257.8	3,948.8	3,711.0	3,594.8
Rheumatic heart	19.5	18.7	21.5	21.0	17.2	25.8	33.3	28.8	29.2	28.6
Hypertensive heart [2].	180.3	154.3	154.9	161.4	159.2	250.8	212.1	223.2	235.7	235.7

[1] Includes persons under 25 years old, not shown separately.   [2] With or without renal disease.
Source: U.S. National Center for Health Statistics, Vital Statistics of the United States, annual; and unpublished data.

Vital Statistics   95

No. 133. Death Rates From Cancer by Sex and Age: 1990 to 1998

[Deaths per 100,000 population in the specified age groups. See headnote, Table 132]

Age at death and selected type of cancer	Male 1990	Male 1995	Male 1996	Male 1997	Male 1998	Female 1990	Female 1995	Female 1996	Female 1997	Female 1998
Total [1]	221.3	219.5	217.2	214.6	213.6	186.0	191.0	190.2	189.2	187.7
25 to 34 years	12.6	11.7	11.5	11.5	10.9	12.6	12.2	12.6	11.7	11.7
35 to 44 years	38.5	36.5	35.6	34.5	34.4	48.1	44.0	42.9	43.1	42.1
45 to 54 years	162.5	143.7	140.7	138.0	136.5	155.5	140.7	135.2	132.3	128.2
55 to 64 years	532.9	480.5	469.1	453.4	441.1	375.2	357.5	349.6	343.2	331.6
65 to 74 years	1,122.2	1,089.9	1,080.9	1,058.4	1,045.5	677.4	690.7	685.2	676.8	675.2
75 to 84 years	1,914.4	1,842.3	1,802.7	1,770.2	1,745.6	1,010.3	1,061.5	1,060.0	1,050.6	1,048.6
85 years old and over	2,739.9	2,837.3	2,733.1	2,712.5	2,562.6	1,372.1	1,429.1	1,426.8	1,439.2	1,412.5
Persons, 35 to 44 years old:										
Respiratory, intrathoracic	9.1	7.6	7.8	7.5	7.5	5.4	5.1	5.3	5.6	5.5
Digestive organs, peritoneum	8.9	8.9	8.7	8.5	8.4	5.5	5.5	5.5	5.7	5.6
Breast	(B)	(B)	(B)	(B)	(B)	17.8	15.0	14.2	14.0	13.4
Genital organs	0.6	0.7	0.6	0.6	0.7	7.3	6.7	6.5	6.3	6.4
Lymphatic and hematopoietic tissues, excl. leukemia	4.5	4.9	4.6	4.3	3.9	2.1	2.3	2.2	2.3	1.9
Urinary organs	1.5	1.5	1.4	1.3	1.5	0.6	0.7	0.6	0.7	0.7
Lip, oral cavity, and pharynx	1.3	1.1	1.1	1.1	1.0	0.3	0.4	0.4	0.4	0.4
Leukemia	2.5	2.4	2.1	2.1	2.5	2.2	1.7	1.7	1.7	1.7
Persons, 45 to 54 years old:										
Respiratory, intrathoracic	63.0	49.9	48.5	45.2	43.6	35.3	30.1	29.0	27.5	26.7
Digestive organs, peritoneum	40.4	37.3	36.6	38.4	39.4	23.3	21.0	20.2	20.1	20.8
Breast	0.3	0.3	0.2	0.2	0.2	45.4	41.4	38.8	37.8	35.8
Genital organs	2.9	2.6	2.9	2.7	2.6	19.4	17.6	16.4	17.1	16.6
Lymphatic and hematopoietic tissues, excl. leukemia	10.9	11.0	10.3	10.9	10.2	6.0	6.2	6.2	5.8	5.6
Urinary organs	7.2	7.1	6.9	7.0	7.2	2.9	2.8	2.8	3.0	2.6
Lip, oral cavity, and pharynx	5.9	5.3	4.9	5.0	4.8	1.6	1.3	1.2	1.4	1.3
Leukemia	5.6	4.8	5.1	4.9	4.6	4.1	3.5	3.5	3.5	3.3
Persons, 55 to 64 years old:										
Respiratory, intrathoracic	232.6	196.1	190.7	182.7	176.4	107.6	104.8	102.2	100.7	99.7
Digestive organs, peritoneum	124.0	120.9	117.1	115.4	112.5	69.3	66.0	63.6	62.7	61.3
Breast	0.6	0.7	0.6	0.7	0.5	78.6	69.8	67.4	64.4	62.2
Genital organs	27.9	23.6	22.2	20.5	20.1	40.1	37.2	37.1	36.1	35.1
Lymphatic and hematopoietic tissues, excl. leukemia	27.2	27.7	27.8	27.6	26.5	16.7	18.6	18.6	18.9	17.2
Urinary organs	23.5	21.9	22.1	21.6	21.7	8.8	9.1	8.7	8.7	8.5
Lip, oral cavity, and pharynx	16.2	12.7	12.8	11.7	12.1	4.7	4.3	4.1	3.7	3.7
Leukemia	14.7	14.5	14.0	13.8	12.8	8.8	8.7	8.5	8.7	7.9
Persons, 65 to 74 years old:										
Respiratory, intrathoracic	447.3	432.4	424.6	418.8	416.4	181.7	205.0	209.0	212.0	215.3
Digestive organs, peritoneum	267.4	256.9	255.0	252.4	250.9	153.0	149.9	147.1	141.8	143.5
Breast	1.1	1.1	1.2	1.2	0.9	111.7	103.3	99.1	94.1	93.3
Genital organs	123.5	110.0	107.8	98.7	92.6	71.0	66.7	65.9	65.6	64.6
Lymphatic and hematopoietic tissues, excl. leukemia	56.8	61.3	61.6	63.5	61.9	39.5	44.0	43.0	43.5	42.8
Urinary organs	50.7	50.9	52.7	51.6	52.2	19.8	19.8	20.0	20.0	19.7
Lip, oral cavity, and pharynx	21.5	19.3	19.1	19.2	18.0	8.3	7.5	6.6	7.0	6.5
Leukemia	36.0	37.2	37.1	37.4	36.8	18.8	18.9	20.0	19.2	18.9
Persons, 75 to 84 years old:										
Respiratory, intrathoracic	594.4	573.4	566.9	562.9	553.2	194.5	245.1	251.1	258.9	262.8
Digestive organs, peritoneum	468.0	418.7	418.7	415.7	412.1	293.3	283.4	280.5	274.2	271.5
Breast	1.6	2.4	2.3	2.1	2.5	146.3	142.0	139.8	132.2	131.4
Genital organs	358.5	333.9	321.7	301.3	291.6	95.3	96.3	95.0	93.5	93.7
Lymphatic and hematopoietic tissues, excl. leukemia	104.5	109.3	113.4	114.1	112.6	71.2	80.3	80.2	80.7	82.4
Urinary organs	107.5	105.4	101.0	102.5	101.3	38.5	39.3	39.9	39.8	39.2
Lip, oral cavity, and pharynx	26.1	23.2	21.1	20.5	21.8	11.6	10.3	10.5	10.4	10.2
Leukemia	71.9	75.1	71.4	71.6	71.9	38.8	39.9	40.8	37.9	39.4
Persons, 85 years old and over:										
Respiratory, intrathoracic	538.0	543.2	543.2	568.8	532.5	142.8	187.5	190.6	203.2	202.5
Digestive organs, peritoneum	699.5	644.0	644.0	628.2	598.8	497.6	478.8	478.3	477.9	469.9
Breast	2.4	4.2	4.2	3.3	4.0	196.8	203.7	204.9	198.5	194.7
Genital organs	750.0	821.5	775.2	767.4	705.0	115.6	120.5	117.5	117.3	114.6
Lymphatic and hematopoietic tissues, excl. leukemia	140.5	154.2	153.7	148.8	153.1	90.0	100.4	98.0	103.9	98.3
Urinary organs	186.3	192.2	192.8	186.0	186.4	68.5	68.4	67.4	70.8	67.8
Lip, oral cavity, and pharynx	37.4	34.1	29.6	29.1	29.9	17.5	17.7	16.3	16.7	18.2
Leukemia	116.0	123.0	120.7	115.7	102.2	65.0	65.5	64.6	65.3	65.8

B Base figure too small to meet statistical standards for reliability.   [1] Includes persons under 25 years of age and malignant neoplasms of other and unspecified sites, not shown separately. *Vital Statistics of the United States*, annual; and unpublished data.

No. 134. Death Rates From Accidents and Violence by Race and Sex: 1990 to 1997

[Rates are per 100,000 population. Excludes deaths of nonresidents of the United States. Deaths classified according to the ninth revision of the *International Classification of Diseases*. See text, this section. See Appendix III]

Cause of death	White						Black					
	Male			Female			Male			Female		
	1990	1995	1997	1990	1995	1997	1990	1995	1997	1990	1995	1997
Motor vehicle accidents.....	26.1	22.6	21.9	11.4	10.8	10.9	28.1	24.6	24.2	9.4	9.0	9.9
All other accidents	23.6	24.7	25.3	12.4	13.5	14.5	32.7	31.6	29.1	13.4	13.5	13.0
Suicide...............	22.0	21.4	20.2	5.3	(NA)	4.9	12.0	(NA)	10.9	2.3	(NA)	1.9
Homicide	9.0	(NA)	6.7	2.8	(NA)	2.3	69.2	56.3	47.1	13.5	(NA)	9.3

NA Not available.

No. 135. Deaths and Death Rates From Accidents by Type: 1980 to 1996

[See headnote, Table 134 and Appendix III]

Type of accident	Deaths (number)					Rate per 100,000 population				
	1980	1990	1994	1995	1996	1980	1990	1994	1995	1996
Total	105,718	91,983	(NA)	(NA)	(NA)	46.7	37.0	(NA)	(NA)	(NA)
Motor vehicle accidents	53,172	46,814	42,524	43,363	43,649	23.5	18.8	16.3	16.5	16.5
Traffic	51,930	45,827	41,507	42,331	42,522	22.9	18.4	15.9	16.1	16.0
Nontraffic	1,242	987	1,017	1,032	1,127	0.5	0.4	0.4	0.4	0.4
Water-transport accidents	1,429	923	723	762	675	0.6	0.4	0.3	0.3	0.3
Air and space transport accidents ..	1,494	941	1,075	851	1,061	0.7	0.4	0.4	0.3	0.4
Railway accidents	632	663	635	569	565	0.3	0.3	0.2	0.2	0.2
Accidental falls	13,294	12,313	13,450	13,986	14,986	5.9	5.0	5.2	5.3	5.6
Accidental drowning...........	6,043	3,979	3,404	3,790	3,488	2.7	1.6	1.3	1.4	1.3
Accidents caused by—										
Fires and flames	5,822	4,175	3,986	3,761	3,741	2.6	1.7	1.5	1.4	1.4
Firearms, unspecified and other ..	1,667	1,175	1,123	992	947	0.7	0.5	0.4	0.4	0.4
Handguns...............	288	241	233	233	187	0.1	0.1	0.1	0.1	0.1
Electric current	1,095	670	561	559	482	0.5	0.3	0.2	0.2	0.2
Accidental poisoning by—										
Drugs and medicines	2,492	4,506	7,828	8,000	8,431	1.1	1.8	3.0	3.0	3.2
Other solid and liquid substances .	597	549	481	461	441	0.3	0.2	0.2	0.2	0.2
Gases and vapors	1,242	748	685	611	638	0.5	0.3	0.3	0.2	0.2
Complications due to medical procedures.............	2,282	2,669	2,616	2,712	2,919	1.0	1.1	1.0	1.0	1.1
Inhalation and ingestion of objects ..	3,249	3,303	3,065	3,185	3,206	1.4	1.3	1.2	1.2	1.2

NA Not available.

Source of Tables 134-135: U.S. National Center for Health Statistics, *Vital Statistics of the United States,* annual; and unpublished data.

No. 136. Death Rates for Injury by Firearms, Sex, Race, and Age: 1997

[Death rate per 100,000 population. Deaths classified according to the ninth revision of the *International Classification of Diseases*]

Item	5-14 yrs old	15-24 yrs old	25-34 yrs old	35-44 yrs old	45-54 yrs old	55-64 yrs old	65-74 yrs old	75-84 yrs old	85 yrs and over
MALE									
Firearms: White	1.8	24.8	23.1	19.5	19.0	20.1	23.9	36.1	49.3
Black	3.9	119.9	84.0	39.5	25.8	19.0	19.0	15.4	(B)
Accidents: White...........	0.5	1.3	0.8	0.5	0.5	0.5	0.5	(B)	(B)
Black................	0.7	2.5	(B)	(B)	(B)	(B)	(B)	(B)	(B)
Suicide: White	0.5	12.4	13.6	13.8	14.8	16.8	21.8	34.6	45.9
Black..................	(B)	11.6	11.4	6.3	5.2	7.1	11.3	11.6	(B)
Homicide: White	0.7	10.8	8.5	5.1	3.6	2.6	1.4	0.8	(B)
Black.................	2.6	104.2	71.1	32.5	20.2	10.9	6.4	(B)	(B)
FEMALE									
Firearms: White	0.5	3.8	4.5	4.9	4.2	3.1	2.9	2.4	1.7
Black	1.5	10.6	9.8	6.2	3.9	2.6	2.7	(B)	(B)
Accidents: White...........	(B)	(B)	(B)	(B)	(B)	(B)	(B)	(B)	(B)
Black................	(B)	(B)	(B)	(B)	(B)	(B)	(B)	(B)	(B)
Suicide: White	0.1	1.8	2.4	3.1	2.9	2.4	2.2	1.7	0.8
Black..................	(B)	1.3	1.2	(B)	(B)	(B)	(B)	(B)	(B)
Homicide: White	0.3	1.8	1.9	1.6	1.1	0.7	0.7	0.6	(B)
Black................	1.1	9.1	8.3	5.4	2.8	1.8	(B)	(B)	(B)

B Does not meet standard of reliability or precision.

Source: U.S. National Center for Health Statistics, *Advance Data from Vital and Health Statistics,* No. 231.

U.S. Census Bureau, Statistical Abstract of the United States: 2000

No. 137. Poisoning Deaths by Cause: 1980 to 1997

[Represents poisoning deaths of 50 or more. ICD-9 = International Classification of Diseases, Ninth Revision]

Item	1980	1985	1990	1992	1993	1994	1995	1996	1997
Total poisoning deaths [1]	12,075	13,173	14,103	16,026	17,658	18,334	18,549	19,177	20,094
Drugs, total [1]	6,313	7,606	9,344	11,611	13,206	13,943	14,213	14,872	16,019
Unintentional poisoning by drugs	2,492	3,612	4,506	5,951	7,382	7,828	8,000	8,431	9,099
Analgesics, antipyretics, and antirheumatics	636	1,209	1,278	1,657	2,094	2,148	2,508	2,490	2,813
Opiates and related narcotics	322	867	931	1,279	1,728	1,732	2,118	2,075	2,377
Aromatic analgesics, n.e.c. (incl. acetaminophen)................	21	41	65	69	88	90	81	80	107
Other nonnarcotic analgesics	117	78	88	79	77	96	86	102	111
Other..........................	97	158	145	167	149	182	179	179	178
Benzodiazepine-based	53	57	38	38	44	41	46	53	61
Other psychotropic agents	161	165	217	269	315	355	373	344	393
Antidepressants	141	128	142	141	152	123	150	143	147
Psychostimulants (amphetamines, caffeine) ...	18	32	71	128	162	228	219	197	243
Drugs acting on central and autonomic nervous system	159	448	821	1,113	1,183	1,393	1,156	1,411	1,336
Local anaesthetics (cocaine, lidocaine, procaine, and tetracaine).............	109	390	743	1,031	1,095	1,311	1,088	1,333	1,245
Other drugs	1,155	1,560	2,017	2,755	3,640	3,789	3,835	4,017	4,374
Agents primarily affecting blood constituents...	17	25	35	33	34	27	26	36	53
Agents primarily affecting cardiovascular system......................	190	225	257	218	213	244	226	227	195
Other	404	550	796	1,328	1,902	1,981	1,986	2,012	2,163
Unspecified	462	596	746	1,021	1,318	1,359	1,478	1,602	1,821
Suicide by drugs	2,761	2,668	2,920	3,215	2,975	3,022	2,874	2,896	3,108
Analgesics, antipyretics, and antirheumatics	310	324	374	405	407	445	417	406	457
Barbiturates.....................	498	220	137	154	115	133	102	98	130
Other specified drugs and medicaments	562	592	765	827	735	807	852	853	958
Unspecified drug or medicament	538	625	655	798	784	715	718	765	857
Undetermined intent-poisoning by drug	826	778	955	1,401	1,742	1,834	1,878	1,864	2,200
Analgesics, antipyretics, and antirheumatics .	202	229	247	491	689	687	750	737	857
Tranquilizers and other psychotropic agents.....	140	102	161	159	168	180	161	166	178
Other specified drugs and medicaments	174	186	324	478	618	657	669	661	780
Unspecified drug or medicament	217	216	206	252	257	291	281	288	371
Nondependent abuse of drugs	219	524	931	1,007	1,073	1,229	1,434	1,645	1,574
Tobacco	46	119	239	230	267	297	310	372	323
Morphine type	1	11	13	42	42	77	148	155	191
Cocaine type..................	1	18	85	146	176	238	300	304	304
Other, mixed or unspecified	167	370	587	574	573	589	646	781	724
Other solid and liquid substances, (E860-E866, E950.6-.9, E962.1, E962.9, E980.6-.9, 305.0)...	1,833	1,557	1,612	1,589	1,575	1,570	1,505	1,529	1,593
Unintentional poisoning by other solid and liquid substances	597	479	549	498	495	481	461	441	488
Alcohol, n.e.c.	385	305	369	332	337	323	318	308	342
Other and unspecified ethyl alcohol and its products.......................	182	171	168	168	146	152	143	140	164
Unspecified	163	98	144	117	140	125	124	131	127
Other and unspecified solid and liquid substances	64	51	51	60	54	53	50	42	55
Suicide by other solid/liquid substances	274	269	223	223	204	207	178	177	202
Other and unspecified solid and liquid substances	159	170	148	163	147	159	124	136	147
Undetermined intent-poisoning by other solids and liquids................................	67	54	51	75	54	39	53	46	54
Other and unspecified solid and liquid substances	55	47	46	63	50	32	45	39	50
Nondependent abuse of alcohol	889	750	784	788	819	838	808	849	832
Gases and vapors, total (E867-E869, E951-952, E962.2, E982)	3,929	4,010	3,147	2,826	2,877	2,821	2,831	2,776	2,482
Unintentional poisoning by gases and vapors .	1,242	1,079	748	633	660	685	611	638	576
Other utility gas and other carbon monoxide	1,006	880	582	504	535	553	506	502	459
Motor vehicle exhaust gas.............	611	488	293	223	245	246	234	219	208
Carbon monoxide from incomplete combustion of other domestic fuels	106	126	85	69	77	59	44	52	50
Unspecified carbon monoxide	219	202	123	141	127	153	140	146	123
Other gases and vapours	175	150	133	108	111	108	78	113	104
Other specified gases and vapors.........	151	125	95	76	72	84	60	87	85
Suicide by gases in domestic use and other gases and vapors	2,418	2,767	2,281	2,057	2,092	2,044	2,095	2,007	1,818
Other gases and vapors..................	2,380	2,729	2,253	2,023	2,067	2,026	2,074	1,981	1,793
Motor vehicle exhaust gas..............	1,998	2,308	1,877	1,706	1,670	1,618	1,659	1,508	1,367
Other carbon monoxide	361	396	348	295	373	393	391	454	407
Undetermined intent-poisoning by other gases.....	246	151	110	112	103	79	107	116	74

N.e.c. = Not elsewhere classified.   [1] Includes other causes not shown separately.

Source: U.S. Public Health Service, Compressed Mortality File, 1979-1998. National Center for Health Statistics, *Public Health.*

98   Vital Statistics

No. 138. Suicides by Race, Age, and Method: 1980 to 1997

Sex, age, and method	1980	1985	1989	1990	1991	1992	1993	1994	1995	1996	1997
All races, both sexes [1]	26,869	29,453	30,232	30,906	30,810	30,484	31,102	31,142	31,284	30,903	30,535
5 to 9 years old	3	3	4	6	1	10	6	4	7	4	4
10 to 14 years old	139	275	236	258	265	304	315	318	330	298	303
15 to 19 years old	1,797	1,849	2,009	1,979	1,899	1,847	1,884	1,948	1,890	1,817	1,802
20 to 24 years old	3,442	3,272	2,861	2,890	2,852	2,846	2,965	3,008	2,894	2,541	2,384
25 to 29 years old	3,228	3,364	3,299	3,192	3,086	2,864	2,979	3,026	2,880	2,816	2,709
30 to 34 years old	2,692	3,012	3,266	3,358	3,428	3,308	3,328	3,328	3,412	3,045	2,963
35 to 39 years old	2,150	2,528	2,937	3,098	3,089	3,177	3,248	3,397	3,332	3,476	3,407
40 to 44 years old	1,785	2,098	2,394	2,619	2,678	2,832	2,922	2,978	3,135	3,265	3,323
White, both sexes [1]	24,829	27,087	27,424	28,086	27,996	27,611	28,035	27,976	28,187	27,856	27,513
5 to 9 years old	2	3	2	4	-	6	4	2	5	4	3
10 to 14 years old	130	243	196	219	228	265	258	269	284	244	252
15 to 19 years old	1,635	1,643	1,743	1,701	1,628	1,531	1,594	1,588	1,587	1,522	1,509
20 to 24 years old	3,057	2,866	2,399	2,481	2,450	2,404	2,443	2,490	2,416	2,117	1,947
25 to 29 years old	2,876	2,985	2,847	2,731	2,629	2,464	2,504	2,557	2,443	2,369	2,306
30 to 34 years old	2,391	2,674	2,850	2,952	3,045	2,895	2,940	2,933	2,977	2,640	2,581
35 to 39 years old	1,979	2,316	2,628	2,779	2,799	2,845	2,902	3,003	2,985	3,123	3,066
40 to 44 years old	1,639	1,948	2,189	2,404	2,470	2,582	2,665	2,719	2,857	2,979	3,043
Black, both sexes [1]	1,607	1,795	2,153	2,111	2,097	2,143	2,259	2,271	2,231	2,164	2,103
5 to 9 years old	1	-	2	2	1	1	2	2	1	-	-
10 to 14 years old	9	22	32	29	31	33	39	39	30	36	40
15 to 19 years old	108	135	175	183	183	223	213	263	229	195	211
20 to 24 years old	307	289	350	282	296	313	395	366	323	328	302
25 to 29 years old	278	294	340	357	344	303	353	325	321	301	278
30 to 34 years old	245	262	349	318	301	331	296	282	312	289	289
35 to 39 years old	133	175	244	252	237	257	265	296	266	267	245
40 to 44 years old	128	115	168	171	153	194	183	201	218	209	208
Method total, both sexes:											
Drugs, medicaments, and biologicals	2,761	2,668	2,988	2,920	3,095	3,215	2,975	3,022	2,874	2,896	3,108
Other solid or liquid substances .	274	269	227	223	219	223	204	207	178	177	202
Gases and vapors . [?]	2,418	2,767	2,228	2,281	2,230	2,057	2,092	2,044	2,095	2,007	1,818
Suicide by hanging [2]	3,691	4,264	4,484	4,444	4,561	4,678	4,627	4,745	5,217	5,330	5,413
Handgun	2,109	2,981	3,120	3,464	3,619	3,455	3,586	3,706	3,700	3,675	3,519
Other & unspecified firearms . . .	13,287	14,382	15,058	15,421	14,907	14,714	15,354	15,059	14,803	14,491	14,047
All other	2,329	2,122	2,127	2,153	2,179	2,142	2,264	2,359	2,417	2,327	2,428
Method, White:											
Drugs, medicaments, and biologicals	2,620	2,503	2,774	2,703	2,894	2,979	2,742	2,756	2,643	2,690	2,857
Other solid or liquid substances .	246	234	195	190	195	194	180	171	153	160	170
Gases and vapors	2,375	2,713	2,154	2,227	2,172	1,994	2,017	1,987	2,018	1,946	1,770
Suicide by hanging [2]	3,288	3,712	3,853	3,812	3,945	4,050	3,943	4,063	4,493	4,584	4,666
Handgun	1,940	2,802	2,904	3,218	3,348	3,194	3,304	3,404	3,392	3,393	3,244
Other & unspecified firearms . . .	12,346	13,318	13,767	14,126	13,626	13,412	13,967	13,603	13,468	13,130	12,770
All other	2,014	1,805	1,777	1,810	1,816	1,788	1,882	1,992	2,020	1,953	2,036
Method, Black:											
Drugs, medicaments, and biologicals	106	120	164	159	144	160	164	188	157	134	166
Other solid or liquid substances .	17	26	23	22	14	12	14	24	13	10	20
Gases and vapors	29	39	53	30	44	46	49	33	57	39	34
Hanging [2]	263	334	408	374	375	379	418	394	406	409	417
Handgun	151	146	171	178	191	185	205	201	213	205	188
Other & unspecified firearms . . .	795	886	1,070	1,085	1,062	1,096	1,160	1,192	1,091	1,120	1,021
All other	246	244	264	263	267	265	249	239	240	247	257

- Represents or rounds to zero. [1] Includes ages not shown separately. [2] Includes strangulation and suffocation.
Source: U.S. National Center for Health Statistics, *Vital Statistics of the United States*, annual, and unpublished data.

No. 139. Homicide Rates by Race, Sex, and Age: 1996 and 1997

[Rate per 100,000 population]

Age	White				Black			
	Male		Female		Male		Female	
	1996	1997	1996	1997	1996	1977	1996	1997
Total [1]	7.0	6.7	2.5	2.3	51.5	47.1	10.2	9.3
Under 1 year	6.5	7.8	6.8	4.6	23.1	18.1	21.1	21.6
1-4 yrs	1.9	1.9	1.7	1.6	6.9	7.1	7.6	5.5
5-9 yrs	0.8	0.7	0.7	0.6	2.0	2.1	1.8	1.9
10-14 yrs	1.5	1.4	0.9	0.6	6.0	5.6	3.1	2.3
15-19 yrs	12.2	11.1	2.9	2.9	100.9	85.3	12.9	10.6
20-24 yrs	15.9	15.4	3.6	3.5	148.7	146.0	16.5	16.4
25-29 yrs	12.0	12.5	3.5	3.3	109.2	99.6	17.8	15.8
30-34 yrs	11.0	10.3	3.5	3.5	70.8	66.9	17.4	15.0
35-39 yrs	9.2	8.3	3.5	3.2	56.1	51.8	16.2	14.2
40-44 yrs	7.5	7.3	2.8	2.5	47.3	41.9	11.4	12.1
45-49 yrs	6.0	6.4	2.6	2.4	37.3	37.1	9.4	8.3
50-54 yrs	5.6	5.2	2.2	1.7	32.5	24.4	3.8	4.8
55-59 yrs	5.2	5.0	1.6	1.8	24.3	19.5	4.4	4.3
60-64 yrs	4.4	4.0	1.5	1.3	20.6	20.7	4.4	5.7
65-69 yrs	3.9	3.4	1.6	1.4	15.3	14.0	3.8	4.3
70-74 yrs	2.8	3.1	1.6	1.9	14.7	14.8	5.0	(B)
75-79 yrs	2.7	3.1	2.0	1.9	14.8	15.4	(B)	(B)
80-84 yrs	3.2	3.1	2.0	2.1	20.2	(B)	(B)	(B)
85 yrs. and over	2.8	5.2	2.4	2.7	(B)	(B)	(B)	(B)

B Base figure too small to meet statistical standards for reliability of a derived figure. [1] Includes persons under 15 years old, not shown separately.
Source: U.S. National Center for Health Statistics, *Vital Statistics of the United States*, annual.

Vital Statistics 99

No. 140. Deaths and Death Rates for Injury by Firearms by Race and Sex: 1980 to 1997

[Age-adjusted rates per 100,000 population]

Year	All races Both sexes	Male	Female	White Both sexes	Male	Female	All other Total Both sexes	Male	Female	Black Both sexes	Male	Female
NUMBER												
1980	33,780	28,322	5,458	24,849	20,714	4,135	8,931	7,608	1,323	8,505	7,265	1,240
1985	31,566	26,382	5,184	24,507	20,389	4,118	7,059	5,993	1,066	6,565	5,584	981
1990	37,155	31,736	5,419	26,299	22,249	4,050	10,856	9,487	1,369	10,175	8,922	1,253
1995	35,957	30,724	5,233	25,438	21,510	3,928	10,519	9,214	1,305	9,643	8,494	1,149
1996	34,040	29,183	4,857	24,114	20,511	3,603	9,926	8,672	1,254	9,175	8,050	1,125
1997	32,436	27,756	4,680	23,270	19,673	3,597	9,166	8,083	1,083	8,389	7,430	959
RATE [1]												
1980	14.8	25.3	4.8	12.4	21.1	4.2	29.1	53.0	8.1	33.5	61.8	9.1
1985	12.7	21.8	4.2	11.4	19.4	3.9	19.7	35.4	5.7	23.2	42.2	6.5
1990	14.6	25.4	4.2	11.9	20.5	3.7	26.9	48.9	6.5	33.4	61.5	7.8
1995	13.9	24.1	4.0	11.3	19.3	3.5	24.4	44.4	5.7	30.3	55.6	6.8
1996	12.9	22.4	3.6	10.5	18.0	3.1	22.6	40.8	5.4	28.5	52.0	6.5
1997	12.2	21.1	3.4	10.0	17.1	3.1	20.6	37.6	4.6	25.7	47.4	5.6

[1] Age-adjusted death rate. For method of computation see source.

No. 141. Deaths and Death Rates for Drug-Induced Causes by Race and Sex: 1980 to 1997

[Age-adjusted rates per 100,000 population]

Year	All races Both sexes	Male	Female	White Both sexes	Male	Female	All other Total Both sexes	Male	Female	Black Both sexes	Male	Female
NUMBER												
1980	6,900	3,771	3,129	5,814	3,088	2,726	1,086	683	403	1,006	648	358
1985	8,663	5,342	3,321	6,946	4,172	2,774	1,717	1,170	547	1,600	1,107	493
1990	9,463	5,897	3,566	7,603	4,646	2,957	1,860	1,251	609	1,703	1,155	548
1995	14,218	9,909	4,309	11,173	7,730	3,443	3,045	2,179	866	2,800	2,011	789
1996	14,843	10,093	4,750	11,903	8,061	3,842	2,940	2,032	908	2,682	1,876	806
1997	15,973	10,991	4,982	12,863	8,821	4,042	3,110	2,170	940	2,816	1,988	828
RATE [1]												
1980	3.0	3.4	2.6	2.9	3.2	2.6	3.7	4.9	2.5	4.1	5.8	2.7
1985	3.5	4.5	2.6	3.3	4.0	2.5	4.9	7.2	2.9	5.9	8.9	3.3
1990	3.6	4.6	2.6	3.3	4.2	2.5	4.6	6.7	2.8	5.7	8.4	3.4
1995	5.1	7.3	3.0	4.8	6.8	2.8	6.7	10.4	3.5	8.5	13.3	4.4
1996	5.2	7.3	3.2	5.0	6.9	3.1	6.3	9.5	3.6	8.0	12.2	4.4
1997	5.6	7.9	3.3	5.4	7.6	3.3	6.5	9.8	3.7	8.2	12.6	4.4

[1] Age-adjusted death rate. For method of computation see source.

No. 142. Deaths and Death Rates for Alcohol-Induced Causes by Race and Sex: 1980 to 1997

[Age-adjusted rates per 100,000 population]

Year	All races Both sexes	Male	Female	White Both sexes	Male	Female	All other Total Both sexes	Male	Female	Black Both sexes	Male	Female
NUMBER												
1980	19,765	14,447	5,318	14,815	10,936	3,879	4,950	3,511	1,439	4,451	3,170	1,281
1985	17,741	13,216	4,525	13,216	9,922	3,294	4,525	3,294	1,231	4,114	3,030	1,084
1990	19,757	14,842	4,915	14,904	11,334	3,570	4,853	3,508	1,345	4,337	3,172	1,165
1995	20,231	15,443	4,788	15,991	12,338	3,653	4,240	3,105	1,135	3,538	2,614	924
1996	19,770	14,926	4,844	15,868	12,057	3,811	3,902	2,869	1,033	3,224	2,400	824
1997	19,576	14,755	4,821	15,962	12,110	3,852	3,614	2,645	969	2,954	2,196	758
RATE [1]												
1980	8.4	13.0	4.3	6.9	10.8	3.5	18.8	29.5	10.0	20.4	32.4	10.6
1985	7.0	11.0	3.4	5.8	9.2	2.8	14.6	23.5	7.2	16.8	27.7	8.0
1990	7.2	11.4	3.4	6.2	9.9	2.8	13.6	22.0	6.8	16.1	26.6	7.7
1995	6.7	10.8	3.0	6.2	9.9	2.7	10.1	16.7	4.8	11.5	19.4	5.3
1996	6.4	10.2	3.0	6.0	9.5	2.8	9.0	14.7	4.3	10.2	17.2	4.7
1997	6.3	9.9	2.9	6.0	9.4	2.7	8.1	13.4	3.9	9.2	15.6	4.2

[1] Age-adjusted death rate. For method of computation see source.

Source of Tables 140-142: U.S. National Center for Health Statistics, *National Vital Statistics Report (NVSR)* (formerly *Monthly Vital Statistics Report*).

No. 143. Deaths—Life Years Lost and Mortality Costs by Age, Sex, and Cause: 1997

[**Life years lost:** Number of years person would have lived in absence of death. **Mortality cost:** value of lifetime earnings lost by persons who die prematurely, discounted at 6 percent]

Characteristic	Num- ber of deaths (1,000)	Life years lost [1] Total (1,000)	Per death	Mortality cost [2] Total (mil.)	Per death	Characteristic	Num- ber of deaths (1,000)	Life years lost [1] Total (1,000)	Per death	Mortality cost [2] Total (mil.)	Per death
Total, 1997 .	**2,314**	**37,749**	**16**	**329,712**	**142,495**	Heart disease . . .	357	4,848	14	68,976	193,454
Under 5 yrs. old . .	34	2,551	76	18,553	553,067	Cancer.	281	4,288	15	44,280	157,521
5 to 14 yrs. old . .	8	555	69	5,934	736,191	Cerebrovascular					
15 to 24 yrs. old .	32	1,839	58	30,076	953,447	diseases.	63	760	12	6,405	102,378
25 to 44 yrs. old .	135	5,791	43	114,770	850,490	Accidents and					
45 to 64 yrs. old .	323	9,734	30	126,003	390,461	adverse effects .	62	2,172	35	39,535	638,979
65 yrs. old and						Other.	392	7,937	20	82,327	210,213
over.	1,783	17,279	10	34,376	19,279						
Heart disease . . .	727	9,155	13	97,462	134,078	**Female**	**1,160**	**17,744**	**15**	**88,190**	**76,018**
Cancer.	540	8,895	17	69,964	129,667	Under 5 yrs. old . .	15	1,161	79	6,915	472,408
Cerebrovascular						5 to 14 yrs. old . .	3	239	72	2,048	620,905
diseases.	160	1,874	12	9,905	61,990	15 to 24 yrs. old .	8	515	63	6,238	757,825
Accidents and						25 to 44 yrs. old .	45	2,067	46	28,228	625,924
adverse effects .	96	3,216	34	49,584	518,965	45 to 64 yrs. old .	93	4,144	44	33,566	359,989
Other.	792	14,610	18	102,797	129,787	65 yrs. old and					
Male	**1,154**	**20,005**	**17**	**241,522**	**209,342**	over.	996	9,618	10	11,195	11,245
Under 5 yrs. old . .	19	1,390	74	11,639	615,504	Heart disease . . .	370	4,308	12	28,486	76,916
5 to 14 yrs. old . .	5	316	66	3,887	816,018	Cancer.	258	4,607	18	25,684	99,373
15 to 24 yrs. old .	23	1,323	57	23,837	1,022,526	Cerebrovascular					
25 to 44 yrs. old .	90	3,724	42	86,542	963,208	diseases.	97	1,113	12	3,500	36,003
45 to 64 yrs. old .	229	5,589	24	92,438	402,843	Accidents and					
65 yrs. old and						adverse effects .	34	1,044	31	10,049	298,440
over.	787	7,661	10	23,180	29,438	Other.	400	6,673	17	20,470	51,122

[1] Based on life expectancy at year of death.   [2] Cost estimates based on the person's age, sex, life expectancy at the time of death, labor force participation rates, annual earnings, value of homemaking services, and a 4 percent discount rate by which to convert to present worth the potential aggregate earnings lost over the years.

Source: Institute for Health and Aging, University of California, San Francisco, CA, unpublished data.

No. 144. Marriages and Divorces: 1970 to 1998

Year	Marriages [1] Number (1,000)	Marriages [1] Rate per 1,000 population Total	Men, 15 yrs. old and over [2]	Women, 15 yrs. old and over [2]	Unmarried women 15 yrs. old and over	15 to 44 yrs. old	Divorces and annulments Number (1,000)	Rate per 1,000 population Total [2]	Married women, 15 yrs. old and over
1970	2,159	10.6	31.1	28.4	76.5	140.2	708	3.5	14.9
1975	2,153	10.0	27.9	25.6	66.9	118.5	1,036	4.8	20.3
1980	2,390	10.6	28.5	26.1	61.4	102.6	1,189	5.2	22.6
1984	2,477	10.5	28.0	25.8	59.5	99.0	1,169	5.0	21.5
1985	2,413	10.1	27.0	24.9	57.0	94.9	1,190	5.0	21.7
1986	2,407	10.0	26.6	24.5	56.2	93.9	1,178	4.9	21.2
1987	2,403	9.9	26.3	24.3	55.7	92.4	1,166	4.8	20.8
1988	2,396	9.8	26.0	24.0	54.6	91.0	1,167	4.8	20.7
1989	2,403	9.7	25.8	23.9	54.2	91.2	1,157	4.7	20.4
1990	2,443	9.8	26.0	24.1	54.5	91.3	1,182	4.7	20.9
1991	2,371	9.4	(NA)	(NA)	54.2	86.8	1,189	4.7	20.9
1992	2,362	9.3	(NA)	(NA)	53.3	88.2	1,215	4.8	21.2
1993	2,334	9.0	(NA)	(NA)	52.3	86.8	1,187	4.6	20.5
1994	2,362	9.1	(NA)	(NA)	51.5	84.0	1,191	4.6	20.5
1995	2,336	8.9	(NA)	(NA)	50.8	83.0	1,169	4.4	19.8
1996	2,344	8.8	(NA)	(NA)	49.7	81.5	1,150	4.3	19.5
1997	2,384	8.9	(NA)	(NA)	(NA)	(NA)	1,163	4.3	(NA)
1998	2,244	8.3	(NA)	(NA)	(NA)	(NA)	1,135	4.2	(NA)

NA Not available.   [1] Beginning 1980, includes nonlicensed marriages registered in California.   [2] Rates for 1981-88 are revised and may differ from rates published previously.

No. 145. Percent Distribution of Marriages by Marriage Order: 1970 to 1988

[Excludes marriages with marriage order not stated]

Marriage order	1970	1980	1981	1982	1983	1984	1985	1986	1987	1988
Total.	**100.0**	**100.0**	**100.0**	**100.0**	**100.0**	**100.0**	**100.0**	**100.0**	**100.0**	**100.0**
First marriage of bride and groom	68.6	56.2	54.7	54.8	54.4	54.4	54.3	53.9	53.9	54.1
First marriage of bride, remarriage of groom . . .	7.6	11.3	11.8	11.6	11.6	11.5	11.5	11.3	11.3	11.1
Remarriage of bride, first marriage of groom . . .	7.3	9.8	10.1	10.3	10.5	10.7	10.9	11.2	11.3	11.4
Remarriage of bride and groom	16.5	22.7	23.4	23.3	23.5	23.4	23.4	23.6	23.5	23.4

Source of Tables 144 and 145: U.S. National Center for Health Statistics, *Vital Statistics of the United States*, annual; *National Vital Statistics Report (NVSR)* (formerly *Monthly Vital Statistics Report*); and unpublished data.

Vital Statistics   101

No. 146. Marital Status of Women 15 to 29 Years Old at First Birth by Race and Hispanic Origin: 1970-74 to 1990-1994

[Data for 1975-79 to 1990-94 are based on the June 1995 Current Population Survey and are shown for first births to women residing in the United States at the time of their first child's birth. Data for 1970-74 to 1990-94, are based on the June 1980 Current Population Survey, and are for all women regardless of their place of residence at the time of the first birth. Data for Hispanics are from the June 1995 CPS and are for first births to women residing in the United States at the time of their child's birth]

Item	Number of first births (1,000)	Percent of first births			Percent of premaritally pregnant women marrying before birth of first child
		Premarital birth	Premaritally conceived birth	Postmaritally conceived birth	
ALL WOMEN					
1970-74	6,438	18.0	17.1	64.8	48.7
1975-79	6,626	25.7	12.0	62.2	31.8
1980-84	6,842	29.6	12.3	58.1	29.4
1985-89	6,364	32.7	10.7	56.5	24.7
1990-94	6,324	40.5	12.3	47.2	23.3
WHITE					
1970-74	5,376	11.1	17.6	71.4	61.3
1990-94	4,994	32.4	12.9	54.6	28.5
BLACK					
1970-74	905	59.0	14.5	26.5	19.7
1990-94	1,016	76.9	8.7	14.4	10.2
HISPANIC ORIGIN [1]					
HISPANIC					
1970-74	442	29.6	16.1	54.3	35.2
1990-94	957	40.2	14.2	45.6	26.1
NON-HISPANIC					
1970-74	6,055	19.5	14.9	65.6	43.3
1990-94	5,367	40.5	11.9	47.5	22.7

[1] People of Hispanic origin may be of any race.
Source: U.S. Census Bureau, *Current Population Reports*, P23-197.

No. 147. Marital Status and Marriage Order of Women 15 to 34 Years Old at First Birth by Age, Race, and Hispanic Origin: 1965-69 to 1990-94

[In thousands, except percents. Women 15 to 34 years old. Limited to women residing in the United States at the time of their first child's birth]

Characteristic	Period of first birth					
	1965-69	1970-74	1975-79	1980-84	1985-89	1990-94
ALL WOMEN						
Number of births, total.	5,689	6,797	7,033	7,559	7,234	7,484
Percent:						
Before first marriage	16.8	19.7	24.8	27.6	30.1	35.1
During first marriage.	81.1	77.5	72.2	65.8	63.4	58.9
Between first and second marriage	0.7	1.2	1.3	2.7	1.9	2.2
During second marriage	1.2	1.5	1.7	3.9	4.5	3.7
After second marriage	-	0.1	0.1	-	0.1	0.1
WHITE						
Number of births	4,809	5,755	5,790	6,132	5,868	5,999
Percent:						
Before first marriage	10.8	13.9	17.4	19.8	22.5	27.6
BLACK						
Number of births	743	862	1,024	1,146	1,069	1,090
Percent:						
Before first marriage	55.8	56.0	66.4	68.8	71.7	73.5
HISPANIC [1]						
Number of births	305	472	621	685	753	1,040
Percent:						
Before first marriage	17.7	29.8	32.0	36.7	34.8	37.6
NON-HISPANIC						
Number of births	5,383	6,326	6,412	6,874	6,481	6,444
Percent:						
Before first marriage	16.8	18.9	24.0	26.7	29.6	34.6

- Represents zero.   [1] Hispanics may be of any race.
Source: U.S. Census Bureau, *Current Population Reports*, P23-197, <http://148.129.129.31:80/prod/99pubs/p23-197.pdf>.

No. 148. Marital Status of Women 15 to 44 Years Old at First Birth by Selected Characteristics: 1990-94

[Based on the June 1995 Current Population Survey and are shown for first births to women residing in the United States at the time of their first child's birth. For composition of regions, see map, inside front cover]

| Characteristic | Number of first births (1,000) | Percent of first births | | | Percent of premaritally pregnant women marrying before birth of first child |
		Premarital birth	Premaritally conceived birth	Postmaritally conceived birth	
All women, total....................	7,859	33.6	11.0	55.3	24.7
Age at first birth:					
15 to 19 years old...................	1,873	75.2	13.8	11.0	15.5
20 to 24 years old...................	2,492	36.9	15.1	48.0	29.0
25 to 29 years old...................	1,959	11.8	7.2	81.0	37.9
30 to 34 years old...................	1,159	5.6	7.0	87.4	55.6
35 to 44 years old...................	376	5.2	2.5	92.3	32.5
Race/ethnicity: [1]					
Non-Hispanic White..................	5,420	24.8	10.9	64.3	30.5
Non-Hispanic Black..................	1,104	71.9	8.2	19.9	10.2
Non-Hispanic other races.............	39	72.2	12.4	15.4	14.7
Hispanic.........................	1,296	36.7	14.1	49.3	27.8
Years of school completed:					
Not a high school graduate............	1,304	63.6	10.5	25.9	14.2
High school graduate (includes GED)....	2,612	38.9	14.0	47.1	26.5
Some college, no degree, or associate degree.....	2,192	30.8	12.2	56.9	28.4
Bachelor's, graduate, or professional degree......	1,751	7.0	5.6	87.4	44.4
Citizenship status:					
Native born......................	6,954	34.3	10.9	54.9	24.1
Naturalized citizen.................	168	25.3	7.6	67.1	23.1
Not a U.S. citizen.................	738	29.5	13.5	57.0	31.4
Metropolitan residence:					
In central cities....................	2,521	42.5	10.7	46.8	20.1
Outside central cities...............	3,904	27.3	10.6	62.1	28.0
Nonmetropolitan...................	1,434	35.3	12.8	51.9	26.6
Region of residence:					
Northeast........................	1,476	31.9	10.4	57.7	24.6
Midwest.........................	1,632	35.8	9.6	54.6	21.1
South...........................	2,823	34.4	11.7	53.9	25.4
West............................	1,928	32.0	11.8	56.2	26.9

[1] People of Hispanic origin may be of any race.
Source: U.S. Census Bureau, *Current Population Reports*, P23-197.

No. 149. Marriage Experience for Women by Age and Race: 1980 and 1990

[In percent. As of June. Based on Current Population Survey; see text, Section 1 Population]

| Martial status and age | All races | | White | | Black | | Hispanic [1] | |
	1980	1990	1980	1990	1980	1990	1980	1990
Ever married 20 to 24 years old.......	49.5	38.5	52.2	41.3	33.3	23.5	55.4	45.8
25 to 29 years old................	78.6	69.0	81.0	73.2	62.3	45.0	80.2	69.6
30 to 34 years old................	89.9	82.2	91.6	85.6	77.9	61.1	88.3	83.0
35 to 39 years old................	94.3	89.4	95.3	91.4	87.4	74.9	91.2	88.9
40 to 44 years old................	95.1	92.0	95.8	93.4	89.7	82.1	94.2	92.8
45 to 49 years old................	95.9	94.4	96.4	95.1	92.5	89.7	94.4	91.7
50 to 54 years old................	95.3	95.5	95.8	96.1	92.1	91.9	95.0	91.8
Divorced after first marriage 20 to 24 years old.....................	14.2	12.5	14.7	12.8	10.5	9.6	9.4	6.8
25 to 29 years old................	20.7	19.2	21.0	19.8	20.2	17.8	13.9	13.5
30 to 34 years old................	26.2	28.1	25.8	28.6	31.4	26.6	21.1	19.9
35 to 39 years old................	27.2	34.1	26.7	34.6	32.9	35.8	21.9	29.7
40 to 44 years old................	26.1	35.8	25.5	35.2	33.7	45.1	19.7	26.6
45 to 49 years old................	23.1	35.2	22.7	35.5	29.0	39.8	23.9	24.6
50 to 54 years old................	21.8	29.5	21.0	28.5	29.0	39.2	22.5	22.9
Remarried after divorce 20 to 24 years old.....................	45.5	38.1	47.0	39.3	(B)	(B)	(B)	(B)
25 to 29 years old................	53.4	51.8	56.4	52.8	27.9	44.4	(B)	49.5
30 to 34 years old................	60.9	59.6	63.3	61.4	42.0	42.0	58.3	45.9
35 to 39 years old................	64.9	65.0	66.9	66.5	50.6	54.0	45.2	51.2
40 to 44 years old................	67.4	67.1	68.6	69.5	58.4	50.3	(B)	53.9
45 to 49 years old................	69.2	65.9	70.4	67.2	62.7	55.0	(B)	51.0
50 to 54 years old................	72.0	63.0	72.6	65.4	72.7	50.2	(B)	62.2
Redivorced after remarriage 20 to 24 years old.....................	8.5	13.1	(NA)	(NA)	(NA)	(NA)	(NA)	(NA)
25 to 29 years old................	15.6	17.8	(NA)	(NA)	(NA)	(NA)	(NA)	(NA)
30 to 34 years old................	19.1	22.7	(NA)	(NA)	(NA)	(NA)	(NA)	(NA)
35 to 39 years old................	24.7	28.5	(NA)	(NA)	(NA)	(NA)	(NA)	(NA)
40 to 44 years old................	28.4	30.6	(NA)	(NA)	(NA)	(NA)	(NA)	(NA)
45 to 49 years old................	25.1	36.4	(NA)	(NA)	(NA)	(NA)	(NA)	(NA)
50 to 54 years old................	29.0	34.5	(NA)	(NA)	(NA)	(NA)	(NA)	(NA)

B Base is less than 75,000.   NA Not available.   [1] Persons of Hispanic origin may be of any race.
Source: U.S. Census Bureau, *Current Population Reports*, P23-180.

Vital Statistics   103

No. 150. Marriages and Divorces—Number and Rate by State: 1990 to 1998

[2443.0 represents 2,443,000. By place of occurrence]

State	Marriages [1]						Divorces [3]					
	Number (1,000)			Rate per 1,000 population [2]			Number (1,000)			Rate per 1,000 population [2]		
	1990	1995	1998	1990	1995	1998	1990	1995	1998	1990	1995	1998
U.S.	2,443.0	2,336.0	2,258.0	9.8	8.9	8.3	1,182.0	1,169.0	850.8	4.7	4.4	4.3
Alabama.	43.3	42.0	49.9	10.6	9.9	11.4	25.3	26.0	26.3	6.1	6.1	5.9
Alaska	5.7	5.5	5.9	10.2	9.0	9.6	2.9	3.0	3.2	5.5	5.0	4.8
Arizona.	37.0	38.9	37.9	10.0	9.2	7.9	25.1	27.6	25.8	6.9	6.6	5.8
Arkansas	35.7	36.6	38.4	15.3	14.7	15.1	16.8	16.0	15.4	6.9	6.5	6.3
California [4]	236.7	199.6	194.1	7.9	6.3	5.9	128.0	(NA)	(NA)	4.3	(NA)	(NA)
Colorado.	31.5	34.3	31.4	9.8	9.2	7.7	18.4	(NA)	(NA)	5.5	(NA)	(NA)
Connecticut.	27.8	22.6	19.9	7.9	6.7	6.1	10.3	10.6	9.6	3.2	2.9	3.2
Delaware	5.6	5.4	5.0	8.4	7.5	6.7	3.0	3.7	3.4	4.4	5.1	4.9
Dist. of Columbia .	4.7	3.5	2.4	8.2	6.4	4.6	2.7	1.9	1.1	4.5	3.4	3.6
Florida	142.3	144.3	139.5	10.9	10.2	9.2	81.7	79.5	80.1	6.3	5.6	5.3
Georgia	64.4	61.5	59.8	10.3	8.5	7.7	35.7	37.2	35.8	5.5	5.2	4.8
Hawaii	18.1	18.8	20.8	16.4	15.8	17.5	5.2	5.5	4.8	4.6	4.6	4.6
Idaho	15.0	15.5	15.5	13.9	13.3	12.4	6.6	6.8	7.0	6.5	5.8	5.4
Illinois	97.1	83.2	84.5	8.8	7.0	7.0	44.3	38.8	40.5	3.8	3.3	3.2
Indiana.	54.3	50.4	34.6	9.6	8.7	5.8	(NA)	(NA)	(NA)	(NA)	(NA)	(NA)
Iowa	24.8	22.0	23.5	9.0	7.8	8.2	11.1	10.5	9.5	3.9	3.7	3.7
Kansas.	23.4	22.1	20.9	9.2	8.6	7.9	12.6	10.7	10.7	5.0	4.2	4.0
Kentucky	51.3	47.6	44.3	13.5	12.3	11.2	21.8	22.9	22.4	5.8	5.9	5.8
Louisiana	41.2	40.8	42.2	9.6	9.4	9.6	(NA)	(NA)	(NA)	(NA)	(NA)	(NA)
Maine.	11.8	10.8	10.5	9.7	8.7	8.4	5.3	5.5	5.1	4.3	4.4	4.4
Maryland	46.1	42.8	37.5	9.7	8.5	7.3	16.1	15.0	16.4	3.4	3.0	2.9
Massachusetts. . .	47.8	43.6	39.2	7.9	7.2	6.4	16.8	13.5	16.5	2.8	2.2	2.2
Michigan.	76.1	71.0	66.1	8.2	7.4	6.7	40.2	39.9	38.9	4.3	4.2	4.0
Minnesota.	33.7	32.8	32.2	7.7	7.1	6.7	15.4	15.8	15.3	3.5	3.4	3.3
Mississippi	24.3	21.5	20.6	9.4	8.0	7.4	14.4	13.1	13.0	5.5	4.8	4.7
Missouri	49.3	44.9	43.8	9.6	8.4	8.0	26.4	26.8	25.8	5.1	5.0	4.9
Montana.	7.0	6.6	6.4	8.6	7.6	7.2	4.1	4.2	3.4	5.1	4.8	4.7
Nebraska	12.5	12.1	12.3	8.0	7.4	7.4	6.5	6.3	6.4	4.0	3.8	3.8
Nevada	123.4	134.8	143.9	99.0	88.1	79.5	13.3	12.4	14.8	11.4	8.1	6.8
New Hampshire . .	10.6	9.6	7.3	9.5	8.4	6.1	5.3	4.9	7.0	4.7	4.2	4.1
New Jersey.	58.0	52.4	48.4	7.6	6.7	5.9	23.6	24.3	25.3	3.0	3.1	3.0
New Mexico	13.2	15.1	13.4	8.8	9.0	7.7	7.7	11.3	8.0	4.9	6.7	6.5
New York	169.3	147.4	115.9	8.6	8.1	6.4	57.9	56.0	45.8	3.2	3.1	3.1
North Carolina . . .	52.1	61.6	63.8	7.8	8.6	8.3	34.0	37.0	36.8	5.1	5.1	4.8
North Dakota. . . .	4.8	4.6	4.2	7.5	7.2	6.6	2.3	2.2	2.1	3.6	3.4	3.5
Ohio	95.8	90.1	85.6	9.0	8.1	7.6	51.0	48.7	46.0	4.7	4.4	4.3
Oklahoma	33.2	28.5	25.9	10.6	8.7	7.7	24.9	21.8	20.0	7.7	6.7	6.5
Oregon.	25.2	25.7	26.0	8.9	8.2	7.9	15.9	15.0	15.2	5.5	4.8	4.5
Pennsylvania. . . .	86.8	75.8	74.2	7.1	6.3	6.2	40.1	39.4	38.5	3.3	3.3	3.3
Rhode Island. . . .	8.1	7.4	7.5	8.1	7.5	7.6	3.8	3.7	3.2	3.7	3.7	3.7
South Carolina. . .	55.8	44.6	41.5	15.9	12.1	10.7	16.1	14.8	14.6	4.5	4.0	3.8
South Dakota . . .	7.7	7.3	6.7	11.1	10.0	9.2	2.6	2.9	2.6	3.7	4.0	3.9
Tennessee	66.6	82.3	81.2	13.9	15.7	14.8	32.3	33.1	34.5	6.5	6.3	6.0
Texas.	182.8	188.5	188.9	10.5	10.1	9.4	94.0	99.9	(NA)	5.5	5.3	5.0
Utah	19.0	21.6	21.5	11.2	11.1	10.1	8.8	8.9	8.8	5.1	4.6	4.2
Vermont.	6.1	6.1	5.9	10.9	10.3	9.9	2.6	2.8	2.6	4.5	4.8	4.7
Virginia.	71.3	67.9	64.3	11.4	10.3	9.4	27.3	28.9	30.0	4.4	4.4	4.2
Washington.	48.6	42.0	41.2	9.5	7.7	7.2	28.8	29.7	28.8	5.9	5.5	5.2
West Virginia. . . .	13.2	11.2	11.7	7.2	6.1	6.5	9.7	9.4	9.3	5.3	5.1	5.2
Wisconsin.	41.2	36.3	35.1	7.9	7.1	6.7	17.8	17.5	17.7	3.6	3.4	3.3
Wyoming.	4.8	5.2	4.7	10.7	10.7	9.7	3.1	3.2	2.8	6.6	6.7	6.7

NA Not available. [1] Data are counts of marriages performed, except as noted. [2] Based on total population residing in area; population enumerated as of April 1 for 1980; estimated as of July 1 for all other years. [3] Includes annulments. [4] Marriage data include nonlicensed marriages registered.

Source: U.S. National Center for Health Statistics, *Vital Statistics of the United States*, annual; *National Vital Statistics Reports (NVSR)* (formerly *Monthly Vital Statistical Report*).

Health and Nutrition

This section presents statistics on health expenditures and insurance coverage, including medicare and medicaid, medical personnel, hospitals, nursing homes and other care facilities, incidence of acute and prevalence of chronic conditions, nutritional intake of the population, and food consumption. Summary statistics showing recent trends on health care and discussions of selected health issues are published annually by the U.S. National Center for Health Statistics (NCHS) in *Health, United States*. Data on national health expenditures, medical costs, and insurance coverage are compiled by the U.S. Health Care Financing Administration (HCFA) and appear in the quarterly *Health Care Financing Review* and in the annual *Medicare and Medicaid Statistical Supplement* to the *Health Care Financing Review*. Statistics on health insurance are also collected by NCHS and are published in Series 10 of *Vital and Health Statistics*. U.S. Census Bureau also publishes data on insurance coverage. Statistics on health facilities are collected by NCHS and are published in Series 14 of *Vital and Health Statistics*. Statistics on hospitals are published annually by the Health Forum, L.L.C., an American Hospital Association Company, in *Hospital Statistics*. Primary sources for data on nutrition are the quarterly *National Food Review* and the annual *Food Consumption, Prices, and Expenditures*, both issued by the U.S. Department of Agriculture. NCHS also conducts periodic surveys of nutrient levels in the population, including estimates of food and nutrient intake, overweight and obesity, hypercholesterolemia, hypertension, and clinical signs of malnutrition.

National health expenditures—HCFA compiles estimates of national health expenditures (NHE) to measure spending for health care in the United States. The NHE accounts are structured to show spending by type of expenditure (i.e., hospital care,

physician care, dental care, and other professional care; home health; drugs and other medical nondurables; vision products and other medical durables; nursing home care and other personal health expenditures; plus nonpersonal health expenditures for such items as public health, research, construction of medical facilities, administration, and the net cost of private health insurance) and by source of funding (e.g., private health insurance, out-of-pocket payments, and a range of public programs including medicare, medicaid, and those operated by the Department of Veterans Affairs (VA)).

Data used to estimate health expenditures come from existing sources which are tabulated for other purposes. The type of expenditure estimates rely upon statistics produced by such groups as the American Hospital Association, the Census Bureau, and the Department of Health and Human Services (HHS). Source of funding estimates are constructed using administrative and statistical records from the medicare and medicaid programs, the Department of Defense and VA medical programs, the Social Security Administration, Census Bureau's *Governmental Finances*, state and local governments, other HHS agencies, and other nongovernment sources. Detailed descriptions of sources and methods are published in an article titled "National health accounts: Lessons from the U.S. experience" in the summer 1992 edition of the *Health Care Financing Review*, Volume 13, Number 4. Revisions to the sources and methods, along with the most recent analysis of health care expenditure estimates, are published in the *Health Care Financing Review's* annual article on national health expenditures.

Medicare and medicaid—Since July 1966, the Federal medicare program has provided two coordinated plans for nearly all people age 65 and over: (1) A hospital insurance plan which covers hospital and related services and (2) a voluntary supplementary medical insurance plan, financed partially by monthly premiums paid by participants, which partly covers physicians' and related medical services. Such insurance also applies, since July 1973, to disabled beneficiaries of any age after 24 months of entitlement to cash benefits under the social security or railroad retirement programs and to persons with end stage renal disease.

Medicaid is a health insurance program for certain low-income people. These include: certain low-income families with children; aged, blind, or disabled people on supplemental security Income; certain low-income pregnant women and children; and people who have very high medical bills. Medicaid is funded and administered through a state-Federal partnership. Although there are broad Federal requirements for medicaid, states have a wide degree of flexibility to design their program. States have authority to establish eligibility standards, determine what benefits and services to cover, and set payment rates. All states, however, must cover these basic services: inpatient and outpatient hospital services, laboratory and X-ray services, skilled nursing and home health services, doctors' services, family planning, and periodic health checkups, diagnosis and treatment for children.

Health resources—Hospital statistics based on data from the American Hospital Association's yearly survey are published annually in *Hospital Statistics* and cover all hospitals accepted for registration by the Association. To be accepted for registration, a hospital must meet certain requirements relating to number of beds, construction, equipment, medical and nursing staff, patient care, clinical records, surgical and obstetrical facilities, diagnostic and treatment facilities, laboratory services, etc. Data obtained from NCHS cover all U.S. hospitals which meet certain criteria for inclusion. The criteria are published in *Vital and Health Statistics* reports, Series 13.

NCHS defines a hospital as a non-Federal short-term general or special facility with six or more inpatient beds with an average stay of less than 60 days.

Statistics on the demographic characteristics of persons employed in the health occupations are compiled by the U.S. Bureau of Labor Statistics and reported in *Employment and Earnings* (monthly) (see Table 669, Section 13, Labor Force). Data based on surveys of health personnel and utilization of health facilities providing long-term care, ambulatory care, and hospital care are presented in NCHS Series 13 and Series 14, *Data on Health Resources Utilization* and *Data on Health Resources: Manpower and Facilities.* Statistics on patient visits to health care providers, as reported in health interviews, appear in NCHS Series 10, *National Health Interview Survey Data.*

The HCFA's *Health Care Financing Review* and its annual *Medicare and Medicaid Statistical Supplement* present data for hospitals and nursing homes as well as extended care facilities and home health agencies. These data are based on records of the medicare program and differ from those of other sources because they are limited to facilities meeting Federal eligibility standards for participation in medicare.

Data on facilities and patients in various mental health organizations and general hospital mental health services are collected by the Center for Mental Health Services, U.S. Substance Abuse and Mental Health Services Administration, and published in *Mental Health, United States*, biennially.

Disability and illness—General health statistics, including morbidity, disability, injuries, preventive care, and findings from physiological testing are collected by NCHS in its National Health Interview Survey and its National Health and Nutrition Examination Surveys and appear in *Vital and Health Statistics*, Series 10 and 11, respectively. The Department of Labor compiles statistics on occupational injuries (see Section 13, Labor Force). Annual incidence data on notifiable diseases are compiled by the

U.S. Census Bureau, Statistical Abstract of the United States: 2000

Public Health Service (PHS) at its Centers for Disease Control and Prevention in Atlanta, Georgia, and are published as a supplement to its *Morbidity and Mortality Weekly Report*. The list of diseases is revised annually and includes those which, by mutual agreement of the states and PHS, are communicable diseases of national importance.

Nutrition—Statistics on annual per capita consumption of food and its nutrient value are estimated by the U.S. Department of Agriculture and published quarterly in *National Food Review*. Historical data can be found in *Food Consumption, Prices, and Expenditures*, issued annually.

Statistics on food insufficiency and food and nutrient intake are collected by NCHS to estimate the diet of the Nation's population. NCHS also collects physical examination data to assess the population's nutritional status, including growth, overweight/obesity, nutritional deficiencies, and prevalence of nutrition-related conditions, such as hypertension, hypercholesterolemia, and diabetes.

Statistical reliability—For discussion of statistical collection, estimation, and sampling procedures and measures of reliability applicable to data from NCHS and HCFA, see Appendix III.

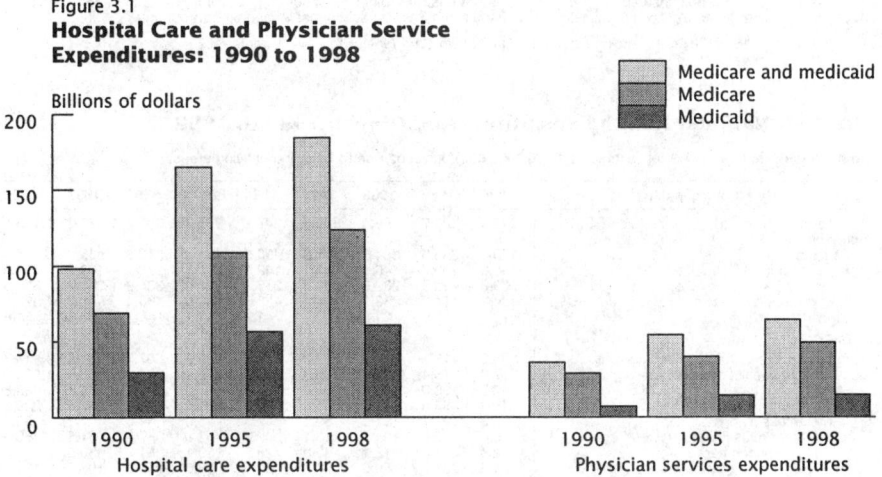

Figure 3.1
Hospital Care and Physician Service Expenditures: 1990 to 1998

Billions of dollars

Source: Chart prepared by U.S. Census Bureau. For data, see Table 157.

No. 151. National Health Expenditures by Type: 1980 to 1998

[In billions of dollars (247.3 represents $247,300,000,000), except percent. Includes Puerto Rico and outlying areas]

Type of expenditure	1980	1985	1990	1993	1994	1995	1996	1997	1998
Total	247.3	428.7	699.4	898.5	947.7	993.3	1,039.4	1,088.2	1,149.1
Annual percent change [1]	14.9	9.9	12.2	7.4	5.5	4.8	4.6	4.7	5.6
Percent of gross domestic product	8.9	10.3	12.2	13.7	13.6	13.7	13.6	13.4	13.5
Private expenditures	142.5	254.5	416.2	513.2	524.7	537.3	559.0	586.0	626.4
Health services and supplies	138.0	248.0	405.9	501.3	513.0	526.3	547.5	572.7	613.4
Out-of-pocket payments	60.3	100.7	145.0	167.1	168.2	170.5	178.1	189.1	199.5
Insurance premiums [2]	69.8	132.8	239.6	306.8	315.3	324.0	334.9	346.7	375.0
Other	8.0	14.5	21.4	27.4	29.5	31.8	34.5	37.0	38.8
Medical research	0.3	0.5	1.0	1.2	1.3	1.3	1.4	1.5	1.6
Medical facilities construction	4.2	6.0	9.3	10.7	10.5	9.6	10.1	11.8	11.5
Public expenditures	104.8	174.2	283.2	385.3	423.0	456.0	480.4	502.2	522.7
Percent federal of public	68.7	70.7	68.9	71.5	71.2	71.5	72.3	72.3	72.1
Health services and supplies	97.6	164.3	268.9	368.2	404.3	436.2	460.0	480.7	500.4
Medicare [3]	37.5	72.1	111.5	148.7	166.9	185.3	199.4	211.3	216.6
Public assistance medical payments [4] . . .	28.0	44.4	80.4	126.8	140.1	151.6	159.5	165.2	175.5
Temporary disability insurance [5]	0.1	0.1	0.1	0.1	0.1	0.1	0.1	0.1	0.1
Workers' compensation (medical) [5]	5.1	8.0	16.1	18.5	18.6	17.9	17.7	17.5	17.0
Defense Dept. hospital, medical.	4.4	7.5	11.6	13.3	13.2	13.4	13.3	13.4	13.6
Maternal, child health programs.	0.9	1.3	1.9	2.2	2.3	2.4	2.4	2.5	2.6
Public health activities	6.7	11.6	19.6	25.3	28.2	29.8	31.3	34.6	36.6
Veterans' hospital, medical care.	5.9	8.7	11.4	14.3	15.3	15.6	16.5	16.5	17.1
Medical vocational rehabilitation.	0.3	0.4	0.6	0.6	0.7	0.7	0.7	0.8	0.8
State and local hospitals [6]	5.6	7.0	10.8	11.8	12.0	11.9	11.5	11.2	11.8
Other [7]	3.1	3.3	5.0	6.6	7.1	7.5	7.5	7.7	8.7
Medical research	5.2	7.3	11.3	13.3	14.6	15.4	15.7	16.4	18.3
Medical facilities construction	2.0	2.6	3.0	3.8	4.1	4.4	4.7	5.2	4.0

[1] Change from immediate prior year. For explanation of average annual percent change, see Guide to Tabular Presentation.
[2] Covers insurance benefits and amount retained by insurance companies for expenses, additions to reserves, and profits (net cost of insurance). [3] Represents expenditures for benefits and administrative cost from Federal hospital and medical insurance trust funds under old-age, survivors, disability, and health insurance programs; see text, of this section. [4] Payments made directly to suppliers of medical care (primarily medicaid). [5] Includes medical benefits paid under public law by private insurance carriers, state governments, and self-insurers. [6] Expenditures not offset by other revenues. [7] Covers expenditures for Substance Abuse and Mental Health Services Administration, Indian Health Service; school health and other programs.

Source: U.S. Health Care Financing Administration, *Health Care Financing Review,* winter 1999.

No. 152. National Health Expenditures by Object: 1980 to 1998

[In billions of dollars (247.3 represents $247,300,000,000). Includes Puerto Rico and outlying areas]

Object of expenditure	1980	1985	1990	1993	1994	1995	1996	1997	1998
Total.	247.3	428.7	699.4	898.5	947.7	993.3	1,039.4	1,088.2	1,149.1
Spent by—									
Consumers	130.0	233.5	384.6	473.9	483.5	494.6	513.0	535.7	574.6
Out-of-pocket	60.3	100.7	145.0	167.1	168.2	170.5	178.1	189.1	199.5
Private insurance.	69.8	132.8	239.6	306.8	315.3	324.0	334.9	346.7	375.0
Government.	104.8	174.2	283.2	385.3	423.0	456.0	480.4	502.2	522.7
Other [1]	12.5	21.0	31.6	39.3	41.2	42.7	46.1	50.3	51.8
Spent for—									
Health services and supplies.	235.6	412.3	674.8	869.5	917.3	962.5	1,007.5	1,053.5	1,113.7
Personal health care expenses	217.0	376.4	614.7	790.5	834.0	879.1	924.0	968.6	1,019.3
Hospital care.	102.7	168.3	256.4	323.0	335.7	347.0	359.4	370.2	382.8
Physician services	45.2	83.6	146.3	185.9	193.0	201.9	208.5	217.8	229.5
Dental services	13.3	21.7	31.6	39.5	42.4	45.0	47.5	51.1	53.8
Other professional services [2]	6.4	16.6	34.7	46.1	49.6	53.6	57.4	61.5	66.6
Home health care.	2.4	5.6	13.1	23.0	26.2	29.1	31.2	30.5	29.3
Drugs/other medical nondurables	21.6	37.1	59.9	76.2	81.5	88.6	98.0	108.6	121.9
Vision products/other med. durables [3] . .	3.8	6.7	10.5	12.3	12.6	13.3	14.1	15.1	15.5
Nursing home care.	17.6	30.7	50.9	66.4	71.1	75.5	80.2	84.7	87.8
Other health services	4.0	6.1	11.2	18.0	21.9	25.1	27.6	29.2	32.1
Net cost of insurance and admin. [4]	11.9	24.3	40.5	53.7	55.2	53.6	52.1	50.3	57.7
Government public health activities.	6.7	11.6	19.6	25.3	28.2	29.8	31.3	34.6	36.6
Medical research [5]	5.5	7.8	12.2	14.5	15.9	16.7	17.2	17.9	19.9
Medical facilities construction	6.2	8.5	12.3	14.5	14.6	14.0	14.8	16.9	15.5

[1] Includes nonpatient revenues, privately funded construction, and industrial inplant. [2] Includes services of registered and practical nurses in private duty, podiatrists, optometrists, physical therapists, clinical psychologists, chiropractors, naturopaths, and Christian Science practitioners. [3] Includes expenditures for eyeglasses, hearing aids, orthopedic appliances, artificial limbs, crutches, wheelchairs, etc. [4] Includes administrative expenses of federally financed health programs. [5] Research and development expenditures of drug companies and other manufacturers and providers of medical equipment and supplies are excluded from research expenditures but are included in the expenditure class in which the product falls.

Source: U.S. Health Care Financing Administration, *Health Care Financing Review,* winter 1999.

No. 153. Health Services and Supplies—Per Capita Consumer Expenditures by Object: 1980 to 1998

[In dollars, except percent. Based on Social Security Administration estimates of total U.S. population as of July 1, including Armed Forces and Federal employees abroad and civilian population of outlying areas. Excludes research and construction]

Object of expenditure	1980	1985	1990	1993	1994	1995	1996	1997	1998
Total, national	**1,002**	**1,668**	**2,594**	**3,242**	**3,389**	**3,524**	**3,656**	**3,787**	**3,968**
Annual percent change [1]	13.9	9.3	11.1	6.4	4.5	4.0	3.7	3.6	4.8
Hospital care	437	681	986	1,204	1,240	1,270	1,304	1,331	1,364
Physicians' services	192	338	563	693	713	739	756	783	818
Dentists' services	57	88	121	147	157	165	173	184	192
Other professional services [2]	27	67	133	172	183	196	208	221	237
Home health care	10	23	50	86	97	107	113	110	104
Drugs and other medical nondurables.	92	150	230	284	301	325	356	390	434
Vision products and other medical durables [2]....	16	27	40	46	46	49	51	54	55
Nursing home care	75	124	196	248	263	276	291	305	313
Other health services.................	17	25	43	67	81	92	100	105	115
Net cost of insurance and administration [2].....	51	98	156	200	204	196	189	181	206
Government public health activities	29	47	75	94	104	109	114	124	131
Total, private consumer [3]	**553**	**945**	**1,478**	**1,767**	**1,786**	**1,811**	**1,861**	**1,926**	**2,047**
Hospital care	178	274	410	462	448	433	434	443	466
Physicians' services	135	234	381	474	481	492	500	515	540
Dentists' services	54	85	117	140	149	157	164	175	183
Other professional services [2]	19	50	99	122	128	136	145	155	169
Home health care	4	8	23	33	34	35	37	36	36
Drugs and other medical nondurables.	85	137	205	249	263	282	307	334	367
Vision products and other medical durables [2]. ...	14	21	29	30	29	29	30	31	32
Nursing home care	32	58	92	102	105	110	111	115	118
Net cost of insurance..................	33	76	122	155	150	138	133	123	135

[1] Change from immediate prior year.   [2] See footnotes for corresponding objects in Table 152.   [3] Represents out-of-pocket payments and private health insurance.

Source: U.S. Health Care Financing Administration, *Health Care Financing Review*, winter 1999.

No. 154. Government Expenditures for Health Services and Supplies: 1998

[In millions of dollars (500,359 represents $500,359,000,000). Includes Puerto Rico and outlying areas. Excludes medical research and construction]

Type of service	Total [1]	Federal	State and local	Medicare [2] (OASDHI)	Public assistance [3]	Other health services Veterans	Defense Dept. [4]	Workers' compensation [5]
Total [1]	**500,359**	**360,399**	**139,960**	**216,588**	**175,547**	**17,093**	**13,584**	**16,992**
Hospital care	232,902	187,377	45,525	123,925	63,424	13,787	10,043	7,672
Physician services	73,289	60,850	12,439	49,382	15,330	175	1,642	5,848
Drugs and other medical nondurables	18,799	10,744	8,055	1,169	16,730	17	520	316
Nursing home care.....	53,023	35,370	17,653	10,439	40,805	1,779	-	-
Administration	18,827	12,617	6,210	6,107	11,032	69	127	1,200
Public health activities. . .	36,636	4,222	32,414	-	-	-	-	-

- Represents zero.   [1] Includes other items not shown separately.   [2] Covers hospital and medical insurance payments and administrative costs under old-age, survivors, disability, and health insurance program.   [3] Covers medicaid and other medical public assistance. Excludes funds paid into medicare trust fund by states to cover premiums for public assistance recipients and medically indigent persons.   [4] Includes care for retirees and military dependents.   [5] Medical benefits.

Source: U.S. Health Care Financing Administration, *Health Care Financing Review*, winter 1999.

No. 155. Personal Health Care—Third Party Payments and Private Consumer Expenditures: 1980 to 1998

[In billions of dollars (217.0 represents $217,000,000,000), except percent. See headnote, Table 156]

Item	1980	1985	1990	1993	1994	1995	1996	1997	1998
Personal health care expenditures.	217.0	376.4	614.7	790.5	834.0	879.1	924.0	968.6	1,019.3
Third party payments, total	**156.8**	**275.8**	**469.6**	**623.5**	**665.8**	**708.6**	**745.9**	**779.6**	**819.8**
Percent of personal health care	72.2	73.3	76.4	78.9	79.8	80.6	80.7	80.5	80.4
Private insurance payments	62.0	114.1	207.7	265.2	274.7	286.3	298.1	312.4	337.0
Government expenditures	87.0	147.7	241.1	331.4	362.2	391.2	414.0	430.9	444.9
Other [1]	7.8	14.0	20.8	26.8	28.8	31.1	33.8	36.3	37.9
Private consumer expenditures [2]	**122.3**	**214.7**	**352.8**	**432.3**	**442.9**	**456.8**	**476.2**	**501.4**	**536.5**
Percent met by private insurance	50.7	53.1	58.9	61.4	62.0	62.7	62.6	62.3	62.8
Hospital care	41.8	67.8	106.6	124.0	121.2	118.2	119.6	123.2	130.9
Percent met by private insurance......	87.2	87.0	89.6	88.6	89.6	90.4	90.2	90.1	90.2
Physicians' services	31.8	57.9	99.0	127.1	130.2	134.5	137.8	143.1	151.7
Percent met by private insurance......	53.9	57.8	67.5	74.1	75.9	77.5	77.4	76.4	76.5
Drugs/other medical nondurables	19.9	34.0	53.4	66.9	71.2	76.9	84.5	92.8	103.1
Percent met by private insurance......	12.2	18.6	24.3	30.1	32.9	37.2	39.7	43.0	46.3

[1] Includes nonpatient revenues and industrial inplant health services.   [2] Includes expenditures not shown separately. Represents out-of-pocket payments and private health insurance benefits. Excludes net cost of insurance.

Source: U.S. Health Care Financing Administration, *Health Care Financing Review*, winter 1999.

Health and Nutrition 109

No. 156. Personal Health Care Expenditures by Object and Source of Payment: 1998

[In millions of dollars (1,019,347 represents $1,019,347,000,000), except as indicated. Includes Puerto Rico and outlying areas. Covers all expenditures for health services and supplies, except net cost of insurance and administration, government public health activities, and expenditures of philanthropic agencies for fund raising activities]

Object of expenditure	Total	Private payments						Govern-ment	Third party pay-ments [2]
		Total	Consumer						
			Total	Out of pocket pay-ments	Private health insur-ance	Other [1]			
Total	1,019,347	574,451	536,542	199,540	337,002	37,909		444,896	819,807
Hospital care.................	382,807	149,905	130,852	12,845	118,007	19,053		232,902	369,962
Physicians' services	229,504	156,215	151,677	35,697	115,979	4,539		73,289	193,806
Dentists' services.............	53,829	51,542	51,293	25,751	25,542	250		2,287	28,078
Other professional services [3]	66,587	52,356	47,377	27,158	20,219	4,979		14,232	39,429
Home health care..............	29,255	13,740	10,045	6,037	4,008	3,695		15,515	23,218
Drugs/other medical nondurables ...	121,906	103,107	103,107	55,353	47,755	-		18,799	66,553
Vision products/other med. durables [3] .	15,499	8,996	8,996	8,191	805	-		6,503	7,308
Nursing home care.............	87,835	34,812	33,196	28,507	4,689	1,616		53,023	59,328
Other health services	32,125	3,777	-	-	-	3,777		28,348	32,125

- Represents zero. [1] Includes nonpatient revenues and industrial plant. [2] Covers private health insurance, other private payments, and government. [3] See footnotes for corresponding items on Table 152.

Source: U.S. Health Care Financing Administration, *Health Care Financing Review*, winter 1999.

No. 157. Hospital Care and Physician Service Expenditures by Source of Payment: 1990 to 1998

[In billions of dollars (256.4 represents $256,400,000,000)]

Source of payment	Hospital care					Physician services				
	1990	1995	1996	1997	1998	1990	1995	1996	1997	1998
Total	256.4	347.0	359.4	370.2	382.8	146.3	201.9	208.5	217.8	229.5
Out-of-pocket payments	11.1	11.4	11.7	12.2	12.8	32.2	30.3	31.1	33.8	35.7
Third-party payments..........	245.4	335.6	347.7	358.0	370.0	114.2	171.6	177.4	184.0	193.8
Private health insurance	95.6	106.8	107.9	111.0	118.0	66.8	104.2	106.7	109.4	116.0
Other private funds	10.2	14.7	16.4	18.1	19.1	2.7	3.8	4.3	4.5	4.5
Government	139.6	214.0	223.4	228.9	232.9	44.7	63.6	66.5	70.1	73.3
Federal................	105.4	170.4	179.3	185.0	187.4	35.6	50.9	53.7	57.4	60.8
State and local..........	34.2	43.6	44.1	43.9	45.5	9.1	12.6	12.7	12.8	12.4
Medicare [1]	68.7	108.9	116.4	122.9	123.9	29.2	39.9	42.0	45.6	49.4
Medicaid [2]	29.4	56.6	58.7	58.4	60.8	7.0	14.5	15.3	15.4	15.0

[1] Medicare expenditures come from federal funds. [2] Medicaid expenditures come from federal and state and local funds.

Source: U.S. Health Care Financing Administration, *Health Care Financing Review*, winter 1999.

No. 158. Retail Prescription Drug Sales: 1995 to 1999

[2,297 represents 2,297,000]

Sales outlet	Number of prescriptions (millions)					Retail sales (bil. dol.)				
	1995	1996	1997	1998	1999	1995	1996	1997	1998	1999
Total	2,297	2,418	2,535	2,726	2,974	68.6	78.1	89.1	103.0	121.7
Traditional chain	883	937	999	1,087	1,203	26.5	30.2	35.0	41.5	49.8
Independent	697	692	685	693	724	20.9	22.2	23.9	26.4	29.9
Mass merchandiser	238	252	254	272	289	7.2	8.1	8.9	10.4	12.0
Food stores	221	242	269	306	357	7.0	8.3	9.8	11.4	13.4
Mail order [1]	258	295	328	368	401	7.0	9.3	11.4	13.4	16.6

[1] Mail converted to retail equivalents: one mail prescription = three retail equivalent prescriptions.

Source: National Association of Chain Drug Stores, Alexandria, VA, *The Chain Pharmacy Industry Profile*, 1999. (Copyright)

No. 159. National Health Expenditures by Source of Payment, 1990 to 1997, and Projections, 1999 to 2005

[In billions of dollars (699.4 represents $699,400,000,000). The health spending projections for 1999 to 2005 were based on the 1997 release of the national health expenditures (NHE). Subsequent releases of the NHE may not be consistent with these projections and should not be substituted for the 1997 historic estimates]

Source of payment	1990	1995	1997	Projections						
				1999	2000	2001	2002	2003	2004	2005
Total	699.4	993.7	1,092.4	1,228.5	1,316.2	1,403.6	1,495.5	1,590.4	1,690.4	1,799.5
Private	416.2	538.5	585.3	669.2	722.6	774.9	825.9	874.3	926.1	982.1
Public	283.2	455.2	507.1	559.3	593.6	628.7	669.6	716.1	764.3	817.5
Medicare	111.5	185.2	214.6	230.1	244.5	257.4	273.2	291.6	309.5	329.0
Medicaid	75.4	146.1	159.9	182.0	193.4	206.7	222.6	240.7	260.9	283.6
Other.................	96.3	123.9	132.6	147.2	155.7	164.6	173.8	183.8	193.9	204.9
Federal	195.2	326.0	367.0	399.8	423.9	447.7	476.2	508.8	542.1	578.7
State and local	88.0	129.2	140.0	159.5	169.7	181.0	193.5	207.2	222.2	238.8

Source: U.S. Health Care Financing Administration, Office of the Actuary, "Table 3a"; published July 1999; <http://www.hcfa.gov/stats/NHE-Proj/proj1998/tables/table3a.htm>.

No. 160. National Health Expenditures by Object, 1990 and 1997, and Projections, 1999 to 2005

[In billions of dollars (699.4 represents $699,400,000,000). The health spending projections for 1999 to 2005 were based on the 1997 release of the national health expenditures (NHE). Subsequent releases of the NHE may not be consistent with these projections and should not be substituted for the 1997 historic estimates]

Object of expenditure	1990	1997	Projections						
			1999	2000	2001	2002	2003	2004	2005
Total	699.4	1,092.4	1,228.5	1,316.2	1,403.6	1,495.5	1,590.4	1,690.4	1,799.5
Health services and supplies........	674.8	1,057.5	1,189.7	1,275.5	1,361.0	1,451.0	1,543.7	1,641.5	1,748.2
Personal health care	614.7	969.0	1,078.3	1,150.9	1,227.3	1,310.0	1,397.9	1,488.6	1,586.4
Hospital care.............	256.4	371.1	401.3	424.0	447.5	473.9	502.5	530.7	560.3
Physician services	146.3	217.6	241.5	258.7	275.9	293.3	310.7	328.7	347.9
Dental services	31.6	50.6	56.6	60.2	63.9	67.7	71.5	75.3	79.3
Other professional services	34.7	61.9	72.1	77.9	83.9	90.1	96.4	102.8	109.7
Home health care..........	13.1	32.3	33.8	36.0	38.3	41.0	43.9	47.4	51.1
Drugs and other medical nondurables	59.9	108.9	132.6	145.5	159.1	173.9	189.9	206.9	225.6
Vision products and other medical durables	10.5	13.9	14.3	15.0	15.8	16.6	17.6	18.5	19.5
Nursing home care.........	50.9	82.8	90.1	94.1	99.2	104.9	111.1	117.6	124.9
Other personal health care.....	11.2	29.9	36.0	39.5	43.7	48.6	54.3	60.7	68.1
Program administration and net cost of private health insurance ..	40.5	50.0	65.1	74.5	79.6	82.9	83.5	85.8	89.5
Government public health activities.	19.6	38.5	46.2	50.2	54.0	58.0	62.4	67.1	72.3
Research and construction	24.5	34.9	38.8	40.7	42.6	44.5	46.6	48.9	51.4
Research [1]	12.2	18.0	19.7	20.6	21.6	22.8	24.0	25.4	26.9
Construction..............	12.3	16.9	19.2	20.1	21.0	21.8	22.6	23.5	24.5

[1] Research and development expenditures of drug companies and other manufacturers and providers of medical equipment and supplies are excluded from research expenditures, but are included in the expenditure class in which the product falls.

Source: U.S. Health Care Financing Administration, Office of the Actuary, "Table 2"; published July 1999; <http://www.hcfa.gov/stats/NHE-Proj/proj1998/tables/table2.htm>.

No. 161. Personal Health Care Expenditures by Source of Payment, 1990 and 1997, and Projections, 1999 to 2005

[In billions of dollars (614.7 represents $614,700,000,000). The health spending projections for 1999 to 2005 were based on the 1997 release of the national health expenditures (NHE). Subsequent releases of the NHE may not be consistent with these projections and should not be substituted for the 1997 historic estimates]

Source of payment	1990	1997	Projections						
			1999	2000	2001	2002	2003	2004	2005
Total	614.7	969.0	1,078.3	1,150.9	1,227.3	1,310.0	1,397.9	1,488.6	1,586.4
Out-of-pocket payments	145.0	187.6	208.8	222.0	236.5	250.7	265.5	280.7	297.0
Third-party payments............	469.6	781.5	869.5	928.8	990.9	1,059.2	1,132.4	1,207.9	1,289.4
Private health insurance	207.7	313.5	357.9	386.3	416.4	447.5	478.3	509.9	543.1
Other private funds	20.8	35.6	40.4	43.3	46.2	49.2	52.4	55.8	59.3
Government	241.1	432.4	471.2	499.2	528.3	562.5	601.7	642.2	687.0
Federal	177.0	337.3	365.1	387.1	408.8	434.9	465.1	495.8	529.7
State and local	64.2	95.1	106.0	112.2	119.5	127.6	136.6	146.4	157.2
Medicare [1]	108.6	208.9	222.8	236.3	248.5	263.6	281.3	298.6	317.5
Medicaid [2]	71.4	152.3	172.2	183.2	196.2	211.3	228.6	247.8	269.6

[1] Medicare expenditures come from federal funds. [2] Medicaid expenditures come from federal and state and local funds.

Source: U.S. Health Care Financing Administration, Office of the Actuary, "Table 3a"; published July 1999; <http://www.hcfa.gov/stats/NHE-Proj/proj1998/tables/table3a.htm>.

Health and Nutrition 111

No. 162. Consumer Price Indexes of Medical Care Prices: 1980 to 1999

[**1982-1984=100.** Indexes are annual averages of monthly data based on components of consumer price index for all urban consumers; for explanation, see text, Section 15, Prices]

Year	Medical care services						Medical care commodities		Annual percent change [3]		
			Professional services			Hospital and related services	Prescription drugs and medical supplies			Medical care services	Medical care commodities
	Medical care	Total [1]	Total [1]	Physicians	Dental		Total [2]		Medical care		
1980 ..	74.9	74.8	77.9	76.5	78.9	69.2	75.4	72.5	11.0	11.3	9.3
1985 ..	113.5	113.2	113.5	113.3	114.2	116.1	115.2	120.1	6.3	6.1	7.2
1990 ..	162.8	162.7	156.1	160.8	155.8	178.0	163.4	181.7	9.0	9.3	8.4
1992 ..	190.1	190.5	175.8	181.2	178.7	214.0	188.1	214.7	7.4	7.6	6.4
1993 ..	201.4	202.9	184.7	191.3	188.1	231.9	195.0	223.0	5.9	6.5	3.7
1994 ..	211.0	213.4	192.5	199.8	197.1	245.6	200.7	230.6	4.8	5.2	2.9
1995 ..	220.5	224.2	201.0	208.8	206.8	257.8	204.5	235.0	4.5	5.1	1.9
1996 ..	228.2	232.4	208.3	216.4	216.5	269.5	210.4	242.9	3.5	3.7	2.9
1997 ..	234.6	239.1	215.4	222.9	226.6	278.4	215.3	249.3	2.8	2.9	2.3
1998 ..	242.1	246.8	222.2	229.5	236.2	287.5	221.8	258.6	3.2	3.2	3.0
1999 ..	250.6	255.1	229.2	236.0	247.2	299.5	230.7	273.4	3.5	3.4	4.0

[1] Includes other services not shown separately.   [2] Includes other commodities not shown separately.   [3] Percent change from the immediate prior year.

Source: U.S. Bureau of Labor Statistics, *CPI Detailed Report,* January 2000.

No. 163. Average Annual Expenditures Per Consumer Unit for Health Care: 1985 to 1998

[**In dollars, except percent.** See text, Section 14, Income, and headnote, Table 732. For composition of regions, see map, inside front cover]

Item	Health care, total					Percent distribution		
	Amount	Percent of total expenditures	Health insurance	Medical services	Drugs and medical supplies [1]	Health insurance	Medical services	Drugs and medical supplies [1]
1985	1,108	4.7	375	496	238	33.8	44.8	21.5
1990	1,480	5.2	581	562	337	39.3	38.0	22.8
1994	1,755	5.5	815	571	369	46.4	32.5	21.0
1995	1,732	5.4	860	512	360	49.7	29.6	20.8
1996	1,770	5.2	827	543	400	46.7	30.7	22.6
1997	1,841	5.3	881	531	428	47.9	28.8	23.2
1998.................	**1,903**	**5.4**	**913**	**542**	**448**	**48.0**	**28.5**	**23.5**
Age of reference person:								
Under 25 years old	445	2.3	206	136	102	46.3	30.6	22.9
25 to 34 years old	1,185	3.4	604	373	209	51.0	31.5	17.6
35 to 44 years old	1,688	4.0	790	557	341	46.8	33.0	20.2
45 to 54 years old	2,186	4.8	941	738	507	43.0	33.8	23.2
55 to 64 years old	2,158	5.8	991	642	525	45.9	29.7	24.3
65 to 74 years old	2,933	10.5	1,549	592	792	52.8	20.2	27.0
75 years old and over	2,938	14.0	1,503	601	835	51.2	20.5	28.4
Race of reference person:								
White and other	2,015	5.5	955	585	476	47.4	29.0	23.6
Black	1,069	4.1	605	226	238	56.6	21.1	22.3
Origin of reference person:								
Hispanic	1,096	3.7	537	303	257	49.0	27.6	23.4
Non-Hispanic	1,977	5.5	948	564	465	48.0	28.5	23.5
Region of residence:								
Northeast	1,773	4.7	909	464	401	51.3	26.2	22.6
Midwest	2,008	5.8	946	550	513	47.1	27.4	25.5
South	1,985	6.0	940	570	475	47.4	28.7	23.9
West	1,774	4.6	839	559	376	47.3	31.5	21.2
Size of consumer unit:								
One person	1,220	5.7	562	350	308	46.1	28.7	25.2
Two or more persons	2,177	5.3	1,054	619	503	48.4	28.4	23.1
Two persons............	2,459	6.7	1,177	646	635	47.9	26.3	25.8
Three persons	1,913	4.6	969	536	408	50.7	28.0	21.3
Four persons	2,061	4.4	985	670	406	47.8	32.5	19.7
Five persons or more......	1,888	4.1	909	600	380	48.1	31.8	20.1
Income before taxes:								
Complete income reporters [2]...	1,973	5.3	926	569	479	46.9	28.8	24.3
Quintiles of income:								
Lowest 20 percent	1,220	7.3	574	304	342	47.0	24.9	28.0
Second 20 percent......	1,971	8.3	972	443	556	49.3	22.5	28.2
Third 20 percent	1,771	5.6	905	434	432	51.1	24.5	24.4
Fourth 20 percent.......	2,086	4.8	968	646	472	46.4	31.0	22.6
Highest 20 percent......	2,815	4.0	1,212	1,015	588	43.1	36.1	20.9
Incomplete reporters of income .	1,660	5.6	865	445	350	52.1	26.8	21.1

[1] Includes prescription and nonprescription drugs.   [2] A complete reporter is a consumer unit providing values for at least one of the major sources of income.

Source: Bureau of Labor Statistics, *Consumer Expenditure Survey,* annual.

No. 164. Medicare Enrollees: 1980 to 1998

[In millions (28.5 represents 28,500,000). As of July 1. Includes Puerto Rico and outlying areas and enrollees in foreign countries and unknown place of residence]

Item	1980	1985	1990	1994	1995	1996	1997	1998
Total	28.5	31.1	34.2	36.9	37.5	38.1	38.4	38.8
Aged	25.5	28.2	30.9	32.8	33.1	33.4	33.6	33.8
Disabled	3.0	2.9	3.3	4.1	4.4	4.6	4.8	5.0
Hospital insurance	28.1	30.6	33.7	36.5	37.1	37.7	38.1	38.4
Aged	25.1	27.7	30.5	32.4	32.7	33.0	33.2	33.4
Disabled	3.0	2.9	3.3	4.1	4.4	4.6	4.8	5.0
Supplementary medical insurance	27.4	30.0	32.6	35.2	35.7	36.1	36.5	36.8
Aged	24.7	27.3	29.7	31.4	31.7	32.0	32.2	32.3
Disabled	2.7	2.7	2.9	3.7	3.9	4.2	4.3	4.5

Source: U.S. Health Care Financing Administration, Office of the Actuary, "Medicare Enrollment Trends 1966-1998"; published 30 June 1999; <http://www.hcfa.gov/stats/enrltrnd.htm>.

No. 165. Medicare Disbursements by Type of Beneficiary: 1980 to 1999

[In millions of dollars (35,025 represents $35,025,000,000). For years ending Sept. 30. Distribution of benefits by type is estimated and subject to change]

Type of beneficiary	1980	1985	1990	1995	1996	1997	1998	1999, proj.
Total disbursements	35,025	71,384	109,709	180,096	194,263	210,342	213,412	211,959
Hospital insurance disbursements [1]	24,288	48,654	66,687	114,883	125,317	137,789	137,140	131,441
Benefits	23,776	47,710	65,721	113,394	123,907	136,007	134,322	129,106
Aged	20,951	42,123	58,503	100,067	109,149	120,044	118,213	113,042
Disabled	2,825	5,587	7,218	13,327	14,758	15,963	16,109	16,064
Disabled	2,654	5,032	6,467	12,359	13,703	14,861	15,007	14,931
ESRD [2]	171	555	751	968	1,055	1,102	1,102	1,133
Peer review activity [3]	14	131	191	189	180	168	188	177
Administrative expenses [3]	497	813	774	1,300	1,229	1,614	1,653	1,978
Supplementary medical insurance disbursements [1]	10,737	22,730	43,022	65,213	68,946	72,553	76,272	80,518
Benefits	10,144	21,808	41,498	63,491	67,176	71,133	75,815	79,187
Aged	8,497	19,077	36,837	54,831	57,783	60,955	65,091	68,137
Disabled	1,647	2,731	4,661	8,660	9,393	10,178	10,724	11,050
Disabled	1,256	2,373	3,758	7,269	7,916	8,594	9,213	9,528
ESRD [2]	391	358	903	1,391	1,477	1,583	1,510	1,523
Administrative expenses	593	922	1,524	1,722	1,771	1,420	1,435	1,510

[1] Beginning 1998 home health agency transfers are excluded from total supplementary medical insurance disbursements and included in total hospital insurance disbursements. [2] Represents persons entitled because of End Stage Renal Disease only. Benefits for those who have ESRD but would be entitled due to their aged or disabled status are included in aged and disabled benefits. [3] Includes costs of experiments and demonstration projects. Includes costs of the health care fraud and abuse control program.

Source: U.S. Health Care Financing Administration, unpublished data.

No. 166. Medicare Trust Funds: 1980 to 1999

[In billions of dollars (23.9 represents $23,900,000,000)]

Type of trust fund	1980	1985	1990	1994	1995	1996	1997	1998	1999
HOSPITAL INSURANCE (HI)									
Net contribution income [1]	23.9	47.7	72.2	97.9	103.3	115.9	119.5	130.7	140.3
Interest received [2]	1.1	[3]3.4	8.5	10.7	10.8	10.2	9.6	9.3	10.1
Benefit payments	25.1	47.5	66.2	103.3	116.4	128.6	137.8	[4]134.0	[4]128.8
Assets, end of year	13.7	[5]20.5	98.9	132.8	130.3	124.9	115.6	120.4	141.4
SUPPLEMENTARY MEDICAL INSURANCE (SMI)									
Net premium income	3.0	5.6	11.3	17.4	19.7	18.8	19.3	[6]20.9	[6]19.0
Transfers from general revenue	7.5	18.3	33.0	36.2	39.0	65.0	60.2	[6]64.1	[6]59.1
Interest received [2]	0.4	1.2	1.6	2.0	1.6	1.8	2.5	2.7	2.8
Benefit payments	10.6	22.9	42.5	58.6	65.0	68.6	72.8	[4]76.1	[4]80.7
Assets, end of year	4.5	10.9	15.5	19.4	13.1	28.3	36.1	46.2	44.8

[1] Includes income from taxation of benefits beginning in 1994. Includes premiums from aged ineligibles enrolled in HI. [2] Includes recoveries of amounts reimbursed from the trust fund. [3] Reflects interest on interfund borrowing. [4] Monies transferred to the SMI trust fund for home health agency costs, as provided for by P.L. 105-33, are included in HI benefit payments but excluded from SMI benefit payments. [5] Excludes $10.6 billion lent to the OASI Trust Fund (see Table 607). [6] Data adjusted to reflect 12 months of premium and general revenue income.

Source: U.S. Health Care Financing Administration, Annual Report of the Board of Trustees of the Federal Hospital Insurance Trust Fund and Annual Report of the Board of Trustees of the Federal Supplementary Medical Insurance Trust Fund.

U.S. Census Bureau, Statistical Abstract of the United States: 2000

No. 167. Medicare—Persons Served and Reimbursements: 1990 to 1998

[24,809 represents 24,809,000. Persons served are enrollees who use covered services, incurred expenses greater than the applicable deductible amounts and for whom medicare paid benefits. Reimbursements are amounts paid to providers for covered services. Excluded are retroactive adjustments resulting from end of fiscal year cost settlements and certain lump-sum interim payments. Also excluded are beneficiary (or third party payor) liabilities for applicable deductibles, coinsurance amounts, and charges for noncovered services. Includes data for enrollees living in outlying territories and foreign countries]

Type of coverage and service	Unit	Persons 65 years old and over			Disabled persons [1]		
		1990	1995	1998	1990	1995	1998
Persons served, total [2]	1,000 ...	24,809	27,379	25,931	2,390	3,333	3,641
Hospital insurance [2]	1,000 ...	6,367	7,147	6,840	680	933	961
Inpatient hospital	1,000 ...	5,906	6,148	6,074	644	844	899
Skilled-nursing services	1,000 ...	615	1,186	1,443	23	54	75
Home health services	1,000 ...	1,818	3,185	2,641	122	272	225
Supplementary medical insurance [2]	1,000 ...	24,687	27,234	25,605	2,365	3,299	3,596
Physicians' and other medical services	1,000 ...	24,193	26,621	25,083	2,249	3,184	3,452
Outpatient services	1,000 ...	14,055	17,597	18,150	1,496	2,281	2,619
Home health services	1,000 ...	38	42	1,339	-	-	131
Persons served per 1,000 enrollees, total [2]	Rate....	802	826	767	734	759	725
Hospital insurance [2]	Rate....	209	218	205	209	212	191
Inpatient hospital	Rate....	194	188	182	198	192	179
Skilled-nursing services	Rate....	20	36	43	7	12	15
Home health services	Rate....	60	97	79	38	62	45
Supplementary medical insurance [2]	Rate....	832	858	793	804	837	804
Physicians' and other medical services	Rate....	815	839	776	764	808	772
Outpatient services	Rate....	474	554	562	508	579	586
Home health services	Rate....	1	1	42	-	-	29
Reimbursements, total	Mil. dol ..	88,778	138,948	146,355	11,239	21,024	23,855
Per person served	Dollars ...	3,578	5,075	5,644	4,703	6,308	6,552
Hospital insurance	Mil. dol .	54,244	89,631	90,511	6,694	12,752	13,624
Inpatient hospital	Mil. dol .	48,952	68,213	71,899	6,346	11,079	12,342
Skilled-nursing services	Mil. dol .	1,886	7,504	11,074	85	374	603
Home health services	Mil. dol .	3,406	13,914	7,534	264	1,300	678
Supplementary medical insurance	Mil. dol .	34,533	49,317	55,844	4,545	8,272	10,231
Physicians' and other medical services	Mil. dol .	27,379	37,069	38,685	2,831	4,888	5,749
Outpatient services	Mil. dol .	7,077	12,045	12,972	1,714	3,384	3,994
Home health services	Mil. dol .	78	203	4,187	-	-	489

- Represents or rounds to zero.   [1] Age under 65; includes persons enrolled because of end-stage renal disease (ESRD) only.
[2] Persons are counted once for each type of covered service used, but are not double counted in totals.

Source: U.S. Health Care Financing Administration, *Medicare Program Statistics*, annual; and unpublished data.

No. 168. Medicare Benefits by Type of Provider: 1980 to 1999

[In millions of dollars (23,776 represents $23,776,000,000). For years ending Sept. 30. Distribution of benefits by type is estimated and subject to change]

Type of provider	1980	1985	1990	1995	1996	1997	1998	1999, proj.
Hospital insurance benefits, total .	23,776	47,710	65,721	113,394	123,908	136,007	134,321	129,107
Inpatient hospital	22,860	44,610	57,012	80,881	84,200	88,292	86,998	85,259
Skilled nursing facility	392	550	2,761	8,761	10,636	12,561	13,630	12,361
Home health agency	524	1,908	3,295	15,851	17,250	18,012	13,806	8,764
Hospice	(NA)	34	318	1,854	1,969	2,082	2,080	2,479
Managed care	(NA)	608	2,335	6,047	9,853	15,059	17,807	20,243
Supplementary medical insurance benefits, total .	10,144	21,808	41,498	63,491	67,176	71,133	75,815	79,187
Physician fee schedule	(NA)	(NA)	(NA)	31,110	31,569	31,960	32,341	33,184
Durable medical equipment	(NA)	(NA)	(NA)	3,576	3,785	4,112	4,108	4,146
Carrier lab [1]	(NA)	(NA)	(NA)	2,819	2,654	2,414	2,168	2,040
Other carrier [2]	(NA)	(NA)	(NA)	4,513	4,883	5,449	5,845	6,245
Hospital [3]	(NA)	(NA)	(NA)	8,449	8,720	9,293	9,056	8,520
Home health	(NA)	(NA)	(NA)	223	257	265	202	761
Intermediary lab [4]	(NA)	(NA)	(NA)	1,437	1,322	1,416	1,470	1,571
Other intermediary [5]	(NA)	(NA)	(NA)	5,111	5,632	6,330	6,492	5,823
Managed care	(NA)	(NA)	(NA)	6,253	8,353	8,353	14,132	16,897

NA Not available.   [1] Lab services paid under the lab fee schedule performed in a physician's office lab or an independent lab.   [2] Includes free-standing ambulatory surgical centers facility costs, ambulance, and supplies.   [3] Includes the hospital facility costs for Medicare Part B services which are predominantly in the outpatient department. The physician reimbursement associated with these services is included on the "Physician Fee Schedule" line.   [4] Lab fee services paid under the lab fee schedule performed in a hospital outpatient department.   [5] Includes ESRD free-standing dialysis facility payments and payments to rural health clinics, outpatient rehabilitation facilities, psychiatric hospitals, and federally qualified health centers.

Source: U.S. Health Care Financing Administration, unpublished data.

No. 169. Medicare—Summary by State and Other Area: 1995 and 1999

[For fiscal year ending in year shown. (37,535 represents 37,535,000)]

State and area	Enrollment [1] (1,000)		Payments [2] (mil. dol.)		State and area	Enrollment [1] (1,000)		Payments [2] (mil. dol.)	
	1995	1999	1995	1999		1995	1999	1995	1999
All areas ..	**37,535**	**39,027**	**176,884**	**208,624**	MO	833	852	3,821	4,062
U.S.....	**36,758**	**38,175**	**175,976**	**207,303**	MT.........	130	135	489	509
					NE.........	249	252	840	1,056
AL.........	642	675	3,042	3,817	NV.........	194	229	894	1,048
AK.........	34	40	133	133	NH.........	156	167	597	557
AZ.........	602	659	2,717	2,828	NJ.........	1,168	1,188	5,603	7,475
AR.........	423	435	1,638	2,044	NM.........	211	229	710	795
CA.........	3,633	3,822	20,406	23,306	NY.........	2,630	2,677	13,904	16,838
CO.........	421	458	1,835	2,328	NC.........	1,027	1,112	4,276	5,809
CT.........	502	510	2,584	2,986	ND.........	103	103	412	459
DE.........	101	110	445	386	OH.........	1,666	1,686	7,262	9,305
DC.........	78	75	1,164	825	OK.........	488	502	2,178	2,066
FL.........	2,628	2,764	14,828	18,389	OR.........	469	483	1,685	1,649
GA.........	833	897	4,090	3,895	PA.........	2,071	2,081	10,796	12,953
HI.........	149	161	580	600	RI.........	168	170	772	973
ID	150	162	463	580	SC.........	509	556	1,926	2,801
IL.........	1,617	1,621	7,276	7,606	SD.........	117	119	563	487
IN	823	843	3,491	4,730	TN.........	771	814	4,083	4,855
IA	474	475	1,527	1,417	TX.........	2,080	2,219	11,504	14,228
KS.........	383	388	1,545	1,739	UT.........	187	201	708	836
KY.........	586	614	2,401	3,120	VT.........	83	88	284	254
LA.........	581	596	3,448	4,258	VA.........	818	875	2,979	4,050
ME.........	201	213	707	660	WA.........	688	723	2,603	2,505
MD.........	602	632	2,868	4,096	WV.........	330	334	1,208	1,653
MA.........	933	950	5,496	4,833	WI.........	762	775	2,673	3,356
MI	1,347	1,384	6,237	6,716	WY.........	60	64	180	211
MN.........	631	647	2,378	2,992	PR	477	524	875	1,264
MS.........	397	413	1,723	2,231	Other areas .	300	328	33	56

[1] Hospital and/or medical insurance enrollment for 1995 as of July and for 1999 as of September.   [2] Benefit payments for all areas represent 100 percent fee for service experience and actual HMO expenditures through the fiscal year and relate to the state of the provider.

Source: U.S. Health Care Financing Administration, "Medicare Beneficiaries Enrolled as of July 1 of each year. Years 1995-1998"; published 29 July 1999; <http://www.hcfa.gov/stats/histenr1.htm> and unpublished data.

No. 170. Medicaid—Selected Characteristics of Persons Covered: 1998

[In thousands, except percent (27,647 represents 27,647,000). Represents number of persons as of March of following year who were enrolled at any time in year shown. Person did not have to receive medical care paid for by medicaid in order to be counted. See headnote, Table 603]

Poverty status	Total [1]	White	Black	Hispanic [2]	Under 18 years old	18-44 years old	45-64 years old	65 years and over
Persons covered, total......	**27,647**	**18,131**	**7,820**	**5,550**	**14,066**	**7,593**	**3,025**	**2,962**
Below poverty level..........	13,996	8,470	4,659	3,170	7,784	3,836	1,372	1,003
Above poverty level	13,651	9,661	3,161	2,380	6,282	3,757	1,653	1,959
Percent of population covered..	10.2	8.1	22.4	17.6	19.7	7.0	5.2	9.1
Below poverty level..........	40.6	36.1	51.3	39.3	57.8	29.6	29.5	29.6
Above poverty level	5.8	4.8	12.3	10.2	10.9	3.9	3.1	6.8

[1] Includes other races not shown separately.   [2] Persons of Hispanic origin may be of any race.

Source: U.S. Census Bureau, Current Population Reports, P60-208, earlier reports; and unpublished data.

No. 171. Medicaid—Selected Utilization Measures: 1980 to 1998

[In thousands (2,255 represents 2,255,000). For year ending September 30. Includes Virgin Islands. See text, this section]

Measure	1980	1985	1990	1994	1995	1996	1997	1998
General hospitals:								
Recipients discharged	2,255	2,390	3,261	3,890	3,743	3,300	3,135	2,793
Total days of care	24,089	29,562	27,471	28,941	25,711	23,072	21,532	19,091
Nursing facilities: [1]								
Total recipients	1,395	1,375	1,461	1,639	1,667	1,594	1,497	1,555
Total days of care	273,497	277,996	360,044	400,785	400,123	409,663	388,985	384,549
Intermediate care facilities: [2]								
Total recipients	121	147	146	159	151	140	146	124
Total days of care	250,124	47,324	49,730	54,105	56,878	56,625	62,423	50,636

[1] Includes skilled nursing facilities and intermediate care facilities for all other than the mentally retarded.   [2] Mentally retarded.

Source: U.S. Health Care Financing Administration, Office of Information Systems, Statistical Report on Medical Care: Eligibles, Recipients, Payments, and Services.

Health and Nutrition   115

No. 172. Medicaid—Recipients and Payments: 1990 to 1998

[For year ending September 30 (25,255 represents 25,255,000). Includes Puerto Rico and outlying areas. Medical vendor payments are those made directly to suppliers of medical care]

Basis of eligibility and type of service	Recipients (1,000)					Payments (mil. dol.)				
	1990	1995	1996	1997	1998	1990	1995	1996	1997	1998
Total [1]	25,255	36,282	36,118	34,872	40,649	64,859	120,141	121,685	124,430	142,318
Age 65 and over	3,202	4,119	4,285	3,955	3,964	21,508	36,527	36,947	37,721	40,602
Blindness	83	92	95	(NA)	(NA)	434	848	869	(NA)	(NA)
Disabled [2]	3,635	5,767	6,126	6,129	6,638	23,969	48,570	51,196	54,130	60,375
AFDC [3] program	17,230	24,767	23,866	22,594	26,872	17,690	31,487	29,819	29,851	37,639
Other and unknown	1,105	1,537	1,746	2,195	3,176	1,257	2,708	2,853	2,727	3,702
Inpatient services in—										
General hospital	4,593	5,561	5,362	4,746	4,273	16,674	26,331	25,176	23,143	21,499
Mental hospital	92	84	93	87	135	1,714	2,511	2,040	2,009	2,801
Intermediate care facilities, mentally retarded	147	151	140	136	126	7,354	10,383	9,555	9,798	9,482
Nursing facility services [4]	1,461	1,667	1,594	1,603	1,646	17,693	29,052	29,630	30,504	31,892
Physicians	17,078	23,789	22,861	21,170	18,555	4,018	7,360	7,238	7,041	6,070
Dental	4,552	6,383	6,208	5,935	4,965	593	1,019	1,028	1,036	901
Other practitioner	3,873	5,528	5,343	5,142	4,342	372	986	1,094	979	587
Outpatient hospital	12,370	16,712	15,905	13,632	12,158	3,324	6,627	6,504	6,169	5,759
Clinic	2,804	5,322	5,070	4,713	5,285	1,688	4,280	4,222	4,252	3,921
Laboratory [5]	8,959	13,064	12,607	11,074	9,381	721	1,180	1,208	1,033	939
Home health [6]	719	1,639	1,727	1,861	1,225	3,404	9,406	10,868	12,237	2,702
Prescribed drugs	17,294	23,723	22,585	20,954	19,338	4,420	9,791	10,697	11,972	13,522
Family planning	1,752	2,501	2,366	2,091	2,011	265	514	474	418	449
Prepaid health care	(NA)	(NA)	(NA)	(NA)	20,203	(NA)	(NA)	(NA)	(NA)	19,296

NA Not available. [1] Recipient data do not add due to small number of recipients that are reported in more than one category. Includes recipients of, and payments for, other care not shown separately. [2] Permanently and totally. Beginning 1997, includes blind. [3] Aid to families with dependent children includes children, adults, and foster care. [4] Nursing facility services includes skilled nursing facility services and intermediate care facility services for all other than the mentally retarded. [5] Includes radiological services. [6] Data for 1998 not comparable with earlier years.

Source: U.S. Health Care Financing Administration, Office of Information Systems, *Statistical Report on Medical Care: Eligibles, Recipients, Payments, and Services.*

No. 173. Medicaid—Summary by State and Other Area: 1995 and 1998

[For year ending September 30 (36,282 represents 36,282,000). Data for 1998 includes managed care recipients and capitation payments]

State and area	Recipients [1] (1,000)		Payments [2] (mil. dol.)		State and area	Recipients [1] (1,000)		Payments [2] (mil. dol.)	
	1995	1998	1995	1998		1995	1998	1995	1998
All areas . .	**36,282**	**40,649**	**120,141**	**142,318**	MO	695	734	2,039	2,570
U.S.	**35,210**	**39,666**	**119,885**	**142,058**	MT	99	101	326	361
					NE	168	211	608	753
AL	539	527	1,455	1,902	NV	105	128	350	462
AK	68	75	252	330	NH	97	94	473	606
AZ	494	508	218	1,644	NJ	790	813	3,813	4,219
AR	353	425	1,376	1,376	NM	287	329	714	862
CA	5,017	7,082	10,521	14,237	NY	3,035	3,073	22,086	24,299
CO	294	345	1,063	1,439	NC	1,084	1,168	3,175	4,014
CT	380	381	2,125	2,421	ND	61	62	297	341
DE	79	101	324	420	OH	1,533	1,291	5,585	6,121
DC	138	166	532	731	OK	394	342	1,055	1,178
FL	1,735	1,905	4,802	5,686	OR	452	511	1,327	1,378
GA	1,147	1,222	3,076	3,012	PA	1,230	1,523	4,633	6,080
HI	52	185	258	507	RI	135	153	673	919
ID	115	123	360	425	SC	496	595	1,438	2,019
IL	1,552	1,364	5,600	6,173	SD	74	90	305	356
IN	559	607	1,878	2,564	TN	1,466	1,844	2,772	3,167
IA	304	315	1,036	1,289	TX	2,562	2,325	6,565	7,140
KS	256	242	831	916	UT	160	216	464	619
KY	641	644	1,945	2,425	VT	100	124	320	351
LA	785	721	2,708	2,384	VA	681	653	1,833	2,118
ME	153	170	760	747	WA	639	1,413	1,461	2,044
MD	414	561	2,019	2,489	WV	389	343	1,169	1,243
MA	728	908	3,972	4,609	WI	460	519	1,894	2,206
MI	1,168	1,363	3,409	4,345	WY	51	46	171	192
MN	473	538	2,550	2,924	PR	1,055	964	244	250
MS	520	486	1,266	1,442	VI	17	20	12	10

[1] Persons who had payments made on their behalf at any time during the fiscal year. [2] Payments are for fiscal year and reflect federal and state contribution payments. Data exclude disproportionate hospital share payments.

Source: U.S. Health Care Financing Administration, Office of Information Systems, *Statistical Report on Medical Care: Eligibles, Recipients, Payments, and Services.*

No. 174. Medicaid Managed Care Enrollment by State and Other Area: 1991 to 1998

[For year ending June 30. (28,280 represents 28,280,000)]

State and area	Total medi-caid (1,000)	Managed care enrollment Number (1,000)	Per cent of total	State and area	Total medi-caid (1,000)	Managed care enrollment Number (1,000)	Per cent of total	State and area	Total medi-caid (1,000)	Managed care enrollment Number (1,000)	Per cent of total
1991	28,280	2,696	9.5	IL	1,309	176	13.4	NC	815	559	68.5
1995	33,373	9,800	29.4	IN	404	233	57.6	ND	42	22	51.8
				IA	207	191	92.1	OH	1,032	293	28.3
1998, total	**30,897**	**16,574**	**53.6**	KS	171	84	49.3	OK	310	154	49.6
				KY	518	325	62.7	OR	338	300	88.6
				LA	753	41	5.4	PA	1,325	905	68.2
U.S	30,010	15,760	52.5	ME	153	16	10.6	RI	118	74	63.2
AL	511	362	70.9	MD	457	306	67.0	SC	443	16	3.5
AK	66	-	-	MA	851	533	62.6	SD	62	44	70.5
AZ	432	368	85.1	MI	1,106	753	68.0	TN	1,269	1,269	100.0
AR	333	186	55.9	MN	429	225	52.5	TX	1,719	438	25.4
CA	4,901	2,246	45.8	MS	384	154	39.9	UT	124	113	91.2
CO	218	216	99.0	MO	607	252	41.5	VT	108	52	48.3
CT	307	221	71.8	MT	67	66	98.4	VA	499	299	60.0
DE	81	62	76.7	NE	152	111	72.7	WA	789	718	91.0
DC	113	51	45.2	NV	91	35	38.7	WV	309	131	42.5
FL	1,418	916	64.5	NH	73	7	10.0	WI	397	195	49.0
GA	883	674	76.3	NJ	643	377	58.6	WY	35	-	-
HI	164	132	80.4	NM	243	194	79.7	PR	870	814	93.5
ID	89	31	34.8	NY	2,140	634	29.6	VI	17	-	-

- Represents zero.
Source: U.S. Health Care Financing Administration, "National Summary of Medicaid Managed Care Programs and Enrollment, June 30, 1998"; published 8 April 1999; <http://32.97.224.53:80/medicaid/trends98.htm>; and "Medicaid Managed Care Penetration Rates by State - 6/30/98"; published 8 April 1999; <http://32.97.224.53:80/medicaid/mcsten98.htm>.

No. 175. Health Maintenance Organizations (HMOs): 1980 to 1999

[As of **January 1, except 1980 as of June 30 (9.1 represents 9,100,000**). An HMO is a prepaid health plan delivering comprehensive care to members through designated providers, having a fixed periodic payment for health care services, and requiring members to be in a plan for a specified period of time (usually 1 year). A group HMO delivers health services through a physician group that is controlled by the HMO unit or contracts with one or more independent group practices to provide health services. An individual practice association (IPA) HMO contracts directly with physicians in independent practice, and/or contracts with one or more associations of physicians in independent practice, and/or contracts with one or more multispecialty group practices. Data are based on a census of HMOs]

Model type	Number of plans					Model type	Enrollment [1] (mil.)				
	1980	1990	1995	1998	1999		1980	1990	1995	1998	1999
Total	235	572	550	651	643	Total	9.1	33.0	46.2	64.8	81.3
I.P.A.	97	360	323	317	309	I.P.A.	1.7	13.7	17.4	24.8	32.8
Group	138	212	107	122	126	Group	7.4	19.3	12.9	13.1	15.9
Mixed	(NA)	(NA)	120	212	208	Mixed	(NA)	(NA)	15.9	26.9	32.6

NA Not available. [1] Prior to 1999, excludes enrollees in open-ended plans.

No. 176. Persons Enrolled in Health Maintenance Organizations (HMOs) by State: 1990 and 1999

[Data are based on a census of health maintenance organizations. Data for 1990 are for pure HMO enrollment at midyear. Data for 1999 are for pure and open-ended enrollment as of January 1]

State	Number 1999 (1,000)	Percent of population 1990	1999	State	Number 1999 (1,000)	Percent of population 1990	1999	State	Number 1999 (1,000)	Percent of population 1990	1999
U.S. [1]	81,333	13.5	30.1	KS	442	7.9	16.8	ND	16	1.7	2.5
				KY	1,281	5.7	32.5	OH	2,843	13.3	25.4
AL	437	5.3	10.0	LA	775	5.4	17.7	OK	476	5.5	14.2
AK	-	-	-	ME	251	2.6	20.2	OR	1,422	24.7	43.3
AZ	1,496	16.2	32.0	MD	2,362	14.2	46.0	PA	4,036	12.5	33.6
AR	312	2.2	12.3	MA	3,252	26.5	52.9	RI	400	20.6	40.5
CA	17,025	30.7	52.1	MI	2,648	15.2	27.0	SC	383	1.9	10.0
CO	1,563	20.0	39.4	MN	1,437	16.4	30.4	SD	45	3.3	6.1
CT	1,272	19.9	38.8	MS	89	-	3.2	TN	2,045	3.7	37.7
DE	340	17.5	45.7	MO	1,860	8.2	34.2	TX	3,676	6.9	18.6
DC	176	(NA)	33.7	MT	58	1.0	6.6	UT	739	13.9	35.2
FL	4,900	10.6	32.9	NE	305	5.1	18.4	VT	23	6.4	4.0
GA	1,239	4.8	16.2	NV	410	8.5	23.5	VA	1,332	6.1	19.6
HI	402	21.6	33.7	NH	413	9.6	34.9	WA	985	14.6	17.3
ID	79	1.8	6.4	NJ	2,391	12.3	29.5	WV	189	3.9	10.5
IL	2,506	12.6	20.8	NM	661	12.7	38.1	WI	1,614	21.7	30.9
IN	777	6.1	13.2	NY	6,940	15.1	38.2	WY	6	-	1.2
IA	139	10.1	4.9	NC	1,416	4.8	18.8				

- Represents zero. NA Not available. [1] Data for 1999 include Guam and Puerto Rico.
Source of Tables 175 and 176: InterStudy Publications, Minneapolis, MN, The InterStudy Competitive Edge, annual (copyright).

Health and Nutrition 117

No. 177. Health Insurance Coverage Status by Selected Characteristics: 1990 to 1998

[Persons as of following year for coverage in the year shown (248.9 represents 248,900,000). Government health insurance includes medicare, medicaid, and military plans. Based on Current Population Survey; see text, Section 1, Population, and Appendix III]

Characteristic	Number (mil.)							Percent			
	Covered by private or government health insurance						Not covered by health insurance	Covered by private or government health insurance			Not covered by health insurance
	Total persons	Total[1]	Private		Government			Total[1]	Private	Medicaid	
			Total	Group health[2]	Medicare	Medicaid					
1990	248.9	214.2	182.1	150.2	32.3	24.3	34.7	86.1	73.2	9.7	13.9
1994[3]	262.1	222.4	184.3	159.6	33.9	31.6	39.7	84.8	70.3	12.1	15.2
1995[3]	264.3	223.7	185.9	161.5	34.7	31.9	40.6	84.6	70.3	12.1	15.4
1996[3]	266.8	225.1	187.4	163.2	35.2	31.5	41.7	84.4	70.2	11.8	15.6
1997[3]	269.1	225.6	188.5	165.1	35.6	29.0	43.4	83.9	70.1	10.8	16.1
1998, total[3][4]	271.7	227.5	190.9	168.6	35.9	27.9	44.3	83.7	70.2	10.3	16.3
Age:											
Under 18 years	72.0	60.9	48.6	45.6	0.3	14.3	11.1	84.6	67.5	19.8	15.4
Under 6 years	23.7	20.0	15.1	14.4	0.1	5.7	3.7	84.5	63.8	23.9	15.5
6 to 11 years	24.6	21.0	16.8	15.9	0.1	4.9	3.6	85.4	68.2	20.0	14.6
12 to 17 years	23.8	20.0	16.8	15.4	0.1	3.7	3.8	84.0	70.5	15.5	16.0
18 to 24 years	26.0	18.2	15.9	13.1	0.1	2.5	7.8	70.1	61.1	9.8	30.0
25 to 34 years	38.5	29.3	26.7	25.1	0.4	2.5	9.1	76.3	69.5	6.4	23.7
35 to 44 years	44.7	37.0	34.1	32.0	0.7	2.6	7.7	82.8	76.3	5.8	17.2
45 to 54 years	35.2	30.4	28.2	26.4	1.1	1.6	4.8	86.4	79.9	4.6	13.6
55 to 64 years	22.9	19.5	17.2	15.2	2.0	1.4	3.4	85.0	75.0	6.2	15.0
65 years and over	32.4	32.0	20.2	11.2	31.1	3.0	0.4	98.9	62.3	9.1	1.1
Sex: Male	132.8	109.7	94.0	84.3	15.5	11.7	23.0	82.7	70.8	8.8	17.3
Female	139.0	117.7	96.9	84.3	20.4	16.2	21.3	84.7	69.7	11.6	15.3
Race: White	223.3	189.7	163.7	143.7	31.2	18.2	33.6	85.0	73.3	8.2	15.0
Black	35.1	27.3	18.7	17.1	3.7	7.9	7.8	77.8	53.2	22.5	22.2
Hispanic origin[5]	31.7	20.5	14.4	13.3	2.0	5.6	11.2	64.7	45.4	17.6	35.3
Household income:											
Less than $25,000	68.4	51.2	27.5	18.8	18.2	18.6	17.2	74.8	40.2	27.3	25.2
$25,000-$49,999	79.0	64.2	56.0	49.2	10.4	6.2	14.8	81.3	70.9	7.9	18.8
$50,000-$74,999	57.3	50.6	48.0	44.7	3.7	1.8	6.7	88.3	83.7	3.1	11.7
$75,000 or more	67.0	61.5	59.4	55.8	3.6	1.2	5.5	91.7	88.7	1.9	8.3
Persons below poverty	34.5	23.3	8.8	6.0	4.5	14.0	11.2	67.7	25.6	40.6	32.3

[1] Includes other government insurance, not shown separately. Persons with coverage counted only once in total, even though they may have been covered by more that one type of policy. [2] Related to employment of self or other family members. [3] Beginning 1994, data based on 1990 census adjusted population controls. [4] Includes other races not shown separately. [5] Persons of Hispanic origin may be of any race.

Source: U.S. Census Bureau, *Current Population Reports*, P60-208; and unpublished data.

No. 178. Persons With and Without Health Insurance Coverage by State: 1998

[227,462 represents 227,462,000. Based on the Current Population Survey and subject to sampling error; see text, Section 1, Population, and Appendix III]

State	Total persons covered (1,000)	Total persons not covered		Children not covered		State	Total persons covered (1,000)	Total persons not covered		Children not covered	
		Number (1,000)	Percent of total	Number (1,000)	Percent of total			Number (1,000)	Percent of total	Number (1,000)	Percent of total
U.S.	227,462	44,281	16.3	11,073	15.4	MO	4,836	570	10.5	123	8.9
						MT	744	181	19.6	53	19.8
AL	3,487	714	17.0	174	17.9	NE	1,561	155	9.0	28	5.5
AK	535	112	17.3	29	13.7	NV	1,468	394	21.2	127	23.1
AZ	3,719	1,187	24.2	370	26.3	NH	1,086	138	11.3	33	9.6
AR	2,084	478	18.7	127	19.0	NJ	6,763	1,329	16.4	273	13.4
CA	26,002	7,373	22.1	1,905	20.4	NM	1,443	386	21.1	97	17.1
CO	3,371	599	15.1	126	12.5	NY	15,243	3,177	17.3	668	13.8
CT	2,871	412	12.6	85	10.1	NC	6,316	1,111	15.0	242	13.2
DE	668	115	14.7	38	17.6	ND	554	92	14.2	30	16.4
DC	425	87	17.0	18	17.9	OH	10,055	1,169	10.4	268	9.1
FL	12,114	2,564	17.5	585	18.0	OK	2,670	599	18.3	186	22.5
GA	6,325	1,341	17.5	397	19.1	OR	2,875	481	14.3	104	11.8
HI	1,080	121	10.0	30	9.5	PA	10,664	1,248	10.5	267	9.1
ID	1,049	225	17.7	69	17.6	RI	872	96	10.0	18	7.6
IL	10,453	1,842	15.0	520	14.6	SC	3,257	594	15.4	147	14.8
IN	5,001	839	14.4	232	15.2	SD	610	102	14.3	29	15.3
IA	2,572	265	9.3	64	8.7	TN	4,849	724	13.0	156	10.7
KS	2,346	270	10.3	57	8.0	TX	15,065	4,880	24.5	1,453	25.4
KY	3,320	545	14.1	133	14.0	UT	1,812	293	13.9	77	11.5
LA	3,493	817	19.0	212	18.4						
ME	1,106	161	12.7	33	10.4	VT	535	58	9.9	9	6.3
MD	4,209	837	16.6	211	17.5	VA	5,742	946	14.1	214	12.9
MA	5,490	627	10.3	119	8.0	WA	5,042	706	12.3	143	9.4
MI	8,712	1,328	13.2	311	10.7	WV	1,448	302	17.2	33	9.6
MN	4,385	448	9.3	141	10.0	WI	4,525	604	11.8	124	9.7
MS	2,208	554	20.0	163	21.2	WY	404	82	16.9	22	16.4

Source: U.S. Census Bureau; "Health Insurance Coverage: 1998 - Table 8"; published 4 October 1999; <http://www.census.gov/hhes/hlthins/hlthin98/hi98t8.html>; and unpublished data.

No. 179. Percent of Private Establishments Offering Health Insurance and Employees Enrolled: 1997

[Health insurance plan: An insurance plan that provides hospital and/or physician coverage to an employee or retiree for a single premium. Based on the Medical Expenditure Panel Survey— Insurance Component; for details on sample survey, see source]

Firm size and industry group	Percent of all establishments offering one or more major health plans	Percent of establishments offering health insurance that offer—				Private employees		
		Any managed care plan [1]	Exclusive provider plan [2]	Preferred provider plan [3]	Insurance to retirees over age 65	Percent working in establishments offering health insurance	Percent of eligible employees that are enrolled in health insurance	Percent enrolled in employer's plan
Total [4]	52.4	84.4	37.8	61.3	19.5	85.7	84.2	66.7
Less than 10 employees. .	32.9	78.8	32.0	50.1	8.5	47.3	82.7	67.0
10 to 24 employees	63.5	84.3	31.8	58.6	11.0	70.4	80.6	65.3
25 to 99 employees	82.7	87.4	36.0	60.8	13.9	86.5	81.2	62.7
100 to 999 employees . . .	93.8	87.0	38.2	68.5	23.2	96.9	83.1	63.9
1,000 or more employees .	98.2	91.1	52.6	78.6	45.2	97.6	86.6	69.5
Agriculture, forestry, and fishing	21.6	68.3	21.4	52.7	10.3	50.5	86.6	61.8
Mining.	42.5	76.1	17.5	61.5	25.1	81.6	97.5	95.1
Construction.	40.4	83.5	29.3	57.3	9.2	70.0	81.4	63.3
Manufacturing.	68.4	86.0	38.9	59.2	15.8	95.5	89.6	82.3
Transportation, communication, and utilities	59.1	84.1	40.9	64.4	36.8	91.7	91.8	81.9
Wholesale trade	65.6	86.2	35.1	63.4	17.5	91.3	89.9	78.5
Retail trade	53.6	85.7	40.7	63.6	23.1	81.2	72.6	45.3
Finance, insurance, and real estate	62.3	86.9	43.3	70.3	36.5	92.3	87.3	76.4
Services	50.5	83.2	37.0	57.3	12.7	84.3	82.1	62.3

[1] Either a preferred provider or exclusive provider plan.   [2] A plan that requires the enrollee to use a limited subset of providers for all nonemergency care in order for costs to be covered.   [3] A plan that allows the enrollee to use any provider but has a costs incentive to use a particular subset of providers.   [4] Includes establishments with unknown characteristics.

Source: U.S. Agency for Healthcare Research and Quality, "Private-Sector Data by Firm Size and Selected Characteristics: United States: 1997"; <http://www.meps.ahrq.gov/mepsdata/ic/1997/Index197.htm>; (accessed 27 April 2000).

No. 180. Medical Care Benefit Coverage and Average Monthly Employee Contributions: 1980 to 1997

[Covers full-time employees in private nonfarm establishments. Based on a sample survey of establishments; for details, see source and headnotes, Tables 703 and 704]

Item	Medium and large establishments					Small establishments			
	1980	1991	1993	1995	1997	1990	1992	1994	1996
Percent of full-time employees participating. . . .	97	83	82	77	76	69	71	66	64
PERCENT DISTRIBUTION OF PARTICIPATING FULL-TIME EMPLOYEES									
Fee arrangement, total.	100	100	100	100	100	100	100	100	100
Traditional fee-for-service [1]	(NA)	67	50	37	27	74	68	55	36
Preferred provider organization [2]	(NA)	16	26	34	40	13	18	24	35
Health maintenance organization [3]	(NA)	17	23	27	33	14	14	19	27
Other	(NA)	-	1	1	1	-	(Z)	1	2
Individual coverage:									
Employee contributions not required.	(NA)	49	37	33	31	(NA)	(NA)	(NA)	48
Employee contributions required	26	51	61	67	69	42	47	52	52
Family coverage:									
Employee contributions not required.	(NA)	31	21	22	20	(NA)	(NA)	(NA)	24
Employee contributions required	46	69	76	78	80	67	73	75	75
AVERAGE MONTHLY EMPLOYEE CONTRIBUTION (dol.)									
Individual coverage:									
Total	(NA)	27	32	34	39	25	37	41	43
Non-HMO [4]	(NA)	26	31	33	42	25	36	39	43
HMO	(NA)	29	32	36	34	25	39	49	41
Family coverage:									
Total	(NA)	97	107	118	130	109	151	160	182
Non-HMO [4]	(NA)	92	102	112	132	104	147	151	181
HMO	(NA)	118	122	133	126	135	168	190	182

- Represents zero.   NA Not available.   Z Less than 0.5 percent.   [1] These plans pay for specific medical procedures as expenses are incurred.   [2] Groups of hospitals and physicians that contract to provide comprehensive medical services at prearranged prices. To encourage use of organization members, the health plan limits reimbursement rates when participants use nonmember services.   [3] Includes federally qualified and other HMOs that deliver comprehensive health care on a prepayment rather than fee-for-service basis.   [4] Includes traditional fee-for-service plans, preferred provider plans, and exclusive provider organization plans.

Source: U.S. Bureau of Labor Statistics, News, USDL 98-240, June 15, 1998; News, USDL 99-02, January 7, 1999; and earlier releases.

Health and Nutrition 119

No. 181. Annual Receipts/Revenue for the Health Service Industries: 1990 to 1998

[In millions of dollars (271,212 represents $271,212,000,000). Unless otherwise noted, receipts estimates are obtained from a sample of employer and nonemployer firms. Revenue estimates are obtained from a sample of employer firms only]

Industry	1987 SIC code [1]	1990	1994	1995	1996	1997	1998
TAXABLE FIRMS—RECEIPTS							
Health services [2]	80	271,212	351,419	376,279	398,353	420,361	444,727
Offices and clinics of medical doctors	801	128,871	159,616	167,969	172,926	179,474	188,835
Offices and clinics of dentists	802	31,502	41,663	44,909	47,411	50,997	54,151
Offices of osteopathic physicians	803	3,254	4,354	4,698	4,749	4,902	5,325
Offices of other health practitioners [2]	804	20,139	25,891	27,357	28,409	29,561	31,334
Offices and clinics of chiropractors	8041	5,467	6,757	6,742	7,003	7,264	7,680
Offices and clinics of optometrists	8042	4,799	6,021	6,113	6,330	6,491	7,007
Offices and clinics of podiatrists	8043	1,811	2,190	2,388	2,443	2,401	2,421
Nursing and personal care facilities	805	30,162	37,320	41,135	44,282	46,848	49,182
Hospitals [3]	806	26,487	35,143	38,417	44,669	50,154	53,807
General medical and surgical hospitals [3]	8062	20,442	27,993	30,704	36,496	40,920	43,059
Psychiatric hospitals [3]	8063	4,129	3,764	3,847	3,508	3,877	4,342
Specialty hospitals, exc. psychiatric [3]	8069	1,916	3,386	3,866	4,665	5,357	6,407
Medical and dental laboratories	807	12,033	15,427	15,524	16,054	16,510	18,321
Medical laboratories	8071	9,996	13,007	12,909	13,277	13,705	15,247
Dental laboratories	8072	2,037	2,420	2,615	2,777	2,805	3,074
Home health care services	808	7,556	15,394	17,987	19,556	19,286	18,548
Health and allied services, n.e.c. [2][4]	809	11,208	16,611	18,283	20,297	22,629	25,223
Kidney dialysis centers	8092	1,451	2,898	3,259	3,391	3,712	4,318
Specialty outpatient clinics, n.e.c. [4]	8093	5,326	7,965	8,616	9,500	10,615	12,537
TAX EXEMPT FIRMS—REVENUE [3]							
Selected health services [2]	80 pt.	267,858	363,112	385,210	401,047	414,990	436,078
Offices and clinics of medical doctors	801	12,888	21,882	24,873	26,153	28,447	31,728
Nursing and personal care facilities	805	12,132	16,564	17,570	18,510	19,712	21,250
Hospitals	806	233,615	308,105	325,033	337,822	347,837	363,655
General medical and surgical hospitals	8062	210,503	281,430	297,407	309,681	319,535	334,330
Psychiatric hospitals	8063	11,008	9,848	9,211	9,291	9,742	9,906
Specialty hospitals, exc. psychiatric	8069	12,104	16,827	18,415	18,850	18,560	19,418
Home health care services	808	3,874	7,428	7,943	8,043	8,083	7,944
Health and allied services, n.e.c. [2][4]	809	5,285	9,025	9,666	10,388	10,770	11,353
Kidney dialysis centers	8092	305	526	620	676	715	788
Specialty outpatient facilities, n.e.c. [4]	8093	3,519	5,320	5,661	5,957	5,896	5,812

[1] Based on the 1987 Standard Industrial Classification code; see text, Section 17, Business.   [2] Includes other industries not shown separately.   [3] Estimates are obtained from a sample of employer firms only.   [4] N.e.c. means not elsewhere classified.

Source: U.S. Census Bureau, *Current Business Reports, Service Annual Survey: 1998*, BS/98.

No. 182. Receipts for Health Service Industries by Source of Revenue: 1996 to 1998

[In millions of dollars (162,420 represents $162,420,000,000). Based on the 1987 Standard Industrial Classification code; see text, Section 17, Business. Based on a sample of taxable employer firms only and do not include nonemployer receipts]

Source of income	Doctors of medicine (SIC 801)			Dentists (SIC 802)			Offices and clinics of other health practitioners (SIC 804)			Nursing and personal care facilities (SIC 805)		
	1996	1997	1998	1996	1997	1998	1996	1997	1998	1996	1997	1998
Total	162,420	169,127	177,782	45,653	49,111	52,147	23,496	24,583	26,068	43,244	45,794	48,106
Medicare	36,992	38,400	39,600	(S)	(S)	(S)	3,011	3,015	2,941	7,601	8,651	8,942
Medicaid	11,913	11,452	12,445	1,299	1,374	1,392	916	1,010	1,027	23,156	23,297	24,757
Other gov't	2,653	2,436	2,312	(S)	(S)	(S)	(S)	(S)	(S)	362	376	362
Private insurance	79,780	83,455	88,106	21,905	23,226	24,745	9,827	10,088	10,496	3,322	3,670	3,857
Patient	20,856	23,234	24,089	20,741	22,957	24,519	6,965	7,611	8,328	7,291	8,125	8,492
Other	10,226	10,150	11,230	(S)	(S)	(S)	2,190	2,237	2,655	1,512	1,675	1,695

S Data do not meet publication standards.

Source: U.S. Census Bureau, *Current Business Reports, Service Annual Survey: 1998*, BS/98.

120 Health and Nutrition

Figure 3.2
Sources of Receipts for Health Service Firms: 1998
(Covers only taxable employer firms)

Offices and clinics of doctors of medicine (SIC 801)
$178 billion dollars

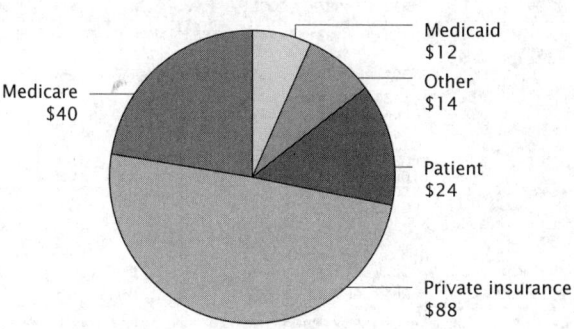

Medicaid $12

Other $14

Medicare $40

Patient $24

Private insurance $88

Offices and clinics of dentists (SIC 802)
$52 billion dollars

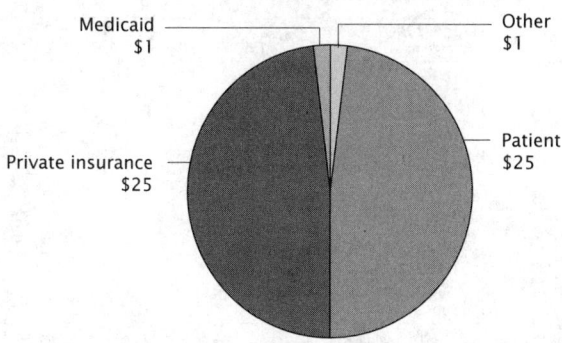

Medicaid $1

Other $1

Private insurance $25

Patient $25

Nursing and personal care facilities (SIC 805)
$48 billion dollars

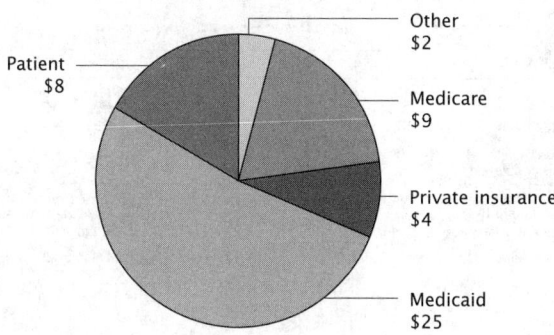

Other $2

Patient $8

Medicare $9

Private insurance $4

Medicaid $25

Source: Chart prepared by U.S. Census Bureau. For data, see Table 182.

No. 183. Receipts for Health Service Industries by Type of Service Performed: 1996 to 1998

[In millions of dollars (162,420 represents $162,420,000,000). Based on the 1987 Standard Industrial Classification code; see text, Section 17, Business. Based on a sample of taxable employer firms only and do not include nonemployer receipts]

Type of service	Doctors of medicine (SIC 8011)			Dentists (SIC 8021)			Chiropractors (SIC 8041)		
	1996	1997	1998	1996	1997	1998	1996	1997	1998
Total [1]	162,420	169,127	177,782	45,653	49,111	52,147	6,223	6,439	6,807
Patient care and other medical professional services [1]	156,501	163,198	171,987	44,033	47,886	51,087	5,932	6,148	6,552
Patient care services	148,442	155,844	163,924	42,974	46,867	50,196	5,739	6,009	6,458
Laboratory services	7,804	7,703	8,009	1,634	1,517	1,609	(S)	(S)	(S)
Inhouse laboratory services ..	6,141	6,327	6,841	862	1,107	1,143	(S)	(S)	(S)
Provider billed independent laboratory services	1,663	1,376	1,168	772	410	465	(S)	(S)	(S)
X-ray services	13,035	12,586	13,005	1,000	832	936	360	332	326
Other patient care services ...	127,603	135,555	142,910	40,340	44,518	47,650	5,298	5,611	6,071
Hospital inpatient services ...	31,940	30,990	32,449	(S)	(S)	(S)	(S)	(S)	(S)
Hospital outpatient services ..	20,110	18,765	20,721	(S)	(S)	(S)	(S)	(S)	(S)
Services delivered in doctor's office	74,303	84,248	88,375	39,719	43,885	47,123	5,268	5,574	6,026
Other services delivered	1,250	1,552	1,364	(S)	(S)	(S)	(S)	(S)	(S)
Merchandise sales	984	1,078	1,126	(S)	(S)	(S)	142	146	153

S Data do not meet publication standards. [1] Includes other types of service, not shown separately.

Source: U.S. Census Bureau, *Current Business Reports, Service Annual Survey: 1998*, BS/98.

No. 184. Employment in the Health Service Industries: 1980 to 1999

[In thousands (5,278 represents 5,278,000). See headnote Table 684]

Industry	1987 SIC code [1]	1980	1990	1995	1997	1998	1999
Health services [2]	80	5,278	7,814	9,230	9,703	9,846	9,973
Offices and clinics of MDs	801	802	1,338	1,609	1,739	1,803	1,865
Offices and clinics of dentists	802	(NA)	513	592	629	646	667
Offices and clinics of other practitioners	804	96	277	397	435	450	452
Nursing and personal care facilities	805	997	1,415	1,691	1,756	1,762	1,755
Skilled nursing care facilities	8051	(NA)	989	1,253	1,335	1,348	1,343
Intermediate care facilities...........	8052	(NA)	200	211	206	201	202
Other, n.e.c. [3]	8059	(NA)	227	227	215	213	211
Hospitals........................	806	2,750	3,549	3,772	3,860	3,926	3,970
General medical and surgical hospitals ...	8062	(NA)	3,268	3,474	3,561	3,625	3,660
Psychiatric hospitals................	8063	(NA)	104	91	83	80	82
Specialty hospitals, exc. psychiatric......	8069	(NA)	176	208	217	222	228
Medical and dental laboratories	807	(NA)	166	190	197	199	202
Home health care services	808	(NA)	291	629	710	672	655

NA Not available. [1] Based on the 1987 Standard Industrial Classification code; see text, Section 17, Business. [2] Includes other industries not shown separately. [3] N.e.c. means not elsewhere classified.

Source: U.S. Bureau of Labor Statistics, Bulletins 2445 and 2481, and *Employment and Earnings*, monthly, March and June issues.

No. 185. Dentists and Nurses: 1980 to 1998

[As of end of year (141 represents 141,000). Excludes Puerto Rico and outlying areas]

Item	Unit	1980	1985	1990	1994	1995	1996	1997	1998
Dentists, number [1]	1,000...	141	156	[2]173	191	194	196	(NA)	(NA)
Active (exc. in Federal service) [3] ..	1,000...	121	134	148	152	153	155	(NA)	149
Rate per 100,000 population [4] ..	Rate ...	53	57	59	58	58	58	(NA)	55
Nurses, number (active registered).	1,000...	1,273	1,538	1,790	2,044	2,116	2,162	2,203	2,239
Rate per 100,000 population [4] ..	Rate ...	560	644	713	785	805	815	823	828

NA Not available. [1] Includes current year's graduates. [2] Revised since originally published. [3] Source: American Dental Association, Bureau of Economic and Behavioral Research, Master Membership file and periodic censuses. [4] Based on Census Bureau estimated resident population as of July 1. Estimates reflect revisions based on the 1990 Census of Population.

Source: Except as noted, U.S. Dept. of Health and Human Services, Health Resources and Services Administration, unpublished data.

No. 186. Physicians by Selected Activity: 1980 to 1998

[In thousands (467.7 represents 467,700). As of Dec. 31, except 1990 as of Jan. 1, and as noted. Includes Puerto Rico and outlying areas]

Activity	1980	1985	1990	1995	1996	1997	1998
Doctors of medicine, total.	**467.7**	**552.7**	**615.4**	**720.3**	**737.8**	**756.7**	**777.9**
Professionally active	435.5	511.1	560.0	646.0	663.9	684.6	707.0
Place of medical education:							
U.S. medical graduates	343.6	398.4	437.2	492.2	505.7	519.7	533.4
Foreign medical graduates [1]	91.8	112.7	122.8	153.8	158.3	164.9	173.7
Sex: Male	386.7	436.3	463.9	505.9	515.6	527.0	538.9
Female.	48.7	74.8	96.1	140.1	148.3	157.7	168.1
Active non-Federal	417.7	489.5	539.5	624.9	643.5	665.2	688.0
Patient care	361.9	431.5	487.8	564.1	580.7	603.7	606.4
Office-based practice	271.3	329.0	359.9	427.3	445.8	458.2	468.8
General and family practice	47.8	53.9	57.6	59.9	61.8	62.0	64.6
Cardiovascular diseases	6.7	9.1	10.7	13.7	14.3	15.0	15.1
Dermatology	4.4	5.3	6.0	7.0	7.2	7.4	7.6
Gastroenterology	2.7	4.1	5.2	7.3	7.6	7.9	7.9
Internal medicine	40.5	52.7	57.8	72.6	77.9	81.4	83.3
Pediatrics	17.4	22.4	26.5	33.9	35.5	36.8	38.4
Pulmonary diseases	2.0	3.0	3.7	5.0	4.9	5.0	4.9
General surgery	22.4	24.7	24.5	24.1	25.4	27.9	27.5
Obstetrics and gynecology	19.5	23.5	25.5	29.1	29.9	30.1	31.2
Ophthalmology	10.6	12.2	13.1	14.6	14.9	15.1	15.6
Orthopedic surgery	10.7	13.0	14.2	17.1	17.6	18.5	18.5
Otolaryngology	5.3	5.8	6.4	7.1	7.2	7.4	7.5
Plastic surgery	2.4	3.3	3.8	4.6	5.0	5.3	5.3
Urological surgery	6.2	7.1	7.4	8.0	8.2	8.4	8.4
Anesthesiology	11.3	15.3	17.8	23.8	24.9	25.6	26.2
Diagnostic radiology	4.2	7.7	9.8	12.8	13.3	14.1	14.2
Emergency medicine	(NA)	(NA)	8.4	11.7	12.3	12.5	13.3
Neurology	3.2	4.7	5.6	7.6	7.9	8.2	8.5
Pathology, anatomical/clinical	6.0	6.9	7.3	9.0	9.7	10.2	10.0
Psychiatry	15.9	18.5	20.0	23.3	24.4	24.5	25.0
Other specialty	31.9	35.8	28.8	35.0	35.8	35.0	35.9
Hospital-based practice [2]	90.6	102.5	127.9	136.8	134.9	145.3	137.6
Residents and interns [2]	59.6	72.2	89.9	93.7	90.6	95.8	92.3
Full-time hospital staff	31.0	30.3	38.0	43.1	44.3	49.5	45.3
Other professional activity [3]	35.2	44.0	39.0	40.3	42.8	41.5	41.6
Not classified	20.6	14.0	12.7	20.6	20.0	20.0	40.0
Federal.	17.8	21.6	20.5	21.1	20.4	19.4	19.0
Patient care	14.6	17.3	16.1	18.1	18.2	16.9	15.3
Other professional activity [3]	3.2	4.3	4.4	3.0	2.2	2.4	3.7
Inactive/unknown address	32.1	41.6	55.4	74.3	73.8	72.1	70.8
Doctors of osteopathy [4]	**18.8**	**24.0**	**30.9**	**35.7**	**37.3**	**38.9**	**40.8**

NA Not available. [1] Foreign medical graduates received their medical education in schools outside the United States and Canada. [2] Includes clinical fellows. [3] Includes medical teaching, administration, research, and other. [4] As of July. Total DOs. Data from American Osteopathic Association, Chicago, IL.
Source: Except as noted, American Medical Association, Chicago, IL, *Physician Characteristics and Distribution in the U.S.*, annual (copyright).

No. 187. Active Non-Federal Physicians and Nurses by State: 1998

[As of **December**. Excludes doctors of osteopathy, federally-employed persons, and physicians with addresses unknown. Includes all physicians not classified according to activity status]

State	Physicians Total	Physicians Rate [1]	Nurses Total	Nurses Rate [1]	State	Physicians Total	Physicians Rate [1]	Nurses Total	Nurses Rate [1]
United States. .	**678,649**	**251**	**2,238,800**	**828**	Missouri	12,528	230	53,160	978
Alabama.	8,609	198	33,560	771	Montana.	1,670	190	7,640	869
Alaska	1,028	167	7,010	1,139	Nebraska	3,624	218	15,040	906
Arizona.	9,411	202	35,760	766	Nevada	3,018	173	10,870	623
Arkansas	4,821	190	19,210	757	New Hampshire	2,807	237	11,010	928
California	80,703	247	177,670	544	New Jersey.	23,908	295	66,550	822
Colorado.	9,433	238	31,070	783	New Mexico	3,679	212	12,260	707
Connecticut.	11,588	354	32,760	1,001	New York	70,257	387	169,980	936
Delaware	1,739	234	8,210	1,103	North Carolina	17,532	232	68,810	912
District of Columbia .	3,844	737	8,340	1,599	North Dakota.	1,419	222	7,360	1,154
Florida	35,551	238	127,680	856	Ohio	26,393	235	103,610	922
Georgia	16,075	211	55,800	731	Oklahoma.	5,654	169	20,260	607
Hawaii	3,156	265	9,290	780	Oregon.	7,378	225	28,470	867
Idaho	1,895	154	7,360	598	Pennsylvania	34,895	291	133,410	1,112
Illinois	31,368	260	108,540	899	Rhode Island.	3,335	338	11,580	1,172
Indiana.	11,495	195	48,430	820	South Carolina.	7,963	207	30,870	804
Iowa	4,961	173	30,690	1,073	South Dakota.	1,348	184	7,480	1,024
Kansas.	5,351	203	23,140	877	Tennessee	13,364	246	48,160	886
Kentucky	8,212	209	32,640	830	Texas.	40,041	203	129,630	658
Louisiana	10,749	246	34,410	789	Utah	4,198	200	13,680	651
Maine.	2,780	223	13,440	1,077	Vermont	1,802	305	5,140	870
Maryland	19,170	374	43,870	855	Virginia.	16,366	241	56,390	831
Massachusetts.	25,320	412	72,480	1,180	Washington	13,352	235	44,270	778
Michigan.	21,982	224	82,710	842	West Virginia.	3,903	215	15,890	877
Minnesota.	11,791	249	50,120	1,060	Wisconsin	11,872	227	47,120	902
Mississippi	4,490	163	21,190	770	Wyoming	821	171	4,750	989

[1] Per 100,000 resident population. Based on U.S. Census Bureau estimates as of July 1, 1998.
Source: Physicians: American Medical Association, Chicago, IL, *Physician Characteristics and Distribution in the U.S.*, annual (copyright); Nurses: U.S. Dept. of Health and Human Services, Health Resources and Services Administration, unpublished data.

Health and Nutrition 123

No. 188. Health Professions Schools—Number, Enrollment, and Graduates: 1980 to 1998

[Data on the number of schools are reported as of the beginning of the academic year; all other data are reported as of the end of the academic year. Data are based on reporting by health professions schools]

| Year | Medi-cine | Oste-opathy | Registered nursing | | | | Licensed practi-cal nursing | Den-tistry | Optom-etry | Phar-macy |
			Total	Bacca-laureate	Associ-ate degree	Diploma				
NUMBER OF SCHOOLS [1]										
1980	126	14	1,385	377	697	311	1,299	60	16	72
1985	127	15	1,473	441	776	256	1,165	60	17	72
1990	126	15	1,470	489	829	152	1,154	58	17	74
1995	125	16	1,516	521	876	119	(NA)	54	17	75
1996	125	17	1,508	523	876	109	(NA)	54	17	79
1997	125	19	(NA)	(NA)	(NA)	(NA)	(NA)	55	17	79
1998	125	19	(NA)	(NA)	(NA)	(NA)	(NA)	55	17	81
FIRST-YEAR ENROLLMENT										
1980	16,930	1,426	105,952	35,414	53,633	16,905	56,316	6,132	1,202	8,035
1985	16,997	1,750	118,224	39,573	63,776	14,875	47,034	5,047	1,187	6,986
1990	16,756	1,844	108,580	29,858	68,634	10,088	52,969	3,979	1,258	8,033
1995	17,085	2,217	127,184	43,451	76,016	7,717	57,906	4,121	1,390	9,157
1996	17,058	2,274	119,205	40,048	72,930	6,227	(NA)	4,237	1,438	8,740
1997	16,935	2,535	(NA)	(NA)	(NA)	(NA)	(NA)	4,255	1,362	8,790
1998	16,867	2,692	(NA)	(NA)	(NA)	(NA)	(NA)	4,347	(NA)	8,571
TOTAL ENROLLMENT										
1980	63,800	4,571	234,659	98,939	92,069	43,651	52,202	22,482	4,517	23,074
1985	67,016	6,547	237,232	95,008	104,968	37,256	48,840	20,588	4,569	18,646
1990	65,016	6,615	201,458	74,865	106,175	20,418	46,720	16,412	4,723	23,013
1995	67,072	8,146	268,350	112,659	135,895	19,796	59,428	16,353	5,201	27,667
1996	66,970	8,475	261,219	109,505	135,235	16,479	56,028	16,552	5,312	28,060
1997	67,276	8,961	238,244	103,213	122,242	12,789	(NA)	16,570	5,210	28,027
1998	66,900	9,434	(NA)	(NA)	(NA)	(NA)	(NA)	16,926	(NA)	28,345
GRADUATES										
1980	15,113	1,059	75,523	24,994	36,034	14,495	41,892	5,256	1,073	7,432
1985	16,318	1,474	82,075	24,975	45,208	11,892	36,955	5,353	1,114	5,735
1990	15,398	1,529	66,088	18,571	42,318	5,199	35,417	4,233	1,258	6,956
1995	15,888	1,843	97,052	31,254	58,749	7,049	44,234	3,908	1,219	7,837
1996	15,907	1,932	94,757	32,413	56,641	5,703	(NA)	3,810	1,210	8,003
1997	15,923	2,009	(NA)	(NA)	(NA)	(NA)	(NA)	3,930	(NA)	7,772
1998	16,114	2,096	(NA)	(NA)	(NA)	(NA)	(NA)	4,041	1,237	7,400
2000, proj.	16,112	1,934	79,660	26,490	47,790	5,380	(NA)	3,242	1,200	7,120

NA Not available.   [1] Some nursing schools offer more than one type of program. Numbers shown for nursing are number of nursing programs.

Source: U.S. National Center for Health Statistics, *Health United States*, annual.

No. 189. Percent Distribution of Number of Visits to Health Care Professionals by Selected Characteristics: 1997 and 1998

[Covers ambulatory visits to doctor's offices and emergency departments, and home health care visits during a 12-month period. Based on the redesigned National Health Interview Survey, a sample survey of the civilian noninstitutionalized population. Data presented in this table are not comparable with data on physician contacts presented in previous editions of the source or the Statistical Abstract]

| Characteristic | None | | 1-3 visits | | 4-9 visits | | 10 or more visits | |
	1997	1998	1997	1998	1997	1998	1997	1998
All persons [1]	16.5	15.9	46.2	46.8	23.6	23.8	13.7	13.5
Age:								
Under 6 years	5.0	4.9	44.9	46.7	37.0	36.6	13.0	11.8
6-17 years	15.3	15.0	58.7	58.4	19.3	20.3	6.8	6.3
18-44 years	21.7	21.6	46.7	47.7	19.0	18.6	12.6	12.2
45-64 years	16.9	15.9	42.9	43.6	24.7	24.3	15.5	16.2
65 years and over	8.9	7.3	34.7	34.1	32.5	35.3	23.8	23.4
Sex: [1]								
Male	21.3	20.7	47.1	47.3	20.6	21.2	11.0	10.8
Female	11.8	11.3	45.4	46.4	26.5	26.3	16.3	16.0
Race and Hispanic origin: [1]								
White, non-Hispanic	14.7	14.2	46.6	47.1	24.4	24.6	14.3	14.0
Black, non-Hispanic	16.9	16.5	46.1	46.5	23.1	23.2	13.8	13.8
Hispanic	24.9	24.0	42.3	44.8	20.3	19.7	12.5	11.5

[1] Estimates are age adjusted to the year 2000 standard using six age groups: Under 18 years, 18-44 years, 45-54 years, 55-64 years, 65-74 years, and 75 years and over.

Source: U.S. National Center for Health Statistics, *Health, United States, 2000*.

No. 190. Medical Practice Characteristics by Selected Specialty: 1985 to 1997

[Dollar figures in thousands (112.2 represents $112,200). Based on a sample telephone survey of 4,000 non-Federal office and hospital based patient care physicians, excluding residents. For details see source. For definition of mean, see Guide to Tabular Presentation]

Specialty	1985	1990	1993	1994	1995	1996	1997
MEAN HOURS IN PATIENT CARE PER WEEK							
All physicians [1]	51.3	53.3	52.9	52.1	51.3	53.4	53.2
General/Family practice	53.6	55.0	54.0	51.9	52.9	53.5	53.1
Internal medicine	52.4	55.7	56.0	56.6	53.9	57.2	56.0
Surgery	51.2	53.1	54.3	53.4	53.2	54.2	55.0
Pediatrics	50.6	52.4	53.8	51.6	50.4	51.0	51.6
Obstetrics/Gynecology	56.9	60.4	58.9	58.1	54.6	60.5	59.9
MEAN NET INCOME							
All physicians [1]	112.2	164.3	189.3	182.4	195.5	199.0	199.6
General/Family practice	77.9	102.7	116.8	121.2	131.2	139.1	140.9
Internal medicine	102.0	152.5	180.8	174.9	185.7	185.7	193.9
Surgery	155.0	236.4	262.7	255.2	269.4	275.2	261.4
Pediatrics	76.2	106.5	135.4	126.2	140.5	140.6	143.5
Obstetrics/Gynecology	124.3	207.3	221.9	200.4	244.3	231.0	228.7
MEAN PROFESSIONAL EXPENSES							
All physicians [1]	102.7	150.0	182.2	183.1	201.6	217.6	228.6
General/Family practice	96.5	134.5	162.4	190.5	179.4	210.7	205.5
Internal medicine	90.0	139.2	185.2	186.4	200.4	192.2	238.2
Surgery	135.7	201.0	245.9	249.9	265.1	307.2	312.5
Pediatrics	87.3	138.0	167.4	157.8	208.5	212.4	224.8
Obstetrics/Gynecology	131.9	212.6	238.1	196.8	266.9	267.1	306.6
MEAN LIABILITY PREMIUM							
All physicians [1]	10.5	14.5	14.4	15.1	15.0	14.1	14.2
General/Family practice	6.8	7.8	7.9	10.2	9.0	8.4	12.0
Internal medicine	5.8	9.2	9.0	8.6	9.4	8.9	9.4
Surgery	16.6	22.8	22.7	22.3	23.3	21.7	19.7
Pediatrics	4.7	7.8	8.6	7.6	7.9	8.3	12.3
Obstetrics/Gynecology	23.5	34.3	33.7	37.4	38.6	35.2	33.0

[1] Includes other specialties not shown separately.

Source: American Medical Association, Chicago IL, *Socioeconomic Characteristics of Medical Practice, 1997/98* (copyright); and *Physician Socioeconomic Statistics, 1999-2000* (copyright).

No. 191. Ambulatory Care Visits to Physicians' Offices and Hospital Outpatient and Emergency Departments: 1998

[1,005.1 represents 1,005,100,000. Based on the annual National Ambulatory Medical Care Survey and National Hospital Ambulatory Medical Care Survey and subject to sampling error; see source for details]

Characteristic	Number of visits (mil.)				Visits per 100 persons			
	Total	Physician offices	Out-patient dept.	Emer-gency dept.	Total	Physician offices	Out-patient dept.	Emer-gency dept.
Total	1,005.1	829.3	75.4	100.4	373	308	28	37
Age:								
Under 15 years old	184.1	145.8	15.9	22.3	307	244	27	37
15 to 24 years old	95.4	71.3	8.1	16.0	255	191	22	43
25 to 44 years old	262.5	211.8	20.5	30.2	316	255	25	36
45 to 64 years old	237.7	203.3	18.0	16.4	419	358	32	29
65 to 74 years old	115.5	102.3	6.9	6.4	643	569	38	35
75 years old and over	109.9	94.8	6.0	9.1	764	659	42	63
Sex:								
Male	406.5	328.9	30.0	47.6	310	251	23	36
Female	598.6	500.4	45.4	52.8	433	362	33	38
Race:								
White	833.7	702.2	54.9	76.6	376	317	25	35
Black	129.2	89.8	18.0	21.4	373	259	52	62
Asian/Pacific Islander	35.6	31.5	2.4	1.8	336	297	22	17
American Indian/Eskimo/Aleut [1]	6.5	5.8	0.2	0.6	272	239	8	25
Region:								
Northeast	212.9	171.3	21.8	19.8	410	330	42	38
Midwest	227.6	181.3	20.3	26.0	341	272	30	39
South	340.3	278.9	23.9	37.5	356	292	25	39
West	224.3	197.7	9.5	17.1	409	361	17	31
Primary source of payment:								
Private insurance	520.7	457.3	25.5	37.9	(X)	(X)	(X)	(X)
Medicare	186.3	159.4	12.2	14.6	(X)	(X)	(X)	(X)
Medicaid	109.1	71.6	19.5	18.0	(X)	(X)	(X)	(X)
Worker's compensation	21.0	17.3	0.6	3.2	(X)	(X)	(X)	(X)
Self pay	78.1	55.9	7.0	15.2	(X)	(X)	(X)	(X)
No charge	11.4	7.9	2.4	1.2	(X)	(X)	(X)	(X)
Other	49.6	42.2	4.5	2.9	(X)	(X)	(X)	(X)
Unknown	28.8	17.6	3.7	7.5	(X)	(X)	(X)	(X)

X Not applicable. [1] Rates do not meet standard of reliability or precision.

Source: U.S. National Center for Health Statistics, *Advance Data,* Nos. 313, 315, and 317; May 10, 2000; July 19, 2000; and July 27, 2000.

Health and Nutrition 125

No. 192. Visits to Office-Based Physicians and Hospital Outpatient Departments by Diagnosis: 1995 and 1998

[307.0 represents 307,000,000. See headnote, Table 191]

MALE

Leading diagnoses [1]	Number (mil.) 1995	1998	Rate per 1,000 persons [2] 1995	1998
All ages	307.0	358.9	2,406	2,734
Under 15 years old [3]	75.2	86.4	2,471	2,820
Routine infant or child health check	10.4	16.9	341	552
Acute upper respiratory infections [4]	7.7	10.6	252	347
Otitis media	9.8	8.0	322	260
Asthma	1.8	3.0	59	97
Acute pharyngitis	2.4	2.1	80	69
15 to 44 years old [3]	90.8	98.9	1,540	1,661
General medical examination	4.5	4.9	76	82
Acute upper respiratory infections [4]	3.7	3.6	63	61
Chronic sinusitis	1.6	2.2	26	37
Chronic and unspecified bronchitis	1.7	2.1	29	36
Diabetes mellitus	1.0	1.9	17	32
45 to 64 years old [3]	69.8	89.3	2,795	3,258
Diabetes mellitus	2.7	5.2	109	190
Essential hypertension	4.3	5.1	172	187
Malignant neoplasms	2.2	2.8	88	104
Ischemic heart disease	2.3	2.8	93	101
General medical examination	1.3	2.5	53	91
65 years old and over [3]	71.2	84.3	5,405	6,168
Essential hypertension	3.8	5.8	286	424
Malignant neoplasms	4.8	5.4	365	394
Ischemic heart disease	3.3	4.3	252	312
Heart disease, excluding ischemic	3.1	3.8	237	275
Diabetes mellitus	2.7	3.7	209	270

FEMALE

Leading diagnoses [1]	Number (mil.) 1995	1998	Rate per 1,000 persons [2] 1995	1998
All ages	457.3	545.8	3,404	3,951
Under 15 years old [3]	71.4	75.4	2,457	2,576
Routine infant or child health check	10.2	13.9	351	476
Acute upper respiratory infections [4]	9.1	8.2	313	281
Otitis media	8.5	6.4	293	220
Acute pharyngitis	2.8	2.8	95	95
Asthma	1.4	2.4	50	80
15 to 44 years old [3]	173.9	212.8	2,888	3,495
Normal pregnancy	22.2	33.5	369	551
Gynecological examination . .	2.6	6.8	44	112
General medical examination .	7.4	6.6	123	109
Acute upper respiratory infections [4]	6.4	6.5	107	107
Complications of pregnancy, childbirth, and the puerperium	2.0	5.2	34	86
45 to 64 years old [3]	104.6	131.9	3,911	4,502
Essential hypertension	5.2	7.7	193	262
Diabetes mellitus	3.5	5.2	131	177
Malignant neoplasms	3.2	3.3	120	112
Gynecological examination . .	1.0	3.1	36	107
Acute upper respiratory infections [4]	2.4	3.1	91	107
65 years old and over [3]	107.5	125.7	5,861	6,722
Essential hypertension	7.7	9.4	421	502
Cataract	4.6	5.7	254	303
Malignant neoplasms	4.3	4.7	234	250
Diabetes mellitus	3.8	4.5	206	240
Heart disease, excluding ischemic	4.2	4.3	227	231

[1] Based on the International Classification of Diseases, 9th Revision, Clinical Modification, (ICD-9-CM).   [2] Based on U.S. Census Bureau estimated civilian population as of July 1.   [3] Includes other first-listed diagnoses, not shown separately.   [4] Excluding pharyngitis.

Source: U.S. National Center for Health Statistics, *Advance Data*, Nos. 315 and 317, July 19, 2000 and July 27, 2000.

No. 193. Visits to Hospital Emergency Departments by Diagnosis: 1998

[47,586 represents 47,586,000. See headnote, Table 191]

MALE

Leading diagnoses [1]	Number (1,000)	Rate per 1,000 persons [2]
All ages	47,586	363
Under 15 years old [3]	12,154	397
Otitis media	1,145	37
Acute upper respiratory infections [4] .	1,073	35
Open wound of head	939	31
Contusions with intact skin surfaces .	574	19
Open wound, excluding head, hand, and fingers	563	18
15 to 44 years old [3]	21,636	363
Contusions with intact skin surfaces .	1,387	23
Open wound, excluding head, hand, and fingers	1,028	17
Open wound of hand and fingers	815	14
Open wound of head	675	11
Chest pain	656	11
45 to 64 years old [3]	7,738	282
Chest pain	447	16
Contusions with intact skin surfaces .	308	11
Abdominal pain	272	10
Open wound of hand and fingers . . .	214	8
Heart disease, excluding ischemic . .	198	7
65 years old and over [3]	6,058	443
Heart disease, excluding ischemic . .	455	33
Chest pain	331	24
Pneumonia	283	21
Ischemic heart disease	275	20
Chronic and unspecified bronchitis . .	157	12

FEMALE

Leading diagnoses [1]	Number (1,000)	Rate per 1,000 persons [2]
All ages	52,798	382
Under 15 years old [3]	10,174	348
Acute upper respiratory infections [4] .	999	34
Otitis media	991	34
Contusions with intact skin surfaces .	511	17
Open wound of head	434	15
Unspecified viral and chlamydial infections	379	13
15 to 44 years old [3]	24,514	403
Abdominal pain	1,363	22
Complications of pregnancy, childbirth, and the puerperium	1,253	21
Contusions with intact skin surfaces .	1,080	18
Acute upper respiratory infections [4] .	792	13
Chest pain	625	10
45 to 64 years old [3]	8,686	296
Chest pain	496	17
Contusions with intact skin surfaces .	304	10
Abdominal pain	300	10
Chronic and unspecified bronchitis . .	252	9
Dorsopathies, excluding intervertebral disc disorders and lumbago . . .	215	7
65 years old and over [3]	9,424	504
Heart disease, excluding ischemic . .	612	33
Contusions with intact skin surfaces .	464	25
Chest pain	383	20
Cerebrovascular disease	382	20
Ischemic heart disease	366	20

[1] Based on the International Classification of Diseases, 9th Revision, Clinical Modification, (ICD-9-CM).   [2] Based on U.S. Census Bureau estimated civilian population as of July 1.   [3] Includes other first-listed diagnoses, not shown separately.   [4] Excluding pharyngitis.

Source: U.S. National Center for Health Statistics, *Advance Data*, No. 313, May 10, 2000.

126   Health and Nutrition

No. 194. Hospitals—Summary Characteristics: 1980 to 1998

[Beds: 1,365 represents 1,365,000. Covers hospitals accepted for registration by the American Hospital Association; see text, this section. Short-term hospitals have an average patient stay of less than 30 days; long-term, an average stay of longer duration. Special hospitals include obstetrics and gynecology; eye, ear, nose, and throat; orthopedic; and chronic and other special hospitals except psychiatric, tuberculosis, alcoholism, and chemical dependency hospitals]

Item	1980	1985	1990	1993	1994	1995	1996	1997	1998
NUMBER									
All hospitals	6,965	6,872	6,649	6,467	6,374	6,291	6,201	6,097	6,021
With 100 beds or more	3,755	3,805	3,620	3,558	3,492	3,376	3,347	3,267	3,216
Non-Federal [1]	6,606	6,529	6,312	6,151	6,067	5,992	5,911	5,812	5,746
Community hospitals [2]	5,830	5,732	5,384	5,261	5,229	5,194	5,134	5,057	5,015
Nongovernmental nonprofit	3,322	3,349	3,191	3,154	3,139	3,092	3,045	3,000	3,026
For profit	730	805	749	717	719	752	759	797	771
State and local government	1,778	1,578	1,444	1,390	1,371	1,350	1,330	1,260	1,218
Long-term general and special	157	128	131	117	110	112	112	125	125
Psychiatric.	534	610	757	741	696	657	636	601	579
Tuberculosis	11	7	4	4	5	3	3	4	3
Federal.	359	343	337	316	307	299	290	285	275
BEDS (1,000)									
All hospitals [3]	1,365	1,318	1,213	1,163	1,128	1,081	1,062	1,035	1,013
Rate per 1,000 population [4]	6.0	5.5	4.9	4.5	4.3	4.1	4.0	3.9	3.7
Beds per hospital	196	190	182	179	177	172	171	170	168
Non-Federal [1]	1,248	1,197	1,113	1,071	1,044	1,004	989	973	956
Community hospitals [2]	988	1,001	927	919	902	873	862	853	840
Rate per 1,000 population [4]	4.3	4.2	3.7	3.6	3.5	3.3	3.3	3.2	3.1
Nongovernmental nonprofit	692	707	657	649	637	610	598	591	588
For profit	87	104	102	99	101	106	109	115	113
State and local government	209	189	169	169	164	157	155	148	139
Long-term general and special	39	31	25	21	19	19	19	17	18
Psychiatric.	215	169	158	131	121	110	106	100	95
Tuberculosis	2	1	(Z)	(Z)	1	(Z)	(Z)	(Z)	(Z)
Federal.	117	112	98	87	84	78	73	62	57
AVERAGE DAILY CENSUS (1,000)									
All hospitals . . . . [2]	1,060	910	844	783	745	710	685	673	662
Community hospitals [2]	747	649	619	592	568	548	531	528	525
Nongovernmental nonprofit.	542	476	455	432	413	393	379	376	377
For profit	57	54	54	51	50	55	56	60	60
State and local government	149	119	111	109	104	100	96	92	87
EXPENSES (bil. dol.) [5]									
All hospitals	91.9	153.3	234.9	301.5	310.8	320.3	330.5	342.3	355.5
Non-Federal [1]	84.0	141.0	219.6	281.9	290.8	300.0	308.3	319.6	332.9
Community hospitals [2]	76.9	130.5	203.7	266.1	275.8	285.6	293.8	305.8	318.8
Nongovernmental nonprofit	55.8	96.1	150.7	197.2	204.2	209.6	216.0	225.3	238.0
For profit	5.8	11.5	18.8	23.1	23.4	26.7	28.4	31.2	31.7
State and local government.	15.2	22.9	34.2	45.8	48.1	49.3	49.4	49.3	49.1
Long-term general and special	1.2	1.9	2.7	2.7	2.3	2.2	2.3	2.5	2.6
Psychiatric.	5.8	8.3	12.9	12.7	12.3	11.7	12.0	11.0	11.2
Tuberculosis	0.1	0.1	0.1	0.1	0.7	0.4	(Z)	0.1	(Z)
Federal.	7.9	12.3	15.2	19.6	20.0	20.2	22.3	22.7	22.6
PERSONNEL (1,000) [6]									
All hospitals	3,492	3,625	4,063	4,289	4,270	4,273	4,276	4,333	4,407
Non-Federal [1]	3,213	3,326	3,760	3,970	3,969	3,971	3,981	4,036	4,071
Community hospitals [2]	2,873	2,997	3,420	3,677	3,692	3,714	3,725	3,790	3,831
Nongovernmental nonprofit	2,086	2,216	2,533	2,711	2,719	2,702	2,711	2,765	2,834
For profit	189	221	273	289	301	343	359	385	383
State and local government.	598	561	614	676	672	670	654	640	614
Long-term general and special	56	58	55	45	38	38	40	37	37
Psychiatric.	275	263	280	242	233	215	212	204	198
Tuberculosis	3	2	1	1	1	1	1	1	1
Federal.	279	299	303	320	301	301	295	296	336
Outpatient visits (mil.)	263.0	282.1	368.2	435.7	453.6	483.2	505.5	520.6	545.5
Emergency	82.0	80.1	92.8	97.4	96.0	99.9	97.6	97.4	99.0

Z Less than 500 beds or $50 million.   [1] Includes hospital units of institutions.   [2] Short term (average length of stay less than 30 days) general and special (e.g., obstetrics and gynecology; eye, ear, nose and throat; rehabilitation etc. except psychiatric, tuberculosis, alcoholism and chemical dependency). Excludes hospital units of institutions.   [3] Beginning 1990, number of beds at end of reporting period; prior years, average number in 12 month period.   [4] Based on Census Bureau estimated resident population as of July 1. Estimates reflect revisions based on the 1990 Census of Population.   [5] Excludes new construction.   [6] Includes full-time equivalents of part-time personnel.

Source: Health Forum, An American Hospital Association Company, Chicago, IL, *Hospital Statistics 2000 Edition*, and prior years (copyright).

Health and Nutrition   127

No. 195. Average Cost to Community Hospitals Per Patient: 1980 to 1998

[In dollars, except percent. Covers non-Federal short-term general or special hospitals (excluding psychiatric or tuberculosis hospitals and hospital units of institutions). Total cost per patient based on total hospital expenses (payroll, employee benefits, professional fees, supplies, etc.). Data have been adjusted for outpatient visits]

Type of expense and hospital	1980	1985	1990	1992	1993	1994	1995	1996	1997	1998
Average cost per day, total......	245	460	687	820	881	931	968	1,006	1,033	1,067
Annual percent change [1].......	12.9	11.9	7.8	9.0	7.4	5.7	4.0	4.0	2.6	3.3
Nongovernmental nonprofit	246	463	692	828	898	950	994	1,042	1,074	1,111
For profit...................	257	501	752	889	914	924	947	946	962	968
State and local government	239	433	635	754	800	859	878	903	914	949
Average cost per stay, total	1,851	3,245	4,947	5,794	6,132	6,230	6,216	6,225	6,262	6,386
Nongovernmental nonprofit	1,902	3,307	5,001	5,809	6,178	6,257	6,279	6,344	6,393	6,526
For profit...................	1,676	3,033	4,727	5,548	5,643	5,529	5,425	5,207	5,219	5,262
State and local government	1,750	3,106	4,838	5,871	6,206	6,513	6,445	6,419	6,475	6,612

[1] Change from immediate prior year.

Source: Health Forum, An American Hospital Association Company, Chicago, IL, *Hospital Statistics 2000 Edition* (copyright).

No. 196. Community Hospitals by State: 1990 to 1998

[Beds: 928.1 represents 928,100. For definition of community hospitals see footnote 2, Table 204]

State	Number of hospitals			Beds (1,000)			Patients admitted (1,000)		Average daily census [1] (1,000)		Outpatient visits (mil.)	
	1990	1995	1998	1990	1995	1998	1995	1998	1995	1998	1995	1998
United States ...	5,384	5,194	5,015	928.1	872.7	840.0	30,945	31,812	547.6	524.5	414.3	474.2
Alabama.........	120	115	110	18.6	18.3	17.0	642	644	10.7	10.0	6.4	6.8
Alaska	16	17	17	1.2	1.3	1.2	40	41	0.7	1.0	0.8	1.0
Arizona..........	61	61	64	9.9	9.9	10.9	427	495	5.6	6.6	4.0	4.6
Arkansas	86	85	82	10.9	10.1	9.9	342	358	6.0	5.8	3.6	4.2
California	445	424	405	80.5	75.0	74.5	3,029	3,170	45.0	45.6	39.5	45.0
Colorado.........	69	69	69	10.4	9.3	9.2	340	373	5.4	5.1	5.5	6.0
Connecticut.......	35	34	33	9.6	7.5	6.9	338	330	5.5	4.8	5.7	6.5
Delaware	8	8	6	2.0	1.9	2.0	81	84	1.5	1.4	1.4	1.3
District of Columbia .	11	12	12	4.5	3.8	3.6	154	140	2.7	2.7	1.2	1.5
Florida	224	212	204	50.7	49.7	49.2	1,772	1,947	29.4	29.7	16.9	19.4
Georgia	163	160	156	25.7	26.1	25.2	859	822	15.8	15.0	9.6	10.3
Hawaii	18	21	20	2.9	3.0	2.8	97	98	2.4	2.1	2.1	2.5
Idaho...........	43	41	42	3.2	3.4	3.4	104	115	1.8	1.9	1.7	2.2
Illinois	210	207	203	45.8	42.0	39.2	1,452	1,466	25.0	23.7	20.6	22.8
Indiana..........	113	115	111	21.8	19.4	19.4	699	704	11.3	11.2	11.8	12.7
Iowa	124	116	116	14.3	12.6	12.2	361	374	7.1	6.9	6.2	7.8
Kansas..........	138	132	129	11.8	10.8	10.9	291	300	5.8	5.9	4.0	4.7
Kentucky	107	104	106	15.9	15.1	15.2	534	551	9.0	8.7	6.1	7.4
Louisiana........	140	130	126	19.1	19.1	17.8	622	638	10.6	9.8	8.0	10.2
Maine...........	39	39	38	4.5	4.0	3.8	142	144	2.6	2.3	2.5	2.7
Maryland	52	50	51	13.6	12.6	12.7	574	565	8.8	8.6	4.9	5.0
Massachusetts.....	101	96	82	21.7	18.9	16.5	751	738	13.0	11.5	13.5	15.4
Michigan.........	176	167	151	33.9	29.6	27.2	1,120	1,105	19.3	17.5	19.2	21.8
Minnesota........	152	142	136	19.4	17.4	16.5	496	516	11.3	11.3	5.7	5.5
Mississippi	103	97	96	12.9	12.6	13.0	388	414	7.6	8.1	3.2	3.4
Missouri	135	126	122	24.3	21.9	20.7	714	742	12.6	11.9	9.9	10.2
Montana.........	55	55	53	4.6	4.2	4.4	96	97	2.7	3.0	1.3	2.3
Nebraska	90	91	86	8.5	7.9	8.1	183	192	4.5	4.9	2.5	2.8
Nevada	21	20	20	3.4	3.6	3.5	149	171	2.2	2.3	1.4	1.6
New Hampshire....	27	29	28	3.5	3.4	2.8	110	109	2.1	1.8	1.8	2.3
New Jersey.......	95	92	83	28.9	29.9	26.4	1,068	1,083	21.4	18.6	12.8	15.3
New Mexico	37	36	36	4.2	3.7	3.5	156	158	2.1	1.9	2.5	3.3
New York	235	230	222	74.7	73.9	68.5	2,398	2,365	59.1	52.5	38.9	43.7
North Carolina.....	120	119	116	22.0	22.7	23.3	833	908	15.5	15.9	8.8	11.1
North Dakota......	50	43	43	4.4	4.2	4.0	89	85	2.7	2.4	1.3	1.4
Ohio	190	180	172	43.1	37.8	35.2	1,375	1,355	22.2	20.0	22.0	24.8
Oklahoma........	111	110	109	12.4	11.5	11.0	368	391	6.1	5.9	3.8	4.4
Oregon..........	70	64	60	8.1	7.2	6.8	296	313	3.8	3.8	5.8	5.8
Pennsylvania......	238	225	212	52.6	48.5	44.7	1,810	1,752	33.8	29.9	26.9	30.6
Rhode Island......	12	11	12	3.2	2.7	2.6	119	117	1.8	1.8	1.7	2.2
South Carolina.....	69	66	65	11.3	11.3	11.5	410	457	7.2	7.6	4.7	5.9
South Dakota	53	50	49	4.2	4.6	4.4	94	96	3.0	2.8	1.0	1.5
Tennessee	134	126	122	23.6	20.9	20.7	740	745	12.5	11.8	7.4	9.2
Texas...........	428	416	400	59.2	57.2	56.6	2,029	2,227	31.1	32.1	22.7	27.3
Utah	42	42	41	4.4	4.2	4.0	171	192	2.2	2.4	3.2	4.2
Vermont	15	14	14	1.7	1.8	1.7	55	50	1.3	1.1	1.0	1.2
Virginia..........	97	96	93	20.0	18.6	17.9	699	717	11.5	11.2	7.2	8.3
Washington.......	91	88	86	12.0	10.8	10.7	467	474	6.0	6.3	8.4	8.7
West Virginia......	59	59	58	8.4	8.1	8.1	271	281	4.9	4.9	4.0	5.0
Wisconsin........	129	127	123	18.6	17.0	16.7	550	554	10.2	9.4	8.2	9.6
Wyoming	27	25	25	2.2	2.0	1.9	43	44	1.1	1.0	0.7	0.8

[1] Inpatients receiving treatment each day; excludes newborn.

Source: Health Forum, An American Hospital Association Company, Chicago, IL, *Hospital Statistics 2000 Edition*, and prior years (copyright).

No. 197. Hospital Use Rates by Type of Hospital: 1980 to 1998

Type of hospital	1980	1985	1990	1994	1995	1996	1997	1998
Community hospitals: [1]								
Admissions per 1,000 population [2]	159	141	125	118	118	117	118	118
Admissions per bed	37	33	34	34	35	36	37	38
Average length of stay [3] (days)	7.6	7.1	7.2	6.7	6.5	6.2	6.1	6.0
Outpatient visits per admission	5.6	6.5	9.7	12.5	13.4	14.1	14.3	14.9
Outpatient visits per 1,000 population [2]	890	919	1,208	1,471	1,577	1,659	1,681	1,754
Surgical operations (million [4])	18.8	20.1	21.9	23.0	23.2	23.6	24.2	25.3
Number per admission	0.5	0.6	0.7	0.7	0.7	0.8	0.8	0.8
Non-Federal psychiatric:								
Admissions per 1,000 population [2]	2.5	2.5	2.9	2.9	2.7	2.7	2.7	2.7
Days in hospital per 1,000 population [2]	295	224	190	136	124	117	109	103

[1] For definition of community hospitals, see footnote 2, Table 194.   [2] Based on U.S. Census Bureau estimated resident population as of July 1. Estimates reflect revisions based on the 1990 Census of Population.   [3] Number of inpatient days divided by number of admissions.   [4] 18.8 represents 18,800,000.

Source: Health Forum, An American Hospital Association Company, Chicago, IL, *Hospital Statistics 2000 Edition*, and prior years (copyright).

No. 198. Hospital Utilization Rates: 1980 to 1998

[37,832 represents 37,832,000. Represents estimates of inpatients discharged from noninstitutional, short-stay hospitals, exclusive of Federal hospitals. Excludes newborn infants. Based on sample data collected from the National Hospital Discharge Survey, a sample survey of hospital records of patients discharged in year shown; subject to sampling variability. Comparisons beginning 1990 with data for earlier years should be made with caution as estimates of change may reflect improvements in the design rather than true changes in hospital use]

Sex	1980	1985	1990	1993	1994	1995	1996	1997	1998
Patients discharged (1,000)	37,832	35,056	30,788	30,825	30,843	30,722	30,545	30,914	31,827
Patients discharged per 1,000 persons, total [1]	168	148	122	118	117	116	114	114	117
Male	139	124	100	97	96	94	92	93	93
Female	194	171	143	139	138	136	135	135	139
Days of care per 1,000 persons, total [1]	1,217	954	784	709	674	620	597	582	589
Male	1,068	849	694	631	599	551	533	508	517
Female	1,356	1,053	869	782	745	686	657	653	658
Average stay (days)	7.3	6.5	6.4	6.0	5.7	5.4	5.2	5.1	5.1
Male	7.7	6.9	6.9	6.5	6.2	5.8	5.8	5.5	5.5
Female	7.0	6.2	6.1	5.6	5.4	5.0	4.9	4.8	4.7

[1] Based on U.S. Census Bureau estimated civilian population as of July 1. Estimates for 1980 and 1985 do not reflect revisions based on the 1990 Census of Population. Beginning with 1990 data, rates are based on the U.S. Census Bureau estimates of the civilian population that have been adjusted for net underenumeration in the 1990 Census.

Source: U.S. National Center for Health Statistics, *Vital and Health Statistics*, Series 13; and unpublished data.

No. 199. Hospital Discharges and Days of Care: 1995 and 1998

[30,722 represents 30,722,000. See headnote, Table 198. For composition of regions, see map, inside front cover]

Age and region	Discharges				Days of care per 1,000 persons [1]		Average stay (days)	
	Number (1,000)		Per 1,000 persons [1]					
	1995	1998	1995	1998	1995	1998	1995	1998
Total	30,722	31,827	116	117	620	589	5.4	5.1
Age:								
Under 1 year old	790	762	198	194	1,083	1,068	5.5	5.5
1 to 4 years old	744	638	46	41	153	133	3.3	3.3
5 to 14 years old	872	899	22	22	99	109	4.5	4.9
15 to 24 years old	2,943	2,919	80	77	271	255	3.4	3.3
25 to 34 years old	4,201	4,004	102	102	354	348	3.5	3.4
35 to 44 years old	3,449	3,454	81	77	381	340	4.7	4.4
45 to 64 years old	6,168	6,696	119	117	657	604	5.5	5.1
65 to 74 years old	4,832	4,876	260	268	1,685	1,596	6.5	6.0
75 years old and over	6,724	7,580	459	477	3,248	3,031	7.1	6.3
Region:								
Northeast	7,051	6,818	136	131	858	757	6.3	5.8
Midwest	6,994	7,366	113	117	586	553	5.2	4.7
South	11,373	12,022	122	124	643	631	5.3	5.1
West	5,303	5,621	91	92	410	418	4.5	4.6

[1] Based on U.S. Census Bureau estimated civilian population that has been adjusted for the net underenumeration in the 1990 Census of Population.

Source: U.S. National Center for Health Statistics, *Vital and Health Statistics*, Series 13; and unpublished data.

U.S. Census Bureau, Statistical Abstract of the United States: 2000

No. 200. Hospital Discharges and Days of Care by Sex: 1998

[**12,469** represents 12,469,000. See headnote, Table 198]

Age and first-listed diagnosis	Discharges		Days of care per 1,000 persons [1]	Aver-age stay (days)	Age and first-listed diagnosis	Discharges		Days of care per 1,000 persons [1]	Aver-age stay (days)
	Num-ber (1,000)	Per 1,000 per-sons [1]				Num-ber (1,000)	Per 1,000 per-sons [1]		
MALE					FEMALE				
All ages [2]	**12,469**	**89.0**	**487**	**5.1**	**All ages** [2]	**19,358**	**117.1**	**530**	**4.3**
Under 15 years [3]	1,303	42.5	201	4.7	Under 15 years [3]	996	34.0	154	4.5
Pneumonia	192	6.3	20	3.3	Pneumonia	147	5.0	18	3.6
Injuries and poisoning	140	4.6	19	4.1	Injuries and poisoning	93	3.2	15	4.8
Asthma	105	3.4	7	2.2	Asthma	61	2.1	5	2.6
15 to 44 years [3]	2,718	44.6	226	5.1	15 to 44 years [3]	7,659	125.4	406	3.2
Injuries and poisoning	481	7.9	36	4.5	Delivery	3,990	65.3	162	2.5
Psychoses.	300	4.9	42	8.4	Psychoses.	323	5.3	43	8.2
Diseases of heart	147	2.4	9	3.5	Injuries and poisoning	312	5.1	20	3.9
Intervertebral disk disorders .	88	1.4	3	2.2					
					45 to 64 years [3]	3,410	115.9	577	5.0
45 to 64 years [3]	3,286	118.8	632	5.3	Diseases of heart	458	15.6	74	4.8
Diseases of heart	790	28.5	128	4.5	Injuries and poisoning	252	8.6	43	5.0
Injuries and poisoning	271	9.8	57	5.8	Malignant neoplasms.	215	7.3	46	6.3
Malignant neoplasms.	187	6.8	47	7.0	Pneumonia	113	3.8	24	6.1
Pneumonia	115	4.2	26	6.3	Diabetes	77	2.6	14	5.3
65 to 74 years [3]	2,284	278.5	1,604	5.8	65 to 74 years [3]	2,592	258.6	1,590	6.1
Diseases of heart	630	76.9	365	4.8	Diseases of heart	525	52.4	265	5.1
Malignant neoplasms.	166	20.2	151	7.5	Injuries and poisoning	185	18.4	123	6.7
Injuries and poisoning	143	17.5	111	6.3	Malignant neoplasms.	178	17.7	147	8.3
Cerebrovascular diseases . .	126	15.3	79	5.2	Cerebrovascular diseases . .	126	12.6	99	7.9
Pneumonia	119	14.5	92	6.3	Pneumonia	112	11.2	88	7.8
75 years old and older [3] . .	2,879	485.6	3,120	6.4	75 years old and older [3] . .	4,701	472.4	2,978	6.3
Diseases of heart	665	112.2	625	5.6	Diseases of heart	1,008	101.3	538	5.3
Pneumonia	226	38.1	271	7.1	Injuries and poisoning	462	46.4	293	6.3
Injuries and poisoning	201	34.0	218	6.4	Pneumonia	309	31.1	208	6.7
Cerebrovascular diseases . .	194	32.8	177	5.4	Cerebrovascular diseases . .	299	30.1	172	5.7
Malignant neoplasms.	169	28.5	232	8.1	Malignant neoplasms.	186	18.7	137	7.3

[1] Based on Census Bureau estimated civilian population as of July 1. Population figures are adjusted for net underenumeration using the 1990 National Population Adjustment Matrix from the US Census Bureau.   [2] Average length of stay and rates per 1,000 population are age-adjusted.   [3] Includes other first-listed diagnoses not shown separately.

Source: U.S. National Center for Health Statistics, *Health, United States, 2000.*

No. 201. Organ Transplants and Grafts: 1985 to 1999

[As of **end of year.** Based on reports of procurement programs and transplant centers in the United States, except as noted]

Procedure	Number of procedures							Number of centers		Num-ber of people waiting, 1999	1-year patient survival rates, 1998 (percent)
	1985	1990	1995	1996	1997	1998	1999	1990	1999		
Transplant: [1]											
Heart	719	2,107	2,361	2,343	2,292	2,345	(NA)	148	141	4,099	83.2
Heart-lung	30	52	70	39	62	47	(NA)	79	88	230	(NA)
Lung	2	204	871	810	928	862	(NA)	70	82	3,572	70.6
Liver	602	2,691	3,925	4,065	4,167	4,487	(NA)	85	116	14,496	85.9
Kidney.	7,695	9,880	11,901	12,152	12,307	13,139	(NA)	232	243	44,010	95.6
Kidney-pancreas .	(NA)	459	918	859	854	973	(NA)	(NA)	(NA)	1,185	(NA)
Pancreas	130	528	1,025	1,024	1,061	1,221	(NA)	84	123	717	95.3
Intestine	(NA)	5	45	45	67	69	(NA)	(NA)	37	116	(NA)
Cornea grafts [2]	26,300	40,631	44,652	46,300	45,493	(NA)	45,765	[3]107	[3]93	1,687	(NA)
Bone grafts	(NA)	350,000	450,000	475,000	(NA)	500,000	600,600	30	(NA)	(X)	(NA)
Skin grafts [4]	(NA)	5,500	5,500	9,000	(NA)	9,000	10,000	25	(NA)	(X)	(NA)

NA Not available.   X Not applicable.   [1] Simultaneous kidney-pancreas transplants are counted twice, both in kidney transplants and in pancreas transplants. Double kidney, double lung, and heart-lung transplants are counted as one transplant.   [2] 1985 and 1990, number of procedures and eye banks include Canada.   [3] Eye banks.   [4] Procedure data are shown in terms of square feet.

Source: Transplants: through 1990, U.S. Department of Health and Human Services, Public Health Service, Division of Organ Transplantation; beginning 1995, United Network for Organ Sharing, Richmond, VA; American Association of Tissue Banks, McLean, VA; and Eye Bank Association of America, Washington, DC; and unpublished data.

No. 202. Procedures for Inpatients Discharged From Short-Stay Hospitals: 1990 to 1998

[23,051 represents 23,051,000. Excludes newborn infants and discharges from federal hospitals. See headnote, Table 198]

Sex and type of procedure	Number of procedures (1,000)				Rate per 1,000 population [1]			
	1990	1995	1997	1998	1990	1995	1997	1998
Surgical procedures, total [2]	**23,051**	**22,530**	**22,927**	**23,780**	**92.4**	**86.2**	**84.8**	**87.1**
Cardiac catheterization	995	1,068	1,112	1,202	4.0	4.1	4.1	4.4
Removal of coronary artery obstruction [3]	285	434	686	926	1.2	1.7	2.5	3.4
Reduction of fracture [4]	609	577	642	610	2.4	2.2	2.4	2.2
Coronary artery bypass graft	392	573	607	553	1.6	2.2	2.2	2.0
Male, total [2]	**8,538**	**8,388**	**8,505**	**8,757**	**70.6**	**65.9**	**64.3**	**65.7**
Cardiac catheterization	620	660	664	716	5.1	5.2	5.0	5.4
Removal of coronary artery obstruction [3]	200	285	459	594	1.7	2.2	3.5	4.4
Coronary artery bypass graft	286	423	420	396	2.4	3.3	3.2	3.0
Female, total [2]	**14,513**	**14,142**	**14,423**	**15,022**	**113.0**	**105.3**	**104.4**	**107.5**
Repair of current obstetric laceration	795	964	1,082	1,093	6.2	7.2	7.8	7.8
Cesarean section	945	785	820	900	7.4	5.8	5.9	6.4
Hysterectomy	591	583	603	645	4.6	4.3	4.4	4.6
Diagnostic and other nonsurgical procedures [5]	**17,455**	**17,278**	**17,582**	**17,720**	**70.0**	**66.1**	**65.0**	**64.9**
Angiocardiography and arteriography [6]	1,735	1,834	1,900	1,961	7.0	7.0	7.0	7.2
Diagnostic ultrasound	1,608	1,181	1,111	1,123	6.4	4.5	4.1	4.1
Respiratory therapy	1,164	1,127	1,088	1,109	4.7	4.3	4.0	4.1
CAT scan [7]	1,506	967	963	986	6.0	3.7	3.6	3.6
Male, total [5]	**7,378**	**7,261**	**7,313**	**7,431**	**61.0**	**57.1**	**55.3**	**55.7**
Angiocardiography and arteriography [6]	1,051	1,076	1,077	1,115	8.7	8.5	8.1	8.4
Respiratory therapy	586	572	561	564	4.9	4.5	4.2	4.2
CAT scan [7]	736	473	473	462	6.1	3.7	3.6	3.5
Female, total [5]	**10,077**	**10,016**	**10,269**	**10,290**	**78.5**	**74.6**	**74.4**	**73.6**
Manual assisted delivery	750	866	1,224	975	5.9	6.5	8.9	7.0
Fetal EKG and fetal monitoring	1,377	935	834	835	10.8	7.0	6.0	6.0
Diagnostic ultrasound	941	682	628	635	7.3	5.1	4.6	4.5

[1] Based on Census Bureau estimated civilian population as of July 1. Beginning 1997 population figures are adjusted for net underenumeration using the 1990 National Population Adjustment Matrix from the Census Bureau.   [2] Includes other types of surgical procedures not shown separately.   [3] Beginning 1997 includes separately coded "insertion of stent".   [4] Excluding skull, nose, and jaw.   [5] Includes other nonsurgical procedures not shown separately.   [6] Using contrast material.   [7] Computerized axial tomography.

Source: U.S. National Center for Health Statistics, *Vital and Health Statistics*, Series 13; and unpublished data.

No. 203. Selected Measures of Hospital Utilization for Patients Discharged With the Diagnosis of Human Immunodeficiency Virus (HIV): 1985 to 1998

[See headnote, Table 198]

Measure of utilization	Unit	1985	1990	1995	1996	1997	1998
Number of patients discharged [1]	1,000	23	146	249	227	178	189
Rate of patient discharges [2]	Rate	1.0	5.8	9.4	8.5	6.6	6.9
Number of days of care	1,000	387	2,188	2,326	2,123	1,448	1,503
Rate of days of care [2]	Rate	16.3	86.9	87.6	79.2	53.5	55.0
Average length of stay [3]	Days	17.1	14.9	9.3	9.4	8.1	8.0

[1] Comparisons beginning 1990 with data for earlier years should be made with caution as estimates of change may reflect improvements in the 1988 sample design rather than true changes in hospital use.   [2] Per 10,000 population. Based on Census Bureau estimated civilian population as of July 1. Population estimates for the 1980's do not reflect revised estimates based on the 1990 Census of Population. Beginning 1900 rates are based on civilian population estimates that have been adjusted for net underenumeration in the 1990 Census.   [3] For similar data on all patients, see Table 198.

Source: National Center for Health Statistics, *Vital and Health Statistics*, Series 13; and unpublished data.

No. 204. Skilled Nursing Facilities: 1980 to 1998

[448 represents 448,000. Covers facilities and beds certified for participation under medicare as of midyear. Includes facilities which have transfer agreements with one or more participating hospitals, and are engaged primarily in providing skilled nursing care and related services for the rehabilitation of injured, disabled, or sick persons]

Item	Unit	1980	1990	1994	1995	1996	1997	1998
Skilled nursing facilities	Number	5,155	9,008	12,584	13,281	14,177	14,860	15,032
Beds	1,000	448	512	649	657	672	685	723
Per 1,000 Medicare enrollees [1]	Rate	16.0	15.2	17.8	17.7	17.8	18.0	18.8

[1] Based on total number of beneficiaries enrolled in the medicare hospital insurance program as of July 1 of year stated.

Source: U.S. Health Care Financing Administration, *Medicare Participating Providers and Suppliers of Health Services, 1980*; and unpublished data.

Health and Nutrition   131

No. 205. Home Health and Hospice Care Agencies by Selected Characteristics: 1998

[In percent, except as indicated (13.3 represents 13,300). Based on the National Home and Hospice Care Survey. Home health care is provided to individuals and families in their place of residence. Hospice care is available in both the home and inpatient settings. See source for details. For composition of regions, see map, inside front cover]

Agency characteristic	Agencies, total	Current patients [1]			Discharges [2]		
		Total	Home health care	Hospice care	Total	Home health care	Hospice care
Total (1,000).................	**13.3**	**1,961.6**	**1,881.8**	**79.8**	**8,117.7**	**7,621.8**	**496.0**
PERCENT DISTRIBUTION							
Ownership:							
Proprietary.....................	53.9	46.1	47.1	23.0	38.4	39.1	26.7
Voluntary nonprofit	36.2	45.4	44.2	73.0	54.3	53.2	69.9
Government and other............	9.9	8.5	8.7	[3]4.1	7.4	7.6	[3]3.4
Certification:							
Medicare.....................	84.3	84.0	83.5	96.6	92.9	92.8	93.9
Medicaid.....................	85.1	85.1	84.8	92.3	89.3	89.3	90.0
Region:							
Northeast.....................	16.7	34.4	35.4	10.7	33.9	34.8	18.7
Midwest......................	25.8	21.5	21.4	23.9	25.6	25.7	22.9
South	42.0	33.9	33.4	44.6	26.4	25.9	33.3
West........................	15.5	10.2	9.7	20.8	14.2	13.5	25.1

[1] Patients on the rolls of the agency as of midnight the day prior to the survey.   [2] Patients removed from the rolls of the agency during the 12 months prior to the day of the survey. A patient could be included more than once if the individual had more than one episode of care during the year.   [3] Figure does not meet standard of reliability or precision.

Source: U.S. National Center for Health Statistics, unpublished data.

No. 206. Home Health and Hospice Care Patients by Selected Characteristics: 1998

[In percent, except as indicated (1,961.6 represents 1,961,600). See headnote, Table 205]

Item	Current patients [1]			Discharges [2]		
	Total	Home health care	Hospice care	Total	Home health care	Hospice care
Total (1,000)..............	**1,961.6**	**1,881.8**	**79.8**	**8,117.7**	**7,621.8**	**496.0**
PERCENT DISTRIBUTION						
Age: [3]						
Under 45 years old	15.1	15.5	4.6	14.7	15.3	5.9
45-54 years old	7.1	7.1	6.4	7.1	7.1	6.7
55-64 years old	8.8	8.7	10.6	8.3	8.1	11.2
65 years old and over	69.1	68.7	78.4	70.0	69.6	76.1
65-69 years old..............	8.2	8.3	7.2	9.7	9.7	9.2
70-74 years old..............	11.6	11.5	15.5	13.0	12.8	16.7
75-79 years old..............	14.5	14.4	16.8	17.0	17.1	16.8
80-84 years old..............	15.5	15.5	16.2	13.9	13.8	15.2
85 years old and over	19.2	19.1	22.7	16.3	16.2	18.2
Sex:						
Male.......................	34.0	33.6	42.7	38.4	37.7	47.9
Female.....................	66.0	66.4	57.3	61.6	62.3	52.1
Race:						
White	70.0	69.5	82.7	67.8	67.0	79.8
Black and other	13.5	13.6	9.9	12.9	13.0	9.3
Black.....................	12.9	13.0	8.9	11.7	11.8	8.0
Unknown...................	16.6	17.0	7.4	19.3	20.0	[4]10.9
Marital status: [3]						
Married.....................	30.3	29.7	44.6	39.7	38.9	48.9
Widowed....................	32.7	32.5	35.8	28.3	28.1	32.0
Divorced or separated	4.9	4.8	8.5	4.5	4.4	5.1
Never married	17.0	17.4	7.5	15.1	15.7	7.2
Unknown....................	15.1	15.6	[4]3.6	12.5	12.9	[4]6.8
Primary admission diagnosis:						
Neoplasms	6.1	3.9	57.5	10.9	7.3	65.7
Endocrine, nutritional and metabolic and immunity disorders	7.9	8.2	([4])	5.1	5.4	([4])
Diseases of the nervous system and sense organs	7.7	7.6	9.5	4.3	4.3	4.9
Diseases of the circulatory system..	23.0	23.5	12.6	24.3	25.2	11.4
Diseases of the respiratory system..	8.0	7.9	10.6	8.3	8.4	6.2
Diseases of the musculoskeletal system and connective tissue	7.9	8.2	([4])	8.3	8.8	([4])
Injuries and poisoning	8.5	8.9	([4])	9.3	9.9	([4])

[1] Patients on the rolls of the agency as of midnight the day prior to the survey.   [2] Patients removed from the rolls of the agency during the 12 months prior to the day of the survey. A patient could be included more than once if the individual had more than one episode of care during the year.   [3] For current patients, current age or marital status; for discharged patients, age or marital status at time of discharge.   [4] Figure does not meet standard of reliability or precision.

Source: U.S. National Center for Health Statistics, unpublished data.

132   Health and Nutrition

No. 207. Elderly Home Health Patients: 1998

[1,293 represents 1,293,000. Covers the civilian population 65 years old and over who are home health care patients. Age of patient is based on age at the time of interview. Home health care is provided to individuals and families in their place of residence. Based on the 1998 National Home and Hospice Care Survey]

Item	Current patients [1] Number (1,000)	Current patients [1] Percent	Discharges [2] Number (1,000)	Discharges [2] Percent	Item	Current patients [1] Number (1,000)	Current patients [1] Percent	Discharges [2] Number (1,000)	Discharges [2] Percent
Total 65 yrs. old & over	**1,293**	**100.0**	**5,301**	**100.0**	Own income.	69	5.4	84	1.6
Received help with—					Medicare.	953	73.8	4,659	87.9
Bathing or showering. .	645	49.9	2,152	40.6	Medicaid	141	10.9	186	3.5
Dressing	554	42.8	1,784	33.7	Services rendered: [5]				
Eating.	115	8.9	330	6.2	Nursing services.	1,015	78.6	4,800	90.5
Transferring in/out of					Social services	151	11.7	714	13.5
a bed or chair.	352	27.2	1,225	23.1	Counseling	70	5.4	191	3.6
Using the toilet room . .	269	20.8	921	17.4	Medications	66	5.1	252	4.8
Doing light housework .	471	36.4	1,173	22.1	Physical therapy	277	21.5	1,664	31.4
Managing money	[3]26	[3]2.0	[3]	[3]					
Shopping for groceries					Homemaker-				
or clothes	176	13.6	192	3.6	household services . .	312	24.2	587	11.1
Using the telephone . .	48	3.7	75	1.4	Nutrition services	49	3.8	118	2.2
Preparing meals	261	20.2	515	9.7	Physician services. . . .	28	2.2	87	1.6
Taking medications . . .	228	17.6	655	12.4	Occupational therapy. .	68	5.3	399	7.5
Primary source of					Speech therapy/				
payment [4]:					audiology.	[3]	[3]	[3]73	[3]1.4
Private insurance	52	4.0	310	5.9					

[1] Patients on the rolls of the agency as of midnight the day prior to the survey. [2] Patients removed from the rolls of the agency during the 12 months prior to the day of the survey. A patient could be included more than once if the individual had more than one episode of care during the year. [3] Figure does not meet standard of reliability or precision. [4] For current patients, the expected source; for discharges the actual source for the entire episode. [5] For current patients, services currently being provided; for discharges services provided during the 30 days prior to discharge.

Source: U.S. National Center for Health Statistics, unpublished data.

No. 208. Nursing Homes by Selected Characteristics: 1985 to 1997

[Beds: 1,624 represents 1,624,000. Covers nursing and related care homes in the conterminous United States that had three or more beds, were staffed for use by residents, and routinely provided nursing and personal care services. Excludes places providing only room and board and places serving specific health problems. Based on the 1997 National Nursing Home Survey, a two-stage survey sample of nursing homes and their residents. Subject to sampling variability. For composition of regions, see map, inside front cover]

Characteristic	Beds Nursing homes	Beds Number (1,000)	Beds Per nursing home	Current residents Number (1,000)	Current residents Occupancy rate [1]	Full-time equivalent employment Administrative, medical, and therapeutic Number (1,000)	Full-time equivalent employment Administrative, medical, and therapeutic Rate per 100 beds	Full-time equivalent employment Nursing Number (1,000)	Full-time equivalent employment Nursing Rate per 100 beds
1985	19,100	1,624	85	1,491	91.8	89.4	5.5	704	43.4
1995	16,700	1,771	106	1,549	87.4	90.5	5.1	916	51.7
1997, total	**17,000**	**1,821**	**107**	**1,609**	**88.4**	**100.0**	**5.5**	**950**	**52.2**
Ownership:									
Proprietary.	11,400	1,214	106	1,054	86.8	66.7	5.5	610	50.3
Voluntary nonprofit	4,400	465	105	423	90.8	26.5	5.7	258	55.4
Government and other	1,200	142	123	132	93.1	6.5	4.6	82	58.0
Certification:									
Medicare and Medicaid									
certified	13,300	1,526	115	1,366	89.5	85.3	5.6	809	53.0
Medicare only.	[2]800	61	76	47	77.6	4.3	7.1	33	54.4
Medicaid only.	2,300	185	80	156	84.6	7.5	4.1	87	46.9
Not certified	[2]700	49	71	39	80.5	2.5	5.2	22	44.6
Bed size:									
Less than 50 beds	2,200	74	34	62	83.7	9.8	13.2	47	63.1
50-99 beds	6,300	451	71	397	88.1	25.8	5.7	232	51.4
100-199 beds.	7,200	942	131	835	88.7	47.8	5.1	491	52.2
200 beds or more	1,300	354	270	314	88.7	16.3	4.6	180	50.9
Region:									
Northeast	2,900	396	135	375	94.6	21.3	5.4	231	58.2
Midwest	5,800	577	99	498	86.3	29.0	5.0	281	48.8
South	5,400	600	111	525	87.5	34.4	5.7	307	51.2
West.	2,900	247	86	211	85.3	14.9	6.0	131	53.1
Affiliation [3]:									
Chain	9,600	1,036	108	909	87.7	57.0	5.5	528	51.0
Independent.	7,400	773	105	690	89.3	42.1	5.5	416	53.9

[1] Number of residents divided by number of available beds multiplied by 100. [2] Figure does not meet standards of reliability or precision. [3] Excludes a small number of homes, beds, and residents with unknown affiliation.

Source: U.S. National Center for Health Statistics, *Advance Data*, No. 311, March 1, 2000 and earlier reports.

Health and Nutrition   133

No. 209. Nursing Home Residents 65 Years Old and Over by Selected Characteristics: 1997

[1,465 represents 1,465,000. Covers nursing and related care homes in the conterminous United States that had three or more beds, were staffed for use by residents, and routinely provided nursing and personal care services. Excludes places providing only room and board and places serving specific health problems. Based on the National Nursing Home Survey, a two-stage survey sample of nursing homes and their residents. Subject to sampling variability]

Characteristic [1]	Number (1,000)	Percent distri-bution	Item	Percent of elderly residents	Functional status	Percent of elderly residents receiving assistance
Total [2]	1,465	100.0	Type of aids used:		ADLs: [9]	
			Wheelchair	62.3	Bathing, showering. . .	96.2
Male	372	25.4	Walker	25.2	Dressing.	87.2
Female.	1,093	74.6			Eating	45.0
					Transferring in or	
65 to 74 years	198	13.5	Vision impaired	27.1	out of beds or chair .	25.4
75 to 84 years	528	36.1	Hearing impaired.	23.7	Using toilet room	56.2
85 years and over	738	50.4				
			Type of nursing care:		IADLs: [10]	
White.	1,295	88.4	Skilled care [3]	47.8	Care of personal	
Black	137	9.4	Intermediate care [4]. . .	47.8	possessions	77.1
			Residential care [5] . . .	3.6	Managing money	72.2
Hispanic	32	2.2			Securing personal . . .	
Non-Hispanic.	1,340	91.5	Primary source of		items	76.2
			payment: [6]		Using telephone	62.2
Living quarters:			Private sources [7]	28.2		
Private residence	472	32.2	Medicare	29.7		
Retirement home	34	2.3	Medicaid	38.2		
Board and care and/or			Other [8].	3.8		
residential facility. . . .	67	4.6				
Nursing home.	179	12.2				
Hospital.	651	44.5				
Mental health facility . .	19	1.3				

[1] At time of admission. [2] Includes other and/or unknown, not shown separately. [3] Skilled care indicates the greatest degree of medical care. Every patient is under the supervision of a physician and the facility has a transfer agreement with a nearby hospital. Twenty-four hour nursing care is provided with a physician on call to furnish medical care in case of emergency. [4] Intermediate care is provided to individuals who do not require the degree of care or treatment normally given by a hospital or skilled nursing facility, but who do require health-related institutionalized care above the level of room and board. [5] Residential care usually means providing residents with room, board, laundry services, some forms of personal care, and recreational activities and social services. [6] In month before interview. [7] Includes private insurance, own income, family support, social security benefits, and retirement funds. [8] Includes supplemental security income, welfare, religious organizations, foundations, agencies, Veterans Administration contract, pensions, or other compensation, payment source not yet determined, and other and unknown sources. [9] Activities of daily living. [10] Instrumental activities of daily living.

Source: U.S. National Center for Health Statistics, *Advance Data*, No. 312, April 25, 2000.

No. 210. Mental Health Facilities—Summary by Type of Facility: 1998

[Beds: 191.1 represents 191,100. Facilities, beds and inpatients as of year-end; Excludes private psychiatric office practice and psychiatric service modes of all types in hospitals or outpatient clinics of federal agencies other than U.S. Dept. of Veterans Affairs. Excludes data from Puerto Rico, Virgin Islands, Guam, and other territories]

Type of facility	Number of facilities	Inpatient beds		Inpatients		Inpatient care episodes [2]
		Total (1,000)	Rate [1]	Total (1,000)	Rate [1]	
Total	3,742	191.1	70.7	150.3	55.7	2,099
Mental hospitals:						
State and county	234	62.2	23.0	56.0	20.7	186
Private [3]	813	63.0	23.3	48.7	18.1	527
General hospitals [4].	1,594	52.5	19.4	35.3	13.1	1,137
Veterans Administration [5]	124	9.3	3.5	7.3	2.7	128
Other [6]	977	4.1	1.5	3.0	1.1	121

[1] Rate per 100,000 population. Based on Census Bureau estimated civilian population as of July 1. [2] "Inpatient care episodes" is defined as the number of residents in inpatient facilities at the beginning of the year plus the total additions to inpatient facilities during the year. [3] Includes residential treatment centers for emotionally disturbed children. [4] Non-Federal hospitals with separate psychiatric services. [5] Includes U.S. Department of Veterans Affairs (VA) neuropsychiatric hospitals, VA general hospitals with separate psychiatric settings and VA freestanding psychiatric outpatient clinics. [6] Includes free-standing psychiatric outpatient facilities that provide only psychiatric outpatient services and other multiservice mental health facilities with two or more settings, which are not elsewhere classified, as well as freestanding partial care facilities which only provide psychiatric partial care services. Number of facilities data also include freestanding psychiatric partial care facilities.

Source: U.S. Substance Abuse and Mental Health Services Administration, Center for Mental Health Services, unpublished data.

No. 211. Days of Disability by Type and Selected Characteristics: 1980 to 1996

[4,165 represents 4,165,000,000. Covers civilian noninstitutional population. Beginning 1985, the levels of estimates may not be comparable to estimates for 1980 because the later data are based on a revised questionnaire and field procedures; for further information, see source. Based on National Health Interview Survey; see Appendix III. For composition of regions, see map, inside front cover]

Item	Total days of disability (millions)						Days per person					
	1980	1985	1990	1994	1995	1996	1980	1985	1990	1994	1995	1996
Restricted-activity days [1]	4,165	3,453	3,669	4,143	4,097	3,825	19.1	14.8	14.9	16.0	15.6	14.5
Male	1,802	1,442	1,558	1,723	1,748	1,587	17.1	12.8	13.1	13.6	13.7	12.3
Female	2,363	2,011	2,111	2,420	2,349	2,237	21.0	16.6	16.7	18.2	17.5	16.5
White	3,518	2,899	3,057	3,375	3,392	3,154	18.7	14.5	14.8	15.7	15.6	14.3
Black	580	489	536	608	558	543	22.7	17.4	17.7	18.4	17.0	16.4
Under 65 years	3,228	2,557	2,734	3,070	3,091	2,857	16.6	12.4	12.6	13.4	13.4	12.3
65 years and over	937	895	936	1,073	1,006	968	39.2	33.1	31.4	34.6	32.0	30.5
Northeast	862	689	656	803	754	716	17.9	13.8	13.2	15.9	14.7	13.3
Midwest	989	744	836	879	865	819	17.2	12.7	14.0	13.9	13.9	12.9
South	1,415	1,308	1,404	1,443	1,561	1,432	19.8	16.3	16.7	16.4	16.9	15.8
West	899	712	773	1,017	917	857	22.0	15.7	14.8	17.6	16.4	15.2
Family income:												
Under $10,000	(NA)	893	662	681	649	554	(NA)	25.8	27.3	29.1	30.0	27.9
$10,000 to $19,999	(NA)	781	758	801	794	779	(NA)	16.7	19.1	21.5	21.0	21.1
$20,000 to $34,999	(NA)	791	715	825	824	702	(NA)	12.1	13.5	15.2	15.1	13.0
$35,000 or more	(NA)	568	912	1,051	1,133	1,083	(NA)	9.9	10.3	10.5	10.6	9.9
Bed-disability days [2]	1,520	1,436	1,521	1,603	1,593	1,566	7.0	6.1	6.2	6.2	6.1	5.9
Male	616	583	625	623	678	626	5.9	5.2	5.2	4.9	5.3	4.9
Female	904	852	896	980	915	940	8.0	7.1	7.1	7.4	6.8	6.9
Under 65 years	1,190	1,064	1,115	1,155	1,181	1,167	6.1	5.1	5.2	5.1	5.1	5.0
65 years and over	330	371	406	448	412	399	13.8	13.7	13.6	14.4	13.1	12.6
Work-loss days [3]	485	575	621	642	657	603	5.0	5.3	5.3	5.2	5.3	4.8
Male	271	287	303	311	307	282	4.9	4.8	4.7	4.6	4.5	4.1
Female	215	288	319	332	349	321	5.1	6.0	5.9	5.9	6.1	5.6
School-loss days [4]	204	217	212	225	229	206	5.3	4.8	4.6	4.5	4.5	4.0
Male	95	100	100	104	107	100	4.8	4.4	4.3	4.1	4.2	3.8
Female	109	117	112	121	122	105	5.7	5.3	5.0	5.0	4.9	4.2

NA Not available.   [1] A day when a person cuts down on his activities for more than half a day because of illness or injury. Includes bed-disability, work-loss, and school-loss days. Total includes other races and unknown income, not shown separately.   [2] A day when a person stayed in bed more than half a day because of illness or injury. Includes those work-loss and school-loss days actually spent in bed.   [3] A day when a person lost more than half a workday because of illness or injury. Computed for persons 17 years of age and over (beginning 1985, 18 years of age and over) in the currently employed population, defined as those who were working or had a job or business from which they were not on layoff during the 2-week period preceding the week of interview.   [4] Child's loss of more than half a school day because of illness or injury. Computed for children 6-16 years of age. Beginning 1985, children 5-17 years old.

Source: U.S. National Center for Health Statistics, *Vital and Health Statistics,* Series 10, No. 200; and earlier reports and unpublished data.

No. 212. Injury and Poisoning Episodes and Conditions by Age and Sex: 1997

[34,383 represents 34,383,000. Covers all medically attended injuries and poisonings occurring during the 3-month period prior to the survey interview. There may be more than one condition per episode. Based on the redesigned National Health Interview Survey, a sample survey of the civilian noninstitutionalized population; see Appendix III. Data presented in this table are not comparable with injury data presented in previous editions]

External cause and nature of injury	Both sexes								
	Total	Total, age-adjusted [1]	Under 12 yrs. old	12 to 21 yrs. old	22 to 44 yrs. old	45 to 64 yrs. old	65 yrs. old and over	Male, total	Female, total
EPISODES									
Number (1,000)	34,383	(X)	5,384	6,542	12,766	5,470	4,221	18,544	15,840
Annual rate per 1,000 population, total [2]	129.0	128.9	112.2	171.4	136.4	99.7	131.9	142.4	116.1
Fall	42.4	43.1	45.7	45.5	30.6	32.1	86.2	36.9	47.7
Struck by or against a person or an object [3]	19.6	19.4	17.3	49.1	18.9	11.5	4.0	27.6	11.9
Transportation [3]	16.7	16.5	8.1	23.8	22.9	11.2	11.5	19.3	14.1
Overexertion	13.9	13.9	[4]2.4	12.3	20.3	17.6	7.8	15.1	12.7
Cutting, piercing instruments	10.0	9.9	8.0	15.4	13.4	5.5	4.4	13.3	6.9
Poisoning	7.3	7.2	13.0	5.6	6.7	5.5	5.4	6.9	7.7
CONDITIONS [5]									
Annual rate per 1,000 population, total [2]	153.6	153.7	118.9	197.3	167.5	120.7	169.1	168.5	139.3
Sprains/strains	38.6	38.5	8.7	58.4	52.0	36.7	24.0	39.9	37.3
Open wounds	29.3	29.0	41.9	40.5	29.0	14.1	24.1	40.3	18.8
Fractures	23.4	23.7	18.5	31.1	19.7	19.5	39.2	25.1	21.8
Contusions	18.7	19.0	12.3	20.7	14.6	20.7	37.2	16.4	20.9

X Not applicable.   [1] Data were age-adjusted by the direct method to the 2000 projected population.   [2] Includes other items not shown separately.   [3] Includes the categories Motor vehicle traffic; Pedal cycle, other; Pedestrian, other; and Transport, other.   [4] Figure does not meet standard of reliability or precision.   [5] Poisoning episodes are assumed to have a single condition resulting from the episode.

Source: U.S. National Center for Health Statistics, *Vital and Health Statistics,* Series 10, No. 202.

Health and Nutrition   135

No. 213. Injuries Associated With Consumer Products: 1997

[For products associated with more than 20,000 injuries in 1997. Estimates calculated from a representative sample of hospitals with emergency treatment departments in the United States. Data are estimates of the number of emergency room treated cases nationwide associated with various products. Product involvement does not necessarily mean the product caused the accident. Products were selected from the U.S. Consumer Product Safety Commission's National Electronic Injury Surveillance System]

Product	Number	Product	Number
Home workshop equipment:		Porches, balconies, open-side floors	114,287
Saws (hand or power)	79,854	Fences or fence posts	110,731
Hammers.	41,518	Handrails, railings, or banisters	34,421
Household packaging and containers:		Glass doors	33,952
Household containers and packaging	184,097	General household appliances:	
Bottles and jars.	81,116	Refrigerators.	25,133
Bags.	21,060	Ranges	23,587
Housewares:		Heating, cooling equipment: [3]	
Knives.	435,276	Pipes (excl. smoking pipes).	26,926
Tableware and flatware.	107,963	Home entertainment equipment:	
Scissors.	30,290	Televisions	37,401
Waste containers, trash baskets, etc.	26,686	Sound recording equipment [4]	22,086
Home furnishing: [1]		Personal use items:	
Beds.	394,939	Footwear.	75,804
Tables.	287,933	Jewelry	54,720
Chairs.	260,055	Razors and shavers.	40,773
Bathtubs and showers	164,749	Hair grooming equipment and accessories .	24,974
Ladders.	143,297	Coins	24,755
Sofas, couches, davenports, etc.	107,812	Yard and garden equipment:	
Carpets, rugs	98,693	Lawn mowers	60,804
Toilets	44,335	Pruning, trimming, and edging equipment .	32,217
Mirrors, mirror glass.	22,623	Chain saws	29,684
Electric lighting equipment.	22,067		
Sinks	20,420	Sports and recreation equipment:	
		Bicycles.	544,561
Home structures, construction: [2]		Trampolines	82,722
Stairs or steps	914,887	Swings or swing sets	73,923
Floors or flooring materials	841,022	Playground climbing equipment	71,828
Other doors (excl. garage)	326,148	Swimming pools	62,812
Ceilings and walls	238,066	All-terrain vehicles	55,400
Household cabinets, racks, and shelves . .	222,621	Skateboards.	48,186
Nails, screws, tacks, or bolts	165,623	Slides or sliding boards	45,767
Windows	131,333	Sleds	26,067

[1] Includes accessories. [2] Includes materials. [3] Includes ventilating equipment. [4] Includes reproducing equipment.

Source: National Safety Council, Itasca, IL, *Injury Facts, 1999 Edition* (copyright).

No. 214. Costs of Unintentional Injuries: 1998

[480.5 represents $480,500,000,000. Covers costs of deaths or disabling injuries together with vehicle accidents and fires]

Cost	Amount (bil. dol.)					Percent distribution				
	Total [1]	Motor vehicle	Work	Home	Other	Total [1]	Motor vehicle	Work	Home	Other
Total	**480.5**	**191.6**	**125.1**	**113.5**	**66.3**	**100.0**	**100.0**	**100.0**	**100.0**	**100.0**
Wage and productivity losses [2]	246.1	67.8	62.9	74.3	44.7	51.2	35.4	50.3	65.5	67.4
Medical expense	77.8	20.7	19.9	23.8	14.5	16.2	10.8	15.9	21.0	21.9
Administrative expenses [3]	81.9	56.3	25.6	4.6	4.1	17.0	29.4	20.4	4.0	6.2
Motor vehicle damage	44.9	44.9	2.2	(NA)	(NA)	9.3	23.4	1.8	(NA)	(NA)
Employer cost [4]	21.4	1.9	12.0	6.2	1.7	4.5	1.0	9.6	5.5	2.5
Fire loss	8.4	(NA)	2.5	4.6	1.3	1.8	(NA)	2.0	4.0	2.0

NA Not available. [1] Excludes duplication between work and motor vehicle ($16.0 billion in 1998). [2] Actual loss of wages and household production, and the present value of future earnings lost. [3] Includes the administrative cost of public and private insurance, and police and legal costs. [4] Estimate of the uninsured costs incurred by employers, representing the money value of time lost by noninjured workers.

Source: National Safety Council, Itasca, IL, *Injury Facts, 1999 Edition* (copyright).

No. 215. Specified Reportable Diseases—Cases Reported: 1980 to 1998

[**190.9 represents 190,900.** Figures should be interpreted with caution. Although reporting of some of these diseases is incomplete, the figures are of value in indicating trends of disease incidence. Includes cases imported from outside the United States]

Disease	1980	1985	1990	1993	1994	1995	1996	1997	1998
AIDS [1]	(²)	8,249	41,595	103,533	78,279	71,547	66,885	58,492	46,521
Botulism [3]	89	122	92	97	143	97	119	132	87
Brucellosis (undulant fever)	183	153	85	120	119	98	112	98	79
Chickenpox [4] (1,000)	190.9	178.2	173.1	134.7	151.2	120.6	83.5	93.6	82.5
Cholera	9	4	6	18	39	23	4	6	17
Cryptosporidiosis	(²)	(²)	(²)	(²)	(²)	(²)	(²)	2,566	3,793
Diphtheria	3	3	4	-	2	-	2	4	1
Escherichia coli 0157:H7	(²)	(²)	(²)	(²)	1,420	2,139	2,741	2,555	3,161
Haemophilus influenza	(²)	(²)	(²)	1,419	1,174	1,180	1,170	1,162	1,194
Hepatitis: B (serum) (1,000)	19.0	26.6	21.1	13.4	12.5	10.8	10.6	10.4	10.3
A (infectious) (1,000)	29.1	23.2	31.4	24.2	29.8	31.6	31.0	30.0	23.2
C/non-A, non-B (1,000) [5]	(²)	4.2	2.6	4.8	4.4	4.6	3.7	3.8	3.5
Legionellosis	(²)	830	1,370	1,280	1,615	1,241	1,198	1,163	1,355
Leprosy (Hansen disease)	223	361	198	187	136	144	112	122	108
Lyme disease	(²)	(²)	(²)	8,257	13,043	11,700	16,455	12,801	16,801
Malaria	2,062	1,049	1,292	1,411	1,229	1,419	1,800	2,001	1,611
Measles (1,000)	13.5	2.8	27.8	0.3	1.0	0.3	0.5	0.1	0.1
Meningococcal infections	2,840	2,479	2,451	2,637	2,886	3,243	3,437	3,308	2,725
Mumps (1,000)	8.6	3.0	5.3	1.7	1.5	0.9	0.8	0.7	0.7
Pertussis [6] (1,000)	1.7	3.6	4.6	6.6	4.6	5.1	7.8	6.6	7.4
Plague [7]	18	17	2	10	17	9	5	4	9
Poliomyelitis, acute [7]	9	7	6	4	8	6	5	3	1
Psittacosis	124	119	113	60	38	64	42	33	47
Rabies, animal	6,421	5,565	4,826	9,377	8,147	7,811	6,982	8,105	7,259
Rabies, human	-	1	1	3	6	5	3	2	1
Rubella [8]	3,904	630	1,125	192	227	128	238	181	364
Salmonellosis [9] (1,000)	33.7	65.3	48.6	41.6	43.3	46.0	45.5	41.9	43.7
Shigellosis [10] (1,000)	19.0	17.1	27.1	32.2	29.8	32.1	26.0	23.1	23.6
Tetanus	95	83	64	48	51	41	36	50	41
Toxic-shock syndrome	(²)	384	322	212	192	191	145	157	138
Trichinosis	131	61	129	16	32	29	11	13	19
Tuberculosis [11] (1,000)	27.7	22.2	25.7	25.3	24.4	22.9	21.3	19.9	18.4
Typhoid fever	510	402	552	440	441	369	396	365	375
Typhus fever:									
Tick-borne (Rocky Mt. spotted fever)	1,163	714	651	456	465	590	831	409	365
Sexually transmitted diseases:									
Gonorrhea (1,000)	1,004	911	690	440	418	393	326	325	356
Syphilis (1,000)	69	68	134	101	82	69	53	47	38
Chlamydia (1,000)	(²)	(²)	(²)	(²)	(²)	478	499	527	604
Chancroid (1,000)	0.8	2.1	4.2	1.4	0.8	0.6	0.4	0.2	0.2

- Represents zero.   [1] Acquired immunodeficiency syndrome was not a notifiable disease until 1984. Figures are shown for years in which cases were reported to the CDC. Beginning 1993, based on revised classification system and expanded surveillance case definition.   [2] Disease was not notifiable.   [3] Includes foodborne, infant, wound, and unspecified cases.   [4] Chickenpox was taken off the nationally notifiable list in 1991 but many states continue to report.   [5] Includes some persons positive for antibody to hepatitis C virus who do not have hepatitis.   [6] Whooping cough.   [7] Revised. Data subject to annual revisions.   [8] German measles.   [9] Excludes typhoid fever.   [10] Bacillary dysentery.   [11] Newly reported active cases.

Source: U.S. Centers for Disease Control and Prevention, Atlanta, GA, *Summary of Notifiable Diseases, United States, 1998, Morbidity and Mortality Weekly Report,* Vol. 47, No. 53, December 31, 1999.

No. 216. Children Immunized Against Specified Diseases: 1995 to 1998

[**In percent.** Covers civilian noninstitutionalized population ages 19 months to 35 months. Based on estimates from the National Immunization Survey. The health care providers of the children are contacted to verify and/or complete vaccination information. Results are based on race/ethnic status of the child]

Vaccination	1995, total	1997, total	1998					
			Total	White non-Hispanic	Hispanic	Black non-Hispanic	American Indian/ Alaskan Native [1]	Asian/ Pacific Islander [1]
Diphtheria-tetanus-pertussis (DPT)/ diphtheria-tetanus:								
3+ doses	95	95	96	97	94	92	92	98
4+ doses	79	82	84	87	81	77	83	89
Polio: 3+ doses	88	91	91	92	89	88	85	93
HiB [2]: 3+ doses	92	93	93	95	92	90	90	92
Measles containing (MCV)	90	91	92	93	91	89	91	92
Hepatitis B: 3+ doses	68	84	87	88	86	84	82	89
Varicella [3]	(NA)	26	43	42	47	42	28	53
4+ DPT/3+ polio/1+ MCV	76	78	81	83	77	74	79	83
4+ DPT/3+ polio/1+ MCV/3+ hiB	74	76	79	82	75	73	78	79

NA Not available.   [1] Non-Hispanic.   [2] Haemophilus B.   [3] Data collection for varicella (chicken pox) began in July 1996.

Source: U.S. Centers for Disease Control and Prevention, Atlanta, GA, *Morbidity and Mortality Weekly Report,* Vol. 47, No. 26, July 10, 1998; and "Vaccination Coverage Levels Among Children Born From February 1995 - May 1997 - United States, January 1998-December 1998"; <http://www.cdc.gov/nip/coverage/nis19981.htm>; (accessed 1 May 2000).

Health and Nutrition   137

No. 217. AIDS Cases Reported by Patient Characteristic: 1981 to 1999

[Provisional. For cases reported in the year shown. Includes Puerto Rico, Virgin Islands, Guam, and U.S. Pacific Islands. For data on AIDS deaths, see Table 131. Data are subject to retrospective changes and may differ from those data in Table 215]

Characteristic	1981-99, total	1990	1995	1996	1997	1998	1999
Total.	733,374	43,164	73,274	68,459	60,088	47,915	46,400
Age:							
Under 5 years old	6,753	612	593	498	316	238	181
5 to 12 years old	1,965	151	204	173	150	143	82
13 to 19 years old	3,725	180	395	399	371	298	312
20 to 29 years old.	123,580	8,451	11,474	10,062	8,478	6,451	6,045
30 to 39 years old.	329,066	19,544	32,884	30,704	26,515	20,465	19,411
40 to 49 years old.	190,087	9,933	19,980	19,251	17,348	14,292	14,207
50 to 59 years old.	56,938	3,013	5,748	5,438	5,096	4,468	4,584
60 years old and over	21,260	1,280	1,996	1,934	1,814	1,560	1,578
Sex:							
Male.	609,329	37,941	59,254	54,453	46,877	36,830	35,482
Female	124,045	5,223	14,020	14,006	13,211	11,085	10,918
Race/ethnic group:							
Non-Hispanic White.	318,354	22,229	29,299	26,055	19,971	15,984	14,813
Non-Hispanic Black.	272,881	13,203	29,005	28,555	26,869	21,617	21,900
Hispanic	133,703	7,312	14,100	12,975	12,417	9,605	9,021
Other/unknown.	8,436	420	870	874	831	709	666
Transmission category:							
Males, 13 years and over.	604,846	37,531	58,870	54,112	46,627	36,638	35,357
Men who have sex with men	341,597	23,938	31,420	28,041	21,763	17,033	15,464
Injecting drug use.	134,356	7,712	14,475	12,772	10,940	8,106	7,207
Men who have sex with men and injecting drug use.	46,582	3,094	4,198	3,604	2,725	2,163	1,806
Hemophilia/coagulation disorder . .	4,803	338	443	326	189	149	139
Heterosexual contact [1]	17,835	297	2,245	2,641	2,581	2,155	2,223
Heterosexual contact with injecting drug user	8,696	478	944	916	835	673	635
Transfusion [2]	4,863	454	324	257	211	149	137
Undetermined [3]	46,114	1,220	4,821	5,555	7,383	6,210	7,746
Females, 13 years and over . . .	119,810	4,870	13,607	13,676	12,995	10,896	10,780
Injecting drug use.	50,073	2,490	5,601	4,979	4,474	3,326	2,931
Hemophilia/coagulation disorder . .	272	17	28	25	34	22	12
Heterosexual contact [1]	28,423	545	3,788	4,141	3,886	3,182	3,126
Heterosexual contact with injecting drug user	19,523	1,149	2,096	2,091	1,634	1,295	1,155
Transfusion [2]	3,668	352	260	263	169	126	119
Undetermined [3]	17,851	317	1,834	2,177	2,798	2,945	3,437

[1] Includes persons who have had heterosexual contact with a person with human immunodeficiency virus (HIV) infection or at risk of HIV infection. [2] Receipt of blood transfusion, blood components, or tissue. [3] Includes persons for whom risk information is incomplete (because of death, refusal to be interviewed, or loss to followup), persons still under investigation, men reported only to have had heterosexual contact with prostitutes, and interviewed persons for whom no specific risk is identified.
Source: U.S. Centers for Disease Control and Prevention, Atlanta, GA, *HIV/AIDS Surveillance Reports*, semiannual.

No. 218. AIDS, Syphilis, Tuberculosis, and Measles Cases Reported by State: 1998

[Diseases selected are those included in the Healthy People 2000 Indicators series]

State	AIDS	Syphilis	Tuber-culosis	Measles	State	AIDS	Syphilis	Tuber-culosis	Measles
U.S. . . .	[1]46,521	37,977	18,361	100	MO	443	375	184	-
AL.	484	1,133	381	1	MT.	29	-	20	-
AK.	29	13	55	33	NE.	72	33	31	-
AZ	645	697	254	11	NV	258	136	128	-
AR	203	506	171	-	NH.	42	14	14	-
CA	5,654	2,618	3,852	9	NJ	2,134	826	640	8
CO.	314	118	79	-	NM.	209	76	68	-
CT	666	177	128	-	NY	8,714	5,145	2,000	4
DE.	174	114	36	1	NC.	788	2,133	498	1
DC.	989	579	107	-	ND.	6	-	10	-
FL.	5,448	2,539	1,302	2	OH.	685	474	230	1
GA.	1,295	1,836	631	2	OK.	285	363	198	-
HI	161	15	181	-	OR.	204	32	156	-
ID	32	15	14	-	PA	1,740	910	448	4
IL.	1,304	2,028	850	1	RI	128	55	63	-
IN	484	509	188	3	SC.	777	871	286	-
IA	75	48	55	-	SD.	15	2	23	-
KS.	126	113	56	-	TN	695	1,750	439	1
KY.	280	339	179	-	TX	3,967	3,955	1,820	-
LA	951	1,651	380	-	UT.	139	55	52	-
ME.	31	4	13	-	VT	20	6	5	1
MD.	1,639	2,156	324	1	VA	998	707	339	2
MA.	924	568	282	2	WA	441	141	265	1
MI	714	686	385	10	WV	86	11	42	-
MN.	190	74	161	-	WI	203	208	109	1
MS.	415	1,161	225	-	WY	6	2	4	-

- Represents zero. [1] Includes 210 cases among persons with unknown state of residence.
Source: U.S. Centers for Disease Control and Prevention, Atlanta, GA, *Summary of Notifiable Diseases, United States, 1998, Morbidity and Mortality Weekly Report*, Vol. 47, No. 53, December 31, 1999.

No. 219. Acute Conditions by Type: 1980 to 1996

[**54 represents 54,000,000.** Covers civilian noninstitutional population. Estimates include only acute conditions which were medically attended or caused at least 1 day of restricted activity. Based on National Health Interview Survey; see Appendix III. See headnote, Table 211. For composition of regions, see map, inside front cover]

Year and characteristic	Number of conditions (mil.)					Rate per 100 population				
	Infective and parasitic	Respiratory Common cold	Respiratory Influenza	Digestive system	Injuries	Infective and parasitic	Respiratory Common cold	Respiratory Influenza	Digestive system	Injuries
1980	54	(NA)	(NA)	25	73	24.6	(NA)	(NA)	11.4	33.4
1985	48	(NA)	(NA)	16	64	20.5	(NA)	(NA)	7.0	27.4
1990	52	61	107	13	60	21.0	25.0	43.4	5.3	24.4
1993	54	68	133	16	62	21.3	26.8	52.2	6.3	24.4
1994	54	66	90	16	62	20.9	25.4	34.8	6.1	23.8
1995	53	61	108	16	65	20.1	23.1	41.2	6.0	24.7
1996, total [1]	**54**	**62**	**95**	**18**	**57**	**20.5**	**23.6**	**36.0**	**6.7**	**21.7**
Under 5 years old.	11	10	11	2	5	57.0	48.6	53.7	9.6	22.9
5 to 17 years old	19	17	23	5	11	37.1	33.8	44.3	9.8	21.4
18 to 24 years old	6	6	10	2	8	23.2	23.8	40.5	6.4	31.5
25 to 44 years old	10	16	32	4	21	12.2	18.7	38.1	5.1	24.9
45 to 64 years old	6	9	14	3	8	11.0	16.4	26.1	5.3	14.6
65 years old and over . . .	2	5	6	2	5	6.5	15.7	18.6	6.6	17.2
Male	23	28	44	8	32	17.9	21.9	34.1	5.9	24.6
Female.	31	34	51	10	26	23.0	25.1	37.8	7.4	18.9
White	46	51	82	15	49	21.0	23.3	37.3	6.8	22.1
Black	6	9	9	2	7	19.0	26.0	28.1	6.9	20.8
Northeast	11	12	15	3	12	21.3	21.7	28.3	4.8	21.9
Midwest	11	16	26	5	15	17.9	26.0	41.5	7.7	24.3
South.	23	17	26	7	18	25.5	19.2	28.8	7.4	20.4
West	8	17	27	3	12	14.7	29.6	48.7	6.1	20.5
Family income:										
Under $10,000	5	6	8	1	6	25.7	30.9	41.8	7.0	28.0
$10,000 to $19,999 . . .	6	7	12	3	10	16.5	18.9	33.7	8.0	25.8
$20,000 to $34,999 . . .	10	12	21	4	12	18.7	23.0	39.7	7.5	21.7
$35,000 or more	26	27	41	7	23	23.5	24.4	37.1	6.0	20.6

NA Not available. [1] Includes other races and unknown income not shown separately.

Source: U.S. National Center for Health Statistics, *Vital and Health Statistics,* Series 10, No. 200, and earlier reports; and unpublished data.

No. 220. Prevalence of Selected Chronic Conditions by Age and Sex: 1996

[**33,638 represents 33,638,000.** Covers civilian noninstitutional population. Conditions classified according to ninth revision of International Classification of Diseases. Based on National Health Interview Survey; see Appendix III. See headnote, Table 211]

Chronic condition	Conditions (1,000)	Rate [1]							
		Male				Female			
		Under 45 years old	45 to 64 years old	65 to 74 years old	75 years old and over	Under 45 years old	45 to 64 years old	65 to 74 years old	75 years old and over
Arthritis.	33,638	26.1	193.0	394.6	437.9	35.8	284.0	500.3	576.4
Dermatitis, including eczema	8,249	24.1	28.6	[2]31.1	[2]34.9	36.4	47.0	[2]23.0	[2]16.0
Trouble with—									
Dry (itching) skin.	6,627	15.0	23.1	[2]37.3	[2]73.0	24.4	34.3	[2]37.7	59.3
Ingrown nails	5,807	21.1	24.4	[2]40.1	[2]41.6	14.4	29.1	[2]29.0	[2]43.4
Corns and calluses	3,778	6.9	19.6	[2]25.4	[2]28.8	9.6	30.9	[2]28.5	[2]35.8
Visual impairments	8,280	21.7	61.0	90.6	125.1	12.2	36.4	52.6	91.4
Cataracts	7,022	[2]1.6	17.3	109.3	189.6	[2]2.1	29.0	186.4	203.9
Hearing impairments.	22,044	34.0	183.4	342.6	457.9	26.4	82.9	184.5	315.5
Tinnitus	7,866	11.0	76.9	119.5	114.1	10.4	43.4	77.1	52.8
Deformities or orthopedic impairments.	29,499	84.8	187.5	165.5	142.0	82.9	168.6	182.8	128.4
Hernia of abdominal cavity.	4,470	7.8	35.0	49.3	59.8	6.6	27.1	[2]29.6	64.0
Frequent indigestion	6,420	20.8	44.7	[2]28.1	[2]7.6	14.0	39.7	46.9	[2]38.1
Diabetes.	7,627	6.1	56.9	117.4	129.0	9.0	59.4	83.1	85.8
Migraine.	11,546	20.2	20.2	[2]1.5	[2]19.4	64.1	93.3	50.6	[2]33.9
Heart conditions.	20,653	30.7	133.5	259.5	394.8	35.5	100.3	221.0	258.7
High blood pressure (Hypertension)	28,314	30.0	214.8	314.6	271.0	30.1	213.3	389.5	437.0
Varicose veins of lower extremities.	7,399	[2]3.8	17.6	[2]38.2	[2]59.2	22.9	74.1	102.9	102.9
Hemorrhoids	8,531	16.7	47.8	[2]46.1	[2]31.2	25.0	59.1	94.3	54.2
Chronic bronchitis.	14,150	48.4	41.0	57.9	[2]34.1	51.9	76.1	63.2	87.7
Asthma.	14,596	49.8	30.4	[2]39.8	[2]33.7	68.1	65.5	46.8	56.8
Hay fever, allergic rhinitis without asthma.	23,721	86.3	85.6	57.9	[2]26.1	92.1	122.8	65.1	106.3
Chronic sinusitis.	33,161	93.5	140.5	119.4	93.7	131.7	205.5	133.1	109.6

[1] Conditions per 1,000 persons. [2] Figure does not meet standards of reliability or precision.

Source: U.S. National Center for Health Statistics, *Vital and Health Statistics,* Series 10, No. 200, and earlier reports; and unpublished data.

U.S. Census Bureau, Statistical Abstract of the United States: 2000

No. 221. Disability Status of Children Under 15 Years Old: 1997

[For period August through November 1997 (11,619 represents 11,619,000). Covers civilian noninstitutional population and members of the Armed Forces living off post or with their families on post. The criteria for presence of disability varied by age. In general, a disability is considered a reduced ability to perform tasks one would normally do at a given stage in life. Based on the Survey of Income and Program Participation; for details, see source]

Age and disability status	Number (1,000)	Percent distribu- tion	Age and disability status	Number (1,000)	Percent distribu- tion
Children under 3 years old	11,619	100.0	Children 6 to 14 years old	35,795	100.0
With a disability	233	2.0	With a disability	3,971	11.1
With a developmental delay	206	1.8	With a severe disability [1]	1,712	4.8
Difficulty moving arms or legs	58	0.5	Difficulty doing regular schoolwork . . .	2,444	6.8
Children 3 to 5 years old	12,192	100.0	With a learning disability	1,781	5.0
With a disability	415	3.4	With a developmental disability [2] . . .	1,615	4.5
With a developmental delay	337	2.8	Difficulty with one or more ADLs [3] . . .	288	0.8
Difficulty running or playing	221	1.8	Needs personal assistance	225	0.6

[1] Children who (1) used an ambulatory aid; (2) had serious difficulty seeing, hearing, or speaking; (3) needed help with one or more ADLs (see Table 223); or had a developmental disability or a developmental condition.   [2] Or condition. Includes mental retardation and other developmental disabilities as well as developmental conditions for which the child had received therapy or diagnostic services.   [3] See headnote, Table 223.

No. 222. Disability Status of Persons 15 Years Old and Over: 1997

[In thousands, except as noted (208,059 represents 208,059,000). See headnote, Table 221]

Disability status	Total	15 to 21 years	22 to 44 years	45 to 54 years	55 to 64 years	65 to 79 years	80 years and over
Total	208,059	26,477	94,307	33,620	21,591	24,827	7,237
Persons with any disability	**47,836**	**2,965**	**12,157**	**7,566**	**7,693**	**12,141**	**5,314**
Percent of total	23.0	11.2	12.9	22.5	35.6	48.9	73.4
With a severe disability	30,576	1,396	7,292	4,647	5,208	7,874	4,160
Difficulty with one or more ADLs [1]	8,661	115	1,364	1,292	1,335	2,616	1,939
Needs personal assistance	4,048	90	613	514	527	1,215	1,089
Difficulty with one or more IADLs [1]	12,912	305	2,291	1,691	1,724	3,925	2,977
Needs personal assistance with one or more ADLs or IADLs [1]	10,224	262	1,788	1,295	1,345	2,923	2,611

[1] See headnote, Table 223.

No. 223. Receipt of Personal Assistance by Persons With Disabilities: 1997

[9,793 represents 9,793,000. See headnote, Table 221. ADLs are activities of daily living and include getting around inside the home, getting in or out of a bed or chair, taking a bath or shower, dressing, eating, and using the toilet. IADLs are instrumental activities of daily living and include going outside the home, keeping track of money and bills, preparing meals, doing light housework, and using the telephone]

Relationship of first helper to person receiving assistance	Persons 15 years old and over				Persons 65 years old and over			
	Receiving assistance with an ADL or an IADL		Receiving assistance with an ADL		Receiving assistance with an ADL or an IADL		Receiving assistance with an ADL	
	Number (1,000)	Percent distribu- tion	Number (1,000)	Percent distribu- tion	Number (1,000)	Percent distribu- tion	Number (1,000)	Percent distribu- tion
Persons receiving assistance	**9,793**	**100.0**	**3,974**	**100.0**	**5,302**	**100.0**	**2,261**	**100.0**
Household member	5,162	52.7	2,479	62.4	2,344	44.2	1,239	54.8
Not a household member	4,631	47.3	1,495	37.6	2,959	55.8	1,023	45.2
Spouse	3,113	31.8	1,558	39.2	1,492	28.1	751	33.2
Daughter	1,790	18.3	703	17.7	1,325	25.0	522	23.1
Son	812	8.3	289	7.3	544	10.3	184	8.1
Parent	965	9.9	234	5.9	(X)	(X)	(X)	(X)
Other relative	1,121	11.4	327	8.2	719	13.6	213	9.4
Nonrelative	1,120	11.4	406	10.2	607	11.4	242	10.7
Paid help	873	8.9	457	11.5	615	11.6	350	15.5

X Not applicable.

Source of Tables 221-223: U.S. Census Bureau, unpublished data.

No. 224. Substance Abuse Treatment Facilities and Clients: 1995 to 1998

[As of **October 1**. Based on the Uniform Facility Data Set (UFDS) survey, a census of all known facilities that provide substance abuse treatment in the United States and associated jurisdictions. Selected missing data for responding facilities were imputed]

Item	Number	Type of care and type of problem	Number of clients, **1998**	Client characteristic	Number of clients, **1998**
FACILITIES		Total	1,038,378	Total	1,038,378
1995	10,746	Outpatient rehab	915,798	Under 18 yrs	100,322
1996	10,641	24-hour rehab.	108,627	18 to 24 yrs	182,986
1997	10,860	24-hour detoxification. . .	13,953	25 to 34 yrs	282,467
1998	13,455			35 to 44 yrs	293,561
				45 to 64 yrs	162,795
CLIENTS				65 yrs and over.	16,247
		Drug only.	279,224		
1995	1,009,127	Alcohol only	245,589	Male	715,479
1996	940,141	Both alcohol & drug	513,565	Female	322,899
1997	929,086				
1998	1,038,378	Total with a drug problem [1].	792,789	White, non-Hispanic. . . .	605,793
				Black, non-Hispanic.	247,840
		Total with an alcohol problem [2].	759,154	Hispanic	140,499
				Asian, Pacific Islander . .	9,300
				American Indian [3]	26,724
				Other	8,222

[1] The sum of clients with a drug problem and clients with both diagnoses.   [2] The sum of clients with an alcohol problem and clients with both diagnoses.   [3] Includes Alaskan native.

Source: U.S. Substance Abuse and Mental Health Services Administration, *Uniform Facility Data Set (UFDS): Annual surveys for 1995, 1996, 1997 and 1998.*

No. 225. Drug Use by Type of Drug and Age Group: 1985 to 1998

[**In percent.** Current users are those who used drugs at least once within month prior to this study. Based on national samples of respondents residing in households. Subject to sampling variability; see source]

Age and type of drug	Ever used					Current user				
	1985	1990	1995	1997	1998	1985	1990	1995	1997	1998
12 YEARS OLD AND OVER										
Any illicit drug	34.4	34.2	34.2	35.6	35.8	12.1	6.7	6.1	6.4	6.2
Marijuana and hashish.	29.4	30.5	31.0	32.9	33.0	9.7	5.4	4.7	5.1	5.0
Cocaine	11.2	11.2	10.3	10.5	10.6	3.0	0.9	0.7	0.7	0.8
Crack	(NA)	1.5	1.8	1.9	2.0	(NA)	0.3	0.2	0.3	0.2
Inhalants	7.9	5.7	5.7	5.7	5.8	0.6	0.4	0.4	0.4	0.3
Hallucinogens	6.9	7.9	9.5	9.6	9.9	1.2	0.4	0.7	0.8	0.7
PCP	2.0	2.0	3.2	3.0	3.5	(NA)	(NA)	-	0.1	-
LSD	4.6	5.8	7.5	7.8	7.9	(NA)	(NA)	0.3	0.2	0.3
Heroin.	0.9	0.8	1.2	0.9	1.1	0.1	-	0.1	0.2	0.1
Stimulants [1]	7.3	5.5	4.9	4.5	4.4	1.8	0.6	0.4	0.3	0.3
Sedatives [1]	4.8	2.8	2.7	1.9	2.1	0.5	0.2	0.2	0.1	0.1
Tranquilizers [1]	7.6	4.0	3.9	3.2	3.5	2.2	0.6	0.4	0.4	0.3
Analgesics [1]	7.6	6.3	6.1	4.9	5.3	1.4	0.9	0.6	0.7	0.8
Alcohol.	84.9	82.2	82.3	81.9	81.3	60.2	52.6	52.2	51.4	51.7
"Binge" alcohol use [2]	(NA)	(NA)	(NA)	(NA)	(NA)	20.2	14.4	15.8	15.3	15.6
Cigarettes	78.0	75.4	71.8	70.5	69.7	38.7	32.6	28.8	29.6	27.7
Smokeless tobacco	(NA)	17.5	17.0	17.3	17.2	(NA)	3.9	3.3	3.2	2.0
12 to 17 YEARS OLD										
Marijuana and hashish	20.1	12.7	16.2	18.9	17.0	10.2	4.4	8.2	9.4	8.3
Cocaine	4.7	2.6	2.0	3.0	2.2	1.5	0.6	0.8	1.0	0.8
Alcohol.	56.1	48.8	40.6	39.7	37.3	41.2	32.5	21.1	20.5	19.1
"Binge" alcohol use [2]	(NA)	(NA)	(NA)	(NA)	(NA)	21.9	(NA)	7.9	8.3	7.7
Cigarettes	50.7	45.1	38.1	38.7	35.8	29.4	22.4	20.2	19.9	18.2
18 TO 25 YEARS OLD										
Marijuana and hashish	57.6	50.4	41.4	41.5	44.6	21.7	12.7	12.0	12.8	13.8
Cocaine	24.3	19.3	9.8	8.9	10.0	8.1	2.3	1.3	1.2	2.0
Alcohol.	(NA)	87.6	84.4	83.5	83.2	70.1	62.8	61.3	58.4	60.0
"Binge" alcohol use [2]	(NA)	(NA)	(NA)	(NA)	(NA)	34.4	(NA)	29.9	28.0	31.7
Cigarettes	75.3	70.7	67.7	67.7	68.8	47.4	40.9	35.3	40.6	41.6
26 TO 34 YEARS OLD										
Marijuana and hashish	54.1	56.5	51.8	47.9	47.9	19.0	9.5	6.7	6.0	5.5
Cocaine	23.6	25.4	21.6	18.4	17.1	6.3	1.9	1.2	0.9	1.2
Alcohol.	(NA)	(NA)	90.1	88.9	88.2	70.6	64.4	63.0	60.2	60.9
Cigarettes	84.7	84.1	75.8	72.8	71.8	45.7	42.4	34.7	33.7	32.5
35 YEARS OLD AND OVER										
Marijuana and hashish	13.9	19.6	25.3	29.4	29.4	2.6	2.4	1.8	2.6	2.5
Cocaine	4.1	5.9	8.6	9.9	10.4	0.5	0.2	0.4	0.5	0.5
Alcohol.	(NA)	83.5	87.1	87.0	86.6	57.5	49.5	52.6	52.8	51.7
Cigarettes	82.2	79.0	77.5	76.0	75.2	35.5	28.9	27.2	27.9	25.1

- Represents or rounds to zero.   NA Not available.   [1] Nonmedical use; does not include over-the-counter drugs.   [2] Binge use is defined as drinking five or more drinks on the same occasion on at least one day in the past 30 days.

Source: U.S. Substance Abuse and Mental Health Services Administration, *National Household Survey on Drug Abuse,* annual.

Health and Nutrition 141

No. 226. Current Cigarette Smoking: 1985 to 1998

[In percent. Prior to 1995, a current smoker is a person who has smoked at least 100 cigarettes and who now smokes. Beginning 1995, definition includes persons who smoke only "some days". Excludes unknown smoking status. Based on the National Health Interview Survey; for details, see Appendix III]

Sex, age, and race	1985	1990	1995	1998	Sex, age, and race	1985	1990	1995	1998
Total smokers, age-adjusted [1]	**29.9**	**25.3**	**24.6**	**24.0**	Black, total	39.9	32.5	28.5	29.0
					18 to 24 years	27.2	21.3	[2]14.6	19.7
Male	32.2	28.0	26.5	25.9	25 to 34 years	45.6	33.8	25.1	25.2
Female	27.9	22.9	22.7	22.1	35 to 44 years	45.0	42.0	36.3	36.2
					45 to 64 years	46.1	36.7	33.9	37.3
White male	31.3	27.6	26.2	26.0	65 years and over	27.7	21.5	28.5	16.3
Black male	40.2	32.8	29.4	29.0	Female, total	27.9	22.8	22.6	21.9
White female	27.9	23.5	23.4	23.0	18 to 24 years	30.4	22.5	21.8	24.5
Black female	30.9	20.8	23.5	21.1	25 to 34 years	32.0	28.2	26.4	24.6
					35 to 44 years	31.5	24.8	27.1	26.4
Total smokers	**30.1**	**25.5**	**24.7**	**24.1**	45 to 64 years	29.9	24.8	24.0	22.5
					65 years and over	13.5	11.5	11.5	11.2
Male, total	32.6	28.4	27.0	26.4	White, total	27.7	23.4	23.1	22.6
18 to 24 years	28.0	26.6	27.8	31.3	18 to 24 years	31.8	25.4	24.9	28.0
25 to 34 years	38.2	31.6	29.5	28.6	25 to 34 years	32.0	28.5	27.3	26.9
35 to 44 years	37.6	34.5	31.5	30.2	35 to 44 years	31.0	25.0	27.0	26.7
45 to 64 years	33.4	29.3	27.1	27.7	45 to 64 years	29.7	25.4	24.3	22.5
65 years and over	19.6	14.6	14.9	10.4	65 years and over	13.3	11.5	11.7	11.2
White, total	31.7	28.0	26.6	26.3	Black, total	31.0	21.2	23.5	21.0
18 to 24 years	28.4	27.4	28.4	34.1	18 to 24 years	23.7	10.0	[2]8.8	8.3
25 to 34 years	37.3	31.6	29.9	29.2	25 to 34 years	36.2	29.1	26.7	21.5
35 to 44 years	36.6	33.5	31.2	29.6	35 to 44 years	40.2	35.5	31.9	30.0
45 to 64 years	32.1	28.7	26.3	27.0	45 to 64 years	33.4	22.6	27.5	25.3
65 years and over	18.9	13.7	14.1	10.0	65 years and over	14.5	11.1	13.3	11.5

[1] Estimates are age adjusted to the year 2000 standard using five age groups: 18-24 years, 25-34 years, 35-44 years, 45-64 years, 65 years and over.   [2] Data have a relative standard error of 20-30 percent.

Source: U.S. National Center for Health Statistics, *Health, United States, 2000.*

No. 227. Current Cigarette Smoking by Sex and State: 1998

[In percent. Current cigarette smoking is defined as persons who reported having smoked 100 or more cigarettes during their lifetime and who currently smoke every day or some days. Based on the Behavioral Risk Factor Surveillance System, a telephone survey of health behaviors of the civilian, noninstitutionalized U.S. population, 18 years old and over; for details, see source]

State	Total	Male	Female	State	Total	Male	Female
U.S. [1]	**22.9**	**25.3**	**21.0**	MO	26.3	29.4	23.6
				MT	21.5	21.5	21.5
AL	24.6	27.2	22.3	NE	22.1	25.2	19.1
AK	26.0	28.3	23.5	NV	30.4	32.6	28.1
AZ	21.9	24.7	19.2	NH	23.3	25.7	21.0
AR	26.0	28.6	23.7				
CA	19.2	21.9	16.6	NJ	19.2	20.9	17.6
				NM	22.6	25.1	20.2
CO	22.8	26.4	19.5	NY	24.3	25.9	22.9
CT	21.1	21.7	20.6	NC	24.7	27.4	22.3
DE	24.5	27.3	21.9	ND	20.0	21.8	18.3
DC	21.6	24.5	19.0				
FL	22.0	23.5	20.6	OH	26.2	29.7	23.0
				OK	23.8	26.7	21.1
GA	23.7	28.0	19.7	OR	21.1	21.6	20.6
HI	19.5	22.3	16.7	PA	23.8	24.0	23.6
ID	20.3	21.9	18.8	RI	22.7	24.1	21.5
IL	23.1	26.0	20.6				
IN	26.0	29.6	22.7	SC	24.7	29.8	20.2
				SD	27.3	36.5	18.5
IA	23.4	25.8	21.1	TN	26.1	30.3	22.4
KS	21.2	23.0	19.5	TX	22.0	25.3	18.9
KY	30.8	33.3	28.5	UT	14.2	15.9	12.5
LA	25.5	28.2	23.1				
ME	22.4	21.2	23.5	VT	22.3	23.6	21.0
				VA	22.9	25.8	20.2
MD	22.4	24.3	20.6	WA	21.4	22.4	20.3
MA	20.9	22.5	19.5	WV	27.9	29.6	26.4
MI	27.4	30.3	24.8	WI	23.4	24.0	22.9
MN	18.0	19.7	16.4	WY	22.8	23.9	21.7
MS	24.1	26.9	21.7				

[1] Represents median value among the states and DC.

Source: U.S. Centers for Disease Control and Prevention, Atlanta, GA, *Morbidity and Mortality Weekly Report,* Vol. 48, No. 45, November 19, 1999.

No. 228. Cancer—Estimated New Cases, 2000, and Survival Rates, 1980-82 to 1989-95

[1,220 represents 1,220,000. The 5-year relative survival rate, which is derived by adjusting the observed survival rate for expected mortality, represents the likelihood that a person will not die from causes directly related to their cancer within 5 years. Survival data shown are based on those patients diagnosed while residents of an area listed below during the time periods shown. Data are based on information collected as part of the National Cancer Institute's Surveillance, Epidemiology and End Results (SEER) program, a collection of population-based registries in Connecticut, New Mexico, Utah, Iowa, Hawaii, Atlanta, Detroit, Seattle-Puget Sound, and San Francisco-Oakland]

Site	Estimated new cases,[1] 2000 (1,000) Total	Male	Female	5-year relative survival rates (percent) White 1980-82	1983-85	1986-88	1989-95	Black 1980-82	1983-85	1986-88	1989-95
All sites[2]	1,220	620	600	52.0	53.8	56.6	60.9	39.7	39.8	42.5	47.7
Lung	164	90	75	13.5	13.9	13.5	14.2	12.2	11.5	11.8	11.3
Breast[3]	184	1	183	77.1	79.2	83.8	86.0	65.9	63.5	69.2	71.0
Colon and rectum	130	64	67	54.8	57.6	60.7	61.8	46.5	47.9	52.1	51.7
Colon	94	43	50	55.6	58.4	61.5	62.4	49.2	49.2	52.5	51.8
Rectum	36	20	16	52.9	55.8	59.1	60.2	38.2	43.8	51.0	51.2
Prostate	180	180	(X)	74.5	76.2	82.6	93.0	64.7	64.1	69.0	83.6
Bladder	53	38	15	78.8	78.2	80.6	81.8	58.3	59.0	62.0	62.2
Corpus uteri	36	(X)	36	83.5	85.2	84.8	86.2	55.5	55.1	57.9	58.0
Non-Hodgkin's lymphoma[4]	55	32	23	51.7	54.3	52.8	51.9	50.0	44.8	49.8	41.3
Oral cavity and pharynx	30	20	10	55.4	55.1	55.1	55.5	30.8	35.1	34.8	33.8
Leukemia[4]	31	17	14	39.3	41.6	43.4	44.4	33.2	33.4	36.8	33.5
Melanoma of skin	48	27	20	83.0	84.6	87.6	87.9	60.9	74.4	65.9	67.6
Pancreas	28	14	15	2.8	2.9	3.0	4.1	4.7	5.4	6.2	3.6
Kidney	31	19	12	51.0	55.7	57.5	61.0	55.4	54.8	53.0	57.7
Stomach	22	13	8	16.5	16.3	19.1	19.3	19.4	18.6	18.9	21.6
Ovary	23	(X)	23	38.6	40.2	41.9	49.9	38.6	41.7	38.6	47.1
Cervix uteri[5]	13	(X)	13	67.9	70.3	71.6	71.4	61.0	59.9	55.4	58.8

X Not applicable. [1] Estimates provided by American Cancer Society are based on rates from the National Cancer Institute's SEER program. [2] Includes other sites not shown separately. [3] Survival rates for female only. [4] All types combined. [5] Invasive cancer only.

Source: U.S. National Institutes of Health, National Cancer Institute, *Cancer Statistics Review,* annual

No. 229. Cancer—Estimated New Cases and Deaths by State: 2000

[In thousands (1,220.1 represents 1,220,100). Excludes basal and squamous cellskin cancers and in situ carcinomas except urinary bladder]

State	New cases[1] Total[2]	Lung	Female breast	Deaths Total[2]	Lung	Female breast
U.S.	1,220.1	164.1	182.8	552.2	156.9	40.8
AL	21.5	3.0	2.7	9.7	2.8	0.6
AK	1.5	0.2	0.2	0.7	0.2	0.1
AZ	20.3	2.8	2.8	9.2	2.6	0.6
AR	13.7	2.2	1.9	6.2	2.1	0.4
CA	113.2	14.0	17.9	51.2	13.4	4.0
CO	13.4	1.5	2.0	6.1	1.4	0.4
CT	15.4	1.9	2.3	7.0	1.9	0.5
DE	3.9	0.6	0.5	1.8	0.5	0.1
DC	2.7	0.3	0.5	1.2	0.3	0.1
FL	88.1	12.6	12.0	39.9	12.0	2.7
GA	29.4	4.2	4.6	13.3	4.0	1.0
HI	4.3	0.5	0.5	2.0	0.5	0.1
ID	4.7	0.6	0.7	2.1	0.5	0.2
IL	55.1	7.3	8.9	24.9	6.9	2.0
IN	27.9	4.0	4.2	12.6	3.9	0.9
IA	14.2	1.9	2.1	6.4	1.8	0.5
KS	11.9	1.6	1.6	5.4	1.6	0.4
KY	20.5	3.4	2.7	9.3	3.2	0.6
LA	20.8	2.9	3.2	9.4	2.7	0.7
ME	6.8	1.0	0.9	3.1	0.9	0.2
MD	22.6	3.1	3.7	10.2	2.9	0.8
MA	30.1	3.9	4.4	13.6	3.7	1.0
MI	44.1	6.1	6.7	20.0	5.8	1.5
MN	19.9	2.3	2.8	9.0	2.2	0.6
MS	13.2	1.9	2.0	6.0	1.8	0.4
MO	27.0	4.0	3.7	12.2	3.8	0.8
MT	4.1	0.5	0.6	1.9	0.5	0.1
NE	7.3	0.9	1.1	3.3	0.9	0.3
NV	8.3	1.2	1.0	3.8	1.2	0.2
NH	5.5	0.7	0.7	2.5	0.7	0.2
NJ	40.0	4.8	6.4	18.1	4.6	1.4
NM	6.6	0.7	1.0	3.0	0.7	0.2
NY	81.5	9.8	13.7	36.9	9.4	3.1
NC	35.7	5.2	5.2	16.2	5.0	1.2
ND	3.0	0.3	0.5	1.3	0.3	0.1
OH	56.1	7.8	8.6	25.4	7.4	1.9
OK	16.1	2.5	2.4	7.3	2.4	0.5
OR	15.8	2.2	2.2	7.1	2.1	0.5
PA	66.6	8.6	10.5	30.1	8.2	2.3
RI	5.4	0.8	0.8	2.4	0.8	0.2
SC	18.0	2.5	2.6	8.2	2.4	0.6
SD	3.5	0.4	0.4	1.6	0.4	0.1
TN	27.3	4.2	3.8	12.4	4.0	0.9
TX	76.1	10.7	11.5	34.4	10.3	2.6
UT	5.1	0.4	0.9	2.3	0.4	0.2
VT	2.7	0.4	0.4	1.2	0.4	0.1
VA	29.3	4.0	4.5	13.3	3.8	1.0
WA	23.6	3.1	3.5	10.7	3.0	0.8
WV	10.5	1.6	1.4	4.8	1.5	0.3
WI	23.6	2.8	3.3	10.7	2.7	0.7
WY	2.0	0.2	0.3	0.9	0.2	0.1

[1] Estimates are offered as a rough guide and should be interpreted with caution. They are calculated according to the distribution of estimated 2000 cancer deaths by state. [2] Includes other types of cancer, not shown separately.

Source: American Cancer Society, Inc., Georgia, *Cancer Facts and Figures—2000* (copyright).

No. 230. Cumulative Percent Distribution of Population by Height and Sex: 1988-94

[**For persons 20 to 79 years old**. Height was measured without shoes. Based on sample and subject to sampling variability; see source]

Height	Males						Females					
	20-29 years	30-39 years	40-49 years	50-59 years	60-69 years	70-79 years	20-29 years	30-39 years	40-49 years	50-59 years	60-69 years	70-79 years
Percent under—												
4'8"	-	-	-	-	-	-	0.6	0.1	-	-	0.2	1.7
4'9"	-	-	-	-	-	-	0.7	0.2	0.3	0.1	0.7	3.3
4'10"	-	-	-	-	0.1	-	1.2	0.7	0.7	1.9	1.7	4.9
4'11"	-	-	-	-	0.1	0.1	3.1	2.6	1.7	3.1	4.4	9.8
5'	0.1	-	0.2	-	0.4	0.1	6.0	5.5	5.3	6.6	9.9	15.4
5'1"	0.1	-	0.4	0.1	0.5	0.6	11.5	10.4	9.9	11.9	19.0	28.9
5'2"	0.5	0.8	0.7	0.2	0.7	1.9	21.8	18.5	18.8	24.4	34.3	45.6
5'3"	1.3	1.4	0.9	1.0	2.2	2.7	34.3	30.7	31.9	38.6	48.3	61.2
5'4"	3.4	2.2	1.7	2.5	5.8	7.8	48.9	42.9	49.2	52.6	65.5	74.5
5'5"	6.9	5.1	5.6	6.0	9.4	16.5	62.7	59.1	64.3	69.9	76.5	85.9
5'6"	11.7	10.1	12.1	11.7	15.8	27.3	74.0	71.8	77.0	81.6	87.8	93.9
5'7"	20.8	18.9	19.6	20.5	27.4	39.5	84.7	84.1	87.0	89.3	92.5	97.3
5'8"	32.0	28.3	28.0	32.6	38.6	53.4	92.4	91.6	94.5	95.6	96.7	99.2
5'9"	46.3	44.3	42.1	43.9	55.1	68.7	96.2	95.6	97.3	99.0	99.3	99.9
5'10"	58.7	58.0	58.1	60.6	68.8	79.5	98.6	98.1	98.9	99.6	99.8	100.0
5'11"	70.1	70.4	71.1	75.2	81.4	89.2	99.5	99.5	99.4	100.0	100.0	100.0
6'	81.2	79.7	81.5	85.4	90.0	94.1	100.0	100.0	100.0	100.0	100.0	100.0
6'1"	87.4	86.2	89.0	92.4	95.2	97.2	100.0	100.0	100.0	100.0	100.0	100.0
6'2"	94.7	92.4	94.4	96.4	98.2	99.3	100.0	100.0	100.0	100.0	100.0	100.0
6'3"	97.9	98.1	97.2	98.2	99.5	99.9	100.0	100.0	100.0	100.0	100.0	100.0

- Represents or rounds to zero.

Source: U.S. National Center for Health Statistics, unpublished data.

No. 231. Percent of U.S. Adults Who Were Overweight and Percent Who Were Obese: 1997

[Percent who are overweight includes those who are obese and represent those who have a body mass index (BMI) equal to or above 25. Percent who are obese represent those who have a BMI equal to or above 30. BMI is a measure that adjusts body weight for height. It is calculated as weight in kilograms divided by height in meters squared. These estimates are based on definitions provided in the *Dietary Guidelines for Americans*, published by the U.S. Dept. of Agriculture and the U.S. Dept. of Health and Human Services. Based on the National Health Interview Survey; for details, see Appendix III]

Characteristic	Both sexes		Males		Females	
	Overweight	Obese	Overweight	Obese	Overweight	Obese
All ages (age-adjusted) [1]	54.3	19.1	62.3	18.8	46.6	19.3
All ages (unadjusted) [1]	54.1	19.0	62.2	18.9	46.4	19.2
18-24 years old	37.4	13.0	41.5	13.9	33.3	12.1
25-44 years old	53.3	18.7	63.7	19.2	42.9	18.2
45-64 years old	62.7	23.8	70.7	23.0	55.0	24.6
65 years old and over	54.5	16.5	59.8	14.4	50.5	18.0
Hispanic	61.0	20.5	64.7	19.5	56.8	21.2
White, Non-Hispanic	52.6	18.0	62.4	18.6	43.0	17.3
Black, Non-Hispanic	64.4	28.6	64.1	22.7	64.5	33.2
Asian/Pacific Islander, Non-Hispanic	29.8	6.0	35.2	5.8	25.2	5.9

[1] Age-specific rates are unadjusted; all other estimates were adjusted to the 2000 projected population.

Source: U.S. National Center for Health Statistics, Percent of U.S. adults who were overweight (including obese) (BMI>= 25) and percent who were obese (BMI>= 30), by selected characteristics, 1997; <http://www.cdc.gov/nchs/products/pubs/pubd/hestats/3and4/overweight.PDF>; (accessed 2 May 2000).

No. 232. Percentage of Adults Engaging in Leisure-Time Physical Activity: 1998

[In percent. Covers **persons 18 years old and over**. Based on response to question about physical activity in prior month. Based on a sample survey of approximately 150,000 persons in 50 states, the District of Columbia and Puerto Rico; for details, contact source]

Characteristic	No partici-pation in physical activity	Partici-pates in regular, sustained activity [1]	Partici-pates in regular, vigorous activity [2]	Characteristic	No partici-pation in physical activity	Partici-pates in regular, sustained activity [1]	Partici-pates in regular, vigorous activity [2]
Total	**28.7**	**20.8**	**13.6**	30 to 44 years old . . .	28.2	19.9	14.8
				45 to 64 years old . . .	31.5	19.8	13.2
Male	26.2	21.9	13.3	65 to 74 years old . . .	35.9	20.3	13.0
Female	31.0	19.7	13.8	75 years old and			
				over	47.1	14.9	12.3
White, non-Hispanic . . .	26.7	21.6	14.0				
Black, non-Hispanic. . . .	33.8	17.8	12.3	School years completed:			
Hispanic	38.4	17.4	11.4	Less than 12 years . .	49.7	14.3	8.2
Other	28.8	21.8	14.3	12 years	33.9	18.2	10.7
				Some college (13-15			
Males:				years)	23.9	22.3	13.9
18 to 29 years old . . .	17.6	26.5	12.2	College (16 or more			
30 to 44 years old . . .	24.9	19.0	11.8	years)	16.3	25.7	19.7
45 to 64 years old . . .	30.6	20.5	14.1				
65 to 74 years old . . .	31.1	24.8	14.2	Household income:			
75 years old and				Less than $10,000. . .	42.4	17.8	10.7
over	39.1	22.2	22.0	$10,000 to $19,999 . .	39.8	16.9	10.5
				$20,000 to $34,999 . .	31.3	19.4	12.1
Females:				$35,000 to $49,999 . .	24.4	21.4	14.0
18 to 29 years old . . .	25.1	20.9	14.2	$50,000 and over . . .	16.9	25.5	17.6

[1] Any type or intensity of activity that occurs 5 times or more per week and 30 minutes or more per occasion. [2] Rhythmic contraction of large muscle groups performed at 50 percent or more of estimated age- and sex-specific maximum cardio-respiratory capacity, 3 times per week or more for at least 20 minutes per occasion.

Source: U.S. National Center for Chronic Disease Prevention and Health Promotion, unpublished data.

No. 233. Households and Persons Having Problems With Access to Food: 1995 to 1998

[100,445 represents 100,445,000. Food secure means that a household had access at all times to enough food for an active healthy life, with no need for recourse to emergency food sources or other extraordinary coping behaviors to meet their basic food needs. A food insecure household did not have this same access to enough food to fully meet basic needs at all times. Food insecure households with hunger were those with one or more household members who were hungry at least sometime during the period due to inadequate resources for food. The omission of homeless persons may be a cause of underreporting. Data are from the Food Security Supplement to the Current Population Survey (CPS); for details about the CPS, see text, Section 1, Population, and Appendix III]

Household food security level	Number (1,000)				Percent distribution			
	1995	1996	1997	1998	1995	1996	1997	1998
Households, total	**100,445**	**101,508**	**102,373**	**103,480**	**100.0**	**100.0**	**100.0**	**100.0**
Food secure	90,097	90,964	93,459	92,972	89.7	89.6	91.3	89.8
Food insecure	10,348	10,544	8,914	10,509	10.3	10.4	8.7	10.2
Without hunger	6,402	6,407	5,760	6,820	6.4	6.3	5.6	6.6
With hunger	3,946	4,137	3,154	3,689	3.9	4.1	3.1	3.6
Adult members	191,063	193,608	195,180	197,423	100.0	100.0	100.0	100.0
Food secure	172,862	175,003	179,420	178,631	90.5	90.4	91.9	90.5
Food insecure	18,200	18,606	15,761	18,792	9.5	9.6	8.1	9.5
Without hunger	11,611	11,582	10,601	12,657	6.1	6.0	5.4	6.4
With hunger	6,589	7,024	5,160	6,135	3.4	3.6	2.6	3.1
Child members	70,279	71,172	70,948	71,463	100.0	100.0	100.0	100.0
Food secure	58,048	58,218	60,589	59,090	82.6	81.8	85.4	82.7
Food insecure	12,231	12,953	10,359	12,373	17.4	18.2	14.6	17.3
Without hunger	8,131	8,537	7,444	9,114	11.6	12.0	10.5	12.8
With hunger	4,100	4,416	2,915	3,259	5.8	6.2	4.1	4.6

Source: U.S. Dept. of Agriculture, Food and Nutrition Service, *Household Food Security in the United States, 1995-1998: Advance Report; July 1999* and *Important User Information/ERRATA Tables 1 & 2D in Household Food Security in The United States 1995-1998 Advance Report;* September 1999.

Health and Nutrition 145

No. 234. Healthy Eating Indexes by Selected Food Groups and Dietary Guidelines: 1996

[Healthy Eating Index is comprised of the sum of 10 dietary component indices for a maximum possible score of 100. A score of 80 or above was judged to reflect a "good" diet. Each of the dietary components has a scoring range of zero to 10. Individuals with an intake at the recommended level received a maximum score of 10 points. A score of zero was assigned when no foods in a particular group were eaten. Intermediate scores were calculated proportionately. The indexes for grains, vegetables, fruits, milk, and meat groups measure the degree to which a person's diet conforms to the U.S. Department of Agriculture's (USDA) "Food Guide Pyramid" serving recommendations. The index was applied to USDA one-day food and nutrient intake data from the Continuing Survey of Food Intakes by Individuals. The data are based on a representative sample of individuals two years old and over excluding women who were pregnant or lactating at the time of the survey]

Food group and dietary guideline	Average score on one day	Percent receiving score of 10	Perfect score of 10 [1]	Score of zero
Healthy Eating Index. . . .	63.8	[2]12.2	(X)	(X)
Grains [3]	6.7	22.2	6-11 servings	No servings
Vegetables [4]	6.3	31.8	3-5 servings	No servings
Fruits [4]	3.8	17.1	2-4 servings	No servings
Milk [5]	5.4	25.5	2-3 servings	No servings
Meat [6]	6.4	26.4	2-3 servings	No servings
Total fat [7]	6.9	37.5	30% or less energy from fat	45% or more energy from fat
Saturated fat [7]	6.4	40.1	Less than 10% energy from saturated fat	15% or more energy from saturated fat
Cholesterol	7.9	71.9	300 mg. or less	450 mg. or more
Sodium	6.3	34.7	2,400 mg. or less	4,800 mg or more
Variety [8]	7.6	53.0	8 different food items over 1 day	Fewer than 4 items over 1 day

X Not applicable.   [1] Depends on recommended energy intake. All amounts listed are based on a per day basis.   [2] Percent receiving a score of 80 or higher.   [3] One serving: a slice of bread, one-half cup of cooked pasta, or one-half cup of cooked cereal grains.   [4] One serving: one-half cup of cooked vegetables, 1 cup of raw leafy vegetables, or one-half cup of raw nonleafy chopped vegetables. Fruits are similar.   [5] One serving: one cup of milk or equivalent.   [6] Includes eggs, nuts, and some legumes. One serving: 2.5 ounces of lean meat or equivalent.   [7] Consumption of specified fat as a percentage of total food energy intake.   [8] Amount of variety in a person's diet over a 1-day period.

Source: U.S. Department of Agriculture, Center for Nutrition Policy and Promotion, unpublished data.

No. 235. Nutrition—Nutrients in Foods Available for Civilian Consumption Per Capita Per Day: 1970 to 1997

[Computed by the Center for Nutrition Policy and Promotion (CNPP). Based on Economic Research Service (ERS) estimates of per capita quantities of food available for consumption from "Food Consumption, Prices, and, Expenditures," on imputed consumption data for foods no longer reported by ERS, and on CNPP estimates of quantities of produce from home gardens. Food supply estimates do not reflect loss of food or nutrients from further marketing or home processing. Enrichment and fortification levels of iron, zinc, thiamin, riboflavin, niacin, vitamin A, vitamin B_6, vitamin B_{12}, and ascorbic acid are included]

Nutrient	Unit	1970-79	1980-89	1990	1995	1997
Food energy	Calories	3,300	3,400	3,600	3,800	3,800
Carbohydrate	Grams	395	423	463	494	509
Dietary fiber	Grams	19	21	23	24	25
Protein	Grams	96	100	106	110	112
Total fat [1]	Grams	149	156	155	157	156
Saturated	Grams	51	52	50	51	50
Monounsaturated	Grams	60	63	64	67	66
Polyunsaturated	Grams	28	31	31	32	33
Cholesterol	Milligrams	440	420	400	410	410
Vitamin A	Micrograms RE [2]	1,540	1,560	1,610	1,650	1,750
Carotenes	Micrograms RE [2]	550	590	630	660	780
Vitamin E	Milligrams α-TE [3] . . .	14.0	15.5	16.3	16.7	16.9
Vitamin C	Milligrams	110	117	115	127	132
Thiamin	Milligrams	2.2	2.6	2.9	3.1	3.1
Riboflavin	Milligrams	2.5	2.8	3.0	3.0	3.0
Niacin	Milligrams	25.0	29.0	31.0	33.0	33.0
Vitamin B_6	Milligrams	2.0	2.2	2.3	2.5	2.5
Folacin	Micrograms	314	348	365	389	396
Vitamin B_{12}	Micrograms	8.9	8.1	8.0	8.1	8.0
Calcium	Milligrams	910	920	960	970	990
Phosphorus	Milligrams	1,490	1,560	1,660	1,700	1,720
Magnesium	Milligrams	340	360	380	390	400
Iron	Milligrams	16.5	20.0	22.8	23.8	24.4
Zinc	Milligrams	13.1	14.2	15.1	15.6	15.7
Copper	Milligrams	1.7	1.8	1.9	2.0	2.0
Potassium	Milligrams	3,520	3,570	3,700	3,790	3,870
Selenium	Milligrams	133	144	152	164	169
Sodium [4]	Milligrams	1,360	1,340	1,370	1,370	1,360

[1] Includes other types of fat not shown separately.   [2] Retinol equivalents.   [3] Alpha-Tocopherol equivalents.   [4] Does not include amount from processed foods; underestimates actual availability.

Source: U.S. Dept. of Agriculture, Center for Nutrition Policy and Promotion. Data published by Economic Research Service in *Food Consumption, Prices, and Expenditures*, annual.

No. 236. Per Capita Consumption of Major Food Commodities: 1980 to 1998

[In pounds, retail weight, except as indicated. Consumption represents the residual after exports, nonfood use and ending stocks are subtracted from the sum of beginning stocks, domestic production, and imports. Based on Census Bureau estimated population]

Commodity	Unit	1980	1985	1990	1995	1996	1997	1998
Red meat, total (boneless, trimmed weight) [1] [2]	Pounds . . .	126.4	124.9	112.3	115.1	112.8	111.0	115.6
Beef.	Pounds . . .	72.1	74.6	63.9	64.4	65.0	63.8	64.9
Veal	Pounds . . .	1.3	1.5	0.9	0.8	1.0	0.9	0.7
Lamb and mutton	Pounds . . .	1.0	1.1	1.0	0.9	0.8	0.8	0.9
Pork	Pounds . . .	52.1	47.7	46.4	49.0	45.9	45.5	49.2
Poultry (boneless, trimmed weight) [2]	Pounds . . .	40.8	45.5	56.3	62.9	64.1	64.2	65.0
Chicken	Pounds . . .	32.7	36.4	42.4	48.8	49.5	50.4	50.8
Turkey	Pounds . . .	8.1	9.1	13.8	14.1	14.6	13.9	14.2
Fish and shellfish (boneless, trimmed weight) . .	Pounds . . .	12.4	15.0	15.0	14.9	14.7	14.5	14.8
Eggs	Number . . .	271	255	234	235	237	239	244
Shell	Number . . .	236	217	186	175	175	173	176
Processed	Number . . .	35	38	48	61	62	66	58
Dairy products, total [3]	Pounds . . .	543.2	593.7	568.4	583.9	574.7	577.7	582.3
Fluid milk products [4]	Gallons . . .	27.9	27.1	26.2	24.9	24.9	24.6	24.3
Beverage milks	Gallons . . .	27.6	26.7	25.7	24.3	24.4	24.0	23.7
Plain whole milk	Gallons . . .	16.5	13.9	10.2	8.4	8.4	8.2	8.0
Plain reduced-fat milk (2%)	Gallons . . .	6.3	7.9	9.1	8.2	8.0	7.7	7.5
Plain light and skim milks.	Gallons . . .	3.1	3.2	4.9	6.2	6.4	6.6	6.6
Flavored whole milk	Gallons . . .	0.6	0.4	0.3	0.3	0.3	0.3	0.3
Flavored milks other than whole	Gallons . . .	0.6	0.7	0.8	0.8	0.9	0.9	1.0
Buttermilk	Gallons . . .	0.5	0.5	0.4	0.3	0.3	0.3	0.3
Yogurt (excl. frozen)	1/2 pints . .	4.6	7.3	7.4	9.4	8.9	9.5	9.3
Fluid cream products [5]	1/2 pints . .	10.5	13.5	14.3	15.9	16.4	17.0	17.3
Cream [6]	1/2 pints . .	6.3	8.2	8.7	9.5	10.2	10.7	10.9
Sour cream and dips	1/2 pints . .	3.4	4.3	4.7	5.5	5.4	5.6	5.7
Condensed and evaporated milks.	Pounds . . .	7.0	7.5	7.9	6.9	6.4	6.6	6.4
Whole milk	Pounds . . .	3.8	3.6	3.2	2.3	2.3	2.6	2.2
Skim milk	Pounds . . .	3.3	3.8	4.8	4.5	4.1	4.0	4.1
Cheese [7]	Pounds . . .	17.5	22.5	24.6	27.3	27.7	28.0	28.4
American	Pounds . . .	9.6	12.2	11.1	11.8	12.0	12.0	12.2
Cheddar	Pounds . . .	6.9	9.8	9.0	9.1	9.2	9.6	9.6
Italian	Pounds . . .	4.4	6.5	9.0	10.4	10.8	11.0	11.3
Mozzarella	Pounds . . .	3.0	4.6	6.9	8.1	8.5	8.4	8.7
Other [8]	Pounds . . .	3.4	3.9	4.5	5.0	5.0	5.0	4.8
Swiss	Pounds . . .	1.3	1.3	1.4	1.1	1.1	1.0	1.0
Cream and Neufchatel	Pounds . . .	1.0	1.2	1.7	2.1	2.2	2.3	2.3
Cottage cheese, total.	Pounds . . .	4.5	4.1	3.4	2.7	2.6	2.7	2.7
Lowfat	Pounds . . .	0.8	1.0	1.2	1.2	1.2	1.3	1.3
Frozen dairy products	Pounds . . .	26.4	27.9	28.4	29.4	28.6	28.8	29.6
Ice cream.	Pounds . . .	17.5	18.1	15.8	15.7	15.9	16.4	16.6
Lowfat ice cream.	Pounds . . .	7.1	6.9	7.7	7.5	7.6	7.9	8.3
Sherbet	Pounds . . .	1.2	1.3	1.2	1.3	1.3	1.3	1.4
Frozen yogurt	Pounds . . .	(NA)	(NA)	2.8	3.5	2.6	2.1	1.9
Fats and oils:								
Total, fat content only	Pounds . . .	56.9	64.1	63.0	66.4	65.3	64.9	65.3
Butter (product weight)	Pounds . . .	4.5	4.9	4.4	4.5	4.3	4.2	4.2
Margarine (product weight)	Pounds . . .	11.3	10.8	10.9	9.2	9.2	8.6	8.3
Lard (direct use)	Pounds . . .	2.3	1.6	1.6	1.7	1.8	1.9	2.0
Edible beef tallow (direct use)	Pounds . . .	1.1	2.0	0.6	2.7	3.0	2.2	3.2
Shortening	Pounds . . .	18.2	22.9	22.2	22.5	22.3	20.9	20.9
Salad and cooking oils	Pounds . . .	21.3	23.6	25.3	26.9	26.2	28.6	27.9
Other edible fats and oils	Pounds . . .	1.5	1.6	1.2	1.6	1.4	1.1	1.3
Flour and cereal products [9]	Pounds . . .	144.7	156.5	181.5	190.7	196.4	197.1	196.8
Wheat flour	Pounds . . .	116.9	124.6	136.0	141.9	148.7	149.5	147.8
Rice, milled	Pounds . . .	9.4	9.1	15.8	18.9	17.8	18.5	18.9
Corn products	Pounds . . .	12.9	17.2	21.9	21.8	21.9	21.8	22.3
Oat products	Pounds . . .	3.9	4.0	6.5	6.5	6.6	6.6	6.6
Breakfast cereals [10]	Pounds . . .	12.0	12.8	15.4	17.1	16.9	16.9	(NA)
Ready-to-eat	Pounds . . .	9.7	10.5	12.6	14.6	14.3	14.3	(NA)
Ready-to-cook	Pounds . . .	2.3	2.3	2.9	2.5	2.5	2.6	(NA)
Caloric sweeteners, total [11]	Pounds . . .	123.0	128.8	137.0	149.8	150.7	154.0	155.1
Sugar, refined cane and beet	Pounds . . .	83.6	62.7	64.4	65.4	66.5	66.5	67.0
Corn sweeteners [12]	Pounds . . .	38.2	64.8	71.1	83.0	82.8	86.2	86.8
High-fructose corn syrup	Pounds . . .	19.0	45.2	49.6	58.4	59.4	62.5	63.8
Other:								
Cocoa beans	Pounds . . .	3.4	4.6	5.4	4.6	5.3	5.1	(NA)
Coffee (green beans).	Pounds . . .	10.3	10.5	10.3	8.0	8.9	9.3	9.5
Peanuts (shelled)	Pounds . . .	4.8	6.3	6.0	5.7	5.7	5.9	5.9
Tree nuts (shelled)	Pounds . . .	1.8	2.5	2.4	1.9	2.0	2.1	2.3

NA Not available.   [1] Excludes edible offals.   [2] Excludes shipments to Puerto Rico and the other U.S. possessions.   [3] Milk-equivalent, milkfat basis. Includes butter.   [4] Fluid milk figures are aggregates of commercial sales and milk produced and consumed on farms.   [5] Includes eggnog, not shown separately.   [6] Heavy cream, light cream, and half and half.   [7] Excludes full-skim American, cottage, pot, and baker's cheese.   [8] Includes other cheeses not shown separately.   [9] Includes rye flour and barley products not shown separately. Excludes quantities used in alcoholic beverages.   [10] Partially overlaps flour and cereal products category.   [11] Dry weight. Includes edible syrups (maple, molasses, etc.) and honey not shown separately.   [12] Includes glucose and dextrose not shown separately.

Source: U.S. Department of Agriculture, Economic Research Service, *Food Consumption, Prices, and Expenditures, 1970-1997*; and *Agricultural Outlook*, monthly.

Health and Nutrition   147

No. 237. Per Capita Utilization of Commercially Produced Fruits and Vegetables: 1980 to 1998

[In pounds, farm weight. Domestic food use of fresh fruits and vegetables reflects the fresh-market share of commodity production plus imports and minus exports]

Commodity	1980	1985	1990	1993	1994	1995	1996	1997	1998
Fruits and vegetables, total [1]	606.0	627.4	656.1	691.3	705.8	694.3	710.9	717.9	699.6
Fruits, total	269.7	269.7	272.6	283.1	291.0	284.8	290.2	296.8	281.4
Fresh fruits	104.8	110.6	116.3	124.5	126.3	124.1	128.1	131.9	131.8
Noncitrus	78.7	89.1	95.0	98.5	101.3	100.0	103.2	104.9	104.7
Apples	19.2	17.3	19.6	19.2	19.6	18.9	19.0	18.4	19.2
Bananas	20.8	23.5	24.4	26.8	28.1	27.4	28.0	27.6	28.6
Cantaloupes	5.8	8.5	9.2	8.7	8.5	9.1	10.4	10.7	11.3
Grapes	4.0	6.8	7.9	7.0	7.3	7.5	6.9	8.0	7.3
Peaches and nectarines	7.1	5.5	5.5	5.9	5.5	5.4	4.4	5.6	4.8
Pears	2.6	2.8	3.2	3.4	3.5	3.4	3.1	3.5	3.4
Pineapples	1.5	1.5	2.1	2.1	2.0	1.9	1.9	2.4	2.8
Plums and prunes	1.5	1.4	1.5	1.3	1.6	0.9	1.5	1.5	1.2
Strawberries	2.0	3.0	3.2	3.6	4.1	4.2	4.4	4.2	4.1
Watermelons	10.7	13.5	13.3	14.3	15.2	15.4	16.8	15.8	14.5
Other [2]	3.5	5.3	5.1	6.2	5.9	5.9	6.8	7.2	7.5
Fresh citrus	26.1	21.5	21.4	26.0	25.0	24.1	24.9	27.0	27.1
Oranges	14.3	11.6	12.4	14.3	13.1	12.0	12.8	14.2	14.9
Grapefruit	7.3	5.5	4.4	6.2	6.1	6.1	5.9	6.3	6.0
Other [3]	4.5	4.4	4.6	5.5	5.8	6.0	6.2	6.5	6.2
Processed fruits	165.0	159.1	156.2	158.5	164.8	160.7	162.0	164.9	149.7
Frozen fruits [4]	3.1	3.3	3.8	3.7	3.8	4.2	4.0	3.7	4.2
Dried fruits [5]	11.2	12.8	12.1	12.6	12.8	12.8	11.3	10.8	12.8
Canned fruits [6]	23.8	20.9	21.0	20.7	21.0	17.5	18.8	20.4	17.3
Fruit juices [7]	126.1	121.8	119.0	121.2	126.7	125.8	127.7	129.3	115.0
Vegetables, total	336.2	357.7	383.5	408.3	414.7	409.5	420.7	421.1	418.1
Fresh vegetables	149.1	156.0	167.1	178.2	184.6	179.1	184.1	190.4	186.5
Asparagus (all uses)	0.3	0.5	0.6	0.6	0.6	0.6	0.6	0.7	0.8
Broccoli	1.4	2.6	3.4	3.4	4.5	4.4	4.6	5.1	5.6
Cabbage	8.1	8.8	8.8	9.5	9.4	8.4	8.6	9.4	8.9
Carrots	6.2	6.5	8.3	10.9	12.8	11.3	12.6	14.4	13.6
Cauliflower	1.1	1.8	2.2	2.1	2.0	1.7	1.7	1.8	1.6
Celery (all uses)	7.4	6.9	7.2	7.3	7.4	6.9	6.4	6.1	6.2
Corn	6.5	6.4	6.7	7.0	8.2	7.9	8.5	8.4	9.0
Cucumbers	3.9	4.4	4.7	5.3	5.4	5.7	6.0	6.5	6.7
Head lettuce	25.6	23.7	27.8	24.6	25.3	22.5	21.9	26.7	22.8
Mushrooms	1.2	1.8	2.0	2.0	2.0	2.1	2.1	2.4	2.5
Onions	11.4	13.6	15.1	17.3	17.1	18.0	18.7	19.1	18.5
Snap beans	1.3	1.3	1.1	1.5	1.6	1.7	1.5	1.4	1.7
Bell peppers (all uses)	2.9	3.8	4.5	6.2	6.5	6.3	7.2	6.6	6.4
Potatoes	51.1	46.3	46.8	50.3	50.2	49.9	50.7	48.5	47.8
Sweetpotatoes (all uses)	4.4	5.4	4.6	3.9	4.7	4.5	4.6	4.5	4.1
Tomatoes	12.8	14.9	15.5	16.4	16.4	17.1	17.7	17.1	17.4
Other fresh vegetables [8]	3.5	7.3	7.8	9.4	10.5	10.1	10.7	11.7	12.9
Processed vegetables	187.1	201.8	216.4	230.1	230.2	230.4	236.6	230.7	231.6
Selected vegetables for freezing	51.5	64.5	66.8	76.0	78.4	79.9	84.7	81.9	82.3
Selected vegetables for canning	102.8	99.2	111.6	112.9	112.4	110.8	109.5	107.8	108.0
Vegetables for dehydrating [9]	10.5	12.8	14.6	15.8	14.3	14.7	17.8	16.8	18.0
Potatoes for chips	16.5	17.6	16.4	17.8	16.7	16.6	16.7	15.9	14.9
Pulses [10]	5.8	7.6	7.1	7.7	8.5	8.4	8.0	8.3	8.4

[1] Excludes wine grapes.   [2] Apricots, avocados, cherries, cranberries, kiwifruit, mangoes, papayas, and honeydew melons.
[3] Lemons, limes, tangerines, and tangelos.   [4] Apples, apricots, blackberries, blueberries, boysenberries, cherries, loganberries, peaches, plums, prunes, raspberries, and strawberries.   [5] Apples, apricots, dates, figs, peaches, pears, prunes, and raisins.
[6] Apples, apricots, cherries, olives, peaches, pears, pineapples, plums, and prunes.   [7] Apple, cranberry, grape, grapefruit, lemon, lime, orange, pineapple, and prunes.   [8] Artichokes, Brussels sprouts, eggplant, escarole, endive, garlic, romaine, leaf lettuce, radishes, and spinach.   [9] Onions and potatoes.   [10] Dry peas, lentils, and dry edible beans.

No. 238. Per Capita Consumption of Selected Beverages by Type: 1980 to 1998

[In gallons. See headnote, Table 236]

Commodity	1980	1985	1990	1993	1994	1995	1996	1997	1998
Nonalcoholic	(NA)	(NA)	128.4	132.4	133.2	133.5	137.0	139.8	(NA)
Milk (plain and flavored)	27.6	26.7	25.7	24.8	24.8	24.3	24.3	24.0	23.7
Whole	17.0	14.3	10.5	9.3	9.2	8.8	8.7	8.5	8.3
Reduced-fat, light, and skim	10.5	12.3	15.2	15.4	15.6	15.6	15.7	15.5	15.4
Tea	7.3	7.1	6.9	8.4	8.2	8.0	7.8	7.4	(NA)
Coffee	26.7	27.4	26.9	23.5	21.1	20.5	22.5	23.5	(NA)
Bottled water	2.4	4.5	8.0	9.4	10.7	11.6	12.5	13.1	(NA)
Carbonated soft drinks	35.1	35.7	46.3	50.1	51.3	51.6	52.0	53.0	(NA)
Diet	5.1	7.1	10.7	11.7	11.8	11.8	11.7	11.6	(NA)
Regular	29.9	28.7	35.6	38.4	39.6	39.8	40.3	41.4	(NA)
Fruit juices	7.4	7.8	7.9	8.5	8.8	8.7	8.9	9.4	8.8
Fruit drinks, cocktails, and ades	(NA)	(NA)	6.3	7.0	7.4	7.8	8.0	8.3	(NA)
Canned iced tea	(NA)	(NA)	0.1	0.4	0.6	0.7	0.7	0.8	(NA)
Vegetable juices	(NA)	(NA)	0.3	0.3	0.3	0.3	0.3	0.3	(NA)
Alcoholic (adult population)	42.8	40.7	39.9	38.2	38.3	38.0	38.6	38.9	(NA)
Beer	36.6	34.6	34.7	33.6	33.8	33.4	33.8	33.9	(NA)
Wine [1]	3.2	3.5	3.0	2.6	2.6	2.7	2.9	3.0	(NA)
Distilled spirits	3.0	2.6	2.2	2.0	1.9	1.9	1.9	1.9	(NA)

NA Not available.   [1] Beginning 1985, includes wine coolers.

Source of Tables 237 and 238: U.S. Dept. of Agriculture, Economic Research Service, *Food Consumption, Prices, and Expenditures,* annual; and *Agricultural Outlook,* monthly.

148   Health and Nutrition

Section 4
Education

This section presents data primarily concerning formal education as a whole, at various levels, and for public and private schools. Data shown relate to the school-age population and school enrollment, educational attainment, education personnel, and financial aspects of education. In addition, data are shown for charter schools, libraries, computer usage in schools, distance education, and adult education. The chief sources are the decennial census of population and the Current Population Survey (CPS), both conducted by the U.S. Census Bureau (see text, Section 1, Population); annual, biennial, and other periodic surveys conducted by the National Center for Education Statistics (NCES), a part of the U.S. Department of Education; and surveys conducted by the National Education Association.

The censuses of population have included data on school enrollment since 1840 and on educational attainment since 1940. The CPS has reported on school enrollment annually since 1945 and on educational attainment periodically since 1947.

The National Center for Education Statistics is continuing the pattern of statistical studies and surveys conducted by the U.S. Office of Education since 1870. The annual *Digest of Education Statistics* provides summary data on pupils, staff, finances, including government expenditures, and organization at the elementary, secondary, and higher education levels. It is also a primary source for detailed information on Federal funds for education, projections of enrollment, graduates, and teachers. *The Condition of Education*, issued annually, presents a summary of information on education of particular interest to policymakers. NCES also conducts special studies periodically.

The census of governments, conducted by the Census Bureau every 5 years (for the years ending in "2" and "7"), provides data on school district finances and state and local government expenditures for education. Reports published by the Bureau of Labor Statistics contain data relating civilian labor force experience to educational attainment (see also Tables 647, 671, and 678 in Section 13, Labor Force).

Types and sources of data—The statistics in this section are of two general types. One type, exemplified by data from the Census Bureau, is based on direct interviews with individuals to obtain information about their own and their family members' education. Data of this type relate to school enrollment and level of education attained, classified by age, sex, and other characteristics of the population. The school enrollment statistics reflect attendance or enrollment in any regular school within a given period; educational attainment statistics reflect the highest grade completed by an individual, or beginning 1992, the highest diploma or degree received.

For enrollment data starting in October 1994, the CPS used 1990 census population controls plus adjustment for undercount. Also the survey changed from paper to computer assisted technology. For years 1981 through 1993, 1980 census population controls were used; 1971 through 1980, 1970 census population controls had been used. These changes had little impact on summary measures (e.g., medians) and proportional measures (e.g., enrollment rates); however, use of the controls may have significant impact on absolute numbers.

Beginning with data for 1986, a new edit and tabulation package for school enrollment has been introduced. In 1988 a new edit and tabulation package was introduced for educational attainment data.

The second type, generally exemplified by data from the National Center for Education Statistics and the National Education Association, is based on reports from administrators of educational institutions and of state and local agencies having jurisdiction over education. Data of this type relate to enrollment, attendance, staff, and finances for the Nation, individual states, and local areas.

Unlike the National Center for Education Statistics, the Census Bureau does not regularly include specialized vocational, trade, business, or correspondence schools in its surveys. The National Center for Education Statistics includes nursery schools and kindergartens that are part of regular grade schools in their enrollment figures. The Census Bureau includes all nursery schools and kindergartens. At the higher education level, the statistics of both agencies are concerned with institutions granting degrees or offering work acceptable for degree-credit, such as junior colleges.

School attendance—All states require that children attend school. While state laws vary as to the ages and circumstances of compulsory attendance, generally they require that formal schooling begin by age 6 and continue to age 16.

Schools—The National Center for Education Statistics defines a school as "a division of the school system consisting of students composing one or more grade groups or other identifiable groups, organized as one unit with one or more teachers to give instruction of a defined type, and housed in a school plant of one or more buildings. More than one school may be housed in one school plant, as is the case when the elementary and secondary programs are housed in the same school plant."

Regular schools are those which advance a person toward a diploma or degree. They include public and private nursery schools, kindergartens, graded schools, colleges, universities, and professional schools.

Public schools are schools controlled and supported by local, state, or Federal governmental agencies; private schools are those controlled and supported mainly by religious organizations or by private persons or organizations.

The Census Bureau defines *elementary* schools as including grades 1 through 8; *high* schools as including grades 9 through 12; and *colleges* as including junior or community colleges, regular 4-year colleges, and universities and graduate or professional schools. Statistics reported by the National Center for Education Statistics and the National Education Association by type of organization, such as elementary level and secondary level, may not be strictly comparable with those from the Census Bureau because the grades included at the two levels vary, depending on the level assigned to the middle or junior high school by the local school systems.

School year—Except as otherwise indicated in the tables, data refer to the school year which, for elementary and secondary schools, generally begins in September of the preceding year and ends in June of the year stated. For the most part, statistics concerning school finances are for a 12-month period, usually July 1 to June 30. Enrollment data generally refer to a specific point in time, such as fall, as indicated in the tables.

Statistical reliability—For a discussion of statistical collection, estimation, and sampling procedures and measures of statistical reliability applicable to the Census Bureau and the National Center for Education Statistics data, see Appendix III.

No. 239. School Enrollment: 1965 to 2009

[In thousands (54,394 represents 54,394,000). As of fall]

Year	All levels			K through grade 8		Grades 9 through 12		College	
	Total	Public	Private	Public	Private	Public	Private	Public	Private
1965	54,394	46,143	8,251	30,563	4,900	11,610	1,400	3,970	1,951
1970	59,838	52,322	7,516	32,558	4,052	13,336	1,311	6,428	2,153
1975	61,004	53,654	7,350	30,515	3,700	14,304	1,300	8,835	2,350
1980	58,305	50,335	7,971	27,647	3,992	13,231	1,339	9,457	2,640
1981	57,916	49,691	8,225	27,280	4,100	12,764	1,400	9,647	2,725
1982	57,591	49,262	8,330	27,161	4,200	12,405	1,400	9,696	2,730
1983	57,432	48,935	8,497	26,981	4,315	12,271	1,400	9,683	2,782
1984	57,150	48,686	8,465	26,905	4,300	12,304	1,400	9,477	2,765
1985	57,226	48,901	8,325	27,034	4,195	12,388	1,362	9,479	2,768
1986	57,709	49,467	8,242	27,420	4,116	12,333	1,336	9,714	2,790
1987	58,254	49,982	8,272	27,933	4,232	12,076	1,247	9,973	2,793
1988	58,485	50,349	8,136	28,501	4,036	11,687	1,206	10,161	2,894
1989	59,436	51,120	8,316	29,152	4,162	11,390	1,193	10,578	2,961
1990	60,267	52,061	8,206	29,878	4,095	11,338	1,137	10,845	2,974
1991	61,605	53,356	8,248	30,506	4,074	11,541	1,125	11,310	3,049
1992	62,686	54,208	8,478	31,088	4,212	11,735	1,163	11,385	3,103
1993	63,241	54,654	8,587	31,504	4,280	11,961	1,191	11,189	3,116
1994	63,986	55,245	8,741	31,898	4,360	12,213	1,236	11,134	3,145
1995	64,764	55,933	8,831	32,341	4,465	12,500	1,197	11,092	3,169
1996	65,694	56,701	8,993	32,764	4,486	12,847	1,297	11,090	3,210
1997	66,332	57,273	9,059	33,073	4,552	13,054	1,308	11,146	3,199
1998 [1]	67,067	57,925	9,142	33,344	4,597	13,191	1,327	11,390	3,218
1999, proj.	68,096	58,846	9,249	33,701	4,622	13,543	1,348	11,602	3,279
2000, proj.	68,611	59,283	9,328	33,875	4,646	13,658	1,360	11,750	3,322
2001, proj.	68,979	59,601	9,379	34,018	4,666	13,767	1,371	11,816	3,342
2002, proj.	69,239	59,833	9,406	34,075	4,674	13,935	1,387	11,823	3,345
2003, proj.	69,490	60,048	9,442	34,035	4,668	14,119	1,406	11,894	3,368
2004, proj.	69,769	60,286	9,482	33,910	4,651	14,376	1,431	12,000	3,400
2005, proj.	70,033	60,511	9,523	33,723	4,625	14,669	1,461	12,119	3,437
2006, proj.	70,239	60,676	9,563	33,550	4,602	14,868	1,480	12,258	3,481
2007, proj.	70,364	60,765	9,599	33,455	4,589	14,907	1,484	12,403	3,526
2008, proj.	70,460	60,822	9,637	33,421	4,584	14,833	1,477	12,568	3,576
2009, proj.	70,510	60,841	9,670	33,427	4,585	14,699	1,464	12,715	3,621

[1] Public elementary and secondary school data are estimated. Data for private schools and higher education are projections.

Source: U.S. National Center for Education Statistics, *Digest of Education Statistics*, annual, and *Projections of Education Statistics*, annual.

No. 240. School Expenditures by Type of Control and Level of Instruction in Constant (1998-99) Dollars: 1960 to 1999

[In millions of dollars (133,616 represents $133,616,000,000). For school years ending in year shown. Total expenditures for public elementary and secondary schools include current expenditures, interest on school debt, and capital outlay. Data deflated by the Consumer Price Index, wage earners, and clerical workers through 1975; thereafter, all urban consumers, on a school year basis (supplied by the National Center for Education Statistics). See also Appendix III]

Year	Elementary and secondary schools			Colleges and universities		
	Total	Total	Public	Private, est.	Total	Public	Private, est.
1960	133,616	93,593	87,433	6,160	40,023	21,860	18,163
1970	298,197	188,100	177,211	10,890	110,097	70,714	39,383
1975	345,223	218,722	206,014	12,708	126,501	85,672	40,829
1980	351,043	218,649	203,389	15,260	132,394	87,819	44,575
1985	385,282	232,422	213,131	19,291	152,860	99,106	53,754
1986	407,488	244,658	224,698	19,960	162,830	105,951	56,879
1987	431,904	259,166	238,012	21,153	172,739	110,281	62,457
1988	445,116	267,034	245,302	21,732	178,083	113,432	64,651
1989	470,961	284,271	262,005	22,266	186,690	118,265	68,425
1990	494,404	299,305	275,720	23,585	195,100	124,904	70,196
1991	507,018	305,857	281,897	23,959	201,162	128,315	72,846
1992	515,488	311,034	286,985	24,049	204,454	129,372	75,081
1993	526,523	316,714	292,008	24,706	209,809	132,960	76,849
1994	537,047	323,539	298,557	24,982	213,508	134,559	78,950
1995	551,279	330,817	305,218	25,599	220,461	139,584	80,877
1996	564,017	338,931	312,733	26,199	225,086	141,380	83,706
1997, prel.	582,372	350,948	324,233	26,715	231,424	144,964	86,460
1998, est.	601,435	362,672	335,509	27,162	238,763	149,240	89,523
1999, est.	618,600	371,900	344,200	27,700	246,700	154,100	92,600

Source: U.S. National Center for Education Statistics, *Digest Education Statistics*, annual.

No. 241. School Enrollment, Faculty, Graduates, and Finances With Projections: 1995 to 2003

[As of fall, except as indicated (50,502 represents 50,502,000)]

Item	Unit	1995	1998, proj.	1999, proj.	2000, proj.	2001, proj.	2002, proj.	2003, proj.
ELEMENTARY AND SECONDARY SCHOOLS								
School enrollment, total	1,000. . .	50,502	52,459	53,215	53,539	53,821	54,071	54,228
Kindergarten through grade 8	1,000. . .	36,806	37,941	38,323	38,521	38,683	38,749	38,703
Grades 9 through 12	1,000. . .	13,697	14,518	14,891	15,018	15,138	15,322	15,525
Public	1,000. . .	44,840	46,535	47,244	47,533	47,785	48,010	48,154
Kindergarten through grade 8 . . .	1,000. . .	32,341	33,344	33,701	33,875	34,018	34,075	34,035
Grades 9 through 12	1,000. . .	12,500	13,191	13,543	13,658	13,767	13,935	14,119
Private	1,000. . .	5,662	5,924	5,971	6,006	6,036	6,061	6,074
Kindergarten through grade 8 . . .	1,000. . .	4,465	4,597	4,622	4,646	4,666	4,674	4,668
Grades 9 through 12	1,000. . .	1,197	1,327	1,348	1,360	1,371	1,387	1,406
Enrollment rate:								
5 and 6 year olds	Percent .	96.0	95.6	(NA)	(NA)	(NA)	(NA)	(NA)
7 to 13 year olds	Percent .	98.9	98.9	(NA)	(NA)	(NA)	(NA)	(NA)
14 to 17 year olds.	Percent .	96.3	96.2	(NA)	(NA)	(NA)	(NA)	(NA)
Classroom teachers, total [1]	1,000. . .	2,978	3,217	3,282	3,108	3,129	3,142	3,149
Public	1,000. . .	2,598	2,826	2,887	2,712	2,731	2,743	2,749
Private	1,000. . .	380	391	395	396	399	400	400
High school graduates, total [2].	1,000. . .	2,540	2,794	2,883	2,895	2,910	2,984	2,982
Public	1,000. . .	2,273	2,503	2,583	2,593	2,607	2,673	2,672
Public schools: [2]								
Average daily attendance (ADA) . . .	1,000. . .	41,502	43,417	43,787	44,055	44,289	44,497	44,631
Constant (**1997-98**) dollars:								
Teachers' average salary	Dol.	39,471	39,889	39,684	39,659	39,812	39,857	39,950
Current school expenditure	Bil. dol. .	267.1	291.9	309.0	294.5	298.3	305.1	309.0
Per pupil in ADA	Dol.	6,435	6,752	6,726	6,771	6,889	6,944	7,033
HIGHER EDUCATION								
Enrollment, total.	1,000. . .	14,262	14,608	14,881	15,072	15,158	15,168	15,262
Male.	1,000. . .	6,343	6,297	6,370	6,432	6,471	6,486	6,525
Full time.	1,000. . .	3,807	3,738	3,801	3,852	3,894	3,907	3,942
Part time	1,000. . .	2,535	2,559	2,569	2,581	2,577	2,579	2,583
Female	1,000. . .	7,919	8,311	8,511	8,639	8,688	8,682	8,736
Full time.	1,000. . .	4,321	4,503	4,649	4,748	4,796	4,795	4,845
Part time	1,000. . .	3,598	3,807	3,863	3,891	3,891	3,887	3,891
Public.	1,000. . .	11,092	11,390	11,602	11,750	11,816	11,823	11,894
Four-year institutions	1,000. . .	5,815	5,937	6,059	6,147	6,193	6,201	6,247
Two-year institutions	1,000. . .	5,278	5,453	5,543	5,602	5,624	5,622	5,647
Private	1,000. . .	3,169	3,218	3,279	3,322	3,342	3,345	3,368
Four-year institutions	1,000. . .	2,955	2,990	3,047	3,086	3,105	3,108	3,129
Two-year institutions	1,000. . .	215	227	232	235	237	237	238
Undergraduate	1,000. . .	12,232	12,577	12,842	13,037	13,137	13,154	13,247
Graduate.	1,000. . .	1,732	1,750	1,760	1,758	1,747	1,740	1,740
First-time professional	1,000. . .	298	280	279	277	275	274	275
Full-time equivalent	1,000. . .	10,335	10,533	10,765	10,930	11,018	11,030	11,118
Public	1,000. . .	7,752	7,923	8,100	8,225	8,292	8,300	8,365
Private.	1,000. . .	2,583	2,610	2,665	2,705	2,726	2,730	2,752
Faculty, total	1,000. . .	932	952	963	971	(NA)	(NA)	(NA)
Public	1,000. . .	657	675	682	688	(NA)	(NA)	(NA)
Private	1,000. . .	275	277	280	283	(NA)	(NA)	(NA)
Degrees conferred, total [2]	1,000. . .	2,248	2,234	2,235	2,231	2,263	2,294	2,317
Associate's	1,000. . .	555	563	568	581	593	601	605
Bachelor's	1,000. . .	1,165	1,166	1,164	1,150	1,174	1,199	1,216
Master's	1,000. . .	406	385	385	383	380	379	381
Doctorate's	1,000. . .	45	44	44	44	44	43	43
First-professional	1,000. . .	77	76	74	73	73	72	71

NA Not available.   [1] Full-time equivalents.   [2] For school year ending June the following year.

Source: U.S. National Center for Education Statistics, *Digest of Education Statistics*, annual, and *Projections of Educational Statistics*, annual.

No. 242. Federal Funds for Education and Related Programs: 1998 to 2000

[In millions of dollars (76,909,200,000), except percent. For fiscal years ending in September. Figures represent on-budget funds]

Level, agency, and program	1998	1999	2000[1]
Total, all programs	**76,909.2**	**83,137.9**	**90,658.9**
Percent of Federal budget outlays	4.7	4.9	5.1
Elementary/secondary education programs	**37,486.2**	**39,937.9**	**43,988.0**
Department of Education[2]	16,001.8	17,026.7	20,757.8
Grants for the disadvantaged	7,817.8	7,554.2	8,379.3
School improvement programs	1,367.8	1,328.0	2,662.7
Indian education	52.7	56.8	80.9
Special education	3,658.4	4,444.1	5,432.3
Vocational and adult education	1,451.3	1,364.0	1,546.9
Education reform—Goals 2000	746.5	887.1	1,124.9
Department of Agriculture[2]	9,090.0	9,367.9	9,856.1
Child nutrition programs	8,564.9	8,877.9	9,354.1
Agricultural Marketing Service— commodities[4]	400.0	400.0	400.0
Special milk program[2]	(3)	(3)	(3)
Department of Defense[2]	1,312.2	1,379.0	1,369.8
Overseas dependents schools	821.8	882.3	864.7
Section VI schools[5]	319.3	329.1	329.3
Department of Health and Human Services	5,137.2	5,429.9	6,039.6
Head Start	4,347.4	4,658.0	5,267.0
Social security student benefits	715.7	709.9	725.6
Department of the Interior[2]	578.8	593.3	670.6
Mineral Leasing Act and other funds	44.5	37.7	52.1
Indian Education	533.3	554.6	617.5
Department of Justice	196.2	204.8	231.6
Inmate programs	195.2	201.8	227.6
Department of Labor	4,644.0	5,402.0	4,524.0
Job Corps[2]	1,188.0	1,253.0	1,003.0
Department of Veterans Affairs[2]	411.3	417.9	423.1
Vocational rehab for disabled veterans	406.0	411.6	416.7
Other agencies and programs	114.7	116.5	115.3
Higher education programs[2]	**15,799.6**	**17,639.5**	**19,887.0**
Department of Education[2]	12,122.3	13,715.6	15,833.9
Student financial assistance	7,878.8	9,124.7	9,363.3
Federal Family Education Loans	2,272.0	2,805.5	4,030.7
Department of Agriculture	36.6	29.7	30.7
Department of Commerce	3.6	3.6	3.7
Department of Defense	934.4	983.2	1,001.7
Tuition assistance for military personnel	286.0	280.5	269.8
Service academies[6]	111.0	115.1	114.7
Senior ROTC	301.0	321.8	337.1
Professional development education	236.4	265.7	280.1
Department of Health and Human Services[2]	788.2	880.2	965.8
Health professions training programs	289.5	301.7	341.9
National Health Service Corps scholarships[7]	30.1	28.5	30.6
National Institutes of Health training grants[7]	428.0	509.2	550.2
Department of the Interior	153.6	132.2	149.3
Shared revenues, Mineral Leasing Act and other receipts—estimated education share	71.0	47.8	60.9
Indian programs	82.6	84.4	88.4
Department of State[2]	283.0	290.0	260.0
Department of Transportation	59.9	60.3	64.2
Department of Veterans Affairs[2]	1,005.7	1,123.2	1,143.1
Post-Vietnam veterans	9.0	3.7	3.1
All-volunteer-force educational assistance	882.2	988.7	991.6
Other agencies and programs[2]	412.2	421.5	434.6
National Endowment for the Humanities	29.7	28.5	29.9
National Science Foundation	359.0	369.0	378.0
United States Information Agency	(8)	(8)	(8)
Other education programs[2]	**5,148.5**	**5,318.0**	**5,766.8**
Department of Education[2]	2,893.7	3,123.3	3,420.0
Administration	403.5	439.9	516.0
Rehabilitative services and handicapped research	2,482.2	2,675.2	2,891.0
Department of Agriculture	410.7	428.3	412.6
Department of Health and Human Services	162.0	181.0	214.0
Department of Justice	32.9	33.8	28.8
Department of State	49.2	56.9	63.3
Department of the Treasury[2]	96.0	65.0	81.0
Other agencies and programs[2]	1,504.0	1,429.7	1,547.0
Agency for International Development	340.3	313.0	340.0
Library of Congress	331.0	350.0	365.0
National Endowment for the Arts	2.2	6.3	4.0
National Endowment for the Humanities	62.6	63.2	63.3
Research programs at universities and related institutions[2]	**18,475.0**	**20,242.5**	**21,017.1**
Department of Agriculture	415.4	536.3	474.8
Department of Defense	1,769.5	1,787.6	1,614.4
Department of Energy	3,499.6	3,713.8	3,945.1
Department of Health and Human Services	7,775.5	9,022.3	9,244.0
National Aeronautics and Space Administration	1,922.1	1,944.1	2,163.8
National Science Foundation	2,147.9	2,359.0	2,518.0

[1] Estimated. [2] Includes other programs and agencies, not shown separately. [3] The Special Milk Program is included in the Child Nutrition Program. [4] Purchased under Section 32 of the Act of August 1935 for use in child nutrition programs. [5] Program provides for the education of dependents of Federal employees residing on Federal property where free public education is unavailable in the nearby community. [6] Instructional costs only including academics, audiovisual, academic computer center, faculty training, military training, physical education, and libraries. [7] Includes alcohol, drug abuse, and mental health training programs. [8] Program transferred to the Department of State in fiscal year 1998.

Source: U.S. National Center for Education Statistics, *Digest of Education Statistics*, 2000.

No. 243. School Expenditures by Source of Funds in Constant (1997-98) Dollars: 1980 to 1997

[For school years ending in year shown. (345.0 represents $345,000,000,000.) Includes nursery, kindergarten, and special programs when provided by school system. Data are deflated by the Consumer Price Index for all urban consumers, on a school year basis (supplied by the U.S. National Center for Education Statistics). Distribution by source of funds is estimated]

Source of funds and control of school	Expenditures (bil. dol.)							Percent distribution		
	1980	1985	1990	1994	1995	1996	1997	1980	1990	1997
Total	345.0	378.8	486.0	527.9	541.9	554.4	572.4	100.0	100.0	100.0
Federal.	39.4	32.6	40.2	46.5	47.0	47.1	48.3	11.4	8.3	8.4
State	134.0	147.0	181.1	181.6	191.3	197.4	205.0	38.8	37.3	35.8
Local	90.2	96.8	124.8	138.3	137.2	139.1	143.3	26.1	25.7	25.0
All other	81.5	102.3	139.9	161.5	166.4	170.7	175.8	23.6	28.8	30.7
Public.	286.3	306.9	393.8	425.7	437.2	446.4	461.2	100.0	100.0	100.0
Federal	30.8	24.2	29.2	35.3	35.6	35.8	36.8	10.8	7.4	8.0
State	133.1	146.0	179.3	180.0	189.6	195.9	203.4	46.5	45.5	44.1
Local	89.8	96.5	124.3	137.7	136.8	138.5	142.7	31.4	31.6	30.9
All other	32.5	40.2	61.0	72.7	75.3	76.2	78.2	11.4	15.5	16.9
Private	58.8	71.9	92.2	102.3	104.6	108.0	111.2	100.0	100.0	100.0
Federal	8.5	8.4	11.0	11.3	11.4	11.3	11.5	14.5	11.9	10.3
State and local	1.3	1.4	2.3	2.2	2.2	2.2	2.2	2.1	2.5	2.0
All other	49.0	62.1	78.9	88.7	91.1	94.5	97.5	83.3	85.6	87.6
Elementary and secondary .	215.0	228.5	294.2	318.0	325.2	333.1	344.9	100.0	100.0	100.0
Federal.	19.6	13.9	16.6	20.7	20.4	20.4	21.0	9.1	5.6	6.1
State	93.1	102.2	128.2	132.5	140.3	146.0	153.0	43.3	43.6	44.3
Local	86.7	93.0	119.7	132.5	131.3	132.8	136.7	40.3	40.7	39.6
All other	15.6	19.6	29.7	32.4	33.2	33.9	34.3	7.3	10.1	9.9
Public.	200.0	209.5	271.0	293.5	300.0	307.4	318.7	100.0	100.0	100.0
Federal	19.6	13.9	16.6	20.7	20.4	20.4	21.0	9.8	6.1	6.6
State.	93.1	102.2	128.2	132.5	140.3	146.0	153.0	46.6	47.3	48.0
Local.	86.7	93.0	119.7	132.5	131.3	132.8	136.7	43.3	44.2	42.9
All other [1].	0.6	0.6	6.6	7.8	8.1	8.2	8.0	0.3	2.4	2.5
Private	15.0	19.0	23.2	24.6	25.2	25.8	26.3	100.0	100.0	100.0
Higher education	130.2	150.3	191.8	209.9	216.7	221.2	227.5	100.0	100.0	100.0
Federal.	19.8	18.7	23.7	25.9	26.7	26.7	27.4	15.2	12.3	12.0
State	40.8	45.0	52.9	49.1	51.0	51.4	52.0	31.4	27.6	22.9
Local	3.5	3.8	5.0	5.9	5.9	6.3	6.6	2.7	2.6	2.9
All other	65.8	82.7	110.2	129.1	133.1	136.8	141.4	50.6	57.4	62.1
Public.	86.3	97.4	122.8	132.3	137.2	139.0	142.5	100.0	100.0	100.0
Federal	11.3	10.2	12.7	14.6	15.2	15.4	15.9	13.0	10.3	11.1
State	40.0	43.9	51.2	47.5	49.3	49.8	50.4	46.4	41.7	35.4
Local.	3.1	3.5	4.5	5.3	5.5	5.8	6.0	3.6	3.7	4.2
All other.	31.9	39.6	54.4	64.9	67.3	68.0	70.1	37.0	44.3	49.2
Private	43.8	52.9	69.0	77.6	79.5	82.3	85.0	100.0	100.0	100.0
Federal	8.5	8.4	11.0	11.3	11.4	11.3	11.5	19.5	15.9	13.5
State and local	1.3	1.4	2.3	2.2	2.2	2.2	2.2	2.9	3.3	2.6
All other.	34.0	43.1	55.7	64.2	65.9	68.8	71.2	77.6	80.8	83.8

[1] Beginning in 1989-90, includes all fees for transportation, books, and food services.

Source: U.S. National Center for Education Statistics, *Digest of Education Statistics*, annual.

No. 244. School Enrollment by Control and Level, With Projections: 1980 to 2009

[In thousands (58,305 represents 58,305,000). As of fall. Data are for regular day schools and exclude independent nursery schools and kindergartens, residential schools for exceptional children, subcollegiate departments of colleges, Federal schools for Indians, and federally operated schools on Federal installations. College data include degree-credit and nondegree-credit enrollment]

Control of school and level	1980	1990	1995	1998 [1]	2000, proj.	2004, proj.	2005, proj.	2006, proj.	2007, proj.	2008, proj.	2009, proj.
Total	58,305	60,267	64,764	67,067	68,611	69,769	70,033	70,239	70,364	70,460	70,510
Public.	50,335	52,061	55,933	57,925	59,283	60,286	60,511	60,676	60,765	60,822	60,841
Private	7,971	8,206	8,831	9,142	9,328	9,482	9,523	9,563	9,599	9,637	9,670
Kindergarten through 8 . .	31,639	33,973	36,806	37,941	38,521	38,561	38,348	38,152	38,044	38,005	38,012
Public	27,647	29,878	32,341	33,344	33,875	33,910	33,723	33,550	33,455	33,421	33,427
Private	3,992	4,095	4,465	4,597	4,646	4,651	4,625	4,602	4,589	4,584	4,585
Grades 9 through 12. . . .	14,570	12,475	13,697	14,518	15,018	15,808	16,129	16,348	16,391	16,310	16,163
Public.	13,231	11,338	12,500	13,191	13,658	14,376	14,669	14,868	14,907	14,833	14,699
Private	1,339	1,137	1,197	1,327	1,360	1,431	1,461	1,480	1,484	1,477	1,464
College.	12,097	13,819	14,262	14,608	15,072	15,400	15,556	15,739	15,929	16,144	16,336
Public	9,457	10,845	11,092	11,390	11,750	12,000	12,119	12,258	12,403	12,568	12,715
Private	2,640	2,974	3,169	3,218	3,322	3,400	3,437	3,481	3,526	3,576	3,621

[1] Public elementary and secondary school data are estimated. Data for private schools and higher education are projections.

Source: U.S. National Center for Education Statistics, *Digest of Education Statistics*, annual; *Projections of Education Statistics*, annual; and unpublished data.

154 Education

No. 245. School Enrollment by Age: 1970 to 1998

[As of **October (60,357 represents 60,357,000).** Covers civilian noninstitutional population enrolled in nursery school and above. Based on Current Population Survey, see text, Section 1, Population]

Age	1970	1980	1985	1990	1993	1994	1995	1996	1997	1998
ENROLLMENT (1,000)										
Total 3 to 34 years old .	60,357	57,348	58,013	60,588	62,730	66,427	66,939	67,317	69,041	69,277
3 and 4 years old	1,461	2,280	2,801	3,292	3,275	3,917	4,042	3,959	4,194	4,164
5 and 6 years old	7,000	5,853	6,697	7,207	7,298	7,752	7,901	7,893	7,964	7,902
7 to 13 years old	28,943	23,751	22,849	25,016	26,110	26,768	27,003	26,936	27,616	27,846
14 and 15 years old.	7,869	7,282	7,362	6,555	7,011	7,519	7,651	7,598	7,744	7,653
16 and 17 years old.	6,927	7,129	6,654	6,098	6,339	6,895	6,997	7,220	7,538	7,456
18 and 19 years old.	3,322	3,788	3,716	4,044	4,063	4,180	4,274	4,539	4,618	4,914
20 and 21 years old.	1,949	2,515	2,708	2,852	2,810	3,133	3,025	3,017	3,231	3,197
22 to 24 years old	1,410	1,931	2,068	2,231	2,579	2,724	2,545	2,605	2,754	2,607
25 to 29 years old	1,011	1,714	1,942	2,013	1,942	2,070	2,216	2,265	2,223	2,216
30 to 34 years old	466	1,105	1,218	1,281	1,303	1,468	1,284	1,286	1,159	1,322
35 years old and over .	(NA)	1,290	1,766	2,439	2,634	2,845	2,830	2,979	2,989	2,831
ENROLLMENT RATE										
Total 3 to 34 years old .	56.4	49.7	48.3	50.2	51.8	53.3	53.7	54.1	55.6	55.8
3 and 4 years old	20.5	36.7	38.9	44.4	40.4	47.3	48.7	48.3	52.6	52.1
5 and 6 years old	89.5	95.7	96.1	96.5	95.4	96.7	96.0	94.0	96.6	95.6
7 to 13 years old	99.2	99.3	99.2	99.6	99.5	99.3	98.9	97.7	99.1	98.9
14 and 15 years old.	98.1	98.2	98.1	99.0	98.9	98.8	98.9	98.0	98.9	98.4
16 and 17 years old.	90.0	89.0	91.7	92.5	94.0	94.4	93.6	92.8	94.3	93.9
18 and 19 years old.	47.7	46.4	51.6	57.3	61.6	60.2	59.4	61.5	61.5	62.2
20 and 21 years old.	31.9	31.0	35.3	39.7	42.7	44.9	44.9	44.4	45.9	44.8
22 to 24 years old	14.9	16.3	16.9	21.0	23.6	24.1	23.2	24.8	26.4	24.9
25 to 29 years old	7.5	9.3	9.2	9.7	10.2	10.8	11.6	11.9	11.8	11.9
30 to 34 years old	4.2	6.4	6.1	5.8	5.9	6.7	6.0	6.1	5.7	6.6
35 years old and over .	(NA)	1.4	1.6	2.1	2.2	2.3	2.2	2.3	2.3	2.1

NA Not available.

Source: U.S. Census Bureau, *Current Population Reports*, P20-521; and earlier reports.

No. 246. School Enrollment by Race, Hispanic Origin, and Age: 1980 to 1998

[See headnote, Table 245. **(47,673 represents 47,673,000)**]

Age	White			Black			Hispanic origin [1]		
	1980	1990	1998	1980	1990	1998	1980	1990	1998
ENROLLMENT (1,000)									
Total 3 to 34 years old	47,673	48,899	44,898	8,251	8,854	10,800	4,263	6,073	9,274
3 and 4 years old	1,844	2,700	2,623	371	452	731	172	249	565
5 and 6 years old	4,781	5,750	4,805	904	1,129	1,321	491	835	1,316
7 to 13 years old	19,585	20,076	17,776	3,598	3,832	4,426	2,009	2,794	4,037
14 and 15 years old	6,038	5,265	5,031	1,088	1,023	1,167	568	739	1,018
16 and 17 years old	5,937	4,858	4,978	1,047	962	1,153	454	592	908
18 and 19 years old	3,199	3,271	3,394	494	596	732	226	329	487
20 and 21 years old	2,206	2,402	2,270	242	305	402	111	213	287
22 to 24 years old.	1,669	1,781	1,772	196	274	298	93	121	275
25 to 29 years old.	1,473	1,706	1,407	187	162	344	84	130	227
30 to 34 years old.	942	1,090	842	124	119	226	54	72	154
35 years old and over	1,104	2,096	2,062	186	238	358	(NA)	145	253
ENROLLMENT RATE									
Total 3 to 34 years old	48.9	49.5	56.0	53.9	51.9	59.2	49.8	47.4	50.3
3 and 4 years old	36.3	44.9	54.2	38.2	41.6	58.3	28.5	29.8	39.7
5 and 6 years old	95.8	96.5	96.0	95.4	96.3	95.3	94.5	94.8	93.3
7 to 13 years old	99.2	99.6	98.9	99.4	99.8	98.6	99.2	99.4	98.9
14 and 15 years old	98.3	99.1	98.9	97.9	99.2	98.8	94.3	99.0	96.8
16 and 17 years old	88.6	92.5	95.1	90.6	91.7	92.9	81.8	85.4	89.1
18 and 19 years old	46.3	57.1	66.8	45.7	55.2	61.1	37.8	44.1	40.3
20 and 21 years old	31.9	41.0	48.9	23.4	28.4	39.9	19.5	27.2	25.6
22 to 24 years old.	16.4	20.2	26.3	13.6	20.0	20.8	11.7	9.9	16.3
25 to 29 years old.	9.2	9.9	11.5	8.8	6.1	13.9	6.9	6.3	8.7
30 to 34 years old.	6.3	5.9	6.3	6.8	4.4	8.8	5.1	3.6	5.5
35 years old and over	1.3	2.1	2.0	1.8	2.1	2.5	(NA)	2.1	2.3

NA Not available.   [1] Persons of Hispanic origin may be of any race.

Source: U.S. Census Bureau, *Current Population Reports*, P20-521; and earlier reports.

Education 155

No. 247. Enrollment in Public and Private Schools: 1960 to 1998

[In millions (39.0 represents 39,000,000), except percent. As of October. For civilian noninstitutional population. For **1960**, 5 to 34 years old; for **1970 to 1985**, 3 to 34 years old; **beginning 1986**, for 3 years old and over]

Year	Public						Private					
	Total	Nursery	Kindergarten	Elementary	High School	College	Total	Nursery	Kindergarten	Elementary	High School	College
1960	39.0	(NA)	(¹)	27.5	9.2	2.3	7.2	(NA)	(¹)	4.9	1.0	1.3
1970	52.2	0.3	2.6	30.0	13.5	5.7	8.1	0.8	0.5	3.9	1.2	1.7
1975	52.8	0.6	2.9	27.2	14.5	7.7	8.2	1.2	0.5	3.3	1.2	2.0
1980	(NA)	0.6	2.7	24.4	(NA)	(NA)	(NA)	1.4	0.5	3.1	(NA)	(NA)
1981	49.7	0.7	2.6	24.8	13.5	8.2	8.7	1.4	0.5	3.0	1.1	2.6
1982	49.2	0.7	2.7	24.4	13.0	8.4	8.2	1.4	0.6	3.0	1.1	2.6
1983	48.7	0.8	2.7	24.2	12.8	8.2	9.0	1.5	0.7	3.0	1.2	2.6
1984	49.0	0.8	3.0	24.1	12.7	8.5	8.3	1.6	0.5	2.7	1.1	2.4
1985 ²	49.0	0.9	3.2	23.8	12.8	8.4	9.0	1.6	0.6	3.1	1.2	2.5
1986 ²	51.2	0.8	3.4	24.2	13.0	9.8	9.4	1.7	0.6	3.0	1.2	2.9
1987 ²	51.7	0.8	3.4	24.8	12.7	10.0	8.9	1.7	0.6	2.8	1.1	2.8
1988 ²	52.2	0.9	3.4	25.5	12.2	10.3	8.9	1.8	0.5	2.8	1.0	2.8
1989 ²	52.5	0.9	3.3	25.9	12.1	10.3	8.9	1.9	0.6	2.7	0.8	2.9
1990 ²	53.8	1.2	3.3	26.6	11.9	10.7	9.2	2.2	0.6	2.7	0.9	2.9
1991 ²	54.5	1.1	3.5	26.6	12.2	11.1	9.4	1.8	0.6	3.0	1.0	3.0
1992 ²	55.0	1.1	3.5	27.1	12.3	11.1	9.4	1.8	0.6	3.1	1.0	3.0
1993 ²	56.0	1.2	3.5	27.7	12.6	10.9	9.4	1.8	0.7	2.9	1.0	3.0
1994 ²	58.6	1.9	3.3	28.1	13.5	11.7	10.7	2.3	0.6	3.4	1.1	3.3
1995 ²	58.7	2.0	3.2	28.4	13.7	11.4	11.1	2.4	0.7	3.4	1.2	3.3
1996 ²	59.5	1.9	3.4	28.1	14.1	12.0	10.8	2.3	0.7	3.4	1.2	3.2
1997 ²	61.6	2.3	3.3	29.3	14.6	12.1	10.5	2.2	0.7	3.1	1.2	3.3
1998 ²	60.8	2.3	3.1	29.1	14.3	12.0	11.3	2.3	0.7	3.4	1.2	3.6
Percent White . .	85.7	(NA)	(¹)	84.3	88.2	92.2	95.7	(NA)	(¹)	95.3	96.7	96.3
1970	84.5	59.5	84.4	83.1	85.6	90.7	93.4	91.1	88.2	94.1	96.1	92.8
1980	(NA)	68.2	80.7	80.9	(NA)	(NA)	(NA)	89.0	87.0	90.7	(NA)	(NA)
1990	79.8	71.7	78.3	78.9	79.2	84.1	87.4	89.6	83.2	88.2	89.4	85.0
1995	78.0	71.3	76.9	77.5	76.9	81.9	85.0	88.7	84.1	86.1	86.0	81.1
1998	77.4	70.6	75.3	77.4	77.0	79.4	83.9	84.4	82.5	85.3	87.9	80.9

NA Not available.   ¹ Included in elementary school.   ² See Table 301 for college enrollment 35 years old and over. Also data beginning 1986 based on a revised edit and tabulation package.

Source: U.S. Census Bureau, *Current Population Reports*, P20-521; and earlier reports.

No. 248. School Enrollment by Sex and Level: 1960 to 1998

[In millions (46.3 represents 46,300,000). As of Oct. For the civilian noninstitutional population. For **1960**, persons 5 to 34 years old; **1970-1979**, 3 to 34 years old; **beginning 1980**, 3 years old and over. Elementary includes kindergarten and grades 1-8; high school, grades 9-12; and college, 2-year and 4-year colleges, universities, and graduate and professional schools. Data for college represent degree-credit enrollment]

Year	All levels ¹			Elementary			High school			College		
	Total	Male	Female	Total	Male	Female	Total	Male	Female	Total	Male	Female
1960	46.3	24.2	22.0	32.4	16.7	15.7	10.2	5.2	5.1	3.6	2.3	1.2
1970	60.4	31.4	28.9	37.1	19.0	18.1	14.7	7.4	7.3	7.4	4.4	3.0
1975	61.0	31.6	29.4	33.8	17.3	16.5	15.7	8.0	7.7	9.7	5.3	4.4
1979	57.9	29.5	28.3	30.9	15.9	15.0	15.1	7.7	7.4	10.0	5.0	5.0
1980 ²	58.6	29.6	29.1	30.6	15.8	14.9	14.6	7.3	7.3	11.4	5.4	6.0
1981 ²	58.4	29.5	28.9	30.1	15.5	14.7	14.4	7.3	7.1	11.8	5.6	6.2
1981 ³	59.9	30.3	29.6	31.0	15.9	15.0	14.7	7.5	7.3	12.1	5.8	6.3
1982	59.4	30.0	29.4	30.7	15.8	14.9	14.2	7.2	7.0	12.3	5.9	6.4
1983	59.3	30.1	29.2	30.6	15.7	14.8	14.1	7.1	7.0	12.4	6.0	6.3
1984	58.9	29.9	29.0	30.3	15.6	14.7	13.9	7.1	6.8	12.3	6.0	6.3
1985	59.8	30.0	29.7	30.7	15.7	15.0	14.1	7.2	6.9	12.5	5.9	6.6
1986	60.1	30.4	29.7	31.1	16.1	15.0	14.0	7.1	6.9	12.4	5.8	6.6
1986 ⁴	60.5	30.6	30.0	31.1	16.1	15.0	14.2	7.2	7.0	12.7	6.0	6.7
1987	60.6	30.7	29.9	31.6	16.3	15.3	13.8	7.0	6.8	12.7	6.0	6.7
1988	61.1	30.7	30.5	32.2	16.6	15.6	13.2	6.7	6.4	13.1	5.9	7.2
1989	61.5	30.8	30.7	32.5	16.7	15.8	12.9	6.6	6.3	13.2	6.0	7.2
1990	63.0	31.5	31.5	33.2	17.1	16.0	12.8	6.5	6.4	13.6	6.2	7.4
1991	63.9	32.1	31.8	33.8	17.3	16.4	13.1	6.8	6.4	14.1	6.4	7.6
1992	64.6	32.2	32.3	34.3	17.7	16.6	13.3	6.8	6.5	14.0	6.2	7.8
1993	65.4	32.9	32.5	34.8	17.9	16.9	13.6	7.0	6.6	13.9	6.3	7.6
1994	69.3	34.6	34.6	35.4	18.2	17.2	14.6	7.4	7.2	15.0	6.8	8.2
1995	69.8	35.0	34.8	35.7	18.3	17.4	15.0	7.7	7.3	14.7	6.7	8.0
1996	70.3	35.1	35.2	35.5	18.3	17.3	15.3	7.9	7.4	15.2	6.8	8.4
1997	72.0	35.9	36.2	36.3	18.7	17.6	15.8	8.0	7.7	15.4	6.8	8.6
1998	72.1	36.0	36.1	36.4	18.7	17.7	15.6	7.9	7.6	15.5	6.9	8.6

¹ Beginning 1970, includes nursery schools, not shown separately.   ² Based on 1970 population controls.   ³ Based on 1980 population controls.   ⁴ Revised. Data beginning 1986, based on a revised edit and tabulation package.

Source: U.S. Census Bureau, *Current Population Reports*, P20-521; and earlier reports.

No. 249. Educational Attainment by Race and Hispanic Origin: 1960 to 1999

[In percent. For persons 25 years old and over. 1960, 1970, and 1980 as of April 1 and based on sample data from the censuses of population. **Other years as of March** and based on the Current Population Survey; see text, Section 1, Population, and Appendix III. See Table 250 for data by sex]

Year	Total [1]	White	Black	Asian and Pacific Islander	Hispanic [2] Total [3]	Mexican	Puerto Rican	Cuban
COMPLETED 4 YEARS OF HIGH SCHOOL OR MORE								
1960	41.1	43.2	20.1	(NA)	(NA)	(NA)	(NA)	(NA)
1965	49.0	51.3	27.2	(NA)	(NA)	(NA)	(NA)	(NA)
1970	52.3	54.5	31.4	(NA)	32.1	24.2	23.4	43.9
1975	62.5	64.5	42.5	(NA)	37.9	31.0	28.7	51.7
1980	66.5	68.8	51.2	(NA)	44.0	37.6	40.1	55.3
1985	73.9	75.5	59.8	(NA)	47.9	41.9	46.3	51.1
1990	77.6	79.1	66.2	80.4	50.8	44.1	55.5	63.5
1995 [4]	81.7	83.0	73.8	(NA)	53.4	46.5	61.3	64.7
1997 [4]	82.1	83.0	74.9	84.9	54.7	48.6	61.1	65.2
1998 [4]	82.8	83.7	76.0	(NA)	55.5	48.3	63.8	67.8
1999 [4]	83.4	84.3	77.0	84.7	56.1	49.7	63.9	70.3
COMPLETED 4 YEARS OF COLLEGE OR MORE								
1960	7.7	8.1	3.1	(NA)	(NA)	(NA)	(NA)	(NA)
1965	9.4	9.9	4.7	(NA)	(NA)	(NA)	(NA)	(NA)
1970	10.7	11.3	4.4	(NA)	4.5	2.5	2.2	11.1
1975	13.9	14.5	6.4	(NA)	(NA)	(NA)	(NA)	(NA)
1980	16.2	17.1	8.4	(NA)	7.6	4.9	5.6	16.2
1985	19.4	20.0	11.1	(NA)	8.5	5.5	7.0	13.7
1990	21.3	22.0	11.3	39.9	9.2	5.4	9.7	20.2
1995 [4]	23.0	24.0	13.2	(NA)	9.3	6.5	10.7	19.4
1997 [4]	23.9	24.6	13.3	42.2	10.3	7.5	10.7	19.7
1998 [4]	24.4	25.0	14.7	(NA)	11.0	7.5	11.9	22.2
1999 [4]	25.2	25.9	15.4	42.4	10.9	7.1	11.1	24.8

NA Not available. [1] Includes other races, not shown separately. [2] Persons of Hispanic origin may be of any race.
[3] Includes persons of other Hispanic origin, not shown separately. [4] Beginning 1995, persons high school graduates and those with a BA degree or higher.

Source: U.S. Census Bureau, *U.S. Census of Population, U.S. Summary*, PC80-1-C1 and *Current Population Reports* P20-455, P20-459, P20-462, P20-465RV, P20-475, P20-476, P20-489, P20-493, P20-505, P20-513, P20-528; and unpublished data.

No. 250. Educational Attainment by Race, Hispanic Origin, and Sex: 1960 to 1999

[In percent. See Table 249 for headnote and totals for both sexes]

Year	All races [1] Male	Female	White Male	Female	Black Male	Female	Asian and Pacific Islander Male	Female	Hispanic [2] Male	Female
COMPLETED 4 YEARS OF HIGH SCHOOL OR MORE										
1960	39.5	42.5	41.6	44.7	18.2	21.8	(NA)	(NA)	(NA)	(NA)
1965	48.0	49.9	50.2	52.2	25.8	28.4	(NA)	(NA)	(NA)	(NA)
1970	51.9	52.8	54.0	55.0	30.1	32.5	(NA)	(NA)	37.9	34.2
1975	63.1	62.1	65.0	64.1	41.6	43.3	(NA)	(NA)	39.5	36.7
1980	67.3	65.8	69.6	68.1	50.8	51.5	(NA)	(NA)	67.3	65.8
1985	74.4	73.5	76.0	75.1	58.4	60.8	(NA)	(NA)	48.5	47.4
1990	77.7	77.5	79.1	79.0	65.8	66.5	84.0	77.2	50.3	51.3
1995 [3]	81.7	81.6	83.0	83.0	73.4	74.1	(NA)	(NA)	52.9	53.8
1997 [3]	82.0	82.2	82.9	83.2	73.5	76.0	(NA)	(NA)	54.9	54.6
1998 [3]	82.8	82.9	83.6	83.8	75.2	76.7	(NA)	(NA)	55.7	55.3
1999 [3]	83.4	83.4	84.2	84.3	76.7	77.2	86.9	82.8	56.0	56.3
COMPLETED 4 YEARS OF COLLEGE OR MORE										
1960	9.7	5.8	10.3	6.0	2.8	3.3	(NA)	(NA)	(NA)	(NA)
1965	12.0	7.1	12.7	7.3	4.9	4.5	(NA)	(NA)	(NA)	(NA)
1970	13.5	8.1	14.4	8.4	4.2	4.6	(NA)	(NA)	7.8	4.3
1975	17.6	10.6	18.4	11.0	6.7	6.2	(NA)	(NA)	8.3	6.4
1980	20.1	12.8	21.3	13.3	8.4	8.3	(NA)	(NA)	9.4	6.0
1985	23.1	16.0	24.0	16.3	11.2	11.0	(NA)	(NA)	9.7	7.3
1990	24.4	18.4	25.3	19.0	11.9	10.8	44.9	35.4	9.8	8.7
1995 [3]	26.0	20.2	27.2	21.0	13.6	12.9	(NA)	(NA)	10.1	8.4
1997 [3]	26.2	21.7	27.0	22.3	12.5	13.9	(NA)	(NA)	10.6	10.1
1998 [3]	26.5	22.4	27.3	22.8	13.9	15.4	(NA)	(NA)	11.1	10.9
1999 [3]	27.5	23.1	28.5	23.5	14.2	16.4	46.2	39.0	10.7	11.0

NA Not available. [1] Includes other races, not shown separately. [2] Persons of Hispanic origin may be of any race.
[3] Beginning 1995, persons high school graduates and those with a BA degree or higher.

Source: U.S. Census Bureau, *U.S. Census of Population, 1960, 1970, and 1980, Vol. 1;* and *Current Population Reports* P20-459, P20-475, P20-476, P20-489, P20-493, P20-505, P20-513, P20-528; and unpublished data.

Education 157

No. 251. Educational Attainment by Selected Characteristics: 1999

[For persons 25 years old and over (173,754 represents 173,754,000). As of March. Based on the Current Population Survey; see text, Section 1, Population, and Appendix III. For composition of regions, see map inside front cover]

Characteristic	Population (1,000)	Percent of population—highest level					
		Not a high school graduate	High school graduate	Some college, but no degree	Associate's degree [1]	Bachelor's degree	Advanced degree
Total persons	173,754	**16.6**	**33.3**	**17.3**	**7.5**	**17.0**	**8.2**
Age:							
25 to 34 years old.	38,474	12.3	30.7	19.6	8.7	22.1	6.6
35 to 44 years old.	44,744	12.0	33.9	17.9	9.2	18.7	8.3
45 to 54 years old.	35,232	11.7	31.7	18.1	8.7	18.2	11.5
55 to 64 years old.	22,909	18.8	36.9	16.3	5.3	13.2	9.5
65 to 74 years old.	17,844	27.6	36.7	14.0	4.6	10.6	6.5
75 years old or over	14,551	37.3	32.6	13.2	3.7	8.6	4.6
Sex:							
Male.	82,917	16.6	31.8	17.1	7.0	17.9	9.6
Female	90,837	16.6	34.8	17.5	8.0	16.2	7.0
Race:							
White.	146,080	15.7	33.5	17.2	7.7	17.4	8.5
Black	19,732	23.0	35.7	19.4	6.4	10.9	4.6
Other	7,942	17.0	24.2	14.4	7.1	24.8	12.6
Hispanic origin:							
Hispanic	16,425	43.9	26.9	13.6	4.7	7.8	3.0
Non-Hispanic	157,329	13.8	34.0	17.7	7.8	17.9	8.8
Region:							
Northeast	34,013	15.4	36.3	13.4	7.3	17.9	9.7
Midwest	40,016	13.8	36.6	17.8	7.8	16.0	8.0
South	61,456	19.3	33.2	17.1	7.0	15.8	7.6
West.	38,269	16.3	27.6	20.7	8.2	19.0	8.2
Marital status:							
Never married	26,052	15.4	29.9	17.8	7.4	21.5	8.0
Married spouse present . . .	108,011	14.0	33.4	17.1	7.9	18.2	9.4
Married spouse absent . . .	6,800	27.6	29.5	15.7	5.4	13.9	8.0
Separated	4,430	24.7	34.2	20.3	7.1	9.5	4.0
Widowed.	13,477	37.1	35.3	12.7	4.1	7.3	3.5
Divorced	19,413	15.2	36.3	20.6	8.5	12.9	6.5
Civilian labor force status:							
Employed	112,514	10.1	32.2	18.5	8.7	20.3	10.1
Unemployed	4,068	22.8	36.6	17.8	6.7	11.8	4.4
Not in the labor force.	56,566	29.3	35.5	14.7	5.1	10.6	4.8

[1] Includes vocational degrees.

Source: U.S. Census Bureau, *Current Population Reports,* P20-528; and unpublished data.

No. 252. Earnings by Highest Degree Earned: 1999

[For persons 25 years old and over with earnings. Persons as of March. Earnings for prior year. Based on Current Population Survey; see text, Section 1, Population, and Appendix III. For definition of mean, see Guide to Tabular Presentation]

Characteristic	Total persons	Level of highest degree							
		Not a high school graduate	High school graduate only	Some college, no degree	Asso-ciate's	Bache-lor's	Master's	Profes-sional	Doctorate
MEAN EARNINGS (dol.)									
All persons [1]	**30,928**	**16,053**	**23,594**	**25,686**	**32,468**	**43,782**	**52,794**	**95,488**	**74,712**
Age:									
25 to 34 years old. . . .	33,084	19,760	26,878	30,515	32,332	42,420	45,930	63,005	65,493
35 to 44 years old. . . .	35,823	18,982	26,228	32,100	35,072	48,842	59,892	105,700	70,673
45 to 54 years old. . . .	39,285	20,734	27,538	34,775	36,635	53,462	56,651	96,479	86,681
55 to 64 years old. . . .	36,410	20,400	26,670	31,998	38,545	47,182	56,078	134,814	85,297
65 years old and over .	23,245	12,481	17,165	23,010	28,449	32,974	21,646	82,060	48,205
Sex:									
Male.	38,134	19,155	28,742	32,005	40,082	55,057	64,533	108,926	82,619
Female	22,818	11,353	17,898	19,327	25,390	31,452	40,429	65,351	54,552
White.	32,057	16,474	24,409	26,357	33,212	44,852	53,497	99,858	77,970
Male.	39,638	19,632	29,782	33,041	41,111	56,620	65,637	112,944	85,837
Female	23,213	11,255	18,327	19,390	25,679	31,406	40,679	67,998	55,793
Black	22,829	13,672	19,236	22,148	26,424	36,373	43,054	53,969	46,848
Male.	26,090	16,013	22,698	25,807	29,532	42,539	47,951	68,693	46,743
Female	20,026	11,372	15,892	19,269	24,187	31,952	39,760	39,109	46,914
Hispanic [2]	22,117	15,832	20,978	22,151	29,933	35,014	55,581	78,353	69,942
Male.	25,534	17,756	24,739	27,145	38,555	40,889	73,362	109,071	90,474
Female	17,461	12,273	15,952	16,941	22,222	29,317	36,589	45,829	33,407

[1] Includes other races, not shown separately. [2] Persons of Hispanic origin may be of any race.

Source: U.S. Census Bureau, *Current Population Reports,* P20-528.

No. 253. Educational Attainment by State: 1990 and 1999

[In percent. As of March 1999 and April 1990. For persons 25 years old and over, except as indicated. Based on the 1990 Census of Population and the Current Population Survey; see text, Section 1, Population, and Appendix III]

State	1990 Not a high school graduate	1990 High school graduate or more	1990 Bachelors degree or more Total	1990 Bachelors degree or more Bachelor's degree	1990 Bachelors degree or more Advanced degree	1990 Drop-outs [1]	1999 High school graduate or more	1999 College graduate or more
United States	24.8	75.2	20.3	13.1	7.2	11.2	83.4	25.2
Alabama................	33.1	66.9	15.7	10.1	5.5	12.6	81.1	21.8
Alaska.................	13.4	86.6	23.0	15.0	8.0	10.9	92.8	25.5
Arizona................	21.3	78.7	20.3	13.3	7.0	14.4	83.1	24.2
Arkansas	33.7	66.3	13.3	8.9	4.5	11.4	78.9	17.3
California	23.8	76.2	23.4	15.3	8.1	14.2	80.4	27.1
Colorado...............	15.6	84.4	27.0	18.0	9.0	9.8	90.4	38.7
Connecticut............	20.8	79.2	27.2	16.2	11.0	9.0	83.7	33.5
Delaware	22.5	77.5	21.4	13.7	7.7	10.4	84.5	24.0
District of Columbia	26.9	73.1	33.3	16.1	17.2	13.9	82.8	42.1
Florida	25.6	74.4	18.3	12.0	6.3	14.3	82.7	21.6
Georgia	29.1	70.9	19.3	12.9	6.4	14.1	80.7	21.5
Hawaii	19.9	80.1	22.9	15.8	7.1	7.5	88.0	26.2
Idaho..................	20.3	79.7	17.7	12.4	5.3	10.4	84.8	20.8
Illinois	23.8	76.2	21.0	13.6	7.5	10.6	85.4	25.6
Indiana................	24.4	75.6	15.6	9.2	6.4	11.4	82.9	18.4
Iowa	19.9	80.1	16.9	11.7	5.2	6.6	89.7	21.7
Kansas................	18.7	81.3	21.1	14.1	7.0	8.7	87.6	26.5
Kentucky	35.4	64.6	13.6	8.1	5.5	13.3	78.2	19.8
Louisiana	31.7	68.3	16.1	10.5	5.6	12.5	78.3	20.7
Maine.................	21.2	78.8	18.8	12.7	6.1	8.3	88.9	22.9
Maryland	21.6	78.4	26.5	15.6	10.9	10.9	84.7	34.7
Massachusetts.........	20.0	80.0	27.2	16.6	10.6	8.5	85.1	31.0
Michigan...............	23.2	76.8	17.4	10.9	6.4	10.0	85.5	21.3
Minnesota.............	17.6	82.4	21.8	15.6	6.3	6.4	91.1	32.0
Mississippi	35.7	64.3	14.7	9.7	5.1	11.8	78.0	19.2
Missouri	26.1	73.9	17.8	11.7	6.1	11.4	85.0	23.0
Montana...............	19.0	81.0	19.8	14.1	5.7	8.1	88.8	24.0
Nebraska	18.2	81.8	18.9	13.1	5.9	7.0	89.3	20.4
Nevada	21.2	78.8	15.3	10.1	5.2	15.2	86.4	20.2
New Hampshire	17.8	82.2	24.4	16.4	7.9	9.4	86.5	27.2
New Jersey.............	23.3	76.7	24.9	16.0	8.8	9.6	87.4	30.5
New Mexico	24.9	75.1	20.4	12.1	8.3	11.7	80.9	24.5
New York	25.2	74.8	23.1	13.2	9.9	9.9	81.9	26.9
North Carolina	30.0	70.0	17.4	12.0	5.4	12.5	79.8	23.9
North Dakota...........	23.3	76.7	18.1	13.5	4.5	4.6	84.9	22.3
Ohio	24.3	75.7	17.0	11.1	5.9	8.9	86.1	25.5
Oklahoma..............	25.4	74.6	17.8	11.8	6.0	10.4	83.5	23.7
Oregon................	18.5	81.5	20.6	13.6	7.0	11.8	86.2	26.8
Pennsylvania...........	25.3	74.7	17.9	11.3	6.6	9.1	86.1	23.9
Rhode Island...........	28.0	72.0	21.3	13.5	7.8	11.1	80.9	26.8
South Carolina.........	31.7	68.3	16.6	11.2	5.4	11.7	78.6	20.9
South Dakota..........	22.9	77.1	17.2	12.3	4.9	7.7	88.7	25.6
Tennessee	32.9	67.1	16.0	10.5	5.4	13.4	79.1	17.7
Texas.................	27.9	72.1	20.3	13.9	6.5	12.9	78.2	24.4
Utah	14.9	85.1	22.3	15.4	6.8	8.7	91.0	27.9
Vermont	19.2	80.8	24.3	15.4	8.9	8.0	89.3	28.3
Virginia................	24.8	75.2	24.5	15.4	9.1	10.0	87.3	31.6
Washington............	16.2	83.8	22.9	15.9	7.0	10.6	91.2	28.6
West Virginia...........	34.0	66.0	12.3	7.5	4.8	10.9	75.1	17.9
Wisconsin..............	21.4	78.6	17.7	12.1	5.6	7.1	86.8	23.6
Wyoming	17.0	83.0	18.8	13.1	5.7	6.9	90.7	22.3

[1] For persons 16 to 19 years old. A dropout is a person who is not in regular school and who has not completed the 12th grade or received a general equivalency degree.

Source: U.S. Census Bureau, 1990 Census of Population, CPH-L-96, and Current Population Reports, P20-528.

Education   159

No. 254. Nonfatal Crimes Against Students: 1996 and 1997

[For students aged 12 through 18 (3,163.0 represents 3,163,000). For crimes occurring at school or going to or from school. Based on the National Crime Victimization Survey; see Appendix III]

Student characteristic	1996				1997			
			Violent				Violent	
	Total	Theft	Total	Serious [1]	Total	Theft	Total	Serious [1]
Total (1,000)............	3,163.0	2,028.7	1,134.0	225.4	2,721.2	1,666.0	1,055.2	201.8
RATE PER 1,000 STUDENTS								
Total [2]...............	121	78	43	9	102	63	40	8
Sex:								
Male..................	134	78	56	11	114	64	50	10
Female................	107	77	30	6	91	61	29	5
Age:								
12 to 14 years old..........	151	91	60	9	123	69	54	10
15 to 18 years old..........	97	67	30	8	86	58	29	6
Race/ethnicity:								
White, non-Hispanic	129	83	45	7	111	67	43	[3]7
Black, non-Hispanic.........	105	73	32	12	95	59	36	[3]8
Hispanic	109	58	51	15	76	44	32	10
Other, non-Hispanic.........	108	72	36	[3]11	91	72	[3]19	[3]5
Urbanity: [4]								
Urban..................	126	76	50	14	105	63	42	12
Suburban	130	82	48	8	111	66	46	[3]8
Rural	95	71	24	[3]4	79	55	24	[3]2
Household income:								
Less than $7,500	86	55	31	[3]8	64	31	32	[3]3
$7,500 to $14,999..........	92	54	38	9	93	53	40	[3]6
$15,000 to $24,999.........	120	68	52	15	107	65	42	9
$25,000 to $34,999.........	130	78	52	10	114	71	43	7
$35,000 to $49,999.........	131	84	48	9	105	56	49	11
$50,000 to $74,999.........	138	95	43	7	110	75	35	[3]8
$75,000 and over	139	104	35	[3]5	125	84	41	[3]7

[1] Includes rape, sexual assault, robbery and aggravated assault. [2] Includes those whose race/ethnicity or incomes are unknown. [3] Estimate based on fewer than 10 cases. [4] Urban: The largest city (or groupings of cities) of an MSA; suburban: those portions of metro areas outside central cities: rural: a place outside MSAs.

Source: U.S. National Center for Education Statistics and U.S. Bureau of Justice Statistics, *Indicators of School Crime and Safety,* September 1999.

No. 255. Public Schools Reporting Criminal Incidents to the Police: 1996-97

[In percent. For crimes that took place in school buildings, on school buses or grounds, and places holding school-sponsored events. Based on the National Center for Education Statistics' Fast Response Survey System; see source for details]

School characteristic	Any incidents					Serious violent incidents [2]				
	Total	City [1]	Urban fringe [1]	Town [1]	Rural [1]	Total	City [1]	Urban fringe [1]	Town [1]	Rural [1]
Total	56.7	59.3	58.4	63.2	46.9	10.1	16.8	11.2	5.4	7.8
Instructional level:										
Elementary school	45.1	46.9	47.0	52.6	34.2	4.2	6.1	3.3	2.0	5.1
Middle school	74.1	86.7	78.8	70.0	62.0	18.7	35.8	21.7	7.0	15.0
High school	76.9	88.8	84.0	84.2	64.1	20.6	48.0	33.0	12.7	9.4
School enrollment:										
Less than 300.............	37.8	(B)	(B)	44.9	38.0	3.9	(B)	(B)	8.8	2.5
300 to 999	59.6	54.2	59.2	67.3	56.8	9.3	12.5	9.0	3.2	13.9
1,000 or more.............	89.1	93.1	86.7	86.5	(B)	32.9	44.2	29.8	15.9	(B)
Minority enrollment:										
Less than 5 percent.........	46.7	(B)	47.2	53.9	40.8	5.8	(B)	5.9	3.3	7.3
5 to 19 percent	57.7	52.0	62.9	64.0	45.0	10.9	14.5	11.3	10.6	6.8
20 to 49 percent	58.1	54.7	58.5	66.7	53.3	11.1	19.1	10.1	5.0	8.0
50 percent or more	68.3	64.8	62.3	81.5	74.9	14.7	17.6	17.8	4.4	11.6
Free/reduced price lunch eligibility:										
Less than 20 percent	54.4	50.6	57.3	64.2	41.2	8.6	12.2	9.9	7.1	5.6
21 to 34 percent	53.2	56.0	65.5	57.2	39.5	11.7	18.4	13.3	7.1	11.6
35 to 49 percent	59.4	76.1	53.3	63.1	52.5	11.6	34.2	8.6	3.0	8.6
50 to 74 percent	58.8	60.8	54.7	66.6	52.0	8.9	22.9	10.3	2.0	2.3
75 percent or more	59.2	58.5	(B)	(B)	(B)	10.2	8.4	(B)	(B)	(B)

B Base figure too small to meet statistical standards for reliability of a derived figure. [1] City: central city of an MSA; urban fringe: a place within an MSA but not its central city; town: a place outside an MSA, with a population greater than or equal to 2,500 and defined as urban by the U.S. Census Bureau; rural: a place with a population under 2,500 and defined as urban by the U.S. Census Bureau. [2] Includes murder, rape or other sexual battery, suicide, physical attack or fight with a weapon, or robbery.

Source: U.S. National Center for Education Statistics and U.S. Bureau of Justice Statistics, *Indicators of School Crime and Safety,* September 1999.

160　Education

No. 256. Children Whose Parents Are Involved in School Activities: 1999

[In percent, except as indicated (23,355 represents 23,355,000). Based on the National Household Education Survey; see source for details]

Parental involvement	Students in grades K to 5					Students in grades 6 to 8				
	Two-parent families	One-parent families				Two-parent families	One-parent families			
	Total	Total	Mother	Father		Total	Total	Mother	Father	
Total students, 1999 (1,000)	**23,355**	**15,841**	**7,514**	**6,634**	**880**	**11,252**	**7,747**	**3,506**	**3,010**	**496**
Any adult attending a meeting....	84.9	88.6	77.1	77.3	75.7	81.1	85.3	72.0	71.2	77.0
Only mother attended.........	39.4	25.7	68.2	77.3	(X)	38.7	28.5	61.2	71.2	(X)
Only father attended.........	5.7	4.1	8.9	(X)	75.7	6.9	5.1	10.9	(X)	77.0
Both attended.............	39.8	58.7	(X)	(X)	(X)	35.6	51.7	(X)	(X)	(X)
Any adult attending a conference..	87.7	89.4	84.1	85.1	76.7	71.1	72.3	68.5	68.1	70.8
Only mother attended.........	52.0	41.0	75.1	85.1	(X)	41.0	33.1	58.8	68.1	(X)
Only father attended.........	6.4	5.1	9.0	(X)	76.7	7.1	5.8	10.0	(X)	70.8
Both attended.............	29.4	43.3	(X)	(X)	(X)	23.0	33.4	(X)	(X)	(X)
Any adult attending a class event..	70.8	74.0	64.1	63.1	71.2	67.8	72.6	57.3	55.9	66.1
Only mother attended.........	31.5	20.0	55.7	63.1	(X)	24.6	14.1	48.0	55.9	(X)
Only father attended.........	5.1	3.6	8.3	(X)	71.2	5.3	3.5	9.3	(X)	66.1
Both attended.............	34.2	50.4	(X)	(X)	(X)	37.9	55.0	(X)	(X)	(X)
Any adult acted as a volunteer ...	48.9	55.5	34.8	36.3	23.1	31.7	36.1	21.9	22.1	20.6
Only mother attended.........	37.0	39.3	32.1	36.3	(X)	21.8	23.0	19.0	22.1	(X)
Only father attended.........	3.2	3.4	2.7	(X)	23.1	3.1	3.1	2.9	(X)	20.6
Both attended.............	8.6	12.7	(X)	(X)	(X)	6.8	9.9	(X)	(X)	(X)
Number of activities at least one parent participated in:										
None..................	3.5	2.2	6.5	6.2	8.3	7.3	4.4	13.7	14.1	11.2
One..................	7.4	5.7	11.0	11.1	10.3	11.7	11.0	13.4	13.9	10.8
Two..................	19.7	17.6	24.3	24.2	25.0	25.8	24.8	27.9	28.0	27.3
Three	32.0	31.7	32.5	31.7	39.0	32.2	33.5	29.2	28.5	33.5
Four	37.4	42.9	25.7	26.8	17.4	23.0	26.2	15.7	15.5	17.2
Number of activities mother participated in: [1]										
None..................	4.6	3.9	6.2	6.2	(X)	8.9	6.9	14.1	14.1	(X)
One..................	8.9	8.1	11.1	11.1	(X)	13.1	12.8	13.9	13.9	(X)
Two..................	20.5	19.0	24.2	24.2	(X)	27.5	27.2	28.0	28.0	(X)
Three	31.2	31.0	31.7	31.7	(X)	30.3	31.0	28.5	28.5	(X)
Four	34.8	38.1	26.8	26.8	(X)	20.2	22.1	15.5	15.5	(X)
Number of activities father participated in: [2]										
None..................	19.7	20.4	8.3	(X)	8.3	21.9	22.6	11.2	(X)	11.2
One..................	19.5	20.0	10.3	(X)	10.3	22.6	23.4	10.8	(X)	10.8
Two..................	26.7	26.8	25.0	(X)	25.0	25.1	24.9	27.3	(X)	27.3
Three	24.4	23.6	39.0	(X)	39.0	23.0	22.3	33.5	(X)	33.5
Four	9.7	9.2	17.4	(X)	17.4	7.4	6.8	17.2	(X)	17.2
Number of activities both parents participated in:										
None..................	24.0	24.0	(X)	(X)	(X)	27.0	27.0	(X)	(X)	(X)
One..................	21.7	21.7	(X)	(X)	(X)	24.8	24.8	(X)	(X)	(X)
Two..................	26.0	26.0	(X)	(X)	(X)	24.2	24.2	(X)	(X)	(X)
Three	21.5	21.5	(X)	(X)	(X)	19.5	19.5	(X)	(X)	(X)
Four	6.7	6.7	(X)	(X)	(X)	4.5	4.5	(X)	(X)	(X)

X Not applicable.   [1] Regardless if father participated.   [2] Regardless if mother participated.

Source: U.S. National Center for Education Statistics, *National Household Education Survey*, 1999.

No. 257. Public Elementary Schools Holding Activities and Parental Attendance: 1996

[In percent. For grades K-8 during school year ending in year shown. Based on survey and subject to sampling error; see source for details]

Type of activity	Schools holding activity	Estimate of typical parental attendance [1]				
		Most or all	More than half	About half	Less than half	Few
Open house or back-to-school night..........	97	49	31	13	6	1
Arts event [2]	96	36	30	16	13	5
Regularly scheduled schoolwide parent-teacher conferences.........................	92	57	21	11	9	3
Sports event [3]	85	12	21	20	30	17
Science fairs or other academic demonstrations or events...........................	84	19	24	20	23	14

[1] Estimated by person most knowledgeable about parental involvement programs.   [2] Such as a play, dance, or musical performance.   [3] Or other athletic demonstration.

Source: U.S. National Center for Education Statistics, Fast Response Survey System, NCES 98-032, *Parent Involvement in Children's Education: Efforts by Public Elementary Schools*, January 1998.

Education 161

No. 258. Children With Difficulty Speaking English: 1979 to 1995

[In percent, except total. For children 5 to 17 years old (1,250 represents 1,250,000). For children reported to speak English less than "very well." Based on the Current Population Survey; see text Section 1, Population, and Appendix III]

Characteristic	1979	1989	1992	1995 [1]
Total with difficulty speaking English (1,000)	**1,250**	**1,850**	**2,178**	**2,431**
Percent of children 5 to 17	2.8	4.4	4.9	5.1
Race and Hispanic origin:				
White, non-Hispanic	0.5	0.8	0.6	0.7
Black, non-Hispanic	0.3	0.5	1.3	0.9
Hispanic [2]	28.7	27.4	29.9	31.0
Other, non-Hispanic [3]	19.8	20.4	21.0	14.1
Region: [4]				
Northeast	2.9	4.8	5.3	5.0
Midwest	1.1	1.3	1.6	2.3
South	2.2	3.8	3.5	3.4
West	6.5	8.8	10.4	11.4
Percent speaking another language at home	32.7	34.9	34.2	36.5
White, non-Hispanic	17.3	22.6	17.2	19.0
Black, non-Hispanic	25.6	22.5	31.0	31.8
Hispanic [2]	38.2	38.5	39.0	41.9
Other, non-Hispanic [3]	44.9	38.1	36.1	31.1

[1] Reflects revised interviewing techniques and/or change in population controls to the 1990 Census-based estimates. [2] Persons of Hispanic origin may be of any race. [3] Includes mostly Asian/Pacific Islander, but also American Indian/Alaska Native children. [4] For composition of regions, see map, inside front cover.

Source: Federal Interagency Forum on Child and Family Statistics, *America's Children: National Indicators of Well-Being, 1998.*

No. 259. Preprimary School Enrollment—Summary: 1970 to 1998

[As of **October. Civilian noninstitutional population (10,949 represents 10,949,000).** Includes public and nonpublic nursery school and kindergarten programs. Excludes 5 year olds enrolled in elementary school. Based on Current Population Survey; see text, Section 1, Population and Appendix III]

Item	1970	1975	1980	1985	1990	1995	1996	1997	1998
NUMBER OF CHILDREN (1,000)									
Population, 3 to 5 years old	**10,949**	**10,183**	**9,284**	**10,733**	**11,207**	**12,518**	**12,378**	**12,121**	**12,078**
Total enrolled [1]	**4,104**	**4,954**	**4,878**	**5,865**	**6,659**	**7,739**	**7,580**	**7,861**	**7,788**
Nursery	1,094	1,745	1,981	2,477	3,378	4,331	4,147	4,438	4,512
Public	332	570	628	846	1,202	1,950	1,830	2,207	2,212
Private	762	1,174	1,353	1,631	2,177	2,381	2,317	2,231	2,300
Kindergarten	3,010	3,211	2,897	3,388	3,281	3,408	3,433	3,422	3,276
Public	2,498	2,682	2,438	2,847	2,767	2,799	2,853	2,847	2,674
Private	511	528	459	541	513	608	580	575	602
White	3,443	4,105	3,994	4,757	5,389	6,144	5,902	6,086	5,985
Black	586	731	725	919	964	1,236	1,245	1,356	1,346
Hispanic [2]	(NA)	(NA)	370	496	642	1,040	1,068	1,142	1,170
3 years old	454	683	857	1,035	1,205	1,489	1,506	1,529	1,498
4 years old	1,007	1,418	1,423	1,765	2,086	2,553	2,454	2,665	2,666
5 years old	2,643	2,852	2,598	3,065	3,367	3,697	3,621	3,667	3,624
ENROLLMENT RATE									
Total enrolled [1]	**37.5**	**48.6**	**52.5**	**54.6**	**59.4**	**61.8**	**61.2**	**64.8**	**64.5**
White	37.8	48.6	52.7	54.7	59.7	63.0	61.2	64.1	63.6
Black	34.9	48.1	51.8	55.8	57.8	58.9	60.8	68.6	68.6
Hispanic [2]	(NA)	(NA)	43.3	43.3	49.0	51.1	52.7	52.5	54.0
3 years old	12.9	21.5	27.3	28.8	32.6	35.9	37.2	38.7	37.6
4 years old	27.8	40.5	46.3	49.1	56.0	61.6	59.2	66.1	66.6
5 years old	69.3	81.3	84.7	86.5	88.8	87.5	86.5	88.6	88.7

NA Not available. [1] Includes races not shown separately. [2] Persons of Hispanic origin may be of any race. The method of identifying Hispanic children was changed in 1980 from allocation based on status of mother to status reported for each child. The number of Hispanic children using the new method is larger.

Source: U.S. Census Bureau, *Current Population Reports*, P20-521.

No. 260. Children's School Readiness Skills: 1993 and 1999

[In percent. For children 3 to 5 years old not yet enrolled in kindergarten. Based on the National Education Household Survey; see source for details. See also Table 326]

Characteristic	Recognizes all letters		Counts to 20 or higher		Writes name		Reads or pretends to read storybooks		Has 3-4 skills	
	1993	1999	1993	1999	1993	1999	1993	1999	1993	1999
Total	21	24	52	57	50	51	72	74	35	39
Age:										
3 years old.............	11	15	37	41	22	24	66	70	15	20
4 years old.............	28	28	62	67	70	70	75	76	49	50
5 years old.............	36	44	78	81	84	87	81	77	65	69
Sex:										
Male	19	21	49	54	47	47	68	70	32	35
Female	23	27	56	60	53	56	76	77	39	43
Race/ethnicity:										
White, non-Hispanic........	23	25	56	60	52	54	76	79	39	42
Black, non-Hispanic........	18	25	53	60	45	49	63	66	31	35
Hispanic...............	10	14	32	41	42	43	59	57	22	25
Other.................	22	30	49	59	52	57	70	79	36	48
Mother's home language:										
English	22	25	55	60	51	53	73	76	37	41
Not English.............	9	8	24	25	38	34	52	45	17	14
Mother's highest education:										
Less than high school........	8	7	30	36	40	32	55	53	19	15
High school	17	17	48	48	48	49	70	69	30	31
Vocational education or some										
college................	23	25	59	60	51	52	79	79	39	42
College degree	31	35	68	73	58	61	84	84	52	54
Graduate/professional training										
or degree	39	40	68	73	59	64	83	83	55	57
Mother's employment status:										
Employed...............	23	24	57	59	52	53	75	75	39	40
Unemployed	17	15	41	53	46	39	67	64	29	32
Not in the labor force	18	24	49	54	47	50	68	73	32	38
Family type:										
Two parents	22	26	54	58	51	53	74	75	37	41
None or one parent	18	19	49	54	47	48	65	69	31	33
Poverty status:										
Above threshold	24	28	57	62	53	56	74	77	40	45
Below threshold...........	12	10	41	39	41	37	64	63	23	19

Source: U.S. National Center for Education Statistics, *Home Literacy Activities and Signs of Children's Emerging Literacy, 1993* and *1999*, NCES 2000-026, November 1999.

No. 261. Charter Schools, Creation Status by Year of Opening: 1999

[Charter schools are public schools that come into existence through a contract with either a state agency or local school board. In 1998-99 they enrolled about 252,000 students in 27 states with open charter schools or 0.8% of students in public schools in those states. Based on a survey; see source for details]

Item		Creation status (percent)			
				Pre-existing	
	Total	All schools	New	Public	Private
All charter schools.	975	100.0	72.2	17.7	10.1
Opened in—					
1998-99	313	100.0	76.4	15.0	8.6
1997-98	252	100.0	82.5	9.9	7.5
1996-97	171	100.0	66.7	17.5	15.8
1995-96	145	100.0	64.1	20.7	15.2
1994-95 or earlier......................	94	100.0	53.2	43.6	3.2

Source: U.S. Department of Education, Office of Education Research and Improvement, *The State of Charter Schools 2000*, Fourth-Year Report, January 2000.

Education 163

No. 262. Public Elementary and Secondary Schools—Summary: 1980 to 1999

[For school year ending in year shown, except as indicated (48,041 represents 48,041,000). Data are estimates]

Item	Unit	1980	1985	1990	1995	1997	1998	1999
School districts, total..........	Number...	16,044	15,812	15,552	14,947	14,889	14,858	14,842
ENROLLMENT								
Population 5-17 years old [1].....	1,000	48,041	44,787	44,949	48,205	49,817	50,504	50,914
Percent of resident population..	Percent...	21.4	19.0	18.2	18.5	18.8	18.9	18.8
Fall enrollment [2].............	1,000	41,778	39,354	40,527	43,898	45,388	45,885	46,286
Percent of population 5-17 years old [3]............	Percent...	87.0	87.9	90.2	91.1	91.1	90.9	90.9
Elementary [3]............	1,000	24,397	23,830	26,253	28,148	28,941	29,228	29,445
Secondary [4]..........	1,000	17,381	15,524	14,274	15,750	16,446	16,657	16,841
Average daily attendance (ADA) ..	1,000	38,411	36,530	37,573	40,792	42,170	42,678	42,970
High school graduates	1,000	2,762	2,424	2,327	2,282	2,352	2,435	2,431
INSTRUCTIONAL STAFF								
Total [5].................	1,000	2,521	2,473	2,685	2,924	3,036	3,116	3,171
Classroom teachers.........	1,000	2,211	2,175	2,362	2,568	2,673	2,745	2,792
Average salaries:								
Instructional staff..........	Dollar	16,715	24,666	32,638	38,339	40,435	41,272	42,459
Classroom teachers.........	Dollar	15,970	23,600	31,367	36,685	38,536	39,454	40,582
REVENUES								
Revenue receipts...........	Mil. dol ..	97,635	141,013	208,656	273,255	303,014	322,501	327,793
Federal.................	Mil. dol ...	9,020	9,533	13,184	18,764	20,202	22,262	22,517
State	Mil. dol ...	47,929	69,107	100,787	129,958	147,855	158,419	163,258
Local	Mil. dol ...	40,686	62,373	94,685	124,533	134,957	141,820	142,018
Percent of total:								
Federal.................	Percent...	9.2	6.8	6.3	6.9	6.7	6.9	6.9
State	Percent...	49.1	49.0	48.3	47.6	48.8	49.1	49.8
Local	Percent...	41.7	44.2	45.4	45.6	44.5	44.0	43.3
EXPENDITURES								
Total	Mil. dol ...	96,105	139,382	209,698	276,584	310,705	327,541	335,243
Current expenditures (day schools)	Mil. dol ...	85,661	127,230	186,583	242,995	269,643	283,283	289,357
Other current expenditures [6]...	Mil. dol ...	1,859	2,109	3,341	5,564	6,195	6,662	7,049
Capital outlay..........	Mil. dol ...	6,504	7,529	16,012	21,646	27,435	29,328	30,326
Interest on school debt	Mil. dol ...	2,081	2,514	3,762	6,379	7,432	8,268	8,511
Percent of total:								
Current expenditures (day schools)	Percent...	89.1	91.3	89.0	87.9	86.8	86.5	86.3
Other current expenditures [6]...	Percent...	1.9	1.5	1.6	2.0	2.0	2.0	2.1
Capital outlay..........	Percent...	6.8	5.4	7.6	7.8	8.8	9.0	9.0
Interest on school debt	Percent...	2.2	1.8	1.8	2.3	2.4	2.5	2.5
In current dollars:								
Revenue receipts per pupil enrolled................	Dollar	2,337	3,583	5,149	6,225	6,676	7,028	7,082
Current expenditures per pupil enrolled................	Dollar	2,050	3,233	4,604	5,535	5,941	6,174	6,251
In constant (1999) dollars: [7]								
Revenue receipts per pupil enrolled................	Dollar	4,954	5,571	6,669	6,808	6,911	7,150	7,082
Current expenditures per pupil enrolled................	Dollar	4,346	5,027	5,963	6,054	6,150	6,281	6,251

[1] Estimated resident population as of July 1 of the previous year. Estimates reflect revisions based on the 1990 Census of Population. [2] Fall enrollment of the previous year. [3] Kindergarten through grade 6. [4] Grades 7 through 12. [5] Full-time equivalent. [6] Current expenses for summer schools, adult education, post-high school vocational education, personnel retraining, etc., when operated by local school districts and not part of regular public elementary and secondary day-school program. [7] Compiled by U.S. Census Bureau. Deflated by the Consumer Price Index, all urban consumers (for school year) supplied by U.S. National Center for Education Statistics.

Source: Except as noted, National Education Association, Washington, DC, Estimates of School Statistics Database (copyright).

No. 263. Public Elementary and Secondary Schools—Conditions and Plans for Repairs: 1999

[In percent. Based on survey and subject to sampling error; see source]

Characteristic	Schools with building features considered less than adequate [1]										Schools with plans for modifying building features in the next 2 years		
	At least one building feature less than adequate	Roofs	Framing, floors, and foundations	Exterior walls, finishes, windows, and doors	Interior finishes, trim	Plumbing	Heating, ventilation and air conditioning	Electric power	Electrical lighting	Life safety features[2]	At least one major repair, renovation or replacement	Major repair or renovation	Replacement
All public schools	**50**	**22**	**14**	**24**	**17**	**25**	**29**	**22**	**17**	**20**	**51**	**41**	**25**
School instructional level:													
Elementary school	49	22	14	23	17	24	28	21	17	19	49	39	23
High school	56	26	16	27	20	28	34	25	19	22	57	48	28
Combined	54	18	15	31	14	25	34	20	20	29	55	37	35
School enrollment size:													
Less than 300	55	24	19	31	20	28	29	23	19	26	45	36	19
300 to 599	50	22	12	21	16	27	32	21	17	21	52	40	26
600 or more	49	22	14	23	18	20	26	22	16	16	53	45	27
Region: [3]													
Northeast	39	16	10	18	14	19	22	14	10	11	49	38	27
Midwest	51	20	15	28	15	25	27	19	15	19	48	39	22
South	51	25	15	22	16	24	28	22	20	22	47	37	23
West	57	27	16	26	25	32	40	32	22	27	62	52	30
Percent minority enrollment:													
5 percent or less	48	21	15	26	14	22	28	18	16	18	45	35	19
6 to 20 percent	49	25	15	23	17	26	29	18	16	22	51	41	28
21 to 50 percent	46	17	12	17	14	23	25	19	15	18	51	40	25
More than 50 percent	59	28	14	29	24	29	34	32	23	24	58	49	30
Percent of students in school eligible for free or reduced-price lunch:													
Less than 20 percent	45	18	14	21	17	23	28	18	14	16	52	41	25
20 to 39 percent	45	21	11	21	14	23	26	20	15	18	44	36	21
40 to 69 percent	53	22	16	25	14	23	29	21	18	22	52	43	25
70 percent or more	63	32	17	30	26	32	35	30	24	27	56	46	30

[1] Based on ratings of fair, poor, and replace by school district respondent. [2] Sprinklers, fire alarms, for example. [3] For composition of regions, see map, inside front cover.

Source: U.S. National Center for Education Statistics, Fast Response Survey System, Condition of America's Public School Facilities, 1999, NCES 2000-032, June 2000.

[**Enrollment in thousands (46,012 represents 46,012,000).** Data reported by schools, rather than school districts]

Enrollment size of school	Number of schools					Enrollment [1]				
	Total	Elementary [2]	Secondary [3]	Combined [4]	Other [5]	Total	Elementary [2]	Secondary [3]	Combined [4]	Other [5]
Total..............	89,508	62,739	21,682	3,120	1,967	46,012	30,013	14,754	1,166	80
PERCENT										
Total..............	100.0	100.0	100.0	100.0	100.0	100.0	100.0	100.0	100.0	100.0
Under 100 students......	9.8	6.2	15.5	33.5	63.6	0.9	0.6	1.0	4.0	21.4
100 to 199 students	9.5	8.7	10.6	15.8	17.7	2.7	2.7	2.2	6.1	20.9
200 to 299 students	11.2	12.2	8.4	9.7	10.2	5.4	6.4	3.0	6.4	20.7
300 to 399 students	13.1	15.3	7.5	7.9	3.2	8.7	11.2	3.7	7.3	9.0
400 to 499 students	13.3	15.9	7.1	6.3	2.6	11.4	14.9	4.5	7.5	9.3
500 to 599 students	11.6	13.8	6.3	6.2	1.2	12.1	15.7	5.0	9.1	5.6
600 to 699 students	8.6	9.8	6.1	4.6	0.2	10.6	13.2	5.7	8.0	0.8
700 to 799 students	6.1	6.7	4.9	3.4	0.2	8.7	10.5	5.2	6.8	0.9
800 to 999 students	7.3	7.0	8.7	5.0	0.5	12.4	13.0	11.1	12.0	3.1
1,000 to 1,499 students ...	6.2	4.0	12.9	4.8	0.6	14.0	9.7	22.5	15.5	5.8
1,500 to 1,999 students ...	2.1	0.5	6.9	1.8	(Z)	6.7	1.6	17.1	8.1	(Z)
2,000 to 2,999 students ...	1.1	0.1	4.4	0.7	0.2	5.1	0.3	14.9	4.4	2.6
3,000 or more students ...	0.2	(Z)	0.8	0.4	(Z)	1.5	(Z)	4.1	4.9	(Z)
Average enrollment......	(X)	(X)	(X)	(X)	(X)	525	478	699	374	121

X Not applicable.   Z Less than .05 percent.   [1] Data for those schools reporting enrollment.   [2] Includes schools beginning with grade 6 or below and with no grade higher than 8.   [3] Includes schools with no grade lower than 7.   [4] Includes schools with both elementary and secondary grades.   [5] Includes special education, alternative, and other schools not classified by grade span.

Source: U.S. National Center for Education Statistics, *Digest of Education Statistics*, annual.

[**In thousands (1,600 represents 1,600,000), except ratios.** As of **fall.** Data are for full-time equivalents. Schools are classified by type of organization, rather than by grade group; elementary includes kindergarten and secondary includes junior high]

Item	Total			Public			Private		
	Total	Elementary	Secondary	Total	Elementary	Secondary	Total	Elementary	Secondary
Number of teachers:									
1960...........	1,600	991	609	1,408	858	550	192	133	59
1970...........	2,292	1,283	1,009	2,059	1,130	929	233	153	80
1975...........	2,453	1,353	1,100	2,198	1,181	1,017	255	172	83
1980...........	2,485	1,401	1,084	2,184	1,189	995	301	212	89
1985...........	2,549	1,483	1,066	2,206	1,237	969	343	246	97
1988...........	2,668	1,604	1,064	2,323	1,353	970	345	251	94
1989...........	2,734	1,662	1,072	2,357	1,387	970	377	275	102
1990...........	2,753	1,683	1,070	2,398	1,429	969	355	254	101
1991...........	2,787	1,722	1,065	2,432	1,468	964	355	254	101
1992...........	2,822	1,752	1,070	2,459	1,492	967	363	260	103
1993...........	2,870	1,775	1,095	2,504	1,513	991	366	262	104
1994...........	2,926	1,791	1,135	2,552	1,525	1,027	374	266	108
1995...........	2,978	1,794	1,184	2,598	1,525	1,073	380	269	111
1996...........	3,054	1,856	1,198	2,667	1,582	1,085	387	274	113
1997...........	3,132	1,889	1,243	2,744	1,614	1,130	388	275	113
1998, prel. [1].....	3,178	1,913	1,266	2,787	1,636	1,152	391	277	114
1999, proj. [1].....	3,095	1,859	1,236	2,700	1,580	1,120	395	279	116
Pupil-teacher ratio:									
1960...........	26.4	29.4	21.4	25.8	28.4	21.7	30.7	36.1	18.6
1970...........	22.4	24.6	19.5	22.3	24.3	19.8	23.0	26.5	16.4
1975...........	20.3	21.7	18.6	20.4	21.7	18.8	19.6	21.5	15.7
1980...........	18.6	20.1	16.6	18.7	20.4	16.8	17.7	18.8	15.0
1985...........	17.6	19.1	15.6	17.9	19.5	15.8	16.2	17.1	14.0
1988...........	17.0	18.6	14.7	17.3	19.0	14.9	15.2	16.1	12.8
1989...........	16.8	18.4	14.3	17.2	19.0	14.6	14.2	15.1	11.7
1990...........	16.9	18.5	14.3	17.2	18.9	14.6	14.7	16.1	11.3
1991...........	17.0	18.4	14.6	17.3	18.8	15.0	14.7	16.0	11.1
1992...........	17.1	18.4	14.8	17.4	18.8	15.2	14.6	16.2	11.3
1993...........	17.1	18.5	14.7	17.4	18.9	15.1	14.8	16.3	11.5
1994...........	17.1	18.6	14.4	17.3	19.0	14.8	14.9	16.4	11.4
1995...........	17.0	18.9	14.0	17.3	19.3	14.4	14.9	16.6	10.8
1996...........	16.8	18.4	14.3	17.1	18.8	14.6	14.9	16.4	11.5
1997...........	16.6	18.3	14.0	16.8	18.6	14.2	15.1	16.6	11.6
1998, prel.	16.6	18.3	14.0	16.8	18.6	14.2	15.2	16.6	11.6
1999, proj........	17.2	19.0	14.5	17.5	19.4	14.8	15.1	16.6	11.6

[1] See revised totals in Table 241; revised data not available by level.

Source: U.S. National Center for Education Statistics, *Digest of Education Statistics*, annual.

No. 266. Public Elementary and Secondary School Enrollment by State: 1980 to 1998

[In thousands (27,647 represents 27,647,000), except rate. As of fall. Includes unclassified students]

State	Enrollment K through grade 8 [1]				Grades 9 through 12				Enrollment rate [2]			
	1980	1990	1997	1998, prel.	1980	1990	1997	1998, prel.	1980	1990	1997	1998, prel.
United States ...	27,647	29,878	33,073	33,344	13,231	11,338	13,054	13,191	86.2	91.3	91.4	91.4
Alabama	528	527	541	542	231	195	208	206	87.6	93.3	95.0	94.8
Alaska	60	85	96	97	26	29	36	38	94.0	97.4	94.5	94.7
Arizona	357	479	596	623	157	161	218	226	88.9	93.3	92.7	94.8
Arkansas	310	314	322	319	138	123	134	133	90.3	95.9	94.5	94.4
California	2,730	3,615	4,196	4,270	1,347	1,336	1,608	1,656	87.1	92.8	92.4	93.4
Colorado	374	420	494	501	172	154	193	198	92.2	94.6	92.3	91.8
Connecticut	364	347	394	399	168	122	141	145	83.3	90.2	93.1	94.0
Delaware	62	73	79	80	37	27	33	33	79.5	87.4	86.8	87.2
District of Columbia	71	61	60	57	29	19	17	15	91.8	100.9	104.7	99.3
Florida	1,042	1,370	1,680	1,704	468	492	614	634	84.4	92.6	91.0	90.4
Georgia	742	849	1,011	1,029	327	303	365	372	86.8	93.6	96.2	96.3
Hawaii	110	123	136	135	55	49	53	53	83.4	87.6	88.5	87.8
Idaho	144	160	169	169	59	61	76	76	95.4	96.9	94.3	94.2
Illinois	1,335	1,310	1,438	1,452	649	512	560	560	82.6	86.9	87.6	87.6
Indiana	708	676	693	697	347	279	294	291	88.0	90.4	89.6	89.3
Iowa	351	345	338	337	183	139	163	162	88.4	92.1	92.4	92.3
Kansas	283	320	328	327	133	117	141	145	88.7	92.6	91.5	91.7
Kentucky	464	459	474	465	206	177	195	191	83.7	90.5	93.0	90.5
Louisiana	544	586	564	558	234	199	213	210	80.2	88.2	87.1	87.5
Maine	153	155	153	151	70	60	59	60	91.6	96.5	93.8	93.8
Maryland	493	527	602	607	258	188	229	235	83.9	89.1	89.2	89.2
Massachusetts	676	604	696	705	346	230	253	258	88.6	88.8	90.4	90.4
Michigan	1,227	1,145	1,236	1,245	570	440	467	475	86.9	90.3	90.3	90.8
Minnesota	482	546	588	586	272	211	266	270	87.2	91.2	91.1	90.8
Mississippi	330	372	365	365	147	131	140	137	79.6	91.3	90.7	90.6
Missouri	567	588	650	651	277	228	261	262	83.8	86.5	87.6	87.5
Montana	106	111	112	110	50	42	50	50	92.9	93.8	93.2	93.2
Nebraska	189	198	202	200	91	76	91	91	86.6	88.7	88.5	88.0
Nevada	101	150	219	229	49	51	78	82	93.4	98.7	94.9	94.0
New Hampshire	112	126	145	147	55	46	56	58	85.3	89.1	90.7	90.8
New Jersey	820	784	921	936	426	306	329	333	81.5	86.1	87.4	87.9
New Mexico	186	208	236	232	85	94	96	96	89.5	94.3	90.1	88.6
New York	1,838	1,828	2,011	2,028	1,033	770	851	849	80.8	86.6	88.3	88.6
North Carolina	786	783	906	921	343	304	330	334	90.1	94.8	91.1	90.1
North Dakota	77	85	80	77	40	33	38	38	85.9	92.8	95.2	93.6
Ohio	1,312	1,258	1,299	1,301	645	514	548	541	84.8	88.0	87.8	87.7
Oklahoma	399	425	445	448	179	154	179	181	92.9	95.1	95.5	96.5
Oregon	319	340	381	380	145	132	160	163	88.5	90.7	90.0	89.2
Pennsylvania	1,231	1,172	1,266	1,267	678	496	549	549	80.4	83.6	85.0	84.9
Rhode Island	98	102	112	112	51	37	42	42	80.1	87.3	88.0	88.0
South Carolina	426	452	473	478	193	170	187	187	88.1	94.0	93.9	94.1
South Dakota	86	95	98	91	42	34	45	42	87.4	89.7	93.9	87.8
Tennessee	602	598	653	665	252	226	240	241	87.8	93.5	92.5	93.4
Texas	2,049	2,511	2,832	2,868	851	872	1,059	1,077	92.4	98.4	98.2	98.3
Utah	250	325	329	329	93	122	154	153	98.2	97.7	97.3	96.7
Vermont	66	71	74	73	29	25	32	32	87.9	93.9	96.6	96.8
Virginia	703	728	807	815	307	270	304	309	90.7	94.2	93.7	93.9
Washington	515	613	694	696	242	227	297	302	91.7	94.0	92.6	91.9
West Virginia	270	224	207	206	113	98	94	92	92.6	95.7	96.8	97.5
Wisconsin	528	566	604	601	303	232	278	279	82.1	86.0	86.9	86.4
Wyoming	70	71	66	64	28	27	32	31	97.3	97.3	96.6	96.6

[1] Data include a small number of prekindergarten students. [2] Percent of persons 5-17 years old. Based on enumerated resident population as of April 1, 1980, and 1990, and estimated resident population as of July 1 for other years. Data not adjusted for revisions based on the 1990 Census of Population.

Source: U.S. National Center for Education Statistics, *Digest of Education Statistics,* annual.

Education 167

No. 267. Public Elementary and Secondary School Enrollment by Grade: 1980 to 1998

[In thousands (40,877 represents 40,877,000). As of fall of year. Kindergarten includes nursery schools]

Grade	1980	1985	1990	1991	1992	1993	1994	1995	1996	1997	1998, prel.
Pupils enrolled	40,877	39,422	41,217	42,047	42,823	43,465	44,111	44,840	45,611	46,127	46,535
Kindergarten and grades 1 to 8 .	27,647	27,034	29,878	30,506	31,088	31,504	31,898	32,341	32,764	33,073	33,344
Kindergarten	2,689	3,192	3,610	3,686	3,817	3,922	4,047	4,173	4,202	4,198	4,171
First	2,894	3,239	3,499	3,556	3,542	3,529	3,593	3,671	3,770	3,755	3,727
Second	2,800	2,941	3,327	3,360	3,431	3,429	3,440	3,507	3,600	3,689	3,682
Third	2,893	2,895	3,297	3,334	3,361	3,437	3,439	3,445	3,524	3,597	3,696
Fourth	3,107	2,771	3,248	3,315	3,342	3,361	3,426	3,431	3,454	3,507	3,592
Fifth	3,130	2,776	3,197	3,268	3,325	3,350	3,372	3,438	3,453	3,458	3,520
Sixth	3,038	2,789	3,110	3,239	3,303	3,356	3,381	3,395	3,494	3,492	3,497
Seventh	3,085	2,938	3,067	3,181	3,299	3,355	3,404	3,422	3,464	3,520	3,530
Eighth	3,086	2,982	2,979	3,020	3,129	3,249	3,302	3,356	3,403	3,415	3,480
Unclassified [1]	924	511	543	545	539	515	494	502	401	442	450
Grades 9 to 12	13,231	12,388	11,338	11,541	11,735	11,961	12,213	12,500	12,847	13,054	13,191
Ninth	3,377	3,439	3,169	3,313	3,352	3,487	3,604	3,704	3,801	3,819	3,856
Tenth	3,368	3,230	2,896	2,915	3,027	3,050	3,131	3,237	3,323	3,376	3,382
Eleventh	3,195	2,866	2,612	2,645	2,656	2,751	2,748	2,826	2,930	2,972	3,018
Twelfth	2,925	2,550	2,381	2,392	2,431	2,424	2,488	2,487	2,586	2,673	2,724
Unclassified [1]	366	303	282	275	269	248	242	245	206	214	211

[1] Includes ungraded and special education.

Source: U.S. National Center for Education Statistics, *Digest of Education Statistics*, annual.

No. 268. Public Elementary and Secondary School Teachers by Selected Characteristics: 1993-94

[For school year. (280 represents 280,000) Based on survey and subject to sampling error; for details, see source. Excludes prekindergarten teachers. See Table 283 for similar data on private school teachers]

Characteristic	Unit	Age				Sex		Race/ethnicity		
		Under 30 yrs. old	30 to 39 yrs. old	40 to 49 yrs. old	Over 50 yrs. old	Male	Fe-male	White [1]	Black [1]	His-panic
Total teachers [2]	1,000 ..	280	573	1,070	637	694	1,067	2,217	188	109
Highest degree held:										
Bachelor's	Percent .	83.9	59.4	46.3	40.9	46.2	54.1	51.8	48.4	62.8
Master's	Percent .	14.5	36.6	47.0	50.4	45.7	40.6	42.5	44.6	29.8
Education specialist	Percent .	1.0	3.0	5.4	6.1	5.1	4.4	4.4	5.4	4.6
Doctorate	Percent .	0.1	0.3	0.7	1.4	1.3	0.5	0.7	0.9	1.4
Full-time teaching experience:										
Less than 3 years	Percent .	47.8	10.5	4.3	1.3	8.9	10.0	9.4	8.5	16.7
3 to 9 years	Percent .	52.2	48.7	16.9	7.3	21.6	26.9	25.5	20.8	32.1
10 to 20 years	Percent .	(X)	40.8	47.5	24.2	29.9	37.0	35.1	35.5	34.1
20 years or more	Percent .	(X)	(X)	31.3	67.1	39.6	26.1	30.0	35.2	17.1
Full-time teachers	1,000 ..	259	518	974	590	643	1,698	2,012	182	103
Earned income	Dol.	27,151	31,596	38,106	42,243	41,031	34,781	36,576	36,200	35,197
Salary	Dol.	24,737	29,270	35,751	39,931	36,182	33,384	34,221	33,889	32,996
Supplemental contract during school year:										
Teachers receiving	1,000 ..	114	205	329	168	349	467	723	49	32
Salary	Dol.	1,777	2,163	2,107	2,109	2,923	1,442	2,067	2,325	1,930
Supplemental contract during summer:										
Teachers receiving	1,000 ..	52	102	161	86	147	254	328	41	24
Salary	Dol.	1,819	1,942	2,053	2,404	2,530	1,803	2,015	2,221	2,477
Teachers with nonschool employment:										
Teaching/tutoring	1,000 ..	12	25	50	32	37	81	100	11	6
Education related	1,000 ..	8	20	34	18	39	41	69	5	4
Not education related	1,000 ..	28	50	101	59	124	113	208	16	7

X Not applicable.   [1] Non-Hispanic.   [2] Includes teachers with no degrees and associates degrees, not shown separately.

Source: U.S. National Center for Education Statistics, *Digest of Education Statistics*, 1997; and unpublished data.

No. 269. Newly Hired Teachers by Selected Characteristics: 1988 to 1994

[**In percent.** Based on sample and subject to sampling error; see source for details]

Characteristic	Public schools			Private schools		
	1988	1991	1994	1988	1991	1994
Total newly hired teachers	100.0	100.0	100.0	100.0	100.0	100.0
First-time teachers	30.6	41.7	45.8	25.2	34.0	42.4
Transfers.....................	36.6	34.3	31.4	38.1	36.1	34.3
Within state and sector................	20.8	21.6	20.2	19.0	18.1	14.6
Across state.....................	8.3	7.1	7.1	8.3	7.0	11.5
Across sector.....................	7.5	5.6	4.1	10.9	11.0	8.1
Reentrants	32.8	24.0	22.9	36.7	30.0	23.3
Main previous year activity:						
First-time teachers.....................	100.0	100.0	100.0	100.0	100.0	100.0
Work in education (nonteaching).........	5.7	5.2	10.7	4.8	7.5	13.6
Work outside education...............	11.0	10.0	11.6	24.5	20.6	19.9
College	66.5	58.4	56.7	51.8	48.7	43.1
Homemaking and childrearing	3.6	4.4	2.1	7.7	5.8	5.8
Other.....................	13.3	22.0	18.9	11.3	17.4	17.6
Substitute teaching................	(NA)	18.0	17.2	(NA)	12.0	15.2
Reentrants.....................	100.0	100.0	100.0	100.0	100.0	100.0
Work in education (nonteaching).........	10.3	19.1	15.0	8.9	11.7	19.9
Work outside education...............	17.4	17.9	19.2	21.2	26.1	26.0
College	18.0	10.4	18.1	20.0	5.6	11.9
Homemaking and childrearing	27.8	19.3	14.6	28.6	23.1	21.4
Other.....................	26.5	33.3	33.1	21.3	33.6	20.9
Substitute teaching................	(NA)	23.8	29.6	(NA)	18.7	18.1

NA Not available.

Source: U.S. National Center for Education Statistics, *Condition of Education, 1996.*

No. 270. Public Elementary and Secondary Schools—Number and Average Salary of Classroom Teachers, 1970 to 1999, and by State, 1999

[Estimates for school year ending in **June of year shown (2,008 represents 2,008,000).** Schools classified by type of organization rather than by grade-group; elementary includes kindergarten]

Year and state	Teachers [1] (1,000)			Avg. salary ($1,000)			Year and state	Teachers [1] (1,000)			Avg. salary ($1,000)		
	Total	Elementary	Secondary	All teachers	Elementary	Secondary		Total	Elementary	Secondary	All teachers	Elementary	Secondary
1970	2,008	1,109	899	8.6	8.4	8.9	LA........	48.7	34.3	14.5	32.5	32.5	32.5
1980	2,211	1,206	1,005	16.0	15.6	16.5	ME........	15.1	10.5	4.6	34.9	34.6	35.7
1985	2,175	1,212	963	23.6	23.2	24.2	MD........	49.2	27.8	21.4	42.5	41.6	43.6
1988	2,282	1,308	974	28.0	27.5	28.8	MA........	65.0	27.9	37.0	45.1	44.9	44.9
1989	2,324	1,354	970	29.6	29.0	30.2	MI	91.2	68.2	23.0	48.2	48.2	48.2
1990	2,362	1,390	972	31.4	30.8	32.0	MN........	54.0	27.3	26.7	39.5	39.8	39.1
1991	2,409	1,436	974	33.1	32.5	33.9	MS........	29.9	16.3	13.6	29.5	29.1	30.1
1992	2,429	1,466	963	34.1	33.5	34.8	MO........	62.3	31.9	30.4	34.7	34.2	35.3
1993	2,466	1,496	970	35.0	34.4	35.9	MT........	10.2	7.0	3.3	31.4	31.0	32.2
1994	2,512	1,517	995	35.7	35.2	36.4	NE........	20.1	11.9	8.2	32.9	32.9	32.9
1995	2,568	1,535	1,033	36.7	36.2	37.5	NV........	16.7	9.6	7.0	38.9	38.6	39.3
1996	2,607	1,562	1,045	37.7	37.3	38.4	NH........	13.3	9.2	4.0	37.4	37.4	37.4
1997	2,673	1,608	1,065	38.5	38.2	39.1	NJ........	93.1	58.6	34.4	51.2	50.1	53.1
1998	2,745	1,652	1,093	39.5	39.1	40.0	NM........	19.9	14.2	5.7	32.4	32.2	32.8
1999, U.S..	**2,792**	**1,679**	**1,114**	**40.6**	**40.3**	**41.2**	NY........	201.2	100.6	100.6	49.4	48.8	50.7
AL........	46.2	27.9	18.3	35.8	35.8	35.8	NC........	78.6	49.2	29.4	36.1	35.9	36.4
AK........	7.7	4.8	2.9	46.8	46.8	46.8	ND........	8.0	5.1	2.9	29.0	29.2	28.6
AZ........	43.2	33.3	9.9	35.0	35.0	35.0	OH........	111.5	74.4	37.0	40.6	40.2	41.3
AR........	28.1	13.8	14.3	32.4	31.4	33.2	OK........	40.6	21.0	19.6	31.1	31.0	31.3
CA........	260.5	192.7	67.8	45.4	44.8	47.3	OR........	29.3	19.9	9.4	42.8	42.5	42.8
CO........	38.1	19.2	18.9	38.0	37.9	38.2	PA........	111.1	57.6	53.4	48.5	48.2	48.8
CT........	39.2	28.0	11.2	51.6	52.4	54.6	RI........	11.9	6.9	5.0	45.7	45.7	45.7
DE........	7.1	3.6	3.5	43.2	43.0	43.3	SC........	42.2	29.4	12.8	34.5	34.2	35.1
DC........	5.5	3.3	2.2	47.2	47.6	46.4	SD........	9.1	6.3	2.8	28.6	28.6	28.4
FL........	129.7	66.2	63.5	35.9	35.9	35.9	TN........	53.6	38.9	14.7	36.5	36.1	37.5
GA........	88.7	52.3	36.4	39.7	39.1	40.5	TX........	261.3	131.9	129.3	35.0	34.4	35.7
HI........	11.0	6.3	4.7	40.4	39.9	39.9	UT........	21.6	11.1	10.5	33.0	33.0	32.9
ID........	13.4	6.8	6.6	34.1	34.2	34.0	VT........	8.1	4.2	3.9	36.8	37.5	36.1
IL........	122.1	85.9	36.2	45.6	43.7	50.1	VA........	79.8	49.1	30.7	37.5	36.3	39.4
IN........	57.8	31.0	26.8	41.2	41.3	41.0	WA........	49.5	28.1	21.4	38.7	38.7	38.7
IA........	33.4	15.5	17.9	34.9	34.1	35.6	WV........	20.6	14.0	6.6	34.2	34.0	34.8
KS........	31.9	16.4	15.5	37.4	37.4	37.4	WI........	56.6	38.6	18.0	40.7	40.4	44.2
KY........	39.0	27.3	11.7	35.5	35.1	36.6	WY........	6.6	3.2	3.5	33.5	33.7	33.3

[1] Full-time equivalent.

Source: National Education Association, Washington, DC, Estimates of School Statistics Database (copyright).

Education 169

No. 271. Average Salary and Wages Paid in Public School Systems: 1980 to 1999

[**In dollars.** For school year ending in year shown. Data reported by a stratified sample of school systems enrolling 300 or more pupils. Data represent unweighted means of average salaries paid school personnel reported by each school system]

Position	1980	1985	1990	1994	1995	1996	1997	1998	1999
ANNUAL SALARY									
Central office administrators:									
Superintendent (contract salary) . . .	39,344	56,954	75,425	87,717	90,198	94,229	98,106	101,519	106,122
Deputy/assoc. superintendent	37,440	52,877	69,623	78,672	81,266	84,077	88,564	90,226	92,936
Assistant superintendent	33,452	48,003	62,698	72,701	75,236	77,007	80,176	82,339	86,005
Administrators for—									
Finance and business	27,147	40,344	52,354	59,997	61,323	63,840	65,797	67,724	71,387
Instructional services	29,790	43,452	56,359	64,676	66,767	68,463	70,788	73,058	75,680
Public relations/information	24,021	35,287	44,926	52,366	53,263	53,860	55,928	57,224	59,214
Staff personnel services	29,623	44,182	56,344	63,690	65,819	67,760	70,088	71,073	73,850
Subject area supervisors	23,974	34,422	45,929	52,837	54,534	56,145	58,776	60,359	61,083
School building administrators:									
Principals:									
Elementary.	25,165	36,452	48,431	56,906	58,589	60,922	62,903	64,653	67,348
Junior high/middle	27,625	39,650	52,163	60,651	62,311	64,452	66,859	68,740	71,499
Senior high.	29,207	42,094	55,722	64,993	66,596	69,277	72,410	74,380	76,768
Assistant principals:									
Elementary.	20,708	30,496	40,916	47,057	48,491	50,537	52,284	53,206	54,306
Junior high/middle	23,507	33,793	44,570	51,518	52,942	54,355	56,451	57,768	59,238
Senior high.	24,816	35,491	46,486	54,170	55,556	57,555	59,739	60,999	62,691
Classroom teachers.	15,913	23,587	31,278	36,531	37,264	38,706	39,580	40,133	41,351
Auxiliary professional personnel:									
Counselors	18,847	27,593	35,979	41,355	42,486	44,073	45,365	46,162	47,287
Librarians	16,764	24,981	33,469	39,319	40,418	41,761	43,315	44,310	45,680
School nurses	13,788	19,944	26,090	30,630	31,066	32,786	33,720	34,619	35,520
Secretarial/clerical personnel:									
Central office:									
Secretaries.	10,331	15,343	20,238	23,495	23,935	24,809	25,709	26,316	27,540
Accounting/payroll clerks.	10,479	15,421	20,088	23,275	24,042	25,009	25,881	26,249	27,630
Typists/data entry clerks	8,359	12,481	16,125	18,296	18,674	19,447	20,726	21,633	22,474
School building level:									
Secretaries.	8,348	12,504	16,184	18,692	19,170	20,076	20,709	21,215	21,831
Library clerks	6,778	9,911	12,152	13,809	14,381	14,791	15,349	15,742	16,033
HOURLY WAGE RATE									
Other support personnel:									
Teacher aides:									
Instructional	4.06	5.89	7.43	8.50	8.77	9.04	9.25	9.46	9.80
Noninstructional	3.89	5.60	7.08	8.14	8.29	8.52	8.88	8.82	9.31
Custodians	4.88	6.90	8.54	9.76	10.05	10.35	10.65	10.79	11.22
Cafeteria workers	3.78	5.42	6.77	7.72	7.89	8.15	8.30	8.56	8.82
Bus drivers	5.21	7.27	9.21	10.35	10.69	11.04	11.50	11.55	12.04

Source: Educational Research Service, Arlington, VA, *National Survey of Salaries and Wages in Public Schools,* annual, Vols. 2 and 3. (All rights reserved. Copyright.)

No. 272. Public School Employment: 1982 and 1996

[**In thousands (3,082 represents 3,082,000).** Covers full-time employment. Excludes Hawaii. 1982 also excludes District of Columbia and New Jersey. 1982 based on sample survey of school districts with 250 or more students. 1996 based on sample survey of school districts with 100 or more employees; see source for sampling variability]

Occupation	1982					1996				
	Total	Male	Female	White [1]	Black [1]	Total	Male	Female	White [1]	Black [1]
All occupations	3,082	1,063	2,019	2,498	432	3,718	1,013	2,705	2,915	506
Officials, administrators	41	31	10	36	3	47	27	19	39	5
Principals and assistant										
principals.	90	72	19	76	11	101	55	45	79	15
Classroom teachers [2]	1,680	534	1,146	1,435	186	2,051	522	1,529	1,735	198
Elementary schools	798	129	669	667	98	1,024	137	887	854	101
Secondary schools	706	363	343	619	67	755	324	431	651	69
Other professional staff	235	91	144	193	35	263	60	203	219	30
Teachers aides [3].	215	14	200	146	45	365	38	327	238	78
Clerical, secretarial staff.	210	4	206	177	19	258	6	252	200	29
Service workers [4]	611	316	295	434	132	633	304	330	407	151

[1] Excludes individuals of Hispanic origin. [2] Includes other classroom teachers, not shown separately. [3] Includes technicians. [4] Includes craftworkers and laborers.

Source: U.S. Equal Employment Opportunity Commission, *Elementary-Secondary Staff Information (EEO-5),* biennial.

No. 273. Public Elementary and Secondary School Price Indexes: 1975 to 1998

[**1983=100**. For years ending **June 30**. Reflects prices paid by public elementary-secondary schools. For explanation of average annual percent change, see Guide to Tabular Presentation]

Year	Personnel compensation					Contracted services, supplies and equipment						
	Index, total	Total	Professional salaries	Nonprofessional salaries	Fringe benefits	Total	Services	Supplies and materials	Equipment replacement	Library materials and textbooks	Utilities	Fixed costs
1975 ..	52.7	53.4	56.0	55.6	40.9	50.4	55.7	58.0	53.7	53.8	34.5	45.2
1980 ..	76.6	75.9	76.7	77.8	71.0	79.2	77.4	85.9	79.6	82.1	71.1	77.9
1984 ..	105.1	106.0	105.7	104.5	108.3	101.7	105.6	99.6	103.4	107.8	94.3	105.4
1985 ..	112.1	113.7	113.4	111.3	117.1	106.0	112.4	103.2	107.2	111.0	96.1	110.8
1986 ..	118.5	121.1	121.4	117.6	123.3	108.3	117.4	103.0	109.3	120.8	93.7	116.2
1987 ..	123.3	127.4	128.4	121.9	128.8	107.5	123.7	101.5	112.9	126.5	75.3	122.7
1988 ..	129.8	134.5	135.5	127.5	137.0	111.7	126.1	105.9	113.4	140.0	78.1	128.4
1989 ..	136.3	141.6	142.2	133.3	147.0	116.1	131.8	112.0	116.0	149.4	75.1	134.6
1990 ..	144.5	150.0	150.1	139.4	159.3	123.5	137.7	119.2	121.2	171.7	82.1	140.3
1991 ..	152.3	158.3	158.1	146.5	169.8	129.6	142.5	122.7	125.7	189.4	92.6	144.9
1992 ..	158.5	165.5	165.9	152.4	175.8	131.9	148.0	122.5	128.5	199.0	90.8	148.9
1993 ..	162.2	169.6	169.3	155.1	184.5	133.9	151.5	121.9	131.8	205.6	90.4	153.8
1994 ..	167.1	175.2	175.1	159.3	190.2	136.5	154.0	122.7	135.4	218.4	90.6	158.8
1995 ..	170.9	179.2	178.9	163.7	194.9	139.3	157.2	124.4	138.7	230.7	89.7	163.9
1996 ..	177.3	185.6	185.7	169.2	200.3	145.9	161.8	138.7	143.2	227.9	91.0	169.1
1997 ..	181.7	190.2	190.2	174.5	204.2	149.4	165.2	137.7	145.2	238.0	100.1	172.9
1998 ..	184.5	193.3	193.3	177.9	207.6	150.8	168.0	137.7	144.2	245.3	98.1	177.0

Source: Research Associates of Washington, Arlington, VA, *Inflation Measures for Schools, Colleges, and Libraries*, annual (copyright).

No. 274. Finances of Public Elementary and Secondary School Systems by Enrollment-Size Group: 1996-97

[**In millions of dollars** (307,471 represents $307,471,000,000), **except as indicated**. Based on the 1997 Census of Governments. For details, see source. See also Appendix III]

Item	All school systems	School systems with enrollment of—						
		50,000 or more	25,000 to 49,999	15,000 to 24,999	7,500 to 14,999	5,000 to 7,499	3,000 to 4,999	Under 3,000
Fall enrollment (1,000)	45,611	8,895	5,205	4,248	6,912	4,212	5,394	10,746
General revenue	307,471	59,243	32,993	26,316	45,464	28,956	37,009	77,489
From Federal sources.	19,737	4,862	2,215	1,593	2,509	1,470	1,880	5,207
Through state	18,078	4,625	2,047	1,484	2,318	1,388	1,719	4,497
Compensatory programs	5,152	1,394	544	388	607	356	444	1,420
Handicapped programs	2,113	448	245	185	321	206	254	453
Child nutrition programs	5,649	1,524	710	514	775	450	563	1,113
Direct.	1,659	237	168	110	191	82	161	711
From state sources [1]	149,946	28,232	16,892	14,644	22,783	13,369	16,650	37,375
General formula assistance	106,557	18,313	11,707	10,781	16,420	9,725	12,260	27,352
Handicapped programs	8,038	1,638	974	747	1,165	665	782	2,066
From local sources.	137,788	26,149	13,887	10,079	20,171	14,117	18,479	34,906
Taxes	93,394	13,785	9,579	6,512	14,183	10,388	13,447	25,501
Contributions from parent gov't	22,952	8,977	2,034	1,774	2,955	1,706	2,439	3,066
From other local governments.	3,220	650	276	222	246	227	410	1,189
Current charges	8,164	1,177	867	713	1,252	782	1,013	2,359
School lunch	4,494	618	474	417	739	465	621	1,161
Other	10,058	1,560	1,130	857	1,535	1,014	1,170	2,791
General expenditure	311,725	59,125	33,251	26,209	45,716	29,061	37,699	80,664
Current spending	271,669	52,535	28,780	22,856	39,865	25,479	32,676	69,477
By function:								
Instruction	165,462	32,298	17,277	14,016	24,515	15,749	20,202	41,405
Support services	90,624	16,914	9,688	7,445	13,046	8,392	10,727	24,411
Other current spending.	15,583	3,324	1,815	1,395	2,304	1,337	1,747	3,661
By object:								
Total salaries and wages	175,782	34,170	19,111	15,158	26,131	16,703	21,248	43,261
Total employee benefits	43,547	8,800	4,355	3,486	6,362	3,930	4,952	11,662
Other	52,340	9,566	5,314	4,212	7,372	4,846	6,475	14,555
Capital outlay	32,434	5,207	3,746	2,733	4,702	2,825	4,012	9,209
Interest on debt	6,573	1,311	703	581	971	622	881	1,503
Payments to other governments	1,050	72	22	39	178	135	130	475
Debt outstanding.	125,667	24,918	13,419	10,786	18,789	12,031	17,168	28,555
Long-term.	123,145	24,857	13,271	10,659	18,389	11,782	16,763	27,424
Short-term	2,523	60	149	127	400	249	406	1,131
Long-term debt issued	22,577	4,438	2,400	1,635	3,434	1,936	3,381	5,352
Long-term debt retired	10,270	2,034	1,024	749	1,519	941	1,436	2,566

[1] Includes other sources, not shown separately.

Source: U.S. Census Bureau, *1997 Census of Governments, Public Education Finances,* GC 97(4)-1; Internet site <http://www.census.gov/govs/www/school.html> (accessed 23 June 2000).

Education 171

No. 275. Public Elementary and Secondary Estimated Finances, 1980 to 1999, and by State, 1999

[In millions of dollars (101,724 represents $101,724,000,000), except as noted. For school years ending in June of year shown]

Year and state	Receipts						Expenditures				
	Revenue receipts					Non-revenue receipts[1]	Current expenditures			Average per pupil in ADA[4]	
		Source							Elementary and secondary day schools		
	Total	Total	Federal	State	Local		Total[2]	Per capita[3] (dol.)		Amount (dol.)	Rank
1980	101,724	97,635	9,020	47,929	40,686	4,089	96,105	427	85,661	2,230	(X)
1985	146,976	141,013	9,533	69,107	62,373	5,963	139,382	591	127,230	3,483	(X)
1990	218,126	208,656	13,184	100,787	94,685	9,469	209,698	850	186,583	4,966	(X)
1993	263,460	247,912	17,381	115,924	114,606	15,548	248,898	976	219,297	5,538	(X)
1994	275,121	259,587	18,434	119,443	121,710	15,534	262,485	1,018	230,773	5,749	(X)
1995	288,501	273,255	18,764	129,958	124,533	15,246	276,584	1,062	242,995	5,957	(X)
1996	305,749	286,521	19,324	137,488	129,709	19,228	292,489	1,113	254,505	6,139	(X)
1997	323,116	303,014	20,202	147,855	134,957	20,102	310,705	1,171	269,643	6,394	(X)
1998	343,347	322,501	22,262	158,419	141,820	20,846	327,541	1,223	283,283	6,638	(X)
1999, total . .	348,548	327,793	22,517	163,258	142,018	20,756	335,243	1,240	289,357	6,734	(X)
Alabama.	3,979	3,901	354	2,557	990	78	4,119	947	3,392	4,818	48
Alaska	1,322	1,180	148	750	282	142	1,298	2,110	1,197	10,611	1
Arizona.	4,849	4,376	332	2,127	1,918	472	4,799	1,028	3,784	4,918	47
Arkansas	2,436	2,367	192	1,443	732	69	2,752	1,084	2,430	5,545	42
California	37,573	36,474	3,244	21,785	11,446	1,098	36,037	1,103	30,976	5,462	43
Colorado.	4,770	4,216	229	1,871	2,116	554	4,476	1,128	3,694	5,697	38
Connecticut. . . .	5,534	5,529	236	2,344	2,950	5	5,534	1,691	5,011	9,589	4
Delaware	1,037	1,013	74	669	269	24	994	1,335	911	8,658	5
District of Columbia	488	443	67	-	375	45	595	1,141	561	7,983	8
Florida	16,732	15,926	1,211	7,690	7,025	806	16,141	1,083	13,028	6,203	33
Georgia	9,715	8,817	584	4,549	3,684	897	9,860	1,291	8,223	6,296	31
Hawaii	1,410	1,317	112	1,173	32	93	1,395	1,172	1,167	6,694	23
Idaho	1,422	1,365	94	856	415	57	1,413	1,148	1,235	5,366	45
Illinois	15,239	13,587	891	3,630	9,066	1,652	14,110	1,169	11,752	6,404	29
Indiana.	8,401	8,065	363	4,110	3,591	336	7,912	1,339	6,564	7,207	19
Iowa	3,640	3,400	135	1,812	1,461	232	3,274	1,144	2,877	6,100	35
Kansas.	3,405	3,166	185	1,931	1,050	239	3,077	1,166	2,765	6,588	26
Kentucky	4,215	4,182	372	2,622	1,188	33	4,030	1,024	3,790	6,662	24
Louisiana	5,082	4,577	522	2,334	1,721	505	4,496	1,030	4,056	5,757	37
Maine.	1,615	1,565	99	734	733	50	1,615	1,295	1,500	7,584	14
Maryland	6,884	6,705	343	2,747	3,614	180	6,790	1,324	5,941	7,553	15
Massachusetts. .	7,529	7,531	387	2,717	4,427	-1	7,312	1,190	6,929	7,854	10
Michigan.	16,882	15,077	998	11,585	2,494	1,805	14,036	1,429	12,704	8,139	7
Minnesota.	7,609	6,618	295	3,718	2,606	991	7,485	1,584	5,949	7,424	16
Mississippi	2,942	2,474	341	1,376	758	468	2,523	917	2,199	4,658	50
Missouri	6,396	5,906	360	2,333	3,213	490	5,495	1,011	4,666	5,614	39
Montana.	1,086	1,056	108	495	453	30	1,065	1,211	952	6,704	22
Nebraska	1,719	1,705	83	676	946	14	1,797	1,082	1,637	6,404	29
Nevada	2,399	2,013	89	688	1,236	386	2,311	1,325	1,692	6,182	34
New Hampshire .	1,576	1,483	54	122	1,306	93	1,474	1,243	1,280	6,839	20
New Jersey. . . .	12,663	12,568	402	4,772	7,394	95	12,671	1,565	12,040	10,420	2
New Mexico . . .	2,137	2,079	274	1,523	282	58	2,036	1,174	1,606	5,429	44
New York	29,885	27,731	1,741	11,122	14,868	2,154	28,638	1,577	25,149	9,786	3
North Carolina . .	8,546	8,050	615	5,570	1,865	496	8,265	1,095	7,191	6,272	32
North Dakota. . .	714	683	79	278	326	31	578	907	527	4,704	49
Ohio	14,932	13,732	796	5,987	6,949	1,200	13,660	1,216	11,463	6,816	21
Oklahoma.	3,778	3,591	319	2,198	1,074	188	3,515	1,053	3,351	5,593	40
Oregon.	4,162	3,818	256	2,426	1,135	344	4,138	1,261	3,604	7,592	13
Pennsylvania. . .	15,344	15,329	851	6,303	8,175	14	13,713	1,143	12,992	7,716	11
Rhode Island. . .	1,268	1,268	71	526	672	-	1,208	1,223	1,169	8,239	6
South Carolina. .	4,917	4,339	351	2,229	1,759	578	4,509	1,174	3,746	6,005	36
South Dakota . .	839	816	80	301	435	23	787	1,077	668	5,281	46
Tennessee	4,661	4,487	357	2,308	1,822	174	4,851	893	4,666	5,579	41
Texas.	28,415	26,019	2,184	11,522	12,313	2,396	28,221	1,432	23,707	6,475	28
Utah	2,296	2,294	152	1,428	714	1	2,253	1,073	1,816	4,059	51
Vermont	833	813	40	228	546	20	796	1,347	723	7,904	9
Virginia.	6,697	6,631	353	2,483	3,794	66	7,699	1,134	6,793	6,550	27
Washington	7,273	7,007	467	4,721	1,818	266	8,544	1,502	6,208	6,633	25
West Virginia. . .	2,590	2,386	257	1,484	645	204	2,446	1,350	2,043	7,401	17
Wisconsin.	7,938	7,348	325	4,002	3,021	590	7,755	1,485	6,389	7,694	12
Wyoming	775	761	47	405	309	14	743	1,548	643	7,305	18

- Represents or rounds to zero. X Not applicable. [1] Amount received by local education agencies from the sales of bonds and real property and equipment, loans, and proceeds from insurance adjustments. [2] Includes interest on school debt and other current expenditures not shown separately. [3] Based on U.S. Census Bureau estimated resident population, as of July 1, the previous year. Estimates reflect revisions based on the 1990 Census of Population. [4] Average daily attendance.

Source: National Education Association, Washington, DC, Estimates of School Statistics Database (copyright).

No. 276. Computers for Student Instruction in Elementary and Secondary Schools: 1999-2000

[(**52,728 represents 52,728,000**) Market Data Retrieval collects student use computer information in elementary and secondary schools nationwide through a comprehensive annual technology survey that utilizes both mail and telephone methods]

Level	Total schools	Total enrollment (1,000)	Number of computers [1] (1,000)	Students per computer	Schools, by location of computer [2] (percent)			Schools with Internet access (percent)	Students per computer with Internet access
					Class-rooms	Computer lab	Library/media center		
U.S. total	110,350	52,728	10,500	5.0	94.4	82.8	76.2	90.7	8.1
Public schools, total	88,571	47,568	9,760	4.9	98.4	83.9	83.9	93.8	7.9
Elementary.	52,068	23,787	4,348	5.5	98.9	78.7	84.1	92.7	9.8
Middle/Junior High.	13,510	8,767	1,783	4.9	97.9	97.1	93.5	96.5	8.0
Senior High	15,912	12,633	3,047	4.1	97.2	92.5	85.3	96.1	6.2
K-12/other	7,081	2,381	582	4.1	98.1	83.3	77.0	92.1	3.9
Catholic schools, total	8,171	2,652	383	6.9	84.5	89.5	64.3	88.1	10.8
Elementary.	6,779	1,966	276	7.1	85.6	88.1	59.3	86.0	16.7
Secondary	1,235	632	98	6.5	87.3	82.5	79.4	98.9	4.2
K-12/other	157	55	10	5.6	77.5	98.4	91.4	94.0	5.7
Other private schools, total	13,608	2,507	357	7.0	82.4	68.0	43.9	75.9	11.2
Elementary.	6,699	1,066	144	7.4	86.3	60.6	38.1	75.7	12.1
Secondary	1,054	224	49	4.5	79.5	75.5	48.5	87.6	12.2
K-12/other	5,855	1,218	164	7.4	64.9	91.2	69.3	74.1	6.3

[1] Includes estimates for schools not reporting number of computers.   [2] Estimates based on responses of those indicating location of computers. Computers may also be in other locations.

Source: Market Data Retrieval, Shelton, CT, unpublished data (copyright).

No. 277. Public Schools with Internet Access: 1995 to 1999

[**In percent.** As of **fall.** Excludes special education, vocational education, and alternative schools. Based on sample and subject to sampling error; see source for details]

School characteristic	Percent of schools with Internet access					Percent of instructional classrooms with Internet access					Students per instructional computer with Internet access, 1999
	1995	1996	1997	1998	1999	1995	1996	1997	1998	1999	
Total [1]	50	65	78	89	95	8	14	27	51	63	9
Instructional level:											
Elementary	46	61	75	88	94	8	13	24	51	62	11
Secondary.	65	77	89	94	98	8	16	32	52	67	7
Size of enrollment:											
Less than 300	39	57	75	87	96	9	15	27	54	71	6
300 to 999.	52	66	78	89	94	8	13	28	53	64	9
1,000 or more	69	80	89	95	96	4	16	25	45	58	10
Percent minority enrollment:											
Less than 6 percent	52	65	84	91	95	9	18	37	57	74	7
6 to 20 percent.	58	72	87	93	97	10	18	35	59	78	8
21 to 49 percent.	54	65	73	91	96	9	12	22	52	64	9
50 percent or more	40	56	63	82	92	3	5	13	37	43	13
Percent of students eligible for free or reduced-price lunch:											
Less than 11 percent.	62	78	88	87	94	9	18	36	62	74	7
11 to 30 percent.	59	72	83	94	96	10	[2]18	32	53	71	8
31 to 49 percent.	[3]47	62	[3]78	94	98	[3]7	[2]12	[3]27	61	68	9
50 to 70 percent.	(NA)	53	(NA)	88	96	(NA)	[2]12	(NA)	40	62	10
71 percent or more	31	53	63	80	90	3	[2]5	14	39	39	16

NA Not available.   [1] Includes combined schools.   [2] Revised since originally published.   [3] 31 to 70 percent.

Source: U.S. National Center for Education Statistics, *"Internet Access in Public Schools and Classrooms: 1994-99,"* Issue Brief, February 1999, NCES 2000-086; and earlier issues and unpublished data.

U.S. Census Bureau, Statistical Abstract of the United States: 2000

No. 278. Student Use of Computers at School: 1984 to 1997

[In percent. As of October. Based on the Current Population Survey and subject to sampling error; see Appendix III and source]

Characteristic	1984, total	1989, total	1993, total	1997					
				Total	Prekinder-garten and kinder-garden	Grades 1-8	Grades 9-12	1st to 4th year of college	5th or later year of college
Total	27.3	42.7	59.0	68.8	36.5	79.3	70.5	64.7	55.5
Sex:									
Male.	29.0	43.5	59.4	70.1	37.1	79.5	71.3	67.8	59.9
Female	25.5	41.9	58.7	67.6	35.7	79.0	69.6	62.2	52.1
Race/ethnicity:									
White [1]	30.0	45.7	61.6	71.1	38.7	84.0	71.9	64.3	53.8
Black [1]	16.8	32.6	51.5	66.3	33.5	71.6	72.9	69.2	55.8
Hispanic	18.6	34.9	52.3	61.5	31.0	68.3	63.1	63.3	54.7
Other	28.6	42.7	59.0	65.3	32.7	74.9	63.6	63.1	68.9
Household income:									
Less than $5,000	18.7	36.7	51.2	62.1	25.4	69.6	67.9	61.1	74.1
$5,000 to $9,999	21.0	36.1	53.3	63.5	35.1	70.1	61.6	69.8	74.8
$10,000 to $14,999 . . .	22.4	38.4	56.4	66.2	33.3	74.1	68.2	64.1	70.5
$15,000 to $19,999 . . .	25.9	41.5	58.1	65.9	33.0	74.9	66.7	62.1	69.4
$20,000 to $24,999 . . .	26.7	42.4	56.4	66.9	34.2	74.9	69.2	64.0	65.8
$25,000 to $29,999 . . .	30.5	46.1	60.0	68.5	38.9	77.7	72.0	63.1	53.7
$30,000 to $34,999 . . .	30.5	44.2	59.1	67.6	34.6	79.9	70.4	55.2	47.7
$35,000 to $39,999 . . .	32.3	45.2	60.7	69.0	34.6	79.9	70.1	61.5	55.2
$40,000 to $49,999 . . .	32.8	44.7	59.3	70.5	34.7	81.6	74.1	63.3	52.0
$50,000 to $74,999 . . .	35.5	47.0	62.6	71.7	39.3	84.0	72.8	67.2	48.5
$75,000 or more	36.0	51.2	64.6	72.1	43.2	85.7	71.6	68.1	50.1
Control of school:									
Public.	27.4	43.3	60.2	70.2	40.1	79.0	70.5	63.4	56.7
Private	26.5	38.9	52.1	60.7	29.6	82.1	69.6	70.4	53.0

[1] Non-Hispanic.

Source: U.S. National Center for Education Statistics, *Digest of Education Statistics*, 1998.

No. 279. Public School Teachers Using Computers or the Internet for Classroom Instruction During Class Time: 1999

[In percent. Based on survey and subject to sampling error; see source]

Characteristic	Teachers using comput-ers or Internet for class-room instruc-tion [1]	Teacher assigns to a moderate or large extent							
		Com-puter applica-tions [2]	Practice drills	Research using the Internet	Solve problems and analyze data	Research using CD-ROM	Produce multi-media reports/ projects	Graphi-cal presen-tation of materials	Demon-stration/ simu-lations
Teachers with access to computers or the Internet at school	66	41	31	30	27	27	24	19	17
School instructional level:									
Elementary school.	68	41	39	25	31	27	22	17	15
Secondary school	60	42	12	41	20	27	27	23	21
Percent of students in school eligible for free or reduced-price school lunch:									
Less than 11 percent	71	55	26	39	25	32	29	26	22
11 to 30 percent	65	45	29	35	29	27	23	18	16
31 to 49 percent	65	39	33	29	26	30	23	16	17
50 to 70 percent	62	33	33	25	27	24	25	19	13
71 percent or more	64	31	35	18	27	19	22	19	16
Hours of professional development:									
0 hours	41	21	19	20	14	16	16	10	8
1-8 hours.	56	36	26	28	24	24	20	16	13
9-32 hours	72	47	35	32	30	31	26	21	19
More than 32 hours	82	55	43	42	41	34	37	31	29

[1] Includes corresponding with others (e.g. authors, experts) via e-mail or Internet, not shown separately.   [2] For example, word processing or spreadsheets.

Source: U.S. National Center for Education Statistics, Fast Response Survey System, "Teacher Use of Computers and the Internet in Public Schools," NCES 2000-090, April 2000.

No. 280. Technology in Public Schools: 1992 to 1998

[For school year ending in year shown (5,781 represents 5,781,000). Based on surveys of school districts conducted in the spring and summer of the school year. For details, see source]

Technology	Number					Percent of total		
	1992	1995	1996	1997	1998	1992	1997	1998
Schools with interactive videodisk								
players [1]	6,502	27,059	29,759	30,417	46,804	8	36	54
Elementary [2]	2,921	14,594	16,200	16,614	25,907	6	32	49
Junior high [3]	1,258	5,460	6,009	6,124	9,202	10	43	64
Senior high [4]	2,106	6,661	7,195	7,322	10,687	14	42	61
Students represented (1,000)	5,781	18,552	20,258	20,706	(NA)	14	45	(NA)
Schools with modems [1]	13,597	35,696	40,147	40,876	61,930	16	48	71
Elementary [2]	5,831	18,858	21,733	22,234	35,066	11	43	66
Junior high [3]	2,608	6,546	7,286	7,417	10,996	20	53	76
Senior high [4]	5,001	9,930	10,682	10,781	14,540	30	63	83
Students represented (1,000)	10,717	22,372	24,688	25,136	(NA)	25	54	(NA)
Schools with networks [1]	4,184	27,805	31,986	32,299	49,178	5	38	56
Elementary [2]	1,583	13,582	16,189	16,441	26,422	3	32	50
Junior high [3]	776	5,194	5,971	6,035	9,003	6	43	62
Senior high [4]	1,736	8,839	9,562	9,565	12,853	10	55	73
Students represented (1,000)	3,754	17,540	19,997	20,193	(NA)	9	44	(NA)
Schools with CD-ROMs [1]	5,706	40,509	45,918	46,388	64,200	7	54	74
Elementary [2]	1,897	22,305	25,965	26,377	37,908	4	51	72
Junior high [3]	1,231	7,501	8,341	8,410	11,023	9	60	76
Senior high [4]	2,543	10,354	11,150	11,140	13,985	15	65	80
Students represented (1,000)	5,298	24,121	27,070	27,347	(NA)	12	59	(NA)
Schools with satellite dishes [1]	1,129	15,400	16,298	16,232	17,457	1	19	20
Elementary [2]	351	5,565	6,014	6,001	6,962	1	11	13
Junior high [3]	166	3,214	3,409	3,377	3,255	1	24	23
Senior high [4]	606	6,550	6,782	6,769	7,052	4	39	40
Students represented (1,000)	1,906	8,963	9,270	9,232	(NA)	4	20	(NA)
Schools with cable [1]	(NA)	63,639	64,310	64,171	66,409	(NA)	75	76
Elementary [2]	(NA)	38,336	38,714	38,678	39,431	(NA)	74	75
Junior high [3]	(NA)	11,518	11,575	11,554	11,862	(NA)	82	82
Senior high [4]	(NA)	13,114	13,282	13,208	13,778	(NA)	77	78
Students represented (1,000)	(NA)	36,284	36,950	36,870	(NA)	(NA)	80	(NA)

NA Not available. [1] Includes schools for special education and adult education, not shown separately. [2] Includes K-12, preschool, preschool through 3, K-6, and K-8. [3] Includes schools with grade spans of 4-8, 7-8, and 7-9. [4] Includes 7-12, 9-12, 10-12, vocational technical, and alternative high schools.

Source: Quality Education Data, Denver, CO, National Education Database.

No. 281. Children and Youth With Disabilities Served by Selected Programs: 1990 to 1999

[For school year ending in year shown (4,210.8 represents 4,210,800). Excludes outlying areas. Through 1994, for persons age 6 to 21 years old served under IDEA (Individuals with Disabilities Act) Part B and Chapter 1 of ESEA (Elementary and Secondary Education Act), SOP (State Operated Programs); beginning 1995, IDEA, Part B only]

Item	1990	1993	1994	1995	1996	1997	1998	1999
All conditions (1,000)	4,210.8	4,586.2	4,730.4	4,859.1	5,028.7	5,177.6	5,338.7	5,486.8
PERCENT DISTRIBUTION								
Specific learning disabilities	48.6	51.3	50.9	51.2	51.3	51.2	51.0	50.8
Speech or language impairments	23.1	21.7	21.4	20.9	20.3	20.1	19.8	19.5
Mental retardation	13.0	11.3	11.3	11.4	11.3	11.2	11.0	10.9
Serious emotional disturbance	9.0	8.7	8.7	8.8	8.7	8.6	8.5	8.4
Hearing impairments	1.3	1.3	1.3	1.3	1.3	1.3	1.3	1.3
Orthopedic impairments	1.1	1.1	1.2	1.2	1.2	1.3	1.3	1.3
Other health impairments	1.2	1.4	1.7	2.2	2.6	3.1	3.6	4.0
Visually impaired	0.5	0.5	0.5	0.5	0.5	0.5	0.5	0.5
Multiple disabilities	2.0	2.2	2.3	1.8	1.8	1.9	2.0	1.9
Deaf/blind	(Z)	(Z)	(Z)	(Z)	(Z)	(Z)	(Z)	(Z)
Autism	(NA)	0.3	0.4	0.5	0.6	0.7	0.8	1.0
Traumatic brain injury	(NA)	0.1	0.1	0.1	0.2	0.2	0.2	0.2
Developmental delay	(NA)	(NA)	(NA)	(NA)	(NA)	(NA)	0.1	0.2

NA Not available. Z less than .05 percent.

Source: U.S. Department of Education, Office of Special Education Programs, Data Analysis System (DANS).

U.S. Census Bureau, Statistical Abstract of the United States: 2000

No. 282. Private Schools: 1997-98

[5,076.1 represents 5,076,100. Based on the Private School Survey, conducted every 2 years; see source for details. For composition of regions, see map, inside front cover]

Characteristic	Schools				Students (1,000)				Teachers (1,000)			
	Number	Elementary	Secondary	Combined	Number	Elementary	Secondary	Combined	Number	Elementary	Secondary	Combined
Total	27,402	16,623	2,487	8,292	5,076.1	2,824.8	798.3	1,452.9	376.5	180.5	60.9	135.2
School type:												
Catholic	8,182	6,800	1,121	262	2,514.7	1,833.1	606.4	75.2	144.6	97.7	40.2	6.7
Parochial	4,778	4,526	204	47	1,346.0	1,245.7	86.2	14.0	72.4	65.4	6.0	1.0
Diocesan	2,556	2,011	480	65	829.3	533.8	278.2	17.3	47.4	28.5	17.5	1.4
Private	848	262	437	150	339.5	53.5	242.1	43.9	24.8	3.8	16.7	4.3
Other religious . . .	13,195	6,830	697	5,668	1,764.4	731.3	112.2	921.0	143.1	55.2	10.2	77.7
Conservative Christian	4,978	1,700	143	3,135	737.0	219.4	22.3	495.3	56.8	15.9	1.7	39.3
Affiliated	3,287	2,166	292	830	551.5	281.8	58.7	211.0	46.4	22.4	5.5	18.4
Unaffiliated . . .	4,929	2,964	262	1,703	475.9	230.1	31.2	214.6	39.9	16.9	3.0	20.0
Nonsectarian	6,025	2,993	670	2,362	797.0	260.5	79.7	456.8	88.8	27.6	10.5	50.8
Regular	2,705	1,523	266	915	553.4	168.9	56.4	328.1	57.4	16.5	7.3	33.6
Special emphasis	2,070	1,290	236	545	158.6	80.6	14.4	63.7	17.0	9.1	1.6	6.3
Special education	1,250	181	168	901	85.0	11.0	9.0	65.0	14.5	2.1	1.6	10.8
Program emphasis:												
Regular elem/sec .	22,363	14,495	1,973	5,895	4,684.0	2,679.9	753.5	1,250.6	330.2	164.5	55.8	109.9
Montessori	1,144	950	(B)	186	69.9	55.7	(B)	13.5	7.5	6.3	0.1	1.2
Special program emphasis	589	273	66	250	100.1	35.4	15.5	49.3	9.8	3.5	1.4	4.8
Special education . .	1,387	204	178	1,005	93.5	12.4	9.7	71.3	16.0	2.3	1.7	12.0
Vocational/tech . .	(B)	(B)	(B)	(B)	(B)	(B)	(B)	(B)	(B)	(B)	(B)	(B)
Early childhood . .	160	148	(B)	(B)	7.9	7.4	-	(B)	0.6	0.5	(B)	(B)
Alternative	1,745	553	253	938	118.8	34.1	17.9	66.9	12.3	3.3	1.8	7.2
Size:												
Less than 150 . . .	15,573	9,041	1,046	5,486	918.9	555.2	58.2	305.5	96.2	50.6	7.7	37.9
150 to 299	6,656	4,860	446	1,349	1,439.3	1,050.7	99.8	289.9	99.3	64.5	9.3	25.5
300 to 499	3,125	1,994	408	722	1,197.2	760.0	159.6	277.7	78.6	42.8	12.8	23.1
500 to 749	1,339	615	297	427	800.4	357.8	181.6	261.0	53.1	17.5	12.9	22.7
750 or more	711	113	290	308	720.2	101.1	300.2	318.9	49.2	5.0	18.2	26.1
Region:												
Northeast	6,325	3,872	795	1,658	1,287.0	751.1	261.1	274.9	100.3	47.7	21.4	31.2
Midwest	7,423	5,299	604	1,520	1,345.6	896.9	240.7	208.0	88.6	53.2	16.7	18.7
South	8,111	4,014	564	3,533	1,510.3	631.8	153.4	725.1	121.9	46.0	12.1	63.7
West	5,542	3,437	524	1,580	933.2	545.0	143.2	245.0	65.7	33.5	10.7	21.5

- Represents zero.   B Does not meet standard of reliability or precision.

Source: U.S. National Center for Education Statistics, Office of Educational Research and Improvement, *Private School Universe Survey, 1997-98*, NCES 1999-319.

No. 283. Private Elementary and Secondary School Teachers by Selected Characteristics: 1993-94

[For school year (65 represents 65,000). Based on survey and subject to sampling error; for details, see source. See Table 268 for similar data on public school teachers]

Characteristic	Unit	Age				Sex		Race/ethnicity		
		Under 30 yrs. old	30 to 39 yrs. old	40 to 49 yrs. old	Over 50 yrs. old	Male	Female	White [1]	Black [1]	Hispanic
Total teachers [2] .	1,000 . . .	65	94	131	88	93	285	348	12	12
Highest degree held:										
Bachelor's	Percent .	78.8	63.1	54.0	47.2	47.3	62.8	59.4	55.8	57.4
Master's.	Percent .	10.8	25.7	35.1	40.5	40.6	26.3	30.2	26.4	19.9
Education specialist .	Percent .	1.0	2.6	3.4	3.8	2.6	3.0	2.6	4.8	4.4
Doctorate	Percent .	0.2	1.4	2.0	2.6	4.3	0.8	1.6	1.0	2.3
Full-time teaching experience:										
Less than 3 years . .	Percent .	54.9	21.7	12.6	7.2	21.7	20.6	20.4	26.9	25.5
3 to 9 years	Percent .	44.9	51.2	29.8	13.4	28.2	34.5	33.6	34.9	41.8
10 to 20 years.	Percent .	0.1	27.1	45.5	30.2	28.7	29.9	30.0	27.9	21.6
20 years or more . . .	Percent .	(Z)	(Z)	12.1	49.2	21.4	13.7	16.0	10.3	11.1
Full-time teachers . .	1,000 . . .	53	82	103	62	70	231	277	9	9
Earned income	Dol.	18,384	21,344	22,190	24,113	27,196	20,007	21,578	23,094	22,912
Salary	Dol.	16,062	19,108	20,631	22,500	23,003	18,815	19,717	20,333	20,740

Z Less than .05 percent.   [1] Non-Hispanic.   [2] Includes teachers with no degrees and associates degrees, not shown separately.

Source: U.S. National Center for Education Statistics, *Digest of Education Statistics*, 1997.

No. 284. Scholastic Assessment Test (SAT) Scores and Characteristics of College-Bound Seniors: 1967 to 1999

[For school year ending in year shown. Data are for the SAT I: Reasoning Tests. SAT I: Reasoning Test replaced the SAT in March 1994. Scores between the two tests have been equated to the same 200-800 scale and are thus comparable. Scores for 1995 and prior years have been recentered and revised]

Type of test and characteristic	Unit	1967	1970	1975	1980	1985	1990	1995	1997	1998	1999
AVERAGE TEST SCORES [1]											
Verbal, total [2]	Point . . .	543	537	512	502	509	500	504	505	505	505
Male	Point . . .	540	536	515	506	514	505	505	507	509	509
Female	Point . . .	545	538	509	498	503	496	502	503	502	502
Math, total [2]	Point . . .	516	512	498	492	500	501	506	511	512	511
Male	Point . . .	535	531	518	515	522	521	525	530	531	531
Female	Point . . .	495	493	479	473	480	483	490	494	496	495
PARTICIPANTS											
Total [3]	1,000 . . .	(NA)	(NA)	996	922	977	1,026	1,068	1,127	1,173	1,229
Male	Percent .	(NA)	(NA)	49.9	48.2	48.3	47.8	46.4	46.1	46.2	46.1
White	Percent .	(NA)	(NA)	86.0	82.1	81.0	73.0	69.2	68.0	67.0	66.9
Black	Percent .	(NA)	(NA)	7.9	9.1	7.5	10.0	10.7	10.8	11.0	11.1
Obtaining scores [1] of— 600 or above:											
Verbal	Percent .	(NA)	(NA)	(NA)	(NA)	(NA)	20.3	21.9	20.9	21.0	21.2
Math	Percent .	(NA)	(NA)	(NA)	(NA)	(NA)	20.4	23.4	23.4	23.7	23.7
Below 400:											
Verbal	Percent .	(NA)	(NA)	(NA)	(NA)	(NA)	17.3	16.4	16.1	16.1	16.1
Math	Percent .	(NA)	(NA)	(NA)	(NA)	(NA)	15.8	16.0	15.2	15.3	15.7
Selected intended area of study:											
Business and commerce	Percent .	(NA)	(NA)	11.5	18.6	21.0	20.9	13.3	12.8	13.6	13.8
Engineering	Percent .	(NA)	(NA)	6.7	11.1	11.7	10.2	8.8	8.4	8.6	8.5
Social science	Percent .	(NA)	(NA)	7.7	7.8	7.5	12.6	11.6	11.0	10.5	10.5
Education	Percent .	(NA)	(NA)	9.1	6.1	4.7	7.5	8.1	8.6	8.9	8.9

NA Not available. [1] Minimum score 200; maximum score, 800. [2] 1967 and 1970 are estimates based on total number of persons taking SAT. [3] 996 represents 996,000.
Source: College Entrance Examination Board, New York, NY, *National College-Bound Senior*, annual (copyright).

No. 285. ACT Program Scores and Characteristics of College-Bound Students: 1970 to 1999

[For academic year ending in year shown. Except as indicated, test scores and characteristics of college-bound students. Through 1980, data based on 10 percent sample; thereafter, based on all ACT tested graduating seniors]

Type of test and characteristic	Unit	1970	1975	1980	1985	1990 [1]	1995 [1]	1996 [1]	1997 [1]	1998 [1]	1999 [1]
TEST SCORES [2]											
Composite	Point . . .	19.9	18.6	18.5	18.6	20.6	20.8	20.9	21.0	21.0	21.0
Male	Point . . .	20.3	19.5	19.3	19.4	21.0	21.0	21.0	21.1	21.2	21.1
Female	Point . . .	19.4	17.8	17.9	17.9	20.3	20.7	20.8	20.8	20.9	20.9
English	Point . . .	18.5	17.7	17.9	18.1	20.5	20.2	20.3	20.3	20.4	20.5
Male	Point . . .	17.6	17.1	17.3	17.6	20.1	19.8	19.8	19.9	19.9	20.0
Female	Point . . .	19.4	18.3	18.3	18.6	20.9	20.6	20.7	20.7	20.8	20.9
Math	Point . . .	20.0	17.6	17.4	17.2	19.9	20.2	20.2	20.6	20.8	20.7
Male	Point . . .	21.1	19.3	18.9	18.6	20.7	20.9	20.9	21.3	21.5	21.4
Female	Point . . .	18.8	16.2	16.2	16.0	19.3	19.7	19.7	20.1	20.2	20.2
Reading [3]	Point . . .	19.7	17.4	17.2	17.4	(NA)	21.3	21.3	21.3	21.4	21.4
Male	Point . . .	20.3	18.7	18.2	18.3	(NA)	21.1	21.0	21.2	21.1	21.1
Female	Point . . .	19.0	16.4	16.4	16.6	(NA)	21.4	21.6	21.5	21.6	21.6
Science reasoning [4]	Point . . .	20.8	21.1	21.1	21.2	(NA)	21.0	21.1	21.1	21.1	21.0
Male	Point . . .	21.6	22.4	22.4	22.6	(NA)	21.6	21.7	21.7	21.8	21.5
Female	Point . . .	20.0	20.0	20.0	20.0	(NA)	20.5	20.5	20.6	20.6	20.6
PARTICIPANTS [5]											
Total [6]	1,000 . . .	788	714	822	739	817	945	925	959	995	1,019
Male	Percent .	52	46	45	46	46	44	44	44	43	43
White	Percent .	(NA)	77	83	82	79	75	77	76	76	76
Black	Percent .	4	7	8	8	9	10	10	10	11	11
Obtaining composite scores of— [7]											
27 or above	Percent .	14	14	13	14	12	13	13	14	14	14
18 or below	Percent .	21	33	33	32	35	34	34	33	33	33
Planned educational major:											
Business [8]	Percent .	18	21	20	21	20	14	13	11	12	11
Engineering	Percent .	8	6	8	9	9	9	9	8	7	7
Social science [9]	Percent .	10	9	6	7	10	9	9	8	9	9
Education	Percent .	16	12	9	6	8	9	9	9	10	10

NA Not available. [1] Beginning 1990, not comparable with previous years because a new version of the ACT was introduced. Estimated average composite scores for prior years: 1989, 20.6; 1988, 1987, and 1986, 20.8. [2] Minimum score, 1; maximum score, 36. [3] Prior to 1990, social studies; data not comparable with previous years. [4] Prior to 1990, natural sciences; data not comparable with previous years. [5] Beginning 1985, data are for seniors who graduated in year shown and had taken the ACT in their junior or senior years. Data by race are for those responding to the race question. [6] 788 represents 788,000. [7] Prior to 1990, 26 or above and 15 or below. [8] Includes political and persuasive (e.g. sales) fields through 1975; 1980 and 1985 business and commerce; thereafter, business and management and business and office. [9] Includes religion through 1975.
Source: ACT, Inc., Iowa City, IA, *High School Profile Report*, annual.

U.S. Census Bureau, Statistical Abstract of the United States: 2000

No. 286. Proficiency Test Scores for Selected Subjects by Characteristic: 1977 to 1998

[Based on The National Assessment of Educational Progress Tests which are administered to a representative sample of students in public and private schools. Test scores can range from 0 to 500, except as indicated. For details, see source]

Test and year	Total	Sex Male	Female	Race White [1]	Black [1]	His-panic origin	Parental education Less than high school	High school	More than high school Total	Some college	College graduate
READING											
9 year olds:											
1979-80	215	210	220	221	189	190	194	213	226	(NA)	(NA)
1987-88	212	208	216	218	189	194	193	211	220	(NA)	(NA)
1995-96	212	207	218	220	190	194	197	207	220	(NA)	(NA)
13 year olds:											
1979-80	259	254	263	264	233	237	239	254	271	(NA)	(NA)
1987-88	258	252	263	261	243	240	247	253	265	(NA)	(NA)
1995-96	259	253	265	267	236	240	241	252	270	(NA)	(NA)
17 year olds:											
1979-80	286	282	289	293	243	261	262	278	299	(NA)	(NA)
1987-88	290	286	294	295	274	271	267	282	300	(NA)	(NA)
1995-96	287	280	294	294	265	265	267	273	297	(NA)	(NA)
WRITING [2]											
4th graders:											
1983-84	204	201	208	211	182	189	179	192	217	208	218
1987-88	206	199	213	215	173	190	194	199	212	211	212
1995-96	207	200	214	216	182	191	190	203	(NA)	205	214
8th graders:											
1983-84	267	258	276	272	247	247	258	261	276	271	278
1987-88	264	254	274	269	246	250	254	258	271	275	271
1995-96	264	251	276	271	242	246	245	258	(NA)	270	274
11th graders:											
1983-84	290	281	299	297	270	259	274	284	299	298	300
1987-88	291	282	299	296	275	274	276	285	298	296	299
1995-96	283	275	292	289	267	269	260	275	(NA)	287	291
MATHEMATICS											
9 year olds:											
1977-78	219	217	220	224	192	203	200	219	231	230	231
1985-86	222	222	222	227	202	205	201	218	231	229	231
1995-96	231	233	229	237	212	215	220	221	(NA)	238	240
13 year olds:											
1977-78	264	264	265	272	230	238	245	263	280	273	284
1985-86	269	270	268	274	249	254	252	263	278	274	280
1995-96	274	276	272	281	252	256	254	267	(NA)	278	283
17 year olds:											
1977-78	300	304	297	306	268	276	280	294	313	305	317
1985-86	302	305	299	308	279	283	279	293	310	305	314
1995-96	307	310	305	313	286	292	281	297	(NA)	307	317
SCIENCE											
9 year olds:											
1976-77	220	222	218	230	175	192	199	223	233	237	232
1985-86	224	227	221	232	196	199	204	220	235	236	235
1995-96	230	232	228	239	201	207	215	222	(NA)	242	240
13 year olds:											
1976-77	247	251	244	256	208	213	224	245	264	260	266
1985-86	251	256	247	259	222	226	229	245	262	258	264
1995-96	256	261	252	266	226	232	232	248	(NA)	260	266
17 year olds:											
1976-77	290	297	282	298	240	262	265	284	304	296	309
1985-86	289	295	282	298	253	259	258	277	300	295	304
1995-96	296	300	292	307	260	269	261	282	(NA)	297	308
HISTORY, 1993-94											
4th graders	205	203	206	215	177	180	177	197	(NA)	214	216
8th graders:	259	259	259	267	239	243	241	251	(NA)	264	270
12th graders	286	288	285	292	265	267	263	276	(NA)	287	296
GEOGRAPHY, 1993-94											
4th graders	206	208	203	218	168	183	186	197	(NA)	216	216
8th graders	260	262	258	270	229	239	238	250	(NA)	265	272
12th graders	285	288	281	291	258	268	263	274	(NA)	286	294
CIVICS, 1997-98 [3]											
4th graders	150	149	151	159	132	126	124	153	(NA)	150	153
8th graders	150	148	152	159	133	127	123	144	(NA)	143	160
12th graders	150	148	152	158	131	130	124	140	(NA)	145	160

NA Not available. [1] Non-Hispanic. [2] Writing scores revised from previous years; previous writing scores were recorded on a 0 to 400 rather than 0 to 500 scale. [3] Civics uses a scale of 0 to 300.

Source: U.S. National Center for Education Statistics, *Digest of Education Statistics*, annual, and *NAEP 1998 Civics Report Card for the Nation.*

178   Education

No. 287. Advanced Placement Program—Summary: 1998 and 1999

[Includes exams taken by candidates abroad. In 1999, this represents 27,101 examinations taken by 18,317 students in 657 schools abroad. Minus sign (-) indicates decrease]

Item	Schools repre- sented, 1999	Exams taken 1998	Exams taken 1999	Percent change, 1998-99	1999 Grade level of test taker 10th grade	11th grade	12th grade	Sex of test taker Male	Female
Exams taken, total [1] .	(X)	1,016,657	1,149,515	13	61,257	393,117	665,013	533,995	615,520
By subject area:									
Art History	773	7,332	9,038	23	953	2,132	5,744	3,259	5,779
Art, Drawing	1,123	3,686	4,204	14	42	836	3,208	1,801	2,403
Art, General	1,887	8,094	8,769	8	91	1,361	7,023	3,301	5,468
Biology	6,162	75,461	82,592	9	5,881	30,727	43,760	35,146	47,446
Calculus AB	9,334	117,671	127,744	9	1,172	16,320	107,624	67,740	60,004
Calculus BC	2,884	27,088	30,724	13	507	5,071	24,544	19,047	11,677
Chemistry	4,672	44,937	48,899	9	2,024	24,429	21,429	27,841	21,058
Computer Science—A . .	1,840	6,478	12,218	89	1,311	4,364	6,227	10,205	2,013
Computer Science—AB .	1,126	4,057	6,619	63	556	2,352	3,538	5,997	622
Economics-Micro	1,224	13,243	14,867	12	226	2,241	11,983	8,773	6,094
Economics-Macro	1,463	17,668	20,014	13	313	2,448	16,738	11,448	8,566
English Language/ Composition	4,922	80,016	97,370	22	1,011	67,989	26,557	36,767	60,603
English Literature/ Composition	9,751	167,194	176,221	5	114	10,076	162,802	64,181	112,040
Environmental Science . .	727	5,163	9,209	78	190	2,759	5,966	4,061	5,148
European History	3,183	48,298	54,759	13	25,410	8,434	19,657	26,152	28,607
French Language	2,814	13,721	15,031	10	691	4,028	9,784	4,569	10,462
French Literature	383	1,618	1,547	-4	68	318	1,119	463	1,084
German Language	1,102	3,493	3,584	3	195	816	2,401	1,712	1,872
Government and Politics—U.S.	3,554	49,934	57,015	14	1,689	5,790	48,356	27,557	29,458
Government and Politics—Comparative . .	806	6,835	7,463	9	389	904	6,026	3,968	3,495
International English Language	72	3,752	4,633	23	3	108	64	1,932	2,701
Latin—Vergil	560	3,311	3,399	3	270	1,604	1,457	1,795	1,604
Latin—Literature	378	2,055	2,212	8	79	911	1,172	1,094	1,118
Music Theory	1,197	4,084	4,820	18	324	1,394	2,970	2,513	2,307
Physics—B	2,713	24,276	27,685	14	436	9,332	17,294	18,065	9,620
Physics—Mechanics	1,793	12,939	14,419	11	100	1,471	12,557	10,649	3,770
Physics—Electricity and Magnetism	1,084	6,415	7,102	11	58	591	6,306	5,572	1,530
Psychology	1,706	21,974	28,291	29	590	7,549	19,514	9,466	18,825
Spanish Language	4,687	51,424	58,340	13	5,182	19,656	31,285	20,932	37,408
Spanish Literature	946	6,975	7,998	15	459	2,384	4,858	2,607	5,391
Statistics	1,795	15,486	25,240	63	908	4,612	19,186	12,952	12,288
U.S. History	7,816	161,979	177,489	10	10,015	150,110	13,864	82,430	95,059
Candidates taking exams [1] .	(X)	635,168	704,298	11	55,452	268,451	358,207	313,987	390,311

X Not applicable.　　[1] Includes candidates and exams taken in other grades not shown separately.

Source: The College Board, New York, NY, Advanced Placement Program, *National Summary Report*, 1999 (copyright).

No. 288. Foreign Language Enrollment in Public High Schools: 1970 to 1994

[In thousands (13,301.9 represents 13,301,900), except percent. As of fall, for grades 9 through 12]

Language	1970	1974	1976	1978	1982	1985	1990	1994
Total enrollment	13,301.9	13,648.9	13,952.1	13,941.4	12,879.3	12,466.5	11,099.6	11,847.5
Enrolled in all foreign languages . . .	3,779.3	3,294.5	3,174.0	3,200.1	2,909.8	4,028.9	4,256.9	5,001.9
Percent of all students	28.4	24.1	22.7	23.0	22.6	32.3	38.4	42.2
Enrolled in modern foreign languages [1] .	3,514.1	3,127.3	3,023.5	3,048.3	2,740.2	3,852.0	4,093.0	4,813.0
Spanish	1,810.8	1,678.1	1,717.0	1,631.4	1,562.8	2,334.4	2,611.4	3,219.8
French	1,230.7	977.9	888.4	856.0	858.0	1,133.7	1,089.4	1,105.9
German	410.5	393.0	352.7	330.6	266.9	312.2	295.4	326.0
Italian	27.3	40.2	45.6	45.5	44.1	47.3	40.4	43.8
Japanese	(NA)	(NA)	(NA)	(NA)	6.2	8.6	25.1	42.3
Russian	20.2	15.1	11.3	8.8	5.7	6.4	16.5	16.4
Percent of all students [1]	26.4	22.9	21.7	21.9	21.3	30.9	36.9	40.6
Spanish	13.6	12.3	12.3	11.7	12.1	18.7	23.5	27.2
French	9.3	7.2	6.4	6.1	6.7	9.1	9.8	9.3
German	3.1	2.9	2.5	2.4	2.1	2.5	2.7	2.8
Italian	0.2	0.3	0.3	0.3	0.3	0.4	0.4	0.4
Japanese	(NA)	(NA)	(NA)	(NA)	0.1	0.1	0.2	0.4
Russian	0.2	0.1	0.1	0.1	(Z)	0.1	0.1	0.1

NA Not available.　　Z Less than .05 percent.　　[1] Includes other foreign languages, not shown separately.

Source: The American Council on the Teaching of Foreign Languages, Yonkers, NY, *Foreign Language Enrollments in Public Secondary Schools, Fall 1994*.

U.S. Census Bureau, Statistical Abstract of the United States: 2000

No. 289. Public High School Graduates by State: 1980 to 1999

[In thousands (2,747.7 represents 2,747,000). For school year ending in year shown]

State	1980	1990	1995	1999, est.	State	1980	1990	1995	1999, est.
United States...	2,747.7	2,320.3	2,273.5	2,502.8	Missouri	62.3	49.0	48.9	51.8
					Montana	12.1	9.4	10.1	10.9
Alabama	45.2	40.5	36.3	39.1	Nebraska	22.4	17.7	18.0	20.2
Alaska	5.2	5.4	5.8	6.5	Nevada	8.5	9.5	10.0	13.3
Arizona	28.6	32.1	31.0	38.3	New Hampshire	11.7	10.8	10.1	10.2
Arkansas	29.1	26.5	24.6	27.7					
California	249.2	236.3	255.2	291.9	New Jersey	94.6	69.8	67.4	66.8
					New Mexico	18.4	14.9	14.9	17.3
Colorado	36.8	33.0	32.4	37.0	New York	204.1	143.3	132.4	140.2
Connecticut	37.7	27.9	26.4	28.6	North Carolina	70.9	64.8	59.5	59.8
Delaware	7.6	5.6	5.2	6.3					
District of Columbia	5.0	3.6	3.0	2.7	North Dakota	9.9	7.7	7.8	8.4
Florida	87.3	88.9	89.8	98.9	Ohio	144.2	114.5	109.4	115.0
					Oklahoma	39.3	35.6	33.3	35.9
Georgia	61.6	56.6	56.7	60.2	Oregon	29.9	25.5	26.7	28.7
Hawaii	11.5	10.3	9.4	10.4	Pennsylvania	146.5	110.5	104.1	112.3
Idaho	13.2	12.0	14.2	15.7					
Illinois	135.6	108.1	105.2	112.6	Rhode Island	10.9	7.8	7.8	8.1
Indiana	73.1	60.0	56.1	58.3	South Carolina	38.7	32.5	30.7	34.0
					South Dakota	10.7	7.7	8.4	9.0
Iowa	43.4	31.8	31.3	34.4	Tennessee	49.8	46.1	43.6	58.6
Kansas	30.9	25.4	26.1	28.6	Texas	171.4	172.5	170.3	203.5
Kentucky	41.2	38.0	37.6	37.0	Utah	20.0	21.2	27.7	31.6
Louisiana	46.3	36.1	36.5	37.4					
Maine	15.4	13.8	11.5	12.7	Vermont	6.7	6.1	5.9	6.5
					Virginia	66.6	60.6	58.3	65.3
Maryland	54.3	41.6	41.4	46.8	Washington	50.4	45.9	49.3	54.5
Massachusetts	73.8	55.9	47.7	50.5	West Virginia	23.4	21.9	20.1	19.5
Michigan	124.3	93.8	84.6	94.2	Wisconsin	69.3	52.0	51.7	58.3
Minnesota	64.9	49.1	49.4	57.0	Wyoming	6.1	5.8	5.9	6.3
Mississippi	27.6	25.2	23.8	24.0					

Source: U.S. National Center for Education Statistics, *Digest of Education Statistics*, annual.

No. 290. High School Dropouts by Race and Hispanic Origin: 1975 to 1998

[In percent. As of October]

Item	1975	1980	1985	1990 [1]	1991	1992	1993	1994	1995	1996	1997	1998
EVENT DROPOUTS [2]												
Total [3]	5.8	6.0	5.2	4.0	4.0	4.3	4.2	5.0	5.4	4.7	4.3	4.4
White	5.4	5.6	4.8	3.8	3.7	4.1	4.1	4.7	5.1	4.5	4.2	4.4
Male	5.0	6.4	4.9	4.1	3.6	3.8	4.1	4.6	5.4	4.8	4.9	4.4
Female	5.8	4.9	4.7	3.5	3.8	4.4	4.1	4.9	4.8	4.1	3.5	4.4
Black	8.7	8.3	7.7	5.1	6.2	4.9	5.4	6.2	6.1	6.3	4.8	5.0
Male	8.3	8.0	8.3	4.1	5.5	3.3	5.7	6.5	7.9	4.6	4.1	4.6
Female	9.0	8.5	7.2	6.0	7.0	6.7	5.0	5.7	4.4	7.8	5.7	5.5
Hispanic [4]	10.9	11.5	9.7	8.0	7.3	7.9	5.4	9.2	11.6	8.4	8.6	8.4
Male	10.1	16.9	9.3	8.7	10.4	5.8	5.7	8.4	10.9	9.2	10.4	8.6
Female	11.6	6.9	9.8	7.2	4.8	8.6	5.0	10.1	12.5	7.6	6.7	8.2
STATUS DROPOUTS [5]												
Total [3]	15.6	15.6	13.9	13.6	14.2	12.7	12.7	13.3	13.9	12.8	13.0	13.9
White	13.9	14.4	13.5	13.5	14.2	12.2	12.2	12.7	13.6	12.5	12.4	13.7
Male	13.5	15.7	14.7	14.2	15.4	13.3	13.0	13.6	14.3	12.9	13.8	15.7
Female	14.2	13.2	12.3	12.8	13.1	11.1	11.5	11.7	13.0	12.1	10.9	11.7
Black	27.3	23.5	17.6	15.1	15.6	16.3	16.4	15.5	14.4	16.0	16.7	17.1
Male	27.8	26.0	18.8	13.6	15.4	15.5	15.6	17.5	14.2	17.4	17.5	20.5
Female	26.9	21.5	16.6	16.2	15.8	17.1	17.2	13.7	14.6	14.7	16.1	14.3
Hispanic [4]	34.9	40.3	31.5	37.3	39.6	33.9	32.7	34.7	34.7	34.5	30.6	34.4
Male	32.6	42.6	35.8	39.8	44.4	38.4	34.7	36.1	34.2	36.2	33.2	39.7
Female	36.8	38.1	27.0	34.5	34.5	29.6	31.0	33.1	35.4	32.7	27.6	28.6

[1] Beginning 1990 reflects new editing procedures for cases with missing data on school enrollment. [2] Percent of students who drop out in a single year without completing high school. For grades 10 to 12. [3] Includes other races, not shown separately. [4] Persons of Hispanic origin may be of any race. [5] Percent of the population who have not completed high school and are not enrolled, regardless of when they dropped out. For persons 18 to 24 years old.

Source: U.S. Census Bureau, *Current Population Reports*, P20-521.

No. 291. High School Dropouts by Age, Race, and Hispanic Origin: 1970 to 1998

[As of **October** (4,670 represents 4,670,000). **For persons 14 to 24 years old.** See Table 293 for definition of dropouts]

Age and race	Number of dropouts (1,000)					Percent of population				
	1970	1980	1990	1995	1998	1970	1980	1990	1995	1998
Total dropouts [1][2]	4,670	5,212	3,854	3,963	4,064	12.2	12.0	10.1	9.9	9.9
16 to 17 years	617	709	418	406	398	8.0	8.8	6.3	5.4	5.0
18 to 21 years	2,138	2,578	1,921	1,980	2,147	16.4	15.8	13.4	14.2	14.3
22 to 24 years	1,770	1,798	1,458	1,491	1,397	18.7	15.2	13.8	13.6	13.3
White [2]	3,577	4,169	3,127	3,098	3,206	10.8	11.3	10.1	9.7	9.8
16 to 17 years	485	619	334	314	310	7.3	9.2	6.4	5.4	4.9
18 to 21 years	1,618	2,032	1,516	1,530	1,663	14.3	14.7	13.1	13.8	13.8
22 to 24 years	1,356	1,416	1,235	1,181	1,147	16.3	14.0	14.0	13.4	13.6
Black [2]	1,047	934	611	605	725	22.2	16.0	10.9	10.0	11.6
16 to 17 years	125	80	73	70	69	12.8	6.9	6.9	5.8	5.4
18 to 21 years	500	486	345	328	433	30.5	23.0	16.0	15.8	19.0
22 to 24 years	397	346	185	194	209	37.8	24.0	13.5	12.5	14.3
Hispanic [2][3]	(NA)	919	1,122	1,355	1,520	(NA)	29.5	26.8	24.7	25.0
16 to 17 years	(NA)	92	89	94	104	(NA)	16.6	12.9	10.7	10.2
18 to 21 years	(NA)	470	502	652	807	(NA)	40.3	32.9	34.6	34.6
22 to 24 years	(NA)	323	523	598	576	(NA)	40.6	42.8	37.4	34.2

NA Not available. [1] Includes other groups not shown separately. [2] Includes persons 14 to 15 years, not shown separately. [3] Persons of Hispanic origin may be of any race.

Source: U.S. Census Bureau, *Current Population Reports*, P20-521; and earlier reports.

No. 292. Enrollment Status by Race, Hispanic Origin, and Sex: 1975 and 1998

[As of October (15,693 represents 15,693,000). For persons 18 to 21 years old. For the civilian noninstitutional population. Based on the Current Population Survey; see text, Section 1, Population, and Appendix III]

Characteristic	Total persons 18 to 21 years old (1,000)		Percent distribution							
			Enrolled in high school		High school graduates				Not high school graduates	
					Total		In college			
	1975	1998	1975	1998	1975	1998	1975	1998	1975	1998
Total [1]	15,693	15,033	5.7	8.9	78.0	76.7	33.5	45.0	16.3	14.3
White	13,448	12,026	4.7	7.7	80.6	78.4	34.6	46.0	14.7	13.8
Black	1,997	2,279	12.5	15.0	60.4	66.1	24.9	35.8	27.0	19.0
Hispanic [2]	899	2,332	12.0	9.4	57.2	55.8	24.4	23.6	30.8	34.6
Male [1]	7,584	7,737	7.4	10.5	76.6	73.2	35.4	41.2	15.9	16.3
White	6,545	6,263	6.2	9.0	79.7	75.1	36.9	42.0	14.1	15.9
Black	911	1,112	15.9	18.3	55.0	59.6	23.9	32.0	29.0	22.0
Hispanic [2]	416	1,234	17.3	9.6	54.6	49.9	25.2	19.1	27.9	40.2
Female [1]	8,109	7,296	4.2	7.3	79.2	80.5	31.8	49.0	16.6	12.1
White	6,903	5,763	3.2	6.2	81.4	82.1	32.4	50.3	15.3	11.6
Black	1,085	1,167	9.7	11.7	65.0	72.2	25.8	39.3	25.4	16.0
Hispanic [2]	484	1,098	7.6	9.0	59.3	62.3	23.6	28.7	33.1	28.3

[1] Includes other races not shown separately. [2] Persons of Hispanic origin may be of any race.

Source: U.S. Census Bureau, *Current Population Reports*, P20-521; and earlier reports.

No. 293. Employment Status of High School Graduates and School Dropouts: 1980 to 1999

[In thousands (11,622 represents 11,622,000), except percent. As of **October**. For civilian noninstitutional population 16 to 24 years old. Based on Current Population Survey; see text, Section 1, Population, and Appendix III]

Employment status, sex, and race	Graduates [1]				Dropouts [3]			
	1980	1990	1995 [2]	1999 [2]	1980	1990	1995 [2]	1999 [2]
Civilian population	11,622	8,370	6,627	6,999	5,254	3,800	3,876	3,829
In labor force	9,795	7,107	5,530	5,933	3,549	2,506	2,443	2,511
Percent of population	84.3	84.9	83.4	84.8	67.5	66.0	63.0	65.6
Employed	8,567	6,279	4,863	5,331	2,651	1,993	1,894	2,129
Percent of labor force	87.5	88.3	87.9	89.9	74.7	79.5	77.5	84.8
Unemployed	1,228	828	667	603	898	513	549	382
Unemployment rate, total [4]	12.5	11.7	12.1	10.2	25.3	20.5	22.5	15.2
Male	13.5	11.1	11.7	9.8	23.5	18.8	19.2	12.8
Female	11.5	12.3	12.5	10.6	28.7	23.5	28.8	19.8
White	10.8	9.0	10.5	11.3	21.6	17.0	19.1	11.3
Black	26.1	26.0	20.3	21.7	43.9	43.3	48.0	35.8
Not in labor force	1,827	1,262	1,097	1,066	1,705	1,294	1,433	1,318
Percent of population	15.7	15.1	16.6	15.2	32.5	34.1	37.0	34.4

[1] For persons not enrolled in college who have completed 4 years of high school only. [2] See footnote 2, Table 643. [3] For persons not in regular school and who have not completed the 12th grade nor received a general equivalency degree. [4] Includes other races not shown separately.

Source: U.S. Bureau of Labor Statistics, Bulletin 2307; *News*, USDL 00-136, May 17, 2000; and unpublished data.

Education 181

No. 294. General Educational Development (GED) Credentials Issued: 1974 to 1998

[GEDs issued in thousands (295 represents 295,000). Includes outlying areas]

Year	GEDs issued	Percent distribution by age of test taker				
		19 years old or under	20 to 24 years old	25 to 29 years old	30 to 34 years old	35 years old and over
1974	295	35	27	13	9	17
1975	342	33	26	14	9	18
1980	488	37	27	13	8	15
1985	427	33	26	15	10	16
1990	419	35	25	14	10	17
1992	465	32	28	13	11	16
1993	476	33	27	14	11	16
1994	499	34	26	13	10	16
1995	513	37	25	13	10	15
1996	514	40	25	13	9	15
1997	471	41	25	12	8	14
1998	496	43	25	11	8	14

Source: U.S. National Center for Education Statistics, *Digest of Education Statistics*, 1999.

No. 295. College Enrollment of Recent High School Graduates: 1960 to 1998

[**High school graduates in thousands (1,679 represents 1,679,000).** For persons 16 to 24 who graduated from high school in the preceeding 12 months. Includes persons receiving GEDs. Based on surveys and subject to sampling error]

Year	Number of high school graduates					Percent enrolled in college [2]				
	Total [1]	Male	Female	White	Black	Total [1]	Male	Female	White	Black
1960	1,679	756	923	1,565	(NA)	45.1	54.0	37.9	45.8	(NA)
1965	2,659	1,254	1,405	2,417	(NA)	50.9	57.3	45.3	51.7	(NA)
1970	2,757	1,343	1,414	2,461	(NA)	51.8	55.2	48.5	52.0	(NA)
1975	3,186	1,513	1,673	2,825	(NA)	50.7	52.6	49.0	51.2	(NA)
1980	3,089	1,500	1,589	2,682	361	49.3	46.7	51.8	49.9	41.8
1982	3,100	1,508	1,592	2,644	384	50.6	49.0	52.1	52.0	36.5
1983	2,964	1,390	1,574	2,496	392	52.7	51.9	53.4	55.0	38.5
1984	3,012	1,429	1,583	2,514	438	55.2	56.0	54.5	57.9	40.2
1985	2,666	1,286	1,380	2,241	333	57.7	58.6	56.9	59.4	42.3
1986	2,786	1,331	1,455	2,307	386	53.8	55.9	51.9	56.0	36.5
1987	2,647	1,278	1,369	2,207	337	56.8	58.4	55.3	56.6	51.9
1988	2,673	1,334	1,339	2,187	382	58.9	57.0	60.8	60.7	45.0
1989	2,454	1,208	1,245	2,051	337	59.6	57.6	61.6	60.4	52.8
1990	2,355	1,169	1,185	1,921	341	59.9	57.8	62.0	61.5	46.3
1991	2,276	1,139	1,137	1,867	320	62.4	57.6	67.1	64.6	45.6
1992	2,398	1,216	1,182	1,900	353	61.7	59.6	63.8	63.4	47.9
1993	2,338	1,118	1,219	1,910	302	62.6	59.7	65.4	62.8	55.6
1994	2,517	1,244	1,273	2,065	318	61.9	60.6	63.2	63.6	50.9
1995	2,599	1,238	1,361	2,088	356	61.9	62.6	61.4	62.6	51.4
1996	2,660	1,297	1,363	2,092	416	65.0	60.1	69.7	65.8	55.3
1997	2,769	1,354	1,415	2,228	394	67.0	63.5	70.3	67.5	59.6
1998	2,810	1,452	1,358	2,227	393	65.6	62.4	69.1	65.8	62.1

NA Not available. [1] Includes other races, not shown separately. [2] As of October.

Source: U.S. National Center for Education Statistics, *Digest of Education Statistics*, annual.

No. 296. College Enrollment by Sex and Attendance Status: 1983 to 1998

[As of **fall. In thousands (12,465 represents 12,465,000)**]

Sex and age	1983		1988		1993		1997		1998, proj.	
	Total	Part time	Total	Part time	Total	Part time	Total	Part time	Total	Part time
Total	12,465	5,204	13,055	5,619	14,305	6,177	14,345	6,023	14,608	6,366
Male	6,024	2,264	6,002	2,340	6,427	2,537	6,330	2,491	6,297	2,559
14 to 17 years old	102	16	55	5	83	10	91	12	98	18
18 to 19 years old	1,256	158	1,290	132	1,224	138	1,376	221	1,402	223
20 to 21 years old	1,241	205	1,243	216	1,294	209	1,249	254	1,238	257
22 to 24 years old	1,158	382	1,106	378	1,260	392	1,136	336	1,077	346
25 to 29 years old	1,115	624	875	485	950	564	969	542	952	550
30 to 34 years old	570	384	617	456	661	484	490	331	499	339
35 years old and over	583	494	816	668	955	739	1,018	796	1,031	824
Female	6,441	2,940	7,053	3,278	7,877	3,640	8,015	3,532	8,311	3,807
14 to 17 years old	142	16	115	17	93	6	117	21	115	17
18 to 19 years old	1,496	179	1,536	195	1,416	172	1,708	243	1,790	256
20 to 21 years old	1,125	204	1,278	218	1,414	279	1,421	262	1,449	277
22 to 24 years old	884	378	932	403	1,263	493	1,097	392	1,088	417
25 to 29 years old	947	658	932	633	1,058	689	1,081	639	1,084	670
30 to 34 years old	721	553	698	499	811	575	699	466	725	500
35 years old and over	1,126	953	1,563	1,313	1,824	1,427	1,893	1,508	2,059	1,670

Source: U.S. National Center for Education Statistics, *Digest of Education Statistics*, annual.

No. 297. Higher Education—Summary: 1970 to 1997

[Institutions, staff, and enrollment as of fall (474 represents 474,000). Finances for fiscal year ending in the following year. Covers universities, colleges, professional schools, junior and teachers colleges, both publicly and privately controlled, regular session. Includes estimates for institutions not reporting. See also Appendix III]

Item	Unit	1970	1980	1985	1990	1993	1994	1995	1996	1997
ALL INSTITUTIONS										
Number of institutions [1]	Number.	2,556	3,231	3,340	3,559	3,632	3,688	3,706	4,009	4,064
4-year	Number .	1,665	1,957	2,029	2,141	2,190	2,215	2,244	2,267	2,309
2-year	Number .	891	1,274	1,311	1,418	1,442	1,473	1,462	1,742	1,755
Instructional staff—										
(Lecturer or above) [2]	1,000. . .	474	686	715	817	915	915	932	932	990
Percent full-time	Percent .	78	66	64	61	60	(NA)	59	59	57
Total enrollment [3]	1,000. . .	8,581	12,097	12,247	13,819	14,305	14,279	14,262	14,368	14,502
Male	1,000. . .	5,044	5,874	5,818	6,284	6,427	6,372	6,343	6,353	6,396
Female	1,000. . .	3,537	6,223	6,429	7,535	7,877	7,907	7,919	8,015	8,106
4-year institutions	1,000. . .	6,262	7,571	7,716	8,579	8,739	8,749	8,769	8,804	8,897
2-year institutions	1,000. . .	2,319	4,526	4,531	5,240	5,566	5,530	5,493	5,563	5,606
Full-time	1,000. . .	5,816	7,098	7,075	7,821	8,128	8,138	8,129	8,303	8,438
Part-time	1,000. . .	2,765	4,999	5,172	5,998	6,177	6,141	6,133	6,065	6,064
Public	1,000. . .	6,428	9,457	9,479	10,845	11,189	11,134	11,092	11,120	11,196
Private	1,000. . .	2,153	2,640	2,768	2,974	3,116	3,145	3,169	3,247	3,306
Undergraduate [4]	1,000. . .	7,376	10,475	10,597	11,959	12,324	12,263	12,232	12,327	12,451
Men	1,000. . .	4,254	5,000	4,962	5,380	5,484	5,422	5,401	5,421	5,469
Women	1,000. . .	3,122	5,475	5,635	6,579	6,840	6,840	6,831	6,906	6,982
First-time freshmen	1,000. . .	2,063	2,588	2,292	2,257	2,161	2,133	2,169	2,274	2,219
First professional	1,000. . .	173	278	274	273	292	295	298	298	298
Men	1,000. . .	159	199	180	167	173	174	174	173	170
Women	1,000. . .	15	78	94	107	120	121	124	126	129
Graduate [4]	1,000. . .	1,031	1,343	1,376	1,586	1,688	1,721	1,732	1,742	1,753
Men	1,000. . .	630	675	677	737	771	776	768	759	758
Women	1,000. . .	400	670	700	849	917	946	965	983	996
Current funds revenues [5]	Mil. dol .	23,879	65,585	100,438	149,766	179,227	189,121	197,973	(NA)	(NA)
Tuition and fees	Mil. dol .	5,021	13,773	23,117	37,434	48,647	51,507	55,260	(NA)	(NA)
Federal government	Mil. dol .	4,190	9,748	12,705	18,236	22,076	23,243	23,939	(NA)	(NA)
State government	Mil. dol .	6,503	20,106	29,912	39,481	41,910	44,343	45,693	(NA)	(NA)
Auxiliary enterprises	Mil. dol .	3,125	7,287	10,674	14,903	17,538	18,336	18,868	(NA)	(NA)
Current funds expenditures [5]	Mil. dol .	23,375	64,053	97,536	146,088	173,351	182,969	190,476	(NA)	(NA)
Educational and general [6]	Mil. dol .	17,616	50,074	76,128	114,140	136,024	144,158	151,446	(NA)	(NA)
Auxiliary enterprises	Mil. dol .	2,988	7,288	10,528	14,272	16,429	17,205	17,599	(NA)	(NA)
Endowment (market value)	Mil. dol .	13,714	23,465	50,281	72,049	96,013	109,707	128,837	(NA)	(NA)
2-YEAR INSTITUTIONS										
Number of institutions [1][7]	Number.	891	1,274	1,311	1,418	1,442	1,473	1,462	1,742	1,755
Public	Number .	654	945	932	972	1,021	1,036	1,047	1,088	1,092
Private	Number .	237	329	379	446	421	437	415	654	663
Instructional staff—										
(Lecturer or above) [2]	1,000. . .	92	192	211	(NA)	290	(NA)	285	285	307
Enrollment [3][4]	1,000. . .	2,319	4,526	4,531	5,240	5,566	5,530	5,493	5,563	5,606
Public	1,000. . .	2,195	4,329	4,270	4,996	5,337	5,308	5,278	5,314	5,361
Private	1,000. . .	124	198	261	244	229	221	215	249	245
Male	1,000. . .	1,375	2,047	2,002	2,233	2,345	2,323	2,329	2,359	2,390
Female	1,000. . .	945	2,479	2,529	3,007	3,220	3,207	3,164	3,204	3,216
Current funds revenue [5]	Mil. dol .	2,504	8,505	12,293	18,021	21,961	22,977	24,614	(NA)	(NA)
Tuition and fees	Mil. dol .	413	1,618	2,618	4,029	5,594	5,643	6,323	(NA)	(NA)
State government	Mil. dol .	926	3,961	5,659	8,001	8,730	9,252	9,848	(NA)	(NA)
Local government	Mil. dol .	701	1,623	2,027	3,044	3,936	4,139	4,324	(NA)	(NA)
Current funds expenditures [5]	Mil. dol .	2,327	8,212	11,976	17,494	21,187	22,078	23,522	(NA)	(NA)
Education and general [6]	Mil. dol .	2,073	7,608	11,118	16,270	19,763	20,616	22,053	(NA)	(NA)
Instruction	Mil. dol .	1,205	3,764	5,398	7,903	9,476	9,829	10,312	(NA)	(NA)

NA Not available.   [1] Beginning 1980, number of institutions includes count of branch campuses. Due to revised survey procedures, data beginning 1990 are not comparable with previous years. Beginning 1996 data reflect a new classification of institutions; this classification includes some additional, primarily 2-year, colleges than before and excludes a few institutions that did not award degrees. Includes institutions that were eligible to participate in Title IV Federal financial aid programs.   [2] Due to revised survey methods, data beginning 1990 not comparable with previous years.   [3] Beginning 1980, branch campuses counted according to actual status, e.g., 2-year branch in 2-year category; previously a 2-year branch included in university category.   [4] Includes unclassified students. (Students taking courses for credit, but are not candidates for degrees.)   [5] Includes items not shown separately.   [6] Data for 1970 are not strictly comparable with later years.   [7] Beginning 1980, includes schools accredited by the National Association of Trade and Technical Schools. See footnote 1 for information pertaining to data beginning 1996.

Source: U.S. National Center for Education Statistics, Digest of Education Statistics, annual; Projections of Education Statistics, annual; and unpublished data.

No. 298. College Enrollment by Selected Characteristics: 1980 to 1997

[In thousands (12,096.9 represents 12,096,900). As of **fall**. Totals may differ from other tables because of adjustments to underreported and nonreported racial/ethnic data. Nonresident alien students are not distributed among racial/ethnic groups]

Characteristic	1980	1990	1992	1993	1994	1995	1996 [1]	1997 [1]
Total	**12,096.9**	**13,818.6**	**14,487.4**	**14,304.8**	**14,278.8**	**14,261.8**	**14,367.5**	**14,502.3**
Male	5,874.4	6,283.9	6,524.0	6,427.5	6,371.9	6,342.5	6,352.8	6,396.0
Female.	6,222.5	7,534.7	7,963.4	7,877.4	7,906.9	7,919.2	8,014.7	8,106.3
Public.	9,457.4	10,844.7	11,384.6	11,189.1	11,133.7	11,092.4	11,120.5	11,196.1
Private	2,639.5	2,973.9	3,102.8	3,115.7	3,145.1	3,169.4	3,247.0	3,306.2
2-year	4,526.3	5,240.1	5,722.4	5,565.9	5,529.7	5,492.5	5,563.3	5,605.6
4-year	7,570.6	8,578.6	8,765.0	8,738.9	8,749.1	8,769.3	8,804.2	8,896.8
Undergraduate.	10,475.5	11,959.2	12,537.7	12,324.0	12,262.6	12,232.0	12,326.9	12,450.6
Graduate	1,342.5	1,586.2	1,668.7	1,688.4	1,721.5	1,732.0	1,742.3	1,753.5
First professional . . .	277.8	273.4	280.9	292.4	294.7	297.6	298.3	298.3
White [2]	9,833.0	10,722.5	10,875.4	10,600.0	10,427.0	10,311.2	10,263.9	10,266.1
Male	4,772.9	4,861.0	4,884.6	4,755.0	4,650.7	4,594.1	4,552.2	4,548.8
Female.	5,060.1	5,861.5	5,990.8	5,845.1	5,776.3	5,717.2	5,711.7	5,717.4
Public.	7,656.1	8,385.4	8,492.8	8,226.6	8,056.3	7,945.4	7,871.9	7,857.8
Private	2,176.9	2,337.0	2,382.6	2,373.4	2,370.6	2,365.9	2,392.0	2,408.3
2-year	3,558.5	3,954.3	4,131.2	3,960.6	3,861.7	3,794.0	3,780.8	3,770.0
4-year	6,274.5	6,768.1	6,744.3	6,639.5	6,565.3	6,517.2	6,483.1	6,496.1
Undergraduate.	8,480.7	9,272.6	9,387.6	9,100.4	8,916.0	8,805.6	8,769.5	8,783.9
Graduate	1,104.7	1,228.4	1,267.2	1,273.8	1,286.8	1,282.3	1,272.6	1,261.8
First professional . . .	247.7	221.5	220.6	225.9	224.2	223.3	221.7	220.4
Black [2]	1,106.8	1,247.0	1,392.9	1,412.8	1,448.6	1,473.7	1,505.6	1,551.0
Male	463.7	484.7	536.9	543.7	549.7	555.9	564.1	579.8
Female.	643.0	762.3	856.0	869.1	898.9	917.8	941.4	971.3
Public.	876.1	976.4	1,100.5	1,114.3	1,144.6	1,160.6	1,177.4	1,205.3
Private	230.7	270.6	292.3	298.5	304.1	313.0	328.1	345.8
2-year	472.5	524.3	601.6	599.0	615.0	621.5	636.0	654.6
4-year	634.3	722.8	791.2	813.7	833.6	852.2	869.6	896.4
Undergraduate.	1,018.8	1,147.2	1,280.6	1,290.4	1,317.3	1,333.6	1,358.6	1,398.1
Graduate	75.1	83.9	94.1	102.2	110.6	118.6	125.5	131.6
First professional . . .	12.8	15.9	18.2	20.2	20.7	21.4	21.5	21.4
Hispanic	471.7	782.4	955.0	988.8	1,045.6	1,093.8	1,166.1	1,218.5
Male	231.6	353.9	427.7	441.2	464.0	480.2	506.6	525.8
Female.	240.1	428.5	527.3	547.6	581.6	613.7	659.5	692.7
Public.	406.2	671.4	822.3	851.3	898.7	937.1	990.7	1,031.6
Private	65.6	111.0	132.7	137.5	146.8	156.8	175.4	186.9
2-year	255.1	424.2	545.0	556.8	582.9	608.4	657.3	688.5
4-year	216.6	358.2	409.9	432.0	462.7	485.5	508.8	530.0
Undergraduate.	433.1	724.6	887.8	918.1	968.3	1,012.0	1,079.4	1,125.9
Graduate	32.1	47.2	55.3	57.9	63.9	68.0	72.8	78.7
First professional . . .	6.5	10.7	12.0	12.8	13.4	13.8	13.9	13.9
American Indian [2] .	83.9	102.8	119.3	121.7	127.4	131.3	137.6	142.5
Male	37.8	43.1	50.2	51.2	53.0	54.8	57.2	59.0
Female.	46.1	59.7	69.1	70.5	74.4	76.5	80.4	83.4
Public.	74.2	90.4	103.3	106.4	110.7	113.8	118.8	123.6
Private	9.7	12.4	15.9	15.3	16.6	17.5	18.8	18.8
2-year	47.0	54.9	64.4	63.2	66.2	65.6	70.2	71.0
4-year	36.9	47.9	54.9	58.5	61.2	65.7	67.3	71.5
Undergraduate.	77.9	95.5	110.9	112.7	117.4	120.7	126.5	130.8
Graduate	5.2	6.2	7.0	7.3	8.1	8.5	8.9	9.4
First professional . . .	0.8	1.1	1.5	1.7	1.8	2.1	2.2	2.3
Asian [2]	286.4	572.4	697.0	724.4	774.3	797.4	828.2	859.2
Male	151.3	294.9	351.5	363.1	385.0	393.3	405.5	417.7
Female.	135.2	277.5	345.6	361.3	389.3	404.1	422.6	441.5
Public.	239.7	461.0	565.9	586.3	622.1	638.0	657.9	680.4
Private	46.7	111.5	131.1	138.2	152.2	159.4	170.3	178.8
2-year	124.3	215.2	289.5	295.0	312.5	314.9	327.0	340.7
4-year	162.1	357.2	407.5	429.4	461.8	482.4	501.1	518.5
Undergraduate.	248.7	500.5	613.0	634.2	674.1	692.2	717.6	743.7
Graduate	31.6	53.2	61.5	65.2	72.6	75.6	79.1	82.6
First professional . . .	6.1	18.7	22.5	25.0	27.6	29.6	31.4	32.9
Nonresident alien .	305.0	391.5	447.7	457.1	455.9	454.4	466.3	465.0
Male	210.8	246.3	273.1	273.4	269.5	264.3	267.2	264.9
Female.	94.2	145.2	174.6	183.7	186.4	190.1	199.0	200.1
Public.	204.2	260.0	299.5	304.3	301.2	297.5	303.8	297.3
Private	100.8	131.4	148.1	152.7	154.7	156.9	162.5	167.7
2-year	64.1	67.1	90.6	91.2	91.4	88.1	92.0	80.7
4-year	240.9	324.3	357.0	365.9	364.5	366.2	374.3	384.3
Undergraduate.	209.9	218.7	257.9	268.2	269.4	267.6	275.3	268.2
Graduate	92.2	167.3	183.6	182.0	179.5	179.5	183.3	189.4
First professional . . .	2.9	5.4	6.2	6.9	7.0	7.3	7.6	7.5

[1] Beginning 1996 data reflect a new classification of institutions; this classification includes some additional, primarily 2-year, colleges than before and excludes a few institutions that did not award degrees.   [2] Non-Hispanic.

Source: U.S. National Center for Education Statistics, *Digest of Education Statistics*, annual.

No. 299. Degree-Granting Institutions, Number, and Enrollment by State: 1997

[Number of institutions beginning in academic year. Opening fall enrollment of resident and extension students attending full time or part time (**14,502 represents 14,502,000**). Excludes students taking courses for credit by mail, radio, or TV, and students in branches of U.S. institutions operated in foreign countries. See Appendix III]

State	Number of institutions [1]	Enrollment (1,000)							Minority enrollment			Non-resident alien
		Total	Male	Female	Public	Private	Full time	White [2]	Total [3]	Black [2]	His-panic	
United States . . .	4,064	14,502	6,396	8,106	11,196	3,306	8,438	10,266	3,771	1,551	1,218	465
Alabama.	79	219	95	123	194	25	152	155	59	54	2	5
Alaska	8	28	11	17	27	1	12	22	6	1	1	(Z)
Arizona.	67	293	131	162	261	32	142	209	76	10	45	8
Arkansas	47	112	47	65	101	11	73	89	21	17	1	2
California	396	1,958	865	1,093	1,664	294	937	956	930	153	406	72
Colorado.	70	252	114	138	213	39	138	200	46	9	25	6
Connecticut.	42	153	67	86	95	58	83	120	27	12	8	6
Delaware	10	45	19	26	36	8	26	35	9	7	1	1
District of Columbia .	17	72	32	40	5	68	50	35	28	21	3	9
Florida	140	658	285	373	535	124	325	421	216	93	99	22
Georgia	104	306	131	175	235	71	209	203	94	79	5	9
Hawaii	20	62	27	34	46	16	36	15	41	2	1	6
Idaho.	15	62	27	34	50	11	42	57	4	(Z)	2	1
Illinois	172	726	317	410	537	190	379	501	206	95	68	19
Indiana.	96	296	134	162	225	71	199	253	33	19	7	10
Iowa	64	181	81	100	128	53	125	161	13	5	3	7
Kansas.	59	178	81	97	160	18	97	148	24	9	8	5
Kentucky	63	179	74	105	146	33	120	158	17	13	1	3
Louisiana	85	219	92	128	189	30	157	143	71	59	5	6
Maine.	35	56	22	34	38	18	32	53	3	1	-	1
Maryland	58	261	109	152	217	44	131	167	84	61	7	10
Massachusetts.	129	413	180	233	175	238	265	315	72	25	19	25
Michigan.	110	550	239	311	459	91	285	436	95	62	12	18
Minnesota.	115	270	120	150	203	67	170	239	24	8	4	7
Mississippi	46	131	55	76	119	12	97	86	43	40	1	2
Missouri	112	303	132	170	191	112	175	253	42	27	6	8
Montana.	28	44	20	24	39	5	34	38	5	(Z)	1	1
Nebraska	37	112	50	61	89	22	69	99	9	4	2	3
Nevada	14	76	34	42	73	3	27	56	18	5	7	2
New Hampshire	26	64	27	37	35	29	39	59	4	1	1	1
New Jersey.	59	326	142	184	261	64	179	218	96	39	33	12
New Mexico	44	109	46	63	101	8	56	58	49	3	37	2
New York	319	1,024	435	590	568	457	670	666	314	138	104	44
North Carolina	121	374	160	214	302	72	236	273	94	77	5	7
North Dakota.	21	39	19	20	35	4	32	35	3	(Z)	(Z)	1
Ohio	177	537	236	301	405	132	341	447	73	52	8	17
Oklahoma.	46	177	80	97	155	23	108	132	37	13	5	8
Oregon.	54	170	78	92	144	26	94	142	22	3	6	6
Pennsylvania.	253	588	263	325	335	253	407	487	84	49	12	18
Rhode Island.	12	72	32	40	37	35	47	60	9	3	3	3
South Carolina.	61	176	73	103	149	28	114	127	47	42	2	3
South Dakota	25	39	18	22	33	6	29	35	4	(Z)	(Z)	1
Tennessee	83	250	108	141	194	56	168	199	46	38	3	5
Texas	194	969	442	527	846	124	534	582	359	98	210	28
Utah	21	158	78	80	119	39	98	142	11	1	5	5
Vermont	25	36	16	21	21	16	26	34	2	(Z)	1	1
Virginia.	92	365	159	206	302	63	208	265	91	62	9	8
Washington	72	315	140	176	275	41	187	247	58	13	13	10
West Virginia.	34	88	39	49	76	12	62	80	6	4	1	2
Wisconsin	66	298	133	166	244	54	183	262	29	13	7	7
Wyoming	9	30	13	17	29	1	17	27	2	(Z)	1	-
U.S. military [4]. . . .	12	83	70	13	83	-	20	66	17	11	3	1

- Represents zero. Z Fewer than 500. [1] Branch campuses counted as separate institutions. [2] Non-Hispanic. [3] Includes other races not shown separately. [4] Service schools.

Source: U.S. National Center for Education Statistics, *Digest of Education Statistics,* annual.

Education 185

Foreign (Nonimmigrant) Student Enrollment in College: 1976 to 1999

[For **fall of the previous year**. (179 represents 179,000)]

Region of origin	Enrollment (1,000)									Engineering		Science[1]		Business	
	1976	1980	1985	1990	1995	1996	1997	1998	1999	1980	1998	1980	1998	1980	1998
All regions . .	179	286	342	387	453	454	458	481	491	25	16	8	8	16	21
Africa	25	36	40	25	21	21	22	23	26	20	14	9	8	19	21
Nigeria	11	16	18	4	2	2	2	2	3	19	14	9	8	22	18
Asia[2]	97	165	200	245	292	290	291	308	308	32	18	8	8	16	21
China: Taiwan . .	11	18	23	31	36	33	30	31	31	17	15	15	6	17	24
Hong Kong	12	10	10	11	13	12	11	10	9	22	15	9	5	26	30
India	10	9	15	26	34	32	31	34	37	31	35	16	8	21	16
Indonesia	1	2	7	9	12	13	12	13	12	27	21	7	2	21	41
Iran	20	51	17	7	3	3	2	2	2	45	30	7	16	11	7
Japan	7	12	13	30	45	46	46	47	46	7	4	5	4	19	19
Malaysia.	2	4	22	14	14	14	15	15	12	13	34	14	3	22	32
Saudi Arabia . . .	3	10	8	4	4	4	4	5	5	30	31	4	4	14	13
South Korea . . .	3	5	16	22	34	36	37	43	39	17	11	11	6	15	14
Thailand.	7	7	7	7	11	12	13	15	12	17	16	6	4	26	38
Europe	14	23	33	46	65	67	68	72	74	15	9	9	9	14	22
Latin America[3] . . .	30	42	49	48	47	47	50	51	55	20	13	8	6	14	25
Mexico.	5	6	6	7	9	9	9	10	10	16	16	7	5	11	25
Venezuela	5	10	10	3	4	4	5	5	5	30	14	8	5	11	24
North America. . . .	10	16	16	19	23	24	24	23	23	8	6	6	8	13	13
Canada	10	15	15	18	23	23	23	22	23	8	6	6	8	12	13
Oceania	3	4	4	4	4	4	4	4	4	5	5	7	6	16	22

[1] Physical and life sciences.   [2] Includes countries not shown separately.   [3] Includes Central America, Caribbean, and South America.

Source: Institute of International Education, New York, NY, *Open Doors*, annual (copyright).

College Enrollment by Sex, Age, Race, and Hispanic Origin: 1980 to 1998

[In thousands (11,387 represents 11,387,000). As of **October** for the civilian noninstitutional population, 14 years old and over. Based on the Current Population Survey; see text, Section 1, Population, and Appendix III]

Characteristic	1980	1985	1990[1]	1991	1992	1993	1994	1995	1996	1997	1998
Total[2]	11,387	12,524	13,621	14,057	14,035	13,898	15,022	14,715	15,226	15,436	15,546
Male[3]	5,430	5,906	6,192	6,439	6,192	6,324	6,764	6,703	6,820	6,843	6,905
18 to 24 years	3,604	3,749	3,922	3,954	3,912	3,994	4,152	4,089	4,187	4,374	4,403
25 to 34 years	1,325	1,464	1,412	1,605	1,392	1,406	1,589	1,561	1,523	1,509	1,500
35 years old and over . .	405	561	772	832	789	873	958	985	1,013	899	953
Female[3]	5,957	6,618	7,429	7,618	7,844	7,574	8,258	8,013	8,406	8,593	8,641
18 to 24 years	3,625	3,788	4,042	4,218	4,429	4,199	4,576	4,452	4,582	4,829	4,919
25 to 34 years	1,378	1,599	1,749	1,680	1,732	1,688	1,830	1,788	1,920	1,760	1,915
35 years old and over . .	802	1,100	1,546	1,636	1,575	1,616	1,766	1,684	1,765	1,892	1,732
White[3]	9,925	10,781	11,488	11,488	11,686	11,710	11,434	12,222	12,021	12,189	12,442	12,401
18 to 24 years	6,334	6,500	6,635	6,813	6,916	6,763	7,118	7,011	7,123	7,495	7,541
25 to 34 years	2,328	2,604	2,698	2,661	2,582	2,505	2,735	2,686	2,644	2,522	2,568
35 years old and over . .	1,051	1,448	2,023	2,107	2,053	2,068	2,267	2,208	2,254	2,297	2,199
Male	4,804	5,103	5,235	5,304	5,210	5,222	5,524	5,535	5,453	5,552	5,602
Female	5,121	5,679	6,253	6,253	6,499	6,212	6,698	6,486	6,735	6,890	6,799
Black[3]	1,163	1,263	1,393	1,477	1,424	1,545	1,800	1,772	1,901	1,903	2,016
18 to 24 years	688	734	894	828	886	861	1,001	988	983	1,085	1,115
25 to 34 years	289	295	258	373	302	386	440	426	519	423	539
35 years old and over . .	156	213	207	257	208	284	323	334	354	372	340
Male	476	552	587	629	527	636	745	710	764	723	770
Female	686	712	807	848	897	909	1,054	1,062	1,136	1,180	1,247
Hispanic origin[3][4]	443	580	748	830	918	995	1,187	1,207	1,223	1,260	1,363
18 to 24 years	315	375	435	516	586	602	662	745	706	806	820
25 to 34 years	118	189	168	196	214	249	312	250	310	254	336
35 years old and over . .	(NA)	(NA)	130	109	102	129	205	193	184	151	198
Male	222	279	364	347	388	442	529	568	529	555	550
Female	221	299	384	483	530	553	659	639	693	704	814

NA Not available.   [1] Beginning 1990, based on a revised edit and tabulation package.   [2] Includes other races not shown separately.   [3] Includes persons 14 to 17 years old, not shown separately.   [4] Persons of Hispanic origin may be of any race.

Source: U.S. Census Bureau, *Current Population Reports*, P20-521; and earlier reports.

No. 302. College Freshmen—Summary Characteristics: 1970 to 1999

[In percent, except as indicated (12 represents $12,000). As of **fall** for first-time full-time freshmen. Based on sample survey and subject to sampling error; see source]

Characteristic	1970	1980	1985	1990	1995	1996	1997	1998	1999
Sex:									
Male	55	49	48	46	46	46	46	46	46
Female	45	51	52	54	54	54	54	54	54
Applied to three or more colleges	[1]15	26	29	36	36	37	36	37	38
Average grade in high school:									
A- to A+	16	21	21	23	28	32	32	33	34
B- to B+	58	60	59	58	56	54	54	54	54
C to C+	27	19	20	19	15	14	14	13	12
D	1	1	1	-	-	-	-	-	-
Political orientation:									
Liberal	34	20	21	23	21	22	22	21	22
Middle of the road	45	60	57	55	54	53	55	57	56
Conservative	17	17	19	20	20	21	19	19	18
Probable field of study:									
Arts and humanities	16	9	8	9	10	10	9	10	11
Biological sciences	4	4	4	4	7	7	6	6	6
Business	16	24	27	21	16	16	16	17	16
Education	11	7	7	10	10	11	10	11	12
Engineering	9	12	11	8	7	8	9	8	8
Physical science	2	3	2	2	2	2	2	2	2
Social science	14	7	8	10	9	9	8	8	9
Professional	(NA)	15	13	15	18	16	15	15	13
Technical	4	6	5	4	4	2	4	4	4
Data processing/computer programming	(NA)	2	2	1	1	1	2	2	2
Other [2]	(NA)	(NA)	16	16	17	19	19	18	19
Communications	(NA)	2	2	2	2	2	2	2	2
Computer science	(NA)	1	2	2	2	3	3	4	4
Recipient of financial aid:									
Pell grant	(NA)	33	19	23	23	20	22	21	20
Supplemental educational opportunity grant	(NA)	8	5	7	6	6	6	6	6
State scholarship or grant	(NA)	16	14	16	16	17	17	17	19
College grant	(NA)	13	19	22	26	29	27	29	29
Federal guaranteed student loan	(NA)	21	23	23	29	26	25	25	24
Perkins loan [3]	(NA)	9	6	8	9	9	9	9	9
College loan	(NA)	4	4	6	10	9	11	10	11
College work-study grant	(NA)	15	10	10	13	12	12	12	12
Attitudes—agree or strongly agree:									
Activities of married women are best confined to home and family	48	27	22	25	24	24	25	(X)	28
Capital punishment should be abolished	56	34	27	22	21	22	24	23	25
Legalize marijuana	38	39	22	19	34	33	35	32	34
There is too much concern for the rights of criminals	52	66	(NA)	(NA)	73	72	70	73	72
Abortion should be legalized	(NA)	54	55	65	58	56	54	51	53
Aspires to an advanced degree	49	49	51	61	64	67	67	65	66
Male	57	50	52	60	61	65	63	61	62
Female	41	47	50	62	66	68	69	67	69
Median family income ($1,000)	12	23	34	43	49	53	53	53	57

- Represents or rounds to zero.   NA Not available.   X Not applicable.   [1] 1969 data.   [2] Includes other fields, not shown separately.   [3] National Direct Student Loan prior to 1990.

Source: The Higher Education Research Institute, University of California, Los Angeles, CA, *The American Freshman: National Norms*, annual.

No. 303. Higher Education Registrations in Foreign Languages: 1970 to 1998

[As of **fall** (1,111.5 represents 1,111,500)]

Item	1970	1974	1977	1980	1983	1986	1990	1995	1998
Registrations [1] (1,000)	1,111.5	946.6	933.5	924.8	966.0	1,003.2	1,184.1	1,138.8	1,193.8
Index (1960=100)	171.8	146.3	144.3	142.9	149.3	155.0	183.0	176.0	184.5
By selected language (1,000):									
Spanish	389.2	362.2	376.7	379.4	386.2	411.3	533.9	606.3	656.6
French	359.3	253.1	246.1	248.4	270.1	275.3	272.5	205.4	199.1
German	202.6	152.1	135.4	126.9	128.2	121.0	133.3	96.3	89.0
Italian	34.2	33.0	33.3	34.8	38.7	40.9	49.7	43.8	49.3
Japanese	6.6	9.6	10.7	11.5	16.1	23.5	45.7	44.7	43.1
Chinese	6.2	10.6	9.8	11.4	13.2	16.9	19.5	26.5	28.5
Latin	27.6	25.2	24.4	25.0	24.2	25.0	28.2	25.9	26.1
Russian	36.1	32.5	27.8	24.0	30.4	34.0	44.6	24.7	23.8
Ancient Greek	16.7	24.4	25.8	22.1	19.4	17.6	16.4	16.3	16.4
Hebrew	16.6	22.4	19.4	19.4	18.2	15.6	13.0	13.1	15.8
American Sign Language	(X)	(X)	(X)	(X)	(X)	(X)	1.6	4.3	11.4
Portuguese	5.1	5.1	5.0	4.9	4.4	5.1	6.2	6.5	6.9
Arabic	1.3	2.0	3.1	3.5	3.4	3.4	3.5	4.4	5.5

X Not applicable.   [1] Includes other foreign languages, not shown separately.

Source: Association of Departments of Foreign Languages, New York, NY, *ADFL Bulletin*, Vol. 31, No. 2, and earlier issues (copyright).

Education   187

No. 304. College Population by Selected Characteristics: 1998

[In thousands (209,831 represents 209,831,000), except percent. As of October. For **persons 15 years old and over.** Based on the Current Population Survey. See text, Section 1, Population, and Appendix III]

| Characteristic | Total popula-tion | Enrolled in college | | | | | | | |
| | | Total | Type of school | | | Percent enrolled full time | Percent employed | | |
			2-year	4-year	Graduate school		Total	Full time	Part time
Total [1]	209,831	15,546	4,234	8,275	3,037	65.5	63.7	33.6	30.1
Male	101,114	6,905	1,845	3,777	1,284	67.6	62.6	34.7	27.9
Female.	108,718	8,641	2,389	4,499	1,754	63.9	64.6	32.8	31.8
White.	175,028	12,401	3,389	6,632	2,379	64.6	65.9	34.1	31.8
Black	25,117	2,016	628	1,063	326	63.7	61.9	39.1	22.8
Hispanic origin [2]	21,817	1,363	640	560	164	58.8	62.1	37.0	25.1
15 to 19 years old	19,752	3,793	1,301	2,447	45	88.9	48.6	9.7	38.9
20 and 21 years old	7,131	3,092	701	2,318	73	86.6	56.7	16.8	39.9
22 to 24 years old	10,474	2,561	619	1,406	537	73.8	64.5	30.3	34.2
25 to 34 years old	38,601	3,414	838	1,261	1,314	45.0	75.2	54.6	20.6
35 years and older	133,871	2,685	772	839	1,070	26.4	77.6	63.3	14.3

[1] Includes other races, not shown separately.   [2] Persons of Hispanic origin may be of any race.

Source: U.S. Census Bureau, *Current Population Reports*, P20-521.

No. 305. Enrollment of Students With Disabilities in Postsecondary Institutions: 1996-97 or 1997-98

[For students who identified themselves as disabled to their institutions. Based on the Postsecondary Education Quick Information System; see source for details]

| Institutional characteristic | Institutions | | Students with disabilities enrolled | | | | | |
	Total	Enrolling students with dis-abilities	With any disability [1]	Hearing impair-ment	Visual impair-ment	Speech or language impair-ment	Mobility/ orthopedic impair-ment	Specific learning disability
Total	5,040	3,630	428,280	23,860	18,650	4,020	59,650	195,870
Public, 2-year	1,240	1,220	230,170	12,680	9,480	2,730	35,650	86,750
Private, 2-year.	1,140	530	5,440	320	200	50	750	2,380
Public, 4-year	610	590	138,860	6,440	7,060	920	20,280	71,160
Private, 4-year.	2,060	1,290	53,810	4,430	1,910	320	2,970	35,580
Less than 3,000 students. . . .	3,830	2,430	75,930	5,840	3,540	840	10,050	36,500
3,000 to 9,999	810	800	149,130	6,460	5,410	1,320	18,320	68,970
10,000 or more	400	400	203,210	11,560	9,700	1,860	31,280	90,390

[1] Includes other disabilities, not shown separately.

Source: National Center for Education Statistics, *An Institutional Perspective on Students with Disabilities in Postsecondary Education*, August 1999, NCES 1999-046.

No. 306. Postsecondary Institutions Offering Distance Education: 1997-98

[Distance education refers to courses delivered to off-campus locations via audio, video or computer technologies. Based on the Postsecondary Education Quick Information System; see source for details]

| Institutional characteristic | Institutions | | Enrollments in distance education courses | | | |
| | | | | In college level credit-granting courses | | |
	Total	Offering distance education	Total	Total	Under-graduate	Graduate [1]
Total [2]	5,010	1,680	1,661,100	1,363,670	1,082,380	281,300
Public, 2-year	1,230	760	714,160	690,700	690,550	(B)
Public, 4-year	610	480	711,350	452,600	289,520	163,080
Private, 4-year.	2,050	390	222,350	208,590	90,520	118,070
Less than 3,000 students.	3,800	730	382,060	270,400	177,150	93,250
3,000 to 9,999	820	610	477,470	461,880	413,770	48,100
10,000 or more	400	350	801,570	631,400	491,460	139,950

B Base too small to meet statistical standards for reliability of a derived figure.   [1] Includes first-professional level courses.   [2] Includes private 2-year institutions, not reported separately. Too few offered distance education to make a reliable estimate.

Source: National Center for Education Statistics, *Distance Education at Postsecondary Education Institutions*, December 1999, NCES 2000-013.

188   Education

No. 307. Higher Education Price Indexes: 1970 to 1998

[1983=100. For years ending June 30. Reflects prices paid by colleges and universities]

Year	Personnel compensation					Contracted services, supplies, and equipment					
	Index, total	Total	Profes-sional salaries	Nonpro-fessional salaries	Fringe benefits	Total	Serv-ices	Supplies and materials	Equip-ment	Library acquisi-tions	Utilities
1970 ..	39.5	42.1	47.7	38.8	24.7	31.9	42.8	37.6	41.9	25.7	16.3
1973 ..	46.7	49.8	54.3	47.6	34.7	37.6	49.9	41.1	46.5	37.7	20.2
1974 ..	49.9	52.8	57.2	50.6	38.6	41.4	52.2	46.5	49.4	41.6	24.8
1975 ..	54.3	56.3	60.3	54.6	42.9	48.5	56.8	58.0	58.3	46.7	31.8
1976 ..	57.8	60.0	63.5	59.0	47.8	51.3	59.1	60.7	61.7	52.1	34.4
1977 ..	61.5	63.5	66.4	63.1	52.8	55.7	62.6	63.8	64.8	56.8	40.5
1978 ..	65.7	67.6	69.9	68.1	58.4	60.2	66.6	66.6	69.3	63.2	45.9
1979 ..	70.5	72.4	74.1	73.4	64.5	65.1	71.2	71.7	74.7	70.0	50.3
1980 ..	77.5	78.4	79.4	80.2	72.6	75.0	77.0	84.6	81.6	77.8	64.1
1981 ..	85.8	85.8	86.3	87.7	81.8	85.9	85.2	95.6	89.6	85.9	79.7
1982 ..	93.9	93.5	93.7	94.6	91.5	94.9	94.2	100.4	96.4	93.5	92.4
1983 ..	100.0	100.0	100.0	100.0	100.0	100.0	100.0	100.0	100.0	100.0	100.0
1984 ..	104.8	105.4	104.7	105.1	108.3	103.0	104.9	99.7	102.3	105.3	102.5
1985 ..	110.8	112.0	111.4	109.2	117.7	107.1	110.8	103.0	104.8	111.3	105.3
1986 ..	116.3	118.8	118.2	112.8	127.7	109.0	115.1	102.6	107.2	121.2	103.1
1987 ..	120.9	125.4	125.0	116.3	137.4	107.4	119.7	99.0	108.9	132.9	91.0
1988 ..	126.2	131.7	130.9	120.6	147.2	109.8	123.0	101.1	120.5	140.5	87.7
1989 ..	132.8	139.6	138.8	125.3	158.8	112.8	128.8	108.3	115.1	153.5	85.3
1990 ..	140.8	148.3	147.6	130.3	171.4	118.7	134.0	114.3	119.6	167.0	90.1
1991 ..	148.2	156.5	155.6	135.4	184.3	123.3	139.8	116.4	123.3	179.8	92.4
1992 ..	153.5	162.4	160.8	140.2	184.3	126.9	145.7	115.2	126.3	193.9	93.3
1993 ..	158.0	167.6	165.0	144.2	204.3	129.4	149.5	113.2	128.6	204.3	94.7
1994 ..	163.3	173.3	170.3	148.2	213.6	133.9	154.8	114.3	130.8	216.2	98.7
1995 ..	168.3	179.1	176.1	152.5	221.4	136.1	158.0	115.7	133.5	228.8	96.8
1996 ..	173.3	184.1	181.7	157.3	224.5	141.3	163.8	130.1	137.0	245.0	93.3
1997 ..	178.6	189.0	187.2	162.1	226.7	148.0	167.3	128.6	139.3	260.9	106.1
1998 ..	184.9	195.9	193.6	168.0	236.7	152.5	172.8	126.2	141.3	275.9	111.1

Source: Research Associates of Washington, Arlington, VA, *Inflation Measures for Schools, Colleges, and Libraries*, annual (copyright).

No. 308. Institutions of Higher Education—Finances: 1980 to 1996

[In millions of dollars (58,520 represents $58,520,000,000). For fiscal years ending in year shown. For coverage, see headnote, Table 297. See also Appendix III]

Item	1980	1985	1990	1993	1994	1995	1996 Total	1996 Public	1996 Private
Current funds revenues	58,520	92,473	139,635	170,881	179,227	189,121	197,973	123,501	74,472
Tuition and fees	11,930	21,283	33,926	45,346	48,647	51,507	55,260	23,257	32,003
Federal government.	8,902	11,509	17,255	21,015	22,076	23,243	23,939	13,672	10,267
State government	18,378	27,583	38,349	41,248	41,910	44,343	45,693	44,243	1,450
Local government	1,588	2,387	3,640	4,445	4,998	5,166	5,608	5,075	533
Private gifts, grants, and con-tracts [1]	2,808	4,896	7,781	9,660	10,203	10,867	11,903	5,089	6,814
Endowment earnings [2]	1,177	2,096	3,144	3,628	3,670	3,988	4,562	721	3,841
Educational activities [2]	1,239	2,127	3,632	5,038	5,294	5,603	5,531	3,529	2,002
Auxiliary enterprises.	6,481	10,100	13,938	16,663	17,538	18,336	18,868	11,595	7,272
Hospitals	(3)	7,475	13,217	18,124	18,960	19,100	18,612	12,276	6,336
Other funds revenues [4].	6,015	3,015	4,753	5,715	5,931	6,967	7,998	4,044	3,954
Current funds expenditures [5]	56,914	89,951	134,656	165,241	173,351	182,969	190,476	119,525	70,952
Educational and general	44,543	70,061	105,585	128,978	136,023	144,158	151,446	96,086	55,360
Instruction.	18,497	28,777	42,146	50,341	52,776	55,720	57,810	38,653	19,157
Institutional support	5,054	8,587	12,674	15,250	15,926	16,845	18,256	10,710	7,545
Research	5,099	7,552	12,506	15,291	16,118	17,110	17,518	12,076	5,442
Plant operation [6]	4,700	7,345	9,458	10,784	11,368	11,746	12,331	8,005	4,326
Academic support	3,876	6,074	9,438	11,073	11,678	12,279	13,297	9,004	4,293
Libraries	1,624	2,362	3,254	3,685	3,908	4,166	4,293	2,691	1,603
Student services	2,567	4,178	6,388	8,165	8,563	9,060	9,631	5,810	3,820
Scholarships and fellowships . . .	2,200	3,670	6,656	10,148	11,238	12,285	13,195	5,085	8,110
Unrestricted funds.	905	1,962	3,854	5,949	6,645	7,329	8,213	2,457	5,756
Restricted funds	1,296	1,709	2,802	4,199	4,593	4,956	4,982	2,628	2,355
Public service	1,817	2,861	4,690	5,935	6,242	6,691	7,007	5,321	1,686
Mandatory transfers [5].	732	1,016	1,630	1,991	2,115	2,423	2,401	1,420	980
Auxiliary enterprises [5]	6,486	10,012	13,204	15,562	16,429	17,205	17,599	11,309	6,290
Hospitals [5]	4,757	8,010	12,679	17,050	17,510	18,071	17,941	11,879	6,062
Independent operations [5]	1,128	1,868	3,187	3,652	3,387	3,534	3,491	251	3,240

[1] Private grants represent nongovernmental revenue for sponsored research and other sponsored programs; includes private contracts.   [2] Sales and services of educational departments only.   [3] Included in other.   [4] Includes sales and services of federally funded research and development centers, and others sources.   [5] Includes mandatory transfers which are primarily current expenditures for plant.   [6] Includes maintenance.

Source: U.S. National Center for Education Statistics, *Digest of Education Statistics*, annual.

Education   189

No. 309. Federal Student Financial Assistance: 1994 to 2000

[For award years July 1 of year shown to the following June 30 (32,650 represents ($32,650,000,000). Funds utilized exclude operating costs, etc., and represent funds given to students]

Award year impact data	1994	1995	1996	1997	1998	1999	2000, est.
FUNDS UTILIZED (mil. dol.)							
Total	32,650	35,450	38,849	38,111	40,477	40,272	42,484
Federal Pell Grants.	5,486	5,445	5,764	6,331	7,236	7,326	7,940
Federal Supplemental Educational Opportunity Grant.	755	764	762	811	855	784	799
Federal Work-Study	757	764	776	906	913	1,044	1,123
Federal Perkins Loan	971	1,029	1,022	1,062	1,070	1,058	1,058
Federal Direct Student Loan (FDSL)	1,790	8,296	9,796	9,838	10,400	9,953	10,605
Federal Family Education Loans (FFEL)	22,891	19,152	20,729	19,163	20,003	20,107	20,959
NUMBER OF AWARDS (1,000)							
Total	13,082	13,667	14,516	14,363	14,828	14,801	15,225
Federal Pell Grants.	3,675	3,612	3,666	3,733	3,856	3,810	3,849
Federal Supplemental Educational Opportunity Grant.	1,057	1,083	1,191	1,116	1,163	1,118	1,139
Federal Work-Study	701	702	691	746	744	930	1,000
Federal Perkins Loan	663	688	674	679	669	698	698
Federal Direct Student Loan (FDSL)	474	2,339	2,762	2,864	3,018	2,891	2,872
Federal Family Education Loans (FFEL)	6,512	5,243	5,531	5,225	5,378	5,354	5,667
AVERAGE AWARD (dol.)							
Total	2,496	2,594	2,676	2,653	2,730	2,721	2,790
Federal Pell Grants.	1,493	1,507	1,572	1,696	1,876	1,923	2,063
Federal Supplemental Educational Opportunity Grant.	715	706	640	727	735	701	701
Federal Work-Study	1,081	1,087	1,123	1,215	1,228	1,123	1,123
Federal Perkins Loan	1,464	1,497	1,516	1,564	1,600	1,516	1,516
Federal Direct Student Loan (FDSL)	3,779	3,548	3,547	3,435	3,445	3,443	3,693
Federal Family Education Loans (FFEL)	3,515	3,653	3,748	3,667	3,719	3,756	3,698
COHORT DEFAULT RATE [1]							
Federal Perkins Loan	10.76	12.57	12.95	12.48	11.54	(X)	(X)
FFEL/FDSL Combined Rates [2]	10.70	10.40	9.60	8.8	(NA)	(X)	(X)

NA Not available.   X Not applicable.   [1] As of June 30. Represents the percent of borrowers entering repayment status in year shown who defaulted in the following year.   [2] Prior to 1995, this rate was FFEL-only.

Source: U.S. Dept. of Education, Office of Postsecondary Education, unpublished data.

No. 310. Finances of Public Colleges, 1990 to 1997, and by State, 1998

[For academic years ending in year shown (7,959.7 represents 7,959,700). Data provided by the state higher education finance officers, except as noted]

State	FTE [1] enroll- ment (1,000)	Appropria- tions for current operations [2] (mil. dol.)	Net tuition reven- ues (mil. dol.)[3]	State	FTE [1] enroll- ment (1,000)	Appropria- tions for current operations [2] (mil. dol.)	Net tuition reven- ues (mil. dol.)[3]
Total, 1990	7,959.7	33,853.9	11,264.7	Michigan	311.1	1,837.3	1,422.0
Total, 1993	8,397.7	35,172.0	15,746.3	Minnesota	156.9	941.6	400.6
Total, 1994	8,334.0	36,497.0	16,623.4	Mississippi	107.4	468.6	228.4
Total, 1995	8,262.7	38,655.2	17,406.8	Missouri	131.2	801.7	493.5
Total, 1996	8,267.1	40,077.5	18,465.2	Montana	33.4	117.4	92.4
Total, 1997	8,304.3	42,143.0	19,443.0	Nebraska	66.4	329.7	128.3
Total, 1998	**8,386.9**	**44,484.6**	**20,210.6**	Nevada	42.0	266.6	61.6
Alabama	168.7	643.1	439.1	New Hampshire	27.0	87.6	175.0
Alaska	17.1	156.0	38.1	New Jersey [4]	181.5	1,149.3	610.2
Arizona.	168.1	865.4	339.1	New Mexico.	67.6	390.1	100.1
Arkansas.	76.8	376.2	181.5	New York	424.3	2,264.5	1,124.8
California.	1,344.6	7,202.8	1,345.6	North Carolina	241.2	1,652.2	375.1
Colorado.	138.5	540.7	462.7	North Dakota	29.8	136.8	63.6
Connecticut	55.7	467.0	223.2	Ohio	335.1	1,578.9	1,165.3
Delaware.	27.4	151.2	186.8	Oklahoma	111.5	612.5	228.8
District of Columbia. . . .	2.9	37.8	9.9	Oregon	102.2	479.0	274.0
Florida	403.5	1,992.1	575.2	Pennsylvania	274.9	1,479.6	1,387.6
Georgia	222.2	1,471.5	449.1	Rhode Island	24.8	141.0	110.9
Hawaii	30.0	201.7	59.1	South Carolina	127.9	550.2	392.0
Idaho	41.0	230.7	59.9	South Dakota	20.8	93.0	70.0
Illinois	364.4	2,078.4	546.9	Tennessee	158.3	723.6	355.1
Indiana	178.4	897.9	586.8	Texas	635.3	3,236.4	1,366.1
Iowa	108.9	615.5	310.5	Utah.	84.6	420.7	153.3
Kansas	100.4	531.7	234.5	Vermont	15.0	47.4	123.2
Kentucky	114.4	512.5	267.6	Virginia	220.2	990.4	688.1
Louisiana	137.6	545.3	340.3	Washington	194.6	978.5	341.5
Maine	26.8	169.8	104.6	West Virginia	62.0	206.0	164.1
Maryland	152.9	763.4	511.4	Wisconsin	184.1	1,085.9	473.6
Massachusetts	114.2	825.9	323.6	Wyoming	21.1	141.5	45.9

[1] Full-time equivalent (FTE). Credit and noncredit program enrollment including summer session. Excludes medical enrollments.   [2] State and local appropriations. Includes aid to students attending in-state public institutions. Excludes sums for research, agriculture stations and cooperative extension, and hospitals and medical schools.   [3] Excludes appropriated aid to students attending in-state public institutions.   [4] Estimated by source.

Source: Research Associates of Washington, Arlington, VA, *State Profiles: Financing Public Higher Education*, annual (copyright).

190 Education

No. 311. Institutions of Higher Education—Charges: 1985 to 1999

[In dollars. Estimated. **For the entire academic year ending in year shown.** Figures are average charges per full-time equivalent student. Room and board are based on full-time students]

Academic control and year	Tuition and required fees [1]				Board rates [2]				Dormitory charges			
	All institutions	2-yr. colleges	4-yr. colleges	Other 4-yr. schools	All institutions	2-yr. colleges	4-yr. colleges	Other 4-yr. schools	All institutions	2-yr. colleges	4-yr. colleges	Other 4-yr. schools
Public:												
1985.....	971	584	1,386	1,117	1,241	1,302	1,276	1,201	1,196	921	1,237	1,200
1990.....	1,356	756	2,035	1,608	1,635	1,581	1,728	1,561	1,513	962	1,561	1,554
1992.....	1,624	937	2,410	1,933	1,780	1,612	1,852	1,745	1,731	1,074	1,789	1,782
1993.....	1,782	1,025	2,604	2,192	1,841	1,668	1,982	1,761	1,756	1,106	1,856	1,787
1994.....	1,942	1,125	2,820	2,360	1,880	1,681	1,993	1,828	1,873	1,190	1,897	1,958
1995.....	2,057	1,192	2,977	2,499	1,949	1,712	2,108	1,866	1,959	1,232	1,992	2,044
1996.....	2,179	1,239	3,151	2,660	2,020	1,681	2,192	1,937	2,057	1,297	2,104	2,133
1997.....	2,271	1,276	3,323	2,778	2,111	1,789	2,282	2,025	2,148	1,339	2,187	2,232
1998.....	2,360	1,314	3,486	2,877	2,228	1,795	2,438	2,130	2,225	1,401	2,285	2,312
1999 est...	2,422	1,328	3,644	2,970	2,345	1,828	2,578	2,241	2,327	1,465	2,407	2,405
Private:												
1985.....	5,315	3,485	6,843	5,135	1,462	1,294	1,647	1,405	1,426	1,424	1,753	1,309
1990.....	8,174	5,196	10,348	7,778	1,948	1,811	2,339	1,823	1,923	1,663	2,411	1,774
1992.....	9,434	5,752	12,192	9,053	2,252	2,090	2,727	2,098	2,221	1,789	2,860	2,038
1993.....	9,942	6,059	13,055	9,533	2,344	1,875	2,825	2,197	2,348	1,970	3,018	2,151
1994.....	10,572	6,370	13,874	10,100	2,434	1,970	2,946	2,278	2,490	2,067	3,277	2,261
1995.....	11,111	6,914	14,537	10,653	2,509	2,023	3,035	2,362	2,587	2,233	3,469	2,347
1996.....	11,864	7,094	15,605	11,297	2,606	2,098	3,218	2,429	2,738	2,371	3,680	2,473
1997.....	12,498	7,236	16,552	11,871	2,663	2,181	3,142	2,520	2,878	2,537	3,826	2,602
1998.....	12,801	7,464	17,229	12,338	2,762	2,785	3,132	2,648	2,954	2,672	3,756	2,731
1999 est...	13,460	7,815	18,237	12,904	2,873	2,860	3,191	2,774	3,077	2,577	3,915	2,851

[1] For in-state students. [2] Beginning 1990, rates reflect 20 meals per week, rather than meals served 7 days a week.

Source: U.S. National Center for Education Statistics, *Digest of Education Statistics,* annual.

No. 312. Voluntary Financial Support of Higher Education: 1990 to 1999

[For school years ending in years shown (9,800 represents $9,800,000,000); enrollment as of fall of preceding year. Voluntary support, as defined in Gift Reporting Standards, excludes income from endowment and other invested funds as well as all support received from Federal, state, and local governments and their agencies and contract research]

Item	Unit	1990	1993	1994	1995	1996	1997	1998	1999
Estimated support, total	**Mil. dol.**	**9,800**	**11,200**	**12,350**	**12,750**	**14,250**	**16,000**	**18,400**	**20,400**
Individuals...............	Mil. dol.	4,770	5,510	6,210	6,540	7,440	8,500	10,000	10,740
Alumni...............	Mil. dol.	2,540	2,980	3,410	3,600	4,040	4,650	5,500	5,930
Business corporations	Mil. dol.	2,170	2,400	2,510	2,560	2,800	3,050	3,250	3,610
Foundations...............	Mil. dol.	1,920	2,200	2,540	2,460	2,815	3,200	3,800	4,530
Fundraising consortia and other organizations	Mil. dol.	700	840	850	940	940	1,000	1,050	1,190
Religious organizations	Mil. dol.	240	250	240	250	255	250	300	330
Current operations	Mil. dol.	5,440	6,300	6,710	7,230	7,850	8,500	9,000	9,900
Capital purposes..........	Mil. dol.	4,360	4,900	5,640	5,520	6,400	7,500	9,400	10,500
Enrollment, higher education...	1,000 ..	13,309	14,257	14,078	14,044	14,021	14,031	14,171	14,313
Support per student.........	Dollars	736	786	877	908	1,016	1,140	1,298	1,425
In **1998-99** dollars	Dollars	954	907	988	993	1,082	1,181	1,320	1,425
Expenditures, higher education .	Bil. dol	150.56	181.73	189.73	201.53	211.35	223.50	233	242
Expenditures per student	Dollars	11,312	12,747	13,477	14,350	15,073	15,929	16,407	16,894
In **1998-99** dollars	Dollars	14,652	14,713	15,180	15,699	16,050	16,490	16,685	16,894
Institutions reporting support	Number.	1,056	1,106	992	1,086	1,104	1,061	1,034	938
Total support reported	**Mil. dol.**	**8,214**	**9,491**	**10,326**	**10,992**	**12,251**	**13,801**	**15,771**	**17,229**
Private 4-year institutions	Mil. dol	5,072	5,767	6,103	6,500	7,163	8,023	9,118	9,848
Public 4-year institutions......	Mil. dol	3,056	3,610	4,138	4,382	4,943	5,654	6,556	7,252
2-year colleges............	Mil. dol	85	115	84	110	145	124	98	129

Source: Council for Aid to Education, New York, NY, *Voluntary Support of Education,* annual.

No. 313. Average Salaries for College Faculty Members: 1997 to 1999

[In thousands of dollars (52.0 represents $52,000). For academic year ending in year shown. Figures are for 9 months teaching for full-time faculty members in 4-year institutions. Fringe benefits averaged in 1997, $12,600 in public institutions and $14,700 in private institutions; in 1998, $13,200 in public institutions and $5,800 in private institutions; and in 1999, $13,200 in public institutions and $16,600 in private institutions]

Type of control and academic rank	1997	1998	1999	Type of control and academic rank	1997	1998	1999
Public: All ranks.............	52.0	53.6	55.9	Private: [1] All ranks...........	59.3	61.5	63.5
Professor	65.8	68.0	71.3	Professor	78.2	81.8	83.9
Associate professor	49.7	51.2	53.4	Associate professor	52.7	54.5	56.3
Assistant professor.........	41.3	42.4	44.1	Assistant professor.........	43.4	44.9	46.8
Instructor	31.8	32.4	33.3	Instructor	33.1	34.5	36.1

[1] Excludes church-related colleges and universities.

Source: American Association of University Professors, Washington, DC, *AAUP Annual Report on the Economic Status of the Profession.*

U.S. Census Bureau, Statistical Abstract of the United States: 2000

No. 314. Employees in Higher Education Institutions by Sex and Occupation: 1976 to 1997

[In thousands (1,863.8 represents 1,863,800). As of **fall**. Based on survey and subject to sampling error; see source]

Year and status		Professional staff									Non-profes-sional staff, total
	Total	Total	Executive, administrative, and managerial		Faculty [1]		Research/ instruction assistants		Other		
			Male	Female	Male	Female	Male	Female	Male	Female	
1976, total	**1,863.8**	**1,073.1**	**74.6**	**26.6**	**460.6**	**172.7**	**106.5**	**53.6**	**87.5**	**91.0**	**790.7**
Full time	1,339.9	709.4	72.0	25.0	326.8	107.2	18.6	9.4	76.2	74.1	630.5
Part time.	523.9	363.7	2.6	1.7	133.7	65.4	87.9	44.2	11.3	16.9	160.2
1991, total	**2,545.2**	**1,595.5**	**85.4**	**59.3**	**525.6**	**300.7**	**119.1**	**78.6**	**165.4**	**261.3**	**949.8**
Full time	1,812.9	1,031.8	82.9	56.2	366.2	169.4	(NA)	(NA)	142.2	214.8	781.1
Part time.	732.3	563.7	2.5	3.1	159.4	131.2	119.1	78.6	23.2	46.4	168.7
1997, total	**2,752.5**	**1,835.9**	**81.9**	**69.4**	**587.4**	**402.4**	**125.9**	**96.9**	**187.6**	**284.4**	**916.6**
Full time	1,828.5	1,104.8	78.9	65.6	363.9	204.8	(NA)	(NA)	159.3	232.3	723.7
Part time.	924.0	731.1	3.0	3.8	223.5	197.6	125.9	96.9	28.3	52.1	192.9

NA Not available.   [1] Instruction and research.

Source: U.S. National Center for Education Statistics, *Fall Staff in Postsecondary Institutions, 1995* and *1997*, March 1998 and January 2000.

No. 315. Faculty in Institutions of Higher Education: 1970 to 1997

[In thousands (474 represents 474,000), except percent. As of **fall**. Based on survey and subject to sampling error; see source]

Year	Total	Employment status		Control		Level		Percent		
		Full time	Part time	Public	Private	4-year	2-year	Part time	Public	2-year
1970	474	369	104	314	160	382	92	22	66	19
1975	628	440	188	443	185	467	161	30	71	26
1980	686	450	236	495	191	494	192	34	72	28
1985	715	459	256	503	212	504	211	36	70	30
1987	793	523	270	553	240	548	246	34	70	31
1989	824	524	300	577	247	584	241	36	70	29
1991	826	536	291	581	245	591	235	35	70	28
1993	915	546	370	650	265	626	289	40	71	32
1995	932	551	381	657	275	647	285	41	70	31
1997	990	569	421	695	295	683	307	43	70	31

Source: U.S. National Center for Education Statistics, *Fall Staff in Postsecondary Institutions, 1995* and *1997*, March 1998 and January 2000.

No. 316. Salary Offers to Candidates for Degrees: 1997 to 1999

[In **dollars**. Data are average beginning salaries based on offers made by business, industrial, government, and nonprofit and educational employers to graduating students. Data from representative colleges throughout the United States]

Field of study	Bachelor's			Master's [1]			Doctor's		
	1997	1998	1999	1997	1998	1999	1997	1998	1999
Accounting	30,154	32,825	34,644	33,636	36,492	38,152	(NA)	(NA)	(NA)
Business, general [2]	29,346	31,454	33,310	42,618	51,231	50,095	(NA)	(NA)	(NA)
Marketing.	28,031	29,231	31,901	[3]47,422	[3]53,563	[3]54,530	(NA)	(NA)	(NA)
Engineering:									
Civil	33,031	35,335	36,076	37,947	41,584	42,265	[3]49,746	[3]54,167	[3]58,571
Chemical	42,802	45,104	46,929	45,469	[3]48,593	[3]52,068	[3]59,536	62,343	67,333
Computer	40,093	43,865	45,666	50,485	51,610	58,673	[3]63,367	[3]64,417	[3]57,471
Electrical.	39,546	43,282	45,180	50,166	53,534	57,162	64,158	66,716	70,848
Mechanical	38,287	41,260	43,275	45,974	48,695	51,879	[3]61,037	[3]58,922	64,283
Nuclear [4]	[3]37,050	[3]41,517	[3]42,986	[3]43,001	[3]45,090	[3]54,000	(NA)	(NA)	(NA)
Petroleum	43,444	49,926	50,440	[3]48,350	[3]50,760	[3]55,375	(NA)	(NA)	(NA)
Engineering technology . .	35,498	39,390	38,182	(NA)	(NA)	(NA)	(NA)	(NA)	(NA)
Chemistry.	34,135	33,892	34,111	[3]37,050	[3]37,145	[3]38,779	[3]54,671	54,219	56,885
Mathematics	32,151	36,203	37,253	[3]38,360	[3]41,186	[3]41,964	[3]53,969	[3]52,368	[3]58,917
Physics	[3]35,554	[3]36,139	40,025	[3]42,500	[3]42,964	[3]50,552	[3]62,403	45,601	[3]60,288
Humanities	25,078	28,447	27,861	(NA)	(NA)	(NA)	(NA)	(NA)	(NA)
Social sciences [5]	25,103	27,149	28,608	(NA)	(NA)	(NA)	(NA)	(NA)	(NA)
Computer science	37,215	41,949	44,649	44,331	52,648	51,438	[3]63,058	[3]62,500	[3]58,688

NA Not available.   [1] Candidates with 1 year or less of full-time nonmilitary employment.   [2] For master's degree, offers are after nontechnical undergraduate degree.   [3] Fewer than 50 offers reported.   [4] Includes engineering physics.   [5] Excludes economics.

Source: National Association of Colleges and Employers, Bethlehem, PA, Salary Survey, *A Study of Beginning Offers*, annual (copyright).

No. 317. Earned Degrees Conferred by Level and Sex: 1960 to 1997

[In thousands (477 represents 477,000), except percent. Includes Alaska and Hawaii]

Year ending	All degrees		Associate's		Bachelor's		Master's		First professional		Doctor's	
	Total	Percent male	Male	Female	Male	Female	Male	Female	Male	Female	Male	Female
1960 [1]	477	65.8	(NA)	(NA)	254	138	51	24	(NA)	(NA)	9	1
1965	660	61.5	(NA)	(NA)	282	212	81	40	27	1	15	2
1970	1,271	59.2	117	89	451	341	126	83	33	2	26	4
1975	1,666	56.0	191	169	505	418	162	131	49	7	27	7
1980	1,731	51.1	184	217	474	456	151	147	53	17	23	10
1981	1,752	50.3	189	228	470	465	147	149	53	19	23	10
1982	1,788	49.8	197	238	473	480	146	150	52	20	22	10
1983	1,815	49.6	204	246	479	490	145	145	51	22	22	11
1984	1,819	49.6	203	250	482	492	144	141	51	23	22	11
1985	1,828	49.3	203	252	483	497	143	143	50	25	22	11
1986	1,830	49.0	196	250	486	502	144	145	49	25	22	12
1987	1,823	48.4	191	245	481	510	141	148	47	25	22	12
1988	1,835	48.0	190	245	477	518	145	154	45	25	23	12
1989	1,873	47.3	186	250	483	535	149	161	45	26	23	13
1990	1,940	46.6	191	264	492	560	154	171	44	27	24	14
1991	2,025	45.8	199	283	504	590	156	181	44	28	25	15
1992	2,108	45.6	207	297	521	616	162	191	45	29	26	15
1993	2,167	45.5	212	303	533	632	169	200	45	30	26	16
1994	2,206	45.1	215	315	532	637	176	211	45	31	27	17
1995	2,218	44.9	218	321	526	634	179	219	45	31	27	18
1996	2,248	44.2	220	336	522	642	179	227	45	32	27	18
1997	2,288	43.6	224	347	521	652	181	238	46	33	27	19

NA Not available.   [1] First-professional degrees are included with bachelor's degrees.

Source: U.S. National Center for Education Statistics, *Digest of Education Statistics*, annual.

No. 318. Degrees Earned by Level and Race/Ethnicity: 1981 to 1997

[For school year ending in year shown. Data exclude some institutions not reporting field of study and are slight undercounts of degrees awarded]

Level of degree and race/ethnicity	Total						Percent distribution	
	1981	1985	1990	1995	1996	1997	1981	1997
Associate's degrees, total	410,174	429,815	450,263	538,545	553,625	563,620	100.0	100.0
White, non-Hispanic	339,167	355,343	369,580	419,323	425,028	424,364	82.7	75.3
Black, non-Hispanic	35,330	35,791	35,327	47,142	51,672	55,260	8.6	9.8
Hispanic	17,800	19,407	22,195	36,013	38,163	42,645	4.3	7.6
Asian or Pacific Islander	8,650	9,914	13,482	20,717	23,091	24,829	2.1	4.4
American Indian/Alaskan Native	2,584	2,953	3,530	5,492	5,556	5,927	0.6	1.1
Nonresident alien	6,643	6,407	6,149	9,858	10,115	10,595	1.6	1.9
Bachelor's degrees, total	934,800	968,311	1,048,631	1,158,788	1,163,036	1,168,023	100.0	100.0
White, non-Hispanic	807,319	826,106	884,376	913,377	904,709	898,224	86.4	76.9
Black, non-Hispanic	60,673	57,473	61,063	87,203	91,166	94,053	6.5	8.1
Hispanic	21,832	25,874	32,844	54,201	58,288	61,941	2.3	5.3
Asian or Pacific Islander	18,794	25,395	39,248	60,478	64,359	67,969	2.0	5.8
American Indian/Alaskan Native	3,593	4,246	4,392	6,606	6,970	7,409	0.4	0.6
Nonresident alien	22,589	29,217	26,708	36,923	37,544	38,427	2.4	3.3
Master's degrees, total	294,183	280,421	322,465	397,052	405,521	414,882	100.0	100.0
White, non-Hispanic	241,216	223,628	251,690	292,784	297,558	302,541	82.0	72.9
Black, non-Hispanic	17,133	13,939	15,446	24,171	25,801	28,224	5.8	6.8
Hispanic	6,461	6,864	7,950	12,907	14,412	15,187	2.2	3.7
Asian or Pacific Islander	6,282	7,782	10,577	16,842	18,161	18,477	2.1	4.5
American Indian/Alaskan Native	1,034	1,256	1,101	1,621	1,778	1,924	0.4	0.5
Nonresident alien	22,057	26,952	35,701	48,727	47,811	48,529	7.5	11.7
Doctor's degrees, total	32,839	32,307	38,113	44,427	44,645	45,394	100.0	100.0
White, non-Hispanic	25,908	23,934	25,880	27,826	27,756	28,344	78.9	62.4
Black, non-Hispanic	1,265	1,154	1,153	1,667	1,636	1,847	3.9	4.1
Hispanic	456	677	788	984	999	1,098	1.4	2.4
Asian or Pacific Islander	877	1,106	1,235	2,690	2,646	2,607	2.7	5.7
American Indian/Alaskan Native	130	119	99	130	158	173	0.4	0.4
Nonresident alien	4,203	5,317	8,958	11,130	11,450	11,325	12.8	24.9
First-professional degrees, total	71,340	71,057	70,744	75,800	76,641	77,815	100.0	100.0
White, non-Hispanic	64,551	63,219	60,240	59,402	59,456	59,852	90.5	76.9
Black, non-Hispanic	2,931	3,029	3,410	4,747	5,016	5,251	4.1	6.7
Hispanic	1,541	1,884	2,427	3,231	3,476	3,553	2.2	4.6
Asian or Pacific Islander	1,456	1,816	3,362	6,397	6,617	7,037	2.0	9.0
American Indian/Alaskan Native	192	248	257	412	463	511	0.3	0.7
Nonresident alien	669	861	1,048	1,611	1,613	1,611	0.9	2.1

Source: U.S. National Center for Education Statistics, *Digest of Education Statistics*, annual.

Education   193

No. 319. Degrees and Awards Earned Below Bachelor's by Field: 1997

[Covers associate degrees and other awards based on postsecondary curriculums of less than 4 years in institutions of higher education]

Field of study	Less than 1-year awards		1- to less than 4-year awards		Associate degrees	
	Total	Women	Total	Women	Total	Women
Total..........................	106,766	58,091	142,446	85,070	571,226	347,278
Agriculture and natural resources	2,566	449	1,704	516	6,463	2,134
Architecture and related programs.............	9	7	40	33	316	260
Area, ethnic, and cultural studies.............	170	128	114	99	84	52
Biological/life sciences.....................	31	7	507	197	2,116	1,347
Business management and administrative services [1].....................	19,879	13,658	26,384	22,159	101,188	73,552
Communications and communications technologies .	613	202	558	218	3,773	1,697
Computer and information sciences............	4,081	2,196	4,013	1,989	10,990	5,130
Construction trades	2,370	180	4,169	251	1,928	99
Consumer and personal services	2,818	2,214	6,686	5,141	8,211	3,096
Education	780	612	743	678	10,526	7,170
Engineering and engineering technologies	2,466	410	7,307	876	35,762	4,629
English language and literature/letters	169	110	22	14	1,455	927
Foreign languages and literatures	307	203	49	37	689	458
Health professions and related sciences.........	33,549	25,861	46,637	39,977	98,921	82,951
Home economics and vocational home economics..	5,313	4,058	4,566	4,125	8,551	7,836
Law and legal studies.....................	663	578	1,779	1,473	8,968	7,863
Liberal/general studies and humanities..........	1,088	740	405	260	181,341	111,769
Library science	108	103	69	55	126	109
Mathematics	9	1	1	-	792	349
Mechanics and repairers	5,064	497	16,386	837	12,180	792
Multi/interdisciplinary studies	385	324	128	63	9,182	4,784
Parks, recreation, leisure, and fitness..........	101	65	147	95	913	359
Physical sciences......................	93	37	97	33	2,526	1,245
Precision production trades	3,984	617	8,588	1,469	10,368	2,335
Protective services.....................	10,399	2,202	3,686	961	19,889	6,301
Psychology...........................	26	21	18	15	1,612	1,235
Public administration and services.............	405	292	375	275	4,270	3,603
R.O.T.C. and military technologies.............	-	-	-	-	556	35
Social sciences and history	7	6	30	21	4,056	2,506
Theological studies, religion and philosophy	96	71	554	259	663	291
Transportation and material moving............	6,309	769	740	111	1,612	263
Visual and performing arts.................	879	426	3,545	1,533	13,593	7,721
Undistributed and unclassified	2,029	1,047	2,399	1,300	7,606	4,380

- Represents zero.   [1] Includes marketing.

Source: U.S. National Center for Education Statistics, *Digest of Education Statistics, 1999.*

No. 320. Bachelor's Degrees Earned by Field: 1971 to 1997

Field of study	1971	1980	1990	1995	1997	Percent female	
						1971	1997
Total......................	839,730	929,417	1,051,344	1,160,134	1,172,879	43.4	55.6
Agriculture and natural resources	12,672	22,802	12,900	19,841	22,602	4.2	39.0
Architecture and environmental design....	5,570	9,132	9,364	8,756	7,944	11.9	35.9
Area, ethnic and cultural studies	2,582	2,840	4,613	5,706	5,839	52.4	65.8
Biological sciences/life sciences	35,743	46,370	37,204	55,984	63,975	29.1	53.9
Business and management	114,729	184,867	248,698	234,323	226,633	9.1	48.6
Communications [1].................	10,802	28,616	51,308	48,803	47,768	35.3	58.8
Computer and information sciences......	2,388	11,154	27,257	24,404	24,768	13.6	27.2
Education	176,307	118,038	105,112	106,079	105,233	74.5	75.0
Engineering [1]	50,046	68,893	81,322	78,154	75,157	0.8	16.6
English language and literature/letters	64,342	32,541	47,519	51,901	49,345	65.6	66.5
Foreign languages and literatures	20,536	12,089	12,386	13,775	13,674	74.0	69.7
Health sciences.................	25,226	63,920	58,302	79,855	85,631	77.1	81.5
Home economics.................	11,167	18,411	14,491	15,345	16,571	97.3	88.4
Law and legal studies..............	545	683	1,592	2,032	2,038	5.0	70.4
Liberal/general studies	7,481	23,196	27,985	33,356	34,776	33.6	61.2
Library and archival sciences	1,013	398	77	50	48	92.0	87.5
Mathematics	24,937	11,378	15,176	13,723	12,820	37.9	46.1
Multi/interdisciplinary studies	6,286	11,277	16,267	26,033	26,137	22.8	65.9
Parks and recreation...............	1,621	5,753	4,582	12,889	15,401	34.7	49.0
Philosophy, religion, and theology	11,890	13,276	12,068	12,854	13,276	25.5	32.2
Physical sciences [1]................	21,412	23,410	16,066	19,177	19,531	13.8	37.4
Protective services................	2,045	15,015	15,354	24,157	25,165	9.2	39.8
Psychology....................	38,187	42,093	53,952	72,083	74,191	44.4	73.9
Public administration and services.......	5,466	16,644	13,908	18,586	20,649	68.4	79.8
R.O.T.C. and military technologies.......	357	38	196	27	4	0.3	-
Social sciences [2]	155,324	103,662	118,083	128,154	124,891	36.8	48.7
Visual and performing arts............	30,394	40,892	39,934	48,690	50,083	59.7	58.6
Unclassified [3]	662	1,535	5,628	5,397	8,729	0.9	31.3

- Represents zero.   [1] Includes technologies.   [2] Includes history.   [3] Includes precision production trades and transportation and materials moving.

Source: U.S. National Center for Education Statistics, *Digest of Education Statistics,* annual.

194   Education

No. 321. Master's and Doctorate's Degrees Earned by Field: 1971 to 1997

Level and field of study	1971	1980	1990	1995	1997	Percent female	
						1971	1997
MASTER'S DEGREES							
Total	230,509	298,081	324,301	397,629	419,401	40.1	56.9
Agriculture and natural resources	2,457	3,976	3,382	4,252	4,516	5.9	42.2
Architecture and related programs.	1,705	3,139	3,499	3,923	4,034	13.8	42.1
Area, ethnic and cultural studies	1,032	852	1,212	1,639	1,651	38.3	55.2
Biological sciences/life sciences	5,728	6,510	4,869	5,393	6,466	33.6	53.1
Business management and administrative services	25,977	54,484	76,676	93,809	97,619	3.9	38.9
Communications and technologies	1,856	3,082	4,362	5,609	5,601	34.6	64.2
Computer and information sciences.	1,588	3,647	9,677	10,326	10,098	10.3	28.2
Education	87,666	101,819	84,881	101,242	110,087	56.2	76.6
Engineering and engineering technologies .	16,443	16,243	24,772	29,670	26,827	1.1	18.3
English language and literature/letters	10,686	6,189	6,567	7,845	7,722	60.6	64.6
Foreign languages	5,217	2,854	2,760	3,136	3,077	64.2	67.4
Health sciences	5,749	15,704	20,321	31,243	35,958	55.3	78.6
Home economics	1,452	2,690	2,100	2,864	2,888	93.9	84.8
Law and legal studies	955	1,817	1,888	2,511	2,886	4.8	37.0
Liberal arts and sciences, general studies and humanities	885	2,646	1,999	2,565	2,661	44.6	66.5
Library science	7,001	5,374	4,341	5,057	4,982	81.3	77.6
Mathematics	5,695	3,382	4,146	4,181	3,783	27.1	40.8
Multi/interdisciplinary studies	821	2,306	2,834	2,457	2,819	25.0	56.9
Parks and recreation.	218	647	529	1,755	1,966	29.8	50.9
Philosophy, religion, and theology	4,036	5,126	6,265	6,620	6,227	27.1	39.5
Physical sciences and science technologies	6,367	5,219	5,449	5,753	5,563	13.3	32.6
Protective services	194	1,805	1,151	1,706	1,845	10.3	40.5
Psychology	5,717	9,938	10,730	13,921	14,353	40.6	73.2
Public administration and services.	7,785	17,560	17,399	23,501	24,781	50.0	71.9
R.O.T.C. and military technologies.	2	46	-	124	136	-	2.9
Social sciences [1]	16,539	12,176	11,634	14,845	14,787	28.5	47.0
Visual and performing arts	6,675	8,708	8,481	10,277	10,627	47.4	57.9
Unclassified [2]	63	142	2,377	1,405	5,441	-	33.0
DOCTORATE'S DEGREES							
Total	32,107	32,615	38,371	44,446	45,876	14.3	40.8
Agriculture and natural resources	1,086	991	1,295	1,264	1,217	2.9	27.4
Architecture and related programs.	36	79	103	141	135	8.3	31.1
Area, ethnic and cultural studies	144	151	131	186	182	16.7	47.8
Biological sciences/life sciences	3,645	3,636	3,844	4,645	4,812	16.3	43.1
Business management and administrative services	757	753	1,093	1,394	1,336	2.8	29.1
Communications and technologies	145	193	273	321	300	13.1	48.3
Computer and information sciences.	128	240	627	884	857	2.3	15.9
Education	6,041	7,314	6,502	6,905	6,751	21.0	62.8
Engineering and engineering technology . .	3,638	2,507	4,981	6,128	6,210	0.6	12.3
English language and literature/letters	1,650	1,294	1,078	1,561	1,575	28.8	57.5
Foreign languages	988	755	724	905	915	34.6	57.9
Health sciences	466	786	1,536	2,069	2,672	16.5	56.0
Home economics	123	192	301	388	382	61.0	75.1
Law and legal studies	20	40	111	88	81	-	27.2
Liberal arts and sciences, general studies and humanities	32	192	63	90	77	31.3	55.8
Library science	39	73	42	55	46	28.2	65.2
Mathematics	1,249	763	966	1,226	1,174	7.6	24.1
Multi/interdisciplinary studies	59	209	272	238	451	6.8	48.6
Parks and recreation.	2	21	35	149	108	50.0	44.4
Philosophy, religion, and theology	866	1,693	1,756	2,098	1,988	5.8	21.5
Physical sciences and science technologies	4,390	3,089	4,164	4,483	4,474	5.6	23.0
Protective services	1	18	38	26	31	-	51.6
Psychology	2,144	3,395	3,811	3,822	4,053	24.0	66.7
Public administration and services.	174	342	508	556	518	24.1	53.1
Social sciences [1]	3,660	3,230	3,010	3,725	3,989	13.9	37.9
Visual and performing arts	621	655	849	1,080	1,060	22.2	50.5
Unclassified [2]	3	4	258	19	482	-	33.6

- Represents zero. [1] Includes history. [2] Includes precision production trades and transportation and materials moving.

Source: U.S. National Center for Education Statistics, *Digest of Education Statistics,* annual.

Education 195

No. 322. First Professional Degrees Earned in Selected Professions: 1970 to 1997

[First professional degrees include degrees which require at least 6 years of college work for completion (including at least 2 years of preprofessional training). See Appendix III]

Type of degree and sex of recipient	1970	1975	1980	1985	1990	1993	1994	1995	1996	1997
Medicine (M.D.):										
Institutions conferring degrees.....	86	104	112	120	124	122	121	119	119	118
Degrees conferred, total.........	8,314	12,447	14,902	16,041	15,075	15,531	15,368	15,537	15,341	15,571
Percent to women	8.4	13.1	23.4	30.4	34.2	37.7	37.9	38.8	40.9	41.4
Dentistry (D.D.S. or D.M.D.):										
Institutions conferring degrees.....	48	52	58	59	57	55	53	53	53	52
Degrees conferred, total.........	3,718	4,773	5,258	5,339	4,100	3,605	3,787	3,897	3,697	3,784
Percent to women	0.9	3.1	13.3	20.7	30.9	33.9	38.5	36.4	35.8	36.9
Law (LL.B. or J.D.):										
Institutions conferring degrees.....	145	154	179	181	182	184	185	183	183	184
Degrees conferred, total.........	14,916	29,296	35,647	37,491	36,485	40,302	40,044	39,349	39,828	40,079
Percent to women	5.4	15.1	30.2	38.5	42.2	42.5	43.0	42.6	43.5	43.7
Theological (B.D., M.Div., M.H.L.):										
Institutions conferring degrees.....	(NA)	(NA)	(NA)	(NA)	(NA)	(NA)	186	192	184	178
Degrees conferred, total.........	5,298	5,095	7,115	7,221	5,851	5,447	5,967	5,978	5,879	5,859
Percent to women	2.3	6.8	13.8	18.5	24.8	24.8	24.8	25.7	25.2	26.2

NA Not available.

Source: U.S. National Center for Education Statistics, *Digest of Education Statistics*, annual.

No. 323. College and University Libraries—Summary: 1982 to 1996

[For school year ending in year shown. For the 50 states and DC. (**567,826 represents 567,826,000**)]

Item	1982	1985	1988	1990	1992	1994	1996
Number of libraries	3,104	3,322	3,438	3,274	3,274	3,303	3,408
COLLECTIONS (1,000)							
Number of volumes	567,826	631,727	706,504	717,042	749,429	776,477	806,717
Volumes added during year..........	19,507	20,658	21,907	19,003	20,982	21,544	21,346
Number of serial subscriptions........	4,890	6,317	6,416	5,748	6,966	6,212	5,709
ELECTRONIC SERVICES (percent)							
Access from within library to electronic catalog of holding's	(NA)	(NA)	(NA)	(NA)	(NA)	(NA)	79.9
Access from within library to Internet. ...	(NA)	(NA)	(NA)	(NA)	(NA)	(NA)	80.9
Reference service by e-mail	(NA)	(NA)	(NA)	(NA)	(NA)	(NA)	40.1
STAFF							
Total	58,476	58,476	67,251	69,359	67,166	67,433	67,581
Librarians and professional	23,816	21,822	25,115	26,101	26,341	26,726	27,268
OPERATING EXPENDITURES ($1,000)							
Total [1]	1,943,769	2,404,524	2,770,075	3,257,813	3,648,654	4,013,333	4,301,815
Salaries......................	1,081,894	1,156,138	1,451,551	1,693,813	1,889,368	2,021,233	2,147,842
Collection....................	561,199	750,282	891,281	1,040,928	1,197,293	1,348,933	1,499,249

NA Not available.   [1] Includes other expenditures, not shown separately.

Source: U.S. National Center for Education Statistics, *Digest of Education Statistics*, annual; and Academic Library Survey, 1994 and 1996.

No. 324. Libraries—Number by Type: 1980 to 1998

Type	1980	1985	1990	1998	Type	1980	1985	1990	1998
Total [1]........	31,564	32,323	34,613	37,519	Academic	4,591	5,034	4,593	4,700
					Junior college	1,191	1,188	1,233	1,270
United States	28,638	29,843	30,761	33,108	Colleges, universities .	3,400	3,846	3,360	3,430
Public............	8,717	8,849	9,060	9,815	Departmental	1,489	1,824	1,454	1,452
Public branches	5,936	6,330	5,833	6,435	Law, medicine,				
Special [2]	7,649	7,530	9,051	9,898	religious	269	531	501	491
Medicine	1,674	1,667	1,861	1,900	Government.........	1,260	1,574	1,735	1,897
Religious	913	839	946	1,010	Armed Forces	485	526	489	363
Law [3]	417	435	647	1,153	Outlying areas	113	114	110	(NA)

NA Not available.   [1] Includes Canadian libraries, and libraries in regions administered by the United States, not shown separately. Data are exclusive of elementary and secondary school libraries. Law libraries with fewer than 10,000 volumes are included only if they specialize in a particular field.   [2] Includes other types of special libraries, not shown separately. Increase between 1980 and 1990 is due mainly to revised criteria for identifying special libraries and improved methods of counting.   [3] Increase in 1998 due to increased effort in identifying special libraries.

Source: R.R. Bowker Co., New York, NY, *The Bowker Annual: Library and Book Trade Almanac* and *American Library Directory*, annual. (Copyright by Reed Elsevier Inc.)

196   Education

No. 325. Public Libraries, Selected Characteristics: 1997

[Based on survey of public libraries (6,267 represents $6,267,000,000). Data are for public libraries in the 50 states and the District of Columbia. The response rates for these items are between 97 and 100 percent]

Population of service area	Number of—		Operating income—			Paid staff [3]		Libraries with Internet access
	Public libraries	Stationary outlets [1]	Total (mil. dol.) [2]	Source (percent)		Total	Librarians with ALA-MLS [4]	
				State government	Local government			
Total........	8,967	16,090	6,267	12.1	77.6	120,750	27,946	7,080
1,000,000 or more ..	21	903	843	10.3	74.5	14,635	4,331	21
500,000 to 999,000 .	51	1,111	1,018	17.7	73.5	17,617	4,572	51
250,000 to 499,999 .	92	1,047	729	11.0	82.0	12,970	3,322	91
100,000 to 249,999 .	318	1,954	1,031	10.2	81.6	19,726	4,644	312
50,000 to 99,999 ...	513	1,604	781	13.3	77.8	15,386	3,478	484
25,000 to 49,999 ...	862	1,632	760	12.2	78.3	15,305	3,485	807
10,000 to 24,999 ...	1,689	2,178	682	10.1	78.8	14,256	2,939	1,524
5,000 to 9,999.....	1,500	1,677	251	11.9	74.0	5,968	855	1,284
2,500 to 4,999.....	1,331	1,373	98	7.6	73.6	2,614	210	997
1,000 to 2,499.....	1,639	1,658	59	5.7	69.2	1,723	93	1,070
Fewer than 1,000...	951	953	17	9.6	66.9	552	18	439

[1] The sum of central and branches libraries. The total number of central libraries was 8,943; the total of branch libraries was 7,147. [2] Includes income from the Federal Government (0.9%) and other sources (9.3%), not shown separately. [3] Full-time equivalents. [4] Librarians with master's degrees from a graduate library education program accredited by the American Library Association (ALA). Total librarians, including those without ALA-MLS, were 40,161.
Source: U.S. National Center for Education Statistics, Public Libraries in the United States: 1997, NCES 2000-316.

No. 326. Children's Involvement in Home Literacy Activities: 1993 and 1999

[In percent, except number of children (8,579 represents 8,579,000). For children 3 to 5 years old not yet enrolled in kindergarten who participated in activities with a family member. Based on the National Education Household Survey; see source. See also Table 260]

Characteristic	Children (1,000)		Read to [1]		Told a story [1]		Taught letters, words, or numbers [1]		Visited a library [2]	
	1993	1999	1993	1999	1993	1999	1993	1999	1993	1999
Total.....................	8,579	8,549	78	81	43	50	58	64	38	36
Race/ethnicity:										
White, non-Hispanic	5,902	5,296	85	89	44	53	58	65	42	39
Black, non-Hispanic.............	1,271	1,258	66	71	39	45	63	68	29	35
Hispanic	1,026	1,421	58	61	38	40	54	55	26	25
Other	381	574	73	81	50	53	59	69	43	43
Mother's highest education: [3]										
Less than high school	1,036	952	60	61	37	36	56	60	22	18
High school	3,268	2,556	76	76	41	48	56	63	31	30
Vocational ed. or some college	2,624	2,586	83	85	45	52	60	67	44	40
College degree..................	912	1,455	90	91	48	55	56	65	55	50
Graduate/professional training or degree .	569	734	90	93	50	54	60	62	59	48
Poverty status:										
Above threshold	6,323	6,575	82	85	44	52	57	66	41	40
Below threshold	2,256	1,975	68	69	39	42	59	58	28	24

[1] Three or more times in the past week. [2] At least once in the past month. [3] Excludes children with no mother in the household and no female guardian.
Source: U.S. National Center for Education Statistics, Statistical Brief, NCES 2000-026, November 1999.

No. 327. Public Library Use of the Internet: 1998

[In percent, except number of outlets. As of spring. Based on sample survey; see source for details]

Item		Metropolitan status [1]			Poverty status [2]		
	Total	Urban	Sub-urban	Rural	Less than 20 percent	20 to 40 percent	More than 40 percent
All libraries outlets [3]	15,718	2,691	4,933	8,094	12,757	2,644	317
Percent of total	100.0	17.1	31.4	51.5	81.2	16.8	2.0
Connected to the Internet...............	83.6	91.0	88.1	78.4	84.1	80.9	83.3
Connected with public access	73.3	84.0	76.7	67.6	73.2	72.8	79.5
Public access services provided—							
Only text-based terminals............	5.8	13.4	5.3	3.2	5.7	5.0	16.1
Some graphical workstations	94.2	86.6	94.7	96.8	94.3	95.0	83.9
Speed of access:							
Less than 28.8 kpbs	4.2	3.6	3.7	4.7	4.8	0.9	3.8
28.8 kpbs to 56 kpbs	28.7	7.7	21.3	42.2	30.6	21.6	11.1
56 kpbs......................	32.7	33.5	35.1	30.7	32.0	34.8	42.6
Greater than 56 kpbs...............	33.7	53.5	39.1	22.2	31.8	42.4	40.9
Special software/hardware for persons with disabilities on—							
All workstations.................	2.9	2.3	1.2	4.2	2.4	5.3	0.8
Some workstations	13.6	24.1	15.1	8.3	12.7	16.9	23.0
No workstations	83.6	73.8	83.7	87.5	84.9	77.9	76.1
Filtering software not used on workstations ..	85.3	82.9	83.3	87.9	85.8	83.1	85.4
With acceptable use policies............	84.8	87.3	85.9	83.1	84.5	86.6	86.3

[1] Urban = inside central city; Suburban = in metro area, outside of a central city; Rural = outside a metro area. [2] Determined by the 1990 poverty status of the service area of the outlet. [3] Central libraries and branches; excludes bookmobiles.
Source: The American Library Association, Washington, D.C., The 1998 National Survey of U.S. Public Library Outlet Internet Connectivity: Final Report, September 1998, by John Carlo Bartot and Charles R. McClure.

Education 197

No. 328. Participation in Adult Education: 1994-95 and 1998-99

[In thousands (189,543 represents 189,543,000), except percent. For the civilian noninstitutional population 17 years old and over not enrolled full time in elementary or secondary school at the time of the survey. Adult education is considered any enrollment in any educational activity at any time in the prior 12 months, except full-time enrollment in a higher education credential program. Based on survey and subject to sampling error; see source for details]

Characteristic		Participants in adult education				
	Adult population (1,000)	Number taking adult ed. courses (1,000)	Percent of total	Reason for taking course (percent) [1]			
				Personal/ social	Advance on the job	Train for a new job	Complete degree or diploma
Total, 1995.	189,543	76,261	40	44	54	11	10
Total, 1999.	194,434	88,809	46	43	54	12	11
Age:							
17 to 24 years old	25,276	13,029	52	34	32	20	23
25 to 34 years old	34,880	19,431	56	38	56	16	11
35 to 44 years old	45,258	23,047	51	41	62	13	9
45 to 54 years old	37,153	18,972	51	44	65	6	7
55 to 64 years old	24,309	9,003	37	49	56	7	9
65 years old and over	27,559	5,328	19	76	22	-	4
Sex:							
Male	92,946	40,204	43	34	59	11	13
Female	101,488	48,605	48	50	50	12	9
Race/ethnicity:							
White [2]	143,679	65,547	46	45	56	11	10
Black [2]	22,129	10,803	49	42	52	15	13
Hispanic	19,491	7,981	41	35	45	14	11
Other races [2]	9,135	4,478	49	35	49	14	19
Marital status:							
Never married	41,530	20,773	50	34	45	17	18
Currently married	118,568	55,966	47	46	58	10	9
Other	34,337	12,070	35	45	55	11	8
Children under 18 in household:							
Yes	83,365	43,060	52	41	55	12	12
No	111,070	45,749	41	44	53	11	10
Educational attainment:							
Up to 8th grade	11,078	1,527	14	41	39	3	21
9th to 12th grade	21,375	5,578	26	35	28	15	21
High school diploma or GED	53,488	19,693	37	39	52	12	7
Vocational school after high school	6,319	2,629	42	44	57	11	5
Some college	35,147	18,220	52	48	46	14	15
Associate's degree	11,377	6,735	59	38	60	15	14
Bachelor's or higher	55,651	34,426	62	45	63	9	8
Labor force status:							
Employed	132,227	70,849	54	37	63	12	11
Unemployed	7,963	3,433	43	39	23	32	22
Not in the labor force	54,244	14,527	27	72	17	7	10
Occupation: [3]							
Professional	21,474	16,460	77	38	73	11	11
Executive, administrative and managerial	26,128	14,692	56	38	72	8	9
Technical and related support	6,940	4,363	63	33	73	16	13
Sales workers	12,472	6,117	49	52	44	12	14
Administrative support [4]	19,162	9,655	50	37	61	14	7
Service	15,570	7,823	50	34	55	14	11
Agriculture, forestry, and fishing	2,028	879	43	29	37	9	18
Precision production, craft and repair	9,857	4,078	41	33	63	7	9
Machine operators, assemblers [5]	8,800	3,359	38	26	61	15	12
Transportation and materials moving	4,732	1,740	37	33	45	22	19
Handlers, equipment cleaners, helpers and laborers	3,207	811	25	28	34	10	21
Nonclassifiable, undetermined	1,858	873	47	67	37	13	3
Household income: [6]							
Under $10,000	22,899	10,551	54	46	32	16	17
$10,001 to $15,000	15,699	6,596	42	41	43	19	14
$15,001 to $20,000	15,965	6,195	39	41	54	12	12
$20,001 to $25,000	17,467	8,657	50	34	56	14	9
$25,001 to $30,000	14,205	8,027	57	34	63	15	10
$30,001 to $40,000	21,452	12,939	60	39	68	11	9
$40,001 to $50,000	14,229	8,736	61	36	74	9	12
$50,001 to $75,000	15,845	9,935	63	40	75	10	10
More than $75,000	11,606	6,836	59	33	72	5	7

- Represents or rounds to zero.   [1] Reason for taking at least one course. Includes duplication. Excludes other reasons, not shown separately.   [2] Non-Hispanic.   [3] For currently employed.   [4] Includes clerical.   [5] Includes inspectors.   [6] For those employed in the 12 months prior to the interview.

Source: U.S. National Center for Education Statistics, *1995* and *1999 National Household Education Surveys.*

198   Education

Section 5

Law Enforcement, Courts, and Prisons

This section presents data on crimes committed, victims of crimes, arrests, and data related to criminal violations and the criminal justice system. The major sources of these data are the Bureau of Justice Statistics (BJS), the Federal Bureau of Investigation (FBI), and the Administrative Office of the U.S. Courts. BJS issues several reports, including *Sourcebook of Criminal Justice Statistics, Criminal Victimization in the United States, Prisoners in State and Federal Institutions, Children in Custody, Census of State Correctional Facilities and Survey of Prison Inmates, Census of Jails and Survey of Jail Inmates, Parole in the United States, Capital Punishment,* and the annual *Expenditure and Employment Data for the Criminal Justice System.* The Federal Bureau of Investigation's major annual report is *Crime in the United States,* which presents data on reported crimes as gathered from state and local law enforcement agencies.

Legal jurisdiction and law enforcement—Law enforcement is, for the most part, a function of state and local officers and agencies. The U.S. Constitution reserves general police powers to the states. By act of Congress, Federal offenses include only offenses against the U.S. Government and against or by its employees while engaged in their official duties and offenses which involve the crossing of state lines or an interference with interstate commerce. Excluding the military, there are 52 separate criminal law jurisdictions in the United States: 1 in each of the 50 states, 1 in the District of Columbia, and the Federal jurisdiction. Each of these has its own criminal law and procedure and its own law enforcement agencies. While the systems of law enforcement are quite similar among the states, there are often substantial differences in the penalties for like offenses.

Law enforcement can be divided into three parts: Investigation of crimes and arrests of persons suspected of committing them; prosecution of those charged with crime; and the punishment or treatment of persons convicted of crime.

Crime—There are two major approaches taken in determining the extent of crime. One perspective is provided by the FBI through its Uniform Crime Reporting Program (UCR). The FBI receives monthly and annual reports from law enforcement agencies throughout the country, currently representing 95 percent of the national population. Each month, city police, sheriffs, and state police file reports on the number of index offenses that become known to them.

The FBI Crime Index offenses are as follows: *Murder and nonnegligent manslaughter* is based on police investigations, as opposed to the determination of a medical examiner or judicial body, includes willful felonious homicides and excludes attempts and assaults to kill, suicides, accidental deaths, justifiable homicides, and deaths caused by negligence; *forcible rape* includes forcible rapes and attempts; *robbery* includes stealing or taking anything of value by force or violence or threat of force or violence and includes attempted robbery; *aggravated assault* includes assault with intent to kill; *burglary* includes any unlawful entry to commit a felony or a theft and includes attempted burglary and burglary followed by larceny; *larceny* includes theft of property or articles of value without use of force and violence or fraud and excludes embezzlement, "con games," forgery, etc.; *motor vehicle theft* includes all cases where vehicles are driven away and abandoned but excludes vehicles taken for temporary use and returned by the taker. Arson was added as the eighth

U.S. Census Bureau, Statistical Abstract of the United States: 2000

Index offense in April 1979 following a Congressional mandate. *Arson* includes any willful or malicious burning or attempt to burn, with or without intent to defraud, a dwelling house, public building, motor vehicle or aircraft, personal property of another, etc.

The monthly Uniform Crime Reports also contain data on crimes cleared by arrest and on characteristics of persons arrested for all criminal offenses. In summarizing and publishing crime data, the FBI depends primarily on the adherence to the established standards of reporting for statistical accuracy, presenting the data as information useful to persons concerned with the problem of crime and criminal-law enforcement.

National Crime Victimization Survey (NCVS)—A second perspective on crime is provided by this survey (formerly known as the National Crime Survey until August 1991) of the Bureau of Justice Statistics. Details about the crimes come directly from the victims. No attempt is made to validate the information against police records or any other source.

The NCVS measures rape, robbery, assault, household and personal larceny, burglary, and motor vehicle theft. The NCVS includes offenses reported to the police, as well as those not reported.

Police reporting rates (percent of victimizations) varied by type of crime. In 1994, for instance, 32 percent of the rapes/sexual assaults were reported; 55 percent of the robberies; 40 percent of assaults; 33 percent of personal thefts; 51 percent of the household burglaries; and 78 percent of motor vehicle thefts.

Murder and kidnaping are not covered. Commercial burglary and robbery were dropped from the program during 1977. The so-called victimless crimes, such as drunkenness, drug abuse, and prostitution, also are excluded, as are crimes for which it is difficult to identify knowledgeable respondents or to locate data records.

Crimes of which the victim may not be aware also cannot be measured effectively. Buying stolen property may fall into this category, as may some instances of embezzlement. Attempted crimes of many types probably are under recorded for this reason. Events in which the victim has shown a willingness to participate in illegal activity also are excluded.

In any encounter involving a personal crime, more than one criminal act can be committed against an individual. For example, a rape may be associated with a robbery or a household offense, such as a burglary, can escalate into something more serious in the event of a personal confrontation. In classifying the survey-measured crimes, each criminal incident has been counted only once—by the most serious act that took place during the incident and ranked in accordance with the seriousness classification system used by the Federal Bureau of Investigation. The order of seriousness for crimes against persons is as follows: Rape, robbery, assault, and larceny.

Personal crimes take precedence over household offenses.

A *victimization*, basic measure of the occurrence of crime, is a specific criminal act as it affects a single victim. The number of victimizations is determined by the number of victims of such acts. Victimization counts serve as key elements in computing rates of victimization. For crimes against persons, the rates are based on the total number of individuals age 12 and over or on a portion of that population sharing a particular characteristic or set of traits. As general indicators of the danger of having been victimized during the reference period, the rates are not sufficiently refined to represent true measures of risk for specific individuals or households.

An *incident* is a specific criminal act involving one or more victims; therefore the number of incidents of personal crimes is lower than that of victimizations.

Courts—Statistics on criminal offenses and the outcome of prosecutions are

U.S. Census Bureau, Statistical Abstract of the United States: 2000

incomplete for the country as a whole, although data are available for many states individually. The only national compilations of such statistics were made by the Census Bureau for 1932 to 1945 covering a maximum of 32 states and by the Bureau of Justice Statistics for 1986, 1988, 1990, and 1992 based on a nationally representative sample survey.

The bulk of civil and criminal litigation in the country is commenced and determined in the various state courts. Only when the U.S. Constitution and acts of Congress specifically confer jurisdiction upon the Federal courts may civil or criminal litigation be heard and decided by them. Generally, the Federal courts have jurisdiction over the following types of cases: Suits or proceedings by or against the United States; civil actions between private parties arising under the Constitution, laws, or treaties of the United States; civil actions between private litigants who are citizens of different states; civil cases involving admiralty, maritime, or prize jurisdiction; and all matters in bankruptcy. The Administrative Office of the United States Courts has compiled statistics on the caseload of the Federal courts annually since 1940.

There are several types of courts with varying degrees of legal jurisdiction. These jurisdictions include original, appellate, general, and limited or special. A court of original jurisdiction is one having the authority initially to try a case and pass judgment on the law and the facts; a court of appellate jurisdiction is one with the legal authority to review cases and hear appeals; a court of general jurisdiction is a trial court of unlimited original jurisdiction in civil and/or criminal cases, also called a "major trial court"; a court of limited or special jurisdiction is a trial court with legal authority over only a particular class of cases, such as probate, juvenile, or traffic cases.

The 94 Federal courts of original jurisdiction are known as the U.S. district courts. One or more of these courts is established in every state and one each in the District of Columbia, Puerto Rico, the Virgin Islands, the Northern Mariana Islands, and Guam. Appeals from the district courts are taken to intermediate appellate courts of which there are 13, known as U.S. courts of appeals and the United States Court of Appeals for the Federal Circuit. The Supreme Court of the United States is the final and highest appellate court in the Federal system of courts.

Juvenile offenders—For statistical purposes, the FBI and most states classify as juvenile offenders persons under the age of 18 years who have committed a crime or crimes.

Delinquency cases are all cases of youths referred to a juvenile court for violation of a law or ordinance or for seriously "antisocial" conduct. Several types of facilities are available for those adjudicated delinquent, ranging from the short-term physically unrestricted environment to the long-term very restrictive atmosphere.

Prisoners—Data on prisoners in Federal and state prisons and reformatories were collected annually by the Census Bureau until 1950, by the Federal Bureau of Prisons until 1971, transferred then to the Law Enforcement Assistance Administration, and, in 1979, to the Bureau of Justice Statistics. Adults convicted of criminal activity may be given a prison or jail sentence. A *prison* is a confinement facility having custodial authority over adults sentenced to confinement of more than 1 year. A *jail* is a facility, usually operated by a local law enforcement agency, holding persons detained pending adjudication and/or persons committed after adjudication to 1 year or less. Nearly every state publishes annual data either for its whole prison system or for each separate state institution.

Statistical reliability—For discussion of statistical collection, estimation and sampling procedures, and measures of statistical reliability pertaining to the National Crime Victimization Survey and Uniform Crime Reporting Program, see Appendix III.

U.S. Census Bureau, Statistical Abstract of the United States: 2000

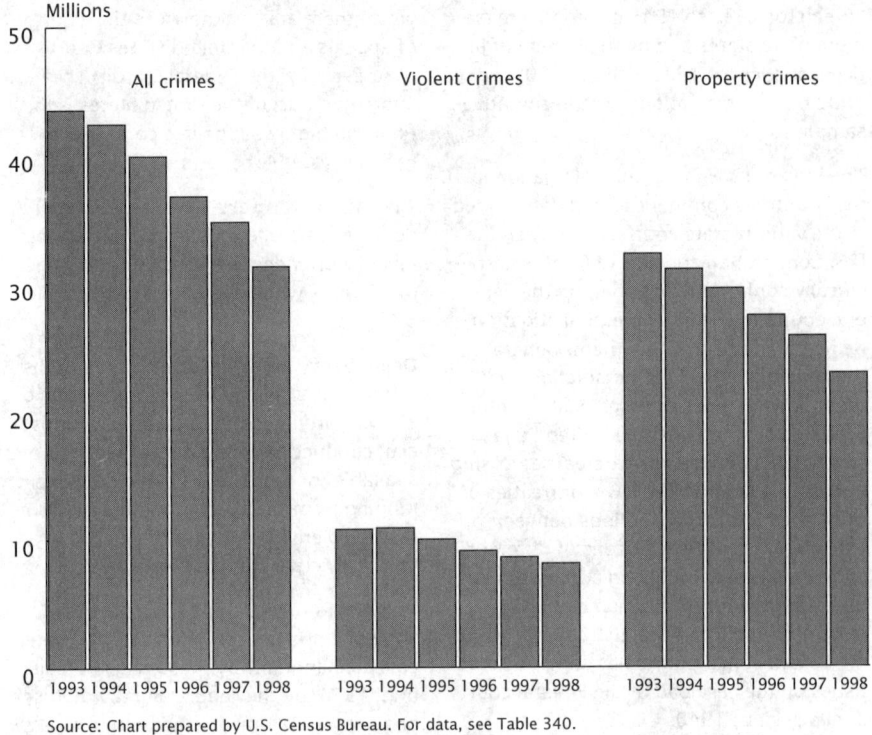

Figure 5.1
Criminal Victimization: 1993 to 1998

Millions

Source: Chart prepared by U.S. Census Bureau. For data, see Table 340.

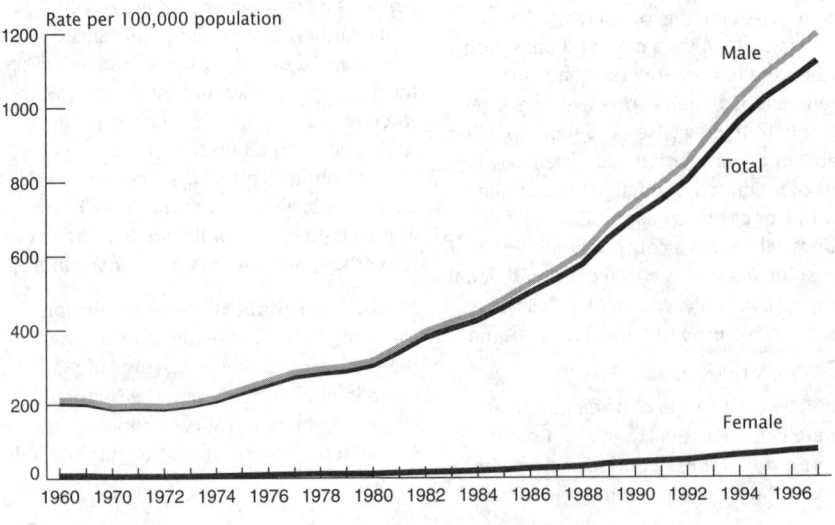

Figure 5.2
Federal and State Prisoners: 1960 to 1997

Rate per 100,000 population

Source: Chart prepared by U.S. Census Bureau. For data, see Table 369.

No. 329. Crimes and Crime Rates by Type of Offense: 1988 to 1998

[13,923 represents 13,923,000. Data refer to offenses known to the police. Rates are based on Census Bureau estimated resident population as of July 1, 1990, enumerated as of April 1. See source for details. Minus sign (-) indicates decrease. For definitions of crimes, see text, this section]

Item and year		Violent crime						Property crime			
	Total	Total	Murder[1]	Forcible rape	Robbery	Aggravated assault	Total	Burglary	Larceny—theft	Motor vehicle theft
Number of offenses (1,000):										
1988.	13,923	1,566	20.7	92.5	543	910	12,357	3,218	7,706	1,433
1989.	14,251	1,646	21.5	94.5	578	952	12,605	3,168	7,872	1,565
1990.	14,476	1,820	23.4	102.6	639	1,055	12,656	3,074	7,946	1,636
1991.	14,873	1,912	24.7	106.6	688	1,093	12,961	3,157	8,142	1,662
1992.	14,438	1,932	23.8	109.1	672	1,127	12,506	2,980	7,915	1,611
1993.	14,145	1,926	24.5	106.0	660	1,136	12,219	2,835	7,821	1,563
1994.	13,990	1,858	23.3	102.2	619	1,113	12,132	2,713	7,880	1,539
1995.	13,863	1,799	21.6	97.5	581	1,099	12,064	2,594	7,998	1,472
1996.	13,494	1,689	19.7	96.3	536	1,037	11,805	2,506	7,905	1,394
1997.	13,195	1,636	18.2	96.2	499	1,023	11,558	2,461	7,744	1,354
1998.	12,476	1,531	16.9	93.1	447	974	10,945	2,330	7,374	1,241
Percent change, number of offenses:										
1988 to 1998	10.4	2.2	18.2	-0.7	17.7	-7.1	11.4	27.6	4.3	13.4
1994 to 1995	-0.9	-3.2	-7.3	-4.6	-6.1	-1.3	-0.6	-4.4	1.5	-4.4
1995 to 1996	-2.7	-6.1	-9.1	-1.3	-7.7	-5.7	-2.1	-3.4	-1.2	-5.3
1996 to 1997	-2.2	-3.1	-7.6	-0.1	-6.9	-1.3	-2.1	-1.8	-2.0	-2.9
1997 to 1998	-5.4	-6.4	-7.1	-3.2	-10.4	-4.8	-5.3	-5.3	-4.8	-8.4
Rate per 100,000 population:										
1988.	5,664.2	637.2	8.4	37.6	220.9	370.2	5,027.1	1,309.2	3,134.9	582.9
1989.	5,741.0	663.1	8.7	38.1	233.0	383.4	5,077.9	1,276.3	3,171.3	630.4
1990.	5,820.3	731.8	9.4	41.2	257.0	424.1	5,088.5	1,235.9	3,194.8	657.8
1991.	5,897.8	758.1	9.8	42.3	272.7	433.3	5,139.7	1,252.0	3,228.8	659.0
1992.	5,660.2	757.5	9.3	42.8	263.6	441.8	4,902.7	1,168.2	3,103.0	631.5
1993.	5,484.4	746.8	9.5	41.1	255.9	440.3	4,737.6	1,099.2	3,032.4	606.1
1994.	5,373.5	713.6	9.0	39.3	237.7	427.6	4,660.0	1,042.0	3,026.7	591.3
1995.	5,275.9	684.6	8.2	37.1	220.9	418.3	4,591.3	987.1	3,043.8	560.4
1996.	5,086.6	636.5	7.4	36.3	201.9	390.9	4,450.1	944.8	2,979.7	525.5
1997.	4,930.0	611.3	6.8	35.9	186.3	382.3	4,318.7	919.4	2,893.4	506.0
1998.	4,615.5	566.4	6.3	34.4	165.2	360.5	4,049.1	862.0	2,728.1	459.0
Percent change, rate per 100,000 population:										
1988 to 1998	-18.5	-11.1	-25.0	-8.5	-25.2	-2.6	-19.5	-34.2	-13.0	-21.3
1994 to 1995	-1.8	-4.1	-8.9	-5.6	-7.1	-2.2	-1.5	-5.3	0.6	-5.2
1995 to 1996	-3.6	-7.0	-9.8	-2.2	-8.6	-6.6	-3.1	-4.3	-2.2	-6.2
1996 to 1997	-3.1	-7.3	-7.4	-4.2	-11.3	-5.7	-6.2	-6.2	-5.7	-9.3
1997 to 1998	-6.4	-7.3	-7.4	-4.2	-11.3	-5.7	-6.2	-6.2	-5.7	-9.3

[1] Includes nonnegligent manslaughter.

Source: U.S. Federal Bureau of Investigation, *Crime in the United States,* annual.

No. 330. Crimes and Crime Rates by Type and Area: 1998

[In thousands (12,476 represents 12,476,000), except rate. Rate per 100,000 population; see headnote, Table 329. Estimated totals based on reports from city and rural law enforcement agencies representing 96 percent of the national population. For definitions of crimes, see text, this section]

Type of crime	United States		Metropolitan areas[1]		Other cities		Rural areas	
	Total	Rate	Total	Rate	Total	Rate	Total	Rate
Total	**12,476**	**4,616**	**10,725**	**4,975**	**1,097**	**4,987**	**654**	**1,998**
Violent crime	1,531	566	1,359	630	98	444	74	227
Murder and nonnegligent manslaughter	17	6	15	7	1	4	1	5
Forcible rape	93	34	78	36	8	36	7	23
Robbery	447	165	423	198	15	66	5	17
Aggravated assault	974	360	840	390	74	339	60	183
Property crime	10,945	4,049	9,366	4,345	1,000	4,543	580	1,771
Burglary	2,330	862	1,940	900	195	885	195	597
Larceny-theft	7,374	2,728	6,276	2,911	755	3,435	342	1,045
Motor vehicle theft	1,241	459	1,149	533	49	223	42	129

[1] For definition, see Appendix II.

Source: U.S. Federal Bureau of Investigation, *Crime in the United States,* annual.

Law Enforcement, Courts, and Prisons 203

No. 331. Crime Rates by State, 1996 to 1998, and by Type, 1998

[**Offenses known to the police per 100,000 population.** Based on Census Bureau estimated resident population as of **July 1.** For definitions of crimes, see text, this section]

State	1996, total	1997, total	1998										
			Total	Violent crime					Property crime			
				Total	Murder[1]	Forcible rape	Robbery	Aggravated assault	Total	Burglary	Larceny—theft	Motor vehicle theft
United States	5,087	4,930	4,616	566	6.3	34.4	165	361	4,049	862	2,728	459
Alabama	4,820	4,890	4,597	512	8.1	33.2	131	340	4,085	964	2,779	342
Alaska.	5,450	5,273	4,777	654	6.7	68.6	87	492	4,123	667	3,031	425
Arizona	7,067	7,195	6,575	578	8.1	31.1	165	374	5,997	1,210	3,922	865
Arkansas	4,699	4,719	4,283	490	7.9	35.2	96	351	3,793	928	2,582	283
California.	5,208	4,865	4,343	704	6.6	30.0	211	457	3,639	824	2,217	599
Colorado	5,119	4,650	4,488	378	4.6	47.4	82	244	4,110	787	2,918	405
Connecticut	4,228	3,984	3,787	366	4.1	22.2	134	206	3,420	666	2,366	388
Delaware [2]	4,895	5,783	5,363	762	2.8	67.1	194	498	4,601	860	3,313	428
District of Columbia [3] . .	11,897	9,839	8,836	1,719	49.7	36.3	690	943	7,117	1,216	4,658	1,243
Florida.	7,497	7,272	6,886	939	6.5	49.6	243	640	5,947	1,362	3,887	699
Georgia	6,310	5,792	5,463	573	8.1	30.4	187	347	4,890	991	3,343	557
Hawaii.	6,585	6,023	5,333	247	2.0	30.0	103	113	5,086	936	3,681	469
Idaho	4,013	3,925	3,715	282	2.9	31.4	22	226	3,433	693	2,554	186
Illinois [4]	5,320	5,141	4,873	808	8.4	34.0	249	517	4,065	826	2,799	440
Indiana	4,498	4,466	4,169	431	7.7	33.1	111	279	3,738	789	2,590	359
Iowa	3,649	3,816	3,501	312	1.9	25.4	51	233	3,189	674	2,307	209
Kansas[4]	4,682	5,152	4,859	397	5.9	42.6	87	262	4,462	893	3,341	228
Kentucky [4]	3,166	3,127	2,889	284	4.6	29.3	75	175	2,605	637	1,750	218
Louisiana.	6,839	6,449	6,098	780	12.8	36.8	198	532	5,319	1,172	3,605	542
Maine	3,394	3,132	3,041	126	2.0	18.1	21	85	2,915	667	2,127	121
Maryland	6,062	5,653	5,366	797	10.0	33.4	299	455	4,569	923	3,097	549
Massachusetts	3,837	3,675	3,436	621	2.0	27.4	97	495	2,815	607	1,778	430
Michigan	5,118	4,917	4,683	621	7.3	50.4	156	407	4,062	838	2,630	594
Minnesota	4,463	4,414	4,047	310	2.6	49.9	93	165	3,736	688	2,724	325
Mississippi	4,523	4,630	4,384	411	11.4	37.3	123	239	3,973	1,145	2,490	339
Missouri.	5,084	4,815	4,826	556	7.3	26.9	149	372	4,271	873	2,948	450
Montana [4]	4,494	4,409	4,071	139	4.1	17.8	20	97	3,932	512	3,192	229
Nebraska.	4,437	4,284	4,405	451	3.1	25.1	77	346	3,954	634	2,972	348
Nevada	5,992	6,065	5,281	644	9.7	52.1	255	327	4,637	1,138	2,711	788
New Hampshire	[4]2,824	2,640	2,420	107	1.5	33.8	22	50	2,313	325	1,863	124
New Jersey	4,333	4,057	3,654	440	4.0	20.0	186	230	3,214	671	2,109	434
New Mexico	6,602	6,907	6,719	961	10.9	55.1	163	732	5,758	1,394	3,744	620
New York.	4,132	3,911	3,589	638	5.1	21.1	270	341	2,951	577	1,999	375
North Carolina	5,526	5,492	5,322	579	8.1	30.6	161	380	4,743	1,325	3,092	326
North Dakota	2,669	2,711	2,681	89	1.1	33.2	10	45	2,592	356	2,059	177
Ohio	4,456	4,510	4,328	363	4.0	41.0	134	185	3,965	810	2,771	384
Oklahoma	5,653	5,495	5,004	539	6.1	45.2	92	396	4,465	1,143	2,916	405
Oregon	5,997	6,270	5,647	420	3.8	39.8	105	271	5,227	928	3,773	526
Pennsylvania	3,556	3,432	3,273	421	5.3	27.0	165	224	2,852	531	1,965	356
Rhode Island	3,994	3,518	3,518	312	2.4	35.5	67	208	3,206	653	2,165	388
South Carolina	6,214	6,134	5,777	903	8.0	45.7	155	695	4,874	1,163	3,295	416
South Dakota	2,970	3,245	2,624	154	1.4	35.0	20	98	2,470	469	1,898	103
Tennessee	5,449	5,512	5,034	715	8.5	45.8	178	483	4,319	1,076	2,726	517
Texas	5,709	5,481	5,112	565	6.8	40.0	145	373	4,547	986	3,072	489
Utah	5,986	5,996	5,506	314	3.1	41.7	66	204	5,192	813	4,012	367
Vermont [4]	3,003	2,828	3,139	106	2.2	27.6	10	67	3,033	671	2,214	148
Virginia	3,968	3,876	3,660	326	6.2	26.7	106	187	3,335	561	2,504	270
Washington	5,909	5,926	5,867	429	3.9	48.2	116	261	5,439	1,063	3,758	619
West Virginia	2,483	2,469	2,547	249	4.3	18.7	37	188	2,299	614	1,498	187
Wisconsin [4]	3,821	3,678	3,543	249	3.6	19.9	86	140	3,294	569	2,453	272
Wyoming	4,254	4,181	3,808	248	4.8	27.7	16	199	3,560	561	2,861	139

[1] Includes nonnegligent manslaughter. [2] Forcible rape figures furnished by the state-level uniform crime reporting (UCR) Program administered by the Delaware State Bureau of Investigation were not in accordance with the national UCR guidelines; therefore, it was necessary that the forcible rape count be estimated. [3] Includes offenses reported by the police at the National Zoo. [4] Complete data were not available; therefore, it was necessary for the crime counts to be estimated for Illinois, Kansas, Kentucky, and Montana for all years shown and for New Hampshire for 1997 and 1998, Vermont for 1997, and Wisconsin for 1998.

Source: U.S. Federal Bureau of Investigation, *Crime in the United States,* annual.

[**Offenses known to the police per 100,000 population.** Based on U.S. Census Bureau estimated resident population as of **July 1.** For definitions of crimes, see text, this section]

City ranked by population size, 1998 [1]	Crime index, total	Violent crime					Property crime			
		Total	Murder	Forcible rape	Rob-bery	Aggra-vated assault	Total	Burglary	Larceny-theft	Motor vehicle theft
New York, NY	4,392	1,167	8.6	27.8	535	596	3,225	628	1,998	599
Los Angeles, CA	5,072	1,359	11.8	38.5	437	871	3,714	720	2,209	785
Chicago, IL	(2)	(2)	25.6	(2)	840	1,336	6,884	1,309	4,418	1,157
Houston. TX	7,112	1,123	14.1	36.4	429	643	5,989	1,283	3,565	1,141
Philadelphia, PA	7,319	1,464	23.3	51.9	789	600	5,854	1,065	3,442	1,347
Phoenix, AZ	8,545	832	15.1	28.2	307	482	7,713	1,528	4,729	1,456
San Diego, CA	4,514	725	3.5	30.8	176	515	3,788	610	2,354	824
San Antonio, TX	7,032	451	8.1	66.7	162	215	6,581	1,089	4,842	650
Dallas, TX	9,236	1,463	23.1	66.5	540	833	7,773	1,722	4,525	1,526
Detroit, MI	11,791	2,443	43.0	85.8	856	1,458	9,349	2,152	4,332	2,865
Las Vegas, NV	5,846	776	12.8	55.1	362	346	5,070	1,258	2,685	1,127
Honolulu, HI	5,425	268	1.9	27.7	120	118	5,157	879	3,735	543
San Jose, CA	3,532	599	3.4	41.5	105	450	2,933	480	2,084	369
Indianapolis, IN	6,257	1,135	18.8	77.1	381	658	5,122	1,482	2,876	764
San Francisco, CA	6,224	990	7.8	32.9	530	419	5,234	905	3,419	910
Jacksonville, FL	7,782	1,154	10.5	74.1	292	777	6,628	1,543	4,333	752
Baltimore, MD	10,947	2,420	47.1	70.8	1,161	1,141	8,527	1,990	5,427	1,111
Columbus, OH	9,468	817	11.8	101.0	395	309	8,652	2,046	5,496	1,111
El Paso, TX	5,730	700	2.7	38.6	132	527	5,030	421	4,183	425
Memphis, TN	8,807	1,499	19.0	119.5	690	670	7,308	2,469	3,459	1,380
Charlotte-Mecklenburg, NC	8,852	1,455	11.0	56.1	405	983	7,398	1,804	4,933	661
Milwaukee, WI	7,843	1,002	18.9	48.6	505	430	6,841	1,199	4,393	1,249
Austin, TX	7,002	540	5.5	39.1	196	300	6,461	1,242	4,669	551
Boston, MA	6,251	1,327	6.1	63.6	417	840	4,924	645	3,141	1,138
Seattle, WA	9,825	832	9.1	45.0	321	456	8,994	1,293	6,193	1,507
Nashville, TN	10,160	1,631	18.5	92.2	424	1,096	8,528	1,431	5,874	1,224
Washington, DC	8,828	1,719	49.7	36.3	689	943	7,110	1,216	4,650	1,243
Denver, CO	5,306	573	10.0	62.8	209	291	4,734	1,158	2,531	1,045
Fort Worth, TX	7,129	870	12.9	58.9	273	525	6,260	1,491	3,942	826
Cleveland, OH	6,981	1,308	16.3	116.2	679	496	5,673	1,382	2,837	1,454
Portland, OR	9,424	1,372	5.3	73.9	335	958	8,052	1,373	5,443	1,236
New Orleans, LA	8,662	1,462	48.8	63.5	629	720	7,200	1,487	3,957	1,755
Tucson, AZ	9,685	1,034	9.6	77.8	318	629	8,652	1,440	5,992	1,220
Oklahoma City, OK	10,077	996	12.1	90.8	274	618	9,082	1,999	6,224	859
Kansas City, MO	12,000	1,868	29.0	85.3	594	1,159	10,132	2,346	6,136	1,650
Virginia Beach, VA	4,050	227	3.2	19.3	112	92	3,823	624	2,987	212
Long Beach, CA	4,437	860	8.8	25.8	410	415	3,577	909	1,842	826
Albuquerque, NM	10,806	1,317	8.8	51.8	401	856	9,489	1,903	6,086	1,501
Atlanta, GA	14,032	3,047	36.0	92.9	1,124	1,794	10,985	2,195	6,883	1,907
Fresno, CA	7,934	1,052	8.9	43.3	345	655	6,881	1,287	4,192	1,403
Tulsa, OK	7,326	1,131	9.8	69.1	220	833	6,194	1,681	3,623	891
Sacramento, CA	8,219	878	8.1	36.7	439	394	7,342	1,691	4,090	1,561
Oakland, CA	9,794	1,862	19.1	90.3	704	1,048	7,932	1,626	4,930	1,377
Miami, FL	12,045	2,549	23.1	37.5	1,018	1,470	9,496	2,100	5,605	1,791
Omaha, NE	7,171	1,315	7.6	47.0	257	1,003	5,857	881	3,954	1,022
Mesa, AZ	6,945	662	3.0	32.9	137	488	6,284	1,082	4,364	838
Minneapolis, MN	9,561	1,525	16.0	126.5	655	728	8,035	1,795	5,002	1,239
Pittsburgh, PA	5,964	876	10.0	53.8	438	374	5,088	1,054	3,249	784
Colorado Springs, CO	5,848	540	2.2	74.6	143	320	5,309	974	3,972	363
Cincinnati, OH	7,350	874	5.8	117.2	391	359	6,476	1,504	4,345	628
St. Louis, MO	14,952	2,571	32.8	48.8	1,017	1,472	12,381	2,627	7,814	1,940
Wichita, KS	7,079	665	9.4	56.8	242	358	6,414	1,433	4,376	605
Toledo, OH.	8,046	905	6.9	56.9	281	560	7,140	1,630	4,437	1,073
Santa Ana, CA	3,687	554	6.7	21.8	270	255	3,134	482	1,866	786
Buffalo, NY	7,232	1,129	12.6	63.8	562	490	6,103	1,670	3,471	962
Arlington, TX	6,380	608	4.2	45.1	165	393	5,773	972	4,152	648
Anaheim, CA	3,495	508	6.0	24.4	184	294	2,987	698	1,744	545
Tampa, FL	12,189	2,557	13.6	90.2	835	1,618	9,632	1,939	5,973	1,720
Corpus Christi, TX	7,833	729	5.9	49.8	122	551	7,104	1,343	5,299	463
Newark, NJ	8,560	2,094	22.3	60.2	1,057	954	6,466	1,270	3,339	1,858
Riverside, CA	4,682	850	6.4	32.9	264	546	3,832	888	2,236	708
St. Paul, MN	7,720	909	8.4	92.6	320	488	6,811	1,502	4,414	895
Aurora, CO	5,536	570	10.7	72.0	182	306	4,966	885	3,381	700
Louisville, KY	6,820	943	14.9	35.4	484	409	5,877	1,750	3,198	929
Birmingham, AL	8,685	1,213	32.8	79.4	373	727	7,472	1,592	4,861	1,019

[1] Resident population estimated by the FBI.   [2] The rates for forcible rape, violent crime, and crime index are not shown because the forcible rape figures were not in accordance with national Uniform Crime Reporting guidelines.

Source: U.S. Federal Bureau of Investigation, *Crime in the United States,* annual.

No. 333. Murder Victims—Circumstances and Weapons Used or Cause of Death: 1990 to 1998

[Based solely on police investigation. For definition of murder, see text, this section]

Characteristic	1990	1995	1997	1998	Characteristic	1990	1995	1997	1998
Murders, total . . .	**20,273**	**20,232**	**15,836**	**14,209**	Other motives.	19.4	21.6	17.2	18.7
Percent distribution . . .	100.0	100.0	100.0	100.0	Unknown	24.8	28.9	31.9	30.9
CIRCUMSTANCES					TYPE OF WEAPON				
Felonies, total.	20.8	17.7	18.7	17.7	OR CAUSE OF DEATH				
Robbery	9.2	9.3	9.5	8.7	Guns	64.3	68.2	67.7	64.9
Narcotics	6.7	5.1	5.1	4.8	Handguns.	49.8	55.8	53.3	52.1
Sex offenses.	1.1	0.2	0.6	0.7	Cutting or stabbing . . .	17.4	12.6	13.0	13.3
Other felonies	3.7	3.2	3.5	3.4	Blunt objects [1]	5.4	4.5	4.6	5.3
Suspected felonies . . .	0.7	0.6	1.0	0.7	Personal weapons [2] . . .	5.5	5.9	6.4	6.7
Argument, total	34.4	31.2	31.2	31.9	Strangulations,				
Property or money . .	2.5	1.7	1.8	1.7	asphyxiations	2.0	1.8	2.0	2.2
Romantic triangle. . .	2.0	1.4	1.1	1.3	Fire.	1.4	0.8	0.9	0.9
Other arguments . . .	29.8	28.2	28.3	29.0	All other [3]	4.0	6.1	5.3	6.7

[1] Refers to club, hammer, etc. [2] Hands, fists, feet, etc. [3] Includes poison, drowning, explosives, narcotics, and unknown.
Source: U.S. Federal Bureau of Investigation, *Crime in the United States,* annual.

No. 334. Murder Victims by Age, Sex, and Race: 1998

Age	Sex				Race			
	Total	Male	Female	Unknown	White	Black	Other	Unknown
Total	**14,209**	**10,678**	**3,466**	**65**	**7,024**	**6,641**	**329**	**215**
Percent distribution	100.0	75.1	24.4	0.5	49.4	46.7	2.3	1.5
Under 18 yrs. old	1,613	1,089	524	-	857	696	44	16
18 yrs. old and over	12,294	9,408	2,882	4	6,058	5,850	281	105
Infant (under 1 yr. old).	224	136	88	-	132	80	5	7
1 to 4 yrs. old	324	177	147	-	176	137	7	4
5 to 8 yrs. old	112	50	62	-	67	40	5	-
9 to 12 yrs. old	100	46	54	-	67	26	7	-
13 to 16 yrs. old	483	356	127	-	242	227	12	2
17 to 19 yrs. old	1,470	1,264	205	1	634	788	39	9
20 to 24 yrs. old	2,526	2,169	356	1	1,035	1,440	36	15
25 to 29 yrs. old	2,026	1,626	399	1	828	1,130	49	19
30 to 34 yrs. old	1,535	1,125	410	-	788	708	28	11
35 to 39 yrs. old	1,462	1,018	444	-	749	667	30	16
40 to 44 yrs. old	1,181	830	351	-	637	495	36	13
45 to 49 yrs. old	768	548	219	1	427	304	26	11
50 to 54 yrs. old	499	376	123	-	306	177	12	4
55 to 59 yrs. old	324	243	81	-	215	99	7	3
60 to 64 yrs. old	229	169	60	-	148	71	8	2
65 to 69 yrs. old	180	130	50	-	123	48	7	2
70 to 74 yrs. old	162	96	66	-	122	33	5	2
75 yrs. old and over	302	138	164	-	219	76	6	1
Age unknown	302	181	60	61	109	95	4	94

- Represents zero.
Source: U.S. Federal Bureau of Investigation, *Crime in the United States,* annual.

No. 335. Homicide Victims by Race and Sex: 1980 to 1997

[**Rates per 100,000 resident population in specified group.** Excludes deaths to nonresidents of United States. Deaths classified according to the ninth revision of the *International Classification of Diseases;* see text, Section 2, Vital Statistics]

Year	Homicide victims					Homicide rate [2]				
		White		Black			White		Black	
	Total [1]	Male	Female	Male	Female	Total [1]	Male	Female	Male	Female
1980	24,278	10,381	3,177	8,385	1,898	10.7	10.9	3.2	66.6	13.5
1981	23,646	9,941	3,125	8,312	1,825	10.3	10.4	3.1	64.8	12.7
1982	22,358	9,260	3,179	7,730	1,743	9.6	9.6	3.1	59.1	12.0
1983	20,191	8,355	2,880	6,822	1,672	8.6	8.6	2.8	51.4	11.3
1984	19,796	8,171	2,956	6,563	1,677	8.4	8.3	2.9	48.7	11.2
1985	19,893	8,122	3,041	6,616	1,666	8.3	8.2	2.9	48.4	11.0
1986	21,731	8,567	3,123	7,634	1,861	9.0	8.6	3.0	55.0	12.1
1987	21,103	7,979	3,149	7,518	1,969	8.7	7.9	3.0	53.3	12.6
1988	22,032	7,994	3,072	8,314	2,089	9.0	7.9	2.9	58.0	13.2
1989	22,909	8,337	2,971	8,888	2,074	9.2	8.2	2.8	61.1	12.9
1990	24,932	9,147	3,006	9,981	2,163	10.0	9.0	2.8	69.2	13.5
1991	26,513	9,581	3,201	10,628	2,330	10.5	9.3	3.0	72.0	14.2
1992	25,488	9,456	3,012	10,131	2,187	10.0	9.1	2.8	67.5	13.1
1993	26,009	9,054	3,232	10,640	2,297	10.1	8.6	3.0	69.7	13.6
1994	24,926	9,055	2,921	10,083	2,124	9.6	8.5	2.6	65.1	12.4
1995	22,895	8,336	3,028	8,847	1,936	8.7	7.8	2.7	56.3	11.1
1996	20,971	7,570	2,747	8,183	1,800	7.9	7.0	2.5	51.5	10.2
1997	19,846	7,343	2,570	7,601	1,652	7.4	6.7	2.3	47.1	9.3

[1] Includes races not shown separately. [2] Rate based on enumerated population figures as of April 1 for 1980 and 1990; July 1 estimates for other years.
Source: U.S. National Center for Health Statistics, *Vital Statistics of the United States,* annual; and *National Vital Statistics Reports (NVSR)* (formerly *Monthly Vital Statistics Report*); and unpublished data.

No. 336. Forcible Rape—Number and Rate: 1980 to 1998

[For definition of rape, see text, this section]

Item	1980	1990	1991	1992	1993	1994	1995	1996	1997	1998
NUMBER										
Total..................	82,990	102,560	106,590	109,060	106,010	102,220	97,460	96,250	96,153	93,103
By force...................	63,599	86,541	91,522	93,825	92,360	89,297	85,249	84,053	84,818	82,758
Attempt	19,391	16,019	15,068	15,235	13,650	12,923	12,211	12,197	11,335	10,345
RATE										
Per 100,000 population........	36.8	41.2	42.3	42.8	41.1	39.3	37.1	36.3	35.9	34.4
Per 100,000 females..........	71.6	80.5	82.5	83.5	80.3	76.7	72.5	71.0	70.4	67.3
Per 100,000 females 12 years old and over	86.3	96.6	100.9	100.5	96.4	92.0	87.1	85.3	84.4	80.6
AVERAGE ANNUAL PERCENT CHANGE IN RATE [1]										
Per 100,000 population........	6.1	8.1	2.7	1.2	-4.0	-4.4	-5.6	-2.2	-1.0	-4.1
Per 100,000 females 12 years old and over	6.0	8.2	4.5	-0.4	-4.1	-4.6	-5.3	-2.1	-1.0	-4.5

[1] Represents annual average from prior year shown except for 1980, from 1979 and for 1990, from 1989.

Source: U.S. Federal Bureau of Investigation, *Population-at-Risk Rates and Selected Crime Indicators*, annual.

No. 337. Robbery and Property Crimes by Type and Selected Characteristics: 1990 to 1998

[For definition of crime, see text, this section]

Characteristic of offenses	Number of offenses (1,000)				Rate per 100,000 inhabitants				Average value lost (dol.)	
	1990	1995	1997	1998	1990	1995	1997	1998	1997	1998
Robbery, total [1] **........**	639	581	498	447	257.0	220.9	186.1	165.2	995	998
Type of crime:										
Street or highway	359	315	249	219	144.2	120.0	93.1	81.2	720	772
Commercial house	73	71	69	61	29.5	27.2	25.6	22.6	1,474	1,350
Gas station	18	13	12	10	7.1	5.1	4.4	3.6	715	546
Convenience store	39	30	28	26	15.6	11.4	10.5	9.6	576	570
Residence	62	63	58	54	25.1	24.0	21.6	20.1	1,133	1,078
Bank	9	9	10	9	3.8	3.5	3.6	3.2	4,802	4,516
Weapon used:										
Firearm..................	234	238	198	171	94.1	90.6	73.9	63.1	(NA)	(NA)
Knife or cutting instrument	76	53	42	39	30.7	20.1	15.9	14.5	(NA)	(NA)
Other dangerous weapon.....	61	53	67	60	24.5	20.2	24.9	22.1	(NA)	(NA)
Strongarm	268	236	191	177	107.7	90.0	71.5	65.6	(NA)	(NA)
Burglary, total	3,074	2,595	2,461	2,330	1,235.9	987.6	919.6	862.0	1,334	1,343
Forcible entry	2,150	1,737	1,615	1,521	864.5	661.2	603.4	562.8	(NA)	(NA)
Unlawful entry.............	678	657	669	649	272.8	250.1	249.9	240.1	(NA)	(NA)
Attempted forcible entry........	245	201	177	160	98.7	76.4	66.3	59.0	(NA)	(NA)
Residence	2,033	1,736	1,640	1,561	817.4	660.6	612.8	577.6	1,305	1,299
Nonresidence	1,041	859	821	769	418.5	327.0	306.8	284.4	1,391	1,432
Occurred during the night	1,135	905	827	776	456.4	344.4	309.1	287.2	(NA)	(NA)
Occurred during the day	1,151	1,000	886	858	462.8	380.5	330.9	317.4	(NA)	(NA)
Larceny-theft, total.......	7,946	8,001	7,744	7,374	3,194.8	3,044.9	2,893.4	2728.1	585	650
Pocket picking.............	81	51	46	44	32.4	19.4	17.1	16.4	466	407
Purse snatching............	82	51	47	42	32.8	19.5	17.4	15.7	403	362
Shoplifting................	1,291	1,205	1,179	1,094	519.1	458.4	440.5	404.8	130	142
From motor vehicles..........	1,744	1,940	1,975	1,936	701.3	738.5	737.8	716.3	584	675
Motor vehicle accessories	1,185	964	770	738	476.3	367.0	287.6	273.0	390	415
Bicycles	443	501	430	375	178.2	190.5	160.7	138.8	293	262
From buildings.............	1,118	1,004	1,051	990	449.4	382.1	392.5	366.3	963	1,028
From coin-operated machines....	63	50	45	44	25.4	18.9	16.7	16.3	453	328
Other....................	1,940	2,235	2,184	2,109	780.0	850.5	816.2	780.4	785	884
Motor vehicles, total [2] **....**	1,636	1,473	1,354	1,241	657.8	560.5	505.8	459.1	5,416	6,030
Automobiles	1,304	1,154	1,042	938	524.3	439.2	389.3	347.0	(NA)	(NA)
Trucks and buses...........	238	240	240	230	95.5	91.2	89.7	85.2	(NA)	(NA)

NA Not available. [1] Includes other crimes not shown separately. [2] Includes other types of motor vehicles not shown separately.

Source: U.S. Federal Bureau of Investigation, *Population-at-Risk Rates and Selected Crime Indicators*, annual.

Law Enforcement, Courts, and Prisons **207**

No. 338. Hate Crimes—Number of Incidents, Offenses, Victims, and Known Offenders by Bias Motivation: 1998

[The FBI collected statistics on hate crimes from 10,461 law enforcement agencies representing over 214 million inhabitants in 1998. Hate crime offenses cover incidents motivated by race, religion, sexual orientation, ethnicity/national origin, and disability]

Bias motivation	Incidents reported	Offenses	Victims [1]	Known offenders [2]
Total bias motivations	7,755	9,235	9,722	7,489
Race, total	4,321	5,360	5,514	4,626
Anti-White	792	989	1,003	1,131
Anti-Black	2,901	3,573	3,663	2,999
Anti-American Indian/Alaskan native	52	66	66	61
Anti-Asian/Pacific Islander	293	359	372	245
Anti-multiracial group	283	373	410	190
Ethnicity/national origin, total	754	919	956	863
Anti-Hispanic	482	595	620	580
Anti-other ethnicity/national origin	272	324	336	283
Religion, total	1,390	1,475	1,720	536
Anti-Jewish	1,081	1,145	1,235	394
Anti-Catholic	61	62	65	15
Anti-Protestant	59	61	62	31
Anti-Islamic	21	22	23	12
Anti-other religious group	125	138	288	71
Anti-multireligious group	41	45	45	12
Anti-atheism/agnosticism/etc	2	2	2	1
Sexual orientation, total	1,260	1,439	1,488	1,408
Anti-male homosexual	850	972	1,005	1,048
Anti-female homosexual	223	265	270	207
Anti-homosexual	158	170	177	129
Anti-heterosexual	12	13	17	7
Anti-bisexual	17	19	19	17
Disability, total	25	27	27	42
Anti-physical	13	14	14	19
Anti-mental	12	13	13	23
Multiple bias	5	15	17	14

[1] The term "victim" may refer to a person, business, institution, or a society as a whole.   [2] The term "known offender" does not imply that the identity of the suspect is known, but only that an attribute of the suspect is identified which distinquishes him/her from an unknown offender.

Source: U.S. Federal Bureau of Investigation, *Hate Crime Statistics,* annual; and <http://www.fbi.gov/ucr/98hate.pdf> (accessed 29 October 1999)

No. 339. Hate Crimes Reported by State: 1998

[See headnote, Table 338]

State	Number of participating agencies	Population	Agencies submitting incidents	Incidents reported	State	Number of participating agencies	Population	Agencies submitting incidents	Incidents reported
U.S.	10,461	214,226,549	1,810	7,755	Missouri	212	4,092,986	24	118
Alabama	(1)	(1)	(1)	(1)	Montana	77	709,382	12	22
Alaska	(1)	(1)	(1)	(1)	Nebraska	202	1,342,201	13	52
Arizona	90	4,441,014	27	283	Nevada	35	1,747,000	9	60
Arkansas	193	2,533,761	2	3	New Hampshire	57	472,857	9	16
California	719	32,651,387	239	1,749	New Jersey	565	8,115,000	255	757
Colorado	233	3,970,717	39	128	New Mexico	59	1,121,146	5	31
Connecticut	94	2,719,192	48	109					
Delaware	50	562,068	9	19	New York	500	18,170,860	33	776
Dist. of Columbia	1	523,000	1	2	North Carolina	434	7,451,189	18	39
Florida	464	14,826,670	63	179	North Dakota	81	495,030	2	2
					Ohio	344	7,394,669	62	172
Georgia	58	1,052,723	10	34	Oklahoma	25	1,317,563	25	57
Hawaii	(1)	(1)	(1)	(1)	Oregon	167	3,264,432	21	93
Idaho	120	1,220,792	26	58	Pennsylvania	1,127	11,744,149	31	168
Illinois	73	4,891,615	68	277	Rhode Island	46	988,000	10	29
Indiana	150	3,717,036	18	50	South Carolina	300	3,830,806	40	94
Iowa	218	2,668,398	-	-					
Kansas	1	329,179	1	54	South Dakota	76	567,373	7	19
Kentucky	264	2,941,256	19	45	Tennessee	260	3,085,684	30	58
Louisiana	134	2,789,979	7	10	Texas	931	19,731,597	97	300
Maine	133	1,219,585	17	57	Utah	101	1,829,393	32	66
Maryland	147	5,130,893	32	282	Vermont	37	418,582	9	13
					Virginia	415	6,791,000	45	160
Massachusetts	177	4,352,318	98	431	Washington	238	5,520,307	51	221
Michigan	546	6,766,382	152	384	West Virginia	112	708,363	16	21
Minnesota	72	2,448,133	72	248	Wisconsin	(1)	(1)	(1)	(1)
Mississippi	90	1,294,255	3	3	Wyoming	33	266,627	3	6

- Represents or rounds to zero.   [1] Did not report.

Source: U.S. Federal Bureau of Investigation, *Hate Crime Statistics,* annual; and <http://www.fbi.gov/ucr/98hate.pdf> (accessed 29 October 1999).

No. 340. Criminal Victimizations and Victimization Rates: 1995 to 1998

[Based on National Crime Victimization Survey; see text, this section and Appendix III]

Type of crime	Number of victimizations (1,000)				Victimization rates [1]			
	1995	1996	1997	1998	1995	1996	1997	1998
All crimes, total	**39,926**	**36,796**	**34,788**	**31,307**	(X)	(X)	(X)	(X)
Personal crimes [2]	**10,436**	**9,443**	**8,971**	**8,412**	**46.2**	**43.5**	**40.8**	**37.9**
Crimes of violence	10,022	9,125	8,614	8,116	44.5	42.0	39.2	36.6
Completed violence	2,960	2,700	2,679	2,564	12.9	12.4	12.2	11.6
Attempted/threatened violence	7,061	6,425	5,935	5,553	31.6	29.6	27.0	25.0
Rape/sexual assault	363	307	311	333	1.6	1.4	1.4	1.5
Rape/attempted rape	252	197	194	200	1.1	0.9	0.9	0.9
Rape	153	98	115	110	0.7	0.4	0.5	0.5
Attempted rape	99	99	79	89	0.4	0.5	0.4	0.4
Sexual assault	112	110	117	133	0.5	0.5	0.5	0.6
Robbery	1,171	1,134	944	886	5.3	5.2	4.3	4.0
Completed/property taken	753	757	607	610	3.5	3.5	2.8	2.7
With injury	224	250	243	170	1.0	1.1	1.1	0.8
Without injury	529	508	363	439	2.4	2.3	1.7	2.0
Attempted to take property	418	377	337	277	1.8	1.7	1.5	1.2
With injury	84	79	73	70	0.4	0.4	0.3	0.3
Without injury	335	298	265	207	1.4	1.4	1.2	0.9
Assault	8,487	7,683	7,359	6,897	37.6	35.4	33.5	31.1
Aggravated	2,050	1,910	1,883	1,674	8.8	8.8	8.6	7.5
With injury	533	513	595	547	2.4	2.4	2.7	2.5
Threatened with weapon	1,517	1,397	1,288	1,126	6.4	6.4	5.9	5.1
Simple	6,437	5,773	5,476	5,224	28.9	26.6	24.9	23.5
With minor injury	1,426	1,240	1,258	1,175	6.0	5.7	5.7	5.3
Without injury	5,012	4,533	4,218	4,048	22.9	20.9	19.2	18.2
Personal theft [3]	414	318	357	296	1.7	1.5	1.6	1.3
Property crimes	**29,490**	**27,353**	**25,817**	**22,895**	**279.5**	**266.3**	**248.3**	**217.4**
Household burglary	5,004	4,845	4,635	4,054	47.4	47.2	44.6	38.5
Completed	4,232	4,056	3,893	3,380	40.0	39.5	37.4	32.1
Attempted forcible entry	773	789	742	674	7.4	7.7	7.1	6.4
Motor vehicle theft	1,717	1,387	1,433	1,138	16.2	13.5	13.8	10.8
Completed	1,163	938	1,007	822	10.8	9.1	9.7	7.8
Attempted	554	449	426	316	5.5	4.4	4.1	3.0
Theft	22,769	21,120	19,749	17,703	215.9	205.7	189.9	168.1
Completed [4]	21,857	20,303	18,960	17,074	207.6	197.7	182.3	162.1
Attempted	911	818	789	629	8.4	8.0	7.6	6.0

X Not applicable. [1] Per 1,000 persons age 12 or older or per 1,000 households. [2] The victimization survey cannot measure murder because of the inability to question the victim. [3] Includes pocket picking, purse snatching, and attempted purse snatching. [4] Includes thefts in which the amount taken was not ascertained.

Source: U.S. Bureau of Justice Statistics, *Criminal Victimization*, annual; and *Criminal Victimization 1998, Changes 1997-98 with Trends 1993-98*, Series NCJ-176353 (revised 25 August 1999).

No. 341. Victimization Rates by Type of Violent Crime and Characteristic of the Victim: 1998

[**Rate per 1,000 persons age 12 years or older.** Based on National Crime Victimization Survey; see text, Section 5, Law Enforcement, and Appendix III]

Characteristic		Crimes of violence						Personal theft
	All crime	All crimes of violence	Rape/ sexual assault	Robbery	Assault			
					Total	Aggra- vated	Simple	
Total	**37.9**	**36.6**	**1.5**	**4.0**	**31.1**	**7.5**	**23.5**	**1.3**
Male	44.3	43.1	0.2	4.6	38.3	10.5	27.8	1.2
Female	31.9	30.4	2.7	3.5	24.3	4.7	19.5	1.5
12 to 15 yrs. old	84.4	82.4	3.5	7.7	71.2	12.2	58.9	2.0
16 to 19 yrs. old	93.4	91.1	5.0	11.4	74.7	19.0	55.7	2.3
20 to 24 yrs. old	69.1	67.3	4.6	7.9	54.8	16.0	38.8	1.8
25 to 34 yrs. old	42.5	41.5	1.7	4.2	35.6	8.4	27.3	1.0
35 to 49 yrs. old	31.1	29.9	0.7	3.2	26.1	6.8	19.3	1.2
50 to 64 yrs. old	17.0	15.4	0.2	1.7	13.5	3.3	10.2	1.6
65 yrs. old and over	3.6	2.8	-	0.5	2.3	0.5	1.8	0.8
White	37.5	36.3	1.5	3.7	31.1	7.0	24.2	1.2
Black	43.8	41.7	2.0	5.9	33.7	11.9	21.8	2.1
Other	29.0	27.6	0.7	4.4	22.5	6.6	15.9	1.4
Hispanic	34.5	32.8	0.8	6.3	25.6	6.1	19.5	1.7
Non-Hispanic	38.1	36.8	1.6	3.7	31.5	7.6	23.9	1.3
Household income:								
Less than $7,500	65.5	63.8	3.2	6.5	54.2	19.6	34.5	1.7
$7,500-$14,999	51.1	49.3	2.4	5.8	41.0	11.8	29.3	1.8
$15,000-$24,999	40.7	39.4	2.3	3.6	33.5	7.9	25.7	1.3
$25,000-$34,999	43.1	42.0	2.4	6.9	32.8	6.3	26.5	1.1
$35,000-$49,999	33.3	31.7	0.5	3.1	28.1	6.2	21.9	1.6
$50,000-$74,999	33.1	32.0	0.7	2.8	28.5	6.2	22.3	1.1
$75,000 or more	34.1	33.1	1.2	2.9	29.0	6.2	22.8	1.0

Source: U.S. Bureau of Justice Statistics, *Criminal Victimization*, annual; and *Criminal Victimization 1998, Changes 1997-98 with Trends 1993-98*, Series NCJ-176353 (revised 25 August 1999).

Law Enforcement, Courts, and Prisons   209

No. 342. Victim-Offender Relationship in Crimes of Violence by Characteristics of the Criminal Incident: 1998

[In percent. Covers only crimes of violence. Based on National Crime Victimization Survey; see text, Section 5, Law Enforcement, and Appendix III]

Characteristic of incident	Total	Rape/ sexual assault	Robbery	Assault		
				Total	Aggra- vated[1]	Simple
Total...................	**100**	**100**	**100**	**100**	**100**	**100**
Victim/offender relationship: [2]						
Relatives......................	17	13	17	12	11	12
Well-known	31	42	15	26	26	26
Casual acquaintance...........	12	20	6	17	12	18
Stranger	40	26	61	45	51	44
Time of day:						
6 a.m. to 6 p.m................	55	34	54	56	51	57
6 p.m. to midnight.............	32	37	31	32	37	30
Midnight to 6 a.m..............	12	22	14	11	12	11
Location of crime:						
At or near victim's home or lodging	29	46	33	28	32	27
Friend's/relative's/neighbor's home.....	7	20	6	7	9	6
Commercial places	12	7	6	13	11	13
Parking lots/garages	8	3	11	8	7	8
School	14	12	9	15	5	17
Streets other than near victim's home...	18	5	27	18	22	16
Other [3]	12	8	9	13	13	13
Victim's activity:						
At work or traveling to or from work	21	12	18	22	19	22
School	13	12	12	13	6	16
Activities at home	24	41	21	23	26	22
Shopping/errands	3	-	7	3	4	3
Leisure activities away from home	22	22	17	23	28	21
Traveling	9	4	16	8	9	8
Other	8	9	9	8	8	8
Distance from victim's home:						
Inside home or lodging	18	44	23	16	17	16
Near victim's home	14	5	13	14	17	13
1 mile or less	18	13	17	18	20	18
5 miles or less	24	21	19	25	21	26
50 miles or less	23	13	22	23	21	24
More than 50 miles	4	3	5	3	4	3
Weapons:						
No weapons present	75	91	58	77	7	100
Weapons present	25	9	42	23	93	-
Firearm	8	4	21	7	27	-
Other type of weapon [4].........	16	5	21	16	66	-

- Represents zero.   [1] An aggravated assault is any assault in which an offender possesses or uses a weapon or inflicts serious injury.   [2] Excludes "don't know" relationships.   [3] Includes areas on public transportation or inside station, in apartment yard, park, field, playground, or other areas.   [4] Includes knives, other sharp objects, blunt objects, and other types of weapons.
Source: U.S. Bureau of Justice Statistics, *Criminal Victimization,* annual; and *Criminal Victimization 1998, Changes 1997-98 with Trends 1993-98,* Series NCJ-176353 (revised 25 August 1999).

No. 343. Property Victimization Rates by Selected Household Characteristic: 1998

[Victimizations per 1,000 households. Based on National Crime Victimization Survey; see text, Section 5, Law Enforcement, and Appendix III]

Characteristic	Total	Burglary	Motor vehicle theft	Theft
Total.................................	**217.4**	**38.5**	**10.8**	**168.1**
Race:				
White........................	212.6	36.3	9.4	166.9
Black........................	248.0	54.8	20.1	173.1
Other........................	224.5	33.2	12.5	178.9
Ethnicity:				
Hispanic......................	267.6	44.9	22.0	200.7
Non-Hispanic..................	212.5	37.7	9.7	165.0
Household income:				
Less than $7,500	209.0	55.4	11.1	142.5
$7,500-$14,999	229.8	57.8	9.0	162.9
$15,000-$24,999	211.0	42.6	12.0	156.5
$25,000-$34,999	233.8	38.2	12.3	183.2
$35,000-$49,999	221.7	32.7	10.8	178.3
$50,000-$74,999	248.6	30.1	10.6	208.0
$75,000 or more	248.6	28.0	11.2	209.4
Residence:				
Urban........................	274.2	49.3	17.8	207.0
Suburban.....................	204.5	32.5	10.2	161.8
Rural........................	173.5	36.6	3.5	133.4
Form of tenure:				
Home owned..................	189.6	31.7	8.5	149.3
Home rented..................	270.6	51.5	15.1	204.0

Source: U.S. Bureau of Justice Statistics, *Criminal Victimization,* annual; and *Criminal Victimization 1998, Changes 1997-98 with Trends 1993-98,* Series NCJ-176353 (revised 25 August 1999).

210   Law Enforcement, Courts, and Prisons

No. 344. Juvenile Arrests for Selected Offenses: 1980 to 1998

[169,439 represents 169,439,000. Juveniles are persons under 18 years of age]

Offense	1980	1990	1991	1992	1993	1994	1995	1996	1997	1998
Number of contributing agencies . .	8,178	10,765	10,148	11,058	10,277	10,693	10,037	10,026	9,472	9,651
Population covered (1,000)	169,439	204,543	189,962	217,754	213,705	208,035	206,762	195,805	194,925	196,083
NUMBER										
Violent crime, total.	77,220	97,103	95,677	118,358	122,434	125,141	123,131	104,455	100,273	90,703
Murder.	1,475	2,661	2,626	3,025	3,473	3,114	2,812	2,184	1,887	1,592
Forcible rape.	3,668	4,971	4,766	5,451	5,490	4,873	4,556	4,228	4,127	4,013
Robbery.	38,529	34,944	35,632	42,639	44,598	47,046	47,240	39,788	36,419	30,047
Aggravated assault	33,548	54,527	52,653	67,243	68,873	70,108	68,523	58,255	57,840	55,051
Weapon law violations	21,203	33,123	37,575	49,903	54,414	52,278	46,506	40,145	39,358	34,210
Drug abuse, total	86,685	66,300	58,603	73,232	90,618	124,931	149,236	148,783	155,444	148,712
Sale and manufacturing	13,004	24,575	22,929	25,331	27,635	32,746	34,077	32,558	30,761	29,475
Heroin/cocaine.	1,318	17,511	16,915	17,881	18,716	20,327	19,187	17,465	15,855	15,189
Marijuana	8,876	4,372	3,579	4,853	6,144	8,812	10,682	11,489	11,208	10,866
Synthetic narcotics	465	346	570	663	455	465	701	614	671	819
Dangerous nonnarcotic drugs .	2,345	2,346	1,865	1,934	2,320	3,142	3,507	2,990	3,027	2,601
Possession.	73,681	41,725	35,674	47,901	62,983	92,185	115,159	116,225	124,683	119,237
Heroin/cocaine.	2,614	15,194	13,747	16,855	17,726	21,004	21,253	17,560	18,328	16,339
Marijuana	64,465	20,940	16,490	25,004	37,915	61,003	82,015	87,712	94,046	91,833
Synthetic narcotics	1,524	1,155	885	897	1,008	1,227	2,047	1,713	1,987	1,920
Dangerous nonnarcotic drugs .	5,078	4,436	4,552	5,145	6,334	8,951	9,844	9,240	10,322	9,145

Source: U.S. Federal Bureau of Investigation, *Crime in the United States*, annual.

No. 345. Persons Arrested by Charge and Selected Characteristics: 1998

[11,231.5 represents 11,231,500. Represents arrests (not charges) reported by approximately 10,000 agencies with a total 1998 population of approximately 200 million as estimated by FBI]

Offense charged	Total arrests (1,000)			American Indian or Alaskan Native	Asian or Pacific Islander	Total arrests (1,000)	Percent—	
	Total	White	Black				Male	Under 18 yrs. old
Total	11,231.5	7,479.6	3,491.0	129.7	131.2	10,295.1	78.2	18.0
Serious crimes [1]:								
Murder and nonnegligent manslaughter	13.3	5.9	7.1	0.1	0.2	12.3	88.8	11.9
Forcible rape.	23.3	13.8	9.0	0.2	0.3	21.9	98.8	17.2
Robbery	106.1	43.9	60.3	0.6	1.3	87.1	90.0	26.9
Aggravated assault	385.5	233.0	143.6	3.8	5.0	359.9	80.4	14.3
Burglary	245.0	166.1	73.4	2.4	3.1	233.4	87.5	35.1
Larceny/theft.	983.6	638.0	316.1	12.3	17.2	940.2	65.3	31.9
Motor vehicle theft	113.0	65.4	44.5	1.2	1.9	107.0	84.3	35.9
Arson	12.3	9.0	3.0	0.1	0.1	12.1	85.3	52.1
All other nonserious crimes:								
Other assaults.	997.6	635.5	338.4	12.5	11.3	947.6	77.6	17.8
Forgery and counterfeiting	87.7	57.1	28.7	0.5	1.3	81.3	61.1	6.2
Fraud	311.2	198.7	107.9	1.4	3.2	268.4	54.2	2.9
Embezzlement	12.8	8.0	4.5	0.1	0.2	12.2	51.2	9.1
Stolen property—buying, receiving, possessing	103.9	59.5	42.4	0.9	1.2	98.5	84.5	24.5
Vandalism.	224.2	163.7	55.2	2.8	2.4	213.5	84.8	42.2
Weapons; carrying, possessing etc.. . .	146.7	85.4	58.8	0.9	1.6	136.0	92.1	23.7
Prostitution and commercialized vice . .	80.3	48.4	29.9	0.5	1.5	68.5	42.2	1.5
Sex offenses (except forcible rape and prostitution)	71.9	52.7	17.4	0.8	1.0	66.0	91.8	17.0
Drug abuse violations	1,263.9	757.7	491.8	6.3	8.1	1,108.8	82.5	13.2
Gambling	15.4	6.5	8.2	-	0.6	9.2	89.6	12.5
Offenses against family and children . .	102.5	69.6	30.2	0.9	1.7	99.8	78.3	7.0
Driving under the influence	977.6	848.2	103.4	14.0	12.0	968.9	84.4	1.5
Liquor laws.	576.1	445.6	112.2	12.3	5.9	448.2	78.6	25.0
Drunkenness.	513.4	421.6	77.8	12.0	2.0	510.3	87.2	3.5
Disorderly conduct	547.3	345.4	191.0	6.5	4.4	501.9	76.7	26.4
Vagrancy	26.8	14.0	11.9	0.6	0.3	22.0	79.4	9.6
Suspicion	3.8	2.8	1.0	0.1	-	3.8	79.6	25.3
Curfew and loitering law violations . . .	139.4	99.9	36.6	1.4	1.6	136.3	69.5	100.0
Runaways	118.6	92.5	20.9	1.2	4.0	117.1	41.8	100.0
All other offenses (except traffic).	3,028.5	1,891.7	1,066.0	33.0	37.8	2,702.9	79.5	11.8

- Represents zero or rounds to zero.   [1] Includes arson.

Source: U.S. Federal Bureau of Investigation, *Crime in the United States*, annual.

Law Enforcement, Courts, and Prisons 211

No. 346. Drug Use by Arrestees in Major U.S. Cities by Type of Drug and Sex: 1998

[Percent testing positive. Based on data from the Arrestee Drug Abuse Monitoring Program]

City	Male				Female			
	Any drug [1]	Marijuana	Cocaine	Heroin	Any drug [1]	Marijuana	Cocaine	Heroin
Albuquerque, NM	64.8	35.9	38.7	8.2	73.1	24.0	59.1	15.4
Atlanta, GA	65.7	26.0	51.3	1.3	(NA)	(NA)	(NA)	(NA)
Chicago, IL	74.2	41.5	44.9	18.3	71.5	19.7	55.5	27.0
Cleveland, OH	65.2	36.8	36.8	6.0	58.1	27.0	40.5	1.4
Dallas, TX	63.4	43.1	29.0	2.3	48.9	24.2	29.5	4.8
Denver, CO	68.8	41.3	39.6	4.2	68.7	29.9	49.9	3.4
Detroit, MI	68.2	46.5	28.2	6.8	60.2	21.5	46.2	21.5
Houston, TX	59.9	35.8	35.8	7.5	51.7	20.1	37.3	7.0
Indianapolis, IN	66.8	45.1	34.2	1.8	67.1	31.2	43.2	4.5
Las Vegas, NV	56.8	25.8	24.2	2.6	70.3	21.6	35.1	13.5
Los Angeles, CA	64.4	27.3	42.7	5.6	71.0	21.8	44.7	8.8
Miami, FL	61.5	29.2	47.3	2.4	(NA)	(NA)	(NA)	(NA)
New Orleans, LA	67.3	38.3	46.0	12.9	50.5	22.1	38.7	3.4
New York, NY	76.9	38.7	47.1	16.2	82.1	23.4	67.0	21.8
Oklahoma City, OK.	69.0	53.1	27.3	1.9	(NA)	(NA)	(NA)	(NA)
Philadelphia, PA.	78.7	44.9	44.5	18.4	77.4	23.7	60.9	14.9
Phoenix, AZ	62.7	32.2	31.1	5.7	70.6	24.9	39.6	7.3
Portland, OR	71.5	36.9	29.2	15.5	74.3	23.2	36.7	25.1
Sacramento, CA.	70.8	44.1	18.2	3.2	72.8	28.2	30.7	8.4
San Antonio, TX.	56.0	41.1	27.0	9.6	37.8	17.5	20.0	8.6
San Diego, CA.	68.6	36.4	19.1	9.3	63.9	26.7	20.4	6.7
San Jose, CA	48.2	24.8	8.0	4.4	41.5	13.6	9.5	4.8
Seattle, WA.	65.4	35.4	35.9	17.4	81.0	37.9	56.9	17.2
Tucson, AZ	63.1	39.2	39.4	6.8	57.0	21.5	41.3	7.4
Washington, DC.	65.3	38.0	33.3	9.7	65.3	28.5	40.4	9.8

NA Not available. [1] Includes other drugs not shown separately.

Source: U.S. National Institute of Justice, *1998 Annual Report on Drug Use Among Adult and Juvenile Arrestees*, April 1999.

No. 347. Drug Arrest Rates for Drug Abuse Violations, 1990 to 1998, and by Region, 1998

[Rate per 100,000 inhabitants. Based on Census Bureau estimated resident population as of July 1, except 1990, enumerated as of April 1. For composition of regions, see map, inside front cover]

Offense				1998				
					Region			
	1990	1995	1997	Total	North-east	Midwest	South	West
Drug arrest rate	435.3	564.7	604.7	608.7	765.4	395.5	565.9	636.6
Sale and/or manufacture	139.0	140.7	136.0	138.6	230.1	107.2	107.0	123.8
Heroin or cocaine [1]	93.7	83.7	75.2	77.1	171.0	24.8	62.7	53.3
Marijuana.	26.4	32.7	34.5	34.0	44.9	33.0	28.4	32.6
Synthetic or manufactured drugs	2.7	3.9	4.3	5.6	3.5	2.7	9.2	4.7
Other dangerous nonnarcotic drugs . .	16.2	20.3	22.0	21.9	10.7	46.7	6.8	33.2
Possession	296.3	423.9	468.7	470.1	535.4	288.3	458.8	542.8
Heroin or cocaine [1]	144.4	157.4	156.5	155.4	215.0	54.1	139.9	188.9
Marijuana.	104.9	192.7	226.5	233.8	291.2	182.4	275.6	172.3
Synthetic or manufactured drugs	6.6	8.5	9.6	10.4	6.3	6.1	13.5	12.7
Other dangerous nonnarcotic drugs . .	40.4	65.4	76.1	70.5	22.9	45.7	29.8	168.9

[1] Includes other derivatives such as morphine, heroin, and codeine.

Source: U.S. Federal Bureau of Investigation, *Crime in the United States*, annual.

No. 348. Federal Drug Seizures by Type of Drug: 1990 to 1999

[In pounds. For fiscal years ending in year shown. Reflects the combined drug seizure effort of the Drug Enforcement Administration, the Federal Bureau of Investigation, the U.S. Customs Services, and beginning October 1993 the U.S. Border Patrol within the jurisdiction of the United States as well as maritime seizures by the U.S. Coast Guard. Based on reports to the Federal-wide Drug Seizure System, which eliminates duplicate reporting of a seizure involving more than one Federal agency]

Drug	1990	1992	1993	1994	1995	1996	1997	1998	1999
Total	1,238,425	1,881,693	1,845,998	2,397,037	2,913,227	3,181,573	3,338,276	3,834,096	4,949,878
Heroin	1,704	2,552	3,516	2,883	2,971	3,373	3,121	3,519	2,791
Cocaine	235,891	304,086	244,315	309,928	233,447	254,437	252,329	265,997	290,756
Cannabis	500,415	787,527	799,083	1,042,113	1,338,405	1,461,881	1,541,413	1,782,290	2,328,166
Marijuana	483,353	783,479	773,004	1,040,999	1,306,528	1,429,786	1,488,362	1,781,694	2,326,484
Hashish	17,062	4,048	26,080	1,114	31,876	32,096	53,051	596	1,681

Source: U.S. Drug Enforcement Administration, unpublished data from Federal-wide Drug Seizure System.

No. 349. Immigration and Naturalization Service Enforcement Activities: 1990 to 1997

[For fiscal years ending in year shown. See text, Section 9, State and Local Government]

Item	Unit	1990	1991	1992	1993	1994	1995	1996	1997
Deportable aliens located.......	1,000	1,169.9	1,197.9	1,258.5	1,327.3	1,094.7	1,394.6	1,650.0	1,536.5
Border Patrol..............	1,000	1,103.4	1,132.9	1,199.6	1,263.5	1,031.7	1,324.2	1,549.9	1,413.0
Southwestern border.....	1,000	(NA)	1,077.9	1,145.6	1,212.9	979.1	1,271.4	1,507.0	1,368.7
Mexican..............	1,000	1,054.8	1,095.1	1,168.9	1,230.1	999.9	1,293.5	1,523.1	1,387.7
Canadian.............	1,000	5.7	6.7	6.2	5.2	3.4	3.5	2.7	2.9
Other	1,000	42.8	31.1	24.4	28.1	28.4	27.2	24.0	22.4
Number of seizures by Border Patrol.................	Number...	17,275	14,261	11,391	10,995	9,134	9,327	11,129	11,792
Value of seizures by Border Patrol.	Mil. dol....	843.6	950.2	1,247.9	1,382.9	1,598.1	2,011.8	1,255.4	1,094.6
Narcotics...............	Mil. dol....	797.8	910.1	1,216.8	1,337.8	1,555.7	1,965.3	1,208.8	1,046.3
Aliens expelled:									
Formal removals [1]........	1,000	30.0	33.2	43.6	42.5	45.5	50.7	69.3	114.1
Voluntary departures [2]......	1,000	1,022.5	1,061.1	1,105.8	1,243.3	1,029.0	1,313.6	1,573.2	1,430.0

NA Not available.   [1] Include deportations, exclusions, and removals.   [2] Includes aliens under docket control required to depart and voluntary departures not under docket control.

Source: U.S. Immigration and Naturalization Service, Statistical Yearbook, annual; and unpublished data.

No. 350. Authorized Intercepts of Communication—Summary: 1980 to 1996

[Data for jurisdictions with statutes authorizing or approving interception of wire or oral communication]

Item	1980	1985	1987	1988	1989	1990	1991	1992	1993	1994	1995	1996
Jurisdictions: [1]												
With wiretap statutes.......	28	32	33	34	37	40	41	41	41	41	41	46
Reporting interceptions	22	22	22	23	25	25	23	23	23	18	19	24
Intercept applications authorized.......	564	784	673	738	763	872	856	919	976	1,154	1,058	1,149
Intercept installations........	524	722	634	678	720	812	802	846	938	1,100	1,024	1,035
Federal	79	235	233	286	305	321	349	332	444	549	527	574
State................	445	487	401	392	415	491	453	514	494	551	497	461
Intercepted communications, average [2]................	1,058	1,320	1,299	1,251	1,656	1,487	1,584	1,861	1,801	2,139	2,028	1,969
Incriminating	315	275	230	316	337	321	290	347	364	373	459	422
Persons arrested [3]..........	1,871	2,469	2,226	2,486	2,804	2,057	2,364	2,685	2,428	2,852	2,577	2,464
Convictions [3]..........	259	660	506	543	706	420	605	607	413	772	494	502
Major offense specified:												
Gambling	199	206	135	126	111	116	98	66	96	86	95	114
Drugs................	282	434	379	435	471	520	536	634	679	876	732	821
Homicide and assault	13	25	18	14	20	21	21	35	28	19	30	41
Other	70	119	141	163	161	215	201	184	173	173	201	173

[1] Jurisdictions include Federal Government, states, and District of Columbia.   [2] Average per authorized installation.
[3] Based on information received from intercepts installed in year shown; additional arrests/convictions will occur in subsequent years but are not shown here.

Source: Administrative Office of the U.S. Courts, Report on Applications for Orders Authorizing or Approving the Interception of Wire, Oral or Electronic Communications (Wiretap Report), annual.

No. 351. Background Checks for Firearm Transfers: 1994 to 1999

[In thousands (22,254 represents 22,254,000), except rates. For "Interim period" of 1994 to November 29, 1998, covered handgun purchases from licensed firearm dealers; beginning November 29, 1998 (effective date for the Brady Handgun Violence Prevention Act, P.L. 103-159,1993) covers the transfer of both handguns and long guns from a Federal firearms licensee, as well as purchases from pawnshops and retail gun shops]

Inquiries and rejections	1994-1999, period	Interim period						Permanent Brady	
		1994	1995	1996	1997	1998 [2]	Dec. 1998 [3]	1999
Applications and rejections:									
Applications received	22,254	2,483	2,706	2,593	2,574	2,384	893	8,621
Applications rejected	536	62	41	70	69	70	20	204
Rejection rate	2.4	2.5	1.5	2.7	2.7	2.9	2.2	2.4

[1] Represents from the Inception of the Brady Act on March 1, 1994, to 1999.   [2] For period January 1 to November 29, 1998.
[3] For period November 30 to December 31, 1999. Counts are from the National Instant Criminal Background Check System and may include multiple transactions for the same application.

Source: U.S. Bureau of Justice Statistics, Background Checks for Firearm Transfers, 1999, Series NCJ 180882, June 2000.

Law Enforcement, Courts, and Prisons   213

No. 352. U.S. Population Who Had Face-to-Face Contact With Police by Race and Ethnicity and Reason for Contact: 1996

[215,529 represents 215,529,000. Persons having multiple contacts or more than one reason for any single contact appear in table more than once; therefore, may not add to total. Covers persons 12 years old and over. Based on the Police-Public Contact Survey of 6,421 persons; data subject to sampling variability]

Reason for contact	Number having contact (1,000)				Percent having contact			
	Total	White	Black	Hispanic [1]	Total	White	Black	Hispanic [1]
Population total	**215,529**	**163,883**	**25,394**	**17,159**	**(X)**	**(X)**	**(X)**	**(X)**
For any reason	44,556	36,262	3,964	2,593	20.7	22.1	15.6	15.1
I reported a crime	12,722	10,640	1,049	634	5.9	6.5	4.1	3.7
I asked police for help	10,087	8,393	744	500	4.7	5.1	2.9	2.9
I reported a problem	7,892	6,449	508	557	3.7	3.9	2.0	3.2
Police ticketed me...........	10,947	8,988	815	865	5.1	5.5	3.2	5.0
I was in a traffic accident	5,454	4,501	501	241	2.5	2.7	2.0	1.4
I witnessed an accident	2,326	2,007	151	102	1.1	1.2	0.6	0.6
I was the victim of a crime	6,755	5,753	343	360	3.1	3.5	1.4	2.1
I witnessed a crime	3,467	2,776	419	179	1.6	1.7	1.6	1.0
Police suspected me of a crime..	2,611	1,945	197	326	1.2	1.2	0.8	1.9
Police asked why I was there ...	2,690	2,070	361	84	1.2	1.3	1.4	0.5
Police had a warrant for my arrest..	492	378	84	30	0.2	0.2	0.3	0.2
I had a casual encounter	8,042	6,901	640	327	3.7	4.2	2.5	1.9
I attended a community meeting ...	2,437	1,986	285	32	1.1	1.2	1.1	0.2
Some other reason	14,066	11,760	1,075	724	6.5	3.9	2.0	3.2

X Not applicable. [1] Persons of Hispanic origin may be of any race.
Source: U.S. Bureau of Justice Statistics, *Police Use of Force, National Collection of Data,* November 1997.

No. 353. Full-Time Sworn Police Officers in State and Local Government—Number and Rate: 1996

[As of **June.** Rate based on Census Bureau estimated resident population as of **July 1**]

State	Number [1]	Rate per 10,000 [2]	Type of agency			State	Number [1]	Rate per 10,000 [2]	Type of agency		
			Local	State	Sheriff				Local	State	Sheriff
U.S. ...	**663,535**	**25**	**410,956**	**54,587**	**152,922**	MO	12,998	24	8,836	996	2,421
AL.....	9,767	23	6,484	581	1,963	MT	1,682	19	690	212	616
AK.....	1,254	21	740	290	-	NE.....	3,297	20	1,929	464	794
AZ.....	10,088	23	6,967	952	1,563	NV.....	4,363	27	2,565	375	935
AR.....	5,819	23	3,244	522	1,410	NH	2,305	20	1,862	245	129
CA.....	69,134	22	35,939	6,219	22,869	NJ.....	28,058	35	19,891	2,702	3,145
CO	9,896	26	5,451	581	3,324	NM	4,134	24	2,462	435	889
CT.....	8,525	26	6,411	1,022	886	NY.....	71,221	39	54,657	3,972	5,852
DE.....	1,660	23	923	540	24	NC	16,953	23	9,505	1,380	5,264
DC	3,909	72	3,587	-	-	ND	1,141	18	561	120	364
FL.....	37,395	26	19,652	1,740	14,124	OH	23,811	21	15,932	1,391	5,179
GA	19,115	26	10,241	878	6,752	OK	7,232	22	4,951	756	1,014
HI	2,989	25	2,746	-	-	OR	6,064	19	3,245	824	1,921
ID	2,524	21	1,142	192	1,053	PA.....	24,873	21	17,655	4,114	1,239
IL	38,192	32	26,151	1,988	8,426	RI	2,422	24	1,958	193	153
IN	10,931	19	6,426	1,207	2,618	SC.....	8,675	23	4,004	892	3,037
IA	5,043	18	3,037	433	1,343	SD.....	1,464	20	847	155	344
KS.....	6,183	24	3,616	552	1,683	TN.....	12,152	23	7,076	768	3,520
KY.....	6,466	17	4,089	984	1,113	TX [3]...	47,767	25	28,269	2,873	11,326
LA.....	16,125	37	5,733	873	8,720	UT.....	3,699	18	1,882	355	1,198
ME	2,318	19	1,426	337	321	VT.....	981	17	548	290	87
MD	13,828	27	8,923	1,625	1,438	VA.....	18,448	28	8,911	1,662	6,605
MA	17,935	29	13,068	2,565	1,540	WA	9,292	17	5,430	906	2,553
MI	20,568	21	13,288	2,164	4,435	WV	2,977	16	1,416	595	726
MN	7,994	17	5,006	484	2,139	WI.....	12,678	25	7,640	497	3,886
MS	5,813	21	3,326	535	1,474	WY	1,377	29	618	151	507

- Represents or rounds to zero. [1] Includes special police not shown separately. [2] Based on resident population as of July 1. [3] Texas includes sworn personnel of constable offices, not shown separately.
Source: U.S. Bureau of Justice Statistics, *Census of State and Local Law Enforcement Agencies, 1996,* Series NCJ 164618, June 1998.

No. 354. General Purpose Law Enforcement Agencies—Number and Employment: 1996

Type of agency	Number of agencies [1]	Number of employees					
		Full time			Part time		
		Total	Sworn	Civilian	Total	Sworn	Civilian
Total	**18,769**	**921,978**	**663,535**	**258,443**	**97,770**	**47,712**	**50,058**
Local police............	13,578	521,985	410,956	111,029	61,453	30,976	30,477
Sheriff................	3,088	257,712	152,922	104,790	22,412	10,845	11,567
State police............	49	83,742	54,587	29,155	1,303	132	1,171
Special police	1,316	56,229	43,082	13,147	12,003	5,202	6,801
Texas constable.........	738	2,310	1,988	322	599	557	42

[1] The number of agencies reported here is the result of a weighted sample and not an exact enumeration.
Source: U.S. Bureau of Justice Statistics, *Census of State and Local Law Enforcement Agencies, 1996,* Series NCJ 164618, June 1998.

No. 355. Law Enforcement Officers Killed and Assaulted: 1990 to 1998

[Covers officers killed feloniously and accidentally in line of duty; includes federal officers. For composition of regions, see map, inside front cover]

Item	1990	1991	1992	1993	1994	1995	1996	1997	1998
OFFICERS KILLED									
Total killed	133	124	130	129	141	133	112	132	142
Northeast	13	16	16	12	17	16	17	14	6
Midwest	20	26	15	27	30	19	21	25	19
South.	69	55	68	57	50	63	46	55	70
West	23	18	23	22	30	32	18	31	36
Puerto Rico.	8	8	8	11	9	2	10	7	9
Outlying areas, foreign countries.	-	1	-	-	5	1	-	-	2
ASSAULTS									
Population (1,000) [1]	199,834	187,866	217,997	211,914	217,935	198,155	166,038	191,303	190,189
Number of—									
Agencies represented	9,512	9,043	10,862	9,858	10,434	8,895	7,808	8,522	8,000
Police officers.	414,037	399,020	460,430	456,565	473,946	440,582	373,575	423,930	445,898
Total assaulted	72,270	62,852	81,252	66,975	64,912	58,063	46,695	49,151	59,545
Firearm	3,665	3,532	4,455	4,002	3,168	2,373	1,887	1,844	2,073
Knife or cutting instrument . . .	1,650	1,493	2,095	1,574	1,513	1,362	871	895	1,077
Other dangerous weapon . . .	7,436	7,014	8,604	7,551	7,210	6,451	5,084	5,389	7,266
Hands, fists, feet, etc	59,519	50,813	66,098	53,848	53,021	47,877	38,853	41,023	49,129

- Represents zero. [1] Represents the number of persons covered by agencies shown.

Source: U.S. Federal Bureau of Investigation, *Law Enforcement Officers Killed and Assaulted*, annual.

No. 356. U.S. Supreme Court—Cases Filed and Disposition: 1980 to 1998

[Statutory term of court begins first Monday in **October**]

Action	1980	1990	1992	1993	1994	1995	1996	1997	1998
Total cases on docket	5,144	6,316	7,245	7,786	8,100	7,565	7,602	7,692	8,083
Appellate cases on docket.	2,749	2,351	2,441	2,442	2,515	2,456	2,430	2,432	2,387
From prior term	527	365	379	342	377	361	375	347	326
Docketed during present term	2,222	1,986	2,062	2,100	2,138	2,095	2,055	2,085	2,061
Cases acted upon [1]	2,324	2,042	2,140	2,099	2,185	2,130	2,124	2,142	2,092
Granted review	167	114	83	78	83	92	74	75	72
Denied, dismissed, or withdrawn .	1,999	1,802	1,920	1,947	2,016	1,945	1,955	1,990	1,940
Summarily decided	90	81	84	34	52	62	66	36	44
Cases not acted upon	425	309	301	343	330	326	306	290	295
Pauper cases on docket	2,371	3,951	4,792	5,332	5,574	5,098	5,165	5,253	5,689
Cases acted upon.	2,027	3,436	4,261	4,621	4,983	4,514	4,613	4,616	4,951
Granted review	17	27	14	21	10	13	13	14	9
Denied, dismissed, or withdrawn .	1,968	3,369	4,209	4,566	4,955	4,439	4,582	4,581	4,926
Summarily decided	32	28	25	30	14	55	15	14	11
Cases not acted upon	344	515	531	711	591	584	552	637	738
Original cases on docket	24	14	12	12	11	11	7	7	7
Cases disposed of during term	7	3	1	1	2	5	2	1	2
Total cases available for argument	264	201	166	145	136	145	140	138	126
Cases disposed of	162	131	120	105	97	93	92	97	94
Cases argued	154	125	116	99	94	90	90	96	90
Cases dismissed or remanded without argument	8	6	4	6	3	3	2	1	4
Cases remaining	102	70	46	40	39	52	48	41	32
Cases decided by signed opinion	144	121	111	93	91	87	87	93	84
Cases decided by per curiam opinion. .	8	4	4	6	3	3	3	1	4
Number of signed opinions.	123	112	107	84	82	75	80	91	75

[1] Includes cases granted review and carried over to next term, not shown separately.

Source: Office of the Clerk, Supreme Court of the United States, unpublished data.

U.S. Census Bureau, Statistical Abstract of the United States: 2000

No. 357. U.S. Courts of Appeals—Cases Commenced and Disposition: 1980 to 1998

[For years ending June 30]

Item	1980	1990	1992	1993	1994	1995	1996	1997	1998
Cases commenced [1]	23,200	40,898	46,032	49,770	48,815	49,671	51,524	52,571	53,328
Criminal	4,405	9,493	10,956	11,885	11,052	10,171	10,653	10,740	10,339
U.S. civil	4,654	6,626	7,113	7,758	7,518	7,761	8,681	8,710	9,803
Private civil	10,200	20,490	22,862	24,030	24,781	25,992	27,188	26,716	27,364
Administrative appeals .	2,950	2,578	3,052	3,824	3,560	3,345	2,858	4,131	3,788
Cases terminated [1]	20,887	38,520	42,933	47,466	48,546	50,085	49,359	51,295	51,348
Criminal	3,993	7,509	9,830	11,043	11,519	11,320	9,995	10,522	10,281
U.S. civil	4,346	6,379	6,797	7,462	7,637	7,710	7,831	8,751	8,993
Private civil	8,942	20,369	21,628	23,437	23,943	25,574	25,999	26,365	26,054
Administrative appeals .	2,643	2,582	2,801	3,464	3,480	3,254	3,131	3,615	4,026
Cases disposed of [2]	10,607	21,006	23,162	25,567	26,475	28,187	26,988	26,287	24,917
Affirmed or granted . . .	8,017	16,629	18,463	20,604	21,371	22,825	21,696	21,170	19,771
Reversed or denied. . .	1,845	2,565	2,681	2,514	2,636	2,679	2,533	2,353	2,267
Other	745	1,812	2,018	2,449	2,468	2,683	2,759	2,764	2,879
Median months [3]	8.9	10.1	10.5	10.4	10.5	10.5	10.3	11.1	11.5

[1] Includes original proceedings and bankruptcy appeals not shown separately. [2] Terminated on the merits after hearing or submission. [3] For 1980, the figure is from filing of complete record to final disposition; beginning 1990, figure is from filing notice of appeal to final disposition. For definition of median, see Guide to Tabular Presentation.

No. 358. U.S. District Courts—Civil Cases Commenced and Pending: 1995 to 1998

[For years ending June 30]

Type of case	Cases commenced				Cases pending			
	1995	1996	1997	1998	1995	1996	1997	1998
Cases total [1]	239,013	272,661	265,151	261,262	224,378	243,703	259,536	269,119
Contract actions [1]	31,619	33,413	38,858	44,205	27,337	26,999	31,613	32,403
Recovery of overpayments [2] . . .	2,099	3,583	8,070	15,188	1,041	2,301	3,881	6,129
Real property actions	7,282	6,276	5,761	5,655	5,073	4,486	3,951	3,971
Tort actions	44,511	67,029	52,710	52,218	52,334	65,823	72,250	84,073
Personal injury	41,102	63,222	48,266	48,356	48,789	62,087	68,154	80,114
Personal injury product liability [1]	17,631	38,170	23,294	28,325	24,166	34,096	36,621	50,838
Asbestos	6,821	6,760	8,184	9,718	3,524	2,037	2,438	1,576
Other personal injury	23,471	25,052	24,972	20,031	24,623	27,991	3,533	29,276
Personal property damage	3,409	3,807	4,444	3,862	3,545	3,736	4,096	3,959
Actions under statutes [1]	155,495	165,922	167,807	159,172	139,487	144,094	151,655	148,630
Civil rights [1]	35,566	40,476	43,166	42,750	37,512	42,545	46,096	46,718
Employment	18,225	22,150	23,707	23,804	20,375	24,212	26,669	27,097
Bankruptcy suits	5,138	4,737	4,217	3,905	4,541	3,938	3,648	2,921
Commerce (ICC rates, etc.) . . .	613	1,622	483	528	446	760	504	510
Environmental matters	1,136	1,158	973	1,007	1,823	1,869	1,630	1,602
Prisoner petitions	62,597	69,352	64,262	55,120	47,382	50,353	50,392	44,905
Forfeiture and penalty	2,670	2,255	2,301	2,431	2,399	1,989	1,905	1,959
Labor laws.	15,030	15,068	15,320	15,039	11,829	11,742	12,199	11,807
Protected property rights [3] . . .	6,990	6,800	7,511	7,660	5,998	6,273	6,765	7,037
Securities commodities and exchanges	1,870	1,741	1,737	2,166	2,969	2,872	2,591	2,998
Social Security laws	10,168	8,517	13,047	13,955	11,310	9,153	12,978	14,844
Tax suits	2,144	2,078	2,294	1,733	1,692	1,646	1,668	1,507
Freedom of information	481	465	400	436	500	496	435	416

[1] Includes other types not shown separately. [2] Includes enforcement of judgments in student loan cases, and overpayments of veterans benefits. [3] Includes copyright, patent, and trademark rights.

Source of Tables 357 and 358: Administrative Office of the U.S. Courts, *Statistical Tables for the Federal Judiciary*, annual.

No. 359. U.S. District Courts—Offenders Convicted and Sentenced to Prison and Length of Sentence: 1998

Most serious offense of conviction	Offenders convicted	Convicted offenders sentenced to prison	Length of sentence (mo.)	Most serious offense of conviction	Offenders convicted	Convicted offenders sentenced to prison	Length of sentence (mo.)
Total [1]	60,958	43,041	58.8	Possession	1,450	1,267	84.2
Violent offenses	3,078	2,808	84.2	Trafficking and			
Property offenses	11,862	7,114	25.4	manufacturing	19,417	18,013	78.5
Fraudulent offenses [2] .	9,752	5,860	22.3	Public-order offenses. . .	14,687	12,218	47.3
Embezzlement. . . .	916	497	15.7	Regulatory offenses . .	1,187	506	27.9
Fraud [3]	7,532	4,584	23.3	Other offenses	13,500	11,712	48.1
Forgery	147	66	17.9	Weapons	3,160	2,914	100.6
Other offenses [2]	2,110	1,254	40.3	Immigration	7,569	6,880	26.4
Larceny	1,344	693	32.6	Tax law violations [4]. .	752	376	18.6
Drug offenses [2]	20,867	19,280	78.8	Misdemeanors	10,375	1,590	11.4

[1] Total may include offenders for whom offense category could not be determined. [2] Includes offenses not shown separately. [3] Excludes tax fraud. [4] Includes tax fraud.

Source: U.S. Bureau of Justice Statistics, *Compendium of Federal Justice Statistics*, annual.

No. 360. U.S. District Courts—Civil Rights-Related Complaints and Disposition: 1990 to 1998

[Covers civil rights complaints related to employment, housing, welfare, or voting rights, but excludes prisoner petitions]

Year	Complaints				Cases disposed	Disposition			
	Jurisdiction					Percent of cases disposed			
	Cases involving U.S. Government			Private cases		Dismissed		Judgment	
	Total	Plaintiff	Defendant			Total	Settled	Total	Trial
1990	18,793	747	1,736	16,310	17,811	65.6	30.7	34.4	7.8
1991	19,892	816	1,532	16,992	17,975	67.2	31.5	32.9	7.6
1992	24,233	639	1,773	21,821	25,094	65.9	31.5	34.1	7.3
1993	27,655	747	1,970	24,938	23,416	67.5	31.5	32.4	6.6
1994	32,622	718	2,268	29,636	26,596	69.4	34.8	30.6	6.7
1995	36,600	668	2,358	33,574	30,175	69.4	33.4	30.6	6.0
1996	42,007	486	2,433	39,088	34,986	69.7	33.7	30.3	5.7
1997	43,278	561	2,356	40,361	38,131	70.5	34.2	29.5	5.2
1998	42,354	672	2,366	38,835	40,185	70.9	35.2	29.2	4.9

Source: U.S. Bureau of Justice Statistics, *Civil Rights Complaints in U.S. District Courts, 1990-98*, Series NCJ 173427, January 2000.

No. 361. Federal Environmental Enforcement Actions Initiated by Type of Violation and Enforcement Action: 1995 to 1997

Type of violation or statute violated	Total			Administrative actions [1]			Civil [2]			Criminal [3]		
	1995	1996	1997	1995	1996	1997	1995	1996	1997	1995	1996	1997
Total actions	3,722	2,902	4,129	2,969	2,171	3,427	207	220	207	546	511	446
Environmental protection	(NA)	(NA)	3,842	(NA)	(NA)	3,427	200	211	204	234	203	211
Clean Air Act	303	338	457	232	242	391	35	56	35	36	40	31
Clean Water Act	1,936	1,167	1,812	1,774	998	1,642	74	72	62	88	97	108
Resource Conservation and Recovery Act (RCRA)	192	336	505	92	238	423	25	21	82	34	37	59
Comprehensive Environmental Response Compensation, and Liability (CERCLA)	320	259	391	280	234	305	66	61	23	15	4	4
Toxic Substances control Act (TSCA)	193	191	191	187	178	185	(NA)	(NA)	(NA)	6	12	6
Other	454	292	486	404	281	481	(NA)	1	-	43	5	3
Wildlife [4]	(NA)	(NA)	287	(NA)	(NA)	(NA)	7	6	2	312	308	235

- Represents or rounds to zero. NA Not available. [1] Represents actions such as requiring the violator to comply with Federal environmental standards, suspending the violator's permit to discharge, and/or assessing a penalty for noncompliance. [2] Represents filing by U.S. attorneys in U.S. district court only. Statistics describing administrative actions for wildlife and conservation offenses were not available. [3] Criminal actions include only those offenses classified as felonies or Class A misdemeanors. [4] Includes Endangered Species Act, Bald and Golden Eagle Protection Act, Migratory Bird Treaty Act, and Lacey Act.

Source: U.S. Bureau of Justice Statistics, *Federal Enforcement of Environmental Laws, 1997*, Series NCJ 175686, November 1999.

No. 362. Federal Prosecutions of Public Corruption: 1980 to 1998

[As of **Dec. 31.** Prosecution of persons who have corrupted public office in violation of Federal Criminal Statutes]

Prosecution status	1980	1985	1989	1990	1991	1992	1993	1994	1995	1996	1997	1998
Total: [1] Indicted	727	1,157	1,348	1,176	1,452	1,189	1,371	1,165	1,051	984	1,057	1,174
Convicted	602	997	1,149	1,084	1,194	1,081	1,362	969	878	902	853	1,014
Awaiting trial	213	256	375	300	346	380	403	332	323	244	327	340
Federal officials: Indicted	123	563	695	615	803	624	627	571	527	456	459	442
Convicted	131	470	610	583	665	532	595	488	438	459	392	414
Awaiting trial	16	90	126	103	149	139	133	124	120	64	83	85
State officials: Indicted	72	79	71	96	115	81	113	99	61	109	51	91
Convicted	51	66	54	79	77	92	133	97	61	83	49	58
Awaiting trial	28	20	18	28	42	24	39	17	23	40	20	37
Local officials: Indicted	247	248	269	257	242	232	309	248	236	219	255	277
Convicted	168	221	201	225	180	211	272	202	191	190	169	264
Awaiting trial	82	49	122	98	88	91	132	96	89	60	118	90

[1] Includes individuals who are neither public officials nor employees but who were involved with public officials or employees in violating the law, not shown separately.

Source: U.S. Department of Justice, *Federal Prosecutions of Corrupt Public Officials, 1970-1980* and *Report to Congress on the Activities and Operations of the Public Integrity Section,* annual.

Law Enforcement, Courts, and Prisons 217

No. 363. Delinquency Cases Disposed by Juvenile Courts by Reason for Referral: 1986 to 1996

[In thousands (1,180 represents 1,180,000), except rate. A delinquency offense is an act committed by a juvenile for which an adult could be prosecuted in a criminal court. Disposition of a case involves taking a definite action such as waiving the case to criminal court, dismissing the case, placing the youth on probation, placing the youth in a facility for delinquents, or such actions as fines, restitution, and community service]

Reason for referral	1986	1987	1988	1989	1990	1991	1992	1993	1994	1995	1996
All delinquency offenses .	**1,180**	**1,181**	**1,190**	**1,236**	**1,320**	**1,413**	**1,484**	**1,515**	**1,605**	**1,703**	**1,758**
Case rate [1]	45.5	46.2	47.0	49.1	51.7	54.4	55.8	55.8	58.2	60.7	61.8
Violent offenses.	71	66	70	80	97	109	121	124	135	141	137
Criminal homicide	2	1	2	2	2	2	2	3	3	3	2
Forcible rape	5	4	4	5	5	6	6	7	6	7	7
Robbery	26	22	22	23	28	31	33	35	37	39	37
Aggravated assault	39	38	43	51	62	70	79	80	88	93	90
Property offenses.	518	519	518	545	564	613	617	593	594	619	623
Burglary	142	134	132	136	146	154	158	149	142	139	141
Larceny	327	331	325	334	341	381	381	374	381	416	422
Motor vehicle theft	43	48	55	68	71	72	71	63	61	53	52
Arson	6	6	7	7	7	7	8	8	9	11	9
Delinquency offenses	590	595	601	611	658	690	746	798	877	943	998
Simple assault	101	105	109	114	128	139	155	171	184	204	217
Vandalism	87	86	84	85	100	112	118	119	124	120	120
Drug law violations	72	72	81	78	71	65	73	91	125	159	176
Obstruction of justice.	72	74	75	77	80	76	80	90	102	109	126
Other [2]	258	258	253	256	278	298	320	328	343	351	359

[1] Number of cases disposed per 1,000 youth (ages 10 to 17) at risk.   [2] Includes such offenses as stolen property offenses, trespassing, weapons offenses, other sex offenses, liquor law violations, disorderly conduct, and miscellaneous offenses.
Source: National Center for Juvenile Justice, Pittsburgh, PA, *Juvenile Court Statistics,* annual.

No. 364. Delinquency Cases and Case Rates by Sex and Race: 1987 to 1996

[A delinquency offense is an act committed by a juvenile for which an adult could be prosecuted in a criminal court. Disposition of a case involves taking a definite action such as waiving the case to criminal court, dismissing the case, placing the youth on probation, placing the youth in a facility for delinquents, or such actions as fines, restitution, and community service. Offenses may not add to total sex and race categories due to rounding]

Sex, race, and offense	Number of cases			Case rate [1]		
	1987	1992	1996	1987	1992	1996
Male, total.	**954,100**	**1,197,100**	**1,359,000**	**72.7**	**87.7**	**92.9**
Person	152,900	243,500	285,800	11.7	17.8	19.5
Property	578,400	693,500	671,100	44.1	50.8	45.9
Drugs.	60,800	63,900	151,100	4.6	4.7	10.3
Public order.	162,000	196,200	251,000	12.3	14.4	17.2
Female, total.	**226,700**	**286,700**	**398,600**	**18.2**	**22.2**	**28.8**
Person	38,000	64,700	95,700	3.0	5.0	6.9
Property	134,000	167,100	203,300	10.7	12.9	14.7
Drugs.	11,300	8,700	25,200	0.9	0.7	1.8
Public order.	43,400	46,100	74,400	3.5	3.6	5.4
White, total.	**831,800**	**975,800**	**1,158,600**	**40.2**	**45.8**	**51.0**
Person	110,200	177,000	224,600	5.3	8.3	9.9
Property	522,100	604,500	611,500	25.2	28.4	26.9
Drugs.	48,200	37,500	114,100	2.3	1.8	5.0
Public order.	151,300	156,700	208,400	7.3	7.4	9.2
Black, total	**315,000**	**453,800**	**530,100**	**82.4**	**113.7**	**124.1**
Person	76,000	121,300	143,100	19.9	30.4	33.5
Property	168,000	221,300	223,700	43.9	55.4	52.3
Drugs.	22,300	33,500	57,800	5.8	8.4	13.5
Public order.	48,700	77,700	105,500	12.7	19.5	24.7
Other races, total	**34,000**	**54,300**	**69,000**	**32.5**	**42.6**	**46.7**
Person	4,700	9,900	13,800	4.5	7.8	9.3
Property	22,400	34,900	39,200	21.4	27.3	26.6
Drugs.	1,600	1,600	4,400	1.5	1.3	3.0
Public order.	5,400	7,900	11,500	5.1	6.2	7.8

[1] Cases per 1,000 youth at risk.

Source: National Center for Juvenile Justice, Pittsburgh, PA, *Juvenile Court Statistics,* annual.

U.S. Census Bureau, Statistical Abstract of the United States: 2000

No. 365. Child Abuse and Neglect Cases Substantiated and Indicated— Victim Characteristics: 1990 to 1998

[Based on reports alleging child abuse and neglect that were referred for investigation by the respective child protective services agency in each state. The reporting period may be either calendar or fiscal year. The majority of states provided duplicated counts. Also, varying number of states reported the various characteristics presented below. A substantiated case represents a type of investigation disposition that determines that there is sufficient evidence under state law to conclude that maltreatment occurred or that the child is at risk of maltreatment. An indicated case represents a type of disposition that concludes that there was a reason to suspect maltreatment had occurred]

Item	1990		1996		1997		1998	
	Number	Percent	Number	Percent	Number	Percent	Number	Percent
TYPES OF SUBSTANTIATED MALTREATMENT								
Victims, total [1] [2]	690,658	(X)	955,516	(X)	790,157	(X)	861,602	(X)
Neglect	338,770	49.1	493,158	51.6	431,563	54.6	461,274	53.5
Physical abuse	186,801	27.0	224,967	23.5	192,872	24.4	195,891	22.7
Sexual abuse	119,506	17.3	117,058	12.3	96,070	12.2	99,278	11.5
Emotional maltreatment	45,621	6.6	55,199	5.8	48,407	6.1	51,618	6.0
Medical neglect.	(NA)	(NA)	25,412	2.7	18,524	2.3	20,338	2.4
SEX OF VICTIM								
Victims, total [2]	742,519	100.0	855,713	100.0	790,395	100.0	760,438	100.0
Male	323,339	43.5	336,315	39.3	315,045	39.9	359,568	47.3
Female	369,919	49.8	371,700	43.4	348,001	44.0	388,187	51.0
AGE OF VICTIM								
Victims, total [2]	731,282	100.0	863,466	100.0	789,303	100.0	767,749	100.0
1 year and younger	97,101	13.3	90,752	10.5	83,819	10.6	105,097	13.7
2 to 5 years old.	172,791	23.6	185,375	21.5	166,523	21.1	187,522	24.4
6 to 9 years old.	157,681	21.6	178,802	20.7	165,845	21.0	193,316	25.2
10 to 13 years old	135,130	18.5	141,009	16.3	130,346	16.5	151,126	19.7
14 to 17 years old	103,383	14.1	110,751	12.8	97,050	12.3	111,894	14.6
18 and over	4,880	0.7	5,995	0.7	2,954	0.4	4,210	0.5

NA Not available.   X Not applicable.   [1] More than one type of maltreatment may be substantiated per child. Therefore, totals for this category will add up to more than 100 percent. Victim totals and maltreatment types are based on subset of states which reported both the number of child victims and maltreatment incidences by type for that year.   [2] Includes other and unknown not shown separately.

No. 366. Child Abuse and Neglect Cases Reported and Investigated by State: 1998

[Based on reports alleging child abuse and neglect that were referred for investigation by the respective child protective services agency in each state. The reporting period may be either calendar or fiscal year. The majority of states provide duplicated counts]

State	Population under 18 years old	Number of reports	Number of children subject of an investi- gation [1]	Number of child victims [2]	State	Population under 18 years old	Number of reports	Number of children subject of an investi- gation [1]	Number of child victims [2]
U.S. [3] . . .	69,872,059	1,851,267	2,972,862	903,395	MO	1,406,616	48,119	75,178	12,556
					MT	224,403	9,676	19,004	3,292
AL	1,084,135	24,413	35,912	16,668	NE	445,642	8,272	14,641	4,219
AK	192,261	11,202	11,326	7,138	NV	467,107	13,705	23,229	8,014
AZ	1,263,404	34,930	60,610	8,983	NH	298,610	6,391	8,974	1,159
AR	653,721	20,511	29,572	8,578	NJ	1,990,439	75,988	75,988	9,851
CA	8,911,372	122,622	413,372	157,683					
CO	1,040,580	28,573	39,141	7,010	NM	504,210	12,781	13,403	4,241
CT	790,715	31,221	40,905	16,923	NY	4,502,611	142,174	240,655	83,537
DE	179,071	6,473	9,693	2,894	NC	1,919,774	125,862	125,862	37,357
DC	102,959	4,077	9,862	4,916	ND	162,611	4,221	7,098	(NA)
FL	3,539,932	125,359	186,967	82,119	OH	2,844,005	84,657	135,628	58,070
GA	2,022,351	47,007	74,180	24,567	OK	879,367	34,790	60,340	16,584
					OR	825,170	17,300	27,680	10,147
HI	298,327	2,129	3,568	2,185	PA	2,859,828	22,589	22,589	5,392
ID	351,158	10,100	26,682	7,936	RI	237,917	8,117	9,863	3,448
IL	3,187,332	64,357	110,658	35,657	SC	959,296	20,000	38,238	8,432
IN	1,517,366	102,155	102,155	18,962					
IA	722,139	19,412	28,072	7,311					
KS	697,452	18,480	26,751	5,312	SD	200,937	5,313	5,313	2,647
KY	988,293	63,439	63,439	22,875	TN	1,331,402	32,286	32,286	9,930
LA	1,191,412	27,117	45,318	13,773	TX	5,629,200	121,183	172,718	39,925
ME	291,585	4,121	9,030	3,579	UT	701,300	16,931	27,222	7,990
MD	1,287,190	31,091	55,964	14,234	VT	141,347	1,883	1,973	887
					VA	1,644,678	32,902	49,026	9,766
MA	1,457,703	37,091	52,899	27,559	WA	1,472,490	32,880	47,281	12,926
MI	2,551,615	62,659	156,425	22,744	WV	404,254	16,350	64,483	7,793
MN	1,259,447	16,197	24,844	10,572	WI	1,351,044	22,232	22,232	8,168
MS	756,875	18,002	32,404	6,079	WY	129,406	1,927	2,209	807

NA Not available.   [1] The number of Children Subject of An Investigation is calculated from the total number of children by Disposition, and is a national estimate for the 50 states and the District of Columbia based on submissions from reporting states.   [2] Victims are defined as children subject of a substantiated or indicated maltreatment. In 1998, Ohio included "In Need of Services," and North Dakota did not use these dispositions.   [3] Includes estimates for states that did not report.

Source of Tables 365 and 366: U.S. Department of Health and Human Services, National Center on Child Abuse and Neglect, National Child Abuse and Neglect Data System, *Child Maltreatment 1998: Reports From the States to the National Child Abuse and Neglect System,* April 2000.

Law Enforcement, Courts, and Prisons   219

No. 367. Jail Inmates by Sex and Race: 1990 to 1999

[Data are for midyear. Excludes Federal and state prisons or other correctional institutions; institutions exclusively for juveniles; state-operated jails in Alaska, Connecticut, Delaware, Hawaii, Rhode Island, and Vermont; and other facilities which retain persons for less than 48 hours. As of **June 30**. Data for 1993 based on National Jail Census; for other years, based on sample survey and subject to sampling variability]

Characteristic	1990	1993	1994	1995	1996	1997	1998	1999
Total inmates [1] . . .	405,320	459,804	486,474	507,044	518,492	567,079	592,462	605,943
Male	368,002	415,600	437,600	455,400	462,500	507,200	(NA)	(NA)
Female.	37,318	44,200	48,800	51,600	55,800	59,900	(NA)	(NA)
White non-Hispanic.	169,600	180,900	190,100	203,300	215,900	230,300	244,900	249,900
Black non-Hispanic.	172,300	203,500	213,400	220,600	213,100	237,900	244,000	251,800
Hispanic	58,100	69,200	74,900	74,400	80,900	88,900	91,800	93,800
Other [1]	5,400	6,200	8,100	8,800	8,600	10,000	11,800	10,400

NA Not available.   [1] Includes American Indians, Alaska Natives, Asians, and Pacific Islanders.

Source: U.S. Bureau of Justice Statistics, through 1994, Jail Inmates, annual; beginning 1995, *Prison and Jail Inmates at Midyear*, annual.

No. 368. State and Federal Correctional Facilities—Inmates and Staff: 1990 and 1995

[Covers all state and Federal correctional institutions or places of confinement such as prisons, prison farms, boot camps, and community based halfway houses and work release centers. Excludes jails and other regional detention centers, private facilities, facilities for the military, Immigration and Naturalization Service, Bureau of Indian Affairs, U.S. Marshall Service, and correctional hospital wards not operated by correctional authorities]

Characteristic	1990	1995	Characteristic	1990	1995
FACILITIES			INMATES		
Total	1,287	1,500	Total	715,649	1,023,572
Type of facility:			Male.	675,624	961,210
Confinement.	1,037	1,196	Female	40,025	62,362
Community.	250	304	Type of facility:		
Federal	80	125	Confinement.	698,570	992,333
State.	1,207	1,375	Community.	17,079	31,239
Size of facility:			Federal	56,821	81,930
Fewer than 500.	816	854	State.	658,828	941,642
500-999.	260	286	Custody level:		
1,000-2,499.	185	306	Maximum/close/high.	150,205	202,174
2,500 or more.	26	54	Medium	292,372	415,688
Age of facility:			Minimum/low	219,907	366,227
Less than 10 years	314	497	Not classified	53,165	39,483
10-19 years old.	163	273			
20-49 years old.	373	366	STAFF		
50-99 years old.	379	310	Total	264,201	347,320
100 years old or more	58	45	Federal.	18,451	25,379
Not reported.	-	9	State	245,750	321,941

- Represents zero.

Source: U.S. Bureau of Justice Statistics, *Census of State and Federal Correctional Facilities, 1995*.

No. 369. Federal and State Prisoners by Sex: 1980 to 1997

[Based on U.S. Census Bureau estimated resident population, as of **December 31**. Includes all persons under jurisdiction of Federal and state authorities rather than those in the custody of such authorities. Represents inmates sentenced to maximum term of more than a year]

Year	Total	Rate [1]	State	Male	Female	Year	Total	Rate [1]	State	Male	Female
1980 . . .	315,974	139	295,363	303,643	12,331	1989 . . .	680,907	276	633,739	643,643	37,264
1981 . . .	353,167	154	331,504	338,940	14,227	1990 . . .	739,980	297	689,577	699,416	40,564
1982 . . .	394,374	171	371,864	378,045	16,329	1991 . . .	789,610	313	732,914	745,808	43,802
1983 . . .	419,820	179	393,015	402,391	17,429	1992 . . .	846,277	332	780,571	799,776	46,501
1984 . . .	443,398	188	415,796	424,193	19,205	1993 . . .	932,074	359	857,675	878,037	54,037
1985 . . .	480,568	202	447,873	458,972	21,296	1994 . . .	1,016,691	389	936,896	956,566	60,125
1986 . . .	522,084	217	485,553	497,540	24,544	1995 . . .	1,085,022	411	1,001,359	1,021,059	63,963
1987 . . .	560,812	231	521,289	533,990	26,822	1996 . . .	1,137,722	427	1,048,907	1,068,123	69,599
1988 . . .	603,732	247	560,994	573,587	30,145	1997 . . .	1,194,581	444	1,099,594	1,120,787	73,794

[1] Rate per 100,000 estimated population.

Source: U.S. Bureau of Justice Statistics, *Prisoners in State and Federal Institutions on December 31*, annual.

No. 370. State Prisons Expenditures by State: 1996

[In millions of dollars (22,033.2 represents $22,033,200,000), except as indicated. For fiscal year ending in year indicated]

State	Total expenditures	Operating expenditures	Capital expenditures	Operating expenditures per inmate (dol.) Per year	Per day	State	Total expenditures	Operating expenditures	Capital expenditures	Operating expenditures per inmate (dol.) Per year	Per day
U.S. ...	22,033.2	20,737.9	1,295.3	20,142	55.18	MO	262.8	249.4	13.4	12,832	35.16
						MT	42.4	41.9	0.6	20,782	56.94
AL	169.0	165.8	3.2	7,987	21.88	NE	69.9	67.9	2.0	22,271	61.02
AK	116.7	112.4	4.3	32,415	88.81	NV	122.0	119.0	2.9	15,370	42.11
AZ	418.1	409.2	8.9	19,091	52.30	NH	43.0	42.4	0.5	20,839	57.09
AR	133.7	124.5	-9.2	13,341	36.55	NJ	839.3	827.1	12.2	30,773	84.31
CA	3,031.0	2,918.8	112.2	21,385	58.59	NM	125.6	123.9	1.7	29,491	80.80
CO	249.8	234.5	15.3	21,020	57.59	NY	2,220.6	1,948.8	271.8	28,426	77.88
CT	497.8	475.4	22.5	31,912	87.43	NC	756.8	733.8	23.1	25,303	69.32
DE	88.0	87.3	0.7	17,987	49.28	ND	10.7	10.6	0.2	17,154	47.00
DC	213.7	212.1	1.6	21,296	58.34	OH	1,014.9	873.6	141.3	19,613	53.74
FL	1,224.9	1,100.7	124.3	17,327	47.47	OK	198.3	193.6	4.7	10,601	29.04
GA	560.4	547.5	12.9	15,933	43.65	OR	254.3	253.4	0.9	31,837	87.22
HI	87.4	83.9	3.5	23,318	63.88	PA	978.8	902.2	76.5	28,063	76.88
ID	57.0	55.0	1.9	16,277	44.60	RI	109.6	108.7	0.9	35,739	97.92
IL	740.4	732.8	7.6	19,351	53.02	SC	315.5	277.9	37.7	13,977	38.29
IN	338.2	325.7	12.5	20,188	55.31	SD	34.2	33.6	0.6	17,787	48.73
IA	146.1	143.8	2.3	24,286	66.54	TN	350.6	349.2	1.4	22,904	62.75
KS	170.8	158.5	12.4	22,242	60.94	TX	1,713.9	1,565.2	148.7	12,215	33.47
KY	208.7	198.8	9.9	16,320	44.71	UT	113.4	111.8	1.6	32,361	88.66
LA	316.2	313.5	2.8	12,304	33.71	VT	33.5	33.4	0.1	31,094	85.19
ME	51.7	48.2	3.5	33,711	92.36	VA	476.7	452.4	24.4	16,306	44.67
MD	520.3	480.9	39.4	22,247	60.95	WA	357.9	311.1	46.7	26,662	73.05
MA	309.7	304.5	5.2	26,002	71.24	WV	46.9	43.7	3.2	17,245	47.25
MI	1,167.6	1,161.1	6.5	28,067	76.89	WI	360.4	313.4	47.1	27,771	76.08
MN	186.0	184.4	1.6	37,825	103.63	WY	29.0	27.0	2.0	19,456	53.30
MS	148.9	143.9	4.9	11,156	30.56						

Source: U.S. Bureau of Justice Statistics, *State Prison Expenditures, 1996*, Series NCJ 172211, August 1999.

No. 371. Prisoners Under Jurisdiction of State and Federal Correctional Authorities—Summary by State: 1980 to 1998

[For years ending December 31]

State	1980	1990	1997	1998, advance Total	Percent change, 1997-1998	State	1980	1990	1997	1998, advance Total	Percent change, 1997-1998
U.S.[1]	329,821	773,919	1,240,962	1,302,019	4.9	MO	5,726	14,943	23,998	24,974	4.1
						MT	739	1,425	2,517	2,734	8.6
AL	6,543	15,665	22,290	23,326	4.6	NE	1,446	2,403	3,402	3,676	8.1
AK[2]	822	2,622	4,165	4,097	-1.6	NV	1,839	5,322	9,024	9,651	6.9
AZ[3]	4,372	14,261	23,484	25,311	7.8	NH	326	1,342	2,164	2,169	0.2
AR	2,911	7,322	10,021	10,638	6.2	NJ	5,884	21,128	28,361	31,121	9.7
CA	24,569	97,309	155,790	161,904	3.9	NM	1,279	3,187	4,688	4,985	6.3
CO	2,629	7,671	13,461	14,312	6.3	NY	21,815	54,895	69,108	72,638	5.1
CT[2]	4,308	10,500	17,241	17,605	2.1	NC	15,513	18,411	31,612	31,811	0.6
DE[2]	1,474	3,471	5,435	5,558	2.3	ND	253	483	797	915	14.8
DC[2]	3,145	9,947	9,353	9,949	6.4	OH[4]	13,489	31,822	48,016	48,450	0.9
FL[3]	20,735	44,387	64,626	67,224	4.0	OK	4,796	12,285	20,542	20,892	1.7
GA[3]	12,178	22,411	36,505	39,262	7.6	OR	3,177	6,492	7,999	8,927	11.6
HI[2]	985	2,533	4,978	4,924	-1.1	PA[2]	8,171	22,290	34,964	36,377	4.0
ID[3]	817	1,961	3,911	4,083	4.4	RI[2]	813	2,392	3,371	3,445	2.2
IL[3]	11,899	27,516	40,788	43,051	5.5	SC	7,862	17,319	21,173	22,115	4.4
IN	6,683	12,736	17,903	19,197	7.2	SD	635	1,341	2,242	2,435	8.6
IA[3]	2,481	3,967	6,938	7,394	6.6	TN	7,022	10,388	16,659	17,738	6.5
KS	2,494	5,775	7,911	8,183	3.4	TX	29,892	50,042	140,351	144,510	3.0
KY	3,588	9,023	14,600	14,987	2.7	UT[2]	932	2,496	4,301	4,391	2.1
LA	8,889	18,599	29,265	32,227	10.1	VT[2]	480	1,049	1,270	1,426	12.3
ME	814	1,523	1,620	1,612	-0.5	VA	8,920	17,593	28,385	28,560	0.6
MD[3,4]	7,731	17,848	22,232	22,572	1.5	WA	4,399	7,995	13,214	14,161	7.2
MA[3,4]	3,185	8,345	11,947	11,832	-1.0	WV	1,257	1,565	3,148	3,478	10.5
MI[3,4]	15,124	34,267	44,771	45,879	2.5	WI	3,980	7,465	16,277	18,451	13.4
MN	2,001	3,176	5,326	5,572	4.6	WY	534	1,110	1,549	1,571	1.4
MS	3,902	8,375	14,296	16,678	16.7						

[1] State-level data excludes Federal inmates.   [2] Includes both jail and prison inmates (state has combined jail and prison system).   [3] Numbers are for custody rather than jurisdiction counts.   [4] Data are for custody counts until 1995 when jurisdiction counts are reported.

Source: U.S. Bureau of Justice Statistics, *Prisoners in 1998*, Series NCJ 175687; and earlier reports.

Law Enforcement, Courts, and Prison   221

No. 372. Adults on Probation, in Jail or Prison, or on Parole: 1980 to 1997

[As of **December 31**, except jail counts as of **June 30**]

Year	Total [1]	Percent of adult population	Probation	Jail	Prison	Parole	Male	Female
1980.........	1,840,400	(NA)	1,118,097	[2]182,288	319,598	220,438	(NA)	(NA)
1981.........	2,006,600	(NA)	1,225,934	[2]195,085	360,029	225,539	(NA)	(NA)
1982.........	2,192,600	(NA)	1,357,264	207,853	402,914	224,604	(NA)	(NA)
1983.........	2,475,100	(NA)	1,582,947	221,815	423,898	246,440	(NA)	(NA)
1984.........	2,689,200	(NA)	1,740,948	233,018	448,264	266,992	(NA)	(NA)
1985.........	3,011,400	1.7	1,968,712	254,986	487,593	300,203	2,606,000	405,500
1986.........	3,239,400	1.8	2,114,621	272,735	526,436	325,638	2,829,100	410,300
1987.........	3,459,600	1.9	2,247,158	294,092	562,814	355,505	3,021,000	438,600
1988.........	3,714,100	2.0	2,356,483	341,893	607,766	407,977	3,223,000	491,100
1989.........	4,055,600	2.2	2,522,125	393,303	683,367	456,803	3,501,600	554,000
1990.........	4,348,000	2.3	2,670,234	403,019	743,382	531,407	3,746,300	601,700
1991.........	4,535,600	2.4	2,728,472	424,129	792,535	590,442	3,913,000	622,600
1992.........	4,762,600	2.5	2,811,611	441,781	850,566	658,601	4,050,300	712,300
1993.........	4,944,000	2.6	2,903,061	455,500	909,381	676,100	4,215,800	728,200
1994.........	5,141,300	2.7	2,981,022	479,800	990,147	690,371	4,377,400	763,900
1995.........	5,335,100	2.8	3,077,861	499,300	1,078,542	679,421	4,546,400	828,100
1996.........	5,482,900	2.8	3,164,996	510,400	1,127,764	679,733	4,663,600	859,400
1997.........	5,692,500	2.8	3,266,837	557,974	1,176,922	690,752	4,797,200	895,300

NA Not available.   [1] Totals may not add due to individuals having multiple correctional statuses.   [2] Estimated.

Source: U.S. Bureau of Justice Statistics, *Correctional Populations in the United States*, annual.

No. 373. Prisoners Under Sentence of Death by Characteristic: 1980 to 1998

[As of **December 31.** Excludes prisoners under sentence of death who remained within local correctional systems pending exhaustion of appellate process or who had not been committed to prison]

Characteristic	1980	1988	1989	1990	1991	1992	1993	1994	1995	1996	1997	1998
Total [1]	**688**	**2,117**	**2,243**	**2,346**	**2,466**	**2,575**	**2,727**	**2,905**	**3,064**	**3,242**	**3,328**	**3,452**
White	418	1,235	1,308	1,368	1,450	1,508	1,575	1,653	1,732	1,833	1,864	1,906
Black and other	270	882	935	978	1,016	1,067	1,152	1,252	1,332	1,409	1,464	1,546
Under 20 years..........	11	11	6	8	14	12	13	19	20	17	16	15
20 to 24 years	173	195	191	168	179	188	211	231	264	288	275	267
25 to 34 years	334	1,048	1,080	1,110	1,087	1,078	1,066	1,088	1,068	1,088	1,077	1,101
35 to 54 years	186	823	917	1,006	1,129	1,212	1,330	1,449	1,583	1,711	1,809	1,899
55 years and over........	10	47	56	64	73	85	96	103	119	138	151	170
Years of school completed:												
7 years or less	68	180	183	178	173	181	185	186	191	196	205	206
8 years	74	184	178	186	181	180	183	198	195	201	206	217
9 to 11 years	204	692	739	775	810	836	885	930	979	1,040	1,069	1,111
12 years	162	657	695	729	783	831	887	939	995	1,037	1,084	1,120
More than 12 years	43	180	192	209	222	232	244	255	272	282	288	297
Unknown	163	231	263	279	313	315	332	382	422	486	476	501
Marital status:												
Never married..........	268	898	956	998	1,071	1,132	1,222	1,320	1,412	1,507	1,555	1,641
Married	229	594	610	632	663	663	671	707	718	739	740	749
Divorced [2]	217	632	684	726	746	780	823	863	924	996	1,033	1,062
Time elapsed since sentencing:												
Less than 12 months	185	293	231	231	252	265	262	280	287	306	262	275
12 to 47 months	389	812	809	753	718	720	716	755	784	816	844	813
48 to 71 months	102	409	408	438	441	444	422	379	423	447	456	482
72 months and over......	38	610	802	934	1,071	1,146	1,316	1,476	1,560	1,673	1,766	1,882
Legal status at arrest:												
Not under sentence	384	1,207	1,301	1,345	1,415	1,476	1,562	1,662	1,764	1,881	1,957	2,029
Parole or probation [3]	115	545	585	578	615	702	754	800	866	894	880	877
Prison or escaped	45	93	94	128	102	101	102	103	110	112	116	127
Unknown	170	279	270	305	321	296	298	325	314	355	375	419

[1] Revisions to the total number of prisoners were not carried to the characteristics except for race.   [2] Includes persons married but separated, widows, widowers, and unknown.   [3] Includes prisoners on mandatory conditional release, work release, leave, AWOL, or bail. Covers 28 prisoners in 1990, 29 in 1991 and 1992, 33 in 1993 and 1995, 31 in 1994 and 1996, and 30 in 1997.

Source: U.S. Bureau of Justice Statistics, *Capital Punishment,* annual.

No. 374. Movement of Prisoners Under Sentence of Death: 1980 to 1998

[Prisoners reported under sentence of death by civil authorities. The term "under sentence of death" begins when the court pronounces the first sentence of death for a capital offense]

Status	1980	1988	1989	1990	1991	1992	1993	1994	1995	1996	1997	1998
Under sentence of death, Jan. 1	595	1,967	2,117	2,243	2,346	2,465	2,580	2,727	2,905	3,064	3,242	3,328
Received death sentence [1] [2]	203	296	251	244	266	265	282	306	310	299	256	285
White	125	196	133	147	163	147	146	162	168	174	146	145
Black	77	91	114	94	101	114	130	136	138	119	106	132
Dispositions other than executions	101	128	102	108	116	124	108	112	105	99	89	93
Executions	-	11	16	23	14	31	38	31	56	45	74	68
Under sentence of death, Dec. 31 [1] [2]	688	2,117	2,243	2,346	2,466	2,575	2,727	2,890	3,054	3,242	3,335	3,452
White	425	1,238	1,308	1,368	1,450	1,508	1,575	1,645	1,730	1,833	1,876	1,906
Black	268	853	898	940	1,016	1,029	1,111	1,197	1,275	1,358	1,406	1,486

- Represents zero. [1] Includes races other than White or Black. [2] Revisions to total number of prisoners under death sentence not carried to this category.

Source: U.S. Bureau of Justice Statistics, *Capital Punishment,* annual.

No. 375. Prisoners Executed Under Civil Authority by Sex and Race: 1930 to 1999

[Excludes executions by military authorities. The Army (including the Air Force) carried out 160 (148 between 1942 and 1950; 3 each in 1954, 1955, and 1957; and 1 each in 1958, 1959, and 1961). Of the total, 106 were executed for murder (including 21 involving rape), 53 for rape, and 1 for desertion. The Navy carried out no executions during the period]

Year or period	Total [1]	Male	Female	White	Black	Executed for murder		
						Total [1]	White	Black
All years, 1930-99	**4,458**	**4,423**	**35**	**1,971**	**2,201**	**3,692**	**1,884**	**1,770**
1930 to 1939	1,667	1,656	11	827	816	1,514	803	687
1940 to 1949	1,284	1,272	12	490	781	1,064	458	595
1950 to 1959	717	709	8	336	376	601	316	280
1960 to 1967	191	190	1	98	93	155	87	68
1968 to 1976	-	-	-	-	-	-	-	-
1977 to 1999	598	595	3	-	-	-	-	-
1985	18	-	-	11	7	18	11	7
1986	18	18	-	11	7	18	11	7
1987	25	25	-	13	12	25	13	12
1988	11	11	-	6	5	11	6	5
1989	16	16	-	8	8	16	8	8
1990	23	23	-	16	7	23	16	7
1991	14	14	-	7	7	14	7	7
1992	31	31	-	19	11	31	19	11
1993	38	38	-	23	14	38	23	14
1994	31	31	-	20	11	31	20	11
1995	56	56	-	33	22	56	33	22
1996	45	45	-	31	14	45	31	14
1997	74	74	-	45	27	74	45	27
1998	68	66	2	48	18	68	48	18
1999	98	98	-	61	33	98	61	33

- Represents zero. [1] Includes races other than White or Black. [2] Includes 25 armed robbery, 20 kidnapping, 11 burglary, 8 espionage (6 in 1942 and 2 in 1953), and 6 aggravated assault.

Source: Through 1978, U.S. Law Enforcement Assistance Administration; thereafter, U.S. Bureau of Justice Statistics, *Correctional Populations in the United States,* annual; and *Capital Punishment,* annual.

No. 376. Prisoners Under Sentence of Death and Executed Under Civil Authority by State: 1977 to 1999

[Alaska, District of Columbia, Hawaii, Iowa, Maine, Massachusetts, Michigan, Minnesota, New York, North Dakota, Rhode Island, Vermont, West Virginia, and Wisconsin are jurisdictions without a death penalty]

State	1977 to 1999	1996	1997	1998	1999	State	1977 to 1999	1996	1997	1998	1999	State	1977 to 1999	1996	1997	1998	1999
U.S.	**598**	**45**	**74**	**68**	**98**	ID	1	-	-	-	-	NC	15	-	-	3	4
						IL	12	1	2	1	1	OK	19	2	1	4	6
AL	19	1	3	1	2	IN	7	1	1	1	1	SC	24	6	2	7	4
AZ	19	2	2	4	7	LA	25	1	1	-	1	TX	199	3	37	20	35
AR	21	1	4	1	4	MD	3	-	1	1	-	UT	6	1	-	-	1
CA	7	2	-	1	2	MS	4	-	-	-	-	VA	73	8	9	13	14
DE	10	3	-	-	2	MO	41	6	6	3	9	WA	3	-	-	1	-
FL	44	2	1	4	1	NE	3	1	1	-	-	WY	1	-	-	-	-
GA	23	2	-	1	-	NV	8	1	-	1	1						

- Represents zero.

Source: Through 1978, U.S. Law Enforcement Assistance Administration; thereafter, U.S. Bureau of Justice Statistics, *Capital Punishment,* annual.

Law Enforcement, Courts, and Prisons   223

No. 377. Fire Losses—Total and Percent Change: 1980 to 1998

[Includes allowance for uninsured and unreported losses but excludes losses to government property and forests. Represents incurred losses]

Year	Total (mil. dol.)	Per capita [1]	Year	Total (mil. dol.)	Per capita [1]	Year	Total (mil. dol.)	Per capita [1]
1980	5,579	24.56	1987	8,504	34.96	1994	12,778	49.09
1981	5,625	24.53	1988	9,626	39.11	1995	11,887	45.24
1982	5,894	25.61	1989	9,514	38.33	1996	12,544	47.30
1983	6,320	27.20	1990	9,495	38.07	1997	12,940	48.33
1984	7,602	32.35	1991	11,302	44.83	1998	12,313	45.55
1985	7,753	32.70	1992	13,588	53.29			
1986	8,488	35.21	1993	11,331	43.96			

[1] Based on Census Bureau resident population as of July 1.

Source: Insurance Information Institute, New York, NY, *Insurance Facts*, annual (copyright).

No. 378. Fires—Number and Loss by Type and Property Use: 1995 to 1998

[**Number: 1,966 represents 1,966,000. Property loss: 8,918 represents 8,918,000.** Based on annual sample survey of fire departments. No adjustments were made for unreported fires and losses. Property loss includes direct property loss only]

Type and property use	Number (1,000)				Property loss (mil. dol.)			
	1995	1996	1997	1998	1995	1996	1997	1998
Fires, total.	**1,966**	**1,975**	**1,795**	**1,755**	**8,918**	**9,406**	**8,525**	**8,629**
Structure	574	578	552	517	7,620	7,933	7,087	6,717
Outside of structure [1]	61	63	57	62	77	91	99	497
Brush and rubbish	778	766	662	653	-	-	-	-
Vehicle.	406	414	397	381	1,152	1,333	1,269	1,337
Other.	147	154	127	142	69	49	70	78
Structure by property use:								
Public assembly	15	16	15	16	336	330	327	354
Educational	9	9	8	8	84	65	58	84
Institutional	9	8	8	9	31	24	25	23
Stores and offices.	29	27	27	25	[2]681	665	612	462
Residential.	426	428	407	381	4,363	4,962	4,585	4,391
1-2 family units [3]	320	324	303	283	3,615	4,121	3,735	3,642
Apartments.	94	93	93	86	649	748	718	631
Other residential [4]	12	11	11	12	99	93	132	118
Storage [5].	39	41	36	36	710	949	577	687
Industry, utility, defense [5] . .	18	18	17	16	[6]1,248	[7]733	723	496
Special structures	29	31	34	26	167	205	180	220

- Represents zero.   [1] Includes outside storage, crops, timber, etc. 1998 property loss data include $390 million loss in timber from Florida wildfires.   [2] Includes an estimated $135 million in property loss that occurred in the explosion and fire in the federal office building in Oklahoma City on April 19, 1995.   [3] Includes mobile homes.   [4] Includes hotels and motels, college dormitories, boarding houses, etc.   [5] Data underreported as some incidents were handled by private fire brigades or fixed suppression systems which do not report.   [6] Includes estimated losses of $500 million in an industrial complex fire in Massachusetts and $200 million in a manufacturing plant in Georgia in 1995.   [7] Includes $280 million in property in a storage property fire in New Orleans, Louisiana in 1996.

Source: National Fire Protection Association, Quincy, MA, "1998 U.S. Fire Loss", *NFPA Journal*, September 1999, and prior issues (copyright 1999).

No. 379. Fires and Property Loss for Incendiary and Suspicious Fires and Civilian Fire Deaths and Injuries by Selected Property Type: 1995 to 1998

[Based on sample survey of fire departments]

Characteristic	1995	1996	1997	1998	Characteristic	1995	1996	1997	1998
NUMBER (1,000)					CIVILIAN FIRE DEATHS				
Structure fires, total .	**574**	**578**	**552**	**517**	**Deaths, total** [3].	**4,585**	**4,990**	**4,050**	**4,035**
Structure fires of incendiary or suspicious origin	91	85	78	76	Residential property.	3,695	4,080	3,390	3,250
					One- and two-family dwellings	3,035	3,470	2,700	2,775
Fires of incendiary origin .	58	52	52	47	Apartments.	605	565	660	445
Fires of suspicious origin.	33	33	26	29	Vehicles	535	710	480	575
PROPERTY LOSS [1] (mil. dol.)					CIVILIAN FIRE INJURIES				
Structure fires, total .	**7,620**	**7,933**	**7,087**	**6,717**	**Injuries, total** [3]	**25,775**	**25,550**	**23,750**	**23,100**
Structure fires of incendiary or suspicious origin	1,647	1,405	1,309	1,249	Residential property.	19,125	19,300	17,775	17,175
					One- and two-family dwellings	13,450	13,700	12,300	11,800
Fires of incendiary origin .	[2]1,116	897	802	816	Apartments.	5,200	5,175	5,000	5,000
Fires of suspicious origin.	531	508	507	433	Vehicles	2,525	2,225	2,125	2,225

[1] Direct property loss only.   [2] Includes $135 million in property loss that occurred in the explosion and fire in the federal office building in Oklahoma City on April 19, 1995.   [3] Includes other not shown separately.

Source: National Fire Protection Association, Quincy, MA, "1998 U.S. Fire Loss", *NFPA Journal*, September 1999, and prior issues (copyright 1999).

224   Law Enforcement, Courts, and Prisons

Geography and Environment

This section presents a variety of information on the physical environment of the United States, starting with basic area measurement data and ending with climatic data for selected weather stations around the country. The subjects covered between those points are mostly concerned with environmental trends but include such related subjects as land use, water consumption, air pollutant emissions, toxic releases, oil spills, hazardous waste sites, municipal waste and recycling, threatened and endangered wildlife, and the environmental industry.

The information in this section is selected from a wide range of Federal agencies that compile the data for various administrative or regulatory purposes, such as the Environmental Protection Agency, U.S. Geological Survey, National Oceanic and Atmospheric Administration, Natural Resources Conservation Service, and General Services Administration.

Area—For the 1990 census, area measurements were calculated by computer based on the information contained in a single, consistent geographic database, the TIGER ™ file (described below), rather than relying on historical, local, and manually calculated information. This especially affects water area figures reported in 1990; these had only included those bodies of water of least 40 acres and those streams with a width of at least one-eighth of a statute mile from 1940 to 1980. Water area figures for 1990 increased because the data reflected all water recorded in the Census Bureau's geographic database including coastal, Great Lakes, and territorial waters.

Geography—The U.S. Geological Survey conducts investigations, surveys, and research in the fields of geography, geology, topography, geographic information systems, mineralogy, hydrology, and geothermal energy resources as well as natural hazards. The U.S. Geological Survey provides United States cartographic data through the Earth Sciences Information Center, water resources data through the National Water Data Exchange (NAWDEX), and a variety of research and Open-File reports which are announced monthly in *New Publications of the U.S. Geological Survey.*

In a joint project with the Census Bureau, the U.S. Geological Survey provided the basic information on geographic features for input into a national geographic and cartographic database prepared by the Census Bureau, called the TIGER ™ (Topologically Integrated Geographic Encoding and Referencing) System. Maps prepared by the Census Bureau show the names and boundaries of various types of legal and statistical entities, such as places, county subdivisions, and larger areas and are available as of the specific decennial census. An inventory is available for the 1990 census, both on computer tape and CD-ROM as the *1990 TIGER/GICS (Geographic Identification Code Scheme)* and for the 1997 economic censuses in the *Geographic Reference Manual* (EC97-R-1). The Census Bureau maintains a current inventory of governmental units and their legal boundaries through its Boundary and Annexation Survey. The TIGER ™ System contains information on the legal and statistical entities used by the Census Bureau, as well as on both manmade and natural features, such as streets, roads, railroads, rivers, and lakes; information is available to the public in the form of machine-readable TIGER extract files.

An inventory of the Nation's land resources by type of use/cover was conducted by the National Resource Recovery Conservation

Geography and Environment **225**

Service (formerly the Soil Conservation Service) every 5 years beginning in 1982. The most recent survey results, which were published in the 1997 National Resources Inventory, cover all non-Federal land in Puerto Rico, the Virgin Islands, and the United States except Alaska. Tables 382 and 383 provide some preliminary results from the survey.

Environment—The principal Federal agency responsible for pollution abatement and control activities is the Environmental Protection Agency (EPA). It is responsible for establishing and monitoring national air quality standards, water quality activities, solid and hazardous waste disposal, and control of toxic substances. Many of these series now appear on the EPA Web site at the Center for Environmental Information and Statistics and can be accessed at <http://www.epa.gov/ceis/>.

National Ambient Air Quality Standards (NAAQS) for suspended particulate matter, sulfur dioxide, photochemical oxidants, carbon monoxide, and nitrogen dioxide were originally set by the EPA in April 1971. Every 5 years, each of the NAAQS is reviewed and revised if new health or welfare data indicates that a change is necessary. The standard for photochemical oxidants, now called ozone, was revised in February 1979. Also, a new NAAQS for lead was promulgated in October 1978 and for suspended particulate matter in 1987. Table 392 gives some of the health-related standards for the six air pollutants having NAAQS. Data gathered from state networks are periodically submitted to EPA's National Aerometric Information Retrieval System (AIRS) for summarization in annual reports on the nationwide status and trends in air quality; for details, see *National Air Quality and Emissions Trends Report, 1998.*

The Toxics Release Inventory (TRI), published by the U.S. EPA, is a valuable source of information regarding toxic chemicals that are being used, manufactured, treated, transported, or released into the environment. Two rules, Section 313 of the Emergency Planning and Community

Right-To-Know Act (EPCRA) and Section 6607 of the Pollution Prevention Act (PPA), mandate that a publicly accessible toxic chemical database be developed and maintained by U.S. EPA. This database, known as the Toxics Release Inventory (TRI), contains information concerning waste management activities and the release of toxic chemicals by facilities that manufacture, process, or otherwise use said materials.

Data on the release of these chemicals are collected from manufacturing facilities and facilities added in 1998 that have the equivalent of 10 or more full-time employees and meet the established thresholds for manufacture, processing, or "otherwise use" of listed chemicals. Facilities must report their releases and other waste management quantities. Federal facilities have been required to report since 1994, regardless of industry classification. In May 1997, EPA added seven new industry sectors that reported to the TRI for the first time in July 1999 for the 1998 reporting year.

Climate—NOAA, through the National Weather Service and the National Environmental Satellite, Data, and Information Service, is responsible for data on climate. NOAA maintains about 11,600 weather stations, of which over 3,000 produce autographic precipitation records, about 600 take hourly readings of a series of weather elements, and the remainder record data once a day. These data are reported monthly in the *Climatological Data* and *Storm Data*, published monthly, and annually in the *Local Climatological Data* (published by location for major cities).

The normal climatological temperatures, precipitation, and degree days listed in this publication are derived for comparative purposes and are averages for the 30-year period, 1961-90. For stations that did not have continuous records for the entire 30 years from the same instrument site, the normals have been adjusted to provide representative values for the current location. The information in all other tables is based on data from the beginning of the record at that location through 1998, except as noted.

No. 380. Land and Water Area of State and Other Area: 1990

[One square mile=2.59 square kilometers. Excludes territorial water, which was included in the 1993 edition of the *Statistical Abstract*]

State and other area	Total area Sq. mi.	Total area Sq. km.	Land area Sq. mi.	Land area Sq. km.	Water area Total Sq. mi.	Water area Total Sq. km.	Inland sq. mi.	Coastal sq. mi.	Great Lakes sq. mi.
United States ...	3,717,796	9,629,091	3,536,278	9,158,960	181,518	470,131	78,937	42,528	60,052
Alabama	52,237	135,293	50,750	131,443	1,486	3,850	968	519	-
Alaska.	615,230	1,593,444	570,374	1,477,268	44,856	116,177	17,501	27,355	-
Arizona	114,006	295,276	113,642	294,333	364	943	364	-	-
Arkansas	53,182	137,742	52,075	134,875	1,107	2,867	1,107	-	-
California.	158,869	411,470	155,973	403,971	2,895	7,499	2,674	222	-
Colorado	104,100	269,618	103,729	268,658	371	960	371	-	-
Connecticut	5,544	14,358	4,845	12,550	698	1,808	161	538	-
Delaware.	2,396	6,206	1,955	5,062	442	1,144	71	371	-
District of Columbia . . .	68	177	61	159	7	18	7	-	-
Florida.	59,928	155,214	53,937	139,697	5,991	15,517	4,683	1,308	-
Georgia.	58,977	152,750	57,919	150,010	1,058	2,740	1,011	47	-
Hawaii.	6,459	16,729	6,423	16,636	36	93	36	-	-
Idaho	83,574	216,456	82,751	214,325	823	2,131	823	-	-
Illinois	57,918	150,007	55,593	143,987	2,325	6,021	750	-	1,575
Indiana	36,420	94,328	35,870	92,904	550	1,424	315	-	235
Iowa	56,276	145,754	55,875	144,716	401	1,038	401	-	-
Kansas	82,282	213,110	81,823	211,922	459	1,189	459	-	-
Kentucky	40,411	104,665	39,732	102,907	679	1,759	679	-	-
Louisiana.	49,651	128,595	43,566	112,836	6,085	15,759	4,153	1,931	-
Maine	33,741	87,388	30,865	79,939	2,876	7,449	2,263	613	-
Maryland	12,297	31,849	9,775	25,316	2,522	6,533	680	1,842	-
Massachusetts	9,241	23,934	7,838	20,300	1,403	3,634	424	979	-
Michigan	96,705	250,465	56,809	147,136	39,895	103,329	1,704	-	38,192
Minnesota	86,943	225,182	79,617	206,207	7,326	18,975	4,780	-	2,546
Mississippi	48,286	125,060	46,914	121,506	1,372	3,553	781	591	-
Missouri.	69,709	180,546	68,898	178,446	811	2,100	811	-	-
Montana	147,046	380,849	145,556	376,991	1,490	3,859	1,490	-	-
Nebraska.	77,358	200,358	76,878	199,113	481	1,245	481	-	-
Nevada.	110,567	286,367	109,806	284,396	761	1,971	761	-	-
New Hampshire	9,283	24,044	8,969	23,231	314	813	314	-	-
New Jersey	8,215	21,277	7,419	19,215	796	2,062	371	425	-
New Mexico	121,598	314,939	121,364	314,334	234	605	234	-	-
New York.	53,989	139,833	47,224	122,310	6,766	17,523	1,888	976	3,901
North Carolina	52,672	136,421	48,718	126,180	3,954	10,241	3,954	-	-
North Dakota	70,704	183,123	68,994	178,695	1,710	4,428	1,710	-	-
Ohio	44,828	116,103	40,953	106,067	3,875	10,036	376	-	3,499
Oklahoma	69,903	181,048	68,679	177,877	1,224	3,171	1,224	-	-
Oregon	97,132	251,571	96,002	248,646	1,129	2,925	1,050	80	-
Pennsylvania	46,058	119,291	44,820	116,083	1,239	3,208	490	-	749
Rhode Island	1,231	3,189	1,045	2,707	186	482	168	18	-
South Carolina	31,189	80,779	30,111	77,988	1,078	2,791	1,006	72	-
South Dakota	77,121	199,744	75,896	196,571	1,225	3,174	1,225	-	-
Tennessee	42,146	109,158	41,219	106,758	926	2,400	926	-	-
Texas	267,277	692,248	261,914	678,358	5,363	13,890	4,959	404	-
Utah	84,904	219,902	82,168	212,815	2,736	7,086	2,736	-	-
Vermont	9,615	24,903	9,249	23,956	366	947	366	-	-
Virginia	42,326	109,625	39,598	102,558	2,729	7,067	1,000	1,728	-
Washington	70,637	182,949	66,581	172,445	4,055	10,503	1,545	2,511	-
West Virginia	24,231	62,759	24,087	62,384	145	375	145	-	-
Wisconsin	65,499	169,643	54,314	140,672	11,186	28,971	1,831	-	9,355
Wyoming	97,818	253,349	97,105	251,501	714	1,848	714	-	-
Other area:									
Puerto Rico.	3,508	9,085	3,427	8,875	81	210	65	16	-
American Samoa . . .	90	233	77	200	13	33	7	6	-
Guam	217	561	210	543	7	18	7	-	-
No. Mariana Islands .	189	490	179	464	10	26	2	8	-
Palau.	241	624	177	458	64	165	40	24	-
Virgin Islands of the U.S	171	443	134	346	37	96	17	20	-

- Represents or rounds to zero.

Source: U.S. Census Bureau, *1990 Census of Population and Housing*, Series CPH-2; and unpublished data from the TIGER/Geographic Information Control System (TIGER/GICS) computer file. Corrections have been made subsequent to the 1990 Census reports.

No. 381. Total and Federally Owned Land by State: 1997

[As of **end of fiscal year;** see text, Section 9. Total land area figures are not comparable with those in Table 393]

State	Total (1,000 acres)	Not owned by Federal Government (1,000 acres)	Owned by Federal Government [1]		State	Total (1,000 acres)	Not owned by Federal Government (1,000 acres)	Owned by Federal Government [1]	
			Acres (1,000)	Per-cent				Acres (1,000)	Per-cent
United States .	**2,271,343**	**1,616,458**	**654,885**	**28.8**	Missouri	44,248	42,111	2,137	4.8
Alabama	32,678	31,569	1,110	3.4	Montana	93,271	67,135	26,136	28.0
Alaska	365,482	117,195	248,287	67.9	Nebraska	49,032	48,293	738	1.5
Arizona	72,688	39,558	33,130	45.6	Nevada	70,264	11,889	58,375	83.1
Arkansas	33,599	30,174	3,260	10.2	New Hampshire . . .	5,769	5,010	759	13.2
California	100,207	55,179	45,027	44.9	New Jersey	4,813	4,648	166	3.4
Colorado	66,486	42,262	24,224	36.4	New Mexico	77,766	51,172	26,594	34.2
Connecticut	3,135	3,120	15	0.5	New York	30,681	30,559	122	0.4
Delaware	1,266	1,239	27	2.1	North Carolina	31,403	28,894	2,508	8.0
District of Columbia.	39	30	9	23.4	North Dakota	44,452	42,603	1,850	4.2
Florida	34,721	31,832	2,889	8.3	Ohio	26,222	25,825	397	1.5
Georgia	37,295	35,215	2,080	5.6	Oklahoma	44,088	42,807	1,281	2.9
Hawaii	4,106	3,500	605	14.7	Oregon	61,599	29,167	32,431	52.6
Idaho	52,933	19,860	33,073	62.5	Pennsylvania	28,804	28,127	678	2.4
Illinois.	35,795	35,167	628	1.8	Rhode Island	677	673	4	0.6
Indiana	23,158	22,648	510	2.2	South Carolina	19,374	18,186	1,188	6.1
Iowa.	35,860	35,626	234	0.7	South Dakota	48,882	46,128	2,754	5.6
Kansas	52,511	51,846	665	1.3	Tennessee	26,728	25,084	1,643	6.1
Kentucky	25,512	24,277	1,236	4.8	Texas	168,218	165,413	2,804	1.7
Louisiana	28,868	27,583	1,285	4.5	Utah	52,697	18,691	34,006	64.5
Maine	19,848	19,656	192	1.0	Vermont	5,937	5,560	376	6.3
Maryland	6,319	6,120	199	3.2	Virginia	25,496	23,197	2,299	9.0
Massachusetts . . .	5,035	4,957	78	1.6	Washington	42,694	30,507	12,186	28.5
Michigan	36,492	32,405	4,087	11.2	West Virginia	15,411	14,233	1,178	7.6
Minnesota	51,206	46,768	4,437	8.7	Wisconsin	35,011	33,054	1,957	5.6
Mississippi	30,223	28,449	1,774	5.9	Wyoming	62,343	31,255	31,088	49.9

[1] Excludes trust properties.

Source: U.S. General Services Administration, *Summary Report on Real Property Owned by the United States Throughout the World,* annual.

No. 382. Urban and Built-Up Land Use by State and Other Area: 1997

State and other area	Total land	Urban land			State and other area	Total land	Urban land		
		Total	Percent of total	Change, 1992-97			Total	Percent of total	Change, 1992-97
Total	**1,944,135**	**80,781**	**4.2**	**15,428**	Montana	94,110	409	0.4	116
United States .	**1,941,827**	**80,276**	**4.1**	**15,286**	Nebraska	49,510	557	1.1	67
Alabama	33,424	1,823	5.5	424	Nevada.	70,763	325	0.5	37
Arizona.	72,964	1,246	1.7	181	New Hampshire . . .	5,941	549	9.2	104
Arkansas	34,037	996	2.9	226	New Jersey	5,216	1,803	34.6	282
California.	101,510	4,952	4.9	685	New Mexico.	77,823	793	1.0	337
Colorado	66,625	1,182	1.8	115	New York	31,361	2,919	9.3	485
Connecticut	3,195	823	25.8	61	North Carolina	33,709	3,556	10.5	755
Delaware.	1,534	213	13.9	34	North Dakota	45,251	271	0.6	37
Florida	37,534	4,867	13.0	925	Ohio.	26,445	3,431	13.0	519
Georgia	37,741	3,534	9.4	1,051	Oklahoma	44,738	1,290	2.9	214
Hawaii	4,163	159	3.8	9	Oregon	62,161	886	1.4	142
Idaho	53,488	445	0.8	109	Pennsylvania	28,995	3,901	13.5	1,103
Illinois.	36,059	2,544	7.1	288	Rhode Island	813	187	22.9	10
Indiana	23,158	1,846	8.0	269	South Carolina	19,939	1,880	9.4	533
Iowa.	36,017	839	2.3	91	South Dakota.	49,358	366	0.7	71
Kansas	52,661	1,070	2.0	167	Tennessee.	26,974	2,182	8.1	597
Kentucky.	25,863	1,418	5.5	341	Texas	171,052	7,126	4.2	1,146
Louisiana	31,377	1,339	4.3	155	Utah.	54,339	505	0.9	99
Maine.	20,966	582	2.8	164	Vermont	6,154	241	3.9	25
Maryland.	7,870	1,189	15.1	219	Virginia	27,087	2,302	8.5	464
Massachusetts. . . .	5,339	1,463	27.4	281	Washington	44,035	1,686	3.8	328
Michigan.	37,349	3,360	9.0	549	West Virginia	15,508	745	4.8	266
Minnesota	54,010	1,535	2.8	300	Wisconsin	35,920	1,844	5.1	271
Mississippi.	30,527	1,094	3.6	298	Wyoming	62,603	261	0.4	42
Missouri	44,614	1,743	3.9	297	Caribbean	2,307	505	21.9	142

Source: U.S. Department of Agriculture, National Resource and Conservation Service, and Iowa State University, Statistical Laboratory, *1997 National Resources Inventory,* issued December 1999.

No. 383. Land Cover/Use by State: 1997

[Preliminary. **In thousands of acres.** Excludes Alaska and District of Columbia]

State	Total surface area [1]	Federal land	Non-Federal land						
			Total	Devel-oped [2]	Rural				
					Total [3]	Crop-land	Pasture land	Range-land	Forest land
Total	**1,944,135**	**1,491,080**	**105,369**	**1,385,711**	**375,044**	**119,573**	**403,114**	**399,031**	**56,253**
United States	1,941,827	1,488,914	104,812	1,384,102	374,690	119,144	402,976	398,409	56,188
Alabama	33,424	31,184	2,410	28,775	2,919	3,527	68	21,073	666
Arizona	72,964	42,330	1,675	40,654	1,204	67	32,114	4,262	3,007
Arkansas	34,037	30,040	1,501	28,539	7,582	5,453	73	14,765	436
California	101,510	52,926	5,687	47,238	9,561	1,065	17,457	14,295	4,687
Colorado	66,625	42,480	1,706	40,775	8,860	1,269	23,855	3,729	1,172
Connecticut	3,195	3,052	897	2,155	199	107	-	1,729	120
Delaware	1,534	1,213	238	975	472	23	-	347	134
Florida	37,534	30,596	5,449	25,147	2,719	4,177	3,193	12,255	2,684
Georgia	37,741	34,564	4,238	30,326	4,661	2,853	-	21,216	999
Hawaii	4,163	3,717	186	3,531	244	89	946	1,514	738
Idaho	53,488	19,368	811	18,557	5,500	1,253	6,478	3,942	600
Illinois	36,059	34,807	3,262	31,546	23,954	2,525	-	3,631	710
Indiana	23,158	22,300	2,356	19,944	13,358	1,818	-	3,638	753
Iowa	36,017	35,354	1,803	33,551	25,262	3,554	-	2,084	912
Kansas	52,661	51,597	2,882	48,715	26,460	2,213	15,179	1,290	724
Kentucky	25,863	24,048	1,955	22,092	5,151	5,613	-	10,440	557
Louisiana	31,377	26,314	1,693	24,622	5,568	2,376	280	13,114	3,143
Maine	20,966	19,509	747	18,762	419	82	-	17,633	599
Maryland	7,870	6,038	1,291	4,747	1,598	454	-	2,331	346
Massachusetts	5,339	4,862	1,549	3,313	271	114	-	2,657	271
Michigan	37,349	32,964	3,764	29,200	8,439	2,004	-	16,238	2,198
Minnesota	54,010	47,526	2,361	45,165	21,328	3,423	-	14,830	4,042
Mississippi	30,527	27,895	1,656	26,239	5,296	3,699	-	16,019	428
Missouri	44,614	41,848	2,653	39,195	13,710	10,947	98	12,118	716
Montana	94,110	65,960	881	65,078	15,086	3,495	37,016	5,279	1,481
Nebraska	49,510	48,371	1,268	47,103	19,421	1,976	22,864	799	799
Nevada	70,763	10,448	416	10,032	711	271	8,300	297	452
New Hampshire	5,941	4,941	642	4,300	132	92	-	3,875	202
New Jersey	5,216	4,537	1,849	2,688	574	109	-	1,625	381
New Mexico	77,823	51,220	1,325	49,896	1,842	207	40,276	4,915	2,189
New York	31,361	29,866	3,373	26,493	5,375	2,627	-	17,533	904
North Carolina	33,709	28,425	4,181	24,244	5,539	1,980	-	15,678	917
North Dakota	45,251	42,417	1,152	41,264	24,991	1,105	10,551	443	1,373
Ohio	26,445	25,664	3,797	21,867	11,504	1,980	-	6,984	1,077
Oklahoma	44,738	42,508	1,997	40,511	9,709	7,933	13,974	7,254	504
Oregon	62,161	30,073	1,296	28,777	3,800	1,905	9,556	12,295	739
Pennsylvania	28,995	27,791	4,336	23,456	5,245	1,812	-	15,306	1,003
Rhode Island	813	659	205	454	20	24	-	381	29
South Carolina	19,939	18,082	2,325	15,757	2,542	1,182	-	10,958	813
South Dakota	49,358	45,367	1,035	44,332	16,738	2,078	21,764	532	1,535
Tennessee	26,974	24,954	2,618	22,336	4,566	4,985	-	11,736	674
Texas	171,052	163,990	8,984	155,006	26,762	15,807	95,323	10,627	2,581
Utah	54,339	18,260	760	17,499	1,676	695	10,720	1,830	2,362
Vermont	6,154	5,495	346	5,149	601	342	-	4,118	87
Virginia	27,087	22,483	2,805	19,678	2,879	3,071	-	13,030	628
Washington	44,035	30,557	2,214	28,344	6,689	1,200	5,744	12,666	1,028
West Virginia	15,508	14,123	986	13,137	848	1,503	-	10,472	314
Wisconsin	35,920	32,778	2,543	30,234	10,537	2,882	-	13,634	2,519
Wyoming	62,603	33,419	716	32,704	2,171	1,181	27,150	995	960
Caribbean	2,307	2,166	557	1,609	355	429	138	622	65

- Represents or rounds to zero.   [1] Includes water area not shown separately.   [2] Includes urban and built-up areas in units of 10 acres or greater and rural transportation.   [3] Includes Conservation Reserve Program land and minor cover/use categories, not shown separately.

Source: U.S. Dept. of Agriculture, National Resource and Conservation Service, and Iowa State University, Statistical Laboratory; *Summary Report, 1997 National Resources Inventory,* issued December 1999.

No. 384. Extreme and Mean Elevations by State and Other Area

[One foot=.305 meter]

State and other area	Highest point Name	Highest Elevation Feet	Highest Elevation Meters	Lowest point Name	Lowest Elevation Feet	Lowest Elevation Meters	Approximate mean elevation Feet	Approximate mean elevation Meters
U.S.....	Mt. McKinley (AK)	20,320	6,198	Death Valley (CA).....	-282	-86	2,500	763
AL........	Cheaha Mountain	2,405	733	Gulf of Mexico	(1)	(1)	500	153
AK........	Mount McKinley........	20,320	6,198	Pacific Ocean........	(1)	(1)	1,900	580
AZ........	Humphreys Peak.......	12,633	3,853	Colorado River.......	70	21	4,100	1,251
AR........	Magazine Mountain	2,753	840	Ouachita River.......	55	17	650	198
CA........	Mount Whitney	14,494	4,419	Death Valley........	-282	-86	2,900	885
CO........	Mt. Elbert...........	14,433	4,402	Arkansas River.......	3,350	1,022	6,800	2,074
CT........	Mt. Frissell on South slope	2,380	726	Long Island Sound	(1)	(1)	500	153
DE........	Ebright Road, [2] New Castle County.....	448	137	Atlantic Ocean	(1)	(1)	60	18
DC........	Tenleytown at Reno Reservoir............	410	125	Potomac River.......	1	(Z)	150	46
FL........	Sec. 30, T6N, R20W, Walton County.............	345	105	Atlantic Ocean	(1)	(1)	100	31
GA........	Brasstown Bald........	4,784	1,459	Atlantic Ocean	(1)	(1)	600	183
HI	Puu Wekiu	13,796	4,208	Pacific Ocean........	(1)	(1)	3,030	924
ID	Borah Peak	12,662	3,862	Snake River.........	710	217	5,000	1,525
IL.........	Charles Mound	1,235	377	Mississippi River......	279	85	600	183
IN	Franklin Twp., Wayne Co .	1,257	383	Ohio River..........	320	98	700	214
IA	Sec. 29, T100N, R41W, Osceola County [3]	1,670	509	Mississippi River......	480	146	1,100	336
KS........	Mount Sunflower.......	4,039	1,232	Verdigris River.......	679	207	2,000	610
KY........	Black Mountain........	4,139	2,162	Mississippi River......	257	78	750	229
LA........	Driskill Mountain	535	163	New Orleans	-8	-2	100	31
ME........	Mount Katahdin.......	5,267	1,606	Atlantic Ocean	(1)	(1)	600	183
MD........	Backbone Mountain	3,360	1,025	Atlantic Ocean	(1)	(1)	350	107
MA........	Mount Greylock........	3,487	1,064	Atlantic Ocean	(1)	(1)	500	153
MI	Mount Arvon..........	1,979	604	Lake Erie...........	571	174	900	275
MN........	Eagle Mountain, Cook Co .	2,301	702	Lake Superior........	600	183	1,200	366
MS........	Woodall Mountain	806	246	Gulf of Mexico	(1)	(1)	300	92
MO........	Taum Sauk Mountain	1,772	540	St. Francis River......	230	70	800	244
MT........	Granite Peak	12,799	3,904	Kootenai River.......	1,800	549	3,400	1,037
NE........	Johnson Twp., Kimball Co .	5,424	1,654	Missouri River.......	840	256	2,600	793
NV........	Boundary Peak	13,140	4,007	Colorado River.......	479	146	5,500	1,678
NH........	Mount Washington......	6,288	1,918	Atlantic Ocean	(1)	(1)	1,000	305
NJ........	High Point	1,803	550	Atlantic Ocean	(1)	(1)	250	76
NM........	Wheeler Peak........	13,161	4,014	Red Bluff Reservoir....	2,842	867	5,700	1,739
NY........	Mount Marcy.........	5,344	1,630	Atlantic Ocean	(1)	(1)	1,000	305
NC........	Mount Mitchell........	6,684	2,039	Atlantic Ocean	(1)	(1)	700	214
ND........	White Butte, Slope Co ...	3,506	1,069	Red River..........	750	229	1,900	580
OH........	Campbell Hill	1,549	472	Ohio River..........	455	139	850	259
OK........	Black Mesa..........	4,973	1,517	Little River.........	289	88	1,300	397
OR........	Mount Hood	11,239	3,428	Pacific Ocean........	(1)	(1)	3,300	1,007
PA........	Mount Davis	3,213	980	Delaware River.......	(1)	(1)	1,100	336
RI	Jerimoth Hill	812	248	Atlantic Ocean	(1)	(1)	200	61
SC........	Sassafras Mountain	3,560	1,086	Atlantic Ocean	(1)	(1)	350	107
SD........	Harney Peak.........	7,242	2,209	Big Stone Lake......	966	295	2,200	671
TN........	Clingmans Dome	6,643	2,026	Mississippi River.....	178	54	900	275
TX........	Guadalupe Peak	8,749	2,668	Gulf of Mexico	(1)	(1)	1,700	519
UT........	Kings Peak	13,528	4,126	Beaverdam Wash	2,000	610	6,100	1,861
VT........	Mount Mansfield	4,393	1,340	Lake Champlain	95	29	1,000	305
VA........	Mount Rogers........	5,729	1,747	Atlantic Ocean	(1)	(1)	950	290
WA........	Mount Rainier........	14,410	4,395	Pacific Ocean........	(1)	(1)	1,700	519
WV........	Spruce Knob.........	4,861	1,483	Potomac River.......	240	73	1,500	458
WI	Timms Hill	1,951	595	Lake Michigan	579	177	1,050	320
WY	Gannett Peak	13,804	4,210	Belle Fourche River....	3,099	945	6,700	2,044
Other areas: Puerto Rico	Cerro de Punta	4,390	1,339	Atlantic Ocean	(1)	(1)	1,800	549
American Samoa...	Lata Mountain.........	3,160	964	Pacific Ocean.......	(1)	(1)	1,300	397
Guam	Mount Lamlam	1,332	406	Pacific Ocean.......	(1)	(1)	330	101
Virgin Is...	Crown Mountain	1,556	475	Atlantic Ocean	(1)	(1)	750	229

Z Less than 0.5 meter. [1] Sea level. [2] At DE-PA state line. [3] "Sec." denotes section; "T," township; "R," range; "N," north; and "W," west.

Source: U.S. Geological Survey, for highest and lowest points, *Elevations and Distances in the United States, 1990*; for mean elevations, 1983 edition.

No. 385. Water Areas for Selected Major Bodies of Water: 1990

[Includes only that portion of body of water under the jurisdiction of the United States, excluding Hawaii. One square mile=2.59 square kilometers]

Body of water and state	Area Sq. mi.	Area Sq. km.	Body of water and state	Area Sq. mi.	Area Sq. km.
Atlantic Coast water bodies:			Leech Lake (MN)	162	419
Chesapeake Bay (MD-VA)	2,747	7,115	Lake St. Clair (MI) [1]	161	416
Pamlico Sound (NC)	1,622	4,200	Eufaula Lake (OK)	157	407
Long Island Sound (CT-NY)	914	2,368			
Delaware Bay (DE-NJ)	614	1,591	Sam Rayburn Reservoir (TX)	150	389
Cape Cod Bay (MA)	598	1,548	Goose Lake (CA-OR)	147	381
Albemarle Sound (NC)	492	1,274	Utah Lake (UT)	139	361
Biscayne Bay (FL)	218	565	Lake Marion (SC)	139	360
Buzzards Bay (MA)	215	558	Lake Francis Case (SD)	134	346
Tangier Sound (MD-VA)	172	445	Lake Pend Oreille (ID)	133	343
Currituck Sound (NC)	116	301	Lake Texoma (OK-TX)	132	342
Pocomoke Sound (MD-VA)	111	286	Yellowstone Lake (WY)	131	339
Chincoteague Bay (MD-VA)	105	272	Livingston Reservoir (TX)	127	330
Great South Bay (NY)	94	243	Franklin D. Roosevelt Lake (WA)	124	322
Core Sound (NC)	88	229	Moosehead Lake (ME)	116	301
			Clark Hill Lake (GA-SC)	105	272
Gulf Coast water bodies:			Lake Maurepas (LA)	91	235
Mississippi Sound (AL-LA-MS)	813	2,105	Lake Moultrie (SC)	89	230
Laguna Madre (TX)	733	1,897	Lake Winnibigoshish (MN)	87	225
Lake Pontchartrain (LA)	631	1,635	Hartwell Lake (GA-SC)	86	224
Florida Bay (FL)	616	1,596	Upper Klamath Lake (OR)	85	221
Breton Sound (LA)	511	1,323	Harry S. Truman Reservoir (MO)	84	217
Mobile Bay (AL)	310	802	Oneida Lake (NY)	80	207
Lake Borgne (LA-MS)	271	702	Malheur Lake (OR)	75	195
Matagorda Bay (TX)	253	656			
Atchafalaya Bay (LA)	245	635	Alaska water bodies:		
Galveston Bay (TX)	236	611	Chatham Strait	1,559	4,039
			Prince William Sound	1,382	3,579
Tampa Bay (FL)	212	549	Clarence Strait	1,199	3,107
Vermilion Bay (LA)	189	489	Iliamna Lake	1,022	2,646
Corpus Christi Bay (TX)	151	392	Frederick Sound	792	2,051
West Cote Blanche Bay (LA)	146	378	Sumner Strait	791	2,048
Trinity Bay (TX)	129	335	Stephens Passage	702	1,819
Choctawhatchee Bay (FL)	122	315	Kvichak Bay	640	1,659
San Antonio Bay (TX)	118	306	Montague Strait	463	1,198
Timbalier Bay (LA)	112	291	Becharof Lake	447	1,158
Charlotte Harbor (FL)	112	291	Icy Strait	436	1,130
Aransas Bay (TX)	104	268	Hotham Inlet	433	1,120
Apalachicola Bay (FL)	101	262	Selawik Lake	403	1,044
Terrebonne Bay (LA)	99	256	Nushagak Bay	393	1,018
East Cote Blanche Bay (LA)	94	243	Baird Inlet	348	902
St. George Sound (FL)	93	240			
Sabine Lake (LA-TX)	89	229	Yakutat Bay	345	894
White Lake (LA)	85	221	Teshekpuk Lake	324	839
Old Tampa Bay (FL)	83	214	Behm Canal	324	839
Bon Secour Bay (AL)	79	204	Turnagain Arm	322	834
Pine Island Sound (FL)	75	194	Kachemak Bay	310	803
			Glacier Bay	310	803
Pacific Coast water bodies:			Stefansson Sound	301	780
Puget Sound (WA)	808	2,092	Revillagigedo Channel	295	764
San Francisco Bay (CA)	264	684	Kasegaluk Lagoon	293	759
Willapa Bay (WA)	125	325	Cordova Bay	241	623
Hood Canal (WA)	117	303	Sitka Sound	229	593
			Naknek Lake	225	582
Interior water bodies:			Eschscholtz Bay	210	543
Lake Michigan (IL-IN-MI-WI)	22,342	57,866	Stepovak Bay	206	534
Lake Superior (MI-MN-WI) [1]	20,557	53,243	Keku Strait	206	534
Lake Huron (MI) [1]	8,800	22,792			
Lake Erie (MI-NY-OH-PA) [1]	5,033	13,036	Port Clarence	187	486
Lake Ontario (NY) [1]	3,446	8,926	Orca Bay	184	476
Great Salt Lake (UT)	1,836	4,756	Knik Arm	169	437
Green Bay (MI-WI)	1,396	3,617	Dall Lake	167	433
Lake Okeechobee (FL)	663	1,717	Knight Island Passage	167	432
Lake Sakakawea (ND)	563	1,459	Scammon Bay	163	423
Lake Oahe (ND-SD)	538	1,394	Port Moller	159	412
Lake of the Woods (MN) [1]	462	1,196	Ernest Sound	158	410
Lake Champlain (NY-VT) [1]	414	1,072	Spafarief Bay	157	405
Fort Peck Lake (MT)	379	981	Pavlov Bay	153	396
Salton Sea (CA)	364	944	Shishmaref Inlet	153	395
Toledo Bend Reservoir (LA-TX)	268	694	Smith Bay	140	363
Lower Red Lake (MN)	257	666	Seymour Canal	140	361
Lake Powell (AZ-UT)	250	649	Sitkalidak Strait	135	349
Kentucky Lake (KY-TN)	234	605	Tlevak Strait	135	349
Lake Mead (AZ-NV)	233	603			
Lake Winnebago (WI)	206	535	Lake Clark	130	336
Mille Lacs Lake (MN)	200	518	Lynn Canal	130	336
Flathead Lake (MT)	191	495	Chignik Bay	119	309
Lake Tahoe (CA-NV)	187	486	Elson Lagoon	119	309
Upper Red Lake (MN)	186	483	Bucareli Bay	119	307
Pyramid Lake (NV)	170	440	Hinchinbrook Entrance	118	306

[1] Area measurements for Lake Champlain, Lake Erie, Lake Huron, Lake Ontario, Lake St. Clair, Lake Superior, and Lake of the Woods include only those portions under the jurisdiction of the United States.

Source: U. S. Census Bureau, unpublished data from the Census TIGER™ database.

Geography and Environment 231

No. 386. Flows of Largest U.S. Rivers—Length, Discharge, and Drainage Area

River	Location of mouth	Source stream (name and location)	Length [1] (miles)	Average discharge at mouth (1,000 cubic ft. per second)	Drainage area (1,000 sq. mi.)
Missouri	Missouri.	Red Rock Creek, MT	2,540	76.2	[2]529
Mississippi	Louisiana.	Mississippi River, MN.	[3]2,340	[4]593	[2][5]1,150
Yukon	Alaska.	McNeil River, Canada	1,980	225	[2]328
St. Lawrence	Canada.	North River, MN	1,900	348	[2]396
Rio Grande	Mexico-Texas	Rio Grande, CO	1,900	-	336
Arkansas	Arkansas	East Fork Arkansas River, CO . . .	1,460	41	161
Colorado.	Mexico	Colorado River, CO	1,450	-	246
Atchafalaya [6]	Louisiana.	Tierra Blanca Creek, NM	1,420	58	95.1
Ohio	Illinois-Kentucky . . .	Allegheny River, PA	1,310	281	203
Red	Louisiana.	Tierra Blanca Creek, NM	1,290	56	93.2
Brazos	Texas	Blackwater Draw, NM.	1,280	-	45.6
Columbia	Oregon-Washington.	Columbia River, Canada.	1,240	265	[2]258
Snake	Washington	Snake River, WY.	1,040	56.9	108
Platte	Nebraska.	Grizzly Creek, CO	990	-	84.9
Pecos	Texas	Pecos River, NM.	926	-	44.3
Canadian	Oklahoma	Canadian River, CO.	906	-	46.9
Tennessee	Kentucky	Courthouse Creek, NC	886	68	40.9
Colorado (of Texas) .	Texas	Colorado River, TX	862	-	42.3
North Canadian	Oklahoma	Corrumpa Creek, NM.	800	-	17.6
Mobile	Alabama	Tickanetley Creek, GA	774	67.2	44.6
Kansas	Kansas	Arikaree River, CO	743	-	59.5
Kuskokwim	Alaska.	South Fork Kuskokwim River, AK .	724	67	48
Yellowstone.	North Dakota	North Folk Yellowstone River, WY	692	-	70
Tanana.	Alaska.	Nabesna River, AK	659	41	44.5
Gila	Arizona	Middle Fork Gila River, NM	649	-	58.2

- Represents zero. [1] From source to mouth. [2] Drainage area includes both the United States and Canada. [3] The length from the source of the Missouri River to the Mississippi River and thence to the Gulf of Mexico is about 3,710 miles. [4] Includes about 167,000 cubic ft. per second diverted from the Mississippi into the Atchafalaya River but excludes the flow of the Red River. [5] Excludes the drainage areas of the Red and Atchafalaya Rivers. [6] In east-central Louisiana, the Red River flows into the Atchafalaya River, a distributary of the Mississippi River. Data on average discharge, length, and drainage area include the Red River, but exclude all water diverted into the Atchafalaya from the Mississippi River.

Source: U.S. Geological Survey, *Largest Rivers in the United States,* Open File Report 87-242, May 1990.

No. 387. U.S. Water Withdrawals and Consumptive Use Per Day by End Use: 1940 to 1995

[Includes Puerto Rico. Withdrawal signifies water physically withdrawn from a source. Includes fresh and saline water; excludes water used for hydroelectric power]

Year	Total (bil. gal.)	Per capita [1] (gal.)	Irrigation (bil. gal.)	Public supply [2] Total (bil. gal.)	Public supply [2] Per capita [3] (gal.)	Rural [4] (bil. gal.)	Industrial and misc. [5] (bil. gal.)	Steam electric utilities (bil. gal.)
WITHDRAWALS								
1940	140	1,027	71	10	75	3.1	29	23
1950	180	1,185	89	14	145	3.6	37	40
1955	240	1,454	110	17	148	3.6	39	72
1960	270	1,500	110	21	151	3.6	38	100
1965	310	1,602	120	24	155	4.0	46	130
1970	370	1,815	130	27	166	4.5	47	170
1975	420	1,972	140	29	168	4.9	45	200
1980	440	1,953	150	34	183	5.6	45	210
1985	399	1,650	137	38	189	7.8	31	187
1990	408	1,620	137	41	195	7.9	30	195
1995	402	1,500	134	43	192	8.9	26	190
CONSUMPTIVE USE								
1960	61	339	52	3.5	25	2.8	3.0	0.2
1965	77	403	66	5.2	34	3.2	3.4	0.4
1970	87	427	73	5.9	36	3.4	4.1	0.8
1975	96	451	80	6.7	38	3.4	4.2	1.9
1980	100	440	83	7.1	38	3.9	5.0	3.2
1985	92	380	74	([6])	([6])	9.2	6.1	6.2
1990	94	370	76	([6])	([6])	8.9	6.7	4.0
1995	100	374	81	([6])	([6])	9.9	4.8	3.7

[1] Based on U.S. Census Bureau resident population as of July 1. [2] Includes commercial water withdrawals. [3] Based on population served. [4] Rural farm and nonfarm household and garden use, and water for farm stock and dairies. [5] For 1940 to 1960, includes manufacturing and mineral industries, rural commercial industries, air-conditioning, resorts, hotels, motels, military and other state and Federal agencies, and miscellaneous; thereafter, includes manufacturing, mining and mineral processing, ordnance, construction, and miscellaneous. [6] Public supply consumptive use included in end-use categories.

Source: 1940-1960, U.S. Bureau of Domestic Business Development, based principally on committee prints, *Water Resources Activities in the United States,* for the Senate Committee on National Water Resources, U.S. Senate, thereafter, U.S. Geological Survey, *Estimated Use of Water in the United States in 1995,* circular 1200, and previous quinquennial issues.

No. 388. Water Withdrawals and Consumptive Use—State and Other Area: 1995

[In millions of gallons per day (401,500 represents 401,500,000,000) except as noted. Figures may not add due to rounding. Withdrawal signifies water physically withdrawn from a source. Includes fresh and saline water]

State or other area	Water withdrawn								Con-sumptive use,[1] fresh water
	Total	Per capita (gal. per day) fresh	Source		Selected major uses				
			Ground water	Surface water	Irrigation	Public supply[2]	Indus-trial	Thermo-electric	
U.S.[2]	401,500	1,280	77,500	324,000	134,000	43,600	26,200	190,000	100,000
Alabama.	7,100	1,670	445	6,650	139	875	753	5,200	532
Alaska	329	350	132	196	0.6	90	197	30	25
Arizona.	6,830	1,620	2,840	3,990	5,670	846	197	62	3,830
Arkansas	8,800	3,540	5,460	3,340	5,940	419	187	1,780	4,140
California	45,900	1,130	14,700	31,300	28,900	5,740	802	9,630	25,500
Colorado.	13,800	3,690	2,270	11,600	12,700	732	191	115	5,230
Connecticut.	4,450	389	166	4,290	28	448	11	3,940	97
Delaware	1,500	1,050	110	1,390	48	101	64	1,270	71
District of Columbia .	10	18	0.5	9.7	-	-	0.5	9.7	15
Florida	18,200	509	4,340	13,800	3,470	2,360	649	11,600	2,780
Georgia	5,820	799	1,190	4,630	722	1,250	676	3,070	1,170
Hawaii	1,930	853	531	1,400	652	218	20	970	542
Idaho	15,100	13,000	2,830	12,300	13,000	254	76	-	4,360
Illinois	19,900	1,680	953	19,000	180	1,950	527	17,100	857
Indiana.	9,140	1,570	709	8,430	116	784	2,410	5,690	505
Iowa	3,030	1,070	528	2,510	39	418	301	2,130	290
Kansas	5,240	2,040	3,510	1,720	3,380	384	77	1,260	3,620
Kentucky	4,420	1,150	226	4,190	12	521	375	3,450	318
Louisiana	9,850	2,270	1,350	8,500	769	677	2,580	5,480	1,930
Maine.	326	178	80	246	27	135	16	136	48
Maryland	7,730	289	246	7,480	57	907	331	6,360	150
Massachusetts.	5,510	189	351	5,160	82	759	88	4,570	180
Michigan.	12,100	1,260	862	11,200	227	1,490	1,910	8,370	667
Minnesota.	3,390	736	714	2,680	157	573	438	2,090	417
Mississippi	3,200	1,140	2,590	614	1,740	377	294	375	1,570
Missouri	7,030	1,320	891	6,140	567	757	63	5,550	692
Montana	8,860	10,200	217	8,640	8,550	161	80	22	1,960
Nebraska	10,500	6,440	6,200	4,350	7,550	328	175	2,350	7,020
Nevada	2,300	1,480	896	1,400	1,640	479	95	27	1,340
New Hampshire	1,320	388	81	1,240	6.3	130	50	1,110	35
New Jersey.	6,110	269	580	5,530	125	1,120	486	4,360	210
New Mexico	3,510	2,080	1,700	1,800	2,990	337	69	55	1,980
New York	16,800	567	1,010	15,800	30	3,140	321	13,100	469
North Carolina	9,290	1,070	535	8,750	239	939	385	7,420	713
North Dakota.	1,120	1,750	122	1,000	117	85	17	819	181
Ohio	10,500	944	905	9,620	27	1,560	650	8,190	791
Oklahoma.	2,040	543	1,220	822	864	597	285	124	716
Oregon.	7,910	2,520	1,050	6,860	6,170	572	379	9.0	3,210
Pennsylvania.	9,680	802	860	8,820	16	1,730	1,930	5,930	565
Rhode Island.	411	138	27	383	2.3	121	7.3	275	19
South Carolina.	6,200	1,690	322	5,880	53	614	703	4,810	321
South Dakota	460	631	187	273	269	97	32	5.3	249
Tennessee	10,100	1,920	435	9,640	24	831	868	8,300	233
Texas.	29,600	1,300	8,780	20,800	9,450	3,420	2,920	13,500	10,500
Utah	4,460	2,200	790	3,670	3,530	506	253	48	2,200
Vermont	565	967	50	515	3.9	66	12	452	24
Virginia.	8,260	826	358	7,900	30	911	622	6,620	218
Washington.	8,860	1,620	1,760	7,100	6,470	1,300	652	376	3,080
West Virginia.	4,620	2,530	146	4,470	-	217	1,330	3,010	352
Wisconsin	7,250	1,420	759	6,490	169	692	453	5,820	443
Wyoming	7,060	14,700	335	6,720	6,590	100	118	220	2,800
Puerto Rico.	2,840	154	135	2,680	107	443	15	2,260	187
Virgin Islands.	202	113	0.7	201	-	7.8	20	173	1.9

- Represents zero. [1] Water that has been evaporated, transpired, or incorporated into products, plant or animal tissue; and therefore, is not available for immediate reuse. [2] Includes Puerto Rico and Virgin Islands.

Source: U.S. Geological Survey, *Estimated Use of Water in the United States in 1995*, circular 1200.

Geography and Environment   233

No. 389. National Ambient Water Quality in Rivers and Streams— Violation Rate: 1980 to 1995

[In percent. Violation level based on U.S. Environmental Protection Agency water quality criteria. Violation rate represents the proportion of all measurements of a specific water quality pollutant which exceeds the "violation level" for that pollutant. "Violation" does not necessarily imply a legal violation. Data based on U.S. Geological Survey's National Stream Quality Accounting Network (NASQAN) data system; for details, see source. Years refer to water years. A water year begins in Oct. and ends in Sept. µg=micrograms; mg=milligrams. For metric conversion, see page ix]

Pollutant	Violation level	1980	1985	1989	1990	1991	1992	1993	1994	1995
Fecal coliform bacteria. . . .	Above 200 cells per 100 ml. .	31	28	30	26	15	28	31	28	35
Dissolved oxygen	Below 5 mg per liter.	5	3	3	2	2	2	(Z)	2	1
Phosphorus, total, as phosporous	Above 1.0 mg per liter	4	3	2	3	2	2	2	2	4
Lead, dissolved	Above 50 µg per liter	(Z)	(Z)	(Z)	(Z)	(Z)	(Z)	(NA)	(NA)	(NA)
Cadmium, dissolved	Above 10 µg per liter	1	(Z)	(Z)	(Z)	(Z)	(Z)	(NA)	(NA)	(NA)

NA Not available.   Z Less than 1.

Source: U.S. Geological Survey, national-level data, unpublished; state-level data, *Water-Data Report*, annual series prepared in cooperation with the state governments.

No. 390. Oil Spills in U.S. Waters—Number and Volume: 1995 to 1998

[Based on reported discharges into U.S. navigable waters, including territorial waters (extending 3 to 12 miles from the coastline), tributaries, the contiguous zone, onto shoreline, or into other waters that threaten the marine environment. Data found in Marine Safety Management System]

Spill characteristic	Number of spills				Spill volume (1,000 gal.)			
	1995	1996	1997	1998	1995	1996	1997	1998
Total	9,038	9,335	8,624	8,315	2,638,229	3,117,831	942,574	885,303
Size of spill (gallons):								
1-100	8,614	8,904	8,299	7,962	48,936	43,434	39,082	38,093
101-1,000	324	322	243	259	115,140	114,831	81,895	86,606
1,001-3,000	52	57	40	54	91,426	102,008	78,117	96,743
3,001-5,000	19	20	14	15	73,598	86,389	58,016	64,609
5,001-10,000	9	12	15	15	63,853	92,163	109,288	108,148
10,001-50,000	15	15	11	8	354,824	351,106	282,176	216,335
50,001-100,000	2	-	1	-	155,950	-	84,000	-
100,000-1,000,000	3	5	1	2	1,734,502	2,327,900	210,000	274,769
1,000,000 and over	-	-	-	-	-	-	-	-
Waterbody:								
Atlantic ocean	267	119	87	109	48,313	27,980	40,857	6,674
Pacific ocean	648	491	505	644	69,053	29,209	32,841	192,775
Gulf of Mexico	1,485	2,403	2,341	2,190	253,040	45,145	105,462	181,372
Great Lakes	282	228	156	119	3,103	3,507	4,311	3,006
Lakes	26	19	29	25	92	52	210,270	63
Rivers and canals	1,849	1,984	1,821	1,944	1,156,002	475,550	182,676	280,651
Bays and sounds	1,109	793	811	891	41,004	1,092,207	46,450	24,234
Harbors.	1,176	992	858	790	148,229	288,252	45,932	97,223
Other	2,196	2,306	2,016	1,603	919,393	1,155,929	273,775	99,305
Source:								
Tankship	148	122	124	104	125,491	219,311	22,429	56,673
Tankbarge	353	313	252	220	1,101,938	1,163,258	165,649	248,089
All other vessels	4,977	5,151	4,971	4,848	396,724	298,451	192,801	316,473
Facilities	586	509	838	937	868,900	406,384	204,935	166,269
Pipelines	30	17	32	45	11,894	978,392	224,122	47,863
All other nonvessels	500	552	486	571	77,428	23,527	72,208	32,584
Unknown	2,444	2,671	1,921	1,590	55,854	28,508	60,430	17,352

- Represents or rounds to zero.

Source: U.S. Coast Guard, <http://www.uscg.mil/hq/g-m/nmc/response/stats/summary.htm> (accessed 09 February 2000).

No. 391. Wastewater Treatment Facilities: 1988 to 1996

[Covers treatment facilities, which are structures designed to treat wastewater, storm water, or combined sewer overflows prior to discharging to the environment. Treatment is accomplished by subjecting the wastewater to a combination of physical, chemical, and/or biological processes that reduce the concentration of contaminants]

Level of treatment	Number of facilities			1996		
				Present design capacity (mgd [1])	Number of persons served	
	1988	1992	1996		Total	Percent of U.S.
Total	15,591	15,613	16,024	42,225	189,710,899	71.8
Nondischarge [2]	1,854	1,981	2,032	1,421	7,660,876	2.9
Less than secondary.	1,789	868	176	3,054	17,177,492	6.5
Secondary	8,536	9,086	9,388	17,734	81,944,349	31.0
Greater than secondary. . . .	3,412	3,678	4,428	20,016	82,928,182	31.4

[1] Millions of gallons per day.   [2] Facilities that do not discharge effluent to surface waters.

Source: U.S. Environmental Protection Agency, Office of Wastewater Management, *1996 Clean Water Needs Survey Report to Congress.*

234   Geography and Environment

No. 392. National Ambient Air Pollutant Concentrations: 1990 to 1998

[Data represent annual composite averages of pollutant based on daily 24-hour averages of monitoring stations, except carbon monoxide is based on the second-highest, nonoverlapping, 8-hour average; ozone, average of the second-highest daily maximum 1-hour value; and lead, quarterly average of ambient lead levels. Based on data from the Aerometric Information Retrieval System. µg/m³=micrograms of pollutant per cubic meter of air; ppm=parts per million]

Pollutant	Unit	Monitoring stations, number	Air quality standard[1]	1990	1993	1994	1995	1996	1997	1998
Carbon monoxide .	ppm. . . .	363	[2]9	5.8	4.9	5.1	4.5	4.2	3.9	3.8
Ozone.	ppm. . . .	661	[3].12	0.112	0.108	0.107	0.112	0.106	0.105	0.11
Sulfur dioxide	ppm. . . .	482	.03	0.0082	0.0072	0.0069	0.0056	0.0056	0.0054	0.0053
Particulates (PM-10)[4]	µg/m³. .	929	50	29.5	26.1	26.1	25	24.1	23.9	23.8
Nitrogen dioxide . .	ppm. . . .	225	.053	0.02	0.019	0.02	0.019	0.019	0.018	0.018
Lead.	µg/m³. . .	189	[5]1.5	0.09	0.05	0.05	0.04	0.04	0.04	0.04

[1] Refers to the primary National Ambient Air Quality Standard that protects the public health. [2] Based on 8-hour standard of 9 ppm. [3] Based on 1-hour standard of .12 ppm. [4] The particulates (PM-10) standard replaced the previous standard for total suspended particulates in 1987. [5] Based on 3-month standard of 1.5 µg/m³
Source: U.S. Environmental Protection Agency, *National Air Quality and Emissions Trends Report,* annual.

No. 393. National Air Pollutant Emissions: 1970 to 1998

[In thousands of tons, except as indicated. PM-10=Particulate matter of less than ten microns. Methodologies to estimate data for 1970 to 1980 period and 1985 to present emissions differ. Beginning with 1985, the estimates are based on a modified National Acid Precipitation Assessment Program inventory]

Year	PM-10	PM-10, fugitive dust[1]	Sulfur dioxide	Nitrogen dioxides	Volatile organic compounds	Carbon monoxide	Lead (tons)
1970	13,042	(NA)	31,161	20,928	30,982	129,444	220,869
1975	7,671	(NA)	28,011	22,632	26,079	116,757	159,659
1980	7,119	(NA)	25,905	24,384	26,336	117,434	74,153
1985	4,831	40,614	23,658	23,198	24,428	117,013	22,890
1986	4,642	46,298	22,886	22,808	23,617	111,688	14,763
1987	4,758	37,711	22,661	23,068	23,470	110,798	7,681
1988	5,598	55,474	23,135	24,124	24,306	118,729	7,053
1989	4,811	48,253	23,293	23,893	22,513	106,439	5,468
1990	5,057	24,905	23,660	24,049	20,936	98,523	4,975
1991	4,725	24,836	23,041	24,249	21,102	100,872	4,169
1992	4,610	24,862	22,806	24,596	20,659	97,630	3,810
1993	4,528	23,478	22,466	24,961	20,868	98,160	3,916
1994	4,751	26,162	21,870	25,372	21,535	102,643	4,047
1995	4,579	22,491	19,181	24,921	20,817	93,353	3,929
1996	4,732	28,309	19,121	24,676	18,736	95,479	3,899
1997	4,743	29,482	19,622	24,824	18,876	94,410	3,952
1998	4,450	30,292	19,647	24,454	17,917	89,454	3,973

NA Not available. [1] Sources such as agricultural tilling, construction, mining and quarrying, paved roads, unpaved roads, and wind erosion.

No. 394. Air Pollutant Emissions by Pollutant and Source: 1998

[In thousands of tons, except as indicated. See headnote, Table 393]

Source	Particulates[1]	Sulfur dioxide	Nitrogen oxides	Volatile organic compounds	Carbon monoxide	Lead (tons)
Total	**34,741**	**19,647**	**24,454**	**17,917**	**89,454**	**3,973**
Fuel combustion, stationary sources.	1,091	16,721	10,189	893	5,374	503
Electric utilities	302	13,217	6,103	54	417	68
Industrial	245	2,895	2,969	161	1,114	19
Other fuel combustion	544	609	1,117	678	3,843	416
Residential	432	127	742	654	3,699	6
Industrial processes	607	1,458	786	1,417	3,624	2,327
Chemical and allied product manufacturing .	65	299	152	396	1,129	175
Metals processing	171	444	88	75	1,495	2,098
Petroleum and related industries	32	345	138	496	368	(NA)
Other	339	370	408	450	632	54
Solvent utilization	6	1	2	5,278	2	(NA)
Storage and transport	94	3	7	1,324	80	(NA)
Waste disposal and recycling	310	42	97	433	1,154	620
Highway vehicles	257	326	7,765	5,325	50,386	19
Light-duty gas vehicles and motorcycles . . .	56	130	2,849	2,832	27,039	12
Light-duty trucks	40	99	1,917	2,015	18,726	7
Heavy-duty gas vehicles.	8	11	323	257	3,067	-
Diesels	152	85.3	2,676	222	1,554	(NA)
Off highway [2] . [3]	461	1,084	5,280	2,461	19,914	503
Miscellaneous [3]	31,916	12	328	786	8,920	(NA)

- Represents or rounds to zero. NA Not available. [1] Represents both PM-10 and PM-10 fugitive dust; see Table 405. [2] Includes emissions from farm tractors and other farm machinery, construction equipment, industrial machinery, recreational marine vessels, and small general utility engines such as lawn mowers. [3] Includes emissions such as from forest fires and other kinds of burning, various agricultural activities, fugitive dust from paved and unpaved roads, and other construction and mining activities, and natural sources.
Source of Tables 393 and 394: U.S. Environmental Protection Agency, *National Air Pollutant Emission Trends, 1900-1998,* EPA-454/R-00-002.

Geography and Environment 235

No. 395. Emissions of Greenhouse Gases by Type and Source: 1990 to 1998

[Emission estimates were mandated by Congress through Section 1605(a) of the Energy Policy Act of 1992 (title XVI). Gases that contain carbon can be measured either in terms of the full molecular weight of the gas or just in terms of their carbon content]

Type and source	Unit	1990	1993	1994	1995	1996	1997	1998
Carbon dioxide:								
Carbon content, total [1]	Mil. metric tons .	1,347.0	1,388.6	1,409.9	1,423.8	1,471.5	1,490.4	1,495.5
Energy sources	Mil. metric tons .	1,345.2	1,378.2	1,398.3	1,411.7	1,460.5	1,480.0	1,485.4
Methane:								
Gas, total [1]	Mil. metric tons .	30.19	29.85	30.05	30.20	29.30	29.27	28.84
Energy sources	Mil. metric tons .	10.77	10.10	10.11	10.34	9.87	10.09	10.09
Landfills	Mil. metric tons .	11.12	11.01	10.90	10.85	10.70	10.36	9.87
Agricultural sources.	Mil. metric tons .	8.18	8.62	8.91	8.87	8.60	8.69	8.74
Nitrous oxide, total [1]	1,000 metric tons	1,167	1,218	1,312	1,257	1,245	1,225	1,220
Agriculture	1,000 metric tons	844	860	929	860	847	865	872
Energy sources	1,000 metric tons	210	240	255	268	265	269	271
Industrial sources.	1,000 metric tons	96	100	110	111	115	73	58
Nitrogen oxide, total [1]	Mil. metric tons .	21.23	21.78	22.05	21.53	21.26	21.36	(NA)
Energy related.	Mil. metric tons .	20.08	20.80	20.91	20.53	20.15	20.22	(NA)
Stationary source fuel combustion.	Mil. metric tons .	9.85	10.05	9.96	9.79	9.52	9.70	(NA)
Transportation	Mil. metric tons .	10.23	10.75	10.95	10.73	10.64	10.52	(NA)
Nonmethane volatile organic compounds (VOCs), total [1]	Mil. metric tons .	18.89	18.79	19.39	18.56	17.42	17.34	(NA)
Energy related.	Mil. metric tons .	8.86	8.71	9.00	8.32	8.13	7.72	(NA)
Transportation	Mil. metric tons .	7.95	7.82	8.11	7.35	7.16	6.95	(NA)
Industrial processes	Mil. metric tons .	8.18	8.65	8.79	8.81	8.21	8.52	(NA)
Solid waste disposal.	Mil. metric tons .	0.89	0.95	0.95	0.97	0.39	0.41	(NA)
Carbon monoxide, total	Mil. metric tons .	86.77	85.62	89.54	80.74	82.34	79.18	(NA)
Energy related.	Mil. metric tons .	71.29	73.91	75.53	69.10	68.48	65.01	(NA)
Transportation	Mil. metric tons .	66.43	68.97	70.65	63.85	63.20	60.79	(NA)
Stationary source fuel combustion	Mil. metric tons .	4.86	4.94	4.87	5.25	5.28	4.22	(NA)
Industrial processes	Mil. metric tons .	4.33	4.22	4.19	4.18	4.19	4.36	(NA)
Chloroflurocarbons (CFCs) gases [2]	1,000 metric tons	202	148	109	102	67	51	32
Hydrofluorocarbons	1,000 metric tons	6	8	13	21	28	34	37
Hydrochlorofluorocarbons (HCFCs) gases [3]	1,000 metric tons	80	82	93	107	119	120	129
Other chemicals:								
Carbon tetrachloride.	1,000 metric tons	32	19	16	5	(Z)	(Z)	(Z)
Methyl Cloroform	1,000 metric tons	158	93	77	46	-	(Z)	(Z)
Sulfur hexafluoride	1,000 metric tons	1	1	1	2	2	2	2

- Represents zero.   NA Not available.   (Z) Less than 0.5.   [1] Includes minor sources not shown separately.   [2] Covers principally CFC-11, CFC-12, and CFC-113.   [3] Covers principally HCFC-22.

Source: U.S. Energy Information Administration, *Emissions of Greenhouse Gases in the United States,* annual.

No. 396. Municipal Solid Waste Generation, Recovery, and Disposal: 1980 to 1998

[In millions of tons (151.5 represents 151,500,000), except as indicated. Covers post-consumer residential and commercial solid wastes which comprise the major portion of typical municipal collections. Excludes mining, agricultural and industrial processing, demolition and constru wastes, sewage sludge, and junked autos and obsolete equipment wastes. Based on material-flows estimating procedure and wet weight as generated]

Item and material	1980	1990	1992	1993	1994	1995	1996	1997	1998
Waste generated	151.5	205.2	208.9	211.8	214.2	211.4	209.2	216.4	220.2
Per person per day (lb.)	3.7	4.5	4.5	4.5	4.5	4.4	4.3	4.4	4.5
Materials recovered.	14.5	33.6	40.6	43.8	50.8	54.9	57.3	59.4	62.2
Per person per day (lb.)	0.35	0.7	0.9	0.9	1.1	1.1	1.2	1.2	1.3
Combustion for energy recovery	2.7	29.7	30.5	30.9	31.2	34.5	36.1	36.7	37.0
Per person per day (lb.)	0.06	0.7	0.7	0.7	0.7	0.7	0.7	0.8	0.8
Combustion without energy recovery .	11.0	2.2	2.2	1.6	1.3	1.0	(1)	(1)	(1)
Per person per day (lb.)	0.27	0.05	0.05	0.03	0.03	0.02	(1)	(1)	(1)
Landfill, other disposal.	123.3	139.7	135.7	135.5	130.9	120.9	115.8	120.4	121.1
Per person per day (lb.)	3.0	3.1	2.9	2.9	2.8	2.5	2.4	2.5	2.5
Percent distribution of generation:									
Paper and paperboard	36.1	35.4	35.5	36.6	37.7	38.6	38.1	38.5	38.2
Glass	9.9	6.4	6.3	6.4	6.2	6.1	5.9	5.5	5.7
Metals	9.6	8.1	7.7	7.5	7.6	7.5	7.7	7.7	7.6
Plastics	5.2	8.3	8.8	9.0	9.0	8.9	9.4	9.9	10.2
Rubber and leather	2.8	2.8	2.8	2.7	2.9	2.9	3.0	3.0	3.1
Textiles	1.7	2.8	3.2	3.2	3.4	3.5	3.7	3.8	3.9
Wood	4.4	6.0	5.9	5.8	5.3	4.9	5.2	5.3	5.4
Food wastes.	8.7	10.1	10.1	10.0	10.0	10.3	10.4	10.1	10.0
Yard wastes	18.2	17.1	16.8	15.7	14.7	14.0	13.3	12.8	12.6
Other wastes	3.4	3.0	2.9	3.0	3.2	3.3	3.3	3.4	3.3

[1] Combustion without energy recovery is no longer available separately.

Source: Franklin Associates, Ltd., Prairie Village, KS, *Characterization of Municipal Solid Waste in the United States: 1998.* Prepared for the U.S. Environmental Protection Agency.

No. 397. Generation and Recovery of Selected Materials in Municipal Solid Waste: 1980 to 1998

[In millions of tons (151.5 represents 151,500,000), except as indicated. Covers post-consumer residential and commercial solid wastes which comprise the major portion of typical municipal collections. Excludes mining, agricultural and industrial processing, demolition and construction wastes, sewage sludge, and junked autos and obsolete equipment wastes. Based on material-flows estimating procedure and wet weight as generated]

Item and material	1980	1990	1992	1993	1994	1995	1996	1997	1998
Waste generated, total	**151.5**	**205.2**	**208.9**	**211.8**	**214.2**	**211.4**	**209.2**	**216.4**	**220.2**
Paper and paperboard	54.7	72.7	74.3	77.4	80.8	81.7	79.7	83.3	84.1
Ferrous metals	11.6	12.6	12.1	11.9	11.8	11.6	11.8	12.3	12.4
Aluminum	1.8	2.8	2.9	2.9	3.0	3.0	3.0	3.0	3.1
Other nonferrous metals.	1.1	1.1	1.1	1.1	1.4	1.3	1.3	1.3	1.4
Glass	15.0	13.1	13.1	13.1	13.6	12.8	12.3	12.0	12.5
Plastics	7.9	17.1	18.4	19.0	19.3	18.9	19.8	21.5	22.4
Yard waste	27.5	35.0	35.0	33.3	31.5	29.7	27.9	27.7	27.7
Other wastes	31.9	50.7	52.1	52.5	53.1	52.4	53.5	55.3	56.7
Materials recovered, total	**14.5**	**33.6**	**40.6**	**43.8**	**50.8**	**54.9**	**57.3**	**59.4**	**62.2**
Paper and paperboard	11.9	20.2	24.5	25.5	29.5	32.7	33.2	33.6	35.0
Ferrous metals	0.4	2.6	3.4	3.9	4.0	4.1	4.4	4.7	4.3
Aluminum	0.3	1.0	1.1	1.0	1.2	0.9	0.9	1.0	0.9
Other nonferrous metals.	0.5	0.7	0.7	0.7	1.0	0.8	0.8	0.8	0.9
Glass	0.8	2.6	2.9	3.0	3.1	3.1	3.2	2.9	3.2
Plastics	-	0.4	0.6	0.7	0.9	1.0	1.1	1.1	1.2
Yard waste	-	4.2	5.4	6.9	8.0	9.0	10.4	11.5	12.6
Other wastes	0.6	1.8	2.0	2.1	3.1	3.2	3.3	3.8	4.1
Percent of generation recovered, total	**9.6**	**16.4**	**19.4**	**20.7**	**23.7**	**26.0**	**27.4**	**27.4**	**28.2**
Paper and paperboard	21.8	27.8	33.0	32.9	36.5	40.0	41.6	40.3	41.6
Ferrous metals	3.4	20.4	27.7	32.8	33.9	35.5	37.2	38.4	35.1
Aluminum	16.7	35.9	38.7	35.7	37.8	31.4	31.5	31.6	27.9
Other nonferrous metals.	45.5	66.4	63.4	63.1	73.3	64.3	66.7	65.4	67.4
Glass	5.3	20.0	22.0	22.1	23.3	24.5	25.8	24.3	25.5
Plastics	-	2.2	3.3	3.5	4.9	5.2	5.4	5.2	5.4
Yard waste	-	12.0	15.4	20.8	25.4	30.3	37.2	41.4	45.3
Other wastes	1.9	3.6	3.9	4.0	5.9	6.1	6.2	6.8	7.3

- Represents zero.

Source: Franklin Associates, Ltd., Prairie Village, KS, *Characterization of Municipal Solid Waste in the United States: 1998.* Prepared for the U.S. Environmental Protection Agency.

No. 398. Curbside Recycling Programs—Number and Population Served by Region: 1995 to 1997

[For composition of regions, see map, inside front cover]

Region	Number of programs			Population served [1]					
				Total (1,000)			Percent		
	1995	1996	1997	1995	1996	1997	1995	1996	1997
Total	**7,375**	**8,817**	**8,969**	**121,335**	**134,630**	**136,229**	**46**	**51**	**51**
Northeast	2,210	3,427	3,406	37,256	43,052	43,200	72	83	83
South	1,281	1,318	1,344	31,521	32,798	36,952	34	35	39
Midwest	2,985	3,198	3,357	25,487	27,454	26,970	41	44	43
West	899	874	862	27,071	31,326	29,107	49	55	50

[1] Calculated using population of states reporting data.

Source: Franklin Associates, Ltd., Prairie Village, KS, *Characterization of Municipal Solid Waste in the United States: 1998.* Prepared for the U.S. Environmental Protection Agency. Also in *Biocycle Magazine.*

U.S. Census Bureau, Statistical Abstract of the United States: 2000

Figure 6.1
Waste Recovery of Selected Materials in Municipal Solid Wastes: 1998

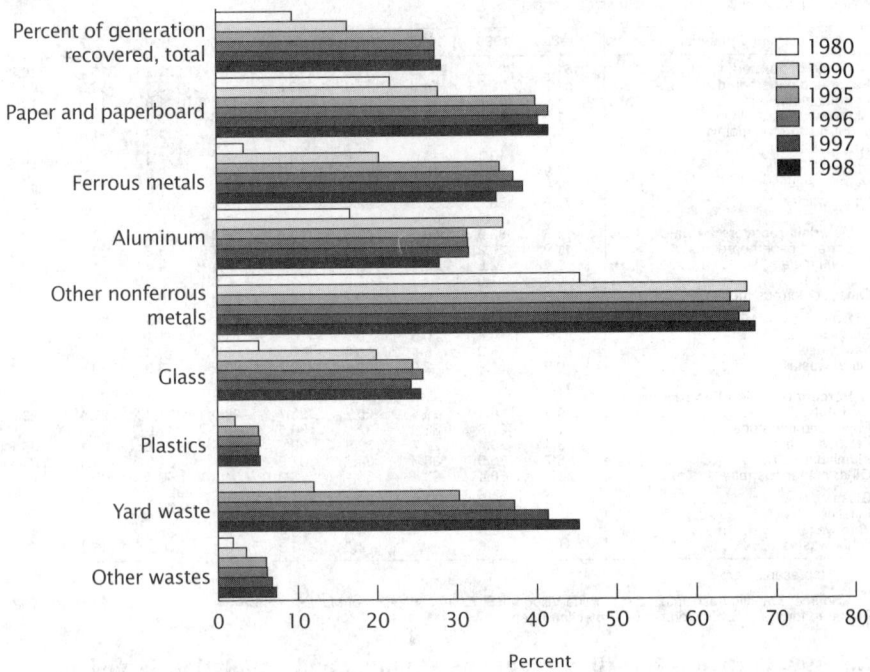

Source: Chart prepared by U.S. Census Bureau. For data, see Table 397.

Figure 6.2
Toxic Chemical Releases, by Industry: 1998

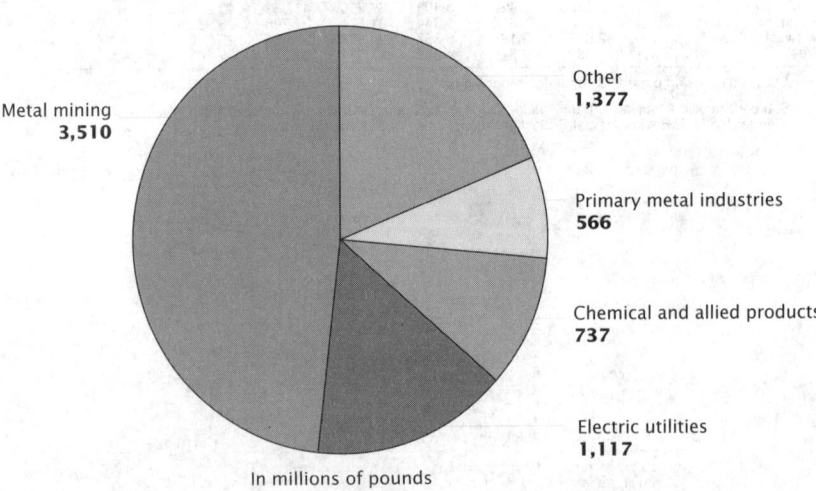

Source: Chart prepared by U.S. Census Bureau. For data, see Table 400.

238 Geography and Environment

No. 399. Toxic Chemical Releases and Transfers by Media: 1988 to 1998

[In millions of pounds (3,396.4 represents 3,396,400,000), except as indicated. Based on reports filed as required by Section 313 of the Emergency Planning and Community Right-to-Know Act (EPCRA, or Title III of the Superfund Amendments and Reauthorization Act of 1986), Public Law 99-499. Owners and operators of facilities that are classified within Standard Classification Code groups 20 through 39, have 10 or more full-time employees, and that manufacture, process, or otherwise uses any listed toxic chemical in quantities greater than the established threshold in the course of a calendar year are covered and required to report]

Media	Core chemicals [1]				Expanded chemical list [2]		
	1988	1996	1997	1998	1996	1997	1998
Total facilities reporting	20,470	20,380	19,999	19,610	22,340	21,927	21,517
Total releases.	**3,396.4**	**1,918.5**	**1,954.0**	**1,856.9**	**2,545.3**	**2,587.0**	**2,496.8**
On-site releases	2,968.4	1,597.6	1,521.2	1,427.0	2,198.0	2,131.2	2,046.6
Air emissions	2,182.6	1,104.9	986.1	920.7	1,470.2	1,336.6	1,257.0
Surface water	164.6	44.6	61.6	44.7	184.7	222.3	223.4
Underground injection	162.0	122.8	131.5	114.6	209.3	221.7	210.6
Releases to land	459.3	325.3	342.0	347.0	333.7	350.6	355.7
Off-site releases	428.0	320.9	432.8	430.0	347.3	455.8	450.1
Total transfers off-site for							
further waste management	(NA)	2,927.2	2,989.4	2,739.5	3,151.3	3,231.8	2,987.8
Transfers to recycling	(NA)	2,154.4	2,144.3	1,945.9	2,200.6	2,189.3	1,989.5
Transfers to energy recovery	(NA)	447.3	469.6	435.7	478.3	507.7	478.8
Transfers to treatment	335.0	185.7	218.6	210.8	226.8	262.4	251.8
Transfers to POTWs [3]	245.4	139.0	156.9	146.1	244.5	272.3	266.7
Other off-site transfers	43.5	0.8	0.0	0.9	1.0	0.0	0.9
Other on-site waste management:							
Recycled on-site	(NA)	6,439.8	6,776.0	7,808.1	7,533.6	8,233.0	9,646.8
Energy recovery on-site	(NA)	2,550.2	2,553.3	2,618.1	2,727.6	2,794.3	2,851.5
Treated on-site	(NA)	4,222.7	4,345.9	4,457.5	5,943.6	6,020.5	6,013.0
Other off-site waste management:							
Recycled off-site	(NA)	2,196.6	2,155.8	2,016.9	2,243.3	2,202.7	2,059.4
Energy recovery off-site	(NA)	486.0	484.0	443.0	512.7	521.8	485.4
Treated off-site	(NA)	364.2	377.3	387.8	511.5	530.9	547.4

NA Not available. [1] Excludes chemicals removed from the list, those added in 1990, 1991, 1994, and 1995, and aluminum oxide, ammonia, hydrochloric acid, and sulfuric acid. Chemicals covered for all reporting years. [2] The Environmental Protection Agency added 286 chemicals and chemical categories to the EPCRA Section 313 list of toxic chemicals. [3] POTW (Publicly Owned Treatment Work) is a wastewater treatment facility that is owned by a state or municipality.

No. 400. Toxic Chemical Releases by Industry: 1998

[In millions of pounds (7,307.3 represents 7,307,300,000), except as indicated. "Original Industries" include owners and operators of facilities that are classified within Standard Classification Code groups 20 through 39, have 10 or more full-time employees, and that manufacture, process, or otherwise uses any listed toxic chemical in quantities greater than the established threshold in the course of a calendar year are covered and required to report. Beginning in 1998, additional industries (listed below as "New Industries") were required to report]

Industry	1987 SIC[1] code	Total facilities (number)	Total on- and off-site releases	Total air emissions	Surface water discharges	On-site land releases Total [2]	Surface impoundments	Total on-site releases	Off-site releases/ transfers off-site to disposal
Total.	(X)	23,487	7,307.3	2,053.5	231.4	4,310.8	1,379.8	6,863.1	444.3
ORIGINAL INDUSTRIES									
Total [3]	(X)	21,517	2,378.8	1,257.0	223.4	355.7	90.2	2,046.6	332.2
Food and kindred products	20	1,995	89.3	63.6	17.1	6.2	0.2	87.0	2.3
Tobacco products	21	21	3.6	3.1	0.2	-	-	3.3	0.3
Textile mill products	22	274	12.0	10.8	0.3	0.2	0.1	11.3	0.7
Apparel and other textile products . .	23	19	0.5	0.5	-	-	-	0.5	-
Lumber and wood products	24	825	34.3	32.5	0.1	0.4	0.1	33.0	1.3
Furniture and fixtures	25	377	17.3	17.2	-	-	-	17.2	0.1
Paper and allied products	26	473	229.9	186.0	21.9	17.1	3.1	225.0	4.9
Printing and publishing	27	225	22.5	22.3	-	-	-	22.3	0.2
Chemical and allied products	28	3,806	737.1	321.7	95.4	73.3	40.7	697.1	39.9
Petroleum and coal products	29	391	63.3	49.0	8.1	0.6	0.3	60.6	2.7
Rubber and misc. plastic products . .	30	1,824	109.7	98.6	-	0.9	-	99.6	10.1
Leather and leather products	31	80	4.8	2.6	0.1	-	-	2.6	2.2
Stone, clay, glass products	32	657	40.4	30.9	0.2	3.2	0.1	34.3	6.1
Primary metal industries	33	1,920	566.4	120.6	53.9	198.0	44.2	373.6	192.8
Fabricated metals products	34	2,897	85.9	61.9	1.3	0.8	-	64.0	21.9
Industrial machinery and equipment .	35	1,117	19.4	14.6	0.1	0.3	-	14.9	4.6
Electronic, electric equipment	36	1,234	29.1	16.6	2.2	0.4	-	19.2	10.0
Transportation equipment	37	1,296	102.5	90.5	0.2	0.4	-	91.1	11.4
Instruments and related products . . .	38	253	12.2	9.6	1.2	0.1	-	10.9	1.3
Miscellaneous	39	316	10.6	9.6	-	0.2	-	9.8	0.7
NEW INDUSTRIES									
Total	(X)	1,970	4,928.5	796.6	8.1	3,955.1	1,289.6	4,816.4	112.0
Metal mining	10	114	3,509.9	4.6	0.5	3,470.5	1,153.8	3,508.6	1.3
Coal mining	12	55	13.3	1.5	0.3	11.5	2.5	13.3	-
Electric utilities	49	612	1,117.1	783.7	6.5	264.2	130.4	1,054.6	62.5
Chemical wholesalers	5169	438	1.6	1.3	-	0.1	-	1.4	0.2
Petroleum bulk terminals	5171	546	4.7	4.3	0.1	0.1	-	4.5	0.2
RCRA/solvent recovery	4953/ 7369	205	281.8	1.3	0.6	208.8	2.9	234.1	47.8

- Represents or rounds to zero. X Not applicable. [1] Standard Industrial Classification, see text, Section 13, Labor Force. [2] Includes items not shown separately. [3] Includes industries with no specific industry identified, not shown separately.
Source of Tables 399 and 400: U.S. Environmental Protection Agency, *1998 Toxics Release Inventory*, EPA report 745-R-98-005.

No. 401. Toxic Releases by State: 1988 to 1998

[In thousands of pounds (3,396.4 represents 3,396,400,000). Excludes delisted chemicals, chemicals added in 1990, 1991, 1994, and 1995, and aluminum oxice, ammonia, hydrochloric acid, and sulfuric acid. See headnote, Table 399]

State and outlying area	Core chemicals 1988	1995	1996	1997	1998	State and outlying area	Core chemicals 1988	1995	1996	1997	1998
Total	3,396.4	1,977.2	1,918.5	1,954.0	1,856.9	MT.........	35.6	42.6	47.2	42.6	50.5
U.S. total...	3,380.9	1,967.1	1,909.3	1,945.6	1,849.4	NE.........	17.1	11.4	8.8	13.9	10.2
AL.........	111.0	100.9	89.9	80.1	75.9	NV.........	2.4	3.4	3.3	4.0	3.7
AK.........	3.7	2.2	1.7	0.8	0.3	NH.........	14.0	2.3	2.2	2.4	2.3
AZ.........	66.3	38.3	45.8	30.6	53.5	NJ.........	48.5	14.1	12.3	13.6	11.5
AR.........	41.2	25.8	30.4	49.1	39.5	NM.........	30.4	43.4	42.7	40.1	23.8
CA.........	110.8	38.2	35.4	28.3	28.2	NY.........	101.4	31.4	27.8	28.7	22.0
CO.........	15.7	3.5	3.2	3.1	3.6	NC.........	132.1	73.3	72.7	63.7	56.6
CT.........	38.7	9.3	7.3	8.5	6.0	ND.........	1.2	1.2	0.8	0.8	1.0
DE.........	8.8	3.0	2.1	2.0	2.3	OH.........	206.0	126.5	123.2	127.0	124.0
DC.........	(Z)	0.1	(Z)	(Z)	(Z)	OK.........	30.6	16.1	15.3	15.2	13.9
FL.........	61.7	52.8	53.9	57.3	41.7	OR.........	21.6	22.3	23.5	24.2	28.0
GA.........	86.7	41.3	41.8	51.9	45.2	PA.........	136.5	97.8	88.2	96.9	89.9
HI.........	0.8	0.6	0.4	0.3	0.3	RI.........	7.8	3.2	2.3	2.0	1.6
ID.........	7.4	12.1	13.9	12.9	13.3	SC.........	66.2	49.1	48.6	47.8	50.0
IL.........	141.2	85.8	82.3	92.0	83.6	SD.........	2.4	1.9	1.4	1.3	1.3
IN.........	185.2	94.0	94.2	105.3	105.5	TN.........	127.0	94.0	90.6	89.9	78.2
IA.........	43.1	22.1	19.1	19.9	24.8	TX.........	322.6	209.0	186.2	179.3	170.0
KS.........	30.6	17.8	17.5	18.9	20.8	UT.........	123.8	69.4	77.7	96.5	99.5
KY.........	66.9	34.1	33.3	35.3	31.1	VT.........	1.8	0.6	0.3	0.3	0.2
LA.........	250.9	125.9	135.4	131.5	120.5	VA.........	112.9	41.0	40.2	40.9	39.5
ME.........	15.6	7.0	5.6	6.4	6.6	WA.........	30.7	22.7	22.3	24.6	24.2
MD.........	20.3	12.0	9.6	9.9	8.8	WV.........	39.7	20.0	17.7	15.3	16.3
MA.........	32.3	8.8	7.0	6.3	6.5	WI.........	62.5	34.8	33.1	33.8	33.8
MI.........	143.5	89.9	81.7	74.6	73.9	WY.........	16.7	1.3	1.4	1.3	1.0
MN.........	56.1	18.4	17.1	15.7	15.0	Guam......	-	(Z)	(Z)	0.0	0.0
MS.........	59.7	40.2	40.6	45.7	40.8	Puerto Rico...	12.9	8.9	7.9	7.2	6.7
MO.........	91.2	50.6	50.1	53.0	48.6	Virgin Island...	2.6	1.2	1.2	1.2	0.9

- Represents zero.   Z Less than 50,000.

Source: U.S. Environmental Protection Agency, *1998 Toxics Release Inventory*.

No. 402. Hazardous Waste Sites on the National Priority List by State: 1999

[As of **December 31**. Includes both proposed and final sites listed on the National Priorities List for the Superfund program as authorized by the Comprehensive Environmental Response, Compensation, and Liability Act of 1980 and the Superfund Amendments and Reauthorization Act of 1986]

State and outlying area	Total sites	Rank	Percent distribution	Federal	Non-Federal	State and outlying area	Total sites	Rank	Percent distribution	Federal	Non-Federal
Total........	1,274	(X)	(X)	166	1,108	Montana.........	11	35	0.9	-	11
						Nebraska	10	38	0.8	1	9
United States ...	1,260	(X)	100.0	163	1,097	Nevada	1	48	0.1	-	1
Alabama........	13	30	1.0	3	10	New Hampshire....	18	21	1.4	1	17
Alaska	7	43	0.6	6	1	New Jersey.......	114	1	9.0	8	106
Arizona.........	10	38	0.8	3	7	New Mexico	11	35	0.9	1	10
Arkansas	12	34	1.0	-	12	New York	86	4	6.8	4	82
California	97	3	7.7	24	73	North Carolina	26	15	2.1	2	24
Colorado........	17	22	1.3	3	14	North Dakota......	-	50	0.0	-	-
Connecticut......	14	29	1.1	1	13	Ohio	36	10	2.9	5	31
Delaware	17	22	1.3	1	16	Oklahoma........	13	30	1.0	1	12
District of Columbia .	1	(X)	0.1	1	-	Oregon.........	10	38	0.8	2	8
Florida.........	51	6	4.0	6	45	Pennsylvania......	98	2	7.8	6	92
Georgia	15	27	1.2	2	13	Rhode Island......	12	32	1.0	2	10
Hawaii	4	45	0.3	3	1	South Carolina.....	26	15	2.1	2	24
Idaho..........	8	41	0.6	2	6	South Dakota	1	48	0.1	1	-
Illinois.........	43	8	3.4	4	39	Tennessee	15	27	1.2	4	11
Indiana.........	29	13	2.3	-	29	Texas...........	36	10	2.9	4	32
Iowa...........	17	22	1.3	1	16	Utah	19	19	1.5	4	15
Kansas.........	11	35	0.9	2	9	Vermont	7	43	0.6	-	7
Kentucky	16	26	1.3	1	15	Virginia.........	29	13	2.3	9	20
Louisiana	17	22	1.3	1	16	Washington.......	46	7	3.7	14	32
Maine..........	12	32	1.0	3	9	West Virginia......	8	41	0.6	2	6
Maryland	19	19	1.5	8	11	Wisconsin........	40	9	3.2	-	40
Massachusetts.....	31	12	2.5	8	23	Wyoming	2	47	0.2	1	1
Michigan........	70	5	5.6	1	69						
Minnesota........	26	15	2.1	2	24	Guam	2	(X)	(X)	1	1
Mississippi	3	46	0.2	-	3	Puerto Rico.......	10	(X)	(X)	-	10
Missouri	25	18	2.0	3	22	Virgin Islands......	2	(X)	(X)	2	-

- Represents zero.   X Not applicable.

Source: U.S. Environmental Protection Agency, *Supplementary Materials: National Priorities List, Proposed Rule*, December 1999.

240   Geography and Environment

No. 403. Environmental Industry—Revenues and Employment by Industry Segment: 1990 to 1999

[59.0 represents $59,000,000,000. 1999 is a projection. Covers approximately 59,000 private and public companies engaged in environmental activities]

Industry segment	Revenue (bil. dol.)					Employment (1,000)				
	1990	1995	1997	1998	1999	1990	1995	1997	1998	1999
Industry total	150.3	179.5	186.1	189.8	197.7	1,174.3	1,327.0	1,351.5	1,357.6	(NA)
Analytical services [1]	1.5	1.2	1.1	1.1	1.1	20.2	14.1	13.0	13.6	(NA)
Wastewater treatment works [2] . . .	20.4	23.4	24.4	25.6	26.3	95.0	101.5	105.7	107.5	(NA)
Solid waste management [3]	26.1	32.5	34.9	36.1	36.9	209.5	243.4	249.3	250.7	(NA)
Hazardous waste management [4] . .	6.3	6.2	5.8	5.7	5.5	56.9	52.5	50.9	46.1	(NA)
Remediation/industrial services . . .	11.1	11.1	11.2	11.0	11.6	107.2	98.1	119.8	113.5	(NA)
Consulting & engineering	12.5	15.5	15.3	15.8	15.9	144.2	180.2	170.1	171.5	(NA)
Water equipment & chemicals	13.5	16.5	18.2	19.1	20.0	97.9	110.2	124.7	128.3	(NA)
Instrument manufacturing	2.0	3.0	3.3	3.3	3.5	18.8	26.2	28.3	27.7	(NA)
Air pollution control equipment [5] . .	13.1	14.8	15.7	16.5	17.1	82.7	107.2	106.7	113.2	(NA)
Waste management equipment [6] . .	8.7	9.9	9.8	9.5	9.7	88.8	93.8	73.2	75.7	(NA)
Process & prevention technology . .	0.4	0.8	0.9	1.0	1.1	8.9	19.5	22.5	26.7	(NA)
Water utilities [7]	19.8	25.3	27.6	28.8	29.4	104.7	118.2	125.7	126.4	(NA)
Resource recovery [8]	13.1	16.9	15.3	13.3	16.4	118.4	136.0	132.8	125.0	(NA)
Environmental energy sources [9] . .	1.8	2.4	2.7	3.0	3.1	21.1	26.1	28.8	31.7	(NA)

NA Not available. [1] Covers environmental laboratory testing and services. [2] Mostly revenues collected by municipal entities. [3] Covers such activities as collection, transportation, transfer stations, disposal, landfill ownership and management for solid waste. [4] Transportation and disposal of hazardous, medical and nuclear waste. [5] Includes stationery and mobile sources. [6] Includes vehicles, containers, liners, processing and remediation equipment. [7] Revenues generated from the sale of water. [8] Revenues generated from the sale of recovered metals, paper, plastic, etc. [9] Includes solar, wind, geothermal and conservation devices.

Source: Environmental Business International, Inc., San Diego, CA, Environmental Business Journal, monthly (copyright).

No. 404. Threatened and Endangered Wildlife and Plant Species—Number: 2000

[As of April. Endangered species: One in danger of becoming extinct throughout all or a significant part of its natural range. Threatened species: One likely to become endangered in the foreseeable future]

Item	Mammals	Birds	Reptiles	Amphibians	Fishes	Snails	Clams	Crustaceans	Insects	Arachnids	Plants
Total listings	339	274	115	27	123	32	71	21	42	6	705
Endangered species, total	**314**	**253**	**79**	**18**	**79**	**21**	**63**	**18**	**34**	**6**	**566**
United States	63	77	14	10	68	20	61	18	30	6	565
Foreign	251	176	65	8	11	1	2	-	4	-	1
Threatened species, total	**25**	**21**	**36**	**9**	**44**	**11**	**8**	**3**	**8**	**-**	**139**
United States	9	15	22	8	44	11	8	3	8	-	139
Foreign	16	6	14	1	-	-	-	-	-	-	-

- Represents zero.

Source: U.S. Fish and Wildlife Service, Endangered Species Technical Bulletin, quarterly.

No. 405. Tornadoes, Floods, Tropical Storms, and Lightning: 1988 to 1998

Weather type	1988	1989	1990	1991	1992	1993	1994	1995	1996	1997	1998
Tornadoes, number [1]	702	856	1,133	1,132	1,298	1,176	1,082	1,235	1,170	1,148	(NA)
Tornado days	156	160	181	179	195	186	199	178	196	196	(NA)
Lives lost, total	32	50	53	39	39	33	69	30	25	67	(NA)
Most in a single tornado	5	21	29	17	12	7	22	6	5	27	(NA)
Floods and flash floods:											
Lives lost	31	85	142	61	62	103	91	80	131	117	(NA)
North Atlantic tropical storms and hurricanes [2]	12	11	14	8	7	8	7	19	13	7	14
Number of hurricanes reaching U.S. mainland	1	3	-	1	1	1	-	2	2	1	3
Total direct deaths from tropical storms and hurricanes	550	84	123	17	28	273	1,175	121	138	4	(NA)
Direct deaths on U.S. mainland .	6	56	10	17	26	9	38	29	33	4	23
Property loss in U.S. (mil. dol.) .	59	7,670	57	1,500	26,500	57	973	3,729	3,600	100	7,299
Lightning:											
Deaths	69	67	74	73	41	43	74	85	52	42	(NA)
Injuries	311	322	252	432	292	295	577	510	309	306	(NA)

- Represents zero. NA Not available. [1] A violent, rotating column of air descending from a cumulonimbus cloud in the form of a tubular- or funnel-shaped cloud, usually characterized by movements along a narrow path and wind speeds from 100 to over 300 miles per hour. Also known as a "twister" or "waterspout." [2] Source: National Hurricane Center, Coral Gables, FL, unpublished data. Tropical storms have maximum winds of 39 to 73 miles per hour; hurricanes have maximum winds of 74 miles per hour or higher.

Source: Except as noted, U.S. National Oceanic and Atmospheric Administration, Storm Data, monthly.

No. 406. Major U.S. Weather Disasters: 1980 to 1999

[1.3 represents $1,300,000,000. Covers only weather related disasters costing $1 billion or more]

Event	Description	Time period	Esti-mated cost (bil. dol.)	Deaths
Hurricane Floyd	Category 2 hurricane in NC, causing severe flooding in NC and some flooding in SC, VA, MD, PA, NY, NJ, DE, RI, CT, MA, and VT.	Sept. 1999	6.0	75
Drought/heat wave	Drought/heatwave over eastern U.S.	Summer 1999	1.0	256
Oklahoma-Kansas tornadoes	Category F4-F5 tornados hit OK, KS, TX, and TN	May 1999	1.0	55
Arkansas-Tennessee tornadoes	Two outbreaks of tornadoes in 6-day period	January 1999	1.3	31
Texas flooding	Severe flooding in southeast Texas from 2 heavy rain events with 10-20 in. totals.	Oct.-Nov. 1998	1.0	31
Hurricane Georges	Category 2 hurricane in Puerto Rico, Florida Keys, and Gulf coasts of LA, MS, AL, and FL.	Sept. 1998	3-4	16
Hurricane Bonnie	Category 3 hurricane in eastern NC and VA	August 1998	1.0	2
Southern drought/heat wave	Severe drought and heat wave from TX/OK eastward to the Carolinas	Summer 1998	6.0	200
Minnesota severe storms/hail.	Very damaging severe thunderstorms with large hail over wide areas of Minnesota	May 1998	1.5	1
Southeast severe weather	Tornadoes and flooding related to strong El Nino in the southeast	Winter/ spring 1998	1.0	Over 130
Northeast ice storm . . .	Intense ice storm hits ME, NH, VT, and NY.	January 1998	1.4	16
Northern plains flooding. .	Severe flooding in Dakotas and Minnesota due to heavy spring snowmelt	April-May 1997	2.0	11
MS and OH valleys flooding and tornadoes .	Tornadoes and severe flooding hit the states of AR, MO, MS, TN, IL, IN, KY, OH, and WV	March 1997	1.0	67
West Coast flooding	Flooding from rains and snowmelt in CA, WA, OR, ID, NV, & MT	Dec. 1996-Jan. 199	2-3	36
Hurricane Fran.	Category 3 hurricane in NC and VA.	Sept. 1996	5.0	37
Southern Plains severe drought	Drought in agricultural areas of TX & OK	Fall 1995-summer 1996	Over 4	(NA)
Pacific Northwest severe flooding	Flooding from heavy rain & snowmelt in OR, WA, ID, and MT	Feb. 1996	1.0	9
Blizzard of '96 followed by flooding	Heavy snowstorm followed by severe flooding in Appalachians, Mid-Atlantic, and Northeast	Jan. 1996	3.0	187
Hurricane Opal	Category 3 hurricane in FL, AL, parts of GA, TN, & Carolinas	Oct. 1995	Over 3	27
Hurricane Marilyn.	Category 2 hurricane in Virgin Islands	Sept. 1995	2.1	13
TX/OK/LA/MS severe weather and flooding. .	Flooding, hail, & tornadoes across TX, OK, parts of LA, MS, Dallas & New Orleans hardest hit	May 1995	5-6	32
California flooding.	Flooding from frequent winter storms across much of CA . .	Jan.-Mar. 1995	3.0	27
Western Fire Season . . .	Severe fire season in western states due to dry weather.	Summer-fall 1994	1.0	(NA)
Texas flooding	Flooding from torrential rain & thunderstorms across southeast TX	Oct. 1994	1.0	19
Tropical Storm Alberto. . .	Flooding due to 10 to 25 inch rain across GA, AL, part of FL	July 1994	1.0	32
Southeast ice storm	Intense ice storm in pts of TX, OK, AR, LA, MS, AL, TN, GA, SC, NC, & VA	Feb. 1994	3.0	9
California wildfires	Out-of-control wildfires over southern CA	Fall 1993	1.0	4
Midwest flooding	Extreme flooding across central U.S.	Summer 1993	15-20	48
Drought/heat wave	Extreme drought/heatwave across southeastern U.S.	Summer 1993	1.0	(NA)
Storm/blizzard	"Storm of the Century" hits entire eastern seaboard	Mar. 1993	3-6	270
Nor'easter of 1992	Slow-moving storm batters northeast U.S. coast, New England hardest hit	Dec. 1992	1-2	19
Hurricane Iniki	Category 4 hurricane hit Hawaiian island of Kauai	Sept. 1992	1.8	7
Hurricane Andrew.	Category 4 hurricane hit FL & LA	Aug. 1992	27.0	58
Oakland Firestorm	Oakland, CA firestorm due to low humidity & high winds . .	Oct. 1991	1.5	25
Hurricane Bob	Category 2 hurricane—mainly coastal NC, Long Island, & New England.	Aug. 1991	1.5	18
TX/OK/LA/AR Flooding . .	Torrential rains cause flooding along Trinity, Red, and Arkansas rivers	May 1990	1.0	13
Hurricane Hugo	Category 4 hurricane hit Puerto Rico & Virgin Islands, devastated NC & SC.	Sept. 1989	Over 9	86
Drought/Heat Wave	Drought/heatwave over central & eastern U.S..	Summer 1988	40.0	5,000-10,000
Hurricane Juan	Category 1 hurricane, flooding most severe problem, hit AL and southeast U.S..	Oct.-Nov. 1985	1.5	63
Hurricane Elena.	Category 3 hurricane across FL to LA	Aug.-Sept. 1985	1.3	4
Florida Freeze	Severe freeze central/northern FL, damage to citrus industry	Jan. 1985	1.2	-
Florida Freeze	Severe freeze central/northern FL, damage to citrus industry	Dec. 1983	2.0	-
Hurricane Alicia	Category 3 hurricane across TX	Aug. 1983	3.0	21
Drought/heat wave	Drought/heatwave over central & eastern U.S..	June-Sept. 1980	20.0	10,000

- Represents zero.   NA Not available or not reported.

Source: U.S. National Oceanic and Atmospheric Administration, National Climatic Data Center. *"Billion Dollar U.S. Weather Disasters,"* (release date April 10, 2000) <http://www.ncdc.noaa.gov/ol/reports/billionz.html>.

242   Geography and Environment

No. 407. Highest and Lowest Temperatures by State Through 1998

State	Highest temperatures Station	Temper-ature (F)	Date	Lowest temperatures Station	Temper-ature (F)	Date
U.S.	Greenland Ranch, CA. .	**134**	**Jul. 10, 1913**	Prospect Creek, AK . . .	**-80**	**Jan. 23, 1971**
AL.	Centerville	112	Sep. 5, 1925	New Market	-27	Jan. 30, 1966
AK.	Fort Yukon	100	[1]Jun. 27, 1915	Prospect Creek Camp . .	-80	Jan. 23, 1971
AZ.	Lake Havasu City	128	Jun. 29, 1994	Hawley Lake	-40	Jan. 7, 1971
AR.	Ozark	120	Aug. 10, 1936	Pond.	-29	Feb. 13, 1905
CA.	Greenland Ranch	134	Jul. 10, 1913	Boca.	-45	Jan. 20, 1937
CO	Bennett	118	Jul. 11, 1888	Maybell	-61	Feb. 1, 1985
CT.	Danbury	106	Jul. 15, 1995	Falls Village	-32	Feb. 16, 1943
DE.	Millsboro	110	Jul. 21, 1930	Millsboro	-17	Jan. 17, 1893
FL.	Monticello	109	Jun. 29, 1931	Tallahassee	-2	Feb. 13, 1899
GA	Greenville	112	Aug. 20, 1983	CCC Camp F-16.	-17	[1]Jan. 27, 1940
HI	Pahala	100	Apr. 27, 1931	Mauna Kea Obs. 111.2. .	12	May 17, 1979
ID	Orofino	118	Jul. 28, 1934	Island Park Dam	-60	Jan. 18, 1943
IL	East St. Louis.	117	Jul. 14, 1954	Elizabeth	-35	[2]Feb. 3, 1996
IN	Collegeville	116	Jul. 14, 1936	New Whiteland	-36	Jan. 19, 1994
IA	Keokuk	118	Jul. 20, 1934	Elkader	-47	[2]Feb. 3, 1996
KS.	Alton (near)	121	[2]Jul. 24, 1936	Lebanon	-40	Feb. 13, 1905
KY.	Greensburg	114	Jul. 28, 1930	Shelbyville	-37	Jan. 19, 1994
LA.	Plain Dealing	114	Aug. 10, 1936	Minden	-16	Feb. 13, 1899
ME	North Bridgton	105	[2]Jul. 10, 1911	Van Buren	-48	Jan. 19, 1925
MD	Cumberland & Frederick.	109	[2]Jul. 10, 1936	Oakland	-40	Jan. 13, 1912
MA	New Bedford & Chester .	107	Aug. 2, 1975	Chester	-35	Jan. 12, 1981
MI	Mio.	112	Jul. 13, 1936	Vanderbilt	-51	Feb. 9, 1934
MN	Moorhead	114	[2]Jul. 6, 1936	Tower	-60	Feb. 2, 1996
MS	Holly Springs	115	Jul. 29, 1930	Corinth	-19	Jan. 30, 1966
MO	Warsaw & Union	118	[2]Jul. 14, 1954	Warsaw	-40	Feb. 13, 1905
MT	Medicine Lake	117	Jul. 5, 1937	Rogers Pass	-70	Jan. 20, 1954
NE.	Minden	118	[2]Jul. 24, 1936	Camp Clarke	-47	Feb. 12, 1899
NV.	Laughlin	125	Jun. 29, 1994	San Jacinto	-50	Jan. 8, 1937
NH	Nashua	106	Jul. 4, 1911	Mt. Washington.	-47	Jan. 29, 1934
NJ	Runyon	110	Jul. 10, 1936	River Vale	-34	Jan. 5, 1904
NM	Waste Isolat Pilot Plt . . .	122	Jun. 27, 1994	Gavilan	-50	Feb. 1, 1951
NY.	Troy	108	Jul. 22, 1926	Old Forge	-52	[2]Feb. 18, 1979
NC	Fayetteville.	110	Aug. 21, 1983	Mt. Mitchell	-34	Jan. 21, 1985
ND	Steele.	121	Jul. 6, 1936	Parshall	-60	Feb. 15, 1936
OH	Gallipolis (near).	113	[2]Jul. 21, 1934	Milligan	-39	Feb. 10, 1899
OK	Tipton	120	[2]Jun. 27, 1994	Watts	-27	Jan. 18, 1930
OR	Pendleton	119	Aug. 10, 1898	Seneca	-54	[2]Feb. 10, 1933
PA.	Phoenixville.	111	[2]Jul. 10, 1936	Smethport	-42	[1]Jan. 5, 1904
RI	Providence.	104	Aug. 2, 1975	Kingston	-23	Jan. 11, 1942
SC.	Camden	111	[2]Jun. 28, 1954	Caesars Head	-19	Jan. 21, 1985
SD.	Gannvalley.	120	Jul. 5, 1936	McIntosh	-58	Feb. 17, 1936
TN.	Perryville	113	[2]Aug. 9, 1930	Mountain City	-32	Dec. 30, 1917
TX.	Seymour	120	Aug. 12, 1936	Seminole	-23	[2]Feb. 8, 1933
UT.	Saint George	117	Jul. 5, 1985	Peter's Sink	-69	Feb. 1, 1985
VT.	Vernon	105	Jul. 4, 1911	Bloomfield	-50	Dec. 30, 1933
VA.	Balcony Falls	110	Jul. 15, 1954	Mtn. Lake Bio. Stn.	-30	Jan. 22, 1985
WA	Ice Harbor Dam	118	[2]Aug. 5, 1961	Mazama & Winthrop . . .	-48	Dec. 30, 1968
WV	Martinsburg	112	[2]Jul. 10, 1936	Lewisburg	-37	Dec. 30, 1917
WI.	Wisconsin Dells	114	Jul. 13, 1936	Couderay.	-55	Feb. 4, 1996
WY	Basin	114	Jul. 12, 1900	Riverside R.S.	-66	Feb. 9, 1933

[1] Estimated.   [2] Also on earlier dates at the same or other places.

Source: U.S. National Oceanic and Atmospheric Administration, <http://www.ncdc.noaa.gov/ol/climate/severeweather/temperatures.html> (released 03 March 2000).

Geography and Environment   243

No. 408. Normal Daily Mean, Maximum, and Minimum Temperatures—Selected Cities

[In **Fahrenheit degrees.** Airport data except as noted. Based on standard 30-year period, 1961 through 1990]

State	Station	Daily mean temperature			Daily maximum temperature			Daily minimum temperature		
		Jan.	July	Annual average	Jan.	July	Annual average	Jan.	July	Annual average
AL	Mobile	49.9	82.3	67.5	59.7	91.3	77.4	40.0	73.2	57.4
AK	Juneau.	24.2	56.0	40.6	29.4	63.9	46.9	19.0	48.1	34.1
AZ	Phoenix	53.6	93.5	72.6	65.9	105.9	85.9	41.2	81.0	59.3
AR	Little Rock.	39.1	81.9	61.8	49.0	92.4	72.5	29.1	71.5	51.0
CA	Los Angeles	56.8	69.1	63.0	65.7	75.3	70.4	47.8	62.8	55.5
	Sacramento	45.2	75.7	60.8	52.7	93.2	73.5	37.7	58.1	48.1
	San Diego.	57.4	71.0	64.2	65.9	76.2	70.8	48.9	65.7	57.6
	San Francisco	48.7	62.7	57.1	55.6	71.6	65.2	41.8	53.9	49.0
CO	Denver.	29.7	73.5	50.3	43.2	88.2	64.2	16.1	58.6	36.2
CT	Hartford	24.6	73.7	49.9	33.2	85.0	60.2	15.8	62.2	39.5
DE	Wilmington	30.6	76.4	54.2	38.7	85.6	63.6	22.4	67.1	44.8
DC	Washington.	34.6	80.0	58.0	42.3	88.5	66.9	26.8	71.4	49.2
FL	Jacksonville.	52.4	81.6	68.0	64.2	91.4	78.9	40.5	71.9	57.1
	Miami.	67.2	82.6	75.9	75.2	89.0	82.8	59.2	76.2	69.0
GA	Atlanta	41.0	78.8	61.3	50.4	88.0	71.2	31.5	69.5	51.3
HI	Honolulu.	72.9	80.5	77.2	80.1	87.5	84.4	65.6	73.5	70.0
ID	Boise	29.0	74.0	50.9	36.4	90.2	62.8	21.6	57.7	39.1
IL	Chicago	21.0	73.2	49.0	29.0	83.7	58.6	12.9	62.6	39.5
	Peoria	21.6	75.5	50.7	29.9	85.7	60.4	13.2	65.4	41.0
IN	Indianapolis.	25.5	75.4	52.3	33.7	85.5	62.1	17.2	65.2	42.4
IA	Des Moines.	19.4	76.6	49.9	28.1	86.7	59.8	10.7	66.5	40.0
KS	Wichita	29.5	81.4	56.2	39.8	92.8	66.7	19.2	69.9	45.0
KY	Louisville	31.7	77.2	56.1	40.3	87.0	66.0	23.2	67.3	46.0
LA	New Orleans	51.3	81.9	68.1	60.8	90.6	77.6	41.8	73.1	58.5
ME	Portland	20.8	68.6	45.4	30.3	78.8	54.9	11.4	58.3	35.8
MD	Baltimore	31.8	77.0	55.1	40.2	87.2	65.0	23.4	66.8	45.2
MA	Boston	28.6	73.5	51.3	35.7	81.8	59.0	21.6	65.1	43.6
MI	Detroit	22.9	72.3	48.6	30.3	83.3	58.1	15.6	61.3	39.0
	Sault Ste. Marie	12.9	63.8	39.7	21.1	76.3	49.6	4.6	51.3	29.8
MN	Duluth	7.0	66.1	38.5	16.2	77.1	47.9	-2.2	55.1	29.0
	Minneapolis-St. Paul. .	11.8	73.6	44.9	20.7	84.0	54.3	2.8	63.1	35.3
MS	Jackson	44.1	81.5	64.2	55.6	92.4	76.4	32.7	70.5	52.0
MO	Kansas City.	25.7	78.5	53.6	34.7	88.7	64.3	16.7	68.2	43.7
	St. Louis.	29.3	79.8	56.1	37.7	89.3	65.4	20.8	70.4	46.7
MT	Great Falls	21.2	68.2	44.8	30.6	83.3	56.4	11.6	53.2	33.1
NE	Omaha.	21.1	76.9	50.6	31.3	87.9	61.5	10.9	65.9	39.5
NV	Reno	32.9	71.6	50.8	45.1	91.9	66.8	20.7	51.3	34.7
NH	Concord	18.6	69.5	45.1	29.8	82.4	57.0	7.4	56.5	33.1
NJ	Atlantic City	30.9	74.7	53.0	40.4	84.5	63.2	21.4	64.8	42.8
NM	Albuquerque	34.2	78.5	56.2	46.8	92.5	70.1	21.7	64.4	42.2
NY	Albany	20.6	71.8	47.4	30.2	84.0	58.1	11.0	59.6	36.6
	Buffalo	23.6	71.1	47.7	30.2	80.2	55.8	17.0	61.9	39.5
	New York [1]	31.5	76.8	54.7	37.6	85.2	62.3	25.3	68.4	47.1
NC	Charlotte.	39.3	79.3	60.1	49.0	88.9	70.4	29.6	69.6	49.7
	Raleigh.	38.9	78.1	59.3	48.9	88.0	70.1	28.8	68.1	48.4
ND	Bismarck	9.2	70.4	41.6	20.2	84.4	53.8	-1.7	56.4	29.4
OH	Cincinnati	28.1	75.1	53.2	36.6	85.5	63.2	19.5	64.8	43.2
	Cleveland	24.8	71.9	49.6	31.9	82.4	58.7	17.6	61.4	40.5
	Columbus	26.4	73.2	51.4	34.1	83.7	61.2	18.5	62.7	41.6
OK	Oklahoma City.	35.9	82.0	60.0	46.7	93.4	71.1	25.2	70.6	48.8
OR	Portland	39.6	68.2	53.6	45.4	79.9	62.6	33.7	56.5	44.5
PA	Philadelphia	30.4	76.7	54.3	37.9	86.1	63.4	22.8	67.2	45.1
	Pittsburgh	26.1	72.1	50.3	33.7	82.6	59.9	18.5	61.6	40.7
RI	Providence	27.9	72.7	50.4	36.6	82.1	59.8	19.1	63.2	41.0
SC	Columbia	43.8	80.8	63.1	55.3	91.6	75.1	32.1	70.0	50.9
SD	Sioux Falls	13.8	74.3	45.5	24.3	86.3	56.8	3.3	62.3	34.2
TN	Memphis.	39.7	82.6	62.3	48.5	92.3	72.1	30.9	72.9	52.4
	Nashville.	36.2	79.3	59.1	45.9	89.5	69.8	26.5	68.9	48.4
TX	Dallas-Fort Worth	43.4	85.3	65.4	54.1	96.5	76.3	32.7	74.1	54.6
	El Paso	42.8	82.3	63.2	56.1	96.1	77.5	29.4	68.4	49.0
	Houston.	50.4	82.6	67.9	61.0	92.7	78.6	39.7	72.4	57.3
UT	Salt Lake City	27.9	77.9	52.0	36.4	92.2	63.6	19.3	63.7	40.3
VT	Burlington	16.3	70.5	44.6	25.1	81.2	54.0	7.5	59.7	35.2
VA	Norfolk	39.1	78.2	59.2	47.3	86.4	67.8	30.9	70.0	50.6
	Richmond.	35.7	78.0	57.7	45.7	88.4	68.8	25.7	67.5	46.6
WA	Seattle-Tacoma	40.1	65.2	52.0	45.0	75.2	59.4	35.2	55.2	44.6
	Spokane.	27.1	68.8	47.3	33.2	83.1	57.5	20.8	54.4	36.9
WV	Charleston	32.1	75.1	55.0	41.2	85.7	65.8	23.0	64.4	44.2
WI	Milwaukee.	18.9	70.9	46.1	26.1	79.9	54.3	11.6	62.0	37.9
WY	Cheyenne	26.5	68.4	45.6	37.7	82.2	58.0	15.2	54.6	33.2
PR	San Juan	77.0	82.6	80.2	83.2	88.5	86.4	70.8	76.8	74.0

[1] City office data.

Source: U.S. National Oceanic and Atmospheric Administration, *Climatography of the United States,* No. 81.

No. 409. Highest Temperature of Record—Selected Cities

[**In Fahrenheit degrees.** Airport data, except as noted. For period of record through 1998]

State	Station	Length of record (yr.)	Jan.	Feb.	Mar.	Apr.	May	June	July	Aug.	Sept.	Oct.	Nov.	Dec.	Annual
AL	Mobile.	57	84	82	90	94	100	102	104	102	99	93	87	81	104
AK	Juneau	54	57	57	61	72	82	86	90	83	73	61	56	54	90
AZ	Phoenix.	61	88	92	100	105	113	122	121	116	118	107	93	88	122
AR	Little Rock	57	83	85	91	95	98	105	112	108	106	97	86	80	112
CA	Los Angeles	63	88	92	95	102	97	104	97	98	110	106	101	94	110
	Sacramento	48	70	76	88	95	105	115	114	110	108	101	87	72	115
	San Diego	58	88	90	93	98	96	101	95	98	111	107	97	88	111
	San Francisco	71	72	78	85	92	97	106	105	100	103	99	85	75	106
CO	Denver	61	73	76	84	90	96	104	104	101	97	89	79	75	104
CT	Hartford.	44	65	73	89	96	99	100	102	101	99	91	81	76	102
DE	Wilmington.	51	75	78	86	94	96	100	102	101	100	91	85	75	102
DC	Washington	57	79	82	89	95	99	101	104	105	101	94	86	79	105
FL	Jacksonville	57	85	88	91	95	100	103	105	102	100	96	88	84	105
	Miami	56	88	89	92	96	96	98	98	98	97	95	89	87	98
GA	Atlanta	50	79	80	89	93	95	101	105	102	98	95	84	79	105
HI	Honolulu	29	88	88	88	91	93	92	94	93	95	94	93	89	95
ID	Boise	59	63	71	81	92	98	109	111	110	102	94	74	65	111
IL	Chicago.	40	65	71	88	91	93	104	104	101	99	91	78	71	104
	Peoria.	59	70	72	86	92	93	105	103	103	100	90	81	71	105
IN	Indianapolis	59	71	74	85	89	93	102	104	102	100	90	81	74	104
IA	Des Moines	59	65	73	91	93	98	103	105	108	101	95	76	69	108
KS	Wichita	46	75	87	89	96	100	110	113	110	107	95	85	83	113
KY	Louisville	51	77	77	86	91	95	102	105	101	104	92	84	76	105
LA	New Orleans	52	83	85	89	92	96	100	101	102	101	94	87	84	102
ME	Portland	58	64	64	88	85	94	98	99	103	95	88	74	71	103
MD	Baltimore.	48	75	79	89	94	98	101	104	105	100	92	83	77	105
MA	Boston	47	66	70	89	94	95	100	102	102	100	90	79	76	102
MI	Detroit.	40	62	65	81	89	93	104	102	100	98	91	77	69	104
	Sault Ste. Marie . . .	58	45	47	75	85	89	93	97	98	95	80	67	60	98
MN	Duluth	57	52	55	78	88	90	94	97	97	95	86	70	55	97
	Minneapolis-St. Paul	60	58	60	83	95	96	102	105	102	98	90	75	68	105
MS	Jackson.	35	82	85	89	94	99	105	106	102	104	95	88	84	106
MO	Kansas City	26	69	77	86	93	95	105	107	109	102	92	82	70	109
	St. Louis	41	76	85	89	93	94	102	107	107	104	94	85	76	107
MT	Great Falls.	61	67	70	78	89	93	101	105	106	98	91	76	69	106
NE	Omaha	62	69	78	89	97	99	105	114	110	104	96	80	72	114
NV	Reno	57	70	75	83	89	96	103	104	105	101	91	77	70	105
NH	Concord	57	68	67	89	95	97	98	102	101	98	90	80	73	102
NJ	Atlantic City	55	78	75	87	94	99	106	104	102	99	90	84	77	106
NM	Albuquerque.	59	69	76	85	89	98	107	105	101	100	91	77	72	107
NY	Albany	52	65	68	89	92	94	99	100	99	100	89	82	71	100
	Buffalo	55	72	70	81	94	90	96	97	99	98	87	80	74	99
	New York [1]	130	72	75	86	96	99	101	106	104	102	94	84	75	106
NC	Charlotte	59	78	81	90	93	100	103	103	103	104	98	85	78	104
	Raleigh	54	79	84	92	95	97	104	105	105	104	98	88	80	105
ND	Bismarck	59	62	69	81	93	98	107	109	109	105	95	75	65	109
OH	Cincinnati.	37	69	73	84	89	93	102	103	102	98	88	81	75	103
	Cleveland	57	73	70	83	88	92	104	103	102	101	90	82	77	104
	Columbus	59	74	73	85	89	94	102	100	101	100	90	80	76	102
OK	Oklahoma City	45	80	92	93	100	104	105	110	110	107	96	87	86	110
OR	Portland	58	63	71	80	90	100	100	107	107	105	92	73	65	107
PA	Philadelphia	57	74	74	87	94	97	100	104	101	100	96	81	73	104
	Pittsburgh	46	69	73	82	89	91	98	103	100	97	87	82	74	103
RI	Providence.	45	69	72	85	98	95	97	102	104	100	86	78	77	104
SC	Columbia.	51	84	84	91	94	101	107	107	107	101	101	90	83	107
SD	Sioux Falls.	53	66	70	87	94	100	110	108	108	104	94	76	63	110
TN	Memphis	57	78	81	85	94	99	104	108	105	103	95	85	81	108
	Nashville	59	78	84	86	91	97	106	107	104	105	94	84	79	107
TX	Dallas-Fort Worth . .	45	88	95	96	95	103	113	110	108	108	102	89	88	113
	El Paso	59	80	83	89	98	104	114	112	108	104	96	87	80	114
	Houston	29	84	91	91	95	99	103	104	107	102	96	89	85	107
UT	Salt Lake City.	70	62	69	78	86	95	104	107	106	100	89	75	69	107
VT	Burlington	55	66	62	84	91	93	100	100	101	94	85	75	67	101
VA	Norfolk	50	78	82	88	97	100	101	103	104	99	95	86	80	104
	Richmond	69	80	83	93	96	100	104	105	102	103	99	86	81	105
WA	Seattle-Tacoma. . . .	54	64	70	75	85	93	96	100	99	98	89	74	64	100
	Spokane	51	59	63	71	90	96	101	103	108	98	86	67	56	108
WV	Charleston.	51	79	78	89	94	93	98	104	101	102	92	85	80	104
WI	Milwaukee	58	62	65	82	91	93	101	103	103	98	89	77	64	103
WY	Cheyenne	63	66	71	74	83	90	100	100	100	96	95	83	73	100
PR	San Juan.	44	92	96	96	97	96	97	95	97	97	98	96	94	98

[1] City office data.

Source: U.S. National Oceanic and Atmospheric Administration, *Comparative Climatic Data*, annual.

U.S. Census Bureau, Statistical Abstract of the United States: 2000

No. 410. Lowest Temperature of Record—Selected Cities

[In Fahrenheit degrees. Airport data, except as noted. For period of record through 1998]

State	Station	Length of record (yr.)	Jan.	Feb.	Mar.	Apr.	May	June	July	Aug.	Sept.	Oct.	Nov.	Dec.	Annual
AL	Mobile	57	3	11	21	32	43	49	60	59	42	30	22	8	3
AK	Juneau	54	-22	-22	-15	6	25	31	36	27	23	11	-5	-21	-22
AZ	Phoenix	61	17	22	25	32	40	50	61	60	47	34	25	22	17
AR	Little Rock	57	-4	-5	11	28	40	46	54	52	37	29	17	-1	-5
CA	Los Angeles	63	23	32	34	39	43	48	49	51	47	41	34	32	23
	Sacramento	48	23	23	26	32	36	41	48	49	43	36	26	18	18
	San Diego	58	29	36	39	41	48	51	55	57	51	43	38	34	29
	San Francisco	71	24	25	30	31	36	41	43	42	38	34	25	20	20
CO	Denver	61	-25	-30	-11	-2	22	30	43	41	17	3	-8	-25	-30
CT	Hartford	44	-26	-21	-6	9	28	37	44	36	30	17	1	-14	-26
DE	Wilmington	51	-14	-6	2	18	30	41	48	43	36	24	14	-7	-14
DC	Washington	57	-5	4	11	24	34	47	54	49	39	29	16	1	-5
FL	Jacksonville	57	7	19	23	34	45	47	61	63	48	36	21	11	7
	Miami	56	30	32	32	46	53	60	69	68	68	51	39	30	30
GA	Atlanta	50	-8	5	10	26	37	46	53	55	36	28	3	-	-8
HI	Honolulu	29	53	53	55	57	60	65	66	67	66	61	57	54	53
ID	Boise	59	-17	-15	6	19	22	31	35	34	23	11	-3	-25	-25
IL	Chicago	40	-27	-19	-8	7	24	36	40	41	28	17	1	-25	-27
	Peoria	59	-25	-19	-10	14	25	39	47	41	26	19	-2	-23	-25
IN	Indianapolis	59	-27	-21	-7	16	28	37	44	41	28	17	-2	-23	-27
IA	Des Moines	59	-24	-26	-22	9	30	38	47	40	26	14	-4	-22	-26
KS	Wichita	46	-12	-21	-2	15	31	43	51	48	31	18	1	-16	-21
KY	Louisville	51	-22	-19	-1	22	31	42	50	46	33	23	-1	-15	-22
LA	New Orleans	52	14	16	25	32	41	50	60	60	42	35	24	11	11
ME	Portland	58	-26	-39	-21	8	23	33	40	33	23	15	3	-21	-39
MD	Baltimore	48	-7	-3	6	20	32	40	50	45	35	25	13	-	-7
MA	Boston	47	-12	-4	6	16	34	45	50	47	38	28	15	-7	-12
MI	Detroit	40	-21	-15	-4	10	25	36	41	38	29	17	9	-10	-21
	Sault Ste. Marie	58	-36	-35	-24	-2	18	26	36	29	25	16	-10	-31	-36
MN	Duluth	57	-39	-39	-29	-5	17	27	35	32	22	8	-23	-34	-39
	Minneapolis-St. Paul	60	-34	-32	-32	2	18	34	43	39	26	13	-17	-29	-34
MS	Jackson	35	2	10	15	27	38	47	51	55	35	26	17	4	2
MO	Kansas City	26	-17	-19	-10	12	30	42	51	43	31	17	1	-23	-23
	St. Louis	41	-18	-12	-5	22	31	43	51	47	36	23	1	-16	-18
MT	Great Falls	61	-37	-35	-29	-6	15	31	40	30	20	-11	-25	-43	-43
NE	Omaha	62	-23	-21	-16	5	27	38	44	43	25	13	-9	-23	-23
NV	Reno	57	-16	-16	-2	13	18	25	33	24	20	8	1	-16	-16
NH	Concord	57	-33	-37	-16	8	21	30	35	29	21	10	-5	-22	-37
NJ	Atlantic City	55	-10	-11	5	12	25	37	42	40	32	20	10	-7	-11
NM	Albuquerque	59	-17	-5	8	19	28	40	52	50	37	21	-7	-7	-17
NY	Albany	52	-28	-21	-21	10	26	36	40	34	24	16	5	-22	-28
	Buffalo	55	-16	-20	-7	12	26	35	43	38	32	20	9	-10	-20
	New York [1]	130	-6	-15	3	12	32	44	52	50	39	28	5	-13	-15
NC	Charlotte	59	-5	5	4	24	32	45	53	53	39	24	11	2	-5
	Raleigh	54	-9	-	11	23	31	38	48	46	37	19	11	4	-9
ND	Bismarck	59	-44	-43	-31	-12	15	30	35	33	11	-10	-30	-43	-44
OH	Cincinnati	37	-25	-11	-11	15	27	39	47	43	31	16	1	-20	-25
	Cleveland	57	-20	-15	-5	10	25	31	41	38	32	19	3	-15	-20
	Columbus	59	-22	-13	-6	14	25	35	43	39	31	20	5	-17	-22
OK	Oklahoma City	45	-4	-3	3	20	37	47	53	51	36	16	11	-8	-8
OR	Portland	58	-2	-3	19	29	29	39	43	44	34	26	13	6	-3
PA	Philadelphia	57	-7	-4	7	19	28	44	51	44	35	25	15	1	-7
	Pittsburgh	46	-22	-12	-1	14	26	34	42	39	31	16	-1	-12	-22
RI	Providence	45	-13	-7	1	14	29	41	48	40	33	20	6	-10	-13
SC	Columbia	51	-1	5	4	26	34	44	54	53	40	23	12	4	-1
SD	Sioux Falls	53	-36	-31	-23	5	17	33	38	34	22	9	-17	-28	-36
TN	Memphis	57	-4	-11	12	29	38	48	52	48	36	25	9	-13	-13
	Nashville	59	-17	-13	2	23	34	42	51	47	36	26	-1	-10	-17
TX	Dallas-Fort Worth	45	4	7	15	29	41	51	59	56	43	29	20	-1	-1
	El Paso	59	-8	8	14	23	31	46	57	56	41	25	1	5	-8
	Houston	29	12	20	22	31	44	52	62	60	48	29	19	7	7
UT	Salt Lake City	70	-22	-30	2	14	25	35	40	37	27	16	-14	-21	-30
VT	Burlington	55	-30	-30	-20	2	24	33	39	35	25	15	-2	-26	-30
VA	Norfolk	50	-3	8	18	28	36	45	54	49	45	27	20	7	-3
	Richmond	69	-12	-10	11	23	31	40	51	46	35	21	10	-1	-12
WA	Seattle-Tacoma	54	-	1	11	29	28	38	43	44	35	28	6	6	-
	Spokane	51	-22	-24	-7	17	24	33	37	35	24	10	-21	-25	-25
WV	Charleston	51	-16	-12	-	19	26	33	46	41	34	17	6	-12	-16
WI	Milwaukee	58	-26	-26	-10	12	21	33	40	44	28	18	-5	-20	-26
WY	Cheyenne	63	-29	-34	-21	-8	16	25	38	36	8	-1	-16	-28	-34
PR	San Juan	44	61	62	60	64	66	69	69	70	69	67	66	63	60

- Represents zero.   [1] City office data.

Source: U.S. National Oceanic and Atmospheric Administration, *Comparative Climatic Data*, annual.

No. 411. Normal Monthly and Annual Precipitation—Selected Cities

[**In inches.** Airport data, except as noted. Based on standard 30-year period, 1961 through 1990]

State	Station	Jan.	Feb.	Mar.	Apr.	May	June	July	Aug.	Sept.	Oct.	Nov.	Dec.	Annual
AL	Mobile.	4.76	5.46	6.41	4.48	5.74	5.04	6.85	6.96	5.91	2.94	4.10	5.31	63.96
AK	Juneau	4.54	3.75	3.28	2.77	3.42	3.15	4.16	5.32	6.73	7.84	4.91	4.44	54.31
AZ	Phoenix.	0.67	0.68	0.88	0.22	0.12	0.13	0.83	0.96	0.86	0.65	0.66	1.00	7.66
AR	Little Rock	3.42	3.61	4.91	5.49	5.17	3.57	3.60	3.26	4.05	3.75	5.20	4.83	50.86
CA	Los Angeles	2.40	2.51	1.98	0.72	0.14	0.03	0.01	0.15	0.31	0.34	1.76	1.66	12.01
	Sacramento	3.73	2.87	2.57	1.16	0.27	0.12	0.05	0.07	0.37	1.08	2.72	2.51	17.52
	San Diego	1.80	1.53	1.77	0.79	0.19	0.07	0.02	0.10	0.24	0.37	1.45	1.57	9.90
	San Francisco	4.35	3.17	3.06	1.37	0.19	0.11	0.03	0.05	0.20	1.22	2.86	3.09	19.70
CO	Denver	0.50	0.57	1.28	1.71	2.40	1.79	1.91	1.51	1.24	0.98	0.87	0.64	15.40
CT	Hartford.	3.41	3.23	3.63	3.85	4.12	3.75	3.19	3.65	3.79	3.57	4.04	3.91	44.14
DE	Wilmington.	3.03	2.91	3.43	3.39	3.84	3.55	4.23	3.40	3.43	2.88	3.27	3.48	40.84
DC	Washington	2.72	2.71	3.17	2.71	3.66	3.38	3.80	3.91	3.31	3.02	3.12	3.12	38.63
FL	Jacksonville	3.31	3.93	3.68	2.77	3.55	5.69	5.60	7.93	7.05	2.90	2.19	2.72	51.32
	Miami	2.01	2.08	2.39	2.85	6.21	9.33	5.70	7.58	7.63	5.64	2.66	1.83	55.91
GA	Atlanta	4.75	4.81	5.77	4.26	4.29	3.56	5.01	3.66	3.42	3.05	3.86	4.33	50.77
HI	Honolulu	3.55	2.21	2.20	1.54	1.13	0.50	0.59	0.44	0.78	2.28	3.00	3.80	22.02
ID	Boise	1.45	1.07	1.29	1.24	1.08	0.81	0.35	0.43	0.80	0.75	1.48	1.36	12.11
IL	Chicago.	1.53	1.36	2.69	3.64	3.32	3.78	3.66	4.22	3.82	2.41	2.92	2.47	35.82
	Peoria.	1.51	1.42	2.91	3.77	3.70	3.99	4.20	3.10	3.87	2.65	2.69	2.44	36.25
IN	Indianapolis	2.32	2.46	3.79	3.70	4.00	3.49	4.47	3.64	2.87	2.63	3.23	3.34	39.94
IA	Des Moines	0.96	1.11	2.33	3.36	3.66	4.46	3.78	4.20	3.53	2.62	1.79	1.32	33.12
KS	Wichita	0.79	0.96	2.43	2.38	3.81	4.31	3.13	3.02	3.49	2.22	1.59	1.20	29.33
KY	Louisville	2.86	3.30	4.66	4.23	4.62	3.46	4.51	3.54	3.16	2.71	3.70	3.64	44.39
LA	New Orleans	5.05	6.01	4.90	4.50	4.56	5.84	6.12	6.17	5.51	3.05	4.42	5.75	61.88
ME	Portland	3.53	3.33	3.67	4.08	3.62	3.44	3.09	2.87	3.09	3.90	5.17	4.55	44.34
MD	Baltimore.	3.05	3.12	3.38	3.09	3.72	3.67	3.69	3.92	3.41	2.98	3.32	3.41	40.76
MA	Boston	3.59	3.62	3.69	3.60	3.25	3.09	2.84	3.24	3.06	3.30	4.22	4.01	41.51
MI	Detroit.	1.76	1.74	2.55	2.95	2.92	3.61	3.18	3.43	2.89	2.10	2.67	2.82	32.62
	Sault Ste. Marie . . .	2.42	1.74	2.30	2.35	2.71	3.14	2.71	3.61	3.69	3.23	3.45	2.88	34.23
MN	Duluth.	1.22	0.80	1.91	2.25	3.03	3.82	3.61	3.99	3.84	2.49	1.80	1.24	30.00
	Minneapolis-St. Paul	0.95	0.88	1.94	2.42	3.39	4.05	3.53	3.62	2.72	2.19	1.55	1.08	28.32
MS	Jackson.	5.24	4.70	5.82	5.57	5.05	3.18	4.51	3.77	3.55	3.26	4.81	5.91	55.37
MO	Kansas City	1.09	1.10	2.51	3.12	5.04	4.72	4.38	4.01	4.86	3.29	1.92	1.58	37.62
	St. Louis	1.81	2.12	3.58	3.50	3.97	3.72	3.85	2.85	3.12	2.68	3.28	3.03	37.51
MT	Great Falls.	0.91	0.57	1.10	1.41	2.52	2.39	1.24	1.54	1.24	0.78	0.66	0.85	15.21
NE	Omaha	0.74	0.77	2.04	2.66	4.52	3.87	3.51	3.24	3.72	2.28	1.49	1.02	29.86
NV	Reno	1.07	0.99	0.71	0.38	0.69	0.46	0.28	0.32	0.39	0.38	0.87	0.99	7.53
NH	Concord	2.51	2.53	2.92	2.91	3.14	3.15	3.23	3.32	2.81	3.23	3.66	3.16	36.37
NJ	Atlantic City	3.46	3.06	3.62	3.56	3.33	2.64	3.83	4.14	2.93	2.82	3.58	3.32	40.29
NM	Albuquerque.	0.44	0.46	0.54	0.52	0.50	0.59	1.37	1.64	1.00	0.89	0.43	0.50	8.88
NY	Albany	2.36	2.27	2.93	2.99	3.41	3.62	3.18	3.47	2.95	2.83	3.23	2.93	36.17
	Buffalo	2.70	2.31	2.68	2.87	3.14	3.55	3.08	4.17	3.49	3.09	3.83	3.67	38.58
	New York [1]	3.42	3.27	4.08	4.20	4.42	3.67	4.35	4.01	3.89	3.56	4.47	3.91	47.25
NC	Charlotte	3.71	3.84	4.43	2.68	3.82	3.39	3.92	3.73	3.50	3.36	3.23	3.48	43.09
	Raleigh	3.48	3.69	3.77	2.59	3.92	3.68	4.01	4.02	3.19	2.86	2.98	3.24	41.43
ND	Bismarck	0.45	0.43	0.77	1.67	2.18	2.72	2.14	1.72	1.49	0.90	0.49	0.51	15.47
OH	Cincinnati.	2.59	2.69	4.24	3.75	4.28	3.84	4.24	3.35	2.88	2.86	3.46	3.15	41.33
	Cleveland	2.04	2.19	2.91	3.14	3.49	3.70	3.52	3.40	3.44	2.54	3.17	3.09	36.63
	Columbus	2.18	2.24	3.27	3.21	3.93	4.04	4.31	3.72	2.96	2.15	3.22	2.86	38.09
OK	Oklahoma City	1.13	1.56	2.71	2.77	5.22	4.31	2.61	2.60	3.84	3.23	1.98	1.40	33.36
OR	Portland	5.35	3.85	3.56	2.39	2.06	1.48	0.63	1.09	1.75	2.67	5.34	6.13	36.30
PA	Philadelphia	3.21	2.79	3.46	3.62	3.75	3.74	4.28	3.80	3.42	2.62	3.34	3.38	41.41
	Pittsburgh	2.54	2.39	3.41	3.15	3.59	3.71	3.75	3.21	2.97	2.36	2.85	2.92	36.85
RI	Providence.	3.88	3.61	4.05	4.11	3.76	3.33	3.18	3.63	3.48	·3.69	4.43	4.38	45.53
SC	Columbia	4.42	4.12	4.82	3.28	3.68	4.80	5.50	6.09	3.67	3.04	2.90	3.59	49.91
SD	Sioux Falls.	0.51	0.64	1.64	2.52	3.03	3.40	2.68	2.85	3.02	1.78	1.09	0.70	23.86
TN	Memphis	3.73	4.35	5.41	5.46	4.98	3.57	3.79	3.43	3.53	3.01	5.10	5.74	52.10
	Nashville	3.58	3.81	4.85	4.37	4.88	3.57	3.97	3.46	3.46	2.62	4.12	4.61	47.30
TX	Dallas-Fort Worth . .	1.83	2.18	2.77	3.50	4.88	2.98	2.31	2.21	3.39	3.52	2.29	1.84	33.70
	El Paso	0.40	0.41	0.29	0.20	0.25	0.67	1.54	1.58	1.70	0.76	0.44	0.57	8.81
	Houston	3.29	2.96	2.92	3.21	5.24	4.96	3.60	3.49	4.89	4.27	3.79	3.45	46.07
UT	Salt Lake City.	1.11	1.23	1.91	2.12	1.80	0.93	0.81	0.86	1.28	1.44	1.29	1.40	16.18
VT	Burlington	1.82	1.63	2.23	2.76	3.12	3.47	3.65	4.06	3.30	2.88	3.13	2.42	34.47
VA	Norfolk	3.78	3.47	3.70	3.06	3.81	3.82	5.06	4.81	3.90	3.15	2.85	3.23	44.64
	Richmond	3.24	3.16	3.61	2.96	3.84	3.62	5.03	4.40	3.34	3.53	3.17	3.26	43.16
WA	Seattle-Tacoma. . . .	5.38	3.99	3.54	2.33	1.70	1.50	0.76	1.14	1.88	3.23	5.83	5.91	37.19
	Spokane	1.98	1.49	1.49	1.18	1.41	1.26	0.67	0.72	0.73	0.99	2.15	2.42	16.49
WV	Charleston	2.91	3.04	3.63	3.31	3.94	3.59	4.99	4.01	3.24	2.89	3.59	3.39	42.53
WI	Milwaukee	1.60	1.45	2.67	3.50	2.84	3.24	3.47	3.53	3.38	2.41	2.51	2.33	32.93
WY	Cheyenne	0.40	0.39	1.03	1.37	2.39	2.08	2.09	1.69	1.27	0.74	0.53	0.42	14.40
PR	San Juan.	2.81	2.15	2.35	3.76	5.93	4.00	4.37	5.32	5.28	5.71	5.94	4.72	52.34

[1] City office data.

Source: U.S. National Oceanic and Atmospheric Administration, *Climatography of the United States*, No. 81.

U.S. Census Bureau, Statistical Abstract of the United States: 2000

No. 412. Average Number of Days With Precipitation of .01 Inch or More—Selected Cities

[Airport data, except as noted. For period of record through 1998]

State	Station	Length of record (yr.)	Jan.	Feb.	Mar.	Apr.	May	June	July	Aug.	Sept.	Oct.	Nov.	Dec.	Annual
AL	Mobile.........	57	11	10	10	8	8	11	16	14	10	6	8	10	122
AK	Juneau	54	18	17	18	17	17	15	17	18	20	23	20	21	222
AZ	Phoenix........	59	4	4	4	2	1	1	4	5	3	3	3	4	36
AR	Little Rock	56	10	9	10	10	10	8	8	7	7	7	8	9	105
CA	Los Angeles......	63	6	6	6	3	1	1	1	(Z)	1	2	3	5	35
	Sacramento	59	10	9	9	5	3	1	(Z)	(Z)	1	3	7	9	58
	San Diego	58	7	6	7	4	2	1	(Z)	-	1	2	4	6	42
	San Francisco	71	11	10	10	6	3	1	(Z)	(Z)	1	4	7	10	63
CO	Denver	61	6	6	9	9	11	9	9	9	6	5	6	5	89
CT	Hartford........	44	11	10	12	11	12	11	10	10	10	9	11	12	128
DE	Wilmington	51	11	9	11	11	11	10	9	9	8	8	9	10	117
DC	Washington	57	10	9	11	10	11	10	10	9	8	7	9	9	113
FL	Jacksonville	57	8	8	8	6	8	12	15	15	13	9	7	8	116
	Miami	56	7	6	6	6	10	15	16	17	17	14	8	7	131
GA	Atlanta	64	12	10	11	9	9	10	12	10	8	7	9	10	116
HI	Honolulu	49	9	9	9	9	7	6	7	6	7	9	9	10	97
ID	Boise	59	12	10	10	8	8	6	3	2	4	6	10	11	90
IL	Chicago.........	40	11	9	12	13	11	10	10	9	9	9	11	11	125
	Peoria.........	59	9	8	11	12	12	10	9	8	9	8	9	10	114
IN	Indianapolis	59	12	10	13	12	12	10	10	9	8	8	10	12	126
IA	Des Moines	59	8	7	10	11	11	11	9	9	9	8	7	8	108
KS	Wichita	45	5	5	8	8	11	9	8	8	8	6	5	6	86
KY	Louisville	51	11	11	13	12	12	10	10	8	8	7	10	11	125
LA	New Orleans	50	10	9	9	7	8	11	14	13	10	6	7	10	115
ME	Portland	58	11	10	11	12	13	11	10	9	9	9	11	12	129
MD	Baltimore.......	48	11	9	11	11	11	9	9	9	8	8	9	10	114
MA	Boston	47	12	10	12	11	12	11	9	10	9	9	11	12	127
MI	Detroit.........	40	13	11	13	13	11	10	10	10	10	10	12	13	135
	Sault Ste. Marie ...	57	19	14	13	11	11	11	10	11	13	14	18	19	166
MN	Duluth	57	12	9	11	10	12	13	12	11	12	10	11	11	134
	Minneapolis-St. Paul	60	9	7	10	10	11	12	10	10	10	8	8	9	116
MS	Jackson........	35	11	9	10	9	9	8	11	10	8	6	8	10	109
MO	Kansas City	26	7	7	10	11	12	10	9	9	8	7	8	7	105
	St. Louis.......	41	9	8	11	11	11	9	9	8	8	8	10	9	111
MT	Great Falls......	61	9	8	9	9	12	12	8	8	7	6	7	8	101
NE	Omaha	62	6	7	9	10	12	11	9	9	8	6	6	6	100
NV	Reno	56	6	6	6	4	5	3	2	2	3	3	5	6	51
NH	Concord	57	11	10	11	12	12	11	10	10	9	9	11	11	126
NJ	Atlantic City	55	11	10	11	11	10	9	9	9	8	7	9	10	113
NM	Albuquerque......	59	4	4	5	3	4	4	9	10	6	5	4	4	61
NY	Albany	52	13	11	12	12	13	11	10	10	10	9	12	12	135
	Buffalo	55	20	17	16	14	13	11	10	10	11	12	16	19	169
	New York [1]......	129	11	10	11	11	11	10	11	10	8	8	9	10	121
NC	Charlotte.......	59	10	10	11	9	10	10	11	10	7	7	8	10	112
	Raleigh........	54	10	10	10	9	10	10	11	10	8	7	8	9	113
ND	Bismarck.......	59	8	7	8	8	10	11	9	8	7	6	7	8	96
OH	Cincinnati.......	51	12	11	13	13	12	11	10	9	8	8	11	12	131
	Cleveland	57	16	14	15	15	13	11	10	10	10	11	14	16	155
	Columbus	59	13	11	14	13	13	11	11	9	8	9	11	13	137
OK	Oklahoma City	59	5	6	7	8	10	8	6	7	7	7	5	6	83
OR	Portland	58	18	16	17	14	12	9	4	5	8	12	18	19	152
PA	Philadelphia......	58	11	9	11	11	11	10	9	9	8	8	9	10	117
	Pittsburgh	46	16	14	16	14	13	12	11	10	10	10	13	16	153
RI	Providence......	45	11	10	12	11	12	11	9	9	9	9	11	12	125
SC	Columbia.......	51	10	10	10	8	9	10	12	11	8	6	7	9	110
SD	Sioux Falls......	53	6	7	9	9	11	11	10	9	8	6	6	6	99
TN	Memphis	48	10	9	11	10	9	9	9	7	7	7	9	10	107
	Nashville.......	57	11	11	12	11	11	10	10	9	8	7	10	11	119
TX	Dallas-Fort Worth ..	45	7	7	7	8	9	7	5	5	7	6	6	7	79
	El Paso........	59	4	3	2	2	2	3	8	8	6	4	3	4	49
	Houston	29	11	9	9	7	8	9	9	9	9	8	8	9	106
UT	Salt Lake City.....	70	10	9	10	10	8	5	5	6	5	6	8	9	91
VT	Burlington	55	15	12	13	12	14	12	12	13	12	12	14	15	155
VA	Norfolk	50	11	10	11	10	10	9	11	10	8	8	8	9	116
	Richmond	61	10	9	11	9	11	9	11	9	8	7	8	9	114
WA	Seattle-Tacoma....	54	19	16	17	14	10	9	5	6	9	13	18	19	155
	Spokane	51	14	11	11	9	10	8	5	5	6	8	13	15	113
WV	Charleston......	51	15	14	15	14	13	12	13	11	9	9	12	14	152
WI	Milwaukee	58	11	10	12	12	12	11	10	9	9	9	10	11	125
WY	Cheyenne	63	6	6	9	10	12	11	11	10	8	6	6	6	101
PR	San Juan........	43	17	13	13	13	16	15	19	18	18	17	19	19	196

- Represents zero.   Z Less than 1/2 day.   [1] City office data.

Source: U.S. National Oceanic and Atmospheric Administration, *Comparative Climatic Data*, annual.

No. 413. Snow and Ice Pellets—Selected Cities

[**In inches.** Airport data, except as noted. For period of record through 1998. T denotes trace]

State	Station	Length of record (yr)	Jan.	Feb.	Mar.	Apr.	May	June	July	Aug.	Sept.	Oct.	Nov.	Dec.	Annual
AL	Mobile	56	0.1	0.1	0.1	T	T	-	T	-	-	-	T	0.1	0.4
AK	Juneau	54	25.7	19	15.2	3.3	-	T	-	-	T	1	12.5	22.3	99
AZ	Phoenix	61	T	-	T	T	T	-	-	-	-	T	-	T	T
AR	Little Rock	56	2.4	1.5	0.5	T	T	T	-	-	-	T	0.2	0.6	5.2
CA	Los Angeles	62	T	T	T	-	-	-	-	-	-	-	-	T	T
	Sacramento	50	T	T	T	-	T	-	-	-	-	-	-	T	T
	San Diego	58	T	-	T	-	-	-	-	-	-	-	-	-	T
	San Francisco	69	-	T	T	-	-	-	-	-	-	-	-	-	T
CO	Denver	61	8.1	7.5	12.5	8.9	1.6	-	T	T	1.6	3.7	9.1	7.3	60.3
CT	Hartford	42	13	12	10	1.5	-	T	-	-	-	0.1	2.1	10.3	49
DE	Wilmington	49	6.8	6.1	3.3	0.2	T	T	T	-	-	0.1	0.9	3.3	20.7
DC	Washington	55	5.5	5.4	2.2	T	T	T	T	T	-	-	0.8	2.8	16.7
FL	Jacksonville	57	T	-	-	T	-	T	T	-	-	-	-	-	T
	Miami	56	-	-	-	-	T	-	-	-	-	-	-	-	T
GA	Atlanta	62	0.9	0.5	0.4	T	-	-	-	-	-	T	-	0.2	2
HI	Honolulu	52	-	-	-	-	-	-	-	-	-	-	-	-	-
ID	Boise	59	6.5	3.7	1.6	0.6	0.1	T	T	T	T	0.1	2.3	5.9	20.8
IL	Chicago	39	10.7	8.2	6.6	1.6	0.1	T	T	T	T	0.4	1.9	8.1	37.6
	Peoria	55	6.6	5.4	4	0.8	-	-	T	-	T	0.1	2	5.9	24.8
IN	Indianapolis	67	6.6	5.6	3.4	0.5	-	T	-	T	-	0.2	1.9	5.1	23.3
IA	Des Moines	57	8.3	7.2	6	1.8	-	T	T	T	-	0.3	3.1	6.7	33.4
KS	Wichita	45	4.3	4.1	2.7	0.2	T	T	T	T	T	-	1.3	3.1	15.7
KY	Louisville	51	5.4	4.6	3.3	0.1	T	T	T	-	-	0.1	1	2.1	16.6
LA	New Orleans	50	-	0.1	T	T	T	-	-	-	-	-	T	0.1	0.2
ME	Portland	58	19.6	16.9	12.9	3	0.2	-	-	-	T	0.2	3.3	14.6	70.7
MD	Baltimore	48	6.2	6.8	3.8	0.1	T	-	T	-	-	-	1	3.2	21.1
MA	Boston	61	12.8	11.8	8	0.9	-	-	-	T	-	-	1.3	7.6	42.4
MI	Detroit	40	10.3	9.2	6.8	1.7	T	-	-	-	T	0.2	2.8	9.7	40.7
	Sault Ste. Marie . .	55	29	18.4	14.7	5.8	0.5	T	T	T	0.1	2.4	15.8	31.1	117.8
MN	Duluth	55	17.9	11.5	13.6	6.6	0.7	T	T	T	0.1	1.5	13	15.6	80.5
	Minneapolis-St. Paul	60	10.2	8.2	10.6	2.8	0.1	T	T	T	T	0.5	7.9	9.4	49.7
MS	Jackson	35	0.5	0.2	0.2	-	-	-	-	-	-	-	-	0.1	1
MO	Kansas City	64	5.7	4.4	3.4	0.8	T	T	T	-	T	0.1	1.2	4.4	20
	St. Louis	62	5.4	4.4	4	0.5	-	T	T	-	-	T	1.4	3.8	19.5
MT	Great Falls	61	9.6	8.3	10.6	7.2	1.7	0.3	T	0.1	1.5	3.4	7.5	8.2	58.4
NE	Omaha	63	7.3	6.6	6.3	1	0.1	T	T	-	T	0.3	2.6	5.6	29.8
NV	Reno	54	5.8	5.2	4.3	1.2	0.8	-	-	-	-	0.3	2.4	4.3	24.3
NH	Concord	57	18	14.4	11.2	2.5	0.1	T	-	-	T	0.1	4	13.7	64
NJ	Atlantic City	51	5	5.3	2.5	0.3	T	T	T	-	-	T	0.4	2.2	15.7
NM	Albuquerque	59	2.5	2.1	1.8	0.6	-	T	T	T	T	0.1	1.2	2.6	10.9
NY	Albany	52	16.4	14.1	11.4	2.5	0.1	T	T	-	T	0.2	4.3	14.6	63.6
	Buffalo	55	23.7	18	11.9	3.2	0.2	T	T	T	T	0.3	11.2	22.8	91.3
	New York [1]	130	7.5	8.6	5.1	0.9	T	-	T	-	-	-	0.9	5.4	28.4
NC	Charlotte	59	2	1.6	1.2	T	T	T	T	-	-	T	0.1	0.5	5.4
	Raleigh	54	2.3	2.5	1.3	-	T	T	T	-	-	-	0.1	0.8	7
ND	Bismarck	59	7.6	7	8.6	4	0.9	T	T	T	0.2	1.8	7	7	44.1
OH	Cincinnati	51	7.2	5.7	4.5	0.5	-	T	T	-	-	0.3	2	3.7	23.9
	Cleveland	57	13.1	12	10.5	2.4	0.1	T	-	-	T	0.6	5.3	11.8	55.8
	Columbus	51	8.7	6.1	4.6	0.9	-	T	T	-	T	0.1	2.2	5.3	27.9
OK	Oklahoma City	59	3.1	2.4	1.5	T	T	T	T	T	T	0.5	1.8	9.3	9.3
OR	Portland	55	3.2	1.1	0.4	T	-	T	T	-	T	-	0.4	1.4	6.5
PA	Philadelphia	56	6	6.6	3.6	0.3	T	-	-	-	-	-	0.7	3.2	20.4
	Pittsburgh	46	11.7	9.2	8.7	1.7	0.1	T	T	T	T	0.4	3.5	8.2	43.5
RI	Providence	45	9.9	9.8	7.3	0.7	0.2	-	-	-	-	0.1	1.1	6.8	35.9
SC	Columbia	51	0.4	0.8	0.2	T	-	-	T	-	-	-	T	0.3	1.7
SD	Sioux Falls	53	6.8	8.2	9.4	2.8	T	T	T	-	-	0.8	5.8	7.2	41
TN	Memphis	48	2.2	1.4	0.8	T	T	T	-	-	-	T	0.1	0.6	5.1
	Nashville	56	3.7	3	1.5	-	-	T	T	-	-	-	0.4	1.4	10
TX	Dallas-Fort Worth . .	43	1.1	0.9	0.2	T	T	-	-	-	-	T	0.1	0.2	2.5
	El Paso	57	1.3	0.8	0.4	0.3	T	T	T	T	-	T	0.9	1.6	5.3
	Houston	64	0.2	0.2	-	T	T	T	T	-	-	-	T	T	0.4
UT	Salt Lake City	70	13.8	10	9.4	4.9	0.6	T	T	T	0.1	1.3	6.8	11.7	58.6
VT	Burlington	55	19.2	16.6	13.2	4.1	0.2	-	T	-	-	0.2	6.8	18	78.3
VA	Norfolk	48	2.8	3	1	-	T	T	T	-	T	-	-	0.9	7.7
	Richmond	60	4.8	4	2.4	0.1	-	T	T	-	-	T	0.4	2	13.7
WA	Seattle-Tacoma	52	4.9	1.6	1.3	0.1	T	-	T	-	T	-	1.1	2.4	11.4
	Spokane	51	15.6	7.5	3.9	0.6	0.1	T	-	-	T	0.4	6.3	14.6	49
WV	Charleston	49	11.1	8.7	5.4	0.9	-	T	T	T	T	0.2	2.4	5.3	34
WI	Milwaukee	58	13.7	9.6	8.3	1.8	0.1	T	T	T	T	0.2	3.2	10.2	47.1
WY	Cheyenne	63	6.6	6.3	11.9	9.2	3.2	0.2	-	T	0.9	3.7	7.1	6.3	55.4
PR	San Juan	43	-	-	-	-	-	-	-	-	-	-	-	-	-

- Represents zero or rounds to zero.   [1] City office data.

Source: U.S. National Oceanic and Atmospheric Administration, *Comparative Climatic Data*, annual.

Geography and Environment   249

No. 414. Sunshine, Average Wind Speed, Heating and Cooling Degree Days, and Average Relative Humidity—Selected Cities

[Airport data, except as noted. For period of record through 1998, except as noted. M=morning. A=afternoon]

State	Station	Avg. pct. of possible sunshine [1] — Length of record (yr.)	Annual	Avg. wind speed (m.p.h.) — Length of record (yr.)	Annual	Jan.	July	Heating degree days	Cooling degree days	Length of record (yr.)	Annual M	Annual A	Jan. M	Jan. A	July M	July A
AL	Mobile	47	60	50	8.8	10.1	6.9	1,702	2,627	36	87	59	82	63	90	62
AK	Juneau	47	23	53	8.3	8.0	7.5	8,897	-	32	79	69	76	73	78	66
AZ	Phoenix	57	81	53	6.2	5.3	7.1	1,350	4,162	38	50	23	65	32	43	20
AR	Little Rock	35	60	56	7.8	8.4	6.7	3,155	2,005	34	83	57	80	62	86	55
CA	Los Angeles	60	72	50	7.5	6.7	7.9	1,458	727	39	79	65	71	61	86	69
	Sacramento	49	73	48	7.9	7.2	8.9	2,749	1,237	12	82	46	90	70	76	29
	San Diego	55	72	58	7.0	6.0	7.5	1,256	984	38	77	63	72	58	82	67
	San Francisco	68	71	71	10.6	7.2	13.6	3,016	145	39	84	62	86	67	86	60
CO	Denver	61	67	47	8.6	8.6	8.3	6,020	679	35	67	40	63	49	68	34
CT	Hartford	41	52	44	8.4	9.0	7.3	6,151	677	39	77	52	72	56	79	51
DE	Wilmington	47	55	50	9.0	9.8	7.8	4,937	1,046	51	78	55	75	60	79	54
DC	Washington	48	55	50	9.4	10.0	8.3	4,047	1,549	38	75	53	70	56	76	53
FL	Jacksonville	47	61	49	7.9	8.1	7.0	1,434	2,551	62	89	56	87	58	89	59
	Miami	46	68	49	9.2	9.5	7.9	200	4,198	34	83	61	84	59	83	63
GA	Atlanta	61	59	60	9.1	10.4	7.7	2,991	1,667	38	82	56	79	60	88	59
HI	Honolulu	47	74	49	11.3	9.4	13.1	-	4,474	29	72	56	81	61	68	51
ID	Boise	56	58	59	8.7	8.0	8.4	5,861	754	59	69	43	80	70	54	22
IL	Chicago	37	52	40	10.4	11.7	8.4	6,536	752	40	80	61	78	69	82	57
	Peoria	52	53	55	9.9	11.0	7.8	6,148	982	39	83	63	80	70	87	61
IN	Indianapolis	64	51	50	9.6	10.9	7.5	5,615	1,014	39	84	62	81	71	87	60
IA	Des Moines	46	55	49	10.7	11.4	8.9	6,497	1,036	37	80	61	77	68	83	59
KS	Wichita	39	62	45	12.2	12.0	11.3	4,791	1,628	45	80	56	79	64	79	50
KY	Louisville	47	53	51	8.3	9.5	6.8	4,514	1,288	38	81	59	77	65	85	58
LA	New Orleans	47	60	50	8.2	9.3	6.1	1,513	2,655	50	88	64	85	67	91	66
ME	Portland	54	55	58	8.7	9.1	7.6	7,378	268	58	79	59	76	61	80	59
MD	Baltimore	45	58	48	8.9	9.6	7.7	4,707	1,137	45	77	54	72	57	80	53
MA	Boston	60	55	41	12.4	13.8	11.0	5,641	678	34	72	58	68	58	74	56
MI	Detroit	37	49	40	10.3	12.0	8.5	6,569	626	40	81	60	80	70	82	54
	Sault Ste. Marie	54	43	57	9.2	9.6	7.8	9,316	131	57	85	67	81	74	89	62
MN	Duluth	47	49	49	11.0	11.6	9.4	9,818	180	37	81	64	77	70	85	60
	Minneapolis-St. Paul	57	54	60	10.5	10.5	9.4	7,981	682	39	79	61	75	68	81	56
MS	Jackson	30	59	35	7.1	8.3	5.5	2,467	2,215	35	91	59	86	65	94	61
MO	Kansas City	23	59	26	10.6	11.2	9.2	5,393	1,288	26	81	61	77	65	85	60
	St. Louis	47	55	49	9.7	10.6	8.0	4,758	1,534	38	82	60	81	67	84	57
MT	Great Falls	57	51	57	12.6	14.9	10.0	7,741	388	37	68	46	67	61	68	31
NE	Omaha	49	59	62	10.5	10.9	8.8	6,300	1,072	34	81	60	79	66	85	60
NV	Reno	53	69	56	6.6	5.6	7.2	5,674	508	35	69	32	79	51	61	19
NH	Concord	54	55	56	6.7	7.3	5.7	7,554	328	33	81	54	76	59	84	51
NJ	Atlantic City	37	56	40	9.9	10.9	8.3	5,169	826	34	82	56	78	59	83	57
NM	Albuquerque	56	76	59	8.9	8.0	8.9	4,425	1,244	38	59	29	68	40	59	27
NY	Albany	57	49	60	8.9	9.8	7.5	6,894	507	33	80	58	78	63	81	55
	Buffalo	52	43	59	11.9	14.0	10.3	6,747	477	38	80	62	79	73	79	55
	New York [2]	42	64	61	9.3	10.7	7.6	4,805	1,096	64	72	56	68	60	75	55
NC	Charlotte	49	59	49	7.4	7.8	6.6	3,341	1,582	38	82	53	78	56	86	56
	Raleigh	47	59	49	7.6	8.4	6.7	3,457	1,417	34	85	54	79	55	89	58
ND	Bismarck	56	55	59	10.2	10.0	9.2	8,968	488	39	81	58	75	70	85	49
OH	Cincinnati	44	49	51	9.0	10.5	7.2	5,248	996	36	82	60	80	69	86	57
	Cleveland	54	45	57	10.5	12.2	8.6	6,201	621	38	80	62	78	70	82	57
	Columbus	46	48	49	8.3	9.8	6.5	5,708	797	39	80	59	77	68	84	56
OK	Oklahoma City	44	64	50	12.3	12.6	10.9	3,659	1,859	33	80	56	78	60	80	51
OR	Portland	47	39	50	7.9	10.0	7.6	4,522	371	58	85	59	85	75	82	45
PA	Philadelphia	55	56	58	9.5	10.3	8.2	4,954	1,101	39	76	55	73	59	79	54
	Pittsburgh	43	46	46	9.0	10.5	7.3	5,968	654	38	79	57	76	66	83	54
RI	Providence	42	55	45	10.4	11.1	9.4	5,884	606	35	75	55	71	57	77	56
SC	Columbia	48	60	50	6.8	7.2	6.3	2,649	1,966	32	87	51	83	55	89	54
SD	Sioux Falls	50	57	50	11.1	10.9	9.8	7,809	744	35	82	62	78	70	84	56
TN	Memphis	43	59	50	8.8	10.0	7.5	3,082	2,118	59	81	58	79	64	84	58
	Nashville	54	57	57	8.0	9.1	6.5	3,729	1,616	33	84	58	80	64	89	58
TX	Dallas-Fort Worth	42	64	45	10.7	11.0	9.8	2,407	2,603	35	82	57	80	61	81	50
	El Paso	53	80	56	8.8	8.3	8.3	2,708	2,094	38	56	27	65	35	61	29
	Houston	26	56	29	7.8	8.2	6.9	1,599	2,700	29	90	61	86	66	93	58
UT	Salt Lake City	69	62	69	8.8	7.5	9.5	5,765	1,047	39	67	43	79	69	52	22
VT	Burlington	52	44	53	9.0	9.8	8.0	7,771	388	33	77	59	73	64	79	53
VA	Norfolk	47	58	50	10.6	11.5	8.9	3,495	1,422	50	78	57	75	59	81	59
	Richmond	50	56	50	7.7	8.1	6.9	3,963	1,348	64	83	53	80	57	85	56
WA	Seattle-Tacoma [3]	51	38	50	8.9	9.6	8.2	4,908	190	39	83	62	81	74	81	49
	Spokane	48	48	51	8.9	8.8	8.6	6,842	398	39	78	52	85	79	65	28
WV	Charleston	47	48	51	5.9	7.1	4.8	4,646	1,031	51	83	56	78	63	90	59
WI	Milwaukee	55	52	58	11.5	12.6	9.7	7,324	479	38	80	65	76	69	82	62
WY	Cheyenne	60	64	41	12.9	15.3	10.4	7,326	285	39	65	45	57	50	70	38
PR	San Juan	40	76	43	8.4	8.4	9.7	-	5,558	43	79	65	82	64	79	67

- Represents zero. [1] Percent of days that are either clear or partly cloudy. Period of record through 1997. [2] Airport data for sunshine. [3] Does not represent airport data.

Source: U.S. National Oceanic and Atmospheric Administration, *Comparative Climatic Data*, annual.

250 Geography and Environment

Section 7

Parks, Recreation, and Travel

This section presents data on national parks and forests, state parks, recreational activities, the arts and humanities, and domestic and foreign travel.

Parks and recreation—The Department of the Interior has responsibility for administering the national parks. As part of this function, issues reports relating to the usage of public parks for recreation purposes. The National Park Service publishes information on visits to national park areas in its annual report, *National Park Statistical Abstract. The National Parks: Index (year)* is a biannual report which has appeared under a variety of Index titles prior to 1985. Beginning with the 1985 edition, the report has appeared under the current title. The Index contains brief descriptions, with acreages, of each area administered by the Service, plus certain "related" areas. A statistical summary of Service-administered areas is also presented. The annual *Federal Recreation Fee Report* summarizes the prior year's recreation fee receipts and recreation visitation statistics for seven Federal land managing agencies.

Statistics for state parks are compiled by the National Association of State Park Directors which issues its *Annual Information Exchange.* The Department of Agriculture's Forest Service, in its *Report of the Forest Service,* issues data on recreational uses of the national forests.

Visitation—Statistics presented on visitation to reporting areas are collected by several different agencies and groups. The methodology used to collect these results may vary accordingly, from visual counts and estimates to the use of electromagnetic traffic counters. In using and comparing these data, one should also be aware of several different definitions that follow: Recreation visit, which is the entry of any person into an area for recreation purposes; nonrecreation visits, which include visits going to and from inholdings, through traffic, tradespeople and personnel with business in the area; and visitor hour, which constitutes the presence of a person in a recreation area or site for recreational purposes for periods of time aggregating 60 minutes.

Recreation and leisure activities—Data on the participation in various recreation and leisure time activities are based on several sample surveys. Data on participation in fishing, hunting, and other forms of wildlife-associated recreation are published periodically by the U.S. Department of Interior, Fish and Wildlife Service. The most recent data are from the 1996 survey. Data on participation in various sports recreation activities are published by the National Sporting Goods Association. Mediamark, Inc. also conducts periodic surveys on sports and leisure activities, as well as other topics.

Travel—Information on foreign travel and personal expenditures abroad, as well as expenditures by foreign citizens traveling in the United States, is compiled annually by the U.S. Bureau of Economic Analysis and published in selected issues of the monthly *Survey of Current Business.* Statistics on arrivals to the United States are reported by the International Trade Administration (ITA). Sources of statistics on departures from the United States include the Department of Transportation's *International Air Travel Statistics* and other sources. Data on domestic travel, business receipts and employment of the travel industry, and travel expenditures are published by the U.S. Travel Data Center, which is the research department of the Travel Industry Association and the national nonprofit center for travel and tourism research which is located in Washington, DC. Other data on household transportation characteristics may be found in Section 21, Land Transportation.

Parks, Recreation, and Travel   251

No. 415. National Park System—Summary: 1990 to 1998

[For fiscal years ending in year shown, except as noted; see text, Section 10, Federal Government (986.1 represents $986,100,000). Includes data for five areas in Puerto Rico and Virgin Islands, one area in American Samoa, and one area in Guam]

Item	1990	1992	1993	1994	1995	1996	1997	1998
Finances (mil. dol.): [1]								
Expenditures reported	986.1	1,268.7	1,429.4	1,404.0	1,445.0	1,391.0	1,473.0	1,553.0
Salaries and wages	459.1	518.1	596.1	627.2	633.0	650.0	683.0	721.0
Improvements, maintenance	160.0	212.1	224.8	222.9	234.0	234.0	246.0	255.0
Construction	108.5	193.3	226.8	205.6	192.0	168.0	188.0	191.0
Other	258.5	345.2	379.7	348.3	386.0	339.0	356.0	386.0
Funds available	1,505.5	2,274.8	2,346.5	2,307.7	2,225.0	2,116.0	2,301.0	2,588.0
Appropriations	1,052.5	1,392.8	1,334.0	1,388.8	1,325.0	1,346.0	1,625.0	1,765.0
Other [2]	453.0	882.0	1,012.5	918.9	900.0	770.0	676.0	823.0
Revenue from operations	78.6	88.3	89.5	97.0	106.3	133.2	174.8	202.8
Recreation visits (millions): [3]								
All areas	258.7	274.7	273.1	268.6	269.6	265.8	275.3	286.7
National parks [4]	57.7	58.7	59.8	63.0	64.8	63.1	65.3	64.5
National monuments	23.9	26.6	26.5	23.6	23.5	23.6	24.1	23.6
National historical, commemorative, archaeological [5]	57.5	63.3	61.9	59.5	56.9	59.0	63.0	74.2
National parkways	29.1	30.7	30.4	29.3	31.3	30.9	31.6	32.8
National recreation areas [4]	47.2	50.3	50.8	52.3	53.7	52.6	51.6	53.0
National seashores and lakeshores	23.3	23.9	24.1	24.0	22.5	20.3	22.4	22.6
National Capital Parks	7.5	8.1	9.1	5.4	5.5	6.1	5.1	4.2
Miscellaneous other areas	12.5	13.1	10.5	11.8	11.4	11.3	12.1	12.0
Recreation overnight stays (millions) [3]	17.6	18.3	17.7	18.3	16.8	16.6	15.8	15.6
In commercial lodgings	3.9	4.1	4.0	3.9	3.8	3.7	3.6	3.6
In Park Service campgrounds	7.9	8.1	7.5	7.6	7.1	6.5	6.3	6.1
In tents	4.1	4.4	4.1	4.2	3.9	3.7	3.6	3.5
In recreation vehicles	3.8	3.7	3.4	3.4	3.2	2.8	2.7	2.6
In backcountry	1.7	2.2	2.4	2.4	2.2	2.1	2.2	2.1
Other	4.2	3.9	3.8	4.4	3.7	3.7	3.8	3.9
Land (1,000 acres): [6]								
Total	76,362	76,492	75,515	74,905	77,355	77,458	77,457	77,654
Parks	46,089	46,208	45,521	48,111	49,307	49,315	49,384	49,416
Recreation areas	3,344	3,347	3,349	3,351	3,353	3,353	3,329	3,361
Other	26,929	26,937	26,645	23,443	24,695	24,790	24,744	24,877
Acquisition, gross	21	23	39	32	27	98	61	94
By purchase	18	21	29	29	25	10	39	21
By gift	2	1	10	1	1	3	3	3
By transfer or exchange	3	1	(Z)	(Z)	1	85	19	70
Exclusion	1	(Z)	(Z)	(Z)	(Z)	(Z)	(Z)	(Z)
Acquisition, net	21	23	39	32	27	98	61	94

Z Less than 500 acres. [1] Financial data are those associated with the National Park System. Certain other functions of the National Park Service (principally the activities absorbed from the former Heritage Conservation and Recreation Service in 1981) are excluded. [2] Includes funds carried over from prior years. [3] For calendar year. [4] For 1990, combined data for North Cascades National Park and two adjacent National Recreation Areas are included in National Parks total. [5] Includes military areas. [6] Federal land only, as of Dec. 31. Federal land acreages, in addition to National Park Service administered lands, also include lands within national park system area boundaries but under the administration of other agencies. Year-to-year changes in the Federal lands figures include changes in the acreages of these other lands and hence often differ from "net acquisition."

Source: U.S. National Park Service, Visits, *National Park Statistical Abstract*, annual; and unpublished data. Other data are unpublished.

No. 416. National Forest Recreation Use—Summary: 1980 to 1996

[Estimated for year ending September 30 (233,549 represents 233,549,000). Represents recreational use of National Forest land and water in states which have a Forest Service recreation program]

Year and activity	Recreation visitor-days [1] (1,000)	Percent	State or other area	Recreation visitor-days [1] 1996 (1,000)	State or other area	Recreation visitor-days [1] 1996 (1,000)
1980	233,549	100.0	U.S.	341,200	NV	3,857
1984	227,554	100.0			NH	3,354
1985	225,407	100.0	AL	689	NM	9,326
1986	226,533	100.0	AK	6,962	NY	39
1987	238,458	100.0	AZ	35,000	NC	6,979
1988	242,316	100.0	AR	2,210	ND	133
1989	252,495	100.0	CA	71,165	OH	524
1990	263,051	100.0	CO	30,971	OK	393
1991	278,849	100.0	FL	2,960	OR	37,030
1992	287,691	100.0	GA	2,925	PA	3,268
1993	295,473	100.0	ID	15,365	SC	1,011
1994	330,348	100.0	IL	1,188	SD	3,571
1995	345,083	100.0	ID	684	TN	3,309
1996, total	341,200	100.0	KS	86	TX	2,302
Mechanized travel and viewing scenery	122,141	35.8	KY	2,326	UT	19,378
Camping, picnicking, and swimming	87,082	25.5	LA	599	VT	1,395
Hiking, horseback riding, and water travel	33,099	9.7	MA	158	VA	4,927
Winter sports	19,708	5.8	MI	4,866	WA	24,797
Hunting	19,384	5.7	MN	5,982	WV	1,499
Resorts, cabins, and organization camps	17,702	5.2	MS	1,828	WI	2,527
Fishing	18,160	5.3	MO	2,518	WY	9,114
Nature studies	3,299	1.0	MT	13,495		
Other [2]	20,627	6.0	NE	320	PR	171

[1] One recreation visitor-day is the recreation use of National Forest land or water that aggregates 12 visitor-hours. This may entail 1 person for 12 hours, 12 persons for 1 hour, or any equivalent combination of individual or group use, either continuous or intermittent. [2] Includes team sports, gathering forest products, attending talks and programs, and other uses.

Source: U.S. Forest Service, *Annual Report*.

No. 417. State Parks and Recreation Areas by State: 1999

[For year ending June 30 (12,916 represents 12,916,000). Data are shown as reported by state park directors. In some states, park agency has under its control forests, fish and wildlife areas, and/or other areas. In other states, agency is responsible for state parks only]

State	Acreage (1,000)	Visitors (1,000) [1]	Revenue Total ($1,000)	Percent of operating expenditures	State	Acreage (1,000)	Visitors (1,000) [1]	Revenue Total ($1,000)	Percent of operating expenditures
United States ...	12,916	766,842	650,864	43.4	Missouri	137	17,709	6,766	23.0
					Montana	54	1,507	1,571	31.5
Alabama	50	5,923	26,160	90.9	Nebraska	133	9,368	13,232	74.5
Alaska	3,291	3,855	2,106	39.3	Nevada	133	2,666	1,822	26.0
Arizona	59	2,180	4,521	31.9	New Hampshire	74	4,361	9,845	208.6
Arkansas	51	6,460	13,311	50.0	New Jersey	343	15,019	7,840	28.0
California	1,376	76,736	68,535	31.3	New Mexico	91	4,725	3,623	24.5
Colorado	346	9,508	12,040	58.1	New York	1,016	61,960	58,924	47.0
Connecticut	180	7,959	3,726	36.5	North Carolina	158	13,269	3,440	14.1
Delaware	20	3,977	6,654	34.3	North Dakota	20	1,068	923	42.2
Florida	513	14,645	25,766	48.9	Ohio	205	60,220	25,180	41.5
Georgia	73	15,344	19,823	45.4	Oklahoma	72	15,546	21,234	52.5
Hawaii	25	15,071	275	4.9	Oregon	94	38,752	14,548	41.8
Idaho	43	2,354	3,182	39.7	Pennsylvania	283	36,019	12,080	18.9
Illinois	411	41,891	951	2.1	Rhode Island	9	6,332	3,684	82.3
Indiana	178	18,652	29,266	73.0	South Carolina	82	9,563	15,265	68.1
Iowa	63	14,736	3,265	31.5	South Dakota	96	6,843	7,522	79.4
Kansas	52	7,100	3,998	53.1	Tennessee	286	31,833	26,192	54.0
Kentucky	43	7,575	47,755	68.2	Texas	628	21,446	26,028	53.3
Louisiana	36	1,469	2,819	20.8	Utah	114	6,958	7,707	37.4
Maine	95	2,454	1,931	29.2	Vermont	84	834	5,623	106.5
Maryland	295	10,780	13,847	41.7	Virginia	75	5,520	7,258	47.3
Massachusetts	287	13,497	5,570	18.1	Washington	262	48,138	10,368	27.5
Michigan	265	27,745	17,724	64.4	West Virginia	196	8,249	17,364	63.3
Minnesota	245	8,406	10,705	44.7	Wisconsin	129	14,181	11,438	67.7
Mississippi	24	4,277	6,706	36.9	Wyoming	121	2,158	751	17.3

[1] Includes overnight visitors.

Source: National Association of State Park Directors, Tuscon, AZ, 2000 Annual Information Exchange.

No. 418. Personal Consumption Expenditures for Recreation: 1990 to 1998

[In billions of dollars (284.9 represents $284,900,000,000), except percent. Represents market value of purchases of goods and services by individuals and nonprofit institutions]

Type of product or service	1990	1993	1994	1995	1996	1997	1998
Total recreation expenditures	**284.9**	**340.1**	**368.7**	**401.6**	**429.6**	**457.8**	**494.7**
Percent of total personal consumption [1]	7.4	7.6	7.8	8.1	8.2	8.3	8.5
Books and maps	16.2	18.8	20.8	23.1	24.9	26.6	27.8
Magazines, newspapers, and sheet music	21.6	23.1	24.9	26.2	27.6	29.5	31.9
Nondurable toys and sport supplies	32.8	39.5	43.4	47.2	50.6	53.7	57.7
Wheel goods, sports and photographic equipment [2]	29.7	32.5	35.2	38.5	40.5	43.2	47.1
Video and audio products, computer equipment, and musical instruments	52.9	62.6	71.0	77.0	80.0	84.0	92.6
Video and audio goods, including and musical instruments	43.9	48.1	53.0	55.9	56.4	57.8	62.2
Computers, peripherals, and software	8.9	14.5	18.0	21.0	23.6	26.2	30.4
Radio and television repair	3.7	3.3	3.3	3.6	3.7	3.9	3.9
Flowers, seeds, and potted plants	10.9	12.5	13.2	13.8	14.9	15.6	16.5
Admissions to specified spectator amusements	14.8	17.5	18.2	19.2	20.7	22.2	23.8
Motion picture theaters	5.1	5.0	5.2	5.5	5.8	6.4	6.8
Legitimate theaters and opera, and entertainments of nonprofit institutions [3]	5.2	6.8	7.2	7.6	8.0	8.7	9.4
Spectator sports [4]	4.5	5.7	5.8	6.1	6.9	7.1	7.6
Clubs and fraternal organizations except insurance [5]	8.7	11.1	11.8	12.7	14.0	14.4	14.9
Commercial participant amusements [6]	24.6	34.0	38.6	43.9	48.3	52.3	56.2
Pari-mutuel net receipts	3.5	3.3	3.4	3.5	3.5	3.6	3.7
Other [7]	65.4	81.9	84.7	93.1	100.8	109.0	118.6

[1] See Table 723. [2] Includes boats and pleasure aircraft. [3] Except athletic. [4] Consists of admissions to professional and amateur athletic events and to racetracks, including horse, dog, and auto. [5] Consists of dues and fees excluding insurance premiums. [6] Consists of billiard parlors; bowling alleys; dancing, riding, shooting, skating, and swimming places; amusement devices and parks; golf courses; sightseeing buses and guides; private flying operations; casino gambling; and other commercial participant amusements. [7] Consists of net receipts of lotteries and expenditures for purchases of pets and pet care services, cable TV, film processing, photographic studios, sporting and recreation camps, video cassette rentals, and recreational services, not elsewhere classified.

Source: U.S. Bureau of Economic Analysis, The National Income and Product Accounts of the United States, 1929-94, Vol.1, and Survey of Current Business, June 2000.

No. 419. Expenditures per Consumer Unit for Entertainment and Reading: 1985 to 1998

[Data are **annual averages. In dollars, except as indicated.** Based on Consumer Expenditure Survey; see text, Section 14, Income, for description of survey. See also headnote, Table 732. For composition of regions, see map, inside front cover]

Year and characteristic	Entertainment and reading		Entertainment				Reading
	Total	Percent of total expenditures	Total	Fees and admissions	Television, radios, and sound equipment	Other equipment and services [1]	
1985...................	1,311	5.6	1,170	320	371	479	141
1989...................	1,581	5.7	1,424	377	429	618	157
1990...................	1,575	5.6	1,422	371	454	597	153
1991...................	1,635	5.5	1,472	378	468	627	163
1992...................	1,662	5.6	1,500	379	492	629	162
1993...................	1,792	5.8	1,626	414	590	621	166
1994...................	1,732	5.5	1,567	439	533	595	165
1995...................	1,775	5.5	1,612	433	542	637	163
1996...................	1,993	5.9	1,834	459	561	814	159
1997...................	1,977	5.7	1,813	471	577	766	164
1998, total	**1,907**	**5.4**	**1,746**	**449**	**535**	**762**	**161**
Age of reference person:							
Under 25 years old.........	1,038	5.3	974	266	403	305	64
25 to 34 years old	1,892	5.4	1,757	421	557	779	135
35 to 44 years old	2,377	5.6	2,215	525	640	1,050	162
45 to 54 years old	2,351	5.2	2,142	628	644	870	209
55 to 64 years old	2,088	5.6	1,904	455	543	907	184
65 to 74 years old	1,492	5.4	1,312	340	378	594	180
75 years old and over........	867	4.1	724	227	298	199	143
Origin of reference person:							
Hispanic.................	1,210	4.0	1,148	234	506	407	62
Non-Hispanic	1,971	5.5	1,801	468	538	795	170
Race of reference person:							
White and other............	2,035	5.5	1,862	486	550	827	173
Black...................	954	3.7	882	175	421	287	72
Region of residence:							
Northeast................	1,973	5.3	1,772	516	603	653	201
Midwest.................	2,020	5.9	1,850	427	513	910	170
South	1,646	5.0	1,521	365	492	665	125
West	2,137	5.5	1,964	545	565	854	173
Size of consumer unit:							
One person...............	1,119	5.2	999	267	346	386	120
Two or more persons	2,221	5.4	2,044	522	610	912	177
Two persons	2,100	5.7	1,907	504	556	847	193
Three persons	2,002	4.8	1,840	470	551	819	162
Four persons.............	2,574	5.5	2,392	599	712	1,081	182
Five persons or more	2,453	5.4	2,304	554	725	1,025	149

[1] Other equipment and services includes pets, toys, and playground equipment; sports, exercise, and photographic equipment; and recreational vehicles.

Source: U.S. Bureau of Labor Statistics, *Consumer Expenditure Survey,* annual.

No. 420. Motion Pictures and Amusement and Recreation Services— Annual Receipts: 1990 to 1998

[**In millions of dollars (39,982 represents $39,982,000,000).** For taxable employer and nonemployer firms. Based on the Service Annual Survey; see Appendix III]

Kind of business	1987 SIC code [1]	1990	1994	1995	1996	1997	1998
Motion pictures.........................	78	39,982	53,504	57,184	60,279	62,865	66,229
Production, distribution, and allied services	781, 782	28,888	40,256	43,264	46,274	48,176	50,393
Theaters	783	6,088	6,233	6,530	7,044	7,582	8,298
Video tape rental..........................	784	5,006	7,015	7,390	6,961	7,107	7,538
Amusement and recreation services...........	79	50,126	68,453	77,452	85,733	92,836	97,512
Dance studios, schools, and halls.............	791	626	906	947	1,046	1,080	1,138
Theatrical producers (except motion picture), bands, orchestras, and entertainers	792	10,735	16,050	17,479	19,597	20,964	22,401
Bowling centers...........................	793	2,800	2,709	2,681	2,751	2,763	2,764
Commercial sports.........................	794	8,636	11,090	13,056	14,589	16,437	17,711
Professional sports clubs and promoters	7941	3,702	6,138	7,695	8,841	9,983	10,732
Racing, including track operation	7948	4,934	4,952	5,360	5,748	6,454	6,979
Miscellaneous amusement and recreation services [2] ..	799	27,329	37,698	43,290	47,748	51,594	53,500
Physical fitness facilities...................	7991	3,623	4,033	4,412	4,975	5,705	6,353
Public golf courses	7992	2,254	3,059	3,584	3,979	4,303	4,619
Coin-operated amusement devices.............	7993	2,146	2,965	3,254	3,491	3,649	3,750
Amusement parks.........................	7996	4,922	5,858	6,298	6,777	7,312	7,478
Membership sports and recreation clubs	7997	4,825	6,379	6,765	7,427	7,653	7,780

[1] 1987 Standard Industrial Classification code; see text, Section 17, Business.   [2] Includes kinds of businesses, not shown separately.

Source: U.S. Census Bureau, *Current Business Reports, Service Annual Survey: 1998,* BS/98, and earlier issues.

No. 421. Quantity of Books Sold and Value of U.S. Domestic Consumer Expenditures: 1982 to 1998

[Includes all titles released by publishers in the United States and imports which appear under the imprints of American publishers. **(1,732 represents 1,732,000,000).** Multi-volume sets, such as encyclopedias, are counted as one unit]

Type of publication and market area	Units sold (mil.)					Consumer expenditures (mil. dol.)				
	1982	1985	1990	1995	1998	1982	1985	1990	1995	1998
Total [1]	1,723	1,788	2,005	2,186	2,254	9,889	12,611	19,043	25,154	28,786
Hardbound, total	646	694	824	827	804	6,190	7,969	11,789	15,011	17,016
Softbound, total	1,077	1,094	1,181	1,359	1,450	3,699	4,642	7,254	10,143	11,770
Trade	459	553	705	813	831	2,484	3,660	6,498	9,340	10,350
Adult	315	360	403	465	476	2,028	2,871	4,777	7,060	7,791
Juvenile	144	193	301	348	355	456	789	1,721	2,280	2,558
Religious	144	134	130	148	161	706	926	1,362	1,792	2,037
Professional	106	110	131	146	150	1,630	2,043	2,957	4,153	4,751
Bookclubs	133	130	108	123	138	510	582	705	949	1,176
Elhi text	233	234	209	237	291	1,067	1,415	1,948	2,384	3,216
College text	115	110	137	142	161	1,388	1,575	2,319	2,708	3,365
Mail order publications	134	121	138	92	76	581	650	752	578	486
Mass market paperbacks— rack sized	382	382	433	470	429	1,102	1,244	1,775	2,322	2,348
General retailers	756	829	1,010	1,145	1,143	3,743	5,103	8,465	11,888	13,102
College stores	224	225	255	274	291	1,910	2,309	3,403	4,311	5,122
Libraries and institutions [2]	80	80	88	97	102	888	1,090	1,592	2,111	2,394
Schools [2]	262	260	244	273	326	1,313	1,685	2,365	2,896	3,780
Direct to consumers	319	300	304	289	293	1,889	2,214	2,901	3,544	3,989
Other	82	94	104	108	99	146	210	316	404	399

[1] Types of publications include university press publications and subscription reference works, not shown separately. [2] Elhi libraries included in schools.

Source: Book Industry Study Group, Inc., New York, NY, *Book Industry Trends, 1999,* annual (copyright).

No. 422. Book Purchasing by Adults: 1991 and 1998

[**In percent.** Excludes books purchased for or by children under age 13. Based on a survey of 16,000 households conducted over 12 months ending in December of year shown. For details, see source]

Characteristic	Total		Mass market [1]		Trade [2]		Hardcover	
	1991	1998	1991	1998	1991	1998	1991	1998
Total	100.0	100.0	100.0	100.0	100.0	100.0	100.0	100.0
Age of purchaser:								
Under 25 years old	4.3	4.8	3.7	4.0	5.2	6.4	4.4	3.9
25 to 34 years old	18.8	15.2	13.9	14.3	25.4	17.0	19.6	14.5
35 to 44 years old	23.7	24.3	22.8	19.2	25.2	27.9	23.7	26.1
45 to 54 years old	22.4	24.4	26.0	24.4	18.5	23.4	20.5	25.5
55 to 64 years old	15.6	15.2	15.8	17.9	13.9	13.1	17.2	14.4
65 years old and over	15.2	16.1	17.8	20.2	11.8	12.2	14.6	15.6
Household income:								
Under $30,000	37.1	30.7	41.7	35.8	32.6	29.1	34.1	26.8
$30,000 to 49,999	27.2	23.2	27.3	23.5	27.7	23.3	26.5	22.6
$50,000 to 59,999	11.0	9.5	9.8	8.5	12.3	10.6	11.5	9.6
$60,000 to 69,999	6.9	11.7	7.0	12.5	7.2	10.6	6.3	11.9
$70,000 and over	17.8	24.9	14.2	19.7	20.2	26.4	21.6	29.1
Household size:								
Singles	20.8	18.5	17.7	19.9	24.1	17.9	22.8	17.7
Families with no children	40.4	44.2	42.3	44.9	38.0	42.4	39.7	45.5
Families with children	38.8	37.3	40.0	35.2	37.9	39.7	37.5	36.8
Age of reader:								
Under 25 years old	7.3	7.8	5.2	5.0	10.1	10.3	7.7	6.4
25 to 34 years old	18.7	15.9	14.1	14.4	24.7	17.8	20.2	15.4
35 to 44 years old	22.9	22.0	22.3	19.1	24.0	26.3	22.7	25.2
45 to 54 years old	20.8	23.4	24.9	23.8	16.5	21.5	18.4	24.2
55 to 64 years old	14.9	14.3	15.9	17.7	12.7	11.4	15.6	13.3
65 years old and over	15.4	16.6	17.6	20.0	12.0	12.7	15.6	15.5
Category of book:								
Popular fiction	54.9	50.9	93.0	93.4	14.9	16.5	31.8	40.2
General nonfiction	10.3	8.1	3.6	2.6	15.6	9.1	16.5	13.1
Cooking/crafts	10.2	9.9	0.4	0.2	20.6	15.3	18.2	14.9
Other	24.6	31.1	3.0	3.8	48.9	59.1	33.5	31.8
Sales outlet:								
Independent	32.5	16.6	26.5	9.8	44.9	24.7	29.0	15.3
Chain book store	22.0	25.3	17.2	22.3	27.4	26.9	25.2	26.9
Book clubs	16.6	18.0	17.8	19.7	9.5	13.4	22.6	21.1
Other [3]	28.9	40.1	38.5	48.2	18.2	35.0	23.2	36.7
Online	(NA)	1.9	(NA)	0.7	(NA)	2.7	(NA)	2.3

NA Not available. [1] "Pocket size" books sold primarily through magazine and news outlets, supermarkets, variety stores, etc. [2] All paperbound books, except mass market. [3] Includes mail order, price clubs, discount stores, food/drug stores, used book stores, and other outlets.

Source: Book Industry Study Group, Inc., New York, NY, *Consumer Research Study on Book Purchasing,* annual (copyright).

Parks, Recreation, and Travel 255

No. 423. Profile of Consumer Expenditures for Sound Recordings: 1990 to 1999

[In percent, except total value (7,541.1 represents $7,541,100,000). Based on monthly telephone surveys of the population 10 years old and over]

Item	1990	1995	1999	Item	1990	1995	1999
Total value (mil. dol.)	**7,541.1**	**12,320.3**	**14,584.5**	Music club	8.9	14.3	7.9
PERCENT DISTRIBUTION [1]				Mail order.............	2.5	4.0	2.5
				Internet [2]	(NA)	(NA)	2.4
Age: 10 to 14 years........	7.6	8.0	8.5	Music type: [3]			
15 to 19 years.........	18.3	17.1	12.6	Rock	36.1	33.5	25.2
20 to 24 years.........	16.5	15.3	12.6	Country	9.6	16.7	10.8
25 to 29 years.........	14.6	12.3	10.5	Rap/Hip Hop..........	8.5	6.7	10.8
30 to 34 years.........	13.2	12.1	10.1	R&B/Urban...........	11.6	11.3	10.5
35 to 39 years.........	10.2	10.8	10.4	Pop................	13.7	10.1	10.3
40 to 44 years.........	7.8	7.5	9.3	Religious	2.5	3.1	5.1
45 years and over	11.1	16.1	24.7	Classical	3.1	2.9	3.5
Sex: Male	54.4	53.0	50.3	Jazz	4.8	3.0	3.0
Female	45.6	47.0	49.7	Soundtracks	0.8	0.9	0.8
Sales outlet:				Oldies	0.8	1.0	0.7
Record store	69.8	52.0	44.5	New age	1.1	0.7	0.5
Other store	18.5	28.2	38.3	Children's............	0.5	0.5	0.4

NA Not available.   [1] Percent distributions exclude nonresponses and responses of don't know.   [2] Excludes record club purchases over the Internet.   [3] As classified by respondent.

Source: Recording Industry Association of America, Inc., Washington, DC, *1999 Consumer Profile.*

No. 424. Household Pet Ownership: 1996

[31.2 represents 31,200,000. Based on a sample survey of 80,000 households in 1996; for details, see source]

Item	Unit	Dog	Cat	Pet bird	Horse
Households owning companion pets [1]	Million	31.2	27.0	4.6	1.5
Percent of all households.....................	Percent ...	31.6	27.3	4.6	1.5
Average number owned.....................	Number...	1.7	2.2	2.7	2.7
Total companion pet population [1]....	Million	52.9	59.1	12.6	4.0
Households obtaining veterinary care [2].............	Percent ...	85.3	67.7	10.8	59.1
Average visits per household per year	Number...	2.6	1.9	0.2	2.3
PERCENT DISTRIBUTION OF HOUSEHOLDS OWNING PETS					
Annual household income:					
Under $12,500	Percent ...	12.7	13.9	17.3	9.5
$12,500 to $24,999.......................	Percent ...	19.1	19.7	20.9	20.3
$25,000 to $39,999.......................	Percent ...	21.6	21.5	22.0	21.8
$40,000 to $59,999	Percent ...	21.5	21.2	17.5	23.1
$60,000 and over	Percent ...	25.2	23.7	22.3	25.4
Family size: [1]					
One person	Percent ...	13.2	16.8	12.7	12.1
Two persons	Percent ...	31.0	32.6	27.9	29.1
Three persons	Percent ...	21.4	20.6	20.4	22.0
Four or more persons	Percent ...	34.5	29.9	38.9	36.7

[1] As of December.   [2] During 1996.

Source: American Veterinary Medical Association, Schaumburg, IL, *U.S. Pet Ownership and Demographics Sourcebook, 1997* (copyright).

No. 425. Retail Sales and Household Participation in Lawn and Garden Activities: 1994 to 1998

[For calendar year (25,897 represents $25,897,000,000). Based on national household sample survey conducted by the Gallup Organization. Subject to sampling variability; see source]

Activity	Retail sales (mil. dol.)					Percent households engaged in activity				
	1994	1995	1996	1997	1998	1994	1995	1996	1997	1998
Total..............	**25,897**	**22,242**	**22,519**	**26,639**	**30,188**	**74**	**72**	**64**	**67**	**65**
Lawn care.............	8,417	7,621	6,925	6,366	8,543	56	53	47	45	47
Indoor houseplants.......	999	864	791	1,107	1,159	37	30	31	29	29
Flower gardening	3,147	2,107	2,987	3,404	3,965	44	38	37	38	39
Insect control...........	1,127	1,049	1,734	1,342	1,671	28	24	24	21	22
Shrub care	1,133	774	1,059	1,441	1,635	30	25	25	24	25
Vegetable gardening......	1,476	1,359	1,341	1,914	2,000	31	28	26	23	24
Tree care	1,408	1,002	1,362	1,892	1,733	22	17	20	18	18
Landscaping	5,797	5,524	3,964	6,153	6,435	26	20	22	23	22
Flower bulbs	635	377	521	573	579	28	21	21	21	21
Fruit trees.............	389	241	349	455	301	14	11	12	11	10
Container gardening	359	377	387	558	783	12	12	10	11	11
Raising transplants [1]......	182	187	238	383	160	11	8	8	7	7
Herb gardening	112	140	144	168	146	10	8	9	8	7
Growing berries	85	55	90	60	82	6	5	5	5	5
Ornamental gardening.....	264	144	158	251	333	5	5	5	6	5
Water gardening	367	421	469	572	659	5	5	4	5	4

[1] Starting plants in advance of planting in ground.

Source: The National Gardening Association, Burlington, VT, *National Gardening Survey,* annual (copyright).

No. 426. Sporting Goods Sales by Product Category: 1990 to 1999

[In millions of dollars (50,725 represents $50,725,000,000), except percent. Based on a sample survey of consumer purchases of 80,000 households, (100,000 beginning 1995), except recreational transport, which was provided by industry associations. Excludes Alaska and Hawaii. Minus sign (-) indicates decrease]

Selected product category	1990	1992	1993	1994	1995	1996	1997	1998	1999, proj.
Sales, all products	**50,725**	**49,633**	**51,900**	**56,162**	**59,794**	**62,818**	**67,333**	**68,680**	**71,300**
Annual percent change [1]	-0.4	-0.3	4.6	8.2	6.5	5.1	7.2	2.0	3.8
Percent of retail sales	2.7	2.5	2.5	2.5	2.5	2.5	2.6	2.5	2.4
Athletic and sport clothing	10,130	8,990	9,096	9,521	10,311	11,127	12,035	12,637	13,390
Athletic and sport footwear [2]	11,654	11,733	11,084	11,120	11,415	12,815	13,319	13,020	13,211
Walking shoes	2,950	2,688	2,673	2,543	2,841	3,079	3,236	3,192	3,204
Gym shoes, sneakers	2,536	2,397	2,016	1,869	1,741	1,996	1,980	2,010	2,050
Jogging and running shoes	1,110	1,232	1,231	1,069	1,043	1,132	1,482	1,469	1,587
Tennis shoes	740	748	599	556	480	541	545	515	499
Aerobic shoes	611	590	500	356	372	401	380	334	307
Basketball shoes	918	984	874	867	999	1,192	1,134	1,000	1,003
Cross training shoes	679	799	877	1,101	1,191	1,417	1,450	1,402	1,486
Golf shoes	226	260	275	238	225	231	239	220	225
Athletic and sport equipment [2]	14,439	15,369	16,651	17,966	18,809	18,988	19,033	18,605	19,212
Archery	265	300	285	306	287	276	270	261	259
Baseball and softball	217	256	323	295	251	277	290	303	321
Camping	1,072	903	906	1,017	1,205	1,127	1,153	1,204	1,240
Exercise equipment	1,824	2,078	2,602	2,781	2,960	3,232	2,968	2,850	3,078
Firearms and hunting	2,202	2,533	2,722	3,523	3,003	2,521	2,562	2,200	2,310
Fishing tackle	1,910	1,906	1,952	1,951	2,010	1,970	1,891	1,903	1,905
Golf	2,514	2,606	2,723	2,747	3,194	3,560	3,703	3,641	3,714
In-line skating and wheel sports	150	268	377	545	646	590	562	515	504
Optics	438	465	493	503	655	673	690	710	739
Pool/billiards	192	238	313	313	304	271	242	251	259
Skiing, alpine	475	521	569	609	562	707	723	718	739
Skin diving and scuba	294	297	315	322	328	340	332	345	356
Tennis	333	310	327	313	297	296	319	313	319
Recreational transport	14,502	13,541	15,069	17,555	19,259	19,888	22,946	24,418	25,487
Pleasure boats	7,644	5,765	6,246	7,679	9,064	9,399	10,208	10,140	10,444
Recreational vehicles	4,113	4,412	4,775	5,690	5,895	6,327	6,904	8,364	9,078
Bicycles and supplies	2,423	2,973	3,534	3,470	3,390	3,187	4,860	4,957	5,007
Snowmobiles	322	391	515	715	910	974	975	957	958

[1] Represents change from immediate prior year.   [2] Includes other products not shown separately.

Source: National Sporting Goods Association, Mt. Prospect, IL, *The Sporting Goods Market in 1999*; and prior issues (copyright).

No. 427. Consumer Purchases of Sporting Goods by Consumer Characteristics: 1998

[In percent. Based on sample survey of consumer purchases of 100,000 households. Excludes Alaska and Hawaii]

Characteristic	Footwear					Equipment					
	Total house-holds	Aero-bic shoes	Gym shoes/ sneak-ers	Jog-ging/ run-ning shoes	Walk-ing shoes	Fish-ing tackle	Camp-ing equip-ment	Exer-cise equip-ment	Hunt-ing equip-ment	Golf equip-ment	Skate board-ing
Total	**100**	**100**	**100**	**100**	**100**	**100**	**100**	**100**	**100**	**100**	**100**
Age of user:											
Under 14 years old	20.1	6.2	43.3	13.5	5.9	5.0	15.0	1.0	3.0	2.0	41.3
14 to 17 years old	5.7	3.7	11.5	11.3	3.1	3.0	9.0	2.0	3.0	2.0	39.6
18 to 24 years old	9.5	9.9	6.9	11.7	4.1	5.0	10.0	6.0	5.0	3.0	6.5
25 to 34 years old	14.2	24.3	11.4	18.5	11.3	22.0	18.0	21.0	21.0	15.0	6.8
35 to 44 years old	16.5	24.3	10.5	19.6	17.3	27.0	18.0	23.0	29.0	23.0	5.1
45 to 64 years old	21.3	27.1	13.0	21.8	39.3	25.0	18.0	34.0	32.0	40.0	0.7
65 years old and over	12.7	4.5	3.4	3.6	19.0	3.0	2.0	11.0	6.0	15.0	-
Multiple ages	-	-	-	-	-	10.0	10.0	2.0	1.0	-	-
Sex of user:											
Male	49.0	11.1	51.4	57.0	38.5	77.0	62.0	39.0	89.0	89.0	76.0
Female	51.0	88.9	48.6	43.0	61.5	11.0	29.0	56.0	8.0	11.0	24.0
Both sexes	-	-	-	-	-	12.0	9.0	5.0	3.0	-	-
Education of household head:											
Less than high school	8.7	4.3	7.6	3.2	6.0	7.0	6.0	5.0	6.0	1.0	0.3
High school	24.1	20.9	26.0	13.7	23.6	23.0	20.0	18.0	30.0	13.0	23.9
Some college	36.2	40.0	36.0	32.9	35.7	44.0	37.0	36.0	40.0	35.0	36.4
College graduate	31.1	34.8	30.4	50.2	34.7	26.0	37.0	41.0	24.0	51.0	39.4
Annual household income:											
Under $15,000	19.6	8.7	13.7	7.9	13.7	9.0	12.0	8.0	7.0	4.0	4.6
$15,000 to $24,999	14.8	13.6	11.6	9.2	12.8	11.0	12.0	8.0	12.0	6.0	8.1
$25,000 to $34,999	14.3	15.4	15.2	11.3	12.5	15.0	13.0	10.0	17.0	7.0	13.9
$35,000 to $49,999	16.0	15.9	17.4	17.2	17.1	26.0	19.0	13.0	21.0	14.0	17.9
$50,000 to $74,999	23.3	29.3	27.0	31.3	28.3	23.0	27.0	33.0	27.0	36.0	43.8
$75,000 and over	12.1	17.1	15.1	23.1	15.6	16.0	17.0	28.0	16.0	33.0	11.7

- Represents or rounds to zero.

Source: National Sporting Goods Association, Mt. Prospect, IL, *The Sporting Goods Market in 1999* (copyright).

Parks, Recreation, and Travel   257

No. 428. Participants in Wildlife Related Recreation Activities: 1996

[In thousands (39,694 represents 39,694,000). For persons 16 years old and over engaging in activity at least once in 1996. Based on survey and subject to sampling error; see source for details]

Participant	Number	Days of participation	Trips	Participant	Number	Days of participation
Total sportsmen [1]	**39,694**	**882,569**	**729,495**	**Wildlife watchers** [1]	**62,868**	**(X)**
Total anglers	35,246	625,893	506,557	Nonresidential [2]	23,652	313,790
Freshwater	29,734	515,115	420,010	Observe wildlife	22,878	278,683
Excluding Great Lakes . .	28,921	485,474	402,814	Photograph wildlife . .	12,038	79,342
Great Lakes	2,039	20,095	17,195	Feed wildlife.	9,976	89,606
Saltwater.	9,438	103,034	86,547			
				Residential [3]	60,751	(X)
Total hunters	13,975	256,676	222,938	Observe wildlife	44,063	(X)
Big game	11,288	153,784	113,971	Photograph wildlife . .	16,021	(X)
Small game	6,945	75,117	63,744	Feed wild birds [4]	54,122	(X)
Migratory birds	3,073	26,501	22,509	Visit public parks. . . .	11,011	(X)
Other animals.	1,521	24,522	22,714	Maintain plantings or natural areas	13,401	(X)

X Not applicable.   [1] Detail does not add to total due to multiple responses and nonresponse.   [2] Persons taking a trip of at least 1 mile for activity.   [3] Activity within 1 mile of home.   [4] Or other wildlife.

No. 429. Expenditures for Wildlife Related Recreation Activities: 1996

[See headnote, Table 428. (37,797 represents $37,797,000,000)]

Type of expenditure	Fishing			Hunting			Wildlife watching		
	Expenditures (mil. dol.)	Spenders		Expenditures (mil. dol.)	Spenders		Expenditures (mil. dol.)	Spenders	
		Number (1,000)	Percent of anglers		Number (1,000)	Percent of hunters		Number (1,000)	Percent of watchers
Total [1]	**37,797**	**34,002**	**96**	**20,613**	**13,769**	**99**	**29,228**	**52,729**	**84**
Food and lodging	5,990	28,452	81	2,512	11,073	79	5,352	17,922	76
Food	4,256	28,267	80	2,078	11,060	79	3,447	17,761	75
Lodging.	1,734	8,020	23	434	1,909	14	1,905	6,783	29
Transportation	3,730	28,741	82	1,780	12,022	86	2,943	20,260	86
Public.	559	1,780	5	145	479	3	811	2,229	9
Private	3,171	28,382	81	1,634	11,926	85	2,132	19,863	84
Other trip-related costs	5,661	28,398	81	864	4,378	31	1,150	9,340	39
Sport specific equipment [2]	5,309	24,726	70	5,519	11,278	81	8,230	47,355	75
Auxiliary equipment [3]	1,037	6,006	17	1,233	5,730	41	858	4,763	8
Special equipment [4]	12,828	3,599	10	4,521	805	6	7,564	1,094	2
Other expenditures [5].	3,242	24,944	71	4,185	12,471	89	3,132	23,827	40

[1] Total not adjusted for multiple responses or nonresponse.   [2] Items owned primarily for each specific activity, such as rods and reels for fishing and guns and rifles for hunting.   [3] Equipment such as camping gear owned for wildlife-associated recreation.   [4] "Big ticket" equipment such as campers and boats owned for wildlife-associated recreation.   [5] Books, magazines, membership dues and contributions, land leasing and ownership, licenses, and plantings.
Source of Tables 428 and 429: U.S. Fish and Wildlife Service, *1996 National Survey of Fishing, Hunting, and Wildlife Associated Recreation.*

No. 430. Participation in NCAA Sports: 1997-98

Sport	Males			Females		
	Teams	Athletes	Average squad	Teams	Athletes	Average squad
Total	**7,723**	**203,686**	**(X)**	**7,859**	**135,110**	**(X)**
Baseball	817	24,806	30.4	(X)	(X)	(X)
Basketball	938	15,079	16.1	956	13,750	14.4
Cross country	790	10,524	13.3	843	10,476	12.4
Fencing [1]	37	616	16.6	44	540	12.3
Field hockey.	(X)	(X)	(X)	234	5,219	22.3
Football.	599	54,793	91.5	(X)	(X)	(X)
Golf	696	7,476	10.7	329	2,700	8.2
Gymnastics	27	403	14.9	91	1,414	15.5
Ice hockey [2]	129	3,613	28.0	30	635	21.2
Lacrosse	186	5,855	31.5	201	4,383	21.8
Rifle [1]	40	339	8.5	11	50	4.5
Rowing [3]	90	3,164	35.2	111	5,009	45.1
Skiing [1]	39	534	13.7	43	522	12.1
Soccer	682	17,204	25.2	724	15,987	22.1
Softball	(X)	(X)	(X)	778	13,750	17.7
Squash [4]	31	491	15.8	26	367	14.1
Swimming/diving	371	7,324	19.7	444	9,413	21.2
Synchronized swimming [2] . .	(X)	(X)	(X)	6	71	11.9
Tennis.	757	7,642	10.1	852	8,099	9.5
Track, indoor	512	16,090	31.4	540	13,548	25.1
Track, outdoor	625	19,349	31.0	649	15,959	24.6
Volleyball	68	965	14.2	915	12,556	13.7
Water polo [2]	43	969	22.5	32	661	20.7
Wrestling	246	6,450	26.2	(X)	(X)	(X)

X Not applicable.   [1] Co-ed championship sport.   [2] Sport recognized by the NCAA but does not have an NCAA championship for women.   [3] Sport recognized by the NCAA but does not have an NCAA championship for men.   [4] Sport recognized by the NCAA but does not have an NCAA championship.
Source: The National Collegiate Athletic Association (NCAA), Indianapolis, IN, 1997-98 Participation Study.

No. 431. High School Students Engaged in Organized Physical Activity: 1999

[In percent. **For students in grades 9 to 12**. Based on the Youth Risk Behavior Survey, a school-based survey and subject to sampling error; for details see source]

Characteristic	Enrolled in physical education class			Played on a sports team
	Total	Attended daily	Exercised 20 minutes or more per class	
All students...........	**56.1**	**29.1**	**76.3**	**55.1**
Male	60.7	31.9	82.1	61.7
Grade 9	82.3	44.0	84.4	63.9
Grade 10...............	65.3	32.8	79.4	62.3
Grade 11...............	44.6	23.5	82.0	58.8
Grade 12...............	43.8	23.6	82.3	60.7
Female..................	51.5	26.3	69.6	48.5
Grade 9	75.6	40.3	72.5	53.4
Grade 10...............	56.6	27.9	70.2	50.9
Grade 11...............	36.8	16.6	68.0	45.8
Grade 12...............	29.4	16.6	60.1	42.3
White, non-Hispanic	56.1	28.3	78.7	56.9
Male...................	60.2	30.8	83.8	63.0
Female	51.7	25.8	72.4	50.5
Black, non-Hispanic	52.9	29.2	67.8	48.7
Male...................	59.2	33.1	78.4	62.0
Female	47.1	25.5	55.8	36.3
Hispanic	59.3	40.4	75.5	50.8
Male...................	65.1	44.6	79.6	57.2
Female	53.6	36.2	70.8	44.5

Source: U.S. Centers for Disease Control and Prevention, Atlanta, GA, *Youth Risk Behavior Surveillance—United States, 1999, Morbidity and Mortality Weekly Report*, Vol. 49, No. SS-5, June 9, 2000.

No. 432. Participation in High School Athletic Programs: 1971 to 1999

[Data based on number of state associations reporting and may underrepresent the number of schools with and participants in athletic programs]

Year	Participants [1]		Sex and sport	Most popular sports, 1998-99 [2]	
	Males	Females		Schools	Participants
1971	3,666,917	294,105	MALES		
1972-73	3,770,621	817,073			
1973-74	4,070,125	1,300,169	Football (11-player)	13,192	983,625
1975-76	4,109,021	1,645,039	Basketball	16,763	549,499
1977-78	4,367,442	2,083,040	Track & field (outdoor)	14,620	477,960
1978-79	3,709,512	1,854,400	Baseball	14,486	455,305
1979-80	3,517,829	1,750,264	Soccer	9,041	321,416
1980-81	3,503,124	1,853,789	Wrestling.............	9,022	235,973
1981-82	3,409,081	1,810,671	Cross country...........	11,855	181,915
1982-83	3,355,558	1,779,972	Golf	12,251	167,781
1983-84	3,303,599	1,747,346	Tennis...............	9,521	142,953
1984-85	3,354,284	1,757,884	Swimming & diving	5,234	83,411
1985-86	3,344,275	1,807,121	FEMALE		
1986-87	3,364,082	1,836,356			
1987-88	3,425,777	1,849,684	Basketball	16,439	456,873
1988-89	3,416,844	1,839,352	Track & field (outdoor)	14,545	405,163
1989-90	3,398,192	1,858,659	Volleyball..............	13,250	380,994
1990-91	3,406,355	1,892,316	Softball (fast pitch)........	12,679	340,480
1991-92	3,429,853	1,940,801	Soccer	7,931	257,586
1992-93	3,416,389	1,997,489	Tennis...............	9,385	156,505
1993-94	3,472,967	2,130,315	Cross country...........	11,341	155,529
1994-95	3,536,359	2,240,461	Swimming & diving	5,450	133,235
1995-96	3,634,052	2,367,936	Competitive spirit squads ...	4,064	74,462
1996-97	3,706,225	2,474,043	Field hockey...........	1,507	57,980
1997-98	3,763,120	2,570,333			
1998-99	3,832,352	2,652,726			

[1] A participant is counted in the number of sports participated in.   [2] Ten most popular sports for each sex in terms of number of participants.

Source: National Federation of State High School Associations, Indianapolis, IN, *The 1998-99 High School Athletics Participation Survey* (copyright).

U.S. Census Bureau, Statistical Abstract of the United States: 2000

No. 433. Selected Spectator Sports: 1985 to 1998

[47,742 represents 47,742,000]

Sport	Unit	1985	1987	1990	1994	1995	1996	1997	1998
Baseball, major leagues: [1]									
Attendance	1,000 . . .	47,742	53,182	55,512	50,010	51,288	61,665	64,921	71,929
Regular season	1,000 . . .	46,824	52,011	54,824	50,010	50,469	60,097	63,168	70,372
National League	1,000 . . .	22,292	24,734	24,492	25,808	25,110	30,379	31,885	38,424
American League	1,000 . . .	24,532	27,277	30,332	24,202	25,359	29,718	31,283	31,948
Playoffs [2]	1,000 . . .	591	784	479	(X)	533	1,300	1,349	1,314
World Series	1,000 . . .	327	387	209	(X)	286	268	404	243
Players' salaries: [3]									
Average	$1,000 . .	371	412	598	1,168	1,111	1,120	1,337	1,399
Basketball: [4] [5]									
NCAA—Men's college:									
Teams	Number .	753	760	767	858	868	866	865	895
Attendance	1,000 . . .	26,584	26,798	28,741	28,390	28,548	28,225	27,738	28,032
NCAA—Women's college:									
Teams	Number .	746	756	782	859	864	874	879	911
Attendance	1,000 . . .	2,072	2,156	2,777	4,557	4,962	5,234	6,734	7,387
Pro: [6]									
Teams	Number .	23	23	27	27	27	29	29	29
Attendance, total [7]	1,000 . . .	11,534	13,190	18,586	19,350	19,883	21,833	21,677	21,801
Regular season	1,000 . . .	10,506	12,065	17,369	17,984	18,516	20,513	20,305	20,373
Average per game . . .	Number .	11,141	12,795	15,690	16,246	16,727	17,252	17,077	17,135
Players' salaries:									
Average.	$1,000 . .	325	440	750	1,700	1,900	2,000	2,200	2,600
Football:									
NCAA College: [5]									
Teams	Number .	509	507	533	568	565	566	581	595
Attendance	1,000 . . .	34,952	35,008	35,330	36,460	35,638	36,083	36,858	37,491
National Football League: [8]									
Teams	Number .	28	28	28	28	30	31	31	31
Attendance, total [9]	1,000 . . .	14,058	[10]15,180	17,666	18,011	19,203	(NA)	19,050	19,742
Regular season	1,000 . . .	13,345	[10]11,406	13,960	14,030	15,044	14,612	14,967	15,365
Average per game . . .	Number .	59,567	[10]54,315	62,321	62,636	62,682	60,885	62,364	64,020
Postseason games [11] . .	1,000 . . .	711	656	848	(NA)	(NA)	(NA)	(NA)	823
Players' salaries: [12]									
Average.	$1,000 . .	194	203	352	637	714	791	725	983
Median base salary	$1,000 . .	140	175	236	325	335	350	340	405
National Hockey League: [13]									
Regular season attendance . .	1,000 . . .	11,621	12,118	12,344	10,646	15,658	16,237	15,701	17,265
Playoffs attendance	1,000 . . .	1,153	1,337	1,442	1,329	1,447	1,423	1,384	1,507
Horseracing: [14] [15]									
Racing days	Number .	13,745	14,208	13,841	13,082	13,243	12,457	11,958	(NA)
Attendance	1,000 . . .	73,346	70,105	63,803	42,065	38,934	43,367	41,846	(NA)
Pari-mutuel turnover	Mil. dol. .	12,222	13,122	7,162	14,143	14,592	14,902	15,220	(NA)
Revenue to government	Mil. dol. .	625	608	624	452	456	444	422	(NA)
Greyhound: [14]									
Total performances.	Number .	9,590	11,156	14,915	17,035	16,110	15,151	14,557	(NA)
Attendance	1,000 . . .	23,853	26,215	28,660	(NA)	(NA)	(NA)	14,306	(NA)
Pari-mutuel turnover.	Mil. dol. .	2,702	3,193	3,422	2,948	2,730	2,433	2,291	(NA)
Revenue to government	Mil. dol. .	201	221	235	183	157	139	114	(NA)
Jai alai: [14]									
Total performances.	Number .	2,736	2,906	3,620	3,146	2,748	2,542	2,648	(NA)
Games played.	Number .	32,260	38,476	(NA)	42,607	37,052	34,346	(NA)	(NA)
Attendance	1,000 . . .	4,722	6,816	5,329	3,684	3,208	(NA)	2,125	(NA)
Total handle	Mil. dol. .	664.0	707.5	545.5	330.7	296.4	273.4	251	(NA)
Revenue to government	Mil. dol. .	50	51	39	22	13	12	10	(NA)
Professional rodeo: [16]									
Rodeos	Number .	617	637	754	782	739	742	729	703
Performances	Number .	1,887	1,832	2,159	2,245	2,217	2,229	2,213	2,125
Members	Number .	5,239	5,342	5,693	6,415	6,894	7,084	7,178	7,301
Permit-holders (rookies)	Number .	2,534	2,746	3,290	3,346	3,835	4,141	4,197	4,117
Total prize money.	Mil. dol. .	15.1	14.9	18.2	23.1	24.5	26.4	28.0	29.9

NA Not available.   X Not applicable.   [1] Source: The National League of Professional Baseball Clubs, New York, NY, *National League Green Book;* and The American League of Professional Baseball Clubs, New York, NY, *American League Red Book.*   [2] Beginning 1996, two rounds of playoffs were played. Prior years had one round.   [3] Source: Major League Baseball Players Association, New York, NY.   [4] Season ending in year shown.   [5] Source: National Collegiate Athletic Assn., Overland Park, KS. For women's attendance total, excludes double-headers with men's teams.   [6] Source: National Basketball Assn., New York, NY. For season ending in year shown.   [7] Includes All-Star game, not shown separately.   [8] Source: National Football League, New York, NY.   [9] Beginning 1987 includes preseason attendance, not shown separately.   [10] Season was interrupted by a strike.   [11] Includes Pro Bowl, a nonchampionship game and Super Bowl.   [12] Source: National Football League Players Association, Washington, DC.   [13] For season beginning in year shown. Source: National Hockey League, Montreal, Quebec. [14] Source: Association of Racing Commissioners International, Inc., Lexington, KY.   [15] Includes thoroughbred, harness, quarter horse, and fairs.   [16] Source: Professional Rodeo Cowboys Association, Colorado Springs, CO, *Official Professional Rodeo Media Guide,* annual (copyright).

Source: Compiled from sources listed in footnotes.

No. 434. Selected Recreational Activities: 1975 to 1998

[26 represents 26,000,000]

Activity	Unit	1975	1980	1985	1990	1995	1996	1997	1998
Softball, amateur: [1]									
Total participants [2]	Million. .	26	30	41	41	42	42	41	41
Youth participants	1,000 . .	450	650	712	1,100	1,350	1,416	1,440	1,500
Adult teams [3]	1,000 . .	66	110	152	188	187	183	178	168
Youth teams [3]	1,000 . .	9	18	31	46	74	79	80	81
Golfers (one round or more) [4][5]	1,000 . .	13,036	15,112	17,520	27,800	25,000	24,737	26,474	26,427
Golf rounds played [4][5]	1,000 . .	308,562	357,701	414,777	502,000	490,200	477,400	547,200	528,500
Golf facilities [4]	Number.	11,370	12,005	12,346	12,846	14,074	14,341	14,602	14,900
Classification:									
Private	Number.	4,770	4,839	4,861	4,810	4,324	4,306	4,257	4,251
Daily fee	Number.	5,014	5,372	5,573	6,024	7,491	7,729	7,984	8,247
Municipal	Number.	1,586	1,794	1,912	2,012	2,259	2,306	2,361	2,402
Tennis: [6]									
Players	1,000 . .	[7]34,000	(NA)	13,000	21,000	17,820	19,499	19,500	(NA)
Courts	1,000 . .	130	(NA)	220	220	240	245	245	(NA)
Indoor	1,000 . .	8	(NA)	14	14	15	15	15	(NA)
Tenpin bowling: [8]									
Participants, total	Million. .	62.5	72.0	67.0	71.0	79.0	91.0	91.0	91.0
Male	Million. .	29.9	34.0	32.0	35.4	36.3	41.8	41.8	41.8
Female	Million. .	32.6	38.0	35.0	35.6	42.6	49.2	49.2	49.2
Establishments	Number.	8,577	8,591	8,275	7,611	7,049	6,880	6,688	6,542
Lanes	1,000 . .	141	154	155	148	139	136	133	131
Membership, total [9]	1,000 . .	8,751	9,664	8,064	6,588	4,925	4,662	4,405	4,156
American Bowling									
Congress	1,000 . .	4,300	4,688	3,657	3,036	2,370	2,261	2,135	2,027
Women's Bowling									
Congress	1,000 . .	3,692	4,187	3,714	2,859	2,036	1,917	1,798	1,678
Young American									
Bowling Alliance [10]	1,000 . .	759	789	693	693	519	484	472	451
Motion picture theaters [11]	1,000 . .	15	18	21	24	28	30	32	34
Four-wall	1,000 . .	11	14	18	23	27	29	31	33
Drive-in	1,000 . .	4	4	3	1	1	1	1	1
Receipts, box office	Mil. dol.	2,115	2,749	3,749	5,022	5,494	5,912	6,366	6,949
Admission, average price . . .	Dollars .	2.05	2.69	3.55	4.23	4.35	4.42	4.59	4.69
Attendance	Million. .	1,033	1,022	1,056	1,189	1,263	1,339	1,388	1,481
Boating: [12]									
Recreational boats owned . . .	1,000 . .	(NA)	11,832	13,778	15,987	15,375	15,830	16,230	16,654
Retail expenditures on									
boating [13]	Mil. dol.	4,800	7,370	13,284	13,731	17,226	17,753	19,344	19,148
Retail units purchased:									
Total all boats [14]	1,000 . .	(NA)	643	675	525	664	635	610	571
Outboard boats	1,000 . .	(NA)	290	305	227	231	215	200	201
Inboard boats	1,000 . .	(NA)	8	17	15	12	11	12	14
Sterndrive boats	1,000 . .	(NA)	56	115	97	94	95	92	91
Jet boats	1,000 . .	(NA)	(NA)	(NA)	(NA)	15	14	12	9
Personal watercraft	1,000 . .	(NA)	(NA)	(NA)	(NA)	200	191	176	130
Sailboats	1,000 . .	(NA)	73	38	21	14	16	14	19
Canoes	1,000 . .	(NA)	105	79	75	98	93	104	108
Inflatable boats	1,000 . .	(NA)	16	34	27	(NA)	(NA)	(NA)	(NA)
Sailboard	1,000 . .	(NA)	21	50	42	(NA)	(NA)	(NA)	(NA)
Boat trailers	1,000 . .	(NA)	176	192	165	207	194	181	174
Outboard motors	1,000 . .	(NA)	315	392	352	317	308	302	314
Sterndrive and inboard									
engines	1,000 . .	(NA)	88	155	134	120	120	116	117

NA Not available. [1] Source: Amateur Softball Association, Oklahoma City, OK. [2] Amateur Softball Association teams and other amateur softball teams. [3] Amateur Softball Association teams only. [4] Source: National Golf Foundation, Jupiter, FL. [5] Prior to 1990, for persons 5 years of age and over; thereafter for persons 12 years of age and over. [6] Source: Tennis Industry Association, Hilton Head, SC. Players for persons 12 years old and over who played at least once. [7] 1974 data. [8] For season ending in year shown. Persons 5 years old and over. Source: Bowling Headquarters, Greendale, WI. [9] Membership totals are for U.S., Canada and for U.S. military personnel worldwide. [10] Prior to 1985, represents American Jr. Bowling Congress and ABC/WIBC Collegiate Division. [11] Source: Motion Picture Association of America, Inc., Encino, CA. For 1975, figures represent theaters; thereafter, screens. [12] Source: National Marine Manufacturers Association, Chicago, IL. (copyright). [13] Represents estimated expenditures for new and used boats, motors and engines, accessories, safety equipment, fuel, insurance, docking, maintenance, launching, storage, repairs, and other expenses. [14] 1980 through 1990 includes other boats, not shown separately.

Source: Compiled from sources listed in footnotes.

U.S. Census Bureau, Statistical Abstract of the United States: 2000

[In thousands (242,884 represents 242,884,000), except rank. For persons 7 years of age or older. Except as indicated, a participant plays a sport more than once in the year]

Activity	All persons Number	All persons Rank	Sex Male	Sex Female	Age 7-11 years	Age 12-17 years	Age 18-24 years	Age 25-34 years	Age 35-44 years	Age 45-54 years	Age 55-64 years	Age 65 years and over	Household income (dol.) Under 15,000	15,000-24,999	25,000-34,999	35,000-49,000	50,000-74,999	75,000 and over
Total	**242,884**	(X)	**118,009**	**124,876**	**19,876**	**23,241**	**25,159**	**38,757**	**44,389**	**34,518**	**22,662**	**34,284**	**36,453**	**32,864**	**37,210**	**45,855**	**48,499**	**42,005**
SERIES I SPORTS [1]																		
Number participated in—																		
Aerobic exercising [2]	25,764	12	5,753	20,011	806	1,916	4,376	6,967	5,255	3,304	1,470	1,672	2,727	2,777	3,900	4,889	5,664	5,807
Backpacking [3]	14,622	18	9,111	5,510	1,459	2,223	2,497	3,797	2,805	1,323	327	190	1,823	1,912	2,281	2,835	3,231	2,540
Badminton	4,826	28	2,046	2,780	925	1,069	613	851	764	363	129	113	685	654	752	1,063	903	769
Baseball	15,856	15	11,980	3,876	4,714	4,307	2,323	1,847	1,647	591	169	257	1,713	1,733	2,451	3,464	3,391	3,104
Basketball	29,417	9	20,166	9,251	6,273	8,246	4,830	4,861	3,318	1,263	397	228	2,845	3,075	4,920	6,100	6,626	5,851
Bicycle riding [2]	43,535	5	22,937	20,598	10,055	7,844	3,588	7,072	7,304	3,893	2,066	1,712	4,172	4,356	6,332	8,573	6,822	9,280
Billiards	32,289	8	20,283	12,006	1,612	3,639	7,914	9,006	5,816	2,830	794	677	3,614	4,526	5,450	6,326	6,903	5,470
Bowling	40,063	6	20,829	19,234	4,865	6,055	7,282	8,161	6,903	3,510	1,486	1,800	3,916	4,469	6,607	8,415	9,541	7,115
Calisthenics [2]	11,779	21	5,838	5,940	1,313	2,335	1,687	2,050	1,865	1,099	569	860	1,448	1,343	1,818	2,677	2,363	2,130
Camping [4]	46,470	3	24,680	21,790	5,529	5,878	6,108	9,204	10,218	5,424	2,445	1,664	4,356	6,086	7,639	10,167	10,635	7,587
Exercise walking [2]	77,645	1	28,368	49,278	2,974	3,781	6,905	13,663	16,099	13,571	8,694	11,960	10,517	9,804	11,640	14,417	16,815	14,454
Exercising with equipment [2]	46,145	4	21,424	24,721	751	4,153	7,033	10,612	9,648	6,801	3,502	3,646	3,939	4,522	6,480	8,516	10,797	11,890
Fishing—fresh water	38,640	7	26,404	12,236	4,627	4,086	4,682	6,898	8,064	5,006	2,941	2,335	4,673	5,575	6,629	7,757	8,106	5,899
Fishing—salt water	11,037	23	7,850	3,187	992	862	796	2,268	2,477	1,498	1,070	1,076	1,251	1,232	1,321	2,184	2,544	2,506
Football—tackle	7,448	27	6,542	906	1,121	3,014	1,692	979	298	120	86	138	985	1,119	1,502	1,577	1,371	894
Football—touch	9,643	24	7,582	2,062	2,182	2,884	1,861	1,558	720	213	78	148	1,020	1,066	1,636	2,124	2,037	1,760
Golf	27,496	10	21,757	5,739	1,264	2,432	3,095	6,092	5,532	4,093	2,349	2,639	1,135	2,368	3,634	4,924	7,207	8,227
Hiking	27,190	11	14,868	12,323	3,080	2,997	3,888	6,004	5,688	3,196	1,381	956	2,520	2,990	4,064	4,928	6,709	5,979
Hunting with firearms	17,285	14	15,439	1,846	489	1,891	2,716	3,853	3,427	2,735	1,322	852	1,897	2,370	3,180	3,850	3,501	2,487
Martial arts	4,560	29	2,749	1,811	1,114	797	639	1,006	512	264	118	110	760	506	685	778	974	858
Racquetball	3,979	30	2,913	1,066	207	349	1,011	1,284	720	224	108	76	373	350	514	842	899	1,001
Running/jogging [2]	22,525	13	12,240	10,285	1,837	3,788	4,455	5,172	3,818	2,234	719	501	2,265	2,355	3,533	3,740	5,187	5,446
Skiing—alpine/downhill	7,680	26	4,582	3,098	548	1,262	1,407	1,715	1,384	948	348	69	264	419	559	1,191	2,006	3,240
Skiing—cross country	2,643	31	1,355	1,287	139	307	335	382	568	538	226	148	203	245	213	396	731	854
Soccer	13,167	19	8,232	4,935	5,489	3,936	1,240	1,337	795	228	56	86	1,252	1,162	1,579	2,340	3,357	3,477
Softball	15,595	16	8,390	7,205	3,040	3,263	2,065	3,379	2,473	989	188	196	1,592	1,383	2,635	3,675	3,578	2,732
Swimming [2]	58,249	2	26,993	31,256	10,067	9,900	6,521	9,473	10,700	5,468	2,697	3,423	5,532	6,055	8,581	11,859	13,448	12,774
Table tennis	8,258	25	4,882	3,376	1,004	1,913	1,217	1,286	1,487	739	321	290	723	859	973	1,500	2,229	1,974
Target shooting	12,755	20	10,029	2,726	745	1,436	2,327	2,943	2,560	1,684	639	420	1,269	2,013	2,263	2,540	3,009	1,661
Tennis	11,227	22	6,202	5,026	1,204	2,011	2,076	2,227	1,981	943	367	418	638	1,153	1,169	1,908	2,970	3,389
Volleyball	14,788	17	6,934	7,854	1,551	3,807	2,765	3,544	1,763	933	282	144	1,565	1,569	2,623	3,245	3,604	2,182

262   Parks, Recreation, and Travel

Activity	All persons Number	All persons Rank	Sex Male	Sex Female	Age 7-11 years	Age 12-17 years	Age 18-24 years	Age 25-34 years	Age 35-44 years	Age 45-54 years	Age 55-64 years	Age 65 years and over	Household income (dol.) Under 15,000	15,000-24,999	25,000-34,999	35,000-49,999	50,000-74,999	75,000 and over
SERIES II SPORTS [5]																		
Total	**242,884**	(X)	**118,011**	**124,877**	**19,876**	**23,241**	**25,159**	**38,757**	**44,390**	**34,519**	**22,662**	**34,899**	**36,596**	**31,576**	**35,746**	**46,800**	**48,994**	**43,175**
Number participating in—																		
Archery (target)	4,768	15	3,662	1,106	789	956	573	836	856	480	145	134	552	621	624	1,090	1,277	604
Boating, motor/power	25,715	3	14,573	11,143	2,368	2,927	2,596	5,480	5,539	3,499	1,895	1,419	1,778	2,293	3,632	5,743	6,311	5,959
Canoeing	7,093	12	3,931	3,162	759	1,086	909	1,285	1,701	796	301	256	426	786	736	1,632	1,772	1,742
Dart throwing	20,821	4	12,768	8,053	1,920	2,351	3,494	5,938	4,455	1,689	640	334	2,777	2,800	3,578	4,287	4,046	3,333
Hunting with bow arrow	5,591	14	5,051	539	174	590	762	1,440	1,452	708	304	175	610	520	1,107	1,381	1,353	619
Ice hockey	2,131	20	1,730	402	365	593	431	384	240	72	14	76	144	201	120	497	615	554
Ice/figure skating	7,799	9	3,151	4,648	1,990	1,785	785	1,179	1,423	406	157	75	571	455	891	1,343	2,227	2,313
Mountain biking-off road	8,610	7	5,685	2,926	1,040	1,224	1,069	2,665	1,646	638	222	106	816	918	985	2,036	2,168	1,687
Mountain biking-on road	15,283	5	8,883	6,399	2,061	1,876	1,955	4,687	2,929	1,181	417	176	1,585	1,506	2,098	3,473	3,602	3,019
Roller hockey	3,093	18	2,568	525	1,009	1,013	447	386	199	14	-	25	102	218	270	617	968	918
Roller skating/in-line	27,033	1	12,973	14,060	9,052	6,892	3,411	3,920	2,743	673	160	183	1,894	2,603	3,356	5,607	7,248	6,325
Roller skating/traditional 2x2 wheel	9,931	6	3,506	6,424	3,639	2,509	746	1,197	1,194	368	131	146	1,542	1,436	1,334	2,405	1,916	1,299
Sailing	3,589	17	1,953	1,637	324	351	218	604	805	695	295	318	305	259	257	693	706	1,368
Scuba (open water)	2,558	19	1,667	891	22	213	285	717	195	389	138	53	160	119	244	464	646	926
Skate boarding	5,782	13	4,474	1,308	2,309	2,253	584	299	195	37	20	85	567	547	704	1,149	1,497	1,318
Snorkeling	7,334	10	3,868	3,466	412	746	585	1,850	1,798	1,365	387	191	328	468	557	1,308	1,887	2,785
Snowboarding	3,635	16	2,778	857	487	1,477	730	551	187	109	55	40	312	280	457	589	1,030	969
Step aerobics	8,463	8	870	7,593	159	314	1,627	2,641	2,145	894	363	321	829	830	1,254	1,947	1,875	1,728
Water skiing	7,215	11	4,467	2,748	632	1,161	1,218	1,959	1,377	721	102	44	249	519	765	1,747	1,804	2,130
Wind surfing	644	21	400	244	22	98	23	154	134	139	35	39	69	57	68	109	147	195
Work out at club	26,544	2	12,379	14,165	282	1,561	4,626	7,057	5,809	3,450	1,663	2,122	2,126	2,031	3,316	5,390	6,062	7,619

- Represents or rounds to zero. X Not applicable. [1] Based on a sampling of 15,000 households. [2] Participant engaged in activity at least six times in the year. [3] Includes wilderness camping. [4] Vacation/overnight. [5] Based on a sampling of 20,000 households.

Source: National Sporting Goods Association, Mt. Prospect, IL, Sports Participation in 1998: Series I and Series II (copyright).

Parks, Recreation, and Travel 263

No. 436. Adult Attendance at Sports Events: 1998

[In thousands (3,576 represents 3,576,000), except percent. For spring 1998. Based on survey and subject to sampling error; see source]

Event	Attend one or more times a month		Attend less than once a month		Event	Attend one or more times a month		Attend less than once a month	
	Number	Percent	Number	Percent		Number	Percent	Number	Percent
Auto racing	3,576	1.8	7,777	4.0	Golf	2,173	1.1	4,346	2.2
Baseball	8,562	4.4	17,808	9.1	High school sports	9,910	5.1	7,089	3.6
Basketball:					Horse racing:				
College games	4,280	2.2	6,615	3.4	Flats, runners	1,131	0.6	3,177	1.6
Professional games	3,009	1.5	7,662	3.9	Trotters/harness	857	0.4	2,339	1.2
Bowling	2,407	1.2	2,876	1.5	Ice hockey	2,934	1.5	7,235	3.7
Boxing	1,313	0.7	2,403	1.2	Motorcycle racing	618	0.3	2,442	1.3
Equestrian events	743	0.4	2,278	1.2	Pro beach volleyball	[1]365	0.2	1,745	0.9
Figure skating	951	0.5	2,748	1.4	Rodeo	1,073	0.5	3,830	2.0
Football:					Soccer	3,394	1.7	3,459	1.8
College games	5,019	2.6	7,942	4.1	Tennis	883	0.5	2,446	1.3
Monday night professional games	1,652	0.8	3,166	1.6	Truck and tractor pull/mud racing	780	0.4	2,693	1.4
Weekend professional games	3,039	1.6	8,250	4.2	Wrestling—professional	1,243	0.6	2,609	1.3

[1] Figure does not meet standards of reliability or precision.

Source: Mediamark Research, Inc., New York, NY *Top-line Reports* (copyright). Internet site <http://www.mediamark.com/mri/docs/TopLineReports.html> (accessed 23 March 2000).

No. 437. Adult Participation in Selected Leisure Activities by Frequency: 1998

[In thousands (13,890 represents 13,890,000), except percent. For spring 1998. Based on sample and subject to sampling error; see source]

Activity	Participated in the last 12 months		Frequency of participation							
			Two or more times a week		Once a week		Two to three times a month		Once a month or less	
	Number	Percent	Number	Percent	Number	Percent	Number	Percent	Number	Percent
Attend auto shows	13,890	7.1	[1]340	0.2	313	0.2	411	0.2	8,275	4.2
Adult education courses	16,006	8.2	3,259	1.7	3,238	1.7	662	0.3	5,958	3.1
Attend horse races	5,951	3.0	[1]188	0.1	369	0.2	[1]418	0.2	3,749	1.9
Attend music performances	42,946	22.0	853	0.4	1,108	0.6	2,616	1.3	31,025	15.9
Attend dance performances	11,862	6.1	[1]185	0.1	552	0.3	644	0.3	7,705	4.0
Backgammon	6,277	3.2	654	0.3	547	0.3	1,077	0.6	2,913	1.5
Baking	40,751	20.9	9,358	4.8	6,477	3.3	9,383	4.8	9,815	5.0
Barbecuing	64,130	32.9	10,827	5.5	11,149	5.7	14,863	7.6	16,430	8.4
Go to bars/night clubs	39,095	20.0	4,372	2.2	5,829	3.0	6,666	3.4	16,756	8.6
Go to beach	48,363	24.8	3,048	1.6	2,362	1.2	5,013	2.6	28,730	14.7
Billiards/pool	22,183	11.4	2,158	1.1	2,272	1.2	2,745	1.4	10,539	5.4
Birdwatching	10,044	5.1	4,506	2.3	951	0.5	1,082	0.6	1,815	0.9
Board games	28,196	14.4	2,488	1.3	2,840	1.5	5,684	2.9	12,958	6.6
Chess	8,677	4.4	780	0.4	865	0.4	1,288	0.7	3,758	1.9
Cooking for fun	36,305	18.6	11,997	6.1	6,597	3.4	5,536	2.8	6,513	3.3
Concerts on radio	10,659	5.5	2,523	1.3	1,193	0.6	1,389	0.7	2,745	1.4
Crossword puzzles	32,058	16.4	14,166	7.3	4,783	2.5	2,568	1.3	5,206	2.7
Dance/go dancing	25,306	13.0	1,963	1.0	3,163	1.6	3,469	1.8	12,021	6.2
Dining out	95,221	48.8	20,155	10.3	21,962	11.3	20,690	10.6	19,023	9.8
Electronic games (not TV)	16,626	8.5	4,934	2.5	2,038	1.0	2,443	1.3	4,150	2.2
Entertain friends or relatives at home	84,886	43.5	10,011	5.1	11,412	5.8	18,663	9.6	32,828	16.8
Fly kites	7,154	3.7	[1]121	0.1	[1]308	0.2	[1]383	0.2	4,756	2.4
Furniture refinishing	9,137	4.7	[1]291	0.1	[1]212	0.1	412	0.2	6,505	3.3
Go to live theater	28,213	14.5	[1]222	0.1	620	0.3	1,397	0.7	20,229	10.3
Model making	4,374	2.2	364	0.2	477	0.2	444	0.2	2,206	1.1
Go to museums	29,632	15.2	500	0.3	575	0.3	701	0.4	22,157	11.3
Painting, drawing	12,544	6.4	2,783	1.4	1,123	0.6	1,829	0.9	4,278	2.2
Photography	21,150	10.8	2,045	1.0	2,185	1.1	3,966	2.0	9,439	4.8
Picnic	30,731	15.7	557	0.3	824	0.4	2,354	1.2	19,484	10.0
Play bingo	12,014	6.2	1,482	0.8	2,037	1.0	959	0.5	5,026	2.6
Play cards	55,661	28.5	8,044	4.1	7,963	4.1	8,957	4.6	21,475	11.0
Play musical instrument	14,814	7.6	6,062	3.1	1,928	1.0	1,577	0.8	3,419	1.8
Reading books	78,581	40.3	45,009	23.1	7,195	3.7	6,286	3.2	9,316	4.8
Word games	15,507	7.9	4,593	2.4	2,106	1.1	1,996	1.0	3,790	2.0
Trivia games	14,196	7.3	1,731	0.9	1,491	0.8	2,056	1.1	6,180	3.2
Video games	24,227	12.4	8,630	4.4	2,510	1.3	2,799	1.4	5,730	2.9
Woodworking	12,026	6.2	2,771	1.4	1,170	0.6	1,821	0.9	4,491	2.3
Zoo attendance	26,563	13.6	[1]90	(Z)	[1]299	0.2	482	0.2	20,491	10.5

Z Less than .05 percent.   [1] Figure does not meet standards of reliability or precision.

Source: Mediamark Research, Inc., New York, NY, *Top-line Reports* (copyright). Internet site <http://www.mediamark.com/mri/docs/TopLineReports.html> (accessed 23 March 2000).

No. 438. Participation in Various Leisure Activities: 1997

[In percent, except as indicated (195.6 represents 195,600,000). Covers activities engaged in at least once in the prior 12 months. See headnote, Table 440. See also Table 441]

Item	Adult population (mil.)	Attendance at—			Participation in—				
		Movies	Sports events	Amusement park	Exercise program	Playing sports	Charity work	Home improvement/repair	Computer hobbies
Total	195.6	66	41	57	76	45	43	66	40
Sex: Male	94.2	66	49	58	75	56	40	71	44
Female	101.4	65	34	57	77	35	46	61	37
Race: Hispanic	19.1	59	35	66	69	35	31	61	25
White	146.1	68	44	56	78	48	45	70	43
African American	22.1	60	35	55	74	34	44	51	37
American Indian	3.0	65	34	59	83	49	34	58	37
Asian	5.3	76	29	58	70	48	41	58	62
Age: 18 to 24 years old	23.7	88	51	76	85	67	35	57	68
25 to 34 years old	40.1	79	51	70	82	63	41	63	51
35 to 44 years old	45.3	73	46	68	79	52	50	76	47
45 to 54 years old	33.7	65	42	53	77	40	46	75	40
55 to 64 years old	20.9	46	33	40	69	19	44	71	23
65 to 74 years old	19.6	38	21	29	65	23	40	55	11
75 years old and over	12.3	28	16	18	56	13	40	44	7
Education: Grade school	13.7	14	13	34	46	13	20	40	1
Some high school	26.9	52	25	54	66	30	31	59	19
High school graduate	62.0	62	38	58	74	41	36	65	35
Some college	50.3	78	48	64	81	54	50	71	52
College graduate	25.2	82	59	61	87	61	55	76	63
Graduate school	17.4	81	55	53	88	57	67	73	59
Income: $10,000 or less	15.0	37	15	39	55	19	32	42	19
$10,001 to $20,000	26.5	46	26	51	69	27	34	53	22
$20,001 to $30,000	29.4	56	28	55	72	40	37	61	30
$30,001 to $40,000	32.1	71	42	64	77	46	47	68	40
$40,001 to $50,000	25.9	73	51	67	80	51	42	75	47
$50,001 to $75,000	35.0	82	54	65	86	60	50	80	54
$75,001 to $100,000	16.2	81	66	64	86	61	51	79	64
Over $100,000	15.5	87	65	56	90	66	59	81	69

Source: U.S. National Endowment for the Arts, *1997 Survey of Public Participation in the Arts*, Research Division Report No. 39, December 1998.

No. 439. Arts and Humanities—Selected Federal Aid Programs: 1980 to 1998

[In millions of dollars (188.1 represents $188,100,000), except as indicated. For fiscal years ending in year shown, see text, Section 9, State and Local Government]

Type of fund and program	1980	1985	1990	1993	1994	1995	1996	1997	1998
National Endowment for the Arts:									
Funds available [1]	188.1	171.7	170.8	159.7	158.1	152.1	86.9	98.4	85.3
Program appropriation	97.0	118.7	124.3	120.0	116.3	109.0	63.5	65.8	64.3
Matching funds [2]	42.9	29.5	32.4	27.4	29.4	28.5	17.2	16.8	16.8
Grants awarded (number)	5,505	4,801	4,475	4,096	3,843	3,685	1,751	1,098	1,460
Funds obligated [3][4]	166.4	149.4	157.6	148.4	145.2	147.9	75.3	94.4	82.3
Partnership agreements	22.1	24.4	26.1	42.0	40.7	39.2	25.9	30.0	33.4
Music	13.6	15.3	16.5	12.4	10.9	10.9	5.4	(X)	(X)
Museums	11.2	11.9	12.1	9.9	9.4	9.0	3.8	(X)	(X)
Theater	8.4	10.6	10.6	8.3	8.8	7.3	5.2	(X)	(X)
Dance	8.0	9.0	9.6	7.9	7.6	7.1	4.2	(X)	(X)
Media arts	8.4	9.9	13.9	10.2	10.9	8.9	3.0	(X)	(X)
Challenge [5]	50.8	20.7	19.7	11.7	9.6	21.1	4.0	(X)	(X)
Visual arts	7.3	6.2	5.9	5.1	4.8	4.4	1.2	(X)	(X)
Other	36.6	41.3	43.1	40.9	42.5	40.0	22.6	(X)	(X)
National Endowment for the Humanities:									
Funds available [1]	186.2	125.6	140.6	158.5	157.9	151.4	93.1	93.9	93.9
Program appropriation	100.3	95.2	114.2	131.9	131.4	125.7	77.2	80.0	80.0
Matching funds [2]	38.4	30.4	26.3	26.5	26.5	25.7	15.9	13.9	13.9
Grants awarded (number)	2,917	2,241	2,195	2,197	1,881	1,871	815	900	852
Funds obligated [3]	185.5	125.7	141.0	160.3	159.0	151.8	93.4	94.8	92.7
Education programs	18.3	17.9	16.3	20.8	19.6	19.2	13.5	10.5	10.8
State programs	26.0	24.4	29.6	32.4	32.2	32.0	29.0	29.5	29.1
Research grants	32.0	24.4	22.5	23.7	23.4	22.2	5.1	8.5	7.7
Fellowship program	18.0	15.3	15.3	18.9	17.7	16.5	5.1	5.6	5.7
Challenge [5]	53.5	19.6	14.6	14.2	14.4	13.8	9.9	9.9	9.9
Public programs	25.1	24.1	25.4	26.7	27.5	25.8	12.5	12.6	11.1
Preservation and access	(X)	(X)	17.5	23.5	24.1	22.2	18.3	18.2	18.4
National Capital Arts and Cultural Affairs Program	(X)	(X)	(X)	(X)	(X)	(X)	(X)	(X)	(X)
Other	12.6	(X)	(X)	(X)	(X)	(X)	(X)	(X)	(X)

X Not applicable. [1] Includes other funds, shown separately. Excludes administrative funds. Gifts are included in 1980; excluded thereafter. [2] Represents federal funds obligated only upon receipt or certification by Endowment of matching non-Federal gifts. [3] Includes obligations for new grants, supplemental awards on previous years' grants, and program contracts. [4] Beginning with 1997 data, the grantmaking structure changed from discipline-based categories to thematic ones. [5] Program designed to stimulate new sources and higher levels of giving to institutions for the purpose of guaranteeing long-term stability and financial independence. Program usually requires a match of at least 3 private dollars to each Federal dollar. Funds for challenge grants are not allocated by program area because they are awarded on a grant-by-grant basis.

Source: U.S. National Endowment for the Arts, *Annual Report;* and U.S. National Endowment for the Humanities, *Annual Report.*

Parks, Recreation, and Travel   265

No. 440. Attendance Rates for Various Arts Activities: 1997

[In percent. For persons 18 years old and over. Excludes elementary and high school performances. Based on the 1997 household survey Public Participation in the Arts. Data are subject to sampling error; see source. See also Tables 438 and 441]

Item	Jazz perfor- mance	Classical music perfor- mance	Opera	Musical play	Non- musical play	Ballet	Art museum	Historic park	Reading litera- ture[1]
Total.	12	16	5	25	16	6	35	47	63
Sex: Male.	13	14	4	22	15	4	34	48	55
Female.	11	17	5	27	17	8	36	46	71
Race: Hispanic	7	8	3	16	10	5	29	33	50
White	12	18	5	27	17	7	36	51	65
African American	16	10	2	22	16	4	31	37	60
American Indian	11	9	5	15	5	1	22	42	56
Asian	10	16	7	20	18	4	42	44	69
Age: 18 to 24 years old . .	15	16	5	26	20	7	38	46	70
25 to 34 years old	13	11	4	23	13	5	37	49	61
35 to 44 years old	14	14	4	26	15	7	37	52	64
45 to 54 years old	13	20	6	29	20	7	40	54	66
55 to 64 years old	9	16	5	23	14	5	30	45	58
65 to 74 years old	8	18	4	24	15	5	28	37	59
75 years old and over . .	4	14	3	15	13	4	20	25	61
Education: Grade school . .	2	2	-	6	3	2	6	13	29
Some high school.	3	4	2	13	7	2	14	27	46
High school graduate . .	7	8	2	16	9	4	25	41	58
Some college	15	18	5	28	19	7	43	56	72
College graduate	21	28	10	44	28	11	58	67	80
Graduate school.	28	45	14	50	37	14	70	73	86
Income: $10,000 or less . .	5	4	2	12	10	2	16	23	45
$10,001 to $20,000. . . .	6	8	2	12	7	3	20	29	53
$20,001 to $30,000. . . .	8	10	2	17	10	4	26	39	62
$30,001 to $40,000. . . .	11	13	3	21	16	5	32	50	62
$40,001 to $50,000. . . .	11	15	5	23	15	6	37	52	64
$50,001 to $75,000. . . .	16	22	8	32	20	8	46	62	72
$75,001 to $100,000. . .	23	26	6	41	27	10	55	65	75
Over $100,000	27	35	13	51	32	13	60	69	76

- Represents or rounds to zero.   [1] Includes novels, short stories, poetry, or and plays.

Source: U.S. National Endowment for the Arts, *1997 Survey of Public Participation in the Arts,* Research Division Report No. 39, December 1998.

No. 441. Participation in Various Arts Activities: 1997

[In percent. Covers activities engaged in at least once in the prior 12 months. See Table 438 and headnote, Table 440]

Item	Playing classical music	Modern dancing[1]	Drawing	Pottery work[2]	Weaving	Photog- raphy[3]	Creative writing	Buying art work	Singing in groups
Total	1	13	16	15	28	17	12	35	10
Sex: Male	9	13	15	16	5	16	10	36	9
Female	13	12	17	14	49	18	14	34	12
Race: Hispanic.	7	14	17	11	17	12	8	33	7
White	12	12	15	16	30	17	12	36	8
African American.	8	11	16	11	25	18	14	43	26
American Indian	9	21	18	25	28	28	10	35	7
Asian	12	17	27	13	28	22	21	19	9
Age: 18 to 24 years old . . .	13	20	39	21	22	28	32	42	14
25 to 34 years old	10	13	18	17	25	18	13	43	9
35 to 44 years old	11	13	15	18	29	18	12	40	9
45 to 54 years old	15	11	13	18	29	18	10	37	13
55 to 64 years old	9	8	9	10	29	10	5	31	11
65 to 74 years old	6	14	7	10	32	10	5	23	10
75 years old and over . .	6	9	4	3	28	5	6	8	7
Education: Grade school . .	2	4	4	7	14	8	2	24	11
Some high school	4	11	13	15	22	12	8	35	9
High school graduate . . .	8	12	15	16	28	13	9	31	9
Some college	14	16	20	18	32	22	17	35	13
College graduate.	18	10	18	13	32	23	14	41	9
Graduate school	20	15	18	13	26	22	19	41	12
Income: $10,000 or less. . .	5	9	15	8	28	11	8	29	13
$10,001 to $20,000	7	10	13	12	27	14	8	27	9
$20,001 to $30,000	8	12	17	16	26	14	12	26	11
$30,001 to $40,000	10	14	15	20	29	18	11	44	13
$40,001 to $50,000	11	12	16	17	29	18	13	35	8
$50,001 to $75,000	15	13	17	18	28	18	17	32	10
$70,001 to $100,000 . . .	15	18	18	17	24	23	13	41	11
Over $100,000	18	12	12	14	23	23	11	46	9

[1] Dancing other than ballet (e.g. folk and tap).   [2] Includes ceramics, jewelry, leatherwork, and metalwork.   [3] Includes making movies or video as an artistic activity.

Source: U.S. National Endowment for the Arts, *1997 Survey of Public Participation in the Arts,* Research Division Report No. 39, December 1998.

No. 442. Performing Arts—Selected Data: 1985 to 1998

[Sales, receipts and expenditures in millions of dollars (209 represents $209,000,000). For season ending in year shown, except as indicated]

Item	1985	1990	1991	1992	1993	1994	1995	1996	1997	1998
Legitimate theater: [1]										
Broadway shows:										
New productions	33	39	28	38	34	38	32	37	37	33
Attendance (mil.)	7.3	8.0	7.3	7.4	7.9	8.1	9.0	9.5	10.6	11.5
Playing weeks [2][3]	1,078	1,070	971	905	1,019	1,066	1,120	1,146	1,349	1,442
Gross ticket sales	209	282	267	293	328	356	406	436	499	558
Broadway road tours:										
Attendance (mil.)	8.2	11.1	12.5	12.9	14.9	16.0	15.6	18.1	17.6	15.2
Playing weeks	993	944	1,152	1,171	1,296	1,249	1,242	1,345	1,334	1,127
Gross ticket sales	226	367	450	503	626	705	701	796	782	721
Nonprofit professional theatres: [4]										
Companies reporting	217	185	184	182	177	231	215	228	197	189
Gross income	234.7	307.6	333.9	359.1	342.5	455.1	444.4	450.7	565.0	570.0
Earned income	146.1	188.4	202.6	222.5	209.7	277.4	281.2	274.0	349.9	342.0
Contributed income	88.6	119.2	131.3	136.6	132.8	177.7	163.1	176.7	215.1	228.0
Gross expenses	239.3	306.3	336.7	365.6	349.3	460.2	444.9	439.5	526.6	518.5
Productions	2,710	2,265	2,277	2,310	2,319	2,929	2,646	3,074	2,295	2,135
Performances	52,341	46,131	48,695	46,184	44,933	59,542	56,608	56,954	51,453	46,628
Total attendance (mil.)	14.2	15.2	16.9	16.0	16.5	20.7	18.6	17.1	17.2	14.6
OPERA America professional member companies: [5]										
Number of companies reporting [6]	97	98	98	100	85	86	88	83	91	89
Expenses [6][7]	216.4	321.2	346.7	371.8	389.5	404.9	435.0	466.7	534.1	556.3
Performances [7]	1,909	2,336	2,283	2,424	1,945	1,982	2,251	2,019	2,137	2,222
Total attendance (mil.) [7][8]	6.7	7.5	7.6	7.3	5.5	6.0	6.5	6.5	6.9	6.6
Main season attendance (mil.) [7][9]	3.3	4.1	4.3	4.3	3.6	3.7	3.9	3.9	4.0	3.7
Symphony orchestras: [10]										
Concerts	19,573	18,931	18,074	19,778	18,389	17,795	29,328	28,887	26,906	31,766
Attendance (mil.)	24.0	24.7	26.7	26.3	24.0	24.4	30.9	31.1	31.9	32.2
Gross revenue	252.4	377.5	394.5	414.0	430.5	442.5	536.2	558.9	575.5	627.6
Concert income	168.6	253.3	273.8	284.1	294.1	303.6	368.6	383.7	390.5	432.9
Endowment income	(NA)	52.1	52.5	55.3	59.7	60.4	76.2	79.9	91.4	111.2
Other earned income	83.8	72.1	68.2	74.6	76.8	78.5	91.4	95.3	93.5	83.4
Operating expenses	426.1	621.7	662.2	683.0	689.9	710.0	858.8	892.4	937.1	1,012.0
Artistic personnel	231.9	327.3	355.8	398.9	378.8	389.9	464.7	473.9	487.1	525.0
Concert production	69.2	104.3	110.3	117.2	114.3	129.3	160.6	166.0	175.1	174.0
Advertising and promotion	32.5	51.3	57.3	58.3	63.1	67.3	75.2	82.9	90.8	99.7
General and administrative	51.3	73.3	75.6	76.2	73.6	74.4	87.2	88.2	91.6	102.4
Other	41.3	65.6	63.2	32.4	60.1	49.1	71.1	81.5	92.5	110.9
Support	188.1	257.8	281.2	279.6	293.0	293.1	351.0	382.8	401.1	459.7
Tax supported grants	42.2	55.6	58.3	49.1	48.0	46.4	55.5	57.6	54.5	54.6
Private sector support	145.9	202.1	222.9	230.5	245.0	246.7	295.5	325.3	346.6	405.1
Development expenses	20.8	31.4	36.7	36.0	38.0	37.9	38.8	42.8	44.9	48.7
Net support	167.3	226.4	244.6	243.6	255.0	255.2	312.2	340.0	356.2	411.0

NA Not available. [1] Source: The League of American Theaters and Producers, Inc, New York, NY. [2] All shows (new productions and holdovers from previous seasons). [3] Eight performances constitute one playing week. [4] Source: Theatre Communications Group, New York, NY. For years ending on or prior to Aug. 31. [5] Source: OPERA America, Washington, DC. For years ending on or prior to Aug 31. [6] United States companies. [7] Prior to 1993, United States and Canadian companies; beginning 1993, U.S. companies only. [8] Includes educational performances, outreach, etc. [9] For paid performances. [10] Source: American Symphony Orchestra League, Inc., Washington, DC. For years ending Aug. 31. Prior to 1995 represents 254 U.S. orchestras; beginning 1995, represents all U.S. orchestras, excluding college/university and youth orchestras. Also, beginning 1995, data based on 1,200 orchestras.

Source: Compiled from sources listed in footnotes.

No. 443. Boy Scouts and Girl Scouts—Membership and Units: 1970 to 1999

[In thousands (6,287 represents 6,287,000). Boy Scouts as of Dec. 31; Girl Scouts as of Sept. 30. Includes Puerto Rico and outlying areas]

Item	1970	1975	1980	1985	1990	1994	1995	1996	1997	1998	1999
BOY SCOUTS OF AMERICA											
Membership	6,287	5,318	4,318	4,845	5,448	5,378	5,457	5,629	5,835	6,049	6,248
Boys	4,683	3,933	3,207	3,755	4,293	4,188	4,256	4,399	4,574	4,756	4,956
Adults	1,604	1,385	1,110	1,090	1,155	1,190	1,201	1,230	1,262	1,293	1,292
Total units (packs, troops, posts, groups)	157	150	129	134	130	129	132	135	139	142	145
GIRL SCOUTS OF THE U.S.A.											
Membership	3,922	3,234	2,784	2,802	3,269	3,363	3,318	3,390	3,525	3,567	3,630
Girls	3,248	2,723	2,250	2,172	2,480	2,561	2,534	2,584	2,671	2,708	2,749
Adults	674	511	534	630	788	802	784	807	855	858	881
Total units (troops, groups)	164	159	154	166	202	218	215	219	223	226	230

Source: Boy Scouts of America, National Council, Irving, TX, *Annual Report;* and Girl Scouts of the United States of America, New York, NY, *Annual Report.*

Parks, Recreation, and Travel 267

No. 444. Travel by U.S. Residents—Summary: 1994 to 1999

[In millions (564.8 represents 564,800,000), except party size. See headnote, Table 445]

Type of trip	1994	1995	1996	1997	1999	1999
All travel:						
Total trips [1]	564.8	577.6	575.7	581.9	594.1	593.3
Person trips	968.0	994.8	994.2	1,026.6	1,035.6	1,042.5
Party size	1.7	1.7	1.7	1.8	1.7	1.8
Auto travel:						
Total trips	386.4	396.2	400.7	402.7	410.5	402.9
Person trips	729.9	751.0	758.6	781.2	784.0	779.8
Party size	1.9	1.9	1.9	1.9	1.9	1.9
Air travel:						
Total trips	136.7	138.6	134.1	136.2	140.8	147.7
Person trips	182.0	185.0	180.9	185.8	192.6	204.3
Party size	1.3	1.3	1.3	1.4	1.4	1.4
Business travel:						
Total trips	168.3	173.9	167.5	165.8	171.7	173.2
Person trips	213.0	219.8	212.8	213.5	219.5	222.0
Party size	1.3	1.3	1.3	1.3	1.3	1.3
Pleasure travel:						
Total trips	335.5	338.5	341.4	347.4	348.1	346.5
Person trips	644.7	653.6	656.2	682.7	681.4	680.7
Party size	1.9	1.9	1.9	2.0	2.0	2.0

[1] Includes other trips (e.g. medical, funerals, weddings), not shown separately.

Source: Travel Industry Association of America, Washington, DC, *TravelScope*, annual (copyright).

No. 445. Characteristics of Pleasure Trips by U.S. Residents: 1994 to 1999

[Represents trips to destinations 50 miles or more, one-way, away from home or one or more overnight trips. (335.5 represents 335,500,000). Based on a monthly mail panel survey of 20,000 U.S. households. For details, see source]

Characteristic	Unit	1994	1995	1996	1997	1998	1999
Total trips	Millions	335.5	338.5	341.4	347.4	348.1	346.5
Average household members on trip	Number	1.9	1.9	1.9	2.0	2.0	2.0
Average nights per trip [1]	Number	3.8	3.7	3.7	3.6	3.6	3.7
Traveled primarily by auto/truck/RV rental car	Percent	77	77	78	78	77	77
Traveled primarily by air	Percent	17	17	16	16	16	17
Used a rental car while on trip [2]	Percent	7	7	7	7	7	8
Stayed in a hotel while on trip	Percent	33	33	33	33	34	35
Household income:							
Less than $40,000	Percent	52	51	49	47	44	41
$40,000 or more	Percent	48	49	51	53	56	59

[1] Includes overnight and nonovernight stays.   [2] As a secondary mode of transportation.

Source: Travel Industry Association of America, Washington, DC, *TravelScope*, annual (copyright).

No. 446. Domestic Travel Expenditures by State: 1998

[426,154 represents $426,154,000,000. Represents U.S. spending on domestic overnight trips and day trips of 50 miles or more, one way, away from home. Excludes spending by foreign visitors and by U.S. residents in U.S. territories and abroad]

State	Total (mil. dol.)	Share of total (percent)	Rank	State	Total (mil. dol.)	Share of total (percent)	Rank	State	Total (mil. dol.)	Share of total (percent)	Rank
U.S., total	426,154	100.0	(X)	KS	3,169	0.7	38	ND	1,033	0.2	50
				KY	4,787	1.1	27	OH	11,580	2.7	11
AL	4,742	1.1	29	LA	7,271	1.7	19	OK	3,496	0.8	34
AK	1,219	0.3	47	ME	1,807	0.4	42	OR	4,769	1.1	28
AZ	7,299	1.7	18	MD	7,117	1.7	20	PA	13,169	3.1	8
AR	3,402	0.8	36	MA	9,655	2.3	14	RI	1,187	0.3	48
CA	54,176	12.7	1	MI	10,048	2.4	13	SC	6,390	1.5	23
CO	8,108	1.9	17	MN	6,088	1.4	24	SD	1,057	0.2	49
CT	4,509	1.1	30	MS	3,982	0.9	31	TN	8,943	2.1	15
DE	974	0.2	51	MO	8,492	2.0	16	TX	28,273	6.6	3
DC	3,806	0.9	33	MT	1,683	0.4	43	UT	3,425	0.8	35
FL	36,865	8.7	2	NE	2,384	0.6	39	VT	1,229	0.3	46
GA	12,753	3.0	9	NV	16,658	3.9	6	VA	11,729	2.8	10
HI	6,961	1.6	22	NH	2,018	0.5	40	WA	7,048	1.7	21
ID	1,840	0.4	41	NJ	13,769	3.2	7	WV	1,585	0.4	44
IL	19,555	4.6	5	NM	3,216	0.8	37	WI	5,706	1.3	25
IN	5,533	1.3	26	NY	25,594	6.0	4	WY	1,364	0.3	45
IA	3,821	0.9	32	NC	10,872	2.6	12				

X Not applicable.

Source: Travel Industry Association of America, Washington, DC, *Impact of Travel on State Economies, 1998* (copyright).

No. 447. International Travelers and Expenditures: 1990 to 1998

[For coverage, see Table 448. **(47,880 represents $47,888,000,000)**]

Year	Travel and passenger fare (mil. dol.)				U.S. net travel and passenger payments (mil. dol.)	U.S. travelers to foreign countries (1,000)	International visitors to the U.S. (1,000)
	Payments by U.S. travelers		Receipts from foreign visitors				
	Total [1]	Expenditures abroad	Total [1]	Travel receipts			
1990	47,880	37,349	58,305	43,007	10,425	44,623	39,363
1991	45,334	35,322	64,237	48,384	18,903	41,566	42,674
1992	49,155	38,552	71,360	54,742	22,205	43,898	47,261
1993	52,123	40,713	74,403	57,875	22,280	44,411	45,779
1994	56,844	43,782	75,414	58,417	18,570	46,450	44,753
1995	59,579	44,916	82,304	63,395	22,725	50,763	43,318
1996	63,866	48,048	90,164	69,751	26,298	52,311	46,489
1997	70,189	52,051	94,090	73,301	23,901	52,944	47,754
1998	75,902	56,105	91,246	71,250	15,344	56,287	46,395

[1] Includes passenger fares not shown separately.

Source: U.S. Dept. of Commerce, International Trade Administration, Tourism Industries, Internet site <http://www.tinet.ita.doc.gov>.

No. 448. Foreign Travel: 1990 to 1998

[In thousands **(44,623 represents 44,623,000)**. U.S. travelers cover residents of the United States, its territories, and possessions. Foreign travelers to the U.S. include travelers for business and pleasure, international travelers in transit through the United States, and students; excludes travel by international personnel and international businessmen employed in the United States]

Item and area	1990	1992	1993	1994	1995	1996	1997	1998
U.S. travelers to foreign countries. . . .	**44,623**	**43,898**	**44,411**	**46,450**	**50,763**	**52,311**	**52,735**	**56,287**
Canada	12,252	11,819	12,024	12,542	12,933	12,909	13,401	14,880
Mexico.	16,381	16,114	15,285	15,759	18,771	19,616	17,700	18,338
Total overseas.	15,990	15,965	17,102	18,149	19,059	19,786	21,634	23,069
Europe	8,043	7,136	7,491	8,167	8,596	8,706	9,800	11,143
Foreign travelers to the U.S..	**39,363**	**47,262**	**45,779**	**44,753**	**43,318**	**46,489**	**47,754**	**46,395**
Canada	17,263	18,598	17,293	14,974	14,663	15,301	15,127	13,422
Mexico.	7,041	10,872	9,824	11,321	8,016	8,530	8,431	9,276
Total overseas.	15,059	17,791	18,662	18,458	20,639	22,658	24,194	23,698
Europe	6,659	8,262	8,630	8,119	8,793	9,727	10,390	10,675
South America	1,328	1,770	2,026	2,112	2,449	2,461	2,831	2,957
Central America	412	481	545	513	509	524	564	697
Caribbean	1,137	1,004	1,098	1,031	1,044	1,133	1,189	1,161
Far East	4,360	5,097	5,165	5,551	6,616	7,500	7,756	6,724
Middle East	365	373	419	403	454	480	552	587
Oceania	662	654	609	556	588	629	680	639
Africa	137	150	169	173	186	205	234	258

Source: U.S. Dept. of Commerce, International Trade Administration, Tourism Industries, Internet site <http://www.tinet.ita.doc.gov>.

No. 449. Top States and Cities Visited by Overseas Travelers: 1998 and 1999

[**23,698 represents 23,698,000.** Includes travelers for business and pleasure, international travelers in transit through the United States, and students; excludes travel by international personnel and international businessmen employed in the United States]

State	Overseas visitors (1,000)		Market share (percent)		City	Overseas visitors (1,000)		Market share (percent)	
	1998	1999	1998	1999		1998	1999	1998	1999
Total overseas travelers [1].	**23,698**	**24,466**	**100.0**	**100.0**					
California	5,972	6,239	25.2	25.5	New York City, NY	5,000	5,505	21.1	22.5
Florida	6,067	5,798	25.6	23.7	Los Angeles, CA	3,555	3,572	15.0	14.6
New York	5,285	5,798	22.3	23.7	Miami, FL	3,270	2,863	13.8	11.7
Hawaii	2,796	2,740	11.8	11.2	Orlando, FL.	2,867	2,863	12.1	11.7
Nevada	1,920	2,373	8.1	9.7	San Francisco, CA	2,583	2,789	10.9	11.4
Illinois	1,256	1,321	5.3	5.4	Las Vegas, NV	1,801	2,251	7.6	9.2
Massachusetts.	1,161	1,321	4.9	5.4	Oahu/Honolulu, HI	2,228	2,202	9.4	9.0
Texas.	1,114	1,052	4.7	4.3	Washington, DC.	1,398	1,297	5.9	5.3
Guam	1,043	1,028	4.4	4.2	Chicago, IL.	1,209	1,272	5.1	5.2
New Jersey.	853	905	3.6	3.7	Boston, MA.	1,043	1,199	4.4	4.9
Arizona.	853	881	3.6	3.6	San Diego, CA.	782	807	3.3	3.3
Georgia	664	612	2.8	2.5	Atlanta, GA	569	538	2.4	2.2
Pennsylvania.	592	538	2.5	2.2	San Jose, CA	474	514	2.0	2.1
Washington.	521	514	2.2	2.1	Tampa/St. Petersburg, FL .	735	489	3.1	2.0
Colorado.	450	465	1.9	1.9	Anaheim, CA.	521	465	2.2	1.9

[1] Includes other states and cities, not shown separately.

Source: U.S. Dept. of Commerce, International Trade Administration, Internet site <http://www.tinet.ita.doc.gov>.

No. 450. Impact of International Travel on States Economies: 1998

[68,750.3 represents $68,750,300,000]

State	Travel expenditures (mil. dol.)	Travel generated payroll (mil. dol.)	Travel generated employment (1,000)	Travel generated tax receipts (mil. dol.)	State	Travel expenditures (mil. dol.)	Travel generated payroll (mil. dol.)	Travel generated employment (1,000)	Travel generated tax receipts (mil. dol.)
U.S., total	68,750.3	18,386.4	937.2	11,731.1	MO	211.2	58.3	3.4	40.0
					MT	87.2	21.0	1.8	12.1
AL	102.6	23.1	1.7	13.9	NE	49.6	13.2	0.9	8.6
AK	144.3	56.8	2.8	28.8	NV	2,061.8	648.3	31.9	284.0
AZ	1,582.9	459.5	26.0	266.7	NH	108.6	25.7	1.7	13.1
AR	45.2	11.7	0.8	6.7	NJ	793.0	208.5	9.6	156.8
CA	12,864.1	3,424.4	169.5	2,058.4	NM	118.6	29.5	2.2	17.3
CO	726.6	232.4	13.0	168.4	NY	8,588.0	2,254.9	96.2	1,795.1
CT	257.3	63.6	3.3	45.2	NC	459.1	138.2	7.7	81.1
DE	78.4	17.5	1.1	12.9	ND	39.3	9.6	0.9	8.8
DC	1,758.2	357.3	15.6	251.7	OH	612.6	167.7	10.1	117.5
FL	16,722.8	4,306.0	231.8	2,653.0	OK	77.6	28.1	1.5	13.9
GA	900.3	319.4	14.6	220.7	OR	361.8	101.2	6.5	59.8
HI	6,807.4	1,669.1	77.8	973.4	PA	1,035.9	299.3	15.7	189.5
ID	96.2	24.0	1.8	18.2	RI	93.5	20.0	1.2	12.3
IL	1,532.6	405.8	20.8	298.5	SC	484.9	117.4	7.9	73.5
IN	215.7	66.0	3.9	39.7	SD	37.7	9.9	0.9	5.1
IA	129.1	31.7	2.4	20.0	TN	342.4	146.6	6.3	79.7
KS	92.9	22.5	1.6	14.0	TX	3,153.6	947.1	48.8	587.2
KY	104.8	40.0	2.1	21.7	UT	309.1	98.3	6.7	62.1
LA	490.6	112.6	7.4	70.0	VT	112.3	27.9	1.9	15.9
ME	195.1	43.1	3.2	26.1	VA	547.8	162.2	9.3	89.8
MD	291.1	85.0	3.9	59.2	WA	922.8	246.2	13.6	173.6
MA	1,685.2	443.1	21.8	279.8	WV	31.2	7.4	0.5	4.8
MI	533.9	143.5	8.5	100.5	WI	288.5	78.2	5.6	50.9
MN	358.0	129.5	6.5	115.7	WY	67.1	17.3	1.5	8.4
MS	39.9	16.7	0.9	6.7					

Source: Travel Industry Association of America, Washington, DC, Impact of Travel on State Economies, 1998 (copyright).

No. 451. Foreign Visitors for Pleasure Admitted by Country of Last Residence: 1985 to 1996

[In thousands (6,609 represents 6,609,000). For years ending September 30. Represents non-U.S. citizens admitted to the country for a temporary period of time (also known as nonimmigrants)]

Country	1985	1990	1995	1996	Country	1985	1990	1995	1996
Total [1]	6,609	13,418	17,612	19,110	Africa [2]	101	105	137	157
					Egypt	16	16	16	19
Europe [2]	2,048	5,383	7,012	7,478	Nigeria	25	11	10	12
Austria	34	87	146	158					
Belgium	39	95	153	170	Oceania [2]	282	562	478	512
Denmark	36	75	78	89	Australia	195	380	327	342
Finland	24	83	47	53	New Zealand	74	153	115	127
France	226	566	738	767	North America	1,664	2,463	2,240	2,314
Greece	34	43	44	43	Canada	79	119	127	121
Ireland	55	81	126	151	Mexico	773	1,061	893	908
Italy	155	308	427	437	Caribbean [2]	584	963	831	907
Netherlands	82	214	308	325	Bahamas, The	211	332	234	292
Norway	41	80	71	80	Barbados	17	34	36	37
Poland	40	55	36	45	Cayman Islands	18	31	31	34
Soviet Union	2	53	54	71	Dominican Republic	57	137	138	140
Spain	64	183	248	262	Haiti	56	57	43	39
Sweden	71	230	142	165	Jamaica	74	132	130	144
Switzerland	110	236	321	337	Netherlands Antilles	27	31	32	27
United Kingdom	598	1,899	2,342	2,495	Trinidad and Tobago	71	81	64	70
Germany [3]	373	969	1,550	1,624	Central America [2]	228	320	387	376
					Costa Rica	41	62	91	87
Asia [2]	1,866	3,830	5,666	5,445	El Salvador	38	46	63	62
China (Mainland China and Taiwan)	83	187	378	363	Guatemala	53	91	99	97
Hong Kong	64	111	162	174	Panama	38	43	54	54
India	52	75	75	84	South America [2]	606	1,016	1,978	2,000
Israel	80	128	160	186	Argentina	66	136	320	339
Japan	1,277	2,846	3,986	3,621	Brazil	148	300	710	723
Korea	26	120	427	513	Chile	28	54	117	121
Philippines	59	76	85	86	Colombia	123	122	174	187
Saudi Arabia	31	33	45	42	Ecuador	42	57	77	78
Singapore	23	32	61	72	Peru	44	97	98	101
					Venezuela	122	199	400	362

[1] Includes countries unknown or not reported.   [2] Includes countries not shown separately.   [3] Data prior to 1995 for former West Germany.

Source: U.S. Immigration and Naturalization Service, Statistical Yearbook, annual.

Section 8

Elections

This section relates primarily to Presidential, congressional, and gubernatorial elections. Also presented are summary tables on congressional legislation; state legislatures; Black, Hispanic, and female officeholders; population of voting age; voter participation; and campaign finances.

Official statistics on Federal elections, collected by the Clerk of the House, are published biennially in *Statistics of the Presidential and Congressional Election* and *Statistics of the Congressional Election.* Federal and state elections data appear also in *America Votes*, a biennial volume published by Congressional Quarterly, Inc., Washington, DC. Federal elections data also appear in the U.S. Congress, *Congressional Directory*, and in official state documents. Data on reported registration and voting for social and economic groups are obtained by the U.S. Census Bureau as part of the Current Population Survey (CPS) and are published in *Current Population Reports*, Series P20 (see text, Section 1).

Almost all Federal, state, and local governmental units in the United States conduct elections for political offices and other purposes. The conduct of elections is regulated by state laws or, in some cities and counties, by local charter. An exception is that the U.S. Constitution prescribes the basis of representation in Congress and the manner of electing the President and grants to Congress the right to regulate the times, places, and manner of electing Federal officers. Amendments to the Constitution have prescribed national criteria for voting eligibility. The 15th Amendment, adopted in 1870, gave all citizens the right to vote regardless of race, color, or previous condition of servitude. The 19th Amendment, adopted in 1919, further extended the right to vote to all citizens regardless of sex. The payment of poll taxes as a prerequisite to voting in Federal elections was banned by the 24th Amendment in 1964. In 1971, as a result of the 26th Amendment, eligibility to vote in national elections was extended to all citizens, 18 years old and over.

Presidential election—The Constitution specifies how the President and Vice President are selected. Each state elects, by popular vote, a group of electors equal in number to its total of members of Congress. The 23d Amendment, adopted in 1961, grants the District of Columbia three presidential electors, a number equal to that of the least populous state. Subsequent to the election, the electors meet in their respective states to vote for President and Vice President. Usually, each elector votes for the candidate receiving the most popular votes in his or her state. A majority vote of all electors is necessary to elect the President and Vice President. If no candidate receives a majority, the House of Representatives, with each state having one vote, is empowered to elect the President and Vice President, again, with a majority of votes required.

The 22d Amendment to the Constitution, adopted in 1951, limits presidential tenure to two elective terms of 4 years each or to one elective term for any person who, upon succession to the Presidency, has held the office or acted as President for more than 2 years.

Congressional election—The Constitution provides that Representatives be apportioned among the states according to their population, that a census of population be taken every 10 years as a basis for apportionment, and that each state have at least one Representative. At the time of each apportionment, Congress decides what the total number of Representatives will be. Since 1912, the total has been 435,

Elections   271

except during 1960 to 1962 when it increased to 437, adding one Representative each for Alaska and Hawaii. The total reverted to 435 after reapportionment following the 1960 census. Members are elected for 2-year terms, all terms covering the same period. The District of Columbia, American Samoa, Guam, and the Virgin Islands each elect one nonvoting Delegate, and Puerto Rico elects a nonvoting Resident Commissioner.

The Senate is composed of 100 members, two from each state, who are elected to serve for a term of 6 years. One-third of the Senate is elected every 2 years. Senators were originally chosen by the state legislatures. The 17th Amendment to the Constitution, adopted in 1913, prescribed that Senators be elected by popular vote.

Voter eligibility and participation— The Census Bureau publishes estimates of the population of voting age and the percent casting votes in each state for Presidential and congressional election years. These voting-age estimates include a number of persons who meet the age requirement but are not eligible to vote, (e.g. aliens and some institutionalized persons). In addition, since 1964, voter participation and voter characteristics data have been collected during November of election years as part of the CPS. These survey data include noncitizens in the voting age population estimates but exclude members of the Armed Forces and the institutional population.

Statistical reliability—For a discussion of statistical collection and estimation, sampling procedures, and measures of statistical reliability applicable to Census Bureau data, see Appendix III.

Figure 8.1
Popular Vote Cast for President, by Major Political Party: 1972 to 1996

Democrat
Republican
Other major candidates[1]

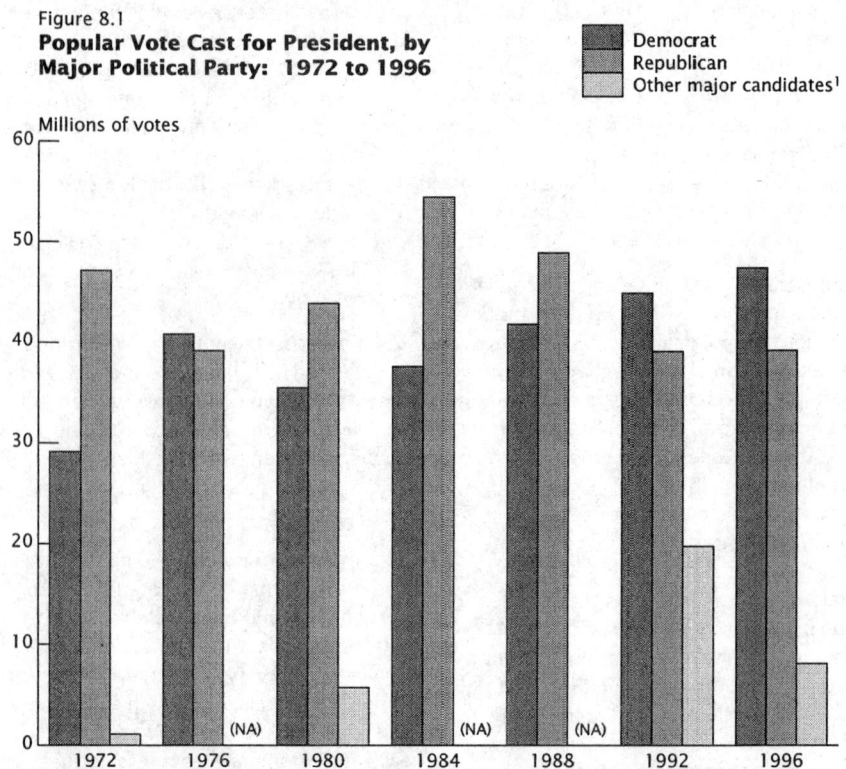

[1]1972—American, John Schmitz; 1980—Independent, John Anderson; 1992—Independent, Ross Perot; 1996—Reform, Ross Perot; Green, Ralph Nader.
Source: Chart prepared by U.S. Census Bureau. For data, see Tables 462 and 463.

No. 452. Vote Cast for President by Major Political Party: 1936 to 1996

[Prior to 1960, excludes Alaska and Hawaii; prior to 1964, excludes DC. Vote cast for major party candidates include the votes of minor parties cast for those candidates]

Year	Candidates for President		Vote cast for President						
	Democratic	Republican	Total popular vote [1] (1,000)	Democratic			Republican		
				Popular vote			Popular vote		
				Number (1,000)	Percent	Electoral vote	Number (1,000)	Percent	Electoral vote
1936	F. D. Roosevelt . .	Landon	45,655	27,757	60.8	523	16,684	36.5	8
1940	F. D. Roosevelt . .	Willkie	49,900	27,313	54.7	449	22,348	44.8	82
1944	F. D. Roosevelt . .	Dewey.	47,977	25,613	53.4	432	22,018	45.9	99
1948	Truman	Dewey.	48,794	24,179	49.6	303	21,991	45.1	189
1952	Stevenson	Eisenhower.	61,551	27,315	44.4	89	33,936	55.1	442
1956	Stevenson	Eisenhower.	62,027	26,023	42.0	73	35,590	57.4	457
1960	Kennedy	Nixon.	68,838	34,227	49.7	303	34,108	49.5	219
1964	Johnson.	Goldwater.	70,645	43,130	61.1	486	27,178	38.5	52
1968	Humphrey	Nixon.	73,212	31,275	42.7	191	31,785	43.4	301
1972	McGovern	Nixon.	77,719	29,170	37.5	17	47,170	60.7	520
1976	Carter	Ford	81,556	40,831	50.1	297	39,148	48.0	240
1980	Carter	Reagan	86,515	35,484	41.0	49	43,904	50.7	489
1984	Mondale.	Reagan	92,653	37,577	40.6	13	54,455	58.8	525
1988	Dukakis	Bush	91,595	41,809	45.6	111	48,886	53.4	426
1992	Clinton.	Bush	104,425	44,909	43.0	370	39,104	37.4	168
1996	Clinton.	Dole	96,278	47,402	49.2	379	39,199	40.7	159

[1] Include votes for minor party candidates, independents, unpledged electors, and scattered write-in votes.

Source: Congressional Quarterly, Inc., Washington, DC, *America at the Polls 2*, 1965, and *America Votes*, biennial, (copyright).

No. 453. Vote Cast for Leading Minority Party Candidates for President: 1936 to 1996

[See headnote, Table 452]

Year	Candidate	Party	Popular vote (1,000)	Candidate	Party	Popular vote (1,000)
1936 . .	William Lemke.	Union	892	Norman Thomas . . .	Socialist	188
1940 . .	Norman Thomas . . .	Socialist	116	Roger Babson	Prohibition.	59
1944 . .	Norman Thomas . . .	Socialist	79	Claude Watson	Prohibition.	75
1948 . .	Strom Thurmond . . .	States' Rights.	1,176	Henry Wallace.	Progressive	1,157
1952 . .	Vincent Hallinan. . . .	Progressive	140	Stuart Hamblen	Prohibition.	73
1956 . .	T. Coleman Andrews.	States' Rights.	111	Eric Hass	Socialist Labor	44
1960 . .	Eric Hass	Socialist Labor	48	Rutherford Decker . .	Prohibition.	46
1964 . .	Eric Hass	Socialist Labor	45	Clifton DeBerry	Socialist Workers	33
1968 . .	George Wallace. . . .	American Independent.	9,906	Henning Blomen . . .	Socialist Labor	53
1972 . .	John Schmitz.	American.	1,099	Benjamin Spock. . . .	People's	79
1976 . .	Eugene McCarthy . .	Independent	757	Roger McBride.	Libertarian.	173
1980 . .	John Anderson	Independent	5,720	Ed Clark.	Libertarian.	921
1984 . .	David Bergland	Libertarian.	228	Lyndon H. LaRouche.	Independent	79
1988 . .	Ron Paul	Libertarian.	432	Lenora B. Fulani . . .	New Alliance	217
1992 . .	H. Ross Perot	Independent	19,742	Andre Marrou	Libertarian.	292
1996 . .	H. Ross Perot	Reform Party	8,085	Ralph Nader	Green.	685

Source: Congressional Quarterly, Inc. Washington, DC, *America at the Polls 1920-1996*, 1997; and *America Votes*, biennial (copyright).

No. 454. Democratic and Republican Percentages of Two-Party Presidential Vote by Selected Characteristics of Voters: 1992 and 1996

[In percent. Covers citizens of voting age living in private housing units in the contiguous United States. Percentages for Democratic Presidential vote are computed by subtracting the percentage Republican vote from 100 percent; third-party or independent votes are not included as valid data. Data are from the National Election Studies and are based on a sample and subject to sampling variability; for details, see source]

| Characteristic | 1992 | | 1996 | | Characteristic | 1992 | | 1996 | |
	Demo- cratic	Repub- lican	Demo- cratic	Repub- lican		Demo- cratic	Repub- lican	Demo- cratic	Repub- lican
Total	**58**	**42**	**58**	**42**	Race:				
Year of birth:					White.	53	47	54	46
1959 or later	58	42	58	42	Black.	94	6	99	1
1943 to 1958	58	42	58	42					
1927 to 1942	56	44	56	44	Education:				
1911 to 1926.	62	38	64	36	Grade school	68	32	82	18
1895 to 1910	58	42	57	43	High school.	62	38	60	40
					College	52	48	49	51
Sex:									
Male	55	45	51	50	Union household.	68	32	75	25
Female	61	39	65	35	Nonunion household . .	57	43	54	46

Source: Center for Political Studies, University of Michigan, Ann Arbor, MI, unpublished data (copyright).

U.S. Census Bureau, Statistical Abstract of the United States: 2000

No. 455. Electoral Vote Cast for President by Major Political Party—States: 1956 to 1996

[D=Democratic, R=Republican. For composition of regions, see map, inside front cover]

State	1956[1]	1960[2]	1964	1968[3]	1972[4]	1976[5]	1980	1984	1988[6]	1992	1996
Democratic	73	303	486	191	17	297	49	13	111	370	379
Republican	457	219	52	301	520	240	489	525	426	168	159
Northeast:											
Democratic	-	121	126	102	14	86	4	-	53	106	106
Republican	133	12	-	24	108	36	118	113	60	-	-
Midwest:											
Democratic	13	71	149	31	-	58	10	10	29	100	100
Republican	140	82	-	118	145	87	135	127	108	29	29
South:											
Democratic	60	101	121	45	3	149	31	3	8	68	80
Republican	105	50	47	77	165	20	138	174	168	116	104
West:											
Democratic	-	10	90	13	-	4	4	-	21	96	93
Republican	79	75	5	82	102	97	98	111	90	23	26
AL	[1]D-10	[2]D-5	R-10	([3])	R-9	D-9	R-9	R-9	R-9	R-9	R-9
AK	(X)	R-3	D-3	R-3	R-3	R-3	R-3	R-3	R-3	R-3	R-3
AZ	R-4	R-4	R-5	R-5	R-6	R-6	R-6	R-7	R-7	R-8	R-8
AR	D-8	D-8	D-6	([3])	R-6	D-6	R-6	R-6	R-6	D-6	D-6
CA	R-32	R-32	D-40	R-40	R-45	R-45	R-45	R-47	R-47	D-54	D-54
CO	R-6	R-6	D-6	R-6	R-7	R-7	R-7	R-8	R-8	D-8	R-8
CT	R-8	D-8	D-8	D-8	R-8	R-8	R-8	R-8	R-8	D-8	D-8
DE	R-3	D-3	D-3	R-3	R-3	D-3	R-3	R-3	R-3	D-3	D-3
DC	(X)	(X)	D-3	D-3	D-3	D-3	D-3	D-3	D-3	D-3	D-3
FL	R-10	R-10	D-14	R-14	R-17	D-17	R-17	R-21	R-21	R-25	D-25
GA	D-12	D-12	R-12	([3])	R-12	D-12	D-12	R-12	R-12	D-13	R-13
HI	(X)	D-3	D-4	D-4	R-4	D-4	D-4	R-4	D-4	D-4	D-4
ID	R-4	R-4	D-4	R-4	R-4	R-4	R-4	R-4	R-4	R-4	R-4
IL	R-27	D-27	D-26	R-26	R-26	R-26	R-26	R-24	R-24	D-22	D-22
IN	R-13	R-13	D-13	R-13	R-13	R-13	R-13	R-12	R-12	R-12	R-12
IA	R-10	R-10	D-9	R-9	R-8	R-8	R-8	R-8	D-8	D-7	D-7
KS	R-8	R-8	D-7	R-7	R-7	R-7	R-7	R-7	R-7	R-6	R-6
KY	R-10	R-10	D-9	R-9	R-9	D-9	R-9	R-9	R-9	D-8	D-8
LA	R-10	D-10	R-10	([3])	R-10	D-10	R-10	R-10	R-10	D-9	D-9
ME	R-5	R-5	D-4	D-4	R-4	R-4	R-4	R-4	R-4	D-4	D-4
MD	R-9	D-9	D-10	D-10	R-10	D-10	D-10	R-10	R-10	D-10	D-10
MA	R-16	D-16	D-14	D-14	D-14	D-14	D-14	R-13	D-13	D-12	D-12
MI	R-20	D-20	D-21	D-21	R-21	R-21	R-21	R-20	R-20	D-18	D-18
MN	R-11	D-11	D-10	D-10	R-10	D-10	D-10	D-10	D-10	D-10	D-10
MS	D-8	([2])	R-7	([3])	R-7	D-7	R-7	R-7	R-7	R-7	R-7
MO	D-13	D-13	D-12	R-12	R-12	D-12	R-12	R-11	R-11	D-11	D-11
MT	R-4	R-4	D-4	R-4	R-4	R-4	R-4	R-4	R-4	D-3	R-3
NE	R-6	R-6	D-5	R-5	R-5	R-5	R-5	R-5	R-5	R-5	R-5
NV	R-3	D-3	D-3	R-3	R-3	R-3	R-3	R-4	R-4	D-4	D-4
NH	R-4	R-4	D-4	R-4	R-4	R-4	R-4	R-4	R-4	D-4	D-4
NJ	R-16	D-16	D-17	R-17	R-17	R-17	R-17	R-16	R-16	D-15	D-15
NM	R-4	D-4	D-4	R-4	R-4	R-4	R-4	R-5	R-5	D-5	D-5
NY	R-45	D-45	D-43	D-43	R-41	D-41	R-41	R-36	D-36	D-33	D-33
NC	D-14	D-14	D-13	[3]R-12	R-13	D-13	R-13	R-13	R-13	R-14	R-14
ND	R-4	R-4	D-4	R-4	R-3	R-3	R-3	R-3	R-3	R-3	R-3
OH	R-25	R-25	D-26	R-26	R-25	D-25	R-25	R-23	R-23	D-21	D-21
OK	R-8	[2]R-7	D-8	R-8	R-8	R-8	R-8	R-8	R-8	R-8	R-8
OR	R-6	R-6	D-6	R-6	R-6	R-6	R-6	R-7	D-7	D-7	D-7
PA	R-32	D-32	D-29	D-29	R-27	D-27	R-27	R-25	R-25	D-23	D-23
RI	R-4	D-4	D-4	D-4	R-4	D-4	D-4	R-4	D-4	D-4	D-4
SC	D-8	D-8	R-8	R-8	R-8	D-8	R-8	R-8	R-8	R-8	R-8
SD	R-4	R-4	D-4	R-4	R-4	R-4	R-4	R-3	R-3	R-3	R-3
TN	R-11	R-11	D-11	R-11	R-10	D-10	R-10	R-11	R-11	D-11	D-11
TX	R-24	D-24	D-25	D-25	R-26	D-26	R-26	R-29	R-29	R-32	R-32
UT	R-4	R-4	D-4	R-4	R-4	R-4	R-4	R-5	R-5	R-5	R-5
VT	R-3	R-3	D-3	R-3	R-3	R-3	R-3	R-3	R-3	D-3	D-3
VA	R-12	R-12	D-12	R-12	[4]R-11	R-12	R-12	R-12	R-12	R-13	R-13
WA	R-9	R-9	D-9	D-9	R-9	[5]R-8	R-9	R-10	D-10	D-11	D-11
WV	R-8	D-8	D-7	D-7	R-6	D-6	D-6	R-6	[6]D-5	D-5	D-5
WI	R-12	R-12	D-12	R-12	R-11	D-11	R-11	R-11	D-11	D-11	D-11
WY	R-3	R-3	D-3	R-3	R-3	R-3	R-3	R-3	R-3	R-3	R-3

- Represents zero.   X Not applicable.   [1] Excludes one electoral vote cast for Walter B. Jones in Alabama.   [2] Excludes 15 electoral votes cast for Harry F. Byrd as follows: AL 6, MS 8, and OK 1.   [3] Excludes 46 electoral votes cast for American Independent George C. Wallace as follows: AL 10, AR 6, GA 12, LA 10, MS 7, and NC 1.   [4] Excludes one electoral vote cast for Libertarian John Hospers in Virginia.   [5] Excludes one electoral vote cast for Ronald Reagan in Washington.   [6] Excludes one electoral vote cast for Lloyd Bentsen for President in West Virginia.

Source: 1956-72, U.S. Congress, Clerk of the House, *Statistics of the Presidential and Congressional Election*, quadrennial; 1976-96, Congressional Quarterly, Inc., Washington DC, *America Votes*, biennial (copyright).

No. 456. Popular Vote Cast for President by Political Party—States: 1992 and 1996

[In thousands 104,425 represents 104,425,000, except percent]

State	1992 Total [1]	1992 Demo-cratic Party	1992 Repub-lican Party	1992 Perot (Reform Party)	1996 Total [1]	1996 Demo-cratic Party	1996 Repub-lican Party	1996 Perot (Reform Party)	Percent of total vote Demo-cratic Party	Percent of total vote Repub-lican Party	Percent of total vote Perot (Reform Party)
United States..	**104,425**	**44,909**	**39,104**	**19,742**	**96,278**	**47,402**	**39,199**	**8,085**	**49.2**	**40.7**	**8.4**
Alabama.........	1,688	690	804	183	1,534	662	769	92	43.2	50.1	6.0
Alaska..........	259	78	102	73	242	80	123	26	33.3	50.8	10.9
Arizona.........	1,487	543	572	354	1,404	653	622	112	46.5	44.3	8.0
Arkansas.......	951	506	337	99	884	475	325	70	53.7	36.8	7.9
California	11,132	5,121	3,631	2,296	10,019	5,120	3,828	698	51.1	38.2	7.0
Colorado........	1,569	630	563	366	1,511	671	692	100	44.4	45.8	6.6
Connecticut......	1,616	682	578	349	1,393	736	483	140	52.8	34.7	10.0
Delaware	290	126	102	59	271	140	99	29	51.8	36.6	10.6
District of Columbia .	228	193	21	10	186	158	17	4	85.2	9.3	1.9
Florida	5,314	2,073	2,173	1,053	5,304	2,547	2,245	484	48.0	42.3	9.1
Georgia	2,321	1,009	995	310	2,299	1,054	1,081	146	45.8	47.0	6.4
Hawaii	373	179	137	53	360	205	114	27	56.9	31.6	7.6
Idaho..........	482	137	203	130	492	165	257	63	33.6	52.2	12.7
Illinois	5,050	2,453	1,734	841	4,311	2,342	1,587	346	54.3	36.8	8.0
Indiana.........	2,306	848	989	456	2,136	887	1,007	224	41.5	47.1	10.5
Iowa	1,355	586	505	253	1,234	620	493	105	50.3	39.9	8.5
Kansas.........	1,157	390	450	312	1,074	388	583	93	36.1	54.3	8.6
Kentucky	1,493	665	617	204	1,389	637	623	120	45.8	44.9	8.7
Louisiana	1,790	816	733	211	1,784	928	713	123	52.0	39.9	6.9
Maine..........	679	263	207	207	606	313	186	86	51.6	30.8	14.2
Maryland	1,985	989	707	281	1,781	966	682	116	54.3	38.3	6.5
Massachusetts.....	2,774	1,319	805	631	2,557	1,572	718	227	61.5	28.1	8.9
Michigan........	4,275	1,871	1,555	825	3,849	1,990	1,481	337	51.7	38.5	8.7
Minnesota.......	2,348	1,021	748	563	2,193	1,120	766	258	51.1	35.0	11.8
Mississippi	982	400	488	86	894	394	440	52	44.1	49.2	5.8
Missouri	2,392	1,054	811	519	2,158	1,026	890	217	47.5	41.2	10.1
Montana........	411	155	144	107	407	168	180	55	41.3	44.1	13.6
Nebraska.......	738	217	344	174	677	237	363	71	35.0	53.7	10.5
Nevada	506	189	176	133	464	204	199	44	43.9	42.9	9.5
New Hampshire....	538	209	202	121	499	246	196	48	49.3	39.4	9.7
New Jersey.......	3,344	1,436	1,357	522	3,076	1,652	1,103	262	53.7	35.9	8.5
New Mexico	570	262	213	92	556	273	233	32	49.2	41.9	5.8
New York	6,927	3,444	2,347	1,091	6,316	3,756	1,933	503	59.5	30.6	8.0
North Carolina	2,612	1,114	1,135	358	2,516	1,108	1,226	168	44.0	48.7	6.7
North Dakota......	308	99	136	71	266	107	125	33	40.1	46.9	12.2
Ohio	4,940	1,985	1,894	1,036	4,534	2,148	1,860	483	47.4	41.0	10.7
Oklahoma........	1,390	473	593	320	1,207	488	582	131	40.4	48.3	10.8
Oregon.........	1,463	621	476	354	1,378	650	538	121	47.2	39.1	8.8
Pennsylvania.....	4,960	2,239	1,792	903	4,506	2,216	1,801	431	49.2	40.0	9.6
Rhode Island......	453	213	132	105	390	233	105	44	59.7	26.8	11.2
South Carolina.....	1,203	480	578	139	1,152	506	573	64	44.0	49.8	5.6
South Dakota	336	125	137	73	324	139	151	31	43.0	46.5	9.7
Tennessee	1,983	934	841	200	1,894	909	864	106	48.0	45.6	5.6
Texas..........	6,154	2,282	2,496	1,355	5,612	2,460	2,736	379	43.8	48.8	6.7
Utah	744	183	323	203	666	222	362	66	33.3	54.4	10.0
Vermont	290	134	88	66	258	138	80	31	53.4	31.1	12.0
Virginia.........	2,559	1,039	1,151	349	2,417	1,091	1,138	160	45.1	47.1	6.6
Washington.......	2,288	993	731	542	2,254	1,123	841	201	49.8	37.3	8.9
West Virginia.....	684	331	242	109	636	328	234	72	51.5	36.8	11.3
Wisconsin.......	2,531	1,041	931	544	2,196	1,072	845	227	48.8	38.5	10.4
Wyoming	201	68	79	51	212	78	105	26	36.8	49.8	12.3

[1] Includes other parties.

Source: Congressional Quarterly, Inc., Washington, DC, *America Votes*, biennial (copyright).

Elections 275

No. 457. Vote Cast for United States Senators, 1996 and 1998, and Incumbent Senators, 1998—States

[D=Democrat; R=Republican]

State	1996 Total [1] (1,000)	1996 Percent for leading party	1998 Total [1] (1,000)	1998 Percent for leading party	Incumbent senators and year term expires — Name, party, and year	Incumbent senators and year term expires — Name, party, and year
Alabama	1,499	R-52.5	1,293	R-63.2	Jeff Sessions (R) 2003	Richard C. Shelby (R) 2005
Alaska	232	R-76.7	222	R-74.5	Frank H. Murkowski (R) 2005	Ted Stevens (R) 2003
Arizona	(X)	(X)	1,013	R-68.7	John McCain (R) 2005	Jon Kyl (R) 2001
Arkansas	846	R-52.7	701	D-55.1	Blanche Lincoln (D) 2005	Tim Hutchinson (R) 2003
California	(X)	(X)	8,315	D-53.1	Barbara Boxer (D) 2005	Dianne Feinstein (D) 2001
Colorado	1,470	R-51.1	1,327	R-62.5	Ben N. Campbell (R) 2005	Wayne Allard (R) 2003
Connecticut . .	(X)	(X)	964	D-65.1	Christopher J. Dodd (D) 2005	Joseph I. Lieberman (D) 2001
Delaware	276	D-60.0	(X)	(X)	Joseph R. Biden Jr. (D) 2003	William V. Roth, Jr. (R) 2001
Florida	(X)	(X)	3,900	D-62.5	Bob Graham (D) 2005	Connie Mack (R) 2001
Georgia	2,259	D-48.9	1,754	R-52.4	Paul Coverdell (R) 2005	Max Cleland (D) 2003
Hawaii	(X)	(X)	398	D-79.2	Daniel K. Akaka (D) 2001	Daniel K. Inouye (D) 2005
Idaho.	497	R-57.0	378	R-69.5	Larry E. Craig (R) 2003	Michael D. Crapo (R) 2005
Illinois	4,251	D-56.1	3,395	D-50.3	Peter Fitzgerald (R) 2005	Richard J. Durbin (D) 2003
Indiana	(X)	(X)	1,589	D-63.7	Evan Bayh (D) 2005	Richard G. Lugar (R) 2001
Iowa	1,224	D-51.8	948	R-68.4	Tom Harkin (D) 2003	Charles E. Grassley (R) 2005
Kansas	[2]1,065	R-53.9	727	R-65.3	Sam Brownback (R) 2005	Pat Roberts (R) 2003
Kentucky	1,307	R-55.5	1,145	R-49.7	Jim Bunning (R) 2005	Mitch McConnell (R) 2003
Louisiana [3] . .	1,700	D-50.2	969	D-64.0	John B. Breaux (D) 2005	Mary Landrieu (D) 2003
Maine	607	R-49.2	(X)	(X)	Susan Collins (R) 2003	Olympia Snowe (R) 2001
Maryland	(X)	(X)	1,507	D-70.5	Barbara A. Mikulski (D) 2005	Paul S. Sarbanes (D) 2001
Massachusetts . . .	2,556	D-52.2	(X)	(X)	Edward M. Kennedy (D) 2001	John F. Kerry (D) 2003
Michigan	3,763	D-58.4	(X)	(X)	Carl Levin (D) 2003	Spencer Abraham (R) 2001
Minnesota . . .	2,183	D-50.3	(X)	(X)	Paul David Wellstone (D) 2003	Rod Grams (R) 2001
Mississippi . . .	879	R-71.0	(X)	(X)	Thad Cochran (R) 2003	Trent Lott (R) 2001
Missouri	(X)	(X)	1,577	R-52.7	Christopher S. Bond (R) 2005	John Ashcroft (R) 2001
Montana	407	D-49.6	(X)	(X)	Max Baucus (D) 2003	Conrad Burns (R) 2001
Nebraska	677	R-56.1	(X)	(X)	Chuck Hagel (R) 2003	J. Robert Kerrey (D) 2001
Nevada	(X)	(X)	436	D-47.9	Harry Reid (D) 2005	Richard H. Bryan (D) 2001
New Hampshire . . .	493	R-49.2	315	R-67.8	Judd Gregg (R) 2005	Robert C. Smith (R) 2003
New Jersey . .	2,884	D-52.7	(X)	(X)	Robert G. Torricelli (D) 2003	Frank R. Lautenberg (D) 2001
New Mexico . .	552	R-64.7	(X)	(X)	Jeff Bingaman (D) 2001	Pete V. Domenici (R) 2003
New York	(X)	(X)	4,671	D-54.6	Daniel P. Moynihan (D) 2001	Charles E. Schumer (D) 2005
North Carolina.	2,556	R-52.6	2,012	D-51.2	John Edwards (D) 2005	Jesse Helms (R) 2003
North Dakota .	(X)	(X)	213	D-63.2	Byron L. Dorgan (D) 2005	Kent Conrad (D) 2001
Ohio	(X)	(X)	3,404	R-56.5	George V. Voinovich (R) 2005	Mike DeWine (R) 2001
Oklahoma . . .	1,183	R-56.7	860	R-66.4	James Inhofe (R) 2003	Don Nickles (R) 2005
Oregon	1,360	R-49.8	1,118	D-61.1	Gordon Smith (R) 2003	Ron Wyden (D) 2005
Pennsylvania .	(X)	(X)	2,958	R-61.3	Rick Santorum (R) 2001	Arlen Specter (R) 2005
Rhode Island .	363	D-63.5	(X)	(X)	Jack Reed (D) 2003	John H. Chafee (R) 2001
South Carolina. . . .	1,161	R-53.4	1,068	D-52.7	Ernest F. Hollings (D) 2005	Strom Thurmond (R) 2003
South Dakota .	324	D-51.3	262	D-62.1	Thomas A. Daschle (D) 2005	Tim Johnson (D) 2003
Tennessee . . .	1,779	R-61.4	(X)	(X)	Fred Thompson (R) 2003	Bill Frist (R) 2001
Texas	5,527	R-54.8	(X)	(X)	Kay Bailey Hutchison (R) 2001	Phil Gramm (R) 2003
Utah	(X)	(X)	495	R-64.0	Robert F. Bennett (R) 2005	Orrin G. Hatch (R) 2001
Vermont	(X)	(X)	214	D-72.2	Patrick J. Leahy (D) 2005	James M. Jeffords (R) 2001
Virginia	2,355	R-52.5	(X)	(X)	Charles S. Robb (D) 2001	John W. Warner (R) 2003
Washington . .	(X)	(X)	1,889	D-58.4	Patty Murray (D) 2005	Slade Gorton (R) 2001
West Virginia .	596	D-76.6	(X)	(X)	Robert C. Byrd (D) 2001	John D. Rockefeller IV (D) 2003
Wisconsin. . . .	(X)	(X)	1,761	D-50.5	Herb Kohl (D) 2001	Russell Feingold (D) 2005
Wyoming	211	R-54.1	(X)	(X)	Mike Enzi (R) 2003	Craig Thomas (R) 2001

X Not applicable.   [1] Includes vote cast for minor parties.   [2] Kansas had elections to fill two Senate seats in 1996. Pat Roberts was elected to fill the full-term seat vacated by the retiring Nancy Kassenbaum. Sam Brownback was elected to fill the short-term seat vacated by Robert Dole, who resigned in 1996 to run for President.   [3] Louisiana holds an open-primary election with candidates from all parties running on the same ballot. Any candidate who receives a majority is elected.

Source: Congressional Quarterly, Inc., Washington, DC. *America Votes*, biennial (copyright).

No. 458. Vote Cast for United States Representatives by Major Political Party—States: 1990 to 1998

[In thousands (61,513 represents 61,513,000), except percent. In each state, totals represent the sum of votes cast in each Congressional District or votes cast for Representative at Large in states where only one member is elected. In all years there are numerous districts within the state where either the Republican or Democratic party had no candidate. In some states the Republican and Democratic vote includes votes cast for the party candidate by endorsing parties]

State	1990 Total[1]	1990 Democratic	1990 Republican	1990 Percent for leading party	1996 Total[1]	1996 Democratic	1996 Republican	1996 Percent for leading party	1998 Total[1]	1998 Democratic	1998 Republican	1998 Percent for leading party
U.S. [2] . . .	61,513	32,565	27,648	D-52.9	89,863	43,626	43,902	R-48.9	65,897	31,482	32,255	R-48.9
AL	1,017	690	315	D-67.9	1,469	656	786	R-53.5	1,215	545	666	R-54.8
AK	192	92	99	R-51.7	234	85	139	R-59.4	223	77	140	R-62.6
AZ [3]	966	345	621	R-64.3	1,356	521	801	R-59.0	1,004	407	574	R-57.1
AR [3]	665	369	296	D-55.5	863	396	456	R-52.8	525	169	320	R-60.9
CA	7,287	3,568	3,347	D-49.0	9,482	4,707	4,292	D-49.6	7,990	4,040	3,510	D-50.6
CO	1,001	504	487	D-50.3	1,461	597	833	R-57.0	1,274	533	716	R-56.2
CT	1,037	489	546	R-52.6	1,294	724	547	D-55.9	954	496	442	D-51.9
DE	177	116	58	D-65.5	267	73	186	R-69.5	181	57	120	R-66.4
DC [3 4]	160	98	42	D-61.7	(NA)	(NA)	(NA)	(NA)	(NA)	(NA)	(NA)	(NA)
FL [4]	2,378	1,213	1,163	D-51.0	4,692	2,037	2,640	R-56.3	1,213	581	558	D-47.9
GA	1,394	855	539	D-61.3	2,163	1,011	1,152	R-53.3	1,632	592	1,040	R-63.7
HI	341	216	118	D-63.3	353	196	136	D-55.5	397	261	119	D-65.7
ID	315	183	131	D-58.2	494	194	290	R-58.7	379	169	205	R-54.0
IL	3,077	1,646	1,349	D-53.5	4,128	2,267	1,813	D-54.9	3,215	1,566	1,625	R-50.5
IN	1,514	831	683	D-54.9	2,105	944	1,119	R-53.1	1,576	673	862	R-54.7
IA	792	401	385	D-50.6	1,201	533	650	R-54.1	901	338	552	R-61.3
KS	781	394	387	D-50.4	1,049	425	591	R-56.4	727	272	450	R-61.9
KY	764	353	397	R-52.0	1,238	507	731	R-59.0	1,099	456	637	R-58.0
LA	106	106	-	D-100.0	660	262	398	R-60.3	310	213	97	D-68.7
ME	517	284	233	D-55.0	600	379	211	D-63.2	415	281	125	D-67.7
MD	1,091	566	517	D-51.9	1,639	877	762	D-53.5	1,482	792	690	D-53.5
MA	2,051	1,420	567	D-69.2	2,409	1,585	781	D-65.8	1,742	1,306	413	D-75.0
MI	2,434	1,321	1,089	D-54.3	3,700	1,945	1,679	D-52.6	2,985	1,469	1,438	D-49.2
MN	1,781	1,042	736	D-58.5	2,141	1,180	895	D-55.1	2,040	1,090	863	D-53.5
MS	369	299	69	D-81.2	904	397	488	R-54.0	551	263	232	D-47.7
MO	1,353	728	625	D-53.8	2,116	1,116	833	D-52.8	1,572	788	748	D-50.1
MT	317	157	160	R-50.5	404	175	212	R-52.4	332	147	176	R-53.0
NE	587	277	309	R-52.7	662	204	450	R-68.0	526	105	393	R-74.7
NV	313	144	151	R-48.2	450	173	249	R-55.3	410	79	275	R-67.1
NH	291	141	149	R-51.2	491	221	247	R-50.3	318	124	190	R-59.8
NJ	1,827	837	911	R-49.9	2,823	1,352	1,399	R-49.6	1,815	902	858	D-49.7
NM	359	146	214	R-59.5	548	271	261	D-49.4	498	228	246	R-49.5
NY	3,662	1,830	1,662	D-50.0	5,551	3,041	2,358	D-54.8	4,267	2,278	1,858	D-53.4
NC	2,011	1,076	935	D-53.5	2,514	1,136	1,340	R-53.3	1,904	827	1,014	R-53.3
ND	234	153	81	D-65.2	263	145	114	D-55.1	213	120	88	D-56.2
OH	3,418	1,807	1,590	D-52.9	4,388	2,031	2,192	R-49.9	3,375	1,594	1,752	R-51.9
OK	857	519	338	D-60.6	1,180	430	723	R-61.3	859	314	538	R-62.7
OR	1,053	667	342	D-63.4	1,335	724	558	D-54.3	1,090	631	402	D-57.9
PA	2,851	1,293	1,552	R-54.5	4,316	2,223	2,038	D-51.5	2,896	1,381	1,472	R-50.8
RI	347	182	165	D-52.5	360	241	108	D-66.9	293	204	77	D-69.5
SC	670	383	275	D-57.2	1,057	345	683	R-64.6	974	370	580	R-59.6
SD	257	174	83	D-67.6	323	120	186	R-57.7	259	64	194	R-75.1
TN	717	369	289	D-51.5	1,784	856	889	R-49.8	914	412	470	R-51.4
TX	3,278	1,763	1,498	D-53.8	5,219	2,323	2,785	R-53.4	3,462	1,531	1,787	R-51.6
UT	442	234	191	D-52.9	664	264	386	R-58.2	471	127	304	R-64.6
VT	210	6	83	I-56.0	255	24	83	I-58.1	215	(X)	71	R-32.9
VA	1,153	663	411	D-57.5	2,199	1,027	1,117	R-50.8	1,149	514	542	R-47.2
WA	1,313	696	596	D-53.0	2,174	1,130	1,021	D-52.0	1,858	980	819	D-52.8
WV	375	251	123	D-67.1	522	458	64	D-87.8	351	283	29	D-80.6
WI	1,256	597	652	R-51.9	2,150	1,012	1,121	R-52.1	1,673	762	880	R-52.6
WY	158	71	87	R-55.1	210	86	116	R-55.2	174	67	101	R-57.8

- Represents zero.   NA Not available.   X Not applicable.   [1] Includes vote cast for minor parties. Total for 1996 includes results from 431 districts, including 14 where members were elected without major party opposition (7 won by the Republicans and 7 by the Democrats). In four districts (three in Louisiana and one in Florida) candidates ran unopposed and no vote was recorded. [2] Includes vote cast for nonvoting Delegate at Large in District of Columbia, except for 1994 and 1996. [3] State law does not require tabulation of votes for unopposed candidates. [4] In 1990 Districts 8, 10, 12, 13, and 16 were unopposed; in 1994 Districts 4, 10, 13, 14, 18, and 23 were unopposed; in 1996 District 4 was unopposed.

Source: Congressional Quarterly, Inc., Washington, DC, *America Votes,* biennial (copyright).

U.S. Census Bureau, Statistical Abstract of the United States: 2000

No. 459. Vote Cast for United States Representatives by Major Political Party—Congressional Districts: 1998

[In some states the Democratic and Republican vote includes votes cast for the party candidate by endorsing parties]

State and district	Democratic candidate Name	Percent of total	Republican candidate Name	Percent of total	State and district	Democratic candidate Name	Percent of total	Republican candidate Name	Percent of total
AL	(X)	(X)	(X)	(X)	44th..	Waite	35.7	Bono	60.1
1st..	(1)	(1)	Callahan	99.4	45th..	Neal	37.3	Rohrabacher	58.7
2d...	Fondren	30.7	Everett	69.3	46th..	Sanchez	56.4	Dornan	39.3
3d...	Turnham	41.9	Riley	58.1	47th..	Avalos	29.5	Cox	67.6
4th..	Bevill	43.5	Aderholt	56.4	48th..	(1)	(1)	Packard	76.9
5th..	Cramer	69.7	Aust	30.3	49th..	Kehoe	46.6	Bilbray	48.8
6th..	Smalley	28.1	Bachus	71.8	50th..	Filner	99.2	(1)	(1)
7th..	Hilliard	98.0	(1)	(1)	51st..	Kripke	34.7	Cunningham	61.0
AK ...	Duncan	34.6	Young	62.6	52d..	(1)	(1)	Hunter	75.7
AZ ...	(X)	(X)	(X)	(X)	CO ...	(X)	(X)	(X)	(X)
1st..	Mendoza	35.4	Salmon	64.6	1st..	DeGette	66.9	McClanahan	30.1
2d...	Pastor	67.8	Barron	28.0	2d...	Udall	49.9	Greenlee	47.4
3d...	Starky	32.7	Stump	67.3	3d...	Kelley	31.5	McInnis	66.1
4th..	Ehst	31.2	Shadegg	64.7	4th..	Kirkpatrick	40.7	Schaffer	59.3
5th..	Volgy	45.2	Kolbe	51.6	5th..	Alford	26.0	Hefley	72.7
6th..	Owens	43.7	Hayworth	53.0	6th..	Strauss	41.5	Tancredo	55.9
AR ...	(X)	(X)	(X)	(X)	CT ...	(X)	(X)	(X)	(X)
1st..	Berry	(1)	(1)	(1)	1st..	Larson	58.1	O'Connor	41.4
2d...	Snyder	58.0	Wyrick	42.0	2d...	Gejdenson	61.0	Koval	35.5
3d...	(1)	(1)	Hutchinson	80.7	3d...	DeLauro	71.3	Reust	27.4
4th..	Smith	42.5	Dickey	57.5	4th..	Kantrowitz	29.9	Shays	69.1
CA ...	(X)	(X)	(X)	(X)	5th..	Maloney	49.9	Nielsen	48.4
1st..	Thompson	61.9	Luce	32.8	6th..	Koskoff	39.6	Johnson	58.1
2d...	Braden	34.5	Herger	62.5	DE ...	Williams	31.8	Castle	66.4
3d...	Dunn	45.0	Ose	52.4	FL ...	(X)	(X)	(X)	(X)
4th..	Shapiro	34.4	Doolittle	62.2	1st..	(1)	(1)	Scarborough	99.5
5th..	Matsui	71.9	Dinsmore	26.0	2d...	Boyd	95.2	(1)	(1)
6th..	Woolsey	68.0	McAuliffe	29.7	3d...	Brown	55.4	Randall	44.6
7th..	Miller	76.7	Reece	23.3	4th..	(1)	(1)	Fowler	(1)
8th..	Pelosi	85.8	Martz	12.0	5th..	Thurman	66.3	(1)	(1)
9th..	Lee	82.8	Sanders	13.2	6th..	(1)	(1)	Stearns	(1)
10th..	Tauscher	53.5	Ball	43.4	7th..	(1)	(1)	Mica	(1)
11th..	Figueroa	36.2	Pombo	61.4	8th..	Krulick	34.2	McCollum	65.8
12th..	Lantos	74.0	Evans Jr.	21.1	9th..	(1)	(1)	Bilirakis	(1)
13th..	Stark	71.2	Goetz	26.6	10th..	(1)	(1)	Young	(1)
14th..	Eshoo	68.6	Haugen	28.4	11th..	Davis	64.9	Chillura	35.1
15th..	Lane	37.9	Campbell	60.5	12th..	(1)	(1)	Canady	(1)
16th..	Lofgren	72.8	Thayn	23.4	13th..	(1)	(1)	Miller	(1)
17th..	Farr	64.5	McCampbell	32.7	14th..	(1)	(1)	Goss	(1)
18th..	Condit	86.8	(1)	(1)	15th..	Golding	36.9	Weldon	63.1
19th..	(1)	(1)	Radanovich	79.4	16th..	(1)	(1)	Foley	(1)
20th..	Dooley	60.7	Unruh	39.3	17th..	Meek	(1)	(1)	(1)
21st..	(1)	(1)	Thomas	78.9	18th..	(1).	(1)	Ros, Lehtin	(1)
22d..	Capps	55.1	Bordonaro	43.0	19th..	Wexler	(1)	(1)	(1)
23d..	Gonzalez	39.9	Gallegly	60.1	20th..	Deutsch	(1)	(1)	(1)
24th..	Sherman	57.3	Hoffman	38.5	21st..	Cusack	25.2	Diaz(1)Balar	74.8
25th..	(1)	(1)	McKeon	74.7	22d..	(1)	(1)	Shaw	(1)
26th..	Berman	82.5	(1)	(1)	23d..	Hastings	(1)	(1)	(1)
27th..	Gordon	46.4	Rogan	50.7	GA ...	(X)	(X)	(X)	(X)
28th..	Nelson	39.3	Dreier	57.6	1st..	(1)	(1)	Kingston	100.0
29th..	Waxman	73.9	Gottlieb	22.6	2d...	Bishop	56.8	McCormick	43.2
30th..	Becerra	81.2	Parker	18.8	3d...	(1)	(1)	Collins	100.0
31st..	Martinez	70.0	Moreno	22.6	4th..	McKinney	61.1	Warren	38.9
32d..	Dixon	86.7	Ardito	11.3	5th..	Lewis	78.5	Lewis Sr.	21.5
33d..	Roybal(1)Allard	87.2	Miller	12.8	6th..	Pelphrey	29.3	Gingrich	70.7
34th..	Napolitano	67.6	Perez	28.6	7th..	Williams	44.6	Barr	55.4
35th..	Waters	89.3	(1)	(1)	8th..	Cain	37.6	Chambliss	62.4
36th..	Hahn- Millender(1)	46.6	Kuykendall	48.9	9th..	(1)	(1)	Deal	100.0
					10th..	Freeman	40.4	Norwood	59.6
37th..	McDonald	85.1	Lankster	14.9	11th..	Littman	30.7	Linder	69.3
38th..	Mathews	44.3	Horn	52.9	HI ...	(X)	(X)	(X)	(X)
39th..	Groom	34.0	Royce	62.6	1st..	Abercrombie	61.6	Ward	36.3
40th..	Conaway	31.9	Lewis	64.9	2d...	Mink	69.4	Douglass	24.3
41st..	Ansari	40.7	Miller	53.2	ID ...	(X)	(X)	(X)	(X)
42d..	Brown	55.3	Pirozzi	40.3	1st..	Williams	44.7	Chenoweth	55.3
43d..	Rayburn	37.8	Calvert	55.7	2d...	Stallings	44.7	Simpson	52.5

See footnotes at end of table.

U.S. Census Bureau, Statistical Abstract of the United States: 2000

[See headnote, p. 278]

State and district	Democratic candidate Name	Percent of total	Republican candidate Name	Percent of total
IL	(X)	(X)	(X)	(X)
1st...	Rush	87.1	Ahimaz	10.6
2d ...	Jackson Jr.	89.4	Gordon III.	9.6
3d ...	Lipinski	72.5	Marshall.	27.5
4th...	Gutierrez	81.7	Birch	15.9
5th...	Blagojevich.	74.0	Spitz	26.0
6th...	Cramer	30.1	Hyde	67.3
7th...	Davis.	92.9	[1]	[1]
8th...	Rothman	31.4	Crane	68.6
9th...	Schakowsky	74.6	Sohn	23.1
10th..	[1]	[1]	Porter	100.0
11th.	Mueller	41.2	Weller	58.8
12th.	Costello	60.4	Price	39.6
13th.	Hynes	39.0	Biggert.	61.0
14th.	Cozzi	30.2	Hastert.	69.8
15th.	Prussing.	38.4	Ewing	61.6
16th.	[1]	[1]	Manzullo	100.0
17th.	Evans	51.6	Baker	48.4
18th.	[1]	[1]	LaHood	100.0
19th.	Phelps	58.3	Winters	41.7
20th.	Verticchio	38.7	Shimkus.	61.3
IN	(X)	(X)	(X)	(X)
1st...	Visclosky	72.5	Petyo	26.2
2d ...	Boles.	38.0	McIntosh	60.6
3d ...	Roemer	58.1	Holtz	41.9
4th...	Wehrle.	36.7	Souder	63.3
5th...	Steele	36.0	Buyer	62.5
6th...	Kern	16.8	Burton	72.0
7th...	Hillenberg.	28.1	Pease	68.9
8th...	Riecken	46.0	Hostettler	52.1
9th...	Hill	50.8	Leising.	47.9
10th..	Carson.	58.3	Hofmeister	39.4
IA	(X)	(X)	(X)	(X)
1st...	Rush	42.3	Leach	56.5
2d ...	Tully	44.0	Nussle.	55.2
3d ...	Boswell	56.9	McKibben.	41.1
4th...	Dvorak.	33.9	Ganske	65.2
5th...	[1]	[1]	Latham	99.2
KS	(X)	(X)	(X)	(X)
1st...	Phillips.	19.3	Moran	80.7
2d ...	Clark.	39.0	Ryun	61.0
3d ...	Moore	52.4	Snowbarger	47.6
4th...	Lawing.	38.6	Tiahrt.	58.3
KY	(X)	(X)	(X)	(X)
1st...	Barlow.	44.8	Whitfield.	55.2
2d ...	Evans	35.3	Lewis.	63.7
3d ...	Gorman	47.5	Northup.	51.5
4th...	Lucas	53.4	Williams.	46.6
5th...	Bailey[1]Barner	21.8	Rogers.	78.2
6th...	Scorsone	46.0	Fletcher.	53.1
LA [2]	(X)	(X)	(X)	(X)
1st...	[1]	[1]	Livingston [3]	[1]
2d ...	Jefferson [3]	86.0	[1]	[1]
3d ...	[1]	[1]	Tauzin [3]	[1]
4th...	[1]	[1]	McCrery [3]	[1]
5th...	[1]	[1]	Cooksey	[1]
6th...	McKeithen	49.3	Baker [3]	50.7
7th...	John [4]	[1]	[1]	[1]
ME	(X)	(X)	(X)	(X)
1st...	Allen	60.3	Connelly.	35.5
2d ...	Baldacci.	76.2	Reisman	23.8
MD	(X)	(X)	(X)	(X)
1st...	Pinder	30.8	Gilchrest	69.2
2d ...	Bosley.	30.7	Ehrlich.	69.3
3d ...	Cardin.	77.6	Harby	22.4
4th...	Wynn.	85.7	Kimble.	14.3
5th...	Hoyer	65.4	Ostrom	34.6
6th...	McCown.	36.6	Bartlett.	63.4
7th...	Cummings	85.7	Kondner.	14.3
8th...	Neas	39.6	Morella.	60.3
MA	(X)	(X)	(X)	(X)
1st...	Olver	71.7	Morgan	28.3
2d ...	Neal	99.0	[1]	[1]
3d ...	McGovern	56.9	Amorello	41.5
4th...	Frank.	98.4	[1]	[1]
5th...	Meehan	70.7	Coleman	29.3
6th...	Tierney	54.6	Torkildsen.	42.4
7th...	Markey	70.6	Long	29.3
8th...	Capuano	81.7	Hyde	11.6
9th...	Moakley.	99.4	[1]	[1]
10th..	Delahunt	70.0	Bleicken.	29.9
MI	(X)	(X)	(X)	(X)
1st...	Stupak.	58.7	McManus	39.5
2d ...	Shrauger	29.8	Hoekstra	68.7
3d ...	Ferguson Jr.	24.7	Ehlers	73.1
4th...	[1]	[1]	Camp	91.3
5th...	Barcia	71.2	Brewster	27.1
6th...	Annen	28.1	Upton	70.1
7th...	Berryman	40.1	Smith.	57.5
8th...	Stabenow.	57.4	Munsell	38.6
9th...	Kildee	55.9	McMillin.	41.9
10th..	Bonior	52.4	Palmer.	45.3
11th..	Reeds	33.7	Knollenberg	63.9
12th..	Levin.	55.9	Tourna.	42.0
13th..	Rivers	58.1	Hickey	39.8
14th..	Conyers Jr.	86.9	Collins	11.1
15th..	Kilpatrick	87.0	Boyd[1]Fields	10.3
16th..	Dingell Jr.	66.6	Morse	31.0
MN	(X)	(X)	(X)	(X)
1st...	Beckman	45.2	Gutknecht	54.7
2d ...	Minge	57.0	Duehring	36.1
3d ...	Leino.	23.5	Ramstad	71.9
4th...	Vento	53.7	Newinski	39.8
5th...	Sabo	66.9	Taylor	27.6
6th...	Luther	50.0	Kline	46.0
7th...	Peterson	71.7	Edin	28.1
8th...	Oberstar	66.0	Shuster	26.5
MS	(X)	(X)	(X)	(X)
1st...	Weathers	30.6	Wicker.	67.2
2d ...	Thompson	71.2	[1]	[1]
3d ...	[1]	[1]	Pickering	84.6
4th...	Shows	53.4	Hosemann	44.9
5th...	Taylor	77.8	McConnell	19.1
MO	(X)	(X)	(X)	(X)
1st...	Clay	72.6	Soluade	24.5
2d ...	Ross	28.3	Talent	70.0
3d ...	Gephardt	55.8	Federer	42.0
4th...	Skelton	71.0	Noland.	27.2
5th...	McCarthy	65.9	Bennett	31.0
6th...	Danner	70.9	Bailey	26.8
7th...	Perkel	24.3	Blunt	72.6
8th...	Heckemeyer	35.7	Emerson [5]	62.6
9th...	Vogt	35.5	Hulshof	62.2
MT	(X)	(X)	(X)	(X)
...	Deschamps	44.4	Hill	53.0
NE	(X)	(X)	(X)	(X)
1st...	Eret.	26.4	Bereuter.	73.5
2d ...	Scott	34.2	Terry	65.5
3d ...	[1]	[1]	Barrett	84.3
NV	(X)	(X)	(X)	(X)
1st...	Berkley	49.2	Chairez	45.7
2d ...	[1]	[1]	Gibbons	81.1
NH	(X)	(X)	(X)	(X)
1st...	Flood.	33.1	Sununu	66.8
2d ...	Rauh.	44.8	Bass	53.1
NJ	(X)	(X)	(X)	(X)
1st...	Andrews.	73.2	Richards	22.6
2d ...	Hunsberger	30.8	LoBiondo	65.9
3d ...	Polansky	35.1	Saxton.	62.0
4th...	Schneider.	35.0	Smith.	62.2
5th...	Schneider.	33.3	Roukema	63.7
6th...	Pallone	57.0	Ferguson	40.3
7th...	Connelly.	44.4	Franks.	52.5
8th...	Pascrell Jr.	62.1	Kirnan	35.4
9th...	Rothman	64.6	Lonegan	33.8
10th..	Payne	83.5	Wnuck.	10.8
11th..	Scollo	29.6	Frelinghuysen.	67.7
12th..	Holt.	50.1	Pappas	47.2
13th..	Menendez	80.1	de Leon.	16.6

See footnotes at end of table.

U.S. Census Bureau, Statistical Abstract of the United States: 2000

No. 459. Vote Cast for United States Representatives by Major Political Party—Congressional Districts: 1998—Continued

[See headnote, p. 278]

State and district	Democratic candidate Name	Democratic Percent of total	Republican Candidate Name	Republican Percent of total	State and district	Democratic candidate Name	Democratic Percent of total	Republican Candidate Name	Republican Percent of total
NM....	(X)......	(X)	(X).....	(X)	12th..	Brown....	32.8	Kasich....	67.2
1st...	Maloof....	41.9	Wilson....	48.4	13th..	Brown....	61.5	Drake....	38.5
2d...	Baca....	42.1	Skeen....	57.9	14th..	Sawyer...	62.7	Watkins...	37.3
3d...	Udall.....	53.2	Redmond..	43.3	15th..	Miller.....	28.5	Pryce....	65.7
NY....	(X)......	(X)	(X).....	(X)	16th..	Ferguson	36.0	Regula..	64.0
1st...	Holst....	35.9	Forbes....	64.1	17th..	Traficant.	68.2	Alberty...	31.8
2d...	Bace....	29.5	Lazio....	66.2	18th..	Burch....	39.7	Ney....	60.3
3d...	Langberg.	34.9	King....	64.3	19th..	Kelley....	33.6	LaTourette.	66.4
4th...	McCarthy.	52.6	Becker....	46.6	OK....	(X)......	(X)	(X)......	(X)
5th...	Ackerman.	65.0	Pinzon....	33.1	1st...	Plowman..	38.2	Largent..	61.8
6th...	Meeks...	100.0	(¹)......	(¹)	2d...	Pharaoh..	39.8	Coburn..	57.7
7th...	Crowley...	69.0	Dillon....	25.6	3d...	Roberts...	38.0	Watkins..	62.0
8th...	Nadler....	86.0	Howard...	14.0	4th...	Odom.....	38.5	Watts....	61.5
9th...	Weiner....	66.4	Telano....	23.4	5th...	Smothermon	31.8	Istook....	68.2
10th...	Towns.....	92.3	Brown....	6.2	6th...	Barby....	33.2	Lucas....	65.0
11th...	Owens....	90.0	Greene....	8.7	OR....	(X)......	(X)	(X)......	(X)
12th...	Velazquez.	83.6	Markgraf..	11.6	1st...	Wu.......	50.1	Bordonaro.	47.1
13th...	Prisco....	34.2	Fossella..	64.8	2d...	Campbell..	34.8	Walden...	61.5
14th...	Maloney...	77.4	Kupferman.	22.6	3d...	Blumenauer.	83.9	(¹)......	(¹)
			Cunning-		4th...	DeFazio...	70.1	Webb....	28.6
15th...	Rangel....	93.1	ham....	5.8	5th...	Hooley...	54.9	Shannon..	40.5
16th...	Serrano...	95.4	Bayley Jr..	3.5	PA....	(X)......	(X)	(X)......	(X)
			Flume-		1st...	Brady....	81.2	Harrison..	16.6
17th...	Engel....	88.0	freddo..	12.0	2d...	Fattah....	86.5	Mulligan...	13.5
18th...	Lowey....	82.8	(¹)......	(¹)	3d...	Borski....	59.3	Dougherty.	40.7
19th...	Collins....	33.6	Kelly....	62.2	4th...	Klink....	63.8	Turzai....	36.2
20th...	Feiner....	38.8	Gilman...	58.3	5th...	(¹)......	(¹)	Peterson..	84.8
21st...	McNulty...	74.2	Ayers....	25.8	6th...	Holden...	61.0	Meckley...	39.0
22d...	Bordewich.	42.1	Sweeney..	55.3	7th...	D'Urso...	28.2	Weldon...	71.8
23d...	(¹)......	(¹)	Boehlert..	80.8	8th...	Tuthill....	32.6	Greenwood	63.2
24th...	Tallon.....	21.0	McHugh...	79.0	9th...	(¹)......	(¹)	Shuster...	99.5
25th...	Rothenberg.	30.6	Walsh....	69.4	10th...	Casey....	48.4	Sherwood.	48.7
26th...	Hinchey...	61.8	Walker....	31.3	11th...	Kanjorski...	66.8	Urban....	33.2
27th...	Cook....	42.7	Reynolds..	57.3	12th...	Murtha....	68.5	Holloway..	31.5
28th...	Slaughter.	64.8	Kaplan...	30.8	13th...	Hoeffel...	51.6	Fox.......	46.6
29th...	LaFalce...	57.0	Collins....	40.7	14th...	Coyne....	60.5	Ravotti...	38.3
30th...	Peoples...	32.2	Quinn....	67.8	15th...	Afflerbach.	45.0	Toomey...	55.0
31st...	Rossiter..	25.3	Houghton.	68.0	16th...	Yorczyk...	29.5	Pitts....	70.5
NC....	(X)......	(X)	(X)......	(X)	17th...	(¹)......	(¹)	Gekas....	99.8
1st...	Clayton....	62.2	Tyler.....	37.0	18th...	Doyle....	67.7	Walker...	32.3
2d...	Etheridge.	57.4	Page....	41.7	19th...	Ropp....	28.5	Goodling..	67.6
3d...	Williams...	37.1	Jones Jr..	81.9	20th...	Mascara...	99.8	(¹)......	(¹)
4th...	Price....	57.4	Roberg...	41.6	21st...	Klemens..	36.6	English...	63.4
5th...	Robinson.	31.7	Burr....	67.6	RI....	(X)......	(X)	(X)......	(X)
6th...	(¹)......	(¹)	Coble....	88.6	1st...	Kennedy..	66.8	Santa....	27.7
7th...	McIntyre..	91.3	(¹)......	(¹)	2d...	Weygand.	72.0	Matson...	24.8
8th...	Taylor....	48.2	Hayes....	50.7	SC....	(X)......	(X)	(X)......	(X)
9th...	Blake....	29.5	Myrick...	69.3	1st...	(¹)......	(¹)	Sanford...	91.0
10th...	(¹)......	(¹)	Ballenger..	85.6	2d...	Frederick...	41.0	Spence...	57.8
11th...	Young....	42.2	Taylor....	56.6	3d...	(¹)......	(¹)	Graham...	99.7
12th...	Watt......	56.0	Keadle...	42.2	4th...	Reese....	40.2	DeMint...	57.7
ND....	Pomeroy.	56.2	Cramer...	41.1	5th...	Spratt....	57.9	Burkhold..	40.4
OH....	(X)......	(X)	(X)......	(X)	6th...	Clyburn....	72.6	McLeod...	25.8
1st...	Qualls.....	47.0	Chabot...	53.0	SD....	Moser....	24.9	Thune....	75.1
2d...	Sanders..	24.2	Portman..	75.8	TN....	(X)......	(X)	(X)......	(X)
3d...	Hall......	69.3	Shondel..	30.7	1st...	White....	30.8	Jenkins...	69.1
4th...	McClain..	36.2	Oxley....	63.8	2d...	(¹)......	(¹)	Duncan Jr..	88.6
5th...	Darrow...	33.3	Gillmor...	66.7	3d...	Lewis Jr....	32.6	Wamp....	66.0
6th...	Strickland.	57.0	Hollister..	43.0	4th...	Cooper....	40.4	Hilleary...	59.6
7th...	Minor....	27.7	Hobson..	67.2	5th...	Clement...	82.8	(¹)......	(¹)
8th...	Griffin....	29.3	Boehner..	70.7	6th...	Gordon....	54.6	Massey...	45.3
9th...	Kaptur....	81.2	Emery....	18.8	7th...	(¹)......	(¹)	Bryant....	99.5
10th...	Kucinich..	66.8	Slovenic..	33.2	8th...	Tanner....	100.0	(¹)......	(¹)
11th...	Tubbs Jones	80.4	Hereford..	13.0	9th...	Ford Jr.....	78.7	Burdikoff..	18.9

See footnotes at end of table.

U.S. Census Bureau, Statistical Abstract of the United States: 2000

No. 459. Vote Cast for United States Representatives by Major Political Party—Congressional Districts: 1998—Continued

[See headnote, p. 278]

State and district	Democratic candidate Name	Percent of total	Republican candidate Name	Percent of total	State and district	Democratic candidate Name	Percent of total	Republican candidate Name	Percent of total
TX	(X)........	(X)	(X)........	(X)	2d ...	Pickett	94.3	(¹)	(¹)
1st...	Sandlin....	59.4	Boerner....	40.6	3d ...	Scott	76.0	(¹)	(¹)
2d ...	Turner	58.4	Babin......	40.8	4th...	Sisisky	97.0	(¹)	(¹)
3d ...	(¹)........	(¹)	Johnson....	91.2	5th...	Goode Jr. ..	98.9	(¹)	(¹)
4th...	Hall	57.6	Lohmeyer...	40.9	6th...	Bowers.....	30.7	Goodlatte ...	69.3
5th...	Morales	43.4	Sessions ...	55.8	7th...	(¹)........	(¹)	Bliley	78.7
6th...	Boothe	25.9	Barton	72.9	8th...	Moran	66.7	Miller	33.1
7th...	(¹)........	(¹)	Archer	93.3	9th...	Boucher....	60.9	Barta	39.1
8th...	(¹).....₇..	(¹)	Brady⁶.....	92.8	10th..	Brooks	25.2	Wolf......	71.6
9th...	Lampson⁷..	63.7	Cottar.....	36.3	11th ..	(¹)........	(¹)	Davis III	81.7
10th..	Doggett....	85.2	(¹)........	(¹)	WA	(X)........	(X)	(X)........	(X)
11th..	Edwards....	82.4	(¹)........	(¹)	1st...	Inslee......	49.8	Smith	44.1
12th..	Hall	36.3	Granger	61.9	2d ...	Cammerm-			
13th..	Harmon	31.0	Thornberry ..	67.9		eyer.......	44.8	Metcalf.....	55.2
14th..	Sneary.....	44.5	Paul.......	55.3	3d ...	Baird	54.7	Benton	45.3
15th..	Hinojosa ...	58.4	Haughey....	41.6	4th...	Pross	24.4	Hastings...	69.1
16th..	Reyes	87.9	(¹)........	(¹)	5th...	Lyons......	38.1	Nethercutt...	56.9
17th..	Stenholm ...	53.6	Izzard	45.3	6th...	Dicks	68.4	Lawrence ...	31.6
18th..	Jackson(¹)Lee	89.9	(¹)........	(¹)	7th...	McDermott ..	88.2	(¹)........	(¹)
19th..	Blakenship ..	16.4	Combest....	83.6	8th...	Behrens(¹)			
20th..	Gonzalez ...	63.2	Walker	35.6		Benedict....	40.3	Dunn	59.7
21st..	(¹)........	(¹)	Smith	91.4	9th...	Smith	64.7	Taber	35.3
22d ...	Kemp......	33.7	DeLay......	65.2	WV	(X)........	(X)	(X)........	(X)
23d ...	Jones......	35.1	Bonilla	63.8	1st...	Mollohan...	84.7	(¹)........	(¹)
24th..	Frost	57.5	Terry	40.9	2d ...	Wise	73.0	Kay	21.4
25th..	Bentsen⁸...	57.9	Sanchez....	41.3	3d ...	Rahall II ...	86.6	(¹)........	(¹)
26th..	(¹)........	(¹)	Armey	88.1	WI	(X)........	(X)	(X)........	(X)
27th..	Ortiz	63.3	Stone......	35.2	1st...	Spottswood..	42.7	Ryan	57.1
28th..	Rodriguez...	90.5	(¹)........	(¹)	2d ...	Baldwin	52.5	Musser.....	46.7
29th..	Green	92.8	(¹)........	(¹)	3d ...	Kind......	71.5	Brechler....	28.4
30th..	Johnson⁹..	72.2	Kelleher	26.8	4th...	Kleczka....	57.9	Reynolds ...	42.0
UT	(X)......	(X)	(X)........	(X)	5th...	Barrett	78.2	Melvin	21.6
1st...	Beierlein....	30.4	Hansen	67.7	6th...	(¹)........	(¹)	Petri......	92.6
2d ...	Eskelsen ...	43.5	Cook	52.8	7th...	Obey	60.6	West	39.3
3d ...	(¹)........	(¹)	Cannon	76.9	8th...	Johnson....	45.4	Green	54.6
VT¹⁰...	(¹)........	(¹)	Candon	32.9	9th...	(¹)........	(¹)	Sensenbren-	
VA	(¹)........	(X)	(X)........	(X)				ner	91.3
1st...	(¹)........	(¹)	Bateman....	76.4	WY	Farris......	38.7	Cubin.....	57.8

X Not applicable. ¹ No candidate. ² Louisiana holds an open-primary election with candidates from all parties running on the same ballot. Any candidate who receives a majority is elected; if no candidate receives 50 percent, there is a run-off election in November between the top two finishers. ³ Candidate listed won seat in open-primary. ⁴ There were two Democratic candidates; Hunter Lundy received 46.9 percent of Democratic votes. ⁵ Jo Ann Emerson ran as an Independent but caucused in the 105th Congress with the Democrats. ⁶ There were two Republican candidates; Gene Fontenot received 38.9 percent of Republican votes. ⁷ There were two Democratic candidates; Geraldine Sam received 9.4 percent of Democratic votes. ⁸ There were two Democratic candidates; Beverly Clark received 16.9 percent of Democratic votes. ⁹ There were two additional Democratic candidates who received a total of 15.7 percent of Democratic candidates. ¹⁰ The winning candidate was Bernard Sanders, an Independent, who received 49.9 percent of the vote.
Source: Congressional Quarterly Inc., *Congressional Quarterly Weekly Report* (copyright).

No. 460. Composition of Congress by Political Party: 1971 to 1999

[D=Democratic, R=Republican. Data for beginning of first session of each Congress (as of January 3), except as noted. Excludes vacancies at beginning of session]

Year	Party and President	Congress	House Majority party	Minority party	Other	Senate Majority party	Minority party	Other
1971 [1]	R (Nixon)........	92d...........	D-254	R-180	-	D-54	R-44	2
1973 [1][2]	R (Nixon)........	93d...........	D-239	R-192	1	D-56	R-42	2
1975 [3]	R (Ford)	94th..........	D-291	R-144	-	D-60	R-37	2
1977 [4]	D (Carter).......	95th..........	D-292	R-143	-	D-61	R-38	1
1979 [4]	D (Carter).......	96th..........	D-276	R-157	-	D-58	R-41	1
1981 [4]	R (Reagan)	97th..........	D-243	R-192	-	R-53	D-46	1
1983	R (Reagan).....	98th..........	D-269	R-165	-	R-54	D-46	-
1985	R (Reagan).....	99th..........	D-252	R-182	-	R-53	D-47	-
1987	R (Reagan).....	100th.........	D-258	R-177	-	D-55	R-45	-
1989	R (Bush).......	101st.........	D-259	R-174	-	D-55	R-45	-
1991 [5]	R (Bush).......	102d..........	D-267	R-167	1	D-56	R-44	-
1993 [5]	D (Clinton)......	103d..........	D-258	R-176	1	D-57	R-43	-
1995 [5]	D (Clinton)......	104th.........	R-230	D-204	1	R-52	D-48	-
1996 [5]	D (Clinton)......	104th.........	R-236	D-197	1	R-53	D-46	-
1997 [5][6]	D (Clinton)......	105th.........	R-226	D-207	2	R-55	D-45	-
1999	D (Clinton)......	106th.........	R-222	D-212	-	R-54	D-45	1

- Represents zero. ¹ Senate had one Independent and one Conservative-Republican. ² House had one Independent-Democrat. ³ Senate had one Independent, one Conservative-Republican, and one undecided (New Hampshire). ⁴ Senate had one Independent. ⁵ House had one Independent-Socialist. ⁶ As of beginning of second session.
Source: U.S. Congress, Joint Committee on Printing, *Congressional Directory*, annual; beginning 1977, biennial.

U.S. Census Bureau, Statistical Abstract of the United States: 2000

No. 461. Composition of Congress by Political Party Affiliation— States: 1989 to 1999

[Figures are for the beginning of the first session (as of January 3), except as noted. Dem.=Democratic; Rep.=Republican]

State	Representatives								Senators							
	102d Cong.,[2] 1991		103rd Cong.,[2] 1993		105th Cong.,[2 3 4] 1997		106th Cong., 1999		102d Cong., 1991		103rd Cong., 1993		104th Cong.,[3 5] 1997		106th Cong.,[1] 1999	
	Dem.	Rep.	Dem.	Rep.	Dem.	Rep.	Dem.	Rep.	Dem.	Rep.	Dem.	Rep.	Dem.	Rep.	Dem.	Rep.
U.S.	267	167	258	176	206	228	212	222	56	44	57	43	46	53	45	55
AL.	5	2	4	3	2	5	2	5	2	-	2	-	-	2	-	2
AK.	-	1	-	1	-	1	-	1	-	2	-	2	-	2	-	2
AZ.	1	4	3	3	1	5	1	5	1	1	1	1	-	2	-	2
AR.	3	1	2	2	2	2	2	2	2	-	2	-	1	1	1	1
CA.	26	19	30	22	29	23	28	24	1	1	2	-	2	-	2	-
CO.	3	3	2	4	2	4	2	4	1	1	1	1	-	2	-	2
CT.	3	3	3	3	4	2	4	2	2	-	2	-	2	-	2	-
DE.	1	-	-	1	-	1	-	1	1	1	1	1	1	1	1	1
FL.	9	10	10	13	8	15	8	15	1	1	1	1	1	1	1	1
GA	9	1	7	4	3	8	3	8	2	-	1	1	1	1	1	1
HI	2	-	2	-	2	-	2	-	2	-	2	-	2	-	2	-
ID	2	-	1	1	-	2	-	2	-	2	-	2	-	2	-	2
IL	15	7	12	8	10	10	10	10	2	-	2	-	2	-	1	1
IN	8	2	7	3	4	6	4	6	-	2	-	2	-	2	1	1
IA	2	4	1	4	1	4	1	4	1	1	1	1	1	1	1	1
KS.	2	3	2	2	-	4	1	3	-	2	-	2	-	2	-	2
KY.	4	3	4	2	1	5	1	5	1	1	1	1	1	1	-	2
LA.	4	4	4	3	2	5	2	5	2	-	2	-	2	-	2	-
ME	1	1	1	1	2	-	2	-	1	1	1	1	-	2	-	2
MD	5	3	4	4	4	4	4	4	2	-	2	-	2	-	2	-
MA	10	1	8	2	10	-	10	-	2	-	2	-	2	-	2	-
MI	11	7	10	6	10	6	10	6	2	-	2	-	1	1	1	1
MN	6	2	6	2	6	2	6	2	1	1	1	1	1	1	1	1
MS	5	-	5	-	2	3	3	2	-	2	-	2	-	2	-	2
MO	6	3	6	3	5	4	5	4	-	2	-	2	-	2	-	2
MT	1	1	1	-	-	1	-	1	1	1	1	1	1	1	1	1
NE.	1	2	1	2	-	3	-	3	2	-	2	-	1	1	1	1
NV.	1	1	1	1	-	2	1	1	2	-	2	-	2	-	2	-
NH	1	1	1	1	-	2	-	2	-	2	-	2	-	2	-2	1
NJ.	8	6	7	6	6	7	7	6	2	-	2	-	2	-	2	-
NM	1	2	1	2	-	3	1	2	1	1	1	1	1	1	1	1
NY.	21	13	18	13	18	13	19	12	1	1	1	1	1	1	2	-
NC	7	4	8	4	6	6	5	7	1	1	-	2	-	2	1	1
ND	1	-	1	-	1	-	1	-	2	-	2	-	2	-	2	-
OH	11	10	10	9	8	11	8	11	2	-	2	-	1	1	-	2
OK	4	2	4	2	-	6	-	6	1	1	1	1	-	2	-	2
OR	4	1	4	1	4	1	4	1	-	2	-	2	1	1	1	1
PA.	11	12	11	10	11	10	11	10	-	2	1	1	-	2	-	2
RI	1	1	1	1	2	-	2	-	1	1	1	1	1	1	1	1
SC.	4	2	3	3	2	4	2	4	1	1	1	1	1	1	1	1
SD.	1	-	1	-	-	1	-	1	1	1	1	1	2	-	2	-
TN.	6	3	6	3	4	5	4	5	2	-	2	-	-	2	-	2
TX.	19	8	21	9	17	13	17	13	1	1	1	1	-	2	-	2
UT.	2	1	2	1	-	3	-	3	-	2	-	2	-	2	1	1
VT.	-	-	-	-	-	-	-	-	1	1	1	1	1	1	1	1
VA.	6	4	7	4	6	5	6	5	1	1	1	1	1	1	1	1
WA	5	3	8	1	3	6	5	4	1	1	1	1	1	1	1	1
WV	4	-	3	-	3	-	3	-	2	-	2	-	2	-	2	-
WI	4	5	4	5	5	4	5	4	1	1	2	-	2	-	2	-
WY	-	1	-	1	-	1	-	1	-	2	-	2	-	2	-	2

- Represents zero.   [1] Alabama and Indiana had one vacancy each.   [2] Vermont had one Independent-Socialist Representative.   [3] As of beginning of second session.   [4] California had one vacancy.   [5] Oregon had one vacancy.

Source: U.S. Congress, Joint Committee on Printing, *Congressional Directory*, biennial; and unpublished data.

Year	Representatives							Senators					
		Incumbent candidates							Incumbent candidates				
			Reelected		Defeated in—				Reelected		Defeated in—		
	Retirements[1]	Total	Number	Percent of candidates	Primary	General election	Retirements[1]	Total	Number	Percent of candidates	Primary	General election	
PRESIDENTIAL-YEAR ELECTIONS													
1964	33	397	344	86.6	8	45	2	33	28	84.8	1	4	
1968	23	409	396	96.8	4	9	6	28	20	71.4	4	4	
1972	40	390	365	93.6	12	13	6	27	20	74.1	2	5	
1976	47	384	368	95.8	3	13	8	25	16	64.0	-	9	
1980	34	398	361	90.7	6	31	5	29	16	55.2	4	9	
1984	22	411	392	95.4	3	16	4	29	26	89.7	-	3	
1988	23	409	402	98.3	1	6	6	27	23	85.2	-	4	
1992	65	368	325	88.3	[2]19	[3]24	7	28	23	82.1	1	4	
1996	50	384	361	94.0	2	21	13	21	19	90.5	1	1	
MIDTERM ELECTIONS													
1966	22	411	362	88.1	8	41	3	32	28	87.5	3	1	
1970	29	401	379	94.5	10	12	4	31	24	77.4	1	6	
1974	43	391	343	87.7	8	40	7	27	23	85.2	2	2	
1978	49	382	358	93.7	5	19	10	25	15	60.0	3	7	
1982	40	393	354	90.1	[2]10	29	3	30	28	93.3	-	2	
1986	40	394	385	97.7	3	6	6	28	21	75.0	-	7	
1990	27	406	390	96.1	1	15	3	32	31	96.9	-	1	
1994	48	387	349	90.2	4	34	9	26	24	92.3	-	2	
1998	23	404	395	97.8	1	6	5	29	26	89.7	-	3	

- Represents zero. [1] Does not include persons who died or resigned before the election. [2] Number of incumbents defeated in primaries by other incumbents due to redistricting: six in 1982 and four in 1992. [3] Five incumbents defeated in general election by other incumbents due to redistricting.

Source: Ornstein, Norman J., Thomas E. Mann, and Michael J. Malbin, *Vital Statistics on Congress, 1993-1994.* Beginning 1995, Congressional Quarterly, Inc., Washington, DC, *America Votes,* biennial (copyright).

No. 463. Members of Congress—Selected Characteristics: 1981 to 1999

[As of beginning of first session of each Congress, (January 3). Figures for Representatives exclude vacancies]

Members of congress and year	Male	Female	Black[1]	API[2]	Hispanic[3]	Age [4] (in years)					Seniority [5]				
						Under 40	40 to 49	50 to 59	60 to 69	70 and over	Less than 2 yrs.	2 to 9 yrs.	10 to 19 yrs.	20 to 29 yrs.	30 yrs. or more
REPRESENTATIVES															
97th Cong., 1981	416	19	[6]17	3	6	94	142	132	54	13	77	231	96	23	8
98th Cong., 1983	413	21	[6]21	3	8	86	145	132	57	14	83	224	88	28	11
99th Cong., 1985	412	22	[7]20	3	10	71	154	131	59	19	49	237	104	34	10
100th Cong., 1987	412	23	[7]23	4	11	63	153	137	56	26	51	221	114	37	12
101st Cong., 1989	408	25	[7]24	5	10	41	163	133	74	22	39	207	139	35	13
102d Cong., 1991	407	28	[7]26	3	11	39	152	134	86	24	55	178	147	44	11
103d Cong., 1993 [8]	388	47	[7]38	4	17	47	151	128	89	15	118	141	132	32	12
104th Cong., 1995	388	47	[9]40	4	17	53	155	135	79	13	92	188	110	36	9
106th Cong., 1999	379	56	[9]39	(NA)	(NA)	23	116	173	87	35	41	236	104	46	7
SENATORS															
97th Cong., 1981	98	2	-	3	-	9	35	36	14	6	19	51	17	11	2
98th Cong., 1983	98	2	-	2	-	7	28	39	20	6	5	61	21	10	3
99th Cong., 1985	98	2	-	2	-	4	27	38	25	6	8	56	27	7	2
100th Cong., 1987	98	2	-	2	-	5	30	36	22	7	14	41	36	7	2
101st Cong., 1989	98	2	-	2	-	-	30	40	22	8	23	22	43	10	2
102d Cong., 1991	98	2	-	2	-	-	23	46	24	7	5	34	47	10	4
103d Cong., 1993 [8]	93	7	1	2	-	1	16	48	22	12	15	30	39	11	5
104th Cong., 1995	92	8	1	2	-	1	14	41	27	17	12	38	30	15	5
106th Cong., 1999	91	9	-	(NA)	(NA)	-	14	38	35	13	8	39	33	14	6

- Represents zero.   NA Not available.   [1] Source: Joint Center for Political and Economic Studies, Washington, DC, *Black Elected Officials: Statistical Summary,* annual (copyright).   [2] Asians and Pacific Islanders. Source: Library of Congress, Congressional Research Service, "Asian Pacific Americans in the United States Congress," Report 94-767 GOV.   [3] Source: National Association of Latino Elected and Appointed Officials, Washington, DC, *National Roster of Hispanic Elected Officials,* annual.   [4] Some members do not provide date of birth.   [5] Represents consecutive years of service.   [6] Does not include District of Columbia or Virgin Islands delegate.   [7] Includes District of Columbia delegate but not Virgin Islands delegate.   [8] Includes members elected to fill vacant seats through June 14, 1993.   [9] Includes District of Columbia and Virgin Islands delegate.

Source: Except as noted, compiled by U.S. Census Bureau from data published in *Congressional Directory,* biennial.

No. 464. U.S. Congress—Measures Introduced and Enacted and Time in Session: 1981 to 1997

[Excludes simple and concurrent resolutions]

Item	97th Cong., 1981-82	98th Cong., 1983-84	99th Cong., 1985-86	100th Cong., 1987-88	101st Cong., 1989-90	102d Cong., 1991-92	103d Cong., 1993-94	104th Cong., 1995-96	105th Cong., 1996-97
Measures introduced	11,490	11,156	9,885	9,588	6,664	6,775	8,544	6,808	7,732
Bills	10,582	10,134	8,697	8,515	5,977	6,212	7,883	6,545	7,532
Joint resolutions	908	1,022	1,188	1,073	687	563	661	263	200
Measures enacted	529	677	483	761	666	609	473	337	404
Public	473	623	466	713	650	589	465	333	394
Private	56	54	17	48	16	20	8	4	10
HOUSE OF REPRESENTATIVES									
Number of days	303	266	281	298	281	280	265	290	251
Number of hours	1,420	1,705	1,794	1,659	1,688	1,796	1,887	2,445	2,001
Number of hours per day. . . .	4.7	6.4	6.4	5.6	6.0	6.4	7.1	8.4	8.0
SENATE									
Number of days	312	281	313	307	274	287	291	343	296
Number of hours	2,158	1,951	2,531	2,341	2,254	2,292	2,514	2,876	2,188
Number of hours per day. . . .	6.9	6.9	8.1	7.6	8.2	8.0	8.6	8.4	7.4

Source: U.S. Congress, *Congressional Record* and *Daily Calendar*, selected issues.

No. 465. Congressional Bills Vetoed: 1961 to 1997

Period	President	Total vetoes	Regular vetoes	Pocket vetoes	Vetoes sustained	Bills passed over veto
1961-63	Kennedy	21	12	9	21	-
1963-69	Johnson	30	16	14	30	-
1969-74	Nixon	43	26	17	36	7
1974-77	Ford	66	48	18	54	12
1977-81	Carter	31	13	18	29	2
1981-89	Reagan	78	39	39	69	9
1989-93	Bush	44	29	15	43	1
1993-97	Clinton	30	30	-	28	2

- Represents zero.

Source: U.S. Congress, Senate Library, *Presidential Vetoes ... 1789-1968*; U.S. Congress, *Calendars of the U.S. House of Representatives and History of Legislation,* annual.

No. 466. Congressional Staff by Location of Employment: 1972 to 1995

[Excludes those persons employed in congressional support agencies such as the U.S. General Accounting Office, the Library of Congress, and the Congressional Budget Office]

Year	Personal staff		Year	Standing committee staff		Location of employment	1985	1990	1991	1993	1995
	House	Senate		House	Senate						
1972. . . .	5,280	2,426	1970 . . .	702	635	Total	18,136	17,625	17,851	(NA)	16,184
1980. . . .	7,371	3,746	1980 . . .	1,917	1,191						
1981. . . .	7,487	3,945	1981 . . .	1,843	1,022	House of Representatives	11,636	11,064	11,041	10,791	9,913
1982. . . .	7,511	4,041	1982 . . .	1,839	1,047	Committee staff [2]	2,146	2,173	2,321	2,070	1,266
1983. . . .	7,606	4,059	1983 . . .	1,970	1,075	Personal staff	7,528	7,496	7,278	7,390	7,186
1984. . . .	7,385	3,949	1984 . . .	1,944	1,095	Leadership staff	144	156	149	137	134
1985. . . .	7,528	4,097	1985 . . .	2,009	1,080	Officers of House, staff.	1,818	1,239	1,293	1,194	1,327
1986. . . .	[1]7,920	[1]3,774	1986 . . .	1,954	1,075						
1987. . . .	7,584	4,075	1987 . . .	2,024	1,074	Senate	6,369	6,425	6,665	6,529	6,163
			1988 . . .	1,976	970	Committee staff [2]	1,178	1,207	1,154	1,032	796
1989. . . .	7,569	3,837	1989 . . .	1,986	1,013	Personal staff	4,097	4,162	4,294	4,200	4,247
1990. . . .	7,496	4,162	1990 . . .	1,993	1,090	Leadership staff	118	94	125	132	126
1991. . . .	7,278	4,294	1991 . . .	2,201	1,030	Officers of Senate, staff	976	962	1,092	1,165	994
1992. . . .	7,597	4,249	1992 . . .	2,178	1,008						
1993. . . .	7,400	4,138	1993 . . .	2,118	897	Joint committee staff . . .	131	136	145	(NA)	108
1994. . . .	7,390	4,200	1994 . . .	2,046	958						
1995. . . .	7,186	4,247	1995 . . .	1,246	732						

NA Not available. [1] House figure is average for year, and Senate figure only covers period following implementation of Gramm-Rudman budget reductions. [2] Covers standing, select, and special committees.

Source: Ornstein, Norman J., Thomas E. Mann, and Michael J. Malbin, *Vital Statistics on Congress, 1993-1994,* Congressional Quarterly, Inc., Washington, DC, 1994, and unpublished data (copyright).

No. 467. Number of Governors by Political Party Affiliation: 1970 to 2000

[Reflects figures after inaugurations for each year]

Year	Demo-cratic	Repub-lican	Indepen-dent/other	Year	Demo-cratic	Repub-lican	Indepen-dent/other	Year	Demo-cratic	Repub-lican	Indepen-dent/other
1970	18	32	-	1989	28	22	-	1995	19	30	1
1975	36	13	1	1990	29	21	-	1996	18	31	1
1980	31	19	-	1991 [1] ...	29	19	2	1997	17	32	1
1985	34	16	-	1992	28	20	2	1998	17	32	1
1987	26	24	-	1993	30	18	2	1999	17	31	2
1988	27	23	-	1994	29	19	2	2000	17	31	2

- Represents zero.   [1] Reflects result of runoff election in Arizona in February 1991.

Source: National Governors' Association, Washington, DC, 1970-87 and 1991-99, *Directory of Governors of the American States, Commonwealths & Territories*, annual; and 1988-90, *Directory of Governors*, annual. (copyright).

No. 468. Vote Cast for and Governor Elected by State: 1990 to 1998

[In thousands (1,216 represents 1,216,000), except percent. D=Democratic, R=Republican, I=Independent]

State	1990 Total vote [1]	1990 Percent leading party	1994 Total vote [1]	1994 Percent leading party	1996 Total vote [1]	1996 Percent leading party	1998 Total vote [1]	1998 Percent leading party	Candidate elected at most recent election
AL.........	1,216	R-52.1	1,202	R-50.3	(X)	(X)	1,318	D-57.7	Donald Siegelman
AK.........	195	I-38.9	213	D-41.1	(X)	(X)	220	D-51.3	Tony Knowles
AZ.........	2,941 [2]	[2] R-52.4	1,129	R-52.5	(X)	(X)	1,018	R-60.9	Jane Dee Hull
AR.........	696	D-57.5	717	D-59.8	(X)	(X)	706	R-59.8	Mike Huckabee
CA.........	7,699	R-49.2	8,659	R-55.2	(X)	(X)	8,385	D-58.0	Gray Davis
CO.........	1,011	D-61.9	1,116	D-55.5	(X)	(X)	1,321	R-49.1	Bill Owens
CT.........	1,141	I-40.4	1,147	R-36.2	(X)	(X)	1,000	R-62.9	John G. Rowland
DE.........	(X)	(X)	(X)	(X)	271	D-69.5	(X)	(X)	Thomas R. Carper
FL.........	3,531	D-56.5	4,206	D-50.8	(X)	(X)	3,964	R-55.3	Jeb Bush
GA	1,450	D-52.9	1,545	D-51.1	(X)	(X)	1,793	D-52.5	Roy Barnes
HI	340	D-59.8	369	D-36.6	(X)	(X)	408	D-50.1	Benjamin J. Cayetano
ID	321	D-68.2	413	R-52.3	(X)	(X)	381	R-67.7	Dirk Kempthorne
IL	3,257	R-50.7	3,107	R-63.9	(X)	(X)	3,359	R-51.0	George Ryan
IN	(X)	(X)	(X)	(X)	2,110	D-51.5	(X)	(X)	Frank L. O'Bannon
IA	976	R-60.6	997	R-56.8	(X)	(X)	956	D-52.3	Tom Vilsack
KS	783	D-48.6	821	R-64.1	(X)	(X)	743	R-73.4	Bill Graves
KY	(X)	(X)	(X)	(X)	984	D-50.9	(X)	(X)	Paul E. Patton
LA.......	(X)	(X)	(X)	(X)	1,550	R-63.5	(X)	(X)	Mike Foster
ME	522	R-46.7	511	I-35.4	(X)	(X)	421	R-18.9	Angus King
MD	1,111	D-59.8	1,410	D-50.2	(X)	(X)	1,536	D-55.1	Parris N. Glendening
MA	2,343	R-50.2	2,164	R-70.9	(X)	(X)	1,903	R-50.8	Argeo Paul Cellucci
MI	2,565	R-49.8	3,088	R-61.5	(X)	(X)	3,027	R-62.2	John Engler
MN	1,807	R-49.6	1,766	R-62.0	(X)	(X)	2,091	R-34.3	Jesse Ventura
MS	(X)	(X)	(X)	(X)	819	R-55.6	(X)	(X)	Kirk Fordice
MO	(X)	(X)	(X)	(X)	2,143	D-57.2	(X)	(X)	Mel Carnahan
MT	(X)	(X)	(X)	(X)	405	R-79.2	(X)	(X)	Marc Racicot
NE	587	D-49.9	580	D-73.0	(X)	(X)	545	R-53.9	Mike Johanns
NV	321	D-64.8	371	D-53.9	(X)	(X)	434	R-51.6	Kenny Guinn
NH	295	R-60.3	312	R-69.9	497	D-57.2	319	D-66.1	Jeanne Shaheen
NJ [3].......	2,254	D-61.2	2,506	R-49.3	(X)	(X)	2,418	R-46.9	Christine Todd Whitman
NM	411	D-54.6	468	R-49.8	(X)	(X)	499	R-54.5	Gary E. Johnson
NY	4,057	D-53.2	5,204	R-48.8	(X)	(X)	4,735	R-54.3	George E. Pataki
NC	(X)	(X)	(X)	(X)	2,566	D-56.0	(X)	(X)	James B. Hunt
ND	(X)	(X)	(X)	(X)	264	R-66.2	(X)	(X)	Edward T. Schafer
OH	3,478	R-55.7	3,346	R-71.8	(X)	(X)	3,354	R-50.0	Bob Taft
OK	911	D-57.4	995	R-46.9	(X)	(X)	874	R-57.9	Frank Keating
OR	1,113	D-45.7	1,221	D-50.9	(X)	(X)	1,113	D-64.4	John Kitzhaber
PA.......	3,053	D-67.7	3,585	R-45.4	(X)	(X)	3,025	R-57.4	Tom Ridge
RI	357	D-74.1	361	R-47.4	(X)	(X)	306	R-51.0	Lincoln C. Almond
SC	761	R-69.5	934	R-50.4	(X)	(X)	1,071	D-53.2	Jim Hodges
SD	257	R-58.9	312	R-55.4	(X)	(X)	260	R-64.0	William J. Janklow
TN	790	D-60.8	1,487	R-54.3	(X)	(X)	976	R-68.6	Don Sundquist
TX	3,893	D-49.5	4,396	R-53.5	(X)	(X)	3,738	R-68.2	George W. Bush
UT	(X)	(X)	(X)	(X)	672	R-75.0	(X)	(X)	Michael O. Leavitt
VT [3].......	211	R-51.8	212	D-68.7	255	D-70.5	218	D-55.7	Howard Dean
VA [3].......	1,789	D-50.1	1,794	R-58.3	(X)	(X)	1,736	R-55.8	James S. Gilmore
WA	(X)	(X)	(X)	(X)	2,237	D-58.0	(X)	(X)	Gary Locke
WV	(X)	(X)	(X)	(X)	629	R-51.6	(X)	(X)	Cecil H. Underwood
WI	1,380	R-58.2	1,563	R-67.3	(X)	(X)	1,756	R-59.7	Tommy G. Thompson
WY	160	D-65.4	201	R-58.7	(X)	(X)	175	R-55.6	Jim Geringer

X Not applicable.   [1] Includes minor party and scattered votes.   [2] Voting years 1987, 1991, and 1995.   [3] Voting years 1989, 1993, and 1997.

Source: Congressional Quarterly Inc., Washington, DC, *America Votes*, biennial; and unpublished data (copyright).

U.S. Census Bureau, Statistical Abstract of the United States: 2000

No. 469. Composition of State Legislatures by Political Party Affiliation: 1992 to 1998

[Data reflect election results in year shown for most states; and except as noted, results in previous year for other states. Figures reflect immediate results of elections, including holdover members in state houses which do not have all of their members running for reelection. Dem.=Democrat, Rep.=Republican. In general, Lower House refers to body consisting of state Representatives; Upper House, of state Senators]

State	Lower House 1992 [1][2] Dem.	Rep.	1994 [3] Dem.	Rep.	1996 [4] Dem.	Rep.	1998 [5] Dem.	Rep.	Upper House 1992 [1] Dem.	Rep.	1994 [3][6] Dem.	Rep.	1996 Dem.	Rep.	1998 [7] Dem.	Rep.
U.S.	**3,186**	**2,223**	**2,817**	**2,603**	**2,886**	**2,539**	**2,903**	**2,580**	**1,132**	**799**	**1,021**	**905**	**998**	**931**	**1,041**	**963**
AL [8]	82	23	74	31	72	33	71	34	27	8	23	12	22	12	22	13
AK [9]	20	18	17	22	16	24	15	25	10	10	8	12	7	13	6	14
AZ [10]	25	35	22	38	22	38	22	38	12	18	11	19	12	18	12	18
AR [9]	88	11	88	12	86	13	86	14	30	5	28	7	28	6	28	7
CA [9]	47	33	39	40	43	37	42	37	21	16	21	17	25	15	23	16
CO [9]	31	34	24	41	24	41	24	41	16	19	16	19	15	20	15	20
CT [10]	85	64	90	61	97	54	96	55	19	17	17	19	19	17	19	17
DE [9]	18	23	14	27	14	27	13	28	15	6	12	9	13	8	13	8
FL [9]	71	49	63	57	59	61	57	63	20	20	19	21	17	23	17	23
GA [10]	128	51	114	65	106	74	102	78	41	15	35	20	34	22	34	22
HI [9]	47	4	44	7	39	12	39	12	22	3	23	2	23	2	23	2
ID [10]	20	50	13	57	11	59	11	59	12	23	8	27	5	30	5	30
IL [9]	67	51	54	64	60	58	60	58	27	32	26	33	28	31	28	31
IN [9]	55	45	44	56	50	50	50	50	22	28	20	30	19	31	19	31
IA [9]	49	51	36	64	46	54	46	54	27	23	27	23	21	29	22	28
KS [9]	59	66	45	80	48	77	48	77	13	27	13	27	13	27	13	27
KY [9]	71	29	64	36	64	36	64	36	25	13	21	17	20	18	20	18
LA [8]	88	16	86	17	76	28	78	27	33	6	33	6	25	14	25	14
ME [10]	93	58	77	74	81	69	81	69	20	15	16	18	19	15	19	15
MD [8]	116	25	100	41	100	41	99	41	38	9	32	15	32	15	32	15
MA [10]	123	34	125	34	134	25	130	29	31	9	30	10	34	6	31	8
MI [9]	55	55	53	56	58	52	58	51	16	22	16	22	16	22	16	22
MN [9]	85	49	71	63	70	64	70	64	45	22	43	21	42	24	42	24
MS [8]	91	29	89	31	86	33	84	36	37	15	36	14	34	18	34	18
MO [9]	98	65	87	76	88	75	85	76	20	14	19	15	19	15	19	15
MT [9]	47	53	33	67	35	65	35	65	30	20	19	31	16	34	16	33
NE.	([11])	([11])	([11])	([11])	([11])	([11])	([11])	([11])	([11])	([11])	([11])	([11])	([11])	([11])	([11])	([11])
NV [9]	27	12	21	21	25	17	25	17	10	11	8	13	9	12	9	12
NH [10]	136	258	112	286	143	255	147	248	11	13	6	18	9	15	9	15
NJ [9]	27	53	28	52	30	50	32	48	16	24	16	24	16	24	16	24
NM [9]	53	17	46	24	42	28	42	28	27	15	27	15	25	17	25	17
NY [10]	100	50	94	56	96	54	95	52	26	35	25	36	26	35	26	35
NC [9]	78	42	52	68	59	61	59	61	39	11	26	24	30	20	30	20
ND [9]	33	65	23	75	26	72	26	71	25	24	20	29	19	30	18	29
OH [9]	53	46	43	56	39	60	39	60	13	20	13	20	12	21	12	20
OK [9]	70	31	65	36	65	36	65	36	37	11	35	13	33	15	33	15
OR [9]	28	32	26	34	29	31	29	31	16	14	11	19	10	20	10	20
PA [9]	105	98	101	102	99	104	99	104	24	25	21	29	20	30	20	30
RI [10]	85	15	84	16	84	16	84	16	39	11	40	10	41	9	42	8
SC [9]	71	52	58	62	53	70	52	71	30	16	29	17	26	20	25	21
SD [10]	28	42	24	46	23	47	22	48	20	15	16	19	13	22	13	22
TN [9]	63	36	59	40	61	38	61	38	19	14	18	15	18	15	18	15
TX [9]	91	58	89	61	82	68	82	68	18	13	17	14	14	16	14	17
UT [9]	26	49	20	55	20	55	21	54	11	18	10	19	9	20	9	20
VT [10]	87	57	86	61	89	57	89	57	14	16	12	18	17	13	17	13
VA [9]	52	47	52	47	53	46	51	48	22	18	22	18	20	20	19	21
WA [9]	65	33	38	60	45	53	41	57	28	21	25	24	23	26	23	26
WV [9]	79	21	69	30	74	25	74	26	32	2	26	8	25	9	25	9
WI [9]	51	47	48	51	47	52	46	51	16	17	16	17	17	16	17	16
WY [9]	19	41	13	47	17	43	17	43	10	20	10	20	9	21	9	21

[1] Status as of November 11, 1993.   [2] Excludes one Independent each for AR, LA, NH, SC, and VA; two Independents each for AK and MS; four Independents for VT; members of political parties other than Democratic, Republican, or Independent (one in MA, two in VT, and four in NH); one vacancy each for GA, NH, TX, and WI; two vacancies each for CT and MA; and three vacancies for NV.   [3] Status as of December 7, 1994.   [4] Excludes one independent each for ME, MA, SC, VT, and VA; three for MS; two for NH; one vacancy each for AR and LA; three for party other than Democratic, Republican, or Independent.   [5] Excludes one Independent each for ME, MA, MO, SC, VA, and VT; two each for MS and NH; and three Progressives for VT.   [6] Excludes one Independent each for CA, ME, and MN; one vacancy each for AL, AR, and TX; and 49 from party other than Democratic, Republican, or Independent.   [7] Excludes one Independent each in CA, ME, and MN; one vacancy each in MA, MO, and OH; and two in ND.   [8] Members of both houses serve 4-year terms.   [9] Upper House members serve 4-year terms and Lower House members serve 2-year terms.   [10] Members of both houses serve 2-year terms.   [11] Single chamber (unicameral body) of 49 members, elected without party designation.

Source: The Council of State Governments, Lexington, KY, *State Elective Officials and the Legislatures*, biennial (copyright); thereafter, National Conference of State Legislatures, Denver, CO, unpublished data.

No. 470. Political Party Control of State Legislatures by Party: 1975 to 1999

[As of **beginning of year.** Until 1972 there were two nonpartisan legislatures in Minnesota and Nebraska. Since then only Nebraska has had a nonpartisan legislature]

Year	Legislatures under— Demo-cratic control	Legislatures under— Split control or tie	Legislatures under— Re-publican control	Year	Legislatures under— Demo-cratic control	Legislatures under— Split control or tie	Legislatures under— Re-publican control	Year	Legislatures under— Demo-cratic control	Legislatures under— Split control or tie	Legislatures under— Re-publican control
1975...	37	7	5	1987...	28	12	9	1995...	18	12	19
1977...	36	8	5	1989 [2].	28	13	8	1996...	16	15	18
1979...	30	7	12	1990...	29	11	9	1997...	20	11	18
1981...	28	6	15	1992...	29	14	6	1999...	20	11	18
1983 [1].	34	4	11	1993...	25	16	8				
1985...	27	11	11	1994...	24	17	8				

[1] Two 1984 midterm recall elections resulted in a change in control of the Michigan State Senate. At the time of the 1984 election, therefore, Democrats controlled 33 legislatures.   [2] A party change during the year by a Democratic representative broke the tie in the Indiana House of Representatives, giving the Republicans control of both chambers.

Source: National Conference of State Legislatures, Denver, CO, *State Legislatures*, periodic.

No. 471. Local Elected Officials by Sex, Race, Hispanic Origin, and Type of Government: 1992

Sex, race, and Hispanic origin	Total	General purpose County	General purpose Municipal	General purpose Town, township	Special purpose School district	Special purpose Special district
Total	**493,830**	**58,818**	**135,531**	**126,958**	**88,434**	**84,089**
Male	324,255	43,563	94,808	76,213	54,443	55,228
Female	100,531	12,525	26,825	27,702	24,730	8,749
Sex not reported	69,044	2,730	13,898	23,043	9,261	20,112
White	405,905	52,705	114,880	102,676	73,894	61,750
Black	11,542	1,715	4,566	369	4,222	670
American Indian, Eskimo, Aleut	1,800	147	776	86	564	227
Asian, Pacific Islander	514	80	97	16	184	137
Hispanic	5,859	906	1,701	216	2,466	570
Non-Hispanic	413,902	53,741	118,618	102,931	76,398	62,214
Race, Hispanic origin not reported	74,069	4,171	15,212	23,811	9,570	21,305

Source: U.S. Census Bureau, *1992 Census of Governments, Popularly Elected Officials,* (GC92(1)-2).

No. 472. Women Holding State Public Offices by Office and State: 1999

[As of **January.** For data on women in U.S. Congress, see Table 463]

State	State-wide elective executive office [1]	State legisla-ture	State	State-wide elective executive office [1]	State legisla-ture	State	State-wide elective executive office [1]	State legisla-ture
United States	**89**	**1,664**	Kentucky	-	16	North Dakota	4	26
Alabama	3	11	Louisiana	1	20	Ohio	2	28
Alaska	1	11	Maine	-	52	Oklahoma	4	15
Arizona	5	32	Maryland	1	55	Oregon	-	27
Arkansas	2	20	Massachusetts	2	52	Pennsylvania	1	32
California	2	31	Michigan	2	36	Rhode Island	-	38
Colorado	1	34	Minnesota	4	57	South Carolina	1	19
Connecticut	4	55	Mississippi	-	21	South Dakota	4	14
Delaware	3	15	Missouri	2	43	Tennessee	1	22
Florida	2	38	Montana	2	37	Texas	2	32
Georgia	2	44	Nebraska	2	12	Utah	2	22
Hawaii	1	17	Nevada	3	23	Vermont	1	57
Idaho	1	26	New Hampshire	1	135	Virginia	-	22
Illinois	2	45	New Jersey	1	19	Washington	4	60
Indiana	3	27	New Mexico	3	31	West Virginia	-	24
Iowa	2	32	New York	1	44	Wisconsin	-	31
Kansas	2	55	North Carolina	3	31	Wyoming	2	18

- Represents zero.   [1] Excludes women elected to the judiciary, women appointed to state cabinet-level positions, women elected to executive posts by the legislature, and elected members of university Board of Trustees or board of education.

Source: Center for the American Woman and Politics, Eagleton Institute of Politics, Rutgers University, New Brunswick, NJ, information releases, copyright.

No. 473. Black Elected Officials by Office, 1970 to 1998, and State, 1998

[As of **January 1998**, no Black elected officials had been identified in Hawaii, Idaho, Montana, North Dakota, or Utah]

State	Total	U.S. and state legisla- tures[1]	City and county offices[2]	Law enforce- ment[3]	Educa- tion[4]	State	Total	U.S. and state legisla- tures[1]	City and county offices[2]	Law enforce- ment[3]	Educa- tion[4]
1970 (Feb.) .	1,469	179	715	213	362	MD	183	38	102	32	11
1980 (July). .	4,890	326	2,832	526	1,206	MA	31	7	19	3	2
1985 (Jan.). .	6,016	407	3,517	661	1,431	MI	348	19	142	56	131
1990 (Jan.). .	7,335	436	4,485	769	1,645	MN	17	1	4	7	5
1995 (Jan.). .	8,385	604	4,954	987	1,840	MS	849	46	574	96	133
1996 (Jan.). .	8,545	606	5,023	994	1,922	MO	209	17	154	14	24
1997 (Jan.). .	8,617	613	5,056	996	1,952	NE	3	1	1	-	1
1998 (Jan.) .	**8,830**	**614**	**5,210**	**998**	**2,008**	NV	13	5	4	2	2
						NH	2	2	-	-	-
AL	733	36	550	51	96	NJ	232	16	127	-	89
AK	1	-	1	-	-	NM	5	2	-	2	1
AZ	16	4	2	5	5	NY	311	32	74	77	128
AR	482	13	272	61	136	NC	513	27	361	29	96
CA	240	10	69	76	85	OH	220	20	127	27	46
CO	19	4	5	9	1	OK	104	6	80	1	17
CT	68	14	43	4	7	OR	7	4	1	2	-
DE	24	4	16	1	3	PA	161	19	53	61	28
DC	148	3	140	-	5	RI	10	9	1	-	-
FL	212	23	142	32	15	SC	554	34	342	11	167
GA	597	48	402	40	107	TN	167	17	104	26	20
ID	1	-	-	1	-	TX	474	18	313	45	98
IL	626	26	314	58	228	UT	1	-	-	1	-
IN	82	14	51	11	6	VT	1	1	-	-	-
IA	12	1	8	1	2	VA	333	16	138	16	163
KS	20	7	6	4	3	WA	21	2	9	9	1
KY	62	5	46	5	6	WV	18	2	13	3	-
LA	666	32	384	115	135	WI	33	8	16	4	5
ME	1	1	-	-	-	WY	-	-	-	-	-

- Represents zero. [1] Includes elected state administrators. [2] County commissioners and councilmen, mayors, vice mayors, aldermen, regional officials, and other. [3] Judges, magistrates, constables, marshals, sheriffs, justices of the peace, and other. [4] Members of state education agencies, college boards, school boards, and other.

Source: Joint Center for Political and Economic Studies, Washington, DC, *Black Elected Officials: A Statistical Summary, 1993-1997*, annual (copyright).

No. 474. Hispanic Public Officials by Office, 1985 to 1994, and by State, 1994

[As of **September**. For states not shown, no Hispanic public officials had been identified]

State	Total	State execu- tives and legisla- tors[1]	County and munici pal officials	Judicial and law enforce- ment	Educa- tion and school boards	State	Total	State execu- tives and legisla- tors[1]	County and munici pal officials	Judicial and law enforce- ment	Educa- tion and school boards
1985 (Sept.). .	3,147	129	1,316	517	1,185	IN	8	1	5	1	1
1986 (Sept.). .	3,202	132	1,352	530	1,188	KS	7	5	1	-	1
1987 (Sept.). .	3,317	138	1,412	568	1,199	LA	12	3	1	8	-
1988 (Sept.). .	3,360	135	1,425	574	1,226	MD	2	-	1	-	1
1989 (Sept.). .	3,783	143	1,724	575	1,341	MA	1	-	-	-	1
1990 (Sept.). .	4,004	144	1,819	583	1,458	MI	8	-	5	1	2
1991 (Sept.). .	4,202	151	1,867	596	1,588	MN	3	2	-	1	-
1992 (Sept.). .	4,994	150	1,908	628	2,308	MO	1	-	1	-	-
1993 (Sept.). .	5,170	182	2,023	633	2,332	MT	2	-	-	1	1
						NE	3	-	2	-	1
1994	**5,459**	**199**	**2,197**	**651**	**2,412**	NV	4	1	-	1	2
						NJ	37	2	17	1	17
AK	1	1	-	-	-	NM	716	50	410	105	151
AZ	341	11	144	50	136	NY	83	12	13	11	47
AR	2	1	-	-	1	OH	4	-	1	2	1
CA	796	16	349	50	381	OK	1	-	1	-	-
CO	201	9	140	10	42	OR	5	-	3	1	1
CT	26	12	9	-	5	PA	8	1	3	1	3
DE	1	-	1	-	-	RI	1	1	-	-	-
DC	1	-	-	1	-	TX	2,215	41	1,022	389	763
FL	64	16	33	12	3	UT	1	1	-	-	-
HI	2	2	-	-	-	WA	14	2	4	2	6
ID	2	1	1	-	-	WI	2	-	2	-	-
IL	881	7	26	3	[2]845	WY	3	1	2	-	-

- Represents zero. [1] Includes U.S. Representatives. [2] Includes local school council members in the Chicago area.

Source: National Association of Latino Elected and Appointed Officials, Washington, DC, *National Roster of Hispanic Elected Officials,* annual.

No. 475. Public Confidence Levels in Selected Public and Private Institutions: 1999

[Based on a sample survey of 2,719 persons 18 years old and over conducted during the spring and subject to sampling variability; see source]

Institution	Level of confidence				
	A great deal	Quite a lot	Some	Very little	Can't say/no answer
Religious organizations	31.9	29.5	26.7	9.7	2.1
Higher education (colleges or univ.)	22.9	35.6	26.6	8.1	6.9
Private elementary or secondary education	17.0	33.8	32.5	10.3	6.4
Youth development and recreation organizations	33.0	38.9	20.1	4.9	3.0
Federated charitable appeals	16.1	28.8	33.2	16.4	5.6
Health organizations	15.0	27.5	35.4	12.8	9.3
Environmental organizations.	13.3	25.7	36.0	15.8	9.2
Human service organizations	29.0	38.7	23.6	5.5	3.2
Recreational organizations (adult)	19.9	38.2	30.2	7.3	4.4
Arts, culture, & humanities organizations	16.6	34.0	32.3	11.1	6.1
Private and community foundations	8.7	26.5	36.2	12.5	16.2
Public /society benefit organizations [1]	10.9	22.5	41.4	18.4	6.8
International/foreign organizations [2]	7.7	19.9	38.5	20.9	13.0
Small businesses	16.4	38.1	33.4	8.7	3.5
Military	22.2	35.0	29.4	10.8	2.6
Public higher educ. (colleges or univ.)	19.1	42.4	28.7	7.4	2.4
Public elementary or secondary education	15.9	35.0	32.6	14.9	1.5
Organized labor	9.9	18.1	39.1	27.5	5.4
Media (e.g. newspapers, TV, radio)	7.6	20.7	37.4	32.5	1.8
Work-related organizations.	6.6	23.5	47.1	14.7	8.2
Major corporations	7.4	21.5	43.5	23.0	4.6
State government.	7.9	23.1	45.0	21.6	2.4
Organizations that lobby for a particular cause.	5.3	15.6	42.6	28.1	8.4
Political organizations, parties.	4.3	14.5	37.3	40.5	3.4
Local government.	8.7	24.1	42.8	22.0	2.4
Federal Government	7.9	19.5	43.4	26.9	2.3
Congress	6.4	15.8	40.2	34.9	2.7

[1] Civil rights, social justice, or community improvement organizations.   [2] Culture exchange or relief organizations.

Source: Saxon-Harold, Susan K.E., Murray Weitzman, and the Gallup Organization, Inc., *Giving & Volunteering in the United States: 1999 Edition.* (Copyright and published by INDEPENDENT SECTOR, Washington, DC, 2000.)

No. 476. Political Party Identification of the Adult Population by Degree of Attachment, 1972 to 1994, and by Selected Characteristics, 1994

[**In percent.** Covers citizens of voting-age living in private housing units in the contiguous United States. Data are from the National Election Studies and are based on a sample and subject to sampling variability; for details, see source]

Year and selected characteristic	Total	Strong Democrat	Weak Democrat	Independent Democrat	Independent	Independent Republican	Weak Republican	Strong Republican	Apolitical
1972	100	15	26	11	13	11	13	10	1
1980	100	18	23	11	13	10	14	9	2
1984	100	17	20	11	11	12	15	12	2
1986	100	18	22	10	12	11	15	11	2
1988	100	18	18	12	11	13	14	14	2
1990	100	20	19	12	11	12	15	10	2
1992	100	18	18	14	12	12	14	11	1
1994 [1]	100	15	19	13	10	12	15	16	1
Age:									
17 to 24 years	100	9	20	22	10	8	19	10	1
25 to 34 years old. . . .	100	11	19	14	12	11	16	16	1
35 to 44 years old. . . .	100	13	18	14	12	11	14	18	-
45 to 54 years old. . . .	100	15	16	15	7	16	12	17	1
55 to 64 years old. . . .	100	18	22	8	8	16	12	15	-
65 to 74 years old. . . .	100	28	17	6	8	13	14	15	-
75 to 99 years old. . . .	100	19	26	9	9	5	17	13	2
Sex:									
Male	100	13	17	12	11	14	14	18	1
Female	100	18	21	13	10	9	15	13	1
Race:									
White	100	12	19	12	10	13	16	17	1
Black	100	38	23	20	8	4	2	3	1
Education:									
Grade school	100	26	26	7	13	7	11	6	4
High school	100	15	22	14	13	10	13	11	1
College	100	14	16	13	7	13	16	21	-

- Represents zero.   [1] Includes other characteristics, not shown separately.

Source: Center for Political Studies, University of Michigan, Ann Arbor, MI, unpublished data. Data prior to 1988 published in Warren E. Miller and Santa A. Traugott, *American National Election Studies Data Sourcebook, 1952-1986,* Harvard University Press, Cambridge, MA, 1989 (copyright).

Elections   289

No. 477. Voting-Age Population, Percent Reporting Registered, and Voted: 1980 to 1998

[As of **November**. Covers civilian noninstitutional population 18 years old and over. Includes aliens. Figures are based on Current Population Survey (see text, Section 1, Population, and Appendix III) and differ from those in Table 479 based on population estimates and official vote counts]

Characteristic	Voting-age population (mil.)							Percent reporting they registered								Percent reporting they voted							
								Presidential election years				Congressional election years				Presidential election years				Congressional election years			
	1980	1988	1990	1992	1994	1996	1998	1980	1988	1992	1996	1986	1990	1994	1998	1980	1988	1992	1996	1986	1990	1994	1998
Total [1]	157.1	178.1	182.1	185.7	190.3	193.7	198.2	66.9	66.6	68.2	65.9	64.3	62.2	62.0	62.1	59.2	57.4	61.3	54.2	46.0	45.0	44.6	41.9
18 to 20 years old	12.3	10.7	10.8	9.7	10.3	10.8	11.4	44.7	44.9	48.3	45.6	35.4	35.4	37.2	32.1	35.7	33.2	38.5	31.2	18.6	18.4	16.5	13.5
21 to 24 years old	15.9	14.8	14.0	14.6	14.9	13.9	14.1	52.7	50.6	55.3	51.2	46.6	43.3	45.5	43.1	43.1	38.3	45.7	33.4	24.2	19.2	22.3	16.6
25 to 34 years old	35.7	42.7	42.7	41.6	41.1	40.1	38.6	62.0	57.8	60.6	56.9	55.8	52.0	51.5	52.4	54.6	48.0	53.2	43.1	35.1	33.8	32.2	29.7
35 to 44 years old	25.6	35.2	37.9	39.7	41.9	43.3	44.4	70.6	69.3	69.2	66.5	67.9	65.5	63.3	62.4	64.4	61.3	63.6	54.9	49.3	48.4	46.0	40.7
45 to 64 years old	43.6	45.9	46.9	49.1	50.9	53.7	57.4	75.8	75.5	75.3	73.5	74.8	71.4	71.0	71.1	69.3	67.9	70.0	(NA)	58.7	58.5	56.0	49.3
65 years old and over	24.1	28.8	29.9	30.8	31.1	31.9	32.3	74.6	78.4	78.0	77.0	76.9	76.5	75.6	75.4	65.1	68.8	70.1	(NA)	60.9	60.3	60.7	59.5
Male	74.1	84.5	86.6	88.6	91.0	92.6	95.2	66.6	65.2	66.9	64.4	63.4	61.2	60.8	60.6	59.1	56.4	60.2	52.8	45.8	44.6	44.4	41.4
Female	83.0	93.6	95.5	97.1	99.3	101.0	103.0	67.1	67.8	69.3	67.3	65.0	63.1	63.2	63.5	59.4	58.3	62.3	55.5	46.1	45.4	44.9	42.4
White	137.7	152.9	155.6	157.8	160.3	162.8	165.8	68.4	67.9	70.1	67.7	65.3	63.8	64.2	63.9	60.9	59.1	63.6	56.0	47.0	46.7	46.9	43.3
Black	16.4	19.7	20.4	21.0	21.8	22.5	23.3	60.0	64.5	63.9	63.5	64.0	58.8	58.3	60.2	50.5	51.5	54.0	50.6	43.2	39.2	37.0	39.6
Hispanic [2]	8.2	12.9	13.8	14.7	17.5	18.4	20.3	36.3	35.5	35.0	35.7	35.9	32.3	30.0	33.7	29.9	28.8	28.9	26.7	24.2	21.0	19.1	20.3
Region: [3]																							
Northeast	35.5	37.9	38.1	38.3	38.4	38.3	38.5	64.8	64.8	67.0	64.7	62.0	61.0	60.9	60.8	58.5	57.4	61.2	54.5	44.4	45.2	45.2	41.2
Midwest	41.5	43.3	43.9	44.4	44.5	45.2	45.9	73.8	72.5	74.6	71.6	70.7	68.2	68.7	68.2	65.8	62.9	67.2	59.3	49.5	48.6	48.8	47.3
South	50.6	60.7	62.4	63.7	66.4	68.1	70.1	64.8	65.6	67.2	65.9	63.0	61.3	60.7	62.7	55.6	55.6	58.5	51.8	48.4	42.4	40.5	38.6
West	29.5	36.2	37.7	39.3	41.0	42.1	43.7	63.3	63.0	63.6	60.8	60.8	57.7	58.1	56.0	57.2	55.6	58.5	51.8	48.4	45.0	46.4	42.3
School years completed:																							
8 years or less	22.7	19.1	17.7	15.4	14.7	14.1	13.3	53.0	47.5	43.9	40.7	50.5	44.0	40.1	40.2	42.6	36.7	35.1	28.1	32.7	27.7	23.2	24.6
High school:																							
1 to 3 years	22.5	21.1	21.0	[4]21.0	[4]20.7	[4]21.0	[4]21.0	54.6	52.8	[4]50.4	[4]47.9	52.4	47.9	[4]44.7	[4]43.4	45.6	41.3	[4]41.2	[4]33.8	33.8	30.9	[4]27.0	[4]25.0
4 years	61.2	70.0	71.5	[5]65.3	[5]64.9	[5]65.2	[5]65.6	66.4	64.6	[5]64.9	[5]62.2	62.9	60.0	[5]58.9	[5]58.6	58.9	54.7	[5]57.5	[5]49.1	44.1	42.2	[5]40.5	[5]37.1
College:																							
1 to 3 years	26.7	34.3	36.3	[6]46.7	[6]50.4	[6]50.9	[6]52.9	74.4	73.5	[6]75.4	[6]72.9	70.0	68.7	[6]68.4	[6]68.3	67.2	64.5	[6]68.7	[6]60.5	49.9	50.0	[6]49.1	[6]46.2
4 years or more	24.0	33.6	35.6	[7]37.4	[7]39.4	[7]42.5	[7]45.4	84.3	83.1	[7]84.8	[7]80.4	77.8	77.3	[7]76.3	[7]75.1	79.9	77.6	[7]81.0	[7]73.0	62.5	62.5	[7]63.1	[7]57.2
Employed	95.0	113.8	115.5	116.3	122.6	125.6	135.7	68.7	67.1	69.9	67.0	64.4	62.6	62.9	62.6	61.8	58.4	63.8	55.2	45.7	45.1	45.2	41.2
Unemployed	6.9	5.8	6.7	8.3	6.5	6.4	5.2	50.3	50.4	53.7	52.5	50.6	44.6	46.4	48.5	41.2	38.6	46.2	37.2	31.2	27.9	28.3	28.4
Not in labor force	55.2	58.5	59.9	61.1	61.2	61.6	62.5	65.8	67.2	66.8	65.1	65.4	63.4	61.9	62.1	57.0	57.3	58.7	54.1	48.2	46.7	45.3	44.5

NA Not available. [1] Includes other races not shown separately. [2] Hispanic persons may be of any race. [3] For composition of regions, see map, inside cover. [4] Represents those who completed 9th to 12th grade, but have no high school diploma. [5] High school graduate. [6] Some college or associate degree. [7] Bachelor's or advanced degree.

Source: U.S. Census Bureaus, *Current Population Reports*, P20-453 and P20-466; and unpublished data.

No. 478. Persons Reported Registered and Voted by State: 1998

[See headnote, Table 477]

State	Voting-age population (1,000)	Percent of voting-age population Registered	Percent of voting-age population Voted
U.S.....	198,228	62.1	41.9
AL	3,252	73.7	51.2
AK	413	72.3	53.8
AZ	3,362	51.1	33.8
AR	1,855	63.2	42.4
CA	23,696	52.1	40.5
CO	2,954	68.5	52.1
CT	2,438	66.6	45.4
DE	555	61.1	36.5
DC	392	65.1	45.4
FL	11,275	59.0	39.0
GA	5,581	62.0	37.4
HI	855	54.1	48.1
ID	881	60.0	45.0
IL	8,659	63.9	44.5
IN	4,377	61.7	40.0
IA	2,102	74.3	51.6
KS	1,868	63.8	40.1
KY	2,956	65.0	44.4
LA	3,114	72.6	38.3
ME	938	75.0	47.9
MD	3,861	60.4	47.3
MA	4,594	64.2	46.2
MI	7,227	72.2	49.7
MN	3,443	80.9	64.2
MS	1,975	73.2	40.2
MO	3,967	71.8	45.8
MT	654	72.3	53.3
NE	1,193	66.2	45.3
NV	1,298	46.7	33.1
NH	874	64.4	40.9
NJ	6,059	60.1	35.5
NM	1,253	60.4	48.2
NY	13,440	57.0	41.4
NC	5,536	62.7	39.4
ND	460	90.5	57.0
OH	8,263	63.7	44.6
OK	2,426	64.1	40.1
OR	2,474	66.1	47.0
PA	8,942	61.0	39.2
RI	726	65.9	48.5
SC	2,817	67.7	47.1
SD	529	68.7	50.7
TN	4,080	63.9	36.2
TX	14,080	59.0	32.9
UT	1,408	55.9	39.9
VT	444	71.2	51.6
VA	4,969	60.3	30.1
WA	4,179	62.8	45.6
WV	1,401	62.8	35.9
WI	3,790	68.7	50.3
WY	346	65.6	54.3

Source: U.S. Census Bureau, unpublished data.

No. 479. Participation in Elections for President and U.S. Representatives: 1932 to 1998

[As of **November**. Estimated resident population 21 years old and over, 1932-70, except as noted, and 18 years old and over thereafter; includes Armed Forces. Prior to 1960, excludes Alaska and Hawaii. District of Columbia is included in votes cast for President beginning 1964 and in votes cast for Representative from 1972 to 1998]

Year	Resident population (incl. aliens) of voting age [1] (1,000)	Votes cast For President [2] (1,000)	Per-cent of voting-age population	Votes cast For U.S. Representatives (1,000)	Per-cent of voting-age population	Year	Resident population (incl. aliens) of voting age [1] (1,000)	Votes cast For President [2] (1,000)	Per-cent of voting-age population	Votes cast For U.S. Representatives (1,000)	Per-cent of voting-age population
1932 . . .	75,768	39,758	52.5	37,657	49.7	1966 . . .	116,638	(X)	(X)	52,908	45.4
1934 . . .	77,997	(X)	(X)	32,256	41.4	1968 . . .	120,285	73,212	60.9	66,288	55.1
1936 . . .	80,174	45,654	56.9	42,886	53.5	1970 . . .	124,498	(X)	(X)	54,173	43.5
1938 . . .	82,354	(X)	(X)	36,236	44.0	1972 . . .	140,777	77,719	55.2	71,430	50.7
1940 . . .	84,728	49,900	58.9	46,951	55.4	1974 . . .	146,338	(X)	(X)	52,495	35.9
1942 . . .	86,465	(X)	(X)	28,074	32.5	1976 . . .	152,308	81,556	53.5	74,422	48.9
1944 . . .	85,654	47,977	56.0	45,103	52.7	1978 . . .	158,369	(X)	(X)	55,332	34.9
1946 . . .	92,659	(X)	(X)	34,398	37.1	1980 . . .	163,945	86,515	52.8	77,995	47.6
1948 . . .	95,573	48,794	51.1	45,933	48.1	1982 . . .	169,643	(X)	(X)	64,514	38.0
1950 . . .	98,134	(X)	(X)	40,342	41.1	1984 . . .	173,995	92,653	53.3	83,231	47.8
1952 . . .	99,929	61,551	61.6	57,571	57.6	1986 . . .	177,922	(X)	(X)	59,619	33.5
1954 . . .	102,075	(X)	(X)	42,580	41.7	1988 . . .	181,956	91,595	50.3	81,786	44.9
1956 . . .	104,515	62,027	59.3	58,426	55.9	1990 . . .	185,812	(X)	(X)	61,513	33.1
1958 . . .	106,447	(X)	(X)	45,818	43.0	1992 . . .	189,524	104,425	55.1	96,239	50.8
1960 . . .	109,672	68,838	62.8	64,133	58.5	1994 . . .	193,650	(X)	(X)	70,781	36.6
1962 . . .	112,952	(X)	(X)	51,267	45.4	1996 . . .	196,928	96,278	49.0	89,863	45.8
1964 . . .	114,090	70,645	61.9	65,895	57.8	1998 . . .	198,228	(X)	(X)	65,897	32.9

X Not applicable.   [1] Population 18 and over in Georgia, 1944-70, and in Kentucky, 1956-70; 19 and over in Alaska; and 20 and over in Hawaii, 1960-70.   [2] Source: 1932-58, U.S. Congress, Clerk of the House, *Statistics of the Presidential and Congressional Election*, biennial.

Source: Except as noted, U.S. Census Bureau, *Current Population Reports*, P25-1085; Congressional Quarterly Inc., Washington, DC, *America Votes*, biennial (copyright).

[As of **November**. **Estimated population, 18 years old and over**. Includes Armed Forces stationed in each state, aliens, and incitutional population]

State	Voting-age population							Percent casting votes for—				
				1998 (1,000)				Presidential electors		U.S. Representatives		
	1992 (1,000)	1994 (1,000)	1996 (1,000)	Total	Female	Black	His-panic[1]	1992	1996	1992	1994	1998
U.S. . . .	189,524	193,650	196,928	198,228	103,042	23,305	20,321	55.1	49.0	50.8	36.0	33.2
AL	3,080	3,138	3,221	3,252	1,693	835	26	54.8	47.7	52.0	35.5	37.4
AK	405	429	423	413	204	11	12	63.8	56.9	59.0	48.5	54.1
AZ	2,812	2,923	3,321	3,362	1,780	121	818	52.9	45.4	50.1	37.6	29.9
AR	1,774	1,817	1,854	1,855	969	318	16	53.6	47.5	50.1	39.0	28.3
CA	22,521	23,225	23,095	23,696	12,047	1,579	6,264	49.4	43.3	46.8	35.9	33.7
CO	2,579	2,713	2,841	2,954	1,489	107	366	60.8	53.1	57.4	38.9	43.1
CT	2,508	2,486	2,471	2,438	1,262	208	229	64.4	56.4	57.2	43.0	39.1
DE	521	534	551	555	281	108	13	55.6	49.6	53.0	36.5	32.5
DC	467	452	428	392	220	248	17	48.7	42.7	42.1	(NA)	(NA)
FL	10,422	10,856	11,055	11,275	5,974	1,417	1,917	51.0	48.0	47.2	26.3	10.8
GA	5,006	5,159	5,432	5,581	2,977	1,744	127	46.4	42.6	44.2	29.0	29.2
HI	866	900	875	855	459	7	28	43.1	40.8	41.4	39.3	46.5
ID	750	803	847	881	431	3	72	64.3	58.2	63.0	49.0	43.0
IL	8,598	8,712	8,703	8,659	4,472	1,179	755	58.7	49.2	56.2	34.9	37.1
IN	4,209	4,298	4,346	4,377	2,279	313	83	54.8	48.9	52.7	36.0	36.0
IA	2,073	2,112	2,135	2,102	1,085	21	24	65.3	57.7	59.9	46.3	42.8
KS	1,840	1,889	1,896	1,868	969	91	71	62.9	56.6	61.1	43.3	38.9
KY	2,798	2,857	2,926	2,956	1,511	175	21	53.4	47.5	48.6	27.5	37.2
LA	3,045	3,100	3,117	3,114	1,606	980	66	58.8	56.9	22.4	(NA)	10.0
ME	932	931	943	938	480	4	3	72.9	64.5	71.8	54.0	44.2
MD	3,705	3,750	3,786	3,861	2,019	931	131	53.6	46.7	48.8	35.9	38.4
MA	4,616	4,564	4,677	4,594	2,365	213	217	60.1	55.3	56.6	43.3	37.9
MI	6,947	6,983	7,177	7,227	3,736	997	196	61.5	54.5	55.9	43.0	41.3
MN	3,272	3,362	3,417	3,443	1,703	61	69	71.8	64.3	69.5	52.0	59.2
MS	1,873	1,905	1,966	1,975	1,089	670	22	52.4	45.6	51.5	32.6	27.9
MO	3,851	3,902	3,981	3,967	2,110	339	66	62.1	54.2	61.0	45.2	39.6
MT	600	623	647	654	331	1	8	68.4	62.9	67.3	56.5	50.7
NE	1,164	1,192	1,211	1,193	619	30	47	63.4	56.1	61.1	47.9	44.1
NV	1,011	1,088	1,204	1,298	644	88	201	50.1	39.3	48.7	34.6	31.6
NH	838	843	869	874	452	6	15	64.2	58.0	61.0	36.7	36.4
NJ	5,964	5,974	6,023	6,059	3,182	886	630	56.1	51.2	50.2	33.6	30.0
NM	1,121	1,167	1,216	1,253	638	16	535	50.8	46.0	49.6	39.6	39.7
NY	13,705	13,646	13,610	13,440	6,953	2,082	1,984	50.5	46.5	43.2	33.8	31.8
NC	5,190	5,364	5,512	5,536	2,872	1,276	112	50.3	45.8	48.7	29.6	34.4
ND	462	467	475	460	234	-	1	66.7	56.3	64.5	50.4	46.3
OH	8,207	8,313	8,334	8,263	4,376	821	98	60.2	54.3	55.8	39.7	40.8
OK	2,352	2,394	2,423	2,426	1,249	213	74	59.1	49.9	54.2	40.5	35.4
OR	2,220	2,311	2,404	2,474	1,250	38	180	65.9	57.5	62.6	51.6	44.1
PA	9,161	9,212	9,150	8,942	4,806	784	245	54.1	49.0	50.1	36.6	32.4
RI	768	764	754	726	392	37	36	59.0	52.0	51.9	44.8	40.4
SC	2,669	2,740	2,792	2,817	1,489	741	24	45.1	41.5	41.8	31.7	34.6
SD	505	522	533	529	260	2	4	66.6	61.1	65.9	58.6	48.9
TN	3,796	3,913	4,009	4,080	2,140	635	20	52.2	47.1	45.5	36.2	22.4
TX	12,681	13,166	13,748	14,080	7,389	1,614	4,057	48.5	41.2	44.3	31.3	24.6
UT	1,169	1,246	1,347	1,408	738	5	86	63.6	50.3	62.2	40.5	33.4
VT	429	429	442	444	225	-	2	67.5	58.6	65.6	49.3	48.5
VA	4,855	4,967	5,058	4,969	2,624	1,054	107	52.7	47.5	48.8	38.4	23.1
WA	3,812	4,000	4,112	4,179	2,102	81	182	60.0	54.7	58.3	42.2	44.5
WV	1,376	1,389	1,401	1,401	745	22	5	49.7	45.0	40.9	29.3	25.1
WI	3,675	3,777	3,819	3,790	1,950	187	25	68.9	57.4	65.0	38.6	44.2
WY	329	343	348	346	171	4	13	61.0	60.1	59.9	57.2	50.4

- Represents or rounds to zero.   NA Not available.   [1] Persons of Hispanic origin may be of any race.

Source: Compiled by U.S. Census Bureau. Population data from U.S. Census Bureau, *Current Population Reports*, P25-1117 and Statistical Brief (SB/96-2); votes cast from Elections Research Center, Chevy Chase, MD, *America Votes*, biennial, (copyright); and 1994, Congressional Quarterly Inc., *Congressional Quarterly Weekly Report*, Vol. 53, No. 15, April 15, 1995 (copyright).

No. 481. Source of Voter Registration Applications: 1995-1996

[Based on a report to the United States Congress on the impact of the National Voter Registration Act of 1993 on the administration of elections for Federal office during the preceding 2-year period, 1995 through 1996. Based on survey results from 43 states and the District of Columbia. Six states are exempt from the provisions of the Act. Vermont is excluded because of state constitutional impediments]

State	Motor vehicle offices				Public assistance offices	Disability services	Armed Forces offices	State designated sites	All other services
	Total	Total	Percent of total	By mail					
United States..	41,452,428	13,722,233	33.1	12,330,015	2,602,748	178,015	76,008	1,732,475	10,810,934
Alabama........	560,500	90,356	16.1	106,199	80,096	3,202	4,730	17,512	258,405
Alaska.........	170,669	55,215	32.4	21,264	3,673	133	8	40,668	49,708
Arizona.........	524,042	81,317	15.5	272,550	17,845	2,662	7,278	57,108	85,282
Arkansas	282,023	114,325	40.5	52,305	28,324	1,570	956	6,670	77,873
California	5,761,575	818,927	14.2	2,372,689	129,273	4,132	2,094	25,219	2,409,241
Colorado........	554,343	303,422	54.7	52,644	12,255	1,460	2,292	3,264	179,006
Connecticut......	338,203	35,323	10.4	97,829	21,061	221	919	9,843	173,007
Delaware	159,302	128,626	80.7	5,956	7,889	2,135	917	632	13,147
District of Columbia ..	320,968	276,653	86.2	13,743	14,268	129	387	15,788	-
Florida	2,723,303	1,202,599	44.2	706,163	158,836	9,396	4,787	56,231	585,291
Georgia	1,469,269	772,419	52.6	295,283	103,942	2,046	231	140,762	154,586
Hawaii.........	139,399	27,370	19.6	103,709	1,040	-	-	2,606	4,674
Idaho [1]........	(X)	(X)	(X)	(X)	(X)	(X)	(X)	(X)	(X)
Illinois	887,874	295,255	33.3	94,681	33,837	26,676	1,706	5,068	430,651
Indiana.........	1,059,666	287,198	27.1	478,351	83,853	8,388	2,697	55,208	143,971
Iowa	731,514	240,316	32.9	142,058	26,345	950	507	-	321,338
Kansas.........	377,279	186,604	49.5	56,228	8,419	1,028	630	11,122	113,248
Kentucky	1,495,553	731,840	48.9	50,505	63,477	4,624	1,061	23,402	620,644
Louisiana	1,345,799	291,805	21.7	226,014	74,636	5,709	4,826	35,605	707,204
Maine..........	269,673	106,434	39.5	46,254	16,849	118	54	7,538	92,426
Maryland	473,449	165,267	34.9	222,233	982	671	188	25,802	58,306
Massachusetts.....	619,966	96,097	15.5	301,088	10,895	2,258	1,043	92,910	115,675
Michigan.	1,493,541	1,211,238	81.1	64,717	79,538	8,371	4,237	-	125,440
Minnesota [1]......	(X)	(X)	(X)	(X)	(X)	(X)	(X)	(X)	(X)
Mississippi	268,459	-	-	77,938	33,203	4,255	1,097	-	151,966
Missouri	937,209	409,323	43.7	135,076	143,135	4,507	1,361	15,851	227,956
Montana.........	90,017	51,690	57.4	21,553	473	211	232	-	15,858
Nebraska	294,282	125,477	42.6	25,784	9,564	1,929	780	204	130,544
Nevada	289,345	150,695	52.1	94,025	13,200	340	512	-	30,573
New Hampshire [1]...	(X)	(X)	(X)	(X)	(X)	(X)	(X)	(X)	(X)
New Jersey.......	1,425,826	172,607	12.1	39,358	54,579	6,790	-	374,686	777,806
New Mexico	203,052	35,650	17.6	78,109	16,668	543	170	6,671	65,241
New York	3,275,102	699,644	21.4	2,020,088	358,105	32,216	892	90,292	73,865
North Carolina.....	1,449,659	539,287	37.2	229,122	74,882	8,097	3,496	139,477	455,298
North Dakota [1].....	(X)	(X)	(X)	(X)	(X)	(X)	(X)	(X)	(X)
Ohio	1,866,048	528,762	28.3	360,675	100,129	4,041	2,155	240,236	630,050
Oklahoma........	554,679	228,138	41.1	124,795	58,811	1,213	178	1,760	139,784
Oregon.........	802,724	199,065	24.8	401,234	38,446	5,174	-	3,432	155,373
Pennsylvania......	1,846,786	597,625	32.4	959,041	59,462	950	4,953	6,342	218,413
Rhode Island......	41,131	-	75.9	5,569	3,822	523	-	-	-
South Carolina.....	117,197	93,881	80.1	-	20,615	2,051	650	-	-
South Dakota	94,117	5,030	5.3	14,993	13,906	648	2,022	3,582	53,936
Tennessee	776,156	186,563	24.0	222,871	147,830	-	4,568	28,126	186,198
Texas..........	3,340,587	1,494,846	44.8	1,050,413	353,550	7,690	5,991	129,066	299,031
Utah	330,169	84,743	25.7	93,404	24,913	754	2,165	47,229	76,961
Vermont[2]	(X)	(X)	(X)	(X)	(X)	(X)	(X)	(X)	(X)
Virginia.........	664,754	181,128	27.3	228,418	54,051	2,428	906	775	197,048
Washington......	883,722	350,304	39.6	330,403	22,859	5,360	2,292	7,313	165,191
West Virginia......	143,497	37,952	26.5	34,683	23,212	2,416	40	4,475	40,719
Wisconsin [1]......	(X)	(X)	(X)	(X)	(X)	(X)	(X)	(X)	(X)
Wyoming [1]......	(X)	(X)	(X)	(X)	(X)	(X)	(X)	(X)	(X)

- Represents zero.   X Not applicable   [1] Exempt from the National Voter Registration Act of 1993.   [2] Has not yet implemented to National Voter Registration Act of 1993.

Source: Federal Election Commission, Executive Summary—*Report to the Congress, June 1997*.

Elections   293

No. 482. Political Party Financial Activity by Major Political Party: 1981 to 1998

[In millions of dollars (39.3 represents $39,300,000). Covers financial activity during 2-year calendar period indicated. Some political party financial activities, such as building funds and state and local election spending, are not reported to the source. Also excludes contributions earmarked to Federal candidates through the party organizations, since some of those funds never passed through the committees' accounts]

Year and type of committee	Democratic				Republican			
	Receipts, net [1]	Disburse-ments, net [1]	Contribu-tions to candi-dates	Monies spent on behalf of party's nomi-nees [2]	Receipts, net [1]	Disburse-ments, net [1]	Contribu-tions to candi-dates	Monies spent on behalf of party's nomi-nees [2]
1981-82	39.3	40.1	1.7	3.3	215.0	214.0	5.6	14.3
1983-84	98.5	97.4	2.6	9.0	297.9	300.8	4.9	20.1
1985-86	64.8	65.9	1.7	9.0	255.2	258.9	3.4	14.3
1987-88	127.9	121.9	1.8	17.9	263.3	257.0	3.4	22.7
1989-90	85.8	90.9	1.5	8.7	206.3	213.5	2.9	10.7
1991-92	177.7	171.9	1.9	28.1	267.3	256.1	3.0	33.9
1993-94, total	143.3	141.8	2.2	21.2	254.4	243.7	3.0	20.6
1995-96, total	281.5	274.8	2.1	22.6	474.0	465.3	3.8	31.0
National committee	108.4	105.6	-	6.7	193.0	192.4	0.5	22.8
Senatorial committee	30.8	30.8	0.5	8.4	64.5	66.1	0.7	0.3
Congressional committee	26.6	26.4	1.0	5.7	74.2	73.6	1.3	7.3
State and local	93.2	88.9	0.6	1.8	128.4	120.2	1.3	0.6
1997-98, total [3]	**189.0**	**184.3**	**1.2**	**27.1**	**319.6**	**310.5**	**2.6**	**15.7**
National committee	64.8	65.3	-	6.0	104.0	105.1	0.4	3.9
Senatorial committee	35.6	35.8	0.3	8.4	53.4	53.7	0.3	-
Congressional committee	25.2	24.7	0.4	3.0	72.7	71.7	0.8	5.1
State and local	63.4	58.5	0.5	9.6	89.4	80.0	1.1	6.7

- Represents zero.   [1] Excludes monies transferred between affiliated committees.   [2] Monies spent in the general election. Minus sign (-) indicates refunds for expenditures.   [3] Excludes "Other national" activity.

Source: U.S. Federal Election Commission, *FEC Reports on Financial Activity, Final Report, Party and Non-Party Political Committees*, biennial.

No. 483. Independent Expenditures for Presidential and Congressional Campaigns: 1985 to 1996

[In thousands of dollars (10,205 represents $10,205,000). Covers campaign finance activity during 2-year calendar period indicated. An "independent expenditure" is money spent to support or defeat a clearly identified candidate. According to Federal election law, such an expenditure must be made without cooperation or consultation with the candidate or his/her campaign. Independent expenditures are not limited, as are contributions]

Type of office and year	All parties			Democrats		Republicans		Others	
	Total	For	Against	For	Against	For	Against	For	Against
TOTAL									
1985-86	10,205	8,832	1,373	3,450	888	5,376	485	6	-
1987-88	21,341	16,654	4,687	2,865	4,248	13,784	439	6	-
1989-90	5,774	4,177	1,597	1,530	735	2,645	862	2	-
1991-92	11,052	8,710	2,342	3,044	1,483	5,548	847	118	12
1993-94	4,980	3,256	1,724	672	1,119	2,571	590	13	15
1995-96	21,744	11,016	10,728	1,186	6,491	9,714	4,228	116	9
PRESIDENTIAL									
1985-86	841	795	45	76	28	719	17	-	-
1987-88	14,127	10,628	3,499	568	3,352	10,054	146	6	-
1989-90	497	322	174	5	169	318	5	-	-
1991-92	4,431	3,695	736	583	561	3,052	163	60	12
1993-94	112	27	85	12	84	15	(Z)	-	1
1995-96	1,436	601	835	111	761	459	74	31	-
SENATE									
1985-86	5,312	4,331	980	988	632	3,343	348	-	-
1987-88	4,401	3,641	761	831	617	2,810	143	(Z)	-
1989-90	3,506	2,362	1,144	756	428	1,604	716	2	-
1991-92	2,604	1,912	692	1,025	462	886	230	1	-
1993-94	2,627	1,612	1,015	261	476	1,351	539	(Z)	-
1995-96	15,765	8,012	7,753	315	5,498	7,697	2,255	-	-
1997-98	2,759	1,964	795	577	111	1,387	685	-	-
HOUSE OF REPRESENTATIVES									
1985-86	4,053	3,706	347	2,386	227	1,314	120	6	-
1987-88	2,813	2,385	427	1,466	279	920	149	(Z)	-
1989-90	1,772	1,493	279	770	138	723	141	-	-
1991-92	4,017	3,103	914	1,436	460	1,610	454	57	-
1993-94	2,241	1,617	624	399	559	1,205	51	13	14
1995-96	5,186	3,349	1,837	808	182	2,540	1,656	-	-
1997-98	6,265	5,584	680	1,816	202	3,768	478	-	-

- Represents zero.   Z Less than $500.

Source: U.S. Federal Election Commission, *FEC Index of Independent Expenditures, 1987-88*, May 1989; press release of May 19, 1989; and unpublished data.

294 Elections

No. 484. Political Action Committees—Number by Committee Type: 1980 to 1999

[As of **December 31**]

Committee type	1980	1985	1990	1994	1995	1996	1997	1998	1999
Total.	2,551	3,992	4,172	3,954	4,016	4,079	3,844	3,798	3,835
Corporate	1,206	1,710	1,795	1,660	1,674	1,642	1,597	1,567	1,548
Labor	297	388	346	333	334	332	332	321	318
Trade/membership/health	576	695	774	792	815	838	825	821	844
Nonconnected	374	1,003	1,062	980	1,020	1,103	931	935	972
Cooperative	42	54	59	53	44	41	42	39	38
Corporation without stock	56	142	136	136	129	123	117	115	115

Source: U.S. Federal Election Commission, press release of January.

No. 485. Political Action Committees—Financial Activity Summary by Committee Type: 1993 to 1998

[**In millions of dollars (391.8 represents $391,800,000).** Covers financial activity during 2-year calendar period indicated. Data have not been adjusted for transfers between affiliated committees]

Committee type	Receipts			Disbursements [1]			Contributions to candidates		
	1993-94	1995-96	1997-98	1993-94	1995-96	1997-98	1993-94	1995-96	1997-98
Total	391.8	437.5	502.6	388.1	430.0	470.8	189.6	217.9	219.9
Corporate	115.0	133.8	144.1	116.8	130.6	137.6	69.6	78.2	78.0
Labor.	90.3	104.1	111.3	88.4	99.8	98.2	41.9	48.0	44.6
Trade/membership/health.	96.4	106.0	119.6	94.1	105.4	114.4	52.9	60.2	62.3
Nonconnected	76.9	81.2	114.3	75.1	81.3	107.8	18.2	24.0	28.2
Cooperative	4.4	3.9	4.5	4.5	4.2	4.3	3.0	3.0	2.4
Corporation without stock.	8.9	8.5	8.8	9.2	8.7	8.5	4.1	4.5	4.4

[1] Comprises contributions to candidates, independent expenditures, and other disbursements.

Source: U.S. Federal Election Commission, *FEC Reports on Financial Activity, Final Report, Party and Non-Party Political Committees,* biennial.

No. 486. Presidential Campaign Finances—Federal Funds for General Election: 1980 to 1996

[**In millions of dollars (62.7 represents $62,700,000).** Based on FEC certifications, audit reports, and Dept. of Treasury reports]

1980		1988		1992		1996	
Candidate	Amount	Candidate	Amount	Candidate	Amount	Candidate	Amount
Total	62.7	Total	92.2	Total.	110.4	Total	152.6
Anderson [1]	4.2	Bush.	46.1	Bush.	55.2	Clinton	61.8
Carter	29.4	Dukakis.	46.1	Clinton	55.2	Dole	61.8
Reagan	29.2	Perot	-	Perot	29.0		

- Represents zero. [1] John Anderson, as the candidate of a new party, was permitted to raise funds privately. Total receipts for the Anderson campaign, including Federal funds, were $17.6 million, and total expenditures were $15.6 million.

Source: U.S. Federal Election Commission, periodic press releases.

No. 487. Presidential Campaign Finances—Primary Campaign Receipts and Disbursements: 1987 to 1996

[**In millions of dollars (213.8 represents $213,000,000).** Covers campaign finance activity during 2-year calendar period indicated. Covers candidates who received Federal matching funds or who had significant financial activity]

Item	Total			Democratic			Republican		
	1987-88 [1]	1991-92 [2]	1995-96	1987-88	1991-92	1995-96	1987-88	1991-92	1995-96
Receipts, total [3]	213.8	125.2	243.9	91.9	70.0	46.2	116.0	49.7	187.0
Individual contributions . .	141.1	82.4	126.4	59.4	44.7	31.3	76.8	34.4	93.1
Federal matching funds . .	65.7	41.5	56.0	30.1	24.4	14.0	34.7	15.0	41.6
Disbursements	210.7	118.7	(NA)	90.2	64.4	(NA)	114.6	48.8	(NA)

NA Not available. [1] Includes a minor party candidate who sought several party nominations and a Democratic candidate who did not receive Federal matching funds, but who had significant financial activity. [2] Includes other parties, not shown separately. [3] Includes other types of receipts, not shown separately.

Source: U.S. Federal Election Commission, *FEC Reports on Financial Activity, Final Report, Presidential Pre-Nomination Campaigns,* quadrennial.

No. 488. Congressional Campaign Finances—Receipts and Disbursements: 1993 to 1998

[Covers all campaign finance activity during 2-year calendar period indicated for primary, general, run-off, and special elections, 1993-94 relates to 2,045 House of Representatives candidates and 331 Senate candidates. Data have been adjusted to eliminate transfers between all committees within a campaign. For further information on legal limits of contributions, see Federal Election Campaign Act of 1971, as amended]

Item	House of representatives						Senate					
	Amount (mil. dol.)			Percent distribution			Amount (mil. dol.)			Percent distribution		
	1993-94	1995-96	1997-98	1993-94	1995-96	1997-98	1993-94	1995-96	1997-98	1993-94	1995-96	1997-98
Total receipts [1]	421.3	505.4	489.2	100	100	100	319.1	285.1	287.1	100	100	100
Individual contributions.	214.9	272.9	253.2	51	55	52	185.2	166.9	166.5	58	59	58
Other committees	132.1	155.0	158.5	31	31	32	47.2	45.6	48.1	15	16	17
Candidate loans	43.7	42.0	46.8	10	8	10	43.1	40.3	52.2	14	14	18
Candidate contributions	9.2	7.0	5.3	2	1	1	24.9	16.4	1.3	8	6	(Z)
Democrats.	216.7	233.1	233.4	51	46	47	133.6	126.5	134.1	42	44	47
Republicans.	201.8	266.9	255.8	48	53	52	183.6	157.7	153.0	58	55	53
Others	2.8	5.4	4.5	1	1	1	2.0	0.9	0.4	1	(Z)	(Z)
Incumbents	140.8	107.5	128.7	53	56	60	113.3	81.8	135.5	36	29	47
Challengers	29.1	73.1	44.5	24	24	19	119.2	79.2	113.9	37	28	40
Open seats [2]	46.8	42.5	60.2	23	14	21	86.6	124.1	37.7	27	44	13
Total disbursements . . .	407.2	477.8	452.5	100	95	100	318.8	287.5	287.9	100	100	100
Democrats.	213.4	221.1	211.1	46	44	47	136.3	127.4	134.6	43	44	47
Republicans.	191.0	251.4	237.2	53	50	52	180.6	159.1	152.9	57	55	53
Others	2.8	5.4	4.2	1	1	1	2.0	0.9	0.4	1	(Z)	(Z)
Incumbents	213.5	258.1	257.2	54	51	57	115.1	85.4	137.3	36	30	48
Challengers	99.1	119.6	94.7	25	24	21	118.3	78.9	112.5	37	27	39
Open seats [2]	94.6	100.2	100.6	21	20	22	85.5	123.1	38.1	27	43	13

Z Less than $50,000 or 0.5 percent.   [1] Includes other types of receipts, not shown separately.   [2] Elections in which an incumbent did not seek reelection.

Source: U.S. Federal Election Commission, *FEC Reports on Financial Activity, Final Report, U.S. Senate and House Campaigns*, biennial.

No. 489. Contributions to Congressional Campaigns by Political Action Committees (PAC) by Type of Committee: 1981 to 1998

[In millions of dollars (61.1 represents $61,100,000). Covers amounts given to candidates in primary, general, run-off, and special elections during the 2-year calendar period indicated. For number of political action committees, see Table 484]

Type of committee	Total [1]	Democrats	Republicans	Incumbents	Challengers	Open seats [2]
HOUSE OF REPRESENTATIVES						
1981-82	61.1	34.2	26.8	40.8	10.9	9.4
1983-84	75.7	46.3	29.3	57.2	11.3	7.2
1985-86	87.4	54.7	32.6	65.9	9.1	12.4
1987-88	102.2	67.4	34.7	82.2	10.0	10.0
1989-90	108.5	72.2	36.2	87.5	7.3	13.6
1991-92	127.4	85.4	41.7	94.4	12.2	20.8
1993-94	132.4	88.2	43.9	101.4	12.7	18.3
1995-96	159.8	79.4	79.7	117.2	21.4	20.1
1997-98, total [3]	158.7	77.6	80.9	123.9	14.8	19.7
Corporate	50.3	16.2	34.1	44.1	2.0	4.2
Trade association [4]	46.5	17.7	28.8	38.1	3.0	5.3
Labor	37.3	34.1	3.1	26.1	5.4	5.7
Nonconnected [5]	20.0	7.6	12.3	11.5	4.2	4.3
SENATE						
1981-82	22.6	11.2	11.4	14.3	5.2	3.0
1983-84	29.7	14.0	15.6	17.9	6.3	5.4
1985-86	45.3	20.2	25.1	23.7	10.2	11.4
1987-88	45.7	24.2	21.5	28.7	8.0	9.0
1989-90	41.2	20.2	21.0	29.5	8.2	3.5
1991-92	51.2	29.0	22.2	31.9	9.4	10.0
1997-98, total [3]	48.1	20.7	27.3	34.3	6.6	7.2
Corporate	20.9	6.9	14.0	15.3	2.6	3.0
Trade association [4]	12.5	4.6	7.9	9.0	1.6	1.9
Labor	6.0	5.4	0.6	4.0	0.9	1.5
Nonconnected [5]	7.1	3.0	4.1	4.9	1.2	1.0

[1] Includes other parties, not shown separately.   [2] Elections in which an incumbent did not seek reelection.   [3] Includes other types of political action committees not shown separately.   [4] Includes membership organizations and health organizations.   [5] Represents "ideological" groups as well as other issue groups not necessarily ideological in nature.

Source: U.S. Federal Election Commission, *FEC Reports on Financial Activity, Party and Non-Party Political Committees, Final Report*, biennial.

Section 9

State and Local Government
Finances and Employment

This section presents data on revenues, expenditures, debt, and employment of state and local governments. Nationwide statistics relating to state and local governments, their numbers, finances, and employment are compiled primarily by the U.S. Census Bureau through a program of censuses and surveys. Every fifth year (for years ending in "2" and "7") the Census Bureau conducts a census of governments involving collection of data for all governmental units in the United States. In addition, the Census Bureau conducts annual surveys which cover all the state governments and a sample of local governments.

Annually, the Census Bureau releases information on the Internet which presents financial data for the Federal Government, nationwide totals for state and local governments, and state-local data by states. Also released annually is a series on state, city, county, and school finances and on state and local public employment. There is also a series of quarterly data releases covering tax revenue and finances of major public employee retirement systems.

Basic information for Census Bureau statistics on governments is obtained by mail canvass from state and local officials; however, financial data for each of the state governments and for many of the large local governments are compiled from their official records and reports by Census Bureau personnel. In over two thirds of the states, all or part of local government financial data are obtained through central collection arrangements with state governments. Financial data on the Federal Government are primarily based on the *Budget* published by the Office of Management and Budget (see

text, Section 10, Federal Government Finances and Employment).

Governmental units—The governmental structure of the United States includes, in addition to the Federal Government and the states, thousands of local governments—counties, municipalities, townships, school districts, and numerous kinds of "special districts." In 1997, 87,453 local governments were identified by the census of governments. As defined by the census, governmental units include all agencies or bodies having an organized existence, governmental character, and substantial autonomy. While most of these governments can impose taxes, many of the special districts—such as independent public housing authorities and numerous local irrigation, power, and other types of districts—are financed from rentals, charges for services, benefit assessments, grants from other governments, and other nontax sources. The count of governments excludes semiautonomous agencies through which states, cities, and counties sometimes provide for certain functions—for example, "dependent" school systems, state institutions of higher education, and certain other "authorities" and special agencies which are under the administrative or fiscal control of an established governmental unit.

Finances—The financial statistics relate to government fiscal years ending June 30 or at some date within the 12 previous months. The following governments are exceptions and are included as though they were part of the June 30 group; ending September 30, the state governments of Alabama and Michigan, the District of Columbia, and Alabama

U.S. Census Bureau, Statistical Abstract of the United States: 2000

school districts; and ending August 31, the state government of Texas and Texas school districts. New York State ends its fiscal year on March 31. The Federal Government ended the fiscal year June 30 until 1976 when its fiscal year, by an act of Congress, was revised to extend from Oct. 1 to Sept. 30. A 3-month quarter (July 1 to Sept. 30, 1976) bridged the transition.

Nationwide government finance statistics have been classified and presented in terms of uniform concepts and categories, rather than according to the highly diverse terminology, organization, and fund structure utilized by individual governments. Accordingly, financial statistics which appear here for the Federal Government and for individual states or local governments have been standardized and may not agree directly with figures appearing in the original sources.

Statistics on governmental finances distinguish among general government, utilities, liquor stores, and insurance trusts. *General government* comprises all activities except utilities, liquor stores, and insurance trusts. Utilities include government water supply, electric light and power, gas supply, and transit systems. Liquor stores are operated by 17 states and by local governments in 6 states. Insurance trusts relate to employee retirement, unemployment compensation, and other social insurance systems administered by the Federal, state, and local governments.

Data for cities or counties relate only to municipal or county and their dependent agencies and do not include amounts for other local governments in the same geographic location. Therefore, expenditure figures for "education" do not include spending by the separate school districts which administer public schools within most municipal or county areas. Variations in the assignment of governmental responsibility for public assistance, health, hospitals, public housing, and other functions to a lesser degree also have an important effect upon reported amounts of city or county expenditure, revenue, and debt. Therefore, any comparisons based upon these figures should be made with caution and with due recognition of variations that exist among areas in the relative role of the municipal corporation.

Employment and payrolls—These data are based mainly on mail canvassing of state and local governments. Payroll includes all salaries, wages, and individual fee payments for the month specified, and employment relates to all persons on governmental payrolls during a pay period of the month covered—including paid officials, temporary help, and (unless otherwise specified) part-time as well as full-time personnel. Beginning 1986, statistics for full-time equivalent employment have been computed with a formula using hours worked by part-time employees. A payroll based formula was used prior to 1985. Full-time equivalent employment statistics were not computed for 1985. Figures shown for individual governments cover major dependent agencies such as institutions of higher education, as well as the basic central departments and agencies of the government.

Statistical reliability—For a discussion of statistical collection and estimation, sampling procedures, and measures of statistical reliability applicable to Census Bureau data, see Appendix III.

U.S. Census Bureau, Statistical Abstract of the United States: 2000

No. 490. Number of Governmental Units by Type: 1942 to 1997

Type of government	1942	1952 [1]	1962	1967	1972	1977	1982	1987	1992	1997
Total	155,116	116,807	91,237	81,299	78,269	79,913	81,831	83,237	85,006	87,504
U.S. Government	1	1	1	1	1	1	1	1	1	1
State government	48	50	50	50	50	50	50	50	50	50
Local governments	155,067	116,756	91,186	81,248	78,218	79,862	81,780	83,186	84,955	87,453
County.	3,050	3,052	3,043	3,049	3,044	3,042	3,041	3,042	3,043	3,043
Municipal	16,220	16,807	18,000	18,048	18,517	18,862	19,076	19,200	19,279	19,372
Township and town	18,919	17,202	17,142	17,105	16,991	16,822	16,734	16,691	16,656	16,629
School district	108,579	67,355	34,678	21,782	15,781	15,174	14,851	14,721	14,422	13,726
Special district.	8,299	12,340	18,323	21,264	23,885	25,962	28,078	29,532	31,555	34,683

[1] Adjusted to include units in Alaska and Hawaii which adopted statehood in 1959.

No. 491. Number of Local Governments by Type—States: 1997

State	All governmental units [1]	County	Municipal	Township [1]	School district	Special district [2] Total [3]	Natural resources	Fire protection	Housing & community development
U.S	87,453	3,043	19,372	16,629	13,726	34,683	6,983	5,601	3,469
Alabama.	1,131	67	446	-	127	491	71	5	154
Alaska	175	12	149	-	-	14	-	-	13
Arizona.	637	15	87	-	231	304	79	152	-
Arkansas	1,516	75	491	-	311	639	232	74	126
California	4,607	57	471	-	1,069	3,010	472	369	79
Colorado.	1,869	62	269	-	180	1,358	168	249	96
Connecticut. . . .	583	-	30	149	17	387	1	65	94
Delaware	336	3	57	-	19	257	236	-	3
District of Columbia	2	-	1	-	-	1	-	-	-
Florida	1,081	66	394	-	95	526	132	56	105
Georgia	1,344	156	535	-	180	473	36	2	206
Hawaii	19	3	1	-	-	15	14	-	-
Idaho	1,147	44	200	-	114	789	182	144	10
Illinois	6,835	102	1,288	1,433	944	3,068	935	827	113
Indiana.	3,198	91	569	1,008	294	1,236	134	2	63
Iowa	1,876	99	950	-	394	433	249	68	26
Kansas.	3,950	105	627	1,370	324	1,524	260	-	204
Kentucky	1,366	119	434	-	176	637	131	144	17
Louisiana	467	60	302	-	66	39	3	-	-
Maine.	832	16	22	467	98	229	16	-	30
Maryland	420	23	156	-	-	241	156	-	20
Massachusetts. .	861	12	44	307	85	413	18	16	252
Michigan	2,775	83	534	1,242	584	332	82	2	-
Minnesota.	3,501	87	854	1,794	360	406	114	-	176
Mississippi	936	82	295	-	164	395	251	-	62
Missouri	3,416	114	944	324	537	1,497	181	273	143
Montana	1,144	54	128	-	362	600	125	159	12
Nebraska	2,894	93	535	455	681	1,130	84	419	126
Nevada	205	16	19	-	17	153	35	16	5
New Hampshire .	575	10	13	221	166	165	10	14	21
New Jersey. . . .	1,421	21	324	243	552	281	16	200	2
New Mexico . . .	881	33	99	-	96	653	609	-	6
New York	3,413	57	615	929	686	1,126	2	912	-
North Carolina. .	952	100	527	-	-	325	155	-	94
North Dakota. . .	2,758	53	363	1,341	237	764	80	289	38
Ohio	3,597	88	941	1,310	666	592	97	60	73
Oklahoma.	1,799	77	592	-	578	552	98	20	105
Oregon.	1,493	36	240	-	258	959	195	263	22
Pennsylvania. . .	5,070	66	1,023	1,546	516	1,919	7	-	91
Rhode Island. . .	119	-	8	31	4	76	3	34	26
South Carolina. .	716	46	269	-	91	310	48	97	45
South Dakota . .	1,810	66	309	956	177	302	107	60	34
Tennessee	940	93	343	-	14	490	112	-	100
Texas.	4,700	254	1,177	-	1,087	2,182	428	103	395
Utah	683	29	230	-	40	384	77	24	17
Vermont	691	14	49	237	279	112	14	20	10
Virginia.	483	95	231	-	1	156	47	-	-
Washington	1,812	39	275	-	296	1,202	163	402	45
West Virginia. . .	704	55	232	-	55	362	15	-	39
Wisconsin.	3,059	72	583	1,266	442	696	184	-	171
Wyoming	654	23	97	-	56	478	119	61	-

- Represents zero. [1] Includes "town" governments in the six New England States and in Minnesota, New York, and Wisconsin. [2] Single function districts. [3] Includes other special districts not shown separately.

Source of Tables 490 and 491: U.S. Census Bureau, *1997 Census of Governments, Government Organization*, Series GC97(1)-1, quinquennial.

State and Local Government Finances and Employment 299

No. 492. County, Municipal, and Township Governments by Population Size: 1997

[Number of governments as of **January 1997**. Population enumerated as of **July 1, 1994.** Consolidated city-county governments are classified as municipal rather than county governments. Township governments include "towns" in the six New England States, Minnesota, New York, and Wisconsin]

Population-size group	County governments			Municipal governments			Township governments		
	Population, **1994**			Population, **1994**			Population, **1994**		
	Number, 1997	Number (1,000)	Percent	Number, 1997	Number (1,000)	Percent	Number, 1997	Number (1,000)	Percent
Total..........	**3,043**	**236,107**	**100**	**19,372**	**161,605**	**100**	**16,629**	**54,662**	**100**
250,000 or more	183	128,741	55	66	46,417	29	4	1,758	3
100,000 to 299,999	264	40,234	17	142	20,687	13	31	4,259	8
50,000 to 99,999	378	26,583	11	346	23,595	15	84	5,626	10
25,000 to 49,999	604	21,543	9	590	20,623	13	257	8,750	16
10,000 to 24,999	908	15,047	6	1,378	21,606	13	744	11,509	21
5,000 to 9,999........	413	3,105	1	1,618	11,504	7	1,064	7,403	14
2,500 to 4,999........	178	668	-	2,096	7,426	5	1,836	6,422	12
1,000 to 2,499........	86	165	-	3,723	5,965	4	3,606	5,766	11
Less than 1,000.......	29	21	-	9,413	3,782	2	9,003	3,169	6

- Represents or rounds to zero.

Source: U.S. Census Bureau, *1997 Census of Governments, Government Organization,* Series GC97(1)-1 quinquennial.

Figure 9.1
Lottery Ticket Sales—Type of Games: 1999

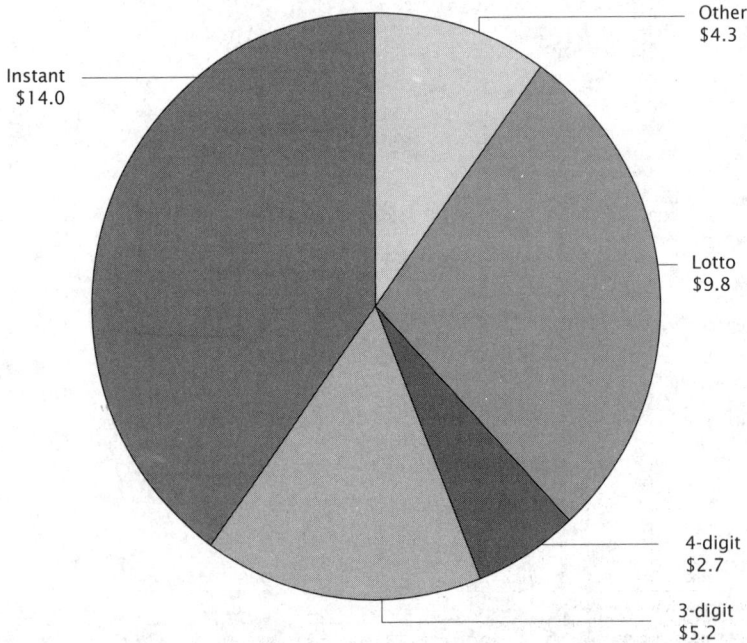

Type of Game
Total ticket sales: $36.0 billiion

Other $4.3

Instant $14.0

Lotto $9.8

4-digit $2.7

3-digit $5.2

Source: Chart prepared by U.S. Census Bureau. For data, see Table 519.

No. 493. All Governments—Revenue, Expenditure, and Debt: 1990 to 1996

[2,047 represents $2,047,000,000,000. For fiscal year ending in year shown; see text, this section. Local government amounts are estimates subject so sampling variation; see Appendix III and source]

Item	All govern-ments (bil. dol.)	Federal[1]		State and local (bil. dol.)			Per capita[2] (dollars)		
		Total (bil. dol.)	Percent of total	Total	State	Local	Total	Federal	State and local
Revenue: [3]									
1990	[4]2,047	1,155	56.4	[4]1,032	632	580	[4]8,229	4,641	4,149
1995	[4]2,759	1,573	57.0	[4]1,418	906	757	[4]10,500	5,986	5,396
1996	(NA)	(NA)	(NA)	[4]1,514	967	804	(NA)	(NA)	5,709
Intergovernmental:									
1990.	(X)	3	(X)	[4]137	126	191	(X)	12	550
1995.	(X)	3	(X)	[4]229	216	259	(X)	12	872
1996.	(X)	(NA)	(X)	[4]235	221	270	(X)	(NA)	886
General, own sources:									
1990.	1,493	780	52.2	713	391	322	6,002	3,137	2,865
1995.	1,956	1,015	51.9	941	523	417	7,444	3,863	3,581
1996.	(NA)	(NA)	(NA)	988	549	439	3,725	(NA)	3,725
Taxes: [3]									
1990	1,134	632	55.7	502	301	201	4,558	2,542	2,016
1995	1,505	844	56.1	661	399	261	5,728	3,212	2,516
1996	(NA)	(NA)	(NA)	689	418	271	2,598	(NA)	2,598
Property:									
1990	156	(X)	(X)	156	6	150	626	(X)	626
1995	203	(X)	(X)	203	10	194	773	(X)	773
1996	(NA)	(X)	(X)	209	10	199	788	(X)	788
Individual income:									
1990	573	467	81.6	106	96	10	2,301	1,877	425
1995	728	590	81.0	138	126	12	2,771	2,245	525
1996	(NA)	(NA)	(NA)	147	134	13	554	(NA)	554
Corporate income:									
1990	117	94	80.3	24	22	2	471	376	95
1995	188	157	83.5	31	29	2	715	598	118
1996	(NA)	(NA)	(NA)	32	29	3	121	(NA)	121
Sales or gross receipts:									
1990	232	[5]54	23.3	178	147	31	932	[5]217	715
1995	312	[5]75	24.0	237	197	40	1,187	[5]285	902
1996	(NA)	(NA)	(NA)	249	206	43	939	(NA)	939
Current charges and miscellaneous:									
1990	359	148	41.3	211	91	120	1,444	596	849
1995	451	171	37.9	280	124	156	1,716	651	1,066
1996	(NA)	(NA)	(NA)	299	131	168	1,127	(NA)	1,127
Expenditures: [3]									
1990	[4]2,219	1,393	62.8	[4]976	572	581	[4]8,921	5,601	3,924
1995	[4]2,820	1,705	60.5	[4]1,351	837	759	[4]11,630	6,491	5,143
1996	(NA)	(NA)	(NA)	[4]1,398	860	794	[4]5,272	(NA)	5,272
Intergovernmental:									
1990.	(X)	147	(X)	[4]3	175	6	(X)	591	13
1995.	(X)	233	(X)	[4]4	241	8	(X)	887	15
1996.	(X)	(NA)	(X)	[4]4	252	8	(X)	(NA)	15
Direct: [3]									
1990.	2,219	1,246	56.2	973	397	575	8,919	5,009	3,911
1995.	2,820	1,472	52.2	1,348	596	751	10,732	5,602	5,130
1996.	(NA)	(NA)	(NA)	1,394	608	786	5,257	(NA)	5,257
Current operation:									
1990	1,190	490	41.2	700	258	442	4,785	1,970	2,814
1995	1,471	486	33.0	986	396	590	5,598	1,850	3,752
1996	(NA)	(NA)	(NA)	1,021	406	616	3,850	(NA)	3,850
Capital outlay:									
1990	221	98	44.3	123	46	78	888	394	495
1995	226	75	33.2	151	58	94	860	285	575
1996	(NA)	(NA)	(NA)	159	59	100	600	(NA)	600
Debt outstanding: [6]									
1990	4,127	3,266	79.2	861	318	542	16,589	13,129	3,459
1995	6,116	5,001	81.8	1,115	427	688	23,276	19,033	4,243
1996	(NA)	(NA)	(NA)	1,170	452	717	4,412	(NA)	4,412

NA Not available.   X Not applicable.   [1] Data adjusted to system for reporting state and local data; therefore, differ from figures in Section 10 tables.   [2] 1980 and 1990 based on enumerated resident population as of April 1, all other years based on estimated resident population as of July 1.   [3] Includes amounts not shown separately.   [4] Excludes duplicate transactions between levels of government; see source.   [5] Includes customs.   [6] End of fiscal year.

Source: U.S. Census Bureau, 1990, Government Finances, GF, No. 5, annual; thereafter, <http://www.census.gov/ftp/pub/govs/www/index. html> (accessed 20 May 1999).

No. 494. All Governments—Detailed Finances: 1996

[In millions of dollars (1,572,588 represents $1,572,588,000,000), except as indicated. For fiscal year ending in year shown; see text, this section. Local government amounts are estimates subject to sampling variation; see Appendix III and source]

Item	Federal [1]	State and local Total	State and local State	State and local Local	Per capita [2] (dol.) Federal	Per capita [2] (dol.) State and local
Revenue	1,572,588	1,513,633	966,808	803,737	5,985	5,708
Intergovernmental revenue	3,060	234,891	221,369	270,480	12	886
Revenue from own sources	1,569,528	1,278,743	745,439	533,257	5,973	4,822
General revenue from own sources	1,015,042	987,930	549,147	438,736	3,863	3,725
Taxes [3]	844,415	689,038	418,390	270,602	3,214	2,598
Property	(X)	209,440	9,974	199,467	(X)	790
Individual income	590,243	146,844	133,547	13,296	2,246	554
Corporation income	157,004	32,009	29,316	2,693	598	121
Sales and gross receipts	75,185	248,993	206,115	42,832	286	939
Customs duties	19,438	(X)	(X)	(X)	74	(X)
General	(X)	169,071	139,363	29,709	(X)	638
Selective [3]	55,747	79,922	66,752	13,123	212	301
Motor fuel	28,669	26,833	25,988	844	109	101
Alcoholic beverages	7,523	3,988	3,667	275	29	15
Tobacco products	5,878	7,520	7,338	183	22	28
Public utilities	9,365	15,920	8,615	7,306	36	60
Motor vehicle and operators' licenses	(X)	14,939	13,848	1,090	(X)	56
Death and gift	14,763	5,352	5,320	32	56	20
Charges and miscellaneous [3]	170,627	298,892	130,757	168,135	649	1,127
Current charges [3]	95,860	182,201	67,259	114,942	365	687
National defense and international relations	9,612	(X)	(X)	(X)	37	(X)
Postal service	53,311	(X)	(X)	(X)	203	(X)
Education [3]	(X)	49,741	37,592	12,150	(X)	188
School lunch sales	(X)	4,307	16	4,290	(X)	16
Higher education	(X)	41,546	37,100	4,445	(X)	157
Natural resources	13,042	2,076	1,573	503	50	8
Hospitals	223	50,544	15,533	35,011	1	191
Sewerage	(X)	21,067	27	21,041	(X)	79
Solid waste management	2	9,019	347	8,672	-	34
Parks and recreation	113	4,916	1,000	3,916	-	19
Housing and community development	2,459	3,605	374	3,231	9	14
Airports	27	8,170	705	7,465	-	31
Sea and inland port facilities	1,491	2,131	600	1,531	6	8
Highways	(X)	5,610	3,517	2,093	(X)	21
Interest earnings	12,973	57,592	28,621	28,971	49	217
Special assessments	(X)	3,123	102	3,021	(X)	12
Sale of property	4,666	856	209	647	18	3
Utility and liquor store revenue	(X)	75,326	7,079	68,247	(X)	284
Insurance trust revenue	554,486	215,487	189,213	26,273	2,110	813
Expenditure	1,705,486	1,397,634	859,599	794,318	6,491	5,270
Intergovernmental expenditure	233,389	3,920	252,005	8,198	888	15
Direct expenditure	1,472,097	1,393,714	607,594	786,120	5,602	5,256
General expenditure [3]	913,806	1,189,356	503,306	686,050	3,478	4,485
Education [3]	26,660	398,859	106,565	292,294	101	1,504
Elementary and secondary education	(X)	279,353	2,447	276,906	(X)	1,053
Higher education	(X)	100,736	85,348	15,388	(X)	380
Public welfare	57,246	40,588	23,118	17,470	218	153
Hospitals	11,990	70,648	29,063	41,585	46	266
Health	14,531	40,166	22,180	17,986	55	151
Highways	731	79,092	47,548	31,545	3	298
Police protection	6,862	44,683	6,499	38,184	26	168
Fire protection	(X)	17,709	(X)	17,709	(X)	67
Corrections	3,065	37,510	25,294	12,216	12	141
Natural resources	39,742	15,819	12,306	3,512	151	60
Sewerage	(X)	24,665	1,527	23,138	(X)	93
Solid waste management	2,711	14,700	1,620	13,080	10	55
Housing and community development	16,278	22,666	2,369	20,297	62	85
Governmental administration	(X)	54,991	23,360	31,631	(X)	207
Parks and recreation	2,250	19,137	3,063	16,073	9	72
Interest on general debt	233,225	58,912	25,410	33,502	888	222
Utility	(X)	92,509	8,043	84,465	(X)	349
Liquor store expenditure	(X)	3,099	2,593	506	(X)	12
Insurance trust expenditure	558,291	108,751	93,652	15,099	2,125	410
By character and object:						
Current operation	486,041	1,021,155	405,527	615,629	1,850	3,851
Capital outlay	74,648	158,911	58,927	99,984	284	599
Construction	9,929	116,076	46,934	69,142	38	438
Equip., land, and existing structures	64,719	42,835	11,994	30,842	246	162
Assistance and subsidies	119,892	36,154	23,313	12,841	456	136
Interest on debt (general and utility)	233,225	68,743	26,175	42,568	888	259
Insurance benefits and repayments	558,291	108,751	93,652	15,099	2,125	410
Expenditure for salaries and wages [4]	162,392	447,638	129,577	318,061	618	1,688

- Represents or rounds to zero.   X Not applicable.   [1] 1995 data.   [2] Based on estimated resident population as of July 1. See Table 2.   [3] Includes amounts not shown separately.   [4] Included in items shown above.

Source: U.S. Census Bureau <http://www.census.gov/pub/ govs/www/index.html> (accessed 20 May 1999), and unpublished data.

No. 495. All Governments—Capital Outlays: 1980 to 1996

[In millions of dollars (99,386 represents $99,386,000,000), except percent. For fiscal year ending in year shown; see text, this section. Local government amounts are subject to sampling variation; see Appendix III and source]

Level and function	1980	1985	1990	1992	1993	1994	1995	1996
Total	99,386	156,912	220,960	227,798	221,227	217,328	226,088	(NA)
Federal government:								
Total.	36,492	77,014	97,891	93,095	85,328	79,827	74,648	(NA)
Annual percent change [1]	10.9	6.3	-1.9	-2.6	-8.3	-6.5	-6.5	(NA)
Direct expenditure	526,330	924,889	1,246,131	889,494	1,364,873	1,412,364	1,472,097	(NA)
Percent of direct expenditure .	6.9	8.3	7.9	10.5	6.3	5.7	5.1	(NA)
By function:								
National defense [2]	28,161	64,154	75,624	69,061	61,754	59,160	53,826	(NA)
Education.	97	39	41	90	86	145	221	(NA)
Highways.	132	121	181	310	210	203	185	(NA)
Health and hospitals	673	916	1,096	1,594	1,703	1,508	1,740	(NA)
Natural resources	4,046	4,092	4,698	5,466	6,122	2,990	3,261	(NA)
Housing [3]	317	1,935	4,343	4,017	3,942	3,557	3,918	(NA)
Air transportation	151	785	664	879	916	909	791	(NA)
Water transportation [4]	1,003	583	385	506	739	495	369	(NA)
Other	1,912	4,389	10,859	11,172	9,856	10,837	10,337	(NA)
State and local governments:								
Total.	62,894	79,898	123,069	134,703	135,899	137,501	151,440	158,911
Annual percent change [1]	7.0	13.1	9.9	2.3	0.9	1.2	10.1	4.9
Direct expenditure	432,328	656,188	972,662	1,146,853	1,213,723	1,115,997	1,347,763	1,393,714
Percent of direct expenditure .	14.5	12.2	12.7	11.7	11.2	12.3	11.2	11.4
By function:								
Education [5]	10,737	13,477	25,997	30,845	31,359	29,012	35,708	40,302
Higher education	2,972	4,629	7,441	9,180	8,949	8,959	10,461	11,006
Elementary and secondary.	7,362	8,358	18,057	21,319	22,102	19,693	24,808	28,868
Highways.	19,133	23,900	33,867	37,031	36,980	39,503	42,561	43,453
Health and hospitals	2,443	2,709	3,848	4,331	5,291	4,464	4,883	5,160
Natural resources	1,052	1,736	2,545	2,266	2,137	2,349	2,891	3,042
Housing [3]	2,248	3,217	3,997	4,182	4,890	4,066	4,527	4,704
Air transportation	1,391	1,875	3,434	4,605	5,413	5,170	3,802	3,814
Water transportation [4]	623	717	924	778	996	1,483	1,101	1,246
Sewerage	6,272	5,926	8,356	8,926	10,261	7,989	8,894	9,326
Parks and recreation	2,023	2,196	3,877	3,934	3,849	3,919	4,085	4,869
Utilities	9,933	13,435	16,601	17,785	15931	18,180	19,028	18,755
Water.	3,335	4,160	6,873	7,567	6,490	6,893	7,466	7,381
Electric.	4,572	5,247	3,976	3,950	3,760	4,030	3,715	3,522
Transit	1,921	3,830	5,443	5,836	5,253	6,966	7,507	7,533
Gas	105	198	310	432	428	290	340	318
Other	7,039	10,711	19,623	20,020	18,793	21,366	23,961	24,239

NA Not available. [1] Change from prior year shown. [2] Includes international relations and U.S. service schools. [3] Includes community development. [4] Includes terminals. [5] Includes other education.

Source: U.S. Census Bureau, 1980-92 *Historical Statistics on Governmental Finances and Employment*; and *Government Finances*, Series GF, No. 5, annual; thereafter, <http://www.census.gov/govs/www/index.html> (accessed 20 May 1999).

No. 496. All Governments—Expenditure for Public Works: 1980 to 1996

[In millions of dollars (72,177 represents $72,177,000,000). Public works include expenditures on highways, airports, water transport terminals, sewerage, solid waste management, water supply, and mass transit systems. Represents direct expenditures excluding intergovernmental grants]

Item	Total	Highways	Airport transpor-tation	Water transport and ter-minals	Sewer-age	Solid waste manage-ment	Water supply	Mass transit
1980: Total.	72,177	33,745	5,071	3,278	9,892	3,322	9,228	7,641
Federal	5,114	434	2,570	2,110	-	-	-	-
State	22,832	20,661	360	360	334	-	91	1,026
Local	44,231	12,650	2,141	808	9,558	3,322	9,137	6,615
Capital expenditures (percent) .	48	57	30	50	63	11	36	25
1990: Total.	146,762	61,913	10,983	4,524	18,309	10,144	22,101	18,788
Federal	7,911	856	4,499	2,556	-	-	-	-
State	43,787	36,464	635	504	636	891	136	4,521
Local	95,064	24,593	5,848	1,464	17,673	9,253	21,966	14,267
Capital expenditures (percent) .	42	55	37	29	46	18	31	29
1994: Total.	180,634	72,758	15,896	5,476	21,624	14,041	26,617	24,221
Federal	10,021	691	6,482	2,848	-	-	-	-
State	52,534	43,812	788	635	1,318	1,370	176	4,434
Local	118,079	28,255	8,626	1,993	20,305	12,671	26,441	19,788
Capital expenditures (percent) .	40	55	38	36	37	13	26	29
1995: Total.	192,985	77,840	15,085	5,016	23,583	17,701	28,041	25,719
Federal	12,837	731	6,688	2,707	-	2,711	-	-
State	56,392	46,893	783	604	1,462	1,658	178	4,814
Local	123,756	30,216	7,614	1,706	22,121	13,331	27,863	20,904
Capital expenditures (percent) .	39	55	30	29	38	11	27	29
1996: Total.	(NA)	(NA)	(NA)	(NA)	(NA)	(NA)	(NA)	(NA)
Federal	(NA)	(NA)	(NA)	(NA)	(NA)	(NA)	(NA)	(NA)
State	89,392	79,092	796	784	1,527	1,620	184	5,388
Local	142,895	47,548	7,997	1,794	23,138	13,080	28,766	20,573
Capital expenditures (percent) .	(NA)	(NA)	(NA)	(NA)	(NA)	(NA)	(NA)	(NA)
Capital expenditures	(NA)	(NA)	(NA)	(NA)	(NA)	(NA)	(NA)	(NA)

- Represents or rounds to zero. NA Not available.

Source: U.S. Census Bureau, 1980-92, *Government Finances,* Series GF, No. 5, annual; thereafter, <http://www.census.gov/govs/www/index.html> (accessed 20 May 1999), *State and Local Government Finance Estimates by State,* annual, and unpublished data.

No. 497. Federal Grants-in-Aid Summary: 1970 to 2000

[24,065 represents $24,065,000,000, except as indicated. For fiscal year ending in year shown; see text, this section. Minus sign (-) indicates decrease]

Year	Current dollars							Constant (1996) dollars	
			Grants to individuals		Grants as percent of—				
	Total grants (mil. dol.)	Annual percent change [1]	Total (mil. dol.)	Percent of total grants	State/local govt. expenditures from own sources [2]	Federal outlays	Gross domestic product	Total grants (bil. dol.)	Annual percent change [1]
1970	24,065	19.3	8,717	36.2	29.1	12.3	2.4	94.0	11.6
1975	49,791	14.8	16,752	33.6	34.8	15.0	3.2	136.6	3.6
1980	91,385	9.6	32,619	35.7	39.8	15.5	3.3	169.0	-1.0
1985	105,852	8.5	49,321	46.6	29.6	11.2	2.6	146.9	4.9
1990	135,325	11.0	75,685	55.9	25.3	10.8	2.4	157.6	6.6
1991	154,519	14.2	90,744	58.7	26.4	11.7	2.6	173.5	10.1
1992	178,065	15.2	110,016	61.8	28.8	12.9	2.9	195.9	12.9
1993	193,612	8.7	121,519	62.8	29.6	13.7	3.0	207.4	5.9
1994	210,596	8.8	131,123	62.3	30.9	14.4	3.0	220.5	6.3
1995	224,991	6.8	141,183	62.8	31.7	14.8	3.1	229.7	4.2
1996	227,811	1.3	142,802	62.7	30.8	14.6	3.0	227.8	-0.8
1997	234,160	2.8	144,189	61.6	30.1	14.6	2.9	229.8	0.9
1998	246,128	5.1	155,854	63.3	30.3	14.9	2.8	238.5	3.8
1999	267,081	8.5	167,677	62.8	31.4	15.7	2.9	253.8	6.4
2000, est ..	284,072	6.4	175,556	61.8	(NA)	15.9	3.0	262.7	3.5

NA Not available. [1] Average annual percent change from prior year shown. For explanation, see Guide to Tabular Presentation. 1970, change from 1969. [2] Outlays as defined in the national income and product accounts.

Source: U. S. Office of Management and Budget, based on *Historical Tables* and *Analytical Prospectives, Budget of the United States Government,* annual.

No. 498. Federal Aid to State and Local Governments: 1970 to 2000

[In millions of dollars (24,065 represents $24,065,000,000). For fiscal year ending in year shown; See text, this section. Includes trust funds]

Program	1970	1980	1990	1995	1997	1998	1999	2000, est.
Grant-in-aid shared revenue [1]	[2]24,065	91,385	135,325	224,991	234,160	246,128	267,081	284,072
National defense	37	93	241	68	-	12	1	(NA)
Energy	25	499	461	492	440	424	462	430
Natural resources and environment	411	5,363	3,745	4,148	3,998	3,758	4,103	4,463
Environmental Protection Agency.........	194	4,603	2,874	2,912	2,907	2,746	2,960	3,260
Agriculture	604	569	1,285	780	634	668	659	831
Commerce and Housing Credit..........	4	3	(-)	5	9	9	5	6
Transportation [1]	4,599	13,022	19,174	25,787	26,846	26,144	28,904	32,344
Airports [3]	83	590	1,220	1,826	1,489	1,511	1,565	1,896
Highways [3]	4,395	9,208	14,171	19,475	20,304	19,791	22,590	25,185
Urban mass transit [3]	104	3,129	3,730	4,353	4,499	4,221	4,188	4,476
Community and regional development [1]	1,780	6,486	4,965	7,230	8,161	7,653	9,332	8,963
Appalachian regional development........	184	335	124	182	236	180	136	144
Community development block grants......	(X)	3,902	2,818	4,333	4,517	4,621	4,804	4,856
Education, employment, training, social services [1]	6,417	21,862	23,359	34,125	34,735	36,502	38,217	43,663
Compensatory education for the disadvantaged	7,187	7,800	7,534	8,354	1,470	3,370	4,437	6,785
School improvement programs	86	523	1,080	1,288	1,187	1,260	1,255	2,385
Bilingual and immigrant education	-	166	152	189	171	204	284	433
Federally affected areas impact aid	622	622	799	803	651	724	1,076	1,021
Vocational and adult education	285	854	1,287	1,449	1,382	1,425	1,338	1,512
Payments to states for Family Support Activities	81	383	265	953	4,047	4,451	4,707	5,495
Social services-block grants to states	574	2,763	2,749	2,797	2,571	2,437	1,993	1,623
Children and family services programs	390	1,548	2,618	4,463	4,876	5,054	5,421	5,906
Training and employment assistance	954	6,191	3,042	3,620	3,324	3,399	3,436	3,690
Office of libraries..................	105	158	127	109	132	121	129	157
Health [1]	3,849	15,758	43,890	93,587	98,974	105,833	113,969	123,340
Alcohol, drug abuse, and mental health [4] ...	146	679	1,241	2,444	1,622	2,236	2,214	2,451
Grants to states for Medicaid [4]	2,727	13,957	41,103	89,070	95,552	101,234	108,042	116,117
Income security [1]	5,795	18,495	35,189	55,122	54,965	58,870	64,178	63,174
Family support payments to states [4].......	4,142	6,888	12,246	17,133	5,345	2,171	2,756	3,053
Food stamps-administration	559	412	2,130	2,740	3,122	3,673	3,362	3,717
Child nutrition and special milk programs [4] ..	380	3,388	4,871	7,387	8,141	8,436	8,740	9,211
Housing assistance [4].................	436	3,435	9,516	18,416	17,717	19,668	22,830	19,806
Veterans benefits and services [4]...........	18	90	134	253	277	288	317	397
Administration of justice...............	42	529	574	1,222	2,845	3,658	4,793	4,166
General government [5].................	479	8,616	2,309	2,172	2,276	2,309	2,141	2,295

- Represents or rounds to zero. NA Not available. X Not applicable. [1] Includes items not shown separately. [2] Includes $5 million for international affairs subsequently provided to a private institution. [3] Trust funds. [4] Includes grants for payments to individuals. [5] Includes general purpose fiscal assistance.

Source: U.S. Office of Management and Budget, *Historical Tables, Budget of the United States Government,* annual.

No. 499. Federal Aid to State and Local Governments—Selected Programs by State: 1999

[In millions of dollars (274,448 represents $274,448,000,000), except per capita. For fiscal year ending September 30]

| State and outlying area | Federal aid, total [1] | Department of Agriculture | | | | | Department of Education | | | | |
| | | Food and nutrition service | | | | | | Office of Special Education and Rehabilitative Services | | | |
		Total	Child nutrition programs [2]	Food stamp program [3]	Special supplemental food program (WIC)	Other	Total	Education for the disadvantaged	Special education	Rehabilitation services & disability research	Other
United States [4] ..	274,448	18,718	8,680	3,392	3,944	2,701	22,768	7,550	4,745	2,672	7,801
Alabama.........	4,165	323	170	30	64	59	388	132	69	52	134
Alaska	1,582	69	24	6	17	21	216	32	17	10	156
Arizona.........	4,290	322	169	21	80	51	456	113	71	44	229
Arkansas	2,504	220	102	18	46	55	225	77	45	35	68
California	32,716	2,188	1,111	221	666	190	2,506	935	432	257	881
Colorado........	2,951	183	86	18	40	39	261	79	60	32	91
Connecticut.......	3,702	136	67	17	34	18	234	74	64	19	76
Delaware	763	51	26	6	8	11	67	19	13	10	26
District of Columbia .	3,028	46	25	5	9	7	140	22	9	21	88
Florida	10,811	870	478	114	189	89	1,021	293	279	123	325
Georgia	6,432	575	333	58	119	65	601	204	125	86	186
Hawaii	1,180	99	40	11	30	18	152	21	18	11	102
Idaho..........	1,109	91	34	7	17	32	101	28	21	15	38
Illinois	10,614	646	334	82	147	83	933	307	220	98	308
Indiana.........	4,535	274	132	28	65	50	410	118	103	54	136
Iowa	2,416	165	73	12	34	45	219	55	50	26	87
Kansas.........	2,174	158	89	9	27	33	225	66	46	28	83
Kentucky	4,312	294	145	27	65	57	386	137	67	83	99
Louisiana	5,069	431	242	40	75	74	467	205	67	53	142
Maine..........	1,626	86	34	8	13	32	116	35	22	16	43
Maryland	4,359	243	126	30	52	36	349	116	74	42	117
Massachusetts.....	7,448	259	147	31	53	28	552	164	133	52	203
Michigan........	9,333	679	225	255	110	89	835	346	153	95	241
Minnesota.......	4,283	290	146	40	47	56	327	90	79	42	115
Mississippi	3,213	303	156	24	51	72	313	130	47	43	94
Missouri	5,227	315	156	36	64	59	491	174	124	56	137
Montana........	1,174	75	29	7	11	28	132	27	17	12	77
Nebraska	1,589	109	58	11	18	22	159	41	37	16	66
Nevada	1,191	78	38	8	20	12	87	24	22	11	30
New Hampshire....	1,039	46	17	4	9	15	79	17	20	11	31
New Jersey......	7,344	330	168	56	73	33	575	168	156	50	201
New Mexico	2,448	184	100	11	33	39	317	65	86	22	144
New York	28,364	1,172	624	162	280	106	1,586	657	328	144	458
North Carolina.....	7,084	494	263	49	94	88	536	147	124	76	190
North Dakota......	1,062	62	23	6	10	23	91	19	11	12	49
Ohio	9,708	519	243	87	117	72	789	284	164	113	228
Oklahoma........	3,191	276	134	28	54	59	306	91	56	35	125
Oregon.........	3,554	323	94	34	46	149	271	80	66	36	89
Pennsylvania.....	12,362	586	261	105	132	89	862	289	167	115	289
Rhode Island......	1,430	53	27	7	12	7	104	28	19	10	46
South Carolina.....	3,610	267	156	20	56	35	274	81	54	39	100
South Dakota	1,085	76	28	8	12	27	133	20	13	15	84
Tennessee	5,742	345	179	30	77	58	424	130	105	63	127
Texas..........	16,646	1,427	846	138	317	127	1,801	674	458	192	478
Utah	1,760	154	71	33	31	19	157	30	42	23	61
Vermont.........	941	48	15	10	9	15	75	19	14	12	31
Virginia.........	4,405	305	125	56	73	51	458	121	110	61	166
Washington.......	5,210	355	141	44	81	89	399	109	78	54	158
West Virginia......	2,315	141	66	10	28	37	193	74	33	27	59
Wisconsin........	4,439	259	112	37	55	55	429	132	84	62	152
Wyoming	894	37	15	2	7	13	80	17	18	8	36
Outlying areas	4,929	1,661	176	1,270	164	52	459	234	54	50	122
Puerto Rico	3,910	1,598	153	1,257	147	41	4	1	1	-	2

See footnotes at end of table.

U.S. Census Bureau, Statistical Abstract of the United States: 2000

No. 499. Federal Aid to State and Local Governments—Selected Programs by State: 1999—Continued

[In millions of dollars (2,693 represents $2,693,000,000). For fiscal year ending September 30]

State and outlying area	FEMA[5], total	Department of Housing and Urban Development							Department of Labor	
			Public housing programs						State unemployment insurance and employment service	Employment & Training Administration workforce Investment Act
		Total	Community development block grants	Low rent block	Section 8 programs	Housing certificate program	Capital programs	Other	Total[6]	
United States[4]	2,693	30,348	4,817	2,966	7,210	7,858	3,089	4,408	7,309	3,315	3,436
Alabama	63	422	65	77	75	74	74	57	98	42	51
Alaska	4	177	14	9	8	16	3	126	46	30	11
Arizona	11	324	52	24	48	71	15	114	114	43	65
Arkansas	16	189	23	19	43	57	20	27	65	32	25
California	548	3,423	634	110	860	1,121	162	536	1,195	487	625
Colorado	8	318	48	11	94	92	24	49	76	42	30
Connecticut	3	516	49	50	163	144	47	63	106	60	34
Delaware	3	81	6	9	32	17	5	12	23	14	6
District of Columbia	1	447	86	50	77	67	102	65	62	20	28
Florida	169	1,055	180	85	216	362	61	151	265	112	145
Georgia	55	753	112	99	132	184	131	93	142	70	56
Hawaii	5	156	17	10	29	56	25	19	50	20	24
Idaho	5	70	14	-	20	23	1	13	41	27	13
Illinois	44	1,692	249	244	487	314	219	179	314	156	129
Indiana	18	449	95	31	99	133	26	65	113	56	47
Iowa	21	178	47	1	52	50	4	24	66	33	25
Kansas	20	140	34	9	39	29	11	18	52	29	18
Kentucky	14	378	60	35	85	90	56	51	93	34	49
Louisiana	39	454	88	52	90	99	68	56	127	43	72
Maine	19	155	22	7	59	39	6	22	44	24	17
Maryland	6	627	69	68	178	157	53	101	129	67	53
Massachusetts	12	1,263	147	87	445	346	94	145	150	76	59
Michigan	26	817	150	54	251	142	91	130	222	126	77
Minnesota	72	470	92	29	137	97	50	66	102	57	29
Mississippi	29	241	43	20	61	60	26	30	64	27	35
Missouri	16	470	100	32	121	98	44	76	110	57	42
Montana	2	95	13	6	15	20	4	38	36	18	14
Nebraska	13	119	23	6	28	32	7	23	35	20	12
Nevada	5	121	13	14	30	35	8	21	55	34	17
New Hampshire	10	114	19	6	35	33	6	15	28	16	11
New Jersey	5	1,234	122	136	364	355	130	127	236	118	110
New Mexico	3	161	31	5	19	46	10	49	56	22	30
New York	62	4,042	407	710	806	1,084	614	421	484	212	247
North Carolina	72	586	91	73	117	153	58	95	161	79	64
North Dakota	87	134	81	3	13	19	1	17	26	15	10
Ohio	25	1,179	191	130	291	312	102	154	245	109	128
Oklahoma	43	373	54	20	56	76	17	150	85	35	42
Oregon	20	289	52	10	58	107	12	50	106	53	42
Pennsylvania	17	1,595	290	215	341	319	253	176	333	169	148
Rhode Island	-	209	17	17	89	51	11	23	34	20	12
South Carolina	6	294	50	26	71	85	22	39	88	39	38
South Dakota	13	118	30	2	21	17	1	47	22	12	9
Tennessee	39	493	67	80	101	113	61	71	103	41	51
Texas	112	1,504	310	89	245	492	137	231	434	163	252
Utah	8	103	23	3	24	30	4	20	62	46	12
Vermont	10	68	14	3	22	18	2	10	25	12	10
Virginia	18	542	80	52	175	133	36	65	137	68	59
Washington	33	464	86	25	63	153	36	102	206	95	92
West Virginia	14	177	35	13	59	39	11	20	65	21	37
Wisconsin	19	403	84	13	117	90	19	79	106	63	34
Wyoming	2	35	7	1	12	5	1	9	19	12	5
Outlying areas	727	628	129	87	134	103	106	69	217	40	163
Puerto Rico	671	556	127	62	129	86	90	61	178	34	134

See footnotes at end of table.

U.S. Census Bureau, Statistical Abstract of the United States: 2000

No. 499. Federal Aid to State and Local Governments—Selected Programs by State: 1999—Continued

[In millions of dollars (148,566 represents $148,566,000,000). For fiscal year ending September 30]

State and outlying area	Department of Health and Human Services						Department of Transportation				
		Administration for children									
	Total	Tempo-rary assis-tance to needy families	Chil-dren & family serv-ices (Head start)	Foster care and adop-tion assis-tance	Health care financ-ing admin-istration	Other	Total	High-way trust fund	Federal transit admin-istration	Other	Federal aid, other
United States [4]	148,566	13,653	5,492	4,706	108,569	16,146	29,523	22,662	4,569	2,291	14,524
Alabama	2,220	92	89	16	1,762	261	436	375	22	38	215
Alaska	492	57	28	13	297	97	341	236	10	95	237
Arizona	2,066	183	118	63	1,445	257	561	461	32	68	435
Arkansas	1,426	44	62	37	1,141	142	295	257	11	27	70
California	18,232	3,294	678	972	11,503	1,785	3,005	2,085	763	157	1,619
Colorado	1,348	50	69	48	941	240	469	313	107	49	287
Connecticut	2,186	257	48	114	1,589	179	414	350	55	9	107
Delaware	370	38	14	9	254	55	120	113	6	2	48
District of Columbia	1,019	79	60	36	640	204	171	75	92	4	1,141
Florida	5,825	577	211	157	4,025	855	1,085	778	212	96	521
Georgia	3,278	271	135	58	2,400	415	797	612	119	65	231
Hawaii	525	96	23	20	316	70	120	84	22	14	73
Idaho	520	20	28	10	392	70	187	162	6	20	94
Illinois	5,594	640	241	352	3,666	695	1,001	686	232	83	391
Indiana	2,528	168	84	64	1,924	288	582	491	53	38	160
Iowa	1,322	119	48	56	945	153	330	273	19	38	115
Kansas	1,112	154	63	29	749	116	354	325	16	14	113
Kentucky	2,546	155	95	52	2,016	228	405	318	32	56	196
Louisiana	2,950	84	123	72	2,398	273	419	348	36	35	183
Maine	956	58	26	34	765	73	162	135	18	9	87
Maryland	2,328	211	79	109	1,589	341	450	339	82	29	228
Massachusetts	4,056	472	105	95	3,029	355	814	610	181	23	342
Michigan	5,470	698	204	208	3,819	541	887	769	46	71	399
Minnesota	2,388	169	75	66	1,775	303	440	351	42	47	195
Mississippi	1,813	24	130	26	1,458	175	303	274	9	21	147
Missouri	3,006	233	102	80	2,280	311	602	454	109	38	217
Montana	419	25	29	10	297	57	278	252	5	21	136
Nebraska	853	76	34	24	622	97	202	174	8	19	98
Nevada	462	41	20	16	300	85	255	204	19	31	130
New Hampshire	541	31	15	15	416	63	139	120	4	15	82
New Jersey	3,832	218	116	62	2,962	474	886	512	340	35	245
New Mexico	1,129	100	53	21	838	116	264	235	6	23	334
New York	18,359	1,559	339	447	14,702	1,312	1,986	1,181	681	125	674
North Carolina	4,197	287	136	82	3,246	446	809	686	43	79	228
North Dakota	364	26	23	12	253	50	189	169	4	15	109
Ohio	5,782	417	218	310	4,186	650	834	637	128	69	335
Oklahoma	1,595	114	87	46	1,146	201	306	259	17	29	206
Oregon	1,810	166	69	45	1,316	214	440	321	92	27	295
Pennsylvania	7,448	725	202	347	5,449	724	1,137	816	200	121	384
Rhode Island	785	106	20	18	580	60	181	145	23	13	63
South Carolina	2,174	65	73	26	1,810	200	342	301	10	32	163
South Dakota	377	16	26	6	273	55	182	168	3	12	164
Tennessee	3,407	190	97	39	2,778	304	570	486	36	48	362
Texas	8,725	324	392	125	6,830	1,054	1,980	1,584	265	131	663
Utah	808	56	38	25	569	120	316	246	57	13	153
Vermont	441	42	17	16	316	51	198	124	68	6	76
Virginia	2,044	183	135	45	1,366	315	661	570	50	41	239
Washington	2,799	277	106	41	2,023	353	632	437	139	55	321
West Virginia	1,262	30	46	21	1,054	111	313	235	11	68	149
Wisconsin	2,491	231	93	102	1,739	326	506	432	35	39	225
Wyoming	195	-	16	4	143	32	205	190	3	12	322
Outlying areas	684	104	149	-	238	193	232	114	81	37	320
Puerto Rico	612	99	129	-	222	162	160	72	78	9	132

- Represents or rounds to zero. [1] Includes programs not shown separately. [2] Includes "special milk program." [3] For Puerto Rico, amount shown is for nutritional assistance grant program, all other amounts are grant payments for food stamp administration. [4] Includes undistributed amounts not shown separately. [5] FEMA = Federal Emergency Management Agency. [6] Includes other not shown separately.

Source: U.S. Census Bureau, Federal Aid to States For Fiscal Year 1999, Series FAS/99.

State and Local Government Finances and Employment 307

No. 500. State and Local Government Receipts and Current Expenditures in the National Income and Product Accounts: 1980 to 1999

[In billions of dollars (316.6 represents $316,600,000,000). For explanation of national income, see text, Section 14, Income, Expenditures, and Wealth]

Item	1980	1990	1991	1992	1993	1994	1995	1996	1997	1998	1999
Receipts	**316.6**	**663.4**	**716.0**	**772.2**	**823.2**	**873.8**	**917.9**	**960.4**	**1,009.0**	**1,070.4**	**1,140.2**
Personal tax and nontax											
receipts	53.9	136.0	145.3	156.4	164.7	174.8	186.5	199.6	217.4	236.9	251.9
Income taxes	42.6	107.7	112.6	119.6	126.0	133.4	142.5	152.9	168.0	184.7	196.8
Nontaxes	5.0	15.6	19.2	22.5	23.4	25.0	27.1	29.2	31.3	33.2	35.3
Other	6.3	12.8	13.4	14.3	15.3	16.4	17.0	17.5	18.2	19.0	19.7
Corporate profits tax accruals. . .	14.5	22.5	23.6	24.4	26.9	30.0	31.7	33.0	34.0	33.8	37.0
Indirect business tax and nontax											
accruals [1]	172.3	383.4	403.8	429.2	454.8	480.1	501.6	524.9	550.9	579.6	614.8
Sales taxes	82.9	183.2	190.0	202.2	216.0	230.9	243.6	255.6	269.3	284.3	307.2
Property taxes	68.8	161.1	172.8	182.8	191.1	197.6	203.5	211.4	218.7	225.5	234.5
Contributions for social											
insurance	3.6	10.0	11.6	13.1	14.1	14.5	13.6	12.5	11.0	10.7	11.1
Federal grants-in-aid	72.3	111.4	131.6	149.1	162.6	174.5	184.5	190.4	195.7	209.3	225.5
Current expenditures	**307.8**	**660.8**	**723.8**	**777.2**	**821.7**	**865.2**	**902.5**	**939.0**	**981.5**	**1,028.7**	**1,089.2**
Consumption expenditures	260.5	545.8	576.1	601.6	629.5	662.6	694.7	726.5	765.9	807.5	857.4
Transfer payments to persons . .	51.2	127.8	156.6	180.1	195.4	206.9	217.8	224.3	227.9	234.8	244.7
Net interest paid	-5.4	-6.3	-2.1	2.8	5.6	4.4	0.5	0.9	-0.6	-2.0	-0.7
Interest received by											
government	24.7	66.7	65.8	62.2	59.1	61.3	67.3	69.5	71.2	72.7	72.1
Less: Dividends received.	0.1	0.2	0.2	0.2	0.2	0.2	0.3	0.3	0.3	0.3	0.3
Subsidies	0.4	0.4	0.4	0.4	0.4	0.3	0.3	0.3	0.4	0.5	0.5
Less: Current surplus of											
government enterprises.	-1.2	6.7	7.0	7.6	8.9	8.8	10.5	12.8	11.8	11.7	12.3
Current surplus or deficit .	**8.8**	**2.6**	**-7.8**	**-4.9**	**1.5**	**8.6**	**15.3**	**21.4**	**27.5**	**41.7**	**51.0**
Social insurance funds	1.3	2.0	2.4	3.1	4.2	4.6	4.0	2.7	1.2	0.9	0.8
Other.	7.5	0.7	-10.2	-8.1	-2.7	4.0	11.4	18.7	26.4	40.8	50.2

[1] Includes other items not shown separately.

Source: U.S. Bureau of Economic Analysis, *National Income and Product Accounts of the United States, 1929-94*, Vol. 1, and *Survey of Current Business,* May 2000.

No. 501. State and Local Government Consumption Expenditures and Transfers in the National Income and Product Accounts: 1980 to 1999

[In billions of dollars (324.4 represents $324,400,000,000). For explanation of national income, see text, Section 14, Income, Expenditures, and Wealth]

Expenditure	1980	1985	1990	1993	1994	1995	1996	1997	1998	1999
Consumption expenditures and gross investment [1] . . .	**324.4**	**464.9**	**673.0**	**765.7**	**806.8**	**850.5**	**890.4**	**943.2**	**991.0**	**1059.4**
Consumption expenditures	260.5	380.5	545.8	629.5	662.6	694.7	726.5	765.9	807.5	857.4
Durable goods [2]	4.7	7.4	10.6	12.1	12.2	12.7	13.1	14.0	15.2	16.2
Nondurable goods	28.3	38.1	53.6	62.5	66.7	72.9	79.9	84.4	86.3	95.3
Services.	227.5	335.0	481.5	554.9	583.7	609.0	633.6	667.5	706.1	746.0
Gross investment	64.0	84.4	127.2	136.2	144.2	155.8	163.8	177.3	183.5	202.0
Structures.	55.1	67.6	98.5	104.5	108.7	117.3	122.5	132.8	135.2	149.7
Equipment	8.9	16.8	28.7	31.7	35.5	38.6	41.3	44.5	48.3	52.3
Transfers	**51.2**	**77.3**	**127.8**	**195.4**	**206.9**	**217.8**	**224.3**	**227.9**	**234.8**	**(NA)**
Benefits from social insurance										
funds.	2.8	4.9	9.2	11.4	11.0	10.7	10.9	10.9	10.8	(NA)
Temporary disability										
insurance	0.8	1.4	2.2	2.3	2.2	2.1	2.0	2.0	2.1	(NA)
Workers' compensation	2.0	3.5	7.0	9.1	8.8	8.6	8.9	8.8	8.7	(NA)
Public assistance.	44.0	67.2	111.1	174.9	185.8	195.8	201.9	205.2	211.2	(NA)
Medical care	24.9	42.4	78.2	135.1	144.9	155.0	163.6	168.7	174.0	(NA)
Medicaid										
Family Assistance [3]	12.5	15.2	19.2	22.8	23.2	22.6	20.3	17.6	17.1	(NA)
Supplemental Security										
Income	2.0	2.3	3.8	3.9	3.8	3.8	3.6	3.7	3.9	(NA)
General assistance	1.4	2.2	2.9	3.7	3.4	3.5	3.3	3.2	3.3	(NA)
Energy assistance	1.3	2.1	1.6	1.5	2.0	1.5	1.3	1.4	1.3	(NA)
Other [4]	1.7	3.0	5.4	7.8	8.6	9.4	9.7	10.7	11.5	(NA)
Education.	2.4	3.5	5.3	6.6	7.6	8.7	9.1	9.1	9.8	(NA)
Employment and training.	1.7	0.9	0.9	1.1	1.1	1.1	0.9	1.0	1.1	(NA)
Other [5]	0.3	0.7	1.2	1.4	1.4	1.5	1.6	1.7	1.8	(NA)

NA Not available. [1] Gross government investment consists of general government and government enterprise expenditures for fixed assets; inventory investment is included in government consumption expenditures. [2] Consumption expenditures for durable goods excludes expenditures classified as investment, except for goods transferred to foreign countries by the Federal Government. [3] Consists of aid to families with dependent children. Beginning with 1996, assistance programs operating under the Personal Responsibility and work opportunity Act of 1996. [4] Consists of emergency assistance and medical insurance premium payments paid on behalf of indigents. [5] Consists largely of foster care, veterans benefits, Alaska dividends, and crime victim payments.

Source: U.S. Bureau of Economic Analysis, *National Income and Product Accounts of the United States 1929-94*, Vol.1, and *Survey of Current Business,* May 2000.

No. 502. State and Local Governments—Summary of Finances: 1980 to 1996

[In millions of dollars (451,537 represents $451,537,000,000), except as indicated. For fiscal year ending in year shown; see text, this section. Local government amounts are estimates subject to sampling variation; see Appendix III and source]

Item	Total (mil. dol.)				Per capita [1] (dol.)			
	1980	1990	1995	1996	1980	1990	1995	1996
Revenue [2]................	451,537	1,032,115	1,417,925	1,513,633	1,993	4,150	5,396	5,708
From Federal Government	83,029	136,802	228,771	234,891	367	550	871	886
Public welfare.................	24,921	59,961	115,799	119,201	110	241	441	449
Highways...................	8,980	14,368	19,879	19,279	40	58	76	73
Education...................	14,435	23,233	34,045	36,224	64	93	130	137
Health and hospitals...........	2,513	5,904	11,113	11,915	11	24	42	45
Housing and community development .	3,905	9,655	15,255	15,585	17	39	58	59
Other and unallocable...........	28,275	23,683	32,681	32,687	125	95	124	123
From state and local sources	368,509	895,313	1,189,153	1,278,742	1,627	3,600	4,526	4,822
General, net intergovernmental......	299,293	712,700	940,733	987,930	1,321	2,865	3,580	3,725
Taxes..................	223,463	501,619	660,577	689,038	986	2,017	2,514	2,598
Property	68,499	155,613	203,451	209,440	302	626	774	790
Sales and gross receipts	79,927	177,885	237,268	248,993	353	715	903	939
Individual income	42,080	105,640	137,931	146,844	186	425	525	554
Corporation income	13,321	23,566	31,406	32,009	59	95	120	121
Other	19,636	38,915	50,521	51,752	87	156	192	195
Charges and miscellaneous	75,830	211,081	280,156	298,892	335	849	1,066	1,127
Utility and liquor stores	25,560	58,642	72,271	75,325	113	236	275	284
Water supply system...........	6,766	17,674	23,879	25,433	30	71	91	96
Electric power system	11,387	29,268	34,627	35,476	50	118	132	134
Transit system	2,397	5,216	6,540	6,889	11	21	25	26
Gas supply system	1,809	3,043	3,588	3,795	8	12	14	14
Liquor stores	3,201	3,441	3,637	3,732	14	14	14	14
Insurance trust revenue [3]	43,656	123,970	176,149	215,487	193	498	670	813
Employee retirement...........	25,441	94,268	122,595	165,411	112	379	467	624
Unemployment compensation.....	13,529	18,441	37,225	33,864	60	74	142	128
Direct expenditure............	432,328	972,662	1,347,763	1,393,714	1,908	3,911	5,129	5,256
By function:								
Direct general expenditure [3]........	367,340	834,786	1,146,188	1,189,356	1,622	3,356	4,362	4,485
Education [3]	133,211	288,148	378,273	398,859	588	1,159	1,440	1,504
Elementary and secondary	92,930	202,009	264,240	279,353	410	812	1,006	1,053
Higher education............	33,919	73,418	97,048	100,736	150	295	369	380
Highways	33,311	61,057	77,109	79,092	147	245	293	298
Public welfare	45,552	110,518	193,110	193,480	201	444	735	730
Health	8,387	24,223	38,020	40,166	37	97	145	151
Hospitals.................	23,787	50,412	67,926	70,648	105	203	259	266
Police protection.............	13,494	30,577	41,055	44,683	60	123	156	168
Fire protection	5,718	13,186	17,009	17,709	25	53	65	67
Natural resources	5,509	12,330	15,251	15,819	24	50	58	60
Sanitation and sewerage	13,214	28,453	38,573	39,365	58	114	147	148
Housing and community development	6,062	15,479	21,509	22,666	27	62	82	85
Parks and recreation..........	6,520	14,326	17,888	19,137	29	58	68	72
Financial administration	6,719	16,217	22,380	22,633	30	65	85	85
Interest on general debt [4]........	14,747	49,739	56,970	58,912	65	200	217	222
Utility and liquor stores [4]	36,191	77,801	94,235	95,608	160	313	359	361
Water supply system..........	9,228	22,101	28,041	28,950	41	89	107	109
Electric power system	15,016	30,997	34,021	34,084	66	125	129	129
Gas supply system	1,715	2,989	25,719	3,514	8	12	98	13
Transit system	7,641	18,788	3,434	25,961	34	76	13	98
Liquor stores	2,591	2,926	3,020	3,099	11	12	11	12
Insurance trust expenditure [3]	28,797	63,321	107,340	108,751	127	255	409	410
Employee retirement...........	14,008	38,355	61,427	68,010	56	154	234	256
Unemployment compensation.....	12,070	16,499	35,204	29,509	53	66	134	111
By character and object:								
Current operation.............	307,811	700,131	985,693	1,021,155	1,359	2,815	3,751	3,851
Capital outlay	62,894	123,069	151,440	158,911	278	495	576	599
Construction	51,492	89,114	110,012	116,076	227	358	419	438
Equipment, land, and existing structures	11,402	33,955	41,429	42,835	50	137	158	162
Assistance and subsidies	15,222	27,227	36,867	36,154	67	109	140	136
Interest on debt (general and utility) ...	17,604	58,914	66,423	68,743	78	237	253	259
Insurance benefits and repayments...	28,797	63,321	107,340	108,751	127	255	409	410
Expenditure for salaries and wages	*163,896*	*341,158*	*430,950*	*447,638*	*723*	*1,372*	*1,640*	*1,688*
Debt outstanding, year end	335,603	860,584	1,115,370	1,169,714	1,481	3,460	4,245	4,411
Long-term	322,456	841,278	1,088,331	1,145,666	1,423	3,382	4,142	4,320
Short-term	13,147	19,306	27,039	24,048	58	78	103	91
Long-term debt:								
Issued	42,364	108,468	129,337	141,087	187	436	492	532
Retired...................	17,404	64,831	95,070	106,501	77	261	362	402

[1] 1980 and 1990 based on enumerated resident population as of April 1. Other years based on estimated resident population as of July 1; see Table 2.   [2] Aggregates exclude duplicative transactions between state and local governments; see source.   [3] Includes amounts not shown separately.   [4] Interest on utility debt included in "utility expenditure." For total interest on debt, see "Interest on debt (general and utility)."

Source: U.S. Census Bureau, 1980-90, *Government Finances,* GF, No. 5, annual; thereafter, <http://www.census.gov/govs/www/estimate.html> (accessed 21 May 1999).

State and Local Government Finances and Employment **309**

No. 503. State and Local Governments—Revenue by State: 1996

[In millions of dollars ($1,513,633 represents $1,513,633,000,000). For fiscal year ending in year shown; see text, this section]

State		General revenue							
			Intergov-ernmental from Federal Govern-ment	Taxes			Charges and miscella-neous	Utility and liquor stores	Insurance trust revenue
	Total revenue [1]	Total		Total	Property	Sales and gross receipts			
United States..	1,513,633	1,222,821	234,891	689,038	209,440	248,993	298,892	75,326	215,487
Alabama.........	19,617	16,214	3,615	7,632	999	3,905	4,967	1,599	1,804
Alaska..........	10,002	8,332	1,121	2,301	680	239	4,910	223	1,446
Arizona.........	20,787	16,873	3,163	10,163	3,114	4,541	3,547	2,042	1,873
Arkansas	11,396	9,319	2,271	4,851	754	2,320	2,197	427	1,651
California	200,998	155,497	31,217	86,215	22,779	30,856	38,066	12,506	32,994
Colorado........	20,785	16,979	3,102	9,244	2,841	3,460	4,633	1,136	2,670
Connecticut......	20,766	18,164	3,015	12,543	4,657	3,932	2,607	388	2,214
Delaware	4,432	3,962	677	2,046	299	246	1,239	136	333
District of Columbia .	5,675	4,910	1,871	2,481	702	794	558	377	388
Florida	74,196	60,703	9,360	33,557	11,813	17,578	17,786	4,174	9,319
Georgia	38,006	31,283	5,805	17,309	4,793	6,822	8,169	2,282	4,441
Hawaii	7,821	6,641	1,342	3,842	613	1,992	1,458	175	1,004
Idaho	5,932	4,740	910	2,542	652	861	1,287	160	1,033
Illinois	63,909	52,928	9,332	32,660	12,510	10,969	10,937	2,239	8,741
Indiana.........	25,793	23,125	3,937	12,980	4,029	3,804	6,209	1,125	1,543
Iowa	14,320	12,715	2,303	6,983	2,384	2,243	3,429	565	1,041
Kansas.........	12,874	11,025	1,760	6,373	1,987	2,325	2,893	805	1,043
Kentucky	18,515	15,562	3,378	8,413	1,411	3,211	3,771	713	2,240
Louisiana	21,458	18,227	4,446	8,466	1,359	4,644	5,315	661	2,570
Maine..........	6,145	5,627	1,330	3,231	1,352	937	1,065	157	361
Maryland	25,843	22,571	3,666	14,132	3,795	3,765	4,774	570	2,702
Massachusetts.....	37,025	32,077	6,243	19,123	6,475	3,954	6,711	1,754	3,194
Michigan........	52,580	43,872	8,184	24,828	7,098	8,380	10,860	1,637	7,071
Minnesota.......	30,794	24,922	3,846	14,569	4,116	4,611	6,508	1,216	4,656
Mississippi	12,516	10,674	2,790	5,143	1,208	2,658	2,740	571	1,271
Missouri........	25,647	20,221	4,013	11,687	2,616	4,870	4,521	1,019	4,407
Montana........	4,505	3,802	1,044	1,782	776	269	976	96	606
Nebraska.......	9,898	7,440	1,291	4,181	1,579	1,401	1,967	1,821	638
Nevada	9,124	7,009	914	4,266	879	2,778	1,829	310	1,806
New Hampshire....	5,589	4,673	915	2,619	1,766	429	1,140	283	633
New Jersey......	53,661	43,694	6,713	27,449	12,815	7,394	9,532	1,164	8,803
New Mexico	10,147	8,086	1,925	3,877	474	2,083	2,283	250	1,811
New York	154,432	122,097	24,889	72,495	23,262	19,402	24,712	5,538	26,798
North Carolina....	35,885	29,864	5,800	16,486	3,458	6,115	7,578	2,658	3,363
North Dakota......	3,439	2,941	703	1,441	412	598	797	64	434
Ohio	64,538	48,318	9,567	27,961	7,967	8,621	10,789	2,072	14,149
Oklahoma.......	14,996	11,971	2,266	6,558	1,014	2,762	3,146	778	2,247
Oregon.........	22,126	16,018	3,926	7,238	2,332	740	4,855	816	5,291
Pennsylvania.....	64,439	52,534	10,574	30,280	8,689	9,037	11,680	2,466	9,439
Rhode Island......	5,769	4,714	1,154	2,711	1,151	784	850	96	958
South Carolina.....	18,369	15,096	3,276	7,328	1,953	2,709	4,492	1,573	1,700
South Dakota	3,446	2,903	754	1,439	558	696	711	135	408
Tennessee	27,197	20,027	4,964	9,992	2,266	6,075	5,071	4,629	2,540
Texas..........	89,318	74,847	13,787	40,705	15,248	20,642	20,355	5,029	9,442
Utah	10,459	8,434	1,910	4,294	1,008	1,787	2,231	1,171	854
Vermont........	3,189	2,869	765	1,518	680	406	586	144	176
Virginia.........	31,667	26,477	3,813	15,627	4,847	4,860	7,037	1,306	3,884
Washington......	37,557	26,810	4,400	15,467	4,673	9,347	6,943	3,281	7,466
West Virginia.....	8,746	7,590	2,164	3,643	727	1,490	1,784	151	1,004
Wisconsin.......	33,829	24,384	3,896	15,205	5,438	4,205	5,283	729	8,717
Wyoming........	3,478	3,058	784	1,165	435	443	1,110	106	314

[1] Includes items not shown separately.

Source: U.S. Census Bureau, <http://www.census.gov/govs/www/esti96.html> (accessed 26 April 1999).

U.S. Census Bureau, Statistical Abstract of the United States: 2000

No. 504. State and Local Governments—Expenditures and Debt by State: 1996

[In millions of dollars (1,397,634 represents $1,397,634,000,000), except as indicated. For fiscal year ending in year shown; see text, this section]

State	General expenditure										
	Total			Selected functions (direct expenditures)							
	Total expendi- ture[1]	Amount	Per capita[2] (dol.)	Direct expendi- tures	Educa- tion	Public welfare	Health and hospi- tals	High- ways	Police protec- tion	Utility expen- ditures	Debt outstand- ing
United States.	1,397,634	1,393,714	5,256	1,189,356	398,859	193,480	110,813	79,092	44,683	92,509	1,169,714
Alabama	19,303	19,303	4,498	16,585	5,796	2,366	2,980	1,147	502	1,529	11,615
Alaska	7,215	7,108	11,745	6,291	1,550	623	244	698	146	305	6,799
Arizona.	20,028	20,028	4,519	16,950	6,148	2,625	835	1,241	777	1,956	19,211
Arkansas.	9,661	9,659	3,856	8,679	3,164	1,587	876	823	254	399	5,812
California.	187,314	185,237	5,832	151,433	43,799	24,103	15,318	6,402	7,209	16,218	143,791
Colorado	19,204	19,197	5,033	16,193	6,072	2,144	1,072	1,177	600	1,456	19,254
Connecticut	19,797	19,797	6,065	17,478	5,332	2,817	1,339	1,017	560	556	25,571
Delaware.	4,218	4,217	5,800	3,783	1,362	463	207	339	128	151	5,508
District of Columbia.	5,817	5,817	10,780	4,184	669	1,172	432	89	248	1,138	4,137
Florida	68,581	68,580	4,754	60,773	18,027	7,383	6,011	4,580	3,034	4,712	65,164
Georgia	35,129	35,129	4,790	30,647	11,150	4,691	3,799	2,052	1,005	2,875	23,701
Hawaii	7,570	7,557	6,365	6,555	1,549	915	492	343	181	285	7,206
Idaho	5,073	5,073	4,277	4,545	1,810	560	402	439	154	108	2,323
Illinois.	59,756	59,754	5,007	50,951	17,013	8,831	3,644	3,602	2,278	3,394	52,419
Indiana	24,272	24,252	4,162	22,044	9,214	3,241	2,048	1,466	621	1,176	15,391
Iowa.	13,467	13,431	4,715	12,218	4,633	1,789	1,339	1,380	333	534	6,355
Kansas	12,214	12,214	4,725	10,826	4,247	1,133	997	1,338	364	762	8,051
Kentucky.	16,653	16,653	4,289	14,634	5,328	2,789	961	1,187	372	769	19,401
Louisiana	20,679	20,679	4,765	18,391	5,652	2,975	2,665	1,286	682	760	16,323
Maine.	6,006	5,999	4,846	5,402	1,788	1,275	292	488	129	93	4,681
Maryland.	24,711	24,711	4,886	21,728	7,724	2,963	1,031	1,306	895	811	22,249
Massachusetts . .	36,639	36,452	5,992	30,730	8,055	5,779	2,814	2,282	1,116	2,785	40,635
Michigan	49,070	49,002	5,034	43,425	17,242	6,768	4,131	2,363	1,461	1,415	31,611
Minnesota	27,891	27,891	6,000	24,715	8,252	4,670	2,253	1,949	652	1,245	22,067
Mississippi.	11,712	11,712	4,322	10,487	3,649	1,607	1,593	995	287	444	6,149
Missouri	21,614	21,614	4,026	19,176	7,132	2,949	1,739	1,566	720	1,160	13,873
Montana	4,199	4,199	4,790	3,723	1,469	525	221	416	102	69	2,928
Nebraska	8,986	8,977	5,447	6,941	2,827	1,018	621	719	177	1,801	6,222
Nevada.	7,951	7,946	4,965	6,867	2,035	698	586	682	342	355	8,166
New Hampshire .	5,192	5,192	4,478	4,724	1,625	1,030	128	333	146	69	6,937
New Jersey	49,032	48,973	6,116	42,022	14,576	7,095	2,021	2,576	1,797	2,079	41,630
New Mexico. . . .	8,598	8,598	5,034	7,818	2,614	1,170	794	839	282	261	5,427
New York	145,293	144,338	7,956	120,189	32,959	25,048	12,322	5,944	4,620	10,554	149,701
North Carolina . .	33,978	33,978	4,649	28,992	10,231	4,584	4,166	1,920	998	2,921	21,501
North Dakota . . .	2,958	2,958	4,602	2,662	1,020	395	80	282	54	88	1,742
Ohio.	55,041	55,038	4,927	45,854	16,628	7,904	3,781	2,821	1,723	2,089	28,954
Oklahoma	13,568	13,527	4,104	11,630	4,525	1,627	1,225	944	402	755	8,967
Oregon	18,459	18,459	5,777	15,090	5,296	2,127	1,256	1,072	532	1,102	12,450
Pennsylvania . . .	60,353	60,227	5,005	51,091	18,025	9,861	3,209	2,968	1,735	2,975	58,490
Rhode Island . . .	5,582	5,562	5,629	4,780	1,496	867	335	265	164	116	6,518
South Carolina . .	17,864	17,864	4,780	15,036	5,289	2,560	2,669	724	448	1,763	12,102
South Dakota . . .	3,082	3,082	4,181	2,833	951	409	143	385	80	111	2,406
Tennessee.	25,759	25,759	4,854	19,975	6,378	3,770	2,569	1,490	660	4,621	22,490
Texas	83,495	83,495	4,387	72,366	27,859	10,243	7,866	5,125	2,582	6,209	75,988
Utah.	9,883	9,882	4,887	8,259	3,428	961	557	544	265	1,115	11,479
Vermont	2,905	2,893	4,934	2,627	1,043	505	65	268	67	122	2,257
Virginia	29,030	29,030	4,354	26,135	10,023	3,288	1,912	2,264	910	1,261	24,233
Washington	34,611	34,581	6,266	27,018	9,428	3,800	2,520	1,995	806	3,967	31,770
West Virginia . . .	8,437	8,437	4,635	7,342	2,653	1,589	438	745	133	130	6,499
Wisconsin	26,742	26,610	5,143	23,862	9,154	3,928	1,437	1,915	873	850	19,692
Wyoming.	3,043	3,042	6,336	2,695	969	256	378	303	78	89	1,870

[1] Includes items not shown separately.   [2] Based on estimated resident population as of July 1.

Source: U.S. Census Bureau, <http://www.census.gov/govs/www/esti96.html> (accessed 17 June 1999).

State and Local Government Finances and Employment   311

No. 505. State and Local Governments—Per Capita Summary of Finances by State: 1996

[In millions of dollars (1,513,633 represents $1,513,633,000,000), except as indicated. For fiscal year ending in year shown; see text, this section]

State	Revenue [1] All revenue	Per capita [2] (dol.)	General revenue	Per capita [2] (dol.)	Intergovernmental From state/local sources	Per capita [2] (dol.)	Expenditures [1] Direct general expenditures	Per capita [2] (dol.)	Debt outstanding Total	Per capita [2] (dol.)
United States..	1,513,633	5,708	1,222,821	4,611	987,930	3,725	1,189,356	4,485	1,169,714	4,411
Alabama.........	19,617	4,572	16,214	3,779	12,599	2,936	16,585	3,865	11,615	2,707
Alaska..........	10,002	16,526	8,332	13,767	7,211	11,915	6,291	10,395	6,799	11,234
Arizona.........	20,787	4,690	16,873	3,807	13,709	3,093	16,950	3,824	19,211	4,334
Arkansas........	11,396	4,549	9,319	3,720	7,047	2,813	8,679	3,465	5,812	2,320
California	200,998	6,328	155,497	4,896	124,281	3,913	151,433	4,768	143,791	4,527
Colorado........	20,785	5,450	16,979	4,452	13,877	3,639	16,193	4,246	19,254	5,048
Connecticut......	20,766	6,362	18,164	5,565	15,150	4,642	17,478	5,355	25,571	7,834
Delaware	4,432	6,095	3,962	5,450	3,285	4,518	3,783	5,203	5,508	7,575
District of Columbia .	5,675	10,516	4,910	9,099	3,039	5,631	4,184	7,752	4,137	7,665
Florida	74,196	5,144	60,703	4,208	51,343	3,559	60,773	4,213	65,164	4,517
Georgia	38,006	5,182	31,283	4,265	25,477	3,474	30,647	4,179	23,701	3,232
Hawaii	7,821	6,587	6,641	5,594	5,300	4,464	6,555	5,521	7,206	6,069
Idaho..........	5,932	5,001	4,740	3,996	3,829	3,228	4,545	3,832	2,323	1,958
Illinois	63,909	5,355	52,928	4,435	43,596	3,653	50,951	4,270	52,419	4,393
Indiana.........	25,793	4,426	23,125	3,968	19,188	3,293	22,044	3,783	15,391	2,641
Iowa	14,320	5,027	12,715	4,463	10,412	3,655	12,218	4,289	6,355	2,231
Kansas.........	12,874	4,981	11,025	4,266	9,266	3,585	10,826	4,188	8,051	3,115
Kentucky	18,515	4,769	15,562	4,008	12,184	3,138	14,634	3,769	19,401	4,997
Louisiana	21,458	4,944	18,227	4,200	13,781	3,175	18,391	4,238	16,323	3,761
Maine..........	6,145	4,963	5,627	4,545	4,296	3,470	5,402	4,363	4,681	3,781
Maryland	25,843	5,110	22,571	4,463	18,906	3,738	21,728	4,296	22,249	4,399
Massachusetts.....	37,025	6,087	32,077	5,273	25,834	4,247	30,730	5,052	40,635	6,680
Michigan........	52,580	5,402	43,872	4,507	35,688	3,666	43,425	4,461	31,611	3,248
Minnesota.......	30,794	6,625	24,922	5,362	21,077	4,535	24,715	5,317	22,067	4,747
Mississippi	12,516	4,618	10,674	3,939	7,884	2,909	10,487	3,870	6,149	2,269
Missouri........	25,647	4,777	20,221	3,766	16,208	3,019	19,176	3,572	13,873	2,584
Montana........	4,505	5,138	3,802	4,337	2,758	3,146	3,723	4,247	2,928	3,339
Nebraska	9,898	6,006	7,440	4,514	6,149	3,731	6,941	4,211	6,222	3,775
Nevada	9,124	5,701	7,009	4,379	6,095	3,808	6,867	4,291	8,166	5,103
New Hampshire....	5,589	4,820	4,673	4,030	3,758	3,241	4,724	4,074	6,937	5,983
New Jersey......	53,661	6,701	43,694	5,456	36,981	4,618	42,022	5,248	41,630	5,199
New Mexico	10,147	5,941	8,086	4,734	6,160	3,607	7,818	4,578	5,427	3,178
New York	154,432	8,512	122,097	6,730	97,207	5,358	120,189	6,625	149,701	8,252
North Carolina....	35,885	4,910	29,864	4,086	24,064	3,293	28,992	3,967	21,501	2,942
North Dakota.....	3,439	5,350	2,941	4,575	2,238	3,482	2,662	4,141	1,742	2,709
Ohio	64,538	5,778	48,318	4,326	38,751	3,469	45,854	4,105	28,954	2,592
Oklahoma........	14,996	4,550	11,971	3,632	9,705	2,944	11,630	3,529	8,967	2,721
Oregon.........	22,126	6,924	16,018	5,013	12,093	3,784	15,090	4,723	12,450	3,896
Pennsylvania.....	64,439	5,355	52,534	4,366	41,960	3,487	51,091	4,246	58,490	4,860
Rhode Island.....	5,769	5,838	4,714	4,771	3,561	3,603	4,780	4,837	6,518	6,596
South Carolina....	18,369	4,915	15,096	4,040	11,820	3,163	15,036	4,024	12,102	3,238
South Dakota	3,446	4,674	2,903	3,938	2,149	2,915	2,833	3,843	2,406	3,263
Tennessee	27,197	5,124	20,027	3,774	15,064	2,838	19,975	3,764	22,490	4,238
Texas..........	89,318	4,693	74,847	3,932	61,059	3,208	72,366	3,802	75,988	3,992
Utah	10,459	5,172	8,434	4,171	6,524	3,226	8,259	4,084	11,479	5,676
Vermont........	3,189	5,439	2,869	4,894	2,104	3,588	2,627	4,481	2,257	3,849
Virginia.........	31,667	4,749	26,477	3,971	22,663	3,399	26,135	3,920	24,233	3,635
Washington.......	37,557	6,805	26,810	4,858	22,410	4,061	27,018	4,896	31,770	5,757
West Virginia......	8,746	4,805	7,590	4,170	5,427	2,981	7,342	4,034	6,499	3,571
Wisconsin........	33,829	6,538	24,384	4,712	20,488	3,960	23,862	4,612	19,692	3,806
Wyoming	3,478	7,246	3,058	6,371	2,275	4,738	2,695	5,613	1,870	3,896

[1] Includes items not shown separately.   [2] Based on estimated resident population as of July 1.

Source: U.S. Census Bureau, <http://www.census.gov/govs/www/esti96.html> (accessed 17 June 1999); and unpublished data.

No. 506. Long-Term Municipal New Issues for State and Local Governments: 1980 to 1999

[In billions of dollars (45.6 represents $45,600,000,000)]

Item	1980	1985	1990	1993	1994	1995	1996	1997	1998	1999
Long-term municipal new issues [1]	**45.6**	**202.4**	**125.9**	**289.9**	**162.2**	**156.2**	**181.4**	**214.3**	**279.7**	**219.2**
General obligation	13.7	39.6	40.2	91.4	55.6	60.2	64.2	72.2	92.6	69.8
Revenue	31.9	162.8	85.7	198.5	106.7	96.0	117.3	142.1	187.1	149.4
Competitive	19.3	27.8	30.2	55.6	49.5	41.0	47.0	47.8	65.2	52.8
Negotiated	26.4	174.6	95.9	234.3	112.8	115.4	134.4	166.5	214.5	166.4
States with largest issuance: [2]										
California	3.6	25.3	15.7	38.3	25.4	20.2	24.9	27.7	33.9	26.5
New York	2.9	12.7	16.9	30.7	18.8	18.8	20.8	27.4	36.3	19.8
Texas	3.8	21.2	6.5	16.3	10.3	10.4	11.6	15.3	18.1	17.7
Florida	2.2	13.2	5.9	17.7	7.7	9.1	10.0	10.5	14.7	10.8
Illinois	2.3	9.2	6.3	11.7	7.9	6.6	8.8	9.6	10.1	12.4
All others	30.8	120.8	74.6	175.2	92.1	91.1	105.3	123.8	166.6	132.0
Type of issuer: [3]										
City, town, or village	8.5	36.5	22.7	51.3	26.6	27.9	30.3	34.8	44.3	33.0
College or university	0.2	2.9	1.5	4.7	2.4	2.5	4.5	3.3	4.6	4.1
County/parish	4.6	15.8	10.0	24.4	17.2	13.3	16.8	15.5	21.2	17.1
Direct issuer	-	0.4	0.2	0.8	0.6	0.4	1.0	0.8	2.1	2.0
District	3.9	15.6	15.2	38.2	21.7	22.4	27.5	33.7	43.6	34.1
Local authority	9.2	51.1	20.7	56.5	26.3	27.9	33.7	41.5	53.9	43.2
State authority	14.1	68.1	40.6	85.7	47.6	47.2	53.2	66.0	85.2	68.1
State	5.1	12.1	15.0	28.2	19.8	14.6	14.3	18.7	24.7	17.6
Refunding	1.6	70.5	25.3	194.6	49.8	47.5	605.2	81.2	120.8	66.3
New capital	45.6	202.4	125.9	289.9	162.3	156.2	181.4	214.3	279.7	219.2
General use of proceeds:										
Airports	0.4	3.0	5.2	5.7	4.3	4.7	5.2	6.4	10.2	5.5
Combined utilities	0.3	2.4	1.0	1.9	1.2	0.7	1.2	1.5	1.8	1.0
Economic development	0.2	2.5	2.1	6.0	4.2	2.5	1.8	2.9	3.5	3.6
Education	4.0	20.4	20.5	43.4	26.9	28.5	35.0	42.7	56.5	47.6
Health care	3.1	30.0	12.6	29.2	13.8	11.5	16.6	22.1	33.4	22.0
Industrial development	1.0	2.9	1.9	2.4	2.1	3.2	2.8	3.5	3.6	3.5
Multifamily housing	2.5	20.2	3.1	6.2	4.9	6.1	6.7	5.4	6.4	6.1
Nursing homes/life care retirement	0.3	1.2	1.6	2.5	2.4	1.9	3.0	3.6	4.8	4.9
Other miscellaneous	11.1	37.3	36.2	82.7	48.8	44.2	55.2	57.0	71.5	58.4
Pollution control	2.3	10.0	2.5	8.1	7.0	5.0	5.5	5.6	9.7	8.9
Electric & public power	4.4	23.2	5.2	27.8	6.3	4.8	5.7	6.5	15.6	4.9
Single family housing	10.6	16.4	12.5	8.2	10.5	10.0	10.4	13.6	12.9	12.6
Solid waste/resource recovery	0.4	3.8	3.0	5.1	3.8	3.3	2.2	3.6	2.4	1.2
Student loans	0.2	4.0	0.4	4.8	3.3	4.4	4.2	3.9	4.9	5.3
Transportation	1.3	11.0	7.6	21.0	9.4	11.3	10.3	16.6	20.5	16.0
Water, sewer, and gas facilities	3.1	13.4	9.3	33.2	12.5	13.2	14.3	18.2	20.9	16.4
Waterfront/seaports	0.5	1.5	0.5	1.6	0.8	0.8	1.3	1.2	0.9	1.2

- Represents or rounds to zero.   [1] Excludes issues with a final maturity of less than 13 months, private placements, and not-for-profit cooperative utilities.   [2] Ranked by 1997 Long-Term Municipal New Issue Volume.   [3] Includes outlying areas.

Source: Thomson Financial Securities Data Company, Newark, NJ, Municipal New Issues Database (copyright).

No. 507. State and Local Governments—Indebtedness: 1980 to 1996

[In billions of dollars (335.6 represents $335,600,000,000), except per capita. For fiscal year ending in year shown; see text, this section. Local government amounts are estimates subject to sampling variation; see Appendix III and source]

Item		Debt outstanding					Long term		
	Total	Per capita [1] (dol.)	Long term			Short term	Net long term	Debt issued	Debt retired
			Local schools [2]	Utilities	All other				
1980: Total	335.6	1,481	32.3	55.2	235.0	13.1	262.9	42.4	17.4
State	122.0	540	3.8	4.6	111.5	2.1	79.8	16.4	5.7
Local	213.6	943	28.5	50.6	123.5	11.0	183.1	25.9	11.7
1985: Total	568.6	2,390	43.8	90.8	414.5	19.6	430.5	101.2	43.5
State	211.9	893	6.7	8.6	193.8	2.8	110.4	41.7	16.4
Local	356.7	1,499	37.1	82.2	220.6	16.8	320.1	59.5	27.2
1990: Total	860.6	3,459	60.4	134.8	646.1	19.3	477.0	108.5	64.8
State	318.3	1,282	4.4	12.3	298.8	2.8	125.5	43.5	22.9
Local	542.3	2,180	56.0	122.4	347.4	16.5	351.5	65.0	42.0
1993: Total	1,016.2	3,943	89.2	157.6	746.8	22.6	617.1	195.0	146.3
State	389.7	1,515	9.4	14.8	361.7	3.9	176.9	77.1	60.7
Local	628.0	2,437	79.8	142.7	385.2	18.9	440.2	118.4	86.3
1994: Total	1,074.7	4,129	143.5	164.9	438.0	26.7	672.8	207.8	166.6
State	411.0	1,582	10.4	16.7	162.0	4.9	200.8	78.5	61.3
Local	663.7	2,550	86.2	148.2	276.0	21.8	472.0	129.3	105.3
1995: Total	1,115.3	4,244	118.2	163.9	756.0	27.0	835.3	129.3	95.1
State	427.2	1,629	11.3	17.0	345.0	6.1	205.3	52.6	37.5
Local	688.1	2,619	107.0	146.9	411.0	20.9	629.9	76.8	57.6
1996: Total	1,169.7	4,411	130.7	170.3	868.8	24.0	890.2	141.1	106.5
State	452.4	1,709	11.2	16.3	424.9	5.8	224.4	60.2	42.4
Local	717.3	2,705	119.5	154.0	443.8	18.2	665.7	80.9	64.1

[1] 1980 and 1990 based on enumerated resident population as of April 1; other years based on estimated resident population as of July 1; see Table 2.   [2] Includes debt for education activities other than higher education.

Source: U.S. Census Bureau, 1980-90, State and Local Government Finance Estimates, annual; thereafter, <http://www.census.gov/govs/www/estimate.html> (accessed 21 May 1999).

State and Local Government Finances and Employment   313

No. 508. Bond Ratings for State Governments by State: 1999

[As of fourth quarter. Key to investment grade ratings is in declining order of quality. The ratings from AA to CCC may be modified by the addition of a plus or minus sign to show relative standing within the major rating categories. **S&P:** AAA, AA, A, BBB, BB, B, CCC, CC, C; **Moody's:** Aaa, Aa, A, Baa, Ba, B, Caa, Ca, C; Numerical modifiers 1, 2, and 3 are added to letter-rating. **Fitch:** AAA, AA, A, BBB, BB, B, CCC, CC, C]

State	Standard & Poor's	Moody's	Fitch	State	Standard & Poor's	Moody's	Fitch
Alabama	AA	Aa3	AA	Montana	AA-	Aa3	[1]
Alaska	[1]	Aa2	AA	Nebraska	[1]	[1]	[1]
Arizona	[1]	[1]	[1]	Nevada	AA	Aa2	AA
Arkansas	AA	Aa3	[1]	New Hampshire	AA+	Aa2	AA+
California	AA-	Aa3	AA-	New Jersey	AA+	Aa1	AA+
Colorado	[1]	[1]	[1]	New Mexico	AA+	Aa1	[1]
Connecticut	AA	Aa3	AA	New York	A+	A2	A+
Delaware	AAA	Aa1	[1]	North Carolina	AAA	Aaa	AAA
Florida	AA+	Aa2	AA	North Dakota	[1]	Aa3	[1]
Georgia	AAA	Aaa	AAA	Ohio	AA+	Aa1	AA+
Hawaii	A+	A1	AA-	Oklahoma	AA	Aa3	AA
Idaho	[1]	[1]	[1]	Oregon	AA	Aa2	AA
Illinois	AA	Aa2	AA	Pennsylvania	AA	Aa3	AA
Indiana	AA+	[1]	[1]	Rhode Island	AA-	Aa3	AA
Iowa	[1]	[1]	[1]	South Carolina	AAA	Aaa	AAA
Kansas	AA+	[1]	[1]	South Dakota	[1]	[1]	[1]
Kentucky	AA	[1]	[1]	Tennessee	AAA	Aaa	AAA
Louisiana	A-	A2	A	Texas	AA	Aa1	AA+
Maine	AA+	Aa2	AA	Utah	AAA	Aaa	AAA
Maryland	AAA	Aaa	AAA	Vermont	AA	Aa1	AA+
Massachusetts	AA-	Aa2	AA-	Virginia	AAA	Aaa	AAA
Michigan	AA+	Aa1	AA+	Washington	AA+	Aa1	AA+
Minnesota	AAA	Aaa	AAA	West Virginia	AA-	Aa3	AA-
Mississippi	AA	Aa3	AA	Wisconsin	AA	Aa2	AA+
Missouri	AAA	Aaa	AAA	Wyoming	AA	[1]	[1]

[1] Not reviewed.

Sources: Standard & Poor's, New York, NY; Moody's Investors Service, New York, NY (copyright); and Fitch IBCA, New York, NY (copyright).

No. 509. Bond Ratings for City Governments by Largest Cities: 1999

[As of fourth quarter. For key to ratings, see headnote in table above]

Cities ranked by 1998 population	Standard & Poor's	Moody's	Fitch IBCA	Cities ranked by 1998 population	Standard & Poor's	Moody's	Fitch IBCA
New York, NY	A-	A3	A	Fresno, CA	A+	[1]	[1]
Los Angeles, CA	AA	Aa2	AA	Honolulu, HI	AA-	Aa3	AA
Chicago, IL	A+	A1	AA-	Tulsa, OK	AA	Aa2	[1]
Houston, TX	AA-	Aa3	AA	Omaha, NE	AAA	Aaa	[1]
Philadelphia, PA	BBB	Baa2	AAA	Miami, FL	BB	Ba1	A+
San Diego, CA	AA	Aa1	AA+	Oakland, CA	A+	A1	A+
Phoenix, AZ	AA+	Aa1	[1]	Mesa, AZ	AA-	A1	AAA
San Antonio, TX	AA+	Aa2	[1]	Minneapolis, MN	AAA	Aaa	[1]
Dallas, TX	AAA	Aaa	[1]	Colorado Springs, CO	AA	Aa3	[1]
Detroit, MI	A-	Baa1	AAA	Pittsburgh, PA	BBB	Baa1	BBB+
San Jose, CA	[1]	[1]	[1]	St. Louis, MO	A-	A3	[1]
San Francisco, CA	AA-	Aa3	AA	Cincinnati, OH	AA+	Aa1	[1]
Indianapolis, IN	AAA	Aaa	AAA	Wichita, KS	AA	Aa2	[1]
Jacksonville, FL	[1]	Aa2	AA	Toledo, OH	A	A3	[1]
Columbus, OH	AAA	Aaa	[1]	Arlington, TX	AA	Aa3	[1]
Baltimore, MD	A	A1	A+	Santa Ana, CA	[1]	[1]	[1]
El Paso, TX	AA	Aa3	AAA	Buffalo, NY	BBB	Baa2	[1]
Memphis, TN	AA	Aa2	AA	Anaheim, CA	AA	Aa2	[1]
Milwaukee, WI	AA+	Aa1	AA+	Tampa, FL	[1]	[1]	[1]
Boston, MA	AA-	Aa3	AA-	Corpus Christi, TX	A+	A3	[1]
Austin, TX	AA	Aa2	[1]	Newark, NJ	BBB+	Baa1	[1]
Seattle, WA	AA+	Aaa	[1]	Riverside, CA	[1]	[1]	[1]
Washington, DC	BBB	Baa3	BBB	Raleigh, NC	AAA	Aaa	AAA
Nashville-Davidson, TN	AA	Aa2	[1]	St. Paul, MN	AA+	Aa2	AA+
Charlotte, NC	AAA	Aaa	[1]	Louisville, KY	AA-	Aa3	[1]
Portland, OR	[1]	Aaa	[1]	Anchorage, AK	AA-	Aa3	[1]
Denver, CO	AA+	Aa2	AA	Birmingham, AL	AA	Aa3	AA
Cleveland, OH	A+	A2	A	Aurora, CO	AA-	Aa3	AAA
Fort Worth, TX	AA	Aa2	[1]	Lexington-Fayette, KY	AA+	[1]	[1]
Oklahoma City, OK	AA	Aa2	[1]	Stockton CA	[1]	[1]	[1]
New Orleans, LA	BBB+	Baa2	[1]	St. Petersburg, FL	A+	[1]	[1]
Tucson, AZ	AA	Aa3	[1]	Jersey City, NJ	BBB	Baa3	[1]
Kansas City, MO	AA	Aa3	[1]	Rochester, NY	AA	A1	[1]
Virginia Beach, VA	AA	Aa1	AA+	Akron, OH	AA-	A1	AA-
Long Beach, CA	AA-	[1]	[1]	Norfolk, VA	AA	A1	[1]
Albuquerque, NM	AA	Aa3	AA	Baton Rouge, LA	[1]	[1]	[1]
Sacramento, CA	AA	Aa2	[1]	Mobile, AL	A+	A2	[1]
Atlanta, GA	AA	Aa3	[1]	Richmond, VA	AA	A1	AA

[1] Not reviewed.

Sources: Standard & Poor's, New York, NY; Moody's Investors Service, New York, NY (copyright); and Fitch IBCA, New York, NY (copyright).

No. 510. State Resources, Expenditures, and Balances: 1999 and 2000

[In millions of dollars (900,613 represents $900,613,000,000). For fiscal year ending in year shown; see text; this section. **General funds** exclude special funds earmarked for particular purposes, such as highway trust funds and Federal funds; they support most on-going broad-based state services and are available for appropriation to support any governmental activity. Minus sign (-) indicates deficit]

State	Expenditures by fund source					State general fund					
	Total, 1999	2000 [1]				Resources [3][4]		Expenditures [4]		Balance [5]	
		Total [2]	General fund	Federal funds	Other state funds	1999	2000 [1]	1999	2000 [1]	1999	2000 [1]
Total	**900,613**	**981,702**	**455,315**	**249,120**	**252,948**	**500,248**	**522,447**	**471,990**	**504,540**	**25,106**	**16,699**
United States	**881,435**	**961,769**	**448,232**	**245,300**	**244,393**	**493,382**	**515,251**	**465,276**	**497,426**	**24,953**	**16,617**
Alabama	13,675	16,725	5,238	5,810	5,377	4,991	5,276	4,919	5,238	72	38
Alaska	5,092	5,165	2,255	1,724	1,186	2,294	305	2,294	2,289	[6]-	[6]-1,984
Arizona	14,803	15,313	5,918	3,895	4,952	6,142	6,198	5,886	6,023	255	175
Arkansas	9,463	10,368	3,175	2,284	4,799	3,050	3,175	3,009	3,175	40	-
California	109,635	124,213	65,856	38,632	16,263	61,535	68,869	57,827	65,856	[6]3,708	[6]3,012
Colorado	6,523	5,097	3,348	1,295	454	6,525	6,685	5,845	5,981	[6]679	[6]704
Connecticut	14,772	14,715	10,599	1,057	1,922	10,616	10,959	10,545	10,718	72	241
Delaware	4,701	5,000	2,306	712	1,864	2,506	2,306	2,153	2,323	[6]305	[6]221
Florida	46,213	48,653	18,705	9,891	18,753	18,318	18,815	17,952	18,815	366	-
Georgia	24,218	23,002	12,184	6,336	3,935	14,174	14,369	13,013	14,203	1,161	166
Hawaii	6,496	6,824	3,168	1,094	2,189	3,440	3,439	3,251	3,182	189	257
Idaho	3,372	3,811	1,685	1,194	927	1,657	1,693	1,611	1,685	47	8
Illinois	31,416	45,718	17,062	8,450	15,722	22,876	24,293	21,525	22,943	1,351	1,350
Indiana	15,014	16,867	7,867	4,844	4,068	10,500	10,729	8,474	9,105	1,467	1,076
Iowa	10,649	11,609	4,778	2,761	4,070	4,810	4,865	4,526	4,770	284	114
Kansas	8,306	8,392	4,430	2,002	1,856	4,737	4,707	4,196	4,389	541	318
Kentucky	14,635	15,712	6,638	4,679	4,395	6,593	6,701	6,537	6,454	64	183
Louisiana	14,984	16,173	5,916	4,612	5,569	5,830	5,823	5,818	5,822	-30	1
Maine	4,479	5,250	2,345	1,595	1,216	2,276	2,612	2,154	2,316	229	297
Maryland	17,116	18,178	8,940	3,853	4,761	9,118	9,835	8,535	9,019	583	816
Massachusetts	24,267	25,682	17,130	5,620	1,932	19,328	20,099	18,370	19,694	215	109
Michigan	33,180	34,915	9,230	9,503	15,897	9,667	9,528	9,422	9,267	[6]-	[6]21
Minnesota	17,592	18,897	11,958	3,924	2,705	12,902	13,957	10,981	11,588	[6]1,921	[6]2,370
Mississippi	8,149	10,132	3,461	3,452	3,015	3,382	3,557	3,138	3,468	124	39
Missouri	15,228	16,674	7,088	4,633	4,871	7,427	7,380	7,063	7,088	364	292
Montana	2,615	2,957	1,105	1,148	704	1,149	1,256	1,039	1,091	110	165
Nebraska	5,358	4,730	2,345	1,216	1,169	2,526	2,575	2,233	2,324	293	120
Nevada	6,947	7,172	1,568	959	4,566	1,721	1,703	1,623	1,601	98	102
New Hampshire	2,549	3,409	1,000	937	1,405	935	1,028	935	1,048	-	-20
New Jersey	26,788	29,367	19,424	6,176	2,872	19,422	20,636	18,070	19,462	[6]1,267	[6]1,174
New Mexico	7,803	7,794	2,660	2,075	2,699	3,402	3,547	3,217	3,404	[6]185	[6]143
New York	74,482	78,369	35,771	22,827	17,910	37,379	38,233	36,487	37,063	[6]892	[6]1,170
North Carolina	23,810	24,413	13,973	5,951	3,839	13,477	14,147	12,962	14,146	297	1
North Dakota	2,123	2,191	772	806	570	837	814	758	773	62	41
Ohio	36,210	43,471	19,339	6,124	16,899	19,204	19,772	18,017	19,339	221	345
Oklahoma	10,000	11,387	4,525	3,335	3,437	4,694	4,844	4,460	4,545	234	299
Oregon	12,891	14,519	4,860	2,748	6,911	4,677	5,345	4,128	4,861	549	484
Pennsylvania	36,863	39,689	19,279	11,899	7,596	18,966	19,701	18,368	19,279	448	444
Rhode Island	4,042	4,616	2,135	1,339	1,035	2,151	2,276	2,036	2,231	114	44
South Carolina	11,121	13,330	4,945	3,532	4,528	5,447	5,798	4,724	5,334	[6]723	[6]464
South Dakota	1,959	2,134	751	822	560	767	785	734	767	-	-
Tennessee	15,722	16,468	7,025	6,250	3,069	6,394	6,820	6,278	6,735	90	47
Texas	44,700	49,641	27,389	14,118	7,982	56,418	57,699	52,939	57,675	3,479	24
Utah	6,543	6,490	3,367	1,489	1,511	3,256	3,364	3,248	3,364	7	-
Vermont	2,020	2,242	833	852	556	840	854	840	854	-	-
Virginia	21,535	23,068	10,288	3,704	8,665	10,679	11,781	10,194	11,272	485	510
Washington	20,357	22,339	10,236	5,315	5,825	10,288	10,632	9,826	10,159	462	474
West Virginia	6,067	6,084	2,192	2,210	1,409	2,767	2,820	2,606	2,804	156	2
Wisconsin	22,797	20,611	10,612	5,076	4,923	10,722	11,987	10,009	11,328	[6]701	[6]659
Wyoming	2,155	2,153	558	540	1,055	575	661	502	558	[6]73	[6]103
Puerto Rico	19,178	19,933	7,083	3,820	8,555	6,866	7,196	6,714	7,114	153	82

- Represents zero. [1] Estimated. [2] Includes bonds not shown separately. [3] Includes funds budgeted, adjustments, and balances from previous year. [4] May or may not include budget stabilization fund transfers, depending on state accounting practices. [5] Resources less expenditures. Total excludes Puerto Rico. [6] Ending balance includes the balance in a budget stabilization fund.

Source: Expenditures by fund from National Association of State Budget Officers, Washington, DC, *1999 State Expenditure Report*, and *State General Fund from National Governors' Association and NASBO, Fiscal Survey of the States*, semiannual (copyright).

State and Local Government Finances and Employment 315

No. 511. State Governments—Summary of Finances: 1980 to 1998

[In millions of dollars (293,356 represents $293,356,000,000), except where indicated. For fiscal year ending in year shown; see text; this section]

Item	Total (mil. dol.)				Per capita [1] (dollars)			
	1980	1990	1997	1998	1980	1990	1997	1998
Borrowing and revenue	293,356	672,994	1,093,486	1,179,301	1,299	2,712	4,092	4,372
Borrowing	16,394	40,532	54,064	83,439	73	163	202	309
Revenue	276,962	632,462	1,039,422	1,095,862	1,226	2,549	3,890	4,063
General revenue	233,592	517,720	814,382	864,863	1,034	2,087	3,048	3,206
Taxes	137,075	300,779	443,335	474,392	607	1,212	1,659	1,759
Sales and gross receipts . . .	67,855	147,404	215,737	227,343	300	594	807	843
General	43,168	99,929	147,069	155,971	191	403	550	578
Motor fuels	9,722	19,379	27,132	28,345	43	78	102	105
Alcoholic beverages	2,478	3,191	3,698	3,765	11	13	14	14
Tobacco products.	3,738	5,541	7,451	7,748	17	22	28	29
Other.	8,750	19,365	30,387	31,513	39	78	114	117
Licenses	8,690	18,849	28,217	29,668	38	76	106	110
Motor vehicles.	4,936	9,850	12,965	13,667	22	40	49	51
Corporations in general. . .	1,388	3,096	5,882	6,135	6	12	22	23
Other.	2,366	5,903	9,370	9,866	10	24	35	37
Individual income	37,089	96,076	144,668	160,746	164	387	541	596
Corporation net income	13,321	21,751	30,662	31,094	59	88	115	115
Property	2,892	5,775	10,297	10,650	13	23	39	39
Other	7,227	10,922	13,754	14,891	32	44	51	55
Charges and miscellaneous . .	32,190	90,612	140,454	149,682	142	365	526	555
Intergovernmental revenue. . . .	64,326	126,329	230,592	240,789	285	509	863	893
From Federal Government . .	61,892	118,353	215,421	224,444	274	477	806	832
Public welfare	24,680	59,397	123,087	127,356	109	239	461	472
Education.	12,765	21,271	33,663	36,138	57	86	126	134
Highways	8,860	13,931	19,346	19,659	39	56	72	73
Health and hospitals.	2,309	5,475	11,676	12,579	10	22	44	47
Other.	13,278	17,279	27,649	28,712	69	96	103	106
From local governments. . . .	2,434	7,976	15,171	16,345	11	32	57	61
Utility revenue	1,304	3,305	4,046	4,205	6	13	15	16
Liquor store revenue	2,765	2,907	3,292	3,483	12	12	12	13
Insurance trust revenue [2]	39,301	108,530	217,703	223,311	174	437	815	828
Employee retirement.	21,146	78,898	168,184	186,885	94	318	629	693
Unemployment compensation . .	13,468	18,370	34,882	23,051	60	74	131	85
Expenditure and debt redemption.	263,494	592,213	935,208	988,507	1,166	2,386	3,500	3,665
Expenditure	257,812	572,318	893,827	930,037	1,141	2,306	3,345	3,448
General expenditure.	228,223	508,284	788,176	827,654	1,010	2,048	2,950	3,068
Education	87,939	184,935	275,821	294,814	389	745	1,032	1,093
Public welfare	44,219	104,971	203,204	207,926	196	423	760	771
Health	6,485	20,029	33,880	35,067	29	81	127	130
Hospitals.	11,370	22,637	29,313	28,928	50	91	110	107
Highways	25,044	44,249	60,204	63,620	111	178	225	236
Police protection.	2,263	5,166	7,501	8,038	10	21	28	30
Correction.	4,449	17,266	29,043	30,601	20	70	109	113
Natural resources	4,346	9,909	12,909	13,541	19	40	48	50
Housing and community development	601	2,856	3,839	3,982	3	12	14	15
Other and unallocable	41,507	96,266	132,462	141,137	184	388	496	523
Utility expenditure	2,401	7,131	7,783	8,365	11	29	29	31
Liquor store expenditure	2,206	2,452	2,697	2,820	10	10	10	10
Insurance trust expenditure [2]	24,981	54,452	95,172	91,198	111	219	356	338
Employee retirement.	10,256	29,562	56,570	63,087	45	119	212	234
Unemployment compensation . .	12,006	16,423	27,475	17,712	53	66	103	66
By character and object:								
Intergovernmental expenditure . . .	84,504	175,028	264,207	278,853	374	705	989	1,034
Direct expenditure	173,307	397,291	629,620	651,183	767	1,601	2,356	2,414
Current operation	108,131	258,046	425,898	446,440	479	1,040	1,594	1,655
Capital outlay.	23,325	45,524	59,658	64,441	103	183	223	239
Construction.	19,736	34,803	46,991	50,542	87	140	176	187
Other capital outlay	(X)	(X)	12,667	13,899	(X)	(X)	47	52
Land and existing structure . .	1,345	3,471	(NA)	(NA)	6	14	(NA)	-
Equipment	2,243	7,250	(NA)	(NA)	10	29	(NA)	-
Assistance and subsidies.	9,818	16,902	21,867	21,515	43	68	82	80
Interest on debt	7,052	22,367	27,025	27,590	31	90	101	102
Insurance benefits [3]	24,981	54,452	95,171	91,198	111	219	356	338
Debt redemption	5,682	19,895	41,381	58,470	25	80	155	217
Debt outstanding, year end . .	121,958	318,254	455,698	483,117	540	1,282	1,705	1,791
Long-term	119,821	315,490	453,556	480,948	530	1,271	1,697	1,783
Full-faith and credit.	49,364	74,972	119,514	124,653	219	302	447	462
Nonguaranteed	70,457	240,518	334,042	356,294	312	969	1,250	1,321
Short-term	2,137	2,764	2,142	2,169	9	11	8	8
Net long-term [4]	79,810	125,524	222,393	237,107	353	506	832	879
Full-faith and credit only	39,357	63,481	109,513	114,890	174	256	410	426

- Represents zero. NA Not available. X Not applicable. [1] 1980 and 1990 based on enumerated resident population as of April 1; other years based on estimated resident population as of July 1. [2] Includes other items not shown separately. [3] Includes repayments. [4] Less cash and investment assets specifically held for redemption of long-term debt.

Source: U.S. Census Bureau, *State Government Finances*, Series GF, No. 3, annual; <http://www.census.gov/ftp/pub/govs/www/state.html>; (released 26 June 2000).

No. 512. State Governments—Revenue by State: 1998

[In millions of dollars (1,095,862 represents $1,095,862,000,000), except as noted. For fiscal year ending in year shown; see text, this section. Includes local shares of state imposed taxes. N.e.c. = Not elsewhere classified]

State	Total revenue [1]	General revenue Total	Per capita [2] Total (dol.)	Rank	Intergovernmental revenue Total	From Federal Government	Charges and miscellaneous Total	Current charges	Miscellaneous general revenue	Insurance trust revenue
United States . .	1,095,862	864,863	3,206	(X)	240,789	224,444	149,682	76,219	73,463	223,311
Alabama	14,844	12,433	2,858	38	4,021	3,975	2,673	1,894	779	2,269
Alaska.	9,039	7,973	12,960	1	1,080	1,076	5,707	306	5,402	1,044
Arizona	16,582	11,814	2,531	47	3,330	3,011	1,534	746	789	4,748
Arkansas	9,487	7,724	3,043	29	2,368	2,358	1,300	817	483	1,763
California	144,985	111,088	3,399	19	30,894	28,414	12,480	7,668	4,813	33,738
Colorado	13,514	10,953	2,760	42	2,789	2,767	2,275	1,292	982	2,561
Connecticut	16,520	14,452	4,416	6	3,016	3,011	2,042	943	1,099	2,045
Delaware	4,594	3,883	5,219	2	725	697	1,177	516	661	702
Florida.	51,752	36,780	2,467	49	8,302	7,922	5,957	2,080	3,878	14,966
Georgia.	25,707	20,165	2,641	45	5,676	5,627	2,899	1,559	1,340	5,542
Hawaii.	6,761	5,474	4,598	4	1,176	1,169	1,122	794	328	1,287
Idaho	4,705	3,592	2,918	33	863	858	671	327	344	1,063
Illinois	40,460	33,787	2,799	41	8,959	8,208	5,056	2,082	2,974	6,674
Indiana	18,508	17,113	2,897	35	3,943	3,785	3,422	2,075	1,347	1,395
Iowa	10,029	8,821	3,083	26	2,216	2,118	1,803	1,114	689	1,114
Kansas	8,444	7,785	2,950	32	1,863	1,832	1,260	770	491	659
Kentucky	15,989	12,969	3,296	22	3,603	3,592	2,251	1,233	1,018	3,020
Louisiana	17,605	13,649	3,128	25	4,026	3,973	3,541	2,123	1,417	3,950
Maine	5,690	4,567	3,661	14	1,411	1,406	786	315	471	1,052
Maryland	20,559	15,589	3,039	30	3,534	3,404	2,865	1,484	1,381	4,875
Massachusetts . . .	28,235	25,801	4,199	7	6,458	5,928	4,854	1,698	3,156	2,357
Michigan	40,069	36,085	3,675	13	8,557	8,186	6,312	3,749	2,563	3,471
Minnesota	24,509	17,856	3,778	11	3,938	3,888	2,414	1,167	1,247	6,653
Mississippi	10,611	8,400	3,053	28	2,947	2,816	1,210	782	428	2,063
Missouri.	19,021	14,884	2,737	43	4,246	4,224	2,416	1,201	1,214	4,137
Montana	3,626	2,980	3,389	20	1,048	1,032	605	296	309	611
Nebraska.	5,636	4,829	2,908	34	1,282	1,261	914	494	420	806
Nevada	7,320	4,615	2,646	44	912	856	590	332	258	2,679
New Hampshire . .	4,010	2,968	2,503	48	1,024	864	936	411	525	788
New Jersey	37,007	28,357	3,503	15	6,392	6,027	6,361	3,058	3,303	8,180
New Mexico	9,059	7,127	4,111	8	1,846	1,796	1,706	637	1,070	1,932
New York.	96,131	80,720	4,445	5	33,791	26,121	10,775	4,450	6,325	13,133
North Carolina . . .	33,327	23,950	3,174	23	6,817	6,281	3,263	1,980	1,283	9,377
North Dakota	3,128	2,533	3,972	9	893	863	562	407	155	595
Ohio	48,133	32,300	2,874	36	8,953	8,691	5,704	3,180	2,523	15,404
Oklahoma	12,186	9,411	2,818	40	2,516	2,436	1,594	1,045	549	2,501
Oregon	15,688	11,273	3,435	17	3,365	3,322	2,909	1,320	1,590	4,215
Pennsylvania	48,503	36,833	3,069	27	9,609	9,537	6,595	3,636	2,959	10,894
Rhode Island	4,438	3,781	3,828	10	1,146	1,065	814	287	526	646
South Carolina . . .	15,203	11,415	2,973	31	3,442	3,312	2,290	1,616	674	3,060
South Dakota	2,874	2,098	2,871	37	764	752	500	199	301	776
Tennessee	16,675	14,086	2,593	46	5,265	5,197	1,825	1,310	515	2,589
Texas	57,807	48,066	2,438	50	14,605	13,998	8,831	4,328	4,503	9,741
Utah	8,762	6,627	3,155	24	1,690	1,673	1,437	935	502	2,032
Vermont	2,373	2,196	3,719	12	730	727	509	306	203	148
Virginia	25,918	19,268	2,838	39	3,781	3,623	4,944	2,946	1,998	6,392
Washington	27,980	19,079	3,354	21	4,247	4,178	3,026	1,902	1,124	8,606
West Virginia	7,808	6,206	3,425	18	2,096	2,069	1,097	584	513	1,556
Wisconsin	21,395	18,169	3,479	16	3,795	3,709	3,224	1,724	1,500	3,226
Wyoming.	2,653	2,337	4,867	3	839	812	642	101	541	278

See footnotes at end of table.

U.S. Census Bureau, Statistical Abstract of the United States: 2000

[See headnote, page 317]

State	All taxes				Sales and gross receipts taxes						
		Per capita [2]					Selective sales taxes [3]				
	Total [1]	Total (dol.)	Rank	Total property taxes	Total [1]	Total general sales taxes	Total [1]	Alcoholic beverages and tobacco sales	Insurance premiums	Motor fuels sales	Public utilities
United States...	474,392	1,759	(X)	10,650	227,343	155,971	71,372	11,513	9,187	28,345	8,796
Alabama	5,739	1,319	46	140	2,994	1,571	1,423	188	172	486	435
Alaska	1,186	1,928	12	49	117	-	117	44	34	35	2
Arizona	6,949	1,489	42	252	4,008	3,050	958	215	148	534	56
Arkansas	4,057	1,598	31	9	2,102	1,514	588	122	67	349	-
California	67,714	2,072	9	3,871	26,512	21,302	5,210	920	1,226	2,875	46
Colorado	5,890	1,484	43	-	2,318	1,531	788	93	115	503	8
Connecticut	9,394	2,870	1	-	4,721	3,032	1,689	178	180	570	205
Delaware	1,981	2,663	3	-	255	-	255	33	45	99	23
Florida	22,521	1,511	40	985	16,928	12,924	4,004	1,032	376	1,497	634
Georgia	11,589	1,518	38	38	4,992	3,993	999	217	224	558	-
Hawaii	3,176	2,668	2	-	1,912	1,425	486	75	89	74	120
Idaho	2,057	1,671	25	-	953	653	300	34	51	207	3
Illinois	19,771	1,638	29	206	9,112	5,596	3,516	521	99	1,301	987
Indiana	9,747	1,650	28	3	4,409	3,156	1,253	122	149	640	5
Iowa	4,803	1,679	24	-	2,214	1,529	686	112	109	326	-
Kansas	4,662	1,767	21	46	2,190	1,619	571	122	96	333	1
Kentucky	7,115	1,808	17	364	3,258	1,981	1,276	82	216	414	-
Louisiana	6,082	1,394	45	23	3,199	1,981	1,218	140	240	531	13
Maine	2,370	1,900	14	43	1,141	831	310	105	43	157	1
Maryland	9,190	1,791	18	242	3,843	2,161	1,682	152	175	677	147
Massachusetts	14,488	2,358	5	-	4,371	2,963	1,408	362	311	621	-
Michigan	21,216	2,160	6	1,569	9,501	7,573	1,929	700	145	1,041	-
Minnesota	11,504	2,434	4	10	4,933	3,244	1,689	246	158	554	-
Mississippi	4,243	1,542	36	2	2,798	2,035	763	97	108	389	-
Missouri	8,222	1,512	39	17	3,800	2,628	1,172	138	194	668	-
Montana	1,328	1,509	41	228	275	-	275	31	38	178	15
Nebraska	2,633	1,586	33	5	1,318	920	398	64	36	266	2
Nevada	3,113	1,785	19	72	2,626	1,657	970	82	111	248	9
New Hampshire	1,009	850	50	1	498	-	498	87	52	115	58
New Jersey	15,605	1,928	13	3	7,650	4,766	2,884	413	310	476	1,143
New Mexico	3,575	2,062	10	37	1,951	1,455	496	60	79	241	7
New York	36,155	1,991	11	-	12,423	7,615	4,808	855	681	495	1,675
North Carolina	13,869	1,838	16	-	5,735	3,273	2,462	203	284	1,114	341
North Dakota	1,078	1,691	23	2	610	309	301	30	20	106	27
Ohio	17,643	1,570	34	17	8,311	5,531	2,780	377	351	1,328	708
Oklahoma	5,301	1,587	32	-	2,010	1,328	681	134	149	355	15
Oregon	4,999	1,523	37	-	672	-	672	216	62	382	10
Pennsylvania	20,629	1,719	22	150	9,688	6,313	3,375	494	390	811	729
Rhode Island	1,821	1,844	15	2	900	526	375	72	42	125	62
South Carolina	5,683	1,480	44	12	2,894	2,163	731	153	82	339	39
South Dakota	834	1,141	49	-	661	443	219	31	33	114	1
Tennessee	6,996	1,288	47	-	5,321	4,028	1,293	156	258	752	5
Texas	24,629	1,249	48	-	19,884	12,474	7,409	1,017	697	2,506	414
Utah	3,501	1,666	26	-	1,773	1,312	461	65	77	307	-
Vermont	958	1,622	30	10	424	195	230	28	20	56	8
Virginia	10,543	1,553	35	21	3,911	2,225	1,686	127	237	761	100
Washington	11,806	2,076	8	2,047	8,683	6,909	1,774	423	229	708	252
West Virginia	3,012	1,663	27	3	1,558	856	702	42	76	233	191
Wisconsin	11,150	2,135	7	76	4,587	3,047	1,540	299	94	846	296
Wyoming	856	1,783	20	99	403	335	67	7	12	45	2

See footnotes at end of table.

U.S. Census Bureau, Statistical Abstract of the United States: 2000

[See headnote, page 317]

State	License taxes					Income			Other taxes	
	Total [1]	Corpora-tion license	Hunting and fishing license	Motor vehicle and opera-tors license	Occu-pancy and business license, n.e.c.	Total	Indi-vidual income	Corpora-tion net income	Total[1]	Death and gift
United States...	29,668	6,135	1,041	14,924	6,163	191,840	160,746	31,094	14,892	6,939
Alabama	434	119	18	193	94	2,042	1,794	249	129	36
Alaska.	94	1	17	38	36	276	-	276	651	5
Arizona	233	7	15	146	56	2,391	1,863	528	64	64
Arkansas	237	12	21	118	69	1,643	1,390	253	65	33
California	3,136	44	69	1,783	1,124	33,372	27,784	5,588	824	787
Colorado	278	5	57	169	41	3,153	2,882	271	141	108
Connecticut	360	11	4	250	84	3,941	3,406	535	372	279
Delaware	649	440	2	31	164	967	761	205	111	45
Florida.	1,451	121	14	948	292	1,271	-	1,271	1,886	578
Georgia	397	34	21	208	70	6,057	5,317	740	106	85
Hawaii.	93	2	-	63	18	1,145	1,083	62	27	20
Idaho	196	1	24	102	39	897	779	118	12	9
Illinois	1,208	123	24	810	240	8,949	6,987	1,962	297	250
Indiana	217	5	14	134	50	4,993	4,065	928	125	125
Iowa	453	37	18	303	69	2,035	1,838	197	100	91
Kansas	214	24	14	137	31	2,050	1,744	306	162	89
Kentucky	447	149	16	182	90	2,752	2,418	334	295	106
Louisiana.	457	255	22	111	63	1,810	1,451	360	593	90
Maine	119	3	13	66	33	1,013	906	107	54	41
Maryland	351	13	10	189	136	4,518	4,139	379	237	125
Massachusetts . . .	451	21	6	306	69	9,387	8,032	1,355	280	191
Michigan	1,105	7	46	764	225	8,671	6,316	2,355	369	110
Minnesota	875	5	40	573	241	5,503	4,750	753	183	62
Mississippi	300	85	12	141	53	1,091	847	244	51	21
Missouri.	575	92	19	262	165	3,730	3,372	358	101	99
Montana	157	1	29	54	29	522	444	78	146	16
Nebraska.	169	6	11	80	54	1,116	974	142	26	18
Nevada	336	17	7	114	110	-	-	-	79	45
New Hampshire . .	125	4	7	67	37	298	62	236	87	43
New Jersey	753	132	12	439	107	6,769	5,591	1,178	430	338
New Mexico	188	2	19	130	32	979	799	180	420	12
New York.	967	56	31	708	96	21,417	18,289	3,128	1,348	1,022
North Carolina . . .	842	227	16	469	111	7,124	6,125	1,000	168	165
North Dakota	80	-	7	43	29	260	178	83	126	5
Ohio	1,457	512	29	616	267	7,734	6,968	766	124	115
Oklahoma	747	44	12	594	86	2,108	1,885	223	437	81
Oregon	506	6	28	326	128	3,718	3,439	279	104	41
Pennsylvania	2,181	1,030	44	746	292	7,588	6,025	1,563	1,024	711
Rhode Island	88	10	1	52	22	805	736	70	27	20
South Carolina . . .	405	42	14	122	95	2,301	2,087	214	71	45
South Dakota	105	2	12	33	49	38	-	38	29	26
Tennessee	656	311	19	242	77	768	161	607	251	113
Texas	3,534	2,005	61	926	464	-	-	-	1,212	327
Utah	120	4	15	76	24	1,559	1,375	185	48	25
Vermont	66	1	5	40	17	412	366	46	47	19
Virginia	455	20	20	310	95	5,851	5,405	446	304	122
Washington	529	12	27	282	155	-	-	-	547	82
West Virginia	159	8	16	87	26	1,088	866	222	205	13
Wisconsin	637	60	62	297	209	5,728	5,048	681	122	80
Wyoming	79	6	22	47	4	-	-	-	275	7

- Represents or rounds to zero.   X Not applicable.   [1] Includes amounts not shown separately.   [2] Based on estimated resident population as of July 1.

Source: U.S. Census Bureau; <http://www.census.gov/govs/www/index.html> (accessed 26 June 2000).

No. 513. State Governments—Expenditures and Debt by State: 1998

[In millions of dollars (930,037 represents $930,037,000,000) except as indicated. For fiscal year ending in year shown; see text, this section]

State	Total expen-diture [1]	General expenditure Total Amount	Per capita [2] (dol.)	Inter-govern-mental	Direct expen-ditures	Educa-tion	Public welfare	Health and hospitals	High-ways	Police protection
United States..	930,037	827,654	3,068	278,853	651,183	294,814	207,926	63,995	63,620	8,038
Alabama	13,728	12,476	2,867	3,420	10,309	5,362	3,027	1,503	882	102
Alaska.	5,803	5,230	8,501	983	4,820	1,208	759	187	550	58
Arizona	13,328	12,070	2,586	5,023	8,305	4,393	2,648	719	1,192	135
Arkansas	8,104	7,572	2,983	2,110	5,994	3,019	1,797	643	779	63
California	120,330	106,681	3,264	51,053	69,276	38,140	30,412	8,820	4,631	1,146
Colorado	11,278	10,105	2,546	3,159	8,118	4,333	2,401	433	989	63
Connecticut	14,516	12,681	3,875	2,628	11,888	3,143	3,036	1,457	686	114
Delaware	3,465	3,203	4,305	591	2,874	1,072	501	241	288	54
Florida.	39,214	36,662	2,459	12,537	26,677	12,595	8,160	2,342	3,254	338
Georgia	21,735	20,281	2,656	6,311	15,425	9,192	4,692	1,382	1,282	151
Hawaii.	5,860	5,261	4,419	147	5,713	1,636	919	502	249	7
Idaho	3,786	3,377	2,743	1,104	2,681	1,403	595	139	397	36
Illinois	35,685	32,005	2,652	9,862	25,823	9,865	8,905	2,541	2,475	332
Indiana	17,223	16,278	2,755	5,883	11,340	6,833	3,298	639	1,721	179
Iowa	9,729	9,030	3,156	2,795	6,935	3,744	1,937	732	1,056	66
Kansas	7,681	7,040	2,668	2,509	5,172	3,237	1,093	579	937	45
Kentucky	13,541	12,284	3,122	3,007	10,534	4,574	3,291	763	1,172	129
Louisiana.	14,919	13,423	3,077	3,451	11,468	4,828	2,958	1,593	981	208
Maine	4,606	4,173	3,345	852	3,755	1,171	1,397	301	326	40
Maryland	16,578	14,481	2,823	3,711	12,868	4,770	3,255	1,110	1,198	274
Massachusetts . . .	27,194	25,153	4,094	6,215	20,979	5,478	6,181	1,921	2,387	307
Michigan	37,410	34,066	3,469	15,430	21,979	15,406	6,835	3,319	2,186	256
Minnesota	18,418	16,662	3,525	6,022	12,396	6,482	4,559	699	1,241	114
Mississippi	9,336	8,526	3,099	2,876	6,460	3,042	1,888	715	868	56
Missouri.	15,313	14,191	2,610	4,177	11,137	5,451	3,301	1,064	1,278	155
Montana	3,262	2,890	3,286	713	2,550	1,059	466	229	349	35
Nebraska.	4,754	4,565	2,749	1,291	3,462	1,683	1,108	358	573	47
Nevada	5,398	4,696	2,693	1,915	3,482	1,835	723	175	389	44
New Hampshire . .	3,477	3,039	2,563	455	3,022	694	925	169	318	33
New Jersey	31,702	25,974	3,208	7,176	24,526	8,460	5,235	1,835	1,865	253
New Mexico	7,540	6,944	4,006	2,187	5,353	2,623	1,277	587	875	55
New York.	87,338	73,869	4,068	27,271	60,067	17,403	28,538	5,698	2,772	419
North Carolina . . .	24,605	22,671	3,004	7,928	16,676	9,496	4,886	1,791	2,076	255
North Dakota	2,527	2,327	3,648	541	1,985	810	462	91	322	11
Ohio	39,209	31,943	2,842	11,214	27,995	11,602	8,147	2,495	2,631	208
Oklahoma	9,953	8,693	2,603	2,803	7,150	3,922	1,749	598	862	27
Oregon	13,466	10,967	3,342	3,707	9,759	4,209	2,351	839	995	138
Pennsylvania	40,804	35,603	2,966	10,158	30,646	11,013	10,516	2,899	3,069	703
Rhode Island	3,964	3,413	3,455	548	3,416	982	1,017	208	190	25
South Carolina . . .	13,575	11,846	3,085	3,142	10,433	4,209	2,955	1,335	711	170
South Dakota	2,245	2,120	2,901	493	1,752	643	410	100	347	17
Tennessee	14,775	13,875	2,554	3,924	10,851	4,920	4,197	1,078	1,374	103
Texas	51,065	46,405	2,354	14,027	37,038	19,770	10,833	3,755	3,520	291
Utah	7,470	6,927	3,298	1,717	5,753	3,179	1,042	537	935	61
Vermont	2,295	2,154	3,647	356	1,940	679	565	67	220	32
Virginia	20,529	19,037	2,804	5,660	14,869	7,490	3,420	1,810	2,232	348
Washington	22,880	19,671	3,458	6,048	16,832	8,198	4,340	1,669	1,528	216
West Virginia	7,149	6,211	3,428	1,530	5,619	2,301	1,648	210	807	44
Wisconsin	19,101	16,980	3,252	7,481	11,620	6,595	3,007	1,012	1,352	61
Wyoming	2,172	1,920	4,000	711	1,461	663	264	107	301	14

See footnotes at end of table.

U.S. Census Bureau, Statistical Abstract of the United States: 2000

[See headnote, page 320]

| State | General expenditure—Con. | | | | | | | | Debt outstanding | | |
| | Selected functions—Con. | | | | | | | | | | |
	Corrections	Natural resources	Parks and recreation	Governmental administration	Interest on general debt	Utility expenditures	Liquor stores expenditures	Insurance trust expenditures	Cash and security holdings	Total	Per capita [2] (dol.)
United States..	30,601	13,541	4,473	30,577	26,776	8,365	2,820	91,198	2,061,508	483,117	1,791
Alabama	257	180	20	318	203	-	146	1,107	23,466	4,167	958
Alaska.	159	265	17	345	225	25	-	548	41,008	3,800	6,177
Arizona	717	156	48	419	151	27	-	1,231	31,571	2,807	601
Arkansas	206	162	49	262	124	-	-	531	13,344	2,384	939
California	3,438	2,082	270	3,728	2,420	85	-	13,564	269,125	50,251	1,538
Colorado	619	156	49	334	237	5	-	1,168	25,068	3,637	916
Connecticut	480	73	42	677	983	200	-	1,635	26,339	17,727	5,417
Delaware	142	43	35	275	213	43	-	219	9,545	3,770	5,067
Florida.	1,932	1,068	133	1,672	1,038	69	-	2,483	77,360	16,969	1,138
Georgia	857	418	163	530	386	-	-	1,454	51,020	6,040	791
Hawaii.	121	87	50	273	346	-	-	599	11,719	5,710	4,796
Idaho	124	118	21	124	111	-	40	369	9,830	1,883	1,530
Illinois	1,066	286	223	1,060	1,614	-	-	3,680	66,724	25,315	2,097
Indiana	447	168	58	435	290	-	-	945	26,047	6,704	1,135
Iowa	227	220	20	345	117	-	65	634	22,073	2,029	709
Kansas	255	158	6	263	79	-	-	641	10,057	1,411	535
Kentucky	304	242	106	501	426	8	-	1,250	28,007	6,814	1,732
Louisiana	448	359	277	423	425	3	-	1,492	29,631	7,093	1,626
Maine	72	118	9	174	168	-	48	385	6,704	3,474	2,785
Maryland	742	307	238	700	614	368	-	1,729	42,235	10,536	2,054
Massachusetts . . .	862	251	141	1,068	1,775	110	-	1,931	46,252	32,833	5,344
Michigan	1,315	377	47	755	874	-	395	2,949	66,027	16,147	1,644
Minnesota	332	396	125	669	309	-	-	1,756	44,816	5,333	1,128
Mississippi	221	191	139	232	156	-	119	690	16,484	2,674	972
Missouri.	461	247	38	551	478	-	-	1,122	35,726	8,091	1,488
Montana	87	148	7	175	134	-	30	342	7,240	2,259	2,568
Nebraska.	119	136	27	128	107	-	-	189	8,301	1,908	1,149
Nevada	206	62	18	205	174	83	-	618	14,245	2,881	1,652
New Hampshire . .	61	33	8	159	385	1	220	218	8,522	5,367	4,526
New Jersey	1,067	303	619	1,175	1,228	1,414	-	4,314	68,959	27,214	3,362
New Mexico	196	85	42	277	152	-	-	596	23,850	2,572	1,484
New York.	2,372	343	376	3,497	3,694	4,954	-	8,515	168,410	73,254	4,034
North Carolina . . .	981	452	135	624	385	-	-	1,934	59,153	6,877	911
North Dakota	32	83	8	71	52	-	-	200	5,321	857	1,344
Ohio	1,369	309	112	1,046	850	-	262	7,004	123,272	14,183	1,262
Oklahoma	416	153	53	368	164	255	-	1,005	18,712	3,951	1,183
Oregon	472	264	34	661	325	1	122	2,376	26,707	5,729	1,746
Pennsylvania	1,229	505	121	1,143	1,203	-	717	4,483	86,783	16,394	1,366
Rhode Island	127	38	34	195	269	38	-	513	9,787	5,352	5,419
South Carolina . . .	423	185	50	289	221	659	-	1,070	22,234	5,191	1,352
South Dakota	58	80	21	88	117	-	-	125	6,342	2,068	2,830
Tennessee	441	177	124	361	205	4	-	896	25,329	3,192	588
Texas	2,598	643	66	1,311	908	-	-	4,660	145,605	14,408	731
Utah	188	133	26	354	161	-	77	467	14,363	3,435	1,635
Vermont	39	64	9	142	122	4	26	111	4,276	2,110	3,573
Virginia	933	149	56	863	659	6	237	1,250	48,807	10,828	1,595
Washington	565	499	77	463	544	-	243	2,967	54,731	10,289	1,809
West Virginia	120	141	48	282	255	4	40	894	8,203	3,433	1,895
Wisconsin	655	309	56	479	637	-	-	2,121	64,258	10,721	2,053
Wyoming	41	119	18	86	63	-	34	218	7,915	1,043	2,173

- Represents or rounds to zero.   [1] Includes items not shown separately.   [2] Based on estimated resident population as of July 1.

Source: U.S. Census Bureau, <http://www.census.gov/govs/www/st98.html> (accessed 26 June 2000).

No. 514. Local Governments—Revenue by State: 1996

[In millions of dollars (803,737 represents $803,737,000,000), except as noted. For fiscal year ending in year shown; see text, this section]

State	General revenue									Utility revenue
	Total revenue [1]	Total	Per capita [2] (dol.)	Intergovernmental revenue		Taxes			Total charges and miscellaneous	
				From Federal Government	From state governments	Total	Property	General sales		
United States..	803,737	709,216	2,674	26,906	243,574	270,602	199,467	29,709	168,135	67,674
Alabama	9,902	8,345	1,945	314	2,980	2,374	864	961	2,677	1,463
Alaska.	2,549	2,314	3,824	109	796	782	624	109	627	207
Arizona	12,698	10,511	2,372	396	4,167	3,753	2,751	731	2,195	2,020
Arkansas	4,278	3,830	1,529	116	1,521	1,148	746	301	1,045	427
California	123,892	103,549	3,260	4,485	43,881	28,468	19,404	4,315	26,715	12,363
Colorado	11,862	10,462	2,743	376	2,924	4,423	2,841	1,289	2,739	1,136
Connecticut	8,687	8,078	2,475	286	2,265	4,713	4,657	-	814	367
Delaware	1,479	1,326	1,823	44	633	362	299	-	286	129
District of Columbia	5,675	4,910	9,099	1,871	-	2,481	702	468	558	377
Florida.	43,455	38,648	2,679	1,189	10,646	13,829	11,058	356	12,985	4,169
Georgia	21,195	18,536	2,527	486	5,497	7,016	4,757	1,525	5,536	2,282
Hawaii.	1,619	1,444	1,216	122	174	762	613	-	386	175
Idaho	2,592	2,479	2,090	67	1,035	687	653	-	690	113
Illinois	36,051	31,755	2,661	1,460	8,889	15,105	12,297	1,135	6,301	2,239
Indiana	13,762	12,579	2,159	313	4,393	4,543	4,026	-	3,331	1,125
Iowa	7,488	6,994	2,455	246	2,330	2,542	2,384	60	1,876	477
Kansas	7,170	6,294	2,435	102	2,124	2,394	1,946	289	1,674	805
Kentucky	7,342	6,607	1,702	237	2,605	1,924	999	-	1,841	713
Louisiana.	10,171	9,403	2,167	362	2,982	3,559	1,338	1,928	2,499	661
Maine	2,614	2,527	2,042	88	733	1,335	1,309	-	371	87
Maryland	13,153	11,911	2,355	540	3,237	5,965	3,569	-	2,169	369
Massachusetts . . .	17,905	15,309	2,517	889	5,603	6,668	6,475	-	2,148	1,686
Michigan	28,031	25,240	2,593	871	12,621	6,128	5,458	-	5,620	1,162
Minnesota	16,751	15,213	3,273	384	6,324	4,327	4,107	25	4,178	1,063
Mississippi	6,182	5,744	2,119	182	2,443	1,283	1,184	1	1,836	437
Missouri.	12,049	10,652	1,984	322	3,432	4,477	2,601	1,015	2,420	1,019
Montana	1,716	1,659	1,892	68	627	571	546	-	393	57
Nebraska.	5,885	3,890	2,360	127	960	1,812	1,574	143	990	1,821
Nevada	4,852	4,588	2,867	150	1,691	1,371	823	83	1,377	264
New Hampshire . .	2,479	2,417	2,085	53	302	1,782	1,765	-	281	60
New Jersey	25,625	24,900	3,109	289	7,582	13,064	12,813	-	3,965	718
New Mexico	3,962	3,712	2,173	176	1,915	816	437	302	806	250
New York.	91,383	82,105	4,526	2,517	25,932	38,345	23,262	6,171	15,311	3,382
North Carolina . . .	19,416	16,736	2,290	500	6,461	4,604	3,446	884	5,171	2,370
North Dakota	1,327	1,253	1,949	71	427	456	410	30	298	74
Ohio	30,204	28,340	2,537	1,198	9,133	12,312	7,950	932	5,698	1,698
Oklahoma	6,764	6,192	1,879	147	2,299	1,941	1,014	813	1,805	532
Oregon	9,649	9,016	2,821	659	3,179	2,887	2,332	-	2,291	632
Pennsylvania	31,499	28,878	2,400	1,511	9,768	11,985	8,468	100	5,614	1,773
Rhode Island	2,103	1,974	1,998	101	552	1,157	1,141	-	164	88
South Carolina . . .	8,328	7,395	1,979	213	2,436	2,215	1,941	54	2,531	929
South Dakota	1,480	1,335	1,811	67	311	708	558	121	249	116
Tennessee	15,715	10,785	2,032	275	3,225	3,813	2,266	1,110	3,472	4,629
Texas	51,020	45,051	2,367	1,175	12,696	19,093	15,248	2,340	12,087	5,029
Utah	5,200	4,116	2,036	198	1,459	1,388	1,008	247	1,071	1,083
Vermont	1,303	1,179	2,011	118	256	677	670	-	127	116
Virginia	15,933	14,199	2,130	436	4,316	6,726	4,828	594	2,721	1,057
Washington	18,651	15,498	2,808	566	5,827	4,880	2,872	1,058	4,225	3,028
West Virginia	3,226	3,101	1,704	85	1,325	878	724	-	813	106
Wisconsin	15,814	14,663	2,834	317	6,068	5,620	5,354	144	2,657	728
Wyoming	1,650	1,574	3,279	31	589	454	352	75	500	72

- Represents or rounds to zero.   [1] Includes items not shown separately.   [2] Based on estimated resident population as of July.

Source: U.S. Census Bureau, <http://www.census.gov/govs/www/esti96.html> (accessed 26 April 19990; and unpublished data.

U.S. Census Bureau, Statistical Abstract of the United States: 2000

[In millions of dollars, (794,318 represents $794,318,000,000), except as indicated. For fiscal year ending in year shown; see text, this section]

State	General expenditure										
	Total			Selected functions (direct expenditures)							
	Total expenditure[1]	Amount	Per capita[2] (dol.)	Direct expenditures	Education	Public welfare	Health and hospitals	Highways	Police protection	Utility expenditures	Debt outstanding
United States ...	794,318	693,946	2,617	686,050	292,953	37,776	60,322	31,600	38,187	84,465	717,322
Alabama.........	10,262	8,680	2,023	8,670	3,556	41	1,669	448	426	1,529	7,970
Alaska..........	2,536	2,244	3,708	2,244	957	17	112	110	99	284	3,622
Arizona.........	12,673	10,650	2,403	10,387	4,574	770	362	516	662	1,931	16,275
Arkansas	4,245	3,835	1,531	3,834	1,999	4	288	250	203	399	3,670
California	121,559	102,738	3,235	101,408	32,996	11,765	10,032	3,317	6,298	16,118	97,932
Colorado........	11,877	10,279	2,695	10,235	3,977	586	728	603	548	1,452	15,677
Connecticut......	8,694	8,169	2,503	8,167	4,206	174	75	325	455	370	4,102
Delaware	1,483	1,372	1,887	1,369	803	1	9	93	82	97	1,229
District of Columbia .	5,817	4,184	7,752	4,184	669	1,172	432	89	248	1,138	4,137
Florida..........	43,383	38,407	2,663	38,293	14,943	281	3,627	1,553	2,742	4,648	49,649
Georgia	20,439	17,378	2,369	17,343	7,858	83	2,919	834	858	2,875	17,501
Hawaii	1,755	1,470	1,238	1,470	-	12	19	73	176	285	2,089
Idaho..........	2,580	2,471	2,083	2,462	1,237	32	311	177	126	108	869
Illinois.........	34,221	29,437	2,467	29,408	13,246	395	1,414	1,678	2,016	3,394	29,742
Indiana.........	14,043	12,818	2,200	12,713	5,967	489	1,493	512	478	1,176	9,275
Iowa	7,331	6,785	2,382	6,708	3,216	127	797	670	272	534	4,291
Kansas.........	7,245	6,410	2,480	6,409	3,198	40	498	474	324	762	6,890
Kentucky	7,638	6,858	1,766	6,856	3,441	37	455	227	269	761	12,371
Louisiana	9,686	8,835	2,036	8,827	3,738	77	1,185	472	548	760	8,871
Maine..........	2,503	2,409	1,946	2,409	1,295	32	59	146	95	93	1,522
Maryland	12,481	11,688	2,311	11,610	5,804	68	282	471	688	418	12,558
Massachusetts.....	17,201	13,633	2,241	13,100	6,074	168	634	634	865	2,697	11,340
Michigan........	27,323	25,184	2,587	25,081	12,352	440	2,137	1,485	1,245	1,415	17,943
Minnesota.......	16,719	15,127	3,254	15,035	6,049	1,064	1,314	1,232	566	1,245	17,208
Mississippi......	6,002	5,557	2,050	5,556	2,629	26	1,009	388	236	444	3,917
Missouri........	12,106	10,758	2,004	10,756	5,495	77	721	651	616	1,160	6,744
Montana........	1,766	1,699	1,938	1,693	988	28	75	92	80	69	683
Nebraska	5,669	3,803	2,307	3,796	2,045	56	252	286	141	1,801	4,820
Nevada	4,741	4,469	2,793	4,467	1,510	70	450	330	303	272	5,908
New Hampshire....	2,405	2,330	2,010	2,275	1,213	180	18	129	120	69	1,104
New Jersey.......	24,761	24,124	3,013	23,758	11,629	1,298	792	843	1,558	657	16,028
New Mexico	3,928	3,667	2,147	3,645	1,633	53	237	203	226	261	3,281
New York	91,534	80,684	4,447	76,740	27,332	11,859	6,629	3,176	4,280	5,897	76,579
North Carolina.....	19,708	16,501	2,258	16,234	7,039	980	3,038	310	803	2,921	16,988
North Dakota......	1,318	1,224	1,905	1,213	605	41	13	118	47	88	923
Ohio	29,700	27,548	2,466	27,415	12,221	1,436	2,177	1,404	1,541	2,089	16,327
Oklahoma........	6,800	6,257	1,899	6,255	3,088	18	701	326	350	524	5,078
Oregon.........	9,714	8,571	2,682	8,567	4,070	53	634	532	430	1,101	6,364
Pennsylvania......	31,216	27,641	2,297	27,631	12,982	1,408	1,254	942	1,117	2,975	43,444
Rhode Island......	2,006	1,885	1,908	1,885	1,049	7	3	55	135	78	1,012
South Carolina.....	8,203	7,096	1,899	7,073	3,331	23	1,434	130	315	1,109	6,777
South Dakota	1,480	1,345	1,824	1,341	673	17	37	140	60	111	702
Tennessee	15,483	10,648	2,006	10,608	4,254	112	1,547	540	578	4,617	19,420
Texas...........	50,226	43,259	2,273	43,212	21,815	296	5,214	1,603	2,291	6,209	61,413
Utah	5,243	4,128	2,041	4,123	2,096	22	158	187	221	1,115	9,015
Vermont	1,147	1,023	1,744	1,023	663	-	4	109	34	120	539
Virginia.........	15,710	14,226	2,134	14,175	6,684	691	504	459	751	1,257	15,440
Washington.......	18,962	14,894	2,699	14,861	6,261	29	1,189	954	687	3,967	22,779
West Virginia......	3,189	3,048	1,674	3,045	1,813	1	242	40	94	125	3,669
Wisconsin........	15,936	14,924	2,884	14,901	6,936	1,115	847	1,209	814	850	10,566
Wyoming	1,668	1,576	3,283	1,575	746	7	290	58	68	89	1,071

- Represents or rounds to zero. [1] Includes items not shown separately. [2] Based on estimated resident population as of July 1.

Source: U.S. Census Bureau, <http://www.census.gov/govs/www/esti96.html>; (accessed 26 April 1999); and unpublished data.

State and Local Government Finances and Employment 323

No. 516. Estimated State and Local Taxes Paid by a Family of Four in Selected Cities: 1998

[Data based on average family of four (two wage earners and two school age children) owning their own home and living in a city where taxes apply. Comprises state and local sales, income, auto, and real estate taxes. For definition of median, see Guide to Tabular Presentation]

City	Total taxes paid by gross family income level (dollars)					Total taxes paid as percent of income				
	$25,000	$50,000	$75,000	$100,000	$150,000	$25,000	$50,000	$75,000	$100,000	$150,000
Albuquerque, NM . . .	1,592	3,637	6,303	8,886	14,261	6.4	7.3	8.4	8.9	9.5
Atlanta, GA	1,742	4,239	7,280	9,990	15,396	7.0	8.5	9.7	10.0	10.3
Baltimore, MD	1,785	5,333	8,410	11,163	16,621	7.1	10.7	11.2	11.2	11.1
Boston, MA.	1,882	4,893	8,001	10,744	16,253	7.5	9.8	10.7	10.7	10.8
Charlotte, NC	1,807	4,115	6,859	9,575	14,630	7.2	8.2	9.1	9.6	9.8
Chicago, IL	2,694	5,272	8,214	10,716	15,701	10.8	10.5	11.0	10.7	10.5
Columbus, OH.	2,067	4,374	7,150	9,863	15,425	8.3	8.7	9.5	9.9	10.3
Denver, CO.	1,408	3,406	5,427	7,184	11,097	5.6	6.8	7.2	7.2	7.4
Detroit, MI.	2,399	5,020	7,953	10,600	15,878	9.6	10.0	10.6	10.6	10.6
Honolulu, HI	2,256	4,967	8,196	11,185	17,221	9.0	9.9	10.9	11.2	11.5
Houston, TX	1,325	2,433	3,808	4,869	6,986	5.3	4.9	5.1	4.9	4.7
Indianapolis, IN	1,992	3,806	5,854	7,701	11,392	8.0	7.6	7.8	7.7	7.6
Jacksonville, FL. . . .	1,220	2,443	3,976	5,167	7,543	4.9	4.9	5.3	5.2	5.0
Kansas City, MO . . .	2,224	4,485	7,196	9,645	14,855	8.9	9.0	9.6	9.6	9.9
Las Vegas, NV	1,499	2,406	3,731	4,688	6,596	6.0	4.8	5.0	4.7	4.4
Los Angeles, CA . . .	1,876	3,849	7,201	10,620	17,454	7.5	7.7	9.6	10.6	11.6
Memphis, TN.	1,509	2,448	3,970	5,171	7,674	6.0	4.9	5.3	5.2	5.1
Milwaukee, WI.	2,469	5,617	8,763	11,589	17,205	9.9	11.2	11.7	11.6	11.5
Minneapolis, MN . . .	1,728	4,523	8,088	11,196	17,434	6.9	9.0	10.8	11.2	11.6
New Orleans, LA . . .	1,475	3,412	5,852	7,943	11,999	5.9	6.8	7.8	7.9	8.0
New York City, NY . .	2,152	5,837	10,073	14,121	22,328	8.6	11.7	13.4	14.1	14.9
Oklahoma City, OK. .	2,032	4,139	6,748	9,138	14,052	8.1	8.3	9.0	9.1	9.4
Omaha, NE.	1,946	4,179	7,082	9,795	15,596	7.8	8.4	9.4	9.8	10.4
Philadelphia, PA. . . .	3,253	6,110	9,160	11,906	17,338	13.0	12.2	12.2	11.9	11.6
Phoenix, AZ	1,984	3,915	6,173	8,208	12,481	7.9	7.8	8.2	8.2	8.3
Portland, ME.	2,670	6,065	10,108	13,735	20,960	10.7	12.1	13.5	13.7	14.0
Seattle, WA.	2,072	3,484	5,369	6,810	9,690	8.3	7.0	7.2	6.8	6.5
Virginia Beach, VA . .	2,138	4,291	6,961	9,269	13,850	8.6	8.6	9.3	9.3	9.2
Washington, DC. . . .	2,141	4,650	7,901	10,937	16,961	8.6	9.3	10.5	10.9	11.3
Wichita, KS.	1,680	3,598	6,222	8,622	13,385	6.7	7.2	8.3	8.6	8.9
Average [1]	2,026	4,274	7,004	9,442	14,376	8.1	8.5	9.3	9.4	9.6
Median [1]	1,918	4,173	7,018	9,575	14,648	7.7	8.3	9.4	9.6	9.8

[1] Based on selected cities and District of Columbia. For complete list of cities, see Table 517.

Source: Government of the District of Columbia, Department of Finance and Revenue, *Tax Rates and Tax Burdens in the District of Columbia: A Nationwide Comparison,* annual.

No. 517. Residential Property Tax Rates in Selected Cities: 1998

[Effective tax rate is amount each jurisdiction considers based upon assessment level used. Assessment level is ratio of assessed value to assumed market value. Nominal rate is announced rates it levied at taxable value of house]

City	Effective tax rate per $100		Assessment level (percent)	Nominal rate per $100	City	Effective tax rate per $100		Assessment level (percent)	Nominal rate per $100
	Rank	Rate				Rank	Rate		
Bridgeport, CT.	1	4.59	70.0	6.55	Memphis, TN	27	1.40	25.0	5.59
Newark, NJ.	2	3.99	16.4	24.28	Houston, TX	27	1.40	100.0	1.40
Manchester, NH.	3	3.33	107.0	3.12	Wilmington, DE	30	1.34	61.0	2.19
Milwaukee, WI.	4	3.00	99.1	3.03	Boston, MA	30	1.34	100.0	1.34
Philadelphia, PA	5	2.64	32.0	8.26	Minneapolis, MN	32	1.31	89.2	1.47
Portland, ME.	6	2.53	100.0	2.53	Billings, MT.	33	1.29	74.0	1.74
Des Moines, IA	7	2.52	54.9	4.59	Little Rock, AR	34	1.28	20.0	6.39
Baltimore, MD	8	2.41	40.0	6.03	Wichita, KS.	35	1.25	11.5	10.85
Sioux Falls, SD	9	2.37	85.0	2.79	Albuquerque, NM. . . .	36	1.20	33.3	3.61
Detroit, MI	10	2.34	40.7	5.76	Seattle, WA.	37	1.19	91.2	1.30
Jacksonville, FL.	11	2.10	100.0	2.10	Oklahoma City, OK . .	38	1.13	11.0	10.25
Providence, RI	12	2.08	65.0	3.20	Louisville, KY	38	1.13	90.0	1.25
Omaha, NE	13	2.04	94.0	2.17	Virginia Beach, VA . . .	40	1.12	91.7	1.22
Fargo, ND	14	2.02	4.2	47.99	Las Vegas, NV	41	1.07	35.0	3.06
Atlanta, GA.	15	1.95	40.0	4.88	Charlotte, NC	42	1.00	86.3	1.16
Burlington, VT.	16	1.88	93.0	2.02	Jackson, MS.	43	0.97	10.0	9.69
Boise City, ID	17	1.82	99.3	1.83	Washington, DC	44	0.93	97.0	0.96
Anchorage, AK	18	1.80	97.5	1.85	Charleston, WV	45	0.92	60.0	1.53
New Orleans, LA	19	1.67	10.0	16.73	New York City, NY . . .	46	0.83	7.6	10.87
Columbus, OH	19	1.67	31.4	5.33	Los Angeles, CA	47	0.79	75.0	1.06
Phoenix, AZ	21	1.66	10.0	16.61	Birmingham, AL.	47	0.79	10.0	7.86
Indianapolis, IN	21	1.66	15.0	11.10	Denver, CO	49	0.78	9.7	8.00
Portland, OR.	23	1.52	76.8	1.98	Cheyenne, WY	50	0.69	9.5	7.25
Kansas City, MO	24	1.49	19.0	7.84	Honolulu, HI	51	0.46	100.0	0.46
Columbia, SC	25	1.45	4.0	36.25					
Chicago, IL.	26	1.41	16.0	8.84	Unweighted average .	(X)	1.67	55.2	6.66
Salt Lake City, UT . . .	27	1.40	99.0	1.42	Median	(X)	1.41	(X)	(X)

X Not applicable

Source: Government of the District of Columbia, Department of Finance and Revenue, Tax Rates and Tax Burdens in the District of Columbia: A Nationwide Comparison, annual.

No. 518. Gross Revenue From Parimutuel and Amusement Taxes and Lotteries by State: 1998

[In millions of dollars (35,834 represents $35,834,000,000). For fiscal years; see text, this section]

State	Gross revenue (mil. dol.)	Amuse- ment taxes [1]	Parimutuel taxes	Lottery revenue Total [2] (mil. dol.)	Apportionment of funds (percent) Prizes	Admini- stration	Proceeds available from ticket sales
United States.	35,834	2,130	405	33,299	19,207	1,927	12,164
Alabama.	4	-	4	-	-	-	-
Alaska	2	2	-	-	-	-	-
Arizona.	238	1	3	234	134	25	76
Arkansas	7	-	7	-	-	-	-
California	2,226	-	83	2,143	1,184	162	797
Colorado.	418	62	7	349	220	32	96
Connecticut.	1,078	260	11	807	474	75	258
Delaware	277	-	-	277	62	5	210
Florida	2,002	-	60	1,942	1,022	124	795
Georgia	1,558	-	-	1,558	902	104	552
Hawaii	-	-	-	-	-	-	-
Idaho	90	-	-	90	52	17	21
Illinois	1,724	275	38	1,412	842	59	510
Indiana.	589	-	4	586	368	32	186
Iowa	294	136	3	154	96	24	34
Kansas.	179	1	4	174	102	20	52
Kentucky	569	-	18	551	358	34	158
Louisiana	276	1	5	270	140	18	112
Maine.	153	-	4	149	85	16	48
Maryland	1,085	11	2	1,073	571	102	399
Massachusetts.	3,034	7	9	3,018	2,205	64	749
Michigan.	1,531	-	13	1,518	851	52	615
Minnesota.	414	62	1	351	225	64	62
Mississippi	249	249	-	-	-	-	-
Missouri	611	148	-	463	273	40	150
Montana	28	-	-	28	15	6	6
Nebraska	82	8	1	74	39	16	19
Nevada	503	503	-	-	-	-	-
New Hampshire	178	2	3	173	110	6	57
New Jersey.	1,858	317	-	1,541	855	48	639
New Mexico	90	4	1	85	43	21	21
New York	3,641	1	38	3,602	1,994	90	1,518
North Carolina.	-	-	-	-	-	-	-
North Dakota.	12	12	-	-	-	-	-
Ohio	2,212	-	16	2,196	1,245	72	879
Oklahoma.	15	11	5	-	-	-	-
Oregon.	1,428	-	1	1,426	650	224	552
Pennsylvania.	1,601	-	25	1,576	846	58	672
Rhode Island.	554	-	6	548	429	6	113
South Carolina.	34	34	-	-	-	-	-
South Dakota	122	-	1	121	16	8	97
Tennessee	-	-	-	-	-	-	-
Texas.	2,836	23	15	2,797	1,648	64	1,085
Utah	-	-	-	-	-	-	-
Vermont	74	-	-	74	43	8	23
Virginia.	878	-	-	878	490	116	272
Washington.	458	-	3	455	280	59	116
West Virginia.	218	-	9	209	98	22	89
Wisconsin.	401	1	4	397	238	33	125
Wyoming	-	-	-	-	-	-	-

- Represents or rounds to zero.   [1] Represents nonlicense taxes.   [2] Excludes commissions.

Source: U.S. Census Bureau, unpublished data; <http://www.census.gov/govs/index.html>.

No. 519. Lottery Sales—Type of Game: 1980 to 1999

[In millions of dollars (2,393 represents $2,393,000,000). For fiscal years]

Game	1980	1985	1990	1995	1996	1997	1998	1999
Total ticket sales	2,393	9,035	20,017	31,931	34,031	35,486	35,588	35,966
Passive [1]	206	88	(NA)	(NA)	(NA)	(NA)	(NA)	(NA)
Instant [2]	527	1,296	5,204	11,511	13,268	14,217	13,882	13,933
Three-digit [3]	1,554	3,376	4,572	5,737	5,680	5,639	5,643	5,237
Four-digit [3]	55	693	1,302	1,941	2,003	2,111	2,232	2,655
Lotto [4]	52	3,583	8,563	10,594	10,227	9,996	9,854	9,794
Other [5]	(NA)	(NA)	409	2,148	2,853	3,523	3,978	4,347
State proceeds (net income) [6]	978	3,735	7,703	11,100	11,576	11,959	12,102	11,255

NA Not available.   [1] Also known as draw game or ticket. Player must match his ticket to winning numbers drawn by lottery. Players cannot choose their numbers.   [2] Player scratches a latex section on ticket which reveals instantly whether ticket is a winner.   [3] Players choose and bet on three or four digits, depending on game, with various payoffs for different straight order or mixed combination bets.   [4] Players typically select six digits out of a large field of numbers. Varying prizes are offered for matching three through six numbers drawn by lottery.   [5] Includes breakopen tickets, spiel, keno, video lottery, etc.   [6] Sales minus prizes and expenses equal net government income.

Source: TLF Publications, Inc., Boyds, MD, *2000 World Lottery Almanac* annual; *LaFleur's Fiscal 1999 Lottery Special Report*; and *LaFleur's Lottery World Government Profits Report* (copyright).

State and Local Government Finances and Employment   325

No. 520. City Governments—Revenue for Largest Cities: 1996

[In millions of dollars (49,292 represents $49,292,000,000). For fiscal years ending in year shown; see text, this section. Cities ranked by size of population estimated as of July 1, 1996, except Honolulu ranked by county population. Data reflect inclusion of fiscal activity of dependent school systems where applicable]

Cities ranked by 1996 population	Total revenue	General revenue — Total	Intergovernmental — Total	Intergov. — From Federal Govt.	Intergov. — From state/local govt.	Intergov. — From local govt.	Gen. rev. from own sources — Total	Taxes — Total	Taxes — Property	Sales and gross receipts — Total	Sales and gross receipts — General sales	Sales and gross receipts — Public utilities	Current charges — Total	Current charges — Parks and recreation	Current charges — Sewerage[1]	Miscellaneous — Total	Miscellaneous — Interest earnings	Utility revenue[2]	Employee retirement revenue[1]
New York City, NY[3]	49,292	41,024	16,419	1,895	14,524	110	24,605	18,182	7,179	3,863	2,742	366	4,769	29	828	1,655	630	2,374	5,893
Los Angeles, CA	8,483	4,437	960	501	458	84	3,477	1,822	607	883	277	450	1,220	44	427	435	294	2,342	1,704
Chicago, IL	5,036	4,057	1,146	349	797	-	2,911	1,723	653	883	154	385	724	-	119	464	286	268	1,711
Houston, TX	2,327	1,644	121	88	33	3	1,523	864	447	388	248	109	485	17	262	174	97	255	428
Philadelphia, PA[3]	4,513	3,495	1,249	366	883	166	2,246	1,686	351	132	82	-	419	15	194	141	105	694	323
San Diego, CA	1,716	1,353	330	170	160	60	1,023	417	130	234	135	30	264	36	194	341	164	179	184
Phoenix, AZ	1,528	1,282	411	98	312	33	871	440	122	288	194	56	287	21	104	181	73	151	95
Dallas, TX	1,628	1,300	88	63	25	3	1,212	555	285	258	151	83	476	30	178	94	71	143	185
San Antonio, TX	1,748	724	115	35	80	11	609	295	144	140	96	13	221	22	141	115	64	962	52
Detroit, MI[3]	2,868	1,805	807	214	593	32	998	632	228	53	-	53	251	15	185	101	47	181	882
Honolulu, HI[3]	1,120	988	142	74	68	-	846	528	417	65	-	19	217	17	180	102	54	132	-
San Jose, CA	1,115	876	121	22	99	1	755	401	121	179	100	67	251	14	146	75	47	12	227
Indianapolis, IN[3]	1,106	1,067	279	72	207	40	788	447	353	25	-	-	266	17	63	354	61	7	32
San Francisco, CA[3]	4,542	3,302	1,285	213	1,072	2	2,017	981	459	271	103	61	682	32	132	194	196	273	967
Jacksonville, FL[3]	1,752	872	141	69	72	-	731	356	219	125	49	68	181	2	100	129	180	770	111
Baltimore, MD[3]	2,395	1,946	1,045	70	974	55	901	674	463	46	-	26	99	4	59	71	67	66	382
Columbus, OH	888	770	124	42	82	6	646	383	26	8	8	-	191	7	121	57	34	118	-
Milwaukee, WI	1,042	690	367	71	296	316	323	163	153	-	-	-	103	3	40	50	38	56	296
Memphis, TN	2,157	1,108	724	20	703	4	385	221	176	34	-	12	114	38	57	44	30	947	102
El Paso, TX	441	343	48	31	17	53	295	167	87	74	58	13	84	4	50	252	29	50	48
Washington, DC[3]	5,101	4,661	1,662	1,609	53	9	2,998	2,481	702	794	468	190	265	25	69	100	57	53	388
Boston, MA[3]	2,296	2,022	906	30	857	1	1,115	771	719	30	-	-	244	-	96	72	36	86	188
Seattle, WA	1,358	895	134	30	103	1	762	434	143	187	93	72	256	30	191	74	54	401	61
Austin, TX	1,444	728	68	68	38	1	661	240	119	106	80	12	347	14	110	140	119	637	78
Nashville-Davidson, TN[3]	1,987	1,236	259	29	256	-	977	628	351	230	199	9	209	3	92	130	97	695	56
Denver, CO[3]	1,612	1,446	343	84	314	1	1,103	489	131	306	270	13	484	32	64	66	46	97	69
Cleveland, OH	898	656	169	83	85	1	486	319	54	12	-	-	101	6	17	95	45	242	-
New Orleans, LA	822	719	147	23	63	-	573	322	23	164	108	28	156	7	63	34	20	56	47
Oklahoma City, OK	547	490	47	38	24	28	443	278	131	249	227	19	131	11	63	71	50	50	8
Fort Worth, TX	604	465	76	23	53	-	389	222	178	60	49	-	95	7	76	102	58	81	58
Portland, OR	656	598	102	38	63	8	496	284	127	41	-	31	111	9	75	100	56	57	-
Kansas City, MO	840	689	80	53	63	96	610	393	67	179	88	66	116	12	35	88	58	60	90
Charlotte, NC	639	588	180	33	147	11	408	178	127	22	-	3	142	-	65	38	20	34	17
Tucson, AZ	576	446	181	49	132	11	265	174	30	135	117	12	54	10	11	78	37	94	35
Long Beach, CA[3]	1,017	850	131	61	70	-	718	190	54	116	31	76	450	3	99	37	27	165	3
Virginia Beach, VA[3]	857	816	299	17	282	12	517	418	284	96	33	26	62	9	37	37	53	41	-
Albuquerque, NM	639	584	201	28	174	73	383	172	56	106	88	11	138	9	72	73	66	55	-
Atlanta, GA	968	751	114	35	79	-	637	241	124	81	-	27	289	19	94	106	66	86	131

- Represents or rounds to zero.   [1] Includes solid waste management.   [2] Includes water, electric, and transit.   [3] Represents, in effect, city-county consolidated government.

Source: U.S. Census Bureau, unpublished data.

[In millions of dollars (48,018 represents $48,018,000,000). For fiscal year ending in year shown; see text, this section. Regarding intercity comparisons, see text, this section]

Cities ranked by 1996 population	Total expenditure	Total direct expenditure	General expenditure — Total	Education	Housing and community development	Public welfare	Health and hospitals	Police protection	Fire protection	Correction	Highways	Parks and recreation	Sewerage	Solid waste management	Governmental administration	General public buildings	Interest on general debt	Utility expenditure	Employee retirement expenditure	Debt outstanding
New York City, NY [1]	48,018	45,184	38,753	8,813	2,487	7,510	4,301	2,519	838	1,071	1,223	373	1,222	712	895	289	1,853	4,569	4,697	44,149
Los Angeles, CA	7,572	7,511	4,655	15	2,362	-	-	806	297	3	170	210	379	144	268	106	344	2,120	797	9,181
Chicago, IL	4,768	4,693	3,890	1	170	132	129	821	270	-	405	43	101	163	114	40	452	285	594	7,448
Houston, TX	2,261	2,238	1,777	-	45	-	79	358	171	14	154	97	297	53	84	-	181	387	96	4,407
Philadelphia, PA [1]	4,310	4,221	3,244	16	140	294	418	358	130	221	105	90	169	97	271	134	160	709	357	3,515
San Diego, CA	1,791	1,787	1,460	-	131	-	2	186	77	5	80	149	408	71	65	17	141	266	65	1,985
Phoenix, AZ	1,479	1,472	1,221	11	73	-	-	193	120	7	74	113	100	51	87	21	203	224	34	2,854
Dallas, TX	1,447	1,416	1,197	-	18	-	18	177	103	5	72	85	83	29	36	28	53	135	116	3,776
San Antonio, TX	1,648	1,645	796	15	15	32	34	136	96	1	67	60	100	42	26	5	94	827	24	3,928
Detroit, MI	2,329	2,239	1,653	5	81	-	98	287	118	1	130	103	198	107	137	10	120	332	345	2,195
Honolulu, HI [1]	1,253	1,253	1,022	-	101	-	11	118	50	-	31	77	121	99	82	20	78	232	-	1,588
San Jose, CA	873	855	790	-	88	-	3	132	67	-	47	64	64	58	38	5	118	21	63	1,504
Indianapolis, IN [1]	1,417	1,406	1,346	1	115	90	241	101	46	32	57	71	189	36	99	78	210	28	43	2,255
San Francisco, CA [1]	3,813	3,710	2,959	71	77	354	685	235	139	66	37	173	47	20	186	13	202	563	290	4,270
Jacksonville, FL [1]	1,859	1,831	1,802	-	61	10	47	104	68	39	84	180	100	64	57	19	81	726	8	4,821
Baltimore, MD [1]	1,999	1,991	1,075	673	102	-	75	202	96	-	55	82	89	42	100	16	63	70	127	1,296
Columbus, OH	851	840	720	-	23	-	29	136	67	7	44	53	64	43	44	7	30	132	-	1,361
Milwaukee, WI	834	798	705	-	78	-	18	147	73	-	36	7	40	52	44	30	23	31	98	532
Memphis, TN	2,097	2,079	1,110	575	22	-	7	109	89	-	22	75	49	37	17	23	29	895	93	818
El Paso, TX	461	458	344	-	9	2	24	69	89	-	89	25	110	17	24	29	29	91	26	568
Washington, DC [1]	4,955	4,771	4,368	669	101	1,172	432	248	96	292	66	60	99	29	256	2	313	91	496	3,824
Boston, MA	2,129	1,912	1,890	560	64	100	266	192	75	70	111	22	96	32	56	53	47	32	207	1,151
Seattle, WA	1,511	1,402	975	-	52	-	20	115	48	12	41	192	47	75	71	14	19	471	65	1,701
Austin, TX	1,434	1,423	691	423	-	-	217	74	62	-	34	52	68	21	32	4	94	716	26	3,302
Nashville-Davidson, TN [1]	1,977	1,977	1,716	-	31	7	119	89	59	31	44	27	55	24	81	19	106	754	79	2,835
Denver, CO [1]	1,867	1,804	1,144	-	61	12	211	107	72	42	52	88	9	22	87	16	332	119	33	5,054
Cleveland, OH	947	944	644	-	88	176	26	149	33	5	21	45	54	30	43	29	29	303	-	1,322
New Orleans, LA	763	763	652	-	13	3	25	63	71	41	32	25	42	20	67	60	60	75	36	968
Oklahoma City, OK	511	511	438	-	8	-	-	82	37	-	66	49	50	17	25	38	38	66	7	702
Fort Worth, TX	495	494	374	-	36	-	-	69	63	-	30	56	136	7	21	55	55	83	38	806
Portland, OR	719	715	624	-	49	-	8	99	50	-	42	50	40	13	43	3	55	53	42	1,155
Kansas City, MO	831	806	720	407	12	1	-	104	36	4	63	47	24	18	61	23	58	66	45	1,005
Charlotte, NC	587	579	423	-	31	5	-	63	35	-	74	42	4	22	13	1	38	133	13	1,353
Tucson, AZ	557	557	412	-	86	-	50	62	51	-	24	44	19	69	44	6	30	174	-	730
Long Beach, CA [1]	1,086	1,086	910	-	3	16	3	154	32	18	53	42	60	17	51	21	81	156	85	1,849
Virginia Beach, VA [1]	856	855	771	-	25	4	1	75	30	24	39	90	65	31	26	4	44	85	-	812
Albuquerque, NM [1]	737	737	658	-	22	2	42	54	54	16	56	22	72	23	27	6	56	80	13	1,183
Baton Rouge, LA [1]	539	539	502	-	12	1	21	54	30	16	39	64	65	32	46	39	59	7	30	859
Atlanta, GA	1,114	1,094	866	-	-	-	44	99	54	19	56	64	72	55	55	-	80	144	103	1,379

-Represents or rounds to zero. [1] Represents, in effect, city-county consolidated government.

Source: U.S. Census Bureau, unpublished data.

State and Local Government Finances and Employment 327

No. 522. County Governments—Revenue for Largest Counties: 1996

[In millions of dollars. For fiscal year ending in year shown; see text, this section]

Counties ranked by 1996 population	Total revenue [1]	General revenue — Total [1]	Intergovernmental — Total [1]	From Federal Gov't — Total	From Federal Gov't — Housing and community development	From state gov't — Total	From state gov't — Public welfare	From state gov't — Health and hospitals	From local government	Own sources — Total	Taxes — Total [1]	Taxes — Property	Sales and gross receipts — Total	Sales and gross receipts — General sales	Current charges — Total	Current charges — Parks and recreation	Current charges — Sewerage [1]	Current charges — Hospitals	Misc. general revenue — Total	Misc. general revenue — Interest earnings
Los Angeles, CA	13,988	11,391	8,100	235	193	7,602	4,392	1,114	263	3,291	1,696	1,532	98	43	903	78	39	448	691	233
Cook, IL	2,267	1,938	376	22	20	352	158	2	-	1,563	1,130	735	382	231	349	33	-	187	84	57
Harris, TX	1,505	1,505	327	23	-	241	126	55	63	1,179	712	655	22	12	195	2	-	65	272	238
San Diego, CA	2,831	2,388	1,701	70	54	1,544	894	201	87	688	405	358	16	8	155	2	64	-	128	33
Orange, CA	2,459	2,132	1,167	24	18	1,079	444	173	64	966	245	216	10	-	261	13	79	154	460	214
Maricopa, AZ	1,408	1,408	770	43	14	707	345	12	20	638	300	288	-	-	237	7	6	570	101	72
Wayne, MI	1,392	1,315	677	112	7	503	83	284	62	637	235	230	-	-	256	7	54	228	146	34
Dade, FL [2]	4,068	3,858	745	352	136	389	-	-	5	3,113	1,127	775	288	73	1,545	18	402	-	441	258
King, WA	911	886	170	2	-	146	31	59	-	716	360	324	3	-	294	15	229	78	62	48
Santa Clara, CA	1,474	1,416	312	44	12	201	-	109	68	1,104	704	344	264	230	315	-	10	38	85	70
San Bernardino, CA	1,640	1,640	1,078	38	5	996	588	69	44	562	336	311	4	3	135	2	47	13	91	47
Cuyahoga, OH	1,848	1,713	1,236	72	15	1,105	723	110	59	477	170	146	16	12	155	7	-	197	152	71
Middlesex, MA	143	61	29	9	-	27	-	-	3	32	11	11	-	-	19	-	4	-	2	-
Broward, FL	1,144	1,144	457	25	7	444	221	125	5	686	372	206	135	127	219	10	131	19	95	79
Riverside, CA	1,496	1,496	964	19	9	878	489	6	9	532	493	407	61	16	137	7	42	36	159	120
Suffolk, NY	1,793	1,703	515	31	10	451	221	100	68	993	236	199	20	593	342	10	10	31	82	87
Allegheny, PA	1,103	1,033	496	18	5	483	137	43	37	1,207	1,011	402	595	88	115	-	-	130	47	50
Alameda, CA	1,505	1,418	921	21	25	869	564	221	-	518	281	275	95	-	185	7	5	128	97	30
Nassau, NY	1,645	1,645	381	4	6	360	181	150	33	1,264	949	476	470	463	236	11	-	53	114	34
Bexar, TX	609	609	123	10	15	108	64	63	11	486	227	207	6	-	145	12	-	-	70	34
Tarrant, TX	554	554	166	7	3	145	52	26	11	388	241	219	7	-	78	3	10	-	46	106
Oakland, MI	725	665	123	17	8	108	51	51	128	389	168	163	-	-	55	6	-	-	158	62
Sacramento, CA	1,793	1,634	396	27	6	261	17	103	23	269	331	180	118	95	282	11	145	53	76	32
Hennepin, MN	1,122	1,122	864	4	14	824	502	80	14	770	351	348	67	-	264	5	46	186	52	88
Franklin, OH	614	612	431	12	3	391	242	56	24	691	245	167	260	60	32	4	3	-	44	48
St. Louis, MO	492	463	284	6	4	255	82	94	12	329	336	70	308	222	27	1	-	-	31	42
Erie, NY	1,255	1,216	322	26	12	306	219	5	10	407	537	220	102	303	284	2	4	189	40	31
Palm Beach, FL	1,003	977	114	28	-	88	3	27	-	894	418	300	6	-	277	1	143	-	73	40
Clark, NV	1,696	1,532	316	44	6	236	4	4	52	863	545	192	7	-	521	14	56	247	168	86
Milwaukee, WI	1,113	952	429	13	-	377	-	114	7	1,216	193	148	-	-	300	23	-	202	150	108
Westchester, NY	1,645	1,640	371	55	11	385	132	60	18	523	666	436	118	95	502	19	16	351	30	10
Fairfax, VA	2,570	2,128	223	43	11	308	239	14	8	1,223	1,389	1,112	67	60	271	3	184	-	55	40
Hillsborough, FL	1,264	1,189	223	29	29	179	27	7	-	1,757	380	288	176	222	438	3	43	220	97	83
Hamilton, OH	634	634	213	14	14	191	62	51	8	966	258	190	81	54	130	3	102	-	147	81
Pinellas, FL	641	599	73	12	5	60	56	51	1	526	298	219	51	48	144	1	86	-	84	58

- Represents or rounds to zero. [1] Includes solid waste management. [2] Represents, in effect, city-county consolidated government.
Source: U.S. Census Bureau, unpublished data. <www/cnty/html>; and unpublished data.

U.S. Census Bureau, Statistical Abstract of the United States: 2000

No. 523. County Governments—Expenditures and Debt for Largest Counties: 1996

[In millions of dollars (12,421 represents $12,421,000,000). For fiscal year ending in year shown; see text, this section]

Counties ranked by 1996 population	Total expenditure	Total direct expenditure	General expenditure Total	Education	Housing and community development	Public welfare	Health	Hospitals	Police protection	Correction	Governmental administration	General public buildings	Highways	Parks and recreation	Natural resources	Sewerage and solid waste management	Interest on general debt	Utility expenditure[1]	Employee retirement expenditure	Debt outstanding
Los Angeles, CA	12,421	11,862	11,545	370	220	4,087	780	1,568	1,072	612	1,099	91	185	202	171	43	343	38	837	5,452
Cook, IL	2,061	2,040	1,926	2	20	1	58	639	62	254	403	55	86	90	-	-	97	-	135	1,611
Harris, TX	1,569	1,569	1,569	83	13	19	97	378	116	215	198	23	128	26	45	-	268	-	-	4,915
San Diego, CA	2,331	2,316	2,223	68	50	879	269	-	99	155	376	-	31	12	7	79	64	10	99	650
Orange, CA	2,079	2,035	1,982	18	21	518	173	38	104	127	328	24	66	57	52	43	259	-	97	3,599
Maricopa, AZ	1,434	1,231	1,239	-	14	94	49	191	54	103	179	-	81	85	36	15	72	10	-	1,152
Wayne, MI	1,310	1,250	1,250	-	8	51	263	-	21	202	131	8	92	6	110	100	63	-	71	1,007
Dade, FL	4,390	4,387	3,961	209	-	51	24	697	311	170	228	2	77	100	19	469	320	429	-	5,713
Dallas, TX	912	908	907	-	5	6	94	396	23	61	108	19	12	-	-	-	44	-	5	763
King, WA	1,558	1,534	1,253	1	13	507	194	40	65	182	184	20	89	74	30	256	128	-	-	1,984
Santa Clara, CA	1,760	1,696	1,760	93	5	673	158	222	37	82	247	41	55	21	2	16	52	305	-	816
San Bernardino, CA	1,917	1,860	1,839	74	1	1	103	323	107	37	148	5	4	14	38	77	57	-	72	1,419
Middlesex, MA	109	64	64	-	1	1	-	14	-	-	-	3	5	-	-	-	-	6	45	5
Cuyahoga, OH	1,096	1,084	1,096	-	10	216	191	319	15	61	128	2	28	-	-	11	80	-	-	1,344
Broward, FL	1,127	1,090	1,021	10	15	21	74	-	125	103	104	18	42	39	11	126	138	106	-	2,103
Riverside, CA	1,482	1,397	1,481	15	25	454	99	99	99	66	156	16	56	7	87	18	98	-	-	1,307
Suffolk, NY	1,777	1,550	1,645	25	31	360	117	-	314	56	92	28	25	22	3	45	69	132	37	1,437
Allegheny, PA	1,034	984	997	80	9	486	180	95	23	115	93	25	35	24	-	-	96	-	76	1,467
Alameda, CA	1,770	1,687	1,694	216	15	303	183	194	31	103	177	101	37	214	78	-	65	-	-	697
Nassau, NY	1,967	1,768	1,965	27	-	44	89	210	318	58	71	5	49	32	5	105	96	2	1	2,696
Bexar, TX	613	571	612	18	8	12	34	256	16	67	58	22	12	2	-	-	106	-	-	1,200
Tarrant, TX	512	512	512	200	-	2	67	172	13	52	68	1	15	5	-	-	55	-	-	927
Oakland, MI	643	631	616	-	6	580	106	7	28	92	81	22	84	4	56	85	20	16	11	336
Sacramento, CA	1,748	1,720	1,672	-	95	165	184	-	60	67	169	11	95	9	19	189	113	8	69	2,208
Hennepin, MN	1,059	1,055	1,059	44	5	145	200	273	39	50	97	13	45	21	4	53	23	-	-	685
Franklin, OH	620	602	619	-	5	2	32	-	16	43	71	13	25	-	-	3	45	1	-	566
St. Louis, MO	496	337	487	-	3	476	46	-	44	61	39	19	51	13	-	2	24	-	10	324
Erie, NY	1,243	996	1,217	67	2	22	25	179	26	70	35	43	37	28	26	25	56	-	-	717
Palm Beach, FL	928	900	879	-	9	44	21	-	107	80	154	2	66	11	38	93	58	26	-	1,672
Clark, NV	1,600	1,587	1,438	-	11	210	30	264	159	99	108	30	194	43	-	27	142	49	-	2,761
Milwaukee, WI	1,060	1,060	898	11	5	443	76	256	15	55	78	23	20	112	1	-	29	162	61	572
Westchester, NY	1,754	1,554	1,725	-	-	113	72	353	16	98	59	-	44	97	-	113	82	101	-	735
Fairfax, VA	2,351	2,320	2,102	1,039	-	57	29	-	94	55	98	-	31	33	10	182	123	28	114	2,406
Hillsborough, FL	1,317	1,307	1,227	47	-	93	126	286	108	49	90	13	64	35	35	36	107	135	-	2,231
Hamilton, OH	708	621	708	17	13	57	29	67	43	39	90	-	23	5	-	117	30	90	-	501
Pinellas, FL	624	594	587	13	7	10	50	-	61	39	105	-	63	20	13	58	44	37	-	802

- Represents or rounds to zero. [1] Includes water, electric, and transit.

Source: U.S. Census Bureau, unpublished data.

State and Local Government Finances and Employment 329

No. 524. Governmental Employment and Payrolls: 1980 to 1998

[Employees in thousands (16,213 represents 16,213,000), payroll in millions of dollars (19,935 represents $19,935,000,000). For 1980 to 1995 as of October; later years as of March. 1996 data are not available. Covers both full-time and part-time employees. Local government data are estimates subject to sampling variation; see Appendix III and source]

Type of government	1980	1985	1990	1991	1992	1993	1994	1995	1997	1998
EMPLOYEES (1,000)										
Total	16,213	16,690	18,369	18,554	18,745	18,823	19,420	19,521	19,540	19,854
Federal (civilian) [1]	2,898	3,021	3,105	3,103	3,047	2,999	2,952	2,895	2,807	2,765
State and local	13,315	13,669	15,263	15,452	15,698	15,824	16,468	16,626	16,733	17,089
Percent of total	82	82	83	83	84	84	85	85	86	86
State	3,753	3,984	4,503	4,521	4,595	4,673	4,694	4,719	4,733	4,758
Local	9,562	9,685	10,760	10,930	11,103	11,151	11,775	11,906	12,000	12,271
Counties	1,853	1,891	2,167	2,196	2,253	2,270	(NA)	(NA)	2,425	(NA)
Municipalities	2,561	2,467	2,642	2,662	2,665	2,644	(NA)	(NA)	2,755	(NA)
School districts	4,270	4,416	4,950	5,045	5,134	(NA)	(NA)	(NA)	455	(NA)
Townships	394	392	418	415	424	(NA)	(NA)	(NA)	5,675	(NA)
Special districts	484	519	585	612	627	(NA)	(NA)	(NA)	691	(NA)
OCTOBER PAYROLLS (mil. dol.)										
Total	19,935	28,945	39,228	41,237	43,120	(NA)	(NA)	(NA)	49,156	51,568
Federal (civilian) [1]	5,205	7,580	8,999	9,687	9,937	(NA)	(NA)	(NA)	9,744	10,115
State and local	14,730	21,365	30,229	31,551	33,183	34,540	36,545	37,714	39,412	41,453
Percent of total	74	74	77	77	77	(NA)	(NA)	(NA)	80	80
State	4,285	6,329	9,083	9,437	9,828	10,288	10,666	10,927	11,413	11,845
Local	10,445	15,036	21,146	22,113	23,355	24,252	25,878	26,787	27,999	29,608
Counties	1,936	2,819	4,192	4,404	4,698	4,839	(NA)	(NA)	5,750	(NA)
Municipalities	2,951	4,191	5,564	5,784	6,207	6,328	(NA)	(NA)	7,146	(NA)
School districts	4,683	6,746	9,551	9,975	10,394	(NA)	(NA)	(NA)	869	(NA)
Townships	330	446	642	664	685	(NA)	(NA)	(NA)	12,579	(NA)
Special districts	546	834	1,197	1,287	1,370	(NA)	(NA)	(NA)	1,654	(NA)

NA Not available.   [1] Includes employees outside the United States.

Source: U.S. Census Bureau, *Historical Statistics on Governmental Finances and Employment*, and *Public Employment*, Series GE, No. 1, annual; <http://www.census.gov/govs/www/apes.html> (accessed 28 August 2000).

No. 525. All Governments—Employment and Payroll by Function: 1999

[Employees in thousands (20,265 represents 20,265,000), payroll in millions of dollars (54,240 represents $54,240,000,000). As of **March 1999**. Covers full-time and part-time employees. Local government data are estimates subject to sampling variation; see Appendix III and source]

Function	Employees (1,000)				October payrolls (mil. dol.)			
	Total	Federal (civilian) [1]	State and local			Total	Federal (civilian) [1]	State and local	
			Total	State	Local			Total	State	Local
Total	20,265	2,799	17,465	4,827	12,639	54,240	10,478	43,763	12,562	31,201
National defense [2]	713	713	(X)	(X)	(X)	2,459	2,459	(X)	(X)	(X)
Postal Service	876	876	(X)	(X)	(X)	2,936	2,936	(X)	(X)	(X)
Space research and technology . .	19	19	(X)	(X)	(X)	106	106	(X)	(X)	(X)
Elem. and secondary educ.	6,729	(X)	6,729	55	6,674	16,313	(X)	16,313	144	16,169
Higher education	2,589	(X)	2,589	2,065	525	5,460	(X)	5,460	4,512	948
Other education	121	11	110	110	(X)	350	49	301	301	(X)
Health	570	135	435	175	260	1,723	598	1,125	507	617
Hospitals	1,180	156	1,024	436	588	3,221	555	2,666	1,161	1,505
Public welfare	519	9	510	228	283	1,320	43	1,277	607	670
Social insurance administration . . .	163	67	96	96	(X)	568	283	285	285	(X)
Police protection	1,019	104	915	100	815	3,524	514	3,010	351	2,659
Fire protection	378	(X)	378	(X)	378	1,109	(X)	1,109	(X)	1,109
Correction	722	31	691	462	228	2,107	118	1,989	1,330	659
Streets & highways	569	3	566	252	314	1,583	17	1,566	750	817
Air transportation	90	50	40	3	37	440	309	132	11	121
Water transport/Terminals	28	14	14	5	9	87	43	44	16	28
Solid waste management	117	(X)	117	2	115	299	(X)	299	7	292
Sewerage	130	(X)	130	2	129	382	(X)	382	6	376
Parks & recreation	369	25	345	39	306	646	86	560	81	479
Natural resources	390	184	206	164	42	1,297	767	530	434	96
Housing & community dev.	143	17	126	-	126	417	79	338	-	338
Water supply	170	-	170	1	169	469	-	469	3	466
Electric power	80	-	80	6	75	312	-	312	29	283
Gas supply	11	-	11	-	11	31	-	31	-	31
Transit	210	(X)	210	29	181	753	(X)	753	118	634
Libraries	171	4	167	1	166	282	20	262	1	261
State liquor stores	8	(X)	8	8	(X)	16	(X)	16	16	(X)
Financial administration	550	137	413	169	244	1,594	516	1,078	493	584
Other government administration . .	460	22	438	60	378	868	86	782	173	610
Judicial and legal	455	56	398	148	250	1,539	280	1,259	534	725
Other & unallocable	716	166	550	213	336	2,027	611	1,416	693	723

- Represents or rounds to zero.   X Not applicable.   [1] Includes employees outside the United States.   [2] Includes international relations.

Source: U.S. Census Bureau; <http://www.census.gov/pub/govs/www/apes.html> (accessed 18 August 2000).

No. 526. State and Local Government—Employer Costs per Hour Worked: 1999

[In dollars. As of March. Based on a sample; see source for details. For additional data, see Table 701]

Item	Total compensation	Wages and salaries	Benefits Total	Paid leave	Supplemental pay	Insurance	Retirement and savings	Legally required benefits	Other[1]
Total workers	28.00	19.78	8.22	2.17	0.24	2.22	1.91	1.64	0.04
Occupational group:									
White-collar occupations	30.99	22.44	8.55	2.24	0.14	2.35	2.02	1.76	0.05
Professional specialty and technical	36.67	27.30	9.36	2.21	0.15	2.51	2.41	2.02	0.07
Professional specialty	38.03	28.45	9.58	2.22	0.13	2.58	2.51	2.07	0.07
Teachers	40.83	30.94	9.89	2.08	0.06	2.73	2.80	2.14	0.08
Technical	22.88	15.70	7.17	2.14	0.35	1.76	1.36	1.54	0.03
Executive, admin., & managerial	35.08	24.58	10.51	3.52	0.17	2.42	2.37	2.02	(Z)
Admin. support including clerical	17.88	11.91	5.97	1.63	0.10	2.02	1.09	1.11	0.02
Blue-collar occupations	21.94	14.47	7.47	2.09	0.34	2.09	1.41	1.53	0.02
Service occupations	21.23	13.74	7.49	1.98	0.51	1.84	1.80	1.33	0.04
Industry group:									
Services	29.45	21.50	7.95	1.96	0.15	2.27	1.86	1.66	0.05
Health services	22.95	15.52	7.43	2.35	0.58	1.72	1.15	1.60	0.03
Hospitals	23.48	15.89	7.59	2.41	0.58	1.75	1.19	1.63	0.03
Educational services	30.67	22.64	8.03	1.89	0.09	2.34	1.98	1.68	0.05
Elementary and secondary education	30.25	22.38	7.87	1.71	0.06	2.46	1.96	1.61	0.07
Higher education	32.35	23.80	8.55	2.41	0.16	2.01	2.08	1.89	(Z)
Public administration	25.39	16.78	8.61	2.53	0.37	2.10	2.03	1.55	0.03

Z Cost per hour worked is less than 1 cent.   [1] Includes severance pay and supplemental unemployment benefits.
Source: U.S. Bureau of Labor Statistics, *Compensation and Working Conditions, Fall 1999.*

No. 527. State and Local Governments—Full-Time Employment and Salary by Sex and Race/Ethnic Group: 1973 to 1997

[As of June 30. (3,809 represents 3,809,000). Excludes school systems and educational institutions. Based on reports from state governments (44 in 1973; 48 in 1975, 1976, and 1979; 47 in 1977 and 1983; 45 in 1978; 42 in 1980; 49 in 1981 and 1984 through 1987; and 50 in 1989 through 1991) and a sample of county, municipal, township, and special district jurisdictions employing 15 or more nonelected, nonappointed full-time employees. Data for 1993 only for state and local governments with 100 or more employees. Data for 1974, 1982, 1988, 1992, and 1994 not available. For definition of median, see Guide to Tabular Presentation]

Year and occupation	Employment (1,000) Total	Male	Female	White[1]	Minority Total[2]	Black[1]	Hispanic[3]	Median annual salary ($1,000) Male	Female	White[1]	Minority Total[2]	Black[1]	Hispanic[3]
1973	3,809	2,486	1,322	3,115	693	523	125	9.6	7.0	8.8	7.5	7.4	7.4
1975	3,899	2,436	1,464	3,102	797	602	147	11.3	8.2	10.2	8.8	8.6	8.9
1976	4,369	2,724	1,645	3,490	880	664	165	11.8	8.6	10.7	9.2	9.1	9.4
1977	4,415	2,737	1,678	3,480	935	705	175	12.4	9.1	11.3	9.7	9.5	9.9
1978	4,447	2,711	1,736	3,481	966	723	181	13.3	9.7	12.0	10.4	10.1	10.7
1979	4,576	2,761	1,816	3,568	1,008	751	192	14.1	10.4	12.8	10.9	10.6	11.4
1980	3,987	2,350	1,637	3,146	842	619	163	15.2	11.4	13.8	11.8	11.5	12.3
1981	4,665	2,740	1,925	3,591	1,074	780	205	17.7	13.1	16.1	13.5	13.3	14.7
1983	4,492	2,674	1,818	3,423	1,069	768	219	20.1	15.3	18.5	15.9	15.6	17.3
1984	4,580	2,700	1,880	3,458	1,121	799	233	21.4	16.2	19.6	17.4	16.5	18.4
1985	4,742	2,789	1,952	3,563	1,179	835	248	22.3	17.3	20.6	18.4	17.5	19.2
1986	4,779	2,797	1,982	3,549	1,230	865	259	23.4	18.1	21.5	19.6	18.7	20.2
1987	4,849	2,818	2,031	3,600	1,249	872	268	24.2	18.9	22.4	20.9	19.3	21.1
1989	5,257	3,030	2,227	3,863	1,394	961	308	26.1	20.6	24.1	22.1	20.7	22.7
1990	5,374	3,071	2,302	3,918	1,456	994	327	27.3	21.8	25.2	23.3	22.0	23.8
1991	5,459	3,110	2,349	3,965	1,494	1,011	340	28.4	22.7	26.4	23.8	22.7	24.5
1993	5,024	2,820	2,204	3,588	1,436	948	341	30.6	24.3	28.5	25.9	24.2	26.8
1995, total	**5,315**	**2,960**	**2,355**	**3,781**	**1,534**	**993**	**379**	**33.5**	**27.0**	**31.4**	**26.3**	**26.8**	**28.6**
Officials/administrators	299	201	98	250	48	31	12	52.7	45.2	50.6	44.9	47.7	49.0
Professionals	1,313	624	689	999	314	183	68	41.4	36.1	38.9	35.8	35.0	36.3
Technicians	481	280	202	359	122	71	34	33.3	27.4	31.1	29.6	27.8	29.2
Protective service	931	788	142	687	244	160	69	34.1	28.9	33.7	32.3	30.5	35.5
Paraprofessionals	380	105	275	231	149	114	26	23.8	21.9	23.1	22.3	21.0	22.2
Admin. support	926	123	803	627	299	187	82	24.6	22.9	23.0	23.1	23.0	23.0
Skilled craft	408	389	19	306	102	62	30	31.1	25.6	30.8	30.7	30.3	31.1
Service/maintenance	578	450	128	321	258	186	59	25.0	19.9	24.1	25.6	22.9	24.5
1997, total	**5,205**	**2,898**	**2,307**	**3,676**	**1,529**	**973**	**392**	**34.6**	**27.9**	**32.2**	**30.2**	**27.4**	**29.5**
Officials/administrators	296	197	99	247	49	31	12	54.8	47.2	52.5	50.7	49.7	50.7
Professionals	1,291	605	686	974	317	183	71	42.3	36.6	39.1	37.3	35.5	37.0
Technicians	456	265	191	338	118	68	33	34.4	27.8	31.7	29.7	28.4	28.7
Protective service	969	813	156	704	265	171	77	35.0	29.2	34.6	32.2	30.5	36.5
Paraprofessionals	369	100	269	221	148	111	27	25.1	22.6	24.1	22.8	21.1	23.0
Admin. support	882	117	765	590	292	179	83	25.3	23.5	23.7	23.6	23.4	23.5
Skilled craft	406	385	21	302	104	62	31	31.9	26.4	31.5	31.2	31.0	32.2
Service/maintenance	536	416	120	299	237	168	56	25.7	19.9	24.9	23.9	22.8	24.4

[1] Non-Hispanic.   [2] Includes other minority groups not shown separately.   [3] Persons of Hispanic origin may be of any race.
Source: U.S. Equal Employment Opportunity Commission, *State and Local Government Information Report,* biennially.

State and Local Government Finances and Employment   331

No. 528. State and Local Government Full-Time Equivalent Employment by Selected Function and State: 1998

[In thousands (1,541.5 represents 1,541,500) for **March**. Local government amounts are estimates subject to sampling variation; see Appendix III and source]

State	Education Total		Elem. & secondary		Higher education		Public welfare		Health		Hospitals	
	Total	Local	State	Local	State	Local	State	Local	State	Local	State	Local
United States.....	1,541.5	6,023.3	44.9	5,720.5	1,398.8	302.8	224.1	261.7	169.4	224.3	415.8	536.5
Alabama.........	36.5	92.7	-	92.7	33.1	-	3.8	1.5	5.3	4.3	11.3	25.0
Alaska..........	7.8	15.5	3.1	15.5	4.2	-	2.0	0.2	0.6	0.6	0.2	0.3
Arizona.........	26.7	98.4	-	87.8	23.8	10.6	5.9	1.9	2.1	2.8	0.7	4.6
Arkansas........	21.1	59.2	-	59.2	18.2	-	3.7	0.1	4.9	0.3	4.6	4.9
California........	127.4	648.4	-	577.2	122.8	71.2	3.5	54.9	10.6	36.9	29.7	60.5
Colorado........	35.7	83.8	-	82.3	34.4	1.5	1.9	5.1	1.1	2.6	3.8	9.6
Connecticut......	20.0	69.7	3.6	69.7	13.5	-	4.7	1.9	2.0	1.4	10.5	-
Delaware........	7.2	14.7	-	14.7	6.9	-	1.6	-	1.7	0.2	2.2	-
District of Columbia...	-	10.2	(X)	9.4	(X)	0.8	(X)	1.0	(X)	1.3	(X)	4.1
Florida..........	48.5	290.1	-	267.7	46.5	22.3	12.5	5.8	18.0	5.5	6.0	28.8
Georgia.........	46.0	186.1	-	186.0	39.2	0.1	9.1	0.6	3.7	14.3	11.9	33.4
Hawaii..........	31.4	-	24.2	-	7.0	-	0.8	0.1	2.9	0.2	3.2	-
Idaho..........	10.3	30.3	-	29.3	9.7	1.0	1.7	0.1	1.3	0.8	1.0	4.7
Illinois.........	55.9	257.4	-	237.3	52.9	20.1	12.5	6.8	3.1	7.1	14.9	14.3
Indiana.........	47.3	126.4	-	126.4	46.1	-	5.0	1.4	1.7	3.0	5.0	23.4
Iowa...........	24.7	72.2	-	66.1	23.5	6.1	2.8	1.3	0.3	2.1	7.4	10.2
Kansas.........	19.3	78.1	-	72.0	18.7	6.1	2.7	0.6	0.9	3.3	2.9	6.1
Kentucky........	27.4	94.3	-	94.3	23.4	-	6.4	0.7	1.7	4.6	4.6	4.3
Louisiana........	31.9	103.9	-	103.5	28.3	0.3	6.0	0.4	6.0	1.2	22.2	16.8
Maine..........	7.1	33.0	0.1	33.0	5.9	-	2.0	0.4	1.2	0.7	0.4	0.8
Maryland........	27.8	109.6	-	100.9	25.8	8.7	7.3	2.7	5.9	4.2	5.8	-
Massachusetts......	23.4	137.1	-	136.1	22.4	1.1	7.4	2.3	7.7	3.0	8.8	3.0
Michigan........	66.0	212.6	-	200.5	65.0	12.0	12.9	2.0	1.7	8.1	12.8	11.0
Minnesota.......	37.2	117.0	-	117.0	33.3	-	2.6	11.1	2.2	3.9	4.8	10.8
Mississippi.......	19.2	76.8	-	70.9	17.6	5.9	3.1	0.8	3.1	0.2	10.6	22.2
Missouri.........	31.5	124.1	-	118.7	29.4	5.4	8.0	2.8	3.3	4.4	13.0	9.3
Montana........	7.7	19.9	-	19.8	7.3	0.1	1.5	0.5	0.9	0.6	0.6	0.6
Nebraska........	10.5	41.6	-	38.8	10.0	2.9	2.8	1.2	0.8	0.6	4.6	3.9
Nevada.........	7.4	29.5	-	29.5	7.2	-	1.0	0.4	1.2	0.7	1.0	5.0
New Hampshire.....	7.0	28.3	-	28.3	6.7	-	1.4	2.2	0.9	0.1	0.8	0.4
New Jersey.......	43.9	187.8	12.8	177.8	27.4	10.0	5.7	11.4	2.7	3.7	15.0	3.7
New Mexico.......	18.4	46.0	-	42.0	17.5	4.0	1.4	0.4	2.2	0.3	5.7	0.7
New York.........	49.4	445.6	-	413.6	44.7	32.1	6.7	49.5	9.5	17.7	48.4	53.1
North Carolina.....	47.1	181.4	-	166.3	44.2	15.2	1.4	13.6	2.6	14.8	15.9	23.3
North Dakota......	6.9	13.6	-	13.6	6.6	-	0.4	1.0	1.2	0.3	1.1	-
Ohio...........	67.0	236.7	-	230.4	64.8	6.3	2.1	24.8	3.6	16.0	12.2	13.9
Oklahoma........	27.0	78.6	-	78.4	24.8	0.3	5.3	0.2	4.1	1.3	4.4	10.1
Oregon.........	16.2	69.3	-	61.5	15.2	7.8	5.4	0.9	1.9	4.0	6.7	2.8
Pennsylvania......	51.9	220.2	-	213.9	49.1	6.2	11.9	21.1	1.4	4.9	14.1	0.2
Rhode Island......	6.6	22.8	0.5	22.8	5.5	-	1.6	0.2	1.4	0.1	1.3	-
South Carolina.....	28.6	87.4	-	87.4	25.9	-	5.0	0.3	7.8	2.0	8.9	21.6
South Dakota......	5.0	18.1	-	17.8	4.6	0.4	0.9	0.3	0.5	0.2	1.0	0.6
Tennessee........	36.1	112.6	-	112.6	34.1	-	5.3	2.7	3.1	3.5	10.0	20.2
Texas..........	93.6	555.8	-	524.4	88.9	31.4	21.5	3.1	14.6	18.2	33.3	45.0
Utah...........	25.9	44.3	-	44.3	24.9	-	3.2	0.5	1.5	1.7	5.1	0.9
Vermont.........	4.7	16.1	-	16.1	4.3	-	1.1	-	0.5	-	0.2	-
Virginia.........	46.7	159.8	-	158.6	43.9	1.3	2.0	6.6	5.2	5.9	13.4	3.5
Washington.......	50.3	87.4	-	87.4	46.8	-	5.0	1.0	5.4	3.3	7.6	9.5
West Virginia......	13.2	41.2	-	41.2	11.7	-	0.1	-	0.7	1.2	1.7	3.6
Wisconsin........	29.6	120.9	-	111.2	28.3	9.8	1.1	13.2	1.9	6.1	3.9	1.6
Wyoming.........	3.2	16.5	-	14.7	3.1	1.8	0.8	-	0.5	0.2	1.0	4.5

See footnote at end of table.

U.S. Census Bureau, Statistical Abstract of the United States: 2000

State and Local Government Full-Time Equivalent Employment by Selected Function and State: 1998—Continued

[In thousands, for March. Local government amounts are estimates subject to sampling variation; see Appendix III and source]

State	Highways		Police protection		Fire protection		Corrections		Parks and recreation		Government administration	
	State	Local	State	Local	State	Local	State	Local	State	Local	State	Local
United States.....	247.2	296.1	98.2	750.8	(X)	289.6	457.2	221.0	32.9	205.4	361.8	640.1
Alabama	3.5	7.0	1.4	11.1	(X)	5.5	4.4	2.6	0.6	3.3	7.1	8.4
Alaska.	2.7	0.8	0.4	1.1	(X)	0.6	1.3	0.1	0.1	0.3	2.7	2.2
Arizona	3.0	4.5	1.8	14.4	(X)	5.1	8.9	3.8	0.4	4.0	5.4	16.2
Arkansas	3.5	3.6	1.1	6.6	(X)	2.4	3.7	1.5	0.7	0.9	2.8	6.1
California	19.5	21.3	12.4	82.4	(X)	29.8	47.1	28.8	3.0	31.7	28.8	91.4
Colorado	3.0	5.1	1.3	10.9	(X)	4.4	5.4	3.3	0.2	6.1	5.8	10.0
Connecticut	3.6	4.0	1.7	8.5	(X)	4.5	8.8	-	0.2	2.3	7.8	4.6
Delaware	1.4	0.4	0.9	1.5	(X)	0.3	2.3	-	0.2	0.3	2.5	1.1
District of Columbia . . .	(X)	0.5	(X)	4.2	(X)	1.6	(X)	2.9	(X)	0.6	(X)	2.0
Florida.	10.3	12.9	4.0	49.4	(X)	19.9	31.9	13.9	1.1	16.0	25.0	37.4
Georgia	6.2	7.6	2.2	20.9	(X)	8.9	18.6	7.2	1.6	4.1	5.0	19.1
Hawaii.	0.9	1.0	-	3.5	(X)	1.7	2.3	-	0.2	1.7	3.9	2.2
Idaho	1.7	1.7	0.5	2.8	(X)	1.0	1.6	1.0	0.2	0.7	2.2	3.2
Illinois	8.3	12.5	3.9	41.3	(X)	15.9	15.8	9.2	0.7	15.2	11.1	31.1
Indiana	4.3	7.1	2.0	14.2	(X)	7.0	6.0	4.6	0.1	3.5	4.3	15.0
Iowa	2.9	5.6	1.0	5.9	(X)	1.7	3.1	1.0	0.1	1.8	4.6	5.8
Kansas	3.4	5.1	1.0	7.9	(X)	2.7	3.5	2.2	0.5	2.0	4.5	6.9
Kentucky	5.4	3.5	2.1	7.6	(X)	5.1	3.5	2.6	1.6	1.4	8.8	6.8
Louisiana.	5.7	5.0	1.1	14.2	(X)	4.4	6.8	5.4	1.2	2.9	5.7	10.7
Maine	2.6	1.8	0.4	2.9	(X)	1.3	1.2	0.6	0.1	0.6	2.1	3.0
Maryland	4.7	5.3	2.4	15.2	(X)	6.1	11.4	2.8	0.6	6.4	8.8	8.9
Massachusetts	4.4	6.4	4.7	18.0	(X)	12.6	6.9	5.4	1.0	2.0	13.3	9.5
Michigan	3.0	9.5	3.2	21.6	(X)	7.9	17.8	5.1	0.5	4.7	6.4	23.3
Minnesota	5.1	7.5	0.9	9.7	(X)	2.1	3.6	4.0	0.6	4.4	6.0	12.9
Mississippi	3.3	5.4	1.2	7.4	(X)	3.1	4.1	1.5	0.4	0.9	2.1	7.7
Missouri.	6.6	7.2	2.4	14.9	(X)	6.9	11.5	2.2	0.6	4.1	7.1	10.8
Montana	1.9	1.2	0.4	1.8	(X)	0.6	1.0	0.5	0.1	0.4	1.6	2.3
Nebraska.	2.3	2.9	0.7	3.8	(X)	1.2	1.9	1.0	0.3	1.0	1.6	4.1
Nevada	1.6	1.6	0.7	5.4	(X)	2.1	3.1	1.6	0.2	2.4	2.7	5.7
New Hampshire	1.9	1.8	0.4	2.8	(X)	1.6	1.2	0.5	0.2	0.4	1.7	1.7
New Jersey	7.3	10.5	3.8	29.3	(X)	7.2	9.4	6.5	1.7	5.0	19.5	18.8
New Mexico	2.4	1.8	0.6	4.7	(X)	1.8	4.2	1.3	0.7	2.0	4.7	4.7
New York.	13.6	26.8	5.7	79.1	(X)	23.4	35.3	26.1	2.7	10.2	36.4	41.7
North Carolina	11.9	4.2	3.4	19.4	(X)	6.3	19.1	3.8	0.9	5.2	10.2	11.1
North Dakota	0.9	1.0	0.2	1.2	(X)	0.3	0.5	0.2	0.1	0.8	1.3	1.4
Ohio	7.5	13.8	2.6	29.2	(X)	15.0	17.9	7.8	0.7	8.4	11.9	33.6
Oklahoma	4.1	6.1	1.8	9.1	(X)	4.2	11.5	1.0	1.8	2.2	5.6	6.2
Oregon	3.5	4.4	1.4	7.0	(X)	3.5	4.3	3.5	0.4	2.7	8.4	7.2
Pennsylvania	13.4	12.0	5.5	25.3	(X)	6.2	14.8	10.9	1.3	3.9	13.6	32.0
Rhode Island	0.8	0.9	0.3	2.8	(X)	2.5	1.8	-	0.1	0.5	2.7	1.6
South Carolina	4.9	2.7	3.2	9.9	(X)	3.8	8.9	1.9	0.6	2.7	3.5	7.7
South Dakota	1.0	1.5	0.3	1.4	(X)	0.4	0.9	0.5	0.1	0.5	1.2	1.6
Tennessee	4.7	6.5	1.9	15.3	(X)	6.6	6.3	4.8	1.1	4.2	5.3	11.0
Texas	14.7	19.7	3.6	54.5	(X)	19.3	46.8	21.6	1.0	12.9	16.8	41.0
Utah	1.8	1.7	0.8	4.7	(X)	1.7	2.9	1.0	0.3	2.5	3.4	4.3
Vermont	1.0	1.2	0.5	0.8	(X)	0.3	0.9	-	0.1	0.2	1.5	0.9
Virginia	10.3	4.4	2.5	15.2	(X)	7.2	15.6	6.3	0.9	6.6	8.0	14.0
Washington	6.4	6.9	2.2	11.6	(X)	6.5	7.5	4.3	0.6	4.2	5.7	15.3
West Virginia	6.2	0.9	1.0	2.6	(X)	1.0	1.2	0.4	0.6	0.8	3.6	3.7
Wisconsin	2.0	8.9	0.9	14.5	(X)	4.5	7.9	3.6	0.2	3.2	6.1	11.2
Wyoming	1.8	0.6	0.2	1.4	(X)	0.4	0.7	0.3	0.1	0.6	1.0	1.0

- Represents or rounds to zero.   X Not applicable.

Source: U.S. Census Bureau; <http://www.census.gov/govs/www/apes/html> (accessed 28 August 2000).

State and Local Government Finances and Employment   333

No. 529. State and Local Government Employment and Average Earnings by State: 1990 and 1998

[In thousands (3,840 represents 3,840,000) except as noted. For 1998 for March; prior years for October]

State	Full-time equivalent employment (1,000)				Full-time equivalent employment per 10,000 population [2]				Average earnings [3] (dol.)			
	State		Local [1]		State		Local [1]		State		Local [1]	
	1990	1998	1990	1998	1990	1998	1990	1998	1990	1998	1990	1998
United States	3,840	3,985	9,239	10,505	154	147	371	389	2,472	3,088	2,364	2,938
Alabama	79	82	148	175	196	190	367	402	2,196	2,553	1,749	2,193
Alaska	22	22	21	22	401	361	385	359	3,543	3,778	3,491	3,801
Arizona	50	62	136	165	137	133	370	353	2,334	2,845	2,540	2,821
Arkansas	43	49	78	94	182	194	330	369	1,922	2,563	1,545	2,022
California	325	335	1,091	1,214	109	103	367	372	3,209	3,988	3,073	3,742
Colorado	54	61	130	159	165	155	395	401	2,765	3,554	2,292	2,885
Connecticut	58	61	98	103	178	186	299	315	3,018	3,654	2,854	3,682
Delaware	21	22	17	19	314	297	250	250	2,245	2,918	2,458	3,168
District of Columbia	(X)	(X)	57	44	(X)	(X)	939	835	(X)	(X)	3,024	3,610
Florida	160	177	497	559	123	119	384	375	2,095	2,845	2,247	2,621
Georgia	112	112	270	329	173	147	418	430	2,037	2,678	1,872	2,387
Hawaii	49	53	13	14	445	441	120	121	2,317	2,737	2,536	3,286
Idaho	19	22	37	49	186	179	372	396	2,100	2,744	1,772	2,282
Illinois	145	139	416	469	127	115	364	390	2,520	3,290	2,463	3,225
Indiana	89	83	196	225	161	140	354	382	2,496	2,679	2,036	2,514
Iowa	57	53	107	115	207	185	387	401	2,936	3,276	2,024	2,513
Kansas	50	44	104	123	200	169	421	467	2,077	2,887	1,979	2,438
Kentucky	75	73	114	139	204	184	310	353	2,141	2,812	1,823	2,187
Louisiana	85	94	155	178	200	216	368	407	2,047	2,475	1,713	2,170
Maine	22	20	42	48	179	161	345	387	2,352	2,808	1,978	2,418
Maryland	89	89	159	179	186	173	333	349	2,609	3,050	2,776	3,204
Massachusetts	93	84	196	217	155	137	325	354	2,541	3,291	2,554	3,227
Michigan	144	136	316	337	155	139	340	343	2,858	3,672	2,646	3,384
Minnesota	70	69	163	199	160	146	374	421	2,936	3,719	2,552	3,078
Mississippi	47	52	105	125	183	188	407	455	1,824	2,483	1,543	1,948
Missouri	74	87	171	211	145	159	334	388	1,965	2,501	2,052	2,445
Montana	17	19	35	33	211	219	434	379	2,072	2,569	1,959	2,259
Nebraska	29	29	68	78	186	175	430	468	2,075	2,402	2,089	2,550
Nevada	19	24	42	59	160	138	348	336	2,502	3,198	2,574	3,377
New Hampshire	16	17	33	40	145	144	301	339	2,352	2,599	2,215	2,694
New Jersey	112	123	304	308	145	152	393	380	2,859	3,779	2,698	3,847
New Mexico	40	43	57	71	262	246	379	411	2,100	2,449	1,783	2,279
New York	285	252	866	898	158	138	482	494	2,997	3,649	2,795	3,608
North Carolina	107	123	244	298	161	163	368	395	2,372	2,832	2,065	2,513
North Dakota	15	15	20	21	234	240	314	332	2,057	2,560	2,138	2,608
Ohio	139	136	385	428	128	121	355	382	2,510	3,184	2,236	2,898
Oklahoma	65	71	116	133	208	213	369	398	1,975	2,051	1,761	2,128
Oregon	52	56	100	120	184	169	353	366	2,302	2,998	2,322	3,092
Pennsylvania	127	149	361	380	107	124	304	316	2,437	3,188	2,403	3,159
Rhode Island	21	20	27	30	205	205	266	300	2,586	3,296	2,656	3,247
South Carolina	79	80	116	157	227	209	333	408	1,956	2,486	1,848	2,339
South Dakota	13	13	24	27	192	177	349	369	1,979	2,559	1,733	2,189
Tennessee	79	81	175	205	163	149	358	377	2,055	2,597	1,883	2,361
Texas	223	268	706	872	131	136	415	441	2,192	2,843	1,952	2,371
Utah	37	46	51	67	216	221	294	321	2,000	2,652	2,092	2,680
Vermont	13	13	18	19	233	212	312	317	2,302	2,787	2,090	2,563
Virginia	117	111	221	258	188	163	356	380	2,267	3,013	2,248	2,681
Washington	91	106	164	190	187	187	336	333	2,459	3,271	2,515	3,527
West Virginia	34	32	59	62	188	177	326	341	1,919	2,430	1,862	2,250
Wisconsin	67	65	183	212	136	124	375	405	2,503	3,345	2,372	3,138
Wyoming	11	11	24	28	239	231	539	573	2,045	2,307	2,110	2,539

X Not applicable.   [1] Estimates subject to sampling variation; see Appendix III and source.   [2] Based on estimated resident population as of July 1.   [3] For full-time employees.

Source: U.S. Census Bureau, *1990 Public Employment,* Series GE, No. 1, annual; thereafter, <http//:www.census.gov/pub/govs/www/apes.html> (accessed 28 August 2000).

No. 530. City Government Employment and Payroll—Largest Cities: 1990 and 1998

[1998 for March; 1990 for October. In thousands, (456.2 represents 456,200). See footnote 3, Table 520, for those areas representing city-county consolidated governments]

Cities ranked by 1996 population	Total employment (1,000)		Full-time equivalent employment [1]				Payroll (mil. dol.)		Average earnings for full-time employees (dol.)	
			Total (1,000)		Per 10,000 [1] population					
	1990	1998	1990	1998	1990	1998	1990	1998	1990	1998
New York, NY [2][3]	456.2	447.0	394.6	416.4	539	564	1,091.7	1,485.9	2,783	3,694
Los Angeles, CA	51.3	47.2	50.8	46.2	146	130	176.5	207.4	3,488	4,534
Chicago, IL	41.6	41.9	41.6	41.9	149	154	124.9	195.8	3,002	4,670
Houston, TX	19.6	22.9	19.6	22.7	120	130	40.4	64.0	2,061	2,813
Philadelphia, PA.	32.4	30.2	31.9	29.4	201	199	89.1	102.4	2,843	3,511
San Diego, CA.	10.4	11.7	9.8	11.0	88	94	28.8	43.8	3,019	4,072
Phoenix, AZ	11.9	13.1	11.4	12.7	116	110	31.7	48.9	2,876	3,909
San Antonio, TX.	13.4	16.5	12.8	15.3	134	144	28.4	43.6	2,227	2,927
Dallas, TX.	14.9	15.4	14.5	15.0	144	143	28.2	49.6	1,945	3,326
Detroit, MI.	22.1	18.5	21.2	18.1	206	181	49.8	59.5	2,390	3,301
Honolulu, HI	9.9	9.7	9.2	9.0	110	103	23.7	30.9	2,600	3,479
San Jose, CA	5.9	7.4	4.9	6.7	62	80	16.0	33.2	3,453	5,227
Indianapolis, IN	12.8	11.4	12.5	11.2	171	150	23.1	30.2	1,910	2,756
San Francisco, CA	25.8	26.7	25.7	26.7	356	363	93.8	119.6	3,648	4,487
Jacksonville, FL	10.8	9.2	9.8	9.2	154	135	23.8	29.7	2,582	3,238
Baltimore, MD [2]	29.7	30.9	29.1	29.5	395	437	73.2	92.4	2,540	3,229
Columbus, OH.	7.7	8.9	7.5	8.6	118	131	17.8	28.5	2,416	3,369
El Paso, TX.	4.9	6.2	4.8	6.1	94	101	9.5	15.6	1,973	2,596
Memphis, TN [2]	21.7	26.3	21.1	25.2	341	422	47.6	73.6	2,287	2,973
Milwaukee, WI	9.0	8.0	8.6	7.9	137	133	20.6	28.6	2,431	3,636
Boston, MA [2]	20.9	22.7	20.9	21.3	363	382	49.8	73.9	2,391	3,526
Washington, DC [2][3]	49.6	36.5	47.9	34.9	789	642	138.7	129.3	2,930	3,725
Austin, TX.	10.0	10.9	9.6	10.1	203	187	20.9	30.9	2,186	3,121
Seattle, WA.	11.2	10.0	10.2	9.6	198	183	32.3	42.8	3,274	4,462
Nashville-Davidson, TN [2] . . .	17.9	24.2	16.9	20.0	347	392	41.8	46.8	2,510	2,353
Cleveland, OH	8.9	9.9	8.2	9.3	163	187	20.6	26.8	2,521	2,899
Denver, CO.	13.0	14.4	11.9	14.0	254	281	31.1	45.9	2,649	3,324
Portland, OR	4.8	6.0	4.5	5.3	97	109	14.6	22.6	3,305	4,390
Fort Worth, TX.	5.5	6.4	5.2	6.1	117	127	11.1	18.5	2,171	3,159
New Orleans, LA	9.8	10.9	9.6	10.7	194	224	15.5	24.5	1,623	2,322
Oklahoma City, OK.	4.8	5.1	4.5	4.8	101	102	10.5	16.0	2,430	3,482
Tucson, AZ	5.0	6.3	4.7	5.4	114	117	11.5	17.0	2,528	3,181
Charlotte, NC	5.0	5.0	4.8	4.9	115	112	11.5	15.6	2,399	3,188
Kansas City, MO	6.4	6.6	6.3	6.6	145	149	14.9	19.7	2,390	3,023
Virginia Beach, VA [2]	14.4	18.3	13.1	16.0	334	372	28.4	41.0	2,232	2,744
Long Beach, CA	5.7	5.9	5.4	5.5	126	131	17.7	24.3	3,413	4,720
Albuquerque, NM	6.9	7.8	6.2	7.1	161	168	12.2	17.2	2,040	2,494
Atlanta, GA	8.3	8.3	8.1	8.2	205	204	18.4	23.2	2,286	2,831
Fresno, CA	2.9	3.6	2.7	3.3	77	82	7.9	12.2	2,944	3,829
Tulsa, OK	4.4	4.5	4.2	4.4	115	115	10.5	13.5	2,555	3,118
Las Vegas, NV	1.9	2.6	2.0	2.5	77	65	4.9	10.8	2,563	4,512
Sacramento, CA.	4.2	4.3	3.9	4.3	105	114	11.3	16.0	3,021	3,733
East Baton Rouge Parish, LA.	6.0	7.1	5.0	6.3	132	170	11.0	15.7	2,255	2,615
Oakland, CA	4.6	5.5	4.1	5.0	111	136	15.3	22.3	3,948	5,084
Omaha, NE.	2.9	3.6	2.7	3.3	79	92	7.9	14.2	3,051	4,398
Minneapolis, MN	6.4	3.2	5.7	2.9	154	79	15.2	10.4	2,815	3,778
Miami, FL	4.3	10.4	4.0	6.3	113	175	14.6	21.7	3,771	3,654
St. Louis, MO	7.8	8.6	7.4	8.1	186	232	17.0	24.6	2,363	3,033
Pittsburgh, PA	5.9	4.4	5.6	4.3	152	123	12.3	15.3	2,240	3,610
Cincinnati, OH	7.0	6.4	6.3	6.3	173	182	16.1	20.5	2,634	3,399
Colorado Springs, CO.	5.9	6.9	5.3	6.6	188	191	13.3	21.5	2,618	3,371
Mesa, AZ	2.3	3.3	2.3	3.2	81	93	6.8	12.0	2,898	3,819
Wichita, KS	2.7	3.4	2.6	3.2	87	99	5.4	9.2	2,083	2,928
Toledo, OH	3.0	3.0	3.0	3.0	91	95	8.6	11.3	2,847	3,751
Buffalo, NY [2]	13.1	12.0	12.4	10.7	379	345	31.3	40.4	2,596	3,999
Santa Ana, CA.	2.0	2.5	1.7	2.1	58	70	6.8	9.3	4,144	5,315
Arlington, TX.	1.8	3.2	1.8	2.6	68	87	4.5	7.4	2,538	3,069
Anaheim, CA.	3.7	3.2	2.6	2.6	99	90	8.6	11.4	3,728	5,038
Tampa, FL	4.3	4.2	4.2	4.1	151	144	10.5	13.3	2,505	3,272
Corpus Christi, TX	3.2	3.4	3.0	3.2	116	115	5.9	7.9	2,009	2,507
Newark, NJ	5.1	5.5	4.9	5.2	177	195	8.3	21.4	1,698	4,177
Louisville, KY.	4.5	5.0	4.3	4.6	159	175	9.1	11.8	2,180	2,674
St. Paul, MN	3.6	3.5	3.4	3.2	124	122	10.5	12.1	3,265	3,961
Birmingham, AL	3.9	4.1	3.8	4.0	142	153	8.4	10.8	2,243	2,735
Riverside, CA	2.0	2.0	2.0	1.8	88	72	7.0	7.5	3,459	4,348
Aurora, CO	1.9	2.4	1.9	2.3	84	93	4.8	8.4	2,586	3,572
Anchorage, AK	8.8	9.8	7.9	8.4	351	334	28.4	29.4	3,706	3,571
Raleigh, NC	3.0	3.2	3.0	2.9	141	120	5.0	8.4	2,297	3,036
Lexington-Fayette, KY.	3.0	3.8	3.0	3.5	133	145	6.0	9.6	1,929	2,827
St. Petersburg, FL	3.0	3.0	3.0	2.8	125	121	7.0	9.3	2,412	3,264
Norfolk, VA [2]	10.5	14.3	9.8	12.0	376	513	21.9	30.8	2,268	2,577
Stockton, CA.	2.0	2.3	1.0	1.9	47	80	5.0	6.5	3,554	3,846
Jersey City, NJ	4.0	4.1	3.0	3.8	131	164	10.0	15.6	3,172	4,301
Rochester, NY	9.0	11.0	8.0	10.5	347	475	27.0	38.2	3,315	3,677
Akron, OH.	6.0	2.9	5.0	2.7	224	127	11.0	9.6	2,255	3,570
Lincoln, NE.	4.0	1.9	3.0	1.9	156	86	7.0	5.4	2,367	2,882
Mobile, AL.	2.0	1.4	2.0	1.4	102	71	5.0	5.1	2,025	3,756

[1] 1990 based on enumerated resident population as of April 1, 1990. Other years based on estimated resident population as of July 1.   [2] Includes city-operated elementary and secondary schools.   [3] Includes city-operated university or college.
Source: U.S. Census Bureau, City Employment, GE-90-2; and unpublished data.

State and Local Government Finances and Employment   335

No. 531. County Government Employment and Payroll—Largest Counties: 1998

[For March. See text, this section. See footnote 2, Table 522]

Counties ranked by 1996 population	Total employment (1,000)	Full-time equivalent employment (1,000)	Per 10,000 population[1]	Payroll (mil. dol.)	Avg. earnings, full-time employees (dol.)	Counties ranked by 1996 population	Total employment (1,000)	Full-time equivalent employment (1,000)	Per 10,000 population[1]	Payroll (mil. dol.)	Avg. earnings, full-time employees (dol.)
Los Angeles, CA	90.3	86.7	95	339.9	3,975	Kent, MI	2.0	2.0	36	6.1	3,198
Cook, IL	25.5	25.4	50	84.5	3,321	Wake, NC	16.9	14.5	271	13.7	806
Harris, TX	19.5	19.2	61	53.1	2,764	San Joaquin, CA	7.2	6.7	126	17.5	2,859
San Diego, CA	19.0	18.1	68	58.6	3,281	Tulsa, OK	1.6	1.6	29	3.2	2,053
Orange, CA	17.7	16.9	64	56.1	3,341	Summit, OH	3.6	3.5	67	8.6	2,453
Maricopa, AZ	8.2	7.9	30	21.3	2,721	Bernalillo, NM	1.5	1.4	27	3.6	2,565
Wayne, MI	6.7	6.6	31	23.1	3,536	Bristol, MA	0.7	0.7	13	1.7	2,568
Metropolitan Dade, FL	35.0	34.0	164	114.7	3,446	Camden, NJ	4.0	3.5	70	11.0	3,133
Dallas, TX	12.6	12.4	62	34.0	2,748	Union, NJ	5.5	4.0	81	15.2	3,926
King, WA	15.4	13.3	82	49.4	3,836	Hidalgo, TX	1.6	1.6	32	3.1	1,950
Santa Clara, CA	14.4	13.5	85	54.2	4,100	Jefferson, CO	2.6	2.4	49	7.1	2,991
San Bernardino, CA	16.5	15.5	97	50.9	3,344	Ramsey, MN	3.8	3.5	72	12.2	3,606
Broward, FL	10.6	10.4	72	31.5	3,067	Lake, IN	2.0	1.8	38	4.0	2,203
Riverside, CA	13.9	13.3	94	46.4	3,542	Gwinnett, GA	3.6	3.4	70	9.5	2,856
Cuyahoga, OH	15.4	15.4	110	43.7	2,842	Ocean, NJ	3.4	3.1	65	7.8	2,598
Alameda, CA	11.5	10.5	79	43.0	4,090	El Paso, CO	2.1	2.0	42	5.3	2,683
Bexar, TX	9.1	8.7	66	21.1	2,445	New Castle, DE	1.6	1.5	31	4.7	3,425
Tarrant, TX	6.4	6.3	49	16.1	2,555	Onondaga, NY	6.1	5.4	117	15.1	2,866
Nassau, NY	17.6	16.5	127	63.5	4,090	Anne Arundel, MD	14.0	12.6	270	16.1	1,168
Allegheny, PA	7.1	7.0	54	16.6	2,408	Passaic, NJ	3.8	3.5	76	7.4	2,149
Oakland, MI	4.8	4.4	38	13.8	3,262	Plymouth, MA	0.6	0.6	12	1.9	3,407
Sacramento, CA	12.3	11.9	107	44.4	3,760	Jefferson, LA	11.4	10.6	233	29.4	2,830
Hennepin, MN	11.2	10.4	98	36.9	3,552	Arapahoe, CO	1.9	1.8	40	5.5	3,008
Clark, NV	14.3	13.1	125	49.0	3,849	Brevard, FL	3.7	3.5	77	8.3	2,463
Franklin, OH	6.5	6.3	63	16.9	2,719	Lucas, OH	3.9	3.8	83	9.9	2,620
St Louis, MO	4.0	3.9	39	11.6	3,010	Lancaster, PA	2.4	2.2	50	5.0	2,413
Palm Beach, FL	8.3	8.2	82	25.0	3,091	Morris, NJ	3.6	3.1	70	8.0	2,674
Erie, NY	12.3	10.6	111	34.1	3,430	Hampden, MA	-	-	-	-	-
Milwaukee, WI	8.2	7.8	84	24.3	3,165	Polk, FL	3.9	3.7	85	9.3	2,532
Fairfax, VA	33.4	31.1	344	102.3	3,434	Douglas, NE	2.1	2.0	45	5.1	2,759
Hillsborough, FL	14.4	12.2	136	29.9	2,707	Genesee, MI	2.2	2.2	50	5.8	2,646
Westchester, NY	10.2	9.8	110	37.2	3,862	Sedgwick, KS	2.2	2.2	50	6.8	3,199
Pinellas, FL	5.5	5.4	62	14.4	2,665	Will, IL	1.8	1.7	40	4.9	2,872
Shelby, TN	13.7	12.6	146	34.0	2,696	Sonoma, CA	5.5	4.9	116	19.6	4,258
Du Page, IL	3.6	3.3	39	10.3	3,133	Stanislaus, CA	5.0	4.7	112	15.4	3,457
Hamilton, OH	5.8	5.7	67	14.5	2,557	Volusia, FL	2.8	2.6	62	5.9	2,383
Bergen, NJ	5.1	3.9	47	11.1	2,786	Burlington, NJ	3.5	3.1	76	5.8	1,855
Salt Lake, UT	5.4	4.1	50	12.2	3,231	Chester, PA	2.4	2.1	52	5.4	2,608
Montgomery, MD	36.5	29.2	358	68.2	2,247	Johnson, KS	3.4	3.0	75	8.7	3,010
Prince Georges, MD	28.6	26.5	343	24.2	823	Spokane, WA	1.7	1.7	41	5.0	3,035
Pima, AZ	7.7	7.0	91	18.3	2,696	Mobile, AL	2.0	2.0	50	3.7	1,839
Orange, FL	9.8	8.6	113	24.3	2,868	Dane, WI	2.4	2.1	54	6.7	3,339
Essex, NJ	6.9	5.8	76	17.3	3,074	Santa Barbara, CA	5.2	4.7	122	17.0	3,688
Fresno, CA	7.3	7.0	93	21.6	3,192	Washington, OR	1.5	1.4	38	4.7	3,297
Macomb, MI	2.9	2.7	37	8.2	3,165	Lee, FL	3.2	3.1	81	7.4	2,411
Monroe, NY	6.8	6.0	83	17.8	3,021	Guilford, NC	12.3	11.3	298	9.3	757
Worcester, MA	0.6	0.6	8	1.7	3,137	Westmoreland, PA	2.3	2.2	59	4.8	2,225
Fulton, GA	6.5	6.3	88	19.1	3,138	Stark, OH	2.7	2.7	71	5.8	2,171
Baltimore, MD	24.0	20.6	287	57.2	2,927	Collin, TX	1.0	1.0	28	2.6	2,492
Ventura, CA	8.2	7.9	111	28.5	3,595	Kane, IL	1.3	1.3	35	3.3	2,542
Montgomery, PA	3.2	3.1	44	8.1	2,640	York, PA	2.0	1.9	50	3.9	2,096
Middlesex, NJ	5.3	4.8	68	12.8	2,798	Solano, CA	2.7	2.5	68	8.3	3,461
San Mateo, CA	5.9	5.7	83	21.5	4,016	Knox, TN	9.2	8.2	225	18.7	2,279
Essex, MA	1.0	0.9	13	2.1	2,391	Hillsborough, NH	0.8	0.7	19	1.7	2,643
El Paso, TX	3.7	3.6	52	8.8	2,529	Polk, IA	2.1	1.9	55	5.9	3,088
Travis, TX	3.8	3.5	51	9.9	2,891	Berks, PA	2.5	2.5	71	5.0	1,993
Jefferson, KY	3.3	3.2	47	7.7	2,430	Pulaski, AR	1.3	1.2	35	2.8	2,283
Jefferson, AL	4.0	3.9	59	11.1	2,839	Tulare, CA	3.8	3.7	105	11.4	3,244
Pierce, WA	3.3	3.2	48	12.4	3,998	Denton, TX	1.1	1.1	31	2.6	2,369
Jackson, MO	2.0	1.8	28	4.0	2,237	Greenville, SC	2.0	1.7	50	3.8	2,307
Suffolk, NY	13.9	12.8	198	47.9	3,836	Waukesha, WI	1.4	1.3	38	3.6	2,803
Norfolk, MA	0.9	0.9	14	2.4	2,755	Monterey, CA	4.6	4.4	128	14.7	3,438
Oklahoma, OK	2.0	1.9	30	3.5	1,920	Seminole, FL	2.2	2.2	65	5.6	2,616
Multnomah, OR	4.1	3.6	58	13.1	3,792	Mercer, NJ	4.0	3.2	96	8.2	2,682
Kern, CA	8.1	7.5	120	26.7	3,611	Dakota, MN	1.6	1.5	45	4.9	3,446
Mecklenburg, NC	22.2	19.5	326	16.3	755	Orange, NY	3.3	3.0	93	8.5	2,819
Monmouth, NJ	5.8	5.1	87	13.8	2,747	Clackamas, OR	2.0	1.7	54	6.0	3,560
Dekalb, GA	6.1	6.0	102	16.9	2,829	Butler, OH	2.2	2.1	64	5.1	2,467
Lake, IL	2.6	2.4	40	7.4	3,112	Luzerne, PA	2.1	2.0	62	4.1	2,073
Bucks, PA	2.3	2.2	38	6.4	2,939	Utah, UT	0.8	0.7	22	1.9	2,822
Montgomery, OH	4.9	4.6	81	13.2	2,904	Nueces, TX	1.5	1.5	47	3.1	2,151
Hudson, NJ	3.8	3.3	60	7.9	2,438	Cameron, TX	1.2	1.2	38	2.0	1,679
Delaware, PA	3.2	3.2	58	7.4	2,328	Pasco, FL	1.2	1.2	39	3.0	2,532
Snohomish, WA	2.3	2.3	43	8.2	3,509	Allen, IN	1.4	1.3	41	2.8	2,295
Cobb, GA	3.9	3.7	68	10.1	2,845	Adams, CO	1.5	1.5	47	4.0	2,752

- Represents or rounds to zero.   [1] 1998 based on estimated resident population as of July 1, 1996.

Source: U.S. Census Bureau, unpublished data.

Section 10
Federal Government Finances and Employment

This section presents statistics relating to the financial structure and the civilian employment of the Federal Government. The fiscal data cover taxes, other receipts, outlays, and debt. The principal sources of fiscal data are *The Budget of the United States Government* and related documents, published annually by the Office of Management and Budget (OMB), and the Department of the Treasury's *United States Government Annual Report* and its *Appendix.* Detailed data on tax returns and collections are published annually by the Internal Revenue Service. The personnel data relate to staffing and payrolls. They are published by the Office of Personnel Management and the Bureau of Labor Statistics. The primary source for data on public lands is *Public Land Statistics*, published annually by the Bureau of Land Management, Department of the Interior. Data on federally owned land and real property are collected by the General Services Administration and presented in its annual *Inventory Report on Real Property Owned by the United States Throughout the World.*

Budget concept—Under the unified budget concept, all Federal monies are included in one comprehensive budget. These monies comprise both Federal funds and trust funds. Federal funds are derived mainly from taxes and borrowing and are not restricted by law to any specific government purpose. Trust funds, such as the Unemployment Trust Fund, collect certain taxes and other receipts for use in carrying out specific purposes or programs in accordance with the terms of the trust agreement or statute. Fund balances include both cash balances with Treasury and investments in U.S. securities. Part of the balance is obligated, part unobligated. Prior to 1985, the budget totals, under provisions of law, excluded some Federal

activities—including the Federal Financing Bank, the Postal Service, the Synthetic Fuels Corporation, and the lending activities of the Rural Electrification Administration. The Balanced Budget and Emergency Deficit Control Act of 1985 (P.L.99-177) repealed the off-budget status of these entities and placed social security (Federal old-age and survivors insurance and the Federal disability insurance trust funds) off-budget. Though social security is now off-budget and, by law, excluded from coverage of the congressional budget resolutions, it continues to be a Federal program.

Receipts arising from the Government's sovereign powers are reported as governmental receipts; all other receipts, i.e., from business-type or market-oriented activities, are offset against outlays. Outlays are reported on a checks-issued (net) basis (i.e., outlays are recorded at the time the checks to pay bills are issued).

Debt concept—For most of U.S. history, the total debt consisted of debt borrowed by the Treasury (i.e., public debt). The present debt series, includes both public debt and agency debt. The *gross Federal debt* includes money borrowed by the Treasury and by various Federal agencies; it is the broadest generally used measure of the Federal debt. *Total public debt* is covered by a statutory debt limitation and includes only borrowing by the Treasury.

Treasury receipts and outlays—All receipts of the Government, with a few exceptions, are deposited to the credit of the U.S. Treasury regardless of ultimate disposition. Under the Constitution, no money may be withdrawn from the Treasury unless appropriated by the Congress.

The day-to-day cash operations of the Federal Government clearing through the

U.S. Census Bureau, Statistical Abstract of the United States: 2000

accounts of the U.S. Treasury are reported in the *Daily Treasury Statement*. Extensive detail on the public debt is published in the *Monthly Statement of the Public Debt of the United States*.

Budget receipts such as taxes, customs duties, and miscellaneous receipts, which are collected by Government agencies, and outlays represented by checks issued and cash payments made by disbursing officers as well as government agencies are reported in the *Daily Treasury Statement of Receipts and Outlays of the United States Government* and in the Treasury's *United States Government Annual Report* and its *Appendix*. These deposits in and payments from accounts maintained by Government agencies are on the same basis as the unified budget.

The quarterly *Treasury Bulletin* contains data on fiscal operations and related Treasury activities, including financial statements of Government corporations and other business-type activities.

Income tax returns and tax collections—Tax data are compiled by the Internal Revenue Service of the Treasury Department. The *Annual Report of the Commissioner and Chief Counsel of the Internal Revenue Service* gives a detailed account of tax collections by kind of tax and by regions, districts, and states. The agency's annual *Statistics of Income* reports present detailed data from individual income tax returns and corporation income tax returns. The quarterly *Statistics of Income Bulletin* has, in general, replaced the supplemental *Statistics of Income* publications which presented data on such diverse subjects as tax-exempt organizations, unincorporated businesses, fiduciary income tax and estate tax returns, sales of capital assets by individuals, international income and taxes reported by corporations and individuals, and estate tax wealth.

Employment and payrolls—The Office of Personnel Management collects employment and payroll data from all departments and agencies of the Federal Government,

except the Central Intelligence Agency, the National Security Agency, and the Defense Intelligence Agency. Employment figures represent the number of persons who occupied civilian positions at the end of the report month shown and who are paid for personal services rendered for the Federal Government, regardless of the nature of appointment or method of payment. Federal payrolls include all payments for personal services rendered during the report month and payments for accumulated annual leave of employees who separate from the service. Since most Federal employees are paid on a biweekly basis, the calendar month earnings are partially estimated on the basis of the number of work days in each month where payroll periods overlap.

Federal employment and payroll figures are published by the Office of Personnel Management in its *Federal Civilian Workforce Statistics—Employment and Trends*. It also publishes biennial employment data for minority groups, data on occupations of white- and blue-collar workers, and data on employment by geographic area; reports on salary and wage distribution of Federal employees are published annually. General schedule is primarily white-collar; wage system primarily blue-collar. Data on Federal employment are also issued by the Bureau of Labor Statistics in its *Monthly Labor Review* and in Employment and Earnings and by the U.S. Census Bureau in its annual *Public Employment*.

Public lands—The data on applications, entries, selections, patents, and certifications refer to transactions which involve the disposal, under the public land laws (including the homestead laws), of Federal public lands to non-Federal owners. In general, original entries and selections are applications to secure title to public lands which have been accepted as properly filed (i.e., allowed). Some types of applications, however, are not reported until issuance of the final certificate, which passes equitable title to the land to the applicant.

No. 532. Federal Budget—Summary: 1945 to 2000

[In millions of dollars (45,159 represents $45,159,000,000), except percent. For fiscal years ending in year shown; see text, Section 9, State and Local Government. The Balanced Budget and Emergency Deficit Control Act of 1985 put all the previously off-budget Federal entities into the budget and moved social security off-budget. Minus sign (-) indicates deficit or decrease]

Year	Receipts	Outlays	Surplus or deficit(-)	Outlays as percent of GDP [1]	Gross Federal debt [2]		Held by the public		
					Total	Federal gov't account	Total	Federal Reserve System	As percent of GDP [1]
1945......	45,159	92,712	-47,553	41.9	260,123	24,941	235,182	21,792	117.5
1950......	39,443	42,562	-3,119	15.6	256,853	37,830	219,023	18,331	93.9
1955......	65,451	68,444	-2,993	17.3	274,366	47,751	226,616	23,607	69.4
1960......	92,492	92,191	301	17.7	290,525	53,686	236,840	26,523	55.9
1965......	116,817	118,228	-1,411	17.2	322,318	61,540	260,778	39,100	46.8
1970......	192,807	195,649	-2,842	19.3	380,921	97,723	283,198	57,714	37.6
1975......	279,090	332,332	-53,242	21.3	541,925	147,225	394,700	84,993	34.8
1980......	517,112	590,947	-73,835	21.6	909,050	197,118	711,932	120,846	33.3
1981......	599,272	678,249	-78,976	22.2	994,845	205,418	789,427	124,466	32.5
1982......	617,766	745,755	-127,989	23.1	1,137,345	212,740	924,605	134,497	35.2
1983......	600,562	808,385	-207,822	23.5	1,371,710	234,392	1,137,318	155,527	39.9
1984......	666,486	851,874	-185,388	22.1	1,564,657	257,611	1,307,046	155,122	40.7
1985......	734,088	946,423	-212,334	22.9	1,817,521	310,163	1,507,357	169,806	43.9
1986......	769,215	990,460	-221,245	22.5	2,120,629	379,878	1,740,750	190,855	48.2
1987......	854,353	1,004,122	-149,769	21.6	2,346,125	456,203	1,889,922	212,040	50.4
1988......	909,303	1,064,489	-155,187	21.2	2,601,307	549,487	2,051,819	229,218	51.9
1989......	991,190	1,143,671	-152,481	21.2	2,868,039	677,084	2,190,956	220,088	53.0
1990......	1,031,969	1,253,198	-221,229	21.8	3,206,564	794,733	2,411,831	234,410	55.9
1991......	1,055,041	1,324,403	-269,361	22.3	3,598,485	909,179	2,689,306	258,591	60.7
1992......	1,091,279	1,381,684	-290,404	22.2	4,002,123	1,002,050	3,000,073	296,397	64.3
1993......	1,154,401	1,409,512	-255,110	21.5	4,351,403	1,102,647	3,248,755	325,653	66.3
1994......	1,258,627	1,461,902	-203,275	21.0	4,643,691	1,210,242	3,433,449	355,150	66.8
1995......	1,351,830	1,515,837	-164,007	20.7	4,921,005	1,316,208	3,604,797	374,114	67.2
1996......	1,453,062	1,560,572	-107,510	20.3	5,181,921	1,447,392	3,734,529	390,924	67.3
1997......	1,579,292	1,601,282	-21,990	19.6	5,369,694	1,596,862	3,772,832	424,507	65.6
1998......	1,721,798	1,652,611	69,187	19.1	5,478,711	1,757,090	3,721,621	458,131	63.4
1999......	1,827,454	1,703,040	124,414	18.7	5,606,087	1,973,160	3,632,927	488,865	61.5
2000, est....	1,956,252	1,789,562	166,690	18.7	5,686,338	2,210,478	3,475,860	(NA)	59.4

NA Not available. [1] Gross domestic product as of fiscal year; for calendar year GDP, see Section 14, Income, Expenditures, and Wealth. [2] See text, this section, for discussion of debt concept.

Source: U.S. Office of Management and Budget, *Historical Tables*, annual.

No. 533. Federal Budget Outlays—Defense, Human and Physical Resources, and Net Interest Payments: 1980 to 2000

[In millions of dollars (590,947 represents $590,947,000,000). For fiscal year ending in year shown. Minus sign (-) indicates offsets]

Outlays	1980	1990	1995	1997	1998	1999	2000, est.
Federal outlays, total	**590,947**	**1,253,198**	**1,515,837**	**1,601,282**	**1,652,611**	**1,703,040**	**1,789,562**
National defense	133,995	299,331	272,066	270,505	268,456	274,873	290,636
Human resources..............	313,374	619,329	923,765	1,002,336	1,033,426	1,058,888	1,124,844
Education, training, employment, and social services	31,843	38,755	54,263	53,008	54,954	56,402	63,397
Health......................	23,169	57,716	115,418	123,843	131,442	141,079	154,227
Medicare...................	32,090	98,102	159,855	190,016	192,822	190,447	202,513
Income security	86,557	147,076	220,493	230,899	233,202	237,707	251,286
Social security	118,547	248,623	335,846	365,257	379,225	390,041	406,625
Veterans benefits and services...................	21,169	29,058	37,890	39,313	41,781	43,212	46,796
Physical resources	65,985	126,039	59,142	59,900	74,695	81,928	86,261
Energy	10,156	3,341	4,936	1,475	1,270	912	-1,640
Natural resources and environment .	13,858	17,080	21,915	21,227	22,300	23,968	24,479
Commerce and housing credit.....	9,390	67,600	-17,808	-14,624	1,014	2,647	5,598
Transportation	21,329	29,485	39,350	40,767	40,335	42,531	46,709
Community and regional development...................	11,252	8,532	10,749	11,055	9,776	11,870	11,115
Net interest	52,538	184,380	232,169	244,016	241,153	229,735	220,314
International affairs	12,714	13,764	16,434	15,228	13,109	15,243	17,078
General science, space/technology .	5,832	14,444	16,724	17,174	18,219	18,125	18,853
Agriculture..................	8,839	11,958	9,778	9,032	12,206	23,011	31,988
Administration of justice	4,584	9,993	16,216	20,173	22,832	25,924	26,771
General government	13,028	10,575	13,998	12,891	15,709	15,758	15,035
Undistributed offsetting receipts	-19,942	-36,615	-44,455	-49,973	-47,194	-40,445	-43,061

Source: U. S. Office of Management and Budget, *Historical Tables*, annual.

Federal Government Finances and Employment   339

Figure 10.1
Federal Budget Summary: 1980 to 1999

Receipts, outlays, and surplus or deficit

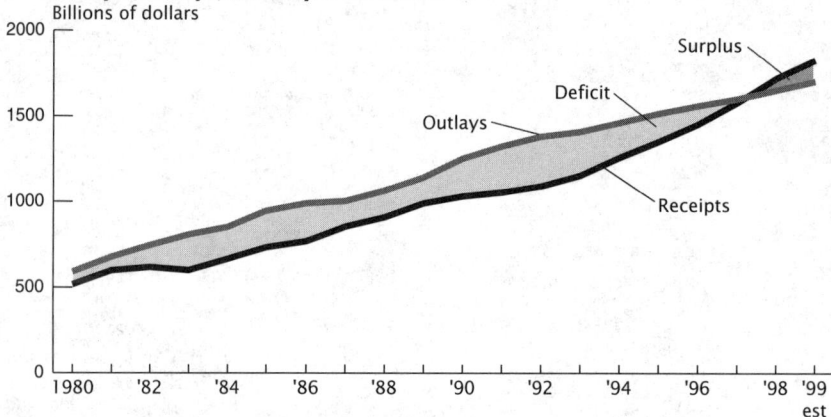

Outlays and Federal debt as a percent of gross domestic product

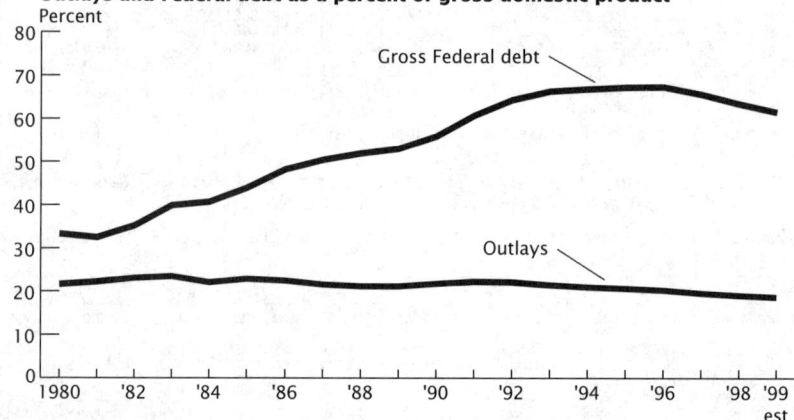

Gross Federal debt

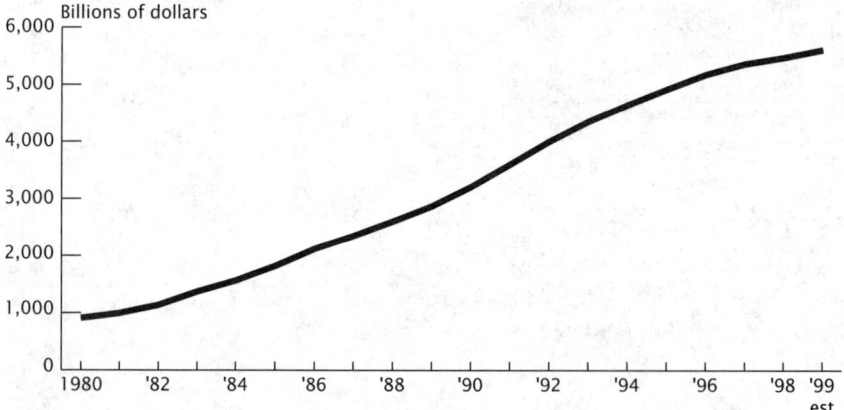

Source: Chart prepared by U.S. Census Bureau. For data, see Table 532.

No. 534. Federal Receipts by Source: 1990 to 2000

[In millions of dollars (1,031,969 represents $1,031,969,000,000). For fiscal years ending in year shown; see text, Section 9, State and Local Government. Receipts reflect collections. Covers both Federal funds and trust funds; see text, this section. Excludes government-sponsored but privately-owned corporations, Federal Reserve System, District of Columbia government, and money held in suspense as deposit funds]

Source	1990	1995	1997	1998	1999	2000, est.
Total receipts [1]	**1,031,969**	**1,351,830**	**1,579,292**	**1,721,798**	**1,827,454**	**1,956,252**
Individual income taxes	466,884	590,244	737,466	828,586	879,480	951,586
Corporation income taxes	93,507	157,004	182,293	188,677	184,680	192,395
Social insurance and retirement receipts	380,047	484,473	539,371	571,831	611,833	650,021
Excise taxes	35,345	57,484	56,924	57,673	70,414	68,384
Social insurance and retirement receipts [1]	380,048	484,473	539,371	571,831	611,833	650,021
Employment and general retirement	353,891	451,045	506,751	540,014	580,880	617,538
Old-age and survivors insurance:						
Trust funds (off-budget)	255,031	284,091	336,729	358,784	383,559	408,583
Disability insurance (off-budget)	26,625	66,988	55,261	57,015	60,909	68,180
Hospital insurance	68,556	96,024	110,710	119,863	132,268	136,515
Railroad retirement/pension fund:						
Trust funds	2,292	2,424	2,440	2,583	2,629	2,621
Railroad social security equivalent account	1,387	1,518	1,611	1,769	1,515	1,639
Unemployment insurance	21,635	28,878	28,202	27,484	26,480	28,188
Trust funds	21,635	28,878	28,202	27,484	26,480	28,188
Total excise taxes [1]	**35,345**	**57,484**	**56,924**	**57,673**	**70,414**	**68,384**
Federal funds	15,591	26,941	27,831	21,665	19,293	23,143
Alcohol	5,695	7,216	7,257	7,215	7,386	7,235
Tobacco	4,081	5,878	5,873	5,657	5,400	7,336
Telephone	2,995	3,794	4,543	4,910	5,185	5,500
Ozone depleting chemicals/products	360	616	130	98	105	73
Transportation fuels	(NA)	8,491	7,107	589	849	787
Trust funds	19,754	30,543	29,093	36,008	51,121	45,241
Highway	13,867	22,611	23,867	26,628	39,299	34,311
Airport and airway	3,700	5,534	4,007	8,111	10,391	9,222
Black lung disability	665	608	614	636	596	577
Inland waterway	63	103	96	91	104	104
Hazardous substance superfund	818	867	71	(NA)	11	204
Oil spill liability	143	211	1	(NA)	(NA)	173
Aquatic resources	218	306	316	290	374	336
Leaking underground storage tank	122	165	-2	136	216	183
Vaccine injury compensation	159	138	123	116	130	131

NA Not available. [1] Totals reflect interfund and intragovernmental transactions and/or other functions, not shown separately.

Source: U.S. Office of Management and Budget, *Historical Tables*, annual.

No. 535. Federal Trust Fund Receipts, Outlays, and Balances: 1996 to 1998

[In billions of dollars (835 represents $835,000,000,000). For fiscal years ending in year shown. Receipts deposited. Outlays on a checks-issued basis less refunds collected. Balances: That which have not been spent. See text, this section, for discussion of the budget concept and trust funds]

Description	Income			Outlays			Balances [1]		
	1996	1997	1998	1996	1997	1998	1996	1997	1998
Total [2]	**835**	**878**	**932**	**720**	**752**	**771**	**1,391**	**1,515**	**1,669**
Airport and airway trust fund	3	5	9	7	6	6	8	6	9
Federal employees health benefits fund	16	16	17	16	17	17	7	7	6
Federal civilian employees retirement funds	68	71	73	40	42	44	402	431	461
Federal old-age, survivors and disability insurance trust funds	418	449	481	352	367	382	550	631	730
Foreign military sales trust fund	15	15	14	14	15	14	6	-	-
Highway trust fund	(NA)	25	29	(NA)	25	25	(NA)	22	18
Health insurance trust funds:									
Medicare: Federal hospital insurance	124	129	138	128	138	137	125	116	117
Federal supplemental medical insurance	82	81	83	69	73	77	27	35	41
Military retirement fund	33	38	38	29	30	31	131	139	146
Railroad retirement trust funds	9	9	10	8	8	8	14	15	17
Unemployment trust funds	32	33	32	26	24	24	54	62	71
Veterans life insurance trust funds	2	2	2	2	2	2	14	14	14
Other trust funds [3]	10	10	10	9	9	9	31	31	33

- Represents or rounds to zero. NA Not available. [1] Balances available on a cash basis (rather than an authorization basis) at the end of the year. Balances are primarily invested in Federal debt securities. [2] Includes funds not shown separately. [3] Effective August 9, 1989, the permanent insurance fund of the FDIC was classified under law as a Federal fund.

Source: U.S. Office of Management and Budget, *Analytical Perspectives*, annual.

No. 536. Federal Budget Outlays in Constant (1996) Dollars: 1980 to 2000

[Dollar amounts in billions of dollars (1,087.9 represents $1,087,900,00,00). For fiscal year ending in year shown; see text, Section 9. Given the inherent imprecision in deflating outlays, the data shown in constant dollars present a reasonable perspective—not precision. The deflators and the categories that are deflated are as comparable over time as feasible. Minus sign (-) indicates offset]

Outlays	1980	1990	1993	1994	1995	1996	1997	1998	1999	2000, est.
Constant (1996) dollar outlays, total	1,087.9	1,478.0	1,507.7	1,530.3	1,550.6	1,560.6	1,572.5	1,604.8	1,626.3	1,670.3
National defense [1]	244.7	354.3	314.1	297.9	281.8	265.8	265.3	260.4	263.1	273.8
Nondefense, total	843.1	1,123.8	1,193.6	1,232.4	1,268.6	1,294.8	1,307.2	1,344.4	1,363.0	1,396.4
Payments for individuals	510.3	683.8	834.0	857.3	892.0	909.4	932.5	948.9	951.9	980.1
Direct payments [2]	450.5	593.5	701.5	716.2	743.3	761.8	786.4	793.9	788.7	813.6
Grants to state and local governments	59.8	90.2	132.5	141.1	148.7	147.6	146.1	155.0	163.2	166.5
All other grants	109.0	67.1	74.7	79.2	80.9	80.2	83.7	83.6	90.6	96.2
Net Interest [2]	93.3	213.6	211.6	211.2	236.6	241.1	239.9	234.1	220.2	208.0
All other [2]	171.9	207.2	115.8	125.6	106.0	101.8	100.3	123.1	138.7	152.3
Undistributed offsetting receipts [2]	-41.4	-47.8	-42.5	-41.0	-46.8	-37.6	-49.3	-45.3	-38.3	-40.2
Total outlays as percent of GDP	21.6	21.8	21.5	21.0	20.7	20.3	19.6	19.1	18.7	18.7
National defense [1]	4.9	5.2	4.4	4.1	3.7	3.5	3.3	3.1	3.0	3.0
Nondefense, total	16.7	16.6	17.0	17.0	17.0	16.8	16.3	16.0	15.7	15.7
Payments for individuals	10.2	10.2	11.9	11.8	11.9	11.8	11.6	11.3	11.0	11.0
Direct payments [2]	9.0	8.8	10.0	9.9	10.0	9.9	9.8	9.5	9.1	9.2
Grants to state and local governments	1.2	1.3	1.9	1.9	2.0	1.9	1.8	1.8	1.9	1.9
All other grants	2.1	1.0	1.1	1.1	1.1	1.0	1.0	1.0	1.1	1.1
Net Interest [2]	1.9	3.2	3.0	2.9	3.2	3.1	3.0	2.8	2.5	2.3
All other [2]	3.2	2.9	1.6	1.7	1.4	1.3	1.2	1.5	1.6	1.7
Percent of outlays, total	100.0	100.0	100.0	100.0	100.0	100.0	100.0	100.0	100.0	100.0
National defense [1]	22.7	23.9	20.7	19.3	17.9	17.0	16.9	16.2	16.1	16.2
Nondefense, total	77.3	76.1	79.3	80.7	82.1	83.0	83.1	83.8	83.9	83.8
Payments for individuals	47.1	46.6	55.5	56.2	57.7	58.3	59.3	59.1	58.6	59.0
Direct payments [2]	41.6	40.5	46.7	47.0	48.1	48.8	50.0	49.4	48.6	49.0
Grants to state and local governments	5.5	6.2	8.8	9.3	9.6	9.5	9.3	9.7	10.0	10.0
All other grants	9.9	4.6	4.9	5.1	5.2	5.1	5.3	5.2	5.6	5.8
Net Interest [2]	8.9	14.7	14.1	13.9	15.3	15.4	15.2	14.6	13.5	12.3
All other [2]	14.8	13.1	7.5	8.1	6.8	6.5	6.3	7.7	8.5	9.0
Undistributed offsetting receipts [2]	-3.4	-2.9	-2.7	-2.6	-2.9	-2.4	-3.1	-2.9	-2.4	-2.4

[1] Includes a small amount of grants to State and local governments and direct payments for individuals.   [2] Includes some off-budget amounts; most of the off-budget amounts are direct payments for individuals (social security benefits).

Source: U.S. Office of Management and Budget, *Historical Tables*, annual.

No. 537. Federal Outlays by Agency: 1990 to 2000

[In millions of dollars (1,253,198 represents $1,253,198,000,000)]

Department or other unit	1990	1995	1998	1999	2000, est.
Total outlays	1,253,198	1,515,837	1,652,611	1,703,040	1,789,562
Legislative Branch	2,241	2,625	2,600	2,609	3,197
The Judiciary Branch	1,646	2,903	3,467	3,790	4,378
Agriculture	46,012	56,665	53,947	62,834	71,096
Commerce	3,734	3,401	4,046	5,036	8,134
Defense-Military	289,755	259,556	256,122	261,380	277,476
Education	22,972	31,205	31,498	32,436	36,444
Energy	12,084	17,617	14,438	16,048	15,269
Health and Human Services	175,531	303,081	350,570	359,701	387,339
Housing and Urban Development	20,167	29,044	30,227	32,734	30,076
Interior	5,825	7,486	7,274	7,815	8,397
Justice	6,507	10,788	16,168	18,317	18,536
Labor	25,215	32,092	30,007	32,461	33,986
State	4,802	6,267	5,382	6,456	8,402
Transportation	28,650	38,777	39,466	41,829	45,925
Treasury	255,172	348,579	390,103	386,698	388,412
Veterans Affairs	28,998	37,771	41,773	43,168	46,723
Corps of Engineers	3,324	3,745	3,845	4,191	4,498
Other Defense-Civil Programs	21,692	27,977	31,216	32,014	33,008
Environmental Protection Agency	5,108	6,351	6,284	6,750	7,040
Executive Office of the President	158	215	237	417	267
Federal Emergency Management Administration	2,183	3,136	2,096	4,039	3,198
General Services Administration	-93	831	1,091	-46	525
International Assistance Programs	10,086	11,129	8,974	10,059	10,498
National Aeronautics and Space Administration	12,429	13,378	14,206	13,664	13,447
National Science Foundation	1,838	2,845	3,188	3,283	3,596
Office of Personnel Management	31,949	41,276	46,305	47,515	49,352
Small Business Administration	692	677	-77	57	107
Social Security Administration (on-budget)	18,147	31,753	38,134	40,575	44,518
Social Security Administration (off-budget)	244,998	330,370	370,069	379,213	394,947
Other Independent Agencies (on-budget)	68,679	-6,102	10,773	6,054	12,503
Other Independent Agencies (off-budget)	1,626	-1,969	217	1,021	1,498
Undistributed offsetting receipts	-98,930	-137,632	-161,035	-159,078	-174,073

Source: U.S. Office of Management and Budget, *Historical Tables*, annual.

342   Federal Government Finances and Employment

No. 538. Federal Outlays by Detailed Function: 1990 to 2000

[In millions of dollars (1,253,198 represents $1,253,198,000,000)]

Superfunction and function	1990	1995	1998	1999	2000, est.
Total outlays	**1,253,198**	**1,515,837**	**1,652,611**	**1,703,040**	**1,789,562**
National defense, total	299,331	272,066	268,456	274,873	290,636
Department of Defense—Military [1]	289,755	259,442	256,122	261,380	277,476
Military personnel	75,622	70,809	68,976	69,503	73,509
Operation and maintenance.	88,340	91,078	93,473	96,418	103,821
Procurement.	80,972	54,982	48,206	48,826	47,972
Research, development, test, and evaluation	37,458	34,594	37,420	37,363	37,400
Military construction	5,080	6,823	6,044	5,521	4,767
Family housing	3,501	3,571	3,871	3,692	3,753
Atomic energy defense activities	8,988	11,777	11,268	12,358	11,947
Defense-related activities	587	847	1,066	1,135	1,213
International affairs, total	13,764	16,434	13,109	15,243	17,078
International develop. & humanitarian assist.	5,498	7,599	5,446	5,654	7,281
International security assistance	8,652	5,252	5,135	5,531	5,354
Conduct of foreign affairs	3,050	4,192	3,262	4,162	5,960
Foreign info. and exchange activities	1,103	1,417	1,159	1,227	821
International financial programs	-4,539	-2,026	-1,893	-1,331	-2,338
General science, space & technology, total	14,444	16,724	18,219	18,125	18,853
General science and basic research.	2,835	4,131	5,353	5,679	6,260
Space flight, research, and supporting activities	11,609	12,593	12,866	12,446	12,593
Energy, total	3,341	4,936	1,270	912	-1,640
Energy supply	1,976	3,584	181	-118	-2,694
Energy conservation	365	671	621	586	690
Emergency energy preparedness.	442	223	233	225	164
Energy information, policy, & regulation.	559	458	235	219	200
Natural resources & environment, total [1].	17,080	21,915	22,300	23,968	24,479
Water resources	4,401	4,628	4,650	4,728	5,562
Conservation and land management	3,553	5,318	5,475	5,679	5,082
Recreational resources	1,876	2,801	2,984	3,498	3,611
Pollution control and abatement.	5,170	6,513	6,422	6,898	7,202
Agriculture, total.	11,958	9,778	12,206	23,011	31,988
Farm income stabilization.	9,761	7,020	9,297	20,020	28,748
Agricultural research and services	2,197	2,758	2,909	2,991	3,240
Commerce and housing credit, total [1]	67,600	-17,808	1,014	2,647	5,598
Mortgage credit	3,845	-1,038	-2,934	364	-4,464
Postal Service	2,116	-1,839	303	1,050	1,598
Deposit insurance	57,891	-17,827	-4,371	-5,280	-1,378
Transportation, total [1]	29,485	39,350	40,335	42,531	46,709
Ground transportation	18,954	25,297	26,004	28,052	31,639
Air transportation	7,234	10,020	10,622	10,720	10,600
Water transportation	3,151	3,732	3,510	3,544	4,208
Community & regional development, total	8,532	10,749	9,776	11,870	11,115
Community development	3,530	4,744	5,118	5,116	5,396
Area and regional development.	2,902	2,723	2,512	2,327	2,527
Disaster relief and insurance	2,100	3,282	2,146	4,427	3,192
Education, training, employ., & social services [1]	38,755	54,263	54,954	56,402	63,397
Elementary, secondary, & vocational education.	9,918	14,694	16,606	17,589	21,313
Higher education	11,107	14,172	12,070	11,783	11,653
Research and general education aids	1,577	2,120	2,271	2,318	2,752
Training and employment	5,619	7,430	6,636	6,781	8,214
Social services	9,723	14,882	16,335	16,853	18,280
Health, total.	57,716	115,418	131,442	141,079	154,227
Health care services	47,642	101,931	116,338	124,526	135,371
Health research and training	8,611	11,569	13,073	14,382	16,501
Consumer & occupational health & safety	1,462	1,918	2,031	2,171	2,355
Medicare	98,102	159,855	192,822	190,447	202,513
Income security, total [1]	147,076	220,493	233,202	237,707	251,286
General retirement & disability insurance [2]	5,148	5,106	4,632	1,940	5,042
Federal employee retirement & disability	52,037	65,882	73,485	75,146	77,710
Unemployment compensation	18,889	23,638	22,070	23,631	24,095
Housing assistance	15,891	27,520	28,741	27,677	29,221
Food and nutrition assistance	23,964	37,594	33,585	33,147	34,174
Social security	248,623	335,846	379,225	390,041	406,625
Veterans benefits and services, total [1]	29,058	37,890	41,781	43,212	46,796
Income security for veterans	15,241	18,966	21,322	22,153	25,052
Veterans educ., training & rehab.	278	1,124	1,102	1,273	1,255
Hospital & medical care for veterans	12,134	16,428	17,545	18,168	18,627
Veterans housing	517	329	837	560	610
Administration of justice, total.	9,993	16,216	22,832	25,924	26,771
General government, total	10,575	13,998	15,709	15,758	15,035
Net interest, total	184,380	232,169	241,153	229,735	220,314
Interest on the public debt	264,724	332,414	363,793	353,504	359,045
Interest received by on-budget trust funds	-46,321	-59,871	-67,208	-66,561	-71,356
Interest received by off-budget trust funds	-15,991	-33,305	-46,630	-52,071	-59,656
Undistributed offsetting receipts, total.	-36,615	-44,455	-47,194	-40,445	-43,061

[1] Includes functions not shown separately. [2] Includes social security.

Source: U.S. Office of Management and Budget, *Historical Tables*, annual.

Federal Government Finances and Employment   343

No. 539. Tax Expenditures Estimates by Function: 1999 to 2002

[In millions of dollars (2,120 represents $2,120,000,000). For years ending **Sept. 30.** Tax expenditures are defined as *revenue losses* attributable to provisions of the Federal tax laws which allow a special exclusion, exemption, or deduction from gross income or which provide a special credit, a preferential rate of tax, or a deferral of liability. Represents tax expenditures of **$2.0 billion or more in 2001**]

Function and provision	1999	2000	2001	2002
National defense:				
Current law tax expenditures	2,120	2,140	2,160	2,180
Exclusion of benefits and allowances to armed forces personnel . .	2,120	2,140	2,160	2,180
International affairs:				
Current law tax expenditures	14,415	15,595	16,685	17,015
Exclusion of income earned abroad by US citizens	2,330	2,550	2,790	3,040
Exclusion of income of foreign sales corporations	3,640	3,890	4,160	4,460
Deferral of income from controlled foreign corporations [1]	5,800	6,200	6,600	7,000
General science, space, and technology:				
Current law tax expenditures	3,595	2,875	5,245	5,675
Commerce and housing:				
Current law tax expenditures	227,870	235,565	247,145	255,305
Exclusion of interest on life insurance savings.	13,920	14,985	16,130	17,365
Deductibility of mortgage interest on owner-occupied homes . . .	56,920	58,815	60,925	63,240
Deductibility of State and local property tax on owner-occupied homes	21,215	22,185	23,075	24,000
Capital gains exclusion on home sales	18,000	18,540	19,095	19,670
Exception from passive loss rules for $25,000 of rental loss . . .	5,315	5,035	4,790	4,555
Credit for low-income housing investment.	2,820	3,055	3,195	3,300
Accelerated depreciation on rental housing [1]	3,710	3,985	4,225	4,500
Capital gains (except agriculture, timber, iron ore, and coal) [1] . .	39,405	40,575	41,780	43,025
Step-up basis of capital gains at death	25,800	27,090	28,240	29,370
Accelerated depreciation of machinery and equipment [1]	26,445	27,740	32,830	33,345
Graduated corporation income tax rate [1]	6,360	6,300	6,275	6,460
Transportation:				
Current law tax expenditures	1,870	1,970	2,080	2,200
Education, training, employment, and social services:				
Current law tax expenditures	34,070	36,030	37,565	38,745
Education:				
HOPE tax credit	4,595	4,925	5,125	5,145
Lifetime Learning tax credit	2,170	2,375	2,420	2,465
Deductibility of charitable contributions (education).	2,525	2,650	2,765	2,910
Deductibility of charitable contributions, other than education and health	19,220	20,015	20,860	21,780
Proposals affecting tax expenditures	-	66	1,363	3,654
Provide College Opportunity tax cut	-	-	395	2,009
Current law tax expenditures	82,880	89,290	95,150	101,690
Exclusion of employer contributions for medical insurance premiums and medical care.	69,610	75,095	80,570	86,175
Workers' compensation insurance premiums	4,420	4,585	4,555	4,935
Deductibility of medical expenses.	3,695	3,910	4,160	4,440
Deductibility of charitable contributions (health).	2,675	2,800	2,930	3,080
Income security:				
Current law tax expenditures	140,290	147,665	153,085	159,305
Exclusion of workmen's compensation benefits.	5,185	5,330	5,785	6,040
Net exclusion of pension contributions and earnings:				
Employer plans	83,780	88,830	92,390	97,085
Individual Retirement Accounts.	13,350	15,050	15,975	17,030
Keogh plans	5,230	5,550	5,895	6,255
Child credit	19,435	19,575	19,480	18,970
Earned income tax credit	4,825	4,700	4,790	4,985
Credit for child and dependent care expenses	2,420	2,390	2,360	2,330
Proposals affecting tax expenditures	-	5	2,648	4,605
Social security:				
Current law tax expenditures	23,300	24,505	25,765	27,295
Exclusion of social security benefits:				
Social security benefits for retired workers	17,135	18,010	18,885	19,995
Social security benefits for disabled	2,390	2,595	2,830	3,090
Social security benefits for dependents and survivors	3,775	3,900	4,050	4,210
Veterans benefits and services:				
Current law tax expenditures	3,120	3,265	3,405	3,545
Exclusion of veterans death benefits and disability compensation .	2,940	3,070	3,200	3,335
General purpose fiscal assistance:				
Current law tax expenditures	63,005	65,805	68,265	70,775
Exclusion of interest on public purpose bonds	22,750	22,975	23,205	23,440
Deductibility of nonbusiness state and local taxes other than on owner-occupied homes	37,740	40,240	42,390	44,735
Tax credit for corporations receiving income from doing business in U.S. possessions	2,515	2,590	2,670	2,600

- Represents zero.   [1] Normal tax method.

Source: U.S. Office of Management and Budget, *Budget of the United States Government*, annual.

No. 540. United States Government—Balance Sheet: 1990 to 1999

[In millions of dollars (70,415 represents $70,415,000,000). For fiscal year ending in year shown]

Item	1990	1995	1997	1998	1999
Assets, total	**70,415**	**89,349**	**121,273**	**135,874**	**170,777**
Cash and monetary assets, total	60,839	84,080	81,242	85,030	103,904
U.S. Treasury operating cash:					
Federal Reserve account	7,638	8,620	7,692	4,952	6,641
Tax and loan note accounts	32,517	29,329	35,930	33,926	49,817
Special drawing rights (SDR):					
Total holdings	10,666	11,035	9,997	10,106	10,284
SDR's certificates issued to					
Federal Reserve banks.	-8,518	-10,168	-9,200	-9,200	-7,200
Monetary assets with IMF [1]	8,883	14,682	14,045	21,155	19,982
Other cash and monetary assets:					
U.S. Treasury monetary assets	1,572	356	87	87	30
Cash and other assets held outside the Treasury					
Account.	8,079	29,697	18,670	18,967	18,795
U.S. Treasury time deposits	(NA)	528	4,021	4,543	5,554
Loan financing accounts:					
Guaranteed loans	(NA)	-12,714	-13,905	-14,362	-18,518
Direct loans	(NA)	19,732	53,816	65,289	83,894
Miscellaneous asset accounts	9,576	-1,748	120	-83	1,497
Total assets and excess of liabilities over assets. . . .	2,479,165	3,674,266	3,834,651	3,781,596	3,691,125
Excess of liabilities over assets at beginning of fiscal					
year	2,188,926	3,421,723	3,691,894	3,715,533	3,645,722
Add: Total deficit for fiscal year	220,388	163,916	-21,957	-69,242	-124,366
Subtotal	(NA)	3,585,639	3,713,850	3,646,292	3,521,356
Deduct: Other transactions not applied to surplus or					
deficit	564	722	472	569	1,009
Excess of liabilities over assets at close of fiscal year . .	2,408,750	3,584,917	3,713,378	3,642,594	3,520,348
Liabilities, total	**2,479,165**	**3,674,266**	**3,834,651**	**3,781,994**	**3,691,125**
Borrowing from the public	2,470,166	3,603,299	3,771,141	3,719,864	3,633,325
Public debt securities outstanding	3,233,313	4,973,985	5,413,147	5,526,194	5,656,272
Premium and discount on public debt securities	59,811	-79,996	-76,633	-76,849	-76,696
Total public debt securities	(NA)	4,893,989	5,336,514	5,449,345	5,577,575
Agency securities outstanding	32,758	26,955	33,187	29,359	28,910
Federal securities, total.	3,266,073	4,920,944	5,369,700	5,478,704	5,606,486
Deduct: Net Federal securities held as investments					
by government accounts.	795,907	1,317,645	1,598,559	1,758,853	1,973,160
Accrued interest payable	43,799	50,611	46,083	45,448	42,603
Special drawing rights allocated by IMF [1]	6,823	7,380	6,689	6,719	6,799
Deposit fund liabilities	8,306	8,186	6,800	3,893	3,977
Miscellaneous liability accounts (checks outstanding,					
etc.)	9,882	4,790	3,938	3,923	4,420

NA Not available.   [1] IMF = International Monetary Funds.

Source: U.S. Dept. of Treasury, *United States Government Annual Report*.

No. 541. Federal Participation in the Credit Market: 1970 to 2000

[In millions of dollars (16.2 represents $16,200,000), except percents]

Item	1970	1980	1990	1995	1996	1997	1998	1999 est.	2000 est.
Total, Federal and federally assisted									
borrowing	**16.2**	**122.5**	**376.9**	**323.2**	**361.1**	**208.7**	**300.3**	**317.4**	**221.7**
Federal borrowing from the public	35.0	69.5	220.8	171.3	129.6	38.2	-51.3	-50.1	-97.9
Guaranteed borrowing.	7.8	31.6	40.7	26.2	89.9	57.8	58.5	102.1	97.9
Government-sponsored enterprise borrowing. . .	4.9	21.4	115.4	125.7	141.5	112.8	293.1	265.3	221.7
Total, Federal and federally assisted									
lending	**15.9**	**79.9**	**133.5**	**90.4**	**255.1**	**178.4**	**341.5**	**423.7**	**332.1**
Direct loans	3.0	24.2	2.8	1.6	4.0	12.8	6.8	14.7	11.1
Guaranteed loans.	7.8	31.6	40.7	26.2	89.9	57.8	58.5	102.1	97.9
Government-sponsored enterprise loans.	5.2	24.1	90.0	68.2	161.2	107.9	276.2	306.9	223.1
Total net borrowing in credit market	88.2	336.9	704.1	705.6	713.7	687.1	933.8	(NA)	(NA)
Federal borrowing participation rate (percent) . .	18.4	36.4	53.5	45.8	50.6	30.4	32.2	(NA)	(NA)
Total net lending in credit market.	88.2	336.9	704.1	705.6	713.7	687.1	933.7	(NA)	(NA)
Federal lending participation rate (percent)	18.0	23.7	19.0	12.8	35.7	26.0	36.6	(NA)	(NA)

NA Not available.

Source: U.S. Office of Management and Budget, *Analytical Perspectives*, annual.

Federal Government Finances and Employment   345

No. 542. Summary of Federal Debt: 1990 to 1999

[In millions of dollars ($3,266,073 represents $3,266,073,000,000). Based on end of fiscal year]

Item	1990	1995	1997	1998	1999
Debt outstanding, total	**3,266,073**	**5,000,945**	**5,446,333**	**5,555,565**	**5,685,181**
Public debt securities	3,233,313	4,973,983	5,413,146	5,526,193	5,656,271
Agency securities	32,758	26,962	33,187	29,372	28,910
Securities held by—					
Government accounts, total	795,907	1,320,800	1,605,557	1,769,497	1,989,705
Public debt securities	795,762	1,320,784	1,598,459	1,765,580	1,989,072
Agency securities	145	16	7,098	3,917	634
The public, total	2,470,166	3,680,145	3,840,776	3,786,068	3,695,476
Public debt securities	2,437,551	3,653,199	3,814,687	3,760,613	3,667,199
Agency securities	32,613	26,946	26,089	25,455	28,276
Interest-bearing public debt, total	**3,210,943**	**4,950,644**	**5,407,528**	**5,518,681**	**5,647,241**
Marketable, total	2,092,759	3,260,447	3,439,616	3,331,030	3,232,998
Treasury bills	482,454	742,462	701,909	637,648	653,165
Treasury notes	1,218,081	1,980,343	2,122,172	2,009,115	1,828,775
Treasury bonds	377,224	522,643	576,151	610,444	643,695
Treasury inflation-indexed notes	(Z)	(Z)	24,384	58,823	92,365
Federal Financing Bank	15,000	15,000	15,000	15,000	15,000
Nonmarketable, total	1,118,184	1,690,197	1,967,912	2,187,651	2,414,242
U.S. savings bonds	122,152	181,181	182,665	180,816	180,019
Foreign series: Government	36,041	40,950	34,909	35,079	30,970
Government account series, total	779,412	1,324,270	1,608,478	1,777,329	2,005,166
Airport and airway trust fund	14,312	11,145	6,360	8,550	12,414
Bank insurance fund	8,438	20,117	26,329	27,445	28,359
Employees life insurance fund	9,561	15,839	18,038	19,377	20,755
Exchange stabilization fund	1,863	2,399	15,460	15,981	12,382
Federal disability insurance trust fund	11,254	35,150	63,513	76,947	92,622
Federal employees retirement funds	223,229	357,539	407,202	440,145	474,692
Federal hospital insurance trust fund	96,249	129,864	116,621	118,250	153,767
Federal Housing Administration	6,678	6,277	13,643	14,518	15,152
Fed. old-age & survivors insurance trust fund	203,717	447,947	567,445	653,282	762,226
Fed. S&L Corp., resolution fund	929	528	1,806	2,087	2,304
Fed. supplementary medical insur. trust fund	14,286	13,513	34,464	39,502	26,528
Government life insurance fund	184	106	(Z)	(Z)	(Z)
Highway trust fund	9,530	8,954	22,341	17,926	28,083
National service life insurance fund	10,917	11,954	12,023	12,008	11,954
Postal Service fund	3,063	1,249	860	1,000	-
Railroad retirement account	8,356	12,129	17,486	19,764	22,347
Treasury deposit funds	304	130	74	71	71
Unemployment trust fund	50,186	47,098	61,880	70,598	77,357
Other	106,376	202,332	222,933	239,878	264,153
State and local government series	161,248	113,368	111,863	164,431	168,091
Domestic series	18,886	29,995	29,995	29,995	29,995
Other	447	432	1	1	1
MATURITY DISTRIBUTION					
Amount outstanding, privately held	**1,841,903**	**2,870,781**	**2,998,846**	**2,856,637**	**2,726,011**
Maturity class:					
Within 1 year	626,297	1,002,875	1,017,913	940,572	915,146
1-5 years	630,144	1,157,492	1,206,993	1,105,175	946,041
5-10 years	267,573	290,111	321,622	319,331	331,115
10-20 years	82,713	87,297	154,205	157,347	149,703
20 years and over	235,176	333,006	298,113	334,212	298,750

- Represents or rounds to zero.   Z Less than $500,000.

Source: U.S. Department of the Treasury, *Treasury Bulletin*, quarterly.

No. 543. U.S. Savings Bonds: 1980 to 1999

[In billions of dollars ($73 represents $73,000,000), except percent. As of end of fiscal year, see text, Section 9, State and Local Government]

Item	1980	1990	1991	1992	1993	1994	1995	1996	1997	1998	1999
Amounts outstanding, total [1]	73	123	134	149	167	177	182	184	183	181	180
Funds from sales	5	8	9	14	17	9	7	6	5	5	6
Accrued discounts	4	8	10	9	9	9	9	10	9	9	9
Redemptions [2]	17	8	8	7	8	9	12	2	2	14	14
Percent of total outstanding	23.0	6.1	5.6	5.0	4.7	5.3	6.5	1.4	1.1	7.9	7.9

[1] Interest-bearing debt only for amounts end of year.   [2] Matured and unmatured bonds.

Source: U.S. Dept. of the Treasury, *Treasury Bulletin*, quarterly.

No. 544. Federal Funds—Summary Distribution by State: 1998

[In millions of dollars ($1,484,177 represents $1,484,177,000,000). For year ending Sept. 30. Data for grants, salaries and wages and direct payments to individuals are on an expenditures basis; procurement is on obligation basis]

State	Federal funds			Non-defense	Direct payments to individuals	Procure-ment	Grants to state and local govern-ments	Salaries and wages
	Total [1]	Per capita [2] (dol.)	Defense					
United States [3]. . . .	1,484,177	5,491	226,444	1,257,733	835,619	209,260	269,128	170,171
Alabama	25,297	5,813	4,501	20,796	15,089	3,104	4,161	2,944
Alaska.	4,767	7,763	1,467	3,300	1,194	863	1,427	1,282
Arizona	24,067	5,155	4,753	19,315	13,595	3,793	4,147	2,533
Arkansas	13,016	5,128	938	12,078	9,048	475	2,440	1,054
California	161,571	4,946	29,072	132,498	86,771	25,365	32,090	17,344
Colorado	21,009	5,291	4,632	16,377	10,164	4,300	3,048	3,496
Connecticut	19,424	5,933	3,920	15,504	10,600	3,814	3,653	1,357
Delaware	3,553	4,776	382	3,172	2,293	215	678	367
District of Columbia . . .	24,034	45,955	2,274	21,761	3,298	5,200	4,101	11,436
Florida.	83,558	5,602	12,201	71,357	58,414	7,128	10,320	7,696
Georgia.	37,144	4,861	8,118	29,026	20,324	4,603	6,233	5,984
Hawaii.	8,442	7,076	3,394	5,048	3,641	1,053	1,190	2,557
Idaho	5,961	4,850	535	5,426	3,235	1,019	1,055	652
Illinois	55,467	4,605	3,313	52,154	35,246	4,576	10,156	5,490
Indiana	26,098	4,424	2,510	23,588	17,796	2,233	4,152	1,917
Iowa	14,535	5,079	719	13,815	10,241	930	2,424	941
Kansas	13,426	5,107	2,061	11,365	8,497	1,316	1,934	1,680
Kentucky	23,161	5,884	3,269	19,892	12,588	3,850	4,236	2,488
Louisiana	22,900	5,242	2,441	20,459	13,839	2,351	4,708	2,002
Maine	7,463	5,999	1,442	6,021	4,088	1,025	1,602	748
Maryland	41,565	8,094	8,738	32,827	18,083	10,417	5,022	8,042
Massachusetts	37,173	6,047	5,103	32,070	20,864	5,451	8,019	2,840
Michigan	41,917	4,270	1,852	40,065	28,613	1,871	8,618	2,814
Minnesota	20,399	4,317	1,591	18,808	12,701	1,795	4,199	1,704
Mississippi	15,314	5,565	2,429	12,885	9,176	1,613	3,025	1,500
Missouri.	32,682	6,009	5,678	27,004	18,221	6,341	5,065	3,055
Montana	5,465	6,210	367	5,098	3,337	376	1,139	614
Nebraska.	8,253	4,963	868	7,385	5,292	487	1,511	963
Nevada	7,566	4,331	955	6,611	4,846	805	1,081	835
New Hampshire	5,272	4,449	702	4,569	3,258	524	1,042	448
New Jersey	40,373	4,975	4,068	36,304	25,715	4,091	7,108	3,458
New Mexico	12,933	7,446	1,605	11,329	5,036	3,769	2,547	1,581
New York.	99,766	5,489	4,746	95,020	58,464	5,995	28,066	7,240
North Carolina	35,677	4,728	5,123	30,554	21,645	2,064	7,133	4,833
North Dakota	4,131	6,475	477	3,654	2,253	258	1,067	554
Ohio	52,006	4,640	4,434	47,571	33,663	4,368	9,733	4,242
Oklahoma	18,205	5,439	2,970	15,234	11,128	1,381	3,059	2,637
Oregon	15,119	4,607	820	14,299	9,646	728	3,275	1,471
Pennsylvania	67,350	5,612	5,417	61,933	44,501	5,163	12,381	5,306
Rhode Island	6,039	6,112	722	5,317	3,644	313	1,368	715
South Carolina	19,870	5,180	3,235	16,635	11,611	2,489	3,525	2,246
South Dakota	4,319	5,852	310	4,009	2,487	317	1,007	508
Tennessee	30,497	5,615	2,272	28,225	17,238	5,116	5,510	2,633
Texas	92,019	4,657	15,994	76,024	51,152	13,893	15,809	11,164
Utah	8,728	4,156	1,305	7,423	4,430	1,180	1,727	1,392
Vermont	2,895	4,898	188	2,706	1,659	154	803	278
Virginia	55,830	8,221	23,079	32,752	21,525	18,523	4,423	11,360
Washington	31,186	5,482	6,416	24,770	16,232	4,920	5,422	4,612
West Virginia	10,697	5,906	364	10,332	6,870	488	2,480	859
Wisconsin	21,883	4,189	986	20,896	14,426	1,295	4,697	1,464
Wyoming	2,743	5,702	283	2,460	1,343	175	850	376

[1] Includes other programs not shown separately.   [2] Based on U.S. Census Bureau resident population as of July 1.
[3] Includes outlying areas, not shown separately.

Source: U.S. Census Bureau, *Federal Expenditures by State for Fiscal Year*, annual.

Federal Government Finances and Employment   347

No. 545. Per Capita Federal Balance of Payments by State: 1990 to 1998

[For year ending Sept. 30. Represents Federal spending within the borders of the 50 states, including defense and excluding interest payments on the Federal debt. Each state runs a balance of payments surplus or deficit with the Federal Government. Put another way, each state indirectly subsidizes or is being subsidized by the other states]

State	1990	1995	1996	1997	1998 Amount	1998 Rank	1998 Spending	1998 Defense	1998 Non-defense	1998 Social Security
Alabama	1,857	1,593	1,453	1,603	1,823	11	6,256	1,222	1,761	1,731
Alaska	1,003	1,057	1,365	2,019	2,108	7	6,888	2,208	3,047	634
Arizona	1,118	803	655	372	482	23	5,153	1,100	1,477	1,454
Arkansas	1,028	934	1,073	1,251	1,501	15	5,622	551	1,608	1,870
California	-463	-208	-283	-366	-587	39	4,880	954	1,376	1,182
Colorado	860	-133	-144	-444	-434	38	5,258	1,404	1,795	1,136
Connecticut	1,693	-2,209	-1,917	-2,272	-2,380	50	5,278	1,110	1,090	1,521
Delaware	-1,913	-1,483	-992	-1,030	-1,027	43	4,637	558	1,307	1,546
District of Columbia	26,381	32,441	33,554	35,520	36,987	(X)	(NA)	(NA)	(NA)	(NA)
Florida	45	375	285	338	125	28	5,915	962	1,299	1,980
Georgia	-180	131	67	-59	-109	32	5,297	1,246	1,494	1,338
Hawaii	769	1,020	1,414	1,788	1,938	10	5,747	2,366	1,307	1,043
Idaho	1,401	611	633	637	799	20	5,104	1,080	1,648	1,373
Illinois	-1,553	-1,680	-1,673	-1,688	-1,502	45	4,588	312	1,447	1,480
Indiana	-449	-747	-679	-511	-366	36	4,591	491	1,267	1,629
Iowa	252	-156	172	131	536	22	5,438	329	2,062	1,784
Kansas	278	-62	-96	-174	183	26	5,464	912	1,730	1,615
Kentucky	1,096	1,450	1,155	1,541	2,029	9	6,405	997	2,016	1,784
Louisiana	1,045	1,423	1,277	1,521	1,283	16	5,633	687	1,622	1,537
Maine	737	1,057	1,147	1,454	1,631	14	5,712	1,228	1,369	1,544
Maryland	1,291	1,600	1,387	1,767	2,101	8	8,299	1,825	3,804	1,300
Massachusetts	22	-244	-365	-518	-776	40	5,304	792	1,444	1,393
Michigan	-1,017	-1,439	-1,416	-1,383	-1,205	44	4,503	244	1,066	1,698
Minnesota	-590	-1,466	-1,343	-1,325	-1,534	47	4,569	417	1,527	1,429
Mississippi	2,185	2,332	2,451	2,234	2,300	6	6,144	1,084	1,673	1,716
Missouri	1,502	1,289	1,904	1,108	1,242	17	6,460	1,255	1,945	1,731
Montana	1,564	1,668	1,721	1,925	2,401	5	6,509	542	3,195	1,569
Nebraska	548	-44	-32	-138	123	29	5,291	645	1,907	1,572
Nevada	-871	-1,165	-909	-1,413	-1,763	48	4,315	894	1,136	1,335
New Hampshire	-1,561	-1,354	-1,375	-1,419	-1,531	46	4,099	628	1,128	1,337
New Jersey	-2,243	-1,983	-1,958	-1,946	-2,009	49	4,366	479	1,053	1,432
New Mexico	3,731	3,473	3,335	3,464	3,697	1	7,642	2,548	2,514	1,340
New York	-961	-1,030	-789	-785	-835	41	4,840	288	1,261	1,443
North Carolina	-196	75	33	134	65	30	5,125	829	1,325	1,630
North Dakota	1,951	1,748	1,577	2,788	2,513	4	6,958	874	3,169	1,545
Ohio	-204	-552	-442	-429	-361	35	4,729	497	1,193	1,623
Oklahoma	919	1,176	1,289	1,539	1,717	13	5,886	1,110	1,749	1,642
Oregon	-5	-360	-373	-387	-431	37	4,683	342	1,536	1,545
Pennsylvania	-194	11	3	44	213	25	5,356	511	1,367	1,765
Rhode Island	136	411	356	633	738	21	5,512	736	1,411	1,597
South Carolina	1,526	1,207	1,052	983	1,134	18	5,601	1,402	1,215	1,642
South Dakota	1,582	1,154	1,223	1,507	1,799	12	6,363	558	2,932	1,606
Tennessee	617	748	749	741	978	19	6,043	711	2,026	1,674
Texas	-52	65	-1	-42	-247	33	5,113	987	1,611	1,251
Utah	1,480	787	273	94	9	31	4,160	665	1,750	974
Vermont	-630	-12	62	-87	164	27	4,723	378	1,580	1,448
Virginia	2,408	2,836	2,353	2,648	2,905	2	8,603	3,646	2,655	1,347
Washington	353	48	-111	-99	-348	34	5,297	1,403	1,435	1,305
West Virginia	1,424	2,005	1,981	2,235	2,651	3	6,492	384	1,936	2,214
Wisconsin	-712	-1,147	-1,061	-965	-867	42	4,400	258	1,255	1,650
Wyoming	880	327	244	622	238	24	5,952	693	2,768	1,431

NA Not available.   X Not applicable.

Source: Jay H. Walder and Herman B. Leonard, *The Federal Budget and the States*, annual.

U.S. Census Bureau, Statistical Abstract of the United States: 2000

No. 546. Tax Returns Filed—Examination Coverage: 1988 to 1998

[In thousands ($103,251 represents $103,251,000), except as indicated. Return classification as Schedule C or C-EZ (nonfarm sole proprietorships) or Schedule F (farm proprietorships) for audit examination purposes was based on the largest source of income on the return and certain other characteristics. Therefore, some returns with business activity are reflected in the nonbusiness individual income tax return statistics in the table below (and vise versa), so that the statistics for the number of returns with Schedule C is not comparable to the number of nonfarm sole proprietorship returns in Table 857. Series completely revised starting with fiscal year 1988]

Year and item	Returns filed [1]	Returns examined					Average tax and penalty per return (dollars)		
		Total	Percent coverage	By—			Revenue agents [3]	Tax auditors	Service centers
				Revenue agents	Tax auditors	Service centers [2]			
INDIVIDUAL RETURNS									
1988.	103,251	1,621	1.57	353	532	736	997,696	2,188	1,950
1989.	107,029	1,385	1.29	243	543	599	246,371	1,827	1,649
1990.	109,868	1,145	1.04	202	517	426	309,566	1,962	2,432
1991.	112,305	1,313	1.17	200	500	613	664,440	2,398	2,738
1992.	113,829	1,206	1.06	210	537	459	1,365,896	2,280	2,539
1993.	114,719	1,059	0.92	251	506	303	103,250	2,625	2,974
1994.	113,754	1,226	1.08	364	456	406	246,785	3,113	1,963
1995.	114,683	1,919	1.67	339	459	1,122	204,616	3,497	1,404
1996.	116,060	1,942	1.67	252	509	1,180	818,753	3,051	1,714
1997.	118,363	1,519	1.28	210	506	804	802,549	3,460	2,963
1998 [4]									
Individual, total	120,342	1,193	0.99	168	383	625	177,830	3,372	2,760
1040A, TPI under $25,000 [5]	45,343	515	1.14	16	104	388	29,096	3,054	3,026
Non 1040, TPI under $25,000 [5]	12,923	104	0.81	11	38	53	32,439	2,184	2,457
TPI $25,000 under $50,000 [5]	28,293	165	0.58	16	78	68	28,927	2,105	1,991
TPI $50,000 under $100,000 [5]	19,444	121	0.62	17	60	43	16,565	2,499	1,450
TPI $100,000 and over [5]	6,045	100	1.66	41	27	31	219,233	6,272	4,379
Sch C—TGR under $25,000 [6]	2,530	60	2.37	9	30	20	11,363	3,140	1,720
Sch C—TGR $25,000 under $100,000 [6]	3,228	59	1.82	16	31	12	37,421	5,535	1,948
Sch C—TGR $100,000 and over [6]	1,836	60	3.25	39	14	7	209,606	10,391	3,633
Sch F—TGR under $100,000 [6]	425	4	0.93	1	2	1	7,141	2,015	865
Sch F—TGR $100,000 and over [6] . .	276	5	1.63	4	1	2	165,237	3,214	2,144
Corporation (except S Corporation). .	2,586	54	2.09	53	(NA)	2	4,367,167	(NA)	20,834
Fiduciary.	3,315	7	0.21	2	(NA)	4	37,779	(NA)	288
Estate.	102	10	10.22	10	(NA)	0.4	141,769	(NA)	8,606
Gift.	256	2	0.79	2	(NA)	0.0001	182,695	(NA)	(NA)
Employment.	29,070	34	0.12	32	2	0.3	142,058	3,080	594
Excise.	801	20	2.48	18	1	(NA)	144,703	364	(NA)
Windfall profit	(NA)	(NA)	(NA)	(NA)	(NA)	(NA)	(NA)	(NA)	(NA)
Misc. taxable		0.4	-	0.04	(NA)	0.0009	1,213,107	(NA)	4,631
Partnerships.	1,738	10	0.58	9	(NA)	2	(NA)	(NA)	(NA)
S Corporations (nontaxable)	2,450	26	1.04	25	(NA)	0.9	(NA)	(NA)	(NA)
Miscellaneous nontaxable [7]	(NA)	0.2	(NA)	0.02	(NA)	(NA)	(NA)	(NA)	(NA)

- Represents zero.   NA Not available.   [1] Returns filed in previous calender year.   [2] Includes taxpayer contacts by correspondence.   [3] Mostly reflects coordinated examination of large corporations and related returns.   [4] Includes activities to protect release of funds in Treasury in response to taxpayer efforts to recoup tax previously assessed and paid with penalty.   [5] Total positive income, i.e., excludes losses.   [6] Total gross receipts.   [7] Includes Domestic International Sales Corporations, Interest Charge Domestic International Sales Corporations, Real Estate Investment Mortgage Conduits, and other.

Source: U.S. Internal Revenue Service, IRS Data Book, 1997, Publication 55B.

No. 547. Internal Revenue Gross Collections by Source: 1980 to 1998

[For fiscal year ending in year shown; see text, Section 9, State and Local Government]

Source of revenue	Collections (bil. dol.)					Percent of total				
	1980	1990	1995	1997	1998	1980	1990	1995	1997	1998
All taxes	519	1,078	1,389	1,623	1,769	100.0	100.0	100.0	100.0	100.0
Individual income taxes	288	540	676	825	928	54.9	50.1	48.7	50.7	52.5
Withheld by employers.	224	388	534	580	647	43.1	36.0	38.4	35.7	36.6
Employment taxes [1]	128	367	465	529	558	24.7	34.0	33.5	32.6	31.5
Old-age and disability insurance.	123	358	455	518	547	23.6	33.2	32.8	31.9	30.9
Unemployment insurance	3	6	6	6	6	0.6	0.6	0.4	0.4	0.4
Corporation income taxes	72	110	174	204	213	13.9	10.2	12.5	12.6	12.0
Estate and gift taxes.	7	12	15	20	25	1.3	1.1	1.1	1.2	1.4
Excise taxes	25	49	59	59	59	4.7	4.5	4.2	3.6	3.3

[1] Includes railroad retirement, not shown separately.

Source: U.S. Internal Revenue Service, Annual Report, and Bureau of Alcohol, Tobacco, and Firearms, Alcohol and Tobacco Tax Collections.

Federal Government Finances and Employment 349

No. 548. Federal Individual Income Tax Returns With Adjusted Gross Income (AGI)—Summary: 1990 and 1997

[Includes Puerto Rico and Virgin Islands. Includes returns of resident aliens, based on a sample of unaudited returns as filed. Data are not comparable for all years because of tax changes and other changes, as indicated. See *Statistics of Income, Individual Income Tax Returns* publications for a detailed explanation. See Appendix III]

Item	Number of returns (1,000)		Amount (mil. dol.)		Average amount (dollars)	
	1990	1997	1990	1997	1990	1997
Total returns	113,717	122,422	3,405,427	4,969,950	29,947	40,597
Adjusted gross income (AGI)	113,717	122,422	3,405,427	4,969,950	29,947	40,597
Salaries and wages	96,730	104,405	2,599,401	3,613,918	26,873	34,614
Taxable interest received	70,370	67,301	227,084	171,700	3,227	2,551
Tax-exempt interest	3,917	4,926	40,228	49,017	10,270	9,951
Dividends in AGI	22,904	29,508	80,169	120,493	3,500	4,083
Business or profession net income	11,222	12,702	161,657	210,585	14,405	16,579
Business or profession net loss	3,416	4,236	20,227	23,844	5,921	5,629
Net capital gain in AGI	9,217	19,497	123,783	364,829	13,430	18,712
Net capital loss in AGI	5,071	7,124	9,552	8,746	1,884	1,228
Sales of property other than capital assets, net gain	866	879	6,300	6,321	7,275	7,191
Sales of property other than capital assets, net loss	825	868	4,829	7,782	5,853	8,965
Pensions and annuities in AGI	17,014	19,497	159,294	259,711	9,363	13,321
Unemployment compensation in AGI	8,014	7,124	15,453	17,230	1,928	2,419
Social security benefits in AGI	5,083	8,308	19,687	61,558	3,873	7,409
Rent net income	3,934	4,393	25,886	39,326	6,580	8,952
Rent net loss	5,163	4,836	33,450	28,320	6,479	5,856
Royalty net income	1,171	1,122	4,534	6,745	3,872	6,012
Royalty net loss	49	45	126	157	2,571	3,489
Partnerships and S Corporations net income [1]	3,210	3,918	112,030	213,559	34,900	54,507
Partnerships and S Corporations net loss [1]	2,767	2,115	45,007	45,236	16,266	21,388
Estate or trust net income	445	458	4,633	9,016	10,411	19,686
Estate or trust net loss	74	50	468	882	6,324	17,640
Farm net income	996	721	11,395	9,222	11,441	12,791
Farm net loss	1,325	1,439	11,829	16,069	8,928	11,167
Statutory adjustments, total	16,648	18,786	33,974	46,955	2,041	2,499
Individual Retirement Arrangements	5,224	4,069	9,858	8,663	1,887	2,129
Self-employed retirement plans	824	1,190	6,778	10,238	8,226	8,603
Deduction for self-employment tax	11,006	13,513	9,921	14,868	901	1,100
Self-employment health insurance	2,754	3,285	1,627	3,870	591	1,178
Exemptions, total [2]	227,549	241,279	465,985	627,825	2,048	2,602
Age 65 or older	(NA)	(NA)	(NA)	(NA)	(NA)	(NA)
Deductions, total	112,796	121,469	789,942	1,062,506	7,003	8,747
Standard deductions	80,621	84,844	331,457	441,696	4,111	5,206
Returns with additional standard deductions for age 65 or older or for blindness	10,954	11,136	10,616	13,333	969	1,197
Itemized deductions, total [3]	32,175	36,625	458,485	620,810	14,250	16,950
Medical and dental expenses	5,091	5,256	21,457	29,284	4,215	5,572
Taxes paid	31,594	36,095	140,011	220,628	4,432	6,112
Interest paid	29,395	30,790	208,354	250,599	7,088	8,139
Home mortgage interest paid	26,679	30,436	189,233	235,970	7,093	7,753
Charitable contributions	29,230	32,613	57,243	99,192	1,958	3,041
Taxable income	93,148	99,315	2,263,661	3,429,109	24,302	34,528
Income tax before credits	93,089	99,226	453,128	739,482	4,868	7,453
Tax credits, total [2]	12,484	16,195	6,831	12,179	547	752
Child care credit	6,144	5,796	2,549	2,464	415	425
Elderly and disabled credit	340	190	62	41	182	216
Foreign tax	772	2,334	1,682	4,073	2,179	1,745
General business credit	263	306	616	826	2,342	2,699
Income tax after credits	89,844	93,450	446,296	727,303	4,967	7,783
Income tax, total [4]	89,862	93,471	447,127	731,321	4,976	7,824
Minimum tax	(NA)	(NA)	(NA)	(NA)	(NA)	(NA)
Alternative minimum tax	132	618	830	4,005	6,288	6,481
Earned income credit	12,555	19,391	7,512	30,389	598	1,567
Used to offset income tax before credits	5,702	8,400	1,617	3,768	284	449
Used to offset other taxes	1,355	3,041	659	2,225	486	732
Excess earned income credit (refundable)	8,698	15,368	5,266	24,396	605	1,587
Tax payments, total	104,816	112,455	495,922	785,183	4,731	6,982
Excess social security tax withheld	931	1,268	905	1,400	972	1,104
Estimated tax payments	12,806	12,766	91,607	162,584	7,153	12,736
Payments with requests for extension of filing time	1,305	1,597	16,704	38,918	12,800	24,369
Taxes due at time of filing	26,987	31,198	56,561	93,910	2,096	3,010
Tax overpayments, total	83,508	88,311	88,479	140,110	1,060	1,587
Overpayment refunds	80,514	85,381	78,103	119,707	970	1,402

NA Not available.   [1] S Corporations are certain small corporations with up to 35 shareholders.   [2] Includes items not shown separately. Beginning 1996, total exemptions amount is after limitation.   [3] Beginning 1996, total itemized deductions are after limitation.   [4] Includes minimum tax or alternative minimum tax. *Statistics of Income Bulletin,* and *Statistics of Income, Individual Income Tax Returns,* annual.

Source: U.S. Internal Revenue Service, *Statistics of Income Bulletin,* and *Statistics of Income, Individual Income Tax Returns,* annual.

No. 549. Individual Income Tax Returns—Number, Income Tax, and Average Tax by Size of Adjusted Gross Income: 1995 and 1997

[In billions of dollars ($4,189.4 represents $4,189,400,000,000), except as indicated]

Size of adjusted gross income	Number of returns (1,000) 1995	Number of returns (1,000) 1997, prel.	Adjusted gross income (AGI) 1995	Adjusted gross income (AGI) 1997, prel.	Taxable income 1995	Taxable income 1997, prel.	Income tax total [1] 1995	Income tax total [1] 1997, prel.	Tax as percent of AGI [2] 1995	Tax as percent of AGI [2] 1997, prel.	Average tax ($1,000) [2] 1995	Average tax ($1,000) [2] 1997, prel.
Total.........[3]	118,218	122,422	4,189.4	4,970.0	2,813.8	3,429.1	588.4	731.3	14.1	14.7	6.8	7.8
Less than $1,000 [3] .	3,204	2,931	-53.9	-52.2	0.1	-	0.1	0.1	-0.2	-0.3	0.2	0.4
$1,000-$2,999	6,526	6,108	13.0	12.1	0.9	1.1	0.2	0.2	1.2	1.5	0.1	0.1
$3,000-$4,999	5,860	5,816	23.2	23.1	1.3	1.6	0.2	0.3	1.0	1.1	0.1	0.1
$5,000-$6,999	5,680	5,467	34.0	32.7	2.9	3.1	0.4	0.5	1.3	1.5	0.2	0.3
$7,000-$8,999	5,593	5,199	44.9	41.6	6.7	5.9	1.0	0.8	2.2	2.0	0.3	0.3
$9,000-$10,999 ...	5,372	5,424	53.7	54.2	10.7	11.2	1.6	1.7	3.0	3.1	0.5	0.5
$11,000-$12,999...	5,555	5,248	66.6	62.9	17.2	15.7	2.6	2.3	3.9	3.6	0.8	0.7
$13,000-$14,999 .	5,344	5,250	74.8	73.4	23.9	21.2	3.2	2.9	4.3	4.0	0.9	0.9
$15,000-$16,999 .	4,837	4,781	77.3	76.4	29.2	26.7	3.8	3.5	4.9	4.6	1.1	1.1
$17,000-$18,999 .	4,402	4,456	79.3	80.2	34.0	31.9	4.3	3.9	5.5	4.9	1.3	1.3
$19,000-$21,999 .	6,507	6,451	133.4	132.1	64.9	61.1	8.6	7.9	6.5	5.9	1.5	1.5
$22,000-$24,999 .	5,610	5,651	131.8	132.8	71.1	69.0	10.1	9.4	7.6	7.1	1.9	1.9
$25,000-$29,999 .	7,848	8,065	215.2	221.4	125.1	128.1	18.5	18.7	8.6	8.4	2.4	2.4
$30,000-$39,999 .	12,380	12,967	430.5	450.3	270.6	279.4	42.4	43.1	9.9	9.6	3.5	3.3
$40,000-$49,999 .	9,099	9,788	406.6	437.6	269.4	288.6	43.6	46.7	10.7	10.7	4.8	4.8
$50,000-$74,999 .	13,679	15,180	823.8	925.0	579.8	646.6	100.3	110.3	12.1	11.9	8.2	7.3
$75,000-$99,999 .	5,374	6,455	458.5	554.0	335.0	404.5	67.7	80.2	14.8	14.5	16.0	12.4
$100,000-$199,999.	4,075	5,378	532.0	707.8	411.6	548.3	97.2	126.3	18.3	17.8	31.3	23.5
$200,000-$499,999.	1,007	1,402	292.1	404.3	249.4	345.7	74.6	99.5	25.6	24.6	95.0	71.0
$500,000-$999,999.	178	262	120.3	176.7	106.6	157.8	36.3	51.3	30.2	29.0	258.2	196.1
$1,000,000 or more.	87	144	227.6	423.5	203.5	381.5	71.5	121.9	31.4	28.8	1,077.0	844.8

- Represents or rounds to zero.   [1] Consists of income after credits, and alternative minimum tax.   [2] Computed using taxable returns only.   [3] In addition to low income taxpayers, this size class (and others) includes taxpayers with "tax preferences," not reflected in adjusted gross income or taxable income which are subject to the "alternative minimum tax" (included in total income tax).

Source: U.S. Internal Revenue Service, *Statistics of Income Bulletin,* quarterly and *Statistics of Income, Individual Income Tax Returns,* annual.

No. 550. Individual Income Tax Returns—Itemized Deductions and Statutory Adjustments by Size of Adjusted Gross Income: 1997

[Preliminary]

Item	Unit	Total	Under $10,000	$10,000 to $19,999	$20,000 to $29,999	$30,000 to $39,999	$40,000 to $49,999	$50,000 to $99,999	$100,000 and over
Returns with itemized deductions:									
Number [1]	1,000 ..	36,625	614	2,049	3,241	4,284	4,602	15,281	6,553
Amount	Mil. dol .	620,810	6,393	21,878	33,462	46,041	54,229	227,239	231,567
Medical and dental expenses:									
Returns	1,000 ..	5,256	360	1,023	1,020	833	697	1,150	172
Amount	Mil. dol .	29,284	2,378	6,396	5,076	3,628	2,956	6,225	2,625
Taxes paid:									
Returns, total	1,000 ..	36,095	539	1,888	3,169	4,236	4,547	15,189	6,528
State, local income taxes ...	1,000 ..	30,820	268	1,293	2,606	3,646	3,906	13,353	5,748
Real estate taxes	1,000 ..	32,250	449	1,498	2,640	3,613	4,016	13,936	6,099
Amount, total	Mil. dol .	220,628	1,015	3,895	7,175	11,610	14,927	75,390	106,617
State, local income taxes..	Mil. dol .	136,965	181	936	2,447	5,387	7,410	42,438	78,165
Real estate taxes	Mil. dol .	74,998	765	2,691	4,174	5,486	6,707	29,317	25,858
Interest paid:									
Returns	1,000 ..	30,790	400	1,304	2,526	3,575	3,950	13,513	5,522
Amount	Mil. dol .	250,599	2,369	7,452	13,873	20,716	24,787	99,970	81,432
Home mortgages interest:									
Returns	1,000 ..	30,436	385	1,288	2,494	3,560	3,934	13,422	5,352
Amount	Mil. dol .	235,970	2,303	7,317	13,660	20,480	24,412	98,219	69,580
Contributions:									
Returns	1,000 ..	32,613	364	1,587	2,669	3,648	3,975	14,087	6,284
Amount	Mil. dol .	99,192	367	2,222	4,048	5,779	6,556	29,946	50,274
Employee business expense:									
Returns.................	1,000 ..	11,414	53	404	913	1,404	1,605	5,335	1,701
Amount.................	Mil. dol .	39,336	156	1,455	2,817	4,068	4,928	16,438	9,474
Returns with statutory adjus'mts: [2]									
Returns.................	1,000 ..	18,786	2,877	3,121	2,479	2,133	1,773	3,996	2,407
Amount of adjustments	Mil. dol .	46,955	2,236	3,804	4,138	3,627	3,661	11,112	18,376
Payments to IRAs: [3]									
Returns.................	1,000 ..	4,069	226	613	841	720	558	708	403
Amount	Mil. dol .	8,663	370	1,121	1,561	1,423	980	1,910	1,297
Payments to Keogh plans:									
Returns.................	1,000 ..	1,190	10	39	49	55	77	400	560
Amount	Mil. dol .	10,238	30	90	126	197	277	2,101	7,416
Alimony paid:									
Returns.................	1,000 ..	624	43	47	70	44	82	188	148
Amount.................	Mil. dol .	6,311	371	246	473	176	510	1,422	3,115

[1] After limitations.   [2] Includes disability income exclusion, employee business expenses, moving expenses, forfeited interest penalty, alimony paid, deduction for expense of living abroad, and other data not shown separately.   [3] Individual Retirement Account.

Source: U.S. Internal Revenue Service, *Statistics of Income, Individual Income Tax Returns,* annual.

Federal Government Finances and Employment 351

No. 551. Federal Individual Income Tax Returns—Adjusted Gross Income (AGI) by Source of Income and Income Class for Taxable Returns: 1997

[In millions of dollars ($93,471 represents $93,471,000,000), except as indicated. Minus sign (-) indicates net loss was greater than net income. See headnote, Table 548]

Item	Total [1]	Under $10,000	$10,000 to $19,999	$20,000 to $29,999	$30,000 to $39,999	$40,000 to $49,999	$50,000 to $99,999	$100,000 and over
Number of returns(1,000)	93,471	10,000	15,722	16,357	12,881	9,739	21,592	7,181
SOURCE OF INCOME								
Adjusted gross income (AGI)	4,765,197	52,478	235,780	407,092	447,342	435,466	1,476,061	1,710,979
Salaries and wages	3,405,123	45,890	169,621	328,754	370,103	359,863	1,186,483	944,408
Percent of AGI for taxable returns	71.5	88.7	71.7	81.2	83.2	83.0	81.1	56.8
Interest received	159,628	4,328	14,926	13,251	11,668	11,466	36,471	67,518
Dividends in AGI	115,739	1,948	5,233	5,608	5,372	5,703	25,226	66,650
Business; profession, net profit less loss.	169,376	1,563	7,718	10,718	12,741	13,273	43,830	79,532
Pensions and annuities in AGI . . .	244,990	3,327	27,915	34,362	28,786	24,326	83,246	43,026
Sales of property, [2] net gain less loss.	350,410	4,555	3,934	5,000	5,224	6,577	36,747	288,373
Rents and royalties, net income less loss. . . . [3]	23,615	68	924	440	454	297	1,645	19,786
Other sources, [3] net.	339,546	-8,731	7,955	12,650	16,565	17,592	73,482	220,033
PERCENT OF ALL RETURNS [4]								
Number of returns.	76.4	8.2	12.8	13.4	10.5	8.0	17.6	5.9
Adjusted gross income.	95.9	1.1	4.7	8.2	9.0	8.8	29.7	34.4
Salaries and wages.	94.2	1.3	4.7	9.1	10.2	10.0	32.8	26.1
Interest received.	93.0	2.5	8.7	7.7	6.8	6.7	21.2	39.3
Dividends in AGI.	96.1	1.6	4.3	4.7	4.5	4.7	20.9	55.3
Business; profession, net profit less loss	90.7	0.8	4.1	5.7	6.8	7.1	23.5	42.6
Pensions and annuities in AGI	94.3	1.3	10.7	13.2	11.1	9.4	32.1	16.6
Sales of property [2] net gain less loss	98.8	1.3	1.1	1.4	1.5	1.9	10.4	81.3

[1] Includes a small number of taxable returns with no adjusted gross income.   [2] Includes sales of capital assets and other property; net gain less loss.   [3] Excludes rental passive losses disallowed in the computation of adjusted gross income; net income less loss.   [4] Without regard to taxability.

Source: U.S. Internal Revenue Service, *Statistics of Income*, annual.

No. 552. Federal Individual Income Tax Returns by State: 1997

State	Number of returns [1] (1,000)	Adjusted gross income [2] (AGI)	Income tax Total [3] (mil. dol.)	Income tax Per capita [4] (dol.)	State	Number of returns [1] (1,000)	Adjusted gross income [2] (AGI)	Income tax Total [3] (mil. dol.)	Income tax Per capita [4] (dol.)
U.S.	**122,422**	**4,969,950**	**731,321**	**2,733**	MO.	2,381	91,067	12,630	2,338
					MT	388	11,082	1,360	1,547
AL	1,938	62,572	8,090	1,873	NE	820	29,688	4,016	2,424
AK	324	10,089	1,479	2,429	NV	816	36,531	5,757	3,433
AZ	2,001	78,158	11,263	2,473	NH	591	25,557	3,875	3,304
AR	1,108	34,146	4,266	1,691	NJ	3,670	197,745	32,921	4,088
CA	14,028	613,757	91,148	2,825	NM	745	23,063	2,761	1,596
CO	1,858	82,028	12,018	3,087	NY	8,097	381,907	62,316	3,436
CT	1,594	90,892	16,358	5,002	NC	3,455	126,772	16,783	2,260
DE	421	17,001	2,385	3,258	ND	245	8,057	1,060	1,654
DC	304	14,075	2,286	4,321	OH	5,310	192,154	26,695	2,386
FL	6,882	272,678	42,307	2,887	OK	1,498	47,298	6,034	1,819
GA	3,405	133,139	18,318	2,447	OR	1,529	59,705	7,896	2,435
HI.	550	18,648	2,327	1,960	PA	5,436	208,798	30,164	2,509
ID.	519	16,152	2,007	1,659	RI.	485	19,236	2,757	2,793
IL.	5,440	241,458	38,251	3,215	SC	1,747	57,529	7,298	1,941
IN.	2,516	99,121	13,915	2,373	SD	354	10,620	1,367	1,852
IA.	1,354	46,437	5,778	2,026	TN	2,523	91,363	13,000	2,422
KS	1,210	45,593	6,303	2,429	TX	8,482	325,363	50,094	2,577
KY	1,656	58,681	7,776	1,990	UT	898	34,357	4,266	2,072
LA	1,664	58,509	8,354	1,920	VT	308	10,690	1,354	2,299
ME	527	17,681	2,191	1,764	VA	3,051	131,693	18,594	2,761
MD	2,531	112,014	15,992	3,139	WA	2,693	116,689	17,575	3,133
MA	3,031	146,298	23,160	3,786	WV	705	21,378	2,561	1,410
MI	4,529	181,296	26,524	2,714	WI	2,550	96,636	13,312	2,575
MN	2,376	101,464	14,609	3,118	WY	198	8,257	1,331	2,773
MS	1,044	32,112	3,747	1,372	Other [5]	636	22,711	2,694	(NA)

NA Not available.   [1] Includes returns constructed by Internal Revenue Service for certain self-employment tax returns.   [2] Less deficit.   [3] Includes additional tax for tax preferences, self-employment tax, tax from investment credit recapture and other income-related taxes.   Total is before earned income credit.   [4] Based on resident population as of July 1.   [5] Includes returns filed from Army Post Office and Fleet Post Office addresses by members of the armed forces stationed overseas; returns by other U.S. citizens abroad; and returns filed by residents of Puerto Rico with income from sources outside of Puerto Rico or with income earned as U.S. Government employees.

Source: U.S. Internal Revenue Service, *Statistics of Income Bulletin.* Quarterly.

No. 553. Federal Individual Income Tax—Tax Liability and Effective and Marginal Tax Rates for Selected Income Groups: 1990 to 1999

[Refers to income after exclusions. Effective rate represents tax liability divided by stated income. The marginal tax rate is the percentage of the first additional dollar of income which would be paid in income tax. Computations assume the low income allowance, standard deduction, zero bracket amount, or itemized deductions equal to 10 percent of adjusted gross income, whichever is greatest. Excludes self-employment tax]

Adjusted gross income	1990	1994	1995	1996	1997	1998	1999
TAX LIABILITY							
Single person, no dependents:							
$5,000	-	-306	-314	-323	-332	-341	-347
$10,000	705	563	540	518	480	455	427
$20,000	2,205	2,063	2,040	2,018	1,980	1,958	1,943
$25,000	2,988	2,813	2,790	2,768	2,730	2,708	2,693
$35,000	5,718	5,093	4,973	4,846	4,692	4,559	4,479
$50,000	9,498	8,957	8,865	8,766	8,654	8,549	8,483
$75,000	16,718	15,555	15,418	15,270	15,107	14,951	14,852
Married couple, two dependents: [1]							
$5,000	-700	-1,500	-1,800	-2,000	-2,000	-2,000	-2,000
$10,000	-953	-2,528	-3,110	-3,556	-3,556	-3,756	-3,816
$20,000	926	-359	-832	-1,324	-1,414	-1,811	-1,958
$25,000	1,703	1,275	929	479	389	-8	-155
$35,000	3,203	2,828	2,768	2,715	2,625	2,565	2,520
$50,000	5,960	5,078	5,018	4,965	4,875	4,815	4,770
$75,000	12,386	11,216	11,030	10,831	10,576	10,371	10,224
EFFECTIVE RATE							
Single person, no dependents:							
$5,000 [2]	-	-6.1	-6.3	-6.5	-6.6	-6.8	-6.9
$10,000	7.1	5.6	5.4	5.2	4.8	4.6	4.3
$20,000	11.0	10.3	10.2	10.1	9.9	9.8	9.7
$25,000	12.0	11.3	11.2	11.1	10.9	10.8	10.8
$35,000	16.3	14.6	14.2	13.8	13.4	13.0	12.8
$50,000	19.0	17.9	17.7	17.5	17.3	17.1	17.0
$75,000	22.3	20.7	20.6	20.4	20.1	19.9	19.8
Married couple, two dependents: [2]							
$5,000 [3]	-14.0	-30.0	-36.0	-40	-40	-40.0	-40.0
$10,000 [4]	-9.5	-25.3	-31.1	-35.6	-35.6	-37.6	38.2
$20,000 [4]	4.6	-1.8	-4.2	-6.6	-7.1	-9.1	-9.8
$25,000	6.8	5.1	3.7	1.9	1.6	-	-0.6
$35,000	9.2	8.1	7.9	7.8	7.5	7.3	7.2
$50,000	11.9	10.2	10.0	9.9	9.8	9.6	9.5
$75,000	16.5	15.0	14.7	14.4	14.1	13.8	13.6
MARGINAL TAX RATE							
Single person, no dependents:							
$5,000	-	7.7	-	-	-	-	-
$10,000	15	15	15	15	15	22.7	22.7
$20,000	15	15	15	15	15	15	15
$25,000	28	15	15	15	15	15	15
$35,000	28	28	28	28	28	28	28
$50,000	28	28	28	28	28	28	28
$75,000	33	31	31	31	31	31	31
Married couple, two dependents: [1]							
$5,000 [3]	-14	-30	-36	-40	-40	-40	-40
$10,000 [4]	-	-	-	-	-	-	-
$20,000 [4]	25	32.7	35.2	36.1	36.1	36.1	36.1
$35,000	15	15	15	15	15	15	15
$50,000	28	15	15	15	15	15	15
$75,000	28	28	28	28	28	28	28

- Represents zero.   [1] Only one spouse is assumed to work.   [2] Beginning 1994, refundable earned income credit.   [3] Refundable earned income credit.   [4] Refundable earned income credit.

Source: U.S. Dept. of the Treasury, Office of Tax Analysis, unpublished data.

U.S. Census Bureau, Statistical Abstract of the United States: 2000

No. 554. Federal Individual Income Tax—Current Income Equivalent to 1995 Constant Income for Selected Income Groups: 1990 to 1998

[Constant 1995 dollar incomes calculated by using the NIPA Chain-Type Price Index for Person Consumption Expenditures (1996 = 100) 1990, 85.63; 1994, 95.70; 1995, 97.90; 1996, 100.0; 1997, 101.98; 1998, 102.93; and 1999, 104.57]

Adjusted gross income	1990	1994	1995	1996	1997	1998	1999
REAL INCOME EQUIVALENT							
Single person, no dependents:							
$5,000	4,280	4,790	4,900	5,000	5,100	5,150	5,230
$10,000	8,560	9,570	9,790	10,000	10,200	10,290	10,460
$20,000	17,130	19,140	19,580	20,000	20,400	20,590	20,910
$25,000	21,410	23,930	24,480	25,000	25,500	25,730	26,140
$35,000	29,970	33,500	34,270	35,000	35,690	36,030	36,600
$50,000	42,820	47,850	48,950	50,000	50,990	51,470	52,290
$75,000	64,220	71,780	73,430	75,000	76,490	77,200	78,430
Married couple, two dependents: [1]							
$5,000	4,280	4,790	4,900	5,000	5,100	5,150	5,230
$10,000	8,560	9,570	9,790	10,000	10,200	10,290	10,460
$20,000	17,130	19,140	19,580	20,000	20,400	20,590	20,910
$25,000	21,410	23,930	24,480	25,000	25,500	25,730	26,140
$35,000	29,970	33,500	34,270	35,000	35,690	36,030	36,600
$50,000	42,820	47,850	48,950	50,000	50,990	51,470	52,290
$75,000	64,220	71,780	73,430	75,000	76,490	77,200	78,430
EFFECTIVE RATE (percent)							
Single person, no dependents:							
$5,000 [2]	-	-6.4	-6.4	-6.5	-6.5	-6.6	-6.6
$10,000	5.7	5.2	5.2	5.2	5.0	4.9	4.9
$20,000	10.4	10.1	10.1	10.1	10.0	9.9	9.9
$25,000	11.3	11.1	11.1	11.1	11.0	10.9	11.0
$35,000	14.6	13.9	13.9	13.8	13.7	13.5	13.5
$50,000	18.0	17.6	17.6	17.5	17.5	17.3	17.3
$75,000	21.0	20.4	20.4	20.4	20.3	20.2	20.2
Married couple, two dependents: [1]							
$5,000 [3]	-14.0	-30.0	-36.0	-40.0	-40.0	-40.0	-40.0
$10,000 [4]	-11.1	-26.4	-31.8	-35.6	-34.9	-36.5	-36.5
$20,000 [4]	1.2	-3.3	-5.0	-6.6	-6.2	-7.8	-7.8
$25,000	5.4	3.9	3.0	1.9	2.2	1.0	1.0
$35,000	8.2	7.8	7.8	7.8	7.6	7.5	7.5
$50,000	10.2	9.9	9.9	9.9	9.9	9.8	9.8
$75,000	15.1	14.5	14.5	14.4	14.3	14.2	14.1
MARGINAL TAX RATE (percent)							
Single person, no dependents:							
$5,000	-	-	-	-	-	-	-
$10,000	15.0	15.0	15.0	15.0	15.0	15.0	15.0
$20,000	15.0	15.0	15.0	15.0	15.0	15.0	15.0
$25,000	15.0	15.0	15.0	15.0	15.0	15.0	15.0
$35,000	28.0	28.0	28.0	28.0	28.0	28.0	28.0
$50,000	28.0	28.0	28.0	28.0	28.0	28.0	28.0
$75,000	33.0	31.0	31.0	31.0	31.0	31.0	31.0
Married couple, two dependents: [1]							
$5,000 [3]	-14.0	-30.0	-36.0	-40.0	-40.0	-40.0	-40.0
$10,000	-	-	-	-	-	-	-
$20,000 [4]	25.0	32.7	35.2	36.1	36.1	36.1	36.1
$25,000	15.0	32.7	35.2	36.1	36.1	36.1	36.1
$35,000	15.0	15.0	15.0	15.0	15.0	15.0	15.0
$50,000	15.0	15.0	15.0	15.0	15.0	15.0	15.0
$75,000	28.0	28.0	28.0	28.0	28.0	28.0	28.0

- Represents zero. [1] Only one spouse is assumed to work. [2] Beginning 1994, refundable earned income credit. [3] Refundable earned income credit. [4] Refundable earned income credit.

Source: U.S. Dept. of the Treasury, Office of Tax Analysis, unpublished data.

No. 555. Paid Full-Time Federal Civilian Employment, All Areas: 1990 to 1999

[As of March 31. Excludes employees of Congress and Federal courts, maritime seamen of Dept. of Commerce, and small number for whom rates were not reported. See text, this section, for explanation of general schedule and wage system]

Compensation authority	Employees (1,000)				Average pay			
	1990	1995	1998	1999	1990	1995	1998	1999
Total	2,697	2,620	2,490	2,483	31,174	(NA)	(NA)	47,569
General Schedule	1,506	1,417	1,258	1,234	31,239	40,568	44,824	46,744
Wage System	369	269	222	214	26,565	32,084	34,763	35,767
Postal pay system [1]	661	753	792	798	29,264	33,665	35,670	36,413
Other	161	181	218	237	41,149	53,839	60,678	62,519

NA Not available. [1] Source: Employees—U.S. Postal Service, *Annual Report of the Postmaster General.* Average pay—U.S. Postal Service, *Comprehensive Statement of Postal Operations,* annual.

Source: Except as noted, U.S. Office of Personnel Management, *Pay Structure of the Federal Civil Service,* annual.

U.S. Census Bureau, Statistical Abstract of the United States: 2000

No. 556. Federal Civilian Employment by Branch and Agency: 1990 to 1999

[For fiscal year ending in year shown; excludes Central Intelligence Agency, National Security Agency; and, as of November 1984, the Defense Intelligence Agency; and, as of October 1996, the National Imagery and Mapping Agency]

Agency	1990	1998	1999	Percent change 1990-95	Percent change 1998-99
Total, all agencies	**3,128,267**	**2,789,532**	**2,749,239**	**-6.6**	**-1.4**
Legislative Branch, total	37,495	30,474	30,353	-11.0	-0.4
Judicial Branch	23,605	31,742	32,196	22.8	1.4
Executive Branch, total	3,067,167	2,727,316	2,686,690	-6.8	-1.5
Executive Departments	2,065,542	1,646,245	1,614,097	-13.7	-2.0
State	25,288	24,713	25,892	-1.7	4.8
Treasury	158,655	140,873	143,088	-1.7	1.6
Defense	1,034,152	717,901	690,706	-19.5	-3.8
Justice	83,932	122,759	124,885	23.0	1.7
Interior	77,679	72,434	72,541	-1.6	0.1
Agriculture	122,594	105,664	104,661	-7.6	-0.9
Commerce	69,920	50,041	60,765	-47.4	21.4
Labor	17,727	15,894	15,913	-8.6	0.1
Health & Human Services	123,959	59,813	61,403	-51.8	2.7
Housing & Urban Development	13,596	10,063	10,273	-13.0	2.1
Transportation	67,364	64,859	64,135	-5.7	-1.1
Energy	17,731	16,156	15,820	10.5	-2.1
Education	4,771	4,677	4,770	4.5	2.0
Veterans Affairs [1]	248,174	240,398	219,245	6.3	-8.8
Independent agencies:	999,894	1,079,469	1,070,961	7.4	-0.8
American Battle Monuments Commission	396	357	362	-5.3	1.4
Armed Forces Retirement Home	966	848	801	(X)	-5.5
Arms Control & Disarmament Agency	216	222	(X)	23.1	-100.0
Board of Gov. Federal Reserve System	1,525	1,669	1,688	11.7	1.1
Commodity Futures Trading Commission	542	583	574	0.4	-1.5
Consumer Product Safety Commission	520	468	483	-6.5	3.2
Environmental Protection Agency	17,123	18,787	18,590	4.6	-1.0
Equal Employment Opportunity Commission	2,880	2,571	2,945	-2.9	14.5
Federal Communications Commission	1,778	1,988	1,978	19.0	-0.5
Federal Deposit Insurance Corporation	17,641	7,778	7,492	-16.3	-3.7
Federal Emergency Managment Agency	3,137	5,812	5,521	67.5	-5.0
Federal Housing Finance Board [2]	65	120	120	73.8	-
Federal Trade Commission	988	1,004	982	0.8	-2.2
General Services Administration	20,277	14,207	14,199	-18.6	-0.1
Int Boun & Wat Commission (U.S. & Mexico)	260	258	286	-9.2	10.9
National Archives & Records Administration	3,120	2,610	2,612	-9.2	0.1
National Aeronautics & Space Administration	24,872	18,899	18,647	-13.0	-1.3
National Labor Relations Board	2,263	1,866	1,897	-9.4	1.7
National Science Foundation	1,318	1,231	1,271	-2.0	3.2
Nuclear Regulatory Commission	3,353	2,995	2,862	-4.2	-4.4
Office of Personnel Management	6,636	3,576	3,689	-34.4	3.2
Panama Canal Commission	8,240	9,966	9,060	10.0	-9.1
Peace Corps	1,178	1,059	1,097	0.1	3.6
Railroad Retirement Board	1,772	1,289	1,252	-12.9	-2.9
Securities & Exchange Commission	2,302	2,826	2,866	23.9	1.4
Small Business Administration	5,128	4,574	4,575	-0.8	-
Smithsonian Institution, summary	5,092	5,166	5,271	6.9	2.0
Social Security Administration	(X)	65,257	64,008	(X)	-1.9
Tennessee Valley Authority	28,392	13,818	13,321	-41.7	-3.6
U.S. Information Agency	8,555	6,378	6,318	-12.6	-0.9
U.S. Postal Service	816,886	871,467	866,342	3.5	-0.6

- Represents zero.   X Not applicable.   [1] Formerly Veterans Administration.   [2] Formerly Federal Home Loan Bank Board.
Source: U.S. Office of Personnel Management, *Federal Civilian Workforce Statistics— Employment and Trends*, bimonthly.

No. 557. Federal Employment Trends by Individual Characteristics: 1990 to 1998

[In percents, except as indicated]

Characteristics	1990	1991	1992	1993	1994	1995	1996	1997	1998
Average age (years) [1]	42.3	42.5	43.0	43.8	44.1	44.3	44.8	45.2	45.6
Average length of service (years) [1]	13.4	13.5	14.1	14.9	15.2	15.5	15.9	16.3	16.6
Retirement eligible:									
Civil Service Retirement System [2]	8.0	8.0	10.0	10.0	10.0	10.0	11.0	12.0	13.0
Federal Employees Retirement System	3.0	3.0	3.0	4.0	5.0	5.0	6.0	7.0	8.0
College-conferred [3]	35.0	35.0	36.0	37.0	38.0	39.0	39.0	40.0	40.0
Gender:									
Men	57.0	56.0	57.0	56.0	56.0	56.0	56.0	56.0	56.0
Women	43.0	44.0	43.0	44.0	44.0	44.0	44.0	44.0	44.0
Race and national origin:									
Total minorities	27.4	27.7	27.9	28.2	28.5	28.9	29.1	29.4	29.7
Disabled	7.0	7.0	7.0	7.0	7.0	7.0	7.0	7.0	7.0
Veterans preference	30.0	28.0	28.0	27.0	27.0	26.0	26.0	25.0	25.0
Vietnam Era veterans	17.0	16.0	16.0	16.0	17.0	17.0	17.0	15.0	14.0
Retired military	4.9	4.7	4.4	4.3	4.3	4.2	4.3	4.2	3.9
Retired officers	0.5	0.5	0.5	0.5	0.5	0.5	0.5	0.5	0.5

[1] Represents full-time permanent employees.   [2] Represents full-time permanent employees under the Civil Service Retirement System (excluding hires since January 1984), and the Federal Employees Retirement System (since January 1984).   [3] Bachelor's degree or higher.
Source: U.S. Office of Personnel Management, Office of Workforce Information, *The Typical Federal Civilian Employee.*

Federal Government Finances and Employment 355

[Employment in thousands (2,997 represents 2,997,000); payroll in millions of dollars ($27,322 represents $27,322,000,000). Average annual employment. **For fiscal year ending in year shown**; see text, Section 9, State and Local Government. Includes employees in U.S. territories and foreign countries. Data represent employees in active-duty status, including intermittent employees. Annual employment figures are averages of monthly figures. Excludes Central Intelligence Agency, National Security Agency, and, as of November 1984, the Defense Intelligence Agency, and as of October 1996, the National Imagery and Mapping Agency.]

Year		Percent of U.S. employed [1]	Employment				Payroll				
	Total		Executive Total	Defense	Legislative	Judicial	Total	Executive Total	Defense	Legislative	Judicial
1970	[2]2,997	3.8	2,961	1,263	29	7	27,322	26,894	11,264	338	89
1971	2,899	3.7	2,861	1,162	31	7	29,475	29,007	11,579	369	98
1972	2,882	3.5	2,842	1,128	32	8	31,626	31,102	12,181	411	112
1973	2,822	3.3	2,780	1,076	33	9	33,240	32,671	12,414	447	121
1974	2,825	3.3	2,781	1,041	35	9	35,661	35,035	12,789	494	132
1975	2,877	3.4	2,830	1,044	37	10	39,126	38,423	13,418	549	154
1976	2,879	3.2	2,831	1,025	38	11	42,259	41,450	14,699	631	179
1977	2,855	3.1	2,803	997	39	12	45,895	44,975	15,696	700	219
1978	2,875	3.0	2,822	987	40	13	49,921	48,899	16,995	771	251
1979	2,897	2.9	2,844	974	40	13	53,590	52,513	18,065	817	260
1980	[3]2,987	3.0	2,933	971	40	14	58,012	56,841	18,795	883	288
1981	2,909	2.9	2,855	986	40	15	63,793	62,510	21,227	922	360
1982	2,871	2.9	2,816	1,019	39	16	65,503	64,125	22,226	980	398
1983	2,878	2.9	2,823	1,033	39	16	69,878	68,420	23,406	1,013	445
1984	2,935	2.8	2,879	1,052	40	17	74,616	73,084	25,253	1,081	451
1985	3,001	2.8	2,944	1,080	39	18	80,599	78,992	28,330	1,098	509
1986	3,047	2.8	2,991	1,089	38	19	82,598	80,941	29,272	1,112	545
1987	3,075	2.7	3,018	1,084	38	19	85,543	83,797	29,786	1,153	593
1988	3,113	2.7	3,054	1,073	38	21	88,841	86,960	29,609	1,226	656
1989	3,133	2.7	3,074	1,067	38	22	92,847	90,870	30,301	1,266	711
1990	[4]3,233	2.7	3,173	1,060	38	23	99,138	97,022	31,990	1,329	787
1991	3,101	2.7	3,038	1,015	38	25	104,273	101,965	32,956	1,434	874
1992	3,106	2.6	3,040	1,004	39	27	108,054	105,402	31,486	1,569	1,083
1993	3,043	2.5	2,976	952	39	28	114,323	111,523	32,755	1,609	1,191
1994	2,993	2.4	2,928	900	37	28	116,138	113,264	32,144	1,613	1,260
1995	2,943	2.4	2,880	852	34	28	118,304	115,328	31,753	1,598	1,379
1996	2,881	2.3	2,819	811	32	29	119,321	116,385	31,569	1,519	1,417
1997	2,816	2.2	2,755	768	31	30	119,603	116,693	31,431	1,515	1,396
1998	2,783	2.1	2,721	730	31	31	121,964	118,800	30,315	1,517	1,647
1999	2,789	2.1	2,726	703	30	32	124,990	121,732	30,141	1,560	1,699

[1] Civilian only. See Table 645. [2] Includes 33,000 temporary census workers. [3] Includes 81,116 temporary census workers. [4] Includes 111,020 temporary census workers.

Source: U.S. Office of Personnel Management, *Federal Civilian Workforce Statistics—Employment and Trends*, bimonthly; and unpublished data.

No. 559. Federal Executive Branch (Nonpostal) Employment by Race and National Origin: 1990 to 1999

[As of **Sept. 30**. Covers total employment for only Executive branch agencies participating in OPMs Central Personnel Data File (CPDF)]

Pay system	1990	1995	1997	1998	1999
All personnel	2,150,359	1,960,577	1,830,300	1,804,591	1,766,298
White, non-Hispanic	1,562,846	1,394,690	1,293,244	1,269,790	1,236,698
General schedule and related	1,218,188	1,101,108	1,027,440	1,010,793	979,803
Grades 1-4 ($13,870 - $24,833)	132,028	79,195	63,775	61,909	58,381
Grades 5-8 ($21,370 - $38,108)	337,453	288,755	264,288	255,344	246,759
Grades 9-12 ($32,380 - $61,040).	510,261	465,908	434,228	425,617	413,989
Grades 13-15 ($55,837 - $100,897) . . .	238,446	267,250	265,149	267,923	260,674
Total executives/senior pay levels [1]	9,337	13,307	13,465	13,634	13,856
Wage pay system.	244,220	186,184	164,755	157,639	151,585
Other pay systems	91,101	94,091	87,584	87,724	91,454
Black.	356,867	327,302	303,415	300,661	298,694
General schedule and related	272,657	258,586	243,932	242,587	241,422
Grades 1-4 ($13,870-$24,833)	65,077	41,381	32,439	30,668	28,530
Grades 5-8 ($21,370 - $38,108)	114,993	112,962	106,037	103,985	101,742
Grades 9-12 ($32,380 - $61,040).	74,985	79,795	79,124	79,999	81,410
Grades 13-15 ($55,837 - $100,897) . . .	17,602	24,448	26,332	27,935	29,740
Total executives/senior pay levels [1]	479	942	1,002	1,044	1,103
Wage pay system.	72,755	55,637	47,261	45,492	44,076
Other pay systems	10,976	12,137	11,220	11,538	12,093
Hispanic	115,170	115,964	114,740	115,545	114,743
General schedule and related	83,218	86,762	87,427	89,155	89,367
Grades 1-4 ($13,870 - $24,833)	15,738	11,081	9,320	9,213	8,874
Grades 5-8 ($21,370 - $38,108)	28,727	31,152	31,843	31,877	31,544
Grades 9-12 ($32,380 - $61,040).	31,615	34,056	34,742	35,864	36,474
Grades 13-15 ($55,837 - $100,897)	7,138	10,473	11,522	12,201	12,475
Total executives/senior pay levels [1]	154	382	409	454	487
Wage pay system.	26,947	22,128	20,565	19,341	17,781
Other pay systems	4,851	6,692	6,339	6,595	7,108
American Indian, Alaska Natives, Asian, and Pacific Islander	115,476	122,621	118,901	118,595	116,163

[1] General schedule pay rates and Senior Pay Levels effective as of January 1999.
Source: Office of Personnel Management, Central Personnel Data File.

No. 560. Paid Civilian Employment in the Federal Government: 1998

[As of **December 31 (2,758 represents 2,758,000).** Excludes Central Intelligence Agency, Defense Intelligence Agency, seasonal and on-call employees, and National Security Agency]

State	Total (1,000)	Percent Defense	Percent change, 1996-98	State	Total (1,000)	Percent Defense	Percent change, 1996-98
United States.	2,758	23.7	0.8	Missouri	57	15.8	-1.7
Alabama	52	42.3	-	Montana	11	9.1	-
Alaska	14	28.6	-	Nebraska	15	20.0	-
Arizona	43	18.6	7.5	Nevada.	13	15.4	8.3
Arkansas.	21	19.0	5.0	New Hampshire	8	12.5	-
California.	265	26.4	-1.5	New Jersey	65	23.1	-4.4
Colorado.	54	20.4	3.8	New Mexico.	26	26.9	-
Connecticut	23	13.0	4.5	New York	139	8.6	-
Delaware.	5	20.0	-	North Carolina	57	29.8	3.6
District of Columbia.	181	7.2	-2.2	North Dakota	8	25.0	-
Florida	116	23.3	3.6	Ohio.	87	27.6	1.2
Georgia	88	35.2	1.1	Oklahoma	43	46.5	2.4
Hawaii	24	70.8	-	Oregon	30	10.0	7.1
Idaho	11	9.1	-	Pennsylvania	113	24.8	0.9
Illinois.	98	14.3	1.0	Rhode Island	11	36.4	-
Indiana	38	23.7	-5.0	South Carolina	27	37.0	3.8
Iowa	20	5.0	-	South Dakota.	10	10.0	-
Kansas	25	20.0	-	Tennessee.	52	13.5	-
Kentucky.	31	22.6	-8.8	Texas	175	25.7	1.7
Louisiana	35	22.9	2.9	Utah.	28	42.9	-3.4
Maine.	13	38.5	-	Vermont	6	8.3	-
Maryland	131	25.2	4.0	Virginia	147	55.8	-2.6
Massachusetts	56	12.5	3.7	Washington	63	34.9	1.6
Michigan	59	13.6	7.3	West Virginia	18	11.1	-
Minnesota	35	5.7	6.1	Wisconsin	31	9.7	6.9
Mississippi.	25	40.0	4.2	Wyoming.	6	16.7	-

- Represents or rounds to zero.

Source: U.S. Office of Personnel Management, *Biennial Report of Employment by Geographic Area.*

No. 561. Federal General Schedule Employee Pay Increases: 1965 to 1999

[Percent change from prior year shown, except 1965, change from 1964. Represents legislated pay increases. For some years data based on range for details see source]

Date	Pay increase	Date	Pay increase	Date	Pay increase
1965	3.6	1976	5.2	1989	4.1
1966	2.9	1977	7.0	1990	3.6
1967	4.5	1978	5.5	1991	4.1
1968	4.9	1979	7.0	1992	4.2
1969	9.1	1980	9.1	1993	3.7
1970	6.0	1981	4.8	1994	-
1971	6.0	1982	4.0	1995	2.0
1972	5.5	1984	4.0	1996	2.0
1972	5.1	1985	3.5	1997	2.3
1973	4.8	1986	-	1998	2.3
1974	5.5	1987	3.0	1999	3.1
1975	5.0	1988	2.0		

- Represents zero.

Source: U.S. Office of Personnel Management, *Pay Structure of the Federal Civil Service,* annual.

No. 562. Turnover Data for the Executive Branch—All Areas: 1984 to 1998

[Turnover data exclude Legislative and Judicial branches, U.S. Postal Service, Postal Rate Commission]

Year	Accessions		Separations		Total employment		
	Total	New hires	Total	Quits	Average	Change from prior year	Percent change
1984	533,865	427,349	496,426	193,195	2,178,273	19,498	0.9
1985	541,787	451,516	484,742	185,453	2,210,487	32,214	1.5
1986	466,191	379,267	478,595	182,124	2,207,807	-2,680	-0.1
1987	515,958	431,687	440,797	176,813	2,207,828	21	(Z)
1988	463,413	375,561	448,025	175,374	2,226,642	18,814	0.9
1989	515,759	435,911	483,850	172,376	2,233,981	7,339	0.3
1990	819,554	716,066	799,237	165,099	2,348,458	114,477	5.1
1991	495,123	351,112	515,673	134,175	2,224,389	-124,069	-5.3
1992	430,021	290,883	446,126	129,167	2,238,635	14,246	0.6
1993	382,399	253,374	423,830	127,140	2,189,416	-49,219	-2.2
1994	317,509	219,026	398,134	111,096	2,114,387	-75,029	-3.4
1995	345,166	222,025	457,246	91,909	2,037,890	-76,542	-3.6
1996	266,473	199,463	356,566	80,922	1,960,892	-76,953	-3.8
1997	283,517	208,725	333,431	81,574	1,895,295	-65,597	-3.3
1998	320,830	242,637	321,292	84,124	1,855,112	-40,183	-2.1

Z Less than .05 percent.

Source: U.S. Office of Personnel Management, *Monthly Report of Federal Civilian Employment.*

No. 563. Accessions to and Separations From Employment in the Federal Government: 1995 and 1999

[As of **September 30**]

Agency	Accessions				Separations			
	Number		Rate		Number		Rate	
	1995	1999	1995	1999	1995	1999	1995	1999
Total, all agencies	**556,695**	**640,928**	**19.2**	**23.4**	**638,733**	**585,131**	**22.1**	**21.4**
Legislative Branch, total [1]	1,074	1,163	6.6	8.6	1,985	1,702	12.2	12.5
General Accounting Office	39	228	0.9	6.8	392	383	8.9	11.5
Government Printing Office	77	138	1.8	4.2	318	319	7.6	9.7
Library of Congress	540	342	11.6	7.8	642	519	13.8	11.9
Judicial Branch	-	-	-	-	-	-	-	-
Executive Branch, total.	555,621	639,765	19.3	23.5	636,748	583,429	22.1	21.4
Executive Office of the President	384	469	24.3	29.2	373	431	23.6	26.8
Executive Departments	257,125	400,462	14.0	24.4	422,606	348,452	23.0	21.3
State	3,338	4,523	13.3	18.1	3,919	2,941	15.6	11.7
Treasury	24,532	49,398	15.0	32.9	52,634	48,369	32.2	32.2
Defense	104,088	95,944	12.2	13.7	155,722	125,129	18.3	17.8
Justice	14,958	11,029	14.9	8.9	7,496	7,223	7.5	5.8
Interior	12,936	18,565	17.1	26.5	16,147	13,774	21.4	19.6
Agriculture	25,365	26,483	23.3	26.5	41,384	26,946	37.9	26.9
Commerce [2]	5,900	148,079	15.8	232.9	6,460	57,721	17.3	90.8
Labor	1,438	1,709	8.7	10.7	2,003	1,711	12.2	10.7
Health & Human Services [3]	8,774	10,795	9.3	17.8	78,780	8,744	83.7	14.4
Housing & Urban Development	489	1,622	4.0	16.0	1,952	1,402	15.8	13.8
Transportation	2,673	2,833	4.2	4.4	4,740	4,214	7.4	6.5
Energy	2,087	1,026	10.5	6.4	2,671	1,272	13.4	7.9
Education	683	523	13.8	11.2	354	237	7.2	5.1
Veterans Affairs [4]	49,864	27,933	19.0	12.1	48,344	48,769	18.5	21.1
Independent agencies [1]	298,112	238,834	28.6	22.0	213,769	234,546	20.5	21.6
Board of Governors, Fed RSRV System .	231	178	13.7	10.6	199	188	11.8	11.2
Environmental Protection Agency	2,232	1,510	12.3	8.1	2,078	1,518	11.5	8.1
Equal Employment Opportunity Comm . .	129	360	4.5	13.5	156	87	5.4	3.3
Federal Deposit Insurance Corporation. .	360	700	2.2	9.3	4,404	1,007	26.8	13.4
Fed Emergency Management Agency . . .	3,165	3,505	60.2	59.1	3,059	3,547	58.2	59.8
General Services Administration	292	653	1.7	4.6	2,552	620	14.8	4.4
National Aeronautics & Space Admin . .	2,004	1,315	8.9	7.0	3,673	1,522	16.2	8.1
National Archives & Records Admin	583	525	20.0	19.8	307	340	10.5	12.8
Nuclear Regulatory Commission	98	168	3.0	5.8	263	314	8.0	10.8
Office of Personnel Management.	506	565	10.3	15.5	1,407	508	28.6	13.9
Panama Canal Comm	1,744	1,461	19.6	15.8	1,246	2,305	14.0	24.9
Railroad Retirement Board	46	46	2.9	3.6	185	85	11.6	6.7
Securities and Exchange Commission . .	584	523	21.1	18.5	356	429	12.8	15.2
Small Business Administration.	1,065	1,747	18.1	36.6	2,799	1,840	47.6	38.6
Smithsonian Institution.	707	588	13.1	13.6	980	603	18.2	13.9
Tennessee Valley Authority	674	655	4.1	4.8	2,873	1,113	17.3	8.2
U.S. Information Agency	356	326	4.7	5.1	836	519	11.0	8.2
U.S. International Dev. Coop. Agency . . .	333	200	8.6	7.3	665	331	17.2	12.1
U.S. Postal Service.	210,447	216,256	25.0	24.6	179,494	210,640	21.3	23.9

- Represents or rounds to zero.   [1] Includes other branches, or other agencies, not shown separately.   [2] 1998 and 1999 include Census Enumerators for the 2000 Decennial Census.   [3] Sizable changes due to the Social Security Administration which was separated from the Department of Health and Human Services to become an independent agency effective April 1995. [4] Formerly Veterans Administration.

Source: U.S. Office of Personnel Management, Federal Civilian Workforce Statistics—*Employment and Trends*, bimonthly.

No. 564. Federal Land and Buildings Owned and Leased and Predominant Land Usage: 1990 to 1998

[**For fiscal years ending in years shown;** see text, Section 9, State and Local Government. Covers Federal real property throughout the world, except as noted. Cost of land figures represent total cost of property owned in year shown. For further details see source. For data on Federal land by state, see Table 381]

Item	Unit	1990	1994	1995	1996	1997	1998
Federally owned:							
Land, worldwide	1,000 acres. .	650,014	677,802	549,670	563,278	563,231	655,042
United States	1,000 acres. .	649,802	676,615	549,474	563,129	563,081	654,885
Buildings	1,000	(NA)	(NA)	(NA)	(NA)	(NA)	(NA)
United States	1,000	446	448	424	430	430	420
Buildings floor area (sq. ft.)	Mil. sq/ft. . . .	(NA)	(NA)	(NA)	(NA)	(NA)	(NA)
United States	Mil. sq/ft. . . .	2,859	2,944	2,793	2,930	2,935	2,911
Costs	Mil. dol.	187,865	209,318	199,387	217,857	222,391	244,273
Land	Mil. dol.	(NA)	20,947	18,972	22,952	22,914	26,450
Buildings	Mil. dol.	(NA)	115,633	113,018	123,897	128,530	130,858
Structures and facilities.	Mil. dol.	(NA)	72,738	67,398	71,008	70,946	86,965
Federally leased:							
Land, worldwide	1,000 acres. .	994	1,119	1,385	1,373	1,374	1,306
United States	1,000 acres. .	938	1,055	1,351	1,339	1,340	1,272
Buildings	1,000	(NA)	(NA)	(NA)	(NA)	(NA)	(NA)
United States	Number	47,291	53,128	77,896	77,232	76,761	76,357
Buildings floor area (sq. ft.)	Mil. sq/ft. . . .	(NA)	(NA)	(NA)	(NA)	(NA)	(NA)
United States	Mil. sq/ft. . . .	234	276	275	277	276	276
Annual rental	Mil. dol.	2,590	3,766	3,633	3,739	3,613	3,628
United States	Mil. dol.	2,125	3,105	3,174	3,214	3,212	3,226

NA Not available.

National Defense and Veterans Affairs

This section presents data on national defense and its human and financial costs; active and reserve military personnel; ships, equipment and aircraft; and federally sponsored programs and benefits for veterans. The principal sources of these data are the annual *Selected Manpower Statistics* and the *Atlas/Data Abstract for the United States and Selected Areas* issued by the Office of the Secretary of Defense; *Annual Report of Secretary of Veterans Affairs, Department of Veterans Affairs*, and *The Budget of the United States Government*, Office of Management and Budget. For more data on expenditures, personnel, and ships, see Section 30.

Department of Defense (DOD)—The Department of Defense is responsible for providing the military forces of the United States. It includes the Office of the Secretary of Defense, the Joint Chiefs of Staff, the Army, the Navy, the Air Force, and the defense agencies. The President serves as Commander in Chief of the Armed Forces; from him, the authority flows to the Secretary of Defense and through the Joint Chiefs of Staff to the commanders of unified and specified commands (e.g., U.S. Strategic Command).

Reserve components—Reserve personnel of the Armed Forces consist of the Army National Guard, Army Reserve, Naval Reserve, Marine Corps Reserve, Air National Guard, Air Force Reserve, and Coast Guard Reserve. They provide trained personnel available for active duty in the Armed Forces in time of war or national emergency and at such other times as authorized by law.

The National Guard has dual Federal-state responsibilities and uses jointly provided equipment, facilities, and budget support. The President is empowered to mobilize the National Guard and to use such of the Armed Forces as he considers necessary to enforce Federal authority in any state.

The ready reserve includes selected reservists who are intended to assist active forces in a war and the individual ready reserve who, in a major war, would be used to fill out active and reserve units and later would be a source of combat replacements; a portion of the ready reserve serves in an active status. The standby reserve cannot be called to active duty unless the Congress gives explicit approval. The retired reserve represents a low potential for mobilization.

Department of Veterans Affairs—The Department of Veterans Affairs administers laws authorizing benefits for eligible former and present members of the Armed Forces and for the beneficiaries of deceased members. Veterans benefits available under various acts of Congress include compensation for service-connected disability or death; pensions for non-service-connected disability or death; vocational rehabilitation, education, and training; home loan insurance; life insurance; health care; special housing and automobiles or other conveyances for certain disabled veterans; burial and plot allowances; and educational assistance to families of deceased or totally disabled veterans, servicemen missing in action, or prisoners of war. Since these benefits are legislated by Congress, the dates they were enacted and the dates they apply to veterans may be different from the actual dates the conflicts occurred.

VA estimates of veterans cover all persons with active duty service during periods of war or armed conflict and until 1982 include those living outside the United States.

U.S. Census Bureau, Statistical Abstract of the United States: 2000

No. 565. National Defense Outlays and Veterans Benefits: 1960 to 2000

[For fiscal year ending in year shown; see text, Section 9, State and Local Government. Includes outlays of Department of Defense, Department of Veterans Affairs, and other agencies for activities primarily related to national defense and veterans programs. For explanation of average annual percent change, see Guide to Tabular Presentation. Minus sign (-) indicates decline]

Year	National defense and veterans outlays				Annual percent change [1]			Defense outlays, percent of—	
		Defense outlays							
	Total outlays (bil. dol.)	Current dollars (bil. dol.)	Constant (1996) dollars (bil. dol.)	Veterans outlays (bil. dol.)	Total outlays	Defense outlays	Veterans outlays	Federal outlays	Gross domestic product [2]
1960	53.5	48.1	280.3	5.4	2.5	2.4	3.1	52.2	9.3
1965	56.3	50.6	267.7	5.7	-6.8	-7.6	0.7	42.8	7.4
1970	90.4	81.7	336.6	8.7	0.3	-1.0	13.6	41.8	8.1
1975	103.1	86.5	239.5	16.6	11.2	9.0	24.0	26.0	5.5
1980	155.1	134.0	244.7	21.1	13.9	15.2	6.3	22.7	4.9
1985	279.0	252.7	329.9	26.3	10.3	11.1	2.7	26.7	6.1
1990	328.4	299.3	354.3	29.1	-1.6	-1.4	-3.2	23.9	5.2
1991	304.6	273.3	309.3	31.3	-7.2	-8.7	7.6	20.6	4.6
1995	310.0	272.1	281.8	37.9	-2.9	-3.4	0.8	17.9	3.7
1996	302.7	265.8	265.8	37.0	-2.3	-2.3	-2.4	17.0	3.5
1997	309.8	270.5	265.3	39.3	2.3	1.8	6.3	16.9	3.3
1998	310.2	268.5	260.4	41.8	0.1	-0.8	6.3	16.2	3.1
1999	320.2	274.9	263.1	43.2	3.2	2.4	3.4	16.1	3.0
2000, est	337.4	290.6	273.8	46.8	5.4	5.7	8.3	16.2	3.0

[1] Change from prior year shown; for 1960, change from 1955. [2] Represents fiscal year GDP; for definition, see text, Section 14, Income, Expenditures, and Wealth.

No. 566. Federal Budget Outlays for Defense Functions: 1980 to 2000

[In billions of dollars ($134.0 represents $134,000,000,000), except percent. For fiscal year ending in year shown; see text, Section 9, State and Local Government. Minus sign (-) indicates decline]

Defense function	1980	1990	1992	1993	1994	1995	1996	1997	1998	1999	2000, est.
Total	134.0	299.3	298.4	291.1	281.6	272.1	265.8	270.5	268.5	274.9	290.6
Percent change [1]	15.2	-1.4	9.2	-2.4	-3.3	-3.4	-2.3	1.8	-0.7	3.1	5.7
Defense Dept., military	130.9	289.8	286.9	278.6	268.6	259.4	253.2	258.3	256.1	261.4	277.5
Military personnel	40.9	75.6	81.2	75.9	73.1	70.8	66.7	69.7	69.0	69.5	73.5
Operation, maintenance	44.8	88.3	92.0	94.1	87.9	91.1	88.8	92.5	93.5	96.4	103.8
Procurement	29.0	81.0	74.9	69.9	61.8	55.0	48.9	47.7	48.2	48.8	48.0
Research and development	13.1	37.5	34.6	37.0	34.8	34.6	36.5	37.0	37.4	37.4	37.4
Military construction	2.5	5.1	4.3	4.8	5.0	6.8	6.7	6.2	6.0	5.5	4.8
Family housing	1.7	3.5	3.3	3.3	3.3	3.6	3.8	4.0	3.9	3.7	3.8
Other [2]	-1.1	-1.2	-3.3	-6.4	2.7	-2.4	1.8	1.2	-1.9	0.1	6.3

[1] Change from immediate year. [2] Revolving and management funds, trust funds, special foreign currency program allowances, and offsetting receipts.

No. 567. National Defense—Budget Authority and Outlays: 1980 to 2000

[In billions of dollars ($143.9 represents $143,900,000,000), except percent. For fiscal year ending in year shown, except as noted; see text, Section 9, State and Local Government]

Item	1980	1990	1993	1994	1995	1996	1997	1998	1999	2000, est.
Budget authority [1]	143.9	303.3	281.1	263.3	266.3	266.0	270.3	271.3	292.1	293.3
Department of Defense-Military [2]	140.7	293.0	267.2	251.4	255.7	254.4	258.0	258.5	278.4	279.9
Atomic energy defense activities [1]	3.0	9.7	12.1	10.9	10.1	10.7	11.4	11.7	12.6	12.2
Defense-related activities	0.2	0.6	1.8	1.1	0.6	0.9	1.0	1.0	1.1	1.2
Outlays (Defense) [1]	134.0	299.3	291.1	281.6	272.1	265.8	270.5	268.5	274.9	290.6
Department of Defense-Military	130.9	289.8	278.6	268.6	259.4	253.2	258.3	256.1	261.4	277.5
Atomic energy defense activities [1]	2.9	9.0	11.0	11.9	11.8	11.6	11.3	11.3	12.4	11.9
Defense-related activities	0.2	0.6	1.5	1.1	0.8	0.9	0.9	1.1	1.1	1.2

[1] Includes defense budget authority, balances, and outlays by other departments. [2] Excluding accruals.

Source of Tables 565-567: U.S. Office of Management and Budget, Historical Tables, annual.

Figure 11.1
National Defense Outlays as a Percent of Federal Expenditures and Gross Domestic Product: 1980 to 1999

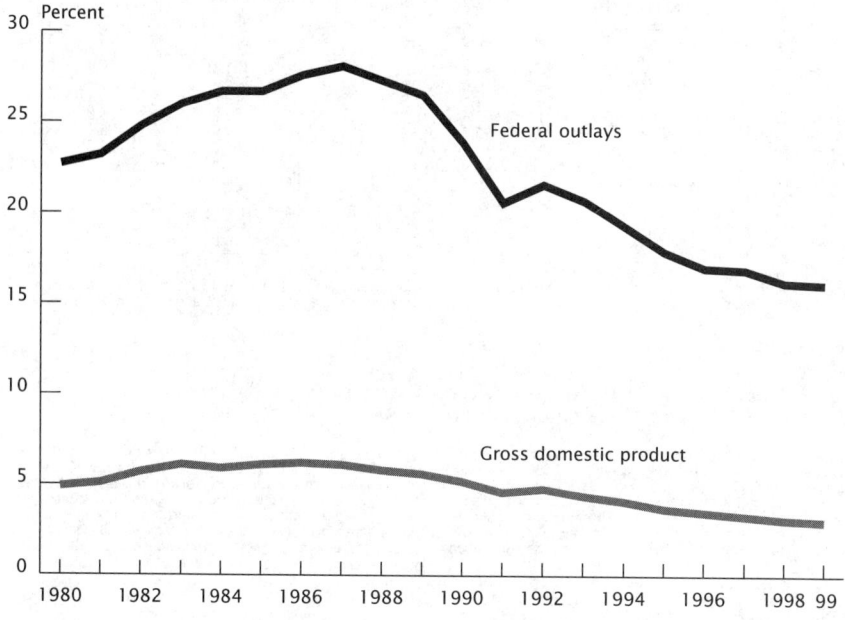

Source: Chart prepared by U.S. Census Bureau. For data, see Table 565.

Figure 11.2
U.S. Military Personnel on Active Duty Abroad: 1998

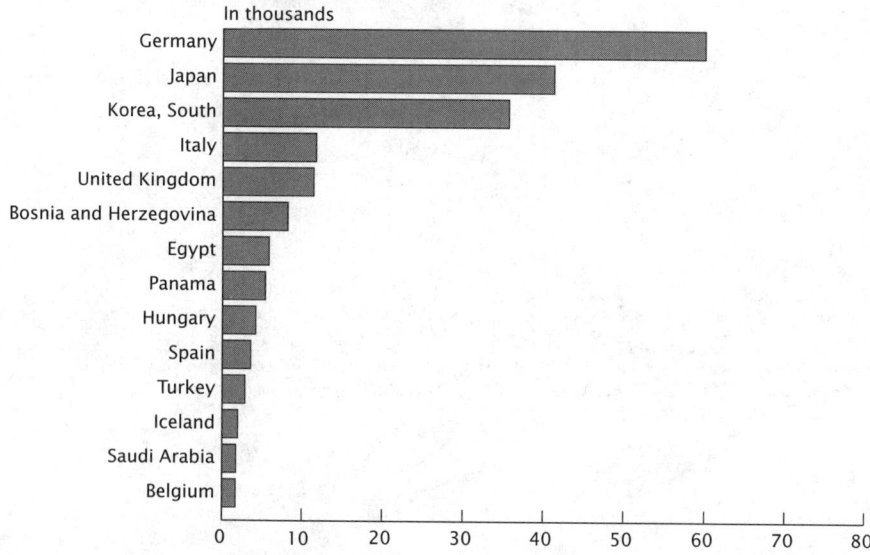

Source: Chart prepared by U.S. Census Bureau. For data, see Table 580.

National Defense and Veterans Affairs 361

No. 568. Military Prime Contract Awards to All Businesses by Program: 1980 to 1998

[In billions of dollars ($83.7 represents $83,700,000,000). Net values for **fiscal year ending in year shown;** see text, Section 9, State and Local Government. Includes all new prime contracts; debit or credit changes in contracts are also included. Actions cover official awards, amendments, or other changes in prime contracts to obtain military supplies, services, or construction. Excludes term contracts and contracts which do not obligate a firm total dollar amount or fixed quantity, but includes job orders, task orders, and delivery orders against such contracts]

DOD procurement program	1980	1990	1992	1993	1994	1995	1996	1997	1998
Total	83.7	144.7	136.3	138.3	132.2	131.4	132.2	128.4	128.8
Intragovernmental [1]	10.2	10.0	9.6	12.9	11.1	12.3	13.0	11.5	9.9
For work outside the U.S.	5.4	7.1	5.9	5.8	5.6	5.6	6.4	6.4	5.6
Educ. and nonprofit institutions	1.5	3.5	3.4	3.4	3.3	3.3	3.3	3.6	3.5
With business firms for work in the U.S. [2] . .	66.7	123.8	117.2	116.0	112.0	110.0	109.5	106.9	109.7
Major hard goods	41.0	79.1	67.1	64.5	59.2	56.0	55.1	52.5	56.0
Aircraft	12.5	24.0	24.1	23.0	23.5	18.8	20.3	18.4	20.8
Electronics and communication equip..	9.6	18.5	14.2	14.2	12.4	12.3	11.5	12.1	10.7
Missiles and space systems	7.9	17.1	13.1	12.1	11.6	10.6	10.2	9.5	9.9
Ships	6.0	10.3	8.3	9.0	6.8	9.1	7.1	6.8	8.6
Tanks, ammo. and weapons	5.1	9.2	7.4	6.2	4.9	5.3	5.9	5.7	6.0
Services	5.9	14.6	17.3	17.5	17.7	18.6	19.2	20.2	21.2

[1] Covers only purchases from other Federal agencies and reimbursable purchases on behalf of foreign governments.
[2] Includes Department of Defense. Includes other business not shown separately. Contracts awarded for work in U.S. possessions and other areas subject to complete sovereignty of United States; contracts in a classified location; and any intragovernmental contracts entered into overseas.

Source: U.S. Dept. of Defense, *Prime Contract Awards*, semiannual.

No. 569. Department of Defense Contract Awards, Payroll, and Civilian and Military Personnel by State: 1998

[For years ending **Sept. 30. Contracts** refer to awards made in year specified; expenditures relating to awards may extend over several years. **Civilian employees** include United States citizen and foreign national direct-hire civilians subject to Office of Management and Budget (OMB) ceiling controls and civilian personnel involved in civil functions in the United States. Excludes indirect-hire civilians and those direct-hire civilian not subject to OMB ceiling controls. **Military personnel** include active duty personnel based ashore. Excludes personnel temporarily shore-based in a transient status or afloat. **Payroll outlays** include the gross earnings of civilian and active duty military personnel for services rendered to the government and for cash allowances for benefits. Excludes employer's share of employee benefits, accrued military retirement benefits, and most permanent change of station costs]

State	Contract awards [1] (mil. dol.)	Payroll (mil. dol.)	Personnel (1,000) Civilian	Personnel (1,000) Military	State	Contract awards [1] (mil. dol.)	Payroll (mil. dol.)	Personnel (1,000) Civilian	Personnel (1,000) Military
U.S.	**109,386**	**97,378**	**645.1**	**1,030.4**	MO	4,653	1,400	9.2	13.5
AL	2,202	2,450	22.1	14.7	MT	107	263	1.1	3.6
AK	617	850	4.0	16.4	NE	233	649	3.4	8.4
AZ	3,003	1,842	8.3	20.8	NV	231	737	2.1	7.7
AR	217	721	3.7	4.8	NH	426	245	1.0	0.3
CA	17,401	11,479	71.8	116.2	NJ	2,661	1,451	15.2	7.1
CO	2,381	2,301	11.2	29.0	NM	633	1,074	7.2	12.2
CT	3,409	533	2.7	4.3	NY	3,062	1,703	11.8	19.6
DE	88	282	1.4	3.8	NC	1,004	4,078	17.0	87.4
DC	1,366	1,131	12.6	13.6	ND	140	345	1.7	7.8
FL	5,464	6,716	27.7	53.7	OH	2,472	2,131	24.5	7.4
GA	3,690	4,565	31.3	62.3	OK	921	2,190	19.8	25.6
HI	890	2,485	16.0	34.6	OR	289	523	2.8	0.6
ID	172	358	1.4	4.3	PA	3,318	2,146	27.8	3.1
IL	1,285	2,059	13.8	31.5	RI	217	469	4.5	3.1
IN	1,649	775	6.4	0.9	SC	969	2,267	9.8	37.7
IA	459	249	1.4	0.4	SD	88	223	1.3	3.1
KS	1,007	1,075	5.6	16.0	TN	1,216	1,050	5.5	2.2
KY	1,637	1,718	6.9	34.2	TX	7,980	8,343	45.7	106.9
LA	1,241	1,198	7.8	15.3	UT	470	915	11.8	4.6
ME	895	537	5.4	1.7	VT	92	91	0.5	0.1
MD	5,220	3,466	33.3	29.5	VA	12,671	10,441	80.0	80.3
MA	4,245	816	7.5	2.7	WA	2,631	3,767	23.3	33.0
MI	1,065	812	7.9	1.0	WV	107	249	1.7	0.5
MN	1,215	408	2.5	0.7	WI	557	379	1.9	0.5
MS	1,352	1,214	9.8	12.1	WY	68	208	0.9	3.4

[1] Military awards for supplies, services, and construction. Net value of contracts of over $25,000 for work in each state and DC. Figures reflect impact of prime contracting on state distribution of defense work. Often the state in which a prime contractor is located in is not the state where the subcontracted work is done. See also headnote, Table 579. Undistributed civilians and military personnel, their payrolls, and prime contract awards for performance in classified locations are excluded.

Source: U.S. Dept. of Defense, *Atlas/Data Abstract for the United States and Selected Areas*, annual.

No. 570. Worldwide Military Expenditures in Current and Constant (1997) Dollars: 1990 to 1997

[In billions of dollars ($1,090 represents $1,090,000,000,000). For military expenditures and Armed Forces by country, see Section 30, Comparative International Statistics. GNP = Gross national product]

Country group	1990	1991	1992	1993	1994	1995	1996	1997
CURRENT DOLLARS								
Expenditures, total [1]	1,090	1,010	856	819	813	798	810	842
United States	306	280	305	298	288	279	271	276
Percent of total.	28.1	27.7	35.6	36.4	35.4	35.0	33.5	32.8
Developed countries [2]	883	817	649	637	628	600	597	610
Developing countries [2]	206	196	207	182	185	198	212	232
NATO countries [3]	488	465	486	477	467	454	451	457
CONSTANT (1997) DOLLARS								
Expenditures, total [1]	1,280	1,150	949	885	860	826	823	842
United States	359	317	338	321	305	289	276	276
Percent of total.	28.0	27.6	35.6	36.3	35.5	35.0	33.5	32.8
Developed countries [2]	1,030	925	719	688	664	621	607	610
Developing countries [2]	242	222	230	197	196	205	216	232
NATO countries [3]	572	527	538	515	494	470	458	457
Percent of GNP	4.5	4.0	3.4	3.1	2.9	2.7	2.6	2.6
United States	5.2	4.7	4.8	4.5	4.1	3.8	3.5	3.3
Developed countries [2]	4.5	4.0	3.3	3.2	3.0	2.7	2.6	2.5
Developing countries [2]	4.6	4.0	3.6	2.9	2.7	2.7	2.7	2.7
NATO countries [3]	4.1	3.7	3.7	3.5	3.2	3.0	2.8	2.7

[1] Includes countries not shown separately. [2] Twenty-eight developed countries; see Table 571 for selected countries; for complete list, see source. [3] North Atlantic Treaty Organization.

No. 571. Arms Trade in Constant (1997) Dollars by Selected Country: 1990 to 1997

[In millions of dollars ($70 represents $70,000,000), except percent. Because some countries exclude arms imports or exports from their trade statistics and their "total" imports and exports are therefore understated, and because arms transfers may be estimated independently of trade data, the ratio of arms to total imports or exports may be overstated and may even exceed 100 percent]

Country	1990	1995	1996	1997	Country	1990	1995	1996	1997
EXPORTERS [1]					IMPORTERS [1]				
Australia	70	52	295	30	Algeria	375	249	132	480
Belarus	(NA)	176	203	490	Australia	1,405	1,346	1,322	925
Belgium.	223	124	325	110	Brazil	199	269	346	430
Bulgaria.	94	145	112	120	China, Mainland	468	854	1,627	500
Canada	732	647	559	550	China, Taiwan.	1,171	1,553	1,728	9,200
China: Mainland	2,694	673	635	1,100	Egypt	1,522	2,174	1,728	1,600
Czech Republic.	(NA)	104	102	90	Germany	2,694	880	915	750
France	6,090	2,692	3,558	5,900	Greece	849	497	661	850
Germany	1,874	1,760	1,322	750	Iran	2,225	342	356	850
India	12	5	5	90	Israel	1,640	802	940	1,100
Israel	820	906	763	370	Italy	492	404	488	430
Italy	234	228	163	700	Japan	1,874	1,864	2,440	2,600
Korea, North.	246	62	112	701	Korea, South	1,113	1,967	1,322	1,100
Netherlands	234	352	366	500	Kuwait.	316	1,346	1,728	2,000
Poland	269	41	71	60	Malaysia	82	854	203	725
Russia.	(NA)	3,935	3,152	2,300	Netherlands	995	425	686	460
					Pakistan	1,405	570	275	600
Singapore	35	31	41	90	Qatar	117	52	5	625
South Africa	59	166	356	370	Saudi Arabia	8,900	10,350	9,862	11,600
Spain	410	414	224	525	Spain	703	425	661	430
Sweden.	849	1,010	1,220	900	Thailand	457	777	635	950
Switzerland	70	145	203	50					
Ukraine	(NA)	249	203	500	Turkey.	1,522	1,760	1,627	1,600
United Arab Emirates .	6	10	81	40	United Arab Emirates .	1,874	1,346	1,118	1,400
United Kingdom	5,387	5,488	6,303	6,600	United Kingdom	1,522	984	1,525	2,100
United States	**25,650**	**23,710**	**23,380**	**31,800**	**United States**	**2,108**	**1,035**	**1,220**	**1,600**

NA Not available. [1] Includes countries not shown separately.

Source of Tables 570 and 571: U.S. Arms Control and Disarmament Agency, *World Military Expenditures and Arms Transfers,* annual.

National Defense and Veterans Affairs 363

No. 572. Arms Transfers—Cumulative Value for Period 1994-96 by Major Supplier and Recipient Country

[In millions of dollars ($119,565 represents $119,565,000,000)]

Recipient	Total [1]	Supplier					
		United States	United Kingdom	Russia	West Germany	France	China: Mainland
World, total [1]	**119,565**	**67,210**	**16,405**	**8,490**	**4,045**	**6,675**	**1,970**
Africa [1]							
North Africa.	990	280	5	305	-	60	15
Algeria	525	20	-	300	-	-	-
Libya	25	-	-	-	-	-	-
Morocco	250	170	-	-	-	-	-
Subsahara Africa	1,880	75	55	625	-	130	70
Angola	920	20	-	550	-	-	-
Nigeria	45	10	-	-	-	-	-
Rwanda	20	5	-	-	-	-	-
Zimbabwe	100	-	-	-	-	50	-
Americas:							
Central America & Caribbean. . .	380	355	-	-	-	10	-
Cuba	-	-	-	-	-	-	-
El Salvador	80	80	-	-	-	-	-
North America (NAFTA).	4,510	875	960	60	320	360	40
Canada	765	525	-	-	-	200	-
Mexico	415	350	-	-	-	-	-
United States.	3,330	-	950	40	320	160	40
South America.	3,370	1,350	210	120	100	265	40
Brazil	770	440	170	-	60	50	-
Chile	710	90	-	-	-	60	-
Colombia	200	160	-	-	-	-	-
Venezuela.	510	370	-	-	-	-	-
Asia:							
Central Asia & Caucasus.	910	80	-	665	30	-	5
Middle East.	44,475	22,505	12,900	1,655	220	3,180	690
Egypt	5,675	5,000	-	210	-	130	-
Iran	1,025	-	-	320	-	-	500
Israel	2,865	2,600	-	-	150	-	-
Kuwait	3,405	1,900	675	750	-	60	-
Saudi Arabia	26,585	11,700	11,200	-	60	2,000	-
Syria	230	-	-	-	-	-	-
United Arab Emirates	2,270	800	260	200	-	750	-
Yemen	480	5	-	-	-	-	-
East Asia	25,580	15,820	1,830	3,270	1,335	920	510
Burma	315	-	-	-	-	-	-
China:							
Mainland	2,565	120	-	2,000	-	-	(X)
Taiwan	4,090	3,300	-	-	-	775	-
Indonesia	1,260	300	725	-	90	-	-
Japan.	6,020	6,000	-	-	-	-	-
Korea, South	4,780	3,200	70	80	1,200	-	-
Malaysia	1,990	360	950	550	-	-	-
Singapore	1,290	950	-	-	-	-	-
Thailand	1,715	1,100	-	-	-	-	110
South Asia	2,605	280	100	740	-	440	480
India	985	110	-	650	-	-	-
Pakistan	1,040	140	70	-	-	440	230
Europe:							
Eastern Europe	2,045	220	20	750	75	20	-
Hungary	90	20	-	-	-	-	-
Western Europe.	24,910	20,255	270	265	1,460	1,215	-
Belgium	890	600	-	-	-	280	-
Denmark.	445	410	-	-	-	-	-
Finland	1,360	1,200	-	70	-	-	-
France	695	550	-	-	-	(X)	-
Germany.	2,710	2,600	-	-	(X)	-	-
Greece	1,770	1,100	-	-	410	50	-
Italy	1,410	1,300	90	-	-	-	-
Netherlands.	1,565	1,500	-	-	-	-	-
Norway.	755	575	-	-	-	130	-
Portugal	555	500	-	-	-	-	-
Spain	1,690	1,400	-	-	-	90	-
Sweden	1,125	850	-	-	270	-	-
Switzerland	570	500	-	-	-	-	-
Turkey	4,985	3,200	-	190	700	350	-
United Kingdom	3,570	3,500	(X)	-	-	-	-
Oceania	4,285	2,020	40	-	500	-	-
Australia.	3,500	1,800	-	-	500	-	-
New Zealand.	760	220	-	-	-	-	-

- Represents $2.5 million or less.   X Not applicable.   [1] Includes countries not shown separately.

Source: U.S. Arms Control and Disarmament Agency, *World Military Expenditures and Arms Transfers,* annual.

No. 573. U.S. Military Sales and Assistance to Foreign Governments: 1990 to 1998

[In millions of dollars, ($16,614 represents $16,614,000,000). For fiscal year ending in year shown; see text, Section 9, State and Local Government. Department of Defense (DOD) sales deliveries cover deliveries against sales orders authorized under Arms Export Control Act, as well as earlier and applicable legislation. For details regarding individual programs, see source]

Item	1990	1991	1992	1993	1994	1995	1996	1997	1998
Military sales agreements	16,614	17,324	13,901	31,109	13,292	8,950	10,295	8,782	8,231
Military constr. sales agrmts	636	799	148	660	58	25	83	30	341
Military sales deliveries [1]	7,718	8,777	10,054	11,314	9,467	11,940	11,574	19,233	13,523
Military sales financing	4,758	4,693	4,274	4,124	3,917	3,712	3,836	3,530	3,420
Military assistance programs [2] . . .	137	177	116	651	328	123	340	70	93
Military assist. program delivery [3] .	27	150	82	60	5	10	25	114	59
IMET program/deliveries [3]	43	46	42	43	22	26	39	43	36

[1] Includes military construction sales deliveries.   [2] Also includes Military Assistance Service Funded (MASF) program data, section 506(a) drawdown authority, and MAP Merger Funds.   [3] Includes Military Assistance Service Funded (MASF) program data and section 506(a) drawdown authority.

No. 574. U.S. Military Sales Deliveries by Country: 1990 to 1998

[In millions of dollars ($8,065 represents $8,065,000,000). For fiscal years ending in year shown. See text, Section 9, State and Local Government. Represents Department of Defense military sales]

Country	1990	1991	1992	1993	1994	1995	1996	1997	1998
Total [1]	8,065	9,191	10,389	11,666	9,736	12,158	11,716	19,331	13,905
Australia	384	205	156	259	354	308	229	197	344
China: Taiwan	455	549	711	818	845	1,353	853	5,696	1,490
Egypt	368	482	1,027	1,239	890	1,536	1,112	1,181	584
Germany	366	476	510	356	152	236	378	211	191
Greece	114	124	163	226	236	221	210	717	414
Israel	146	238	720	782	412	328	386	504	1,618
Italy	61	61	52	72	181	54	77	51	43
Japan	272	518	571	380	785	753	786	512	420
Kuwait	52	75	815	840	217	476	628	1,391	325
Netherlands	397	387	236	114	140	157	397	174	347
Saudi Arabia	874	2,742	2,387	3,453	1,992	3,568	2,854	4,660	3,959
South Korea	328	230	309	306	381	442	342	483	956
Turkey	761	627	703	756	937	374	483	1,167	541

[1] Includes countries not shown.

Source of Tables 573 and 574: U.S. Defense Security Assistance Agency, *Foreign Military Sales, Foreign Military Construction Sales,* and *Military Assistance Facts,* annual.

No. 575. Defense-Related Employment and Spending: 1977 to 1996, and Projections to 2006

[Dollar amounts in billions of chain-weighted 1992 dollars ($4,279.3 represents $4,279,300,000,000)]

Item	1977	1987	1996	2002	2006	Change 1977-87	Change 1987-96	Change 1996-2002	Change 1996-2006	Change 1997-2006
Spending (bil. dol.):										
Gross domestic product (GDP). .	4,279.3	5,648.4	6,911.0	7,739.9	8,539.1	1,369.1	1,262.6	828.9	1,628.1	2,890.7
Defense purchases	266.4	409.2	314.9	265.4	257.3	142.8	-94.3	-49.5	-57.6	-151.9
As percent of GDP:										
Defense purchases	6.2	7.2	4.6	3.4	3.0	1.0	-2.7	-1.1	-1.5	-4.2
Employment, total [1] (1,000).	95,588	116,523	133,884	144,646	152,370	20,935	17,361	10,762	18,485	35,847
Defense-related	4,767	6,942	4,492	3,744	3,595	2,175	-2,450	-748	-897	-3,347
As percent of total employment:										
Defense related	4.99	5.96	3.36	2.59	2.36	0.97	-2.60	-0.77	-1.00	-3.60

[1] Total employed, including resident Armed Forces, plus Department of Defense estimates of Armed Forces abroad.

Source: U.S. Bureau of Labor Statistics, *Monthly Labor Review, July 1998.*

No. 576. Military and Civilian Personnel and Expenditures: 1990 to 1998

Item	1990	1994	1995	1996	1997	1998
Personnel, total [1] (1,000)	**3,693**	**3,623**	**3,391**	**3,252**	**3,081**	**2,943**
Active duty military	1,185	1,131	1,085	1,056	1,045	1,004
Expenditures, total (mil. dol.) [2]	**209,904**	**210,138**	**209,695**	**211,740**	**205,764**	**208,843**
Prime contract awards [3] (mil. dol.)	121,254	110,316	109,005	109,408	106,561	109,386
Major area of work (mil. dol.):						
Aircraft, fixed wing	6,329	6,277	7,543	8,950	5,432	12,904
Guided missiles	928	494	495	625	2,831	417

[1] Includes those based ashore and excludes those temporarily shore-based, in a transient status, or afloat.   [2] Includes expenditures not shown separately.   [3] Represents contract awards over $25,000.

Source: U.S. Dept. of Defense, *Atlas/Data Abstract for the United States and Selected Areas,* annual.

National Defense and Veterans Affairs   365

No. 577. Department of Defense Manpower: 1950 to 1997

[In thousands (1,459 represents 1,459,000. As of end of fiscal year; see text, Section 9, State and Local Government. Includes National Guard, Reserve, and retired regular personnel on extended or continuous active duty. Excludes Coast Guard. Other officer candidates are included under enlisted personnel]

Year	Total¹ ²	Army Total²	Army White	Army Black	Army Officers	Army Enlisted	Navy³ Total²	Navy White	Navy Black	Navy Officers	Navy Enlisted	Marine corps Total²	Marine White	Marine Black	Marine Officers	Marine Enlisted	Air Force Total²	AF White	AF Black	AF Officers	AF Enlisted
1950	1,459	593	(NA)	(NA)	73	519	381	(NA)	(NA)	45	333	74	(NA)	(NA)	7	67	411	(NA)	(NA)	57	354
1955	2,935	1,109	(NA)	(NA)	122	986	661	(NA)	(NA)	75	583	205	(NA)	(NA)	18	187	960	(NA)	(NA)	137	823
1960	2,475	873	(NA)	(NA)	101	770	617	(NA)	(NA)	70	545	171	(NA)	(NA)	16	154	815	(NA)	(NA)	130	683
1965	2,654	969	(NA)	(NA)	112	855	670	(NA)	(NA)	78	588	190	(NA)	(NA)	17	173	825	(NA)	(NA)	132	690
1966	3,092	1,200	(NA)	(NA)	118	1,080	743	(NA)	(NA)	80	659	262	(NA)	(NA)	21	241	887	(NA)	(NA)	131	753
1967	3,375	1,442	(NA)	(NA)	144	1,297	750	(NA)	(NA)	82	664	285	(NA)	(NA)	24	262	897	(NA)	(NA)	135	759
1968	3,546	1,570	(NA)	(NA)	166	1,402	764	(NA)	(NA)	85	674	307	(NA)	(NA)	25	283	905	(NA)	(NA)	140	762
1969	3,458	1,512	(NA)	(NA)	173	1,337	774	(NA)	(NA)	85	684	310	(NA)	(NA)	26	284	862	(NA)	(NA)	135	723
1970	3,065	1,323	(NA)	(NA)	167	1,153	691	(NA)	(NA)	81	606	260	(NA)	(NA)	25	235	791	(NA)	(NA)	130	657
1971	2,713	1,124	(NA)	(NA)	149	972	622	(NA)	(NA)	75	542	212	(NA)	(NA)	22	191	755	(NA)	(NA)	126	625
1972	2,322	811	(NA)	(NA)	121	687	587	(NA)	(NA)	73	511	198	(NA)	(NA)	20	178	726	(NA)	(NA)	122	600
1973	2,252	801	(NA)	(NA)	116	682	564	(NA)	(NA)	71	490	196	(NA)	(NA)	19	177	691	(NA)	(NA)	115	572
1974	2,162	783	(NA)	(NA)	106	674	546	(NA)	(NA)	67	475	189	(NA)	(NA)	19	170	644	(NA)	(NA)	110	529
1975	2,128	784	(NA)	(NA)	103	678	535	(NA)	(NA)	66	466	196	(NA)	(NA)	19	177	613	(NA)	(NA)	105	503
1976	2,082	779	(NA)	(NA)	99	678	525	(NA)	(NA)	64	458	192	(NA)	(NA)	19	174	585	(NA)	(NA)	100	481
1977	2,075	782	(NA)	(NA)	98	680	530	(NA)	(NA)	63	462	192	(NA)	(NA)	19	173	571	(NA)	(NA)	96	470
1978	2,062	772	(NA)	(NA)	98	670	530	(NA)	(NA)	63	463	191	(NA)	(NA)	18	172	570	(NA)	(NA)	95	470
1979	2,027	759	(NA)	(NA)	97	657	523	(NA)	(NA)	62	457	185	(NA)	(NA)	18	167	559	(NA)	(NA)	96	459
1980	2,051	777	503	229	99	674	527	436	55	63	460	188	142	39	18	170	558	460	80	98	456
1981	2,083	781	502	232	102	675	540	443	58	65	470	191	145	39	18	172	570	468	83	99	467
1982	2,109	780	504	230	103	673	553	450	62	67	481	192	149	38	19	173	583	476	87	102	476
1983	2,123	780	512	220	106	669	558	462	66	68	485	194	152	37	20	174	592	483	88	105	483
1984	2,138	780	520	215	108	668	565	455	67	69	491	196	153	36	20	176	597	486	89	106	486
1985	2,151	781	523	211	110	667	571	459	70	71	495	198	152	37	20	178	602	488	90	108	489
1986	2,169	781	524	210	110	667	581	464	75	72	504	199	151	38	20	179	608	491	92	109	495
1987	2,174	781	519	212	108	668	587	467	81	72	510	200	150	38	20	179	607	489	92	107	495
1988	2,138	772	507	213	107	660	593	466	85	72	516	197	147	38	20	177	576	462	88	105	467
1989	2,130	770	497	218	107	658	593	461	91	72	516	197	146	38	20	177	571	458	87	104	463
1990	2,044	732	466	213	104	624	579	446	93	72	503	197	145	38	20	177	535	428	82	100	431
1991	1,986	711	452	204	104	603	570	439	92	71	495	194	144	36	20	174	510	409	77	97	409
1992	1,807	610	388	173	95	511	542	415	88	69	468	185	138	32	19	165	470	377	70	90	376
1993	1,705	572	365	158	88	480	510	390	84	66	439	178	134	30	18	160	444	357	65	84	356
1994	1,610	541	344	147	85	452	469	355	78	62	403	174	131	28	18	156	426	341	62	81	341
1995	1,518	509	322	137	83	422	435	326	75	59	372	175	130	(NA)	18	157	400	318	58	78	318
1996	1,472	491	(NA)	(NA)	81	407	417	(NA)	(NA)	57	355	175	(NA)	(NA)	18	157	389	(NA)	(NA)	76	309
1997	1,439	492	(NA)	(NA)	79	408	396	(NA)	(NA)	56	335	174	(NA)	(NA)	18	156	377	(NA)	(NA)	74	299

NA Not available. ¹ Beginning 1980, excludes Navy Reserve personnel on active duty for Training and Administration of Reserves (TARS). From 1969, the full-time Guard and Reserve. ² Includes Cadets and other not shown separately. ³ Prior to 1980, includes Navy Reserve personnel on active duty for Training and Administration of Reserves (TARS).

Source: U.S. Dept. of Defense, Selected Manpower Statistics, annual.

No. 578. United States Military and Civilian Personnel in Installations: 1997

[As of **September 30.** MC represents Marine Corps]

State	Military personnel				Civilian personnel			
	Total	Army	Navy/MC	Air Force	Total [1]	Army	Navy/MC	Air Force
U.S.	**1,056,173**	**398,528**	**342,647**	**314,998**	**689,187**	**224,770**	**193,959**	**164,489**
AL	15,570	9,581	916	5,073	22,104	17,436	28	2,688
AK	16,069	6,561	259	9,249	4,689	2,609	23	1,729
AZ	22,297	5,952	4,290	12,055	8,350	3,534	425	3,384
AR	5,161	497	116	4,548	3,703	2,702	24	859
CA	121,971	7,985	89,148	24,838	78,963	7,877	41,906	17,463
CO	29,433	14,796	967	13,670	11,501	3,277	35	4,854
CT	5,713	26	5,573	114	2,778	474	1,188	245
DE	3,889	9	20	3,860	1,462	179	-	1,202
DC	14,501	4,560	6,140	3,801	12,782	4,756	6,636	1,078
FL	57,426	2,488	28,472	26,466	28,294	2,399	14,146	8,380
GA	62,947	47,892	5,444	9,611	31,827	12,155	4,870	11,419
HI	34,826	15,249	15,963	3,614	17,216	4,779	9,361	1,951
ID	4,524	20	80	4,424	1,431	650	60	671
IL	30,399	713	23,663	6,023	14,732	7,888	1,884	3,264
IN	1,251	652	428	171	9,910	1,622	3,235	1,170
IA	462	225	132	105	1,453	873	4	509
KS	16,659	13,361	219	3,079	5,684	4,121	3	1,058
KY	33,875	33,301	265	309	7,839	5,726	296	221
LA	17,511	8,495	3,261	5,755	7,952	4,156	1,612	1,683
ME	2,036	241	1,618	177	5,229	284	4,273	287
MD	30,453	8,874	15,176	6,403	33,900	12,985	15,584	2,374
MA	3,256	458	588	2,210	7,392	1,885	410	3,568
MI	1,239	589	391	259	7,946	4,900	21	1,565
MN	884	365	371	148	2,512	1,358	27	786
MS	12,362	500	3,063	8,799	9,677	3,799	2,604	2,939
MO	15,078	10,022	1,688	3,368	10,525	6,707	234	1,260
MT	3,574	21	18	3,535	1,151	418	2	666
NE	8,953	74	501	8,378	3,583	1,583	18	1,544
NV	7,813	28	1,158	6,627	2,138	246	406	1,258
NH	404	10	258	136	1,264	528	268	294
NJ	7,472	1,015	1,024	5,433	18,112	10,777	4,350	1,652
NM	13,154	471	394	12,289	8,092	3,443	94	3,917
NY	18,853	15,701	2,301	851	12,287	7,598	182	2,530
NC	91,855	41,320	41,240	9,295	17,255	6,126	7,695	1,235
ND	8,698	23	5	8,670	1,674	412	1	1,138
OH	8,174	582	647	6,945	26,122	1,468	107	13,290
OK	27,060	16,150	758	10,152	19,421	4,082	86	13,639
OR	889	239	399	251	2,815	2,045	11	723
PA	3,566	1,661	1,555	350	29,933	9,246	9,426	1,624
RI	3,271	83	3,028	160	4,525	270	3,921	248
SC	33,653	11,455	12,696	9,502	10,155	2,819	4,139	1,759
SD	3,102	92	12	2,998	1,260	484	-	705
TN	1,864	323	1,245	296	5,049	2,709	502	952
TX	110,956	63,578	6,995	40,383	49,680	18,366	1,966	24,008
UT	4,896	298	154	4,444	12,421	2,168	24	8,259
VT	125	22	19	84	545	267	1	231
VA	84,463	26,921	43,200	14,342	81,998	21,230	36,922	4,354
WA	37,896	20,809	9,315	7,772	23,824	5,624	14,854	1,885
WV	547	227	285	35	1,820	1,320	83	388
WI	689	357	101	231	3,247	2,209	11	884
WY	3,534	4	11	3,519	965	201	1	699

- Represents zero. [1] Includes other DOD organizations not shown separately.

Source: U.S. Dept. of Defense, *Selected Manpower Statistics*, annual.

No. 579. Military Personnel on Active Duty by Location: 1980 to 1998

[In thousands (2,051 represents 2,051,000). As of end of fiscal year; see text, Section 9, State and Local Government]

Item	1980	1985	1990	1991	1992	1993	1994	1995	1996	1997	1998
Total	2,051	2,151	2,044	1,986	1,807	1,705	1,611	1,518	1,472	1,439	1,407
Shore-based [1]	1,840	1,920	1,794	1,743	1,589	1,505	1,431	1,351	1,317	1,294	1,267
Afloat [2]	211	231	252	243	218	200	180	167	155	145	140
United States [3]	1,562	1,636	1,437	1,539	1,463	1,397	1,324	1,280	1,231	1,211	1,147
Foreign countries	488	516	609	448	344	308	287	238	240	227	260

[1] Includes Navy personnel temporarily on shore.   [2] Includes Marine Corps.   [3] Includes outlying areas.

Source: U.S. Dept. of Defense, *Selected Manpower Statistics*, annual.

No. 580. U.S. Military Personnel on Active Duty in Selected Foreign Countries: 1998

[As of end of fiscal year]

Country	1998	Country	1998	Country	1998
In foreign countries [1] .	259,871	Egypt	5,846	Norway	107
Ashore	218,957	El Salvador	28	Oman	28
Afloat	40,914	France	74	Pakistan	29
		Germany	60,053	Panama	5,400
Antarctica	22	Greece	498	Peru	29
Argentina	27	Greenland	131	Philippines	35
Australia	333	Haiti	239	Portugal	1,066
Austria	34	Honduras	427	Qatar	26
Bahamas, The	24	Hungary	4,220	Rep. of Korea	35,663
Bahrain	748	Iceland	1,960	Russia	68
Belgium	1,679	India	25	Saudi Arabia	1,722
Bolivia	26	Indonesia	48	Singapore	168
Bosnia and Herzegovina . . .	8,170	Israel	40	South Africa	25
Brazil	45	Italy	11,677	Spain	3,575
Canada	179	Jamaica	11	Switzerland	22
Chile	25	Japan	41,257	Thailand	126
China	58	Jordan	30	Tunisia	193
Colombia	32	Kenya	31	Turkey	2,864
Croatia	866	Korea, Republic of	35,663	Ukraine	10
Cuba (Guantanamo)	1,527	Kuwait	1,640	United Arab Emirates	22
Cyprus	25	Macedonia	518	United Kingdom	11,379
Denmark	39	Mexico	27	Venezuela	35
Diego Garcia	705	Netherlands	703	Zambabwe	11
Ecuador	164	New Zealand	25		

[1] Includes areas not shown separately.

Source: U.S. Department of Defense, *Selected Manpower Statistics*, annual.

No. 581. Coast Guard Personnel on Active Duty: 1980 to 1998

[As of end of fiscal year; see text, Section 9, State and Local Government]

Year	Total	Officers	Cadets	Enlisted	Year	Total	Officers	Cadets	Enlisted
1980	39,381	6,463	877	32,041	1994	37,802	7,656	881	29,265
1985	38,595	6,775	733	31,087	1995	36,731	7,462	841	28,401
1990	36,939	6,876	927	29,136	1996	35,229	7,270	830	27,129
1991	38,377	7,192	900	30,285	1997	34,890	7,100	845	26,945
1992	39,388	7,507	919	30,962	1998	35,293	7,119	811	27,363
1993	39,234	7,628	907	30,699					

Source: U.S. Dept. of Transportation, *Annual Report of the Secretary of Transportation*.

No. 582. U.S. Active Duty Military Deaths by Manner of Death: 1980 to 1999

Manner of death	1980-99	1980	1990	1991	1992	1993	1994	1995	1996	1997	1998	1999
Deaths, total	32,912	2,391	1,526	1,787	1,332	1,245	1,109	1,055	1,008	864	815	761
Accident	19,488	1,577	864	931	712	672	548	572	518	463	420	411
Illness	5,974	401	275	323	253	215	217	167	180	177	156	126
Homicide	1,803	161	71	108	112	89	86	59	65	43	28	34
Self-inflicted	4,539	236	250	233	222	246	231	242	210	159	155	110
Pending/undetermined . .	545	15	42	44	32	13	8	9	14	22	53	80
Hostile deaths	563	1	24	148	1	10	19	6	21	-	3	-
Deaths per 100,000 . .	(X)	116.6	74.7	90.0	73.7	73.0	68.9	69.5	68.5	60.1	57.9	54.9
Nonhostile deaths per 100,000 . .	(X)	116.5	73.5	82.5	73.7	72.4	67.7	69.1	67.1	60.1	57.7	54.9
Accidents per 100,000 . .	(X)	76.9	42.3	46.9	39.4	39.4	34.0	37.7	35.2	32.2	29.9	29.7
Illnesses per 100,000 . .	(X)	19.6	13.5	16.3	14.0	12.6	13.5	11.0	12.2	12.3	11.1	9.1
Homicides per 100,000 . .	(X)	7.9	3.5	5.4	6.2	5.2	5.3	3.9	4.4	3.0	2.0	2.5
Self-inflicted per 100,000 .	(X)	11.5	12.2	11.7	12.3	14.4	14.3	15.9	14.3	11.1	11.0	7.9

- Represents zero.   X Not applicable.

Source: U.S. Dept. of Defense, *DoD Worldwide U.S. Active Duty Military Personnel*

No. 583. Armed Forces Personnel—Summary of Major Conflicts

[For Revolutionary War, number of personnel serving not known, but estimates range from 184,000 to 250,000; for War of 1812, 286,730 served; for Mexican War, 78,718 served. Dates of the major conflicts may differ from those specified in various laws providing benefits for veterans]

Item	Unit	Civil War [1]	Spanish-American War	World War I	World War II	Korean conflict	Vietnam conflict
Personnel serving [2]	1,000....	2,213	307	4,735	[3]16,113	[4]5,720	[5]8,744
Average duration of service	Months...	20	8	12	33	19	23
Service abroad: Personnel serving	Percent ..	(NA)	[6]29	53	73	[7]56	(NA)
Average duration [8]	Months...	(NA)	1.5	6	16	13	(NA)
Casualties: [9]							
Battle deaths [2]	1,000....	140	(Z)	53	292	34	[10]47
Other deaths	1,000....	224	2	63	114	3	11
Wounds not mortal [2]	1,000....	282	2	204	671	103	[10]153
Draftees:							
Classified	1,000....	777	(X)	24,234	36,677	9,123	[5]75,717
Examined	1,000....	522	(X)	3,764	17,955	3,685	[5]8,611
Rejected	1,000....	160	(X)	803	6,420	1,189	[5]3,880
Inducted	1,000....	46	(X)	2,820	10,022	1,560	[5]1,759

NA Not available. X Not applicable. Z Fewer than 500. [1] Union forces only. Estimates of the number serving in Confederate forces range from 600,000 to 1.5 million. [2] Source: U.S. Department of Defense, *Selected Manpower Statistics*, annual. [3] Covers Dec. 1, 1941, to Dec. 31, 1946. [4] Covers June 25, 1950, to July 27, 1953. [5] Covers Aug. 4, 1964, to Jan. 27, 1973. [6] Army and Marines only. [7] Excludes Navy. Covers July 1950 through Jan. 1955. Far East area only. [8] During hostilities only. [9] For periods covered, see footnotes 3, 4, and 5. [10] Covers Jan. 1, 1961, to Jan. 27, 1973. Includes known military service personnel who have died from combat related wounds.

Source: Except as noted, the President's Commission on Veterans' Pensions, Veterans' *Benefits in the United States*, Vol. I, 1956; and U.S. Dept. of Defense, unpublished data.

No. 584. Enlisted Military Personnel Accessions: 1990 to 1997

[In thousands (461.1 represents 461,100). For years ending Sept. 30]

Branch of service	1990	1995	1996	1997	Branch of service	1990	1995	1996	1997
Total	461.1	357.3	367.6	380.1	First enlistments	62.1	36.4	39.2	43.7
First enlistments	216.4	160.0	174.6	184.6	Reenlistments	58.6	41.4	40.6	41.6
Reenlistments	237.0	180.8	181.0	187.4	Marine Corps	47.7	46.7	48.7	50.0
Reserves to active duty	15.6	16.6	12.0	8.1	First enlistments	32.9	34.4	34.5	35.1
Army	181.7	135.9	146.0	162.3	Reenlistments	14.4	11.9	0.4	14.7
First enlistments	84.8	57.7	69.7	75.3	Air Force	104.4	81.3	81.6	74.5
Reenlistments	96.5	77.7	76.2	87.0	First enlistments	36.6	31.4	31.2	30.5
Navy	135.3	93.4	91.3	93.3	Reenlistments	67.5	49.7	50.3	44.0

Source: U.S. Dept. of Defense, *Selected Manpower Statistics*, annual.

No. 585. Military Personnel on Active Duty: 1990 to 1997

[In thousands (2,043.7 represents 2,043,700). As of Sept. 30]

Rank/grade	1990	1992	1993	1994	1995	1996	1997
Total [1]	**2,043.7**	**1,807.2**	**1,705.1**	**1,610.5**	**1,518.2**	**1,471.7**	**1,438.6**
Recruit—E-1	97.6	83.2	75.4	73.3	63.4	69.3	74.1
Private—E-2	140.3	110.9	114.1	108.2	99.7	99.0	100.8
Pvt. 1st class—E-3	280.1	233.5	214.6	208.4	197.1	200.4	196.0
Corporal—E-4	427.8	383.5	352.2	322.2	317.2	283.8	264.8
Sergeant—E-5	361.5	305.1	295.6	281.0	261.4	254.8	250.6
Staff Sgt.—E-6	239.1	227.4	214.6	198.1	180.5	172.6	169.6
Sgt. 1st class—E-7	134.1	130.5	124.7	119.7	109.3	107.7	104.7
Master Sgt.—E-8	38.0	33.2	31.6	29.9	28.8	28.8	27.6
Sgt. Major—E-9	15.3	13.5	12.8	12.1	11.1	10.7	10.8
Warrant Officer—W-1	3.2	2.2	2.4	2.4	2.0	2.1	2.0
Chief Warrant—W-4	3.0	2.7	2.4	2.4	2.2	2.0	1.9
2d Lt.—O-1	31.9	25.8	25.0	24.8	25.6	25.2	24.8
1st Lt.—O-2	37.9	33.5	29.7	27.3	26.1	25.8	25.5
Captain—O-3	106.6	100.2	93.0	89.2	84.3	81.0	78.3
Major—O-4	53.2	50.4	48.0	44.8	43.9	43.9	43.1
Lt. Colonel—O-5	32.3	30.9	29.5	29.0	28.7	28.2	28.0
Colonel—O-6	14.0	13.2	12.5	12.2	11.7	11.6	11.4
Brig. General—O-7	0.5	0.5	0.4	0.5	0.4	0.4	0.4
Major General—O-8	0.4	0.3	0.3	0.3	0.3	0.3	0.3
Lt. General—O-9	0.1	0.1	0.1	0.1	0.1	0.1	0.1
General—O-10	(Z)	(Z)	(Z)	(Z)	(Z)	(Z)	(Z)

Z Fewer than 50. [1] Includes cadets and midshipmen and warrant officers, W-2 and W-3.

Source: U.S. Dept. of Defense, *Selected Manpower Statistics*, annual, and Office of the Comptroller, unpublished data.

National Defense and Veterans Affairs 369

No. 586. Military Reserve Personnel: 1980 to 1999

[In thousands (1,349 represents 1,349,000). As of **end of fiscal year**; see text, Section 9, State and Local Government. Excludes U.S. Coast Guard Reserve. The ready reserve includes selected reservists who are intended to assist active forces in a war and the individual ready reserve who, in a major war, would be used to fill out active and reserve units and later would be a source of combat replacements; a portion of the ready reserve serves in an active status. The standby reserve cannot be called to active duty unless the Congress gives its explicit approval. The retired reserve represents a low potential for mobilization]

Reserve status and branch of service	1980	1985	1990	1991	1992	1993	1994	1995	1996	1997	1998	1999
Total reserves [1]	1,349	1,610	1,671	1,786	1,883	1,867	1,805	1,659	1,550	1,461	1,369	1,304
Ready reserve	1,263	1,566	1,641	1,758	1,858	1,841	1,779	1,633	1,523	1,438	1,341	1,276
Standby reserve	86	44	29	28	25	26	26	26	28	23	29	28
Retired reserve	338	372	462	474	442	461	482	506	530	550	562	564
Army [2]	804	1,045	1,050	1,124	1,156	1,132	1,077	1,001	921	862	799	753
Navy	207	214	252	271	297	302	317	280	262	238	218	202
Marine Corps	94	92	83	96	107	112	109	104	102	100	99	99
Air Force [3]	243	259	286	295	323	321	302	274	265	261	253	249

[1] Less retired reserves.   [2] Includes Army national guard.   [3] Includes Air national guard.

Source: U.S. Dept. of Defense, *Official Guard and Reserve Manpower Strengths and Statistics*, quarterly.

No. 587. Ready Reserve Personnel Profile by Race and Sex: 1990 to 1999

Item	Race					Percent distribution			
	Total	White	Black	Asian	American Indian	White	Black	Asian	American Indian
1990	1,641,475	1,289,367	271,470	14,616	7,695	78.5	16.5	0.9	0.5
1993	1,840,650	1,425,255	309,699	21,089	9,068	77.4	16.8	1.1	0.5
1994	1,779,436	1,366,387	297,519	22,190	8,870	76.8	16.7	1.2	0.5
1995	1,633,497	1,254,592	273,847	21,792	8,591	76.8	16.8	1.3	0.5
1996	1,522,451	1,166,628	249,114	21,240	8,226	76.6	16.4	1.4	0.5
1997	1,437,722	1,102,234	229,950	21,412	8,115	76.7	16.0	1.5	0.6
1998	1,340,557	1,022,851	209,814	21,411	7,531	76.3	15.7	1.6	0.6
1999, total [1]	1,276,190	969,248	201,969	22,293	7,349	75.9	15.8	1.7	0.6
Male	1,065,979	833,945	145,969	18,714	5,846	78.2	13.7	1.8	0.5
Officers	164,885	139,328	11,188	2,270	456	84.5	6.8	1.4	0.3
Enlisted	901,094	694,617	134,781	16,444	5,390	77.1	15.0	1.8	0.6
Female	209,830	135,291	55,996	3,578	1,503	64.5	26.7	1.7	0.7
Officers	38,135	28,153	5,956	564	123	73.8	15.6	1.5	0.3
Enlisted	171,695	107,138	50,040	3,014	1,380	62.4	29.1	1.8	0.8

[1] Includes unknown sex.

Source: U.S. Dept. of Defense, *Official Guard and Reserve Manpower Strengths and Statistics*, annual.

No. 588. Military Reserve Costs: 1980 to 1996

[In millions of dollars ($7,969 represents $7,969,000,000). As of **end of fiscal year**; see text, Section 9, State and Local Government. Army and Air Force data include National Guard]

Type of cost	1980	1985	1990	1991	1992	1993	1994	1995	1996
Total	7,969	19,414	21,526	21,811	21,867	22,825	20,269	20,424	21,539
Operations and maintenance	3,526	5,734	6,687	7,398	7,714	8,095	8,173	8,832	8,782
Personnel	2,456	7,703	8,621	8,543	9,272	9,062	9,564	9,258	9,322
Procurement	1,459	5,009	4,914	4,480	3,533	4,398	1,168	1,102	2,292
Active-duty support	408	566	638	700	731	682	632	658	715
Construction	120	402	666	690	617	588	732	574	428

Source: U.S. Dept. of Defense, unpublished data.

No. 589. National Guard—Summary: 1980 to 1998

[As of **end of fiscal year**; see text, Section 9, State and Local Government. Includes Puerto Rico]

Item	Unit	1980	1985	1990	1993	1994	1995	1996	1997	1998
Army National Guard:										
Units	Number . . .	3,379	4,353	4,055	6,339	6,000	5,872	5,643	5,500	5,415
Personnel [1]	1,000	368	438	444	410	397	375	373	370	362
Funds obligated [2]	Bil. dol. . . .	1.8	4.4	5.2	6.3	6.0	6.0	5.9	5.7	6.0
Value of equipment	Bil. dol. . . .	7.6	18.8	29.0	31.0	31.0	33.0	33.0	33.0	33.0
Air National Guard:										
Units	Number . . .	1,054	1,184	1,339	1,330	1,665	1,604	1,588	(NA)	1,541
Personnel [1]	1,000	96	109	118	117	114	110	110	108	108
Funds obligated [2]	Bil. dol. . . .	1.7	2.8	3.2	2.6	3.1	4.2	4.6	4.5	4.4
Value of equipment (est.) [3]	Bil. dol. . . .	5.2	21.4	26.4	41.7	40.2	38.3	40.1	42.0	41.0

NA Not available.   [1] Officers and enlisted personnel.   [2] Federal funds; includes personnel, operations, maintenance, and military construction.   [3] Beginning 1985, increase due to repricing of aircraft to current year dollars to reflect true replacement value. Beginning 1993 includes value of aircraft and support equipment.

Source: National Guard Bureau, *Annual Review of the Chief, National Guard Bureau;* and unpublished data.

370 National Defense and Veterans Affairs

No. 590. Summary of U.S. Military Force Structure: 1993 to 1999, and Projections to 2001

Item	1993	1994	1995	1996	1997	1998	1999	2000	2001
DEPARTMENT OF DEFENSE (DOD) STRATEGIC FORCES [1]									
Land-based ICBMs: [2]									
Minuteman II (1 warhead each) plus Minuteman III (3 warheads each)	737	625	535	530	530	500	500	500	500
Peacekeeper (10 warheads each)	50	50	50	50	50	50	50	50	34
Heavy bombers (PAI): [3]									
B-52	84	64	74	56	56	56	56	56	56
B-1 [4]	84	84	60	60	60	70	74	80	82
B-2.	-	3	6	9	10	12	13	16	16
Submarine-launched ballistic missiles: [2]									
Poseidon (C-3) and Trident (C-4) missiles on pre-Ohio-class submarines .	96	48	-	-	-	-	-	-	-
Trident (C-4 and D-5) missiles on Ohio-class submarines	312	336	360	384	408	432	432	432	432
DOD AIRLIFT AND SEALIFT FORCES									
Intratheater Airlift (PMAI): [5]									
C-5.	109	107	104	104	104	104	104	104	104
C-141	214	214	199	187	163	143	136	104	88
KC-10 [6]	57	54	54	54	54	54	54	54	54
C-17.	2	9	17	22	24	30	37	46	58
Intratheater Airlift (PMAI): [5]									
C-130 [7]	380	424	428	432	430	425	425	425	425
Sealift ships (Active): [8]									
Tankers.	20	18	18	12	13	10	10	10	10
Cargo	40	51	51	49	48	43	49	52	57
Sealift ships, reserve:									
RRF [9]	97	93	77	82	87	88	87	87	69
SPECIAL OPERATIONS FORCES									
Army:									
Special forces groups, (Active)	5	5	5	5	5	5	5	5	5
Special forces groups, (National Guard) .	2	2	2	2	2	2	2	2	2
Special forces groups, (Reserve)	2	-	-	-	-	-	-	-	-
Psychological operations groups (Active).	1	1	1	1	1	1	1	1	1
Special operations aviation regiments. . .	1	1	1	1	1	1	1	1	1
Ranger regiments	1	1	1	1	1	1	1	1	1
Civil affairs battalions (Active)	1	1	1	1	1	1	1	1	1
Civil affairs brigades (Reserve)	9	9	9	9	9	8	8	8	8
Civil affairs commands (Reserve).	3	3	3	3	3	4	4	4	4
Air Force:									
Special operations wings/groups:									
Active	3	3	3	3	3	3	3	3	3
National Guard	1	1	1	1	1	1	1	1	1
Special operations wing (Reserve)	1	1	1	1	1	1	1	1	1
Special tactics groups	1	1	1	1	1	1	1	1	1
Naval:									
Special boat squadrons	2	2	2	2	2	2	2	2	2

- Represents or rounds to zero.   [1] Force levels shown are for the ends of the fiscal years in question. The actual force levels for FY 2000 and FY 2001 will depend on future decisions.   [2] Number of operational missiles. Not in maintenance or overhaul status.   [3] PAI=Primary aircraft inventory. PAI excludes backup and attrition reserve aircrafts as well as aircraft in depot maintenance. Total inventory counts will be higher than the PAI figures given here.   [4] B-1 are accountable under START I but will not be accountable under START II.   [5] PMAI = Primary mission aircraft inventory for active and reserve components. The numbers shown reflect only combat support and industrial funded PMAI aircraft and not developments/test or training aircraft.   [6] Includes 37 KC-10s allocated to an airlift code.   [7] Does not include Department of the Navy aircraft.   [8] Includes fast sea lift (FSS), afloat prepositioning, and common-user (charter) ships, plus (through FY 1998) aviation support ships. For FY 1999 on, includes LMSR and and ready reserve force (RRF) ships tendered to the Military sealift command (MSC). FSS and LMSR vessels are maintained in a reserve, four-day ready status.   [9] The RRF includes vessels assigned to 4-, 5-, 10-, or 20-day reactivation readiness groups. The ship counts shown exclude RRF vessels tendered to the MSC. Inventory figures for FY 1999, FY 2000, and FY 2001 include aviation support ships.

Source: U.S. Dept. of Defense, *Annual Report to the President and the Congress.*

No. 591. Veterans by State: 1999

[In thousands (24,679 represents 24,679,000). Data were estimated starting with veteran's place of residence as of April 1, 1980, based on 1980 Census of Population data, extended to later years on the basis of estimates of veteran interstate migration, separations from the Armed Forces, and mortality; not directly comparable with earlier estimates previously published by the VA. Excludes 602,000 whose active-duty military service occurred since 1980, and who failed to satisfy the minimum service requirement. Also excludes a small indeterminate number of National Guard personnel or reservists who incurred service-connected disabilities while on an initial tour of active duty for training only]

State	Total veterans [1] Both sexes	Male	Female	World War I	World War II	Korean conflict	Vietnam era [2]	Persian Gulf War
United States........	24,679	23,445	1,234	3	5,922	4,034	8,079	2,188
Alabama..............	408	387	21	-	95	72	133	49
Alaska...............	63	58	5	-	6	7	29	4
Arizona..............	443	416	27	-	113	78	146	32
Arkansas	246	234	12	-	62	41	79	28
California	2,666	2,514	152	-	608	444	925	185
Colorado.............	363	340	23	-	72	59	140	31
Connecticut...........	313	299	15	-	82	51	96	21
Delaware	75	71	4	-	18	12	24	7
District of Columbia	46	42	3	-	12	9	14	5
Florida	1,652	1,559	93	-	501	301	491	126
Georgia	661	624	36	-	121	98	244	67
Hawaii...............	112	104	8	-	22	18	42	10
Idaho................	107	101	5	-	25	16	35	11
Illinois	999	960	39	-	249	160	310	89
Indiana..............	564	541	23	-	128	88	178	55
Iowa	273	263	10	-	68	47	84	28
Kansas...............	246	236	10	-	60	41	84	20
Kentucky	350	336	14	-	82	56	116	37
Louisiana	349	332	17	-	86	57	113	41
Maine................	148	140	8	-	32	23	50	15
Maryland	505	473	32	-	106	77	170	42
Massachusetts..........	549	522	26	-	151	92	162	36
Michigan.............	898	858	40	-	205	132	284	91
Minnesota............	437	420	17	-	95	69	147	35
Mississippi	221	210	11	-	55	39	66	30
Missouri..............	556	533	24	-	132	94	180	52
Montana.............	89	84	5	-	21	15	30	10
Nebraska............	158	150	8	-	37	29	50	16
Nevada	184	174	10	-	40	35	65	10
New Hampshire.........	130	122	8	-	27	20	45	11
New Jersey............	682	655	27	-	190	118	196	47
New Mexico	165	154	11	-	37	26	59	16
New York	1,422	1,360	62	-	370	228	404	133
North Carolina	684	647	37	-	151	110	230	66
North Dakota...........	55	52	3	-	12	10	18	6
Ohio	1,124	1,076	48	-	275	173	347	112
Oklahoma.............	324	310	14	-	81	58	114	27
Oregon...............	356	337	19	-	85	54	124	30
Pennsylvania...........	1,283	1,229	54	-	356	207	373	113
Rhode Island...........	102	97	5	-	29	17	31	8
South Carolina..........	367	347	20	-	78	58	128	41
South Dakota	70	67	4	-	16	13	21	9
Tennessee	495	474	21	-	110	79	169	50
Texas................	1,556	1,475	81	-	341	251	567	145
Utah	129	124	5	-	33	22	43	11
Vermont	60	56	4	-	12	9	20	6
Virginia..............	676	629	48	-	135	110	254	60
Washington...........	607	570	37	-	125	95	229	49
West Virginia..........	188	181	6	-	50	33	58	20
Wisconsin............	481	460	21	-	112	75	149	44
Wyoming.............	43	41	2	-	10	7	16	4

- Represents or rounds to zero. [1] Veterans who served in more than one wartime period are counted only once. "All veterans" includes Vietnam era (no prior wartime service), Korean conflict (no prior wartime service), World War 11, post Vietnam era, Persian Gulf War era, and other. [2] Excludes reservists.

Source: U.S. Dept. of Veterans Affairs, Management Sciences Service (008B2), *Annual Report of the Secretary of Veterans Affairs.*

No. 592. Veterans Living in the United States and Puerto Rico by Age and Service: 1999

[In thousands, except as indicated. As of July 1. Estimated. Excludes 73,000 whose active military service of less than 2 years occurred since Sept. 30, 1980. See headnote, table 591]

Age	Total veterans	Wartime veterans							Peace-time veterans
		Total [1]	Persian Gulf	Vietnam era	Korean conflict	World War II	World War I		
All ages.......	26,178	18,945	2,200	8,113	4,064	5,940	3		5,858
Under 30 years old . . .	833	773	773	-	-	-	-		60
30-34 years old	1,108	589	589	-	-	-	-		519
35-39 years old	1,387	286	274	12	-	-	-		1,101
40-44 years old	1,749	691	222	518	-	-	-		1,009
45-49 years old	2,391	1,996	202	1,949	-	-	-		240
50-54 years old	3,546	3,330	99	3,310	-	-	-		137
55-59 years old	2,472	1,494	30	1,485	-	-	-		957
60-64 years old	2,363	899	9	385	583	-	-		1,386
65 years old and over .	10,330	8,887	2	455	3,481	5,940	3		449
Female, total.......	1,273	791	263	234	88	239	-		449

- Represents or rounds to zero. [1]Veterans who served in more than one wartime period are counted only once.

Source: U.S. Dept. of Veterans Affairs, Office of Policy & Planning, *Veteran Population*, annual.

No. 593. Disabled Veterans Receiving Compensation: 1980 to 1999

[In thousands (2,274 represents 2,274,000), except as indicated. As of end of fiscal year; see text, Section 9, State and Local Government. Represents veterans receiving compensation for service-connected disabilities. Totally disabled refers to veterans with any disability, mental or physical, deemed to be total and permanent which prevents the individual from maintaining a livelihood and are rated for disability at 100 percent]

Military service	1980	1990	1992	1993	1994	1995	1996	1997	1998	1999
Disabled, all periods [1]	2,274	2,184	2,181	2,198	2,218	2,236	2,253	2,263	2,277	2,294
Peace-time	262	444	500	471	492	514	529	539	550	561
World War I [1]	30	3	2	1	1	1	(Z)	(Z)	(Z)	(Z)
World War II.	1,193	876	805	769	731	692	655	616	578	541
Korea	236	209	202	198	195	191	187	182	179	175
Vietnam.	553	652	671	682	694	705	714	724	729	736
Persian Gulf.	(X)	(X)	(X)	76	106	134	168	202	241	282
Totally disabled, all periods [1] .	121	131	132	135	138	143	150	156	161	166
Peace-time	20	27	28	28	29	30	32	33	34	35
World War I [1]	3	(Z)	(Z)	(Z)	(Z)	(Z)	(Z)	(Z)	(Z)	(Z)
World War II.	51	43	39	37	36	34	33	31	30	29
Korea	16	16	15	15	15	15	15	15	14	14
Vietnam.	31	44	49	52	56	61	67	73	78	82
Persian Gulf.	(X)	(X)	(X)	2	2	3	3	4	5	6
Compensation (mil. dol.).	6,104	9,284	10,031	10,545	11,056	11,644	11,072	13,004	13,795	(NA)

NA Not available.   X Not applicable.   Z Less than 500.   [1] Includes Spanish-American War and Mexican Border service, not shown separately.

Source: U.S. Dept. of Veterans Affairs, *Annual Report of the Secretary of Veterans Affairs;* and unpublished data.

No. 594. Veterans Benefits—Expenditures by Program: 1980 to 1998

[In millions of dollars ($23,187 represents $23,187,000,000). For fiscal years ending in year shown; see text, Section 9, State and Local Government. Beginning with fiscal year 1990, data are for outlays]

Program	1980	1990	1992	1993	1994	1995	1996	1997	1998
Total	23,187	28,998	33,900	35,460	37,401	37,775	36,915	39,277	41,776
Medical programs	6,042	11,582	13,815	14,603	15,430	16,255	16,337	16,900	17,575
Construction.	300	661	639	622	695	641	698	597	515
General operating expenses . . .	605	811	920	904	906	954	961	1,063	877
Compensation and pension. . . .	11,044	14,674	16,282	16,882	17,188	17,765	17,056	19,284	20,289
Vocational rehabilitation and education.	2,350	452	695	863	1,119	1,127	1,212	1,287	1,310
All other [1]	2,846	818	1,549	1,586	2,062	1,034	652	145	1,209

[1] Includes insurance and indemnities, and miscellaneous funds and expenditures. (Excludes expenditures from personal funds of patients.)

Source: U.S. Dept. of Veterans Affairs, *Trend Data*, annual.

No. 595. Veterans Compensation and Pension Benefits—Number on Rolls by Period of Service and Status: 1980 to 1999

[As of **Sept. 30. In thousands.** Living refers to veterans receiving compensation for disability incurred or aggravated while on active duty and war veterans receiving pension and benefits for nonservice connected disabilities. Deceased refers to deceased veterans whose dependents were receiving pensions and compensation benefits]

Period of service and veteran status	1980	1990	1995	1996	1997	1998	1999
Total	**4,646**	**3,584**	**3,330**	**3,308**	**3,281**	**3,263**	**3,252**
Living veterans	3,195	2,746	2,669	2,671	2,667	2,668	2,673
Service connected	2,273	2,184	2,236	2,253	2,263	2,277	2,294
Nonservice connected	922	562	433	418	404	391	379
Deceased veterans	1,451	838	662	637	614	595	579
Service connected	358	320	307	306	305	303	304
Nonservice connected	1,093	518	355	332	309	291	274
Prior to World War I	14	4	2	2	2	1	1
Living	(Z)	(Z)	(Z)	(Z)	(Z)	(Z)	(Z)
World War I	692	198	89	74	61	51	42
Living	198	18	3	2	1	1	(Z)
World War II	2,520	1,723	1,307	1,237	1,165	1,097	1,031
Living	1,849	1,294	961	902	842	785	730
Korean conflict [1]	446	390	368	360	351	342	333
Living	317	305	290	285	278	271	264
Peacetime	312	495	559	574	582	592	602
Living	262	444	514	529	539	550	561
Vietnam era [2]	662	774	868	889	913	932	953
Living	569	685	766	784	804	819	835
Persian Gulf War [3]	(X)	(X)	138	173	207	247	290
Living	(X)	(X)	134	169	203	242	283

X Not applicable.   Z Fewer than 500.   [1] Service during period June 27, 1950, to Jan. 31, 1955.   [2] Service from Aug. 5, 1964, to May 7, 1975.   [3] Service from August 2, 1990, to the present.

Source: U.S. Dept. of Veterans Affairs, *Annual Report of the Secretary of Veterans Affairs;* and unpublished data.

No. 596. Veterans Administration Health Care Summary: 1990 to 1999

[For years ending **Sept. 30**]

Item	Unit	1990	1995	1999	Item	Unit	1990	1995	1999
Facilities operating:					Obligations [2]	Mil. dol.	11,827	15,982	17,876
Hospitals	Number	172	173	172	Prescriptions dispensed	Millions	58.6	66.1	(NA)
Domiciliaries	Number	32	39	40	Laboratory	Millions	188	(NA)	(NA)
Outpatient clinics	Number	339	391	527	Inpatients treated [3]	1,000	1,113	1,035	752
Nursing home units	Number	126	131	134	Average daily	1,000	88	81	60
Employment [1]	1,000	199	200	183	Outpatient visits	Millions	22.6	28.0	36.9

NA Not available.   [1] Net full-time equivalent.   [2] 1980, cost basis; thereafter, obligation basis.   [3] Based on the number of discharges and deaths during the fiscal year, plus the number on the rolls (bed occupants and patients on authorized leave of absence) at the end of the fiscal year. Excludes interhospital transfers.

Source: U.S. Dept. of Veterans Affairs, *Annual Report of the Secretary of Veterans Affairs; Directory of VA Facilities,* biennial; and unpublished data.

No. 597. Veterans Assistance—Education and Training: 1980 to 1999

[In thousands (1,107 represents 1,107,000), except where indicated. For fiscal years ending in year shown; see text, Section 9, State and Local Governments. Represents persons in training during year]

Program	1980	1990	1994	1995	1996	1997	1998	1999
Veteran Education Assistance [1]	1,107	102	284	292	296	297	297	288
Institutions of higher education	842	94	258	264	270	267	265	256
Resident schools other than college	149	6	19	19	18	18	18	18
Correspondence schools	42	1	4	(NA)	3	4	4	3
On-the-job training	74	1	3	4	5	8	9	11
Children's Educational Assistance	82.6	37.5	35.7	34.8	35.7	36.2	37.2	38.7
Institutions of higher education	75.5	35.3	33.7	33.1	34	34.4	35.3	36.8
Schools other than college	6.5	2.1	1.9	1.7	1.6	1.7	1.8	1.8
Special restorative training	0.1	(Z)	(Z)	(Z)	(Z)	(Z)	(Z)	(Z)
On-the-job training	0.5	0.1	(Z)	(Z)	(Z)	0.1	0.1	0.1
Spouses, Widows/Widowers Educational Assistance Program	13.0	4.5	4.6	4.6	5.0	5.2	5.5	5.7
Institutions of higher education	10.8	4.1	4.1	4.2	4.5	4.7	5.0	5.2
Schools other than college	2.2	0.4	0.4	0.4	0.4	0.4	0.4	0.4
Disabled Veterans Vocational Rehab.	25.5	27.8	44.2	47.9	51.8	53.8	53.4	(NA)
Guaranteed and insured loans	297.4	196.6	602.2	263.1	320.8	258.8	344	485.6
Guaranteed and insured loans (mil. dol.)	14,815	15,779	55,141	25,341	32,609	27,042	37,906	54,088
Guaranty and insurance (mil. dol.)	6,370	5,561	18,332	8,383	10,525	8,632	11,757	16,660

NA Not available.   Z Fewer than 50.   [1] Data for 1980 are for Post-Korean Conflict GI Bill (Title 38 USC Chapter 34). Data for 1990-99 are for the Active Duty Montgomery GI Bill (Title 38 USC Chapter 30).

Source: U.S. Dept. of Veterans Affairs, *Annual Report of the Secretary of Veterans Affairs;* and unpublished data.

Social Insurance and
Human Services

This section presents data related to governmental expenditures for social welfare; governmental programs for old-age, survivors, disability, and health insurance (OASDHI); governmental employee retirement; private pension plans; government unemployment and temporary disability insurance; Federal supplemental security income payments and aid to the needy; child and other welfare services; and Federal food programs. Also included here are selected data on workers' compensation and vocational rehabilitation, child support, child care, charity contributions, and philanthropic trusts and foundations.

The principal sources for these data are the Social Security Administration's quarterly *Social Security Bulletin* and the *Annual Statistical Supplement to the Social Security Bulletin* which present current data on many of the programs.

Social insurance under the Social Security Act— Programs established by the Social Security Act provide protection against wage loss resulting from retirement, prolonged disability, death, or unemployment, and protection against the cost of medical care during old age and disability. The Federal OASDI program provides monthly benefits to retired or disabled insured workers and their dependents and to survivors of insured workers. To be eligible, a worker must have had a specified period of employment in which OASDI taxes were paid. The age of eligibility for full retirement benefits has been 65 years old for many years. However, for persons born in 1938 or later that age will gradually increase until it reaches age 67 for those born after 1959. Reduced benefits may be obtained as early as age 62. The worker's spouse is under the same limitations. Survivor benefits are payable to dependents of deceased insured workers.

Disability benefits are payable to an insured worker under age 65 with a prolonged disability and to the disabled worker's dependents on the same basis as dependents of retired workers. Disability benefits are provided at age 50 to the disabled widow or widower of a deceased worker who was fully insured at the time of death. Disabled children, aged 18 or older, of retired, disabled, or deceased workers are also eligible for benefits. A lump sum benefit is generally payable on the death of an insured worker to a spouse or minor children. For information on the medicare program, see Section 3, Health.

Retirement, survivors, disability, and hospital insurance benefits are funded by a payroll tax on annual earnings (up to a maximum of earnings set by law) of workers, employers, and the self-employed. The maximum taxable earnings are adjusted annually to reflect increasing wage levels (see Table 606). Effective January 1994, there is no dollar limit on wages and self-employment income subject to the hospital insurance tax. Tax receipts and benefit payments are administered through Federal trust funds. Special benefits for uninsured persons; hospital benefits for persons aged 65 and over with specified amounts of social security coverage less than that required for cash benefit eligibility; and that part of the cost of supplementary medical insurance not financed by contributions from participants are financed from Federal general revenues.

Unemployment insurance is presently administered by the U.S. Employment and Training Administration and each state's employment security agency. By agreement with the U.S. Secretary of Labor, state agencies also administer unemployment compensation for eligible ex-military personnel and Federal employees. Under state unemployment insurance laws, benefits related to the individual's past earnings are paid to unemployed eligible workers. State laws vary concerning the length of time benefits are paid and their amount. In most states, benefits are payable for 26 weeks and, during periods of high unemployment, extended benefits are payable under a Federal-state program to those who have exhausted their regular state benefits. Some states also supplement the basic benefit with allowances for dependents.

Unemployment insurance is funded by a Federal unemployment tax levied on the taxable payrolls of most employers. Taxable payroll under the Federal act and 12 state laws is the first $7,000 in wages paid each worker during a year. Forty-one states have taxable payrolls above $7,000. Employers are allowed a percentage credit of taxable payroll for contributions paid to states under state unemployment insurance laws. The remaining percent of the Federal tax finances administrative costs, the Federal share of extended benefits, and advances to states. About 97 percent of wage and salary workers are covered by unemployment insurance.

Retirement programs for government employees—The Civil Service Retirement System (CSRS) and the Federal Employees' Retirement System (FERS) are the two major programs providing age and service, disability, and survivor annuities for Federal civilian employees. In general, employees hired after December 31, 1983, are covered under FERS and the social security program (OASDHI), and employees on staff prior to that date are members of CSRS and are covered under medicare. CSRS employees were offered the option of transferring to FERS during 1987 and 1998. There are separate retirement systems for the uniformed services (supplementing OASDHI) and for certain special groups of Federal employees. State and local government employees are covered for the most part by state and local retirement systems similar to the Federal Civil Service Retirement System. In many jurisdictions these benefits supplement OASDHI coverage.

Workers' compensation—All states provide protection against work-connected injuries and deaths, although some states exclude certain workers (e.g., domestic help). Federal laws cover Federal employees, private employees in the District of Columbia, and longshoremen and harbor workers. In addition, the Social Security Administration and the Department of Labor administer "black lung" benefits programs for coal miners disabled by pneumoconiosis and for specified dependents and survivors. Specified occupational diseases are compensable to some extent. In most states, benefits are related to the worker's salary. The benefits may or may not be augmented by dependents' allowances or automatically adjusted to prevailing wage levels.

Income support—Income support programs are designed to provide benefits for persons with limited income and resources. The Supplemental Security Income (SSI) program and Temporary Assistance for Needy Families (TANF) program are the major programs providing monthly payments. In addition, a number of programs provide money payments or in-kind benefits for special needs or purposes. Several programs offer food and nutritional services. Also, various Federal-state programs provide energy assistance, public housing, and subsidized housing to individuals and families with low incomes. General assistance may also be available at the state or local level.

The SSI program, administered by the Social Security Administration, provides income support to persons aged 65 or older and blind or disabled adults and children. Eligibility requirements and Federal payment standards are nationally uniform. Most states supplement the basic SSI payment for all or selected categories of persons.

The Personal Responsibility and Work Opportunity Reconciliation Act of 1996 contained provisions that replaced the Aid to Families With Dependent Children (AFDC), Job Opportunities and Basic Skills

U.S. Census Bureau, Statistical Abstract of the United States: 2000

(JOBS), and Emergency Assistance programs with the Temporary Assistance for Needy Families block grant program. This law contains strong work requirements, comprehensive child support enforcement, support for families moving from welfare to work, and other features. The TANF became effective as soon as each state submitted a complete plan implementing TANF, but no later than July 1, 1997. The AFDC program provided cash assistance based on need, income, resources, and family size.

Federal Food Stamp program—Under the food stamp program, single persons and those living in households meeting nationwide standards for income and assets may receive coupons redeemable for food at most retail food stores. The monthly amount of coupons a unit receives is determined by household size and income. Households without income receive the determined monthly cost of a nutritionally adequate diet for their household size. This amount is updated to account for food price increases. Households with income receive the difference between the amount of a nutritionally adequate diet and 30 percent of their income, after certain allowable deductions.

To qualify for the program, a household must have less than $2,000 in disposable assets ($3,000 if one member is aged 60 or older), gross income below 130 percent of the official poverty guidelines for the household size, and net income below 100 percent of the poverty guidelines. Households with a person aged 60 or older or a disabled person receiving SSI, social security, state general assistance, or veterans' disability benefits may have gross income exceeding 130 percent of the poverty guidelines. All households in which all members receive TANF or SSI are categorically eligible for food stamps without meeting these income or resource criteria. Households are certified for varying lengths of time, depending on their income sources and individual circumstances.

Health and welfare services—Programs providing health and welfare services are aided through Federal grants to states for child welfare services, vocational rehabilitation, activities for the aged, maternal and child health services, maternity and infant care projects, comprehensive health services, and a variety of public health activities. For information about the medicaid program, see Section 3, Health.

Noncash benefits—The U.S. Census Bureau annually collects data on the characteristics of recipients of noncash (in-kind) benefits to supplement the collection of annual money income data in the Current Population Survey (see text, Section 1, Population, and Section 15, Prices). Noncash benefits are those benefits received in a form other than money which serve to enhance or improve the economic well-being of the recipient. As for money income, the data for noncash benefits are for the calendar year prior to the date of the interview. The major categories of noncash benefits covered are public transfers (e.g., food stamps, school lunch, public housing, and medicaid) and employer or union-provided benefits to employees.

Statistical reliability— For discussion of statistical collection, estimation, and sampling procedures and measures of statistical reliability applicable to HHS and Census Bureau data, see Appendix III.

U.S. Census Bureau, Statistical Abstract of the United States: 2000

No. 598. Social Welfare Expenditures Under Public Programs: 1980 to 1995

[In billions of dollars (493 represents $493,000,000,000), except percent. See headnote, Table 600]

Year	Total	Social insur-ance	Public aid	Health and medical programs [1]	Veterans pro-grams	Educa-tion	Housing	Other social welfare	All health and medical care [2]
Total:									
1980..............	493	230	73	27	21	121	7	14	100
1985..............	732	370	98	39	27	172	13	14	171
1990..............	1,049	514	147	61	31	258	19	18	274
1992..............	1,267	619	208	70	36	292	21	22	353
1993..............	1,367	659	221	75	36	332	21	23	382
1994..............	1,436	684	238	80	38	344	27	25	409
1995..............	1,505	705	254	86	39	366	29	27	435
Federal:									
1980..............	303	191	49	13	21	13	6	9	69
1985..............	451	310	63	18	27	14	11	8	122
1990..............	617	422	93	27	30	18	17	9	190
1992..............	750	496	139	32	35	20	17	11	250
1993..............	805	534	152	33	36	20	19	11	276
1994..............	853	557	163	35	37	24	25	12	295
1995..............	888	580	170	37	38	23	27	12	308
State and local:									
1980..............	190	39	23	14	(Z)	108	1	5	31
1985..............	281	59	35	21	(Z)	158	2	6	49
1990..............	432	92	54	34	(Z)	240	3	9	84
1992..............	517	123	69	38	1	272	3	11	103
1993..............	561	125	69	42	1	312	2	12	106
1994..............	583	126	75	45	1	320	2	13	114
1995..............	617	126	83	49	1	342	2	14	127
Percent Federal:									
1980..............	62	83	68	47	99	11	91	65	69
1985..............	62	84	64	46	99	8	88	56	71
1990..............	59	82	63	44	98	7	85	50	69
1993..............	59	81	69	44	98	6	91	48	72
1994..............	59	82	68	43	98	7	92	48	72
1995..............	59	82	67	43	98	6	93	47	71
Per capita (current dollars):									
1980..............	2,126	990	314	118	92	523	30	59	434
1985..............	3,009	1,516	405	161	111	708	52	56	705
1990..............	4,123	2,017	579	243	120	1,018	77	71	1,081
1993..............	5,238	2,523	849	287	137	1,275	80	87	1,466
1994..............	5,446	2,591	905	305	141	1,308	103	94	1,554
1995..............	5,622	2,632	949	320	144	1,368	109	99	1,628
Per capita (constant (1995) dollars): [3][4]									
1980..............	3,788	1,764	560	210	164	932	53	105	764
1985..............	4,131	2,081	556	223	152	972	71	77	969
1990..............	4,741	2,319	665	279	138	1,170	89	81	1,243
1993..............	5,487	2,644	889	301	144	1,335	84	91	1,536
1994..............	5,570	2,650	925	312	144	1,338	105	96	1,589
1995..............	5,622	2,632	949	320	144	1,368	109	99	1,628

Z Less than $500 million.   [1] Excludes program parts of social insurance, public aid, veterans, and other social welfare.   [2] Combines "health and medical programs" with medical services included in social insurance, public aid, veterans, vocational rehabilitation, and antipoverty programs.   [3] Excludes payments within foreign countries for education, veterans, OASDHI, and civil service retirement.   [4] Constant dollar figures are based on implicit price deflators for personal consumption expenditures published by U.S. Bureau of Economic Analysis in *Survey of Current Business.*

No. 599. Social Welfare Expenditures Under Public Programs as Percent of GDP and Total Government Outlays: 1980 to 1995

[493 represents $493,000,000,000. See headnote, Table 600]

Year	Total expenditures				Federal				State and local government			
			Percent of—				Percent of—				Percent of—	
	Total (bil. dol.)	Percent change [1]	Total GDP [2]	Total govt. outlays	Total (bil. dol.)	Percent change [1]	Total GDP [2]	Total Federal outlays	Total (bil. dol.)	Percent change [1]	Total GDP [2]	Total state and local outlays
1980....	493	14.7	18.6	57.2	303	15.2	11.4	54.4	190	13.8	7.2	62.9
1985....	732	8.0	18.4	54.4	451	7.1	11.3	48.7	281	9.3	7.1	68.8
1990....	1,049	9.6	18.5	58.2	617	9.1	10.9	51.4	432	10.3	7.6	74.0
1992....	1,267	9.2	20.6	63.7	750	10.8	12.2	57.4	517	7.0	8.4	77.6
1993....	1,367	7.8	21.1	66.6	805	7.2	12.4	60.0	561	8.5	8.7	80.7
1994....	1,436	5.1	21.0	64.5	853	6.1	12.5	57.4	583	3.7	8.5	80.4
1995....	1,505	4.8	20.9	67.5	888	4.1	12.4	60.2	617	5.8	8.6	83.6

[1] Percent change from immediate prior year.   [2] Gross domestic product.

Source of Tables 598 and 599: U.S. Social Security Administration, *Social Security Bulletin*, Vol. 62, No. 2, 1999; and unpublished data.

No. 600. Social Welfare Expenditures by Source of Funds and Public Program: 1990 to 1995

[In millions of dollars (616,639 represents $616,639,000,000). For fiscal years ending in year shown; see text, Section 9, State and Local Government. Represents outlays from trust funds (mostly social insurance funds built up by earmarked contributions from insured persons, their employers, or both) and budgetary outlays from general revenues. Includes administrative expenditures, capital outlay, and some expenditures and payments outside the United States]

Program	Federal				State and local			
	1990	1993	1994	1995	1990	1993	1994	1995
Total	616,639	805,336	852,876	888,358	432,167	561,418	582,944	616,779
Social insurance	422,257	534,212	557,321	579,804	91,565	124,998	126,458	125,680
Old-age, survivors, disability, health	355,264	449,277	477,340	496,356	(X)	(X)	(X)	(X)
Health insurance (medicare)	109,709	148,094	161,393	164,713	(X)	(X)	(X)	(X)
Public employee retirement [1]	53,541	61,632	63,733	67,022	36,851	50,928	55,520	60,980
Railroad employee retirement	7,230	7,921	8,025	8,106	(X)	(X)	(X)	(X)
Unemployment insurance and employment services [2]	3,096	12,124	4,972	5,156	16,878	28,597	26,279	21,146
Other railroad employee insurance [3]	105	86	83	78	(X)	(X)	(X)	(X)
State temporary disability insurance [4]	(X)	(X)	(X)	(X)	3,224	3,316	3,201	3,189
Workers' compensation [5]	3,021	3,173	3,168	3,085	34,613	42,157	41,458	40,365
Hospital and medical benefits	457	597	688	668	13,849	17,116	15,512	16,032
Public aid	92,858	151,850	162,675	170,260	53,953	69,149	75,351	83,270
Public assistance [6]	54,747	95,340	100,209	107,599	50,347	65,285	71,546	79,620
Medical assistance payments [7]	40,690	77,367	81,192	89,113	35,485	47,771	53,012	61,756
Social services	2,065	2,785	2,734	2,797	688	928	911	932
Supplemental security income	13,625	22,642	26,281	26,488	3,605	3,864	3,805	3,650
Food stamps	16,254	24,497	25,274	25,319	(X)	(X)	(X)	(X)
Other [8]	8,232	9,372	10,911	10,854	(X)	(X)	(X)	(X)
Health and medical programs	27,204	33,189	34,770	36,767	34,282	41,528	45,465	48,740
Hospital and medical care	14,816	18,575	18,601	19,373	11,155	12,042	12,962	12,531
Civilian programs	3,654	5,166	5,466	5,951	11,155	12,042	12,962	12,531
Defense Department [9]	11,162	13,409	13,134	13,422	(X)	(X)	(X)	(X)
Maternal and child health programs	492	595	615	612	1,374	1,590	1,657	1,736
Medical research	9,172	10,690	11,739	12,544	1,676	2,090	2,249	2,438
Medical facilities construction	413	166	102	429	1,922	2,878	3,137	3,369
School health	(X)	(X)	(X)	(X)	1,113	1,320	1,489	1,667
Other	2,311	3,164	3,714	3,809	17,043	21,608	23,971	26,999
Veterans programs	30,428	35,806	37,262	38,385	488	572	633	687
Pensions and compensation	15,793	17,205	17,481	18,070	(X)	(X)	(X)	(X)
Health and medical programs	12,004	15,410	16,231	16,654	(X)	(X)	(X)	(X)
Education	523	938	1,098	1,118	(X)	(X)	(X)	(X)
Life insurance [10]	1,038	905	972	946	(X)	(X)	(X)	(X)
Welfare and other	1,070	1,348	1,479	1,596	488	572	633	687
Education [11]	18,374	20,455	24,084	23,472	240,011	311,542	320,007	342,153
Elementary and secondary [12]	9,944	13,238	15,514	15,301	189,333	239,268	245,492	262,574
Construction [13]	23	5	9	2	10,613	22,283	19,684	24,808
Higher	6,747	5,285	6,577	6,164	50,678	72,273	74,514	79,580
Construction [13]	-	35	23	29	3,953	8,955	8,959	10,461
Vocational and adult [13]	1,293	1,495	1,504	1,508	([12])	([12])	([12])	([12])
Housing	16,612	18,985	24,987	27,276	2,856	1,798	2,045	2,085
Other social welfare	8,905	10,838	11,777	12,394	9,012	11,832	12,985	14,164
Vocational rehabilitation	1,661	1,830	1,963	2,031	466	549	597	599
Medical services and research	415	458	491	508	116	137	149	150
Institutional care [14]	143	143	150	152	486	579	633	722
Child nutrition [15]	5,470	7,139	7,626	7,992	1,696	2,253	2,473	2,661
Child welfare [16]	253	295	295	292	(NA)	(NA)	(NA)	(NA)
Special CSA and ACTION programs [17]	169	208	204	222	(X)	(X)	(X)	(X)
Welfare, not elsewhere classified [18]	1,209	1,223	1,540	1,704	6,365	8,451	9,282	10,182

- Represents zero. NA Not available. X Not applicable. [1] Excludes refunds to those leaving service. Federal data include military retirement. [2] Includes compensation for Federal employees and ex-servicemen, trade adjustment and cash training allowance, and payments under extended, emergency, disaster, and special unemployment insurance programs. [3] Unemployment and temporary disability insurance. [4] Cash and medical benefits in five areas. Includes private plans where applicable. [5] Benefits paid by private insurance carriers, state funds, and self-insurers. Federal includes black lung benefit programs. [6] Includes payments under state general assistance programs and work incentive activities, not shown separately. [7] Medicaid payments and state and local general assistance medical payments. [8] Refugee assistance, surplus food for the needy, and work-experience training programs under the Comprehensive Employment and Training Act. Includes low-income energy assistance program. [9] Includes medical care for military dependent families. [10] Excludes servicemen's group life insurance. [11] Federal expenditures include administrative costs (Department of Education) and research, not shown separately. [12] All state and local vocational education costs included with elementary-secondary. [13] Construction costs of vocational and adult education programs included under elementary-secondary expenditures. [14] Federal expenditures represent primarily surplus foods for nonprofit institutions. [15] Surplus food for schools and programs under National School Lunch and Child Nutrition Acts. [16] Represents primarily child welfare services under Title V of the Social Security Act. [17] Represents domestic volunteer programs under ACTION. [18] Federal expenditures include administrative expenses of the Secretary of Health and Human Services; Indian welfare and guidance; and aging and juvenile delinquency activities. State and local include antipoverty and manpower programs, child care and adoption services, legal assistance, and other unspecified welfare services.

Source: U.S. Social Security Administration, *Social Security Bulletin*, Vol. 62, No. 2, 1999; and unpublished data.

No. 601. Public Income-Maintenance Programs—Cash Benefit Payments: 1980 to 1995

[In billions of dollars (228.1 represents $228,100,000,000). Includes payments outside the United States and benefits to dependents, where applicable]

Program	1980	1985	1988	1989	1990	1991	1992	1993	1994	1995
Total [1]	228.1	335.2	393.8	421.9	457.5	504.2	544.9	557.7	584.4	608.3
Percent of personal income [2]	10.1	9.9	9.7	9.6	9.5	10.2	10.4	10.2	10.1	10.0
OASDI [3]	120.3	186.1	216.4	229.6	245.6	265.6	284.3	302.4	316.8	332.6
Public employee retirement [4]	40.6	63.0	78.0	83.8	90.4	97.3	103.7	112.6	119.3	128.0
Railroad retirement	4.9	6.3	6.7	6.9	7.2	7.5	7.7	7.9	8.0	8.1
Veterans' pensions, compensation	11.4	14.1	14.7	15.3	15.8	16.3	16.5	17.2	17.5	18.1
Unemployment benefits [5]	18.9	14.4	13.2	16.4	20.0	31.3	37.3	21.5	21.6	22.0
Temporary disability benefits	1.4	1.8	2.8	2.9	3.2	3.9	4.0	3.3	3.2	3.2
Workers' compensation [6]	9.7	22.3	30.3	33.8	37.6	41.7	45.7	45.3	44.6	43.4
Public assistance	12.1	15.3	17.0	17.4	19.3	20.1	22.4	21.0	23.3	22.8
Supplemental security income	7.9	11.1	14.7	14.9	17.2	19.6	23.4	26.5	30.1	30.1

[1] Includes lump sum death benefits, not shown separately. Lump sum death benefits for state and local government employee retirement systems are not available beginning 1988.   [2] For base data, see Table 724.   [3] Old-age, survivors, and disability insurance under Federal Social Security Act; see text for this section.   [4] Excludes refunds of contributions to employees who leave service.   [5] Beginning 1985, covers state unemployment insurance, Ex-Servicemen's Compensation Act and railroad unemployment insurance only.   [6] Includes black lung benefits.

Source: U.S. Social Security Administration, *Social Security Bulletin*, quarterly; and unpublished data.

No. 602. Number of Families Receiving Specified Sources of Income by Characteristic of Householder and Family Income: 1997

[In thousands (70,884 represents 70,884,000). Families as of **March 1998.** Based on Current Population Survey; see text, Sections 1, Population and 14, Income, and Appendix III]

Source of income	Total families [1]	Under 65 years old	65 years old and over	White	Black	His- panic origin [2]	Under $15,000	$15,000 to $24,999	$25,000 to $34,999
Total [1]	70,884	59,614	11,270	59,515	8,408	6,961	8,870	9,250	9,079
Earnings	60,607	56,071	4,536	50,858	7,087	6,071	5,225	6,539	7,512
Wages and salary	58,587	54,515	4,072	49,034	6,989	5,927	4,836	6,163	7,241
Social security, railroad retirement	16,371	5,912	10,459	14,252	1,717	973	2,322	3,699	2,965
Supplemental security income (SSI)	2,460	1,938	523	1,699	621	379	974	603	317
Public assistance	2,682	2,624	58	1,632	928	621	1,956	427	133
Veterans payments	1,541	889	652	1,359	143	72	134	206	212
Unemployment compensation	4,230	4,020	210	3,465	574	483	409	591	593
Workers compensation	1,523	1,404	119	1,325	151	165	124	169	260
Retirement income	9,920	4,174	5,746	8,971	699	344	367	1,470	1,847
Private pensions	6,296	2,380	3,916	5,745	416	215	266	1,124	1,310
Military retirement	959	595	364	827	95	28	17	61	79
Federal employee pensions	1,137	403	734	1,031	77	43	26	114	186
State or local employee pensions	1,880	726	1,154	1,689	139	63	53	177	299
Alimony	235	222	13	219	6	15	20	22	62
Child support	4,305	4,286	19	3,527	694	371	892	673	691
Education assistance	4,836	4,707	129	3,891	690	360	445	525	517

[1] Includes other items not shown separately.   [2] Persons of Hispanic origin may be of any race.

Source: U.S. Census Bureau, "09 Table of Contents"; published 17 December 1998; <http://ferret.bls.census.gov/macro/031998/faminc/09000.htm>.

No. 603. Households Receiving Means-Tested Noncash Benefits: 1980 to 1998

[In thousands (82,368 represents 82,368,000), **except percent**. Households as of **March** of following year. Covers civilian noninstitutional population, including persons in the Armed Forces living off post or with their families on post. A means-tested benefit program requires that the household's income and/or assets fall below specified guidelines in order to qualify for benefits. There are general trends toward underestimation of noncash beneficiaries. Households are classified according to poverty status of family or nonfamily householder; for explanation of poverty level, see text, Section 14, Income. Data for 1980 and 1990 based on 1980 census population controls; beginning 1995, based on 1990 census population controls. Based on Current Population Survey; see text, Section 1, Population, and Appendix III]

Type of benefit received	1980	1990	1995	1997	1998 Total	1998 Below poverty level Number	1998 Below poverty level Percent of total	1998 Above poverty level
Total households	82,368	94,312	99,627	102,528	103,874	12,714	100	91,160
Food stamps	6,769	7,163	8,388	7,256	6,357	4,293	34	2,064
School lunch	5,532	6,252	8,607	7,585	8,120	3,398	27	4,722
Public housing	2,777	4,339	4,846	4,778	4,808	2,709	21	2,099
Medicaid	8,287	10,321	14,111	13,589	13,363	5,676	45	7,687

Source: U.S. Census Bureau, "Current Population Survey, Annual Demographic Survey, March Supplement"; published 24 September 1998; <http://ferret.bls.census.gov/macro/031999/noncash/1001.htm> and *Current Population Reports*, P-60 reports.

No. 604. Government Expenditures for Income-Tested Benefits by Type of Benefit: 1980 to 1998

[In millions of dollars (104,676 represents $104,676,000,000). For years ending September 30. Programs covered provide cash, goods, or services in return. In case of many programs, including family cash welfare, food and housing programs, job and training programs and some educational programs, some recipients must work or study. Most of the programs base eligibility on individual, household, or family income, but some use group or area income tests; and a few offer help on the basis of presumed need. Constant dollar figures are based on the Consumer Price Index for all Urban Consumers]

Level of government and year	Total spending		Constant (1998) dollars							
	Current dollars	Constant (1998) dollars	Medical benefits	Cash aid	Food benefits	Housing benefits	Education benefits	Jobs/training	Services	Energy aid
TOTAL										
1980	104,676	207,231	64,537	56,865	26,818	19,017	10,247	17,235	9,103	3,407
1985	143,294	217,245	74,955	57,059	30,914	21,396	15,115	6,028	8,302	3,475
1990	212,578	265,405	108,397	67,738	31,345	21,909	17,966	5,296	10,597	2,158
1991	251,896	301,724	131,652	73,813	35,117	22,712	18,458	5,783	11,892	2,298
1992	296,403	344,585	157,919	81,173	39,820	28,160	16,527	6,387	12,538	2,061
1993	312,331	352,697	161,546	84,468	41,034	28,553	17,028	6,023	12,233	1,812
1994	348,770	383,854	177,654	95,002	41,687	28,351	17,103	6,070	15,792	2,195
1995	366,669	392,253	186,816	97,989	41,323	29,176	17,215	5,817	12,119	1,800
1996	370,769	385,319	184,923	96,083	40,617	29,052	17,020	4,868	11,454	1,301
1997	379,971	385,910	189,008	94,537	37,932	29,347	17,809	4,036	11,813	1,428
1998	391,733	391,729	196,389	94,562	35,511	29,511	18,126	3,856	12,453	1,321
FEDERAL										
1980	80,043	158,464	38,405	37,571	25,913	19,017	9,681	17,075	7,394	3,407
1985	105,064	159,285	42,268	37,123	29,354	21,396	14,427	5,905	5,384	3,428
1990	151,514	189,166	62,708	45,502	29,803	21,909	17,181	4,963	5,099	2,003
1991	177,953	213,154	74,805	50,634	33,545	22,712	17,803	5,257	6,236	2,163
1992	208,273	242,129	91,470	56,635	38,142	25,486	15,813	5,834	6,790	1,959
1993	223,595	252,492	96,044	60,245	39,266	27,051	16,163	5,388	6,604	1,732
1994	246,374	271,158	103,112	69,774	39,739	26,574	16,109	5,350	8,389	2,110
1995	258,457	276,491	108,489	72,662	39,365	26,689	16,193	4,949	6,431	1,713
1996	263,550	273,893	108,003	72,758	38,622	26,497	16,028	4,199	6,560	1,225
1997	269,754	273,971	109,471	72,971	35,927	26,853	16,767	3,855	6,764	1,363
1998	277,332	277,330	113,779	73,872	33,451	26,897	16,989	3,785	7,300	1,257
STATE AND LOCAL										
1980	24,633	48,767	26,132	19,294	905	-	566	160	1,709	-
1985	38,230	57,960	32,687	19,936	1,560	-	688	123	2,918	47
1990	61,064	76,239	45,689	22,236	1,542	-	785	333	5,498	155
1991	73,943	88,570	56,847	23,179	1,572	-	655	526	5,656	135
1992	88,130	102,456	66,449	24,538	1,678	2,674	714	553	5,629	102
1993	88,736	100,204	65,502	24,223	1,768	1,502	865	635	5,748	80
1994	102,396	112,696	74,542	25,228	1,948	1,777	994	720	7,403	85
1995	108,212	115,762	78,327	25,327	1,958	2,487	1,022	868	5,688	87
1996	107,219	111,426	76,920	23,325	1,995	2,555	992	669	4,894	76
1997	110,216	111,938	79,537	21,566	2,005	2,494	1,042	181	5,049	65
1998	114,401	114,399	82,610	20,690	2,060	2,614	1,137	71	5,153	64

- Represents or rounds to zero.

Source: Library of Congress, Congressional Research Service, "Cash and Noncash Benefits for Persons With Limited Income: Eligibility Rules, Recipient and Expenditure Data, FY1996-FY1998"; CRS Report RL 30401; December 15, 1999.

Social Insurance and Human Services 381

No. 605. Cash and Noncash Benefits for Persons With Limited Income: 1997 and 1998

[For years ending September 30, except as noted (379,971 represents $379,971,000,000). Programs covered provide cash, goods, or services to persons who make no payment and render no service in return. In case of many programs, including family cash welfare, food and housing programs, job and training programs and some educational programs, some recipients must work or study. Most of the programs base eligibility on individual, household, or family income, but some use group or area income tests; and a few offer help on the basis of presumed need]

Program	Average monthly recipients (1,000)		Expenditures (mil. dol.)					
			Total		Federal		State and local	
	1997	1998	1997	1998	1997	1998	1997	1998
Total	(X)	(X)	379,971	391,733	269,754	277,332	110,216	114,401
Medical care[1]	(X)	(X)	186,100	196,391	107,787	113,779	78,313	82,612
Medicaid[2,3]	40,160	41,360	167,359	177,364	94,738	100,177	72,621	77,187
Veterans[4,5]	(NA)	153	9,220	9,603	9,220	9,603	-	-
General assistance[5,2,3]	(NA)	(NA)	5,268	4,956	-	-	5,268	4,956
Indian health services[2,3]	1,430	1,458	2,057	2,099	2,057	2,099	-	-
Maternal and child health services . . .	23,900	(NA)	1,105	1,102	681	678	424	424
Consolidated health centers[2]	8,300	8,450	802	825	802	825	-	-
Cash aid[1]	(X)	(X)	93,082	94,562	71,848	73,872	21,234	20,690
Supplemental security income[3,6]	6,984	7,199	32,395	33,601	28,667	29,656	3,728	3,945
TANF/AFDC[3,7]	10,936	8,770	23,179	21,513	12,494	11,286	10,685	10,227
Earned income tax credit (refunded portion)[8]	58,143	58,197	23,200	25,300	23,200	25,300	-	-
Foster care	289	306	6,794	7,033	3,692	3,730	3,102	3,303
General assistance[8]	700	(NA)	3,200	2,625	-	-	3,200	2,625
Pensions for needy veterans[9,10]	747	712	3,066	3,071	3,066	3,071	-	-
Food benefits[1]	(X)	(X)	37,348	35,511	35,374	33,451	1,974	2,060
Food stamps[3,11]	24,200	21,000	24,772	22,384	22,868	20,397	1,904	1,987
School lunch program[12,13]	15,100	15,300	5,044	5,196	5,044	5,196	(NA)	(NA)
Women, infants and children[3,14]	7,400	7,400	3,846	3,896	3,846	3,896	-	-
School breakfast[12]	6,000	6,100	1,180	1,266	1,180	1,266	-	-
Child and adult care food program[15] . . .	(NA)	1,800	1,199	1,404	1,199	1,404	-	-
Nutrition program for elderly[16]	(NA)	(NA)	685	700	615	627	70	73
Housing benefits[1]	(X)	(X)	28,896	29,511	26,440	26,897	2,456	2,614
Low-income housing asst. (Sec. 8)[17] . .	2,943	3,001	16,393	16,114	16,393	16,114	-	-
Low-rent public housing[17,18] . .	1,372	1,295	4,384	3,899	4,384	3,899	(NA)	(NA)
Rural housing loans[19,20]	41	55	2,706	3,830	2,706	3,830	-	-
Interest reduction payments[17]	494	477	604	618	604	618	-	-
Home investment partnerships[3,20,21] . .	73	75	3,817	4,062	1,373	1,461	2,444	2,601
Education aid[1]	(X)	(X)	17,535	18,128	16,509	16,991	1,026	1,137
Pell grants[22,23]	3,665	3,732	5,660	6,274	5,660	6,274	-	-
Head Start	794	822	4,976	5,434	3,981	4,347	995	1,087
Stafford loans[22]	4,882	4,956	4,610	3,770	4,610	3,770	-	-
Federal Work-Study Program[22,23] . . .	691	945	617	830	617	830	-	-
Services[1]	(X)	(X)	11,631	12,453	6,660	7,300	4,971	5,153
Social services (Title 20)[24]	(NA)	(NA)	6,400	5,885	2,500	2,299	3,900	3,586
Child care and development block grant[25]	(NA)	(NA)	3,378	4,690	2,307	3,123	1,071	1,567
Jobs and training[1]	(X)	(X)	3,973	3,857	3,796	3,785	178	71
Training for disadvantaged adults and youth[26]	483	499	1,022	1,085	1,022	1,085	-	-
Job Corps	65	70	1,154	1,246	1,154	1,246	-	-
Summer youth employment program[27] . . .	493	530	871	871	871	871	-	-
Energy assistance[1]	(X)	(X)	1,406	1,321	1,342	1,257	64	64
Low-income energy assistance[3,28] . .	(NA)	(NA)	1,221	1,132	1,221	1,132	(NA)	(NA)

- Represents zero. NA Not available. X Not applicable. [1] Includes other programs not shown separately. [2] Recipient data represent unduplicated annual number. [3] Expenditures include administrative expenses. [4] Medical care for veterans with a nonservice-connected disability. [5] Estimated expenditures. [6] Includes state-administered SSI supplements. [7] Aid to families with dependent children program and its successor, Temporary Assistance for Needy Families (TANF). Excludes data for foster care program and child support operations (cost and collections). [8] Estimated expenditures. [9] Estimated recipients as of September. [10] Includes dependents and survivors. [11] Includes Puerto Rico's nutritional assistance program. [12] Free and reduced-price segments. [13] Includes estimate of commodity assistance. [14] Special supplemental food program for women, infants and children. [15] Recipient data are numbers of children receiving free or reduced price meals and snacks in child care centers and estimates of children in family day care homes with incomes below 185 percent of poverty. [16] No income test required but preference given to those with greatest need. [17] Recipient data represent units eligible for payment at end of year. [18] Includes operating subsidies and HUD-administered Indian housing. [19] Recipient data represent total families or dwelling units during year. [20] Expenditure data represent amounts obligated. [21] Recipient data are housing units provided or rehabilitated. [22] Recipient data are total numbers for the school year ending in year shown. [23] Expenditure data are appropriations available for school year ending the fiscal year named. [24] Non-Federal expenditure data are rough estimates. [25] Recipient data are estimated number of children served. P.L. 104-193 ended AFDC and its related child care programs and established a new mandatory child care block grant. [26] Recipient data are total number of participants. [27] Total participants (June-August). [28] Households served during the year with heating and winter crisis aid. Federal funds include amounts transferred to other programs serving the needy.

Source: Library of Congress, Congressional Research Service, "Cash and Noncash Benefits for Persons With Limited Income: Eligibility Rules, Recipient and Expenditure Data, FY 1996-FY 1998"; CRS Report RL30401; December 15, 1999.

No. 606. Social Security—Covered Employment, Earnings, and Contribution Rates: 1980 to 1999

[140.4 represents 140,400,000. Includes Puerto Rico, Virgin Islands, American Samoa, and Guam. Represents all reported employment. Data are estimated. OASDHI=Old-age, survivors, disability, and health insurance; SMI=Supplementary medical insurance]

Item	Unit	1980	1985	1990	1993	1994	1995	1996	1997	1998	1999
Workers with insured status [1]	Million	140.4	150.9	164.0	169.1	170.7	172.9	174.8	177.5	179.5	181.8
Male	Million	76.6	80.7	86.5	88.5	89.1	90.0	90.9	92.0	92.8	93.8
Female	Million	63.8	70.1	77.5	80.6	81.6	82.9	84.0	85.5	86.7	88.0
Under 25 years old	Million	25.7	22.0	21.3	19.5	19.0	18.8	18.5	18.8	19.2	19.6
25 to 34 years old	Million	36.5	40.1	41.6	40.3	39.8	39.4	38.8	38.2	37.4	36.7
35 to 44 years old	Million	23.0	29.9	36.4	38.9	39.7	40.5	41.3	41.8	42.2	42.5
45 to 54 years old	Million	18.6	19.2	22.8	26.8	28.2	29.5	30.7	31.9	33.1	34.5
55 to 59 years old	Million	9.3	9.0	8.7	9.3	9.5	9.7	10.1	10.7	11.3	11.8
60 to 64 years old	Million	8.2	8.8	8.8	8.5	8.4	8.4	8.5	8.8	8.9	9.1
65 to 69 years old	Million	7.0	7.5	8.2	8.2	8.1	8.1	8.1	8.0	7.9	7.9
70 years old and over	Million	12.1	14.3	16.3	17.7	18.1	18.5	18.8	19.3	19.6	19.8
Workers reported with—											
Taxable earnings [2]	Million	113	120	134	136	138	141	144	147	149	152
Maximum earnings [2]	Million	10	8	8	8	8	8	9	9	9	9
Earnings in covered employment [2]	Bil. dol	1,329	1,942	2,704	3,023	3,169	3,359	3,568	3,848	4,141	4,409
Reported taxable [2]	Bil. dol	1,178	1,725	2,359	2,636	2,785	2,920	3,076	3,287	3,517	3,748
Percent of total	Percent	88.6	88.8	87.2	87.2	87.9	86.9	86.2	85.4	84.9	85.0
Average per worker:											
Total earnings [2]	Dollars	11,761	16,125	20,227	22,205	22,929	23,814	24,863	26,236	27,697	29,082
Taxable earnings [2]	Dollars	10,430	14,326	17,642	19,364	20,152	20,700	21,431	22,415	23,525	24,707
Annual maximum taxable earnings [3]	Dollars	25,900	39,600	51,300	57,600	60,600	61,200	62,700	65,400	68,400	72,600
Contribution rates for OASDHI: [4]											
Each employer and employee	Percent	6.13	7.05	7.65	7.65	7.65	7.65	7.65	7.65	7.65	7.65
Self-employed [5]	Percent	8.10	14.10	15.30	15.30	15.30	15.30	15.30	15.30	15.30	15.30
SMI, monthly premium [6]	Dollars	9.60	15.50	28.60	36.60	41.10	46.10	42.50	43.80	43.80	45.50

[1] Estimated number fully insured for retirement and/or survivor benefits as of end of year.   [2] Includes self-employment.   [3] The maximum taxable earnings for HI was $135,000 in 1993. Beginning 1994 upper limit on earnings subject to HI taxes was repealed.   [4] As of January 1, 2000, each employee and employer pays 7.65 percent and the self-employed pay 15.3 percent.   [5] Self-employed pays 11.8 percent in 1985. The additional amount is supplied from general revenues. Beginning 1990, self-employed pays 15.3 percent, and half of the tax is deductible for income tax purposes and for computing self-employment income subject to social security tax.   [6] 1980, as of July 1; beginning 1985, as of January 1. As of January 1, 2000, the monthly premium is $45.50.

Source: U.S. Social Security Administration, *Annual Statistical Supplement* to the *Social Security Bulletin;* and unpublished data.

No. 607. Social Security Trust Funds: 1980 to 1999

[In billions of dollars (103.5 represents $103,500,000,000)]

Type of trust fund	1980	1985	1990	1994	1995	1996	1997	1998	1999
Old-age and survivors insurance (OASI):									
Net contribution income [1]	103.5	180.2	272.4	298.3	310.1	328.0	357.4	380.4	407.3
Interest received [2]	1.8	1.9	16.4	29.9	32.8	35.7	39.8	44.5	49.8
Benefit payments [3]	105.1	167.2	223.0	279.1	291.6	302.9	316.3	326.8	334.4
Assets, end of year	22.8	[4]35.8	214.2	413.5	458.5	514.0	589.1	681.6	798.8
Disability insurance (DI):									
Net contribution income [1]	13.3	17.4	28.7	51.7	54.7	57.7	56.5	59.5	63.9
Interest received [2]	0.5	0.9	0.9	1.2	2.2	3.0	4.0	4.8	5.7
Benefit payments [3]	15.5	18.8	24.8	37.7	40.9	44.2	45.7	48.2	51.4
Assets, end of year	3.6	[5]6.3	11.1	22.9	37.6	52.9	66.4	80.8	97.3

[1] Includes deposits by states and deductions for refund of estimated employee-tax overpayment. Beginning in 1985, includes government contributions on deemed wage credits for military service in 1957 and later. Includes tax credits on net earnings from self-employment in 1985-89. Includes taxation of benefits beginning in 1985.   [2] In 1985-90, includes interest on advance tax transfers. Beginning 1985, includes interest on reimbursement for unnegotiated checks. Data for 1985 reflect interest on interfund borrowing.   [3] Includes payments for vocational rehabilitation services furnished to disabled persons receiving benefits because of their disabilities. Beginning in 1985, amounts reflect deductions for unnegotiated benefit checks.   [4] Includes $13.2 billion borrowed from the DI and HI Trust Funds (see Table 166).   [5] Excludes $2.5 billion lent to the OASI Trust Fund.

Source: U.S. Social Security Administration, *Annual Report of Board of Trustees, OASI, DI, HI, and SMI Trust Funds.* Also published in *Social Security Bulletin,* quarterly.

Social Insurance and Human Services   383

No. 608. Social Security (OASDI)—Benefits by Type of Beneficiary: 1980 to 1999

[**35,585 represents 35,585,000.** A person eligible to receive more than one type of benefit is generally classified or counted only once as a retired-worker beneficiary. OASDI=Old-age, survivors, and disability insurance. See also headnote, Table 606 and Appendix III]

Type of beneficiary	1980	1985	1990	1993	1994	1995	1996	1997	1998	1999
Number of benefits [1] (1,000) .	**35,585**	**37,058**	**39,832**	**42,246**	**42,883**	**43,387**	**43,737**	**43,971**	**44,246**	**44,596**
Retired workers [2] (1,000)	19,562	22,432	24,838	26,104	26,408	26,673	26,898	27,275	27,511	27,775
Disabled workers [3] (1,000)	2,859	2,657	3,011	3,726	3,963	4,185	4,386	4,508	4,698	4,879
Wives and husbands [2][4] (1,000) . .	3,477	3,375	3,367	3,367	3,337	3,290	3,194	3,129	3,054	2,987
Children (1,000)	4,607	3,319	3,187	3,527	3,654	3,734	3,803	3,772	3,769	3,795
Under age 18	3,423	2,699	2,497	2,777	2,887	2,956	3,010	2,970	2,963	2,970
Disabled children [5].	450	526	600	656	673	686	697	705	713	721
Students [6]	733	94	89	94	94	92	96	97	93	104
Of retired workers	639	457	422	436	440	442	443	441	439	442
Of deceased workers	2,610	1,917	1,776	1,836	1,864	1,884	1,898	1,893	1,884	1,885
Of disabled workers	1,358	945	989	1,255	1,350	1,409	1,463	1,438	1,446	1,468
Widowed mothers [7] (1,000).	562	372	304	289	283	275	242	230	221	212
Widows and widowers [2][8] (1,000). .	4,411	4,863	5,111	5,224	5,232	5,226	5,210	5,053	4,990	4,944
Parents [2] (1,000)	15	10	6	5	4	4	4	4	3	3
Special benefits [9] (1,000)	93	32	7	2	2	1	1	(Z)	(Z)	(Z)
AVERAGE MONTHLY BENEFIT, CURRENT DOLLARS										
Retired workers [2]	341	479	603	674	697	720	745	765	780	804
Retired worker and wife [2]	567	814	1,027	1,145	1,184	1,221	1,262	1,295	1,318	1,357
Disabled workers [3]	371	484	587	642	661	682	704	722	733	754
Wives and husbands [2][4]	164	236	298	332	343	354	369	379	386	398
Children of retired workers	140	198	259	297	309	322	337	349	358	373
Children of deceased workers	240	331	406	443	456	469	487	500	510	526
Children of disabled workers	110	142	164	173	178	183	194	201	208	216
Widowed mothers [7]	246	332	409	448	464	478	515	532	545	566
Widows and widowers, nondisabled [2]	311	433	556	630	655	680	699	731	749	775
Parents [2]	276	378	482	547	570	591	614	636	651	674
Special benefits [9]	105	138	167	183	187	192	197	201	204	209
AVERAGE MONTHLY BENEFIT, CONSTANT (1999) DOLLARS [10]										
Retired workers [2]	665	738	758	778	784	789	791	798	801	804
Retired worker and wife [2]	1,106	1,253	1,292	1,322	1,331	1,339	1,339	1,351	1,353	1,357
Disabled workers [3]	724	745	738	741	743	748	747	753	753	754
Wives and husbands [2][4]	320	363	375	383	386	388	392	395	397	398
Children of deceased workers	468	510	511	511	513	514	517	522	523	526
Widowed mothers [7]	480	511	514	517	522	524	546	555	560	566
Number of benefits awarded (1,000)	**4,215**	**3,796**	**3,717**	**4,001**	**3,940**	**3,882**	**3,793**	**3,866**	**3,800**	**3,917**
Retired workers [2]	1,620	1,690	1,665	1,661	1,625	1,609	1,581	1,719	1,631	1,690
Disabled workers [3]	389	377	468	635	632	646	624	587	608	620
Wives and husbands [2][4]	469	440	379	365	345	322	302	319	311	322
Children	1,174	714	695	816	824	809	798	757	763	773
Widowed mothers [7]	108	72	58	56	55	52	49	44	42	42
Widows and widowers [2][8]	452	502	452	466	459	445	438	440	444	470
Parents [2]	1	(Z)	(Z)	(Z)	(Z)	(Z)	(Z)	(Z)	(Z)	(Z)
Special benefits [9]	1	1	(Z)	(Z)	(Z)	(Z)	(Z)	(Z)	(Z)	(Z)
BENEFIT PAYMENTS DURING YEAR (bil. dol.)										
Total [11]	**120.5**	**186.2**	**247.8**	**302.4**	**316.8**	**332.6**	**347.1**	**362.0**	**375.0**	**385.8**
Monthly benefits [12]	120.1	186.0	247.6	302.2	316.6	332.4	346.9	361.8	374.8	385.6
Retired workers [2]	70.4	116.8	156.8	188.4	196.4	205.3	213.4	223.6	232.3	238.5
Disabled workers [3]	12.8	16.5	22.1	30.9	33.7	36.6	39.6	41.1	43.5	46.5
Wives and husbands [2][4]	7.0	11.1	14.5	16.9	17.4	17.9	18.2	18.6	18.9	18.8
Children	10.5	10.7	12.0	14.6	15.4	16.1	17.1	17.6	18.1	18.6
Under age 18	7.4	8.5	9.0	10.8	11.4	11.9	12.6	13.0	13.3	13.6
Disabled children [5]	1.0	1.8	2.5	3.3	3.4	3.6	3.8	4.0	4.2	4.4
Students [6]	2.1	0.4	0.5	0.5	0.6	0.6	0.6	0.6	0.7	0.7
Of retired workers.	1.1	1.1	1.3	1.6	1.6	1.7	1.8	1.9	1.9	2.0
Of deceased workers	7.4	7.8	8.6	9.9	10.3	10.7	11.2	11.7	11.9	12.1
Of disabled workers	2.0	1.8	2.2	3.1	3.4	3.7	4.0	4.1	4.2	4.4
Widowed mothers [7]	1.6	1.5	1.4	1.5	1.6	1.6	1.5	1.5	1.4	1.4
Widows and widowers [2][8]	17.6	29.3	40.7	49.7	52.1	54.8	57.0	59.3	60.5	61.8
Parents [2]	0.1	0.1	(Z)	(Z)	(Z)	(Z)	(Z)	(Z)	(Z)	(Z)
Special benefits [9]	0.1	0.1	(Z)	(Z)	(Z)	(Z)	(Z)	(Z)	(Z)	(Z)
Lump sum	0.4	0.2	0.2	0.2	0.2	0.2	0.2	0.2	0.2	0.2

Z Fewer than 500 or less than $50 million. [1] Number of benefit payments in current-payment status, i.e., actually being made at a specified time with no deductions or with deductions amounting to less than a month's benefit. [2] 62 years and over. [3] Disabled workers under age 65. [4] Includes wife beneficiaries with entitled children in their care and entitled divorced wives. [5] 18 years old and over. Disability began before age 18 and, beginning 1973, before age 22. [6] Full-time students aged 18-21 through 1984 and aged 18 and 19 beginning 1985. [7] Includes surviving divorced mothers with entitled children in their care and widowed fathers with entitled children in their care. [8] Includes widows aged 60-61, surviving divorced wives aged 60 and over, disabled widows and widowers aged 50 and over; and widowers aged 60-61. [9] Benefits for persons aged 72 and over not insured under regular or transitional provisions of Social Security Act. [10] Constant dollar figures are based on the consumer price index (CPI-U) for December as published by the U.S. Bureau of Labor Statistics. [11] Represents total disbursements of benefit checks by the U.S. Dept. of the Treasury during the years specified. [12] Distribution by type estimated.

Source: U.S. Social Security Administration, *Annual Statistical Supplement* to the *Social Security Bulletin;* and unpublished data.

No. 609. Social Security—Beneficiaries, Annual Payments, and Average Monthly Benefit, 1990 to 1999 and by State and Other Area, 1999

[Number of beneficiaries in current-payment status **(39,832 represents 39,832,000)** and average monthly benefit as of **December**. Data based on 10-percent sample of administrative records. See also headnote, Table 608, and Appendix III]

Year, state, and other area	Number of beneficiaries (1,000)				Annual payments [2] (mil. dol.)				Average monthly benefit (dol.)		
	Total	Retired workers and dependents [1]	Survivors	Disabled workers and dependents	Total	Retired workers and dependents [1]	Survivors	Disabled workers and dependents	Retired workers [3]	Disabled workers	Widows and widowers [4]
1990	39,832	28,369	7,197	4,266	247,796	172,042	50,951	24,803	603	587	557
1995	43,380	30,139	7,379	5,862	332,581	224,381	67,302	40,898	720	682	680
1996	43,737	30,314	7,347	6,077	347,088	232,938	69,976	44,174	745	705	707
1997	43,976	30,649	7,171	6,156	361,970	243,590	72,721	45,659	765	722	731
1998	44,247	30,819	7,091	6,338	374,772	252,659	73,940	48,173	780	734	749
1999, total [5]	**44,599**	**31,035**	**7,038**	**6,526**	**385,525**	**258,885**	**75,309**	**51,331**	**804**	**755**	**775**
United States...	43,530	30,384	6,820	6,326	379,483	255,617	73,754	50,114	(NA)	(NA)	(NA)
Alabama	811	503	149	159	6,546	3,933	1,440	1,173	757	724	698
Alaska	52	33	9	10	423	263	88	72	786	743	729
Arizona	769	556	105	108	6,702	4,699	1,129	875	816	784	798
Arkansas	511	326	87	98	4,046	2,489	832	725	739	711	683
California	4,111	2,958	600	553	35,933	24,815	6,604	4,514	813	767	806
Colorado	523	364	79	81	4,423	2,938	847	638	783	750	780
Connecticut	567	427	73	68	5,401	3,972	873	556	880	780	864
Delaware	132	94	19	19	1,191	820	217	154	837	779	832
District of Columbia	74	51	13	10	555	365	112	78	675	704	644
Florida	3,141	2,338	416	388	27,253	19,564	4,581	3,108	802	760	799
Georgia	1,078	688	185	205	8,884	5,517	1,791	1,576	770	734	711
Hawaii	179	139	22	18	1,517	1,148	229	140	793	781	747
Idaho	190	136	28	25	1,592	1,102	299	191	783	737	788
Illinois	1,817	1,295	293	229	16,708	11,457	3,372	1,878	845	782	833
Indiana	979	682	155	141	8,917	6,003	1,787	1,126	842	766	824
Iowa	537	393	83	60	4,694	3,278	943	472	805	737	795
Kansas	434	312	68	54	3,858	2,678	766	414	825	733	818
Kentucky	730	431	130	169	5,886	3,317	1,282	1,287	753	749	696
Louisiana	703	421	156	126	5,618	3,168	1,515	936	746	758	710
Maine	247	167	34	45	1,964	1,293	353	318	741	691	730
Maryland	703	501	116	86	6,216	4,233	1,256	727	807	782	785
Massachusetts	1,049	745	142	161	9,220	6,336	1,614	1,270	807	747	808
Michigan	1,619	1,116	264	239	15,085	10,010	3,067	2,009	865	812	831
Minnesota	725	533	109	84	6,266	4,396	1,213	657	794	737	778
Mississippi	507	297	93	117	3,859	2,213	828	818	722	703	653
Missouri	987	675	156	157	8,415	5,569	1,644	1,202	792	738	767
Montana	155	109	24	22	1,309	878	257	174	782	746	769
Nebraska	283	206	43	33	2,422	1,691	485	246	791	712	799
Nevada	270	199	34	37	2,365	1,675	369	321	810	794	808
New Hampshire	195	141	25	28	1,728	1,216	288	223	818	754	817
New Jersey	1,326	975	191	160	12,748	9,118	2,253	1,377	886	807	857
New Mexico	274	184	46	43	2,163	1,408	437	317	752	729	727
New York	2,964	2,105	424	435	27,250	18,833	4,783	3,634	854	799	824
North Carolina	1,321	883	195	243	10,930	7,158	1,901	1,872	773	727	706
North Dakota	114	81	22	12	937	619	227	91	752	717	738
Ohio	1,902	1,314	331	257	16,955	11,121	3,776	2,059	822	761	807
Oklahoma	586	400	101	85	4,886	3,176	1,052	657	766	742	748
Oregon	560	412	78	70	4,951	3,508	877	566	818	750	812
Pennsylvania	2,333	1,690	377	267	21,130	14,620	4,358	2,152	828	768	815
Rhode Island	190	138	23	29	1,657	1,183	252	222	804	735	808
South Carolina	673	435	107	130	5,544	3,520	1,011	1,013	772	739	698
South Dakota	135	96	23	16	1,075	731	233	111	737	686	728
Tennessee	975	623	166	186	8,015	4,961	1,643	1,411	769	727	718
Texas	2,576	1,749	480	347	21,486	13,907	4,935	2,644	780	748	752
Utah	236	171	35	30	2,023	1,425	374	224	811	735	824
Vermont	103	72	14	17	872	591	154	127	793	718	776
Virginia	1,008	680	163	165	8,471	5,504	1,675	1,293	778	751	734
Washington	826	602	115	109	7,452	5,237	1,320	895	837	758	827
West Virginia	388	231	77	80	3,337	1,866	820	652	795	798	742
Wisconsin	888	654	129	104	7,955	5,640	1,477	838	825	753	814
Wyoming	75	54	10	10	650	455	115	81	804	770	791
Puerto Rico	654	354	121	179	3,700	1,820	797	1,084	527	637	478
Guam	10	6	2	1	56	34	17	6	565	622	532
American Samoa	5	2	2	2	26	8	9	9	470	553	402
Virgin Islands	13	9	2	2	89	61	16	12	669	697	598
Northern Mariana Islands	2	1	1	(Z)	7	4	3	1	440	422	348
Abroad	383	277	90	16	2,139	1,324	707	107	496	655	532

NA Not available. Z Fewer than 500. [1] Includes special benefits for persons aged 72 and over not insured under regular or transitional provisions of Social Security Act. [2] Unnegotiated checks not deducted. Through 1997 includes lump-sum payments to survivors of deceased workers. [3] Excludes persons with special benefits. [4] Nondisabled only. [5] Includes those with state or area unknown.

Source: U.S. Social Security Administration, *Social Security Bulletin*, quarterly.

Social Insurance and Human Services 385

No. 610. Public Employee Retirement Systems—Participants and Finances: 1980 to 1999

[For fiscal year of retirement system, except data for the Thrift Savings Plan are for calendar year (4,629 represents 4,629,000)]

Retirement plan	Unit	1980	1985	1990	1994	1995	1996	1997	1998, proj.	1999, proj.
TOTAL PARTICIPANTS [1]										
Federal retirement systems:										
Defined benefit:										
Civil Service Retirement System	1,000	4,629	4,919	4,167	3,808	3,731	3,663	3,578	(NA)	(NA)
Federal Employees Retirement System [2]	1,000	(X)	(X)	1,180	1,764	1,512	1,615	1,679	(NA)	(NA)
Military Service Retirement System [3]	1,000	3,380	3,672	3,763	3,451	3,387	3,372	3,367	(NA)	(NA)
Thrift Savings Plan [4]	1,000	(X)	(X)	1,625	2,119	2,195	2,254	2,303	(NA)	(NA)
State and local retirement systems [5][6]	1,000	(NA)	15,234	16,858	13,290	14,734	15,153	15,192	(NA)	(NA)
ACTIVE PARTICIPANTS										
Federal retirement systems:										
Defined benefit:										
Civil Service Retirement System	1,000	2,700	2,800	1,826	1,443	1,525	1,343	1,189	(NA)	(NA)
Federal Employees Retirement System [2]	1,000	(X)	(X)	1,136	1,375	1,318	1,447	1,497	(NA)	(NA)
Military Service Retirement System [3]	1,000	2,050	2,192	2,130	1,666	1,572	1,525	1,491	(NA)	(NA)
Thrift Savings Plan [4]	1,000	(X)	(X)	1,419	1,876	1,930	1,987	2,011	(NA)	(NA)
State and local retirement systems [5][6]	1,000	(NA)	10,364	11,345	11,849	12,524	13,051	12,815	(NA)	(NA)
ASSETS										
Total	Bil. dol.	258	529	1,047	1,519	1,655	1,854	2,105	(NA)	(NA)
Federal retirement systems	Bil. dol.	73	154	326	494	537	581	625	668	(NA)
Defined benefit	Bil. dol.	73	154	318	468	502	534	564	591	616
Civil Service Retirement System	Bil. dol.	73	142	220	294	311	328	344	360	374
Federal Employees Retirement System [2]	Bil. dol.	(X)	(X)	18	50	60	71	77	84	91
Military Service Retirement System [3]	Bil. dol.	(7)	12	80	124	131	135	143	147	151
Thrift Savings Plan [4]	Bil. dol.	(X)	(X)	8	26	35	47	61	77	(NA)
State and local retirement systems [5]	Bil. dol.	185	374	721	1,025	1,118	1,273	1,480	(NA)	(NA)
CONTRIBUTIONS										
Total	Bil. dol.	83	106	103	121	127	129	139	(NA)	(NA)
Federal retirement systems	Bil. dol.	19	54	61	67	67	66	73	73	(NA)
Defined benefit	Bil. dol.	19	54	59	62	61	60	66	65	65
Civil Service Retirement System	Bil. dol.	19	27	28	31	31	32	33	33	33
Federal Employees Retirement System [2]	Bil. dol.	(X)	(X)	4	6	6	6	7	6	6
Military Service Retirement System [3]	Bil. dol.	(7)	27	27	25	24	22	26	26	26
Thrift Savings Plan [4]	Bil. dol.	(X)	(X)	2	5	6	6	7	8	(NA)
State and local retirement systems [5]	Bil. dol.	64	52	42	54	60	63	66	(NA)	(NA)
BENEFITS										
Total	Bil. dol.	39	62	89	124	125	131	142	(NA)	(NA)
Federal retirement systems	Bil. dol.	27	40	53	65	66	66	73	76	(NA)
Defined benefit	Bil. dol.	27	40	53	64	65	69	72	74	(NA)
Civil Service Retirement System	Bil. dol.	15	23	31	36	37	39	41	42	43
Federal Employees Retirement System [2]	Bil. dol.	(X)	(X)	(Z)	(Z)	1	1	1	1	1
Military Service Retirement System [3]	Bil. dol.	12	17	22	28	28	29	30	31	(NA)
Thrift Savings Plan [4]	Bil. dol.	(X)	(X)	(Z)	1	1	1	1	2	(NA)
State and local retirement systems [5]	Bil. dol.	12	22	36	59	59	65	69	(NA)	(NA)

NA Not available.   X Not applicable.   Z Less than $500 million.   [1] Includes active, separated vested, retired employees, and survivors.   [2] The Federal Employees Retirement System was established June 6, 1986.   [3] Includes nondisability and disability retirees, surviving families, and all active personnel with the exception of active reserves.   [4] The Thrift Savings Plan (a defined contribution plan) was established April 1, 1987.   [5] Excludes state and local plans that are fully supported by employee contributions.   [6] Not adjusted for double counting of individuals participating in more than one plan.   [7] The Military Retirement System was unfunded until October 1, 1984.

Source: Employee Benefit Research Institute, Washington, DC, *EBRI Databook on Employee Benefits, Fourth Edition*, and unpublished data (copyright).

No. 611. Federal Civil Service Retirement: 1980 to 1999

[As of **Sept. 30** or for **year ending Sept. 30** (2,720 represents 2,720,000). Covers both Civil Service Retirement System and Federal Employees Retirement System]

Item	Unit	1980	1985	1990	1994	1995	1996	1997	1998	1999
Employees covered [1]	1,000	2,720	2,750	2,945	2,778	2,668	2,629	2,681	2,658	2,668
Annuitants, total	1,000	1,675	1,955	2,143	2,263	2,311	2,333	2,352	2,369	2,368
Age and service	1,000	905	1,122	1,288	1,398	1,441	1,459	1,474	1,488	1,491
Disability	1,000	343	332	297	268	263	260	257	253	246
Survivors	1,000	427	501	558	597	607	614	621	628	631
Receipts, total [2]	Mil. dol	24,389	40,790	52,689	63,390	65,684	67,339	70,227	72,156	74,522
Employee contributions	Mil. dol	3,686	4,679	4,501	4,610	4,498	4,398	4,358	4,274	4,381
Federal government contributions	Mil. dol	15,562	22,301	27,368	32,434	33,130	33,991	35,386	36,188	36,561
Disbursements, total [3]	Mil. dol	14,977	23,203	31,416	36,532	38,435	39,711	41,722	43,058	43,932
Age and service annuitants [4]	Mil. dol	12,639	19,414	26,495	30,440	32,070	32,970	34,697	35,806	36,492
Survivors	Mil. dol	1,912	3,158	4,366	5,607	5,864	6,221	6,518	6,763	6,978
Average monthly benefit:										
Age and service	Dollars	992	1,189	1,369	1,587	1,643	1,698	1,749	1,796	1,830
Disability	Dollars	723	881	1,008	1,141	1,164	1,184	1,204	1,216	1,221
Survivors	Dollars	392	528	653	789	819	849	881	905	923
Cash and security holdings	Bil. dol	73.7	142.3	238.0	344.3	366.2	394.1	422.2	451.3	481.3

[1] Excludes employees in leave without pay status.   [2] Includes interest on investments.   [3] Includes refunds, death claims, and administration.   [4] Includes disability annuitants.

Source: U.S. Office of Personnel Management, *Civil Service Retirement and Disability Trust Fund Annual Report*.

No. 612. State and Local Government Retirement Systems—Beneficiaries and Finances: 1980 to 1998

[In billions of dollars, except as indicated (37.3 represents $37,300,000,000). For fiscal years closed during the 12 months ending June 30]

Year and level of government	Number of beneficiaries (1,000)	Receipts					Benefits and withdrawals			Cash and security holdings
		Employee contributions		Government contributions		Earnings on investments	Total	Benefits	Withdrawals	
		Total		State	Local					
1980										
All systems	(NA)	37.3	6.5	7.6	10.0	13.3	14.0	12.2	1.8	185
State-administered	(NA)	28.6	5.3	7.4	5.6	10.3	10.3	8.8	1.4	145
Locally administered	(NA)	8.7	1.2	0.2	4.3	3.0	3.8	3.4	0.4	41
1990										
All systems	4,026	111.3	13.9	14.0	18.6	64.9	38.4	36.0	2.4	721
State-administered	3,232	89.2	11.6	14.0	11.5	52.0	29.6	27.6	2.0	575
Locally administered	794	22.2	2.2	(Z)	7.0	12.9	8.8	8.4	0.4	145
1995										
All systems	4,979	148.8	18.6	16.6	24.4	89.2	61.4	58.8	2.7	1,118
State-administered	4,025	123.3	15.7	16.2	15.4	76.0	48.0	45.8	2.2	914
Locally administered	954	25.5	2.9	0.4	9.0	13.3	13.5	13.0	0.5	204
1998										
All systems	5,381	263.4	21.8	18.9	23.5	199.2	80.5	76.5	4.0	1,717
State-administered	4,423	213.7	18.3	18.6	16.2	160.7	63.0	59.7	3.3	1,423
Locally administered	958	49.6	3.5	0.3	7.3	38.5	17.5	16.8	0.7	293

NA Not available. Z Less than $50 million.

Source: U.S. Census Bureau, Through 1995, *Finances of Employee-Retirement Systems of State and Local Governments*, Series GF, No. 2, annual; 1998, "Employee-Retirement Systems of State and Local Governments"; published 3 February 2000; <http://www.census.gov/govs/www/retire.html>.

No. 613. Private Pension Plans—Summary by Type of Plan: 1980 to 1996

[488.9 represents 488,900. "Pension plan" is defined by the Employee Retirement Income Security Act (ERISA) as "any plan, fund, or program which was heretofore or is hereafter established or maintained by an employer or an employee organization, or by both, to the extent that such plan (a) provides retirement income to employees, or (b) results in a deferral of income by employees for periods extending to the termination of covered employment or beyond, regardless of the method of calculating the contributions made to the plan, the method of calculating the benefits under the plan, or the method of distributing benefits from the plan." A defined benefit plan provides a definite benefit formula for calculating benefit amounts - such as a flat amount per year of service or a percentage of salary times years of service. A defined contribution plan is a pension plan in which the contributions are made to an individual account for each employee. The retirement benefit is dependent upon the account balance at retirement. The balance depends upon amounts contributed, investment experience, and, in the case of profit sharing plans, amounts which may be allocated to the account due to forfeitures by terminating employees. Employee Stock Ownership Plans (ESOP) and 401(k) plans (see Table 616) are included among defined contribution plans. Data are based on Form 5500 series reports filed with the Internal Revenue Service]

Item	Unit	Total				Defined contribution plan				Defined benefit plan			
		1980	1990	1995	1996	1980	1990	1995	1996	1980	1990	1995	1996
Number of plans [1]	1,000. . .	488.9	712.3	693.4	696.2	340.8	599.2	623.9	632.6	148.1	113.1	69.5	63.7
Total participants [2][3] . .	Million . .	57.9	76.9	87.5	91.7	19.9	38.1	47.7	50.6	38.0	38.8	39.7	41.1
Active participants [2][4] .	Million . .	49.0	61.8	66.2	67.9	18.9	35.5	42.7	44.6	30.1	26.3	23.5	23.3
Contributions [5]	Bil. dol. .	66.2	98.8	158.8	169.5	23.5	75.8	117.4	133.7	42.6	23.0	41.4	35.8
Benefits [6]	Bil. dol. .	35.3	129.4	183.0	213.4	13.1	63.0	97.9	116.5	22.1	66.4	85.1	96.9

[1] Excludes all plans covering only one participant. [2] Includes double counting of workers in more than one plan. [3] Total participants include active participants, vested separated workers, and retirees. [4] Any workers currently in employment covered by a plan and who are earning or retaining credited service under a plan. Includes any nonvested former employees who have not yet incurred breaks in service. [5] Includes both employer and employee contributions. [6] Benefits paid directly from trust and premium payments made from plan to insurance carriers. Excludes benefits paid directly by insurance carriers.

Source: U.S. Dept. of Labor, Pension and Welfare Benefits Administration, *Private Pension Plan Bulletin*, winter 1996 and unpublished data.

No. 614. Percent of Full-Time Employees Participating in Retirement Plans: 1991 to 1997

[In percent. Covers full-time employees in medium and large private nonfarm establishments. Based on a sample survey of establishments; for details, see source and headnote, Table 703]

Type of retirement plan	1991	1993	1995	1997
Total [1]	78	78	80	79
Defined benefit	59	56	52	50
Defined contribution	48	49	55	57
401(k) plans [2]	44	43	54	55

[1] Some employees participate in both defined benefit and defined contribution plans, but are counted just once in total. [2] A 401(k) plan is a qualified retirement plan that allows participants to have a portion of their compensation (otherwise payable in cash) contributed pretax to a retirement account on their behalf.

Source: U.S. Bureau of Labor Statistics, *News*, USDL 99-02, January 7, 1999.

Social Insurance and Human Services 387

No. 615. Pension Plan Coverage of Workers by Selected Characteristics: 1998

[64,009 represents 64,009,000. Covers workers as of **March 1999** who had earnings in 1998. Based on Current Population Survey; see text, Section 1, Population and Appendix III]

Sex and age	Number with coverage (1,000)				Percent of total workers			
	Total [1]	White	Black	Hispanic [2]	Total [1]	White	Black	Hispanic [2]
Total	64,009	54,474	6,763	4,176	43.8	44.4	40.7	28.4
Male.	35,428	30,727	3,204	2,326	45.8	46.6	41.6	27.5
Under 65 years old	34,690	30,064	3,163	2,296	46.6	47.5	42.0	27.7
15 to 24 years old	1,783	1,548	150	172	14.1	14.4	10.9	9.6
25 to 44 years old	19,188	16,393	1,906	1,411	50.2	51.2	45.4	29.6
45 to 64 years old	13,718	12,123	1,107	712	58.3	58.9	56.5	40.7
65 years old and over	739	663	41	31	25.4	24.9	25.2	20.9
Female.	28,581	23,748	3,559	1,850	41.5	41.8	39.9	29.6
Under 65 years old	28,031	23,252	3,522	1,833	42.0	42.4	40.3	29.7
15 to 24 years old	1,380	1,108	181	134	11.6	11.4	11.3	10.0
25 to 44 years old	15,461	12,651	2,089	1,146	45.8	46.6	43.0	33.6
45 to 64 years old	11,190	9,493	1,252	553	53.2	53.1	55.2	38.8
65 years old and over	550	496	37	16	24.4	24.6	19.9	22.6

[1] Includes other races, not shown separately.   [2] Hispanic persons may be of any race.

Source: U.S. Census Bureau, unpublished data.

No. 616. 401(k) Plans—Summary: 1985 to 1996

[10,339 represents 10,339,000. A 401(k) plan is a qualified retirement plan that allows participants to have a portion of their compensation (otherwise payable in cash) contributed pretax to a retirement account on their behalf]

Item	1985	1990	1991	1992	1993	1994	1995	1996
Number of plans [1]	29,869	97,614	111,314	139,704	154,527	174,945	200,813	230,808
Active participants [2] (1,000)	10,339	19,548	19,126	22,404	23,138	26,206	28,061	30,843
Assets (bil. dol.).	144	385	440	553	616	675	864	1,062
Contributions (bil. dol.)	24	49	52	64	69	76	87	104
Benefits (bil. dol.)	16	32	33	43	44	51	62	78
Percentage of all private defined contribution plans:								
Assets	34	54	53	58	58	62	65	(NA)
Contributions	46	65	64	69	68	72	74	(NA)
Benefits	35	51	51	58	57	62	64	(NA)

NA Not available.   [1] Excludes single-participant plans.   [2] May include some employees who are eligible to participate in the plan but have not elected to join. 401(k) participants may participate in one or more additional plans.

Source: Employee Benefit Research Institute, Washington, DC, *EBRI Databook on Employee Benefits, Fourth Edition* (copyright).

No. 617. State Unemployment Insurance by State and Other Area: 1998

[7,332 represents 7,332,000. See headnote, Table 618. For state data on insured unemployment, see Table 680]

State or other area	Benefi- ciaries, first pay- ments (1,000)	Benefits paid (mil. dol.)	Avg. weekly unem- ploy- ment benefits (dol.)	State or other area	Benefi- ciaries, first pay- ments (1,000)	Benefits paid (mil. dol.)	Avg. weekly unem- ploy- ment benefits (dol.)	State or other area	Benefi- ciaries, first pay- ments (1,000)	Benefits paid (mil. dol.)	Avg. weekly unem- ploy- ment benefits (dol.)
Total .	7,332	19,433	200	KY	110	218	186	OH. . . .	263	680	215
AL	145	201	152	LA	68	144	148	OK. . . .	47	93	189
AK	44	113	176	ME. . . .	40	86	149	OR. . . .	148	416	215
AZ	68	141	149	MD. . . .	101	304	202	PA	419	1,403	238
AR	86	177	186	MA. . . .	183	733	261	RI	47	135	227
CA	1,075	2,583	154	MI	408	983	235	SC	102	164	174
CO. . . .	57	152	225	MN. . . .	107	336	257	SD	8	16	162
CT	109	341	214	MS. . . .	60	104	146	TN	165	312	174
DE. . . .	25	66	197	MO. . . .	140	275	164	TX	338	932	208
DC. . . .	18	65	231	MT. . . .	27	54	173	UT	37	85	195
FL	240	666	205	NE	28	45	164	VT	19	42	181
GA	175	249	180	NV	63	175	208	VA	101	187	183
HI	37	150	269	NH	16	25	183	WA. . . .	178	772	260
ID	46	95	195	NJ	266	1,092	266	WV. . . .	52	119	187
IL	300	1,091	227	NM. . . .	33	84	169	WI	220	463	215
IN	128	272	201	NY	471	1,605	206	WY. . . .	11	25	189
IA. . . .	72	152	214	NC	223	390	207	PR	146	247	99
KS	49	136	215	ND	12	35	190	VI. . . .	2	4	154

Source: U.S. Employment and Training Administration, unpublished data.

388   Social Insurance and Human Services

No. 618. State Unemployment Insurance—Summary: 1980 to 1998

[3,356 represents 3,356,000. Includes unemployment compensation for state and local government employees where covered by state law]

Item	Unit	1980	1985	1990	1992	1993	1994	1995	1996	1997	1998
Insured unemployment, avg. weekly. .	1,000 . .	3,356	2,617	2,522	3,245	2,751	2,670	2,572	2,596	2,323	2,222
Percent of covered employment [1] . .	Percent .	3.9	2.9	2.4	3.1	2.6	2.5	2.3	2.3	2.0	1.9
Percent of civilian unemployed. .	Percent .	43.9	31.5	35.8	33.8	30.8	33.4	34.7	35.9	34.5	35.8
Unemployment benefits, avg. weekly .	Dollars .	100	128	162	174	180	182	187	189	193	200
Percent of weekly wage	Percent .	36.6	35.3	36.0	35.4	36.0	35.7	35.5	34.5	33.5	32.9
Weeks compensated	Million . .	149.0	119.3	116.0	150.2	125.6	123.4	118.3	119.0	106.6	101.4
Beneficiaries, first payments [2]	1,000 . .	9,992	8,372	8,629	9,243	7,884	7,959	8,035	7,990	7,325	7,332
Average duration of benefits [2]	Weeks. .	14.9	14.2	13.4	16.2	15.9	15.5	14.7	14.9	14.6	13.8
Claimants exhausting benefits.	1,000 . .	3,072	2,572	2,323	3,838	3,204	2,977	2,662	2,739	2,485	2,266
Percent of first payment [3]	Percent .	33.2	31.2	29.4	39.9	39.2	36.3	34.3	33.4	32.8	31.8
Contributions collected [4]	Bil. dol. .	11.4	19.3	15.2	17.0	19.8	21.8	22.0	21.6	21.2	19.8
Benefits paid	Bil. dol. .	14.2	14.7	18.0	25.1	21.8	21.5	21.2	21.8	19.7	19.4
Funds available for benefits [5]	Bil. dol. .	6.6	10.1	37.9	25.8	28.0	31.3	35.4	38.6	43.8	48.0
Average employer contribution rate [6] .	Percent .	2.4	3.1	2.0	2.2	2.5	2.6	2.4	2.3	2.1	1.9

[1] Insured unemployment as percent of average covered employment in preceding year.   [2] Weeks compensated divided by first payment.   [3] Based on first payments for 12-month period ending June 30.   [4] Contributions from employers; also employees in states which tax workers.   [5] End of year. Sum of balances in state clearing accounts, benefit-payment accounts, and state accounts in Federal unemployment trust funds.   [6] As percent of taxable wages.
Source: U.S. Employment and Training Administration, unpublished data.

No. 619. Persons With Work Disability by Selected Characteristics: 1999

[In thousands, except percent (16,993 represents 16,993,000). As of March. Covers civilian noninstitutional population and members of Armed Forces living off post or with their families on post. Persons are classified as having a work disability if they (1) have a health problem or disability which prevents them from working or which limits the kind or amount of work they can do; (2) have a service-connected disability or ever retired or left a job for health reasons; (3) did not work in survey reference week or previous year because of long-term illness or disability; or (4) are under age 65, and are covered by medicare or receive supplemental security income. Based on Current Population Survey; see text, Section 1, Population, and Appendix III]

Age and participation status in assistance programs	Total [1]	Male	Female	White	Black	Hispanic [2]
Persons with work disability.	**16,993**	**8,289**	**8,704**	**12,879**	**3,418**	**1,723**
16 to 24 years old.	1,292	655	637	903	329	176
25 to 34 years old.	2,132	1,013	1,119	1,521	537	237
35 to 44 years old.	3,928	2,010	1,918	2,905	867	396
45 to 54 years old.	4,532	2,227	2,305	3,517	806	438
55 to 64 years old.	5,108	2,383	2,726	4,034	878	475
Percent work disabled of total population.	9.7	9.7	9.8	9.0	15.5	8.7
16 to 24 years old.	3.8	3.9	3.8	3.4	6.5	3.5
25 to 34 years old.	5.6	5.4	5.7	5.0	10.3	4.3
35 to 44 years old.	8.8	9.2	8.5	7.9	15.6	8.6
45 to 54 years old.	12.9	13.0	12.7	11.8	20.9	15.3
55 to 64 years old.	22.3	21.7	22.8	20.5	38.4	27.9
Percent of work disabled—						
Receiving social security income	31.1	32.2	30.1	31.7	30.4	29.1
Receiving food stamps	18.2	14.4	21.9	15.5	27.6	26.4
Covered by medicaid.	32.0	27.2	36.6	28.6	44.7	42.2
Residing in public housing	6.8	5.3	8.3	5.0	13.6	9.6
Residing in subsidized housing	3.6	3.0	4.1	2.8	6.5	4.8

[1] Includes other races not shown separately.   [2] Hispanic persons may be of any race.
Source: U.S. Census Bureau, unpublished data.

No. 620. Vocational Rehabilitation—Summary: 1980 to 1998

[For year ending September 30 (1,076 represents $1,076,000,000). Includes Puerto Rico, Guam, Virgin Islands, American Samoa, Northern Mariana Islands, and the Republic of Palau. State agencies, using matching state and Federal funds, provide vocational rehabilitation services to eligible individuals with disabilities to enable them to prepare for and engage in gainful employment. Services may include counseling, guidance and work related placement services, physical and mental restoration, training and rehabilitation technology]

Item	Unit	1980	1985	1990	1993	1994	1995	1996	1997	1998
Federal and state expenditures [1]	Mil. dol . .	1,076	1,452	1,910	2,241	2,517	2,714	2,844	3,046	3,080
Federal expenditures	Mil. dol . .	817	1,100	1,525	1,691	1,891	2,054	2,104	2,164	2,232
Applicants processed for program eligibility .	1,000 . . .	717	594	625	713	675	625	578	617	624
Percent accepted into program	Percent .	58	60	57	61	72	76	76	79	79
Total persons rehabilitated [2]	1,000 . . .	277	228	216	194	203	210	213	212	224
Rehabilitation rate [3]	Percent .	64	64	62	56	49	46	61	61	62
Severely disabled persons rehabilitated [2][4] .	1,000 . . .	143	135	146	139	149	159	166	168	185
Rehabilitation rate [3]	Percent .	61	62	62	55	49	46	60	60	61
Percent of total persons rehabilitated . . .	Percent .	51	59	68	72	74	76	78	79	83
Persons served, total [5]	1,000 . . .	1,095	932	938	1,049	1,194	1,250	1,226	1,267	1,211
Persons served, severely disabled [4][5]	1,000 . . .	606	581	640	762	882	940	951	1,005	988
Percent of total persons served	Percent .	55	62	68	73	74	75	78	79	82

[1] Includes expenditures only under the basic support provisions of the Rehabilitation Act.   [2] Persons successfully placed into gainful employment.   [3] Persons rehabilitated as a percent of all active case closures (whether rehabilitated or not); beginning 1996, as a percent of persons who required services.   [4] An individual with a severe disability is an individual whose severe physical or mental impairment seriously limits one or more functional capacities in terms of an employment outcome, and whose vocational rehabilitation can be expected to require multiple vocational rehabilitation services over an extended period of time.   [5] Includes active cases accepted for rehabilitation services during year plus active cases on hand at beginning of year.
Source: U.S. Dept. of Education, Rehabilitation Services Administration, Caseload Statistics of State Vocational Rehabilitation Agencies in Fiscal Years, and State Vocational Rehabilitation Agency Program Data in Fiscal Years, both annual.

Social Insurance and Human Services   389

No. 621. Workers' Compensation Payments: 1980 to 1998

[In billions of dollars, except as indicated (79 represents 79,000,000). See headnote, Table 622]

Item	1980	1985	1990	1992	1993	1994	1995	1996	1997	1998
Workers covered [1] (mil.)	79	84	106	104	106	109	113	115	118	121
Premium amounts paid [2]	22.3	29.2	53.1	57.4	60.8	60.5	57.1	55.1	52.0	52.1
Private carriers [2]	15.7	19.5	35.1	34.5	35.6	34.0	31.6	30.3	29.1	29.7
State funds	3.0	3.5	8.0	9.6	10.9	11.2	10.5	10.1	9.4	9.7
Federal programs [3]	1.1	1.7	2.2	2.5	2.5	2.5	2.6	2.6	2.6	2.7
Self-insurers	2.4	4.5	7.9	10.8	11.8	12.8	12.5	12.0	11.0	10.0
Annual benefits paid [2]	13.6	22.2	38.2	45.7	45.3	44.6	43.4	42.1	40.6	41.7
By private carriers [2]	7.0	12.3	22.2	25.3	24.1	22.3	21.1	20.5	20.6	22.2
From state funds [4]	4.3	5.7	8.8	10.7	10.6	10.8	11.0	10.7	10.1	10.4
Employers' self-insurance [5]	2.3	4.1	7.2	9.7	10.6	11.5	11.2	10.9	9.9	9.1
Percent of covered payroll: [1]										
Workers' compensation costs [6][7]	1.96	1.82	2.13	2.13	2.17	2.05	1.83	1.67	1.46	1.35
Benefits [7]	1.07	1.30	1.49	1.66	1.58	1.52	1.39	1.28	1.14	1.08

[1] Data for years 1980 and 1985 not comparable with later years. [2] Premium and benefit amounts include estimated payments under insurance policy deductible provisions. Deductible benefits are allocated to private carriers and state funds. [3] Includes Federal employer compensation program and that portion of Federal black lung benefits program financed from employer contributions. [4] Net cash and medical benefits paid by competitive and exclusive state funds and by Federal workers' compensation programs, including black lung benefit program. [5] Cash and medical benefits paid by self-insurers, plus value of medical benefits paid by employers carrying workers' compensation policies that exclude standard medical coverage. [6] Premiums written by private carriers and state funds, and benefits paid by self-insurers increased by 5-10 percent prior to 1992 and by 11 percent for 1992-98 for administrative costs. Also includes benefits paid and administrative costs of Federal system for government employees. [7] Excludes programs financed from general revenue—black lung benefits and supplemental pensions in some states.

Source: 1980-1993, U.S. Social Security Administration, *Annual Statistical Supplement* to the *Social Security Bulletin*. Beginning 1994, National Academy of Social Insurance, Washington, DC, *Workers' Compensation: Benefits, Coverage, and Costs*, *1997-1998 New Estimates*.

No. 622. Workers' Compensation Payments by State: 1990 to 1998

[In millions of dollars (38,238 represents $38,238,000,000). Calendar-year data, except fiscal-year data for Federal civilian and other programs and for some states with state funds. Payments represent compensation and medical benefits and include insurance losses paid by private insurance carriers (compiled from state workers' compensation agencies and A.M. Best Co); disbursements of state funds (compiled from the A.M. Best Co., and state workers' compensation agencies); and self-insurance payments based on information from the National Association of Insurance Commissioners and the source's estimates. Includes benefit payments under Longshore and Harbor Workers' Compensation Act for states in which such payments are made]

State	1990	1995	1996	1997	1998	State	1990	1995	1996	1997	1998
Total [1]	38,238	43,373	42,065	40,586	41,706	Nebraska	137	141	199	185	164
						Nevada.	339	365	383	341	288
Alabama	444	516	525	530	615	New Hampshire	169	169	188	155	164
Alaska	113	115	122	115	111	New Jersey	844	[2]972	931	1,064	955
Arizona	371	386	459	404	418	New Mexico.	228	145	151	120	117
Arkansas	229	187	160	157	161	New York	1,752	[2]2,780	2,559	2,618	2,557
California.	6,065	[2]7,177	6,830	7,074	7,374	North Carolina	480	495	501	610	766
Colorado.	595	584	679	627	657	North Dakota	60	71	67	77	81
Connecticut	694	[2]733	672	732	711	Ohio.	1,960	2,162	2,146	2,033	2,335
Delaware.	75	[2]103	115	121	119	Oklahoma	369	580	645	547	520
District of Columbia. .	86	113	90	89	71	Oregon.	573	463	506	471	493
Florida	1,976	2,518	2,707	2,318	2,208	Pennsylvania	2,019	[2]2,663	2,534	2,471	2,448
Georgia	735	699	822	703	808	Rhode Island	219	138	122	167	104
Hawaii	216	326	288	255	195	South Carolina	277	[2]353	372	459	484
Idaho	105	148	128	139	166	South Dakota.	56	70	82	74	73
Illinois	1,607	1,438	1,643	1,577	1,687	Tennessee.	463	396	432	433	518
Indiana	350	361	410	399	439	Texas	2,896	[2]2,006	1,820	1,352	1,465
Iowa.	231	233	261	273	292	Utah.	187	140	155	122	169
Kansas	266	[2]290	270	313	318	Vermont	61	65	74	82	88
Kentucky.	383	498	507	483	511	Virginia	507	557	560	534	591
						Washington	883	1,129	1,182	1,386	1,482
Louisiana	575	516	557	420	365	West Virginia	389	529	524	464	464
Maine.	380	286	314	249	288	Wisconsin	561	651	648	594	622
Maryland.	505	[2]522	597	568	511	Wyoming.	49	74	74	68	74
Massachusetts	1,235	[2]775	700	653	641						
Michigan	1,205	[2]1,585	1,559	1,332	1,367	Federal programs:					
Minnesota	582	[2]733	740	738	732	Civilian employees.	1,448	1,880	1,912	1,901	1,955
Mississippi	198	[2]218	224	231	235	Black lung					
Missouri	496	733	619	471	528	benefits [3]	1,435	1,222	1,154	1,103	1,035
Montana	150	140	150	184	155	Other [4]	11	(NA)	(NA)	(NA)	13

NA Not available. [1] Total for 1995 includes an amount for benefits under deductible provisions not distributed by state. [2] Includes benefits under deductible provisions. [3] Includes payments by Social Security Administration and by Department of Labor. [4] Primarily payments made to dependents of reservists who died while on active duty in the Armed Forces.

Source: 1990, U.S. Social Security Administration, *Social Security Bulletin*, summer 1995, and selected prior issues. Beginning 1995, National Academy of Social Insurance, Washington, DC, *Workers' Compensation: Benefits, Coverage, and Costs*, *1997-1998, New Estimates*.

No. 623. Supplemental Security Income—Recipients and Payments: 1980 to 1998

[As of December, except total payments, calendar year (4,142 represents 4,142,000). See also Appendix III]

Program	Unit	1980	1985	1990	1993	1994	1995	1996	1997	1998
Recipients, total [1]	1,000...	4,142	4,138	4,817	5,984	6,296	6,514	6,614	6,495	6,566
Aged	1,000...	1,808	1,504	1,454	1,475	1,466	1,446	1,413	1,363	1,332
Blind	1,000...	78	82	84	85	85	84	82	81	80
Disabled	1,000...	2,256	2,551	3,279	4,424	4,745	4,984	5,119	5,052	5,154
Payments, total [2]	Mil. dol.	7,941	11,060	16,599	24,557	25,877	27,628	28,792	29,052	30,216
Aged	Mil. dol.	2,734	3,035	3,736	4,248	4,367	4,467	4,507	4,532	4,425
Blind	Mil. dol.	190	264	334	375	372	376	372	375	366
Disabled	Mil. dol.	5,014	7,755	12,521	19,928	21,131	22,779	23,906	24,006	25,305
Average monthly payment, total [1]	Dollars.	168	226	299	345	351	358	363	351	359
Aged	Dollars	128	164	213	237	243	251	261	268	277
Blind	Dollars	213	274	342	359	364	370	379	382	390
Disabled	Dollars	198	261	337	381	384	389	391	373	380

[1] Persons with a Federal SSI payment and/or federally administered state supplementation. [2] Includes payments not distributed by reason for eligibility.

No. 624. Supplemental Security Income (SSI)—Recipients and Payments by State and Other Area: 1995 to 1998

[Recipients as of December; payments for calendar year (6,514 represents 6,514,000). Data cover Federal SSI payments and/or federally-administered state supplementation. For explanation of methodology, see Appendix III]

State and other area	Recipients (1,000)			Payments for year (mil. dol.)			State and other area	Recipients (1,000)			Payments for year (mil. dol.)		
	1995	1997	1998	1995	1997	1998		1995	1997	1998	1995	1997	1998
Total..	6,514	6,495	6,566	27,037	28,371	29,408	MO	114	113	112	431	453	459
							MT	14	14	14	53	54	55
U.S.	6,513	6,494	6,563	27,035	28,368	29,405	NE	21	21	21	76	81	83
AL	165	163	163	600	633	651	NV	21	22	23	79	88	95
AK	7	7	8	27	30	32	NH	11	11	11	39	44	46
AZ	73	76	78	288	316	329	NJ	144	144	145	594	628	646
AR	94	91	90	326	335	340	NM	45	45	46	166	177	183
CA	1,032	1,023	1,042	5,391	5,513	5,769	NY	589	598	608	2,724	2,932	3,055
CO	57	56	56	217	230	231	NC	191	193	194	639	699	717
CT	45	46	47	181	195	203	ND	9	9	9	29	30	30
DE	11	11	12	40	46	48	OH	248	247	249	1,044	1,111	1,132
DC	20	20	20	83	85	89	OK	74	74	73	266	283	293
FL	338	353	362	1,300	1,449	1,515	OR	47	48	49	183	198	206
GA	199	199	199	692	744	767	PA	265	269	276	1,159	1,235	1,306
HI	19	19	20	82	89	94	RI	24	25	26	100	109	117
ID	17	17	17	63	69	71	SC	111	110	110	384	410	420
IL	267	253	255	1,160	1,145	1,180	SD	14	13	13	47	49	50
IN	89	89	90	348	370	378	TN	180	172	170	648	658	670
IA	42	41	41	148	153	157	TX	404	407	409	1,391	1,491	1,542
KS	38	36	37	141	146	148	UT	20	20	20	80	86	87
KY	165	168	172	635	676	708	VT	13	13	13	50	50	51
LA	182	175	174	717	728	740	VA	130	131	133	471	507	525
ME	31	28	29	96	100	107	WA	92	94	97	398	432	453
MD	82	85	86	332	364	383	WV	68	69	71	276	297	313
MA	164	168	167	700	740	772	WI	112	91	90	487	370	371
MI	210	209	213	896	945	975	WY	6	6	6	21	23	23
MN	62	63	64	235	253	262	N. Mariana...	1	1	1	2	3	3
MS	141	136	135	504	518	528							

Source of Tables 623 and 624: U.S. Social Security Administration, Social Security Bulletin, quarterly, and Annual Statistical Supplement to the Social Security Bulletin.

No. 625. Temporary Assistance for Needy Families (TANF)—Families and Recipients: 1980 to 1999

[In thousands (3,712 represents 3,712,000). Average monthly families and recipients for calendar year, except 1999 for Jan.-Sept. period. Prior to TANF, the cash assistance program to families was called Aid to Families with Dependent Children (1980-1996). Under the new welfare law (Personal Responsibility and Work Opportunity Reconciliation Act of 1996), the program became TANF. See text, this section. Includes Puerto Rico, Guam, and Virgin Islands

Year	Families	Recipients	Year	Families	Recipients
1980	3,712	10,774	1990	4,057	11,695
1981	3,835	11,079	1991	4,467	12,930
1982	3,542	10,258	1992	4,829	13,773
1983	3,686	10,761	1993	5,012	14,205
1984	3,714	10,831	1994	5,033	14,161
1985	3,701	10,855	1995	4,791	13,418
1986	3,763	11,038	1996	4,434	12,321
1987	3,776	11,027	1997	3,734	10,381
1988	3,749	10,915	1998	3,027	8,358
1989	3,799	10,993	1999	2,582	7,018

Source: U.S. Administration for Children and Families, "Temporary Assistance for Needy Families (TANF) 1936-1999"; <http://www.acf.dhhs.gov/news/stats/3697.htm>; (accessed 20 September 1999) and unpublished data..

Social Insurance and Human Services 391

No. 626. Temporary Assistance for Needy Families (TANF)—Recipients by State and Other Area: 1995 and 1999

[In thousands (4,791 represents 4,791,000). Average monthly families and recipients for calendar year, except as noted. See headnote, Table 625]

State or other area	Families 1995	Families 1999 [1]	Recipients 1995	Recipients 1999 [1]	State or other area	Families 1995	Families 1999 [1]	Recipients 1995	Recipients 1999 [1]
Total	4,791	2,582	13,418	7,018	MT	11	5	33	13
U.S.	4,734	2,543	13,242	6,901	NE	15	11	41	33
AL	45	20	114	47	NV	16	8	41	19
AK	12	8	36	26	NH	10	6	27	15
AZ	68	34	185	89	NJ	110	61	310	160
AR	24	12	62	29	NM	34	26	103	79
CA	916	616	2,675	1,764	NY	452	290	1,241	801
CO	38	14	106	37	NC	123	56	305	127
CT	61	34	169	85	ND	5	3	14	8
DE	11	6	24	16	OH	222	110	592	279
DC	26	19	72	50	OK	44	19	120	53
FL	224	79	606	188	OR	38	17	101	45
GA	138	60	378	151	PA	201	103	582	290
HI	22	16	66	45	RI	22	18	60	50
ID	9	1	24	3	SC	48	18	127	42
IL	233	117	684	352	SD	6	3	17	8
IN	62	37	177	110	TN	102	57	271	149
IA	35	22	97	59	TX	269	111	730	300
KS	28	13	77	32	UT	16	10	44	29
KY	74	42	184	96	VT	10	7	27	18
LA	77	37	251	103	VA	70	36	179	88
ME	21	13	59	35	WA	101	62	283	168
MD	80	33	220	84	WV	38	11	102	31
MA	97	52	263	125	WI	71	8	202	26
MI	195	92	578	251	WY	5	1	14	2
MN	61	43	178	127	PR	54	35	164	105
MS	51	16	140	37	GU	2	3	8	9
MO	88	50	249	130	VI	1	1	5	3

[1] January-September period only.

Source: U.S. Administration for Children and Families, unpublished data.

No. 627. Federal Food Programs: 1980 to 1999

[For fiscal years ending in year shown; see text, Section 9, State and Local Government. Program data include Puerto Rico, Virgin Islands, Guam, American Samoa, Northern Marianas, and the former Trust Territory when a Federal food program was operated in these areas. Participation data are average monthly figures except as noted (21.1 represents 21,100,000). Participants are not reported for the commodity distribution programs. Cost data are direct Federal benefits to recipients; they exclude Federal administrative payments and applicable state and local contributions. Federal costs for commodities and cash-in-lieu of commodities are shown separately from direct cash benefits for those programs receiving both]

Program	Unit	1980	1985	1990	1995	1996	1997	1998	1999
Food Stamp:									
Participants	Million . .	21.1	19.9	20.1	26.6	25.5	22.9	19.8	18.2
Federal cost.	Mil. dol. .	8,721	10,744	14,187	22,765	22,440	19,550	16,889	15,782
Monthly average coupon value per recipient .	Dollars . .	34.47	44.99	58.92	71.27	73.21	71.27	71.12	72.33
Nutrition assistance program for Puerto Rico: [1]									
Federal cost.	Mil. dol. .	(X)	825	937	1,131	1,143	1,174	1,204	1,236
National school lunch program (NSLP):									
Free lunches served	Million . .	1,671	1,657	1,662	2,090	2,128	2,194	2,197	2,206
Reduced-price lunches served	Million . .	308	255	273	309	326	347	362	393
Children participating [2]	Million . .	26.6	23.6	24.1	25.7	25.9	26.3	26.6	27.0
Federal cost.	Mil. dol. .	2,279	2,578	3,214	4,467	4,662	4,934	5,101	5,314
School breakfast (SB):									
Children participating [2]	Million . .	3.6	3.4	4.1	6.3	6.6	6.9	7.1	7.4
Federal cost.	Mil. dol. .	288	379	596	1,048	1,119	1,214	1,272	1,344
Special supplemental food program (WIC): [3]									
Participants	Million . .	1.9	3.1	4.5	6.9	7.2	7.4	7.4	7.3
Federal cost.	Mil. dol. .	584	1,193	1,637	2,516	2,690	2,815	2,808	2,852
Child and adult care (CC): [4]									
Participants [5]	Million . .	0.7	1.0	1.5	2.4	2.4	2.5	2.6	2.7
Federal cost. . . . . [6]	Mil. dol. .	207	390	720	1,296	1,360	1,393	1,372	1,438
Federal cost of commodities donated to— [6]									
Child nutrition (NSLP, CC, SF, and SB)	Mil. dol. .	930	840	646	733	734	661	774	754

X Not applicable. [1] Puerto Rico was included in the food stamp program until June 30, 1982. [2] Average monthly participation (excluding summer months of June through August). Includes children in public and private elementary and secondary schools and in residential child care institutes. [3] WIC serves pregnant and postpartum women, infants, and children up to age five. [4] Program provides year-round subsidies to feed preschool children in child care centers and family day care homes. Certain care centers serving disabled or elderly adults also receive meal subsidies. [5] Average quarterly daily attendance at participating institutions. [6] Includes the Federal cost of commodity entitlements, cash-in-lieu of commodities, and bonus foods. SF=summer feeding program.

Source: U.S. Dept. of Agriculture, Food and Nutrition Service. In "Annual Historical Review of FNS Programs" and unpublished data.

No. 628. Selected Characteristics of Food Stamp Households and Participants: 1990 to 1998

[For years ending September 30. Data for 1990-1992 exclude Guam and the Virgin Islands. Based on a sample of 47,145 households from the Food Stamp Quality Control System]

Year	Households				Participants		
		Percent of total				Percent of total	
	Total (1,000)	With children	With elderly [1]	With disabled [2]	Total (1,000)	Children	Elderly [1]
1990	7,803	60.3	18.1	8.9	20,411	49.6	7.7
1991	8,855	60.4	16.4	9.0	22,963	52.0	7.0
1992	10,049	62.2	15.4	9.5	25,743	51.9	6.6
1993	10.791	62.1	15.5	10.7	27,595	51.5	6.8
1994	11,091	61.1	15.8	12.5	28,009	51.4	7.0
1995	10,883	59.7	16.0	18.9	26,955	51.5	7.1
1996	10,552	59.5	16.2	20.2	25,926	51.0	7.3
1997	9,452	58.3	17.6	22.3	23,117	51.4	7.9
1998	8,246	58.3	18.2	24.4	19,969	52.8	8.2

[1] Persons 60 years old and over. [2] Beginning 1995, disabled households are defined as households with at least one member under age 65 who received SSI, or at least one member age 18 to 61 who received Social Security, veterans benefits, or other government benefits as a result of a disability. For years prior to 1995, disabled households are defined as households with SSI but no members over age 59. The substantial increase in the percentage of households with a disabled member between 1994 and 1995 is due in part to the change in the definition of disabled households. Using the previous definition, 13.3 percent of households included a disabled person in fiscal year 1995.

No. 629. Food Stamp Households and Participants—Summary: 1998

[For year ending September 30. Based on a sample of 47,145 households from the Food Stamp Quality Control System]

Household type and income source	Households		Age, sex, race, and Hispanic origin	Participants	
	Number (1,000)	Percent		Number (1,000)	Percent
Total	**8,246**	**100.0**	**Total [1]**	**19,969**	**100.0**
With children	4,803	58.2	Children	10,546	52.8
Single-parent households	3,264	39.6	Under 5 years old	3,509	17.6
Married-couple households	712	8.6	5 to 17 years old	7,037	35.2
Other	830	10.0	Adults	9,409	47.1
With elderly	1,500	18.2	18 to 35 years old	4,292	21.5
Living alone	1,184	14.4	36 to 59 years old	3,480	17.4
Not living alone	316	3.8	60 years old and over	1,637	8.2
Disabled	2,015	24.4			
Living alone	1,113	13.5	Male	7,926	39.7
Not living alone	903	10.9	Female	11,967	59.9
Earned income	2,167	26.3	White, non-Hispanic	8,008	40.1
Wages and salaries	2,047	24.8	Black, non-Hispanic	7,248	36.3
Unearned income	6,495	78.8	Hispanic	3,652	18.3
TANF [2]	2,591	31.4	Asian	605	3.0
Supplemental Security Income . . .	2,315	28.1	Native American	311	1.6
Social Security	1,924	23.3	Other	145	0.7
No income	724	8.8			

[1] Includes persons of unknown age not shown separately. [2] Temporary Assistance for Needy Families (TANF) program.
Source of Tables 628 and 629: U.S. Dept. of Agriculture, Food and Nutrition Service, *Characteristics of Food Stamp Households: Fiscal Year 1998 (Advance Report)*, July 1999.

No. 630. Federal Food Stamp Program by State: 1995 and 1999

[Participation data are average monthly number (26,619 represents 26,619,000). For years ending Sept. 30. Food stamp costs are for benefits only and exclude administrative expenditures]

State	Persons (1,000)		Benefits (mil. dol.)		State	Persons (1,000)		Benefits (mil. dol.)		State	Persons (1,000)		Benefits (mil. dol.)	
	1995	1999	1995	1999		1995	1999	1995	1999		1995	1999	1995	1999
Total [1] .	**26,619**	**18,183**	**22,765**	**15,782**	IA	184	129	141	103	NC . . .	614	505	495	435
U.S. . .	**26,579**	**18,146**	**22,714**	**15,729**	KS. . . .	184	115	144	80	ND . . .	41	33	32	26
					KY. . . .	520	396	413	337	OH . . .	1,155	640	1,017	552
AL. . . .	525	405	441	346	LA. . . .	711	516	629	463	OK . . .	375	271	315	221
AK. . . .	45	41	50	49	ME . . .	132	109	112	89	OR . . .	289	224	254	190
AZ. . . .	480	257	414	233	MD . . .	399	264	365	237	PA. . . .	1,173	835	1,006	704
AR. . . .	272	253	212	210	MA . . .	410	261	315	205	RI	93	76	82	61
CA. . . .	3,175	2,027	2,473	1,804	MI	971	683	806	515	SC. . . .	364	309	297	251
CO . . .	252	173	217	145	MN . . .	308	208	240	171	SD. . . .	50	44	40	37
CT. . . .	226	178	169	150	MS . . .	480	288	383	232	TN. . . .	662	511	554	425
DE. . . .	57	39	47	32	MO . . .	576	408	488	348	TX. . . .	2,558	1,401	2,246	1,255
DC . . .	94	84	93	80	MT . . .	71	61	57	52	UT. . . .	119	88	90	73
FL. . . .	1,395	933	1,307	819	NE. . . .	105	92	77	66	VT. . . .	59	44	46	34
GA . . .	816	617	700	514	NV. . . .	99	62	91	56	VA. . . .	546	362	450	282
HI	125	125	177	180	NH . . .	58	37	44	31	WA . . .	476	307	417	260
ID	80	57	59	45	NJ	551	385	506	346	WV . . .	309	247	253	208
IL	1,151	820	1,056	767	NM . . .	239	178	196	144	WI	320	182	220	124
IN	470	298	382	255	NY. . . .	2,183	1,541	2,065	1,464	WY . . .	34	23	28	19

[1] Includes Guam and the Virgin Islands. Several outlying areas receive nutrition assistance grants in lieu of food stamp assistance (e.g., Puerto Rico, American Samoa and the Northern Marianas).
Source: U.S. Dept. of Agriculture, Food and Nutrition Service. In "Annual Historical Review of FNS Programs" and unpublished data.

Social Insurance and Human Services   393

No. 631. Child Support—Award and Recipiency Status of Custodial Parent: 1995

[In thousands except as noted (13,739 represents 13,739,000). Custodial parents 15 years and older with own children under 21 years of age present from absent parents as of spring 1996. Covers civilian noninstitutional population. Based on Current Population Survey; see text, Section 1, Population and Appendix III. For definition of mean, see Guide to Tabular Presentation]

Award and recipiency status	All custodial parents				Custodial parents below poverty level			
	Total				Total			
	Number	Percent distribu- tion	Mothers	Fathers	Number	Percent distribu- tion	Mothers	Fathers
Total.	**13,739**	**(X)**	**11,634**	**2,105**	**4,172**	**(X)**	**3,871**	**301**
With child support agreement or award . . .	7,967	(X)	7,123	844	2,103	(X)	1,979	124
Supposed to receive payments in 1995. .	6,966	100.0	6,233	733	1,761	100.0	1,654	108
Actually received payments in 1995 . .	4,769	68.5	4,353	416	1,067	60.6	1,024	44
Received full amount	2,718	39.0	2,482	236	432	24.5	415	17
Received partial payments.	2,051	29.4	1,871	180	635	36.1	609	26
Did not receive payments in 1995. . . .	2,198	31.6	1,880	318	694	39.4	630	64
Child support not awarded	5,772	(X)	4,511	1,261	2,069	(X)	1,892	177
MEAN INCOME AND CHILD SUPPORT								
Received child support payments in 1995:								
Mean total money income (dol.).	22,543	(X)	21,829	30,030	6,855	(X)	6,855	(B)
Mean child support received (dol.)	3,732	(X)	3,767	3,370	2,531	(X)	2,519	(B)
Received the full amount due:								
Mean total money income (dol.) . . .	25,092	(X)	24,355	32,839	6,734	(X)	6,695	(B)
Mean child support received (dol.). .	5,044	(X)	5,086	4,606	4,082	(X)	4,135	(B)
Received partial payments:								
Mean total money income (dol.) . . .	19,166	(X)	18,477	26,338	6,937	(X)	6,964	(B)
Mean child support received (dol.). .	1,993	(X)	2,016	1,746	1,477	(X)	1,420	(B)
Received no payments in 1995:								
Mean total money income (dol.).	17,398	(X)	16,093	25,122	6,043	(X)	6,160	(B)
Without child support agreement or award:								
Mean total money income (dol.).	18,927	(X)	14,068	36,312	5,660	(X)	5,614	(B)

B Base too small to meet statistical standards for reliability.   X Not applicable.
Source: U.S. Census Bureau, *Current Population Reports*, P60-196.

No. 632. Child Support Enforcement Program—Caseload and Collections: 1980 to 1998

[For years ending Sept. 30 (5,432 represents 5,432,000). Includes Puerto Rico, Guam, and the Virgin Islands. The child support enforcement program locates absent parents, establishes paternity of children born out-of-wedlock, and establishes and enforces support orders. By law, these services are available to all families that need them. The program is operated at the state and local government level but 68 percent of administrative costs are paid by the Federal Government. Child support collected for families not receiving Aid to Families with Dependent Children (AFDC) goes to the family to help it remain self-sufficient. Most of the child support collected on behalf of AFDC families goes to Federal and state governments to offset AFDC payments. Based on data reported by state agencies. Minus sign (-) indicates net outlay]

Item	Unit	1980	1985	1990	1994	1995	1996	1997	1998
Total cases	1,000 . . .	**5,432**	**8,401**	**12,796**	**18,610**	**19,162**	**19,319**	**19,057**	**19,419**
AFDC and AFDC arrears only caseload . . .	1,000 . . .	(NA)	(NA)	7,953	10,420	10,379	9,971	9,109	8,506
AFDC cases	1,000 . . .	4,583	6,242	5,872	7,986	7,880	7,380	6,462	5,658
AFDC arrears only cases [1]	1,000 . . .	(NA)	(NA)	2,082	2,434	2,499	2,591	2,648	2,847
Non-AFDC cases	1,000 . . .	849	2,159	4,843	8,190	8,783	9,348	9,947	10,914
Cases for which a collection was made:									
AFDC cases	1,000 . . .	503	684	701	926	976	940	865	789
AFDC arrears only cases [1]	1,000 . . .	(NA)	(NA)	224	308	343	402	493	608
Non-AFDC cases	1,000 . . .	243	654	1,363	2,169	2,408	2,612	2,850	3,070
Percentage of cases with collections:									
AFDC cases	Percent .	11.0	11.0	11.9	11.6	12.4	12.7	13.4	13.9
AFDC arrears only cases [1]	Percent .	(NA)	(NA)	10.8	12.7	13.7	15.5	18.6	21.4
Non-AFDC cases	Percent .	28.7	30.3	28.1	26.5	27.4	27.9	28.7	28.1
Absent parents located, total	1,000 . . .	643	878	2,062	4,204	4,950	5,808	6,441	6,585
Paternities established, total.	1,000 . . .	144	232	393	592	659	734	814	848
Support orders established, total [2]	1,000 . . .	374	669	1,022	1,025	1,051	1,093	1,260	1,148
FINANCES									
Collections, total [3]	Mil. dol .	**1,478**	**2,694**	**6,010**	**9,850**	**10,827**	**12,020**	**13,364**	**14,348**
AFDC collections	Mil. dol . .	603	1,090	1,750	2,550	2,689	2,855	2,843	2,650
State share	Mil. dol . .	274	415	620	891	939	1,014	1,159	1,089
Incentive payments to states	Mil. dol . .	72	145	264	407	400	409	410	396
Federal share	Mil. dol . .	246	341	533	762	822	888	1,046	961
Payments to AFDC families [4]	Mil. dol . .	10	189	334	457	474	480	157	152
Non-AFDC collections	Mil. dol . .	874	1,604	4,260	7,300	8,138	9,165	10,521	11,698
Administrative expenditures, total	Mil. dol . .	466	814	1,606	2,556	3,012	3,049	3,428	3,585
State share	Mil. dol . .	117	243	545	816	918	1,014	1,100	1,200
Federal share.	Mil. dol . .	349	571	1,061	1,741	2,095	2,035	2,328	2,385
Program savings, total.	Mil. dol . .	127	86	-190	-496	-852	-738	-813	-1,139
State share	Mil. dol . .	230	317	338	482	421	409	469	286
Federal share.	Mil. dol . .	-103	-231	-528	-978	-1,273	-1,147	-1,282	-1,424
Total fees and costs recovered for non-AFDC cases	Mil. dol . .	5	3	22	33	33	37	41	49

NA Not available.   [1] Reflects cases that are no longer receiving AFDC but still have outstanding child support due.
[2] Through 1990 includes modifications to orders.   [3] Beginning 1994 includes medical support payments not shown separately.
[4] Beginning 1985, states were required to pass along to the family the first $50 of any current child support collected each month. Beginning 1997 excludes payments to families that are no longer required since the passage of the welfare reform laws.
Source: U.S. Department of Health and Human Services, Office of Child Support Enforcement, *Annual Report to Congress*.

No. 633. Regular Child Care Arrangements for Children Under 6 Years Old by Type of Arrangement: 1995

[In percent, except as indicated (21,421 represents 21,421,000). Estimates are based on children under 6 years old who have yet to enter kindergarten. Based on 14,064 interviews from a sample survey of the civilian, noninstitutional population in households with telephones; see source for details]

Characteristic	Children		Type of nonparental arrangement				
	Number (1,000)	Percent distribution	Total [1]	In relative care	In non-relative care	In center-based program [2]	No non-parental arrange-ment
Total................	21,421	100	60	21	18	31	40
Race/ethnicity:							
White, non-Hispanic	13,996	65	62	18	21	33	38
Black, non-Hispanic.........	3,344	16	66	31	12	33	34
Hispanic	2,838	13	46	23	12	17	54
Other	1,243	6	58	25	13	28	42
Mother's employment status: [3]							
35 or more hours per week....	7,101	34	88	33	32	39	12
Less than 35 hours per week ..	4,034	19	75	30	26	35	25
Looking for work..........	1,635	8	42	16	4	25	58
Not in labor force	8,354	40	32	7	6	22	68
Household income:							
Less than $10,001	4,502	21	50	22	10	25	50
$10,001 to $20,000.........	2,909	14	54	27	12	24	46
$20,001 to $30,000.........	3,385	16	53	22	14	25	47
$30,001 to $40,000.........	3,047	14	60	23	20	27	40
$40,001 to $50,000.........	2,304	11	63	19	22	32	37
$50,001 to $75,000.........	3,063	14	74	20	26	40	26
$75,001 or more...........	2,211	10	77	14	30	49	23

[1] Columns do not add to total because some children participated in more than one type of nonparental arrangement. [2] Center-based programs include day care centers, head start programs, preschool, prekindergartens, and other early childhood programs. [3] Children without mothers are not included.

Source: U.S. National Center for Education Statistics, *Statistics in Brief*, October 1995 (NCES 95-824).

No. 634. Licensed Child Care Centers and Family Child Care Providers by State: 1999

[Centers for the period October 1998 through January 1999; family child care providers as of August]

State	Licensed child care centers	Licensed family child care providers	State	Licensed child care centers	Licensed family child care providers
United States......	101,773	290,375	Missouri	1,515	2,570
			Montana	251	1,541
Alabama	1,353	3,015	Nebraska	783	3,475
Alaska	225	1,707	Nevada	399	659
Arizona............	1,910	1,769	New Hampshire	1,200	403
Arkansas...........	1,935	1,654			
California...........	13,051	35,819	New Jersey.........	3,500	5,100
			New Mexico.........	600	278
Colorado...........	2,503	5,781	New York	3,411	20,857
Connecticut	1,638	4,506	North Carolina	3,825	5,180
Delaware...........	267	1,952	North Dakota	109	2,536
District of Columbia....	354	234			
Florida	6,052	8,435	Ohio..............	3,760	6,563
			Oklahoma	1,912	4,170
Georgia	1,244	6,895	Oregon	970	10,748
Hawaii	384	525	Pennsylvania	3,508	4,942
Idaho	526	1,282	Rhode Island	360	810
Illinois............	2,907	9,821			
Indiana	656	3,268	South Carolina.......	1,731	1,968
			South Dakota........	164	1,061
Iowa..............	1,526	4,775	Tennessee..........	3,033	2,826
Kansas............	1,385	7,766	Texas	7,733	13,583
Kentucky...........	1,974	4,647	Utah..............	320	1,820
Louisiana	1,808	11,000			
Maine.............	904	2,400	Vermont	515	1,420
			Virginia	2,402	5,015
Maryland...........	2,284	12,007	Washington	1,883	7,401
Massachusetts.......	2,295	11,005	West Virginia	320	4,716
Michigan...........	4,746	16,437	Wisconsin	2,295	6,845
Minnesota..........	1,574	15,559	Wyoming...........	218	678
Mississippi.........	1,555	951			

Source: Children's Foundation, Washington, DC, *1999 Child Care Licensing Study and Family Child Care Licensing Study* (copyright).

Social Insurance and Human Services 395

No. 635. Head Start—Enrollment and Congressional Appropriations: 1980 to 1998

[For fiscal years ending in year shown; see text, Section 9, State and Local Government (376 represents 376,000)]

Year	Enrollment (1,000)	Appropriation (mil. dol.)	Year	Enrollment (1,000)	Appropriation (mil. dol.)	Age and race	Enrollment, 1998 (percent)
1980	376	735	1990	541	1,552	Under 3 years old	4
1981	387	819	1991	583	1,952	3 years old	31
1982	396	912	1992	621	2,202	4 years old	59
1983	415	912	1993	714	2,776	5 years old and over . . .	6
1984	442	996	1994	740	3,326		
1985	452	1,075				White	32
1986	452	1,040	1995	751	3,534	Black	36
1987	447	1,131	1996	752	3,569	Hispanic	26
1988	448	1,206	1997	794	3,981	American Indian	3
1989	451	1,235	1998	822	4,347	Asian	3

Source: U.S. Administration for Children and Families, "1999 Head Start Fact Sheet"; published 19 Nov. 1999; <http://ww2.acf.dhhs.gov/programs/hsb/research/99_hsfs.htm>.

No. 636. Community Service Participation of Students in Grades 6 Through 12: 1996 and 1999

[12,627 represents 12,627,000. Based on the National Household Education Survey, a sample survey of approximately 55,000 households with telephones in the civilian, noninstitutional population; for details, see source

Characteristics	Students participating in community service (1,000)		Percent of students participating community service		Characteristics	Students participating in community service (1,000)		Percent of students participating community service	
	1996	1999	1996	1999		1996	1999	1996	1999
Total [1]	12,627	14,063	49	52	Parent's highest level of education:				
Student's grade:					Less than high school . . .	834	1,013	34	37
Grades 6 through 8	5,462	5,610	47	48	High school graduate or				
Grades 9 and 10	3,370	3,955	45	50	equivalent	3,273	3,125	42	45
Grades 11 and 12	3,795	4,486	56	61	Voc/tech education after high school or some				
Sex:					college	3,617	3,930	48	50
Male	5,971	6,446	45	47	College graduate	2,250	2,710	58	62
Female	6,656	7,617	53	57	Graduate or professional				
Race/ethnicity:					school	2,653	3,285	64	65
White, non-Hispanic	9,113	9,759	53	56	School type:				
Black, non-Hispanic	1,761	1,993	43	47	Public	11,056	12,331	47	50
Hispanic	1,246	1,587	38	39	Private:				
Other race/ethnicity	506	724	50	53	Church related	1,270	1,286	69	72
					Not church related	301	446	57	68

[1] Includes students with no grade reported.

Source: U.S. National Center for Education Statistics, *Statistics in Brief*, November 1999 (NCES 2000-028).

No. 637. Percent of Adult Population Doing Volunteer Work: 1998

[Volunteers are persons who worked in some way to help others for no monetary pay during the previous year. Based on a sample survey of 2,553 persons 18 years old and over conducted during the spring of the following year and subject to sampling variability; see source]

Age, sex, race, and Hispanic origin	Percent of population volunteering	Average hours volunteered per week	Educational attainment and household income	Percent of population volunteering	Average hours volunteered per week	Type of activity	Percent of population involved in activity
Total.	55.5	3.5	Elementary school . . .	29.4	(B)	Arts, culture, humanities. .	8.6
			Some high school. . . .	43.0	3.9	Education	17.3
18-24 years old	48.5	3.0	High school graduate . .	43.2	2.8	Environment	9.2
25-34 years old	54.9	3.5	Technical, trade, or			Health.	11.4
35-44 years old	67.3	3.7	business school	53.5	3.5	Human services	15.9
45-54 years old	62.7	3.8	Some college	67.2	4.8		
55-64 years old	50.3	3.3	College graduate . . .	67.7	3.1	Informal	24.4
65-74 years old	46.6	3.6				International, foreign	2.5
75 years old and over.	43.0	3.1	Under $10,000.	42.1	3.4	Political organizations . . .	4.6
			$10,000-$19,999	42.2	2.9	Private, community	
Male	49.4	3.6	$20,000-$29,999	43.7	4.0	foundations	3.4
Female	61.7	3.4	$30,000-$39,999	54.4	3.4		
			$40,000-$49,999	67.5	3.6	Public and societal benefit.	7.9
White.	58.6	3.5	$50,000-$59,999	62.8	4.3	Recreation - adults	8.6
Black.	46.6	4.7	$60,000-$74,999	71.2	2.9	Religion	22.8
			$75,000-$99,999	64.2	3.5	Work-related organizations	10.3
Hispanic [1]	46.4	2.1	$100,000 or more. . . .	70.5	3.5	Youth development	17.5

B Base figure too small to meet statistical standards for reliability. [1] Hispanic persons may be of any race.

Source: Saxon-Harrold, Susan K.E., Murray Weitzman, and the Gallup Organization, Inc., *Giving and Volunteering in the United States: 1999 Edition*. (Copyright and published by INDEPENDENT SECTOR, Washington, DC, 2000.)

396   Social Insurance and Human Services

No. 638. Charity Contributions—Average Dollar Amount and Percent of Household Income, 1991 to 1998, and by Age of Respondent and Household Income, 1998

[Estimates cover households' contribution activity (both cash and in-kind) for the year and are based on respondents' replies as to contribution and volunteer activity of household. For 1998, based on a sample survey of 2,553 persons 18 years old and over conducted during the spring of the following year and subject to sampling variability; see source]

Year, age, race, and Hispanic origin	All contributing households		Contributors and volunteers		Household income	All contributing households		Contributors and volunteers	
	Average amount (dol.)	Percent of household income	Average amount (dol.)	Percent of household income		Average amount (dol.)	Percent of household income	Average amount (dol.)	Percent of household income
1991	899	2.2	1,155	2.6	**1998—**				
1995	1,017	2.2	1,279	2.6	Under $10,000 . . .	329	5.2	419	6.3
					$10,000-$19,999 . .	495	3.3	633	4.2
1998, total	**1,075**	**2.1**	**1,339**	**2.5**	$20,000-$29,999 . .	552	2.2	650	2.6
18-24 years	478	1.2	598	1.4	$30,000-$39,999 . .	734	2.1	886	2.5
25-34 years	768	1.5	875	1.8	$40,000-$49,999 . .	951	2.1	1,073	2.4
35-44 years	1,071	1.9	1,273	2.2	$50,000-$59,999 . .	1,041	1.9	1,189	2.2
45-54 years	1,375	2.2	1,720	2.6	$60,000-$74,999 . .	1,696	2.6	1,948	3.0
55-64 years	1,345	2.5	1,716	3.2	$75,000-$99,999 . .	1,394	1.6	1,748	2.0
65-74 years	897	2.5	1,212	3.0	$100,000 and over.	2,550	2.2	3,029	2.6
75 years and over .	1,242	4.6	1,781	5.7					
					Itemizers [1]	1,509	2.4	1,791	2.8
					Claimed charitable				
White.	1,174	2.2	1,466	2.7	deduction . .	1,798	2.7	2,084	3.1
Black.	658	1.8	789	2.1	Didn't claim chari-				
					table deduction . .	426	0.9	487	1.1
Hispanic [2].	504	1.1	500	1.2	Nonitemizers	619	1.7	774	2.0

[1] Persons who itemized their deductions on their 1998 Federal tax returns. [2] Hispanic persons may be of any race.

Source: Saxon-Harrold, Susan K.E., Murray Weitzman, and the Gallup Organization, Inc., *Giving and Volunteering in the United States: 1999 Edition.* (Copyright and published by INDEPENDENT SECTOR, Washington, DC, 2000.)

No. 639. Charity Contributions—Percent of Households Contributing by Dollar Amount, 1991 to 1998, and Type of Charity, 1998

[In percent, except as noted. Estimates cover households' contribution activity (both cash and in-kind) for the year and are based on respondents' replies as to contribution and volunteer activity of household. For 1998 based on a sample survey of 2,553 persons 18 years old and over conducted during the spring of the following year and subject to sampling variability; see source]

Annual amount of household contributions	All households			Givers			Type of charity	1998	
	1991	1995	1998	1991	1995	1998		Percentage of households	Average contribution [1] (dol.)
None	27.8	31.5	29.9	(X)	(X)	(X)	Arts, culture, humanities .	11.4	221
Givers	72.2	68.5	70.1	100.0	100.0	100.0	Education	12.6	382
$1 to $100. . . .	14.9	15.2	15.6	24.9	24.3	22.2	Environment.	12.4	194
$101 to $200 . .	8.1	7.2	8.8	13.5	11.6	12.5	Health.	20.8	234
$201 to $300 . .	7.3	5.7	6.9	12.2	9.2	9.9	Human services	27.3	250
$301 to $400 . .	3.3	4.7	5.6	5.6	7.5	8.0	International	4.5	279
$401 to $500 . .	3.2	5.2	4.3	5.4	8.3	6.1	Private, community		
$501 to $600 . .	2.6	3.0	3.3	4.4	4.7	4.7	foundations	4.8	271
$601 to $700 . .	2.5	2.6	2.6	4.2	4.1	3.7	Public, societal benefit . .	11.1	134
$701 to $999 . .	3.4	3.7	4.3	5.7	6.0	6.1	Recreation - adults	5.0	144
$1,000 or more.	14.5	15.2	18.8	24.2	24.3	26.8	Religion.	45.2	1,002
Not reported . .	12.4	5.9	(X)	(X)	(X)	(X)	Youth development	21.4	174

X Not applicable.   [1] Average contribution per contributing household.

Source: Hodgkinson, Virginia, Murray Weitzman, and the Gallup Organization, Inc., *Giving and Volunteering in the United States: 1992 and 1996 Editions* (Copyright and published by INDEPENDENT SECTOR, Washington, DC, fall 1992 and 1996.) and Saxon-Harrold, Susan K.E., Murray Weitzman, and the Gallup Organization, Inc., *Giving and Volunteering in the United States: 1999 Edition.* (Copyright and published by INDEPENDENT SECTOR, Washington, DC, 2000.)

Social Insurance and Human Services   397

No. 640. Private Philanthropy Funds by Source and Allocation: 1980 to 1998

[In billions of dollars (48.6 represents $48,600,000,000).] Estimates for sources of funds based on U.S. Internal Revenue Service reports of individual charitable deductions, household surveys of giving by Independent Sector, and, for 1980 and 1985, an econometric model. For corporate giving, data are those prepared by the Council for Aid to Education. Data about foundation donations are based upon surveys of foundations and data provided by the Foundation Center. Estimates of the allocation of funds were derived from surveys of nonprofits conducted by source and other groups]

Source and allocation	1980	1985	1989	1990	1991	1992	1993	1994	1995	1996	1997	1998
Total funds	48.6	71.7	98.4	101.4	105.0	110.4	116.5	119.2	124.0	138.6	157.7	174.5
Individuals	40.7	57.4	79.5	81.0	84.3	87.7	92.0	92.5	95.4	107.6	122.9	134.8
Foundations [1]	2.8	4.9	6.6	7.2	7.7	8.6	9.5	9.7	10.6	12.0	13.9	17.1
Corporations	2.3	4.6	5.5	5.5	5.2	5.9	6.5	7.0	7.3	7.5	8.2	9.0
Charitable bequests	2.9	4.8	7.0	7.6	7.8	8.2	8.5	10.0	10.7	10.7	11.5	13.6
Allocation:												
Religion	22.2	38.2	47.8	49.8	50.0	54.9	56.3	60.2	66.3	70.7	72.7	76.1
Health	5.3	7.7	9.9	9.9	9.7	10.2	10.8	11.5	12.6	13.9	14.0	16.9
Education	5.0	8.2	11.0	12.4	13.5	14.3	15.4	16.6	17.6	19.2	22.2	24.6
Human service	4.9	8.5	11.4	11.8	11.1	11.6	12.5	11.7	11.7	12.2	12.7	16.1
Arts, culture and humanities . .	3.2	5.1	7.5	7.9	8.8	9.3	9.6	9.7	10.0	10.9	10.6	10.5
Public/societal benefit	1.5	2.2	3.8	4.9	4.9	5.0	5.4	6.1	7.1	7.6	8.4	10.5
Environment/wildlife	(2)	(2)	1.9	2.5	2.8	2.9	3.0	3.3	3.8	3.8	4.1	5.2
International	(2)	(2)	1.0	1.3	1.5	1.5	1.6	1.9	1.8	1.7	2.0	2.1
Unallocated [3]	4.6	-2.9	-0.3	-3.0	-1.7	-4.4	-4.3	-8.2	-15.2	-13.9	-3.5	-4.8
Gifts to foundations [1]	2.0	4.7	4.4	3.8	4.5	5.0	6.3	6.3	8.5	12.6	14.6	16.9

[1] Data, except for 1998, are from the Foundation Center. [2] Included in "Unallocated." [3] Money received by charities but not allocated to sources.

Source: AAFRC Trust for Philanthropy, New York, NY, *Giving USA*, annual, (copyright).

No. 641. Foundations—Number and Finances by Asset Size: 1998

[Figures are for latest year reported by foundations (385,052 represents $385,052,000,000). Covers nongovernmental nonprofit organizations with funds and programs managed by their own trustees or directors, whose goals were to maintain or aid social, educational, religious, or other activities deemed to serve the common good. Excludes organizations that make general appeals to the public for funds, act as trade associations for industrial or other special groups, or do not currently award grants]

Asset size	Number	Assets (mil. dol.)	Gifts received (mil. dol.)	Expend-itures (mil. dol.)	Grants (mil. dol.)	Percent distribution				
						Number	Assets	Gifts received	Expend-itures	Grants
Total	46,832	385,052	22,574	24,211	19,457	100.0	100.0	100.0	100.0	100.0
Under $50,000.	7,413	127	336	427	392	15.8	(Z)	1.5	1.8	1.9
$50,000-$99,999	3,335	245	109	169	149	7.1	0.1	0.5	0.7	0.8
$100,000-$249,999.	6,479	1,079	251	309	269	13.8	0.3	1.1	1.3	1.4
$250,000-$499,999.	5,914	2,142	343	367	306	12.6	0.6	1.5	1.5	1.6
$500,000-$999,999.	6,107	4,390	568	598	492	13.0	1.1	2.5	2.5	2.5
$1,000,000-$4,999,999	11,216	25,091	2,823	2,312	1,928	23.9	6.5	12.5	9.6	9.9
$5,000,000-$9,999,999	2,637	18,512	1,821	1,570	1,255	5.6	4.8	8.1	6.5	6.5
$10,000,000-$49,999,999 . . .	2,820	59,493	4,033	4,480	3,612	6.0	15.5	17.9	18.5	18.6
$50,000,000-$99,999,999 . . .	435	30,688	1,798	2,019	1,607	0.9	8.0	8.0	8.3	8.3
$100,000,000-$249,999,999. .	286	43,524	2,460	2,714	2,167	0.6	11.3	10.9	11.2	11.1
$250,000,000 or more.	190	199,761	8,033	9,247	7,279	0.4	51.9	35.6	38.2	37.4

Z Less than 0.05 percent.

Source: The Foundation Center, New York, NY, *Guide to U.S. Foundations*, annual.

No. 642. Foundations—Grants Reported by Subject Field and Recipient Organization: 1998

[Covers grants of $10,000 or more in size. Based on reports of 1,009 foundations. Grant sample dollar value ($9,711,000,000) represented half of all grant dollars awarded by private, corporate, and community foundations. For definition of foundations, see headnote, Table 641]

Subject field	Number of grants		Dollar value		Recipient organization [1]	Number of grants		Dollar value	
	Num-ber	Per-cent distri-bution	Amount (mil. dol.)	Per-cent distri-bution		Num-ber	Per-cent distri-bution	Amount (mil. dol.)	Per-cent distri-bution
Total	97,220	100.0	9,711	100.0	Arts/humanities org.	3,575	3.7	346	3.6
Arts and culture	14,105	14.5	1,439	14.8	Community improvement				
Education	20,080	20.7	2,367	24.4	organizations	4,984	5.1	440	4.5
Environment & animals . .	5,871	6.0	540	5.6	Educational institutions.	26,360	27.1	3,580	36.9
Health	11,816	12.2	1,602	16.5	Colleges & universities . . .	12,674	13.0	2,137	22.0
Human services.	22,923	23.6	1,456	15.0	Educational support				
International affairs,					agencies.	5,968	6.1	650	6.7
development & peace . .	2,918	3.0	313	3.2	Schools	5,389	5.5	435	4.5
Public/societal benefit . . .	12,076	12.4	1,149	11.8	Environmental agencies	3,898	4.0	340	3.5
Science and technology . .	2,451	2.5	369	3.8	Hospitals/medical care				
Social sciences	1,688	1.7	243	2.5	facilities	3,856	4.0	455	4.7
Religion	3,153	3.2	221	2.3	Human service agencies. . . .	18,053	18.6	1,060	10.9
Other	139	0.1	12	0.1	Museums/historical societies .	4,007	4.1	511	5.3

[1] Grants may be awarded to multiple types of recipient organizations and would thereby be double-counted.

Source: The Foundation Center, New York, NY, *The Foundation Grants Index*, 1999.

Section 13

Labor Force, Employment, and Earnings

This section presents statistics on the labor force; its distribution by occupation and industry affiliation; and the supply of, demand for, and conditions of labor. The chief source of these data is the Current Population Survey (CPS) conducted by the U.S. Census Bureau for the Bureau of Labor Statistics (BLS). Comprehensive historical and current data are available from the BLS Internet site <http://stats.bls.gov/cpshome.htm>. These data are published on a current basis by the BLS monthly publication *Employment and Earnings*. Detailed data on the labor force are also available from the Census Bureau's decennial census of population.

Types of data—Most statistics in this section are obtained by two methods: household interviews or questionnaires and reports of establishment payroll records. Each method provides data which the other cannot suitably supply. Population characteristics, for example, are readily obtainable only from the household survey, while detailed industrial classifications can be readily derived only from establishment records.

Household data are obtained from a monthly sample survey of the population. The CPS is used to gather data for the calendar week including the 12th of the month and provides current comprehensive data on the labor force (see text, Section 1, Population). The CPS provides information on the work status of the population without duplication since each person is classified as employed, unemployed, or not in the labor force. Employed persons holding more than one job are counted only once, according to the job at which they worked the most hours during the survey week.

Monthly, quarterly, and annual data from the CPS are published by the Bureau of

Labor Statistics in *Employment and Earnings*. Data presented include national totals of the number of persons in the civilian labor force by sex, race, Hispanic origin, and age; the number employed; hours of work; industry and occupational groups; and the number unemployed, reasons for, and duration of unemployment. Annual data shown in this section are averages of monthly figures for each calendar year, unless otherwise specified.

The CPS also produces annual estimates of employment and unemployment for each state, 50 large metropolitan statistical areas, and selected cities. These estimates are published by BLS in its annual *Geographic Profile of Employment and Unemployment*. More detailed geographic data (e.g., for counties and cities) are provided by the decennial population censuses.

Data based on establishment records are compiled by BLS and cooperating state agencies as part of an ongoing Current Employment Statistics program. Survey data, gathered monthly from a sample of employers through mail questionnaires or electronic interviewing, are supplemented by data from other government agencies and adjusted at intervals to data from government social insurance program reports. The estimates exclude self-employed persons, private household workers, unpaid family workers, agricultural workers, and the Armed Forces. In March 1999, reporting establishments employed 8 million manufacturing workers (41 percent of the total manufacturing employment at the time), 19 million workers in private nonmanufacturing industries (21 percent of the total in private nonmanufacturing), and 15 million Federal, state, and local government employees (75 percent of total government).

U.S. Census Bureau, Statistical Abstract of the United States: 2000

The establishment survey counts workers each time they appear on a payroll during the reference period (as with the CPS, the week including the 12th of the month). Thus, unlike the CPS, a person with two jobs is counted twice. The establishment survey is designed to provide detailed industry information for the Nation, states, and metropolitan areas on nonfarm wage and salary employment, average weekly hours, and average hourly and weekly earnings. Establishment survey data also are published in *Employment and Earnings*. Historical national data are available on the site <http://stats.bls.gov/ceshome.htm>.

Labor force—According to the CPS definitions, the civilian labor force comprises all civilians in the noninstitutional population 16 years and over classified as "employed" or "unemployed" according to the following criteria: Employed civilians comprise (a) all civilians, who, during the reference week, did any work for pay or profit (minimum of an hour's work) or worked 15 hours or more as unpaid workers in a family enterprise and (b) all civilians who were not working but who had jobs or businesses from which they were temporarily absent for noneconomic reasons (illness, weather conditions, vacation, labor-management dispute, etc.) whether they were paid for the time off or were seeking other jobs. Unemployed persons comprise all civilians who had no employment during the reference week, who made specific efforts to find a job within the previous 4 weeks (such as applying directly to an employer, or to a public employment service, or checking with friends) and who were available for work during that week, except for temporary illness. Persons on layoff from a job and expecting recall also are classified as unemployed. All other civilian persons, 16 years old and over, are "not in the labor force."

Beginning in 1982, changes in the estimation procedures and the introduction of 1980 census data caused substantial increases in the population and estimates of persons in all labor force categories. Rates on labor force characteristics, however,

were essentially unchanged. In order to avoid major breaks in series, some 30,000 labor force series were adjusted back to 1970. The effect of the 1982 revisions on various data series and an explanation of the adjustment procedure used are described in "Revisions in the Current Population Survey in January 1982," in the February 1982 issue of *Employment and Earnings*. The revisions did not, however, smooth out the breaks in series occurring between 1972 and 1979, and data users should make allowances for them in making certain data comparisons.

Beginning in January 1985, and again in January 1986, the CPS estimation procedures were revised due to the implementation of a new sample design (for the 1985 revision) and to reflect an explicit estimate of the number of undocumented immigrants (for the 1986 revision). The greatest impact of these revisions was on estimates of persons of Hispanic origin. Where possible these estimates were revised back to January 1980. A description of the changes and an indication of their effect on the national estimates of labor force characteristics appear in the February 1985 and February 1986 issues of *Employment and Earnings*, respectively.

Beginning in January 1994, several changes were introduced into the CPS that effect all data comparisons with prior years. These changes include the results of a major redesign of the survey questionnaire and collection methodology, revisions to some of the labor force concepts and definitions, and the introduction of 1990 census population controls, adjusted for the estimated undercount. An explanation of the changes and their effects on the labor force data appears in "Revisions in the Current Population Survey Effective January 1994" in the February 1994 issue of *Employment and Earnings*.

Beginning 1996, 1990 census population controls, adjusted for the estimated undercount, were extended back to January 1990. A discussion of the changes and their effects on the labor force data appears in "Revisions In Household Survey

Data Effective February 1996" in the March 1996 issue of *Employment and Earnings.*

Beginning in January 1997, the CPS reflects updated 1990 census-based population controls. The greatest impact of the new population controls was on estimates for persons of Hispanic origin. An explanation of the changes and their effects on labor force estimates appear in "Revisions in the Current Population Survey Effective January 1997" in the February 1997 issue of *Employment and Earnings.*

Beginning in January 1998, the CPS reflects the introduction of new composite estimation procedures and revised 1990 census-based population controls. An explanation of the changes and their effects on labor force estimates appear in "Revisions in the Current Population Survey Effective January 1998" in the February 1998 issue of *Employment and Earnings.*

Beginning in January 1999, the CPS reflects the introduction of revised 1990 census-based population controls that incorporate newly updated information on immigration. An explanation of the changes and their effects on labor force estimates appear in "Revisions in the Current Population Survey Effective January 1999" in the February 1999 issue of *Employment and Earnings.*

Hours and earnings—Average hourly earnings, based on establishment data, are gross earnings (i.e., earnings before payroll deductions) and include overtime premiums; they exclude irregular bonuses and value of payments in kind. Hours are those for which pay was received. Wages and salaries from the CPS consist of total monies received for work performed by an employee during the income year. It includes wages, salaries, commissions, tips, piece-rate payments, and cash bonuses earned before deductions were made for taxes, bonds, union dues, etc. Persons who worked 35 hours or more are classified as working full time.

Industry and Occupational groups—Industry data derived from the CPS for 1983-91 utilize the 1980 census industrial

classification developed from the 1972 SIC. CPS data from 1971 to 1982 were based on the 1970 census classification system which was developed from the 1967 SIC. Most of the industry categories were not affected by the change in classification.

Establishments responding to the establishment survey are classified according to the *Standard Industrial Classification (SIC) Manual.* See text, Section 17, Business, for information about the SIC manual.

The occupational classification system used in the 1980 census and in the CPS for 1983-91, evolved from the 1980 Standard Occupational Classification (SOC) system, first introduced in 1977. Occupational categories used in the 1980 census classification system are so radically different from the 1970 census system used in the CPS through 1982, that their implementation represented a break in historical data series. In cases where data have not yet been converted to the 1980 classifications and still reflect the 1970 classifications (e.g., Table 704), comparisons between the two systems should not be made. To help users bridge the data gap, a limited set of estimates was developed for the 1972-82 period based on the new classifications. The estimates were developed by means of applying conversion factors created by double coding a 20-percent sample of CPS occupational records for 6 months during 1981-82. For further details, contact BLS.

Beginning in January 1992, the occupational and industrial classification system used in the 1990 census were introduced into the CPS. (These systems were largely based on the 1980 Standard Occupational Classification and the 1987 Standard Industrial Classification.) There were a few breaks in comparability between the 1980 and 1990 census-based systems, particularly within the "technical, sales, and administrative support" categories. The most notable changes in industry classification were the shift of several industries from "business services" to "professional services" and the splitting of some industries into smaller, more detailed categories.

A number of industry titles were changed as well, with no change in content.

Productivity—BLS publishes data on productivity as measured by output per hour (labor productivity), output per combined unit of labor and capital input (multifactor productivity), and, for manufacturing industries, output per combined unit of capital, labor, energy, materials, and purchased service inputs. Labor productivity and related indexes are published for the business sector as a whole and its major subsectors: nonfarm business, manufacturing, nonfinancial corporations, and over 450 specific industries. Multifactor productivity and related measures are published for the private business sector and its major subsectors. Productivity indexes which take into account capital, labor, energy, materials, and service inputs are published for the 18 major industry groups which comprise the manufacturing sector, the utility services industry group, and for the following industries: cotton and synthetic broadwoven fabrics, household furniture, tire and inner tubes, footwear, steel, metal stampings, farm and garden machinery, refrigeration and heating equipment, motor vehicles, and railroad transportation. The major sector data are published in the BLS quarterly news release, *Productivity and Costs* and in the annual *Multifactor Productivity Measures* release. Industry productivity measures are published annually in the news releases *Productivity and Costs, Manufacturing Industries,* and *Productivity and Costs, Services - Producing and Mining Industries.* Detailed information on methods, limitations, and data sources appears in the BLS *Handbook of Methods,* BLS Bulletin 2490 (1997), Chapters 10 and 11.

Unions—As defined here, unions include traditional labor unions and employee associations similar to labor unions. Data on union membership status provided by BLS are for employed wage and salary workers and relate to their principal job. Earnings by union membership status are usual weekly earnings of full-time wage and salary workers. The information is collected through the Current Population Survey. Collective bargaining settlements data are available for bargaining situations involving 1,000 or more workers in private industry and state and local government.

Work stoppages—Work stoppages include all strikes and lockouts known to BLS which last for at least 1 full day or shift and involve 1,000 or more workers. All stoppages, whether or not authorized by a union, legal or illegal, are counted. Excluded are work slowdowns and instances where employees report to work late or leave early to attend mass meetings or mass rallies.

Seasonal adjustment—Many economic statistics reflect a regularly recurring seasonal movement which can be estimated on the basis of past experience. By eliminating that part of the change which can be ascribed to usual seasonal variation (e.g., climate or school openings and closings), it is possible to observe the cyclical and other nonseasonal movements in the series. However, in evaluating deviations from the seasonal pattern—that is, changes in a seasonally adjusted series—it is important to note that seasonal adjustment is merely an approximation based on past experience. Seasonally adjusted estimates have a broader margin of possible error than the original data on which they are based, since they are subject not only to sampling and other errors, but also are affected by the uncertainties of the adjustment process itself.

Statistical reliability—For discussion of statistical collection, estimation, sampling procedures, and measures of statistical reliability applicable to Census Bureau and BLS data, see Appendix III.

[In thousands (104,995 represents 104,995,000), except as indicated. For the civilian noninstitutional population 16 years old and over. Annual averages of monthly figures. Based on Current Population Survey; see text, Section 1, Population, and Appendix III]

Year	Civilian noninstitutional population	Civilian labor force			Employ-ment/population ratio [1]	Unemployed		Not in labor force	
		Total	Percent of population	Employed		Number	Percent of labor force	Number	Percent of population
1950	104,995	62,208	59.2	58,918	56.1	3,288	5.3	42,787	40.8
1960	117,245	69,628	59.4	65,778	56.1	3,852	5.5	47,617	40.6
1970	137,085	82,771	60.4	78,678	57.4	4,093	4.9	54,315	39.6
1980	167,745	106,940	63.8	99,303	59.2	7,637	7.1	60,806	36.2
1981	170,130	108,670	63.9	100,397	59.0	8,273	7.6	61,460	36.1
1982	172,271	110,204	64.0	99,526	57.8	10,678	9.7	62,067	36.0
1983	174,215	111,550	64.0	100,834	57.9	10,717	9.6	62,665	36.0
1984	176,383	113,544	64.4	105,005	59.5	8,539	7.5	62,839	35.6
1985	178,206	115,461	64.8	107,150	60.1	8,312	7.2	62,744	35.2
1986	180,587	117,834	65.3	109,597	60.7	8,237	7.0	62,752	34.7
1987	182,753	119,865	65.6	112,440	61.5	7,425	6.2	62,888	34.4
1988	184,613	121,669	65.9	114,968	62.3	6,701	5.5	62,944	34.1
1989	186,393	123,869	66.5	117,342	63.0	6,528	5.3	62,523	33.5
1990 [2]	189,164	125,840	66.5	118,793	62.8	7,047	5.6	63,324	33.5
1991	190,925	126,346	66.2	117,718	61.7	8,628	6.8	64,578	33.8
1992	192,805	128,105	66.4	118,492	61.5	9,613	7.5	64,700	33.6
1993	194,838	129,200	66.3	120,259	61.7	8,940	6.9	65,638	33.7
1994 [2]	196,814	131,056	66.6	123,060	62.5	7,996	6.1	65,758	33.4
1995	198,584	132,304	66.6	124,900	62.9	7,404	5.6	66,280	33.4
1996	200,591	133,943	66.8	126,708	63.2	7,236	5.4	66,647	33.2
1997 [2]	203,133	136,297	67.1	129,558	63.8	6,739	4.9	66,837	32.9
1998 [2]	205,220	137,673	67.1	131,463	64.1	6,210	4.5	67,547	32.9
1999 [2]	207,753	139,368	67.1	133,488	64.3	5,880	4.2	68,385	32.9

[1] Civilian employed as a percent of the civilian noninstitutional population. [2] Data not strictly comparable with data for earlier years. See text, this section, and February 1994, March 1996, February 1997, February 1998, and February 1999 issues of Employment and Earnings.

Source: U.S. Bureau of Labor Statistics, Bulletin 2307; and Employment and Earnings, monthly.

No. 644. Civilian Labor Force and Participation Rates With Projections: 1970 to 2008

[For civilian noninstitutional population 16 years old and over (82.8 represents 82,800,000). Annual averages of monthly figures. Rates are based on annual average civilian noninstitutional population of each specified group and represent proportion of each specified group in the civilian labor force. Based on Current Population Survey; see text, Section 1, Population, and Appendix III]

Race, sex, and age	Civilian labor force (millions)						Participation rate (percent)					
	1970	1980	1990 [1]	1995	1999 [1]	2008, proj.	1970	1980	1990 [1]	1995	1999 [1]	2008, proj.
Total [2]	82.8	106.9	125.8	132.3	139.4	154.6	60.4	63.8	66.5	66.6	67.1	67.6
White	73.6	93.6	107.4	112.0	116.5	126.7	60.2	64.1	66.9	67.1	67.3	67.9
Male	46.0	54.5	59.6	61.1	63.4	67.7	80.0	78.2	77.1	75.7	75.6	74.5
Female	27.5	39.1	47.8	50.8	53.1	59.0	42.6	51.2	57.4	59.0	59.6	61.5
Black	[3]9.2	10.9	13.7	14.8	16.4	19.1	61.8	61.0	64.0	63.7	65.8	66.3
Male	5.2	5.6	6.8	7.2	7.7	8.9	76.5	70.3	71.0	69.0	68.7	68.3
Female	4.0	5.3	6.9	7.6	8.7	10.2	49.5	53.1	58.3	59.5	63.5	64.6
Hispanic [4]	(NA)	6.1	10.7	12.3	14.7	19.6	(NA)	64.0	67.4	65.8	67.7	67.7
Male	(NA)	3.8	6.5	7.4	8.5	11.0	(NA)	81.4	81.4	79.1	79.8	77.9
Female	(NA)	2.3	4.2	4.9	6.1	8.6	(NA)	47.4	53.1	52.6	55.9	57.9
Male	51.2	61.5	69.0	71.4	74.5	81.1	79.7	77.4	76.4	75.0	74.7	73.7
16 to 19 years	4.0	5.0	4.1	4.0	4.3	4.8	56.1	60.5	55.7	54.8	52.9	52.9
20 to 24 years	5.7	8.6	7.9	7.3	7.3	8.3	83.3	85.9	84.4	83.1	81.9	81.4
25 to 34 years	11.3	17.0	19.9	18.7	17.3	17.1	96.4	95.2	94.1	93.0	93.3	93.2
35 to 44 years	10.5	11.8	17.5	19.2	20.4	18.3	96.9	95.5	94.3	92.3	92.8	92.3
45 to 54 years	10.4	9.9	11.1	13.4	15.4	19.0	94.3	91.2	90.7	88.8	88.8	88.8
55 to 64 years	7.1	7.2	6.6	6.5	7.5	10.8	83.0	72.1	67.8	66.0	67.9	69.4
65 years and over	2.2	1.9	2.0	2.2	2.3	2.8	26.8	19.0	16.3	16.8	16.9	17.8
Female	31.5	45.5	56.8	60.9	64.9	73.4	43.3	51.5	57.5	58.9	60.0	61.9
16 to 19 years	3.2	4.4	3.7	3.7	4.0	4.6	44.0	52.9	51.6	52.2	51.0	52.4
20 to 24 years	4.9	7.3	6.8	6.3	6.6	7.5	57.7	68.9	71.3	70.3	73.2	74.6
25 to 34 years	5.7	12.3	16.1	15.5	14.8	15.3	45.0	65.5	73.5	74.9	76.4	79.0
35 to 44 years	6.0	8.6	14.7	16.6	17.5	16.6	51.1	65.5	76.4	77.2	77.2	80.0
45 to 54 years	6.5	7.0	9.1	11.8	14.0	17.8	54.4	59.9	71.2	74.4	76.7	80.0
55 to 64 years	4.2	4.7	4.9	5.4	6.2	9.8	43.0	41.3	45.2	49.2	51.5	57.7
65 years and over	1.1	1.2	1.5	1.6	1.7	1.9	9.7	8.1	8.6	8.8	8.9	9.1

NA Not available. [1] See footnote 2, Table 643. [2] Beginning 1980, includes other races, not shown separately. [3] For 1970, Black and other. [4] Persons of Hispanic origin may be of any race.

Source: U.S. Bureau of Labor Statistics, Employment and Earnings, monthly, January issues; Monthly Labor Review, November 1999; and unpublished data.

Labor Force, Employment, and Earnings   403

No. 645. Employment Status of the Civilian Population: 1970 to 1999

[In thousands (137,085 represents 137,085,000), except as indicated. For the civilian noninstitutional population 16 years old and over. Annual averages of monthly figures. Based on Current Population Survey; see text, Section 1, Population, and Appendix III]

Year, sex, race, and Hispanic origin	Civilian noninstitutional population	Civilian labor force							Not in labor force	
		Total	Percent of population	Employed	Employment/population ratio [1]	Unemployed			Number	Percent of population
						Number	Percent of labor force			

Year, sex, race, and Hispanic origin	Civilian noninstitutional population	Total	Percent of population	Employed	Employment/population ratio [1]	Number	Percent of labor force	Number	Percent of population
Total: [2]									
1970.........	137,085	82,771	60.4	78,678	57.4	4,093	4.9	54,315	39.6
1980.........	167,745	106,940	63.8	99,303	59.2	7,637	7.1	60,806	36.2
1985. [3] ...	178,206	115,461	64.8	107,150	60.1	8,312	7.2	62,744	35.2
1990 [3]	189,164	125,840	66.5	118,793	62.8	7,047	5.6	63,324	33.5
1995.........	198,584	132,304	66.6	124,900	62.9	7,404	5.6	66,280	33.4
1997 [3]	203,133	136,297	67.1	129,558	63.8	6,739	4.9	66,837	32.9
1998 [3]	205,220	137,673	67.1	131,463	64.1	6,210	4.5	67,547	32.9
1999 [3]	207,753	139,368	67.1	133,488	64.3	5,880	4.2	68,385	32.9
Male:									
1970.........	64,304	51,228	79.7	48,990	76.2	2,238	4.4	13,076	20.3
1980.........	79,398	61,453	77.4	57,186	72.0	4,267	6.9	17,945	22.6
1985. [3] ...	84,469	64,411	76.3	59,891	70.9	4,521	7.0	20,058	23.7
1990 [3]	90,377	69,011	76.4	65,104	72.0	3,906	5.7	21,367	23.6
1995.........	95,178	71,360	75.0	67,377	70.8	3,983	5.6	23,818	25.0
1997 [3]	97,715	73,261	75.0	69,685	71.3	3,577	4.9	24,454	25.0
1998 [3]	98,758	73,959	74.9	70,693	71.6	3,266	4.4	24,799	25.1
1999 [3]	99,722	74,512	74.7	71,446	71.6	3,066	4.1	25,210	25.3
Female:									
1970.........	72,782	31,543	43.3	29,688	40.8	1,855	5.9	41,239	56.7
1980.........	88,348	45,487	51.5	42,117	47.7	3,370	7.4	42,861	48.5
1985. [3] ...	93,736	51,050	54.5	47,259	50.4	3,791	7.4	42,686	45.5
1990 [3]	98,787	56,829	57.5	53,689	54.3	3,140	5.5	41,957	42.5
1995.........	103,406	60,944	58.9	57,523	55.6	3,421	5.6	42,462	41.1
1997 [3]	105,418	63,036	59.8	59,873	56.8	3,162	5.0	42,382	40.2
1998 [3]	106,462	63,714	59.8	60,771	57.1	2,944	4.6	42,748	40.1
1999 [3]	108,031	64,855	60.0	62,042	57.4	2,814	4.3	43,175	40.0
White:									
1970.........	122,174	73,556	60.2	70,217	57.5	3,339	4.5	48,618	39.8
1980.........	146,122	93,600	64.1	87,715	60.0	5,884	6.3	52,523	35.9
1985. [3] ...	153,679	99,926	65.0	93,736	61.0	6,191	6.2	53,753	35.0
1990 [3]	160,625	107,447	66.9	102,261	63.7	5,186	4.8	53,178	33.1
1995.........	166,914	111,950	67.1	106,490	63.8	5,459	4.9	54,965	32.9
1997 [3]	169,993	114,693	67.5	109,856	64.6	4,836	4.2	55,301	32.5
1998 [3]	171,478	115,415	67.3	110,931	64.7	4,484	3.9	56,064	32.7
1999 [3]	173,085	116,509	67.3	112,235	64.8	4,273	3.7	56,577	32.7
Black:									
1973.........	14,917	8,976	60.2	8,128	54.5	846	9.4	5,941	39.8
1980.........	17,824	10,865	61.0	9,313	52.2	1,553	14.3	6,959	39.0
1985. [3] ...	19,664	12,364	62.9	10,501	53.4	1,864	15.1	7,299	37.1
1990 [3]	21,477	13,740	64.0	12,175	56.7	1,565	11.4	7,737	36.0
1995.........	23,246	14,817	63.7	13,279	57.1	1,538	10.4	8,429	36.3
1997 [3]	24,003	15,529	64.7	13,969	58.2	1,560	10.0	8,474	35.3
1998 [3]	24,373	15,982	65.6	14,556	59.7	1,426	8.9	8,391	34.4
1999 [3]	24,855	16,365	65.8	15,056	60.6	1,309	8.0	8,490	34.2
Hispanic: [4]									
1980.........	9,598	6,146	64.0	5,527	57.6	620	10.1	3,451	36.0
1985.........	11,915	7,698	64.6	6,888	57.8	811	10.5	4,217	35.4
1990 [3]	15,904	10,720	67.4	9,845	61.9	876	8.2	5,184	32.6
1995.........	18,629	12,267	65.8	11,127	59.7	1,140	9.3	6,362	34.2
1997 [3]	20,321	13,796	67.9	12,726	62.6	1,069	7.7	6,526	32.1
1998 [3]	21,070	14,317	67.9	13,291	63.1	1,026	7.2	6,753	32.1
1999 [3]	21,650	14,665	67.7	13,720	63.4	945	6.4	6,985	32.3
Mexican:									
1986.........	7,377	4,941	67.0	4,387	59.5	555	11.2	2,436	33.0
1990 [3]	9,752	6,707	68.8	6,146	63.0	561	8.4	3,045	31.2
1995.........	11,609	7,765	66.9	7,016	60.4	750	9.7	3,844	33.1
1997 [3]	12,443	8,546	68.7	7,884	63.4	662	7.7	3,897	31.3
1998 [3]	13,216	9,096	68.8	8,431	63.8	664	7.3	4,121	31.2
1999 [3]	13,582	9,267	68.2	8,656	63.7	611	6.6	4,315	31.8
Puerto Rican:									
1986.........	1,494	804	53.8	691	46.3	113	14.0	690	46.2
1990 [3]	1,718	960	55.9	870	50.6	91	9.5	758	44.1
1995.........	1,896	1,098	57.9	974	51.4	123	11.2	798	42.1
1997 [3]	2,139	1,293	60.4	1,166	54.5	127	9.8	846	39.6
1998 [3]	2,080	1,249	60.0	1,145	55.0	104	8.3	832	40.0
1999 [3]	2,058	1,269	61.6	1,165	56.6	104	8.2	789	38.3
Cuban:									
198..........	842	570	67.7	533	63.3	36	6.4	272	32.3
1990 [3]	918	603	65.7	559	60.9	44	7.2	315	34.3
1995.........	1,019	613	60.2	568	55.7	45	7.4	406	39.8
1997 [3]	1,025	646	63.0	603	58.8	43	6.6	379	37.0
1998 [3]	1,062	651	61.3	612	57.6	39	6.0	411	38.7
1999 [3]	1,141	714	62.6	681	59.7	33	4.6	427	37.4

[1] Civilian employed as a percent of the civilian noninstitutional population. [2] Includes other races, not shown separately. [3] See footnote 2, Table 643. [4] Persons of Hispanic origin may be of any race. Includes persons of other Hispanic origin, not shown separately.

Source: U.S. Bureau of Labor Statistics, Bulletin 2307; and *Employment and Earnings*, monthly, January issues.

No. 646. Civilian Labor Force—Percent Distribution by Sex and Age: 1970 to 1999

[For civilian noninstitutional population 16 years old and over (82,771 represents 82,771,000). Annual averages of monthly figures. Based on Current Population Survey; see text, Section 1, Population, and Appendix III]

Year and sex	Civilian labor force (1,000)	Percent distribution						
		16 to 19 years	20 to 24 years	25 to 34 years	35 to 44 years	45 to 54 years	55 to 64 years	65 yrs. and over
Total: 1970	82,771	8.8	12.8	20.6	19.9	20.5	13.6	3.9
1980	106,940	8.8	14.9	27.3	19.1	15.8	11.2	2.9
1990 [1]	125,840	6.2	11.7	28.6	25.5	16.1	9.2	2.7
1995	132,304	5.9	10.3	25.8	27.0	19.1	9.0	2.9
1998 [1]	137,673	6.0	9.9	23.8	27.3	20.6	9.6	2.8
1999 [1]	139,368	6.0	10.0	23.1	27.2	21.1	9.8	2.9
Male: 1970	51,228	7.8	11.2	22.1	20.4	20.3	13.9	4.2
1980	61,453	8.1	14.0	27.6	19.3	16.1	11.8	3.1
1990 [1]	69,011	5.9	11.4	28.8	25.3	16.1	9.6	2.9
1995	71,360	5.7	10.3	26.2	26.9	18.8	9.1	3.1
1998 [1]	73,959	5.7	9.8	24.1	27.4	20.2	9.8	3.0
1999 [1]	74,512	5.8	9.8	23.2	27.4	20.7	10.0	3.1
Female: 1970	31,543	10.3	15.5	18.1	18.9	20.7	13.2	3.3
1980	45,487	9.6	16.1	26.9	19.0	15.4	10.4	2.6
1990 [1]	56,829	6.5	12.0	28.3	25.8	16.1	8.7	2.6
1995	60,944	6.1	10.4	25.5	27.2	19.4	8.8	2.7
1998 [1]	63,714	6.3	10.1	23.6	27.1	21.0	9.4	2.5
1999 [1]	64,855	6.2	10.2	22.9	27.0	21.6	9.6	2.6

[1] See footnote 2, Table 643.
Source: U.S. Bureau of Labor Statistics, Bulletin 2307, and *Employment Earnings*, monthly, January issues.

No. 647. Civilian Labor Force and Participation Rates by Educational Attainment, Sex, Race, and Hispanic Origin: 1992 to 1999

[As of **March**. For the civilian noninstitutional population 25 to 64 years of age (102,387 represents 102,387,000). See Table 678 for unemployment data. Based on Current Population Survey; see text, Section 1, Population, and Appendix III]

Year, sex, and race	Civilian labor force					Participation rate [1]				
		Percent distribution								
	Total (1,000)	Less than high school diploma	High school graduate, no degree	Less than a bachelor's degree	College graduate	Total	Less than high school diploma	High school graduates, no degree	Less than a bachelor's degree	College graduate
Total: [2]										
1992	102,387	12.2	36.2	25.2	26.4	79.0	60.3	78.3	83.5	88.4
1995	106,519	10.8	33.1	27.8	28.3	79.3	59.8	77.3	83.2	88.7
1996	108,037	10.9	32.9	27.7	28.5	79.4	60.2	77.9	83.7	87.8
1997 [3]	110,514	10.9	33.0	27.4	28.6	80.1	61.7	82.5	83.7	88.5
1998 [3]	111,857	10.7	32.8	27.4	29.1	80.2	63.0	78.4	83.5	88.0
1999 [3]	112,542	10.3	32.3	27.4	30.0	80.0	62.7	78.1	83.0	87.6
Male:										
1992 . . .	55,917	13.9	34.7	23.8	27.5	88.6	75.1	89.0	91.8	93.7
1995 . . .	57,454	12.2	32.3	25.7	29.7	87.4	72.0	86.9	90.1	93.8
1996 . . .	58,121	12.7	32.2	26.0	29.1	87.5	74.3	86.9	90.0	92.9
1997 [3] . .	59,268	12.8	32.2	25.8	29.2	87.7	75.2	86.4	90.6	93.5
1998 [3] . .	59,905	12.3	32.3	25.8	29.6	87.8	75.3	86.7	90.0	93.4
1999 [3] . .	60,030	11.7	32.0	25.8	30.5	87.5	74.4	86.6	89.4	93.0
Female:										
1992 . . .	46,469	10.2	37.9	26.9	25.0	70.0	45.6	69.1	76.2	82.2
1995 . . .	49,065	9.1	34.1	30.2	26.6	71.5	47.2	68.9	77.3	82.8
1996 . . .	49,916	8.8	33.7	29.7	27.8	71.8	45.7	69.8	78.1	82.3
1997 [3] . .	51,246	8.7	34.0	29.3	28.0	72.8	47.1	71.4	77.6	83.2
1998 [3] . .	51,953	8.8	33.3	29.3	28.6	73.0	49.8	70.9	77.8	82.3
1999 [3] . .	52,512	8.7	32.7	29.2	29.5	72.8	50.5	70.4	77.4	81.9
White:										
1992 . . .	87,656	11.3	36.1	25.5	27.1	79.8	61.5	78.7	83.8	88.7
1995 . . .	90,192	10.0	32.8	27.8	29.3	80.1	61.6	77.9	83.4	88.8
1996 . . .	91,506	10.4	32.8	27.5	29.3	80.4	62.5	78.6	83.9	88.2
1997 [3] . .	93,179	10.4	32.8	27.3	29.5	81.0	63.8	79.2	83.9	89.0
1998 [3] . .	93,527	10.2	32.7	27.4	29.8	80.6	63.8	78.6	83.5	88.3
1999 [3] . .	94,216	9.8	32.2	27.2	30.8	80.6	64.2	78.5	83.3	87.9
Black:										
1992 . . .	10,936	19.2	40.3	24.9	15.6	74.4	55.4	76.9	83.4	89.1
1995 . . .	11,695	14.1	38.6	29.6	17.7	74.2	51.0	74.5	82.8	90.9
1996 . . .	11,891	14.2	37.2	31.2	17.4	73.7	50.1	74.3	83.0	87.9
1997 [3] . .	12,253	14.3	37.8	31.3	16.6	74.9	52.9	75.0	83.8	89.0
1998 [3] . .	12,893	14.3	37.3	30.1	18.2	77.7	59.3	77.0	85.0	88.8
1999 [3] . .	12,945	13.0	37.2	30.4	19.5	76.5	55.1	76.5	82.9	88.6
Hispanic: [4]										
1992 . . .	7,702	39.1	30.2	19.3	11.4	73.8	64.6	77.5	84.2	87.1
1995 . . .	9,298	38.9	28.2	21.3	11.6	73.2	64.7	75.9	81.9	87.9
1996 . . .	9,683	38.9	28.5	21.2	11.3	74.2	65.0	78.2	83.7	87.2
1997 [3] . .	10,556	37.4	28.1	22.1	12.4	75.9	66.4	79.4	85.3	87.7
1998 [3] . .	10,922	37.3	29.1	20.3	13.3	75.8	67.9	78.8	82.3	86.9
1999 [3] . .	11,129	36.5	29.2	21.4	12.9	75.7	67.0	79.0	84.0	85.0

[1] See headnote, Table 644.   [2] Includes other races, not shown separately.   [3] See footnote 2, Table 643.   [4] Persons of Hispanic origin may be of any race.
Source: U.S. Bureau of Labor Statistics, unpublished data.

Labor Force, Employment, and Earnings   405

No. 648. Characteristics of the Civilian Labor Force by State: 1999

[In thousands (139,368 represents 139,368,000), except ratio and rate. Preliminary. For civilian noninstitutional population 16 years old and over. Annual averages of monthly figures. Because of separate processing and weighting procedures, the totals for the United States may differ from results obtained by aggregating totals for states]

State	Total		Employed		Em-ployed/popula-tion ratio [1]	Unemployed					Participation rate [3]	
						Total		Rate [2]				
	Number	Female	Total	Female		Num-ber	Female	Total	Male	Female	Male	Female
United States .	**139,368**	**64,855**	**133,488**	**62,042**	**64.3**	**5,880**	**2,814**	**4.2**	**4.1**	**4.3**	**74.7**	**60.0**
Alabama	2,145	1,007	2,043	955	60.3	102	51	4.8	4.5	5.1	70.5	56.7
Alaska	315	145	295	136	68.8	20	8	6.4	7.0	5.6	80.6	66.6
Arizona	2,364	1,093	2,260	1,039	63.3	104	54	4.4	3.9	4.9	74.8	58.4
Arkansas	1,222	570	1,167	546	60.0	55	25	4.5	4.6	4.3	69.7	56.4
California	16,586	7,471	15,722	7,068	62.8	864	404	5.2	5.1	5.4	74.9	58.1
Colorado	2,264	1,032	2,198	1,002	71.4	66	30	2.9	2.9	3.0	80.1	66.9
Connecticut	1,692	810	1,638	787	65.4	53	22	3.2	3.5	2.7	73.9	61.7
Delaware	389	185	375	180	64.7	14	5	3.5	4.1	2.9	73.1	61.5
Dist. of Columbia .	282	145	264	135	63.4	18	10	6.3	5.5	7.0	71.6	64.3
Florida	7,366	3,425	7,082	3,279	60.1	284	146	3.9	3.5	4.3	70.3	55.4
Georgia	4,088	1,956	3,925	1,863	66.8	163	93	4.0	3.3	4.7	76.8	63.1
Hawaii	595	298	561	285	63.2	33	13	5.6	6.8	4.4	70.7	63.6
Idaho.	655	292	621	278	66.1	34	15	5.2	5.3	5.0	77.5	62.0
Illinois	6,385	3,005	6,112	2,875	66.7	274	130	4.3	4.2	4.3	76.9	63.0
Indiana	3,078	1,428	2,985	1,382	66.2	93	46	3.0	2.8	3.2	76.0	61.1
Iowa	1,574	733	1,534	717	70.1	40	16	2.5	2.8	2.2	77.8	66.1
Kansas	1,434	678	1,392	659	70.0	43	19	3.0	3.2	2.8	78.3	66.3
Kentucky	1,970	897	1,882	857	61.5	88	41	4.5	4.4	4.5	72.5	56.7
Louisiana	2,052	991	1,948	935	59.4	104	56	5.1	4.5	5.6	70.3	56.0
Maine	672	321	644	309	65.1	28	12	4.1	4.4	3.8	73.8	62.4
Maryland	2,766	1,338	2,668	1,293	67.3	98	45	3.5	3.7	3.4	75.1	64.9
Massachusetts . .	3,278	1,552	3,173	1,500	66.5	105	52	3.2	3.1	3.4	74.8	63.0
Michigan	5,136	2,344	4,942	2,252	66.0	194	92	3.8	3.6	3.9	76.3	61.2
Minnesota	2,699	1,275	2,623	1,240	73.0	75	35	2.8	2.9	2.7	80.4	69.9
Mississippi	1,270	604	1,205	573	58.0	65	31	5.1	5.0	5.2	69.7	53.9
Missouri	2,847	1,303	2,751	1,266	66.4	96	37	3.4	3.8	2.9	76.4	61.4
Montana	474	221	449	209	65.6	25	11	5.2	5.3	5.1	74.9	63.6
Nebraska	911	430	885	418	71.0	26	13	2.9	2.8	3.0	80.0	66.6
Nevada	942	425	900	406	66.0	42	19	4.4	4.5	4.4	76.6	61.7
New Hampshire . .	666	311	648	304	70.3	18	8	2.7	2.9	2.5	78.7	66.2
New Jersey	4,207	1,950	4,013	1,856	64.1	193	95	4.6	4.4	4.9	75.5	59.5
New Mexico	810	379	764	358	58.5	46	20	5.6	5.9	5.4	69.3	55.3
New York	8,883	4,171	8,424	3,958	59.7	459	213	5.2	5.2	5.1	70.9	55.8
North Carolina. . .	3,874	1,814	3,752	1,746	65.1	122	68	3.2	2.6	3.7	74.8	60.3
North Dakota . . .	337	160	325	155	68.1	11	5	3.4	3.6	3.2	76.1	65.2
Ohio	5,749	2,717	5,503	2,602	64.0	246	116	4.3	4.3	4.3	74.1	60.3
Oklahoma	1,648	774	1,591	745	62.9	57	29	3.4	3.2	3.7	72.6	58.4
Oregon	1,760	806	1,660	759	64.3	100	47	5.7	5.6	5.8	76.2	60.6
Pennsylvania . . .	5,969	2,812	5,707	2,692	61.6	262	119	4.4	4.5	4.2	72.1	57.5
Rhode Island . . .	504	240	483	231	64.4	21	10	4.1	4.3	4.0	74.3	60.8
South Carolina . .	1,962	936	1,874	890	62.7	88	46	4.5	4.1	4.9	72.9	59.2
South Dakota . . .	400	190	388	185	71.1	12	6	2.9	2.9	3.0	78.5	68.2
Tennessee	2,819	1,336	2,705	1,287	63.6	114	49	4.0	4.4	3.6	73.6	59.7
Texas	10,206	4,622	9,734	4,389	65.6	472	233	4.6	4.3	5.0	77.9	60.3
Utah	1,084	490	1,043	471	69.6	40	19	3.7	3.6	3.9	81.8	63.3
Vermont	336	160	326	156	69.9	10	4	3.0	3.5	2.6	77.9	66.5
Virginia	3,522	1,651	3,424	1,596	65.6	98	55	2.8	2.3	3.3	75.1	60.6
Washington	3,076	1,434	2,931	1,364	66.9	145	69	4.7	4.6	4.8	77.6	63.3
West Virginia . . .	817	382	763	360	52.7	54	23	6.6	7.2	5.9	65.0	49.1
Wisconsin.	2,892	1,359	2,804	1,321	70.1	88	39	3.0	3.2	2.8	77.6	67.2
Wyoming	262	122	249	116	67.8	13	6	4.9	5.0	4.7	78.5	64.3

[1] Civilian employment as a percent of civilian noninstitutional population.   [2] Percent unemployed of the civilian labor force.
[3] Percent of civilian noninstitutional population of each specified group in the civilian labor force.

Source: U.S. Bureau of Labor Statistics, "Local Area Unemployment Statistics, Geographic Profile" Internet site <http://stats.bls.gov./lauhome.htm>.

No. 649. Civilian Labor Force by Selected Metropolitan Area: 1998

[For the civilian noninstitutional population 16 years old and over (137,673 represents 137,673,000). Annual averages of monthly figures. Data are derived from the Local Area Unemployment Statistics Program. For composition of metropolitan areas, see Appendix II]

Metropolitan areas ranked by labor force size, 1998	Civilian labor force (1,000)	Unemployment rate [1]	Metropolitan areas ranked by labor force size, 1998	Civilian labor force (1,000)	Unemployment rate [1]
U.S. total	137,673	4.5	Indianapolis, IN MSA	835	2.5
Los Angeles-Long Beach, CA PMSA . . .	4,641	6.5	Columbus, OH MSA	812	2.7
Chicago, IL PMSA	4,164	4.3	Milwaukee-Waukesha, WI PMSA	809	3.3
New York, NY PMSA	4,092	7.3	San Antonio, TX MSA.	759	3.7
Washington, DC-MD-VA-WV PMSA. . . .	2,559	3.2	Sacramento, CA PMSA.	758	4.9
Philadelphia, PA-NJ PMSA	2,493	4.3	Fort Lauderdale, FL PMSA	757	4.5
Detroit, MI PMSA.	2,255	3.5	Charlotte-Gastonia-Rock Hill,		
Houston, TX MSA	2,129	4.1	NC-SC MSA	746	2.7
Atlanta, GA MSA	2,123	3.3	Norfolk-Virginia Beach-Newport News,		
Dallas, TX PMSA.	1,870	3.2	VA-NC MSA	735	3.5
Boston, MA-NH PMSA	1,817	2.8	Las Vegas, NV-AZ MSA	698	4.2
Minneapolis-St. Paul, MN-WI MSA	1,678	2.0	Austin-San Marcos, TX MSA	682	2.6
Phoenix-Mesa, AZ MSA	1,507	2.7	Salt Lake City-Ogden, UT MSA	681	3.6
Orange County, CA PMSA.	1,435	2.9	Bergen-Passaic, NJ PMSA	673	4.4
Nassau-Suffolk, NY PMSA	1,399	3.2	Nashville, TN MSA.	642	2.7
Riverside-San Bernardino, CA PMSA . .	1,382	6.1	Middlesex-Somerset-Hunterdon,		
Seattle-Bellevue-Everett, WA PMSA . . .	1,382	3.1	NJ PMSA	633	3.3
St. Louis, MO-IL MSA.	1,321	4.3	Greensboro-Winston-Salem-High Point,		
San Diego, CA MSA.	1,319	3.5	NC MSA.	632	2.7
Baltimore, MD PMSA	1,299	5.1	Raleigh-Durham-Chapel Hill, NC MSA . .	622	1.7
Oakland, CA PMSA	1,191	3.9	New Orleans, LA MSA	621	4.9
Tampa-St. Petersburg-Clearwater,			Grand Rapids-Muskegon-Holland,		
FL MSA	1,173	3.0	MI MSA	595	3.0
Pittsburgh, PA MSA	1,151	4.6	Hartford, CT MSA	581	3.5
Denver, CO PMSA.	1,128	3.2	Rochester, NY MSA.	575	4.0
Cleveland-Lorain-Elyria, OH PMSA	1,106	4.4	Buffalo-Niagara Falls, NY MSA.	575	5.3
Portland-Vancouver, OR-WA PMSA. . . .	1,048	4.2	Providence-Fall River-Warwick,		
Miami, FL PMSA	1,037	6.5	RI-MA MSA.	573	4.9
Newark, NJ PMSA.	1,010	4.5	Memphis, TN-AR-MS MSA	552	3.7
Kansas City, MO-KS MSA.	967	3.8	Louisville, KY-IN MSA.	549	3.3
San Jose, CA PMSA	963	3.2	Oklahoma City, OK MSA.	534	3.8
San Francisco, CA PMSA	949	3.0	Jacksonville, FL MSA	534	3.1
Fort Worth-Arlington, TX PMSA	879	3.3	Monmouth-Ocean, NJ PMSA	515	4.3
Orlando, FL MSA.	842	3.0	West Palm Beach-Boca Raton, FL MSA.	508	5.5
Cincinnati, OH-KY-IN PMSA	839	3.4	Richmond-Petersburg, VA MSA	507	2.6

[1] Percent unemployed of the civilian labor force.

Source: U.S. Bureau of Labor Statistics, Local Area Unemployment Statistics program.

No. 650. School Enrollment and Labor Force Status: 1980 and 1999

[In thousands (37,103 represents 37,103,000), except percent. As of October. For the civilian noninstitutional population 16 to 24 years old. Based on Current Population Survey; see text, Section 1, Population, and Appendix III]

Characteristic	Population		Civilian labor force		Employed		Unemployed		
							1980, total	1999 [1]	
	1980	1999 [1]	1980	1999 [1]	1980	1999 [1]		Total	Rate [2]
Total, 16 to 24 years [3].	37,103	34,173	24,918	22,135	21,454	20,044	3,464	2,091	9.4
Enrolled in school [3]	15,713	18,371	7,454	9,199	6,433	8,380	1,021	819	8.9
16 to 19 years	11,126	12,451	4,836	5,510	4,029	4,892	807	618	11.2
20 to 24 years	4,587	5,920	2,618	3,688	2,404	3,488	214	200	5.4
Sex:									
Male	7,997	9,217	3,825	4,516	3,259	4,065	566	452	10.0
Female	7,716	9,154	3,629	4,682	3,174	4,315	455	367	7.8
College level	7,664	9,400	3,996	5,503	3,632	5,194	364	309	5.6
Full time.	6,396	7,976	2,854	4,258	2,554	4,022	300	236	5.6
Race:									
White	13,242	14,523	6,687	7,762	5,889	7,166	798	596	7.7
Below college	6,566	6,990	3,095	3,153	2,579	2,765	516	388	12.3
College level	6,678	7,533	3,592	4,609	3,310	4,401	282	208	4.5
Black.	2,028	2,654	595	963	406	776	189	187	19.4
Below college	1,282	1,470	294	391	174	276	120	115	29.3
College level	747	1,183	300	572	230	499	70	72	12.7
Not enrolled [3]	21,390	15,801	17,464	12,936	15,021	11,664	2,443	1,272	9.8
White	18,103	12,700	15,121	10,593	13,318	9,757	1,803	836	7.9
Black	2,864	2,463	2,055	1,865	1,451	1,485	604	380	20.4

[1] See footnote 2, Table 643. [2] Percent of civilian labor force in each category. [3] Includes other races, not shown separately.

Source: U.S. Bureau of Labor Statistics, Bulletin 2307; News, USDL 00-136, May 17, 2000; and unpublished data.

Labor Force, Employment, and Earnings   407

No. 651. Labor Force Participation Rates by Marital Status, Sex, and Age: 1960 to 1999

[Annual averages of monthly figures. See Table 648 for definition of participation rate. Based on Current Population Survey; see text, Section 1, Population, and Appendix III]

Marital status and year	Male participation rate							Female participation rate						
	Total	16-19 years	20-24 years	25-34 years	35-44 years	45-64 years	65 and over	Total	16-19 years	20-24 years	25-34 years	35-44 years	45-64 years	65 and over
Single:														
1960	69.8	42.6	80.3	91.5	88.6	80.1	31.2	58.6	30.2	77.2	83.4	82.9	79.8	24.3
1970	65.5	54.6	73.8	87.9	86.2	75.7	25.2	56.8	44.7	73.0	81.4	78.6	73.0	19.7
1980	72.6	59.9	81.3	89.2	82.2	66.9	16.8	64.4	53.6	75.2	83.3	76.9	65.6	13.9
1985	73.8	56.3	81.5	89.4	84.6	65.5	15.6	66.6	52.3	76.3	82.4	80.8	67.9	9.8
1990 [1]	74.8	55.1	81.6	89.9	84.5	67.3	15.7	66.7	51.7	74.5	80.9	80.8	66.2	12.1
1994 [1]	73.9	53.6	80.5	88.4	83.1	67.8	17.8	66.7	51.4	73.6	78.9	78.7	68.8	12.7
1995	73.7	54.4	80.3	88.7	81.4	67.0	17.9	66.8	52.2	72.9	80.2	79.5	67.3	11.6
1996	73.3	52.8	79.8	89.1	82.1	67.4	18.2	67.1	51.5	73.3	80.9	79.4	68.5	12.2
1997 [1]	73.1	51.9	80.1	89.0	82.1	68.5	14.8	67.9	51.0	75.1	82.3	80.1	70.8	11.5
1998 [1]	73.3	52.9	79.7	89.1	82.5	70.2	15.2	68.5	52.4	75.3	83.0	80.9	69.9	9.7
1999 [1]	73.4	52.5	79.7	89.5	83.5	70.6	17.3	68.7	51.1	76.1	84.2	80.8	69.6	9.9
Married: [2]														
1960	89.2	91.5	97.1	98.8	98.6	93.7	36.6	31.9	27.2	31.7	28.8	37.2	36.0	6.7
1970	86.1	92.3	94.7	98.0	98.1	91.2	29.9	40.5	37.8	47.9	38.8	46.8	44.0	7.3
1980	80.9	91.3	96.9	97.5	97.2	84.3	20.5	49.8	49.3	61.4	58.8	61.8	46.9	7.3
1985	78.7	91.0	95.6	97.4	96.8	81.7	16.8	53.8	49.6	65.7	65.8	68.1	49.4	6.6
1990 [1]	78.6	92.1	95.6	96.9	96.7	82.6	17.5	58.4	49.5	66.1	69.6	74.0	56.5	8.5
1994 [1]	77.4	88.7	94.2	95.9	95.6	81.9	18.1	60.7	48.9	65.8	71.6	75.8	61.9	9.4
1995	77.5	89.2	94.9	96.3	95.4	82.4	18.0	61.0	51.6	64.7	72.0	75.7	62.7	9.1
1996	77.6	84.4	94.5	96.4	95.4	83.2	18.3	61.2	48.6	66.0	71.7	75.8	63.7	9.0
1997 [1]	77.7	84.6	94.9	96.1	95.7	83.6	18.3	61.6	50.1	66.1	71.9	76.0	64.6	8.9
1998 [1]	77.6	83.8	95.0	96.4	95.8	83.7	17.5	61.2	49.8	66.1	71.6	74.5	64.9	8.9
1999 [1]	77.5	83.2	93.7	96.5	95.9	83.4	18.3	61.2	49.8	64.5	70.9	74.6	65.3	9.6
Other: [3]														
1960	63.1	(B)	96.9	95.2	94.4	83.2	22.7	41.6	43.5	58.0	63.1	70.0	60.0	11.4
1970	60.7	(B)	90.4	93.7	91.1	78.5	19.3	40.3	48.6	60.3	64.6	68.8	61.9	10.0
1980	67.5	(B)	92.6	94.1	91.9	73.3	13.7	43.6	50.0	68.4	76.5	77.1	60.2	8.2
1985	68.7	(B)	95.1	93.7	91.8	72.8	11.4	45.1	51.9	66.2	76.9	81.6	61.0	7.5
1990 [1]	68.9	(B)	93.1	93.0	90.7	74.9	12.0	47.2	53.9	65.4	77.0	82.1	65.0	8.4
1994 [1]	66.8	(B)	91.0	90.3	88.6	72.6	11.9	47.5	46.2	66.6	74.3	80.4	67.6	8.7
1995	66.2	(B)	92.7	90.9	88.2	72.4	12.1	47.4	55.8	67.2	77.1	80.7	67.2	8.4
1996	66.4	(B)	90.6	92.0	88.8	73.1	11.5	48.1	42.6	70.7	78.5	82.1	67.7	8.0
1997 [1]	67.4	60.8	89.9	92.1	89.6	74.7	13.2	48.6	49.7	70.4	80.2	81.9	68.6	8.1
1998 [1]	66.9	66.2	89.1	93.0	89.1	73.7	13.1	48.8	50.4	73.7	81.0	82.8	68.6	8.4
1999 [1]	65.9	(B)	90.2	92.3	88.7	73.4	12.3	49.1	45.3	73.6	82.4	83.4	69.1	8.4

B For 1960, percentage not shown where base is less than 50,000; beginning 1970, 35,000. [1] See footnote 2, Table 643. [2] Spouse present. [3] Widowed, divorced, and married (spouse absent).

Source: U.S. Bureau of Labor Statistics, Bulletins 2217 and 2340; and unpublished data.

No. 652. Marital Status of Women in the Civilian Labor Force: 1960 to 1999

[Annual averages of monthly figures (23,240 represent 23,240,000). For civilian noninstitutional population 16 years old and over. Based on the Current Population Survey; see text, Section 1, Population, and Appendix III]

Year	Female labor force (1,000)				Female participation rate [3]			
	Total	Single	Married [1]	Other [2]	Total	Single	Married [1]	Other [2]
1960	23,240	5,410	12,893	4,937	37.7	58.6	31.9	41.6
1970	31,543	7,265	18,475	5,804	43.3	56.8	40.5	40.3
1975	37,475	9,125	21,484	6,866	46.3	59.8	44.3	40.1
1980	45,487	11,865	24,980	8,643	51.5	64.4	49.9	43.6
1982	47,755	12,460	25,971	9,324	52.6	65.1	51.1	44.8
1983	48,503	12,659	26,468	9,376	52.9	65.0	51.8	44.4
1984	49,709	12,867	27,199	9,644	53.6	65.6	52.8	44.7
1985	51,050	13,163	27,894	9,993	54.5	66.6	53.8	45.1
1986	52,413	13,512	28,623	10,277	55.3	67.2	54.9	45.6
1987	53,658	13,885	29,381	10,393	56.0	67.4	55.9	45.7
1988	54,742	14,194	29,921	10,627	56.6	67.7	56.7	46.2
1989	56,030	14,377	30,548	11,104	57.4	68.0	57.8	47.0
1990 [4]	56,829	14,612	30,901	11,315	57.5	66.7	58.4	47.2
1991	57,178	14,681	31,112	11,385	57.4	66.2	58.5	46.8
1992	58,141	14,872	31,700	11,570	57.8	66.2	59.3	47.1
1993	58,795	15,031	31,980	11,784	57.9	66.2	59.4	47.2
1994 [4]	60,239	15,333	32,888	12,018	58.8	66.7	60.7	47.5
1995	60,944	15,467	33,359	12,118	58.9	66.8	61.0	47.4
1996	61,857	15,842	33,618	12,397	59.3	67.1	61.2	48.1
1997 [4]	63,036	16,492	33,802	12,742	59.8	67.9	61.6	48.6
1998 [4]	63,714	17,087	33,857	12,771	59.8	68.5	61.2	48.8
1999 [4]	64,855	17,575	34,372	12,909	60.0	68.7	61.2	49.1

[1] Husband present. [2] Widowed, divorced, or separated. [3] See Table 648 for definition of participation rate. [4] See footnote 2, Table 643.

Source: U.S. Bureau of Labor Statistics, Bulletin 2307; and unpublished data.

No. 653. Employment Status of Women by Marital Status and Presence and Age of Children: 1970 to 1999

[As of **March (7.0 represents 7,000,000).** For the civilian noninstitutional persons 16 years and over, thereafter 16 years old and over. Based on the Current Population Survey; see text, Section 1, Population, and Appendix III]

Item	Total			With any children								
				Total			Children 6 to 17 only			Children under 6		
	Single	Mar-ried [1]	Other [2]	Single	Mar-ried [1]	Other [2]	Single	Mar-ried [1]	Other [2]	Single	Mar-ried [1]	Other [2]
IN LABOR FORCE (mil.)												
1970	7.0	18.4	5.9	(NA)	10.2	1.9	(NA)	6.3	1.3	(NA)	3.9	0.6
1980	11.2	24.9	8.8	0.6	13.7	3.6	0.2	8.4	2.6	0.3	5.2	1.0
1985	12.9	27.7	10.3	1.1	14.9	4.0	0.4	8.5	2.9	0.7	6.4	1.1
1990	14.0	31.0	11.2	1.5	16.5	4.2	0.6	9.3	3.0	0.9	7.2	1.2
1995	15.0	33.6	12.0	2.1	18.0	4.6	0.8	10.2	3.3	1.3	7.8	1.3
1996	15.4	33.4	12.4	2.2	17.8	4.7	0.9	10.2	3.4	1.4	7.6	1.3
1997 [3]	16.2	33.9	12.8	2.8	18.2	4.7	1.0	10.6	3.4	1.8	7.6	1.3
1998 [3]	16.9	34.1	12.9	3.0	18.1	4.5	1.2	10.5	3.3	1.8	7.7	1.2
1999 [3]	17.5	34.3	13.0	3.1	17.9	4.6	1.2	10.6	3.3	1.8	7.2	1.3
PARTICIPATION RATE [4]												
1970	53.0	40.8	39.1	(NA)	39.7	60.7	(NA)	49.2	66.9	(NA)	30.3	52.2
1980	61.5	50.1	44.0	52.0	54.1	69.4	67.6	61.7	74.6	44.1	45.1	60.3
1985	65.2	54.2	45.6	51.6	60.8	71.9	64.1	67.8	77.8	46.5	53.4	59.7
1990	66.4	58.2	46.8	55.2	66.3	74.2	69.7	73.6	79.7	48.7	58.9	63.6
1995	65.5	61.1	47.3	57.5	70.2	75.3	67.0	76.2	79.5	53.0	63.5	66.3
1996	65.2	61.1	48.2	60.5	70.0	77.0	71.8	76.7	80.6	55.1	62.7	69.2
1997 [3]	66.8	62.1	48.7	68.1	71.1	79.1	74.0	77.6	81.1	65.1	63.6	74.2
1998 [3]	68.1	61.8	49.4	72.5	70.6	79.7	81.2	76.8	82.7	67.3	63.7	72.5
1999 [3]	68.1	61.6	49.4	73.4	70.1	80.4	82.6	77.1	81.8	68.1	61.8	77.1
EMPLOYMENT (mil.)												
1970	6.5	17.5	5.6	(NA)	9.6	1.8	(NA)	6.0	1.2	(NA)	3.6	0.6
1980	10.1	23.6	8.2	0.4	12.8	3.3	0.2	8.1	2.4	0.2	4.8	0.9
1985	11.6	26.1	9.4	0.9	13.9	3.5	0.3	8.1	2.6	0.5	5.9	0.9
1990	12.9	29.9	10.5	1.2	15.8	3.8	0.5	8.9	2.7	0.7	6.9	1.1
1995	13.7	32.3	11.3	1.8	17.2	4.2	0.7	9.8	3.1	1.1	7.3	1.2
1996	14.1	32.3	11.7	1.8	17.1	4.4	0.7	9.8	3.2	1.1	7.3	1.2
1997 [3]	14.7	32.8	12.1	2.3	17.5	4.3	0.9	10.3	3.1	1.4	7.3	1.1
1998 [3]	15.6	33.0	12.2	2.5	17.4	4.2	1.1	10.1	3.1	1.4	7.3	1.1
1999 [3]	16.2	33.4	12.3	2.7	17.3	4.3	1.1	10.4	3.1	1.6	7.0	1.1
UNEMPLOY-MENT RATE [5]												
1970	7.1	4.8	4.8	(NA)	6.0	7.2	(NA)	4.8	5.9	(NA)	7.9	9.8
1980	10.3	5.3	6.4	23.2	5.9	9.2	15.6	4.4	7.9	29.2	8.3	12.8
1985	10.2	5.7	8.5	23.8	6.6	12.1	15.4	5.5	10.6	28.5	8.0	16.1
1990	8.2	3.5	5.7	18.4	4.2	8.5	14.5	3.8	7.7	20.8	4.8	10.2
1995	8.7	3.9	5.8	16.6	4.3	8.1	11.8	3.6	7.1	19.5	5.3	10.8
1996	8.6	3.4	5.5	18.5	3.5	6.4	15.7	3.2	5.1	20.3	3.9	9.7
1997 [3]	8.8	3.2	5.8	16.9	3.5	9.0	13.5	2.9	7.9	18.8	4.4	11.7
1998 [3]	7.5	3.2	5.0	15.1	3.8	6.7	11.8	3.2	5.3	17.5	4.5	10.6
1999 [3]	7.4	2.8	5.0	11.7	2.9	6.2	8.9	2.4	4.5	13.6	3.7	10.7

NA Not available. [1] Husband present. [2] Widowed, divorced, or separated. [3] See footnote 2, Table 643. [4] Percent of women in each specific category in the labor force. [5] Unemployed as a percent of civilian labor force in specified group.
Source: U.S. Bureau of Labor Statistics, Bulletin 2307; and unpublished data.

No. 654. Labor Force Participation Rates for Wives, Husband Present by Age of Own Youngest Child: 1975 to 1999

[As of **March. For civilian noninstitutional population, 16 years old and over.** For definition of participation rate, see Table 653. Based on Current Population Survey; see text, Section 1, Population, and Appendix III]

Presence and age of child	Total			White			Black		
	1975	1985	1999 [1]	1975	1985	1999 [1]	1975	1985	1999 [1]
Wives, total	44.4	54.2	61.6	43.6	53.3	60.7	54.1	63.8	71.6
No children under 18	43.8	48.2	54.4	43.6	47.5	53.8	47.6	55.2	60.7
With children under 18	44.9	60.8	70.1	43.6	59.9	69.2	58.4	71.7	83.0
Under 6, total..........	36.7	53.4	61.8	34.7	52.1	60.6	54.9	69.6	80.1
Under 3..........	32.7	50.5	59.2	30.7	49.4	58.2	50.1	66.2	77.4
1 year or under	30.8	49.4	59.2	29.2	48.6	57.6	50.0	63.7	83.5
2 years...........	37.1	54.0	61.2	35.1	52.7	60.8	56.4	69.9	79.5
3 to 5 years	42.2	58.4	65.7	40.1	56.6	64.2	61.2	73.8	83.5
3 years...........	41.2	55.1	63.2	39.0	52.7	61.9	62.7	72.3	81.2
4 years...........	41.2	59.7	69.0	38.7	58.4	68.0	64.9	70.6	80.3
5 years...........	44.4	62.1	65.8	43.8	59.9	63.2	56.3	79.1	88.0
6 to 13 years	51.8	68.2	76.4	50.7	67.7	75.6	65.7	73.3	87.0
14 to 17 years	53.5	67.0	78.7	53.4	66.6	79.1	52.3	74.4	79.7

[1] See footnote 2, Table 643.
Source: U.S. Bureau of Labor Statistics, Bulletin 2340; and unpublished data.

Labor Force, Employment, and Earnings **409**

No. 655. Families With Own Children—Employment Status of Parents: 1995 and 1999

[Annual average of monthly figures (33,544 represents 33,544,000). For families with own children. Based on the Current Population Survey, see text, Section 1, Population, and Appendix III]

Characteristic	Number (1,000) 1995	Number (1,000) 1999	Percent distribution 1995	Percent distribution 1999	Characteristic	Number (1,000) 1995	Number (1,000) 1999	Percent distribution 1995	Percent distribution 1999
WITH OWN CHILDREN UNDER 18					Father employed, not mother	2,921	3,061	22.5	22.6
					Neither parent employed	517	390	4.0	2.9
Total families	33,544	34,340	100.0	100.0					
Parent(s) employed	29,659	31,493	88.4	91.7	Families maintained by women [1]	4,360	4,722	100.0	100.0
No parent employed	3,886	2,847	11.6	8.3	Mother employed	3,142	3,737	72.1	79.1
					Mother not employed	1,219	985	27.9	20.9
Married-couple families	24,604	24,904	100.0	100.0					
Parent(s) employed	23,643	24,243	96.1	97.3	Families maintained by men [1]	908	1,077	100.0	100.0
Mother employed	16,629	16,995	67.6	68.2	Father employed	766	913	84.3	84.8
Both parents employed	15,491	15,958	63.0	64.1	Father not employed	143	164	15.7	15.2
Mother employed, not father	1,137	1,037	4.6	4.2	WITH OWN CHILDREN UNDER 6				
Father employed, not mother	7,014	7,249	28.5	29.1	Total families	15,275	14,976	100.0	100.0
Neither parent employed	962	662	3.9	2.7	Parent(s) employed	13,267	13,670	86.9	91.3
					No parent employed	2,007	1,307	13.1	8.7
Families maintained by women [1]	7,433	7,653	100.0	100.0	Married-couple families	11,604	11,340	100.0	100.0
Mother employed	4,755	5,713	64.0	74.7	Parent(s) employed	11,159	11,070	96.2	97.6
Mother not employed	2,678	1,940	36.0	25.3	Mother employed	7,066	6,882	60.9	60.7
					Both parents employed	6,646	6,512	57.3	57.4
Families maintained by men [1]	1,507	1,782	100.0	100.0	Mother employed, not father	421	370	3.6	3.3
Father employed	1,261	1,537	83.7	86.3	Father employed, not mother	4,092	4,188	35.3	36.9
Father not employed	245	245	16.3	13.7	Neither parent employed	445	270	3.8	2.4
WITH OWN CHILDREN 6 to 17					Families maintained by women [1]	3,073	2,931	100.0	100.0
Total families	18,270	19,364	100.0	100.0	Mother employed	1,613	1,976	52.5	67.4
Parent(s) employed	16,391	17,825	89.7	92.1	Mother not employed	1,460	956	47.5	32.6
No parent employed	1,878	1,539	10.3	7.9					
					Families maintained by men [1]	598	705	100.0	100.0
Married-couple families	13,001	13,565	100.0	100.0	Father employed	496	624	82.8	88.5
Parent(s) employed	12,484	13,175	96.0	97.1	Father not employed	102	81	17.1	11.5
Mother employed	9,562	10,113	73.6	74.6					
Both parents employed	8,846	9,446	68.0	69.6					
Mother employed, not father	717	668	5.5	4.9					

[1] No spouse present.

Source: U.S. Bureau of Labor Statistics, *News,* USDL 97-195, June 16, 1997; and USDL 00-172, June 22, 2000.

No. 656. Employed Civilians and Weekly Hours: 1970 to 1999

[In thousands (78,678 represents 78,678,000, except as indicated. For civilian noninstitutional population 16 years old and over. Annual averages of monthly figures. Based on Current Population Survey; see text, Section 1, Population, and Appendix III]

Item	1970	1980	1990 [1]	1995	1996	1997 [1]	1998 [1]	1999 [1]
Total employed	78,678	99,303	118,793	124,900	126,708	129,558	131,463	133,488
Age:								
16 to 19 years old	6,144	7,710	6,581	6,419	6,500	6,661	7,051	7,172
20 to 24 years old	9,731	14,087	13,401	12,443	12,138	12,380	12,557	12,891
25 to 34 years old	16,318	27,204	33,935	32,356	32,077	31,809	31,394	30,865
35 to 44 years old	15,922	19,523	30,817	34,202	35,051	35,908	36,278	36,728
45 to 54 years old	16,473	16,234	19,525	24,378	25,514	26,744	27,587	28,635
55 to 64 years old	10,974	11,586	11,189	11,435	11,739	12,296	12,872	13,315
65 years old and over	3,118	2,960	3,346	3,666	3,690	3,761	3,725	3,882
Class of worker:								
Nonagriculture	75,215	95,938	115,570	121,460	123,264	126,159	128,085	130,207
Wage and salary worker	69,491	88,525	106,598	112,448	114,171	116,983	119,019	121,323
Self-employed	5,221	7,000	8,719	8,902	8,971	9,056	8,962	8,790
Unpaid family workers	502	413	253	110	122	120	103	95
Agriculture	3,463	3,364	3,223	3,440	3,443	3,399	3,378	3,281
Wage and salary worker	1,154	1,425	1,740	1,814	1,869	1,890	2,000	1,944
Self-employed	1,810	1,642	1,378	1,580	1,518	1,457	1,341	1,297
Unpaid family workers	499	297	105	45	56	51	38	40
Weekly hours:								
Nonagriculture:								
Wage and salary workers	38.3	38.1	39.2	39.2	39.2	39.4	39.2	39.5
Self-employed	45.0	41.2	40.8	39.4	39.6	39.7	39.6	40.1
Unpaid family workers	37.9	34.7	34.0	33.5	34.1	32.6	34.0	33.4
Agriculture:								
Wage and salary workers	40.0	41.6	41.2	41.1	41.5	41.6	40.6	41.1
Self-employed	51.0	49.3	46.8	43.5	43.1	42.7	43.3	43.3
Unpaid family workers	40.0	38.6	38.5	42.0	38.0	44.3	36.2	36.6

[1] See footnote 2, Table 643.

Source: U.S. Bureau of Labor Statistics, *Employment and Earnings,* monthly, January issues; and unpublished data.

No. 657. Employed Workers Actively Seeking a New Job: 1999

[As of **February. In thousands (117,930 represents 117,930,000), except rate.** For employed wage and salary workers 16 old and over (except as indicated) responding to the question on actively seeking work in the prior 3 months. Based on the Current Population Survey; see text, Section 1, Population, and Appendix III]

Characteristic	Total employed	Persons responding to search question			Characteristic	Total employed	Persons responding to search question		
		Total	Actively seeking work	Per-cent			Total	Actively seeking work	Per-cent
Total	117,930	114,898	5,131	4.5	Professional specialty . .	18,617	18,265	839	4.6
					Technical and related				
Age:					support	4,079	4,029	194	4.8
16 to 19 years old	6,600	6,360	377	5.9	Sales	13,324	12,912	686	5.3
20 to 24 years old	12,108	11,692	855	7.3	Administrative support,				
25 to 34 years old	28,836	28,126	1,631	5.8	including clerical	18,241	17,787	774	4.3
35 to 44 years old	32,390	31,649	1,387	4.4	Private household.	614	482	28	5.8
45 to 54 years old	24,518	23,966	672	2.8	Protective service	2,490	2,405	81	3.4
55 to 64 years old	10,754	10,475	177	1.7	Service, except private				
65 years old and over . .	2,724	2,629	32	1.2	households and pro-				
Sex: Male.	61,095	59,541	2,712	4.6	tective	13,368	12,923	633	4.9
Female.	56,835	55,357	2,419	4.4	Precision production,				
Educational attainment: [1]					craft, and repair	12,576	12,287	476	3.9
Less than high school					Machine operators,				
diploma.	9,644	9,275	246	2.7	assemblers, and				
High school diploma, no					inspectors	7,189	7,003	255	3.6
college	31,207	30,425	897	2.9	Transportation and				
Some college or associ-					material moving				
ate degree.	28,075	27,486	1,262	4.6	occupations	4,859	4,734	188	4.0
Bachelor's degree or					Handlers, equipment				
more	30,297	29,660	1,493	5.0	cleaners, helpers and				
Occupation:					laborers	4,754	4,585	227	5.0
Executive, administra-					Farming, forestry and				
tive, and managerial . .	16,237	15,957	671	4.2	fishing	1,582	1,529	78	5.1

[1] Persons 25 years old and over.
Source: U.S. Bureau of Labor Statistics, Current Population Survey, February 1999, unpublished data.

No. 658. Persons at Work by Hours Worked: 1999

[**For civilian noninstitutional population 16 years old and over (128,081 represents 128,081,000).** Annual averages of monthly figures. Based on Current Population Survey; see text, Section 1, Population, and Appendix III]

Hours of work	Persons at work (1,000)			Percent distribution		
	Total	Agriculture industries	Non-agriculture industries	Total	Agriculture industries	Non-agriculture industries
Total.	**128,081**	**3,132**	**124,948**	**100.0**	**100.0**	**100.0**
1 to 34 hours.	30,913	913	30,000	24.1	29.2	24.0
1 to 4 hours	1,230	67	1,164	1.0	2.1	0.9
5 to 14 hours	4,844	197	4,647	3.8	6.3	3.7
15 to 29 hours	15,339	436	14,903	12.0	13.9	11.9
30 to 34 hours	9,500	213	9,286	7.4	6.8	7.4
35 hours and over	97,167	2,219	94,948	75.9	70.8	76.0
35 to 39 hours	8,670	160	8,510	6.8	5.1	6.8
40 hours	47,955	826	47,129	37.4	26.4	37.7
41 hours and over.	40,542	1,234	39,309	31.7	39.4	31.5
41 to 48 hours	14,722	231	14,491	11.5	7.4	11.6
49 to 58 hours	14,986	366	14,620	11.7	11.7	11.7
60 hours and over	10,834	637	10,198	8.5	20.3	8.2
Average weekly hours:						
Total at work	39.6	41.9	39.5	(X)	(X)	(X)
Persons usually working full time . . .	43.4	48.1	43.3	(X)	(X)	(X)

X Not applicable.
Source: U.S. Bureau of Labor Statistics, *Employment and Earnings,* monthly, January, 2000 issue.

No. 659. Persons With a Job but Not at Work: 1980 to 1999

[**In thousands (5,881 represents 5,881,000), except percent. For civilian noninstitutional population 16 years old and over.** Annual averages of monthly figures. Based on Current Population Survey; see text, Section 1, Population, and Appendix III]

Reason for not working	1980	1985	1990 [1]	1992	1993	1994 [1]	1995	1996	1997 [1]	1998 [1]	1999 [1]
All industries, number	**5,881**	**5,789**	**6,160**	**6,088**	**6,041**	**5,619**	**5,582**	**5,768**	**5,555**	**5,586**	**5,407**
Percent of employed	5.9	5.4	5.2	5.1	5.0	4.6	4.5	4.6	4.3	4.2	4.1
Reason for not working:											
Vacation	3,320	3,338	3,529	3,409	3,328	2,877	2,982	3,085	2,942	3,033	2,899
Illness	1,426	1,308	1,341	1,259	1,295	1,184	1,084	1,090	1,114	1,095	1,096
Bad weather	155	141	90	128	153	165	122	256	146	130	104
Industrial dispute	105	42	24	19	24	15	21	11	20	10	7
All other	876	960	1,177	1,272	1,241	1,378	1,373	1,325	1,334	1,318	1,300

[1] See footnote 2, Table 643.
Source: U.S. Bureau of Labor Statistics, *Employment and Earnings,* monthly, January issues; and unpublished data.

Labor Force, Employment, and Earnings 411

No. 660. Self-Employed Workers by Industry and Occupation: 1980 to 1999

[In thousands (8,642 represents 8,642,000). For civilian noninstitutional population 16 years old and over. Annual averages of monthly figures. Data from 1994 forward are not fully comparable with data for prior years because of the introduction of the occupational and industrial classification used in the 1990 census. Based on the Current Population Survey; see text, Section 1, Population, and Appendix III]

Item	1980	1990 [1]	1994 [1]	1995	1996	1997 [1]	1998 [1]	1999 [1]
Total self-employed.	8,642	10,097	10,648	10,482	10,490	10,513	10,303	10,087
Industry:								
Agriculture.	1,642	1,378	1,645	1,580	1,518	1,457	1,341	1,297
Nonagriculture	7,000	8,719	9,003	8,902	8,971	9,056	8,962	8,790
Mining.	28	24	13	16	15	14	21	16
Construction.	1,173	1,457	1,506	1,460	1,496	1,492	1,519	1,545
Manufacturing.	358	427	426	433	406	422	428	380
Transportation and public utilities	282	301	385	396	432	438	430	429
Trade	1,899	1,851	1,906	1,772	1,760	1,761	1,640	1,621
Finance, insurance, and real estate	458	630	625	660	674	629	609	661
Services	2,804	4,030	4,142	4,166	4,189	4,300	4,317	4,138
Occupation:								
Managerial and professional specialty.	(NA)	3,050	3,106	3,147	3,288	3,432	3,400	3,298
Technical, sales, and administrative support. .	(NA)	2,240	2,380	2,341	2,304	2,219	2,117	2,111
Service occupations	(NA)	1,207	1,178	1,190	1,198	1,179	1,198	1,136
Precision production, craft, and repair.	(NA)	1,675	1,740	1,618	1,595	1,651	1,697	1,665
Operators, fabricators, and laborers	(NA)	567	639	631	634	629	584	607
Farming, forestry, and fishing	(NA)	1,358	1,605	1,556	1,471	1,403	1,307	1,270

NA Not available.   [1] See footnote 2, Table 643.

Source: U.S. Bureau of Labor Statistics, Bulletin 2307; *Employment and Earnings,* monthly, January issues; and unpublished data.

No. 661. Self-Employed Persons With Home-Based Businesses: 1997

[As of **May (4,125 represents 4,125,000)**. For persons at work 16 years and over in nonagricultural industries who worked in home-based businesses as part of their primary job. Based on the Current Population Survey; see text, Section 1, Population, and Appendix III]

Characteristic	Total [1] (1,000)	Percent distribution by hours worked at home			Mean hours	
		Less than 8 hours	8 hours or more		Worked at home	Total at work on primary job
			Total	35 hours or more		
Total	4,125	30.4	69.6	29.3	23.0	37.3
SEX						
Male.	2,157	36.2	63.8	25.5	20.4	42.1
Female.	1,968	24.2	75.8	33.5	25.9	31.9
RACE AND HISPANIC ORIGIN						
White	3,868	30.5	69.5	29.0	22.9	36.9
Black	135	29.2	70.8	47.0	29.1	42.7
Hispanic origin [2].	156	27.8	72.2	31.3	23.8	35.9
OCCUPATION						
Managerial and professional.	1,714	28.3	71.7	28.2	23.1	37.0
Exec., admin., and managerial.	1,014	28.3	71.7	29.0	23.8	39.6
Professional.	700	28.3	71.7	27.1	22.1	33.2
Technical, sales and administrative [3]	1,016	33.4	66.6	22.5	19.5	32.0
Sales	722	34.4	65.6	24.1	20.2	35.8
Administrative support	259	33.1	66.9	15.5	16.7	20.1
Service	616	12.0	88.0	58.3	36.9	42.1
Precision production, craft, and repair.	564	50.1	49.9	15.1	14.8	41.9
Operators, fabricators, and laborers	215	36.1	63.9	22.4	20.0	38.0
INDUSTRY						
Construction	726	49.5	50.5	14.3	14.3	44.3
Manufacturing.	193	13.6	86.4	38.5	29.1	36.5
Transportation and public utilities.	132	52.8	47.2	18.0	14.9	35.7
Wholesale trade.	185	28.9	71.1	30.2	22.3	39.4
Retail trade	532	38.9	61.1	19.2	19.1	30.5
Finance, insurance, and real estate	291	22.5	77.5	23.6	20.9	34.5
Services	2,054	23.0	77.0	37.8	27.4	36.8

[1] Includes persons who worked at home but did not report the number of hours worked. These persons are excluded from the distribution.   [2] Persons of Hispanic origin may be of any race.   [3] Includes other occupations, not shown separately.

Source: U.S. Bureau of Labor Statistics, *News,* USDL 98-93, March 11, 1998.

412   Labor Force, Employment, and Earnings

No. 662. Multiple Jobholders: 1999

[Annual average of monthly figures (7,802 represents 7,802,000). For the civilian noninstitutional population 16 years old and over. Multiple jobholders are employed persons who, either 1) had jobs as wage or salary workers with two employers or more; 2) were self-employed and also held a wage and salary job; or 3) were unpaid family workers on their primary jobs but also held wage and salary job. Based on the Current Population Survey; see text, Section 1, Population, and Appendix III]

Characteristic	Total		Male		Female	
	Number (1,000)	Percent of employed	Number (1,000)	Percent of employed	Number (1,000)	Percent of employed
Total [1]	**7,802**	**5.8**	**4,104**	**5.7**	**3,698**	**6.0**
Age:						
16 to 19 years old	343	4.8	153	4.1	190	5.5
20 to 24 years old	751	5.8	341	5.1	410	6.7
25 to 54 years old	5,886	6.1	3,146	6.1	2,740	6.1
55 to 64 years old	701	5.3	387	5.3	314	5.2
65 years old and over	122	3.1	77	3.4	45	2.7
Race and Hispanic origin:						
White	6,674	5.9	3,514	5.7	3,159	6.2
Black	831	5.5	442	6.3	389	4.8
Hispanic origin [2]	490	3.6	280	3.5	210	3.7
Marital status:						
Married, spouse present	4,309	5.6	2,566	5.9	1,744	5.2
Widowed, divorced, or separated	1,356	6.5	490	5.8	866	7.0
Single, never married	2,137	5.9	1,048	5.3	1,089	6.7
Full- or part-time status:						
Primary job full time, secondary job part time . .	4,293	(X)	2,497	(X)	1,796	(X)
Both jobs part time	1,657	(X)	519	(X)	1,138	(X)
Both jobs full time	298	(X)	204	(X)	94	(X)
Hours vary on primary or secondary job	1,513	(X)	861	(X)	652	(X)

X Not applicable.   [1] Includes a small number of persons who work part time on their primary job and full time on their secondary job(s), not shown separately. Includes other races, not shown separately.   [2] Persons of Hispanic origin may be of any race.

Source: U.S. Bureau of Labor Statistics, *Employment and Earnings*, monthly, January 2000 issue.

No. 663. Reasons for Multiple Jobholding: 1997

[As of **May (8,751 represents 8,751,000).** See headnote, Table 662]

Characteristic	Percent distribution by reason								
	Total (1,000)	Meet regular houshold expenses	To pay off debts	To save for the future	To get experi- ence or build up a busi- ness	To help out a friend or relative	To get extra money to buy some- thing special	Enjoys the work on the second job	Other reasons
Total [1]	**8,751**	**30.9**	**10.5**	**8.7**	**7.7**	**3.2**	**7.9**	**14.5**	**16.6**
Age:									
16 to 24 years old	1,274	24.7	18.2	11.4	5.2	2.3	13.0	6.5	18.5
25 to 54 years old	6,648	33.0	9.8	8.4	8.5	3.3	6.7	14.4	15.7
55 years old and over. . .	829	23.6	4.6	6.2	5.0	3.7	9.4	26.9	20.7
Race and Hispanic origin:									
White.	7,566	29.7	9.8	8.8	8.0	3.5	8.0	15.2	17.1
Black.	874	38.9	14.1	7.9	5.6	1.4	7.0	11.4	13.8
Hispanic origin [2]	557	39.5	9.5	9.7	5.4	3.1	11.1	4.7	17.1
Males	4,720	29.4	10.4	10.1	8.4	2.8	7.4	15.9	15.7
Single	1,238	24.5	15.6	11.1	8.0	2.3	10.2	10.3	18.0
Married, spouse present .	2,910	31.2	8.1	10.1	8.2	3.0	6.3	19.2	13.9
Widowed, divorced, or separated	573	30.6	10.5	7.9	9.8	2.8	7.2	11.0	20.3
Females	4,031	32.7	10.7	6.9	7.0	3.7	8.5	12.8	17.6
Single	1,145	28.7	15.5	9.4	3.6	2.5	12.9	9.0	18.3
Married, spouse present .	1,941	28.8	7.2	6.5	9.9	4.1	7.4	16.5	19.5
Widowed, divorced, or separated	946	45.4	12.2	4.9	5.1	4.3	5.4	9.9	12.8
Women who maintain families.	577	52.5	12.0	5.0	1.6	2.1	6.1	8.3	12.5

[1] Due to estimation procedures, the number of multiple jobholders differs from the regularly published monthly data. Includes other races, not shown separately.   [2] Persons of Hispanic origin may be of any race.

Source: U.S. Bureau of Labor Statistics, unpublished data.

Labor Force, Employment, and Earnings   413

No. 664. Distribution of Workers by Tenure With Current Employer and by Selected Characteristic: 1998

[As of **February (115,892 represents 115,892,000. For employed wage and salary workers 16 years old and over**. Based on the Current Population Survey and subject to sampling error; see source and Appendix III]

Characteristic	Number employed (1,000)	Percent distribution by tenure with current employer								
		12 months or less	13 to 23 months	2 years	3 to 4 years	5 to 9 years	10 to 14 years	15 to 19 years	20 years or more	Median years [1]
Total [2]	**115,892**	**27.8**	**7.9**	**4.9**	**15.8**	**17.9**	**10.7**	**6.1**	**9.0**	**3.6**
AGE AND SEX										
16 to 19 years old.	6,461	77.9	10.2	6.1	5.5	0.3	-	-	-	0.7
20 years old and over	109,431	24.8	7.7	4.8	16.4	18.9	11.3	6.5	9.5	4.0
20 to 24 years old	11,967	53.5	13.1	9.1	18.4	5.9	(Z)	-	-	1.1
25 to 34 years old	29,291	31.3	10.4	6.0	21.9	21.5	8.0	0.9	-	2.7
35 to 44 years old	31,684	20.5	6.7	4.0	15.6	22.0	15.9	9.7	5.6	5.0
45 to 54 years old	23,482	14.7	5.2	3.4	12.5	18.7	13.6	10.2	21.7	8.1
55 to 64 years old	10,377	11.6	4.0	2.6	11.0	17.3	14.2	10.4	28.9	10.1
65 years old and over.	2,631	16.1	3.5	3.6	13.1	18.6	13.9	9.5	21.7	7.8
Male	60,113	26.9	7.5	4.7	15.9	17.4	10.5	6.2	10.9	3.8
16 to 19 years old	3,143	78.3	10.4	5.0	5.9	0.4	-	-	-	0.7
20 years old and over.	56,970	24.1	7.3	4.7	16.4	18.3	11.1	6.6	11.5	4.2
20 to 24 years old	6,270	52.1	12.1	10.3	19.4	6.0	(Z)	-	-	1.2
25 to 34 years old	15,637	30.6	9.6	5.7	22.6	22.2	8.4	1.0	-	2.8
35 to 44 years old	16,568	19.2	6.5	3.5	14.7	21.8	16.7	10.8	6.8	5.5
45 to 54 years old	11,866	14.3	4.6	3.1	12.2	16.2	11.5	10.7	27.5	9.4
55 to 64 years old	5,333	11.3	3.9	2.6	10.1	15.9	12.2	8.3	35.8	11.2
65 years old and over . . .	1,297	16.5	4.9	4.3	14.2	17.7	15.1	6.3	20.9	7.1
Female	55,779	28.7	8.3	5.1	15.8	18.3	10.9	6.0	6.9	3.4
16 to 19 years old	3,318	77.4	10.0	7.2	5.2	0.2	-	-	-	0.7
20 years old and over.	52,461	25.6	8.2	5.0	16.4	19.5	11.6	6.3	7.4	3.8
20 to 24 years old	5,697	55.0	14.2	7.7	17.3	5.7	(Z)	-	-	1.1
25 to 34 years old	13,654	32.2	11.3	6.4	21.2	20.8	7.4	0.7	-	2.5
35 to 44 years old	15,116	21.9	6.8	4.5	16.6	22.3	15.0	8.6	4.2	4.5
45 to 54 years old	11,616	15.2	5.8	3.8	12.8	21.3	15.7	9.7	15.8	7.2
55 to 64 years old	5,044	11.9	4.2	2.6	11.9	18.9	16.3	12.6	21.6	9.6
65 years old and over . . .	1,334	15.7	2.1	3.0	12.0	19.6	12.6	12.6	22.4	8.7
RACE AND HISPANIC ORIGIN										
White	97,341	27.5	8.0	4.8	15.7	18.0	10.8	6.2	9.2	3.6
Male	51,234	26.6	7.5	4.6	15.7	17.3	10.7	6.4	11.2	3.9
Female	46,108	28.4	8.6	5.0	15.6	18.7	11.0	5.9	6.9	3.4
Black	13,298	29.1	6.3	5.4	16.6	16.8	10.0	6.4	9.4	3.5
Male	6,123	28.7	6.1	5.2	16.5	17.3	9.2	6.0	11.1	3.6
Female	7,175	29.5	6.5	5.6	16.6	16.3	10.7	6.7	8.0	3.4
Hispanic origin [3]	12,695	31.4	8.4	6.5	19.6	17.4	8.6	3.6	4.4	2.8
Male	7,468	30.7	7.9	6.1	19.9	18.1	8.1	4.0	5.2	3.0
Female	5,227	32.5	9.1	7.0	19.0	16.5	9.3	3.2	3.3	2.6

- Represents zero.   Z Less than 0.05 percent.   [1] For definition of median, see Guide to Tabular Presentation.   [2] Includes other races, not shown separately.   [3] Persons of Hispanic origin may be of any race.

Source: U. S. Bureau of Labor Statistics, *News,* USDL 98-387, September 23, 1998, and unpublished data.

No. 665. Part-Time Workers by Reason: 1999

[**In thousands (30,913 represents 30,913,000), except hours.** For persons working 1 to 34 hours per per week. **For civilian noninstitutional population 16 years old and over.** Annual average of monthly figures. Based on the Current Population Survey and subject to sampling error; see text, Section 1, Population, and Appendix III]

Reason	All industries			Nonagricultural industries		
		Usually work—			Usually work—	
	Total	Full time	Part time	Total	Full time	Part time
Total working fewer than 35 hours	**30,913**	**10,079**	**20,834**	**30,000**	**9,807**	**20,193**
Economic reasons	3,357	1,281	2,076	3,189	1,193	1,996
Slack work or business conditions	1,968	1,021	947	1,861	962	899
Could find only part-time work	1,079	-	1,079	1,056	-	1,056
Seasonal work	147	97	50	115	74	41
Job started or ended during the week	162	162	-	157	157	-
Noneconomic reasons	27,556	8,798	18,758	26,811	8,614	18,197
Child-care problems.	856	86	770	843	84	759
Other family or personal obligations	5,629	746	4,882	5,476	727	4,749
Health or medical limitations	712	-	712	674	-	674
In school or training	6,463	100	6,363	6,320	97	6,223
Retired or Social Security limit on earnings . . .	1,984	-	1,984	1,863	-	1,863
Vacation or personal day	3,239	3,239	-	3,188	3,188	-
Holiday, legal, or religious	966	966	-	956	956	-
Weather related curtailment.	824	824	-	781	781	-
Other	6,884	2,837	4,047	6,710	2,781	3,929
Average hours per week:						
Economic reasons.	23.1	24.0	22.5	23.2	24.1	22.6
Noneconomic reasons	21.5	25.7	19.6	21.6	25.8	19.6

- Represents or rounds to zero.

Source: U.S. Bureau of Labor Statistics, *Employment and Earnings,* monthly, January 2000 issue.

No. 666. Displaced Workers by Selected Characteristics: 2000

[In percent, except total (3,275 represents 3,275,000). As of February. For persons 20 years old and over with tenure of 3 years or more who lost or left a job between January 1997 and December 1999 because of plant closings or moves, slack work, or the abolishment of their positions. Data revised since originally published. Based on Current Population Survey and subject to sampling error; see source and Appendix III]

Characteristic	Total (1,000)	Employment status			Reason for job loss		
		Employed	Unem-ployed	Not in the labor force	Plant or company closed down or moved	Slack work	Position or shift abolished
Total [1]	**3,275**	**73.5**	**10.4**	**16.1**	**49.4**	**21.6**	**29.0**
20 to 24 years old	100	87.7	3.7	8.7	49.8	29.5	20.7
25 to 54 years old	2,503	79.5	10.3	10.2	48.3	22.1	29.6
55 to 64 years old	517	56.0	13.6	30.4	56.6	15.3	28.1
65 years old and over	155	26.3	5.2	68.6	43.1	29.0	27.9
Males	1,765	78.9	9.6	11.5	47.1	24.0	28.9
20 to 24 years old	75	86.6	4.9	8.4	43.4	36.1	20.5
25 to 54 years old	1,331	85.1	9.1	5.8	46.2	24.0	29.8
55 to 64 years old	279	62.9	13.3	23.8	56.3	17.4	26.3
65 years old and over	80	23.6	10.0	66.4	33.5	34.6	31.9
Females	1,511	67.3	11.3	21.4	52.1	18.7	29.1
20 to 24 years old	25	(2)	(2)	(2)	(2)	(2)	(2)
25 to 54 years old	1,172	73.2	11.7	15.1	50.7	19.9	29.4
55 to 64 years old	238	47.9	14.0	38.1	57.0	12.8	30.2
65 years old and over	75	29.1	-	70.9	53.4	23.0	23.6
White	2,778	74.4	9.9	15.7	48.9	20.9	30.3
Black	363	72.2	12.8	15.0	53.2	26.5	20.3
Hispanic origin [3]	346	69.7	13.0	17.3	50.4	32.1	17.5

- Represents zero. [1] Includes other races, not shown separately. [2] Data not shown where base is less than 75,000. [3] Persons of Hispanic origin may be of any race.
Source: U.S. Bureau of Labor Statistics, *News*, USDL 00-223, August 9, 2000.

No. 667. Labor Force Status of Persons With a Work Disability by Age: 1999

[In percent, except as indicated. As of March. For civilians 16 to 74 who have a condition which prevents then from working or limits the amount of work they can do. Data from the Current Population Survey and subject to sampling error; see text, Section 1, Population, and Appendix III]

Labor force status	Total	Age						
		16 to 24 years old	25 to 34 years old	35 to 44 years old	45 to 54 years old	55 to 64 years old	65 to 69 years old	70 to 74 years old
Number (1,000)	21,412	1,292	2,132	3,928	4,532	5,108	2,202	2,218
In labor force	25.4	36.9	40.6	35.5	30.8	17.8	11.0	6.7
Employed	22.7	28.6	34.5	31.7	28.6	16.5	10.3	6.5
Full-time	13.9	11.1	22.7	21.0	20.8	9.3	3.00	2.1
Not in labor force	74.6	63.1	59.4	64.5	69.2	82.2	89.0	93.3
Unemployment rate	10.5	22.5	15.0	10.7	7.1	7.0	6.4	3.9

Source: U.S. Census Bureau Internet site <http://www.census.gov/hhes/www/disable.html> (accessed 30 March 2000).

No. 668. Persons Not in the Labor Force: 1999

[In thousands (68,385 represents 68,385,000). Annual average of monthly figures. For the civilian noninstitutional population 16 years old and over. Based on the Current Population Survey; see text, Section 1, Population, and Appendix III]

Status and reason	Total	Age			Sex	
		16 to 24 years old	25 to 54 years old	55 years old and over	Male	Female
Total not in the labor force	**68,385**	**11,740**	**18,785**	**37,861**	**25,210**	**43,175**
Do not want a job now [1]	63,818	9,938	16,814	37,066	23,307	40,511
Want a job now	4,568	1,802	1,971	795	1,903	2,665
In the previous year—						
Did not search for a job.	2,723	981	1,144	599	1,083	1,640
Did search for a job [2]	1,844	822	827	196	820	1,024
Not available for work now	644	345	258	41	249	395
Available for work now, not looking for work. . .	1,201	477	569	155	571	629
Reason for not currently looking for work:						
Discouraged over job prospects [3]	273	86	146	41	161	113
Family responsibilities.	132	29	92	11	29	103
In school or training	214	176	34	4	110	104
Ill health or disability.	97	13	57	26	39	58
Other [4].	485	173	239	73	234	251

[1] Includes some persons who are not asked if they want a job. [2] Persons who had a job in the prior 12 months must have searched since the end of that job. [3] Includes such things as believes no work available, could not find work, lacks necessary schooling or training, employer thinks too young or old, and other types of discrimination. [4] Includes such things as child care and transportation problems.
Source: U.S. Bureau of Labor Statistics, *Employment and Earnings,* monthly, January 2000 issue.

Labor Force, Employment, and Earnings   415

No. 669. Employed Civilians by Occupation, Sex, Race, and Hispanic Origin: 1983 and 1999

[For civilian noninstitutional population 16 years old and over (100,834 represents 100,834,000). Annual average of monthly figures. Based on Current Population Survey; see text, Section 1, Population, and Appendix III. Persons of Hispanic origin may be of any race. See headnote, Table 660]

Occupation	1983				1999 [1]			
	Total em- ployed (1,000)	Percent of total			Total em- ployed (1,000)	Percent of total		
		Fe- male	Black	His- panic		Fe- male	Black	His- panic
Total....................................	100,834	43.7	9.3	5.3	133,488	46.5	11.3	10.3
Managerial and professional specialty	23,592	40.9	5.6	2.6	40,467	49.5	8.0	5.0
Executive, administrative, and managerial [2]..........	10,772	32.4	4.7	2.8	19,584	45.1	7.6	5.6
Officials and administrators, public	417	38.5	8.3	3.8	655	51.1	14.0	4.9
Financial managers	357	38.6	3.5	3.1	753	51.1	7.0	5.4
Personnel and labor relations managers	106	43.9	4.9	2.6	196	60.4	10.9	6.3
Purchasing managers.........................	82	23.6	5.1	1.4	138	47.4	8.9	5.6
Managers, marketing, advertising and public relations ..	396	21.8	2.7	1.7	739	37.6	4.8	2.7
Administrators, education and related fields	415	41.4	11.3	2.4	821	62.5	15.0	4.8
Managers, medicine and health	91	57.0	5.0	2.0	716	77.4	8.9	6.6
Managers, properties and real estate	305	42.8	5.5	5.2	577	49.4	6.6	8.9
Management-related occupations	2,966	40.3	5.8	3.5	4,879	57.8	9.8	5.3
Accountants and auditors	1,105	38.7	5.5	3.3	1,658	58.6	9.6	4.9
Professional specialty [2]	12,820	48.1	6.4	2.5	20,883	53.5	8.4	4.5
Architects..	103	12.7	1.6	1.5	194	15.7	2.3	4.4
Engineers [2]	1,572	5.8	2.7	2.2	2,081	10.6	4.6	3.5
Aerospace engineers	80	6.9	1.5	2.1	79	11.5	7.5	4.8
Chemical engineers	67	6.1	3.0	1.4	82	16.3	2.7	5.0
Civil engineers...........................	211	4.0	1.9	3.2	287	9.5	5.5	3.3
Electrical and electronic.	450	6.1	3.4	3.1	639	10.1	6.1	4.1
Industrial engineers	210	11.0	3.3	2.4	260	16.8	4.1	3.2
Mechanical	259	2.8	3.2	1.1	340	7.1	1.9	2.4
Mathematical and computer scientists [2].........	463	29.6	5.4	2.6	1,847	31.1	7.5	3.6
Computer systems analysts, scientists	276	27.8	6.2	2.7	1,549	28.5	7.4	3.4
Operations and systems researchers and analysts ...	142	31.3	4.9	2.2	241	46.6	8.4	5.2
Natural scientists [2]........................	357	20.5	2.6	2.1	578	30.1	3.7	3.6
Chemists, except biochemists................	98	23.3	4.3	1.2	136	27.4	5.7	3.5
Biological and life scientists	55	40.8	2.4	1.8	109	43.8	3.2	4.1
Medical scientists	(3)	(3)	(3)	(3)	100	44.9	6.1	5.3
Health diagnosing occupations [2]...............	735	13.3	2.7	3.3	1,071	24.1	4.4	4.1
Physicians	519	15.8	3.2	4.5	720	24.5	5.7	4.8
Dentists	126	6.7	2.4	1.0	173	16.5	1.9	3.1
Health assessment and treating occupations	1,900	85.8	7.1	2.2	3,019	85.7	9.1	3.4
Registered nurses	1,372	95.8	6.7	1.8	2,128	92.9	9.6	3.1
Pharmacists	158	26.7	3.8	2.6	216	49.0	5.6	3.5
Dietitians	71	90.8	21.0	3.7	92	84.0	19.5	4.6
Therapists [2]	247	76.3	7.6	2.7	517	75.8	7.5	4.5
Respiratory therapists	69	69.4	6.5	3.7	90	60.6	17.6	3.3
Physical therapists	55	77.0	9.7	1.5	144	73.2	5.3	5.3
Speech therapists	51	90.5	1.5	-	99	93.1	1.1	4.2
Physicians' assistants	51	36.3	7.7	4.4	67	52.6	4.3	2.6
Teachers, college and university..............	606	36.3	4.4	1.8	978	42.4	6.5	4.2
Teachers, except college and university [2].........	3,365	70.9	9.1	2.7	5,277	74.9	9.9	5.4
Prekindergarten and kindergarten	299	98.2	11.8	3.4	600	98.4	13.4	8.2
Elementary school.......................	1,350	83.3	11.1	3.1	2,072	83.8	10.3	5.1
Secondary school........................	1,209	51.8	7.2	2.3	1,342	57.5	7.9	5.0
Special education........................	81	82.2	10.2	2.3	369	84.4	9.1	2.8
Counselors, educational and vocational............	184	53.1	13.9	3.2	247	68.7	18.1	5.7
Librarians, archivists, and curators	213	84.4	7.8	1.6	264	82.9	7.6	4.8
Librarians	193	87.3	7.9	1.8	236	83.7	7.7	4.8
Social scientists and urban planners [2]............	261	46.8	7.1	2.1	460	58.4	8.1	3.1
Economists.............................	98	37.9	6.3	2.7	141	51.2	6.1	1.9
Psychologists	135	57.1	8.6	1.1	266	64.9	9.9	3.5
Social, recreation, and religious workers [2]	831	43.1	12.1	3.8	1,435	56.4	18.5	6.3
Social workers..........................	407	64.3	18.2	6.3	813	71.4	24.2	7.4
Recreation workers.......................	65	71.9	15.7	2.0	128	66.4	18.0	7.0
Clergy	293	5.6	4.9	1.4	352	14.2	10.3	5.2
Lawyers and judges........................	651	15.8	2.7	1.0	964	28.9	5.2	3.9
Lawyers	612	15.3	2.6	0.9	923	28.8	5.1	4.0
Writers, artists, entertainers, and athletes [2]	1,544	42.7	4.8	2.9	2,454	49.9	6.6	5.3
Authors	62	46.7	2.1	0.9	148	55.2	7.3	2.3
Technical writers	(3)	(3)	(3)	(3)	71	60.2	5.7	0.1
Designers	393	52.7	3.1	2.7	722	56.2	3.7	5.5
Musicians and composers	155	28.0	7.9	4.4	172	35.6	9.2	7.1
Actors and directors	60	30.8	6.6	3.4	129	38.8	10.7	5.1
Painters, sculptors, craft-artists, and artist printmakers	186	47.4	2.1	2.3	252	54.8	5.2	3.8
Photographers...........................	113	20.7	4.0	3.4	166	34.5	7.1	8.2
Editors and reporters	204	48.4	2.9	2.1	290	49.8	4.5	2.7
Public relations specialists	157	50.1	6.2	1.9	190	61.0	7.5	4.9
Announcers.............................	(3)	(3)	(3)	(3)	50	21.4	8.9	9.2
Athletes	58	17.6	9.4	1.7	110	28.0	19.0	3.4

See footnotes at end of table.

No. 669. Employed Civilians by Occupation, Sex, Race, and Hispanic Origin: 1983 and 1999—Continued

[See headnote, page 416]

Occupation	1983				1999 [1]			
	Total employed (1,000)	Percent of total			Total employed (1,000)	Percent of total		
		Female	Black	Hispanic		Female	Black	Hispanic
Technical, sales, and administrative support	**31,265**	**64.6**	**7.6**	**4.3**	**38,921**	**63.8**	**11.2**	**8.4**
Technicians and related support	3,053	48.2	8.2	3.1	4,355	51.9	10.7	6.4
Health technologists and technicians [2]	1,111	84.3	12.7	3.1	1,701	81.2	14.4	7.3
Clinical laboratory technologists and technicians	255	76.2	10.5	2.9	338	78.5	19.4	5.6
Dental hygienists	66	98.6	1.6	-	106	99.1	2.8	1.5
Radiologic technicians	101	71.7	8.6	4.5	167	74.4	9.7	4.1
Licensed practical nurses	443	97.0	17.7	3.1	357	95.1	18.4	5.8
Engineering and related technologists and technicians [2]	822	18.4	6.1	3.5	973	19.1	9.7	6.2
Electrical and electronic technicians	260	12.5	8.2	4.6	437	14.5	11.3	6.5
Drafting occupations	273	17.5	5.5	2.3	235	18.3	6.5	5.6
Surveying and mapping technicians	(3)	(3)	(3)	(3)	67	11.0	4.5	7.9
Science technicians [2]	202	29.1	6.6	2.8	293	40.8	11.0	7.3
Biological technicians	52	37.7	2.9	2.0	106	64.1	6.8	4.8
Chemical technicians	82	26.9	9.5	3.5	79	28.9	14.9	9.9
Technicians, except health, engineering, and science [2]	917	35.3	5.0	2.7	1,388	41.5	7.0	5.3
Airplane pilots and navigators	69	2.1	-	1.6	143	3.1	2.7	4.3
Computer programmers	443	32.5	4.4	2.1	665	26.3	6.4	3.8
Legal assistants	128	74.0	4.3	3.6	403	83.9	8.7	7.1
Sales occupations	11,818	47.5	4.7	3.7	16,118	50.1	8.7	7.9
Supervisors and proprietors	2,958	28.4	3.6	3.4	4,896	40.9	6.1	6.8
Sales representatives, finance and business services [2]	1,853	37.2	2.7	2.2	2,735	43.9	7.2	5.0
Insurance sales	551	25.1	3.8	2.5	585	44.0	5.8	4.6
Real estate sales	570	48.9	1.3	1.5	769	53.2	5.5	5.0
Securities and financial services sales	212	23.6	3.1	1.1	541	28.5	6.8	3.7
Advertising and related sales	124	47.9	4.5	3.3	187	57.1	11.9	4.1
Sales representatives, commodities, except retail	1,442	15.1	2.1	2.2	1,526	26.8	2.9	5.4
Sales workers, retail and personal services	5,511	69.7	6.7	4.8	6,866	63.9	12.5	10.4
Cashiers	2,009	84.4	10.1	5.4	3,014	77.0	16.7	12.0
Sales-related occupations	54	58.7	2.8	1.3	95	67.7	8.6	3.0
Administrative support, including clerical	16,395	79.9	9.6	5.0	18,448	78.7	13.5	9.4
Supervisors	676	53.4	9.3	5.0	675	57.5	17.5	8.2
Computer equipment operators	605	63.9	12.5	6.0	356	57.3	13.9	7.2
Computer operators	597	63.7	12.1	6.0	350	57.3	13.9	7.3
Secretaries, stenographers, and typists [2]	4,861	98.2	7.3	4.5	3,457	97.9	10.4	7.8
Secretaries	3,891	99.0	5.8	4.0	2,781	98.6	9.5	7.7
Typists	906	95.6	13.8	6.4	556	95.5	15.6	8.5
Information clerks	1,174	88.9	8.5	5.5	2,143	88.3	10.7	11.0
Receptionists	602	96.8	7.5	6.6	1,091	95.4	10.2	10.3
Records processing occupations, except financial [2]	866	82.4	13.9	4.8	1,047	77.8	16.9	10.8
Order clerks	188	78.1	10.6	4.4	270	72.7	21.5	12.0
Personnel clerks, except payroll and time keeping	64	91.1	14.9	4.6	70	83.3	24.6	5.4
Library clerks	147	81.9	15.4	2.5	151	74.4	9.8	11.1
File clerks	287	83.5	16.7	6.1	345	79.2	16.2	11.2
Records clerks	157	82.8	11.6	5.6	202	82.0	15.2	10.3
Financial records processing [2]	2,457	89.4	4.6	3.7	2,181	90.8	8.9	6.4
Bookkeepers, accounting, and auditing clerks	1,970	91.0	4.3	3.3	1,691	91.4	7.6	5.6
Payroll and time keeping clerks	192	82.2	5.9	5.0	146	88.2	8.7	9.3
Billing clerks	146	88.4	6.2	3.9	179	92.0	15.9	8.7
Cost and rate clerks	96	75.6	5.9	5.3	60	83.6	7.9	13.7
Billing, posting, and calculating machine operators	(3)	(3)	(3)	(3)	105	88.1	12.1	7.4
Duplicating, mail and other office machine operators	68	62.6	16.0	6.1	63	56.7	20.2	8.4
Communications equipment operators	256	89.1	17.0	4.4	158	81.7	18.6	13.7
Telephone operators	244	90.4	17.0	4.3	142	83.7	20.2	12.2
Mail and message distributing occupations	799	31.6	18.1	4.5	990	42.2	21.1	8.4
Postal clerks, except mail carriers	248	36.7	26.2	5.2	313	50.8	28.4	7.5
Mail carrier, postal service	259	17.1	12.5	2.7	332	31.8	15.0	5.6
Mail clerks, except postal service	170	50.0	15.8	5.9	194	60.5	24.6	13.5
Messengers	122	26.2	16.7	5.2	151	23.3	15.2	9.6
Material recording, scheduling, and distributing [2][4]	1,562	37.5	10.9	6.6	1,959	45.5	13.2	12.8
Dispatchers	157	45.7	11.4	4.3	274	52.6	14.2	9.2
Production coordinators	182	44.0	6.1	2.2	208	60.2	10.0	4.4
Traffic, shipping, and receiving clerks	421	22.6	9.1	11.1	646	33.7	14.8	17.9
Stock and inventory clerks	532	38.7	13.3	5.5	459	41.8	12.5	11.2
Expediters	112	57.5	8.4	4.3	264	68.1	11.1	13.6
Adjusters and investigators	675	69.9	11.1	5.1	1,802	75.5	18.1	7.9
Insurance adjusters, examiners, and investigators	199	65.0	11.5	3.3	472	71.3	15.4	7.6
Investigators and adjusters, except insurance	301	70.1	11.3	4.8	1,054	77.4	17.8	7.6
Eligibility clerks, social welfare	69	88.7	12.9	9.4	102	85.4	20.8	16.1
Bill and account collectors	106	66.4	8.5	6.5	175	69.8	24.9	6.3
Miscellaneous administrative support [2]	2,397	85.2	12.5	5.9	3,616	83.4	14.4	11.0
General office clerks	648	80.6	12.7	5.2	728	81.4	13.4	12.0
Bank tellers	480	91.0	7.5	4.3	425	87.7	13.3	8.1
Data entry keyers	311	88.9	18.6	5.6	746	81.3	15.6	10.9
Statistical clerks	96	75.7	7.5	3.4	94	83.6	18.2	10.2
Teachers' aides	348	93.7	17.8	12.6	689	91.0	13.8	14.9

See footnotes at end of table.

Labor Force, Employment, and Earnings **417**

No. 669. Employed Civilians by Occupation, Sex, Race, and Hispanic Origin: 1983 and 1999—Continued

[See headnote, page 416]

Occupation	1983 Total employed (1,000)	1983 Percent of total Female	1983 Percent of total Black	1983 Percent of total Hispanic	1999[1] Total employed (1,000)	1999[1] Percent of total Female	1999[1] Percent of total Black	1999[1] Percent of total Hispanic
Service occupations	13,857	60.1	16.6	6.8	17,915	60.4	18.3	15.2
Private household [2]	980	96.1	27.8	8.5	831	95.2	15.1	29.3
Child care workers	408	96.9	7.9	3.6	295	97.4	10.2	21.5
Cleaners and servants	512	95.8	42.4	11.8	521	94.4	17.6	33.9
Protective service	1,672	12.8	13.6	4.6	2,440	18.9	19.8	8.2
Supervisors, protective service	127	4.7	7.7	3.1	181	13.2	10.6	5.0
Supervisors, police and detectives	58	4.2	9.3	1.2	96	17.3	8.8	4.8
Firefighting and fire prevention	189	1.0	6.7	4.1	241	2.8	10.6	6.5
Firefighting occupations	170	1.0	7.3	3.8	223	1.9	11.1	5.4
Police and detectives	645	9.4	13.1	4.0	1,108	16.9	18.2	8.1
Police and detectives, public service	412	5.7	9.5	4.4	618	14.2	15.1	9.1
Sheriffs, bailiffs, and other law enforcement officers	87	13.2	11.5	4.0	175	14.4	17.3	3.6
Correctional institution officers	146	17.8	24.0	2.8	315	23.5	24.9	8.7
Guards	711	20.6	17.0	5.6	910	26.7	26.1	9.4
Guards and police, except public service	602	13.0	18.9	6.2	763	20.7	29.0	9.6
Service except private household and protective	11,205	64.0	16.0	6.9	14,644	65.4	18.2	15.5
Food preparation and service occupations [2]	4,860	63.3	10.5	6.8	6,091	57.7	11.8	16.5
Bartenders	338	48.4	2.7	4.4	316	48.4	4.1	12.9
Waiters and waitresses	1,357	87.8	4.1	3.6	1,431	77.4	5.1	10.2
Cooks	1,452	50.0	15.8	6.5	2,078	44.0	17.4	19.9
Food counter, fountain, and related occupations	326	76.0	9.1	6.7	360	64.5	10.3	13.7
Kitchen workers, food preparation	138	77.0	13.7	8.1	293	70.4	13.2	12.6
Waiters' and waitresses' assistants	364	38.8	12.6	14.2	538	49.5	10.6	19.4
Health service occupations	1,739	89.2	23.5	4.8	2,521	89.2	31.7	9.9
Dental assistants	154	98.1	6.1	5.7	213	96.1	6.7	10.4
Health aides, except nursing	316	86.8	16.5	4.8	338	80.5	25.0	10.0
Nursing aides, orderlies, and attendants	1,269	88.7	27.3	4.7	1,970	89.9	35.6	9.8
Cleaning and building service occupations [2]	2,736	38.8	24.4	9.2	3,021	45.5	21.9	23.2
Maids and housemen	531	81.2	32.3	10.1	663	82.7	25.4	28.1
Janitors and cleaners	2,031	28.6	22.6	8.9	2,118	35.8	21.0	22.1
Personal service occupations [2]	1,870	79.2	11.1	6.0	3,011	80.8	16.1	10.5
Barbers	92	12.9	8.4	12.1	81	20.3	25.1	11.3
Hairdressers and cosmetologists	622	88.7	7.0	5.7	784	90.8	11.7	10.1
Attendants, amusement and recreation facilities	131	40.2	7.1	4.3	247	39.7	11.5	6.9
Public transportation attendants	63	74.3	11.3	5.9	111	83.5	13.1	7.1
Welfare service aides	77	92.5	24.2	10.5	97	83.8	30.2	10.7
Family child care providers	(NA)	(NA)	(NA)	(NA)	469	98.0	13.9	15.5
Early childhood teachers' assistants	(NA)	(NA)	(NA)	(NA)	509	95.3	20.3	10.8
Precision production, craft, and repair	12,328	8.1	6.8	6.2	14,593	9.0	8.0	12.8
Mechanics and repairers	4,158	3.0	6.8	5.3	4,868	4.8	8.2	10.0
Mechanics and repairers, except supervisors [2]	3,906	2.8	7.0	5.5	4,604	4.5	8.1	10.2
Vehicle and mobile equipment mechanics/repairers [2]	1,683	0.8	6.9	6.0	1,768	1.6	7.2	11.3
Automobile mechanics	800	0.5	7.8	6.0	837	1.4	8.2	13.8
Aircraft engine mechanics	95	2.5	4.0	7.6	147	4.2	7.8	10.4
Electrical and electronic equipment repairers [2]	674	7.4	7.3	4.5	966	11.1	9.3	8.7
Data processing equipment repairers	98	9.3	6.1	4.5	315	15.2	9.4	6.3
Telephone installers and repairers	247	9.9	7.8	3.7	249	13.2	13.2	6.9
Construction trades	4,289	1.8	6.6	6.0	5,801	2.5	7.0	15.0
Construction trades, except supervisors	3,784	1.9	7.1	6.1	4,985	2.6	7.4	16.0
Carpenters	1,160	1.4	5.0	5.0	1,398	1.2	5.1	15.0
Extractive occupations	196	2.3	3.3	6.0	130	0.9	6.3	11.6
Precision production occupations	3,685	21.5	7.3	7.4	3,793	24.3	9.6	13.2
Operators, fabricators, and laborers	16,091	26.6	14.0	8.3	18,167	24.1	15.7	16.6
Machine operators, assemblers, and inspectors [2]	7,744	42.1	14.0	9.4	7,386	37.2	15.5	18.5
Textile, apparel, and furnishings machine operators [2]	1,414	82.1	18.7	12.5	872	70.8	18.1	28.9
Textile sewing machine operators	806	94.0	15.5	14.5	461	79.9	15.0	33.2
Pressing machine operators	141	66.4	27.1	14.2	79	78.2	20.1	39.0
Fabricators, assemblers, and hand working occupations	1,715	33.7	11.3	8.7	1,995	33.7	14.9	14.7
Production inspectors, testers, samplers, and weighers	794	53.8	13.0	7.7	716	48.3	14.5	19.9
Transportation and material moving occupations	4,201	7.8	13.0	5.9	5,516	9.9	15.9	11.9
Motor vehicle operators	2,978	9.2	13.5	6.0	4,202	11.5	16.1	12.4
Trucks drivers	2,195	3.1	12.3	5.7	3,116	4.9	14.1	12.7
Transportation occupations, except motor vehicles	212	2.4	6.7	3.0	163	2.4	15.0	3.9
Material moving equipment operators	1,011	4.8	12.9	6.3	1,152	5.2	15.5	11.4
Industrial truck and tractor operators	369	5.6	19.6	8.2	544	7.1	21.8	17.4
Handlers, equipment cleaners, helpers, and laborers [2]	4,147	16.8	15.1	8.6	5,265	20.5	15.7	18.8
Freight, stock, and material handlers	1,488	15.4	15.3	7.1	2,060	24.3	17.6	14.7
Laborers, except construction	1,024	19.4	16.0	8.6	1,286	21.6	16.2	17.0
Farming, forestry, and fishing	3,700	16.0	7.5	8.2	3,426	19.7	5.0	23.1
Farm operators and managers	1,450	12.1	1.3	0.7	1,134	24.7	1.0	2.9
Other agricultural and related occupations	2,072	19.9	11.7	14.0	2,135	18.1	7.1	35.1
Farm workers	1,149	24.8	11.6	15.9	757	18.6	5.4	46.0
Forestry and logging occupations	126	1.4	12.8	2.1	107	7.0	5.2	8.0
Fishers, hunters, and trappers	53	4.5	1.8	2.5	50	6.4	5.6	2.3

- Represents or rounds to zero.   NA Not available.   [1] See footnote 2, Table 643.   [2] Includes other occupations, not shown separately.   [3] Level of total employment below 50,000.   [4] Includes clerks.

Source: U.S. Bureau of Labor Statistics, *Employment and Earnings,* monthly, January issues; and unpublished data.

No. 670. Employment Projections by Occupation: 1998 and 2008

[In thousands (299 represents 299,000), except percent and rank. Estimates based on the Current Employment Statistics estimates; the Occupational Employment Statistics estimates; and the Current Population Survey. See source for methodological assumptions]

Occupation	Employment (1,000)		Change		Quartile rank by 1997 median hourly earnings [1]	Education and training category
	1998	2008	Number (1,000)	Percent		
FASTEST GROWING						
Computer engineers	299	622	323	108	1	Bachelor's degree
Computer support specialists	429	869	439	102	1	Associate degree
Systems analysts	617	1,194	577	94	1	Bachelor's degree
Database administrators	87	155	67	77	1	Bachelor's degree
Desktop publishing specialists	26	44	19	73	2	Long-term on-the-job training
Paralegals and legal assistants	136	220	84	62	2	Associate degree
Personal care and home health aides	746	1,179	433	58	4	Short-term on-the-job training
Medical assistants	252	398	146	58	3	Moderate-term on-the-job training
Social and human service assistants	268	410	141	53	3	Moderate-term on-the-job training
Physician assistants	66	98	32	48	1	Bachelor's degree
Data processing equipment repairers	79	117	37	47	2	Postsecondary vocational training
Residential counselors	190	278	88	46	3	Bachelor's degree
Electronic semiconductor processors	63	92	29	45	2	Moderate-term on-the-job training
Medical records and health information technicians	92	133	41	44	3	Associate degree
Physical therapy assistants and aides	82	118	36	44	3	Associate degree
Engineering, natural science, and computer and information systems managers	326	468	142	43	1	Work experience plus bachelors or higher degree
Respiratory therapists	86	123	37	43	2	Associate degree
Dental assistants	229	325	97	42	3	Moderate-term on-the-job training
Surgical technologists	54	77	23	42	2	Postsecondary vocational training
Securities, commodities, and financial services sales agents	303	427	124	41	1	Bachelor's degree
Dental hygienists	143	201	58	41	1	Associate degree
Occupational therapy assistants and aides .	19	26	7	40	2	Associate degree
Cardiovascular technologists and technicians	21	29	8	39	2	Associate degree
Correctional officers	383	532	148	39	2	Long-term on-the-job training
Speech-language pathologists and audiologists	105	145	40	38	1	Masters degree
Social workers	604	822	218	36	2	Bachelor's degree
Bill and account collectors	311	420	110	35	3	Short-term on-the-job training
LARGEST JOB GROWTH						
Systems analysts	617	1,194	577	94	1	Bachelor's degree
Retail salespersons	4,056	4,620	563	14	4	Short-term on-the-job training
Cashiers	3,198	3,754	556	17	4	Short-term on-the-job training
General managers and top executives	3,362	3,913	551	16	1	Work experience plus bachelors or higher degree
Truck drivers light and heavy	2,970	3,463	493	17	2	Short-term on-the-job training
Office clerks, general	3,021	3,484	463	15	3	Short-term on-the-job training
Registered nurses	2,079	2,530	451	22	1	Associate degree
Computer support specialists	429	869	439	102	1	Associate degree
Personal care and home health aides	746	1,179	433	58	4	Short-term on-the-job training
Teacher assistants	1,192	1,567	375	31	4	Short-term on-the-job training
Janitors and cleaners, including maids and housekeeping cleaners	3,184	3,549	365	11	4	Short-term on-the-job training
Nursing aides, orderlies, and attendants . . .	1,367	1,692	325	24	4	Short-term on-the-job training
Computer engineers	299	622	323	108	1	Bachelor's degree
Teachers, secondary school	1,426	1,749	322	23	1	Bachelor's degree
Office and administrative support supervisors and managers	1,611	1,924	313	19	2	Work experience in a related occupation
Receptionists and information clerks	1,293	1,599	305	24	3	Short-term on-the-job training
Waiters and waitresses	2,019	2,322	303	15	4	Short-term on-the-job training
Guards	1,027	1,321	294	29	4	Short-term on-the-job training
Marketing and sales worker supervisors . . .	2,584	2,847	263	10	2	Work experience in a related occupation
Food counter, fountain, and related workers	2,025	2,272	247	12	4	Short-term on-the-job training
Child care workers	905	1,141	236	26	4	Short-term on-the-job training
Laborers, landscaping and groundskeeping.	1,130	1,364	234	21	3	Short-term on-the-job training
Social workers	604	822	218	36	2	Bachelor's degree
Hand packers and packagers	984	1,197	213	22	4	Short-term on-the-job training
Teachers, elementary school	1,754	1,959	205	12	1	Bachelor's degree
Blue-collar worker supervisors	2,198	2,394	196	9	1	Work experience in a related occupation
College and university faculty	865	1,061	195	23	1	Doctoral degree

[1] Quartile ranks based on the Occupational Employment Statistics hourly earnings. Ranks: 1 = $16.25 and over; 2 = $10.89 to $16.14; 3 = $7.78 to $10.88; 4 = below $7.77.

Source: U.S. Bureau of Labor Statistics, *Monthly Labor Review,* November 1999.

Labor Force, Employment, and Earnings   419

No. 671. Occupations of the Employed by Selected Characteristics: 1999

[In thousands (58,770 represents 58,770,000). Annual averages of monthly figures. For civilian noninstitutional population 25 to 64 years old. Based on Current Population Survey; see text, Section 1, Population, and Appendix III]

Sex, race, and educational attainment	Total employed	Managerial/ profes- sional	Tech./ sales/ adminis- trative	Service [1]	Precision produc- tion [2]	Oper- ators/ fabrica- tors [3]	Farming, forestry, fishing
Male, total [4]	58,770	18,641	11,124	4,782	11,581	10,693	1,949
Less than a high school diploma	6,477	326	438	818	1,864	2,405	625
High school graduates, no college	18,493	2,174	2,977	1,797	5,372	5,448	724
Less than a bachelor's degree	15,328	3,707	3,872	1,555	3,518	2,291	388
College graduates	18,472	12,434	3,837	611	827	550	213
White	50,125	16,451	9,493	3,558	10,295	8,551	1,776
Less than a high school diploma	5,503	281	370	597	1,678	2,016	561
High school graduates, no college	15,610	1,947	2,557	1,270	4,835	4,351	650
Less than a bachelor's degree	12,934	3,296	3,243	1,201	3,075	1,758	361
College graduates	16,079	10,926	3,323	491	707	427	205
Black	5,870	1,149	1,031	922	907	1,738	124
Less than a high school diploma	694	28	42	147	130	299	48
High school graduates, no college	2,305	158	318	425	409	939	56
Less than a bachelor's degree	1,750	286	446	270	304	426	16
College graduates	1,120	677	224	79	64	74	3
Female, total [4]	50,773	18,273	19,356	7,794	1,145	3,670	535
Less than a high school diploma	4,090	226	845	1,695	196	999	128
High school graduates, no college	16,232	2,487	7,630	3,543	529	1,842	201
Less than a bachelor's degree	15,045	4,496	7,435	2,019	297	673	127
College graduates	15,406	11,065	3,446	537	122	156	78
White	41,700	15,571	16,202	5,726	918	2,780	503
Less than a high school diploma	3,122	190	695	1,201	152	770	115
High school graduates, no college	13,420	2,186	6,593	2,605	439	1,405	192
Less than a bachelor's degree	12,252	3,813	6,087	1,510	233	488	122
College graduates	12,905	9,383	2,828	410	93	117	74
Black	6,631	1,817	2,355	1,656	144	642	16
Less than a high school diploma	701	26	108	392	24	144	7
High school graduates, no college	2,245	223	830	782	65	338	6
Less than a bachelor's degree	2,224	541	1,085	415	43	142	1
College graduates	1,460	1,027	333	68	12	19	2

[1] Includes private household workers. [2] Includes craft and repair. [3] Includes laborers. [4] Includes other races, not shown separately.

Source: U.S. Bureau of Labor Statistics, unpublished data.

No. 672. Employment by Industry: 1980 to 1999

[In thousands (99,303 represents 99,303,000), except percent. See headnote, Table 646. Data for 1990, and also beginning 1995, not strictly comparable with other years due to changes in industrial classification]

Industry	1980	1990 [1]	1995 [1]	1998 [1]	1999 [1] Total	1999 [1] Percent Female	1999 [1] Percent Black	1999 [1] Percent His- panic [2]
Total employed	99,303	118,793	124,900	131,463	133,488	46.5	11.3	10.3
Agriculture	3,364	3,223	3,440	3,378	3,281	25.9	3.6	22.4
Mining	979	724	627	620	565	12.3	4.3	10.1
Construction	6,215	7,764	7,668	8,518	8,987	9.9	6.2	13.5
Manufacturing	21,942	21,346	20,493	20,733	20,070	32.0	10.6	11.2
Transportation, communication, and other public utilities	6,525	8,168	8,709	9,307	9,554	28.7	15.4	9.3
Wholesale and retail trade	20,191	24,622	26,071	27,203	27,572	47.6	9.6	11.5
Wholesale trade	3,920	4,669	4,986	5,090	5,189	32.0	7.2	11.1
Retail trade	16,270	19,953	21,086	22,113	22,383	51.2	10.2	11.6
Finance, insurance, real estate	5,993	8,051	7,983	8,605	8,815	58.0	10.7	7.4
Services [3]	28,752	39,267	43,953	47,212	48,687	62.0	12.7	8.9
Business and repair services [3]	3,848	7,485	7,526	8,708	9,046	36.3	11.5	11.2
Advertising	191	277	267	308	284	56.4	7.7	8.1
Services to dwellings and buildings	370	827	829	791	820	47.6	17.9	25.6
Personnel supply services	235	710	853	1,027	1,066	58.9	21.3	11.8
Computer and data processing	221	805	1,136	1,780	2,079	30.0	6.3	4.4
Detective/protective services	213	378	506	573	593	24.9	27.9	9.5
Automobile services	952	1,457	1,459	1,536	1,583	14.8	9.3	14.8
Personal services [3]	3,839	4,733	4,375	4,451	4,488	70.7	13.9	18.0
Private households	1,257	1,036	971	967	940	91.6	16.0	27.5
Hotels and lodging places	1,149	1,818	1,495	1,371	1,541	56.2	14.5	19.5
Entertainment and recreation [3]	1,047	1,526	2,238	2,530	2,649	42.8	10.0	8.0
Professional and related services [3]	19,853	25,351	29,661	31,392	32,370	69.7	13.1	7.1
Hospitals	4,036	4,700	4,961	5,116	5,117	76.5	16.7	5.8
Health services, except hospitals	3,345	4,673	5,967	6,388	6,529	78.9	15.6	8.0
Elementary, secondary schools	5,550	5,994	6,653	7,131	7,451	75.8	11.9	7.8
Colleges and universities	2,108	2,637	2,768	2,792	2,919	52.1	10.7	6.5
Social services	1,590	2,239	2,979	3,240	3,426	82.7	19.5	9.9
Legal services	776	1,215	1,335	1,356	1,365	56.6	7.0	6.4
Public administration [4]	5,342	5,627	5,957	5,887	5,958	44.6	16.7	6.8

[1] See footnote 2, Table 643. [2] Persons of Hispanic origin may be of any race. [3] Includes industries not shown separately. [4] Includes workers involved in uniquely governmental activities, e.g., judicial and legislative.

Source: U.S. Bureau of Labor Statistics, Employment and Earnings, monthly, January issues; and unpublished data.

No. 673. Employment Projections by Industry: 1998 to 2008

[140,515 represents 140,515,000. Estimates based on the Current Employment Statistics estimates; the Occupational Employment Statistics estimates; and the Current Population Survey. See source for methodological assumptions. Minus sign (-) indicates decline]

Industry	1987 SIC code [1]	Employment (1,000)		Change (1,000), 1998-2008	Average annual rate of change, 1998-2008
		1998	2008		
Total	(X)	140,515	160,795	20,281	1.4
MOST RAPID GROWTH					
Computer and data processing services	737	1,599	3,472	1,872	8.1
Health services, n.e.c. [2]	807-809	1,209	2,018	809	5.3
Residential care	836	747	1,171	424	4.6
Management and public relations	874	1,034	1,500	466	3.8
Personnel supply services	736	3,230	4,623	1,393	3.7
Miscellaneous equipment rental and leasing	735	258	369	111	3.6
Museums, botanical and zoological gardens	84	93	131	39	3.6
Research and testing services	873	614	861	247	3.4
Miscellaneous transportation services	473,474,478	236	329	94	3.4
Security and commodity brokers	62	645	900	255	3.4
Miscellaneous business services	732,733,738	2,278	3,172	893	3.4
Offices of health practitioners	801-804	2,949	4,098	1,150	3.3
Automobile parking, repair, and services.	752-754	944	1,300	356	3.2
Amusement and recreation services, n.e.c. [2] . . .	791,9	1,217	1,653	436	3.1
Water and sanitation	494-497	196	263	67	3.0
Local and interurban passenger transit	41	468	622	154	2.9
Individual and miscellaneous social services	832,839	923	1,223	300	2.9
Child day care services	835	605	800	196	2.8
Job training and related services.	833	369	484	114	2.7
Landscape and horticultural services	078	460	603	142	2.7
Veterinary services	074	196	255	59	2.7
Producers, orchestras, and entertainers	792	176	225	49	2.5
Cable and pay television services	484	181	230	49	2.4
Commercial sports	794	127	160	34	2.4
Engineering and architectural services	871	905	1,140	235	2.3
Nondepository; holding and investment offices. . . .	61,67	906	1,141	235	2.3
Miscellaneous transportation equipment	375,379	76	96	20	2.3
Nursing and personal care facilities	805	1,762	2,213	451	2.3
Automotive rentals, without drivers	751	200	250	50	2.3
Services to buildings.	734	950	1,187	237	2.3
MOST RAPID DECLINE					
Crude petroleum, natural gas, and gas liquids	131,132	143	77	-66	-6.0
Apparel	231-238	547	350	-197	-4.4
Coal mining.	12	92	59	-32	-4.2
Footwear except rubber and plastic	313,4	38	25	-13	-4.1
Federal electric utilities	(X)	30	20	-10	-4.1
Metal cans and shipping containers	341	37	25	-12	-3.8
Watches, clocks and parts	387	7	5	-2	-3.7
Tobacco products	21	41	30	-11	-3.1
Metal mining	10	50	37	-13	-3.0
Luggage, handbags, and leather products, n.e.c. [2] . .	311,315-317,319	45	34	-11	-2.7
Blast furnaces and basic steel products	331	232	177	-55	-2.7
Petroleum refining	291	96	75	-21	-2.5
Weaving, finishing, yarn and thread mills	221-224, 226,228	320	251	-69	-2.4
Private households	88	962	759	-203	-2.3
Forestry, fishing, hunting, and trapping	08,09	48	38	-10	-2.3
Hydraulic cement	324	17	14	-4	-2.3
Electrical industrial apparatus	362	153	122	-31	-2.3
Railroad transportation	40	231	185	-46	-2.2
Knitting mills	225	159	128	-32	-2.2
Primary nonferrous smelting and refining	333	39	32	-8	-2.1
Service industries for the printing trade.	279	50	41	-9	-2.0
Engines and turbines	351	84	69	-15	-1.9
Household appliances	363	117	96	-20	-1.9
Household audio and video equipment.	365	82	67	-14	-1.9
Combined utilities	493	159	131	-27	-1.9
Jewelry, silverware, and plated ware	391	50	42	-8	-1.8
Ordnance and ammunition	348	41	34	-7	-1.8
Tires and inner tubes	301	79	66	-13	-1.8
Electric distribution equipment	361	82	70	-13	-1.7
Photographic equipment and supplies	386	81	69	-12	-1.6

NA Not available.   X Not applicable.   [1] Based on the 1987 Standard Industrial Classification; see text, Section 17, Business.   [2] N.e.c. means not elsewhere classified.

Source: U.S. Bureau of Labor Statistics, *Monthly Labor Review,* November 1999.

Labor Force, Employment, and Earnings   421

No. 674. Unemployed Workers—Summary: 1980 to 1999

[In thousands (7,637 represents 7,637,000), except as indicated. For civilian noninstitutional population 16 years old and over. Annual averages of monthly figures. For data on unemployment insurance, see Table 618]

Age, sex, race, Hispanic origin	1980	1985	1990 [1]	1995	1996	1997 [1]	1998 [1]	1999 [1]
UNEMPLOYED								
Total [2]	7,637	8,312	7,047	7,404	7,236	6,739	6,210	5,880
16 to 19 years old	1,669	1,468	1,212	1,346	1,306	1,271	1,205	1,162
20 to 24 years old	1,835	1,738	1,299	1,244	1,239	1,152	1,081	1,042
25 to 44 years old	2,964	3,681	3,323	3,390	3,262	2,989	2,677	2,432
45 to 64 years old	1,075	1,331	1,109	1,269	1,289	1,199	1,125	1,120
65 years and over	94	93	105	153	139	127	122	124
Male	4,267	4,521	3,906	3,983	3,880	3,577	3,266	3,066
16 to 19 years old	913	806	667	744	733	694	686	633
20 to 24 years old	1,076	944	715	673	675	636	583	562
25 to 44 years old	1,619	1,950	1,803	1,776	1,689	1,504	1,308	1,195
45 to 64 years old	600	766	662	697	707	674	621	606
65 years and over	58	55	59	94	76	69	69	70
Female	3,370	3,791	3,140	3,421	3,356	3,162	2,944	2,814
16 to 19 years old	755	661	544	602	573	577	519	529
20 to 24 years old	760	794	584	571	564	516	498	480
25 to 44 years old	1,345	1,732	1,519	1,615	1,574	1,486	1,370	1,238
45 to 64 years old	473	566	447	574	582	525	503	513
65 years and over	36	39	46	60	63	58	53	54
White [3]	5,884	6,191	5,186	5,459	5,300	4,836	4,484	4,273
16 to 19 years old	1,291	1,074	903	952	939	912	876	844
20 to 24 years old	1,364	1,235	899	866	854	765	731	720
Black [3]	1,553	1,864	1,565	1,538	1,592	1,560	1,426	1,309
16 to 19 years old	343	357	268	325	310	302	281	268
20 to 24 years old	426	455	349	311	327	327	301	273
Hispanic [3][4]	620	811	876	1,140	1,132	1,069	1,026	945
16 to 19 years old	145	141	161	205	199	197	214	196
20 to 24 years old	138	171	167	209	217	206	194	171
Full-time workers	6,269	6,793	5,677	5,909	5,803	5,395	4,916	4,669
Part-time workers	1,369	1,519	1,369	1,495	1,433	1,344	1,293	1,211
UNEMPLOYMENT RATE (percent) [5]								
Total [2]	7.1	7.2	5.6	5.6	5.4	4.9	4.5	4.2
16 to 19 years old	17.8	18.6	15.5	17.3	16.7	16.0	14.6	13.9
20 to 24 years old	11.5	11.1	8.8	9.1	9.3	8.5	7.9	7.5
25 to 44 years old	6.0	6.2	4.9	4.8	4.6	4.2	3.8	3.5
45 to 64 years old	3.7	4.5	3.5	3.4	3.3	3.0	2.7	2.6
65 years and over	3.1	3.2	3.0	4.0	3.6	3.3	3.2	3.1
Male	6.9	7.0	5.7	5.6	5.4	4.9	4.4	4.1
16 to 19 years old	18.3	19.5	16.3	18.4	18.1	16.9	16.2	14.7
20 to 24 years old	12.5	11.4	9.1	9.2	9.5	8.9	8.1	7.7
25 to 44 years old	5.6	5.9	4.8	4.7	4.4	3.9	3.4	3.2
45 to 64 years old	3.5	4.5	3.7	3.5	3.4	3.1	2.8	2.6
65 years and over	3.1	3.1	3.0	4.3	3.4	3.0	3.1	3.0
Female	7.4	7.4	5.5	5.6	5.4	5.0	4.6	4.3
16 to 19 years old	17.2	17.6	14.7	16.1	15.2	15.0	12.9	13.2
20 to 24 years old	10.4	10.7	8.5	9.0	9.0	8.1	7.8	7.2
25 to 44 years old	6.4	6.6	4.9	5.0	4.9	4.6	4.2	3.8
45 to 64 years old	4.0	4.6	3.2	3.3	3.3	2.8	2.6	2.5
65 years and over	3.1	3.3	3.1	3.7	4.0	3.6	3.3	3.2
White [3]	6.3	6.2	4.8	4.9	4.7	4.2	3.9	3.7
16 to 19 years old	15.5	15.7	13.5	14.5	14.2	13.6	12.6	12.0
20 to 24 years old	9.9	9.2	7.3	7.7	7.8	6.9	6.5	6.3
Black [3]	14.3	15.1	11.4	10.4	10.5	10.0	8.9	8.0
16 to 19 years old	38.5	40.2	30.9	35.7	33.6	32.4	27.6	27.9
20 to 24 years old	23.6	24.5	19.9	17.7	18.8	18.3	16.8	14.6
Hispanic [3][4]	10.1	10.5	8.2	9.3	8.9	7.7	7.2	6.4
16 to 19 years old	22.5	24.3	19.5	24.1	23.6	21.6	21.3	18.6
20 to 24 years old	12.1	12.6	9.1	11.5	11.8	10.3	9.4	8.3
Experienced workers [6]	6.9	6.8	5.3	5.4	5.2	4.7	4.3	4.0
Women maintaining families	9.2	10.4	8.3	8.0	8.2	8.1	7.2	6.4
Married men, wife present [2]	4.2	4.3	3.4	3.3	3.0	2.7	2.4	2.2
White	3.9	4.0	3.1	3.0	2.8	2.5	2.2	2.1
Black	7.4	8.0	6.2	5.0	4.9	4.3	3.9	3.8
Percent without work for—								
Fewer than 5 weeks	43.2	42.1	46.3	36.5	36.4	37.7	42.2	43.7
5 to 10 weeks	23.4	22.2	23.5	22.0	21.8	21.9	22.1	21.8
11 to 14 weeks	9.0	8.0	8.5	9.6	9.8	9.9	9.3	9.3
15 to 26 weeks	13.8	12.3	11.7	14.6	14.6	14.8	12.3	12.8
27 weeks and over	10.7	15.4	10.0	17.3	17.4	15.8	14.1	12.3
Unemployment duration, average (weeks)	11.9	15.6	12.0	16.6	16.7	15.8	14.5	13.4

[1] See footnote 2, Table 643. [2] Includes other races, not shown separately. [3] Includes other ages, not shown separately. [4] Persons of Hispanic origin may be of any race. [5] Unemployed as percent of civilian labor force in specified group. [6] Wage and salary workers.

Source: U.S. Bureau of Labor Statistics, *Employment and Earnings*, monthly, January issues; and unpublished data.

No. 675. Unemployed Persons by Sex and Reason: 1980 to 1999

[In thousands (4,267 represents 4,267,000). **For civilian noninstitutional population 16 years old and over.** Annual averages of monthly figures. Based on Current Population Survey; see text, Section 1, Population, and Appendix III]

Sex and reason	1980	1985	1990 [1]	1991	1992	1993	1994 [1]	1995	1996	1997 [1]	1998 [1]	1999 [1]
Male, total	4,267	4,521	3,906	4,946	5,523	5,055	4,367	3,983	3,880	3,577	3,266	3,066
Job losers [2]	2,649	2,749	2,257	3,172	3,593	3,150	2,416	2,190	2,158	1,902	1,703	1,563
Job leavers	438	409	528	507	495	507	408	407	372	414	368	389
Reentrants	776	876	806	891	978	939	1,265	1,113	1,076	1,004	931	895
New entrants	405	487	315	375	457	459	278	273	273	257	264	219
Female, total	3,370	3,791	3,140	3,683	4,090	3,885	3,629	3,421	3,356	3,162	2,944	2,814
Job losers [2]	1,297	1,390	1,130	1,522	1,796	1,699	1,399	1,286	1,212	1,135	1,119	1,059
Job leavers	453	468	513	497	507	469	383	417	402	381	366	394
Reentrants	1,152	1,380	1,124	1,247	1,307	1,259	1,521	1,412	1,435	1,334	1,201	1,111
New entrants	468	552	373	416	480	459	326	306	307	312	257	250

[1] See footnote 2, Table 643. [2] Beginning 1994, persons who completed temporary jobs are identified separately and are included as job losers.

Source: U.S. Bureau of Labor Statistics, *Employment and Earnings,* monthly, January issues; and Bulletin 2307; and unpublished data.

No. 676. Unemployment Rates by Industry, 1980 to 1999, and by Sex, 1980 and 1999

[In percent. **For civilian noninstitutional population 16 years old and over.** Annual averages of monthly figures. Rate represents unemployment as a percent of labor force in each specified group. Data for 1985-90 not strictly comparable with other years due to changes in industrial classification]

Industry	1980	1985	1990 [1]	1995 [1]	1998 [1]	1999 [1]	Male 1980	Male 1999 [1]	Female 1980	Female 1999 [1]
All unemployed [2]	7.1	7.2	5.6	5.6	4.5	4.2	6.9	4.1	7.4	4.3
Industry: [3]										
Agriculture	11.0	13.2	9.8	11.1	8.3	8.9	9.7	8.6	15.1	9.6
Mining	6.4	9.5	4.8	5.2	3.2	5.7	6.7	5.8	4.5	5.4
Construction	14.1	13.1	11.1	11.5	7.5	7.0	14.6	7.1	8.9	5.8
Manufacturing	8.5	7.7	5.8	4.9	3.9	3.6	7.4	3.1	10.8	4.7
Transportation and public utilities	4.9	5.1	3.9	4.5	3.4	3.0	5.1	3.0	4.4	3.2
Wholesale and retail trade	7.4	7.6	6.4	6.5	5.5	5.2	6.6	4.5	8.3	6.0
Finance, insurance, and real estate	3.4	3.5	3.0	3.3	2.5	2.3	3.2	2.4	3.5	2.3
Services	5.9	6.2	5.0	5.4	4.5	4.1	6.3	4.2	5.8	4.0
Government	4.1	3.9	2.7	2.9	2.1	2.1	3.9	2.1	4.3	2.1

[1] See footnote 2, Table 643. [2] Includes the self-employed, unpaid family workers, and persons with no previous work experience, not shown separately. [3] Covers unemployed wage and salary workers.

Source: U.S. Bureau of Labor Statistics, *Employment and Earnings,* monthly, January issues.

No. 677. Unemployment by Occupation, 1990 to 1999, and by Sex, 1999

[For civilian noninstitutional population 16 years old and over (7,047 represents 7,047,000). Annual averages of monthly data. Rate represents unemployment as a percent of the labor force for each specified group. Based on Current Population Survey; see text, Section 1, Population, and Appendix III. See also headnote, Table 660]

Occupation	Number (1,000) 1990 [1]	Number (1,000) 1995 [1]	Number (1,000) 1999 [1]	Unemployment rate 1990 [1]	Unemployment rate 1995 [1]	1999 [1] Total	1999 [1] Male	1999 [1] Female
Total [2]	7,047	7,404	5,880	5.6	5.6	4.2	4.1	4.3
Managerial and professional specialty	666	880	770	2.1	2.4	1.9	1.8	1.9
Executive, administrative, and managerial	350	420	376	2.3	2.4	1.9	1.7	2.0
Professional specialty	316	460	394	2.0	2.5	1.9	1.8	1.9
Technical sales, and administrative support	1,641	1,744	1,477	4.3	4.5	3.7	3.2	3.9
Technicians and related support	116	113	101	2.9	2.8	2.3	2.6	1.9
Sales occupations	720	795	714	4.8	5.0	4.2	3.0	5.4
Administrative support, including clerical	804	836	662	4.1	4.3	3.5	3.7	3.4
Service occupations	1,139	1,378	1,081	6.6	7.5	5.7	5.5	5.8
Private household	47	99	67	5.6	10.7	7.4	6.0	7.5
Protective service	74	86	72	3.6	3.7	2.9	2.4	4.9
Service except private household and protective	1,018	1,193	943	7.1	7.9	6.0	6.7	5.7
Precision production, craft, and repair	861	860	607	5.9	6.0	4.0	3.9	5.2
Mechanics and repairers	175	182	136	3.8	4.0	2.7	2.6	4.8
Construction trades	483	501	330	8.5	9.0	5.4	5.3	8.8
Other precision production, craft, and repair	202	177	142	4.7	4.2	3.5	3.1	4.7
Operators, fabricators, and laborers	1,714	1,618	1,207	8.7	8.2	6.2	5.9	7.3
Machine operators, assemblers, inspectors	727	629	440	8.1	7.4	5.6	4.7	7.2
Transportation and material moving occupations	329	329	235	6.3	6.0	4.1	4.0	5.3
Handlers, equipment cleaners, helpers, laborers	657	660	532	11.6	11.7	9.2	9.4	8.4
Construction laborers	177	179	140	18.1	18.7	13.2	13.0	18.2
Farming, forestry, and fishing	237	311	249	6.4	7.9	6.8	6.2	9.0

[1] See footnote 2, Table 643. [2] Includes persons with no previous work experience and those whose last job was in the Armed Forces.

Source: U.S. Bureau of Labor Statistics, *Employment and Earnings,* monthly, January issues.

Labor Force, Employment, and Earnings   423

No. 678. Unemployed and Unemployment Rates by Educational Attainment, Sex, Race, and Hispanic Origin: 1992 to 1999

[As of **March (6,846 represents 6,846,000). For the civilian noninstitutional population 25 to 64 years old.** See Table 647 for civilian labor force and participation rate data. Based on Current Population Survey; see text, Section 1, Population, and Appendix III]

Year, sex, and race	Unemployed (1,000)					Unemployment rate [1]				
	Total	Less than high school diploma	High school graduates, no degree	Less than a bachelor's degree	College graduate	Total	Less than high school diploma	High school graduate, no degree	Less than a bachelor's degree	College graduate
Total: [2]										
1992	6,846	1,693	2,851	1,521	782	6.7	13.5	7.7	5.9	2.9
1995	5,065	1,150	1,833	1,329	753	4.8	10.0	5.2	4.5	2.5
1998 [3] . . .	4,463	1,018	1,751	1,111	582	4.0	8.5	4.8	3.6	1.8
1999 [3] . . .	3,942	895	1,445	961	640	3.5	7.7	4.0	3.1	1.9
Male:										
1992	4,207	1,151	1,709	854	493	7.5	14.8	8.8	6.4	3.2
1995	2,925	765	1,064	656	440	5.1	10.9	5.7	4.4	2.6
1998 [3]	2,461	592	989	575	306	4.1	8.0	5.1	3.7	1.7
1999 [3]	2,121	491	782	495	353	3.5	7.0	4.1	3.2	1.9
Female:										
1992	2,639	542	1,142	666	289	5.7	11.4	6.5	5.3	2.5
1995	2,140	385	770	673	313	4.4	8.6	4.6	4.5	2.4
1998 [3]	2,002	426	762	537	276	3.9	9.3	4.4	3.5	1.9
1999 [3]	1,821	404	663	466	287	3.5	8.8	3.9	3.0	1.9
White:										
1992	5,247	1,285	2,146	1,176	641	6.0	12.9	6.8	5.3	2.7
1995	3,858	831	1,362	1,054	612	4.3	9.2	4.6	4.2	2.3
1998 [3]	3,282	711	1,283	814	474	3.5	7.5	4.2	3.2	1.7
1999 [3]	2,886	651	1,034	716	484	3.1	7.0	3.4	2.8	1.7
Black:										
1992	1,353	361	619	291	81	12.4	17.2	14.1	10.7	4.8
1995	905	225	377	218	86	7.7	13.7	8.4	6.3	4.1
1998 [3]	948	248	402	248	50	7.3	13.4	8.4	6.4	2.1
1999 [3]	810	201	321	204	84	6.3	12.0	6.7	5.2	3.3
Hispanic: [4]										
1992	757	408	224	88	36	9.8	13.6	9.6	5.9	4.2
1995	746	393	211	102	40	8.0	10.9	8.1	5.2	3.7
1998 [3]	647	337	176	94	41	5.9	8.3	5.5	4.2	2.8
1999 [3]	620	315	179	89	36	5.6	7.8	5.5	3.7	2.5

[1] Percent unemployed of the civilian labor force. [2] Includes other races, not shown separately. [3] See footnote 2, Table 643. [4] Persons of Hispanic origin may be of any race.

Source: U.S. Bureau of Labor Statistics, unpublished data.

No. 679. Unemployed Persons by Reason of Unemployment: 1999

[**Annual averages of monthly data (5,880 represents 5,880,000).** Based on Current Population Survey; see text, Section 1, Population, and Appendix III]

Age, sex, and reason	Total unemployed (1,000)	Percent distribution by duration				
		Less than 5 weeks	5 to 14 weeks	15 weeks and over		
				Total	15 to 26 weeks	27 weeks or longer
Total 16 years old and over	5,880	43.7	31.2	25.2	12.8	12.3
16 to 19 years old	1,162	53.1	32.2	14.7	8.5	6.2
Total 20 years old and over	**4,718**	**41.3**	**30.9**	**27.8**	**13.9**	**13.8**
Males	**2,433**	**40.1**	**30.8**	**29.0**	**14.2**	**14.8**
Job losers and persons who completed						
temporary jobs	1,459	41.4	32.0	26.6	15.2	11.4
On temporary layoff	475	51.8	34.3	13.9	10.6	3.3
Not on temporary layoff	984	36.3	30.9	32.7	17.4	15.4
Permanent job losers	685	33.8	30.4	35.7	18.9	16.8
Persons who completed temporary jobs	299	42.0	32.1	25.9	13.8	12.1
Job leavers	336	48.2	28.7	23.1	11.1	11.9
Reentrants	592	33.0	29.5	37.5	14.1	23.4
New entrants	46	33.5	27.1	39.4	9.0	30.4
Females	**2,285**	**42.6**	**31.0**	**26.4**	**13.6**	**12.8**
Job losers and persons who completed						
temporary jobs	990	43.5	30.7	25.8	15.1	10.7
On temporary layoff	310	56.9	30.1	13.1	8.2	4.8
Not on temporary layoff	680	37.3	31.0	31.6	18.2	13.4
Permanent job losers	481	35.1	31.4	33.5	20.0	13.5
Persons who completed temporary jobs	199	42.6	30.3	27.1	13.6	13.4
Job leavers	333	49.2	30.3	20.5	11.4	9.1
Reentrants	866	40.1	31.6	28.3	12.5	15.8
New entrants	96	34.1	29.3	36.7	16.1	20.6

Source: U.S. Bureau of Labor Statistics, *Employment and Earnings*, monthly, January 2000 issue.

[For civilian noninstitutional population 16 years old and over (7,637 represents 7,637,000). Annual averages of monthly figures. Total unemployment estimates based on the Current Population Survey; see text, Section 1, Population, and Appendix III. U.S. totals derived by independent population controls; therefore, state data may not add to U.S. totals]

State	Total unemployed								Insured unemployed [3]			
	Number (1,000)				Percent [1]				Number (1,000)		Percent [4]	
	1980	1985	1990 [2]	1999 [2]	1980	1985	1990 [2]	1999 [2]	1997	1998	1997	1998
United States ...	7,637	8,312	7,047	5,880	7.1	7.2	5.6	4.2	[5]2,322.6	2,221.7	[5]2.0	[5]1.9
Alabama	147	160	130	102	8.8	8.9	6.9	4.8	30.1	30.3	1.7	1.7
Alaska	18	24	19	20	9.7	9.7	7.0	6.4	12.1	12.1	5.0	5.0
Arizona	83	96	99	104	6.7	6.5	5.5	4.4	21.0	19.0	1.1	1.0
Arkansas	76	91	78	55	7.6	8.7	7.0	4.5	28.2	26.2	2.7	2.5
California	790	934	874	864	6.8	7.2	5.8	5.2	386.5	365.5	3.0	2.7
Colorado	88	101	89	66	5.9	5.9	5.0	2.9	18.9	16.7	1.0	0.9
Connecticut	94	83	95	53	5.9	4.9	5.2	3.2	33.9	30.8	2.2	2.0
Delaware	22	17	19	14	7.7	5.3	5.2	3.5	6.1	6.1	1.7	1.6
District of Columbia	24	27	22	18	7.3	8.4	6.6	6.3	8.2	6.8	2.0	1.7
Florida	251	320	390	284	5.9	6.0	6.0	3.9	79.5	74.3	1.3	1.2
Georgia	163	188	182	163	6.4	6.5	5.5	4.0	37.0	33.0	1.1	1.0
Hawaii	21	27	16	33	4.9	5.6	2.9	5.6	13.4	12.6	2.7	2.5
Idaho	34	37	29	34	7.9	7.9	5.9	5.2	12.7	13.0	2.6	2.6
Illinois	459	513	369	274	8.3	9.0	6.2	4.3	115.4	103.6	2.1	1.9
Indiana	252	215	149	93	9.6	7.9	5.3	3.0	31.4	30.9	1.2	1.1
Iowa	82	112	62	40	5.8	8.0	4.3	2.5	19.0	16.4	1.4	1.2
Kansas	53	62	57	43	4.5	5.0	4.5	3.0	14.1	13.1	1.2	1.1
Kentucky	133	161	104	88	8.0	9.5	5.9	4.5	27.0	26.1	1.7	1.6
Louisiana	121	229	117	104	6.7	11.5	6.3	5.1	23.7	22.7	1.4	1.3
Maine	39	30	33	28	7.8	5.4	5.2	4.1	12.8	11.3	2.5	2.1
Maryland	140	104	122	98	6.5	4.6	4.7	3.5	37.8	34.5	1.8	1.6
Massachusetts	162	120	195	105	5.6	3.9	6.0	3.2	63.5	63.4	2.2	2.1
Michigan	534	433	350	194	12.4	9.9	7.6	3.8	89.4	90.7	2.1	2.1
Minnesota	125	133	117	75	5.9	6.0	4.9	2.8	34.0	31.2	1.4	1.3
Mississippi	79	116	90	65	7.5	10.3	7.6	5.1	19.9	18.7	1.9	1.8
Missouri	167	158	151	96	7.2	6.4	5.8	3.4	40.8	41.3	1.7	1.7
Montana	23	31	24	25	6.1	7.7	6.0	5.2	8.7	8.2	2.6	2.4
Nebraska	31	44	18	26	4.1	5.5	2.2	2.9	7.2	6.8	0.9	0.8
Nevada	27	41	33	42	6.2	8.0	4.9	4.4	17.4	17.9	2.1	2.1
New Hampshire	22	21	36	18	4.7	3.9	5.7	2.7	4.8	3.8	0.9	0.7
New Jersey	260	217	206	193	7.2	5.7	5.1	4.6	96.1	90.7	2.8	2.6
New Mexico	42	57	46	46	7.5	8.8	6.5	5.6	11.9	11.4	1.9	1.7
New York	597	544	467	459	7.5	6.5	5.3	5.2	188.7	173.1	2.5	2.2
North Carolina	187	168	144	122	6.6	5.4	4.2	3.2	47.8	50.4	1.4	1.4
North Dakota	15	20	13	11	5.0	5.9	4.0	3.4	4.2	3.6	1.5	1.2
Ohio	426	455	310	246	8.4	8.9	5.7	4.3	75.7	72.1	1.5	1.4
Oklahoma	66	112	86	57	4.8	7.1	5.7	3.4	12.4	12.7	1.0	1.0
Oregon	107	116	83	100	8.3	8.8	5.6	5.7	41.2	43.0	2.9	2.9
Pennsylvania	425	443	315	262	7.8	8.0	5.4	4.4	146.5	140.6	2.9	2.7
Rhode Island	34	25	35	21	7.2	4.9	6.8	4.1	15.8	13.3	3.7	3.1
South Carolina	96	107	83	88	6.9	6.8	4.8	4.5	25.1	24.7	1.5	1.5
South Dakota	16	18	13	12	4.9	5.1	3.9	2.9	2.4	2.3	0.7	0.7
Tennessee	152	180	126	114	7.3	8.0	5.3	4.0	43.0	42.0	1.8	1.7
Texas	352	565	544	472	5.2	7.0	6.3	4.6	114.8	110.5	1.4	1.3
Utah	40	43	35	40	6.3	5.9	4.3	3.7	8.5	9.4	1.0	1.0
Vermont	16	13	15	10	6.4	4.8	5.0	3.0	6.6	5.8	2.5	2.2
Virginia	128	160	141	98	5.0	5.6	4.3	2.8	24.6	24.1	0.8	0.8
Washington	156	170	125	145	7.9	8.1	4.9	4.7	72.8	77.1	3.1	3.2
West Virginia	74	100	64	54	9.4	13.0	8.4	6.6	16.8	15.9	2.6	2.5
Wisconsin	167	171	114	88	7.2	7.2	4.4	3.0	52.7	51.2	2.1	2.0
Wyoming	9	18	13	13	4.0	7.1	5.5	4.9	3.4	3.2	1.7	1.5

[1] Total unemployment as percent of civilian labor force. [2] See footnote 2, Table 643. [3] Source: U.S. Employment and Training Administration, *Unemployment Insurance, Financial Handbook,* annual updates. [4] Insured unemployment as percent of average covered employment in the previous year. [5] Includes 56,900 in Puerto Rico and the Virgin Islands in 1997 and 58,000 in 1998.

Source: Except as noted, U.S. Bureau of Labor Statistics, *Geographic Profile of Employment and Unemployment,* annual.

No. 681. Job Openings and Placements and Help-Wanted Advertising: 1980 to 1998

[8,122 represents 8,122,000. Openings 1980, for years ending **Sept. 30**; beginning 1985, for years ending **June 30**]

Item	1980	1985	1990	1994	1993	1995	1996	1997	1998
Job openings: [1]									
Received (1,000)	8,122	7,529	5,651	6,343	6,619	5,917	6,039	6,559	7,264
Average per month	677	627	471	529	552	493	503	547	605
Nonagricultural placements [1] (1,000)	5,610	3,270	3,714	3,375	3,360	2,859	2,687	2,456	2,196
Index of help-wanted advertising in newspapers [2] (1987=100)	84	91	84	69	83	85	83	87	89

[1] As reported by state employment agencies. Beginning 1985, all placements. Placements include duplication for individuals placed more than once. [2] Source: The Conference Board, New York, NY (copyright). Index based on the number of advertisements in classified sections of 51 newspapers, each in a major employment area.

Source: Except as noted, U.S. Employment and Training Administration, unpublished data.

Labor Force, Employment, and Earnings **425**

No. 682. Nonfarm Establishments—Employees, Hours, and Earnings by Industry: 1980 to 1999

[Based on data from establishment reports. Includes all full- and part-time employees who worked during or received pay for any part of the pay period reported. Excludes proprietors, the self-employed, farm workers, unpaid family workers, private household workers, and Armed Forces. Establishment data shown here conform to industry definitions in the 1987 Standard Industrial Classification and are adjusted to March 1998 employment benchmarks and reflect historical corrections to previously published data. Based on the Current Employment Statistics Program; see Appendix III]

Item and year		Goods producing				Service producing						
	Total	Total	Mining	Con-struc-tion	Manu-factur-ing	Total	Trans-portation and public utilities	Whole-sale trade	Retail trade	Finance, insur-ance, and real estate	Serv-ices	Govern-ment
EMPLOYEES (1,000)												
1980	90,406	25,658	1,027	4,346	20,285	64,748	5,146	5,292	15,018	5,160	17,890	16,241
1985	97,387	24,842	927	4,668	19,248	72,544	5,233	5,727	17,315	5,948	21,927	16,394
1990	109,403	24,905	709	5,120	19,076	84,497	5,777	6,173	19,601	6,709	27,934	18,304
1992	108,601	23,231	635	4,492	18,104	85,370	5,718	5,997	19,356	6,602	29,052	18,645
1993	110,713	23,352	610	4,668	18,075	87,361	5,811	5,981	19,773	6,757	30,197	18,841
1994	114,163	23,908	601	4,986	18,321	90,256	5,984	6,162	20,507	6,896	31,579	19,128
1995	117,191	24,265	581	5,160	18,524	92,925	6,132	6,378	21,187	6,806	33,117	19,305
1996	119,608	24,493	580	5,418	18,495	95,115	6,253	6,482	21,597	6,911	34,454	19,419
1997	122,690	24,962	596	5,691	18,675	97,727	6,408	6,648	21,966	7,109	36,040	19,557
1998	125,826	25,347	590	5,985	18,772	100,480	6,600	6,831	22,296	7,407	37,526	19,819
1999	128,615	25,240	535	6,273	18,432	103,375	6,792	7,004	22,787	7,632	39,000	20,160
PERCENT DISTRIBUTION												
1980	100.0	28.4	1.1	4.8	22.4	71.6	5.7	5.9	16.6	5.7	19.8	18.0
1985	100.0	25.5	1.0	4.8	19.8	74.5	5.4	5.9	17.8	6.1	22.5	16.8
1990	100.0	22.8	0.6	4.7	17.4	77.2	5.3	5.6	17.9	6.1	25.5	16.7
1992	100.0	21.4	0.6	4.1	16.7	78.6	5.3	5.5	17.8	6.1	26.8	17.2
1993	100.0	21.1	0.6	4.2	16.3	78.9	5.2	5.4	17.9	6.1	27.3	17.0
1994	100.0	20.9	0.5	4.4	16.0	79.1	5.2	5.4	18.0	6.0	27.7	16.8
1995	100.0	20.7	0.5	4.4	15.8	79.3	5.2	5.4	18.1	5.8	28.3	16.5
1996	100.0	20.5	0.5	4.5	15.5	79.5	5.2	5.4	18.1	5.8	28.8	16.2
1997	100.0	20.3	0.5	4.6	15.2	79.7	5.2	5.4	17.9	5.8	29.4	15.9
1998	100.0	20.1	0.5	4.8	14.9	79.9	5.2	5.4	17.7	5.9	29.8	15.8
1999	100.0	19.6	0.4	4.9	14.3	80.4	5.3	5.4	17.7	5.9	30.3	15.7
WEEKLY HOURS [1]												
1980	35.3	(NA)	43.3	37.0	39.7	(NA)	39.6	38.4	30.2	36.2	32.6	(NA)
1985	34.9	(NA)	43.4	37.7	40.5	(NA)	39.5	38.4	29.4	36.4	32.5	(NA)
1990	34.5	(NA)	44.1	38.2	40.8	(NA)	38.4	38.1	28.8	35.8	32.5	(NA)
1992	34.4	(NA)	43.9	38.0	41.0	(NA)	38.3	38.2	28.8	35.8	32.5	(NA)
1993	34.5	(NA)	44.3	38.5	41.4	(NA)	39.3	38.2	28.8	35.8	32.5	(NA)
1994	34.7	(NA)	44.8	38.9	42.0	(NA)	39.7	38.4	28.9	35.8	32.5	(NA)
1995	34.5	(NA)	44.7	38.9	41.6	(NA)	39.4	38.3	28.8	35.9	32.4	(NA)
1996	34.4	(NA)	45.3	39.0	41.6	(NA)	39.6	38.3	28.8	35.9	32.4	(NA)
1997	34.6	(NA)	45.4	39.0	42.0	(NA)	39.7	38.4	28.9	36.1	32.6	(NA)
1998	34.6	(NA)	43.9	38.8	41.7	(NA)	39.5	38.4	29.0	36.4	32.6	(NA)
1999	34.5	(NA)	43.8	39.0	41.7	(NA)	38.7	38.4	29.0	36.2	32.6	(NA)
HOURLY EARNINGS [1]												
1980	6.66	(NA)	9.17	9.94	7.27	(NA)	8.87	6.95	4.88	5.79	5.85	(NA)
1985	8.57	(NA)	11.98	12.32	9.54	(NA)	11.40	9.15	5.94	7.94	7.90	(NA)
1990	10.01	(NA)	13.68	13.77	10.83	(NA)	12.92	10.79	6.75	9.97	9.83	(NA)
1992	10.57	(NA)	14.54	14.15	11.46	(NA)	13.43	11.39	7.12	10.82	10.54	(NA)
1993	10.83	(NA)	14.60	14.38	11.74	(NA)	13.55	11.74	7.29	11.35	10.78	(NA)
1994	11.12	(NA)	14.88	14.73	12.07	(NA)	13.78	12.06	7.49	11.83	11.04	(NA)
1995	11.43	(NA)	15.30	15.09	12.37	(NA)	14.13	12.43	7.69	12.32	11.39	(NA)
1996	11.82	(NA)	15.62	15.47	12.77	(NA)	14.45	12.87	7.99	12.80	11.79	(NA)
1997	12.28	(NA)	16.15	16.04	13.17	(NA)	14.92	13.45	8.33	13.34	12.28	(NA)
1998	12.78	(NA)	16.90	16.59	13.49	(NA)	15.31	14.06	8.73	14.06	12.85	(NA)
1999	13.24	(NA)	17.04	17.13	13.91	(NA)	15.67	14.59	9.08	14.61	13.38	(NA)
WEEKLY EARNINGS [1]												
1980	235	(NA)	397	368	289	(NA)	351	267	147	210	191	(NA)
1985	299	(NA)	520	464	386	(NA)	450	351	175	289	257	(NA)
1990	345	(NA)	603	526	442	(NA)	496	411	194	357	319	(NA)
1992	364	(NA)	638	538	470	(NA)	514	435	205	387	343	(NA)
1993	374	(NA)	647	554	486	(NA)	533	448	210	406	350	(NA)
1994	386	(NA)	667	573	507	(NA)	547	463	216	424	359	(NA)
1995	394	(NA)	684	587	515	(NA)	557	476	221	442	369	(NA)
1996	407	(NA)	708	603	531	(NA)	572	493	230	460	382	(NA)
1997	425	(NA)	733	626	553	(NA)	592	516	241	482	400	(NA)
1998	442	(NA)	742	644	563	(NA)	605	540	253	512	419	(NA)
1999	457	(NA)	746	668	580	(NA)	606	560	263	529	436	(NA)

NA Not available. [1] Average hours and earnings. Private production and related workers in mining, manufacturing, and construction; nonsupervisory employees in other industries.

Source: U.S. Bureau of Labor Statistics, *Employment and Earnings*, monthly, June issues and Internet site <http://stats.bls.gov/ceshome.htm>.

No. 683. Employees in Nonfarm Establishments by State: 1990 to 1999

[In thousands (109,404 represents 109,403,000). For coverage, see headnote, Table 682. National totals differ from the sum of the state figures because of differing benchmarks among States and differing industrial and geographic stratification. Based on 1987 *Standard Industrial Classification Manual*, see text, Section 17, Business]

State	1990	1995	1999 Total [1]	Construction	Manufacturing	Transportation and public utilities	Wholesale and retail trade	Finance, insurance, and real estate	Services	Government
United States	109,403	117,191	128,615	6,273	18,432	6,792	29,791	7,632	39,000	20,160
Alabama.	1,636	1,804	1,924	104	369	95	446	92	457	352
Alaska	238	262	278	14	14	26	57	13	71	74
Arizona.	1,483	1,796	2,160	155	211	104	511	140	680	349
Arkansas	924	1,069	1,142	50	253	69	262	46	271	188
California	12,500	12,422	13,972	679	1,923	719	3,194	822	4,378	2,235
Colorado.	1,521	1,834	2,134	148	204	139	507	141	653	329
Connecticut.	1,624	1,562	1,672	61	269	78	360	141	527	236
Delaware	348	366	412	24	60	17	90	49	116	55
District of Columbia	686	643	616	9	12	17	48	31	276	223
Florida	5,387	5,996	6,877	365	488	350	1,721	449	2,531	967
Georgia	2,992	3,402	3,890	199	599	258	969	203	1,066	589
Hawaii	528	533	534	[2]22	17	41	133	35	174	113
Idaho.	385	477	540	35	77	27	136	24	133	106
Illinois	5,288	5,593	5,955	252	956	347	1,344	407	1,812	827
Indiana.	2,522	2,787	2,968	148	690	147	702	143	729	403
Iowa	1,226	1,358	1,467	65	261	72	356	85	386	239
Kansas.	1,089	1,198	1,327	66	213	78	319	63	343	240
Kentucky	1,471	1,643	1,795	87	321	105	426	71	463	301
Louisiana	1,590	1,772	1,898	130	188	113	443	85	523	369
Maine.	535	538	586	28	86	24	146	31	174	96
Maryland	2,171	2,183	2,382	151	177	111	550	140	814	438
Massachusetts.	2,985	2,977	3,236	119	433	139	738	226	1,161	418
Michigan	3,970	4,274	4,528	190	978	177	1,063	208	1,240	667
Minnesota.	2,127	2,379	2,609	112	440	131	619	160	752	388
Mississippi	937	1,075	1,155	56	245	56	252	42	270	229
Missouri	2,345	2,521	2,725	138	411	172	642	166	771	420
Montana.	297	351	381	20	25	22	101	18	112	79
Nebraska	730	816	891	43	118	57	215	61	243	152
Nevada	621	786	985	91	42	52	202	44	426	118
New Hampshire	508	540	605	24	107	21	160	33	178	81
New Jersey.	3,635	3,601	3,866	138	467	263	906	257	1,262	571
New Mexico	580	682	730	44	42	35	171	33	211	180
New York	8,212	7,892	8,454	311	893	419	1,710	748	2,926	1,442
North Carolina	3,118	3,460	3,866	224	803	177	873	186	994	607
North Dakota.	266	302	323	17	24	18	81	16	92	72
Ohio	4,882	5,221	5,548	236	1,088	245	1,334	307	1,552	773
Oklahoma.	1,196	1,316	1,462	58	184	82	337	73	417	283
Oregon.	1,247	1,418	1,572	83	241	78	388	95	425	261
Pennsylvania.	5,170	5,253	5,577	236	931	293	1,250	324	1,813	710
Rhode Island.	451	440	464	18	75	16	104	30	159	63
South Carolina.	1,545	1,646	1,833	114	345	88	441	82	447	315
South Dakota	289	344	373	17	50	17	91	25	101	72
Tennessee	2,193	2,499	2,674	124	509	171	628	131	716	391
Texas.	7,095	8,023	9,155	528	1,086	562	2,179	518	2,597	1,540
Utah	724	908	1,050	73	133	59	249	57	293	179
Vermont	258	270	290	15	48	12	67	13	88	47
Virginia.	2,896	3,070	3,408	197	396	178	749	184	1,084	610
Washington.	2,143	2,347	2,643	153	364	139	636	138	736	473
West Virginia.	630	688	726	34	82	38	163	30	217	141
Wisconsin.	2,292	2,559	2,777	121	616	131	628	146	735	398
Wyoming	199	219	233	17	11	14	53	8	54	59

[1] Includes mining, not shown separately.   [2] Hawaii includes mining with construction.

Source: U.S. Bureau of Labor Statistics, *Employment and Earnings,* monthly, May issues. Compiled from data supplied by cooperating state agencies.

Labor Force, Employment and Earnings   427

No. 684. Nonfarm Industries—Employees and Earnings: 1980 to 1999

[Annual averages of monthly figures (90,406 represents 90,406,000). Covers all full- and part-time employees who worked during or received pay for any part of the pay period including the 12th of the month. For mining and manufacturing, data refer to production and related workers; for construction, to employees engaged in actual construction work; and for other industries, to nonsupervisory employees and working supervisors. See also headnote, Table 682]

Industry	1987 SIC [1] code	All employees (1,000)			Production workers					
					Total (1,000)			Average hourly earnings (dollars)		
		1980	1990	1999	1980	1990	1999	1980	1990	1999
Total	(X)	90,406	109,403	128,615	(NA)	(NA)	(NA)	(NA)	(NA)	(NA)
Private sector [2]	(X)	74,166	91,098	108,455	60,331	73,774	88,725	6.66	10.01	13.24
Mining	(B)	1,027	709	535	762	509	404	9.17	13.68	17.04
Metal mining	10	98	58	49	74	46	37	10.26	14.05	18.24
Coal mining	12	246	147	85	204	119	70	10.86	16.71	19.28
Oil and gas extraction.	13	560	395	293	389	261	214	8.59	12.94	16.86
Nonmetallic minerals, except fuels	14	123	110	109	96	83	82	7.52	11.58	15.11
Construction.	(C)	4,346	5,120	6,273	3,421	3,974	4,849	9.94	13.77	17.13
General building contractors	15	1,173	1,298	1,434	900	938	999	9.22	13.01	16.49
Heavy construction, except building . . .	16	895	770	862	720	643	719	9.20	13.34	16.74
Special trade contractors.	17	2,278	3,051	3,978	1,802	2,393	3,131	10.63	14.20	17.43
Manufacturing.	(D)	20,285	19,076	18,432	14,214	12,947	12,662	7.27	10.83	13.91
Durable goods [3]	(X)	12,159	11,109	10,985	8,416	7,363	7,511	7.75	11.35	14.40
Lumber and wood products [3]	24	704	733	826	587	603	678	6.57	9.08	11.46
Logging	241	88	85	77	71	70	61	8.64	11.22	13.24
Sawmills and planing mills	242	215	198	180	190	172	157	6.70	9.22	11.40
Millwork, plywood, and structural members.	243	206	262	325	170	210	260	6.44	9.04	11.59
Wood containers	244	43	45	55	37	38	47	4.95	6.64	9.23
Mobile homes	2451	46	41	77	36	33	64	6.08	8.67	11.79
Furniture and fixtures [3]	25	466	506	540	376	400	431	5.49	8.52	11.23
Household furniture	251	301	289	286	253	241	243	5.12	7.87	10.67
Office furniture	252	51	68	69	40	51	50	5.91	9.64	11.89
Partitions and fixtures . . . . . . [3] . .	254	63	78	95	47	57	71	6.68	9.77	11.84
Stone, clay, and glass products [3]	32	629	556	569	486	432	445	7.50	11.12	13.90
Flat glass	321	18	17	17	14	13	14	9.65	15.15	18.30
Glass and glassware, pressed and blown	322	124	83	70	105	72	57	7.97	12.40	15.75
Products of purchased glass	323	45	60	63	32	46	48	6.50	9.75	12.50
Cement, hydraulic.	324	31	18	18	25	14	13	10.55	13.90	19.17
Structural clay products	325	46	36	34	34	28	26	6.14	9.55	12.32
Pottery and related products.	326	47	39	37	39	31	29	6.25	9.62	12.00
Concrete, gypsum, and plaster	327	204	206	238	157	157	185	7.45	10.76	13.52
Primary metal industries [3]	33	1,142	756	690	878	574	538	9.77	12.92	15.85
Blast furnaces and basic steel products	331	512	276	222	396	212	172	11.39	14.82	18.87
Iron and steel foundries	332	209	132	126	167	105	103	8.20	11.55	14.69
Primary nonferrous metals	333	71	46	37	53	34	29	10.63	14.36	17.58
Nonferrous rolling and drawing	335	211	172	168	151	124	127	8.81	12.29	14.52
Nonferrous foundries (castings).	336	90	84	91	72	66	74	7.30	10.21	12.81
Fabricated metal products [3]	34	1,609	1,419	1,489	1,194	1,045	1,119	7.45	10.83	13.46
Metal cans and shipping containers . . .	341	75	50	36	63	43	30	9.84	14.27	16.73
Cutlery, handtools, and hardware . . .	342	164	131	124	125	96	95	7.02	10.78	12.41
Plumbing and heating, exc. electric . .	343	71	60	58	52	43	42	6.59	9.75	12.07
Fabricated structural metal products	344	506	427	468	351	303	341	7.27	10.16	12.94
Screw machine products	345	109	96	104	84	73	81	6.96	10.70	13.85
Metal forgings and stampings . . . [3] .	346	260	225	257	205	178	202	8.56	12.70	15.73
Industrial machinery and equipment [3] . .	35	2,517	2,095	2,129	1,614	1,260	1,343	8.00	11.77	15.01
Engines and turbines	351	135	89	84	87	58	56	9.73	14.55	18.06
Farm and garden machinery.	352	169	106	96	116	78	67	8.78	10.99	13.86
Construction and related machinery . .	353	389	229	243	255	141	154	8.60	11.92	14.16
Metalworking machinery	354	398	330	339	290	236	242	8.13	12.27	15.92
Special industry machinery.	355	194	159	170	125	94	91	7.53	11.90	15.68
General industrial machinery	356	300	247	261	196	158	166	7.95	11.32	14.35
Computer and office equipment.	357	420	438	360	181	137	144	6.75	11.51	16.42
Refrigeration and service machinery . . . . [3]	358	175	177	201	120	125	143	7.23	10.93	13.55
Electronic and other elec. equip. [3] . . .	36	1,771	1,673	1,661	[4]	1,055	1,035	[4]	10.30	13.45
Electric distribution equipment.	361	117	97	82	82	67	56	6.96	10.15	13.06
Electrical industrial apparatus	362	232	169	147	163	119	101	[4]	10.00	12.93
Household appliances	363	162	124	118	128	99	97	6.95	10.26	12.98
Electric lighting and wiring equip . . .	364	211	189	177	157	136	127	6.43	10.12	13.01
Household audio and video equip . . .	365	109	85	82	79	59	53	6.42	9.68	12.67
Communications equipment	366	[4]	264	275	[4]	133	122	[4]	11.03	14.05
Electronic components and accessories . . . . [3] .	367	539	582	639	325	329	378	6.05	10.00	13.72
Transportation equipment [3]	37	1,881	1,989	1,855	1,220	1,224	1,230	9.35	14.08	18.10
Motor vehicles and equipment	371	789	812	1,000	575	617	762	9.85	14.56	18.48
Aircraft and parts	372	633	712	490	344	345	241	9.28	14.79	19.76
Ship and boat building and repairing	373	221	188	164	176	141	121	8.22	10.94	13.82
Railroad equipment.	374	71	33	35	53	25	25	9.93	13.41	16.54
Guided missiles, space vehicles, and parts	376	111	185	87	35	57	23	9.22	14.39	20.24

See footnotes at end of table.

U.S. Census Bureau, Statistical Abstract of the United States: 2000

[See headnote, p. 428]

Industry	1987 SIC [1] code	All employees (1,000)			Production workers					
					Total (1,000)			Average hourly earnings (dollars)		
		1980	1990	1999	1980	1990	1999	1980	1990	1999
Durable goods—Continued										
Instruments and related products	38	1,022	1,006	839	[4]	499	424	[4]	11.29	14.17
Search and navigation equipment . . .	381	[4]	284	155	[4]	94	41	[4]	14.62	17.53
Measuring and controlling devices. . .	382	[4]	323	294	[4]	180	149	[4]	10.68	14.31
Medical instruments and supplies . . .	384	[4]	246	277	[4]	144	166	[4]	9.85	12.90
Ophthalmic goods	385	44	43	33	31	30	24	5.30	8.18	10.78
Photographic equipment and supplies	386	135	100	73	67	43	40	8.83	14.08	17.78
Watches, clocks, watchcases, and parts	387	22	11	6	17	8	5	5.24	7.70	10.75
Misc. manufacturing industries [3]	39	418	375	387	313	272	268	5.46	8.61	11.33
Jewelry, silverware, and plated ware.	391	56	52	50	40	37	34	5.76	9.23	11.95
Toys and sporting goods	394	117	104	101	88	76	68	5.01	7.94	10.90
Pens, pencils, office and art supplies	395	37	34	30	27	24	21	5.58	8.89	11.41
Costume jewelry and notions	396	[4]	33	21	[4]	25	15	[4]	7.40	10.20
Nondurable goods [3] **. . . . .**	(X)	**8,127**	**7,968**	**7,446**	**5,798**	**5,584**	**5,151**	**6.56**	**10.12**	**13.17**
Food and kindred products [3]	20	1,708	1,661	1,685	1,175	1,194	1,257	6.85	9.62	12.10
Meat products	201	358	422	501	298	359	427	6.99	7.94	9.96
Dairy products	202	175	155	141	96	95	97	6.86	10.56	14.06
Preserved fruits and vegetables	203	246	247	227	202	206	190	5.94	8.95	11.65
Grain mill products	204	144	128	124	99	89	88	7.67	11.52	15.00
Bakery products.	205	230	213	207	139	133	143	7.14	10.85	13.02
Sugar and confectionery products . . .	206	108	99	93	81	78	73	6.56	10.26	13.81
Fats and oils	207	44	31	34	32	22	24	7.03	10.10	13.40
Beverages	208	234	184	183	105	78	90	8.12	13.51	16.18
Tobacco products	21	69	49	39	54	36	28	7.74	16.23	19.07
Cigarettes.	211	46	35	26	35	26	18	9.23	19.57	24.59
Textile mill products [3]	22	848	691	562	737	593	475	5.07	8.02	10.71
Broadwoven fabric mills, cotton. . .	221	150	91	65	135	82	58	5.25	8.31	11.05
Broadwoven fabric mills, synthetics . .	222	116	77	60	104	68	51	5.30	8.63	11.49
Broadwoven fabric mills, wool.	223	19	17	10	16	14	9	5.21	8.61	11.20
Narrow fabric mills	224	23	24	21	20	20	17	4.63	7.39	9.81
Knitting mills	225	224	205	143	194	179	121	4.77	7.37	9.91
Textile finishing, except wool.	226	74	62	61	62	50	51	5.39	8.45	10.80
Carpets and rugs	227	54	61	66	44	50	54	5.20	8.25	10.75
Yarn and thread mills	228	125	103	83	113	92	73	4.76	7.68	10.45
Apparel and other textile products [3] . . .	23	1,264	1,036	685	1,079	869	545	4.56	6.57	8.86
Men's and boys' suits and coats	231	77	50	23	67	42	18	5.34	7.34	8.94
Men's and boys' furnishings	232	362	274	157	310	235	130	4.23	6.06	8.28
Women's and misses outerwear	233	417	328	203	360	274	158	4.61	6.26	8.41
Women's and children's undergarments	234	90	62	27	76	51	22	4.15	6.18	8.37
Girls' and children's outerwear	236	64	56	21	55	47	17	4.20	5.95	8.37
Paper and allied products [3]	26	685	697	659	519	522	500	7.84	12.31	15.97
Papermills.	262	178	180	149	133	136	116	9.05	15.10	20.46
Paperboard mills	263	65	52	47	51	40	36	9.28	15.26	20.48
Paperboard containers and boxes . . .	265	205	209	215	157	162	167	6.94	10.39	13.44
Misc. converted paper products . . .	267	220	241	237	163	174	172	6.89	10.79	13.96
Printing and publishing [3]	27	1,252	1,569	1,553	699	871	828	7.53	11.24	13.83
Newspapers	271	420	474	442	164	166	147	7.72	11.17	13.61
Periodicals	272	90	129	141	16	47	44	7.16	11.95	15.31
Books	273	101	121	123	52	66	56	6.76	10.10	13.50
Commercial printing	275	410	552	578	304	401	410	7.85	11.52	14.02
Blankbooks and bookbinding	278	62	72	61	51	56	46	5.78	8.83	10.87
Chemicals and allied products [3]	28	1,107	1,086	1,035	626	600	583	8.30	13.54	17.47
Industrial inorganic chemicals	281	161	138	112	88	70	59	9.07	14.66	19.41
Plastics materials and synthetics. . . .	282	205	180	151	137	116	99	8.21	13.97	18.27
Drugs.	283	196	237	290	97	105	133	7.69	12.90	17.22
Soap, cleaners, and toilet goods	284	141	159	152	86	98	99	7.67	11.71	14.82
Paints and allied products	285	65	61	53	33	31	28	7.39	11.99	14.90
Industrial organic chemicals	286	174	155	134	88	86	78	9.67	15.97	20.59
Agricultural chemicals	287	72	56	52	45	34	31	8.12	13.73	17.48
Petroleum and coal products [3]	29	198	157	137	125	103	90	10.10	16.24	21.46
Petroleum refining	291	155	118	92	93	75	59	10.94	17.58	24.41
Asphalt paving and roofing materials.	295	31	27	30	24	21	23	7.69	12.87	16.36
Rubber and misc. plastics products [3]. . .	30	764	888	1,019	588	687	790	6.58	9.76	12.31
Tires and inner tubes	301	115	84	77	81	62	57	9.74	15.42	19.28
Rubber and plastics footwear	302	22	11	5	20	9	4	4.43	6.66	10.29
Leather and leather products [3]	31	233	133	74	197	109	55	4.58	6.91	9.69
Leather tanning and finishing	311	19	15	11	16	12	9	6.10	9.04	12.53
Footwear, except rubber	314	144	74	31	123	63	25	4.42	6.61	9.32
Luggage	316	16	11	8	12	8	6	4.90	6.91	8.91
Handbags and personal leather goods.	317	30	15	8	25	12	4	4.33	6.08	8.48

See footnotes at end of table.

Labor Force, Employment, and Earnings   **429**

[See headnote, p. 428]

Industry	1987 SIC [1] code	All employees (1,000)			Production workers					
					Total (1,000)			Average hourly earnings (dollars)		
		1980	1990	1999	1980	1990	1999	1980	1990	1999
Transp. and public utilities [3]	(E)	5,146	5,777	6,792	4,293	4,781	5,630	8.87	12.92	15.67
Railroad transportation	40	532	279	230	(4)	(4)	(4)	(4)	(4)	(4)
Class I railroads, plus Amtrak [5] . . .	4011	482	241	204	(4)	(4)	(4)	[6]9.92	16.08	17.79
Local and interurban passenger transit .	41	265	338	482	244	308	441	6.34	9.23	11.63
Trucking and warehousing	42	(4)	1,395	1,813	(NA)	1,215	1,589	(4)	11.68	13.95
Water transportation	44	211	177	181	(4)	(4)	(4)	(4)	(4)	(4)
Transportation by air	45	(4)	968	1,237	(4)	(4)	(4)	(4)	(4)	(4)
Pipelines, except natural gas	46	21	19	13	15	14	11	10.50	17.04	21.79
Transportation services	47	(4)	336	469	159	270	384	6.94	10.38	14.15
Communication [3]	48	1,357	1,309	1,522	1,014	978	1,098	8.50	13.51	17.38
Telephone communication	481	1,072	913	1,048	779	658	727	8.72	14.13	17.70
Radio and television broadcasting . . .	483	192	234	248	154	193	202	7.44	12.71	18.35
Cable and other pay television services	484	(4)	126	189	(4)	105	154	(4)	10.50	14.57
Electric, gas, and sanitary services [3] . . .	49	829	957	845	678	759	678	8.90	15.23	20.61
Electric services	491	391	454	362	316	351	291	9.12	15.80	21.69
Gas production and distribution	492	168	165	132	138	129	104	8.27	14.25	18.87
Combination utility services	493	197	193	153	162	156	122	9.64	17.58	24.69
Sanitary services	495	50	115	164	44	99	136	7.16	11.55	16.77
Wholesale trade	(F)	5,292	6,173	7,004	4,328	4,959	5,615	6.95	10.79	14.59
Retail trade [3]	(G)	15,018	19,601	22,787	13,484	17,358	20,040	4.88	6.75	9.08
General merchandise stores	53	2,245	2,540	2,775	2,090	2,380	2,594	4.77	6.83	8.97
Food stores	54	2,384	3,215	3,483	2,202	2,953	3,152	6.24	7.31	9.29
Automotive dealers and service stations.	55	1,689	2,063	2,406	1,430	1,718	1,999	5.66	8.92	12.54
Apparel and accessory stores	56	957	1,183	1,180	820	991	988	4.30	6.25	8.84
Furniture and home furnishings stores . .	57	606	820	1,085	502	670	896	5.53	8.53	12.24
Eating and drinking places.	58	4,626	6,509	7,904	4,256	5,905	7,100	3.69	4.97	6.62
Finance, insurance, real estate . .	(H)	5,160	6,709	7,632	3,907	4,860	5,589	5.79	9.97	14.61
Depository institutions.	60	(4)	2,251	2,047	(4)	1,632	1,472	(4)	8.43	11.25
Nondepository institutions	61	(4)	373	714	(4)	270	483	(4)	10.40	15.33
Security and commodity brokers	62	227	424	679	(4)	(4)	(4)	(4)	(4)	(4)
Insurance carriers	63	1,224	1,462	1,635	854	982	1,250	6.29	11.18	17.01
Insurance, agents, brokers, service	64	464	663	767	(4)	(4)	(4)	(4)	(4)	(4)
Real estate.	65	989	1,315	1,525	(4)	(4)	(4)	(4)	(4)	(4)
Holding and other investment offices . . .	67	115	221	266	(4)	(4)	(4)	(4)	(4)	(4)
Services [3]	(I)	17,890	27,934	39,000	15,921	24,387	33,937	5.85	9.83	13.38
Hotels and other lodging places	70	1,076	1,631	1,799	(4)	(4)	(4)	(4)	(4)	(4)
Hotels and motels.	701	1,038	1,578	1,737	954	1,398	1,524	4.45	6.98	9.22
Personal services [3]	72	818	1,104	1,206	(4)	(4)	(4)	(4)	(4)	(4)
Laundry, cleaning, garment services .	721	356	426	434	318	379	382	4.47	6.82	8.76
Beauty shops	723	284	372	420	264	333	370	4.26	7.10	9.81
Business services [3]	73	2,564	5,139	9,123	(4)	4,522	8,057	(4)	9.48	13.23
Advertising	731	153	235	281	116	169	200	8.07	13.51	18.58
Personnel supply services	736	543	1,535	3,405	(4)	(4)	(4)	(4)	(4)	(4)
Employment agencies	7361	(4)	246	388	(4)	(4)	(4)	(4)	(4)	(4)
Help supply services	7363	(4)	1,288	3,017	(4)	1,245	2,912	(4)	8.09	10.57
Computer and data processing services	737	304	772	1,781	254	603	1,426	7.16	15.11	22.34
Prepackaged software	7372	(4)	113	293	(4)	(4)	(4)	(4)	(4)	(4)
Data processing and preparation . .	7374	(4)	197	277	(4)	(4)	(4)	(4)	(4)	(4)
Auto repair, services, and parking	75	571	914	1,185	488	756	963	6.10	8.77	11.48
Automotive repair shops	753	350	524	663	297	429	524	6.52	9.67	12.85
Motion pictures [3]	78	(4)	408	600	(4)	344	507	(4)	10.95	15.69
Motion picture theaters	783	124	112	144	(4)	(4)	(4)	(4)	(4)	(4)
Amusement and recreation services . . .	79	(4)	1,076	1,696	(4)	944	1,481	(4)	8.11	9.81
Health services [3]	80	5,278	7,814	9,973	4,712	6,948	8,832	5.68	10.41	14.21
Offices and clinics of medical doctors	801	802	1,338	1,865	(4)	1,105	1,535	(4)	10.58	14.85
Nursing and personal care facilities . .	805	997	1,415	1,755	898	1,279	1,577	4.17	7.24	10.18
Hospitals.	806	2,750	3,549	3,970	2,522	3,248	3,638	6.06	11.79	15.97
Home health care services.	808	(4)	291	655	(4)	269	602	(4)	8.72	12.01
Legal services.	81	498	908	1,002	427	748	801	7.35	14.16	19.00
Educational services.	82	1,138	1,661	2,270	(4)	(4)	(4)	(4)	(4)	(4)
Social services	83	1,134	1,734	2,782	990	1,494	2,403	4.26	7.11	9.59
Membership organizations.	86	1,539	1,946	2,402	(4)	(4)	(4)	(4)	(4)	(4)
Engineering and management services .	87	(4)	2,478	3,420	(4)	1,886	2,563	(4)	13.56	18.51
Government	(J)	16,241	18,304	20,160	(NA)	(NA)	(NA)	(NA)	(NA)	(NA)
Federal Government	(X)	2,866	3,085	2,669	(NA)	(NA)	(NA)	(NA)	(NA)	(NA)
State government	(X)	3,610	4,305	4,695	(NA)	(NA)	(NA)	(NA)	(NA)	(NA)
Local government	(X)	9,765	10,914	12,796	(NA)	(NA)	(NA)	(NA)	(NA)	(NA)

NA Not available.   X Not applicable.   [1] 1987 Standard Industrial Classification, see text, Section 17, Business   [2] Excludes government.   [3] Includes industries not shown separately.   [4] Included in totals; not available separately.   [5] For changes in "Class I" classification, see text, Section 21, Land Transportation.   [6] Includes all employees except executives, officials, and staff assistants who received pay during the month.

Source: U.S. Bureau of Labor Statistics, *Employment and Earnings*, monthly, June issues and Internet site <http://stats.bls.gov/ceshome.htm>.

No. 685. Employers With Selected Work-Based Learning Activities by Establishment Size and Type: 1997

[In percent. Based on survey of private establishments with 20 or more employees. Excludes nonprofits, government, and corporate headquarters. Subject to sampling error; see source]

Establishment	All activities	At least one activity	Internship	Job shadowing	Cooperative education	Mentoring	Registered apprenticeship
Total	**0.8**	**41.9**	**20.6**	**14.8**	**14.4**	**9.5**	**7.8**
20 to 49 employees	1.3	35.2	17.0	14.6	12.2	9.2	8.1
50 to 99 employees	-	47.1	18.9	13.0	15.4	7.7	7.4
100 to 249 employees	0.2	54.2	29.3	14.9	19.1	10.6	7.4
250 employees or more	0.4	68.5	48.6	24.6	24.0	19.4	7.4
Construction, manufacturing and transportation	-	39.7	16.6	9.0	11.1	5.2	12.3
Wholesale/retail trade	1.7	38.3	17.1	13.9	18.0	11.4	7.7
Services	0.1	50.5	31.0	22.6	11.6	11.1	3.1

- Represents zero.

Source: U.S. National Center for Education Statistics, *Vocational Education in the United States: Toward 2000*, NCES 2000-029.

No. 686. Employees Receiving Employer-Provided Training: 1995

[In percent, except hours. For May through October. For private establishments with 50 or more employees. Formal training is structured, planned in advances and with a defined curriculum. Based on the 1995 Survey of Employer-Provided Training; see source for details]

Employee characteristic	Employees receiving formal training [1]	Hours of training per employee		Employee characteristic	Employees receiving formal training [1]	Hours of training per employee	
		Formal training [2]	Informal training [2]			Formal training [2]	Informal training [2]
Total	**69.8**	**13.4**	**31.1**	Occupation: Managerial and professional	80.2	4.3	22.4
Age: 24 years old and under.	63.4	2.7	21.4	Professional, para-			
25 to 34 years old	78.5	14.0	32.5	professional and tech. ..	84.8	22.3	38.7
35 to 44 years old	74.7	15.4	30.3	Sales, clerical, and			
45 to 54 years old	64.7	17.2	39.0	admin. support	72.5	10.2	23.2
55 years old and over ...	50.7	5.7	17.1	Service	49.8	5.6	22.1
Sex: Male	66.5	12.2	35.4	Production [3]	66.3	15.2	38.5
Female	73.1	14.6	26.9				
				Tenure in current job:			
Education: High school				2 years or less	67.5	8.9	56.5
graduate or less	60.1	10.9	24.8	2 to 5 years	56.8	4.5	19.5
Some college	67.8	14.3	37.0	5 to 10 years	79.7	19.5	27.0
BA degree or more	89.7	16.1	31.8	More than 10 years	75.3	21.1	20.5

[1] In the prior 12 months, measured by the employee survey. [2] Measured by the employee survey. [3] Includes construction, operating, maintenance, and material handling.

Source: U.S. Bureau of Labor Statistics, *Monthly Labor Review*, June 1998.

No. 687. Adults Taking Work-Related Adult Education Classes: 1999

[In thousands (183,498 represents 183,498,000), except percent. For the civilian noninstitutional population 16 years old and over not enrolled in elementary or secondary school. Excludes retired persons over 70 who did not work for pay in the prior year. Excludes classes such as basic skills, personal development, etc. See also Table 328]

Occupation	Total population	Participants		Occupation	Total population	Participants	
		Number	Percent			Number	Percent
Total.	**183,498**	**44,815**	**24**	Service	18,192	3,393	19
Health assessment, treatment	3,034	2,207	73	Precision production, craft and repair.	11,179	1,634	15
Health diagnosing	884	578	65	Transportation and materials			
Teacher, below college	6,778	3,512	52	moving.	5,476	959	18
Other professional [1]	9,864	4,991	51	Machine operators, assemblers			
Executive, admin., managerial	28,665	10,704	37	and inspectors.	10,121	1,873	19
College teacher.	2,582	1,080	42	Agriculture, forestry and fishing ...	2,532	394	16
Technical and related support	7,314	3,021	41	Handlers, equipment cleaning,			
Miscellaneous.	2,161	337	16	helpers and laborers.	3,874	206	5
Admin. support, incl. clerical	22,276	5,789	26				
Sales workers.	14,626	3,325	23	No job in the past year	33,939	814	2

[1] For example, includes engineers, scientists, and social scientists.

Source: U.S. National Center for Education Statistics, National Household Education Survey, spring 1999.

No. 688. Annual Indexes of Output Per Hour for Selected Three-Digit SIC Industries: 1988 to 1998

[See text, this section. Minus sign (-) indicates decrease]

Industry	1987 SIC code [1]	Indexes (1987=100) 1988	1990	1995	1996	1997	1998	Average annual percent change [2]
Mining:								
Bituminous coal and lignite mining	122	111.7	118.7	155.9	168.0	176.6	187.3	5.9
Crude petroleum and natural gas	131	101.0	97.0	119.4	123.9	125.2	128.7	2.3
Manufacturing:								
Meat products.	201	100.1	97.1	102.3	97.4	103.2	(NA)	0.3
Dairy products	202	108.4	107.3	116.4	116.0	119.5	(NA)	1.8
Preserved fruits and vegetables	203	97.0	95.6	109.1	109.2	111.8	(NA)	1.1
Grain mill products.	204	101.3	105.4	115.4	108.0	118.7	(NA)	1.7
Bakery products	205	96.8	92.7	97.3	95.6	99.3	(NA)	-0.1
Sugar and confectionery products	206	99.5	103.2	108.3	113.8	117.1	(NA)	1.6
Beverages	208	106.0	117.7	134.3	135.7	136.3	(NA)	3.1
Miscellaneous food and kindred products.	209	107.0	99.3	103.1	109.2	103.9	(NA)	0.4
Broadwoven fabric mills, cotton	221	99.6	103.1	134.0	137.3	130.9	(NA)	2.7
Knitting mills.	225	96.3	107.5	138.6	150.5	150.2	(NA)	4.1
Yarn and thread mills	228	102.1	110.2	137.4	147.4	155.5	(NA)	4.5
Men's and boys' furnishings	232	100.1	102.1	123.4	134.7	152.4	(NA)	4.3
Women's and misses' outerwear	233	101.4	104.1	135.5	141.6	151.5	(NA)	4.2
Miscellaneous fabricated textile products	239	96.6	99.9	109.2	105.6	117.0	(NA)	1.6
Logging	241	93.7	86.3	86.0	85.4	71.9	(NA)	-3.3
Sawmills and planing mills	242	100.7	99.8	110.2	115.6	117.5	(NA)	1.6
Millwork, plywood, and structural members. . . .	243	98.8	98.0	92.7	92.4	89.9	(NA)	-1.1
Wood buildings and mobile homes	245	97.8	103.1	97.0	96.7	101.1	(NA)	0.1
Miscellaneous wood products	249	95.9	107.7	115.4	114.4	123.1	(NA)	2.1
Household furniture	251	99.4	104.5	116.9	121.6	121.8	(NA)	2.0
Partitions and fixtures.	254	95.7	95.6	101.2	97.5	121.4	(NA)	2.0
Paper mills.	262	103.9	102.3	118.6	111.6	107.0	(NA)	0.7
Paperboard containers and boxes	265	99.7	101.3	105.1	106.3	110.1	(NA)	1.0
Miscellaneous converted paper products	267	101.1	101.4	113.3	113.6	121.7	(NA)	2.0
Newspapers	271	96.9	90.6	79.0	77.4	79.0	(NA)	-2.3
Periodicals	272	97.9	93.9	87.8	89.1	100.1	(NA)	(Z)
Books	273	99.1	96.6	101.6	99.3	102.2	(NA)	0.2
Miscellaneous publishing	274	96.7	92.2	94.8	93.6	114.5	(NA)	1.4
Blankbooks and bookbinding	278	95.6	99.4	108.7	114.5	115.3	(NA)	1.4
Industrial inorganic chemicals	281	105.7	106.8	109.3	110.1	116.1	(NA)	1.5
Plastics materials and synthetics	282	98.8	100.9	128.3	125.3	133.8	(NA)	3.0
Drugs	283	101.0	103.8	108.7	112.1	112.6	(NA)	1.2
Soaps, cleaners, and toilet goods.	284	102.0	103.8	118.6	120.9	130.4	(NA)	2.7
Industrial organic chemicals.	286	109.9	101.4	98.6	99.0	112.9	(NA)	1.2
Miscellaneous chemical products	289	95.4	97.3	107.8	110.1	120.2	(NA)	1.9
Petroleum refining	291	105.3	109.2	132.3	142.0	149.2	(NA)	4.1
Tires and inner tubes	301	102.9	103.0	131.1	138.8	148.5	(NA)	4.0
Fabricated rubber products, n.e.c. [3]	306	104.2	109.0	121.5	121.0	125.4	(NA)	2.3
Miscellaneous plastics products, n.e.c. [3]	308	100.5	105.7	120.9	124.7	130.1	(NA)	2.7
Glass and glassware, pressed or blown.	322	100.6	104.8	115.7	121.4	128.2	(NA)	2.5
Concrete, gypsum, and plaster products	327	100.8	102.3	104.5	107.3	109.2	(NA)	0.9
Miscellaneous nonmetallic mineral products . . .	329	103.0	95.4	107.8	110.4	112.7	(NA)	1.2
Blast furnace and basic steel products	331	112.6	109.6	142.7	155.1	160.9	(NA)	4.9
Iron and steel foundries	332	104.0	106.1	112.7	116.2	121.7	(NA)	2.0
Nonferrous rolling and drawing.	335	95.5	92.7	99.2	104.0	112.3	(NA)	1.2
Nonferrous foundries (castings)	336	102.6	104.0	117.8	122.3	126.4	(NA)	2.4
Cutlery, handtools, and hardware	342	97.8	97.3	111.3	118.2	113.1	(NA)	1.2
Fabricated structural metal products	344	100.4	98.8	105.8	106.5	110.0	(NA)	1.0
Metal forgings and stampings	346	101.5	95.6	109.3	113.6	120.2	(NA)	1.9
Metal services, n.e.c. [3]	347	108.3	104.7	127.7	128.4	123.5	(NA)	2.1
Miscellaneous fabricated metal products	349	101.4	97.5	106.6	108.3	106.2	(NA)	0.6
Engines and turbines	351	106.8	106.5	122.7	136.6	134.2	(NA)	3.0
Farm and garden machinery	352	106.3	116.5	134.7	137.2	141.0	(NA)	3.5
Construction and related machinery	353	106.5	107.0	122.1	123.3	131.8	(NA)	2.8
Metalworking machinery	354	101.0	101.1	114.8	114.9	118.6	(NA)	1.7
Special industry machinery	355	104.6	107.5	132.3	134.0	130.1	(NA)	2.7
General industrial machinery	356	105.9	101.5	109.0	109.4	110.1	(NA)	1.0
Computer and office equipment	357	121.4	138.1	469.4	681.3	937.0	(NA)	25.1
Refrigeration and service machinery	358	102.1	103.6	112.7	114.7	114.8	(NA)	1.4
Industrial machinery, n.e.c. [3]	359	106.5	107.3	138.8	141.4	129.7	(NA)	2.6

See footnotes, end of table.

U.S. Census Bureau, Statistical Abstract of the United States: 2000

[See headnote, page 432]

Industry	1987 SIC code [1]	Indexes (1987=100)						Annual average percent change [2]
		1988	1990	1995	1996	1997	1998	
Manufacturing—Continued:								
Electric distribution equipment	361	105.4	106.3	143.0	143.9	143.9	(NA)	3.7
Electrical industrial apparatus	362	104.6	107.7	150.8	154.3	163.9	(NA)	5.1
Household appliances	363	103.0	105.8	127.3	127.4	138.1	(NA)	3.3
Electric lighting and wiring equipment	364	101.9	99.9	113.7	116.9	121.4	(NA)	2.0
Communications equipment	366	110.5	121.4	170.9	190.3	221.0	(NA)	8.3
Electronic components and accessories	367	109.0	133.4	401.5	514.9	610.5	(NA)	19.8
Miscellaneous electrical equipment & supplies	369	102.8	90.6	114.1	123.1	124.6	(NA)	2.2
Motor vehicles and equipment	371	103.2	102.4	106.7	107.2	116.5	(NA)	1.5
Aircraft and parts	372	100.6	98.9	107.8	113.0	114.0	(NA)	1.3
Ship and boat building and repairing	373	99.4	103.7	98.0	99.2	104.3	(NA)	0.4
Guided missiles, space vehicles, parts	376	104.1	116.5	121.0	129.4	126.6	(NA)	2.4
Search and navigation equipment	381	104.8	112.7	149.5	142.2	148.9	(NA)	4.1
Measuring and controlling devices	382	103.9	107.0	147.8	151.9	144.3	(NA)	3.7
Medical instruments and supplies	384	105.2	116.9	131.5	139.8	146.3	(NA)	3.9
Photographic equipment & supplies	386	105.6	107.8	129.5	128.7	121.6	(NA)	2.0
Toys and sporting goods	394	104.8	108.1	113.6	119.9	139.6	(NA)	3.4
Miscellaneous manufactures	399	102.1	106.5	108.1	112.8	109.3	(NA)	0.9
Transportation:								
U.S. postal service [4]	431	99.9	104.0	106.5	104.7	108.3	109.5	0.8
Air transportation [5]	4512, 13, 22 (pts.)	99.5	92.9	108.6	111.1	111.6	108.5	0.7
Utilities:								
Telephone communications	481	106.2	113.3	148.1	159.5	160.9	171.2	5.0
Radio and television broadcasting	483	103.1	104.9	109.6	105.8	101.1	100.8	0.1
Cable and other pay TV services	484	102.0	92.5	86.7	84.4	87.6	88.0	-1.2
Electric utilities	491, 3 (pt.)	104.9	110.1	135.0	146.5	150.5	157.2	4.2
Gas utilities	492, 3 (pt.)	108.3	105.8	137.1	145.9	158.6	153.4	4.0
Trade:								
Lumber and other building materials dealers	521	101.0	103.6	117.6	121.7	122.2	133.0	2.6
Paint, glass, and wallpaper stores	523	102.8	106.0	135.3	140.2	143.8	166.0	4.7
Hardware stores	525	108.6	110.5	108.5	112.1	111.2	125.3	2.1
Retail nurseries, lawn and garden supply stores	526	106.7	83.9	117.2	136.6	128.1	136.1	2.8
Department stores	531	99.2	94.2	110.9	118.4	123.5	129.4	2.4
Variety stores	533	101.9	151.2	203.2	229.2	247.6	262.5	9.2
Miscellaneous general merchandise stores	539	100.8	116.4	163.9	164.9	168.2	189.9	6.0
Grocery stores	541	98.9	94.6	91.2	89.4	89.2	90.2	-0.9
Retail bakeries	546	89.8	89.7	86.8	81.7	75.4	65.0	-3.8
New and used car dealers	551	103.4	106.1	107.1	108.2	107.8	108.0	0.7
Auto and home supply stores	553	103.2	102.7	105.7	104.6	104.2	107.0	0.6
Gasoline service stations	554	103.0	102.6	126.3	125.1	125.0	130.6	2.5
Men's and boy's wear stores	561	106.0	113.7	117.5	125.7	132.2	145.5	3.5
Women's clothing stores	562	97.8	105.1	128.5	142.3	145.8	154.8	4.1
Family clothing stores	565	102.0	104.5	133.8	138.8	142.1	145.6	3.5
Shoe stores	566	102.7	106.1	134.8	146.9	143.5	136.4	2.9
Furniture and homefurnishings stores	571	98.6	101.8	112.0	118.6	119.4	121.6	1.8
Household appliance stores	572	98.5	102.8	138.7	141.8	155.5	184.5	5.7
Radio, television, computer, and music stores	573	118.6	119.6	196.7	204.6	215.1	258.9	9.0
Eating and drinking places	581	102.8	104.0	100.9	99.5	100.5	101.1	0.1
Drug and proprietary stores	591	101.9	103.6	106.9	109.6	115.4	117.7	1.5
Liquor stores	592	98.2	105.2	103.7	112.8	108.9	113.9	1.2
Used merchandise stores	593	105.3	100.3	117.3	129.8	138.0	158.4	4.3
Miscellaneous shopping goods stores	594	100.7	104.2	117.8	120.0	123.7	131.5	2.5
Nonstore retailers	596	105.6	108.8	146.1	165.5	177.2	193.5	6.2
Fuel dealers	598	95.6	84.4	114.2	115.8	113.4	112.0	1.0
Retail stores, n.e.c. [3]	599	105.9	113.7	126.2	139.5	147.3	157.6	4.2
Finance and services:								
Commercial banks	602	102.8	107.7	126.4	129.7	133.0	133.0	2.6
Hotels and motels	701	97.6	96.1	110.1	109.7	107.9	108.8	0.8
Laundry, cleaning, and garment services	721	97.2	101.8	105.5	108.7	108.0	113.5	1.2
Photographic studios, portrait	722	100.1	96.6	129.3	126.6	133.7	153.4	4.0
Beauty shops	723	95.1	96.8	103.5	106.3	107.5	108.4	0.7
Funeral services and crematories	726	102.5	90.9	99.7	97.1	101.3	107.0	0.6
Automotive repair shops	753	105.7	106.9	115.9	114.1	115.2	121.2	1.8
Motion picture theaters	783	107.1	115.8	101.4	100.5	99.8	101.3	0.1

NA Not available.   Z Less than .05.   [1] 1987 Standard Industrial Classification; see text, Section 17, Business.   [2] Average annual percent change, 1987 to current year, based on compound rate formula.   [3] N.e.c. means not elsewhere classified.   [4] Refers to output per full-time equivalent employee years on fiscal basis.   [5] Refers to output per employee.

Source: U.S. Bureau of Labor Statistics, Internet site <http://stats.bls.gov/iprhome.htm>.

No. 689. Productivity and Related Measures: 1980 to 1999

[See text, this section. Minus sign (-) indicates decrease]

Item	1980	1985	1990	1994	1995	1996	1997	1998	1999
INDEXES (1992=100)									
Output per hour, business sector	80.6	88.8	95.1	101.8	102.5	105.4	107.4	110.5	114.0
Nonfarm business	82.1	89.3	95.3	101.8	102.7	105.4	107.1	110.1	113.5
Manufacturing	70.4	82.8	93.0	105.3	109.4	113.8	119.6	125.9	134.0
Output, [1] business sector	69.8	83.1	97.6	108.1	111.5	116.4	122.2	128.5	134.6
Nonfarm business	70.2	83.0	97.8	108.2	111.8	116.7	122.4	128.8	135.0
Manufacturing	75.7	86.6	97.5	109.1	113.8	118.0	126.1	132.3	137.8
Hours, [2] business sector	86.7	93.5	102.6	106.2	108.8	110.4	113.8	116.3	118.1
Nonfarm business	85.5	93.0	102.7	106.3	108.9	110.7	114.3	117.0	119.0
Manufacturing	107.5	104.6	104.8	103.6	104.0	103.7	105.5	105.1	102.9
Compensation per hour, [3] business sector	54.3	72.9	90.6	104.5	106.7	110.1	114.2	120.4	126.4
Nonfarm business	54.7	73.3	90.5	104.3	106.5	109.8	113.8	119.8	125.4
Manufacturing	55.6	75.1	90.8	105.6	107.9	109.3	113.4	120.0	125.9
Real hourly compensation, [3] business sector	89.6	92.8	96.4	99.7	99.3	99.7	101.2	105.3	108.3
Nonfarm business	90.2	93.2	96.3	99.5	99.1	99.5	100.8	104.7	107.5
Manufacturing	91.7	95.6	96.6	100.8	100.4	99.0	100.5	104.9	107.9
Unit labor costs, [4] business sector	67.4	82.1	95.3	102.6	104.1	104.5	106.4	109.0	110.9
Nonfarm business	66.6	82.0	95.0	102.5	103.7	104.2	106.2	108.7	110.5
Manufacturing	78.9	90.7	97.6	100.3	98.6	96.0	94.8	95.3	94.0
ANNUAL PERCENT CHANGE [5]									
Output per hour, business sector	-0.3	1.9	1.3	1.3	0.7	2.8	1.9	2.9	3.2
Nonfarm business	-0.3	1.3	1.1	1.3	0.9	2.6	1.6	2.8	3.0
Manufacturing	0.3	3.8	2.5	3.1	3.9	4.1	5.0	5.3	6.4
Output, [1] business sector	-1.1	4.2	1.5	4.9	3.1	4.4	5.0	5.2	4.7
Nonfarm business	-1.1	3.9	1.4	4.7	3.4	4.3	4.9	5.2	4.8
Manufacturing	-4.3	3.0	0.4	5.3	4.3	3.7	6.9	4.9	4.2
Hours, [2] business sector	-0.9	2.2	0.2	3.5	2.4	1.5	3.1	2.2	1.5
Nonfarm business	-0.8	2.5	0.3	3.3	2.4	1.7	3.2	2.4	1.7
Manufacturing	-4.6	-0.7	-2.1	2.2	0.4	-0.4	1.8	-0.4	-2.1
Compensation per hour, [3] business sector	10.8	4.9	5.7	2.0	2.1	3.2	3.7	5.4	5.0
Nonfarm business	10.8	4.6	5.5	2.1	2.1	3.1	3.6	5.3	4.7
Manufacturing	12.0	5.5	4.8	2.8	2.1	1.3	3.7	5.8	5.0
Real hourly compensation, [3] business sector	-0.3	1.5	0.6	-0.2	-0.4	0.5	1.5	4.0	2.8
Nonfarm business	-0.3	1.3	0.4	-0.1	-0.4	0.4	1.4	3.9	2.6
Manufacturing	0.8	2.1	-0.2	0.6	-0.4	-1.4	1.5	4.4	2.8
Unit labor costs, [4] business sector	11.1	2.9	4.3	0.7	1.4	0.4	1.8	2.4	1.8
Nonfarm business	11.1	3.3	4.3	0.8	1.2	0.5	1.9	2.4	1.6
Manufacturing	11.7	1.6	2.2	-0.2	-1.7	-2.6	-1.3	0.5	-1.4

[1] Refers to gross sectoral product, annual weighted. [2] Hours at work of all persons engaged in the business and nonfarm business sectors (employees, proprietors, and unpaid family workers); employees' and proprietors' hours in manufacturing. [3] Wages and salaries of employees plus employers' contributions for social insurance and private benefit plans. Also includes an estimate of same for self-employed. Real compensation deflated by the consumer price index for all urban consumers, see text, Section 15, Prices. [4] Hourly compensation divided by output per hour. [5] All changes are from the immediate prior year.
Source: U.S. Bureau of Labor Statistics, News USDL 00-125, Productivity and Costs; and Internet site <http://stats.bls.gov. lprhome.htm>.

No. 690. Workers Using Computers on the Job: 1993 and 1997

[In percent, except as indicated (51,106 represents 51,106,000). For workers 18 years old and over. Based on the Current Population Survey and subject to sampling error; see Appendix III and source]

Characteristic	Number using computers [1] (1,000)	Percent of total	Type of application						
			Analysis/ spread-sheets	Book-keeping/ inven-tory	Com-munica-tions [2]	Data-bases	Desktop publish-ing	Sales and telemar-keting	Word proces-sing
Total, 1993	51,106	45.8	36.1	45.0	38.7	34.5	22.3	16.2	44.4
Total, 1997	63,885	49.8	40.9	66.4	47.0	34.1	26.1	22.1	57.0
Age:									
18 to 24 years old	6,007	37.1	28.2	70.3	35.3	23.4	18.4	23.5	43.1
25 to 29 years old	7,984	52.5	41.7	69.8	46.6	35.0	25.8	23.4	58.3
30 to 39 years old	18,864	53.3	44.0	67.0	49.1	35.4	28.3	24.0	58.5
40 to 49 years old	18,182	54.9	43.6	65.8	48.6	36.9	27.1	20.6	58.9
50 to 59 years old	10,092	50.7	39.1	62.8	49.0	33.5	26.1	19.6	58.8
60 years old and over	2,755	32.6	33.5	62.1	42.2	28.8	21.6	21.3	54.1
Sex:									
Male	30,336	44.1	46.5	64.3	51.4	36.8	29.4	24.6	53.9
Female	33,549	56.5	35.8	68.3	43.1	31.6	23.1	19.9	59.8
Occupation:									
Executive, admin., managerial	14,528	77.5	60.1	76.3	61.4	47.2	32.6	30.9	74.5
Professional specialty	13,900	71.7	44.4	45.1	55.8	37.8	40.3	9.8	68.7
Teachers, below college	2,961	60.3	33.1	31.9	39.7	27.5	42.3	4.6	73.6
Teachers, college and univ.	759	79.9	51.5	27.1	74.6	40.2	41.3	5.4	83.5
Technical/related support	3,226	75.1	42.9	51.8	49.4	36.9	26.1	7.7	49.6
Sales workers	8,277	54.8	38.4	83.0	43.0	31.3	21.0	57.2	46.1
Admin. support, inc. clerical	14,235	77.6	31.4	75.0	39.4	28.3	17.0	15.9	56.2
Service workers	2,752	16.4	15.7	52.3	27.6	17.4	9.6	11.0	34.4
Precision prod., craft/repair	3,501	25.0	29.6	62.8	31.6	22.5	18.2	11.1	29.0
Operators, laborers [3]	3,154	17.3	19.1	63.1	21.3	14.6	12.6	9.2	17.4
Farming, forestry and fishing	311	9.3	40.2	79.3	22.8	33.0	11.2	19.1	33.7

[1] Includes other applications, not shown separately. A person may be counted in more than one application. [2] Includes bulletin boards and electronic mail. [3] Includes fabricators.
Source: U.S. National Center for Education Statistics, *Digest of Education Statistics, 1994* and *1998*.

No. 691. Annual Total Compensation and Wages and Salary Accruals Per Full-Time Equivalent Employee by Industry: 1990 to 1998

[In dollars. Wage and salary accruals include executives' compensation, bonuses, tips, and payments-in-kind; total compensation includes in addition to wages and salaries, employer contributions for social insurance, employer contributions to private and welfare funds, director's fees, jury and witness fees, etc. Based on the 1987 Standard Industrial Classification Code (SIC); See text, Section 17, Business]

Industry	Annual total compensation				Annual wages and salary			
	1990	1995	1997	1998	1990	1995	1997	1998
Domestic industries	31,940	37,742	40,119	41,881	26,259	30,911	33,339	35,021
Private industries	30,822	36,322	38,708	40,567	25,853	30,310	32,825	34,594
Agriculture, forestry, and fishing.	18,475	21,022	23,242	23,506	15,996	18,166	20,333	20,730
Mining.	45,872	56,523	60,255	62,449	38,024	46,583	50,428	52,465
Construction	33,833	37,285	39,497	40,987	27,871	30,431	32,924	34,524
Manufacturing	36,958	44,713	47,281	49,420	30,054	35,779	38,965	40,928
Transportation	36,459	40,732	42,562	43,723	28,900	32,349	34,439	35,621
Communications	46,281	59,952	63,339	67,151	38,751	48,979	52,620	56,177
Electric, gas, and sanitary services.	48,097	59,478	63,283	66,299	39,557	48,751	52,484	55,246
Wholesale trade	37,031	44,508	48,038	50,617	31,499	37,808	41,166	43,549
Retail trade	18,626	21,189	22,398	23,426	15,990	18,246	19,496	20,508
Finance, insurance, and real estate	37,501	49,272	56,175	60,606	31,982	41,661	48,176	52,210
Services	28,807	34,043	36,125	37,830	24,697	29,084	31,118	32,746
Government	37,218	44,951	47,650	49,050	28,176	33,962	36,082	37,349

Source: U.S. Bureau of Economic Analysis, *National Income and Product Accounts of the United States, 1929-94*, Vol.2; and *Survey of Current Business*, June 2000.

No. 692. Average Hourly and Weekly Earnings by Private Industry Group: 1980 to 1999

[Average earnings include overtime. Data are for production and related workers in mining, manufacturing, and construction, and nonsupervisory employees in other industries. Excludes agriculture. See headnote, Table 682]

Private industry group	Current dollars					Constant (1982) dollars [1]				
	1980	1985	1990	1995	1999	1980	1985	1990	1995	1999
AVERAGE HOURLY EARNINGS										
Total.	6.66	8.57	10.01	11.43	13.24	7.78	7.77	7.52	7.39	7.86
Mining	9.17	11.98	13.68	15.30	17.04	10.71	10.86	10.28	9.90	10.12
Construction	9.94	12.32	13.77	15.09	17.13	11.61	11.17	10.35	9.76	10.17
Manufacturing	7.27	9.54	10.83	12.37	13.91	8.49	8.65	8.14	8.00	8.26
Transportation, public utilities	8.87	11.40	12.92	14.13	15.67	10.36	10.34	9.71	9.14	9.31
Wholesale trade	6.95	9.15	10.79	12.43	14.59	8.12	8.30	8.11	8.04	8.66
Retail trade	4.88	5.94	6.75	7.69	9.08	5.70	5.39	5.07	4.97	5.39
Finance, insurance, real estate	5.79	7.94	9.97	12.32	14.61	6.76	7.20	7.49	7.97	8.68
Services	5.85	7.90	9.83	11.39	13.38	6.83	7.16	7.39	7.37	7.95
AVERAGE WEEKLY EARNINGS										
Total.	235	299	345	394	457	275	271	259	255	271
Mining	397	520	603	684	746	464	471	453	442	443
Construction	368	464	526	587	668	430	421	395	380	397
Manufacturing	289	386	442	515	580	337	350	332	333	344
Transportation, public utilities	351	450	496	557	606	410	408	373	360	360
Wholesale trade	267	351	411	476	560	312	319	309	308	333
Retail trade	147	175	194	221	263	172	158	146	143	156
Finance, insurance, real estate	210	289	357	442	529	245	262	268	286	314
Services	191	257	319	369	436	223	233	240	239	259

[1] Earnings in current dollars divided by the Consumer Price Index (CPI-W) on a 1982 base; see text, Section 15, Prices.

Source: U.S. Bureau of Labor Statistics, *Employment and Earnings*, monthly, March and June issues; and Internet site <http://stats.bls.gov/ceshome.htm>.

No. 693. Annual Percent Changes in Earnings and Compensation: 1980 to 1999

[Annual percent change from immediate prior year. Minus sign (-) indicates decrease]

Item	1980	1985	1990	1994	1995	1996	1997	1998	1999
Current dollars:									
Hourly earnings, total [1]	8.1	3.0	3.6	2.7	2.8	3.4	3.9	4.1	3.6
Hourly earnings, manufacturing [2]	8.5	3.8	3.3	2.8	2.5	3.2	3.1	2.4	3.1
Compensation per employee-hour [3]	10.7	4.6	5.5	2.1	2.1	3.1	3.6	5.3	4.7
Constant (1982) dollars:									
Hourly earnings, total [1]	-4.8	-0.4	-1.6	0.1	-0.1	0.5	1.6	2.6	1.4
Hourly earnings, manufacturing [2]	-4.5	0.3	-1.7	0.2	-0.4	0.4	0.9	1.1	0.9
Compensation per employee-hour [3]	-0.4	1.2	0.4	-0.1	-0.4	0.4	1.4	3.9	2.6

[1] Production or nonsupervisory workers on private nonfarm payrolls.   [2] Production and related workers.   [3] Nonfarm business sector.

Source: U.S. Bureau of Labor Statistics, News USDL 00-125, Productivity and Costs; and Internet site <http://stats.bls.gov/lprhome.htm>.

Labor Force, Employment, and Earnings   435

No. 694. Average Annual Pay by State: 1997 and 1998

[**In dollars, except percent change.** For workers covered by state unemployment insurance laws and for Federal civilian workers covered by unemployment compensation for Federal employees, approximately 98 percent of wage and salary civilian employment in 1998. Excludes most agricultural workers on small farms, all Armed Forces, elected officials in most states, railroad employees, most domestic workers, most student workers at school, employees of certain nonprofit organizations, and most self-employed individuals. Pay includes bonuses, cash value of meals and lodging, and tips and other gratuities]

State	Average annual pay		Percent change, 1997-98	State	Average annual pay		Percent change, 1997-98
	1997	1998 [1]			1997	1998 [1]	
United States.	30,353	31,908	5.1	Missouri	27,780	28,907	4.1
Alabama	26,139	27,035	3.4	Montana	21,946	22,644	3.2
Alaska	33,156	33,839	2.1	Nebraska	24,565	25,535	3.9
Arizona	27,659	29,317	6.0	Nevada	28,672	30,201	5.3
Arkansas	23,277	24,422	4.9	New Hampshire	29,296	30,943	5.6
California	33,525	35,349	5.4	New Jersey	37,514	(NA)	(NA)
Colorado	30,066	32,246	7.3	New Mexico	24,684	25,716	4.2
Connecticut	38,941	40,915	5.1	New York	38,543	40,678	5.5
Delaware	32,188	33,996	5.6	North Carolina	26,684	28,107	5.3
District of Columbia	46,761	48,727	4.2	North Dakota	22,049	22,990	4.3
Florida	26,673	28,143	5.5	Ohio	29,094	30,395	4.5
Georgia	29,037	30,873	6.3	Oklahoma	24,226	25,122	3.7
Hawaii	28,357	29,029	2.4	Oregon	28,411	29,542	4.0
Idaho	24,062	24,866	3.3	Pennsylvania	30,163	31,582	4.7
Illinois	33,024	34,704	5.1	Rhode Island	28,662	30,148	5.2
Indiana	27,635	29,107	5.3	South Carolina	24,995	26,151	4.6
Iowa	24,803	26,035	5.0	South Dakota	21,648	22,754	5.1
Kansas	25,694	26,842	4.5	Tennessee	27,248	28,457	4.4
Kentucky	25,577	26,689	4.3	Texas	29,699	31,512	6.1
Louisiana	25,755	26,905	4.5	Utah	25,736	26,869	4.4
Maine	24,899	25,875	3.9	Vermont	25,496	26,615	4.4
Maryland	31,763	33,306	4.9	Virginia	29,548	31,384	6.2
Massachusetts	35,716	37,787	5.8	Washington	30,769	33,076	7.5
Michigan	32,780	34,542	5.4	West Virginia	24,716	25,269	2.2
Minnesota	30,231	32,073	6.1	Wisconsin	27,337	28,542	4.4
Mississippi	22,778	23,822	4.6	Wyoming	23,866	24,747	3.7

NA Not available. [1] Preliminary. 1998 U.S. total includes an estimate for New Jersey.

Source: U.S. Bureau of Labor Statistics, *News* USDL 99-357, December 15, 1999, *Average Annual Pay by State and Industry.*

No. 695. Average Annual Pay by Selected Metropolitan Area: 1997 and 1998

[**In dollars.** Metropolitan areas ranked by average pay 1997. Includes data for metropolitan statistical areas and primary metropolitan statistical areas defined as of June 30, 1996. In the New England areas, the New England county metropolitan area (NECMA) definitions were used. See source for details. See also headnote, Table 694]

Metropolitan area	1997	1998 [1]	Metropolitan area	1997	1998 [1]
Metropolitan areas	**31,734**	**33,381**	Saginaw-Bay City-Midland, MI.	32,063	33,274
San Jose, CA.	48,655	51,409	Portland-Vancouver, OR-WA	31,590	32,846
New York, NY	47,378	50,395	Rochester, MN	31,551	33,142
San Francisco, CA	42,698	45,670	Monmouth-Ocean, NJ	31,510	(NA)
New Haven-Bridgeport-Stamford-			Rochester, NY	31,345	32,087
Waterbury-Danbury, CT	42,551	44,853	Baltimore, MD	31,317	32,752
Middlesex-Somerset-Hunterdon, NJ . .	41,794	(NA)	Springfield, IL.	31,175	32,608
Newark, NJ	40,413	(NA)	Dutchess County, NY	31,136	33,581
Trenton, NJ	39,834	(NA)	Cleveland-Lorain-Elyria, OH	31,086	32,375
Bergen-Passaic, NJ.	38,513	(NA)	Austin-San Marcos, TX	31,061	35,488
Washington, DC-MD-VA-WV	38,461	40,695	Sacramento, CA	31,003	33,001
Jersey City, NJ.	38,459	(NA)	St. Louis, MO-IL	30,989	32,263
Detroit, MI	37,164	39,520	Raleigh-Durham-Chapel Hill, NC	30,923	32,332
Hartford, CT.	36,662	38,504	Yolo, CA	30,868	32,024
Oakland, CA	36,410	38,535	Charlotte-Gastonia-Rock Hill, NC-SC .	30,834	32,884
Seattle-Bellevue-Everett, WA	36,315	39,848	Milwaukee-Waukesha, WI	30,689	32,136
Boston-Worcester-Lawrence-Lowell-			Lansing-East Lansing, MI	30,672	30,943
Brockton, MA-NH	36,218	38,357	Bloomington-Normal, IL	30,584	31,410
Chicago, IL	35,892	37,752	Indianapolis, IN	30,514	32,495
Kokomo, IN	35,880	37,517	Ventura, CA.	30,489	31,962
Dallas, TX	35,015	37,323	Cincinnati, OH-KY-IN	30,484	32,220
Los Angeles-Long Beach, CA	34,958	36,608	Pittsburgh, PA	30,366	31,379
Houston, TX	34,938	36,732	San Diego, CA	30,357	32,221
Wilmington-Newark, DE-MD	34,843	36,758	Racine, WI	30,346	31,371
Anchorage, AK.	34,787	35,441	Dayton-Springfield, OH	30,304	31,210
Philadelphia, PA-NJ.	34,367	(NA)	Fort Worth-Arlington, TX	30,054	31,660
Nassau-Suffolk, NY.	34,338	35,752	Richmond-Petersburg, VA	29,986	31,442
Orange County, CA.	33,750	35,714	Nashville, TN	29,904	30,685
Flint, MI	33,654	34,612	Kansas City, MO-KS	29,809	31,278
Minneapolis-St. Paul, MN-WI	33,581	35,626	West Palm Beach-Boca Raton, FL. . .	29,808	31,735
Denver, CO	33,359	35,628	Albany-Schenectady-Troy, NY	29,724	31,086
Atlanta, GA	33,254	35,433	Allentown-Bethlehem-Easton, PA	29,706	30,685
Boulder-Longmont, CO	33,199	37,821	Birmingham, AL	29,636	30,604
New London-Norwich, CT.	33,053	34,612	Grand Rapids-Muskegon-Holland, MI .	29,627	31,178
Ann Arbor, MI.	32,606	34,350	Decatur, IL	29,533	31,234
Huntsville, AL.	32,588	33,798	Honolulu, HI.	29,512	30,248
Brazoria, TX	32,206	32,901	Columbus, OH	29,488	31,180

NA Not available. [1] Preliminary. 1998 U.S. total includes an estimate for New Jersey.

Source: U.S. Bureau of Labor Statistics, *News* USDL 99-374, December 30, 1999 *Average Annual Pay Levels in Metropolitan Areas.*

No. 696. Full-Time Wage and Salary Workers—Number and Earnings: 1985 to 1999

[In current dollars of usual weekly earnings. Data represent annual averages (77,002 represents 77,002,000). See text, this section, and headnote Table 660, for a discussion of occupational data. Based on Current Population Survey; see text, Section 1, Population, and Appendix III. For definition of median, see Guide to Tabular Presentation]

Characteristic	Number of workers (1,000)				Median weekly earnings (dol.)			
	1985	1990 [1]	1995 [1]	1999 [1]	1985	1990 [1]	1995 [1]	1999 [1]
All workers [2]	77,002	85,804	89,282	97,626	343	412	479	549
Male	45,589	49,564	51,222	55,181	406	481	538	618
16 to 24 years old	6,956	6,824	6,118	6,444	240	282	303	356
25 years old and over	38,632	42,740	45,104	48,738	442	512	588	668
Female.	31,414	36,239	38,060	42,444	277	346	406	473
16 to 24 years old	5,621	5,227	4,366	4,830	210	254	275	324
25 years old and over	25,793	31,012	33,695	37,615	296	369	428	497
White	66,481	72,811	74,874	80,849	355	424	494	573
Male	40,030	42,797	43,747	46,825	417	494	566	638
Female	26,452	30,014	31,127	34,024	281	353	415	483
Black	8,393	9,820	10,596	12,190	277	329	383	445
Male	4,367	4,983	5,279	5,846	304	361	411	488
Female	4,026	4,837	5,317	6,344	252	308	355	409
Hispanic origin [3]	(NA)	7,812	8,719	10,950	(NA)	304	329	385
Male	(NA)	5,000	5,597	6,788	(NA)	318	350	406
Female	(NA)	2,812	3,122	4,162	(NA)	278	305	348
Occupation, male:								
Managerial and professional	11,078	12,255	13,684	15,537	583	729	829	952
Exec., admin., managerial	5,835	6,389	7,172	7,981	593	740	833	967
Professional specialty	5,243	5,866	6,512	7,556	571	719	827	939
Technical, sales, and administrative support. .	8,803	9,677	9,894	10,525	420	493	556	626
Tech. and related support	1,563	1,762	1,688	1,802	472	567	641	728
Sales	4,227	4,692	5,000	5,402	431	502	579	666
Admin. support, incl. clerical	3,013	3,224	3,206	3,322	391	436	489	539
Service	3,947	4,602	4,779	5,209	272	317	357	402
Private household	13	12	15	17	(B)	(B)	(B)	(B)
Protective	1,327	1,531	1,691	1,791	391	477	552	613
Other service	2,607	3,059	3,073	3,400	230	271	300	336
Precision production [4]	10,026	10,259	10,046	10,861	408	486	534	606
Mechanics and repairers	3,752	3,687	3,658	4,057	400	475	538	622
Construction trades	3,308	3,650	3,541	4,059	394	478	507	571
Other	2,966	2,922	2,847	2,745	433	508	574	634
Operators, fabricators and laborers	10,585	11,464	11,529	11,685	325	375	413	472
Machine operators, assemblers, and inspectors.	4,403	4,594	4,576	4,371	341	387	421	487
Transportation and material moving	3,459	3,752	3,870	4,083	369	416	482	522
Handlers, equipment cleaners, helpers, and laborers	2,724	3,118	3,083	3,230	261	306	328	377
Farming, forestry, and fishing	1,150	1,306	1,290	1,364	216	261	294	341
Occupation, female:								
Managerial and professional	8,302	10,575	12,609	15,167	399	510	605	681
Exec., admin., managerial	3,492	4,758	5,803	6,992	383	484	570	652
Professional specialty	4,810	5,816	6,806	8,175	408	534	632	707
Technical, sales, and administrative support. .	14,622	16,290	16,004	16,863	269	331	383	431
Tech. and related support	1,200	1,476	1,506	1,749	331	417	480	528
Sales	2,929	3,554	3,862	4,326	226	290	330	399
Admin. support, incl. clerical	10,494	11,260	10,636	10,788	270	332	384	427
Service	3,963	4,577	4,838	5,632	185	230	264	304
Private household	330	305	324	367	130	171	193	240
Protective	156	217	246	347	278	405	438	492
Other service	3,477	4,055	4,249	4,918	188	230	264	302
Precision production [4]	906	900	957	1,066	268	316	371	428
Mechanics and repairers	144	139	150	206	392	458	550	592
Construction trades	53	50	66	85	265	393	400	423
Other	709	711	741	776	253	299	346	403
Operators, fabricators, and laborers	3,482	3,722	3,462	3,498	216	261	297	337
Machine operators, assemblers, and inspectors.	2,778	2,878	2,559	2,444	216	259	296	340
Transportation and material moving	189	227	261	317	252	314	354	394
Handlers, equipment cleaners, helpers and laborers	514	616	642	737	209	249	284	314
Farming, forestry, and fishing	138	175	190	218	185	216	249	283

B Data not shown where base is less than 50,000. NA Not available. [1] See footnote 2, Table 643. [2] Includes other races, not shown separately. [3] Persons of Hispanic origin may be of any race. [4] Includes craft and repair.

Source: U.S. Bureau of Labor Statistics, Bulletin 2307, and *Employment and Earnings*, monthly, January issues; and unpublished data.

Labor Force, Employment, and Earnings 437

No. 697. Workers With Earnings by Occupation of Longest Held Job and Sex: 1998

[Covers persons 15 years old and over as of March 1999 (68,846 represents 68,846,000). Based on Current Population Survey; see text, Section 1, Population, and Appendix III. For definition of median, see Guide to Tabular Presentation]

	All workers				Year round full-time			
	Women		Men		Women		Men	
Major occupation of longest job held	Number (1,000)	Median earnings	Number (1,000)	Median earnings	Number (1,000)	Median earnings	Number (1,000)	Median earnings
Total [1]	68,846	17,716	77,295	28,755	38,785	25,862	56,951	35,345
Executive, administrators, and managerial . . .	9,251	30,868	10,818	48,902	7,125	34,755	9,438	51,351
Professional specialty.	11,577	30,489	9,793	46,981	6,922	36,261	7,768	51,654
Technical and related support	2,399	24,547	2,132	36,903	1,612	27,849	1,737	40,546
Sales	9,268	11,432	8,788	30,332	4,182	23,197	6,397	37,248
Admin. support, incl. clerical	16,041	18,696	4,236	24,450	9,697	23,835	3,004	31,153
Precision production, craft and repair	1,436	18,346	14,131	28,860	927	23,907	11,064	31,631
Machine operators, assemblers, and inspectors	3,095	15,155	5,170	25,495	1,955	19,015	3,953	27,890
Transportation and material moving	620	14,471	5,100	25,986	268	21,449	3,671	30,422
Handlers, equipment cleaners, helpers, and laborers.	1,284	10,112	5,049	13,915	544	16,550	2,633	21,871
Service workers	13,011	9,203	8,168	14,205	5,262	15,647	4,881	22,515
Private household.	937	4,822	53	(B)	245	11,840	9	(B)
Service, except private household.	12,074	9,564	8,115	14,268	5,017	15,801	4,872	22,557
Farming, forestry, and fishing.	785	5,934	3,184	12,045	235	15,865	1,739	18,855

B Base less than 75,000. [1] Includes people whose longest job was in the Armed Forces.

Source: U.S. Census Bureau, *Current Population Reports* P60-206.

No. 698. Employment Cost Index (ECI), Compensation by Industry and Occupation: 1982 to 1999

[As of **December.** The ECI is a measure of the rate of change in employee compensation (wages, salaries, and employer costs for employee benefits). Data are not seasonally adjusted: 1982 and 1985 based on fixed employment counts from 1970 Census of Population; 1990 based on fixed employment counts from the 1980 Census of Population; Beginning 1995 based primarily on 1990 Occupational Employment Survey]

Item	Indexes (June 1989=100)						Percent change for 12 months ending Dec.—				
	1982	1985	1990	1995	1998	1999	1985	1990	1995	1998	1999
Civilian workers [1]	74.8	86.8	107.6	127.2	139.8	144.6	4.3	4.9	2.7	3.4	3.4
Workers, by occupational group:											
White-collar occupations	72.9	85.8	108.3	128.0	141.4	146.3	4.9	5.2	2.9	3.6	3.5
Blue-collar occupations	78.2	88.4	106.5	125.8	136.1	140.6	3.3	4.4	2.5	2.8	3.3
Service occupations	74.3	87.2	108.0	127.4	140.0	144.8	3.9	5.1	2.5	3.2	3.4
Workers, by industry division:											
Manufacturing	76.9	87.8	107.2	128.3	138.9	143.6	3.3	5.1	2.6	2.7	3.4
Nonmanufacturing	73.9	86.4	107.8	126.8	139.9	144.7	4.7	4.9	2.8	3.6	3.4
Service industries . . . [2]	70.5	84.1	110.2	129.4	141.7	146.5	4.7	6.3	2.4	3.0	3.4
Public administration [2]	71.9	85.4	108.7	128.3	139.9	144.4	4.9	5.3	3.3	3.6	3.2
State and local government. . .	70.8	84.6	110.4	129.3	139.8	144.6	5.6	5.8	2.9	3.0	3.4
Workers, by occupational group:											
White-collar occupations	70.4	84.2	110.9	129.1	139.3	144.0	5.8	6.0	2.9	2.8	3.4
Blue-collar workers	73.9	86.7	108.7	128.0	137.8	142.5	5.3	4.8	2.6	2.7	3.4
Workers, by industry division:											
Service industries.	70.0	84.0	111.3	129.6	139.7	144.5	5.9	6.3	2.8	2.7	3.4
Schools.	69.0	83.6	111.6	129.8	139.9	144.7	6.2	6.0	2.8	2.7	3.4
Elementary and secondary	68.6	83.6	112.1	130.1	139.3	144.1	6.4	6.3	2.8	2.6	3.4
Colleges and universities [3]	(NA)	(NA)	110.2	128.7	141.5	146.5	(NA)	5.3	2.5	3.1	3.5
Services, excluding schools [3]	73.1	85.2	110.2	129.4	138.8	143.8	4.7	6.8	3.0	2.6	3.6
Public administration [2]	71.9	85.4	108.7	128.3	139.9	144.4	4.9	5.3	3.3	3.6	3.2
Private industry workers [4]	75.8	87.3	107.0	126.7	139.8	144.6	3.9	4.6	2.6	3.5	3.4
Workers, by occupational group:											
White-collar occupations	73.7	86.4	107.4	127.6	142.0	146.9	4.9	4.9	2.8	3.9	3.5
Blue-collar occupations	78.4	88.5	106.4	125.6	135.9	140.5	3.1	4.4	2.4	2.7	3.3
Service occupations	76.3	88.4	107.3	125.2	138.0	142.6	3.0	4.7	1.9	2.9	3.3
Workers, by industry division:											
Manufacturing	76.9	87.8	107.2	128.3	138.9	143.6	3.3	5.1	2.6	2.7	3.4
Nonmanufacturing	75.1	87.0	106.9	125.9	139.7	144.5	4.3	4.5	2.7	3.7	3.4
Service industries	(NA)	84.1	109.3	129.4	142.7	147.6	(NA)	6.2	2.2	3.0	3.4
Business services	(NA)	(NA)	107.4	126.3	145.9	151.9	(NA)	6.0	2.7	5.3	4.1
Health services	(NA)	83.7	110.8	132.2	139.0	144.2	(NA)	6.8	2.7	0.7	3.7
Hospitals	(NA)	(NA)	110.7	131.3	139.9	144.6	(NA)	7.0	2.1	2.5	3.4
Workers by bargaining status:											
Union.	79.6	90.1	106.2	127.7	137.5	141.2	2.6	4.3	2.8	3.0	2.7
Nonunion	74.3	86.3	107.3	126.5	140.1	145.2	4.6	4.8	2.7	3.5	3.6

NA Not available. [1] Includes private industry and state and local government workers and excludes farm, household, and federal government workers. [2] Consists of legislative, judicial, administrative, and regulatory activities. [3] Includes library, social, and health services. Formerly called hospitals and other services. [4] Excludes farm and household workers.

Source: U.S. Bureau of Labor Statistics, *News, Employment Cost Index,* quarterly; and Internet site <http://stats.bls.gov/ecthome.htm>.

438 Labor Force, Employment, and Earnings

No. 699. Federal Minimum Wage Rates: 1950 to 1998

Year	Value of the minimum wage		Year	Value of the minimum wage	
	Current dollars	Constant (1998) dollars [1]		Current dollars	Constant (1998) dollars [1]
1950	0.75	5.07	1975	2.10	6.36
1951	0.75	4.70	1976	2.30	6.59
1952	0.75	4.61	1977	2.30	6.19
1953	0.75	4.58	1978	2.65	6.63
1954	0.75	4.54	1979	2.90	6.51
1955	0.75	4.56	1980	3.10	6.13
1956	1.00	5.99	1981	3.35	6.01
1957	1.00	5.80	1982	3.35	5.66
1958	1.00	5.64	1983	3.35	5.48
1959	1.00	5.60	1984	3.35	5.26
1960	1.00	5.51	1985	3.35	5.07
1961	1.15	6.27	1986	3.35	4.98
1962	1.15	6.21	1987	3.35	4.81
1963	1.25	6.66	1988	3.35	4.62
1964	1.25	6.57	1989	3.35	4.40
1965	1.25	6.47	1990	3.80	4.74
1966	1.25	6.29	1991	4.25	5.09
1967	1.40	6.83	1992	4.25	4.94
1968	1.60	7.49	1993	4.25	4.79
1969	1.60	7.11	1994	4.25	4.67
1970	1.60	6.72	1995	4.25	4.55
1971	1.60	6.44	1996	4.75	4.93
1972	1.60	6.24	1997	5.15	5.23
1973	1.60	5.87	1998	5.15	5.15
1974	2.00	6.61			

[1] Adjusted for inflation using the CPI-U; see text, Section 15, Prices.

Source: U.S. Employment Standards Administration, Internet site: <http://www.dol.gov/esa/public/minwage/main.htm> (accessed 20 July 2000).

No. 700. Workers Paid Hourly Rates by Selected Characteristics: 1999

[Data are annual averages (72,306 represents 72,306,000). For employed wage and salary workers. Based on Current Population Survey; see text, Section 1, Population, and Appendix III]

Characteristic	Number of workers [1] (1,000)			Percent of all workers paid hourly rates			Median hourly earnings of workers paid hourly rates [2]
	Total paid hourly rates	At or below $5.15			At or below $5.15		
		Total	At $5.15	Below $5.15	Total	At $5.15	Below $5.15	

Characteristic	Total paid hourly rates	Total	At $5.15	Below $5.15	Total	At $5.15	Below $5.15	Median
Total, 16 years and over [3]	72,306	3,340	1,146	2,194	4.6	1.6	3.0	$9.53
16 to 24 years	16,636	1,695	632	1,064	10.2	3.8	6.4	6.87
16 to 19 years	6,600	1,006	429	577	15.2	6.5	8.7	6.08
25 years and over	55,670	1,644	514	1,130	3.0	0.9	2.0	10.47
Male, 16 years and over ..	36,073	1,214	446	768	3.4	1.2	2.1	10.31
16 to 24 years	8,556	699	289	410	8.2	3.4	4.8	7.12
16 to 19 years	3,346	428	195	233	12.8	5.8	7.0	6.18
25 years and over	27,517	515	157	358	1.9	0.6	1.3	12.00
Women, 16 years and over.	36,233	2,126	700	1,426	5.9	1.9	3.9	8.64
16 to 24 years	8,080	996	343	654	12.3	4.2	8.1	6.60
16 to 19 years	3,254	577	233	344	17.7	7.2	10.6	5.98
25 years and over	28,153	1,129	357	772	4.0	1.3	2.7	9.53
White	58,999	2,698	895	1,803	4.6	1.5	3.1	9.74
Black	10,126	516	217	298	5.1	2.1	2.9	8.85
Hispanic origin [4]	9,402	513	238	275	5.5	2.5	2.9	8.07
Full-time workers	54,931	1,320	372	948	2.4	0.7	1.7	10.22
Part-time workers [5]	17,227	2,011	772	1,238	11.7	4.5	7.2	6.86
Private sector industries...	63,557	3,108	1,028	2,080	4.9	1.6	3.3	9.19
Goods-producing [6]	19,165	308	129	179	1.6	0.7	0.9	10.87
Service-producing [7]	44,392	2,801	899	1,902	6.3	2.0	4.3	8.49
Public sector	8,749	230	117	113	2.6	1.3	1.3	11.48

[1] Excludes the incorporated self-employed.   [2] For definition of median, see Guide to Tabular Presentation.   [3] Includes races not shown separately. Also includes a small number of multiple jobholders whose full- part-time status can not be determined for their principal job.   [4] Persons of Hispanic origin may be of any race.   [5] Working fewer than 35 hours per week.   [6] Includes agriculture, mining, construction, and manufacturing.   [7] Includes transportation and public utilities; wholesale trade; finance, insurance, and real estate; private households; and other service industries.

Source: U.S. Bureau of Labor Statistics, unpublished data.

Labor Force, Employment, and Earnings   439

No. 701. Employer Costs for Employee Compensation Per Hour Worked: 2000

[In dollars. As of March, for private industry workers. Based on a sample of establishments; see source for details]

Compensation component	Total	Goods producing[1]	Service producing[2]	Manufacturing	Non-manufacturing	Union members	Non-union members	Full-time workers	Part-time workers
Total compensation . . .	**19.85**	**23.55**	**18.72**	**23.41**	**19.12**	**25.88**	**19.07**	**22.62**	**10.75**
Wages and salaries	14.49	16.25	13.95	16.01	14.18	16.87	14.18	16.25	8.70
Total benefits.	5.36	7.30	4.77	7.40	4.94	9.01	4.89	6.37	2.04
Paid leave	1.28	1.51	1.20	1.74	1.18	1.75	1.22	1.56	0.33
Vacation.	0.63	0.76	0.59	0.86	0.58	0.91	0.59	(NA)	(NA)
Holiday	0.44	0.56	0.40	0.65	0.40	0.58	0.42	(NA)	(NA)
Sick	0.15	0.11	0.16	0.13	0.15	0.18	0.15	(NA)	(NA)
Other	0.06	0.08	0.05	0.10	0.05	0.08	0.05	(NA)	(NA)
Supplemental pay	0.60	1.02	0.47	1.04	0.51	1.05	0.54	0.73	0.17
Premium pay	0.24	0.54	0.15	0.58	0.17	0.68	0.18	(NA)	(NA)
Nonproduction bonuses . .	0.31	0.41	0.29	0.36	0.30	0.22	0.33	(NA)	(NA)
Shift pay	0.05	0.08	0.04	0.10	0.04	0.15	0.04	(NA)	(NA)
Insurance	1.19	1.77	1.02	1.85	1.06	2.37	1.04	1.47	0.28
Health insurance	1.09	1.62	0.92	1.69	0.96	2.17	0.95	(NA)	(NA)
Retirement and savings . . .	0.59	0.83	0.51	0.75	0.56	1.49	0.47	0.72	0.16
Defined benefit	0.23	0.41	0.18	0.34	0.21	1.07	0.12	(NA)	(NA)
Defined contributions . . .	0.36	0.43	0.34	0.41	0.35	0.41	0.35	(NA)	(NA)
Legally required	1.67	2.09	1.54	1.92	1.62	2.25	1.59	1.84	1.11
Social Security	1.20	1.38	1.15	1.38	1.17	1.45	1.17	(NA)	(NA)
Federal unemployment . .	0.03	0.03	0.03	0.03	0.03	0.03	0.03	(NA)	(NA)
State unemployment . . .	0.10	0.12	0.09	0.11	0.10	0.13	0.10	(NA)	(NA)
Workers compensation . .	0.33	0.56	0.27	0.40	0.32	0.64	0.29	(NA)	(NA)
Other benefits[3]	0.03	0.07	-	0.09	-	0.10	0.02	0.03	-

- Represents or rounds to zero. NA Not available. [1] Mining, construction, and manufacturing. [2] Transportation, communications, and public utilities, wholesale and retail trade, finance, insurance, and real estate, and services. [3] Includes severance pay, and supplemental unemployment benefits.

Source: U.S. Bureau of Labor Statistics, *News, Employer Costs for Employee Compensation*, USDL, 00-186, June 29, 2000.

No. 702. Employees With Employer- or Union-Provided Pension Plans or Group Health Plans: 1998

[**Total in thousands (146,273 represents 146,273,000). For wage and salary workers 15 years old and over as of March 1999.** Based on Current Population Survey; see text, Section 1, Population, and Appendix III. Data based on 1990 population controls]

Occupation	Total (1,000)	Percent—Included in pension plan	Percent—With group health plan	Characteristic	Total (1,000)	Percent—Included in pension plan	Percent—With group health plan
Total	**146,273**	**43.8**	**53.3**	AGE			
Executive, admin., managerial . . .	20,074	58.2	68.8	**Total . . . .**	**146,273**	**43.8**	**53.3**
Professional specialty	21,375	61.5	67.4	15 to 24 years	24,596	12.9	20.8
				25 to 44 years old	71,948	48.2	58.7
Technical/related support	4,530	56.4	66.8	45 to 64 years	44,560	55.9	64.0
Sales workers	18,071	32.1	42.9	65 years and over	5,168	24.9	39.8
Admin. support, inc. clerical	20,342	48.5	55.7	WORK EXPERIENCE			
				Worked.	146,273	43.8	53.3
Precision prod., craft/repair	15,572	45.3	57.8	Full time	116,489	51.4	62.3
				50 weeks or more	95,776	56.4	67.4
Mach. operators, assemblers [1] . . .	8,266	46.6	60.1	27 to 49 weeks	12,156	36.0	49.2
Transportation/material moving . . .	5,722	40.8	56.0	26 weeks or fewer	8,558	18.1	24.7
Handlers, equipment cleaners [2] . .	6,337	26.6	38.2	Part time	29,783	13.8	17.8
				50 weeks or more	13,609	19.3	23.9
Service workers	21,194	23.5	32.0	27 to 49 weeks	6,538	14.0	18.1
Private households	990	2.8	7.4	26 weeks or fewer	9,636	6.0	9.0
Other	20,204	24.5	33.2	EMPLOYER SIZE			
				Under 25 persons	42,707	16.1	29.3
Farming, forestry and fishing	3,984	11.7	22.3	25 to 99 persons	18,431	37.0	52.9
				100 to 499 persons	20,304	51.3	62.6
Armed Forces	804	73.2	40.6	500 to 999 persons	8,174	59.0	66.9
				Over 1,000 persons	56,657	61.9	66.2

[1] Includes inspectors.   [2] Includes helpers and laborers.

Source: U.S. Census Bureau, unpublished data.

No. 703. Employee Benefits in Medium and Large Establishments: 1997

[In percent. Covers full-time employees in private industry. Medium and large establishments exclude establishments with fewer than 100 workers. Covers only benefits for which the employer pays part or all of the premium or expenses involved, except unpaid family leave. Based on a sample survey of establishments; for details, see source. For data on employee benefits in small establishments, see Table 704]

Employee benefit program	All employees	Professional, technical and related	Clerical and sales	Blue collar and service	Employee benefit program	All employees	Professional, technical and related	Clerical and sales	Blue collar and service
Paid time off:					Tax-deferred savings:				
Holidays	89	89	91	88	With employer contribution	46	56	51	38
Vacations	95	96	97	94	With no employer contribution	9	11	8	8
Personal leave	20	23	33	13	Income continuation plans:				
Funeral leave	81	84	85	76	Severance pay	36	48	43	26
Jury duty leave	87	92	89	83	Supplemental unemployment benefits	5	2	2	7
Military leave	47	60	50	38					
Sick leave	56	73	73	38	Family benefits:				
Family leave	2	3	3	1	Child care	10	14	10	7
					Adoption assistance	10	16	12	6
Unpaid family leave	93	95	96	91	Long-term care insurance	7	10	11	4
					Flexible workplace	2	5	3	(Z)
Disability benefits:									
Short-term disability	55	54	52	58	Health promotion programs:				
Long-term disability	43	62	52	28	Wellness programs	36	44	36	32
					Employee assistance programs	61	75	63	52
Insurance:					Fitness center	21	31	19	16
Medical care	76	79	78	74					
Dental care	59	64	59	56	Miscellaneous benefits:				
Vision care	26	28	25	24	Job-related travel accident insurance	42	56	46	32
Life insurance	87	94	91	81	Nonproduction bonuses	42	43	43	40
					Subsidized commuting	6	10	7	3
Retirement	79	89	81	72	Educational assistance:				
Defined benefit	50	52	49	50	Job related	67	81	68	58
Defined contribution	57	70	63	46	Nonjob related	20	25	18	18
Savings and thrift	39	49	45	30					
Deferred profit sharing	13	15	15	12					
Employee stock ownership	4	6	6	3					
Money purchase pension	8	12	6	6					

Z Less than 0.5 percent.
Source: U.S. Bureau of Labor Statistics, News, USDL 99-02, January 7, 1999.

No. 704. Employee Benefits in Small Establishments: 1996

[In percent. Covers full-time employees in private industry. Small establishments are establishments with fewer than 100 workers. Covers only benefits for which the employer pays part or all of the premium or expenses involved, except certain tax deferred earnings arrangements. Based on a sample survey of establishments; for details, see sources. For data on employee benefits in medium and large establishments, see Table 703]

Employee benefit program	All employees	Professional, technical and related	Clerical and sales	Blue collar and service	Employee benefit program	All employees	Professional, technical and related	Clerical and sales	Blue collar and service
Paid time off:					Income contribution plans:				
Holidays	80	86	91	71	Severance pay	15	23	19	9
Vacations	86	90	95	79	Supplemental unemployment benefits	(Z)	(NA)	(Z)	(Z)
Personal leave	14	21	18	8	Family benefits:				
Funeral leave	51	60	60	42	Employer assistance for child care	2	4	2	(Z)
Jury duty leave	59	74	68	47	Employer provided funds	1	2	2	(Z)
Military leave	18	25	22	12	On-site child care	1	2	(Z)	(Z)
Sick leave	50	66	64	35	Off-site child care	1	2	(Z)	(Z)
Family leave	2	3	3	1					
Insurance:					Health promotion programs:				
Short-term disability	29	32	33	25	Wellness programs	8	11	9	5
Long-term disability	22	39	30	10	Employee assistance programs	14	18	19	10
Medical care	64	76	69	56	Fitness center	4	6	5	3
Fee-for-service [1]	36	31	34	41					
HMO [1]	27	27	28	25	Miscellaneous benefits:				
PPO [1]	35	41	36	32	Job-related travel accident insurance	12	17	16	7
Dental care	31	40	35	24	Nonproduction bonuses	44	44	46	43
Life insurance	62	72	68	54	Subsidized commuting	1	3	2	1
Retirement	46	56	53	37	Educational assistance:				
Defined benefit	15	12	16	15	Job related	38	56	45	27
Defined contribution	38	51	46	28	Nonjob related	5	6	6	4
Tax deferred earnings arrangements:									
With employer contribution	24	30	31	17					
With no employer contribution	4	8	4	3					

NA Not available.   Z Less than 0.5 percent.   [1] Percent of participants receiving medical care insurance.
Source: U.S. Bureau of Labor Statistics, News, USDL 98-240, June 15, 1998.

Labor Force, Employment, and Earnings   441

No. 705. Workers Killed or Disabled on the Job: 1960 to 1998

[Data for **1998** are preliminary estimates **(13.8 represents 13,800)**. Excludes homicides and suicides. Estimates based on data from the U.S. National Center for Health Statistics, State vital statistics departments, state industrial commissions and beginning 1992, Bureau of Labor Statistics, Census of Occupational Fatalities. Numbers of workers based on data from the U.S. Bureau of Labor Statistics]

Year	Total		Manufacturing		Non-manufacturing		Dis-abling injuries [2] (mil.)	Year and industry group	Deaths		Dis-abling injuries [2] (1,000)
	Number (1,000)	Rate [1]	Number (1,000)	Rate [1]	Number (1,000)	Rate [1]			Number	Rate [1]	
1960 ..	13.8	21	1.7	10	12.1	25	2.0	**Total, 1998** [3]	5,100	3.8	3,800
1965 ..	14.1	20	1.8	10	12.3	24	2.1	Agriculture [4]	780	22.1	140
1970 ..	13.8	18	1.7	9	12.1	21	2.2	Mining and quarrying [5] . .	150	24.3	30
1975 ..	13.0	15	1.6	9	11.4	17	2.2	Construction	1,120	13.9	410
1980 ..	13.2	13	1.7	8	11.5	15	2.2	Manufacturing	660	3.2	650
1990 ..	10.1	9	1.0	5	9.1	9	3.9	Transportation and			
1994 ..	5.3	4	0.7	4	4.3	4	3.5	utilities	920	11.9	380
1995 ..	5.0	4	0.6	4	4.3	4	3.6	Trade [6]	450	1.7	730
1996 ..	5.0	4	0.7	3	4.3	4	3.9	Services [7]	680	1.5	900
1997 ..	5.1	4	0.7	3	4.4	4	3.8	Government	340	1.7	560
1998 ..	5.1	4	0.7	3	4.4	4	3.8				

[1] Per 100,000 workers. [2] Disabling injury defined as one which results in death, some degree of physical impairment, or renders the person unable to perform regular activities for a full day beyond the day of the injury. Due to change in methodology, data beginning 1990 not comparable with prior years. [3] Includes deaths where industry is not known. [4] Includes forestry and fishing. [5] Includes oil and gas extraction. [6] Includes wholesale and retail trade. [7] Includes finance, insurance, and real estate.

Source: National Safety Council, Itasca, IL, *Injury Facts*, annual (copyright).

No. 706. Worker Deaths, Injuries, and Production Time Lost: 1995 to 1998

[**45.7 represents 45,700**. Data may not agree with Table 705 because data here are not revised]

Item	Deaths (1,000)			Disabling injuries [1] (mil.)			Production time lost (mil. days)					
							In the current year			In future years [2]		
	1995	1997	1998	1995	1997	1998	1995	1997	1998	1995	1997	1998
All accidents	45.7	43.3	42.7	9.9	9.6	9.5	225	220	220	455	420	420
On the job	5.3	5.1	5.1	3.6	3.8	3.8	75	80	80	65	60	60
Off the job	40.4	38.2	37.6	6.3	5.8	5.7	150	140	140	390	360	360
Motor vehicle	22.9	22.0	21.0	1.2	1.2	1.1	(NA)	(NA)	(NA)	(NA)	(NA)	(NA)
Public nonmotor vehicle .	7.5	6.8	7.0	2.3	2.3	2.3	(NA)	(NA)	(NA)	(NA)	(NA)	(NA)
Home	10.0	9.4	9.6	2.8	2.3	2.3	(NA)	(NA)	(NA)	(NA)	(NA)	(NA)

NA Not available. [1] See footnote 2, Table 705, for a definition of disabling injuries. [2] Based on an average of 5,850 days lost in future years per fatality and 565 days lost in future years per permanent injury.

Source: National Safety Council, Itasca, IL, *Injury Facts*, annual (copyright).

No. 707. Industries With the Highest Total Case Incidence Rates for Nonfatal Injuries and Illnesses: 1997 and 1998

[Rates per 100 full-time employees. Industries shown are those with the highest rates for 1998. For nonfarm employment data, see Table 684. Rates refer to any occupational injury or illness resulting in (1) lost workday cases, or (2) nonfatal cases without lost workdays. Incidence rates were calculated as: Number of injuries and illnesses divided by total hours worked by all employees during year multiplied by 200,000 as base for 100 full-time equivalent workers (working 40 hours per week, 50 weeks a year)]

Industry	1987 SIC [1] code	1997	1998	Industry	1987 SIC [1] code	1997	1998
Private industry	(X)	7.1	6.7	Aluminum die-castings	3363	17.4	17.6
Meat packing plants	2011	32.1	29.3	Fabricated structural metal	3441	16.8	17.6
Gray and ductile iron foundries	3321	26.6	25.1	Flat glass	321	15.9	17.5
Motor vehicles and car bodies	3711	25.5	23.9	Steel pipe and tubes	3317	16.3	17.4
Truck trailers	3715	21.3	23.4	Boat building and repairing	3732	17.6	17.0
Ship building and repairing	3731	21.4	22.4	Poultry slaughtering and processing . .	2015	16.6	16.8
Vitreous plumbing fixtures	3261	23.9	22.2	Fresh and frozen prepared fish	2092	16.8	16.8
Mobile homes	2451	22.6	21.3	Iron and steel forgings	3462	17.3	16.7
Automotive stampings [2]	3465	20.0	21.1	Primary aluminum	3334	18.8	16.3
Steel foundries, n.e.c. [2]	3325	19.1	20.8	Construction machinery	3531	17.0	16.3
Metal sanitary ware	3431	24.4	20.0	Transportation equipment, n.e.c. [2] . .	3799	18.6	16.3
Truck and bus bodies	3713	16.6	19.6	Industrial trucks and tractors	3537	14.5	16.2
Aluminum foundries	3365	19.8	18.2	Air transportation, scheduled	451	17.7	15.9
Commerical laundry equipment	3582	(NA)	18.0	Concrete products, n.e.c. [2]	3272	14.7	15.8

NA Not available. X Not applicable. [1] 1987 Standard Industrial Classification; see text, Section 17, Business. [2] N.e.c. means not elsewhere classified.

Source: U.S. Bureau of Labor Statistics, *Occupational Injuries and Illnesses in the United States by Industry*, annual.

No. 708. Nonfatal Occupational Injury and Illness Incidence Rates: 1997 and 1998

[Rates per 100 full-time employees. For nonfarm employment data, see Table 707. Rates refer to any occupational injury or illness resulting in (1) lost workday cases, or (2) nonfatal cases without lost workdays. Incidence rates were calculated as: Number of injuries and illnesses divided by total hours worked by all employees during year multiplied by 200,000 as base for 100 full-time equivalent workers (working 40 hours per week, 50 weeks a year)]

Industry	1987 SIC [1] code	1997	1998	Industry	1987 SIC [1] code	1997	1998
Private sector [2]	(X)	**7.1**	**6.7**	Trucking and warehousing	42	10.0	8.4
Agriculture, forestry, fishing [2]	A	**8.4**	**7.9**	Water transportation	44	8.6	7.5
Mining [3]	B	**5.9**	**4.9**	Transportation by air	45	16.4	14.5
Metal mining [3]	10	4.9	5.2	Pipelines, except natural gas	46	3.7	2.2
Coal mining [3]	12	7.8	8.2	Transportation services	47	3.9	3.4
Oil and gas extraction	13	5.9	4.1	Communications	48	3.4	3.0
Nonmetallic minerals, exc. fuels	14	4.7	4.6	Electric, gas, sanitary services	49	6.9	6.3
Construction	C	**9.5**	**8.8**	**Wholesale and retail trade**	F, G	**6.7**	**6.5**
General building contractors	15	8.5	8.4	Wholesale trade	F	6.5	6.5
Heavy construction, except building	16	8.7	8.2	Retail trade	G	6.8	6.5
Special trade contractors	17	10.0	9.1	**Finance, insurance, real estate**	H	**2.2**	**1.9**
Manufacturing	D	**10.3**	**9.7**	Depository institutions	60	1.8	1.5
Durable goods	(X)	11.3	10.7	Nondepository institutions	61	1.2	1.2
Lumber and wood products	24	13.5	13.2	Security and commodity brokers	62	0.7	0.6
Furniture and fixtures	25	12.0	11.4	Insurance carriers	63	2.2	1.9
Stone, clay, and glass products	32	11.8	11.8	Insurance agents, brokers, and service	64	1.3	1.1
Primary metal industries	33	15.0	14.0	Real estate	65	4.7	4.0
Fabricated metal products	34	14.2	13.9	Holding and other investment offices	67	2.0	1.7
Industrial machinery and equip	35	10.0	9.5	**Services [4]**	I	**5.6**	**5.2**
Electronic/other electric equip	36	6.6	5.9	Hotels and other lodging places	70	8.4	7.3
Transportation equipment	37	15.4	14.6	Personal services	72	3.8	3.1
Instruments/related products	38	4.8	4.0	Business services	73	3.6	3.6
Miscellaneous manufacturing industries	39	8.9	8.1	Auto repair, services, and parking	75	6.3	5.2
Nondurable goods	(X)	8.8	8.2	Miscellaneous repair services	76	7.4	6.4
Food and kindred products	20	14.5	13.6	Motion pictures	78	3.1	3.5
Tobacco products	21	5.9	6.4	Amusement and recreation services	79	8.1	8.2
Textile mill products	22	6.7	6.7	Health services	80	8.4	7.7
Apparel and other textile products	23	7.0	6.2	Legal services	81	0.8	0.8
Paper and allied products	26	7.3	7.1	Educational services	82	2.9	3.1
Printing and publishing	27	5.7	5.4	Social services	83	6.4	6.4
Chemicals and allied products	28	4.8	4.2	Museums, botanical, zoological gardens	84	7.4	8.1
Petroleum and coal products	29	4.3	3.9	Membership organizations	86	3.4	2.9
Rubber and misc. plastics products	30	11.9	11.2	Engineering and management services	87	1.9	2.1
Leather and leather products	31	10.6	9.8	Services, n.e.c. [5]	89	1.3	(NA)
Transportation/public utilities [3][4]	E	**8.2**	**7.3**				
Railroad transportation [3]	40	3.4	3.4				
Local passenger transit	41	8.0	8.8				

NA Not available. X Not applicable. [1] 1987 Standard Industrial Classification; see text, Section 17, Business. [2] Excludes farms with fewer than 11 employees. [3] Data conforming to OSHA definitions for employers in the railroad industry and for mining operators in coal, metal, and nonmetal mining. Independent mining contractors are excluded from the coal, metal, and nonmetal mining industries. [4] Includes categories not shown separately. [5] N.e.c means not elsewhere classified.

Source: U.S. Bureau of Labor Statistics, *Occupational Injuries and Illnesses in the United States by Industry*, annual.

No. 709. Fatal Work Injuries by Cause: 1998

[For the 50 states and DC. Based on the 1998 census of fatal occupational injuries. Due to methodological differences, data differ from those in Table 705. For details, see source]

Cause	Number of fatalities	Percent distribution	Cause	Number of fatalities	Percent distribution
Total	**6,026**	**100**	Contacts with objects and equipment [1]	941	16
			Struck by object [1]	517	9
Transportation accidents [1]	2,630	44	Struck by falling objects	317	5
Highway accidents [1]	1,431	24	Struck by flying object	58	1
Collision between vehicles, mobile equipment	701	12	Caught in or compressed by—		
Noncollision accidents	373	6	Equipment or objects	266	4
Nonhighway accident (farm, industrial premises)	384	6	Collapsing materials	140	2
Aircraft accidents	223	4	Falls	702	12
Workers struck by a vehicle	413	7	Exposure to harmful substances or environments [1]	572	9
Water vehicle accidents	112	2	Contact with electric current	334	6
Railway accidents	60	1	Exposure to caustic, noxious or allergenic substances	104	2
Assaults and violent acts [1]	960	16	Oxygen deficiency	87	1
Homicides [1]	709	12	Drowning, submersion	75	1
Shooting	569	9			
Stabbing	61	1	Fires and explosions	205	3
Self-inflicted injury	223	4	Other events and exposures	16	(Z)

Z Less than 0.5 percent. [1] Includes other causes, not shown separately.

Source: U.S. Bureau of Labor Statistics, *USDL News*, Bulletin 99-208, August 4, 1999.

Labor Force, Employment, and Earnings   443

No. 710. Fatal Occupational Injuries by Industry and Event: 1998

[For the 50 states and DC. Based on the 1998 census of fatal occupational injuries. Due to methodological differences, data differ from those in Table 705. For details, see source]

Industry	1987 SIC[1] code	Event or exposure—Percent distribution						
		Fatal- ities[2]	Transpor- tation incidents	Assaults/ violent acts	Contact with objects[3]	Falls	Expo- sure[4]	Rate[5]
Total	(X)	6,026	43.6	15.9	15.6	11.6	9.5	4.5
Private industry	(X)	5,428	42.1	15.2	16.8	12.5	9.9	4.8
Agriculture, forestry, fishing	A	831	53.9	5.8	21.8	7.0	10.1	23.3
Mining[6].....................	B	146	28.1	3.4	32.2	11.0	9.6	23.6
Coal mining...............	12	30	23.3	-	60.0	-	-	-
Oil and gas extraction..........	13	76	23.7	-	18.4	14.5	14.5	20.4
Construction.................	C	1,171	25.7	3.2	17.8	32.7	18.2	14.5
General building contractors......	15	212	19.3	3.8	20.8	41.5	12.7	-
Heavy construction, except building..................	16	271	49.1	1.1	22.5	8.1	16.2	-
Special trade contractors........	17	679	18.1	3.8	15.3	39.9	20.8	-
Manufacturing[6]............	D	694	29.1	9.5	35.4	8.1	10.1	3.3
Food and kindred products.......	20	72	37.5	8.3	26.4	8.3	16.7	4.3
Lumber and wood products	24	170	26.5	2.4	60.0	4.7	4.1	19.7
Transportation and public utilities[6] ...	E	909	71.4	8.9	8.4	3.2	5.8	11.8
Local passenger transit..........	41	85	38.8	61.2	-	-	-	15.4
Trucking and warehousing.......	42	562	79.7	4.1	8.9	2.7	3.0	21.8
Transportation by air...........	45	74	93.2	-	4.1	-	-	8.9
Electric, gas, sanitary services	49	83	42.2	-	12.0	6.0	28.9	7.8
Wholesale trade	F	228	52.2	13.2	19.7	7.5	3.1	4.5
Retail trade[6]	G	569	28.3	57.1	4.6	5.3	2.6	2.6
Food stores..................	54	135	10.4	82.2	2.2	3.0	-	3.7
Automotive dealer and service stations	55	119	47.1	37.8	7.6	4.2	-	5.4
Eating and drinking places.......	58	107	15.9	71.0	-	5.6	3.7	1.6
Finance, insurance, real estate......	H	92	39.1	33.7	3.3	15.2	7.6	1.1
Services[6]	I	757	41.9	25.6	9.6	9.2	9.5	2.0
Business services.............	73	194	45.4	21.6	7.2	10.8	11.3	3.0
Auto repair, services, and parking ..	75	132	32.6	28.8	23.5	3.8	3.0	8.6
Government.................	J	598	57.5	22.7	5.0	4.0	5.9	3.0

- No data reported or data do not meet publication standards.   X Not applicable.   [1] 1987 Standard Industrial Classification code, see text, Section 17, Business.   [2] Includes 31 fatalities for which there was insufficient information to determine industry classification. Includes fatalities caused by other events and exposures, not shown separately.   [3] Includes equipment.   [4] Exposure to harmful substances or environments.   [5] Rate per 100,000 employed civilians 16 years old and over.   [6] Includes other industries, not shown separately.

Source: U.S. Bureau of Labor Statistics, USDL News, 99-208, August 4, 1999; and unpublished data.

No. 711. Work Stoppages: 1960 to 1999

[Excludes work stoppages involving fewer than 1,000 workers and lasting less than 1 day. (896 represents 896,000). Information is based on reports of labor disputes appearing in daily newspapers, trade journals, and other public sources. The parties to the disputes are contacted by telephone, when necessary, to clarify details of the stoppages]

Year	Number of work stop- pages[1]	Workers involved[2] (1,000)	Days idle		Year	Number of work stop- pages[1]	Workers involved[2] (1,000)	Days idle	
			Number[3] (1,000)	Percent estimated working time[4]				Number[3] (1,000)	Percent estimated working time[4]
1960......	222	896	13,260	0.09	1984......	62	376	8,499	0.04
1965......	268	999	15,140	0.10	1985......	54	324	7,079	0.03
1970......	381	2,468	52,761	0.29	1986......	69	533	11,861	0.05
1971......	298	2,516	35,538	0.19	1987......	46	174	[5]4,481	0.02
1972......	250	975	16,764	0.09	1988......	40	118	[5]4,381	0.02
1973......	317	1,400	16,260	0.08	1989......	51	452	16,996	0.07
1974......	424	1,796	31,809	0.16	1990......	44	185	5,926	0.02
1975......	235	965	17,563	0.09	1991......	40	392	4,584	0.02
1976......	231	1,519	23,962	0.12	1992......	35	364	3,989	0.01
1977......	298	1,212	21,258	0.10	1993......	35	182	3,981	0.01
1978......	219	1,006	23,774	0.11	1994......	45	322	5,020	0.02
1979......	235	1,021	20,409	0.09	1995......	31	192	5,771	0.02
1980......	187	795	20,844	0.09	1996......	37	273	4,889	0.02
1981......	145	729	16,908	0.07	1997......	29	339	4,497	0.01
1982......	96	656	9,061	0.04	1998......	34	387	5,116	0.02
1983......	81	909	17,461	0.08	1999......	17	73	1,996	0.01

[1] Beginning in year indicated.   [2] Workers counted more than once if involved in more than one stoppage during the year.   [3] Resulting from all stoppages in effect in a year, including those that began in an earlier year.   [4] Agricultural and government employees are included in the total working time; private household and forestry and fishery employees are excluded.   [5] Revised since originally published.

Source: U.S. Bureau of Labor Statistics, Compensation and Working Conditions, monthly through 1995; thereafter, quarterly.

No. 712. Labor Union Membership by Sector: 1983 to 1999

[See headnote, Table 714. **(17,717.4 represents 17,717,400)**]

Sector	1983	1985	1990	1994	1995	1996	1997	1998	1999
TOTAL (1,000)									
Wage and salary workers:									
Union members	17,717.4	16,996.1	16,739.8	16,740.3	16,359.6	16,269.4	16,109.9	16,211.4	16,476.7
Covered by unions	20,532.1	19,358.1	19,057.8	18,842.5	18,346.3	18,158.1	17,923.0	17,918.3	18,182.3
Public sector workers:									
Union members.	5,737.2	5,743.1	6,485.0	7,091.0	6,927.4	6,854.4	6,746.7	6,905.3	7,058.1
Covered by unions. . . .	7,112.2	6,920.6	7,691.4	8,191.8	7,986.6	7,829.7	7,668.0	7,814.7	7,966.3
Private sector workers:									
Union members.	11,980.2	11,253.0	10,254.8	9,649.4	9,432.1	9,415.0	9,363.3	9,306.1	9,418.6
Covered by unions. . . .	13,419.9	12,437.5	11,366.4	10,650.6	10,359.8	10,328.4	10,255.0	10,103.6	10,216.0
PERCENT									
Wage and salary workers:									
Union members	20.1	18.0	16.1	15.5	14.9	14.5	14.1	13.9	13.9
Covered by unions	23.3	20.5	18.3	17.4	16.7	16.2	15.6	15.4	15.3
Public sector workers:									
Union members.	36.7	35.7	36.5	38.7	37.7	37.6	37.2	37.5	37.3
Covered by unions. . . .	45.5	43.1	43.3	44.7	43.5	43.0	42.3	42.5	42.1
Private sector workers:									
Union members.	16.5	14.3	11.9	10.8	10.3	10.0	9.7	9.5	9.4
Covered by unions. . . .	18.5	15.9	13.2	11.9	11.3	11.0	10.6	10.3	10.2

Source: The Bureau of National Affairs, Inc., Washington, DC, *Union Membership and Earnings Data Book: Compilations from the Current Population Survey (2000 edition)*, (copyright by BNA PLUS); authored by Barry Hirsch of Trinity University, San Antonio, TX, and David Macpherson of Florida State University. Internet site: <http://www.bna.com/bnaplus/databook.html>

No. 713. Union Members by Selected Characteristics: 1999

[**Annual averages of monthly data (118,963 represents 118,963,000).** Covers employed wage and salary workers 16 years old and over. Excludes self-employed workers whose businesses are incorporated although they technically qualify as wage and salary workers. Based on Current Population Survey, see text, Section 1, Population, and Appendix III]

Characteristic	Employed wage and salary workers			Median usual weekly earnings [3] (dol.)			
		Percent					
	Total (1,000)	Union members [1]	Represented by unions [2]	Total	Union members [1]	Represented by unions [2]	Not represented by unions
Total [4]	**118,963**	**13.9**	**15.3**	**549**	**672**	**667**	**516**
16 to 24 years old	19,606	5.7	6.3	341	437	433	335
25 to 34 years old	28,657	11.9	13.2	518	604	601	506
35 to 44 years old	32,438	15.2	16.7	611	691	687	594
45 to 54 years old	24,665	19.8	21.8	652	750	745	617
55 to 64 years old	10,880	17.8	19.4	604	696	697	582
65 years and over	2,718	8.1	9.1	404	616	623	381
Men.	61,914	16.1	17.4	618	711	708	599
Women	57,050	11.4	13.0	473	608	606	449
White.	**99,147**	**13.5**	**14.8**	**573**	**692**	**689**	**534**
Men.	52,492	15.7	16.9	638	731	730	615
Women	46,655	10.9	12.4	483	619	618	461
Black.	**14,346**	**17.2**	**19.2**	**445**	**575**	**575**	**415**
Men.	6,585	20.5	22.2	488	588	589	459
Women	7,760	14.4	16.7	409	548	545	388
Hispanic [5].	**12,810**	**11.9**	**13.1**	**385**	**561**	**559**	**363**
Men.	7,457	13.0	14.1	406	604	597	384
Women	5,353	10.4	11.8	348	490	490	329
Full-time workers	97,626	15.3	16.9	549	672	667	516
Part-time workers	21,065	6.9	7.8	(X)	(X)	(X)	(X)
Managerial and professional specialty	34,693	13.2	15.4	797	826	819	792
Technical sales, and admin. support	35,514	9.0	10.2	488	583	580	477
Service occupations	16,829	12.8	13.9	336	536	529	314
Precision, production, craft, and repair	12,474	22.4	23.5	594	755	747	546
Operators, fabricators, and laborers.	17,514	20.7	21.9	429	591	584	398
Farming, forestry, and fishing	1,940	5.8	6.4	331	512	514	322
Agricultural wage and salary workers.	1,721	2.5	2.8	340	(B)	(B)	337
Private nonagri. wage and salary workers. .	98,304	9.5	10.3	525	634	628	513
Mining.	531	10.6	11.4	734	710	731	735
Construction	6,230	19.1	19.6	552	778	772	509
Manufacturing	19,323	15.6	16.6	576	614	611	561
Transportation and public utilities	7,317	25.5	26.7	651	748	742	613
Wholesale and retail trade, total.	24,671	5.2	5.7	421	499	492	418
Finance, insurance, and real estate	7,588	2.1	2.5	598	582	587	599
Services	32,645	5.5	6.5	517	554	563	515
Government	18,938	37.3	42.1	641	714	709	585

B Data not shown where base is less than 50,000. X Not applicable. [1] Members of a labor union or an employee association similar to a labor union. [2] Members of a labor union or an employee association similar to a union as well as workers who report no union affiliation but whose jobs are covered by a union or an employee association contract. [3] For full-time employed wage and salary workers. [4] Includes races not shown separately. Also includes a small number of multiple jobholders whose full- part-time status can not be determined for their principal job. [5] Persons of Hispanic origin may be of any race.
Source: U.S. Bureau of Labor Statistics, *Employment and Earnings*, monthly, January 2000 issue.

Labor Force, Employment, and Earnings 445

No. 714. Labor Union Membership by State: 1983 and 1999

[Annual averages of monthly figures (17,717.4 represents 17,717,400). For wage and salary workers in agriculture and nonagriculture. Data represent union members by place of residence. Based on the Current Population Survey and subject to sampling error. For methodological details, see source]

| State | Union members (1,000) | | Workers covered by unions (1,000) | | Percent of workers— | | | | | |
| | | | | | Union members | | Covered by unions | | Private manufacturing sector union members | |
	1983	1999	1983	1999	1983	1999	1983	1999	1983	1999
United States..	17,717.4	16,476.7	20,532.1	18,182.3	20.1	13.9	23.3	15.3	27.8	15.6
Alabama [1]	228.2	201.0	268.2	224.9	16.9	11.0	19.8	12.3	25.9	16.5
Alaska	41.7	51.0	49.2	59.2	24.9	20.4	29.3	23.6	23.3	10.8
Arizona [1]	125.0	137.3	156.4	168.1	11.4	6.7	14.3	8.2	7.8	3.1
Arkansas [1]	82.2	78.8	103.2	90.6	11.0	7.5	13.8	8.6	18.7	10.2
California	2,118.9	2,286.0	2,505.2	2,526.5	21.9	16.6	25.9	18.3	21.0	8.5
Colorado	177.9	180.6	209.6	199.5	13.6	9.4	16.0	10.4	13.1	6.6
Connecticut	314.0	264.4	345.1	278.9	22.7	18.2	25.0	19.2	28.1	15.1
Delaware	49.2	46.8	54.1	52.7	20.1	13.8	22.1	15.5	27.3	22.8
District of Columbia	52.4	32.1	69.4	37.8	19.5	13.1	25.9	15.4	17.6	22.1
Florida [1]	393.7	409.8	532.9	543.4	10.2	6.5	13.8	8.7	11.3	3.7
Georgia [1]	267.0	252.6	345.1	313.0	11.9	7.3	15.3	9.0	16.9	10.4
Hawaii	112.6	114.5	124.9	123.6	29.2	23.2	32.4	25.0	35.6	24.8
Idaho [1]	41.3	48.4	53.7	59.4	12.5	9.2	16.2	11.3	19.0	10.5
Illinois	1,063.8	993.3	1,205.1	1,053.7	24.2	18.0	27.4	19.1	32.4	21.7
Indiana	503.3	424.1	544.5	453.9	24.9	15.7	27.0	16.8	48.7	25.8
Iowa [1]	185.9	184.4	231.3	208.8	17.2	13.8	21.5	15.7	40.3	25.8
Kansas [1]	125.2	119.2	170.4	140.6	13.7	9.7	18.7	11.5	25.5	23.7
Kentucky	223.7	192.1	259.8	213.4	17.9	11.6	20.8	12.9	37.4	20.8
Louisiana [1]	204.2	144.9	267.8	179.5	13.8	8.1	18.1	10.0	24.9	21.5
Maine	88.0	84.0	100.4	93.1	21.0	15.4	24.0	17.1	24.8	27.4
Maryland	346.5	366.6	423.1	438.2	18.5	15.0	22.6	17.9	29.2	20.9
Massachusetts	603.2	465.1	661.4	492.0	23.7	16.2	26.0	17.1	26.7	14.5
Michigan	1,005.4	963.2	1,084.6	1,009.4	30.4	21.5	32.8	22.5	46.2	30.2
Minnesota	393.9	443.9	439.4	471.2	23.2	19.3	25.9	20.5	22.3	14.0
Mississippi [1]	79.4	67.2	99.7	93.5	9.9	6.2	12.5	8.6	18.9	9.2
Missouri	374.4	353.2	416.7	375.8	20.8	14.4	23.2	15.3	36.6	19.3
Montana	49.5	55.4	55.5	62.2	18.3	15.3	20.5	17.2	33.0	17.8
Nebraska [1]	80.6	65.6	94.8	91.5	13.6	8.8	16.0	12.2	19.1	10.6
Nevada [1]	90.0	160.8	106.7	172.2	22.4	19.5	26.6	20.9	10.8	9.8
New Hampshire	48.5	60.0	60.8	69.0	11.5	10.6	14.4	12.2	10.6	6.8
New Jersey	822.1	740.6	918.2	806.9	26.9	20.5	30.0	22.4	31.4	15.8
New Mexico	52.6	65.3	70.6	78.2	11.8	9.9	15.8	11.8	11.9	8.2
New York	2,155.6	1,896.9	2,385.9	1,986.4	32.5	25.3	36.0	26.5	31.0	18.2
North Carolina [1]	178.7	108.9	238.1	131.9	7.6	3.2	10.2	3.9	6.9	1.6
North Dakota [1]	28.4	24.8	35.1	27.0	13.2	9.3	16.3	10.1	27.4	15.1
Ohio	1,011.0	896.2	1,125.0	955.5	25.1	17.9	27.9	19.1	40.9	28.1
Oklahoma	131.5	123.6	168.2	140.0	11.5	8.8	14.7	10.0	25.2	13.0
Oregon	222.9	216.4	261.9	234.2	22.3	15.2	26.2	16.5	28.7	12.2
Pennsylvania	1,195.7	895.9	1,350.0	959.7	27.5	17.4	31.1	18.6	42.3	21.2
Rhode Island	85.8	76.8	93.7	81.5	21.5	17.7	23.5	18.8	16.9	13.3
South Carolina [1]	69.6	60.9	100.6	64.9	5.9	3.5	8.6	3.8	5.5	7.3
South Dakota [1]	26.8	19.9	34.8	25.9	11.5	6.0	14.9	7.8	19.0	7.4
Tennessee [1]	252.4	181.2	300.9	212.8	15.1	7.5	18.0	8.8	21.4	9.8
Texas [1]	583.7	519.8	712.8	610.9	9.7	6.0	11.9	7.0	16.1	8.0
Utah [1]	81.6	60.1	100.9	70.1	15.2	6.4	18.9	7.5	14.9	3.7
Vermont	25.9	26.4	31.5	29.5	12.6	9.7	15.3	10.8	13.5	5.5
Virginia	268.3	203.7	346.1	249.2	11.7	6.6	15.1	8.0	21.2	10.5
Washington	419.9	534.8	499.7	609.5	27.1	20.7	32.3	23.6	35.5	25.0
West Virginia	142.7	106.5	160.6	113.3	25.3	15.2	28.5	16.1	41.3	28.9
Wisconsin	465.5	452.4	526.7	476.4	23.8	18.1	26.9	19.0	36.0	18.8
Wyoming [1]	27.1	19.2	31.8	22.9	13.9	9.1	16.2	10.8	14.6	11.2

[1] Right to work state.

Source: The Bureau of National Affairs, Inc., Washington, DC, *Union Membership and Earnings Data Book: Compilations from the Current Population Survey (2000 edition)*, (copyright by BNA PLUS); authored by Barry Hirsch of Trinity University, San Antonio, TX, and David Macpherson of Florida State University. Internet site: <http://www.bna.com/bnaplus/databook.html>.

Section 14

Income, Expenditures, and Wealth

This section presents data on gross domestic product (GDP), gross national product (GNP), national and personal income, saving and investment, money income, poverty, and national and personal wealth. The data on income and expenditures measure two aspects of the U.S. economy. One aspect relates to the national income and product accounts (NIPAs), a summation reflecting the entire complex of the Nation's economic income and output and the interaction of its major components; the other relates to the distribution of money income to families and individuals or consumer income.

The primary source for data on GDP, GNP, national and personal income, gross saving and investment, and fixed reproducible tangible wealth is the *Survey of Current Business*, published monthly by the Bureau of Economic Analysis (BEA). A comprehensive revision to the NIPAs was released beginning in October 1999. Discussions of the revision appeared in the August, September, October, December 1999, and the April 2000 issues of the *Survey of Current Business*. Summary historical estimates appeared in the August 2000 issue of the *Survey of Current Business*. Detailed historical data will appear in forthcoming *National Income and Product Accounts of the United States, 1929-97* report to be issued in 2001.

Sources of income distribution data are the decennial censuses of population and the Current Population Survey (CPS), both products of the U.S. Census Bureau (see text, Section 1). Annual data on income of families, individuals, and households are presented in *Current Population Reports, Consumer Income,* P60 series.

Data on individuals' saving and assets are published by the Board of Governors of the Federal Reserve System in the quarterly *Flow of Funds Accounts*. The Board also periodically conducts the *Survey of Consumer Finances,* which presents financial information on family assets and net worth. Detailed information on personal wealth is published periodically by the Internal Revenue Service (IRS) in *SOI Bulletin*.

National income and product—Gross domestic product is the total output of goods and services produced by labor and property located in the United States, valued at market prices. GDP can be viewed in terms of the expenditure categories that comprise its major components—purchases of goods and services by consumers and government, gross private domestic investment, and net exports of goods and services. The goods and services included are largely those bought for final use (excluding illegal transactions) in the market economy. A number of inclusions, however, represent imputed values, the most important of which is rental value of owner-occupied housing. GDP, in this broad context, measures the output attributable to the factors of production located in the United States. Gross state product (GSP) is the gross market value of the goods and services attributable to labor and property located in a state. It is the state counterpart of the Nation's gross domestic product.

As part of the comprehensive revision released in January 1996, BEA replaced its fixed-weighted index as the featured measure of real GDP with an index based on chain-type annual weights. Changes in the new featured measures of real output and prices are calculated as the average of changes based on weights for the current and preceding years. (Components of real output are weighted by price, and components of prices are weighted by output.)

These annual changes are "chained" (multiplied) together to form a time series that allows for the effects of changes in relative prices and changes in the composition of output over time. Quarterly and monthly changes are also based on annual weights. The new output indexes are expressed as 1996= 100, and for recent years, in 1996 dollars; the new price indexes are based to 1996=100.

Chained (1996) dollar estimates of most components of GDP are not published for periods prior to 1987, because during periods far from the base period, the levels of the components may provide misleading information about their contributions to an aggregate. Values are published in index form (1996=100) for 1929 to the present to allow users to calculate the percent changes for all components, changes which are accurate for all periods. In addition, the Bureau of Economic Analysis publishes estimates of the contribution of major components to the percent change in GDP for all periods.

Gross national product measures the output attributable to all labor and property supplied by United States residents. GNP differs from "national income" mainly in that GNP includes allowances for depreciation and for indirect business taxes (sales and property taxes); see Table 721.

In December 1991, the Bureau of Economic Analysis began featuring gross domestic product rather than gross national product as the primary measure of U.S. production. GDP is now the standard measure of growth because it is the appropriate measure for much of the short-term monitoring and analysis of the economy. In addition, the use of GDP facilitates comparisons of economic activity in the United States with that in other countries.

National income is the aggregate of labor and property earnings which arises in the current production of goods and services. It is the sum of employee compensation, proprietors' income, rental income of persons, corporate profits, and net interest. It measures the total factor costs of the goods and services produced by the economy. Income is measured before deduction of taxes.

Capital consumption adjustment for corporations and for nonfarm sole proprietorships and partnerships is the difference between capital consumption based on income tax returns and capital consumption measured using empirical evidence on prices of used equipment and structures in resale markets, which have shown that depreciation for most types of assets approximates a geometric pattern. The tax return data are valued at historical costs and reflect changes over time in service lives and depreciation patterns as permitted by tax regulations. *Inventory valuation adjustment* represents the difference between the book value of inventories used up in production and the cost of replacing them.

Personal income is the current income received by persons from all sources minus their personal contributions for social insurance. Classified as "persons" are individuals (including owners of unincorporated firms), nonprofit institutions that primarily serve individuals, private trust funds, and private noninsured welfare funds. Personal income includes transfers (payments not resulting from current production) from government and business such as social security benefits, public assistance, etc., but excludes transfers among persons. Also included are certain nonmonetary types of income—chiefly estimated net rental value to owner-occupants of their homes and the value of services furnished without payment by financial intermediaries. Capital gains (net losses) are excluded.

Disposable personal income is personal income less personal tax and nontax payments. It is the income available to persons for spending or saving. Personal tax and nontax payments are tax payments (net of refunds) by persons (except personal contributions for social insurance) that are not chargeable to business expense and certain personal payments to general government that are treated like taxes. Personal taxes include income, estate and gift, and personal property taxes and motor vehicle licenses. Nontax payments include passport fees, fines and forfeitures, and donations.

Consumer Expenditure Survey—The Consumer Expenditure Survey program was begun in late 1979. The principal objective of the survey is to collect current consumer expenditure data which provide a continuous flow of data on the buying habits of American consumers. The data are necessary for future revisions of the Consumer Price Index.

The survey conducted by the Census Bureau for the Bureau of Labor Statistics consists of two components: (1) An interview panel survey in which the expenditures of consumer units are obtained in five interviews conducted every 3 months, and (2) a diary or recordkeeping survey completed by participating households for two consecutive 1-week periods.

Each component of the survey queries an independent sample of consumer units representative of the U.S. total population.

Over 52 weeks of the year, 5,000 consumer units are sampled for the diary survey. Each consumer unit keeps a diary for two 1-week periods yielding approximately 10,000 diaries a year. The interview sample is selected on a rotating panel basis, targeted at 5,000 consumer units per quarter. Data are collected in 88 urban and 16 rural areas of the country that are representative of the U.S. total population. The survey includes students in student housing. Data from the two surveys are combined; integration is necessary to permit analysis of total family expenditures because neither the diary nor quarterly interview survey was designed to collect a complete account of consumer spending.

Distribution of money income to families and individuals—Money income statistics are based on data collected in various field surveys of income conducted since 1936. Since 1947, the Census Bureau has collected the data on an annual basis and published them in *Current Population*

Reports, P60 series. In each of the surveys, field representatives interview samples of the population with respect to income received during the previous year. Money income as defined by the Bureau of the Census differs from the BEA concept of "personal income."

Data on consumer income collected in the CPS by the Census Bureau cover money income received (exclusive of certain money receipts such as capital gains) before payments for personal income taxes, social security, union dues, medicare deductions, etc. Therefore, money income does not reflect the fact that some families receive part of their income in the form of noncash benefits (see Section 12) such as food stamps, health benefits, and subsidized housing; that some farm families receive noncash benefits in the form of rent-free housing and goods produced and consumed on the farm; or that noncash benefits are also received by some nonfarm residents which often take the form of the use of business transportation and facilities, full or partial payments by business for retirement programs, medical and educational expenses, etc. These elements should be considered when comparing income levels. For data on noncash benefits, see Section 12. None of the aggregate income concepts (GDP, national income, or personal income) is exactly comparable with money income, although personal income is the closest.

In October 1983, the Census Bureau began to collect data under the new Survey of Income and Program Participation (SIPP). The information supplied by this survey is expected to provide better measures of the status and changes in income distribution and poverty of households and persons in the United States. The data collected in SIPP will be used to study Federal and state aid programs (such as food stamps, welfare, medicaid, and subsidized housing), to estimate program costs and coverage, and to assess the effects of proposed changes in program eligibility rules or benefit levels. The core questions are repeated at each interview and cover labor force

Income, Expenditures, and Wealth 449

activity, the types and amounts of income received, and participation status in various programs. The core also contains questions covering attendance in post-secondary schools and private health insurance coverage. Various supplements or topical modules covering areas such as educational attainment, assets and liabilities, and pension plan coverage are periodically included.

Poverty—Families and unrelated individuals are classified as being above or below the poverty level using the poverty index originated at the Social Security Administration in 1964 and revised by Federal Interagency Committees in 1969 and 1980.

The poverty index is based solely on money income and does not reflect the fact that many low-income persons receive noncash benefits such as food stamps, medicaid, and public housing. The index is based on the Department of Agriculture's 1961 Economy Food Plan and reflects the different consumption requirements of families based on their size and composition. The poverty thresholds are updated every year to reflect changes in the Consumer Price Index. The following technical changes to the thresholds were made in 1981: (1) distinctions based on sex of householder have been eliminated; (2) separate thresholds for farm families have been dropped; and (3) the matrix has been expanded to families of nine or more persons from the old cutoff of seven or more persons. These changes have been incorporated in the calculation of poverty data beginning with 1981. In the recent past, the Census Bureau has published a number of technical papers that presented experimental poverty estimates based on income definitions that counted the value of selected government noncash benefits. The Census Bureau has also published annual reports on after-tax income (see Tables 739 and 740). The annual income and poverty reports (P60 Series) have brought together the benefit and tax data that previously appeared in the separate reports. These reports have shown the distribution of income among households and the prevalence of poverty under the official definition of money income and under definitions that add or subtract income components. In addition, in July 1999, the Census Bureau released a report (P60-205) that showed the effect of using experimental poverty following the recommendations of a National Academy of Sciences panel on redefining our Nation's poverty measure.

Statistical reliability—For a discussion of statistical collection and estimation, sampling procedures, and measures of statistical reliability pertaining to Census Bureau data, see Appendix III.

No. 715. Gross Domestic Product in Current and Real (1996) Dollars: 1960 to 1999

[In billions of dollars (527.4 represents $527,400,000,000). For explanation of gross domestic product and chained dollars, see text, Section 14, Income]

Item	1960	1970	1980	1985	1986	1987	1988	1989	1990	1991	1992	1993	1994	1995	1996	1997	1998	1999
CURRENT DOLLARS																		
Gross domestic product	**527.4**	**1,039.7**	**2,795.6**	**4,213.0**	**4,452.9**	**4,742.5**	**5,108.3**	**5,489.1**	**5,803.2**	**5,986.2**	**6,318.9**	**6,642.3**	**7,054.3**	**7,400.5**	**7,813.2**	**8,300.8**	**8,759.9**	**9,256.1**
Personal consumption expenditures	332.3	648.9	1,762.9	2,712.6	2,895.2	3,105.3	3,356.6	3,596.7	3,831.5	3,971.2	4,209.7	4,454.7	4,716.4	4,969.0	5,237.5	5,524.4	5,848.6	6,257.3
Durable goods	43.3	85.0	214.2	363.3	401.3	419.7	450.2	467.8	467.6	443.0	470.8	513.4	560.8	589.7	616.5	642.9	698.2	758.6
Nondurable goods	152.9	272.0	696.1	928.8	958.5	1,015.3	1,082.9	1,165.4	1,246.1	1,278.8	1,322.9	1,375.2	1,438.0	1,497.3	1,574.1	1,641.7	1,708.9	1,843.1
Services	136.1	292.0	852.7	1,420.6	1,535.4	1,670.3	1,823.5	1,963.5	2,117.8	2,249.4	2,415.9	2,566.1	2,717.6	2,882.0	3,047.0	3,239.8	3,441.5	3,655.6
Gross private domestic investment	78.9	152.4	477.9	736.3	747.2	781.5	821.1	872.9	861.7	800.4	866.6	955.1	1,097.1	1,143.8	1,242.7	1,383.7	1,531.2	1,622.7
Fixed investment	75.7	150.4	484.2	714.5	740.7	754.3	802.7	845.2	847.2	800.2	851.6	934.0	1,034.6	1,110.7	1,212.7	1,315.4	1,460.0	1,578.0
Change in business inventories	3.2	2.0	-6.3	21.8	6.6	27.1	18.5	27.7	14.5	-0.2	15.0	21.1	62.6	33.0	30.0	68.3	71.2	44.6
Net exports of goods and services	2.4	1.2	-14.9	-114.2	-131.9	-142.3	-106.3	-80.7	-71.4	-20.7	-27.9	-60.5	-87.1	-84.3	-89.0	-88.3	-149.6	-253.9
Exports	25.3	57.0	278.9	303.0	320.3	365.6	446.9	509.0	557.2	601.6	636.8	658.0	725.1	818.6	874.2	968.0	966.3	998.3
Imports	22.8	55.8	293.8	417.2	452.2	507.9	553.2	589.7	628.6	622.3	664.6	718.5	812.1	902.8	963.1	1,056.3	1,115.9	1,252.2
Government consumption expenditures and gross investment	113.8	237.1	569.7	878.3	942.3	997.9	1,036.9	1,100.2	1,181.4	1,235.5	1,270.5	1,293.0	1,327.9	1,372.0	1,421.9	1,481.0	1,529.7	1,630.1
Federal	65.9	116.4	245.3	413.4	438.7	460.4	462.6	482.6	508.4	527.4	534.5	527.3	521.1	521.5	531.6	537.8	538.7	570.6
National defense	55.2	90.9	169.6	312.4	332.2	351.2	355.9	363.2	374.9	384.5	378.5	364.9	355.1	350.6	357.0	352.5	348.6	364.5
State and local	47.9	120.7	324.4	464.9	503.6	537.5	574.3	617.7	673.0	708.1	736.0	765.7	806.8	850.5	890.4	943.2	991.0	1,059.4
CHAINED (1996) DOLLARS																		
Gross domestic product	**2,376.7**	**3,578.0**	**4,900.9**	**5,717.1**	**5,912.4**	**6,113.3**	**6,368.4**	**6,591.8**	**6,707.9**	**6,676.4**	**6,880.0**	**7,062.6**	**7,347.7**	**7,543.8**	**7,813.2**	**8,144.8**	**8,495.7**	**8,848.2**
Personal consumption expenditures	1,510.8	2,317.5	3,193.0	3,820.9	3,981.2	4,113.4	4,279.5	4,393.7	4,474.5	4,466.6	4,594.5	4,748.9	4,928.1	5,075.6	5,237.5	5,417.3	5,681.8	5,983.6
Durable goods	(NA)	(NA)	(NA)	(NA)	(NA)	455.2	481.5	491.7	487.1	454.9	479.0	518.3	557.7	583.5	616.5	657.4	731.5	815.7
Nondurable goods	(NA)	(NA)	(NA)	(NA)	(NA)	1,274.5	1,315.1	1,351.0	1,369.6	1,364.0	1,389.7	1,430.3	1,485.1	1,529.0	1,574.1	1,619.9	1,685.3	1,776.1
Services	(NA)	(NA)	(NA)	(NA)	(NA)	2,379.3	2,477.2	2,546.0	2,616.2	2,651.8	2,729.7	2,802.5	2,886.2	2,963.4	3,047.0	3,140.3	3,268.0	3,400.1
Gross private domestic investment	272.8	436.2	655.3	863.4	857.7	879.3	902.8	936.5	907.3	829.5	899.8	977.9	1,107.0	1,140.6	1,242.7	1,385.8	1,547.4	1,637.7
Fixed investment	(NA)	(NA)	(NA)	(NA)	(NA)	856.0	887.1	911.2	894.6	832.5	886.5	958.4	1,045.9	1,109.2	1,242.7	1,316.0	1,471.8	1,590.5
Change in business inventories	(NA)	(NA)	(NA)	(NA)	(NA)	29.6	-18.4	29.6	16.5	-1.0	-17.1	20.0	66.8	30.4	30.0	69.1	-74.3	42.2
Net exports of goods and services	(NA)	(NA)	(NA)	(NA)	(NA)	-156.2	-112.1	-79.4	-56.5	-15.8	-19.8	-59.1	-86.5	-78.4	-89.0	-112.1	-217.6	-323.0
Exports	87.5	159.3	334.8	341.6	366.6	408.0	473.5	529.4	575.7	613.2	651.0	672.7	732.8	808.2	874.2	983.1	1,004.6	1,042.3
Imports	108.0	223.1	324.8	490.7	531.9	564.2	585.6	608.8	632.2	629.0	670.8	731.8	819.4	886.6	963.1	1,095.2	1,222.2	1,365.4
Government consumption expenditures and gross investment	661.3	931.1	1,020.9	1,190.5	1,255.2	1,292.5	1,307.5	1,343.5	1,387.3	1,403.4	1,410.0	1,398.8	1,400.1	1,406.4	1,421.9	1,453.7	1,478.8	1,534.1
Federal	(NA)	(NA)	(NA)	(NA)	(NA)	597.8	586.9	594.7	606.8	604.9	595.1	572.0	551.3	536.5	531.6	530.7	525.9	540.8
National defense	(NA)	(NA)	(NA)	(NA)	(NA)	450.2	446.8	443.3	443.2	438.4	417.1	394.7	375.9	361.9	357.0	348.3	341.7	347.8
State and local	(NA)	(NA)	(NA)	(NA)	(NA)	695.6	721.4	749.5	781.1	798.9	815.3	827.0	848.9	869.9	890.4	923.0	952.7	993.1

NA Not available.

Source: U.S. Bureau of Economic Analysis, *Survey of Current Business*, May 2000.

Income, Expenditures, and Wealth   451

No. 716. Gross Domestic Product in Current and Real (1996) Dollars by Industry: 1990 to 1998

[In billions of dollars (5,803.2 represents 5,803,200,000,000). Data are based on the 1987 SIC. Data include nonfactor charges (capital consumption allowances, indirect business taxes, etc.) as well as factor charges against gross product; corporate profits and capital consumption allowances have been shifted from a company to an establishment basis]

Industry	Current dollars				Chained (1996) dollars			
	1990	1995	1997	1998	1990	1995	1997	1998
Gross domestic product [1]	5,803.2	7,400.5	8,300.8	8,759.9	6,707.9	7,543.8	8,144.8	8,495.7
Private industries.	4,996.7	6,411.1	7,241.4	7,659.8	5,736.8	6,508.7	7,146.1	7,510.5
Agriculture, forestry, and fishing	108.3	109.8	129.7	125.2	118.5	123.1	143.1	142.9
Farms	79.6	73.2	88.0	80.2	84.2	85.5	103.3	100.7
Agricultural services	28.7	36.7	41.6	45.0	34.6	37.6	40.0	41.9
Mining	111.9	95.7	121.0	105.9	105.8	113.0	119.4	126.4
Metal mining	5.2	6.5	5.8	5.0	4.4	5.5	6.4	7.2
Coal mining	11.8	10.7	11.1	11.6	7.5	10.1	11.6	12.7
Oil and gas extraction	87.1	69.3	92.8	77.0	87.5	88.6	90.4	94.5
Nonmetallic minerals, except fuels	7.8	9.1	11.4	12.3	8.1	9.1	10.9	12.0
Construction	248.7	290.3	343.1	373.2	290.7	299.6	329.3	342.9
Manufacturing	1,040.6	1,289.1	1,377.2	1,432.8	1,102.3	1,284.7	1,385.5	1,448.7
Durable goods	586.6	729.8	798.7	842.6	585.1	714.9	820.2	906.5
Lumber and wood products	32.2	42.3	41.9	43.9	45.1	41.6	40.3	42.2
Furniture and fixtures	15.6	19.5	22.8	25.2	18.1	20.7	22.2	23.8
Stone, clay, and glass products	25.3	32.4	38.0	42.1	29.4	32.8	37.3	39.7
Primary metal industries	43.2	53.0	51.8	54.8	43.7	49.6	51.7	55.5
Fabricated metal products	69.4	87.2	99.6	104.7	76.1	90.8	98.1	99.3
Industrial machinery	118.2	132.8	143.8	153.3	93.5	124.7	159.1	193.5
Electronic & other electric equipment	105.7	146.9	166.0	168.3	68.6	128.7	182.4	222.1
Motor vehicles and equipment	47.3	98.2	99.5	105.0	68.7	103.2	100.2	104.8
Other transportation equipment	60.5	47.7	55.6	59.7	75.7	49.4	54.9	57.8
Instruments and related products	49.3	47.2	54.1	59.0	62.8	52.6	50.0	49.7
Misc. manufacturing industries	19.8	22.7	25.6	26.6	22.8	23.3	25.1	25.3
Nondurable goods	454.0	559.2	578.5	590.1	520.2	570.3	565.9	546.4
Food and kindred products	96.4	121.1	119.3	122.0	109.5	133.3	114.5	113.5
Tobacco manufactures	11.9	15.1	16.1	17.9	14.5	15.7	14.5	11.6
Textile mill products	22.0	24.8	25.7	25.6	22.8	26.0	25.1	24.4
Apparel and other textile products	25.4	27.3	26.1	25.4	27.3	28.0	26.0	24.7
Paper and allied products	45.0	58.9	53.6	54.9	52.5	52.2	58.3	55.4
Printing and publishing	73.1	80.8	90.2	96.3	102.9	89.2	85.6	86.6
Chemicals and allied products	109.9	150.8	158.8	158.7	131.1	148.0	158.5	149.5
Petroleum and coal products	31.7	29.0	31.5	30.1	22.9	26.9	25.8	24.0
Rubber and misc. plastic products	33.9	46.1	52.7	54.9	34.0	47.0	53.8	53.6
Leather and leather products	4.7	5.3	4.5	4.4	5.2	5.3	4.5	4.2
Transportation and public utilities	490.9	642.6	713.2	759.1	525.0	634.5	700.1	726.0
Transportation	177.4	233.4	262.8	283.9	180.6	225.1	256.8	261.6
Railroad transportation	19.8	23.6	23.2	24.2	18.1	22.7	23.0	22.7
Local & interurban passenger transit	9.1	12.4	14.8	16.0	12.8	13.2	14.8	15.3
Trucking and warehousing	69.4	89.0	99.5	106.5	68.1	86.6	97.5	96.6
Water transportation	10.0	11.6	13.3	13.9	10.2	11.3	13.4	13.4
Transportation by air	45.3	67.7	79.2	87.8	46.9	62.9	75.5	78.1
Pipelines, except natural gas	5.5	5.5	5.9	6.5	5.7	5.0	6.4	6.9
Transportation services	18.2	23.5	26.9	29.0	19.5	23.4	26.3	28.7
Communications	148.1	202.3	243.1	258.7	155.2	202.4	240.1	256.6
Telephone and telegraph	119.4	151.6	189.5	201.7	117.1	147.6	190.8	209.1
Radio and television broadcasting	28.7	50.7	53.7	57.0	37.5	55.2	49.7	48.5
Electric, gas, and sanitary services	165.4	206.9	207.2	216.6	190.0	207.2	203.2	208.0
Wholesale trade	376.1	500.6	572.3	613.8	395.1	483.0	589.3	664.0
Retail trade	507.8	646.8	734.1	781.9	559.5	641.4	739.2	795.7
Finance, insurance, and real estate	1,010.3	1,347.2	1,561.6	1,674.2	1,250.6	1,393.0	1,510.5	1,606.7
Depository institutions	171.3	227.4	271.2	289.6	244.0	242.4	241.7	257.9
Nondepository institutions	23.3	34.1	51.6	78.5	26.3	33.4	55.6	87.6
Security and commodity brokers	42.3	77.7	117.3	117.1	42.0	76.5	124.2	136.3
Insurance carriers	64.6	120.2	141.4	143.1	112.2	129.9	131.0	129.6
Insurance agents, brokers & services	37.7	47.2	51.3	53.7	61.4	49.9	48.8	49.3
Real estate	665.7	832.6	919.2	967.9	763.4	852.8	902.9	932.4
Services	1,071.5	1,462.4	1,692.5	1,841.3	1,361.9	1,510.4	1,634.4	1,708.1
Hotels and other lodging places	46.3	61.7	70.6	76.3	55.2	62.7	66.2	63.7
Personal services	38.0	46.7	50.1	53.0	46.4	48.1	48.3	49.9
Business services	203.9	302.0	395.5	454.1	241.3	313.9	383.1	421.5
Auto repair, services, and garages	50.3	65.1	72.0	77.6	61.9	65.9	69.4	72.0
Motion pictures	17.7	22.4	25.2	27.2	21.2	23.6	24.7	26.1
Amusement and recreation services	36.5	53.5	64.8	70.5	45.0	55.6	62.9	66.1
Health services	314.4	433.1	476.2	495.5	423.2	444.3	463.4	467.0
Legal services	82.7	101.1	108.5	116.5	108.8	105.1	103.8	107.1
Educational services	39.6	55.7	61.1	66.4	50.3	58.5	58.6	60.9
Social services & membership organizations .	30.1	47.4	53.2	57.8	38.0	49.3	51.0	52.4
Other services	149.2	194.4	229.6	254.1	191.3	199.9	221.6	238.3
Government	806.6	989.5	1,059.4	1,100.1	1,008.2	1,017.1	1,035.7	1,047.0
Federal	300.2	342.3	355.0	360.9	384.7	354.3	349.1	349.8
State and local	506.4	647.2	704.4	739.3	624.1	662.9	686.5	697.2

[1] Includes private households and statistical discrepancy, not shown separately.

Source: U.S. Bureau of Economic Analysis, *National Income and Product Accounts, 1929-94*, and *Survey of Current Business* June 2000.

No. 717. Gross Domestic Product in Current and Real (1996) Dollars by Type of Product and Sector: 1990 to 1999

[In billions of dollars (5,803.2 represents 5,803,200,000,000). For explanation of chained dollars, see text, this section]

Item	1990	1992	1993	1994	1995	1996	1997	1998	1999
CURRENT DOLLARS									
Gross domestic product	5,803.2	6,318.9	6,642.3	7,054.3	7,400.5	7,813.2	8,300.8	8,759.9	9,256.1
PRODUCT									
Goods	2,266.4	2,391.4	2,503.2	2,680.2	2,798.1	2,951.3	3,142.4	3,310.3	3,482.2
Durable goods	1,002.0	1,026.5	1,107.8	1,197.3	1,273.3	1,351.0	1,460.3	1,567.8	1,644.5
Nondurable goods	1,264.4	1,364.9	1,395.4	1,482.9	1,524.8	1,600.3	1,682.1	1,742.5	1,837.7
Services	3,010.8	3,416.0	3,593.5	3,782.6	3,985.1	4,191.0	4,434.7	4,664.5	4,932.0
Structures	526.0	511.5	545.6	591.6	617.3	670.9	723.7	785.1	842.0
SECTOR									
Business	4,842.0	5,242.1	5,518.0	5,886.6	6,190.1	6,556.0	6,996.8	7,402.0	7,828.9
Nonfarm	4,762.4	5,161.6	5,444.4	5,803.0	6,116.9	6,463.8	6,908.8	7,321.9	7,746.4
Farm	79.6	80.5	73.6	83.6	73.2	92.2	88.0	80.2	82.5
Households and institutions	237.9	279.5	297.0	313.3	330.3	348.6	366.2	385.6	408.3
General government	723.3	797.3	827.3	854.5	880.1	908.7	937.8	972.3	1,019.0
Federal	259.7	282.8	287.0	287.4	286.8	292.0	293.7	296.9	308.2
State and local	463.6	514.5	540.3	567.0	593.3	616.7	644.0	675.4	710.7
CHAINED (1996) DOLLARS									
Gross domestic product	6,707.9	6,880.0	7,062.6	7,347.7	7,543.8	7,813.2	8,144.8	8,495.7	8,848.2
PRODUCT									
Goods	2,404.2	2,455.0	2,548.2	2,708.3	2,813.8	2,951.3	3,141.3	3,330.5	3,509.0
Durable goods	1,007.1	1,015.0	1,093.5	1,179.0	1,264.8	1,351.0	1,481.0	1,625.0	1,742.1
Nondurable goods	1,400.4	1,444.9	1,457.3	1,531.1	1,549.3	1,600.3	1,660.8	1,708.1	1,771.8
Services	3,692.3	3,847.3	3,916.8	4,010.3	4,097.5	4,191.0	4,304.2	4,429.3	4,579.1
Structures	614.8	584.9	602.5	630.7	632.9	670.9	700.2	738.9	766.4
SECTOR									
Business	5,523.5	5,668.9	5,838.3	6,111.8	6,295.9	6,556.0	6,868.5	7,202.4	7,534.4
Nonfarm	5,440.8	5,575.3	5,753.4	6,013.7	6,210.3	6,463.8	6,765.9	7,100.8	7,432.9
Farm	84.2	95.7	85.8	100.3	85.5	92.2	103.3	100.7	99.5
Households and institutions	291.5	308.6	319.7	330.9	341.5	348.6	360.5	369.0	376.3
General government	895.1	904.9	906.2	905.6	906.7	908.7	915.9	924.8	939.1
Federal	331.4	326.2	319.7	309.9	299.1	292.0	287.8	285.8	284.8
State and local	564.7	579.4	587.1	596.1	607.7	616.7	628.2	638.9	654.1

Source: U.S. Bureau of Economic Analysis, *National Income and Product Accounts of the United States, 1929-94*, Vol. 1; and *Survey of Current Business*, May 2000.

No. 718. GDP Components in Current Dollars—Annual Percent Change: 1990 to 1999

[Change from previous year; for 1990, change from 1989. Minus sign (-) indicates decrease]

Item	1990	1991	1992	1993	1994	1995	1996	1997	1998	1999
Gross domestic product (GDP)	5.7	3.2	5.6	5.1	6.2	4.9	5.6	6.2	5.5	5.7
Personal consumption expenditures	6.5	3.6	6.0	5.8	5.9	5.4	5.4	5.5	5.9	7.0
Durable goods	-	-5.3	6.3	9.1	9.2	5.2	4.5	4.3	8.6	8.7
Nondurable goods	6.9	2.6	3.5	3.9	4.6	4.1	5.1	4.3	4.1	7.9
Services	7.9	6.2	7.4	6.2	5.9	6.0	5.7	6.3	6.2	6.2
Gross private domestic investment	-1.3	-7.1	8.3	10.2	14.9	4.2	8.7	11.3	10.7	6.0
Fixed investment	0.2	-5.5	6.4	9.7	10.8	7.4	9.2	8.5	11.0	8.1
Nonresidential	2.8	-3.4	2.8	9.0	9.7	10.2	9.0	9.6	10.7	6.9
Structures	4.7	-9.4	-6.1	4.2	4.5	9.1	9.9	12.9	7.4	0.2
Producers' durable equipment	1.9	-0.6	6.7	10.8	11.6	10.6	8.7	8.5	11.8	9.1
Residential	-6.5	-11.7	17.7	11.7	13.6	-0.1	9.7	5.1	12.0	11.5
Exports of goods and services	9.5	8.0	5.8	3.3	10.2	12.9	6.8	10.7	-0.2	3.3
Exports of goods	7.2	7.0	5.2	2.5	10.8	14.6	5.9	11.4	-1.1	2.6
Exports of services	15.5	10.5	7.4	5.4	8.7	8.9	9.0	9.1	2.2	5.0
Imports of goods and services	6.6	-1.0	6.8	8.1	13.0	11.2	6.7	9.7	5.6	12.2
Imports of goods	4.9	-1.4	8.8	8.8	14.2	12.0	6.7	9.5	5.1	12.8
Imports of services	14.6	0.8	-1.5	5.0	7.7	7.2	6.6	10.6	8.4	9.5
Govt. consumption expenditures and gross investment	7.4	4.6	2.8	1.8	2.7	3.3	3.6	4.2	3.3	6.6
Federal	5.4	3.7	1.4	-1.4	-1.2	0.1	1.9	1.2	0.2	5.9
National defense	3.2	2.6	-1.6	-3.6	-2.7	-1.3	1.8	-1.3	-1.1	4.6
Nondefense	12.0	7.0	9.2	4.1	2.2	3.0	2.1	6.1	2.6	8.4
State and local	9.0	5.2	3.9	4.0	5.4	5.4	4.7	5.9	5.1	6.9

- Represents or rounds to zero.

Source: U.S. Bureau of Economic Analysis, *National Income and Product Accounts of the United States, 1929-94*, Vol. 1; and *Survey of Current Business*, May 2000.

Income, Expenditures, and Wealth **453**

No. 719. Gross State Product in Current and Real (1992) Dollars: 1990 to 1997

[In billions of dollars (5,659.8 represents 5,659,800,000,000). For definition of gross state product or chained dollars, see text, this section]

State	Current dollars					Chained (1992) dollars [1]				
	1990	1994	1995	1996	1997	1990	1994	1995	1996	1997
United States . . .	5,659.8	6,868.0	7,231.8	7,629.5	8,103.2	6,046.5	6,535.6	6,726.6	6,965.5	7,262.9
Alabama	71.1	89.3	94.9	98.5	103.1	75.5	85.5	88.1	90.0	92.8
Alaska	25.4	21.9	23.2	24.0	24.5	25.2	21.5	22.2	21.8	21.8
Arizona.	68.5	95.4	103.6	111.9	121.2	72.9	91.3	97.0	103.5	110.5
Arkansas	37.9	50.4	53.1	56.1	58.5	40.0	48.3	49.7	51.4	53.2
California	792.7	876.0	918.9	966.8	1,033.0	845.2	836.2	857.8	883.6	927.5
Colorado.	74.4	100.7	108.3	116.2	126.1	79.0	96.7	101.1	105.8	112.7
Connecticut.	98.5	112.6	118.6	124.6	134.6	105.2	107.2	109.5	112.6	118.5
Delaware	21.0	24.1	27.8	29.2	31.6	23.2	25.3	25.8	26.7	27.4
District of Columbia .	40.7	48.1	49.5	50.3	52.4	45.3	45.6	44.6	44.0	44.1
Florida	255.2	321.7	338.7	360.3	380.6	273.0	306.2	313.6	326.8	338.1
Georgia	140.5	186.0	200.2	214.4	229.5	150.0	178.4	186.6	196.1	206.1
Hawaii	32.4	35.2	36.7	37.0	38.0	34.9	35.0	34.2	33.8	33.7
Idaho	17.5	24.5	26.9	27.8	29.1	18.5	23.5	25.5	26.1	27.3
Illinois	273.4	336.9	353.6	370.4	393.5	290.8	325.5	332.4	343.1	358.1
Indiana	109.6	141.4	147.4	154.2	161.7	116.3	135.1	138.2	142.9	148.0
Iowa	55.0	68.7	70.9	76.5	80.5	58.0	66.1	67.1	70.8	74.3
Kansas.	51.3	61.9	63.5	67.4	71.7	54.3	59.4	59.5	61.5	64.6
Kentucky	67.7	86.1	90.1	94.5	100.1	72.3	83.5	85.8	88.5	92.6
Louisiana	91.1	103.9	112.5	117.6	124.4	93.7	100.7	106.6	106.0	109.8
Maine.	23.2	26.2	27.8	28.7	30.2	24.8	24.9	25.4	25.9	26.8
Maryland	113.7	132.9	138.1	144.8	153.8	122.3	126.0	127.0	130.2	135.0
Massachusetts.	158.9	186.0	195.7	207.3	221.0	169.9	177.5	182.2	189.4	197.8
Michigan.	188.0	240.6	247.7	259.2	272.6	202.1	229.1	230.7	237.4	246.4
Minnesota.	99.5	124.6	131.1	140.9	149.4	105.1	118.7	121.5	128.1	133.8
Mississippi	38.7	50.8	53.7	55.8	58.3	40.8	48.5	50.4	51.3	52.9
Missouri	104.1	129.1	137.7	143.7	152.1	111.3	123.4	128.2	131.2	136.7
Montana	13.3	16.9	17.6	18.3	19.2	13.9	16.1	16.4	16.7	17.2
Nebraska	33.2	42.1	43.6	47.0	48.8	34.9	40.4	41.0	42.9	44.2
Nevada	31.3	44.5	48.4	53.4	57.4	33.1	42.3	44.4	48.0	50.2
New Hampshire	23.7	29.3	32.2	35.1	38.1	25.2	28.1	30.3	32.7	35.2
New Jersey.	214.1	255.8	266.7	279.2	294.1	227.7	243.3	247.1	253.8	260.9
New Mexico	26.7	40.9	41.0	42.6	45.2	27.9	40.0	40.2	41.1	43.5
New York	498.3	565.2	589.5	621.2	651.7	535.6	544.4	547.3	565.5	579.7
North Carolina	142.5	182.3	193.6	203.5	218.9	154.5	178.1	185.3	191.3	202.1
North Dakota	11.4	13.7	14.2	15.6	15.8	11.9	13.2	13.4	14.3	14.4
Ohio	227.1	276.7	292.1	303.6	320.5	241.6	265.2	273.1	280.0	291.4
Oklahoma.	56.9	66.0	68.3	72.7	76.6	59.5	63.5	64.5	66.6	69.2
Oregon.	57.0	74.7	80.7	90.9	98.4	60.8	70.8	74.9	83.9	90.2
Pennsylvania.	245.8	296.8	312.3	322.8	339.9	261.9	282.8	290.3	295.5	305.3
Rhode Island.	21.5	23.9	25.1	26.0	27.8	23.1	22.8	23.3	23.6	24.7
South Carolina.	65.4	80.7	85.1	88.3	93.3	69.5	77.7	79.8	81.8	85.2
South Dakota	12.9	17.5	18.5	19.5	20.2	13.7	16.8	17.2	17.6	17.9
Tennessee	94.2	127.9	134.5	138.8	147.0	100.5	122.1	125.4	127.2	132.6
Texas.	388.9	484.1	515.9	554.7	601.6	404.1	467.6	488.7	509.3	544.0
Utah	31.1	42.0	46.0	51.2	55.4	32.9	40.2	42.7	46.6	49.6
Vermont	11.6	13.6	13.9	14.6	15.2	12.3	13.0	13.1	13.5	13.9
Virginia.	148.1	178.8	188.0	198.6	211.3	160.6	172.9	176.6	182.5	189.7
Washington.	114.1	144.7	150.5	160.1	172.3	122.2	137.3	138.7	144.4	152.3
West Virginia.	28.0	34.5	35.9	37.2	38.2	29.3	33.4	34.1	34.9	35.3
Wisconsin.	99.2	125.8	132.2	139.7	147.3	105.0	120.9	123.6	128.8	134.6
Wyoming	13.5	14.9	15.6	17.0	17.6	13.4	15.0	15.5	16.0	16.5

[1] For chained (1992) dollar estimates, states will not add to U.S. total.

Source: U.S. Bureau of Economic Analysis, *Survey of Current Business*, June 2000.

No. 720. Gross State Product in Chained (1992) Dollars by Industry: 1997

[In billions of dollars (7,262.9 represents 7,262,900,000,000). For definition of gross state product or chained dollars, see text, this section. Industries based on 1987 Standard Industrial Classification]

State	Total [1]	Farms, forestry, fisher-ies [2]	Con-struction	Manu-facturing	Trans-portation, public utilities	Whole-sale trade	Retail trade	Finance, insur-ance, real estate	Services	Govern-ment [3]
United States [4]	**7,262.9**	**127.6**	**274.4**	**1,369.9**	**644.3**	**532.0**	**713.5**	**1,286.0**	**1,398.6**	**827.1**
Alabama	92.8	2.1	3.6	21.1	8.8	6.3	10.5	11.0	14.4	13.4
Alaska	21.8	0.3	0.8	1.0	4.1	0.7	1.7	2.3	2.6	4.2
Arizona	110.5	1.9	5.8	19.7	8.7	7.7	12.6	19.3	21.1	12.9
Arkansas	53.2	2.7	1.9	13.4	5.9	3.5	6.2	5.7	7.4	6.0
California	927.5	20.9	29.1	149.2	68.3	67.3	91.4	199.3	200.6	98.9
Colorado	112.7	2.1	5.8	13.8	13.1	7.8	12.2	18.4	23.6	13.6
Connecticut	118.5	0.8	3.6	22.0	7.5	8.9	9.9	31.5	24.6	9.8
Delaware	27.4	0.3	0.9	5.5	1.5	1.1	1.8	10.2	3.8	2.4
District of Columbia	44.1	-	0.4	1.1	2.6	0.6	1.3	8.0	14.3	16.0
Florida	338.1	6.4	14.9	28.5	31.6	27.0	42.5	69.6	76.8	40.1
Georgia	206.1	4.0	7.4	38.6	24.1	19.8	20.6	30.7	35.9	24.4
Hawaii	33.7	0.4	1.4	1.1	3.7	1.4	4.3	7.5	7.1	6.9
Idaho	27.3	1.7	1.4	6.5	2.4	1.7	3.0	3.0	4.1	3.3
Illinois	358.1	5.0	13.7	73.4	34.3	29.3	31.9	66.8	69.7	33.1
Indiana	148.0	2.8	6.5	49.5	11.8	9.5	14.8	17.3	21.6	13.5
Iowa	74.3	5.6	2.7	20.6	5.9	5.4	6.6	9.4	10.4	7.8
Kansas	64.6	2.9	2.5	12.0	7.4	5.5	7.0	7.7	10.4	8.4
Kentucky	92.6	2.7	3.4	27.2	7.8	5.7	9.0	9.5	12.8	11.4
Louisiana	109.8	1.3	4.5	18.0	10.5	6.7	10.2	13.6	16.9	11.9
Maine	26.8	0.4	1.1	4.8	2.1	1.7	3.5	4.7	4.9	3.5
Maryland	135.0	1.2	6.5	12.5	10.9	9.2	13.3	28.4	30.7	22.4
Massachusetts	197.8	1.2	6.0	33.0	13.2	15.3	17.5	45.0	49.3	17.4
Michigan	246.4	2.6	9.2	67.9	17.4	19.7	25.8	34.3	43.6	25.1
Minnesota	133.8	3.6	5.6	27.2	11.0	11.9	13.0	22.4	25.2	13.5
Mississippi	52.9	1.6	2.0	12.8	5.6	3.2	6.0	5.6	8.1	7.5
Missouri	136.7	2.8	6.0	29.6	14.8	10.9	14.0	18.7	25.1	14.4
Montana	17.2	1.0	0.8	1.3	2.2	1.2	2.0	2.1	3.2	2.6
Nebraska	44.2	3.5	1.7	6.6	5.4	3.6	4.2	5.9	7.3	6.0
Nevada	50.2	0.4	4.2	2.4	4.1	2.7	5.6	8.9	15.6	4.9
New Hampshire	35.2	0.2	1.1	10.4	2.6	2.3	3.4	7.0	5.9	2.7
New Jersey	260.9	1.4	8.7	38.4	26.5	25.8	21.3	57.9	54.4	26.5
New Mexico	43.5	0.9	1.7	11.1	3.2	1.9	4.1	5.2	6.6	6.6
New York	579.7	2.6	15.4	69.2	46.5	38.1	44.5	177.9	125.3	60.2
North Carolina	202.1	5.0	8.0	59.6	15.8	13.5	19.4	26.8	29.0	24.3
North Dakota	14.4	1.1	0.7	1.4	1.6	1.4	1.5	1.7	2.4	2.1
Ohio	291.4	3.9	10.4	82.7	22.9	22.1	29.7	41.6	48.7	28.5
Oklahoma	69.2	2.1	2.0	13.0	7.2	4.4	7.7	7.8	11.4	10.4
Oregon	90.2	2.4	4.3	25.9	6.6	7.3	8.2	12.2	14.4	9.5
Pennsylvania	305.3	3.0	11.1	67.4	28.2	19.6	30.0	52.5	62.4	29.5
Rhode Island	24.7	0.2	0.8	4.3	1.8	1.5	2.4	5.7	5.1	2.9
South Carolina	85.2	1.2	3.8	23.2	6.7	5.3	10.0	10.6	12.3	11.9
South Dakota	17.9	1.7	0.7	2.8	1.5	1.3	1.9	3.0	2.8	2.1
Tennessee	132.6	1.7	5.0	30.4	11.1	10.7	16.3	17.4	25.1	14.6
Texas	544.0	8.3	21.6	98.5	62.5	42.9	52.0	71.0	94.0	58.0
Utah	49.6	0.6	2.6	8.2	4.5	3.2	5.8	7.4	9.1	6.6
Vermont	13.9	0.3	0.6	3.0	1.2	0.9	1.5	2.3	2.7	1.6
Virginia	189.7	1.9	7.9	31.2	17.2	11.2	17.3	32.1	36.9	32.9
Washington	152.3	4.0	7.1	19.7	14.0	12.3	16.6	26.0	31.4	21.1
West Virginia	35.3	0.3	1.5	6.0	4.6	1.9	3.4	3.6	5.4	4.6
Wisconsin	134.6	2.8	5.3	41.2	9.6	9.0	12.9	19.6	20.8	13.4
Wyoming	16.5	0.4	0.6	0.9	2.4	0.6	1.2	1.9	1.4	1.9

- Represents zero. [1] Includes mining not shown separately. [2] Includes agricultural services. [3] Includes Federal civilian and military and state and local government. [4] States will not add to U.S. total as chained-dollar estimates are usually not additive.

Source: U.S. Bureau of Economic Analysis, *Survey of Current Business*, June 2000.

Income, Expenditures, and Wealth   455

No. 721. Relation of GDP, GNP, Net National Product, National Income, Personal Income, Disposable Personal Income, and Personal Saving: 1990 to 1999

[In billions of dollars ($5,803.2 represents $5,803,200,000,000). For definitions, see text, this section]

Item	1990	1993	1994	1995	1996	1997	1998	1999
Gross domestic product...........	5,803.2	6,642.3	7,054.3	7,400.5	7,813.2	8,300.8	8,759.9	9,256.1
Plus: Receipts of factor income from the rest of the world [1]............	188.3	154.4	184.3	232.3	245.6	282.6	285.3	302.3
Less: Payments of factor income to the rest of the world [2]............	159.3	130.1	167.5	211.9	227.5	278.4	295.2	322.3
Equals: Gross national product.....	5,832.2	6,666.7	7,071.1	7,420.9	7,831.2	8,305.0	8,750.0	9,236.2
Less: Consumption of fixed capital.....	711.3	812.8	874.9	911.7	956.2	1,009.1	1,064.6	1,135.8
Equals: Net national product [3]......	5,120.9	5,853.9	6,196.2	6,509.1	6,875.0	7,295.9	7,685.4	8,100.4
Less: Indirect business tax and nontax liability....................	447.3	540.1	575.3	594.6	620.0	645.8	677.0	716.3
Plus: Subsidies [4]...............	25.3	29.6	25.2	22.2	22.6	19.0	20.8	26.5
Equals: National income [3]........	4,642.1	5,251.9	5,556.8	5,876.7	6,210.4	6,635.5	7,038.8	7,496.3
Less: Corporate profits [5]...........	408.6	510.5	573.2	668.8	754.0	838.5	848.4	892.7
Net interest..................	452.4	374.3	380.5	389.8	386.3	412.5	435.7	467.5
Contributions for social insurance	410.1	477.8	508.4	533.2	555.8	588.2	621.9	658.2
Wage accruals less disbursements ...	0.1	6.4	17.6	16.4	3.6	-4.1	3.5	-
Plus: Personal interest income........	772.4	725.5	742.4	792.5	810.6	854.9	897.8	931.3
Personal dividend income	165.4	203.0	234.7	254.0	297.4	333.4	348.3	364.3
Government transfer payments to persons	573.1	776.5	810.1	860.1	902.4	934.5	954.8	988.6
Business transfer payments to persons......................	21.3	22.1	23.7	25.8	26.4	27.9	28.8	29.6
Equals: Personal income	4,903.2	5,610.0	5,888.0	6,200.9	6,547.4	6,951.1	7,358.9	7,791.8
Less: Personal tax and nontax payments.	609.6	674.6	722.6	778.3	869.7	968.3	1,072.6	1,152.1
Equals: Disposable personal income..	4,293.6	4,935.3	5,165.4	5,422.6	5,677.7	5,982.8	6,286.2	6,639.7
Less: Personal outlays.............	3,959.3	4,584.5	4,849.9	5,120.2	5,405.6	5,711.7	6,056.6	6,483.3
Equals: Personal saving...........	334.3	350.8	315.5	302.4	272.1	271.1	229.7	156.3

- Represents zero or rounds to zero. [1] Consists largely of receipts by U.S. residents of interest and dividends and reinvested earnings of foreign affiliates of U.S. corporations. [2] Consists largely of payments to foreign residents of interest and dividends and reinvested earnings of U.S. affiliates of foreign corporations. [3] Includes items not shown separately. [4] Less current surplus of government enterprises. [5] With inventory valuation and capital consumption adjustments.

Source: U.S. Bureau of Economic Analysis, National Income and Product Accounts of the United States, 1929-94, Vol. 1; and Survey of Current Business, May 2000.

No. 722. Selected Per Capita Income and Product Items in Current and Real (1996) Dollars: 1960 to 1999

[In dollars. Based on Census Bureau estimated population including Armed Forces abroad; based on quarterly averages. For explanation of chained dollars, see text, Section 14, Income]

Year	Current dollars					Chained (1996) dollars				
	Gross domestic product	Gross national product	Personal income	Dispos-able per-sonal income	Personal consump-tion expendi-tures	Gross domestic product	Gross national product	Dispos-able personal income	Personal consump-tion expendi-tures
1960	2,918	2,935	2,283	2,026	1,838	13,148	13,232	9,210	8,358
1970	5,069	5,101	4,101	3,591	3,164	17,446	17,556	12,823	11,300
1971	5,434	5,471	4,358	3,860	3,382	17,804	17,925	13,218	11,581
1972	5,909	5,950	4,736	4,138	3,671	18,570	18,701	13,692	12,149
1973	6,537	6,597	5,254	4,619	4,022	19,456	19,633	14,496	12,626
1974	7,017	7,091	5,730	5,013	4,359	19,163	19,366	14,268	12,407
1975	7,571	7,632	6,166	5,470	4,771	18,911	19,065	14,393	12,551
1976	8,363	8,442	6,765	5,960	5,272	19,771	19,953	14,873	13,155
1977	9,221	9,315	7,432	6,519	5,803	20,481	20,685	15,256	13,583
1978	10,313	10,412	8,302	7,253	6,425	21,383	21,584	15,845	14,035
1979	11,401	11,547	9,247	8,033	7,091	21,821	22,096	16,120	14,230
1980	12,276	12,431	10,205	8,869	7,741	21,521	21,791	16,063	14,021
1981	13,614	13,765	11,301	9,773	8,453	21,830	22,066	16,265	14,069
1982	14,035	14,192	11,922	10,364	8,954	21,184	21,418	16,328	14,105
1983	15,085	15,242	12,576	11,036	9,757	21,902	22,126	16,673	14,741
1984	16,636	16,786	13,853	12,215	10,569	23,288	23,494	17,799	15,401
1985	17,664	17,771	14,738	12,941	11,373	23,970	24,112	18,229	16,020
1986	18,501	18,565	15,425	13,555	12,029	24,565	24,649	18,641	16,541
1987	19,529	19,585	16,317	14,246	12,787	25,174	25,246	18,870	16,938
1988	20,845	20,920	17,433	15,312	13,697	25,987	26,080	19,522	17,463
1989	22,188	22,271	18,593	16,235	14,539	26,646	26,742	19,833	17,760
1990	23,215	23,331	19,614	17,176	15,327	26,834	26,962	20,058	17,899
1991	23,691	23,789	20,126	17,710	15,717	26,423	26,529	19,919	17,677
1992	24,741	24,833	21,105	18,616	16,482	26,938	27,039	20,318	17,989
1993	25,735	25,829	21,735	19,121	17,259	27,363	27,461	20,384	18,399
1994	27,068	27,132	22,593	19,820	18,097	28,194	28,257	20,709	18,910
1995	28,131	28,208	23,571	20,613	18,888	28,676	28,753	21,055	19,294
1996	29,428	29,496	24,660	21,385	19,727	29,428	29,496	21,385	19,727
1997	30,968	30,983	25,932	22,320	20,610	30,386	30,409	21,887	20,210
1998	32,373	32,336	27,195	23,231	21,614	31,396	31,367	22,569	20,998
1999	33,885	33,812	28,525	24,307	22,907	32,392	32,328	23,244	21,905

Source: U.S. Bureau of Economic Analysis, National Income and Product Accounts of the United States, 1929-94, Vol. 2; and Survey of Current Business, May 2000.

456   Income, Expenditures, and Wealth

No. 723. Personal Consumption Expenditures in Current and Real (1996) Dollars by Type: 1990 to 1998

[In billions of dollars ($3,831.5 represents $3,831,500,000,000). For definition of "chained" dollars, see text, this section]

Expenditure	Current dollars				Chained (1996) dollars			
	1990	1995	1997	1998	1990	1995	1997	1998
Total expenditures [1]	3,831.5	4,969.0	5,524.4	5,848.6	4,474.5	5,075.6	5,417.3	5,681.8
Food and tobacco [1]	677.9	802.5	866.3	907.4	774.4	825.1	846.2	866.2
Food purchased for off-premise consumption	401.6	459.8	489.5	509.4	452.4	473.7	480.5	494.0
Purchased meals and beverages [2]	227.8	287.5	318.5	334.7	261.8	294.6	309.8	317.6
Tobacco products	41.0	46.7	49.3	54.0	52.0	48.1	47.1	45.8
Clothing, accessories, and jewelry [1]	261.7	317.3	348.2	367.9	258.2	312.9	348.8	375.8
Shoes	31.5	37.1	40.0	41.6	32.0	36.8	40.1	42.0
Clothing	172.4	210.4	230.9	244.4	165.1	207.2	230.7	249.8
Jewelry and watches	30.3	38.1	41.2	44.2	30.1	36.7	42.8	47.7
Personal care	53.7	67.4	76.1	80.5	60.1	68.3	75.1	78.2
Housing [1]	585.6	740.8	809.8	855.9	696.2	763.7	786.5	805.6
Owner-occupied nonfarm dwellings-space rent	410.7	529.3	585.5	622.6	488.3	546.1	569.0	586.6
Tenant-occupied nonfarm dwellings-space rent	148.7	177.0	186.0	193.6	174.6	181.6	180.9	182.6
Household operation [1]	433.6	555.0	617.5	646.5	476.8	564.2	611.2	643.7
Furniture [3]	38.4	47.5	54.1	57.0	42.2	48.1	54.2	57.2
Semidurable house furnishings [4]	22.5	29.7	32.6	34.6	21.8	29.0	33.3	36.2
Cleaning and polishing preparations	38.9	47.3	51.5	54.3	42.4	48.5	51.0	52.9
Household utilities	141.1	175.0	188.6	186.8	162.8	180.8	184.6	187.1
Electricity	74.2	91.0	93.8	95.9	83.2	92.5	93.3	99.3
Gas	26.8	31.5	36.6	32.2	29.5	32.8	34.2	30.7
Water and other sanitary services	27.1	38.4	43.0	45.4	37.1	39.8	42.0	42.9
Fuel oil and coal	12.9	14.1	15.2	13.2	13.1	15.7	15.1	14.5
Telephone and telegraph	60.5	87.8	103.9	113.1	62.6	88.1	103.7	114.6
Medical care [1]	619.7	888.6	977.6	1,032.3	807.6	907.8	956.6	987.4
Drug preparations and sundries [5]	65.4	92.1	108.1	116.8	80.3	94.1	106.5	112.6
Physicians	140.4	192.4	206.9	219.6	183.3	193.8	204.1	212.2
Dentists	32.4	46.5	52.0	54.8	44.8	48.7	49.7	50.2
Hospitals and nursing homes [6]	265.0	370.9	408.5	428.4	340.5	381.5	400.8	410.4
Health insurance	37.7	58.0	57.6	59.8	66.0	58.9	56.0	57.9
Medical care [7]	31.7	46.4	46.9	49.7	47.9	47.1	45.0	46.3
Personal business [1]	284.7	406.8	488.3	528.6	363.2	424.4	460.8	488.5
Expense of handling life insurance [8]	55.0	81.8	89.0	91.3	71.2	87.0	84.5	82.4
Legal services	40.9	48.0	55.0	58.5	51.9	49.7	52.9	53.8
Funeral and burial expenses	9.5	13.3	15.3	16.0	12.9	14.0	14.6	14.7
Transportation [1]	455.4	560.3	623.7	647.4	532.2	574.7	616.4	653.8
User-operated transportation [1]	419.0	517.8	575.6	598.0	493.5	532.3	570.3	606.1
New autos	89.7	82.2	82.8	90.6	104.0	83.5	82.7	91.2
Net purchases of used autos	29.3	50.0	53.4	55.5	42.0	51.2	54.8	57.6
Tires, tubes, accessories, etc.	29.9	36.9	39.7	41.7	29.7	36.8	39.9	42.3
Repair, greasing, washing, parking, storage, rental, and leasing	84.9	122.2	145.9	153.8	100.8	124.5	143.9	149.0
Gasoline and oil	107.3	113.3	126.2	112.9	113.1	120.2	126.2	127.7
Purchased local transportation	8.4	10.4	11.8	12.1	10.8	11.4	11.6	12.0
Mass transit systems	5.8	7.1	8.1	8.4	7.4	7.8	8.0	8.3
Taxicab	2.6	3.2	3.7	3.7	3.4	3.6	3.6	3.7
Purchased intercity transportation [1]	28.1	32.1	36.3	37.2	28.1	31.0	34.5	35.7
Railway (commutation)	0.7	0.6	0.7	0.7	0.9	0.7	0.7	0.7
Bus	1.3	1.6	1.8	1.8	1.3	1.6	1.8	1.8
Airline	22.7	25.5	29.0	29.5	22.0	24.3	27.4	28.3
Recreation [1][9]	284.9	401.6	457.8	494.7	292.6	398.7	464.6	512.2
Magazines, newspapers, and sheet music	21.6	26.2	29.5	31.9	27.2	27.2	29.2	30.9
Nondurable toys and sport supplies	32.8	47.2	53.7	57.7	33.7	47.4	54.2	61.1
Video and audio products, including musical instruments and computer goods	52.9	77.0	84.0	92.6	33.0	67.3	97.0	124.5
Computers, peripherals, and software	8.9	21.0	26.2	30.4	2.1	14.6	38.1	63.9
Education and research	83.7	114.5	130.7	139.2	107.6	119.2	126.1	130.1
Higher education	43.8	62.9	69.2	71.8	60.1	65.6	66.7	66.7
Religious and welfare activities	97.1	134.9	150.3	163.5	115.3	138.7	145.9	154.7
Foreign travel and other, net	-6.3	-20.7	-21.8	-15.3	-5.3	-21.4	-20.7	-11.8
Foreign travel by U.S. residents	42.7	54.1	63.4	68.2	51.7	55.3	62.3	68.5
Less: Expenditures in the United States by nonresidents	51.6	75.4	86.5	85.4	60.1	77.4	84.7	82.7

[1] Includes other expenditures not shown separately.　[2] Consists of purchases (including tips) of meals and beverages from retail, service, and amusement establishments; hotels; dining and buffet cars; schools; school fraternities; institutions; clubs; and industrial lunch rooms. Includes meals and beverages consumed both on and off premise.　[3] Includes mattresses and bedsprings.　[4] Consists largely of textile house furnishings including piece goods allocated to house furnishing use. Also includes lamp shades, brooms, and brushes.　[5] Excludes drug preparations and related products dispensed by physicians, hospitals, and other medical services.　[6] Consists of (1) current expenditures (including consumption of fixed capital) of nonprofit hospitals and nursing homes and (2) payments by patients to proprietary and government hospitals and nursing homes.　[7] Consists of (1) premiums, less benefits and dividends, for health hospitalization and accidental death and dismemberment insurance provided by commercial insurance carriers and (2) administrative expenses (including consumption of fixed capital) of Blue Cross and Blue Shield plans and of other independent prepaid and self-insured health plans.　[8] Consists of (1) operating expenses of life insurance carriers and private noninsured pension plans and (2) premiums less benefits and dividends of fraternal benefit societies. Excludes expenses allocated by commercial carriers to accident and health insurance.　[9] For additional details, see Table 418.

Source: U.S. Bureau of Economic Analysis, *National Income and Product Accounts of the United States, 1929-94,* Vol. 1; and *Survey of Current Business,* June 2000.

Income, Expenditures, and Wealth　457

No. 724. Personal Income and Its Disposition: 1990 to 1999

[In billions of dollars (4,903.2 represents 4,903,200,000,000), except as indicated. For definition of personal income and chained dollars, see text, Section 14, Income]

Item	1990	1993	1994	1995	1996	1997	1998	1999
Personal income	**4,903.2**	**5,610.0**	**5,888.0**	**6,200.9**	**6,547.4**	**6,951.1**	**7,358.9**	**7,791.8**
Wage and salary disbursements	2,754.6	3,085.2	3,236.7	3,424.7	3,626.5	3,888.9	4,186.0	4,472.3
Goods-producing industries [1]	754.4	780.6	824.0	863.6	908.2	975.5	1,038.7	1,082.4
Manufacturing.	561.4	592.4	620.3	647.5	673.7	718.8	757.5	779.7
Distributive industries [2]	633.6	697.3	738.4	782.1	822.4	879.1	944.6	1,005.8
Service industries [3]	849.9	1,022.4	1,070.4	1,156.3	1,254.9	1,369.8	1,509.9	1,657.6
Government	516.7	584.9	603.9	622.7	641.0	664.4	692.8	726.5
Other labor income.	390.0	482.8	507.5	497.0	490.0	500.9	515.7	535.8
Proprietors' income [4]	381.0	461.8	476.6	497.7	544.7	578.6	606.1	658.5
Rental income of persons [5]	49.1	90.9	110.3	117.9	129.7	130.2	137.4	145.9
Personal dividend income	165.4	203.0	234.7	254.0	297.4	333.4	348.3	364.3
Personal interest income	772.4	725.5	742.4	792.5	810.6	854.9	897.8	931.3
Transfer payments to persons	594.4	798.6	833.9	885.9	928.8	962.4	983.6	1,018.2
Less: Personal contributions for								
social insurance	*203.7*	*237.8*	*254.1*	*268.8*	*280.4*	*298.1*	*315.9*	*334.6*
Less: Personal tax and nontax payments.	*609.6*	*674.6*	*722.6*	*778.3*	*869.7*	*968.3*	*1,072.6*	*1,152.1*
Equals: Disposable personal income. .	**4,293.6**	**4,935.3**	**5165.4**	**5422.6**	**5677.7**	**5982.8**	**6,286.2**	**6639.7**
Less: Personal outlays.	*3,959.3*	*4,584.5*	*4,849.9*	*5,120.2*	*5,405.6*	*5,711.7*	*6,056.6*	*6,483.3*
Personal consumption expenditures . .	3,831.5	4,454.7	4,716.4	4,969.0	5,237.5	5,524.4	5,848.6	6,257.3
Interest paid by persons	115.8	115.4	117.9	134.7	149.9	166.7	185.7	201.7
Personal transfer payments to								
the rest of the world (net).	12.0	14.4	15.6	16.5	18.2	20.6	22.3	24.3
Equals: Personal saving.	**334.3**	**350.8**	**315.5**	**302.4**	**272.1**	**271.1**	**229.7**	**156.3**
Addenda:								
Disposable personal income:								
Total, billions of chained								
(1996) dollars.	5,014.2	5,261.3	5,397.2	5,539.1	5,677.7	5,866.7	6,107.1	6,349.4
Per capita (dollars):								
Current dollars	17,176.0	19,121.0	19,820.0	20,613.0	21,385.0	22,320.0	23,231.0	24,307.0
Chained (1996) dollars	20,058.0	20,384.0	20,709.0	21,055.0	21,385.0	21,887.0	22,569.0	23,244.0
Personal saving as percentage of								
disposable personal income	7.8	7.1	6.1	5.6	4.8	4.5	3.7	2.4

[1] Comprises agriculture, forestry, fishing, mining, construction, and manufacturing.   [2] Comprises transportation, communication, public utilities, and trade.   [3] Comprises finance, insurance, real estate, services, and rest of world.   [4] With capital consumption and inventory valuation adjustments.   [5] With capital consumption adjustment.

Source: U.S. Bureau of Economic Analysis, *National Income and Product Accounts of the United States, 1929-94,* Vol. 1; and *Survey of Current Business,* May 2000.

No. 725. Gross Saving and Investment: 1990 to 1999

[In billions of dollars (977.7 represents $977,700,000,000)]

Item	1990	1993	1994	1995	1996	1997	1998	1999
Gross saving	**977.7**	**1,039.4**	**1,155.9**	**1,257.5**	**1,349.3**	**1,521.3**	**1,646.0**	**1,727.1**
Gross private saving	1,016.2	1,159.4	1,199.3	1,266.0	1,290.4	1,362.0	1,371.2	1,364.7
Personal saving	334.3	350.8	315.5	302.4	272.1	271.1	229.7	156.3
Undistributed corporate profits [1]	102.4	142.0	151.6	203.6	232.7	266.6	259.6	268.6
Undistributed profits	95.3	141.9	151.8	203.3	205.0	223.9	193.1	224.4
Inventory valuation adjustment . . .	-12.9	-4.0	-12.4	-18.3	3.1	7.4	20.9	-13.0
Capital consumption adjustment . . .	19.9	4.1	12.2	18.6	24.6	35.3	45.6	57.2
Corporate consumption of fixed								
capital	391.1	448.5	482.7	512.1	543.5	578.8	616.9	661.1
Noncorporate consumption of fixed								
capital	188.4	211.6	231.9	231.5	238.5	249.8	261.5	278.6
Wage accruals less disbursements . . .	-	6.4	17.6	16.4	3.6	-4.1	3.5	-
Gross government saving	-38.6	-120.0	-43.4	-8.5	58.9	159.3	274.8	362.5
Federal	-104.3	-195.4	-130.9	-108.0	-51.5	37.7	134.3	206.3
State and local	65.7	75.4	87.5	99.4	110.4	121.5	140.5	156.2
Gross investment	**1,008.2**	**1,103.2**	**1,214.4**	**1,284.0**	**1,382.1**	**1,518.1**	**1,598.4**	**1,602.0**
Gross private domestic investment	861.7	955.1	1,097.1	1,143.8	1,242.7	1,383.7	1,531.2	1,622.7
Gross government investment	215.8	220.9	225.6	238.2	250.1	258.1	268.7	297.8
Net foreign investment	-69.2	-72.9	-108.3	-98.0	-110.7	-123.7	-201.5	-318.5
Statistical discrepancy	**30.6**	**63.8**	**58.5**	**26.5**	**32.8**	**-3.2**	**-47.6**	**-125.1**

- Represents or rounds to zero.   [1] With inventory valuation and capital consumption adjustments.

Source: U.S. Bureau of Economic Analysis, *National Income and Product Accounts of the United States, 1929-94,* Vol. 1; and *Survey of Current Business,* May 2000.

No. 726. Personal Income in Current and Constant (1996) Dollars by State: 1990 to 1999

[In billions of dollars ($4,885.5 represents $4,885,500,000,000), except percent. 1999 preliminary. Represents a measure of income received from all sources during the calendar year by residents of each state. Data exclude Federal employees overseas and U.S. residents employed by private U.S. firms on temporary foreign assignment. Totals may differ from those in Tables 721, 722, and 724. For definition of average annual percent change, see Guide to Tabular Presentation]

State	Current dollars				Constant (1996) dollars [1]				Average annual percent change		Percent distribution	
	1990	1995	1998	1999	1990	1995	1998	1999	1990-98	1998-99	1990	1999
United States..	4,885.5	6,192.2	7,351.5	7,776.5	5,705.4	6,325.1	7,142.3	7,435.9	2.2	4.1	100.0	100.0
Alabama	64.1	83.9	96.0	100.3	74.9	85.7	93.2	95.9	2.3	2.9	1.3	1.3
Alaska.	12.6	15.5	17.1	17.7	14.7	15.8	16.6	16.9	1.1	1.8	0.3	0.2
Arizona	63.3	88.9	113.0	120.9	73.9	90.8	109.8	115.6	4.1	5.3	1.3	1.6
Arkansas	34.2	46.0	53.7	56.4	39.9	47.0	52.2	53.9	2.9	3.3	0.7	0.7
California	655.6	771.5	920.5	988.3	765.6	788.0	894.3	945.1	1.3	5.7	13.4	12.7
Colorado	65.1	92.9	119.0	128.5	76.0	94.9	115.7	122.9	4.4	6.2	1.3	1.7
Connecticut	87.9	104.3	122.2	128.5	102.7	106.6	118.7	122.9	1.3	3.5	1.8	1.7
Delaware	14.5	18.2	21.9	23.1	16.9	18.6	21.2	22.1	2.1	4.2	0.3	0.3
District of Columbia	16.1	18.2	19.0	19.8	18.8	18.6	18.4	19.0	-0.3	3.3	0.3	0.3
Florida.	258.5	333.5	400.2	423.5	301.9	340.7	388.8	404.9	2.5	4.1	5.3	5.4
Georgia	115.4	159.8	197.3	211.8	134.8	163.2	191.7	202.5	3.7	5.6	2.4	2.7
Hawaii.	24.9	30.2	31.9	33.0	29.1	30.8	30.9	31.6	0.7	2.3	0.5	0.4
Idaho	16.1	22.9	27.2	29.3	18.7	23.4	26.4	28.1	3.6	6.4	0.3	0.4
Illinois	237.6	304.8	360.3	379.4	277.5	311.3	350.1	362.7	2.4	3.6	4.9	4.9
Indiana	97.9	126.5	148.7	155.1	114.3	129.2	144.4	148.3	2.4	2.7	2.0	2.0
Iowa	48.3	60.2	70.8	73.8	56.4	61.5	68.8	70.6	2.1	2.6	1.0	0.9
Kansas	45.1	56.6	67.4	70.7	52.7	57.8	65.5	67.6	2.2	3.2	0.9	0.9
Kentucky	57.2	74.1	87.3	91.7	66.8	75.7	84.8	87.7	2.5	3.4	1.2	1.2
Louisiana	64.2	84.6	96.9	99.6	75.0	86.4	94.1	95.3	2.4	1.3	1.3	1.3
Maine	21.5	25.0	29.3	31.3	25.1	25.6	28.5	29.9	1.1	4.9	0.4	0.4
Maryland	110.4	135.1	156.8	166.3	129.0	138.0	152.3	159.1	1.5	4.5	2.3	2.1
Massachusetts . . .	139.8	170.1	205.8	220.7	163.2	173.7	200.0	211.0	1.9	5.5	2.9	2.8
Michigan	177.1	231.6	264.0	274.6	206.8	236.6	256.5	262.6	2.3	2.4	3.6	3.5
Minnesota	87.8	113.2	138.3	146.2	102.5	115.6	134.4	139.8	2.7	4.0	1.8	1.9
Mississippi	33.9	46.2	54.4	56.8	39.6	47.2	52.9	54.3	3.1	2.6	0.7	0.7
Missouri.	91.0	117.6	136.8	143.2	106.3	120.2	132.9	136.9	2.5	3.0	1.9	1.8
Montana	12.4	16.3	18.7	19.7	14.5	16.6	18.1	18.8	2.2	3.9	0.3	0.3
Nebraska.	28.6	36.3	43.1	45.7	33.4	37.1	41.8	43.7	2.3	4.5	0.6	0.6
Nevada	25.2	39.4	50.9	54.9	29.4	40.2	49.5	52.5	5.9	6.1	0.5	0.7
New Hampshire . .	23.0	28.6	35.0	37.1	26.9	29.3	34.0	35.5	2.2	4.4	0.5	0.5
New Jersey	192.1	233.2	278.3	294.0	224.4	238.2	270.4	281.1	1.7	4.0	3.9	3.8
New Mexico	22.7	31.7	36.7	38.4	26.6	32.4	35.6	36.7	3.2	3.1	0.5	0.5
New York.	419.7	503.2	583.1	617.7	490.2	514.0	566.5	590.7	1.3	4.3	8.6	7.9
North Carolina . . .	115.6	157.6	190.0	200.6	135.0	161.0	184.6	191.8	3.4	3.9	2.4	2.6
North Dakota	10.1	12.2	14.6	14.9	11.8	12.5	14.2	14.3	1.3	0.7	0.2	0.2
Ohio	204.1	255.3	293.0	304.8	238.4	260.8	284.7	291.5	1.8	2.4	4.2	3.9
Oklahoma	51.0	63.3	73.3	76.6	59.6	64.7	71.3	73.2	1.8	2.7	1.0	1.0
Oregon	52.2	71.2	85.0	90.0	60.9	72.7	82.6	86.0	3.4	4.1	1.1	1.2
Pennsylvania	235.8	285.9	329.7	343.9	275.4	292.1	320.3	328.9	1.4	2.7	4.8	4.4
Rhode Island	20.3	23.8	27.9	29.4	23.7	24.3	27.1	28.2	1.2	4.1	0.4	0.4
South Carolina . . .	56.2	72.1	85.9	91.3	65.6	73.6	83.5	87.3	2.4	4.6	1.2	1.2
South Dakota	11.3	14.5	17.3	18.4	13.2	14.8	16.8	17.6	2.5	4.8	0.2	0.2
Tennessee	82.3	114.3	132.8	140.3	96.1	116.7	129.0	134.1	3.2	4.0	1.7	1.8
Texas	297.6	402.1	500.1	531.7	347.5	410.7	485.9	508.4	3.4	4.6	6.1	6.8
Utah	25.9	37.3	46.7	49.7	30.3	38.1	45.4	47.6	4.4	4.8	0.5	0.6
Vermont	10.2	12.4	14.5	15.4	11.9	12.7	14.1	14.7	1.6	4.3	0.2	0.2
Virginia	127.6	161.4	190.5	202.6	149.0	164.9	185.1	193.8	2.2	4.7	2.6	2.6
Washington	98.1	129.7	163.3	174.4	114.6	132.5	158.7	166.8	3.3	5.1	2.0	2.2
West Virginia	26.1	32.6	36.6	37.7	30.5	33.3	35.5	36.1	1.6	1.7	0.5	0.5
Wisconsin	89.0	116.0	137.3	143.9	104.0	118.4	133.3	137.6	2.5	3.2	1.8	1.9
Wyoming	8.2	10.3	11.7	12.5	9.5	10.5	11.3	11.9	2.0	5.3	0.2	0.2

[1] Implicit price deflator for personal consumption expenditures is used as a deflator.

Source: U.S. Bureau of Economic Analysis, *Survey of Current Business*, May 2000, and unpublished data.

Income, Expenditures, and Wealth   459

No. 727. Personal Income Per Capita in Current and Constant (1996) Dollars by State: 1990 to 1999

[1999 preliminary. See headnote, Table 726]

State	Current dollars				Constant (1996) dollars [1]				Income rank	
	1990	1995	1998	1999	1990	1995	1998	1999	1990	1999
United States ...	**19,584**	**23,562**	**27,203**	**28,518**	**22,870**	**24,067**	**26,429**	**27,269**	(X)	(X)
Alabama.........	15,832	19,683	22,054	22,946	18,489	20,105	21,426	21,941	42	43
Alaska	22,719	25,798	27,835	28,523	26,532	26,351	27,043	27,274	6	17
Arizona.........	17,211	20,634	24,206	25,307	20,099	21,077	23,517	24,199	35	35
Arkansas	14,509	18,546	21,167	22,114	16,944	18,944	20,564	21,146	49	47
California	21,889	24,496	28,163	29,819	25,562	25,021	27,361	28,513	8	13
Colorado........	19,703	24,865	29,994	31,678	23,009	25,398	29,140	30,291	19	6
Connecticut......	26,736	31,947	37,338	39,167	31,223	32,632	36,275	37,452	1	1
Delaware	21,636	25,391	29,383	30,685	25,267	25,936	28,547	29,341	9	9
District of Columbia .	26,627	33,045	36,415	38,228	31,095	33,754	35,378	36,554	(X)	(X)
Florida	19,855	23,512	26,845	28,023	23,187	24,016	26,081	26,796	17	18
Georgia	17,738	22,230	25,839	27,198	20,715	22,707	25,103	26,007	29	23
Hawaii	22,391	25,584	26,759	27,842	26,149	26,133	25,997	26,623	7	20
Idaho..........	15,866	19,630	22,079	23,445	18,529	20,051	21,451	22,418	41	40
Illinois.........	20,756	25,643	29,853	31,278	24,239	26,193	29,003	29,908	10	7
Indiana.........	17,625	21,845	25,163	26,092	20,583	22,314	24,447	24,949	30	30
Iowa	17,380	21,181	24,745	25,727	20,297	21,635	24,041	24,600	33	33
Kansas.........	18,182	21,889	25,537	26,633	21,233	22,359	24,810	25,467	23	26
Kentucky	15,484	19,215	22,183	23,161	18,082	19,627	21,552	22,147	44	42
Louisiana	15,223	19,541	22,206	22,792	17,778	19,960	21,574	21,794	45	45
Maine..........	17,479	20,240	23,499	24,960	20,412	20,674	22,830	23,867	31	37
Maryland	23,023	26,896	30,557	32,166	26,887	27,473	29,687	30,757	5	5
Massachusetts.....	23,223	28,051	33,496	35,733	27,120	28,653	32,543	34,168	4	3
Michigan........	19,022	23,975	26,885	27,844	22,214	24,489	26,120	26,625	20	19
Minnesota.......	20,011	24,583	29,263	30,622	23,369	25,110	28,430	29,281	16	10
Mississippi	13,164	17,185	19,776	20,506	15,373	17,554	19,213	19,608	50	50
Missouri	17,751	22,094	25,150	26,187	20,730	22,568	24,434	25,040	28	29
Montana........	15,524	18,764	21,229	22,314	18,129	19,166	20,625	21,337	43	46
Nebraska	18,088	22,196	25,924	27,437	21,123	22,672	25,186	26,235	25	21
Nevada	20,674	24,810	29,200	30,351	24,143	26,362	28,369	29,022	12	11
New Hampshire	20,713	25,008	29,480	30,905	24,189	25,544	28,641	29,552	11	8
New Jersey......	24,766	29,277	34,383	36,106	28,922	29,905	33,404	34,525	2	2
New Mexico	14,960	18,852	21,164	22,063	17,471	19,256	20,562	21,097	47	48
New York	23,315	27,721	32,108	33,946	27,228	28,316	31,194	32,459	3	4
North Carolina	17,367	21,938	25,181	26,220	20,281	22,409	24,464	25,072	34	28
North Dakota......	15,880	19,084	22,892	23,518	18,545	19,493	22,240	22,488	40	38
Ohio	18,792	22,887	26,073	27,081	21,946	23,378	25,331	25,895	21	25
Oklahoma........	16,214	19,394	21,964	22,801	18,935	19,810	21,339	21,802	38	44
Oregon.........	18,253	22,668	25,912	27,135	21,316	23,154	25,174	25,947	22	24
Pennsylvania......	19,823	23,738	27,469	28,676	23,150	24,247	26,687	27,420	18	16
Rhode Island......	20,194	24,046	28,262	29,720	23,583	24,562	27,457	28,418	14	14
South Carolina.....	16,050	19,473	22,372	23,496	18,743	19,891	21,735	22,467	39	39
South Dakota	16,238	19,848	23,715	25,107	18,963	20,274	23,040	24,007	37	36
Tennessee	16,821	21,800	24,437	25,581	19,644	22,268	23,741	24,461	36	34
Texas..........	17,458	21,526	25,369	26,525	20,388	21,988	24,647	25,363	32	27
Utah	14,996	18,858	22,240	23,356	17,513	19,263	21,607	22,333	46	41
Vermont	18,055	21,359	24,602	25,892	21,085	21,817	23,902	24,758	26	32
Virginia.........	20,538	24,456	28,063	29,484	23,985	24,981	27,264	28,193	13	15
Washington.......	20,026	23,878	28,719	30,295	23,387	24,390	27,901	28,968	15	12
West Virginia......	14,579	17,913	20,185	20,888	17,026	18,297	19,610	19,973	48	49
Wisconsin.......	18,160	22,573	26,284	27,412	21,208	23,057	25,536	26,212	24	22
Wyoming	17,996	21,514	24,312	26,003	21,016	21,975	23,620	24,864	27	31

X Not applicable.   [1] Implicit price deflator for personal consumption expenditures is used as a deflator.

Source: U.S. Bureau of Economic Analysis, *Survey of Current Business,* May 2000, and unpublished data.

No. 728. Disposable Personal Income Per Capita in Current and Constant (1996) Dollars by State: 1990 and 1999

[In dollars. 1999 preliminary]

State	Current dollars 1990	Current dollars 1999	Constant (1996) dollars[1] 1990	Constant (1996) dollars[1] 1999	State	Current dollars 1990	Current dollars 1999	Constant (1996) dollars[1] 1990	Constant (1996) dollars[1] 1999
United States...	17,146	24,297	20,023	23,233	Missouri	15,611	22,469	18,231	21,485
					Montana........	13,785	19,590	16,098	18,732
Alabama........	14,097	20,068	16,463	19,189	Nebraska	16,071	23,805	18,768	22,762
Alaska	19,937	24,978	23,283	23,884	Nevada.........	18,112	26,205	21,151	25,057
Arizona........	15,247	21,855	17,806	20,898	New Hampshire ...	18,450	26,732	21,546	25,561
Arkansas.......	12,988	19,412	15,168	18,562	New Jersey......	21,503	30,251	25,112	28,926
California..;....	19,027	25,100	22,220	24,001					
					New Mexico......	13,396	19,396	15,644	18,547
Colorado.......	17,251	26,801	20,146	25,627	New York	19,899	28,072	23,238	26,843
Connecticut.....	23,279	31,797	27,186	30,404	North Carolina....	15,257	22,424	17,817	21,442
Delaware.......	18,612	25,714	21,735	24,588	North Dakota	14,320	20,842	16,723	19,929
District of Columbia.	22,921	31,457	26,767	30,079	Ohio...........	16,442	23,018	19,201	22,010
Florida	17,731	24,201	20,707	23,141					
Georgia	15,537	23,225	18,144	22,208	Oklahoma.......	14,264	19,800	16,658	18,933
					Oregon........	16,003	22,964	18,689	21,958
Hawaii	19,428	24,305	22,688	23,241	Pennsylvania....	17,433	24,498	20,359	23,425
Idaho	14,071	20,419	16,432	19,525	Rhode Island	17,795	25,686	20,781	24,561
Illinois.........	18,042	26,519	21,070	25,358	South Carolina....	14,199	20,491	16,582	19,594
Indiana........	15,398	22,223	17,982	21,250					
Iowa..........	15,295	22,252	17,862	21,277	South Dakota.....	14,846	22,443	17,337	21,460
					Tennessee.......	15,193	22,626	17,743	21,635
Kansas........	16,009	22,880	18,696	21,878	Texas.........	15,600	23,223	18,218	22,206
Kentucky.......	13,623	19,930	15,909	19,057	Utah..........	13,219	20,013	15,437	19,137
Louisiana......	13,681	20,016	15,977	19,139	Vermont.......	15,838	22,308	18,496	21,331
Maine.........	15,414	21,530	18,001	20,587					
Maryland.......	19,712	26,686	23,020	25,517	Virginia........	17,899	25,010	20,903	23,915
					Washington.....	17,761	26,203	20,742	25,055
Massachusetts....	19,915	29,589	23,257	28,293	West Virginia.....	12,997	18,977	15,178	17,572
Michigan.......	16,589	23,684	19,373	22,647	Wisconsin	15,817	23,213	18,471	22,196
Minnesota......	17,328	26,003	20,236	24,864	Wyoming........	16,077	22,244	18,775	21,270
Mississippi......	11,927	18,241	13,929	17,442					

[1] Constant dollars based on the implicit price deflator for personal consumption expenditures.
Source: U.S. Bureau of Economic Analysis, *Survey of Current Business*, May 2000, unpublished data.

No. 729. Personal Income by Selected Large Metropolitan Area: 1996 to 1998

[As defined **June 30, 1994.** CMSA=Consolidated Metropolitan Statistical Area; MSA=Metropolitan Statistical Area. See Appendix II]

Metropolitan area ranked by 1997 population	Personal income 1996 (mil. dol.)	Personal income 1997 (mil. dol.)	Personal income 1998 (mil. dol.)	Annual percent change, 1997-98	Per capita personal income 1996 (dol.)	Per capita personal income 1997 (dol.)	Per capita personal income 1998 (dol.)	Percent of national average, 1998
United States	6,538,103	6,942,114	7,351,547	5.9	24,651	25,924	27,203	100.0
New York-No. New Jersey-Long Island, NY-NJ-CT-PA CMSA	656,669	691,794	731,539	5.7	33,119	34,749	36,582	134.5
Los Angeles-Riverside-Orange County, CA CMSA	377,560	396,704	422,989	6.6	24,566	25,491	26,778	98.4
Chicago-Gary-Kenosha, IL-IN-WI CMSA .	254,130	269,815	285,768	5.9	29,201	30,795	32,389	119.1
Washington-Baltimore, DC-MD-VA-WV CMSA.................	218,231	230,658	244,282	5.9	30,564	32,019	33,602	123.5
San Francisco-Oakland-San Jose, CA CMSA...................	219,438	237,395	254,915	7.4	33,161	35,333	37,414	137.5
Philadelphia-Wilmington-Atlantic City, PA-NJ-DE-MD CMSA.............	167,458	176,777	186,297	5.4	28,014	29,576	31,119	114.4
Boston-Worcester-Lawrence-Lowell-Brockton, MA-NH (NECMA).........	174,216	187,231	200,107	6.9	30,096	32,133	34,127	125.5
Detroit-Ann Arbor-Flint, MI CMSA......	145,721	154,172	162,363	5.3	26,863	28,330	29,775	109.5
Dallas-Fort Worth, TX CMSA........	123,313	134,468	146,431	8.9	27,089	28,785	30,541	112.3
Houston-Galveston-Brazoria, TX CMSA..	112,191	122,128	132,134	8.2	26,551	28,352	30,026	110.4
Atlanta, GA MSA...............	98,182	106,039	115,272	8.7	27,803	29,194	30,788	113.2
Miami-Fort Lauderdale, FL CMSA	85,943	89,340	94,488	5.8	24,209	24,755	25,826	94.9
Seattle-Tacoma-Bremerton, WA CMSA ..	93,370	102,812	112,135	9.1	28,241	30,528	32,762	120.4
Cleveland-Akron, OH CMSA	75,742	80,003	83,577	4.5	25,954	27,434	28,694	105.5
Phoenix-Mesa, AZ MSA	64,964	71,417	78,210	9.5	23,593	25,134	26,686	98.1
Minneapolis-St. Paul, MN-WI MSA	82,373	88,381	94,991	7.5	29,836	31,621	33,561	123.4
San Diego, CA MSA	66,403	71,126	76,502	7.6	24,836	26,129	27,657	101.7
St. Louis, MO-IL MSA	67,326	71,492	74,516	4.2	26,406	27,951	29,089	106.9
Pittsburgh, PA MSA..............	60,346	63,488	66,013	4.0	25,422	26,909	28,149	103.5
Denver-Boulder-Greeley, CO CMSA	66,080	72,406	79,121	9.3	29,116	31,236	33,485	123.1
Tampa-St. Petersburg-Clearwater, FL MSA	53,581	57,542	61,373	6.7	24,408	25,861	27,224	100.1
Portland-Salem, OR-WA CMSA	53,575	57,945	61,184	5.6	25,848	27,391	28,453	104.6
Cincinnati-Hamilton, OH-KY-IN CMSA...	48,223	51,501	54,505	5.8	25,132	26,624	27,975	102.8
Kansas City, MO-KS MSA...........	44,001	46,864	49,464	5.5	25,946	27,278	28,473	104.7
Sacramento-Yolo, CA CMSA	40,520	43,160	46,278	7.2	24,487	25,701	27,102	99.6
Milwaukee-Racine, WI CMSA	44,336	47,230	49,779	5.4	26,936	28,718	30,258	111.2

U.S. Bureau of Economic Analysis, *Survey of Current Business*, June 2000.

Income, Expenditures, and Wealth   461

No. 730. Flow of Funds Accounts—Composition of Individuals' Savings: 1990 to 1999

[In billions of dollars (567.7 represents 567,700,000,000). Combined statement for households, farm business, and nonfarm noncorporate business. Minus sign (-) indicates decrease]

Composition of savings	1990	1992	1993	1994	1995	1996	1997	1998	1999
Increase in financial assets	567.7	448.4	439.7	502.4	485.9	497.0	441.2	586.6	556.6
Foreign deposits	1.4	1.2	-1.1	3.1	4.6	12.4	6.3	-0.3	4.3
Checkable deposits and currency	-19.4	103.7	56.4	-24.2	-53.9	-50.7	-32.8	59.2	-14.2
Time and savings deposits	48.5	-76.9	-106.5	-4.0	173.2	175.7	190.2	202.3	115.6
Money market fund shares	26.9	-40.9	-0.3	13.5	98.8	56.6	89.7	145.4	103.9
Securities	179.0	179.3	140.8	151.4	-129.4	-107.2	-277.9	-275.0	-81.4
Open market paper	6.2	-3.3	15.6	1.2	1.3	7.4	3.6	4.2	5.3
U.S. government securities	114.2	78.9	-16.3	290.2	-48.0	27.7	-161.8	-153.8	100.7
Municipal securities	27.7	-27.0	-32.1	-50.2	-43.5	-22.2	53.6	15.3	48.3
Corporate and foreign bonds	43.1	2.3	31.3	30.5	95.0	46.2	75.4	60.4	32.3
Corporate equities [1]	-39.6	-5.6	-62.8	-187.6	-228.8	-347.2	-507.1	-462.7	-401.7
Mutual fund shares	27.5	133.9	205.1	67.4	94.7	180.8	258.4	261.6	133.6
Life insurance reserves	26.5	29.1	37.1	35.5	45.8	44.5	59.3	53.3	58.6
Pension fund reserves	249.4	244.3	267.9	254.4	235.4	247.6	304.4	303.9	287.4
Investment in bank personal trusts	32.9	-7.1	0.9	17.8	4.0	-8.6	-56.3	-48.0	-31.1
Miscellaneous assets	22.4	15.7	44.5	54.9	107.3	126.7	158.2	145.8	113.6
Gross investment in tangible assets	806.3	793.8	864.4	958.8	979.9	1,061.1	1,092.5	1,206.1	1,364.1
Minus: Consumption of fixed capital	593.5	639.0	649.2	690.6	709.3	729.6	755.7	784.7	840.7
Equals: Net investment in tangible assets . . .	212.9	154.8	215.2	268.2	270.5	331.5	336.9	421.4	523.4
Net increase in liabilities	241.5	168.6	246.2	324.8	407.3	484.7	533.9	641.7	757.3
Mortgage debt on nonfarm homes	212.3	168.9	159.4	182.6	179.5	241.2	251.0	382.3	431.7
Other mortgage debt [2]	1.4	-39.4	-29.4	-29.6	-8.5	53.6	83.7	79.3	89.8
Consumer credit	11.9	6.1	58.4	124.9	138.9	88.8	52.5	67.6	94.4
Policy loans	4.1	5.7	5.6	7.8	10.5	4.5	3.2	0.1	-5.3
Security credit	-3.7	-1.6	22.6	-1.1	3.5	15.8	36.8	21.6	69.7
Other liabilities [2]	15.5	28.9	29.6	40.2	83.5	80.8	106.7	90.7	77.0
Personal saving with consumer durables [3] . . .	539.1	434.7	408.7	445.7	349.1	343.8	244.2	366.3	322.7
Personal saving, without consumer durable [3] . .	466.3	379.6	323.0	332.7	223.8	202.7	88.3	170.7	101.7
Personal saving (NIPA, excludes consumer durables) [4]	334.3	413.7	350.8	315.6	302.4	272.1	271.1	229.7	156.3

[1] Only directly held and those in closed-end funds. Other equities are included in mutual funds, life insurance and pension reserves, and bank personal trusts.   [2] Includes corporate farms.   [3] Flow of Funds measure.   [4] National Income and Product Accounts measure.

Source: Board of Governors of the Federal Reserve System, *Flow of Funds Accounts*, quarterly.

No. 731. Annual Expenditure Per Child by Husband-Wife Families by Family Income and Expenditure Type: 1999

[In dollars. Expenditures based on data from the 1990-92 Consumer Expenditure Survey updated to 1998 dollars using the Consumer Price Index. Excludes expenses for college. For more on the methodology, see report cited below]

Age of child	Expenditure type							
	Total	Housing	Food	Trans- por- tation	Clothing	Health care	Child care and educa- tion	Miscel- lan- eous [1]
INCOME: LESS THAN $36,800								
Less than 2 yrs. old	6,080	2,320	860	730	380	430	760	600
3 to 5 yrs. old	6,210	2,290	960	700	370	410	860	620
6 to 8 yrs. old	6,310	2,210	1,240	820	410	470	510	650
9 to 11 yrs. old	6,330	2,000	1,480	890	460	510	310	680
12 to 14 yrs. old	7,150	2,230	1,560	1,000	770	510	220	860
15 to 17 yrs. old	7,050	1,800	1,680	1,350	680	550	360	630
INCOME: $36,800-$61,900								
Less than 2 yrs. old	8,450	3,140	1,030	1,090	450	560	1,250	930
3 to 5 yrs. old	8,660	3,110	1,190	1,060	440	530	1,380	950
6 to 8 yrs. old	8,700	3,030	1,520	1,180	480	610	890	990
9 to 11 yrs. old	8,650	2,820	1,790	1,250	530	660	580	1,020
12 to 14 yrs. old	9,390	3,050	1,800	1,360	900	670	420	1,190
15 to 17 yrs. old	9,530	2,620	2,000	1,720	800	700	730	960
INCOME: MORE THAN $61,900								
Less than 2 yrs. old	12,550	4,990	1,370	1,520	590	640	1,880	1,560
3 to 5 yrs. old	12,840	4,960	1,550	1,500	580	620	2,050	1,580
6 to 8 yrs. old	12,710	4,880	1,870	1,610	630	700	1,410	1,610
9 to 11 yrs. old	12,600	4,670	2,170	1,680	690	760	980	1,650
12 to 14 yrs. old	13,450	4,900	2,280	1,800	1,140	760	750	1,820
15 to 17 yrs. old	13,800	4,470	2,400	2,180	1,030	800	1,330	1,590

[1] Expenses include personal care items, entertainment, and reading materials.

Source: Dept. of Agriculture, Center for Nutrition Policy and Promotion, *Expenditures on Children by Families, 1999 Annual Report*.

No. 732. Average Annual Expenditures of All Consumer Units by Race, Hispanic Origin, and Age of Householder: 1998

[In dollars. Based on Consumer Expenditure Survey. Data are averages for the noninstitutional population. Expenditures reported here are out-of-pocket]

Item	All consumer units	Black	Hispanic	Age Under 25 yrs.	25 to 34 yrs.	35 to 44 yrs.	45 to 54 yrs.	55 to 64 yrs.	65 yrs. and over
Expenditures, total	**35,535**	**25,796**	**30,013**	**19,436**	**34,779**	**42,154**	**45,475**	**37,329**	**24,721**
Food	4,810	3,725	5,099	3,075	4,577	5,753	5,999	4,900	3,456
Food at home	2,780	2,399	3,366	1,518	2,547	3,314	3,388	2,831	2,264
Cereals and bakery products	425	340	463	226	386	521	502	410	362
Cereals and cereal products	146	134	172	83	150	187	171	121	113
Bakery products	278	206	291	142	237	334	331	289	249
Meats, poultry, fish, and eggs	723	812	1,036	356	643	864	896	769	587
Beef	218	192	339	118	196	263	269	232	170
Pork	146	188	213	66	114	171	179	169	131
Other meats	92	84	125	45	86	110	113	90	77
Poultry	137	181	185	64	136	172	170	134	96
Fish and seafood	98	131	114	40	82	113	127	107	84
Eggs	32	36	60	22	29	35	37	37	30
Dairy products	301	203	346	173	284	373	343	299	246
Fresh milk and cream	120	84	154	70	117	154	126	115	101
Other dairy products	181	120	192	103	167	219	217	184	146
Fruits and vegetables	472	412	594	246	412	521	585	512	427
Fresh fruits	149	121	207	74	124	158	189	170	141
Fresh vegetables	145	119	201	69	130	158	181	158	130
Processed fruits	101	102	107	63	90	112	125	105	90
Processed vegetables	76	70	79	40	68	92	90	79	66
Other food at home	858	631	928	517	822	1,035	1,062	841	642
Nonalcoholic beverages	231	186	285	146	216	287	289	223	164
Food away from home	2,030	1,326	1,733	1,557	2,030	2,439	2,611	2,069	1,192
Alcoholic beverages	309	152	276	311	372	328	346	314	194
Housing	11,713	9,280	10,089	6,151	12,015	14,181	14,154	11,979	8,388
Shelter	6,680	5,224	6,148	3,795	7,232	8,400	8,095	6,316	4,271
Owned dwellings	4,245	2,390	2,592	414	3,519	5,955	5,874	4,494	2,817
Mortgage interest and charges	2,455	1,525	1,642	255	2,487	4,008	3,535	2,249	662
Property taxes	1,015	504	487	75	613	1,161	1,404	1,247	1,085
Rented dwellings	1,978	2,644	3,337	3,144	3,434	2,033	1,433	1,214	1,092
Other lodging	458	191	218	237	279	412	788	608	362
Utilities, fuels, and public services	2,405	2,471	2,090	1,145	2,221	2,688	2,893	2,602	2,171
Natural gas	284	337	274	95	257	309	329	320	290
Electricity	921	933	729	416	803	1,019	1,111	1,011	884
Fuel oil and other fuels	85	41	33	13	54	85	106	114	106
Telephone	830	915	811	560	888	947	993	835	595
Water and other public services	285	245	243	61	219	328	355	323	296
Household operations	546	326	347	196	679	727	498	433	464
Personal services	260	207	214	136	493	441	141	60	117
Other household expenses	286	119	133	60	186	285	357	374	347
Housekeeping supplies	482	244	392	188	366	549	547	755	393
Household furnishings and equipment	1,601	1,015	1,111	826	1,517	1,817	2,121	1,873	1,089
Household textiles	105	44	98	41	89	106	140	138	91
Furniture	377	264	300	158	440	465	439	425	221
Floor coverings	144	109	18	28	47	147	278	133	159
Major appliances	164	165	131	101	134	195	203	194	128
Miscellaneous household equipment	729	394	496	448	742	813	958	882	431
Apparel and services	1,674	1,675	1,934	1,134	1,781	2,193	2,199	1,498	820
Men and boys	399	403	356	243	420	558	530	339	175
Women and girls	651	560	722	412	585	854	931	583	360
Children under 2 years old	73	84	118	96	143	91	49	41	22
Footwear	281	376	465	205	290	397	348	242	131
Other apparel products and services	270	252	273	176	343	294	342	293	132
Transportation	6,616	4,752	5,934	4,149	6,728	7,873	8,509	7,101	4,025
Vehicle purchases (net outlay)	2,964	2,175	2,834	2,084	3,090	3,703	3,730	3,075	1,593
Cars and trucks, new	1,383	998	1,104	480	1,195	1,777	1,925	1,641	809
Cars and trucks, used	1,532	1,178	1,690	1,491	1,855	1,891	1,755	1,420	716
Gasoline and motor oil	1,017	743	970	654	1,016	1,203	1,308	1,077	645
Other vehicle expenses	2,206	1,541	1,777	1,176	2,253	2,572	2,928	2,372	1,382
Vehicle finance charges	319	264	275	211	421	393	423	284	111
Maintenance and repair	641	451	523	357	568	750	844	696	473
Vehicle insurance	739	564	662	383	683	815	1,008	810	551
Public transportation	429	293	352	235	369	394	543	577	405
Health care [1]	1,903	1,069	1,096	445	1,185	1,688	2,186	2,158	2,936
Entertainment [2]	1,746	882	1,148	974	1,757	2,215	2,142	1,904	1,044
Personal care products and services	401	388	333	262	371	435	515	413	330
Reading	161	72	62	64	135	162	209	184	163
Education	580	349	319	1,139	499	597	1,051	388	102
Tobacco products and smoking supplies	273	194	138	186	252	344	338	334	151
Miscellaneous	860	595	703	300	772	972	1,026	1,164	694
Cash contributions	1,109	575	537	206	673	997	1,503	1,252	1,529
Personal insurance and pensions	3,381	2,089	2,348	1,040	3,662	4,415	5,297	3,740	888
Life and other personal insurance	398	279	178	64	255	429	576	627	324
Pensions and Social Security	2,982	1,811	2,169	976	3,407	3,986	4,721	3,114	564
Personal taxes	**3,264**	**1,517**	**1,862**	**866**	**3,352**	**4,132**	**5,448**	**3,404**	**1,118**

[1] For additional health care expenditures, see Table 163.   [2] For additional recreation expenditures, see Table 419.

Source: U.S. Bureau of Labor Statistics, *Consumer Expenditures in 1998*.

Income, Expenditures, and Wealth   463

No. 733. Average Annual Expenditures of All Consumer Units by Region and Size of Unit: 1998

[See headnote, page 463. For composition of regions, see map, inside front cover]

Item	Region				Size of consumer unit				
	North-east	Mid west	South	West	One person	Two per-sons	Three per-sons	Four per-sons	Five or more
Expenditures, total	**37,535**	**34,513**	**32,958**	**38,938**	**21,483**	**36,973**	**41,388**	**47,020**	**45,569**
Food	5,146	4,737	4,450	5,159	2,640	4,672	5,701	6,623	7,488
Food at home	2,917	2,725	2,592	3,016	1,408	2,604	3,307	3,935	4,797
Cereals and bakery products	461	431	386	448	214	387	491	633	747
Cereals and cereal products	158	150	128	162	71	121	162	229	299
Bakery products	303	281	258	286	143	266	330	404	448
Meats, poultry, fish, and eggs	785	687	710	729	332	673	863	979	1,423
Beef	234	226	207	215	88	208	256	291	462
Pork	146	149	153	131	63	141	181	199	268
Other meats	105	99	83	87	44	84	105	128	182
Poultry	155	112	137	146	63	119	162	204	272
Fish and seafood	113	73	97	112	56	91	123	114	179
Eggs	33	27	32	38	18	30	35	43	61
Dairy products	324	301	273	327	152	275	366	434	524
Fresh milk and cream	121	121	112	132	58	102	144	184	228
Other dairy products	203	180	161	196	94	173	222	250	296
Fruits and vegetables	514	445	425	539	258	469	549	643	726
Fresh fruits	161	145	126	180	86	151	166	200	225
Fresh vegetables	161	129	131	171	78	148	167	191	228
Processed fruits	113	96	92	111	59	95	125	140	152
Processed vegetables	80	75	75	77	35	76	92	113	121
Other food at home	833	862	798	973	451	800	1,037	1,246	1,376
Nonalcoholic beverages	226	234	222	247	118	217	279	329	382
Food away from home	2,229	2,011	1,859	2,144	1,232	2,067	2,394	2,689	2,691
Alcoholic beverages	368	284	249	378	298	364	310	253	245
Housing	13,173	11,035	10,321	13,354	7,843	12,059	13,149	15,228	14,379
Shelter	8,042	6,043	5,392	8,198	4,817	6,687	7,438	8,551	8,121
Owned dwellings	5,105	4,108	3,387	4,989	2,073	4,337	5,080	6,457	5,696
Mortgage interest and charges	2,616	2,168	2,051	3,259	1,000	2,216	3,223	4,125	3,752
Property taxes	1,662	1,090	687	884	561	1,148	1,137	1,380	1,194
Maintenance, repair, insurance, other	828	851	649	845	512	973	720	952	751
Rented dwellings	2,356	1,517	1,638	2,675	2,471	1,749	1,878	1,576	2,002
Other lodging	581	417	368	534	272	601	480	518	423
Utilities, fuels, and public services	2,460	2,401	2,519	2,179	1,536	2,481	2,770	3,025	3,186
Natural gas	373	401	171	258	181	289	318	358	402
Electricity	831	854	1,143	723	570	959	1,040	1,176	1,251
Fuel oil and other fuels	225	70	48	36	54	97	90	115	88
Telephone	814	801	858	828	581	839	990	991	1,022
Water and other public services	217	274	299	334	149	296	332	385	422
Household operations	504	496	551	627	271	427	756	1,018	693
Personal services	254	273	251	264	58	92	465	665	451
Other household expenses	250	224	300	364	213	335	291	353	241
Housekeeping supplies	446	475	488	514	267	568	501	613	601
Household furnishings and equipment	1,721	1,620	1,371	1,837	952	1,898	1,684	2,021	1,778
Household textiles	105	96	85	148	67	115	99	156	121
Furniture	411	351	317	471	203	437	437	519	396
Floor coverings	157	233	103	101	96	222	68	169	118
Major appliances	189	149	172	145	106	178	190	194	201
Small appliances, misc. housewares	81	73	78	91	45	92	99	95	91
Miscellaneous household equipment	778	717	616	881	436	853	791	888	851
Apparel and services	1,848	1,624	1,623	1,652	961	1,541	2,064	2,398	2,488
Men and boys	462	414	352	399	203	339	507	608	682
Women and girls	686	638	655	628	395	637	764	929	854
Children under 2 years old	57	59	88	79	12	40	134	138	167
Footwear	299	298	268	266	159	236	340	412	493
Other apparel products and services	345	215	258	281	192	290	319	311	291
Transportation	6,540	6,290	6,612	7,039	3,331	6,684	8,609	9,198	8,925
Vehicle purchases (net outlay)	2,816	2,774	3,242	2,860	1,362	2,768	4,162	4,439	4,132
Cars and trucks, new	1,475	1,107	1,518	1,385	590	1,379	2,124	1,986	1,611
Cars and trucks, used	1,323	1,618	1,656	1,430	721	1,368	1,965	2,399	2,437
Gasoline and motor oil	896	1,034	1,035	1,077	529	1,050	1,227	1,377	1,460
Other vehicle expenses	2,216	2,149	2,024	2,545	1,144	2,300	2,834	2,947	2,885
Vehicle finance charges	247	318	368	308	115	309	446	495	482
Maintenance and repair	574	615	629	746	392	678	778	796	794
Vehicle insurance	822	680	683	816	393	780	918	989	955
Public transportation	612	333	311	557	297	565	386	436	447
Health care [1]	1,773	2,008	1,985	1,774	1,220	2,459	1,913	2,061	1,888
Entertainment [2]	1,772	1,850	1,521	1,964	999	1,907	1,840	2,392	2,304
Personal care products and services	395	368	402	441	250	441	425	510	510
Reading	201	170	125	173	120	193	162	182	149
Education	815	598	409	622	399	465	745	838	823
Tobacco products and smoking supplies	301	315	274	202	175	272	338	338	359
Miscellaneous	887	855	723	1,059	676	900	851	1,073	978
Cash contributions	888	1,089	1,113	1,322	923	1,389	1,072	963	1,040
Personal insurance and pensions	3,427	3,291	3,152	3,798	1,648	3,628	4,210	4,963	3,995
Life and other personal insurance	445	397	416	330	153	497	442	554	505
Pensions and Social Security	2,982	2,894	2,736	3,468	1,496	3,131	3,768	4,409	3,490
Personal taxes	**3,319**	**3,294**	**2,622**	**4,115**	**2,040**	**3,609**	**4,185**	**4,252**	**2,945**

[1] For additional health care expenditures, see Table 163.   [2] For additional recreation expenditures, see Table 419.

Source: U.S. Bureau of Labor Statistics, *Consumer Expenditures in 1998*.

No. 734. Average Annual Expenditures of All Consumer Units by Type of Expenditure: 1990 to 1998

[In dollars. See headnote, Table 732]

Type	1990	1992	1993	1994	1995	1996	1997	1998
Number of consumer units (1,000)	96,968	100,019	100,049	102,210	103,024	104,212	105,576	107,182
Total expenditures	**28,381**	**29,846**	**30,692**	**31,751**	**32,277**	**33,797**	**34,819**	**35,535**
Food	4,296	4,273	4,399	4,411	4,505	4,698	4,801	4,810
Food at home	2,485	2,643	2,735	2,712	2,803	2,876	2,880	2,780
Meats, poultry, fish, and eggs	668	687	734	732	752	737	743	723
Dairy products	295	302	295	289	297	312	314	301
Fruits and vegetables	408	428	444	437	457	490	476	472
Other food at home	746	814	827	825	856	889	895	858
Food away from home	1,811	1,631	1,664	1,698	1,702	1,823	1,921	2,030
Alcoholic beverages	293	301	268	278	277	309	309	309
Housing	8,703	9,477	9,636	10,106	10,465	10,747	11,272	11,713
Shelter	4,836	5,411	5,415	5,686	5,932	6,064	6,344	6,680
Fuels, utilities, public services	1,890	1,984	2,112	2,189	2,193	2,347	2,412	2,405
Apparel and services	1,618	1,710	1,676	1,644	1,704	1,752	1,729	1,674
Transportation	5,120	5,228	5,453	6,044	6,016	6,382	6,457	6,616
Vehicle purchase	2,129	2,189	2,319	2,725	2,639	2,815	2,736	2,964
Gasoline and motor oil	1,047	973	977	986	1,006	1,082	1,098	1,017
Other transportation	1,944	1,776	1,843	1,953	2,016	2,058	2,230	2,206
Health care	1,480	1,634	1,776	1,755	1,732	1,770	1,841	1,903
Entertainment	1,422	1,500	1,626	1,567	1,612	1,834	1,813	1,746
Reading	153	162	166	165	163	159	164	161
Tobacco products, smoking supplies	274	275	268	259	269	255	264	273
Personal insurance and pensions	2,593	2,750	2,908	2,957	2,967	3,060	3,223	3,381
Life and other personal insurance	345	353	399	398	374	353	379	398
Pensions and Social Security	2,248	2,397	2,509	2,559	2,593	2,707	2,844	2,982

Source: U.S. Bureau of Labor Statistics, *Consumer Expenditures in 1998*.

No. 735. Average Annual Expenditures of All Consumer Units by Metropolitan Area: 1997-98

[In dollars. Metropolitan areas defined June 30, 1983, CMSA=Consolidated Metropolitan Statistical Area; MSA=Metropolitan Statistical Area; PMSA=Primary Metropolitan Statistical Area. See text, Section 1, Population, and Appendix II. See headnote, Table 738]

Metropolitan area	Total expenditures [1]	Food	Housing Total [1]	Shelter	Utility fuels [2]	Transportation Total [1]	Vehicle purchases	Gasoline and motor oil	Health care
Anchorage, AK MSA	$49,510	6,469	16,306	9,805	2,557	9,617	4,152	1,284	2,030
Atlanta, GA MSA	$39,315	4,010	13,481	7,716	3,040	8,787	4,287	1,158	1,872
Baltimore, MD MSA	$35,552	4,793	11,949	7,304	2,361	5,493	2,236	952	1,600
Boston-Lawrence-Salem, MA-NH CMSA	$38,029	4,542	14,799	9,370	2,536	6,145	2,274	1,020	1,693
Chicago-Gary-Lake County, IL-IN-WI CMSA	$36,497	4,978	13,071	7,695	2,598	5,859	2,557	982	1,976
Cincinnati-Hamilton, OH-KY-IN CMSA	$36,772	5,055	12,091	6,784	2,389	6,481	2,704	1,109	2,312
Cleveland-Akron-Lorain, OH CMSA	$36,450	5,027	11,721	6,345	2,604	6,658	3,030	939	1,518
Dallas-Fort Worth, TX CMSA	$44,182	5,994	13,315	7,200	2,907	8,985	4,701	1,290	2,102
Denver-Boulder-Greeley, CO CMSA	$42,862	5,119	14,997	8,733	2,128	7,846	2,781	1,099	1,713
Detroit-Ann Arbor, MI CMSA	$35,658	5,057	11,789	6,809	2,505	7,069	2,629	1,055	1,604
Honolulu, HI MSA	$42,636	6,206	14,775	10,233	2,011	6,845	2,394	1,111	1,905
Houston-Galveston-Brazoria, TX CMSA	$40,017	4,906	12,231	6,536	2,802	9,118	4,657	1,254	1,935
Kansas City, MO-Kansas City, KS CMSA	$35,890	5,490	11,334	6,036	2,667	6,686	3,005	1,144	2,056
Los Angeles-Long Beach, CA PMSA	$41,597	5,060	15,562	10,078	2,321	7,696	2,870	1,185	1,590
Miami-Fort Lauderdale, FL CMSA	$35,131	4,317	12,911	7,815	2,662	6,973	2,819	952	1,418
Milwaukee, WI PMSA	$36,310	4,537	13,333	8,114	2,224	6,176	2,599	1,036	1,806
Minneapolis-St. Paul, MN-WI MSA	$47,198	5,607	14,766	8,135	2,292	9,129	4,117	1,258	2,184
New York-Northern New Jersey-Long Island, NY-NJ-CT CMSA	$41,103	6,090	15,153	9,711	2,501	6,293	2,030	870	1,873
Philadelphia-Wilmington-Trenton, PA-NJ-DE-MD CMSA	$38,131	4,134	14,713	9,428	2,821	7,159	2,978	1,015	1,682
Phoenix-Mesa, AZ MSA	$37,504	4,744	12,958	7,477	2,577	7,236	3,277	1,025	1,736
Pittsburgh-Beaver Valley, PA CMSA	$36,239	5,029	11,170	5,329	2,609	6,572	2,909	946	1,798
Portland-Vancouver, OR-WA CMSA	$40,685	5,648	13,315	8,074	2,044	7,266	3,559	993	1,845
San Diego, CA MSA	$39,917	4,979	15,388	10,037	1,990	6,713	2,394	1,091	1,791
San Francisco-Oakland-San Jose, CA CMSA	$47,458	6,377	16,052	10,467	2,276	7,754	2,799	1,179	1,781
Seattle-Tacoma, WA CMSA	$43,251	5,461	15,310	9,637	2,272	7,880	3,306	1,221	1,644
St. Louis-East St. Louis-Alton, MO-IL CMSA	$36,968	5,310	11,157	5,911	2,789	6,693	2,859	1,064	1,807
Tampa-St. Petersburg-Clearwater, FL MSA	$33,036	4,670	10,964	5,761	2,430	6,123	2,686	911	1,844
Washington, DC-MD-VA MSA	$46,679	5,296	17,129	10,865	2,732	7,721	3,318	1,112	2,240

[1] Includes expenditures not shown separately. [2] Includes public services.

Source: U.S. Bureau of Labor Statistics, *Consumer Expenditures,* annual; and Internet http://stats.bls.gov:80/csxmsa. htm#y9797 (released 16 November 1999).

Income, Expenditures, and Wealth   465

No. 736. Money Income of Households—Percent Distribution by Income Level, Race, and Hispanic Origin in Constant (1998) Dollars: 1970 to 1998

[Constant dollars based on CPI-U deflator. Households as of **March of following year.** Based on Current Population Survey; see text, Sections 1 and 14, and Appendix III. For definition of median, see Guide to Tabular Presentation]

Year	Number of house-holds (1,000)	Percent distribution							Median income (dollars)
		Under $10,000	$10,000-$14,999	$15,000-$24,999	$25,000-$34,999	$35,000-$49,999	$50,000-$74,999	$75,000 and over	
ALL HOUSEHOLDS [1]									
1970	64,778	13.2	7.5	14.9	15.4	21.5	18.1	9.4	34,471
1980	82,368	12.1	8.2	15.6	14.0	19.0	18.6	12.6	35,076
1985	88,458	12.2	7.8	15.3	13.9	17.7	18.1	15.0	35,778
1990	94,312	11.4	7.7	14.5	13.8	17.6	18.3	16.7	37,343
1995	99,627	11.1	8.4	15.1	13.8	16.7	17.8	17.0	36,446
1996	101,018	11.3	8.2	15.1	13.4	16.2	18.1	17.7	36,872
1997	102,528	10.8	8.0	14.8	13.2	16.3	18.0	18.9	37,581
1998	103,874	10.3	7.8	14.0	13.2	16.0	18.6	20.1	38,885
WHITE									
1970	57,575	12.0	7.0	14.3	15.4	22.2	19.0	10.1	35,903
1980	71,872	10.6	7.7	15.2	14.1	19.5	19.6	13.4	37,005
1985	76,576	10.5	7.4	14.9	14.0	18.2	18.9	16.1	37,732
1990	80,968	9.6	7.3	14.3	14.0	17.9	19.2	17.8	38,949
1995	84,511	9.5	8.0	14.9	13.8	17.0	18.6	18.2	38,254
1996	85,059	9.6	7.8	14.8	13.5	16.6	18.9	18.8	38,606
1997	86,106	9.3	7.7	14.4	13.1	16.5	18.7	20.2	39,579
1998	87,212	8.7	7.4	13.7	13.2	16.3	19.3	21.3	40,912
BLACK									
1970	6,180	23.9	12.1	20.7	15.3	15.1	9.6	3.2	21,853
1980	8,847	24.9	12.9	19.0	13.5	14.6	10.5	4.7	21,319
1985	9,797	25.0	11.2	19.0	13.6	14.0	11.3	5.9	22,449
1990	10,671	25.6	11.2	16.2	13.1	15.0	11.7	7.1	23,291
1995	11,577	22.4	11.3	17.9	14.2	14.6	12.1	7.7	23,951
1996	12,109	22.2	11.5	17.6	13.6	14.2	12.8	7.9	24,395
1997	12,474	21.2	10.3	18.0	14.2	14.8	13.4	8.1	25,440
1998	12,579	21.4	10.6	17.4	13.5	14.3	13.2	9.6	25,351
HISPANIC [2]									
1970	(NA)	(NA)	(NA)	(NA)	(NA)	(NA)	(NA)	(NA)	(NA)
1980	3,906	15.9	10.5	20.1	16.3	17.2	13.8	6.4	27,037
1985	5,213	17.0	11.5	19.0	15.4	16.6	13.0	7.5	26,457
1990	6,220	16.2	11.3	18.4	15.6	17.2	13.0	8.4	27,848
1995	7,939	18.3	12.0	20.7	14.9	14.4	12.5	7.2	24,450
1996	8,225	16.5	11.7	20.8	14.6	15.5	12.4	8.5	25,874
1997	8,590	16.5	10.5	19.6	15.3	16.5	12.3	9.3	27,043
1998	9,060	15.0	10.9	17.9	16.3	15.8	14.0	10.2	28,330

NA Not Available. [1] Includes other races not shown separately. [2] Persons of Hispanic origin may be of any race.

No. 737. Money Income of Households—Median Income by Race and Hispanic Origin in Current and Constant (1998) Dollars: 1970 to 1998

[In dollars. See headnote, Table 736]

Year	Median income in current dollars					Median income in constant (1998) dollars				
	All house-holds [1]	White	Black	Asian, Pacific Islander	His-panic [2]	All house-holds [1]	White	Black	Asian, Pacific Islander	His-panic [2]
1970	8,734	9,097	5,537	(NA)	(NA)	34,471	35,903	21,853	(NA)	(NA)
1980	17,710	18,684	10,764	(NA)	13,651	35,076	37,005	21,319	(NA)	27,037
1985	23,618	24,908	14,819	(NA)	17,465	35,778	37,732	22,449	(NA)	26,457
1986	24,897	26,175	15,080	(NA)	18,352	37,027	38,928	22,427	(NA)	27,294
1987 [3]	26,061	27,458	15,672	(NA)	19,336	37,394	39,398	22,487	(NA)	27,744
1988	27,225	28,781	16,407	32,267	20,359	37,512	39,656	22,606	44,459	28,052
1989	28,906	30,406	18,083	36,102	21,921	37,997	39,969	23,770	47,457	28,816
1990	29,943	31,231	18,676	38,450	22,330	37,343	38,949	23,291	47,952	27,848
1991	30,126	31,569	18,807	36,449	22,691	36,054	37,781	22,508	43,621	27,156
1992 [4]	30,636	32,209	18,755	37,801	22,597	35,593	37,420	21,789	43,917	26,253
1993	31,241	32,960	19,533	38,347	22,886	35,241	37,180	22,034	43,256	25,816
1994	32,264	34,028	21,027	40,482	23,421	35,486	37,426	23,127	44,525	25,760
1995	34,076	35,766	22,393	40,614	22,860	36,446	38,254	23,951	43,439	24,450
1996	35,492	37,161	23,482	43,276	24,906	36,872	38,606	24,395	44,958	25,874
1997	37,005	38,972	25,050	45,249	26,628	37,581	39,579	25,440	45,954	27,043
1998	38,885	40,912	25,351	46,637	28,330	38,885	40,912	25,351	46,637	28,330

NA Not available. [1] Includes other races not shown separately. [2] Persons of Hispanic origin may be of any race. [3] Beginning 1987, data based on revised processing procedures and not directly comparable with prior years. [4] Based on 1990 census population controls.

Source of Tables 736 and 737: U.S. Census Bureau, *Current Population Reports,* P60-206; and Internet site <http://www.census.gov/hhes/income/histinc/ho5.html> (accessed 17 May 2000).

No. 738. Money Income of Households—Distribution by Income Level and Selected Characteristics: 1998

[See headnote, Table 736]

Characteristic	Number of house-holds (1,000)	Number (1,000)							Median income (dollars)
		Under $10,000	$10,000-$14,999	$15,000-$24,999	$25,000-$34,999	$35,000-$49,999	$50,000-$74,999	$75,000 and over	
Total [1]	103,874	10,705	8,093	14,587	13,698	16,660	19,272	20,860	38,885
Age of householder:									
15 to 24 years	5,770	1,075	668	1,325	944	932	551	274	23,564
25 to 34 years	18,819	1,506	1,193	2,521	2,932	3,502	4,192	2,973	40,069
35 to 44 years	23,968	1,494	1,132	2,426	2,950	4,387	5,529	6,051	48,451
45 to 54 years	20,158	1,288	790	1,831	2,119	3,123	4,621	6,387	54,148
55 to 64 years	13,571	1,507	863	1,590	1,681	2,086	2,494	3,350	43,167
65 years and over	21,589	3,836	3,448	4,893	3,071	2,631	1,886	1,824	21,729
White	87,212	7,615	6,468	11,937	11,480	14,230	16,862	18,619	40,912
Black	12,579	2,691	1,338	2,183	1,700	1,795	1,659	1,215	25,351
Hispanic [2]	9,060	1,353	989	1,620	1,477	1,432	1,271	919	28,330
Region:									
Northeast	19,877	2,155	1,580	2,614	2,358	3,007	3,582	4,580	40,634
Midwest	24,489	2,187	1,834	3,304	3,353	3,940	5,032	4,840	40,609
South	36,959	4,380	2,925	5,683	5,100	5,907	6,473	6,491	35,797
West	22,549	1,982	1,755	2,985	2,887	3,806	4,185	4,948	40,983
Size of household:									
One person	26,606	6,237	4,151	5,273	3,926	3,406	2,297	1,314	20,154
Two persons	34,262	2,182	2,051	5,115	4,991	5,936	6,871	7,115	41,512
Three persons	17,386	1,072	844	1,941	2,014	2,999	3,971	4,544	49,069
Four persons	15,030	636	544	1,241	1,567	2,536	3,723	4,784	55,886
Five persons	6,962	371	310	622	729	1,161	1,680	2,089	53,706
Six persons	2,367	141	126	256	299	383	473	690	49,080
Seven or more persons . .	1,261	66	66	138	171	239	256	324	46,646
Type of household:									
Family households	71,535	4,187	3,653	8,639	8,996	12,192	15,676	18,191	47,469
Married-couple	54,770	1,541	1,841	5,488	6,329	9,454	13,301	16,816	54,276
Male householder, wife absent	3,976	235	209	641	675	759	845	612	39,414
Female householder, husband absent	12,789	2,411	1,603	2,510	1,992	1,979	1,530	764	24,393
Nonfamily households	32,339	6,518	4,440	5,948	4,701	4,468	3,596	2,668	23,441
Male householder	14,368	2,084	1,364	2,475	2,237	2,415	2,128	1,665	30,414
Female householder . .	17,971	4,435	3,076	3,473	2,464	2,053	1,467	1,003	18,615
Educational attainment of householder: [3]									
Total	98,104	9,630	7,425	13,262	12,754	15,727	18,721	20,585	40,296
Less than 9th grade	7,047	1,987	1,327	1,537	918	668	402	208	16,154
9th to 12th grade (no diploma)	9,407	2,059	1,346	2,056	1,304	1,289	890	463	20,724
High school graduate	30,613	3,268	2,613	4,840	4,831	5,534	5,729	3,797	34,373
Some college, no degree . .	17,833	1,208	1,126	2,357	2,579	3,330	3,852	3,381	41,658
Associate degree	7,468	392	387	772	918	1,376	1,875	1,748	48,604
Bachelor's degree or more . .	25,738	717	626	1,700	2,204	3,531	5,973	10,987	66,474
Bachelor's degree	16,781	514	422	1,251	1,616	2,465	4,070	6,442	62,188
Master's degree	5,961	131	134	340	429	805	1,337	2,784	71,086
Professional degree	1,623	42	51	64	81	132	282	971	95,309
Doctorate degree	1,373	30	18	45	77	129	284	789	84,100
Work experience of householder:									
Total	103,874	10,705	8,093	14,587	13,698	16,660	19,272	20,860	38,885
Worked	74,296	3,215	3,571	8,487	9,867	13,421	16,937	18,798	48,179
Worked at full-time jobs	64,566	1,869	2,485	6,882	8,626	11,941	15,419	17,344	50,562
50 weeks or more . .	54,963	731	1,676	5,302	7,240	10,323	13,853	15,838	53,033
27 to 49 weeks	6,194	361	447	998	968	1,136	1,103	1,181	39,041
26 weeks or less . . .	3,409	776	363	581	418	482	463	325	24,525
Worked at part-time jobs	9,730	1,346	1,086	1,605	1,241	1,480	1,518	1,454	31,470
50 weeks or more . .	4,867	481	561	872	667	721	763	802	32,276
27 to 49 weeks	2,325	306	234	384	268	407	371	356	33,945
26 weeks or less . . .	2,538	560	290	349	306	352	384	296	27,249
Did not work	29,578	7,490	4,522	6,100	3,831	3,239	2,335	2,061	19,093

[1] Includes other races not shown separately.   [2] Persons of Hispanic origin may be of any race.   [3] Persons 25 years old and over.

Source: U.S. Census Bureau, *Current Population Reports*, P60-206, *Money Income in the United States: 1998.*

No. 739. Household Income Before and After Taxes in Current and Constant (1997) Dollars: 1980 to 1997

[In dollars, except as indicated. Households as of **March of the following year**. Income in current and 1997 CPI-U-X1 adjusted dollars]

Year	Number of house-holds (1,000)	Current dollars				Constant (1997) dollars			
		Mean		Median		Mean		Median	
		Before taxes	After taxes	Before taxes	After taxes	Before taxes	After taxes	Before taxes	After taxes
1980	82,368	21,063	16,272	17,710	14,551	41,077	31,733	34,538	28,377
1985 [1]	88,458	29,066	22,646	23,618	19,401	43,356	33,780	35,229	28,939
1990	94,312	37,403	29,188	29,943	24,546	45,931	35,843	36,770	30,143
1991	95,669	37,922	29,640	30,126	24,955	44,688	34,928	35,501	29,407
1992 [2]	96,426	38,840	30,425	30,636	25,474	44,432	34,806	35,047	29,142
1993 [3]	97,107	41,428	32,092	31,241	26,112	46,015	35,645	34,700	29,003
1994 [4]	98,990	43,133	33,315	32,264	26,973	46,713	36,080	34,942	29,212
1995 [5]	99,627	44,938	34,592	34,076	28,249	47,326	36,431	35,887	29,750
1996	101,018	47,123	36,008	35,492	29,312	48,204	36,834	36,306	29,985
1997	102,528	49,692	37,656	37,005	30,648	49,692	37,656	37,005	30,648

[1] Recording of amounts for earnings from longest job increased to $299,999. Full implementation of 1980 census-based sample design.   [2] Implementation of 1990 census population controls.   [3] Data collection method changed from paper and pencil to computer assisted interviewing. In addition, the March 1994 income supplement was revised to allow for the coding of different income amounts on selected questionnaire items. Limits either increased or decreased in the following categories: earnings increased to $999,999; social security increased to $49,999; supplemental security income and public assistance increased to $24,999; veterans' benefits increased to $99,999; child support and alimony decreased to $49,999.   [4] Introduction of 1990 census sample design.   [5] Full implementation of the 1990 census-based sample design and metropolitan definitions, 7,000 household sample reduction, and revised race edits.

Source: U.S. Census Bureau, Internet site <http://www.census.gov/hhes/income/histinc/rdi02.html> (accessed 8 June 1999).

No. 740. Mean-Taxes Paid and Taxes Paid as a Percentage of Total Mean Before-Tax Income by Type of Tax in Current and Constant (1997) Dollars: 1980 to 1997

[Households as of **March of the following year**. Mean taxes paid in current and 1997 CPI-U-X1 adjusted dollars]

Type of tax and year	Mean taxes paid				Type of tax and year	Mean taxes paid			
	Num-ber (1,000)	Current dollars (dol-lars)	Con-stant 1997 dollars (dol-lars)	As a per-cent of mean before-tax income		Num-ber (1,000)	Current dollars (dol-lars)	Con-stant 1997 dollars (dol-lars)	As a per-cent of mean before-tax income
One or more taxes paid:					1993 [3]	62,459	2,045	2,271	4.4
1980	76,171	5,180	10,102	23.1	1994 [4]	63,626	2,194	2,376	4.1
1985	81,943	6,947	10,362	22.5	1995 [5]	64,827	2,296	2,418	4.2
1990	87,597	8,896	10,924	22.4	1996	65,856	2,467	2,524	4.3
1991	88,636	9,007	10,614	22.3	1997	67,164	2,674	2,674	4.5
1992	89,232	9,178	10,499	22.2	FICA payroll taxes:				
1993	89,561	10,217	11,348	23.1	1980	62,061	1,114	2,173	4.6
1994	91,540	10,768	11,662	23.4	1985 [1]	66,090	1,894	2,825	5.6
1995	92,754	11,292	11,892	23.7	1990	70,942	2,692	3,306	6.2
1996	94,236	12,118	12,396	24.3	1991	71,466	2,807	3,308	6.3
1997	95,850	13,077	13,077	24.9	1992 [2]	72,516	2,889	3,305	6.3
Federal income taxes:					1993 [3]	72,264	2,961	3,289	6.1
1980	61,316	4,011	7,822	15.3	1994 [4]	74,050	3,107	3,365	6.1
1985 [1]	68,019	4,675	6,973	13.2	1995 [5]	75,096	3,193	3,363	6.1
1990	70,255	5,806	7,130	12.4	1996	76,724	3,330	3,406	6.0
1991	69,842	5,901	6,954	12.3	1997	77,999	3,508	3,508	6.1
1992 [2]	68,957	6,029	6,897	12.1	Property taxes on own home:				
1993 [3]	68,786	7,098	7,884	13.3	1980	52,328	575	1,121	2.3
1994 [4]	69,501	7,591	8,221	13.5	1985 [1]	53,298	811	1,210	2.3
1995 [5]	70,926	7,935	8,357	13.7	1990	58,472	1,125	1,382	2.5
1996	72,009	8,637	8,835	14.3	1991	59,403	1,119	1,319	2.5
1997	73,941	9,445	9,445	14.9	1992 [2]	59,838	1,213	1,388	2.6
State income taxes:					1993 [3]	60,554	1,230	1,366	2.5
1980	52,591	859	1,675	3.3	1994 [4]	62,121	1,257	1,361	2.4
1985 [1]	57,033	1,330	1,984	3.8	1995 [5]	63,377	1,361	1,433	2.5
1990	61,875	1,710	2,100	3.8	1996	64,559	1,433	1,466	2.6
1991	62,314	1,761	2,075	3.8	1997	65,998	1,390	1,390	2.3
1992 [2]	62,247	1,837	2,101	3.9					

[1] See footnote 1, Table 739.   [2] See footnote 2, Table 739.   [3] See footnote 3, Table 739.   [4] See footnote 4, Table 739.   [5] See footnote 5, Table 739.

Source: U.S. Census Bureau, Internet site <http://www.census.gov/hhes/income/histinc/rdi02.html (accessed 8 June 1999).

No. 741. Money Income of Households—Median Income and Income Level by Household Type: 1998

[See headnote, Table 736]

Item	All house-holds	Family households				Nonfamily households		
		Total	Married couple	Male house-holder, wife absent	Female house-holder, husband absent	Total [1]	Single-person household	
							Male house-holder	Female house-holder
MEDIAN INCOME (dollars)								
All households	38,885	47,469	54276	39,414	24,393	23,441	30,414	18,615
White.	40,912	49,781	54,845	41,384	27,542	24,582	31,659	19,239
Black	25,351	30,636	47,382	30,360	17,737	16,071	20,673	13,608
Hispanic [2].	28,330	30,812	35,207	32,239	18,452	16,805	23,427	11,669
NUMBER (1,000)								
All households	103,874	71,535	54,770	3,976	12,789	32,339	14,368	17,971
Under $5,000	3,373	1,650	627	98	926	1,724	725	998
$5,000 to $9,999	7,332	2,537	914	138	1,486	4,795	1,358	3,436
$10,000 to $14,999	8,093	3,653	1,841	209	1,603	4,440	1,365	3,075
$15,000 to $19,999	7,316	4,150	2,515	284	1,351	3,166	1,196	1,970
$20,000 to $24,999	7,271	4,489	2,973	356	1,160	2,782	1,279	1,503
$25,000 to $34,999	13,698	8,997	6,329	675	1,992	4,702	2,237	2,464
$35,000 to $49,999	16,660	12,192	9,455	759	1,979	4,468	2,417	2,053
$50,000 to $74,999	19,272	15,675	13,304	844	1,531	3,597	2,129	1,467
$75,000 to $99,999	9,935	8,489	7,739	320	433	1,445	850	595
$100,000 and over	10,926	9,702	9,077	293	333	1,224	816	408

[1] Includes other nonfamily households not shown separately.   [2] Persons of Hispanic origin may be of any race.

Source: U.S. Census Bureau, *Current Population Reports*, P60-206.

No. 742. Money Income of Households—Median Income by State in Constant (1998) Dollars: 1988 to 1998

[Constant dollars based on the CPI-U-X1 deflator. Data based on the Current Population Survey; see text, Sections 1 and 14, and Appendix III. The CPS is designed to collect reliable data on income primarily at the national level and secondarily at the regional level. When the income data are tabulated by state, the estimates are considered less reliable and, therefore, particular caution should be used when trying to interpret the results]

State	1988	1990	1995 [1]	1997	1998	State	1988	1990	1995 [1]	1997	1998
U.S.	**$37,512**	**$37,343**	**$36,446**	**$37,581**	**$38,885**						
						MO	32,301	34,087	37,247	37,122	40,201
AL	27,485	29,129	27,799	32,436	36,266	MT	30,631	29,152	29,688	29,667	31,577
AK	45,611	49,010	51,289	48,742	50,692	NE	34,665	34,274	35,219	35,232	36,413
AZ	36,424	36,446	33,010	33,250	37,090	NV	38,556	39,937	38,594	39,459	39,756
AR	27,794	28,417	27,609	26,569	27,665	NH	47,708	50,889	41,895	41,637	44,958
CA	41,731	41,517	39,583	40,312	40,934						
						NJ	49,998	48,306	46,979	48,769	49,826
CO	36,119	38,328	43,537	43,906	46,599	NM	26,587	31,227	27,799	30,555	31,543
CT	49,896	48,476	43,042	44,670	46,508	NY	39,841	39,398	35,325	36,356	37,394
DE	42,031	38,417	37,357	43,703	41,458	NC	33,640	32,836	34,203	36,398	35,838
DC	36,845	34,161	32,887	32,356	33,433	ND	33,195	31,508	31,112	32,154	30,304
FL	35,006	33,280	31,814	32,961	34,909						
						OH	38,222	37,430	37,371	36,697	38,925
GA	36,604	34,372	36,471	37,234	38,665	OK	32,610	30,410	28,141	31,839	33,727
HI	45,502	48,540	45,831	41,572	40,827	OR	38,233	36,517	38,904	37,827	39,067
ID	32,311	31,559	34,949	33,924	36,680	PA	36,847	36,173	36,925	38,101	39,015
IL	40,680	40,584	40,719	41,926	43,178	RI	41,118	39,868	37,818	35,339	40,686
IN	36,228	33,583	35,707	39,495	39,731						
						SC	35,181	35,836	31,093	34,796	33,267
IA	33,489	34,032	37,989	34,309	37,019	SD	30,718	30,643	31,635	30,157	32,786
KS	35,226	37,310	32,451	37,039	36,711	TN	28,737	28,175	31,033	31,113	34,091
KY	27,429	30,904	31,883	33,973	36,252	TX	34,395	35,204	34,267	35,621	35,783
LA	28,242	27,942	29,893	33,778	31,735	UT	36,255	37,591	39,017	43,441	44,299
ME	36,378	34,251	36,213	33,282	35,640						
						VT	39,941	38,783	36,177	35,599	39,372
MD	50,363	48,460	43,896	47,412	50,016	VA	44,984	43,741	38,741	43,626	43,354
MA	45,763	45,205	41,257	42,678	42,345	WA	44,542	40,048	38,042	45,256	47,421
MI	40,608	37,335	38,960	39,345	41,821	WV	26,666	27,608	26,611	27,916	26,704
MN	40,078	39,241	40,571	43,227	47,926	WI	40,750	38,301	43,804	40,212	41,327
MS	25,030	25,165	28,384	28,943	29,120	WY	36,401	36,740	33,722	33,944	35,250

[1] Full implementation of the 1990 census-based sample design and metropolitan definitions, 7,000 household sample reduction, and revised race edits.

Source: U.S. Census Bureau, *Current Population Reports*, P60-206; and <http://www.census.gov/hhes/income/histinc/h08.html (released 09 November 1999).

Income, Expenditures, and Wealth   469

No. 743. Money Income of Families—Percent Distribution by Income Level, Race, and Hispanic Origin in Constant (1998) Dollars: 1970 to 1998

[Constant dollars based on CPI-U deflator. Families as of **March of following year.** Beginning with 1980, based on householder concept and restricted to primary families. Based on Current Population Survey; see text, Sections 1 and 14, and Appendix III. For definition of median, see Guide to Tabular Presentation]

Year	Number of families (1,000)	Under $10,000	$10,000-$14,999	$15,000-$24,999	$25,000-$34,999	$35,000-$49,999	$50,000-$74,999	$75,000 and over	Median income (dollars)
ALL FAMILIES [1]									
1970	52,227	6.9	6.1	14.3	16.2	24.4	21.1	11.1	38,942
1980	60,309	6.5	6.1	14.0	14.1	21.1	22.5	15.6	41,637
1985	63,558	7.5	5.8	13.8	13.8	19.1	21.5	18.5	42,015
1990	66,322	6.9	5.7	12.5	13.4	18.8	21.6	21.0	44,090
1995	69,597	6.8	6.1	13.3	13.5	17.9	21.1	21.3	43,436
1996	70,241	7.3	5.8	13.1	13.2	17.5	21.4	21.8	43,945
1997	70,884	6.7	5.6	12.9	12.7	17.5	21.2	23.5	45,262
1998	71,551	6.5	5.3	12.3	12.7	16.8	21.6	25.0	46,737
WHITE									
1970	46,535	5.7	5.4	13.5	16.2	25.3	22.2	11.8	40,399
1980	52,710	5.2	5.3	13.3	14.2	21.7	23.7	16.8	43,382
1985	54,991	5.8	5.1	13.2	13.8	19.6	22.5	20.0	44,161
1990	56,803	5.2	4.9	12.1	13.5	19.2	22.7	22.4	46,038
1995	58,872	5.1	5.4	12.8	13.5	18.2	22.1	22.8	45,612
1996	58,934	5.5	5.0	12.5	13.2	18.0	22.4	23.3	46,496
1997	59,515	5.2	5.0	12.3	12.6	17.7	22.0	25.2	47,482
1998	60,077	4.9	4.7	11.6	12.6	17.1	22.4	26.5	49,023
BLACK									
1970	4,928	16.9	12.0	22.0	16.9	17.1	11.5	3.7	24,782
1980	6,317	17.2	13.2	19.6	14.4	16.6	13.1	6.0	25,102
1985	6,921	19.7	10.9	19.2	14.3	15.3	13.5	7.1	25,429
1990	7,471	20.0	11.7	15.9	13.2	16.5	13.8	9.0	26,717
1995	8,055	18.0	10.4	17.7	14.4	15.9	14.0	9.7	27,776
1996	8,455	18.4	10.4	17.6	13.9	15.4	14.9	9.6	27,553
1997	8,408	16.7	9.4	17.9	14.0	15.5	16.1	10.2	29,048
1998	8,452	16.0	9.5	17.9	13.6	14.7	16.0	12.4	29,404
HISPANIC ORIGIN [2]									
1970	(NA)	(NA)	(NA)	(NA)	(NA)	(NA)	(NA)	(NA)	(NA)
1980	3,235	12.0	10.5	20.0	17.3	18.5	15.1	6.7	29,146
1985	4,206	13.5	11.4	19.2	15.7	17.4	14.5	8.3	28,823
1990	4,981	13.4	11.2	18.9	15.3	17.8	14.0	9.3	29,222
1995	6,287	14.6	11.7	22.0	15.6	14.8	13.5	7.9	26,279
1996	6,631	13.9	11.3	21.3	15.1	16.0	13.0	9.4	27,197
1997	6,961	13.4	10.8	19.9	15.6	17.1	12.9	10.3	28,580
1998	7,273	11.9	10.4	18.9	17.1	16.1	15.0	10.7	29,608

[1] Includes other races not shown separately.   [2] Persons of Hispanic origin may be of any race.

No. 744. Money Income of Families—Median Income by Race and Hispanic Origin in Current and Constant (1998) Dollars: 1970 to 1998

[See headnote, Table 736]

Year	Median income in current dollars					Median income in constant (1998) dollars				
	All families [1]	White	Black	Asian, Pacific Islander	His-panic [2]	All families [1]	White	Black	Asian, Pacific Islander	His-panic [2]
1970	9,867	10,236	6,279	(NA)	(NA)	38,942	40,399	24,782	(NA)	(NA)
1980	21,023	21,904	12,674	(NA)	14,716	41,637	43,382	25,102	(NA)	29,146
1985 [3]	27,735	29,152	16,786	(NA)	19,027	42,015	44,161	25,429	(NA)	28,823
1986	29,458	30,809	17,604	(NA)	19,995	43,811	45,820	26,181	(NA)	29,737
1987 [4]	30,970	32,385	18,406	(NA)	20,300	44,438	46,468	26,410	(NA)	29,128
1988	32,191	33,915	19,329	36,560	21,769	44,354	46,730	26,633	50,374	29,994
1989	34,213	35,975	20,209	40,351	23,446	44,974	47,290	26,565	53,042	30,820
1990	35,353	36,915	21,423	42,246	23,431	44,090	46,038	26,717	52,686	29,222
1991	35,939	37,783	21,548	40,974	23,895	43,011	45,218	25,788	49,036	28,597
1992 [5]	36,573	38,670	21,103	42,255	23,555	42,490	44,927	24,517	49,092	27,366
1993 [6]	36,959	39,300	21,542	44,456	23,654	41,691	44,332	24,300	50,148	26,682
1994 [7]	38,782	40,884	24,698	46,122	24,318	42,655	44,967	27,164	50,728	26,747
1995 [8]	40,611	42,646	25,970	46,356	24,570	43,436	45,612	27,776	49,580	26,279
1996	42,300	44,756	26,522	49,105	26,179	43,945	46,496	27,553	51,014	27,197
1997	44,568	46,754	28,602	51,850	28,142	45,262	47,482	29,048	52,658	28,580
1998	46,737	49,023	29,404	52,826	29,608	46,737	49,023	29,404	52,826	29,608

NA Not available.   [1] Includes other races not shown separately.   [2] Persons of Hispanic origin may be of any race. [3] Recording of amounts for earnings from longest job increased to $299,999.   [4] Implementation of a new March CPS processing system.   [5] Implementation of 1990 census population controls.   [6] See text, Section 14, for information on data collection change.   [7] Introduction of 1990 census sample design.   [8] Full implementation of the 1990 census-based sample design and metropolitan definitions, 7,000 household sample reduction, and revised race edits.
Source of Tables 743 and 744: U.S. Census Bureau, *Current Population Reports*, P60-206.

No. 745. Share of Aggregate Income Received by Each Fifth and Top 5 Percent of Families: 1970 to 1998

[Families as of **March of the following year**. Income in constant 1998 CPI-U adjusted dollars]

Year	Num-ber of fami-lies (1,000)	Income at selected positions (dollars)					Percent distribution of aggregate income					
		Upper limit of each fifth					Low-est 5th	Sec-ond 5th	Third 5th	Fourth 5th	Highest 5th	Top 5 percent
		Lowest	Sec-ond	Third	Fourth	Top 5 percent						
1970.......	51,948	20,128	32,837	44,594	61,297	95,708	5.4	12.2	17.6	23.8	40.9	15.6
1980.......	60,309	20,598	34,680	49,118	68,923	108,931	5.3	11.6	17.6	24.4	41.1	14.6
1985.......	63,558	20,125	34,669	50,221	73,061	119,622	4.8	11.0	16.9	24.3	43.1	16.1
1990.......	66,322	21,009	36,222	52,429	76,686	127,654	4.6	10.8	16.6	23.8	44.3	17.4
1991 [1]...	67,173	20,345	34,839	51,461	75,386	123,057	4.5	10.7	16.6	24.1	44.2	17.1
1992 [2]..	68,216	19,417	34,475	51,119	74,413	123,164	4.3	10.5	16.5	24.0	44.7	17.6
1993 [3]..	68,506	19,143	33,841	50,795	75,346	127,672	4.1	9.9	15.7	23.3	47.0	20.3
1994 [3]..	69,313	19,732	34,426	51,694	76,988	132,031	4.2	10.0	15.7	23.3	46.9	20.1
1995.......	69,597	20,396	35,279	52,392	77,286	132,257	4.4	10.1	15.8	23.2	46.5	20.0
1996.......	70,241	20,445	35,649	53,072	78,244	132,976	4.2	10.0	15.8	23.1	46.8	20.3
1997.......	70,884	20,907	36,561	54,451	81,246	139,215	4.2	9.9	15.7	23.0	47.2	20.7
1998.......	71,551	21,600	37,692	56,020	83,693	145,199	4.2	9.9	15.7	23.0	47.3	20.7

[1] Based on 1990 census population controls. [2] See text, Section 14, for explanation of changes in data collection method. [3] Introduction of new 1990 census sample design. [4] Persons of Hispanic origin may be of any race.

Source: U.S. Census Bureau, Current Population Reports, P60-206; and <http://www.census.gov/hhes/income/histinc/f02.html> (accessed 26 October 1999).

No. 746. Money Income of Families—Distribution by Family Characteristics and Income Level: 1998

[See headnote, Table 743. For composition of regions, see text, inside front cover]

Characteristic	Number of fami-lies (1,000)	Income level (1,000)								Median income (dollars)
		Under $10,000	$10,000 to $14,999	$15,000 to $24,999	$25,000 to $34,999	$35,000 to $49,999	$50,000 to $74,999	$75,000 and over		
All families	**71,551**	**4,593**	**3,799**	**8,811**	**9,052**	**11,995**	**15,427**	**17,874**	**46,737**
Age of householder:									
15 to 24 years old............	3,242	747	372	722	491	456	316	138	21,918
25 to 34 years old............	13,226	1,214	873	1,694	1,860	2,329	3,048	2,209	41,074
35 to 44 years old............	18,823	1,011	787	1,776	2,059	3,361	4,537	5,291	51,883
45 to 54 years old............	15,127	526	442	1,050	1,319	2,225	3,865	5,699	61,833
55 to 64 years old............	9,635	462	386	978	1,112	1,576	2,120	3,001	52,577
65 years old and over	11,498	634	937	2,590	2,213	2,047	1,540	1,536	31,568
White.......................	60,077	2,993	2,844	6,996	7,570	10,268	13,460	15,944	49,023
Black......................	8,452	1,351	803	1,511	1,145	1,245	1,351	1,044	29,404
Hispanic origin [1].............	7,273	866	758	1,371	1,247	1,168	1,090	774	29,608
Northeast	13,384	839	634	1,523	1,489	2,122	2,819	3,958	50,567
Midwest	16,875	903	750	1,826	2,200	2,839	4,108	4,251	49,552
South.....................	25,894	1,856	1,567	3,602	3,463	4,413	5,314	5,678	42,711
West	15,398	996	847	1,860	1,900	2,621	3,186	3,988	46,819
Type of family:									
Married-couple families	54,778	1,553	1,842	5,515	6,345	9,452	13,303	16,769	54,180
Male householder, wife absent	3,977	317	237	707	690	756	777	494	35,681
Female householder, husband absent...................	12,796	2,724	1,720	2,589	2,017	1,788	1,347	612	22,163
Unrelated subfamilies	525	197	81	108	59	44	29	7	13,691
Education attainment of householder: [2]									
Total....................	68,309	3,846	3,427	8,088	8,562	11,539	15,111	17,736	48,194
Less than 9th grade	4,464	658	689	1,153	812	600	359	194	22,328
9th to 12th grade (no diploma)	6,227	911	652	1,364	1,005	1,110	772	414	26,707
High school graduate (includes equivalency)	21,689	1,300	1,190	2,998	3,459	4,365	4,984	3,394	41,302
Some college, no degree..........	12,612	574	508	1,349	1,664	2,434	3,149	2,935	48,495
Associate degree	5,420	165	180	474	557	998	1,538	1,508	54,719
Bachelor's degree or more........	17,896	241	207	750	1,064	2,033	4,309	9,291	76,999
Bachelor's degree	11,593	178	144	565	777	1,480	3,029	5,420	71,680
Master's degree	4,093	35	43	140	186	404	924	2,362	83,052
Professional degree	1,228	17	18	26	55	77	184	851	100,000
Doctorate degree	982	11	3	19	47	72	172	658	96,945

[1] Persons of Hispanic origin may be of any race. [2] Persons 25 years old and over.

Source: U.S. Census Bureau, Current Population Reports, P60-206.

Income, Expenditures, and Wealth   471

No. 747. Money Income of Families—Work Experience by Income Level: 1998

[See headnote, Table 743]

Characteristic	Number of families (1,000)	Under $10,000	$10,000 to $14,999	$15,000 to $24,999	$25,000 to $34,999	$35,000 to $49,999	$50,000 to $74,999	$75,000 and over	Median income (dollars)
All families.............	**71,551**	**4,593**	**3,799**	**8,811**	**9,052**	**11,995**	**15,427**	**17,874**	**46,737**
Number of earners:									
No earners................	9,692	2,134	1,236	2,517	1,624	1,091	606	483	20,689
One earner................	21,023	2,039	1,973	4,046	3,637	3,678	3,120	2,728	31,483
Two earners or more	40,638	420	590	2,247	3,792	7,226	11,700	14,663	61,675
Two earners	31,787	388	549	2,065	3,287	6,146	9,140	10,213	58,397
Three earners	6,642	32	40	173	447	924	2,020	3,006	70,339
Four earners or more	2,209	1	-	9	59	156	541	1,444	88,031
Work experience of householder:									
Total...................	**71,551**	**4,593**	**3,799**	**8,811**	**9,052**	**11,995**	**15,427**	**17,874**	**46,737**
Worked	54,167	2,077	2,091	5,053	6,120	9,368	13,425	16,033	53,500
Worked at full-time jobs	47,366	1,237	1,598	4,156	5,288	8,204	12,118	14,766	55,605
50 weeks or more	40,470	419	1,054	3,148	4,428	7,098	10,812	13,511	58,274
27 to 49 weeks	4,465	254	302	666	581	757	916	990	43,709
26 weeks or less	2,430	563	242	343	278	350	389	265	26,912
Worked at part-time jobs.........	6,801	841	493	896	833	1,164	1,308	1,267	39,038
50 weeks or more	3,347	245	273	471	448	571	651	689	40,571
27 to 49 weeks	1,604	217	85	195	175	323	301	306	41,279
26 weeks or less	1,851	379	134	230	209	271	356	272	33,755

- Represents zero.

No. 748. Median Income of Families by Type of Family in Current and Constant (1998) Dollars: 1970 to 1998

[See headnote, Table 743]

Year	Current dollars						Constant (1998) dollars					
		Married-couple families				Female house-holder, no hus-band present		Married-couple families				Female house-holder, no hus-band present
	Total	Total	Wife in paid labor force	Wife not in paid labor force	Male house-holder, no wife present		Total	Total	Wife in paid labor force	Wife not in paid labor force	Male house-holder, no wife present	
1970	9,867	10,516	12,276	9,304	9,012	5,093	38,942	41,504	48,450	36,720	35,568	20,101
1980	21,023	23,141	26,879	18,972	17,519	10,408	41,637	45,832	53,235	37,575	34,697	20,614
1985	27,735	31,100	36,431	24,556	22,622	13,660	42,015	47,112	55,188	37,199	34,269	20,693
1990	35,353	39,895	46,777	30,265	29,046	16,932	44,090	49,754	58,337	37,744	36,224	21,116
1991 [1]	35,939	40,995	48,169	30,075	28,351	16,692	43,011	49,062	57,647	35,993	33,930	19,976
1992 [1]	36,573	41,890	49,775	30,174	27,576	17,025	42,490	48,668	57,828	35,056	32,038	19,780
1993 [2]	36,959	43,005	51,204	30,218	26,467	17,443	41,691	48,511	57,760	34,087	29,856	19,676
1994 [2]	38,782	44,959	53,309	31,176	27,751	18,236	42,655	49,449	58,633	34,289	30,522	20,057
1995 [3]	40,611	47,062	55,823	32,375	30,358	19,691	43,436	50,335	59,706	34,627	32,470	21,061
1996	42,300	49,707	58,381	33,748	31,600	19,911	43,945	51,640	60,651	35,060	32,829	20,685
1997	44,568	51,591	60,669	36,027	32,960	21,023	45,262	52,395	61,614	36,588	33,473	21,350
1998	46,737	54,180	63,751	37,161	35,681	22,163	46,737	54,180	63,751	37,161	35,681	22,163

[1] Based on 1990 census population controls.   [2] See text, Section 14, for information on data collection change.
[3] Introduction of 1990 census sample design.

No. 749. Married-Couple Families—Number and Median Income by Work Experience of Husbands and Wives and Presence of Children: 1998

[As of March 1999. Based on Current Population Survey; see text, Sections 1 and 14, and Appendix III]

Work experience of husband or wife	Number (1,000)		One or more related children under 18 years old			Median income (dollars)		One or more related children under 18 years old		
	All mar-ried-couple fami-lies	No related chil-dren	Total	One child	Two chil-dren or more	All mar-ried-couple fami-lies	No related chil-dren	Total	One child	Two children or more
All married-couple families...	54,778	28,552	26,226	10,077	16,150	54,180	51,323	57,022	59,033	55,674
Husband worked	43,705	18,822	24,883	9,429	15,454	60,867	64,090	58,730	60,784	57,118
Wife worked................	32,873	14,289	18,584	7,459	11,125	65,411	68,878	62,817	65,261	61,561
Wife year-round, full-time worker.	19,132	9,139	9,993	4,421	5,572	70,918	73,284	68,438	71,474	66,482
Wife did not work	10,832	4,532	6,300	1,970	4,329	45,541	49,128	42,079	42,063	42,084
Husband year-round, full-time worker.	36,285	14,576	21,709	8,155	13,554	63,750	68,930	60,883	62,429	59,910
Wife worked................	27,799	11,555	16,244	6,491	9,753	68,075	72,342	65,140	67,325	63,693
Wife year-round, full-time worker.	16,703	7,774	8,929	3,932	4,997	72,930	76,459	70,515	73,502	68,203
Wife did not work	8,486	3,021	5,465	1,663	3,801	48,514	52,355	45,372	43,373	45,996
Husband did not work	11,073	9,730	1,343	647	696	28,488	28,819	26,196	27,388	25,168
Wife worked................	3,019	2,230	789	393	396	38,818	41,883	31,098	35,727	28,875
Wife year-round, full-time worker.	1,666	1,194	472	230	242	43,080	45,437	36,102	40,107	32,030
Wife did not work	8,055	7,500	554	254	300	25,657	26,029	19,116	19,903	17,312

Source of Tables 747-749: U.S. Census Bureau, Current Population Reports, P60-206; and <http://www.census.gov/hhes/income/histinc/index.htm> (accessed 17 May 2000).

No. 750. Money Income of Persons—Selected Characteristics by Income Level: 1998

[Persons as of **March of following year. Covers persons 15 years old and over.** For definition of median, see Guide to Tabular Presentation. For composition of regions, see map, inside front cover]

Characteristic	All persons (1,000)	Persons with income									Median income (dollars)
		Number (1,000)									
		Total (1,000)	Under $5,000 [1]	$5,000 to $9,999	$10,000 to $14,999	$15,000 to $24,999	$25,000 to $34,999	$35,000 to $49,999	$50,000 to $74,999	$75,000 and over	
MALE											
Total	102,048	94,948	8,360	9,142	9,548	17,620	14,718	15,234	11,763	8,562	26,492
15 to 24 years old. . . .	19,131	14,079	5,019	2,778	2,057	2,557	971	477	160	61	8,190
25 to 34 years old. . . .	18,923	18,330	893	1,104	1,639	4,117	3,955	3,604	2,085	931	28,117
35 to 44 years old. . . .	22,156	21,539	786	1,232	1,245	3,482	3,944	4,600	3,668	2,582	35,177
45 to 54 years old. . . .	17,144	16,821	608	938	995	2,196	2,648	3,424	3,341	2,671	38,922
55 to 64 years old. . . .	10,967	10,678	556	908	913	1,705	1,510	1,826	1,678	1,583	32,776
65 yr. old and over . . .	13,727	13,501	499	2,182	2,699	3,562	1,690	1,303	831	734	18,166
Northeast.	19,308	18,024	1,658	1,710	1,648	3,114	2,713	2,962	2,343	1,876	27,521
Midwest.	23,687	22,551	2,020	1,986	2,083	3,973	3,743	3,844	2,965	1,937	27,668
South	35,895	33,002	2,832	3,455	3,451	6,556	5,176	5,172	3,733	2,625	25,297
West.	23,158	21,370	1,850	1,991	2,366	3,977	3,085	3,256	2,721	2,124	26,358
White	85,750	80,896	6,588	7,072	8,017	14,744	12,592	13,434	10,551	7,898	27,646
Black	11,483	9,776	1,275	1,605	1,120	2,022	1,541	1,219	718	276	19,321
Hispanic [2]	10,937	9,617	912	1,431	1,686	2,436	1,332	952	579	289	17,257
Education attainment of householder : [3]											
Total	82,917	80,869	3,342	6,364	7,491	15,063	13,747	14,757	11,603	8,501	30,654
Less than 9th grade. . .	5,990	5,641	405	1,600	1,357	1,381	495	255	95	54	12,571
9th to 12th grade [4] . .	7,736	7,366	592	1,174	1,280	2,078	1,169	660	305	108	17,462
High school graduate [5].	26,368	25,636	1,090	2,031	2,637	5,940	5,540	4,964	2,585	848	26,542
Some college, no degree.	14,201	13,935	520	753	1,063	2,671	2,784	2,966	2,229	949	31,627
Associate degree	5,841	5,766	195	235	393	855	1,066	1,455	1,082	484	35,962
Bachelor's degree or more	22,781	22,525	540	571	762	2,137	2,693	4,457	5,306	6,058	50,272
Bachelor's degree . .	14,808	14,614	394	390	522	1,554	2,046	3,164	3,392	3,153	45,749
Master's degree. . . .	4,811	4,772	94	114	157	359	439	897	1,291	1,421	55,784
Professional degree .	1,700	1,695	32	40	35	123	114	194	292	866	76,362
Doctorate degree. . .	1,463	1,443	20	27	49	102	94	202	331	618	65,319
FEMALE											
Total	109,628	98,694	18,146	18,463	14,113	19,018	12,504	9,149	5,094	2,208	14,430
15 to 24 years old. . . .	18,791	13,875	5,761	3,100	1,944	2,106	686	203	49	27	6,534
25 to 34 years old. . . .	19,551	17,773	2,860	2,174	2,384	4,135	3,137	1,976	844	263	18,257
35 to 44 years old. . . .	22,588	20,970	3,271	2,457	2,594	4,197	3,378	2,884	1,517	671	20,285
45 to 54 years old. . . .	18,088	16,915	2,138	2,016	1,948	3,383	2,834	2,319	1,622	653	21,588
55 to 64 years old. . . .	11,943	10,968	2,089	2,114	1,367	2,026	1,331	1,068	617	355	14,675
65 yr. old and over . . .	18,667	18,193	2,027	6,602	3,876	3,171	1,137	699	444	239	10,504
Northeast.	21,546	19,601	3,398	3,657	2,840	3,632	2,368	1,920	1,218	568	14,811
Midwest.	25,089	23,391	4,370	4,152	3,457	4,641	3,089	2,103	1,119	458	14,523
South	38,986	34,618	6,427	6,961	4,750	6,925	4,450	2,961	1,528	615	13,977
West.	24,007	21,085	3,951	3,692	3,066	3,819	2,596	2,164	1,229	567	14,672
White	90,463	82,063	15,136	14,891	11,766	15,698	10,601	7,700	4,309	1,962	14,617
Black	13,964	12,272	2,101	2,833	1,812	2,444	1,395	1,075	484	128	13,137
Hispanic [2]	11,058	8,405	1,945	1,955	1,473	1,534	766	464	194	74	10,862
Education attainment of householder: [3]											
Total	90,837	84,819	12,385	15,363	12,169	16,912	11,818	8,946	5,045	2,181	16,258
Less than 9th grade. . .	6,408	5,419	1,153	2,367	1,065	628	109	40	31	27	7,914
9th to 12th grade [4] . .	8,707	7,559	1,461	2,493	1,681	1,356	348	127	70	23	9,582
High school graduate [5].	31,566	29,330	4,731	5,959	5,078	7,009	3,700	1,855	752	246	13,786
Some college, no degree.	15,901	15,173	2,095	2,140	2,083	3,518	2,636	1,738	682	280	18,445
Associate degree	7,233	6,931	823	813	856	1,501	1,274	1,067	471	127	21,290
Bachelor's degree or more	21,022	20,409	2,124	1,591	1,406	2,900	3,751	4,120	3,038	1,479	30,692
Bachelor's degree . .	14,687	14,218	1,672	1,296	1,113	2,226	2,782	2,634	1,693	803	27,415
Master's degree. . . .	4,955	4,837	357	235	227	554	830	1,212	1,024	396	36,888
Professional degree .	802	788	57	43	48	62	82	147	180	168	43,490
Doctorate degree. . .	577	567	38	18	17	57	57	127	141	111	46,275

[1] Includes persons with income deficit.   [2] Persons of Hispanic origin may be of any race.   [3] Persons 25 years and over.
[4] No diploma attained.   [5] Includes high school equivalency.

Source: U.S. Census Bureau, *Current Population Reports*, P60-206.

Income, Expenditures, and Wealth   473

No. 751. Median Income of Persons with Income in Constant (1998) Dollars by Sex, Race, and Hispanic Origin: 1980 to 1998

[Persons as of **March of following year. Persons 15 years old and over.** Constant dollars based on CPI-U deflator]

Item	Male					Female				
	1980	1990	1995	1997	1998	1980	1990	1995	1997	1998
NUMBER WITH INCOME (1,000)										
All races	78,661	88,220	92,066	94,168	94,948	80,826	92,245	96,007	97,447	98,694
White	69,420	76,480	79,022	80,400	80,896	70,573	78,566	80,608	81,352	82,063
Black	7,387	8,820	9,339	9,671	9,776	8,596	10,687	11,607	11,961	12,272
Asian and Pacific Islander.	(NA)	2,235	3,095	3,330	3,500	(NA)	2,333	3,025	3,415	3,591
Hispanic [1]	3,996	6,767	8,577	9,585	9,617	3,617	5,903	7,478	8,055	8,405
Non-Hispanic White.	65,564	69,987	70,754	71,150	71,707	67,084	72,939	73,506	73,709	74,106
MEDIAN INCOME IN CONSTANT (1998) DOLLARS										
All races	24,816	25,308	24,131	25,605	26,492	9,744	12,559	12,974	13,916	14,430
White	26,397	26,402	25,557	26,522	27,646	9,798	12,867	13,173	14,007	14,617
Black	15,862	16,048	17,119	18,378	19,321	9,071	10,386	11,723	13,251	13,137
Asian and Pacific Islander.	(NA)	24,187	23,703	25,436	25,124	(NA)	13,826	13,757	14,535	15,228
Hispanic [1]	19,130	16,799	15,872	16,469	17,257	8,724	9,393	9,549	10,420	10,862
Non-Hispanic White.	27,096	27,385	27,253	27,988	29,862	9,863	13,196	13,698	14,613	15,217

NA Not available.   [1] Persons of Hispanic origin may be of any race.

No. 752. Average Earnings of Year-Round, Full-Time Workers by Educational Attainment: 1998

[In dollars. For persons 18 years old and over as of March 1999]

Age and sex	All workers	Less than 9th grade	High school		College		
			9th to 12th grade (no diploma)	High school graduate (includes equivalency)	Some college, no degree	Associate degree	Bachelor's degree or more
Male, total	44,898	23,925	25,168	32,647	39,820	43,668	69,065
18 to 24 years old	22,201	34,684	16,586	21,096	20,681	31,296	32,460
25 to 34 years old	36,079	16,443	22,924	29,281	34,492	36,660	49,874
35 to 44 years old	47,642	23,578	27,094	34,786	43,819	46,537	70,871
45 to 54 years old	53,049	26,620	28,896	36,867	45,223	43,639	78,479
55 to 64 years old	54,709	26,264	32,109	37,257	45,145	60,350	87,371
65 years old and over. . . .	56,364	19,120	22,028	38,510	74,479	(B)	74,670
Female, total	30,671	17,335	17,218	23,841	27,610	31,959	43,810
18 to 24 years old	18,395	(B)	15,729	17,162	17,553	19,171	24,653
25 to 34 years old	28,634	15,362	16,309	22,519	25,267	27,279	37,628
35 to 44 years old	33,579	18,289	17,291	24,569	29,692	34,128	50,606
45 to 54 years old	33,535	18,114	17,766	25,381	31,498	37,153	46,749
55 to 64 years old	30,502	16,140	18,089	26,419	30,590	34,618	43,023
65 years old and over. . . .	26,714	(B)	(B)	21,858	28,685	(B)	39,840

B Base figure too small to meet statistical standards for reliability of derived figure.

No. 753. Per Capita Money Income in Current and Constant (1998) Dollars by Race and Hispanic Origin: 1970 to 1998

[In dollars. Constant dollars based on CPI-U deflator. As of March of following year]

Year	Current dollars					Constant (1998) dollars				
	All races [1]	White	Black	Asian, Pacific Islander	His-panic [2]	All races [1]	White	Black	Asian, Pacific Islander	His-panic [2]
1970	3,177	3,354	1,869	(NA)	(NA)	12,539	13,237	7,376	(NA)	(NA)
1980 [3]	7,787	8,233	4,804	(NA)	4,865	15,423	16,306	9,515	(NA)	9,635
1985 [3]	11,013	11,671	6,840	(NA)	6,613	16,683	17,680	10,362	(NA)	10,018
1990	14,387	15,265	9,017	(NA)	8,424	17,942	19,037	11,245	(NA)	10,506
1991	14,617	15,510	9,170	(NA)	8,662	17,493	18,562	10,974	(NA)	10,366
1992 [4]	14,847	15,785	9,239	(NA)	8,591	17,249	18,339	10,734	(NA)	9,981
1993	15,777	16,800	9,863	15,691	8,830	17,797	18,951	11,126	17,700	9,960
1994	16,555	17,611	10,650	16,902	9,435	18,208	19,370	11,714	18,590	10,377
1995	17,227	18,304	10,982	16,567	9,300	18,425	19,576	11,746	17,719	9,947
1996	18,136	19,181	11,899	17,921	10,048	18,841	19,927	12,362	18,618	10,439
1997	19,241	20,425	12,351	18,226	10,773	19,541	20,743	12,543	18,510	10,941
1998	20,120	21,394	12,957	18,709	11,434	20,120	21,394	12,957	18,709	11,434

NA Not available.   [1] Includes other races not shown separately.   [2] Persons of Hispanic origin may be of any race.   [3] Beginning 1985, data based on revised Hispanic population controls.   [4] Based on 1990 population controls.

Source of Tables 751-753: U.S. Census Bureau, *Current Population Reports*, P60-206; and Internet site, <http://www.census.gov/hhes/income/histinc/index.html> (accessed 17 May 2000).

No. 754. Persons Below Poverty Level and Below 125 Percent of Poverty Level: 1970 to 1998

[Persons as of **March of the following year**. Based on Current Population Survey; see text, Sections 1 and 14, and Appendix III]

Year	Number below poverty level (1,000)					Percent below poverty level					Below 125 percent of poverty level	
	All races[1]	White	Black	Asian and Pacific Islander	His-panic[2]	All races[1]	White	Black	Asian and Pacific Islander	His-panic[2]	Number (1,000)	Percent of total popula-tion
1970	25,420	17,484	7,548	(NA)	(NA)	12.6	9.9	33.5	(NA)	(NA)	35,624	17.6
1975	25,877	17,770	7,545	(NA)	2,991	12.3	9.7	31.3	(NA)	26.9	37,182	17.6
1976	24,975	16,713	7,595	(NA)	2,783	11.8	9.1	31.1	(NA)	24.7	35,509	16.7
1977	24,720	16,416	7,726	(NA)	2,700	11.6	8.9	31.3	(NA)	22.4	35,659	16.7
1978	24,497	16,259	7,625	(NA)	2,607	11.4	8.7	30.6	(NA)	21.6	34,155	15.8
1979 [3]	26,072	17,214	8,050	(NA)	2,921	11.7	9.0	31.0	(NA)	21.8	36,616	16.4
1980	29,272	19,699	8,579	(NA)	3,491	13.0	10.2	32.5	(NA)	25.7	40,658	18.1
1981	31,822	21,553	9,173	(NA)	3,713	14.0	11.1	34.2	(NA)	26.5	43,748	19.3
1982	34,398	23,517	9,697	(NA)	4,301	15.0	12.0	35.6	(NA)	29.9	46,520	20.3
1983 [4]	35,303	23,984	9,882	(NA)	4,633	15.2	12.1	35.7	(NA)	28.0	47,150	20.3
1984	33,700	22,955	9,490	(NA)	4,806	14.4	11.5	33.8	(NA)	28.4	45,288	19.4
1985	33,064	22,860	8,926	(NA)	5,236	14.0	11.4	31.3	(NA)	29.0	44,166	18.7
1986	32,370	22,183	8,983	(NA)	5,117	13.6	11.0	31.1	(NA)	27.3	43,486	18.2
1987 [5]	32,221	21,195	9,520	1,021	5,422	13.4	10.4	32.4	16.1	28.0	43,032	17.9
1988	31,745	20,715	9,356	1,117	5,357	13.0	10.1	31.3	17.3	26.7	42,551	17.5
1989	31,528	20,785	9,302	939	5,430	12.8	10.0	30.7	14.1	26.2	42,653	17.3
1990	33,585	22,326	9,837	858	6,006	13.5	10.7	31.9	12.2	28.1	44,837	18.0
1991	35,708	23,747	10,242	996	6,339	14.2	11.3	32.7	13.8	28.7	47,527	18.9
1992 [6]	38,014	25,259	10,827	985	7,592	14.8	11.9	33.4	12.7	29.6	50,592	19.7
1993	39,265	26,226	10,877	1,134	8,126	15.1	12.2	33.1	15.3	30.6	51,801	20.0
1994	38,059	25,379	10,196	974	8,416	14.5	11.7	30.6	14.6	30.7	50,401	19.3
1995	36,425	24,423	9,872	1,411	8,574	13.8	11.2	29.3	14.6	30.3	48,761	18.5
1996	36,529	24,650	9,694	1,454	8,697	13.7	11.2	28.4	14.5	29.4	49,310	18.5
1997	35,574	24,396	9,116	1,468	8,308	13.3	11.0	26.5	14.0	27.1	47,853	17.8
1998	34,476	23,454	9,091	1,360	8,070	12.7	10.5	26.1	12.5	25.6	46,036	17.0

NA Not available.   [1] Includes other races not shown separately.   [2] Persons of Hispanic origin may be of any race. [3] Population controls based on 1980 census; see text, sections 1 and 14.   [4] Beginning 1983, data based on revised Hispanic population controls and not directly comparable with prior years.   [5] Beginning 1987, data based on revised processing procedures and not directly comparable with prior years.   [6] Beginning 1992, based on 1990 population controls.

Source: U.S. Census Bureau, *Current Population Reports,* P60-207.

No. 755. Children Below Poverty Level by Race and Hispanic Origin: 1970 to 1998

[Persons as of **March of the following year**. Covers only related children in families under 18 years old. Based on Current Population Survey; see text, Sections 1 and 14, and Appendix III]

Year	Number below poverty level (1,000)				Percent below poverty level			
	All races[1]	White	Black	Hispanic[2]	All races[1]	White	Black	Hispanic[2]
1970	10,235	6,138	3,922	(NA)	14.9	10.5	41.5	(NA)
1975	10,882	6,748	3,884	1,619	16.8	12.5	41.4	33.1
1976	10,081	6,034	3,758	1,424	15.8	11.3	40.4	30.1
1977	10,028	5,943	3,850	1,402	16.0	11.4	41.6	28.0
1978	9,722	5,674	3,781	1,354	15.7	11.0	41.2	27.2
1979	9,993	5,909	3,745	1,505	16.0	11.4	40.8	27.7
1980	11,114	6,817	3,906	1,718	17.9	13.4	42.1	33.0
1981	12,068	7,429	4,170	1,874	19.5	14.7	44.9	35.4
1982	13,139	8,282	4,388	2,117	21.3	16.5	47.3	38.9
1983 [3]	13,427	8,534	4,273	2,251	21.8	17.0	46.2	37.7
1984	12,929	8,086	4,320	2,317	21.0	16.1	46.2	38.7
1985	12,483	7,838	4,057	2,512	20.1	15.6	43.1	39.6
1986 [4]	12,257	7,714	4,037	2,413	19.8	15.3	42.7	37.1
1987	12,275	7,398	4,234	2,606	19.7	14.7	44.4	38.9
1988	11,935	7,095	4,148	2,576	19.0	14.0	42.8	37.3
1989	12,001	7,164	4,257	2,496	19.0	14.1	43.2	35.5
1990	12,715	7,696	4,412	2,750	19.9	15.1	44.2	37.7
1991	13,658	8,316	4,637	2,977	21.1	16.1	45.6	39.8
1992 [5]	14,521	8,752	5,015	3,440	21.6	16.5	46.3	39.0
1993	14,961	9,123	5,030	3,666	22.0	17.0	45.9	39.9
1994	14,610	8,826	4,787	3,956	21.2	16.3	43.3	41.1
1995	13,999	8,474	4,644	3,938	20.2	15.5	41.5	39.3
1996	13,764	8,488	4,411	4,090	19.8	15.5	39.5	39.9
1997	13,422	8,441	4,116	3,865	19.2	15.4	36.8	36.4
1998	12,845	7,935	4,073	3,670	18.3	14.4	36.4	33.6

NA Not available.   [1] Includes other races not shown separately.   [2] Persons of Hispanic origin may be of any race. [3] Beginning 1983, data based on revised Hispanic population controls and not directly comparable with prior years.   [4] Beginning 1987, data based on revised processing procedures and not directly comparable with prior years.   [5] Beginning 1992, based on 1990 population controls.

Source: U.S. Census Bureau, *Current Population Reports,* P60-207.

Income, Expenditures, and Wealth   475

No. 756. Weighted Average Poverty Thresholds: 1980 to 1998

[Official poverty thresholds; see text, Section 14]

Size of unit	1980[1]	1990	1992	1993	1994	1995	1996	1997	1998
One person (unrelated individual) . . .	$4,190	$6,652	$7,143	$7,363	$7,547	$7,763	7,995	8,183	8,316
Under 65 years	4,290	6,800	7,299	$7,518	7,710	7,929	8,163	8,350	8,480
65 years and over	3,949	6,268	6,729	6,930	7,108	7,309	7,525	7,698	7,818
Two persons	5,363	8,509	9,137	9,414	9,661	9,933	10,233	10,473	10,634
Householder under 65 years	5,537	8,794	9,443	9,728	9,976	10,259	10,564	10,805	10,972
Householder 65 years and over . . .	4,983	7,905	8,487	8,740	8,967	9,219	9,491	9,712	9,862
Three persons	6,565	10,419	11,186	11,522	11,821	12,158	12,516	12,802	13,003
Four persons	8,414	13,359	14,335	14,763	15,141	15,569	16,036	16,400	16,660
Five persons	9,966	15,792	16,952	17,449	17,900	18,408	18,952	19,380	19,680
Six persons	11,269	17,839	19,137	19,718	20,235	20,804	21,389	21,886	22,228
Seven persons	12,761	20,241	21,594	22,383	22,923	23,552	24,268	24,802	25,257
Eight persons	14,199	22,582	24,053	24,838	25,427	26,237	27,091	27,593	28,166
Nine or more persons	16,896	26,848	28,745	29,529	30,300	31,280	31,971	32,566	33,339

[1] Poverty levels for nonfarm families.

Source: U.S. Census Bureau, *Current Population Reports*, P60-207; and <http://www.census.gov/hhes/poverty/hispov/hstpov1.html> (accessed 19 October 1999).

No. 757. Persons Below Poverty Level by Selected Characteristics: 1998

[Persons as of **March 1999.** Based on Current Population Survey; see text, Sections 1 and 14, and Appendix III. For composition of regions, see map, inside front cover]

Age and region	Number below poverty level (1,000)				Percent below poverty level			
	All races [1]	White	Black	Hispanic [2]	All races [1]	White	Black	Hispanic [2]
Total	34,476	23,454	9,091	8,070	12.7	10.5	26.1	25.6
Under 18 years old	13,467	8,443	4,151	3,837	18.9	15.1	36.7	34.4
18 to 24 years old	4,312	3,023	1,043	1,010	16.6	14.6	27.2	25.6
25 to 34 years old	4,582	3,171	1,113	1,225	11.9	10.3	21.2	22.1
35 to 44 years old	4,082	2,906	998	938	9.1	7.9	17.8	20.3
45 to 54 years old	2,444	1,754	551	418	6.9	5.9	14.3	14.6
55 to 59 years old	1,165	853	266	158	9.2	7.9	21.3	16.2
60 to 64 years old	1,039	749	252	128	10.1	8.4	24.2	17.6
65 years old and over . . .	3,386	2,555	718	356	10.5	8.9	26.4	21.0
65 to 74 years old	1,616	1,135	411	224	9.1	7.3	25.6	20.5
75 years old and over .	1,770	1,420	307	132	12.2	10.8	27.4	21.9
Northeast	6,357	4,081	1,949	1,436	12.3	9.5	29.9	29.6
Midwest	6,501	4,475	1,751	486	10.3	8.1	27.2	20.3
South	12,992	7,761	4,807	2,430	13.7	10.7	25.3	23.5
West	8,625	7,137	584	3,717	14.0	13.8	20.3	26.7

[1] Includes other races not shown separately. [2] Persons of Hispanic origin may be of any race.

Source: U.S. Census Bureau, *Current Population Reports*, P60-207. and unpublished data.

No. 758. Persons 65 Years Old and Over Below Poverty Level: 1980 to 1998

[Persons as of **March of following year.** Based on the Current Population Survey, see text, Sections 1 and 14, and Appendix III]

Characteristic	Number below poverty level (1,000)					Percent below poverty level				
	1980	1990	1995	1997	1998	1980	1990	1995	1997	1998
Total	3,871	3,658	3,318	3,376	3,386	15.7	12.2	10.5	10.5	10.5
White	3,042	2,707	2,572	2,569	2,555	13.6	10.1	9.0	9.0	8.9
Black	783	860	629	700	718	38.1	33.8	25.4	26.0	26.4
Asian and Pacific Islander.	(NA)	62	89	87	97	(NA)	12.1	14.3	12.3	12.4
Hispanic [1]	179	245	342	384	356	30.8	22.5	23.5	23.8	21.0
In families	(NA)	1,172	1,058	1,143	1,234	(NA)	5.8	5.0	5.3	5.7
Unrelated individuals	(NA)	2,479	2,260	2,233	2,150	(NA)	24.7	21.4	21.0	20.4

NA Not available. [1] Persons of Hispanic origin may be of any race.

Source: U.S. Census Bureau, *Current Population Reports*, P60-207; and earlier reports.

No. 759. Persons Below Poverty Level by State: 1980 to 1998

[Based on the Current Population Survey; see text, Sections 1 and 14, and Appendix III. The CPS is designed to collect reliable data on income primarily at the national level and secondarily at the regional level. When the income data are tabulated by state, the estimates are considered less reliable and, therefore, particular caution should be used when trying to interpret the results; for additional detail, see source]

State	Number below poverty level (1,000)					Percent below poverty level				
	1980	1990 [1]	1995	1997	1998	1980	1990 [1]	1995	1997	1998
United States	29,272	33,585	36,425	35,574	34,476	13.0	13.5	13.8	13.3	12.7
Alabama.	810	779	882	665	609	21.2	19.2	20.1	15.7	14.5
Alaska	36	57	45	56	60	9.6	11.4	7.1	8.8	9.4
Arizona.	354	484	700	797	812	12.8	13.7	16.1	17.2	16.6
Arkansas	484	472	376	515	377	21.5	19.6	14.9	19.7	14.8
California	2,619	4,128	5,342	5,459	5,118	11.0	13.9	16.7	16.6	15.4
Colorado.	247	461	335	320	363	8.6	13.7	8.8	8.2	9.2
Connecticut.	255	196	318	282	310	8.3	6.0	9.7	8.6	9.5
Delaware	68	48	74	72	80	11.8	6.9	10.3	9.6	10.3
District of Columbia	131	120	122	113	114	20.9	21.1	22.2	21.8	22.3
Florida	1,692	1,896	2,321	2,056	1,923	16.7	14.4	16.2	14.3	13.1
Georgia	727	1,001	878	1,109	1,034	13.9	15.8	12.1	14.5	13.6
Hawaii	81	121	122	164	131	8.5	11.0	10.3	13.9	10.9
Idaho	138	157	167	183	165	14.7	14.9	14.5	14.7	13.0
Illinois	1,386	1,606	1,459	1,349	1,234	12.3	13.7	12.4	11.2	10.1
Indiana.	645	714	545	515	547	11.8	13.0	9.6	8.8	9.4
Iowa	311	289	352	270	257	10.8	10.4	12.2	9.6	9.1
Kansas.	215	259	273	250	250	9.4	10.3	10.8	9.7	9.6
Kentucky	701	628	572	623	521	19.3	17.3	14.7	15.9	13.5
Louisiana	868	952	849	691	821	20.3	23.6	19.7	16.3	19.1
Maine.	158	162	138	124	131	14.6	13.1	11.2	10.1	10.4
Maryland	389	468	520	422	359	9.5	9.9	10.1	8.4	7.2
Massachusetts.	542	626	665	732	528	9.5	10.7	11.0	12.2	8.7
Michigan.	1,194	1,315	1,174	1,006	1,099	12.9	14.3	12.2	10.3	11.0
Minnesota.	342	524	427	457	498	8.7	12.0	9.2	9.6	10.4
Mississippi	591	684	630	455	486	24.3	25.7	23.5	16.7	17.6
Missouri	625	700	484	627	531	13.0	13.4	9.4	11.8	9.8
Montana.	102	134	133	139	153	13.2	16.3	15.3	15.6	16.6
Nebraska	199	167	159	163	211	13.0	10.3	9.6	9.8	12.3
Nevada	70	119	173	190	195	8.3	9.8	11.1	11.0	10.6
New Hampshire	63	68	60	109	119	7.0	6.3	5.3	9.1	9.8
New Jersey.	659	711	617	737	693	9.0	9.2	7.8	9.3	8.6
New Mexico	268	319	457	387	371	20.6	20.9	25.3	21.2	20.4
New York	2,391	2,571	3,020	2,979	3,068	13.8	14.3	16.5	16.5	16.7
North Carolina	877	829	877	839	1,039	15.0	13.0	12.6	11.4	14.0
North Dakota.	99	87	76	87	97	15.5	13.7	12.0	13.6	15.1
Ohio	1,046	1,256	1,285	1,231	1,253	9.8	11.5	11.5	11.0	11.2
Oklahoma.	406	481	548	456	458	13.9	15.6	17.1	13.7	14.1
Oregon.	309	267	360	382	503	11.5	9.2	11.2	11.6	15.0
Pennsylvania.	1,142	1,328	1,464	1,337	1,338	9.8	11.0	12.2	11.2	11.2
Rhode Island.	97	71	102	120	112	10.7	7.5	10.6	12.7	11.6
South Carolina.	534	548	744	500	527	16.8	16.2	19.9	13.1	13.7
South Dakota	127	93	103	117	77	18.8	13.3	14.5	16.5	10.8
Tennessee	884	833	846	791	749	19.6	16.9	15.5	14.3	13.4
Texas.	2,247	2,684	3,270	3,297	2,994	15.7	15.9	17.4	16.7	15.1
Utah	148	143	168	185	190	10.0	8.2	8.4	8.9	9.0
Vermont	62	61	61	54	58	12.0	10.9	10.3	9.3	9.9
Virginia.	647	705	648	858	589	12.4	11.1	10.2	12.7	8.8
Washington.	538	434	677	529	512	12.7	8.9	12.5	9.2	8.9
West Virginia.	297	328	300	286	312	15.2	18.1	16.7	16.4	17.8
Wisconsin.	403	448	449	422	449	8.5	9.3	8.5	8.2	8.8
Wyoming	49	51	59	66	51	10.4	11.0	12.2	13.5	10.6

[1] Beginning 1990, data based on revised processing procedures and not directly comparable with prior years.

Source: U.S. Census Bureau, Current Population Reports, P60-207, and <http://www.census.gov/hhes/poverty/histpov/hstpov21.html> (accessed 17 May 2000).

Income, Expenditures, and Wealth   477

Figure 14.1
Percent of Persons Below Poverty Level: 1980 to 1998

Percent

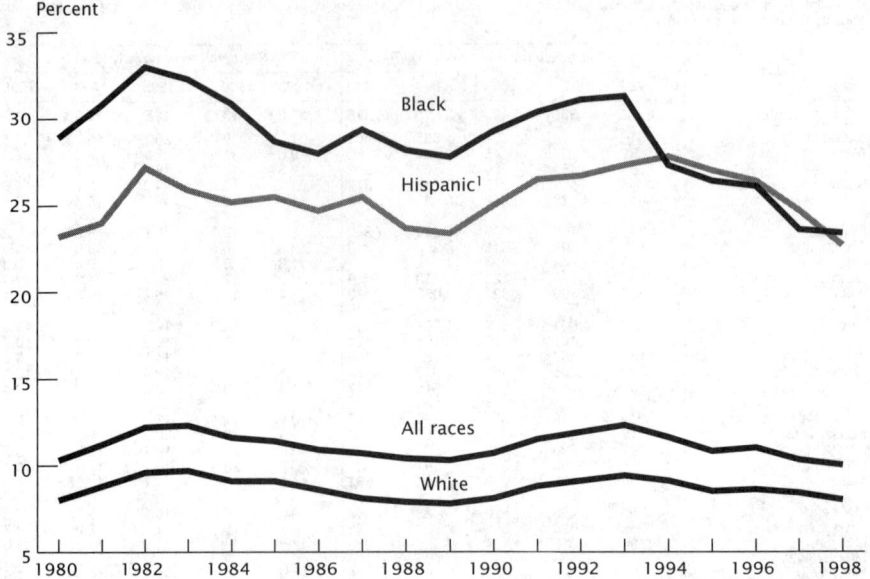

¹ Persons of Hispanic origin may be of any race.
Source: Chart prepared by U.S. Census Bureau. For data, see Table 760.

No. 760. Families Below Poverty Level and Below 125 Percent of Poverty Level: 1970 to 1998

[Families as of **March of the following year.** Based on Current Population Survey, see text, Sections 1 and 14, and Appendix III]

Year	Number below poverty level (1,000)				Percent below poverty level				Below 125 percent of poverty level	
	All races [1]	White	Black	His-panic [2]	All races [1]	White	Black	His-panic [2]	Number (1,000)	Percent
1970	5,260	3,708	1,481	(NA)	10.1	8.0	29.5	(NA)	7,516	14.4
1975	5,450	3,838	1,513	627	9.7	7.7	27.1	25.1	7,974	14.2
1976	5,311	3,560	1,617	598	9.4	7.1	27.9	23.1	7,647	13.5
1977	5,311	3,540	1,637	591	9.3	7.0	28.2	21.4	7,713	13.5
1978	5,280	3,523	1,622	559	9.1	6.9	27.5	20.4	7,417	12.8
1979 [3]	5,461	3,581	1,722	614	9.2	6.9	27.8	20.3	7,784	13.1
1980	6,217	4,195	1,826	751	10.3	8.0	28.9	23.2	8,764	14.5
1981	6,851	4,670	1,972	792	11.2	8.8	30.8	24.0	9,568	15.7
1982	7,512	5,118	2,158	916	12.2	9.6	33.0	27.2	10,279	16.7
1983 [4]	7,647	5,220	2,161	981	12.3	9.7	32.3	25.9	10,358	16.7
1984	7,277	4,925	2,094	991	11.6	9.1	30.9	25.2	9,901	15.8
1985	7,223	4,983	1,983	1,074	11.4	9.1	28.7	25.5	9,753	15.3
1986	7,023	4,811	1,987	1,085	10.9	8.6	28.0	24.7	9,476	14.7
1987 [5]	7,005	4,567	2,117	1,168	10.7	8.1	29.4	25.5	9,338	14.3
1988	6,874	4,471	2,089	1,141	10.4	7.9	28.2	23.7	9,284	14.1
1989	6,784	4,409	2,077	1,133	10.3	7.8	27.8	23.4	9,267	14.0
1990	7,098	4,622	2,193	1,244	10.7	8.1	29.3	25.0	9,564	14.4
1991	7,712	5,022	2,343	1,372	11.5	8.8	30.4	26.5	10,244	15.3
1992 [6]	8,144	5,255	2,484	1,529	11.9	9.1	31.1	26.7	10,959	16.1
1993	8,393	5,452	2,499	1,625	12.3	9.4	31.3	27.3	11,203	16.4
1994	8,053	5,312	2,212	1,724	11.6	9.1	27.3	27.8	10,771	15.5
1995	7,532	4,994	2,127	1,695	10.8	8.5	26.4	27.0	10,223	14.7
1996	7,708	5,059	2,206	1,748	11.0	8.6	26.1	26.4	10,476	14.9
1997	7,324	4,990	1,985	1,721	10.3	8.4	23.6	24.7	10,032	14.2
1998	7,186	4,829	1,981	1,648	10.0	8.0	23.4	22.7	9,714	13.6

NA Not available. [1] Includes other races not shown separately. [2] Persons of Hispanic origin may be of any race. [3] Population controls based on 1980 census; see text, this section. [4] Beginning 1983, data based on revised Hispanic population controls and not directly comparable with prior years. [5] Beginning 1987, data based on revised processing procedures and not directly comparable with prior years. [6] Beginning 1992, based on 1990 population controls.

Source: U.S. Bureau of the Census, *Current Population Reports*, P60-207.

478 Income, Expenditures, and Wealth

No. 761. Families Below Poverty Level by Selected Characteristics: 1998

[See headnote, Table 760]

Characteristic	Number below poverty level (1,000)				Percent below poverty level			
	All races [1]	White	Black	His-panic [2]	All races [1]	White	Black	His-panic [2]
Total	7,186	4,829	1,981	1,648	10.0	8.0	23.4	22.7
Age of householder:								
15 to 24 years old	963	609	305	213	31.1	25.3	54.7	34.1
25 to 34 years old	2,073	1,360	609	550	15.7	12.9	29.9	27.4
35 to 44 years old	1,909	1,278	548	494	10.1	8.2	23.6	23.2
45 to 54 years old	833	573	190	187	5.5	4.5	11.6	15.7
55 to 64 years old	615	453	127	94	6.4	5.4	14.1	13.6
65 years old and over	734	513	188	93	6.4	5.0	19.6	15.8
Education of householder: [3]								
No high school diploma	2,469	1,716	628	909	23.1	20.1	35.8	31.5
High school diploma, no college	2,146	1,427	640	312	9.9	7.8	23.7	18.1
Some college, less than bachelor's degree	1,189	784	322	146	6.6	5.2	14.1	11.4
Bachelor's degree or more	360	252	73	52	2.0	1.6	6.5	7.1
Work experience of householder:								
Total [4]	6,447	4,312	1,792	1,554	10.7	8.7	23.9	23.3
Worked during year	3,853	2,643	1,028	981	7.4	6.1	16.9	17.7
Year-round, full-time	1,426	1,016	341	445	3.6	3.0	7.7	11.0
Not year-round, full-time	2,427	1,627	688	535	20.1	16.6	40.7	35.5
Did not work	2,594	1,669	764	573	31.4	25.7	54.8	50.9

[1] Includes other races not shown separately.   [2] Hispanic persons may be of any race.   [3] Householder 25 years old and over.   [4] Persons 16-64 years old.

Source: U.S. Census Bureau, *Current Population Reports*, P60-207; and unpublished data.

No. 762. Monthly Measures of Poverty Status by Selected Characteristics: 1993-94 Period

[**Covers 2-year calendar period.** Based on Survey of Income and Program Participation, see text, Section 14]

Characteristic	Persons poor in an average month of 1994		Persons poor 2 or more months of 1994		Persons poor all 24 months of 1993-94		Median duration of poverty spells (months)
	Number (1,000)	Percent	Number (1,000)	Percent	Number (1,000)	Percent	
Total [1]	40,009	15.4	54,800	21.4	13,105	5.3	4.5
Under 18 years old	17,169	24.5	22,529	32.4	6,489	9.4	5.3
18 to 64 years old	19,652	12.3	28,317	18.1	5,156	3.4	4.0
65 years old and over	3,188	10.2	3,954	13.5	1,459	5.4	6.7
White	27,543	12.7	38,861	18.3	7,793	3.8	4.2
Black	10,304	31.2	13,059	40.2	4,461	14.1	6.8
Hispanic origin [2]	8,555	31.4	10,940	41.8	3,262	13.5	5.0
Region: [3]							
Northeast	7,303	14.1	9,892	19.3	2,822	5.5	4.4
Midwest	8,740	13.2	12,069	18.4	2,571	4.0	3.9
South	14,701	16.8	20,044	23.3	5,085	6.1	5.6
West	9,265	16.8	12,795	24.3	2,628	5.2	4.4
Educational attainment: [4]							
Less than 4 years of high school	9,507	24.8	12,221	33.0	3,736	10.5	6.4
High school graduate, no college	8,263	11.6	11,973	17.3	2,120	3.1	4.0
One or more years of college	5,071	6.3	8,077	10.1	759	1.0	3.7
Disability status: [5]							
With a work disability	7,059	21.6	8,991	29.8	2,519	8.6	5.8
With no work disability	15,539	10.5	23,445	15.9	3,444	2.4	4.0

[1] Includes other characteristics not shown separately.   [2] Persons of Hispanic origin may be of any race.   [3] For composition of regions, see map, inside front cover.   [4] Persons 18 years old and over.   [5] Persons 15 to 69 years old.

Source: U.S. Census Bureau, unpublished data from the Survey of Income and Program Participation.

Income, Expenditures, and Wealth   479

No. 763. Nonfinancial Assets Held by Families by Type of Asset: 1998

[Median value in thousands of dollars. Constant dollar figures are based on consumer price index for all urban consumers published by U.S. Bureau of Labor Statistics. Families include one-person units and, as used in this table, are comparable to the U.S. Census Bureau household concept. For definition of family, see text, Section 1, Population. Based on Survey of Consumer Finance; see Appendix III. For data on financial assets, see Table 792. For definition of median, see Guide to Tabular Presentation]

Age of family head, and family income	Total	Vehicles	Primary residence	Other residential property	Equity in nonresidential property	Business equity	Other	Any nonfinancial asset
PERCENT OF FAMILIES OWNING ASSET								
All families, total	96.8	82.8	66.2	12.8	8.6	11.5	8.5	89.9
Age of family head:								
Under 35 years old	94.8	78.3	38.9	3.5	2.7	7.2	7.3	83.3
35 to 44 years old.	97.6	85.8	67.1	12.2	7.5	14.7	8.8	92.0
45 to 54 years old.	96.7	87.5	74.4	16.2	12.2	16.2	9.2	92.9
55 to 64 years old.	98.2	88.7	80.3	20.4	10.4	14.3	8.5	93.8
65 to 74 years old.	98.5	83.4	81.5	18.4	15.3	10.1	10.3	92.0
75 years old and over	96.4	69.8	77.0	13.6	8.1	2.7	7.0	87.2
Family income:								
Less than $10,000	83.8	51.3	34.5	(B)	(B)	3.8	2.6	62.7
$10,000 to $24,999	96.4	78.0	51.7	5.8	5.0	5.0	5.6	85.9
$25,000 to $49,999	99.2	89.6	68.2	11.4	7.6	10.3	9.4	95.6
$50,000 to $99,999	100.0	93.6	85.0	19.0	12.0	15.0	10.2	98.0
$100,000 and more	100.0	88.7	93.3	37.3	22.6	34.7	17.1	98.9
Current work status of householder:								
Working for someone else	98.2	87.6	63.5	10.6	6.7	5.5	8.8	92.4
Self-employed	99.2	89.5	81.3	25.3	17.7	63.4	13.3	98.1
Retired	94.7	73.3	72.4	14.3	10.1	3.6	6.4	85.2
Other not working	85.7	58.5	35.8	4.5	(B)	3.7	(B)	66.3
Tenure:								
Owner occupied	100.0	90.6	100.0	16.8	11.3	14.5	9.5	100.0
Renter occupied or other	90.7	67.6	(X)	5.1	3.3	5.4	6.4	70.1
MEDIAN VALUE [1]								
All families, total	123.5	10.8	100.0	65.0	38.0	60.0	10.0	97.8
Age of family head:								
Under 35 years old	28.9	8.9	84.0	42.5	25.0	34.0	5.0	22.7
35 to 44 years old.	128.0	11.4	101.0	45.0	20.0	62.5	8.0	103.5
45 to 54 years old.	178.9	12.8	120.0	74.0	45.0	100.0	14.0	126.8
55 to 64 years old.	198.2	13.5	110.0	70.0	54.0	62.5	28.0	126.9
65 to 74 years old.	165.2	10.8	95.0	75.0	45.0	61.1	10.0	109.9
75 years old and over	135.0	7.0	85.0	103.0	54.0	40.0	10.0	96.1
Family income:								
Less than $10,000	11.7	4.0	51.0	(B)	(B)	37.5	5.0	16.3
$10,000 to $24,999	46.2	5.7	71.9	70.0	25.0	31.1	5.0	43.7
$25,000 to $49,999	112.0	10.2	85.0	50.0	28.0	37.5	6.0	83.5
$50,000 to $99,999	233.2	16.6	130.0	60.0	30.0	56.0	12.0	156.3
$100,000 and more	665.6	26.8	240.0	132.0	114.1	230.0	36.0	380.0
Current work status of householder:								
Working for someone else	112.4	11.2	98.0	50.0	24.0	30.0	7.0	89.6
Self-employed	329.3	15.5	150.0	85.0	80.0	100.0	50.0	256.6
Retired	134.5	8.6	89.0	100.0	50.0	50.0	10.0	97.8
Other not working	18.0	7.2	90.0	64.6	(B)	39.0	(B)	28.5
Tenure:								
Owner occupied	193.3	13.2	100.0	65.0	45.0	75.0	13.0	130.6
Renter occupied or other	11.6	6.2	(X)	64.6	15.0	31.0	5.0	7.2

B Base too small to meet statistical standards for reliability of derived figure.   X Not applicable.   [1] Median value of financial asset for families holding such assets.

Source: Board of Governors of the Federal Reserve System, *Federal Reserve Bulletin*, January 2000, and unpublished revisions.

No. 764. Family Net Worth—Mean and Median Net Worth in Constant (1998) Dollars by Selected Family Characteristics: 1992 to 1998

[Net worth in thousands of constant (1998) dollars (212.7 represents $212,700). Constant dollar figures are based on consumer price index for all urban consumers published by U.S. Bureau of Labor Statistics. Families include one-person units and as used in this table are comparable to the Census Bureau household concept. Based on Survey of Consumer Finance; see Appendix III. For definition of median, see Guide to Tabular Presentation]

Family characteristic	1992 Percent of families	1992 Net worth Mean	1992 Net worth Median	1995 Percent of families	1995 Net worth Mean	1995 Net worth Median	1998 Percent of families	1998 Net worth Mean	1998 Net worth Median
All families	100.0	212.7	56.5	100.0	224.8	60.9	100.0	282.5	71.6
Age of family head:									
Under 35 years old.	25.8	53.1	10.4	24.8	47.4	12.7	23.3	65.9	9.0
35 to 44 years old	22.8	152.7	50.9	23.0	152.8	54.9	23.3	196.2	63.4
45 to 54 years old	16.2	304.4	89.3	17.9	313.0	100.8	19.2	362.7	105.5
55 to 64 years old	13.2	384.9	130.2	12.5	404.7	122.4	12.8	530.2	127.5
65 to 74 years old	12.6	326.1	112.3	12.0	369.3	117.9	11.2	465.5	146.5
75 years old and over.	9.4	244.4	99.2	9.8	273.8	98.8	10.2	310.2	125.6
Family income in constant (1998) dollars:[1]									
Less than $10,000	14.8	32.1	2.9	15.1	46.6	4.8	12.6	40.0	3.6
$10,000 to $24,999	27.0	69.8	27.1	25.4	80.3	31.0	24.8	85.6	24.8
$25,000 to $49,999	29.8	131.4	55.6	31.0	124.0	56.7	28.8	135.4	60.3
$50,000 to $99,999	20.7	245.6	129.9	21.0	258.1	126.6	25.2	275.5	152.0
$100,000 and more	7.6	1,300.8	481.9	7.4	1,411.9	511.4	8.6	1,727.8	510.8
Education of householder:									
No high school diploma.	20.4	80.2	21.3	18.5	89.6	24.0	16.5	79.1	20.9
High school diploma.	30.0	127.7	43.9	31.7	141.3	54.7	31.9	157.8	53.8
Some college	17.8	195.8	65.9	19.0	201.2	49.7	18.5	237.8	73.9
College degree	31.9	387.0	112.1	30.7	407.2	110.9	33.2	528.2	146.4
Current work status of householder:									
Working for someone else. . . .	54.8	139.6	44.7	58.3	145.2	51.9	59.2	168.9	52.4
Self-employed	10.9	682.3	164.7	10.3	742.0	165.5	11.3	919.8	248.1
Retired.	26.0	214.0	80.7	25.0	239.4	86.2	24.4	307.2	113.0
Other not working	8.3	72.2	4.5	6.5	62.9	3.9	5.1	76.5	3.6
Region:									
Northeast	20.2	240.0	73.2	19.8	266.9	88.0	19.3	302.4	94.2
Midwest	24.4	198.0	65.0	23.9	210.0	69.2	23.6	248.8	80.3
South	34.6	160.4	39.4	35.1	197.6	46.6	35.7	267.5	61.3
West	20.9	290.2	81.4	21.2	247.1	58.1	21.3	327.1	61.3
Tenure:									
Owner occupied	63.9	307.4	112.8	64.7	321.3	110.5	66.2	403.5	132.1
Renter occupied or other. . . .	36.1	45.1	3.7	35.3	47.9	5.2	33.8	45.1	4.2

[1] Income for year preceding the survey.

Source: Board of Governors of the Federal Reserve System, *Federal Reserve Bulletin*, January 2000, and unpublished data.

Figure 14.2
Family Net Worth: 1998

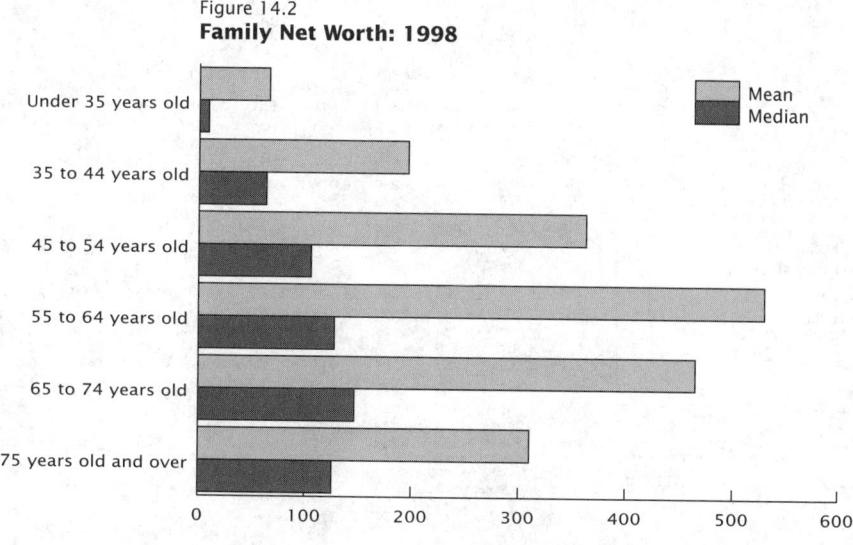

Source: Chart prepared by U.S. Census Bureau. For data, see Table 764.

Income, Expenditures, and Wealth 481

No. 765. Household and Nonprofit Organization Sector Balance Sheet: 1980 to 1999

[In billions of dollars ($10,932 represents $10,932,000,000,000). As of **December 31**. For details of financial assets and liabilities, see Table 800]

Item	1980	1985	1990	1993	1994	1995	1996	1997	1998	1999
Assets	**10,932**	**16,640**	**24,290**	**28,429**	**29,477**	**32,610**	**35,483**	**39,697**	**43,509**	**48,889**
Tangible assets [1]	4,368	6,540	9,327	9,975	10,308	10,777	11,300	12,069	12,926	13,941
Real estate	3,422	5,235	7,405	7,805	8,018	8,398	8,833	9,517	10,238	11,088
Consumer durable goods	921	1,269	1,869	2,103	2,218	2,305	2,389	2,470	2,604	2,763
Financial assets [1]	6,563	10,100	14,963	18,454	19,169	21,834	24,184	27,628	30,583	34,948
Deposits	1,517	2,484	3,265	3,183	3,157	3,366	3,540	3,807	4,165	4,338
Checkable deposits and currency.	251	342	409	593	564	505	446	445	461	442
Time and savings deposits .	1,203	1,941	2,477	2,236	2,224	2,388	2,553	2,725	2,924	3,013
Money market fund shares .	62	193	365	338	351	449	505	595	738	838
Credit market instruments [1]	425	849	1,503	1,637	1,930	1,885	1,994	1,873	1,781	1,960
U.S. government securities. . .	165	270	529	591	913	822	896	721	552	659
Treasury	160	251	462	585	782	700	688	511	391	347
Savings bonds.	73	80	126	172	180	185	187	187	187	186
Corporate equities	875	1,058	1,807	3,242	3,071	4,122	4,642	5,690	6,339	8,009
Mutual fund shares.	46	198	468	991	1,052	1,265	1,586	2,057	2,501	3,104
Pension fund reserves	971	2,087	3,462	4,675	4,948	5,768	6,642	7,894	9,079	10,360
Equity in noncorporate business .	2,154	2,607	3,230	3,184	3,405	3,640	3,833	4,172	4,395	4,630
Liabilities	**1,426**	**2,326**	**3,679**	**4,290**	**4,613**	**4,982**	**5,333**	**5,708**	**6,206**	**6,841**
Credit market instruments	1,374	2,236	3,554	4,108	4,427	4,783	5,108	5,438	5,910	6,467
Home mortgages	905	1,408	2,461	2,893	3,070	3,252	3,464	3,698	4,058	4,480
Consumer credit.	355	604	805	859	984	1,123	1,212	1,264	1,332	1,429
Net worth	**9,506**	**14,313**	**20,612**	**24,139**	**24,864**	**27,628**	**30,151**	**33,989**	**37,303**	**42,048**

[1] Includes types of assets and/or liabilities not shown separately.

Source: Board of Governors of the Federal Reserve System, *Balance Sheets for the U.S. Economy*.

No. 766. Net Stock of Fixed Reproducible Tangible Wealth in Current and Real (1996) Dollars: 1980 to 1998

[In billions of dollars ($10,297 represents $10,297,000,000,000). As of December 31]

Item	1980	1990	1991	1992	1993	1994	1995	1996	1997	1998
CURRENT DOLLARS										
Net stock	**10,297**	**18,225**	**18,649**	**19,411**	**20,418**	**21,637**	**22,630**	**23,707**	**24,826**	**26,179**
Private	7,213	12,760	13,022	13,583	14,318	15,204	15,909	16,723	17,573	18,643
Nonresidential equipment	1,420	2,542	2,623	2,708	2,829	2,992	3,183	3,352	3,518	3,736
Information processing and related equipment.	225	663	687	720	760	803	850	906	969	1,045
Industrial equipment.	525	893	917	937	964	1,011	1,075	1,119	1,158	1,203
Transportation equipment. . . .	306	472	497	522	557	604	651	690	721	781
Other equipment	319	513	522	530	547	575	607	637	669	707
Nonresidential structures.	2,256	4,081	4,138	4,279	4,499	4,739	4,941	5,175	5,437	5,714
Nonresidential buildings, excluding farm	1,169	2,514	2,576	2,676	2,817	2,992	3,125	3,286	3,489	3,722
Utilities	695	1,005	1,021	1,051	1,109	1,148	1,190	1,229	1,262	1,271
Residential	3,537	6,138	6,261	6,596	6,991	7,472	7,784	8,195	8,619	9,193
Housing units.	2,898	4,963	5,047	5,315	5,653	6,059	6,302	6,625	6,960	7,451
Government.	2,151	3,612	3,732	3,895	4,086	4,322	4,533	4,725	4,928	5,118
Equipment.	300	559	590	619	645	672	686	692	692	696
Structures.	1,952	3,053	3,142	3,276	3,441	3,651	3,847	4,033	4,236	4,422
Federal	653	1,087	1,130	1,176	1,229	1,279	1,314	1,343	1,364	1,380
Defense	483	743	773	807	842	874	885	891	890	888
State and local	1,498	2,525	2,603	2,719	2,857	3,043	3,219	3,382	3,565	3,737
Consumer durable goods	934	1,853	1,895	1,934	2,014	2,111	2,189	2,259	2,325	2,419
Motor vehicles.	257	574	567	574	599	629	647	663	669	699
Furniture and household equipment.	459	861	887	908	946	987	1,024	1,059	1,095	1,135
Other.	203	417	441	452	470	495	519	537	560	585
CHAINED (1996) DOLLARS										
Net stock	**14,269**	**20,657**	**20,996**	**21,361**	**21,808**	**22,303**	**22,840**	**23,457**	**24,112**	**24,884**
Private	9,950	14,562	14,790	15,033	15,345	15,694	16,075	16,521	17,005	17,570
Nonresidential equipment	1,855	2,723	2,770	2,826	2,915	3,036	3,183	3,354	3,550	3,799
Nonresidential structures.	3,177	4,704	4,775	4,828	4,887	4,939	5,008	5,094	5,194	5,304
Residential	4,921	7,142	7,251	7,384	7,547	7,720	7,884	8,074	8,263	8,478
Government.	3,127	4,192	4,284	4,371	4,445	4,512	4,585	4,668	4,743	4,822
Federal	969	1,291	1,308	1,322	1,327	1,326	1,326	1,334	1,329	1,327
State and local	2,156	2,901	2,976	3,049	3,117	3,185	3,259	3,334	3,415	3,495
Consumer durable goods	1,198	1,906	1,927	1,962	2,021	2,099	2,180	2,268	2,365	2,498

Source: U.S. Bureau of Economic Analysis, *Fixed Assets and Consumer Durable Goods in the United States, 1925-97* (forthcoming in early 2001); and *Survey of Current Business*, April 2000.

Section 15
Prices

This section presents indexes of producer and consumer prices, actual prices for selected commodities, and energy prices. The primary sources of these data are monthly publications of the Department of Labor, Bureau of Labor Statistics (BLS), which include *Monthly Labor Review, Consumer Price Index, Detailed Report, Producer Price Indexes*, and *U.S. Import and Export Price Indexes*. The Department of Commerce, Bureau of Economic Analysis is the source for gross domestic product measures.

Producer price index (PPI)—This index, dating from 1890, is the oldest continuous statistical series published by BLS. It is designed to measure average changes in prices received by producers of all commodities, at all stages of processing, produced in the United States.

The index has undergone several revisions (see *Monthly Labor Review*, February 1962, April 1978, and August 1988). It is now based on approximately 10,000 individual products and groups of products along with about 100,000 quotations per month. Indexes for the net output of manufacturing and mining industries have been added in recent years. Prices used in constructing the index are collected from sellers and generally apply to the first significant large-volume commercial transaction for each commodity—i.e., the manufacturer's or other producer's selling price or the selling price on an organized exchange or at a central market.

The weights used in the index represent the total net selling value of commodities produced or processed in this country. Values are f.o.b. (free-on-board) production point and are exclusive of excise taxes. Effective with the release of data for January 1988, many important producer price indexes were changed to a new reference base year, 1982=100, from 1967=100. The

reference year of the PPI shipment weights has been taken primarily from the 1987 Census of Manufactures. For further detail regarding the PPI, see the BLS *Handbook of Methods*, Bulletin 2490 (April 1997), Chapter 16. The PPI web page is <http://stats.bls.gov/ppihome.htm>.

Consumer price indexes (CPI)—The CPI is a measure of the average change in prices over time in a "market basket" of goods and services purchased either by urban wage earners and clerical workers or by all urban consumers. In 1919, BLS began to publish complete indexes at semiannual intervals, using a weighting structure based on data collected in the expenditure survey of wage-earner and clerical-worker families in 1917-19 (BLS Bulletin 357, 1924). The first major revision of the CPI occurred in 1940, with subsequent revisions in 1953, 1964, 1978, 1987, and 1998.

Beginning with the release of data for January 1988 in February 1988, most Consumer Price Indexes shifted to a new reference base year. All indexes previously expressed on a base of 1967=100, or any other base through December 1981, have been rebased to 1982-84=100. The expenditure weights are based upon data tabulated from the Consumer Expenditure Surveys for 1993, 1994, and 1995.

BLS publishes CPIs for two population groups: (1) a CPI for all urban consumers (CPI-U) which covers approximately 80 percent of the total population; and (2) a CPI for urban wage earners and clerical workers (CPI-W) which covers 32 percent of the total population. The CPI-U includes, in addition to wage earners and clerical workers, groups which historically have been excluded from CPI coverage, such as professional, managerial, and technical workers; the self-employed; short-term workers;

U.S. Census Bureau, Statistical Abstract of the United States: 2000

the unemployed; and retirees and others not in the labor force.

The current CPI is based on prices of food, clothing, shelter, fuels, transportation fares, charges for doctors' and dentists' services, drugs, etc. purchased for day-to-day living. Prices are collected in 87 areas across the country from over 50,000 housing units and 23,000 establishments. Area selection was based on the 1990 census. All taxes directly associated with the purchase and use of items are included in the index. Prices of food, fuels, and a few other items are obtained every month in all 87 locations. Prices of most other commodities and services are collected monthly in the three largest geographic areas and every other month in other areas.

In calculating the index, each item is assigned a weight to account for its relative importance in consumers' budgets. Price changes for the various items in each location are then averaged. Local data are then combined to obtain a U.S. city average. Separate indexes are also published for regions, area size-classes, cross-classifications of regions and size-classes, and for 26 local areas, usually consisting of the Metropolitan Statistical Area (MSA); see Appendix II. Area definitions are those established by the Office of Management and Budget in 1983. Definitions do not include revisions made since 1992. Area indexes do not measure differences in the level of prices among cities; they only measure the average change in prices for each area since the base period. For further detail regarding the CPI, see the BLS *Handbook of Methods*, Bulletin 2490, Chapter 17; the *Consumer Price Index*, and the CPI home page: <http://stats.bls.gov/cpihome.htm>. In January 1983, the method of measuring home-ownership costs in the CPI-U was changed to a rental equivalence approach. This treatment calculates homeowner costs of shelter based on the implicit rent owners would pay to rent the homes they own. The rental equivalence approach was introduced into the CPI-W in 1985. The CPI-U was used to prepare the consumer price tables in this section.

Other price indexes—Chain-weighted price indexes, produced by the Bureau of Economic Analysis (BEA), are weighted averages of the detailed price indexes used in the deflation of the goods and services that make up the gross domestic product (GDP) and its major components. Growth rates are constructed for years and quarters using quantity weights for the current and preceding year or quarter; these growth rates are used to move the index for the preceding period forward a year or quarter at a time. The gross domestic purchases chained price index measures the average price of goods and services purchased in the United States. It differs from the GDP chained price index, which measures of the average price of goods produced in the United States, by excluding net exports. All chain-weighted price indexes are expressed in terms of the reference year value 1996=100.

Measures of inflation—Inflation is defined as a time of generally rising prices for goods and factors of production. The Bureau of Labor Statistics samples prices of items in a representative market basket and publishes the result as the CPI. The media invariably announce the inflation rate as the percent change in the CPI from month to month. A much more meaningful indicator of inflation is the percent change from the same month of the prior year. The Producer Price Index measures prices at the producer level only. The PPI shows the same general pattern of inflation as does the CPI but is more volatile. The PPI can be roughly viewed as a leading indicator. It often tends to foreshadow trends that later occur in the CPI.

Other measures of inflation include the gross domestic purchases chain-weighted price index, the index of industrial materials prices; the Dow Jones Commodity Spot Price Index; Futures Price Index; the Employment Cost Index, the Hourly Compensation Index, or the Unit Labor Cost Index as a measure of the change in cost of the labor factor-of production; and changes in long-term interest rates that are often used to measure changes in the cost of the capital factor of production.

International price indexes—The BLS International Price Program produces export and import price indexes for nonmilitary goods traded between the United States and the rest of the world.

The export price index provides a measure of price change for all products sold by U.S. residents to foreign buyers. The import price index provides a measure of price change for goods purchased from other countries by U.S. residents. The reference period for the indexes is 1995=100, unless otherwise indicated. The product universe for both the import and export indexes includes raw materials, agricultural products, semifinished manufactures, and finished manufactures, including both capital and consumer goods. Price data for these items are collected primarily by mail questionnaire. In nearly all cases, the data are collected directly from the exporter or importer, although in a few cases, prices are obtained from other sources.

To the extent possible, the data gathered refer to prices at the U.S. border for exports and at either the foreign border or the U.S. border for imports. For nearly all products, the prices refer to transactions completed during the first week of the month. Survey respondents are asked to indicate all discounts, allowances, and rebates applicable to the reported prices, so that the price used in the calculation of the indexes is the actual price for which the product was bought or sold.

In addition to general indexes for U.S. exports and imports, indexes are also published for detailed product categories of exports and imports. These categories are defined according to the five-digit level of detail for the Bureau of Economic Analysis End-use Classification, the three-digit level of detail for the Standard International Trade Classification (SITC), and the four-digit level of detail for the Harmonized System. Aggregate import indexes by country or region of origin are also available.

No. 767. Purchasing Power of the Dollar: 1950 to 1999

[Indexes: PPI, 1982=$1.00; CPI, 1982-84=$1.00. Producer prices prior to 1961 and consumer prices prior to 1964, exclude Alaska and Hawaii. Producer prices based on finished goods index. Obtained by dividing the average price index for the 1982=100, PPI; 1982-84=100, CPI base periods (100.0) by the price index for a given period and expressing the result in dollars and cents. Annual figures are based on average of monthly data]

Year	Annual average as measured by—		Year	Annual average as measured by—		Year	Annual average as measured by—	
	Producer prices	Consumer prices		Producer prices	Consumer prices		Producer prices	Consumer prices
1950	$3,546	$4,151	1967	2.809	2.993	1984	0.964	0.961
1951	3.247	3.846	1968	2.732	2.873	1985	0.955	0.928
1952	3.268	3.765	1969	2.632	2.726	1986	0.969	0.913
1953	3.300	3.735	1970	2.545	2.574	1987	0.949	0.880
1954	3.289	3.717				1988	0.926	0.846
			1971	2.469	2.466	1989	0.880	0.807
1955	3.279	3.732	1972	2.392	2.391	1990	0.839	0.766
1956	3.195	3.678	1973	2.193	2.251	1991	0.822	0.734
1957	3.077	3.549	1974	1.901	2.029	1992	0.812	0.713
1958	3.012	3.457	1975	1.718	1.859	1993	0.802	0.692
1959	3.021	3.427	1976	1.645	1.757	1994	0.797	0.675
1960	2.994	3.373				1995	0.782	0.656
			1977	1.546	1.649	1996	0.762	0.638
1961	2.994	3.340	1978	1.433	1.532	1997	0.759	0.623
1962	2.985	3.304	1979	1.289	1.380	1998	0.766	0.614
1963	2.994	3.265	1980	1.136	1.215	1999	0.752	0.600
1964	2.985	3.220	1981	1.041	1.098			
1965	2.933	3.166	1982	1.000	1.035			
1966	2.841	3.080	1983	0.984	1.003			

Source: U.S. Bureau of Labor Statistics. Monthly data in U.S. Bureau of Economic Analysis, *Survey of Current Business.*

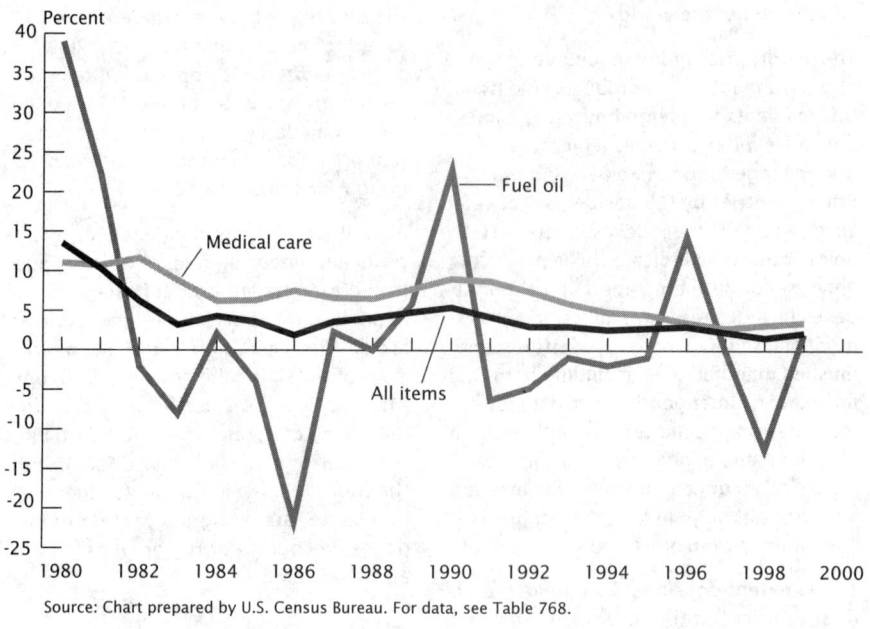

Figure 15.1
**Annual Percent Change in Consumer
Price Indexes: 1980 to 1999**

Percent

Medical care

Fuel oil

All items

Source: Chart prepared by U.S. Census Bureau. For data, see Table 768.

Figure 15.2
**Annual Percent Change in Producer Price Indexes
by Stage of Processing: 1980 to 1999**

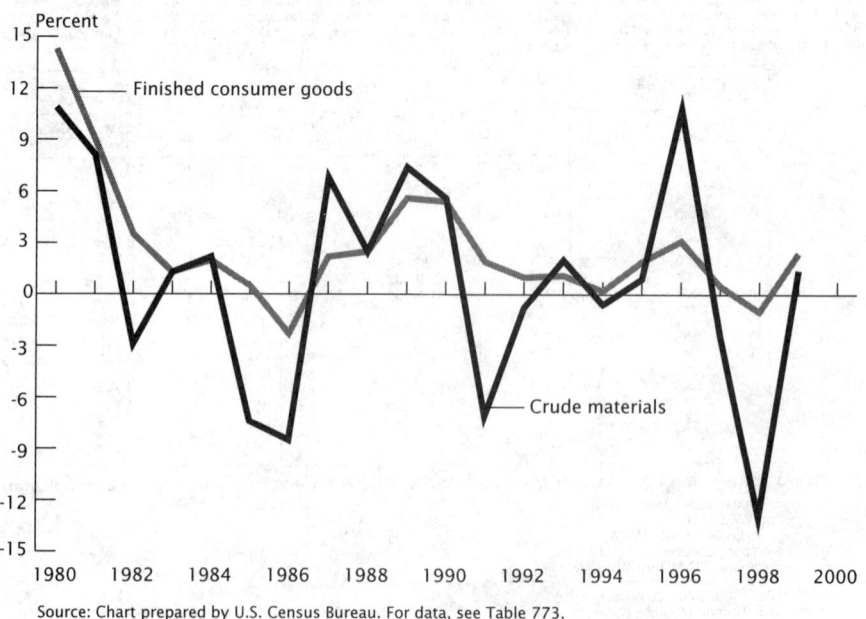

Percent

Finished consumer goods

Crude materials

Source: Chart prepared by U.S. Census Bureau. For data, see Table 773.

486 Prices

No. 768. Consumer Price Indexes (CPI-U) by Major Groups: 1980 to 1999

[1982-84=100. Represents annual averages of monthly figures. Reflects buying patterns of all urban consumers. Minus sign (-) indicates decrease. See text, this section]

Year	All items	Com-modi-ties	Energy	Food	Shelter	Apparel and upkeep	Trans-porta-tion	Medi-cal care	Fuel oil	Elec-tricity	Utility (piped) gas	Tele-phone services
1980	82.4	86.0	86.0	86.8	81.0	90.9	83.1	74.9	87.7	75.8	65.7	77.7
1985	107.6	105.4	101.6	105.6	109.8	105.0	106.4	113.5	94.6	108.9	104.8	111.7
1986	109.6	104.4	88.2	109.0	115.8	105.9	102.3	122.0	74.1	110.4	99.7	117.2
1987	113.6	107.7	88.6	113.5	121.3	110.6	105.4	130.1	75.8	110.0	95.1	116.5
1988	118.3	111.5	89.3	118.2	127.1	115.4	108.7	138.6	75.8	111.5	94.5	116.0
1989	124.0	116.7	94.3	125.1	132.8	118.6	114.1	149.3	80.3	114.7	97.1	117.2
1990	130.7	122.8	102.1	132.4	140.0	124.1	120.5	162.8	98.6	117.4	97.3	117.7
1991	136.2	126.6	102.5	136.3	146.3	128.7	123.8	177.0	92.4	121.8	98.5	119.7
1992	140.3	129.1	103.0	137.9	151.2	131.9	126.5	190.1	88.0	124.2	100.3	120.4
1993	144.5	131.5	104.2	140.9	155.7	133.7	130.4	201.4	87.2	126.7	106.5	121.2
1994	148.2	133.8	104.6	144.3	160.5	133.4	134.3	211.0	85.6	126.7	108.5	123.1
1995	152.4	136.4	105.2	148.4	165.7	132.0	139.1	220.5	84.8	129.6	102.9	124.0
1996	156.9	139.9	110.1	153.3	171.0	131.7	143.0	228.2	97.0	131.8	107.2	125.9
1997	160.5	141.8	111.5	157.3	176.3	132.9	144.3	234.6	96.9	132.5	114.6	127.7
1998	163.0	141.9	102.9	160.7	182.1	133.0	141.6	242.1	84.8	127.4	112.4	100.7
1999	166.6	144.4	106.6	164.1	187.3	131.3	144.4	250.6	86.6	126.5	113.0	100.1
PERCENT CHANGE [1]												
1980	13.5	12.3	30.9	8.6	17.6	7.1	17.9	11.0	39.0	15.5	19.2	2.5
1985	3.6	2.1	0.7	2.3	5.6	2.8	2.6	6.3	-4.0	3.4	-0.7	3.9
1986	1.9	-0.9	-13.2	3.2	5.5	0.9	-3.9	7.5	-21.7	1.4	-4.9	4.9
1987	3.6	3.2	0.5	4.1	4.7	4.4	3.0	6.6	2.3	-0.4	-4.6	-0.6
1988	4.1	3.5	0.8	4.1	4.8	4.3	3.1	6.5	-	1.4	-0.6	-0.4
1989	4.8	4.7	5.6	5.8	4.5	2.8	5.0	7.7	5.9	2.9	2.8	1.0
1990	5.4	5.2	8.3	5.8	5.4	4.6	5.6	9.0	22.8	2.4	0.2	0.4
1991	4.2	3.1	0.4	2.9	4.5	3.7	2.7	8.7	-6.3	3.7	1.2	1.7
1992	3.0	2.0	0.5	1.2	3.3	2.5	2.2	7.4	-4.8	2.0	1.8	0.6
1993	3.0	1.9	1.2	2.2	3.0	1.4	3.1	5.9	-0.9	2.0	6.2	0.7
1994	2.6	1.7	0.4	2.4	3.1	-0.2	3.0	4.8	-1.9	0.0	1.9	1.6
1995	2.8	1.9	0.6	2.8	3.2	-1.0	3.6	4.5	-0.9	2.3	-5.2	0.7
1996	3.0	2.6	4.7	3.3	3.2	-0.2	2.8	3.5	14.4	1.7	4.2	1.5
1997	2.3	1.4	1.3	2.6	3.1	0.9	0.9	2.8	-0.1	0.5	6.9	1.4
1998	1.6	0.1	-7.7	2.2	3.3	0.1	-1.9	3.2	-12.5	-3.8	-1.9	-
1999	2.2	1.8	3.6	2.1	2.9	-1.3	2.0	3.5	2.1	-0.7	0.5	-0.6

- Represents zero.   [1] Change from prior year.
Source: Bureau of Labor Statistics, Monthly Labor Review and Handbook of Labor Statistics, periodic.

No. 769. Consumer Price Indexes (CPI-U) by Selected Area: 1999

[1982-84=100, except as indicated. Represents annual averages of monthly figures. Local area CPI indexes are byproducts of the national CPI program. Each local index has a smaller sample size than the national index and is therefore, subject to substantially more sampling and other measurement error. As a result, local area indexes show greater volatility than the national index, although their long-term trends are similar. Area definitions are those established by the Office of Management and Budget in 1983. For further detail see the U.S. Bureau of Labor Statistics Handbook of Methods, Bulletin 2285, Chapter 19, the Consumer Price Index, and Report 736, the CPI: 1987 Revision. See text, this section]

Area	All items	Food and bever-ages	Food	Housing	Apparel and upkeep	Trans-porta-tion	Medical care	Fuel and other utilities
U.S. city average	166.6	164.6	164.1	163.9	131.3	144.4	250.6	128.8
Anchorage, AK MSA	148.4	148.4	148.7	132.7	125.8	143.7	260.8	144.6
Atlanta, GA MSA	164.8	167.6	172.1	165.1	132.4	130.3	254.0	143.1
Boston, MA MSA	176.0	170.6	171.0	170.3	143.6	142.3	330.2	117.4
Chicago-Gary, IL-IN CMSA	168.4	168.4	167.7	168.0	117.2	140.5	253.6	117.4
Cincinnati-Hamilton, OH-KY-IN CMSA	159.2	152.0	150.4	153.1	130.1	140.9	233.0	126.3
Cleveland-Akron-Lorain, OH CMSA	162.5	169.5	171.4	160.2	124.1	143.6	224.9	127.8
Dallas-Fort Worth, TX CMSA	158.0	165.1	162.7	146.8	140.7	141.0	233.2	127.8
Denver-Boulder-Greely, CO CMSA	166.6	157.0	159.2	161.9	94.0	169.5	289.4	129.2
Detroit-Ann Arbor-Flint, MI CMSA	163.9	158.3	157.6	156.3	133.4	152.1	245.2	127.8
Honolulu, HI MSA	173.3	162.9	163.0	175.8	105.4	162.2	231.3	133.4
Houston-Galveston-Brazoria, TX CMSA	148.7	152.8	152.1	132.1	139.9	135.7	238.5	106.1
Kansas City, MO-KS CMSA	160.1	161.0	162.1	154.6	121.6	139.2	229.1	134.3
Los Angeles-Anaheim-Riverside, CA CMSA	166.1	169.9	168.0	164.5	118.2	146.8	244.5	145.4
Miami-Fort Lauderdale, FL CMSA	162.4	171.0	171.3	155.2	138.2	148.8	231.3	115.8
Milwaukee, WI PMSA	163.7	163.7	164.6	162.6	116.8	142.5	251.5	112.4
Minneapolis-St. Paul, MN-WI MSA	163.3	172.1	168.7	149.2	139.3	148.6	241.1	123.5
New York-Northern New Jersey-Long Island, NY-NJ-CT CMSA	177.0	170.5	169.6	179.6	125.5	152.3	265.3	116.1
Philadelphia-Wilmington-Trenton, PA-NJ-DE-MD CMSA	171.9	159.4	158.6	172.5	107.5	152.2	264.8	130.4
Pittsburgh, PA MSA	162.5	156.0	154.7	162.2	144.5	131.9	244.4	142.5
Portland, OR MSA	172.6	157.3	157.7	174.5	134.8	152.1	229.8	139.5
San Diego, CA MSA	172.8	166.5	164.5	178.2	131.6	152.1	247.2	120.8
San Francisco-Oakland-San Jose, CA CMSA	172.5	170.8	171.5	185.6	114.2	135.8	232.6	145.3
Seattle-Tacoma, WA CMSA	172.8	169.6	170.0	177.3	125.5	149.9	240.3	123.6
St. Louis-East St. Louis, MO-IL CMSA	157.6	161.9	160.2	149.0	123.5	141.7	245.7	122.5
Tampa-St. Petersburg-Clearwater, FL MSA [1]	140.6	137.7	136.8	135.3	148.2	126.3	191.9	120.1
Washington-Baltimore, DC-MD-VA-WV CMSA [2]	104.2	103.1	103.1	105.5	[2]98.3	[2]100.3	106.9	108.1

[1] 1987=100.   [2] 1997=100; except "Apparel and upkeep" and "Transportation," 1996=100.
Source: U.S. Bureau of Labor Statistics, Monthly Labor Review and CPI Detailed Report, January issues.

Prices   487

No. 770. Consumer Price Indexes for All Urban Consumers (CPI-U) for Selected Items and Groups: 1980 to 1999

[1982-84 = 100. Annual averages of monthly figures. See headnote, Table 768]

Item	1980	1990	1993	1994	1995	1996	1997	1998	1999
All items	**82.4**	**130.7**	**144.5**	**148.2**	**152.4**	**156.9**	**160.5**	**163.0**	**166.6**
Food and beverages	86.7	132.1	141.6	144.9	148.9	153.7	157.7	161.1	164.6
Food	86.8	132.4	140.9	144.3	148.4	153.3	157.3	160.7	164.1
Food at home	88.4	132.3	140.1	144.1	148.8	154.3	158.1	161.1	164.2
Cereals and bakery products	83.9	140.0	156.6	163.0	167.5	174.0	177.6	181.1	185.0
Cereals and cereal products	84.2	141.1	157.9	164.8	167.1	168.9	169.5	171.5	175.0
Cereals	76.3	158.6	183.3	190.6	192.5	190.0	187.5	189.9	195.2
Rice, pasta, and cornmeal	90.9	122.0	129.7	139.7	140.2	144.2	148.8	150.5	151.9
Bakery products	83.8	139.2	155.7	161.9	167.4	176.1	181.1	185.4	189.4
White bread	85.9	136.4	152.2	159.0	165.5	177.5	183.8	187.3	192.5
Cookies, cakes, and cupcakes	81.5	142.7	159.3	165.1	169.1	174.1	179.2	181.2	185.0
Meats, poultry, fish and eggs	92.0	130.0	135.5	137.2	138.8	144.8	148.5	147.3	147.9
Meats	92.7	128.5	134.6	135.4	135.5	140.2	144.4	141.6	142.3
Beef and veal	98.4	128.8	137.1	136.0	134.9	134.5	136.8	136.5	139.2
Ground beef excl. canned	104.6	118.1	121.7	119.7	116.1	114.3	116.4	116.1	118.4
Chuck roast	99.8	130.3	141.9	140.3	138.7	140.0	142.3	(NA)	(NA)
Round steak	98.9	125.1	134.4	133.0	130.4	129.3	130.1	(NA)	(NA)
Sirloin steak	96.2	130.6	138.5	137.5	138.7	137.6	139.0	(NA)	(NA)
Pork	81.9	129.8	131.7	133.9	134.8	148.2	155.9	148.5	145.9
Bacon	73.5	113.4	110.8	118.1	120.0	148.9	164.0	152.0	151.5
Chops	82.9	140.2	144.6	144.2	144.2	153.0	155.2	146.8	143.5
Ham	85.5	132.4	137.9	139.3	139.6	149.2	156.3	150.0	147.0
Poultry	93.7	132.5	136.9	141.5	143.5	152.4	156.6	157.1	157.9
Fresh whole chicken	94.4	134.9	138.0	140.1	142.2	152.6	158.5	159.6	161.8
Fresh, frozen chicken parts	91.7	135.9	140.1	145.6	146.0	155.0	157.4	157.2	156.8
Fish and seafood	87.5	146.7	156.6	163.7	171.6	173.1	177.1	181.7	185.3
Canned fish and seafood	93.7	119.5	121.5	123.8	125.5	125.9	128.4	132.6	131.5
Fresh, frozen fish, seafood	84.1	161.4	174.5	183.6	194.1	196.0	200.7	(NA)	(NA)
Eggs	88.6	124.1	117.1	114.3	120.5	142.1	140.0	135.4	128.1
Dairy products	90.9	126.5	129.4	131.7	132.8	142.1	145.5	150.8	159.6
Fruits and vegetables	82.1	149.0	159.0	165.0	177.7	183.9	187.5	198.2	203.1
Fresh fruits and vegetables	81.8	(NA)	(NA)	186.7	206.0	211.8	215.4	231.2	237.2
Fresh fruits	84.8	170.9	188.8	201.2	219.0	234.4	236.3	246.5	266.3
Apples	92.1	147.5	169.0	174.0	183.5	202.3	199.6	202.3	200.1
Bananas	91.5	138.2	135.5	143.6	153.8	159.0	159.6	160.9	159.4
Oranges, tangerines	72.6	160.6	190.1	189.9	224.5	239.3	226.1	251.5	337.0
Fresh vegetables	79.0	151.1	168.7	172.3	193.1	189.2	194.6	215.8	209.3
Potatoes	81.0	162.6	154.6	174.3	174.7	180.6	174.2	185.2	193.1
Lettuce	77.8	150.3	178.2	170.3	221.2	185.7	200.1	229.1	208.3
Tomatoes	81.9	160.8	168.0	173.5	188.3	198.2	213.6	239.2	224.1
Processed fruits and vegetables	82.6	(NA)	(NA)	134.5	137.5	144.4	147.9	(NA)	(NA)
Processed fruits	82.1	136.9	132.3	133.1	137.2	145.2	148.8	(NA)	(NA)
Processed vegetables	83.1	127.5	130.8	136.6	138.3	143.9	147.2	(NA)	(NA)
Coffee	111.6	117.5	109.8	140.4	163.1	149.2	168.0	163.4	154.8
Food away from home	83.4	(NA)	(NA)	145.7	149.0	152.7	157.0	161.1	165.1
Lunch	83.8	133.9	144.0	146.4	149.6	153.3	157.7	(NA)	(NA)
Dinner	84.2	132.3	141.3	143.8	147.1	150.7	154.7	(NA)	(NA)
Alcoholic beverages	86.4	129.3	149.6	151.5	153.9	158.5	162.8	165.7	169.7
Alcoholic beverages at home	87.3	123.0	142.2	142.5	143.1	146.8	149.5	150.6	153.7
Beer and ale	84.8	123.6	143.2	143.4	143.9	147.4	148.2	148.5	151.9
Distilled spirits	89.8	125.7	143.2	144.3	145.7	147.5	150.8	152.7	156.2
Wine	89.5	114.4	134.0	133.3	134.6	138.6	139.3	145.5	147.3	149.4
Alcoholic beverages away from home	82.9	144.4	167.4	171.6	176.5	182.7	189.4	195.0	201.0
Housing	81.1	128.5	141.2	144.8	148.5	152.8	156.8	160.4	163.9
Shelter	81.0	140.0	155.7	160.5	165.7	171.0	176.3	182.1	187.3
Renters' cost	(NA)	146.7	165.0	169.4	174.3	180.2	186.4	(NA)	(NA)
Rent, residential	80.9	138.4	150.3	154.0	157.8	162.0	166.7	(NA)	(NA)
Tenants' insurance	78.9	130.6	140.8	145.8	150.9	154.7	159.2	(NA)	(NA)
Homeowners' costs	(NA)	144.6	160.2	165.5	171.0	176.5	181.5	(NA)	(NA)
Owners' equivalent rent	(NA)	144.8	160.5	165.8	171.3	176.8	181.9	187.8	192.9
Household insurance	(NA)	135.3	146.9	152.3	157.4	161.0	165.3	(NA)	(NA)
Maintenance and repair	82.4	122.2	130.6	130.8	135.0	139.0	143.7	(NA)	(NA)
Fuels and other utilities	75.4	111.6	121.3	122.8	123.7	127.5	130.8	128.5	128.8
Fuels	74.8	104.5	111.2	111.7	111.5	115.2	117.9	113.7	113.5
Fuel oil and other	86.1	99.3	90.3	88.8	88.1	99.2	99.8	90.0	91.4
Fuel oil	87.7	98.6	87.2	85.6	84.8	97.0	96.9	84.8	86.6
Gas (piped) and electricity	71.4	109.3	118.5	119.2	119.2	122.1	125.1	121.2	120.9
Electricity	75.8	117.4	126.7	126.7	129.6	131.8	132.5	127.4	126.5
Utility (piped) gas	65.7	97.3	106.5	108.5	102.9	107.2	114.6	112.4	113.0
Telephone services	77.7	117.7	121.2	123.1	124.0	125.9	127.7	(NA)	(NA)
Local charges	72.8	149.3	156.4	156.9	160.4	160.8	163.1	165.7	168.7
Interstate toll charges	83.3	68.2	69.6	75.2	74.9	77.9	77.3	75.5	73.4
Intrastate toll charges	85.2	95.1	90.7	90.2	86.0	89.4	93.9	95.7	94.7
Water and sewerage maintenance	74.0	150.2	181.4	190.6	196.5	204.5	210.0	217.3	222.0
Cable television	(NA)	158.4	198.9	197.4	200.7	212.6	228.7	245.2	254.6
Refuse collection	(NA)	171.2	220.5	231.4	241.2	246.0	250.5	256.7	263.8

See footnotes at end of table.

U.S. Census Bureau, Statistical Abstract of the United States: 2000

No. 770. Consumer Price Indexes for All Urban Consumers (CPI-U) for Selected Items and Groups: 1980 to 1999—Continued

[1982-84=100. Annual averages of monthly figures. See headnote, Table 768]

Item	1980	1990	1993	1994	1995	1996	1997	1998	1999
Household furnishings and operations	86.3	113.3	119.3	121.0	123.0	124.7	125.4	126.6	126.7
Housefurnishings	88.5	106.7	109.5	111.0	111.2	111.3	110.6	(NA)	(NA)
Furniture and bedding	88.0	115.7	123.5	128.2	130.9	134.1	134.5	135.0	134.9
Bedroom furniture	83.5	118.5	132.5	135.1	136.4	139.3	141.5	141.3	141.0
Sofas	(NA)	118.4	120.1	125.2	132.8	141.5	142.0	(NA)	(NA)
Living room chairs and tables	(NA)	116.7	125.0	132.7	136.6	136.9	136.7	(NA)	(NA)
Appliances and electronic equip.	93.5	87.8	83.4	82.3	80.0	77.8	75.3	(NA)	(NA)
Video and audio equipment	100.7	80.8	77.1	76.0	73.9	71.3	99.4	101.1	100.7
Television	104.6	74.6	70.7	69.9	68.1	64.5	61.7	59.2	54.9
Video products other than TV	(NA)	91.5	78.5	73.8	70.3	66.3	63.4	(NA)	(NA)
Audio products	97.7	93.2	93.9	93.8	92.1	90.7	88.9	85.2	81.7
Housekeeping supplies	83.2	125.2	130.7	132.3	137.1	141.1	143.1	145.7	148.1
Housekeeping services	84.3	120.1	135.8	138.5	143.7	148.0	151.9	(NA)	(NA)
Postage	76.2	125.1	145.3	145.3	160.3	160.3	160.3	160.3	165.1
Apparel and upkeep	90.9	124.1	133.7	133.4	132.0	131.7	132.9	133.0	131.3
Apparel commodities	92.9	122.0	131.0	130.4	128.7	128.2	129.1	(NA)	(NA)
Apparel commodities less footwear	93.0	122.8	131.9	131.2	129.3	128.5	129.4	129.3	127.8
Men's and boy's apparel	89.4	120.4	127.5	126.4	126.2	127.7	130.1	131.8	131.1
Women's and girl's apparel	96.0	122.6	132.6	130.9	126.9	124.7	126.1	126.0	123.3
Infants' and toddlers'	85.5	125.8	127.1	128.1	127.2	129.7	129.0	126.1	129.0
Footwear	91.8	117.4	125.9	126.0	125.4	126.6	127.6	128.0	125.7
Transportation	83.1	120.5	130.4	134.3	139.1	143.0	144.3	141.6	144.4
Private transportation	84.2	118.8	127.5	131.4	136.3	140.0	141.0	137.9	140.5
New vehicles	88.5	121.4	132.7	137.6	141.0	143.7	144.3	143.4	142.9
New cars	88.4	121.0	131.5	136.0	139.0	141.4	141.7	140.7	139.6
New trucks	(NA)	121.6	135.7	141.7	145.9	149.5	151.4	151.1	152.0
Used cars	62.3	117.6	133.9	141.7	156.5	157.0	151.1	150.6	152.0
Motor fuel	97.4	101.2	98.0	98.5	100.0	106.3	106.2	92.2	100.7
Automobile maintenance and repair	81.5	130.1	145.9	150.2	154.0	158.4	162.7	167.1	171.9
Automobile insurance	82.0	177.9	216.7	224.8	234.3	243.9	251.6	254.3	253.8
Automobile finance charges	86.4	99.6	78.6	83.8	99.0	94.4	93.6	(NA)	(NA)
Vehicle rental, registration, other	78.3	148.1	169.8	174.2	177.9	181.1	185.4	102.5	103.8
Public transportation	69.0	142.6	167.0	172.0	175.9	181.9	186.7	190.3	197.7
Airline fares	68.0	148.4	178.7	185.5	189.7	192.5	199.2	205.3	218.8
Other intercity transportation	73.1	143.3	150.9	152.8	153.3	156.0	155.1	160.4	160.6
Intracity transportation	69.7	133.5	150.7	152.7	157.5	173.2	175.8	174.2	172.4
Medical care	74.9	162.8	201.4	211.0	220.5	228.2	234.6	242.1	250.6
Medical care commodities	75.4	163.4	195.0	200.7	204.5	210.4	215.3	221.8	230.7
Prescription drugs	72.5	181.7	223.0	230.6	235.0	242.9	249.3	258.6	273.4
Nonprescription drugs, medical sup.	(NA)	120.6	135.5	138.1	140.5	143.1	145.4	147.7	176.7
Medical care services	74.8	162.7	202.9	213.4	224.2	232.4	239.1	246.8	255.1
Professional medical services	77.9	156.1	184.7	192.5	201.0	208.3	215.4	222.2	229.2
Physicians' services	76.5	160.8	191.3	199.8	208.8	216.4	222.9	229.5	236.0
Dental services	78.9	155.8	188.1	197.1	206.8	216.5	226.6	236.2	247.2
Eye care	(NA)	117.3	130.4	133.0	137.0	139.3	141.5	144.1	145.5
Hospital and related services	69.2	178.0	231.9	245.6	257.8	269.5	278.4	287.5	299.5
Hospital rooms	68.0	175.4	226.4	239.2	251.2	261.0	(NA)	(NA)	(NA)
Entertainment	83.6	132.4	145.8	150.1	153.9	159.1	162.5	(NA)	(NA)
Entertainment commodities	84.5	124.0	133.4	136.1	138.7	143.0	144.2	(NA)	(NA)
Reading materials	77.7	136.2	156.2	161.3	168.1	176.4	179.0	184.1	186.1
Newspapers	79.4	134.6	161.1	168.2	178.7	188.9	191.3	(NA)	(NA)
Magazines, periodicals, and books	75.9	137.9	151.8	155.1	158.4	165.0	167.8	(NA)	(NA)
Sporting goods, equipment	88.5	114.9	120.1	122.2	123.5	123.4	122.6	121.9	120.3
Sport vehicles, including bicycles	87.9	116.3	120.6	122.3	125.3	125.7	124.5	125.3	128.7
Toys, hobbies; other entertainment	86.5	121.5	126.0	127.4	127.8	131.9	133.3	(NA)	(NA)
Pet supplies and expenses	83.3	124.6	128.8	130.9	132.3	139.0	142.7	143.5	144.5
Entertainment services	82.3	143.2	160.8	166.8	172.0	178.1	183.8	(NA)	(NA)
Club membership	(NA)	117.0	128.4	130.7	132.8	133.3	132.1	(NA)	(NA)
Admissions	83.8	151.2	167.3	175.2	182.3	192.1	198.9	205.5	216.5
Tobacco and smoking products	72.0	181.5	228.4	220.0	225.7	232.8	243.7	274.8	355.8
Personal care	81.9	130.4	141.5	144.6	147.1	150.1	152.7	156.7	161.1
Personal care services	83.7	132.8	144.0	147.3	147.9	151.5	156.6	162.4	171.4
Beauty parlor services for women	83.4	133.0	143.6	147.7	150.9	155.9	161.4	(NA)	(NA)
Haircuts, etc. for men	84.4	131.5	144.6	147.9	153.4	158.5	165.5	(NA)	(NA)
Personal and educational expenses	70.9	170.2	210.7	223.2	235.5	247.5	259.7	(NA)	(NA)
School books and supplies	71.4	171.3	197.6	205.5	214.4	226.9	238.4	250.8	261.7
Personal and educational services	70.8	170.4	211.9	224.8	237.3	249.3	261.6	(NA)	(NA)
Tuition and other school fees	71.2	175.7	225.3	239.8	253.8	267.1	280.4	294.2	308.4
College tuition	70.8	175.0	233.5	249.8	264.8	279.8	294.1	306.5	318.7
Elementary and high school tuition	72.3	182.8	228.9	242.6	259.2	272.8	288.1	307.9	327.3
Day care and nursery school	(NA)	(NA)	113.6	119.6	124.5	129.4	134.3	140.9	148.1
All commodities	86.0	122.8	131.5	133.8	136.4	139.9	141.8	141.9	144.4
All commodities less food	85.7	117.4	126.3	127.9	129.8	132.6	133.4	132.0	134.0
Energy	86.0	102.1	104.2	104.6	105.2	110.1	111.5	102.9	106.6

NA Not available.

Source: U.S. Bureau of Labor Statistics, *Monthly Labor Review* and *CPI Detailed Report*, January issues.

Prices   489

No. 771. Cost of Living Index—Selected Metropolitan Areas: Fourth Quarter 1999

[Measures relative price levels for consumer goods and services in participating areas for a mid-management standard of living. The nationwide average equals 100, and each index is read as a percent of the national average. The index does not measure inflation but compares prices at a single point in time. Excludes taxes. Metropolitan areas as defined by the Office of Management and Budget. For definitions and components of MSAs, see source for details]

Metropolitan area (MA)	Composite index (100%)	Grocery items (16%)	Housing (28%)	Utilities (8%)	Transportation (10%)	Health care (5%)	Misc. goods and services (33%)
Birmingham, AL MSA	97.7	96.4	96.2	103.8	97.3	91.6	99.1
Decatur, AL MSA	95.1	96.5	90.1	92.0	100.3	91.6	98.3
Dothan, AL MSA	92.0	95.8	81.4	95.4	93.4	87.0	98.7
Florence, AL MSA	93.7	97.3	87.3	94.4	92.0	89.4	98.5
Gadsden, AL MSA	92.1	97.5	74.2	107.6	90.4	89.4	101.8
Huntsville, AL MSA	96.0	96.1	86.5	88.5	102.5	97.0	103.7
Mobile, AL MSA	93.4	97.5	86.2	103.0	96.5	83.3	95.9
Montgomery, AL MSA	96.7	92.0	93.8	103.1	103.1	90.7	98.9
Tuscaloosa, AL MSA	102.1	99.1	101.6	99.0	101.6	98.7	105.4
Anchorage, AK MSA	122.9	124.3	137.1	87.6	102.7	162.8	118.7
Nonmetropolitan areas:							
Fairbanks, AK	123.4	113.9	124.6	162.4	113.0	164.1	114.5
Juneau, AK	130.3	127.2	132.8	148.5	127.6	153.4	122.6
Kodiak, AK	136.2	139.3	137.2	168.6	111.1	156.3	130.5
Flagstaff, AZ-UT MSA	108.3	107.7	122.6	92.6	107.4	119.4	99.0
Las Vegas, NV-AZ MSA:							
Lake Havasu City, AZ	98.3	110.6	86.1	112.6	98.8	104.9	98.1
Phoenix-Mesa, AZ MSA:							
Phoenix, AZ	102.4	101.7	100.9	102.4	108.7	115.7	100.0
Tucson, AZ MSA	96.8	102.3	91.9	131.9	84.1	97.4	93.5
Yuma, AZ	101.2	101.6	92.9	145.3	100.9	103.0	97.2
Fayetteville-Springdale-Rogers, AR MSA	89.8	88.9	85.3	88.4	93.7	87.6	93.6
Fort Smith, AR-OK MSA	88.9	84.8	79.0	92.3	89.7	92.1	97.6
Jonesboro, AR MSA	89.4	93.5	85.0	94.5	83.9	84.2	92.4
Little Rock-North Little Rock, AR MSA	98.2	107.8	88.7	115.7	104.9	99.8	95.1
Fresno, CA MSA	107.6	116.0	97.4	134.2	113.2	111.2	103.4
Los Angeles-Long Beach, CA PMSA	123.0	115.8	152.1	116.8	109.8	113.5	108.6
Modesto, CA MSA	109.5	113.3	112.5	106.1	108.7	135.2	102.3
Riverside-San Bernardino, CA PMSA:							
Riverside City, CA	113.0	109.1	118.0	120.5	109.4	123.8	108.2
Sacramento, CA PMSA	109.0	121.3	96.2	113.3	116.8	141.5	105.5
San Diego, CA MSA	126.7	126.2	161.3	101.2	128.0	120.2	104.5
Visalia-Tulare-Porterville, CA MSA	105.6	108.8	93.9	117.1	106.2	112.8	109.9
Colorado Springs, CO MSA	102.7	103.3	117.7	82.2	101.3	117.1	93.0
Denver, CO PMSA	110.3	108.9	126.8	84.7	111.4	119.8	101.5
Fort Collins-Loveland, CO MSA:							
Fort Collins, CO	103.4	111.5	112.0	79.0	103.5	114.6	96.4
Grand Junction, CO MSA	99.9	102.9	104.2	84.8	106.9	105.3	95.6
Pueblo, CO MSA	91.7	110.2	79.6	83.5	92.1	102.9	93.2
Hartford, CT MSA	118.8	113.4	128.7	142.6	113.0	136.5	106.4
New Haven-Meriden, CT PMSA	125.0	113.9	147.6	167.6	104.7	122.0	107.4
Dover, DE MSA	102.7	107.9	97.4	126.8	99.5	85.8	102.3
Wilmington-Newark, DE-MD PMSA	109.7	112.8	115.6	132.9	99.5	94.7	102.8
Washington DC-MD-VA-WV PMSA	131.6	101.3	181.2	94.5	129.8	118.3	115.9
Daytona Beach, FL MSA	94.0	101.7	83.9	112.4	93.0	95.4	94.6
Fort Walton Beach FL, MSA	97.7	107.2	85.0	93.9	98.9	93.7	105.1
Jacksonville, FL MSA	95.7	101.4	89.5	96.5	103.7	87.7	96.9
Orlando, FL MSA	98.9	103.4	98.9	98.9	97.8	112.0	95.2
Panama City, FL MSA	98.7	101.4	91.5	101.6	103.0	99.1	101.4
Pensacola, FL MSA	96.9	106.1	85.2	94.3	100.0	96.1	102.2
Sarasota-Bradenton, FL MSA:							
Sarasota, FL	104.3	101.4	112.0	92.7	100.1	97.6	104.3
Tallahassee, FL MSA	109.7	107.7	113.0	120.9	103.8	99.0	108.5
Tampa-St. Petersburg-Clearwater, FL MSA	99.4	101.7	101.1	112.4	100.9	89.5	94.7
West Palm Beach-Boca Raton, FL MSA	107.8	106.9	111.9	113.5	110.0	103.7	103.2
Albany, GA MSA	90.3	97.6	75.4	107.2	92.9	85.4	95.3
Atlanta, GA MSA:							
Atlanta, GA	104.3	103.7	109.2	106.5	101.5	108.5	100.1
Augusta-Aiken, GA-SC MSA	94.5	105.7	82.3	96.2	95.9	94.5	98.5
Macon, GA MSA	98.0	106.1	87.7	104.8	88.6	94.9	104.6
Boise City, ID MSA	96.7	97.2	93.9	83.5	105.2	107.4	97.8
Pocatello, ID	98.6	106.0	87.0	79.6	108.4	98.1	106.5
Bloomington-Normal, IL MSA	107.2	105.2	114.0	102.9	103.5	97.7	105.9
Champaign-Urbana, IL MSA	104.7	97.0	113.6	98.8	101.6	98.4	104.1
Chicago, IL PMSA:							
Homewood, IL	117.9	108.1	129.6	110.7	127.3	124.2	110.8
Joliet/Will County, IL	108.2	110.5	110.0	114.4	112.0	110.9	102.6
Davenport-Moline-Rock Island, IA-IL MSA	97.7	100.7	91.8	98.9	101.3	95.8	100.3
Decatur, IL MSA	100.5	103.0	105.0	103.0	96.4	84.4	98.5
Rockford, IL MSA	99.0	99.7	95.6	100.2	101.2	102.3	100.0
Springfield, IL MSA	93.2	99.7	93.1	82.4	93.3	94.7	92.4
Bloomington, IN MSA	101.8	108.8	96.3	100.5	99.5	108.8	102.9
Elkhart-Goshen, IN MSA	97.5	96.0	99.8	100.5	96.7	93.0	96.4
Evansville-Henderson, IN-KY MSA	94.8	88.6	104.7	85.2	93.5	87.1	93.2
Indianapolis, IN MSA:							
Indianapolis/Marion County, IN	96.6	99.0	95.2	96.8	93.8	93.6	97.9
Lafayette, IN MSA	98.4	97.3	101.7	106.5	98.2	97.3	94.4

See footnote at end of table.

U.S. Census Bureau, Statistical Abstract of the United States: 2000

[See headnote, page 490]

Metropolitan area	Com- posite index (100%)	Grocery items (16%)	Housing (28%)	Utilities (8%)	Trans- por- tation (10%)	Health care (5%)	Misc. goods and services (33%)
Muncie, IN MSA	97.5	95.3	100.1	100.8	99.2	92.4	95.7
South Bend, IN MSA	92.0	91.1	90.0	91.4	91.4	100.6	93.3
Terre Haute, IN MSA	97.0	95.7	93.2	106.8	95.3	91.9	99.7
Cedar Rapids, IA MSA	97.2	87.5	95.9	118.5	98.3	93.2	98.1
Des Moines, IA MSA	95.4	91.8	87.8	103.3	97.5	100.3	100.3
Iowa City, IA MSA	97.8	97.9	90.4	103.4	104.5	96.0	100.9
Waterloo-Cedar Falls, IA MSA	97.9	97.4	100.9	95.0	97.3	89.5	97.7
Lawrence, KS MSA	99.5	96.1	105.3	87.1	97.0	87.9	101.8
Wichita, KS MSA	97.7	96.8	91.7	106.2	98.5	105.9	99.8
Cincinnati, OH-KY-IN PMSA:							
Covington, KY	93.3	98.3	87.1	94.5	92.3	95.6	95.9
Clarksville-Hopkinsville, TN-KY MSA:							
Hopkinsville, KY	94.6	95.0	85.9	101.0	90.7	87.8	102.6
Evansville-Henderson, IN-KY MSA	90.1	101.2	80.1	85.3	88.5	89.9	95.0
Lexington, KY MSA	96.9	103.1	95.2	88.6	88.7	99.4	99.6
Louisville, KY-IN MSA	97.5	99.0	93.1	95.5	109.8	88.5	98.5
Alexandria, LA MSA	94.3	89.4	92.2	100.5	98.1	85.0	97.3
Baton Rouge, LA MSA	102.9	109.1	97.7	127.3	109.4	95.9	97.4
Lafayette, LA MSA	97.5	96.7	103.5	88.6	101.9	90.3	94.7
Lake Charles, LA MSA	94.1	89.2	90.6	108.8	99.5	89.2	95.0
Monroe, LA MSA	96.7	89.1	88.2	114.0	101.1	89.5	103.1
New Orleans, LA MSA	102.4	102.1	96.5	143.1	108.3	99.0	96.4
Shreveport-Bossier City, LA MSA	93.0	83.7	96.1	96.7	92.5	96.5	93.6
Baltimore, MD PMSA	96.0	94.0	92.6	105.6	98.7	94.0	96.9
Cumberland, MD-WV MSA	98.9	96.5	104.4	110.0	90.7	93.0	96.1
Boston, MA-NH PMSA:							
Boston PMSA (MA Part)	136.9	114.5	185.9	134.5	120.1	127.0	113.3
Fitchburg-Leominster, MA PMSA	105.6	102.5	114.3	109.3	98.4	112.4	100.1
Springfield, MA MSA	120.3	118.0	129.5	149.9	111.6	119.9	109.2
Grand Rapids-Muskegon-Holland, MI MSA	105.5	102.5	120.8	87.0	112.6	88.4	99.0
Lansing-East Lansing, MI MSA	103.3	100.9	122.8	82.0	93.7	91.5	97.9
Minneapolis-St Paul, MN-WI MSA:							
Minneapolis, MN	106.3	101.1	105.0	101.1	113.7	127.0	105.7
St Cloud, MN MSA	100.1	100.0	97.1	102.4	99.3	100.5	102.2
Hattiesburg, MS MSA	94.3	92.5	91.3	103.8	87.8	88.9	98.3
Jackson, MS MSA	92.0	88.9	95.0	87.6	94.9	81.9	92.7
Columbia, MO MSA	97.5	96.0	94.9	92.8	98.6	96.9	101.2
Joplin, MO MSA	86.7	89.8	76.2	86.1	82.8	97.1	94.0
St Joseph, MO MSA	93.2	87.7	94.6	92.9	87.0	96.3	96.3
St Louis, MO-IL MSA	97.5	100.7	96.2	95.2	95.9	104.7	96.9
Springfield, MO MSA	91.6	91.5	89.8	77.5	93.2	97.5	95.3
Billings, MT MSA	101.7	99.4	100.4	93.7	108.7	104.8	103.3
Great Falls, MT MSA	99.6	101.3	101.0	94.2	95.6	103.1	99.7
Missoula, MT MSA	103.8	110.7	105.9	89.3	100.8	98.4	104.0
Lincoln, NE MSA	104.0	101.3	116.7	86.5	100.3	93.5	101.4
Omaha, NE-IA MSA	94.3	96.1	91.2	97.0	97.4	93.2	94.7
Las Vegas, NV-AZ MSA:							
Las Vegas, NV MSA	106.4	117.1	102.2	87.6	123.2	124.1	101.6
Reno, NV MSA	113.7	111.3	124.5	93.9	117.3	124.6	107.7
Manchester, NH PMSA	112.3	104.8	119.0	148.0	107.5	113.0	103.0
Albuquerque, NM MSA:							
Albuquerque, NM	105.0	102.7	113.8	98.2	101.4	98.2	102.5
Las Cruces, NM MSA	98.9	102.1	108.4	95.9	89.5	97.3	93.1
Santa Fe, NM MSA:							
Santa Fe, NM	113.6	103.5	139.2	94.4	110.8	104.0	103.7
Binghamton, NY MSA	99.1	104.4	89.8	131.2	101.4	90.1	97.2
Buffalo-Niagara Falls, NY MSA	99.8	111.3	88.2	145.4	98.2	89.7	94.9
Glens Falls, NY MSA	101.6	100.9	86.1	153.3	112.6	94.2	100.3
New York, NY PMSA	240.1	148.4	486.3	173.3	120.9	185.1	136.2
Syracuse,NY MSA	100.1	112.7	84.4	130.3	107.9	103.0	97.1
Asheville, NC MSA	103.8	98.8	118.1	105.8	103.3	90.4	95.9
Charlotte-Gastonia-Rock Hill, NC-SC MSA	100.6	98.1	99.8	102.1	99.0	92.7	103.9
Fayetteville, NC MSA	100.8	102.2	94.1	107.1	98.3	109.1	103.8
Greensboro-Winston-Salem-High Point, NC MSA	96.4	94.1	98.8	102.7	92.5	85.8	96.7
Hickory-Morganton-Lenior, NC MSA	97.3	99.1	91.6	100.7	96.2	81.3	103.3
Jacksonville, NC MSA	94.0	98.1	86.1	102.7	88.5	98.3	97.7
Raleigh-Durham-Chapel Hill, NC MSA:							
Raleigh, NC	103.6	104.5	109.6	106.6	96.9	103.8	99.2
Wilmington, NC MSA	102.6	101.6	111.9	101.1	88.9	100.2	100.0
Bismarck, ND MSA	99.3	98.3	101.5	91.3	90.0	94.9	103.4
Fargo-Moorhead, ND-MN MSA	96.7	93.4	97.0	90.6	96.2	104.8	98.4
Akron, OH PMSA	100.3	105.1	91.5	119.3	101.3	101.9	100.3
Cincinnati, OH-KY-IN PMSA:							
Cincinnati, OH	99.3	99.2	97.5	108.6	96.4	93.9	100.2
Cleveland-Lorain-Elyria, OH PMSA	110.3	109.3	116.5	127.1	108.9	117.7	100.9
Dayton-Springfield, OH MSA	98.8	91.4	103.5	101.6	101.8	96.3	97.2
Lima, OH MSA	94.4	100.7	93.3	89.0	93.2	90.2	94.6
Mansfield, OH MSA	96.5	100.7	91.7	125.9	90.5	87.5	94.6
Toledo, OH MSA	101.7	104.7	95.6	125.4	95.2	102.1	101.5
Youngstown-Warren, OH MSA	93.7	98.2	90.9	119.1	85.6	84.5	91.7

See footnote at end of table.

U.S. Census Bureau, Statistical Abstract of the United States: 2000

[See headnote, page 490]

Metropolitan area	Com-posite index (100%)	Grocery items (16%)	Housing (28%)	Utilities (8%)	Trans-por-tation (10%)	Health care (5%)	Misc. goods and services (33%)
Enid, OK MSA	92.3	92.1	79.6	94.1	95.1	87.0	102.7
Lawton, OK MSA	91.2	96.7	75.1	87.2	101.5	94.6	99.5
Oklahoma City, OK MSA	92.8	95.5	77.7	96.5	97.2	96.3	101.4
Tulsa, OK MSA	94.2	102.9	85.2	83.2	89.9	94.6	101.6
Corvallis, OR MSA	110.4	99.3	127.6	89.6	110.7	126.3	103.6
Portland-Vancover, OR-WA PMSA	111.7	102.4	124.6	80.3	114.7	123.7	110.2
Salem, OR PMSA	105.7	100.4	111.0	83.6	102.2	122.2	107.6
Altoona, PA MSA	97.9	101.7	95.8	118.5	88.2	84.6	97.9
Harrisburg-Lebanon-Carlisle, PA MSA	94.7	96.0	83.8	104.2	104.9	94.6	97.8
Lancaster, PA MSA	106.3	95.9	113.4	114.8	106.4	94.0	105.0
Philadelphia, PA-NJ PMSA	116.2	105.1	133.6	130.0	109.2	97.7	108.4
Pittsburgh, PA MSA	117.3	104.6	135.5	134.8	105.7	107.2	108.7
Scranton-Wilkes Barre-Hazelton, PA MSA	94.8	95.3	82.2	114.3	99.2	96.4	99.0
Williamsport, PA MSA	98.9	93.3	99.5	111.3	94.6	88.0	101.1
York, PA MSA	95.4	96.7	82.9	114.9	109.6	91.7	96.9
Charleston-North Charleston, SC MSA	103.0	100.6	111.1	104.2	92.9	103.0	100.1
Columbia, SC MSA	95.2	98.0	91.4	111.8	89.1	94.3	95.1
Myrtle Beach, SC MSA	103.8	102.7	106.5	101.8	94.8	94.9	106.7
Sumter, SC MSA	93.6	99.4	80.1	105.4	93.5	90.8	99.7
Sioux Falls, SD MSA	97.3	95.3	96.6	95.5	99.3	104.0	97.6
Chattanooga, TN-GA MSA	99.3	98.2	99.7	95.4	93.5	91.3	103.4
Clarksville-Hopkinsville, TN-KY MSA: Clarksville, TN.	93.4	95.3	90.5	89.2	98.8	86.7	95.3
Johnson City-Kingsport-Bristol, TN-VA MSA:							
Johnson City, TN	94.3	93.8	101.8	97.3	86.8	85.3	91.2
Kingsport, TN	87.7	93.2	86.1	78.8	87.8	88.7	88.3
Knoxville, TN MSA	94.3	94.7	85.8	94.2	97.7	95.5	100.1
Memphis, TN-AR-MS MSA	92.5	95.6	89.9	84.0	94.7	94.4	94.3
Nashville, TN MSA:							
Nashville-Franklin, TN	95.5	100.0	94.6	87.5	95.1	86.8	97.5
Abilene, TX MSA	94.8	86.8	90.3	95.2	101.7	95.9	100.2
Amarillo, TX MSA	91.3	90.8	90.1	72.2	101.4	87.8	94.7
Austin-San Marcos, TX MSA:							
Austin, TX	105.0	93.2	115.9	103.6	98.0	108.3	103.5
Beaumont-Port Arthur, TX MSA	95.2	89.4	89.4	90.4	96.2	109.8	101.7
Brownsville-Harlingen-San Benito, TX MSA	94.3	95.2	83.3	109.2	100.8	95.5	97.5
Bryan-College Station, TX MSA	86.0	85.7	79.1	80.4	91.9	87.2	91.4
Dallas, TX PMSA	100.3	98.5	96.1	106.5	106.3	104.2	100.7
El Paso, TX MSA	90.5	93.4	77.5	88.0	107.8	99.9	94.1
Fort Worth-Arlington, TX PMSA:							
Arlington, TX	96.9	95.7	87.6	117.5	103.1	97.1	98.4
Houston, TX PMSA:							
Houston, TX PMSA	95.1	92.8	85.6	99.8	106.4	110.8	97.4
Killeen-Temple, TX MSA	92.0	85.2	81.5	111.7	97.7	102.8	96.1
Lubbock, TX MSA	90.4	89.7	86.3	69.8	97.4	102.6	95.2
McAllen-Edinburg-Mission, TX MSA	91.7	85.5	77.6	113.0	94.5	110.7	97.8
Odessa-Midland, TX MSA:							
Odessa, TX	88.3	85.5	75.2	88.1	95.0	93.9	97.9
San Angelo, TX MSA	92.1	90.5	77.1	91.3	100.5	97.1	102.6
San Antonio, TX MSA:							
San Antonio, TX	90.6	90.0	84.2	85.9	88.1	94.4	97.5
Sherman-Denison, TX MSA	93.7	90.2	88.9	99.7	100.5	104.3	94.4
Texarkana, TX-AR MSA	87.2	87.0	75.6	96.7	95.6	95.2	91.2
Tyler, TX MSA	93.2	88.9	83.5	100.1	93.3	95.1	101.6
Victoria, TX MSA	88.6	81.7	84.8	100.0	95.1	85.8	90.8
Waco, TX MSA	91.6	88.8	77.2	110.1	101.7	100.3	96.2
Wichita Falls, TX MSA	90.6	97.1	74.3	93.9	94.3	100.5	97.9
Provo-Orem, UT MSA	96.5	99.0	96.7	77.7	110.6	87.0	96.9
Salt Lake City-Ogden, UT MSA	106.5	106.4	117.6	78.1	105.8	108.8	104.0
Burlington, VT MSA	115.1	106.2	127.7	132.9	100.5	114.0	108.9
Lynchburg, VA	96.6	99.7	97.2	83.3	91.8	96.8	99.2
Norfolk-Virginia Beach-Newport News VA-NC MSA	99.2	96.6	97.2	120.3	109.0	96.3	94.5
Richmond-Petersburg, VA MSA	104.8	96.0	111.1	116.3	101.5	100.2	102.7
Roanoke, VA MSA	92.1	95.6	90.9	77.9	89.1	96.1	95.1
Washington DC-MD-VA-WV PMSA:							
Fredericksburg, VA	108.3	107.1	102.2	115.3	136.2	112.4	103.4
Bellingham, WA MSA	107.8	102.5	118.9	83.8	104.7	122.5	105.6
Bremerton, WA PMSA	105.3	104.1	108.7	95.5	103.1	135.4	101.6
Olympia, WA PMSA	106.4	105.3	115.7	81.7	106.1	131.1	101.5
Richland-Kennewick-Pasco, WA MSA	99.5	98.5	100.8	72.6	103.3	125.6	100.3
Spokane, WA MSA	104.0	104.1	114.2	65.7	100.7	121.7	102.8
Tacoma, WA MSA	104.1	111.1	100.8	70.8	115.2	123.5	105.2
Yakima, WA MSA	107.8	104.8	119.7	77.6	100.1	125.7	106.1
Charleston, WV MSA	98.7	98.9	102.4	91.7	102.4	93.4	96.7
Washington DC-MD-VA-WV MSA	92.4	92.5	85.9	98.4	99.4	88.4	94.9
Appleton-Oshkosh-Neenah, WI MSA	96.9	95.2	106.8	91.0	93.2	94.8	92.2
Eau Claire, WI MSA	100.5	100.4	100.7	119.4	103.3	108.3	93.9
Green Bay, WI MSA	99.9	96.6	103.6	97.5	103.9	100.8	97.7
Sheboygan, WI MSA	100.2	96.6	102.8	96.5	106.3	95.8	99.5
Wausau, WI MSA	98.5	100.2	96.9	90.5	98.7	104.0	100.0
Cheyenne, WY MSA	99.1	101.6	95.1	81.3	101.5	102.4	104.3

Source: ACCRA, 4232 King St., Alexandria, VA 22302-1507, *ACCRA Cost of Living Index*, Fourth Quarter 1999 (copyright).

No. 772. Annual Percent Changes From Prior Year in Consumer Prices— United States and OECD Countries: 1990 to 1998

[Covers member countries of Organization for Economic Cooperation (OECD). For consumer price indexes for OECD countries, see Section 30, Comparative International Statistics]

Country	1990	1992	1993	1994	1995	1996	1997	1998
United States	5.4	3.0	3.0	2.6	2.8	2.9	2.3	1.6
OECD	5.8	5.0	4.2	4.4	5.5	5.1	4.2	(NA)
Australia	7.3	1.0	1.8	1.9	4.6	2.6	0.2	0.8
Canada	4.8	1.5	1.9	0.2	2.2	1.6	1.6	1.0
Japan	3.1	1.7	1.2	0.7	-0.1	0.1	1.7	(NA)
New Zealand.	6.1	1.0	1.3	1.8	3.8	2.3	1.2	1.3
Austria	3.3	4.0	3.6	3.0	2.2	1.5	1.3	0.9
Belgium	3.4	2.4	2.8	2.4	1.5	2.1	1.6	1.0
Denmark.	2.7	2.1	1.3	2.0	2.1	2.1	2.2	1.9
Finland.	6.1	2.9	2.2	1.1	0.8	0.6	1.2	1.4
France	3.4	2.4	2.1	1.7	1.8	2.0	1.2	0.7
Greece.	20.4	15.9	14.4	10.7	8.9	8.2	5.5	4.8
Ireland	3.3	3.1	1.4	2.3	2.5	1.7	1.4	2.4
Italy [1]	6.1	5.3	4.2	3.9	5.4	3.8	1.8	1.7
Luxembourg	3.7	3.2	3.6	2.2	1.9	1.3	1.4	1.0
Netherlands	2.5	3.2	2.6	2.8	1.9	2.0	2.2	2.0
Norway.	4.1	2.3	2.3	1.4	2.5	1.3	2.6	2.3
Portugal [2]	13.4	9.4	6.7	5.4	4.2	3.1	2.3	2.8
Spain	6.7	5.9	4.6	4.7	4.7	3.6	2.0	1.8
Sweden	10.5	2.6	4.7	2.4	2.9	0.8	0.9	(NA)
Switzerland.	5.4	4.0	3.3	0.9	1.8	0.8	0.5	-
Turkey [2]	60.3	70.1	66.1	105.2	89.1	80.3	85.7	84.6
United Kingdom	9.5	3.7	1.6	2.5	3.4	2.5	3.1	3.4
Germany	2.7	5.1	4.5	2.7	1.8	1.5	1.7	1.0

- Represents or rounds to zero.   NA Not available.   [1] Households of wage and salary earners.   [2] Excludes rent.
Source: Organization for Economic Cooperation and Development, Paris, France, *Main Economic Indicators,* monthly (copyright).

No. 773. Producer Price Indexes by Stage of Processing: 1980 to 1999

[1982=100. Minus sign (-) indicates decline. See text this section]

Year	Crude materials				Interme- diate materi- als, sup- plies, and com- ponents	Finished goods		Consumer foods		
	Total	Food- stuffs and feed- stuffs	Fuel	Crude nonfood materials except fuel		Con- sumer goods	Capital equip- ment	Crude	Pro- cessed	Finished consumer goods excl. food
1980	95.3	104.6	69.4	91.8	90.3	88.6	85.8	93.9	92.3	87.1
1981	103.0	103.9	84.8	109.8	98.6	96.6	94.6	104.4	97.2	96.1
1982	100.0	100.0	100.0	100.0	100.0	100.0	100.0	100.0	100.0	100.0
1983	101.3	101.8	105.1	98.8	100.6	101.3	102.8	102.4	100.9	101.2
1984	103.5	104.7	105.1	101.0	103.1	103.3	105.2	111.4	104.9	102.2
1985	95.8	94.8	102.7	94.3	102.7	103.8	107.5	102.9	104.8	103.3
1986	87.7	93.2	92.2	76.0	99.1	101.4	109.7	105.6	107.4	98.5
1987	93.7	96.2	84.1	88.5	101.5	103.6	111.7	107.1	109.6	100.7
1988	96.0	106.1	82.1	85.9	107.1	106.2	114.3	109.8	112.7	103.1
1989	103.1	111.2	85.3	95.8	112.0	112.1	118.8	119.6	118.6	108.9
1990	108.9	113.1	84.8	107.3	114.5	118.2	122.9	123.0	124.4	115.3
1991	101.2	105.5	82.9	97.5	114.4	120.5	126.7	119.3	124.4	118.7
1992	100.4	105.1	84.0	94.2	114.7	121.7	129.1	107.6	124.4	120.8
1993	102.4	108.4	87.1	94.1	116.2	123.0	131.4	114.4	126.5	121.7
1994	101.8	106.5	82.4	97.0	118.5	123.3	134.1	111.3	127.9	121.6
1995	102.7	105.8	72.1	105.8	124.9	125.6	136.7	118.8	129.8	124.0
1996	113.8	121.5	92.6	105.7	125.7	129.5	138.3	129.2	133.8	127.6
1997	111.1	112.2	101.3	103.5	125.6	130.2	138.2	126.6	135.1	128.2
1998	96.8	103.9	86.7	84.5	123.0	128.9	137.6	127.2	134.8	126.4
1999	98.2	98.7	91.2	91.1	123.2	132.0	137.6	125.5	135.9	130.5
PERCENT CHANGE [1]										
1980	10.9	4.6	21.1	22.0	15.2	14.3	10.7	1.7	6.3	18.5
1981	8.1	-0.7	22.2	21.6	9.2	9.0	10.3	11.2	5.3	10.3
1982	-2.9	-3.8	17.9	19.6	1.4	3.5	5.7	-4.2	2.9	4.1
1983	1.3	1.8	5.1	-8.9	0.6	1.3	2.8	2.4	0.9	1.2
1984	2.2	2.8	-	-1.2	2.5	2.0	2.3	8.8	4.0	1.0
1985	-7.4	-9.5	-2.3	2.2	-0.4	0.5	2.2	-7.6	-0.1	1.1
1986	-8.5	-1.7	-10.2	-6.6	-3.5	-2.3	2.0	2.6	2.5	-4.6
1987	6.8	3.2	-8.8	-19.4	2.4	2.2	1.8	1.4	2.0	2.2
1988	2.5	10.3	-2.4	16.4	5.5	2.5	2.3	2.5	2.8	2.4
1989	7.4	4.8	3.9	-2.9	4.6	5.6	3.9	8.9	5.2	5.6
1990	5.6	1.7	-0.6	12.0	2.2	5.4	3.5	2.8	4.9	5.9
1991	-7.1	-6.7	-2.2	-9.1	-0.1	1.9	3.1	-3.0	-	2.9
1992	-0.8	-0.4	1.3	-3.4	0.3	1.0	1.9	-9.8	-	1.8
1993	2.0	3.1	3.7	-0.1	1.3	1.1	1.8	6.3	1.7	0.7
1994	-0.6	-1.8	-5.4	3.1	2.0	0.2	2.1	-2.7	1.1	-0.1
1995	0.9	-0.7	-12.5	9.1	5.4	1.9	1.9	6.7	1.5	2.0
1996	10.8	14.8	28.4	-0.1	0.6	3.1	1.2	8.8	3.1	2.9
1997	-2.4	-7.7	9.4	-2.1	-0.1	0.5	-0.1	-2.0	1.0	0.5
1998	-12.9	-7.4	-14.4	-18.4	-2.1	-1.0	-0.4	0.5	-0.2	-1.4
1999	1.4	-5.0	5.2	7.8	0.2	2.4	0.0	-1.3	0.8	3.2

- Represents or rounds to zero.   [1] Change from prior year.
Source: U.S. Bureau of Labor Statistics, *Producer Price Indexes,* monthly and annual.

Prices   493

No. 774. Producer Price Indexes by Stage of Processing: 1990 to 1999

[1982=100, except as indicated]

Stage of processing	1990	1993	1994	1995	1996	1997	1998	1999
Finished goods	**119.2**	**124.7**	**125.5**	**127.9**	**131.3**	**131.8**	**130.7**	**133.0**
Finished consumer goods	**118.2**	**123.0**	**123.3**	**125.6**	**129.5**	**130.2**	**128.9**	**132.0**
Finished consumer foods	**124.4**	**125.7**	**126.8**	**129.0**	**133.6**	**134.5**	**134.3**	**135.1**
Fresh fruits and melons	118.1	84.5	82.7	85.8	100.8	99.4	90.5	103.6
Fresh and dry vegetables	118.1	135.2	129.0	144.4	135.0	123.1	139.5	118.0
Eggs for fresh use (Dec. 1991=100)	(NA)	86.6	80.9	86.3	105.1	97.1	90.1	77.9
Bakery products	141.0	156.6	160.0	164.3	169.8	173.9	175.8	178.0
Milled rice	102.5	101.3	118.3	113.1	129.4	127.3	124.9	121.3
Pasta products (June 1985=100)	114.1	121.5	127.1	125.0	127.4	125.1	122.6	122.1
Beef and veal	116.0	112.9	103.6	100.9	100.2	102.8	99.4	106.3
Pork	119.8	105.7	101.4	101.5	120.9	123.1	96.6	96.0
Processed young chickens	111.0	109.5	113.3	113.5	121.5	118.6	125.2	113.4
Processed turkeys	107.6	101.0	108.5	104.9	105.5	101.0	95.2	94.8
Finfish and shellfish	147.2	156.5	161.4	170.8	165.9	178.1	183.2	190.9
Dairy products	117.2	118.1	119.4	119.7	130.4	128.1	138.2	139.2
Processed fruits and vegetables	124.7	118.2	121.1	122.4	127.6	126.4	125.7	128.1
Confectionery end products	140.0	154.1	156.9	160.7	166.9	168.3	168.7	170.4
Soft drinks	122.3	126.2	127.0	133.1	134.0	133.2	134.8	137.9
Roasted coffee	113.0	100.5	128.2	146.5	129.2	152.9	143.9	134.7
Shortening and cooking oils	123.2	122.9	138.6	142.5	138.5	137.8	143.4	140.4
Finished consumer goods excluding food	**115.3**	**121.7**	**121.6**	**124.0**	**127.6**	**128.2**	**126.4**	**130.5**
Alcoholic beverages	117.2	126.0	124.8	125.8	132.8	135.1	135.2	136.7
Women's apparel	116.1	120.2	119.7	119.6	119.9	120.5	122.3	123.9
Men's and boy's apparel	120.2	127.7	128.5	130.3	132.1	132.7	133.2	133.1
Girls', children's, and infants' apparel	115.3	120.1	119.9	121.6	122.4	122.9	121.8	118.2
Textile house furnishings	109.5	115.8	117.3	119.5	122.3	122.6	123.1	122.7
Footwear	125.6	134.4	135.5	139.2	141.6	143.7	144.7	144.5
Residential electric power (Dec. 1990=100)	(NA)	109.8	109.8	111.8	112.8	112.8	110.7	109.5
Residential gas (Dec. 1990=100)	(NA)	107.3	108.8	104.4	110.4	116.5	114.0	114.3
Gasoline	78.7	63.9	61.7	63.7	72.8	71.9	53.4	64.7
Fuel oil No. 2	73.3	59.1	56.0	56.6	69.5	64.8	48.1	56.1
Pharmaceutical preps, ethical (Prescription)	200.8	242.2	250.0	257.0	265.4	273.5	322.9	335.0
Pharmaceutical preps, proprietary (Overcounter)	156.8	180.0	183.2	186.5	185.1	184.8	184.5	186.0
Soaps and synthetic detergents	117.7	122.2	121.4	122.9	125.2	126.4	126.1	126.3
Cosmetics and other toilet preparations	121.6	129.1	128.7	129.0	130.2	130.6	132.9	135.4
Tires, tubes, and tread	96.8	98.9	98.6	100.2	97.0	95.2	94.0	92.9
Sanitary papers and health products	135.3	134.6	133.2	144.4	149.9	147.1	145.1	144.3
Newspaper circulation	144.1	169.5	174.9	185.6	198.8	201.9	202.9	207.1
Periodical circulation	150.3	164.8	171.1	176.6	180.6	188.1	193.8	196.9
Book publishing	153.4	169.1	175.8	185.0	193.9	200.1	205.9	213.0
Household furniture	125.1	133.4	138.0	141.8	144.5	146.2	148.4	150.5
Floor coverings	119.0	120.2	121.5	123.7	126.6	128.0	128.3	127.2
Household appliances	110.8	112.9	112.8	112.4	112.7	110.1	108.9	108.5
Home electronic equipment	82.7	80.2	80.3	78.9	79.0	77.1	75.9	73.7
Household glassware	132.5	142.9	147.4	153.2	157.3	161.3	162.7	163.9
Household flatware	122.1	130.7	133.9	138.3	138.4	138.5	139.2	139.7
Lawn and garden equipment, except tractors	123.0	126.2	128.4	130.4	132.3	132.2	131.7	132.0
Passenger cars	118.3	129.8	133.9	134.1	135.4	133.6	131.9	131.3
Toys, games, and children's vehicles	118.1	121.5	122.4	124.3	125.3	125.2	124.4	123.1
Sporting and athletic goods	112.6	118.6	120.1	122.0	123.3	124.7	126.2	126.2
Tobacco products	221.4	260.3	224.7	231.3	237.4	248.9	283.6	374.0
Mobile homes	117.5	127.8	137.0	145.6	149.8	152.2	154.3	158.4
Jewelry, platinum, and karat gold	122.8	125.6	127.3	127.8	129.4	129.2	128.1	127.1
Costume jewelry and novelties	125.3	133.2	134.1	135.1	136.9	139.9	139.6	140.1
Capital equipment	**122.9**	**131.4**	**134.1**	**136.7**	**138.3**	**138.2**	**137.6**	**137.6**
Agricultural machinery and equipment	121.7	133.6	137.0	142.9	146.8	149.0	150.4	152.1
Construction machinery and equipment	121.6	132.0	133.7	136.7	139.8	142.2	145.2	147.2
Metal cutting machine tools	129.8	141.1	143.1	148.0	152.6	156.0	159.9	160.7
Metal forming machine tools	128.7	138.4	141.9	145.7	149.6	153.9	157.6	159.7
Tools, dies, jigs, fixtures, and industrial molds	117.2	128.4	131.4	133.8	136.2	138.1	138.8	139.8
Pumps, compressors, and equipment	119.2	132.8	135.2	139.4	143.5	146.5	149.0	151.7
Industrial material handling equipment	115.0	120.2	122.4	125.3	127.4	129.7	131.3	132.9

See footnote at end of table.

494 Prices

[1982=100, except as indicated]

Stage of processing	1990	1993	1994	1995	1996	1997	1998	1999
Capital equipment—Continued								
Electronic computers (Dec. 1990=100)	(NA)	62.9	58.0	51.8	42.4	33.2	113.2	87.2
Textile machinery	128.8	143.7	144.9	146.7	148.4	152.1	152.8	154.2
Paper industries machinery (June 1982=100)	134.8	144.9	147.5	151.0	153.8	157.4	160.0	162.6
Printing trades machinery	124.9	129.5	130.9	133.6	136.8	138.8	140.9	141.0
Transformers and power regulators	120.9	123.0	125.3	128.9	129.7	129.5	130.8	132.6
Communic'tn/related equip. (Dec. 1985=100)	106.1	109.1	110.8	112.1	113.0	114.0	114.1	112.7
X-ray and electromedical equipment	109.8	114.0	112.4	111.8	109.9	107.4	106.6	104.3
Oil field and gas field machinery	102.4	108.2	110.8	114.1	117.8	122.8	125.9	126.5
Mining machinery and equipment	121.0	129.5	131.1	135.6	139.0	140.3	142.2	144.2
Office and store machines and equipment	109.5	111.0	111.3	111.5	112.0	112.4	112.3	112.3
Commercial furniture	133.4	140.5	144.7	148.2	151.7	154.3	155.2	156.6
Light motor trucks	130.0	150.3	157.1	159.0	160.3	158.9	155.2	157.5
Heavy motor trucks	120.3	133.9	138.7	144.1	144.5	144.5	140.4	146.5
Truck trailers	110.8	118.2	122.2	131.7	130.7	130.3	135.0	136.3
Civilian aircraft (Dec. 1985=100)	115.3	131.5	135.4	141.8	147.3	150.0	150.2	151.7
Ships (Dec. 1985=100)	110.1	129.1	131.1	132.8	138.7	143.7	145.7	145.8
Railroad equipment	118.6	125.2	129.2	134.8	137.2	134.7	135.0	135.2
Intermediate materials, supplies, and components	**114.5**	**116.2**	**118.5**	**124.9**	**125.7**	**125.6**	**123.0**	**123.2**
Intermediate foods and feeds	**113.3**	**112.7**	**114.8**	**114.8**	**128.1**	**125.4**	**116.2**	**111.1**
Flour	103.6	108.9	110.4	123.0	136.8	118.7	109.2	104.3
Refined sugar	122.7	118.2	118.2	119.3	123.7	123.6	119.9	121.0
Confectionery materials	101.2	98.9	112.4	109.1	107.9	105.4	93.7	94.0
Crude vegetable oils	115.8	110.5	135.0	130.0	118.1	116.6	131.1	90.2
Prepared animal feeds	107.4	111.0	111.3	109.1	135.3	132.9	108.0	98.3
Intermediate materials less foods and feeds	**120.9**	**123.8**	**127.1**	**135.2**	**134.0**	**134.2**	**133.5**	**133.1**
Synthetic fibers	106.7	103.6	104.1	109.4	111.3	111.1	109.9	103.8
Processed yarns and threads	112.6	107.8	108.4	112.8	114.7	114.0	112.7	108.6
Gray fabrics	117.2	118.6	116.8	121.2	121.4	121.2	121.6	114.4
Leather	177.5	168.6	179.6	191.4	177.9	182.7	178.4	176.3
Liquefied petroleum gas	77.4	63.6	58.2	65.1	84.7	84.5	60.1	73.7
Commercial electric power	115.3	127.2	128.8	131.7	131.6	131.7	130.4	129.1
Industrial electric power	119.6	130.6	129.2	130.8	131.6	130.8	130.0	128.9
Commercial natural gas (Dec. 1990=100)	(NA)	102.7	103.7	96.5	103.2	109.8	106.4	108.1
Industrial natural gas (Dec. 1990=100)	(NA)	101.6	99.5	90.9	98.9	109.3	103.6	103.3
Natural gas to electric utilities (Dec. 1990=100)	(NA)	93.5	90.2	87.7	90.4	96.9	80.0	81.6
Jet fuels	76.0	59.0	53.9	55.0	66.7	62.9	46.1	52.5
No. 2 Diesel fuel	74.1	60.5	56.0	57.0	70.0	64.5	47.4	57.3
Residual fuel	57.7	49.6	48.2	52.6	59.8	59.5	43.8	51.5
Industrial chemicals	113.2	110.4	114.3	128.4	126.7	126.4	121.4	118.9
Prepared paint	124.8	133.2	135.3	142.1	147.2	152.1	154.9	157.4
Paint materials	136.3	131.5	132.1	139.4	141.3	141.5	143.8	144.1
Medicinal and botanical chemicals	102.2	120.7	125.4	128.3	128.6	133.4	135.0	142.2
Fats and oils, inedible	88.1	95.6	110.6	126.9	133.3	132.3	116.7	88.4
Mixed fertilizers	103.3	99.0	105.7	111.1	114.7	113.6	115.3	113.7
Nitrogenates	92.3	99.3	112.3	129.4	130.5	132.3	108.2	94.6
Phosphates	96.5	82.8	95.5	109.1	116.3	110.4	112.6	112.0
Other agricultural chemicals	119.9	134.7	140.8	144.3	146.1	147.8	148.4	144.5
Plastic resins and materials	124.1	117.1	122.4	143.5	133.1	137.3	125.3	125.8
Synthetic rubber	111.9	105.7	108.9	126.3	122.2	119.3	117.2	113.9
Plastic construction products	117.2	116.6	122.9	133.8	130.9	128.2	128.2	128.0
Unsupported plastic film, sheet, and shapes	119.0	121.4	122.8	135.6	132.7	131.7	128.0	127.5
Plastic parts and components for manufacturing	112.9	113.9	113.5	115.9	117.5	117.2	117.1	117.4
Softwood lumber	123.8	193.0	198.1	178.5	189.5	206.5	182.7	196.0
Hardwood lumber	131.0	163.3	168.3	167.0	163.9	174.1	178.7	177.3
Millwork	130.4	156.6	162.4	163.8	166.6	170.9	171.1	174.7
Plywood	114.2	152.8	158.6	165.3	156.4	159.3	157.3	176.4
Woodpile	151.3	104.2	115.9	183.2	133.1	128.6	122.6	119.7
Paper	128.8	123.8	126.0	159.0	149.4	143.9	145.4	141.8
Paperboard	135.7	130.0	140.5	183.1	155.1	144.4	151.6	153.2
Paper boxes and containers	129.9	129.9	136.1	163.8	153.9	144.7	154.7	158.0
Building paper and board	112.2	132.7	144.1	144.9	137.2	129.6	132.9	141.6

See footnotes at end of table.

U.S. Census Bureau, Statistical Abstract of the United States: 2000

[1982=100, except as indicated]

Stage of processing	1990	1993	1994	1995	1996	1997	1998	1999
Intermediate materials less foods and feeds—Continued								
Commercial printing (June 1982=100)	128.0	134.8	136.5	144.5	148.3	148.7	152.0	152.2
Foundry and forge shop products	117.2	121.3	123.9	129.3	132.6	134.1	135.0	135.1
Steel mill products	112.1	108.2	113.4	120.1	115.6	116.4	113.8	105.3
Primary nonferrous metals	133.4	98.1	115.7	146.8	126.2	126.2	106.7	101.5
Aluminum mill shapes	127.9	120.4	127.7	160.4	144.8	147.5	142.0	138.1
Copper and brass mill shapes	174.6	150.7	167.3	195.2	179.0	177.3	153.0	151.2
Nonferrous wire and cable	142.6	133.1	139.8	151.5	147.5	148.1	141.1	135.6
Metal containers.	114.0	109.7	108.1	117.2	110.0	108.1	108.3	106.4
Hardware	125.9	135.2	137.5	141.1	143.8	145.6	147.0	148.7
Plumbing fixtures and brass fittings	144.3	155.9	159.6	166.0	171.1	174.5	175.1	176.7
Heating equipment	131.6	140.4	142.5	147.5	151.2	152.4	153.3	154.0
Fabricated structural metal products	121.8	123.2	127.3	135.1	137.8	140.3	142.5	143.3
Fabricated ferrous wire products (June 1982=100) . .	114.6	119.3	122.6	125.7	126.8	128.0	130.1	130.6
Other miscellaneous metals	120.7	121.4	122.7	124.9	125.7	126.2	126.2	125.5
Mechanical power transmission equipment	125.3	136.2	140.5	146.9	151.5	154.8	157.7	161.1
Air conditioning and refrigeration equipment	122.1	126.0	127.0	130.2	132.7	132.6	134.6	135.5
Metal valves, excluding fluid power (Dec. 1982=100) .	125.3	137.2	140.3	145.3	149.8	153.3	156.7	160.2
Ball and roller bearings	130.6	141.9	145.7	152.0	157.8	162.9	165.2	166.8
Wiring devices	132.2	138.6	141.5	147.2	151.2	154.0	154.0	152.5
Motors, generators, motor generator sets	132.9	138.6	140.2	143.9	145.6	144.7	145.8	145.9
Switchgear and switchboard equipment	124.4	134.6	136.8	140.3	142.6	145.6	148.4	151.0
Electronic components and accessories	118.4	117.7	116.6	113.6	108.9	104.0	100.0	98.2
Internal combustion engines.	120.2	130.2	132.9	135.6	138.8	140.1	140.7	143.0
Machine shop products	124.3	128.0	129.7	131.3	133.6	135.2	136.4	136.8
Flat glass	107.5	107.3	110.5	113.2	110.0	108.4	107.1	106.4
Cement	103.7	111.7	119.5	128.1	134.0	139.4	145.7	150.6
Concrete products	113.5	120.2	124.6	129.4	133.2	136.0	140.0	143.7
Asphalt felts and coatings	97.1	96.8	95.3	100.0	100.0	99.9	99.5	99.2
Gypsum products	105.2	108.3	136.1	154.5	154.0	170.8	177.6	208.0
Glass containers	120.4	125.8	127.5	130.5	129.1	125.7	125.9	125.9
Motor vehicle parts	111.2	113.8	114.3	116.0	116.2	115.4	114.7	114.0
Aircraft engines and engine parts (Dec. 1985=100) .	113.5	127.7	130.7	132.8	134.7	135.7	137.1	138.5
Aircraft parts and auxiliary equipment, NEC (June 1985=100).	117.7	131.2	134.0	135.7	139.3	141.3	142.9	143.7
Photographic supplies	127.6	124.3	124.7	126.8	129.8	130.0	128.9	128.3
Medical/surgical/personal aid devices.	127.3	137.8	140.4	141.3	143.1	143.1	143.4	144.6
Crude materials for further processing	108.9	102.4	101.8	102.7	113.8	111.1	96.8	98.2
Crude foodstuffs and feedstuffs.	113.1	108.4	106.5	105.8	121.5	112.2	103.9	98.7
Wheat	87.6	98.4	104.8	118.6	136.6	108.2	87.8	79.5
Corn	100.9	92.9	100.1	109.0	158.5	110.1	91.7	78.2
Slaughter cattle	122.5	116.7	105.8	99.5	95.8	97.9	92.5	97.6
Slaughter hogs	94.1	76.1	65.9	70.2	88.6	87.0	52.2	53.8
Slaughter broilers/fryers.	119.5	125.9	127.7	129.1	148.0	137.2	151.8	134.5
Slaughter turkeys	116.9	113.1	119.6	120.3	121.5	112.9	110.4	120.0
Fluid milk	100.8	94.1	95.7	93.6	107.9	97.5	112.9	106.3
Soybeans	100.8	104.8	106.0	102.2	127.9	131.0	103.4	80.1
Cane sugar, raw.	119.2	113.2	115.2	119.7	118.6	116.8	117.2	113.7
Crude nonfood materials	101.5	94.7	94.8	96.8	104.5	106.4	88.4	94.3
Raw cotton	118.2	91.9	121.3	156.2	130.0	116.5	111.0	87.4
Leaf tobacco	95.8	100.3	100.2	102.5	105.1	(NA)	105.1	101.6
Cattle hides.	217.8	180.2	200.9	209.9	186.5	196.1	153.6	141.9
Coal.	97.5	96.1	96.7	95.0	94.5	96.3	93.6	90.7
Natural gas	80.4	84.7	78.8	66.6	91.2	101.7	83.9	91.2
Crude petroleum	71.0	51.4	47.1	51.1	62.6	57.5	35.7	50.3
Logs and timber.	142.8	212.3	219.1	220.4	206.8	214.4	208.1	202.0
Wastepaper.	138.9	117.4	209.5	371.1	141.6	163.3	145.4	183.6
Iron ore	83.3	82.7	82.7	91.8	96.7	96.3	95.4	94.9
Iron and steel scrap	166.0	172.5	192.9	202.7	191.1	188.9	165.0	139.2
Nonferrous metal ores (Dec. 1983=100)	98.3	67.2	81.4	100.5	90.2	82.2	66.6	63.1
Copper base scrap	181.3	136.1	155.5	193.5	166.3	157.7	116.2	108.2
Aluminum base scrap	172.6	129.2	172.9	209.4	173.4	195.1	162.5	161.7
Construction sand, gravel, and crushed stone	125.4	134.0	137.9	142.3	145.6	148.2	152.8	157.2

NA Not available.

Source: U.S. Bureau of Labor Statistics, *Producer Price Indexes, Producer Price Indexes,* monthly and annual.

No. 775. Producer Price Indexes for the Net Output of Selected Industries: 1995 to 1999

[Indexes are based on selling prices reported by establishments of all sizes by probability sampling. Manufacturing industries selected by shipment value. N.e.c.= not elsewhere classified]

Industry	SIC code [1]	Index base [2]	1995	1996	1997	1998	1999
MINING							
Iron ores.	1011	12/84	91.0	95.7	95.3	94.5	94.0
Copper ores	1021	06/88	157.1	117.0	110.4	76.8	71.3
Lead and zinc ores.	1031	12/85	103.1	109.4	138.6	107.0	111.8
Gold ores	1041	06/85	115.9	117.0	100.9	90.0	85.6
Metal mining services	1081	12/85	111.4	112.5	116.8	122.2	120.2
Metal ores, n.e.c.	1099	12/85	119.3	110.5	100.8	89.9	82.9
Bituminous coal and lignite.	1211	12/81	95.3	95.0	95.9	93.0	90.6
Anthracite mining	1231	12/79	158.9	158.6	159.0	160.1	158.7
Coal Mining Services	1241	06/85	105.7	109.2	108.1	108.1	107.7
Crude petroleum and natural gas liquids.	1331	06/96	(X)	(X)	115.6	86.1	102.6
Drilling oil and gas wells	1381	12/85	104.2	115.1	143.7	154.6	133.1
Oil and gas exploration services	1382	12/85	103.4	103.7	105.6	114.5	92.7
Oil and gas field services, n.e.c.	1389	12/85	111.0	108.2	112.7	113.6	112.9
Dimension stone	1411	06/85	126.4	132.2	138.2	142.2	145.9
Crushed and broken limestone	1422	12/83	130.9	132.4	134.5	137.4	140.6
Crushed and broken granite, n.e.c.	1423	12/83	153.6	156.5	159.7	166.4	172.5
Crushed and broken stone, n.e.c.	1429	12/83	137.1	143.0	145.4	147.9	149.9
Construction sand and gravel.	1442	06/82	146.6	151.1	155.3	163.0	169.0
Industrial sand.	1446	06/82	134.2	136.6	138.9	142.2	145.2
Kaolin and ball clay	1455	06/84	115.2	116.5	117.1	115.8	113.3
Clay and related minerals, n.e.c.	1459	06/84	128.8	130.2	131.7	133.4	133.5
Potash, soda, and borate minerals	1474	12/84	113.7	121.2	117.4	118.9	113.6
Chemicals and fertilizer mineral mining, n.e.c.	1479	12/89	95.1	91.8	92.7	93.4	95.0
Nonmetallic minerals (except fuels) services	1481	06/85	100.0	103.4	104.7	104.7	106.5
Miscellaneous nonmetallic minerals	1499	06/85	126.8	130.3	133.5	136.7	138.0
MANUFACTURING							
Meat packing plants	2011	12/80	105.9	110.9	113.5	101.4	104.2
Sausage and other prepared meats.	2013	12/82	108.5	115.5	118.8	113.3	113.8
Poultry slaughtering and processing	2015	12/81	120.5	127.1	124.7	127.1	119.8
Natural and processed cheese	2022	06/81	110.8	119.6	115.7	126.1	124.3
Dry, condensed, and evaporated milk products	2023	12/83	131.1	139.5	138.7	146.4	142.4
Ice cream and frozen desserts	2024	06/83	125.8	130.5	135.1	142.6	150.0
Fluid milk	2026	12/82	123.3	134.3	133.6	140.4	145.9
Canned specialties	2032	12/82	154.3	157.7	163.0	165.6	168.6
Canned fruits, vegetables, preserves, jams, and jellies	2033	06/81	131.8	138.4	137.7	136.9	138.2
Pickled fruits/veg./veg. sauces/seasonings/salad dressings	2035	06/81	157.0	160.9	161.2	162.2	163.2
Frozen fruits and vegetables	2037	06/81	134.8	141.5	139.2	138.6	141.8
Frozen specialties	2038	12/82	133.2	135.7	136.8	137.0	137.4
Flour and other grain mill products	2041	06/83	116.0	133.3	114.3	103.3	97.1
Cereal breakfast foods	2043	12/83	169.4	174.5	168.2	161.4	159.5
Wet corn milling.	2046	06/85	124.5	133.6	123.6	107.1	101.3
Dog and cat food	2047	12/85	124.6	130.7	132.1	132.3	132.2
Prepared animal feeds, n.e.c.	2048	12/80	98.3	119.8	112.2	95.2	86.7
Bread and other bakery products, except cookies and crackers	2051	06/80	189.4	195.7	199.7	201.4	204.5
Cookies and crackers	2052	06/83	156.5	161.4	167.0	170.3	171.0
Candy and other confectionery products, and chewing gum.	2064	06/83	137.8	143.8	146.2	146.8	149.4
Soybean oil mill products.	2075	12/79	87.7	98.6	103.2	86.7	68.0
Malt beverages	2082	06/82	124.0	127.7	128.0	128.1	131.4
Bottled and canned soft drinks	2086	06/81	140.2	141.2	140.5	142.4	145.7
Flavoring extracts and syrups, n.e.c.	2087	12/85	125.5	127.7	130.7	131.4	133.6
Fresh or frozen packaged fish	2092	12/82	149.4	140.0	145.2	151.7	160.9
Coffee	2095	06/81	152.6	138.7	161.8	153.3	145.8
Potato and corn chips, and similar snacks	2096	06/91	104.3	106.5	109.4	111.1	112.7
Macaroni, spaghetti, and noodles	2098	06/85	125.0	127.4	125.5	122.7	122.3
Food preparations, n.e.c.	2099	12/85	121.4	124.1	127.5	128.5	128.9
Cigarettes.	2111	12/82	204.3	210.5	223.3	260.4	356.7
Cigars	2121	12/82	186.5	201.8	228.5	242.7	259.6
Cotton broadwoven fabric	2211	12/80	118.6	119.1	118.5	117.4	114.1
Manmade fiber and silk broadwoven fabric	2221	06/81	112.4	113.0	115.0	114.8	108.6
Narrow fabric mills	2241	06/84	119.7	121.2	122.7	123.8	124.3
Knit outerwear.	2253	12/84	116.7	117.9	118.6	118.9	116.4
Carpet and rugs.	2273	06/90	102.2	104.4	105.9	106.4	105.6
Spun yarn.	2281	12/82	105.8	106.1	104.7	102.5	96.9
Men's and boys' separate trousers and slacks.	2325	12/81	130.7	133.1	133.4	136.5	137.0
Women's, misses', and juniors' dresses	2335	12/80	124.9	125.4	126.0	127.0	126.3
Women's, misses', and juniors' outerwear, n.e.c.	2339	06/83	106.6	108.4	110.9	111.2	112.6
House furnishings, n.e.c.	2392	06/83	116.8	120.4	120.5	119.5	118.8
Automotive trimmings, apparel findings, and related products	2396	12/83	110.2	117.2	120.1	124.0	122.6
Logging camps and logging contractors	2411	12/81	194.3	185.8	191.2	188.2	182.8
Sawmills and planing mills	2421	12/80	150.8	152.0	163.1	151.7	157.4
Millwork	2431	06/83	152.1	153.6	156.4	157.2	160.0
Wood kitchen cabinets	2434	06/84	144.3	147.3	150.4	153.1	155.7
Softwood plywood	2436	12/80	158.0	139.5	142.4	142.5	164.7
Mobile homes	2451	06/81	151.0	155.3	157.8	159.9	164.2
Wood household furniture, except upholstered.	2511	12/79	186.3	189.7	192.3	195.8	200.5
Upholstered wood household furniture	2512	06/82	132.9	136.3	138.1	140.1	142.0
Nonwood office furniture	2522	12/79	188.1	192.4	193.5	191.6	191.8
Public building and related furniture.	2531	12/84	130.0	133.7	135.9	135.9	136.8

See footnotes at end of table.

U.S. Census Bureau, Statistical Abstract of the United States: 2000

[See headnote, page 497]

Industry	SIC code [1]	Index base	1995	1996	1997	1998	1999
Paper mills	2621	06/81	164.8	152.2	143.2	144.4	139.7
Paperbord mills	2631	12/82	203.2	169.8	158.2	165.1	167.0
Corrugated and solid fiber boxes.	2653	03/80	186.5	168.7	154.9	168.8	175.5
Folding paperboard boxes	2657	12/83	141.4	143.4	142.2	143.6	142.3
Paper coated and laminated, n.e.c.	2672	06/93	108.2	110.5	110.1	109.6	109.8
Plastics, foil and coated paper bags	2673	12/83	161.4	158.6	160.9	156.6	159.0
Sanitary Paper Products	2676	06/83	149.5	150.3	147.8	146.0	145.1
Newspaper publishing.	2711	12/79	286.7	306.9	317.7	328.6	339.3
Periodical publishing.	2721	12/79	246.3	253.2	263.2	276.9	284.9
Book Publishing	2731	12/80	214.3	224.7	232.1	238.8	247.6
Miscellaneous publishing	2741	06/84	167.1	174.5	181.1	187.7	194.5
Commercial printing, lithographic.	2752	06/82	145.0	149.0	149.8	153.3	153.2
Commercial printing, n.e.c..	2759	06/82	154.4	158.2	159.4	160.9	162.6
Manifold business forms	2761	12/83	163.9	168.4	165.8	167.0	170.5
Industrial inorganic chemicals, n.e.c.	2819	12/82	125.2	136.0	135.5	132.3	129.2
Plastic materials and resins	2821	12/80	159.0	149.6	153.9	139.2	142.8
Noncellulosic manmade fibers	2824	06/81	107.9	109.3	107.7	106.7	98.9
Medicinal chemicals and botanical products (in bulk)	2833	06/82	129.2	129.8	134.2	136.3	143.2
Pharmaceutical preparations	2834	06/81	249.9	253.9	259.1	290.1	298.5
In vivo and In vitro diagnostics	2835	03/80	165.3	166.6	167.4	177.9	184.5
Biological products, except diagnostics.	2836	06/91	109.9	111.2	112.3	116.4	126.1
Soap and other detergents.	2841	06/83	121.7	123.8	124.6	125.1	125.9
Specialty cleaning, polishing and sanitation preparations	2842	06/83	129.2	129.6	130.8	132.6	135.1
Toilet preparations	2844	03/80	167.1	168.5	168.9	171.6	174.8
Paints and Allied Products	2851	06/83	143.1	147.4	152.1	154.9	157.3
Cyclic (coal tar) crudes and intermediates, organic dyes and pigments.	2865	12/82	125.0	118.3	115.2	109.4	110.1
Industrial organic chemicals, n.e.c.	2869	12/82	163.0	171.2	171.5	167.7	169.1
Agricultural chemicals, n.e.c.	2879	06/82	135.2	136.5	137.6	138.5	135.4
Adhesives and sealants.	2891	12/83	145.1	146.1	148.8	151.4	151.7
Printing ink	2893	06/84	135.7	138.2	136.4	136.7	135.8
Chemicals and chemical preparations, n.e.c..	2899	06/85	128.9	130.3	133.2	134.7	134.8
Petroleum Refining.	2911	06/85	74.5	85.3	83.1	62.3	73.6
Tires and inner tubes	3011	06/81	108.5	105.2	103.4	102.0	100.4
Fabricated rubber products, n.e.c.	3069	06/83	128.6	130.6	132.1	132.4	132.2
Unsupported plastic film and sheet	3081	06/93	112.4	108.9	108.3	103.7	103.2
Plastic bottles	3085	06/93	110.3	107.0	107.1	105.7	106.1
Plastic foam products	3086	06/93	110.6	110.7	109.7	108.7	108.6
Custom compounding of purchased plastic resins	3087	06/93	108.2	108.1	106.7	107.5	104.2
Plastic products n.e.c.	3089	06/93	105.8	106.4	106.3	106.3	106.7
Products of purchased glass	3231	06/83	126.8	126.3	127.1	127.5	128.4
Concrete products	3272	12/79	144.4	148.1	151.6	156.6	161.0
Ready-mixed concrete.	3273	06/81	131.3	135.2	138.0	142.3	145.6
Blast furnaces and steel mills	3312	06/82	118.5	114.0	114.2	111.3	102.0
Cold finishing of steel shapes - mfpm.	3316	06/82	122.0	116.4	116.7	114.5	110.3
Steel pipe and tubes - mfpm	3317	06/82	127.0	126.7	131.8	132.7	127.1
Gray iron foundries.	3321	12/80	137.7	141.5	143.0	143.4	144.5
Primary copper	3331	06/80	194.4	144.8	137.3	106.2	102.2
Secondary nonferrous metals	3341	06/80	102.1	94.0	94.5	85.9	84.8
Rolling, drawing and extruding of copper	3351	12/80	161.6	151.1	149.9	131.8	130.0
Aluminum sheet, plate, foil and welded tube products . . .	3353	06/81	165.6	148.4	152.9	145.4	139.5
Nonferrous wire drawing and insulating	3357	12/82	157.4	153.7	154.5	148.2	143.7
Metal cans	3411	06/81	118.7	112.0	110.4	109.8	107.8
Hardware, n.e.c..	3429	06/85	121.7	123.7	125.0	126.0	127.4
Fabricated structural metal.	3441	06/82	126.2	130.7	132.8	136.9	139.1
Metal doors, sash and trim.	3442	06/83	148.5	151.1	152.5	152.9	153.6
Fabricated plate work (boiler shops)	3443	03/80	155.6	159.1	161.9	164.7	167.2
Sheet metal work	3444	12/82	137.6	137.7	138.6	139.9	140.1
Bolts, nuts, screws, rivets, and washers	3452	06/82	122.2	124.2	125.6	126.9	126.4
Automotive stampings.	3465	12/82	111.7	112.5	112.8	111.9	110.4
Metal stampings, n.e.c.	3469	06/84	126.6	127.3	128.5	128.9	128.6
Metal coating and allied services.	3479	12/84	116.6	118.0	119.4	119.1	118.8
Industrial Valves.	3491	06/91	111.7	114.8	117.3	119.8	122.4
Fabricated metal products, n.e.c.	3499	06/85	127.4	128.5	129.9	131.8	131.8
Turbines and turbine generator sets.	3511	06/82	148.1	145.7	146.9	146.9	148.7
Internal combustion engines, n.e.c.	3519	12/82	131.2	134.3	135.7	136.2	138.1
Farm machinery and equipment	3523	12/82	133.2	136.7	138.8	140.4	142.2
Lawn and garden equipment	3524	12/82	124.1	125.9	126.0	124.9	124.5
Construction machinery.	3531	12/80	157.2	161.6	164.4	167.8	170.8
Special tools, dies, jigs, fixtures and industrial molds . . .	3544	06/81	140.1	142.5	144.1	144.9	145.8
Special industry machinery, n.e.c.	3559	12/81	156.5	160.5	163.3	165.9	168.2
Pumps and pumping equipment	3561	12/83	141.3	146.1	150.4	153.4	156.2
General industrial machinery, n.e.c.	3569	12/84	143.4	147.0	149.5	151.3	153.8
Electronic computers.	3571	12/90	53.8	45.2	36.5	109.1	91.1
Computer storage devices	3572	12/92	67.2	57.6	51.1	107.1	95.0
Computer peripheral equipment, n.e.c.	3577	12/93	95.7	93.1	90.5	84.6	80.1
Refrigeration and heating equipment	3585	12/82	126.0	128.2	129.2	131.3	131.5
Service industry machinery, n.e.c.	3589	06/82	150.6	154.6	159.3	161.8	164.0
Machinery, except electrical, n.e.c.	3599	06/84	121.4	123.4	125.4	127.0	127.6
Switchgear and switchboard apparatus	3613	06/85	132.4	133.6	135.0	138.2	141.0
Electric motors and generators	3621	06/83	137.5	139.1	138.6	139.8	139.9
Relays and industrial controls.	3625	06/85	130.7	133.6	137.8	140.4	142.8

See footnotes at end of table.

No. 775. Producer Price Indexes for the Net Output of Selected Industries: 1995 to 1999—Continued

[See headnote, page 497]

Industry	SIC code [1]	Index base	1995	1996	1997	1998	1999
Household audio & video equipment	3651	03/80	82.6	82.4	80.5	79.5	77.8
Telephone & telegraph apparatus	3661	12/85	118.2	119.7	119.4	118.0	115.8
Radio and television broadcast and communication equipment.	3663	12/91	103.5	104.2	105.7	105.5	104.1
Printed circuit boards	3672	06/91	95.1	95.9	95.0	93.2	92.2
Semiconductors and related devices	3674	06/81	91.3	84.8	76.7	101.7	97.4
Electrical equipment for internal combustion engines . . .	3694	12/82	126.7	128.2	128.8	127.8	127.4
Motor vehicles and passenger car bodies	3711	06/82	139.1	140.4	138.7	136.8	137.6
Truck and bus bodies	3713	12/82	145.5	149.9	153.5	155.3	157.0
Motor vehicle parts and accessories	3714	12/82	113.5	114.0	113.1	112.6	112.0
Aircraft	3721	12/85	137.3	140.5	142.3	142.7	144.1
Aircraft engines and engine parts	3724	12/85	130.9	133.4	134.8	135.8	136.8
Ship building and repairing.	3731	12/85	127.6	130.1	133.3	134.8	135.4
Railroad equipment.	3743	06/84	127.6	129.6	127.4	127.5	128.1
Search/detection/navigation/&guidance sys & aero/nautical nav syst	3812	12/91	104.8	105.5	107.0	109.1	109.0
Industrial process control instruments.	3823	06/83	138.2	142.2	147.7	150.1	151.0
Electrical measuring and integrating instruments	3825	12/83	133.8	134.2	135.0	135.2	135.5
Laboratory analytical instruments	3826	12/85	114.6	115.9	117.5	118.3	116.9
Surgical and medical instruments and apparatus	3841	06/82	129.7	130.9	129.0	127.9	127.4
Surgical, orthopedic and prosthetic appliances and supplies	3842	06/83	154.8	156.1	158.1	160.5	163.0
Dental equipment and supplies.	3843	06/85	138.4	141.9	147.8	155.7	166.5
Electromedical equipment	3845	06/85	109.7	107.9	104.7	103.7	101.4
Photographic equipment and supplies	3861	12/83	113.8	114.9	113.5	109.7	106.7
Sporting and athletic goods, n.e.c..	3949	12/85	123.6	125.3	127.5	129.0	128.8
Signs and advertising displays	3993	12/85	129.6	132.1	134.3	136.4	139.1
Burial caskets	3995	12/84	143.5	148.3	152.8	157.8	162.2
SERVICES							
Railroads, line haul operations	4011	12/84	111.7	111.5	112.1	113.4	113.0
Local trucking without storage.	4212	06/93	102.9	102.9	104.6	104.9	106.3
Trucking, except local	4213	06/92	105.1	107.6	110.7	114.1	118.0
Local trucking with storage.	4214	06/93	110.7	11.9	112.2	113.0	113.2
Courier services, except by air	4215	12/92	109.5	113.0	116.4	122.1	126.0
Farm product warehousing and storage	4221	12/92	104.0	102.4	102.9	104.1	107.1
Refrigerated warehousing and storage	4222	12/91	104.2	104.6	105.1	105.4	106.4
General warehousing and storage.	4225	06/93	103.1	104.3	105.5	107.5	111.5
United States Postal Service	4311	06/89	132.2	132.3	132.3	132.3	135.3
Deep sea foreign transportation of freight	4412	06/88	113.3	114.1	113.1	116.7	134.0
Domestic deep sea transportation of freight	4424	06/88	121.5	122.0	124.5	121.1	124.3
Marine cargo handling.	4491	12/91	102.1	101.6	103.7	104.9	106.7
Tugging and towing services	4492	12/92	107.2	110.9	113.3	115.6	119.7
Air transportation, scheduled	4512	12/89	137.8	148.1	153.9	152.6	161.2
Air courier services.	4513	12/89	109.5	113.9	115.1	113.2	117.3
Air transportation, nonscheduled	4522	06/92	103.6	105.0	104.5	106.0	109.2
Airports, flying fields, and airport services	4581	06/92	102.8	106.6	109.7	112.5	116.2
Crude petroleum pipelines	4612	06/86	113.4	104.7	96.0	96.8	95.5
Refined petroleum pipelines	4613	06/86	104.6	104.3	105.3	104.8	104.9
Travel agencies	4724	12/89	111.3	109.9	114.5	112.1	112.0
Freight transportation arrangement	4731	12/94	99.8	101.5	101.4	99.7	99.2
Telephone communications, except radiotelephone. . . .	4813	06/95	(X)	99.9	99.6	98.4	96.0
Radio broadcasting.	4832	06/88	128.8	140.6	148.5	151.1	162.3
Cable and other pay television services	4841	06/93	98.5	103.3	108.3	112.5	116.2
Electric power and natural gas utilities	4981	12/90	109.4	111.1	112.0	110.4	109.5
Scrap and waste materials.	5093	12/86	181.8	147.6	152.7	131.6	127.9
Operators and lessors of nonresidential buildings.	6512	12/95	(X)	99.6	101.0	103.3	105.9
Real estate agents and managers.	6531	12/95	(X)	99.6	100.8	102.4	104.4
Hotels and motels	7011	06/93	106.1	110.1	115.6	119.9	124.9
Advertising agencies.	7311	06/95	(X)	101.7	103.8	105.3	107.4
Building cleaning and maintenance services, n.e.c.	7349	12/94	101.0	102.4	104.5	105.6	108.0
Employment agencies.	7361	06/94	102.0	103.0	104.5	106.6	109.9
Help supply services.	7363	06/94	103.1	105.1	106.9	109.1	111.1
Prepackaged software.	7372	12/97	(X)	(X)	(X)	100.7	100.1
Truck rental and leasing, without drivers.	7513	06/91	103.7	106.5	104.5	104.7	104.2
Passenger car rental, without drivers	7514	12/91	123.8	119.3	130.5	132.6	129.4
Offices and clinics of doctors of medicine	8011	12/93	106.8	107.6	109.0	111.3	113.8
Skilled and intermediate care facilities	8053	12/94	103.7	110.0	114.7	119.6	124.1
General medical and surgical hospitals.	8062	12/92	109.9	112.5	113.6	114.6	116.6
Psychiatric hospitals	8063	12/92	110.4	113.7	112.0	108.4	109.2
Specialty hospitals, except psychiatric	8069	12/92	110.9	113.6	114.7	117.0	120.0
Medical laboratories	8071	06/94	104.0	105.3	106.1	106.4	105.9
Home health care services.	8082	12/96	(X)	(X)	103.3	106.2	107.1
Legal services	8111	12/96	(X)	(X)	102.5	106.1	108.7
Engineering design, analysis, and consulting services. . .	8711	12/96	(X)	(X)	102.3	105.0	107.9
Architectural design, analysis, and consulting services . .	8712	12/96	(X)	(X)	102.0	105.8	111.8
Accounting, auditing, and bookkeeping services.	8721	06/95	(X)	102.9	105.7	108.2	111.9

NA Not available. N.e.c. Not elsewhere classified. X Not applicable. [1] Standard Industrial Classification code. [2] Index base year equals 100.

Source: U.S. Bureau of Labor Statistics, *Producer Price Indexes,* monthly.

Prices 499

No. 776. Chain-Type Price Indexes for Personal Consumption Expenditures (PCE): 1980 to 1999

[**1996=100.** For explanation of "chain-type," see text, Section 14, Income]

Item	1980	1985	1990	1995	1997	1998	1999
Personal consumption expenditures.............	**55.2**	**71.0**	**85.6**	**97.9**	**102.0**	**102.9**	**104.6**
Durable goods...................	76.5	88.6	96.0	101.1	97.8	95.5	93.0
Motor vehicles and parts.......	61.0	74.2	83.8	98.4	99.7	99.1	99.3
Furniture and household equipment...	106.3	116.3	113.6	104.5	95.2	90.4	85.0
Nondurable goods	65.3	77.3	91.0	97.9	101.4	101.4	103.8
Food.........................	60.8	72.9	88.2	97.3	102.2	104.0	106.1
Clothing and shoes..............	86.5	93.3	103.5	101.4	100.1	98.0	96.4
Gasoline, fuel oil, and other energy goods........................	90.6	93.3	95.2	93.7	100.1	88.8	96.0
Gasoline and oil	91.4	92.8	94.8	94.2	100.0	88.5	96.4
Fuel oil and coal	87.4	97.6	98.6	89.6	100.9	91.7	93.0
Services.......................	45.9	64.4	81.0	97.3	103.2	105.3	107.5
Housing......................	47.1	66.7	84.1	97.0	103.0	106.2	109.3
Household operation	56.3	81.8	87.6	98.1	101.7	100.7	100.7
Transportation	51.9	65.5	81.8	98.4	103.6	104.7	105.8
Medical care	37.2	55.9	76.0	97.9	102.3	104.7	107.4
Recreation...................	53.7	67.9	83.3	96.8	103.1	105.9	108.0
Addenda:							
Energy goods and services........	75.5	90.3	92.5	95.6	101.1	93.6	97.1
PCE less food and energy	52.4	69.2	84.7	98.2	102.0	103.3	104.8

Source: U.S. Bureau of Economic Analysis, *The National Income and Product Accounts of the United States*, 1929-94, Vol. 2; and *Survey of Current Business*, May 1999.

No. 777. Chain-Type Price Indexes for Gross Domestic Product: 1980 to 1999

[**1996=100.** For explanation of "chain-type," see text Section 14, Income]

Item	1980	1985	1990	1995	1997	1998	1999
Gross domestic product.........	**57.1**	**73.7**	**86.5**	**98.1**	**101.9**	**103.1**	**104.6**
Personal consumption expenditures......	55.2	71.0	85.6	97.9	102.0	102.9	104.6
Durable goods................	76.5	88.6	96.0	101.1	97.8	95.5	93.0
Nondurable goods...............	65.3	77.3	91.0	97.9	101.4	101.4	103.8
Services....................	45.9	64.4	81.0	97.3	103.2	105.3	107.5
Gross private domestic investment	73.0	85.3	95.1	100.3	99.8	99.0	98.8
Fixed investment................	71.8	84.5	94.7	100.1	100.0	99.2	99.2
Nonresidential	77.4	89.6	98.2	100.9	99.0	97.2	96.0
Structures.................	60.0	74.1	85.8	97.4	104.1	107.4	110.2
Producers' durable equipment	86.6	96.3	102.9	102.1	97.4	94.0	91.6
Residential..................	58.7	72.2	85.5	97.9	102.7	105.3	109.4
Exports of goods and services	83.3	88.7	96.8	101.3	98.5	96.2	95.8
Exports of goods	94.7	95.6	101.4	102.7	97.3	94.3	93.0
Exports of services.............	58.4	73.4	86.5	98.0	101.4	101.1	102.9
Imports of goods and services	90.5	85.0	99.4	101.8	96.5	91.3	91.6
Imports of goods	95.9	88.8	102.0	102.5	95.9	90.2	90.2
Imports of services.............	69.0	69.5	88.3	98.3	99.5	97.3	99.6
Government consumption expenditures [1] ..	55.8	73.8	85.2	97.6	101.9	103.4	106.2
Federal......................	57.5	75.7	83.8	97.2	101.3	102.4	105.5
National defense...............	57.9	77.2	84.6	96.9	101.2	102.0	104.8
Nondefense.................	56.0	71.5	82.0	97.9	101.6	103.2	106.9
State and local.................	67.1	72.4	87.7	97.7	103.7	107.0	111.5

[1] And gross investment.

Source: U.S. Bureau of Economic Analysis, *The National Income and Product Accounts of the United States, 1929-94*; and *Survey of Current Business*, May 2000.

No. 778. Commodity Research Bureau Futures Price Index: 1980 to 1999

[**1967=100.** Index computed daily. Represents unweighted geometric average of commodity futures prices (through 6 months forward) of 17 major commodity futures markets. Represents end of year index]

Item	1980	1985	1990	1991	1992	1993	1994	1995	1996	1997	1998	1999
All commodities....	**308.5**	**229.2**	**222.6**	**208.0**	**205.9**	**212.4**	**229.7**	**237.1**	**247.9**	**229.1**	**191.2**	**205.1**
Softs [1].............	426.0	398.2	276.0	264.4	232.4	246.9	352.3	354.4	322.2	408.7	344.8	280.9
Industrials..........	324.6	211.7	245.5	217.2	224.7	235.0	263.6	272.5	266.3	210.9	185.3	192.9
Grains and oilseeds [2]	312.1	198.5	171.2	196.1	196.9	193.8	191.2	218.6	284.7	210.7	172.8	156.6
Energy	(NA)	96.5	246.0	182.2	192.6	151.8	173.8	180.0	224.0	180.4	135.0	221.0
Oilseeds [3]...........	314.6	245.4	223.6	195.4	218.8	239.8	259.9	277.5	307.9	(3)	(3)	(3)
Livestock and meats.....	217.4	206.9	226.2	174.0	179.8	201.4	192.3	192.4	241.7	238.1	186.7	239.6
Metals (precious)	531.4	256.6	257.8	226.0	228.5	242.2	273.9	276.0	271.3	249.3	234.3	253.4

NA Not available   [1] Prior to 1997, reported as Imported.   [2] Prior to 1997, reported as grains.   [3] Beginning 1997, incorporated into grains and oilseeds.

Source: Bridge Commodity Research Bureau (CRB), Chicago, IL, *CRB Commodity Index Report*, weekly (copyright).

No. 779. Indexes of Spot Primary Market Prices: 1980 to 1999

[1967=100. Computed weekly for 1980; daily thereafter. Represents unweighted geometric average of price quotations of 23 commodities; much more sensitive to changes in market conditions than is a monthly producer price index]

Item and number of commodities	1980	1985	1990	1992	1993	1994	1995	1996	1997	1998	1999
All commodities (23)	265.1	251.4	279.2	242.3	237.7	261.5	290.6	297.7	271.8	235.2	227.3
Foodstuffs (10).	260.9	248.1	231.5	201.3	208.3	215.5	229.1	251.3	227.3	197.5	178.1
Raw industrials (13)	268.0	253.6	317.0	275.5	260.4	299.2	348.2	334.9	307.5	265.3	268.9
Livestock and products (5)	250.5	284.5	306.9	276.4	291.3	296.9	314.6	338.4	306.1	232.3	265.7
Metals (5)	257.9	220.2	313.9	262.7	236.2	262.1	306.7	296.7	269.8	218.5	261.6
Textiles and fibers (4)	234.7	220.8	259.4	218.6	205.3	252.6	286.0	274.6	261.5	237.5	223.8
Fats and oils (4)	229.5	273.1	193.3	180.7	190.1	209.6	228.3	245.7	257.1	236.0	174.8

Source: Bridge Commodity Research Bureau, Chicago, IL, *CRB Commodity Index Report,* weekly (copyright).

No. 780. Average Prices of Selected Fuels and Electricity: 1980 to 1999

[In dollars per unit, except electricity, in cents per kWh. Represents price to end-users, except as noted]

Type	Unit [1]	1980	1990	1992	1993	1994	1995	1996	1997	1998	1999
Crude oil, composite [2]. . .	Barrel	28.07	22.22	18.43	16.41	15.59	17.23	20.71	19.04	12.52	17.46
Motor gasoline: [3]											
Unleaded regular	Gallon.	1.25	1.16	1.13	1.11	1.11	1.15	1.23	1.23	1.06	1.17
Unleaded premium . . .	Gallon.	(NA)	1.35	1.32	1.30	1.31	1.34	1.41	1.42	1.25	1.36
No. 2 heating oil.	Gallon.	0.97	1.06	0.93	0.91	0.88	0.87	0.99	0.98	0.85	0.88
No. 2 diesel fuel.	Gallon.	0.82	0.73	0.62	0.60	0.55	0.56	0.68	0.64	0.49	0.58
Residual fuel oil	Gallon.	0.61	0.44	0.34	0.34	0.35	0.39	0.46	0.42	0.31	0.38
Natural gas, residential . . .	1,000 cu/ft. .	3.68	5.80	5.89	6.16	6.41	6.06	6.34	6.94	6.82	6.63
Electricity, residential. . . .	kWh	5.36	7.83	8.21	8.32	8.38	8.40	8.36	8.43	8.26	8.17

NA Not available. [1] See headnote. [2] Refiner acquisition cost. [3] Average, all service.

Source: U.S. Energy Information Administration, *Monthly Energy Review.*

No. 781. Weekly Food Cost by Type of Family: 1990 and 1999

[In dollars. Assumes that food for all meals and snacks is purchased at the store and prepared at home. See source for details on estimation procedures]

Family type	December 1990				October 1999			
	Thrifty-plan	Low-cost plan	Moderate-cost plan	Liberal-plan	Thrifty-plan	Low-cost plan	Moderate-cost plan	Liberal-plan
FAMILIES								
Family of two:								
20-50 years.	48.10	60.60	74.70	92.70	59.10	75.40	93.00	115.60
51 years and over	45.60	58.30	71.80	85.80	55.70	72.50	89.80	107.60
Family of four:								
Couple, 20-50 years and children—								
1-2 and 3-5 years	70.10	87.30	106.60	131.00	86.20	108.90	133.20	163.90
6-8 and 9-11 years	80.10	102.60	128.30	154.40	99.30	128.30	159.90	192.70
INDIVIDUALS [1]								
Child:								
1-2 years	12.70	15.40	18.00	21.80	15.60	19.30	22.60	27.50
3-5 years	13.70	16.80	20.70	24.90	16.90	21.10	26.10	31.30
6-8 years	16.60	22.20	27.90	32.50	20.90	28.00	34.90	40.60
9-11 years	19.80	25.30	32.50	37.60	24.70	31.80	40.50	47.00
Male:								
12-14 years.	20.60	28.60	35.70	42.00	25.60	35.80	44.50	52.20
15-19 years.	21.40	29.60	36.80	42.60	26.30	36.90	46.00	53.00
20-50 years.	22.90	29.30	36.60	44.30	28.20	36.60	45.60	55.20
51 years and over	20.90	27.90	34.30	41.10	25.50	34.80	42.90	51.50
Female:								
12-14 years.	20.80	24.80	30.10	36.30	25.60	30.90	37.50	45.30
20-50 years.	20.80	25.80	31.30	40.00	25.50	31.90	38.90	49.90
51 years and over	20.60	25.10	31.00	36.90	25.10	31.10	38.70	46.30

[1] The costs given are for individuals in four-person families. For individuals in other size families, the following adjustments are suggested: one-person, add 20 percent; two-person, add 10 percent; three-person, add 5 percent; five- or six-person, subtract 5 percent; seven- (or more) person, subtract 10 percent.

Source: U.S. Dept. of Agriculture, *Agricultural Research Service,* monthly.

U.S. Census Bureau, Statistical Abstract of the United States: 2000

No. 782. Food—Retail Prices of Selected Items: 1990 to 1999

[In dollars per pound, except as indicated. As of December]

Food	1990	1992	1993	1994	1995	1996	1997	1998	1999
Cereals and bakery products:									
Flour, white, all purpose	0.24	0.23	0.22	0.23	0.24	0.30	0.28	0.28	0.27
Rice, white, lg. grain, raw	0.49	0.53	0.50	0.53	0.55	0.55	0.58	0.54	0.50
Spaghetti and macaroni	0.85	0.86	0.84	0.87	0.88	0.84	0.88	0.88	0.88
Bread, whole wheat	(NA)	1.09	1.12	1.12	1.15	1.30	1.30	1.32	1.36
Meats, poultry, fish and eggs:									
Ground beef, 100% beef	1.63	1.50	1.57	1.38	1.40	1.42	1.39	1.39	1.53
Ground beef, lean and extra lean	(NA)	2.16	2.25	2.14	2.04	2.05	2.06	2.08	2.15
Sirloin steak, bone-in	3.65	3.75	3.69	(NA)	(NA)	(NA)	(NA)	(NA)	(NA)
T-bone steak.	5.45	5.39	5.77	5.86	5.92	5.87	6.07	6.40	6.71
Pork:									
Bacon, sliced	2.28	1.86	2.02	1.89	2.17	2.64	2.61	2.58	2.75
Chops, center cut, bone-in.	3.32	3.15	3.24	3.03	3.29	3.44	3.39	3.03	3.21
Sausage	2.42	2.14	1.99	1.85	1.92	2.15	2.08	2.43	2.50
Poultry:									
Chicken, fresh, whole	0.86	0.88	0.91	0.90	0.94	1.00	1.00	1.06	1.05
Chicken breast, bone-in	2.00	2.08	2.17	1.91	1.95	2.09	1.99	2.11	2.08
Turkey, frozen, whole	0.96	0.93	0.95	0.98	0.99	1.02	0.98	0.95	0.98
Tuna, light, chunk, canned.	2.11	1.96	2.04	2.02	2.00	2.03	2.03	2.22	2.03
Eggs, Grade A, large, (dozen)	1.00	0.93	0.87	0.87	1.16	1.31	1.17	1.09	0.92
Dairy products:									
Milk, fresh, whole, fortified (1/2 gal . . .	1.39	1.39	1.43	1.44	1.48	1.65	1.61	(NA)	(NA)
Butter, salted, grade AA, stick	1.92	1.64	1.61	1.54	1.73	2.17	2.46	3.18	2.27
Ice cream, prepack., bulk,reg.(1/2 gal .	2.54	2.49	2.59	2.62	2.68	2.94	3.02	3.30	3.40
Fresh fruits and vegetables:									
Apples, red Delicious	0.77	0.76	0.78	0.72	0.83	0.89	0.90	0.85	0.92
Bananas	0.43	0.40	0.41	0.46	0.45	0.48	0.46	0.51	0.49
Oranges, navel	0.56	0.52	0.56	0.55	0.64	0.59	0.58	0.61	0.64
Grapefruit.	0.56	0.52	0.50	0.47	0.49	0.55	0.53	0.55	0.58
Grapes, thompson seedless.	(NA)	(NA)	1.96	2.13	1.86	(NA)	2.19	(NA)	2.40
Lemons	0.97	0.90	1.05	1.04	1.12	1.14	1.06	1.37	1.41
Pears, Anjou	0.79	0.80	0.89	(NA)	(NA)	1.06	0.85	0.98	1.03
Potatoes, white	0.32	0.31	0.36	0.34	0.38	0.33	0.37	0.38	0.40
Tomatoes, field grown.	0.86	1.23	1.31	1.43	1.51	1.21	1.62	1.80	1.41
Cabbage	0.39	0.38	0.37	0.45	0.41	0.40	0.46	0.42	0.42
Carrots, short trimmed and topped . . .	0.44	0.44	0.41	0.48	0.53	0.54	0.50	0.54	0.52
Celery	0.49	0.48	0.49	0.52	0.54	0.44	0.57	0.53	0.56
Cucumbers.	0.56	0.51	0.93	0.69	0.53	0.60	0.58	(NA)	0.84
Onions, dry yellow	(NA)	0.42	0.48	0.43	0.41	0.46	0.46	(NA)	(NA)
Peppers, sweet	(NA)	1.15	1.26	1.52	1.32	0.81	1.54	1.46	1.53

NA Not available.

Source: U.S. Bureau of Labor Statistics, *Monthly Labor Review* and *CPI Detailed Report,* January issues.

No. 783. Import Price Indexes by Selected Commodity: 1990 to 1999

[1995 = 100. Indexes are weighted by the 1990 Tariff Schedule of the United States Annotated, a scheme for describing and reporting product composition and value of U.S. imports. Import prices are based on U.S. dollar prices paid by importer. F.o.b. = Free on board; c.i.f. = Cost, insurance, and freight; n.e.s = Not elsewhere specified]

Commodity	1990	1993	1994	1995 [1]	1996	1997	1998	1999
All commodities.	**90.3**	**94.4**	**95.8**	**100.8**	**100.1**	**98.2**	**92.6**	**92.4**
Food and live animals.	84.9	87.0	93.9	100.1	94.7	103.7	98.0	93.3
Meat.	116.3	115.6	105.9	99.1	90.4	101.9	98.3	94.5
Fish.	77.9	86.9	97.6	101.6	97.5	103.6	109.4	104.3
Crustaceans; fresh, chilled, frozen, salted or dried. .	73.3	80.1	97.7	103.4	95.0	103.5	106.4	99.0
Beverages and tobacco.	86.1	97.7	98.2	99.7	103.6	107.5	109.6	110.4
Crude materials.	82.4	77.1	86.3	99.8	94.3	97.4	87.7	90.3
Mineral fuels and related products.	92.9	101.6	96.9	105.1	110.6	104.6	77.6	92.7
Crude petroleum and petroleum products	91.7	100.8	96.4	105.4	111.0	104.0	73.4	91.3
Natural gas	112.7	113.8	105.4	101.2	108.2	113.3	111.9	106.5
Chemicals and related products	88.3	92.1	92.0	100.7	98.8	96.4	93.6	90.6
Intermediate manufactured products	88.8	88.6	90.2	99.8	99.2	96.8	94.0	92.0
Machinery and transport equipment.	90.2	95.9	97.6	100.6	98.6	95.7	91.8	90.3
Computer equipment and office machines	119.2	109.7	104.0	100.4	91.7	81.2	70.4	63.1
Computer equipment	143.0	121.9	109.1	99.7	93.0	80.8	66.5	54.7
Telecommunications [2]	102.0	99.9	99.2	100.5	97.3	93.4	89.4	87.6
Electrical machinery and equipment	92.0	96.9	98.9	101.6	95.5	90.2	84.5	82.7
Road vehicles	84.3	92.8	96.6	100.0	100.4	100.8	101.1	102.3
Miscellaneous manufactured articles	92.1	97.9	98.2	100.4	100.7	100.2	98.6	97.8
Plumbing, heating & lighting fixtures.	95.3	98.8	96.4	100.4	99.5	96.2	96.0	93.0
Furniture and parts	93.7	98.4	98.2	100.7	100.8	102.9	100.2	98.7
Articles of apparel and clothing	97.6	99.2	99.2	100.1	101.5	102.6	102.7	101.8
Footwear.	97.2	99.4	98.4	100.0	101.3	101.1	100.7	100.7

[1] June 1995 may not equal 100 because indexes were reweighted to an "average" trade value in 1995.   [2] Includes sound recording and reproducing equipment.

Source: U.S. Bureau of Labor Statistics, *U.S. Import and Export Price Indexes,* monthly.

No. 784. Export Price Indexes by Selected Commodity: 1990 to 1999

[1995=100. Indexes are weighted by 1980 export values according to the Schedule B classification system of the U.S. Census Bureau. Prices used in these indexes were collected from a sample of U.S. manufacturers of exports and are factory transaction prices, except as noted. F.a.s. = free alongside ship. N.e.s. = not elsewhere specified. F.o.b. = free on board]

Commodity	1990	1993	1994	1995 [1]	1996	1997	1998	1999
All commodities.	91.5	93.2	94.8	100.5	101.4	99.3	96.1	94.5
Food and live animals.	89.0	83.5	88.7	97.4	122.0	98.5	90.9	89.2
Meat.	84.9	96.2	92.5	99.9	101.6	95.3	97.8	91.5
Fish	83.6	82.0	83.3	103.2	89.4	85.3	80.7	118.5
Cereals and cereal preparations	90.6	75.7	84.9	95.4	145.6	92.3	82.6	75.9
Wheat	80.4	67.4	65.4	91.1	129.3	87.1	75.4	69.7
Maize	97.6	78.8	94.9	98.0	165.3	90.4	80.9	73.3
Fruits and vegetables	83.6	84.4	89.8	96.2	105.7	101.6	98.4	98.5
Feeding stuff for animals	93.2	96.2	101.4	98.3	122.5	127.2	95.0	86.7
Miscellaneous food products.	100.4	100.8	98.3	101.3	103.2	103.5	105.0	107.0
Beverages and tobacco.	86.4	98.4	98.7	99.9	100.6	100.8	99.9	101.2
Tobacco and tobacco manufactures	86.6	98.3	98.6	100.0	100.6	100.9	99.7	101.2
Crude materials	80.4	79.6	86.4	104.1	90.3	93.4	82.0	74.9
Raw hides and skins	105.1	79.1	94.3	103.4	95.7	100.8	84.8	79.0
Oil seeds and oleaginous fruits	97.0	97.8	112.7	96.6	127.0	134.6	102.6	79.2
Cork and wood.	66.4	105.1	97.3	102.1	94.7	93.2	82.0	82.0
Pulp and waste paper	64.7	45.4	61.1	111.6	56.8	65.9	64.0	66.0
Textile fibers.	81.8	66.6	83.7	106.9	91.1	83.4	79.3	68.6
Cotton textile fibers	83.4	62.2	81.4	107.9	90.2	80.6	78.7	65.6
Crude fertilizers and minerals	101.9	96.7	97.3	99.4	96.8	97.8	97.0	93.5
Metalliferous ores and metal scrap.	83.4	70.1	76.2	104.2	89.3	91.7	76.6	70.7
Ferrous waste and scrap	85.2	84.5	81.6	99.6	93.3	93.5	74.2	63.2
Nonferrous base metal waste and scrap	85.3	62.0	79.6	100.2	86.8	89.2	70.1	66.3
Mineral fuels and related materials	100.1	96.6	96.0	102.0	109.1	110.9	103.2	102.0
Coal, coke and briquettes.	103.2	96.8	96.8	100.3	103.1	102.0	100.1	98.3
Crude petroleum and petroleum products	99.9	96.0	95.7	103.6	113.7	119.4	106.8	107.6
Animal and vegetable oils, fats and waxes	86.6	82.7	92.5	96.5	95.4	94.7	107.9	76.6
Chemicals and related products	85.6	84.4	86.9	102.6	97.1	96.5	92.6	91.2
Organic chemicals.	81.7	77.9	79.8	106.8	87.8	84.9	77.1	75.2
Hydrocarbons, n.e.s. and derivatives, f.a.s.	82.9	71.2	82.0	115.7	90.8	95.0	75.0	78.4
Alcohols, phenols, phenol-alcohols, & deriv., f.a.s. . .	77.4	75.0	71.8	105.9	88.0	81.5	80.2	73.6
Chemical materials and products, n.e.s.	85.9	91.9	94.6	100.0	102.0	103.9	100.6	99.6
Intermediate manufactured products	86.9	87.7	90.9	100.8	97.9	98.2	97.9	96.8
Rubber manufactures	84.9	93.1	93.7	99.8	102.8	103.2	101.9	105.5
Paper and paperboard products	81.1	76.5	78.4	100.3	87.3	83.5	83.8	83.4
Textiles	89.7	96.2	96.1	101.1	103.8	103.3	103.2	99.2
Nonmetallic mineral manufactures	91.1	96.4	98.1	100.1	101.2	104.3	106.7	106.3
Nonferrous metals.	88.4	71.7	81.6	99.7	93.4	93.4	88.1	85.0
Manufactures of metals, n.e.s..	88.0	92.7	94.7	100.1	101.5	104.4	107.0	108.7
Machinery and transport equipment [2].	95.3	99.8	99.4	100.0	100.9	100.6	98.7	97.6
Power generating machinery [3]	86.5	95.9	97.7	99.4	104.3	106.0	107.1	109.6
Rotating electric plant and parts thereof, n.e.s.	89.2	95.0	96.2	100.4	102.4	103.1	103.1	102.7
Machinery specialized for particular industries	88.0	95.8	97.3	99.9	102.7	104.2	105.2	106.1
Agricultural machinery and parts [4]	90.3	96.8	98.7	100.3	102.0	102.8	103.1	103.8
Civil engineering and contractors, plant and equip. .	87.6	93.5	97.1	100.2	101.5	103.1	105.8	107.5
Metalworking machinery.	89.0	99.1	98.8	100.0	102.3	104.3	108.4	108.8
General industrial machines, parts, n.e.s.	89.2	96.8	98.4	99.4	102.5	105.2	106.1	107.3
Computer equipment and office machines	132.0	115.3	106.5	100.8	93.7	84.7	76.5	71.6
Computer equipment	148.1	123.2	111.0	101.5	90.1	79.1	73.8	67.0
Telecommunications [5]	94.1	102.9	100.9	100.3	101.1	99.6	98.7	96.9
Electrical machinery and equipment	96.8	100.2	99.9	100.7	99.1	96.5	92.1	88.6
Electronic valves, diodes, transistors & integr. cir. . .	101.6	103.3	101.0	101.7	97.9	91.8	84.4	79.1
Road vehicles	92.1	97.3	98.4	99.8	101.0	101.8	101.9	102.5
Miscellaneous manufactured articles	91.7	99.0	99.1	99.9	100.8	101.7	100.8	101.0

[1] June 1995 may not equal 100 because indexes were reweighted to an "average" trade value in 1995.   [2] Excludes military and commercial aircraft.   [3] Includes equipment.   [4] Excludes tractors.   [5] Includes sound recording and reproducing equipment.

Source: U.S. Bureau of Labor Statistics, *U.S. Import and Export Price Indexes*, monthly.

Prices   503

No. 785. Refiner/Reseller Sales Price of Gasoline by State: 1996 to 1998

[**In cents per gallon. As of March.** Represents all refinery and gas plant operators' sales through company-operated retail outlets. Gasoline prices exclude excise taxes]

State	Gasoline excise taxes 1998	Average, all grades			Midgrade			Premium		
		1996	1997	1998	1996	1997	1998	1996	1997	1998
United States	(NA)	71.5	70.3	53.0	76.0	75.1	57.9	80.4	79.4	61.8
Alabama	18	69.5	67.6	51.0	72.7	70.3	53.7	77.3	75.7	58.9
Alaska	8	90.0	90.8	75.5	103.7	101.7	85.1	102.5	101.9	86.1
Arizona	18	80.3	78.5	60.0	85.6	85.3	65.5	91.1	90.1	71.1
Arkansas	19	67.7	66.2	49.3	70.7	68.9	51.6	75.4	73.6	56.5
California	18	78.0	79.4	62.5	81.1	84.4	67.4	87.7	90.4	73.1
Colorado	22	73.3	72.4	54.1	78.1	76.0	57.2	80.5	79.7	61.0
Connecticut	36	74.7	73.4	56.2	78.2	78.0	60.8	83.6	82.0	63.8
Delaware	23	73.5	71.6	53.4	76.1	74.7	56.5	81.7	80.5	62.0
District of Columbia . .	20	85.4	82.1	66.9	83.8	80.7	66.7	91.2	86.7	70.7
Florida	13	71.2	70.0	51.5	73.6	72.9	53.9	80.4	79.3	60.0
Georgia	8	68.2	66.2	49.8	70.8	69.1	52.6	76.0	74.0	57.5
Hawaii	16	103.7	102.5	97.5	106.7	106.2	99.5	112.7	111.7	105.6
Idaho	25	77.8	79.6	60.4	80.0	82.7	63.7	84.7	88.2	68.9
Illinois	19	73.8	71.0	54.2	82.8	78.6	60.7	84.0	81.6	65.1
Indiana	15	70.2	67.8	51.5	75.2	71.6	55.1	78.6	76.6	60.1
Iowa	20	70.2	68.8	51.4	75.9	72.6	56.4	76.8	75.3	58.4
Kansas	18	67.6	66.5	49.0	73.5	72.0	53.9	74.6	73.2	55.5
Kentucky	16	70.8	69.2	52.4	74.6	73.2	55.5	77.9	77.2	60.3
Louisiana	20	66.2	65.8	48.0	70.2	70.4	53.6	74.2	72.1	53.7
Maine	19	71.4	71.1	53.5	77.0	75.8	57.9	78.7	79.2	61.6
Maryland	24	77.0	73.7	57.7	79.1	76.2	60.7	85.0	81.1	64.9
Massachusetts	21	75.2	74.6	55.8	80.3	80.5	61.9	82.9	83.2	63.9
Michigan	19	71.8	68.3	51.9	76.0	72.6	57.0	79.9	76.9	60.6
Minnesota	20	72.6	71.6	55.9	78.7	74.4	57.4	79.7	78.2	62.0
Mississippi	18	66.4	65.5	49.2	70.1	69.9	54.0	74.2	73.6	56.5
Missouri	17	69.8	68.9	51.9	75.9	75.0	56.3	77.1	77.0	60.3
Montana	28	79.9	77.4	60.0	81.9	79.9	62.5	88.4	86.6	69.1
Nebraska	25	69.9	68.7	51.1	74.0	73.0	56.8	77.1	76.0	58.5
Nevada	24	78.6	78.1	58.4	82.6	81.7	63.4	88.0	87.3	68.0
New Hampshire	18	77.8	76.7	56.8	80.8	81.3	62.2	86.8	86.7	66.5
New Jersey	11	71.6	70.7	53.1	79.9	79.2	61.4	80.9	80.6	63.5
New Mexico	19	74.7	73.0	53.8	78.7	76.0	57.2	82.4	80.9	61.5
New York	23	74.3	74.4	56.3	79.5	79.4	61.6	84.5	83.8	65.9
North Carolina	22	68.5	67.3	50.0	70.9	70.1	53.3	76.2	75.2	57.3
North Dakota	20	72.5	70.4	52.0	77.7	75.9	58.3	81.6	79.1	60.6
Ohio	22	70.6	68.4	53.2	74.5	72.2	57.3	79.3	77.6	62.8
Oklahoma	17	65.5	64.4	47.2	72.8	70.7	53.6	72.9	71.5	53.5
Oregon	24	77.2	75.7	57.1	82.9	82.4	62.9	88.0	86.8	67.6
Pennsylvania	26	70.7	69.1	51.1	73.7	72.3	55.0	78.7	77.4	58.4
Rhode Island	29	73.3	72.6	53.9	76.7	77.3	57.6	81.7	81.6	62.0
South Carolina	16	68.5	66.6	48.9	71.3	69.2	51.5	76.8	74.7	56.4
South Dakota	21	72.6	70.9	52.8	77.0	73.4	55.9	80.4	79.1	60.5
Tennessee	20	68.9	67.5	50.3	71.3	70.5	53.4	76.5	75.3	57.6
Texas	20	65.3	63.8	46.7	71.4	69.9	52.0	73.7	72.2	54.7
Utah	25	77.3	79.3	59.5	79.9	81.9	62.8	83.3	85.7	66.2
Vermont	19	78.8	77.6	58.7	81.6	81.9	63.5	87.7	86.5	67.9
Virginia	18	71.6	69.4	52.9	73.9	72.0	56.0	80.0	77.2	60.6
Washington	23	79.8	76.5	59.5	84.6	81.8	64.6	90.7	87.6	69.1
West Virginia	21	73.6	71.3	56.3	76.4	74.3	59.2	81.9	79.8	65.0
Wisconsin	25	71.8	68.6	51.8	75.9	73.2	57.0	79.2	76.5	60.2
Wyoming	9	76.0	75.4	56.8	80.7	81.9	62.4	83.5	83.8	65.0

NA Not available.

Source: U.S. Energy Information Administration, *Petroleum Marketing Monthly.*

Section 16
Banking, Finance, and Insurance

This section presents data on the Nation's finances, various types of financial institutions, money and credit, securities, and insurance. The primary sources of these data are publications of several departments of the Federal Government, especially the Treasury Department, and independent agencies such as the Federal Deposit Insurance Corporation, the Federal Reserve System, and the Securities and Exchange Commission. National data on insurance are available primarily from private organizations, such as the American Council of Life Insurance.

Flow of funds—The flow of funds accounts of the Federal Reserve System bring together statistics on all of the major forms of financial instruments to present an economy-wide view of asset and liability relationships. In flow form, the accounts relate borrowing and lending to one another and to the nonfinancial activities that generate income and production. Each claim outstanding is included simultaneously as an asset of the lender and as a liability of the debtor. The accounts also indicate the balance between asset totals and liability totals over the economy as a whole. Several publications of the Board of Governors of the Federal Reserve System contain information on the flow of funds accounts: Summary data on flows and outstandings, in the *Federal Reserve Bulletin,* and *Flow of Funds Accounts of the United States* (quarterly); and concepts and organization of the accounts, in *Guide to the Flow of Funds Accounts* (2000). Data are also available at the Board's web site <http://www.federalreserve.gov/releases>.

Banking system—Banks in this country are organized under the laws of both the states and the Federal Government and are regulated by several bank supervisory agencies. National banks are supervised by the Comptroller of the Currency. *Reports of Condition* have been collected from national banks since 1863. Summaries of these reports are published in the Comptroller's *Annual Report,* which also presents data on the structure of the national banking system.

The Federal Reserve System was established in 1913 to exercise central banking functions, some of which are shared with the U.S. Treasury. It includes national banks and such state banks that voluntarily join the system. Statements of state bank members are consolidated by the Board of Governors of the Federal Reserve System with data for national banks collected by the Comptroller of the Currency into totals for all member banks of the system. Balance sheet data for member banks and other commercial banks are published quarterly in the *Federal Reserve Bulletin.* The Federal Deposit Insurance Corporation (FDIC), established in 1933, insures each depositor up to $100,000. Major item balance sheet and income data for all commercial banks are published in the *FDIC Quarterly Banking Profile.* This publication is also available on the Internet at the following address: <http://www.fdic.gov>. Balance sheet and income data for individual institutions are also available at this site in the Institution Directory (ID) system.

The FDIC is the primary Federal regulator of state-chartered banks that are not members of the Federal Reserve System and of most savings banks insured by the Bank Insurance Fund (BIF). The agency also has certain backup supervisory authority, for safety and soundness purposes, over state-chartered banks that are members of the Federal Reserve System, national banks, and savings associations.

Savings institutions—Savings institutions are primarily involved in credit extension in the form of mortgage loans. Statistics on savings institutions are collected by the U.S. Office of Thrift Supervision and the

U.S. Census Bureau, Statistical Abstract of the United States: 2000

FDIC. The Financial Institutions Reform, Recovery, and Enforcement Act of 1989 (FIRREA) authorized the establishment of the Resolution Trust Corporation (RTC) which was responsible for the disposal of assets from failed savings institutions. FIRREA gave the FDIC the job of managing the Federal deposit insurance fund for savings institutions (SAIF=Savings Association Insurance Fund). Major balance sheet and income data for all insured savings institutions are published in the *FDIC Quarterly Banking Profile.*

Credit unions—Federally chartered credit unions are under the supervision of the National Credit Union Administration. State-chartered credit unions are supervised by the respective state supervisory authorities. The Administration publishes comprehensive program and statistical information on all Federal and federally insured state credit unions in the *Annual Report of the National Credit Union Administration.* Deposit insurance (up to $100,000 per account) is provided to members of all Federal and those state credit unions that are federally-insured by the National Credit Union Share Insurance Fund which was established in 1970. Deposit insurance for state chartered credit unions is also available in some states under private or state-administered insurance programs.

Other credit agencies—Insurance companies, finance companies dealing primarily in installment sales financing, and personal loan companies represent important sources of funds for the credit market. Statistics on loans, investments, cash, etc., of life insurance companies are published principally by the American Council of Life Insurance in its *Life Insurance Fact Book* and in the *Federal Reserve Bulletin.* Consumer credit data are published currently in the *Federal Reserve Bulletin.*

Government corporations and credit agencies make available credit of specified types or to specified groups of private borrowers, either by lending directly or by insuring or guaranteeing loans made by private lending institutions. Data on operations of government credit agencies, along with other government corporations, are available in reports of individual agencies; data on their debt outstanding are published in the *Federal Reserve Bulletin.*

Currency—Currency, including coin and paper money, represents about 46 percent of all media of exchange in the United States, with most payments made by check. All currency is now issued by the Federal Reserve Banks.

Securities—The Securities and Exchange Commission (SEC) was established in 1934 to protect the interests of the public and investors against malpractices in the securities and financial markets and to provide the fullest possible disclosure of information regarding securities to the investing public. Statistical data are published in the *SEC Annual Report.*

Insurance—Insuring companies, which are regulated by the various states or the District of Columbia, are classified as either life or property. Companies that underwrite accident and health insurance only and those that underwrite accident and health insurance in addition to one or more property lines are included with property insurance. Insuring companies, other than those classified as life, are permitted to underwrite one or more property lines provided they are so licensed and have the necessary capital or surplus.

There are a number of published sources for statistics on the various classes of insurance—life, health, fire, marine, and casualty. Organizations representing certain classes of insurers publish reports for these classes. The American Council of Life Insurance publishes statistics on life insurance purchases, ownership, benefit payments, and assets in its *Life Insurance Fact Book.*

No. 786. Gross Domestic Product in Finance, Insurance, and Real Estate, in Current and Real (1996) Dollars: 1990 to 1998

[In billions of dollars, except percent (1,010.3 represents $1,010,300,000,000). For definition of gross domestic product, see text, Section 14, Income. Based on 1987 Standard Industrial Classification; see text, Section 17, Business]

Industry	Current dollars				Chained (1996) dollars [1]			
	1990	1995	1997	1998	1990	1995	1997	1998
Finance, insurance, real estate, total	1,010.3	1,347.2	1,561.6	1,674.2	1,250.6	1,393.0	1,510.5	1,606.7
Percent of gross domestic product	17.4	18.2	18.8	19.1	18.6	18.5	18.5	18.9
Depository institutions	171.3	227.4	271.2	289.6	244.0	242.4	241.7	257.9
Nondepository institutions	23.3	34.1	51.6	78.5	26.3	33.4	55.6	87.6
Security and commodity brokers	42.3	77.7	117.3	117.1	42.0	76.5	124.2	136.3
Insurance carriers.	64.6	120.2	141.4	143.1	112.2	129.9	131.0	129.6
Insurance agents, brokers, and service	37.7	47.2	51.3	53.7	61.4	49.9	48.8	49.3
Real estate	665.7	832.6	919.2	967.9	763.4	852.8	902.9	932.4
Nonfarm housing services	488.3	628.9	680.2	711.9	580.1	648.0	662.0	671.0
Other real estate.	177.3	203.7	239.0	256.1	182.9	204.9	241.2	262.6
Holding and other investment offices	5.5	8.0	9.7	24.2	10.2	9.9	7.5	16.4

[1] See text, Section 14, Income.

Source: U.S. Bureau of Economic Analysis, *Survey of Current Business*, June 2000.

No. 787. Finance, Insurance, and Real Estate Establishments—Number, Revenues, Payroll, and Employees: 1992 and 1997

[586 represents 586,000. Covers only establishments with payroll]

Kind of business	1987 SIC code [1]	Establishments (1,000)		Revenue (bil. dol.)		Annual payroll (bil. dol.)		Paid employees (1,000)	
		1992	1997	1992	1997	1992	1997	1992	1997
Finance, insurance, and real estate .	(H)	586	661	1,832	2,475	212	308	6,510	7,314
Depository institutions	60	105	110	532	(D)	57	(D)	2,100	[2]
Nondepository institutions	61	39	52	135	(D)	15	(D)	446	[2]
Security and commodity brokers	62	31	45	109	(D)	34	(D)	406	[2]
Insurance carriers	63	39	41	796	997	51	67	1,517	1,614
Insurance agents, brokers, & service . . .	64	122	132	52	75	19	25	636	713
Real estate	65	229	252	142	180	26	33	1,231	1,340
Holding and other investment offices. . . .	67	20	30	66	139	9	14	174	258

D Data withheld to avoid disclosure. [1] Standard Industrial Classification; see text, Section 17, Business. [2] 100,000 or more employees.

Source: U.S. Census Bureau, *1997 Economic Census, Core Business Statistics Series, Comparative Statistics*, EC97X-CS2.

No. 788. Finance, Insurance, and Real Estate—Establishments, Employees, and Payroll: 1990 and 1997

[544.7 represents 544,700. Covers establishments with payroll. Employees are for the week including March 12. Most government employees are excluded. For statement on methodology, see Appendix III]

Kind of business	1987 SIC code [1]	Establishments (1,000)		Employees (1,000)		Payroll (bil. dol.)	
		1990	1997	1990	1997	1990	1997
Finance, insurance, and real estate .	(H)	544.7	676.8	6,957	7,367	197.4	313.3
Depository institutions [2][3]	60	81.2	115.1	2,033	2,067	48.4	72.5
Commercial banks	602	52.3	75.8	1,472	1,513	35.6	53.3
Savings institutions . . [2][3]	603	21.7	16.4	417	258	8.8	8.3
Nondepository institutions [2][3]	61	42.0	53.0	506	567	14.0	24.0
Mortgage bankers and brokers	616	10.9	26.0	153	259	4.6	11.0
Security and commodity brokers [2]	62	25.2	49.4	411	675	26.6	68.3
Security brokers and dealers	621	15.9	28.8	308	468	20.8	48.8
Security and commodity services	628	7.1	18.9	76	185	4.5	18.0
Insurance carriers [2]	63	43.3	41.7	1,407	1,561	41.5	64.8
Life insurance . . . . [2] .	631	14.1	11.2	572	514	16.3	20.2
Medical service and health insurance [2] . . .	632	2.1	3.6	188	333	5.1	12.9
Hospital and medical service plans	6324	1.0	2.6	139	276	3.8	10.7
Fire, marine, and casualty insurance	633	18.3	20.6	533	624	17.0	28.1
Insurance agents, brokers, and service	64	110.8	131.9	712	719	20.3	26.2
Real estate [2]	65	217.0	256.1	1,374	1,418	28.5	36.3
Real estate operators and lessors.	651	95.7	102.4	509	480	8.7	10.1
Real estate agents and managers.	653	72.2	129.3	585	784	13.3	21.9
Holding and other investment offices.	67	22.6	27.9	263	269	10.0	15.7
Administrative and auxiliary	(X)	2.6	1.7	251	91	8.2	5.5

X Not applicable. [1] Standard Industrial Classification; see text, Section 17, Business. [2] Includes industries not shown separately. [3] Includes government employees.

Source: U.S. Census Bureau, *County Business Patterns*, annual.

U.S. Census Bureau, Statistical Abstract of the United States: 2000

No. 789. Flow of Funds Accounts—Financial Assets of Financial and Nonfinancial Institutions by Holder Sector: 1980 to 1999

[In billions of dollars (13,976 represents $13,976,000,000,000). As of Dec. 31]

Sector	1980	1985	1990	1993	1994	1995	1996	1997	1998	1999
All sectors	13,976	23,913	36,484	45,228	47,556	53,812	59,974	68,301	76,576	86,989
Households [1]	6,563	10,100	14,963	18,454	19,169	21,834	24,184	27,628	30,583	34,948
Nonfinancial business	1,541	2,847	3,977	4,586	4,901	5,441	5,998	6,560	6,975	7,687
Farm business	24	33	47	57	59	61	61	62	65	65
Nonfarm noncorporate	145	435	486	514	581	660	748	826	907	991
Nonfinancial corporations	1,373	2,379	3,444	4,015	4,261	4,719	5,189	5,672	6,003	6,632
State and local government	301	645	963	1,083	1,026	994	1,008	1,033	1,150	1,230
U.S. Government	229	372	440	489	436	438	437	432	437	559
U.S. Govt.-sponsored enterprises	195	324	478	631	782	897	989	1,099	1,404	1,720
Federally-related mortgage pools	114	369	1,020	1,357	1,472	1,570	1,711	1,826	2,018	2,292
Monetary authorities	174	243	342	424	452	472	495	534	567	697
Commercial banking [2]	1,482	2,376	3,337	3,892	4,160	4,494	4,710	5,175	5,642	5,994
U.S.-chartered commercial banks	1,266	1,990	2,644	2,932	3,123	3,322	3,445	3,742	4,094	4,433
Foreign banking offices in U.S.	98	144	367	542	590	666	715	811	806	758
Bank holding companies	103	219	298	388	414	467	511	575	686	741
Nonbank finance [2]	2,884	5,688	8,999	11,712	12,303	14,243	16,310	19,151	22,181	25,556
Funding corporations	16	135	247	327	365	373	480	594	711	932
Savings institutions	792	1,275	1,323	1,020	1,009	1,013	1,032	1,029	1,088	1,151
Credit unions	68	135	217	282	294	311	330	354	391	415
Life insurance	464	796	1,351	1,755	1,863	2,064	2,246	2,515	2,770	3,105
Other insurance	182	299	533	642	678	740	770	841	890	891
Private pension funds	513	1,228	1,608	2,252	2,352	2,755	3,155	3,706	4,331	4,998
State and local govt. retirement funds	197	399	884	1,103	1,185	1,465	1,790	2,308	2,698	3,047
Finance companies	197	338	547	557	600	672	715	757	828	956
Real estate investment trusts	3	10	28	30	31	33	38	64	71	67
Mutual funds	62	246	608	1,375	1,477	1,853	2,342	2,989	3,611	4,515
Closed-end investment funds	8	8	53	116	118	134	145	149	143	143
Money market funds	76	242	493	560	603	745	891	1,049	1,334	1,585
Security brokers, dealers	45	156	262	479	455	568	636	779	921	999
Asset-backed securities issuers	-	37	270	492	568	709	858	1,067	1,382	1,622
Bank personal trusts, estates	245	358	522	661	670	775	842	918	976	1,092
Rest of the world	493	950	1,965	2,601	2,856	3,430	4,132	4,862	5,618	6,305

- Represents zero. [1] Includes nonprofit organizations. [2] Includes other sectors not shown separately.

No. 790. Flow of Funds Accounts—Credit Market Debt Outstanding: 1980 to 1999

[In billions of dollars (4,733 represents $4,733,000,000,000). As of Dec. 31. N.e.c.=Not elsewhere classified]

Item	1980	1985	1990	1993	1994	1995	1996	1997	1998	1999
Credit market debt	4,733	8,628	13,752	16,169	17,204	18,444	19,806	21,251	23,364	25,614
U.S. Government	735	1,590	2,498	3,336	3,492	3,637	3,782	3,805	3,752	3,680
Non-Federal domestic nonfinancial	3,223	5,543	8,352	9,101	9,519	10,087	10,678	11,429	12,493	13,705
Households [1]	1,374	2,236	3,554	4,108	4,427	4,783	5,108	5,438	5,910	6,467
Corporations	912	1,613	2,522	2,569	2,707	2,937	3,120	3,402	3,807	4,286
Nonfarm noncorporate business	431	843	1,148	1,119	1,122	1,152	1,236	1,314	1,412	1,531
Farm business	161	173	135	138	142	145	150	156	164	169
State and local government	344	678	992	1,168	1,122	1,070	1,063	1,119	1,200	1,252
Rest of the world	197	237	286	386	370	441	519	570	604	622
Financial sectors	578	1,258	2,616	3,346	3,822	4,279	4,828	5,447	6,516	7,607
Commercial banking	91	188	198	208	228	251	264	309	382	452
Thrift institutions [2]	55	111	140	100	113	115	141	161	214	262
Life insurance companies	-	-	-	-	1	1	2	2	2	3
Government-sponsored enterprises [3]	163	264	399	528	701	807	897	995	1,274	1,592
Federally-related mortgage pools	114	369	1,020	1,357	1,472	1,570	1,711	1,826	2,018	2,292
Asset-backed securities issuers	-	37	271	494	570	713	866	1,078	1,395	1,632
Finance companies	127	224	374	385	434	484	530	554	598	654
Mortgage companies	12	17	25	30	19	17	21	16	18	18
Real estate investment trusts	4	8	28	30	40	45	56	96	159	167
Security brokers, dealers	-	1	15	34	34	29	27	35	43	25
Funding corporations	13	39	147	180	211	249	313	374	414	511
CORPORATE CREDIT MARKET DEBT OUTSTANDING, BY TYPE OF INSTRUMENT										
Total	912	1,613	2,522	2,569	2,707	2,937	3,120	3,402	3,807	4,286
Commercial paper	28	72	117	118	139	157	156	169	193	230
Municipal securities [4]	46	127	115	125	132	135	138	142	148	153
Corporate bonds	366	578	1,008	1,230	1,253	1,344	1,460	1,611	1,830	2,059
Bank loans, n.e.c.	230	424	545	478	521	588	627	695	778	850
Other loans and advances	110	248	473	388	421	454	472	521	568	615
Savings institutions	1	15	17	5	5	6	8	9	12	15
Finance companies	78	135	241	224	247	271	279	287	313	366
U.S. Government	8	14	9	8	8	10	9	8	8	8
Acceptance liabilities to banks	17	28	29	17	15	14	13	11	7	4
Rest of the world	5	56	172	114	122	122	126	143	142	117
Asset-backed securities issuers	-	-	4	19	24	30	38	62	86	104
Mortgages	132	163	264	230	241	259	266	264	292	379

- Represents or rounds to zero. [1] Includes nonprofit organizations. [2] Covers savings institutions and credit unions. [3] U.S. Government. [4] Industrial revenue bonds. Issued by state and local governments to finance private investment and secured in interest and principal by the industrial user of the funds.

Source of Tables 789 and 790: Board of Governors of the Federal Reserve System, *"Federal Reserve Statistical Release, Z.1, Flow of Funds Accounts of the United States"*; published: 10 March 2000; <http://www.bog.frb.fed.us/releases/Z1/20000310/data.htm>.

No. 791. Flow of Funds Accounts—Assets of Households: 1980 to 1999

[As of **December 31 (6,563 represents $6,563,000,000,000)**. Includes nonprofit organizations]

Type of instrument	Total (bil. dol.)							Percent distribution		
	1980	1985	1990	1995	1997	1998	1999	1980	1990	1999
Total financial assets	**6,563**	**10,100**	**14,963**	**21,834**	**27,628**	**30,583**	**34,948**	**100.0**	**100.0**	**100.0**
Deposits	1,517	2,484	3,265	3,366	3,807	4,165	4,338	23.1	21.8	12.4
Foreign deposits	-	8	13	23	42	42	45	-	0.1	0.1
Checkable deposits and currency . .	251	342	409	505	445	461	442	3.8	2.7	1.3
Time and savings deposits	1,203	1,941	2,477	2,388	2,725	2,924	3,013	18.3	16.6	8.6
Money market fund shares	62	193	365	449	595	738	838	0.9	2.4	2.4
Credit market instruments	425	849	1,503	1,885	1,873	1,781	1,960	6.5	10.0	5.6
Open-market paper	38	35	63	48	59	63	69	0.6	0.4	0.2
U.S. Government securities	165	270	529	822	721	552	659	2.5	3.5	1.9
Treasury issues	160	251	462	700	511	391	347	2.4	3.1	1.0
Savings bonds	73	80	126	185	187	187	186	1.1	0.8	0.5
Other Treasury	88	171	335	515	325	204	160	1.3	2.2	0.5
Agency issues	5	19	67	122	209	162	312	0.1	0.4	0.9
Municipal securities	104	346	574	458	464	475	528	1.6	3.8	1.5
Corporate and foreign bonds	30	77	192	448	521	581	596	0.5	1.3	1.7
Mortgages	87	120	144	109	109	109	110	1.3	1.0	0.3
Corporate equities [1]	875	1,058	1,807	4,122	5,690	6,339	8,009	13.3	12.1	22.9
Mutual fund shares	46	198	468	1,265	2,057	2,501	3,104	0.7	3.1	8.9
Security credit	16	35	62	128	215	277	319	0.2	0.4	0.9
Life insurance reserves	221	264	392	566	665	718	772	3.4	2.6	2.2
Pension fund reserves [2]	971	2,087	3,462	5,768	7,894	9,079	10,360	14.8	23.1	29.6
Investment in bank personal trusts . . .	265	384	552	803	943	1,001	1,117	4.0	3.7	3.2
Equity in noncorporate business	2,154	2,607	3,230	3,640	4,172	4,395	4,630	32.8	21.6	13.2
Miscellaneous assets	74	133	224	292	312	327	339	1.1	1.5	1.0

- Represents zero.   [1] Only those directly held and those in closed-end funds. Other equities are included in mutual funds, life insurance and pension reserves, and bank personal trusts.   [2] See also Table 846.

Source: Board of Governors of the Federal Reserve System, *"Federal Reserve Statistical Release, Z.1, Flow of Funds Accounts of the United States"*; published: 10 March 2000; <http://www.bog.frb.fed.us/releases/Z1/20000310/data.htm>.

No. 792. Financial Assets Held by Families by Type of Asset: 1992 to 1998

[**Median value in thousands of constant 1998 dollars (13.1 represents $13,100)**. Constant dollar figures are based on consumer price index data published by U.S. Bureau of Labor Statistics. Families include one-person units; for definition of family, see text, Section 1, Population. Based on Survey of Consumer Finance; see Appendix III. For definition of median, see Guide to Tabular Presentation]

Age of family head and family income	Any financial asset [1]	Trans-action accounts [2]	Certifi-cates of deposit	Savings bonds	Stocks [3]	Mutual funds [4]	Retirement accounts [5]	Life insur-ance [6]	Other man-aged [7]
PERCENT OF FAMILIES OWNING ASSET									
1992, total	90.2	86.9	16.7	22.3	17.0	10.4	39.6	34.9	4.0
1995, total	91.0	87.0	14.3	22.8	15.2	12.3	45.2	32.0	3.9
1998, total	**92.9**	**90.5**	**15.3**	**19.3**	**19.2**	**16.5**	**48.8**	**29.6**	**5.9**
Under 35 years old	88.6	84.6	6.2	17.2	13.1	12.2	39.8	18.0	1.9
35 to 44 years old	93.3	90.5	9.4	24.9	18.9	16.0	59.5	29.0	3.9
45 to 54 years old	94.9	93.5	11.8	21.8	22.6	23.0	59.2	32.9	6.5
55 to 64 years old	95.6	93.9	18.6	18.1	25.0	15.2	58.3	35.8	6.5
65 to 74 years old	95.6	94.1	29.9	16.1	21.0	18.0	46.1	39.1	11.8
75 years old and over	92.1	89.7	35.9	12.0	18.0	15.1	16.7	32.6	11.6
Less than $10,000	70.6	61.9	7.7	3.5	3.8	1.9	6.4	15.7	(B)
$10,000 to $24,999	89.9	86.5	16.8	10.2	7.2	7.6	25.4	20.9	4.9
$25,000 to $49,999	97.3	95.8	15.9	20.4	17.7	14.0	54.2	28.1	3.9
$50,000 to $99,999	99.8	99.3	16.4	30.6	27.7	25.8	73.5	39.8	8.0
$100,000 and more	100.0	100.0	16.8	32.3	56.6	44.8	88.6	50.1	15.8
MEDIAN VALUE [8]									
1992, total	13.1	2.6	12.6	0.7	9.1	18.3	16.0	3.5	22.8
1995, total	16.5	2.3	10.6	1.1	9.6	21.2	18.1	5.3	31.9
1998, total	**22.4**	**3.1**	**15.0**	**1.0**	**17.5**	**25.0**	**24.0**	**7.3**	**31.5**
Under 35 years old	4.5	1.5	2.5	0.5	5.0	7.0	7.0	2.7	19.4
35 to 44 years old	22.9	2.8	8.0	0.7	12.0	14.0	21.0	8.5	25.0
45 to 54 years old	37.8	4.5	11.5	1.0	24.0	30.0	34.0	10.0	39.3
55 to 64 years old	45.6	4.1	17.0	1.5	21.0	58.0	46.8	9.5	65.0
65 to 74 years old	45.8	5.6	20.0	2.0	50.0	60.0	38.0	8.5	41.3
75 years old and over	36.6	6.1	30.0	5.0	50.0	59.0	30.0	5.0	30.0
Less than $10,000	1.1	0.5	7.0	1.8	14.0	6.0	7.5	3.0	(B)
$10,000 to $24,999	4.8	1.3	20.0	1.0	10.0	26.0	8.0	5.0	30.0
$25,000 to $49,999	17.6	2.5	14.5	0.6	8.0	11.0	13.0	5.0	15.0
$50,000 to $99,999	57.2	6.0	13.3	1.0	15.0	25.0	31.0	9.5	32.0
$100,000 and more	244.3	19.0	22.0	1.5	50.0	65.0	93.0	18.0	100.0

B Base figure too small.   [1] Includes other types of financial assets, not shown separately.   [2] Checking, savings, and money market deposit accounts, money market mutual funds, and call accounts at brokerages.   [3] Covers only those stocks that are directly held by families outside mutual funds, retirement accounts and other managed assets.   [4] Excludes money market mutual funds and funds held through retirement accounts, or other managed assets.   [5] Covers IRAs, Keogh accounts, and certain employer-sponsored accounts.   [6] Cash value.   [7] Includes personal annuities and trusts with an equity interest and managed investment accounts.   [8] Median value of financial asset for families holding such assets.

Source: Board of Governors of the Federal Reserve System, *Federal Reserve Bulletin*, January 2000, and unpublished revisions.

Banking, Finance, and Insurance   509

No. 793. Flow of Funds Accounts—Liabilities of Households: 1980 to 1999

[As of **December 31** (**1,426 represents $1,426,000,000,000**). Includes nonprofit organizations]

Type of instrument	Total (bil. dol.)							Percent distribution		
	1980	1985	1990	1995	1997	1998	1999	1980	1990	1999
Total liabilities	1,426	2,326	3,679	4,982	5,708	6,206	6,841	100.0	100.0	100.0
Credit market instruments	1,374	2,236	3,554	4,783	5,438	5,910	6,467	96.4	96.6	94.5
Home mortgages	905	1,408	2,461	3,252	3,698	4,058	4,480	63.5	66.9	65.5
Consumer credit	355	604	805	1,123	1,264	1,332	1,429	24.9	21.9	20.9
Municipal securities	17	81	87	98	115	127	137	1.2	2.4	2.0
Bank loans, n.e.c. [1]	28	31	18	57	67	73	65	2.0	0.5	1.0
Other loans	55	79	101	160	191	204	219	3.8	2.7	3.2
Commercial mortgages	15	33	83	92	104	117	137	1.0	2.2	2.0
Security credit	25	51	39	79	131	153	222	1.7	1.1	3.3
Trade payables	14	24	69	103	120	126	133	1.0	1.9	1.9
Unpaid life insurance premiums [2]	13	15	16	18	19	17	19	0.9	0.4	0.3

[1] Not elsewhere classified.   [2] Includes deferred premiums.
Source: Board of Governors of the Federal Reserve System, *"Federal Reserve Statistical Release, Z.1, Flow of Funds Accounts of the United States"*; published: 10 March 2000; <http://www.bog.frb.fed.us/releases/Z1/20000310/data.htm>.

No. 794. Financial Debt Held by Families by Type of Debt: 1992 to 1998

[**Median debt in thousands of constant 1998 dollars** (**19.9 represents $19,900**). See headnote, Table 792]

Age of family head and family income	Any debt	Home-secured debt [1]	Installment	Other lines of credit	Credit card balances [2]	Other residential property	Other debt [3]
PERCENT OF FAMILIES HOLDING DEBTS							
1992, total	73.2	39.1	46.0	2.3	43.7	5.7	8.4
1995, total	74.5	41.0	45.9	1.9	47.3	4.7	8.5
1998, total	74.1	43.1	43.7	2.3	44.1	5.1	8.8
Under 35 years old	81.2	33.2	60.0	2.4	50.7	2.0	9.6
35 to 44 years old	87.6	58.7	53.3	3.6	51.3	6.7	11.4
45 to 54 years old	87.0	58.8	51.2	3.6	52.5	6.7	11.1
55 to 64 years old	76.4	49.4	37.9	1.6	45.7	7.8	8.3
65 to 74 years old	51.4	26.0	20.2	(B)	29.2	5.1	4.1
75 years old and over	24.6	11.5	4.2	(B)	11.2	1.8	2.0
Less than $10,000	41.7	8.3	25.7	(B)	20.6	(B)	3.6
$10,000 to $24,999	63.7	21.3	34.4	1.2	37.9	1.8	7.0
$25,000 to $49,999	79.6	43.7	50.0	2.9	49.9	4.1	7.7
$50,000 to $99,999	89.4	71.0	55.0	3.3	56.7	7.7	12.2
$100,000 and more	87.8	73.4	43.2	2.6	40.4	16.4	14.8
MEDIAN DEBT [4]							
1992, total	19.9	50.2	5.3	2.3	1.1	28.5	2.9
1995, total	23.4	54.9	6.4	3.7	1.6	31.9	2.1
1998, total	33.3	62.0	8.7	2.5	1.7	40.0	3.0
Under 35 years old	19.2	71.0	9.1	1.0	1.5	55.0	1.7
35 to 44 years old	55.7	70.0	7.7	1.4	2.0	40.0	3.0
45 to 54 years old	48.4	68.8	10.0	3.0	1.8	40.0	5.0
55 to 64 years old	34.6	49.4	8.3	4.9	2.0	41.0	5.0
65 to 74 years old	11.9	29.0	6.5	(B)	1.1	56.0	4.5
75 years old and over	8.0	21.2	8.9	(B)	0.7	29.8	1.7
Less than $10,000	4.1	16.0	4.0	(B)	1.1	(B)	0.6
$10,000 to $24,999	8.0	34.2	6.0	1.1	1.0	34.0	1.3
$25,000 to $49,999	27.1	47.0	8.0	3.0	1.9	20.0	2.2
$50,000 to $99,999	75.0	75.0	11.3	2.8	2.4	42.0	3.8
$100,000 and more	135.4	123.8	15.4	5.0	3.2	60.0	10.0

B Base figure too small.   [1] First and second mortgages and home equity loans and lines of credit secured by the primary residence.   [2] Families that had an outstanding balance on any of their credit cards after paying their most recent bills.
[3] Includes loans on insurance policies, loans against pension accounts, borrowing on margin accounts and unclassified loans.
[4] Median amount of financial debt for families holding such debts.

No. 795. Percent Distribution of Amount of Debt Held by Families: 1995 and 1998

[See headnote, Table 796]

Type of debt	1995	1998	Purpose of debt	1995	1998	Type of lending institution	1995	1998
Total	100.0	100.0	**Total**	100.0	100.0	**Total**	100.0	100.0
Home-secured debt . . .	73.3	71.9	Home purchase	70.4	68.1	Commercial bank	35.1	32.6
Installment loans	11.8	12.8	Home improvement . .	2.0	2.0	Savings and loan	10.8	9.6
Credit card balances . .	3.9	3.8	Investment, excluding			Credit union	4.5	4.2
Other lines of credit . . .	0.6	0.3	real estate	1.0	3.2	Finance or loan company.	3.2	4.2
Other residential			Vehicles	7.5	7.5	Brokerage	1.9	3.7
property	7.5	7.4	Goods and services . .	5.7	6.0	Real estate lender	32.7	35.9
Other debt	2.8	3.7	Investment real estate.	8.2	7.8	Individual lender	5.0	3.4
			Education	2.7	3.4	Other nonfinancial	0.8	1.3
			Other loans	2.4	1.9	Government	1.3	0.6
						Credit and store cards . .	3.9	3.8
						Other loans	0.9	0.7

Source of Tables 794 and 795: Board of Governors of the Federal Reserve System, *Federal Reserve Bulletin*, January 2000, and unpublished data.

No. 796. Ratios of Debt Payments to Family Income: 1992 to 1998

[In percent. Constant dollar figures are based on consumer price index data published by U.S. Bureau of Labor Statistics. Families include one-person units; for definition of family, see text, Section 1, Population. Based on Survey of Consumer Finance; see Appendix III. For definition of median, see Guide to Tabular Presentation]

Age of family head and family income (constant (1998) dollars)	Ratio of debt payments to family income						Percent of debtors with—					
	Aggregate			Median			Ratios above 40 percent			Any payment 60 days or more past due		
	1992	1995	1998	1992	1995	1998	1992	1995	1998	1992	1995	1998
All families	**14.1**	**13.6**	**14.5**	**16.1**	**16.1**	**17.6**	**10.9**	**10.5**	**12.7**	**6.0**	**7.1**	**8.1**
Under 35 years old	16.5	17.1	16.6	16.6	16.9	17.4	10.5	11.0	11.8	8.3	8.7	11.1
35 to 44 years old	17.8	16.6	17.0	19.0	18.1	19.4	11.6	9.2	11.6	6.8	7.7	8.4
45 to 54 years old	14.6	14.6	16.3	16.1	16.6	17.8	10.2	10.4	11.6	5.4	7.4	7.4
55 to 64 years old	11.4	11.5	12.9	14.5	14.0	16.7	14.3	14.5	13.9	4.7	3.2	7.5
65 to 74 years old	7.8	6.9	8.5	10.6	12.2	13.9	7.8	7.8	17.5	1.0	5.3	3.1
75 years old and over	3.4	2.9	3.9	5.0	3.4	8.9	8.7	8.9	20.9	1.8	5.4	1.1
Less than $10,000	16.8	19.5	19.4	19.5	15.4	20.3	28.4	27.6	32.0	11.6	8.4	15.1
$10,000 to $24,999	14.8	16.1	16.2	15.3	17.7	17.8	15.5	17.3	19.9	9.3	11.3	12.3
$25,000 to $49,999	16.5	16.2	17.4	16.3	16.6	18.1	9.6	8.0	13.8	6.3	8.6	9.2
$50,000 to $99,999	15.3	16.0	17.4	17.0	16.9	18.3	4.4	4.2	5.7	2.2	2.7	4.5
$100,000 and more	10.7	8.7	10.0	13.7	11.1	13.1	2.2	1.7	2.1	0.5	1.3	1.5

Source: Board of Governors of the Federal Reserve System, *Federal Reserve Bulletin*, January 2000, and unpublished data.

No. 797. Household Debt-Service Payments as a Percentage of Disposable Personal Income: 1980 to 1999

[In **percent**. As of **end of year**. Seasonally adjusted. The household debt-service burden is an estimate of the ratio of debt payments to disposable personal income. Debt payments consist of the estimated required payments on outstanding mortgage and consumer debt]

Year	Total	Consumer	Mortgage
1980	12.41	7.99	4.42
1981	12.34	7.62	4.72
1982	12.33	7.47	4.85
1983	12.33	7.46	4.88
1984	12.83	7.80	5.03
1985	13.74	8.29	5.44
1986	14.18	8.50	5.69
1987	13.71	7.92	5.79
1988	13.34	7.58	5.77
1989	13.51	7.57	5.94
1990	13.24	7.11	6.14
1991	12.56	6.51	6.05
1992	11.70	6.03	5.67
1993	11.59	6.13	5.46
1994	12.01	6.52	5.49
1995	12.70	7.05	5.65
1996	13.09	7.44	5.65
1997	13.17	7.47	5.70
1998	13.29	7.57	5.72
1999	13.51	7.58	5.93

Source: Board of Governors of the Federal Reserve System, "Household Debt Service Burden;" published: 24 March 2000; <http://www.bog.frb.fed.us/releases/housedebt/default.htm>.

No. 798. Banking Offices by Type of Bank: 1980 to 1999

[As of **December 31**. Includes Puerto Rico and outlying areas. Covers all FDIC-insured commercial banks and savings institutions. Commercial banks include insured branches of foreign banks. Data for 1980 include automatic teller machines which were reported by many banks as branches]

Item	1980	1985	1990	1994	1995	1996	1997	1998	1999
All banking offices	**(NA)**	**82,367**	**84,332**	**81,135**	**81,273**	**82,466**	**83,514**	**84,332**	**85,404**
Number of banks	(NA)	18,033	15,192	12,641	12,002	11,478	10,945	10,483	10,238
Number of branches	(NA)	64,334	69,140	68,494	69,271	70,988	72,569	73,849	75,166
Commercial banks	53,172	57,660	62,710	65,055	65,827	66,733	68,691	69,873	71,142
Number of banks	14,434	14,407	12,377	10,489	9,972	9,553	9,165	8,794	8,598
Number of branches	38,738	43,253	50,333	54,566	55,855	57,180	59,526	61,079	62,544
Savings institutions	(NA)	24,707	21,622	16,080	15,446	15,733	14,823	14,459	14,262
Number of banks	(NA)	3,626	2,815	2,152	2,030	1,925	1,780	1,689	1,640
Number of branches	(NA)	21,081	18,807	13,928	13,416	13,808	13,043	12,770	12,622

NA Not available.

Source: U.S. Federal Deposit Insurance Corporation, *Statistics on Banking*, annual and *The FDIC Quarterly Banking Profile Graph Book*.

No. 799. Selected Financial Institutions—Number and Assets by Asset Size: 1999

[As of **December** (5,734.8 represents $5,734,800,000,000). FDIC=Federal Deposit Insurance Corporation]

Asset size	Number of institutions			Assets (bil. dol.)		
	F.D.I.C.-insured			F.D.I.C.-insured		
	Commercial banks	Savings institutions	Credit unions [1]	Commercial banks [2]	Savings institutions	Credit unions [1]
Total.................	**8,580**	**1,640**	**10,628**	**5,734.8**	**1,148.7**	**411.4**
Less than $5.0 million.........	(3)	(3)	4,511	(3)	(3)	8.5
$5.0 million to $9.9 million......	(3)	(3)	1,683	(3)	(3)	12.0
$10.0 million to $24.9 million....	[3]1,161	[3]139	1,872	[3]19.1	[3]2.2	30.1
$25.0 million to $49.9 million....	1,839	198	1,054	68.3	7.4	37.3
$50.0 million to $99.9 million....	2,157	327	688	155.1	24.1	48.3
$100.0 million to $499.9 million...	2,729	705	698	547.9	159.5	144.6
$500.0 million to $999.9 million...	300	124	86	206.6	85.2	57.3
$1.0 billion to $2.9 billion.......	216	96	32	357.4	161.5	49.2
$3.0 billion or more...........	178	51	4	4,380.4	708.9	24.1
	Percent distribution			Percent distribution		
Total.................	**100.0**	**100.0**	**100.0**	**100.0**	**100.0**	**100.0**
Less than $5.0 million.........	(3)	(3)	42.4	(3)	(3)	2.1
$5.0 million to $9.9 million......	(3)	(3)	15.8	(3)	(3)	2.9
$10.0 million to $24.9 million....	[3]13.5	[3]8.5	17.6	[3]0.3	[3]0.2	7.3
$25.0 million to $49.9 million....	21.4	12.1	9.9	1.2	0.6	9.1
$50.0 million to $99.9 million....	25.1	19.9	6.5	2.7	2.1	11.7
$100.0 million to $499.9 million...	31.8	43.0	6.6	9.6	13.9	35.1
$500.0 million to $999.9 million...	3.5	7.6	0.8	3.6	7.4	13.9
$1.0 billion to $2.9 billion.......	2.5	5.9	0.3	6.2	14.1	12.0
$3.0 billion or more...........	2.1	3.1	(Z)	76.4	61.7	5.9

Z Less than 0.05 percent.   [1] Source: National Credit Union Administration, *National Credit Union Administration Yearend Statistics 1999*. Excludes nonfederally insured state chartered credit unions and federally insured corporate credit unions.   [2] Includes foreign branches of U.S. banks.   [3] Data for institutions with assets less than $10 million included with those with assets of $10.0 million to $24.9 million.

Source: Except as noted, U.S. Federal Deposit Insurance Corporation, *Statistics on Banking, 1999*.

No. 800. Insured Commercial Banks—Assets and Liabilities: 1980 to 1999

[In billions of dollars, except as indicated (1,856 represents $1,856,000,000,000). As of **Dec. 31**. Includes outlying areas. Except as noted, includes foreign branches of U.S. banks]

Item	1980	1985	1990	1994	1995	1996	1997	1998	1999 [1]
Number of banks reporting.......	14,435	14,417	12,343	10,450	9,940	9,528	9,142	8,774	8,580
Assets, total............	**1,856**	**2,731**	**3,389**	**4,011**	**4,313**	**4,578**	**5,015**	**5,441**	**5,735**
Net loans and leases.........	1,006	1,608	2,055	2,306	2,550	2,758	2,916	3,181	3,433
Real estate loans	269	438	830	998	1,080	1,139	1,245	1,346	1,510
Home equity loans [2]........	(NA)	(NA)	61	76	79	85	98	97	102
Commercial and industrial loans...	391	578	615	589	661	710	795	899	971
Loans to individuals..........	187	309	404	487	535	562	561	571	558
Credit cards and related plans ..	(NA)	(NA)	134	187	216	232	231	229	212
Farm loans................	32	36	33	39	40	41	45	46	45
Other loans and leases........	158	288	242	251	292	364	329	381	410
Less: Reserve for losses.......	10	23	56	52	53	53	55	57	59
Less: Unearned income	21	18	14	6	6	5	4	4	4
Investment securities..........	325	439	605	823	811	801	872	980	1,046
Other	524	684	730	881	952	1,020	1,227	1,280	1,256
Domestic office assets..........	1,533	2,326	2,999	3,483	3,728	3,906	4,267	4,733	4,995
Foreign office assets...........	323	406	390	527	585	672	748	708	739
Liabilities and capital, total ...	**1,856**	**2,731**	**3,389**	**4,011**	**4,313**	**4,578**	**5,015**	**5,441**	**5,735**
Noninterest-bearing deposits [3]......	432	471	489	572	612	664	677	720	703
Interest-bearing deposits [4]........	1,049	1,646	2,162	2,302	2,416	2,533	2,745	2,961	3,128
Subordinated debt.............	7	15	24	41	44	51	62	73	76
Other liabilities................	260	429	496	783	892	955	1,113	1,225	1,348
Equity capital.................	108	169	219	312	350	375	418	462	480
Domestic office deposits.........	1,187	1,796	2,357	2,443	2,573	2,724	2,896	3,109	3,175
Foreign office deposits..........	294	322	293	432	454	474	526	572	656

NA Not available.   [1] Preliminary.   [2] For one- to four-family residential properties.   [3] Prior to 1984, demand deposits.   [4] Prior to 1984, time and savings deposits.

Source: U.S. Federal Deposit Insurance Corporation, *The FDIC Quarterly Banking Profile, Annual Report*, and *Statistics on Banking*, annual.

No. 801. Insured Commercial Banks—Income and Selected Measures of Financial Condition: 1980 to 1999

[In billions of dollars, except as indicated (177.4 represents $177,400,000,000). Includes outlying areas. Includes foreign branches of U.S. banks]

Item	1980	1985	1990	1994	1995	1996	1997	1998	1999 [1]
Interest income	177.4	248.2	320.5	257.8	302.4	312.7	339.5	362.0	367.3
Interest expense.	120.1	157.3	204.9	111.3	148.2	150.0	165.0	179.3	175.1
Net interest income	57.3	90.9	115.5	146.6	154.2	162.8	174.5	182.8	192.2
Provisions for loan losses.	4.5	17.8	32.1	11.0	12.6	16.3	19.9	22.2	21.7
Noninterest income	13.3	31.1	54.9	76.3	82.4	93.6	104.5	123.7	144.5
Percent of net operating revenue [2]	18.8	25.5	32.2	34.2	34.8	36.5	37.5	40.4	42.9
Noninterest expense	46.7	82.4	115.7	144.2	149.7	160.7	170.0	194.1	204.2
Income taxes	5.0	5.6	7.7	22.4	26.1	28.2	31.9	32.0	39.4
Net income.	14.0	18.0	16.0	44.6	48.7	52.4	59.2	61.8	71.7
From domestic operations	11.9	16.3	14.2	39.3	43.1	46.0	53.1	56.6	65.0
From foreign operations.	2.0	1.7	1.8	5.3	5.7	6.3	6.1	5.2	6.7
PERFORMANCE RATIOS									
Return on assets [3] (percent).	0.80	0.70	0.48	1.15	1.17	1.19	1.23	1.19	1.31
Return on equity [4] (percent).	13.66	11.31	7.45	14.61	14.66	14.45	14.69	13.93	15.34
Net interest margin [5] (percent)	3.66	4.09	3.94	4.36	4.29	4.27	4.21	4.07	4.07
Net charge-offs [6]	3.6	13.6	29.7	11.2	12.2	15.5	18.3	20.7	20.3
Net charge-offs to loans and leases, total (percent).	0.36	0.84	1.43	0.50	0.49	0.58	0.64	0.67	0.61
Net charge-off rate, credit card loans (percent) . .	(NA)	2.95	3.86	3.00	3.98	4.66	5.34	5.26	4.49
CONDITION RATIOS									
Equity capital to assets (percent).	5.80	6.20	6.45	7.78	8.11	8.20	8.33	8.49	8.37
Noncurrent assets plus other real estate owned to assets [7] (percent).	(NA)	1.87	2.94	1.01	0.85	0.75	0.66	0.65	0.63
Percentage of banks losing money	3.7	17.1	13.4	4.0	3.6	4.3	4.8	6.1	7.2

NA Not available. [1] Preliminary. [2] Net operating revenue equals net interest income plus noninterest income. [3] Net income (including securities transactions and nonrecurring items) as a percentage of average total assets. [4] Net income as a percentage of average total equity capital. [5] Interest income less interest expense as a percentage of average earning assets (i.e. the profit margin a bank earns on its loans and investments). [6] Total loans and leases charged off (removed from balance sheet because of uncollectibility), less amounts recovered on loans and leases previously charged off. [7] The sum of loans, leases, debt securities and other assets that are 90 days or more past due, or in nonaccrual status plus foreclosed property.

No. 802. Insured Commercial Banks—Selected Measures of Financial Condition by Asset Size and Region: 1999

[In percent, except as indicated. Preliminary. See headnote, Table 801]

Asset size and region	Number of banks	Return on assets	Return on equity	Equity capital to assets	Net charge-offs to loans and leases	Percentage of banks losing money
Total.	**8,580**	**1.31**	**15.34**	**8.37**	**0.61**	**7.2**
Less than $100 million . .	5,157	1.01	9.07	10.68	0.37	10.5
$100 million to $1 billion .	3,029	1.36	14.24	9.26	0.36	2.4
$1 billion to $10 billion. . .	318	1.49	16.02	9.09	0.68	1.3
$10 billion or more	76	1.28	15.97	7.87	0.66	1.3
Northeast [1].	678	1.24	15.76	7.71	0.79	10.2
Southeast [2].	1,450	1.29	14.75	8.60	0.45	12.4
Central [3].	1,858	1.28	15.46	8.03	0.37	5.2
Midwest [4].	2,205	1.50	16.94	8.86	0.75	3.2
Southwest [5].	1,456	1.15	13.18	8.53	0.46	6.5
West [6].	933	1.64	15.54	10.30	0.95	11.9

[1] CT, DE, DC, ME, MD, MA, NH, NJ, NY, PA, PR, RI, and VT. [2] AL, FL, GA, MS, NC, SC, TN, VA, and WV. [3] IL, IN, KY, MI, OH, and WI. [4] IA, KS, MN, MO, NE, ND, and SD. [5] AR, LA, NM, OK, and TX. [6] AK, AZ, CA, CO, HI, ID, MT, NV, OR, Pacific Islands, UT, WA, and WY.

Source of Tables 801 and 802: U.S. Federal Deposit Insurance Corporation, *Annual Report; Statistics on Banking*, annual; and *FDIC Quarterly Banking Profile.*

No. 803. Insured Commercial Banks—Delinquency Rates on Loans: 1990 to 1999

[In percent. Annual averages. Delinquent loans are those past due 30 days or more and still accruing interest as well as those in nonaccrual status. They are measured as a percentage of end-of-period loans]

Type of loan	1990	1992	1993	1994	1995	1996	1997	1998	1999
Total loans.	**5.34**	**5.23**	**3.97**	**2.78**	**2.48**	**2.41**	**2.27**	**2.19**	**2.13**
Real estate	6.26	6.58	5.07	3.59	2.99	2.71	2.40	2.19	1.93
Residential [1]	(NA)	3.11	2.71	2.29	2.20	2.31	2.32	2.16	1.98
Commercial [2]	(NA)	10.74	8.12	5.37	4.05	3.22	2.45	2.10	1.73
Consumer	3.82	3.78	3.27	2.78	3.09	3.53	3.73	3.73	3.61
Credit cards	(NA)	5.00	4.26	3.35	3.74	4.34	4.70	4.71	4.55
Other	(NA)	3.13	2.73	2.44	2.68	3.00	3.09	3.13	3.08
Leases	2.06	2.17	1.47	0.97	0.83	1.10	1.12	1.07	1.30
Commercial and industrial	5.24	4.97	3.51	2.23	1.94	1.88	1.67	1.69	1.91
Agricultural	5.35	4.45	3.60	2.84	2.71	3.20	2.74	2.76	3.03

NA Not available. [1] Residential real estate loans include loans secured by one- to four-family properties, including home equity lines of credit. [2] Commercial real estate loans include construction and land development loans, loans secured by multifamily residences, and loans secured by nonfarm, nonresidential real estate.

Source: Federal Financial Institutions Examination Council (FFIEC), *Consolidated Reports of Condition and Income* (FFIEC 031 through 034).

Banking, Finance, and Insurance   513

No. 804. U.S. Banking Offices of Foreign Banks—Summary: 1980 to 1999

[In billions of dollars, except as indicated (201 represents $201,000,000,000). As of December. Data cover foreign-bank branches and agencies in the 50 states and the District of Columbia, New York investment companies (through September 1996) and U.S. commercial banks of which more than 25 percent is owned by foreign banks, and International Banking Facilities]

Item	1980	1985	1990	1995	1996	1997	1998	1999	Share [1] 1980	1990	1995	1999
Assets	201	441	791	984	991	1,126	1,118	1,228	11.9	21.4	21.7	19.0
Loans, total	121	247	398	461	461	495	494	499	13.4	18.0	17.3	13.4
Business	60	109	193	249	265	282	280	279	18.2	30.8	35.1	25.4
Deposits	80	237	384	523	535	603	558	697	6.6	14.5	17.6	17.1

[1] Percent of "domestically owned" commercial banks plus U.S. offices of foreign banks.

Source: Board of Governors of the Federal Reserve System, "Selected Assets and Liabilities of U.S. Offices of Foreign Banks"; <http://www.bog.frb.fed.us/releases/lba/Share/SHRTBL1.html>; accessed 27 March 2000; and "Selected Assets and Liabilities of Domestically Owned Commercial Banks plus U.S. Offices of Foreign Banks"; <http://www.bog.frb.fed.us/releases/lba/Share/SHRTBL10.html> accessed 27 March 2000.

No. 805. Foreign Lending by U.S. Banks by Type of Borrower and Country: 1999

[In millions of dollars (323,508 represents $323,508,000,000). As of December. Covers 104 U.S. banking organizations which do nearly all of the foreign lending in the country. Data represent claims on foreign residents and institutions held at all domestic and foreign offices of covered banks. Data cover only cross-border and nonlocal currency claims. These result from a U.S. bank's office in one country lending to residents of another country or lending in a currency other than that of the borrower's country. Excludes local currency loans and other claims and local currency liabilities held by banks' foreign offices on residents of the country in which the office was located (e.g. Deutsche mark loans to German residents booked at the German branch of the reporting U.S. bank). Criteria for country selection is $3.3 billion or more]

Country	Total	Bank	Public	All other	Country	Total	Bank	Public	All other
Total [1]	323,508	93,915	76,690	152,903	Germany	26,819	12,115	9,385	5,319
					Italy	20,502	3,992	14,759	1,751
Argentina	7,521	795	1,903	4,823	Japan	20,734	3,418	8,769	8,547
Australia	5,511	1,154	701	3,656	Korea, South	4,868	2,077	1,118	1,673
Belgium	9,180	5,055	2,026	2,099	Mexico	12,539	324	5,055	7,160
Bermuda	5,545	4	20	5,521	Netherlands	19,248	8,053	2,750	8,445
Brazil	10,749	2,076	2,574	6,099	Netherlands Antilles	4,243	24	-	4,219
Canada	12,050	3,956	2,484	5,610	Spain	4,607	1,735	1,223	1,649
Cayman Islands	14,536	5,541	73	8,922	Sweden	3,911	1,176	1,889	846
Chile	3,293	139	714	2,440	Switzerland	7,113	2,792	459	3,862
France	18,585	9,009	4,455	5,121	United Kingdom	45,052	15,076	645	29,331

- Represents zero. [1] Includes other countries, not shown separately.

Source: Board of Governors of the Federal Reserve System, Federal Financial Institutions Examination Council, Statistical Release, Country Exposure Lending Survey: December 31, 1999.

No. 806. Insured Commercial Banks by State and Other Area: 1999

[In billions of dollars, except number of banks (5,734.8 represents $5,734,800,000,000). As of December 31. Includes foreign branches of U.S. banks]

State	Number	Assets	Deposits	State	Number	Assets	Deposits
Total	8,580	5,734.8	3,830.8	Nevada	27	32.2	11.4
United States	8,562	5,687.7	3,803.2	New Hampshire	19	22.0	15.5
Alabama	156	177.8	122.5	New Jersey	75	107.9	82.3
Alaska	6	5.4	4.0	New Mexico	54	16.0	11.1
Arizona	45	47.7	25.9	New York	150	1,170.3	729.8
Arkansas	195	26.7	22.5	North Carolina	71	936.9	604.0
California	325	286.8	226.3	North Dakota	114	11.6	8.4
Colorado	188	41.6	33.8	Ohio	219	309.3	187.0
Connecticut	24	3.2	2.5	Oklahoma	300	39.6	31.0
Delaware	33	133.2	64.3	Oregon	44	7.2	5.7
District of Columbia	6	0.6	0.5	Pennsylvania	193	195.3	135.3
Florida	272	86.3	64.9	Rhode Island	6	103.0	50.6
Georgia	345	86.2	50.8	South Carolina	77	20.8	16.3
Hawaii	10	23.6	16.8	South Dakota	102	32.0	12.0
Idaho	17	2.1	1.8	Tennessee	201	90.4	64.8
Illinois	725	328.7	228.4	Texas	754	181.2	143.2
Indiana	158	65.0	45.3	Utah	51	59.2	29.9
Iowa	439	44.9	35.8	Vermont	20	7.6	6.1
Kansas	387	34.8	29.0	Virginia	147	80.7	54.5
Kentucky	248	51.4	37.2	Washington	81	13.4	10.9
Louisiana	153	50.8	40.5	West Virginia	82	23.1	17.3
Maine	16	5.1	3.8	Wisconsin	337	74.2	53.5
Maryland	77	45.4	34.4	Wyoming	50	7.5	6.1
Massachusetts	45	169.7	115.6				
Michigan	171	123.3	88.1	American Samoa	1	0.1	0.1
Minnesota	497	157.4	105.6	Puerto Rico	12	46.2	26.7
Mississippi	99	29.5	22.8	Guam	2	0.8	0.7
Missouri	365	80.4	61.7	Federated States of			
Montana	85	10.1	8.2	Micronesia	1	0.1	(Z)
Nebraska	301	28.5	23.0	Virgin Islands	2	0.1	0.1

Z Less than $50 million.

Source: U.S. Federal Deposit Insurance Corporation, Statistics on Banking, annual.

514 Banking, Finance, and Insurance

No. 807. Retail Fees and Services of Banks: 1997 and 1998

[In dollars, except as noted. As of June. For most services, fees are reported in terms of (1) the proportion of those banks offering a service that charge for the service and (2) the average fee charged by the institutions that charge for the service. Based on a random sample of depository institutions belonging to the Bank Insurance Fund, whose members are predominantly commercial banks]

Type of account or service	1997	1998	Type of account or service	1997	1998
NONINTEREST CHECKING ACCOUNT			AUTOMATED TELLER MACHINES (ATMs)		
Percent offering.	98.7	98.5	Percent offering.	79.4	86.5
Single-balance, single-fee account: [1]			Annual fee:		
Percent offering	39.3	35.6	Percent charging	16.7	15.1
Monthly fee (low balance)	6.09	6.43	Average	11.51	13.11
Minimum balance to avoid fee	479	499	Fees for customer transactions on us: [4]		
Minimum balance to open	124	115	Withdrawals:		
			Percent charging.	7.4	6.4
Fee-only account: [2]			Average	0.65	0.68
Percent offering.	33.3	36.3			
Monthly fee (low balance)	4.49	4.73	Balance inquiries:		
Check charge:			Percent charging.	6.7	5.7
Percent charging.	32.4	45.0	Average	0.65	0.67
Average	0.38	0.40	Fees for customer transactions on others: [4]		
Minimum balance to open	61	76	Withdrawals:		
			Percent charging.	67.0	74.4
NOW ACCOUNTS [3]			Average	1.06	1.10
Percent offering.	97.6	94.3	Balance inquiries:		
Single-fee account: [1]			Percent charging.	55.2	63.2
Percent offering	56.7	50.8	Average	0.99	1.05
Monthly fee (low balance)	7.81	8.07	Surcharge: [5]		
Minimum balance to avoid fee	1,052	1,109	Percent charging	60.1	77.9
Minimum balance to open	663	616	Average	1.14	1.20

[1] A monthly fee for balances below the minimum, no monthly fee for balances above the minimum, and no other charges. [2] A monthly fee, no minimum balance to eliminate the fee, and a charge per check in some cases. [3] NOW (negotiable order of withdrawal) accounts are checking accounts that pay interest and often have fee structures that differ from those of noninterest checking accounts. [4] An institution's "customer" is one who has an account at the institution. A customer's ATM transactions in which the machine used is that of the customer's institution are called "on us"; a customer's transactions in which the machine used is that of another institution are called "on others". [5] An ATM surcharge is a fee imposed by the ATM's institution, typically on every transaction by the machine's noncustomer users.

Source: Board of Governors of the Federal Reserve Systems, *Annual Report to the Congress on Retail Fees and Services of Depository Institutions*, June 1999.

No. 808. Insured Savings Institutions—Financial Summary: 1985 to 1999

[In billions of dollars, except number of institutions (1,263 represents $1,263,000,000,000). As of December 31. Includes Puerto Rico, Guam, and Virgin Islands. Covers SAIF- (Savings Association Insurance Fund) and BIF- (Bank Insurance Fund) insured savings institutions. Excludes institutions in Resolution Trust Corporation conservatorship and, beginning 1992, excludes one self-liquidating institution. Minus sign (-) indicates loss]

Item	1985	1990	1992	1993	1994	1995	1996	1997	1998	1999
Number of institutions	3,626	2,815	2,390	2,262	2,152	2,030	1,925	1,780	1,689	1,640
Assets, total	1,263	1,259	1,030	1,001	1,009	1,026	1,028	1,026	1,088	1,149
Loans and leases, net . . .	821	812	648	626	635	648	681	692	714	755
Liabilities, total.	1,218	1,192	956	922	929	940	942	937	994	1,054
Deposits	1,023	987	828	774	737	742	728	704	705	707
Equity capital.	45	68	74	78	80	86	86	89	95	95
Interest and fee income.	119	117	78	66	63	71	72	69	71	74
Interest expense	101	91	46	35	33	43	42	41	42	43
Net interest income.	17	26	32	32	30	28	30	29	29	31
Net income	6	-5	7	7	6	8	7	9	10	11

Source: U.S. Federal Deposit Insurance Corporation, *Statistics on Banking*, annual and *FDIC Quarterly Banking Profile*.

No. 809. Federal and State-Chartered Credit Unions—Summary: 1980 to 1999

[Except as noted, as of December 31 (24,519 represents 24,519,000). Federal data include District of Columbia, Puerto Rico, Canal Zone, Guam, and Virgin Islands. Excludes state-insured, privately-insured, and noninsured state-chartered credit unions and corporate central credit unions which have mainly other credit unions as members]

Year	Operating credit unions		Number of failed institu- tions [1]	Members (1,000)		Assets (mil. dol.)		Loans outstanding (mil. dol.)		Savings (mil. dol.)	
	Federal	State		Federal	State	Federal	State	Federal	State	Federal	State
1980 . . .	12,440	4,910	239	24,519	12,338	40,092	20,870	26,350	14,582	36,263	18,469
1990 . . .	8,511	4,349	164	36,241	19,454	130,073	68,133	83,029	44,102	117,892	62,082
1995 . . .	7,329	4,358	26	42,163	24,927	193,781	112,860	120,514	71,606	170,300	99,838
1998 . . .	6,814	4,181	17	43,865	29,674	231,890	156,811	144,849	100,890	202,651	137,348
1999 . . .	6,566	4,062	23	44,076	31,308	239,316	172,086	155,578	116,366	207,614	149,305

[1] Through 1990 for year ending September 30; 1995 reflects 15-month period from October 1994 through December 1995; beginnning 1998 reflects calendar year. A failed institution is defined as a credit union which has ceased operation because it was involuntarily liquidated or merged with assistance from the National Credit Union Share Insurance Fund. Assisted mergers were not identified until 1981.

Source: National Credit Union Administration, *Annual Report of the National Credit Union Administration*, and unpublished data.

No. 810. Characteristics of Conventional First Mortgage Loans for Purchase of Single-Family Homes: 1990 to 1999

[In percent, except as indicated (154.1 represents $154,100). Annual averages. Covers fully amortized conventional mortgage loans used to purchase single-family nonfarm homes. Excludes refinancing loans, nonamortized and balloon loans, loans insured by the Federal Housing Administration, and loans guaranteed by the Veterans Administration. Based on a sample of mortgage lenders, including savings and loans associations, savings banks, commercial banks, and mortgage companies]

Loan characteristics	New homes						Previously occupied homes					
	1990	1995	1996	1997	1998	1999	1990	1995	1996	1997	1998	1999
Contract interest rate, [1]												
all loans	9.7	7.7	7.6	7.6	6.9	6.9	9.8	7.7	7.6	7.5	7.0	7.2
Fixed-rate loans	10.1	8.0	7.8	7.7	7.1	7.3	10.1	8.0	7.8	7.7	7.1	7.3
Adjustable-rate loans [2]	8.9	7.2	7.0	6.9	6.4	6.3	8.9	7.0	6.9	6.7	6.3	6.5
Initial fees, charges [3]	1.98	1.20	1.21	1.01	0.88	0.76	1.74	0.93	0.93	0.97	0.84	0.73
Effective interest rate, [4]												
all loans	10.1	7.9	7.8	7.7	7.1	7.0	10.1	7.8	7.7	7.7	7.1	7.3
Fixed-rate loans	10.4	8.2	8.0	7.9	7.2	7.4	10.4	8.2	8.0	7.9	7.2	7.4
Adjustable-rate loans [2]	9.2	7.4	7.2	7.0	6.5	6.3	9.2	7.1	7.1	6.9	6.5	6.6
Term to maturity (years)	27.3	27.7	27.1	28.2	28.4	28.8	27.0	27.4	26.8	27.3	27.7	28.1
Purchase price ($1,000)	154.1	175.4	182.6	181.4	195.0	210.7	140.3	137.3	150.2	161.0	169.5	179.3
Loan to price ratio	74.9	78.6	78.1	80.4	80.1	78.8	74.9	80.1	79.1	79.2	78.7	78.4
Percent of number of loans with adjustable rates.	31	37	26	21	17	35	27	31	27	22	12	18

[1] Initial interest rate paid by the borrower as specified in the loan contract. [2] Loans with a contractual provision for periodic adjustments in the contract interest rate. [3] Includes all fees, commissions, discounts and "points" paid by the borrower, or seller, in order to obtain the loan. Excludes those charges for mortgage, credit, life or property insurance; for property transfer; and for title search and insurance. [4] Contract interest rate plus fees and charges amortized over a 10-year period.

Source: U.S. Federal Housing Finance Board, *Rates & Terms on Conventional Home Mortgages, Annual Summary.*

No. 811. Mortgage Debt Outstanding by Type of Property and Holder: 1980 to 1999

[In billions of dollars (1,465 represents $1,465,000,000,000). As of Dec. 31. Includes Puerto Rico and Guam]

Type of property and holder	1980	1985	1990	1992	1993	1994	1995	1996	1997	1998	1999
Mortgage debt, total.	1,465	2,378	3,808	4,073	4,212	4,391	4,593	4,881	5,185	5,683	6,319
Residential nonfarm	1,110	1,738	2,932	3,254	3,413	3,596	3,784	4,011	4,261	4,657	5,131
One- to four-family homes.	969	1,533	2,647	2,984	3,147	3,330	3,510	3,722	3,960	4,328	4,760
Savings institutions	487	554	600	490	470	478	482	514	521	534	549
Mortgage pools or trusts [1]	125	407	1,046	1,400	1,519	1,658	1,771	1,941	2,106	2,381	2,697
Government National Mortgage Association	92	207	392	411	405	441	461	494	523	522	565
Federal Home Loan Mortgage Corp . .	13	100	308	402	443	488	512	552	577	643	745
Federal National Mortgage Assoc	(X)	54	291	436	487	521	570	633	688	804	925
Private mortgage conduits [2]	4	24	55	152	185	209	228	262	318	411	463
Commercial banks	160	211	430	479	532	590	647	678	746	797	879
Individuals and others [3]	117	239	403	411	387	367	372	363	367	392	421
Federal and related agencies	61	110	153	194	230	228	229	220	213	217	206
Federal National Mortgage Assoc. . . .	52	92	94	124	151	159	164	155	150	148	141
Life insurance companies	18	12	13	11	9	9	9	7	7	7	7
Five or more units	141	205	286	270	266	266	273	289	302	329	371
Commercial	258	534	797	740	718	712	725	783	833	930	1,086
Farm	97	106	79	80	81	83	85	87	90	97	103
TYPE OF HOLDER											
Savings institutions	603	760	802	628	598	596	597	628	632	644	669
Commercial banks	264	431	849	901	948	1,013	1,090	1,145	1,245	1,337	1,496
Life insurance companies	131	172	268	242	224	216	213	208	207	214	229
Individuals and others [3]	206	408	562	564	534	523	532	560	574	608	649
Mortgage pools or trusts [1]	146	440	1,088	1,453	1,581	1,728	1,852	2,044	2,241	2,588	2,955
Government National Mortgage Assoc	94	212	404	420	414	451	472	506	537	537	582
Federal Home Loan Mortgage Corp	17	100	316	408	447	491	515	554	579	646	749
Federal National Mortgage Association . . .	(X)	55	300	445	496	530	583	651	710	835	961
Farmers Home Administration [4]	32	48	(Z)	(Z)	(Z)	(Z)	(Z)	(Z)	(Z)	(Z)	-
Private mortgage conduits	4	25	68	181	225	256	282	333	415	570	662
Federal and related agencies	115	167	239	286	326	316	309	295	286	293	322
Federal National Mortgage Association . . .	57	98	105	137	166	174	179	169	161	158	153
Farmers Home Administration [4]	3	1	41	42	41	42	42	42	41	41	74
Federal Land Banks.	38	47	29	29	28	29	28	30	31	33	35
Federal Home Loan Mortgage Corp	5	14	22	34	47	42	44	47	48	57	57
Federal Housing and Veterans Admin . . .	6	5	9	13	12	11	10	6	4	4	4
Government National Mortgage Assoc. . . .	5	1	(Z)	(Z)	(Z)	(Z)	(Z)	(Z)	(Z)	(Z)	(Z)
Federal Deposit Insurance Corp	(X)	(X)	(X)	(X)	14	8	4	2	1	(Z)	(Z)
Resolution Trust Corporation	(X)	(X)	33	32	17	10	2	(X)	(X)	(X)	(X)

- Represents zero. X Not applicable. Z Less than $500 million. [1] Outstanding principal balances of mortgage pools backing securities insured or guaranteed by the agency indicated. Includes other pools not shown separately. [2] Includes securitized home equity loans. [3] Includes mortgage companies, real estate investment trusts, state and local retirement funds, noninsured pension funds, state and local credit agencies, credit unions, and finance companies. [4] FmHA-guaranteed securities sold to the Federal Financing Bank were reallocated from FmHA mortgage pools to FmHA mortgage holdings in 1986 because of accounting changes by the Farmers Home Administration.

Source: Board of Governors of the Federal Reserve System, *Federal Reserve Bulletin,* monthly.

No. 812. Estimated Home Equity Debt Outstanding by Type and Source of Credit: 1990 to 1998

[In billions of dollars (258 represents $258,000,000,000). A "traditional home equity loan" is a closed-end loan extended for a specific period that generally requires repayment of interest and principal in equal monthly installments. Such a loan typically has a fixed interest rate. A "home equity line of credit" is a revolving account that permits borrowing from time to time, at the home-owner's discretion, up to the amount of the credit line. It usually has a more flexible repayment schedule and a variable interest rate. Based on reports from lending institutions and data from the Survey of Consumers, a sample survey of households]

Year		Home equity lines of credit			Traditional home equity loans		
	Total	All lenders	Commercial banks	Other sources	All lenders	Commercial banks	Other sources
1990	258	105	61	44	153	54	99
1992	258	114	73	41	144	50	94
1993	261	110	73	37	151	49	102
1994	274	116	76	40	158	54	104
1995	299	123	79	44	176	61	115
1996	347	132	85	47	215	69	146
1997	420	152	98	54	268	76	192
1998	470	153	96	57	317	80	237

Source: Board of Governors of the Federal Reserve System, *Federal Reserve Bulletin*, July 1994 and April 1998; and unpublished data.

No. 813. Home Equity Lending—Percentage of Homeowners With Credit, Sources of Credit, and Uses for Funds Borrowed: 1993-94 and 1997

[In percent. See headnote, Table 812]

Item	Home equity lines of credit		Traditional home equity loans		Uses for funds borrowed	1997[1]	
	1993-94	1997	1993-94	1997		Home equity lines of credit	Traditional home equity loans
Percentage of homeowners with home equity credit . .	8	8	5	5	Home improvement	69	45
					Repayment of other debts .	49	61
					Education.	19	2
SOURCE OF HOME EQUITY CREDIT							
Total.	100	100	100	100	Real estate.	9	10
Commercial banks	60	61	29	44	Auto or truck.	37	6
Savings institutions [2]	21	16	30	20	Medical expenses	10	2
Credit unions	13	16	11	13	Business expenses	18	4
Other creditors [3]	7	7	29	24	Vacation.	13	1
					Other [4]	1	1

[1] Percentages sum to more than 100 because respondents were allowed to cite multiple uses for a single loan or drawdown and more than one draw for one line of credit. [2] Includes savings banks and savings and loan associations. [3] Includes finance and loan companies, brokerage firms, mortgage companies, and individuals. [4] Includes purchase of furniture or appliance, purchase of boat or other recreational vehicle, payment of taxes, and personal financial investments.

Source: Board of Governors of the Federal Reserve System, *Federal Reserve Bulletin*, April 1998.

No. 814. Mortgage Delinquency and Foreclosure Rates: 1980 to 1999

[In percent, except as indicated (30,033 represents 30,033,000). Covers one- to four-family residential nonfarm mortgage loans]

Item	1980	1985	1990	1994	1995	1996	1997	1998	1999
Number of mortgage loans outstanding (1,000)	30,033	34,004	40,638	47,462	48,854	49,633	50,438	51,500	52,121
Delinquency rates: [1]									
Total.	5.0	5.8	4.7	4.1	4.3	4.3	4.3	4.4	4.1
Conventional loans.	3.1	4.0	3.0	2.6	2.8	2.8	2.8	2.9	2.6
VA loans.	5.3	6.6	6.4	6.3	6.4	6.7	6.9	7.1	6.8
FHA loans	6.6	7.5	6.7	7.3	7.6	8.1	8.1	8.5	8.6
Foreclosure rates: [2]									
Total.	0.5	1.0	0.9	0.9	0.9	1.0	1.1	1.1	1.1
Conventional loans.	0.2	0.7	0.7	0.7	0.7	0.7	0.7	0.7	0.7
VA loans.	0.6	1.1	1.2	1.3	1.3	1.6	1.8	1.8	1.8
FHA loans	0.7	1.3	1.3	1.5	1.4	1.6	2.0	2.2	2.2

[1] Number of loans delinquent 30 days or more as percentage of mortgage loans serviced in survey. Annual average of quarterly figures. [2] Percentage of loans in the foreclosure process at yearend, not seasonally adjusted.

Source: Mortgage Bankers Association of America, Washington, DC, *National Delinquency Survey,* quarterly.

Banking, Finance, and Insurance **517**

No. 815. Consumer Credit Outstanding and Finance Rates: 1980 to 1999

[In billions of dollars, except percent (349.4 represents $349,400,000,000). Estimated amounts of seasonally adjusted credit outstanding as of end of year; finance rates, annual averages]

Type of credit	1980	1985	1990	1993	1994	1995	1996	1997	1998	1999
Total...................	349.4	593.2	789.3	839.2	960.7	1,096.0	1,182.4	1,234.1	1,300.5	1,395.4
Revolving ...¡...............	55.1	124.7	238.6	310.0	365.6	443.2	499.5	531.3	560.7	596.0
Nonrevolving [1]............	294.3	468.5	550.7	529.2	595.1	652.8	682.9	702.8	739.8	799.4
FINANCE RATES (percent)										
Commercial banks:										
New automobiles (48 months) [2]...	14.32	12.91	11.78	8.09	8.12	9.57	9.05	9.02	8.72	8.44
Other consumer goods (24 months)	15.48	15.94	15.46	13.47	13.19	13.94	13.54	13.90	13.74	13.39
Credit-card plans............	17.31	18.69	18.17	16.83	16.04	15.90	15.63	15.77	15.71	15.21
Finance companies:										
New automobiles............	14.82	11.98	12.54	9.48	9.79	11.19	9.83	7.12	6.30	6.66
Used automobiles...........	19.10	17.58	15.99	12.79	13.49	14.48	13.53	13.27	12.64	12.60

[1] Comprises automobile loans and all other loans not included in revolving credit, such as loans for mobile homes, trailers, or vacations. These loans may be secured or unsecured. [2] For 1980, maturities were 36 months for new car loans.

Source: Board of Governors of the Federal Reserve System, *Federal Reserve Bulletin*, monthly.

No. 816. Credit Cards—Holders, Numbers, Spending, and Debt, 1990 and 1998, and Projections, 2000

[122 represents 122,000,000]

Type of credit card	Cardholders (mil.)			Number of cards (mil.)			Credit card spending (bil. dol.)			Credit card debt outstanding (bil. dol.)		
	1990	1998	2000, proj.	1990	1998	2000, proj.	1990	1998	2000, proj.	1990	1998	2000, proj.
Total [1]...............	122	154	157	1,012	1,420	1,480	467	1,157	1,391	243	564	620
Bank [2]	79	102	106	213	429	456	243	751	929	154	404	445
Oil company.............	85	79	79	123	113	113	28	37	43	3	4	4
Phone.................	97	119	126	141	175	183	14	20	21	2	2	3
Store ....₃....	96	110	114	459	617	640	75	108	108	51	84	84
Travel and entertainment [3]...	16	21	22	28	29	30	85	177	215	20	35	43
Other [4]...............	10	7	7	49	56	58	22	66	76	13	34	40

[1] Cardholders may hold more than one type of card. [2] Visa and MasterCard credit cards. Excludes debit cards. [3] Includes American Express and Diners Club. [4] Includes Air Travel Card, JCB, automobile rental, other airline including business aviation, hotel, restaurant, and club cards, Discover (except for cardholders), and miscellaneous cards.

Source: HSN Consultants Inc., Oxnard, CA, *The Nilson Report*, twice-monthly. (Copyright used by permission.)

No. 817. Usage of General Purpose Credit Cards by Families: 1989 to 1998

[General purpose credit cards include Mastercard, Visa, Optima, and Discover cards. Excludes cards used only for business purposes. All dollar figures are given in constant 1998 dollars based on consumer price index data as published by U.S. Bureau of Labor Statistics. Families include one-person units; for definition of family, see text, Section 1, Population. Based on Survey of Consumer Finance; see Appendix III. For definition of median, see Guide to Tabular Presentation]

Age of family head and family income	Percent having a general purpose credit card	Median number of cards	Median new charges on last month's bills	Percent having a balance after last month's bills	Median balance [1]	Percent of cardholding families who—		
						Almost always pay off the balance	Some-times pay off the balance	Hardly ever pay off the balance
1989, total........	56.0	2	$100	52.1	$1,300	52.9	21.2	25.8
1992, total........	62.4	2	100	52.6	1,100	53.0	19.6	27.4
1995, total........	66.4	2	200	56.0	1,600	52.4	20.1	27.5
1998, total	67.5	2	200	54.7	1,900	53.8	19.3	26.9
Under 35 years old.....	58.3	2	200	71.6	1,500	39.0	22.5	38.5
35 to 44 years old	71.3	2	200	62.5	2,000	46.5	19.1	34.4
45 to 54 years old	75.3	2	200	59.2	2,000	48.2	22.7	29.1
55 to 64 years old	76.0	2	200	48.8	2,300	61.0	20.1	18.9
65 to 74 years old	71.2	2	200	33.9	1,000	74.0	14.9	11.1
75 years old and over...	50.8	1	100	16.7	700	86.3	7.8	5.9
Less than $10,000	23.2	2	100	64.0	900	46.4	19.9	33.8
$10,000 to $24,999	50.8	2	100	56.9	1,200	52.3	19.3	28.4
$25,000 to $49,999	73.2	2	100	58.2	1,700	48.3	20.5	31.2
$50,000 to $99,999	89.6	2	200	55.9	2,400	53.9	20.2	25.9
$100,000 and more	97.9	2	800	36.4	3,100	72.0	13.8	14.1

[1] Among families having a balance.

Source: Board of Governors of the Federal Reserve System, unpublished data.

No. 818. Consumer Payment Systems by Method of Payment, 1990 and 1998, and Projections, 2000

[98.3 represents 98,300,000,000]

Method of payment	Transactions				Volume					
	Number (bil.)		Percent distribution		Amount (bil. dol.)			Percent distribution		
	1998	2000, proj.	1998	2000, proj.	1990	1998	2000, proj.	1990	1998	2000, proj.
Total	98.3	111.4	100.0	100.0	2,972	4,551	5,131	100.0	100.0	100.0
Paper	74.2	80.8	75.4	72.6	2,511	3,255	3,399	84.6	71.5	66.2
Checks [1]	29.4	28.7	29.9	25.8	1,821	2,243	2,211	61.3	49.3	43.1
Cash	42.8	50.3	43.5	45.1	582	858	1,031	19.6	18.9	20.1
Money orders	1.2	1.2	1.2	1.1	61	106	113	2.1	2.3	2.2
Travelers cheques	0.3	0.3	0.3	0.3	22	19	17	0.7	0.4	0.3
Official checks [2]	0.1	0.1	0.1	0.1	11	20	22	0.4	0.4	0.4
Food stamps............	0.4	0.2	0.4	0.2	14	9	5	0.5	0.2	0.1
Cards	23.0	28.6	23.3	25.8	441	1,164	1,525	14.8	25.6	29.7
Credit cards [3]	17.1	18.3	17.4	16.5	432	973	1,173	14.5	21.4	22.9
Debit cards [4]	4.9	8.6	4.9	7.8	9	168	310	0.3	3.7	6.0
Stored value cards [5]........	0.7	1.2	0.7	1.1	-	15	30	-	0.3	0.6
EBT cards [6]	0.3	0.5	0.3	0.4	-	8	12	-	0.2	0.2
Electronic	1.3	2.0	1.3	1.7	20	132	208	0.7	2.9	4.0
Preauthorized payments [7]....	1.0	1.5	1.0	1.3	18	106	160	0.6	2.3	3.1
Remote payments [8]	0.3	0.5	0.3	0.4	2	26	48	0.1	0.6	0.9

- Represents zero. [1] Excludes repayments and prepayments involving other payment systems. [2] Official checks include cashier's checks, teller checks, and certified checks purchased from financial institutions. Excludes those purchased by businesses. [3] Credit cards include general purpose cards usable at all kinds of merchants and proprietary cards usable only at selected outlets. Includes purchases on commercial cards and business-related spending on personal cards. Cash advances are excluded. [4] Debit cards include general purpose cards carrying the Visa or MasterCard brand, electronic funds transfer (EFT) brands of regional EFT systems, proprietary commercial cards issued by private firms to drivers in the long-haul trucking and business aviation industry, and proprietary merchant cards issued by supermarkets and gasoline marketers. Cash withdrawals at ATMs and cash back over the counter are excluded. [5] Stored value cards are used primarily for gift certificates and telephone calls. [6] Electronic benefits transfer (EBT) cards are being issued to replace paper scrip food stamps used at participating merchants. [7] Preauthorized payments are handled electronically through an automated clearing house. Mortgages are excluded. [8] Remote payments are made using a telephone, on-line computer service, or the internet. Also included are point-of-service check conversions and utility-bill payments made by clerk-assisted electronic banking machines at supermarkets, ATMs, and self-service kiosks.

Source: HSN Consultants Inc., Oxnard, CA, *The Nilson Report*, twice-monthly. (Copyright used by permission.)

No. 819. Debit Cards—Numbers, Transactions, and Volume, 1990 to 1998, and Projections, 2000

[164 represents 164,000,000]

Type of debit card	Number of cards (mil.)				Number of transactions (mil.)				Volume (bil. dol.)			
	1990	1995	1998	2000, proj.	1990	1995	1998	2000, proj.	1990	1995	1998	2000, proj.
Total [1]...............	164	201	217	230	274	1,558	5,731	9,901	12	62	239	423
Bank [2]	9	40	100	126	127	829	3,765	6,655	8	36	171	309
EFT systems [3]	160	190	206	219	129	672	1,908	3,186	3	23	65	110
Other [4]	4	11	11	11	17	57	58	60	1	3	3	3

[1] Increasingly, bank cards and EFT cards are the same pieces of plastic that carry multiple brands. The total card figure shown does not include any duplication. [2] Visa Check Card and MasterCard MasterMoney. [3] Cards issued by financial institution members of regional and national switches. EFT=Electronic funds transfer. [4] Commercial fuel cards issued by private-label firms plus retail cards such as those issued by supermarkets and oil companies.

Source: HSN Consultants Inc., Oxnard, CA, *The Nilson Report*, twice-monthly. (Copyright used by permission.)

No. 820. Electronic Funds Transfer Volume: 1980 to 1999

[Electronic funds transfer cover automated teller machine (ATM) transactions and transactions at point-of-sale (POS) terminals. Point-of-sale terminals are electronic terminals in retail stores that allow a customer to pay for goods through a direct debit to a customer's account at the bank]

Item	Unit	1980	1985	1990	1994	1995	1996	1997	1998	1999
Total number of transactions	Million. .	(NA)	3,579	5,942	9,078	10,464	11,780	12,580	13,160	13,316
ATM transactions	Million . .	(NA)	3,565	5,751	8,454	9,689	10,684	10,980	11,160	10,889
POS transactions	Million . .	(NA)	14	191	624	775	1,096	1,600	2,000	2,428
ATM terminals, total [1]...........	1,000. . .	18.5	60.0	80.2	109.1	122.7	139.1	165.0	187.0	227.0
Monthly transactions per terminal ..	Number .	5,405	4,951	5,980	6,459	6,580	6,399	5,515	4,973	3,997
POS terminals, total [2]...........	1,000. . .	(NA)	(NA)	53	344	529	875	1,300	1,700	2,350

NA Not available. [1] As of September through 1995; 1996, as of August; 1997 and 1998 as of June; and 1999 as of March. [2] As of June.

Source: Faulkner & Gray, Chicago, IL, *Bank Network News*, August 11, 1999, (copyright).

U.S. Census Bureau, Statistical Abstract of the United States: 2000

No. 821. Money Stock: 1980 to 1999

[In billions of dollars (408 represents $408,000,000,000). As of **December**. Seasonally adjusted averages of daily figures]

Item	1980	1982	1983	1984	1985	1986	1987	1988	1989	1990	1991	1992	1993	1994	1995	1996	1997	1998	1999
M1, total	**408**	**474**	**521**	**551**	**619**	**724**	**750**	**786**	**793**	**824**	**896**	**1,024**	**1,130**	**1,150**	**1,127**	**1,081**	**1,074**	**1,097**	**1,124**
Currency [1]	115	133	146	156	168	181	197	212	223	247	268	293	322	354	373	394	425	460	516
Travelers checks [2]	3	4	4	4	5	5	6	6	6	7	8	8	7	8	8	8	8	8	8
Demand deposits [3]	261	234	238	243	267	303	288	287	279	277	289	340	386	384	389	402	395	379	356
Other checkable deposits [4]	28	104	132	147	180	236	260	281	285	294	332	384	415	404	357	276	246	250	244
M2, total	**1,600**	**1,911**	**2,128**	**2,312**	**2,498**	**2,734**	**2,833**	**2,997**	**3,161**	**3,281**	**3,381**	**3,436**	**3,491**	**3,505**	**3,650**	**3,823**	**4,041**	**4,397**	**4,652**
M1	408	474	521	551	619	724	750	786	793	824	896	1,024	1,130	1,150	1,127	1,081	1,074	1,097	1,124
Non-M1 components in M2	1,192	1,437	1,607	1,760	1,878	2,010	2,084	2,211	2,369	2,457	2,485	2,411	2,361	2,355	2,523	2,742	2,967	3,300	3,526
Money market funds, retail	64	186	138	167	177	211	225	247	324	360	375	357	360	389	458	524	602	749	839
Savings deposits (including MMDAs [5])	400	400	685	705	815	941	937	926	894	923	1,044	1,186	1,219	1,150	1,134	1,271	1,397	1,599	1,735
Commercial banks	186	190	363	389	457	534	535	542	541	581	664	754	785	753	775	904	1,020	1,185	1,286
Thrift institutions	215	210	322	315	359	407	403	384	353	342	379	433	434	397	360	367	377	414	443
Small time deposits [6]	729	851	784	889	886	858	921	1,037	1,151	1,173	1,066	868	782	816	931	947	968	952	955
Commercial banks	286	380	351	388	386	369	392	451	534	611	602	508	468	503	575	593	625	626	634
Thrift institutions	442	471	433	501	499	489	529	586	618	563	463	360	314	314	357	354	343	326	321
M3, total	**1,996**	**2,461**	**2,699**	**2,993**	**3,210**	**3,501**	**3,692**	**3,936**	**4,091**	**4,156**	**4,208**	**4,219**	**4,280**	**4,354**	**4,617**	**4,952**	**5,402**	**5,997**	**6,469**
M2	1,600	1,911	2,128	2,312	2,498	2,734	2,833	2,997	3,161	3,281	3,381	3,436	3,491	3,505	3,650	3,823	4,041	4,397	4,652
Non-M2 components in M3	396	550	571	681	712	767	859	939	930	875	827	783	789	849	967	1,129	1,361	1,600	1,817
Large time deposits [7]	260	325	316	403	422	420	467	518	541	482	418	354	334	364	421	492	574	628	732
Commercial banks [8]	215	261	220	256	271	270	304	344	380	361	334	287	273	299	346	414	488	539	610
Thrift institutions	45	64	97	147	152	150	163	175	161	121	83	67	62	65	74	78	86	89	91
Repurchase agreements [9]	58	72	97	107	121	146	178	197	169	151	131	142	173	196	198	211	256	301	335
Eurodollars [9]	61	104	117	109	104	116	121	132	109	103	92	80	73	86	94	115	151	153	173
Money market funds, institution only	16	49	41	62	64	85	92	92	110	138	186	208	209	202	254	312	381	518	607

[1] Currency outside U.S. Treasury, Federal Reserve Banks and the vaults of depository institutions. [2] Outstanding amount of nonbank issuers. [3] At commercial banks and foreign-related institutions. [4] Consists of negotiable order of withdrawal (NOW) and automatic transfer service (ATS) accounts at all depository institutions, credit union share draft balances, and demand deposits at thrift institutions. [5] Money market deposit accounts (MMDA). [6] Issued in amounts of less than $100,000. [7] Includes retail repurchase agreements. Excludes individual retirement accounts (IRAs) and Keogh accounts. Issued in amounts of $100,000 or more. Excludes those booked at international banking facilities. [8] Excludes those held by money market mutual funds, depository institutions, U.S. Government, foreign banks and official institutions. [9] Excludes those held by depository institutions and money market mutual funds.

Source: Board of Governors of the Federal Reserve System, *Federal Reserve Bulletin*, monthly, and *Money Stock, Liquid Assets, and Debt Measures, Federal Reserve Statistical Release H.6*, weekly.

No. 822. Money Market Interest Rates and Mortgage Rates: 1980 to 1999

[Percent per year. Annual averages of monthly data, except as indicated]

Type	1980	1985	1988	1989	1990	1991	1992	1993	1994	1995	1996	1997	1998	1999
Federal funds, effective rate	13.35	8.10	7.57	9.21	8.10	5.69	3.52	3.02	4.21	5.83	5.30	5.46	5.35	4.97
Prime rate charged by banks	15.26	9.93	9.32	10.87	10.01	8.46	6.25	6.00	7.15	8.83	8.27	8.44	8.35	8.00
Eurodollar deposits, 3-month [1]	14.00	8.27	7.85	9.16	8.16	5.86	3.70	3.18	4.63	5.93	5.38	5.61	5.45	5.31
Bankers acceptances, 3-month [1]	12.67	7.91	7.56	8.87	7.93	5.70	3.62	3.13	4.56	5.81	5.31	5.54	5.39	5.24
Bankers acceptances, 6-month [1]	12.20	7.95	7.60	8.67	7.80	5.67	3.67	3.21	4.83	5.80	5.31	5.57	5.30	5.30
Large negotiable CDs:														
3-month, secondary market	13.07	8.05	7.73	9.09	8.15	5.83	3.68	3.17	4.63	5.92	5.39	5.62	5.47	5.19
6-month, secondary market	12.94	8.24	7.91	9.08	8.17	5.91	3.76	3.28	4.96	5.98	5.47	5.73	5.44	5.33
Taxable money market funds [2]	12.68	7.71	7.11	8.87	7.82	5.71	3.36	2.70	3.75	5.48	4.95	5.10	5.04	4.64
Tax-exempt money market funds [2]	(NA)	4.90	4.79	5.90	5.45	4.13	2.58	1.97	2.38	3.39	2.99	3.14	2.94	2.72
Certificates of deposit (CDs): [3]														
6-month	(NA)	8.05	7.34	8.55	7.79	5.80	3.51	2.88	3.42	4.92	4.68	4.86	4.58	4.27
1-year	(NA)	8.53	7.66	8.65	7.92	6.03	3.78	3.16	4.01	5.39	4.95	5.15	4.81	4.56
2½-year	(NA)	9.32	7.99	8.58	7.96	6.46	4.56	3.80	4.58	5.69	5.14	5.40	4.93	4.74
5-year	(NA)	9.99	8.35	8.56	8.06	7.02	5.76	4.98	5.42	6.00	6.46	5.66	5.08	4.93
U.S. Government securities:														
Secondary market: [4]														
3-month Treasury bill	11.39	7.47	6.67	8.11	7.50	5.38	3.43	3.00	4.25	5.49	5.01	5.06	4.78	4.64
6-month Treasury bill	11.32	7.65	6.91	8.03	7.46	5.44	3.54	3.12	4.64	5.56	5.08	5.18	4.83	4.75
1-year Treasury bill	10.85	7.81	7.13	7.92	7.35	5.52	3.71	3.29	5.02	5.60	5.22	5.36	4.80	4.81
Auction average: [5]														
3-month Treasury bill	11.51	7.47	6.68	8.12	7.51	5.42	3.45	3.02	4.29	5.51	5.02	5.07	4.81	4.66
6-month Treasury bill	11.37	7.64	6.92	8.04	7.47	5.49	3.57	3.14	4.66	5.59	5.09	5.18	4.85	4.76
1-year Treasury bill	10.75	7.76	7.17	7.91	7.36	5.54	3.75	3.33	4.98	5.69	5.23	5.36	4.85	4.78
Home mortgages:														
HUD series: [6]														
FHA insured, secondary market [7]	13.44	12.24	10.49	10.24	10.17	9.25	8.46	7.46	8.68	8.18	8.19	7.89	7.04	7.74
Conventional, new-home [8]	13.95	12.28	10.30	10.21	10.08	9.20	8.43	7.37	8.58	8.05	8.03	7.76	7.00	7.45
Conventional, existing-home [8]	13.95	12.29	10.31	10.22	10.08	9.20	8.43	7.37	8.59	8.05	8.03	7.76	7.01	7.47
Conventional, 15 yr. fixed [3]	(NA)	11.48	10.14	10.03	9.73	8.76	7.80	6.65	7.77	7.39	7.28	7.16	6.58	7.09
Conventional, 30 yr. fixed [3]	(NA)	11.85	10.38	10.25	9.97	9.09	8.27	7.17	8.28	7.86	7.76	7.57	6.92	7.46

NA Not available. [1] Yields are quoted on a bank-discount basis, rather than an investment yield basis (which would give a higher figure). Based on representative closing yields. From Jan. 1, 1981, rates of top-rated banks only. [2] 12 month return for period ending December 31. Source: IBC Financial Data, Inc., Ashland, MA, *IBC's Money Market Insight*, monthly (copyright). [3] Annual averages. Source: Financial Rates, Inc., North Palm Beach, FL, *Bank Rate Monitor*, weekly (copyright). [4] Averages based on daily closing bid yields in secondary market, bank discount basis. [5] Averages computed on an issue-date basis; bank discount basis. [6] HUD=Housing and Urban Development. Averages based on quotations for 1 day each month as compiled by FHA. [7] Primary market. [8] Average contract rates on new commitments.

Source: Except as noted, Board of Governors of the Federal Reserve System, *Federal Reserve Bulletin*, monthly, and *Annual Statistical Digest*.

No. 823. Bond Yields: 1980 to 1999

[**Percent per year**. Annual averages of daily figures, except as indicated]

Type	1980	1985	1990	1992	1993	1994	1995	1996	1997	1998	1999
U.S. Treasury, constant maturities: [1][2]											
1-year	12.00	8.42	7.89	3.89	3.43	5.32	5.94	5.52	5.63	5.05	5.08
2-year	11.73	9.27	8.16	4.77	4.05	5.94	6.15	5.84	5.99	5.13	5.43
3-year	11.51	9.64	8.26	5.30	4.44	6.27	6.25	5.99	6.10	5.14	5.49
5-year	11.45	10.12	8.37	6.19	5.14	6.69	6.38	6.18	6.22	5.15	5.55
7-year	11.40	10.50	8.52	6.63	5.54	6.91	6.50	6.34	6.33	5.28	5.79
10-year	11.43	10.62	8.55	7.01	5.87	7.09	6.57	6.44	6.35	5.26	5.65
20-year	(NA)	(NA)	(NA)	(NA)	6.29	7.47	6.95	6.83	6.69	5.72	6.20
30-year	11.27	10.79	8.61	7.67	6.59	7.37	6.88	6.71	6.61	5.58	5.87
U.S. Govt., long-term bonds [2][3]	10.81	10.75	8.74	7.52	6.45	7.41	6.93	6.80	6.67	5.69	6.14
State and local govt. bonds, Aaa	7.86	8.60	6.97	6.09	5.38	5.77	5.80	5.52	5.32	4.93	5.29
State and local govt. bonds, Baa	9.02	9.58	7.30	6.48	5.83	6.17	6.10	5.79	5.50	5.14	5.70
Municipal (Bond Buyer, 20 bonds)	8.59	9.10	7.27	6.44	5.60	6.18	5.95	5.76	5.52	5.09	5.43
Corporate Aaa seasoned [4]	11.94	11.37	9.32	8.14	7.22	7.97	7.59	7.37	7.27	6.53	7.05
Corporate Baa seasoned [4]	13.67	12.72	10.36	8.98	7.93	8.63	8.20	8.05	7.87	7.22	7.88
Corporate (Moody's) [4][5]	12.75	12.05	9.77	8.55	7.54	8.26	7.83	7.66	7.54	6.87	7.44
Industrials (49 bonds) [6]	12.35	11.80	9.77	8.52	7.51	8.21	7.76	7.58	7.47	6.79	7.33
Public utilities (51 bonds) [7]	13.15	12.29	9.76	8.57	7.56	8.30	7.90	7.74	7.63	7.00	7.54

NA Not available.   [1] Yields on the more actively traded issues adjusted to constant maturities by the U.S. Treasury.   [2] Yields are based on closing bid prices quoted by at least five dealers.   [3] Averages (to maturity or call) for all outstanding bonds neither due nor callable in less than 10 years, including several very low yielding "flower" bonds.   [4] Source: Moody's Investors Service, New York, NY.   [5] For 1980 and 1985 includes railroad bonds which were discontinued as part of composite in 1989.   [6] Covers 40 bonds for 1980 and 38 bonds for 1985.   [7] Covers 40 bonds for 1980 and 1985.

Source: Except as noted, Board of Governors of the Federal Reserve System, *Federal Reserve Bulletin*, monthly.

No. 824. Volume of Debt Markets by Type of Security: 1990 to 1999

[**In billions of dollars (2,780 represents $2,780,000,000,000)**. Covers debt markets as represented by the source]

Type of security	1990	1994	1995	1996	1997	1998	1999
NEW ISSUE VOLUME							
Total	**2,780**	**5,296**	**6,772**	**8,188**	**9,414**	**10,451**	**11,135**
U.S. Treasury securities [1]	1,531	2,112	2,331	2,485	2,169	1,969	2,028
Federal agency debt	637	2,256	3,531	4,525	5,751	6,348	7,074
Municipal	163	205	198	227	267	321	263
Mortgage-backed securities [2]	235	359	269	371	368	727	687
Asset-backed securities [3]	42	75	107	152	185	196	197
Corporate debt [4]	173	289	336	428	674	890	886
DAILY TRADING VOLUME							
Total	**111.2**	**237.7**	**246.3**	**274.0**	**300.5**	**352.8**	**316.6**
U.S. Treasury securities [1][5]	111.2	191.3	193.2	203.7	212.1	226.6	186.5
Federal agency debt [5]	(NA)	16.0	23.7	31.1	40.2	47.6	54.6
Municipal [6]	(NA)	(NA)	(NA)	1.1	1.1	7.7	8.5
Mortgage-backed securities [2][5]	(NA)	30.4	29.4	38.1	47.1	70.9	67.1
VOLUME OF SECURITIES OUTSTANDING							
Total	**7,434**	**9,645**	**10,422**	**11,297**	**12,225**	**13,411**	**14,727**
U.S. Treasury securities [1]	2,196	3,126	3,307	3,460	3,457	3,356	3,281
Federal agency debt [7]	435	739	845	926	1,023	1,297	1,500
Municipal	1,184	1,342	1,294	1,296	1,368	1,464	1,533
Mortgage-backed securities [2]	1,024	1,442	1,570	1,711	1,826	2,018	2,292
Asset-backed securities [3][7]	87	206	292	388	514	633	744
Money market instruments [8]	1,157	1,035	1,177	1,394	1,693	1,978	2,338
Corporate debt [4][7]	1,350	1,756	1,938	2,122	2,346	2,666	3,040

NA Not available.   [1] Marketable public debt.   [2] Includes only Government National Mortgage Association (GNMA), Federal National Mortgage Association (FNMA), and Federal Home Loan Mortgage Corporation (FHLMC) mortgage-backed securities.   [3] Excludes mortgage-backed assets.   [4] Includes nonconvertible corporate debt, Yankee bonds, and MTNs (Medium-Term Notes), but excludes Federal and agency debt.   [5] Primary dealer transactions.   [6] Beginning September 1998 includes customer-to-dealer and dealer-to-dealer transactions.   [7] The Bond Market Association estimates.   [8] Commercial paper, bankers acceptances, and large time deposits.

Source: The Bond Market Association, New York, NY. Copyright. Based on data supplied by Board of Governors of the Federal Reserve System, U.S. Dept. of Treasury, Securities Data Company, FHLMC, FNMA, GNMA, Federal Home Loan Banks, Student Loan Marketing Association, Federal Farm Credit Banks, Tennessee Valley Authority, and Municipal Securities Rulemaking Board.

No. 825. Commercial Paper Outstanding by Type of Company: 1980 to 1999

[**In billions of dollars (124 represents $124,000,000,000)**. As of **December 31**. Seasonally adjusted. Commercial paper is an unsecured promissory note having a fixed maturity of no more than 270 days]

Type of company	1980	1985	1990	1992	1993	1994	1995	1996	1997	1998	1999
All issuers	**124**	**299**	**563**	**546**	**555**	**595**	**675**	**775**	**967**	**1,163**	**1,403**
Financial companies [1][2]	88	214	415	398	399	431	487	591	766	936	1,124
Dealer-placed paper [2]	20	78	215	227	219	223	276	361	513	614	787
Directly-placed paper [3]	68	135	200	172	180	208	211	230	253	322	337
Nonfinancial companies [4]	37	85	148	148	156	165	188	185	201	227	279

[1] Institutions engaged primarily in commercial, savings, and mortgage banking; sales, personal, and mortgage financing; factoring, finance leasing, and other business lending; insurance underwriting; and other investment activities.   [2] Includes all financial company paper sold by dealers in the open market.   [3] As reported by financial companies that place their paper directly with investors.   [4] Includes public utilities and firms engaged primarily in such activities as communications, construction, manufacturing, mining, wholesale and retail trade, transportation, and services.

Source: Board of Governors of the Federal Reserve System, *Federal Reserve Bulletin*, monthly.

No. 826. Total Returns of Stocks, Bonds, and Treasury Bills: 1950 to 1999

[In percent. Average annual percent change. Stock return data are based on the Standard & Poor's 500 index]

Period	Stocks				Treasury bills, total return	Bonds (10-year), total return
	Total return	Capital gains	Dividends and reinvestment	Total return after inflation		
1950 to 1959.	19.28	13.58	5.02	16.69	2.02	0.73
1960 to 1969.	7.78	4.39	3.62	5.13	4.06	2.42
1970 to 1979.	5.82	1.60	4.15	-0.14	6.42	5.84
1980 to 1989.	17.54	12.59	4.42	11.87	9.21	13.06
1990 to 1999.	18.17	15.31	2.48	15.09	5.01	7.96

Source: Global Financial Data, Los Angeles, CA, "Stocks, Bills, Bonds And Inflation Sector Total Returns In The United States, 1871-1996"; <http://www.globalfindata.com/sector.pdf>; (accessed: 26 June 2000); and unpublished data. (copyright).

No. 827. Equities, Corporate Bonds, and Municipal Securities—Holdings and Net Purchases by Type of Investor: 1990 to 1999

[In billions of dollars (3,543 represents $3,543,000,000,000). Holdings as of Dec. 31. Minus sign (-) indicates net sales]

Type of investor	Holdings					Net purchases				
	1990	1995	1997	1998	1999	1990	1995	1997	1998	1999
EQUITIES [1]										
Total [2]	3,543	8,496	13,181	15,413	18,877	-45.7	-16.0	-99.6	-198.1	-67.8
Household sector [3]	1,807	4,122	5,690	6,339	8,009	-39.6	-228.8	-507.1	-455.3	-380.1
State and local governments	5	26	79	102	125	1.5	12.1	16.8	9.7	13.1
Rest of the world [4]	244	528	920	1,115	1,203	-16.0	16.6	66.8	43.8	96.2
Bank personal trusts and estates . .	190	225	305	308	336	0.5	1.6	-14.5	-59.0	-35.9
Life insurance companies	82	315	559	723	952	-5.7	18.6	86.3	107.4	96.6
Other insurance companies.	80	134	186	201	214	-7.0	-0.6	3.0	-5.2	-1.8
Private pension funds	595	1,238	1,864	2,232	2,500	-4.1	5.9	-16.1	-52.7	-80.3
State and local retirement funds. . .	271	791	1,432	1,758	2,042	18.5	65.3	100.7	88.0	93.4
Mutual funds	233	1,025	2,019	2,509	3,359	14.4	87.4	166.8	143.3	136.9
CORPORATE & FOREIGN BONDS										
Total [2]	1,706	2,841	3,563	4,099	4,551	125.2	336.7	406.7	535.6	452.5
Household sector [3]	192	448	521	581	596	44.9	95.0	68.9	60.3	14.8
Rest of the world [4]	217	369	537	660	817	5.3	58.1	84.0	122.4	157.5
Commercial banking	89	111	143	181	220	4.6	8.4	27.8	38.0	38.9
Savings institutions	76	79	59	89	112	-19.3	-8.2	-9.9	29.9	23.2
Life insurance companies	567	870	1,046	1,130	1,202	56.5	90.7	86.8	84.5	71.1
Other insurance companies.	89	123	160	176	174	10.4	12.7	18.9	16.7	-1.9
Private pension funds	146	207	256	301	336	14.9	5.6	27.7	45.4	34.6
State and local retirement funds. . .	180	191	245	280	305	8.5	5.6	30.1	35.1	25.6
Money market mutual funds	2	22	36	81	124	-1.7	6.4	12.5	44.8	42.5
Mutual funds	59	196	274	339	369	4.7	23.3	44.4	65.5	29.3
MUNICIPAL SECURITIES [5]										
Total [2]	1,184	1,293	1,367	1,464	1,532	49.3	-48.2	71.4	96.8	68.2
Household sector [3]	574	458	464	475	528	27.7	-43.5	44.9	11.8	52.1
Other insurance companies.	137	161	192	211	209	1.8	7.0	2.6	19.2	-1.9
Money market mutual funds	84	128	167	193	210	13.9	14.3	22.5	26.0	17.5
Mutual funds	113	210	220	243	241	13.9	3.2	6.5	22.8	-1.1

[1] Excludes mutual fund shares. [2] Includes other types not shown separately. [3] Includes nonprofit organizations.
[4] Holdings of U.S. issues by foreign residents. [5] Includes loans.

Source: Board of Governors of the Federal Reserve System, "Federal Reserve Statistical Release, Z.1, Flow of Funds Accounts of the United States"; published: 10 March 2000; <http://www.bog.frb.fed.us/releases/Z1/20000310/data.htm>.

No. 828. New Security Issues of Corporations by Type of Offering: 1985 to 1999

[In billions of dollars (254.6 represents $254,600,000,000). Represents gross proceeds of issues maturing in more than one year. Figures are the principal amount or the number of units multiplied by the offering price. Excludes secondary offerings, employee stock plans, investment companies other than closed-end, intracorporate transactions, equities sold abroad, and Yankee bonds. Stock data include ownership securities issued by limited partnerships]

Type of offering	1985	1990	1992	1993	1994	1995	1996	1997	1998	1999
Total	254.6	339.1	559.8	768.3	582.6	672.7	751.8	861.1	1,047.0	990.0
Bonds, total	203.7	298.9	471.5	645.8	498.0	573.0	592.7	695.0	846.8	778.7
Public, domestic	119.7	188.8	378.1	486.2	364.8	408.5	465.6	536.8	731.0	627.6
Private placement, domestic . . .	46.2	87.0	65.9	121.2	76.1	87.5	43.7	55.0	37.8	28.5
Sold abroad	37.8	23.1	27.6	38.4	56.8	76.8	83.4	103.2	78.0	122.6
Stocks, total	50.9	40.2	88.3	122.5	84.6	99.7	159.1	166.1	200.2	211.3
Preferred	6.5	4.0	21.3	18.9	12.2	11.3	32.2	29.5	38.4	19.3
Common	29.0	19.4	57.1	82.7	47.6	56.3	82.4	81.4	82.9	105.7
Private placement	15.4	16.7	9.9	20.9	24.8	32.1	44.5	55.2	78.9	86.3

Source: Board of Governors of the Federal Reserve System, *Federal Reserve Bulletin*, monthly.

No. 829. Purchases and Sales by U.S. Investors of Foreign Bonds and Stocks, 1980 to 1999, and by Selected Country, 1999

[In billions of dollars (3.1 represents $3,100,000,000). See headnote, Table 830. Minus sign (-) indicates net sales by U.S. Investors or a net inflow of capital into the United States]

Year and country	Net purchases			Total transactions [1]			Bonds		Stocks	
	Total	Bonds	Stocks	Total	Bonds	Stocks	Pur-chases	Sales	Pur-chases	Sales
1980	3.1	1.0	2.1	53	35	18	18	17	10	8
1985	7.9	4.0	3.9	212	166	46	85	81	25	21
1990	31.2	21.9	9.2	907	652	255	337	315	132	123
1991	46.8	14.8	32.0	949	675	273	345	330	153	121
1992	47.9	15.6	32.3	1,375	1,043	332	529	514	182	150
1993	143.1	80.4	62.7	2,126	1,572	554	826	746	308	245
1994	57.3	9.2	48.1	2,526	1,706	820	858	848	434	386
1995	98.7	48.4	50.3	2,569	1,827	741	938	890	396	346
1996	110.6	51.4	59.3	3,239	2,279	960	1,165	1,114	510	450
1997	89.1	48.1	40.9	4,505	2,952	1,553	1,500	1,452	797	756
1998	11.1	17.3	-6.2	4,527	2,674	1,853	1,346	1,328	923	930
1999, total [2] **. . . . . .**	**-10.0**	**5.7**	**-15.6**	**3,941**	**1,602**	**2,339**	**804**	**798**	**1,162**	**1,177**
United Kingdom	-39.8	-1.3	-38.5	1,751	845	907	422	423	434	473
Japan	43.6	-2.5	46.1	406	50	356	24	26	201	155
Canada	1.0	0.1	0.9	253	155	98	78	78	49	48
Bermuda	1.0	1.2	-0.2	181	135	46	68	67	23	23
British West Indies	1.4	0.1	1.3	169	52	117	26	26	59	58
Germany	2.2	4.7	-2.4	113	22	91	13	9	44	47
Hong Kong	-4.2	-1.5	-2.8	98	11	87	5	6	42	45
Netherlands Antilles	-4.2	-0.2	-4.0	94	24	70	12	12	33	37
France	-1.0	0.4	-1.4	73	18	55	9	9	27	28
Switzerland	-4.2	-0.7	-3.5	72	8	64	4	4	30	34

[1] Total purchases plus total sales.   [2] Includes other countries, not shown separately.

Source: U.S. Dept. of Treasury, *Treasury Bulletin*, quarterly.

No. 830. Foreign Purchases and Sales of U.S. Securities by Type of Security, 1980 to 1999, and by Selected Country, 1999

[In billions of dollars (15.8 represents $15,800,000,000). Covers transactions in all types of long-term domestic securities by foreigners as reported by banks, brokers, and other entities in the United States (except nonmarketable U.S. Treasury notes, foreign series; and nonmarketable U.S. Treasury bonds and notes, foreign currency series). Data cover new issues of securities, transactions in outstanding issues, and redemptions of securities. Includes transactions executed in the United States for the account of foreigners, and transactions executed abroad for the account of reporting institutions and their domestic customers. Data by country show the country of domicile of the foreign buyers and sellers of the securities; in the case of outstanding issues, this may differ from the country of the original issuer. The term "foreigner" covers all institutions and individuals domiciled outside the United States, including U.S. citizens domiciled abroad, and the foreign branches, subsidiaries and other affiliates abroad of U.S. banks and businesses; the central governments, central banks, and other official institutions of foreign countries; and international and regional organizations. "Foreigner" also includes persons in the United States to the extent that they are known by reporting institutions to be acting on behalf of foreigners. Minus sign (-) indicates net sales by foreigners or a net outflow of capital from the United States]

Year and country	Net purchases					Total transactions [4]				
	Total	Trea-sury bonds and notes [1]	U.S. Govt. corpora-tions [2] bonds	Corpo-rate bonds [3]	Corpo-rate stocks	Total	Trea-sury bonds and notes [1]	U.S. Govt. corpora-tions [2] bonds	Corpo-rate bonds [3]	Corpo-rate stocks
1980	15.8	4.9	2.6	2.9	5.4	198	97	17	9	75
1985	78.3	29.2	4.3	39.8	4.9	1,256	968	46	84	159
1990	18.7	17.9	6.3	9.7	-15.1	4,204	3,620	104	117	362
1991	58.1	19.9	10.2	16.9	11.1	4,706	4,016	124	155	411
1992	73.2	39.3	18.3	20.8	-5.1	5,282	4,444	204	187	448
1993	111.1	23.6	35.4	30.6	21.6	6,314	5,195	263	239	618
1994	140.4	78.8	21.7	38.0	1.9	6,562	5,343	297	222	699
1995	231.9	134.1	28.7	57.9	11.2	7,243	5,828	222	278	915
1996	370.2	232.2	41.7	83.7	12.5	8,965	7,134	241	422	1,169
1997	388.0	184.2	49.9	84.4	69.6	12,759	9,546	469	617	2,126
1998	277.8	49.0	56.8	121.9	50.0	14,989	10,259	992	641	3,097
1999, total [5] **. . . . . .**	**351.7**	**-10.0**	**94.2**	**159.9**	**107.5**	**12,618**	**8,586**	**882**	**577**	**2,574**
United Kingdom	128.4	-20.2	14.0	91.7	42.9	5,442	4,083	174	317	867
British West Indies	20.9	-7.0	10.5	9.1	8.2	1,732	411	283	49	989
Bermuda	30.9	4.0	13.2	15.2	-1.5	1,223	399	73	48	704
Japan	43.4	20.1	11.6	5.9	5.7	867	587	77	17	186
France	2.4	-3.3	0.3	1.6	3.8	789	465	3	7	314
Canada	13.1	7.3	2.4	3.6	-0.3	670	469	10	21	169
Netherlands Antilles	-11.9	-9.5	0.4	0.8	-3.5	564	259	13	11	282
Ireland	3.0	-3.0	0.8	3.0	2.1	315	237	19	10	50
Switzerland	8.4	-1.8	0.7	3.9	5.7	301	73	10	8	210
Germany	23.4	2.3	2.9	4.8	13.4	271	131	8	11	121

[1] Marketable bonds and notes.   [2] Includes federally-sponsored agencies.   [3] Includes transactions in directly placed issues abroad by U.S. corporations and issues of states and municipalities.   [4] Total purchases plus total sales.   [5] Includes other countries, not shown separately.

Source: U.S. Dept. of Treasury, *Treasury Bulletin*, quarterly.

No. 831. Stock Prices and Yields: 1990 to 1999

[Closing values as of end of December, except as noted]

Index	1990	1994	1995	1996	1997	1998	1999
STOCK PRICES							
Standard & Poor's indices: [1]							
S&P 500 composite (1941-43=10)	330.9	460.9	614.5	740.5	970.4	1,229.2	1,469.3
Industrials	387.1	548.9	719.7	870.0	1,121.4	1,479.2	1,841.9
Utilities	144.8	151.9	201.7	198.8	235.8	259.6	227.2
S&P 400 MidCap Index (1982=100)	100.0	169.4	217.8	255.6	333.4	392.3	444.7
Russell indices: [2]							
Russell 1000 (Dec. 31, 1986=130).	171.22	244.65	328.89	393.75	513.79	642.87	767.97
Russell 2000 (Dec. 31, 1986=135).	132.16	250.36	315.97	362.61	437.02	421.96	504.75
Russell 3000 (Dec. 31, 1986=140).	180.85	263.44	351.91	419.44	543.05	664.27	793.31
N.Y. Stock Exchange common stock index							
Composite (Dec. 31, 1965=50)	180.49	250.94	329.51	392.30	511.19	596.05	650.30
Yearly high	201.55	267.78	331.73	401.08	515.24	601.76	663.50
Yearly low.	161.76	241.79	249.86	320.90	386.36	462.69	572.40
Industrial (Dec. 31, 1965=50).	223.60	318.10	413.29	494.38	630.38	743.65	828.21
Transportation (Dec. 31, 1965=50)	141.49	222.46	301.96	352.30	466.25	482.38	466.70
Utility (Dec. 31, 1965=100)	182.60	198.41	252.90	259.91	335.19	445.94	511.15
Finance (Dec. 31, 1965=50)	122.07	195.80	274.25	351.17	495.96	521.42	516.61
American Stock Exchange Composite Index							
(Dec. 29, 1995=550).	(NA)	(NA)	550.00	572.34	684.61	688.99	876.97
NASDAQ composite index (Feb. 5, 1971=100)	373.8	752.0	1,052.1	1,291.0	1,570.4	2,192.7	4,069.3
Nasdaq-100 (Sept. 25, 1985=100)	200.5	404.3	576.2	821.4	990.8	1,836.0	3,708.0
Industrial (Feb. 5, 1971=100)	406.1	753.8	964.7	1,109.6	1,221.0	1,304.3	2,239.0
Insurance (Feb. 5, 1971=100)	451.8	925.9	1,292.6	1,465.4	1,798.0	1,796.8	1,896.3
Bank (Feb. 5, 1971=100)	254.9	697.1	1,009.4	1,273.5	2,083.2	1,838.0	1,691.3
Dow-Jones and Co., Inc.:							
Composite (65 stocks).	920.6	1,274.4	1,693.2	2,025.8	2,607.4	2,870.8	3,214.4
Industrial (30 stocks)	2,633.7	3,834.4	5,117.1	6,448.3	7,908.3	9,181.4	11,497.1
Transportation (20 stocks).	910.2	1,455.0	1,981.0	2,255.7	3,256.5	3,149.3	2,977.2
Utility (15 stocks).	209.7	181.5	225.4	232.5	273.1	312.3	283.4
Wilshire 5000 Total Market Index [3]							
(Dec. 31, 1980=1404.596).	3,101.4	4,540.6	6,057.2	7,198.3	9,298.2	11,317.6	13,812.7
COMMON STOCK YIELDS (percent)							
Standard & Poor's composite index (500 stocks): [4]							
Dividend-price ratio [5]	3.61	2.82	2.56	2.19	1.77	1.49	1.25
Earnings-price ratio [6]	6.47	5.83	6.09	5.24	4.57	3.46	3.17

NA Not available. [1] Standard & Poor's Indices are market-value weighted. The S&P 500 index represents the 500 largest publicly traded companies, as determined by Standard & Poor's and represent a broad range of industry segments within the U.S. economy. The S&P MidCap Index tracks mid-cap companies. [2] The Russell 1000 and 3000 indices show respectively the 1000 and 3000 largest capitalization stocks in the United States. The Russell 2000 index shows the 2000 largest capitalization stocks in the United States after the first 1000. [3] The Wilshire 5000 Total Market Index measures the performance of all U.S. headquartered equity securities with readily available prices. [4] Source: U.S. Council of Economic Advisors, *Economic Report of the President*, annual. [5] Aggregate cash dividends (based on latest known annual rate) divided by aggregate market value based on Wednesday closing prices. Averages of monthly figures. [6] Averages of quarterly ratios which are ratio of earnings (after taxes) for 4 quarters ending with particular quarter to price index for last day of that quarter.

Source: Except as noted, Global Financial Data, Los Angeles, CA, "GFD Standard and Poor's Sectors"; <http://www.globalfindata.com/freesp.pdf>; "Global Financial Data Dow Jones Industrial Average"; <http://www.globalfindata.com/freedjia.htm>; (all accessed 27 June 2000) and unpublished data (copyright).

No. 832. Dow-Jones U.S. Equity Market Index by Industry: 1990 to 1999

[As of end of year]

Industry	1990	1994	1995	1996	1997	1998	1999
U.S. Equity Market Index, total	305.59	432.95	581.27	700.37	922.34	1,169.34	1,390.32
Basic materials	299.67	456.87	540.85	615.06	680.77	630.44	831.36
Consumer, cyclical	325.98	533.68	636.36	712.53	961.83	1,340.80	1,611.47
Consumer, noncyclical.	543.87	740.55	1,053.32	1,287.85	1,738.25	2,192.39	2,013.60
Independents.	354.20	634.77	886.93	1,222.07	1,794.92	2,463.15	3,675.32
Energy	262.85	286.86	358.95	442.36	533.72	522.82	603.11
Financial services.	233.04	408.70	612.43	810.66	1,203.36	1,303.63	1,314.02
Industrial.	288.12	399.58	499.69	581.66	700.74	737.60	782.85
Technology	242.10	406.36	570.39	730.24	891.62	1,446.78	2,419.30
Utilities	248.91	272.72	362.52	359.53	473.01	631.38	672.03

Source: Dow Jones & Company, Inc., New York, NY, *Wall Street Journal*, selected issues (copyright).

No. 833. NASDAQ—Securities Listed and Volume of Trading: 1980 to 1999

Item	Unit	1980	1985	1990	1993	1994	1995	1996	1997	1998	1999
Member firms	Number. . .	2,932	6,307	5,827	5,296	5,426	5,451	5,553	5,597	5,592	5,482
Branch offices	Number. . .	7,555	15,375	24,457	44,181	57,105	58,119	60,151	62,966	70,752	80,035
Companies listed	Number. . .	2,894	4,136	4,132	4,611	4,902	5,112	5,556	5,487	5,068	4,829
Issues	Number. . .	3,050	4,784	4,706	5,393	5,761	5,955	6,384	6,208	5,583	5,210
Shares traded	Billion	6.7	20.7	33.4	66.5	74.4	101.2	138.1	163.9	202.0	272.6
Value of shares traded . . .	Bil. dol. . . .	69	234	452	1,350	1,449	2,398	3,302	4,482	5,759	11,013

Source: National Association of Securities Dealers, Washington, DC, *1999 Nasdaq-Amex Fact Book & Company Directory*.

No. 834. Sales of Stocks and Options on Registered Exchanges: 1980 to 1998

[522 represents $522,000,000,000. Excludes over-the-counter trading]

Exchange	Unit	1980	1985	1990	1992	1993	1994	1995	1996	1997	1998
Market value of all sales,											
all exchanges [1][2]	**Bil. dol. .**	**522**	**1,260**	**1,752**	**2,149**	**2,734**	**2,966**	**3,690**	**4,735**	**6,879**	**8,698**
New York	Bil. dol . .	398	1,024	1,394	1,759	2,278	2,483	3,078	4,013	5,848	7,275
American.	Bil. dol . .	47	38	65	69	83	83	105	131	204	355
Chicago	Bil. dol . .	21	79	74	87	107	98	114	136	213	326
CBOE [3]	Bil. dol . .	28	38	81	63	65	87	107	130	179	214
Pacific.	Bil. dol . .	13	40	53	65	70	70	94	108	151	182
Philadelphia.	Bil. dol . .	11	23	41	49	55	51	59	68	89	97
STOCKS [4]											
Shares sold, all exchanges [2] . . .	Billion. . .	15.5	37.0	53.3	65.5	82.8	90.5	106.4	125.7	159.7	206.4
New York	Billion. . .	12.4	30.2	43.8	53.3	68.7	76.7	90.1	108.2	138.8	178.9
American	Billion. . .	1.7	2.1	3.1	3.6	4.5	4.3	4.8	5.3	6.2	7.6
Chicago.	Billion. . .	0.6	2.3	2.5	3.0	3.8	3.5	3.9	4.2	6.0	9.5
Pacific	Billion. . .	0.4	1.4	1.7	2.1	2.3	2.1	2.7	3.0	3.2	4.0
Market value, all exchanges [2] . .	Bil. dol . .	476	1,200	1,612	2,032	2,610	2,817	3,507	4,511	6,559	8,307
New York	Bil. dol . .	398	1,023	1,390	1,758	2,276	2,482	3,076	4,011	5,847	7,274
American	Bil. dol . .	35	26	36	42	54	56	73	86	139	280
Chicago.	Bil. dol . .	21	79	74	87	107	98	114	136	213	326
Pacific.	Bil. dol . .	11	37	45	58	62	59	79	92	123	148

[1] Includes market value of stocks, rights, warrants, and options trading beginning 1990. [2] Includes other registered exchanges, not shown separately. [3] Chicago Board Options Exchange, Inc. [4] Includes voting trust certificates, American Depository Receipts, and certificate of deposit for stocks.

Source: U.S. Securities and Exchange Commission, *SEC Monthly Statistical Review* (discontinued Feb. 1989); and unpublished data.

No. 835. Volume of Trading on New York Stock Exchange: 1980 to 1999

[11,562 represents 11,562,000,000. **Round lot**: A unit of trading or a multiple thereof. On the NYSE the unit of trading is generally 100 shares in stocks. For some inactive stocks, the unit of trading is 10 shares. **Odd lot**: An amount of stock less than the established 100-share unit or 10-share unit of trading]

Item	Unit	1980	1985	1990	1993	1994	1995	1996	1997	1998	1999
Shares traded	**Million .**	**11,562**	**27,774**	**39,946**	**67,461**	**74,003**	**87,873**	**105,477**	**134,404**	**171,188**	**206,299**
Round lots	Million. .	11,352	27,511	39,665	66,923	73,420	87,218	104,636	133,312	169,745	203,914
Average daily shares	Million . .	45	109	157	265	291	346	412	527	674	809
High day	Million. .	84	181	292	379	483	653	681	1,201	1,216	1,350
Low day	Million. .	16	62	57	90	114	118	130	155	247	312
Odd lots	Million. .	209	263	282	538	583	656	841	1,091	1,443	2,384
Value of shares traded . .	**Bil. dol .**	**382**	**981**	**1,336**	**2,305**	**2,477**	**3,110**	**4,102**	**5,833**	**7,395**	**9,073**
Round lots	Bil. dol. .	375	970	1,325	2,283	2,454	3,083	4,064	5,778	7,318	8,945
Odd lots	Bil. dol. .	8	10	11	22	22	27	38	56	77	128
Bond volume [1] **. . . . .**	**Mil. dol .**	**5,190**	**9,047**	**10,893**	**9,743**	**7,197**	**6,979**	**5,529**	**5,046**	**3,838**	**3,221**
Daily average	Mil. dol .	20.5	35.9	43.1	38.5	28.6	27.7	21.8	19.9	15.2	12.8

[1] Par value.

Source: New York Stock Exchange, Inc., New York, NY, *Fact Book,* annual (copyright).

No. 836. Securities Listed on New York Stock Exchange: 1980 to 1999

[As of **December 31**, except **cash dividends** are for **calendar year** (602 represents $602,000,000,000)]

Item	Unit	1980	1985	1990	1992	1993	1994	1995	1996	1997	1998	1999
BONDS												
Number of issuers	Number .	1,045	1,010	743	636	574	583	564	563	533	474	416
Number of issues.	Number .	3,057	3,856	2,912	2,354	2,103	2,141	2,097	2,064	1,965	1,858	1,736
Face value	Bil. dol . .	602	1,327	1,689	2,009	2,342	2,526	2,773	2,845	2,625	2,554	2,402
STOCKS												
Companies	Number .	1,570	1,541	1,774	2,088	2,361	2,570	2,675	2,907	3,047	3,114	3,025
Number of issues.	Number .	2,228	2,298	2,284	2,658	2,904	3,060	3,126	3,285	3,358	3,382	3,286
Shares listed	Billion. . .	33.7	52.4	90.7	115.8	131.1	142.3	154.7	176.9	207.1	239.3	280.9
Market value	Bil. dol . .	1,243	1,950	2,820	4,035	4,541	4,448	6,013	7,300	9,413	10,864	12,296
Average price	Dollars . .	36.87	37.20	31.08	34.83	34.65	31.26	38.86	41.26	45.45	45.40	43.77
Cash dividends on common stock [1]	Bil. dol . .	53.1	74.2	103.2	109.7	120.2	130.0	147.0	150.6	159.4	179.0	174.7

[1] Beginning 1990 estimate based on average annual yield of the NYSE composite index.

Source: New York Stock Exchange, Inc., New York, NY, *Fact Book,* annual (copyright).

No. 837. Stock Ownership by Age of Head of Family and Family Income: 1992 to 1998

[**Median value in thousands of constant 1998 dollars (12.0 represents $12,000).** Constant dollar figures are based on consumer price index data published by U.S. Bureau of Labor Statistics. Families include one-person units; for definition of family, see text, Section 1, Population. Based on Survey of Consumer Finance; see Appendix III. For definition of median, see Guide to Tabular Presentation]

Age of family head and family income (constant (1998) dollars)	Families having direct or indirect stock holdings [1] (percent)			Median value among families with holdings			Stock holdings' share of group's financial assets (percent)		
	1992	1995	1998	1992	1995	1998	1992	1995	1998
All families	**36.7**	**40.4**	**48.8**	**12.0**	**15.4**	**25.0**	**33.7**	**40.0**	**53.9**
Under 35 years old	28.3	36.6	40.7	4.0	5.4	7.0	24.8	27.2	44.8
35 to 44 years old.	42.4	46.4	56.5	8.6	10.6	20.0	31.0	39.5	54.7
45 to 54 years old.	46.4	48.9	58.6	17.1	27.6	38.0	40.6	42.9	55.7
55 to 64 years old.	45.3	40.0	55.9	28.5	32.9	47.0	37.3	44.4	58.3
65 to 74 years old.	30.2	34.4	42.6	18.3	36.1	56.0	31.6	35.8	51.3
75 years old and over	25.7	27.9	29.4	28.5	21.2	60.0	25.4	39.8	48.7
Less than $10,000	6.8	5.4	7.7	6.2	3.2	4.0	15.9	12.9	24.8
$10,000 to $24,999.	17.8	22.2	24.7	4.6	6.4	9.0	15.3	26.7	27.5
$25,000 to $49,999.	40.2	45.4	52.7	7.2	8.5	11.5	23.7	30.3	39.1
$50,000 to $99,999	62.5	65.4	74.3	15.4	23.6	35.7	33.5	39.9	48.8
$100,000 and more.	78.3	81.6	91.0	71.9	85.5	150.0	40.2	46.4	63.0

[1] Indirect holdings are those in mutual funds, retirement accounts, and other managed assets.

Source: Board of Governors of the Federal Reserve System, *Federal Reserve Bulletin*, January 2000, and unpublished data.

No. 838. Household Ownership of Equities: 1999

[**49.2 represents 49,200,000.** Based on a national probability sample of 4,842 household financial decisionmakers. Of these, 2,336 decisionmakers who indicated they owned equities were asked further questions about equity ownership]

Type of holding	Households owning equities		Number of individual investors (mil.)
	Number (mil.)	Percent of all households	
Any type of equity (net) [1]	49.2	48.2	78.7
Any equity inside employer-sponsored retirement plans	32.5	31.8	52.0
Any equity outside employer-sponsored retirement plans	36.3	35.5	61.6
Individual stock (net) [1]	26.7	26.1	40.0
Individual stock inside employer-sponsored retirement plans.	10.7	10.5	14.0
Individual stock outside employer-sponsored retirement plans.	21.9	21.4	32.8
Stock mutual funds (net) [1]	41.8	40.9	66.8
Stock mutual funds inside employer-sponsored retirement plans	28.5	27.9	39.9
Stock mutual funds outside employer-sponsored retirement plans . . .	27.8	27.2	44.4

[1] Multiple responses included.

No. 839. Characteristics of Equity Owners: 1999

[**In percent, except as indicated.** See headnote, Table 838. For definition of median, see Guide to Tabular Presentation]

Item		Age				Household income		
	Total	19 to 35 years old	36 to 54 years old	55 to 74 years old	75 years old and over	Less than $50,000	$50,000 to $99,999	$100,000 and over
Median age (years).	47	29	44	61	78	45	44	48
Median household income (dol.)	60,000	47,000	62,500	53,000	30,000	34,000	65,000	125,000
Median household financial assets [1] (dol.).	85,000	25,000	88,000	200,000	200,000	42,500	89,000	300,000
Equity investments owned:								
Individual stock (net) [2]	54	45	52	58	63	44	52	67
Inside employer-sponsored retirement plans . .	20	21	23	17	6	15	20	29
Outside employer-sponsored retirement plans .	44	35	43	51	59	34	44	61
Stock mutual funds (net) [2].	85	83	88	84	80	81	89	88
Inside employer-sponsored retirement plans . .	58	64	67	47	12	49	66	69
Outside employer-sponsored retirement plans .	57	45	57	62	72	51	55	66
Nonequity investments owned: [2]								
Savings accounts, MMDAs, or CDs [3]	83	82	84	82	86	79	84	86
Bond investments (net) [2]	22	14	21	24	44	15	19	31
Individual bonds.	9	4	8	11	25	4	7	15
Bond mutual funds.	16	11	16	19	30	12	15	23
Fixed or variable annuities	21	9	20	30	35	17	20	25
Hybrid mutual funds.	39	33	42	41	35	33	42	46
Money market mutual funds	26	17	26	32	30	20	26	38
Investment real estate	26	17	26	34	24	18	26	40
Have employer-sponsored retirement plan coverage.	80	83	86	73	49	73	86	84
Have Individual Retirement Account (IRA).	53	37	53	67	39	41	55	67

[1] Includes assets in employer-sponsored retirement plans but excludes value of primary residence. [2] Multiple responses included. [3] MMDA=money market deposit account; CD=certificate of deposit.

Source of Tables 838 and 839: Investment Company Institute, Washington, DC, and Securities Industry Association, New York, NY, *Equity Ownership in America*, fall 1999 (copyright).

Banking, Finance, and Insurance 527

No. 840. Household Ownership of Mutual Funds by Age and Income: 1999

[In percent. Includes money market, stock, bond and hybrid, variable annuity, IRA, Keogh, and employer-sponsored retirement plan fund owners. An estimated 48,400,000 households own mutual funds. Based on a sample survey of 3,000 households; for details, see source]

Age of household head and household income	All house-holds, percent distribution	Households owning mutual funds		Age of household head and household income	All house-holds, percent distribution	Households owning mutual funds	
		Percent distribution	Percent of all house-holds			Percent distribution	Percent of all house-holds
Total	100	100	47				
Less than 25 years old .	5	3	28	Less than $25,000	24	8	15
25 to 34 years old.	19	19	47	$25,000 to $34,999. . . .	15	9	30
35 to 44 years old.	23	27	55	$35,000 to $49,999. . . .	18	18	49
45 to 54 years old.	19	23	58	$50,000 to $74,999. . . .	22	30	62
55 to 64 years old.	13	13	50	$75,000 to $99,999. . . .	10	16	78
65 years old and over . .	21	15	34	$100,000 and over	11	19	78

Source: Investment Company Institute, Washington, DC, *Fundamentals, Investment Company Institute Research in Brief*, Vol. 8, No. 5, September 1999 (copyright).

No. 841. Characteristics of Mutual Fund Owners: 1998

[In percent, except as indicated. Mutual fund ownership includes holdings of money market, stock, bond, and hybrid mutual funds; and funds owned through variable annuities, Individual Retirement Accounts (IRAs), Keoghs, and employer-sponsored retirement plans. Based on a national probability sample of 1,470 primary financial decisionmakers in households with mutual fund investments. For definition of median, see Guide to Tabular Presentation]

Characteristic	Total	Age			Household income		
		18 to 33 years old	34 to 52 years old	53 years old and over	Less than $50,000	$50,000 to $100,000	Over $100,000
Median age (years)	44	29	43	61	41	43	46
Median household income (dol.).	55,000	44,000	62,000	47,000	35,000	69,000	125,000
Median household financial assets [1] (dol.)	80,000	26,000	90,000	200,000	37,000	100,000	325,000
Own an IRA	57	45	56	73	49	59	71
Household has a defined contribution retirement plan(s), net [2]	77	85	83	59	70	86	89
401(k) plan	60	73	66	39	52	68	77
403(k) plan	12	12	12	13	10	14	19
State, local, or Federal Government plan	24	21	26	23	24	27	20
Median mutual fund assets (dol.)	25,000	10,000	25,000	62,500	10,000	30,000	70,000
Median number of mutual funds owned.	4	3	4	4	2	4	6
Own: [2]							
Equity funds	88	87	88	90	79	91	96
Bond funds	42	34	42	52	34	40	53
Hybrid funds	35	29	36	40	30	33	43
Money market mutual funds.	48	43	47	53	45	40	53
Own mutual funds bought: [2]							
Outside employer-sponsored retirement plan(s).	54	45	55	59	43	53	65
Inside employer-sponsored retirement plan(s) . .	62	66	70	46	53	73	78

[1] Includes assets in employer-sponsored retirement plans but excludes value of primary residence. [2] Multiple responses included.

Source: Investment Company Institute, Washington, DC, *1998 Profile of Mutual Fund Shareholders*, 1999 (copyright).

No. 842. Mutual Funds—Summary: 1980 to 1999

[Number of funds and assets as of December 31 (135 represents $135,000,000,000). A mutual fund is an open-end investment company that continuously issues and redeems shares that represent an interest in a pool of financial assets. Excludes data for funds that invest in other mutual funds. Minus sign (-) indicates net redemptions]

Type of fund	Unit	1980	1985	1990	1994	1995	1996	1997	1998	1999
Number of funds, total	Number. .	[1]564	1,527	3,081	5,330	5,728	6,254	6,684	7,314	7,791
Equity funds.	Number. .	277	579	1,100	1,887	2,140	2,572	2,951	3,513	3,952
Hybrid funds.	Number. .	(NA)	87	194	365	414	470	501	525	533
Bond funds	Number. .	(NA)	404	1,046	2,115	2,177	2,224	2,219	2,250	2,261
Money market funds, taxable [2] . . .	Number. .	96	346	506	646	674	666	682	685	702
Money market funds, tax-exempt [3] . .	Number. .	10	111	235	317	323	322	331	341	343
Assets, total	Bil. dol . .	[1]135	495	1,065	2,155	2,811	3,526	4,468	5,525	6,846
Equity funds.	Bil. dol. . .	44	117	239	853	1,249	1,726	2,368	2,978	4,042
Hybrid funds.	Bil. dol. . .	(NA)	12	36	164	211	253	317	365	383
Bond funds	Bil. dol. . .	(NA)	123	291	527	599	645	724	831	808
Money market funds, taxable [2] . . .	Bil. dol. . .	75	208	415	501	630	762	898	1,163	1,409
Money market funds, tax-exempt [3] . .	Bil. dol. . .	2	36	84	110	123	140	161	189	204
Equity, hybrid and bond funds:										
Sales.	Bil. dol. . .	10	114	149	472	476	681	869	1,058	1,274
Redemptions.	Bil. dol. . .	8	34	98	329	313	398	541	748	1,021
Net sales	Bil. dol. . .	2	80	51	143	163	284	328	310	252
Money market funds, taxable [2]:										
Sales.	Bil. dol. . .	232	730	1,219	2,234	2,729	3,524	4,395	5,534	7,083
Redemptions.	Bil. dol. . .	204	732	1,183	2,229	2,617	3,415	4,265	5,289	6,866
Net sales	Bil. dol. . .	28	-2	36	5	112	108	129	244	217
Money market funds, tax-exempt [3]:										
Sales.	Bil. dol. . .	5	109	197	369	396	467	536	639	687
Redemptions.	Bil. dol. . .	4	99	190	370	385	453	518	612	675
Net sales	Bil. dol. . .	2	11	7	-1	11	13	18	27	12

NA Not available. [1] Includes "income and bond funds," a category subsequently discontinued. [2] Funds invest in short-term, high-grade securities sold in the money market. [3] Funds invest in municipal securities with relatively short maturities.

Source: Investment Company Institute, Washington, DC, *Mutual Fund Fact Book*, annual (copyright).

No. 843. Mutual Fund Shares—Holdings and Net Purchases by Type of Investor: 1990 to 1999

[In billions of dollars (608 represents $608,000,000,000). Holdings as of **Dec. 31**. Minus sign (-) indicates net sales]

Type of investor	Holdings					Net purchases				
	1990	1995	1997	1998	1999	1990	1995	1997	1998	1999
Total.	**608**	**1,853**	**2,989**	**3,611**	**4,515**	**53.7**	**147.4**	**265.1**	**274.6**	**191.3**
Households, nonprofit organizations . .	468	1,265	2,057	2,501	3,104	27.5	94.7	258.4	261.4	147.6
Nonfinancial corporate business	10	46	69	91	112	-1.0	4.6	-8.2	7.3	8.0
State and local governments	5	35	34	26	31	3.3	5.9	-7.4	-7.3	4.3
Commercial banking.	2	2	8	9	11	-0.3	0.3	0.8	-0.4	1.2
Credit unions.	1	3	2	4	3	0.2	0.2	-0.2	1.2	-1.1
Bank personal trusts and estates	63	254	342	397	489	9.7	9.5	-7.2	9.4	8.7
Life insurance companies	31	28	38	19	14	12.6	13.5	-7.2	-28.2	-8.0
Private pension funds	29	221	438	564	752	1.6	18.6	36.2	31.2	30.8

Source: Board of Governors of the Federal Reserve System, "Federal Reserve Statistical Release, Z.1, Flow of Funds Accounts of the United States"; published: 10 March 2000; <http://www.bog.frb.fed.us/releases/Z1/20000310/data.htm>.

No. 844. Mutual Fund Retirement Assets: 1990 to 1999

[In billions of dollars, except percent (208 represents $208,000,000,000). Based on data from the Institute's Annual Questionnaire for Retirement Statistics. The 1999 survey gathered data from over 8,000 mutual fund share classes representing 83 percent of equity funds, 75 percent of bond and hybrid funds, and 69 percent of money market funds. Assets were estimated for all nonreporting funds. Reporting funds were grouped by investment objective and a percentage increase (from previous data) by investment objective was determined. These ratios were used to estimate data for nonreporting funds. Estimates of retirement assets in street name and omnibus accounts were derived from data reported on the Annual Survey of Retirement Statistics and the Annual Institutional Shareholder survey]

Type of account	1990	1993	1994	1995	1996	1997	1998	1999
Mutual fund retirement assets . . .	**208**	**587**	**666**	**918**	**1,172**	**1,509**	**1,881**	**2,426**
Percent of total retirement assets .	5	10	11	13	15	16	17	19
Individual retirement accounts (IRAs) . . .	141	324	352	479	602	764	944	1,222
Employer-sponsored defined								
contribution retirement plans	67	263	314	439	570	745	937	1,204
401(k) plans [1]	35	140	184	266	349	471	598	777
Percent of total 401(k) assets	9	23	27	31	33	37	41	45
403(b) plans [2]	15	86	90	119	146	183	227	281
457 plans [3]	2	4	6	8	11	16	22	30
Other defined contribution plans [4]	15	33	35	46	64	75	90	116
Percent of all mutual funds:								
Mutual fund retirement assets	20	28	31	33	33	34	34	35
Individual retirement accounts (IRAs) . . .	13	16	16	17	17	17	17	18
Employer-sponsored retirement plans . . .	6	13	15	16	16	17	17	18

[1] See headnote, Table 616. May also include some profit-sharing plan assets that do not have a 401(k) feature. [2] Section 403(b) of the Internal Revenue Code permits employees of certain charitable organizations, nonprofit hospitals, universities, and public schools to establish tax-sheltered retirement programs. These plans may invest in either annuity contracts or mutual fund shares. [3] These plans are deferred compensation arrangements for government employees and employees of certain tax-exempt organizations. [4] Includes thrift savings, stock bonus, target benefit, money purchase, and all other defined contribution plans.

No. 845. Individual Retirement Accounts (IRA) Plans—Value by Institution: 1990 to 1999

[As of **December 31** (635 represents $635,000,000,000). Estimated]

Institution	Amount (bil. dol.)									Percent distribution		
	1990	1992	1993	1994	1995	1996	1997	1998	1999	1990	1995	1999
Total IRA assets.	**635**	**866**	**993**	**1,056**	**1,288**	**1,467**	**1,728**	**2,029**	**2,473**	**100**	**100**	**100**
Bank and thrift deposits [1]	266	275	263	255	261	258	254	249	244	42	20	10
Life insurance companies	53	56	70	79	94	110	160	190	220	8	7	9
Mutual funds	141	239	324	352	479	602	764	944	1,222	22	37	49
Securities directly held												
through brokerage accounts .	176	297	336	370	454	496	550	646	787	28	35	32

[1] Includes Keogh deposits.

Source of Tables 844 and 845: Investment Company Institute, Washington, DC, *Fundamentals, Investment Company Institute Research in Brief, "Mutual Funds and the Retirement Market"*; Vol. 9, No. 2, May 2000 <http://www.ici.org> (copyright).

No. 846. Assets of Private and Public Pension Funds by Type of Fund: 1980 to 1999

[In billions of dollars. As of end of year. Except for corporate equities, represents book value. Excludes social security trust funds and U.S. Government pension funds; see Tables 607 and 611]

Type of pension fund	1980	1985	1990	1994	1995	1996	1997	1998	1999
Total, all types	882	1,887	3,089	4,422	5,222	6,039	7,247	8,385	9,623
Private funds	685	1,488	2,205	3,237	3,757	4,249	4,939	5,687	6,576
Insured	172	260	596	885	1,002	1,095	1,234	1,356	1,578
Noninsured [1] [2]	513	1,228	1,608	2,352	2,755	3,155	3,706	4,331	4,998
Credit market instruments [2]	151	331	491	661	717	769	835	953	1,044
U.S. Government securities . . .	51	196	289	402	444	470	503	562	602
Treasury	32	129	137	158	177	189	204	218	233
Agency	18	67	152	244	268	281	299	344	369
Corporate and foreign bonds . .	78	97	146	201	207	228	256	301	336
Corporate equities	232	516	595	996	1,238	1,491	1,864	2,232	2,500
Mutual fund shares	7	11	29	150	221	321	438	564	752
Unallocated insurance contracts [3] .	(NA)	132	189	210	211	220	235	262	280
State and local pension funds [2]	197	399	884	1,185	1,465	1,790	2,308	2,698	3,047
Credit market instruments [2]	147	252	440	497	531	568	632	698	746
U.S. Government securities	40	124	231	268	291	308	340	360	374
Corporate and foreign bonds	92	107	180	185	191	214	245	280	305
Corporate equities	44	120	271	557	791	1,032	1,432	1,758	2,042

NA Not available. [1] Private defined benefit plans and defined contribution plans (including 401(k) type plans). Also includes Federal Employees Retirement System (FERS) Thrift Savings Plan. [2] Includes other types of assets not shown separately. [3] Assets held at life insurance companies (e.g., guaranteed investment contracts (GICs), variable annuities).

Source: Board of Governors of the Federal Reserve System, "Federal Reserve Statistical Release, Z.1, Flow of Funds Accounts of the United States"; published: 10 March 2000; <http://www.bog.frb.fed.us/releases/Z1/20000310/data.htm>.

No. 847. Securities Industry—Revenues and Expenses: 1980 to 1998

[In millions of dollars (19,829 represents $19,829,000,000)]

Type	1980	1985	1990	1992	1993	1994	1995	1996	1997	1998
Revenues, total	19,829	49,844	71,356	90,584	108,844	112,758	143,414	172,411	207,245	234,964
Commissions.	6,777	10,955	12,032	16,249	19,905	19,847	23,215	27,866	32,662	36,696
Trading/investment gains	5,091	14,549	15,746	21,838	25,427	20,219	28,963	30,768	35,958	32,754
Underwriting profits.	1,571	4,987	3,728	8,300	11,249	6,844	8,865	12,613	14,611	16,237
Margin interest.	2,151	2,746	3,179	2,690	3,235	4,668	6,470	7,386	10,630	12,732
Mutual fund sales.	278	2,754	3,242	5,950	8,115	6,887	7,434	10,081	12,422	14,845
Other	3,960	13,854	33,428	35,557	40,913	54,293	68,468	83,697	100,961	121,700
Expenses, total	16,668	43,342	70,566	81,467	95,805	109,266	132,089	155,433	187,281	217,780
Interest expense	3,876	11,470	28,093	24,576	26,616	40,250	56,877	64,698	80,659	98,095
Compensation	7,619	18,112	22,931	32,071	39,125	37,595	41,541	51,033	58,558	65,027
Commissions/clearance paid .	1,055	2,314	2,959	3,722	5,338	5,360	5,700	7,364	8,864	10,326
Other	4,119	11,446	16,583	21,098	24,726	26,060	27,970	32,338	39,200	44,332
Net income, pretax. . . .	3,160	6,502	790	9,117	13,039	3,492	11,325	16,978	19,964	17,184

Source: U.S. Securities and Exchange Commission, Annual Report.

No. 848. Health Insurance—Premium Income and Benefit Payments of Insurance Companies: 1980 to 1996

[In billions of dollars (43.7 represents $43,700,000,000). Includes Puerto Rico and other U.S. outlying areas. Represents premium income of and benefits paid by insurance companies only. Excludes Blue Cross-Blue Shield plans, medical-society sponsored plans, and all other independent plans]

Item	1980	1985	1988	1989	1990	1991	1992	1993	1994	1995	1996
Premiums [1]	43.7	75.2	98.2	108.0	112.9	116.4	125.0	124.7	129.3	133.9	137.1
Group policies [2]	36.8	64.4	87.6	96.1	100.2	103.0	110.4	110.2	114.1	116.4	116.3
Individual and family policies . . .	6.9	10.8	10.6	11.8	12.7	13.3	14.6	14.5	15.2	17.5	20.8
Benefit payments	37.0	60.0	83.0	89.4	92.5	97.6	104.8	103.6	106.3	110.1	113.8
Group policies [2]	33.0	53.7	76.4	82.2	84.4	88.8	95.2	94.1	95.9	98.1	99.0
Individual and family policies . . .	4.0	6.3	6.6	7.2	8.2	8.8	9.6	9.3	10.4	12.0	14.8
Type of coverage:											
Loss of income	5.3	5.6	6.4	7.2	7.4	7.5	8.3	8.1	7.8	8.2	9.2
Medical expense	27.9	47.2	66.4	72.0	73.8	77.9	82.9	81.4	84.0	85.8	(NA)
Dental	2.8	5.3	6.3	6.5	6.4	6.4	7.1	7.0	7.0	7.7	(NA)
Medicare supplement	1.0	1.9	3.8	3.7	5.0	5.8	6.4	6.9	7.5	8.4	(NA)

NA Not available. [1] Earned premiums. [2] Insurance company group premiums and benefit payments include administrative service agreements and minimum premium plans.

Source: Health Insurance Association of America, Washington, DC, Source Book of Health Insurance Data, annual.

No. 849. Property and Casualty Insurance—Summary: 1990 to 1998

[In billions of dollars (217.8 represents $217,800,000,000). Minus sign (-) indicates loss]

Item	1990	1992	1993	1994	1995	1996	1997	1998
Premiums, net written	217.8	227.8	241.7	250.7	259.8	268.6	276.4	281.5
Automobile, private [1]	78.4	88.4	93.4	96.8	102.0	107.7	113.6	117.3
Automobile, commercial [1]	17.0	16.1	16.3	16.7	17.2	17.6	18.0	18.1
Liability other than auto	22.1	21.1	22.1	23.6	23.4	24.5	25.0	24.2
Fire and allied lines	7.1	7.1	7.9	8.7	9.4	9.9	8.4	8.4
Homeowners' multiple peril	18.6	20.5	21.5	22.6	24.0	25.4	26.9	29.0
Commercial multiple peril	17.7	16.4	17.3	17.8	18.8	18.9	19.0	19.0
Workers' compensation	31.0	29.7	30.3	28.9	26.2	25.1	24.1	23.2
Marine, inland and ocean	5.7	5.5	6.1	6.7	7.1	7.5	7.6	7.6
Accident and health	5.0	5.4	6.8	7.2	7.8	7.8	8.3	9.8
Other lines	15.2	17.6	20.0	21.7	23.9	24.2	25.5	24.9
Losses and expenses	234.7	259.6	250.7	263.3	268.4	277.1	272.6	289.7
Underwriting gain/loss	-20.9	-33.3	-15.1	-19.0	-14.2	-16.7	-5.8	-16.7
Net investment income	32.9	33.7	32.6	33.7	36.8	38.0	41.5	39.9
Operating earnings after taxes	9.0	5.8	19.3	10.9	20.6	24.4	36.8	30.8
Assets	556.3	637.3	671.5	704.6	765.2	806.1	870.1	908.8
Policyholders' surplus	138.4	163.1	182.3	193.3	230.0	255.5	308.5	333.3

[1] Includes premiums for automobile liability and physical damage.

Source: Insurance Information Institute, New York, NY, *The Fact Book, Property/Casualty Insurance Facts*, annual (copyright).

No. 850. Automobile Insurance—Average Expenditures Per Insured Vehicle by State: 1995 to 1998

[In dollars. The average expenditures for automobile insurance in a state are affected by a number of factors, including the underlying rate structure, the coverages purchased, the deductibles and limits selected, the types of vehicles insured, and the distribution of driver characteristics]

State	1995	1997	1998	State	1995	1997	1998	State	1995	1997	1998
U.S.	**667**	**706**	**699**	KS	474	516	532	ND	381	436	452
				KY	555	597	617	OH	531	572	581
AL	549	616	632	LA	788	841	830	OK	526	566	575
AK	730	776	771	ME	472	478	492	OR	565	621	630
AZ	727	819	818	MD	732	772	769	PA	667	718	722
AR	500	566	589	MA	898	803	816	RI	870	866	852
CA	794	776	718	MI	645	736	737	SC	582	629	655
CO	722	774	764	MN	628	671	680	SD	428	470	479
CT	881	909	901	MS	579	648	653	TN	519	586	587
DE	784	828	845	MO	573	614	611	TX	711	740	731
DC	959	1,039	1,033	MT	468	501	471	UT	547	610	619
FL	739	759	771	NE	452	505	518	VT	512	519	534
GA	597	653	672	NV	759	848	843	VA	553	566	564
HI	963	912	797	NH	609	616	622	WA	650	693	710
ID	447	479	494	NJ	1,013	1,126	1,138	WV	646	707	725
IL	612	666	607	NM	639	690	676	WI	506	548	552
IN	542	571	583	NY	906	953	960	WY	433	477	492
IA	429	456	459	NC	501	556	564				

Source: National Association of Insurance Commissioners, Kansas City, MO, *State Average Expenditures and Premiums for Personal Automobile Insurance*, annual (copyright).

No. 851. Life Insurance in Force in the United States—Summary: 1980 to 1998

[As of **December 31** or **calendar year,** as applicable (**402 represents 402,000,000**). Covers life insurance with life insurance companies only. Represents all life insurance in force on lives of U.S. residents whether issued by U.S. or foreign companies. For definition of household, see text, Section 1, Population]

Year	Number of policies, total (mil.)	Life insurance in force					Average size policy in force (dollars)				Average amount ($1,000)		Disposable personal income per household ($1,000)
		Value (bil. dol.)					Ordinary	Group	Industrial	Credit [1]	Per household	Per insured household	
		Total	Ordinary	Group	Industrial	Credit [1]							
1980	402	3,541	1,761	1,579	36	165	11,920	13,410	620	2,110	41.9	51.1	24.4
1985	386	6,053	3,247	2,562	28	216	22,780	19,720	640	3,100	66.6	82.2	34.6
1990	389	9,393	5,367	3,754	24	248	37,910	26,630	670	3,500	98.4	124.5	44.6
1993	363	11,105	6,428	4,456	20	200	45,770	31,430	700	3,850	111.6	143.1	49.7
1994	390	11,057	6,407	4,442	19	189	45,870	26,338	659	3,609	113.9	146.3	51.7
1995	393	11,638	6,816	4,603	18	201	49,090	27,051	664	3,554	119.1	148.9	54.3
1996	355	12,704	7,408	5,068	18	211	52,912	36,459	695	4,215	128.6	157.3	56.6
1997	351	13,364	7,855	5,279	18	212	57,333	37,176	720	4,516	134.1	167.6	58.1
1998	358	14,471	8,506	5,735	17	213	62,543	37,732	724	4,629	141.1	178.6	58.8

[1] Insures borrower to cover consumer loan in case of death.

Source: American Council of Life Insurance, Washington, DC, *Life Insurance Fact Book*, annual (copyright).

U.S. Census Bureau, Statistical Abstract of the United States: 2000

No. 852. Life Insurance Purchases in the United States—Number and Amount: 1980 to 1998

[29,007 represents 29,007,000. Excludes revivals, increases, dividend additions, and reinsurance acquired. Includes long-term credit insurance (life insurance on loans of more than 10 years' duration). See also headnote, Table 851]

Year	Number of policies purchased (1,000)				Amount purchased (bil. dol.)			
	Total	Ordinary	Group	Industrial	Total	Ordinary	Group	Industrial
1980	29,007	14,750	11,379	2,878	573	386	183	4
1985	33,880	17,104	16,243	533	[1]1,231	911	[1]320	1
1990	28,791	14,066	14,592	133	1,529	1,070	459	(Z)
1993	31,238	13,574	17,574	90	1,678	1,101	577	(Z)
1994	32,225	13,675	18,390	160	1,611	1,051	560	(Z)
1995	31,999	12,466	19,404	129	1,543	1,005	538	(Z)
1996	30,783	11,926	18,761	96	1,704	1,089	615	(Z)
1997	31,708	11,667	19,973	68	1,893	1,204	689	(Z)
1998	31,891	11,522	20,332	37	2,065	1,325	740	(Z)

Z Less than $500 million.   [1] Includes Federal Employees' Group Life Insurance: $11 billion in 1985.

Source: American Council of Life Insurance, Washington, DC, *Life Insurance Fact Book*, annual (copyright).

No. 853. U.S. Life Insurance Companies—Summary: 1980 to 1998

[As of **December 31** or **calendar year**, as applicable **(130.9 represents $130,900,000,000)**. Covers domestic and foreign business of U.S. companies. Beginning 1994 includes annual statement data for companies that primarily are health insurance companies]

Item	Unit	1980	1985	1990	1992	1993	1994	1995	1996	1997	1998
U.S. companies [1]	Number .	1,958	2,261	2,195	1,944	1,844	2,136	2,079	1,679	1,620	1,563
Income	**Bil. dol.**	**130.9**	**234.0**	**402.2**	**426.9**	**466.4**	**492.6**	**528.1**	**561.1**	**610.6**	**663.4**
Life insurance premiums	Bil. dol .	40.8	60.1	76.7	83.9	94.4	98.9	102.8	107.6	115.0	119.9
Annuity considerations	Bil. dol .	22.4	53.9	129.1	132.6	156.4	153.0	158.4	178.4	197.5	229.5
Health insurance premiums	Bil. dol .	29.4	41.8	58.3	65.5	68.7	86.2	90.0	92.2	92.7	94.9
Investment and other	Bil. dol .	38.3	78.2	138.2	144.9	146.8	154.5	176.9	182.9	205.3	219.1
Payments to life insurance beneficiaries	Bil. dol .	12.9	18.2	24.6	27.2	28.8	32.6	34.5	36.3	37.5	40.1
Payments under life insurance and annuity contracts	Bil. dol .	25.2	48.3	63.8	67.8	71.2	168.2	193.1	210.7	239.1	261.8
Surrender values under life insurance [2]	Bil. dol .	6.7	15.6	18.0	16.8	16.9	18.0	19.5	24.5	24.0	26.8
Surrender values under annuity policies [2]	Bil. dol .	(NA)	(NA)	(NA)	(NA)	(NA)	92.8	105.4	115.7	140.8	154.5
Policy dividends	Bil. dol .	6.8	10.1	12.0	12.2	12.7	15.9	17.8	18.1	18.0	18.9
Annuity payments	Bil. dol .	10.2	21.3	32.6	37.6	40.3	40.4	48.5	51.1	55.1	60.4
Matured endowments	Bil. dol .	0.9	0.8	0.7	0.6	0.6	0.6	1.0	0.7	0.6	0.6
Other payments	Bil. dol .	0.6	0.5	0.6	0.6	0.6	0.5	0.9	0.6	0.6	0.6
Health insurance benefit payments	Bil. dol .	23.0	27.3	40.0	45.0	46.0	60.1	64.7	66.7	67.4	70.0
BALANCE SHEET											
Assets	**Bil. dol.**	**479**	**826**	**1,408**	**1,665**	**1,839**	**1,942**	**2,144**	**2,328**	**2,579**	**2,827**
Government securities	Bil. dol .	33	125	211	320	384	396	409	411	391	379
Corporate securities	Bil. dol .	227	374	711	863	982	1,072	1,241	1,416	1,658	1,896
Percent of total assets	Percent .	47.4	45.3	50.5	51.8	53.4	55.2	57.9	60.8	64.3	67.1
Bonds	Bil. dol .	180	297	583	670	730	791	869	962	1,060	1,140
Stocks	Bil. dol .	47	77	128	192	252	282	372	454	598	758
Mortgages	Bil. dol .	131	172	270	247	229	215	212	212	210	216
Real estate	Bil. dol .	15	29	43	51	54	54	52	50	46	41
Policy loans	Bil. dol .	41	54	63	72	78	85	96	102	105	105
Other	Bil. dol .	32	72	110	112	112	120	133	137	169	187
Interest earned on assets [3]	Percent .	8.02	9.63	8.89	8.08	7.52	7.14	7.34	7.25	7.35	6.95
Obligations and surplus funds [4]	Bil. dol .	479	826	1,408	1,665	1,839	1,942	2,144	2,328	2,579	2,827
Policy reserves [5]	**Bil. dol.**	**390**	**665**	**1,197**	**1,407**	**1,550**	**1,644**	**1,812**	**1,966**	**2,165**	**2,377**
Annuities [6]	Bil. dol .	172	400	798	940	1,041	1,095	1,213	1,312	1,455	1,608
Group	Bil. dol .	140	303	516	560	602	612	619	690	762	845
Individual	Bil. dol .	32	97	282	381	439	482	594	622	693	763
Life insurance	Bil. dol .	198	236	349	402	436	468	511	556	606	656
Health insurance	Bil. dol .	11	19	33	45	51	58	63	70	75	82
Asset valuation reserve	Bil. dol .	6	11	15	21	25	25	30	33	36	38
Capital and surplus	Bil. dol .	34	57	91	115	128	137	151	147	160	173

NA Not available.   [1] Beginning 1994 includes life insurance companies that sell accident and health insurance.   [2] Beginning with 1994, "surrender values" include annuity withdrawals of funds, which were not included in prior years.   [3] Net rate.   [4] Includes other obligations not shown separately.   [5] Includes the business of health insurance departments of life companies. Includes reserves for supplementary contracts with and without life contingencies, not shown separately.   [6] Beginning 1996 data are not comparable with prior years' data due to a change in the treatment of separate account annuities.

Source: American Council of Life Insurance, Washington, DC, *Life Insurance Fact Book*, annual (copyright).

Section 17
Business Enterprise

This section relates to the place and behavior of the business firm and to business initiative in the American economy. It includes data on the number, type, and size of businesses; financial data of domestic and multinational U.S. corporations; business investments, expenditures, and profits; sales and inventories; and business failures.

The principal sources of these data are the *Survey of Current Business*, published by the Bureau of Economic Analysis (BEA), the *Federal Reserve Bulletin*, issued by the Board of Governors of the Federal Reserve System, the annual *Statistics of Income* (SOI) reports of the Internal Revenue Service (IRS), *The Business Failure Record* and *the Business Starts Record* issued by the Dun & Bradstreet Corporation, Murray Hill, NJ. ; and the *Quarterly Financial Report for Manufacturing, Mining, and Trade Corporations (QFR)*.

Business firms—A firm is generally defined as a business organization under a single management and may include one or more establishments. The terms firm, business, company, and enterprise are used interchangeably throughout this section. A firm doing business in more than one industry is classified by industry according to the major activity of the firm as a whole. The industrial classification is based on the Standard Industrial Classification (SIC) Manual.

The IRS concept of a business firm relates primarily to the legal entity used for tax reporting purposes. A **sole proprietorship** is an unincorporated business owned by one person including large enterprises with many employees and hired managers and part-time operations in which the owner is the only person involved. A **partnership** is an unincorporated business owned by two or more persons, each of whom has a financial interest in the business. A **corporation** is a business that is legally incorporated under state laws. While many corporations file consolidated tax returns, most corporate tax returns represent individual corporations, some of which are affiliated through common ownership or control with other corporations filing separate returns.

Economic censuses—The economic censuses constitute comprehensive and periodic canvasses of the Nation's industrial and business activities. The first economic census of the United States was conducted as part of the 1810 decennial census, when inquiries on manufacturing were included with the census of population. Minerals data were collected in 1840. The first censuses of construction and business were taken for 1929. An integrated economic census program was begun for 1954. In that year, the censuses covered the retail and wholesale trades, selected service industries, manufactures, and mineral industries. In 1992, coverage was expanded to 95 percent of the private U.S. economy. The economic censuses are taken at 5-year intervals covering years ending in "2" and "7." Special surveys are conducted every 5 years as part of the economic censuses to determine the extent of business ownership by specific minority groups and women.

Industrial groups—Establishments are classified into industries on the basis of their principal product or activity in accordance with the 1987 *Standard Industrial Classification (SIC) Manual*, Office of Management and Budget. The SIC is a classification structure for the entire national economy. The structure provides data on a division and industry code basis, according to the level of industrial detail. For example, manufacturing is a major industrial division; food and kindred products (Code

U.S. Census Bureau, Statistical Abstract of the United States: 2000

20) is one of its major groups. One of the ways this group is further divided is into meat products (Code 201) and meat packing plants (Code 2011).

Changes in industry presentation—The country detail in this presentation is identical to that in the 1989 benchmark survey and in the intervening annual surveys. However, three changes have affected the industry detail. First, beginning with the publication of the preliminary 1994 benchmark survey results, the data for nonbank U.S. parents and foreign affiliates exclude savings institutions and credit unions. The change in coverage reflects the reclassification of savings institutions and credit unions from the "finance, except banking" industry (which is covered by the nonbank data) to the industry "depository institutions" (which will replace the industry "banking" in the publication of the final 1994 benchmark results). This change will not materially affect the comparisons of the data for 1993 with the data for 1994, because in 1993, only one U.S. parent and no foreign affiliates were classified as a savings institution or credit union.

Second, beginning with the preliminary 1994 benchmark survey results, the "communication and public utilities" group was disaggregated and the "metal mining" and "nonmetallic minerals mining" groups were aggregated in the industry table stub. Third, beginning with the revised 1993 annual estimates, the names of two industry groups were changed; the group "machinery, except electrical" is now called "industrial machinery and equipment," and the group "electric and electronic equipment" is now called "electronic and other electric equipment."

North American Industry Classification System (NAICS) Implementation—The various statistical agencies and statistical programs in the United States will convert to the new classification system on a variable time schedule. For example, most of the 1997 Economic Census data are issued on a NAICS basis as seen in the industry and geographic series from the census. Other related census reports remain on an SIC basis due to use of administrative records and other methodological and data processing issues. Noncensuses or current survey data from the Census Bureau, as well as, most of the other statistical agencies will convert to NAICS after benchmarking to the 1997 Economic Census where appropriate or implementation of data collection on a NAICS basis over a sufficient time period to provide reliable statistical results.

No. 854. Number of Returns and Business Receipts by Type of Business Size of Receipts: 1980 to 1997

[2,711 represents 2,711,000. Covers active enterprises only. Figures are estimates based on sample of unaudited tax returns; see Appendix III. The industrial distribution is based on data collected from companies; see text, this section]

Size-class of receipts	Returns (1,000)					Business receipts [1] (bil. dol.)				
	1980	1990	1995	1996	1997	1980	1990	1995	1996	1997
Corporations	2,711	3,717	4,474	4,631	4,710	6,172	10,914	13,969	14,890	15,890
Under $25,000 [2]	557	879	1,030	1,060	1,106	4	5	4	5	4
$25,000 to $49,999	208	252	288	286	306	8	9	11	11	11
$50,000 to $99,999	323	359	447	480	453	22	26	33	35	33
$100,000 to $499,999	926	1,162	1,393	1,444	1,450	224	291	350	364	363
$500,000 to $999,999	280	416	513	521	533	197	294	361	368	376
$1,000,000 or more	418	649	803	841	862	5,717	10,289	13,210	14,107	15,102
Partnerships	1,380	1,554	1,581	1,654	1,759	286	541	854	1,042	1,297
Under $25,000 [2]	638	963	931	956	987	5	4	4	4	4
$25,000 to $49,999	182	126	133	141	151	7	5	5	5	5
$50,000 to $99,999	184	133	142	146	165	13	10	10	10	12
$100,000 to $499,999	290	222	245	268	294	64	51	56	61	68
$500,000 to $999,999	48	52	59	64	68	33	36	42	45	48
$1,000,000 or more	37	57	69	80	94	164	435	738	917	1,160
Nonfarm proprietorships [3]	9,730	14,783	16,424	16,956	17,176	411	731	807	844	870
Under $25,000 [2]	6,916	10,196	11,317	11,577	11,703	44	69	76	78	79
$25,000 to $49,999	1,079	1,660	1,983	2,091	2,111	39	58	71	74	75
$50,000 to $99,999	836	1,282	1,393	1,473	1,491	59	91	99	105	107
$100,000 to $499,999	796	1,444	1,514	1,579	1,637	159	296	310	319	332
$500,000 to $999,999	74	143	147	165	160	50	97	100	110	107
$1,000,000 or more	29	57	70	71	75	60	119	151	158	170

[1] Excludes investment income except for partnerships and corporations in finance, insurance, and real estate. Starting 1990, investment income no longer included for S corporations. S corporations are certain small companies with 35 shareholders (15 in 1980), mostly individuals, electing to be taxed through shareholders. [2] Includes firms with no receipts. [3] Number of businesses for 1980. Number of nonfarm sole proprietorship returns is not available by size prior to 1981. However, the number of returns and the number of businesses are very closely related. The ratio of number of returns to the number of businesses is approximately 1 to 1.3.

Source: U.S. Internal Revenue Service, *Statistics of Income; Statistics of Income Bulletin;* and unpublished data.

No. 855. Number of Returns, Receipts, and Net Income by Type of Business and Industry: 1980 to 1997

[8,932 represents 8,932,000. See headnote, Table 854. Minus sign (-) indicates net loss]

Item	Number of returns (1,000)			Business receipts [2] (bil. dol.)			Net income (less loss) [3] (bil. dol.)		
	Nonfarm propri- etor- ships [1]	Partner- ships	Corpora- tions	Nonfarm propri- etor- ships [1]	Partner- ships	Corpora- tions	Nonfarm propri- etor- ships [1]	Partner- ships	Corpora- tions
1980	8,932	1,380	2,711	411	286	6,172	55	8	239
1985	11,929	1,714	3,277	540	349	8,050	79	-9	240
1988	13,679	1,654	3,563	672	516	9,804	126	15	413
1989	14,298	1,635	3,628	693	524	10,440	133	14	389
1990	14,783	1,554	3,717	731	541	10,914	141	17	371
1991 [4]	15,181	1,515	3,803	713	539	10,963	142	21	345
1992	15,495	1,485	3,869	737	571	11,272	154	43	402
1993	15,848	1,468	3,965	757	627	11,814	156	67	498
1994	16,154	1,493	4,342	791	731	12,858	167	83	577
1995 [4]	16,424	1,581	4,474	807	854	13,969	169	107	714
1996 [4]	16,955	1,654	4,631	843	1,042	14,890	177	145	806
1997 [4]	17,176	1,759	4,710	870	1,297	15,890	187	168	915
Agriculture, forestry, fishing [5]	565	127	163	24	16	108	4	2	3
Mining	124	28	33	6	34	134	(Z)	7	10
Construction	1,883	72	488	118	53	768	25	3	21
Manufacturing	480	40	325	33	182	4,794	4	11	306
Transportation, public utilities	781	31	209	46	130	1,248	7	-2	71
Wholesale and retail trade [6]	3,133	173	1,149	255	292	4,589	17	5	82
Wholesale	348	27	371	39	116	2,163	5	2	36
Retail	2,784	144	774	215	175	2,417	12	3	46
Finance, insurance, real estate	1,314	974	745	76	295	2,711	24	95	373
Services	8,408	311	1,593	299	294	1,537	106	47	50

Z Less than $500 million. [1] In 1980, represents individually owned businesses, including farms; thereafter, represents only nonfarm proprietors, i.e., business owners. [2] Excludes investment income except for partnerships and corporations in finance, insurance, and real estate. Starting 1985, investment income no longer included for S corporations. [3] Net income (less loss) is defined differently by form of organization, basically as follows: (a) Proprietorships: Total taxable receipts less total business deductions, including cost of sales and operations, depletion, and certain capital expensing, excluding charitable contributions and owners' salaries; (b) Partnerships: Total taxable receipts (including investment income except capital gains) less deductions, including cost of sales and operations and certain payments to partners, excluding charitable contributions, oil and gas depletion, and certain capital expensing; (c) Corporations: Total taxable receipts (including investment income, capital gains, and income from foreign subsidiaries deemed received for tax purposes, except for S corporations beginning 1985) less business deductions, including cost of sales and operations, depletion, certain capital expensing, and officers' compensation (except S corporation charitable contributions and investment expenses starting 1985; net income is before income tax. [4] Includes businesses not allocable to individual industries. [5] Represents agricultural services only. [6] Includes trade business not identified as wholesale or retail.

Source: U.S. Internal Revenue Service, *Statistics of Income,* various publications.

U.S. Census Bureau, Statistical Abstract of the United States: 2000

No. 856. Number of Returns and Business Receipts by Industry, Type of Business, and Size of Business Receipts: 1997

[Number of returns in thousands (17,176 represents 17,176,000); receipts and net income in billions of dollars (870 represents $870,000,000,000). Covers active enterprises only. Figures are estimates based on a sample of unaudited tax returns; see Appendix III. The industrial distribution is based on data collected from establishments; see text, this section]

Industry	Nonfarm proprietor-ships	Partner-ships	Corporations				
			Under $1 mil. [1]	$1 mil.-$4.9 mil.	$5 mil.-$9.9 mil.	$10 mil.-$49.9 mil.	$50 mil. or more
Total: [2]							
Number	17,176	1,759	3,848	636	106	97	23
Business receipts [3]	870	1,297	788	1,357	735	1,972	11,037
Net income (less loss)	187	168	5	32	25	86	767
Agriculture, forestry, fishing:							
Number	565	127	147	13	2	1	(Z)
Business receipts [3]	24	16	26	28	11	16	27
Mining:							
Number	124	28	28	4	(Z)	1	(Z)
Business receipts [3]	6	34	4	8	3	13	106
Construction:							
Number	1,883	72	372	89	15	10	1
Business receipts [3]	118	53	102	192	105	191	178
Manufacturing:							
Number	480	40	205	76	18	19	6
Business receipts [3]	33	182	50	173	128	395	4,049
Transportation, public utilities:							
Number	781	31	167	32	6	3	1
Business receipts [3]	46	130	33	70	43	70	1,031
Wholesale and retail trade:							
Number	3,133	173	823	237	39	42	9
Business receipts [3]	255	292	222	509	270	885	2,703
Finance, insurance, real estate:							
Number	1,314	974	686	38	8	8	4
Business receipts [3]	76	295	73	85	57	171	2,325
Services:							
Number	8,408	311	1,415	146	18	12	2
Business receipts [3]	299	294	279	291	119	230	618

Z Less than 500 returns.   [1] Includes businesses without receipts.   [2] Includes businesses not allocable to individual industries.   [3] Excludes investment income except for partnerships and corporations (other than S corporations) in finance, insurance, and real estate.

Source: U.S. Internal Revenue Service, Statistics of Income, various publications, and unpublished data.

No. 857. Sole Proprietorships—Selected Income and Deduction Items: 1980 to 1997

[In millions of dollars, (21,996 represents $21,996,000,000) except as indicated. Covers nonfarm sole proprietorships. All figures are estimates based on sample. Tax law changes have affected the comparability of the data over time; see Statistics of Income reports for a description]

Item	1980	1985	1990	1992	1993	1994	1995	1996	1997
Number of returns (1,000)	8,932	11,929	14,783	15,495	15,848	16,154	16,424	16,955	17,176
Businesses with net income (1,000)	(NA)	8,641	11,222	11,720	11,872	12,187	12,213	12,524	12,703
Inventory, end of year	21,996	24,970	30,422	29,898	31,795	33,602	33,356	33,785	33,223
Business receipts	411,206	540,045	730,606	737,082	757,215	790,630	807,364	843,234	870,392
Income from sales and operations	407,169	528,675	719,008	725,666	746,306	778,494	796,597	831,546	858,453
Business deductions [1]	356,258	461,273	589,250	583,147	600,765	623,833	638,127	666,461	683,872
Cost of goods sold/operations [1]	209,890	232,294	291,010	274,220	289,578	301,004	306,959	316,421	319,557
Purchases	168,302	(NA)	210,225	204,317	210,260	216,365	219,305	220,029	224,259
Labor costs	10,922	14,504	22,680	18,838	20,685	23,497	24,383	26,002	24,941
Materials and supplies	12,909	(NA)	30,195	28,825	32,701	34,304	34,427	40,473	37,552
Commissions	3,333	(NA)	8,816	10,457	8,707	9,029	9,592	10,792	10,986
Salaries and wages (net)	26,561	38,266	46,998	52,316	52,046	53,649	54,471	56,322	57,746
Car and truck expenses	13,378	17,044	21,766	23,920	26,714	30,845	32,785	36,700	38,728
Rent paid	9,636	15,259	23,392	25,148	25,008	26,769	27,503	28,516	29,326
Repairs	5,032	(NA)	8,941	9,706	9,847	10,385	10,172	10,715	10,897
Taxes paid	7,672	(NA)	10,342	12,618	13,062	13,600	13,471	13,736	13,774
Utilities	4,790	(NA)	13,539	14,547	16,069	16,918	17,206	18,162	18,575
Insurance	6,003	(NA)	13,358	13,260	13,173	13,289	12,978	13,195	13,299
Interest paid	7,190	11,914	13,312	10,406	9,431	9,170	10,057	10,567	10,884
Depreciation	13,953	26,291	23,735	23,274	24,964	26,158	26,738	27,883	28,625
Pension and profit sharing plans	141	311	586	528	636	605	649	707	728
Net income (less loss)	54,947	78,773	141,430	153,960	156,459	166,799	169,262	176,756	186,644
Businesses with net income	68,010	98,776	161,657	173,473	176,983	187,845	191,729	200,124	210,465

NA Not available.   [1] Includes other amounts not shown separately.

Source: U.S. Internal Revenue Service, Statistics of Income Bulletin.

No. 858. Partnerships—Selected Items by Industry: 1980 to 1997

[In millions of dollars, (597,504 represents $597,504,000,000) except number of partners and partnerships in thousands. Covers active partnerships only. Includes partnerships not allocable by industry. Figures are estimates based on samples. See Appendix III]

Year	Number of partnerships (1,000)			Number of partners	Total assets [1]	Business receipts [2][3]	Total deductions [3]	Net income less loss [3]	Net income [3]	Net loss [3]
	Total	With net income	With net loss							
All industries:										
1980	1,380	774	605	8,420	597,504	285,967	283,749	8,249	45,062	36,813
1985	1,714	876	838	13,245	1,269,434	349,169	376,001	-8,884	77,045	85,928
1990	1,554	854	700	17,095	1,735,285	540,647	549,603	16,610	116,318	99,708
1994	1,494	890	604	14,990	2,295,212	731,834	680,052	82,183	150,928	68,745
1995	1,581	955	626	15,606	2,718,648	853,831	783,603	106,829	178,651	71,822
1996	1,654	1,010	644	15,662	3,368,166	1,042,136	943,352	145,218	228,158	82,939
1997	1,759	1,092	667	16,184	4,171,499	1,296,865	1,186,199	168,241	262,373	94,132
Agriculture, forestry, fishing:										
1980.	126	72	54	381	24,595	21,611	22,859	472	2,539	2,067
1985.	136	76	60	585	27,027	6,529	10,495	-1,049	2,797	3,846
1990.	125	77	48	503	27,580	9,497	11,805	1,667	3,905	2,238
1994.	123	72	51	575	41,517	11,324	13,682	1,608	3,985	2,377
1995.	129	75	54	603	43,481	13,270	16,207	1,330	4,183	2,853
1996.	131	80	51	594	46,605	14,716	17,835	1,357	4,394	3,036
1997.	127	73	54	576	54,450	16,336	19,286	1,926	4,738	2,813
Mining:										
1980.	35	15	20	722	24,742	13,201	18,248	-4,208	3,920	8,128
1985.	62	33	30	2,207	66,930	19,922	21,920	1,482	7,884	6,402
1990.	41	29	14	2,149	58,246	19,967	20,869	2,183	7,009	4,825
1994.	27	17	10	1,010	45,532	15,902	17,323	984	5,076	4,092
1995.	26	15	11	828	55,503	17,813	19,004	1,111	5,272	4,161
1996.	25	16	9	746	68,122	23,545	21,846	4,865	8,737	3,872
1997.	28	19	9	775	84,066	34,247	31,727	6,652	10,815	4,164
Construction:										
1980.	67	51	16	160	9,811	18,407	17,202	1,560	2,119	559
1985.	57	41	16	134	15,008	21,476	20,080	2,207	2,743	536
1990.	59	45	15	162	17,989	30,716	29,672	1,908	3,020	1,112
1994.	66	48	18	159	15,171	31,140	29,065	2,654	3,127	474
1995.	71	48	22	167	16,653	35,881	33,936	2,527	3,338	810
1996.	74	51	23	179	20,592	45,117	43,055	3,114	4,036	922
1997.	72	52	20	171	25,088	53,239	50,687	3,204	4,244	1,041
Transportation, public utilities:										
1980.	20	11	10	73	9,291	5,868	5,821	248	1,092	844
1985.	25	15	10	186	26,468	11,253	14,814	-3,066	1,360	4,426
1990.	25	14	11	503	63,334	32,800	35,989	-117	5,887	6,004
1994.	23	12	11	635	126,351	66,407	64,863	5,627	11,118	5,491
1995.	26	14	12	656	158,869	76,796	75,538	6,750	13,209	6,459
1996.	30	16	13	647	200,208	101,127	101,891	7,051	18,121	11,070
1997.	31	19	12	621	244,181	129,698	141,323	-1,637	18,283	19,920
Manufacturing:										
1980.	30	20	10	92	11,252	15,327	16,142	-472	1,199	1,671
1985.	30	12	18	105	24,838	22,588	24,225	-1,085	1,228	2,314
1990.	28	15	13	246	59,789	65,354	65,833	1,166	4,791	3,626
1994.	30	18	12	224	93,494	107,569	104,551	6,584	9,853	3,268
1995.	30	19	12	223	108,926	124,007	120,741	9,221	13,034	3,812
1996.	34	19	15	233	127,699	149,775	146,680	9,696	14,088	4,392
1997.	40	23	18	252	156,313	182,374	178,914	11,066	17,069	6,003
Wholesale and retail trade:										
1980.	200	123	77	487	17,727	65,793	63,988	2,475	3,374	900
1985.	201	113	88	493	20,568	69,079	68,119	1,977	3,467	1,490
1990.	176	100	77	481	28,423	98,120	97,131	2,610	4,717	2,107
1994.	153	87	66	443	44,367	142,116	140,295	4,301	6,344	2,043
1995.	164	93	71	501	59,436	171,905	170,756	3,996	7,171	3,175
1996.	168	91	72	534	80,882	212,077	210,482	5,464	9,330	3,866
1997.	173	93	80	584	104,358	292,127	292,622	5,330	10,114	4,784
Finance, insurance, and real estate:										
1980.	637	313	325	5,566	454,531	87,133	91,382	-4,249	15,169	19,418
1985.	844	369	475	7,755	979,787	92,309	118,237	-25,929	30,383	56,311
1990.	822	401	422	10,846	1,329,452	64,313	87,011	-19,213	47,577	66,790
1994.	810	465	345	9,881	1,750,671	161,365	137,240	24,125	65,369	41,245
1995.	849	505	344	10,317	2,074,641	196,234	151,712	44,522	82,871	38,349
1996.	892	548	344	10,262	2,587,697	246,681	176,958	69,724	112,749	43,025
1997.	974	614	361	10,555	3,214,105	294,486	199,944	94,922	134,095	39,173
Services:										
1980.	263	169	94	938	45,510	58,627	48,106	12,424	15,649	3,224
1985.	341	207	134	1,713	106,597	104,197	96,202	16,541	26,942	10,400
1990.	267	173	96	2,153	150,063	161,702	145,789	26,453	39,383	12,930
1994.	261	170	91	2,060	177,992	195,933	172,926	36,318	46,048	9,730
1995.	282	186	96	2,297	200,562	217,684	195,402	37,394	49,561	12,168
1996.	297	187	110	2,455	235,679	248,883	224,417	43,883	56,614	12,731
1997.	311	198	113	2,642	287,829	293,864	271,571	46,696	62,923	16,227

[1] Total assets are understated because not all partnerships file complete balance sheets. [2] Includes investment income for partnerships in finance, insurance, and real estate. [3] Beginning 1985, only net (not gross) income from farming, rents, and royalties are included.

Source: U.S. Internal Revenue Service, *Partnership Returns—1978-1997.*

U.S. Census Bureau, Statistical Abstract of the United States: 2000

No. 859. Partnerships—Selected Income and Balance Sheet Items: 1980 to 1997

[In billions of dollars (1,380 represents $1,380,000,000,000). Covers active partnerships only. All figures are estimates based on samples. See Appendix III]

Item	1980	1985	1990	1992	1993	1994	1995	1996	1997
Number of returns (1,000)	1,380	1,714	1,554	1,485	1,468	1,494	1,581	1,654	1,759
Number with net income (1,000). . .	774	876	854	856	870	890	955	1,010	1,092
Number of partners (1,000).	8,420	13,245	17,095	15,735	15,627	14,990	15,606	15,662	16,184
Assets [1] [2]	598	1,269	1,735	1,907	2,118	2,295	2,719	3,368	4,171
Depreciable assets (net).	239	696	681	701	698	712	767	848	980
Inventories, end of year	33	27	57	62	71	76	88	137	147
Land.	70	152	215	213	207	208	221	232	257
Liabilities [1] [2]	489	1,069	1,415	1,508	1,620	1,662	1,886	2,235	2,658
Accounts payable	34	41	67	79	80	81	91	121	159
Short-term debt [3].	48	103	88	115	131	126	124	126	127
Long-term debt [4]	178	382	498	486	489	508	544	607	706
Nonrecourse loans. . . . :	119	328	470	476	478	463	466	474	492
Partners' capital accounts [2]	109	200	320	399	499	633	832	1,133	1,513
Receipts [1]	292	367	566	597	656	762	890	1,089	1,354
Business receipts	271	303	483	515	561	732	854	1,042	1,297
Interest received	11	21	21	16	16	19	31	33	41
Deductions [1]	284	376	550	554	589	680	784	943	1,186
Cost of goods sold/operations	114	146	243	249	273	335	395	486	625
Salaries and wages	22	34	56	62	65	70	80	94	115
Taxes paid	10	8	9	10	11	12	13	15	18
Interest paid	28	29	30	25	27	36	43	49	60
Depreciation	22	54	60	60	60	22	23	29	38
Net income (less loss)	8	-9	17	43	67	82	107	145	168
Net income.	45	77	116	122	137	151	179	228	262

[1] Includes items not shown separately.   [2] Assets, liabilities, and partners' capital accounts are understated because not all partnerships file complete balance sheets.   [3] Mortgages, notes, and bonds payable in less than 1 year.   [4] Mortgages, notes, and bonds payable in 1 year or more.

Source: U.S. Internal Revenue Service, *Statistics of Income,* various issues.

No. 860. Corporate Funds—Sources and Uses: 1980 to 1999

[In billions of dollars (183 represents $183,000,000,000). Covers nonfarm nonfinancial corporate business. See text this section]

Item	1980	1985	1990	1992	1993	1994	1995	1996	1997	1998	1999
Profits before tax (book)	183	173	236	257	305	381	422	460	503	490	540
-Profit tax accruals	67	70	95	91	105	128	136	150	158	152	168
-Dividends	45	72	118	134	149	158	178	201	219	244	259
+Consumption of fixed capital	159	323	371	391	408	445	474	506	540	583	630
=U.S. internal funds, book	231	354	393	423	459	540	581	615	666	676	743
+Foreign earnings retained abroad.	19	26	51	45	56	39	59	60	59	66	75
+Inventory valuation adjustment (IVA) . . .	-42	-	-13	-3	-4	-12	-18	3	7	21	-12
=Internal funds + IVA.	207	380	431	465	511	567	622	678	733	763	806
Gross investment [1]	165	212	355	402	593	583	645	653	700	740	798
Capital expenditures [1]	262	381	430	439	497	573	635	678	759	832	888
Fixed investment [2]	261	365	419	429	472	524	588	652	688	760	846
Net financial investment	-97	-169	-76	-37	95	10	10	-25	-59	-92	-90
Net acquisition of financial assets	125	211	108	124	313	251	401	373	287	262	615
Foreign deposits	-	3	-	-1	-1	1	2	11	-6	1	-2
Checkable deposits and currency	3	11	16	7	14	19	31	37	-7	16	48
Time and savings deposits	-	12	-16	-15	22	-7	-25	1	6	-7	15
Money market fund shares	4	-2	10	16	-3	7	25	10	24	45	36
Security RPs.	1	-1	-1	3	-3	-	-	1	-1	-1	-
Commercial paper	-	1	-	2	2	-1	1	11	4	-8	19
U.S. government securities	1	3	-20	21	-1	3	10	-5	-8	10	15
Municipal securities	5	3	-8	1	9	2	-20	-6	5	6	-2
Mortgages	9	6	-2	1	-8	4	2	-4	-4	-4	-4
Consumer credit	1	4	3	3	7	9	-2	-7	1	-4	5
Trade receivables	50	45	29	28	51	72	78	88	37	9	90
Mutual fund shares	-	4	-1	5	7	2	5	3	-8	7	8
Miscellaneous assets . . . . [3] . . .	52	122	97	53	217	140	293	233	244	192	386
U.S. direct investment abroad [3] . . .	20	14	35	42	58	79	91	78	90	114	133
Net increase in liabilities [1]	222	380	184	161	218	242	391	398	346	354	705
Net funds raised in markets.	83	102	64	72	67	90	176	85	171	139	301
Net new equity issues.	10	-85	-63	27	21	-45	-58	-70	-114	-267	-143
Credit market instruments [1]	73	186	127	45	45	135	235	155	286	406	444
Commercial paper.	4	15	10	9	10	21	18	-1	14	24	37
Municipal securities [4]	11	23	-	4	7	7	3	3	4	6	5
Corporate bonds [3]	28	83	47	68	75	23	91	116	151	219	230
Bank loans n.e.c.	29	32	3	-19	-11	43	67	39	69	82	72

- Represents or rounds to zero.   [1] Includes other not shown separately.   [2] Nonresidential plant and equipment plus residential construction.   [3] Through 1992:Q4, corporate bonds include net issues by Netherlands Antillean financial subsidiaries, and U.S. direct investment abroad excludes net inflows from those bond issues.   [4] Industrial revenue bonds. Issued by state and local governments to finance private investment and secured in interest and principal by industrial user of the funds.

Source: Board of Governors of the Federal Reserve System. Data derived from *Flow of Funds Accounts,* annual.

538 Business Enterprise

No. 861. Nonfinancial Corporate Business-Sector Balance Sheet: 1990 to 1998

[In billions of dollars (9,828 represents $9,828,000,000,000). Represents year-end outstandings]

Item	1990	1991	1992	1993	1994	1995	1996	1997	1998
Assets	**9,828**	**9,808**	**9,793**	**10,147**	**10,775**	**11,581**	**12,362**	**13,455**	**14,310**
Tangible assets (current cost)	6,194	6,043	5,861	5,858	6,208	6,523	6,802	7,380	7,876
Real estate [1]	3,440	3,255	3,012	2,901	3,074	3,203	3,350	3,776	4,184
Equipment [2]	1,828	1,876	1,925	1,994	2,092	2,214	2,317	2,426	2,486
Inventories [2]	925	913	924	963	1,042	1,105	1,135	1,177	1,206
Financial assets	3,634	3,764	3,932	4,289	4,567	5,059	5,560	6,075	6,434
Checkable deposits and currency	167	183	189	203	222	253	303	311	348
Time and savings deposits	73	67	52	74	67	43	45	51	80
Trade receivables	967	961	989	1,035	1,107	1,185	1,247	1,277	1,336
Liabilities	4,729	4,830	5,110	5,389	5,627	6,010	6,349	6,690	7,084
Credit market instruments [3]	2,488	2,430	2,475	2,536	2,687	2,913	3,113	3,366	3,709
Municipal securities [4]	115	114	118	125	132	135	138	142	148
Corporate bonds [5]	1,008	1,087	1,155	1,230	1,253	1,326	1,399	1,490	1,622
Mortgages	229	213	194	197	220	253	311	339	389
Net worth (market value)	5,099	4,978	4,683	4,758	5,148	5,572	6,013	6,765	7,226

[1] At market value. [2] At replacement (current) cost. [3] Includes items not shown separately. [4] Industrial revenue bonds. Issued by state and local governments to finance private investment and secured in interest and principal by the industrial user of the funds. [5] Through 1992, corporate bonds include net issues by Netherlands Antillean financial subsidiaries, and U.S. direct investment abroad excludes net inflows from those bond issues.

Source: Board of Governors of the Federal Reserve System, *Balance Sheets for the U.S. Economy.*

No. 862. Corporations—Selected Financial Items: 1980 to 1997

[In billions of dollars (7,617 represents $7,617,000,000,000), except as noted. Covers active corporations only. All corporations are required to file returns except those specifically exempt. See source for changes in law affecting comparability of historical data. Based on samples; see Appendix III]

Item	1980	1985	1990	1992	1993	1994	1995	1996	1997
Number of returns (1,000)	2,711	3,277	3,717	3,869	3,965	4,342	4,474	4,631	4,710
Number with net income (1,000)	1,597	1,820	1,911	2,064	2,145	2,392	2,455	2,588	2,647
S Corporation returns [1] (1,000)	545	725	1,575	1,785	1,902	2,024	2,153	2,304	2,452
Assets [2]	7,617	12,773	18,190	20,002	21,816	23,446	26,014	28,642	33,030
Cash	529	683	771	806	812	853	962	1,097	1,299
Notes and accounts receivable	1,985	3,318	4,198	4,169	4,532	4,768	5,307	5,783	6,632
Inventories	535	715	894	915	947	1,126	1,045	1,079	1,114
Investments in Govt. obligations	266	917	921	1,248	1,290	1,309	1,363	1,339	1,343
Mortgage and real estate	894	1,259	1,538	1,567	1,627	1,661	1,713	1,825	2,029
Other investments	1,214	2,414	4,137	4,971	5,701	6,265	7,429	8,657	10,756
Depreciable assets	2,107	3,174	4,318	4,755	4,969	5,284	5,571	5,923	6,208
Depletable assets	72	112	129	131	137	148	154	169	177
Land	93	141	210	221	230	239	242	254	262
Liabilities [2]	7,617	12,773	18,190	20,002	21,816	23,446	26,014	28,642	33,030
Accounts payable	542	892	1,094	1,605	1,466	1,606	1,750	1,905	2,111
Short-term debt [3]	505	1,001	1,803	1,560	1,569	1,831	2,034	2,328	2,582
Long-term debt [4]	987	1,699	2,665	2,742	2,871	3,100	3,335	3,651	4,072
Capital stock	417	920	1,585	1,881	2,042	2,132	2,194	2,278	2,951
Paid-in or capital surplus	532	1,421	2,814	3,656	4,223	4,790	5,446	6,427	7,253
Retained earnings [5]	1,070	1,366	1,410	1,431	1,662	1,698	2,191	2,519	3,113
Net worth	1,944	3,304	4,739	5,700	(NA)	7,031	8,132	9,495	11,353
Receipts [3][6]	6,361	8,398	11,410	11,742	12,270	13,360	14,539	15,526	16,610
Business receipts [6][7]	5,732	7,370	9,860	10,360	10,866	11,884	12,786	13,659	14,461
Interest [8]	367	635	977	829	808	882	1,039	1,082	1,140
Rents and royalties	54	105	133	140	130	132	145	156	176
Deductions [3][6]	6,125	8,158	11,033	11,330	11,765	12,775	13,821	14,728	15,704
Cost of sales and operations [7]	4,205	4,894	6,611	6,772	7,052	7,625	8,206	8,707	9,114
Compensation of officers	109	171	205	221	226	282	304	319	336
Rent paid on business property	72	135	185	196	201	223	232	248	265
Taxes paid	163	201	251	274	290	322	326	341	350
Interest paid	345	569	825	597	546	611	744	771	866
Depreciation	157	304	333	346	364	403	437	474	513
Advertising	52	92	126	134	140	157	163	177	188
Net income (less loss) [6][9]	239	240	371	402	498	577	714	806	915
Net income	297	364	553	570	659	740	881	987	1,118
Deficit	58	124	182	168	161	162	166	180	202
Income subject to tax	247	266	366	378	437	494	565	640	684
Income tax before credits [10]	104	109	119	126	149	168	194	224	239
Tax credits [3]	42	48	32	30	35	37	42	53	51
Foreign tax credit	25	24	25	22	23	25	30	40	42
Income tax after credits [11]	62	61	96	102	(NA)	136	156	171	184

NA Not available. [1] Represents certain small corporations with up to 35 shareholders (15 in 1980), mostly individuals, electing to be taxed at the shareholder level. [2] Includes items not shown separately. [3] Payable in less than 1 year. [4] Payable in 1 year or more. [5] Appropriated and unappropriated. [6] Except for 1980, receipts, deductions, and net income of S corporations are limited to those from trade or business. Those from investments are excluded. [7] Beginning 1990, includes gross sales and cost of sales of securities, commodities, and real estate by exchanges, brokers, or dealers selling on their own accounts. Previously, net gain included in total receipts only. Excludes investment income. [8] Includes tax-exempt interest in state and local government obligations. [9] Excludes regulated investment companies. [10] Consists of regular (and alternative tax) only. [11] Includes minimum tax, alternative minimum tax, adjustments for prior year credits, and other income-related taxes.

Source: U.S. Internal Revenue Service, *Statistics of Income, Corporation Income Tax Returns,* annual.

U.S. Census Bureau, *Statistical Abstract of the United States: 2000*

No. 863. Corporations—Selected Financial Items by Industry: 1980 to 1997

[In billions of dollars (40.7 represents $40,700,000,000), except as indicated. Covers active corporations only. Industrial distribution based on data collected from companies; see text, this section. Excludes corporations not allocable by industry]

Industry	1980	1985	1990	1993	1994	1995	1996	1997
Agriculture, forestry, and fishing:								
Returns (1,000)	81	103	126	141	147	148	159	163
Assets	40.7	52.7	68.3	74.6	79.9	86.3	94.1	92
Liabilities [1]	29.3	37.2	45.0	46.9	50.6	56.2	61.4	59
Receipts [2]	52.1	70.5	88.1	98.3	100.9	107.6	119.7	117.4
Deductions [2]	51.4	70.6	86.9	96.7	99.6	106.0	117.2	114.7
Net income (less loss) [2]	0.7	-0.1	1.2	1.6	1.3	1.6	2.6	2.7
Mining:								
Returns (1,000)	26	41	40	35	35	35	36	33
Assets	126.9	240.8	219.2	224.0	239.7	268.7	299.1	324.3
Liabilities [1]	72.9	136.0	108.9	112.6	121.1	136.6	147.4	159.2
Receipts [2]	176.7	142.0	111.4	112.1	115.7	126.8	141.3	150.3
Deductions [2]	169.1	145.4	106.5	109.6	112.3	121.4	133.4	141.0
Net income (less loss) [2]	7.8	-2.5	5.3	2.6	3.6	5.5	8.2	9.7
Construction:								
Returns (1,000)	272	318	407	417	433	450	471	488
Assets	132.9	215.3	243.8	240.4	249.1	265.8	284.6	314.6
Liabilities [1]	100.1	160.6	180.0	164.6	170.9	179.3	192.2	215.4
Receipts [2]	267.2	387.2	534.7	538.3	592.8	637.1	710.5	779.0
Deductions [2]	262.1	382.8	527.8	530.7	581.2	622.6	692.6	758.4
Net income (less loss) [2]	5.3	4.4	6.8	7.5	11.6	14.5	17.9	20.5
Manufacturing:								
Returns (1,000)	243	277	302	307	312	320	326	325
Assets	1,709.5	2,644.4	3,921.3	4,225.1	4,525.5	4,941.1	5,425.2	5,966.3
Liabilities [1]	960.3	1,544.7	2,529.1	2,784.4	2,936.6	3,201.5	3,458.3	3,855.6
Receipts [2]	2,404.3	2,831.1	3,688.7	3,890.7	4,218.8	4,585.5	4,902.7	5,177.7
Deductions [2]	2,290.6	2,733.1	3,545.1	3,741.6	4,024.3	4,354.6	4,653.0	4,910.7
Net income (less loss) [2]	125.7	113.8	171.4	173.2	219.1	260.9	286.1	306.0
Transportation and public utilities:								
Returns (1,000)	111	138	160	176	187	194	206	209
Assets	758.4	1,246.4	1,522.0	1,770.7	1,826.3	1,903.2	2,069.5	2,219.0
Liabilities [1]	467.7	755.9	1,013.4	1,190.9	1,207.2	1,270.1	1,355.3	1,456.9
Receipts [2]	523.8	772.4	936.3	1,037.2	1,103.2	1,156.7	1,257.0	1,330.7
Deductions [2]	504.0	747.8	901.0	984.9	1,036.1	1,084.7	1,182.4	1,260.9
Net income (less loss) [2]	20.0	25.1	35.4	52.9	68.3	72.9	75.4	71.0
Wholesale and retail trade:								
Returns (1,000)	800	917	1,023	1,073	1,106	1,132	1,142	1,149
Assets	646.9	1,010.0	1,447.3	1,702.8	1,795.2	1,919.7	2,016.2	1,947.9
Liabilities [1]	424.6	723.7	1,092.5	1,254.2	1,303.1	1,385.8	1,447.6	1,334.4
Receipts [2]	1,955.5	2,473.9	3,309.0	3,709.5	4,052.2	4,310.3	4,490.1	4,703.8
Deductions [2]	1,919.5	2,440.4	3,279.1	3,659.8	3,984.0	4,247.6	4,418.3	4,624.2
Net income (less loss) [2]	38.3	33.1	30.1	49.7	68.5	63.6	73.4	81.6
Finance, insurance, and real estate:								
Returns (1,000)	493	518	609	641	682	683	724	745
Assets	4,022.2	7,029.5	10,193.3	12,831.7	13,895.3	15,677.3	17,360.1	20,905.6
Liabilities [1] [3]	3,491.7	5,867.5	8,051.3	9,288.5	10,053.1	11,008.7	11,754.8	13,750.0
Receipts [2]	697.5	1,182.0	1,954.7	1,940.3	1,976.5	2,278.1	2,406.9	2,711.3
Deductions [2]	652.6	1,104.6	1,809.9	1,723.3	1,773.1	1,985.8	2,076.6	2,304.3
Net income (less loss) [2]	33.1	60.7	109.9	185.2	169.3	256.8	299.1	373.5
Services:								
Returns (1,000)	671	939	1,029	1,158	1,424	1,504	1,557	1,593
Assets	178.2	331.0	572.8	744.8	833.9	950.7	1,092.3	1,259.4
Liabilities [1]	125.3	241.1	429.7	508.6	570.3	643.1	729.2	845.7
Receipts [2]	279.9	534.6	779.3	941.6	1,198.0	1,335.7	1,496.2	1,638.6
Deductions [2]	271.8	528.7	769.0	916.5	1,162.5	1,297.5	1,453.2	1,589.0
Net income (less loss) [2]	8.2	5.9	10.6	25.4	35.6	38.4	44.0	50.5
ANNUAL PERCENT CHANGE RECEIPTS [4]								
Agriculture, forestry, and fish	-2.4	5.9	1.7	2.8	2.6	6.6	11.2	-2.0
Mining	33.3	15.0	8.8	-0.6	3.1	9.6	11.4	6.4
Construction	5.7	14.4	3.3	7.8	10.1	7.5	11.5	11.5
Manufacturing	11.7	2.3	4.5	3.5	8.4	8.7	6.9	9.6
Transportation and public utilities	17.5	6.4	3.3	4.0	6.3	4.8	8.6	5.9
Wholesale and retail trade	11.6	7.2	3.9	5.9	9.2	6.4	4.1	4.8
Finance, insurance, and real estate	24.3	14.4	4.6	2.1	1.8	15.3	5.6	12.6
Services	14.2	9.0	6.0	8.3	27.2	11.5	12.0	9.5

[1] Liabilities does not include net worth.   [2] Beginning 1990, receipts, deductions, and net income of S corporations are limited to those from trade or business; those from investments are generally excluded. S corporations are certain small corporations with up to 35 shareholders (15 in 1980), mostly individuals, electing to be taxed at the shareholder level.   [3] Beginning 1990, includes gross sales (previously net sales) of securities, commodities, and real estate by exchanges, brokers, or dealers selling on their own account.   [4] Change from preceding year.

Source: U.S. Internal Revenue Service, *Statistics of Income, Corporation Income Tax Returns*, annual.

No. 864. Corporations by Asset-Size Class and Industry: 1997

[In millions of dollars (91,984 represents $91,984,000,000), except number of returns and percent distribution. Covers active corporations only. Excludes corporations not allocable by industry. The industrial distribution is based on data collected from companies; see text, this section. Detail may not add to total because of rounding]

Industry	Total	Under $10 mil. [1]	Asset-size class				
			$10-$24.9 mil.	$25-$49.9 mil.	$50-$99.9 mil.	$100-$249.9 mil.	$250 mil. and over
Agriculture, forestry, and fishing:							
Returns.	163,114	162,383	454	155	58	46	17
Assets	91,984	59,385	6,676	5,362	4,145	6,901	9,516
Receipts	117,388	82,276	8,107	5,767	5,392	9,032	6,815
Deductions	114,674	80,604	7,888	5,660	5,381	8,829	6,312
Net income (less loss)	2,674	1,641	206	96	8	201	523
Mining:							
Returns.	32,996	31,824	600	196	123	96	157
Assets	324,294	16,147	8,844	6,858	8,906	16,430	267,110
Receipts	150,318	21,151	7,577	4,037	4,948	8,265	104,340
Deductions	141,046	20,333	7,119	3,732	4,698	7,926	97,239
Net income (less loss)	9,726	806	452	305	249	331	7,586
Construction:							
Returns.	487,783	484,616	2,289	517	208	94	58
Assets	314,551	181,361	33,851	17,632	14,510	14,603	52,594
Receipts	779,014	542,355	74,509	38,474	27,669	30,592	65,416
Deductions	758,429	527,723	72,505	37,536	26,947	30,011	63,707
Net income (less loss)	20,522	14,588	1,985	936	713	577	1,723
Manufacturing:							
Returns.	325,045	310,365	7,102	2,968	1,758	1,325	1,529
Assets	5,966,306	233,820	110,905	104,267	123,103	207,067	5,187,143
Receipts	5,177,664	610,377	199,371	164,800	175,782	263,750	3,763,584
Deductions	4,910,704	591,930	191,160	159,138	168,664	251,243	3,548,569
Net income (less loss)	305,958	18,806	8,177	5,676	7,100	12,636	253,564
Transportation and public utilities:							
Returns.	209,412	206,268	1,529	521	327	304	463
Assets	2,219,019	72,705	23,428	17,990	22,726	47,562	2,034,609
Receipts	1,330,726	222,077	31,390	21,592	23,373	37,479	994,815
Deductions	1,260,912	217,818	30,909	21,205	23,128	37,749	930,103
Net income (less loss)	70,985	4,239	473	381	255	-293	65,930
Wholesale and retail trade:							
Returns.	1,149,132	1,135,526	8,768	2,378	1,098	742	618
Assets	1,947,932	500,100	133,045	81,559	77,023	116,744	1,039,461
Receipts	4,703,817	1,880,377	421,262	226,237	192,337	257,753	1,725,850
Deductions	4,624,196	1,856,337	414,634	222,095	189,181	252,975	1,688,975
Net income (less loss)	81,585	23,896	6,623	4,130	3,146	4,762	39,027
Finance, insurance, and real estate:							
Returns.	744,545	717,434	7,364	4,750	4,416	4,852	5,728
Assets	20,905,620	307,864	117,610	172,066	316,477	768,001	19,223,603
Receipts [2]	2,711,270	294,356	31,288	29,988	42,335	92,174	2,221,129
Deductions	2,304,340	281,306	31,060	26,499	36,017	71,529	1,857,929
Net income (less loss)	373,482	12,222	-13	2,973	4,920	16,782	336,597
Services:							
Returns.	1,592,854	1,586,221	3,653	1,250	745	540	447
Assets	1,259,382	279,747	56,774	43,747	54,049	84,631	740,433
Receipts	1,638,588	895,818	80,843	51,284	62,492	80,741	467,409
Deductions	1,589,011	872,970	80,599	51,359	61,303	79,338	443,442
Net income (less loss)	50,470	22,747	236	-66	1,125	1,426	25,003
PERCENT DISTRIBUTION RECEIPTS							
Agriculture, forestry, and fishing	100.0	70.1	6.9	4.9	4.6	7.7	5.8
Mining	100.0	14.1	5.0	2.7	3.3	5.5	69.4
Construction	100.0	69.6	9.6	4.9	3.6	3.9	8.4
Manufacturing	100.0	11.8	3.9	3.2	3.4	5.1	72.7
Transportation and public utilities	100.0	16.7	2.4	1.6	1.8	2.8	74.8
Wholesale and retail trade	100.0	40.0	9.0	4.8	4.1	5.5	36.7
Finance, insurance, and real estate [2] . .	100.0	10.9	1.2	1.1	1.6	3.4	81.9
Services	100.0	54.7	4.9	3.1	3.8	4.9	28.5

[1] Includes returns with zero assets. [2] Includes investment income.

Source: U.S. Internal Revenue Service, *Statistics of Income, Corporation Income Tax Returns,* annual.

No. 865. Advance Comparative Statistics for the United States (1987 Basis): 1992 and 1997

[162.1 represents $162,100,000,000. These data are preliminary and are subject to change; they will be superceded by data released in later reports. Includes only establishments with payroll. For meaning of abbreviations and symbols, see text this section]

Industry	1987 SIC[1] code	Establishments (number)		Sales/receipts revenues/shipments (bil. dol.)		Annual payroll (bil. dol.)		Paid employees (1,000)	
		1992	1997	1992	1997	1992	1997	1992	1997
MINERAL INDUSTRIES									
Total	(X)	30,787	25,251	162.1	174.5	24.2	22.1	638.2	550.1
Metal mining	10	1,023	696	9.9	11.5	2.1	2.2	52.9	50.2
Coal mining	12	3,069	1,820	27.1	24.0	5.5	4.3	134.5	95.6
Oil & gas extraction	13	20,891	17,219	111.5	122.2	13.4	12.0	344.9	304.7
Nonmetallic minerals, except fuels	14	5,804	5,516	13.6	16.8	3.2	3.6	105.9	99.6
CONSTRUCTION INDUSTRIES									
Total	(X)	572,851	639,482	539.1	834.8	117.7	170.3	4,668.3	5,616.8
Building construction—general contractors & operative builders	15	168,407	184,517	220.2	365.6	27.1	39.2	1,096.9	1,266.2
Heavy construction other than buildings construction	16	37,180	39,542	98.5	126.9	23.7	29.3	799.4	858.2
Construction—special trade contractors	17	367,263	415,423	220.3	342.4	66.9	101.9	2,772.0	3,492.3
MANUFACTURES									
Total	(X)	370,912	377,776	3,004.7	3,958.1	494.1	596.2	16,948.9	17,634.0
Food & kindred products	20	20,798	20,878	407.0	480.8	36.8	43.1	1,502.7	1,567.2
Tobacco products	21	114	105	35.2	36.2	1.5	1.6	38.0	34.5
Textile mill products	22	5,886	6,155	70.8	82.4	12.4	13.6	616.4	557.8
Apparel & other textile products	23	23,093	23,411	71.7	81.2	15.3	15.5	985.3	840.5
Lumber & wood products	24	35,807	36,735	81.6	111.9	13.9	18.7	655.8	756.9
Furniture & fixtures	25	11,658	12,095	43.8	61.5	10.2	13.3	471.1	522.9
Paper & allied products	26	6,416	6,496	133.2	159.2	20.5	23.8	626.3	623.8
Printing & publishing	27	65,392	62,355	166.2	210.9	41.1	49.1	1,492.1	1,519.8
Chemicals & allied products	28	12,004	12,371	305.4	400.1	32.5	38.4	848.6	843.5
Petroleum & coal products	29	2,124	2,147	150.2	175.8	5.0	5.4	114.4	106.9
Rubber & miscellaneous plastics products	30	15,842	16,892	113.6	160.7	23.2	30.0	906.7	1,031.2
Leather & leather products	31	2,040	1,839	9.7	10.1	1.8	1.8	101.1	84.0
Stone, clay, & glass products	32	16,254	16,393	62.5	87.2	13.1	16.5	468.8	509.7
Primary metal industries	33	6,501	6,275	138.3	188.8	22.2	26.9	662.1	692.9
Fabricated metal products	34	36,429	37,985	166.5	231.7	39.0	51.1	1,362.3	1,555.7
Industrial machinery & equipment	35	53,956	56,383	258.7	407.4	57.2	75.0	1,738.9	2,001.7
Electronic & other electric equipment	36	16,922	17,104	216.8	348.6	44.2	57.9	1,438.8	1,573.9
Transportation equipment	37	11,287	12,387	399.3	515.9	62.7	68.5	1,646.9	1,587.1
Instruments & related products	38	11,354	11,727	134.9	156.6	33.1	35.6	907.1	832.4
Miscellaneous mfg. industries	39	17,035	18,043	39.5	60.0	8.4	10.5	365.5	391.7
TRANSPORTATION, COMMUNICATIONS, & UTILITIES									
Total	(X)	252,953	293,575	791.2	1,144.9	152.5	204.7	4,934.2	5,822.7
Passenger transportation	41	17,805	19,621	12.6	18.7	5.2	7.7	354.9	455.2
Motor freight transportation & warehousing	42	110,908	133,373	143.8	197.4	39.9	55.8	1,580.1	1,963.5
Water transportation	44	8,147	9,214	29.2	35.2	5.2	6.3	171.3	180.3
Transportation by air	45	9,363	11,455	33.0	47.4	7.4	10.4	272.6	360.0
Pipelines, except natural gas	46	844	861	7.1	7.2	-	0.1	16.8	14.9
Transportation services	47	46,593	52,409	23.9	41.0	7.9	12.7	329.2	433.8
Communications	48	39,244	44,319	230.7	349.2	47.1	68.7	1,294.2	1,570.2
Electric, gas, & sanitary services	49	20,049	22,323	311.0	447.9	39.2	42.2	915.0	844.8
WHOLESALE TRADE									
Total	(X)	495,457	521,127	3,238.5	4,235.4	173.3	234.4	5,791.3	6,507.0
Durable goods	50	313,464	337,277	1,593.9	2,299.5	105.2	147.5	3,349.1	3,879.5
Nondurable goods	51	181,993	183,850	1,644.6	1,935.9	68.1	86.9	2,442.2	2,627.5
Merchant wholesalers:									
Total	(X)	414,836	444,003	1,847.3	2,500.0	128.0	177.9	4,587.9	5,295.4
Durable goods	50	264,611	288,043	902.8	1,325.7	78.3	114.0	2,714.0	3,235.5
Nondurable goods	51	150,225	155,960	944.5	1,174.3	49.7	63.9	1,873.9	2,059.9
RETAIL TRADE									
Total	(X)	1,526,215	1,561,195	1,894.9	2,545.9	222.9	293.6	18,407.5	21,349.1
Building materials, hardware, garden supply, & mobile home dlr	52	69,483	67,469	98.8	146.2	11.8	17.5	665.7	854.5
General merchandise stores	53	34,606	34,899	245.3	328.2	24.5	30.6	2,078.5	2,494.9
Food stores	54	180,568	171,057	369.2	416.0	37.2	43.4	2,969.3	3,147.0
Automotive dealers & gasoline service stations	55	201,707	202,237	529.9	788.2	39.4	55.7	1,942.6	2,290.8
Apparel & accessory stores	56	145,490	126,863	101.7	116.6	12.0	13.7	1,144.6	1,121.5
Home furniture, furnishings, & equipment stores	57	110,073	115,124	93.2	136.1	11.9	16.4	702.2	868.3
FINANCIAL, INSURANCE, AND REAL ESTATE INDUSTRIES									
Total	(X)	585,580	661,388	1,831.5	2,474.9	211.6	-	6,509.6	-
Depository institutions	60	104,505	109,851	532.1	612.2	57.3	76.9	2,100.1	2,130.1
Nondepository credit institutions	61	39,439	52,074	135.4	216.0	15.5	24.3	445.6	588.9
Security & commodity brokers, dealers, exchanges, & services	62	31,177	45,029	108.9	255.3	33.8	67.1	406.4	642.9
Insurance carriers	63	38,977	40,717	796.0	997.4	50.5	65.7	1,516.6	1,586.6
Insurance agents, brokers, & services	64	121,662	131,582	51.7	75.3	18.9	25.8	635.5	720.4
Real estate	65	229,493	252,292	141.7	180.0	26.2	35.3	1,231.5	1,393.6

See footnotes at end of table.

U.S. Census Bureau, Statistical Abstract of the United States: 2000

No. 865. Advance Comparative Statistics for the United States (1987 Basis): 1992 and 1997—Continued

[**162.1 represents $162,100,000,000.** These data are preliminary and are subject to change; they will be superceded by data released in later reports. Includes only establishments with payroll. For meaning of abbreviations and symbols, see text this section]

Industry	1987 SIC [1] code	Establishments (number)		Sales/receipts revenues/shipments (bil. dol.)		Annual payroll (bil. dol.)		Paid employees (1,000)	
		1992	1997	1992	1997	1992	1997	1992	1997
SERVICE INDUSTRIES									
Total.	(X)	2,034,346	2,077,666	1,648.9	1,843.8	639.4	921.9	27,399.3	34,223.9
Hotels, rooming houses, camps, & other lodging places	70	51,817	55,992	70.0	97.9	19.8	-	1,506.7	-
Personal services.	72	197,101	204,455	43.3	53.1	14.4	17.9	1,217.6	1,311.4
Business services.	73	306,551	397,264	274.9	528.5	109.3	215.5	5,542.4	8,749.9
Automotive repair, services, & parking .	75	171,970	191,907	70.0	99.6	15.5	22.9	863.9	1,109.6
Miscellaneous repair services.	76	71,576	66,607	30.7	37.3	9.7	11.6	428.1	426.8
Motion pictures	78	41,857	46,017	44.0	67.9	9.8	13.7	478.1	568.9
Amusement & recreation services	79	83,871	81,225	57.8	81.8	18.9	29.5	1,119.6	1,529.5
Health services	80	465,356	466,421	623.5	398.5	274.6	346.7	10,017.2	11,369.7
Legal services	81	153,462	165,757	102.3	122.6	40.0	48.2	945.0	977.9
Educational services.	82	21,018	21,283	10.2	12.9	3.4	5.5	196.3	256.4
Social services.	83	140,849	162,365	67.0	94.3	24.8	34.4	1,912.3	2,273.1
Museums, art galleries, & botanical & zoological gardens	84	3,553	4,781	3.4	6.3	1.2	1.8	69.6	88.5
Membership organizations	86	72,386	65,075	36.3	41.1	10.2	12.6	602.5	597.2
Eng., acctg., research, mgt., & rel. serv. (exc. noncomm research org.) . .	87	238,392	3,543	207.6	15.4	84.6	129.3	2,418.9	3,139.2
Services, n.e.c.	89	14,587	(S)	8.0	-	3.1	-	81.1	-
AUXILIARIES									
Total	(X)	47,250	(S)	-	-	137.1	-	3,229.7	-

- Represents zero.   S Figure does not meet publication standards.   X Not applicable.   [1]1987 Standard Industrial Classification (SIC).

Source: U.S. Census Bureau, 1997 Economic Census: Advancement Summary Statistics for the United States, 1997 NAICS Basis.

Figure 17.1
Industry Sales/Receipts/Revenue/Shipments (1987 Basis): 1992 to 1997

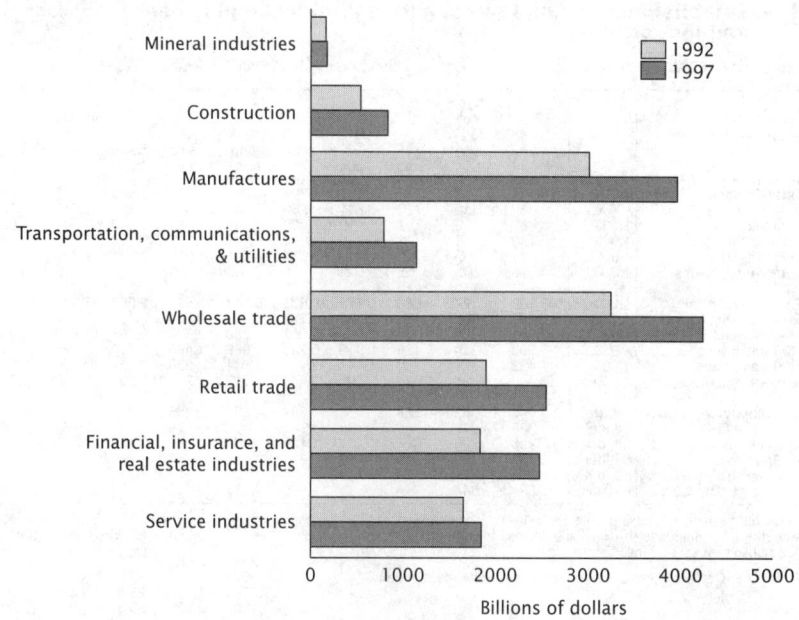

Source: Chart prepared by U.S. Census Bureau. For data, see Table 865.

Business Enterprise 543

No. 866. Employees and Payroll by Employment-Size Class: 1980 to 1997

[1,035 represents $1,035,000,000. Excludes government employees, railroad employees, self-employed persons, etc. See "General Explanation" in source for definitions and statement on reliability of data. An **establishment** is a single physical location where business is conducted or where services or industrial operations are performed]

Employment-size class	Unit	1980	1985	1990	1992	1993	1994	1995	1996	1997
Employees, total [1]	1,000. .	74,844	81,111	93,476	92,801	94,789	96,733	100,335	102,199	105,299
Under 20 employees	1,000. .	19,423	21,810	24,373	25,000	25,233	25,373	25,785	26,115	26,883
20 to 99 employees	1,000. .	21,168	23,539	27,414	27,030	27,443	28,138	29,202	29,697	30,631
100 to 499 employees	1,000. .	17,840	19,410	22,926	22,227	23,195	24,048	25,364	26,086	26,993
500 to 999 employees	1,000. .	5,689	5,716	6,551	6,270	6,449	6,663	7,021	7,274	7,422
1,000 or more employees	1,000. .	10,716	10,645	12,212	12,275	12,470	12,513	12,962	13,026	13,370
Annual payroll, total [1] . .	Bil. dol	1,035	1,514	2,104	2,272	2,363	2,488	2,666	2,849	3,048
Under 20 employees	Bil. dol.	231	352	485	536	554	579	608	647	688
20 to 99 employees	Bil. dol.	261	388	547	586	611	650	696	747	796
100 to 499 employees	Bil. dol.	249	362	518	550	582	621	675	730	786
500 to 999 employees	Bil. dol.	91	126	174	186	191	202	219	240	254
1,000 or more employees	Bil. dol.	208	286	381	413	424	436	467	485	524

[1] Prior to 1990, totals for employees and annual payroll have been revised. Detail may not add to totals because revisions for size class are not available.

Source: U.S. Census Bureau, *County Business Patterns,* annual.

No. 867. Establishments, Employees, and Payroll by Industry: 1980 to 1997

[4,543 represents 4,543,000] Beginning 1990, data are based on the 1987 Standard Industrial Classification (SIC). Prior to 1990, data are based on the 1972 SIC]

Industry	Establishments (1,000)				Employees (1,000)				Payroll (bil. dol.)			
	1980	1990	1995	1997	1980	1990	1995	1997	1980	1990	1995	1997
All industries [1] . . .	**4,543**	**6,176**	**6,613**	**6,895**	**74,844**	**93,476**	**100,335**	**105,299**	**1,035**	**2,104**	**2,666**	**3,048**
Agricultural services [2] . . .	46	85	108	117	290	531	630	727	3	9	12	15
Mining	30	30	27	27	994	723	627	586	22	27	26	28
Construction	418	578	634	667	4,473	5,239	5,039	5,513	75	132	147	176
Manufacturing	319	378	390	393	21,165	19,173	18,613	18,633	355	544	631	689
Transportation [3]	168	235	285	301	4,623	5,592	5,924	6,247	88	166	201	226
Wholesale trade	385	476	518	530	5,211	6,328	6,606	6,810	89	181	227	256
Retail trade	1,223	1,530	1,568	1,589	15,047	19,815	21,085	22,003	124	242	300	330
Finance and insurance [4] .	421	545	628	677	5,295	6,956	6,998	7,367	77	197	256	313
Services	1,278	2,059	2,386	2,544	17,186	28,800	34,707	37,380	197	599	864	1,014

[1] Includes nonclassifiable establishments not shown separately.   [2] Includes forestry and fisheries.   [3] Includes public utilities.   [4] Includes real estate.

Source: U.S. Census Bureau, *County Business Patterns,* annual.

No. 868. Establishments, Employees, and Payroll by Employment-Size Class and Industry: 1997

[6,895 represents 6,895,000. See headnote, Table 866. Data are based on the 1987 Standard Industrial Classification]

Employment size-class	Unit	All industries [1]	Agricultural services [2]	Mining	Construction	Manufacturing	Transportation [3]	Wholesale trade	Retail trade	Finance and insurance [4]	Services
Establishments, total .	1,000 . .	**6,895**	**117**	**27**	**667**	**393**	**301**	**530**	**1,589**	**677**	**2,544**
Under 20 employees	1,000 . .	6,467	110	22	611	263	249	455	1,327	619	2,261
20 to 99 employees	1,000 . .	767	6	4	50	92	42	66	232	49	226
100 to 499 employees	1,000 . .	143	1	1	5	33	9	8	29	8	49
500 to 999 employees	1,000 . .	11	(Z)	(Z)	(Z)	4	1	(Z)	1	1	4
1,000 or more employees . . .	1,000 . .	6	(Z)	(Z)	(Z)	2	(Z)	(Z)	(Z)	(Z)	3
Employees, total	1,000 . .	**105,299**	**727**	**586**	**5,513**	**18,633**	**6,247**	**6,810**	**22,003**	**7,367**	**37,380**
Under 20 employees	1,000 . .	26,883	405	101	2,360	1,530	1,092	2,304	7,137	2,424	9,502
20 to 99 employees	1,000 . .	30,641	(D)	(D)	1,893	4,057	1,730	2,532	9,093	1,889	9,066
100 to 499 employees	1,000 . .	26,993	(D)	186	946	6,740	1,696	1,445	5,050	1,525	9,316
500 to 999 employees	1,000 . .	7,422	(D)	(D)	147	2,495	511	280	457	580	2,879
1,000 or more employees . . .	1,000 . .	13,370	21	75	166	3,811	1,217	249	265	949	6,617
Annual payroll, total . .	Bil. dol	**3,048**	**15,062**	**28**	**176**	**689**	**226**	**256**	**330**	**313**	**1,014**
Under 20 employees	Bil. dol	688	8,246	4	38	45	32	79	103	84	268
20 to 99 employees	Bil. dol	796	(D)	(D)	64	129	57	92	126	79	236
100 to 499 employees	Bil. dol	786	(D)	10	36	231	64	59	81	70	233
500 to 999 employees	Bil. dol	254	(D)	(D)	6	94	22	13	11	28	78
1,000 or more employees . . .	Bil. dol	524	544	4	6	190	51	13	9	52	199

D Withheld to avoid disclosing data for individual companies; data are included in higher-level totals.   Z Less than 500 establishments.   [1] Includes nonclassifiable establishments not shown separately.   [2] Includes forestry and fisheries.   [3] Includes public utilities.   [4] Includes real estate.

Source: U.S. Census Bureau, *County Business Patterns,* annual.

No. 869. Major Industries—Private Firms, Establishments, Annual Payroll, and Estimated Receipts by Firm Size: 1997

[5,541.9 represents 5,541,900. Firms are an aggregation of all establishments owned by a parent company within an industry. Employment is measured in March and payroll is annual leading to some firms with zero employment]

Industry and data type	Unit	All industries employment size of firm								
		Total	0	1 to 4	5 to 9	10 to 19	20 to 99	100 to 499	Less than 500	More than 500
Total:										
Firms...........	1,000 ..	5,541.9	720.0	2,638.1	1,006.9	593.7	487.5	79.7	5,525.8	16.1
Establishments....	1,000 ..	6,894.9	721.8	2,642.6	1,022.9	639.1	682.6	308.6	6,017.6	877.2
Employment......	1,000 ..	105,299.1	-	5,546.3	6,610.4	7,962.1	19,109.7	15,316.9	54,545.4	50,753.8
Annual payroll	Bil. dol .	3,047.9	29.7	128.7	150.9	193.8	494.6	418.5	1,416.2	1,631.7
Receipts, estimated.	Bil. dol.	18,242.6	190.6	848.1	797.2	951.1	2,519.8	2,161.6	7,468.2	10,774.4
Agricultural services, forestry, and fishing:										
Firms............	1,000 ..	115.0	24.9	52.6	20.6	11.3	5.1	0.4	114.9	0.1
Establishments........	1,000 ..	117.0	24.9	52.6	20.6	11.4	5.3	0.7	115.4	1.6
Employment..........	1,000 ..	727.5	-	109.7	135.3	148.9	(D)	(D)	(D)	(D)
Annual payroll.........	Bil. dol .	15.1	0.5	2.0	2.4	2.9	(D)	(D)	(D)	(D)
Receipts, estimated.....	Bil. dol .	51.4	3.0	9.6	8.7	9.1	(D)	(D)	(D)	(D)
Mining:										
Firms	1,000 ..	20.7	2.3	9.7	3.1	2.3	2.3	0.5	20.3	0.4
Establishments........	1,000 ..	26.9	2.3	9.8	3.3	2.5	3.1	1.5	22.5	4.3
Employment..........	1,000 ..	586.2	-	19.6	20.8	31.0	86.3	75.8	233.5	352.7
Annual payroll.........	Bil. dol .	27.8	0.2	0.6	0.6	1.0	3.2	3.3	8.8	19.0
Receipts, estimated.....	Bil. dol .	172.8	1.3	3.1	3.5	4.9	16.9	16.0	45.7	127.1
Construction:										
Firms	1,000 ..	663.1	103.8	322.9	116.9	66.4	47.4	5.1	662.4	0.7
Establishments........	1,000 ..	669.4	103.8	322.9	116.9	66.4	48.1	6.4	664.6	4.8
Employment..........	1,000 ..	5,513.4	-	678.3	764.4	886.7	1,761.0	832.1	4,922.5	590.9
Annual payroll.........	Bil. dol .	176.0	3.3	15.5	18.6	25.0	58.4	30.6	151.4	24.6
Receipts, estimated.....	Bil. dol .	835.1	22.9	101.4	89.2	109.2	250.6	138.5	711.8	123.3
Manufacturing:										
Firms	1,000 ..	333.7	29.1	100.9	60.7	53.0	67.8	17.2	328.7	5.0
Establishments........	1,000 ..	393.8	29.2	100.9	60.8	53.2	72.5	29.1	345.7	48.1
Employment..........	1,000 ..	18,633.1	-	229.0	407.5	723.3	2,803.8	3,113.6	7,277.1	11,355.9
Annual payroll.........	Bil. dol .	688.7	2.1	5.3	9.9	19.5	83.3	97.4	217.5	471.1
Receipts, estimated.....	Bil. dol .	3,991.0	17.8	24.5	42.3	78.8	344.6	481.2	989.3	3,001.7
Transportation, communications & public utilities:										
Firms	1,000 ..	218.7	30.5	103.3	35.4	22.5	21.1	4.2	217.0	1.7
Establishments........	1,000 ..	301.6	30.5	103.5	35.9	24.0	28.5	14.9	237.3	64.3
Employment..........	1,000 ..	6,247.0	-	211.2	231.9	303.4	806.5	663.9	2,216.8	4,030.2
Annual payroll.........	Bil. dol .	226.1	1.2	4.4	5.1	7.2	21.6	20.1	59.5	166.5
Receipts, estimated.....	Bil. dol .	1,264.0	7.4	24.2	23.8	31.0	92.9	97.2	276.3	987.6
Wholesale trade:										
Firms	1,000 ..	413.7	40.6	181.2	78.5	54.1	47.4	8.5	410.3	3.4
Establishments........	1,000 ..	531.0	40.7	181.6	80.2	59.2	71.7	30.0	463.3	67.7
Employment..........	1,000 ..	6,810.4	-	386.8	518.8	721.0	1,709.5	1,076.5	4,412.6	2,397.8
Annual payroll.........	Bil. dol .	255.9	1.9	12.0	16.0	23.1	57.8	38.5	149.3	106.6
Receipts, estimated.....	Bil. dol .	4,222.6	35.7	235.8	231.7	285.5	685.8	500.0	1,974.6	2,248.0
Retail trade:										
Firms	1,000 ..	1,097.7	133.2	460.6	225.3	143.2	118.4	13.9	1,094.5	3.2
Establishments........	1,000 ..	1,592.3	134.4	461.8	230.0	157.8	177.0	82.1	1,243.0	349.3
Employment..........	1,000 ..	22,003.6	-	1,034.2	1,487.9	1,909.5	4,436.5	2,281.0	11,149.2	10,854.5
Annual payroll.........	Bil. dol .	330.4	3.8	13.5	19.1	25.1	67.7	38.1	167.3	163.1
Receipts, estimated.....	Bil. dol .	2,578.2	33.6	135.6	148.7	175.2	540.3	322.6	1,356.0	1,222.2
Finance, insurance & real estate:										
Firms	1,000 ..	460.6	58.7	278.5	60.6	29.0	24.4	6.1	457.3	3.3
Establishments........	1,000 ..	678.1	58.8	279.3	63.3	35.1	50.3	33.8	520.6	157.5
Employment..........	1,000 ..	7,367.2	-	536.8	388.8	382.2	929.3	860.4	3,097.4	4,269.8
Annual payroll.........	Bil. dol .	313.3	2.9	13.4	11.7	13.2	33.5	32.7	107.4	205.8
Receipts, estimated.....	Bil. dol .	2,468.1	19.1	95.3	58.9	62.2	176.8	227.6	640.0	1,828.1
Services:										
Firms	1,000 ..	2,224.3	273.3	1,122.6	405.7	214.7	164.8	34.3	2,215.4	8.9
Establishments........	1,000 ..	2,553.6	273.8	1,124.1	410.9	229.1	226.1	110.1	2,374.0	179.6
Employment..........	1,000 ..	37,384.6	-	2,330.1	2,648.1	2,852.8	6,400.0	6,351.5	20,582.4	16,802.2
Annual payroll.........	Bil. dol .	1,014.2	13.5	62.0	67.4	76.8	165.5	156.6	541.7	472.5
Receipts, estimated.....	Bil. dol .	2,657.0	48.4	218.0	190.1	195.1	400.8	374.7	1,427.1	1,230.0
Unclassified:										
Firms	1,000 ..	31.2	23.6	6.2	1.1	0.3	0.1	-	31.2	-
Establishments........	1,000 ..	31.2	23.6	6.2	1.1	0.3	0.1	-	31.2	-
Employment..........	1,000 ..	26.1	-	10.6	6.9	3.5	(D)	(D)	(D)	(D)
Annual payroll.........	Bil. dol .	0.6	0.3	0.1	0.1	-	(D)	(D)	(D)	(D)
Receipts, estimated.....	Bil. dol .	2.5	1.6	0.5	0.2	0.1	(D)	(D)	(D)	(D)

- Represents or rounds to zero.   D Withheld to avoid disclosing data for individual companies; data are included in higher-level totals.

Source: U.S. Small business Administration, Office of Advocacy, based on data provided by the U.S. Department of Commerce, U.S. Census Bureau, *Statistics of U.S. Businesses.*

Business Enterprise   545

No. 870. Private Employer Firms, Establishments, Employment, Annual Payroll and Estimated Receipts by Firm Size: 1990 to 1997

[Firms are an aggregation of all establishments owned by a parent company. Employment is measured in March and payroll is annual leading to some firms with zero employment. This table illustrates the changing importance of firm sizes over time, not job growth as firms can grow or decline and change firm size cells over time]

Item	Total	All industries—employment size of firm						
		0-4	5-9	10-19	20-99	100-499	Less than 500	More than 500
Employer firms:								
1990	5,073,795	3,020,935	952,030	562,610	453,732	70,465	5,059,772	14,023
1991	5,051,025	3,036,304	941,296	551,299	439,811	68,338	5,037,048	13,977
1992	5,095,356	3,075,280	945,802	551,912	439,084	69,156	5,081,234	14,122
1993	5,193,642	3,139,518	962,481	559,602	445,900	71,512	5,179,013	14,629
1994	5,276,964	3,208,235	964,985	563,097	452,383	73,267	5,261,967	14,997
1995	5,369,068	3,249,573	981,094	576,866	469,869	76,222	5,353,624	15,444
1996	5,478,047	3,327,783	996,356	585,844	476,312	76,136	5,462,431	15,616
1997	5,541,918	2,638,070	1,006,897	593,696	487,491	79,707	5,525,839	16,079
Establishments:								
1990	6,175,559	3,032,253	970,580	599,529	590,496	254,747	5,447,605	727,954
1991	6,200,859	3,048,830	961,391	593,302	593,248	260,595	5,457,366	743,493
1992	6,319,300	3,082,325	964,863	606,276	634,713	283,719	5,571,896	747,404
1993	6,401,233	3,147,991	980,865	608,922	631,873	285,184	5,654,835	746,398
1994	6,509,065	3,218,076	982,695	608,804	631,324	283,782	5,724,681	784,384
1995	6,612,721	3,259,795	998,264	618,268	638,616	283,993	5,798,936	813,785
1996	6,738,476	3,338,051	1,013,353	624,610	636,285	280,635	5,892,934	845,542
1997	6,894,869	2,642,590	1,022,901	639,090	682,580	308,633	6,017,638	877,231
Employment:								
1990	93,469,275	5,116,914	6,251,632	7,543,360	17,710,042	13,544,849	50,166,797	43,302,478
1991	92,307,559	5,151,143	6,174,730	7,386,939	17,146,411	13,143,390	49,002,613	43,304,946
1992	92,825,797	5,178,909	6,202,861	7,390,874	17,121,010	13,307,187	49,200,841	43,624,956
1993	94,773,913	5,258,195	6,313,651	7,498,345	17,420,634	13,825,238	50,316,063	44,457,850
1994	96,721,594	5,318,961	6,332,580	7,543,777	17,693,995	14,118,375	51,007,688	45,713,906
1995	100,314,946	5,395,432	6,440,349	7,734,080	18,422,228	14,660,421	52,652,510	47,662,436
1996	102,187,297	5,485,712	6,541,288	7,854,502	18,643,192	14,649,808	53,174,502	49,012,795
1997	105,299,123	5,546,306	6,610,374	7,962,136	19,109,691	15,316,863	54,545,370	50,753,753
Annual payroll ($mil.):								
1990	2,103,971	116,857	114,006	144,451	352,391	279,452	1,007,156	1,096,815
1991	2,145,016	118,234	116,794	146,517	352,033	279,437	1,013,014	1,132,002
1992	2,272,392	124,592	122,382	152,831	368,969	298,174	1,066,948	1,205,444
1993	2,363,208	128,968	127,133	159,153	385,005	316,184	1,116,443	1,246,765
1994	2,487,960	134,649	131,667	166,476	408,053	335,574	1,176,419	1,311,541
1995	2,665,922	141,538	137,083	175,388	437,065	361,061	1,252,135	1,413,787
1996	2,848,623	150,825	144,692	185,491	465,230	384,020	1,330,258	1,518,365
1997	3,047,907	128,716	150,877	193,805	494,617	418,453	1,416,200	1,631,707
Receipts (est.) ($mil.):								
1990	9,450,656	626,679	569,640	681,192	1,715,443	1,316,747	4,909,700	4,540,956
1991	12,961,444	777,738	680,216	829,025	2,207,715	1,618,187	6,112,880	6,848,564
1992	13,605,184	820,739	705,147	859,446	2,292,331	1,717,788	6,395,452	7,209,732
1993	14,098,572	846,812	730,360	891,635	2,394,813	1,816,355	6,679,975	7,418,597
1994	14,840,452	880,764	752,675	928,380	2,531,403	1,930,758	7,023,980	7,816,472
1995	15,751,365	919,735	778,864	965,259	2,678,293	2,062,235	7,404,386	8,346,979
1996	16,654,636	979,261	818,958	1,006,930	2,817,214	2,168,503	7,790,866	8,863,770
1997	18,242,633	848,057	797,162	951,050	2,519,757	2,161,616	7,468,212	10,774,421

Source: U.S. Small Business Administration, Office of Advocacy, based on data provided by the Department of Commerce, U.S. Census Bureau, unpublished data.

No. 871. Employer Firm Births and Deaths by Employment Size of Firms: 1989-96

[Longitudinal data for establishments active (payroll) in first quarter of the year (establishments with 0 employment in the first quarter were excluded). New firm births are classified by their employment size at the first quarter. Represents private establishments excluding railroad, domestic and farms. The number of continuing firms was calculated from static and longitudinal data. Existing firms with ownership changes are considered continuing firms]

Item	New firms (original locations)				Deaths (original locations)			
	Total	Less than 20	Less than 500	More than 500	Total	Less than 20	Less than 500	More than 500
Firms:								
1989-1990	584,892	558,478	584,660	232	531,400	502,685	530,991	409
1990-1991	541,141	515,870	540,889	252	546,518	516,964	546,149	369
1991-1992	544,596	519,014	544,278	318	521,606	492,746	521,176	430
1992-1993	564,504	539,601	564,093	411	492,651	466,550	492,266	385
1993-1994	570,587	546,437	570,337	250	503,563	476,667	503,125	438
1994-1995	594,369	568,896	594,119	250	497,246	472,441	496,874	372
1995-1996	597,792	572,442	597,503	289	512,402	485,509	512,024	378
Employment:								
1989-1990	3,211,064	1,886,311	3,090,643	120,421	3,198,829	1,683,174	2,988,436	210,393
1990-1991	3,105,363	1,712,856	2,907,351	198,012	3,208,099	1,723,159	3,044,470	163,629
1991-1992	3,200,969	1,703,491	2,863,799	337,170	3,126,463	1,602,579	2,894,127	232,336
1992-1993	3,438,106	1,750,662	3,053,765	384,341	2,906,260	1,515,896	2,697,656	208,604
1993-1994	3,105,753	1,760,322	2,889,507	216,246	3,077,307	1,549,072	2,800,933	276,374
1994-1995	3,322,001	1,836,153	3,049,456	272,545	2,822,627	1,516,552	2,633,587	189,040
1995-1996	3,255,676	1,844,516	3,055,596	200,080	3,099,589	1,559,598	2,808,493	291,096

Source: U.S. Small Business Administration, Office of Advocacy, from data provided by Department of Commerce, U.S. Census Bureau, unpublished data.

546 Business Enterprise

No. 872. Small Establishments, Employees, and Payroll by Employment-Size Class and Industry: 1997

[Data are based on the 1987 Standard Industrial Classification (SIC)]

Employment size-class	Unit	All industries [1]	Agricultural services [2]	Manufacturing	Transportation [3]	Wholesale trade	Retail trade	Finance and insurance [4]	Services
Establishments, total....	Number.	6,894,869	116,588	393,091	300,644	529,993	1,588,717	676,799	2,543,677
1 to 4 employees	Number.	3,757,627	77,601	135,131	162,768	264,055	705,461	429,866	1,493,572
5 to 9 employees	Number.	1,354,488	21,001	66,215	49,766	111,167	372,908	122,067	487,741
10 to 19 employees...	Number.	856,118	11,831	61,214	36,205	79,840	248,575	67,182	279,606
20 + employees	Number.	926,636	6,155	130,531	51,905	74,931	261,773	57,684	282,758
Employees, total	1,000 ..	105,299	727	18,633	6,247	6,810	22,003	7,367	37,380
1 to 4 employees	1,000 ..	6,433	111	242	270	487	1,314	729	2,562
5 to 9 employees	1,000 ..	8,950	138	446	329	740	2,485	802	3,200
10 to 19 employees...	1,000 ..	11,501	156	843	494	1,077	3,338	893	3,739
20 + employees	1,000 ..	78,416	(D)	17,102	5,154	4,581	14,866	4,943	27,878
Annual payroll	Mil. dol .	3,047,907	15,062	688,629	226,026	255,865	330,334	313,257	1,013,965
1 to 4 employees	Mil. dol .	196,234	2,617	8,824	8,566	18,537	24,515	26,972	85,479
5 to 9 employees	Mil. dol .	209,651	2,515	11,598	8,820	24,088	34,203	25,613	82,692
10 to 19 employees...	Mil. dol .	282,352	3,114	24,138	14,473	36,842	44,531	31,459	99,940
20 + employees	Mil. dol .	2,359,670	(D)	644,071	51,303	176,399	227,085	229,213	745,855

D Withheld to avoid disclosing data for individual companies; data are included in higher-level totals. [1] Includes establishments not shown separately. [2] Includes forestry and fisheries. [3] Includes public utilities. [4] Includes real estate.

Source: U.S. Census Bureau, County Business Patterns, annual.

No. 873. Women-Owned Firms by Major Industry Group: 1992

[Based on the 1987 SIC system. Includes individual proprietorships, partnerships and subchapter S corporations. Detail may not add to total due to rounding]

Major industry group	All firms		Firms with paid employees			
	Firms (number)	Sales and receipts ($1,000)	Firms (number)	Sales and receipts ($1,000)	Employees (number)	Annual payroll ($1,000)
All industries	5,888,883	642,484,352	817,773	550,425,116	6,252,029	104,786,488
Agric. services, forestry, & fishing...	82,526	4,987,572	15,254	3,787,251	69,542	1,002,688
Mining..................	37,205	6,905,374	2,731	5,940,020	30,563	841,127
Construction.............	183,695	45,978,168	64,746	41,579,094	371,788	8,827,641
Manufacturing............	152,346	90,634,753	41,038	88,751,252	803,428	18,574,330
Transportation & public utilities	141,623	25,822,193	31,049	23,026,912	290,081	5,841,177
Wholesale trade	154,542	12,487,093	45,591	120,625,000	385,814	9,846,339
Retail trade	1,093,342	155,852,751	244,488	139,694,945	1,850,074	19,926,963
Finance, insurance, and real estate .	602,802	51,748,279	56,040	33,084,796	295,871	6,347,967
Services	3,158,444	130,745,314	307,443	92,823,096	2,145,482	33,415,073
Industries not classified	282,358	4,962,855	9,394	1,112,750	9,386	163,185

Source: U.S. Census Bureau, Women-Owned Businesses Enterprises, Series WB92-1.

No. 874. Minority-Owned Firms—Comparison of Business Ownership by Minority Group and Gender: 1987 and 1992

[Based on the 1987 Standard Industrial Classification (SIC). Data includes individual proprietorships, partnerships and subchapter S corporations. Detail may not add to total due to rounding]

Sex and race	Firms		Percent change, 1987-1992	Percent of total		Sales/receipts		Percent change, 1987-1992	Percent of total	
	1987	1992		1987	1992	1987 (mil. dol.)	1992 (mil. dol.)		1987	1992
All minorities .	1,213,750	1,965,565	61.9	(X)	(X)	77,840	202,011	160.0	(X)	(X)
Men	825,441	1,248,130	51.2	68.0	63.5	59,847	152,245	154.9	76.9	75.4
Women........	388,309	717,435	84.8	32.0	36.5	17,993	49,767	176.6	23.1	24.6
Black	424,165	620,912	46.4	34.9	31.6	19,763	32,197	62.9	25.4	15.9
Men	265,887	343,666	29.3	21.9	17.5	13,232	23,688	77.1	17.0	11.7
Women	158,278	277,246	75.2	13.0	14.1	6,531	8,510	30.3	8.4	4.2
Hispanic	422,373	771,708	82.7	34.8	39.3	24,732	72,824	194.5	31.8	36.0
Men	307,348	525,330	70.9	25.3	26.7	20,403	55,645	172.2	26.2	27.5
Women	115,025	246,378	114.2	9.5	12.5	4,328	17,180	297.0	5.6	8.5
API/AIAN: [1]										
Men	258,514	397,779	53.9	21.3	20.2	26,700	74,856	180.4	34.3	37.1
Women	118,197	208,647	76.5	9.7	10.6	7,336	24,853	238.8	9.4	12.3

X Not applicable. [1] API/AIAN = Asian, Pacific Islander, American Indian, and Alaska Native.

Source: U.S. Census Bureau, Survey of Minority-Owned Businesses, Summary 1992, Series MB92-4.

Business Enterprise 547

No. 875. Business Starts and Employment Associated With Start: 1990 to 1999

[647 represents 647,000]

Item	1990	1992	1993	1994	1995	1996	1997	1998	1999
New incorporations (1,000).......	647	667	707	742	767	786	799	761	(NA)
Failures,[1] total	60,747	97,069	86,133	71,558	71,128	71,931	84,342	71,857	(NA)
Rate per 10,000 concerns.......	74	110	109	86	82	80	89	76	(NA)
Current liabilities [2] (mil. dol.)	56,130	94,318	47,756	28,978	37,284	29,569	24,802	(NA)	(NA)
Business starts, total	**158,930**	**164,086**	**166,154**	**188,387**	**168,158**	**170,475**	**166,740**	**155,141**	**151,016**
Agriculture, forestry & fishing	2,295	2,160	2,195	2,644	2,199	2,295	2,275	2,451	2,732
Mining	1,054	805	772	680	564	589	655	588	467
Construction	20,801	18,259	17,533	18,213	16,980	18,624	18,513	17,016	15,775
Manufacturing	15,315	14,043	13,789	12,927	12,172	12,908	13,144	11,876	11,292
Transportation & public utilities	6,281	6,578	6,846	7,683	7,161	7,993	8,741	8,559	8,932
Wholesale trade	18,170	18,419	17,958	16,409	14,956	16,019	15,780	13,983	12,233
Retail trade	43,109	40,318	38,707	38,949	36,381	38,407	36,377	33,151	29,263
Finance, insurance & real estate	9,550	9,581	10,314	11,746	10,362	11,222	12,198	12,317	11,783
Services	38,471	40,555	41,349	49,328	44,586	50,077	50,253	48,500	47,643
Unclassifiable establishments	3,884	13,368	16,691	29,808	22,797	12,341	8,804	6,700	10,896
Employment, total	**827,012**	**800,827**	**780,804**	**758,134**	**738,606**	**846,973**	**939,310**	**906,105**	**926,899**
Agriculture, forestry & fishing	8,518	7,422	5,198	7,099	6,146	7,794	10,001	10,105	11,090
Mining	8,431	6,519	6,164	4,312	3,184	4,697	4,248	6,790	4,575
Construction	80,096	59,361	53,432	54,210	53,118	64,478	82,336	78,920	80,558
Manufacturing	139,506	122,483	119,487	105,255	104,660	108,644	125,007	111,507	114,248
Transportation & public utilities	45,373	45,227	44,885	41,617	43,583	50,072	59,144	59,972	70,284
Wholesale trade	75,914	79,247	78,924	66,186	59,933	69,001	73,281	70,297	67,802
Retail trade	207,752	203,698	191,484	174,270	176,159	200,354	211,007	195,802	183,907
Finance. insurance & real estate	54,872	56,665	57,199	55,857	54,610	61,185	70,982	75,113	73,139
Services	205,481	219,120	222,054	243,296	233,482	278,292	299,137	294,331	316,065
Unclassifiable establishments	1,069	1,085	1,977	6,032	3,731	2,456	4,167	3,268	5,231

NA Not available.   [1] Includes concerns discontinued following assignment, voluntary or involuntary petition in bankruptcy, attachment, execution, foreclosure, etc.   [2] Liabilities exclude long-term publicly held obligations; offsetting assets are not taken into account.

Source: The Dun & Bradstreet Corporation, Murray Hill, NJ 07974-0027. *Business Starts Record,* annual; and *Monthly Failure Report* (copyright).

No. 876. Business Starts and Business Failures by State: 1997 and 1998

State	Business starts		Number of failures		State	Business starts		Number of failures	
	1997	1998	1997	1998		1997	1998	1997	1998
United States.....	**166,740**	**155,141**	**84,342**	**71,857**	Missouri	2,435	2,163	1,555	1,321
					Montana	419	397	191	201
Alabama	2,480	2,645	632	546	Nebraska	648	565	491	383
Alaska	267	271	179	177	Nevada.............	1,672	1,465	628	677
Arizona.............	3,110	2,868	1,219	1,225	New Hampshire	718	708	432	322
Arkansas............	1,183	1,091	1,131	748					
California............	22,497	21,582	20,277	17,679	New Jersey	7,481	6,412	2,649	2,024
					New Mexico..........	961	887	647	585
Colorado............	3,276	3,041	3,117	2,483	New York	14,450	13,403	5,093	4,233
Connecticut	2,123	2,069	640	530	North Carolina	4,578	4,371	1,051	846
Delaware............	602	508	33	28	North Dakota	255	229	138	144
District of Columbia....	696	537	91	75					
Florida	13,032	13,029	2,597	2,047	Ohio...............	5,122	4,829	2,862	2,524
					Oklahoma	1,499	1,367	1,559	990
Georgia	5,383	5,471	1,186	800	Oregon	1,837	1,823	1,201	1,109
Hawaii	696	593	647	781	Pennsylvania	6,450	5,525	3,154	2,641
Idaho	784	639	685	441	Rhode Island	511	544	188	150
Illinois	6,525	5,542	3,527	3,291					
Indiana	2,928	2,611	856	473	South Carolina	2,014	2,023	418	410
					South Dakota........	286	281	284	275
Iowa...............	1,199	1,020	528	244	Tennessee...........	3,239	2,835	1,746	1,369
Kansas	1,109	967	1,272	1,140	Texas	11,859	10,936	7,329	6,785
Kentucky............	1,859	1,824	568	270	Utah...............	1,527	1,417	586	388
Louisiana	2,028	1,849	303	377					
Maine	570	577	398	259	Vermont	291	261	150	80
					Virginia.............	3,779	3,502	903	860
Maryland............	3,668	3,139	1,502	1,283	Washington	3,223	2,956	3,015	2,528
Massachusetts	3,766	3,425	1,687	1,200	West Virginia	555	623	320	305
Michigan	4,881	4,293	1,949	1,551	Wisconsin	2,515	2,357	1,221	1,005
Minnesota...........	2,336	2,111	1,220	1,711	Wyoming............	247	213	140	166
Mississippi..........	1,171	1,347	147	177					

Source: The Dun & Bradstreet Corporation, Murray Hill, NJ, 07974-0027. *A Decade of Business Starts,* monthly; (copyright), and *Business Failure Record,* annual, (copyright).

548   Business Enterprise

No. 877. Business Failures by Industry: 1990 to 1998

Industry	Number					Rate per 10,000 firms				
	1990	1995	1996	1997	1998	1990	1995	1996	1997	1998
Total	60,747	71,128	71,931	84,342	71,857	74	82	80	89	76
Agriculture, forestry, fishing	1,733	2,231	2,723	2,977	2,547	50	85	102	103	47
Mining	388	200	189	163	173	88	57	60	52	58
Construction	8,162	9,158	9,801	11,057	9,568	91	106	112	118	102
Manufacturing	4,740	4,383	4,093	4,224	3,314	92	88	83	81	64
Food and kindred products	232	216	230	221	176	91	91	93	86	70
Textile mill products	102	117	126	126	90	97	122	139	131	93
Apparel, other textile products	318	394	359	358	274	114	151	141	134	103
Lumber and wood products	420	318	375	397	127	97	89	107	107	33
Furniture and fixtures	258	229	184	161	43	151	144	120	100	27
Paper and allied products	68	51	57	46	(NA)	105	76	84	63	(NA)
Printing and publishing	734	815	696	772	605	74	81	69	74	60
Chemicals and allied products	139	126	123	112	82	86	81	78	66	47
Petroleum refining and coal prod..	21	14	14	13	9	83	67	64	56	38
Rubber and misc. products	158	128	156	121	94	101	80	98	74	58
Leather and leather products	40	28	32	32	27	113	92	110	105	88
Stone, clay, and glass products	161	125	106	122	84	80	74	64	70	47
Primary metal products	115	59	59	67	57	123	69	71	79	67
Fabricated metal products	397	354	311	311	242	90	83	73	71	55
Machinery, exc. electric	656	565	486	511	456	84	75	65	66	58
Electric and electronic	287	255	217	228	189	114	104	88	87	72
Transportation equipment	242	160	154	140	104	147	114	109	93	69
Instruments and related equipment	120	121	92	116	70	68	68	52	60	36
Miscellaneous	272	308	316	368	310	74	76	74	78	64
Transportation, public utilities	2,630	2,733	3,362	4,402	3,824	94	90	107	132	115
Wholesale trade	4,423	4,149	3,957	3,912	3,138	77	71	69	67	56
Retail trade	12,972	12,952	13,476	15,132	12,640	65	73	72	79	70
Finance, insurance, real estate	3,819	4,293	4,138	4,634	3,261	60	60	57	62	43
Services	16,119	21,850	22,928	29,752	28,547	49	54	59	73	72
Public administration	10	24	23	27	25	(NA)	(NA)	(NA)	(NA)	(NA)
Nonclassifiable establishments	5,751	9,221	7,241	8,062	4,820	(NA)	(NA)	(NA)	(NA)	(NA)

NA Not available.

Source: The Dun and Bradstreet Corporation, Murray Hill, NJ 07974-0027; *Business Failure Record,* annual (copyright).

No. 878. Bankruptcy Cases Filed by State: 1995 to 1999

[In thousands (858.1 represents 858,100). For years ending June 30. Includes outlying areas, not shown separately. Covers only bankruptcy cases filed under the Bankruptcy Reform Act of 1978. **Bankruptcy:** legal recognition that a company or individual is insolvent and must restructure or liquidate. Petitions "filed" means the commencement of a proceeding through the presentation of a petition to the clerk of the court]

State	1995	1997	1998	1999	State	1995	1997	1998	1999
United States...	858.1	1,317.0	1,429.5	1,392.0	Missouri	15.1	24.2	27.4	27.9
Alabama	24.3	33.3	33.8	31.2	Montana	2.1	3.2	3.7	3.7
Alaska	0.9	1.3	1.4	1.5	Nebraska	3.4	5.7	6.1	5.8
Arizona	14.8	23.2	24.7	23.7	Nevada	7.3	12.3	14.4	15.5
Arkansas	7.9	14.7	16.5	16.8	New Hampshire	3.1	4.3	5.1	4.5
California	140.4	200.1	211.3	200.2					
					New Jersey	25.5	38.8	44.5	44.1
Colorado	13.1	17.9	18.9	17.3	New Mexico	3.7	6.8	7.9	7.7
Connecticut	8.5	12.7	13.5	13.2	New York	48.8	69.8	76.9	74.4
Delaware	1.4	2.4	2.7	3.9	North Carolina	14.0	24.9	26.5	26.8
District of Columbia	1.4	2.2	2.8	2.8	North Dakota	1.2	1.9	2.1	2.2
Florida	43.4	67.4	76.4	79.2					
					Ohio	32.4	50.1	55.5	55.3
Georgia	42.1	59.9	62.6	59.3	Oklahoma	13.2	20.8	22.5	21.3
Hawaii	1.8	3.8	5.1	5.9	Oregon	13.2	17.9	17.9	18.2
Idaho	3.7	6.2	7.5	7.3	Pennsylvania	22.0	38.3	45.2	45.7
Illinois	39.2	60.3	64.6	66.6	Rhode Island	3.0	5.1	5.4	5.3
Indiana	22.3	33.7	38.5	38.9					
					South Carolina	6.9	10.7	11.3	11.6
Iowa	5.9	9.6	9.7	8.9	South Dakota	1.3	2.1	2.3	2.3
Kansas	8.5	12.5	13.2	12.3	Tennessee	35.5	52.1	52.6	48.2
Kentucky	13.0	20.6	22.1	21.4	Texas	43.8	69.5	72.0	68.6
Louisiana	13.4	22.6	23.2	22.5	Utah	6.9	10.6	13.5	14.0
Maine	1.9	3.6	4.4	4.5					
					Vermont	0.9	1.7	1.9	1.9
Maryland	16.3	28.8	34.5	34.1	Virginia	25.5	40.7	43.4	41.2
Massachusetts	14.3	22.5	22.1	20.9	Washington	18.6	31.7	33.6	32.4
Michigan	22.7	36.1	41.2	38.8	West Virginia	3.8	7.6	8.8	8.4
Minnesota	14.1	19.9	19.5	17.4	Wisconsin	11.8	17.9	19.6	18.9
Mississippi	10.6	18.2	19.1	18.1	Wyoming	1.2	2.0	2.1	2.2

Source: Administrative Office of the U.S. Courts, unpublished data.

U.S. Census Bureau, Statistical Abstract of the United States: 2000

No. 879. Bankruptcy Petitions Filed and Pending by Type and Chapter: 1985 to 1999

[**For years ending June 30.** Covers only bankruptcy cases filed under the Bankruptcy Reform Act of 1978. **Bankruptcy:** legal recognition that a company or individual is insolvent and must restructure or liquidate. Petitions "filed" means the commencement of a proceeding through the presentation of a petition to the clerk of the court; "pending" is a proceeding in which the administration has not been completed]

Item	1985	1990	1993	1994	1995	1996	1997	1998	1999
Total filed . . .	**364,536**	**725,484**	**918,734**	**845,257**	**858,104**	**1,042,110**	**1,316,999**	**1,429,451**	**1,391,964**
Business [1]	66,651	64,688	66,428	56,748	51,288	52,938	53,993	50,202	39,934
Nonbusiness [2] . . .	297,885	660,796	852,306	788,509	806,816	989,172	1,263,006	1,379,249	1,352,030
Voluntary.	362,939	723,886	917,350	844,087	856,991	1,040,915	1,315,782	1,428,550	1,391,130
Involuntary	1,597	1,598	1,384	1,170	1,113	1,195	1,217	901	834
Chapter 7 [3]	244,650	505,337	638,916	578,903	581,390	712,129	917,274	1,015,453	993,414
Chapter 9 [4]	3	7	9	17	12	10	9	5	3
Chapter 11 [5]	21,425	19,591	20,579	17,098	13,221	12,859	11,159	9,613	8,684
Chapter 12 [6]	(X)	1,351	1,434	976	904	1,063	1,006	845	829
Chapter 13 [7]	98,452	199,186	257,777	248,246	262,551	316,024	387,521	403,501	389,004
Section 304 [8]. . . .	6	12	19	17	26	24	29	34	30
Total pending .	**608,945**	**961,919**	**1,183,009**	**1,134,036**	**1,090,446**	**1,169,112**	**1,331,290**	**1,389,917**	**1,401,862**

X Not applicable.   [1] Business bankruptcies include those filed under chapters 7, 9, 11, or 12.   [2] Bankruptcies include those filed under chapters 7, 11, or 13.   [3] Chapter 7, liquidation of nonexempt assets of businesses or individuals.   [4] Chapter 9, adjustment of debts of a municipality.   [5] Chapter 11, individual or business reorganization.   [6] Chapter 12, adjustment of debts of a family farmer with regular income, effective November 26, 1986.   [7] Chapter 13, adjustment of debts of an individual with regular income.   [8] Chapter 11 U.S.C., Section 304, cases ancillary to foreign proceedings.

Source: Administrative Office of the U.S. Courts, *Statistical Tables for the Federal Judiciary.*

No. 880. Small Business Administration Loans to Small Businesses: 1980 to 1996

[**For fiscal year ending in year shown;** see text, Section 9, State and Local Government. A small business must be independently owned and operated, must not be dominant in its particular industry, and must meet standards set by the Small Business Administration as to its annual receipts or number of employees]

Loans approved	Unit	1980	1985	1990	1991	1992	1993	1994	1995	1996
Loans, all businesses	1,000. . .	31.7	19.3	18.8	20.6	26.4	29.4	40.4	60.1	52.7
Loans, minority-owned businesses. .	1,000. . .	6.0	2.8	2.4	3.1	3.9	4.5	6.8	10.4	9.1
Percent of all business loans	Percent .	19	15	13	15	15	15	18	19	19
Value of total loans [1]	Mil. dol. .	3,858	3,217	4,354	4,861	6,596	7,591	9,527	9,854	10,177
Minority business loans [2]	Mil. dol. .	470	324	473	764	1,033	1,178	1,754	1,885	2,124

[1] Includes both SBA and bank portions of loans.   [2] SBA direct loans and guaranteed portion of bank loans only.

Source: U.S. Small Business Administration, Management Information Summary, unpublished data.

No. 881. Venture Capital Commitments by Source: 1980 to 1999

[Investment in venture capital partnerships]

Source	1980	1985	1990	1993	1994	1995	1996	1997	1998	1999
Capital commitments (bil. dol.) . .	**2.02**	**2.92**	**2.65**	**3.94**	**7.17**	**8.22**	**10.55**	**15.59**	**27.73**	**46.10**
PERCENT DISTRIBUTION										
Corporations	19.2	11.8	6.8	8.3	9.1	4.2	18.9	24.0	11.7	15.0
Endowments & Foundations	13.9	7.8	12.6	10.6	21.4	19.6	11.3	16.0	6.2	21.0
Foreign Investors	8.3	23.5	7.5	4.3	2.4	3.8	5.6	4.0	1.1	6.0
Individuals & Families	15.4	13.0	11.4	7.3	11.9	16.2	6.5	12.0	11.2	22.0
Financial & Insurance	13.3	10.9	9.3	10.5	9.5	19.3	2.9	6.0	10.2	13.0
Pension Funds	29.8	33.0	52.5	59.0	45.8	37.0	54.8	38.0	59.4	23.0

Source: Venture Economics Investor Services, Boston, MA, *Venture Capital Journal,* monthly.

No. 882. Mergers and Acquisitions—Summary: 1985 to 1999

[Covers transactions valued at $5 million or more. Values based on transactions for which price data revealed. **All activity** includes mergers, acquisitions, acquisitions of partial interest that involve a 40% stake in the target or an investment of at least $100 million, divestitures, and leveraged transactions that result in a change in ownership. **Divestiture:** sale of a business, division, or subsidiary by corporate owner to another party. **Leveraged buyout:** acquisition of a business in which buyers use mostly borrowed money to finance purchase price and incorporate debt into capital structure of business after change in ownership]

Item	Unit	1985	1990	1993	1994	1995	1996	1997	1998	1999
All activity:										
Number.	Number . .	1,719	4,239	3,722	4,383	4,981	5,639	8,770	9,634	9,599
Value	Bil. dol. . . .	149.6	205.6	420.4	524.9	895.8	1,059.3	1,610.3	2,480.2	3,401.6
Divestitures:										
Number	Number . .	780	1,907	1,993	2,005	2,227	2,423	3,189	3,304	3,184
Value	Bil. dol. . . .	51	90.8	213.4	236.9	365.3	319.0	616.2	554.8	677.7
Leveraged buyouts:										
Number	Number . .	154	177	621	173	206	169	198	238	344
Value	Bil. dol. . . .	16.3	17.6	1.64	10.6	23.6	17.4	24.1	27.2	58.1
Foreign acquisitions of U.S. companies:										
Number	Number . .	259	773	(NA)	(NA)	80	73	441	483	566
Value	Bil. dol. . . .	27.9	56.4	(NA)	(NA)	3.5	2.9	64.8	232.5	282.6
U.S. acquisitions overseas:										
Number	Number . .	91	392	197	207	317	364	539	746	651
Value	Bil. dol. . . .	3.7	20.5	19.5	21.1	62.6	59.3	87.8	127.8	166.1

NA Not available.

No. 883. Mergers and Acquisitions by Industry: 1998

[See headnote Table 882]

Industry	U.S. Company acquiring U.S. company		Foreign company acquiring U.S. company		U.S. company acquiring foreign company	
	Number	Value (mil. dol.)	Number	Value (mil. dol.)	Number	Value (mil. dol.)
Total activity [1]	3,882	1,378,564.6	483	232,505.1	746	127,760.9
Construction firms	76	3,494.9	6	1,314.3	8	344.0
Food and kindred products	56	11,089.3	10	359.1	23	5,380.5
Tobacco products	(NA)	(NA)	1	729.3	1	12.0
Textile and apparel products.	32	3,648.9	8	479.1	2	584.8
Wood products, furniture, and fixtures	20	2,914.5	5	631.1	4	61.1
Paper and allied products	19	16,637.0	9	911.6	10	3,460.9
Chemicals and allied products	37	14,275.9	13	2,327.2	15	2,824.1
Drugs.	52	9,071.8	16	2,734.0	13	1,428.2
Stone, clay, glass and concrete products	23	3,843.7	3	792.5	9	3,846.1
Metal and metal products.	84	12,155.2	10	2,008.5	24	1,408.0
Machinery.	90	24,549.5	7	228.4	19	1,369.7
Computer and office equipment	39	12,139.8	11	9,746.3	13	1,490.9
Prepackaged software.	160	19,782.5	36	3,059.4	38	2,793.9
Electronic and electrical equipment	101	26,438.6	25	2,938.6	29	11,996.4
Communications equipment.	47	5,006.3	15	6,005.5	20	1,615.4
Transportation equipment	34	21,649.7	9	43,520.0	19	2,497.2
Aerospace and aircraft	16	1,296.7	2	85.0	4	354.9
Measuring, medical, photo equip; clocks.	104	28,158.3	24	3,676.3	25	3,336.0
Transportation and shipping (except air).	8	1,788.9	2	222.0	6	5,666.9
Air transportation and shipping	60	2,613.3	10	4,065.5	21	1,681.9
Telecommunications	101	206,600.2	15	13,086.6	29	4,904.3
Radio & television broadcasting stations.	137	108,477.3	5	341.7	11	4,872.3
Printing, publishing, and allied services	39	8,007.2	11	9,751.8	7	411.6
Electric, gas, water distribution	57	29,988.7	6	16,767.4	30	19,649.0
Sanitary services	26	23,760.0	1	14.5	2	486.4
Hotels and casinos.	122	18,939.7	8	489.4	21	1,840.8
Amusement and recreation services	46	5,411.5	3	140.6	7	245.4
Motion picture production and distribution	27	3,474.4	1	420.0	4	146.4
Personal services.	7	1,977.4	1	11.0	1	68.6
Business services.	433	75,834.2	37	6,305.8	81	5,506.2
Advertising services	31	3,194.3	4	54.4	10	2,163.6
Repair services	18	2,657.0	1	14.8	3	1,411.5
Wholesale trade—durable goods.	93	6,612.4	7	296.8	16	1,250.9
Retail trade—general merchandise and apparel. .	23	20,812.6	1	6.0	2	220.0
Commercial banks, bank holding companies . . .	253	241,677.7	1	9,082.1	13	1,878.2
Real estate, mortgage bankers and brokers . . .	482	46,668.9	46	4,577.5	24	5,275.9
Investment & commodity firms, dealers, exchanges	120	37,363.9	18	3,407.2	34	4,797.7
Insurance	96	61,680.2	16	7,068.5	23	4,289.8
Agriculture, forestry, and fishing	17	4,087.3	3	415.0	10	1,477.4
Mining	28	6,415.8	7	2,108.6	16	1,034.7
Oil and gas; petroleum refining	147	118,128.6	19	56,178.8	38	7,594.3
Holding companies, except banks	2	640.8	1	27.6	2	164.0
Public administration.	4	109.8	1	1,100.0	2	169.7

NA Not available.   [1] Includes other items not shown separately.

Source of Tables 882 and 883: Thomson Financial Securities Data, Newark, NJ, Merger & Corporate Transactions Database (copyright).

No. 884. Patents and Trademarks: 1980 to 1998

[In thousands (113.0 represents 113,000). Calendar year data. Covers patents issued to citizens of the United States and residents of foreign countries. For data on foreign countries, see Table 1382]

Type	1980	1990	1992	1993	1994	1995	1996	1997	1998
Patent applications filed..........	113.0	176.7	187.2	189.4	206.9	226.6	211.6	233.0	261.5
Inventions..................	104.3	164.6	173.1	174.7	189.9	212.4	195.2	215.3	243.1
Designs...................	7.8	11.3	13.1	13.6	15.8	15.4	15.2	16.5	17.1
Botanical plants.............	0.2	0.4	0.4	0.4	0.5	0.5	0.7	0.6	0.7
Reissues..................	0.6	0.5	0.6	0.6	0.7	0.6	0.6	0.6	0.6
Patents issued................	66.2	99.2	107.4	109.7	113.6	113.8	121.7	124.1	163.1
Inventions.................	61.8	90.4	97.4	98.3	101.7	101.4	109.6	112.0	147.5
Individuals..............	13.8	17.3	17.3	16.5	17.3	17.4	18.2	17.6	22.5
Corporations:									
United States............	27.7	36.1	40.3	41.8	44.0	44.0	48.7	50.2	66.1
Foreign [1]............	19.1	36.0	38.7	38.8	38.8	39.1	41.5	42.9	57.9
U.S. Government...........	1.2	1.0	1.2	1.2	1.3	1.0	0.9	0.9	1.0
Designs..................	3.9	8.0	9.3	10.6	11.1	11.7	11.4	11.4	14.8
Botanical plants............	0.1	0.3	0.3	0.4	0.5	0.4	0.4	0.4	0.6
Reissues.................	0.3	0.4	0.4	0.3	0.3	0.3	0.3	0.3	0.3
U.S. residents [2]............	40.8	52.8	58.7	61.1	64.2	64.4	69.3	69.9	90.6
Foreign country residents [2].......	25.4	46.2	48.7	48.7	49.3	49.4	52.4	54.2	72.5
Percent of total.............	38.4	46.7	45.3	44.3	43.4	43.4	43.0	43.7	44.4
Other published documents [3].......	(Z)	0.1	0.1	0.1	0.1	0.1	0.1	0.1	0.1
Trademarks:									
Applications filed..............	46.8	127.3	127.8	150.4	161.1	188.9	212.5	234.6	246.6
Issued	24.7	60.8	85.8	86.9	70.1	92.5	102.5	145.2	136.1
Trademarks	18.9	53.6	80.2	80.6	63.9	85.6	93.7	138.2	129.9
Trademark renewals..........	5.9	7.2	5.6	6.3	6.2	6.9	8.8	7.0	6.2

Z Less than 50. [1] Includes patents to foreign governments. [2] Includes patents for inventions, designs, botanical plants, and reissues. [3] Includes Defensive Publications, a practice which began in November 1968 and ended in July 1986; and Statutory Invention Registrations, the current practice, which began May 1985. These documents are patent applications, which are published to provide the defensive properties of a patent, but do not have the enforceable rights of a patent.

Source: U.S. Patent and Trademark Office. Fiscal-year figures are published in the *Commissioner of Patents and Trademarks Annual Report.*

No. 885. Patents by State: 1998

[Includes only U.S. patents granted to residents of the United States and territories]

State	Total	Inventions	Designs	Botanical plants	Reissues	State	Total	Inventions	Designs	Botanical plants	Reissues
U.S. [1].......	90,645	80,292	9,913	245	195	Mississippi.....	202	175	24	3	-
						Missouri.......	1,049	900	143	4	2
Alabama......	422	365	54	2	1	Montana......	149	130	19	-	-
Alaska.......	76	64	12	-	-	Nebraska......	233	204	29	-	-
Arizona.......	1,677	1,513	161	-	3	Nevada.......	332	270	59	-	3
Arkansas.....	184	145	38	-	1	New Hampshire..	649	611	37	-	1
California.....	17,821	15,791	1,889	112	29						
						New Jersey....	4,198	3,767	418	3	10
Colorado......	1,916	1,750	161	1	4	New Mexico....	363	343	20	-	-
Connecticut...	2,071	1,798	267	1	5	New York.....	7,113	6,319	777	2	15
Delaware.....	422	394	27	-	1	North Carolina...	1,840	1,614	218	-	8
District of Columbia.........	85	74	9	-	2	North Dakota ...	69	65	4	-	-
Florida........	3,114	2,668	413	28	5	Ohio.........	3,890	3,272	604	4	10
						Oklahoma....	542	488	51	3	-
Georgia.......	1,495	1,290	199	2	4	Oregon	1,560	1,184	347	27	2
Hawaii........	93	84	9	-	-	Pennsylvania ...	3,759	3,370	373	5	11
Idaho........	897	854	33	-	10	Rhode Island ...	357	280	77	-	-
Illinois........	4,364	3,726	633	-	5						
Indiana.......	1,561	1,373	185	1	2	South Carolina ..	682	570	105	3	4
						South Dakota...	57	50	7	-	-
Iowa........	720	645	75	-	-	Tennessee.....	912	783	124	2	3
Kansas.......	404	349	52	-	3	Texas.........	5,972	5,576	377	7	12
Kentucky.....	404	349	53	1	1	Utah.........	731	666	63	1	1
Louisiana.....	543	486	42	12	3						
Maine........	143	122	20	-	1	Vermont.......	343	323	20	-	-
						Virginia.......	1,157	1,051	104	-	2
Maryland.....	1,569	1,443	122	4	-	Washington	1,998	1,774	219	2	3
Massachusetts..	3,735	3,413	314	3	5	West Virginia ...	210	189	20	1	-
Michigan......	3,825	3,507	295	9	14	Wisconsin......	1,878	1,567	306	1	4
Minnesota....	2,779	2,473	300	1	5	Wyoming......	49	45	4	-	-

- Represents zero. [1] Includes U.S. territories not shown separately.

Source: U.S. Patent and Trademark Office, Technology Assessment and Forecast Data Base.

No. 886. Patents by Industry: 1980 to 1998

[Based on the 1972 Standard Industrial Classification (SIC). Includes all patents for inventions granted to residents of the United States, its territories, and foreign citizens. Individual industries may not add to total since a patent may be recorded in more than one industry category. Except for total, data for all years have been revised to reflect the U.S. Patent Classification System as of 1993]

Industry	SIC code	1980	1985	1990	1995	1997	1998
Total.	(X)	**61,819**	**71,661**	**90,364**	**101,419**	**111,983**	**147,518**
Durable goods:							
Stone, clay, and glass products	32	1,221	1,307	1,638	1,575	1,859	2,117
Primary metals	33, 3462-3	706	780	913	902	751	964
Fabricated metal products [1]	34	5,012	5,560	6,771	5,908	5,920	7,697
Machinery, except electrical	35	14,325	16,841	19,144	21,148	23,541	33,000
Electronic and other electric equipment.	36, 3825	10,737	13,892	19,088	25,302	27,595	37,682
Transportation equipment	37, 348	3,107	3,743	4,727	4,466	4,505	5,781
Instruments and related products [2]	38	7,443	8,938	12,297	14,502	15,755	21,271
Nondurable goods:							
Food and kindred products	20	484	546	730	601	544	650
Textile mill products	22	420	494	501	609	643	794
Chemicals and allied products	28	9,880	10,274	12,487	13,566	17,179	20,475
Oil and gas extraction, petroleum products . .	13, 29	595	802	664	643	461	573
Rubber and miscellaneous plastics products .	30	2,611	3,045	3,818	3,958	4,067	4,959
Other industries	(X)	5,279	5,440	7,586	8,241	9,163	11,557

X Not applicable.   [1] Excludes SIC groups 3462, 3463, and 348.   [2] Excludes SIC group 3825.

Source: U.S. Patent and Trademark Office, *Patenting Trends in the United States, State Country Report, 1963-1998.*

No. 887. Academic Patenting—Number of U.S. Universities and Colleges With Patent Awards and Number of Academic Patent Awards: 1985 to 1998

Year	Number of universities and colleges with patent award			Number of academic patents granted		
	Total	Public	Private	Total	Public	Private
1985	111	64	47	589	311	232
1986	119	74	45	670	356	262
1987	122	70	52	819	399	363
1988	120	68	52	814	407	368
1989	147	87	60	1,228	661	526
1990	145	88	57	1,183	676	479
1991	152	94	58	1,342	798	511
1992	150	92	58	1,542	909	599
1993	159	98	61	1,620	939	648
1994	166	100	66	1,780	1,068	677
1995	164	101	63	1,879	1,191	654
1996	176	105	71	2,154	1,341	774
1997	172	106	66	2,436	1,510	880
1998	173	102	71	3,151	1,828	1,278

Source: U.S. Patent and Trademark Office, *Technology Assessment and For Report, U.S. Universities and Colleges, 1969-97;* National Science Foundation, special tabulation.

U.S. Census Bureau, Statistical Abstract of the United States: 2000

No. 888. Net Stock of Fixed Private Capital by Industry: 1990 to 1998

[In billions of dollars (12,760 represents $12,760,000,000,000). Estimates as of **Dec. 31**. Based on the 1987 Standard Industrial Classification (SIC)]

Industry	1990	1994	1995	1996	1997	1998
Fixed private capital	**12,760**	**15,204**	**15,908**	**16,723**	**17,573**	**18,643**
Agriculture, forestry, and fishing	481	535	551	569	589	614
Farms	447	486	498	511	525	544
Housing	161	182	187	192	198	206
Other	285	304	311	319	327	338
Agricultural services, forestry, and fishing	35	49	53	59	63	70
Mining	431	433	455	483	501	530
Metal mining	29	33	34	36	36	37
Coal mining	32	36	39	41	44	47
Oil and gas extraction	350	344	360	384	397	420
Nonmetallic minerals, except fuels	19	20	21	22	24	26
Construction	82	93	101	109	118	129
Manufacturing	1,217	1,387	1,457	1,521	1,590	1,660
Durable goods	636	709	747	782	821	861
Lumber and wood products	25	27	29	31	32	33
Furniture and fixtures	11	13	13	14	14	15
Stone, clay, and glass products	40	42	44	46	50	55
Primary metal industries	116	122	126	129	131	134
Fabricated metal products	70	77	81	84	87	91
Industrial machinery and equipment	110	121	126	130	137	143
Electronic and other electric equipment	92	108	120	133	143	153
Motor vehicles and equipment	64	78	85	90	96	102
Other transportation equipment	51	54	55	55	57	60
Instruments and related products	45	53	54	56	59	59
Miscellaneous manufacturing industries	12	13	14	15	15	15
Nondurable goods	581	679	711	738	769	800
Food and kindred products	119	138	146	151	159	166
Tobacco products	9	9	9	10	10	10
Textile mill products	34	37	38	39	40	41
Apparel and other textile products	11	13	13	14	14	14
Paper and allied products	84	94	98	101	104	108
Printing and publishing	52	58	59	61	63	66
Chemicals and allied products	157	190	200	210	221	229
Petroleum and coal products	75	90	93	95	96	96
Rubber and miscellaneous plastics products	38	48	52	55	60	65
Leather and leather products	3	3	3	3	3	3
Transportation and public utilities	1,855	2,140	2,232	2,313	2,398	2,477
Transportation	582	661	692	721	748	776
Railroad transportation	304	329	337	349	353	349
Local and interurban passenger transit	21	24	25	27	27	28
Trucking and warehousing	71	89	99	104	114	126
Water transportation	35	37	37	38	39	40
Transportation by air	85	108	115	122	131	147
Pipelines, except natural gas	38	44	44	45	47	47
Transportation services	26	30	34	36	37	40
Communications	436	519	549	587	618	660
Telephone and telegraph	377	439	458	484	505	534
Radio and television	59	80	91	103	113	126
Electric, gas, and sanitary services	837	959	991	1,005	1,033	1,041
Electric services	609	675	696	701	715	721
Gas services	165	200	205	212	222	223
Sanitary services	63	84	89	92	95	97
Wholesale trade	286	351	379	405	433	463
Retail trade	391	482	514	550	583	617
Finance, insurance, and real estate	7,466	9,088	9,481	9,986	10,518	11,239
Depository institutions	236	266	268	275	285	301
Nondepository institutions	114	151	166	192	208	239
Security and commodity brokers	40	59	63	69	75	84
Insurance carriers	89	124	139	146	155	165
Insurance agents, brokers, and service	8	12	13	14	16	17
Real estate	6,944	8,429	8,779	9,232	9,714	10,359
Owner-occupied housing	4,337	5,459	5,718	6,050	6,394	6,843
Tenant-occupied housing	1,640	1,831	1,880	1,953	2,026	2,145
Other	967	1,139	1,182	1,229	1,293	1,372
Holding and other investment offices	35	46	52	59	65	73
Services	552	695	739	786	843	913
Hotels and other lodging places	105	121	125	136	148	161
Personal services	27	26	27	27	29	31
Business services	99	122	131	139	147	161
Auto repair, services, and parking	62	101	111	119	125	131
Miscellaneous repair services	9	11	12	13	14	16
Motion pictures	16	24	28	31	35	39
Amusement and recreation services	34	43	47	50	55	59
Other services	200	246	257	272	291	314
Health services	98	128	135	143	153	165
Legal services	18	19	19	20	20	21
Educational services	11	13	14	15	16	17
Other [1]	73	86	90	94	102	111

[1] Consists of social services, membership organizations, and miscellaneous professional services.

Source: U.S. Bureau of Economic Analysis, *Survey of Current Business,* April 2000.

No. 889. New Product Introductions of Consumer Packaged Goods: 1980 to 1997

[**Consumer packaged goods:** consumable products packaged by the manufacturer for retail sale primarily through grocery and drug stores. **New product:** a product not previously offered for sale by a particular manufacturer including new varieties, formats, sizes, and packaging for existing products]

Item	Food	Beverages	Health and beauty	Household products	Pet products	Miscellaneous products
Domestic and imports:						
1980	1,192	256	834	331	86	197
1985	2,327	585	1,222	463	139	294
1990	3,453	630	1,531	432	164	154
1995	3,891	809	2,419	314	123	134
1996	3,889	977	3,051	369	160	148
1997, total	3,793	1,205	3,492	366	216	122
Percent:						
New brands [1]	19.8	30.8	20.1	22.7	31.9	34.4
Brand extensions [2]	1.6	1.3	1.1	2.5	-	-
Line extensions [3]	78.6	67.9	78.8	74.8	68.1	65.6
Types of new product innovation (percent): [4]						
Formulation [5]	56.5	61.6	48.4	50.0	47.1	46.9
New market [6]	1.0	-	0.7	3.1	-	3.1
Packaging [7]	14.0	20.2	9.7	17.2	11.8	9.4
Positioning [8]	24.6	18.2	39.8	29.7	41.2	25.0
Technology [9]	-	-	1.4	-	-	12.5
Merchandising	3.9	-	-	-	-	3.1
CUMULATIVE						
Domestic, except imports, 1980-97	47,796	10,093	29,520	6,447	2,575	2,965
Imports, 1980-97 [10]	4,075	1,314	1,389	261	75	178
International, 1985-97 [11]	18,206	5,712	15,534	3,043	2,914	985

- Represents or rounds to zero.   [1] Product introduced under completely or partly new brand name.   [2] Product introduced in a category with an existing brand name which has not been used in the category before.   [3] Introduction of a new variety, format, size, or package of an existing product/brand name.   [4] Product which offers consumers something significantly different from existing products.   [5] Added or new ingredient which offers a benefit not previously provided by existing products in its category.   [6] Special category for new products which do not compete with any existing category of products.   [7] New product packaged in a way that makes it easier to store, handle, prepare, or dispense than others in its category.   [8] New product presented for new users or uses compared to existing products in its category.   [9] New product with added consumer benefits resulting from use of a new technology.   [10] New products introduced in the United States by foreign companies.   [11] New products introduced by U.S. and foreign companies outside the United States.

Source: Marketing Intelligence Service Ltd., Naples, NY, *Product Alert Weekly.* Publication contains extract from database, Product scan.

No. 890. Gross Private Domestic Investment in Current and Real (1996) Dollars: 1990 to 1998

[In billions of dollars 861.7 represents $861,700,000,000]

Item	1990	1992	1993	1994	1995	1996	1997	1998
CURRENT DOLLARS								
Gross private domestic investment	861.7	866.6	955.1	1,097.1	1,143.8	1,242.7	1,383.7	1,531.2
Less: Consumption of fixed capital	579.5	642.2	660.1	714.6	743.6	781.9	828.5	878.4
Equals: Net private domestic investment .	282.2	224.4	295.0	382.5	400.1	460.8	555.1	652.8
Fixed investment	847.2	851.6	934.0	1,034.6	1,110.7	1,212.7	1,315.4	1,460.0
Less: Consumption of fixed capital . . .	579.5	642.2	660.1	714.6	743.6	781.9	828.5	878.4
Equals: Net fixed investment	267.7	209.4	273.9	320.0	367.1	430.8	486.8	581.6
Nonresidential	630.3	626.1	682.2	748.6	825.1	899.4	986.1	1,091.3
Residential	216.8	225.5	251.8	286.0	285.6	313.3	329.2	368.7
Change in business inventories	14.5	15.0	21.1	62.6	33.0	30.0	68.3	71.2
Gross government investment	215.8	223.1	220.9	225.6	238.2	250.1	258.1	268.7
Federal	19.8	13.4	6.0	-0.1	-1.7	1.0	-5.8	-2.2
State and local	64.1	64.4	62.3	65.3	71.7	74.9	83.4	84.7
CHAINED (1996) DOLLARS								
Gross private domestic investment	907.3	899.8	977.9	1,107.0	1,140.6	1,242.7	1,385.8	1,547.4
Net private domestic investment	894.6	886.5	958.4	1,045.9	1,109.2	1,212.7	1,316.0	1,471.8
Fixed investment	612.6	667.9	677.7	724.3	742.6	781.9	830.0	887.5
Nonresidential	641.7	630.6	683.6	744.6	817.5	899.4	995.7	1,122.5
Residential	253.5	257.2	276.0	302.7	291.7	313.3	320.6	350.2
Gross government investment [1]	238.9	242.0	235.0	234.5	240.8	250.1	256.3	266.4
Federal	19.0	12.5	5.1	-0.7	-2.0	1.0	-4.9	-0.8

[1] See text, Section 14, Income.

Source: U.S. Bureau of Economic Analysis, *National Income and Product Accounts, Volume 1, 1929-94,* and *Survey of Current Business,* May 2000.

No. 891. Capital Expenditures: 1997 and 1998

[In millions of dollars (870,221 represents $870,221,000,000). Based on 1987 Standard Industrial Classification code (SIC)]

Item	SIC code	Capital expenditures					
		All companies		Companies with employees		Nonemployer businesses	
		1997	1998	1997	1998	1997	1998
STRUCTURES AND EQUIPMENT							
Total	(X)	871,765	973,587	772,343	879,041	99,422	94,546
Structures	(X)	273,298	328,146	236,166	290,353	37,132	37,793
New	(X)	254,451	283,526	225,107	250,814	29,344	32,712
Used	(X)	18,849	44,620	11,060	39,539	7,789	5,081
Equipment	(X)	598,466	645,441	536,177	588,687	62,289	56,753
New	(X)	562,019	609,864	515,965	564,769	46,054	45,095
Used	(X)	36,447	35,576	20,212	23,919	16,235	11,658
CAPITAL LEASE AND CAPITALIZED INTEREST EXPENSES							
Capital leases	(X)	16,066	16,533	14,549	15,323	1,517	1,210
Capitalized interest	(X)	(NA)	(NA)	7,273	8,965	(NA)	(NA)
INDUSTRY							
Total expenditures	(X)	(NA)	(NA)	772,343	879,041	(NA)	(NA)
Mining	(X)	(NA)	(NA)	38,957	40,346	(NA)	(NA)
Construction	15-17	(NA)	(NA)	15,531	18,289	(NA)	(NA)
Manufacturing industries	20-39	(NA)	(NA)	192,345	207,304	(NA)	(NA)
Durable goods	24, 25, 32-39	(NA)	(NA)	108,405	118,991	(NA)	(NA)
Nondurable goods	20-23, 26-31	(NA)	(NA)	83,940	88,312	(NA)	(NA)
Transportation	40-42, 44-47	(NA)	(NA)	45,045	51,843	(NA)	(NA)
Communications	48	(NA)	(NA)	68,467	78,491	(NA)	(NA)
Utilities	49	(NA)	(NA)	38,719	42,319	(NA)	(NA)
Electric and gas services	491, 493	(NA)	(NA)	26,503	28,632	(NA)	(NA)
Gas, water, and other utilities	492, 494-497	(NA)	(NA)	12,216	13,687	(NA)	(NA)
Wholesale trade	50, 51	(NA)	(NA)	28,847	31,164	(NA)	(NA)
Retail trade	52-59	(NA)	(NA)	55,868	63,063	(NA)	(NA)
Finance	60-62, 67	(NA)	(NA)	91,328	110,064	(NA)	(NA)
Insurance and real estate	63-65	(NA)	(NA)	29,270	50,325	(NA)	(NA)
Services	07-09, 70-89	(NA)	(NA)	164,975	182,440	(NA)	(NA)

NA Not available. X Not applicable.

Source: U.S. Census Bureau, *Annual Capital Expenditures.*

No. 892. Composite Indexes of Economic Cyclical Indicators: 1980 to 1998

Item	Unit	1980	1990	1995	1996	1997	1998
Leading index, composite	1992=100	89.5	99.2	100.8	102.1	103.9	105.5
Average weekly hours, manufacturing	Hours	39.7	40.8	41.6	41.5	42.0	41.8
Average weekly initial claims for unemployment insurance	1,000	488.9	385.9	358.3	351.6	319.4	315.4
Manufacturers' new orders, consumer goods and materials (1992 dol.)	Mil. dol.	96,153	118,017	139,592	142,199	151,576	154,552
Vendor performance, slower deliveries diffusion index	Percent	40.6	47.9	52.8	50.5	53.9	51.1
Manufacturers' new orders, nondefense capital goods (1992 dol.)	Mil. dol.	27,142	34,598	38,743	42,066	45,195	48,437
Building permits, new private housing units	1,000	1,246.4	1,155.1	1,335.8	1,419.1	1,444.6	1,612.8
Stock prices, 500 common stocks	1941-43=10	118.8	334.6	541.6	670.8	872.7	1,084.3
Money supply, M2 (1992 dol.)	Bil. dol.	2,534	3,433	3,333	3,425	3,536	3,761
Interest rate spread, 10-year Treasury bonds less Federal funds	Percent	-1.9	0.5	0.7	1.1	0.9	-0.1
Index of consumer expectations	1966:1=100	56.8	70.2	83.2	85.7	97.7	98.3
Coincident index, composite	1992=100	80.2	100.3	109.3	112.5	116.7	120.9
Employees on nonagricultural payrolls	1,000	90,418	109,404	117,189	119,594	122,673	125,803
Personal income less transfer payments (1992 dol.)	Bil. dol.	3,361	4,580	4,974	5,140	5,382	5,683
Industrial production	1992=100	79.7	98.9	114.4	119.4	127.0	132.4
Manufacturing and trade sales (1992 dol.)	Mil. dol.	434,290	562,978	652,755	675,345	714,249	756,217
Lagging index, composite	1992=100	104.6	106.8	104.0	105.1	105.6	107.2
Average duration of unemployment	Weeks	11.9	12.0	16.6	16.7	15.8	14.5
Inventories to sales ratio, manufacturing and trade (1992 dol.)	Ratio	1.5	1.5	1.4	1.4	1.4	1.4
Change in labor cost per unit of output, manufacturing	Percent	11.1	2.8	-2.4	-3.6	-1.2	0.8
Average prime rate	Percent	15.3	10.0	8.8	8.3	8.4	8.4
Commercial and industrial loans outstanding (1992 dol.)	Mil. dol.	332,044	570,099	529,373	547,333	571,390	649,907
Consumer installment credit to personal income ratio	Percent	15.0	16.1	16.6	17.6	17.5	17.2
Change in consumer price index for services	Percent	14.6	5.8	3.4	3.3	2.9	2.6

Source: The Conference Board, New York, NY 10022-6601, *Business Cycle Indicators,* monthly (copyright).

No. 893. Business Cycle Expansions and Contractions—Months of Duration: 1919 to 1999

[A trough is the low point of a business cycle; a peak is the high point. Contraction, or recession, is the period from peak to subsequent trough; expansion is the period from trough to subsequent peak. Business cycle reference dates are determined by the National Bureau of Economic Research, Inc.]

Business cycle reference date				Contraction (trough from previous peak)	Expansion (trough to peak)	Length of cycle	
Trough		Peak				Trough from previous trough	Peak from previous peak
Month	Year	Month	Year				
March	1919	January	1920	[1]7	10	[2]51	[1]17
July	1921	May	1923	18	22	28	40
July	1924	October	1926	14	27	36	41
November	1927	August	1929	13	21	40	34
March	1933	May	1937	43	50	64	93
June	1938	February	1945	13	80	63	93
October	1945	November	1948	8	37	88	45
October	1949	July	1953	11	45	48	56
May	1954	August	1957	10	39	55	49
April	1958	April	1960	8	24	47	32
February	1961	December	1969	10	106	34	116
November	1970	November	1973	11	36	117	47
March	1975	January	1980	16	58	52	74
July	1980	July	1981	6	12	64	18
November	1982	July	1990	16	92	28	108
March	1991	(X)	(X)	8	(X)	100	(X)
Average, all cycles:							
1854 to 1991 (31 cycles)				18	35	53	[3]53
1854 to 1919 (16 cycles)				22	27	48	[4]49
1919 to 1945 (6 cycles)				18	35	53	53
1945 to 1991 (9 cycles)				11	50	61	61
Average, peacetime cycles:							
1854 to 1991 (26 cycles)				19	29	48	[5]48
1854 to 1919 (14 cycles)				22	24	46	[6]47
1919 to 1945 (5 cycles)				20	26	46	45
1945 to 1991 (7 cycles)				11	43	53	53

X Not applicable.   [1] Previous peak: August 1918.   [2] Previous trough: December 1914.   [3] 30 cycles.   [4] 15 cycles.   [5] 25 cycles.   [6] 13 cycles.

Source: National Bureau of Economic Research, Inc., Cambridge, MA, unpublished data.

No. 894. Manufacturing and Trade—Sales and Inventories: 1990 to 1998

[In billions of dollars, except ratios]

Item	1990	1991	1992	1993	1994	1995	1996	1997	1998
Sales, average monthly	**546**	**543**	**567**	**595**	**639**	**684**	**717**	**752**	**778**
Manufacturing	243	240	250	261	279	300	310	327	338
Retail trade	154	155	163	174	188	197	209	218	229
Merchant wholesalers	150	148	154	161	172	188	199	207	211
Inventories [1]	**841**	**835**	**843**	**870**	**934**	**995**	**1,013**	**1,060**	**1,095**
Manufacturing	405	391	383	384	405	431	437	456	467
Retail trade	240	243	252	269	294	310	321	330	341
Merchant wholesalers	196	200	208	217	235	254	256	274	287
Inventory-sales ratios [2]	**1.52**	**1.53**	**1.48**	**1.44**	**1.41**	**1.43**	**1.41**	**1.38**	**1.39**
Manufacturing	1.65	1.65	1.54	1.47	1.41	1.41	1.40	1.37	1.38
Retail trade	1.56	1.54	1.52	1.51	1.50	1.55	1.51	1.49	1.46
Merchant wholesalers	1.29	1.33	1.32	1.32	1.31	1.32	1.29	1.28	1.33

[1] Seasonally adjusted end-of-year data. See text, this section.   [2] End-of-year seasonally adjusted inventories to seasonally adjusted sales.

Source: U.S. Council of Economic Advisors, Economic Report of the President, annual.

No. 895. Manufacturing Corporations—Number, Assets, and Profits by Asset Size: 1980 to 1999

[Corporations and assets as of **end of 4th quarter**; profits for **entire year.** Based on complete canvass. The asset value for complete canvass was raised in 1980 to $25 million, in 1988 to $50 million, and in 1995 to $250 million. Asset sizes less than these values are sampled, except as noted. For details regarding methodology, see source for first quarter, 1988]

Year	Unit	Total	Asset-size						
			Under [1] $10 mil.	$10-$25 mil.	$25-$50 mil.	$50-$100 mil.	$100-$250 mil.	$250 mil.-$1 bil.	$1 bil. and over
Corporations:									
1980.......	Number...	(NA)	(NA)	1,777	941	590	491	369	244
1985.......	Number...	(NA)	(NA)	(NA)	896	744	608	428	281
1990.......	Number...	(NA)	(NA)	(NA)	(NA)	834	774	597	367
1995.......	Number...	(NA)	(NA)	(NA)	(NA)	574	639	727	447
1997.......	Number...	(NA)	(NA)	(NA)	(NA)	470	615	748	529
1998.......	Number...	(NA)	(NA)	(NA)	(NA)	416	531	753	549
1999.......	Number...	(NA)	(NA)	(NA)	(NA)	438	486	730	601
Assets:									
1980.......	Mil. dol ...	1,384,474	126,639	43,569	34,930	41,963	75,284	179,959	882,129
1985.......	Mil. dol ...	1,932,766	153,883	64,324	52,669	58,019	96,748	208,403	1,298,720
1990.......	Mil. dol ...	2,629,458	142,498	74,477	55,914	72,554	123,967	287,512	1,872,536
1995.......	Mil. dol ...	3,345,229	155,618	87,011	68,538	87,262	159,133	370,263	2,417,403
1997.......	Mil. dol ...	3,746,797	167,921	87,398	76,034	85,186	157,130	397,559	2,775,570
1998.......	Mil. dol ...	3,967,309	170,068	87,937	69,627	86,816	148,060	419,153	2,985,647
1999.......	Mil. dol ...	4,307,317	171,007	86,377	67,560	100,642	138,638	401,804	3,341,289
Net profit: [2]									
1980.......	Mil. dol ...	92,443	7,770	2,235	1,904	2,479	4,532	11,485	62,041
1985.......	Mil. dol ...	87,647	8,601	2,551	2,305	2,819	3,628	7,312	60,431
1990.......	Mil. dol ...	110,128	8,527	5,160	2,769	2,661	3,525	7,110	80,377
1995.......	Mil. dol ...	198,151	13,224	5,668	3,767	5,771	7,000	16,549	146,172
1997.......	Mil. dol ...	244,505	17,948	8,383	4,153	4,675	7,074	18,433	183,836
1998.......	Mil. dol ...	234,386	18,350	6,421	3,790	4,681	5,610	14,364	181,170
1999.......	Mil. dol ...	260,577	17,372	7,639	3,479	4,854	4,663	13,540	209,032

NA Not available.   [1] Beginning 1986, excludes estimates for corporations with less than $250,000 in assets at time of sample selection. Prior periods include estimates for corporations in this size category.   [2] After taxes.

Source: U.S. Census Bureau, *Quarterly Financial Report for Manufacturing, Mining and Trade Corporations.*

No. 896. 1,000 Largest Industrial Corporations—Selected Financial Items by Industry: 1996 and 1997

[Data are medians. for explanation of terms, see source. Minus sign (-) indicates decrease. For definition of median, see Guide to Tabular Presentation]

Industry	Revenue, percent change from 1996	Profits					Total return to investors (percent)	
		Percent change from 1996	As percent of revenue	As percent of assets	As percent of stockholders' equity	Earnings per share, 1987-97 ann. rate	1987-97 ann. rate	1997
Aerospace	13	18	5	6	21	7	21	20
Apparel	7	24	7	9	19	6	12	-1
Beverages	4	17	6	8	17	9	21	32
Building materials, glass	9	66	7	8	23	-2	14	3
Chemicals................	2	3	6	6	17	7	14	19
Computer and data services.......	11	15	5	7	14	14	17	35
Computer peripherals	13	70	7	12	22	13	22	33
Computers, office equipment	12	21	5	5	16	10	12	24
Diversified outsourcing services	15	21	2	6	21	14	19	64
Electronics, electrical equip	10	11	5	7	15	9	17	20
Electronics, network communications..	33	25	14	17	22	27	21	-15
Electronics, semiconductors.......	4	6	12	10	16	23	15	7
Food	4	18	3	7	17	10	18	43
Food services	7	12	2	4	12	15	18	19
Forest and paper products	1	-59	2	2	4	-4	10	6
Industrial and farm equipment.......	10	17	5	6	16	9	15	31
Insurance: Life, health (stock)......	9	36	8	1	11	12	23	42
Insurance: property and casualty (stock)	7	28	9	3	12	9	20	41
Metal products...............	8	20	8	7	17	12	17	36
Metals	3	19	4	5	13	8	14	-5
Motor vehicles and parts	6	36	4	4	17	6	14	37
Petroleum refining	-	6	5	6	14	7	14	22
Pharmaceuticals................	8	12	14	13	27	14	23	34
Pipelines...................	37	-19	3	2	8	6	20	16
Publishing, printing.............	8	-	7	7	15	8	14	38
Savings institutions.............	10	20	10	1	11	5	22	61
Scientific, photo, and control equip ...	8	-	7	7	14	10	14	13
Securities..................	22	25	10	1	19	15	29	81
Soaps, cosmetics..............	6	17	7	10	27	13	23	32
Utilities, gas and electric	6	-	8	3	11	1	14	27
Wholesalers.................	11	14	1	3	11	9	15	18

- Represents or rounds to zero.

Source: Time Warner, New York, NY, *The Fortune Directories* (copyright).

No. 897. Corporate Profits, Taxes, and Dividends: 1990 to 1999

[In billions of dollars (372 represents $372,000,000,000). Covers corporations organized for profit and other entities treated as corporations. Represents profits to U.S. residents, without deduction of depletion charges and exclusive of capital gains and losses; intercorporate dividends from profits of domestic corporations are eliminated; net receipts of dividends, reinvested earnings of incorporated foreign affiliates, and earnings of unincorporated foreign affiliates are added]

Item	1990	1994	1995	1996	1997	1998	1999
Profits before tax	402	573	669	726	796	782	849
Profits tax liability	141	187	211	224	238	240	259
Profits after tax	261	387	458	503	558	542	589
Dividends	166	235	254	298	334	349	365
Undistributed profits	95	152	203	205	224	193	224
Inventory valuation adjustment (IVA)	-13	-12	-18	3	7	21	-13
Capital consumption adjustment	20	12	19	25	35	46	57
Net interest	452	381	390	386	413	436	468
Addenda:							
Corporate profits after tax with IVA/CCA [1]	268	387	458	530	600	608	633
Net cash flow with inventory IVA/CCA [1]	494	634	716	776	845	877	930
Undistributed profits with IVA/CCA [1]	102	152	204	233	267	260	269
Consumption of fixed capital	391	483	512	544	579	617	661
Less: Inventory valuation adjustment (IVA)	-13	-12	-18	3	7	21	-13
Equals: Net cash flow	506	647	734	773	838	856	943

[1] Inventory valuation adjustment/capital consumption adjustment.

Source: U.S. Bureau of Economic Analysis, *National Income and Product Accounts of the United States, 1929-94*, forthcoming, and *Survey of Current Business*, August 2000.

No. 898. Corporate Profits Before Taxes by Industry: 1990 to 1999

[In millions of dollars (401,534 represents $401,534,000,000). Profits are without inventory valuation and capital consumption adjustments. Minus sign (-) indicates loss. See headnote, Table 897]

Industry	1990	1993	1994	1995	1996	1997	1998	1999
Corporate profits before tax	401,534	510,375	573,406	668,454	726,345	792,396	758,172	822,976
Domestic industries [1]	328,812	433,634	496,168	576,442	625,492	681,706	654,672	711,560
Agriculture, forestry, and fishing	1,638	1,911	1,385	1,842	2,950	3,059	3,104	4,355
Agricultural services, forestry, and fishing	574	706	990	1,281	1,592	1,453	(NA)	(NA)
Mining	2,502	1,509	3,348	4,517	8,124	10,972	3,184	2,376
Manufacturing	113,552	107,711	144,709	172,518	175,789	192,312	167,600	183,909
Transportation and public utilities	45,931	69,300	82,954	85,894	92,023	83,991	82,532	89,700
Transportation	954	6,368	10,316	11,613	16,157	18,639	22,148	24,470
Communications	20,049	33,202	36,837	33,604	35,012	25,570	22,966	26,641
Electric, gas, and sanitary services	24,928	29,730	35,801	40,677	40,854	39,782	37,418	38,589
Wholesale trade	21,201	30,614	36,883	35,546	41,588	46,315	50,905	58,455
Retail trade	24,896	41,831	49,187	47,471	54,806	62,648	76,512	84,784
Finance, insurance, and real estate	88,334	129,104	117,726	160,062	171,827	195,658	180,922	190,752
Services	19,836	41,506	46,326	51,327	56,453	61,055	57,155	61,000
Rest of the world	72,722	76,741	77,238	92,012	100,853	110,690	103,500	111,416

NA Not Not available. [1] Consists of receipts by all U.S. residents, including both corporations and persons, of earnings of unincorporated foreign affiliates, dividends from their incorporated foreign affiliates, and their share of their incorporated foreign affiliates, net of corresponding outflows.

No. 899. Corporate Profits With Inventory Valuation and Capital Consumption Adjustments—Financial and Nonfinancial Industries: 1990 to 1999

[In billions of dollars (408.6 represents $408,600,000,000). See headnote, Table 897]

Item	1990	1993	1994	1995	1996	1997	1998	1999
Corporate profits with IVA/CCA [1]	408.6	510.5	573.2	668.8	754.0	838.5	848.4	892.7
Domestic industries	335.9	433.7	496.0	576.8	653.2	730.4	748.4	789.4
Rest of the world	72.7	76.7	77.2	92.0	100.9	108.1	100.0	103.3
Corporate profits with IVA [1]	388.6	506.4	561.0	650.2	729.4	803.2	802.8	835.6
Domestic industries	315.9	429.6	483.7	558.2	628.6	695.1	702.8	732.2
Financial	91.6	127.9	114.7	154.3	165.3	184.2	191.3	208.1
Nonfinancial	224.3	301.7	369.0	403.8	463.3	510.9	511.5	524.2
Manufacturing	109.2	108.4	139.6	166.1	181.2	185.6	168.4	165.6
Transportation and public utilities	44.4	69.6	82.9	85.8	91.4	104.7	109.0	116.3
Wholesale trade	19.1	28.2	33.1	29.4	42.6	46.8	47.2	42.4
Retail trade	21.0	39.7	46.6	44.1	52.9	63.7	69.8	72.9
Other	30.6	55.9	66.8	78.5	95.2	110.1	117.1	127.1

[1] Inventory valuation adjustment and capital consumption adjustment.

Source of Tables 898-899: U.S. Bureau of Economic Analysis, *National Income and Product Accounts of the United States, 1929-94*, forthcoming, and *Survey of Current Business*, August 2000.

Business Enterprise   559

No. 900. Manufacturing, Mining, and Trade Corporations—Profits and Stockholders' Equity Ratios: 1990 to 1999

[Averages of quarterly figures at annual rates. Beginning 1990, manufacturing data exclude estimates for corporations with less than $250,000 in assets at time of sample selection. Data are not necessarily comparable from year to year due to changes in accounting procedures, industry classifications, sampling procedures, etc.; for detail, see source. Based on sample; see source for discussion of methodology. Minus sign (-) indicates loss]

Industry	Ratio of profits to stockholders' equity (percent)				Profits per dollar of sales (cents)				Ratio of stockholders' equity to debt			
	1990	1995	1998	1999	1990	1995	1998	1999	1990	1995	1998	1999
Manufacturing corporations	10.6	16.0	15.8	16.7	3.9	5.6	6.0	6.3	1.3	1.4	1.4	1.3
Durable goods	7.9	15.4	16.4	16.9	3.0	5.2	5.9	6.3	1.6	1.8	1.7	1.6
Lumber and wood products	(NA)	12.6	14.9	24.5	(NA)	3.5	3.8	5.4	(NA)	1.8	1.3	1.1
Furniture and fixtures	(NA)	7.9	19.1	17.4	(NA)	2.2	4.7	4.1	(NA)	1.7	1.4	1.1
Stone, clay, and glass products	5.2	12.2	15.2	20.5	1.7	4.4	5.2	7.3	0.8	1.1	1.1	1.0
Primary metal industries	9.2	19.0	10.0	6.5	2.5	5.4	3.5	2.3	1.1	1.3	1.3	1.2
Iron and steel	6.1	14.8	7.4	1.9	0.9	3.9	2.3	0.6	0.6	1.3	1.2	1.0
Nonferrous metals	10.2	22.1	12.1	10.3	3.9	6.7	4.6	4.1	1.7	1.3	1.4	1.3
Fabricated metal products	11.7	13.0	18.5	18.0	3.3	3.5	5.6	5.7	1.3	1.2	1.2	1.2
Machinery, exc. electrical	8.1	12.1	13.8	16.1	4.3	4.3	5.1	6.3	2.2	1.8	1.8	1.8
Electrical and electronic equipment	7.5	18.8	12.3	14.8	3.0	8.3	6.3	8.2	1.6	2.4	2.4	2.3
Transportation equipment	3.8	17.4	33.2	23.8	1.2	4.5	7.8	5.8	1.9	2.1	1.7	1.6
Motor vehicles and equipment	-1.0	21.0	44.0	25.1	-0.5	4.7	9.1	5.5	2.2	2.6	2.1	1.8
Aircraft, guided missiles, and parts	11.5	10.6	17.9	21.7	3.4	3.6	5.0	6.5	1.6	1.7	1.3	1.3
Instruments and related products	12.8	13.7	9.0	16.0	6.5	7.6	5.2	9.1	1.6	2.3	1.6	1.4
Miscellaneous manufacturing	(NA)	11.1	12.0	13.1	(NA)	3.2	4.1	4.2	(NA)	1.7	1.3	1.0
Nondurable goods	13.1	16.6	15.1	16.5	4.8	6.0	6.0	6.3	1.2	1.2	1.2	1.1
Food and kindred products [1]	16.1	18.4	19.9	21.1	4.0	5.4	5.6	5.7	0.8	1.0	0.9	0.8
Textile mill products	2.7	4.9	10.8	4.5	0.6	1.3	3.2	1.3	0.7	0.9	1.1	0.8
Apparel (includes leather)	(NA)	12.5	17.6	13.6	(NA)	2.7	3.5	2.9	(NA)	1.1	1.0	1.0
Paper and allied products	10.6	20.9	7.6	11.0	4.2	6.9	2.8	4.1	1.1	0.9	0.9	0.9
Printing and publishing	8.2	14.8	20.1	20.6	3.6	6.1	7.5	7.6	1.2	1.3	1.1	1.0
Chemicals and allied products	16.8	21.0	20.0	18.9	7.9	9.1	9.8	9.0	1.4	1.2	1.2	1.1
Industrial	13.1	16.2	11.9	11.2	6.6	6.6	5.2	5.0	1.4	1.0	0.8	0.8
Drugs	27.1	26.7	29.1	28.2	15.7	14.4	15.9	14.3	2.2	1.4	1.5	1.4
Residual of chemicals	(NA)	20.3	17.6	15.5	(NA)	7.6	8.5	7.3	(NA)	1.3	1.3	1.2
Petroleum and coal products	12.7	10.6	5.2	11.5	5.6	4.9	3.1	5.9	1.7	1.7	2.1	2.0
Rubber and misc. plastics products	6.9	15.3	15.7	13.4	1.8	4.1	4.4	3.8	1.0	1.3	1.1	1.0
Mining corporations [2]	8.2	2.1	-5.7	2.1	5.8	1.9	-5.3	2.1	1.3	1.4	1.2	1.1
Retail trade corporations [2]	8.4	10.0	14.4	14.1	1.0	1.6	2.5	2.5	0.6	1.0	1.1	1.1
Wholesale trade corporations [2]	5.0	9.1	8.5	9.8	0.6	1.2	1.3	1.5	1.0	0.8	1.0	1.0

NA Not available.   [1] Tobacco included in food and kindred products.   [2] Includes estimates for corporations with assets of $50 million and over at time of sample selection.

No. 901. Manufacturing Corporations—Selected Finances: 1980 to 1999

[In billions of dollars (1,913 represents $1,913,000,000,000). Data are not necessarily comparable from year to year due to changes in accounting procedures, industry classifications, sampling procedures, etc.; for detail, see source]

Year	All manufacturing corps.					Durable goods industries					Nondurable goods industries				
		Profits [1]		Stock holders' equi- ty [1]	Debt [2]		Profits [1]		Stock holders' equi- ty [1]	Debt [2]		Profits [1]		Stock holders' equi- ty [1]	Debt [2]
	Sales	Before taxes	After taxes			Sales	Before taxes	After taxes			Sales	Before taxes	After taxes		
1980	1,913	146	93	668	292	889	57	36	318	143	1,024	88	57	350	149
1982	2,039	108	71	770	371	913	35	22	356	177	1,126	74	49	415	193
1983	2,114	133	86	813	368	974	49	30	372	168	1,141	84	56	440	200
1984	2,335	166	108	864	405	1,108	76	49	396	166	1,228	90	59	469	239
1985	2,331	137	88	866	454	1,143	62	39	421	167	1,189	76	49	445	267
1986	2,221	129	83	875	501	1,126	52	33	436	168	1,095	77	51	438	298
1987	2,378	173	116	901	553	1,178	78	53	444	229	1,200	95	63	457	324
1988	2,596	215	154	958	622	1,285	92	67	469	265	1,312	124	87	489	357
1989	2,745	188	135	999	733	1,357	75	56	501	308	1,389	113	80	498	425
1990	2,811	158	110	1,044	782	1,357	57	41	515	328	1,454	101	69	529	453
1991	2,761	99	66	1,064	814	1,304	14	7	507	338	1,457	85	59	557	476
1992 [3]	2,890	31	22	1,035	819	1,390	-34	-24	474	335	1,500	65	46	561	485
1993	3,015	118	83	1,040	819	1,490	39	27	483	327	1,525	79	56	557	492
1994	3,256	244	175	1,110	815	1,658	121	87	533	316	1,598	123	88	577	500
1995	3,528	275	198	1,241	862	1,808	131	94	614	333	1,721	144	104	627	529
1996	3,758	307	225	1,348	920	1,942	147	106	674	366	1,816	160	119	674	554
1997	3,922	331	244	1,464	953	2,076	167	121	744	386	1,847	164	123	721	566
1998	3,949	315	234	1,487	1,065	2,169	175	128	794	458	1,781	140	107	694	607
1999	4,137	356	261	1,629	1,179	2,281	200	144	896	524	1,856	156	117	733	656

[1] Beginning 1998, profits before and after income taxes reflect inclusion of minority stockholders' interest in net income before and after income taxes.   [2] Annual data are average equity for the year (using four end-of-quarter figures).   [3] Data for 1992 (most significantly 1992: 1st qtr.) reflect the early adoption of Financial Accounting Standards Board Statement 106 (Employer's Accounting for Post-Retirement Benefits Other Than Pensions) by a large number of companies during the fourth quarter of 1992. Data for 1993: 1st qtr. also reflect adoption of Statement 106. Corporations must show the cumulative effect of a change in accounting principle in the first quarter of the year in which the change is adopted.

Source of Tables 900 and 901: Through 1981, U.S. Federal Trade Commission; thereafter, U.S. Bureau of Census, Quarterly Financial Report for Manufacturing, Mining, and Trade Corporations. In U.S. Council of Economic Advisers, Economic Report of the President, annual.

No. 902. U.S. Multinational Companies—Gross Product: 1995 and 1997

[In millions of dollars (1,831,046 represents $1,831,046,000,000). Gross product measures valued added by a firm. Consists of nonbank U.S. parent companies and their nonbank foreign affiliates. A U.S. parent comprises the domestic operations of a multinational and is a U.S. person that owns or controls 10 percent or more of the voting securities, or the equivalent, of a foreign business enterprise. A U.S. person can be an incorporated business enterprise. A majority-owned foreign affiliate is a foreign business enterprise in which a U.S. parent company owns or controls 50 percent or more of the voting securities]

Industry	U.S. multinationals		U.S. parents		Majority-owned foreign affiliates	
	1995	1997	1995	1997	1995	1997
All industries	1,831,046	2,089,796	1,365,470	1,570,490	462,959	519,306
Petroleum	205,044	229,602	110,014	125,214	95,030	104,388
Manufacturing	1,023,697	1,080,824	723,182	765,122	300,515	315,702
Food and kindred products	119,282	107,813	78,223	69,852	41,059	37,961
Chemical and allied products	182,827	199,911	116,949	126,931	65,878	72,980
Primary and fabricated metals	59,387	55,242	39,937	41,926	19,450	13,316
Industrial machinery and equipment [1]	139,767	148,586	88,818	92,094	50,949	56,492
Electronic and other electric equipment [1]	103,693	127,535	77,286	94,413	26,407	33,122
Transportation equipment	202,108	220,862	152,834	167,277	49,274	53,585
Other	216,632	220,876	169,135	172,630	47,497	48,246
Wholesale trade	39,127	69,184	30,853	51,621	8,274	17,563
Finance (exc. dep. inst.), insurance & real estate	72,489	106,548	52,813	81,872	19,676	24,676
Finance, except depository institutions	22,370	(NA)	18,205	40,919	4,165	7,904
Insurance	41,677	(NA)	32,815	39,523	8,862	11,194
Real estate	(D)	(NA)	1,667	1,726	31	243
Holding companies	5,286	(NA)	127	-296	5,159	4,364
Services	118,328	160,626	97,623	130,070	20,705	30,558
Hotels and other lodging places	9,178	(NA)	7,557	10,051	1,621	1,065
Business services	51,915	(NA)	38,667	60,592	13,248	21,797
Advertising	5,181	(NA)	2,820	4,303	2,361	2,774
Equipment rental (exc. auto, computers)	1,288	(NA)	1,100	1,184	188	126
Computer and data processing	24,094	(NA)	18,481	31,578	5,613	12,216
Business services, n.e.c.	21,352	(NA)	16,266	23,526	5,086	6,680
Automotive rental and leasing	3,717	(NA)	3,346	3,247	371	442
Motion pictures, television tape and film	11,613	(NA)	10,126	13,107	1,487	(D)
Health services	17,569	(NA)	17,218	17,244	351	186
Engineering and architectural services [1]	6,077	(NA)	5,301	5,666	776	1,039
Management and public relations	5,210	(NA)	3,621	6,844	1,589	1,939
Other	13,051	(NA)	11,788	13,320	1,263	(D)
Other industries	372,360	443,012	350,984	416,591	21,376	26,421

D Figure withheld to avoid disclosure pertaining to a specific organization or individual.   NA Not available.   [1] For changes in industry definition, see text, this section.

Source: U.S. Bureau of Economic Analysis, *Survey of Current Business*, September 1998.

No. 903. U.S. Multinational Companies—Selected Characteristics: 1997

[Preliminary. In billions of dollars (8,567.3 represents $8,567,300,000,000), except as indicated. Consists of nonbank U.S. parent companies and their nonbank foreign affiliates. U.S. parent is a U.S. person that owns or controls directly or indirectly, 10 percent or more of the voting securities of an incorporated foreign business enterprise, or an equivalent interest in an unincorporated foreign business enterprise. A U.S. person can be an incorporated business enterprise. A foreign affiliate is a foreign business enterprise owned or controlled by a U.S. parent company]

Industry [1]	U.S. parents				Foreign affiliates				U.S. exports shipped to foreign affiliates	U.S. imports shipped from foreign affiliates
	Total assets	Sales	Employment (1,000)	Employee compensation	Total assets	Sales	Employment (1,000)	Employee compensation		
All industries	8,567.3	4,859.6	19,867.4	894.8	3,397.3	2,356.4	8,018.0	261.2	215.8	178.7
Petroleum	459.9	412.8	483.2	30.9	295.3	360.5	226.1	11.4	5.0	13.4
Manufacturing	2,695.2	2,233.1	8,622.7	464.2	884.1	1,086.1	4,592.9	142.4	138.6	150.2
Food and kindred products	223.6	226.9	732.8	29.8	112.9	127.7	598.0	14.1	3.0	3.6
Chemicals and allied products	479.9	331.1	966.8	67.2	220.9	208.0	622.4	24.9	16.7	10.7
Primary and fabricated metals	129.3	126.9	611.4	26.9	47.2	44.7	244.7	7.7	2.9	3.9
Industrial machinery and equipment	293.5	296.2	1,103.8	59.9	123.3	178.3	634.1	25.0	20.9	30.0
Electronic and electric equipment	438.1	307.5	1,175.1	60.3	84.5	110.6	774.5	15.0	22.6	25.0
Transportation equipment	640.2	524.9	1,657.6	108.9	131.6	244.2	724.2	26.4	56.9	61.6
Other	490.6	419.6	2,375.2	111.2	163.8	172.7	995.0	29.4	15.7	15.4
Wholesale trade	217.0	396.2	756.9	32.6	223.5	422.3	588.0	27.1	65.4	12.7
Finance (except depository institutions), insurance, real estate	3,514.5	552.9	1,052.1	79.8	1,498.1	135.3	218.8	12.6	0.3	0.1
Services	335.1	249.3	3,024.3	90.2	154.2	128.6	988.9	35.7	2.4	0.3
Other industries	1,345.6	1,015.2	5,928.3	197.1	342.0	223.6	1,403.3	32.1	4.3	2.1

[1] Represents industry of U.S. parent or industry of foreign affiliate.

Source: U.S. Bureau of Economic Analysis, *Survey of Current Business*, July 1999.

No. 904. Gross Product, Employment, and Capital Expenditures of Nonbank U.S. MNCs, U.S. Parents, and Foreign Affiliates: 1990 to 1997

[Gross product and capital expenditures in millions of dollars; employees in thousands. MNC=Multinational company. MOFA=Majority-owned foreign affiliate]

Item	1990	1993	1994	1995	1996	1997 [1]	Percent change at annual rates		
							1989-94	1995-96	1996-97
GROSS PRODUCT									
MNCs worldwide:									
Parents and all affiliates .	(NA)	(NA)	(NA)	(NA)	(NA)	(NA)	(NA)	(NA)	(NA)
Parents and MOFAs [2] . . .	(NA)	(NA)	1,717,488	1,831,046	1,965,438	2,089,796	4.7	8.1	5.6
Parents	(NA)	(NA)	1,313,792	1,365,470	1,466,999	1,570,490	4.7	8.4	6.1
Affiliates, total	(NA)	(NA)	(NA)	(NA)	(NA)	(NA)	(NA)	(NA)	(NA)
MOFAs	356,033	359,179	403,696	465,576	498,310	519,306	4.8	7.0	4.2
Other	(NA)	(NA)	(NA)	(NA)	(NA)	(NA)	(NA)	(NA)	(NA)
EMPLOYEES									
MNCs worldwide:									
Parents and all affiliates .	25,264	24,222	25,670	25,921	26,334	27,885	0.2	1.6	5.9
Parents and MOFAs	23,786	22,760	24,273	24,500	24,867	26,392	0.3	1.5	6.1
Parents	18,430	17,537	18,565	18,576	18,790	19,867	-0.2	1.2	5.7
Affiliates, total	6,834	6,685	7,105	7,345	7,544	8,018	1.4	2.7	6.3
MOFAs	5,356	5,223	5,707	5,924	6,077	6,525	2.2	2.6	7.4
Other	1,478	1,461	1,398	1,421	1,467	1,493	-1.5	3.2	1.8
CAPITAL EXPENDITURES									
MNCs worldwide:									
Parents and all affiliates .	(NA)	(NA)	328,240	(NA)	(NA)	(NA)	3.7	(NA)	(NA)
Parents and MOFAs	274,614	271,661	303,364	323,616	340,510	387,148	3.5	5.2	13.7
Parents	213,079	207,437	231,917	248,017	260,048	298,902	3.1	4.9	14.9
Affiliates, total	(NA)	(NA)	96,323	(NA)	(NA)	(NA)	5.1	(NA)	(NA)
MOFAs	61,535	64,224	71,447	75,599	80,462	88,246	4.6	6.4	9.7
Other	(NA)	(NA)	24,876	(NA)	(NA)	(NA)	6.7	(NA)	(NA)

NA Not available.   [1] Break-in-series. See source, appendix for details.   [2] Majority-owned foreign affiliate.

Source: U.S. Bureau of Economic Analysis, *Survey of Current Business*, July 1999.

No. 905. Nonbank U.S. MNCs, U.S. Parents, and MOFAs by Industry of U.S. Parent: 1989 and 1997

[In billions of dollars (1,364.9 represents $1,364,900,000,000). MNC=Multinational company. MOFA=Majority-owned foreign affiliate]

Item	MNCs			Parents			MOFAs		
	Gross product	Profit-type return	Capital expen-ditures	Gross product	Profit-type return	Capital expen-ditures	Gross product	Profit-type return	Capital expendi-tures
1989: All industries	1,364.9	251.4	260.5	1,044.9	164.9	201.8	320.0	86.5	58.7
Petroleum	165.7	31.3	41.5	93.1	15.8	26.8	72.6	15.5	14.7
Manufacturing	793.8	147.0	133.2	586.6	86.2	98.7	207.2	60.7	34.5
Food and kindred products	79.5	19.5	12.0	60.3	14.6	9.4	19.2	5.0	2.6
Chemicals and allied products	141.0	38.4	29.3	97.1	23.4	20.3	43.9	15.0	9.0
Primary and fabricated metals	45.8	9.6	7.2	37.6	6.3	5.4	8.2	3.3	1.8
Industrial machinery and equip. . . .	116.1	16.2	18.4	70.9	1.8	11.5	45.3	14.4	6.9
Electronic/other electric equip	68.5	12.4	13.6	56.1	9.2	11.0	12.4	3.2	2.6
Transportation equipment	160.3	22.0	24.3	121.1	11.6	18.6	39.2	10.4	5.7
Other manufacturing	182.6	28.8	28.3	143.4	19.3	22.4	39.2	9.5	5.9
Wholesale trade	28.8	5.6	6.1	22.6	3.2	5.0	6.2	2.5	1.1
Finance (except banking), insurance and real estate	62.7	20.2	10.0	50.5	16.4	7.6	12.2	3.8	2.4
Services	67.0	7.8	16.7	57.1	5.9	13.6	9.9	1.8	3.0
Other industries	246.9	39.5	53.1	235.0	37.4	50.2	12.0	2.1	2.9
1997: All industries	2,089.8	485.0	387.1	1,570.5	337.0	298.9	519.3	148.0	88.2
Petroleum	229.6	53.6	49.2	125.2	24.2	30.2	104.4	29.4	19.0
Manufacturing	1,080.8	248.8	166.8	765.1	154.5	116.3	315.7	94.3	50.5
Food and kindred products	107.8	31.7	12.7	69.9	20.1	9.2	38.0	11.6	3.6
Chemicals and allied products	199.9	61.6	34.8	126.9	33.2	23.3	73.0	28.4	11.6
Primary and fabricated metals	55.2	10.0	7.2	41.9	6.9	5.6	13.3	3.0	1.6
Industrial machinery and equip. . . .	148.6	36.4	20.7	92.1	19.0	14.1	56.5	17.3	6.6
Electronic and other electric equipment	127.5	37.3	28.3	94.4	26.0	21.2	33.1	11.3	7.0
Transportation equipment	220.9	36.6	32.2	167.3	24.3	18.8	53.6	12.3	13.3
Other manufacturing	220.9	35.4	30.9	172.6	25.0	24.1	48.2	10.4	6.8
Wholesale trade	69.2	13.5	12.2	51.6	8.0	9.9	17.6	5.5	2.3
Finance (except depository institutions), insurance and real estate	106.5	54.0	16.0	81.9	44.0	13.1	24.7	10.0	2.9
Services	160.6	24.6	25.0	130.1	20.0	21.5	30.6	4.6	3.5
Other industries	443.0	90.5	118.0	416.6	86.3	108.0	26.4	4.2	10.0

Source: U.S. Bureau of Economic Analysis, *Survey of Current Business*, September 1998 and April 1999.

Section 18

Communications and Information Technology

This section presents statistics on the various communications media: telephone, computers, Internet, telegraph, radio, television, newspapers, and periodicals and the usage, finances, and operations of the Postal Service. Expenditure data for advertising in the media are also included.

Communication media—The U.S. Census Bureau's *Annual Survey of Communication Services* (ASCS) covers all employer firms with one or more establishments that are primarily engaged in providing point-to-point communication services, whether by wire or radio, and whether intended to be received aurally or visually. This includes telephone communications, including cellular and other radiotelephone services; telegraph and other message communications, such as electronic mail services, facsimile transmission services, telex services, etc.; radio and television broadcasting stations and networks; cable and other pay television services; and other communication services, such as radar station operations, satellite earth stations, satellite or missile tracking stations, etc. The report presents statistics that are summarized by kind-of-business classification based on the 1987 edition of the *Standard Industrial Classification Manual*. See text, Section 17, Business.

The Federal Communications Commission (FCC), established in 1934, regulates wire and radio communications. Only the largest carriers and holding companies file annual or monthly financial reports. The FCC has jurisdiction over interstate and foreign communication services but not over intrastate or local services. The gross operating revenues of the telephone carriers reporting annually to the FCC, however, are estimated to cover about 90 percent of the revenues of all U.S. telephone companies. Data are not comparable with Census Bureau *Annual Survey of Communication Services* because of coverage (ASCS includes all domestic long-distance telephone companies, all local exchange carriers, and all cellular telephone companies) and different accounting practices for those telephone companies which report to the FCC.

Reports filed by the broadcasting industry cover all radio and television stations operating in the United States. The private radio services represent the largest and most diverse group of licensees regulated by the FCC. These services provide voice, data communications, point-to-point, and point-to-multipoint radio communications for fixed and mobile communicators. Major users of these services are small businesses, the aviation industry, the maritime trades, the land transportation industry, manufacturing industry, state and local public safety and governmental authorities, emergency medical service providers, amateur radio operators, and personal radio operations (CB and the General Mobile Radio Service). The FCC also licenses entities as private and common carriers. Private and common carriers provide fixed and land mobile communications service on a for-profit basis. Principal sources of wire, radio, and television data are the FCC's *Annual Report* and its annual *Statistics of Communications Common Carriers*.

Statistics on publishing are available from the Census Bureau, as well as from various private agencies. The censuses of manufactures (conducted by the Census Bureau every 5 years, through 1992, for the years ending in "2" and "7") provide statistics on newspapers, periodicals, books, and pamphlets. Beginning 1997, these data are collected in the information

Communications and Information Technology 563

sector of the economic census. See Section 32. Editor & Publisher Co., New York, NY, presents annual data on the number and circulation of daily and Sunday newspapers in its *International Year Book*. Monthly data on new books and new editions appear in *Publishers Weekly*, issued by R. R. Bowker Company, New York. (See Table 928 for annual data.)

Advertising—Data on advertising expenditures are compiled primarily by McCann-Erickson, Inc., which compiles certain of the data shown (see Table 937). Monthly index figures of advertising in certain media are also published periodically by McCann-Erickson in *Advertising Age*.

The Broadcast Advertisers Reports distinguishes between spot and local advertising primarily on the basis of the type of advertiser to whom the time is sold, rather than how and by whom it is sold. In general, time purchased on behalf of retail or service establishments in the market is considered local, even though the establishments may be part of a national or regional chain. That is, spot advertising promotes a product, while local advertising promotes a given establishment. Network advertising, mutually exclusive of spot and local, is broadcast through the network system.

Postal Service—The Postal Service provides mail processing and delivery services within the United States. The Postal Reorganization Act of 1970 created the Postal Service, effective July 1971, as an independent establishment of the Federal Executive Branch.

Revenue and cost analysis describes the Postal Service's system of attributing revenues and costs to classes of mail and service. This system draws primarily upon probability sampling techniques to develop estimates of revenues, volumes, and weights, as well as costs by class of mail and special service. The costs attributed to classes of mail and special services are primarily incremental costs which vary in response to changes in volume; they account for roughly 60 percent of the total costs of the Postal Service. The balance represents "institutional costs." Statistics on revenues, volume of mail, and distribution of expenditures are presented in the Postal Service's annual report, *Cost and Revenue Analysis*, and its *Annual Report of the Postmaster General* and its annual *Comprehensive Statement on Postal Operations*.

Statistical reliability—For a discussion of statistical collection and estimation, sampling procedures, and measures of statistical reliability applicable to Census Bureau data, see Appendix III.

U.S. Census Bureau, Statistical Abstract of the United States: 2000

No. 906. Gross Domestic Income in Information Technologies (IT) Industries: 1992 to 2000

[In millions of dollars (371,080 represents $371,080,000,000), except as noted]

Industry	1987 SIC [1] code	1992	1995	1998 est.	1999 est.	2000 est.
Total all IT industries	(X)	371,080	491,292	665,530	746,092	814,727
Percent share of the economy	(X)	5.9	6.7	7.6	8.0	8.3
Hardware	(X)	110,050	155,409	210,914	226,214	243,506
Computers and equipment, calc. machines	3571,2,5,7pt., 3578,9pt	24,102	31,036	39,211	42,622	46,330
Computers and equipment wholesale sales	5045pt	39,743	51,114	75,084	81,106	88,162
Computers and equipment retail sales	5734pt	1,915	2,861	3,407	3,687	4,008
Electron tubes	3671	1,053	1,206	1,317	1,402	1,493
Printed circuit boards	3672	3,556	4,406	5,527	5,604	5,683
Semiconductors	3674	18,308	40,836	57,055	60,763	64,713
Passive electronic components	3675,6,7,8,9pt, 3661pt	13,494	15,310	12,072	12,881	13,744
Industrial instruments for measurement	3823	2,552	2,526	4,874	5,215	5,580
Instruments for measuring electricity	3825pt	3,493	3,981	8,383	8,953	9,562
Laboratory analytical instruments	3826	1,835	2,134	3,986	3,982	4,233
Software/services [2]	(X)	75,490	111,350	185,609	213,986	245,644
Computer programming services	7371	18,624	26,120	47,796	55,013	62,715
Prepackaged software	7372	14,555	22,768	34,497	40,016	46,419
Computer integrated systems design	7373	11,814	13,599	24,692	28,420	32,598
Computer processing and data preparation	7374	12,554	21,844	28,062	32,300	37,048
Information retrieval services	7375	2,879	3,910	8,977	10,333	11,852
Computer services management	7376	1,910	2,090	2,942	3,386	3,884
Computer rental leasing	7377	1,528	1,880	2,944	3,389	3,887
Computer maintenance and repair	7378	4,989	6,949	10,029	11,544	13,241
Computer related services, n.e.c. [3]	7379	4,406	9,305	21,261	24,472	28,069
Communications hardware [2]	(X)	23,970	30,775	46,710	49,151	51,816
Telephone and telegraph equipment	3661pt,3577pt,3679pt	10,251	12,139	21,807	22,592	23,405
Radio and TV and communications equip	3663, 3679pt,3699	10,134	14,310	20,642	22,252	23,987
Communications services [2]	(X)	161,570	193,758	222,298	256,740	273,761
Telephone and telegraph communications	481, 2, 9	129,960	145,491	159,712	189,400	199,109
Television broadcasting	4833	11,649	18,442	22,740	23,520	26,551
Cable and other pay TV services	4841	14,992	21,778	29,798	32,266	35,231

X Not applicable.   [1] 1987 Standard Industrial Classification code. See text, Section 17, Business.   [2] Includes other industries, not shown separately.   [3]N.e.c. means not elsewhere classified.

No. 907. Information Technologies (IT)—Employment and Wages: 1992 to 1998

[89,956 represents 89,956,000]

Industry	1987 SIC [1] code	Employment (1,000)			Annual wages per worker (dol.)		
		1992	1995	1998	1992	1995	1998
Total private	(X)	89,956	97,885	106,007	25,400	27,200	31,400
Total IT-producing industries	(X)	3,875	4,240	5,156	41,300	46,400	58,000
Hardware	(X)	1,436	1,475	1,708	42,400	46,300	58,000
Electronic computers	3571	242	190	200	52,400	59,600	83,900
Computers and equipment wholesalers	5045pt	277	285	367	52,500	54,300	69,700
Computers and equipment retailers	5734pt	75	94	126	32,200	33,800	40,400
Computer storage devices & peripheral equipment	3572,7	91	105	119	41,200	46,500	57,400
Computer terminals, office & accounting, machines, & office machines, n.e.c. [2]	3575,8,9	58	58	61	43,300	46,600	56,900
Electron tubes	3671	27	24	20	38,400	41,900	46,400
Semiconductors	3674	217	235	284	44,500	53,800	64,400
Printed circuit boards, electronic capacitors	3672,5-8	157	187	208	25,700	28,300	32,900
Electronic components, n.e.c. [2]	3679	127	135	148	29,700	32,900	37,500
Industrial instruments for measurement	3823	61	64	67	35,100	38,400	46,400
Instruments for measuring electricity	3825	76	71	77	42,500	51,600	62,900
Analytical instruments	3826	28	28	32	38,700	44,200	54,300
Software/services [3]	(X)	854	1,110	1,625	44,300	50,700	65,300
Computer programming services	7371	169	245	370	46,200	52,700	64,700
Prepackaged software	7372	131	181	252	57,000	63,700	94,100
Computer integrated systems design	7373	103	130	178	48,600	54,700	65,400
Computer processing & data preparation	7374	204	223	254	34,400	39,700	45,800
Information retrieval services	7375	45	57	98	36,700	42,200	63,700
Computer maintenance & repair	7378	43	49	60	36,600	37,800	41,200
Computer services management, rental & leasing, & maintenance & repair	7376,7,9	141	205	387	46,000	51,800	64,100
Communications equipment [3]	(X)	317	337	353	38,900	43,200	53,700
Telephone and telegraph equipment	3661	110	112	126	42,400	49,900	62,400
Radio and TV communications equipment & communications equipment, n.e.c. [2]	3663,9	129	153	156	39,100	42,700	52,100
Communication services [3]	(X)	1,269	1,318	1,469	38,600	43,700	50,900
Telephone communications	481	885	900	1,007	41,400	46,800	53,700
Telephone & telegraph communications	482,489	26	27	35	41,700	48,500	56,200
Television broadcasting	4833	115	123	131	41,400	47,200	54,600
Cable & other pay TV services	4841	131	156	181	29,600	34,600	42,200

X Not applicable.   [1] 1987 Standard Industrial Classification code. See text, Section 17, Business.   [2] N.e.c. means not elsewhere classified.   [3] Includes other industries, not shown separately.
Source of Tables 906 and 907: U.S. Department of Commerce, Economics and Statistics Administration, *The Digital Economy*, June 2000.

Communications and Information Technology   565

No. 908. Communications Industry—Finances: 1995 to 1998

[In millions of dollars (165,783 represents $165,783,000,000). Covers publicly reporting media and communications companies with revenues of over $1 million in 13 media and communication industry segments]

Industry	Revenue				Operating income			
	1995	1996	1997	1998	1995	1996	1997	1998
Total	165,783	192,471	219,237	242,386	22,223	23,947	27,952	30,840
Television broadcasting	21,634	25,287	27,760	30,763	3,531	4,521	5,233	5,565
Television network companies	15,805	18,275	19,547	22,030	2,117	2,630	2,998	3,244
Television station broadcasters......	5,829	7,013	8,212	8,733	1,414	1,891	2,234	2,322
Radio broadcasting	2,370	3,384	5,160	6,799	399	576	981	1,377
Radio station broadcasters	2,219	3,207	4,913	6,537	385	558	956	1,353
Radio network companies	151	177	247	262	14	18	25	25
Subscription video services.........	24,989	30,722	38,602	40,498	3,280	3,055	4,037	3,688
Subscription video services operators .	18,949	23,041	28,991	29,842	2,578	1,966	2,694	2,175
Cable and pay-per-view networks	6,039	7,682	9,611	10,656	702	1,089	1,343	1,513
Entertainment.....................	30,549	39,168	42,996	46,671	3,786	3,503	3,511	4,375
Newspaper publishing	20,692	21,946	24,053	25,962	2,865	3,464	4,846	5,107
Consumer book publishing	3,490	3,525	3,278	3,065	432	177	238	75
Consumer magazine publishing	6,638	7,091	7,294	7,557	659	641	811	856
The Internet	1,187	2,642	3,902	4,737	-84	-245	-826	-967
Business-to-business communications. . .	2,696	2,999	3,226	3,564	346	408	481	457
Professional and educational publishing .	12,358	10,728	12,070	13,593	1,360	1,246	1,007	1,430
Business information services	21,351	24,665	27,495	31,151	3,871	4,489	5,199	5,807
Financial information.	10,942	12,337	13,609	15,091	2,249	2,336	2,710	2,880
Marketing information	2,112	2,473	3,012	3,339	202	295	365	398
Technology information	366	496	650	832	50	93	120	167
Health-care information.	1,587	1,843	1,653	1,946	191	286	258	287
Other business information companies.	6,344	7,516	8,570	9,944	1,180	1,479	1,748	2,075
Advertising agencies	10,941	12,911	14,639	16,914	1,108	1,364	1,508	1,943
Specialty media	6,889	7,403	8,764	11,114	672	750	925	1,127

Source: Veronis, Suhler & Associates Inc., New York, NY, Communications Industry Report, annual (copyright).

No. 909. Media Usage and Consumer Spending: 1993 to 2003

[Estimates of time spent were derived using rating data for television and radio, survey research and consumer purchase data for recorded music, newspapers, magazines, books, home video, admissions for movies, and consumer online/Internet access services. Adults 18 and older except for recorded music, movies in theaters, and video games where estimates include persons 12 and older]

Item	1993	1994	1995	1996	1997	1998	1999, proj.	2000, proj.	2001, proj.	2002, proj.	2003, proj.
HOURS PER PERSON PER YEAR											
Total.	3,295	3,393	3,391	3,393	3,371	3,426	3,448	3,491	3,523	3,555	3,587
Television.	1,535	1,560	1,575	1,567	1,561	1,573	1,579	1,591	1,595	1,605	1,610
Broadcast TV.	1,082	1,091	1,019	980	926	884	840	805	773	751	729
Network stations [1]	920	919	836	803	748	708	660	627	596	570	548
Independent stations	162	172	183	177	178	176	180	178	177	181	181
Subscription video services . .	453	469	556	587	635	689	739	786	822	854	881
Basic networks [2]	375	388	468	498	537	582	632	675	712	738	762
Premium channels.	78	81	88	89	98	107	107	111	110	116	119
Radio.	1,082	1,102	1,091	1,091	1,082	1,050	1,037	1,024	1,014	1,003	992
Recorded music	248	294	289	289	265	284	288	294	300	308	319
Daily newspapers	170	169	165	161	159	156	154	152	151	150	149
Consumer books	99	102	99	99	95	95	94	95	97	98	99
Consumer magazines.	85	84	84	83	82	82	81	80	79	79	78
Home video [3]	43	45	45	49	50	56	57	60	62	64	66
Movies in theaters	12	12	12	12	13	13	13	14	14	14	15
Home video games	19	22	24	26	36	43	48	59	65	66	67
Consumer online Internet access	2	3	7	16	28	74	97	122	146	168	192
CONSUMER SPENDING PER PERSON PER YEAR (dol.)											
Total.	428.55	450.94	472.90	504.65	533.38	576.90	622.31	674.60	722.87	767.28	814.12
Television.	110.12	111.08	125.19	139.13	154.01	168.78	188.55	206.53	225.01	243.89	263.66
Broadcast TV.	-	-	-	-	-	-	-	-	-	-	-
Subscription video services . .	110.12	111.08	125.19	139.13	154.01	168.78	188.55	206.53	225.01	243.89	263.66
Radio	-	-	-	-	-	-	-	-	-	-	-
Recorded music	47.42	56.35	56.92	57.34	55.42	61.54	63.07	66.21	68.92	72.72	76.60
Daily newspapers	48.25	49.12	50.08	50.90	50.90	51.39	51.85	52.76	53.46	54.65	55.72
Consumer books	72.75	77.62	79.23	81.00	80.69	84.35	88.73	93.33	98.13	102.77	107.13
Consumer magazines.	35.27	36.36	36.10	36.95	38.03	38.30	39.51	40.36	41.34	42.37	43.39
Home video [3]	73.30	78.09	80.01	86.09	85.82	92.14	97.51	106.14	114.86	120.27	126.77
Movies in theaters	24.33	25.20	25.38	27.05	28.83	31.16	32.18	33.60	35.14	36.68	38.22
Home video games	12.56	11.75	10.54	11.45	16.42	18.45	21.01	26.59	29.50	30.18	30.59
Consumer online Internet access.	4.54	5.38	9.44	14.74	23.26	30.78	39.89	49.07	56.52	63.74	72.03

- Represents zero. [1] Includes affiliates of the Fox network and, beginning 1995, UPN and WB. [2] Includes TBS. [3] Playback of prerecorded tapes only.

Source: Veronis, Suhler & Associates Inc., New York, NY, Communications Industry Report, annual (copyright).

No. 910. Utilization of Selected Media: 1970 to 1998

[62.0 represents 62,000,000]

Item	Unit	1970	1980	1985	1990	1993	1994	1995	1996	1997	1998
Households with—											
Telephone service [1]	Percent .	87.0	93.0	91.8	93.3	94.2	93.9	93.9	93.8	93.9	94.1
Radio [2]	Millions .	62.0	78.6	87.1	94.4	97.3	98.0	98.0	98.0	98.0	(NA)
Percent of total households . .	Percent .	98.6	99.0	99.0	99.0	99.0	99.0	99.0	99.0	99.0	99.0
Average number of sets	Number .	5.1	5.5	5.5	5.6	5.6	5.6	5.6	5.6	5.6	5.6
Television [3]	Millions .	59	76	85	92	93	94	95	96	97	98
Percent of total households . .	Percent .	95.3	97.9	98.1	98.2	98.3	98.3	98.3	98.3	98.4	98.3
Television sets in homes	Millions .	81	128	155	193	201	211	217	223	229	235
Average number of sets per home	Number .	1.4	1.7	1.8	2.1	2.2	2.2	2.3	2.3	2.4	2.4
Color set households	Millions .	21	63	78	90	92	93	94	95	97	98
Cable television [4]	Millions .	4	15	36	52	57	59	60	63	64	66
Percent of TV households . . .	Percent .	6.7	19.9	42.8	56.4	61.4	62.4	63.4	65.3	66.5	67.2
VCRs [4]	Millions .	(NA)	1	18	63	72	74	77	79	82	83
Percent of TV households . . .	Percent .	(NA)	1.1	20.8	68.6	77.1	79.0	81.0	82.2	84.2	84.6
Commercial radio stations: [2]											
AM	Number .	4,323	4,589	[5]4,718	4,987	4,994	4,913	4,150	4,857	4,762	4,793
FM	Number .	2,196	3,282	[5]3,875	4,392	4,971	5,109	5,730	5,419	5,542	5,662
Television stations: [6] Total	Number .	862	1,011	1,197	1,442	1,506	1,512	1,532	1,533	1,574	1,572
Commercial	Number .	677	734	883	1,092	1,138	1,145	1,161	1,174	1,205	1,204
VHF	Number .	501	516	520	547	552	561	562	554	560	562
UHF	Number .	176	218	363	545	586	584	599	620	645	642
Cable television:											
Systems [7]	Number .	2,490	4,225	6,844	9,575	11,217	11,214	11,218	11,119	10,950	10,845
Households served [8]	Millions .	4.5	17.7	39.9	54.9	58.8	60.5	63.0	64.6	65.9	67.4
Daily newspaper circulation [9]	Millions .	62.1	62.2	62.8	62.3	59.8	59.3	58.2	57.0	56.7	55.9

NA Not available. [1] For occupied housing units. 1970 and 1980 as of April 1; all other years as of March. Source: U.S. Census Bureau, 1970 and 1980 Census of Housing, Vol. 1; thereafter Federal Communications Commission, Trends in Telephone Service, annual. [2] As of December 31, except as noted. Source: Radio Advertising Bureau, New York, NY, through 1990, Radio Facts, annual, (copyright); beginning 1993, Radio Marketing Guide and Fact Book for Advertisers, annual, (copyright). Number of stations on the air compiled from Federal Communications Commission reports. [3] 1970, as of September of prior year; all other years as of January of year shown. Excludes Alaska and Hawaii. Source: Television Bureau of Advertising, Inc., Trends in Television, annual (copyright). [4] As of February. Excludes Alaska and Hawaii. Source: See footnote 3. [5] As of February 1986. [6] As of January 1. Source: See footnote 3. [7] As of January 1. Source: Warren Publishing, Washington DC, Television and Cable Factbook (copyright). [8] Source: Nielsen Media Research, New York, NY. Nielsen Station Index, November diary estimates (copyright). [9] As of September 30. Source: Editor & Publisher, Co., New York, NY, Editor & Publisher International Year Book, annual (copyright).

Source: Compiled from sources mentioned in footnotes.

No. 911. Multimedia Audiences—Summary: 2000

[In percent, except total (199,438 represents 199,438,000). As of spring. For persons 18 years old and over. Represents the percent of persons participating during the prior week, except as indicated. Based on sample and subject to sampling error; see source for details]

Item	Total population (1,000)	Television viewing	Television prime time viewing	Cable viewing [1]	Radio listening	Newspaper reading	Accessed Internet [2]
Total	199,438	93.5	82.1	71.3	84.0	79.3	45.4
18 to 24 years old.	25,691	92.2	73.8	68.6	90.6	73.3	58.7
25 to 34 years old.	39,066	92.4	81.3	71.1	90.6	77.0	53.3
35 to 44 years old.	44,791	92.4	81.1	71.9	89.7	80.5	53.8
45 to 54 years old.	34,774	93.7	83.5	74.7	87.5	83.5	54.8
55 to 64 years old.	22,711	94.7	85.6	76.4	80.8	82.4	35.1
65 years old and over	32,404	96.5	86.7	65.4	61.1	78.1	10.7
Male.	95,691	94.3	82.3	72.0	85.3	79.3	47.1
Female	103,747	92.8	81.8	70.6	82.8	79.2	43.8
White	167,002	93.4	82.0	72.6	84.4	80.0	46.8
Black	23,628	95.9	84.9	67.3	84.1	77.3	33.1
Asian	5,507	92.2	77.4	49.8	74.6	68.3	53.5
Other	3,301	88.3	74.4	68.2	78.1	72.0	46.4
Spanish speaking	21,359	93.5	81.6	55.9	84.6	66.3	34.1
Not high school graduate	35,260	94.8	82.7	56.6	73.0	60.0	11.6
High school graduate	66,360	94.5	84.6	71.8	82.7	78.8	31.0
Attended college.	52,878	93.6	80.6	76.2	89.3	83.7	59.5
College graduate	44,940	91.1	79.4	76.1	88.1	89.7	76.5
Employed:							
Full time	113,259	92.7	81.0	74.6	91.1	82.0	56.8
Part time	17,176	92.2	78.7	70.9	89.2	82.1	55.1
Not employed.	69,003	95.3	84.6	65.9	71.0	74.1	24.2
Household income:							
Less than $10,000.	14,292	93.6	81.6	47.7	68.0	58.7	14.6
$10,000 to $19,999	24,406	95.3	84.2	55.8	71.2	68.6	14.2
$20,000 to $29,999	25,327	94.8	84.3	63.8	78.7	73.9	24.5
$30,000 to $39,999	24,055	94.0	82.2	70.4	84.7	77.2	37.5
$40,000 to $49,999	21,816	92.8	82.6	73.9	86.4	79.5	44.1
$50,000 or more	89,542	92.7	80.7	80.9	90.7	87.5	67.1

[1] In the past 7 days. [2] In the last 30 days.

Source: Mediamark Research Inc., New York, NY, Multimedia Audiences, spring 2000 (copyright).

No. 912. Use of Home Computers: 1997

[In percent, except persons using computers (81,013 represents 81,013,000). As of **October.** Based on the Current Population Survey and subject to sampling error; see text, Section 1, Population, and Appendix III]

Characteristic	Persons using computers (1,000)	Percent of total	Frequency of use per week				Computer capabilities [1]			
			6 or 7 days	4 or 5 days	2 or 3 days	1 day or less	CD-ROM drive	Printer	Modem	Internet
Total [2]	81,013	30.3	23.4	20.1	32.6	24.0	71.3	85.5	71.1	52.1
Sex:										
Male	41,260	31.6	27.1	20.1	30.6	22.2	72.1	85.5	71.7	52.9
Female	39,753	29.1	19.6	20.0	34.6	25.8	70.6	85.6	70.5	51.2
Age:										
Under 5 years old	1,675	8.5	12.2	16.3	38.1	33.5	71.9	83.3	74.5	53.8
5 to 9 years old	7,599	37.1	11.8	17.6	44.2	26.4	74.7	83.8	71.5	50.5
10 to 14 years old	9,500	48.7	21.1	21.8	38.0	19.1	75.5	87.9	70.6	50.3
15 to 19 years old	8,395	43.1	24.7	22.4	32.4	20.5	73.7	88.0	69.9	52.3
20 to 24 years old	4,975	28.5	28.3	20.2	28.9	22.6	69.5	83.4	69.8	53.0
25 to 29 years old	5,963	31.7	26.1	22.3	30.0	21.7	70.1	80.4	75.8	58.4
30 to 39 years old	15,393	35.8	24.2	20.6	32.0	23.2	71.9	84.5	72.8	53.5
40 to 49 years old	15,346	38.3	24.3	18.8	30.3	26.6	73.9	87.4	73.0	54.4
50 to 59 years old	7,679	28.5	26.6	19.8	28.0	25.7	66.5	86.2	67.6	50.7
60 to 69 years old	3,162	16.2	29.7	17.5	24.1	28.6	61.0	86.8	63.5	42.3
70 years old and over.	1,327	5.9	29.4	17.8	25.4	27.5	59.0	86.1	60.4	38.6
Race/ethnicity:										
White, non-Hispanic	68,026	35.5	23.5	20.2	32.1	24.3	72.4	87.1	72.8	53.7
Black, non-Hispanic	4,943	14.7	20.8	20.5	37.6	21.2	58.2	75.2	57.7	40.3
Hispanic.	4,081	13.5	23.3	17.3	36.4	23.1	69.1	78.2	60.8	44.4
Family income: Less than $5,000. . .	1,517	13.3	31.1	16.7	26.8	25.3	63.2	81.9	66.2	44.6
$5,000 to $9,999	1,575	8.1	24.8	19.6	29.4	26.1	59.6	81.0	56.7	40.5
$10,000 to $14,999	2,197	9.7	26.2	17.7	31.4	24.8	55.9	74.5	54.7	38.7
$15,000 to $19,999	2,084	12.0	25.9	20.4	29.9	23.8	60.5	77.8	60.0	42.7
$20,000 to $24,999	3,645	17.1	25.1	18.9	31.4	24.5	59.9	80.9	58.1	38.8
$25,000 to $29,999	4,174	21.0	23.3	19.3	33.3	24.1	62.2	77.6	61.0	42.0
$30,000 to $34,999	5,003	25.7	22.5	20.5	32.9	24.1	66.4	82.6	64.1	43.7
$35,000 to $39,999	5,367	29.1	22.7	18.5	34.1	24.7	65.9	84.3	66.3	46.1
$40,000 to $49,999	9,627	35.4	22.2	19.5	33.3	25.1	68.2	86.0	67.6	46.4
$50,000 to $74,999	21,685	44.6	22.1	20.2	32.5	25.1	73.9	87.2	74.3	53.9
$75,000 and over.	24,138	58.0	24.1	21.1	32.8	22.0	80.9	89.8	81.1	64.5

[1] For the most recently purchased computers for those with more than one.   [2] Includes other races, not shown separately.
Source: U.S. National Center for Education Statistics, *Digest of Education Statistics, 1999.*

No. 913. Internet Access and Usage and Online Service Usage: 2000

[For persons 18 years old and over (199,438 represents 199,438,000). As of **spring.** Based on sample and subject to sampling error; see source for details]

Item	Total adults	Any online/ Internet usage	Have Internet access			Used the Internet in the last 30 days			Used any online service in the past 30 days
			Home or work	Home only	Work only	Home or work	Home only	Work only	
Total adults (1,000)	199,438	90,458	112,949	77,621	50,476	86,289	65,471	40,449	75,409
PERCENT DISTRIBUTION									
Age:									
18 to 34 years old.	32.5	39.7	37.9	35.1	34.9	39.8	36.6	34.6	40.3
35 to 54 years old	39.9	47.7	46.0	49.4	55.4	47.7	49.6	56.3	47.4
55 years old and over	27.6	12.7	16.2	15.5	9.7	12.5	13.8	9.1	12.3
Sex:									
Male.	48.0	49.8	48.5	49.3	52.3	49.8	50.1	52.7	49.3
Female	52.0	50.2	51.5	50.7	47.7	50.2	49.9	47.3	50.7
Household size:									
1 to 2 persons	47.9	40.2	41.0	37.9	41.8	40.4	39.0	42.6	39.5
3 to 4 persons	36.9	44.4	43.3	45.9	44.6	44.3	45.6	44.4	44.5
5 or more persons.	15.2	15.4	15.7	16.2	13.6	15.3	15.4	13.0	16.1
Any child in household. . . .	42.1	47.7	47.0	48.7	48.0	47.3	48.3	46.7	47.9
Marital status:									
Single	23.7	27.5	26.0	23.4	22.6	27.7	24.5	23.3	28.4
Married	57.2	61.6	61.1	66.2	65.3	61.4	65.7	65.1	60.6
Other	19.1	10.9	12.9	10.3	12.0	10.9	9.7	11.6	10.9
Educational attainment:									
Graduated college plus . . .	22.5	38.0	33.6	38.6	49.2	38.8	41.6	53.1	37.8
Attended college.	26.5	34.8	33.7	34.0	30.6	35.0	34.4	30.2	35.0
Did not attend college	51.0	27.2	32.8	27.3	20.3	26.2	24.1	16.7	27.2
Household income:									
Less than $50,000	55.1	33.6	38.3	29.9	23.3	32.9	28.4	20.8	32.9
$50,000 to $74,999	20.7	26.2	25.7	26.9	27.4	26.2	26.5	26.8	26.0
$75,000 to $149,999	20.1	32.6	29.4	34.7	39.6	33.1	36.4	41.8	33.1
$150,000 or more	4.1	7.6	6.7	8.5	9.7	7.8	8.7	10.7	8.0

Source: Mediamark Research Inc., New York, NY, *CyberStats,* spring 2000 (copyright). Internet site <http://www.mediamark.com> (accessed 23 May 2000).

No. 914. Households With Computers and Internet Access by Selected Characteristic: 1998

[In percent. Based on survey and subject to sampling error; for details, see source]

Characteristic	Households with computers				Households with Internet			
	Total	Rural [1]	Urban [1]	Central city [1]	Total	Rural [1]	Urban [1]	Central city [1]
All households	**42.1**	**39.9**	**42.9**	**38.5**	**26.2**	**22.2**	**27.5**	**24.5**
Age of householder:								
Under 25 years old	32.3	27.7	33.3	34.0	20.5	13.3	22.0	22.8
25 to 34 years old	46.0	42.4	46.9	43.5	30.1	24.2	31.6	28.8
35 to 44 years old	54.9	55.2	54.8	48.5	34.1	30.2	35.4	31.3
45 to 54 years old	54.7	52.8	55.3	49.2	35.0	30.8	36.5	30.7
55 years old or over	25.8	23.3	26.7	23.0	14.6	12.4	15.4	13.8
Householder race/ethnicity:								
White [2]	46.6	42.0	48.5	47.4	29.8	23.7	32.4	32.3
Black [2]	23.2	17.9	23.8	21.8	11.2	7.1	11.7	10.2
Asian, Indian, Eskimo, Aleut [2]	34.3	26.8	38.7	[3]35.6	18.9	[3]12.8	22.5	[3]20.2
Asian or Pacific Islander [2]	55.0	[3]40.6	55.6	50.5	36.0	[3]24.7	36.5	33.3
Hispanic	25.5	23.2	25.7	21.4	12.6	9.8	12.9	10.2
Education of householder:								
Elementary	7.9	6.3	8.7	7.7	3.1	1.8	3.7	3.4
Some high school	15.7	17.2	15.0	12.7	6.3	6.1	6.4	5.2
High school graduate of GED	31.2	33.2	30.3	25.6	16.3	15.5	16.6	13.7
Some college	49.3	51.7	48.6	43.7	30.2	29.6	30.4	26.4
BA degree or more	68.7	69.7	68.5	65.8	48.9	47.0	49.4	47.7
Household income:								
Under $5,000	15.9	11.9	16.9	15.7	8.1	4.3	9.1	9.5
$5,000 to $9,000	12.3	8.1	13.6	12.9	6.1	2.9	7.2	6.8
$10,000 to $14,999	15.9	13.8	16.6	17.9	7.4	6.0	7.9	8.1
$15,000 to $19,999	21.2	22.1	20.8	21.8	9.8	8.4	10.3	11.0
$20,000 to $24,999	25.7	24.7	26.1	26.6	12.1	10.0	12.9	14.4
$25,000 to $34,999	35.8	34.0	36.5	38.3	19.1	15.4	20.4	22.5
$35,000 to $49,999	50.2	51.0	50.0	50.2	29.5	26.4	30.6	31.8
$50,000 to $74,999	66.3	64.2	67.1	65.4	43.9	38.7	45.7	44.0
$75,000 and over	79.9	76.5	80.8	77.3	60.3	53.7	62.0	59.7
Region of residence: [4]								
Northeast	41.3	47.8	39.5	30.4	26.7	29.7	25.9	18.7
Midwest	42.9	41.1	43.6	37.7	25.4	21.5	26.9	24.0
South	38.0	34.6	39.6	36.7	23.5	19.0	25.6	22.6
West	48.9	47.0	49.2	47.4	31.3	26.2	32.0	31.8

[1] See text, Section 1, Population, and Appendix II. [2] Non-Hispanic. [3] Figure does not meet standards of reliability or precision. [4] For composition of regions, see map inside front cover.

Source: U.S. Dept. of Commerce, National Telecommunications and Information Administration, *Falling Through the Net: Defining the Digital Divide,* July 1999.

No. 915. Households With Telephones, Computers, or Internet Access: 1998

[In percent. Based on survey and subject to sampling error; for details, see source]

State	Telephones	Computers	Internet access	State	Telephones	Computers	Internet access
United States	**94.1**	**42.1**	**26.2**	Missouri	96.2	41.8	24.3
Alabama	93.6	34.3	21.6	Montana	94.7	40.9	21.5
Alaska	95.7	62.4	44.1	Nebraska	95.8	42.9	22.9
Arizona	92.9	44.3	29.3	Nevada	93.1	41.6	26.5
Arkansas	88.7	29.8	14.7	New Hampshire	95.6	54.2	37.1
California	95.1	47.5	30.7	New Jersey	95.1	48.1	31.3
Colorado	95.4	55.3	34.5	New Mexico	87.1	42.2	25.8
Connecticut	95.1	43.8	31.8	New York	95.1	37.3	23.7
Delaware	96.6	40.5	25.1	North Carolina	93.6	35.0	19.9
District of Columbia	91.0	41.4	24.2	North Dakota	97.5	40.2	20.6
Florida	92.3	39.5	27.8	Ohio	95.8	40.7	24.6
Georgia	91.4	35.8	23.9	Oklahoma	89.6	37.8	20.4
Hawaii	93.2	42.3	27.9	Oregon	96.0	51.3	32.7
Idaho	94.1	50.0	27.4	Pennsylvania	96.7	39.3	24.9
Illinois	91.8	42.7	26.5	Rhode Island	94.6	41.0	27.1
Indiana	93.9	43.5	26.1	South Carolina	92.6	35.7	21.4
Iowa	96.0	41.4	21.8	South Dakota	91.0	41.6	23.9
Kansas	94.5	43.7	25.7	Tennessee	93.4	37.5	21.3
Kentucky	92.9	35.9	21.1	Texas	91.6	40.9	24.5
Louisiana	91.1	31.1	17.8	Utah	94.6	60.1	35.8
Maine	96.5	43.4	26.0	Vermont	94.8	48.7	31.8
Maryland	97.2	46.3	31.0	Virginia	92.3	46.4	27.9
Massachusetts	95.5	43.4	28.1	Washington	95.5	56.3	36.6
Michigan	94.9	44.0	25.4	West Virginia	93.5	28.3	17.6
Minnesota	98.0	47.6	29.0	Wisconsin	96.4	43.0	25.1
Mississippi	90.3	25.7	13.6	Wyoming	94.0	46.1	22.7

Source: U.S. Department of Commerce, National Telecommunications and Information Administration, *Falling Through the Net: Defining the Digital Divide,* July 1999.

Communications and Information Technology 569

No. 916. Telecommunications Industry—Carriers and Revenue: 1994 to 1998

[Revenue in millions of dollars (174,890 represents $174,890,000,000). Data based on carrier filings to the FCC. Because of reporting changes, data beginning 1997 are not strictly comparable with previous years; see source for details]

Category	Carriers					Telecommunications revenue				
	1994	1995	1996	1997	1998	1994	1995	1996	1997	1998
Total [1]	2,847	3,058	3,832	3,604	4,144	174,890	190,076	211,782	231,168	246,392
Local service providers.	1,574	1,675	2,028	2,066	2,239	99,011	103,792	109,273	108,568	113,369
Incumbent local exchange carriers (ILECs)[2]	1,347	1,347	1,376	1,410	1,348	98,431	102,820	107,905	105,154	108,234
Pay telephone providers	197	271	533	509	615	300	349	357	933	1,101
Competitors of ILECs	30	57	119	147	276	281	623	1,011	2,481	4,034
CAPs and CLECs [3]	30	57	94	129	212	281	623	1,011	1,919	3,348
Local resellers	(4)	(4)	8	11	54	(4)	(4)	(4)	206	410
Other local exchange carriers .	(4)	(4)	13	3	10	(4)	(4)	(4)	157	36
Private carriers.	(4)	(4)	(4)	2	(4)	(4)	(4)	(4)	112	147
Shared tenant service providers.	(4)	(4)	4	2	(4)	(4)	(4)	(4)	87	93
Wireless service providers [5]	907	930	1,217	969	1,258	14,197	18,627	25,900	33,030	37,032
Telephony [6]	790	792	853	732	808	13,259	17,208	23,778	29,944	33,139
Paging service providers	117	138	200	137	303	(4)	(4)	(4)	2,861	3,161
Toll service providers	366	453	587	569	647	70,466	76,447	86,896	89,570	95,992
Interexchange carriers	97	130	149	151	171	66,381	70,938	79,057	79,080	83,443
Operator service providers.	29	25	27	32	24	536	500	461	603	590
Prepaid service providers	(4)	8	16	18	20	(4)	16	238	519	888
Satellite service carriers	(4)	(4)	22	13	13	(4)	(4)	(4)	1,011	475
Toll resellers	206	260	345	340	388	2,840	4,220	6,564	8,010	9,885
Other toll carriers	34	30	28	15	31	709	773	577	348	710

[1] Revenue data include adjustments, not shown separately. Through 1996, revenue data include some nontelecommunications revenue, formerly reported as local exchange wireless revenue. [2] Fewer ILECs filed in 1998 than in 1997 because of consolidation of study areas. [3] Competitive access providers and competitive local exchange carriers. [4] Data not available separately. [5] Includes specialized mobile radio services and other services, not shown separately. [6] Cellular service, personal communications service, and specialized mobile radio.

Source: U.S. Federal Communications Commission, *Trends in Telephone Service*, March 2000.

No. 917. Telephone Systems—Summary: 1985 to 1998

[112 represents 112,000,000. Covers principal carriers filing annual reports with Federal Communications Commission]

Item	Unit	1985	1990	1992	1993	1994	1995	1996	1997	1998
LOCAL EXCHANGE CARRIERS [1]										
Carriers [2]	Number .	55	51	54	53	52	53	51	51	52
Access lines.	Millions. .	112	130	140	149	157	166	178	194	205
Business access lines.	Millions. .	31	36	39	41	42	46	49	53	57
Residential access lines	Millions. .	79	89	93	96	98	101	104	108	110
Other access lines (public, mobile, special)	Millions. .	2	6	8	13	17	19	25	33	38
Number of local calls (originating).	Billions . .	365	402	434	447	465	484	504	522	544
Number of toll calls (originating).	Billions . .	(NA)	63	72	78	83	94	95	101	97
Gross book cost of plant.	Bil. dol. .	191	240	254	264	272	284	296	309	325
Depreciation and amortization reserves. .	Bil. dol. .	49	89	99	107	116	127	138	149	163
Net plant	Bil. dol. .	142	151	155	156	157	157	158	160	161
Total assets	Bil. dol. .	162	180	187	192	196	197	198	198	200
Total stockholders equity	Bil. dol. .	63	74	77	73	72	72	74	72	70
Operating revenues	Bil. dol. .	73	84	87	90	93	96	101	103	108
Local revenues	Bil. dol. .	32	37	40	42	43	46	50	52	55
Operating expenses [3]	Bil. dol. .	48	62	64	66	70	72	74	75	78
Net operating income [4]	Bil. dol. .	13	14	14	14	13	14	16	16	18
Net income	Bil. dol. .	9	11	9	5	9	11	13	12	12
Employees.	(1,000) . .	(NA)	569	527	507	474	447	437	435	436
Compensation of employees	Bil. dol. .	(NA)	23	22	23	22	21	23	22	23
Average monthly residential local telephone rate [5]	Dollars . .	(NA)	19.24	19.72	19.95	19.81	20.01	19.95	19.88	19.76
Average monthly single-line business telephone rate [5]	Dollars . .	(NA)	41.21	42.29	42.57	41.64	41.80	41.81	41.67	41.28
LONG DISTANCE CARRIERS										
Number of carriers with presubscribed lines	Number .	(NA)	325	414	436	511	583	621	(NA)	(NA)
Number of presubscribed lines.	Millions. .	(NA)	132	139	143	148	153	159	(NA)	(NA)
Total toll service revenues.	Bil. dol. .	43	52	58	62	67	74	82	89	94
Interstate switched access minutes.	Bil. min. .	167	307	350	371	401	432	468	497	519
INTERNATIONAL TELEPHONE SERVICE [6]										
Number of U.S. billed calls	Millions. .	411	984	1,643	1,926	2,313	2,821	3,485	4,229	4,547
Number of U.S. billed minutes	Millions. .	3,446	8,030	10,156	11,393	13,393	15,837	19,119	22,586	24,369
U.S. billed revenues.	Mil. dol. .	3,487	8,042	10,179	11,353	12,255	13,990	14,079	15,125	14,320
U.S. carrier revenue net of settlements with foreign carriers	Mil. dol. .	2,358	5,280	6,835	7,649	7,966	9,053	8,433	9,689	9,561
Revenue from private-line service.	Mil. dol. .	172	201	313	356	440	506	649	840	936
Revenue from resale service	Mil. dol. .	(NA)	167	511	593	1,120	1,687	3,457	4,088	4,794

NA Not available. [1] Gross operating revenues, gross plant, and total assets of reporting carriers estimated at more than 90 percent of total industry. New accounting rules became effective in 1990; prior years may not be directly comparable on a one-to-one basis. Includes Virgin Islands, and prior to 1992, Puerto Rico. [2] The reporting threshold for carriers is $100 million. [3] Excludes taxes. [4] After tax deductions. [5] Based on surveys conducted by FCC. [6] Beginning 1992, includes calls to and from Alaska, Hawaii, Puerto Rico, Canada, and Mexico.

Source: U.S. Federal Communications Commission, *Statistics of Communications Common Carriers*, annual.

570 Communications and Information Technology

No. 918. Telephone Communications—Finances: 1990 to 1998

[Based on a sample of employer firms with one or more establishments that are primarily engaged in providing telephone, voice, and data communication services **(160,482 represents $160,482,000,000).** For SIC 481. Based on the 1987 Standard Industrial Classification code; see text, Section 17, Business]

Item	Total (mil. dol.)					Percent distribution		
	1990	1995	1996	1997	1998	1990	1995	1998
Operating revenue.	**160,482**	**216,296**	**238,063**	**256,116**	**284,515**	**100.0**	**100.0**	**100.0**
Local service	40,180	49,349	53,403	57,065	63,276	25.0	22.8	22.3
Long-distance service	67,698	86,834	94,039	98,528	104,149	42.2	40.1	36.6
Network access	30,044	34,131	36,101	37,447	40,430	18.7	15.8	14.2
Cellular and other radio/telephone	6,002	22,837	28,520	33,453	41,908	3.7	10.6	14.7
Directory advertising	8,373	9,850	10,214	10,764	11,982	5.2	4.6	4.2
Other	8,185	13,295	15,786	18,859	22,771	5.1	6.1	8.0
Operating expenses	**131,493**	**180,538**	**192,349**	**212,490**	**239,657**	**100.0**	**100.0**	**100.0**
Annual payroll.	34,903	40,721	42,087	44,524	49,194	26.5	22.6	20.5
Employer contributions to Social Security and other supplemental benefits.	8,121	9,184	9,611	10,263	11,423	6.2	5.1	4.8
Access charges	23,214	33,748	36,018	39,781	43,964	17.7	18.7	18.3
Depreciation.	22,927	31,651	32,937	37,589	42,448	17.4	17.5	17.7
Lease and rental	3,543	3,919	4,492	5,310	6,496	2.7	2.2	2.7
Purchased repairs	2,977	4,907	5,243	6,533	7,001	2.3	2.7	2.9
Insurance	193	304	336	371	397	0.1	0.2	0.2
Tele. and other purchased comm. serv. . . .	504	1,858	2,030	2,373	2,791	0.4	1.0	1.2
Purchased utilities	1,106	1,770	1,961	2,174	2,372	0.8	1.0	1.0
Purchased advertising	2,328	3,607	4,534	5,624	6,431	1.8	2.0	2.7
Taxes	5,086	7,539	7,978	9,021	9,953	3.9	4.2	4.1
Other	26,591	41,330	45,122	48,927	57,187	20.2	22.9	23.9

Source: U.S. Census Bureau, *Annual Survey of Communication Services.*

No. 919. Cellular Telephone Industry: 1990 to 1999

[**Calendar year data, except as noted (5,283 represents 5,283,000).** Based on a survey mailed to all cellular, personal communications services, and enhanced special mobile radio systems. For 1999 data, the universe was 3,518 systems and the response rate was 91 percent]

Item	Unit	1990	1993	1994	1995	1996	1997	1998	1999
Systems	Number .	751	1,529	1,581	1,627	1,740	2,228	3,073	3,518
Subscribers	1,000 . . .	5,283	16,009	24,134	33,786	44,043	55,312	69,209	86,047
Cell sites [1]	Number .	5,616	12,805	17,920	22,663	30,045	51,600	65,887	81,698
Employees	Number .	21,382	39,775	53,902	68,165	84,161	109,387	134,754	155,817
Service revenue	Mil. dol. .	4,548	10,891	14,229	19,081	23,635	27,486	33,133	40,018
Roamer revenue [2]	Mil. dol. .	456	1,360	1,830	2,542	2,781	2,974	3,501	4,085
Capital investment	Mil. dol. .	6,282	13,946	18,939	24,080	32,574	46,058	60,543	71,265
Average monthly bill [3]	Dollars .	80.90	61.48	56.21	51.00	47.70	42.78	39.43	41.24
Average length of call [3]	Minutes .	2.20	2.41	2.24	2.15	2.32	2.31	2.39	2.38

[1] The basic geographic unit of a wireless PCS or cellular system. A city or county is divided into smaller "cells," each of which is equipped with a low-powered radio transmitter/receiver. The cells can vary in size depending upon terrain, capacity demands, etc. By controlling the transmission power, the radio frequencies assigned to one cell can be limited to the boundaries of that cell. When a wireless PCS or cellular phone moves from one cell toward another, a computer at the Switching Office monitors the movement and at the proper time, transfers or hands off the phone call to the new cell and another radio frequency. [2] Service revenue generated by subscribers' calls outside of their system areas. [3] As of December 31.
Source: Cellular Telecommunications Industry Association, Washington, DC, *Semi-annual Wireless Survey* (copyright).

No. 920. Radio and Television Broadcasting Services—Finances: 1990 to 1998

[**In millions of dollars (28,017 represents $28,017,000,000).** Based on a sample of taxable employer firms with one or more establishments primarily engaged in broadcasting to the public, except cable and other pay television services. Based on the 1987 Standard Industrial Classification Code; see text, Section 17, Business]

Item	Total (SIC 483)			Radio (SIC 4832)			Television (SIC 4833)		
	1990	1995	1998	1990	1995	1998	1990	1995	1998
Operating revenue	**28,017**	**34,319**	**42,462**	**6,954**	**8,518**	**11,206**	**21,063**	**25,801**	**31,256**
Station time sales	19,019	22,450	27,672	6,397	7,779	10,253	12,622	14,671	17,419
Network compensation	549	564	645	105	71	83	444	493	563
National/regional advertising.	7,226	8,166	9,700	1,522	1,765	2,274	5,704	6,401	7,426
Local advertising	11,244	13,720	17,326	4,770	5,943	7,896	6,474	7,777	9,430
Network time sales.	7,905	10,319	12,721	305	464	638	7,600	9,855	12,083
Other	1,093	1,550	2,069	252	275	316	841	1,275	1,754
Operating expenses	**24,145**	**28,038**	**33,618**	**6,317**	**6,997**	**8,747**	**17,828**	**21,041**	**24,870**
Annual payroll	6,333	7,933	9,897	2,428	2,864	3,462	3,905	5,069	6,435
Employer contributions to social security & other supplemental benefits	998	1,303	1,540	326	361	431	672	942	1,109
Broadcast rights	7,642	8,260	9,923	264	304	352	7,378	7,956	9,571
Music license fees	373	405	500	159	204	272	214	201	228
Depreciation	1,345	1,324	1,636	477	403	583	868	921	1,053
Lease and rental	469	538	673	197	226	282	272	312	391
Purchased repairs	232	300	317	79	76	90	153	224	227
Insurance	143	168	158	64	69	72	79	99	86
Tele. and other purchased comm. serv. .	240	278	344	115	123	156	125	155	188
Purchased utilities	246	281	288	99	104	110	147	177	178
Purchased advertising	947	1,115	1,429	368	409	468	579	706	961
Taxes	176	217	233	60	71	88	116	146	145
Other [1]	5,001	5,916	6,680	1,681	1,783	2,381	3,320	4,133	4,298

[1] Includes network compensation fees.
Source: U.S. Census Bureau, *Annual Survey of Communication Services.*

Communications and Information Technology   **571**

No. 921. Copyright Registration by Subject Matter: 1990 to 1999

[In thousands (643.5 represents 643,500). For years ending **September 30.** Comprises claims to copyrights registered for both U.S. and foreign works]

Subject matter	1990	1995	1998	1999	Subject matter	1990	1995	1998	1999
Total	**643.5**	**609.2**	**558.6**	**594.5**	Sound recordings	37.5	34.0	31.6	38.0
Monographs [1]	179.7	196.0	189.3	207.5	Renewals.	51.8	30.6	25.4	23.8
Semiconductor chip products. .	1.0	0.8	0.9	0.5	Musical works [2]	185.3	163.6	142.4	155.2
Serials................	111.5	88.7	72.6	75.6	Works of the visual arts [3]	76.7	95.5	96.0	93.6

[1] Includes computer software and machine readable works. [2] Includes dramatic works, accompanying music, choreography, pantomimes motion pictures, and filmstrips. [3] Two-dimensional works of fine and graphic art, including prints and art reproductions; sculptural works; technical drawings and models; photographs; commercial prints and labels; works of applied arts, cartographic works, and multimedia works.

Source: The Library of Congress, Copyright Office, *Annual Report.*

No. 922. Public Television Programming: 1984 to 1996

[**For October through September seasons.** General programming is directed at the general community. Instructional programming is directed at students in the classroom or otherwise in the general context of formal education]

Item	1984	1986	1988	1990	1992	1994	1996
Stations broadcasting	303	305	322	341	349	349	352
Number of broadcasters [1]	169	178	186	193	198	198	201
Average annual hours per broadcaster...............	5,542	5,650	6,135	6,392	6,303	6,500	6,758
BROADCAST HOURS, PERCENT DISTRIBUTION							
Program content	100	100	100	100	100	100	100
General......................	88	86	85	86	90	92	92
News and public affairs [2]	14	16	16	18	17	19	19
Information and skills................	26	30	32	32	29	27	29
Cultural.....................	20	21	18	19	18	16	17
General children's and youth's..........	8	7	6	6	15	20	20
Sesame Street	15	11	12	11	11	9	8
Other	6	2	1	1	1	1	1
Instructional [3]...................	13	15	16	14	12	9	8
Children and youth	12	(NA)	(NA)	(NA)	9	6	5
Adult.....................	1	(NA)	(NA)	(NA)	3	3	3
Producer	100	100	100	100	100	100	100
Local	6	5	5	5	4	5	5
Any public TV source...............	44	38	27	32	31	33	36
U.S. Coproduction [4]	3	3	10	10	6	6	6
Children's TV Workshop............	16	[5]29	16	15	14	12	9
Independent producer	9	([5])	19	19	25	26	27
Foreign producer, international coproduction	13	15	14	12	11	10	10
Commercial producer...............	3	6	4	4	5	5	4
Other	5	4	4	3	4	4	4
Distributor.......................	100	100	100	100	100	100	100
Local distribution only	6	5	6	6	5	4	5
Public broadcasting service................	65	64	62	59	63	63	63
Regional public television network	13	14	18	24	23	23	25
Other	16	17	14	11	9	9	8

NA Not available. [1] Beginning 1988, only broadcasters in the 50 U.S. States were surveyed. In prior years, the stations in the outlying areas were also included. [2] Beginning 1986, this category includes "Business or Consumer." [3] Some general audience programs with instructional applications were double counted if aired during school hours when school was in session. "The Electric Company" was one such program. [4] Prior to 1986, "Consortium." [5] Independent producer included with Children's TV Workshop for 1986.

Source: Corporation for Public Broadcasting, Washington, DC, *Programming Survey,* biennial.

No. 923. Public Broadcasting Systems—Income by Source: 1990 to 1998

[In millions of dollars (1,581 represents $1,581,000,000), except number of stations and percents. Stations as of **Dec. 31;** fiscal year data for income.] Includes nonbroadcast income]

Number of stations and income source	1990	1993	1994	1995	1996 [1]	1997	1998, prel.	Percent distribution		
								1990	1995	1998
CPB-qualified public radio stations [2] . .	318	400	403	407	408	694	(NA)	(X)	(X)	(X)
Public television stations	341	352	351	351	352	352	(NA)	(X)	(X)	(X)
Total revenue...............	1,581	1,790	1,795	1,917	1,956	1,935	2,041	100	100	100
Corporation for Public Broadcasting...	229	253	275	286	275	260	250	15	15	12
Federal grants and contracts	38	116	55	53	64	62	70	2	3	3
State and local tax based [3]	474	475	510	560	518	536	560	30	29	27
Private	840	945	955	1,018	1,099	1,077	1,162	53	53	57

NA Not available. X Not applicable. [1] Not comparable with previous years due to different reporting standards. [2] Through 1996 includes CPB-supported developmental grantees/stations and excludes repeater stations; beginning 1997 reflects a count of full-powered transmitters. [3] Includes income received from state and other public colleges and universities.

Source: Corporation for Public Broadcasting (CPB), Washington, DC, *Public Broadcasting Revenue,* Internet site <http://www.cpb.org/research/reports/revenuereports/fy1998/> (accessed 08 May 2000); and unpublished data.

No. 924. Recording Media—Manufacturers' Shipments and Value: 1982 to 1999

[577.4 represents 577,400,000. Domestic shipments based on reports of manufacturers representing more than 85 percent of the market. Domestic value data based on list prices of records and other media]

Medium	1982	1985	1990	1994	1995	1996	1997	1998	1999
UNIT SHIPMENTS [1] (mil.)									
Total [2]	577.4	653.0	865.7	1,122.7	1,112.7	1,137.2	1,063.4	1,124.3	1,160.6
CDs.	(X)	22.6	286.5	662.1	722.9	778.9	753.1	847.0	938.9
CD singles.	(X)	(X)	1.1	9.3	21.5	43.2	66.7	56.0	55.9
Cassettes	182.3	339.1	442.2	345.4	272.6	225.3	172.6	158.5	123.6
Cassette singles	(X)	(X)	87.4	81.1	70.7	59.9	42.2	26.4	14.2
Albums—LPs and EPs.	243.9	167.0	11.7	1.9	2.2	2.9	2.7	3.4	2.9
Vinyl singles	137.2	120.7	27.6	11.7	10.2	10.1	7.5	5.4	5.3
Music video	(X)	(X)	9.2	11.2	12.6	16.9	18.6	27.2	19.8
DVDs [3]	(X)	(X)	(X)	(X)	(X)	(X)	(X)	0.5	2.5
VALUE (mil. dol.)									
Total [2]	3,641.6	4,378.8	7,541.1	12,068.0	12,320.3	12,533.8	12,236.8	13,723.5	14,584.5
CDs.	(X)	389.5	3,451.6	8,464.5	9,377.4	9,934.7	9,915.1	11,416.0	12,816.3
CD singles.	(X)	(X)	6.0	56.1	110.9	184.1	272.7	213.2	222.4
Cassettes	1,384.5	2,411.5	3,472.4	2,976.4	2,303.6	1,905.3	1,522.7	1,419.9	1,061.6
Cassette singles	(X)	(X)	257.9	274.9	236.3	189.3	133.5	94.4	48.0
Albums—LPs and EPs.	1,925.1	1,280.5	86.5	17.8	25.1	36.8	33.3	34.0	31.8
Vinyl singles	283.0	281.0	94.4	47.2	46.7	47.5	35.6	25.7	27.9
Music video	(X)	(X)	172.3	231.1	220.3	236.1	323.9	508.0	376.7
DVDs [3]	(X)	(X)	(X)	(X)	(X)	(X)	(X)	12.2	66.3

X Not applicable. [1] Net units, after returns. [2] Includes discontinued media. [3] Included in music videos for 1999.
Source: Recording Industry Association of America, Washington, DC, Internet site <http://www.riaa.com> (accessed 02 August 2000).

No. 925. Cable Television—Systems and Subscribers: 1970 to 2000

[Subscribers in thousands (4,500 represents 4,500,000), except percent. Estimated]

Year (As of Jan. 1)	Sys-tems	Sub-scrib-ers	Year (As of Jan. 1)	Sys-tems	Sub-scrib-ers	Subscriber size-group	Number of [1]—		Percent of [1]—	
							Sys-tems	Sub-scrib-ers	Sys-tems	Sub-scribers
1970.	2,490	4,500	1991	10,704	51,000	1999, total [2].	10,466	66,054	100	100
1975.	3,506	9,800	1992	11,075	53,000	50,000 and over . . .	279	33,600	3	51
1980.	4,225	16,000	1993	11,100	55,000	20,000 to 49,999. . .	442	13,976	4	21
1984.	6,200	30,000	1994	11,200	57,000	10,000 to 19,999. . .	481	6,982	5	11
1985.	6,600	32,000	1995	11,126	58,000	5,000 to 9,999	651	4,516	6	7
1986.	7,600	37,500	1996	11,119	60,280	3,500 to 4,999	394	1,740	4	3
1987.	7,900	41,100	1997	10,950	64,050	1,000 to 3,499	1,842	3,469	18	5
1988.	8,500	44,000	1998	10,845	64,170	500 to 999	1,324	956	13	1
1989.	9,050	47,500	1999	10,700	65,500	250 to 499	1,290	463	12	1
1990.	9,575	50,000	2000	10,400	66,500	Less than 250	3,051	352	29	1

[1] As of October 1. [2] Total number of systems includes 712 not available by subscriber size-group.
Source: Warren Communications News, Inc., Washington, DC, Television & Cable Factbook, annual, (copyright).

No. 926. Cable and Pay TV—Revenue and Expenses: 1990 to 1998

[In millions of dollars (22,165 represents $22,165,000,000), except percent. Based on a sample of taxable employer firms with one or more establishments that are primarily engaged in the dissemination of visual and textual television programs on a subscription or fee basis. For SIC 4841. Based on the 1987 Standard Industrial Classification code; see text, Section 17, Business]

Item	Total					Percent distribution		
	1990	1995	1996	1997	1998	1990	1995	1998
Total and other pay TV revenue.	22,165	32,541	37,027	41,499	46,945	100.0	100.0	100.0
Advertising	1,882	4,466	5,007	5,627	6,643	8.5	13.7	14.2
Program revenue.	3,816	4,843	5,438	6,313	7,473	17.2	14.9	15.9
Basic service.	10,933	16,310	18,621	21,134	24,255	49.3	50.1	51.7
Pay-per-view and other premium service	4,351	5,068	5,696	5,906	5,994	19.6	15.6	12.8
Installation fees	302	445	508	555	619	1.4	1.4	1.3
Other cable and pay TV revenue.	881	1,409	1,757	1,964	1,960	4.0	4.3	4.2
Total operating expenses	19,354	26,428	30,471	35,060	41,606	100.0	100.0	100.0
Annual payroll	2,816	4,519	5,061	6,027	7,337	14.5	17.1	17.6
Employer contributions to Social Security and other supplemental benefits	588	1,000	1,150	1,293	1,581	3.0	3.8	3.8
Program and production costs [1]	5,926	9,442	11,239	12,839	14,920	30.6	35.7	35.9
Depreciation	3,611	4,433	4,990	6,117	7,246	18.7	16.8	17.4
Lease and rental payments	513	682	764	836	998	2.7	2.6	2.4
Purchased repairs	343	555	615	648	740	1.8	2.1	1.8
Insurance	110	175	190	213	236	0.6	0.7	0.6
Telephone, other purchased communications . .	133	283	321	350	389	0.7	1.1	0.9
Purchased utilities	188	215	241	265	318	1.0	0.8	0.8
Purchased advertising.	467	891	1,062	1,153	1,402	2.4	3.4	3.4
Taxes.	310	429	436	470	499	1.6	1.6	1.2
Other operating expenses	4,349	3,804	4,402	4,849	5,941	22.5	14.4	14.3

[1] Includes costs from basic cable, pay-per-view, premium services, in-house programs, and other program and production costs.
Source: U.S. Census Bureau, Annual Survey of Communication Services.

Communications and Information Technology 573

No. 927. Cable and Pay TV—Summary: 1975 to 1999

[Cable TV for calendar year (9,800 represents 9,800,000). Pay TV as of Dec. 31 of year shown]

Year	Cable TV Avg. basic subscribers (1,000)	Avg. monthly basic rate (dol.)	Revenue [1] (mil. dol.) Total	Revenue [1] (mil. dol.) Basic	Pay TV Units [2] (1,000) Total pay [3]	Pay cable	Noncable delivered premium	Monthly rate (dol.) All pay weighted average [3]	Pay cable	Noncable delivered premium
1975	9,800	6.50	804	764	194	194	(NA)	(NA)	7.85	(NA)
1976	11,000	6.45	932	851	611	568	(NA)	7.96	7.87	(NA)
1977	12,200	6.86	1,207	1,004	1,138	1,047	(NA)	8.03	7.92	(NA)
1978	13,400	7.13	1,513	1,147	2,473	2,182	(NA)	8.16	8.01	(NA)
1979	15,000	7.40	1,942	1,332	5,157	4,480	(NA)	8.54	8.24	(NA)
1980	17,500	7.69	2,609	1,615	8,581	7,336	(NA)	8.91	8.62	(NA)
1981	21,100	7.99	3,675	2,023	14,310	12,239	(NA)	9.16	8.92	(NA)
1982	25,250	8.30	5,032	2,515	19,395	17,007	(NA)	9.49	9.30	(NA)
1983	29,430	8.61	6,485	3,041	24,515	22,818	(NA)	9.82	9.70	(NA)
1984	32,800	8.98	7,738	3,534	28,815	27,754	(NA)	10.03	9.96	(NA)
1985	35,440	9.73	8,831	4,138	29,885	29,418	(NA)	10.29	10.25	(NA)
1986	38,170	10.67	9,955	4,887	31,033	30,668	(NA)	10.35	10.31	(NA)
1987	41,160	12.18	11,563	6,016	33,528	33,232	(NA)	10.25	10.23	(NA)
1988	44,160	13.86	13,409	7,345	37,085	36,777	(NA)	10.24	10.17	(NA)
1989	47,500	15.21	15,378	8,670	39,055	38,916	(NA)	10.25	10.20	(NA)
1990	50,520	16.78	17,582	10,174	39,902	39,751	(NA)	10.35	10.30	(NA)
1991	52,570	18.10	19,426	11,418	39,983	36,569	(NA)	10.35	10.27	(NA)
1992	54,300	19.08	21,079	12,433	40,893	36,879	(NA)	10.29	10.17	(NA)
1993	56,200	[4]19.39	22,809	13,528	42,010	37,113	(NA)	9.27	9.11	(NA)
1994	58,450	21.62	23,160	15,164	46,428	41,628	4,800	8.23	8.37	6.99
1995	60,900	23.07	25,556	16,860	53,273	44,473	8,800	8.28	8.54	6.99
1996	62,800	24.41	27,951	18,395	59,457	46,057	13,400	8.04	8.35	6.99
1997	64,410	26.48	30,744	20,383	65,200	46,400	18,800	7.92	8.29	6.99
1998, est. . .	65,420	27.81	33,503	21,830	71,485	47,685	23,800	7.80	8.20	6.99
1999, est. . .	66,700	28.92	36,919	23,146	77,700	49,200	28,500	7.65	8.09	6.99

NA Not available. [1] Includes installation revenue, subscriber revenue, and nonsubscriber revenue; excludes telephony and high-speed access. [2] Individual program services sold to subscribers. [3] Includes multipoint distribution service (MDS), satellite TV (STV), multipoint multichannel distribution service (MMDS), satellite master antenna TV (SMATV, C-band satellite, and DBS satellite. [4] Weighted average representing 8 months of unregulated basic rate and 4 months of FCC rolled-back rate.

Source: Paul Kagan Associates Inc., Carmel, CA, *The Cable TV Financial Databook*, annual, 1999 (copyright); and *The Pay TV Newsletter*, May 31, 1999.

No. 928. New Books and Editions Published and Imports by Subject: 1990 to 1998

[Covers listings in Bowker's American Book Publishing Record in year shown, plus titles issued in that year which were listed in following 6 months. Comprises new books (published for first time) and new editions (with changes in text or format). Excludes government publications; books sold only by subscription; dissertations; periodicals and quarterlies; and pamphlets under 49 pages, unless they are juvenile, poetry, bibliographies, or drama titles]

Subject	New books and new editions 1990	1995	1996	1997	1998, prel.	Imports 1990	1995	1996	1997	1998, prel.
Total	46,738	62,039	68,175	65,796	56,129	6,414	8,539	9,271	8,369	5,769
Agriculture	514	673	675	871	801	86	97	72	119	65
Art	1,262	2,168	2,033	1,912	1,685	94	273	203	205	124
Biography	1,957	2,658	3,007	3,069	2,657	115	142	221	189	114
Business	1,191	1,843	1,788	1,657	1,456	134	268	238	188	130
Education	1,039	1,526	1,595	1,438	1,224	234	285	280	190	158
Fiction	5,764	7,605	8,573	7,963	7,096	166	251	280	273	148
General works	1,760	2,751	3,027	3,159	2,237	266	367	424	380	248
History	2,243	2,999	3,576	3,713	3,108	329	462	536	512	296
Home economics	758	1,395	1,447	1,593	1,200	19	41	22	22	8
Juvenile.	5,172	5,678	5,353	3,683	3,381	103	63	47	54	22
Language	649	732	898	1,056	840	202	263	313	345	223
Law	896	1,230	1,357	1,390	1,189	138	215	264	296	223
Literature	2,049	2,525	3,082	2,729	2,369	242	308	428	331	214
Medicine	3,014	3,510	4,223	4,136	3,676	588	611	720	706	517
Music	289	479	461	433	408	52	73	67	46	40
Philosophy, psychology .	1,683	2,068	2,333	2,321	2,104	284	346	393	380	359
Poetry and drama	874	1,407	1,566	1,545	1,125	119	206	231	196	93
Religion	2,285	3,324	3,803	3,857	3,153	176	235	310	278	174
Science	2,742	3,323	3,725	3,942	3,432	1,030	1,068	1,058	996	663
Sociology, economics. . .	7,042	9,362	10,528	10,064	8,970	1,368	2,198	2,392	1,954	1,548
Sports, recreation	973	1,591	1,751	1,691	1,367	75	118	136	127	69
Technology	2,092	2,470	2,629	2,765	1,999	546	487	520	501	294
Travel	495	722	745	809	652	48	162	116	81	39

Source: R. R. Bowker Co., New Providence, NJ, *Publishers Weekly*. (Copyright by R.R. Bowker, A Division of Elsevier, Inc.)

No. 929. Books—Average Retail Prices: 1980 to 1998

[**In dollars.** Covers listings in Bowker's American Book Publishing Record in year shown, plus titles issued in that year which were listed in following 6 months. Comprises new books (published for first time) and new editions (with changes in text or format)]

Subject	1980	1985	1990	1993	1994	1995	1996	1997	1998
Hardcover [1]	24.64	31.46	42.12	34.98	44.65	47.15	50.00	50.22	49.60
Agriculture	27.55	36.77	54.24	41.84	58.10	49.00	45.00	47.54	43.60
Art.	27.70	35.15	42.18	39.99	39.97	41.23	53.40	46.00	43.22
Biography	19.77	22.20	29.58	28.37	30.43	30.01	31.67	33.50	33.15
Business	22.45	28.84	45.48	37.95	42.72	46.90	52.62	52.89	54.77
Education	17.01	27.28	38.72	38.60	47.98	43.00	47.09	45.57	49.49
Fiction	12.46	15.29	19.83	19.50	20.95	21.47	22.89	21.41	22.25
General works	29.84	37.91	54.77	45.41	60.41	54.11	68.36	59.39	59.65
History	22.78	27.02	36.43	40.78	40.20	42.19	45.62	43.51	43.39
Home economics	13.31	17.50	23.80	20.55	20.49	22.53	23.39	23.32	24.04
Juvenile	8.16	9.95	13.01	13.87	14.59	14.55	15.97	15.64	16.12
Language	22.16	28.68	42.98	34.02	52.09	54.89	58.81	57.59	58.52
Law	33.25	41.70	60.78	53.94	72.32	73.09	88.51	89.15	79.32
Literature	18.70	24.53	35.80	35.30	37.77	38.49	43.28	44.89	45.05
Medicine.	34.28	44.36	72.24	49.78	76.30	75.80	81.48	85.92	81.77
Music.	21.79	28.79	41.86	41.44	39.27	43.27	39.21	43.58	47.25
Philosophy, psychology . .	21.70	28.11	40.58	39.44	44.71	45.26	48.40	48.06	50.40
Poetry and drama	17.85	22.14	32.19	31.06	31.56	34.96	34.15	36.76	36.02
Religion	17.61	19.13	31.31	29.16	30.73	34.27	36.62	40.52	35.08
Science	37.45	51.19	74.39	52.71	90.12	93.52	90.63	78.14	72.39
Sociology, economics . . .	31.76	33.33	42.10	41.32	50.24	55.51	53.82	55.05	58.36
Sports, recreation.	15.92	23.43	30.52	32.28	33.39	32.14	34.71	32.35	37.21
Technology	33.64	50.37	76.80	56.31	81.03	88.28	91.59	89.96	85.47
Travel	16.80	24.66	30.41	26.22	32.13	38.30	33.91	30.58	36.59
Paperbacks:									
Mass market [2]	(NA)	3.63	4.57	5.82	5.70	6.53	6.57	9.31	9.31
Trade	8.60	13.98	17.45	20.56	20.56	21.71	21.41	22.67	22.86

NA Not available. [1] Excludes publications of the United States and other governmental units, books sold only by subscription, and dissertations. [2] "Pocket-sized" books sold primarily through magazine and news outlets, supermarkets, variety stores, etc.

Source: R.R. Bowker Co., New Providence, NJ, *The Bowker Annual: Library and Book Trade Almanac.* (Copyright by R.R. Bowker, A Division of Elsevier, Inc.)

No. 930. Periodicals—Average Retail Prices: 1994 to 1998

[**In dollars**]

Subject	1994	1995	1996	1997	1998
Agriculture	293.56	326.02	383.21	417.56	419.04
Anthropology.	143.20	157.10	176.07	189.79	207.45
Art and architecture	87.17	92.24	97.99	101.06	102.30
Astronomy	746.36	840.93	993.03	1,071.36	1,087.53
Biology.	556.93	620.18	731.84	824.81	891.40
Botany.	422.25	475.10	556.14	607.42	644.47
Business and economics	194.94	227.43	271.13	307.21	339.55
Chemistry	1,006.70	1,106.09	1,319.23	1,467.35	1,577.13
Education	125.39	136.45	150.99	165.03	178.53
Engineering and technology	523.24	575.28	695.69	785.93	866.99
Food science.	272.22	308.20	352.20	385.11	440.44
General science.	369.40	416.28	487.86	548.10	607.80
General works.	63.09	66.73	76.04	80.66	80.53
Geography	305.27	340.79	391.43	452.85	493.93
Geology	469.41	516.08	628.26	703.95	740.14
Health sciences	367.24	403.28	461.07	517.24	573.79
History	76.83	83.27	91.45	95.62	99.26
Language and literature.	71.24	77.83	87.34	90.60	92.55
Law.	97.22	105.21	119.16	123.80	138.78
Library and information science.	136.23	153.58	172.45	181.35	202.30
Math and computer science	566.94	619.31	728.84	805.26	859.91
Military and naval science	133.50	153.75	168.00	184.13	209.50
Music.	52.75	57.50	60.89	65.27	67.93
Philosophy and religion	81.48	91.30	101.25	105.99	107.14
Physics	1,035.81	1,144.93	1,358.19	1,510.45	1,601.03
Political science	105.37	119.91	138.24	151.75	166.05
Psychology	163.91	182.67	207.48	234.12	257.69
Recreation	59.82	61.30	68.73	71.54	75.94
Sociology	149.41	156.42	181.84	201.66	222.23
Technology	457.94	519.93	621.97	702.67	775.05
Zoology	421.74	471.55	539.72	594.28	641.06

Source: Library Journal, New York, NY, *Library Journal,* April 15, 1998. (Copyright by R.R. Bowker, A Division of Elsevier, Inc.)

Communications and Information Technology 575

No. 931. Newspapers and Periodicals—Number by Type: 1980 to 1999

[Data refer to year of compilation of the directory cited as the source, i.e., generally to year preceding year shown. Data for 1995 and prior years include Canada and Mexico]

Type	1980	1985	1990	1993	1994	1995	1996	1997	1998	1999
Newspapers [1] . .	9,620	9,134	11,471	12,597	12,513	12,246	10,466	10,042	10,504	10,521
Semiweekly.	537	517	579	639	661	705	612	558	557	560
Weekly.	7,159	6,811	8,420	9,177	9,067	9,011	7,655	7,191	7,267	7,471
Daily	1,744	1,701	1,788	1,850	1,831	1,710	1,537	1,582	1,461	1,647
Periodicals [1] . . .	10,236	11,090	11,092	11,863	12,136	11,179	9,843	8,530	12,448	9,893
Weekly.	1,716	1,367	553	485	487	513	442	350	382	388
Semimonthly [2]	645	801	435	199	209	216	307	139	262	260
Monthly	3,985	4,088	4,239	4,545	4,494	4,067	3,554	3,067	3,378	3,447
Bimonthly	1,114	1,361	2,087	2,359	2,475	2,568	2,216	1,943	2,184	2,220
Quarterly	1,444	1,759	2,758	3,199	3,370	3,621	3,280	2,893	3,386	3,429

[1] Includes other items not shown separately. [2] Includes fortnightly (every 2 weeks).

Source: Gale Research Inc., Detroit, MI, *2000 Gale Directory of Publications and Broadcast Media,* 133rd edition; and earlier editions (copyright).

No. 932. Daily and Sunday Newspapers—Number and Circulation: 1970 to 1999

[Number of newspapers as of **February 1** the following year. Circulation figures as of **September 30** of year shown **(62.1 represents 62,100,000).** For English language newspapers only]

Type	1970	1975	1980	1985	1990	1993	1994	1995	1996	1997	1998	1999
NUMBER												
Daily: Total [1]	1,748	1,756	1,745	1,676	1,611	1,556	1,548	1,533	1,520	1,509	1,489	1,483
Morning	334	339	387	482	559	623	635	656	686	705	721	736
Evening	1,429	1,436	1,388	1,220	1,084	954	935	891	846	816	781	760
Sunday	586	639	736	798	863	884	886	888	890	903	898	905
CIRCULATION (mil.)												
Daily: Total [1]	62.1	60.7	62.2	62.8	62.3	59.8	59.3	58.2	57.0	56.7	56.2	56.0
Morning	25.9	25.5	29.4	36.4	41.3	43.1	43.4	44.3	44.8	45.4	45.6	46.0
Evening	36.2	35.2	32.8	26.4	21.0	16.7	15.9	13.9	12.2	11.3	10.5	10.0
Sunday	49.2	51.1	54.7	58.8	62.6	62.6	62.3	61.5	60.8	60.5	60.1	59.9
PER CAPITA CIRCULATION [2]												
Daily: Total [1]	0.30	0.28	0.27	0.26	0.25	0.23	0.23	0.22	0.21	0.21	0.21	0.21
Morning	0.13	0.12	0.13	0.15	0.17	0.17	0.17	0.17	0.17	0.17	0.17	0.17
Evening	0.18	0.16	0.14	0.11	0.08	0.06	0.06	0.05	0.05	0.04	0.04	0.04
Sunday	0.24	0.24	0.24	0.25	0.25	0.24	0.24	0.23	0.23	0.23	0.22	0.22

[1] All-day newspapers are counted in both morning and evening columns but only once in total. Circulation is divided equally between morning and evening. [2] Based on U.S. Census Bureau estimated resident population as of July 1.

Source: Editor & Publisher Co., New York, NY, *Editor & Publisher International Year Book,* annual (copyright).

No. 933. Daily Newspapers—Number and Circulation by Size of City: 1980 to 1999

[Number of newspapers as of **February 1** the following year. Circulation as of **September 30 (29,413 represents 29,413,000).** For English language newspapers only. See Table 38 for number of cities by population size. All-day newspapers are counted in both morning and evening columns; circulation is divided equally between morning and evening]

Type of daily and population-size class	Number					Net paid circulation (1,000)				
	1980	1985	1990	1995	1999	1980	1985	1990	1995	1999
Morning dailies, total . .	387	482	559	656	736	29,413	36,361	41,311	44,310	45,997
In cities of—										
1,000,001 or more	20	22	18	25	27	8,795	9,367	6,508	10,173	10,658
500,001 to 1,000,000.	27	24	22	22	27	5,705	6,897	4,804	5,587	6,481
100,001 to 500,000	99	121	138	153	155	8,996	12,197	20,051	17,214	16,506
50,001 to 100,000	75	87	100	138	158	2,973	3,653	4,373	5,602	5,827
25,001 to 50,000	64	83	102	115	138	1,701	2,145	3,209	3,150	3,593
Less than 25,000	102	145	179	203	231	1,243	2,099	2,365	2,584	2,933
Evening dailies, total . .	1,388	1,220	1,084	891	760	32,788	26,407	21,017	13,883	9,982
In cities of—										
1,000,001 or more	11	8	7	3	1	2,984	2,169	1,423	390	1
500,001 to 1,000,000.	23	14	12	7	4	4,101	1,626	1,350	1,017	733
100,001 to 500,000	123	102	71	45	36	8,178	6,987	4,687	2,529	1,756
50,001 to 100,000	156	127	94	72	61	4,896	3,942	2,941	2,029	1,571
25,001 to 50,000	246	229	204	158	131	5,106	4,606	4,278	2,819	2,117
Less than 25,000	829	740	696	606	527	7,523	7,075	6,338	5,099	3,803

Source: Editor & Publisher Co., New York, NY, *Editor & Publisher International Year Book,* annual (copyright).

No. 934. Daily and Sunday Newspapers—Number and Circulation, by State: 1999

[Number of newspapers as of **February 1** the following year. Circulation as of **September 30 (55,979 represents 55,979,000).** For English language newspapers only. New York, Massachusetts, and Virginia Sunday newspapers include national circulation]

State	Daily Number	Daily Circulation [1] Net paid (1,000)	Daily Circulation [1] Per capita [2]	Sunday Number	Sunday Net paid circulation [1] (1,000)	State	Daily Number	Daily Circulation [1] Net paid (1,000)	Daily Circulation [1] Per capita [2]	Sunday Number	Sunday Net paid circulation [1] (1,000)
U.S. . . .	1,483	55,979	0.21	905	59,894	MO	43	963	0.18	23	1,236
AL	24	664	0.15	20	736	MT	11	186	0.21	7	190
AK	7	109	0.18	5	127	NE	17	445	0.27	6	418
AZ	16	778	0.16	11	903	NV	9	300	0.17	4	324
AR	30	473	0.19	16	530	NH	12	228	0.19	8	232
CA	91	6,154	0.19	59	6,264	NJ	19	1,383	0.17	16	1,684
CO	29	1,203	0.30	16	1,430	NM	18	290	0.17	13	292
CT	17	746	0.23	13	836	NY	59	6,380	0.35	36	5,442
DE	2	142	0.19	2	171	NC	47	1,349	0.18	38	1,494
DC	2	861	1.66	2	1,136	ND	10	171	0.27	7	176
FL	42	3,007	0.20	37	3,822	OH	84	2,462	0.22	41	2,744
GA	34	1,045	0.13	27	1,352	OK	43	645	0.19	36	792
HI	6	222	0.19	5	255	OR	19	687	0.21	10	720
ID	12	215	0.17	8	236	PA	85	2,773	0.23	40	3,185
IL	68	2,347	0.19	30	2,502	RI	6	229	0.23	3	268
IN	68	1,319	0.22	22	1,279	SC	15	627	0.16	14	738
IA	38	637	0.22	12	646	SD	11	159	0.22	4	136
KS	46	447	0.17	15	405	TN	25	858	0.16	17	1,049
KY	23	614	0.16	14	661	TX	87	2,936	0.15	84	3,933
LA	26	745	0.17	21	825	UT	6	327	0.15	6	368
ME	7	239	0.19	4	197	VT	8	125	0.21	3	99
MD	14	611	0.12	8	889	VA	28	2,692	0.39	18	1,203
MA	32	1,663	0.27	15	1,610	WA	24	1,140	0.20	18	1,283
MI	49	1,740	0.18	26	2,000	WV	22	365	0.20	12	375
MN	25	855	0.18	14	1,154	WI	35	946	0.18	17	1,087
MS	23	391	0.14	18	395	WY	9	87	0.18	4	65

[1] Circulation figures based on the principal community served by a newspaper which is not necessarily the same location as the publisher's office.   [2] Per capita based on estimated resident population as of July 1.

Source: Editor & Publisher Co., New York, NY, *Editor & Publisher International Year Book,* annual (copyright).

No. 935. U.S. Postal Service Rates for Letters and Post Cards: 1958 to 1999

[Domestic airmail letters discontinued in 1973 at 13 cents per ounce; superseded by express mail. Prior to February 3, 1991, international airmail rates were based on international zones which have been discontinued. Rates exclude Canada and Mexico]

Domestic mail date rate of change	Surface mail Letters Each ounce	Surface mail Letters First ounce	Surface mail Letters Each added ounce	Post cards	Express mail [1]	International air mail date of rate change	Letters First 1/2 ounce	Letters Second 1/2 ounce	Letters Each added 1/2 ounce	Post cards	Aero-gram-mes
1958 (Aug. 1) . .	$0.04	(X)	(X)	$0.03	(X)	1961 (July 1) . .	(X)	(X)	(X)	$0.11	$0.11
1963 (Jan. 7). . .	$0.05	(X)	(X)	$0.04	(X)	1967 (May 1) . .	(X)	(X)	(X)	$0.13	$0.13
1968 (Jan. 7). . .	$0.06	(X)	(X)	$0.05	(X)	1971 (July 1) . .	(X)	(X)	(X)	$0.13	$0.13
1971 (May 16). .	$0.08	(X)	(X)	$0.06	(X)	1974 (Mar. 2) . .	(X)	(X)	(X)	$0.18	$0.18
1974 (Mar. 2). . .	$0.10	(X)	(X)	$0.08	(X)	1976 (Jan. 3) . .	(X)	(X)	(X)	$0.21	$0.22
1975 (Sept. 14) .	(X)	$0.10	$0.09	$0.07	(X)	1981 (Jan. 1) . .	(X)	(X)	(X)	$0.28	$0.30
1975 (Dec. 31). .	[2](X)	[2]$0.13	[2]$0.11	[2]$0.09	(X)	1985 (Feb. 17) .	(X)	(X)	(X)	$0.33	$0.36
1978 (May 29). .	(X)	$0.15	$0.13	$0.10	(X)	1988 (Apr. 17) .	(X)	(X)	[3](X)	$0.36	$0.39
1981 (Mar. 22). .	(X)	$0.18	$0.17	$0.12	(X)	1991 (Feb. 3) . .	$0.50	$0.45	[3]$0.39	$0.40	$0.45
1981 (Nov. 1) . .	(X)	$0.20	$0.17	$0.13	$9.35	1995 (July 9) . .	$0.60	[3]$0.40	(X)	$0.40	$0.45
1985 (Feb.17) . .	(X)	$0.22	$0.17	$0.14	$10.75	1999 (Jan. 10) .	$0.60	[3]$0.40	(X)	$0.50	$0.50
1988 (Apr. 3). . .	(X)	$0.25	$0.20	$0.15	[4]$12.00						
1991 (Feb. 3) . .	(X)	$0.29	$0.23	$0.19	[4]$13.95						
1995 (Jan. 1). . .	(X)	$0.32	$0.23	$0.20	[4]$15.00						
1999 (Jan. 10). .	(X)	$0.33	$0.22	$0.20	[4]$15.75						

X Not applicable.   [1] Post Office to addressee rates. Rates shown are for weights up to 2 pounds, all zones. Beginning Feb. 17, 1985, for weights between 2 and 5 lbs, $12.85 is charged. Prior to Nov. 1, 1981, rate varied by weight and distances. Over 5 pounds still varies by distance.   [2] As of October 11, 1975, surface mail service upgraded to level of airmail.   [3] Up to the limit of 64 ounces.   [4] Over 8 ounces and up to 2 pounds.

Source: U.S. Postal Service, "United States Domestic Postage Rate: Recent History," and unpublished data.

Communications and Information Technology   577

No. 936. U.S. Postal Service—Summary: 1980 to 1999

[For fiscal years; see text, Section 9, State and Local Government. (106,311 represents 106,311,000,000). Includes Puerto Rico and all outlying areas. See text, this Section]

Item	1980	1990	1995	1996	1997	1998	1999
Offices, stations, and branches	**39,486**	**40,067**	**39,149**	**38,212**	**38,019**	**38,159**	**38,169**
Number of post offices	30,326	28,959	28,392	28,189	28,060	27,952	27,893
Number of stations and branches	9,160	11,108	10,757	10,023	9,959	10,207	10,276
Pieces of mail handled (mil.)	**106,311**	**166,301**	**180,734**	**183,440**	**190,888**	**196,905**	**201,576**
Domestic [1]	105,348	165,503	179,933	182,386	189,881	195,961	200,613
First class [2]	60,276	89,270	96,296	98,216	99,660	100,434	101,937
Express Mail	17	59	57	58	64	66	69
Priority Mail	248	518	869	937	1,068	1,174	1,190
Periodicals (formerly 2d class)	10,220	10,680	10,194	10,126	10,411	10,317	10,274
Standard A (formerly 3d class)	30,381	63,725	71,112	71,686	77,254	82,508	85,662
Standard B (formerly 4th class)	633	663	936	949	988	1,023	1,043
Mailgram	39	14	5	4	5	4	4
U.S. Postal Service	(NA)	538	412	360	377	380	382
Free for the blind	28	35	52	50	53	53	53
International surface	450	166	106	105	97	96	103
International air	513	632	696	949	910	848	860
Employees, total (1,000)	**667**	**843**	**875**	**886**	**893**	**905**	**906**
Career	643	761	753	761	765	792	798
Headquarters	3	2	2	2	2	2	2
Headquarters support	(NA)	6	4	4	4	4	4
Inspection Service	5	4	4	4	4	4	4
Inspector General	(X)	(X)	(X)	(X)	(Z)	(Z)	(Z)
Field Career	635	747	745	748	755	781	786
Postmasters	29	27	27	26	26	26	26
Supervisors/managers	36	43	35	35	36	37	39
Professional, administrative, and technical	5	10	11	11	11	12	11
Clerks	263	290	274	277	281	294	292
Mail handlers	37	51	57	58	59	62	62
City carriers	187	236	240	238	234	241	242
Motor vehicle operators	6	7	8	8	9	9	9
Rural carriers	33	42	46	48	50	52	55
Special delivery messengers	3	2	2	1	1	(X)	(X)
Building and equipment maintenance . .	27	33	38	39	40	41	42
Vehicle maintenance	5	5	5	5	6	6	6
Other [3]	4	1	2	2	2	2	2
Noncareer	25	83	122	125	128	113	108
Casuals	5	27	26	25	33	26	25
Transitional	(X)	(X)	32	33	27	17	12
Rural substitutes	20	43	50	54	55	56	57
Relief/leave replacements	(X)	12	13	13	13	13	12
Nonbargaining temporary	(X)	(Z)	1	1	1	1	1
Compensation and employee benefits (mil. dol.)	16,541	34,214	41,931	42,676	43,835	45,588	47,322
Avg. salary per employee (dol.) [4]	24,799	37,570	45,001	44,718	48,793	50,117	48,111
Pieces of mail per employee, (1,000)	159	197	207	207	214	218	222
Total revenue (mil. dol.) [5]	**19,253**	**40,074**	**54,509**	**56,544**	**58,331**	**60,116**	**62,755**
Operating postal revenue	17,143	39,201	54,176	56,309	58,133	60,005	62,655
Mail revenue [6]	16,377	37,892	52,490	54,538	56,267	58,033	60,418
First class mail	10,146	24,023	31,955	33,117	33,398	33,861	34,933
Priority mail [7]	612	1,555	3,075	3,322	3,857	4,187	4,533
Express mail [8]	184	630	711	737	825	855	942
Mailgram	15	8	2	2	2	2	2
Periodicals (formerly 2d class)	863	1,509	1,972	2,014	2,068	2,072	2,115
Standard mail A (formerly 3d class)	2,412	8,082	11,792	12,175	12,876	13,702	14,436
Standard mail B (formerly 4th class) . . .	805	919	1,525	1,524	1,628	1,754	1,829
International surface	154	222	205	199	192	184	194
International air	442	941	1,254	1,450	1,423	1,416	1,434
Service revenue	765	1,310	1,687	1,771	1,866	1,972	2,237
Registry [9]	157	174	118	113	95	89	95
Certified [9]	120	310	560	559	343	386	377
Insurance [9]	55	47	52	49	61	73	92
Collection-on-delivery	21	26	21	21	22	18	20
Special delivery [10]	73	6	3	4	1	(X)	(X)
Money orders	95	155	196	221	212	210	228
Other [9]	244	592	737	803	1,131	1,197	1,425
Operating expenses (mil. dol.) [11]	19,413	40,490	50,730	53,113	54,873	57,778	60,631

NA Not available.   X Not applicable.   Z Fewer than 500.   [1] Data for 1980 includes penalty and franked mail, not shown separately.   [2] Items mailed at 1st class rates and weighing 11 ounces or less.   [3] Includes discontinued operations, area offices, and nurses.   [4] For career bargaining unit employees. Includes fringe benefits.   [5] Net revenues after refunds of postage. Includes operating reimbursements, stamped envelope purchases, indemnity claims, and miscellaneous revenue and expenditure offsets. Shown in year which gave rise to the earnings.   [6] For 1980, includes penalty and franked mail, not shown separately. Later years have that mail distributed into the appropriate class.   [7] Provides 2 to 3 day delivery service.   [8] Overnight delivery of packages weighing up to 70 pounds.   [9] Beginning 1997, return receipt revenue broken out from registry, certified, and insurance and included in "other."   [10] Special delivery discontinued June 8, 1997.   [11] Shown in year in which obligation was incurred.

Source: U.S. Postal Service, *Annual Report of the Postmaster General* and *Comprehensive Statement on Postal Operations*, annual; and unpublished data.

No. 937. Advertising—Estimated Expenditures, Through Medium: 1990 to 1999

[In millions of dollars (129,590 represents $129,590,000,000). See text, this Section for definitions of types of advertising]

Medium	1990	1992	1993	1994	1995	1996	1997	1998	1999, prel.
Total.	129,590	132,650	139,540	151,680	162,930	175,230	187,529	201,594	215,229
National	73,380	76,710	80,795	88,250	95,360	103,040	110,232	118,966	127,565
Local	56,210	55,940	58,745	63,430	67,570	72,190	77,297	82,628	87,664
Newspapers	32,281	30,737	32,025	34,356	36,317	38,402	41,670	44,292	46,582
National	3,867	3,602	3,620	3,906	3,996	4,400	5,016	5,402	5,942
Local	28,414	27,135	28,405	30,450	32,321	34,002	36,654	38,890	40,640
Magazines	6,803	7,000	7,357	7,916	8,580	9,010	9,821	10,518	11,096
Broadcast TV	26,616	27,249	28,020	31,133	32,720	36,046	36,893	39,173	41,036
Four TV networks . . .	9,863	10,249	10,209	10,942	11,600	13,081	13,020	13,736	14,698
(Three TV networks) . . .	9,383	9,549	9,369	9,959	10,263	11,423	11,324	12,105	12,890
Syndication	1,109	1,370	1,576	1,734	2,016	2,218	2,438	2,609	2,818
Spot (National)	7,788	7,551	7,800	8,993	9,119	9,803	9,999	10,659	10,925
Spot (Local)	7,856	8,079	8,435	9,464	9,985	10,944	11,436	12,169	12,595
Cable TV	2,457	3,201	3,678	4,302	5,108	6,438	7,237	8,301	9,807
Cable TV networks	1,860	2,227	2,586	3,052	3,535	4,472	5,067	5,827	6,992
Spot (Local)	597	974	1,092	1,250	1,573	1,966	2,170	2,474	2,815
Radio	8,726	8,654	9,457	10,529	11,338	12,269	13,491	15,073	16,930
Network	482	424	458	463	480	523	560	622	655
Spot (National)	1,635	1,505	1,657	1,902	1,959	2,135	2,455	2,823	3,135
Local (Local)	6,609	6,725	7,342	8,164	8,899	9,611	10,476	11,628	13,140
Yellow Pages	8,926	9,320	9,517	9,825	10,236	10,849	11,423	11,990	12,666
National	1,132	1,188	1,230	1,314	1,410	1,555	1,711	1,870	2,000
Local	7,794	8,132	8,287	8,511	8,826	9,294	9,712	10,120	10,666
Direct mail	23,370	25,392	27,266	29,638	32,866	34,509	36,890	39,620	41,601
Business papers	2,875	3,090	3,260	3,358	3,559	3,808	4,109	4,232	4,443
Billboards.	1,084	1,030	1,090	1,167	1,263	1,339	1,455	1,576	1,688
National	640	610	605	648	701	743	795	845	895
Local	444	421	485	519	562	596	660	731	793
Internet	(NA)	(NA)	(NA)	(NA)	(NA)	(NA)	600	1,050	1,840
Miscellaneous.	16,452	16,977	17,870	19,456	20,943	22,560	23,940	25,769	27,540
National	11,956	12,503	13,171	14,384	15,539	16,783	17,751	19,153	20,525
Local	4,496	4,474	4,699	5,072	5,404	5,777	6,189	6,616	7,015

NA Not available.
Source: McCann-Erickson, Inc., New York, NY. Compiled for Crain Communications, Inc. in *Advertising Age,* (copyright).

No. 938. Magazine Advertising Revenue by Category: 1998 and 1999

[13,751.5 represents $13,751,500,000. Represents the volume of advertising in the consumer magazines belonging to the Publishers Information Bureau]

Category	Pages		Volume (mil. dol.)	
	1998	1999	1998	1999
Total [1]	242,419	255,146	13,751.5	15,508.4
Automotive	23,560	24,753	1,699.4	1,843.7
Automotive accessories and equipment	23,333	24,502	1,690.2	1,833.0
Technology [1]	21,253	22,009	1,217.5	1,384.7
Telecommunications	4,047	4,734	237.8	312.2
Computers and software	12,851	13,252	788.8	893.8
Home furnishings and supplies	16,543	17,273	1,035.0	1,185.3
Toiletries and cosmetics [1]	17,572	15,857	1,215.8	1,143.3
Cosmetics and beauty aids [2]	9,357	8,484	597.6	578.5
Personal hygiene and health [2]	3,521	3,238	299.0	286.9
Hair products and accessories [2]	3,173	2,589	230.6	185.0
Direct response companies	24,729	22,163	1,204.1	1,121.4
Apparel and accessories [1]	24,891	24,776	1,056.8	1,119.8
Ready-to-wear	13,243	12,771	496.7	499.5
Footwear.	3,405	3,349	148.8	158.2
Jewelry and watches	4,212	4,214	207.5	209.9
Financial, insurance and real estate.	14,331	16,253	818.1	1,023.0
Financial	11,067	12,557	593.3	756.8
Food and food products [1]	9,876	9,894	945.0	1,003.3
Ingredients, mixes and seasonings.	1,715	1,615	183.5	181.6
Prepared foods.	1,752	1,919	159.8	194.2
Dairy, produce, meat and bakery goods	3,076	2,809	297.4	287.8
Beverages	1,773	1,854	153.1	165.5
Drugs and remedies	10,491	11,759	824.0	977.3
Medicines and proprietary remedies	9,152	10,272	719.7	849.5
Media and advertising.	9,328	11,418	675.1	846.0
Retail [1]	11,745	15,798	536.9	825.8
Retail [3]	8,568	12,786	385.7	670.8
Department stores	2,132	1,852	108.4	90.4
Public transportation, hotels, and resorts	13,647	15,231	605.5	705.2
Cigarettes, tobacco, and accessories	5,044	6,034	366.3	481.2
Beer, wine and liquor	4,752	4,565	277.5	299.4
Liquor.	3,759	3,600	220.6	235.2
Local services and amusements	4,177	5,424	185.4	276.9
Sporting goods	10,389	10,503	222.7	240.0
Schools, camps, seminars	2,276	2,353	65.8	76.4

[1] Includes other categories, not shown separately. [2] Women's, men's, and unisex. [3] Includes apparel, business, drugs and toiletries, and food and beverage.
Source: Publishers Information Bureau, Inc., New York, NY, as compiled by Competitive Media Reporting.

Communications and Information Technology 579

No. 939. Television—Expenditures for Network Advertising: 1997 to 1999

[In millions of dollars (15,225 represents $15,225,000,000). See text, this section, for a definition of network advertising]

Product	1997	1998	1999	Product	1997	1998	1999
Total.	15,225	16,272	18,003	Financial products and services . . .	230	288	570
Cars and light trucks, factory	2,214	2,130	2,332	Games, toys, hobbycraft (no			
Apparel	310	281	243	software)	253	304	297
Audio and video equipment and				Hair care	388	415	341
supplies	232	293	251	Household equipment, supplies			
Beer and wine.	436	468	434	and furnishings	403	467	538
Candy, gum, snacks.	434	441	508	Household soaps, cleansers and			
Carbonated soft drinks	313	309	355	polishes	265	319	282
Other beverages (nonalcoholic) . . .	331	334	301	Insurance	184	228	249
Cereals	284	237	249	Medications and supplements:			
Other foods and food products	744	711	704	over-the-counter	1,290	1,141	1,128
Computers—hardware and				Motion pictures	718	780	741
software	262	341	401	Pets, pet foods and supplies	128	134	148
Cosmetics	359	382	450	Prescription medications	97	391	522
Credit cards and travelers check. . .	330	343	393	Restaurants, national	1,216	1,131	1,189
Apparel retailers	134	269	325	Telephone companies and services.	502	578	811
Department stores	361	284	260	Toiletries	633	601	589
Discount department stores	157	209	268	Travel, hotels, and resorts	155	149	192
Other retail	311	350	497	All other	1,555	1,963	2,435

Source: Television Bureau of Advertising, Inc., New York, NY (copyright). Data compiled by Competitive Media Reporting, New York, NY.

No. 940. Television—Estimated Time Charges for National Spot Advertising: 1997 to 1999

[In millions of dollars (10,203 represents $10,203,000,000). Data represent activity in the top 75 markets monitored by Competitive Media Reporting, currently covering approximately 474 stations. See text, this section, for definitions of types of advertising]

Product	1997	1998	1999	Product	1997	1998	1999
Total.	10,203	11,024	10,776	Household equipment, supplies and			
Cars and light trucks, factory [1]	1,880	2,059	2,404	furnishings	146	131	120
Car and Truck Dealer Assn. [1]				Insurance	306	380	362
(consumer)	1,032	1,087	981	Internet—ISPs, Web hosts and			
Beer and wine.	129	117	134	support	36	39	79
Building materials, equipment				Medications and supplements:			
and fixtures.	82	88	88	over-the-counter	188	182	185
Candy, gum, snacks.	107	101	98	Motion pictures	381	373	386
Carbonated soft drinks	137	124	140	Organizations	31	88	109
Other beverages (nonalcoholic) . . .	106	92	112	Prescription medications	22	55	90
Bakery goods (fresh, frozen,				Print and Internet media	84	90	149
refrig. etc.)	98	112	105	Restaurants, local	59	67	76
Cereals	200	201	173	Restaurants, national	1,212	1,255	1,282
Other foods	350	340	314	Schools, camps, seminars.	153	172	207
Cosmetics	81	82	86	Telephone companies and services.	611	603	631
Dairy products and substitutes	148	151	154	Television, cable, satellite, and			
Financial products and services . . .	421	482	419	radio	234	226	217
Fitness and diet programs and				Toiletries	108	112	95
spas	119	112	99	Travel, hotels, and resorts	402	434	447
Government (nonpolitical)	111	114	120	All other.	1,229	1,557	912

[1] Sales and leasing.

Source: Television Bureau of Advertising, Inc., New York, NY (copyright). Data compiled by Competitive Media Reporting, New York, NY, in the top 75 markets.

No. 941. Television—Expenditures for Retail/Local Advertising: 1997 to 1999

[In millions of dollars (4,331 represents $4,331,000,000). See headnote, Table 940]

Product	1997	1998	1999	Product	1997	1998	1999
Total	4,331	4,461	4,611	Home and building retailers	779	783	846
Amusements and events	290	280	299	Home and building services	184	206	177
Apparel retailers	250	269	289	Hospitals, clinics, and medical			
Automotive services and				centers	203	208	177
gas stations	149	132	115	Legal services	158	162	173
Automotive supply retailers.	57	58	51	Miscellaneous services	114	102	92
Business retailers	50	70	74	Optical goods and services.	53	50	47
Car and truck dealers [1]	446	456	516	Pet stores and services	23	19	38
Card, gift and book shops	7	16	29	Pharmacies, health, and beauty			
Consumer electronics stores.	209	207	204	supply retailers.	119	112	109
Consumer retail—other	89	89	101	Shopping centers and associations . .	35	29	32
Department stores	262	264	275	Sporting goods stores	32	29	32
Direct response	55	81	103	Video rental, CD, tape, and			
Discount department stores	229	241	238	record stores	67	113	110
Food and beverage retailers	365	372	359	Other	105	112	123

[1] Sales and leasing.

Source: Television Bureau of Advertising, Inc., New York, NY (copyright). Data compiled by Competitive Media Reporting, New York, NY, in the top 75 markets.

Section 19

Energy

This section presents statistics on fuel resources, energy production and consumption, electric energy, hydroelectric power, nuclear power, solar energy, wood energy and the electric and gas utility industries. The principal sources are the U.S. Department of Energy's Energy Information Administration (EIA), the Edison Electric Institute, Washington, DC, and the American Gas Association, Arlington, VA. The Department of Energy was created in October 1977 and assumed and centralized the responsibilities of all or part of several agencies including the Federal Power Commission (FPC), the U.S. Bureau of Mines, the Federal Energy Administration, and the U.S. Energy Research and Development Administration. For additional data on transportation, see Section 21; on fuels, see Section 24; and on energy-related housing characteristics, see Section 25.

The EIA, in its *Annual Energy Review*, provides statistics and trend data on energy supply, demand, and prices. Information is included on petroleum and natural gas, coal, electricity, hydroelectric power, nuclear power, solar, wood, and geothermal energy. Among its annual reports are *Annual Energy Review, Electric Power Annual, Natural Gas Annual, Petroleum Supply Annual, State Energy Data Report, State Energy Price and Expenditure Report, Financial Statistics of Selected Electric Utilities, Performance Profiles of Major Energy Producers, Annual Energy Outlook,* and *International Energy Annual.* These various publications contain state, national, and international data on production of electricity, net summer capability of generating plants, fuels used in energy production, energy sales and consumption, and hydroelectric power. The EIA also issues the *Monthly Energy Review*, which presents current supply, disposition, and price data and monthly publications on petroleum, coal, natural gas, and electric power. Data on residential energy consumption,

expenditures, and conservation activities are available from EIA's Residential Energy Consumption Survey and are published triennially in *Residential Energy Consumption Survey: Consumption and Expenditures,* and *Residential Energy Consumption Survey: Housing Characteristics*, and other reports.

The Edison Electric Institute's monthly bulletin and annual *Statistical Year Book of the Electric Utility Industry for the Year* contain data on the distribution of electric energy by public utilities; information on the electric power supply, expansion of electric generating facilities, and the manufacture of heavy electric power equipment is presented in the annual *Year-End Summary of the Electric Power Situation in the United States.* The American Gas Association, in its monthly and quarterly bulletins and its yearbook, *Gas Facts*, presents data on gas utilities, financial and operating statistics.

Btu conversion factors—Various energy sources are converted from original units to the thermal equivalent using British thermal units (Btu). A Btu is the amount of energy required to raise the temperature of 1 pound of water 1 degree Fahrenheit (F) at or near 39.2 degrees F. Factors are calculated annually from the latest final annual data available; some are revised as a result. The following list provides conversion factors used in 1995 for production and consumption, in that order, for various fuels: Petroleum, 5.800 and 5.586 mil. Btu per barrel; total coal, 21.278 and 20.852 mil. Btu per short ton; and natural gas (dry), 1,028 Btu per cubic foot for both. The factors for the production of nuclear power and geothermal power were 10,676 and 20,914 Btu per kilowatt-hour, respectively. The fossil fuel steam-electric power plant generation factor of 10,272 Btu per kilowatt-hour was used for hydroelectric power generation and for wood and waste, wind, photovoltaic, and solar thermal energy consumed at electric utilities.

Energy 581

Figure 19.1
Energy Production, Trade, and Consumption: 1980 to 1999

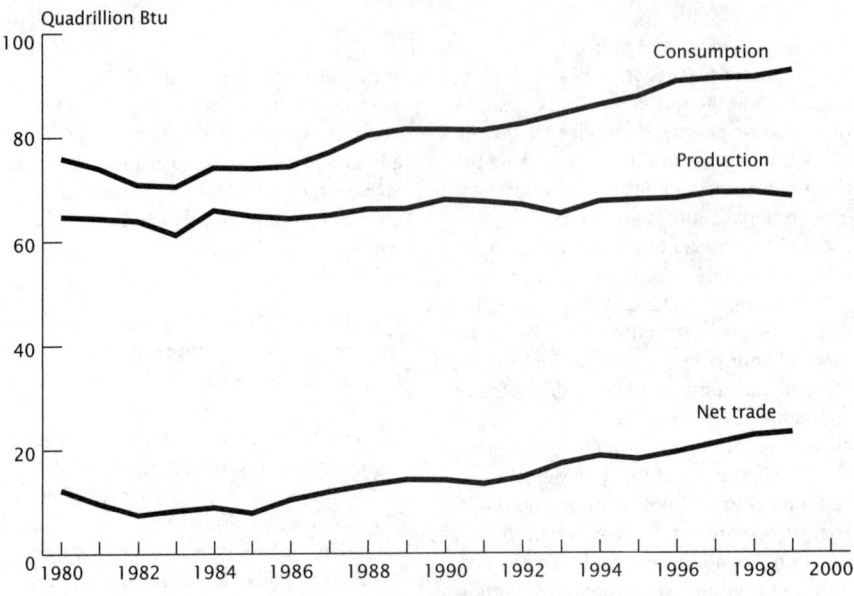

Source: Chart prepared by U.S. Census Bureau. For data, see Table 942.

Figure 19.2
Energy Consumption, by End-Use Sector: 1980 to 1999

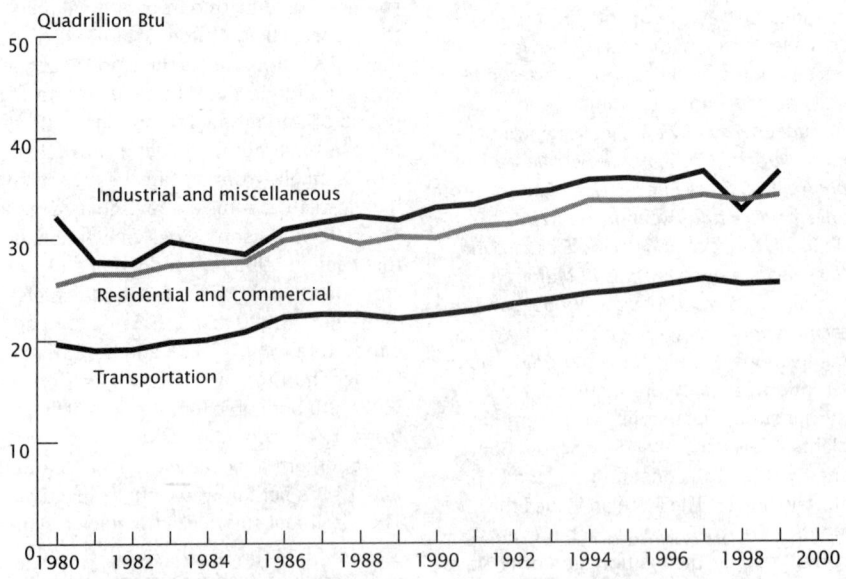

Source: Chart prepared by U.S. Census Bureau. For data, see Table 945.

Energy Supply and Disposition by Type of Fuel: 1970 to 1999

[In quadrillion British thermal units (Btu). For Btu conversion factors, see text, this section]

Type of fuel	1970	1973	1975	1980	1985	1990	1995	1996	1997	1998	1999
Production	63.50	63.58	61.36	67.24	67.72	[1]70.85	71.29	72.58	72.53	72.55	72.52
Crude oil [2]	20.40	19.49	17.73	18.25	18.99	15.57	13.89	13.72	13.66	13.24	12.54
Natural gas liquids	2.51	2.57	2.37	2.25	2.24	2.18	2.44	2.53	2.50	2.42	2.51
Natural gas	21.67	22.19	19.64	19.91	16.98	18.36	19.10	19.36	19.39	19.29	19.30
Coal	14.61	13.99	14.99	18.60	19.33	22.46	22.03	22.68	23.21	23.72	23.33
Nuclear electric power	0.24	0.91	1.90	2.74	4.15	6.16	7.18	7.17	6.68	7.16	7.73
Renewable energy:											
Hydroelectric power	2.63	2.86	3.16	2.90	2.97	3.05	3.21	3.59	3.72	3.35	3.23
Geothermal	0.01	0.04	0.07	0.11	0.20	0.35	0.32	0.34	0.33	0.33	0.33
Biofuels (wood & waste) [3]	1.43	1.53	1.50	2.48	2.86	2.67	3.04	3.10	2.98	2.99	3.51
Net trade [4]	-5.73	12.68	11.75	12.25	7.87	14.08	18.00	19.33	20.94	22.51	23.08
Exports	2.66	2.05	2.36	3.72	4.23	4.87	4.54	4.66	4.57	4.34	3.82
Coal	1.94	1.43	1.76	2.42	2.44	2.77	2.32	2.37	2.19	2.05	1.53
Natural gas	0.07	0.08	0.07	0.05	0.06	0.09	0.16	0.16	0.16	0.16	0.16
Petroleum (crude oil)	0.55	0.49	0.44	1.16	1.66	1.82	1.99	2.06	2.10	1.97	1.96
Imports	8.39	14.73	14.11	15.97	12.10	18.95	22.54	23.99	25.52	26.86	26.92
Coal	(Z)	(Z)	0.02	0.03	0.05	0.07	0.24	0.20	0.19	0.22	0.23
Natural gas	0.85	1.06	0.98	1.01	0.95	1.55	2.90	3.00	3.06	3.22	3.64
Petroleum [5]	7.47	13.47	12.95	14.66	10.61	17.12	18.86	20.27	21.74	22.91	22.53
Consumption	67.86	75.81	72.04	78.43	76.78	84.19	90.94	93.91	94.32	94.57	96.60
Petroleum [6]	29.52	34.84	32.73	34.20	30.92	33.55	34.55	35.76	36.27	36.93	37.71
Natural gas [7]	21.80	22.51	19.95	20.39	17.83	19.30	22.16	22.56	22.53	21.92	22.10
Coal	12.27	12.97	12.66	15.42	17.48	19.10	20.02	20.94	21.44	21.59	21.70
Nuclear electric power	0.24	0.91	1.90	2.74	4.15	6.16	7.18	7.17	6.68	7.16	7.73
Renewable energy	2.67	3.06	3.29	3.23	3.61	[1]6.17	6.85	7.39	(NA)	(NA)	(NA)
Hydroelectric power [8]	2.65	3.01	3.22	3.12	3.40	[9]3.14	3.47	3.92	3.94	3.55	3.42
Geothermal	0.01	0.04	0.07	0.11	0.20	[1]0.36	0.34	0.35	0.33	0.34	0.33
Other [3]	(Z)	-	-	0.01	0.02	[1]0.02	0.02	0.02	0.02	0.02	(NA)

- Represents or rounds to zero. NA Not available. Z Less than 50 trillion. [1] There is a discontinuity in this time series between 1989 and 1990 due to the expanded coverage of nonelectric utility use of renewable energy beginning in 1990. [2] Includes lease condensate. [3] Includes wood, wood waste, peat, wood liquors, railroad ties, pitch, wood sludge, municipal solid waste, agricultural waste, straw, tires, landfill gases, fish oils, and/or other waste. [4] Exports minus imports. [5] Includes imports of crude oil for the Strategic Petroleum Reserve, which began in 1977. Includes imports of unfinished oils and natural gas plant liquids. [6] Petroleum products supplied, including natural gas plant liquids and crude oil burned as fuel. [7] Includes supplemental gaseous fuels. [8] Includes net imports of electricity. [9] There is a discontinuity in this time series between 1989 and 1990; beginning in 1990, pumped storage is removed and expanded coverage of industrial use of hydroelectric power is included.

Source: U.S. Energy Information Administration, *Annual Energy Review* through 1985; thereafter, *Monthly Energy Review*, March.

Energy Supply and Disposition by Type of Fuel—Estimates, 1997 to 1999, and Projections, 2005 to 2020

[In quadrillion British thermal units (Btu). Projections are "reference" or mid-level forecasts. See report for methodology and assumptions used in generating projections]

Type of fuel	1997	1998	1999	Projections			
				2005	2010	2015	2020
Production, total	73.30	73.46	73.05	74.85	77.61	80.35	82.18
Crude oil and lease condensate	13.66	13.23	12.72	11.35	10.96	11.01	11.13
Natural gas plant liquids	2.57	2.49	2.50	2.57	2.90	3.21	3.36
Natural gas	19.43	19.40	18.88	20.25	23.09	25.73	27.13
Coal	23.28	23.89	23.48	25.79	26.18	26.63	27.36
Nuclear power	8.71	7.19	7.46	7.20	6.70	5.45	4.56
Imports, total	25.34	26.85	27.49	34.36	37.50	40.16	42.67
Crude oil [1]	17.88	18.60	19.02	21.49	24.91	24.97	25.22
Petroleum products [2]	3.89	3.99	4.01	5.37	6.80	8.88	10.87
Natural gas	3.06	3.37	3.68	4.52	4.91	5.31	5.61
Other imports [3]	0.54	0.59	0.78	0.99	0.88	0.89	0.97
Exports, total	4.45	4.16	3.79	3.76	3.89	3.75	3.76
Petroleum [4]	2.09	1.94	2.00	1.94	1.97	1.95	1.93
Natural gas	0.16	0.17	0.18	0.24	0.29	0.35	0.35
Coal	2.19	2.05	1.60	1.59	1.63	1.44	1.46
Consumption, total	94.41	94.88	96.39	105.26	111.26	116.66	120.95
Petroleum products [5]	36.43	37.21	37.94	41.21	43.98	46.65	48.05
Natural gas	22.60	21.99	22.05	24.57	27.69	30.68	32.38
Coal	21.34	21.50	21.89	24.72	25.12	25.84	26.60
Nuclear power	6.71	7.19	7.46	7.20	6.70	5.46	4.65
Renewable energy/other [6]	7.00	8.67	6.56	7.08	7.41	7.71	7.99

[1] Includes imports of crude oil for the Strategic Petroleum Reserve. [2] Includes imports of finished petroleum products, imports of unfinished oils, alcohols, ethers, and blending components. [3] Includes coal, coal coke (net), and electricity (net). [4] Includes crude oil and petroleum products. [5] Includes natural gas plant liquids, crude oil consumed as a fuel, and nonpetroleum based liquids for blending, such as ethanol. [6] Includes net electricity imports, methanol, and liquid hydrogen.

Source: U.S. Energy Information Administration, *Annual Energy Outlook*.

No. 944. Selected Energy Indicators—Summary: 1970 to 1999

[Btu=British thermal unit. For Btu conversion factors, see text, this section. Minus sign (-) indicates decrease]

Item	1970	1973	1975	1980	1985	1990	1993	1994	1995	1996	1997	1998	1999
AVERAGE ANNUAL PERCENT CHANGE [1]													
Gross domestic product [2]	4.3	1.9	-0.2	-	0.8	1.7	2.6	4.0	2.6	3.5	4.2	4.2	4.1
Energy production, total [3]	4.6	-0.2	-0.8	0.9	1.4	2.0	-2.4	3.6	0.6	1.8	-0.1	-	1
Crude oil [4]	4.2	-0.9	-2.3	0.2	0.2	-3.4	-4.9	-2.7	-1.5	-1.2	-0.5	-3.1	-5.4
Natural gas.	6.4	-	-3.8	13.7	-1.2	2.8	1.1	4.0	-1.3	1.4	0.2	-0.5	-
Coal	2.2	-0.2	3.4	1.2	-0.4	5.1	-6.6	8.8	-0.4	2.9	2.3	2.2	-1.7
Energy consumption, total [3] . . .	4.6	1.4	-1.4	-0.7	-0.1	-0.5	2.1	2.2	1.9	3.2	0.4	0.3	2.1
Petroleum products	4.8	1.9	-1.1	-1.6	-0.1	-1.9	0.9	2.4	-0.3	3.4	1.4	1.8	2.1
Natural gas (dry)	6.4	-	-6.1	13.7	-1.2	2.8	1.1	4.0	-1.3	1.4	0.2	-0.5	-
Coal	4.8	1.9	-3.1	-1.6	-0.1	-1.9	0.9	2.4	-0.3	3.4	1.4	1.8	2.1
PER CAPITA [5] (mil. Btu)													
Energy production	304	294	278	290	289	284	265	272	271	274	271	268	266
Energy consumption	326	351	334	345	323	337	339	343	346	354	352	350	354
Energy consumption per dollar of GDP [2] (1,000 Btu) . . .	0.1	0.1	0.1	0.1	0.1	0.1	0.1	0.1	0.1	0.1	0.1	0.1	0.1

- Represents zero. [1] Represents percent change from immediate prior year; for example, 1970, change from 1965. Percent change derived from Btu values. [2] Gross domestic product in chained (1996) dollars. For definition of chained, see text, Section 14, Income. [3] Includes types of fuel or power, not shown separately. [4] Includes lease condensate. [5] Based on resident population estimated as of July 1.

Source: U.S. Energy Information Administration, *Annual Energy Review*, and *Monthly Energy Review*.

No. 945. Energy Consumption by End-Use Sector: 1970 to 1999

[There exits a discontinuity in the series between 1989 and 1990 due to the expanded coverage of nonelectric utility use of renewable energy beginning 1990. Btu=British thermal units. For Btu conversion factors, see text, this section]

Year	Total consumption (quad. Btu)	Residential and commercial (quad. Btu)	Industrial and miscel- laneous (quad. Btu)	Transpor- tation (quad. Btu)	Percent of total		
					Residential and commercial	Industrial and miscel- laneous	Trans- portation
1970	67.86	22.11	29.65	16.10	32.6	43.7	23.7
1973	75.81	24.50	32.69	18.61	32.3	43.1	24.5
1975	72.04	24.33	29.46	18.25	33.8	40.9	25.3
1976	76.07	25.51	31.46	19.10	33.5	41.4	25.1
1977	78.12	25.94	32.36	19.82	33.2	41.4	25.4
1978	80.12	26.72	32.79	20.61	33.3	40.9	25.7
1979	81.04	26.55	34.02	20.47	32.8	42.0	25.3
1980	78.43	25.53	32.21	19.69	32.6	41.1	25.1
1981	76.57	26.13	30.93	19.50	34.1	40.4	25.5
1982	73.44	26.59	27.78	19.07	36.2	37.8	26.0
1983	73.32	26.57	27.60	19.14	36.2	37.6	26.1
1984	76.97	27.42	29.75	19.81	35.6	38.7	25.7
1985	76.78	27.62	29.09	20.07	36.0	37.9	26.1
1986	77.06	27.75	28.50	20.82	36.0	37.0	27.0
1987	79.63	28.49	29.68	21.46	35.8	37.3	26.9
1988	83.07	29.83	30.92	22.31	35.9	37.2	26.9
1989	84.59	30.43	31.58	22.57	36.0	37.3	26.7
1990	84.19	29.48	32.15	22.54	35.0	38.2	26.8
1991	84.06	30.14	31.80	22.13	35.9	37.8	26.3
1992	85.51	30.03	33.01	22.47	35.1	38.6	26.3
1993	87.31	31.12	33.30	22.89	35.6	38.1	26.2
1994	89.23	31.37	34.35	23.52	35.2	38.5	26.4
1995	90.94	32.26	34.70	23.97	35.5	38.2	26.4
1996	93.91	33.67	35.71	24.52	35.9	38.0	26.1
1997	94.32	33.64	35.85	24.82	35.7	38.0	26.3
1998	94.57	33.68	35.54	25.36	35.6	37.6	26.8
1999	96.60	34.17	36.50	25.92	35.4	37.8	26.8

Source: U.S. Energy Information Administration, *Annual Energy Review*.

No. 946. Energy Consumption—End-Use Sector and Selected Source by State: 1997

[In trillions of Btu (94,063.6 represents 94,063,600,000,000,000), except as indicated. For Btu conversion factors, see text, this section]

State	Total[1]	Per capita[2] (mil. Btu)	End-use sector				Source				
			Resi-dential	Com-mercial	Indus-trial	Trans-portation	Petro-leum	Natural gas (dry)	Coal	Hydro-electric power	Nuclear electric power
United States.....	**94,063.6**	**351.3**	**18,402.5**	**14,918.1**	**[3]35,797.4**	**24,945.6**	**36,382.5**	**22,691.1**	**20,986.4**	**3,880.4**	**6,678.1**
Alabama......	1,977.5	457.7	333.7	219.1	983.5	441.2	546.6	335.5	858.8	121.2	314.2
Alaska.......	697.3	1,145.3	48.8	64.7	398.8	184.9	244.8	425.4	11.7	11.3	-
Arizona......	1,152.4	253.2	262.4	250.6	240.1	399.3	432.1	134.0	369.4	127.9	311.4
Arkansas	1,030.2	408.2	190.0	118.9	446.2	275.1	316.7	267.0	246.8	36.3	150.9
California	7,727.5	239.9	1,338.1	1,249.5	2,322.5	2,817.4	3,281.2	1,982.0	49.2	447.5	324.1
Colorado......	1,133.4	291.3	260.5	242.7	298.3	331.8	397.9	309.6	356.0	21.6	-
Connecticut....	795.8	243.5	247.0	193.2	139.0	216.6	439.5	140.7	28.0	11.8	-1.3
Delaware	267.2	363.5	54.4	43.8	103.2	65.7	130.2	48.1	48.6	-	-
District of Columbia	176.6	334.0	35.7	109.2	3.5	28.2	34.5	34.8	1.0	-	-
Florida.......	3,614.7	246.2	991.0	778.5	565.1	1,280.1	1,691.4	509.0	697.3	10.6	244.0
Georgia	2,588.4	345.8	533.6	400.7	840.3	813.7	980.6	371.4	771.9	45.9	323.1
Hawaii.......	239.5	201.4	21.2	24.1	77.3	117.0	217.8	2.7	3.3	1.2	-
Idaho.......	497.7	411.1	92.4	81.8	205.7	117.9	163.4	69.0	6.4	151.0	-
Illinois	3,900.2	324.7	937.7	719.2	1,398.5	844.8	1,293.6	1,099.7	964.2	1.1	542.5
Indiana.......	2,683.6	457.0	486.6	300.0	1,278.1	618.9	878.3	563.3	1,427.3	5.8	-
Iowa........	1,136.4	398.1	234.9	158.3	472.5	270.7	375.5	257.1	390.0	8.3	44.1
Kansas.......	1,033.1	394.9	194.9	173.1	390.4	274.7	371.7	334.5	310.8	0.1	89.6
Kentucky	1,809.6	463.1	318.6	215.3	841.2	434.6	642.4	239.3	985.2	34.9	-
Louisiana	4,093.0	940.6	327.1	230.2	2,754.4	777.4	1,592.1	1,855.0	225.4	15.3	143.5
Maine........	553.4	444.4	100.0	57.9	283.5	112.0	261.7	6.3	4.8	68.7	-
Maryland	1,360.0	267.0	360.7	323.8	302.6	372.9	529.4	214.5	290.2	16.4	140.4
Massachusetts..	1,534.1	250.9	419.4	382.7	301.7	430.3	746.0	388.6	122.9	14.0	45.8
Michigan......	3,259.1	333.1	770.4	572.3	1,123.7	792.7	1,051.7	995.4	774.6	26.9	232.8
Minnesota.....	1,685.8	359.6	357.5	225.5	656.8	446.0	647.5	360.5	341.2	95.4	114.9
Mississippi	1,123.7	411.3	198.9	138.6	434.3	351.9	453.5	264.1	132.2	-	114.9
Missouri	1,748.9	323.4	447.6	337.9	375.6	587.8	729.9	286.4	666.7	15.2	95.1
Montana......	377.5	429.6	70.8	54.7	148.5	103.6	175.4	61.7	160.7	138.3	-
Nebraska.....	617.1	372.6	140.2	121.8	170.5	184.6	239.4	131.9	193.3	17.2	98.5
Nevada	584.4	348.8	113.7	91.9	199.2	179.6	210.6	132.1	166.3	26.7	-
New Hampshire .	303.9	259.0	82.7	55.9	77.0	88.3	162.1	21.1	44.5	24.2	84.8
New Jersey.....	2,585.4	321.0	547.0	523.4	669.5	845.5	1,253.0	642.8	75.0	[4]-0.9	147.7
New Mexico	647.1	375.6	91.0	105.6	215.8	234.7	215.7	274.4	288.4	2.7	-
New York	4,093.2	225.6	1,056.3	1,168.8	905.6	962.4	1,531.9	1,260.3	306.1	337.2	314.1
North Carolina...	2,425.2	326.5	556.3	418.4	792.1	658.4	889.1	221.9	733.1	61.2	344.7
North Dakota...	355.8	555.1	57.1	44.3	177.5	76.8	121.2	58.9	386.5	35.3	-
Ohio	4,144.3	369.6	892.2	651.9	1,673.0	927.3	1,299.2	939.2	1,409.7	5.2	162.9
Oklahoma.....	1,405.2	424.0	267.1	203.7	553.3	381.2	466.6	566.7	367.4	29.1	-
Oregon.......	1,132.9	349.3	230.2	185.0	406.0	311.7	368.0	179.5	16.4	486.3	-
Pennsylvania...	3,900.7	324.6	898.5	592.4	1,463.7	946.1	1,350.0	717.9	1,462.1	16.9	718.7
Rhode Island...	235.1	238.2	70.6	51.5	47.3	65.7	104.1	84.9	0.1	7.4	-
South Carolina..	1,474.2	389.0	274.4	193.0	661.8	345.1	469.0	158.7	361.6	21.7	477.1
South Dakota ..	241.9	331.0	59.1	40.6	63.6	78.6	115.2	36.1	42.4	92.9	-
Tennessee	2,084.2	387.5	443.0	339.2	748.5	553.4	703.6	291.1	673.5	107.0	261.8
Texas........	11,396.1	588.8	1,324.1	1,130.7	6,551.0	2,390.4	5,247.0	4,061.2	1,507.1	24.8	396.9
Utah	691.2	334.7	125.2	114.7	249.7	201.7	261.8	172.1	365.5	14.0	-
Vermont	167.1	283.9	45.4	28.6	41.7	51.4	88.7	8.2	0.1	32.1	45.3
Virginia.......	2,126.4	315.8	499.4	451.1	543.8	632.1	819.9	252.0	384.8	2.1	287.7
Washington....	2,164.2	386.2	426.5	321.7	779.3	636.8	852.5	241.9	80.5	1,058.7	66.3
West Virginia...	809.2	445.7	145.6	95.7	389.1	178.8	277.7	169.9	922.5	11.8	-
Wisconsin.....	1,835.4	352.9	384.2	279.1	768.4	403.7	562.0	405.0	488.4	25.6	41.6
Wyoming	428.3	892.2	38.7	42.8	243.0	103.8	149.0	107.9	466.5	14.2	-

- Represents zero.   [1] Sources of energy includes geothermal, wood and waste, and net interstate sales of electricity, including losses, not shown separately.   [2] Based on estimated resident population as of July 1.   [3] Includes net imports of coal coke not allocated by state.   [4] A negative number occurs when more electricity is expended than is created to provide electricity during peak demand periods.

Source: U.S. Energy Information Administration, *State Energy Data Report*, annual.

Energy 585

No. 947. Energy Expenditures—End-Use Sector and Selected Source by State: 1996

[In millions of dollars ($567,318 represents $567,318,000,000). End-use sector and electric utilities exclude expenditure sources such as hydropower, solar, wind, and geothermal. Also excludes expenditures for reported amounts of energy consumed by the energy industry for production, transportation, and processing operations]

State		End-use sector				Source			
	Total [1]	Resi-dential	Com-mercial	Industrial	Trans-portation	Petroleum products	Natural gas	Coal	Electricity sales
U.S.	567,318	138,691	100,209	119,786	208,632	266,595	91,769	27,522	213,645
AL.	9,816	2,234	1,342	2,557	3,682	4,312	1,298	1,345	3,884
AK.	2,180	334	344	235	1,266	1,520	252	26	485
AZ.	8,574	2,125	1,711	1,069	3,669	4,005	574	534	4,019
AR.	5,812	1,363	728	1,400	2,322	2,625	981	406	2,216
CA.	55,187	11,970	10,748	8,617	23,853	25,651	8,879	87	21,568
CO	6,881	1,563	1,250	1,013	3,054	3,521	1,097	362	2,244
CT.	7,248	2,387	1,699	797	2,366	3,605	932	54	2,991
DE.	1,692	463	293	350	585	822	232	75	704
DC	1,334	288	763	17	266	306	281	2	747
FL.	25,117	7,515	4,916	2,265	10,421	12,121	1,928	1,205	12,588
GA	15,642	3,906	2,702	3,006	6,028	7,017	1,995	1,234	6,484
HI	2,288	417	415	482	973	1,338	42	6	1,152
ID	2,550	466	338	608	1,138	1,471	226	13	821
IL	25,089	7,064	4,814	5,504	7,706	9,879	5,382	1,492	9,688
IN	14,106	3,178	1,691	4,145	5,092	6,257	2,743	1,782	4,668
IA	6,649	1,650	915	1,701	2,383	3,166	1,220	402	2,157
KS.	5,850	1,344	1,029	1,374	2,104	2,802	1,083	318	2,025
KY.	9,045	1,780	1,074	2,509	3,682	4,755	1,036	1,107	3,067
LA.	15,120	2,237	1,480	6,641	4,762	7,643	3,751	333	4,442
ME	3,158	915	487	654	1,103	1,923	43	12	1,137
MD	9,583	2,851	2,091	1,086	3,554	4,471	1,220	432	3,928
MA	13,087	3,875	3,223	1,790	4,199	5,871	2,622	211	4,993
MI	19,758	5,033	3,726	4,316	6,684	8,499	4,264	1,102	6,806
MN	9,869	2,310	1,252	2,311	3,996	5,176	1,537	391	3,090
MS	5,963	1,334	867	1,276	2,486	3,091	749	205	2,326
MO	11,532	2,996	1,940	1,670	4,927	5,884	1,615	635	4,002
MT	2,171	403	289	490	989	1,290	258	113	611
NE.	3,814	830	631	717	1,635	1,999	612	120	1,196
NV.	3,637	727	504	792	1,614	1,812	590	232	1,338
NH	2,525	817	512	324	871	1,328	146	73	1,059
NJ.	18,764	5,075	4,303	2,925	6,461	8,382	3,532	132	6,925
NM	3,427	658	653	493	1,623	1,824	512	385	1,172
NY.	34,089	11,118	10,342	3,805	8,825	12,117	7,913	463	14,682
NC	15,823	4,277	2,571	3,117	5,858	7,332	1,275	1,067	7,068
ND	1,699	332	226	494	647	894	163	411	466
OH	25,556	6,604	4,407	6,288	8,257	10,321	5,139	1,898	9,831
OK	7,333	1,661	1,068	1,651	2,954	3,390	1,884	349	2,398
OR	6,058	1,232	874	1,114	2,838	3,200	610	21	2,197
PA.	25,810	7,598	4,428	5,465	8,318	10,656	4,314	2,113	10,157
RI	2,044	669	443	268	664	941	473	-	716
SC.	8,177	1,993	1,167	2,133	2,884	3,545	741	539	3,771
SD.	1,629	398	231	277	723	981	158	42	483
TN.	11,604	2,621	1,938	2,380	4,664	5,507	1,340	789	4,587
TX.	55,070	9,509	6,834	21,307	17,420	30,027	10,365	1,900	17,386
UT.	3,708	707	550	601	1,849	2,125	529	374	1,042
VT.	1,368	429	239	186	514	794	40	-	525
VA.	13,451	3,710	2,500	1,784	5,457	6,544	1,448	525	5,349
WA	10,330	2,086	1,446	1,647	5,151	5,806	909	136	3,531
WV	4,002	881	520	1,155	1,446	2,062	568	1,119	1,308
WI	10,156	2,553	1,499	2,255	3,849	4,908	2,014	562	3,113
WY	1,873	206	193	656	818	1,075	250	389	499

- Represents zero.   [1] Includes sources not shown separately. Total expenditures are the sum of purchases for each source (including electricity sales) less electric utility purchases of fuel.

Source: U.S. Energy Information Administration, *State Energy Price and Expenditure Report*, annual.

No. 948. Energy Expenditures and Average Fuel Prices by Source and Sector: 1970 to 1997

[82,862 represents $82,862,000,000. For definition of Btu, see text, this section. End-use sector and electric utilities exclude expenditures and prices on energy sources such as hydropower, solar, wind, and geothermal. Also excludes expenditures for reported amounts of energy consumed by the energy industry for production, transportation, and processing operations]

Source and sector	1970	1973	1975	1980	1985	1990	1993	1994	1995	1996	1997
EXPENDITURES (mil. dol.)											
Total [1][2]	82,862	111,591	171,828	374,359	437,292	471,786	491,904	505,518	515,321	561,473	567,318
Natural gas	10,891	13,933	20,061	51,061	72,938	64,102	75,941	77,716	74,150	85,634	91,769
Petroleum products [2] .	47,942	65,257	103,372	237,628	223,591	235,224	222,936	229,804	236,937	268,071	266,595
Motor gasoline . . .	31,596	39,667	59,446	124,408	118,043	126,454	126,401	129,897	136,475	148,230	149,549
Coal	4,594	6,251	13,047	22,648	29,723	28,372	27,763	27,186	26,861	27,368	27,522
Electricity sales	23,345	33,780	50,680	98,095	149,233	176,737	196,579	200,883	205,932	211,011	213,645
Residential sector . . .	20,151	27,078	36,988	69,523	99,009	110,057	125,019	126,963	128,423	137,628	138,691
Commercial sector. . .	10,654	15,107	22,839	46,888	70,267	78,828	86,474	89,409	91,587	95,798	100,209
Industrial sector	16,678	23,502	41,068	94,268	106,835	102,336	105,563	109,112	107,732	120,005	119,786
Transportation sector [2]	35,379	45,904	70,933	163,680	161,182	180,565	174,847	180,034	187,578	208,041	208,632
Motor gasoline . . .	30,525	38,598	57,992	121,809	115,199	123,742	124,549	127,942	134,471	145,993	147,046
Electric utilities	-4,316	7,817	-16,396	-37,435	-42,558	-38,276	-36,692	-36,166	-34,810	-36,614	-37,815
AVERAGE FUEL PRICES (dol. per mil. Btu)											
All sectors	1.65	2.02	3.33	6.89	8.36	8.29	8.27	8.31	8.29	8.77	8.82
Residential sector . . .	2.11	2.73	3.81	7.44	10.93	11.91	12.29	12.63	12.57	12.68	13.24
Commercial sector. . .	1.96	2.56	4.09	7.88	11.71	12.02	12.68	12.87	12.75	12.88	13.15
Industrial sector	0.98	1.09	2.12	5.15	6.27	5.25	4.99	4.92	4.74	5.49	5.20
Transportation sector .	2.31	2.57	4.02	8.61	8.26	8.27	7.87	7.88	8.04	8.72	8.65
Electric utilities	0.32	0.46	0.96	1.75	1.85	1.46	1.35	1.30	1.23	1.28	1.30

[1] Includes electricity sales; excludes electricity generation.   [2] Includes sources or fuel types not shown separately.

Source: U.S. Energy Information Administration, *State Energy Price and Expenditure Report*, annual.

No. 949. Residential Energy Consumption, Expenditures, and Average Price, 1980 to 1997

[For period April to March for 1980-1985; January to December for 1987 to 1997. Excludes Alaska and Hawaii in 1980. Covers occupied units only. Excludes household usage of gasoline for transportation and the use of wood or coal. Based on Residential Energy Consumption Survey; see source. Btu=British thermal unit; see text, this section]

Type of fuel	Unit	1980	1983	1985	1987	1990	1993	1997
CONSUMPTION								
Total.	Quad. Btu	9.74	8.62	9.04	9.13	9.22	10.01	10.25
Avg. per household	Mil. Btu . . .	126	103	105	101	98	103.6	101.5
Natural gas	Quad. Btu	5.31	4.77	4.98	4.83	4.86	5.27	5.28
Electricity	Quad. Btu	2.42	2.42	2.48	2.76	3.03	3.28	3.54
Fuel oil, kerosene	Quad. Btu	1.71	1.14	1.26	1.22	1.04	1.07	1.07
Liquid petroleum gas.	Quad. Btu	0.31	0.29	0.31	0.32	0.28	0.38	0.36
EXPENDITURES								
Total.	Bil. dol.	63.2	87.8	97.0	97.7	110.2	123.91	135.79
Avg. per household	Dollars	(NA)	(NA)	(NA)	1,080	1,172	1,282	1,338
Natural gas	Bil. dol.	17.8	27.1	29.8	26.1	27.3	32.04	35.81
Electricity	Bil. dol.	32.6	48.4	54.5	61.6	71.5	81.08	88.33
Fuel oil, kerosene	Bil. dol.	10.7	9.6	9.6	7.2	8.3	6.98	7.61
Liquid petroleum gas.	Bil. dol.	2.1	2.7	3.1	2.8	3.1	3.81	4.04
AVERAGE PRICE								
Total.	Dol./mil. Btu . .	6.49	10.18	10.73	10.71	12.00	12.38	13.25
Natural gas	Dol./mil. Btu . . .	3.36	5.67	5.97	5.41	5.60	6.07	6.78
Electricity	Dol./mil. Btu . . .	13.46	19.98	21.94	22.34	23.60	24.69	24.97
Fuel oil, kerosene	Dol./mil. Btu . . .	6.29	8.42	7.64	5.89	7.90	6.52	15.56
Liquid petroleum gas.	Dol./mil. Btu . . .	6.71	9.42	9.91	8.91	11.20	10.04	11.23

NA Not available.

Source: U.S. Energy Information Administration, *Residential Energy Consumption Survey: Consumption and Expenditures*, annual through 1983 beginning 1985, triennial. For 1987 and 1993, *Household Energy Consumption and Expenditures*, 1987, 1990, 1993, and 1997.

Energy   587

No. 950. Residential Energy Consumption and Expenditures by Type of Fuel and Selected Household Characteristic: 1997

[For period January through December. Quad.=quadrillion. See headnote, Table 949]

Characteristic	Consumption (Btu)					Expenditures				
	Total [1] (quad.)	Avg. per house-hold[1] (mil.)	Natural gas (quad.)	Elec-tricity (quad.)	Fuel oil[2] (quad.)	Total[1] (bil. dol.)	Avg. per house-hold[1] (dol.)	Natural gas (bil. dol.)	Elec-tricity (bil. dol.)	Fuel oil[2] (bil. dol.)
Total households . .	10.25	101	5.28	3.54	1.01	135.8	1,338	35.81	88.33	7.11
Single family	8.46	115	4.46	2.84	0.83	110.0	1,492	29.97	70.33	6.13
2- to 4-unit building.	0.51	92	0.34	0.12	0.05	6.2	1,108	2.36	3.47	0.35
5 or more unit building . .	0.77	49	0.32	0.32	0.12	11.9	755	2.46	8.84	0.59
Mobile home	0.50	80	0.16	0.25	(B)	7.6	1,206	1.02	5.68	(B)
Year house built:										
1949 or earlier	3.48	125	2.05	0.74	0.54	39.6	1,420	14.15	20.03	3.77
1950 to 1959	1.33	106	0.77	0.39	0.15	16.8	1,340	5.30	10.14	1.08
1960 to 1969	1.39	96	0.73	0.47	0.14	18.3	1,264	4.88	11.85	0.97
1970 to 1979	1.71	87	0.74	0.80	0.09	25.3	1,291	4.75	19.03	0.63
1980 to 1989	1.41	82	0.56	0.74	0.06	22.5	1,302	3.83	17.62	0.44
1990 to 1997	0.92	95	0.43	0.41	0.03	13.3	1,369	2.91	9.66	0.22
1997 family income:										
Less than $10,000 . . .	1.02	76	0.53	0.33	0.11	13.3	2,013	(NA)	(NA)	(NA)
$10,000 to $24,999 . . .	2.54	87	1.30	0.89	0.22	33.7	3,478	(NA)	(NA)	(NA)
$25,000 to $49,999 . . .	3.19	103	1.65	1.08	0.31	41.6	2,670	(NA)	(NA)	(NA)
$50,000 or more	3.49	125	1.80	1.24	0.37	47.3	3,434	(NA)	(NA)	(NA)

B Base figure too small to meet statistical standards for reliability of a derived figure.   NA Not available.   [1] Includes liquid petroleum gas, not shown separately.   [2] Includes kerosene.

Source: U.S. Energy Information Administration, *Household Energy Consumption and Expenditures, 1987, 1990, 1993*, and *1997*.

No. 951. Manufacturing Primary Energy Consumption for All Purposes by Type of Fuel and Major Industry Group: 1994

[In trillions of Btu (21,663 represents 21,663,000,000,000). Estimates represented in this table are for the primary consumption of energy for heat and power and as feedstocks or raw material inputs. Primary consumption is defined as the consumption of the energy that was originally produced off-site or was produced on-site from input materials not classified as energy. Examples of the latter are hydrogen produced from the electrolysis of brine; the output of captive (on-site) mines or wells; woodchips, bark, and woodwaste from wood purchased as a raw material input; and waste materials such as wastepaper and packing materials. Primary consumption excludes quantities of energy that are produced from other energy inputs and, therefore, avoids double counting. Based on the 1994 Manufacturing Energy Consumption Survey and subject to sampling variability]

Industry	SIC [1] code	Total	Net elec-tricity [2]	Residual fuel oil	Distil-late fuel oil [3]	Natural gas [4]	LPG	Coal	Coke and breeze	Other [5]
All industries	(X)	21,663	2,656	490	158	6,835	1,631	2,105	449	7,926
Food and kindred products	20	1,193	198	30	19	631	(D)	165	(D)	141
Tobacco products	21	(D)	3	1	(D)	(D)	(D)	(D)	-	(D)
Textile mill products.	22	310	111	17	7	117	4	40	-	14
Apparel and other textile products .	23	(D)	26	(D)	1	25	(D)	(D)	-	(D)
Lumber and wood products	24	491	68	2	25	48	(D)	(D)	-	341
Furniture and fixtures	25	69	22	(Z)	1	24	1	3	-	18
Paper and allied products.	26	2,665	223	173	9	575	5	307	-	1,373
Printing and publishing	27	112	59	(D)	2	48	(D)	-	-	2
Petroleum and coal products	2813	104	80	-	(D)	23	(D)	(Z)	1	1
Rubber and misc. plastic products .	30	287	149	10	4	110	3	5	-	6
Leather and leather products	31	(D)	3	2	(D)	(D)	(D)	-	-	(Z)
Stone, clay, and glass products . . .	32	944	123	7	23	432	4	274	8	73
Primary metal industries.	33	2,462	493	43	13	811	5	922	424	85
Industrial machinery & equipment .	35	246	109	(D)	4	111	3	11	(D)	5
Electric and electronic equipment .	36	243	113	3	2	88	2	(D)	(D)	(S)
Transportation equipment.	37	363	132	11	7	157	3	28	2	23
Instruments and related products. .	38	107	46	4	1	29	(D)	(D)	-	3
Misc. manufacturing industries . . .	39	(D)	19	1	1	19	1	1	-	(D)

- Represents or rounds to zero.   D Withheld to avoid disclosing data for individual establishments.   S Withheld because Relative Standard Error is greater than 50 percent.   X Not applicable.   Z Less than 0.5 trillion Btu.   [1] Standard Industrial Classification Code; see text, Section 17, Business.   [2] Net electricity is obtained by aggregating purchases, transfers in, and generation from noncombustible renewable resources minus quantities sold and transferred out. Excludes electricity inputs from on-site cogeneration or generation from combustible fuels because that energy has already been included as generating fuel (for example, coal).   [3] Includes Nos.1, 2, and 4 fuel oils and Nos. 1, 2, and 4 diesel fuels.   [4] Includes natural gas obtained from utilities, transmission pipelines, and any other supplier such as brokers and producers.   [5] Includes net steam, and other energy that respondents indicated was used to produce heat and power or as feedstock/raw material inputs.

Source: U.S. Energy Information Administration, *Manufacturing Energy Consumption: 1994*.

No. 952. Commercial Buildings—Energy Consumption and Expenditures: 1995

[Covers buildings using one or more major fuel. Excludes industrial buildings, predominantly residential buildings, and buildings of less than 1,000 sq. ft. Based on a sample survey of building representatives and energy suppliers; therefore, subject to sampling variability. For characteristics of commercial buildings, see tables in Section 25, Construction and Housing. For composition of regions, see map, inside front cover]

Building characteristic	All buildings using any major fuel		Consumption (tril. Btu)			Expenditures (mil. dol.)		
	Number (1,000)	Square feet (mil.)	Major fuel, total [1]	Electricity	Natural gas	Major fuel, total [1]	Electricity	Natural gas
All buildings	**4,579**	**58,772**	**5,321**	**2,608**	**1,946**	**69,918**	**56,621**	**9,018**
Region:								
Northeast	725	11,883	1,035	436	297	16,479	13,059	1,739
Midwest	1,139	14,322	1,497	558	750	15,076	10,946	2,947
South	1,750	20,830	1,684	1,027	528	22,211	19,009	2,560
West.	964	11,736	1,106	587	371	16,152	13,607	1,772
Year constructed:								
1919 or before	353	3,673	292	99	135	3,310	2,290	655
1920 to 1945	562	6,710	508	173	210	5,665	4,012	966
1946 to 1959	867	9,298	826	325	391	9,813	7,395	1,796
1960 to 1969	718	10,858	1,024	472	375	13,135	10,405	1,750
1970 to 1979	813	11,333	1,125	615	393	15,366	13,005	1,695
1980 to 1989	846	12,252	1,059	648	288	15,895	13,844	1,397
1990 to 1992	218	2,590	297	163	100	4,011	3,318	510
1993 to 1995	202	2,059	190	113	54	2,722	2,353	249
Principal activity within building:								
Assembly [2]	682	8,011	677	252	232	7,876	5,688	1,145
Education	309	7,740	614	221	245	7,129	5,168	1,117
Food sales	137	642	137	119	18	2,634	2,532	97
Food service	285	1,353	332	166	158	4,817	3,931	851
Health care	105	2,333	561	211	258	5,261	3,901	838
Lodging.	158	3,618	461	187	213	5,114	3,838	966
Mercantile/services	1,289	12,728	973	508	395	14,025	11,655	1,979
Office	705	10,478	1,019	676	239	15,849	14,020	1,150
Warehouse and storage	580	8,481	325	176	106	4,709	3,934	559
Other	67	1,004	173	75	55	1,865	1,473	197
Vacant	261	2,384	51	18	26	638	481	119
Square footage:								
1,001 to 5,000	2,399	6,338	708	380	264	11,577	9,696	1,483
5,001 to 10,000	1,035	7,530	624	238	272	8,063	6,055	1,439
10,001 to 25,000	745	11,617	824	384	356	11,099	8,911	1,775
25,001 to 50,000	213	7,676	630	316	231	8,676	7,005	1,159
50,001 to 100,000.	115	7,968	698	363	243	8,824	7,194	1,091
100,001 to 200,000.	48	6,776	687	337	244	7,859	6,283	958
200,001 to 500,000.	19	5,553	636	307	211	7,291	5,908	729
500,001 and over	6	5,313	514	282	125	6,530	5,568	385

[1] Includes fuel oil, propane, and purchased steam not shown separately. [2] Includes public assembly, public order and safety, and religious worship.

Source: U.S. Energy Information Administration, *Commercial Buildings Energy Consumption and Expenditures, 1995.*

No. 953. Energy Prices: 1980 to 1998

Product	Unit	1980	1990	1992	1993	1994	1995	1996	1997	1998
Crude oil domestic first purchase price:										
Nominal.	Dol/bbl	21.6	20.0	16.0	14.3	13.2	14.6	18.5	17.2	10.87
Real [1]	Dol/bbl	37.9	23.2	17.4	15.2	13.7	14.9	18.5	16.9	10.54
Motor gasoline	Cents/gal.	122.1	121.7	119.0	117.3	117.4	120.5	128.8	129.1	112.0
Leaded regular	Cents/gal.	119.1	114.9	(NA)	(NA)	(NA)	(NA)	(NA)	(NA)	(NA)
Unleaded regular.	Cents/gal.	124.5	116.4	112.7	110.8	111.2	114.7	123.1	123.4	106
Premium	Cents/gal.	(NA)	134.9	131.6	130.2	130.5	133.6	141.3	141.6	125.0
Natural gas, residential	Dol/1,000 cu. ft. . .	3.7	5.8	5.9	6.2	6.4	6.1	6.3	6.9	6.8
Heating oil, residential	Cents/gal.	97.4	106.3	93.4	91.7	88.4	86.7	98.9	98.4	85.2
Coal, all	Dol/short tons. . . .	24.7	21.8	21.0	19.9	19.4	18.8	18.5	26.2	17.7
Electricity, total	Cents/kilowatthour.	4.7	6.6	6.8	6.9	6.9	6.9	6.9	6.9	6.74
Uranium, domestic purchases . . .	Dol/lb	(NA)	15.7	13.5	13.1	10.3	11.1	13.8	12.9	12.3

NA Not available. [1] In chained (1992) dollars, calculated by using gross domestic product implicit price deflators.

Source: U.S. Energy Information Administration, *Annual Energy Review.*

Energy 589

No. 954. Fossil Fuel Prices in Current and Constant (1996) Dollars: 1970 to 1999

[In cents per million British thermal units (Btu). All fuel prices taken as close to the point of production as possible. See text, this section, for explanation of Btu conversions from mineral fuels]

Fuel	1970	1973	1975	1980	1985	1990	1993	1994	1995	1996	1997	1998	1999
CURRENT DOLLARS													
Composite [1]	0.32	0.40	0.82	2.04	2.51	1.84	1.67	1.53	1.47	1.82	1.81	1.41	1.63
Crude oil	0.55	0.67	1.32	3.72	4.15	3.45	2.46	2.27	2.52	3.18	2.97	1.87	2.68
Natural gas	0.15	0.20	0.40	1.45	2.26	1.55	1.84	1.67	1.40	1.96	2.10	1.75	1.86
Bituminous coal [2]	0.27	0.37	0.84	1.10	1.15	1.00	0.93	0.91	0.88	0.87	0.85	0.83	0.83
CONSTANT (1996) DOLLARS													
Composite [1]	1.09	1.18	2.05	3.58	3.41	2.13	1.78	1.59	1.50	1.82	1.77	1.36	1.55
Crude oil	1.89	2.00	3.30	6.52	5.64	3.99	2.61	2.37	2.57	3.18	2.92	1.82	2.56
Natural gas	0.53	0.60	1.00	2.54	3.06	1.79	1.96	1.74	1.43	1.96	2.06	1.70	1.78
Bituminous coal [2]	0.92	1.09	2.11	1.93	1.56	1.15	0.99	0.94	0.90	0.87	0.84	0.81	0.80

[1] Weighted by relative importance of individual fuels in total fuels production.   [2] Includes subbituminous and lignite.

Source: U.S. Energy Information Administration, *Annual Energy Review*.

No. 955. Energy Imports and Exports by Type of Fuel: 1970 to 1998

[In quadrillion of Btu. For definition of Btu, see text, this section]

Type of fuel	1970	1973	1975	1980	1985	1990	1993	1994	1995	1996	1997	1998
Net imports:[1]												
Coal	-0.96	-1.01	-3.24	-4.60	-4.39	-4.42	-2.83	-2.58	-3.24	-3.41	-3.13	-2.75
Natural gas (dry)	0.23	0.32	1.06	3.98	2.79	2.71	4.41	4.50	3.86	5.33	6.02	5.82
Petroleum	0.98	2.93	5.76	10.42	12.57	12.67	7.59	7.78	6.39	11.01	9.37	7.33
Other [2]	-0.08	0.01	0.08	-0.08	-0.03	0.02	0.11	0.23	0.27	0.18	0.20	0.25
Imports:												
Coal	(Z)	(Z)	0.02	0.03	0.07	0.09	0.22	0.23	0.25	0.24	0.26	0.28
Natural gas (dry)	0.26	0.36	1.15	4.21	3.05	2.97	4.77	4.90	4.23	5.79	6.50	6.33
Petroleum	1.48	3.50	6.77	12.54	17.47	16.90	11.74	11.14	9.95	15.27	16.93	13.01
Other [2]	(Z)	0.04	0.16	0.05	0.04	0.07	0.12	0.13	0.16	0.11	0.12	0.14
Exports:												
Coal	0.96	1.01	3.26	4.63	4.47	4.51	3.09	2.85	3.57	3.69	3.39	3.00
Natural gas (dry)	0.03	0.04	0.09	0.23	0.26	0.27	0.36	0.40	0.37	0.46	0.47	0.42
Petroleum	0.50	0.57	1.01	2.12	4.90	4.23	4.15	3.36	3.56	4.25	7.55	5.67
Other [2]	0.08	0.03	0.07	0.13	0.08	0.05	0.06	0.04	0.05	0.06	0.05	0.04

Z Less than .005 quadrillion Btu.   [1] Net imports equals imports minus exports.   Minus sign (-) denotes an excess of exports over imports.   [2] Coal coke and small amounts of electricity transmitted across U.S. borders with Canada and Mexico.

Source: U.S. Energy Information Administration, *Annual Energy Review*.

No. 956. U.S. Foreign Trade in Selected Mineral Fuels: 1973 to 1998

[Minus sign (-) indicates an excess of imports over exports]

Mineral fuel	Unit	1973	1975	1980	1985	1990	1994	1995	1996	1997	1998
NATURAL GAS											
Imports	Bil. cu. ft.	1,033	953	985	950	1,532	2,624	2,841	2,937	2,994	3,152
Exports	Bil. cu. ft.	77	73	49	55	86	162	154	153	157	159
Net trade	Bil. cu. ft.	-956	-880	-936	-894	-1,446	-2,462	-2,687	-2,784	-2,837	-2,993
CRUDE OIL											
Imports [1]	Mil. bbl.	1,184	1,498	1,926	1,168	2,151	2,578	2,639	2,740	3,002	3,178
Exports	Mil. bbl.	1	2	105	75	40	36	35	40	39	40
Net trade	Mil. bbl.	-1,183	-1,496	-1,821	-1,093	-2,112	-2,542	-2,604	-2,700	-2,963	-3,138
PETROLEUM PRODUCTS											
Imports	Mil. bbl.	1,099	712	603	681	775	706	586	719	707	731
Exports	Mil. bbl.	84	74	94	211	273	308	312	318	318	327
Net trade	Mil. bbl.	-1015	-638	-509	-470	-502	-398	-274	-402	-389	-404
COAL											
Imports	1,000 sh. tons	127	940	1,194	1,952	2,699	8,870	9,473	8,115	7,487	8,724
Exports	1,000 sh. tons	53,587	66,309	91,742	92,680	105,804	71,359	88,547	90,473	83,545	78,048
Net trade	1,000 sh. tons	53,460	65,369	90,548	90,728	103,105	62,489	79,074	82,358	76,058	69,324

[1] Beginning 1980, includes strategic petroleum reserve imports.

Source: U.S. Energy Information Administration, *Annual Energy Review*.

No. 957. Crude Oil Imports Into the United States by Country of Origin: 1970 to 1998

[In millions of barrels (483 represents 483,000,000). Barrels contain 42 gallons]

Country of origin	1970	1973	1975	1980	1985	1990	1992	1993	1994	1995	1996	1997	1998
Total imports . . .	483	1,184	1,498	1,921	1,168	2,151	2,220	2,477	2,578	2,643	2,748	3,002	3,178
Total OPEC[1]	183	765	1,172	1,410	479	1,283	1,243	1,317	1,307	1,303	1,280	1,376	1,518
Persian Gulf[2], total. . .	23	293	409	550	89	657	597	598	589	539	544	597	746
Arab OPEC.	52	258	404	713	110	680	608	607	597	549	547	599	746
Algeria	2	44	96	166	31	23	9	9	8	10	3	2	(NA)
Iraq[3]	-	1	1	10	17	188	-	-	-	-	-	33	123
Kuwait[3]	12	15	1	10	1	29	14	126	112	78	86	92	109
Qatar	-	3	7	8	-	1	-	-	-	-	-	-	1
Saudi Arabia[3]	15	169	256	456	48	436	585	468	473	460	457	472	512
United Arab Emirates. .	23	26	43	63	13	3	-	4	4	1	1	-	1
Other OPEC[2], total	160	472	763	860	390	625	646	720	717	764	735	779	772
Indonesia	26	73	138	115	107	36	26	24	34	23	16	19	18
Nigeria	17	164	272	307	102	286	243	264	228	226	218	252	251
Venezuela	98	126	144	57	112	243	302	369	377	421	477	509	503
Non-OPEC[4], total. . . .	245	419	326	511	689	869	977	1,160	1,271	1,340	1,410	1,624	1,656
Canada	245	365	219	73	171	235	292	329	359	380	394	437	462
Ecuador[5].	44	44	14	23	28	33	36	35	42	36			
Gabon	-	-	10	9	19	23	45	55	71	84	67	84	(NA)
Malaysia.	(NA)	(NA)	(NA)	(NA)	(NA)	(NA)	(NA)	4	2	2	2	3	9
Mexico.	-	(Z)	26	185	261	251	288	315	343	375	442	496	482
Norway.	-	-	4	53	11	35	43	50	69	95	107	105	81
Trinidad and Tobago	(Z)	22	42	42	36	28	26	20	23	23	21	20	19
United Kingdom	-	-	(Z)	63	101	57	73	114	145	125	79	62	59

- Represents zero.   NA Not available.   Z Represents less than half the unit of measure.   [1] OPEC (Organization of Petroleum Exporting Countries) includes the Persian Gulf nations shown below, except Bahrain, which is not a member of OPEC, and also includes nations shown under "Other OPEC".   [2] Excludes petroleum imported into the United States indirectly from members of the OPEC countries.   [3] Imports from the Neutral Zone between Kuwait and Saudi Arabia are included in Saudi Arabia.   [4] Includes petroleum imported into the United States indirectly from member of OPEC, primarily from Caribbean and West European areas, as petroleum products that were refined from crude oil produced by OPEC.   [5] Ecuador withdrew from OPEC on Dec. 31, 1992; therefore, it is included under OPEC for the period 1973 to 1992.

Source: 1970, U.S. Bureau of Mines, *Minerals Yearbooks*, Vol. I; thereafter, U.S. Energy Information Administration, *Petroleum Supply Annual*, Vol. I.

No. 958. Crude Oil and Refined Products—Summary: 1973 to 1999

[Barrels of 42 gallons. Data are averages]

Year	Crude Oil (1,000 bbl. per day)					Refined oil products (1,000 bbl. per day)			Total oil imports[2] (1,000 bbl. per day)	Crude oil stocks[3] (mil. bbl.)	
	Input to refineries	Domestic produc-tion	Imports Total[1]	Imports Strategic reserve	Ex-ports	Domestic demand	Imports	Ex-ports		Total	Strategic reserve
1973	12,431	9,208	3,244	(X)	2	17,308	3,012	229	6,256	242	(X)
1974	12,133	8,774	3,477	(X)	3	16,653	2,635	218	6,112	265	(X)
1975	12,442	8,375	4,105	(X)	6	16,322	1,951	204	6,056	271	(X)
1976	13,416	8,132	5,287	(X)	8	17,461	2,026	215	7,313	285	(X)
1977	14,602	8,245	6,615	21	50	18,431	2,193	193	8,807	348	7
1978	14,739	8,707	6,356	161	158	18,847	2,008	204	8,363	376	67
1979	14,648	8,552	6,519	67	235	18,513	1,937	236	8,456	430	91
1980	13,481	8,597	5,263	44	287	17,056	1,646	258	6,909	466	108
1981	12,470	8,572	4,396	256	228	16,058	1,599	367	5,996	594	230
1982	11,774	8,649	3,488	165	236	15,296	1,625	579	5,113	644	294
1983	11,685	8,688	3,329	234	164	15,231	1,722	575	5,051	723	379
1984	12,044	8,879	3,426	197	181	15,726	2,011	541	5,437	796	451
1985	12,002	8,971	3,201	118	204	15,726	1,866	577	5,067	814	493
1986	12,716	8,680	4,178	48	154	16,281	2,045	631	6,224	843	512
1987	12,854	8,349	4,674	73	151	16,665	2,004	613	6,678	890	541
1988	13,246	8,140	5,107	51	155	17,283	2,295	661	7,402	890	560
1989	13,401	7,613	5,843	56	142	17,325	2,217	717	8,061	921	580
1990	13,409	7,355	5,894	27	109	16,988	2,123	748	8,018	908	586
1991	13,301	7,417	5,782	-	116	16,714	1,844	885	7,627	893	569
1992	13,411	7,171	6,083	10	89	17,003	1,805	861	7,888	893	575
1993	13,613	6,847	6,787	15	98	17,237	1,833	904	8,620	922	587
1994	13,866	6,662	7,063	12	99	17,718	1,933	843	8,996	929	592
1995	13,973	6,560	7,230	-	95	17,725	1,605	855	8,835	895	592
1996	14,195	6,465	7,508	-	110	18,309	1,971	871	9,478	850	566
1997	14,662	6,452	8,225	-	108	18,620	1,936	896	10,162	868	563
1998	14,889	6,252	8,706	-	110	18,917	2,002	835	10,708	895	571
1999	14,807	5,925	8,588	6	118	19,389	1,964	822	10,551	852	567

- Represents zero.   X Not applicable.   [1] Includes Strategic Petroleum Reserve.   [2] Crude oil (including Strategic Petroleum Reserve imports) plus refined products.   [3] End of year.

Source: U.S. Energy Information Administration, *Monthly Energy Review*.

No. 959. Petroleum and Coal Products Corporations—Sales, Net Profit, and Profit Per Dollar of Sales: 1980 to 1999

[Represents SIC Group 29. Profit rates are averages of quarterly figures at annual rates. Beginning 1990, excludes estimates for corporations with less than $250,000 in assets]

Item	Unit	1980	1985	1990	1991	1992	1993	1994	1995	1996	1997	1998	1999
Sales	Bil. dol.	333.2	320.9	318.5	282.2	278.0	266.1	268.2	283.1	323.5	320.0	250.4	288.4
Net profit:													
Before income taxes	Bil. dol.	39.1	17.7	23.1	12.1	2.0	14.9	17.2	16.5	32.6	36.8	9.7	20.7
After income taxes	Bil. dol.	25.5	12.7	17.8	10.8	3.1	13.0	14.9	13.9	26.6	29.4	8.3	17.7
Depreciation[1]	Bil. dol.	11.6	22.1	18.7	18.0	18.3	17.4	17.1	16.7	15.9	15.6	14.7	14.0
Profits per dollar of sales:													
Before income taxes	Cents	11.7	5.5	7.3	4.3	0.4	5.6	6.3	5.8	10.1	11.5	3.5	7.0
After income taxes	Cents	7.7	4.0	5.6	3.8	0.9	4.9	5.5	4.9	8.2	9.2	3.1	5.9
Profits on stockholders' equity:													
Before income taxes	Percent	30.7	11.7	16.4	8.6	1.6	11.8	13.2	12.6	23.2	23.5	6.0	13.5
After income taxes	Percent	20.0	8.5	12.7	7.6	2.5	10.2	11.4	10.6	18.9	18.9	5.2	11.5

[1] Includes depletion and accelerated amortization of emergency facilities.
Source: 1980, U.S. Federal Trade Commission; thereafter, U.S. Census Bureau, *Quarterly Financial Report for Manufacturing, Mining and Trade Corporations.*

No. 960. Major Petroleum Companies—Financial Data Summary: 1973 to 1999

[Data represent a composite of approximately 42 major worldwide petroleum companies aggregated on a consolidated total company basis]

Item	1973	1975	1980	1985	1990	1994	1995	1996	1997	1998	1999
FINANCIAL DATA (bil. dol.)											
Net income	11.8	11.6	32.9	19.4	26.8	20.3	24.3	39.7	40.0	14.5	35.0
Depreciation, depletion, etc	10.5	11.3	32.5	53.0	38.7	38.9	43.1	44.4	46.0	61.0	45.9
Cash flow[1]	22.3	22.8	65.4	72.4	65.5	59.2	67.4	84.1	86.0	75.5	80.9
Dividends paid	4.0	4.7	9.3	12.0	15.9	16.4	17.6	18.9	20.1	20.9	23.2
Net internal funds available for investment or debt repayment[2]	18.3	18.1	56.1	60.4	49.6	42.8	49.8	65.2	65.9	54.6	57.7
Capital and exploratory expenditures	16.3	26.9	62.1	58.3	59.6	51.5	59.8	59.3	75.3	83.9	66.2
Long-term capitalization	102.9	121.1	211.4	272.1	300.0	299.0	304.3	336.6	372.5	382.0	402.3
Long-term debt	22.5	28.9	49.8	93.5	90.4	89.1	85.4	80.8	86.1	103.9	106.8
Preferred stock	0.4	0.4	2.0	3.3	5.2	5.4	5.7	5.8	5.1	3.9	3.9
Common stock and retained earnings[3]	80.0	91.9	159.6	175.3	204.4	204.5	213.2	250.0	281.3	274.2	291.6
Excess of expenditures over cash income[4]	-2.0	8.9	6.0	-2.1	10.0	8.7	10.0	-5.9	9.4	29.3	8.5
RATIOS[5] (percent)											
Long-term debt to long-term capitalization	22.0	23.8	23.6	34.4	30.1	29.8	28.1	24.0	23.1	27.2	26.5
Net income to total average capital	12.0	10.0	17.0	7.0	9.1	6.8	8.1	12.4	11.3	3.8	8.9
Net income to average common equity	15.6	13.1	22.5	10.8	13.5	10.1	11.6	17.1	15.1	5.2	12.4

[1] Generally represents internally-generated funds from operations. Sum of net income and noncash charges such as depreciation, depletion, and amortization.   [2] Cash flow minus dividends paid.   [3] Includes common stock, capital surplus, and earned surplus accounts after adjustments.   [4] Capital and exploratory expenditures plus dividends paid minus cash flow.
[5] Represents approximate year-to-year comparisons because of changes in the makeup of the group due to mergers and other corporate changes.
Source: Carl H. Pforzheimer & Co., New York, NY, *Comparative Oil Company Statements,* annual.

No. 961. Electric Utility Sales and Average Prices by End-Use Sector: 1970 to 1999

[Prior to 1980, covers Class A and B privately-owned electric utilities; thereafter, Class A utilities whose electric operating revenues were $100 million or more during the previous year]

Year	Sales (bil. kWh)				Average price of electricity sold (cents per kWh)							
					Current dollars				Chained (1996) dollars [2]			
	Total [1]	Resi- dential	Com- mercial	Indus- trial	Total [1]	Resi- dential	Com- mercial	Indus- trial	Total [1]	Resi- dential	Com- mercial	Indus- trial
1970	1,392	466	307	571	1.7	2.2	2.1	1.0	5.8	7.6	7.2	3.4
1973	1,713	579	388	686	2.0	2.5	2.4	1.3	6.0	7.4	7.1	3.9
1975	1,747	588	403	688	2.9	3.5	3.5	2.1	7.2	8.7	8.7	5.2
1980	2,094	717	488	815	4.7	5.4	5.5	3.7	8.2	9.5	9.6	6.5
1985	2,324	794	606	837	6.4	7.39	7.27	4.97	8.7	10.0	9.9	6.7
1986	2,369	819	631	831	6.4	7.42	7.20	4.93	8.6	9.8	9.6	6.6
1987	2,457	850	660	858	6.4	7.45	7.08	4.77	8.2	9.6	9.1	6.2
1988	2,578	893	699	896	6.4	7.48	7.04	4.70	7.9	9.3	8.8	5.9
1989	2,647	906	726	926	6.5	7.65	7.20	4.72	7.8	9.2	8.6	5.7
1990	2,713	924	751	946	6.6	7.83	7.34	4.74	7.6	9.0	8.5	5.5
1991	2,762	955	766	947	6.8	8.04	7.53	4.83	7.5	9.0	8.4	5.4
1992	2,763	936	761	973	6.8	8.21	7.66	4.83	7.4	8.9	8.3	5.3
1993	2,861	995	795	977	6.9	8.32	7.74	4.85	7.4	8.8	8.2	5.2
1994	2,935	1,008	820	1,008	6.9	8.38	7.73	4.77	7.2	8.7	8.0	5.0
1995	3,013	1,043	863	1,013	6.9	8.40	7.69	4.66	7.0	8.6	7.8	4.8
1996	3,098	1,082	887	1,030	6.9	8.36	7.64	4.60	6.9	8.4	7.6	4.6
1997	3,140	1,076	928	1,033	6.9	8.43	7.59	4.53	6.7	8.3	7.4	4.4
1998	3,240	1,128	969	1,040	6.7	8.26	7.41	4.48	6.5	8.0	7.2	4.3
1999	3,265	1,139	975	1,050	6.6	8.17	7.20	4.42	6.3	7.8	6.9	4.2

[1] Includes other sectors not shown separately.   [2] Based on the GDP implicit price deflator.
Source: U.S. Energy Information Administration, *Annual Energy Review.*

592   Energy

No. 962. Electric Utility Industry—Net Generation, Net Summer Capability, Generating Units, and Consumption of Fuels: 1980 to 1998

[Net generation for **calendar years;** other data as of **December 31**]

Item	Unit	1980	1990	1992	1993	1994	1995	1996	1997	1998
RETAIL SALES										
Retail sales, total	Bil. kWh . .	2,094	2,713	2,763	2,861	2,935	3,013	3,098	3,140	3,240
Net generation by electric utilities. . .	Bil. kWh. . .	2,286	2,808	2,797	2,883	2,911	2,995	3,077	3,123	3,212
Purchases by utilities from nonutility purchasers.	Bil. kWh. . .	1	116	166	189	209	222	229	243	259
Imports	Bil. kWh. . .	25	23	37	39	52	47	47	(NA)	(NA)
Exports	Bil. kWh. . .	4	21	9	11	8	9	9	(NA)	(NA)
Losses and unaccounted for	Bil. kWh. . .	214	214	229	238	223	232	277	(NA)	(NA)
NET GENERATION										
Total	Bil. kWh . .	2,286	2,808	2,797	2,883	2,911	2,995	3,077	3,123	3,212
Average annual change [1]	Percent . . .	3.5	0.9	-1.0	3.0	1.0	2.8	2.7	1.5	2.9
Net generation, kWh per kW of net summer capability [2].	Rate	3,951	4,067	4,024	4,119	4,147	4,248	4,333	(NA)	(NA)
Source of energy:										
Coal [3]	Percent . . .	50.8	55.6	56.3	56.9	56.2	55.2	57.0	57.3	56.3
Nuclear	Percent . . .	11.0	20.5	22.1	21.2	22.0	22.5	22.0	20.1	21.0
Oil	Percent . . .	10.8	4.2	3.2	3.5	3.1	2.0	2.0	2.5	3.4
Gas	Percent . . .	15.1	9.4	9.4	9.0	10.0	10.3	9.0	9.1	9.6
Hydro	Percent . . .	12.1	10.1	8.7	9.3	8.5	9.9	11.0	10.9	9.6
Type of prime mover: [4]										
Hydro	Bil. kWh. . .	276	280	240	265	244	294	328	337	304
Steam conventional [5]	Bil. kWh. . .	1,726	1,919	1,908	1,964	1,982	1,977	2,018	2,094	2,158
Gas turbine and internal combustion.	Bil. kWh. . .	28	14	21	25	36	44	49	55	69
Steam nuclear	Bil. kWh. . .	251	577	619	610	640	673	675	629	674
Other	Bil. kWh. . .	6	11	10	10	9	6	7	(NA)	(NA)
NET SUMMER CAPABILITY										
Total [6]	Mil. kW . . .	579	691	695	700	702	705	710	(NA)	687
Average annual change [1]	Percent . . .	3.3	0.8	0.3	0.7	0.3	0.4	0.7	(NA)	(NA)
Hydro	Mil. kW . . .	82	91	93	96	96	97	94	(NA)	94
Steam conventional [7]	Mil. kW . . .	397	448	447	447	446	446	442	(NA)	423
Gas turbine	Mil. kW . . .	43	46	50	52	55	57	53	(NA)	53
Steam nuclear	Mil. kW . . .	52	100	99	99	99	99	101	(NA)	97
Internal combustion.	Mil. kW . . .	5	5	5	5	5	5	5	(NA)	5
Geothermal and other	Mil. kW . . .	1	2	2	2	2	2	2	(NA)	2
Combined cycle	Mil. kW . . .	(NA)	(NA)	(NA)	(NA)	(NA)	(NA)	14	(NA)	14
NUMBER OF GENERATING UNITS										
Total [8]	Number	11,084	10,296	10,221	10,471	10,427	10,396	10,422	(NA)	10,207
Hydro	Number . .	3,275	3,479	3,497	3,388	3,362	3,337	3,480	3,346	3,406
Steam conventional.	Number . .	2,862	2,354	2,307	2,221	2,170	2,157	2,153	(NA)	2,022
Gas turbine	Number . .	1,447	1,460	1,501	1,411	1,446	1,486	1,542	(NA)	1,490
Steam nuclear	Number . .	74	111	109	109	109	109	110	110	104
Internal combustion.	Number . .	3,410	2,847	2,807	2,976	2,953	2,920	2,884	(NA)	2,929
CONSUMPTION OF FOSSIL FUELS										
Net generation by fuel [9]	Quad. Btu .	18.56	20.32	19.99	20.58	20.92	20.92	21.44	(NA)	(NA)
Coal	Quad. Btu .	12.12	16.19	6.21	16.79	16.90	16.99	17.91	18.44	18.72
Percent of total	Percent . . .	65.30	79.68	81.09	81.58	80.78	81.21	83.5	(NA)	(NA)
Petroleum	Quad. Btu .	2.63	1.25	0.95	1.05	0.97	0.66	0.73	0.84	1.17
Gas	Quad. Btu .	3.81	2.88	2.83	2.74	3.05	3.28	2.81	3.03	3.32
Fuel consumed:										
Coal	Mil. sh. tons	569	774	780	814	817	829	875	900	911
Oil	Mil. bbl. . . .	421	200	152	169	155	102	113	125	179
Gas	Bil cu. ft. . . .	3,682	2,787	2,766	2,682	2,987	3,197	2,732	2,968	3,258

NA Not available.   [1] Change from immediate prior year, except for 1980, change from 1975. For explanation of average annual percent change, see Guide to Tabular Presentation.   [2] Net summer capability is the steady hourly output that generating equipment is expected to supply to system load, exclusive of auxiliary power as demonstrated by test at the time of summer peak demand.   [3] Includes small percentage (.5 percent) from wood and waste, geothermal, and petroleum coke.   [4] A prime mover is the engine, turbine, water wheel, or similar machine which drives an electric generator.   [5] Fossil fuels only.   [6] Includes wind, solar thermal, and photovoltaic, not shown separately.   [7] Includes fossil steam, wood, and waste.   [8] Each prime mover type in combination plants counted separately. Includes geothermal, wind, and solar, not shown separately.   [9] Includes small amounts of wood, waste, wind, geothermal, solar thermal, and photovoltaic.

Source: U.S. Energy Information Administration, 1980, *Power Production, Fuel Consumption, and Installed Capacity Data-Annual,* and unpublished data; thereafter, *Electric Power Annual, Annual Energy Review,* and unpublished data.

Energy   593

No. 963. Electric Utility Industry—Capability, Peak Load, and Capacity Margin: 1980 to 1998

[Excludes Alaska and Hawaii. Capability represents the maximum kilowatt output with all power sources available and with hydraulic equipment under actual water conditions, allowing for maintenance, emergency outages, and system operating requirements. Capacity margin is the difference between capability and peak load]

| Year | Capability at the time of— | | | | Noncoincident peak load | | Capacity margin | | | |
| | Summer peak load (1,000 kW) | | Winter peak load (1,000 kW) | | | | Summer | | Winter | |
	Amount	Change from prior year	Amount	Change from prior year	Summer	Winter	Amount (1,000 kW)	Percent of capability	Amount (1,000 kW)	Percent of capability
1980	558,237	13,731	572,195	17,670	427,058	384,567	131,179	23.5	187,628	32.8
1981	572,219	13,982	586,569	14,374	429,349	397,800	142,870	25.0	188,769	32.2
1982	586,142	13,923	598,066	11,497	415,618	373,985	170,524	29.1	224,081	37.5
1983	596,449	10,307	612,453	14,387	447,526	410,779	148,923	25.0	201,674	32.9
1984	604,240	7,791	622,125	9,672	451,150	436,374	153,090	25.3	185,751	29.9
1985	621,597	17,357	636,475	14,350	460,503	423,660	161,094	25.9	212,815	33.4
1986	633,291	11,694	646,721	10,246	476,320	422,857	156,971	24.8	223,864	34.6
1987	648,118	14,827	662,977	16,256	496,185	448,277	151,933	23.4	214,700	32.4
1988	661,580	13,462	676,940	13,963	529,460	466,533	132,120	20.0	210,407	31.1
1989	673,316	11,736	685,249	8,309	523,432	496,378	149,884	22.3	188,871	27.6
1990	685,091	11,775	696,757	11,508	545,537	484,014	139,554	20.4	212,743	30.5
1991	690,915	5,824	703,212	6,455	551,320	485,435	139,595	20.2	217,777	31.0
1992	695,436	4,521	707,752	4,540	548,707	492,983	146,729	21.1	214,769	30.3
1993	694,250	1,186	711,957	4,205	575,356	521,733	118,894	17.1	190,224	26.7
1994	702,985	8,735	715,090	3,133	585,320	518,253	117,665	16.7	196,837	27.5
1995	714,222	11,237	727,679	12,589	620,249	544,684	93,973	13.2	182,995	25.1
1996	723,571	9,349	740,526	12,847	615,529	545,061	108,042	14.9	195,465	26.4
1997	729,079	5,508	743,774	3,248	631,355	560,228	97,724	13.4	183,546	24.7
1998	727,242	-1,837	742,391	-1,383	648,694	573,107	78,548	10.8	169,284	22.8

Source: Edison Electric Institute, Washington, DC, *Statistical Yearbook of the Electric Utility Industry,* annual.

No. 964. Electric Energy Sales by Class of Service and by State, 1999

[In billions of kilowatt-hours (3,265.4 represents 3,265,400,000,000)]

State	Total [1]	Residential	Commercial	Industrial	State	Total [1]	Residential	Commercial	Industrial
Total [2]	3,265.4	1,139.5	975.2	1,050.4	Missouri	68.0	27.5	23.9	15.7
					Montana	9.4	3.6	3.1	2.5
Alabama	78.9	26.7	15.3	36.2	Nebraska	23.0	8.0	6.7	6.9
Alaska	5.3	1.9	2.4	0.9	Nevada	26.0	8.3	6.0	10.8
Arizona	57.2	22.6	20.1	11.7	New Hampshire ...	9.7	3.6	3.5	2.5
Arkansas	39.1	13.9	8.3	16.2	New Jersey	70.6	24.6	32.3	13.3
California	230.4	75.6	90.0	60.3					
					New Mexico	17.9	4.6	6.0	5.8
Colorado	40.9	13.2	17.4	9.3	New York	126.9	41.7	46.9	25.4
Connecticut	29.7	11.6	11.8	6.0	North Carolina	114.5	43.4	34.7	34.3
Delaware	10.7	3.6	3.4	3.8	North Dakota	8.2	3.3	2.6	1.8
Dist. of Columbia ..	10.4	1.6	8.1	0.2	Ohio	161.3	46.5	38.9	71.7
Florida	186.4	93.6	70.0	17.1					
					Oklahoma	46.4	18.2	12.6	12.9
Georgia	109.6	40.9	33.5	33.8	Oregon	49.4	17.9	14.3	16.6
Hawaii	9.4	2.7	2.9	3.7	Pennsylvania	132.4	44.5	38.2	48.4
Idaho	21.9	6.8	6.4	8.3	Rhode Island	7.1	2.7	2.9	1.4
Illinois	131.6	39.4	40.3	43.3	South Carolina	72.4	23.3	16.6	31.5
Indiana	95.7	28.7	19.7	46.8					
					South Dakota	7.9	3.3	2.3	1.9
Iowa	36.9	11.8	8.0	15.7	Tennessee	93.0	35.3	12.6	44.1
Kansas	33.4	11.5	9.7	9.7	Texas	298.7	107.3	79.7	98.3
Kentucky	75.9	22.2	12.0	38.5	Utah	22.0	6.3	7.4	7.5
Louisiana	77.9	26.3	17.5	31.3	Vermont	5.4	2.0	1.9	1.5
Maine	11.9	3.7	3.5	4.7					
					Virginia	92.3	35.5	26.8	20.0
Maryland	59.4	23.5	25.1	10.0	Washington	93.2	33.0	23.1	33.5
Massachusetts	50.6	17.3	22.5	10.2	West Virginia	27.1	9.4	6.5	11.1
Michigan	102.8	30.7	35.0	36.3	Wisconsin	63.9	19.6	17.0	26.6
Minnesota	56.8	18.2	11.1	26.8	Wyoming	12.3	2.1	2.6	7.1
Mississippi	43.3	16.0	9.8	16.7					

[1] Includes other service not shown separately.　[2] Estimated.

Source: U.S. Energy Information Administration, *Electric Power Annual.*

No. 965. Electric Energy—Net Generation and Net Summer Capability by State: 1990 to 1998

[Capacity as of **Dec. 31. (2,808.2 represents 2,808,200,000,000).** Covers utilities for public use]

State	Net generation (bil. kWh) 1990	1995	1998 Total	1998 Percent from coal	Net summer capability (mil. kW) 1995	1998
U.S.	2,286.4	2,994.5	3,212.2	56.3	706.1	711.9
AL	78.3	99.6	113.4	63.0	20.5	20.8
AK	3.1	4.8	4.6	3.7	1.7	1.8
AZ	36.9	69.0	81.3	44.6	15.2	15.2
AR	19.7	39.5	43.2	53.6	9.6	9.7
CA	140.3	121.9	114.9	-	43.3	43.7
CO	23.6	32.7	35.5	93.3	6.6	6.9
CT	24.7	26.9	15.1	9.8	6.7	6.3
DE	6.7	8.3	6.3	60.3	2.2	2.3
DC	0.7	0.2	0.2	-	0.8	0.8
FL	95.9	147.2	169.4	38.6	35.9	36.7
GA	63.3	102.0	108.7	64.3	22.3	23.1
HI	6.5	6.2	6.3	-	1.6	1.6
ID	9.5	10.1	12.0	-	2.6	2.6
IL	103.4	145.2	131.3	53.6	33.1	33.5
IN	70.6	105.2	112.8	98.2	20.7	20.2
IA	21.8	33.5	37.1	86.0	8.2	8.2
KS	25.1	38.2	41.5	67.6	9.7	9.8
KY	57.1	86.2	86.2	95.7	15.4	15.7
LA	45.7	65.6	66.1	31.4	17.0	17.1
ME	7.9	2.7	3.5	-	2.4	1.5
MD	32.2	44.7	48.5	59.9	11.0	11.1
MA	34.8	27.0	26.0	31.4	9.3	9.4
MI	74.8	92.5	85.1	81.2	22.0	21.9
MN	31.5	42.5	44.0	68.0	8.9	9.2
MS	18.5	26.4	32.0	36.7	7.2	7.2
MO	48.9	65.4	74.9	83.4	15.7	16.2
MT	15.5	25.4	27.6	59.8	4.9	4.9
NE	16.3	25.3	28.7	63.8	5.5	5.8
NV	14.1	20.0	26.6	64.6	5.6	5.6
NH	6.0	13.9	14.2	24.7	2.5	2.5
NJ	29.4	27.1	35.9	15.6	13.8	13.7
NM	24.7	29.4	31.4	87.6	5.1	5.2
NY	108.6	101.2	115.8	20.3	32.1	30.0
NC	72.1	96.1	113.1	61.0	20.6	21.1
ND	15.8	28.8	30.5	92.3	4.5	4.7
OH	110.2	137.9	146.4	87.9	27.4	26.6
OK	44.6	48.0	51.5	60.3	12.9	12.9
OR	36.6	44.0	46.4	7.2	10.4	10.5
PA	122.5	168.9	173.9	61.3	33.7	33.8
RI	1.0	0.7	2.1	-	0.4	0.4
SC	41.9	78.4	84.4	38.4	16.7	17.4
SD	8.6	8.8	9.1	34.0	3.0	2.9
TN	60.2	82.3	94.1	58.5	16.1	17.4
TX	203.0	261.7	293.1	45.3	64.4	64.9
UT	32.1	35.2	94.4	4.8	4.9	
VT	3.8	4.8	4.4	-	1.1	1.1
VA	34.3	52.7	63.8	49.3	14.3	15.3
WA	92.3	95.7	97.1	9.6	24.3	25.3
WV	70.8	77.3	89.6	99.3	14.5	14.5
WI	37.8	51.0	52.5	75.7	11.5	11.8
WY	22.4	39.7	44.7	96.8	6.0	6.0

- Represents zero.

Source: U.S. Energy Information Administration, *Electric Power Annual, Electric Power Monthly,* December issues, and *Inventory of Power Plants in the United States,* annual.

No. 966. Nuclear Power Plants—Number of Units, Net Generation, and Net Summer Capability by State: 1998

State	Number of units	Net generation Total (mil. kWh)	Net generation Percent of total[1]	Net summer capability Total (mil. kW)	Net summer capability Percent of total[1]
U.S.	107	673,702	21	99.7	14.0
AL	5	28,663	25	4.9	23.4
AZ	3	30,301	37	3.8	24.9
AR	2	13,097	30	1.7	17.5
CA	4	34,594	30	4.3	9.9
CT	3	3,243	21	2.6	41.8
FL	5	31,115	18	3.9	10.6
GA	4	31,380	29	4.0	17.1
IL	13	55,596	42	12.6	37.6
IA	1	3,768	10	0.5	6.5
KS	1	10,411	25	1.2	11.9
LA	2	16,428	25	2.0	11.8
ME	-	(NA)	(NA)	-	-
MD	2	13,331	28	1.7	15.1
MA	1	5,698	22	0.7	7.1
MI	4	12,494	15	3.9	17.9
MN	3	11,644	25	1.6	17.1
MS	1	9,191	29	1.2	16.8
MO	1	8,517	11	1.1	7.1
NE	2	8,259	29	1.3	21.7
NH	1	8,387	59	1.2	46.3
NJ	4	27,132	76	3.9	28.2
NY	6	31,314	27	5.0	16.5
NC	5	38,778	34	4.7	22.6
OH	2	16,476	11	2.0	7.7
PA	9	61,149	35	9.0	26.6
SC	7	48,759	58	6.4	36.8
TN	3	28,388	30	3.4	19.3
TX	4	38,685	13	4.8	7.4
VT	1	3,358	76	0.5	45.3
VA	4	27,234	43	3.4	22.2
WA	1	6,916	7	1.2	4.6
WI	3	9,397	18	1.4	12.1

- Represents zero.   NA Not available.   [1] For total capability and generation, see Table 965.

Source: U.S. Energy Information Administration, *Electric Power Annual* and *Electric Power Monthly,* December issues.

U.S. Census Bureau, Statistical Abstract of the United States: 2000

No. 967. Nuclear Power Plants—Number, Capacity, and Generation: 1980 to 1999

Item	1980	1985	1990	1991	1992	1993	1994	1995	1996	1997	1998	1999
Operable generating units [1]	71	96	112	111	109	110	109	109	109	107	104	104
Net summer capability [1][2] (mil. kW)	51.8	79.4	99.6	99.6	99.0	99.1	99.1	99.5	100.8	99.7	97.1	97.2
Net generation (bil. kWh)	251.1	383.7	577.0	612.6	618.8	610.4	640.5	673.4	674.7	628.6	673.7	727.9
Percent of total electric utility generation	11.0	15.5	19.1	19.9	20.1	19.1	19.7	20.1	19.6	18.0	18.6	19.8
Capacity factor [3]	56.3	58.0	66.0	70.2	70.9	70.5	73.8	77.4	76.2	71.1	78.2	85.5

[1] As of year-end.   [2] Net summer capability is the peak steady hourly output that generating equipment is expected to supply to system load, exclusive of auxiliary and other power plant, as demonstrated by test at the time of summer peak demand. [3] Weighted average of monthly capacity factors. Monthly factors are derived by dividing actual monthly generation by the maximum possible generation for the month (hours in month times net maximum dependable capacity).

Source: U.S. Energy Information Administration, *Annual Energy Review.*

No. 968. Uranium Supply and Discharged Commercial Reactor Fuel: 1980 to 1998

[Years ending **Dec. 31.** For additional data on uranium, see Section 24, Natural Resources on mining]

Item	Unit	1980	1985	1990	1993	1994	1995	1996	1997	1998, prel.
URANIUM CONCENTRATE										
Production	Mil. lb	43.70	11.31	8.89	3.06	3.35	6.04	6.32	5.64	4.71
Exports	Mil. lb	5.8	5.3	2.0	3.0	17.7	9.8	11.5	17.0	15.1
Imports	Mil. lb	3.6	11.7	23.7	21.0	36.6	41.3	45.4	43.0	43.7
Utility purchases from domestic suppliers	Mil. lb	(NA)	21.7	20.5	15.5	22.7	22.3	22.9	18.7	20.3
Loaded into U.S. nuclear reactors [1]	Mil. lb	(NA)	(NA)	45.1	40.4	51.1	46.2	48.2	38.3
Inventories, total	Mil. lb	(NA)	176.9	129.1	105.7	86.9	72.5	80.0	106.2	137.6
At domestic suppliers	Mil. lb	(NA)	23.7	26.4	24.5	21.5	13.7	13.9	40.4	70.7
At electric utilities	Mil. lb	(NA)	153.2	102.7	81.2	65.4	58.7	66.1	65.9	66.9
Average prices:										
Purchased imports	Dol. per lb	(NA)	20.08	12.55	10.53	8.95	10.20	13.15	11.81	11.19
Domestic purchases	Dol. per lb	(NA)	31.43	15.70	13.14	10.30	11.11	13.81	12.87	12.31
DISCHARGED COMMERCIAL REACTOR FUEL [2]										
Annual discharge	Metric tons	1,193	1,330	2,084	2,102	1,809	2,292	2,174	(NA)	(NA)
Inventory, year-end [3]	Metric tons	6,434	12,481	21,029	27,039	28,848	31,140	(NA)	(NA)	(NA)

NA Not available.   [1] Does not include any fuel rods removed from reactors and later reloaded into the reactor.   [2] Uranium content. Source: Nuclear Assurance Corporation, Atlanta, GA.   [3] Reprocessed fuel not included as inventory.

Source: Except as noted, U.S. Energy Information Administration, *Annual Energy Review, Uranium Industry Annual* and unpublished data.

No. 969. Electric Utilities—Generation, Sales, Revenue, and Customers: 1980 to 1998

[Sales and revenue are to and from ultimate customers]

Class	Unit	1980	1985	1990	1993	1994	1995	1996	1997	1998
Generation [1]	Bil. kWh	2,286	2,470	2,808	2,883	2,911	2,995	3,077	3,123	(NA)
Sales [2]	Bil. kWh	2,126	2,306	2,684	2,850	2,935	3,013	3,098	3,140	3,240
Residential or domestic	Bil. kWh	734	793	916	994	1,008	1,043	1,082	1,076	1,128
Percent of total	Percent	34.5	34.4	34.1	34.9	34.3	34.6	34.9	34.4	34.8
Commercial [3]	Bil. kWh	524	606	739	803	820	863	887	928	969
Industrial [4]	Bil. kWh	794	820	932	957	1,008	1,013	1,030	1,033	1,040
Revenue [2]	Bil. dol	95.5	149.2	176.5	197.9	202.7	207.7	212.5	215.1	218.3
Residential or domestic	Bil. dol	37.6	58.6	71.7	82.4	84.6	87.6	90.5	90.7	93.2
Percent of total	Percent	39.4	39.3	40.7	41.7	41.7	42.2	42.6	42.2	42.7
Commercial [3]	Bil. dol	27.4	44.1	54.2	62.0	63.4	66.4	67.8	71.8
Industrial [4]	Bil. dol	27.3	41.4	44.9	46.6	48.1	47.2	47.4	46.8	46.5
Ultimate customers, Dec. 31 [2]	Million	92.7	101.6	110.1	115.2	116.5	118.3	120.0	122.1	124.0
Residential or domestic	Million	82.2	89.8	97.0	101.3	102.3	103.9	105.3	107.0	108.7
Commercial [3]	Million	9.7	10.9	12.1	12.5	12.7	13.0	13.2	13.5	13.8
Industrial [4]	Million	0.5	0.5	0.5	0.5	0.6	0.6	0.6	0.6	0.5
Avg. kWh used per customer	1,000	23.2	22.9	24.6	24.9	25.2	(NA)	25.8	25.7	(NA)
Residential	1,000	9.0	8.9	9.5	9.9	9.9	(NA)	10.3	10.1	(NA)
Commercial [3]	1,000	54.5	56.1	61.3	64.4	65.7	(NA)	78.0	68.7	(NA)
Avg. annual bill per customer	Dollar	1,040	1,482	1,614	1,727	1,741	(NA)	1,769	1,761	(NA)
Residential	Dollar	462	658	744	818	827	(NA)	859	849	(NA)
Commercial [3]	Dollar	2,848	4,080	4,494	4,977	5,076	(NA)	5,140	5,209	(NA)
Avg. revenue per kWh sold	Cents	4.49	6.47	6.57	6.94	6.91	6.89	6.86	6.85	6.74
Residential	Cents	5.12	7.39	7.83	8.29	8.38	8.40	8.36	8.43	8.26
Commercial [3]	Cents	5.22	7.27	7.33	7.73	7.73	7.69	7.64	7.59	7.41
Industrial [4]	Cents	3.44	5.04	4.81	4.87	4.77	4.66	4.60	4.53	4.48

NA Not available.   [1] Source: U.S. Energy Information Administration, *Monthly Energy Review*, monthly.   [2] Includes other types not shown separately.   [3] Small light and power.   [4] Large light and power.

Source: Except as noted, Edison Electric Institute, Washington, DC, *Statistical Yearbook of the Electric Utility Industry*, annual.

596 Energy

No. 970. Major Investor-Owned Electric Utilities—Balance Sheet and Income Account of Privately Owned Companies: 1993 to 1998

[In millions of dollars ($193,638 represents $193,638,000,000). As of **Dec. 31.** Covers approximately 180 investor-owned electric utilities that during each of the last 3 years met any one or more of the following conditions—1 mil. megawatt-hours of total sales; 100 megawatt-hours of sales for resale, 500 megawatt-hours of gross interchange out, and 500 megawatt-hours of wheeling for other]

Item	1993	1994	1995	1996	1997	1998
COMPOSITE INCOME ACCOUNTS						
Operating revenue	193,638	196,282	199,967	207,459	215,083	217,818
Electric	176,354	179,307	183,655	188,901	195,898	201,613
Gas	16,687	16,222	15,580	17,869	18,663	15,735
Other utility	597	753	731	689	522	470
Operating expenses	161,908	164,207	165,321	173,920	182,796	186,103
Electric	146,118	148,663	150,599	156,938	165,443	171,294
Operation	91,328	93,108	91,881	97,207	104,337	110,807
Maintenance	12,447	12,022	11,767	12,050	12,368	12,451
Depreciation	18,099	18,679	19,885	21,194	23,072	23,890
Taxes other than income taxes	13,040	13,275	13,519	13,569	13,612	12,836
Regulatory debits (net)	429	706	1,142	683	616	-585
Income taxes	8,297	9,626	11,480	11,195	11,862	13,078
Deferred income tax	2,993	1,832	1,474	1,617	25	-535
Investment tax credit (net)	-516	-585	-550	-577	-448	-649
Gas	15,235	14,878	14,073	16,258	16,925	14,396
Income taxes	252	465	532	224	585	668
Other	14,983	14,413	13,541	16,034	16,341	13,718
Operating income	31,730	32,074	34,646	33,539	32,286	31,715
Electric	30,236	30,645	33,057	31,963	30,454	30,319
Gas	1,452	1,344	1,507	1,612	1,737	1,339
Other utility	41	86	82	-36	95	57
Total income before interest charges	33,076	33,884	36,457	35,153	34,100	32,827
Net interest charges	14,700	14,162	14,421	13,990	14,086	13,963
Interest expense	14,567	13,915	14,170	13,646	13,768	13,654
Less allow. for borrowed funds used during const'n.	555	421	435	326	331	323
Other charges, net	689	667	687	671	649	632
Net income before extraordinary charges	18,376	19,722	22,036	21,162	20,014	18,864
Less extraordinary items after taxes	484	-165	-25	-66	3,151	1,344
Net income	17,891	19,888	22,061	21,228	16,863	17,521
Dividends declared - preferred stock	1,765	1,582	1,519	1,248	1,005	756
Earnings available for common stocks	16,126	18,306	20,542	19,980	15,857	16,764
Dividends declared - common stock.	15,334	15,876	16,250	16,810	17,756	17,361
Additions total earnings	296	2,063	4,282	2,193	-1,960	-17
COMPOSITE BALANCE SHEET						
Total assets and other debits	**566,641**	**574,512**	**578,934**	**581,991**	**586,241**	**598,951**
Utility plant, net	393,829	397,812	397,383	396,438	385,258	363,015
Electric utility plant, net	363,829	366,936	366,116	363,854	351,427	328,215
Electric utility plant	519,207	535,928	553,858	569,969	579,042	574,716
Construction work in progress	18,049	17,148	13,523	11,396	11,164	11,353
Less accumulated depreciation	173,427	186,140	201,265	217,510	238,779	257,854
Nuclear fuel, net	5,964	5,657	5,286	5,444	5,219	4,791
Other utility plant, net.	24,036	25,219	25,981	27,140	28,613	30,009
Other property and investments	20,064	23,479	27,988	33,120	43,248	48,398
Current and accrued assets	42,410	41,263	44,140	43,515	47,639	54,491
Deferred debits	110,338	111,957	109,423	108,918	110,096	133,048
CAPITALIZATION AND LIABILITIES						
Liabilities and other credits.	**566,641**	**574,512**	**578,934**	**581,991**	**586,241**	**598,951**
Capitalization	360,455	364,725	365,775	365,783	369,079	366,814
Common stock equity (end of year)	(NA)	164,483	170,497	174,325	174,467	172,351
Common stock	107,471	109,522	111,302	112,633	113,890	113,169
Retained earnings (adjusted)	52,826	54,961	59,195	61,692	60,577	59,182
Preferred stock.	25,304	24,860	21,569	18,830	16,080	14,337
Long-term debt.	174,854	175,382	173,708	172,627	178,532	180,126
Current liabilities and deferred credits	206,186	209,787	213,159	216,208	217,162	232,137
Other noncurrent liabilities	11,478	13,453	14,352	15,309	17,086	18,004
Current and accrued liabilities	48,879	48,035	49,929	49,342	51,594	57,743
Deferred credits	145,829	148,299	148,877	151,557	148,482	156,389
Accumulated deferred income taxes	104,964	107,055	108,615	110,537	106,394	106,550
Accumulated deferred investment tax credit	13,429	12,784	12,139	11,491	10,783	9,793
Other deferred credits (adjusted)	27,436	28,460	28,123	29,529	31,305	40,047
COMPOSITE FINANCIAL INDICATORS						
Activity:						
1. Electric fixed asset (net plant) turnover	0.48	0.49	0.50	0.52	0.56	0.61
2. Total asset turnover	0.34	0.34	0.35	0.36	0.37	0.36
Leverage:						
3. Current assets to current liabilities	0.87	0.86	0.88	0.88	0.92	0.94
4. Long term debt to capitalization	48.51	48.09	47.49	47.19	48.37	49.11
5. Preferred stock to capitalization	7.02	6.82	5.90	5.15	4.36	3.91
6. Common stock equity to capitalization	44.47	45.10	46.61	47.66	47.27	46.99
7. Total debt to total assets	32.48	32.35	31.89	31.57	32.23	32.00
8. Common stock equity to total assets	28.29	28.63	29.45	29.95	29.76	28.78
9. Interest coverage before taxes without AFUDC	2.78	3.10	3.37	3.36	3.33	3.37
Profitability:						
10. Profit margin	9.24	10.13	11.03	10.23	7.84	8.04
11. Return on average common stock equity	22.32	12.24	13.17	12.31	9.67	10.10
12. Return on investment	3.16	3.46	3.81	3.65	2.88	2.93

NA Not available.

Source: U.S. Energy Information Administration, *Electric Power Annual.*

No. 971. Nonutility Electric Power Producers—Summary by Type of Fuel: 1990 to 1998

Type of fuel	1990	1991	1992	1993	1994	1995	1996	1997	1998
Installed capacity (megawatts)......	45,271	49,998	56,814	60,778	68,461	70,254	73,189	74,004	98,085
Coal [1]	6,937	7,351	8,503	9,772	10,372	10,877	11,370	11,027	13,712
Petroleum [2]	1,038	1,514	1,730	2,043	2,262	2,116	2,251	2,924	2,629
Natural gas	17,430	20,694	21,542	23,463	26,925	27,906	30,166	31,092	37,325
Other gas [3]	(4)	(4)	(4)	(4)	1,130	1,217	327	35	205
Petroleum/natural gas (combined)	6,468	5,292	8,478	8,505	9,820	10,479	10,912	10,029	23,105
Hydroelectric	1,968	2,072	2,684	2,741	3,364	3,399	3,419	3,770	4,136
Geothermal	1,086	1,103	1,254	1,318	1,335	1,295	1,346	1,303	1,449
Solar	360	360	360	360	360	354	354	354	385
Wind	1,405	1,652	1,822	1,813	1,737	1,723	1,670	1,566	1,689
Wood [5]	6,049	6,708	6,805	7,046	7,416	6,885	7,263	7,282	6,887
Waste [6]	2,323	2,741	3,006	3,131	3,150	3,430	3,463	3,394	3,488
Gross generation (mil. kilowatthours)	220,058	251,747	296,001	325,226	354,925	375,901	382,423	384,496	421,364
Coal [1]	32,131	40,587	47,363	53,367	59,035	60,234	61,375	59,211	70,369
Petroleum [2]	7,330	7,814	10,963	13,364	15,069	15,049	14,959	15,930	17,533
Natural gas	116,969	131,820	158,798	174,282	179,735	196,633	198,555	207,527	238,747
Other gases [3]	(4)	(4)	(4)	(4)	12,480	13,984	14,750	11,687	8,866
Hydroelectric	8,153	8,180	9,446	11,511	13,227	14,774	16,555	17,902	14,633
Geothermal	7,235	8,014	8,578	9,749	10,122	9,912	10,198	9,382	9,882
Solar	663	779	746	897	824	824	903	893	887
Wind	2,251	2,606	2,916	3,052	3,482	3,185	3,400	3,248	3,015
Wood [5]	30,812	33,785	36,255	37,421	38,595	37,283	37,525	34,898	32,596
Waste [6]	11,688	14,475	17,352	18,325	18,789	20,231	20,412	20,246	21,086

[1] Includes coal, anthracite, culm and coal waste.   [2] Includes petroleum, petroleum coke, diesel, kerosene, and petroleum sludge and tar.   [3] Includes butane, ethane, propane, and other gases.   [4] Included in "Natural gas."   [5] Includes wood, wood waste, peat, wood liquors, railroad ties, pitch and wood sludge.   [6] Includes municipal solid waste, agricultural waste, straw, tires, landfill gases and other waste.

Source: Energy Information Administration, *Annual Nonutility Power Producer Report.*

No. 972. Water Power—Developed and Undeveloped Capacity by Division: 1980 to 1998

[In millions of kilowatts. (64.4 represents 64,400,000). As of Dec. 31. Excludes all capacity of reversible equipment at pumped storage projects. Also excludes capacity precluded from development due to wild and scenic river legislation. For composition of divisions, see map, inside front cover]

Division	Developed installed capacity							Estimated undeveloped capacity						
	1980	1990	1994	1995	1996	1997	1998	1980	1990	1994	1995	1996	1997	1998
United States	64.4	73.0	74.1	74.2	74.8	73.5	73.8	129.9	73.9	73.5	71.0	70.0	64.1	64.1
New England..........	1.5	1.9	1.9	1.9	2.0	2.0	2.0	4.7	4.4	4.4	4.4	4.4	3.9	3.9
Middle Atlantic........	4.3	4.9	4.9	4.9	5.0	5.6	5.6	5.1	5.1	4.9	4.9	4.8	3.6	3.6
East North Central	0.9	1.1	1.2	1.2	1.2	1.2	1.2	2.0	1.7	1.7	1.7	1.6	1.5	1.5
West North Central.....	2.8	3.1	3.1	3.1	3.0	3.0	3.0	3.4	3.1	3.1	3.1	3.0	2.8	2.8
South Atlantic	5.9	6.7	6.7	6.7	6.8	6.8	6.8	9.6	7.0	7.2	7.2	7.3	6.8	6.8
East South Central	5.6	5.9	5.9	5.9	5.9	5.9	5.9	3.3	2.4	2.4	2.3	2.0	2.0	2.0
West South Central	2.3	2.7	2.7	2.7	2.7	2.8	2.8	4.7	4.6	4.6	4.6	4.0	4.0	4.0
Mountain	7.4	9.2	9.5	9.5	10.0	10.0	10.0	34.2	19.4	19.1	18.8	19.1	18.0	18.0
Pacific	33.7	37.5	38.2	38.3	38.3	36.2	36.5	62.9	26.2	26.1	24.0	22.9	21.5	21.5

Source: U.S. Federal Energy Regulatory Commission (formerly U.S. Federal Power Commission), *Hydroelectric Power Resources of the United States, Developed and Undeveloped,* January 1, 1988; and unpublished data.

No. 973. Solar Collector Shipments by Type, End Use, and Market Sector: 1986 to 1998

[In thousands of square feet, except number of manufacturers. Solar collector is a device for intercepting sunlight, converting the light to heat, and carrying the heat to where it will be either used or stored]

Year	Number of manufac- turers	Total ship- ments [1]	Collector type		End use			Market sector		
			Low tem- perature	Medium tempera- ture, spe- cial, other	Pool heating	Hot water	Space heating	Resi- dential	Com- mercial	Industrial
1986 [2]	98	9,360	3,751	1,111	3,494	1,181	127	4,131	703	13
1987 [2]	59	7,269	3,157	957	3,111	964	23	3,775	305	11
1988 [2]	51	8,174	3,326	732	3,304	726	7	3,796	255	7
1989 [2]	44	11,482	4,283	1,989	4,688	1,374	205	5,804	424	42
1990	51	11,409	3,645	2,527	5,016	1,091	2	5,835	294	22
1991	48	6,574	5,585	989	5,535	989	24	6,322	225	13
1992	45	7,086	6,187	897	6,210	801	35	6,832	204	27
1993	41	6,968	6,025	931	6,040	880	15	6,694	215	31
1994	41	7,627	6,823	803	6,813	790	19	7,026	583	16
1995	36	7,666	6,813	840	6,763	755	132	6,966	604	82
1996	28	7,616	6,821	785	6,787	765	57	6,873	682	54
1997	29	8,138	7,524	606	7,528	595	10	7,360	768	7
1998	28	7,756	7,292	443	7,201	463	67	7,165	517	62

[1] Includes high temperature collectors, end uses such process heating, and utility and other market sectors not shown separately.   [2] Declines between 1986 and 1989 are primarily due to the expiration of the Federal energy tax credit and industry consolidation.

Source: U.S. Energy Information Administration, *Solar Collector Manufacturing Activity,* annual.

No. 974 Renewable Energy Consumption Estimates by Type: 1990 to 1999

[**In quadrillion Btu**. Renewable energy is obtained from sources that are essentially inexhaustible unlike fossil fuels of which there is a finite supply]

Source and sector	1990	1995	1996	1997	1998	1999
Consumption, total	**6.26**	**6.96**	**7.48**	**7.36**	**6.98**	**7.37**
Residential and commercial	0.68	0.72	0.72	0.56	0.50	0.54
Biomass [1]	0.62	0.64	0.64	0.48	0.42	0.46
Geothermal energy [2]	0.01	0.01	0.01	0.01	0.02	0.02
Solar [3]	0.06	0.07	0.07	0.07	0.07	0.06
Industrial [4]	2.24	2.69	2.80	2.81	2.84	3.37
Biomass [5]	1.94	2.28	2.37	2.39	2.44	2.92
Geothermal energy [6]	0.16	0.21	0.22	0.20	0.21	0.28
Conventional hydroelectric power [7]........	0.10	0.15	0.17	0.19	0.15	0.13
Solar energy...................	0.01	0.01	0.01	0.01	0.01	0.01
Wind energy...................	0.03	0.03	0.04	0.03	0.03	0.04
Transportation						
Biomass [8]	0.08	0.10	0.07	0.10	0.11	0.11
Electric utilities [9].................	3.25	3.46	3.89	3.89	3.53	3.35
Biomass [5]	0.02	0.02	0.02	0.02	0.02	0.02
Geothermal energy [10].............	0.19	0.12	0.12	0.12	0.11	0.04
Conventional hydroelectric power [7,11].......	3.04	3.32	3.74	3.75	3.40	3.29
Solar and wind energy	(Z)	(Z)	(Z)	(Z)	(Z)	(Z)

Z Less than 0.005 quadrillion Btu. [1] Wood. [2] Geothermal heat pump and direct use energy. [3] The solar thermal component of 0.06 quadrillion Btu for residential and commercial use is calculated by presuming an overall efficiency of 50 percent for all three categories of solar thermal collectors, a 1,500-Btu per square foot average daily insulation, and the potential thermal energy production from the 219 million square feet of thermal collectors produced between 1980 and 1999. [4] Generation of electricity by nonutility power producers is included in the industrial sector, not the electric utility sector. Covers facilities of 1 megawatt or greater capacity. [5] Wood, wood waste, wood liquors, peat, railroad ties, wood sludge, spent sulfite liquors, agricultural waste, straw, tires, fish oils, tall oil, sludge waste, waste alcohol, municipal solid waste, landfill gases, and other waste. [6] Geothermal electricity generation, heat pump, and direct use energy. [7] Hydroelectricity generated by pumped storage is not included in renewable energy. [8] Ethanol blended into motor gasoline. [9] For Btu conversion rates, see source Appendix Table 6. [10] Includes electricity from Mexico that are derived from geothermal energy. [11] Includes electricity net imports from Canada that are derived from hydroelectric power.

Source: U.S. Energy Information Administration, *Renewable Energy Annual.*

No. 975. Privately Owned Gas Utility Industry—Balance Sheet and Income Account: 1980 to 1998

[**In millions of dollars (75,851 represents $75,851,000,000).** The gas utility industry consists of pipeline and distribution companies. Excludes operations of companies distributing gas in bottles or tanks]

Item	1980	1985	1990	1993	1994	1995	1996	1997	1998
COMPOSITE BALANCE SHEET									
Assets, total	75,851	104,478	121,686	135,813	137,911	141,965	121,328	134,715	119,715
Total utility plant...........	67,071	88,121	112,863	135,859	139,372	143,636	135,179	140,268	135,092
Depreciation and amortization. ...	26,162	36,377	49,483	60,152	61,140	62,723	58,815	62,554	61,226
Utility plant (net).............	40,909	51,744	63,380	75,707	78,232	80,912	76,364	77,714	73,866
Investment and fund accounts ...	15,530	23,871	23,872	23,342	22,658	26,489	13,207	22,812	12,337
Current and accrued assets	17,243	24,771	23,268	21,451	20,728	18,564	17,393	19,084	17,348
Deferred debits [1]	2,169	4,092	9,576	13,369	14,234	13,923	11,983	12,844	13,721
Liabilities, total	75,851	104,478	121,686	135,813	137,911	141,965	121,328	134,775	119,715
Capitalization, total...........	51,382	65,799	74,958	82,755	85,728	90,581	77,440	78,887	71,718
Capital stock	29,315	39,517	43,810	49,051	50,394	54,402	43,555	42,530	37,977
Long-term debts	22,067	26,282	31,148	33,693	35,296	35,548	33,644	35,971	33,386
Current and accrued liabilities....	18,119	26,125	29,550	27,321	25,438	28,272	22,098	33,507	26,953
Deferred income taxes [2]	4,149	7,769	11,360	13,070	13,787	14,393	13,326	13,636	13,239
Other liabilities and credits	2,201	4,785	5,818	12,667	12,955	8,715	8,464	8,745	7,806
COMPOSITE INCOME ACCOUNT									
Operating revenues, total ..	85,918	103,945	66,027	69,966	63,446	58,390	63,600	62,617	57,117
Operating expenses [3]	81,789	98,320	60,137	62,977	56,789	50,760	56,695	59,375	50,896
Operation and maintenance ...	74,508	88,572	51,627	50,468	43,879	37,966	43,742	46,070	41,026
Federal, state, and local taxes..	4,847	6,590	4,957	6,185	6,613	6,182	6,362	7,182	5,429
Operating income.............	4,129	5,625	5,890	6,988	6,657	7,630	6,905	3,242	6,220
Utility operating income........	4,471	6,030	6,077	7,177	6,851	7,848	7,013	3,337	6,361
Income before interest charges. ..	6,929	7,636	8,081	8,754	8,200	9,484	8,030	4,193	7,779
Net income	4,194	3,785	4,410	5,589	5,011	5,139	4,797	48	4,379
Dividends	2,564	4,060	3,191	3,149	3,928	4,037	4,138	6,258	2,263

[1] Includes capital stock discount and expense and reacquired securities. [2] Includes reserves for deferred income taxes. [3] Includes expenses not shown separately.

Source: American Gas Association, Arlington, VA, *Gas Facts,* annual (copyright).

Energy 599

No. 976. Gas Utility Industry—Summary: 1980 to 1998

[Covers natural, manufactured, mixed, and liquid petroleum gas. Based on questionnaire mailed to all privately and municipally owned gas utilities in United States, except those with annual revenues less than $25,000]

Item	Unit	1980	1985	1990	1994	1995	1996	1997	1998
End users [1]	1,000	47,223	49,971	54,261	57,960	58,728	59,820	59,802	60,437
Residential	1,000	43,489	45,929	49,802	53,243	53,955	54,968	54,998	55,642
Commercial	1,000	3,498	3,816	4,246	4,474	4,530	4,616	4,593	4,595
Industrial and other	1,000	187	179	166	181	181	183	173	162
Sales [2]	Tril. Btu [3]	15,413	12,616	9,842	9,480	9,094	9,532	8,913	8,341
Residential	Tril. Btu	4,826	4,513	4,468	4,972	4,736	5,198	5,021	4,693
Percent of total	Percent	31.3	35.8	45.4	52.4	52.0	54.5	56.3	56.3
Commercial	Tril. Btu	2,453	2,338	2,192	2,351	2,204	2,395	2,244	2,043
Industrial	Tril. Btu	7,957	5,635	3,010	2,009	1,930	1,791	1,524	1,489
Other	Tril. Btu	177	130	171	148	224	148	124	116
Revenues [2]	Mil. dol	48,303	63,293	45,153	49,864	46,381	51,115	51,517	46,924
Residential	Mil. dol	17,432	26,864	25,000	30,563	28,741	32,022	33,068	30,671
Percent of total	Percent	36.1	42.4	55.4	61.3	61.9	62.6	64.2	65.4
Commercial	Mil. dol	8,183	12,722	10,604	12,254	11,410	12,726	12,666	11,189
Industrial	Mil. dol	22,215	23,086	8,996	6,475	5,652	5,821	5,284	4,678
Other	Mil. dol	473	621	553	572	579	546	498	387
Prices per mil. Btu [3]	Dollars	3.13	5.02	4.59	5.23	5.10	5.37	5.78	5.63
Residential	Dollars	3.61	5.95	5.60	6.14	6.06	6.17	6.59	6.54
Commercial	Dollars	3.34	5.44	4.84	5.21	5.18	5.31	5.64	5.48
Industrial	Dollars	2.79	4.10	2.99	3.17	3.00	3.32	3.53	3.28
Gas mains mileage	1,000	1,052	1,119	1,207	1,267	1,262	1,269	1,258	1,280
Field and gathering	1,000	84	94	90	72	62	58	46	45
Transmission	1,000	266	271	280	276	265	260	257	254
Distribution	1,000	702	754	837	919	935	952	955	981
Construction expenditures [4]	Mil. dol	5,350	5,671	7,899	9,282	10,829	7,722	7,189	11,941
Transmission	Mil. dol	1,583	1,562	2,886	3,065	3,384	1,316	1,334	2,892
Distribution	Mil. dol	1,869	2,577	3,714	4,550	5,448	4,234	4,404	6,852
Production and storage	Mil. dol	1,150	790	309	230	366	651	347	572

[1] Annual average.   [2] Excludes sales for resale.   [3] For definition of Btu, see text, this section.   [4] Includes general.

Source: American Gas Association, Arlington, VA, *Gas Facts*, annual (copyright).

No. 977. Gas Utility Industry—Customers, Sales, and Revenues by State: 1998

[See headnote, Table 986. For definition of Btu, see text, this section]

State	Customers [1] (1,000) Total [2]	Customers [1] Resi-dential	Sales [3] (tril. Btu) Total [2]	Sales [3] Resi-dential	Revenues [3] (mil. dol.) Total [2]	Revenues [3] Resi-dential	State	Customers [1] (1,000) Total [2]	Customers [1] Resi-dential	Sales [3] (tril. Btu) Total [2]	Sales [3] Resi-dential	Revenues [3] (mil. dol.) Total [2]	Revenues [3] Resi-dential
U.S.	60,437	55,642	8,341	4,693	46,924	30,671	MO	1,425	1,289	186	119	1,122	772
							MT	245	217	31	20	157	102
AL	823	759	117	52	678	392	NE	504	444	80	44	392	240
AK	99	86	24	16	82	58	NV	483	454	51	29	311	203
AZ	716	674	70	31	454	268	NH	89	76	16	7	105	49
AR	618	547	80	38	430	255	NJ	2,434	2,218	489	207	2,332	1,457
CA	9,536	9,099	756	513	4,615	3,474							
CO	1,338	1,213	182	111	844	577	NM	496	453	57	35	270	187
CT	486	439	89	39	689	398	NY	4,379	4,050	600	358	4,615	3,214
DE	120	110	23	9	145	75	NC	876	766	140	54	860	447
DC	145	131	24	11	203	101	ND	117	102	23	11	97	52
FL	594	544	67	16	451	166	OH	3,169	2,930	408	304	2,458	1,879
GA	1,707	1,581	291	157	1,158	723	OK	956	865	118	68	597	388
HI	37	34	3	1	49	16	OR	538	475	77	36	421	232
ID	239	211	28	17	133	85	PA	2,467	2,274	326	216	2,387	1,725
IL	3,803	3,521	523	397	2,660	2,078	RI	228	207	28	17	233	160
IN	1,686	1,539	251	150	1,448	955	SC	498	443	97	27	531	216
IA	866	774	136	81	722	471	SD	150	132	24	13	126	74
KS	909	824	114	73	623	442	TN	894	797	144	57	790	369
KY	703	632	107	58	597	354	TX	3,878	3,545	509	226	2,551	1,364
LA	740	693	268	39	717	242	UT	632	589	91	59	438	315
ME	23	16	5	1	35	7	VT	32	27	8	3	42	18
MD	882	822	90	63	686	516	VA	915	829	123	62	876	534
MA	1,303	1,201	174	101	1,435	946	WA	763	685	133	63	613	346
MI	3,247	3,009	514	370	2,547	1,876	WV	392	357	47	33	321	237
MN	1,268	1,156	244	114	1,107	618	WI	1,406	1,278	256	128	1,321	777
MS	454	407	77	28	354	162	WY	135	120	23	13	96	57

[1] Averages for the year.   [2] Includes other service, not shown separately.   [3] Excludes sales for resale.

Source: American Gas Association, Arlington, VA, *Gas Facts*, annual (copyright).

Section 20
Science and Technology

This section presents statistics on scientific, engineering, and technological resources, with emphasis on patterns of research and development (R&D) funding and on scientific, engineering, and technical personnel; education; and employment. Also included are statistics on space program outlays and accomplishments. Principal sources of these data are the National Science Foundation (NSF) and the National Aeronautics and Space Administration (NASA).

NSF gathers data chiefly through recurring surveys. Current NSF publications containing data on funds for research and development and on scientific and engineering personnel include detailed statistical tables, issue briefs, and annual, biennial, triennial, and special reports. Titles or the areas of coverage of these reports include the following: *Science and Engineering Indicators; National Patterns of R&D Resources; Women, Minorities, and Persons with Disabilities in Science and Engineering*—science and technology data presented in chart and tabular form in a pocket-sized publication—*Federal Funds for Research and Development; Federal R&D Funding by Budget Function; Federal Support to Universities, Colleges, and Selected Nonprofit Institutions; Research and Development in Industry*; R&D expenditures and graduate enrollment and support in academic science and engineering; and characteristics of doctoral scientists and engineers and of recent graduates in the United States. Statistical surveys in these areas pose problems of concept and definition and the data should therefore be regarded as broad estimates rather than precise, quantitative statements. See sources for methodological and technical details.

The National Science Board's biennial *Science and Engineering Indicators* contains data and analysis of international and domestic science and technology, including measures of inputs and outputs. The *Budget of the United States Government*, published by the U.S. Office of Management and Budget, contains summary financial data on Federal R&D programs.

Research and development outlays— NSF defines research as "systematic study directed toward fuller scientific knowledge of the subject studied" and development as "the systematic use of scientific knowledge directed toward the production of useful materials, devices, systems, or methods, including design and development of prototypes and processes." National coverage of R&D expenditures is developed primarily from periodic surveys in four principal economic sectors: (1) *Government*, made up primarily of Federal executive agencies; (2) *industry*, consisting of manufacturing and nonmanufacturing firms and the federally funded research and development centers (FFRDCs) they administer; (3) *universities and colleges*, composed of universities, colleges, and their affiliated institutions, agricultural experiment stations, and associated schools of agriculture and of medicine, and FFRDCs administered by educational institutions; and (4) *other nonprofit institutions*, consisting of such organizations as private philanthropic foundations, nonprofit research institutes, voluntary health agencies, and FFRDCs administered by nonprofit organizations. The R&D funds reported consist of current operating costs, including planning and administration costs, except as otherwise noted. They exclude funds for routine testing, mapping

Science and Technology 601

and surveying, collection of general-purpose data, dissemination of scientific information, and training of scientific personnel.

Scientists, engineers, and technicians—Scientists and engineers are defined as persons engaged in scientific and engineering work at a level requiring a knowledge of sciences equivalent at least to that acquired through completion of a 4-year college course. Technicians are defined as persons engaged in technical work at a level requiring knowledge acquired through a technical institute, junior college, or other type of training less extensive than 4-year college training. Craftsmen and skilled workers are excluded.

Figure 20.1
Research and Development Expenditures: 1980 to 1999

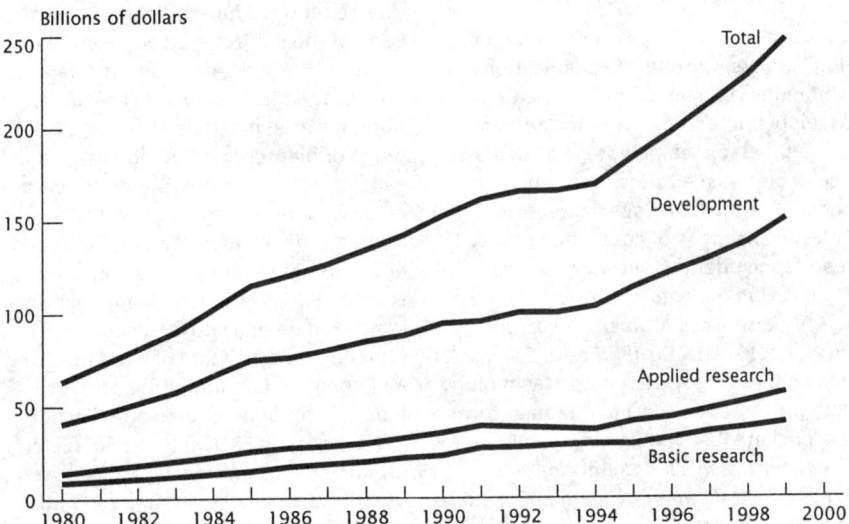

Billions of dollars

Source: Chart prepared by U.S. Census Bureau. For data, see Table 978.

No. 978. R&D Expenditures: 1960 to 1999

[In millions of dollars (13,711 represents $13,711,000,000) except as indicated. For calendar years]

Year	Total	Sources of funds					Objective (percent of total)			Character of work		
		Federal Government	Industry	Universities/colleges	Non-profit	Non-Federal Government[1]	Defense related[2]	Space related[3]	Other	Basic research	Applied research	Development
1960....	13,711	8,915	4,516	67	123	90	53	3	44	1,286	3,065	9,360
1961....	14,564	9,484	4,757	75	148	101	50	6	44	1,512	3,123	9,930
1962....	15,636	10,138	5,124	84	179	112	46	9	45	1,824	3,698	10,116
1963....	17,519	11,645	5,456	96	197	125	41	15	43	2,115	3,865	11,540
1964....	19,103	12,764	5,888	114	200	138	37	20	43	2,396	4,201	12,506
1965....	20,252	13,194	6,549	136	225	150	33	22	45	2,664	4,374	13,215
1966....	22,072	14,165	7,331	165	252	160	32	21	47	2,930	4,653	14,490
1967....	23,346	14,563	8,146	200	271	168	32	18	49	3,168	4,848	15,332
1968....	24,666	14,964	9,008	221	290	185	32	17	52	3,376	5,137	16,154
1969....	25,996	15,228	10,011	233	316	208	31	15	54	3,491	5,454	17,051
1970....	26,271	14,984	10,449	259	343	237	30	14	56	3,594	5,752	16,925
1971....	26,952	15,210	10,824	290	366	262	29	12	59	3,720	5,833	17,399
1972....	28,740	16,039	11,715	312	393	282	30	11	59	3,850	6,147	18,743
1973....	30,952	16,587	13,299	343	422	302	29	10	62	4,099	6,655	20,197
1974....	33,365	17,287	14,886	393	480	320	27	9	64	4,515	7,347	21,503
1975....	35,686	18,533	15,825	432	548	348	26	8	65	4,880	8,098	22,708
1976....	39,458	20,292	17,702	480	616	369	26	9	66	5,376	8,990	25,092
1977....	43,456	22,155	19,645	569	695	394	26	7	67	6,075	9,690	27,691
1978....	48,822	24,468	22,462	679	771	443	25	6	69	7,001	10,731	31,090
1979....	55,521	27,303	26,103	785	850	482	24	6	70	7,867	12,148	35,506
1980....	63,332	30,035	30,940	920	919	519	24	5	71	8,825	13,773	40,734
1981....	72,307	33,714	35,967	1,058	988	581	25	5	70	9,827	16,421	46,059
1982....	80,837	37,233	40,718	1,207	1,059	621	28	4	68	10,803	18,303	51,730
1983....	90,030	41,576	45,295	1,357	1,145	658	30	3	67	12,018	20,408	57,603
1984....	102,308	46,571	52,245	1,514	1,258	721	30	3	67	13,403	22,540	66,365
1985....	114,747	52,748	58,049	1,743	1,373	834	31	3	66	14,772	25,437	74,538
1986....	120,297	54,711	61,097	2,019	1,502	969	32	3	65	17,152	27,292	75,853
1987....	126,255	58,548	62,683	2,262	1,697	1,065	32	3	65	18,393	27,968	79,894
1988....	133,903	60,179	68,102	2,527	1,931	1,165	30	3	66	19,637	29,621	84,646
1989....	141,909	60,488	75,118	2,852	2,177	1,274	28	4	68	21,712	32,381	87,816
1990....	152,039	61,668	83,382	3,186	2,405	1,399	25	4	70	22,837	35,095	94,107
1991....	160,863	60,821	92,490	3,457	2,614	1,482	23	4	73	26,915	38,764	95,184
1992....	165,212	60,922	96,411	3,568	2,787	1,524	22	4	74	27,258	38,066	99,889
1993....	165,442	60,524	96,700	3,719	2,950	1,550	22	4	74	28,312	37,379	99,751
1994....	168,854	60,881	99,326	3,960	3,076	1,611	20	4	76	29,046	36,689	103,119
1995....	183,232	63,220	111,005	4,139	3,126	1,741	19	5	77	28,909	41,085	113,239
1996....	196,540	63,547	123,561	4,375	3,218	1,839	18	4	78	32,012	43,156	121,372
1997....	211,586	65,016	136,394	4,842	3,436	1,898	17	4	79	35,495	47,453	128,638
1998....	226,984	64,853	151,105	5,366	3,686	1,974	15	4	81	37,695	51,722	137,566
1999....	247,000	65,853	169,312	5,838	3,913	2,085	14	3	83	40,224	56,462	150,315

[1] Non-Federal R&D expenditures to university and college performers.   [2] R&D spending by the Department of Defense, including space activities, and a portion of the Department of Energy funds.   [3] For the National Aeronautics and Space Administration only.

Source: U.S. National Science Foundation, *National Patterns of R&D Resources*, annual.

No. 979. Federal Obligations for R&D by Agency: 1980 to 2000

[In millions of dollars (29,830 represents $29,830,000,000). For fiscal years ending in year shown; see text, Section 9, State and Local Government. Includes those agencies with obligations of $1 billion or more in 2000]

Agency	1980	1985	1990	1995	1996	1997	1998	1999, prel.	2000, prel.
CURRENT DOLLARS									
Obligations, total[1]	29,830	48,360	63,559	68,187	67,653	69,827	71,903	75,351	75,104
Dept. of Defense	13,981	29,792	37,268	33,796	34,535	34,788	35,286	35,637	34,441
Dept. of Health and Human Services .	3,780	5,451	8,406	11,455	11,951	12,785	13,704	15,629	16,148
National Aeronautics and Space Administration................	3,234	3,327	6,533	9,015	8,570	9,327	9,568	9,308	9,370
Dept. of Energy	4,754	4,966	5,631	6,145	5,345	5,604	5,874	6,499	6,518
National Science Foundation.......	882	1,346	1,690	2,149	2,188	2,249	2,289	2,513	2,698
Dept. of Agriculture	688	943	1,108	1,380	1,300	1,389	1,441	1,637	1,597
CONSTANT (1996) DOLLARS [2]									
Obligations, total[1]	66,338	65,510	73,615	69,500	67,653	68,660	69,809	72,217	70,920
Dept. of Defense	31,402	40,357	43,164	34,447	34,535	34,207	34,258	34,155	32,522
Dept. of Health and Human Services .	8,354	7,384	9,736	11,676	11,951	12,572	13,305	14,979	15,248
National Aeronautics and Space Administration................	10,676	4,507	7,567	9,189	8,570	9,171	9,289	8,921	8,848
Dept. of Energy	7,132	6,727	6,522	6,263	5,345	5,510	5,703	6,229	6,155
National Science Foundation.......	2,073	1,823	1,957	2,191	2,188	2,211	2,223	2,408	2,548
Dept. of Agriculture	1,463	1,277	1,283	1,407	1,300	1,365	1,399	1,569	1,508

[1] Includes other agencies, not shown separately.   [2] Based on gross domestic product implicit price deflator.

Source: U.S. National Science Foundation, *Federal Funds for Research and Development*, annual.

Science and Technology   603

No. 980. Performance Sector of R&D Expenditures: 1994 to 1999

[In millions of dollars (168,854 represents $168,854,000,000). For calendar year. FFRDCs are federally funded research and development centers. For most academic institutions and the Federal Government before 1997 began on July 1 instead of October 1]

Year	Total	Federal Government	Industry — Total	Industry — Funded by Federal Government	Industry — Funded by Industry[1]	Industry — Industry FFRDCs	Universities and colleges — Total	Univ. — Funded by Federal Government	Univ. — Non-Federal government[2]	Univ. — Industry	Univ. — Universities & colleges	Univ. — Nonprofits	Univ. — Universities & colleges FFRDCs[3]	Other nonprofit institutions — Total	Other — Funded by Federal Government	Other — Industry	Other — Nonprofits	Other — Nonprofit FFRDCs
RESEARCH AND DEVELOPMENT TOTAL																		
1994	168,854	16,432	117,392	20,261	97,131	2,202	21,626	13,009	1,611	1,448	3,960	1,598	5,317	5,125	2,900	747	1,478	759
1995	183,232	17,131	129,830	21,178	108,652	2,273	22,647	13,604	1,741	1,539	4,139	1,624	5,372	5,165	2,848	814	1,502	812
1996	196,540	16,627	142,371	21,356	121,015	2,297	23,720	14,180	1,839	1,655	4,375	1,672	5,410	5,343	2,906	891	1,546	771
1997	211,586	16,814	155,409	21,798	133,611	2,130	25,136	14,805	1,898	1,805	4,842	1,785	5,612	5,665	3,036	978	1,651	820
1998, prelim	226,984	17,189	168,291	20,249	148,042	1,979	26,684	15,446	1,974	1,983	5,366	1,915	5,913	6,105	3,254	1,079	1,771	823
1999, prelim	247,000	17,362	185,892	19,937	165,955	2,166	28,256	16,137	2,085	2,163	5,838	2,032	6,169	6,319	3,246	1,194	1,880	836
BASIC RESEARCH																		
1994	29,046	2,553	6,514	436	6,078	503	14,472	9,186	988	888	2,429	980	2,870	2,060	1,126	343	591	74
1995	28,909	2,695	5,569	190	5,379	530	15,233	9,683	1,068	945	2,540	997	2,661	2,146	1,170	375	601	76
1996	32,012	2,689	7,498	650	6,848	708	16,129	10,201	1,143	1,028	2,719	1,039	2,632	2,277	1,249	410	619	79
1997	35,495	2,735	9,795	1,029	8,766	625	17,030	10,740	1,157	1,099	2,947	1,087	2,788	2,428	1,317	450	660	95
1998, prelim	37,695	2,920	10,669	956	9,713	581	17,832	11,241	1,158	1,163	3,147	1,123	2,958	2,625	1,420	496	709	111
1999, prelim	40,224	3,100	11,778	890	10,888	601	18,758	11,743	1,207	1,252	3,379	1,176	3,086	2,795	1,494	549	752	107
APPLIED RESEARCH																		
1994	36,689	5,003	22,988	3,616	19,372	503	5,357	2,625	511	459	1,255	507	980	1,746	960	254	532	112
1995	41,085	5,007	26,919	3,164	23,755	535	5,622	2,758	551	487	1,311	514	1,117	1,753	935	277	541	131
1996	43,156	4,874	29,010	3,640	25,370	231	5,816	2,854	571	514	1,358	519	1,284	1,819	960	303	557	122
1997	47,453	5,079	32,430	2,648	29,782	213	6,229	2,917	608	579	1,554	572	1,442	1,937	1,010	333	594	123
1998, prelim	51,722	5,421	35,458	2,460	32,998	198	6,864	3,054	669	672	1,820	649	1,633	2,045	1,040	367	638	104
1999, prelim	56,462	5,494	39,367	2,376	36,991	212	7,401	3,216	720	747	2,016	702	1,729	2,156	1,073	406	677	101
DEVELOPMENT																		
1994	103,119	8,876	87,890	16,209	71,681	1,196	1,798	1,198	112	101	276	111	1,467	1,319	815	149	355	573
1995	113,239	9,431	97,342	17,824	79,518	1,209	1,792	1,163	121	107	288	113	1,593	1,266	743	163	361	606
1996	121,372	9,064	105,863	17,066	88,797	1,358	1,775	1,125	125	113	298	114	1,495	1,247	697	178	371	570
1997	128,638	9,001	113,184	18,120	95,064	1,292	1,876	1,149	133	127	341	126	1,382	1,300	708	196	396	603
1998, prelim	137,566	8,848	122,164	16,833	105,331	1,200	1,988	1,152	147	148	399	142	1,322	1,435	794	216	425	608
1999, prelim	150,315	8,768	134,747	16,671	118,076	1,353	2,096	1,178	158	164	443	154	1,354	1,369	679	239	451	628

[1] Includes all non-Federal sources. [2] Because of limitations in the survey information, data on non-Federal government funding to other performers are not available but included in other sectors' support for their own R&D performance. [3] Includes all R&D expenditures of FFRDCs administered by academic institutions. In 1997, 99 percent of total funds used were from Federal sources.

Source: National Science Foundation, Research and Development in Industry, annual; Academic Research and Development Expenditures, annual; and Federal Funds For Research and Development, annual.

No. 981. Performance Sector of R&D Expenditures by State: 1998

[In millions of dollars (226,984 represents $226,984,000,000). Industry R&D data refer to calendar years; other R&D data refer to fiscal years but may serve as approximation to calendar year data]

State	Industry					Universities and colleges						Other nonprofit institutions funded by Federal Government [5]
	Total R&D [1]	Federal Government [2]	Funded by—			Total	Funded by—					
			Total	Federal Government [3]	Industry [4]		Federal Government	Non-Federal government	Industry	U&Cs	Nonprofits	
U.S.	226,984	17,189	168,291	20,249	148,042	26,684	15,446	1,974	1,983	5,366	1,915	3,254
AL......	1,926	753	707	180	527	442	282	7	30	82	40	24
AK......	(D)	44	(D)	(D)	9	76	32	4	16	24	-	4
AZ......	2,318	138	1,727	490	1,237	406	210	12	22	147	15	8
AR......	283	46	118	(D)	(D)	117	41	33	8	27	7	2
CA......	43,919	1,595	35,568	3,803	31,764	3,345	2,009	146	213	702	274	519
CO	4,565	202	3,565	1,237	2,329	489	332	26	27	68	36	55
CT......	3,559	18	3,113	179	2,935	404	262	13	26	67	35	24
DE......	2,556	4	2,476	13	2,463	73	36	5	4	19	9	3
DC......	2,606	1,718	503	90	413	233	166	2	19	26	19	150
FL......	4,773	750	3,300	889	2,411	713	356	81	52	184	40	11
GA	2,492	236	1,444	86	1,358	802	370	70	86	246	30	10
HI	242	55	17	(D)	(D)	148	87	37	11	13	-	22
ID	1,127	25	1,028	(D)	(D)	72	25	22	8	16	1	1
IL	8,830	72	6,892	136	6,755	1,046	587	57	60	262	81	62
IN	3,089	38	2,622	(D)	(D)	425	214	26	40	126	19	3
IA	1,054	33	634	(D)	(D)	358	167	53	31	89	18	4
KS......	1,518	25	1,279	(D)	(D)	213	80	47	12	56	17	1
KY......	645	7	427	(D)	(D)	210	80	15	19	86	9	2
LA......	542	84	102	14	87	352	144	78	23	87	20	4
ME	159	11	82	(D)	(D)	35	14	2	7	11	1	31
MD	8,019	4,766	1,744	655	1,089	1,330	1,014	63	42	143	69	179
MA	13,382	301	10,604	2,419	8,185	1,343	987	32	107	99	118	707
MI	13,655	111	12,648	(D)	(D)	878	472	56	59	221	69	18
MN	3,818	38	3,321	334	2,986	365	206	48	25	56	29	94
MS	366	133	73	17	57	153	80	29	10	31	2	8
MO	1,868	49	1,313	(D)	(D)	484	278	24	30	109	43	22
MT......	191	33	82	(D)	(D)	72	36	14	8	13	1	3
NE......	315	29	93	(D)	(D)	186	63	47	17	55	5	7
NV......	571	49	434	(D)	(D)	84	45	5	5	24	4	4
NH	1,340	34	1,187	(D)	(D)	117	71	8	6	17	14	2
NJ......	11,368	393	10,415	134	10,282	485	228	40	27	150	39	17
NM	3,032	396	1,205	(D)	(D)	229	152	13	13	46	5	15
NY	13,514	192	11,176	2,216	8,960	1,925	1,224	82	96	286	236	221
NC	4,560	236	3,362	12	3,350	899	516	129	121	96	36	64
ND	119	27	34	-	34	57	23	1	4	26	4	1
OH	6,970	698	5,338	605	4,732	808	444	74	88	152	49	125
OK	513	51	245	2	243	209	84	37	13	60	15	8
OR	1,910	88	1,492	26	1,467	310	203	33	10	38	25	21
PA	8,762	133	7,083	485	6,598	1,342	873	44	156	199	70	174
RI	1,677	222	1,320	(D)	(D)	112	78	3	2	26	3	23
SC......	989	45	695	(D)	(D)	246	113	27	11	83	11	3
SD......	60	28	5	-	5	25	12	8	-	3	2	2
TN......	2,503	38	2,040	(D)	(D)	346	208	37	20	54	28	28
TX......	10,774	597	8,408	223	8,185	1,698	910	179	140	290	179	69
UT......	1,495	135	1,109	181	928	249	165	18	14	43	10	1
VT......	175	4	112	32	80	58	31	3	6	12	6	1
VA......	4,934	1,480	2,707	1,614	1,093	491	289	49	46	77	30	44
WA	8,466	184	7,476	(D)	(D)	534	384	13	42	77	19	122
WV	421	97	225	(D)	(D)	63	25	3	5	27	4	1
WI	2,501	38	1,919	(D)	(D)	536	300	44	20	111	61	8
WY	65	12	2	-	2	49	18	5	3	21	1	3
Unknown ..	12,449	700	4,820	4,177	37,478	1,043	418	70	118	380	55	319

- Represents or rounds to zero.   D Data withheld to avoiding disclosing information about individual companies.   [1] Includes university and college Federally Funded Research and Development Centers (FFRDCs). Nonprofit FFRDCs not shown separately.   [2] For R&D funded by the Federal Government.   [3] Includes performance at industry Federally Funded Research and Development Centers (FFRDCs). Nonprofit FFRDCs not shown separately.   [3] Includes performance at university and college FFRDCs.   [4] Includes all non-Federal sources.   [5] Data by state are for R&D funded by the Federal Government.

Source: National Science Foundation. Data derived from *Research and Development in Industry*, annual; *Academic Research and Development Expenditures*, annual; and *Federal Funds For Research and Development*, annual.

U.S. Census Bureau, Statistical Abstract of the United States: 2000

No. 982. Federal Funding for R&D by Selected Budget Functions: 1970 to 2000

[In millions of dollars (15,339 represents $15,339,000,000). For fiscal years ending in year shown; see text, Section 9, State and Local Government. Excludes R&D plant. Represents budget authority. Functions shown are those for which $1 billion or more was authorized since 1995]

Function	1970	1980	1985	1990	1995	1997	1998	1999, prel.	2000, prel.
CURRENT DOLLARS									
Total [1]	15,339	29,739	49,887	63,781	68,791	71,653	73,569	76,886	75,415
Eight functions, percent of total ..	96.6	96.5	98.3	98.0	97.7	98.1	97.7	97.6	97.5
National defense.	7,981	14,946	33,698	39,925	37,204	39,591	39,823	40,387	37,710
Health.	1,084	3,694	5,418	8,308	11,407	12,670	13,576	15,479	15,824
Space research and technology [2] . . .	3,606	2,738	2,725	5,765	7,916	7,844	8,198	8,239	8,422
Energy [2].	574	3,603	2,389	2,726	2,844	2,372	948	1,164	1,348
General science	452	1,233	1,862	2,410	2,794	2,944	4,360	4,739	4,951
Natural resources and environment ..	340	999	1,059	1,386	1,988	1,886	1,855	1,928	1,944
Transportation	535	887	1,030	1,045	1,833	1,785	1,833	1,731	1,840
Agriculture.	238	585	836	950	1,194	1,203	1,249	1,352	1,522
CONSTANT (1996) DOLLARS [3]									
Total [1].	53,446	52,804	67,579	73,872	70,116	70,455	71,426	73,688	71,213
National defense.	27,808	26,538	45,649	46,242	37,921	38,929	38,663	38,707	35,609
Health.	3,777	6,559	7,339	9,622	11,627	12,458	13,181	14,835	14,942
Space research and technology [2] . . .	12,564	4,862	3,691	6,677	8,068	7,713	7,959	7,896	7,953
Energy [2].	2,000	6,397	3,236	3,157	2,899	2,332	920	1,116	1,273
General science	1,575	2,189	2,522	2,791	2,848	2,895	4,233	4,542	4,675
Natural resources and environment ..	1,185	1,774	1,435	1,605	2,026	1,854	1,801	1,848	1,836
Transportation	1,864	1,575	1,395	1,210	1,868	1,755	1,780	1,659	1,737
Agriculture.	829	1,039	1,132	1,100	1,217	1,183	1,213	1,296	1,437

[1] Includes other functions, not shown separately.   [2] Beginning in FY 1998, a number of DOE programs were reclassified from energy (270).   [3] Based on gross domestic product implicit price deflator.
Source: U.S. National Science Foundation, *Federal R&D Funding by Budget Function*, annual.

No. 983. National R&D Expenditures as a Percent of Gross Domestic Product by Country: 1981 to 1998

Year	Total R&D						Nondefense R&D [1]					
	United States	Japan	Unified Germany	France	United Kingdom	Italy	United States	Japan	Unified Germany	France	United Kingdom	Italy
1981 ..	2.32	(NA)	2.43	1.97	2.37	0.88	(NA)	2.34	1.57	1.84	0.85	1.21
1985 ..	2.74	2.58	2.72	2.25	2.23	1.13	2.56	2.60	1.87	1.76	1.07	1.40
1990 ..	2.65	2.85	2.75	2.41	2.18	1.30	2.83	2.62	1.95	1.84	1.26	1.41
1993 ..	2.52	2.68	2.42	2.45	2.15	1.14	2.65	2.34	2.10	1.86	1.09	1.56
1994 ..	2.43	2.63	2.32	2.38	2.11	1.06	2.60	2.25	2.05	1.84	1.01	(NA)
1995 ..	2.52	2.77	2.31	2.34	2.02	1.01	2.73	2.23	2.04	1.78	0.98	1.55
1996 ..	2.57	2.83	2.30	2.32	1.95	1.02	2.80	2.21	2.03	1.72	1.01	(NA)
1997 ..	2.60	2.92	2.31	2.23	1.87	1.08	(NA)	2.23	(NA)	1.65	1.07	1.57
1998 ..	2.67	(NA)	2.33	(NA)	(NA)	1.11	(NA)	(NA)	(NA)	(NA)	(NA)	1.57

NA Not available.   [1] Estimated.
Source: National Science Foundation, *National Patterns of R&D Resources*, annual; and Organization for Economic Cooperation and Development.

No. 984. R&D Expenditures in Science and Engineering at Universities and Colleges: 1981 to 1998

[In millions of dollars (6,847 represents $6,847,000,000)]

Characteristic	1981	1990	1998	Characteristic	1981	1990	1998
CURRENT DOLLARS				**CONSTANT (1996) DOLLARS** [1]			
Total	6,847	16,286	25,735	Total	11,090	18,863	24,985
Basic research	4,594	10,643	17,382	Basic research	7,441	12,327	16,876
Applied R&D	2,253	5,643	8,353	Applied R&D	3,649	6,536	8,110
Source of funds:				Source of funds:			
All governments	5,117	10,962	17,005	All governments	8,288	12,696	16,510
Institutions' own funds . . .	1,004	3,006	4,999	Institutions' own funds . . .	1,626	3,482	4,853
Industry.	291	1,127	1,870	Industry.	471	1,305	1,816
Other	435	1,191	1,861	Other	705	1,379	1,807
Fields:				Fields:			
Physical sciences	765	1,807	2,440	Physical sciences	1,239	2,093	2,369
Environmental sciences ..	550	1,069	1,615	Environmental sciences ..	891	1,238	1,568
Mathematical sciences . . .	87	222	308	Mathematical sciences ..	141	257	299
Computer sciences	144	515	754	Computer sciences	233	596	732
Life sciences	3,695	8,726	14,547	Life sciences	5,985	10,107	14,123
Psychology	127	253	437	Psychology	206	293	424
Social sciences	366	703	1,121	Social sciences	593	814	1,088
Other sciences	145	336	460	Other sciences	235	389	447
Engineering	967	2,656	4,054	Engineering	1,566	3,076	3,936

[1] Based on gross domestic product implicit price deflator.
Source: U.S. National Science Foundation, *Survey of Research and Development Expenditures at Universities and Colleges*, annual.

No. 985. Federal Obligations to Universities and Colleges: 1970 to 1998

[In millions of dollars (3,237 represents $3,237,000,000) except percent. For fiscal years ending in year shown; see text, Section 9, State and Local Government. Minus sign (-) indicates decrease]

Item	1970	1980	1985	1990	1995	1996	1997	1998
CURRENT DOLLARS								
Federal obligations, total	3,237	8,299	10,972	15,226	(NA)	(NA)	(NA)	(NA)
Annual percent change [1]	-6.5	9.1	9.3	-1.8	(NA)	(NA)	(NA)	(NA)
Academic science/engineering obligations	2,188	4,791	7,258	10,471	14,461	14,450	15,096	16,032
Percent of total	67.6	57.7	66.2	68.8	(NA)	(NA)	(NA)	(NA)
Research and development	1,447	4,161	6,246	9,017	12,181	12,346	13,019	13,847
Research and development plant	45	38	114	142	341	248	276	157
Other science/engineering activities	696	593	898	1,312	1,939	1,856	1,801	2,028
Nonscience/engineering activities	1,049	3,508	3,714	4,755	(NA)	(NA)	(NA)	(NA)
CONSTANT (1996) DOLLARS [2]								
Federal obligations, total	11,277	14,735	14,863	17,634	(NA)	(NA)	(NA)	(NA)
Annual percent change [1]	-11.3	0.5	5.9	-5.4	(NA)	(NA)	(NA)	(NA)
Academic science/engineering obligations	7,622	8,507	9,832	12,127	14,740	14,450	14,844	15,565
Percent of total	67.6	57.7	66.2	68.8	(NA)	(NA)	(NA)	(NA)
Research and development	5,040	7,387	8,461	10,443	12,416	12,346	12,802	13,444
Research and development plant	156	67	154	164	348	248	271	152
Other science/engineering activities	2,426	1,052	1,216	1,520	1,976	1,856	1,771	1,969
Nonscience/engineering activities	3,655	6,228	5,031	5,507	(NA)	(NA)	(NA)	(NA)

NA Not available. [1] Percent change from immediate prior year. [2] Based on gross domestic product implicit price deflator.
Source: U.S. National Science Foundation, *Survey of Federal S&E Support to Universities, Colleges, and Nonprofit Institutions*, annual.

No. 986. Federal R&D Obligations to Selected Universities and Colleges: 1981 to 1998

[In millions of dollars (4,410.9 represents $4,410,900,000), except rank. For fiscal years ending in year shown; see text, Section 9, State and Local Government. For the top 45 institutions receiving Federal R&D funds in 1998. Awards to the administrative offices of university systems are excluded from totals for individual institutions because that allocation of funds is unknown, but those awards are included in "total all institutions"]

Major institution ranked by total 1998 Federal R&D obligations	Obligations				Rank			
	1981	1985	1995	1998	1981	1985	1995	1998
Total, all institutions [1]	4,410.9	6,246.2	12,180.9	13,847.4	(X)	(X)	(X)	(X)
45 institutions, percent of total	61.6	60.1	58.6	59.3	(X)	(X)	(X)	(X)
Johns Hopkins University	363.4	297.4	569.3	618.4	1	1	1	1
University of Washington	100.0	146.2	299.7	335.5	4	4	2	2
Stanford University	106.1	175.0	266.7	329.7	3	3	4	3
University of Michigan	74.0	108.0	243.6	288.6	11	11	5	4
University of Pennsylvania	76.1	103.1	202.3	273.6	10	15	10	5
University of California—San Diego	91.4	103.6	239.2	262.2	6	13	6	6
University of California—Los Angeles	94.9	122.8	216.4	246.4	5	5	7	7
Massachusetts Institute of Technology	146.0	189.6	280.3	242.7	2	2	3	8
Harvard University	87.8	109.4	191.5	229.5	7	9	13	9
University of California—San Francisco	64.8	98.5	201.8	221.4	15	16	12	10
Columbia University—Main Division	83.7	127.3	185.7	220.6	9	6	14	11
Yale University	73.5	109.2	179.5	216.1	12	10	15	12
University of Colorado	46.1	71.4	165.4	214.9	22	23	17	13
Washington University	54.2	72.0	165.4	212.8	17	22	18	14
University of Wisconsin—Madison	86.9	124.6	207.7	210.9	8	7	8	15
Duke University	44.3	69.2	155.0	198.8	23	26	20	16
University of Minnesota	72.0	103.3	202.8	198.8	14	14	9	17
Cornell University	72.7	120.0	202.2	196.0	13	8	11	18
University of Pittsburgh	38.5	58.6	166.3	193.5	29	28	16	19
University of North Carolina at Chapel Hill	38.4	63.1	156.3	182.7	30	27	19	20
Pennsylvania State University	47.1	76.7	152.5	176.5	21	19	21	21
University of California—Berkeley	64.1	106.7	142.4	173.3	16	12	23	22
University Southern California	49.2	89.7	152.2	167.1	20	17	22	23
University of Alabama—Birmingham	30.0	44.1	120.2	160.7	44	46	26	24
Case Western Reserve University	33.7	48.0	127.4	151.1	38	40	25	25
California Institute of Technology	33.0	55.1	113.7	133.8	40	32	29	26
University of Illinois—Urbana Champaign	53.6	83.1	115.7	130.9	19	18	28	27
University of Rochester	43.0	70.4	107.6	129.8	25	25	30	28
University of Arizona	36.3	49.7	137.1	129.8	33	37	24	29
Boston University	27.0	46.2	86.1	125.0	51	43	41	30
University of Chicago	54.0	71.2	106.7	121.6	18	24	31	31
Northwestern University	32.4	48.3	101.9	119.7	47	39	32	32
University of California—Davis	31.8	43.2	98.9	118.5	42	47	33	33
Baylor College of Medicine	35.1	45.8	84.1	115.2	35	45	43	34
The Scripps Research Institute	-	-	83.2	113.2	(NA)	(NA)	44	35
University of Iowa	35.3	55.1	93.9	112.6	34	31	36	36
Emory University	17.4	27.0	75.8	109.6	72	70	49	37
Vanderbilt University	27.4	39.9	94.4	108.3	49	48	35	38
University of Texas at Austin	43.8	72.4	115.9	107.4	24	21	27	39
Indiana University	29.3	39.1	89.0	105.9	45	49	39	40
New York University	40.6	74.6	85.5	104.3	28	20	42	41
Ohio State University	42.9	56.1	96.5	101.3	26	30	34	42
University of Virginia	24.3	37.4	79.0	100.6	52	52	48	43
University of Florida	30.8	47.7	82.5	98.5	43	41	45	44
University of Utah	38.2	50.9	93.8	97.3	31	36	37	45

NA Not available. X Not applicable. [1] Includes other institutions, not shown separately.
Source: U.S. National Science Foundation, *Federal S&E Support to Universities and Colleges and Nonprofit Institutions*, annual.

U.S. Census Bureau, Statistical Abstract of the United States: 2000

No. 987. Percentage of U.S. Scientific and Technical Articles Which Are Coauthored and Internationally Coauthored: 1986 to 1997

[Coauthorships are based on authors' corporate address. The database consists of the Institute of Scientific Information's Science and Social Science Citation Indexes (SCI, SSCI)]

Science field	Percentage coauthored				Percentage internationally coauthored			
	1986-88	1989-91	1992-94	1995-97	1986-88	1989-91	1992-94	1995-97
Science and engineering, total.....	46.4	49.4	52.9	56.8	9.8	11.8	14.9	18.0
Physics......................	43.5	47.9	54.3	59.3	16.1	19.1	24.7	30.1
Chemistry....................	31.2	34.5	38.6	42.6	10.0	11.6	14.5	16.9
Earth & space science...........	48.8	53.3	58.2	63.1	16.7	20.2	24.2	28.7
Mathematics..................	40.0	42.8	46.8	49.6	19.7	21.0	24.3	26.8
Biology......................	37.9	42.5	46.0	50.1	8.7	11.1	13.1	15.9
Biomedical research	51.1	54.7	58.8	61.8	11.8	14.0	17.0	19.5
Clinical medicine...............	59.6	61.4	63.3	66.4	7.8	9.5	12.2	15.0
Engineering..................	35.5	39.3	43.3	47.0	9.8	11.5	13.8	16.5
Psychology	36.5	38.5	41.3	43.6	4.3	5.7	6.9	8.9
Social science	29.6	30.8	32.9	35.8	6.4	7.0	8.8	10.3
Health & professional fields.........	32.9	34.9	36.1	39.6	3.3	3.8	4.6	6.5

Source: CHI Research, Inc., Haddon Heights, NJ, Science Indicators Database; and U.S. National Science Foundation, special tabulation.

No. 988. Citations on U.S. Patents to the U.S. Scientific and Technical Literature by Cited Field: 1990 to 1998

[Citations to articles with authors in different sectors are assigned fractionally to participating sectors. Citations are to articles published in a 12-year period, lagged by three years from the patent data. For example, 1997 citations are to articles published in 1993-95]

Science field	1990	1991	1992	1993	1994	1995	1996	1997	1998
Total.....................	12,936	15,720	19,425	26,721	27,437	32,536	47,142	74,839	108,335
Physics.....................	2,169	2,424	2,667	3,024	3,589	3,366	3,506	4,150	4,719
Chemistry....................	1,673	1,921	2,451	3,027	3,114	3,689	4,535	6,218	6,900
Earth & space science...........	76	123	94	93	122	134	195	207	285
Mathematics..................	3	2	18	21	14	19	25	30	35
Biology.....................	306	437	436	548	677	812	1,349	1,508	2,426
Biomedical research	3,818	5,199	6,945	10,735	10,332	12,719	20,646	36,397	55,891
Clinical medicine...............	3,415	4,205	5,293	7,393	7,215	9,173	13,637	22,649	33,437
Engineering technology	1,443	1,401	1,492	1,850	2,346	2,593	3,207	3,589	4,452
Psychology	30	2	24	26	15	25	11	52	91
Social sciences	-	-	1	-	-	-	1	-	10
Health & professional fields	1	2	1	-	10	2	24	33	88

- Represents zero.

Source: CHI Research, Inc., Haddon Heights, NJ, Science Indicators Database; and U.S. National Science Foundation, special tabulation.

No. 989. Percentage of Citations to Foreign Articles in U.S. Scientific and Technical Public Publications: 1990 to 1997

[Citations are to 3 years' articles with 2 year lag. For example, 1997 citations are to articles published in 1993-1995]

Science field	1990	1991	1992	1993	1994	1995	1996	1997
Total science & engineering......	29.6	29.9	30.4	31.0	31.7	32.1	32.9	33.5
Physics.....................	34.4	34.9	34.6	35.5	36.9	38.0	39.4	40.9
Chemistry....................	36.4	36.1	37.3	37.6	38.6	38.1	39.3	40.7
Earth & space science...........	28.8	28.7	28.5	29.7	29.7	29.6	31.2	32.0
Mathematics..................	29.5	31.0	30.9	29.9	29.8	31.7	32.5	32.7
Biology......................	28.7	29.4	29.5	29.9	29.5	30.4	32.3	33.4
Biomedical research	29.8	29.9	30.4	30.9	31.5	31.6	32.0	32.3
Clinical medicine...............	30.0	30.4	31.4	32.0	32.8	33.4	34.2	34.5
Engineering technology	26.7	27.5	26.9	26.7	29.4	28.7	29.6	31.8
Psychology	17.8	17.7	17.5	17.7	17.7	18.2	19.2	20.2
Social science	14.7	14.9	14.4	14.7	15.1	15.6	16.9	17.2
Health & professional fields.........	9.5	9.3	9.3	9.8	9.9	9.9	10.1	10.7

Source: CHI Research, Inc., Haddon Heights, NJ, Science Indicators Database; and U.S. National Science Foundation, special tabulation.

No. 990. Funds for Performance of Industrial R&D by Source of Funds and Selected Industries: 1980 to 1998

[In millions of dollars (44,505 represents $44,505,000,000). For calendar years. Covers basic research, applied research, and development]

Industry	1987 SIC[1] code	1980	1985	1990	1995	1997	1998
CURRENT DOLLARS							
Total funds	(X)	44,505	84,239	109,727	132,103	157,539	169,180
Chemicals and allied products	28	4,636	8,540	13,291	17,547	(D)	21,764
Petroleum refining and extraction	13,29	1,552	(D)	2,306	1,760	(D)	1,808
Machinery	35	5,901	12,216	14,446	(D)	18,499	14,919
Electrical equipment	36	9,175	14,432	13,400	18,751	24,585	25,990
Motor vehicles and motor vehicles equipment	371	4,955	6,984	(D)	(D)	(D)	(D)
Aircraft and missiles	372,376	9,198	22,231	20,635	16,951	16,296	14,449
Professional and scientific instruments	38	3,029	5,013	7,055	11,976	13,458	(D)
All other[2]	(X)	6,059	(D)	(D)	(D)	(D)	(D)
Company funds	(X)	30,476	57,043	81,602	108,652	133,611	145,016
Chemicals and allied products	28	4,264	8,310	13,168	17,337	18,628	21,282
Petroleum refining and extraction	13,29	1,401	2,194	2,289	1,754	1,612	1,802
Machinery	35	5,254	10,721	13,575	9,676	18,393	14,846
Electrical equipment	36	5,431	9,271	9,267	17,060	22,747	24,378
Motor vehicles and motor vehicles equipment	371	4,300	6,164	8,594	13,590	13,758	13,502
Aircraft and missiles	372,376	2,570	5,649	5,649	5,387	5,677	5,108
Professional and scientific instruments	38	2,456	4,622	6,318	8,516	8,958	9,625
All other[2]	(X)	4,800	10,112	23,004	35,230	43,838	54,473
CONSTANT (1996) DOLLARS[3]							
Total funds	(X)	77,535	113,683	126,414	134,524	154,906	164,412
Chemicals and allied products	28	8,077	11,525	15,312	17,869	(D)	21,151
Petroleum refining and extraction	13,29	2,704	(D)	2,657	1,792	(D)	1,757
Machinery	35	10,280	16,486	16,643	(D)	18,190	14,499
Electrical equipment	36	15,984	19,476	15,438	19,095	24,174	25,258
Motor vehicles and motor vehicles equipment	371	8,632	9,425	(D)	(D)	(D)	(D)
Aircraft and missiles	372,376	16,024	30,001	23,773	17,262	16,024	14,042
Professional and scientific instruments	38	5,277	6,765	8,128	12,196	13,233	(D)
All other[2]	(X)	10,556	(D)	(D)	(D)	(D)	(D)
Company funds	(X)	53,094	76,981	94,012	110,644	131,378	140,929
Chemicals and allied products	28	7,429	11,215	15,171	17,655	18,317	20,682
Petroleum refining and extraction	13,29	2,441	2,961	2,637	1,786	1,585	1,751
Machinery	35	9,153	14,468	15,639	9,853	18,086	14,428
Electrical equipment	36	9,462	12,511	10,676	17,373	22,367	23,691
Motor vehicles and motor vehicles equipment	371	7,491	8,318	9,901	13,839	13,528	13,121
Aircraft and missiles	372,376	4,477	7,623	6,206	5,590	5,582	4,964
Professional and scientific instruments	38	4,279	6,238	7,279	8,672	8,808	9,354
All other[2]	(X)	8,362	13,646	26,502	35,876	43,105	52,938

D Figure withheld to avoid disclosure of information pertaining to a specific organization or individual.   X Not applicable.
[1] Prior to 1993, 1972 Standard Industrial Classification; beginning 1993, 1987 Standard Industrial Classification; see text, Section 17, Business.   [2] All other manufacturing and nonmanufacturing.   [3] Based on gross domestic product implicit price deflator.

Source: U.S. National Science Foundation, *Research and Development in Industry,* annual.

No. 991. R&D Funds in R&D-Performing Manufacturing Companies by Industry: 1980 to 1998

Industry	1987 SIC[1] code	Total R&D funds as a percent of net sales					Company R&D funds as a percent of net sales				
		1980	1990	1995	1997	1998	1980	1990	1995	1997	1998
Total[2]	(X)	3.0	4.2	3.6	3.9	3.6	2.1	3.1	2.9	2.9	3.1
Food and kindred products[3]	20	0.4	(D)	0.5	0.5	0.4	(D)	0.5	0.5	0.5	0.4
Paper and allied products	26	1.0	1.0	(D)	(D)	(D)	1.0	1.0	1.0	1.1	1.0
Chemicals and allied products	28	3.6	5.3	4.7	(D)	6.5	3.3	5.3	4.7	5.3	6.4
Petroleum refining and extraction	13,29	0.6	0.9	0.7	(D)	0.8	0.5	0.9	0.7	0.6	0.8
Rubber products	30	2.2	(D)	(D)	(D)	(D)	(D)	2.1	1.6	1.4	2.1
Stone, clay, and glass products	32	1.4	(D)	1.5	1.8	(D)	1.3	1.7	1.5	1.8	1.4
Primary metals	33	0.7	0.8	0.5	0.7	(D)	0.5	0.8	0.5	0.6	0.6
Fabricated metal products	34	1.4	1.4	1.1	1.6	1.4	1.2	1.1	1.1	1.5	1.4
Machinery	35	5.0	7.7	(D)	5.6	5.1	4.5	7.2	3.6	5.6	5.1
Electrical equipment	36	6.6	6.5	6.0	6.2	7.1	3.9	4.5	5.4	5.7	6.6
Motor vehicles and motor vehicle equipment	371	4.9	(D)	(D)	(D)	(D)	4.2	3.7	3.6	3.8	2.2
Aircraft and missiles	372,376	13.7	11.8	12.9	11.2	9.3	3.8	3.1	4.2	3.9	3.3
Professional and scientific instruments	38	7.5	8.0	10.3	11.6	(D)	6.1	7.1	7.3	7.7	8.0

D Figure withheld to avoid disclosure of information pertaining to a specific organization or individual.   X Not applicable.
[1] Prior to 1994, 1972 Standard Industrial Classification; beginning 1994, 1987 Standard Industrial Classification; see text, Section 17, Business.   [2] Includes all manufacturing industries.   [3] Includes tobacco products (SIC 21) beginning 1985.

Source: U.S. National Science Foundation, *Research and Development in Industry,* annual.

Figure 20.2
Federal Obligations for Research, by Field of Science in Current and Constant (1996) dollars: 2000

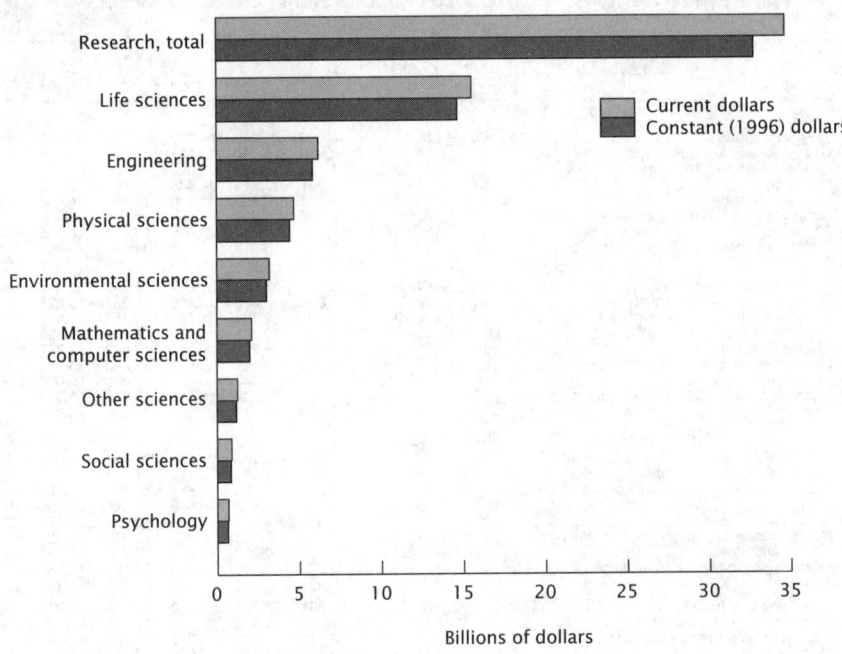

Source: Chart prepared by U.S. Bureau of the Census. For data, see Table 992.

Figure 20.3
R&D Scientists and Engineers Employment and Cost: 1980 to 1998

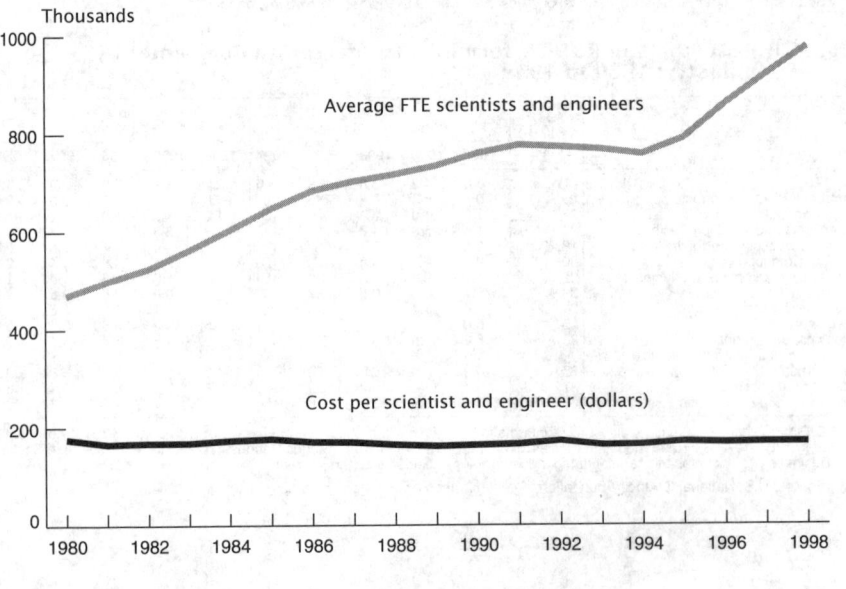

Source: Chart prepared by U.S. Bureau of the Census. For data, see Table 993.

U.S. Census Bureau, Statistical Abstract of the United States: 2000

No. 992. Federal Obligations for Research by Field of Science: 1980 to 2000

[In millions of dollars (11,597 represents $11,597,000,000). **For fiscal years ending in year shown;** see text, Section 9, State and Local Government. Excludes R&D plant]

Field	1980	1985	1990	1995	1996	1997	1998	1999, prel.	2000, prel.
CURRENT DOLLARS									
Research, total	**11,597**	**16,133**	**21,622**	**28,434**	**28,260**	**29,365**	**30,922**	**33,822**	**34,680**
Life sciences	4,192	6,363	8,830	11,811	12,064	12,661	13,558	15,385	15,562
Psychology	199	327	449	623	525	545	591	662	686
Physical sciences	2,001	3,046	3,809	4,278	3,923	4,149	4,210	4,457	4,719
Environmental sciences	1,261	1,404	2,174	2,854	3,020	3,046	3,062	3,171	3,209
Mathematics and computer sciences . . .	241	575	841	1,579	1,572	1,672	1,837	2,008	2,131
Engineering	2,830	3,618	4,227	5,708	5,681	5,690	5,895	6,092	6,219
Social sciences	524	460	630	679	655	696	806	895	890
Other sciences, n.e.c. [1]	350	342	664	902	821	905	964	1,153	1,264
CONSTANT (1996) DOLLARS [2]									
Research, total	**20,592**	**21,855**	**25,043**	**28,982**	**28,260**	**28,874**	**30,022**	**32,427**	**32,747**
Life sciences	7,444	8,619	10,227	12,039	12,064	12,450	13,163	14,751	14,695
Psychology	353	443	520	635	525	536	574	634	648
Physical sciences	3,552	4,126	4,412	4,361	3,923	4,080	4,087	4,273	4,456
Environmental sciences	2,239	1,902	2,518	2,909	3,020	2,995	2,973	3,040	3,030
Mathematics and computer sciences . . .	428	779	974	1,610	1,572	1,644	1,783	1,925	2,012
Engineering	5,025	4,901	4,895	5,818	5,681	5,595	5,724	5,840	5,872
Social sciences	930	623	730	692	655	685	783	858	840
Other sciences, n.e.c. [1]	621	463	769	919	821	890	936	1,105	1,193

[1] N.e.c. = Not elsewhere classified. [2] Based on gross domestic product implicit price deflator.

Source: U.S. National Science Foundation, *Federal Funds for Research and Development*, annual.

No. 993. R&D Scientists and Engineers—Employment and Cost by Industry: 1980 to 1998

[469.2 represents 469,200. Data are estimates; on average full-time-equivalent (FTE) basis]

Industry	1987 SIC [1] code	1980	1985	1990	1993	1994	1995	1996	1997	1998
EMPLOYED SCIENTISTS										
Average FTE of scientists and engineers (1,000) [2][3]	(X)	469.2	646.8	758.5	766.6	757.3	789.5	859.3	918.6	974.6
Chemicals [4]	28	53.1	73.5	81.0	89.8	96.4	97.0	91.7	89.3	90.1
Machinery	35	65.7	85.7	111.5	83.9	69.5	78.0	88.0	100.4	104.1
Electrical equipment [5]	36	100.7	115.6	100.55	92.9	99.9	114.6	130.9	153.8	172.7
Motor vehicles	371	36.7	31.3	47.35	48.1	51.1	54.1	60.4	64.0	63.5
Aircraft and missiles	372,376	90.6	137.5	107.75	85.4	68.2	79.5	95.1	85.8	71.7
CONSTANT (1996) DOLLARS [6]										
Cost per scientist or engineer ($1,000) [3][7]	(X)	176.4	175.7	162.8	162.8	163.8	170.4	168.4	168.6	168.7
Chemicals [4]	28	162.5	157.0	183.2	(D)	(D)	184.3	(D)	(D)	235
Machinery	35	167.1	192.3	159.6	106.8	(D)	(D)	152.9	181.2	139.2
Electrical equipment [5]	36	169.3	168.6	164.5	153.6	158.8	166.6	171.9	157.2	146.2
Motor vehicles	371	251.3	301.1	(D)	(D)	(D)	(D)	(D)	(D)	(D)
Aircraft and missiles	372,376	188.8	218.2	246.2	187.3	194.5	217.2	170.7	186.8	195.8

D Withheld to avoid disclosure.   X Not applicable.   [1] Prior to 1992, 1972 Standard Industrial Classification; beginning 1992, 1987 Standard Industrial Classification; see text, Section 17, Business.   [2] The mean number of FTE R&D scientists and engineers employed in January of the year shown and the following January.   [3] Includes industries not shown separately.   [4] Includes allied products.   [5] Includes communication.   [6] Based on gross domestic product implicit price deflator.   [7] Represents the arithmetic mean of the numbers of R&D scientists and engineers reported in each industry for January in 2 consecutive years divided into total R&D expenditures in each industry.

Source: U.S. National Science Foundation, *Research and Development in Industry*, annual.

Science and Technology 611

No. 994. Civilian Employment of Scientists, Engineers, and Technicians by Occupation and Industry: 1998

[In thousands (5,818.5 represents 5,818,500). Based on sample and subject to sampling error. For details, see source]

Occupation	Total [1]				Wage and salary workers						Self employed [5]
		Min- ing [2]	Con- struc- tion	Manu- factur- ing	Trans- por- tation [3]	Trade	Fire [4]	Serv- ices	Govern- ment	
Scientists, engineers, and technicians	5,818.5	45.4	82.8	1,427.9	260.6	308.6	311.7	2,316.1	692.7	356.5
Scientists	711.9	8.3	0.3	57.9	6.7	8.6	13.8	274.2	198.5	120.7
Physical scientists	200.6	8.2	0.2	54.2	3.6	3.0	0.4	75.4	45.7	8.0
Life scientists.	176.7	0.1	(NA)	(NA)	1.0	1.6	0.5	69.5	73.5	6.6
Mathematical scientists	14.0	(NA)	(NA)	2.0	0.1	-	1.0	6.9	4.0	(NA)
Social scientists	320.6	(NA)	(NA)	1.7	2.0	1.0	11.9	122.4	75.3	106.1
Computer systems analysts, engineers and scientists	1,530.1	4.9	3.5	214.5	66.8	100.6	211.5	714.1	124.2	114.0
Engineers [6]	1,464.0	15.0	35.4	667.0	77.3	47.4	13.2	390.4	166.1	49.9
Civil engineers.	195.0	0.7	13.5	5.9	4.2	0.9	11.3	93.6	63.6	12.0
Electrical/electronics	357.0	0.4	6.8	163.4	35.4	14.9	1.5	87.1	32.1	15.6
Mechanical engineers	219.7	0.6	5.6	127.8	3.2	7.2	1.4	58.0	11.6	4.5
Engineering and science technicians	1,354.2	13.3	39.6	428.9	75.2	103.8	6.9	490.5	151.7	33.3
Electrical/electronics technicians	334.8	0.9	15.6	113.7	29.2	71.9	2.0	78.0	16.2	5.8
Engineering technicians.	771.3	2.7	6.5	259.8	54.4	91.0	2.6	227.1	101.1	8.2
Drafters	285.0	1.0	17.0	84.2	13.0	7.4	1.1	130.4	9.7	17.6
Science technicians	228.8	8.7	0.4	84.7	(NA)	5.4	2.8	86.3	28.6	4.6
Surveyors [7]	110.1	2.1	2.8	0.2	(NA)	-	0.2	75.9	18.2	7.8
Computer programmers	648.2	1.8	1.2	59.4	34.9	48.2	66.1	371.0	34.0	30.8

- Represents zero.   NA Not available.   [1] Includes agriculture, forestry, and fishing not shown separately.   [2] Includes oil and gas extraction. [3] Includes communications and public utilities. [4] Finance, insurance, and real estate. [5] Includes secondary jobs. [6] Includes kinds of engineers and technicians not shown separately. [7] Includes cartographers, photogramnotrists, and surveying and mapping technicians.

Source: U.S. Bureau of Labor Statistics, *Monthly Labor Review*, November 1999; and unpublished data. (Data collected biennially.)

No. 995. Graduate Science/Engineering Students in Doctorate-Granting Colleges: 1985 to 1998

[355.8 represents 355,800. As of fall. Includes outlying areas]

Field of science or engineering	Total (1,000)			Percent—							
				Female			Foreign		Part time		
	1985	1990	1998	1985	1990	1998	1990	1998	1985	1990	1998
Total, all surveyed fields	355.8	398.8	422.8	34.5	37.6	44.4	25.4	24.1	32.4	31.1	28.7
Science/engineering	317.2	351.7	356.9	29.5	32.4	38.9	27.7	27.2	30.7	28.9	27.0
Engineering, total	90.2	99.8	93.8	11.5	13.6	19.0	36.6	39.3	39.7	35.9	32.0
Sciences, total	226.9	251.9	263.1	36.6	39.8	45.9	24.1	22.9	27.2	26.1	25.2
Physical sciences	29.4	32.5	29.1	20.5	23.4	28.1	37.0	35.7	11.9	11.3	11.6
Environmental.	14.1	12.9	12.8	25.3	29.1	38.0	20.1	19.0	23.8	23.6	22.0
Mathematical sciences . .	15.4	17.5	14.4	22.9	30.6	34.8	35.5	35.1	27.6	24.5	22.9
Computer sciences	24.2	28.1	31.1	25.2	23.2	27.2	32.7	40.1	48.6	47.2	43.8
Agricultural sciences . . .	10.9	10.6	11.0	25.8	29.3	39.6	28.8	23.1	18.4	17.9	22.6
Biological sciences. . . .	42.2	46.4	52.7	42.5	45.5	50.3	24.2	21.2	16.1	14.8	14.5
Psychology.	30.8	35.9	39.8	59.7	65.6	69.7	4.6	5.0	30.6	29.0	27.0
Social sciences	59.9	68.0	72.2	39.8	42.8	49.5	21.7	19.6	34.4	32.9	31.0
Health fields, total.	38.7	47.2	65.9	75.7	76.9	74.3	8.6	7.4	46.2	47.4	37.8

Source: U.S. National Science Foundation, *Survey of Graduate Science Engineering Students and Postdoctorates*, annual.

No. 996. Science and Engineering Degree Recipients in 1995 and 1996

[**In thousands (708.9 represents 708,900) except for percent.** Based on survey a and subject to sampling error; see source for details]

Degree and field	Graduates 1995 and 1996 (1,000)	1996 [1] Percent distribution				Median salary [4] ($1,000)
		In school [2]	Employed In S&E [3]	In other	Not employed or not FT students	
Bachelor's recipients.	**708.9**	**21**	**21**	**53**	**5**	**28.2**
All science fields	593.8	23	12	60	5	26.0
Computer and information sciences	41.0	6	57	34	3	37.7
Mathematical sciences	26.8	19	15	63	3	29.8
Life and related sciences	139.0	31	11	53	5	22.8
Physical and related sciences	36.6	38	26	33	3	27.3
Psychology	138.0	24	6	65	5	22.3
Social and related sciences	212.4	18	6	70	6	26.4
All engineering fields	115.1	13	65	18	3	37.7
Aerospace and related engineering	3.0	22	48	27	2	34.0
Chemical engineering	11.6	17	65	14	4	39.3
Civil and architectural engineering	20.7	14	63	20	3	34.4
Electrical, electronics, computer and communications engineering	32.9	10	70	16	4	40.5
Industrial engineering	5.8	8	66	24	2	37.6
Mechanical engineering	27.9	11	71	15	3	38.2
Other engineering	13.2	21	52	25	3	34.1
Master's recipients	**149.5**	**21**	**49**	**27**	**3**	**41.5**
All science fields	102.5	23	36	36	4	37.2
Computer and mathematical sciences	18.2	6	74	18	2	51.2
Mathematical sciences	7.9	27	37	32	3	39.7
Life and related sciences	15.3	32	37	27	4	32.4
Physical and related sciences	9.7	37	42	18	3	33.6
Psychology	26.4	22	29	43	5	29.7
Social and related sciences	25.1	26	15	54	5	35.0
All engineering fields	47.0	15	75	9	2	49.9
Aerospace and related engineering	1.5	31	54	15	1	48.8
Chemical engineering	2.0	33	61	4	2	47.6
Civil and architectural engineering	6.5	11	76	11	1	41.9
Electrical, electronics, computer and communications engineering	16.2	15	77	7	1	55.0
Industrial engineering	3.2	13	70	16	1	49.9
Mechanical engineering	7.2	16	72	10	2	47.7
Other engineering	10.4	10	78	9	4	49.0

[1] As of April. [2] Full-time students. [3] In science and engineering. [4] For the principal job. Excludes full-time students, the self-employed, and persons whose principal job is less than 35 hours per week.

Source: National Science Foundation/SRS, *National Survey of Recent College Graduates: 1997.*

No. 997. Doctorates Conferred by Recipients' Characteristics: 1990 and 1998

[In percent, except as indicated]

Characteristic	1990, total	1998									
		All fields [1]	Engineering	Physical sciences [2]	Earth sciences	Mathematics	Computer sciences	Biological sciences [3]	Agricultural	Social sciences [4]	Psychology
Total conferred (number)	**36,068**	**42,683**	**5,919**	**3,801**	**838**	**1,177**	**923**	**6,646**	**1,192**	**3,394**	**3,681**
Male	63.7	58.0	87.0	77.0	73.0	75.0	83.0	56.0	72.0	59.0	33.0
Female	36.3	42.0	13.0	23.0	27.0	25.0	17.0	44.0	28.0	41.0	67.0
Median age [5]	33.9	33.7	31.6	29.8	33.7	30.7	33.2	31.1	34.6	33.8	32.5
CITIZENSHIP [6]											
Total conferred (number)	**34,697**	**39,556**	**5,413**	**3,526**	**781**	**1,085**	**860**	**5,509**	**1,102**	**3,113**	**3,410**
U.S. citizen	71.8	78.2	55.8	68.5	73.9	61.4	64.1	77.7	56.7	75.6	95.6
Foreign citizen	28.2	21.8	44.2	31.5	26.1	38.6	35.9	22.3	43.3	24.4	4.4
RACE/ETHNICITY [7]											
Total conferred (number)	**26,604**	**30,914**	**3,021**	**4,211**	**577**	**666**	**551**	**4,279**	**625**	**2,352**	**3,259**
White [8]	86.5	78.1	71.5	78.3	82.8	78.4	73.7	75.4	76.8	78.1	80.7
Black [8]	3.8	5.1	2.8	2.2	1.6	2.4	2.5	2.5	3.7	6.2	4.8
Asian/Pacific [8]	4.9	8.8	18.4	12.9	8.8	10.7	16.5	15.4	9.3	7.9	3.5
Indian/Alaskan [8]	0.4	0.6	0.4	0.5	0.5	0.5	0.5	0.3	1.4	0.5	1.0
Hispanic	3.1	4.2	3.6	2.6	2.8	4.1	2.5	3.9	6.1	4.5	6.4
Other/unknown	1.4	3.1	3.3	3.5	3.5	4.1	4.2	2.5	2.7	2.9	3.7

[1] Includes other fields, not shown separately. [2] Astronomy, physics, and chemistry. [3] Biochemistry, botany, microbiology, physiology, zoology, and related fields. [4] Anthropology, sociology, political science, economics, international relations and related fields. [5] For definition of median, see Guide to Tabular Presentation. [6] For those with known citizenship. Includes those with temporary visas. [7] Excludes those with temporary visas. [8] Non-Hispanic.

Source: U.S. National Science Foundation, Division of Science Resources Studies, Survey of Earned Doctorates, *Selected Data on Science and Engineering Doctorate Awards,* annual.

Science and Technology 613

No. 998. Space Vehicle Systems—Net Sales and Backlog Orders: 1965 to 1999

[In millions of dollars (2,449 represents $2,449,000,000). Backlog orders as of Dec. 31. Based on data from major companies engaged in manufacture of aerospace products. Includes parts but excludes engines and propulsion units]

Year	Net sales			Backlog orders			Year	Net sales			Backlog orders		
	Total	Military	Non-military	Total	Military	Non-military		Total	Military	Non-military	Total	Military	Non-military
1965 .	2,449	602	1,847	2,203	503	1,700	1994 .	10,594	5,707	4,887	12,888	6,732	6,156
1970 .	1,956	1,025	931	1,184	786	398	1995 .	11,314	4,782	6,532	15,650	5,872	9,778
1975 .	2,119	1,096	1,023	1,304	1,019	285	1996 .	11,698	5,613	6,085	23,004	9,125	13,879
1980 .	3,483	1,461	2,022	1,814	951	863	1997 .	13,410	4,916	8,494	23,357	8,790	14,567
1985 .	6,300	4,241	2,059	6,707	4,941	1,766	1998 .	9,490	4,227	5,264	20,371	7,970	12,402
1990 .	9,691	6,556	3,135	12,462	8,130	4,332	1999 .	9,022	5,107	3,915	21,026	10,036	10,989

Source: U.S. Census Bureau, *Current Industrial Reports*, MA-37D, *Aerospace Industry (Orders, Sales, and Backlog)* and, beginning 1994, Internet site <http://www.census.gov/cir/www>.

No. 999. Federal Outlays for General Science, Space, and Other Technology: 1980 to 1999, and Projections 2000 to 2005

[In billions of dollars (5.8 represents $5,800,000,000). For fiscal years ending in year shown; see text, Section 9, State and Local Government]

Year	Current dollars			Constant (1996) dollars		
	Total	General science/basic research	Space and other technologies	Total	General science/basic research	Space and other technologies
1980	5.8	1.4	4.5	11.5	2.7	8.8
1985	8.6	2.0	6.6	12.8	3.0	9.8
1990	14.4	2.8	11.6	18.2	3.6	14.7
1995	16.7	4.1	12.6	17.3	4.3	13.0
1996	16.7	4.0	12.7	16.7	4.0	12.7
1997	17.2	4.1	13.1	17.0	4.1	12.9
1998	18.2	5.4	12.9	17.6	5.1	12.5
1999	18.1	5.7	12.4	17.3	5.4	11.9
2000, est.	18.9	6.3	12.6	17.7	5.8	11.9
2001, est.	19.6	6.9	12.7	18.1	6.3	11.8
2002, est.	20.5	7.4	13.1	18.6	6.7	11.9
2003, est.	21.2	7.7	13.5	18.8	6.8	12.1
2004, est.	21.6	7.7	13.9	18.9	6.7	12.2
2005, est.	22.2	7.8	14.3	19.0	6.7	12.3

Source: U.S. Office of Management and Budget, *Budget of the United States, Historical Tables, Fiscal Year 2001*, annual.

No. 1000. U.S. Commercial Space Industry Revenue by Type: 1996 to 2000

[In billions of dollars (19.6 represents $19,600,000,000). For calendar years]

Industry	1996	1997	1998	1999	2000, est.
Total	19.6	26.7	30.5	31.9	37.5
Satellite manufacturing [1]	7.3	10.3	11.8	10.0	10.0
Launch industry	3.2	3.6	3.5	3.5	5.8
Satellite services [2]	4.8	6.3	7.4	9.8	12.2
Ground equipment manufacturing [3]	4.3	6.5	7.8	8.6	9.5

[1] Includes revenues from the construction and sale of satellites to both commercial and government. [2] Includes revenues derived from transponder leasing and subscription/retail services such as direct-to-home television and satellite mobile and data communications. [3] Includes revenues from the manufacture of gateways and satellite control stations, satellite news-gathering trucks, very small aperture terminals, direct-to-home television equipment and mobile satellite phones.

No. 1001. Worldwide Commercial Space Industry Revenue by Type: 1996 to 2000

[In billions of dollars (44.8 represents $44,800,000,000). For calendar years]

Industry	1996	1997	1998	1999	2000, est.
Total	44.8	57.5	63.9	69.1	82.6
Satellite manufacturing [1]	12.4	15.9	18.5	15.8	18.3
Launch industry	6.9	7.9	7.0	6.6	9.6
Satellite services [2]	15.8	21.2	24.5	30.7	37.0
Ground equipment manufacturing [3]	9.7	12.5	13.9	16.0	17.7

[1] Includes revenues from the construction and sale of satellites to both commercial and government. [2] Includes revenues derived from transponder leasing and subscription/retail services such as direct-to-home television and satellite mobile and data communications. [3] Includes revenues from the manufacture of gateways and satellite control stations, satellite news-gathering trucks, very small aperture terminals, direct-to-home television equipment and mobile satellite phones.

Source of Tables 1000 and 1001: Satellite Industry Association/Futron Corporation, Bethesda, MD, *1999 Satellite Survey* (copyright).

614   Science and Technology

No. 1002. National Aeronautics and Space Administration—Budget Summary: 1999 and Projections 2000 to 2005

[In millions of dollars (13,653.0 represents $13,653,000,000)]

Item	1999	2000	2001	2002	2003	2004	2005
Total	13,653.0	13,600.8	14,035.3	14,465.4	14,769.2	15,305.4	15,570.3
Human space flight.	5,480.0	5,467.7	5,499.9	5,387.6	4,939.0	4,817.4	4,686.3
International space station	2,299.7	2,323.1	2,114.5	1,858.5	1,452.5	1,327.0	1,275.0
Space flight operations (space shuttle) . . .	2,998.3	2,979.5	3,165.7	3,307.8	3,264.9	3,253.3	3,169.5
Payload utilization and operations	182.0	165.1	(NA)	(NA)	(NA)	(NA)	(NA)
Payload and elv support.	(X)	(X)	90.2	90.3	91.5	97.0	101.7
Investments and support	(X)	(X)	129.5	131.0	130.1	140.1	140.1
Science, aeronautics and technology	5,653.9	5,580.9	5,929.4	6,388.9	6,993.9	7,571.3	7,913.5
Space science	2,119.2	2,192.8	2,398.8	2,606.4	2,961.4	3,298.8	3,577.9
Life and microgravity sciences and applications	263.5	274.7	302.4	300.3	304.1	323.2	326.0
Earth science	1,413.8	1,443.4	1,405.8	1,332.5	1,293.3	1,303.4	1,306.3
Aerospace technology	1,338.9	1,124.9	1,193.0	1,548.9	1,948.8	2,244.7	2,302.6
Mission communication services	380.0	406.3	(NA)	(NA)	(NA)	(NA)	(NA)
Space operations	(X)	(X)	529.4	500.8	386.3	301.2	300.7
Academic programs.	138.5	138.8	100.0	100.0	100.0	100.0	100.0
Mission support	2,499.5	2,532.2	2,584.0	2,666.2	2,812.7	2,892.2	2,945.1
Safety, mission assurance, engineering and advanced concepts	35.6	43.0	47.5	51.5	51.5	51.5	51.5
Space communication services	185.8	89.7	(NA)	(NA)	(NA)	(NA)	(NA)
Research and program management	2,109.6	2,217.6	2,290.6	2,383.7	2,482.2	2,569.7	2,662.6
Construction of facilities	168.5	181.9	245.9	231.0	279.0	271.0	231.0
Inspector General.	19.6	20.0	22.0	22.7	23.6	24.5	25.4

NA Not available.   X Not applicable.

Source: U.S. National Aeronautics and Space Administration, Internet site <http://ifmp.nasa.gov/codeb/budget/2000?HTML/MYB.htm>.

No. 1003. NASA Space Shuttle Operations Expenditures: 1996 to 2001

[In millions of dollars (2,485.4 represents $2,485,400,000). Data are funding requirements fiscal years shown]

Operation	1996	1997	1998	1999	2000	2001
Total	2,485.4	2,464.9	2,369.4	2,998.3	2,979.5	3,165.7
Shuttle operations.	2,485.4	2,464.9	2,369.4	2,426.7	2,490.7	2,672.8
Orbiter and integration	521.0	492.6	502.9	608.0	698.8	724.5
Propulsion	1,061.5	1,124.7	1,061.8	1,071.2	1,053.1	1,167.4
External tank.	327.5	352.4	341.3	363.2	355.2	349.7
Space shuttle main engine.	185.0	208.3	204.6	200.0	187.5	261.9
Reusable solid rocket motor.	395.7	412.8	380.4	339.0	356.7	418.3
Solid rocket booster	153.3	151.2	135.5	169.0	153.7	137.5
Mission and launch operations.	902.9	847.6	804.7	747.5	738.8	780.9
Safety and performance upgrades	(X)	(X)	(X)	571.6	488.8	492.9
Orbiter improvements.	(X)	(X)	(X)	234.8	183.7	327.2
Propulsion upgrades	(X)	(X)	(X)	175.7	213.2	60.2
Flight operations and launch site equipment. . .	(X)	(X)	(X)	147.6	80.9	90.0
Construction of facilities	(X)	(X)	(X)	13.5	11.0	15.5

X Not applicable.

Source: U.S. National Aeronautics and Space Administration, NASA, 1996-97, Pocket Statistics, annual; thereafter, <http://ifmp.nasa.gov/codeb/budget2001/html>.

No. 1004. World-Wide Successful Space Launches: 1957 to 1999

[Criterion of success is attainment of Earth orbit or Earth escape]

Country	Total, 1957-99	1957-64	1965-69	1970-74	1975-79	1980-84	1985-89	1990-94	1995-99	1998	1999
Total	4,042	289	586	555	607	605	550	466	384	77	73
Soviet Union/Russia [1]	2,598	82	302	405	461	483	447	283	135	24	26
United States	1,188	207	279	139	126	93	61	122	161	34	30
Japan	54	-	-	5	10	12	11	9	7	2	-
ESA [2]	117	-	-	-	1	8	21	33	54	11	10
China	59	-	-	2	6	6	9	15	21	6	4
France.	10	-	4	3	3	-	-	-	-	-	-
India	9	-	-	-	-	3	-	3	3	-	1
Israel.	3	-	-	-	-	-	1	1	1	-	-
Ukraine [1]	2	(NA)	(NA)	(NA)	(NA)	(NA)	(NA)	(NA)	2	(NA)	2
Australia.	1	-	1	-	-	-	-	-	-	-	-
United Kingdom.	1	-	-	1	-	-	-	-	-	-	-

- Represents zero.   NA Not available.   [1] Since Commonwealth of Independent States (CIS) barely exists, now show Russia as the successor to the Soviet space program and Ukraine separately.   [2] European Space Agency. Includes launches by Arianespace.

Source: Library of Congress, Congressional Research Service, Science Policy Research Division, Space Activities of the United States, CIS, and Other Launching Countries/Organizations 1957-1994, July 31, 1995; and forthcoming report.

Science and Technology   615

No. 1005. Space Shuttle Launches—Summary: 1981 to May 2001

Flight number	Mission date	Orbiter name	Crew size (up/down)	Days/hours duration	Flight number	Mission date	Orbiter name	Crew size (up/down)	Days/hours duration
1	04/12/81	Columbia	2	2	55	04/26/93	Columbia	7	10
2	11/12/81	Columbia	2	2	57	06/21/93	Endeavour	6	10
3	03/22/82	Columbia	2	8	51	09/12/93	Discovery	5	10
4	06/27/82	Columbia	2	7	58	10/18/93	Columbia	7	14
5	11/11/82	Columbia	4	5	61	12/02/93	Endeavour	7	11
6	04/04/83	Challenger	4	5	60	02/03/94	Discovery	6	8
7	06/18/83	Challenger	5	6	62	03/04/94	Columbia	5	14
8	08/30/83	Challenger	5	6	59	04/09/94	Endeavour	6	11
9	11/28/83	Columbia	6	10	65	07/08/94	Columbia	7	15
10	02/03/84	Challenger	5	8	64	09/09/94	Discovery	6	11
11	04/06/84	Challenger	5	7	68	09/30/94	Endeavour	6	11
12	08/30/84	Discovery	6	7	66	11/03/94	Atlantis	6	11
13	10/05/84	Challenger	7	8	63	02/03/95	Discovery	6	8
14	11/08/84	Discovery	5	8	67	03/02/95	Endeavour	7	17
15	01/24/85	Discovery	5	4	71	06/27/95	Atlantis	7/8	10
16	04/12/85	Discovery	7	7	70	07/13/95	Discovery	5	9
17	04/29/85	Challenger	7	7	69	09/07/95	Endeavour	5	11
18	06/17/85	Discovery	7	7	73	10/20/95	Columbia	7	16
19	07/29/85	Challenger	7	8	74	11/08/95	Atlantis	5	8
20	08/27/85	Discovery	5	7	72	01/11/96	Endeavour	6	9
21	10/03/85	Atlantis	5	4	75	02/22/96	Columbia	7	16
22	10/30/85	Challenger	8	7	76	03/22/96	Atlantis	6/5	9
23	11/26/85	Atlantis	7	7	77	05/19/96	Endeavour	6	10
24	01/12/86	Columbia	7	6	78	06/20/96	Columbia	7	17
25	01/28/86	Challenger	7	-	79	09/16/96	Atlantis	6	10
26	09/29/88	Discovery	5	4	80	11/20/96	Columbia	5	18
27	12/02/88	Atlantis	5	4	81	01/12/97	Atlantis	6	10/5
29	03/13/89	Discovery	5	5	82	02/11/97	Discovery	7	10/0
30	05/04/89	Atlantis	5	4	83	04/04/97	Columbia	7	3/23
28	08/08/89	Columbia	5	5	84	05/15/97	Atlantis	7/7	9/5
34	10/18/89	Atlantis	5	5	94	07/01/97	Columbia	7	15/7
33	11/22/89	Discovery	5	5	85	08/07/97	Discovery	5	11/20
32	01/09/90	Columbia	5	11	86	09/25/97	Atlantis	7/7	10/19
36	02/28/90	Atlantis	5	4	87	11/19/97	Columbia	6	15/17
31	04/24/90	Discovery	5	5	89	01/22/98	Endeavor	7/7	8/20
41	10/06/90	Discovery	5	4	90	04/17/98	Columbia	7	15/22
38	11/15/90	Atlantis	5	5	91	06/02/98	Discovery	6/7	9/19
35	12/02/90	Columbia	7	9	95	11/20/98	Discovery	7	8/22
37	04/05/91	Atlantis	5	6	88	12/04/98	Endeavor	6	11/19
39	04/28/91	Discovery	7	8	96	05/27/99	Discovery	7	9/19
40	06/05/91	Columbia	7	9	93	07/23/99	Columbia	5	4/24
43	08/02/91	Atlantis	5	9	103	12/19/99	Atlantis	7	7/23
48	09/12/91	Discovery	5	5	99	02/11/00	Endeavor	6	11/4
44	11/24/91	Atlantis	6	7	101	05/19/00	Atlantis	7	10/19
42	01/22/92	Discovery	7	8					
45	03/24/92	Atlantis	7	9	FUTURE				
49	05/07/92	Endeavour	7	9	MISSIONS				
50	06/25/92	Columbia	7	14	IN WORK				
46	07/31/92	Atlantis	7	8					
47	09/12/92	Endeavour	7	8	92	10/05/00	Discovery	7	10
52	10/22/92	Columbia	6	10	97	11/30/00	Endeavor	5	9
53	12/02/92	Discovery	5	7	98	01/18/01	Atlantis	5	10
54	01/13/93	Endeavour	5	6	102	02/15/01	Discovery	10	11
56	04/08/93	Discovery	5	9	100	04/19/01	Atlantis	5	11

- Represents zero.

Source: U.S. National Aeronautics and Space Administration, Internet site <http://www.ksc.nasa.gov/shuttle/missions/missions.html> (accessed 1 August 2000).

No. 1006. Nobel Prize Laureates in Selected Sciences: 1901 to 1998

[Presented by location of award-winning research and by date of award]

Country	1901-1997				1901-1930	1931-1945	1946-1960	1961-1975	1976-1990	1991-1997	1998
	Total	Physics	Chemistry	Physiology/ Medicine							
Total	456	157	131	168	93	49	74	92	98	42	8
United States	198	70	46	82	6	14	38	41	63	28	8
United Kingdom	71	21	26	24	15	11	14	20	9	2	-
Germany [1]	61	17	29	15	27	11	4	8	7	3	-
France	25	11	7	7	13	2	-	5	2	3	-
Soviet Union	10	7	1	2	2	-	4	3	1	-	-
Japan	4	3	1	-	-	-	1	2	1	-	-
Other countries	87	28	21	38	30	11	13	13	15	6	-

- Represents zero.   [1] Between 1946 and 1991, data are for the former West Germany only.

Source: U.S. National Science Foundation, unpublished data.

Section 21
Transportation—Land

This section presents statistics on revenues, passenger and freight traffic volume, and employment in various revenue-producing modes of the transportation industry, including motor vehicles, trains, and pipelines. Data are also presented on commuting travel, highway mileage and finances, motor vehicle travel, accidents, sales, and registrations; automobile operating costs; and characteristics of public transit, railroads, and pipelines.

The principal compiler of data on public roads and on operation of motor vehicles is the U.S. Department of Transportation's (DOT) Federal Highway Administration (FHWA). These data appear in FHWA's annual *Highway Statistics* and other publications.

The U.S. National Highway Traffic Safety Administration issues data on traffic accident deaths and death rates in two annual reports: the *Fact Book* and the *Fatal Accident Reporting System Annual Report*. DOT's Federal Railroad Administration presents data on accidents involving railroads in its annual *Accident/Incident Bulletin*, and the *Rail-Highway Crossing Accident/Incident and Inventory Bulletin*.

The results of the censuses of transportation are presented in the *Truck Inventory and Use Survey*. The *Annual Survey of Manufactures* and reports of the censuses of manufactures, wholesale and retail trade, and service industries contain statistics on the motor vehicle and equipment industry and on retail, wholesale, and services aspects of this industry. Data on persons commuting to work were collected as part of the 1980 census and are in various census reports.

Data are also presented in many nongovernment publications. Among them are the weekly and annual *Cars of Revenue Freight Loaded* and the annual *Yearbook of Railroad Facts*, both published by the

Association of American Railroads, Washington, DC; *Transit Fact Book*, containing electric railway and motorbus statistics, published annually by the American Public Transit Association, Washington, DC.; *Accident Facts*, issued by the National Safety Council, Chicago, IL; and *Transportation in America*, issued by the Eno Foundation for Transportation, Westport, Connecticut.

Federal-aid highway systems—The Intermodal Surface Transportation Efficiency Act (ISTEA) of 1991 eliminated the historical Federal-Aid Highway Systems and created the National Highway System (NHS) and other Federal-aid highway categories. The final NHS was approved by Congress in December of 1995 under the National Highway System Designation Act.

Functional systems—Roads and streets are assigned to groups according to the character of service intended. The functional systems are (1) arterial highways that generally handle the long trips, (2) collector facilities that collect and disperse traffic between the arterials and the lower systems, and (3) local roads and streets that primarily serve direct access to residential areas, farms, and other local areas.

Regulatory bodies—The ICC, created by the U.S. Congress to regulate transportation in interstate commerce, has jurisdiction over railroads, trucking companies, bus lines, freight forwarders, water carriers, coal slurry pipelines, and transportation brokers. The Federal Energy Regulatory Commission is responsible for setting rates and charges for transportation and sale of natural gas and for establishing rates or charges for transportation.

Motor carriers—For 1960-73, Class I for-hire motor carriers of freight were classified by the ICC as those with $1 million or more of gross annual operating revenue;

U.S. Census Bureau, Statistical Abstract of the United States: 2000

1974-79, the class minimum was $3 million. Effective January 1, 1980, Class I carriers are those with $5 million or more in revenue. For 1960-68, Class I motor carriers of passengers were classified by the ICC as those with $200,000 or more of gross annual operating revenue; for 1969-76, as those with revenues of $1 million or more; and since 1977, as those with $3 million or more. Effective January 1, 1988, Class I motor carriers of passengers are those with $5 million or more in operating revenues; Class II less than $5 million in operating revenues.

Railroads—Railroad companies reporting to the ICC are divided into specific groups as follows: (1) Regular line-haul (interstate) railroads (and their nonoperating subsidiaries), (2) switching and terminal railroads, (3) private railroads prior to 1964 (identified by ICC as "circular" because they reported on brief circulars), and (4) unofficial railroads, so designated when their reports are received too late for tabulation. For the most part, the last three groups are not included in the statistics shown here.

For years prior to 1978, Class I railroads were those with annual revenues of $1 million or more for 1950-55; $3 million or more for 1956-64; $5 million or more for 1965-75; and $10 million or more for 1976-77. In 1978, the classification became Class I, those having more than $50 million gross annual operating revenue; Class II, from $10 million to $50 million+; and Class III, less than $10 million. Effective January 1, 1982, the ICC adopted a procedure to adjust the threshold for inflation by restating current revenues in constant 1978 dollars. In 1988, the criteria for Class I and Class II railroads were $92.0 million and $18.4 million, respectively. Also effective January 1, 1982, the ICC adopted a Carrier Classification Index Survey Form for carriers not filing annual report Form R-1 with the commission. Class II and Class III railroads are currently exempted from filing any financial report with the Commission. The form is used for reclassifying carriers.

The Surface Transportation Board (STB) was established pursuant to the ICC Termination Act of 1995, Pub. L. No. 104-88, 109 Stat. 803 (1995) (ICCTA), to assume certain of the regulatory functions that had been administered by the Interstate Commerce Commission. The Board has broad economic regulatory oversight of railroads, addressing such matters as rate reasonableness, car service and interchange, mergers and line acquisitions, line construction, and line abandonments. 49 U.S.C. 10101-11908. Other ICC regulatory functions were either eliminated or transferred to the Federal Highway Administration or the Bureau of Transportation Statistics within DOT.

Class I Railroads are regulated by the STB and subject to the Uniform System of Accounts and required to file annual and periodic reports. Railroads are classified based on their annual operating revenues. The class to which a carrier belongs is determined by comparing its adjusted operating revenues for 3 consecutive years to the following scale: Class I, $250 million or more, Class II $20 million to $250 million, and Class III $0 to 20 million.

The formula below is used to adjust a railroad's operating revenues to eliminate the effects of inflation:

Current year's revenues * (1991 avg. index/current year's avg. index)

The average index (deflator factor) is based on the annual average Railroad Freight Price Index for all commodities. The factor for 1991 is 1.00; for 1997, 0.9750.

Statistical reliability—For a discussion of statistical collection and estimation, sampling procedures, and measures of statistical reliability, see Appendix III.

No. 1007. Passenger and Freight Transportation Outlays by Type of Transport: 1980 to 1997

[In billions of dollars (338.1 represents $338,100,000,000). Freight data include outlays for mail and express. ICC=Interstate Commerce Commission]

Type of transport	1980	1985	1990	1992	1993	1994	1995	1996	1997
Total outlays [1]	338.1	492.2	630.4	644.6	683.7	715.2	763.4	800.9	833.0
Passenger:									
Private transportation	284.8	418.2	528.3	538.2	575.9	604.8	644.0	675.9	701.3
Automobiles [2]	276.7	410.3	518.0	529.3	566.5	594.4	633.5	664.2	687.6
New and used cars	73.3	139.3	165.5	152.9	165.0	184.4	181.8	185.7	189.2
Tires, tubes, accessories	22.2	29.6	25.4	32.8	34.8	31.7	40.2	42.8	43.1
Gasoline and oil	99.7	106.6	120.4	116.1	118.9	117.9	128.4	138.3	140.6
Insurance less claims	11.5	11.6	20.1	28.1	29.5	31.5	32.7	32.6	32.6
Interest on debt	17.5	26.7	35.5	25.7	28.1	34.5	40.7	41.8	38.2
Auto registration fees	2.9	4.8	6.1	7.1	7.4	7.4	7.0	7.1	7.2
Operators' permit fees	0.4	0.5	0.6	0.8	0.7	0.8	0.8	0.8	0.8
Repair, greasing, washing, parking, leasing, rentals [3]	38.0	58.1	91.8	103.8	112.2	116.4	128.7	143.6	154.9
Air	8.1	7.9	10.3	8.9	9.5	10.4	10.5	11.7	13.7
For-hire transportation	53.4	73.9	102.1	106.4	107.8	110.4	119.4	125.0	131.7
Local [4]	19.8	27.3	34.2	36.0	37.4	38.9	43.2	44.3	46.4
Bus and transit [5]	9.3	13.5	16.7	17.9	18.7	20.0	21.6	21.9	22.8
School bus	3.8	5.9	7.6	8.1	7.6	7.8	9.1	10.4	10.8
Taxi	5.2	5.6	7.1	7.3	7.6	7.8	8.1	8.2	9.0
Railroad commutation	1.5	2.2	2.8	2.7	3.5	3.1	4.5	3.7	3.8
Intercity	28.3	39.5	53.0	53.1	52.8	53.8	57.7	62.4	65.7
Air	25.1	35.9	49.5	49.2	49.3	50.5	54.0	58.6	61.8
Rail [6]	1.5	1.6	1.7	1.9	1.8	1.8	2.2	2.2	2.2
Bus	1.7	2.0	1.8	1.9	1.7	1.4	1.5	1.5	1.6
International	5.3	7.1	14.9	17.3	17.6	17.7	18.4	18.4	19.6
Freight, total [4]	213.7	273.6	350.9	375.1	396.3	419.9	444.5	467.2	504.4
Highway	155.3	205.6	270.8	292.9	311.9	330.7	348.1	368.5	401.7
Truck, intercity	94.6	123.2	162.3	176.8	189.7	204.9	219.6	235.4	257.8
Truck, local	60.5	82.2	108.4	116.0	122.1	125.7	128.4	133.0	143.7
Rail	27.9	29.2	30.1	30.5	30.8	33.1	34.3	35.1	35.3
Water	15.5	18.4	20.1	19.9	20.8	21.2	24.9	25.0	25.3
Oil pipeline	7.5	8.9	8.5	8.5	8.4	8.3	9.1	8.6	8.7
Air carrier	4.0	6.8	13.7	15.0	15.8	17.2	18.7	20.1	22.7

[1] Total outlays less than sum of passenger and freight totals, as estimated freight costs included in costs of new cars, gasoline, oil, tires, and tubes have been excluded to prevent duplication. [2] Includes business-owned vehicles. [3] Includes storage. [4] Includes items not shown separately. [5] Includes Federal, state, and local government operating subsidies and capital grants. [6] Includes Federal operating subsidies and capital grants for Amtrak.

Source: Eno Transportation Foundation, Inc., Lansdowne, VA, *Transportation in America*, annual (copyright).

No. 1008. Volume of Domestic Intercity Freight and Passenger Traffic by Type of Transport: 1980 to 1997

[Freight traffic in bil. ton-miles; passenger traffic in bil. passenger-miles. A ton-mile is the movement of 1 ton (2,000 pounds) of freight for the distance of 1 mile. A passenger-mile is the movement of one passenger for the distance of 1 mile. Comprises public and private traffic, both revenue and nonrevenue]

Type of transport	Traffic volume						Percent distribution					
	1980	1985	1990	1995	1996	1997	1980	1985	1990	1995	1996	1997
Freight traffic, total . .	2,487	2,458	2,895	3,407	3,540	3,622	100.0	100.0	100.0	100.0	100.0	100.0
Railroads	932	895	1,091	1,375	1,426	1,421	37.5	38.0	35.6	37.9	37.6	38.1
Truck:												
ICC truck	242	250	311	401	428	466	9.7	9.9	10.4	11.0	11.3	11.8
Non-ICC truck	313	360	424	520	549	585	12.6	11.8	14.9	15.1	15.6	16.0
Water:												
Rivers/canals	311	306	390	406	408	413	12.5	12.8	13.0	13.3	13.0	12.0
Great Lakes	96	76	85	91	90	95	3.9	4.0	2.7	2.5	2.5	2.7
Oil pipelines	588	564	584	601	631	628	23.6	23.2	23.1	19.9	19.5	19.1
Domestic airways [1]	5	7	10	13	13	14	0.2	0.2	0.3	0.3	0.4	0.4
Passenger traffic, total	1,468	1,636	2,034	2,337	2,405	2,476	100.0	100.0	100.0	100.0	100.0	100.0
Private automobiles	1,210	1,310	1,639	1,881	1,917	1,968	82.5	82.7	79.4	81.3	81.3	81.3
Domestic airways [2]	15	12	13	10	11	13	1.0	14.7	-	0.6	0.5	0.5
Air, public carrier	204	278	346	404	435	453	13.9	-	-	16.3	16.5	16.5
Bus [3]	27	24	23	28	29	30	1.9	1.8	1.4	1.1	1.1	1.1
Railroads [4]	11	11	13	14	13	14	0.7	0.7	0.7	0.7	0.7	0.6

- Represents zero. [1] Revenue service only for scheduled and nonscheduled carriers, with small section 418 all-cargo carriers included. Includes express mail, and excess baggage. [2] Includes general aviation (mostly private business) flying. [3] Excludes school and urban transit buses. [4] Includes intercity (Amtrak) and rail commuter service.

Source: Eno Transportation Foundation, Inc., Lansdowne VA, *Transportation in America*, annual (copyright).

No. 1009. Transportation Industry Summary: 1992

[Includes only establishments with payroll]

Kind of business	SIC code [1]	Establish-ments (number)	Revenue ($1,000)	Annual payroll ($1,000)	First-quarter payroll	Paid employees for pay period including March 12 (number)
Total transportation, except U.S. Post Office.	(X)	(NA)	**327,623**	**92,211**	(NA)	**3,356,872**
Railroad transportation [2]	40	(NA)	28,349	8,753	(NA)	197,421
Passenger transportation	41	17,805	12,649	5,191	1,246	354,913
Local and suburban passenger transportation	411	8,275	5,968	2,624	613	153,278
Taxicabs	412	3,337	992	306	75	26,338
Other bus transport. and terminal service	413, 4, 5, 7	6,193	5,689	2,261	558	175,297
Motor freight transportation and warehousing	42	110,908	143,794	39,896	9,196	1,580,095
Trucking and courier services, except air.	421	101,169	135,437	37,760	8,691	1,484,655
Local trucking with storage	4214	4,512	4,191	1,346	303	64,417
Public warehousing and storage	422	9,718	8,330	2,127	504	95,145
Trucking terminal facilities.	423	21	27	8	2	295
Pipelines, except natural gas	46	844	7,063	821	203	16,779
Transportation services	47	46,593	23,890	7,850	1,854	329,202

NA Not available.   X Not applicable.   [1] 1987 Standard Industrial Classification, see Section 13, Labor Force.   [2] Includes Class I Freight railroads only. Source: Association of American Railroads, Washington, DC, *Railroad Facts*, annual.
Source: Except as noted, U.S. Census Bureau, *Census of Transportation, Communications and Utilities: 1992.*

No. 1010. Employment and Earnings in Transportation by Industry: 1980 to 1999

[Annual averages of monthly figures. Based on Current Employment Statistics program; see Appendix III]

Industry	SIC code [1]	1980	1985	1990	1995	1996	1997	1998	1999
NUMBER (1,000)									
Total transportation	(X)	**2,960**	**2,997**	**3,511**	**3,904**	**4,019**	**4,123**	**4,276**	**4,425**
Railroads.	40	532	359	279	238	231	227	231	230
Local and interurban passengers.	41	265	277	338	419	437	452	468	482
Trucking and warehousing	42	211	(NA)	1,395	1,587	1,637	1,677	1,745	1,813
Water transportation	44	211	185	177	175	174	179	180	181
Air transportation	45	(NA)	(NA)	968	1,068	1,107	1,134	1,183	1,237
Pipelines, exc. natural gas	46	21	19	19	15	15	14	14	13
Transportation services	47	(NA)	(NA)	336	401	418	441	455	469
AVG. WEEKLY EARNINGS (dol.)									
Class I railroads	4011	427	595	727	811	850	892	845	797
Local and interurban passengers.	41	217	261	310	358	367	375	387	398
Trucking and warehousing	42	(NA)	(NA)	450	504	515	532	545	561
Pipelines, exc. natural gas	46	441	629	711	888	909	902	918	944

NA Not available.   X Not applicable.   [1] 1987 Standard Industrial Classification, see text, Section 13, Labor Force.
Source: U.S. Bureau of Labor Statistics, Bulletin 2445 and 2481, Employment and Earnings, March and June issues.

No. 1011. Transportation Accidents, Deaths, and Injuries: 1990 and 1998

[For related data, see also Table 1043]

Year and casualty			Type of transport									
	Motor ve-hicle [1] (1,000)	Rail-road [2]	Air carriers				General aviation	Recre-ational boat-ing [6]	Gas pipe-lines [7]	Water-borne [8]	Rail Rapid Trans-it [9]	Hazard-ous materi-als [10]
			Total	Air-lines [3]	Com-muter air car-riers [4]	On demand air car-riers [5]						
Accidents:												
1990. . . .	6,471	2,879	146	24	15	106	2,215	6,411	198	3,613	12,178	8,880
1998. . . .	6,335	2,575	135	48	8	79	1,709	8,175	232	2,837	(NA)	15,349
Deaths:												
1990. . . .	44.6	599	97	39	7	50	767	865	6	85	117	8
1998. . . .	41.5	577	46	1	-	45	621	813	17	31	(NA)	13
Injuries:												
1990. . . .	3,231	22,736	76	29	11	36	402	3,822	69	175	10,036	423
1998. . . .	3,192	10,156	41	28	2	11	332	4,613	73	83	(NA)	198

- Represents or rounds to zero.   NA Not available.   [1] Data on deaths are from U.S. National Highway Traffic Safety Administration and are based on 30 day definition. Includes only police reported crashes.   [2] Accidents which result in damages to railroad property. Grade crossing accidents are also included when classified as a train accident. Deaths exclude fatalities in railroad-highway grade crossing accidents.   [3] Includes scheduled and nonscheduled (charter) air carriers. Represents serious injuries.   [4] All scheduled service. Represents serious injuries.   [5] All nonscheduled service. Represents serious injuries.   [6] Accidents resulting in death; injury or requiring medical treatment beyond first aid; damages exceeding $500; or a person's disappearance.   [7] Pipeline accidents/incidents are credited to year of occurrence; prior data are credited to the year filed.   [8] Covers accidents involving commercial vessels which must be reported to U.S. Coast Guard if there is property damage exceeding $25,000; material damage affecting the seaworthiness or efficiency of a vessel; stranding or grounding; loss of life; or injury causing a person's incapacity for more than 3 days.   [9] Reporting criteria and source of data changed between 1989 and 1990; these data from 1990 to present are not comparable to earlier years.   [10] Accidents, deaths, and injuries involving hazardous materials cover all types of transport.
Source: U.S. Bureau of Transportation Statistics, *National Transportation Statistics*, annual.

620   Transportation—Land

No. 1012. Commodity Shipments—Value, Tons, and Ton-Miles: 1993 and 1997

Mode of transportation	Value 1993	Value 1997	Tons 1993	Tons 1997	Ton-miles 1993	Ton-miles 1997
All modes	**5,846,334**	**6,943,988**	**9,688,493**	**11,089,733**	**2,420,915**	**2,661,363**
Single modes	**4,941,452**	**5,719,558**	**8,922,286**	**10,436,538**	**2,136,873**	**2,383,473**
Truck [1]	4,403,494	4,981,531	6,385,915	7,700,675	869,536	1,023,506
For-hire truck	2,625,093	2,901,345	2,808,279	3,402,605	629,000	741,117
Private truck	1,755,837	2,036,528	3,543,513	4,137,294	235,897	268,592
Rail	247,394	319,629	1,544,148	1,549,817	942,561	1,022,547
Water	61,628	75,840	505,440	563,369	271,998	261,747
Shallow draft	40,707	53,897	362,454	414,758	164,371	189,284
Great Lakes	(S)	1,504	33,041	38,421	12,395	13,415
Deep draft	19,749	20,439	109,945	110,191	95,232	59,047
Air (includes truck and air)	139,086	229,062	3,139	4,475	4,009	6,233
Pipeline [2]	89,849	113,497	483,645	618,202	(S)	(S)
Multiple modes	**662,603**	**945,874**	**225,676**	**216,673**	**191,461**	**204,514**
Parcel, U.S. Postal Service or courier	563,277	855,897	18,892	23,689	13,151	7,994
Truck and rail	83,082	75,695	40,624	54,246	37,675	55,561
Truck and water	9,392	8,241	67,995	33,215	40,610	34,767
Rail and water	3,636	1,771	79,222	79,275	70,219	71,590
Other multiple modes	3,216	4,269	18,943	26,248	(S)	18,603
Other and unknown modes	242,279	278,555	540,530	436,521	92,581	73,376

S Data do not meet publication standards due to high sampling variability or other reasons. [1] Truck as a single mode includes shipments that went by private truck only, for-hire truck only, or a combination of private truck and for-hire truck.
[2] Excludes most shipments of crude oil.

Source: U.S. Bureau of Transportation Statistics, *Transportation 1997 Commodity Flow Survey.*

No. 1013. Hazardous Material Shipment Characteristics: 1997

Item	Value Number (mil. dol.)	Value Percent	Tons Number (1,000)	Tons Percent	Ton-miles Number (mil.)	Ton-miles Percent	Average miles per shipment
MODE OF TRANSPORTATION							
All modes	**466,407**	**100.0**	**1,565,196**	**100.0**	**263,809**	**100.0**	**113**
Single modes	**452,727**	**97.1**	**1,541,716**	**98.5**	**258,912**	**98.1**	**95**
Truck [1]	298,173	63.9	869,796	55.6	74,939	28.4	73
For-hire truck	134,308	28.8	336,363	21.5	45,234	17.1	260
Private truck	160,693	34.5	522,666	33.4	28,847	10.9	35
Rail	33,340	7.1	96,626	6.2	74,711	28.3	853
Water	26,951	5.8	143,152	9.1	68,212	25.9	(S)
Air (includes truck and air)	8,558	1.8	66	(Z)	95	(Z)	1,462
Pipeline [2]	85,706	18.4	432,075	27.6	(S)	(S)	(S)
Multiple modes	**5,735**	**1.2**	**6,022**	**0.4**	**3,061**	**1.2**	**645**
Parcel, U.S. Postal Service or courier	2,874	0.6	143	(Z)	78	(Z)	697
Other multiple modes	2,861	0.6	5,879	0.4	2,982	1.1	(S)
Other and unknown modes	**7,945**	**1.7**	**17,459**	**1.1**	**1,837**	**0.7**	**38**
HAZARDOUS CLASS AND DESCRIPTION							
Total	466,407	100.0	1,565,196	100.0	263,809	100.0	113
Class 1, explosives	4,342	0.9	1,517	0.1	(S)	(S)	549
Class 2, gases	40,884	8.8	115,021	7.3	21,842	8.3	66
Class 3, flammable liquids	335,619	72.0	1,264,281	80.8	159,979	60.6	73
Class 4, flammable solids	3,898	0.8	11,804	0.8	9,618	3.6	838
Class 5, oxidizers and organic peroxides	4,485	1.0	9,239	0.6	4,471	1.7	193
Class 6, toxic (poison)	10,086	2.2	6,366	0.4	2,824	1.1	402
Class 7, radioactive materials	2,722	0.6	87	(Z)	48	(Z)	445
Class 8, corrosive materials	40,423	8.7	91,564	5.9	41,161	15.6	201
Class 9, misc. dangerous goods	23,946	5.1	65,317	4.2	22,727	8.6	323

S Data do not meet publication standards because of high sampling variability or other reasons.   Z Represents or rounds to zero.   [1] "Truck" as a single mode includes shipments which went by private truck only, for-hire truck only or a combination of private truck and for-hire truck.   [2] Commodity Flow Survey data exclude most shipments of crude oil.

Source: U.S. Census Bureau, 1997 Economic Census, *Commodity Flow Survey.*

Transportation—Land 621

No. 1014. Highway Mileage—Functional Systems and Urban/Rural: 1998

[As of **Dec. 31.** For definition of urban, rural, see text, this section]

State		Functional systems				Urban	Rural
	Total [1]	Interstate	Other arterial	Collector	Local		
U.S	**3,906,292**	**46,084**	**378,794**	**792,619**	**2,679,632**	**841,643**	**3,064,649**
AL	94,227	905	8,754	20,310	64,237	20,630	73,597
AK	12,680	1,083	1,505	2,744	7,348	1,810	10,870
AZ	53,968	1,168	4,746	8,554	39,400	17,318	36,650
AR	95,110	542	6,841	20,133	67,480	9,988	85,122
CA	165,948	2,426	26,669	31,874	103,582	83,535	82,413
CO	85,270	952	8,168	16,600	59,329	14,000	71,270
CT	20,726	346	2,849	2,979	14,355	11,742	8,984
DE	5,733	41	618	944	4,119	1,984	3,749
DC	1,421	12	254	156	981	1,421	-
FL	115,415	1,472	12,049	14,395	87,079	48,336	67,079
GA	113,554	1,244	13,116	23,155	75,874	27,370	86,184
HI	4,218	55	749	822	2,558	1,874	2,344
ID	46,108	611	3,752	9,825	31,920	3,915	42,193
IL	137,963	2,165	13,897	21,511	100,308	35,905	102,058
IN	93,344	1,172	7,914	22,632	61,491	19,859	73,485
IA	112,810	782	9,465	31,506	71,057	9,464	103,346
KS	133,825	872	9,187	33,296	90,335	10,080	123,745
KY	73,635	762	5,474	17,626	49,682	11,023	62,612
LA	60,747	894	5,301	12,538	41,968	13,929	46,818
ME	22,638	367	2,314	5,940	13,999	2,629	20,009
MD	30,188	481	3,555	5,018	20,900	14,235	15,953
MA	35,254	566	5,645	5,485	23,353	23,061	12,193
MI	121,482	1,241	12,226	25,761	82,031	29,737	91,745
MN	131,188	913	12,539	29,644	87,947	15,747	115,441
MS	73,295	685	7,070	15,556	49,943	7,923	65,372
MO	122,847	1,178	9,380	24,971	86,998	16,367	106,480
MT	69,890	1,191	6,008	16,395	46,296	2,485	67,405
NE	92,743	482	7,873	20,800	63,571	5,132	87,611
NV	35,413	566	2,867	5,278	26,665	5,693	29,720
NH	15,124	224	1,548	2,670	10,642	2,930	12,194
NJ	35,920	420	5,412	4,587	25,189	24,212	11,708
NM	59,914	1,000	4,514	7,002	47,395	6,145	53,769
NY	112,525	1,499	13,642	20,533	76,026	40,824	71,701
NC	98,608	988	8,933	17,774	70,625	23,090	75,518
ND	86,603	572	5,873	11,499	68,659	1,834	84,769
OH	116,221	1,573	10,612	22,142	81,509	33,465	82,756
OK	112,524	930	7,839	25,387	78,234	13,158	99,366
OR	68,478	727	6,807	17,428	43,461	10,689	57,789
PA	119,281	1,751	13,166	19,767	84,111	34,138	85,143
RI	6,048	68	835	857	4,220	4,704	1,344
SC	64,895	828	6,812	13,391	43,796	10,608	54,287
SD	83,412	678	6,296	19,272	57,166	1,979	81,433
TN	86,601	1,073	8,657	18,067	58,690	17,591	69,010
TX	296,581	3,233	28,399	63,171	200,555	82,286	214,295
UT	41,341	938	3,332	7,815	29,248	7,248	34,093
VT	14,251	320	1,297	3,117	9,498	1,371	12,880
VA	69,860	1,118	8,174	14,204	46,156	18,828	51,032
WA	80,229	764	7,297	16,796	55,059	17,653	62,576
WV	35,829	549	3,236	8,780	23,255	3,190	32,639
WI	111,951	744	11,663	21,416	77,953	16,231	95,720
WY	28,456	913	3,665	10,496	13,379	2,277	26,179

- Represents zero.   [1] Includes freeways and expressways not shown separately.
Source: U.S. Federal Highway Administration, *Highway Statistics*, annual.

No. 1015. Highway Mileage—Urban and Rural by Type and Control and Federal-Aid Highway System: 1980 to 1998

[**In thousands, except percent (3,995 represents 3,995,000).** As of **Dec. 31.** Data for urban and rural mileage are not comparable to years prior to 1980 because of classification changes; see text, this section]

Type and control	1980	1985	1990	1993	1994	1995	1996	1997	1998
Total mileage [1]	[2]3,955	3,862	3,880	3,905	3,906	3,912	3,934	3,959	3,906
Urban mileage	624	691	757	803	814	814	834	843	842
Under State control	79	111	96	106	110	(NA)	113	113	110
Under local control	543	578	661	696	702	(NA)	719	589	730
Rural mileage	[2]3,331	3,171	3,123	3,102	3,093	3,093	3,100	3,116	3,065
Percent surfaced [3]	77.5	88.1	88.6	88.7	91.3	(NA)	89	(NA)	(NA)
Under state control	702	773	703	675	690	(NA)	693	677	661
Under local control	2,270	2,173	2,242	2,247	2,229	(NA)	2,238	2,140	2,285
Under Federal control	262	225	178	180	174	(NA)	169	(NA)	118

NA Not available.   [1] Beginning 1985, includes only public road mileage as defined 23 USC 402.   [2] Includes 98,000 miles of nonpublic road mileage previously contained in other rural categories.   [3] Covers soil-surfaced roads and roads with slag, gravel, stone, bituminous, or concrete surfaces.
Source: U.S. Federal Highway Administration, *Highway Statistics*, annual.

No. 1016. Bridge Inventory—Nondeficient and Deficient, 1992 to 1998, and by State, 1998

State and year	Number of bridges	Deficient and obsolete					
		Total number	Percent	Structurally deficient		Functionally obsolete	
				Number	Percent	Number	Percent
1992, total	572,453	199,219	34.8	118,757	20.7	80,462	14.1
1993, total	574,191	191,574	33.4	111,543	19.4	80,031	13.9
1994, total	576,472	187,321	32.5	107,512	18.6	79,809	13.8
1995, total	577,919	183,853	31.8	103,636	17.9	80,217	13.9
1996, total	582,043	182,761	31.4	101,544	17.4	81,217	14.0
1997, total	583,207	175,987	30.2	98,521	16.9	77,466	13.3
U.S. total, 1998	**583,414**	**172,686**	**29.6**	**93,119**	**16.0**	**79,567**	**13.6**
Alabama	15,591	4,965	31.8	2,767	17.7	2,198	14.1
Alaska	1,368	396	28.9	157	11.5	239	17.5
Arizona	6,713	660	9.8	203	3.0	457	6.8
Arkansas	12,523	3,320	26.5	1,653	13.2	1,667	13.3
California	23,267	6,309	27.1	1,462	6.3	4,847	20.8
Colorado	7,882	1,477	18.7	655	8.3	822	10.4
Connecticut	4,146	1,198	28.9	374	9.0	824	19.9
Delaware	799	149	18.6	65	8.1	84	10.5
District of Columbia	246	169	68.7	41	16.7	128	52.0
Florida	11,028	2,330	21.1	306	2.8	2,024	18.4
Georgia	14,339	3,935	27.4	1,964	13.7	1,971	13.7
Hawaii	1,060	541	51.0	127	12.0	414	39.1
Idaho	4,035	783	19.4	338	8.4	445	11.0
Illinois	25,267	5,439	21.5	3,373	13.3	2,066	8.2
Indiana	17,908	4,562	25.5	2,560	14.3	2,002	11.2
Iowa	24,735	7,027	28.4	4,711	19.0	2,316	9.4
Kansas	25,962	7,294	28.1	3,760	14.5	3,534	13.6
Kentucky	13,273	4,149	31.3	1,273	9.6	2,876	21.7
Louisiana	13,515	4,934	36.5	2,769	20.5	2,165	16.0
Maine	2,354	872	37.0	412	17.5	460	19.5
Maryland	4,814	1,424	29.6	462	9.6	962	20.0
Massachusetts	4,974	2,467	49.6	661	13.3	1,806	36.3
Michigan	10,631	3,490	32.8	2,059	19.4	1,431	13.5
Minnesota	12,614	2,264	17.9	1,522	12.1	742	5.9
Mississippi	16,656	5,574	33.5	4,163	25.0	1,411	8.5
Missouri	22,856	9,458	41.4	6,920	30.3	2,538	11.1
Montana	5,000	1,154	23.1	574	11.5	580	11.6
Nebraska	15,541	4,727	30.4	2,850	18.3	1,877	12.1
Nevada	1,307	224	17.1	73	5.6	151	11.6
New Hampshire	2,339	825	35.3	414	17.7	411	17.6
New Jersey	6,317	2,476	39.2	1,075	17.0	1,401	22.2
New Mexico	3,647	670	18.4	294	8.1	376	10.3
New York	17,282	8,928	51.7	6,684	38.7	2,244	13.0
North Carolina	16,493	5,512	33.4	2,826	17.1	2,686	16.3
North Dakota	4,568	1,244	27.2	954	20.9	290	6.3
Ohio	27,832	7,538	27.1	3,799	13.6	3,739	13.4
Oklahoma	22,827	9,466	41.5	8,014	35.1	1,452	6.4
Oregon	7,215	1,617	22.4	395	5.5	1,222	16.9
Pennsylvania	21,956	9,158	41.7	5,510	25.1	3,648	16.6
Rhode Island	751	366	48.7	182	24.2	184	24.5
South Carolina	9,039	1,913	21.2	1,044	11.5	869	9.6
South Dakota	6,055	1,561	25.8	1,154	19.1	407	6.7
Tennessee	19,122	4,878	25.5	2,109	11.0	2,769	14.5
Texas	47,173	10,592	22.5	3,812	8.1	6,780	14.4
Utah	2,692	579	21.5	325	12.1	254	9.4
Vermont	2,697	1,028	38.1	578	21.4	450	16.7
Virginia	12,584	3,690	29.3	1,254	10.0	2,436	19.4
Washington	7,440	1,933	26.0	513	6.9	1,420	19.1
West Virginia	6,640	2,853	43.0	1,352	20.4	1,501	22.6
Wisconsin	13,326	2,939	22.1	1,950	14.6	989	7.4
Wyoming	3,024	662	21.9	405	13.4	257	8.5
Puerto Rico	1,991	967	48.6	222	11.2	745	37.4

Source: U.S. Federal Highway Administration, Office of Technology, unpublished data.

U.S. Census Bureau, Statistical Abstract of the United States: 2000

No. 1017. Highway Pavement Condition by Type of Road System: 1996

Condition	Urban areas						Rural areas				
			Other						Other		
	Total	Inter-state	Free-ways and ex-press-ways	Prin-cipal arter-ial	Minor arter-ial	Collec-tor	Total	Inter-state	Other prin-cipal arter-ial	Minor arter-ial	Major collec-tor
Percent of road mileage rated—											
Above average...........	35	38	33	25	42	34	42	55	43	39	40
Average...............	42	53	55	49	37	39	42	41	49	51	38
Below average...........	23	9	12	26	21	27	17	4	7	11	22

Source: U.S. Federal Highway Administration, *Highway Statistics,* annual.

No. 1018. Funding for Federal, State and Local Highways: 1980 to 1998

[In millions of dollars (39,834 represents $39,834,000,000). Data compiled from reports of state and local authorities]

Type	1980	1985	1990	1994	1995	1996	1997	1998
Total receipts...............	**39,834**	**61,373**	**75,444**	**91,312**	**96,269**	**102,771**	**107,421**	**109,881**
Current income................	37,723	55,297	69,880	84,017	87,620	94,972	98,667	100,975
Imposts on highway users [1].......	22,647	35,768	44,346	55,387	59,331	64,052	66,266	69,227
Other taxes and fees	12,004	15,231	19,827	21,598	21,732	23,830	25,424	24,274
Investment income, other receipts ...	3,072	4,298	5,707	7,032	6,557	7,090	6,977	7,474
Bond issue proceeds [2]............	2,111	6,076	5,564	7,295	8,649	7,799	8,754	8,906
Intergovernmental payments [3]	(X)	(X)	(X)	(X)	(X)	(X)	(X)	(X)
Funds from (+) or to (-) reserves [3].......	1,929	-3,901	-36	-1,120	-2,791	-4,689	-5,468	-2,689
Total funds available...............	41,763	57,472	75,408	90,192	93,478	98,082	101,953	107,192
Total disbursements..........	**41,763**	**57,472**	**75,408**	**90,192**	**93,478**	**98,082**	**101,953**	**107,192**
Current disbursements.............	40,052	54,697	72,457	85,645	88,994	93,492	97,320	101,995
Capital outlay	20,305	26,583	35,151	42,379	44,228	46,810	48,360	51,614
Maintenance and traffic services.....	11,445	16,589	20,365	23,553	24,319	25,564	26,777	27,235
Administration and research	3,022	4,175	6,501	8,376	8,419	8,445	8,256	8,519
Law enforcement and safety	3,824	5,241	7,235	7,673	8,218	8,897	9,761	10,155
Interest on debt................	1,456	2,109	3,205	3,664	3,810	3,776	4,166	4,472
Debt retirement [2]	1,711	2,775	2,951	4,547	4,484	4,590	4,633	5,197

X Not applicable.   [1] Excludes amounts later allocated for nonhighway purposes.   [2] Excludes issue and redemption of short-term notes or refunding bonds.   [3] Plus sign (+) indicates net receipt of funds from other levels of government; minus sign (-) indicates net disbursement of funds to other levels.

Source: U.S. Federal Highway Administration, *Highway Statistics,* annual; and releases.

No. 1019. Public Highway Debt—State and Local Governments: 1980 to 1998

[In millions of dollars (2,381 represents $2,381,000,000). Long-term obligations. Data are for varying calendar and fiscal years. Excludes duplicated and interunit obligations]

Item	1980	1985	1990	1992	1993	1994	1995	1996	1997	1998
Total debt issued	2,381	8,194	5,708	12,988	14,178	10,833	11,305	9,728	12,347	(NA)
State	1,160	5,397	3,147	9,460	10,035	5,739	4,718	6,653	8,174	9,789
Local	1,221	2,797	2,561	3,528	4,143	5,094	6,587	3,075	4,173	(NA)
Total debt redeemed ..	1,987	5,294	3,120	7,809	11,554	6,178	5,634	6,380	7,043	(NA)
State	1,114	3,835	1,648	5,532	8,813	3,698	2,939	4,161	4,228	6,466
Local	873	1,459	1,472	2,277	2,741	2,480	2,695	2,219	2,815	(NA)
Total debt outstanding .	27,616	32,690	46,586	53,539	58,373	63,062	68,733	72,197	77,501	(NA)
Local	7,406	11,413	18,224	19,353	22,965	25,613	29,505	30,477	31,835	(NA)

NA Not available.

Source: U.S. Federal Highway Administration, *Highway Statistics,* annual.

No. 1020. Disbursement of State Highway Funds by State: 1990 to 1998

[In millions of dollars (53,580 represents $53,580,000,000). Comprises disbursement from current revenues or loans for construction, maintenance, interest and principal payments on highway bonds, transfers to local units, and miscellaneous. Includes transactions by state toll authorities. Excludes amounts allocated for collection expenses and nonhighway purposes, and bonds redeemed by refunding]

State	1990	1995	1998	State	1990	1995	1998	State	1990	1995	1998
U.S.	53,580	67,261	80,518	KS	697	1,019	1,306	ND	189	270	306
				KY	1,008	1,342	1,481	OH	2,271	2,637	3,327
AL	866	1,002	1,053	LA	923	1,195	1,400	OK	827	828	944
AK	336	438	404	ME	332	379	485	OR	765	888	1,051
AZ	1,525	1,199	1,430	MD	1,464	1,289	1,492	PA	2,885	3,153	3,902
AR	456	666	815	MA	1,055	2,501	3,351	RI	214	290	339
CA	4,294	5,966	6,574	MI	1,526	1,974	2,745	SC	585	668	766
CO	714	922	1,166	MN	1,228	1,210	1,377	SD	232	286	305
CT	1,204	1,153	1,427	MS	529	662	843	TN	1,174	1,230	1,420
DE	315	441	647	MO	937	1,313	1,438	TX	3,001	3,593	4,295
DC	273	140	259	MT	302	388	378	UT	355	431	1,129
FL	1,677	3,402	4,024	NE	449	578	589	VT	165	194	222
GA	1,278	1,437	1,613	NV	309	484	446	VA	1,874	2,107	2,619
HI	297	307	326	NH	299	328	371	WA	1,251	1,842	1,805
ID	300	350	414	NJ	1,831	2,102	2,513	WV	650	781	893
IL	2,645	2,985	3,306	NM	409	535	570	WI	979	1,252	1,398
IN	1,218	1,368	1,652	NY	2,874	4,515	6,051	WY	297	272	321
IA	869	1,078	1,177	NC	1,428	1,871	2,352				

Source: U.S. Federal Highway Administration, *Highway Statistics*, annual.

No. 1021. Federal Grants to State and Local Governments for Highway Trust Fund and Federal Transit Administration (FTA) by State: 1997

[Year ending Sept. 30]

State	Highway trust fund		FTA		State	Highway trust fund		FTA		State	Highway trust fund		FTA	
	Total (mil. dol.)	Per capita [1]	Total (mil. dol.)	Per capita [1]		Total (mil. dol.)	Per capita [1]	Total (mil. dol.)	Per capita [1]		Total (mil. dol.)	Per capita [1]	Total (mil. dol.)	Per capita [1]
U.S.	20,467	75.4	4,555	16.8	KS . . .	186	71.7	5	2.1	ND . . .	141	220.5	4	6.8
					KY . . .	293	74.9	16	4.1	OH . . .	763	68.2	94	8.4
AL . . .	299	69.3	10	2.4	LA . . .	256	58.8	48	11.1	OK . . .	270	81.4	13	4.0
AK . . .	240	394.0	2	2.9	ME . . .	118	94.9	3	2.8	OR . . .	340	104.7	164	50.6
AZ . . .	334	73.2	35	7.7	MD . . .	419	82.3	90	17.6	PA . . .	934	77.7	256	21.3
AR . . .	285	113.1	9	3.6	MA . . .	1,025	167.5	225	36.8	RI . . .	106	107.4	7	7.1
CA . . .	2,097	65.0	675	20.9	MI . . .	605	61.9	68	6.9	SC . . .	252	67.0	10	2.8
CO . . .	207	53.3	20	5.2	MN . . .	302	64.5	13	2.7	SD . . .	146	197.3	5	6.6
CT . . .	368	112.7	72	21.9	MS . . .	195	71.4	7	2.6	TN . . .	378	70.5	40	7.4
DE . . .	86	116.9	6	7.6	MO . . .	444	82.2	62	11.5	TX . . .	1,179	60.7	173	8.9
DC . . .	94	178.0	117	220.6	MT . . .	171	195.1	3	2.9	UT . . .	153	74.4	43	20.9
FL . . .	736	50.3	154	10.5	NE . . .	167	101.0	6	3.3	VT . . .	89	151.6	7	12.5
GA . . .	473	63.2	119	15.8	NV . . .	148	88.5	22	13.3	VA . . .	442	65.6	37	5.5
HI . . .	207	174.2	10	8.1	NH . . .	105	89.3	3	2.9	WA . . .	467	83.2	92	16.3
ID . . .	161	133.0	4	3.2	NJ . . .	644	80.0	352	43.7	WV . . .	219	120.3	13	7.1
IL . . .	704	59.1	281	23.6	NM . . .	201	116.3	11	6.6	WI . . .	329	63.7	40	7.7
IN . . .	429	73.1	40	6.8	NY . . .	1,201	66.2	752	41.4	WY . . .	134	279.2	1	2.9
IA . . .	229	80.3	20	6.9	NC . . .	448	60.3	35	4.8					

[1] Based on U.S. Census Bureau resident population as of July 1; excluding population of the territories.
Source: U.S. Census Bureau, *Federal Expenditures by State for Fiscal Year*, annual.

No. 1022. State Gasoline Tax Rates, 1995 and 1998, and Motor Fuel Tax Receipts, 1998

State	Rate [1] (cents/gal.)		Receipts, [2] 1998 (mil. dol.)	State	Rate [1] (cents/gal.)		Receipts, [2] 1998 (mil. dol.)	State	Rate [1] (cents/gal.)		Receipts, [2] 1998 (mil. dol.)
	1995	1998			1995	1998			1995	1998	
AL	18.0	18.0	541	KY	16.4	16.4	452	ND	18.0	20.0	94
AK	8.0	8.0	23	LA	20.0	20.0	529	OH	22.0	22.0	1,417
AZ	18.0	18.0	507	ME	19.0	19.0	152	OK	17.0	17.0	387
AR	18.7	18.6	344	MD	23.5	23.5	617	OR	24.0	24.0	382
CA	(NA)	18.0	2,770	MA	21.0	21.0	600	PA	22.4	25.9	1,649
CO	22.0	22.0	477	MI	15.0	19.0	997	RI	29.0	29.0	130
CT	34.0	36.0	519	MN	20.0	20.0	535	SC	16.0	16.0	396
DE	23.0	23.0	102	MS	18.4	18.4	363	SD	18.0	21.0	107
DC	20.0	20.0	31	MO	15.0	17.0	644	TN	20.0	20.0	690
FL	12.3	13.0	1,446	MT	27.0	27.0	166	TX	20.0	20.0	2,420
GA	7.5	7.5	417	NE	25.4	24.6	270	UT	19.0	24.5	294
HI	16.0	16.0	66	NV	24.0	24.8	290	VT	16.0	20.0	84
ID	21.0	25.0	193	NH	18.7	19.5	126	VA	17.5	17.5	746
IL	19.0	19.0	1,138	NJ	10.5	10.5	487	WA	23.0	23.0	697
IN	15.0	15.0	710	NM	18.0	18.9	242	WV	25.4	35.4	295
IA	20.0	20.0	353	NY	21.9	22.7	1,440	WI	23.4	25.4	728
KS	18.0	18.0	320	NC	21.6	22.3	1,000	WY	9.0	9.0	60

NA Not available.   [1] In effect Dec. 31.   [2] Represents net receipts.
Source: U.S. Federal Highway Administration, *Highway Statistics*, annual.

No. 1023. Selected Motor Vehicle Indicators by Model Year: 1992 to 1999

[In thousands of units (13,118 represents 13,118,000), except as indicated. A model year begins on Oct.1, and ends on Sept. 30. It covers the fourth quarter of one calendar year and the first three quarters of the next calendar year]

Sales and expenditures	1992	1993	1994	1995	1996	1997	1998	1999
New motor vehicle sales.	13,118	14,199	15,413	15,118	15,456	15,498	15,963	17,414
New-car sales.	8,214	8,518	8,990	8,636	8,527	8,273	8,142	8,697
Domestic	6,277	6,734	7,255	7,129	7,254	6,906	6,764	6,982
Import	1,938	1,784	1,735	1,507	1,273	1,366	1,378	1,715
New-truck sales.	4,903	5,681	6,422	6,481	6,929	7,226	7,821	8,717
Light	4,629	5,346	6,034	6,053	6,519	6,797	7,297	8,072
Domestic.	4,233	4,981	5,638	5,663	6,088	6,226	6,651	7,310
Import.	396	365	396	391	431	571	646	763
Other	275	336	388	428	411	429	524	645
Domestic-car production.	5,666	5,979	6,614	6,350	6,080	5,927	5,547	5,641
Avg. expenditure per new car [1] (dollar) . .	16,336	16,871	17,903	17,959	18,777	19,551	20,849	21,022
Domestic (dollar)	15,644	15,976	16,930	16,864	17,468	17,838	18,579	18,725
Import (dollar)	18,593	20,261	21,989	23,202	26,205	28,193	31,986	30,350

[1] BEA estimate based on the manufacturer's suggested retail price.
Source: U.S. Bureau of Economic Analysis, *Survey of Current Business,* November 1997. Data from American Automobile Manufacturers Assoc., Inc., Washington, DC, and Ward's Automotive Reports; seasonally adjusted by BEA.

No. 1024. New and Used Car Sales and Leases: 1990 to 1998

[In thousands, except as indicated]

Item	1990	1991	1992	1993	1994	1995	1996	1997	1998
Total car sales.	**46,830**	**45,465**	**45,163**	**46,575**	**49,132**	**50,393**	**49,355**	**48,542**	**48,372**
New passenger car sales [1]	9,300	8,175	8,213	8,518	8,991	8,635	8,527	8,272	8,142
Used passenger car sales [2]	37,530	37,290	36,950	38,057	40,141	41,758	40,828	40,270	40,230
Value of transactions (bil. dol.).	219	230	247	279	312	338	337	338	336
Average price (dol.).	5,830	6,157	6,693	7,335	7,781	8,093	8,257	8,399	8,353
New passenger car leases [3]	**534**	**667**	**882**	**1,197**	**1,715**	**1,795**	**1,808**	**2,062**	**1,985**

[1] Includes leased cars. [2] Includes sales from franchised dealers, independent dealers, and casual sales. [3] Consumer leases only.
Source: New passenger car sales: 1970-97, American Automobile Manufacturers Association, *Motor Vehicle Facts & Figures, 1998,* Detroit, MI; 1998, Ward's Communications, personal communication, Apr. 7, 1999; Used passenger car sales: ADT Automotive, *1999 Used Car Market Report* Nashville, TN; Leased passenger cars: CNW Marketing/Research, Bandon, OR, personal communication, Jan. 25, 1999.

No. 1025. Number of Households Leasing Vehicles and Number of Vehicles Leased per Household: 1989 to 1998

Item	Share of households leasing a vehicle for personal use (percents)				Average number of leased vehicles, among households having such vehicles			
	1989	1992	1995	1998	1989	1992	1995	1998
All households	**2.5**	**2.9**	**4.5**	**6.4**	**1.1**	**1.1**	**1.1**	**1.2**
Household income:								
Less than $10,000	(Z)	(Z)	(Z)	(Z)	(Z)	(Z)	(Z)	1.2
$10,000 to $24,999	(Z)	(Z)	1.5	4.0	(Z)	(Z)	1.0	1.1
$25,000 to $49,999	(Z)	3.3	3.4	5.0	(Z)	1.1	1.0	1.1
$50,000 to $99,999	6.1	4.1	9.4	9.5	1.1	1.1	1.2	1.2
$100,000 and over.	5.0	9.6	14.2	14.8	1.2	1.1	1.3	1.3
Age of household head:								
Less than 35 years	4.2	3.2	4.8	8.2	1.1	1.0	1.0	1.1
35 to 44 years.	3.0	4.2	5.4	8.3	1.0	1.1	1.1	1.1
45 to 54 years.	3.3	3.2	7.8	7.6	1.1	1.2	1.2	1.3
55 to 64 years.	(Z)	3.2	4.1	4.4	1.6	1.2	1.2	1.1
65 to 74 years.	(Z)	1.0	1.3	2.9	(Z)	1.0	1.1	1.2
75 years and over	(Z)	(Z)	0.5	1.9	(Z)	(Z)	1.0	1.0
Race/ethnicity of respondent:								
White non-Hispanic	2.7	3.1	4.4	6.3	1.1	1.1	1.1	1.1
Non-White and Hispanic	(Z)	2.3	4.9	6.5	(Z)	1.1	1.1	1.3
Work status of household head:								
Work for someone else	3.5	3.4	6.0	8.1	1.1	1.1	1.1	1.2
Self employed	3.4	7.2	5.2	9.0	1.0	1.1	1.3	1.1
Retired.	(Z)	0.7	1.3	1.5	(Z)	1.3	1.0	1.2
Other not working	(Z)	(Z)	3.0	(Z)	(Z)	(Z)	1.0	(Z)
Homeownership status:								
Owner	2.2	3.5	5.8	7.2	1.1	1.1	1.2	1.2
Renter or other	3.0	1.8	2.3	4.8	1.1	1.1	1.1	1.1
Net worth percentile:								
Bottom 25%	(Z)	2.1	2.7	4.8	(Z)	1.1	1.1	1.1
25-49.9%	2.8	(Z)	4.2	5.4	1.1	(Z)	1.0	1.1
50-74.9%	2.5	3.1	4.2	6.8	1.1	1.1	1.1	1.2
75-89.9%	2.9	3.5	6.2	7.8	1.0	1.0	1.2	1.2
Top 10%	2.5	6.4	8.3	9.5	1.3	1.2	1.3	1.2

Z Ten or fewer observations.
Source: Board of Governors of the Federal Reserve System, *Survey of Consumer Finances.*

626 Transportation—Land

No. 1026. Motor Vehicle Registrations, 1980 to 1998, and Drivers Licenses and Motorcycle Registrations 1998 by State

[In thousands (155,796 represents 155,796,000). Motor vehicle registrations cover publicly, privately, and commercially owned vehicles. For uniformity, data have been adjusted to a calendar-year basis as registration years in states differ; figures represent net numbers where possible, excluding re-registrations and nonresident registrations]

| State | Automobiles, trucks, and buses [1] | | | | | | 1998 | | 1998 | |
	1980	1985	1990	1995	1996	1997	Total	Auto-mobiles (incl. taxis)	Motor-cycle registra-tion (incl. official)	Drivers licenses
U.S	155,796	171,654	188,798	201,530	206,365	207,754	211,617	131,839	3,839	184,980
AL......	2,938	3,338	3,744	3,553	3,324	3,669	3,859	2,063	44	3,434
AK......	262	353	477	542	531	542	546	232	14	457
AZ......	1,917	2,235	2,825	2,873	2,983	3,143	2,944	1,728	54	3,198
AR......	1,574	1,384	1,448	1,613	1,633	1,634	1,754	929	21	1,918
CA......	16,873	18,899	21,926	22,432	25,214	24,945	25,600	16,174	390	20,499
CO	2,342	2,759	3,155	2,812	3,433	3,523	3,466	1,843	97	2,946
CT......	2,147	2,465	2,623	2,622	2,609	2,660	2,701	1,998	50	2,349
DE......	397	465	526	592	593	614	616	417	10	546
DC	268	326	262	243	237	234	229	192	1	350
FL......	7,614	9,865	10,950	10,369	10,889	10,874	11,276	7,438	216	12,027
GA	3,818	4,580	5,489	6,120	6,283	6,242	6,893	4,033	85	5,316
HI	570	651	771	802	786	693	704	450	20	746
ID	834	854	1,054	1,043	1,061	1,081	1,119	502	34	863
IL	7,477	7,727	7,873	8,973	8,817	8,443	9,307	6,425	204	7,701
IN	3,826	4,024	4,366	5,072	5,216	5,346	5,372	3,273	102	3,976
IA	2,329	2,696	2,632	2,814	2,869	2,851	3,053	1,738	128	1,950
KS......	2,007	2,148	2,012	2,085	2,110	2,152	2,121	1,127	47	1,851
KY......	2,593	2,615	2,909	2,631	2,696	2,781	2,845	1,716	40	2,640
LA......	2,779	3,012	2,995	3,286	3,318	3,411	3,431	1,967	39	2,736
ME	724	840	977	967	959	1,059	930	565	28	913
MD	2,803	3,276	3,607	3,654	3,635	3,786	3,750	2,622	43	3,178
MA	3,749	3,738	3,726	4,502	4,702	5,070	5,159	3,783	100	4,394
MI......	6,488	6,727	7,209	7,674	8,010	8,024	8,128	5,105	153	6,803
MN	3,091	3,385	3,508	3,882	3,861	3,927	4,178	2,412	128	2,868
MS	1,577	1,746	1,875	2,144	2,182	2,234	2,256	1,250	31	1,758
MO	3,271	3,558	3,905	4,255	4,350	4,351	4,378	2,601	54	3,798
MT	680	652	783	968	973	980	988	458	21	647
NE......	1,254	1,257	1,384	1,467	1,479	1,507	1,526	834	18	1,186
NV......	655	709	853	1,047	1,096	1,146	1,220	666	24	1,246
NH	704	974	946	1,122	1,112	1,127	1,038	688	46	907
NJ......	4,761	4,909	5,652	5,906	5,822	5,817	5,780	4,215	100	5,563
NM	1,068	1,176	1,301	1,484	1,545	1,514	1,595	821	32	1,204
NY......	8,002	9,042	10,196	10,274	10,636	10,873	10,422	7,664	138	10,554
NC	4,532	4,450	5,162	5,682	5,759	5,786	5,862	3,531	75	5,534
ND	627	655	630	695	679	695	672	330	16	455
OH	7,771	8,102	8,410	9,810	9,770	10,108	10,039	6,664	229	7,941
OK	2,583	2,864	2,649	2,856	3,082	2,884	2,919	1,549	53	2,305
OR	2,081	2,204	2,445	2,785	2,851	2,891	2,980	1,588	64	2,417
PA......	6,926	7,209	7,971	8,481	8,640	8,825	8,979	6,132	190	8,405
RI	623	610	672	699	696	710	715	522	18	682
SC......	1,996	2,222	2,521	2,833	2,791	2,850	2,893	1,823	41	2,679
SD......	601	650	704	709	751	718	769	382	25	535
TN......	3,271	3,754	4,444	5,400	4,830	4,535	4,469	2,696	59	4,073
TX......	10,475	12,444	12,800	13,682	13,487	12,923	13,324	7,456	144	13,323
UT......	992	1,099	1,206	1,447	1,445	1,530	1,532	850	24	1,393
VT......	347	398	462	492	503	496	496	296	17	497
VA......	3,626	4,253	4,938	5,613	5,576	5,709	5,818	3,774	57	4,787
WA	3,225	3,526	4,257	4,503	4,603	4,702	4,824	2,776	106	4,079
WV	1,320	1,143	1,225	1,425	1,406	1,355	1,378	777	22	1,281
WI......	2,941	3,187	3,815	3,993	3,972	4,233	4,203	2,544	170	3,710
WY	467	500	528	601	562	553	559	219	16	359

[1] Excludes vehicles owned by military services.

Source: U.S. Federal Highway Administration, *Highway Statistics*, annual; and *Selected Highway Statistics and Charts*, annual.

No. 1027. Motor Vehicle Registrations: 1980 to 1998

[In thousands (155,796 represents 155,796,000). Compiled principally from information obtained from state authorities, but it was necessary to draw on other sources and to make numerous estimates in order to complete series. Includes Alaska and Hawaii]

Item	1980	1990	1994	1995	1996	1997	1998
All motor vehicles	155,796	188,798	198,045	201,530	206,365	207,754	211,617
Private and commercial	153,265	185,541	194,532	197,941	202,714	204,079	207,841
Publicly owned	2,531	3,257	3,514	3,589	3,651	3,674	3,776
Automobiles [1]	121,601	133,700	127,883	128,387	129,728	129,749	131,839
Private and commercial	120,743	132,164	126,397	126,900	128,439	128,450	130,500
Publicly owned	857	1,536	1,486	1,487	1,289	1,299	1,339
Buses	529	627	670	686	697	698	716
Private and commercial	254	275	283	288	291	294	302
Publicly owned	275	351	388	398	406	403	413
Trucks [1]	33,667	54,470	69,491	72,458	75,940	77,307	79,062
Private and commercial	32,268	53,101	67,852	70,754	73,984	75,335	77,039
Publicly owned	1,399	1,369	1,639	1,704	1,956	1,972	2,024

[1] Trucks include pickups, panels and delivery vans. Beginning 1985, personal passenger vans, passenger minivans, and utility-type vehicles are no longer included in automobiles but are included in trucks.

Source: U.S. Federal Highway Administration, *Highway Statistics*, annual.

No. 1028. Alternative Fueled Vehicles in Use by Fuel Type: 1998 to 2000

Fuel	Alternative fueled vehicles			Fuel consumption (1,000) gasoline-equivalent gallons)		
	1998	1999	2000	1998	1999	2000
Fuels	383,847	407,542	430,219	324,826	341,346	368,076
Liquified petroleum gases (LPG)	266,000	268,000	270,000	241,583	243,648	249,550
Compressed natural gas (CNG)	78,782	89,633	101,991	73,251	86,073	104,501
Liquified natural gas (LNG)	1,172	1,422	1,682	5,343	6,062	7,460
M85 (Mixture: 85% methanol + 15% gasoline) . . .	19,648	19,497	18,725	1,212	1,108	1,062
Neat methanol (M100)	200	200	200	449	449	449
E85 (Mixture: 85% ethanol+15% gasoline)	12,788	22,359	30,017	1,727	2,489	3,283
E95 (Mixture: 95% ethanol + 5% gasoline)	14	14	14	59	59	59
Electricity	5,243	6,417	7,590	1,202	1,458	1,712

Source: Energy Information Administration, *Alternatives to Traditional Transportation Fuels: 1998*.

No. 1029. Recreational Vehicles—Number and Retail Value of Shipments: 1980 to 1997

[181.4 represents 181,400]

Item	1980	1985	1988	1989	1990	1991	1992	1993	1994	1995	1996	1997
NUMBER (1,000)												
Total	181.4	351.7	420.0	388.3	347.3	293.7	382.7	420.2	518.8	475.2	466.8	438.8
Motorized homes	99.9	233.5	277.1	261.6	226.5	172.6	226.3	243.8	306.7	281.0	274.6	239.3
Travel trailers	52.0	75.4	89.6	82.9	80.4	77.6	102.5	113.6	128.0	121.2	123.9	131.6
Folding camping trailers	24.5	35.9	42.3	33.9	30.7	33.9	43.3	51.9	61.7	61.1	57.3	57.6
Truck campers	5.0	6.9	11.0	9.9	9.7	9.6	10.6	10.9	11.4	11.9	11.0	10.3
RETAIL VALUE (mil. dol.)												
Total	1,952	6,904	9,061	9,019	8,101	6,623	8,774	9,518	12,196	12,104	12,365	11,928
Motorized homes	1,381	5,724	7,543	7,420	6,660	5,284	6,963	7,544	9,897	9,768	9,788	9,139
Travel trailers	485	997	1,254	1,252	1,220	1,107	1,523	1,644	1,912	1,927	2,171	2,356
Folding camping trailers	69	137	175	147	134	146	189	(NA)	276	290	284	309
Truck campers	17	46	88	81	86	87	99	(NA)	112	119	122	124

NA Not available.

Source: Recreation Vehicle Industry Association, Reston, VA, *RVIA Industry Profile 1997*. Data also in American Automobile Manufacturers Association of the United States, Inc., Washington, DC, *Motor Vehicle Facts and Figures*, annual (copyright).

628 Transportation—Land

No. 1030. Motor Vehicle Production and Trade: 1980 to 1996

[8,010 represents 8,010,000]

Item	Unit	1980	1990	1992	1993	1994	1995	1996
United States	1,000 . .	8,010	9,784	9,702	10,898	12,263	11,985	11,799
Passenger car production	1,000 . .	6,376	6,078	5,664	5,981	6,614	6,351	6,083
Truck and bus production	1,000 . .	1,634	3,706	4,038	4,917	5,649	5,635	5,716
Imports:								
Passenger cars (new) [1][2]	1,000 . .	3,116	3,945	3,575	3,808	4,097	4,114	4,064
Canada	1,000 . .	595	1,220	1,200	1,468	1,591	1,678	1,688
Germany, Federal Republic of.	1,000 . .	339	245	206	184	188	207	234
Japan.	1,000 . .	1,992	1,868	1,637	1,597	1,593	1,387	1,191
Trucks and buses (new) [2]	1,000 . .	747	766	777	722	708	662	688
Japan.	1,000 . .	483	302	197	154	170	90	52
All-terrain vehicles.	1,000 . .	(NA)	100	(NA)	(NA)	(NA)	(NA)	(NA)
Motorcycles, total [3].	1,000 . .	1,120	169	(NA)	(NA)	(NA)	(NA)	(NA)
Import value:								
Passenger cars (new) [1].	Mil. dol. .	16,675	45,716	46,729	52,208	61,367	64,526	66,916
Trucks and buses, (new) [1].	Mil. dol. .	1,985	8,155	10,000	10,104	10,909	11,792	12,381
Motorcycles [3][4]	Mil. dol. .	1,142	361	(NA)	(NA)	(NA)	(NA)	(NA)
Exports, number:								
Passenger cars (new) [1].	1,000 . .	617	794	851	864	1,019	989	974
Trucks and buses (new) exports	1,000 . .	186	159	161	181	274	254	316
Export value [1][5]	Mil. dol. .	16,015	38,086	(NA)	(NA)	(NA)	(NA)	(NA)
Passenger cars (new) [5].	Mil. dol. .	3,932	9,708	11,893	12,476	14,591	14,251	14,392
Trucks and buses (new) [5]	Mil. dol. .	2,977	2,845	3,073	3,399	5,238	5,209	6,246
Parts and accessories [6]	Mil. dol. .	9,106	24,996	(NA)	(NA)	(NA)	(NA)	(NA)
Factory sales:								
Passenger cars	1,000 . .	6,400	6,050	5,685	5,962	6,549	6,310	6,140
Trucks and buses	1,000 . .	1,667	3,725	4,062	4,895	5,640	5,713	5,776
Retail sales:								
Passenger cars (new) [1].	1,000 . .	8,979	9,300	8,213	8,518	8,991	8,635	8,527
Domestics [7].	1,000 . .	6,581	6,897	6,277	6,742	7,255	7,129	7,254
Imports [8].	1,000 . .	2,398	2,403	1,937	1,776	1,735	1,506	1,273
Trucks and buses [9]	1,000 . .	2,232	4,261	4,247	5,000	5,658	5,691	6,132
Light duty (up to 14,000 GVW) [10] .	1,000 . .	1,964	3,984	4,264	5,015	5,673	5,703	(NA)
Med. duty (14,001-26,000 GVW) [10] .	1,000 . .	92	71	57	64	69	80	(NA)
Heavy duty (over 26,000 GVW) [10] .	1,000 . .	176	207	192	239	284	308	(NA)
Under 6,000 pounds	1,000 . .	985	2,866	3,212	3,754	4,132	4,031	4,398
Utility	1,000 . .	51	490	666	721	1,130	1,258	1,392
Van.	1,000 . .	79	31	21	18	12	12	18
Minivan (cargo).	1,000 . .	(X)	83	63	70	82	73	64
Station wagon (truck chassis) . . .	1,000 . .	(X)	112	201	321	-	-	-
Mini-passenger carrier	1,000 . .	(X)	750	840	1,002	1,132	1,113	1,098
6,000 to 10,000 pounds [11]	1,000 . .	975	1,097	1,021	1,232	1,506	1,631	1,690
Utility	1,000 . .	108	68	51	60	72	144	243
Van.	1,000 . .	172	254	241	279	275	274	254
Pickup, conventional	1,000 . .	546	568	524	647	883	967	936
Station wagon (truck chassis) . . .	1,000 . .	39	85	80	115	125	109	137
10,001 pounds and over	1,000 . .	271	298	275	330	388	428	(NA)

- Represents or rounds to zero.   NA Not available.   X Not applicable.   [1] Based on data from U.S. Dept. of Commerce.
[2] Includes other countries, not shown separately.   [3] Source: Motorcycle Industry Council, Inc., Irvine, CA. Data from U.S. Dept. of Commerce. Excludes mopeds/motorized bicycles and all-terrain vehicles. Excludes moped imports (motorcycle imports less than 51 cc's) from all countries (except Japan).   [4] Represents c.i.f. value.   [5] Covers assembled and unassembled vehicles. [6] Includes rubber tires and tubes and used vehicles.   [7] Includes domestic models produced in Canada and Mexico.   [8] Excludes domestic models produced in Canada.   [9] Excludes motorcoaches and light-duty imports from foreign manufactures. Includes imports sold by franchised dealers of U.S. manufacturers. Starting in 1987, includes sales of trucks over 10,000 lbs. GVW by foreign manufacturers.   [10] Gross vehicle weight (fully loaded vehicle).   [11] Includes vehicles, not shown separately.

No. 1031. Motor Vehicles in Use by Age of Vehicle: 1980 to 1995

[104.6 represents 104,600,000]

Item	Unit	1980	1985	1990	1991	1992	1993	1994	1995
Cars in use, total	Million. .	104.6	114.7	123.3	123.3	120.3	121.1	122.0	123.2
Under 5 years	Million . .	52.3	48.7	56.5	54.6	50.4	47.0	45.4	46.2
6-8 years.	Million . .	25.2	27.8	22.6	25.5	27.5	28.7	27.7	26.9
9-11 years.	Million . .	14.6	17.2	19.1	16.7	16.0	22.5	25.1	23.3
12 years and over.	Million . .	12.5	21.0	25.1	26.6	26.4	31.1	31.4	26.8
Average age	Years. . .	6.6	7.6	7.8	7.9	8.1	8.3	8.4	8.3
Cars retired from use [1]	1,000. . .	8,405	7,729	8,897	8,565	11,194	7,366	7,824	7,414
Trucks in use, total.	Million. .	35.2	42.4	56.0	58.2	61.2	82.5	71.4	70.2
Under 3 years	Million . .	8.8	9.0	12.8	12.0	11.3	12.1	13.7	15.4
3-5 years.	Million . .	8.1	6.3	13.2	14.0	14.0	12.9	12.7	12.4
6-8 years.	Million . .	7.4	10.2	8.0	9.9	11.9	14.0	13.6	13.1
9-11 years.	Million . .	4.4	6.2	6.6	5.3	5.6	11.7	11.3	10.7
12 years and over.	Million . .	6.5	10.7	15.5	17.0	18.3	23.2	20.1	18.6
Average age	Years. . .	7.1	8.1	8.0	8.1	8.4	8.6	8.4	8.4
Trucks retired from use [1]	1,000. . .	1,732	2,100	2,177	2,284	1,587	1,048	4,545	2,918

[1] For years ending June 30. Represents vehicles failing to re-register.

Source of Tables 1030 and 1031: Except as noted, American Automobile Manufacturers Association Inc., Detroit, MI, *Motor Vehicle Facts and Figures*, annual (copyright); and *World Motor Vehicle Data*, annual (copyright).

Transportation—Land   629

No. 1032. Travel in the United States by Selected Trip Characteristics: 1995

[Trips of 100 miles or more, one way. U.S. destinations only. Data based on a sample and subject to sampling variability; see text. For definition of terms, see text, this section]

Trip characteristic	Household trips Number (1,000)	Household trips Per-cent	Person trips Number (1,000)	Person trips Per-cent	Person miles Number (1,000)	Person miles Per-cent	Personal use vehicle trips Number (1,000)	Personal use vehicle trips Per-cent	Personal use vehicle miles Number (1,000)	Personal use vehicle miles Per-cent
Total.	656,462	100.0	1,001,319	100.0	826,804	100.0	505,154	100.0	280,127	100.0
Principal means of transportation:										
Personal use vehicles.	505,154	77.0	813,858	81.3	451,590	54.6	505,154	100.0	280,127	100.0
Airplane	129,164	19.7	161,165	16.1	355,286	43.0	(X)	(X)	(X)	(X)
Commercial airplane	124,884	19.0	155,936	15.6	347,934	42.1	(X)	(X)	(X)	(X)
Bus	17,340	2.6	20,445	2.0	13,309	1.6	(X)	(X)	(X)	(X)
Intercity bus.	2,755	0.4	3,244	0.3	2,723	0.3	(X)	(X)	(X)	(X)
Charter or tour bus	11,890	1.8	14,247	1.4	9,363	1.1	(X)	(X)	(X)	(X)
Train	4,200	0.6	4,994	0.5	4,356	0.5	(X)	(X)	(X)	(X)
Ship, boat, or ferry	391	0.1	614	0.1	1,834	0.2	(X)	(X)	(X)	(X)
Other.	213	-	243	-	429	0.1	(X)	(X)	(X)	(X)
Round trip distance:										
Less than 300 miles	194,098	29.6	306,433	30.6	74,658	9.0	185,418	36.7	45,159	16.1
300 to 499 miles	174,389	26.6	274,045	27.4	106,007	12.8	159,743	31.6	61,779	22.1
500 5o 999 miles	140,046	21.3	214,006	21.4	146,631	17.7	106,846	21.2	72,114	25.7
1,000 to 1,999 miles	76,110	11.6	108,331	10.8	153,316	18.5	36,722	7.3	49,953	17.8
2,000 miles or more	71,819	10.9	98,503	9.8	346,192	41.9	16,425	3.3	51,123	18.3
Mean (miles)	872	(X)	827	(X)	(X)	(X)	555	(X)	(X)	(X)
Median (miles)	438	(X)	425	(X)	(X)	(X)	368	(X)	(X)	(X)
Calendar quarter:										
1st quarter	130,963	19.9	200,331	20.0	155,603	18.8	99,549	19.7	50,801	18.1
2d quarter	168,669	25.7	258,400	25.8	208,266	25.2	130,135	25.8	72,421	25.9
3d quarter	193,913	29.5	304,542	30.4	261,463	31.6	152,862	30.3	90,558	32.3
4th quarter	162,917	24.8	238,047	23.8	201,471	24.4	122,607	24.3	66,346	23.7
Main purpose of trip:										
Business	192,537	29.3	224,835	22.5	212,189	25.7	125,036	24.8	61,929	22.1
Pleasure	372,586	56.8	630,110	62.9	506,971	61.3	305,571	60.5	177,698	63.4
Visit friends or relatives	195,468	29.8	330,755	33.0	264,769	32.0	159,981	31.7	92,190	32.9
Leisure [1]	177,119	27.0	299,355	29.9	242,201	29.3	145,590	28.8	85,508	30.5
Rest or relaxation	65,017	9.9	115,154	11.5	100,838	12.2	53,780	10.6	33,598	12.0
Sightseeing	24,272	3.7	42,649	4.3	50,781	6.1	18,069	3.6	14,654	5.2
Outdoor recreation	39,899	6.1	65,418	6.5	41,620	5.0	35,987	7.1	19,407	6.9
Entertainment	37,456	5.7	58,757	5.9	42,929	5.2	27,920	5.5	14,531	5.2
Personal business	91,319	13.9	146,338	14.6	107,621	13.0	74,532	14.8	40,490	14.5
Other.	19	-	36	-	23	-	16	-	9	-
Vacation or weekend trips:										
Vacation trip	301,197	45.9	515,383	51.5	484,144	58.6	236,055	46.7	154,167	55.0
Weekend trip.	270,231	41.2	441,385	44.1	325,864	39.4	216,743	42.9	118,290	42.2
1 or 2 nights away from home. .	151,377	23.1	252,581	25.2	132,782	16.1	133,147	26.4	60,906	21.7
3 to 5 nights away from home. .	118,854	18.1	188,804	18.9	193,083	23.4	83,597	16.5	57,384	20.5
Travel party type and size:										
One adult, no children under 18 . .	386,479	58.9	386,510	38.6	352,350	42.6	275,034	54.4	144,795	51.7
Two or more adults, no children under 18.	155,148	23.6	299,485	29.9	248,762	30.1	133,163	26.4	79,273	28.3
One adult, 1 or more children under 18.	29,436	4.5	67,959	6.8	48,083	5.8	24,879	4.9	13,827	4.9
Two or more adults, 1 or more children under 18	66,086	10.1	225,875	22.6	158,334	19.2	60,497	12.0	34,758	12.4
No adult, 1 or more children under 18.	19,313	2.9	21,489	2.1	19,275	2.3	11,581	2.3	7,472	2.7
Mean travel party size (household members)	1.6	(X)	2.2	(X)	(X)	(X)	1.7	(X)	(X)	(X)
Nights away from home:										
None.	164,032	25.0	239,727	23.9	104,444	12.6	140,914	27.9	49,619	17.7
1 to 3 nights	321,227	48.9	502,465	50.2	331,504	40.1	259,354	51.3	131,559	47.0
4 to 7 nights	121,279	18.5	184,766	18.5	243,546	29.5	76,380	15.1	61,317	21.9
8 or more nights	49,924	7.6	74,361	7.4	147,309	17.8	28,506	5.6	37,631	13.4
Mean excluding none (nights)	4.5	(X)	4.3	(X)	(X)	(X)	4.0	(X)	(X)	(X)
Type of lodging at destination:										
Friend's or relative's home.	211,832	43.6	345,506	45.9	290,428	41.0	170,271	47.3	103,180	45.7
Hotel, motel, or resort	201,264	41.4	282,929	37.6	318,323	44.9	126,160	35.1	82,447	36.5
Rented cabin, condo, or vacation home.	17,607	3.6	30,648	4.1	31,161	4.4	14,631	4.1	10,809	4.8
Owned cabin, condo, or vacation home.	20,205	4.2	38,572	5.1	26,269	3.7	18,103	5.0	9,819	4.3
Camper, trailer, recreational vehicle, tent	11,944	2.5	22,208	3.0	15,836	2.2	11,663	3.2	8,204	3.6
Other type of lodging	23,452	4.8	32,095	4.3	27,080	3.8	18,917	5.3	11,542	5.1
Nights at destination:										
Mean nights at destination	4.2	(X)	4.0	(X)	(X)	(X)	3.8	(X)	(X)	(X)
Friend's or relative's home	4.3	(X)	4.0	(X)	(X)	(X)	3.6	(X)	(X)	(X)
Hotel, motel, or resort	3.0	(X)	3.0	(X)	(X)	(X)	2.8	(X)	(X)	(X)

- Represents zero or a value too small to report.   X Not applicable.   [1] Includes other leisure activities not shown separately.

Source: U.S. Bureau of Transportation Statistics, *1995 American Travel Survey.*

630 Transportation—Land

No. 1033. National Personal Transportation Survey (NPTS)— Summary of Travel Trends: 1969 to 1995

[**62,504 represents 62,504,000.** Data obtained by collecting information on all trips taken by the respondent on a specific day (known as travel day), combined with longer trips taken over a 2-week period (known as travel period). Contains data from previous NPTS surveys. For compatibility with previous survey data, all data are based only on trips taken during travel day. Be aware that terminology changes from survey to survey. See source for details]

Characteristics	Unit	1969	1983	1990	1995	Percent change, 1969-90	Percent change, 1969-95
Households, total	1,000	62,504	85,371	93,347	98,990	49.0	58.4
1 person	1,000	10,980	19,354	22,999	24,732	109.0	125.2
2 persons	1,000	18,448	27,169	30,114	31,834	63.0	72.6
3 persons	1,000	10,746	14,756	16,128	16,827	50.0	56.6
4 persons or more	1,000	22,330	24,092	24,106	25,597	8.0	14.6
Persons, total	1,000	197,213	229,453	[1]239,416	259,994	21.0	31.8
Under 16 yrs. old	1,000	60,100	53,682	54,303	61,411	-10.0	2.2
16-19 yrs. old	1,000	14,598	15,268	13,851	14,074	-5.0	-3.6
20-34 yrs. old	1,000	40,060	60,788	59,517	59,494	49.0	48.5
35-64 yrs. old	1,000	62,982	75,353	82,480	93,766	31.0	48.9
65 yrs. old and over	1,000	19,473	24,362	26,955	31,249	38.0	60.5
5 yrs. old and over	1,000	(NA)	212,932	222,101	241,675	12.0	(NA)
Males	1,000	94,465	111,514	114,441	126,553	21.0	34.0
16 yrs. old and over	1,000	66,652	83,645	86,432	95,627	30.0	43.5
Females	1,000	102,748	117,939	124,975	133,441	22.0	29.9
16 yrs. old and over	1,000	73,526	92,080	96,371	102,956	31.0	40.0
Licensed drivers	1,000	102,986	147,015	163,025	176,330	58.0	71.2
Male	1,000	57,981	75,639	80,289	88,480	38.0	52.6
Female	1,000	45,005	71,376	82,707	87,851	84.0	95.2
Workers	1,000	75,758	103,244	118,343	131,697	56.0	73.8
Male	1,000	48,487	58,849	63,996	71,105	32.0	46.6
Female	1,000	27,271	44,395	54,334	60,593	99.0	122.2
Households with—							
No vehicle	1,000	12,876	11,548	8,573	7,989	-33.0	-38.0
One vehicle	1,000	30,252	28,780	30,654	32,064	1.0	6.0
Two vehicles	1,000	16,501	28,632	35,872	40,024	117.0	142.6
Three or more vehicles	1,000	2,875	16,411	18,248	18,914	535.0	557.9
All vehicles available	1,000	72,500	143,714	165,221	176,067	128.0	142.9
Vehicle trips	Millions [2]	87,284	126,874	158,927	229,745	82.0	163.2
Vehicle miles of travel (VMT)	Millions [2]	775,940	1,002,139	1,409,600	2,068,368	82.0	166.6
Person trips	Millions [2]	145,146	224,385	249,562	378,930	72.0	161.1
Person miles of travel	Millions	1,404,137	1,946,662	2,315,300	3,411,122	65.0	142.9
Ratios:							
Persons per household	Number	[3]3.16	2.69	2.56	2.63	(NA)	(NA)
Vehicles per household	Number	[3]1.16	1.68	1.77	1.78	(NA)	(NA)
Licensed drivers per household	Number	[3]1.65	1.72	1.75	1.78	(NA)	(NA)
Vehicles per licensed driver	Number	[3]0.70	0.98	1.01	1.00	(NA)	(NA)
Workers per household	Number	[3]1.21	1.21	1.27	1.33	(NA)	(NA)
Vehicles per worker	Number	[3]0.96	1.39	1.40	1.34	(NA)	(NA)
Daily vehicle trips per household	Number	[2][3]3.83	4.07	4.66	6.36	(NA)	(NA)
Daily VMT per driver	Number	[2][3]20.64	18.68	23.69	32.14	(NA)	(NA)
Average vehicle trip length (miles)	Number	[3]8.89	7.90	8.87	9.06	(NA)	(NA)
Average annual VMT	Miles	[2]12,423	11,739	15,100	20,895	22.0	(NA)
Home to work	Miles	[2]4,183	3,538	4,853	6,492	16.0	(NA)
Shopping	Miles	[2]929	1,567	1,743	2,807	88.0	(NA)
Other family or personal business	Miles	[2]1,270	1,816	3,014	4,307	137.0	(NA)
Social and recreational	Miles	[2]4,094	3,534	4,060	4,764	-1.0	(NA)
Average annual vehicle trips	Number	[2]1,396	1,486	1,702	2321	22.0	(NA)
Home to work	Number	[2]445	414	448	553	0.7	(NA)
Shopping	Number	[2]213	297	345	501	62.0	(NA)
Other family or personal business	Number	[2]195	272	411	626	111.0	(NA)
Social and recreational	Number	[2]312	335	349	427	12.0	(NA)
Average vehicle trip length	Miles	[2]8.9	7.9	9.0	9.06	1.0	(NA)
Home to work	Miles	[2]9.4	8.5	11.0	11.80	17.0	(NA)
Shopping	Miles	[2]4.4	5.3	5.1	5.64	16.0	(NA)
Other family or personal business	Miles	[2]6.5	6.7	7.4	6.93	14.0	(NA)
Social and recreational	Miles	[2]13.1	10.5	11.8	11.24	-10.0	(NA)
Average vehicle occupancy [4]	Persons	(NA)	1.75	1.64	1.59	[5]-1.3	(NA)
Home to work	Persons	(NA)	1.14	1.1	1.14	[5]-1.3	(NA)
Shopping	Persons	(NA)	1.71	1.7	1.74	[5]-1.6	(NA)
Other family or personal business	Persons	(NA)	1.81	1.84	1.78	[5]-0.8	(NA)
Social and recreational	Persons	(NA)	2.12	2.08	2.04	[5]-1.0	(NA)
Workers by usual mode to work	Percent	100.0	100.0	100.0	100.0	(NS)	(NS)
Auto	Percent	90.8	92.4	87.8	91.0	(NS)	(NS)
Public transit	Percent	8.4	5.8	5.3	5.1	(NS)	(NS)
Other	Percent	0.8	1.8	6.9	3.9	(NS)	(NS)

NA Not available. NS Percent change irrelevant. [1] Includes "don't know" and "refusals." [2] Changes in summary methodology in 1995 reflects higher results in 1995 than would be had the survey been done exactly as in 1990. [3] Excludes pickups and other light-trucks as household vehicles. [4] Includes other purposes not shown separately. [5] Change from 1977.

Source: Federal Highway Administration, *National Personal Transportation Survey, Summary of Travel Trends, 1969, 1977, 1983, 1990, and 1995.*

Transportation—Land 631

No. 1034. Roadway Congestion: 1997

[Various Federal, state, and local information sources were used to develop the data base with the primary source being the Federal Highway Administration's Highway Performance Monitoring System]

Urbanized areas	Freeway daily vehicle miles of travel		Annual person hours of delay		Annual congestion cost		
	Total miles (1,000)	Per lane-mile of freeway	Total hours	Per 1,000 persons	Per driver (dol.)	Per capita (dol.)	Delay and fuel cost (mil. dol.)
Total, average	15,030	15,240	63,560	35	585	755	1,060
Albany-Schenectady-Troy NY	4,975	9,475	3,265	7	140	110	55
Albuquerque NM	3,730	14,920	17,020	30	650	505	285
Allentown-Bethlehem-Easton PA-NJ.	(NA)	(NA)	(NA)	(NA)	(NA)	(NA)	(NA)
Atlanta GA	38,650	17,410	136,590	53	1,125	880	2,270
Austin TX	7,540	13,835	26,175	42	880	685	430
Bakersfield CA.	1,630	10,190	2,205	6	155	105	40
Baltimore MD	20,775	14,425	79,250	37	780	620	1,330
Beaumont TX	1,600	12,800	1,350	10	225	180	25
Boston MA	21,800	16,640	159,030	53	1,095	875	2,635
Boulder CO.	475	9,500	535	5	110	90	10
Brownsville TX.	260	8,665	345	2	50	35	5
Buffalo-Niagara Falls NY	5,790	9,265	5,640	5	115	90	95
Charlotte NC	6,200	13,780	18,010	31	680	520	300
Chicago IL-Northwestern IN	46,800	17,830	266,895	33	720	550	4,400
Cincinnati OH-KY.	14,900	15,280	30,445	24	525	405	515
Cleveland OH	16,660	13,940	29,925	16	345	270	505
Colorado Springs CO	2,470	10,290	4,985	12	275	205	85
Columbus OH	11,515	14,130	23,780	23	515	400	405
Corpus Christi TX.	2,740	9,785	1,775	6	110	80	25
Dallas TX	28,550	14,640	102,155	44	975	740	1,715
Denver CO	15,700	15,245	62,745	35	760	585	1,050
Detroit MI	29,355	16,400	191,910	48	1,010	785	3,145
El Paso TX-NM	3,460	12,355	5,390	9	205	150	90
Eugene-Springfield OR	1,185	10,775	1,315	6	120	95	20
Fort Worth TX	14,615	12,765	37,230	29	640	480	625
Fresno CA	1,905	11,205	7,270	13	315	220	120
Ft. Lauderdale-Hollywood-Pompano FL	11,350	15,655	36,740	24	515	405	605
Harrisburg PA	(NA)	(NA)	(NA)	(NA)	(NA)	(NA)	(NA)
Hartford-Middletown CT.	7,570	12,410	11,395	18	390	305	195
Honolulu HI.	5,730	14,325	16,070	23	510	395	280
Houston TX.	35,900	14,865	132,470	43	960	715	2,210
Indianapolis IN.	10,640	14,185	40,025	40	865	660	665
Jacksonville FL	8,650	13,105	21,600	26	580	435	360
Kansas City MO-KS	17,310	10,275	28,815	21	475	360	485
Laredo TX.	360	6,000	645	4	90	60	10
Las Vegas NV	5,400	14,400	29,830	26	575	440	505
Los Angeles CA.	116,920	22,315	739,245	60	1,370	1,010	12,405
Louisville KY-IN	9,475	14,250	27,040	32	680	540	455
Memphis TN-AR-MS.	5,920	12,870	21,465	22	480	360	350
Miami-Hialeah FL.	12,250	17,255	93,270	45	930	730	1,515
Milwaukee WI	8,750	14,345	24,595	20	425	325	410
Minneapolis-St. Paul MN	24,485	16,005	60,420	26	570	450	1,030
Nashville TN	9,450	13,035	22,350	35	765	595	375
New Orleans LA.	5,470	13,340	21,700	19	400	315	350
New York NY-Northeastern NJ . . .	94,755	14,465	532,190	31	640	520	8,885
Norfolk VA	6,850	11,050	27,150	27	570	440	450
Oklahoma City OK	8,665	11,870	13,705	14	305	235	235
Omaha NE-IA	2,955	10,190	13,080	23	510	385	215
Orlando FL	8,305	12,215	33,640	31	670	520	555
Philadelphia PA-NJ.	23,540	13,605	111,175	21	445	345	1,825
Phoenix AZ.	13,925	16,005	63,185	26	580	440	1,050
Pittsburgh PA	10,540	8,855	22,695	12	245	195	370
Portland-Vancouver OR-WA	11,900	17,245	54,275	41	885	695	930
Providence-Pawtucket RI-MA	7,300	11,585	15,255	17	360	285	255
Rochester NY	5,235	10,470	5,325	9	200	155	95
Sacramento CA	10,470	15,395	34,955	28	645	480	595
Salem OR.	1,060	11,160	2,030	11	215	160	30
Salt Lake City UT.	6,650	14,000	14,875	17	400	285	255
San Antonio TX	13,730	12,890	23,765	19	435	320	395
San Bernardino-Riverside CA. . . .	14,940	16,880	45,885	34	815	580	790
San Diego CA	28,515	15,930	72,535	28	635	485	1,265
San Francisco-Oakland CA	42,565	18,670	177,890	46	995	785	3,065
San Jose CA	17,170	14,800	55,820	34	765	590	955
Seattle-Everett WA.	22,795	18,020	106,560	54	1,165	920	1,805
Spokane WA.	1,335	10,680	2,770	8	200	150	50
St. Louis MO-IL	24,195	14,445	80,255	40	845	645	1,310
Tacoma WA	5,100	17,000	13,065	22	500	380	225
Tampa FL	5,675	13,045	26,750	32	650	520	430
Tucson AZ	1,775	10,145	13,935	21	450	345	225
Washington DC-MD-VA	33,340	18,170	216,110	62	1,260	1,025	3,560

NA Not available.

Source: Texas Transportation Institute, College Station, Texas; *Roadway Congestion in Major Urban Areas*, annual (copyright).

No. 1035. Motor Vehicle Accidents—Number and Deaths: 1972 to 1998

[17.0 represents 17,000,000]

Item	Unit	1972 [1]	1980	1985	1990	1994	1995	1996	1997	1998
Motor vehicle accidents [2]	Million . .	17.0	17.9	19.3	11.5	11.2	10.7	11.2	13.8	12.7
Cars	Million . .	24.5	22.8	25.6	14.3	13.5	12.3	13.3	16.0	13.8
Trucks.	Million . .	3.5	5.5	6.1	4.4	5.2	4.5	4.8	7.7	7.3
Motorcycles	1,000 . .	343	560	480	180	178	152	135	138	100
Motor vehicle deaths within 1 yr. [3] . .	1,000 . .	56.3	53.2	45.9	46.8	42.5	43.4	43.6	42.4	41.2
Noncollision accidents	1,000 . .	15.8	14.7	12.6	4.9	4.4	4.4	4.6	4.2	4.1
Collision accidents:										
With other motor vehicles	1,000 . .	23.9	23.0	19.9	19.9	18.9	19	19.6	20.7	19.5
With pedestrians	1,000 . .	10.3	9.7	8.5	7.3	6.3	6.4	6.1	5.9	5.9
With fixed objects.	1,000 . .	3.9	3.7	3.2	13.1	11.5	12.1	12.1	10.3	10.5
Deaths within 30 days [4]	1,000 . .	54.6	51.1	43.8	44.6	40.7	41.8	41.9	41.9	(NA)
Vehicle occupants	1,000 . .	41.4	36.8	31.5	33.9	32	33.1	33.4	33.6	(NA)
Pedestrians	1,000 . .	10.2	8.1	6.8	6.5	5.5	5.6	5.4	5.3	(NA)
Motorcyclists [5]	1,000 . .	3.0	5.1	4.6	3.2	2.3	2.2	2.2	2.1	(NA)
Bicyclists	1,000 . .	1.0	1.0	0.9	0.9	0.8	0.8	0.8	0.8	(NA)
Traffic death rates: [4] [6]										
Per 100,000 resident population. .	Rate . . .	26.2	22.5	18.4	17.9	15.6	15.9	15.8	15.7	15.3
Per 100,000 registered vehicles . .	Rate . . .	44.5	34.8	26.5	24.3	21.2	21.2	20.8	20.6	(NA)
Per 100 million vehicle miles	Rate . . .	4.3	3.3	2.5	2.1	1.7	1.7	1.7	1.6	1.6
Per 100,000 licensed drivers	Rate . . .	46.1	35.2	27.9	26.7	23.2	23.2	23.6	23.3	(NA)

NA Not available. [1] Represents peak year for deaths from motor vehicle accidents. [2] Covers only accidents occurring on the road. [3] Deaths that occur within 1 year of accident. Includes collision categories not shown separately. [4] Within 30 days of accident. Source: U.S. National Highway Traffic Safety Administration, unpublished data from Fatal Accident Reporting System. [5] Includes motor scooters and motorized bicycles (mopeds). [6] Based on 30-day definition of traffic deaths.

Source: Except as noted, National Safety Council, Itasca, IL, *Accident Facts,* annual (copyright).

No. 1036. Motor Vehicle Deaths by State: 1995 to 1998

[Includes both traffic and nontraffic motor vehicle deaths. See source for definitions]

State	1995	1996	1997	1998	Mileage rate [1] 1995	Mileage rate [1] 1998	State	1995	1996	1997	1998	Mileage rate [1] 1995	Mileage rate [1] 1998
U.S. . .	43,363	43,300	42,400	41,200	1.8	1.6	MO	1,110	1,148	1,192	1,169	1.9	1.8
							MT	215	198	265	237	2.3	2.5
AL.	1,111	1,142	1,181	1,069	2.2	2.0	NE.	254	293	302	315	1.6	1.8
AK.	86	80	77	72	2.0	1.6	NV.	312	348	347	360	2.4	2.2
AZ.	1,040	993	961	980	2.6	2.2	NH	118	134	125	129	1.1	1.1
AR.	631	615	660	625	2.5	2.2	NJ.	776	818	(NA)	755	1.3	1.2
CA.	4,165	3,972	3,377	3,161	1.5	1.1	NM	485	481	484	424	2.3	1.9
CO	645	434	516	524	1.9	1.4	NY.	1,668	1,562	1,625	1,405	1.4	1.1
CT.	318	310	337	329	1.1	1.1	NC	1,438	1,492	1,484	1,574	2.0	1.9
DE.	123	120	147	115	1.7	1.4	ND	74	85	105	92	1.1	1.3
DC	(NA)	(NA)	(NA)	58	(NA)	1.7	OH	1,357	1,393	1,439	1,421	1.4	1.3
FL.	2,812	2,813	2,847	2,804	2.3	2.0	OK	674	775	842	769	1.8	1.6
GA	1,494	1,578	1,584	1,580	1.8	1.7	OR	572	524	521	538	1.9	1.6
HI	127	145	131	120	1.6	1.5	PA.	1,480	1,470	1,562	1,485	1.6	1.5
ID	263	258	259	265	2.2	2.0	RI	69	69	75	74	1.0	1.0
IL	1,589	1,475	1,404	1,392	1.7	1.4	SC.	882	930	903	1,001	2.3	2.4
IN	960	981	(NA)	978	1.5	1.4	SD.	158	175	148	165	2.0	2.0
IA	527	465	468	444	2.0	1.6	TN.	1,240	1,211	1,223	1,208	2.2	2.0
KS.	438	491	483	493	1.7	1.8	TX.	3,172	3,738	3,476	3,516	1.7	1.7
KY.	856	844	865	868	2.1	1.9	UT.	321	321	367	346	1.7	1.7
LA.	880	809	840	812	2.3	2.0	VT.	106	88	96	104	1.7	1.6
ME	189	168	192	184	1.5	1.4	VA.	900	869	981	934	1.3	1.3
MD	682	614	609	606	1.5	1.3	WA	654	690	659	665	1.4	1.3
MA	448	417	443	406	0.9	0.8	WV	376	344	372	351	2.2	1.9
MI	1,537	1,505	1,446	1,367	1.8	1.5	WI	739	759	721	709	1.4	1.3
MN	597	576	598	650	1.4	1.3	WY	170	143	137	154	2.5	2.0
MS	868	811	861	948	3.0	2.9							

NA Not available. [1] Deaths per 100 million vehicle miles.

Source: National Safety Council, Itasca, IL, *Accident Facts,* annual (copyright).

Transportation—Land 633

No. 1037. Fatal Motor Vehicle Accidents—National Summary: 1980 to 1998

[Based on data from the Fatal Accident Reporting System (FARS). FARS gathers data on accidents that result in loss of human life. FARS is operated and maintained by National Highway Traffic Safety Administration's (NHTSA) National Center for Statistics and Analysis (NCSA). FARS data are gathered on motor vehicle accidents that occurred on a roadway customarily open to the public, resulting in the death of a person within 30 days of the accident. Collection of these data depend on the use of police, hospital, medical examiner/coroner, and Emergency Medical Services reports; state vehicle registration, driver licensing, and highway department files; and vital statistics documents and death certificates. See source for further detail]

Item	1980	1985	1990	1994	1995	1996	1997	1998
Fatal accidents, total	45,284	39,196	39,836	36,254	37,241	37,494	37,324	37,081
One vehicle involved	28,306	22,875	23,445	20,526	21,250	21,134	20,807	20,897
Two or more vehicles involved	16,978	16,321	16,391	15,728	15,991	16,360	16,517	16,184
Persons killed in fatal accidents	51,091	43,825	44,599	40,716	41,817	42,065	42,013	41,471
Occupants [1]	41,927	36,043	37,134	34,318	35,291	35,695	35,725	35,359
Drivers	28,816	25,337	25,750	23,691	24,390	24,534	24,667	24,729
Passengers	12,972	10,619	11,276	10,518	10,782	11,058	10,944	10,519
Nonmotorists [1]	9,164	7,782	7,465	6,398	6,526	6,370	6,288	6,112
Pedestrians	8,070	6,808	6,482	5,489	5,584	5,449	5,321	5,220
Pedalcyclists	965	890	859	802	833	765	814	761
Other	129	84	124	107	109	156	153	131
Occupant fatalities by type of vehicle:								
Passenger cars:								
Mini-compact (95 inches)	3,141	3,571	3,556	2,339	2,207	2,037	1,763	1,488
Subcompact (95 to 99 inches)	4,158	4,422	4,753	4,721	4,584	4,581	4,457	4,022
Compact (100 to 104 inches)	927	2,635	5,310	6,322	6,899	7,288	7,195	7,002
Intermediate (105 to 109 inches)	3,878	4,391	4,849	4,407	4,666	4,670	4,794	4,788
Full size (110 to 114 inches)	4,831	2,974	2,386	2,074	2,116	2,147	2,242	2,290
Largest (115 inches and over)	6,746	3,612	2,249	1,486	1,297	1,270	1,239	1,098
Motorcycles	4,961	4,417	3,129	2,190	2,114	2,046	2,028	2,177
Other motorized cycles	183	147	115	130	113	115	88	107
Light trucks	7,378	6,286	8,347	8,904	9,568	9,932	10,249	10,647
Pickup	5,483	4,640	5,979	5,574	5,938	5,904	5,887	5,900
Utility	895	855	1,214	1,757	1,935	2,147	2,380	2,701
Van	1,000	791	1,154	1,508	1,639	1,832	1,914	2,015
Other	(NA)	(NA)	(NA)	65	56	49	68	31
Medium trucks	285	157	134	109	96	87	122	91
Heavy trucks	977	820	571	561	552	534	601	637
Buses	46	57	32	18	33	21	18	36
Persons involved in fatal accidents	113,289	104,045	107,777	98,945	102,102	103,347	102,197	100,978
Occupants [1]	103,049	95,482	99,297	91,644	94,621	96,159	95,050	94,127
Drivers	62,957	57,883	58,893	54,549	56,164	57,001	56,688	56,543
Passengers	39,892	37,477	40,229	36,898	38,252	38,913	38,184	37,388
Nonoccupants	10,240	8,563	8,480	7,301	7,481	7,188	7,147	6,851
Vehicle miles traveled (VMT) (100 million)	15,273	17,742	21,444	23,576	24,227	24,858	25,617	26,254
Licensed drivers (1,000)	145,295	156,868	167,015	175,403	176,628	179,539	182,709	184,980
Registered vehicles (1,000)	161,490	177,098	192,915	192,497	197,065	201,631	203,568	207,588
Fatalities by road type:								
Interstate	4,427	4,148	4,993	4,713	4,835	5,245	5,332	5,367
Federal-aid primary	(NA)	14,526	14,203	(NA)	(NA)	(NA)	(NA)	(NA)
Federal-aid secondary	(NA)	6,429	6,892	(NA)	(NA)	(NA)	(NA)	(NA)
Federal-aid urban	(NA)	8,116	8,432	(NA)	(NA)	(NA)	(NA)	(NA)
Non-Federal aid	(NA)	10,408	10,039	(NA)	(NA)	(NA)	(NA)	(NA)
Fatal accidents by the highest blood alcohol concentration (BAC) in accident:								
0.00 percent	(NA)	48.5	50.6	59.1	58.7	59.1	61.5	61.5
0.01 to 0.09 percent	(NA)	10.3	9.7	8.4	8.6	8.7	8.1	8.2
0.10 percent and over	(NA)	41.2	39.7	32.5	32.6	32.1	30.3	30.3
Fatality rate by age group:								
Under 5 years old	6.9	5.2	4.9	4.8	4.3	4.6	4.1	4.0
5 years to 15 years old	8.7	7.4	6.4	6.0	6.0	5.7	5.6	5.2
16 years to 24 years old	46.0	37.1	35.2	30.7	30.8	30.7	29.3	28.5
25 years to 44 years old	24.6	19.6	19.7	16.3	17.2	17.0	16.6	16.4
45 years to 64 years old	17.2	14.5	14.9	13.3	13.6	13.8	14.2	14.0
65 years to 79 years old	19.6	18.0	18.8	18.7	18.5	18.7	19.2	18.7
80 years old and over	25.3	25.1	26.8	28.0	28.0	27.8	29.2	28.3
Fatalities per 100 million VMT	3.3	2.5	2.1	1.7	1.7	1.7	1.6	1.6
Fatalities per 100,000 licensed drivers	35.2	27.9	26.7	23.2	23.7	23.4	23.0	22.4
Licensed driver per person	0.6	0.7	0.7	0.7	0.7	0.7	0.7	0.7
VMT per registered vehicle	9,458	10,018	11,107	12,247	12,294	12,329	12,584	12,647
Fatalities per 100,000 registered vehicles	31.6	24.8	23.1	21.2	21.2	20.9	20.6	20.0
Fatal crashes per 100 million VMT	2.9	2.2	1.9	1.5	1.5	1.5	1.5	1.4
Involved vehicles per fatal crash	1.4	1.5	1.5	1.5	1.5	1.5	1.5	1.5
Fatalities per fatal crash	1.2	1.1	1.1	1.1	1.1	1.1	1.1	1.1
Average occupants per fatal crash	2.3	2.4	2.5	2.7	2.7	2.8	2.7	2.7
Fatalities per 100,000 population	22.5	18.4	17.9	15.6	15.9	15.9	15.7	15.3

NA Not available. [1] Includes items not shown separately.

Source: National Highway Traffic Safety Administration, *Fatal Accident Reporting System*, annual.

No. 1038. Motor Vehicle Occupants and Nonoccupants Killed and Injured: 1985 to 1998

[Vehicle occupants accounted for almost 84 percent of traffic fatalities in 1995. The remaining 16 percent were pedestrians, pedalcyclists, and other nonoccupants]

Year		Occupants							Nonoccupants			
	Total	Total	Passenger cars	Light trucks	Large trucks	Motor-cycles	Buses	Other/ unknown	Total	Pedes-trian	Pedal-cyclist	Other
KILLED												
1985	43,825	36,043	23,212	6,689	977	4,564	57	544	7,782	6,808	890	84
1986	46,087	38,234	24,944	7,317	926	4,566	39	442	7,853	6,779	941	133
1987	46,390	38,565	25,132	8,058	852	4,036	51	436	7,825	6,745	948	132
1988	47,087	39,170	25,808	8,306	911	3,662	54	429	7,917	6,870	911	136
1989	45,582	38,087	25,063	8,551	858	3,141	50	424	7,495	6,556	832	107
1990	44,599	37,134	24,092	8,601	705	3,244	32	460	7,465	6,482	859	124
1991	41,508	34,740	22,385	8,391	661	2,806	31	466	6,768	5,801	843	124
1992	39,250	32,880	21,387	8,098	585	2,395	28	387	6,370	5,549	723	98
1993	40,150	33,574	21,566	8,511	605	2,449	18	425	6,576	5,649	816	111
1994	40,716	34,318	21,997	8,904	670	2,320	18	409	6,398	5,489	802	107
1995	41,817	35,291	22,423	9,568	648	2,227	33	392	6,526	5,584	833	109
1996	41,907	35,581	22,416	9,901	621	2,160	21	462	6,326	5,412	761	153
1997	42,013	35,725	22,199	10,249	723	2,116	18	420	6,288	5,321	814	153
1998	41,471	35,359	21,164	10,647	728	2,284	36	500	6,112	5,220	761	131
INJURED (1,000)												
1988	3,416	3,224	2,585	478	37	105	15	4	192	110	75	8
1989	3,284	3,088	2,431	511	43	83	15	5	196	112	73	11
1990	3,231	3,044	2,376	505	42	84	33	4	187	105	75	7
1991	3,097	2,931	2,235	563	28	80	21	4	166	88	67	11
1992	3,070	2,908	2,232	545	34	65	20	12	162	89	63	10
1993	3,125	2,958	2,257	590	32	58	17	4	166	93	65	9
1994	3,215	3,056	2,332	619	30	56	15	3	159	90	60	9
1995	3,386	3,232	2,416	709	30	55	18	4	154	84	61	9
1996	3,511	3,360	2,478	768	33	56	20	4	151	82	59	11
1997	3,348	3,201	2,341	755	31	53	17	6	131	77	58	11
1998	3,192	3,061	2,201	763	29	49	16	4	146	69	53	8

Source: U.S. National Highway Traffic Safety Administration, *Traffic Safety Facts 1995, Overview,* annual.

No. 1039. Large Truck Involvement in Fatal Crashes by State: 1998

[Medium/heavy trucks represents trucks over 10,000 pounds GVW, including single unit trucks]

State and other area	Large trucks involved in fatal crashes				State and other area	Large trucks involved in fatal crashes			
	Total vehicles involved in fatal crashes	Number	Per-centage of total vehicles	Per-cent-age of U.S. total for large trucks		Total vehicles involved in fatal crashes	Number	Per-centage of total vehicles	Per-cent-age of U.S. total for large trucks
United States [1] .	56,865	4,935	8.7	100.0	Missouri	1,573	155	9.9	3.1
					Montana	277	18	6.5	0.4
Alabama	1,465	149	10.2	3.0	Nebraska	402	41	10.2	0.8
Alaska	87	1	1.1	-	Nevada	487	34	7.0	0.7
Arizona	1,291	98	7.6	2.0	New Hampshire	171	10	5.8	0.2
Arkansas	836	105	12.6	2.1					
California	4,762	365	7.7	7.4	New Jersey	1,024	64	6.3	1.3
Colorado	848	52	6.1	1.1	New Mexico	508	44	8.7	0.9
Connecticut	455	29	6.4	0.6	New York	2,039	134	6.6	2.7
Delaware	170	18	10.6	0.4	North Carolina	2,211	228	10.3	4.6
District of Columbia . .	81	1	1.2	-	North Dakota	109	8	7.3	0.2
Florida	4,114	317	7.7	6.4	Ohio	1,983	189	9.5	3.8
					Oklahoma	988	106	10.7	2.1
Georgia	2,192	195	8.9	4.0	Oregon	715	68	9.5	1.4
Hawaii	178	4	2.2	0.1	Pennsylvania	2,052	178	8.7	3.6
Idaho	325	23	7.1	0.5	Rhode Island	98	3	3.1	0.1
Illinois	1,945	185	9.5	3.7					
Indiana	1,376	179	13.0	3.6	South Carolina	1,353	118	8.7	2.4
Iowa	649	83	12.8	1.7	South Dakota	215	14	6.5	0.3
Kansas	667	79	11.8	1.6	Tennessee	1,711	136	7.9	2.8
Kentucky	1,192	97	8.1	2.0	Texas	4,894	422	8.6	8.6
Louisiana	1,263	140	11.1	2.8	Utah	443	44	9.9	0.9
Maine	253	21	8.3	0.4	Vermont	124	10	8.1	0.2
					Virginia	1,227	109	8.9	2.2
Maryland	877	65	7.4	1.3	Washington	904	69	7.6	1.4
Massachusetts	561	37	6.6	0.7	West Virginia	468	41	8.8	0.8
Michigan	2,020	147	7.3	3.0	Wisconsin	965	90	9.3	1.8
Minnesota	893	78	8.7	1.6	Wyoming	173	30	17.3	0.6
Mississippi	1,251	104	8.3	2.1	Puerto Rico	716	33	4.6	-

- Represents zero. [1]Excludes outlying area.

Source: U.S. National Highway Traffic Safety Administration, *Traffic Safety Facts,* annual.

No. 1040. Speeding-Related Traffic Fatalities and Costs by Road Type and Speed Limit: 1998

[Includes fatalities that occurred on roads for which the speed limit was unknown. Includes costs for crashes that occurred on unknown road types. Totals may not equal sum of components due to independent rounding]

State	Traffic fatalities, total	Speeding-related fatalities by road type and speed							
		Interstate		Noninterstate					
		Over 55 mph	55 mph	55 mph	50 mph	45 mph	40 mph	35 mph	Under 35 mph
United States......	41,471	1,331	418	3,777	472	1,451	770	1,235	1,275
Alabama..............	1,071	42	3	96	10	108	32	49	30
Alaska...............	71	-	6	6	-	3	2	1	4
Arizona..............	980	74	15	83	21	52	37	34	32
Arkansas	625	14	4	83	-	15	10	6	8
California	3,494	170	17	315	49	85	86	123	126
Colorado.............	628	19	22	41	13	31	21	25	38
Connecticut...........	329	1	17	10	3	10	9	8	34
Delaware	115	-	1	1	5	1	8	2	2
District of Columbia	54	-	3	-	-	5	-	2	15
Florida	2,824	70	15	102	19	113	35	60	69
Georgia	1,569	22	13	115	8	67	16	43	21
Hawaii	120	-	4	8	-	5	-	8	19
Idaho................	265	13	-	7	10	5	1	5	2
Illinois	1,393	52	40	191	1	44	15	65	45
Indiana..............	978	8	10	63	11	15	19	15	30
Iowa	449	2	-	37	2	3	1	2	9
Kansas..............	493	13	1	50	2	4	6	9	14
Kentucky	858	10	6	148	1	9	2	19	5
Louisiana	922	9	4	70	4	32	5	15	11
Maine................	192	4	1	5	16	25	13	7	7
Maryland	606	5	8	31	20	12	40	23	36
Massachusetts..........	406	12	3	10	3	9	22	21	68
Michigan.............	1,367	27	5	182	7	21	15	28	42
Minnesota............	650	8	10	78	8	10	6	1	23
Mississippi	948	26	-	75	34	39	1	17	12
Missouri	1,169	62	15	151	4	28	10	38	37
Montana.............	237	6	1	29	-	6	-	4	9
Nebraska	315	5	1	9	20	-	-	9	3
Nevada	361	38	2	8	7	19	4	16	13
New Hampshire..........	128	-	-	1	4	3	7	5	14
New Jersey............	743	1	9	5	9	12	6	6	23
New Mexico	424	27	7	27	10	9	5	12	10
New York	1,498	7	17	135	2	41	40	21	77
North Carolina..........	1,596	41	21	302	6	106	6	56	10
North Dakota...........	92	3	1	30	-	1	3	2	3
Ohio	1,422	49	2	200	8	22	12	43	32
Oklahoma.............	755	40	1	71	6	51	16	8	18
Oregon...............	538	8	4	114	1	17	8	16	13
Pennsylvania...........	1,481	30	29	127	14	100	69	88	36
Rhode Island...........	74	5	3	-	4	2	2	1	16
South Carolina..........	1,002	58	16	155	9	83	27	48	17
South Dakota	165	4	1	22	3	2	3	6	5
Tennessee	1,216	19	10	93	20	59	37	29	35
Texas................	3,577	202	51	222	36	85	65	105	114
Utah	350	33	-	12	6	1	7	6	6
Vermont	104	10	1	-	20	2	6	11	1
Virginia..............	935	24	17	90	1	31	4	22	9
Washington............	660	33	-	26	34	20	12	63	30
West Virginia..........	354	3	-	26	-	7	12	13	9
Wisconsin.............	714	13	1	110	-	8	5	16	27
Wyoming	154	9	-	5	1	13	2	3	6

- Represents or rounds to zero.

Source: U.S. National Highway Traffic Safety Administration, *Traffic Safety Facts, Speeding*, annual.

U.S. Census Bureau, Statistical Abstract of the United States: 2000

No. 1041. Traffic Fatalities by State and Highest Blood Alcohol Concentration in the Crash: 1998

State	Traffic fatalities, total	No alcohol (BAC=0.00 g/dl)		Any alcohol (BAC>=0.01 g/dl)					
				Total		Low alcohol (BAC=0.01-0.0)		High alcohol (BAC=0.10 g/dl)	
		Number	Percent	number	Percent	Number	Percent	Number	Percent
United States	41,471	25,536	62	15,935	38	3,479	8	12,456	30
Alabama............	1,071	665	62	406	38	77	7	329	31
Alaska.............	71	40	56	31	44	3	4	28	39
Arizona............	980	557	57	423	43	89	9	334	34
Arkansas	625	432	69	193	31	48	8	146	23
California	3,494	2,170	62	1,324	38	315	9	1,009	29
Colorado...........	628	396	63	232	37	43	7	189	30
Connecticut........	329	187	57	142	43	29	9	112	34
Delaware	115	70	61	45	39	7	6	37	33
District of Columbia	54	27	49	27	51	8	16	19	35
Florida	2,824	1,899	67	925	33	210	7	715	25
Georgia	1,569	1,060	68	509	32	130	8	380	24
Hawaii	120	64	53	56	47	14	12	42	35
Idaho.............	265	175	66	90	34	15	6	75	28
Illinois	1,393	794	57	599	43	122	9	477	34
Indiana............	978	599	61	379	39	72	7	307	31
Iowa	449	285	64	164	36	43	9	121	27
Kansas............	493	319	65	174	35	42	8	132	27
Kentucky	858	573	67	285	33	60	7	225	26
Louisiana	922	496	54	426	46	103	11	323	35
Maine.............	192	138	72	54	28	8	4	45	24
Maryland	606	403	66	203	34	59	10	144	24
Massachusetts.......	406	214	53	192	47	59	15	134	33
Michigan...........	1,367	831	61	536	39	120	9	416	30
Minnesota..........	650	370	57	280	43	64	10	216	33
Mississippi	948	597	63	351	37	57	6	294	31
Missouri	1,169	644	55	525	45	139	12	386	33
Montana...........	237	133	56	104	44	23	10	81	34
Nebraska	315	196	62	119	38	31	10	88	28
Nevada	361	184	51	177	49	49	14	127	35
New Hampshire......	128	67	53	61	47	25	20	36	28
New Jersey.........	743	472	64	271	36	77	10	194	26
New Mexico........	424	231	55	193	45	41	10	152	36
New York	1,498	1,133	76	365	24	115	8	250	17
North Carolina......	1,596	1,083	68	513	32	91	6	422	26
North Dakota........	92	48	53	44	47	4	4	40	43
Ohio	1,422	958	67	464	33	83	6	381	27
Oklahoma..........	755	503	67	252	33	44	6	208	28
Oregon............	538	305	57	233	43	50	9	183	34
Pennsylvania.......	1,481	862	58	619	42	103	7	516	35
Rhode Island.......	74	39	52	35	48	9	13	26	35
South Carolina......	1,002	698	70	304	30	50	5	254	25
South Dakota	165	98	59	67	41	13	8	54	33
Tennessee	1,216	717	59	499	41	105	9	394	32
Texas.............	3,577	1,785	50	1,792	50	383	11	1,408	39
Utah	350	300	86	50	14	12	3	39	11
Vermont...........	104	66	63	38	37	7	7	31	30
Virginia............	935	592	63	343	37	76	8	267	29
Washington.........	660	353	54	307	46	62	9	244	37
West Virginia........	354	209	59	145	41	17	5	128	36
Wisconsin..........	714	412	58	302	42	58	8	244	34
Wyoming	154	86	56	68	44	13	8	55	36

Source: U.S. National Highway Traffic Safety Administration, *Traffic Safety Facts, 1998 — Alcohol*, annual.

No. 1042. Fatalities by Highest Blood Alcohol Concentration (BAC) in Highway Crashes: 1985 to 1998

Item	1985	1990	1991	1992	1993	1994	1995	1996	1997	1998
Total fatalities...........	43,825	44,599	41,508	39,250	40,150	40,716	41,817	42,065	42,013	41,471
Fatalities in alcohol-related crashes................	22,716	22,084	19,887	17,858	17,473	16,580	17,247	17,218	16,189	15,935
Percent.................	51.8	49.5	47.9	45.5	43.5	40.7	41.2	40.9	38.5	38.4
BAC = 0.01-0.09:										
Number	4,604	4,434	3,957	3,625	3,496	3,480	3,746	3,774	3,480	3,479
Percent................	10.5	9.9	9.5	9.2	8.7	8.5	9.0	9.0	8.3	8.4
BAC = 0.10+:										
Number	18,111	17,650	15,930	14,234	13,977	13,100	13,501	13,444	12,710	12,456
Percent................	41.3	39.6	38.4	36.3	34.8	32.2	32.3	32.0	30.3	30.0
BAC = 0.00 (no alcohol content):										
Number	21,109	22,515	21,621	21,392	22,677	24,136	24,570	24,847	25,824	25,536
Percent................	48.2	50.5	52.1	54.5	56.5	59.3	58.8	59.1	61.5	61.6

Source: U.S. National Highway Traffic Safety Administration, *Traffic Safety Facts 1998*.

No. 1043. Highway Travel—Mileage and Accident Summary: 1980 to 1998

Item	1980	1985	1990	1993	1994	1995	1996	1997	1998
Highway mileage (1,000)	3,857	3,862	3,880	3,905	3,907	3,912	3,919	3,945	3,906
Vehicle miles of travel (bil.)	1,527	1,775	2,144	2,296	2,358	2,423	2,486	2,560	2,619
Daily vehicle miles per mile.	1,082	1,259	1,516	1,611	1,655	(NA)	(NA)	(NA)	(NA)
Fatal accidents:									
Number	45,284	39,168	39,779	35,750	36,223	37,221	37,351	37,280	37,081
Rate per 100 mil. vehicle mi. of travel .	2.96	2.21	1.85	1.56	1.53	1.54	1.50	1.46	1.41
Nonfatal injury accidents:									
Number (1,000)	2,008	2,219	2,122	2,022	2,123	2,217	2,238	2,149	2,029
Rate per 100 mil. vehicle mi. of travel .	131	125	116	(NA)	(NA)	96	97	94	(NA)
Fatalities [1]:									
Number	51,091	43,825	44,599	40,150	40,716	41,817	42,065	42,013	41,471
Rate per 100 mil. vehicle mi. of travel .	3.35	2.47	2.07	1.75	1.72	1.73	1.69	1.64	1.60
Rate per 100,000 population	22.48	18.42	17.88	15.58	15.64	15.91	15.86	15.69	15.34
Licensed drivers (1,000)	145,295	156,868	167,015	173,149	175,403	176,628	179,539	182,709	(NA)
Rate per 100,000 licensed drivers . .	35.16	27.94	26.70	23.19	23.21	23.68	23.43	22.99	(NA)
Registered motor vehicles (1,000). . . .	146,845	166,047	184,275	188,350	192,497	197,065	201,631	203,568	(NA)
Rate per 100,000 registered vehicles	34.79	26.39	24.20	21.32	21.15	21.22	21.22	20.86	20.64	(NA)

NA Not available. [1] Represents fatalities occurring within 30 days of accident. Excludes nontraffic accidents which, for example, occur outside the rights-of-way or other boundaries of roads that are open for public use.
Source: U.S. Federal Highway Administration, *Fatal and Injury Accident Rates on Public Roads in the United States,* annual.

No. 1044. Alcohol Involvement for Drivers in Fatal Crashes: 1995 and 1998

[BAC = blood alcohol concentration]

Drivers involved in fatal crashes	1995		1998	
	Numbers of drivers	Percentage with BAC of .10% or greater	Numbers of drivers	Percentage with BAC of .10% or greater
Total drivers [1]	**56,155**	**19.3**	**56,543**	**18**
Drivers by age group:				
16 to 20 years old.	7,738	12.7	7,755	14
21 to 24 years old.	6,268	27.8	5,599	28
25 to 34 years old.	13,029	26.8	11,895	24
35 to 44 years old.	10,664	22.8	11,220	21
45 to 64 years old.	10,884	14.3	12,151	13
65 years old and over	6,238	5.0	6,680	5
Drivers by sex:				
Male.	41,216	21.8	40,746	20
Female	14,179	11.2	15,061	10
Drivers by vehicle type:				
Passenger cars	30,692	19.2	28,857	18
Light trucks	17,420	22.4	19,104	20
Large trucks.	4,391	1.3	4,883	1
Motorcycles	2,257	29.1	2,323	31

[1] Does not add, due to unknown or other data not included.
Source: National Safety Council, Itasca, IL, *Accident Facts,* 1997 edition.

No. 1045. Age of Driver and Number in Accidents: 1998

[185,450 represents 185,450,000]

Age group	Drivers (1,000)	Percent	Drivers in accidents						
			Fatal		All		Per number of drivers	
			Number licensed	Percent licenced	Drivers (1,000)	Percent	Fatal [1]	All [2]
Total	**185,450**	**100.0**	**56,100**	**100.0**	**21,300**	**100.0**	**30**	**11**
Under 16 years old.	31	(Z)	500	0.9	120	0.6	([3])	([3])
16 years old	1,708	0.9	1,200	2.1	620	2.9	70	36
17 years old	2,436	1.3	1,200	2.1	720	3.4	49	30
18 years old	2,868	1.5	1,900	3.4	780	3.7	66	27
19 years old	2,941	1.6	1,600	2.9	700	3.3	54	24
19 years old and under	9,984	5.4	6,400	11.4	2,940	13.8	64	29
20 years old	3,048	1.6	1,500	2.7	630	3.0	49	21
21 years old	3,093	1.7	1,500	2.7	600	2.8	48	19
22 years old	3,022	1.6	1,500	2.7	550	2.6	50	18
23 years old	3,209	1.7	1,300	2.3	520	2.4	41	16
24 years old	3,157	1.7	1,300	2.3	500	2.3	41	16
20 to 24 years old	15,529	8.4	7,100	12.7	2,800	13.1	46	18
25 to 34 years old	37,265	20.1	11,900	21.2	4,900	23.0	32	13
35 to 44 years old	41,857	22.6	11,300	20.1	4,440	20.8	27	11
45 to 54 years old	33,662	18.2	7,700	13.7	2,940	13.8	23	9
55 to 64 years old	21,337	11.5	4,600	8.2	1,570	7.4	22	7
65 to 74 years old	15,244	8.2	3,600	6.4	1,010	4.7	24	7
75 years old and over	10,570	5.7	3,500	6.2	710	3.3	33	7

Z Less than .05. [1] Per 100,000 licensed drivers. [2] Per 100 licensed drivers. [3] Rates for drivers under age 16 are substantially overstated due to the high proportion of unlicensed drivers involved.
Source: National Safety Council, Itasca, IL, *Accident Facts,* 1997 edition (copyright).

638 Transportation—Land

No. 1046. State Legislation—Alcohol and Road Safety Laws: Various Years

State	Alcohol legislation				Mandatory belt-use law		Graduated licensing law			
	Administrative license revocation since [1]	BAC limit [2]	Zero tolerance limit for minors [3]	Alcohol ignition interlock device [4]	Enforcement	Seating positions	Graduated licensing law	Minimum instructional permit period	Night-time driving restrictions	Unrestricted license minimum age
Alabama	1996	.08	.02	No	Secondary	Front	No	None	No	16 yrs.
Alaska	1983	.10	.00	Yes	Secondary	All	Yes	None	No	16 yrs.
Arizona	1992	.10	.00	No	Secondary	Front	No	None	No	16 yrs.
Arkansas	1995	[5].10	.02	No	Secondary	Front	No	None	No	16 yrs.
California	1989	[5].08	.01	[6]Yes	Standard	All	Yes	6 mo.	Yes	17 yrs.
Colorado	1983	.10	.02	[6]Yes	Secondary	Front	Yes	3 mo.	No	16 yrs.
Connecticut	1990	.10	.02	No	Standard	[7]Front	Yes	6 mo.	No	16 yrs. & 4 mo.
Delaware	Yes	.10	.02	[6]Yes	Secondary	Front	Yes	6 mo.	Yes	16 yrs. & 10 mo.
District of Columbia	Yes	.08	.00	No	Standard	All	[8]No	None	No	16 yrs.
Florida	1990	.08	.02	Yes	Secondary	Front	Yes	6 mo.	Yes	18 yrs.
Georgia	1995	.10	.02	[6]Yes	Standard	[7]Front	Yes	12 mo.	Yes	18 yrs.
Hawaii	1990	.08	.02	No	Standard	Front	No	None	No	15 yrs. & 3 mo.
Idaho	1994	.08	.02	Yes	Secondary	Front	No	None	No	16 yrs.
Illinois	1986	.08	.00	Yes	Secondary	Front	Yes	3 mo.	Yes	17 yrs.
Indiana	Yes	.10	.02	Yes	Standard	Front	Yes	2 mo.	Yes	18 yrs.
Iowa	1963	.10	.02	Yes	Standard	Front	Yes	6 mo.	Yes	17 yrs.
Kansas	1988	.08	.02	Yes	Secondary	Front	No	None	No	16 yrs.
Kentucky	No	.10	.02	No	Secondary	All	No	None	No	16 yrs. & 6 mo.
Louisiana	1984	.10	.02	Yes	Standard	[7]Front	Yes	3 mo.	Yes	17 yrs.
Maine	1984	[10].08	.00	[6]Yes	[9]Secondary	All	No	None	No	16 yrs.
Maryland	1989	[10].10	.01	Yes	Standard	[7][11]Front	[12]Yes	4 mo.	Yes	17 yrs. & 7 mo.
Massachusetts	1994	.08	.02	No	Standard	All	Yes	6 mo.	Yes	18 yrs.
Michigan	No	.10	.02	Yes	Secondary	[7]Front	Yes	6 mo.	Yes	17 yrs.
Minnesota	1976	.10	.01	No	Secondary	[7]Front	Yes	6 mo.	No	17 yrs.
Mississippi	1983	.10	.02	No	Secondary	Front	No	None	No	16 yrs.
Missouri	1987	.10	.02	[6]Yes	Standard	[7]Front	No	None	No	16 yrs.
Montana	No	.10	.02	Yes	Secondary	All	No	None	No	15 yrs.
Nebraska	1993	.10	.02	Yes	Secondary	Front	No	None	Yes	17 yrs.
Nevada	1983	.10	.02	[6]Yes	Secondary	All	No	None	No	16 yrs.
New Hampshire	1994	.08	.02	No	No	(NA)	Yes	3 mo.	Yes	18 yrs.
New Jersey	No	.10	.01	No	Secondary	Front	[13]Yes	6 mo.	[14]Yes	18 yrs.
New Mexico	1984	.08	.02	Yes	Standard	[15]Front	[8]No	None	No	15 yrs.
New York	[16]1994	.10	.02	[6]Yes	Standard	[7]Front	Yes	(NA)	Yes	17 yrs.
North Carolina	1983	.08	.00	Yes	Standard	Front	Yes	12 mo.	Yes	16 yrs. & 6 mo.
North Dakota	1983	.10	.02	Yes	Secondary	Front	No	3 mo.	No	16 yrs.
Ohio	1993	.10	.02	Yes	Secondary	Front	Yes	6 mo.	Yes	17 yrs.
Oklahoma	1983	.10	.00	Yes	Standard	Front	No	None	No	16 yrs.
Oregon	1983	.08	.00	Yes	Standard	All	No	None	No	16 yrs.
Pennsylvania	No	.10	.02	No	Secondary	Front	Yes	(NA)	Yes	17 yrs.
Rhode Island	No	.10	.02	[6]Yes	Secondary	All	Yes	6 mo.	Yes	17 yrs. & 6 mo.
South Carolina	1998	.10	.02	No	Secondary	[7]Front	Yes	3 mo.	Yes	16 yrs. & 3 mo.
South Dakota	No	.10	.02	No	Secondary	Front	Yes	6 mo.	Yes	16 yrs.
Tennessee	No	.10	.02	Yes	Secondary	[7]Front	No	3 mo.	No	16 yrs.
Texas	1995	.10	.00	[6]Yes	Standard	Front	No	None	No	16 yrs.
Utah	1983	.08	.00	Yes	Secondary	Front	No	None	No	16 yrs.
Vermont	[16]1969	.08	.02	No	Secondary	All	No	None	No	16 yrs.
Virginia	1995	.08	.02	Yes	Secondary	Front	Yes	6 mo.	No	18 yrs.
Washington	[17]1994	.08	.02	Yes	Secondary	All	No	None	No	16 yrs.
West Virginia	1981	.10	.02	Yes	Secondary	[11]Front	No	None	No	16 yrs.
Wisconsin	1988	[18].10	.00	[6]Yes	Secondary	[7]Front	No	None	No	16 yrs.
Wyoming	1973	.10	.02	No	Secondary	Front	No	None	No	16 yrs.

NA Not available. [1] Year original law became effective, not when grandfather clauses expired. [2] Blood alcohol concentration that constitutes the threshold of legal intoxication. [3] Blood alcohol concentration that constitutes "zero tolerance" threshold for minors less than 21 years old unless noted. [4] Legislation for instruments designed to prevent drivers from starting their cars when breath alcohol content is at or above a set point. [5] Commercial driver with BAC of .04 or more. [6] Primarily for repeat offenders, but may also be applied to first time offenders under certain circumstances. [7] Required for certain ages at all seating positions. [8] Legislation pending. [9] Secondary for 19 and older, standard for under 19. [10] BAC of .07 is prima facie evidence of DUI (MD); BAC of .05-.10 constitutes driving while ability impaired (NY). [11] Excluding front center seat. [12] Legislation becomes effective 7/1/99. [13] Legislation becomes effective 1/1/01. [14] Waived for new drivers age 21 and older. [15] Belt use required in rear seat if lap/shoulder belt is available. [16] Revocation by judicial action (NY) or Department of Motor Vehicles (VT). [17] Updated law effective 1/1/99. [18] .08 after second DUI conviction.

Source: National Safety Council, Itasca, IL, *Accident Facts* (copyright).

No. 1047. Motor Vehicle Safety Defect Recalls by Domestic and Foreign Manufacturers: 1980 to 1996

[Covers manufacturers reporting to U.S. National Highway Traffic Administration under Section 151 of National Traffic and Motor Vehicle Safety Act of 1966, as amended]

Manufacturer	Unit	1980	1985	1989	1990	1991	1992	1993	1994	1995	1996
MOTOR VEHICLES											
Total recall campaigns [1]. . .	Number .	167	173	237	208	220	187	221	244	266	265
Domestic	Number .	129	137	182	159	168	142	178	178	190	197
Foreign.	Number .	38	36	55	49	52	45	43	66	76	68
Total vehicles recalled . . .	1,000 . . .	4,868	5,629	7,137	5,985	8,279	10,122	10,922	6,063	18,295	17,084
Domestic	1,000 . . .	3,943	4,995	6,173	4,070	6,646	6,545	7,655	4,280	9,041	15,104
Foreign.	1,000 . . .	925	634	964	1,915	1,633	3,577	3,267	1,784	9,259	1,980
MOTOR VEHICLE TIRES											
Recall campaigns [1]	Number .	24	19	11	13	12	7	5	5	3	1
Tires recalled.	1,000 . . .	7,070	28	115	172	153	8	6	93	10	6

[1] A recall campaign is the notification to the Secretary of the U.S. Dept. of Transportation and to owners, purchasers, and dealers of motor vehicles and motor vehicle equipment.

Source: U.S. National Highway Traffic Safety Administration, *Motor Vehicles Recall Campaigns*, annual.

No. 1048. Cost of Owning and Operating an Automobile: 1980 to 1997

Item	Unit	1980	1990	1992	1993	1994	1995	1996	1997
Cost per mile [1]	Cents	27.95	40.96	45.77	45.14	46.65	48.91	51.43	53.08
Cost per 10,000 miles [1]. . .	Dollars. . . .	2,795	4,096	4,577	4,514	4,665	4,891	5,143	5,308
Variable cost	Cents/mile .	7.62	8.40	9.10	9.30	9.20	10.00	10.10	10.80
Gas and oil	Cents/mile .	5.86	5.40	6.00	6.00	5.60	6.00	5.90	6.60
Maintenance.	Cents/mile .	1.12	2.10	2.20	2.40	2.50	2.60	2.80	2.80
Tires	Cents/mile .	0.64	0.90	0.90	0.90	1.10	1.40	1.40	1.40
Fixed cost	Dollars. . . .	(NA)	(NA)	3,667	3,584	3,745	3,891	4,133	4,228
Insurance.	Dollars. . . .	490	675	747	724	697	716	782	809
License and registration	Dollars. . . .	82	165	179	183	204	211	229	220
Depreciation.	Dollars. . . .	1,038	2,357	2,780	2,883	2,988	3,099	3,208	3,268
Finance charge.	Dollars. . . .	423	680	832	696	695	729	778	793

NA Not available.   [1] Beginning 1990, not comparable to previous data.

Source: American Automobile Manufacturers Association Inc., Detroit, MI, *Motor Vehicle Facts and Figures*, annual (copyright).

No. 1049. Domestic Motor Fuel Consumption by Type of Vehicle: 1970 to 1998

[Comprises all fuel types used for propulsion of vehicles under state motor fuels laws. Excludes Federal purchases for military use. Minus sign (-) indicates decrease]

Year	Fuel consumption					Avg. fuel consumption per vehicle (gal.)			Avg. miles per gallon		
	All vehicles (bil. gal.)	Avg. annual percent change [1]	Cars [2] (bil. gal.)	Buses (incl. school buses) (bil. gal.)	Trucks [3] (bil. gal.)	Cars [2]	Buses	Trucks [3]	Cars [2]	Buses (incl. school buses)	Trucks [3]
1970 . .	92.3	5.4	67.7	0.8	11.3	688	2,172	2,467	13.5	5.5	5.5
1975 . .	109.0	2.5	74.1	1.1	14.6	619	2,279	2,722	14.0	5.6	5.6
1980 . .	115.0	-5.9	70.0	1.0	20.0	507	1,926	3,447	16.0	6.0	5.4
1981 . .	114.5	-0.4	69.1	1.1	20.3	496	1,938	3,565	16.4	5.9	5.3
1982 . .	113.4	-0.9	69.1	1.0	20.4	496	1,756	3,647	16.8	5.9	5.5
1983 . .	116.1	2.4	70.3	0.9	20.8	497	1,507	3,769	17.0	5.9	5.6
1984 . .	118.7	2.3	70.6	0.8	21.4	495	1,398	3,967	17.3	5.7	5.7
1985 . .	121.3	2.2	71.5	0.8	21.4	505	1,405	3,570	17.5	5.4	5.8
1986 . .	125.2	3.2	73.2	0.9	21.8	507	1,496	3,821	17.4	5.3	5.8
1987 . .	127.5	1.8	73.3	0.9	22.5	500	1,527	3,937	18.0	5.8	5.9
1988 . .	130.1	2.0	73.3	0.9	22.9	487	1,524	3,736	18.7	5.8	6.0
1989 . .	131.9	1.4	73.9	0.9	23.5	486	1,519	3,776	18.9	6.0	6.1
1990 . .	130.8	-0.8	69.6	0.9	24.5	461	1,428	3,953	20.2	6.4	6.0
1991 . .	128.6	-1.7	64.3	0.9	25.0	443	1,369	4,047	21.1	6.7	6.0
1992 . .	132.9	3.3	65.4	0.9	25.5	455	1,362	4,210	20.9	6.6	6.0
1993 . .	137.3	3.3	67.0	0.9	26.2	462	1,420	4,309	20.5	6.6	6.1
1994 . .	140.8	2.5	67.9	1.0	27.7	462	1,438	4,102	20.7	6.6	6.1
1995 . .	143.8	2.1	68.1	1.0	29.0	530	1,412	4,315	21.1	6.6	6.1
1996 . .	146.7	2.0	68.9	1.0	29.5	531	1,414	4,205	21.3	6.6	6.2
1997 . .	150.3	2.5	69.9	1.0	29.9	538	1,471	4,217	21.5	6.7	6.4
1998 . .	154.9	3.1	72.2	1.0	30.8	548	1,466	4,257	21.4	6.7	6.4

[1] From prior year, except 1970, change from 1965.   [2] Includes taxicabs. The format used to report some vehicle types was changed. In previous years, some other two-axle four-tire vehicles were included in the passenger car category. Other two-axle four-tire vehicles are now separate from the truck category.   [3] Includes combinations.

Source: U.S. Federal Highway Administration, *Highway Statistics Summary to 1985*, and *Highway Statistics*, annual.

No. 1050. Motor Vehicle Travel by Type of Vehicle and by Speed: 1970 to 1998

[Travel in billions of vehicle-miles, except as indicated (1,110 represents 1,110,000,000,000). Travel estimates based on automatic traffic recorder data. Speed trend data for 1970 were collected by several state highway agencies, normally during summer months; beginning Oct. 1975 all states have monitored speeds at locations on several highway systems Monitoring Program]

Year	Vehicle-miles of travel (bil.)				Avg. miles per vehicle (1,000)			Motor vehicle speed on rural interstate				
					Passenger vehicles			Citations recorded (1,000)[2]	Avg. speed (miles per hour)	Percent of vehicles exceeding—		
	Total	Cars[1]	Buses	Trucks	Cars[1]	Buses	Trucks			55 mph	60 mph	65 mph
1970	1,110	917	4.5	186	10.3	12.0	9.9	200	63.8	87	69	44
1980	1,527	1,122	6.1	291	8.8	11.5	10.4	667	57.5	66	25	7
1985	1,775	1,256	4.5	391	9.4	7.5	10.5	8,449	59.5	75	44	17
1986	1,835	1,280	4.7	424	9.5	7.9	10.8	8,549	59.7	76	46	18
1987	1,921	1,325	5.3	457	9.7	8.9	11.1	7,992	59.7	74	46	19
1988	2,026	1,380	5.5	502	10.0	8.9	11.5	7,566	59.5	74	46	19
1989	2,096	1,412	5.7	536	10.2	9.1	11.7	7,488	60.1	77	49	22
1990	2,144	1,418	5.7	575	10.3	9.1	11.9	7,511	60.4	78	50	23
1991	2,172	1,367	5.8	649	10.3	9.1	12.2	7,594	59.9	76	48	21
1992	2,247	1,381	5.8	707	10.6	9.0	12.4	7,004	61.2	81	56	28
1993	2,296	1,385	6.1	746	10.5	9.4	12.4	6,433	60.8	78	51	24
1994	2,358	1,416	6.4	765	10.8	9.6	12.2	(NA)	(NA)	(NA)	(NA)	(NA)
1995	2,423	1,448	6.4	790	11.0	9.3	12.0	(NA)	(NA)	(NA)	(NA)	(NA)
1996	2,486	1,480	6.6	817	11.3	9.4	11.8	(NA)	(NA)	(NA)	(NA)	(NA)
1997	2,560	1,512	6.8	850	11.6	9.8	12.1	(NA)	(NA)	(NA)	(NA)	(NA)
1998	2,625	1,545	6.9	866	11.7	9.7	12.1	(NA)	(NA)	(NA)	(NA)	(NA)

NA Not available. [1] Includes motorcycles. [2] Citations issued for 55 mph violations.

Source: U.S. Federal Highway Administration, *Highway Statistics Summary, annual.*

No. 1051. Passenger Transit Industry—Summary: 1985 to 1998

[Includes Puerto Rico. Includes aggregate information for all transit systems in the United States. Excludes nontransit services such as taxicab, school bus, unregulated jitney, sightseeing bus, intercity bus, and special application mass transportation systems (e.g., amusement parks, airports, island, and urban park ferries are excluded). Includes active vehicles only]

Item	Unit	1985	1990	1995	1996	1997	1998
Operating systems	Number. . .	4,972	5,078	5,973	5,973	5,973	6,000
Motor bus systems	Number. . .	2,631	2,688	2,250	2,250	2,250	2,262
Passenger vehicles, active [1].	Number. . .	94,368	92,961	115,874	122,362	126,360	128,970
Motor bus	Number. . .	64,258	58,714	67,107	71,678	72,770	74,641
Trolley bus.	Number. . .	676	832	885	871	859	880
Heavy rail	Number. . .	9,326	10,419	10,157	10,201	10,242	10,301
Light rail	Number. . .	717	913	999	1,140	1,229	1,205
Commuter rail	Number. . .	4,035	4,415	4,565	4,665	4,943	4,907
Demand response.	Number. . .	14,490	16,471	29,352	30,804	32,509	32,899
Operating funding, total	Mil. dol . . .	12,195	16,053	18,241	19,151	19,515	18,897
Passenger funding	Mil. dol . . .	4,575	5,891	6,801	7,416	7,546	7,717
Other operating funding [2]	Mil. dol . . .	702	895	2,812	2,928	3,308	2,875
Operating assistance	Mil. dol . . .	6,918	9,267	8,628	8,807	8,661	8,305
Federal	Mil. dol . . .	940	970	817	596	647	726
Local [3].	Mil. dol . . .	[4]5,979	5,327	3,981	4,129	4,095	3,820
State [3].	Mil. dol . . .	([4])	2,970	3,830	4,082	3,919	3,759
Total expense	Mil. dol . . .	14,077	17,979	21,540	22,260	23,159	23,715
Operating expense	Mil. dol . . .	12,381	15,742	17,849	18,341	18,936	19,249
Reconciling expense	Mil. dol . . .	1,696	2,237	3,691	3,919	4,223	4,466
Capital expenditure, Federal.	Mil. dol . . .	2,559	2,428	5,534	4,180	4,125	4,225
Capital expenditures	Million. . . .	(NA)	(NA)	7,230	7,084	7,850	7,143
Vehicle-miles operated [1]	Million. . . .	2,791	3,242	3,550	3,650	3,746	3,932
Motor bus	Million. . . .	1,863	2,130	2,184	2,221	2,245	2,291
Trolley bus.	Million. . . .	16	14	14	14	14	14
Heavy rail	Million. . . .	451	537	537	543	558	566
Light rail	Million. . . .	17	24	35	38	41	43
Commuter rail	Million. . . .	183	213	238	242	251	265
Demand response.	Million. . . .	247	306	507	548	585	698
Passengers carried [1]	Million. . . .	8,636	8,799	7,763	7,948	8,374	8,746
Motor bus	Million. . . .	5,675	5,677	4,848	4,887	5,013	5,387
Trolley bus.	Million. . . .	142	126	119	117	121	117
Heavy rail	Million. . . .	2,290	2,346	2,033	2,157	2,430	2,393
Light rail	Million. . . .	132	175	251	261	262	275
Commuter rail	Million. . . .	275	328	344	352	357	382
Demand response.	Million. . . .	59	68	88	93	99	95
Avg. funding per passenger	Cents	53.0	66.9	87.6	93.0	90.1	88.2
Employees, number (avg.) [5]	1,000 . . .	270	273	311	327	334	332
Payroll, employee.	Mil. dol . . .	5,843	7,226	8,213	8,438	8,772	9078
Fringe benefits, employee	Mil. dol . . .	2,868	3,986	4,484	4,401	4,504	4728

NA Not available. [1] Includes other not shown separately. [2] Beginning 1994, includes taxes levied directly by transit agency and other dedicated funds, formerly included in local. [3] Includes other operating revenue, nonoperating revenue, and auxiliary income. [4] For 1985, state and local combined. [5] Through 1992, represents employee equivalents of 2,080 hours = one employee; beginning 1993, equals actual employees.

Source: American Public Transportation Association, Washington, DC, *Public Transportation Fact Book, annual.* <http://www.apta.com/pubs/stats/index.htm>.

[Carriers subject to ICC regulations. See text, this section. Minus sign (-) indicates deficit]

Item	Unit	1980	1985	1989	1990	1991	1992	1993	1994	1995	1996	1997
Carriers reporting [1]	Number.	48	43	20	21	21	21	21	20	20	17	17
Number of employees, average....	1,000 ..	31	24	(NA)	(NA)	(NA)	(NA)	(NA)	(NA)	(NA)	(NA)	(NA)
Compensation of employees......	Mil. dol .	599	518	(NA)	(NA)	(NA)	(NA)	(NA)	(NA)	(NA)	(NA)	(NA)
Operating revenue ...	Mil. dol .	1,397	1,233	1,205	943	980	938	928	870	917	912	1,000
Passenger revenue [2]	Mil. dol .	947	836	890	738	793	755	751	721	770	772	835
Special bus revenue and other ..	Mil. dol .	215	184	165	90	187	183	177	149	147	140	165
Operating expenses	*Mil. dol .*	*1,318*	*1,168*	*1,133*	*1,015*	*967*	*874*	*880*	*919*	*899*	*878*	*948*
Net operating revenue	Mil. dol .	79	65	72	-72	13	64	48	-49	18	33	52
Ordinary income:												
Before income taxes	Mil. dol .	107	65	(NA)	(NA)	(NA)	(NA)	(NA)	(NA)	(NA)	(NA)	(NA)
After income taxes.	Mil. dol .	90	53	12	-180	162	21	14	-67	-9	13	-2
Passenger vehicles in service [2]....	1,000 ..	8.6	8.4	(NA)	(NA)	(NA)	(NA)	(NA)	(NA)	(NA)	(NA)	(NA)
Vehicle-miles, passenger	Million..	781	567	(NA)	(NA)	(NA)	(NA)	(NA)	(NA)	(NA)	(NA)	(NA)
Revenue passengers carried	Million..	134	88	54	43	42	41	40	41	43	37	52
Expense per vehicle-mile	Dollar .	1.69	2.06	(NA)	(NA)	(NA)	(NA)	(NA)	(NA)	(NA)	(NA)	(NA)

NA Not available. [1] Excludes carriers preponderantly in local or suburban service and carriers engaged in transportation of both property and passengers. [2] Regular route intercity and local.

Source: Through 1993, U.S. Interstate Commerce Commission, *Transport Statistics in the United States*, Part 2, annual, thereafter, Bureau of Transportation Statistics, *Selected Earnings Data, Class I Motor Carriers of Passengers.*

No. 1053. Passenger Transportation Arrangement: 1995 to 1997

[In millions of dollars, except percent. Represents SIC 4722]

Source of receipts	1995	1996	1997	Operating expenses	1995	1996	1997
Receipts, total [1] ...	**12,754**	**13,725**	**14,812**	Expenses, total [1]	**11,258**	**12,238**	**13,166**
Air carriers	7,174	7,689	8,332	Payroll, annual	4,745	5,114	5,460
Water carriers	679	653	649	Employer contributions [2].	718	791	802
Hotels and motels	951	1,045	1,151	Lease and rental payments	786	850	898
Motor coaches........	342	421	466	Advertising and promotion	607	697	691
Railroads	122	147	156	Taxes and licenses	160	152	181
Rental cars	335	363	402	Utilities	505	544	553
Package tours	2,539	2,706	2,875	Depreciation.........	393	412	506
Other..............	612	701	781	Office supplies	324	337	370
				Repair services.......	151	161	195
				Other	2,869	3,180	3,510

[1] Receipts for firms primarily engaged in arranging passenger transportation. These estimates exclude receipts of transportation companies (airlines, railroads, etc.). [2] Includes contributions to social security and other supplemental benefits.

Source: U.S. Census Bureau, *Service Annual Survey.*

No. 1054. Motor Freight Transportation and Warehousing Services— Revenues, Expenses, and Payroll: 1995 and 1997

[In millions of dollars (172,727 represents $172,727,000,000)]

Kind of business	SIC [1] code	Operating revenue		Operating expenses		Annual payroll	
		1995	1997	1995	1997	1995	1997
Motor freight transport and warehousing services [2].........	42	172,727	195,979	160,321	181,332	49,373	55,835
Trucking and courier services, except by air [3]	421	161,806	183,153	151,628	170,998	46,478	52,438
Local trucking without storage	4212	43,830	49,972	38,695	43,871	9,885	11,624
Trucking, except local	4213	91,675	103,847	88,061	98,570	26,635	29,594
Local trucking with storage	4214	5,154	5,860	4,817	5,439	1,633	1,801
Courier services, except by air	4215	21,147	23,474	20,055	23,118	8,325	9,419
Public warehousing and storage	422	10,874	12,750	8,652	10,268	2,883	3,376
Farm product warehousing and storage .	4221	749	710	595	576	182	179
Refrigerated warehousing and storage ..	4222	2,107	2,321	1,747	1,884	588	629
General warehousing and storage	4225	6,143	7,457	4,777	5,840	1,613	1,953
Special warehousing and storage [4]	4226	1,875	2,262	1,533	1,968	500	615

[1] Standard Industrial Classification. [2] Includes terminal and joint terminal maintenance facilities for motor carrier transportation (SIC 4231) not shown separately. [3] Excludes private motor carriers that operate as auxiliary establishments to nontransportation companies and independent owner-operators with no paid employees. [4] Includes household goods warehousing.

Source: U.S. Census Bureau, *Current Business Reports, Transportation Annual Survey.*

No. 1055. Bus Profile: 1980 to 1997

Item	Unit	1980	1990	1995	1996	1997
FINANCIAL						
Expenditures, school bus	Mil. dol. .	3,833	7,605	9,082	10,404	10,820
Operating revenues, intercity bus, Class I.	Mil. dol. .	1,397	943	917	912	1,000
Operating expenses, intercity bus, Class I	Mil. dol. .	1,318	1,026	899	878	948
INVENTORY						
Operating companies, intercity bus, Class I.	Number .	61	31	28	27	(NA)
Vehicles:						
Commercial & Federal bus.	Number .	110,576	118,726	125,057	127,214	129,435
School & other bus.	Number .	418,225	508,261	560,447	596,395	568,113
PERFORMANCE						
Vehicle-miles, all buses:						
Rural & urban highway	Millions .	6,059	5,726	6,383	6,563	6,836
Revenue:						
Passenger miles, intercity bus.	Millions .	(NA)	121,400	136,104	139,136	144,923
Passengers, intercity bus.	1,000. . .	370,000	334,000	366,500	347,900	350,600
Avg. miles traveled per vehicle, all buses.	Miles . . .	11,458	9,133	9,312	9,446	9,799
Avg. annual fuel consumption, all buses.	Gallon . .	1,926	1,428	1,412	1,425	1,471
Avg. miles per gallon, all buses	Mpg . . .	6.0	6.4	6.6	6.6	6.7
Average revenue per passenger mile	Cents . .	7.3	11.6	12.2	12.3	12.6
SAFETY						
Fatalities:						
School bus related	Number .	150	115	122	136	128
School bus occupants	Number .	9	11	13	10	10
Other vehicle occupants	Number .	88	64	72	101	95
Nonoccupants	Number .	53	40	37	25	23
Fatalities in vehicular accidents, all buses	Number .	390	340	306	297	(NA)
Occupant fatality rate:						
Per 100 million vehicle-miles, all buses.	Rate . . .	0.8	0.5	0.5	0.4	0.2
Per 10,000 registered vehicles, all buses	Rate . . .	0.9	0.5	0.5	0.4	0.2

NA Not available.

No. 1056. Truck Profile: 1980 to 1997

Item	Unit	1980	1990	1995	1996	1997
FINANCIAL						
Revenues:						
Local intercity.	Mil. dol . . .	(NA)	127,314	161,806	172,743	183,153
Operating expenses, total.	Mil. dol . . .	29,012	118,968	151,628	162,825	170,998
INVENTORY						
Truck registrations, total	1,000	5,791	6,196	6,719	7,013	7,083
Single-unit 2-axle 6-tire vehicle	1,000	4,374	4,487	5,024	5,266	5,293
Combination trucks	1,000	1,417	1,709	1,696	1,747	1,790
PERFORMANCE						
Vehicle miles, total	Millions . . .	108,491	146,242	178,156	182,971	191,345
Rural highway, total.	Millions . . .	68,776	89,692	106,031	109,480	114,562
Urban highway, total	Millions . . .	39,715	56,550	72,125	73,491	76,783
Single unit 2-axle 6-tire vehicle	Millions . . .	39,813	51,901	62,705	64,072	66,845
Combination trucks	Millions . . .	68,678	94,341	115,451	118,899	124,500
Passenger miles:						
Single unit 2-axle 6-tire vehicle	Millions . . .	39,813	51,901	62,705	64,072	66,845
Combination trucks	Millions . . .	68,678	94,341	115,451	118,899	124,500
Average miles traveled per vehicle:						
All trucks, total	Avg. miles .	18,736	23,603	26,514	26,092	27,013
Single unit 2-axle 6-tire vehicle.	Avg. miles .	9,103	11,567	12,482	12,167	12,628
Combination trucks	Avg. miles .	48,472	55,206	68,083	68,075	69,554
Ton-miles, intercity.	Millions . . .	555,000	735,000	921,000	972,000	1,051,000
Fuel consumed, all trucks.	Mil. gal . . .	19,960	24,490	28,993	29,601	29,867
Single unit 2-axle 6-tire vehicle.	Mil. gal . . .	6,923	8,357	9,216	9,409	9,573
Combination trucks	Mil. gal . . .	13,037	16,133	19,777	20,193	20,294
Average fuel consumption per vehicle.	Gallons . . .	3,447	3,953	4,315	4,221	4,217
Single unit 2-axle 6-tire vehicle.	Gallons . . .	1,583	1,862	1,835	1,787	1,808
Combination trucks	Gallons . . .	9,201	9,441	11,663	11,561	11,338
Highway-user taxes, total	Mil. dol . . .	9,888	19,356	25,116	(NA)	(NA)
SAFETY						
Occupant fatalities	Number. . .	8,748	9,306	10,216	10,522	10,941
Light trucks	Number. . .	7,486	8,601	9,568	9,901	10,224
Large trucks.	Number. . .	1,262	705	648	621	717
Vehicle involvement, total (per 100 million vehicle-miles)	Rate	4.5	2.9	2.4	2.4	2.3

NA Not available.

Source of Tables 1055 and 1056: U.S. Bureau of Transportation Statistics, *National Transportation Statistics*, annual.

Transportation—Land   643

No. 1057. Trucks by Use, Body Type, and Annual Miles: 1992 and 1997

[In thousands (59,200.8 represents 59,200,800), except percent change. Minus sign (-) indicates decrease]

Vehicular and operational characteristics	All trucks			Trucks, excluding pickups, panels, vans, sport utilities, and station wagons		
	1992	1997	Percent change 1992-97	1992	1997	Percent change 1992-97
MAJOR USES						
Total.............................	59,200.8	72,800.3	23.0	5,112.4	5,664.7	10.8
Agriculture.........................	3,554.6	3,377.8	-5.0	898.7	854.7	-4.9
Forestry and lumbering	264.5	276.7	4.6	100.6	112.1	11.4
Mining and quarrying..................	220.4	250.7	13.7	79.2	82.1	3.7
Construction	4,986.3	6,033.9	21.0	1,015.4	1,161.8	14.4
Manufacturing	786.7	729.4	-7.3	257.6	258.6	0.4
Wholesale trade.....................	1,136.1	1,264.6	11.3	438.3	440.4	0.5
Retail trade	1,950.9	2,243.8	15.0	434.9	469.3	7.9
For-hire transportation	889.2	1,059.4	19.1	769.6	938.2	21.9
Utilities	541.2	663.8	22.7	183.4	204.9	11.7
Services	3,123.3	4,233.5	35.5	421.2	591.4	40.4
Daily rental	307.6	508.0	65.1	90.6	171.2	89.0
One-way rental......................	17.1	31.2	82.5	14.1	28.3	100.7
Personal transportation	40,441.9	50,934.5	25.9	231.0	183.0	-20.8
Not in use.........................	981.0	1,193.1	21.6	177.8	168.6	-5.2
BODY TYPE						
Pickup	33,659.6	36,191.8	7.5	(X)	(X)	(X)
Minivan...........................	6,129.6	9,837.9	60.5	(X)	(X)	(X)
Panel or van	5,701.0	5,572.7	-2.3	(X)	(X)	(X)
Utility vehicles	7,140.2	13,762.5	92.7	(X)	(X)	(X)
Station wagon	1,457.9	1,770.7	21.5	(X)	(X)	(X)
Multistop or stepvan	408.4	560.4	37.2	408.4	560.4	37.2
Platform with added devices.............	295.7	308.2	4.2	295.7	308.2	4.2
Low boy or depressed center	89.8	111.1	23.7	89.8	111.1	23.7
Basic platform	1,183.3	1,176.1	-0.6	1,183.3	1,176.1	-0.6
Livestock truck......................	48.3	39.1	-19.0	48.3	39.1	-19.0
Insulated nonrefrigerated van	23.3	34.5	48.1	23.3	34.5	48.1
Insulated refrigerated van...............	204.8	234.0	14.3	204.8	234.0	14.3
Drop-frame van	60.1	54.9	-8.7	60.1	54.9	-8.7
Open-top van.......................	20.1	20.8	3.5	20.1	20.8	3.5
Basic enclosed van...................	785.4	1,009.0	28.5	785.4	1,009.0	28.5
Beverage	73.0	70.2	-3.8	73.0	70.2	-3.8
Utility	157.0	152.0	-3.2	157.0	152.0	-3.2
Winch or crane......................	58.8	55.0	-6.5	58.8	55.0	-6.5
Wrecker	104.1	111.9	7.5	104.1	111.9	7.5
Pole or logging......................	53.9	55.7	3.3	53.9	55.7	3.3
Auto transport	22.3	20.1	-9.9	22.3	20.1	-9.9
Service truck	144.1	168.6	17.0	144.1	168.6	17.0
Yard tractor	8.1	10.8	33.3	8.1	10.8	33.3
Oilfield truck	26.5	26.1	-1.5	26.5	26.1	-1.5
Grain body	310.8	299.1	-3.8	310.8	299.1	-3.8
Garbage hauler	72.4	91.6	26.5	72.4	91.6	26.5
Dump truck	611.9	670.8	9.6	611.9	670.8	9.6
Tank truck (liquids or gases).............	231.9	249.4	7.5	231.9	249.4	7.5
Tank truck (dry bulk)	33.8	39.7	17.5	33.8	39.7	17.5
Concrete mixer......................	61.0	73.1	19.8	61.0	73.1	19.8
Other	23.7	22.6	-4.6	23.7	22.6	-4.6
ANNUAL MILES						
Less than 5,000	12,284.3	13,045.1	6.2	1,663.1	1,554.2	-6.5
5,000 to 9,999	12,273.1	13,465.5	9.7	751.9	753.4	0.2
10,000 to 19,999	22,656.5	29,974.6	32.3	978.6	1,128.8	15.3
20,000 to 29,999	7,499.5	10,198.5	36.0	512.6	585.4	14.2
30,000 to 49,999	3,215.3	4,349.9	35.3	458.8	571.1	24.5
50,000 to 74,999	717.0	951.3	32.7	284.9	374.5	31.4
75,000 or more	554.9	815.5	47.0	462.3	697.3	50.8
VEHICLE ACQUISITION						
Purchased new	26,967.2	30,052.9	11.4	2,091.2	2,323.6	11.1
Purchased used.....................	30,417.3	37,834.5	24.4	2,601.1	2,762.6	6.2
Leased from someone else	1,397.1	4,039.3	189.1	373.6	522.2	39.8
Other and not reported	419.1	873.6	108.4	46.5	56.3	21.1

X Not applicable.

Source: U.S. Census Bureau, *Vehicle Inventory and Use Survey, 1997.*

No. 1058. Trucking and Courier Services—Summary: 1990 to 1998

[Represents SIC 421]

Item	1990	1991	1992	1993	1994	1995	1996	1997	1998
OPERATING REVENUE (mil. dol.)									
All carriers:									
Operating revenue, total	127,314	126,772	135,437	142,547	155,713	161,806	172,743	183,153	197,490
Motor carrier	117,122	117,732	127,049	135,000	148,002	153,881	163,786	173,884	187,451
Local trucking	28,017	27,281	31,120	36,649	43,592	48,731	52,301	59,354	66,968
Long-distance trucking	89,105	90,451	95,929	98,351	104,410	105,150	111,485	114,530	120,483
Commodities handled:									
Agricultural and food products	17,103	17,850	19,390	19,518	20,937	21,668	22,546	23,972	23,132
Mining products, unrefined	1,954	1,748	1,890	2,293	2,668	3,116	3,513	3,977	4,123
Building materials	6,269	5,966	7,247	9,044	10,195	10,495	11,051	12,516	14,045
Forestry, wood, and paper prod.	7,261	7,559	8,441	8,518	9,150	8,653	9,064	9,718	10,910
Chemicals and allied products	5,964	6,071	6,350	6,225	6,232	6,131	6,431	6,826	7,548
Petroleum and petroleum prod.	4,126	3,954	3,734	3,704	3,980	3,765	4,029	4,007	4,272
Metals and metal products	10,794	10,697	11,038	11,797	12,648	13,112	13,927	14,646	15,452
Household goods	7,512	7,416	8,144	8,586	9,737	10,893	11,426	12,852	13,637
Other manufactured products	15,320	15,733	17,109	19,710	23,997	25,234	27,191	28,759	28,407
Other goods	40,819	40,738	43,706	45,605	48,458	50,814	54,608	56,611	65,926
Origin and destination of shipments:									
U.S. to U.S.	(NA)	(NA)	(NA)	(NA)	145,489	151,118	160,603	170,420	183,661
U.S. to Canada	(NA)	(NA)	(NA)	(NA)	1,025	1,155	1,303	1,454	1,454
Canada to U.S.	(NA)	(NA)	(NA)	(NA)	588	617	661	669	671
Other	(NA)	(NA)	(NA)	(NA)	900	900	1,219	1,341	1,665
Operating expenses, total	118,968	118,855	127,687	133,857	145,216	151,628	162,825	170,998	179,908
INVENTORIES (est.) (1,000)									
All carriers:									
Trucks, total	230	235	246	264	297	311	332	346	395
Owned	193	197	211	233	267	280	298	301	349
Leased	37	38	(S)	(S)	(S)	(S)	(S)	(S)	(S)

NA Not available.   S Does not meet publication standards.
Source: U.S. Census Bureau, *Transportation Annual Survey* (formerly known as *Motor Freight Transportation and Warehousing Survey*).

No. 1059. Class I Intercity Motor Carriers of Property by Carrier: 1980 to 1993

[Common carriers are carriers offering regular scheduled service. Contract carriers provide service at request of user. Minus sign (-) indicates loss]

Item	Unit	1980	1985	1989	1990	1991	1992	1993
Common carriers, gen. freight reporting	Number...	298	237	192	191	201	208	220
Number of employees, average	1,000	413	376	461	465	474	490	511
Compensation of employees	Mil. dol ...	9,803	10,217	12,854	13,556	14,032	14,967	15,987
Operating revenues	Mil. dol ...	19,725	22,314	27,405	29,682	31,619	34,594	37,600
Operating expenses	Mil. dol ...	18,870	21,037	26,242	28,340	30,269	32,977	35,729
Ordinary income before taxes	Mil. dol ...	701	1,198	988	1,146	1,180	1,453	1,641
Net income	Mil. dol ...	-72	658	659	746	749	878	985
Intercity vehicle-miles	Million	6,547	5,760	6,557	6,804	7,615	8,674	9,770
Intercity revenue freight carried	Mil. ton ...	178	136	145	157	169	196	225
Common carriers, other reporting [1]	Number...	441	397	337	322	295	330	304
Number of employees, average	1,000	101	76	84	87	74	88	83
Compensation of employees	Mil. dol ...	1,931	1,783	2,105	2,236	1,920	2,358	2,333
Operating revenues	Mil. dol ...	8,792	7,962	8,321	9,042	7,761	9,367	9,315
Operating expenses	Mil. dol ...	8,426	7,752	8,081	8,702	7,509	8,942	8,875
Ordinary income before taxes	Mil. dol ...	230	123	117	198	122	309	354
Net income	Mil. dol ...	14	94	88	153	85	221	250
Intercity vehicle-miles	Million	6,889	5,714	6,320	6,566	5,372	6,696	6,295
Intercity revenue freight carried	Mil. ton ...	324	303	278	302	253	298	296
Contract carrier, other [1]	Number...	69	64	77	87	83	113	115
Number of employees, average	1,000	14	22	29	34	34	42	40
Compensation of employees	Mil. dol ...	336	630	893	1,082	989	1,325	1,321
Operating revenues	Mil. dol ...	1,272	1,942	2,946	3,486	3,644	4,501	4,581
Operating expenses	Mil. dol ...	1,207	1,807	2,888	3,422	3,547	4,333	4,367
Ordinary income before taxes	Mil. dol ...	48	103	15	3	53	127	181
Net income	Mil. dol ...	28	69	3	-13	20	80	123
Intercity vehicle-miles	Million	934	1,227	1,826	2,044	2,339	2,933	2,913
Intercity revenue freight carried	Mil. ton ...	37	41	80	80	76	110	99
Carriers of household goods reporting	Number...	28	40	36	36	36	32	31
Number of employees, average	1,000	10	11	12	13	12	12	10
Compensation of employees	Mil. dol ...	157	240	276	296	298	291	252
Operating revenues	Mil. dol ...	1,824	2,684	3,114	3,152	3,026	3,180	3,274
Intercity freight	Mil. dol ...	1,676	2,388	2,703	2,702	2,318	2,787	2,834
Operating expenses	Mil. dol ...	1,781	2,635	3,059	3,129	2,973	3,159	3,198
Ordinary income before taxes	Mil. dol ...	74	79	41	12	27	-1	48
Net income	Mil. dol ...	42	54	28	8	17	8	62
Power units, intercity service	1,000	25	35					
Intercity vehicle-miles	Million	969	1,171	1,229	1,366	1,086	1,136	949
Intercity revenue freight carried	Mil. ton ...	5	7	7	8	7	9	5

[1] Other than general freight.
Source: Through 1992, U.S. Interstate Commerce Commission, Transport Statistics in the United States, Part 2, annual; thereafter, Bureau of Transportation Statistics, *National Transportation Statistics*, annual.

No. 1060. Railroads, Class I—Summary: 1990 to 1998

[As of **Dec. 31**, or **calendar year** data, except as noted. Compiled from annual reports of class I railroads only except where noted. Financial data are not comparable with earlier years due to change in method of accounting for track and related structures. Minus sign (-) indicates deficit]

Item	Unit	1990	1991	1992	1993	1994	1995	1996	1997	1998
Class I line-hauling companies [1]...	Number.	14	14	13	13	13	11	10	9	9
Employees [2]................	1,000 ..	216	206	197	193	190	188	182	178	178
Compensation.............	Mil. dol	8,654	8,695	8,753	8,732	8,874	9,070	9,202	9,235	9,938
Average per hour........	Dollars .	15.8	16.8	17.8	17.9	18.5	19.0	20.1	20.3	21.3
Average per year........	Dollars .	39,987	42,131	44,336	45,354	46,714	48,188	50,611	51,882	55,764
Mileage:										
Railroad line owned [3]........	1,000 ..	146	144	141	140	138	137	136	133	132
Railroad track owned [4]......	1,000 ..	244	242	238	236	232	228	228	225	224
Equipment:										
Locomotives in service......	Number.	18,835	18,344	18,004	18,161	18,505	18,812	19,269	19,684	20,261
Average horsepower.......	1,000 lb	2,665	2,714	2,750	2,777	2,832	2,927	2,985	3,060	3,126
Cars in service:										
Freight train [5]...........	1,000 ..	1,212	1,190	1,173	1,173	1,192	1,219	1,241	1,270	1,316
Freight cars [6]...........	1,000 ..	659	633	605	587	591	583	571	568	576
Income and expenses:										
Operating revenues	Mil. dol.	28,370	27,845	28,349	28,825	30,809	32,279	32,693	33,118	33,151
Operating expenses	Mil. dol.	24,652	28,061	25,325	24,517	25,511	27,897	26,331	27,291	27,916
Net revenue from operations ..	Mil. dol .	3,718	-216	3,024	4,308	5,298	4,383	6,361	5,827	5,235
Income before fixed charges ...	Mil. dol .	4,627	928	4,127	4,990	6,184	5,016	7,055	6,168	5,803
Provision for taxes [7]........	Mil. dol .	1,088	-156	1,092	1,810	1,935	1,556	2,056	1,886	1,573
Ordinary income...........	Mil. dol .	1,961	-91	2,055	2,258	3,315	2,439	3,885	3,156	2,807
Net income	Mil. dol .	1,977	-281	1,800	2,240	3,298	2,324	3,885	3,156	2,807
Net railway operating income ...	Mil. dol .	2,648	-37	1,955	2,517	3,392	2,858	4,338	3,984	3,698
Total taxes [8]............	Mil. dol .	3,780	2,649	3,732	4,343	4,512	4,075	4,669	4,514	4,411
Indus. return on net investment..	Percent.	8.1	1.3	6.3	7.1	9.4	7.0	9.4	7.6	7.0
Gross capital expenditures.....	Mil. dol .	3,591	3,439	3,680	4,504	5,035	5,720	6,550	6,737	7,357
Balance sheet:										
Total property investment......	Mil. dol .	70,348	71,622	72,677	75,217	78,384	86,186	90,046	96,058	102,171
Accrued depreciation and amortization..........	Mil. dol .	22,222	23,057	23,378	23,892	24,200	23,439	23,932	21,862	23,338
Net investment............	Mil. dol .	48,126	48,565	49,299	51,325	54,184	62,746	66,113	74,196	78,832
Shareholder's equity........	Mil. dol .	23,662	22,603	23,115	24,658	27,389	31,419	32,255	34,996	32,976
Net working capital.........	Mil. dol .	-3,505	-3,988	-4,372	-3,295	-3,059	-2,634	-2,942	-3,434	-4,443
Cash dividends	Mil. dol .	2,074	915	830	1,054	1,398	1,518	3,937	995	1,521
AMTRAK passenger traffic:										
Passenger revenue.........	Mil. dol .	941.9	962.3	933.2	777.6	717.9	734.1	756.2	792.1	821.5
Revenue passengers carried ...	1,000 ..	22,382	21,693	21,678	21,511	21,239	20,349	19,700	20,200	21,248
Revenue passenger miles	Million..	6,125	6,249	6,181	6,068	5,869	5,401	5,066	5,166	5,325
Averages:										
Revenue per passenger.....	Dollars .	42.1	44.4	43.0	36.1	33.8	36.1	38.4	39.2	38.7
Revenue per passenger mile..	Cents ..	15.4	15.4	15.1	12.8	12.2	13.6	14.9	15.3	15.4
Trip per passenger	Miles ..	273.7	288.0	285.1	277.7	(NA)	(NA)	(NA)	(NA)	(NA)
Freight service:										
Freight revenue	Mil. dol .	24,471	26,949	27,508	27,991	29,931	31,356	31,889	32,322	32,247
Per ton-mile.............	Cents ..	2.7	2.6	2.6	2.5	2.5	2.4	2.4	2.4	2.3
Per ton originated..........	Dollar .	19.3	19.5	19.7	20.0	20.4	20.2	19.8	20.4	19.6
Revenue-tons originated	Million..	1,425	1,383	1,399	1,397	1,470	1,550	1,611	1,585	1,649
Revenue-tons carried	Million..	2,024	1,987	2,022	2,047	2,185	2,322	2,229	2,114	2,158
Tons carried one mile	Billion ..	1,034	1,039	1,067	1,109	1,201	1,306	1,356	1,349	1,377
Average miles of road operated .	1,000 ..	133	130	126	124	123	125	127	122	120
Revenue ton-miles per mile of road................	1,000 ..	7,763	8,001	8,451	8,965	9,735	10,439	10,704	11,087	11,491
Revenue per ton-mile	Cents ..	3	3	3	3	2	2	2	2	2
Train miles	Million..	380	375	390	405	441	458	469	475	475
Net ton-miles per train-mile [9] ...	Number.	2,755	2,796	2,759	2,759	2,746	2,870	2,912	2,861	2,923
Net ton-miles per loaded car-mile [9]	Number.	69.1	71.6	70.9	71.6	72.2	73.6	75.0	74.0	73.2
Train-miles per train-hour......	Miles ..	23.7	23.7	23.7	23.1	22.4	21.8	22.0	19.2	19.0
Haul per ton, U.S. as a system..	Miles ..	726	751	763	794	817	843	842	851	835
Accident: [10]										
All railroads..............	Number.	26,440	24,662	22,553	20,400	18,038	15,586	13,597	12,830	12,467
Persons killed..........	Number.	1,297	1,194	1,170	1,279	1,226	1,146	1,039	1,063	1,008
Persons injured.........	Number.	25,143	23,468	21,383	19,121	16,812	14,440	12,558	11,767	11,459
Class I railroads...........	Number.	20,450	18,728	17,055	15,058	12,428	10,565	8,735	8,334	8,432
Persons killed..........	Number.	1,166	1,069	1,047	1,124	1,080	994	896	895	900
Persons injured.........	Number.	19,284	17,659	16,008	13,934	11,348	9,571	7,839	7,439	7,532

NA Not available. [1] See text, this section, for definition of Class I. [2] Average midmonth count. [3] Represents the aggregate length of roadway of all line-haul railroads. Excludes yard tracks, sidings, and parallel lines. (Includes estimate for Class II and III railroads). [4] Includes multiple main tracks, yard tracks, and sidings owned by both line-haul and switching and terminal. (Includes estimate for Class II and III railroads). [5] Includes cars owned by all railroads, private car companies, and shippers. [6] Class I railroads only. [7] Includes State income taxes. [8] Includes payroll, income, and other taxes. [9] Revenue and nonrevenue freight. [10] Source: Federal Railroad Admin., *Accident Bulletin*, annual. Includes highway grade crossing casualties.

Source: Except as noted, Association of American Railroads, Washington, DC, *Railroad Facts*, *Statistics of Railroads of Class I*, annual, and *Analysis of Class I Railroads*, annual.

No. 1061. Railroads, Class I-Cars of Revenue Freight Loaded, 1970 to 1999, and by Commodity Group, 1998 and 1999

[In thousands (27,160 represents 27,160,000). Figures are 52-week totals. N.e.c.= Not elsewhere classified]

Year	Carloads Total	Carloads Piggy-back	Commodity group	Carloads 1998	Carloads 1999	Commodity group	Carloads 1998	Carloads 1999
1970	27,160	1,450	Coal	6,927	6,773	Metals and products	641	651
1975	23,217	1,308	Metallic ores	345	291	Stone, clay, and glass products	483	494
1980	22,598	1,661	Chemicals, allied products	1,560	1,603	Crushed stone, gravel, sand	754	813
1985	19,574	2,863	Grain	1,184	1,271	Nonmetalic minerals, n.e.c	497	450
1990	16,177	(NA)	Motor vehicles and equipment	1,212	1,265	Waste and scrap materials	466	468
1993	15,911	(NA)	Pulp, paper, allied products	511	504	Lumber, wood products, n.e.c. [1]	272	287
1994	16,763	(NA)	Primary forest products	311	283	Coke	209	190
1995	16,763	(NA)	Food and kindred prod., n.e.c.	408	426	Petroleum product	283	295
1996	16,521	(NA)	Grain mill products	507	504	All other carloads	344	344
1997	16,568	(NA)						
1998	16,914	(NA)						
1999, prel	16,913	(NA)						

NA Not available. [1] Excludes furniture.

Source: Association of American Railroads, Washington, DC, *Weekly Railroad Traffic*, annual.

No. 1062. Railroads, Class I Line-Haul-Revenue Freight Originated by Commodity Group: 1990 to 1998

[21,401 represents 21,401,000]

Commodity group	1990	1991	1992	1993	1994	1995	1996	1997	1998
Carloads (1,000) [1]	21,401	20,868	21,205	21,683	23,179	23,726	24,159	25,016	25,705
Coal	5,912	5,683	5,572	5,310	5,681	6,095	6,746	6,703	7,027
Farm products	1,689	1,605	1,646	1,636	1,459	1,692	1,530	1,408	1,404
Chemicals, allied products	1,531	1,556	1,568	1,606	1,695	1,642	1,639	1,674	1,653
Food and kindred products	1,307	1,316	1,352	1,380	1,381	1,377	1,302	1,295	1,282
Nonmetallic minerals [2]	1,202	1,075	1,029	1,044	1,138	1,159	1,176	1,160	1,256
Transportation equipment	1,091	1,068	1,181	1,355	1,448	1,473	1,442	1,485	1,671
Lumber and wood products [3]	780	716	726	710	771	719	682	669	645
Pulp, paper, allied products	611	616	618	620	651	628	589	582	547
Petroleum and coal products	573	533	583	584	602	596	567	534	510
Stone, clay, and glass products	539	479	483	487	512	516	491	485	475
Metallic ores	508	499	489	443	440	463	443	327	311
Primary metal products	477	469	481	528	579	575	597	604	644
Waste and scrap materials	439	433	487	558	604	623	605	608	581
Machinery, exc. electrical	39	39	39	37	40	41	40	43	37
Fabricated metal products [4]	31	34	32	37	37	32	29	29	27
Tons (mil.) [1]	1,425	1,383	1,399	1,397	1,470	1,550	1,611	1,585	1,649
Coal	579	560	554	534	574	627	705	705	749
Farm products	147	144	149	147	131	154	142	126	129
Chemicals, allied products	126	127	130	134	142	138	139	140	139
Nonmetallic minerals [2]	109	99	94	96	106	110	113	109	120
Food and kindred products	81	83	86	88	88	91	87	86	87
Lumber and wood products [3]	53	48	50	49	54	51	49	48	47
Metallic ores	47	45	45	41	40	44	42	32	31
Stone, clay, and glass products	44	39	40	40	42	43	42	41	41
Petroleum and coal products	40	37	41	41	43	43	42	39	38
Primary metal products	38	37	39	43	47	47	49	50	53
Pulp, paper, allied products	33	33	34	34	37	36	33	32	31
Waste and scrap materials	28	27	30	35	37	38	38	37	36
Transportation equipment	23	22	25	29	30	30	29	31	36
Machinery, exc. electrical	1	1	1	1	1	1	1	1	1
Fabricated metal products [4]	1	1	1	1	1	1	1	1	1
Gross revenue (mil. dol.) [1]	29,775	29,319	29,777	30,376	32,424	33,782	34,310	34,964	34,898
Coal	6,954	6,903	6,717	6,481	7,021	7,356	7,706	7,698	7,997
Chemicals, allied products	3,933	4,043	4,123	4,277	4,520	4,553	4,660	4,764	4,610
Transportation equipment	3,100	2,633	2,753	3,021	3,257	3,269	3,390	3,462	3,339
Farm products	2,422	2,332	2,454	2,528	2,407	3,020	2,807	2,645	2,529
Food and kindred products	2,188	2,254	2,308	2,336	2,427	2,464	2,378	2,385	2,378
Pulp, paper, allied products	1,486	1,502	1,508	1,511	1,510	1,543	1,485	1,507	1,472
Lumber and wood products [3]	1,390	1,282	1,342	1,324	1,421	1,385	1,409	1,471	1,487
Primary metal products	979	977	970	1,021	1,114	1,199	1,254	1,294	1,304
Stone, clay, and glass products	931	878	911	944	1,009	1,044	1,033	1,063	1,056
Petroleum and coal products	918	888	943	929	967	997	1,013	1,028	991
Nonmetallic minerals [2]	885	824	812	818	862	875	895	899	920
Waste and scrap materials	504	515	558	613	655	685	702	711	693
Metallic ores	408	400	409	385	378	394	382	399	373
Machinery, exc. electrical	67	62	61	59	65	69	70	73	64
Fabricated metal products [4]	42	48	45	50	50	44	41	41	37

[1] Includes commodity groups and small packaged freight shipments, not shown separately. [2] Except fuels. [3] Except furniture. [4] Except ordnance, machinery, and transport.

Source: Association of American Railroads, Washington, DC, *Freight Commodity Statistics*, annual.

U.S. Census Bureau, Statistical Abstract of the United States: 2000

No. 1063. Railroad Freight—Producer Price Indexes: 1990 to 1999

[Dec. 1984=100. Reflects prices for shipping a fixed set of commodities under specified and unchanging conditions]

Commodity	1990	1993	1994	1995	1996	1997	1998	1999
Total railroad freight	107.5	110.9	111.8	111.7	111.5	112.1	113.4	113.0
Coal.	104.2	106.6	107.5	107.3	106.7	107.0	108.7	107.3
Farm products	110.4	113.7	114.5	115.6	115.7	120.4	123.9	121.7
Food products	105.4	109.0	111.0	111.2	108.5	107.6	107.4	99.7
Metallic ores	106.5	106.7	104.6	101.9	103.5	103.4	104.4	103.8
Chemicals or allied products	111.7	116.2	117.6	120.0	119.2	119.6	120.1	119.1
Nonmetallic minerals	111.7	119.3	119.7	119.5	119.2	120.6	121.5	121.7
Wood or lumber products	107.5	109.7	110.0	110.0	112.8	111.0	110.3	109.8
Transportation equipment.	107.5	113.1	115.3	112.8	114.0	113.2	113.4	113.3
Pulp, paper, or allied products.	108.0	112.6	111.1	108.7	(NA)	111.2	113.7	115.5
Primary metal products	113.1	116.3	115.6	115.6	115.4	114.0	116.1	118.4
Clay, concrete, glass, or stone products .	114.1	117.9	120.1	121.4	121.1	119.8	121.8	122.6
Petroleum and coal products	109.2	110.6	114.8	114.3	114.1	120.5	122.5	123.0

NA Not available.

Source: U.S. Bureau of Labor Statistics, Producer Price Indexes, monthly and annual.

No. 1064. Petroleum Pipeline Companies—Characteristics: 1980 to 1998

[173 represents 173,000. Covers pipeline companies operating in interstate commerce and subject to jurisdiction of Federal Energy Regulatory Commission]

Item	Unit	1980	1985	1990	1993	1994	1995	1996	1997	1998
Miles of pipeline, total	1,000.	173	171	168	164	159	177	169	160	157
Gathering lines	1,000.	36	35	32	29	30	35	32	31	21
Trunk lines.	1,000.	136	136	136	135	128	142	137	130	136
Total deliveries	Mil. bbl.	10,600	10,745	11,378	12,219	12,159	12,862	12,635	12,481	12,914
Crude oil	Mil. bbl.	6,405	6,239	6,563	6,708	6,785	6,952	6,975	6,795	7,639
Products	Mil. bbl.	4,195	4,506	4,816	5,511	5,373	5,910	5,660	5,686	5,275
Total trunk line traffic	Bil. bbl-miles.	3,405	3,342	3,500	3,051	3,566	3,619	3,734	3,683	3,475
Crude oil	Bil. bbl-miles.	1,948	1,842	1,891	1,382	1,823	1,899	1,912	1,901	1,747
Products	Bil. bbl-miles.	1,458	1,500	1,609	1,669	1,743	1,720	1,822	1,782	1,696
Carrier property value	Mil. dol.	19,752	21,605	25,828	31,625	26,363	27,460	28,043	30,655	30,181
Operating revenues.	Mil. dol.	6,356	7,461	7,149	6,931	7,281	7,711	7,321	7,215	6,890
Net income	Mil. dol.	1,912	2,431	2,340	1,763	2,148	2,670	2,372	2,255	2,051

Source: PennWell Publishing Co., Houston, Texas, Oil & Gas Journal, annual (copyright).

No. 1065. Major Interstate Natural Gas Pipeline Companies—Summary: 1985 to 1991

[The classification of A and B interstate natural gas pipeline companies changed to major companies and nonmajor companies. Major natural gas pipleline companies are those whose combined sales for resale and natural gas transported or stored for a fee exceed 50 billion cubic feet. They account for more than 85 percent of all interstate natural gas]

Item	Unit	1985	1986	1987	1988	1989	1990	1991
Sales.	Tril. cu. ft . .	11.3	7.8	6.5	6.4	5.6	4.5	3.9
Residential.	Tril. cu. ft . .	0.3	0.2	0.2	0.3	0.1	0.2	0.2
Commercial, industrial	Tril. cu. ft . .	1.1	0.5	0.4	0.5	0.5	0.4	0.3
For resale	Tril. cu. ft . .	9.9	7.1	5.8	5.6	4.9	3.9	3.3
Operating revenues	Mil. dol . . .	49,106	33,859	27,565	27,501	25,695	22,574	21,420
From sales [1]	Mil. dol . . .	44,996	29,508	22,942	22,512	19,786	15,981	14,135
From transportation of gas of others.	Mil. dol . . .	2,272	3,027	3,622	4,059	4,959	5,505	6,117
Other	Mil. dol . . .	1,838	1,325	1,002	929	950	1,088	1,167
Operation, maintenance expenses. . . .	Mil. dol . . .	42,528	27,460	21,794	22,742	20,829	17,446	17,335
Production.	Mil. dol . . .	36,739	22,208	16,955	17,625	15,257	12,124	11,663
Storage.	Mil. dol . . .	418	420	409	436	458	417	460
Transmission	Mil. dol . . .	3,409	2,984	2,598	2,589	2,589	2,720	2,880
Distribution	Mil. dol . . .	132	80	80	127	94	112	133
Administrative, general, and other . .	Mil. dol . . .	1,830	1,768	1,752	1,966	2,430	2,074	2,048
Pipeline mileage.	1,000	230.2	217.3	249.5	246.9	253.2	230.2	249.5
Transmission lines	1,000	189.7	184.6	181.2	191.6	194.1	195.5	146.8
Field lines	1,000	69.6	64.5	62.9	55.5	55.1	54.0	50.7
Storage.	1,000	4.8	4.6	4.3	4.8	4.8	5.0	4.7

[1] Includes other ultimate customers not shown separately.

Source: U.S. Energy Information Administration, Statistics of Interstate Natural Gas Pipeline Companies, annual.

Section 22

Transportation—Air and Water

This section presents data on civil air transportation, both passenger and cargo, and on water transportation, including inland waterways, oceanborne commerce, the merchant marine, cargo and vessel tonnages, and shipbuilding. Comparative data on various types of transportation carriers are presented in Section 21, Land Transportation.

Principal sources of these data are the annual *National Transportation Statistics*, issued by the U.S. Bureau of Transportation Statistics; the *Annual Report* issued by the Air Transport Association of America, Washington, DC; and the annual *Waterborne Commerce of the United States* issued by the Corps of Engineers of the Department of the Army. In addition, the U.S. Census Bureau in its commodity transportation survey (part of the census of transportation, taken every 5 years through 1992, for years ending in "2" and "7") provides data on the type, weight, and value of commodities shipped by manufacturing establishments in the United States, by means of transportation, origin, and destination. See text, Section 17, Business, for a discussion of the 1997 Economic Census. See also Section 32.

Additional sources of data on water transportation include *Merchant Fleets of the World,* issued periodically by the U.S. Maritime Administration; *The Bulletin,* issued monthly by the American Bureau of Shipping, New York, NY; and the annual *World Fleet Statistics* and the *Register Book,* published by Lloyd's Register of Shipping, London, England.

Civil aviation—Federal promotion and regulation of civil aviation have been carried out by the FAA and the Civil Aeronautics Board (CAB). The CAB promoted and regulated the civil air transportation industry within the United States and between the United States and foreign countries.

The Board granted licenses to provide air transportation service, approved or disapproved proposed rates and fares, and approved or disapproved proposed agreements and corporate relationships involving air carriers. In December 1984, the CAB ceased to exist as an agency. Some of its functions were transferred to the Department of Transportation (DOT), as outlined below. The responsibility for investigation of aviation accidents resides with the National Transportation Safety Board.

The Office of the Secretary, DOT aviation activities include: negotiation of international air transportation rights, selection of U.S. air carriers to serve capacity controlled international markets, oversight of international rates and fares, maintenance of essential air service to small communities, and consumer affairs. DOT's Bureau of Transportation Statistics (BTS) handles aviation information functions formerly assigned to CAB. Prior to BTS, the Research and Special Programs Administration handled these functions.

The principal activities of the FAA include: the promotion of air safety; controlling the use of navigable airspace; prescribing regulations dealing with the competency of airmen, airworthiness of aircraft and air traffic control; operation of air route traffic control centers, airport traffic control towers, and flight service stations; the design, construction, maintenance, and inspection of navigation, traffic control, and communications equipment; and the development of general aviation.

The CAB published monthly and quarterly financial and traffic statistical data for the certificated route air carriers. BTS continues these publications, including both certificated and noncertificated (commuter) air carriers. The FAA publishes annually data on the use of airway facilities; data related to the location of airmen, aircraft, and

Transportation—Air and Water 649

airports; the volume of activity in the field of nonair carrier (general aviation) flying; and aircraft production and registration.

General aviation comprises all civil flying (including such commercial operations as small demand air taxis, agriculture application, powerline patrol, etc.) but excludes certificated route air carriers, supplemental operators, large-aircraft commercial operators, and commuter airlines.

Air carriers and service—The CAB previously issued "certificates of public convenience and necessity" under Section 401 of the Federal Aviation Act of 1958 for scheduled and nonscheduled (charter) passenger services and cargo services. It also issued certificates under Section 418 of the Act to cargo air carriers for domestic all-cargo service only. The DOT Office of the Secretary now issues the certificates under a "fit, willing, and able" test of air carrier operations. Carriers operating only a 60-seat-or-less aircraft are given exemption authority to carry passengers, cargo, and mail in scheduled and nonscheduled service under Part 298 of the DOT (formerly CAB) regulations. Exemption authority carriers who offer scheduled passenger service to an essential air service point must meet the "fit, willing, and able" test.

Vessel shipments, entrances, and clearances—Shipments by dry cargo vessels comprise shipments on all types of watercraft, except tanker vessels; shipments by tanker vessels comprise all types of cargo, liquid and dry, carried by tanker vessels.

A vessel is reported as entered only at the first port which it enters in the United States, whether or not cargo is unloaded at that port. A vessel is reported as cleared only at the last port at which clearance is made to a foreign port, whether or not it takes on cargo. Army and Navy vessels entering or clearing without commercial cargo are not included in the figures.

Units of measurement—Cargo (or freight) tonnage and shipping weight both represent the gross weight of the cargo including the weight of containers, wrappings, crates, etc. However, shipping weight excludes lift and cargo vans and similar substantial outer containers. Other tonnage figures generally refer to stowing capacity of vessels, 100 cubic feet being called 1 ton. Gross tonnage comprises the space within the frames and the ceiling of the hull, together with those closed-in spaces above deck available for cargo, stores, passengers, or crew, with certain minor exceptions. Net or registered tonnage is the gross tonnage less the spaces occupied by the propelling machinery, fuel, crew quarters, master's cabin, and navigation spaces. Substantially, it represents space available for cargo and passengers. The net tonnage capacity of a ship may bear little relation to weight of cargo. Deadweight tonnage is the weight in long tons required to depress a vessel from light water line (that is, with only the machinery and equipment on board) to load line. It is, therefore, the weight of the cargo, fuel, etc., which a vessel is designed to carry with safety.

No. 1066. Air and Water Transportation Industries—Summary: 1992 and 1997

[For establishments with payroll. (10,405 represents $10,405,000,000). See Table 865 in Section 17, Business, for more comparative economic census data]

Industry	1987 SIC code [1]	Establishments	Revenue (mil. dol.)	Annual payroll (mil. dol.)	Paid employees [2] (1,000)
1997 ECONOMIC CENSUS DATA					
Air transportation: [3]	45				
1997.........................		11,445	47,387	10,405	362
Water transportation:	44				
1997.........................		9,214	35,179	6,330	179
1992.........................		8,147	29,207	5,170	171
1992 ECONOMIC CENSUS DATA					
Air transportation [4]....................	**45**	(NA)	82,670	24,530	707
Air transportation, including air courier services [4]	451,2	(NA)	76,503	22,734	627
Scheduled and air courier services [4]	451	(NA)	73,070	22,026	604
Scheduled [4]	4512	(NA)	62,057	19,090	505
Air courier services...................	4513	2,639	11,013	2,935	99
Nonscheduled.......................	452	1,791	3,433	708	23
Airport terminal services...................	458	3,252	6,168	1,796	80
Water transportation.....................	**44**	8,147	29,207	5,170	171
Water transportation of freight............	441,2,3,4	836	14,704	1,523	37
Deep sea foreign and domestic freight	441, 2	615	11,948	1,148	27
Other water transportation of freight	443,4	221	2,756	375	10
Great Lakes-St. Lawrence Seaway freight	4432	26	559	81	1
Water transportation of freight, n.e.c. [5]	4449	195	2,197	293	9
Water transportation of passengers	448	1,033	4,133	508	23
Ferries............................	4482	118	155	51	2
Water transportation of passengers, except by ferry	4481,9	915	3,978	457	22
Services incidental to water transportation........	449	6,278	10,370	3,140	111
Marinas............................	4493	3,348	1,651	346	18
Other services incidental to water transportation ..	4491,2,9	2,930	8,719	2,794	93

NA Not available.   [1] 1987 Standard Industrial Classification code; see text, Section 17, Business.   [2] For the pay period including March 12.   [3] Excludes large certificated air passenger carriers which are out of scope for the 1997 Economic Census. Comparable data for 1992 are not available.   [4] Revenue for scheduled air transportation includes revenues for large certificated passenger carriers that was reported to the Office of Airline Statistics, U.S. Dept. of Transportation, as published in *Air Carrier Financial Statistics Quarterly*.   [5] N.e.c. means not elsewhere classified.

Source: U.S. Census Bureau, *Census of Transportation, Communications, and Utilities: 1992*, UC92-A-1 and *1997 Economic Census, Core Business Statistics, Comparative Statistics Series*, EC97X-CS2.

No. 1067. U.S. Scheduled Airline Industry—Summary: 1990 to 1998

[For calendar years or Dec. 31 (465.6 represents 465,600,000). For domestic and international operations. Covers carriers certificated under Section 401 of the Federal Aviation Act. Minus sign (-) indicates loss]

Item	Unit	1990	1992	1993	1994	1995	1996	1997	1998
SCHEDULED SERVICE									
Revenue passengers enplaned .	Mil.	465.6	475.1	488.5	528.8	547.8	581.2	599.1	614.2
Revenue passenger miles.....	Bil......	457.9	478.6	489.7	519.4	540.7	578.7	605.6	619.5
Available seat miles.........	Bil......	733.4	752.8	771.6	784.3	807.1	835.1	860.8	874.2
Revenue passenger load factor .	Percent .	62.4	63.6	63.5	66.2	67.0	69.3	70.3	70.9
Mean passenger trip length [1]..	Miles ...	984	1,007	1,002	982	987	996	1,011	1,009
Freight and express ton miles ..	Mil.	10,546	11,130	11,944	13,792	14,578	15,301	17,959	18,116
Aircraft departures..........	1,000 ...	6,924	7,051	7,245	7,531	8,062	8,230	8,192	8,309
FINANCES									
Total operating revenue [2] ..	**Mil. dol.** ..	**76,142**	**78,140**	**84,559**	**88,313**	**94,578**	**101,938**	**109,568**	**113,346**
Passenger revenue	Mil. dol.	58,453	59,828	63,945	65,422	69,594	75,286	79,471	80,986
Freight and express revenue...	Mil. dol.	5,432	5,916	6,662	7,284	8,616	9,679	10,477	10,651
Mail revenue	Mil. dol.	970	1,184	1,212	1,183	1,266	1,279	1,362	1,690
Charter revenue	Mil. dol.	2,877	2,801	3,082	3,548	3,485	3,447	3,575	3,811
Total operating expense	Mil. dol. .	78,054	80,585	83,121	85,600	88,718	95,729	100,982	104,034
Operating profit...........	Mil. dol. .	-1,912	-2,444	1,438	2,713	5,860	6,209	8,586	9,312
Interest expense	Mil. dol. .	1,978	1,743	2,027	2,347	2,424	1,981	1,733	1,826
Net profit	Mil. dol. .	-3,921	-4,791	-2,136	-344	2,314	2,804	5,170	4,894
Revenue per passenger mile...	Cents...	12.8	12.5	13.1	12.6	12.9	13.0	13.1	13.1
Rate of return on investment...	Percent .	-6.0	-9.3	-0.4	5.2	11.9	11.5	14.7	12.0
Operating profit margin.......	Percent .	-2.5	-3.1	1.7	3.1	6.2	6.1	7.8	8.2
Net profit margin	Percent .	-5.1	-6.1	-2.5	-0.4	2.4	2.8	4.7	4.3
EMPLOYEES [3]									
Total................	1,000 ...	**545.8**	**540.4**	**537.1**	**539.8**	**547.0**	**564.4**	**586.5**	**621.1**
Pilots and copilots...........	1,000 ...	47.1	51.1	52.1	52.9	55.4	57.6	60.4	64.1
Other flight personnel........	1,000 ...	8.9	8.2	8.1	7.7	8.6	8.9	10.7	11.1
Flight attendants	1,000 ...	83.4	86.3	85.0	86.5	86.7	89.1	96.2	97.6
Mechanics	1,000 ...	61.0	58.6	57.5	55.8	50.5	50.8	65.5	69.9
Aircraft and traffic servicing personnel	1,000 ...	251.2	243.1	242.8	247.2	251.1	266.5	269.6	290.1
All other..................	1,000 ...	94.2	93.2	91.7	89.7	94.8	91.6	84.1	88.3

[1] For definition of mean, see Guide to Tabular Presentation.   [2] Includes other types of revenues, not shown separately.   [3] Average number of full time equivalents.

Source: Air Transport Association of America, Washington, DC, *Air Transport*, annual, and *Air Transport, Facts and Figures*, annual.

No. 1068. Airline Cost Indexes: 1980 to 1998

[Covers U.S. major and national service carriers. Major carriers have operating revenues of $1 billion or more; nationals have operating revenues from $75 million to $1 billion]

Index	Index (1982=100)								Percent distribution of total operating expenses [1]			
	1980	1985	1990	1994	1995	1996	1997	1998	1980	1990	1995	1998
Composite index	86.8	102.8	122.6	129.9	131.3	136.6	137.4	134.8	100.0	100.0	100.0	100.0
Labor costs:												
Passenger carriers.	85.8	110.5	121.7	148.7	155.7	159.4	163.0	164.5	35.2	31.6	35.5	35.5
Cargo carriers.	78.3	116.0	148.8	145.4	151.7	159.6	156.0	159.1	27.3	30.0	40.0	31.1
Fuel	89.7	79.6	77.2	54.4	55.3	64.6	62.5	49.4	30.0	17.3	12.0	9.9
Aircraft fleet [2][3]	88.1	123.7	177.0	217.5	222.8	230.3	223.4	228.2	5.2	7.9	9.7	9.2
Interest [2][4]	88.1	98.0	96.0	87.6	93.5	86.9	72.1	67.4	3.2	2.6	3.1	1.8
Insurance	80.4	155.3	68.2	110.8	111.6	111.5	96.0	64.5	0.3	0.3	0.8	0.4
Maintenance material.	104.9	119.9	190.5	157.2	153.4	169.4	191.0	201.2	2.5	3.4	2.8	3.4
Landing fee . . . . . [2]	87.2	99.9	139.0	171.6	176.6	181.5	184.0	177.4	1.7	1.8	2.2	1.9
Traffic commissions [2].	75.4	112.9	169.2	163.3	139.4	130.7	126.9	113.0	4.9	9.4	8.6	6.9
Communication [2] . . . . . [2] . .	65.8	96.6	111.2	118.2	116.0	114.8	110.4	119.0	1.1	1.4	1.6	1.5
Advertising and promotion [2] . .	67.1	96.2	97.8	69.7	63.6	58.4	54.7	59.2	1.6	2.0	1.5	1.4
Passenger food [2]	90.6	98.9	128.4	120.6	110.9	104.0	102.8	105.2	2.9	3.5	3.4	3.2
All other	86.3	111.3	130.6	144.5	147.6	150.4	152.9	154.7	11.8	19.1	22.7	25.8

[1] Total operating expenses plus interest on long term debt, less depreciation and amortization. [2] Passenger airlines only. [3] Includes lease, aircraft and engine rentals, depreciation and amortization. [4] Interest on debt.
Source: Air Transport Association of America, Washington, DC, Air Transport, annual; and unpublished data.

No. 1069. Top 40 Airports in 1998—Passengers Enplaned: 1988 and 1998

[In thousands (421,683 represents 421,683,000), except rank. For calendar year. Airports ranked by total passengers enplaned by large certificated air carriers, 1998]

Airport	1988		1998		Airport	1988		1998	
	Total	Rank	Total	Rank		Total	Rank	Total	Rank
All airports, total. .	421,683	(X)	571,834	(X)	Philadelphia, PA.	6,637	23	10,279	19
Top 40 airports	329,475	(X)	456,887	(X)	Charlotte (Douglas Munici-				
Atlanta (Hartsfield Intl), GA.	21,824	2	34,945	1	pal), NC	6,620	24	10,238	20
Chicago (O'Hare), IL	26,597	1	32,565	2	New York (John F.				
Dallas/Ft. Worth, TX	21,014	3	27,718	3	Kennedy), NY	10,660	9	9,927	21
Los Angeles, CA	18,643	4	22,747	4	Salt Lake City, UT	4,730	26	9,088	22
Denver, CO.	14,442	5	16,837	5	Pittsburgh, PA	8,379	16	8,957	23
San Francisco, CA	13,348	6	16,657	6	Honolulu, HI	8,396	15	8,598	24
Detroit (Wayne County),					Cincinnati, OH	3,543	35	7,770	25
MI	9,214	14	15,110	7	Washington (National), DC .	7,259	19	7,041	26
Phoenix (Sky Harbor Intl),					San Diego, CA.	5,181	25	6,959	27
AZ.	9,455	13	15,034	8	Baltimore, MD	4,370	30	6,828	28
Newark, NJ	10,838	8	14,552	9	Tampa, FL	4,495	28	6,241	29
St. Louis (Lambert-St					Portland, OR	2,823	39	6,180	30
Louis), MO	9,554	11	14,212	10	Cleveland, OH	3,547	34	5,686	31
Las Vegas (McCarran Intl),					Ft. Lauderdale, FL	3,899	32	5,474	32
NV.	6,865	21	14,017	11	Washington (Dulles Intl),				
Minneapolis/St. Paul, MN. .	8,171	17	13,901	12	DC.	4,327	31	5,357	33
Houston (Intercontinental),					Kansas City, MO	4,470	29	5,279	34
TX	6,872	20	13,783	13	Chicago (Midway), IL	3,174	38	5,024	35
Miami, FL	9,462	12	12,469	14	San Jose, CA	2,774	40	4,992	36
Seattle-Tacoma, WA	6,826	22	12,228	15	San Juan PR.	3,264	36	4,411	37
Orlando, FL.	7,473	18	11,862	16	Oakland, CA	1,826	41	4,410	38
Boston (Logan Intl), MA. . .	10,141	10	10,637	17	New Orleans, LA	3,200	37	4,353	39
New York (La Guardia),					Houston (William P.				
NY.	11,322	7	10,338	18	Hobby), TX	3,840	33	4,183	40

X Not applicable.
Source: U.S. Bureau of Transportation Statistics, Office of Airline Information, Airport Activity Statistics of Certificates Route Air Carriers, Calendar Year 1998 and the Federal Aviation Administration, Airport Activity Statistics, 1988.

No. 1070. Domestic Airline Markets: 1998

[In thousands. (3,625 represents 3,625,000). For calendar year. Data are for the 30 top markets and include all commercial airports in each metro area. Data do not include connecting passengers]

Market	Passengers	Market	Passengers
New York to—from Los Angeles	3,625	Honolulu to—from Lihue, Kauai	1,637
New York to—from Chicago	3,069	New York to—from West Palm Beach. . . .	1,560
New York to—from Miami.	2,834	Honolulu to—from Kona, Hawaii	1,467
New York to—from San Francisco	2,683	Chicago to—from Atlanta	1,467
New York to—from Boston	2,651	Los Angeles to—from Oakland	1,459
Honolulu to—from Kahului, Maui	2,541	Chicago to—from Detroit	1,458
New York to—from Orlando	2,521	New York to—from Dallas/Ft. Worth	1,457
New York to—from Atlanta	2,377	Los Angeles to—from Phoenix	1,344
New York to—from Washington	2,372	Boston to—from Washington.	1,340
Dallas/Ft. Worth to—from Houston.	2,213	Los Angeles to—from Honolulu	1,335
Los Angeles to—from Las Vegas	2,055	Chicago to—from Dallas/Ft. Worth	1,329
Los Angeles to—from San Francisco	2,020	Chicago to—from Minneapolis/St. Paul . . .	1,278
New York to—from Ft. Lauderdale	1,808	Los Angeles to—from Seattle	1,246
New York to—from San Juan	1,798	New York to—from Detroit	1,229
Chicago to—from Los Angeles	1,680	Chicago to—from San Francisco	1,193

Source: Air Transport Association of America, Washington, DC, Air Transport 1999.

No. 1071. Worldwide Airline Fatalities: 1987 to 1999

[For scheduled air transport operations]

Year	Fatal accidents	Passenger deaths	Death rate[1]	Death rate[2]	Year	Fatal accidents	Passenger deaths	Death rate[1]	Death rate[2]
1987	25	900	0.09	0.06	1994	27	1,171	0.09	0.06
1988	29	742	0.07	0.04	1995	25	711	0.05	0.03
1989	29	879	0.08	0.05	1996	24	1,146	0.07	0.05
1990	27	544	0.05	0.03	1997	26	929	0.06	0.04
1991	29	638	0.06	0.03	1998	20	904	0.05	0.03
1992	28	1,076	0.09	0.06	1999	20	489	0.03	0.02
1993	33	864	0.07	0.04					

[1] Rate per 100 million passenger miles flown.   [2] Rate per 100 million passenger kilometers flown.

Source: International Civil Aviation Organization, Montreal, Canada, *Civil Aviation Statistics of the World,* annual.

No. 1072. Airline Passenger Screening Results: 1980 to 1998

[Calendar year data (585 represents 585,000,000)]

Item	1980	1985	1990	1995	1996	1997	1998
Persons screened (mil.).	585	993	1,145	1,263	1,497	1,660	1,903
WEAPONS DETECTED							
Firearms, total	1,914	2,913	2,549	2,390	2,155	2,067	1,515
Handguns	1,878	2,823	2,490	2,230	1,999	1,905	1,401
Long guns	36	90	59	160	156	162	114
Other/other dangerous articles	108	74	304	(X)	(X)	(X)	(X)
Explosive/incendiary devices	8	12	15	(X)	(X)	(X)	(X)
Persons arrested:							
Carrying firearms/explosives	1,031	1,310	1,336	1,194	999	924	660
Giving false information	32	42	18	68	131	72	86
Bomb threats received:							
Against airports.	1,179	477	448	346	(X)	(NA)	(NA)
Against aircraft	268	153	338	327	(X)	(NA)	(NA)

NA Not available.   X Not applicable.

Source: U.S. Bureau of Transportation Statistics, *National Transportation Statistics,* 1999, Internet site <http://www.bts.gov/ntda/nts/NTS99/ch3index.html> (accessed 14 August 2000).

No. 1073. Aircraft Accidents: 1982 to 1999

[For years ending December 31]

Item	Unit	1982	1985	1990	1995	1997	1998	1999, prel.
Air carrier accidents, all services [1]	Number. . .	18	21	24	36	49	50	52
Fatal accidents	Number. . .	5	7	6	3	4	1	2
Fatalities	Number. . .	235	526	39	168	8	1	12
Aboard.	Number. . .	223	525	12	162	6	-	11
Rates per 100,000 flight hours:								
Accidents	Rate	0.241	0.241	0.198	0.267	0.309	0.297	0.298
Fatal accidents	Rate	0.057	0.080	0.049	0.022	0.025	0.006	0.011
Commuter air carrier accidents [2]	Number. . .	26	18	15	12	16	8	13
Fatal accidents	Number. . .	5	7	4	2	5	-	5
Fatalities	Number. . .	14	37	7	9	46	-	12
Aboard.	Number. . .	14	36	5	9	46	-	12
Rates per 100,000 flight hours:								
Accidents	Rate	2.000	1.036	0.641	0.457	1.628	2.261	4.833
Fatal accidents	Rate	0.385	0.403	0.171	0.076	0.509	-	1.859
On-demand air taxi accidents [3]	Number. . .	132	157	107	75	82	77	76
Fatal accidents	Number. . .	31	35	29	24	15	18	12
Fatalities	Number. . .	72	76	51	52	39	48	38
Aboard.	Number. . .	72	75	49	52	39	44	38
Rates per 100,000 flight hours:								
Accidents	Rate	4.39	6.11	4.76	4.39	3.64	3.03	2.71
Fatal accidents	Rate	1.03	1.36	1.29	1.41	0.67	0.71	0.43
General aviation accidents [4]	Number. . .	3,233	2,739	2,215	2,053	1,853	1,909	1,908
Fatal accidents	Number. . .	591	498	443	412	353	365	342
Fatalities	Number. . .	1,187	956	767	734	643	623	628
Aboard.	Number. . .	1,170	945	762	727	637	617	622
Rates per 100,000 flight hours:								
Accidents	Rate	10.90	9.66	7.77	8.23	7.28	7.12	7.05
Fatal accidents	Rate	1.99	1.75	1.55	1.64	1.41	1.36	1.26

- Represents zero.   [1] U.S. air carriers operating under 14 CFR 121. Beginning 1997, includes aircraft with 10 or more seats, previously operating under 14 CFR 135.   [2] All scheduled service of U.S. air carriers operating under 14 CFR 135. Beginning 1997, only aircraft with fewer than 10 seats.   [3] All nonscheduled service of U.S. air carriers operating under 14 CFR 135.   [4] U.S. civil registered aircraft not operated under 14 CFR 121 or 135.

Source: U.S. National Transportation Safety Board, Internet site <http://www.ntsb.gov/aviation/stats.htm> (accessed 14 August 2000).

No. 1074. On-Time Flight Arrivals and Departures at Major U.S. Airports: 1999

[In percent. Quarterly, based on gate arrival and departure times for domestic scheduled operations of U.S. major airlines. All U.S. airlines with 1 percent or more of total U.S. domestic scheduled airline passenger revenues are required to report on-time data. A flight is considered on time if it operated less than 15 minutes after the scheduled time shown in the carrier's computerized reservation system. Cancelled and diverted flights are considered late. See source for data on individual airlines]

Airport	On-time arrivals				On-time departures			
	1st. qtr.	2d. qtr.	3d. qtr.	4th. qtr.	1st. qtr.	2d. qtr.	3d. qtr.	4th. qtr.
Total, all airports	**74.81**	**74.26**	**75.47**	**79.81**	**78.41**	**79.62**	**79.80**	**83.08**
Total 29 major airports.	74.09	73.71	74.91	79.59	76.94	78.35	78.15	82.40
Atlanta, Hartsfield International	74.29	73.30	73.89	74.29	77.79	77.48	77.73	80.38
Baltimore/Washington International	75.67	74.58	72.83	78.03	77.07	77.48	75.40	79.07
Boston, Logan International	64.83	70.39	67.58	75.68	72.83	80.14	75.30	82.11
Charlotte Douglas.	75.78	79.11	75.09	83.58	75.28	78.33	73.42	83.19
Chicago, O'Hare	67.86	65.05	73.36	76.44	70.89	71.99	76.84	80.33
Cincinnati International	79.16	78.68	82.57	86.67	82.68	84.02	85.95	89.57
Dallas/Ft. Worth Regional	78.35	72.20	82.66	86.48	76.52	73.44	82.03	86.53
Denver International	80.88	77.10	78.26	84.94	83.28	81.57	82.10	87.60
Detroit, Metro Wayne	74.81	80.59	81.62	85.78	72.51	80.30	79.75	83.61
Houston George Bush.	82.79	75.36	78.81	83.60	84.59	79.49	81.95	86.49
Las Vegas, McCarran International	76.58	76.49	75.03	76.97	77.99	77.91	73.78	75.89
Los Angeles International.	74.30	72.04	72.22	78.39	79.30	79.13	77.15	80.06
Miami International.	74.64	69.17	68.24	77.32	77.56	76.69	74.70	82.34
Minneapolis/St. Paul International	78.95	80.22	81.39	86.22	79.15	82.42	81.78	85.73
Newark International.	67.75	66.81	65.35	69.78	73.82	77.60	73.60	78.68
New York, Kennedy International.	75.34	73.72	74.93	79.18	79.02	84.04	83.15	86.44
New York, LaGuardia	67.94	68.04	65.75	72.61	75.04	79.12	75.32	80.75
Orlando International	76.84	76.03	74.99	79.73	81.38	82.36	82.31	86.06
Philadelphia International.	66.82	67.96	65.11	73.77	66.30	72.93	68.82	77.65
Phoenix, Sky Harbor International	76.65	76.21	73.38	80.28	77.40	76.39	72.80	77.22
Pittsburgh, Greater International	72.31	77.21	73.74	81.61	73.13	78.62	72.92	82.22
Portland International	76.87	77.80	78.69	79.44	84.91	84.48	85.04	84.42
Ronald Reagan International	73.37	75.03	72.78	81.85	78.29	82.80	80.54	87.49
St. Louis, Lambert	75.51	77.85	84.39	85.50	75.73	77.20	82.49	85.64
Salt Lake City International	79.77	81.72	83.09	85.27	84.70	85.96	85.55	86.93
San Diego International, Lindbergh	73.34	74.49	77.46	80.56	79.64	81.38	81.80	81.95
San Francisco International	66.04	70.17	66.09	76.70	75.45	79.94	76.08	81.96
Seattle-Tacoma International	71.35	71.34	71.20	69.17	79.64	78.13	76.27	75.94
Tampa International	74.12	73.13	72.10	76.87	79.21	80.59	80.92	84.97

Source: U.S. Department of Transportation, Office of Consumer Affairs, *Air Travel Consumer Report*, monthly.

No. 1075. Consumer Complaints Against U.S. Airlines: 1990 to 1999

[Calendar year data. See source for data on individual airlines]

Complaint category	1990	1992	1993	1994	1995	1996	1997	1998	1999
Total	**7,703**	**5,639**	**4,438**	**5,179**	**4,629**	**5,782**	**6,394**	**7,980**	**17,381**
Flight problems [1]	3,034	1,624	1,211	1,586	1,133	1,628	1,699	2,270	6,469
Customer service [2]	758	695	599	805	667	999	1,418	1,716	3,664
Ticketing/boarding [3]	624	680	577	598	666	857	904	805	1,328
Disability [4]	(NA)	(NA)	(NA)	(NA)	(NA)	(NA)	(NA)	331	526
Baggage.	1,329	752	627	761	628	882	826	1,105	2,353
Refunds	701	721	482	393	576	521	531	601	940
Oversales [5]	399	265	257	301	263	353	414	387	673
Fares [6]	312	573	398	267	185	180	195	276	584
Advertising	96	54	51	94	66	61	57	39	57
Tours	29	12	16	127	18	16	13	23	28
Smoking	74	25	30	20	15	13	5	(7)	(7)
Credit.	5	10	4	2	4	3	1	(7)	(7)
Other	342	228	186	225	408	269	331	427	759

NA Not available. [1] Cancellations, delays, etc. from schedule. [2] Unhelpful employees, inadequate meals or cabin service, treatment of delayed passengers. [3] Errors in reservations and ticketing; problems in making reservations and obtaining tickets. [4] Prior to 1998, included in ticketing/boarding. [4] All bumping problems, whether or not airline complied with DOT regulations. [5] Incorrect or incomplete information about fares, discount fare conditions, and availability, etc. [7] Included in "Other" beginning 1998.

Source: U.S. Dept. of Transportation, Office of Consumer Affairs, *Air Travel Consumer Report*, monthly.

No. 1076. Commuter/Regional Airline Operations—Summary: 1980 to 1998

[Calendar year data (14.8 represents 14,800,000). Commuter/regional airlines operate primarily aircraft of predominately 75 passengers or less and 18,000 pounds of payload capacity serving short haul and small community markets. Represents operations within all North America by U.S. Regional Carriers. Averages are means. For definition of mean, see Guide to Tabular Presentation]

Item	Unit	1980	1985	1990	1994	1995	1996	1997	1998
Passenger carriers operating	Number	214	179	150	125	124	109	104	97
Passengers enplaned	Millions	14.8	[1]26.0	42.1	57.1	57.2	61.9	66.3	71.1
Average passengers enplaned per carrier	1,000	69.2	152.4	277.5	457.0	461.4	568.3	637.5	733.0
Revenue passenger miles (RPM)	Billions	1.92	[1]4.41	7.61	12.02	12.75	14.22	15.30	17.42
Average RPMs per carrier	Millions	8.97	[1]24.64	50.75	96.15	102.80	130.49	147.09	179.64
Airports served	Number	732	854	811	806	780	782	766	773
Average trip length	Miles	129	173	183	210	223	230	231	245
Passenger aircraft operated	Number	1,339	1,745	1,917	2,172	2,138	2,127	2,104	2,150
Average seating capacity (seats)	Number	13.9	19.2	22.1	23.7	24.6	25.1	25.9	27.7
Fleet flying hours [2]	1,000	1,740	2,854	3,447	4,565	4,659	4,568	4,695	4,631
Average annual utilization per aircraft	Hours	1,299	1,635	1,798	2,102	2,179	2,148	2,231	2,154

[1] Adjusted to exclude a merger in 1986. [2] Prior to 1994, utilization results reflected airborne rather than block hours. Data inclusive of carriers which may have operated during only part of calendar year 1996.

Source: Regional Airline Association and AvStat Associates, Washington, DC, Annual Report of the Regional Airline Industry (copyright).

No. 1077. Civil Flying—Summary: 1970 to 1997

[As of Dec. 31 or for years ending Dec. 31, except as noted (50.5 represents $50,500,000)]

Item	Unit	1970	1980	1985	1990	1995	1996	1997
Airports in operation [1]	Number	11,261	15,161	16,318	17,490	18,224	18,292	18,345
Heliports	Number	790	2,336	3,120	4,085	4,559	4,596	4,626
Private	Number	7,001	10,347	10,457	12,412	13,092	13,163	13,211
Airports with runway lights	Number	3,554	4,738	4,941	4,822	4,838	4,847	4,832
Airports with paved runways [2]	Number	3,805	5,833	6,721	7,694	8,195	8,218	8,248
Airport Improvement Program [2]	Mil. dol.	50.5	639.0	842.1	1,244.7	1,418.1	1,379.9	1,475.9
Total civil aircraft [3]	1,000	154.5	259.4	274.9	275.9	(NA)	(NA)	(NA)
Active aircraft [3]	1,000	134.5	214.8	215.4	218.9	195.5	198.6	200.0
Air carriers, total [4]	1,000	2.8	3.8	4.7	6.7	7.4	7.5	7.6
General aviation aircraft [5]	1,000	131.7	211.0	210.7	212.2	188.1	191.1	192.4
Fixed-wing aircraft: Multi-engine	1,000	18.4	31.7	33.6	32.7	24.6	25.6	26.2
Single-engine	1,000	109.5	168.4	164.4	165.1	137.7	138.1	140.7
Rotorcraft [6]	1,000	2.2	6.0	6.4	7.4	5.8	6.6	6.8
Balloons, blimps, gliders, etc	1,000	1.6	5.0	6.3	7.0	4.7	4.2	4.1
Airman certificates held	1,000	1,002	1,195	1,105	1,195	1,290	1,157	1,157
Pilot [7]	1,000	733	827	710	703	639	622	616
Held by women	Percent	4.0	6.4	6.1	5.8	6.0	5.9	5.8
Airline transport	1,000	34	70	83	108	124	127	131
Commercial	1,000	187	183	152	149	134	129	125
Private	1,000	304	357	311	299	261	254	248
Student	1,000	196	200	147	128	101	95	96
Nonpilot [8]	1,000	269	368	395	492	651	534	541
Ground technicians [9]	1,000	241	321	341	421	574	459	464
FAA employees: Total	Number	53,125	55,340	47,245	51,269	48,324	48,618	49,531
Air traffic control specialists [10]	Number	(NA)	27,190	23,580	24,339	23,208	22,823	22,985
Full performance [11]	Number	(NA)	16,317	11,672	12,985	14,845	15,799	14,630
Developmental [11]	Number	(NA)	4,387	4,304	5,042	2,272	1,999	2,312
Assistants [11]	Number	(X)	(X)	1,465	1,153	355	335	319
Traffic management coordinators [12]	Number	(X)	(X)	(X)	370	561	542	584
Electronic technicians/ATSS [13]	Number	(NA)	8,871	6,856	6,458	6,749	6,927	7,021
Aviation safety inspectors	Number	(NA)	2,038	1,897	2,984	2,991	3,265	3,577
Engineers	Number	(NA)	2,436	2,457	2,745	2,810	2,860	2,860
Other	Number	(NA)	14,805	12,455	14,743	12,566	12,743	13,088
General aviation: [5]								
Hours flown	Million	26.0	41.0	34.1	34.8	26.6	26.9	27.7
Fuel consumed: [14] Gasoline	Mil. gal.	362	520	420	353	287	289	292
Jet fuel [15]	Mil. gal.	415	766	691	663	560	608	642

NA Not available. X Not applicable. [1] Existing airports, heliports, seaplane bases, etc. recorded with FAA. Includes military airports with joint civil and military use. Includes U.S. outlying areas. Airport-type definitions: Public—publicly owned and under control of a public agency; private—owned by a private individual or corporation. May or may not be open for public use. [2] Fiscal year data. Does not include System Planning Grants. Includes U.S. outlying areas. 1970-1980 data are obligated Federal funds for the Airport Development Aid Program. Thereafter, data are appropriated Federal funds under the Airport and Airway Improvement Act of 1982. [3] Registered aircraft that flew 1 or more hours during the year. [4] Includes helicopters. [5] See text, this Section. Beginning 1995, excludes commuters and includes experimental aircraft, not shown separately. Prior to 1995, experimental aircraft were included in the appropriate type. Data beginning 1995 may not be comparable to data for earlier years due to revisions in survey procedures. [6] Includes autogyros; excludes air carrier helicopters. [7] Includes all active pilots. An active pilot is one with a pilot certificate and a valid medical certificate. Also includes pilots who hold a recreational certificate or only a helicopter, glider, or lighter than air certificate, not shown separately. [8] Includes dispatchers, flight navigators and engineers, and ground technicians—mechanics, parachute riggers, and ground and ground instructors. Data for 1996 on mechanics, repairmen, parachute riggers, ground instructors, and dispatchers are limited to those ages 70 years and less. [9] No medical examinations are required, therefore, data represent all certificates on record and include retired or otherwise inactive technicians. See footnote 8. [10] Includes all air traffic control specialists (staff positions, managers, supervisors, and for 1970-1985 traffic management coordinators, not shown separately) and air traffic assistants. [11] Serving in-flight service stations, towers, and centers. [12] Prior to 1990, included in total air traffic control specialists. [13] Airway Transportation Systems Specialists [14] Source: 1970, U.S. Bureau of Mines; thereafter, FAA General Aviation Activity and Avionics Survey. Data for 1996 are estimated using new information on survey nonresponse and so are not strictly comparable to earlier years. [15] Includes kerosene-type and naphtha-type jet fuels.

Source: Except as noted, U.S. Federal Aviation Administration, FAA Statistical Handbook of Aviation, annual, last published in 1993. Internet site <http://www.api.faa.gov/handbook96/toc96.htm>; and unpublished data.

Transportation—Air and Water   655

No. 1078. Net Orders for U.S. Civil Jet Transport Aircraft: 1985 to 1999

[1985 and 1990 are net new firm orders; beginning beginning 1994, net announced orders. Minus sign (-) indicates net cancellations. In 1997 Boeing acquired McDonnell Douglas]

Type of aircraft and customer	1985	1990	1994	1995	1996	1997	1998	1999
Total number [1]	468	670	79	421	595	501	601	346
U.S. customers	242	259	12	138	408	258	392	192
Foreign customers	226	411	67	283	187	243	209	70
McDonnell Douglas MD-11, total	-	52	2	-6	9	11	12	-
U.S. customers	-	16	2	3	1	-	3	-
Foreign customers	-	36	-	-9	8	11	9	-
McDonnell Douglas MD-80/90, total	114	116	1	51	29	-14	26	-20
U.S. customers	37	91	-8	-	18	-11	24	-
Foreign customers	77	25	9	51	11	-3	2	-20
McDonnell Douglas MD-95, total	-	-	-	50	-	-	65	15
U.S. customers	-	-	-	50	-	-	50	-
Foreign customers	-	-	-	-	-	-	15	15
Boeing 737, total	253	189	49	189	349	280	350	258
U.S. customers	146	38	9	85	284	120	207	155
Foreign customers	107	151	40	104	65	160	143	45
Boeing 747, total	37	153	-5	35	66	37	-4	22
U.S. customers	13	24	-1	2	22	15	1	1
Foreign customers	24	129	-4	33	44	22	-5	19
Boeing 757, total	51	66	5	-7	44	45	47	18
U.S. customers	39	33	-1	-6	35	25	34	7
Foreign customers	12	33	6	-1	9	20	13	2
Boeing 767, total	10	60	27	26	10	96	40	32
U.S. customers	4	23	11	4	11	85	31	21
Foreign customers	6	37	16	22	-1	11	9	1
Boeing 777, total	-	34	-	83	88	46	65	21
U.S. customers	-	34	-	-	37	24	42	8
Foreign customers	-	-	-	83	51	22	23	8

- Represents zero. [1] Includes types of aircraft not shown separately. Beginning 1999, includes unidentified customers.

Source: Aerospace Industries Association of America, Washington, DC, Research Center, Statistical Series 23, Internet site <http://www.aia-aerospace.org>.

No. 1079. U.S. Aircraft Shipments: 1980 to 1999

[Value in millions of dollars (18,929 represents $18,929,000,000)]

Year	Total		Civil						Military	
			Large transports		General aviation [1]		Helicopters			
	Units	Value	Units	Value	Units	Value	Units	Value	Units	Value
1980	14,677	18,929	387	9,895	11,877	2,486	1,366	656	1,047	5,892
1985	3,610	27,269	278	8,448	2,029	1,431	384	506	919	16,884
1990	3,321	38,585	521	22,215	1,144	2,007	603	254	1,053	14,109
1994	2,309	36,568	309	18,124	928	2,357	308	185	764	15,902
1995	2,436	33,658	256	15,263	1,077	2,842	292	194	811	15,359
1996	2,235	36,247	269	17,564	1,130	3,127	278	193	558	15,363
1997	2,777	45,883	374	25,810	1,569	4,674	346	231	488	15,168
1998, est.	3,554	55,398	559	35,890	2,213	5,646	363	252	419	13,610
1999, est.	3,976	60,895	620	39,000	2,496	6,895	345	200	515	14,800

[1] Excludes off-the-shelf military aircraft.

Source: U.S. Department of Commerce, International Trade Administration, Internet site <http://www.ita.doc.gov/td/aerospace/inform/information.htm>.

No. 1080. Employment and Earnings in Aircraft Industries: 1985 to 1999

[Annual averages of monthly figures (794 represents 794,000). See headnote, Table 682]

Item	1987 SIC [1] code	Unit	1985	1990	1995	1998	1999
Employment:							
Total	(X)	1,000	794	898	549	616	576
Aircraft	3721	1,000	326	381	244	270	248
Aircraft engines and engine parts	3724	1,000	148	152	93	103	100
Aircraft equipment, n.e.c. [2]	3728	1,000	143	180	114	151	141
Guided missiles, space vehicles, and parts	376	1,000	177	185	98	92	87
Average weekly earnings: [3]	(X)						
Aircraft engines and parts[2]	3724	Dollars	542	637	770	840	871
Aircraft equipment, n.e.c. [2]	3728	Dollars	506	570	677	752	739
Guided missiles, space vehicles, and parts	376	Dollars	515	612	765	840	836
Average hourly earnings: [3]	(X)						
Aircraft, excluding lump sum benefits	3721	Dollars	13.18	15.66	19.97	21.08	21.78
Aircraft with lump sum benefits	3721	Dollars	13.40	16.32	20.02	21.14	21.84
Aircraft engines and parts[2]	3724	Dollars	12.85	14.84	17.34	18.93	19.67
Aircraft equipment, n.e.c. [2]	3728	Dollars	11.66	13.37	15.93	17.06	17.47
Guided missiles, space vehicles, and parts	376	Dollars	12.14	14.39	17.74	19.96	20.24

X Not applicable. [1] 1987 Standard Industrial Classification; see text, Section 17, Business. [2] N.e.c. means not elsewhere classified. [3] For production workers.

Source: U.S. Bureau of Labor Statistics, Employment and Earnings, monthly, June issues and Internet site <http://stats.bls.gov/ceshome.htm>.

No. 1081. Aerospace—Sales, New Orders, and Backlog: 1990 to 1998

[In billions of dollars (136.6 represents $136,600,000,000), except as indicated. Reported by establishments in which the principal business is the development and/or production of aerospace products]

Item	1990	1993	1994	1995	1996	1997	1998
Net sales.	136.6	109.9	104.3	102.8	103.1	114.9	120.7
Percent U.S. Government	53.8	49.9	54.8	49.5	49.8	44.7	36.9
Complete aircraft and parts [1]	49.9	48.9	43.3	42.5	41.8	54.5	62.9
Aircraft engines and parts	16.4	12.2	11.3	12.5	15.7	12.1	12.8
Missiles and space vehicles, parts	22.0	18.1	18.4	18.4	18.5	21.4	20.7
Other products, services	48.3	30.7	31.3	29.4	27.1	27.1	24.3
Net, new orders	146.0	79.7	88.7	109.1	126.3	119.0	111.2
Backlog, Dec. 31	250.1	211.8	192.6	202.6	229.9	219.0	206.7

[1] Except engines sold separately.
Source: U.S. Census Bureau, Current Industrial Reports, Aerospace Industries, Internet site <http://www.census.gov/cir/www/alpha.html> (accessed 15 August 2000).

No. 1082. Aerospace Industry Sales by Product Group and Customer: 1985 to 2000

[In billions of dollars (96.6 represents $96,600,000,000). Due to reporting practices and tabulating methods, figures may differ from those in Table 1081]

Item	Current dollars					Constant (1987) dollars [3]				
	1985	1990	1995	1999 [1]	2000 [2]	1985	1990	1995	1999 [1]	2000 [2]
Total sales.	96.6	134.4	107.8	155.3	149.4	97.8	121.6	85.7	118.3	111.2
PRODUCT GROUP										
Aircraft, total	50.5	71.4	55.0	90.3	83.2	51.1	64.6	43.8	68.8	62.0
Civil [4]	13.7	31.3	24.0	54.5	45.7	13.9	28.3	19.1	41.5	34.1
Military	36.8	40.1	31.1	35.8	37.5	37.2	36.3	24.7	27.3	27.9
Missiles	11.4	14.2	7.4	8.0	8.7	11.6	12.8	5.9	6.1	6.5
Space	18.6	26.4	27.4	31.1	32.6	18.8	23.9	21.8	23.7	24.3
Related products and services [5]	16.1	22.4	18.0	25.9	24.9	16.3	20.3	14.3	19.7	18.5
CUSTOMER GROUP										
Aerospace, total.	80.5	112.0	89.8	129.5	124.5	81.5	101.3	71.5	98.6	92.7
DOD [6]	53.2	60.5	42.4	44.2	46.5	53.9	54.8	33.7	33.6	34.6
NASA [7] and other agencies	6.3	11.1	11.4	11.4	11.6	6.3	10.0	9.1	8.7	8.6
Other customers [8]	21.0	40.4	36.0	73.9	66.4	21.3	36.5	28.6	56.3	49.4
Related products and services [5]	16.1	22.4	18.0	25.9	24.9	16.3	20.3	14.3	19.7	18.5

[1] Preliminary.   [2] Estimate.   [3] Based on AIA's aerospace composite price deflator.   [4] All civil sales of aircraft (domestic and export sales of jet transports, commuters, business, and personal aircraft and helicopters).   [5] Electronics, software, and ground support equipment, plus sales of nonaerospace products which are produced by aerospace-manufacturing use technology, processes, and materials derived from aerospace products.   [6] Department of Defense.   [7] National Aeronautics and Space Administration.   [8] Includes civil aircraft sales (see footnote 4), commercial space sales, all exports of military aircraft and missiles and related propulsion and parts.
Source: Aerospace Industries Association of America, Inc., Washington, DC, 1999 Year-end Review and Forecast, Internet site <http://www.aia-aerospace.org>.

No. 1083. Aerospace Industry—Net Profits After Taxes: 1980 to 1999

[For calendar year (2,588 represents $2,588,000,000). Minus sign (-) indicates loss]

Year	Aerospace industry profits				All manufacturing corporations profits as a percent of—		
	Total (mil. dol.)	As percent of—			Sales	Assets	Equity
		Sales	Assets	Equity			
1980	2,588	4.3	5.2	16.0	4.8	6.9	13.9
1985	3,274	3.1	3.6	11.1	3.8	4.6	10.1
1986	3,093	2.8	3.1	9.4	3.7	4.2	9.5
1987	4,582	4.1	4.4	14.6	4.9	5.6	12.8
1988	4,883	4.3	4.4	14.9	6.0	6.9	16.2
1989	3,866	3.3	3.3	10.7	5.0	5.6	13.7
1990	4,487	3.4	3.4	11.5	4.0	4.3	10.7
1991	[1]2,484	1.8	1.9	6.1	2.5	2.6	6.4
1992	[1]-1,836	-1.4	-1.2	-5.2	1.0	1.0	2.6
1993	4,621	3.6	3.5	13.2	2.8	2.9	8.1
1994	5,655	4.7	4.3	14.8	5.4	5.8	15.6
1995	4,633	3.8	3.5	11.1	5.7	6.2	16.2
1996	7,150	5.6	5.1	17.1	6.0	6.5	16.8
1997	7,221	5.2	4.8	17.3	6.2	6.6	16.6
1998	7,701	5.0	4.8	18.0	6.0	6.1	15.7
1999, prel.	[2]10,800	6.7	6.7	23.8	6.3	6.2	16.8

[1] Reflects unusually large nonoperating expenses totalling $3.4 billion in 1991 and $8.7 billion in 1992 due to the initial implementation of a change in accounting for future retirement benefit costs and defense-downsizing restructuring charges. Many large aerospace corporations chose to write off against first quarter earnings amounts required to comply with FASB 106.   [2] Includes nonoperating income totaling an estimated $5.7 billion.
Source: Aerospace Industries Association of America, Washington, DC, 1999 Year-end Review and Forecast, Internet site <http://www.aia-aerospace.org>.

Transportation—Air and Water   657

No. 1084. United States Total and Aerospace Foreign Trade: 1970 to 1998

[In millions of dollars (3,225 represents $3,225,000,000), except percent. Data are reported as exports of domestic merchandise, including Department of Defense shipments and undocumented exports to Canada, f.a.s. (free alongside ship) basis, and imports for consumption, customs value basis. Minus sign (-) indicates deficit]

Year	Merchandise trade			Aerospace trade						
						Exports				
								Civil		
	Trade balance	Imports	Exports	Trade balance	Imports	Total	Percent of U.S. exports	Total	Trans-ports	Military
1970	3,225	39,952	43,176	3,097	308	3,405	7.9	2,516	1,283	889
1971	-1,476	45,563	44,087	3,830	373	4,203	9.5	3,080	1,567	1,123
1972	-5,729	55,583	49,854	3,230	565	3,795	7.6	2,954	1,119	841
1973	2,390	69,476	71,865	4,360	782	5,142	7.2	3,788	1,664	1,354
1974	-3,884	103,321	99,437	6,350	745	7,095	7.1	5,273	2,655	1,822
1975	9,551	99,305	108,856	7,045	747	7,792	7.2	5,324	2,397	2,468
1976	-7,820	124,614	116,794	7,267	576	7,843	6.7	5,677	2,468	2,166
1977	-28,353	151,534	123,182	6,850	731	7,581	6.2	5,049	1,936	2,532
1978	-30,205	176,052	145,847	9,058	943	10,001	6.9	6,018	2,558	3,983
1979	-23,922	210,285	186,363	10,123	1,624	11,747	6.3	9,772	4,998	1,975
1980	-19,696	245,262	225,566	11,952	3,554	15,506	6.9	13,248	6,727	2,258
1981	-22,267	260,982	238,715	13,134	4,500	17,634	7.4	13,312	7,180	4,322
1982	-27,510	243,952	216,442	11,035	4,568	15,603	7.2	9,608	3,834	5,995
1983	-52,409	258,048	205,639	12,619	3,446	16,065	7.8	10,595	4,683	5,470
1984	-106,703	330,678	223,976	10,082	4,926	15,008	6.7	9,659	3,195	5,350
1985	-117,712	336,526	218,815	12,593	6,132	18,725	8.6	12,942	5,518	5,783
1986	-138,279	365,438	227,159	11,826	7,902	19,728	8.7	14,851	6,276	4,875
1987	-152,119	406,241	254,122	14,575	7,905	22,480	8.8	15,768	6,377	6,714
1988	-118,526	440,952	322,426	17,860	9,087	26,947	8.4	20,298	8,766	6,651
1989	-109,399	473,211	363,812	22,083	10,028	32,111	8.8	25,619	12,313	6,492
1990	-101,718	495,311	393,592	27,282	11,801	39,083	9.9	31,517	16,691	7,566
1991	-66,723	488,453	421,730	30,785	13,003	43,788	10.4	35,548	20,881	8,239
1992	-84,501	532,665	448,164	31,356	13,662	45,018	10.0	36,906	22,379	8,111
1993	-115,568	580,659	465,091	27,235	12,183	39,418	8.5	31,823	18,146	7,596
1994	-150,630	663,256	512,626	25,010	12,363	37,373	7.3	30,050	15,931	7,322
1995	-158,801	743,543	584,742	21,561	11,509	33,071	5.7	25,079	10,606	7,991
1996	-170,214	795,289	625,075	26,602	13,668	40,270	6.4	29,477	13,624	10,792
1997	-181,488	870,671	689,182	32,239	18,134	50,374	7.3	40,075	21,028	10,299
1998	-231,100	913,597	682,497	40,960	23,110	64,071	9.4	51,999	29,168	12,072

Source: Aerospace Industries Association of America, Washington, DC, *Air Transport Facts and Figures*, annual.

No. 1085. International Transportation Transactions of the United States: 1990 to 1999

[In millions of dollars (37,339 represents $37,339,000,000). Data are international transportation transactions recorded for balance of payment purposes (see Table 1307). Receipts include freight on exports carried by U.S.-operated carriers and foreign carrier expenditures in U.S. ports. Payments include freight on imports carried by foreign carriers and U.S. carrier port expenditures abroad. Freight on exports carried by foreign carriers is excluded since such payments are directly or indirectly for foreign account. Similarly, freight on U.S. imports carried by U.S. carriers is a domestic rather than an international transaction. Minus sign (-) indicates excess of payments over receipts]

Item	1990	1992	1993	1994	1995	1996	1997	1998	1999
Total receipts	37,339	38,147	38,486	40,751	44,990	46,496	47,874	45,702	46,809
Ocean passenger fares	154	176	237	287	285	338	296	394	360
Other ocean transportation	12,141	11,328	11,533	12,404	13,581	12,502	12,230	10,930	11,735
Freight	4,326	4,136	4,056	4,506	5,282	4,703	4,571	3,786	3,929
Port expenditures	7,815	7,192	7,477	7,898	8,299	7,799	7,659	7,144	7,806
Air passenger fares [1]	15,144	16,442	16,291	16,710	18,624	20,084	20,572	19,704	19,416
Other air transportation	8,174	8,374	8,568	9,311	10,016	10,928	12,013	12,010	12,439
Freight	2,432	2,589	2,815	3,175	3,654	3,958	4,610	4,757	5,046
Port expenditures	5,742	5,785	5,753	6,136	6,362	6,970	7,403	7,253	7,393
Miscellaneous receipts	1,726	1,827	1,857	2,039	2,484	2,644	2,763	2,664	2,859
Total payments	35,497	34,372	35,934	39,081	41,697	43,212	47,097	50,334	55,542
Ocean passenger fares	248	301	341	353	353	444	358	399	369
Other ocean transportation	13,078	11,781	12,473	13,694	14,068	13,492	14,094	15,582	17,701
Import freight	10,904	9,752	10,462	11,369	11,514	11,259	11,907	13,652	15,727
Port expenditures	2,174	2,029	2,011	2,325	2,554	2,233	2,187	1,930	1,974
Air passenger fares [1]	10,283	10,302	11,069	12,709	14,310	15,365	17,780	19,572	21,036
Other air transportation	9,881	10,468	10,497	10,525	11,061	11,751	12,575	12,559	13,990
Import freight	2,207	2,376	2,580	2,914	3,113	3,201	3,541	3,624	4,138
Port expenditures	7,674	8,092	7,917	7,611	7,948	8,550	9,034	8,935	9,852
Miscellaneous payments	2,007	1,520	1,554	1,800	1,905	2,160	2,290	2,222	2,446
Balance	1,842	3,775	2,552	1,670	3,293	3,284	777	-4,632	-8,733

[1] Includes interairline settlements.

Source: U.S. Bureau of Economic Analysis, *Survey of Current Business*, July 2000; and unpublished data.

No. 1086. Federal Expenditures for Civil Functions of the Corps of Engineers, United States Army: 1970 to 1998

[In millions of dollars (1,128 represents $1,128,000,000). For fiscal years ending in year shown, see text, Section 9, State and Local Government. These expenditures represent the work of the Corps of Engineers to plan, design, construct, operate, and maintain civil works projects and activities, particularly in the management and improvement of rivers, harbors, and waterways for navigation, flood control, and multiple purposes. The amounts listed below do not include the expenditure of funds contributed, advanced, or reimbursed by other government agencies or local interests. Includes Puerto Rico and outlying areas]

Fiscal year	Total program [1]	Navigation	Flood control	Multiple purpose	Fiscal year	Total program [1]	Navigation	Flood control	Multiple purpose
1970	1,128	398	379	331	1991	3,511	1,473	1,447	443
1980	3,061	1,225	1,228	551	1992	3,675	1,562	1,469	469
1985	2,956	1,234	1,187	419	1993	3,335	1,461	1,243	464
1986	3,163	1,345	1,300	402	1994	3,727	1,607	1,436	521
1987	2,937	1,135	1,272	411	1995	3,796	1,620	1,399	598
1988	3,086	1,271	1,271	423	1996	3,627	1,566	1,349	557
1989	3,252	1,395	1,253	462	1997	3,745	1,620	1,430	545
1990	3,297	1,391	1,397	375	1998	4,091	1,660	1,523	618

[1] Includes expenditures which are not associated with a specific purpose (e.g., headquarters staff supervision, management, and administration activities, and some research and development activities).

Source: U.S. Army Corps of Engineers, *Report of Civil Works Expenditures by State and Fiscal Year*, annual.

No. 1087. Freight Carried on Major U.S. Waterways: 1980 to 1998

[In millions of tons (4.0 represents 4,000,000)]

Item	1980	1985	1990	1993	1994	1995	1996	1997	1998
Atlantic intracoastal waterway	4.0	3.1	4.2	3.8	3.7	3.5	4.3	3.6	3.8
Great Lakes.	183.5	148.1	167.1	159.6	175.3	177.7	181.8	188.6	192.2
Gulf intracoastal waterway	94.5	102.5	115.5	114.9	117.6	117.9	118.0	118.1	113.6
Mississippi River system [1]	584.2	527.8	659.6	660.4	693.3	710.1	701.8	707.1	707.4
Mississippi River mainstem	441.5	384.0	475.6	475.1	496.8	520.2	505.6	504.7	503.9
Ohio River system [2]	179.3	203.9	260.0	257.2	270.5	267.6	270.9	274.9	277.9
Columbia River.	49.2	42.4	51.4	51.2	50.9	57.1	51.2	52.7	49.1
Snake River.	5.1	3.5	4.8	5.3	5.9	6.8	5.7	6.1	5.8

[1] Main channels and all tributaries of the Mississippi, Illinois, Missouri and Ohio Rivers. [2] Main channels and all navigable tributaries and embayments of the Ohio, Tennessee, and Cumberland Rivers.

Source: U.S. Army Corps of Engineers, *Waterborne Commerce of the United States,* annual.

No. 1088. Waterborne Commerce, by Type of Commodity: 1990 to 1998

[In millions of short tons (2,163.9 represents 2,163,900,000). Domestic trade includes all commercial movements between United States ports and on inland rivers, Great Lakes, canals, and connecting channels of the United States, Puerto Rico, and Virgin Islands]

Commodity	1990	1995	1997	1998 Total	1998 Domestic	1998 Foreign imports	1998 Foreign exports
Total [1]	2,163.9	2,240.4	2,333.1	2,339.5	1,094.1	840.7	404.7
Coal.	339.9	324.5	326.0	316.1	229.4	12.0	74.7
Petroleum and petroleum products	923.2	907.1	988.2	987.5	382.5	552.1	52.9
Crude petroleum.	485.7	504.6	553.3	539.7	103.2	433.4	3.1
Petroleum products [1]	437.5	402.5	434.9	447.7	279.3	118.7	49.7
Gasoline	116.9	114.4	114.7	109.0	86.8	17.4	4.8
Distillate fuel oil.	77.4	76.7	88.2	94.2	66.3	23.3	4.6
Residual fuel oil.	145.2	111.9	114.4	127.2	82.6	35.3	9.3
Chemicals and related products	123.8	153.7	156.7	156.4	77.7	27.4	51.3
Crude material, inedible [1]	374.7	381.7	400.9	394.3	245.6	95.1	53.6
Forest products, wood and chips	55.7	47.2	44.0	39.1	17.7	4.4	16.9
Pulp and waste paper	11.8	14.9	11.9	11.3	0.2	1.2	10.0
Soil, sand, gravel, rock, and stone	144.2	152.5	167.8	173.1	139.8	27.2	6.0
Primary manufactured goods [1]	76.0	106.3	117.0	141.0	41.2	86.7	13.1
Papers products	10.7	13.1	14.3	13.3	0.9	4.5	7.9
Lime, cement and glass	28.3	33.9	38.4	46.1	16.5	28.0	1.5
Primary iron and steel products	25.1	44.1	48.0	63.5	16.8	45.3	1.5
Food and farm products [1]	267.5	303.2	271.7	265.7	91.5	28.8	145.4
Fish	3.2	3.6	2.1	2.0	0.1	1.2	0.7
Grain [1]	157.3	167.9	131.0	132.3	49.6	1.8	80.9
Corn	96.1	105.0	77.1	78.1	34.4	0.1	43.7
Wheat	44.5	48.5	40.6	41.3	11.3	0.3	29.7
Oilseeds	36.0	46.1	53.4	45.6	23.7	0.3	21.6
Soybeans.	32.2	42.0	48.4	38.6	18.1	(Z)	20.5
Vegetables products	6.7	9.0	8.9	10.4	1.9	2.9	5.5
Processed grain and animal feed.	28.2	33.0	30.8	30.4	8.1	0.9	21.4

Z Rounds to zero. [1] Includes categories not shown separately.

Source: U.S. Army Corps of Engineers, *Waterborne Commerce of the United States,* annual.

U.S. Census Bureau, Statistical Abstract of the United States: 2000

No. 1089. Cargo-Carrying U.S. Flag Fleet by Area of Operation: 1999

[As of July 1. Tons in thousands of metric tons. (68,941 represents 68,941,000). One ton equals 100 cubic feet of space. Represents active vessels]

Area of operation	Total fleet Number	Total fleet Tons	Liquid carriers Number	Liquid carriers Tons	Dry bulk carriers Number	Dry bulk carriers Tons	Containerships Number	Containerships Tons	Other freighters [1] Number	Other freighters [1] Tons
Total.	29,077	68,941	3,496	19,470	21,419	37,908	118	3,265	4,044	8,298
Total commercial fleet	28,891	65,256	3,468	18,586	21,419	37,908	113	3,179	3,891	5,583
Foreign trade	395	7,240	85	2,624	201	1,086	64	2,461	45	1,069
Self-propelled	159	6,393	39	2,353	11	510	64	2,461	45	1,069
Less than 1,000 gross tons.	-	-	-	-	-	-	-	-	-	-
Greater than or equal to 1,000 gross tons	159	6,393	39	2,353	11	510	64	2,461	45	1,069
Non-self-propelled	236	847	46	271	190	576	-	-	-	-
Less than 1,000 gross tons.	197	577	7	1	190	576	-	-	-	-
Greater than or equal to 1,000 gross tons	39	270	39	270	-	-	-	-	-	-
Domestic trade	28,496	58,016	3,383	15,962	21,218	36,822	49	718	3,846	4,514
Coastal (including noncontiguous).	2,596	13,291	574	9,368	537	1,530	49	718	1,436	1,675
Self-propelled	182	6,454	97	5,759	-	-	23	557	62	138
Less than 1,000 gross tons.	73	31	18	12	-	-	-	-	55	19
Greater than or equal to 1,000 gross tons	109	6,423	79	5,747	-	-	23	557	7	119
Non-self-propelled.	2,414	6,837	477	3,609	537	1,530	26	161	1,374	1,537
Less than 1,000 gross tons.	1,701	1,457	86	100	389	675	-	-	1,226	682
Greater than or equal to 1,000 gross tons	713	5,380	391	3,509	148	855	26	161	148	855
Internal waterways	25,709	42,405	2,788	6,500	20,600	33,214	-	-	2,321	2,691
Self-propelled.	26	18	-	-	-	-	-	-	26	18
Less than 1,000 gross tons.	26	18	-	-	-	-	-	-	26	18
Greater than or equal to 1,000 gross tons	-	-	-	-	-	-	-	-	-	-
Non-self-propelled.	25,683	42,387	2,788	6,500	20,600	33,214	-	-	2,295	2,673
Less than 1,000 gross tons.	24,122	37,013	1,527	2,344	20,374	32,269	-	-	2,221	2,400
Greater than or equal to 1,000 gross tons	1,561	5,374	1,261	4,156	226	945	-	-	74	273
Great Lakes	191	2,320	21	94	81	2,078	-	-	89	148
Self-propelled.	62	1,913	4	20	54	1,873	-	-	4	20
Less than 1,000 gross tons.	9	3	2	1	4	2	-	-	3	-
Greater than or equal to 1,000 gross tons	53	1,910	2	19	50	1,871	-	-	1	20
Non-self-propelled.	129	407	17	74	27	205	-	-	85	128
Less than 1,000 gross tons.	101	144	3	4	18	26	-	-	80	114
Greater than or equal to 1,000 gross tons	28	263	14	70	9	179	-	-	5	14
National Defense Reserve Fleet. . .	179	3,427	28	884	-	-	5	86	146	2,457
Ready Reserve Force(RRF). . . .	90	1,892	10	303	-	-	3	50	77	1,539
Other Reserve.	89	1,535	18	581	-	-	2	36	69	918
Other government: Sealift vessels .	7	258	-	-	-	-	-	-	7	258

- Represents or rounds to zero.   [1] Includes general cargo, Ro-Ro, multi-purpose, LASH (Lighter Aboard Ship) vessels, and deck barges; excludes offshore supply vessels.
Source: U.S. Maritime Administration, Office of Statistical & Economic Analysis.

No. 1090. Private Shipyards—Summary: 1980 to 2000

[For calendar year, unless noted. (178.0 represents 178,000)]

Item	Unit	1980	1985	1990	1995	1996	1997	1998	1999	2000 [1]
Employment [2]	1,000. . .	178.0	138.3	130.8	105.0	100.4	98.6	104.4	99.1	98.1
Production workers	1,000. . .	138.8	101.2	93.6	77.8	73.5	70.8	74.9	67.7	67.6
Building activity:										
Merchant vessels: [3]										
Under construction [4] . . .	Number .	69	10	-	3	10	14	12	5	9
Ordered	Number .	7	-	3	8	5	6	1	6	-
Delivered	Number .	23	3	-	1	1	4	5	2	-
Cancelled.	Number .	4	-	-	-	-	4	3	-	-
Under contract [5]	Number .	49	7	3	10	14	12	5	9	9
Naval vessels: [3]										
Under construction [4] . . .	Number .	99	100	95	57	46	46	42	50	44
Ordered	Number .	11	11	7	6	11	4	20	-	2
Delivered	Number .	19	26	15	17	11	8	12	6	-
Under contract [5]	Number .	91	85	87	46	46	42	50	44	46
Unfinished work: [4]										
Commercial ships	Mil. dol. .	2,070	450	-	93.4	365.4	572.1	746.5	594.6	1917.0
Naval ships	Mil. dol. .	7,107	12,091	24,495	20,768	17,734	20,116	19,097	22,385.6	21,589.5

- Represents zero.   [1] As of June 1.   [2] Annual average of monthly data.   [3] Vessels of 1,000 tons or larger.   [4] As of Jan. 1.
[5] As of Dec. 31.
Source: 1980 and 1985, Shipbuilders Council of America, Arlington, VA., unpublished data; beginning 1990, U.S. Maritime Administration, unpublished data.

No. 1091. Employees in Government and Private Shipyards: 1960 to 1999

[In thousands (208 represents 208,000). Annual average employment in establishments primarily engaged in building and repairing of ships, barges, and lighters, whether self-propelled or towed by other craft. Includes all full- and part-time employees]

Year	Total	Private yards	Federal yards	Year	Total	Private yards	Federal yards	Year	Total	Private yards	Federal yards
1960	208	112	96	1990	198	130	68	1995	139	106	33
1970	216	134	83	1991	193	131	62	1996	127	103	24
1975	220	154	66	1992	183	125	58	1997	124	102	22
1980	250	178	72	1993	163	113	50	1998	128	106	22
1985	218	138	80	1994	148	107	41	1999	121	100	21

Source: U.S. Bureau of Labor Statistics, *Employment and Earnings*, monthly, March and June issues; and Internet site <http://stats.bls.gov/ceshome.htm>.

No. 1092. Employment on U.S. Flag Merchant Vessels and Basic Monthly Wage Scale for Able-Bodied Seamen: 1975 to 1999

[Employment in thousands (20.5 represents 20,500)]

Year	Employ-ment [1]	Year	Employ-ment [1]	Year	East coast wage rate [2]	West coast wage rate [2]	Year	East coast wage rate [2]	West coast wage rate [2]
1975	20.5	1994	9.1	1975	612	900	1994	1,790	2,536
1980	19.6	1995	7.9	1980	967	1,414	1995	1,918	2,637
1985	13.1	1996	7.5	1985	1,419	2,029	1996	2,014	2,769
1990	11.1	1997	8.6	1990	1,505	2,218	1997	2,094	2,879
1992	9.2	1998	7.9	1992	1,655	2,438	1998	2,178	2,994
1993	9.3	1999	7.3	1993	1,721	2,438	1999	2,265	3,114

[1] As of June 30, except beginning 1980, as of Sept. 30. Estimates of personnel employed on merchant ships, 1,000 gross tons and over. Excludes vessels on inland waterways, Great Lakes, and those owned by, or operated for, U.S. Army and Navy, and special types such as cable ships, tugs, etc.   [2] As of January. Basic monthly wage, over and above subsistence (board and room); excludes overtime and fringe pay benefits. West coast incorporates extra pay for Saturdays and Sundays at sea into base wages but east coast does not.

Source: U.S. Maritime Administration, *U.S. Merchant Marine Data Sheet*, monthly; and unpublished data.

No. 1093. Worldwide Tanker Casualties: 1980 to 1999

[136 represents 136,000. Data for 1980 covers tankers, ore/oil carriers and bulk/oil vessels of 6,000 deadweight tons and over; beginning 1985, 10,000 deadweight tons and over; excludes liquid gas carriers. Incident is counted in the year it is reported. Based on data from "Lloyd's List" published by Lloyd's of London. "Casualties" include weather damage, strandings, collisions and other contact, fires and explosions, machinery damage, and other mishaps]

Item	Unit	1980	1985	1990	1993	1994	1995	1996	1997	1998	1999
Casualties	Number	(NA)	340	541	314	270	280	241	270	201	231
Total losses [1]	Number	15	12	10	9	11	6	2	9	2	2
Deaths	Number	132	53	119	26	88	8	15	(NA)	(NA)	(NA)
Oil spills	Number	32	9	31	24	29	18	24	22	22	14
Amount	1,000 tons	136	80	61	120	110	4	72	50	9	36
Amount	Mil. gallons	42	25	19	37	33	1	22	15	3	11

NA Not available.   [1] Excludes losses due to hostilities.

Source: Tanker Advisory Center, Inc., New York, NY, "Worldwide Tanker Casualty Returns," quarterly.

No. 1094. Merchant Vessels—World and United States: 1970 to 1996

[20,980 represents 20,980,000. Through 1992, as of mid-year; thereafter for year-end. For propelled sea-going merchant ships of not less than 100 gross tonnage]

Year	World completed Number	World completed Gross tonnage (1,000)	World owned Number	World owned Gross tonnage (1,000)	U.S. completed Number	U.S. completed Gross tonnage (1,000)	U.S. registered Number	U.S. registered Gross tonnage (1,000)
1970	2,814	20,980	52,444	227,490	156	375	2,983	18,463
1980	2,412	13,101	73,832	419,911	205	555	5,579	18,464
1985	1,964	18,157	76,395	416,269	66	180	6,447	19,518
1990	1,672	15,885	78,336	423,627	16	15	6,348	21,328
1992	1,506	18,633	79,845	444,305	27	54	5,737	18,228
1993	1,505	20,025	80,655	457,915	30	14	5,646	14,087
1994	1,789	19,612	80,676	475,859	28	29	5,270	13,655
1995	1,856	22,565	82,890	490,662	30	14	5,292	12,760
1996	1,745	25,881	84,264	507,873	29	24	5,289	12,024

Source: Through 1992, Lloyd's Register of Shipping, London, England, *Statistical Tables*, annual; and *Annual Summary of Merchant Ships Completed in the World*; thereafter, *World Fleet Statistics*, annual.

No. 1095. Merchant Vessels—Ships and Tonnage Lost Worldwide: 1980 to 1996

[For merchant vessels of 100 gross tonnage and above (1,791 represents 1,791,000). Excludes ships which have been declared constructive losses but have undergone repair during the year. Loss counted in the year the casualty occurred, providing that information was available at time of relevant publication]

Type of ship	Ships lost					Gross tonnage lost (1,000)				
	1980	1990	1994	1995	1996	1980	1990	1994	1995	1996
Total	363	160	171	190	151	1,791	1,047	1,532	1,055	836
Tankers	24	8	16	12	12	707	138	638	172	179
Ore/bulk carriers [1]	21	15	19	19	18	458	687	590	447	303
General cargo	211	87	76	88	77	478	202	237	218	240
Container ships	2	-	-	-	6	6	-	-	-	94
Passenger [2]	9	-	2	1	-	112	-	26	185	-
Fishing	96	50	58	70	38	30	20	41	33	20

- Represents zero. [1] Includes ore/bulk/oil carriers. [2] Includes passenger cargo/ships.

Source: Lloyd's Register of Shipping, London, England, *Casualty Return,* annual.

No. 1096. Merchant Fleets of the World: 1999

[**Vessels of 1,000 gross tons and over.** As of **Oct. 1.** Specified countries have 100 or more ships]

Country of registry, 1999	Total	Tanker	Dry bulk [1]	Container-ship	Roll-on/roll-off	Cruise/passenger	Other [2]
World total, 1999	28,202	6,953	5,709	2,442	1,478	284	11,336
United States	469	158	14	92	58	11	136
Privately-owned	283	130	14	87	26	1	25
Government-owned	186	28	-	5	32	10	111
Foreign total	27,733	6,795	5,695	2,350	1,420	273	11,200
Panama	4,616	1,033	1,361	489	264	46	1,423
Liberia	1,657	682	438	209	58	37	233
Russia	1,496	274	104	24	9	8	1,077
China	1,449	251	336	91	15	4	752
Malta	1,425	382	401	50	62	3	527
Cyprus	1,385	173	469	125	29	9	580
Bahamas	1,031	245	159	52	64	59	452
Singapore	880	399	139	161	38	-	143
Saint Vincent	813	97	144	31	35	4	502
Greece	693	272	266	41	20	15	79
Japan	661	273	162	26	118	6	76
Norway (NIS) [3]	657	305	102	5	72	11	162
Turkey	537	84	167	20	19	3	244
Philippines	501	67	189	10	41	1	193
Indonesia	488	120	25	14	13	-	316
Antigua & Barbuda	464	11	16	125	20	-	292
Netherlands	450	62	5	44	14	7	318
Germany	447	17	-	245	15	2	168
Belize	438	71	25	6	3	-	333
Korea (South)	432	110	96	47	8	3	168
Italy	375	203	37	19	68	6	42
Malaysia	356	111	59	49	9	2	126
Denmark (DIS) [3]	311	68	11	62	10	-	160
India	295	99	125	6	-	-	65
Thailand	294	97	35	12	-	1	149
Ukraine	247	16	8	5	10	6	202
Honduras	241	32	15	5	5	1	183
Hong Kong	218	19	117	44	3	-	35
Cambodia	201	-	19	1	5	-	176
Taiwan	179	17	53	73	1	-	35
Sweden	177	64	8	-	62	-	43
Brazil	159	75	41	6	9	-	28
Isle of Man	148	73	20	18	16	-	21
United Kingdom	147	52	4	32	21	9	29
Romania	145	6	16	2	6	-	115
Syria	128	-	4	-	1	-	123
Norway	126	41	7	-	11	-	67
Marshall Islands	124	47	46	21	3	-	7
Iran	123	24	44	3	2	-	50
Vietnam	118	13	9	1	1	-	94
Egypt	111	15	22	1	9	1	63
Portugal (MAR) [3]	109	25	9	1	10	-	64
Netherlands Antillies & Aruba	103	10	-	15	3	1	74
Bermuda	101	30	23	19	11	-	18
All other	2,677	730	359	140	227	28	1,193

- Represents zero. [1] Includes bulk/oil, ore/oil, and ore/bulk/oil carriers. [2] Breakbulk ships, partial containerships, refrigerated cargo ships, barge and specialized cargo ships. [3] International Shipping Registry which is an open registry under which the ship flies the flag of the specified nation but is exempt from certain taxation and other regulations.

Source: U.S. Maritime Administration, *Merchant Fleets of the World,* summary report, annual; and unpublished data.

This section presents statistics on farms and farm operators; land use; farm income, expenditures, and debt; farm output, productivity, and marketings; foreign trade in agricultural products; specific crops; and livestock, poultry, and their products.

The principal sources are the reports issued by the National Agricultural Statistics Service (NASS) and the Economic Research Service (ERS) of the U.S. Department of Agriculture. The information from the 1997 Census of Agriculture is available in printed form in the Volume 1, Geographic Area Series; in electronic format on CD-ROM; and on the Internet site <http://www.nass.usda.gov/census/>. The Department of Agriculture publishes annually *Agricultural Statistics*, a general reference book on agricultural production, supplies, consumption, facilities, costs, and returns. The Economic Research Service publishes data on farm assets, debt, and income on the Internet site <http://www.ers.usda.gov/briefing/fbe/>. Sources of current data on agricultural exports and imports include *Foreign Agricultural Trade of the United States*, published by the ERS, and the reports of the U.S. Census Bureau, particularly *U.S. Imports of Merchandise on CD-ROM*, and *U.S. Exports of Merchandise on CD-ROM*.

The 45 field offices of the NASS collect data on crops, livestock and products, agricultural prices, farm employment, and other related subjects mainly through sample surveys. Information is obtained on some 75 crops and 50 livestock items as well as scores of items pertaining to agricultural production and marketing. State estimates and supporting information are sent to the Agricultural Statistics Board of NASS which reviews the estimates and issues reports containing state and national data. Among these reports are annual summaries such as *Crop Production, Crop*

Values, Agricultural Prices, and *Livestock Production, Disposition and Income.* For more information about concepts and methods underlying USDA's statistical series, see *Major Statistical Series of the U.S. Department of Agriculture* (Agricultural Handbook No. 671), a 12-volume set of publications.

Farms and farmland—The definitions of a farm have varied through time. Since 1850, when minimum criteria defining a farm for census purposes first were established, the farm definition has been changed nine times. The current definition, first used for the 1974 census, is any place from which $1,000 or more of agricultural products were produced and sold, or normally would have been sold, during the census year.

Acreage designated as "land in farms" consists primarily of agricultural land used for crops, pasture, or grazing. It also includes woodland and wasteland not actually under cultivation or used for pasture or grazing, provided it was part of the farm operator's total operation. Land in farms includes acres set aside under annual commodity acreage programs as well as acres in the Conservation Reserve and Wetlands Reserve Programs for places meeting the farm definition. Land in farms is an operating unit concept and includes land owned and operated as well as land rented from others. All grazing land, except land used under government permits on a per-head basis, was included as "land in farms" provided it was part of a farm or ranch.

Since 1945, an evaluation of census coverage has been conducted for each census of agriculture to provide estimates of the completeness of census farm counts. According to coverage evaluation results, the past five censuses of agriculture included an average of 92 percent of U.S. farms and

98 percent of agriculture production. The 1997 coverage evaluation program was designed to measure four components of error in the census farm counts. These components include undercount due to farms not on the mail list; overcount due to farms duplicated or enumerated more than once; undercount due to farms incorrectly classified as nonfarms; and overcount due to nonfarms incorrectly classified as farms. The first component, mail list undercount, is by far the largest component of coverage error. The percentage of farms missed in the census varies considerably by state. In general, farms not on the mail list tended to be small in acreage, production, and sales of agricultural products. For more explanation about mail list compilation and census coverage, see Appendixes A and C, *1997 Census of Agriculture*, Volume 1, reports.

Farm income—The final agricultural sector output comprises cash receipts from farm marketings of crops and livestock, Federal government payments made directly to farmers for farm-related activities, rental value of farm homes, value of farm products consumed in farm homes, and other farm-related income such as machine hire and custom work. Farm marketings represent quantities of agricultural products sold by farmers multiplied by prices received per unit of production at the local market. Information on prices received for farm products is generally obtained by the NASS Agricultural Statistics Board from surveys of firms (such as grain elevators, packers, and processors) purchasing agricultural commodities directly from producers. In some cases, the price information is obtained directly from the producers.

Crops—Estimates of crop acreage and production by the NASS are based on

current sample survey data obtained from individual producers and objective yield counts, reports of carlot shipments, market records, personal field observations by field statisticians, and reports from other sources. Prices received by farmers are marketing year averages. These averages are based on U.S. monthly prices weighted by monthly marketings during specific periods. U.S. monthly prices are state average prices weighted by marketings during the month. Marketing year average prices do not include allowances for outstanding loans, government purchases, deficiency payments or disaster payments.

All state prices are based on individual state marketing years, while U.S. marketing year averages are based on standard marketing years for each crop. For a listing of the crop marketing years and the participating states in the monthly program, see *Crop Values*. Value of production is computed by multiplying state prices by each state's production. The U.S. value of production is the sum of state values for all states. Value of production figures shown in Tables 1126-1129, 1133, and 1134 should not be confused with cash receipts from farm marketings which relate to sales during a calendar year, irrespective of the year of production.

Livestock—Annual inventory numbers of livestock and estimates of livestock, dairy, and poultry production prepared by the Department of Agriculture are based on information from farmers and ranchers obtained by probability survey sampling methods.

Statistical reliability—For a discussion of statistical collection and estimation, sampling procedures, and measures of statistical reliability pertaining to Department of Agriculture data, see Appendix III.

No. 1097. Farms—Number and Acreage by Size of Farm: 1987 to 1997

[2,088 represents 2,088,000]

Size of farm	Number of farms (1,000)			Land in farms (mil. acres)			Cropland harvested (mil. acres)			Percent distribution, 1997		
	1987	1992	1997	1987	1992	1997	1987	1992	1997	Num- ber of farms	All land in farms	Crop- land har- vested
Total	2,088	1,925	1,912	964.5	945.5	931.8	282.2	295.9	309.4	100.0	100.0	100.0
Under 10 acres......	183	166	154	0.7	0.7	0.6	0.2	0.2	0.2	8.1	0.1	0.1
10 to 49 acres	412	388	411	11.1	10.3	11.0	3.9	3.5	3.6	21.5	1.2	1.2
50 to 99 acres	311	283	295	22.5	20.4	21.2	7.9	7.2	7.0	15.4	2.3	2.3
100 to 179 acres.....	334	301	298	45.3	40.7	40.2	17.1	15.4	14.3	15.6	4.3	4.6
180 to 259 acres.....	192	172	165	41.5	37.2	35.5	17.2	15.5	14.0	8.6	3.8	4.5
260 to 499 acres.....	286	255	238	103.0	91.7	85.4	47.3	43.6	39.3	12.4	9.2	12.7
500 to 999 acres.....	200	186	176	138.5	129.3	122.1	67.4	68.6	65.4	9.2	13.1	21.1
1,000 to 1,999 acres ..	102	102	101	138.8	139.0	138.8	61.1	69.3	73.8	5.3	14.9	23.9
2,000 acres and over..	67	71	75	463.2	476.3	476.9	60.2	72.5	91.8	3.9	51.2	29.7

No. 1098. Farms—Number and Acreage by Tenure of Operator: 1987 to 1997

[2,088 represents 2,088,000. *Full owners* own all the land they operate. *Part owners* own a part and rent from others the rest of the land they operate]

Item and year	Unit					Percent distribution			
		Total	Full owner	Part owner	Tenant	Total	Full owner	Part owner	Tenant
NUMBER OF FARMS									
1987	1,000....	2,088	1,239	609	240	100.0	59.3	29.2	11.5
1992	1,000....	1,925	1,112	597	217	100.0	57.7	31.0	11.3
1997	1,000....	1,912	1,147	574	191	100.0	60.0	30.0	10.0
Under 50 acres	1,000....	564	460	57	48	100.0	81.6	10.1	8.5
50 to 179 acres	1,000....	593	409	131	53	100.0	69.0	22.1	8.9
180 to 499 acres	1,000....	403	189	169	45	100.0	46.9	41.9	11.2
500 to 999 acres	1,000....	176	50	103	23	100.0	28.4	58.5	13.0
1,000 acres or more	1,000....	176	40	114	22	100.0	22.7	64.8	12.5
LAND IN FARMS									
1987	Mil. acres.	964	318	520	127	100.0	32.9	53.9	13.2
1992	Mil. acres.	946	296	527	123	100.0	31.3	55.7	13.0
1997	Mil. acres.	932	316	508	108	100.0	33.9	54.5	11.6

No. 1099. Farm Operators—Tenure and Characteristics: 1992 and 1997

[In thousands, except as indicated (1,925 represents 1,925,000)]

Characteristic	All farms		Farms with sales of $10,000 and over		Characteristic	All farms		Farms with sales of $10,000 and over	
	1992	1997	1992	1997		1992	1997	1992	1997
Total operators	1,925	1,912	1,019	949	Full owner	1,112	1,147	422	404
					Part owner	597	574	448	419
White	1,882	1,865	1,003	932	Tenant.................	217	191	148	126
Black................	19	18	5	4	Principal occupation:				
American Indian, Eskimo,					Farming	1,053	962	754	675
and Aleut	8	10	3	4	Other...............	872	950	265	274
Asian or Pacific Islander....	8	9	5	5	Place of residence: [2]				
Other	8	10	3	3	On farm operated.......	1,379	1,362	736	681
Operators of Hispanic					Not on farm operated	409	413	215	201
origin [1].............	21	28	8	11	Years on present farm: [2]				
					2 years or less........	95	93	41	35
Female	145	165	50	52	3 to 4 years	133	127	58	46
Under 25 years old	28	21	17	12	5 to 9 years	259	264	121	109
25 to 34 years old.......	179	128	112	72	10 years or more	1,113	1,114	648	616
35 to 44 years old.......	382	371	217	200	Days worked off farm: [2]				
45 to 54 years old.......	429	467	223	232	None	802	755	536	476
55 to 64 years old.......	430	427	229	212	Less than 100 days	165	165	104	98
65 years old and over	478	497	220	222	100 to 199 days.......	162	168	76	76
Average age (years)	53.3	54.3	51.9	53.2	200 days or more.......	666	709	226	229

[1] Operators of Hispanic origin may be of any race.   [2] Excludes not reported.

Source of Tables 1097-1099: U.S. Dept. of Agriculture, National Agricultural Statistics Service, *Census of Agriculture: 1992*, Vol. 1; and *1997*, Vol. 1.

Agriculture   665

No. 1100. Farms—Number, Acreage, and Value by Type of Organization: 1992 and 1997

[1,925 represents 1,925,000]

Item	Unit	Total [1]	Indi-vidual or family	Partner-ship	Corpo-ration	Total [1]	Indi-vidual or family	Partner-ship	Corpo-ration
						Percent distribution			
ALL FARMS									
Number of farms:									
1992	1,000 ...	1,925	1,653	187	73	100.0	85.9	9.7	3.8
1997	1,000 ...	1,912	1,643	169	84	100.0	85.9	8.8	4.4
Land in farms:									
1992	Mil. acres.	946	604	153	123	100.0	63.9	16.2	13.0
1997	Mil. acres.	932	585	149	131	100.0	62.8	16.0	14.1
Value of land and buildings: [2]									
1992	Bil. dol...	687	474	109	85	100.0	69.0	15.8	12.4
1997	Bil. dol...	860	593	133	114	100.0	69.0	15.5	13.3
Value of farm products sold:									
1992	Bil. dol...	163	88	29	44	100.0	54.1	18.0	27.2
1997	Bil. dol...	197	103	36	57	100.0	52.6	18.4	29.1
FARMS WITH SALES OF $10,000 AND OVER									
Number of farms:									
1992	1,000 ...	1,019	820	131	61	100.0	80.5	12.8	6.0
1997	1,000 ...	949	758	114	70	100.0	79.9	12.0	7.4
Land in farms:									
1992	Mil. acres.	822	512	143	119	100.0	62.2	17.4	14.4
1997	Mil. acres.	802	485	138	126	100.0	60.5	17.2	15.7

[1] Includes other types, not shown separately. [2] Based on a sample of farms.

No. 1101. Corporate Farms—Characteristics by Type: 1997

[131.5 represents 131,500,000]

Item	Unit	All corpora-tions	Family held corporations			Other corporations		
			Total	1-10 stock-holders	11 or more stock-holders	Total	1-10 stock-holders	11 or more stock-holders
Farms	Number...	84,002	76,103	74,308	1,795	7,899	6,870	1,029
Percent distribution	Percent...	100.0	90.6	88.5	2.1	9.4	8.2	1.2
Land in farms	Mil. acres..	131.5	119.6	109.6	10.0	11.9	8.8	3.1
Average per farm	Acres	1,565	1,571	1,474	5,571	1,507	1,284	2,994
Value of—								
Land and buildings [1]	Bil. dol. ...	113.7	99.3	91.6	7.7	14.4	9.3	5.1
Average per farm	$1,000 ...	1,380	1,338	1,264	4,429	1,769	1,288	5,450
Farm products sold	Bil. dol. ...	56.9	45.9	40.8	5.1	11.0	7.3	3.8
Average per farm	$1,000 ...	677	603	548	2,862	1,395	1,057	3,649

[1] Based on a sample of farms.

No. 1102. Farms—Number, Acreage, and Value of Sales by Size of Sales: 1997

[1,912 represents 1,912,000]

Value of products sold	Farms (1,000)	Acreage		Value of sales		Percent distribution		
		Total (mil.)	Average per farm	Total (mil. dol.)	Average per farm (dol.)	Farms	Acreage	Value of sales
Total	1,912	931.8	487	196,865	102,970	100.0	100.0	100.0
Less than $10,000	963	129.5	134	2,937	3,050	50.4	13.9	1.5
Less than $2,500	497	63.8	128	424	854	26.0	6.8	0.2
$2,500-$4,999	228	26.3	115	820	3,591	12.0	2.8	0.4
$5,000-$9,999	238	39.4	166	1,693	7,113	12.4	4.2	0.9
$10,000 or more	949	802.3	846	193,928	204,373	49.6	86.1	98.5
$10,000-$24,999	274	75.3	275	4,372	15,955	14.3	8.1	2.2
$25,000-$49,999	171	82.0	481	6,084	35,642	8.9	8.8	3.1
$50,000-$99,999	158	118.0	746	11,347	71,741	8.3	12.7	5.8
$100,000-$249,999	189	207.5	1,095	30,143	159,137	9.9	22.3	15.3
$250,000-$499,999	88	138.4	1,577	30,505	347,531	4.6	14.9	15.5
$500,000-$999,999	43	91.3	2,129	29,365	685,140	2.2	9.8	14.9
$1,000,000 or more	26	89.8	3,464	82,110	3,166,152	1.4	9.6	41.7

Source of Tables 1100-1102: U.S. Dept. of Agriculture, National Agricultural Statistics Service. *1997 Census of Agriculture*, Vol. 1.

No. 1103. Farms—Number, Acreage, and Value by State: 1992 and 1997

[1,925 represents 1,925,000]

State	Number of farms (1,000) 1992	Number of farms (1,000) 1997	Land in farms (mil. acres) 1992	Land in farms (mil. acres) 1997	Average size of farm (acres) 1992	Average size of farm (acres) 1997	Total value [1] (mil. dol.) 1992	Total value [1] (mil. dol.) 1997	Farms with sales of $10,000 or more, 1997 — Number of farms (1,000)	Farms with sales of $10,000 or more, 1997 — Land in farms (mil. acres)	Farms with sales of $10,000 or more, 1997 — Average size of farm (acres)
United States .	**1,925**	**1,912**	**945.5**	**931.8**	**491**	**487**	**687,432**	**859,839**	**949**	**802.3**	**846**
Alabama	38	41	8.5	8.7	223	210	8,350	12,340	13	5.2	406
Alaska	1	1	0.9	0.9	1,803	1,608	249	267	(Z)	0.7	3,088
Arizona	7	6	35.0	26.9	5,173	4,379	10,984	10,360	3	25.5	8,681
Arkansas	44	45	14.1	14.4	322	318	12,407	16,255	20	11.4	556
California	78	74	29.0	27.7	373	374	63,689	69,768	42	25.2	605
Colorado	27	28	34.0	32.6	1,252	1,154	14,568	19,993	15	28.9	1,943
Connecticut	3	4	0.4	0.4	105	97	2,138	2,104	1	0.2	159
Delaware	3	2	0.6	0.6	224	236	1,351	1,499	2	0.5	319
Florida	35	35	10.8	10.5	306	300	21,801	23,048	15	8.8	596
Georgia	41	40	10.0	10.7	246	265	11,437	15,842	16	7.5	468
Hawaii	5	5	1.6	1.4	298	263	3,854	3,460	2	1.3	572
Idaho	22	22	13.5	11.8	609	530	9,077	11,983	12	10.3	866
Illinois	78	73	27.3	27.2	351	372	41,844	56,475	50	25.6	515
Indiana	63	58	15.6	15.1	249	261	21,732	30,853	33	13.5	415
Iowa	97	91	31.3	31.2	325	343	38,063	51,438	67	29.2	435
Kansas	63	62	46.7	46.1	738	748	21,725	26,517	39	42.6	1,099
Kentucky	90	82	13.7	13.3	151	162	14,775	18,943	36	9.7	268
Louisiana	26	24	7.8	7.9	306	331	7,474	9,077	10	6.3	661
Maine	6	6	1.3	1.2	218	209	1,396	1,456	2	0.8	337
Maryland	13	12	2.2	2.2	171	178	6,570	6,825	6	1.8	295
Massachusetts . .	5	6	0.5	0.5	100	93	2,421	2,535	3	0.3	130
Michigan	47	46	10.1	9.9	217	215	11,517	16,490	23	8.1	359
Minnesota	75	73	25.7	26.0	342	354	23,319	29,927	47	23.0	486
Mississippi	32	31	10.2	10.1	318	323	7,952	10,555	10	6.9	658
Missouri	98	99	28.5	28.8	291	292	22,070	30,589	44	22.2	505
Montana	23	24	59.6	58.6	2,613	2,414	13,578	16,970	15	52.3	3,499
Nebraska	53	51	44.4	45.5	839	885	22,713	29,200	40	43.6	1,092
Nevada	3	3	9.3	6.4	3,205	2,266	2,347	2,474	1	6.2	4,209
New Hampshire . .	2	3	0.4	0.4	158	141	836	945	1	0.2	222
New Jersey	9	9	0.8	0.8	93	91	5,590	5,403	4	0.6	179
New Mexico	14	14	46.8	45.8	3,281	3,249	9,220	8,801	5	41.6	7,593
New York	32	32	7.5	7.3	231	228	9,130	9,117	17	5.7	334
North Carolina . . .	52	49	8.9	9.1	172	185	13,950	18,566	23	7.2	314
North Dakota . . .	31	31	39.4	39.4	1,267	1,290	13,163	15,635	23	36.4	1,590
Ohio	71	69	14.2	14.1	201	206	20,626	28,450	36	11.8	328
Oklahoma	67	74	32.1	33.2	480	448	15,754	20,188	30	26.7	899
Oregon	32	34	17.6	17.4	552	513	11,824	16,316	13	15.5	1,193
Pennsylvania . . .	45	45	7.2	7.2	160	158	14,752	16,891	25	5.4	221
Rhode Island . . .	1	1	0.1	0.1	76	75	313	325	(Z)	(Z)	107
South Carolina . .	20	20	4.5	4.6	221	228	5,093	6,558	6	2.9	470
South Dakota . . .	34	31	44.8	44.4	1,316	1,418	12,264	15,237	24	40.2	1,669
Tennessee	75	77	11.2	11.1	149	145	13,977	20,066	21	6.7	315
Texas	181	194	130.9	131.3	725	676	65,060	77,351	65	108.0	1,662
Utah	14	14	9.6	12.0	712	848	4,704	6,894	6	11.0	1,776
Vermont	5	6	1.3	1.3	235	217	1,730	1,876	3	1.0	321
Virginia	42	41	8.3	8.2	197	200	13,534	15,813	16	5.9	364
Washington	30	29	15.7	15.2	520	523	14,178	18,410	14	12.8	913
West Virginia . . .	17	18	3.3	3.5	192	194	2,810	3,790	4	1.5	401
Wisconsin	68	66	15.5	14.9	228	227	14,285	18,504	40	12.4	309
Wyoming	9	9	32.9	34.1	3,772	3,692	5,242	7,460	6	30.9	5,349

Z Less than 500 farms or 50,000 acres.   [1] Value of land and buildings. Based on reports for a sample of farms.

Source: U.S. Dept. of Agriculture, National Agricultural Statistics Service, *1997 Census of Agriculture*, Vol. 1.

Agriculture   667

No. 1104. Farms—Number and Acreage: 1980 to 1999

[As of **June 1 (2,440 represents 2,440,000)**. Based on 1974 census definition; for definition of farms and farmland, see text of this section. Data for census years (indicated by italics) have been adjusted for underenumeration and are used as reference points along with data from acreage and livestock surveys in estimating data for other years. Minus sign (-) indicates decrease]

Year	Farms Number (1,000)	Annual change [1] (1,000)	Land in farms Total (mil. acres)	Average per farm (acres)	Year	Farms Number (1,000)	Annual change [1] (1,000)	Land in farms Total (mil. acres)	Average per farm (acres)
1980......	2,440	3	1,039	426	1994......	2,198	-4	966	440
1985......	2,293	-41	1,012	441	1995......	2,196	-1	963	438
1990......	2,146	-29	987	460	1996......	2,191	-6	959	438
1991......	2,117	-29	982	464	*1997......*	*2,191*	-	*956*	*436*
1992......	*2,108*	*-9*	*979*	*464*	1998......	2,191	1	954	435
1993......	2,202	94	969	440	1999......	2,194	3	947	432

- Represents or rounds to zero.   [1] Annual change from immediate preceding year.

No. 1105. Farms—Number and Acreage by State: 1990 and 1999

[**2,146 represents 2,146,000**. See headnote, Table 1104]

State	Farms (1,000) 1990	Farms (1,000) 1999	Acreage (mil.) 1990	Acreage (mil.) 1999	Acreage per farm 1990	Acreage per farm 1999	State	Farms (1,000) 1990	Farms (1,000) 1999	Acreage (mil.) 1990	Acreage (mil.) 1999	Acreage per farm 1990	Acreage per farm 1999
U.S	2,146	2,194	987	947	460	432	Missouri	108	110	30	30	281	274
							Montana	25	28	61	57	2,449	2,036
Alabama.....	47	48	10	9	215	192	Nebraska	57	55	47	46	826	844
Alaska......	1	1	1	1	1,707	1,596	Nevada	3	3	9	7	3,560	2,267
Arizona......	8	8	36	28	4,641	3,571	New Hampshire .	3	3	(Z)	(Z)	163	135
Arkansas	47	49	16	15	330	302	New Jersey....	8	10	1	1	107	86
California	85	89	31	28	362	312	New Mexico ...	14	16	45	45	3,296	2,884
Colorado.....	27	29	33	32	1,249	1,097	New York	39	39	8	8	218	200
Connecticut....	4	4	(Z)	(Z)	108	93	North Carolina..	62	58	10	9	156	160
Delaware	3	3	1	1	207	223	North Dakota...	34	31	41	39	1,209	1,292
Florida	41	45	11	10	266	231	Ohio	83	80	16	15	188	186
Georgia	48	50	13	11	260	224	Oklahoma.....	70	84	33	34	471	405
Hawaii	5	6	2	1	357	262	Oregon.......	37	41	18	17	488	425
Idaho.......	22	25	14	12	628	486	Pennsylvania...	53	59	8	8	153	131
Illinois	83	79	28	28	342	351	Rhode Island...	1	1	(Z)	(Z)	95	86
Indiana......	68	65	16	16	240	238	South Carolina..	25	25	5	5	208	194
Iowa........	104	96	34	33	322	344	South Dakota...	35	33	44	44	1,266	1,354
Kansas.......	69	65	48	48	694	731	Tennessee	87	91	12	12	139	131
Kentucky	93	91	14	14	152	149	Texas........	196	227	132	131	673	575
Louisiana	32	30	9	8	278	272	Utah........	13	16	11	12	856	748
Maine.......	7	7	1	1	201	184	Vermont	7	7	1	1	222	200
Maryland	15	12	2	2	148	169	Virginia.......	46	50	9	9	193	172
Massachusetts..	6	6	1	1	100	93	Washington....	37	40	16	16	432	393
Michigan......	54	53	11	10	200	196	West Virginia...	21	21	4	4	180	176
Minnesota.....	89	81	30	29	337	356	Wisconsin.....	80	78	18	16	220	209
Mississippi	40	43	13	11	325	265	Wyoming	9	9	35	35	3,899	3,761

Z Less than 500,000 acres.

Source of Tables 1104 and 1105: U.S. Dept. of Agriculture, National Agricultural Statistics Service, *Farm Numbers, 1975-80; Farms and Land in Farms, Final Estimates by States, 1979-1987; Farms and Land in Farms, Final Estimates, 1988-1992; Farms and Land in Farms, Final Estimates, 1993-1997;* and *Farms and Land In Farms,* February releases.

No. 1106. Certified Organic Farmland Acreage and Livestock: 1992 to 1997

Item	Unit	1992	1995	1997	Crop	Certified organic acreage, 1997 Total (1,000)	Percent of total cropland
Certified growers...........	Number.	3,587	4,856	5,021	Total...............	1,347	0.16
					Pastureland and rangeland ...	496	0.11
Certified organic acreage, total ..	1,000 ..	935	918	1,347	Cropland................	850	0.23
Pastureland and rangeland ..	1,000 ..	532	279	496			
Cropland	1,000 ..	403	639	850	Corn	43	0.1
					Wheat	126	0.2
Certified animals:					Oats	30	1.1
Beef cows	Number.	6,796	(NA)	4,429	Barley	30	0.5
Milk cows	Number.	2,265	(NA)	12,897	Spelt	2	36.7
Hogs and pigs...........	Number.	1,365	(NA)	482	Buckwheat	8	30.1
Sheep and lambs.........	Number.	1,221	(NA)	705	Soybeans	82	0.1
Layer hens	Number.	43,981	(NA)	537,826	Alfalfa	62	0.3
Broilers	Number.	17,382	(NA)	38,285	Grapes.................	19	1.9
Unclassified/other	Number.	(NA)	(NA)	226,105	Trees for maple syrup	14	11.5

NA Not available.

Source: U.S. Dept. of Agriculture, Economic Research Service, "U.S. certified organic farmland acreage and livestock, 1992-97"; published 4 April 2000; <http://www.ers.usda.gov/whatsnew/issues/organic/table4.htm>; and "Certified organic and total U.S. acreage, selected crops, 1995-1997"; published 4 April 2000; <http://www.ers.usda.gov/whatsnew/issues/organic/table5.htm>.

No. 1107. Gross Farm Product—Summary: 1980 to 1999

[In billions of dollars (142.9 represents $142,900,000,000). For definition of gross product, see text, Section 14, Income. Minus sign (-) indicates decrease]

Item	1980	1985	1990	1992	1993	1994	1995	1996	1997	1998	1999
CURRENT DOLLARS											
Farm output, total...................	142.9	152.7	185.3	187.9	187.4	203.3	197.9	222.6	226.3	214.6	208.4
Cash receipts from farm marketings......	140.3	136.3	172.1	172.3	182.0	181.0	194.2	201.2	208.6	198.2	190.7
Farm housing.....................	5.1	5.0	5.1	5.3	5.6	5.9	6.0	6.2	6.4	6.7	7.0
Farm products consumed on farms	1.2	0.9	0.7	0.6	0.6	0.6	0.5	0.5	0.5	0.5	0.5
Other farm income	2.4	4.6	4.9	4.7	5.1	5.1	6.3	6.8	7.8	8.6	10.4
Change in farm inventories...........	-6.1	5.8	2.4	5.0	-5.9	10.8	-9.2	7.9	2.9	0.6	-0.2
Less: Intermediate goods and services purchased [1].....................	86.8	85.6	105.7	107.4	113.9	119.8	124.7	130.4	138.1	133.9	134.2
Equals: **Gross farm product**............	56.1	67.1	79.6	80.5	73.6	83.6	73.2	92.2	88.3	80.8	74.2
Less: Consumption of fixed capital	18.6	21.0	22.1	23.4	23.5	23.7	24.6	25.4	26.3	27.4	29.2
Indirect business tax [2]...........	3.0	3.3	4.3	4.6	4.4	4.7	5.0	5.0	5.2	5.2	5.6
Plus: Subsidies to operators.............	1.0	6.3	7.5	7.7	11.3	6.6	6.1	6.2	6.3	10.3	17.6
Equals: **Farm national income**	35.5	49.1	60.8	60.2	56.9	61.8	49.7	68.1	63.1	58.5	56.9
CHAINED (**1996**) DOLLARS [3]											
Farm output, total..................	(NA)	(NA)	200.8	213.6	208.3	227.1	217.9	222.6	237.5	238.4	243.9
Cash receipts from farm marketings......	(NA)	(NA)	186.3	195.9	202.6	202.9	214.7	201.2	218.7	220.5	224.3
Farm housing.....................	(NA)	(NA)	6.9	6.8	6.6	6.4	6.3	6.2	6.0	5.9	5.7
Farm products consumed on farms	(NA)	(NA)	0.6	0.6	0.6	0.6	0.5	0.5	0.5	0.5	0.5
Other farm income	(NA)	(NA)	5.7	5.6	6.0	5.8	7.0	6.8	8.2	9.6	12.4
Change in farm inventories...........	(NA)	(NA)	2.6	6.1	-7.9	13.0	-12.3	7.9	3.2	1.2	-
Less: Intermediate goods and services purchased [1].....................	(NA)	(NA)	117.0	118.8	122.8	127.7	132.3	130.4	134.4	138.0	138.4
Equals: **Gross farm product**............	(NA)	(NA)	84.2	95.7	85.8	100.3	85.5	92.2	103.6	100.2	106.3

- Represents or rounds to zero.   NA Not available.   [1] Includes rent paid to nonoperator landlords.   [2] Includes nontax liability.   [3] See text, Section 14, Income.

Source: U.S. Bureau of Economic Analysis, *National Income and Product Accounts of the United States 1929-94*, Vol. 2, and *Survey of Current Business*, August 2000.

No. 1108. Value Added to Economy by Agricultural Sector: 1980 to 1998

[In billions of dollars (148.0 represents $148,000,000,000). Data are consistent with the net farm income accounts and include income and expenses related to the farm operator dwellings. The concept presented is consistent with that employed by the Organization for Economic Cooperation and Development]

Item	1980	1985	1990	1991	1992	1993	1994	1995	1996	1997	1998
Final agricultural sector output .	**148.0**	**153.5**	**188.8**	**183.7**	**191.4**	**191.4**	**208.2**	**203.5**	**228.4**	**231.2**	**220.8**
Final crop output (sales) [1].........	64.4	74.1	83.3	81.0	89.0	82.3	100.4	95.8	115.4	112.1	102.0
Final animal output (sales) [1]........	70.3	68.7	90.2	87.3	87.1	92.0	89.7	87.7	92.1	96.5	94.3
Services and forestry	13.3	10.7	15.3	15.4	15.3	17.1	18.1	19.9	20.8	22.5	24.6
Machine hire and customwork.....	0.7	1.5	1.8	1.8	1.8	1.9	2.1	1.9	2.1	2.6	2.3
Forest products sold	1.0	1.4	1.9	1.8	2.2	2.5	2.7	2.8	2.6	2.9	2.8
Other farm income	0.6	3.2	4.5	4.7	4.1	4.6	4.3	5.8	6.2	6.9	8.7
Gross imputed rental value of farm dwellings	11.0	4.7	7.2	7.2	7.2	8.1	9.0	9.4	9.9	10.1	10.8
Less: Intermediate consumption outlays .... [2]	77.0	73.5	92.9	94.6	93.4	100.7	104.9	109.7	113.2	120.9	118.7
Farm origin [2]	34.9	29.3	39.5	38.6	38.6	41.3	41.3	41.8	42.7	46.9	44.9
Feed purchased	21.0	16.9	20.4	19.3	20.1	21.4	22.6	23.8	25.2	26.3	25.0
Livestock and poultry purchased .	10.7	9.2	14.6	14.1	13.6	14.7	13.3	12.5	11.3	13.8	12.7
Manufactured inputs [2]	22.4	20.2	22.0	23.2	22.7	23.1	24.4	26.2	28.6	29.2	28.3
Fertilizers and lime...........	9.5	7.5	8.2	8.7	8.3	8.4	9.2	10.0	10.9	10.9	10.7
Pesticides	3.5	4.3	5.4	6.3	6.5	6.7	7.2	7.7	8.5	9.0	9.1
Other intermediate expenses [2]	19.7	24.1	31.4	32.8	32.1	36.2	39.2	41.7	41.8	44.9	45.5
Repair and maintenance of capital items	7.1	6.4	8.6	8.6	8.5	9.2	9.1	9.5	10.3	10.4	10.4
Plus: Net government transactions [3] ..	-2.8	2.9	3.1	2.1	2.7	6.9	1.1	0.2	0.2	0.2	4.6
Direct Government payments	1.3	7.7	9.3	8.2	9.2	13.4	7.9	7.3	7.3	7.5	12.2
Property taxes	3.9	4.5	5.9	5.8	6.1	6.2	6.3	6.6	6.7	6.9	7.2
Equals: **Gross value added.**	**68.2**	**82.9**	**98.9**	**91.2**	**100.6**	**97.5**	**104.5**	**94.0**	**115.4**	**110.4**	**106.7**
Less: Capital consumption	21.5	19.4	18.1	18.2	18.3	18.4	18.6	18.9	19.2	19.3	19.4
Equals: Net value added	46.7	63.5	80.7	73.0	82.3	79.2	85.8	75.1	96.2	91.1	87.2
Less: Employee compensation	8.3	8.5	12.5	12.3	12.3	13.2	13.5	14.3	15.3	16.0	16.9
Less: Net rent received by nonoperator landlords	6.1	7.7	10.0	9.9	11.1	10.7	11.5	11.0	13.0	12.9	12.6
Less: Real estate and nonreal estate interest......................	16.3	18.6	13.4	12.1	11.0	10.6	11.5	12.6	13.0	13.5	13.6
Equals: **Net farm income**	**16.1**	**28.6**	**44.7**	**38.7**	**47.9**	**44.5**	**49.2**	**37.2**	**54.9**	**48.6**	**44.1**

[1] Includes home consumption and value of inventory adjustment.   [2] Includes other outlays not shown separately.   [3] Direct Government payments minus motor vehicle registration and licensing fees and property taxes.

Source: U.S. Dept. of Agriculture, Economic Research Service, *Agricultural Income and Finance Situation and Outlook*, September 1999, and "United States and State Farm Income Data"; published 1 October 1999; <http://www.ERS.USDA.gov/briefing/farmincome/finfidmu.htm>.

Agriculture   669

No. 1109. Farm Income—Cash Receipts From Farm Marketings: 1995 to 1998

[In millions of dollars (188,055 represents $188,055,000,000). Represents gross receipts from commercial market sales as well as net Commodity Credit Corporation loans. The source estimates and publishes individual cash receipt values only for major commodities and major producing states. The U.S. receipts for individual commodities, computed as the sum of the reported states, may understate the value of sales for some commodities. The degree of underestimation in some of the minor commodities can be substantial]

Commodity	1995	1996	1997	1998	Commodity	1995	1996	1997	1998
Total	**188,055**	**199,138**	**207,611**	**196,761**	Soybeans	13,868	14,802	18,034	15,447
					Sunflower	470	375	454	479
Livestock and products [1]	87,101	92,956	96,535	94,539	Vegetables [1]	15,040	14,439	14,961	15,337
Cattle and calves	34,044	30,977	36,000	33,724	Beans, dry	567	715	545	594
Hogs	10,255	12,565	13,054	9,396	Potatoes	2,495	2,580	2,226	2,455
Sheep and lambs	566	612	628	484	Broccoli	443	422	487	554
Dairy products	19,880	22,785	20,940	24,312	Carrots	545	465	535	494
Broilers	11,762	13,905	14,159	15,147	Corn, sweet	649	656	673	686
Chicken eggs	3,893	4,776	4,540	4,350	Lettuce	2,004	1,325	1,818	1,577
Turkeys	2,769	3,124	2,881	2,662	Onions	755	735	774	889
Horses/mules	662	753	1,778	1,895	Peppers, green	446	466	480	483
Aquaculture [2]	802	821	838	876	Tomatoes	1,584	1,658	1,646	1,640
					Fruits/nuts [1]	11,097	11,928	13,074	11,727
Crops [1]	100,954	106,182	111,076	102,222	Oranges	1,749	1,844	1,888	1,955
Rice	1,282	1,568	1,681	1,741	Apples	1,579	1,844	1,540	1,411
Wheat	9,115	9,133	8,438	6,968	Grapes	2,045	2,372	3,115	2,637
Barley	825	969	795	642	Strawberries	812	769	904	1,029
Corn	18,893	20,669	19,878	17,096	Almonds	881	1,018	1,161	699
Hay	3,291	3,886	4,741	4,117	Sugarbeets	1,071	1,211	1,162	1,258
Sorghum grain	1,377	1,508	1,561	972	Cane for sugar	893	864	848	913
Cotton	6,851	6,983	6,346	6,013	Christmas trees	416	422	442	460
Tobacco	2,548	2,795	2,874	2,989	Greenhouse/nursery	10,316	10,819	11,841	12,115
Peanuts	1,014	1,030	1,003	1,018	Mushrooms	758	753	782	800

[1] Includes other commodities not shown separately.   [2] See also Table 1159.

No. 1110. Cash Receipts for Selected Commodities—Leading States: 1998

[33,724 represents $33,724,000,000. See headnote, Table 1109]

State	Value of receipts (mil. dol.)	Percent of total receipts	Rank	State	Value of receipts (mil. dol.)	Percent of total receipts	Rank
Cattle and calves	33,724	100.0	(X)	Corn	17,096	100.0	(X)
Texas	5,845	17.3	1	Iowa	3,168	18.5	1
Nebraska	4,266	12.6	2	Illinois	2,922	17.0	2
Kansas	4,026	11.9	3	Nebraska	2,176	12.7	3
Colorado	2,149	6.3	4	Indiana	1,420	8.3	4
Oklahoma	1,836	5.4	5	Minnesota	1,261	7.3	5
Dairy products	24,312	100.0	(X)	Soybeans	15,447	100.0	(X)
California	4,290	17.6	1	Iowa	2,837	18.3	1
Wisconsin	3,496	14.3	2	Illinois	2,644	17.1	2
New York	1,787	7.3	3	Minnesota	1,428	9.2	3
Pennsylvania	1,731	7.1	4	Indiana	1,337	8.6	4
Minnesota	1,426	5.8	5	Ohio	1,108	7.1	5

X Not applicable.

No. 1111. Balance Sheet of the Farming Sector: 1980 to 1998

[In billions of dollars, except as indicated (983 represents $983,000,000,000). As of December 31]

Item	1980	1985	1990	1991	1992	1993	1994	1995	1996	1997	1998
Assets	**983**	**773**	**841**	**844**	**868**	**910**	**935**	**967**	**1,004**	**1,052**	**1,064**
Real estate	783	586	619	625	641	678	704	740	770	808	823
Livestock and poultry [1]	61	46	71	68	71	73	68	58	60	67	62
Machinery, motor vehicles [2]	80	83	86	86	85	86	88	89	89	89	89
Crops [3]	33	23	23	22	24	23	23	27	32	32	30
Purchased inputs	(NA)	1	3	3	4	4	5	3	4	5	5
Financial assets	27	33	38	41	43	46	48	49	49	50	55
Claims	**983**	**773**	**841**	**844**	**868**	**910**	**935**	**967**	**1,004**	**1,052**	**1,064**
Debt	167	178	138	139	139	142	147	151	156	165	173
Real estate debt	90	100	75	75	75	76	78	79	82	85	90
Nonreal estate debt [4]	77	78	63	64	64	66	69	71	74	80	83
Equity	816	595	703	705	729	768	789	816	848	886	891
Farm debt/equity ratio (percent)	20.4	29.8	19.6	19.8	19.1	18.5	18.6	18.5	18.4	18.7	19.4
Farm debt/asset ratio (percent)	17.0	23.0	16.4	16.5	16.0	15.6	15.7	15.6	15.6	15.7	16.2

NA Not available.   [1] Excludes horses, mules, and broilers.   [2] Include only farm share value for trucks and autos.   [3] All non-CCC crops held on farms plus the value above loan rate for crops held under Commodity Credit Corporation.   [4] Excludes debt for nonfarm purposes.

Source of Tables 1109-1111: U.S. Dept. of Agriculture, Economic Research Service, *Agricultural Income and Finance Situation and Outlook*, September 1999, and "United States and State Farm Income Data"; published 1 October 1999; <http://www.ERS. USDA.gov/briefing/farmincome/finfidmu.htm>.

No. 1112. Farm Assets, Debt, and Income by State: 1997 and 1998

[**Assets and debt**, as of **December 31 (1,051,572 represents $1,051,572,000,000)**. Farm income data are after inventory adjustment and include income and expenses related to the farm operator's dwelling]

State	Assets (mil. dol.)		Debt (mil. dol.)		Debt/asset ratio (percent)		Final agricultural sector output (mil. dol.)		Net farm income (mil. dol.)	
	1997	1998	1997	1998	1997	1998	1997	1998	1997	1998
United States . . .	1,051,572	1,064,298	165,413	172,862	15.7	16.2	231,173	220,839	48,623	44,089
Alabama.	14,423	14,895	1,745	1,887	12.1	12.7	3,884	4,026	1,093	1,209
Alaska	614	632	19	21	3.2	3.3	53	52	26	20
Arizona.	27,808	28,662	1,347	1,398	4.8	4.9	2,432	2,493	567	700
Arkansas	20,219	20,670	4,003	4,196	19.8	20.3	6,406	5,923	1,843	1,595
California	78,780	80,098	15,558	16,522	19.8	20.6	27,642	25,854	6,437	5,366
Colorado.	23,016	23,027	3,555	3,630	15.4	15.8	4,893	4,880	613	760
Connecticut.	2,135	2,233	242	252	11.4	11.3	559	566	107	129
Delaware	1,646	2,168	357	367	21.7	16.9	840	876	86	118
Florida	26,074	27,050	4,376	4,518	16.8	16.7	6,811	7,029	2,114	2,226
Georgia	18,883	18,075	3,363	3,503	17.8	19.4	6,332	6,142	1,996	1,901
Hawaii	3,553	3,949	251	265	7.1	6.7	551	542	41	34
Idaho	14,816	15,316	2,903	2,986	19.6	19.5	3,624	3,698	615	840
Illinois	66,510	68,039	8,848	9,346	13.3	13.7	9,695	8,769	2,145	1,484
Indiana.	34,734	34,918	5,319	5,579	15.3	16.0	6,189	5,633	1,264	802
Iowa	67,991	67,032	12,080	12,663	17.8	18.9	13,734	12,142	3,767	2,277
Kansas.	34,143	33,848	6,695	6,918	19.6	20.4	9,555	8,662	1,755	1,496
Kentucky	22,283	22,189	3,206	3,371	14.4	15.2	4,275	4,459	1,315	1,313
Louisiana	8,015	11,119	1,629	1,723	20.3	15.5	2,416	2,091	566	374
Maine.	1,837	1,934	366	371	19.9	19.2	536	557	40	63
Maryland	6,858	7,619	1,042	1,078	15.2	14.2	1,727	1,777	233	310
Massachusetts.	2,930	3,534	333	357	11.4	10.1	604	558	182	130
Michigan.	19,174	20,811	3,070	3,121	16.0	15.0	4,114	3,902	401	308
Minnesota.	41,567	41,687	8,664	9,239	20.8	22.2	8,931	8,791	954	1,260
Mississippi	13,840	13,553	2,584	2,688	18.7	19.8	3,912	3,835	938	927
Missouri	36,623	36,139	5,662	6,086	15.5	16.8	6,125	5,393	1,371	763
Montana.	20,490	19,892	2,692	2,718	13.1	13.7	2,250	2,084	297	355
Nebraska	39,438	39,492	8,459	8,941	21.5	22.6	10,522	9,777	2,011	1,759
Nevada	2,879	2,934	244	258	8.5	8.8	356	380	23	47
New Hampshire	920	1,868	87	94	9.4	5.1	179	176	16	12
New Jersey.	5,722	6,736	587	477	10.3	7.1	900	876	156	117
New Mexico	11,343	11,830	1,280	1,351	11.3	11.4	2,118	2,093	505	571
New York	12,280	13,006	2,352	2,419	19.2	18.6	3,090	3,398	196	447
North Carolina	21,643	21,101	3,514	3,678	16.2	17.4	9,803	8,930	3,326	2,361
North Dakota.	22,087	21,355	3,970	4,070	18.0	19.1	3,197	3,663	128	746
Ohio	32,798	33,204	3,916	4,131	11.9	12.4	6,292	5,792	1,807	1,299
Oklahoma.	24,589	24,008	4,291	4,392	17.5	18.3	4,765	4,337	948	901
Oregon.	17,225	18,223	2,373	2,540	13.8	13.9	3,975	3,797	598	515
Pennsylvania.	20,432	22,000	2,658	2,710	13.0	12.3	4,542	4,686	552	662
Rhode Island.	392	467	37	39	9.3	8.3	71	74	21	24
South Carolina.	8,096	7,800	937	974	11.6	12.5	1,896	1,684	493	330
South Dakota.	21,522	21,790	3,937	4,143	18.3	19.0	4,215	4,208	1,009	1,158
Tennessee	22,835	22,429	2,337	2,517	10.2	11.2	2,767	2,712	492	343
Texas.	88,464	86,678	11,140	11,417	12.6	13.2	15,835	14,713	3,226	3,125
Utah	9,628	9,956	767	787	8.0	7.9	1,104	1,126	190	219
Vermont	2,423	2,622	377	385	15.6	14.7	568	615	108	142
Virginia.	18,141	18,001	1,943	1,995	10.7	11.1	2,699	2,800	508	496
Washington.	20,431	20,502	3,284	3,468	16.1	16.9	6,036	5,996	870	1,050
West Virginia.	4,053	4,096	400	409	9.9	10.0	506	529	32	35
Wisconsin.	26,251	26,497	5,629	5,817	21.5	22.0	6,511	6,813	435	908
Wyoming	9,015	8,614	984	1,051	10.9	12.2	1,136	934	208	60

Source: U.S. Dept. of Agriculture, Economic Research Service, "Farm Business Balance Sheet and Financial Ratios"; published 15 October 1999; <http://www.ers.usda.gov/briefing/farmincome/fbsdmu.htm>; and "United States and State Farm Income Data"; published 1 October 1999; <http://www.ers.usda.gov/briefing/farmincome/finfidmu.htm>.

Agriculture 671

No. 1113. Farm Income—Farm Marketings, 1997 and 1998, and Principal Commodities, 1998 by State

[In millions of dollars (207,611 represents $207,611,000,000). Cattle include calves and greenhouse includes nursery]

State	1997 Total	1997 Crops	1997 Live-stock and products	1998 Total	1998 Crops	1998 Live-stock and products	State rank for total farm marketings and four principal commodities in order of marketing receipts
U.S. . . .	207,611	111,076	96,535	196,761	102,222	94,539	Cattle, dairy products, corn, soybeans
AL	3,216	788	2,428	3,283	696	2,587	25-Broilers, cattle, chicken eggs, greenhouse
AK	49	21	28	47	20	27	50-Greenhouse, dairy products, cattle, hay
AZ	2,183	1,276	906	2,368	1,425	943	29-Cattle, lettuce, dairy products, cotton
AR	5,724	2,379	3,346	5,422	2,172	3,250	12-Broilers, rice, soybeans, cotton
CA	26,137	19,827	6,310	24,616	17,771	6,845	1-Dairy products, greenhouse, grapes, cattle
CO	4,177	1,303	2,875	4,310	1,453	2,857	17-Cattle, corn, wheat, dairy products
CT	501	278	223	509	281	228	43-Greenhouse, dairy products, chicken eggs, tobacco
DE	754	176	579	774	164	609	40-Broilers, soybeans, greenhouse, dairy products
FL	6,516	5,116	1,400	6,762	5,355	1,407	9-Oranges, greenhouse, tomatoes, sugar
GA	5,752	2,350	3,402	5,454	2,047	3,408	11-Broilers, cotton, peanuts, chicken eggs
HI	510	424	86	510	418	92	42-Pineapples, sugar, greenhouse, macadamia nuts
ID	3,283	1,878	1,405	3,320	1,735	1,585	24-Dairy products, cattle, potatoes, wheat
IL	8,984	7,055	1,928	7,742	6,167	1,575	6-Corn, soybeans, hogs, cattle
IN	5,766	3,838	1,928	4,885	3,245	1,639	15-Corn, soybeans, hogs, dairy products
IA	12,944	7,331	5,613	10,994	6,217	4,778	3-Corn, soybeans, hogs, cattle
KS	8,544	3,609	4,936	7,784	3,247	4,537	5-Cattle, wheat, corn, soybeans
KY	3,543	1,571	1,972	3,920	1,787	2,134	19-Tobacco, horses/mules, cattle, broilers
LA	2,168	1,510	659	1,891	1,245	645	33-Sugar, rice, cotton, cattle
ME	489	213	276	506	224	282	45-Potatoes, dairy products, chicken eggs, aquaculture
MD	1,535	607	928	1,520	571	949	35-Broilers, greenhouse, dairy products, soybeans
MA	531	417	114	507	395	112	44-Greenhouse, cranberries, dairy products, sweet corn
MI	3,598	2,234	1,365	3,480	2,158	1,323	22-Dairy products, greenhouse, soybeans, corn
MN	7,998	4,006	3,992	7,680	3,925	3,755	7-Soybeans, dairy products, corn, hogs
MS	3,480	1,476	2,004	3,454	1,285	2,169	23-Broilers, cotton, soybeans, aquaculture
MO	5,402	2,631	2,771	4,682	2,262	2,420	16-Soybeans, cattle, corn, hogs
MT	2,023	1,058	965	1,799	934	865	34-Cattle, wheat, barley, hay
NE	9,803	4,295	5,508	8,848	3,725	5,124	4-Cattle, corn, soybeans, hogs
NV	322	136	187	337	143	194	47-Cattle, hay, dairy products, greenhouse
NH	153	84	68	151	82	69	48-Dairy products, greenhouse, apples, cattle
NJ	794	626	168	828	650	178	39-Greenhouse, horses/mules, dairy products, cranberries
NM	1,917	551	1,366	1,950	513	1,437	32-Cattle, dairy products, hay, greenhouse
NY	2,836	1,007	1,828	3,146	1,054	2,092	26-Dairy products, greenhouse, apples, cattle
NC	8,230	3,507	4,723	7,164	3,247	3,917	8-Broilers, hogs, tobacco, greenhouse
ND	3,267	2,668	598	3,004	2,455	549	28-Wheat, cattle, sunflower, soybeans
OH	5,237	3,361	1,875	4,973	3,124	1,848	14-Soybeans, corn, dairy products, greenhouse
OK	4,174	1,138	3,036	3,900	1,062	2,838	20-Cattle, wheat, broilers, hogs
OR	3,229	2,427	803	3,092	2,330	762	27-Greenhouse, cattle, hay, dairy products
PA	4,132	1,324	2,808	4,175	1,261	2,914	18-Dairy products, greenhouse, cattle, chicken eggs
RI	63	54	9	65	56	9	49-Greenhouse, dairy products, sweet corn, potatoes
SC	1,687	885	802	1,511	748	763	36-Broilers, greenhouse, tobacco, turkeys
SD	4,182	2,401	1,781	3,508	1,951	1,557	21-Cattle, soybeans, corn, wheat
TN	2,273	1,245	1,028	2,216	1,177	1,038	31-Cattle, broilers, dairy products, tobacco
TX	13,208	5,060	8,147	13,206	4,986	8,220	2-Cattle, cotton, greenhouse, dairy products
UT	962	256	706	981	245	736	37-Cattle, dairy products, hay, hogs
VT	500	85	414	557	84	472	41-Dairy products, cattle, greenhouse, hay
VA	2,406	864	1,542	2,328	768	1,561	30-Broilers, dairy products, cattle, turkeys
WA	5,370	3,747	1,622	5,155	3,424	1,730	13-Dairy products, apples, cattle, wheat
WV	397	69	328	405	69	336	46-Broilers, cattle, dairy products, turkeys
WI	5,787	1,721	4,066	6,193	1,701	4,492	10-Dairy products, corn, cattle, soybeans
WY	876	191	686	850	170	681	38-Cattle, hay, sugar beets, sheep/lambs

Source: U.S. Dept. of Agriculture, Economic Research Service, *Agricultural Income and Finance Situation and Outlook*, September 1999.

672 Agriculture

No. 1114. Indexes of Prices Received and Paid by Farmers: 1990 to 1999

[1990-92=100, except as noted]

Item	1990	1995	1998	1999	Item	1990	1995	1998	1999
Prices received, all products.	104	102	101	96	**Prices paid, total [2]**.	99	109	115	115
					Production	99	108	113	112
					Feed	103	103	110	100
					Livestock & poultry	102	82	88	95
Crops	103	112	106	96	Seed	102	110	122	121
Food grains	100	134	103	91	Fertilizer.	97	121	112	105
Feed grains and hay.	105	112	100	86	Agricultural chemicals	95	116	122	121
Cotton	107	127	107	85	Fuels.	100	89	84	93
Tobacco	97	103	104	103	Supplies & repairs	96	112	119	121
Oil-bearing crops	105	104	107	83	Autos and trucks	97	115	119	119
Fruits and nuts [1]	97	97	111	114	Farm machinery.	96	120	132	136
Commercial vegetables [1]. . . .	102	121	121	108	Building materials.	99	114	118	120
Potatoes & dry beans	133	107	99	101	Farm services	96	115	115	115
					Rent	(NA)	117	120	117
Livestock and products.	105	92	97	95	Interest	107	102	104	106
Meat animals	105	85	79	83	Taxes	95	109	119	120
Dairy products	105	98	119	110	Wage rates	96	114	129	135
Poultry and eggs	105	107	117	111	Parity ratio (1910-14=100) [3] . . .	51	45	38	36

NA Not available. [1] Excludes potatoes and dry beans. [2] Includes production items, interest, taxes, wage rates, and a family living component. The family living component is the Consumer Price Index for all urban consumers from the Bureau of Labor Statistics. See text, Section 15, Prices, and Table 768. [3] Ratio of prices received by farmers to prices paid.

Source: U.S. Dept. of Agriculture, National Agricultural Statistics Service, *Agricultural Prices: Annual Summary*.

No. 1115. Value of Selected Commodities Produced Under Contracts: 1998

[67,090 represents $67,090,000,000. Marketing contracts refer to verbal or written agreements between a buyer and a grower that set a price and determine an outlet for a specified quantity of a commodity before harvest or before the farmer markets the commodity. Production contracts involve paying the farmer a fee for providing management, labor, facilities, and equipment, while assigning ownership of the product to the contractor. Survey based estimates (see source) exclude Alaska and Hawaii and do not represent official U.S. Dept. of Agriculture estimates of farm sector activity]

Commodity	Value of production under contract (mil. dol.)	Percent of total production [1]	Commodity	Value of production under contract (mil. dol.)	Percent of total production [1]
Total	**67,090**	[2]**35**	Sugar beets	984	76
Marketing contracts [3]. . .	39,878	[2]21	Vegetables	3,939	[2]36
Cattle	1,472	5	Production contracts [3]. .	27,212	[2]14
Corn	2,385	13	Poultry and eggs [4]. . .	15,051	88
Cotton	2,031	51	Cattle	6,406	21
Fruits	5,605	55	Hogs.	3,437	40
Soybeans	2,078	12	Vegetables.	1,085	10

[1] Represents percent of production under contract as percent of total commodity production, except as noted. [2] Percent of total value of agricultural production. [3] Includes other commodities not shown separately. [4] Data not available to estimate value of production for broilers.

Source: U.S. Dept. of Agriculture, Economic Research Service, unpublished data from 1998 Agricultural Resource Management Study, Phase 3, Version 1.

No. 1116. Civilian Consumer Expenditures for Farm Foods: 1980 to 1998

[In billions of dollars, except percent (264.4 represents $264,400,000,000). Excludes imported and nonfarm foods, such as coffee and seafood, as well as food consumed by the military, or exported]

Item	1980	1985	1990	1991	1992	1993	1994	1995	1996	1997	1998
Consumer expenditures, total . .	264.4	345.4	449.8	465.1	474.5	489.2	512.2	529.5	546.7	566.5	584.6
Farm value, total	81.7	86.4	106.2	101.6	105.1	109.6	109.6	113.8	122.2	121.9	118.8
Marketing bill, total [1]	182.7	259.0	343.6	363.5	369.4	379.6	402.6	415.7	424.5	444.6	465.8
Percent of total consumer expenditures.	69.1	75.0	76.4	78.2	77.9	77.6	78.6	78.5	77.6	78.5	79.7
At-home expenditures [2]	180.1	220.8	276.2	286.1	289.6	294.9	308.7	316.9	328.0	339.2	347.4
Farm value	65.9	66.6	80.2	76.7	76.9	76.4	75.3	76.1	81.6	79.0	77.5
Marketing bill [1]	114.2	154.2	196.0	209.4	212.7	218.5	233.4	240.8	246.4	260.2	269.9
Away-from-home expenditures. . . .	84.3	124.6	173.6	179.0	184.9	194.3	203.5	212.6	218.7	227.3	237.2
Farm value	15.8	19.8	26.0	24.9	28.2	33.2	34.3	37.7	40.6	42.9	41.3
Marketing bill [1]	68.5	104.8	147.6	154.1	156.7	161.1	169.2	174.9	178.1	184.4	195.9
Marketing bill cost components:											
Labor cost	81.5	115.6	154.0	160.9	168.4	178.0	186.1	196.6	204.6	216.9	227.9
Packaging materials	21.0	26.9	36.5	38.1	40.1	40.9	43.3	48.2	47.7	48.7	50.4
Rail and truck transport.	13.0	16.5	19.8	20.4	20.6	21.2	21.8	22.3	22.9	23.6	24.4
Corporate profits before taxes . . .	9.9	10.4	13.2	15.2	15.7	18.1	20.9	19.5	20.7	21.3	22.2
Fuels and electricity	9.0	13.1	15.2	16.3	16.7	17.2	17.9	18.6	19.6	20.2	20.7
Advertising	7.3	12.5	17.1	17.5	18.0	18.6	19.3	19.8	20.9	21.5	22.0
Depreciation	7.8	15.4	16.3	15.8	16.2	17.2	18.1	18.9	20.1	20.7	21.2
Net interest.	3.4	6.1	13.5	12.2	10.9	10.1	11.0	11.6	11.4	12.2	13.0
Net rent	6.8	9.3	13.9	15.9	17.2	17.9	18.9	19.8	21.0	21.8	22.5
Repairs	3.6	4.8	6.2	6.4	6.6	7.2	7.8	7.9	8.5	8.8	9.0
Taxes	8.3	11.7	15.7	16.5	17.5	18.2	18.7	19.1	19.4	20.0	20.6
Other.	11.0	16.7	22.2	28.3	21.5	15.0	18.8	13.4	7.7	8.9	11.9

[1] The difference between expenditures for domestic farm-originated food products and the farm value or payment farmers received for the equivalent farm products. [2] Food primarily purchased from retail food stores for use at home.

Source: U.S. Dept. of Agriculture, Economic Research Service, *Food Cost Review*, annual; *Food Review*, periodic; and *Agricultural Statistics*, annual.

No. 1117. Indexes of Farm Production, Input Use, and Productivity: 1980 to 1996

[1992=100]

Item	1980	1985	1988	1989	1990	1991	1992	1993	1994	1995	1996
Farm output [1]	79	89	82	89	94	94	100	94	107	101	106
Livestock and products [2]	85	89	94	94	95	98	100	101	107	110	109
Meat animals	98	94	97	97	96	99	100	100	103	104	100
Dairy products	85	94	96	95	98	98	100	99	114	115	115
Poultry and eggs	64	71	83	86	92	96	100	104	109	114	119
Crops [2]	75	89	75	86	92	92	100	89	106	96	103
Feed crops	76	100	62	85	88	86	100	76	102	83	98
Food grains	94	95	76	83	107	82	100	96	97	90	93
Oil crops	81	96	72	88	87	94	100	85	115	99	107
Cotton and cottonseed	68	82	96	75	96	109	100	100	122	110	117
Tobacco	102	87	78	80	94	96	100	94	85	93	80
Vegetables and melons	70	82	81	85	93	97	100	97	113	108	112
Fruits and nuts	90	86	102	98	97	96	100	107	111	102	102
Other crops	57	69	86	89	94	97	100	99	105	110	110
Farm input [3]	119	106	100	100	101	102	100	101	104	105	102
Farm labor	123	108	103	104	102	106	100	96	96	92	100
Farm real estate	113	107	99	101	100	100	100	98	100	99	101
Durable equipment	166	139	113	108	105	103	100	97	94	92	89
Energy	121	98	102	101	100	101	100	100	103	109	104
Agricultural chemicals [4]	119	97	91	94	95	100	100	105	106	90	97
Other purchased inputs [5]	117	99	99	103	103	104	100	110	117	121	116
Farm output per unit of input	66	84	83	90	93	92	100	94	103	97	104

[1] Annual production available for eventual human use. [2] Includes items not shown separately. [3] Based on physical quantities of resources used in production. [4] Includes fertilizer, lime, and pesticides. [5] Includes purchased services and miscellaneous inputs.

Source: U.S. Dept. of Agriculture, Economic Research Service, *Agricultural Outlook*, monthly. Also published in the U.S. Council of Economic Advisors, *Economic Report of the President*, annual.

No. 1118. Agricultural Exports and Imports—Volume by Principal Commodities: 1990 to 1999

[In thousands of metric tons (2,707 represents 2,707,000)]

Exports	1990	1995	1998	1999	Imports	1990	1995	1998	1999
Animal products [1]	2,707	5,606	6,153	6,158	Fruits, nuts, vegetables	4,696	6,213	8,171	8,709
Wheat and products [2]	28,247	33,458	27,546	29,367	Bananas	3,094	3,664	3,913	4,295
Feed grains and products	61,526	67,403	47,278	58,932	Green coffee	1,174	953	1,140	1,234
Rice	2,534	3,275	3,722	2,938	Cocoa and products	716	620	863	924
Feeds and fodders	10,974	13,338	11,775	11,945	Meat and products [5]	1,169	1,050	1,302	1,439
Protein meal	5,079	6,404	8,225	6,843					
Oilseeds and products [3]	15,820	23,596	21,479	24,147	Vegetable oils	1,199	1,561	1,949	1,775
Vegetable oils	1,213	2,510	3,074	2,429	Rubber, crude natural	840	1,044	1,200	1,144
Fruits, nuts, vegetables [4]	5,553	6,918	7,157	6,846	Sugar	1,858	1,599	2,047	1,612
Cotton and linters	1,733	2,118	1,663	754	Spices	129	155	197	211
Tobacco, unmanufactured	223	209	212	189	Tobacco, unmanufactured	172	190	224	222

[1] Includes meat and products, poultry meats, dairy products, and fats, oils and greases. Excludes live animals, hides, skins, and eggs. [2] Includes flour and bulgur. [3] Includes soybeans, sunflowerseeds, peanuts, cottonseed, safflowerseed, flaxseed, and nondefatted soybean flour. [4] Excludes fruit juices. [5] Excludes poultry.

Source: U.S. Dept. of Agriculture, Economic Research Service, *U.S. Agricultural Trade Update*, February 29, 2000; and *Foreign Agricultural Trade of the United States*, calendar year supplements.

No. 1119. Agricultural Exports and Imports—Value: 1980 to 1999

[In billions of dollars, except percent (23.9 represents $23,900,000,000). Includes Puerto Rico. Excludes forest products and distilled liquors; includes crude rubber and similar gums (now mainly plantation products). Includes shipments under foreign aid programs]

Year	Trade balance	Exports, domestic products	Percent of all exports	Imports for consumption	Percent of all imports	Year	Trade balance	Exports, domestic products	Percent of all exports	Imports for consumption	Percent of all imports
1980	23.9	41.2	18	17.4	7	1994	19.2	46.2	10	27.1	4
1985	9.1	29.0	13	20.0	6	1995	26.0	56.3	10	30.3	4
1990	16.6	39.5	11	22.9	5	1996	26.8	60.4	10	33.7	4
1991	16.5	39.4	10	22.9	5	1997	21.0	57.2	9	36.3	4
1992	18.3	43.1	10	24.8	5	1998	14.8	51.8	8	37.1	4
1993	17.7	42.9	10	25.2	4	1999	10.4	48.3	8	37.9	4

Source: U.S. Dept. of Agriculture, Economic Research Service, *U.S. Agricultural Trade Update*, February 29, 2000; and *Foreign Agricultural Trade of the United States*, calendar year supplements. Also in *Agricultural Statistics*, annual.

No. 1120. Agricultural Imports—Value by Selected Commodity, 1990 to 1999, and by Leading Countries of Origin, 1999

[In millions of dollars (22,910 represents $22,910,000,000)]

Commodity	1990	1995	1996	1997	1998	1999	Leading countries of origin, 1999
Total	22,910	30,336	33,655	36,300	37,073	37,867	Canada, Mexico, France
Competitive products	17,336	21,873	25,448	26,948	28,090	29,878	Canada, Mexico, France
Cattle, live	978	1,413	1,121	1,124	1,144	1,000	Canada, Mexico, Australia
Beef and veal	1,872	1,447	1,341	1,609	1,842	2,135	Canada, Australia, New Zealand
Pork	938	686	728	754	682	753	Canada, Denmark, Poland
Dairy products	891	1,118	1,274	1,225	1,465	1,556	New Zealand, Canada, Italy
Fruits and preparations . .	2,218	2,249	2,834	2,847	2,852	3,540	Mexico, Chile, Brazil
Vegetables and preparations	2,317	3,189	3,526	3,707	4,375	4,583	Mexico, Canada, Spain
Wine	917	1,153	1,430	1,711	1,876	2,186	France, Italy, Australia
Malt beverages	923	1,166	1,316	1,495	1,712	1,893	Mexico, Netherlands, Canada
Grains and feeds	1,188	2,312	2,657	2,963	2,878	2,991	Canada, Italy, Thailand
Sugar and related products	1,213	1,335	1,889	1,852	1,682	1,589	Canada, Mexico, Brazil
Oilseeds and products . .	947	1,800	2,147	2,242	2,211	1,971	Canada, Malaysia, Italy
Noncompetitive products . .	5,574	8,464	8,207	9,353	8,984	7,989	Indonesia, Colombia, Brazil
Coffee and products . . .	1,915	3,263	2,788	3,886	3,431	2,899	Colombia, Brazil, Mexico
Rubber, crude natural . . .	707	1,629	1,468	1,229	977	704	Indonesia, Thailand, Malaysia
Cocoa and products	1,072	1,106	1,400	1,471	1,666	1,522	Canada, Cote d'Ivoire, Indonesia
Bananas and plantains . .	939	1,140	1,184	1,220	1,202	1,209	Costa Rica, Ecuador, Colombia

Source: U.S. Dept. of Agriculture, Economic Research Service, *U.S. Agricultural Trade Update*, February 29, 2000; and *Foreign Agricultural Trade of the United States*, calendar year supplements.

No. 1121. Imports Share of Food Consumption by Commodity: 1990 to 1998

[In percent. Import share is the total quantity imported divided by the quantity available for domestic human food consumption. Calculated from supply and utilization balance sheets. A portion of the imports of some commodities is exported; therefore, the ratios presented here may overstate the importance of imports in domestic consumption for some commodity groups. Similarly, a portion of the imports of some commodities is diverted to such nonfood uses as feed, seed, alcohol and fuel production, and industrial uses. This too can overstate the importance of imports]

Commodity	1990	1995	1997	1998	Commodity	1990	1995	1997	1998
Red meat	8.1	6.5	7.1	7.7	Grapes	37.6	38.8	41.2	43.7
Beef	9.8	8.3	9.2	10.1	Fruit juice	47.6	27.7	27.3	30.5
Pork	5.6	3.8	3.8	3.9	Orange	46.3	14.0	17.7	18.5
Fish and shellfish	56.3	55.3	62.1	(NA)	Apple	63.9	53.7	60.1	64.1
Dairy products [1]	1.9	1.9	1.9	2.4	Fresh vegetables	7.5	9.5	10.3	12.0
Cheese [2]	4.8	4.7	4.1	4.5	Cucumbers	33.7	38.3	38.1	39.7
Salad and cooking oils [3]	5.9	12.1	11.8	12.2	Peppers	19.7	19.1	22.5	25.2
Fresh fruits	30.6	33.5	34.4	35.9	Tomatoes	20.5	30.5	35.8	39.7
Citrus	3.4	7.1	6.9	8.4	Wheat [4]	4.6	7.7	10.3	10.3
Apples	4.7	7.7	7.2	6.6	Rice [5]	8.1	12.1	15.0	12.6
Bananas	99.8	99.8	99.8	99.7	Cane and beet sugar [6]	24.9	19.1	27.9	22.0

NA Not available. [1] Milk equivalent of all dairy products calculated on a milkfat basis. [2] Natural equivalent of cheese and cheese products. Includes all types of cheese except full-skim American and cottage, pot, and baker's cheeses. [3] Olive and canola oil imports. [4] Flour and other wheat products included. Grain equivalent. [5] Rough equivalent. Includes milled rice converted to rough basis at annual extraction rate. [6] Import share is the quantity of imports for domestic consumption (net of re-exports) divided by domestic food consumption.

Source: U.S. Dept. of Agriculture, Economic Research Service, *Food Consumption, Prices, and Expenditures*, annual.

No. 1122. Selected Farm Products—United States and World Production and Exports: 1995 to 1999

[In metric tons, except as indicated (59 represents 59,000,000). Metric ton=1.102 short tons or .984 long tons]

Commodity	Unit	Amount						United States as percent of world		
		United States			World					
		1995	1998	1999	1995	1998	1999	1995	1998	1999
PRODUCTION [1]										
Wheat	Million	59	69	63	539	589	586	11.0	11.8	10.7
Corn for grain	Million	188	248	240	515	606	605	36.5	40.9	39.6
Soybeans	Million	59	75	72	125	160	156	47.4	46.7	46.1
Rice, milled	Million	5.6	5.9	6.6	371	394	403	1.5	1.5	1.6
Cotton [2]	Million bales [3] .	19.7	18.8	13.9	85.9	91.6	84.5	23.0	20.5	16.4
EXPORTS [4]										
Wheat [5]	Million	33.7	29.0	29.5	99.5	101.4	106.3	33.9	28.6	27.7
Corn	Million	52.7	51.9	47.0	64.9	68.5	69.9	81.1	75.8	67.2
Soybeans	Million	23.1	21.9	26.5	31.9	38.6	46.3	72.4	56.7	57.3
Rice, milled basis	Million	3.1	3.2	2.7	21.0	27.3	25.1	14.8	11.6	10.6
Cotton [2]	Million bales [3] .	9.4	7.5	4.3	28.4	26.7	23.6	33.0	28.1	18.2

[1] Production years vary by commodity. In most cases, includes harvests from July 1 of the year shown through June 30 of the following year. [2] For production and trade years ending in year shown. [3] Bales of 480 lb. net weight. [4] Trade years may vary by commodity. Wheat, corn and soybean data are for trade year beginning in year shown. Rice data are for calendar year shown. [5] Includes wheat flour on a grain equivalent.

Source: U.S. Dept. of Agriculture, Foreign Agricultural Service, *Foreign Agricultural Commodity Circular Series*, periodic.

Agriculture 675

No. 1123. Agricultural Exports—Value by Principal Commodities: 1980 to 1999

[In millions of dollars, except percent (41,234 represents $41,234,000,000). See headnote, Table 1119]

Commodity	Value (mil. dol.)							Percent		
	1980	1990	1995	1996	1997	1998	1999	1980	1990	1999
Total agricultural exports [1].	41,234	39,517	56,348	60,445	57,245	51,829	48,299	100.0	100.0	100.0
Grains and feeds [1]	19,126	14,409	18,644	20,863	15,368	14,008	14,001	46.4	36.5	29.0
Feed grains and products.	9,852	7,150	8,341	9,575	6,219	5,210	5,745	23.9	18.1	11.9
Corn	8,492	6,026	7,304	8,404	5,180	4,382	4,916	20.6	15.2	10.2
Wheat and products	6,660	4,035	5,734	6,466	4,302	3,905	3,806	16.2	10.2	7.9
Rice	1,289	801	996	1,029	932	1,208	944	3.2	2.0	2.0
Oilseeds and products [1]	9,394	5,705	8,921	10,792	12,057	9,462	8,141	22.8	14.4	16.9
Soybeans	5,880	3,548	5,400	7,324	7,379	4,835	4,517	14.3	9.0	9.4
Soybean oilcake and meal	1,666	979	986	1,430	1,865	1,604	1,070	4.1	2.5	2.2
Vegetable oils and waxes. . . .	1,216	810	1,820	1,375	1,766	2,239	1,597	3.0	2.1	3.3
Animals and animal products [1] . .	3,768	6,696	11,018	11,254	11,468	10,674	10,286	9.2	16.9	21.3
Hides and skins, incl. furskins . .	1,046	1,751	1,748	1,675	1,651	1,259	1,141	2.6	4.4	2.4
Cattle hides	637	1,369	1,465	1,327	1,337	993	927	1.6	3.5	1.9
Meats and meat products.	890	2,558	4,522	4,590	4,597	4,371	4,682	2.2	6.5	9.7
Beef and veal	249	1,580	2,647	2,429	2,497	2,326	2,666	0.6	4.0	5.5
Fats, oils, and greases.	769	424	827	614	562	664	525	1.9	1.1	1.1
Poultry and poultry products . . .	603	906	2,345	2,828	2,779	2,530	2,089	1.5	2.3	4.3
Cotton, excluding linters	2,864	2,783	3,681	2,715	2,682	2,545	968	7.0	7.0	2.0
Tobacco, unmanufactured	1,334	1,441	1,400	1,390	1,553	1,459	1,294	3.3	3.6	2.7
Fruits and preparations	1,335	2,379	3,300	3,291	3,451	3,200	3,263	3.3	6.0	6.8
Fresh fruits	739	1,486	1,973	1,971	2,100	1,838	1,821	1.8	3.8	3.8
Vegetables and preparations	1,188	2,225	3,637	3,822	4,144	4,222	4,297	2.9	5.6	8.9
Nuts and preparations.	757	976	1,410	1,626	1,446	1,360	1,184	1.9	2.5	2.5
Other	1,468	2,903	4,337	4,692	5,075	4,899	4,865	3.6	7.3	10.1

[1] Includes commodities not shown separately.

Source: U.S. Dept. of Agriculture, Economic Research Service, *U.S. Agricultural Trade Update*, February 29, 2000; and *Foreign Agricultural Trade of the United States*, calendar year supplements. Also in *Agricultural Statistics*, annual.

No. 1124. Agricultural Exports—Value by Selected Countries of Destination: 1980 to 1999

[41,234 represents $41,234,000,000. See headnote, Table 1119. Totals include transshipments through Canada, but transshipments are not distributed by country prior to 1982 and beginning 1996]

Country	Value (mil. dol.)								Percent		
	1980	1985	1990	1995	1996	1997	1998	1999	1980	1990	1999
Total agricultural exports [1] .	41,234	29,041	39,517	56,348	60,445	57,245	51,829	48,299	100.0	100.0	100.0
Asia [1]	15,046	11,191	17,712	28,212	28,560	25,705	20,988	20,235	36.5	44.8	41.9
Japan	6,133	5,409	8,145	11,170	11,704	10,536	9,110	8,944	14.9	20.6	18.5
Korea, South	1,797	1,413	2,650	3,759	3,871	2,863	2,268	2,461	4.4	6.7	5.1
Taiwan [2]	1,095	1,231	1,663	2,601	2,965	2,616	1,801	1,956	2.7	4.2	4.0
China [2]	2,277	157	818	2,635	2,092	1,613	1,359	862	5.5	2.1	1.8
Hong Kong	437	389	703	1,503	1,490	1,712	1,492	1,209	1.1	1.8	2.5
Indonesia	414	170	274	817	852	772	454	547	1.0	0.7	1.1
Philippines	319	292	381	766	892	873	721	788	0.8	1.0	1.6
Western Europe [1][3]	12,917	7,002	7,385	9,061	9,702	9,728	8,267	7,146	31.3	18.7	14.8
European Union [4]	12,177	6,542	7,102	8,701	9,322	9,105	7,961	6,607	29.5	18.0	13.7
Belgium-Luxembourg	697	387	386	650	749	678	658	565	1.7	1.0	1.2
Netherlands	3,476	1,869	1,585	2,146	2,218	2,040	1,559	1,612	8.4	4.0	3.3
Germany	2,373	1,009	1,165	1,237	1,489	1,355	1,243	969	5.8	2.9	2.0
Spain [5]	1,488	837	937	1,270	1,124	1,157	1,046	711	3.6	2.4	1.5
United Kingdom	996	604	836	1,067	1,233	1,312	1,315	1,084	2.4	2.1	2.2
Italy	1,203	669	714	720	796	764	704	497	2.9	1.8	1.0
Latin America [1]	6,154	4,224	5,121	8,042	10,486	10,417	11,473	10,080	14.9	13.0	20.9
Mexico	2,469	1,439	2,560	3,540	5,447	5,184	6,163	5,637	6.0	6.5	11.7
Canada	1,908	1,622	4,224	5,812	6,146	6,795	7,016	7,073	4.6	10.7	14.6
Soviet Union (former)	1,138	1,923	2,262	1,347	1,747	1,483	1,153	922	2.8	5.7	1.9
Russia	(X)	(X)	(X)	1,046	1,328	1,204	835	524	(X)	(X)	1.1
Eastern Europe	1,644	414	537	293	439	284	272	171	4.0	1.4	0.4
Africa [1]	2,237	2,488	1,935	3,074	2,877	2,282	2,118	2,187	5.4	4.9	4.5
Egypt	774	891	692	1,448	1,319	964	914	1,061	1.9	1.8	2.2

X Not applicable. [1] Includes areas not shown separately. [2] See text, Section 30, International Statistics. [3] Includes Canary Islands and Madeira Islands. [4] Includes France, Denmark, Greece, Ireland, and Portugal. Beginning 1995, also includes Austria, Finland, and Sweden. As of Jan. 1, 1981, Greece became a member of the European Union. As of Jan. 1, 1986, Spain and Portugal became members of the European Union. For consistency, data for all years are shown on same basis. [5] As of Jan. 1, 1984, includes Canary Islands and Spanish Africa, not elsewhere classified.

Source: U.S. Dept. of Agriculture, Economic Research Service, *Foreign Agricultural Trade of the United States*, calendar year supplements. Also in *Agricultural Statistics*, annual.

No. 1125. Cropland Used for Crops and Acreages of Crops Harvested: 1980 to 1999

[In millions of acres, except as indicated (382 represents 382,000,000)]

Item	1980	1985	1990	1993	1994	1995	1996	1997	1998	1999
Cropland used for crops.....	382	372	341	330	339	332	346	349	345	344
Index (1977=100).........	101	98	90	87	90	88	92	92	91	91
Cropland harvested [1].........	342	334	310	297	310	302	314	321	315	316
Crop failure...............	10	7	6	11	7	8	10	7	10	8
Cultivated summer fallow......	30	31	25	22	22	22	22	21	20	20
Acres of crops harvested [2]...	352	342	322	308	321	314	326	332	326	327

[1] Land supporting one or more harvested crops. [2] Area in principal crops harvested as reported by Crop Reporting Board plus acreages in fruits, vegetables for sale, tree nuts, and other minor crops.

Source: U.S. Dept. of Agriculture, Economic Research Service, *Economic Indicators of the Farm Sector: Production and Efficiency Statistics*, annual. Also in *Agricultural Statistics*, annual. Beginning 1993 *Agricultural Resources and Environmental Indicators*, periodic, and *AREI Updates: Cropland Use*, No. 12, annual.

No. 1126. Principal Crops—Production, Supply, and Disappearance: 1990 to 1999

[74.2 represents 74,200,000. Marketing year beginning May 1 for hay, June 1 for wheat, August 1 for cotton, September 1 for soybeans and corn. Acreage, production, and yield of all crops periodically revised on basis of census data]

Crop and year	Acreage (mil.)—		Yield per acre	Pro- duction	Farm price [1]	Farm value (mil. dol.)	Total supply [2]	Disappearance			Ending stocks
	Planted	Har- vested						Total [3]	Exports		
Corn for grain:			Bu.	Mil. bu.	$/bu.			Mil. bu.			
1990.........	74.2	67.0	119	7,934	2.28	18,192	9,282	7,761	1,725		1,521
1995.........	71.5	65.2	114	7,400	3.24	24,118	8,974	8,548	2,228		426
1997.........	79.5	72.7	127	9,207	2.43	22,352	10,099	8,791	1,504		1,308
1998.........	80.2	72.6	134	9,759	1.94	18,922	11,085	9,298	1,981		1,787
1999.........	77.4	70.5	134	9,437	1.90	17,950	11,239	9,500	1,950		1,739
Soybeans:			Bu.	Mil. bu.	$/bu.			Mil. bu.			
1990.........	57.8	56.5	34.1	1,926	5.74	11,042	2,169	1,840	557		329
1995.........	62.5	61.5	35.3	2,174	6.72	14,617	2,516	2,333	851		183
1997.........	70.0	69.1	38.9	2,689	6.47	17,373	2,826	2,626	873		200
1998.........	72.4	70.4	38.9	2,741	4.93	13,494	2,944	2,596	801		348
1999.........	73.8	72.5	36.5	2,643	4.75	12,451	2,994	2,694	940		300
Hay:			Sh. tons	Mil. sh. tons	$/ton			Mil. sh. tons			
1990.........	(NA)	61.0	2.40	146	[4][5]80.60	10,462	173	146	(NA)		27
1995.........	(NA)	59.8	2.58	154	[4][5]82.20	11,042	175	154	(NA)		21
1997.........	(NA)	61.1	2.50	153	[4][5]100.00	13,250	170	148	(NA)		22
1998.........	(NA)	60.1	2.53	152	[4][5]84.60	11,607	174	149	(NA)		25
1999.........	(NA)	63.2	2.52	159	[4][5]77.00	10,901	184	(NA)	(NA)		(NA)
Wheat:			Bu.	Mil. bu.	$/bu.			Mil. bu.			
1990.........	77.0	69.1	39.5	2,730	2.61	7,184	3,303	2,435	1,069		868
1995.........	69.0	61.0	35.8	2,183	4.55	9,787	2,757	2,381	1,241		376
1997.........	70.4	62.8	39.5	2,481	3.38	8,287	3,020	2,298	1,040		722
1998.........	65.8	59.0	43.2	2,547	2.65	6,781	3,373	2,427	1,042		946
1999.........	62.8	53.9	42.7	2,302	2.55	5,904	3,343	2,346	1,050		997
Cotton:			Lb.	Mil. bales [6]	cents/lb.			Mil. bales [6]			
1990.........	12.3	11.7	634	[7]15.5	68.2	5,076	18.5	16.5	7.8		[8]2.3
1995.........	16.9	16.0	537	[7]17.9	76.5	6,575	21.0	18.3	7.7		[8]2.6
1997.........	13.9	13.4	673	[7]18.8	66.2	5,976	22.8	22.8	7.5		[8]3.9
1998.........	13.4	10.7	625	[7]13.9	61.7	4,120	18.2	18.2	4.3		[8]3.9
1999.........	14.9	13.4	608	[7]17.0	47.1	3,836	21.0	21.0	5.7		[8]4.6
Potatoes:			Cwt.	Mil. cwt.	$/cwt.			Mil. cwt.			
1990.........	1.4	1.4	293	402	6.08	2,431	347	[9]310	[10]17		20
1995.........	1.4	1.4	323	445	6.77	2,992	424	[9]365	[10]37		22
1997.........	1.4	1.4	345	467	5.64	2,623	441	[9]379	[10]38		23
1998.........	1.4	1.4	343	476	5.56	2,633	447	[9]381	[10]43		23
1999.........	1.4	1.3	359	478	5.84	2,783	466	[9]388	[10]55		23
Tobacco: [11]			Lb.	Mil. lb.	$/lb.			Mil. lb.			
1990.........	(NA)	0.7	2,218	1,626	[5]1.74	2,827	3,969	1,796	631		2,149
1995.........	(NA)	0.7	1,914	1,270	[5]1.82	2,305	3,742	1,516	534		2,226
1997.........	(NA)	0.8	2,137	1,787	[5]1.80	3,217	3,744	1,494	532		2,250
1998.........	(NA)	0.7	2,062	1,480	[5]1.83	2,701	3,739	1,440	539		2,298
1999.........	(NA)	0.6	1,980	1,275	[5]1.83	2,329	3,566	(NA)	(NA)		(NA)

NA Not available. [1] Except as noted, marketing year average price. U.S. prices are computed by weighting U.S. monthly prices by estimated monthly marketings and do not include an allowance for outstanding loans and government purchases and payments. [2] Comprises production, imports, and beginning stocks. [3] Includes feed, residual, and other domestic uses not shown separately. [4] Prices are for hay sold baled. [5] Season average prices received by farmers. U.S. prices are computed by weighting state prices by estimated sales and include an allowance for outstanding loans and government purchases, if any, for crops under government programs. [6] Bales of 480 pounds, net weight. [7] State production figures, which conform with annual ginning enumeration with allowance for cross-state ginnings, rounded to thousands and added for U.S. totals. [8] Stock estimates based on U.S. Census Bureau data which results in an unaccounted difference between supply and use estimates and changes in ending stocks. [9] Covers potatoes used for table use, frozen and canned products, chips, and dehydration. [10] Covers fresh potatoes, chips, frozen and dehydrated products. [11] Flue-cured and cigar wrapper, crop year July-June; all other types October-September. Farm-sales-weight basis.

Source: Production—U.S. Dept. of Agriculture, National Agricultural Statistics Service. In *Crop Production*, annual; and *Crop Values*, annual. Supply and disappearance—U.S. Dept. of Agriculture, Economic Research Service, *Feed Situation*, quarterly; *Fats and Oils Situation*, quarterly; *Wheat Situation*, quarterly; *Tobacco Situation*, quarterly; *Cotton and Wool Outlook Statistics*, periodic; and *Agricultural Supply and Demand Estimates*, periodic. Data are also in *Agricultural Statistics*, annual; and *Agricultural Outlook*, monthly.

Agriculture   677

No. 1127. Corn—Acreage, Production, and Value by Leading States: 1997 to 1999

[72,671 represents 72,671,000. One bushel of corn=56 pounds]

State	Acreage harvested (1,000 acres)			Yield per acre (bu.)			Production (mil. bu.)			Price ($/bu.)			Farm value (mil. dol.)		
	1997	1998	1999	1997	1998	1999	1997	1998	1999	1997	1998	1999	1997	1998	1999
U.S. [1] .	72,671	72,589	70,537	127	134	134	9,207	9,759	9,437	2.43	1.94	1.90	22,352	18,922	17,950
IA	11,900	12,200	11,800	138	145	149	1,642	1,769	1,758	2.33	1.86	1.80	3,826	3,290	3,165
IL	11,050	10,450	10,650	129	141	140	1,425	1,473	1,491	2.53	2.04	2.05	3,606	3,006	3,057
NE	8,600	8,550	8,300	132	145	139	1,135	1,240	1,154	2.32	1.85	1.85	2,634	2,331	2,134
MN	6,450	6,750	6,600	132	153	150	851	1,033	990	2.15	1.71	1.70	1,831	1,766	1,683
IN	5,750	5,550	5,670	122	137	132	702	760	748	2.53	2.11	1.95	1,775	1,604	1,459
KS	2,600	2,850	2,980	143	147	141	372	419	420	2.47	1.96	1.90	918	821	798
WI	3,050	2,950	2,850	132	137	143	403	404	408	2.34	1.84	1.85	942	744	754
OH	3,550	3,340	3,200	134	141	126	476	471	403	2.48	2.03	2.00	1,180	956	806
SD	3,400	3,550	3,250	96	121	113	326	430	367	2.15	1.61	1.60	702	692	588
MI	2,180	2,050	1,950	117	111	130	255	228	254	2.40	1.90	1.85	612	432	469
MO	2,600	2,500	2,550	115	114	97	299	285	247	2.45	1.92	1.95	733	547	482
TX	1,750	1,850	1,770	138	100	129	242	185	228	2.74	2.26	2.25	662	418	514
CO	980	1,070	1,120	146	145	142	143	155	159	2.59	1.96	1.95	371	304	310
KY	1,150	1,180	1,180	103	115	105	118	136	124	2.62	2.17	2.15	310	294	266
ND	590	825	655	99	107	117	58	88	77	2.12	1.71	1.60	124	151	123
PA	1,010	1,050	880	98	111	70	99	117	62	2.92	2.48	2.55	289	289	157
NY	600	580	590	110	114	101	66	66	60	2.62	2.21	2.15	173	146	128
TN	620	620	570	102	96	102	63	60	58	2.65	2.13	1.95	168	127	113
NC	870	770	460	89	70	80	77	54	51	2.83	2.33	2.25	219	126	115
OK	170	220	310	138	130	145	23	29	45	2.66	2.10	2.00	62	60	90
LA	417	540	330	117	81	121	49	44	40	2.70	2.05	2.05	132	90	82

[1] Includes other states, not shown separately.

Source: U.S. Dept. of Agriculture, National Agricultural Statistics Service, *Crop Production*, annual; and *Crop Values*, annual.

No. 1128. Soybeans—Acreage, Production, and Value by Leading States: 1997 to 1999

[69,110 represents 69,110,000. One bushel of soybeans=60 pounds]

State	Acreage harvested (1,000 acres)			Yield per acre (bu.)			Production (mil. bu.)			Price ($/bu.)			Farm value (mil. dol.)		
	1997	1998	1999	1997	1998	1999	1997	1998	1999	1997	1998	1999	1997	1998	1999
U.S. [1] .	69,110	70,441	72,476	39	39	37	2,689	2,741	2,643	6.47	4.93	4.75	17,373	13,494	12,451
IA	10,400	10,350	10,750	46	48	45	478	497	478	6.33	4.79	4.65	3,028	2,380	2,224
IL	9,950	10,550	10,550	43	44	42	428	464	443	6.56	5.01	4.95	2,807	2,326	2,193
MN	6,550	6,800	6,900	39	42	41	255	286	283	6.20	4.65	4.55	1,584	1,328	1,287
IN	5,300	5,500	5,550	44	42	39	231	231	216	6.59	5.05	4.75	1,519	1,167	1,028
NE	3,550	3,750	4,250	41	44	43	144	165	181	6.28	4.83	4.60	903	797	831
OH	4,340	4,390	4,500	44	44	36	191	193	162	6.49	4.99	4.80	1,239	964	778
MO	4,850	5,000	5,350	36	34	28	175	170	147	6.39	4.90	4.80	1,116	833	706
SD	3,250	3,400	4,070	35	39	36	114	133	147	6.11	4.60	4.40	695	610	645
AR	3,600	3,400	3,350	31	25	28	110	85	94	6.88	5.38	4.95	755	457	464
KS	2,350	2,500	2,800	37	30	28	87	75	78	6.42	4.98	4.65	558	374	365
MI	1,860	1,890	1,940	39	39	40	72	74	78	6.47	4.99	4.70	463	368	365
WI	1,000	1,100	1,300	44	47	46	44	52	60	6.38	4.85	4.65	281	251	278
ND	1,140	1,475	1,340	30	32	35	34	47	47	6.10	4.64	4.10	205	219	192
MS	2,070	2,000	1,900	31	24	24	64	48	45	6.90	5.63	5.10	443	270	228

[1] Includes other states, not shown separately.

Source: U.S. Dept. of Agriculture, National Agricultural Statistics Service, *Crop Production*, annual; and *Crop Values*, annual.

No. 1129. Wheat—Acreage, Production, and Value by Leading States: 1997 to 1999

[62,840 represents 62,840,000. One bushel of wheat= 60 pounds]

State	Acreage harvested (1,000 acres)			Yield per acre (bu.)			Production (mil. bu.)			Price ($/bu.)			Farm value (mil. dol.)		
	1997	1998	1999	1997	1998	1999	1997	1998	1999	1997	1998	1999	1997	1998	1999
U.S. [1] .	62,840	59,002	53,909	39.5	43.2	42.7	2,481	2,547	2,302	3.38	2.65	2.55	8,287	6,781	5,904
KS	10,900	10,100	9,200	46.0	49.0	47.0	501	495	432	3.16	2.53	2.35	1,584	1,252	1,016
ND	11,095	9,610	8,657	24.3	32.0	28.0	269	308	242	3.82	3.03	2.95	1,019	931	716
MT	5,840	5,280	5,320	31.1	32.0	29.0	182	169	154	3.62	3.03	3.20	652	513	493
OK	5,300	5,100	4,300	32.0	39.0	35.0	170	199	151	3.21	2.57	2.35	544	511	354
WA	2,580	2,565	2,290	64.0	61.4	54.2	165	157	124	3.39	2.63	3.05	561	414	379
TX	4,100	3,900	3,400	29.0	35.0	36.0	119	137	122	3.25	2.66	2.35	386	363	288
SD	3,419	3,294	3,024	28.7	36.7	39.9	98	121	121	3.41	2.74	2.70	335	327	317
CO	2,750	2,610	2,450	32.8	39.6	43.8	90	103	107	3.17	2.49	2.50	286	257	268

[1] Includes other states, not shown separately.

Source: U.S. Dept. of Agriculture, National Agricultural Statistics Service, *Crop Production*, annual; and *Crop Values*, annual.

678 Agriculture

No. 1130. Greenhouse and Nursery Crops—Summary by Type of Product: 1990 to 1998

[In millions of dollars, except per capita (8,677 represents $8,677,000,000). Based on a survey of 36 commercial floriculture states and estimates by source]

Item	Total	Cut flowers	Potted flowering plants	Foliage plants	Bedding plants	Cut cultivated greens	Other [1]
Domestic production: [2]							
1990...................	8,677	529	701	693	1,032	121	5,601
1995...................	10,294	479	868	728	1,689	128	6,402
1997...................	11,841	494	894	761	1,953	119	7,621
1998...................	12,115	509	918	788	2,116	130	7,654
Imports:							
1990...................	526	326	18	25	(NA)	14	143
1995...................	855	512	30	53	(NA)	24	236
1997...................	1,003	595	22	68	(NA)	28	289
1998...................	1,079	614	31	91	(NA)	32	311
RETAIL EXPENDITURES [3]							
Total:							
1990...................	38,624	5,567	2,980	2,764	3,096	779	23,439
1995...................	46,583	6,662	3,728	3,092	5,067	888	27,147
1997...................	53,433	7,358	3,797	3,336	5,858	853	32,230
1998...................	54,786	7,626	3,932	3,527	6,347	920	32,433
Per capita (dol.): [4]							
1990...................	155	22	12	11	12	3	94
1995...................	177	25	14	12	19	3	103
1997...................	200	27	14	12	22	3	120
1998...................	203	28	15	13	23	3	120

NA Not available. [1] Includes turfgrass (sod), bulbs, nursery stock, groundcovers, and other greenhouse and nursery products except the following: seeds, cut Christmas trees, and food crops grown under cover. [2] Equivalent wholesale values. [3] Retail sales values of green goods and associated products and accessories through all marketing channels including delivery, installation, landscaping, and related services. [4] Based on U.S. Census Bureau estimated resident population as of July 1.

Source: U.S. Dept. of Agriculture, Economic Research Service, *Floriculture and Environmental Horticulture Situation and Outlook Report*, October 1999.

No. 1131. Fresh Fruits and Vegetables—Supply and Use: 1990 to 1999

[In millions of pounds, except per capita in pounds (7,327 represents 7,327,000,000)]

Year	Utilized production [1]	Imports [2]	Supply, [1] total	Consumption Total	Consumption Per capita	Exports [2]
FRUITS						
Citrus:						
1990..................	7,327	184	7,510	5,331	21.4	2,179
1995..................	8,635	449	9,084	6,333	24.1	2,751
1998..................	9,055	591	9,646	7,142	26.6	2,504
1999..................	8,502	200	8,702	6,283	23.2	2,410
Noncitrus: [3]						
1990..................	12,122	7,852	19,974	17,978	70.4	1,995
1995..................	12,983	9,388	22,371	19,521	74.3	2,850
1998..................	12,312	10,526	22,836	20,305	75.2	2,531
1999..................	12,769	10,005	22,873	20,109	73.8	2,752
VEGETABLES & MELONS						
1990..................	34,629	3,265	38,774	34,574	138.5	2,685
1995..................	38,692	4,698	44,470	39,208	149.3	3,525
1998..................	40,839	6,478	48,411	42,932	158.6	3,686
1999..................	43,724	6,470	51,357	45,645	166.7	3,892
POTATOES						
1990..................	11,335	684	12,019	11,691	46.8	327
1995..................	13,020	685	13,704	13,121	49.9	584
1998..................	12,514	1,061	13,575	12,924	47.8	651
1999..................	12,865	923	13,789	13,190	48.3	599

[1] Crop-year basis for fruits. [2] Fiscal year for fruits; calendar year for vegetables and potatoes. [3] Includes bananas.

No. 1132. Nuts—Supply and Use: 1990 to 1998

[In millions of pounds (shelled) (326.2 represents 326,200,000)]

Year	Beginning stocks	Marketable production [1]	Imports	Supply, total	Con-sumption	Exports	Ending stocks
1990	326.2	961.5	198.4	1,486.1	609.6	522.6	354.0
1995	334.1	770.1	204.0	1,308.2	512.5	543.8	251.9
1997	156.4	1,214.4	241.3	1,612.2	579.9	683.6	348.7
1998	348.7	848.7	259.6	1,457.1	622.8	620.9	213.4

[1] Utilized production minus inedibles and noncommercial usage.

Source of Tables 1131 and 1132: U.S. Dept. of Agriculture, Economic Research Service, *Fruit and Tree Nuts Situation and Outlook Yearbook* and *Vegetables and Specialties Situation and Outlook Yearbook*.

Agriculture   679

No. 1133. Commercial Vegetable and Other Specified Crops— Area, Production, and Value, 1997 to 1999, and Leading Producing States, 1999

[74 represents 74,000. Except as noted, relates to commercial production for fresh market and processing combined. Includes market garden areas but excludes minor producing acreage in minor producing states. Excludes production for home use in farm and nonfarm gardens. Value is for season or crop year and should not be confused with calendar-year income]

Crop	Area [1] (1,000 acres)			Production [2] (1,000 short tons)			Value [3] (mil. dol.)			Leading states in order of production, 1999
	1997	1998	1999	1997	1998	1999	1997	1998	1999	
Asparagus	74	74	76	101	99	110	183	199	234	CA, WA, MI
Beans, snap	290	287	313	919	975	1,005	282	464	391	WI, OR, MI [4]
Beans, dry edible. .	1,759	1,918	1,877	1,469	1,521	1,662	577	567	588	ND, MI, NE
Broccoli	131	134	137	844	868	996	481	512	455	CA, AZ
Cabbage	80	83	81	1,447	1,370	1,281	281	312	239	NY, CA, TX [5]
Cantaloupes	103	101	110	1,042	1,075	1,149	374	383	393	CA, AZ, TX
Carrots	133	136	130	2,498	2,411	2,478	535	483	682	CA, CO, MI [5]
Cauliflower	44	44	46	344	345	387	218	227	217	CA, AZ
Celery	27	27	28	906	900	936	266	221	220	CA, MI, TX
Corn, sweet	702	704	709	4,524	4,572	4,660	669	691	693	(NA)
Fresh market. .	236	237	242	1,182	1,316	1,362	419	452	459	CA, FL, GA
Processed.	466	467	467	3,342	3,256	3,298	250	239	234	WA, MN, WI
Cucumbers.	160	160	163	1,199	1,157	1,209	350	367	365	MN, NC, TX [4]
Lettuce, head	203	198	199	3,440	3,170	3,640	1,202	1,023	971	CA, AZ, CO
Lettuce, leaf	49	46	42	519	515	476	299	296	230	CA, AZ, OH
Mushrooms [6]	136	145	150	388	404	424	730	774	829	(NA)
Onions.	166	166	169	3,438	3,301	3,569	770	826	654	CA, OR, WA
Peppers, green . . .	56	57	58	748	728	766	480	507	466	FL, CA, NJ
Potatoes	1,354	1,388	1,333	23,355	23,789	23,920	2,623	2,633	2,783	ID, WA, WI
Strawberries	44	45	46	814	820	906	903	1,002	1,118	CA, FL, OR
Sweet potatoes . . .	82	84	83	666	619	599	211	190	216	NC, LA, CA
Tomatoes	398	422	482	11,612	11,033	14,611	1,645	1,764	1,833	(NA)
Fresh market. . .	115	122	132	1,639	1,631	1,775	1,040	1,150	920	FL, CA, VA
Processed.	283	300	350	9,973	9,402	12,836	605	614	913	CA, IN, OH
Watermelons.	179	169	176	1,996	1,849	2,066	305	285	268	FL, TX, CA

NA Not available.   [1] Area of crops for harvest for fresh market, including any partially harvested or not harvested because of low prices or other factors, plus area harvested for processing.   [2] Excludes some quantities not marketed.   [3] Fresh market vegetables valued at f.o.b. shipping point. Processing vegetables are equivalent returns at packinghouse door.   [4] Processed only.   [5] Fresh market only.   [6] Area is shown in million square feet. All data are for marketing year ending June 30.

Source: U.S. Dept. of Agriculture, National Agricultural Statistics Service, *Vegetables*, annual summary. Also in *Agricultural Statistics*, annual.

No. 1134. Fruits and Nuts—Utilized Production and Value, 1997 to 1999, and Leading Producing States, 1999

[10,254 represents 10,254,000,000]

Fruit or nut	Unit	Utilized production [1]			Farm value (mil. dol.)			Leading states in order of production, 1999
		1997	1998	1999	1997	1998	1999	
Apples (36 states) [2]	Mil. lb	10,254	10,761	10,519	1,575	1,322	1,679	WA, NY, MI
Apricots	1,000 tons . .	130	108	91	43	35	35	CA, WA, UT
Avocados	1,000 tons . .	178	156	(NA)	278	332	(NA)	CA, FL
Cherries, sweet	1,000 tons . .	223	208	223	279	226	243	WA, OR, CA
Cherries, tart	Mil. lb	283	306	253	45	44	(NA)	MI, NY, UT, WA
Cranberries	1,000 bbl. [3]	5,497	5,444	6,389	350	211	(NA)	WI, MA, NJ
Dates (CA)	1,000 tons . .	21	25	22	23	30	28	CA
Grapefruit (4 states)	Mil. boxes [4]	70	63	61	285	269	339	FL, CA, TX
Grapes (13 states)	1,000 tons . .	7,287	5,816	6,168	3,126	2,642	2,945	CA, WA, NY
Kiwifruit (CA)	1,000 tons . .	32	33	23	16	25	(NA)	CA
K-Early citrus	1,000 tons .	7	2	4	592	45	382	FL
Lemons (2 states).	Mil. boxes [5]	25	24	20	303	241	260	CA, AZ
Nectarines (CA)	1,000 tons . .	264	224	276	99	105	113	CA
Olives (CA)	1,000 tons [6]	104	90	145	67	41	67	CA
Oranges and tangerines (4 states). .	Mil. boxes [6]	303	324	234	1,959	2,062	1,926	FL, CA, AZ
Peaches (31 states)	Mil. lb	2,508	2,326	2,426	444	447	465	CA, SC, GA
Pears	1,000 tons . .	1,042	953	979	288	278	297	WA, CA, OR
Pineapples	1,000 tons . .	324	332	352	92	93	99	HI
Plums (CA)	1,000 tons . .	246	188	196	77	99	82	CA
Prunes (dried basis) (CA)	1,000 tons . .	205	103	173	181	79	(NA)	CA
Almonds (shelled basis) (CA)	Mil. lb	759	520	830	1,161	704	677	CA
Hazelnuts (in the shell)	1,000 tons . .	47	16	38	42	15	34	OR, WA
Macadamia nuts	Mil. lb	58	58	53	44	37	36	HI
Pecans (in the shell) (11 states) . . .	Mil. lb	335	146	325	259	177	274	GA, TX, NM
Pistachios	Mil. lb	180	188	122	203	194	160	CA
Walnuts, English (in the shell)	1,000 tons . .	269	227	280	385	328	(NA)	CA

NA Not available.   [1] Excludes quantities not harvested or not marketed.   [2] Production in commercial orchards with 100 or more bearing age trees.   [3] Barrels of 100 pounds.   [4] Approximate average, net weight, is 67 lb. in AZ and CA; 85 in FL; and 80 in TX.   [5] About 76 lb. net.   [6] Net contents of box varies. In CA and AZ approximate average for oranges and tangerines is 75 lb.; FL oranges, 90 lb.; TX oranges, 85 lb.; and FL tangerines, 95 lb.

Source: U.S. Dept. of Agriculture, National Agricultural Statistics Service, *Noncitrus Fruits and Nuts*, annual; and *Citrus Fruits*, annual.

680 Agriculture

No. 1135. Meat Supply and Use: 1980 to 1999

[In millions of pounds (carcass weight equivalent) (53,151 represents 53,151,000,000). Carcass weight equivalent is the weight of the animal minus entrails, head, hide, and internal organs; includes fat and bone. Covers Federal and state inspected, and farm slaughter]

Year and type of meat	Production	Imports	Supply, [1] total	Consumption [2]	Exports	Ending stocks
RED MEAT AND POULTRY						
1980	53,151	2,668	57,036	54,695	1,124	1,217
1985	56,271	3,255	60,631	58,651	926	1,054
1990	62,255	3,295	66,673	62,937	2,472	1,263
1995	74,070	2,837	78,637	69,912	6,956	1,769
1998	78,637	3,467	84,027	73,060	8,951	2,016
1999	81,537	3,820	87,372	76,061	9,340	1,972
ALL RED MEATS						
1980	38,978	2,668	42,481	41,170	429	882
1985	39,409	3,255	43,505	42,311	461	733
1990	38,787	3,295	42,742	40,784	1,250	707
1995	43,677	2,831	47,512	43,968	2,614	930
1998	45,284	3,461	49,639	45,239	3,407	994
1999	46,284	3,813	51,092	46,476	3,701	914
Beef:						
1980	21,643	2,064	24,166	23,560	173	432
1985	23,728	2,071	26,271	25,523	328	420
1990	22,743	2,356	25,434	24,031	1,006	397
1995	25,222	2,103	27,873	25,533	1,821	519
1998	25,760	2,643	28,868	26,305	2,171	393
1999	26,493	2,874	29,760	26,938	2,411	411
Pork:						
1980	16,617	550	17,521	16,838	252	431
1985	14,807	1,128	16,283	15,865	128	289
1990	15,354	898	16,565	16,031	238	296
1995	17,849	664	18,951	17,768	787	396
1998	19,011	705	20,124	18,309	1,230	584
1999	19,308	827	20,720	18,945	1,285	489
Veal:						
1980	400	21	432	420	2	9
1985	515	20	549	533	4	11
1990	327	(NA)	331	325	(NA)	6
1995	319	(NA)	326	319	(NA)	7
1998	262	(NA)	270	265	(NA)	5
1999	235	(NA)	240	235	(NA)	5
Lamb and mutton:						
1980	318	33	362	351	1	9
1985	359	36	403	389	1	13
1990	363	41	412	397	6	8
1995	287	64	362	348	6	8
1998	251	112	377	360	6	12
1999	248	113	372	358	5	9
POULTRY, TOTAL						
1980	14,173	-	14,555	13,525	695	334
1985	16,862	-	17,126	16,340	465	321
1990	23,468	-	23,931	22,153	1,222	556
1995	30,393	6	31,125	25,944	4,342	839
1998	33,352	6	34,387	27,821	5,545	1,022
1999	35,252	7	36,281	29,585	5,638	1,058
Broilers:						
1980	11,252	-	11,364	10,682	567	115
1985	13,520	-	13,646	13,072	417	158
1990	18,430	-	18,651	17,266	1,143	242
1995	24,827	1	25,287	20,832	3,894	560
1998	27,612	5	28,225	22,841	4,673	711
1999	29,468	4	30,183	24,521	4,866	796
Mature chicken:						
1980	551	-	581	507	53	21
1985	525	-	537	503	21	13
1990	523	-	530	496	25	9
1995	496	3	513	406	99	7
1998	525	-	533	101	426	6
1999	554	2	562	162	393	8
Turkeys:						
1980	2,370	-	2,610	2,337	75	198
1985	2,817	-	2,943	2,765	27	150
1990	4,514	-	4,750	4,390	54	306
1995	5,069	2	5,326	4,706	348	271
1998	5,215	-	5,630	4,880	446	304
1999	5,230	1	5,535	4,902	379	254

- Represents zero.   NA Not available.   [1] Total supply equals production plus imports plus ending stocks of previous year.
[2] Includes shipments to territories.

Source: U.S. Department of Agriculture, Economic Research Service, *Food Consumption, Prices, and Expenditures, 1970-1997*; and *Agricultural Outlook*, monthly.

Agriculture 681

No. 1136. Livestock Inventory and Production: 1980 to 2000

[Production in live weight (111.2 represents 111,200,000); includes animals for slaughter market, younger animals shipped to other states for feeding or breeding purposes, farm slaughter and custom slaughter consumed on farms where produced, minus livestock shipped into states for feeding or breeding with an adjustment for changes in inventory]

Type of livestock	Unit	1980	1985	1990	1994	1995	1996	1997	1998	1999	2000
ALL CATTLE [1]											
Inventory: [2] Number on farms	Mil	111.2	109.6	95.8	101.0	102.8	103.5	101.7	99.7	99.1	98.0
Total value	Bil. dol. .	55.8	44.0	59.0	66.5	63.2	52.1	53.4	60.2	58.8	67.0
Value per head	Dol. . . .	502	402	616	659	615	503	525	603	594	683
Production: Quantity	Bil. lb . .	40.3	40.1	39.2	41.6	42.5	40.9	40.9	41.6	42.3	(NA)
Beef, price per 100 lb . .	Dol . . .	62.40	53.70	74.60	66.70	61.80	58.70	63.10	59.60	63.40	(NA)
Calves, price per 100 lb .	Dol	76.80	62.10	95.60	87.20	73.10	58.40	78.90	78.80	87.70	(NA)
Value of production	Bil. dol. .	25.5	21.2	29.3	26.5	24.7	22.1	24.8	24.2	26.0	(NA)
HOGS AND PIGS											
Inventory: [3] Number on farms	Mil	67.3	54.1	53.8	57.9	59.7	58.2	56.1	61.2	62.2	59.4
Total value	Bil. dol. .	3.8	4.1	4.3	4.3	3.2	4.1	5.3	5.0	2.8	4.3
Value per head	Dol	56.00	75.00	79.10	75.00	53.00	71.00	94.00	82.00	44.00	72.00
Production: Quantity	Bil. lb . .	23.4	20.2	21.3	24.4	24.4	23.1	24.0	25.7	25.6	(NA)
Price per 100 lb	Dol	38.00	44.00	53.70	39.90	40.50	51.90	52.90	34.40	30.30	(NA)
Value of production	Bil. dol. .	8.9	8.9	11.3	9.7	9.8	11.9	12.6	8.7	7.7	(NA)
SHEEP AND LAMBS											
Inventory: [2] Number on farms	Mil	12.7	10.7	11.4	9.8	9.0	8.5	8.0	7.8	7.2	7.0
Total value	Mil. dol .	993	654	901	681	663	732	762	798	638	668
Value per head	Dol	78.20	61.10	79.30	69.90	74.70	86.50	96.00	102.00	88.00	95.00
Production: Quantity	Mil. lb . .	746	704	781	637	602	572	603	555	533	(NA)
Sheep, price per 100 lb .	Dol	21.30	23.90	23.20	30.90	28.00	29.90	37.90	30.60	31.10	(NA)
Lambs, price per 100 lb .	Dol	63.60	67.70	55.50	65.60	78.20	88.20	90.30	72.30	74.50	(NA)
Value of production	Mil. dol	403	434	374	366	414	441	490	354	348	(NA)

NA Not available. [1] Includes milk cows. [2] As of Jan. 1. [3] As of Dec. 1 of preceding year.
Source: U.S. Dept. of Agriculture, National Agricultural Statistics Service, *Meat Animals—Production, Disposition, and Income*, annual; and annual livestock summaries. Also in *Agricultural Statistics*, annual.

No. 1137. Livestock Operations by Size of Herd: 1995 to 1999

[In thousands (1,191 represents 1,191,000). An operation is any place having one or more head on hand at any time during the year]

Size of herd	1995	1998	1999	Size of herd	1995	1998	1999
CATTLE [1]				**MILK COWS** [2]			
Total operations	1,191	1,116	1,096	Total operations	140	117	111
1 to 49 head.	746	695	686	1 to 49 head.	79	61	57
50 to 99 head.	208	195	186	50 to 99 head.	39	34	33
100 to 499 head	210	199	197	100 or more head	21	21	21
500 to 999 head	18	18	18	**HOGS AND PIGS**			
1,000 head or more	9	9	9	Total operations	168	113	98
BEEF COWS [2]				1 to 99 head.	97	62	53
Total operations	898	855	843	100 to 499 head	44	27	23
1 to 49 head.	716	678	666	500 to 999 head	15	11	9
50 to 99 head.	105	101	101	1,000 to 1,999 head.	7	7	7
100 to 499 head	70	70	71	2,000 to 4,999 head.	4	5	5
500 head or more	6	5	5	5,000 head or more	1	2	2

[1] Includes calves. [2] Included in operations with cattle.
Source: U.S. Dept. of Agriculture, National Agricultural Statistics Service, *Cattle Final Estimates, 1994-1998*, January 1999; *Milk Cows and Production Final Estimates 1993-1997*, January 1999; and *Hogs and Pigs Final Estimates 1993-1997*, December 1998; and *Agricultural Statistics*, annual.

No. 1138. Hogs and Pigs—Number, Production, and Value by State: 1997 to 1999

[61,158 represents 61,158,000. See headnote, Table 1136]

State	Number on farms [1] (1,000)			Quantity produced (mil. lb.)			Value of production (mil. dol.)			Commercial slaughter [2] (mil. lb.)	
	1997	1998	1999	1997	1998	1999	1997	1998	1999	1998	1999
U.S. [3]	61,158	62,206	59,407	23,979	25,715	25,600	12,552	8,674	7,660	25,898	26,256
IA.	14,600	15,300	15,400	5,420	6,301	6,498	2,801	1,998	1,892	7,481	7,693
NC	9,600	9,700	9,500	3,828	3,751	3,658	2,072	1,320	1,149	2,383	2,456
MN	5,700	5,700	5,500	2,081	2,403	2,472	1,112	837	739	2,027	2,169
IL.	4,700	4,850	4,100	1,820	1,895	1,865	929	625	560	2,409	2,470
NE	3,500	3,400	3,000	1,425	1,451	1,551	785	535	489	1,606	1,643
IN.	3,950	4,050	3,250	1,533	1,633	1,326	775	531	332	1,580	1,566
MO	3,550	3,300	3,150	1,411	1,421	1,238	713	480	379	999	1,013

[1] As of December 1. [2] Includes slaughter in federally inspected and other slaughter plants; excludes animals slaughtered on farms. [3] Includes other states not shown separately.
Source: U.S. Dept. of Agriculture, National Agricultural Statistics Service, *Meat Animals-Production, Disposition and Income*, annual.

682 Agriculture

No. 1139. Cattle and Calves—Number, Production, and Value by State: 1997 to 2000

[99,744 represents 99,744,000. Includes milk cows. See headnote, Table 1136]

State	Number on farms [1] (1,000)			Quantity produced (mil. lb.)			Value of production (mil. dol.)			Commercial slaughter [2] (mil. lb.)	
	1998	1999	2000	1997	1998	1999	1997	1998	1999	1998	1999
U.S. [3]	99,744	99,115	98,048	40,892	41,620	42,344	24,804	24,153	25,961	43,088	44,099
TX	14,500	14,100	13,900	7,005	7,443	7,417	4,370	4,404	4,638	7,749	7,760
NE	6,750	6,700	6,650	4,030	4,257	4,326	2,429	2,344	2,519	9,052	9,231
KS	6,550	6,550	6,550	3,695	3,764	3,963	2,257	2,188	2,437	8,950	9,632
CO	3,250	3,200	3,150	1,871	1,986	2,069	1,189	1,176	1,292	2,941	3,235
OK	5,400	5,300	5,200	1,960	1,850	2,045	1,354	1,234	1,446	33	38
CA	4,900	5,100	5,100	1,937	1,850	1,972	896	852	862	1,295	1,275
IA	3,700	3,700	3,700	1,888	1,749	1,851	1,090	949	1,004	1,125	1,037
SD	3,700	3,900	3,900	1,296	1,439	1,546	863	914	1,094	327	389
MO	4,350	4,400	4,350	1,165	1,129	1,143	826	777	828	92	102
MN	2,500	2,500	2,550	1,135	1,070	1,083	672	602	625	901	872
WI	3,500	3,400	3,400	1,061	1,055	1,068	548	518	581	2,148	2,254

[1] As of January 1.   [2] Data cover cattle only. Includes slaughter in federally inspected and other slaughter plants; excludes animals slaughtered on farms.   [3] Includes other states not shown separately.

Source: U.S. Dept. of Agriculture, National Agricultural Statistics Service, Meat Animals-Production, Disposition and Income, annual.

No. 1140. Milk Cows—Number, Production, and Value by State: 1997 to 1999

[9,252 represents 9,252,000]

State	Number on farms [1] (1,000)			Milk produced on farms (mil. lb.)			Value of production [2] (mil. dol.)		
	1997	1998	1999	1997	1998	1999	1997	1998	1999
United States [3]	9,252	9,154	9,156	156,091	157,348	162,711	21,126	24,332	23,402
California	1,391	1,420	1,466	27,582	27,654	30,475	3,633	4,151	4,099
Wisconsin	1,393	1,369	1,365	22,368	22,842	23,071	2,982	3,541	3,198
New York	699	701	701	11,530	11,750	12,040	1,547	1,810	1,758
Pennsylvania	629	623	616	10,662	10,847	10,931	1,527	1,736	1,716
Minnesota	569	551	545	9,210	9,275	9,478	1,215	1,442	1,326
Idaho	272	292	318	5,193	5,765	6,453	639	836	839
Texas	378	352	345	5,768	5,605	5,620	790	880	843
Washington	253	248	247	5,305	5,326	5,535	732	847	825
Michigan	306	299	299	5,410	5,365	5,455	738	821	807

[1] Average number during year. Represents cows and heifers that have calved, kept for milk; excluding heifers not yet fresh.   [2] Valued at average returns per 100 pounds of milk in combined marketings of milk and cream. Includes value of milk fed to calves.   [3] Includes other states not shown separately.

Source: U.S. Dept. of Agriculture, National Agricultural Statistics Service, Dairy Products, annual; and Milk: Production, Disposition, and Income, annual.

No. 1141. Milk Production and Manufactured Dairy Products: 1980 to 1999

[334 represents 334,000]

Item	Unit	1980	1985	1990	1994	1995	1996	1997	1998	1999
Number of farms with milk cows	1,000	334	269	193	148	140	131	124	117	111
Cows and heifers that have calved, kept for milk.	Mil. head . .	10.8	11.0	10.0	9.5	9.5	9.4	9.3	9.2	9.2
Milk produced on farms	Bil. lb	128	143	148	154	155	154	156	157	163
Production per cow	1,000 lb. . . .	11.9	13.0	14.8	16.2	16.4	16.4	16.9	17.2	17.8
Whole milk sold from farms [1]	Bil. lb	126	141	146	152	154	153	155	156	161
Value of milk produced	Bil. dol. . . .	16.9	18.4	20.4	20.2	20.1	23.0	21.1	24.3	23.4
Gross farm income, dairy products	Bil. dol. . . .	16.7	18.1	20.2	20.0	19.9	22.8	21.0	24.2	23.2
Cash receipts from marketing of milk and cream [1]	Bil. dol. . . .	16.6	18.1	20.1	20.0	19.9	22.8	20.9	24.1	23.2
Number of dairy manufacturing plants	Number . . .	2,257	2,061	1,723	1,532	1,495	1,422	1,384	1,323	1,258
Manufactured dairy products:										
Butter (incl. whey butter)	Mil. lb	1,145	1,248	1,302	1,296	1,264	1,174	1,151	1,168	1,275
Cheese, total [2]	Mil. lb	3,984	5,081	6,059	6,735	6,917	7,218	7,330	7,492	7,944
American (excl. full-skim American) . . .	Mil. lb	2,376	2,855	2,894	2,974	3,131	3,281	3,286	3,315	3,577
Cream and Neufchatel	Mil. lb	229	294	431	573	544	575	615	621	647
All Italian varieties	Mil. lb	983	1,491	2,207	2,626	2,674	2,812	2,881	3,005	3,143
Cottage cheese: Creamed [3]	Mil. lb	825	716	832	731	711	690	706	728	722
Condensed bulk milk	Mil. lb	952	1,232	1,426	1,593	1,372	1,270	1,275	1,263	1,365
Nonfat dry milk [4]	Mil. lb	1,168	1,398	902	1,242	1,243	1,068	1,223	1,140	1,383
Dry whey [5]	Mil. lb	690	987	1,143	1,212	1,147	1,117	1,137	1,178	1,164
Yogurt, plain and fruit flavored	Mil. lb	(NA)	(NA)	(NA)	1,393	1,646	1,588	1,574	1,639	1,746
Ice cream, regular	Mil. gal . . .	830	901	824	876	862	879	914	935	954
Ice cream, lowfat [6]	Mil. gal . . .	293	301	352	359	357	366	386	407	394

NA Not available.   [1] Comprises sales to plants and dealers, and retail sales by farmers direct to consumers.   [2] Includes varieties not shown separately.   [3] Includes partially creamed (low fat).   [4] Includes dry skim milk for animal feed.   [5] Includes animal but excludes modified whey production.   [6] Includes freezer-made milkshake in most states.

Source: U.S. Dept. of Agriculture, National Agricultural Statistics Service, Dairy Products, annual; and Milk: Production, Disposition, and Income, annual.

Agriculture   683

No. 1142. Milk Production and Commercial Use: 1980 to 1999

[In billions of pounds milkfat basis (128.4 represents 128,400,000,000)]

Year	Production	Farm use	Commercial Farm marketings	Commercial Beginning stock	Imports	Commercial supply, total	CCC net removals [1]	Commercial Ending stock	Commercial Disappearance	Milk price per 100 lb. [2] (dol.)
1980	128.4	2.3	126.1	5.3	2.1	133.5	8.8	5.6	119.0	13.1
1985	143.0	2.5	140.6	4.8	2.8	148.2	13.2	4.5	130.5	12.8
1990	147.7	2.0	145.7	4.1	2.7	152.5	8.5	5.1	138.8	13.7
1995	155.3	1.6	153.7	4.3	2.9	160.9	2.1	4.1	154.7	12.8
1997	156.1	1.4	154.7	4.7	2.7	162.1	1.1	4.9	156.1	13.4
1998	157.3	1.4	156.0	4.9	4.6	165.5	0.4	5.3	159.8	15.4
1999	162.7	1.3	161.4	5.3	4.8	171.4	0.3	6.1	164.9	14.4

[1] Removals from commercial supply by Commodity Credit Corporation.   [2] Wholesale price received by farmers for all milk delivered to plants and dealers.

Source: U.S. Dept. of Agriculture, Economic Research Service, *Agricultural Outlook*, monthly.

No. 1143. Broiler, Turkey, and Egg Production: 1980 to 1999

[For year ending November 30 (392 represents 392,000,000)]

Item	Unit	1980	1985	1990	1993	1994	1995	1996	1997	1998	1999
Chickens: [1]											
Number [2]	Million . .	392	370	353	380	386	388	393	410	424	436
Value per head [2]	Dollars . .	1.88	1.90	2.29	2.37	2.34	2.41	2.65	2.72	2.69	2.65
Value, total [2]	Mil. dol. .	737	704	808	898	902	935	1,039	1,113	1,144	1,155
Number sold [3]	Million . .	238	220	208	198	197	180	174	191	194	205
Price per lb. [3]	Cents . .	11.0	14.8	9.6	10.0	7.4	6.5	6.6	7.7	8.1	7.0
Value of sales [3]	Mil. dol. .	129	152	94	96	73	60	59	71	76	68
PRODUCTION											
Broilers: [4]											
Number.	Million . .	3,963	4,470	5,864	6,694	7,018	7,326	7,597	7,764	7,934	8,146
Weight	Bil. lb. . .	15.5	18.9	25.6	30.6	32.5	34.2	36.5	37.5	38.6	40.8
Price per lb	Cents . .	27.7	30.1	32.6	34.0	35.0	34.4	38.1	37.7	39.3	37.1
Production value.	Mil. dol. .	4,303	5,668	8,366	10,417	11,372	11,762	13,903	14,159	15,145	15,129
Turkeys:											
Number.	Million . .	165	185	282	288	287	292	303	301	285	273
Weight	Bil. lb. . .	3.1	3.7	6.0	6.4	6.5	6.8	7.2	7.2	7.1	6.9
Price per lb	Cents . .	41.3	49.1	39.6	39.0	40.4	41.0	43.3	39.9	38.0	40.8
Production value.	Mil. dol. .	1,272	1,820	2,393	2,509	2,643	2,769	3,124	2,884	2,679	2,835
Eggs:											
Number.	Billion . .	69.7	68.4	68.1	71.9	73.9	74.8	76.4	77.5	79.8	82.7
Price per dozen	Cents . .	56.3	57.2	70.8	63.4	61.5	62.5	75.0	70.3	66.8	62.7
Production value.	Mil. dol. .	3,268	3,262	4,021	3,800	3,790	3,893	4,776	4,540	4,439	4,323

[1] Excludes commercial broilers.   [2] As of December 1.   [3] Data for 1980 represent number produced and production value.   [4] Young chickens of the heavy breeds and other meat-type birds, to be marketed at 2-5 lbs. live weight and from which no pullets are kept for egg production.

Source: U.S. Dept. of Agriculture, National Agricultural Statistics Service, *Poultry—Production and Value*, annual; *Turkeys*, annual; and *Layers and Egg Production*, annual.

No. 1144. Broiler and Turkey Production by State: 1997 to 1999

[In millions of pounds, liveweight production (37,541 represents 37,541,000,000)]

State	Broilers 1997	Broilers 1998	Broilers 1999	Turkeys 1997	Turkeys 1998	Turkeys 1999	State	Broilers 1997	Broilers 1998	Broilers 1999	Turkeys 1997	Turkeys 1998	Turkeys 1999
U.S. [1] . .	37,541	38,554	40,830	7,225	7,051	6,947	MO	1,075	1,097	1,124	563	598	616
AL	4,350	4,517	4,953	(NA)	(NA)	(NA)	NC	3,658	3,592	3,866	1,354	1,270	1,130
AR	5,590	5,619	5,861	525	496	491	OH	229	235	263	218	179	172
CA	1,210	(NA)	(NA)	481	443	429	OK	869	994	1,017	(NA)	(NA)	(NA)
CO	(NA)	(NA)	(NA)	147	(NA)	(NA)	OR	109	(NA)	(NA)	(NA)	(NA)	(NA)
DE	1,413	1,429	1,410	(NA)	(NA)	(NA)	PA	690	691	704	235	233	222
FL	596	632	648	(NA)	(NA)	(NA)	SC	830	848	924	368	356	326
GA	5,914	5,892	6,199	6	(NA)	(NA)	SD	(NA)	(NA)	(NA)	115	123	137
IN	(NA)	(NA)	(NA)	360	352	377	TN	624	716	724	(NA)	(NA)	(NA)
IA	(NA)	(NA)	(NA)	188	(NA)	233	TX	2,094	2,160	2,387	(NA)	(NA)	(NA)
KY	498	843	982	(NA)	(NA)	(NA)	VA	1,219	1,264	1,317	504	533	526
MD	1,417	1,367	1,472	13	15	15	WA	194	(NA)	(NA)	(NA)	(NA)	(NA)
MN	241	207	217	1,015	1,028	1,066	WV	381	358	358	87	88	95
MS	3,313	3,468	3,676	(NA)	(NA)	(NA)	WI	158	164	159	(NA)	(NA)	(NA)

NA Not available.   [1] Includes other states not shown separately.

Source: U.S. Dept. of Agriculture, National Agricultural Statistics Service, *Poultry—Production and Value*, annual; and *Turkeys*, annual.

Section 24
Natural Resources

This section presents data on the area, ownership, production, trade, reserves, and disposition of natural resources. Natural resources is defined here as including forestry, fisheries, and mining and mineral products.

Forestry—Presents data on the area, ownership, and timber resource of commercial timberland; forestry statistics covering the National Forests and Forest Service cooperative programs; product data for lumber, pulpwood, woodpulp, paper and paperboard, and similar data.

The principal sources of data relating to forests and forest products are *Forest Resources of the United States, 1992; Timber Demand and Technology Assessment, 1996; U.S. Timber Production, Trade, Consumption, and Price Statistics; Land Areas of the National Forest System*, issued annually by the Forest Service of the Department of Agriculture; *Agricultural Statistics* issued by the Department of Agriculture; and reports of the census of manufactures (taken every 5 years, see Table 1149) and the annual *Current Industrial Reports*, issued by the Census Bureau issued on the Internet, and in print in the annual *Manufacturing Profiles*. Additional information is published in the monthly *Survey of Current Business* of the Bureau of Economic Analysis; and the annual *Wood Pulp and Fiber Statistics* and *The Statistics of Paper, Paperboard, and Wood Pulp* of the American Forest and Paper Association, Washington, DC.

The completeness and reliability of statistics on forests and forest products vary considerably. The data for forest land area and stand volumes are much more reliable for areas which have been recently surveyed than for those for which only estimates are available. In general, more data are available for lumber and other manufactured products such as particle board and softwood panels, etc., than for the primary forest products such as poles and piling and fuelwood.

Fisheries—The principal source of data relating to fisheries is *Fisheries of the United States*, issued annually by the National Marine Fisheries Service (NMFS), National Oceanic and Atmospheric Administration (NOAA). The NMFS collects and disseminates data on commercial landings of fish and shellfish. Annual reports include quantity and value of commercial landings of fish and shellfish disposition of landings, and number and kinds of fishing vessels and fishing gear. Reports for the fish-processing industry include annual output for the wholesaling and fish processing establishments, annual and seasonal employment. The principal source for these data is the annual *Fisheries of the United States*.

Mining and mineral products—Presents data relating to mineral industries and their products, general summary measures of production and employment, and more detailed data on production, prices, imports and exports, consumption, and distribution for specific industries and products. Data on mining and mineral products may also be found in Sections 26 and 30 of this Abstract; data on mining employment may be found in Section 13.

Mining comprises the extraction of minerals occurring naturally (coal, ores, crude petroleum, natural gas) and quarrying, well operation, milling, refining and processing, and other preparation customarily done at the mine or well site or as a part of extraction activity. (Mineral preparation plants are usually operated together with mines or quarries.) Exploration for minerals is included as is the development of mineral properties.

Natural Resources   685

The principal governmental sources of these data are the *Minerals Yearbook* and *Mineral Commodity Summaries*, published by the U.S. Geological Survey, Department of the Interior, and various monthly and annual publications of the Energy Information Administration, Department of Energy. See text, Section 19, for a list of Department of Energy publications. In addition, the Census Bureau conducts a census of mineral industries every 5 years (for 1997 results, see Table 1162).

Nongovernment sources include the *Annual Statistical Report* of the American Iron and Steel Institute, Washington, DC; *Metals Week* and the monthly *Engineering and Mining Journal*, issued by the McGraw-Hill Publishing Co., New York, NY; *The Iron Age*, issued weekly by the Chilton Co., Philadelphia, PA; and the *Joint Association Survey of the U.S. Oil and Gas Industry*, conducted jointly by the American Petroleum Institute, Independent Petroleum Association of America, and Mid-Continent Oil and Gas Association.

Mineral statistics, with principal emphasis on commodity detail, have been collected by the U.S. Geological Survey and the former Bureau of Mines since 1880. Current data in U.S. Geological Survey publications include quantity and value of nonfuel minerals produced, sold or used by producers, or shipped; quantity of minerals stocked; crude materials treated and prepared minerals recovered; and consumption of mineral raw materials.

Censuses of mineral industries have been conducted by the Census Bureau at various intervals since 1840. Beginning with the 1967 census, legislation provides for a census to be conducted every 5 years for years ending in "2" and "7." The censuses provide, for the various types of mineral establishments, information on operating costs, capital expenditures, labor, equipment, and energy requirements in relation to their value of shipments and other receipts. Commodity statistics on many manufactured mineral products are also collected by the Census Bureau at monthly, quarterly, or annual intervals and issued in its *Current Industrial Reports* series.

In general, figures shown in the individual commodity tables include data for outlying areas and may therefore not agree with summary tables. Except for crude petroleum and refined products, the export and import figures include foreign trade passing through the customs districts of United States and Puerto Rico but exclude shipments between U.S. territories and the customs districts.

No. 1145. Gross Domestic Product of Agriculture, Forestry, Fishing, Mining, and Timber-Related Industries in Current and Real (1996) Dollars by Industry: 1990 to 1998

[In billions of dollars (5,803.3 represents $5,803,200,000,000), except as indicated. Industry classifications based on the 1987 Standard Industrial Classification (SIC). Data include nonfactor charges (capital consumption allowances, indirect business taxes, etc.) as well as factor charges against gross product; corporate profits and capital consumption allowances have been shifted from a company to an establishment basis]

Industry	Current dollars				Chained (1996) dollars			
	1990	1995	1997	1998	1990	1995	1997	1998
All industries, total [1]	5,803.2	7,400.5	8,300.8	8,759.9	6,707.9	7,543.8	8,144.8	8,495.7
Industries covered	297.3	306.7	346.2	330.0	321.9	329.9	361.1	366.9
Percent of all industries	5.12	4.14	4.17	3.77	4.80	4.37	4.43	4.32
Agriculture, forestry, and fishing	108.3	109.8	129.7	125.2	118.5	123.1	143.1	142.9
Farms	79.6	73.2	88.0	80.2	84.2	85.5	103.3	100.7
Agricultural services	28.7	36.7	41.6	45.0	34.6	37.6	40.0	41.9
Mining [1]	111.9	95.7	121.0	105.9	105.8	113.0	119.4	126.4
Metal mining	5.2	6.5	5.8	5.0	4.4	5.5	6.4	7.2
Coal mining	11.8	10.7	11.1	11.6	7.5	10.1	11.6	12.7
Oil and gas extraction	87.1	69.3	92.8	77.0	87.5	88.6	90.4	94.5
Nonmetallic minerals, except fuels . . .	7.8	9.1	11.4	12.3	8.1	9.1	10.9	12.0
Timber-related manufacturing	77	101	95	99	98	94	99	98
Lumber and wood products	32.2	42.3	41.9	43.9	45.1	41.6	40.3	42.2
Paper and allied products	45.0	58.9	53.6	54.9	52.5	52.2	58.3	55.4

[1] For additional industries, see Table 716.

Source: U.S. Bureau of Economic Analysis, *Survey of Current Business*, June 2000.

No. 1146. National Forest System—Summary: 1980 to 1998

[For fiscal years ending in year shown; see text, Section 9, State and Local Government. Includes Alaska and Puerto Rico, except as noted]

Item	Unit	1980	1990	1992	1993	1994	1995	1996	1997	1998
Timber cut, total value . . . . . . [1]	Mil. dol . . .	737	1,192	939	919	787	620	548	502	450
Commercial and cost sales: [1]										
Volume	Mil. bd. ft . .	9,178	10,500	7,290	5,917	4,815	3,866	3,725	3,285	3,298
Value	Mil. dol . . .	730	1,188	935	915	783	616	544	498	446
Free use:										
Volume	Mil. bd. ft . .	2,070	151	80	80	80	80	80	80	80
Value [2]	Mil. dol . . .	5.7	1.0	0.8	0.8	0.8	0.8	0.8	1.0	1.0
Misc. forest products:										
Value	Mil. dol . . .	1.1	2.6	2.7	2.8	3.1	2.9	3.2	3.0	3.0
Livestock grazing: [3]										
Cattle and horses [4]	1,000	1,521	1,236	1,408	1,318	1,224	1,311	1,167	1,225	1,208
Sheep and goats	1,000	1,328	958	1,183	1,111	925	1,068	859	932	909
Roads and trails:										
Road construction [5]	Miles	925	857	853	816	487	424	418	359	200
Trail construction [5][6]	Miles	2,419	1,635	1,976	1,976	2,113	2,139	1,696	(NA)	(NA)
Receipts, total	Mil. dol . . .	703	971	614	504	515	387	273	285	294
Timber use	Mil. dol . . .	625	849	520	425	432	303	195	197	208
Grazing use	Mil. dol . . .	16	10	11	11	11	9	7	7	7
Special land use, etc	Mil. dol . . .	62	112	84	68	72	75	71	81	79
Payments to local govt. [7]	Mil. dol . . .	240	368	322	323	309	273	256	234	229

NA Not available. [1] Includes land exchanges. [2] Includes some free use timber not reducible to board feet. [3] Covers number actually grazed. Excludes Puerto Rico. [4] Excludes animals under 6 months of age. [5] Includes reconstruction. [6] Includes work accomplished by Human Resource Programs and volunteers. [7] Payments made in following year.

Source: U.S. Forest Service, *Timber Demand and Technology Assessment*, RWU-4861. Also in *Agricultural Statistics*, annual.

Natural Resources 687

No. 1147. National Forest System Land—State and Other Area: 1998

[In thousands of acres (231,860 represents 231,860,000). As of Sept. 30]

State and other area	Gross area within unit boundaries [1]	National Forest System Land [2]	Other lands within unit boundaries	State and other area	Gross area within unit boundaries [1]	National Forest System Land [2]	Other lands within unit boundaries
Total	231,680	191,938	40,848	Montana	19,104	16,886	2,218
				Nebraska	442	352	90
United States .	231,624	191,910	40,820	Nevada	6,275	5,826	449
Alabama	1,288	665	623	New Hampshire . . .	1,554	827	727
Alaska	24,355	21,974	2,381	New Jersey	-	-	-
Arizona	11,891	11,255	636	New Mexico	10,367	9,327	1,040
Arkansas	3,539	2,579	960	New York	-	-	-
California	24,403	20,653	3,750	North Carolina	3,166	1,244	1,922
Colorado	16,052	14,509	1,543	North Dakota	-	1,106	-
Connecticut	-	-	-	Ohio	835	229	606
Delaware	-	-	-	Oklahoma	772	397	375
Florida	1,379	1,147	232	Oregon	17,496	15,656	1,840
Georgia	1,856	865	991	Pennsylvania	743	513	230
Hawaii	-	-	-	Rhode Island	-	-	-
Idaho	21,655	20,459	1,196	South Carolina	1,375	613	762
Illinois	856	292	564	South Dakota	2,367	2,012	355
Indiana	644	196	448	Tennessee	1,212	634	578
Iowa	-	-	-	Texas	1,994	755	1,239
Kansas	116	108	8	Utah	9,211	8,111	1,100
Kentucky	2,102	693	1,409	Vermont	817	368	449
Louisiana	1,024	604	420	Virginia	3,224	1,659	1,565
Maine	93	53	40	Washington	10,088	9,202	886
Maryland	-	-	-	West Virginia	1,870	1,033	837
Massachusetts	-	-	-	Wisconsin	2,023	1,521	502
Michigan	4,895	2,857	2,038	Wyoming	9,704	9,238	466
Minnesota	5,467	2,838	2,629				
Mississippi	2,310	1,159	1,151	Puerto Rico	56	28	28
Missouri	3,060	1,495	1,565	Virgin Islands	-	-	-

- Represents zero or rounds to zero.   [1] Comprises all publicly and privately owned land within authorized boundaries of national forests, purchase units, national grasslands, land utilization projects, research and experimental areas, and other areas.   [2] Federally owned land within the "gross area within unit boundaries."

Source: U.S. Forest Service, *Land Areas of the National Forest System,* annual.

No. 1148. Forest and Timberland Area, Sawtimber, and Stock: 1970 to 1996

[As of Jan. 1. (754 acres represents 754,000,000 acres)]

Year and region	Total forest land (mil. acres)	Timberland, ownership [1]				Sawtimber, net volume [3]		Growing stock, net volume [4]	
		All owner-ships (mil. acres)	Federally owned or man-aged [2] (mil. acres)	State, county, and municipal (mil. acres)	Private (mil. acres)	Total (bil. bd. ft.)	Softwood (bil. bd. ft.)	Total (bil. cu. ft.)	Softwood (bil. cu. ft.)
United States, 1970 . .	754	504	116	29	360	2,587	2,035	694	458
North	(NA)	154	11	18	126	295	81	146	39
South	(NA)	203	15	3	185	569	302	191	87
Rocky Mountains	(NA)	65	42	2	20	398	384	101	95
Pacific Coast	(NA)	82	47	5	29	1,325	1,268	257	238
United States, 1987 . .	731	485	97	34	354	2,853	2,040	766	453
North	165	154	11	19	124	459	126	190	48
South	203	197	16	4	177	781	388	245	106
Rocky Mountains	142	61	39	3	20	411	394	108	100
Pacific Coast	220	72	31	8	32	1,202	1,132	223	199
United States, 1992 . .	737	490	97	35	358	2,992	2,047	786	450
North	168	158	11	19	127	540	137	207	51
South	212	199	16	4	179	842	389	251	103
Rocky Mountains	140	63	40	3	20	415	397	110	101
Pacific Coast	217	70	30	8	32	1,196	1,124	218	195
United States, 1996 . .	746	518	124	35	357	3,227	2,231	860	503
North	170	180	32	21	127	574	146	213	49
South	214	201	16	5	180	858	393	256	105
Rocky Mountains	143	68	44	2	21	482	457	141	126
Pacific Coast	219	69	32	7	29	1,313	1,235	250	223

NA Not available.   [1] Timberland is forest land that is producing or is capable of crops of industrial wood and not withdrawn from timber utilization by statute or administrative regulation. Areas qualifying as timberland have the capability of producing in excess of 20 cubic feet per acre per year of industrial wood in natural stands. Currently inaccessible and inoperable areas are included.   [2] Includes Indian lands.   [3] Sawtimber is timber suitable for sawing into lumber. Live trees of commercial species containing at least one 12-foot sawlog or two noncontiguous 8-foot logs, and meeting regional specifications for freedom from defect. Softwood trees must be at least 9.0-inches diameter, and hardwood trees must be at least 11.0-inches diameter at 4 1/2 feet above ground. International 1/4-inch rule.   [4] Live trees of commercial species meeting specified standards of quality or vigor. Cull trees are excluded. Includes only trees 5.0-inches diameter or larger at 4 1/2 feet above ground.

Source: U.S. Forest Service, *Forest Resources of the United States, 1992;* and *Timber Demand and Technology Assessment, 1996,* RWU-4851.

No. 1149. Timber-Based Industries—Summary of Manufactures: 1992 and 1997

Selected industries	1987 SIC code	Establishments		Paid employees		Annual payroll (mil. dol.)		Value of shipments (mil. dol.)	
		1992	1997	1992	1997	1992	1997	1992	1997
Lumber and wood products	**24**	**35,807**	**36,735**	**655,799**	**757,267**	**13,882**	**18,669**	**81,565**	**111,931**
Logging	241	13,063	13,533	83,202	83,212	1,689	2,014	13,592	13,626
Sawmills & planing mills	242	6,845	6,270	168,448	178,575	3,585	4,478	23,294	32,750
Sawmills & planing mills, general	2421	5,815	5,176	137,620	143,292	3,040	3,742	21,061	29,414
Hardwood dimension & flooring mills	2426	833	992	28,919	33,940	510	708	2,085	3,207
Millwork, plywood, & structural members	243	8,947	9,373	224,061	260,726	5,004	6,599	24,744	33,201
Millwork	2431	3,176	2,745	85,804	92,259	1,967	2,345	9,649	12,013
Wood kitchen cabinets	2434	4,355	5,096	63,159	79,579	1,315	1,867	4,968	7,483
Hardwood veneer & plywood	2435	316	332	19,918	22,151	392	526	2,238	2,856
Softwood veneer & plywood	2436	203	155	30,877	28,843	815	913	5,350	5,763
Structural wood members, n.e.c.	2439	897	1,045	24,303	37,894	516	949	2,539	5,085
Wood containers	244	2,466	2,922	40,084	49,580	645	937	2,942	4,332
Nailed wood boxes & shook	2441	308	318	5,850	4,885	101	109	439	406
Wood pallets & skids	2448	1,929	2,347	28,705	38,994	451	718	2,147	3,449
Wood buildings & mobile homes	245	950	1,028	55,997	91,234	1,234	2,363	6,645	13,179
Miscellaneous wood products	249	3,536	3,609	84,007	93,940	1,725	2,278	10,348	14,842
Wood preserving	2491	488	451	10,783	11,668	232	298	2,701	4,462
Reconstituted wood products	2493	288	316	22,847	25,269	616	798	3,986	5,274
Wood products, n.e.c.	2499	2,760	2,842	50,377	57,003	878	1,182	3,660	5,107
Paper and allied products	**26**	**6,416**	**6,496**	**626,348**	**(¹)**	**20,492**	**(D)**	**133,201**	**(D)**
Pulp mills	261	45	39	15,893	10,247	689	524	5,466	4,073
Paper mills	262	280	256	130,556	107,552	5,421	5,380	32,786	35,514
Paperboard mills	263	204	217	51,529	54,643	2,136	2,685	16,140	19,829
Paperboard containers & boxes	265	2,787	2,842	199,403	208,071	5,722	6,952	32,655	40,085
Corrugated & solid fiber boxes	2653	1,651	1,732	112,262	124,537	3,276	4,244	19,834	25,532
Folding paperboard boxes	2657	590	588	52,594	50,921	1,591	1,766	7,929	9,003
Miscellaneous converted paper products	267	3,100	3,142	228,967	(¹)	6,523	(D)	46,154	(D)
Sanitary paper products	2676	150	160	40,601	(²)	1,454	(D)	15,647	(D)

D Data withheld to avoid disclosing data of individual companies. ¹ 100,000 or more employees. ² 25,000 to 49,9999 employees.

Source: U.S. Census Bureau, *1997 Economic Census, Core Business Statistics Series,* Series EC97X-CS2, June 2000.

No. 1150. Timber Products—Production, Foreign Trade, and Consumption by Type of Product: 1980 to 1997

[In millions of cubic feet (12,123 represents 12,123,000,000), roundwood equivalent]

Item	Unit	1980	1990	1991	1992	1993	1994	1995	1996	1997
Industrial roundwood:										
Domestic production	Mil. cu. ft.	12,123	14,674	14,051	14,455	14,184	14,515	14,501	14,664	14,610
Imports	Mil. cu. ft.	2,570	3,121	2,841	3,122	3,516	3,701	3,988	4,045	4,154
Exports	Mil. cu. ft.	1,857	2,207	2,287	2,226	2,044	2,042	2,214	2,182	2,314
Consumption	Mil. cu. ft.	12,836	15,587	14,605	15,351	15,656	16,174	16,275	16,527	17,201
Lumber:										
Domestic production	Mil. cu. ft.	5,305	7,404	6,858	7,058	6,870	7,082	6,826	7,072	7,120
Imports	Mil. cu. ft.	1,545	1,893	1,698	1,947	2,227	2,384	2,515	2,615	2,620
Exports	Mil. cu. ft.	395	573	604	548	519	501	481	471	602
Consumption	Mil. cu. ft.	6,455	8,725	7,953	8,457	8,577	8,965	8,861	9,215	9,139
Plywood and veneer:										
Domestic production	Mil. cu. ft.	1,175	1,422	1,271	1,299	1,300	1,327	1,314	1,297	1,211
Imports	Mil. cu. ft.	120	97	83	100	100	94	107	97	114
Exports	Mil. cu. ft.	45	109	95	106	100	100	86	87	103
Consumption	Mil. cu. ft.	1,250	1,410	1,259	1,293	1,300	1,334	1,333	1,307	1,222
Pulp products:										
Domestic production	Mil. cu. ft.	4,390	5,285	5,370	5,488	5,393	5,531	5,847	5,795	5,794
Imports	Mil. cu. ft.	880	1,083	1,017	1,036	1,128	1,181	1,304	1,262	1,352
Exports	Mil. cu. ft.	579	673	773	823	753	795	943	925	858
Consumption	Mil. cu. ft.	4,691	5,696	5,614	5,702	5,768	5,917	6,208	6,132	6,288
Logs:										
Imports	Mil. cu. ft.	25	4	2	7	15	18	13	18	20
Pulpwood chips, exports	Mil. cu. ft.	278	178	214	225	211	230	250	278	422
Fuelwood consumption	Mil. cu. ft.	3,105	3,177	3,187	3,202	3,244	3,297	3,360	3,420	2,542

Source: U.S. Forest Service, *Timber Demand and Technology Assessment,* RWU-4861. Also in *Agricultural Statistics,* annual.

U.S. Census Bureau, Statistical Abstract of the United States: 2000

No. 1151. Selected Timber Products—Imports and Exports: 1980 to 1998

Product	Unit	1980	1990	1992	1993	1994	1995	1996	1997	1998
IMPORTS [1]										
Lumber, total [2]	Mil. bd. ft..	9,866	13,063	13,426	15,368	16,534	17,524	18,363	18,237	19,012
From Canada	Percent...	97.5	91.2	98.4	98.0	97.4	97.0	97.1	96.2	95.9
Logs, total	Mil. bd. ft.[3]..	128	23	43	94	110	80	115	128	185
From Canada	Percent...	95.2	83.5	93.8	95.1	77.0	70.0	82.3	82.9	90.9
Paper and board [4]	1,000 tons.	8,013	12,195	11,730	12,990	13,651	14,292	13,023	14,525	14,538
Woodpulp	1,000 tons.	4,051	4,893	5,029	5,413	5,650	5,969	5,692	6,398	5,984
Plywood	Mil. sq. ft.[5].	1,235	1,687	1,776	1,786	1,693	1,951	1,780	2,111	2,429
EXPORTS										
Lumber, total [2]	Mil. bd. ft..	2,507	4,614	3,513	3,280	3,115	2,958	2,898	2,933	2,189
To: Canada	Percent...	25.2	14.3	16.3	17.3	19.6	22.0	22.9	24.3	26.3
Japan	Percent...	25.9	27.5	31.7	36.0	33.9	33.1	33.2	27.2	16.2
Europe	Percent...	23.7	14.9	20.9	16.7	17.5	17.4	16.7	20.2	25.6
Logs, total	Mil. bd. ft.[3]..	3,261	4,213	3,279	2,876	2,684	2,820	2,636	2,398	1,978
To: Canada	Percent...	9.7	9.4	12.7	13.6	16.2	25.4	19.7	29.6	39.4
Japan	Percent...	78.0	62.3	62.3	65.4	67.9	61.3	68.6	56.2	50.8
China: Mainland	Percent...	2.7	8.6	7.2	4.6	2.8	0.7	0.6	0.8	0.9
Paper and board [4]	1,000 tons.	4,241	5,163	7,021	6,835	7,536	7,621	9,118	10,368	9,103
Woodpulp	1,000 tons.	3,806	5,905	7,222	6,499	6,728	8,261	7,170	6,990	6,025
Plywood	Mil. sq. ft.[5].	413	1,766	1,760	1,677	1,455	1,517	1,499	1,802	970

[1] Customs value of imports; see text, Section 28, Foreign Commerce. [2] Includes railroad ties. [3] Log scale. [4] Includes paper and board products. Excludes hardboard. [5] 3/8 inch basis.
Source: U.S. Forest Service, *Timber Demand and Technology Assessment*, RWU-4851. Also in *Agricultural Statistics*, annual.

No. 1152. Lumber Consumption by Species Group and End Use: 1994 to 1998

[In million board feet (56.9 represents 56,900,000), except per capita in board feet. Per capita consumption based on estimated resident population as of July 1]

Item	1994	1995	1996	1997	1998	End-use	1994	1995	1996	1997	1998
Total.....	59.8	59.3	62.2	63.0	65.1	New housing	16.1	15.9	19.0	(NA)	(NA)
						Residential upkeep and					
Per capita.....	229	225	234	235	241	improvements.......	12.3	12.4	17.7	(NA)	(NA)
						New nonresidential					
Species group:						construction [1]	5.7	5.8	4.6	(NA)	(NA)
Softwoods...	48.2	47.6	50.2	50.9	52.1	Manufacturing........	5.5	5.5	7.6	(NA)	(NA)
Hardwoods..	11.6	11.7	12.0	12.1	13.0	Shipping	8.5	8.5	6.3	(NA)	(NA)
						Other [2]	8.9	8.8	6.8	(NA)	(NA)

NA Not available. [1] In addition to new construction, includes railroad ties laid as replacements in existing track and lumber used by railroads for railcar repair. [2] Includes upkeep and improvement of nonresidential buildings and structures; made-at-home projects, such as furniture, boats, and picnic tables; made-on-the-job items such as advertising and display structures; and miscellaneous products and uses.
Source: U.S. Forest Service, *Timber Demand and Technology Assessment*, RWU-4851. Also in *Agricultural Statistics*, annual.

No. 1153. Selected Timber Products—Producer Price Indexes: 1990 to 1999

[1982=100]

Product	1990	1992	1993	1994	1995	1996	1997	1998	1999
Lumber and wood products	129.7	146.6	174.0	180.0	178.1	176.1	183.8	179.1	183.6
Lumber..........................	124.6	144.7	183.4	188.4	173.4	179.8	194.5	179.5	188.2
Softwood lumber...............	123.8	148.6	193.0	198.1	178.5	189.5	206.5	182.7	196.0
Hardwood lumber..............	131.0	140.7	163.3	168.3	167.0	163.9	174.1	178.7	177.3
Millwork.	130.4	143.3	156.6	162.4	163.8	166.6	170.9	171.1	174.7
General millwork..............	132.0	146.3	158.5	163.6	165.4	167.9	171.1	172.4	175.6
Prefabricated structural members	122.3	132.7	159.7	169.3	163.5	167.5	177.8	170.1	178.1
Plywood..........................	114.2	133.3	152.8	158.6	165.3	156.4	159.3	157.3	176.4
Softwood plywood..............	119.6	147.2	169.7	176.8	188.1	173.7	175.5	174.9	207.0
Hardwood plywood and related products.	102.7	106.9	115.4	122.3	122.2	124.9	127.1	126.9	128.6
Other wood products	114.7	124.5	135.3	137.7	143.7	127.5	128.4	135.2	131.1
Boxes..........................	119.1	127.5	138.2	141.3	145.0	147.1	149.2	150.7	152.3
Pulp, paper, and allied products	141.2	145.2	147.3	152.5	172.2	168.7	167.9	171.7	174.1
Pulp, paper, and prod, ex bldg paper ...	132.9	129.2	127.6	133.1	163.4	149.7	144.7	147.0	147.9
Woodpulp..................	151.3	118.9	104.2	115.9	183.2	133.1	128.6	122.6	119.7
Wastepaper....................	138.9	117.5	117.4	209.5	371.1	141.6	163.3	145.4	183.6
Paper..........................	128.8	123.2	123.8	126.0	159.0	149.4	143.9	145.4	141.8
Writing and printing papers	129.1	120.2	120.5	121.7	158.4	144.6	140.0	139.9	137.8
Newsprint.....................	119.6	108.9	112.1	116.7	161.8	159.5	133.9	143.4	(NA)
Paperboard	135.7	134.3	130.0	140.5	183.1	155.1	144.4	151.6	153.2
Converted paper & paperboard products......................	135.2	134.8	133.7	136.7	157.0	153.4	148.4	152.2	153.5
Office supplies and accessories	121.4	116.4	115.3	116.9	134.9	132.9	131.0	131.2	129.5
Building paper & building board mill products	112.2	119.6	132.7	144.1	144.9	137.2	129.6	132.9	141.6

NA Not available.
Source: U.S. Bureau of Labor Statistics, *Producer Price Indexes*, monthly.

No. 1154. Selected Species—Stumpage Prices In Current and Constant (1992) Dollars: 1990 to 1998

[In dollars per 1,000 board feet. Stumpage prices are based on sales of sawtimber from National Forests]

Species	1990	1991	1992	1993	1994	1995	1996	1997	1998
CURRENT DOLLARS									
Softwoods:									
Douglas fir [1]	432	466	477	318	652	454	436	331	254
Southern pine [2]	155	127	198	217	266	248	241	307	288
Sugar pine [3]	667	285	492	598	625	397	318	234	200
Ponderosa pine [3][4]	206	218	292	535	291	150	274	270	205
Western hemlock [5]	213	203	165	364	335	297	248	211	161
Hardwoods:									
All eastern hardwoods [6]	52	146	167	264	352	309	259	287	241
Oak, white, red, and black [6]	66	188	211	195	317	297	237	265	270
Maple, sugar [7]	70	135	145	220	313	286	238	357	395
CONSTANT (1992) DOLLARS [8]									
Softwoods:									
Douglas fir [1]	564	470	477	313	635	426	400	305	230
Southern pine [2]	202	128	198	214	259	233	221	282	261
Sugar pine [3]	871	287	492	589	609	373	292	215	181
Ponderosa pine [3][4]	269	220	292	527	283	141	251	248	186
Western hemlock [5]	278	205	165	359	326	279	227	194	146
Hardwoods:									
All eastern hardwoods [6]	147	161	167	260	343	295	287	264	219
Oak, white, red, and black [6]	190	165	211	192	309	279	243	243	245
Maple, sugar [7]	136	121	145	216	305	268	196	328	358

[1] Western Washington and western Oregon.   [2] Southern region.   [3] Pacific Southwest region (formerly California region).
[4] Includes Jeffrey pine.   [5] Pacific Northwest region.   [6] Eastern and Southern regions.   [7] Eastern region.   [8] Deflated by the producer price index, all commodities.

Source: U.S. Forest Service, *Timber Demand and Technology Assessment*, RWU-4851. Also in *Agricultural Statistics*, annual.

No. 1155. Paper and Paperboard—Production and New Supply: 1980 to 1999

[In thousands of short tons (63,600 represents 63,600,000)]

Item	1980	1990	1993	1994	1995	1996	1997	1998	1999, prel.
Production, total	63,600	80,445	86,693	90,897	91,325	92,199	96,846	96,343	96,902
Paper, total	30,116	39,361	41,745	43,356	42,868	42,481	44,697	44,777	46,012
Paperboard, total	30,926	39,318	43,113	45,724	46,640	47,901	50,332	49,749	50,890
Unbleached kraft	15,295	20,357	21,447	22,469	22,697	22,178	23,222	23,199	22,958
Semichemical	4,724	5,640	5,672	5,943	5,662	5,619	6,047	5,894	5,954
Bleached kraft	3,836	4,399	4,583	5,029	5,304	5,236	5,548	5,487	5,712
Recycled	7,071	8,921	11,410	12,283	12,977	14,868	15,514	15,170	16,266
Wet machine board E	138	96	95	96	96	96	96	96	(NA)
Building paper E	1,369	723	797	787	787	787	787	787	(NA)
Insulating board E	1,051	946	943	934	934	934	934	934	(NA)
New supply, all grades, excluding products	67,783	87,683	93,146	97,448	98,164	95,896	101,201	102,869	(NA)
Paper, total	37,126	49,485	51,246	53,077	52,769	50,687	54,149	55,068	(NA)
Newsprint	11,377	13,412	12,750	12,889	12,762	11,768	12,612	12,721	(NA)
Printing/writing papers	16,124	25,456	27,846	29,444	29,550	28,300	30,751	31,384	(NA)
Packaging and ind. conv. papers	5,243	4,718	4,628	4,640	4,241	4,325	4,265	4,285	(NA)
Tissue	4,382	5,899	6,022	6,105	6,215	6,294	6,521	6,680	(NA)
Paperboard, total	27,689	36,301	39,950	42,435	43,448	43,214	45,061	45,597	(NA)
Construction and other	2,968	1,897	1,949	1,935	1,947	1,994	1,991	2,203	(NA)

NA Not available.

Source: American Forest and Paper Association, Washington, DC, *Monthly Statistical Summary of Paper, Paperboard and Woodpulp.*

Natural Resources   691

No. 1156. Fishery Products—Domestic Catch, Imports, and Disposition: 1980 to 1998

[Live weight, in millions of pounds (11,357 represents 11,357,000,000). For data on commercial catch for selected countries, see Table 1381, Section 30, Comparative International Statistics]

Item	1980	1990	1992	1993	1994	1995	1996	1997	1998
Total	11,357	16,349	16,106	20,334	19,309	16,484	16,474	17,131	16,897
For human food	8,006	12,662	13,242	13,821	13,714	13,584	13,625	13,739	14,175
For industrial use	3,351	3,687	2,864	6,513	5,595	2,900	2,848	3,392	2,722
Domestic catch	6,482	9,404	9,637	10,467	10,461	9,788	9,565	9,845	9,194
For human food	3,654	7,041	7,618	8,214	7,936	7,667	7,476	7,248	7,174
For industrial use	2,828	2,363	2,019	2,253	2,525	2,121	2,090	2,597	2,020
Imports [1]	4,875	6,945	6,469	9,867	8,848	6,696	6,909	7,286	7,703
For human food	4,352	5,621	5,624	5,607	5,778	5,917	6,150	6,491	7,001
For industrial use [2] . . .	523	1,324	845	4,260	3,070	779	759	795	702
Disposition of domestic catch	6,482	9,404	9,637	10,467	10,461	9,788	9,565	9,846	9,194
Fresh and frozen	2,621	6,501	7,288	7,744	7,475	7,099	7,054	6,877	6,870
Canned	1,161	751	543	649	622	769	678	648	516
Cured.	96	126	100	115	95	90	93	108	129
Reduced to meal, oil, etc.	2,604	2,026	1,696	1,959	2,269	1,830	1,740	2,213	1,679

[1] Excludes imports of edible fishery products consumed in Puerto Rico; includes landings of tuna caught by foreign vessels in American Samoa. [2] Fish meal and sea herring.

No. 1157. Fisheries—Quantity and Value of Domestic Catch: 1980 to 1998

Year	Quantity (mil. lb. [1])			Value (mil. dol.)	Average price per lb. (cents)	Year	Quantity (mil. lb. [1])			Value (mil. dol.)	Average price per lb. (cents)
	Total	For human food	For industrial products [2]				Total	For human food	For industrial products [2]		
1980	6,482	3,654	2,828	2,237	34.5	1990	9,404	7,041	2,363	3,522	37.5
1981	5,977	3,547	2,430	2,388	40.0	1991	9,484	7,031	2,453	3,308	34.9
1982	6,367	3,285	3,082	2,390	37.5	1992	9,637	7,618	2,019	3,678	38.2
1983	6,439	3,238	3,201	2,355	36.6	1993	[3]10,467	8,214	2,253	3,471	33.2
1984	6,438	3,320	3,118	2,350	36.5	1994	10,461	7,936	2,525	3,807	36.8
1985	6,258	3,294	2,964	2,326	37.2	1995	9,788	7,667	2,121	3,770	38.5
1986	6,031	3,393	2,638	2,763	45.8	1996	9,565	7,474	2,091	3,487	36.5
1987	6,896	3,946	2,950	3,115	45.2	1997	9,842	7,244	2,598	3,448	35.0
1988	7,192	4,588	2,604	3,520	48.9	1998	9,194	7,173	2,021	3,128	34.0
1989	8,463	6,204	2,259	3,238	38.3						

[1] Live weight. [2] Meal, oil, fish solubles, homogenized condensed fish, shell products, bait, and animal food. [3] Represents record year.

No. 1158. Domestic Fish and Shellfish Catch and Value by Species: 1990 to 1998

Species	Quantity (1,000 lb.)				Value ($1,000)			
	1990	1995	1997	1998	1990	1995	1997	1998
Total	9,403,571	9,787,554	9,843,247	9,193,970	3,521,995	3,735,615	3,447,603	3,128,469
Fish, total [1]	8,091,068	8,520,086	8,397,286	7,888,020	1,900,097	1,915,642	1,722,145	1,446,942
Cod:								
Atlantic	95,881	29,631	28,619	24,514	61,329	28,184	24,464	25,474
Pacific.	526,396	591,399	661,314	142,429	91,384	109,680	142,429	87,717
Flounder.	254,519	423,443	566,353	391,178	112,921	150,239	130,769	96,804
Halibut	70,454	44,796	69,864	73,260	96,700	66,781	117,362	103,974
Menhaden	1,962,160	1,846,959	2,027,802	1,705,677	93,896	99,131	112,050	103,836
Pollock, Alaska	3,108,031	2,852,618	2,512,455	2,716,458	268,344	259,614	242,589	190,152
Sablefish	89,802	65,904	52,925	43,500	58,865	123,694	108,776	91,823
Salmon.	733,146	1,020,765	567,658	644,434	612,367	486,107	270,370	257,456
Tuna	62,393	63,864	82,855	84,999	105,040	102,638	109,794	94,462
Shellfish, total [1]	1,312,503	1,267,468	1,445,961	1,305,950	1,621,898	1,819,973	1,725,458	1,681,527
Clams	139,198	134,224	114,184	107,959	130,194	140,414	129,686	135,237
Crabs.	499,416	363,639	429,963	552,716	483,837	511,987	429,547	473,378
Lobsters: American.	61,017	66,406	83,921	79,642	154,677	214,838	267,216	253,636
Oysters	29,193	40,380	37,115	33,538	93,718	101,574	92,243	88,627
Scallops:								
Calico.	(NA)	957	1,613	(NA)	(NA)	1,219	3,601	(NA)
Sea	39,917	18,316	13,789	13,061	153,696	92,826	90,291	79,606
Shrimp	346,494	306,869	290,255	277,757	491,433	570,034	544,056	515,616

NA Not available. [1] Includes other types of fish and shellfish, not shown separately.

Source of Tables 1156-1158: U.S. National Oceanic and Atmospheric Administration, National Marine Fisheries Service, *Fisheries of the United States*, annual.

No. 1159. U.S. Private Aquaculture—Trout and Catfish Production and Value: 1990 to 1999

[67.8 represents 67,800,000. Periods are from **Sept. 1** of the previous year to **Aug. 31** of stated year. Data are for foodsize fish, those over 12 inches long]

Item	Unit	1990	1993	1994	1995	1996	1997	1998	1999
TROUT FOODSIZE									
Number sold	Millions . .	67.8	60.9	58.3	60.2	56.5	59.3	57.6	61.0
Total weight	Mil. lb . .	56.8	54.6	52.1	55.6	53.6	56.9	57.9	60.3
Total value of sales	Mil. dol. .	64.6	54.3	52.7	60.8	57.0	60.7	60.3	65.0
Average price received	Dol./lb . .	1.14	0.99	1.01	1.09	1.06	1.07	1.04	1.08
Percent sold to processors	Percent . .	58	63	68	68	67	63	62	64
CATFISH FOODSIZE									
Number sold	Millions . .	272.9	379.1	347.6	321.8	375.4	391.8	409.8	424.3
Total weight	Mil. lb . .	392.4	495.8	479.4	481.5	526.3	569.6	601.4	634.9
Total value of sales	Mil. dol. .	305.1	352.9	373.6	378.1	403.3	406.8	445.4	464.5
Average price received	Dol./lb . .	0.78	0.71	0.78	0.79	0.77	0.71	0.74	0.73
Fish sold to processors	Mil. lb . .	360.4	459.0	439.3	446.9	472.1	524.9	564.4	596.6
Avg. price paid by processors	Cents/lb . .	75.8	70.9	78.4	78.6	77.3	71.2	74.3	73.7
Processor sales	Mil. lb . . .	183.1	233.5	216.5	227.0	237.2	261.8	281.4	292.7
Avg. price received by processors . . .	Cents/lb . .	224.1	218.6	238.5	240.3	236.9	226.0	229.0	234.0
Inventory (Jan. 1)	Mil. lb . . .	9.4	9.5	11.6	10.9	11.9	11.9	10.8	12.6

Source: U.S. Dept. of Agriculture, National Agricultural Statistics Service, *Trout Production* released September; *Catfish Production* released February; and *Catfish Processing* released February. Also in *Agricultural Statistics*, annual.

No. 1160. Supply of Selected Fishery Items: 1980 to 1998

[In millions of pounds (425 represents 425,000,000). Totals available for U.S. consumption are supply minus exports plus imports. Round weight is the complete or full weight as caught]

Species	Unit	1980	1990	1992	1993	1994	1995	1996	1997	1998
Shrimp	Heads-off weight. .	425	734	820	808	847	832	842	923	1,002
Tuna, canned	Canned weight . . .	666	856	922	835	850	875	859	829	912
Snow crab	Round weight. . . .	54	37	88	66	40	42	46	110	254
Clams	Meat weight.	102	152	155	156	144	144	134	124	119
American lobster	Round weight. . . .	69	95	95	92	101	94	97	112	110
Spiny lobster	Round weight. . . .	127	89	81	76	76	89	81	76	100
Salmon, canned	Canned weight . . .	126	148	73	114	117	147	104	82	86
King crab	Round weight. . . .	133	19	15	8	12	21	30	45	62
Oysters	Meat weight.	71	56	50	48	50	63	58	58	61
Scallops	Meat weight.	51	74	69	66	76	62	71	66	58
Sardines, canned	Canned weight . . .	69	61	41	41	48	44	46	49	50
Crab meat, canned	Canned weight . . .	9	9	9	9	9	12	13	15	22

Source: U.S. National Oceanic and Atmospheric Administration, National Marine Fisheries Service, *Fisheries of the United States*, annual.

No. 1161. Canned, Fresh, and Frozen Fishery Products: 1990 to 1998

[Fresh fishery products exclude Alaska and Hawaii. Canned fishery products data are for natural pack only]

Product	Production (mil. lb.)					Value (mil. dol.)				
	1990	1995	1996	1997	1998	1990	1995	1996	1997	1998
Canned [1]	1,178	1,927	1,877	1,565	1,531	1,562	1,887	1,800	1,593	1,766
Tuna	581	667	676	627	681	902	939	957	919	983
Salmon	196	244	197	162	163	366	419	284	253	274
Clam products	110	129	129	125	113	76	110	117	115	105
Sardines, Maine	13	14	18	16	12	17	24	30	29	19
Shrimp	1	1	1	1	1	3	7	6	5	1
Crabs	1	(Z)	(Z)	(Z)	(Z)	4	(Z)	(Z)	(Z)	(Z)
Oysters [2]	1	(Z)	(Z)	(Z)	(Z)	1	(Z)	(Z)	(Z)	(Z)
Fish fillets and steaks [3] . .	441	385	423	410	439	843	841	904	961	1,002
Cod	65	65	67	79	67	132	152	158	179	162
Flounder	54	35	29	27	24	154	86	80	79	71
Haddock	7	3	4	7	6	24	11	14	24	22
Ocean perch, Atlantic	1	(Z)	(Z)	1	1	1	1	1	2	2
Rockfish	33	25	20	17	16	53	38	42	33	32
Pollock, Atlantic	12	4	2	1	4	21	10	5	2	7
Pollock, Alaska	164	135	136	112	161	174	184	158	129	190
Other	105	118	165	166	160	284	359	446	513	516

Z Less than 500,000 pounds or $500,000.   [1] Includes other products, not shown separately.   [2] Includes oyster specialties.   [3] Fresh and frozen.

Source: U.S. National Oceanic and Atmospheric Administration, National Marine Fisheries Service, *Fisheries of the United States*, annual.

U.S. Census Bureau, Statistical Abstract of the United States: 2000

No. 1162. Mining Summary by Industry: 1992 and 1997

Industry	1987 SIC code	Establishments 1992	Establishments 1997	Paid employees 1992	Paid employees 1997	Annual payroll (mil. dol.) 1992	Annual payroll (mil. dol.) 1997	Value of shipments (mil. dol.) 1992	Value of shipments (mil. dol.) 1997
Total	(X)	30,787	25,251	638,167	512,016	24,199	20,907	162,095	174,520
Metal mining.	10	1,023	696	52,936	48,533	2,111	2,103	9,864	11,546
Iron ores	101	40	32	8,716	7,920	348	394	1,715	1,938
Copper ores	102	62	49	14,912	13,745	550	551	3,375	4,018
Lead & zinc ores	103	44	31	2,829	2,127	113	89	472	531
Gold & silver ores	104	426	316	19,179	18,292	825	810	3,555	4,073
Gold ores	1041	402	300	18,174	17,512	784	778	3,440	3,952
Silver ores.	1044	24	16	1,005	780	41	33	115	122
Metal mining services	108	266	203	3,280	3,066	117	110	350	342
Miscellaneous metal ores	109	185	65	4,020	3,383	157	149	398	644
Coal mining.	12	3,069	1,820	134,482	92,958	5,461	4,157	27,134	24,005
Bituminous coal & lignite mining . . .	122	2,635	1,443	128,542	86,824	5,282	3,947	26,435	23,244
Anthracite mining.	123	76	68	1,365	1,141	39	36	160	183
Coal mining services	124	358	309	4,575	4,993	141	174	538	578
Oil & gas extraction	13	20,891	17,219	344,876	272,764	13,397	11,138	111,523	122,156
Crude petroleum & natural gas. . . .	131	9,391	7,784	174,825	100,333	8,422	4,969	72,245	78,009
Natural gas liquids	132	591	528	12,166	10,548	518	542	27,214	24,828
Oil & gas field services	138	10,909	8,907	157,885	161,883	4,456	5,628	12,064	19,318
Drilling oil & gas wells	1381	2,125	1,628	47,749	52,858	1,371	1,901	3,584	7,298
Oil & gas exploration services . . .	1382	1,490	1,197	13,711	7,039	460	216	965	819
Oil & gas field services, n.e.c. . . .	1389	7,294	6,082	96,425	101,986	2,626	3,511	7,515	11,201
Nonmetallic minerals, except fuels . . .	14	5,804	5,516	105,873	97,761	3,230	3,508	13,574	16,812
Dimension stone	141	166	178	1,401	1,658	30	38	99	126
Crushed & broken stone, including riprap.	142	2,142	2,184	41,641	42,300	1,207	1,510	5,002	7,242
Sand & gravel	144	2,677	2,507	30,323	29,640	888	997	3,160	3,983
Clay, ceramic, & refractory minerals	145	200	167	10,048	7,412	318	265	1,400	1,558
Chemical & fertilizer mineral mining	147	160	92	15,048	10,823	579	495	3,127	3,081
Nonmetallic minerals services, except fuels	148	178	172	1,956	1,874	52	64	189	191
Miscellaneous nonmetallic minerals, except fuels	149	281	216	5,456	4,054	156	140	596	632

X Not applicable.

Source: U.S. Census Bureau, *1997 Economic Census, Core Business Statistics Series*, Series EC97X-CS2, June 2000.

No. 1163. Mining and Primary Metal Production Indexes: 1980 to 1999

[Index 1992=100]

Industry group	1980	1990	1992	1993	1994	1995	1996	1997	1998	1999
Mining	111.5	104.8	100.0	100.0	102.5	102.1	103.7	105.9	103.8	98.0
Coal	83.4	103.7	100.0	94.0	103.0	102.6	105.0	108.2	109.7	108.1
Oil and gas extraction.	124.4	106.4	100.0	101.1	101.7	100.5	101.8	103.1	99.5	92.5
Crude oil and natural gas. . . .	115.1	101.6	100.0	98.0	98.1	96.5	95.9	95.7	94.2	90.6
Oil and gas drilling	236.8	151.1	100.0	122.5	126.9	126.4	137.9	149.3	134.6	106.8
Metal mining.	65.2	93.1	100.0	98.8	100.5	101.6	104.0	110.3	109.1	97.1
Iron ore	128.5	101.4	100.0	100.0	104.3	112.3	111.3	113.6	112.7	103.3
Nonferrous ores.	52.8	91.9	100.0	98.6	99.9	100.1	103.0	110.0	108.7	96.2
Copper ore	65.6	89.4	100.0	102.0	104.7	104.8	108.7	109.9	105.4	91.2
Primary metals, manufacturing . .	108.0	104.0	100.0	105.1	113.8	116.2	119.6	126.7	125.6	126.6
Nonferrous metals	92.4	100.9	100.0	104.0	113.0	115.7	120.5	128.1	129.4	130.9
Copper.	75.9	81.6	100.0	116.7	111.7	121.9	103.5	111.0	107.2	96.4
Aluminum	115.1	100.4	100.0	91.7	81.8	83.7	88.5	89.4	92.1	93.7
Iron and steel	119.0	106.4	100.0	106.1	114.4	116.5	118.9	125.6	122.6	123.2

Source: Board of Governors of the Federal Reserve System, *Federal Reserve Bulletin*, monthly; and *Industrial Production and Capacity Utilization*, Statistical Release G.17, monthly.

No. 1164. Mineral Industries—Employment, Hours, and Earnings: 1990 to 1999

Item	Unit	1990	1995	1999	Item	Unit	1990	1995	1999
All mining:					Avg. weekly hours	Number .	43.9	44.2	42.5
All employees	1,000 . . .	709	581	535	Avg. weekly earnings . .	Dollars . .	568	642	717
Production workers	1,000 . . .	509	424	404	Metal mining:				
Avg. weekly hours	Number .	44.1	44.7	43.8	All employees	1,000 . . .	58	51	45
Avg. weekly earnings . .	Dollars . .	603	684	746	Production workers	1,000 . . .	46	41	37
Coal mining:					Avg. weekly hours	Number .	42.8	43.8	44.5
All employees	1,000 . . .	147	104	85	Avg. weekly earnings . .	Dollars . .	601	735	812
Production workers	1,000 . . .	119	84	70	Nonmetallic minerals,				
Avg. weekly hours	Number .	44.0	44.9	44.8	except fuels:				
Avg. weekly earnings . .	Dollars . .	735	828	864	All employees	1,000 . . .	110	105	112
Oil and gas extraction:					Production workers	1,000 . . .	83	80	82
All employees	1,000 . . .	395	320	293	Avg. weekly hours	Number .	45.3	46.6	46.3
Production workers	1,000 . . .	261	218	214	Avg. weekly earnings . .	Dollars . .	525	624	700

Source: U.S. Bureau of Labor Statistics, *Bulletin 2370* and *Employment and Earnings*, March and June issues.

No. 1165. Mineral Production: 1990 to 1999

[Data represent production as measured by mine shipments, mine sales or marketable production]

Mineral	Unit	1990	1995	1998	1999, est.
FUEL MINERALS					
Coal, total	Mil. sh. tons	1,029.1	1,033.0	1,117.5	1,099.1
Bituminous	Mil. sh. tons	693.2	613.8	631.7	621.3
Subbituminous	Mil. sh. tons	244.3	328.0	394.8	388.3
Lignite	Mil. sh. tons	88.1	86.5	85.8	84.4
Anthracite	Mil. sh. tons	3.5	4.7	5.3	5.2
Natural gas (marketed production)	Tril. cu. ft.	18.59	19.51	19.65	19.67
Petroleum (crude)	Mil. bbl. [1]	2,686	2,394	2,281	2,164
Uranium (recoverable content)	Mil. lb.	8.9	6.0	4.71	4.71
NONFUEL MINERALS					
Asbestos (sales)	1,000 metric tons . .	(D)	9	6	6
Asphalt and related bitumens (native) [3] . .	Mil. metric tons	25	(3)	(3)	(3)
Barite, primary, sold/used by producers . .	1,000 metric tons . .	430	543	476	375
Boron minerals, sold or used by producers	1,000 metric tons . .	1,090	1,190	1,170	(NA)
Bromine, sold or used by producers	1,000 metric tons . .	177	218	230	231
Cement:					
Portland	Mil. metric tons	67	73	80	82
Masonry	Mil. metric tons	3	4	4	4
Clays	1,000 metric tons . .	42,900	43,100	41,600	42,200
Diatomite	1,000 metric tons . .	631	722	725	720
Feldspar [4]	1,000 metric tons . .	630	880	820	900
Fluorspar, finished shipments	1,000 metric tons . .	64	51	-	-
Garnet (abrasive)	1,000 metric tons . .	47	53	(NA)	(NA)
Gypsum, crude	Mil. metric tons	15	17	19	19
Helium [5]	Mil. cu. meters	85	101	112	118
Lime, sold or used by producers	Mil. metric tons	16	19	20	21
Mica, scrap & flake, sold/used by producers	1,000 metric tons . .	109	108	87	94
Peat, sales by producers	1,000 metric tons . .	721	660	785	775
Perlite, processed, sold or used	1,000 metric tons . .	576	700	685	726
Phosphate rock (marketable)	Mil. metric tons	46	44	44	42
Potash (K_2O equivalent) sales	1,000 metric tons . .	1,710	1,480	1,300	1,300
Pumice & pumicite, producer sales	1,000 metric tons . .	443	529	583	617
Salt, common, sold/used by producers . .	Mil. metric tons	37	41	41	41
Sand & gravel, sold/used by producer . .	Mil. metric tons	855	935	1,108	1,108
Construction	Mil. metric tons	829	907	1,080	1,080
Industrial	Mil. metric tons	26	28	28	28
Silica [2]	Metric tons	3,710	979	(NA)	(NA)
Sodium carbonate (natural) (soda ash) . .	1,000 metric tons . .	9,100	10,100	10,100	10,100
Sodium sulfate (natural)	1,000 metric tons . .	349	327	(D)	(D)
Stone [6]	Mil. metric tons	1,110	2,420	2,630	2,600
Crushed and broken	Mil. metric tons	1,110	1,260	1,510	1,560
Dimension	1,000 metric tons . .	1,120	1,160	1,120	1,040
Sulfur: Total shipments	1,000 metric tons . .	11,500	12,100	12,100	10,900
Sulfur: Frasch mines (shipments)	1,000 metric tons . .	3,680	(D)	(D)	(D)
Talc, and pyrophyllite, crude	1,000 metric tons . .	1,270	1,060	971	954
Vermiculite concentrate	1,000 metric tons . .	209	171	(D)	(D)
METALS					
Antimony ore and concentrate	Metric tons	(D)	262	242	480
Aluminum	1,000 metric tons . .	4,048	3,375	3,713	3,800
Bauxite (dried)	1,000 metric tons . .	(D)	(D)	(NA)	(NA)
Copper (recoverable content)	1,000 metric tons . .	1,590	1,850	1,860	1,660
Gold (recoverable content)	Metric tons	294	317	366	340
Iron ore (gross weight) [7]	Mil. metric tons	57	61	63	56
Lead (recoverable content)	1,000 metric tons . .	484	394	493	520
Magnesium metal	1,000 metric tons . .	139	142	106	(D)
Manganiferous ore (gross weight) [8]	1,000 metric ton . . .	(D)	(D)	(D)	(D)
Mercury [9]	Metric tons	562	(D)	(D)	(D)
Molybdenum (concentrate)	1,000 metric tons . .	62	61	53	44
Nickel	1,000 metric tons . .	-	2	-	-
Palladium metal	Kilograms	5,930	5,260	10,600	10,200
Platinum metal	Kilograms	1,810	1,590	3,240	3,200
Silicon (silicon content)	1,000 metric tons . .	418	396	429	425
Silver (recoverable content)	Metric tons	2,120	1,560	2,060	1,860
Titanium concentrate: Ilmenite (gross weight)	1,000 metric tons . .	(D)	(D)	(D)	(D)
Tungsten ore and concentrate [9]	Metric tons	(D)	(D)	(D)	(D)
Zinc (recoverable content)	1,000 metric tons . .	515	614	722	775

- Represents zero.   D Withheld to avoid disclosing individual company data.   NA Not available.   [1] 42 gal. bbl.
[2] 1990 includes aplite.   [3] Refined only.   [4] Includes grindstones, oilstones, whetstones, and deburring media. Excludes grinding pebbles, and tubemill liners.   [5] Excludes abrasive stone, bituminous limestone and sandstone, and ground soapstone, all included elsewhere in table; 1993 excludes dimension stone. Includes calcareous marl and slate.   [6] Represents shipments; includes byproduct ores.   [7] 5 to 35 percent manganiferous ore.   [8] Mercury produced as a byproduct of gold ores only.   [9] Content of ore and concentrate.

Source: Nonfuels, 1990, U.S. Bureau of Mines, thereafter, U.S. Geological Survey, *Minerals Yearbook* and *Mineral Commodities Summaries*, annual; fuels, U.S. Energy Information Administration, *Annual Energy Review* and *Uranium Industry Annual*.

U.S. Census Bureau, *Statistical Abstract of the United States: 2000*

No. 1166. Mineral Production Value: 1990 to 1998

[In millions of dollars (141,608 represents $141,608,000,000). Value derived by multiplying production times price at source of production]

Mineral	1990	1995	1996	1997	1998, est.
Mineral production, total...............	141,608	123,486	145,206	147,204	(NA)
Mineral fuels, total.....................	**108,144**	**84,783**	**106,197**	**106,524**	**83,601**
Coal, total [1]........................	22,415	19,469	19,691	19,777	19,668
Bituminous	19,014	15,688	15,875	16,110	16,036
Anthracite	138	187	177	165	174
Natural gas (wellhead)	31,789	30,241	42,858	46,098	39,082
Petroleum (crude).....................	53,801	35,006	43,561	40,576	24,792
Uranium U_3O_8.....................	140	67	87	73	58
Industrial minerals, total	**21,022**	**24,679**	**25,994**	**27,606**	**(NA)**
Asbestos (sales)	(5)	(5)	(5)	(5)	(5)
Asphalt, related bitumens (native) [2]....	3,480	(NA)	(NA)	(NA)	(NA)
Barite, primary, sold/used by producers ...	16	10	15	16	15
Boron minerals, sold/used by producers...	436	560	519	580	(NA)
Bromine, sold/used by producers	173	186	150	198	227
Cement:[3]					
Portland	3,683	4,920	5,310	5,710	(NA)
Masonry	225	307	321	339	(NA)
Clays.............................	1,620	1,730	1,710	1,670	(NA)
Diatomite	138	171	176	184	182
Feldspar [4]	28	37	39	43	40
Fluorspar, finished shipments...........	(5)	(5)	(5)	(5)	(5)
Garnet (abrasive)....................	7	4	6	6	(NA)
Gemstones (estimate).................	53	49	43	25	23
Gypsum, crude	100	121	124	132	137
Helium [6]...........................	113	196	193	206	(NA)
Lime, sold/used by producers..........	902	1,100	1,170	1,200	(NA)
Mica, scrap and flake, sold/used by producers.......	6	6	8	9	9
Peat (sales by producers)	19	17	19	18	(NA)
Perlite, processed, sold/used by producers........	17	22	21	23	(NA)
Phosphate rock (marketable)	1,075	947	1,060	1,076	1,131
Potash (K_2O equivalent).............	303	284	299	320	(NA)
Pumice and pumicite (sales by producers)	11	13	15	16	15
Salt (common), sold/used by producers	827	1,000	1,060	993	(NA)
Sand and gravel, sold/used by producers.........	3,686	4,400	4,500	4,778	(NA)
Silica, special [7].....................	(Z)	1	1	(NA)	(NA)
Sodium carbonate (natural) (soda ash)...........	836	829	926	915	(NA)
Sodium sulfate (natural)...............	34	28	27	35	(NA)
Stone [8]...........................	5,822	6,970	7,410	8,295	(NA)
Crushed and broken	5,591	6,740	7,180	8,070	(NA)
Dimension	231	233	234	225	205
Sulfur: Frasch mines (shipments)	335	(4)	(4)	(4)	(NA)
Talc and pyrophyllite, crude [9]	31	32	31	(NA)	(NA)
Tripoli............................	3	11	18	16	(NA)
Vermiculite concentrate	19	(4)	(4)	(4)	(NA)
Industrial minerals, undistributed	504	725	820	803	(NA)
Metals, total	**12,442**	**14,024**	**13,015**	**13,074**	**(NA)**
Antimony ore and concentrate [10]........	(11)	(11)	(11)	(11)	(NA)
Bauxite (dried equivalent)	(11)	(11)	(11)	(11)	(NA)
Copper (recoverable content)	4,311	5,640	4,610	4,580	(NA)
Gold (recoverable content).............	3,650	3,950	4,090	3,850	(NA)
Iron ore (gross weight) [12]	1,741	1,730	1,770	1,890	(NA)
Lead (recoverable content)	491	359	459	460	(NA)
Magnesium metal....................	433	476	455	400	(NA)
Manganiferous ore (gross weight) [13]	(11)	(11)	(11)	(11)	(NA)
Mercury [14].........................	(11)	(11)	(11)	(11)	(NA)
Molybdenum (concentrate).............	348	651	456	(D)	(NA)
Palladium metal.....................	22	22	26	50	(NA)
Platinum metal......................	27	21	24	33	(NA)
Silver (recoverable content)	329	259	262	338	(NA)
Titanium concentrate: Ilmenite (gross weight)	(11)	(11)	(11)	(11)	(NA)
Tungsten ore and concentrate	(11)	(11)	(11)	(11)	(NA)
Vanadium (recoverable content)	(11)	(11)	(11)	(11)	(NA)
Zinc mine production (recoverable content)	847	756	674	860	(NA)
Metals, undistributed.................	242	161	190	614	(NA)

D Withheld to avoid disclosing individual company data.   NA Not available.   Z Less than $500,000.   [1] Includes subbituminous and lignite.   [2] Excluded from industrial minerals total.   [3] Value of shipments, 1990; value of production, 1995-96.   [4] Includes aplite.   [5] Included in "Industrial minerals, undistributed."   [6] Refined only.   [7] Includes grindstones, oilstones, whetstones, and deburring media.   [8] Excludes abrasive stone, bituminous limestone, sandstone, and ground soapstone; 1993 excludes dimension stone.   [9] 1990, talc only.   [10] Antimony content.   [11] Included with "Metals, undistributed."   [12] Represents shipments; includes byproduct ores.   [13] 5 to 35 percent manganiferous ore.   [14] Mercury produced as a byproduct of gold ores only.

Source: Nonfuels, 1990, U.S. Bureau of Mines, thereafter, U.S. Geological Survey, *Minerals Yearbook* and *Mineral Commodities Summaries*, annual; fuels, U.S. Energy Information Administration, *Annual Energy Review*.

No. 1167. Nonfuel Mineral Commodities—Summary: 1998

[Preliminary estimates. Average price in dollars per metric tons except as noted]

Mineral	Unit	Mineral disposition				Average price per unit (dollars)	Employment (number)
		Production	Exports	Net import reliance [1] (percent)	Consumption, apparent		
Aluminum	1,000 metric tons	3,713	1,590	27	7,090	[2]65.5	[4]18,200
Antimony (contained)	Metric tons	[3]242	4,170	81	4,270	[2]72	[4]80
Asbestos	1,000 metric tons	6	3	6	16	(D)	[4]30
Barite	1,000 metric tons	476	15	80	2,340	[4]22.70	410
Bauxite and alumina	1,000 metric tons	(NA)	1,500	100	5,000	[4]23.00	-
Beryllium (contained)	Metric tons	243	60	8	260	[2][6]327	25
Bismuth (contained)	Metric tons	-	245	100	(NA)	[2]3.60	-
Boron (B$_2$O$_3$ content)	1,000 metric tons	587	106	([5])	412	[4][7]340.00	900
Bromine (contained)	1,000 metric tons	230	12	-	235	[8][9]70.00	1,700
Cadmium (contained)	Metric tons	[3]1,880	606	20	2,350	[2][10]0.28	140
Cement	1,000 metric tons	83,931	743	19	102,457	[4]76.46	17,900
Chromium	1,000 metric tons	[11]105	62	80	531	[4][12]145.00	-
Clays	1,000 metric tons	41,600	5,230	([5])	36,500	(NA)	13,700
Cobalt (contained)	Metric tons	[11]-	1,680	73	11,500	[2]21.43	-
Copper (Mine, contained)	1,000 metric tons	1,860	(NA)	14	3,010	(NA)	13
Diamond (industrial)	Million carats	(NA)	104	90	267	[14]0.44	-
Diatomite	1,000 metric tons	725	138	([5])	589	[4]248.00	1,000
Feldspar	1,000 metric tons	820	13	([5])	814	[4]49.76	400
Fluorspar	1,000 metric tons	(NA)	44	100	572	(NA)	-
Garnet (industrial)	Metric tons	74,000	12,000	([5])	39,900	[4]50-2000	230
Germanium (contained)	Kilograms	22,000	(NA)	(NA)	(NA)	[8][16](NA)	100
Gold (contained)	Metric tons	366	522	([5])	(NA)	[17]295.00	13,400
Gypsum (crude)	1,000 short tons	(NA)	19,000	28	30,500	[4]7.20	6,000
Iodine	Metric tons	(NA)	1,490	2,790	4,950	[8][21]16.45	40
Iron ore (usable)	Million metric tons	63	6	12	71	[4][22]31.14	7,290
Iron and steel slag (metal)	1,000 metric tons	18,400	10	4	19,000	[4]8.00	2,700
Lead (contained)	1,000 metric tons	(NA)	72	18	1,700	[2]45.30	-
Lime	1,000 metric tons	20,100	56	1	20,300	(NA)	5,600
Magnesium compounds	1,000 metric tons	366	49	45	661	(NA)	600
Magnesium metal	1,000 metric tons	(NA)	35	25	185	(NA)	800
Mercury	Metric tons	[11](NA)	63	(NA)	(NA)	[26]139.84	(NA)
Mica, scrap and flake	1,000 metric tons	87	8	24	137	[4]87.00	367
Molybdenum (contained)	Metric tons	53,300	46,300	([5])	24,500	[5]5.90	600
Nickel (contained)	Metric tons	4,290	8,440	64	149,000	[2][27]4,630.00	7
Nitrogen (fixed)-ammonia	1,000 metric tons	14,700	614	18	18,100	[4][28]121.00	2,500
Peat	1,000 metric tons	676	30	52	1,420	[4]24.07	800
Perlite	1,000 metric tons	685	42	14	793	[4]31.91	140
Phosphate rock	1,000 metric tons	44,200	378	3	(NA)	[4]25.46	5,000
Platinum-group metals	Kilograms	13,840	51,811	(NA)	(NA)	(NA)	620
Potash (K$_2$O equivalent)	1,000 metric tons	1,300	480	80	5,700	[4][30]145.00	1,510
Pumice and pumicite	1,000 metric tons	583	22	31	847	[4]21.90	75
Salt	1,000 metric tons	41,200	731	17	48,800	[4][31]114.93	4,150
Silicon (contained)	1,000 metric tons	429	47	30	616	(NA)	(NA)
Silver (contained)	Metric tons	2,060	3,330	14	4,300	[17]5.54	1,550
Sodium carbonate (soda ash)	1,000 metric tons	10,100	3,660	([5])	6,560	[33]105.00	2,700
Sodium sulfate	1,000 metric tons	(D)	90	4	555	[34]114.00	(D)
Stone (crushed)	Million metric tons	1,510	4	-	1,520	[4]5.39	78,500
Sulfur (all forms)	1,000 metric tons	11,600	940	18	14,100	[4][35]29.14	3,100
Talc	1,000 metric tons	971	146	([5])	990	[4]126.00	700
Thallium (contained)	Kilograms	-	(NA)	100	100	[8]1,280.00	-
Tin (contained)	Metric tons	[11]16,100	5,020	85	60,620	[2]2.64	11,100
Titanium dioxide	1,000 metric tons	1,330	398	([5])	1,130	[2][36]0.98	5
Tungsten (contained)	Metric tons	-	49	77	12,300	[37]52.00	-
Vermiculite	1,000 metric tons	(D)	11	(D)	(D)	(D)	230
Zinc (contained)	1,000 metric tons	722	554	35	1,580	[2]51.40	2,400
Zirconium (Z$_r$0$_2$) content	Metric tons	(D)	28,356	(D)	(D)	[4][39]320.00	-

- Represents or rounds to zero. D Withheld to avoid disclosure. NA Not available. [1] Calculated as a percent of apparent consumption. [2] Dollars per pound. [3] Refinery production. [4] Dollars per metric ton. [5] Net exporter. [6] Metal, vacuum-cast ingot. [7] Granulated pentahydrate borax in bulk, f.o.b mine. [8] Dollars per kilogram. [9] Bulk, purified bromine. [10] 1- to 5-short ton lots. [11] Secondary production. [12] Turkish, chromite price. [13] Columbite price. [14] Value of imports, dollars per carat. [15] Reported consumption. [16] Zone refined. [17] Dollars per troy ounce. [18] Price of flake imports. [19] Includes employment at calcining plants. [20] 99.97% indium. [21] C.i.f. value, crude, per kilogram. [22] Price of eastern Canadian ore. [23] Delivered, No. 1 Heavy Melting composite price. [24] Year-end price. [25] 46%-48% Mn metallurgical ore, per unit contained Mn, c.i.f. U.S. ports. [26] Dollars per 76-pound flask. [27] London Metal Exchange cash price. [28] F.o.b. gulf coast. [29] Dealer price of platinum. [30] Price of K20, muriate. [31] Vacuum and open pan, bulk, pellets and packaged, f.o.b. mine and plant. [32] Ferrosilicon, 50% Si. [33] Quoted year-end price, dense, bulk, f.o.b. Green River, WY, dollars per short ton. [34] Quoted price, bulk, f.o.b. works, East, dollars per short ton. [35] Elemental sulfur, f.o.b. mine and/or plant. [36] Rutile, list, year-end. [37] Dollars per unit W03 (7.93 kilograms of contained tungsten per unit). [38] All forms. [39] Price for imported zircon, f.o.b. U.S. east coast.

Source: U.S. Geological Survey, *Mineral Commodity Summaries*, annual.

U.S. Census Bureau, Statistical Abstract of the United States: 2000

No. 1168. Selected Mineral Products—Average Prices: 1980 to 1999

[Excludes Alaska and Hawaii, except as noted]

Year	Nonfuels								Fuels		
	Copper, electro-lytic (cents per lb.)	Plati-num[1] (dol./ troy oz.)	Gold (dol./ fine oz.)	Silver (dol./ fine oz.)	Lead (cents per lb.)	Tin (New York) (cents per lb.)	Zinc (cents per lb.)	Sulfur, crude[2] (dol./ metric ton)	Bitumi-nous coal[3][4] (dol./ short ton)	Crude petro-leum[3] (dol./ bbl.)	Natural gas[3] (dol./ 1,000 cu. ft.)
1980	101	677	613	20.63	43	846	37	89.06	29.17	21.59	1.59
1981	84	446	460	10.52	37	733	45	111.48	31.51	31.77	1.98
1982	73	327	376	7.95	26	654	39	108.27	32.15	28.52	2.46
1983	77	424	424	11.44	22	655	41	87.24	31.11	26.19	2.59
1984	67	357	361	8.14	26	624	49	94.31	30.63	25.88	2.66
1985	67	291	318	6.14	19	596	40	106.46	30.78	24.09	2.51
1986	66	461	368	5.47	22	383	38	105.22	28.84	12.51	1.94
1987	83	553	478	7.01	36	419	42	89.78	28.19	15.40	1.67
1988	121	523	438	6.53	37	441	60	85.95	27.66	12.58	1.69
1989	131	507	383	5.50	39	520	82	86.62	27.40	15.86	1.69
1990	123	467	385	4.82	46	386	75	80.14	27.43	20.03	1.71
1991	109	371	363	4.04	34	363	53	71.45	27.49	16.54	1.64
1992	107	360	345	3.94	35	402	58	48.14	26.78	15.99	1.74
1993	92	375	361	4.30	32	350	46	31.86	26.15	14.25	2.04
1994	111	411	385	5.29	37	369	49	28.60	25.68	13.19	1.85
1995	138	425	386	5.15	42	416	56	44.46	25.56	14.62	1.55
1996	109	398	389	5.19	49	412	51	34.11	25.17	18.46	2.17
1997	107	397	332	4.90	47	384	65	36.06	24.64	17.23	2.32
1998	79	373	295	5.50	45	381	51	29.14	24.87	10.87	1.94
1999	76	365	285	5.20	44	329	51	30.00	(NA)	15.56	2.07

NA Not available. [1] Average annual dealer prices. [2] F.o.b. works. [3] Average value at the point of production or domestic first purchase price. [4] Includes lignite.

Source: Nonfuels, through 1994, U.S. Bureau of Mines, thereafter, U.S. Geological Survey, *Minerals Yearbook* and *Mineral Commodities Summaries,* annual; fuels, U.S. Energy Information Administration, *Annual Energy Review* and *Monthly Energy Review.*

No. 1169. Value of Domestic Nonfuel Mineral Production by State: 1990 to 1999

[In millions of dollars (33,445 represents $33,445,000,000). Data may not add due to rounding]

State	1990	1995	1998	1999, prel.	State	1990	1995	1998	1999, prel.
United States	33,445	38,506	39,600	39,100	Missouri	1,105	1,140	1,320	1,380
					Montana	573	574	502	491
Alabama	559	706	1,010	1,080	Nebraska	90	146	199	163
Alaska	577	538	999	1,090	Nevada	2,621	3,060	3,170	2,780
Arizona	3,085	4,190	2,770	2,510	New Hampshire.	36	50	168	64
Arkansas	381	492	484	518	New Jersey	229	243	290	300
California	2,771	2,760	2,980	3,200					
					New Mexico	1,103	1,130	888	671
Colorado	377	570	650	555	New York	773	886	972	935
Connecticut	122	93	199	103	North Carolina.	586	735	750	761
Delaware [2]	10	9	112	10	North Dakota	25	31	38	38
Florida.	1,574	1,540	1,810	1,930	Ohio	733	891	1,030	1,040
Georgia	1,504	1,690	1,720	1,840					
					Oklahoma	259	357	460	475
Hawaii	106	114	85	89	Oregon	205	239	301	303
Idaho.	375	510	453	420	Pennsylvania	1,031	1,080	1,230	1,270
Illinois	667	828	875	913	Rhode Island	18	31	125	25
Indiana	428	589	691	717	South Carolina	450	447	562	574
Iowa	310	456	518	537					
					South Dakota	319	332	258	226
Kansas	349	498	551	566	Tennessee	663	665	705	710
Kentucky	359	432	498	483	Texas	1,459	1,680	1,820	1,780
Louisiana	368	434	347	374	Utah	1,335	1,850	1,320	1,260
Maine	55	68	92	101	Vermont.	87	60	174	83
Maryland	368	324	352	336					
					Virginia	507	515	636	667
Massachusetts	128	190	204	204	Washington	483	582	609	631
Michigan	1,440	1,520	1,670	1,660	West Virginia	133	181	170	180
Minnesota	1,482	1,530	1,740	1,580	Wisconsin.	215	416	323	334
Mississippi	111	131	149	190	Wyoming	911	973	1,070	956

[1] Partial data only. [2] Includes District of Columbia.

Source: 1990, U.S. Bureau of Mines, *Minerals Yearbook,* annual, and *Mineral Commodities Summaries,* annual; thereafter, U.S. Geological Survey.

698 Natural Resources

No. 1170. Principal Fuels, Nonmetals, and Metals—World Production and the U.S. Share: 1980 to 1998

Mineral	Unit	World production				Percent U.S. of world			
		1980	1990	1995	1998	1980	1990	1995	1998
Fuels: [1]									
Coal	Mil. sh. ton	4,193	5,356	5,126	5,042	19.8	19.2	20.2	22.2
Petroleum (crude)	Bil. bbl	21.8	22.1	22.8	24.0	14.4	12.2	10.5	9.3
Natural gas (dry, marketable).	Tril. cu. ft	53.5	73.6	78.0	82.8	36.3	24.2	23.9	22.6
Natural gas plant liquids	Bil. bbl	1.3	1.7	2.0	2.1	45.7	33.7	32.1	30.0
Nonmetals:									
Asbestos	1,000 metric tons	4,699	4,003	2,420	1,840	2	(D)	(Z)	(Z)
Barite	1,000 metric tons	7,495	5,633	4,300	5,890	27	8	13	8
Feldspar	1,000 metric tons	3,202	5,456	6,780	8,080	20	12	13	10
Fluorspar	1,000 metric tons	5,006	5,131	4,050	4,670	2	1	1	-
Gypsum.	Mil. metric tons .	78	100	97	107	14	15	17	18
Mica (incl. scrap).	1,000 metric tons	228	215	253	288	46	51	43	30
Nitrogen, (fixed) - ammonia . .	Mil. metric tons .	74	97	96	106	20	13	14	14
Phosphate rock, gross wt. . . .	Mil. metric tons .	144	162	130	145	38	29	33	31
Potash (K_2O equivalent)	Mil. metric tons .	28	28	25	25	8	6	6	5
Sulfur, elemental	Mil. metric tons .	55	58	53	58	22	20	22	20
Metals, mine basis:									
Bauxite	Mil. metric tons .	89	109	107	125	2	(D)	(D)	(D)
Columbian concentrates (Nb content)	1,000 metric tons	15	15	18	19	-	-	-	-
Copper	1,000 metric tons	7,405	9,017	10,100	12,200	16	18	18	15
Gold	Metric tons	1,219	2,133	2,220	2,460	2	14	14	15
Iron ore	Mil. metric tons .	891	982	1,027	1,020	8	6	6	6
Lead [2]	1,000 metric tons	3,470	3,353	2,780	3,100	17	15	14	16
Mercury	Metric tons	6,806	4,523	3,160	2,320	16	12	(D)	(D)
Molybdenum.	1,000 metric tons	111	128	141	135	62	48	43	40
Nickel [2]	1,000 metric tons	779	965	1,030	1,140	2	(Z)	(Z)	(Z)
Silver	1,000 metric tons	11	16	15	16	9	13	10	13
Tantalum concentrates	Metric tons	544	400	362	454	-	-	-	-
Titanium concentrates:									
Ilmenite	1,000 metric tons	3,726	4,072	3,970	3,860	14	(D)	(D)	13
Rutile	1,000 metric tons	436	481	416	406	(D)	(D)	(D)	(D)
Tungsten [2]	1,000 metric tons	52	43	39	32	5	14	(D)	(D)
Vanadium [2]	1,000 metric tons	37	31	35	42	12	(D)	(D)	(D)
Zinc [2]	1,000 metric tons	5,954	7,184	7,240	7,550	6	8	9	10
Metals, smelter basis:									
Aluminum.	1,000 metric tons	15,383	19,292	19,900	22,100	30	21	17	17
Cadmium.	1,000 metric tons	18	20	19	20	9	8	7	10
Copper	1,000 metric tons	7,649	9,472	10,200	11,900	14	15	16	18
Iron, pig.	Mil. metric tons .	514	532	533	541	12	9	10	9
Lead [3]	1,000 metric tons	5,430	5,763	5,590	3,080	23	23	25	25
Magnesium [4]	1,000 metric tons	316	354	389	369	49	39	37	39
Raw Steel	Mil. metric tons .	717	771	755	783	14	12	13	13
Tin [5]	1,000 metric tons	251	223	201	206	1	-	-	-
Zinc	1,000 metric tons	6,049	7,060	7,550	7,550	6	5	5	10

- Represents or rounds to zero.   D Withheld to avoid disclosing company data.   Z Less than half the unit of measure. [1] Source: Energy Information Administration, *International Energy Annual.*   [2] Content of ore and concentrate.   [3] Refinery production.   [4] Primary production; no smelter processing necessary.   [5] Production from primary sources only.

Source: Nonfuels, through 1994, U.S. Bureau of Mines, thereafter, U.S. Geological Survey, *Minerals Yearbook,* annual, and *Mineral Commodities Summaries,* annual; fuels, U.S. Energy Information Administration, *Annual Energy Review. International Energy Annual 1997,* and *Monthly Energy Review.*

No. 1171. Federal Strategic and Critical Materials Inventory: 1990 to 1999

[As of **Dec. 31.** Covers strategic and critical materials essential to military and industrial requirements in time of national emergency]

Mineral	Unit	Quantity [1]				Value (mil. dol.) [2]			
		1990	1995	1998	1999	1990	1995	1998	1999
Bauxite [3]	1,000 lg. ton . . .	18,033	16,032	12,288	9,492	888	203	95	71
Chromium [4].	1,000 sh. ton . . .	1,074	1,192	1,070	1,068	917	839	715	628
Cobalt	Mil. lb.	53	44	32	28	443	1,121	504	295
Diamonds: Stones . .	Carat 1,000. . . .	7,777	5,135	3,097	2,497	267	52	31	25
Industrial, bort . . .	Carat 1,000. . . .	17,353	1,967	62	-	16	9	-	-
Lead	1,000 sh. ton . . .	(NA)	(NA)	337	277	(NA)	(NA)	198	140
Manganese [5].	1,000 sh. ton . . .	4,017	2,817	2,251	2,144	962	464	284	270
Palladium	1,000 troy oz. . . .	(NA)	(NA)	1,247	1,099	(NA)	(NA)	183	343
Platinum.	1,000 troy oz . . .	453	453	440	342	186	154	162	120
Silver.	1,000 troy oz . . .	92,151	46,667	35,121	26,203	374	158	105	86
Tantalum Group	1,000 lb	(NA)	(NA)	82,313	2,689	(NA)	(NA)	127	126
Tin.	1,000 metric ton.	169	130	84	72	962	908	461	391
Titanium [6]	1,000 sh. ton . . .	37	37	35	35	402	221	122	124
Tungsten [6]	Mil. lb.	82	82	82	79	253	253	316	174
Zinc	1,000 sh. ton . . .	379	301	213	198	483	281	220	203

- Represents or rounds to zero.   NA Not available.   [1] Consists of stockpile and nonstockpile grades and reflects uncommitted balances.   [2] Market values are estimated trade values of similar materials and not necessarily amounts that would be realized at time of sale.   [3] Consists of abrasive grade, metallic grade Jamaica, metallic grade Suriname, and refractory.   [4] Consists of ferro-high carbon, ferro-low carbon, ferro-silicon, and metal.   [5] Consists of chemical grade, dioxide battery natural, dioxide battery synthetic, electrolytic, ferro-high carbon, ferro-med. carbon, ferro-silicon, and metal.   [6] Consists of carbide powder, ferro, metal powder, and ores and concentrates.

Source: U.S. Defense Logistics Agency, *Statistical Supplement, Stockpile Report to the Congress* (AP-3).

Natural Resources   699

No. 1172. Net U.S. Imports of Selected Minerals and Metals as Percent of Apparent Consumption: 1980 to 1999

[In percent. Based on net imports which equal the difference between imports and exports plus or minus Government stockpile and industry stock changes]

Mineral	1980	1990	1993	1994	1995	1996	1997	1998	1999
Bauxite [1]	94	98	100	99	99	100	100	100	100
Columbium	100	100	100	100	100	100	100	100	100
Manganese	98	100	100	100	100	100	100	100	100
Mica (sheet) . . .	100	100	100	100	100	100	100	100	100
Strontium	100	100	100	100	100	100	100	100	100
Tin.	79	71	84	83	84	83	86	85	85
Barite.	44	71	72	64	65	70	76	80	67
Cobalt	93	86	85	80	79	76	76	73	73
Potash	65	68	72	76	75	77	80	80	80
Tantalum	90	71	81	75	80	80	75	80	80
Tungsten	53	81	81	95	90	89	84	77	81
Chromium.	91	84	79	81	80	79	75	80	80
Nickel.	76	64	63	64	60	59	56	64	63
Titanium	32	(3)	(D)	(D)	64	50	63	49	(NA)
Zinc [2]	60	41	36	35	35	33	35	35	30
Aluminum	(3)	36	31	31	23	22	23	27	30
Cadmium	55	(3)	19	30	23	32	16	20	19
Gypsum	35	46	64	3	30	29	28	28	29
Copper.	16	15	12	12	27	14	13	14	27
Iron and steel . .	13	13	15	22	21	20	20	27	22
Sulfur.	14	21	14	18	21	13	13	18	17
Iron ore	25	3	7	13	14	14	14	12	17
Silver.	7	(NA)	(NA)	(NA)	(NA)	(NA)	(3)	14	14
Platinum group .	87	88	(NA)	(NA)	(NA)	(NA)	(NA)	(NA)	(NA)
Mercury	27	(D)	(D)	(D)	(NA)	(NA)	(D)	(NA)	(NA)
Selenium	59	46	39	31	31	38	(D)	(D)	(D)
Vanadium	35	(D)	(D)	(D)	84	(D)	(D)	78	80

D Withheld to avoid disclosure.   NA Not available.   [1] Includes alumina.   [2] Beginning 1990, effect of sharp rise in exports of concentrates. If calculated on a refined zinc-only basis, reliance would be about the same as pre-1990 level; 1990, 64%; 1993, 67%; 1994, 70%; 1995, 71%; 1996 and 1997, 70%, 1998, 69%; and 1999, 71%.   [3] Net exports.

Source: Through 1994, U.S. Bureau of Mines; thereafter, U.S. Geological Survey, *Mineral Commodity Summaries;* import and export data from U.S. Census Bureau.

No. 1173. Federal Offshore Leasing, Exploration, Production, and Revenue: 1990 to 1999

[See source for explanation of terms and for reliability statement]

Item	Unit	1990	1993	1994	1995	1996	1997	1998	1999
Tracts offered	Number . . .	10,459	10,164	10,861	10,995	12,230	9,870	8,205	7,453
Tracts leased.	Number . . .	825	336	560	835	1,537	1,780	1,157	333
Acres offered.	Millions . . .	56.79	55.07	58.90	59.70	70.00	26.24	44.10	40.23
Acres leased	Millions . . .	4.30	1.71	2.78	4.34	8.15	9.62	6.34	1.77
Bonus paid for leased tracts.	Bil. dol. . . .	0.6	0.1	0.3	0.4	0.9	(NA)	1.3	0.3
New wells being drilled:									
Active	Number . . .	120	129	120	124	835	186	173	219
Suspended	Number . . .	266	193	222	247	1,323	244	122	110
Cumulative wells (since 1953):									
Wells completed	Number . . .	13,167	13,181	13,342	13,475	13,583	13,546	13,702	13,676
Wells plugged and abandoned .	Number . . .	14,677	16,709	17,427	18,008	18,268	18,728	21,050	22,134
Revenue, total [1]	Bil. dol. . . .	3.4	2.8	2.9	2.7	4.3	5.3	4.3	3.2
Bonuses	Bil. dol. . . .	0.8	0.1	0.3	0.4	0.8	1.4	1.3	0.3
Oil and gas royalties [1]	Bil. dol. . . .	2.6	2.5	2.3	2.1	3.1	3.4	2.7	2.6
Rentals	Bil. dol. . . .	0.09	0.08	0.06	0.09	0.16	0.23	0.26	0.21
Sales value [2]	Bil. dol. . . .	17.0	16.4	15.0	13.8	27.6	31.1	17.6	17.4
Crude oil	Bil. dol. . . .	5.9	4.9	4.4	5.4	6.4	7.5	5.2	5.4
Condensate	Bil. dol. . . .	1.1	0.9	0.7	0.9	1.3	1.4	1.1	1.1
Natural gas	Bil. dol. . . .	9.5	9.9	9.8	7.5	11.8	13.3	11.4	10.9
Sales volume: [3]									
Crude oil	Mil. bbls. . .	274	307	319	357	373	404	401	434
Condensate	Mil. bbls. . .	51	55	51	52	65	75	75	78
Natural gas	Bil. cu. ft . .	5,093	4,533	4,700	4,692	5,024	5,077	4,836	4,994

NA Not available.   [1] Includes condensate royalties.   [2] Production value is value at time of production, not current value.   [3] Excludes sales volumes for gas lost, gas plant products or sulfur.

Source: U.S. Dept. of the Interior, Minerals Management Service, *Federal Offshore Statistics,* annual.

No. 1174. Petroleum Industry—Summary: 1980 to 1999

[Includes all costs incurred for drilling and equipping wells to point of completion as productive wells or abandonment after drilling becomes unproductive. Based on sample of operators of different size drilling establishments]

Item	Unit	1980	1990	1993	1994	1995	1996	1997	1998	1999
Crude oil producing wells (Dec. 31).	1,000. . .	548	602	584	582	574	574	573	562	554
Daily output per well	Bbl.	15.9	12.2	11.7	11.4	11.4	11.3	11.3	11.1	10.7
Completed wells drilled, total	1,000. . .	57.7	26.5	21.2	17.9	17.8	19.7	24.4	21.4	17.0
Crude oil.	1,000. . .	30.8	11.5	7.9	6.2	7.1	7.8	10.0	6.8	4.7
Gas	1,000. . .	15.2	10.4	9.5	8.8	7.8	8.7	10.8	11.5	9.9
Dry	1,000. . .	11.6	4.6	3.9	2.9	2.9	3.2	3.6	3.1	2.4
Average depth per well [1]	Feet . . .	4,171	4,653	5,388	5,731	5,505	5,506	5,552	6,060	6,067
Average cost per well [1]	$1,000 . .	368	384	427	483	513	496	604	769	(NA)
Average cost per foot [1]	Dollars. .	77.02	76.07	75.30	79.49	87.22	88.92	107.83	128.97	(NA)
Crude oil production, total	Mil. bbl. .	3,138	2,685	2,499	2,432	2,394	2,360	2,355	2,282	2,163
Value at wells	Bil. dol . .	67.7	53.8	35.6	32.1	35.0	43.6	40.6	24.8	33.7
Average price per barrel	Dollars. .	21.59	20.03	14.25	13.19	14.62	18.46	17.23	10.87	15.56
Lower 48 states	Mil. bbl. .	2,548	2,037	1,921	1,863	1,853	1,851	1,882	1,853	1,779
Alaska	Mil. bbl. .	590	647	577	569	542	508	473	429	383
Onshore	Mil. bbl. .	2,760	2,290	2,046	1,931	1,838	1,789	1,753	1,664	1,650
Offshore	Mil. bbl. .	377	395	453	500	557	570	602	618	513
Imports: Crude oil	Mil. bbl. .	1,921	2,151	2,477	2,578	2,639	2,740	3,002	3,178	3,135
Refined petroleum products	Mil. bbl. .	601	775	669	706	586	719	707	731	717
Exports: Crude oil	Mil. bbl. .	104.8	39.8	35.8	36.1	34.7	40.2	39.4	40.2	43.1
Proved reserves	Bil. bbl. .	29.8	26.3	23.0	22.5	22.40	22.02	22.55	21.03	(NA)
Operable refineries	Number .	319	205	187	179	175	170	164	163	159
Capacity (Jan. 1)	Mil. bbl. .	6,566	5,683	5,519	5,486	5,632	5,595	5,639	5,734	5,935
Refinery input, total.	Mil. bbl. .	5,117	5,325	5,482	5,482	5,555	5,654	5,807	5,891	5,880
Crude oil	Mil. bbl. .	4,920	4,895	4,968	5,063	5,099	5,179	5,351	5,435	5,406
Natural gas plant liquids	Mil. bbl. .	168	172	179	172	172	164	153	146	135
Other liquids	Mil. bbl. .	29	259	336	252	285	307	303	310	339
Refinery output, total	Mil. bbl. .	5,336	5,574	5,763	5,763	5,836	5,957	6,117	6,216	6,209
Motor gasoline	Mil. bbl. .	2,369	2,540	2,665	2,621	2,723	2,759	2,825	2,880	2,898
Jet fuel	Mil. bbl. .	365	544	518	529	518	555	566	558	573
Distillate fuel oil	Mil. bbl. .	971	1,066	1,142	1,168	1,153	1,212	1,237	1,248	1,245
Residual fuel oil	Mil. bbl. .	577	347	307	303	288	266	259	277	256
Liquefied petroleum gases . . .	Mil. bbl. .	120	183	215	223	237	241	252	245	252
Utilization rate	Percent .	75.4	87.1	91.5	92.6	92.0	94.1	95.2	95.6	92.7

NA Not available.   [1] Source: American Petroleum Institute, *Joint Association Survey on Drilling Costs*, annual.

Source: Except as noted, U.S. Energy Information Administration, *Annual Energy Review, Petroleum Supply Annual; U.S. Crude Oil, Natural Gas,* and *Natural Gas Liquids Reserves;* and *Monthly Energy Review.*

No. 1175. U.S. Petroleum Balance: 1980 to 1999

[In millions of barrels (6,242 represents 6,242,000,000)]

Item	1980	1990	1993	1994	1995	1996	1997	1998	1999
Petroleum products supplied for domestic use	**6,242**	**6,201**	**6,291**	**6,467**	**7,087**	**6,701**	**6,796**	**6,905**	**7,125**
Production of products	5,765	5,934	6,182	6,244	6,940	6,511	6,671	6,733	6,774
Crude input to refineries	4,934	4,894	4,969	5,061	5,718	5,195	5,351	5,434	5,403
Oil, field production	3,138	2,685	2,499	2,431	2,406	2,366	2,355	2,282	2,147
Alaska	592	647	577	569	542	510	473	429	383
Lower 48 States	2,555	2,037	1,922	1,863	1,853	1,856	1,882	1,853	1,764
Net imports	1,821	2,112	2,441	2,542	2,604	2,708	2,963	3,137	3,144
Imports (gross excluding SPR) [1]	1,910	2,142	2,472	2,574	2,639	2,748	3,002	3,178	3,184
SPR [1] imports	16	10	5	4	-	-	-	-	3
Exports	-105	40	36	36	35	40	39	40	43
Other sources	33	98	28	88	102	122	34	15	113
Natural gas liquids (NGL), supply	577	574	664	694	708	716	721	717	757
Other liquids	253	465	550	489	514	599	599	582	614
Net imports of refined products	484	326	134	217	101	181	154	225	252
Imports	578	598	461	518	407	491	469	508	537
Exports	94	272	327	302	307	310	315	283	284
Stock withdrawal, refined products	-7	-59	-24	6	46	9	-29	-53	98
TYPE OF PRODUCT SUPPLIED									
Total products supplied for domestic use	**6,242**	**6,201**	**6,291**	**6,467**	**6,469**	**6,701**	**6,796**	**6,905**	**7,125**
Finished motor gasoline	2,407	2,641	2,729	2,774	2,843	2,888	2,926	3,012	3,077
Distillate fuel oil.	1,049	1,103	1,110	1,154	1,170	1,232	1,254	1,263	1,304
Residual fuel oil	918	449	394	373	311	311	291	324	303
Liquefied petroleum gases [2]	414	568	633	686	693	736	744	713	801
Other	1,454	1,440	1,425	1,480	1,452	1,535	1,582	1,593	1,639
ENDING STOCKS									
Ending stocks, all oils	**1,392**	**1,621**	**1,647**	**1,653**	**1,563**	**1,052**	**1,560**	**1,647**	**1,493**
Crude oil and lease condensate	358	323	335	337	303	284	305	324	284
Strategic Petroleum Reserve (SPR) [1]	108	586	587	592	592	566	563	571	567
Other	926	712	725	724	668	202	692	752	641

- Represents zero.   [1] SPR=Strategic petroleum reserve. For more information, see Table 958.   [2] Includes ethane.

Source: U.S. Energy Information Administration, *Petroleum Supply Annual.*

Natural Resources   701

No. 1176. Crude Petroleum and Natural Gas—Production and Value by Major Producing States: 1990 to 1998

[2,685 mil. bbl. represents 2,685,000,000 bbl. or 18,594 bil. cu. ft. represents 18,594,000,000,000 cu. ft.]

State	Crude petroleum						Natural gas marketed production [1]					
	Quantity (mil. bbl.)			Value (mil. dol.)			Quantity (bil. cu. ft.)			Value (mil. dol.)		
	1990	1995	1998	1990	1995	1998	1990	1995	1998	1990	1995	1998
Total [2] ...	2,685	2,406	2,282	53,772	35,004	24,804	18,594	19,506	19,646	31,658	30,160	38,206
AL......	18	19	12	387	306	150	135	520	564	373	948	1,237
AK......	658	542	429	10,086	6,088	3,669	403	470	467	554	771	614
AR......	10	9	8	222	132	89	175	187	188	360	565	738
CA......	322	279	284	5,732	3,906	2,709	363	280	315	857	483	621
CO.....	31	29	22	722	466	281	243	523	696	377	497	1,323
FL......	6	6	6	(NA)	(NA)	(NA)	6	6	6	15	8	(NA)
IL......	20	16	14	467	274	175	1	-	-	1	(Z)	(NA)
IN......	3	3	2	73	47	28	(Z)	-	1	1	-	1
KS......	59	44	36	1,359	709	433	574	721	604	893	985	1,027
KY......	5	3	3	124	57	34	75	75	82	169	123	196
LA......	148	131	134	3,409	2,096	1,690	5,242	5,108	5,288	9,587	8,048	10,555
MI......	20	11	9	458	189	111	140	238	278	420	399	491
MS.....	30	20	22	630	294	228	95	96	108	167	118	153
MT.....	20	17	16	429	247	186	50	50	58	90	68	88
NE......	5	4	3	119	58	37	1	2	2	2	3	2
NM.....	66	65	72	1,472	1,080	894	965	1,626	1,501	1,629	2,056	2,649
NY......	(Z)	-	-	9	-	3	25	18	17	55	42	43
ND......	39	29	36	849	457	405	52	49	53	93	(NA)	114
OH.....	8	8	7	196	138	80	155	126	109	393	294	243
OK.....	117	88	78	2,690	1,459	988	2,258	1,812	1,645	3,548	2,616	2,915
PA......	2	2	2	54	33	27	178	111	68	417	315	-
TX......	674	560	505	15,060	9,167	6,197	6,343	6,330	6,319	9,939	10,208	13,003
UT......	23	20	19	524	354	240	146	241	277	249	277	479
WV.....	2	2	1	43	32	18	178	186	178	568	414	-
WY.....	103	79	65	2,169	1,223	693	736	674	761	856	1,198	1,352

- Represents zero. NA Not available. Z Less than 500 million cubic feet or less than $500,000. [1] Excludes nonhydrocarbon gases. [2] Includes other states not shown separately. State production does not include state offshore production.

Source: U.S. Energy Information Administration, *Petroleum Supply Annual,* and *Petroleum Marketing Annual; and Natural Gas Annual,* and *Natural Gas Monthly.*

No. 1177. Crude Oil, Natural Gas, and Natural Gas Liquids—Reserves by State: 1990 and 1998

[As of **December 31.** Proved reserves are estimated quantities of the mineral, which geological and engineering data demonstrate with reasonable certainty, to be recoverable in future years from known reservoirs under existing economic and operating conditions. Indicated reserves of crude oil are quantities other than proved reserves, which may become economically recoverable from existing productive reservoirs through the application of improved recovery techniques using current technology. Based on a sample of operators of oil and gas wells]

Area	1990				1998			
	Crude oil		Natural gas (bil. cu. ft.)	Natural gas liquids (mil. bbl.)	Crude oil		Natural gas (bil. cu. ft.)	Natural gas liquids (mil. bbl.)
	Proved (mil. bbl.)	Indicated (mil. bbl.)			Proved (mil. bbl.)	Indicated (mil. bbl.)		
United States	26,254	3,483	169,346	7,586	21,034	3,160	164,041	7,524
Lower 48 States.....	19,730	2,514	160,046	7,246	15,982	2,328	154,114	7,204
Alabama............	44	(Z)	[1]4,125	170	39	-	4,604	81
Alaska.............	6,524	969	9,300	340	5,052	832	9,927	320
Arkansas...........	60	1	1,731	9	47	-	1,328	5
California	[2]4,658	[2]1,425	[2]3,185	[2]105	3,843	1,297	2,244	72
Colorado...........	305	8	4,555	169	212	21	7,881	260
Florida	(NA)	(NA)	(NA)	(NA)	71	-	88	18
Illinois	(NA)	(NA)	(NA)	(NA)	81	-	(NA)	(NA)
Indiana............	131	-	(NA)	(NA)	13	-	(NA)	(NA)
Kansas............	(NA)	(NA)	(NA)	(NA)	246	-	6,402	334
Kentucky	321	(Z)	9,614	313	23	-	1,222	54
Louisiana	33	-	1,016	25	551	309	9,147	411
Michigan...........	(NA)	(NA)	(NA)	(NA)	44	-	2,328	51
Mississippi.........	(NA)	(NA)	(NA)	(NA)	141	-	658	8
Montana...........	(NA)	(NA)	(NA)	(NA)	167	-	782	5
Nebraska	221	-	899	15	18	-	(NA)	(NA)
New Mexico	(NA)	(NA)	(NA)	(NA)	620	168	14,987	929
New York	687	256	17,260	990	(NA)	(NA)	218	(NA)
North Dakota.......	285	-	586	60	245	1	447	48
Ohio..............	65	-	1,214	(NA)	40	-	890	(NA)
Oklahoma..........	734	37	16,151	657	599	59	13,645	698
Pennsylvania........	22	-	1,720	(NA)	15	-	1,840	(NA)
Texas.............	[2]7,106	618	[2]38,192	2,575	4,927	400	37,584	2,544
Utah	249	44	1,510	([3])	201	56	2,388	(NA)
Virginia............	(NA)	(NA)	138	86	(NA)	(NA)	1,973	(NA)
West Virginia	31	-	2,207	72	17	-	2,868	72
Wyoming	794	42	9,944	[4]812	547	10	13,650	675
Federal offshore......	2,805	49	31,433	619	3,261	7	26,902	931

- Represents or rounds to zero. NA Not available. Z Less than 500,000 barrels. [1] Includes state offshore. [2] Excludes Federal offshore. [3] Included with Wyoming. [4] Includes Utah.

Source: Energy Information Administration, *U.S. Crude Oil, Natural Gas, and Natural Gas Liquids Reserves, Annual Report 1998,* December 1999.

702 Natural Resources

No. 1178. World Daily Crude Oil Production by Major Producing Country: 1980 to 1998

[In thousands of barrels per day (59,600 barrels represents 59,600,000 barrels)]

Country	1980	1990	1992	1993	1994	1995	1996	1997	1998
World, total [1]	59,600	60,566	60,213	60,236	60,991	62,335	63,711	65,690	66,962
Saudi Arabia	9,900	6,410	8,332	8,198	8,120	8,231	8,218	8,362	8,389
United States	8,597	7,355	7,171	6,847	6,662	6,560	6,465	6,452	6,252
Russia	(X)	(X)	7,632	6,730	6,135	5,995	5,850	5,920	5,854
Iran	1,662	3,088	3,429	3,540	3,618	3,643	3,686	3,664	3,634
China	2,114	2,774	2,845	2,890	2,939	2,990	3,131	3,200	3,198
Venezuela	2,168	2,137	2,371	2,450	2,588	2,750	2,938	3,280	3,167
Mexico	1,936	2,553	2,669	2,673	2,685	2,618	2,855	3,023	3,070
Norway	528	1,704	2,229	2,350	2,521	2,768	3,104	3,143	3,017
United Kingdom	1,622	1,820	1,825	1,915	2,375	2,489	2,568	2,518	2,616
United Arab Emirates	1,709	2,117	2,266	2,159	2,193	2,233	2,278	2,316	2,345
Nigeria	2,055	1,810	1,943	1,960	1,931	1,993	2,001	2,132	2,153
Iraq	2,514	2,040	425	512	553	560	579	1,155	2,150
Kuwait	1,656	1,175	1,058	1,852	2,025	2,057	2,062	2,007	2,085
Canada	1,435	1,553	1,605	1,679	1,746	1,805	1,837	1,922	1,981
Indonesia	1,577	1,462	1,504	1,511	1,510	1,503	1,547	1,520	1,518
Libya	1,787	1,375	1,433	1,361	1,378	1,390	1,401	1,446	1,390
Algeria	1,106	1,175	1,214	1,162	1,180	1,202	1,242	1,277	1,246
Brazil	182	631	626	643	671	695	795	841	969
Oman	282	685	740	776	810	851	883	904	900
Argentina	491	483	553	594	650	715	756	834	847
Egypt	595	873	881	890	896	920	922	856	834
Angola	150	475	526	509	536	646	709	714	735
Malaysia	283	619	653	640	645	682	695	700	733
Colombia	126	440	433	456	450	585	623	652	733
Qatar	472	406	423	413	415	442	510	550	696
India	182	660	561	534	590	703	651	675	661
Syria	164	388	481	554	560	575	582	561	553
Australia	380	575	535	503	536	562	570	588	544
Kazakhstan	(X)	(X)	444	408	352	362	403	466	476
Yemen	-	193	182	220	335	345	340	362	388

- Represents zero.   X Not applicable.   [1] Includes countries not shown separately.

Source: U.S. Energy Information Administration, *International Energy Review, 1998.*

No. 1179. Liquefied Petroleum Gases—Summary: 1980 to 1999

[In millions of 42-gallon barrels (561 barrels represents 561,000,000 barrels). Includes ethane]

Item	1980	1990	1993	1994	1995	1996	1997	1998	1999
Production	561	638	850	734	760	789	799	775	811
At natural gas plants	441	456	634	511	521	547	547	529	559
At refineries	121	182	216	223	234	242	252	246	251
Imports	79	68	70	67	53	61	62	71	64
Refinery input	85	107	179	108	105	102	96	92	87
Exports	9	14	16	14	21	19	18	15	18
Stocks, Dec. 31	116	98	117	99	93	86	89	115	88

Source: U.S. Energy Information Administration, *Petroleum Supply Annual.*

No. 1180. Natural Gas Plant Liquids—Production and Value: 1980 to 1998

[Barrels of 42 gallons (576 barrels represents 576,000,000 barrels)]

Item	Unit	1980	1990	1992	1993	1994	1995	1996	1997	1998
Field production [1]	Mil. bbl	576	566	621	634	630	643	670	663	642
Pentanes plus	Mil. bbl	126	112	121	122	119	122	123	116	113
Liquefied petroleum gases	Mil. bbl	441	454	500	512	511	521	547	547	529
Natural gas processed	Tril. cu. ft.	15	15	16	16	16	17	17	17	17

[1] Includes other finished petroleum products, not shown separately.

Source: U.S. Energy Information Administration, *Energy Data Reports, Petroleum Statement Annual, Petroleum Supply Annual,* and *Natural Gas Annual.*

No. 1181. Natural Gas—Supply, Consumption, Reserves, and Marketed Production: 1980 to 1998

[182 represents 182,000 wells]

Item	Unit	1980	1990	1991	1992	1993	1994	1995	1996	1997	1998
Producing wells (year-end)	1,000	182	269	276	276	282	292	299	302	311	316
Production value at wells	Bil. dol	32.1	31.8	30.3	32.6	38.7	36.5	30.2	42.9	46.1	38.1
Avg. per 1,000 cu. ft	Dollars	1.59	1.71	1.64	1.74	2.04	1.85	1.55	2.17	2.32	1.94
Proved reserves [1]	Tril. cu. ft	199	169	167	165	162	164	165	166	167	(NA)
Marketed production [2]	**Tril. cu. ft**	**20.2**	**18.6**	**18.5**	**18.7**	**19.0**	**19.7**	**19.5**	**19.8**	**19.9**	**19.6**
Minus: Extraction losses [3]	Tril. cu. ft	0.8	0.8	0.8	0.9	0.9	0.9	0.9	1.0	1.0	0.9
Equals: Dry production	Tril. cu. ft	19.4	17.8	17.7	17.8	18.1	18.8	18.6	18.8	18.9	18.9
Plus: Withdrawals from storage	Tril. cu. ft	2.0	2.0	2.8	2.8	2.7	2.5	3.0	2.9	2.8	(NA)
Plus: Imports [4]	Tril. cu. ft	1.0	1.5	1.8	2.1	2.4	2.6	2.8	2.9	3.0	(NA)
Plus: Balancing item	Tril. cu. ft	-0.6	-0.2	-0.5	-0.5	-0.1	-0.4	-0.2	0.3	0.1	(NA)
Equals: Total supply	Tril. cu. ft	21.9	21.3	21.8	22.8	23.6	24.2	24.8	25.6	25.5	(NA)
Minus: Exports	Tril. cu. ft	0.5	0.9	0.1	0.2	0.1	0.2	0.2	0.2	0.2	(NA)
Minus: Additions to storage [5]	Tril. cu. ft	1.9	2.5	2.7	2.6	2.8	2.9	2.6	3.0	2.9	(NA)
Equals: Consumption, total	**Tril. cu. ft**	**19.9**	**18.7**	**19.0**	**19.5**	**20.3**	**20.7**	**21.6**	**22.0**	**22.0**	**21.3**
Lease and plant fuel	Tril. cu. ft	1.0	1.2	1.1	1.2	1.2	1.1	1.2	1.3	1.2	1.2
Pipeline fuel	Tril. cu. ft	0.6	0.7	0.6	0.6	0.6	0.7	0.7	0.7	0.8	0.6
Residential	Tril. cu. ft	4.8	4.4	4.6	4.7	5.0	4.8	4.9	5.2	5.0	4.5
Commercial [6]	Tril. cu. ft	2.6	2.6	2.7	2.8	2.9	2.9	3.0	3.2	3.2	3.0
Industrial	Tril. cu. ft	7.2	7.0	7.2	7.5	8.0	8.2	8.6	8.9	8.8	8.7
Vehicle fuel	Tril. cu. ft	(NA)	(Z)	(Z)	(Z)	1.0	1.7	2.7	2.9	4.4	-
Electric utilities	Tril. cu. ft	3.7	2.8	2.8	2.8	2.7	3.0	3.2	2.7	3.0	3.3
World production (dry)	Tril. cu. ft	53.5	73.6	74.8	74.8	76.4	76.9	78.0	81.6	81.6	83.0
U.S. production (dry)	Tril. cu. ft	19.4	17.8	17.7	17.8	18.1	18.8	18.6	18.8	18.9	18.9
Percent U.S. of world	Percent	36.3	24.2	23.7	23.8	23.7	24.5	23.9	23.0	23.2	22.7

- Represents or rounds to zero.   NA Not available.   Z Less than .05 trillion cubic feet.   [1] Estimated, end of year. Source: U.S. Energy Information Administration, *U.S. Crude Oil, Natural Gas,* and *Natural Gas Liquids Reserves,* annual.   [2] Marketed production includes gross withdrawals from reservoirs less quantities used for reservoir repressuring and quantities vented or flared. For 1980 and thereafter, it excludes the nonhydrocarbon gases subsequently removed.   [3] Volumetric reduction in natural gas resulting from the extraction of natural gas constituents at natural gas processing plants.   [4] Includes imports of liquefied natural gas.   [5] Includes liquefied natural gas (LNG) storage in above ground tanks.   [6] Includes deliveries to municipalities and public authorities for institutional heating and other purposes.

Source: Except as noted, U.S. Energy Information Administration, *Annual Energy Review, International Energy Annual, Natural Gas Annual,* Volume I and II, and *Monthly Energy Review.*

No. 1182. World Natural Gas Production by Major Producing Country: 1980 to 1998

[In trillion cubic feet (53.45 represents 53,450,000,000,000)]

Country	1980	1990	1992	1993	1994	1995	1996	1997	1998
World, total [1]	**53.35**	**73.57**	**74.84**	**76.36**	**76.93**	**77.96**	**81.64**	**81.61**	**82.96**
Russia	(X)	(X)	22.62	21.81	21.45	21.01	21.23	20.17	20.87
United States	**19.40**	**17.81**	**17.84**	**18.10**	**18.82**	**18.60**	**18.79**	**18.90**	**18.86**
Canada	2.76	3.85	4.52	4.91	5.27	5.60	5.78	5.85	6.04
United Kingdom	1.32	1.75	1.96	2.31	2.47	2.67	3.18	3.03	3.17
Netherlands	3.40	2.69	3.06	3.11	2.95	2.98	3.37	2.99	2.84
Algeria	0.41	1.79	1.97	1.90	1.81	2.05	2.19	2.43	2.60
Indonesia	0.63	1.53	1.79	1.97	2.21	2.24	2.35	2.37	2.24
Uzbekistan	(X)	(X)	1.51	1.59	1.67	1.70	1.70	1.74	1.94
Iran	0.25	0.84	0.88	0.96	1.12	1.25	1.42	1.66	1.77
Saudi Arabia	0.33	1.08	1.20	1.27	1.33	1.34	1.46	1.60	1.65
Norway	0.92	0.98	1.04	0.97	1.04	1.08	1.45	1.62	1.63
Malaysia	0.06	0.65	0.80	0.88	0.92	1.02	1.23	1.36	1.44
United Arab Emirates	0.20	0.78	1.02	0.94	0.91	1.11	1.19	1.28	1.31
Mexico	0.90	0.90	0.88	0.95	0.97	0.96	1.06	1.16	1.27
Australia	0.31	0.72	0.80	0.86	0.93	1.03	1.05	1.07	1.10
Argentina	0.28	0.63	0.71	0.76	0.79	0.88	0.94	0.97	1.05
Venezuela	0.52	0.76	0.76	0.82	0.88	0.89	0.96	0.99	0.99
China	0.51	0.51	0.53	0.56	0.59	0.60	0.67	0.75	0.78
Germany	0.93	0.72	0.68	0.68	0.70	0.74	0.80	0.79	0.77
India	0.05	0.40	0.48	0.53	0.59	0.63	0.70	0.72	0.76
Pakistan	0.29	0.48	0.55	0.58	0.63	0.65	0.70	0.70	0.71
Qatar	0.18	0.28	0.40	0.48	0.48	0.48	0.48	0.61	0.69
Italy	0.44	0.61	0.64	0.69	0.73	0.72	0.71	0.68	0.67
Ukraine	(X)	(X)	0.74	0.68	0.64	0.62	0.64	0.64	0.64
Thailand	-	0.21	0.25	0.31	0.34	0.37	0.43	0.54	0.57
Romania	1.20	1.00	0.78	0.75	0.69	0.68	0.63	0.61	0.52
Egypt	0.03	0.29	0.35	0.40	0.42	0.44	0.47	0.48	0.49
Turkmenistan	-	-	2.02	2.29	1.26	1.14	1.31	0.90	0.47
Trinidad and Tobago	0.08	0.18	0.19	0.22	0.25	0.27	0.30	0.33	0.37
Kuwait	0.24	0.19	0.09	0.19	0.21	0.21	0.33	0.33	0.33

- Represents or rounds to zero.   X Not applicable.   [1] Includes countries not shown separately.

Source: U. S. Energy Information Administration, *International Energy Annual, 1998.*

704   Natural Resources

No. 1183. Coal and Coke—Summary: 1980 to 1999

[**830 short tons represents 830,000,000 short tons.** Includes coal consumed at mines. Demonstrated coal reserve base for United States on Jan. 1, 1997, was an estimated 508 billion tons. Recoverability varies between 40 and 90 percent for individual deposits; 50 percent or more of overall U.S. coal reserve base is believed to be recoverable]

Item	Unit	1980	1990	1994	1995	1996	1997	1998	1999, prel.
COAL									
Coal production, total [1] . . .	**Mil. sh. tons** . .	**830**	**1,029**	**1,034**	**1,033**	**1,064**	**1,090**	**1,118**	**1,099**
Value	Bil. dol.	20.45	22.39	20.06	19.45	19.68	19.77	19.75	19.42
Anthracite production	Mil. sh. tons . . .	6.1	3.5	4.6	4.7	4.8	4.7	5.3	5.2
Bituminous coal and lignite.	Mil. sh. tons . . .	824	1,026	1,029	1,028	1,059	1,085	1,112	1,094
Underground	Mil. sh. tons . . .	337	425	399	396	410	421	417	411
Surface	Mil. sh. tons . . .	487	605	634	637	654	669	700	688
Exports	Mil. sh. tons . . .	92	106	71	89	90	84	78	59
Imports.	Mil. sh. tons . . .	1	3	8	7	7	7	9	9
Consumption [2]	Mil. sh. tons . . .	703	896	930	941	1,006	1,029	1,039	1,041
Electric power utilities	Mil. sh. tons . . .	569	774	817	829	875	900	911	897
Industrial.	Mil. sh. tons . . .	126	115	107	106	103	101	96	94
Number of mines	Number.	5,598	3,243	2,354	2,104	1,903	1,828	1,726	(NA)
Daily employment.	1,000	225	131	98	90	83	82	81	(NA)
Production, by state:									
Alabama	Mil. sh. tons . . .	26	29	23	25	25	24	23	20
Illinois.	Mil. sh. tons . . .	63	60	53	48	47	41	40	40
Indiana	Mil. sh. tons . . .	31	36	31	26	30	35	37	34
Kentucky.	Mil. sh. tons . . .	150	173	162	154	152	156	150	139
Montana	Mil. sh. tons . . .	30	38	42	39	38	41	43	41
Ohio.	Mil. sh. tons . . .	39	35	30	26	29	29	28	23
Pennsylvania	Mil. sh. tons . . .	93	71	62	62	68	76	81	76
Virginia	Mil. sh. tons . . .	41	47	37	34	36	36	34	32
West Virginia	Mil. sh. tons . . .	122	169	162	163	170	174	171	156
Wyoming.	Mil. sh. tons . . .	95	184	237	264	278	282	314	335
Other states.	Mil. sh. tons . . .	140	187	195	192	192	195	196	203
World production	Mil. sh. tons . . .	4,200	5,356	5,008	5,126	5,185	5,172	5,043	(NA)
Percent U.S. of world.	Percent	19.8	19.2	20.6	20.2	20.5	21.1	22.2	(NA)
COKE									
Coke production [3]	Mil. sh. tons . . .	46.13	27.62	22.69	23.75	23.08	22.12	20.04	20.02
Imports.	Mil. sh. tons . . .	0.66	0.77	3.34	3.82	2.54	3.14	3.83	3.22
Exports	Mil. sh. tons . . .	2.07	0.57	0.99	1.36	1.62	1.27	1.13	0.90
Consumption.	Mil. sh. tons . . .	41.28	27.82	25.56	25.90	23.97	24.02	23.03	22.44

NA Not available. [1] Includes bituminous coal, subbituminous coal, lignite, and anthracite. [2] Includes some categories not shown separately. [3] Includes beehive coke.

Source: U.S. Energy Information Administration, *Coal Industry,* annual; *Annual Energy Review, International Energy Annual,* and *Quarterly Coal Report.*

No. 1184. World Coal Production by Major Producing Country: 1980 to 1998

[In millions of short tons (4,200 represents 4,200,000,000)]

Country	1980	1990	1992	1993	1994	1995	1996	1997	1998
World, total	**4,200**	**5,356**	**5,019**	**4,921**	**5,008**	**5,126**	**5,185**	**5,172**	**5,043**
China.	684	1,190	1,229	1,304	1,404	1,537	1,515	1,461	1,351
United States	**830**	**1,029**	**998**	**945**	**1,034**	**1,033**	**1,064**	**1,090**	**1,119**
India.	126	233	270	281	291	301	340	353	359
Australia	116	226	249	248	248	267	272	293	314
Russia	(X)	(X)	406	364	313	296	304	290	272
South Africa	132	193	203	207	216	227	227	246	247
Germany	532	514	346	315	292	273	265	252	229
Poland	254	237	218	218	220	220	222	221	198
Czech Republic	(X)	(X)	(X)	94	85	82	84	84	83
Canada	40	75	72	76	80	83	83	87	83
Ukraine	(X)	(X)	147	128	105	92	79	86	83
Kazakhstan.	(X)	(X)	139	123	115	92	84	80	77
Korea, North	51	71	74	78	78	78	79	68	68
Turkey	20	52	57	54	60	61	62	62	67
Indonesia	1	9	24	30	34	46	55	60	66
Greece.	26	57	61	60	63	64	66	65	65
Serbia and Montenegro.	(X)	(X)	44	41	42	44	42	45	48
United Kingdom	144	104	94	75	54	52	55	54	45
Colombia	5	23	26	23	25	28	33	36	38
Bulgaria	40	39	33	32	32	34	34	33	33
Spain.	41	40	37	35	33	31	31	29	29
Romania.	39	42	42	44	45	45	46	37	29
Thailand.	2	14	17	17	19	20	24	26	22
Hungary	28	19	17	16	16	15	13	14	16
Vietnam	6	5	5	7	6	9	11	13	12
Mexico.	4	9	7	8	10	10	11	10	11
Venezuela.	-	2	3	4	5	4	5	6	8
Macedonia (Former Yugoslav Republic) . . .	(X)	(X)	8	8	8	8	8	7	7
France	25	15	13	12	10	9	9	8	6
Zimbabwe.	3	6	6	6	6	6	5	6	6

- Represents zero. X Not applicable.
Source: U.S. Energy Information Administration, *International Energy Annual.*

No. 1185. Demonstrated Coal Reserves by Type of Coal and Major Producing State: 1997

[In millions of short tons. As of January 1. The demonstrated reserve base represents the sum of coal in both measured and indicated resource categories of reliability. Measured resources of coal are estimates that have a high degree of geologic assurance from sample analyze and measurements from closely spaced and geological well known sample sites. Indicated resources are estimates based partly from sample and analyses and measurements and partly from reasonable geologic projections. For more information on the classification of coal resources and related terminology, see report cited below]

State	Total reserves	Type of coal				Method of mining	
		Anthracite	Bituminous	Sub-bituminous	Lignite	Under ground	Surface
United States.	**507,740**	**7,477**	**270,910**	**185,118**	**44,235**	**341,775**	**165,965**
Alabama.	4,547	-	3,464	-	1,083	1,290	3,256
Alaska	6,126	-	698	5,414	14	5,423	703
Colorado.	16,756	26	8,711	3,830	4,190	11,979	4,777
Illinois	105,069	-	105,069	-	-	88,461	16,608
Indiana.	9,917	-	9,917	-	-	8,860	1,057
Iowa	2,190	-	2,190	-	-	1,733	457
Kentucky	32,041	-	32,041	-	-	18,508	13,533
Kentucky, Eastern. . . .	12,086	-	12,086	-	-	2,247	9,839
Kentucky, Western . . .	19,954	-	19,954	-	-	16,261	3,694
Missouri	5,994	-	5,994	-	-	1,479	4,515
Montana.	119,677	-	1,385	102,531	15,760	70,958	48,718
New Mexico	12,483	2	3,706	8,774	-	6,204	6,279
North Dakota.	9,395	-	-	-	9,395	-	9,395
Ohio	23,664	-	23,664	-	-	17,789	5,875
Oklahoma.	1,575	-	1,575	-	-	1,237	338
Pennsylvania.	28,646	7,220	21,427	-	-	24,232	4,414
Anthracite	7,220	7,220	-	-	-	3,850	3,370
Bituminous	21,427	-	21,427	-	-	20,382	1,044
Texas.	12,931	-	-	-	12,931	-	12,931
Utah	5,850	-	5,849	1	-	5,583	268
Virginia.	2,202	126	2,077	-	-	1,528	674
Washington.	1,390	-	304	1,078	8	1,332	57
West Virginia.	35,397	-	35,397	-	-	30,968	4,429
Wyoming	67,815	-	4,343	63,472	-	42,516	25,299
East of the MS River. . . .	243,156	7,345	234,728	-	1,083	192,939	50,217
West of the MS River . . .	264,584	132	36,182	185,118	43,152	148,836	115,747

- Represents or rounds to zero.

Source: U.S. Energy Information Administration, *U.S. Coal Reserves: 1997 Update*, February 1999.

No. 1186. Uranium Concentrate (U₃O₈) Industry—Summary: 1990 to 1999

[See also Table 968]

Item	Unit	1990	1992	1993	1994	1995	1996	1997	1998	1999
Exploration and development, surface drilling.	Mil. ft.	1.7	1.1	1.1	0.7	1.3	3.0	4.9	4.6	2.5
Expenditures.	Mil. dol.	17.1	14.5	11.3	3.7	6.0	10.1	30.4	21.7	9.0
Number of mines operated	Number.	39	17	12	12	12	13	14	15	14
Underground.	Number.	27	4	-	-	-	1	1	4	3
Openpit	Number.	2	1	-	-	-	-	-	-	-
In situ leaching	Number.	7	4	5	5	5	6	7	6	6
Other sources	Number.	3	8	7	7	7	6	6	5	5
Mine production	1,000 pounds . .	5,876	986	2,050	2,526	3,528	4,705	4,710	4,782	4,548
Underground.	1,000 pounds . .	(D)	(D)	-	-	-	(D)	(D)	(D)	(D)
Openpit	1,000 pounds . .	1,881	(D)	-	-	-	-	-	-	-
In situ leaching	1,000 pounds . .	(D)	(D)	(D)	2,448	3,372	4,379	4,084	3,721	3,830
Other sources	1,000 pounds . .	3,995	986	2,050	78	156	326	626	1,062	718
Uranium concentrate production.	1,000 pounds . .	8,886	5,645	3,063	3,352	6,043	6,321	5,643	4,705	4,611
Concentrate shipments from mills and plants.	1,000 pounds . .	12,957	6,853	3,374	6,319	5,500	5,982	5,817	4,863	5,527
Employment.	Person-years . .	1,335	682	871	980	1,107	1,118	1,097	1,120	848

- Represents or rounds to zero.   D Data withheld to avoid disclosing figures for individual companies.

Source: U.S. Department of Energy, *Uranium Industry*, annual.

Section 25
Construction and Housing

This section presents data on the construction industry and on various indicators of its activity and costs; on housing units and their characteristics and occupants; and on the characteristics and vacancy rates for commercial buildings. This edition contains data from the 1997 American Housing Survey.

The principal source of these data is the U.S. Census Bureau, which issues a variety of current publications. Construction statistics compiled by the Census Bureau appear in its monthly *Current Construction Reports* series with various quarterly or annual supplements; *Housing Starts* and *Housing Completions* present data by type of structure and by four major census regions; *New One-Family Houses Sold and For Sale* also provides statistics annually on physical and financial characteristics for all new housing by the four major census regions; *Price Index of New One-Family Houses Sold* presents quarterly figures and annual regional data; and *Housing Units Authorized by Building Permits* covers approximately 19,000 permit-issuing jurisdictions in the United States (prior to 1995, 17,000 places). Statistics on expenditures by owners of residential properties are issued quarterly and annually in *Expenditures for Residential Upkeep and Improvements. Value of New Construction Put in Place* presents data on all types of construction and includes monthly composite cost indexes. Reports of the censuses of construction industries (see below) are also issued on various topics.

Other Census Bureau publications include the *Current Housing Reports* series, which comprises the quarterly *Housing Vacancies*, the quarterly *Market Absorption of Apartments*, the biennial *American Housing Survey* (formerly *Annual Housing Survey*), and reports of the censuses of housing and of construction industries.

Construction Review, published quarterly by the International Trade Administration, U.S. Department of Commerce, contains many of the census series and other construction statistics series from the Federal Government and private agencies.

Other sources include the monthly *Dodge Construction Potentials* of F. W. Dodge Division, McGraw-Hill Information Systems Company, New York, NY, which presents national and state data on construction contracts; the National Association of Home Builders with state-level data on housing starts; the National Association of REALTORS, which presents data on existing home sales; the Society of Industrial and Office Realtors and Oncor International on commercial office and industrial space; the Bureau of Economic Analysis, which presents data on residential capital and gross housing product; and the U.S. Energy Information Administration , which provides data on commercial buildings through its periodic sample surveys.

Censuses and surveys—Censuses of the construction industry were first conducted by the Census Bureau for 1929, 1935, and 1939; beginning in 1967, a census has been taken every 5 years (through 1992, for years ending in "2" and "7"). The latest complete reports are for 1992. The 1997 census results, part of the 1997 Economic Census, are being released on a flow basis. See Table 1187 and Section 32.

The census of construction industries, covers all employer establishments primarily engaged in (1) building construction by general contractors or operative builders; (2) heavy (nonbuilding) construction by general contractors; and (3) construction by special trade contractors. The 1997 census was conducted in accordance with the 1997 *North American Industry Classification System* (NAICS); the 1992

Construction and Housing 707

census was conducted in accordance with the 1987 *Standard Industrial Classification* (SIC). This sector now includes construction management and land subdividers and developers, not included previously. See text, Section 17, Business, for general information on the SIC and NAICS.

From 1850 through 1930, the Census Bureau collected some housing data as part of its censuses of population and agriculture. Beginning in 1940, separate censuses of housing have been taken at 10-year intervals. For the 1970 and 1980 censuses, data on year-round housing units were collected and issued on occupancy and structural characteristics, plumbing facilities, value, and rent; for 1990 such characteristics were presented for all housing units.

The American Housing Survey (*Current Housing Reports* Series H-150 and H-170), which began in 1973, provided an annual and ongoing series of data on selected housing and demographic characteristics until 1983. In 1984, the name of the survey was changed from the Annual Housing Survey. Currently, national data are collected every other year, and data for selected metropolitan areas are collected on a rotating basis. All samples represent a cross section of the housing stock in their respective areas. Estimates are subject to both sampling and nonsampling errors; caution should therefore be used in making comparisons between years.

Data on residential mortgages were collected continuously from 1890 to 1970, except 1930, as part of the decennial census by the Census Bureau. Since 1973, mortgage status data, limited to single family homes on less than 10 acres with no business on the property, have been presented in the American Housing Survey. Data on mortgage activity are covered in Section 16, Banking.

Housing units—In general, a housing unit is a group of rooms or a single room occupied or intended for occupancy as separate living quarters; that is, the occupants do not live and eat with any other persons in the structure, and there is direct access from the outside or through a common hall. Transient accommodations, barracks for workers, and institutional-type quarters are not counted as housing units.

Statistical reliability—For a discussion of statistical collection and estimation, sampling procedures, and measures of statistical reliability applicable to Census Bureau data, see Appendix III.

U.S. Census Bureau, Statistical Abstract of the United States: 2000

No. 1187. Construction—Summary (SIC Basis): 1992 and 1997

[For establishments with payroll (539,085 represents $539,085,000,000). See Table 865 in Section 17, Business, for more comparative economic census data]

Industry	1987 SIC code [1]	Establishments		Value of business done (mil. dol.)		Annual payroll (mil. dol.)		Paid employees [2] (1,000)	
		1992	1997	1992	1997	1992	1997	1992	1997
Construction, total	C	572,851	639,482	539,085	834,795	117,730	170,962	4,668	5,567
Building construction—general contractors and operative builders . .	15	168,407	184,517	220,231	365,551	27,078	39,852	1,097	1,269
Heavy construction contractors other than buildings construction	16	37,180	39,542	98,528	126,864	23,728	29,218	799	852
Special trade contractors	17	367,263	415,423	220,325	342,379	66,924	101,892	2,772	3,446

[1] 1987 Standard Industrial Classification System code; see text, Section 17, Business.   [2] Average for the pay periods including March, May, August, and November 12.

Source: U.S. Census Bureau, *1997 Economic Census, Core Business Statistics Series, Comparative Statistics Series,* EC97X-CS2.

No. 1188. Construction Materials—Producer Price Indexes: 1990 to 1999

[1982=100, except as noted. For discussion of producer price index, see text, Section 15, Prices. This index, more formally known as the special commodity grouping index for construction materials, covers materials incorporated as integral part of a building or normally installed during construction and not readily removable. Excludes consumer durables such as kitchen ranges, refrigerators, etc. This index is not the same as the stage-of-processing index of intermediate materials and components for construction]

Commodity	1990	1992	1993	1994	1995	1996	1997	1998	1999
Construction materials	119.6	122.5	128.6	133.8	138.8	139.6	142.1	141.4	142.8
Interior solvent based paint	133.0	141.7	142.9	148.1	164.5	175.6	180.5	185.7	188.0
Plastic construction products	117.2	112.7	116.6	122.9	133.8	130.9	128.2	126.2	128.0
Douglas fir, dressed	138.4	169.5	237.6	236.2	198.8	227.1	221.3	186.1	212.1
Southern pine, dressed	111.2	130.6	168.8	182.6	166.9	177.9	201.2	177.3	185.7
Millwork	130.4	143.3	156.6	162.4	163.8	166.6	170.9	171.1	174.7
Softwood plywood	119.6	147.2	169.7	176.8	188.1	173.7	175.5	174.9	207.0
Hardwood plywood and related products	102.7	106.9	115.4	123.3	122.2	124.9	127.1	126.9	128.6
Softwood plywood veneer, ex. reinforced/backed . . .	142.3	168.3	216.0	207.8	203.5	189.3	201.7	180.1	197.4
Building paper and building board mill products	112.2	119.6	132.7	144.1	144.9	137.2	129.6	132.9	141.6
Steel pipe and tubes [1]	102.6	94.1	92.8	96.9	104.4	103.2	106.9	109.4	102.5
Builders hardware	133.0	141.4	144.9	148.0	153.2	156.5	158.4	160.8	161.9
Plumbing fixtures and brass fittings	144.3	153.1	155.9	159.6	166.0	171.1	174.5	175.1	176.7
Heating equipment	131.6	137.3	140.4	142.5	147.5	151.2	152.4	153.3	154.0
Metal doors, sash, and trim	131.4	135.0	136.6	142.0	156.5	159.3	161.0	161.3	162.2
Siding, aluminum [2]	(NA)	116.7	117.2	119.4	132.4	125.5	132.1	134.5	135.4
Outdoor lighting equipment [3]	113.0	115.3	115.5	115.4	120.8	122.9	123.2	122.8	122.3
Commercial fluorescent fixtures [4]	113.0	117.6	117.4	116.2	121.0	123.4	122.8	119.0	118.7
Architectural and ornamental metalwork [5]	118.7	117.7	119.5	123.4	128.0	131.3	133.5	135.4	136.2
Fabricated ferrous wire products [1]	114.6	117.5	119.3	122.6	125.7	126.8	128.0	130.1	130.6
Elevators, escalators, and other lifts.	110.1	109.4	110.7	112.4	113.0	113.7	114.8	116.0	117.5
Stamped metal outlet box	158.0	166.5	172.9	179.1	183.5	186.3	189.0	191.5	192.8
Concrete ingredients and related products	115.3	119.4	123.4	128.7	134.7	138.8	142.5	147.6	152.1
Concrete products	113.5	117.2	120.2	124.6	129.4	133.2	136.0	140.0	143.7
Clay construction products exc. refractories.	129.9	132.0	135.1	138.3	141.3	142.3	143.5	144.9	148.3
Prep. asphalt and tar roofing and siding products. . .	95.8	94.3	94.9	92.9	97.8	97.4	96.5	95.7	95.2
Gypsum products	105.2	99.9	108.3	136.1	154.5	154.0	170.8	177.6	208.0
Insulation materials.	108.4	102.3	105.8	111.9	118.8	118.9	117.7	119.7	131.7
Paving mixtures and blocks	101.2	100.2	102.0	103.2	105.8	107.6	113.2	112.5	112.9

NA Not available.   [1] June 1982=100.   [2] December 1982=100.   [3] June 1985=100.   [4] Recessed nonair.   [5] December 1983=100.

Source: U.S. Bureau of Labor Statistics, *Producer Price Indexes,* monthly and annual.

No. 1189. Price and Cost Indexes for Construction: 1980 to 1999

[**1996=100.** Excludes Alaska and Hawaii. Indexes of certain of these sources are published on bases different from those shown here]

Name of index	1980	1985	1990	1994	1995	1996	1997	1998	1999
U.S. Census Bureau Composite:									
Fixed-weighted [1]	59.3	71.8	85.5	93.9	97.7	99.9	103.2	106.0	110.3
Implicit price deflator [2]	59.0	71.1	85.0	93.9	97.8	100.0	103.3	106.1	110.4
U.S. Census Bureau houses under construction: [3]									
Fixed-weighted	58.0	69.8	84.6	94.1	98.1	100	102.9	105.6	110.4
Price deflator	57.0	68.3	83.4	94	98.1	100	102.9	105.6	110.4
Federal Highway Administration, composite [4]	79.7	83.6	88.9	94.3	99.8	100.0	107.5	105.2	112.7
Bureau of Reclamation composite [5]	62	75	85	94	98	100	103	105	107
Turner Construction Co.;									
Building construction [6]	54	74	87	94	97	100	104	109	113
Engineering News-Record: [7]									
Buildings	60.6	75.8	84.4	97.1	97.1	100.0	105.0	105.8	107.9
Construction	57.6	74.6	84.2	96.2	97.3	100.0	103.6	105.3	107.8
Handy-Whitman public utility: [8]									
Buildings	66	76	85	94	97	100	103	104	107
Electric [9]	60	74	86	95	98	100	102	104	105
Gas [10]	60	75	86	97	99	100	102	104	107
Water [10]	64	76	85	95	98	100	102	104	107
C. A. Turner Telephone Plant [11]	79	77	87	90	96	100	102	102	101

[1] Weighted average of the various indexes used to deflate the Construction Put in Place series. In calculating the index, the weights (i.e., the composition of current dollar estimates in 1996 by category) are held constant. [2] Derived ratio of total current to constant dollar Construction Put in Place (multiplied by 100). [3] Excludes value of site. [4] Based on average contract unit bid prices for composite mile (involving specific average amounts of excavation, paving, reinforcing steel, structural steel, and structural concrete). [5] Derived from the four quarterly indexes which are weighted averages of costs of labor, materials, and equipment for the construction of dams and reclamation projects. [6] Based on firm's cost experience with respect to labor rates, materials prices, competitive conditions, efficiency of plant and management, and productivity. [7] Building construction index computed on the basis of a hypothetical unit of construction requiring 6 bbl. of portland cement, 1,088 M bd. ft. of 2" x 4" lumber, 2,500 lb. of structural steel, and 68.38 hours of skilled labor. General construction index based on same materials components combined with 200 hours of common labor. [8] Based on data covering public utility construction costs in six geographic regions. Covers skilled and common labor. [9] As derived by U.S. Census Bureau. Covers steam generation plants only. [10] As derived by U.S. Census Bureau. Reflects costs for structures and improvements at water pumping and treatment plants. [11] Computed by the Census Bureau by averaging the weighted component indexes published for six geographic regions.

Source: U.S. Census Bureau. In U.S. Department of Commerce, International Trade Administration, *Construction Review*, quarterly.

No. 1190. Value of New Construction Put in Place: 1964 to 1999

[**In millions of dollars (75,097 represents $75,097,000,000).** Represents value of construction put in place during year; differs from building permit and construction contract data in timing and coverage. Includes installed cost of normal building service equipment and selected types of industrial production equipment (largely site fabricated). Excludes cost of shipbuilding, land, and most types of machinery and equipment. For methodology, see Appendix III]

Year	Current dollars					Constant (1996) dollars				
		Private					Private			
	Total	Total [1]	Residential buildings	Nonresidential buildings	Public	Total	Total [1]	Residential buildings	Nonresidential buildings	Public
1964	75,097	54,893	30,526	17,385	20,203	405,864	300,372	169,635	96,497	105,492
1970	105,890	77,982	35,863	28,171	27,908	429,041	321,940	155,113	115,372	107,101
1975	152,635	109,342	51,581	35,409	43,293	404,132	298,555	149,410	96,407	105,577
1980	273,936	210,290	100,381	72,480	63,646	464,144	364,101	175,822	129,275	100,043
1981	289,070	224,378	99,241	85,569	64,691	455,260	361,069	162,706	140,569	94,191
1982	279,332	216,268	84,676	92,690	63,064	423,729	333,894	134,605	145,054	89,835
1983	311,887	248,437	125,833	87,069	63,450	465,073	375,193	195,028	131,289	89,880
1984	370,190	299,952	155,015	107,680	70,238	534,557	437,325	231,396	155,261	97,232
1985	403,416	325,601	160,520	127,466	77,815	567,689	463,854	234,955	178,925	103,835
1986	433,454	348,872	190,677	120,917	84,582	588,804	479,623	266,481	163,740	109,182
1987	446,643	355,994	199,652	123,247	90,648	585,103	470,575	267,063	160,363	114,528
1988	462,012	367,277	204,496	130,854	94,735	583,396	467,599	263,385	164,191	115,797
1989	477,502	379,328	204,255	139,953	98,174	579,583	463,541	252,745	169,173	116,042
1990	476,778	369,300	191,103	143,506	107,478	560,802	436,999	228,943	167,896	123,803
1991	432,592	322,483	166,251	116,570	110,109	503,711	378,245	197,526	135,389	125,467
1992	463,661	347,814	199,393	105,646	115,847	533,322	401,567	232,134	120,921	131,755
1993	493,260	377,300	225,067	110,635	115,960	546,757	418,037	249,757	122,222	128,720
1994	539,232	419,038	258,561	120,289	120,193	574,302	445,460	274,956	127,593	128,842
1995	555,591	425,658	247,351	136,541	129,933	567,900	434,450	251,937	139,711	133,450
1996	613,535	474,273	281,115	153,912	139,263	613,454	474,307	281,229	153,866	139,147
1997	656,630	501,749	289,014	172,990	154,882	635,765	486,273	280,748	166,754	149,493
1998	711,759	552,236	314,607	190,711	159,523	670,859	520,613	297,886	177,639	150,246
1999	764,233	591,561	348,826	195,776	172,673	692,477	535,625	315,757	175,048	156,852

[1] Includes other types of private construction, not shown separately.

Source: U.S. Census Bureau, *Current Construction Reports*, Series C30, *Value of Construction*, monthly.

No. 1191. Value of New Construction Put in Place by Type: 1990 to 1999

[In millions of dollars (476,778 represents $476,778,000,000). Represents value of construction put in place during year; differs from building permit and construction contract data in timing and coverage. Includes installed cost of normal building service equipment and selected types of industrial production equipment (largely site fabricated). Excludes cost of shipbuilding, land, and most types of machinery and equipment. For methodology, see Appendix III]

Type of construction	Current dollars					Constant (1996) dollars				
	1990	1995	1997	1998	1999	1990	1995	1997	1998	1999
Total new construction	476,778	555,591	656,630	711,759	764,233	560,802	567,900	635,765	670,859	692,477
Private construction	369,300	425,658	501,749	552,236	591,561	436,999	434,450	486,273	520,613	535,625
Residential buildings	191,103	247,351	289,014	314,607	348,826	228,943	251,937	280,748	297,886	315,757
New housing units	132,137	171,404	198,063	223,983	249,536	158,319	174,585	192,386	212,068	225,896
1 unit	112,886	153,515	175,179	199,409	222,280	135,253	156,363	170,154	188,785	201,210
2 or more units	19,250	17,889	22,883	24,574	27,256	23,066	18,222	22,232	23,283	24,686
Improvements	58,966	75,947	90,951	90,624	99,290	70,625	77,352	88,362	85,818	89,860
Nonresidential buildings	143,506	136,541	172,990	190,711	195,776	167,896	139,711	166,754	177,639	175,048
Industrial	33,636	34,024	36,739	40,484	34,894	39,350	34,814	35,411	37,715	31,214
Office	35,055	25,613	34,305	42,226	46,570	41,027	26,218	33,058	39,333	41,643
Hotels, motels	10,679	7,112	12,898	14,816	15,939	12,497	7,274	12,438	13,794	14,262
Other commercial	40,047	42,654	51,809	53,598	57,143	46,847	43,636	49,948	49,915	51,067
Religious	3,566	4,326	5,777	6,594	7,497	4,169	4,426	5,565	6,139	6,701
Educational	4,616	5,493	8,693	9,698	9,784	5,398	5,621	8,375	9,039	8,743
Hospital and institutional	10,868	11,248	13,546	13,793	13,624	12,710	11,512	13,066	12,853	12,183
Miscellaneous [1]	5,040	6,071	9,223	9,501	10,327	5,897	6,209	8,892	8,850	9,235
Farm nonresidential	2,801	3,014	3,815	4,284	4,451	3,276	3,084	3,675	3,989	3,977
Public utilities	28,933	35,859	33,638	40,028	39,607	33,505	36,740	32,884	38,616	38,166
Telecommunications	9,803	11,093	12,416	13,328	15,223	11,346	11,556	12,159	13,036	15,142
Other public utilities	19,130	24,766	21,222	26,700	24,384	22,159	25,184	20,725	25,581	23,024
Railroads	2,600	3,509	4,922	5,736	4,918	2,969	3,609	4,745	5,463	4,540
Electric light and power	11,299	14,049	11,325	12,381	14,057	13,083	14,310	11,122	11,885	13,393
Gas	4,820	6,279	4,006	7,318	3,920	5,627	6,329	3,911	7,020	3,690
Petroleum pipelines	411	929	969	1,265	1,489	480	936	947	1,213	1,401
All other private [2]	2,957	2,893	2,292	2,606	2,901	3,379	2,979	2,212	2,482	2,678
Public construction	107,478	129,933	154,882	159,523	172,673	123,803	133,450	149,493	150,246	156,852
Buildings	43,615	57,754	71,867	73,277	77,690	51,117	59,074	69,319	68,334	69,497
Housing and redevelopment	3,808	4,698	5,230	5,124	5,618	4,560	4,786	5,084	4,853	5,088
Industrial	1,434	1,508	999	1,010	925	1,677	1,544	965	941	828
Educational	16,055	25,783	34,385	36,234	39,725	18,772	26,374	33,136	33,743	35,497
Hospital	2,860	4,236	5,152	3,906	3,968	3,348	4,335	4,970	3,642	3,548
Other [3]	19,458	21,528	26,100	27,004	27,454	22,760	22,034	25,164	25,155	24,537
Highways and streets	32,105	37,616	44,105	48,515	53,532	35,879	38,952	42,535	45,877	48,827
Military facilities	2,665	3,011	2,556	2,529	2,111	3,050	3,102	2,466	2,377	1,909
Conservation and development	4,686	6,308	5,739	5,447	6,003	5,482	6,443	5,541	5,219	5,602
Sewer systems	10,276	8,420	10,392	10,168	11,181	12,010	8,600	10,034	9,743	10,438
Water supply facilities	4,909	4,709	6,419	6,830	7,602	5,730	4,809	6,275	6,552	7,142
Miscellaneous public [4]	9,223	12,116	13,803	12,755	14,555	10,535	12,468	13,323	12,145	13,436

[1] Includes amusement and recreational buildings, bus and airline terminals, animal hospitals and shelters, etc.   [2] Includes privately owned streets and bridges, parking areas, sewer and water facilities, parks and playgrounds, golf courses, airfields, etc.   [3] Includes general administrative buildings, prisons, police and fire stations, courthouses, civic centers, passenger terminals, space facilities, postal facilities, etc.   [4] Includes open amusement and recreational facilities, power generating facilities, transit systems, airfields, open parking facilities, etc.

Source: U.S. Census Bureau, *Current Construction Reports*, Series C30, *Value of Construction*, monthly.

Construction and Housing   711

No. 1192. Construction Contracts—Value of Construction and Floor Space of Buildings by Class of Construction: 1980 to 1999

[151.8 represents $151,800,000,000. Building construction includes new structures and additions; nonbuilding construction includes major alterations to existing structures which affect only valuation, since no additional floor area is created by "alteration"]

Year	Total	Resi-dential build-ings	Nonresidential buildings									Non-build-ing con-struc-tion
			Total	Com-mer-cial [1]	Manu-fac-turing	Educa-tional [2]	Health	Public build-ings	Reli-gious	Social and recrea-tional	Mis-cella-neous	
VALUE (bil. dol.)												
1980	151.8	60.4	56.9	27.7	9.2	7.4	5.4	1.6	1.2	2.7	1.7	34.5
1985	235.6	102.1	92.1	54.6	8.1	10.0	7.8	3.1	2.0	4.0	2.5	41.4
1989	271.3	116.2	106.1	53.6	12.7	15.9	8.8	5.2	2.0	5.0	2.9	49.0
1990	246.0	100.9	95.4	44.8	8.4	16.6	9.2	5.7	2.2	5.3	3.1	49.7
1991	230.8	94.4	86.2	32.7	8.3	19.0	9.6	6.2	2.4	5.1	3.0	50.2
1992	252.2	110.6	87.0	32.8	8.9	17.6	10.9	5.8	2.5	5.5	3.1	54.6
1993	271.5	123.9	88.8	34.2	9.0	19.3	10.5	3.9	2.4	6.8	2.6	58.9
1994	296.7	133.6	101.5	40.8	11.2	21.0	10.5	6.1	2.5	6.5	3.0	61.6
1995	306.5	127.9	114.2	46.6	13.8	22.9	10.8	6.3	2.8	7.1	3.8	64.4
1996	332.0	146.5	120.5	51.9	13.1	23.0	11.1	6.3	2.9	8.1	4.1	65.1
1997	362.6	153.6	139.2	59.9	14.2	28.4	11.9	7.0	3.8	10.0	4.0	69.9
1998	404.6	179.7	153.8	73.9	11.8	30.0	12.9	6.6	4.3	10.8	3.6	71.1
1999	444.1	194.8	167.9	76.7	10.7	37.1	13.9	8.2	4.5	11.7	5.1	81.4
FLOOR SPACE (mil. sq. ft.)												
1980	3,102	1,839	1,263	738	220	103	55	18	28	49	52	(X)
1985	3,853	2,324	1,529	1,039	165	111	73	28	32	44	38	(X)
1989	3,516	2,115	1,400	867	158	151	72	41	27	48	35	(X)
1990	3,020	1,817	1,203	694	128	152	69	47	29	51	32	(X)
1991	2,634	1,653	981	476	100	177	72	50	29	45	33	(X)
1992	2,799	1,864	936	462	95	156	77	41	30	42	32	(X)
1993	3,062	2,091	971	481	110	165	75	30	30	51	29	(X)
1994	3,411	2,267	1,144	600	143	172	72	45	30	51	31	(X)
1995	3,454	2,172	1,281	700	163	186	70	40	33	56	33	(X)
1996	3,776	2,479	1,297	723	155	177	77	41	32	60	33	(X)
1997	4,127	2,586	1,541	856	191	204	89	48	42	77	35	(X)
1998	4,807	3,012	1,795	1,106	165	219	97	42	47	85	34	(X)
1999	5,086	3,251	1,835	1,109	138	262	102	49	48	88	39	(X)

X Not applicable.   [1] Includes nonindustrial warehouses.   [2] Includes science.

Source: F.W. Dodge, a Division of the McGraw-Hill Companies, New York, NY (copyright).

No. 1193. Construction Contracts—Value by State: 1990 to 1999

[In millions of dollars (246,022 represents $246,022,000,000). Represents value of construction in states in which work was actually done. See headnote, Table 1192]

State	1990	1995	1999 Total [1]	1999 Resi-den-tial	1999 Non-resi-den-tial	State	1990	1995	1999 Total [1]	1999 Resi-den-tial	1999 Non-resi-den-tial
U.S.	246,022	306,527	444,080	194,762	167,933	MO	3,833	6,438	7,862	3,133	3,238
AL	2,939	4,308	5,482	2,368	2,055	MT	332	865	927	346	297
AK	1,919	1,660	1,353	426	449	NE	1,318	1,694	2,872	950	1,179
AZ	4,553	8,784	13,500	8,270	3,476	NV	3,334	5,555	5,626	2,988	1,716
AR	1,438	2,903	3,353	1,514	983	NH	1,021	1,039	1,666	760	673
CA	37,318	29,045	45,949	21,856	16,099	NJ	6,141	6,454	9,574	3,697	4,632
CO	3,235	6,476	11,775	6,370	3,825	NM	1,124	2,108	2,378	914	801
CT	3,058	3,124	4,448	1,561	2,167	NY	14,137	13,380	19,306	5,606	8,754
DE	787	871	1,036	545	324	NC	6,614	10,599	17,080	9,405	5,656
DC	795	656	1,203	168	785	ND	506	791	1,391	252	319
FL	16,975	21,453	32,243	16,866	11,770	OH	9,885	12,430	17,100	6,938	7,083
GA	7,120	12,156	18,592	9,750	6,514	OK	2,164	2,968	4,404	1,878	1,303
HI	2,831	2,273	1,837	576	756	OR	3,101	5,451	5,907	2,695	2,029
ID	986	1,864	2,380	1,293	746	PA	10,117	9,348	14,188	4,563	6,083
IL	10,796	11,744	16,823	6,821	6,419	RI	594	465	1,083	381	559
IN	6,350	7,896	10,437	5,127	3,775	SC	3,664	4,580	7,236	3,854	2,305
IA	2,034	2,883	3,825	1,418	1,333	SD	468	706	931	347	274
KS	2,193	3,264	4,388	1,958	1,654	TN	4,388	7,167	10,101	4,633	3,976
KY	3,174	4,464	6,676	2,810	2,696	TX	13,197	23,022	40,157	15,984	14,830
LA	3,191	4,354	5,045	1,647	2,113	UT	1,884	4,218	4,489	2,106	1,854
ME	897	1,076	1,653	590	585	VT	515	484	648	253	273
MD	6,056	6,299	7,659	2,980	3,531	VA	7,180	8,794	12,776	5,762	4,921
MA	5,135	7,411	8,922	2,913	4,281	WA	6,185	7,334	10,714	4,645	4,544
MI	7,646	9,947	14,709	6,065	5,985	WV	1,253	1,215	1,537	231	617
MN	4,953	5,607	8,775	3,739	3,345	WI	4,654	5,652	7,472	3,331	2,937
MS	1,569	2,718	3,873	1,252	1,253	WY	462	532	721	227	161

[1] Includes nonbuilding construction, not shown separately.

Source: F.W. Dodge, a Division of the McGraw-Hill Companies, New York, NY (copyright).

No. 1194. New Privately-Owned Housing Units Authorized by State: 1998 and 1999

[1,612.3 represents 1,612,300. Based on about 19,000 places in United States having building permit systems]

State	Housing units (1,000) 1998	1999 Total	1999 One unit	Valuation (mil. dol.) 1998	1999 Total	1999 One unit	State	Housing units (1,000) 1998	1999 Total	1999 One unit	Valuation (mil. dol.) 1998	1999 Total	1999 One unit
U.S .	1,612.3	1,663.5	1,246.7	165,266	181,246	157,123	MO . . .	25.7	26.8	20.7	2,425	2,739	2,426
AL . . .	20.5	19.0	14.9	1,791	1,883	1,655	MT . . .	2.6	2.6	1.6	217	226	176
AK . . .	2.9	2.2	1.5	385	307	233	NE . . .	9.6	8.7	6.6	787	828	731
AZ . . .	63.9	65.1	53.2	6,766	7,350	6,696	NV . . .	37.0	32.6	24.3	2,807	2,977	2,508
AR . . .	10.0	11.5	7.7	798	966	826	NH . . .	5.8	6.3	5.7	658	782	739
CA . . .	124.0	138.0	102.8	18,230	21,031	18,321	NJ . . .	31.3	32.0	25.1	2,936	3,162	2,802
CO . . .	51.2	49.3	38.4	5,777	6,036	5,304	NM . . .	10.3	9.7	8.6	979	1,080	1,026
CT . . .	11.9	10.6	9.2	1,394	1,466	1,373	NY . . .	38.4	42.6	24.7	3,826	4,411	3,386
DE . . .	5.3	5.3	4.8	499	492	476	NC . . .	80.5	84.8	64.1	8,062	8,617	7,665
DC . . .	0.4	0.7	0.3	35	53	36	ND . . .	3.0	2.6	1.4	245	223	168
FL. . . .	148.6	164.7	106.6	14,123	16,102	12,259	OH . . .	48.0	55.9	40.0	5,410	6,401	5,642
GA . . .	85.4	89.6	71.5	7,859	8,749	7,861	OK . . .	14.4	14.2	11.1	1,286	1,430	1,287
HI . . .	3.3	4.2	3.4	484	633	560	OR . . .	25.9	23.2	16.6	2,827	2,653	2,252
ID	11.7	12.2	10.5	1,251	1,357	1,269	PA . . .	41.6	42.7	36.6	4,219	4,635	4,295
IL.	48.0	54.0	39.2	5,618	6,538	5,475	RI. . . .	2.6	3.4	2.7	284	336	301
IN	40.7	41.5	33.4	4,333	4,748	4,325	SC . . .	33.6	36.2	27.2	3,087	3,615	3,100
IA	13.1	13.4	9.7	1,292	1,400	1,192	SD . . .	3.5	3.7	2.9	297	330	285
KS . . .	15.3	15.7	11.3	1,516	1,667	1,443	TN . . .	34.1	37.0	29.9	3,428	3,835	3,495
KY . . .	20.6	21.6	16.5	1,731	1,909	1,694	TX . . .	156.7	146.6	101.8	13,682	14,041	12,101
LA . . .	16.5	17.8	14.6	1,541	1,767	1,569	UT . . .	20.9	20.5	16.6	2,210	2,287	2,029
ME . . .	6.3	5.7	5.4	642	623	602	VT . . .	2.2	2.6	2.2	234	305	271
MD . . .	30.9	29.8	24.2	2,903	3,102	2,825	VA . . .	50.2	53.2	42.1	4,744	5,142	4,621
MA . . .	19.3	19.0	15.5	2,519	2,666	2,324	WA . . .	45.7	42.8	28.1	4,745	4,578	3,596
MI. . . .	54.5	54.3	45.4	5,880	6,205	5,676	WV . . .	3.8	4.2	3.6	323	381	354
MN . . .	30.4	33.3	26.7	3,485	4,053	3,554	WI. . . .	35.4	35.6	24.8	3,556	3,863	3,199
MS . . .	12.9	12.9	9.6	890	990	874	WY . . .	1.9	1.9	1.5	251	279	247

Source: U.S. Census Bureau, *Construction Reports*, Series C40, *Building Permits*, monthly.

No. 1195. New Privately-Owned Housing Units Started—Selected Characteristics: 1970 to 1999

[In thousands (1,434 represents 1,434,000). For composition of regions, see map inside front cover]

Year	Total units	Structures with— One unit	Two to four units	Five or more units	Region North-east	Midwest	South	West	Condominium units [1] Total	Single-family	Multi-family
1970	1,434	813	85	536	218	294	612	311	(NA)	(NA)	(NA)
1972	2,357	1,309	141	906	330	443	1,057	527	(NA)	(NA)	(NA)
1973	2,045	1,132	118	795	277	440	899	429	241	69	172
1974	1,338	888	68	382	183	317	553	285	175	46	130
1975	1,160	892	64	204	149	294	442	275	65	20	45
1976	1,538	1,162	86	289	169	400	569	400	95	30	64
1977	1,987	1,451	122	414	202	465	783	538	118	41	77
1978	2,020	1,433	125	462	200	451	824	545	156	42	114
1979	1,745	1,194	122	429	178	349	748	470	198	43	156
1980	1,292	852	110	331	125	218	643	306	186	35	150
1981	1,084	705	91	288	117	165	562	240	181	36	145
1982	1,062	663	80	320	117	149	591	205	170	40	130
1983	1,703	1,068	113	522	168	218	935	382	276	77	199
1984	1,750	1,084	121	544	204	243	866	436	291	96	194
1985	1,742	1,072	93	576	252	240	782	468	225	79	146
1986	1,805	1,179	84	542	294	296	733	483	214	80	134
1987	1,621	1,146	65	409	269	298	634	420	196	73	123
1988	1,488	1,081	59	348	235	274	575	404	148	53	95
1989	1,376	1,003	55	318	179	266	536	396	118	37	82
1990	1,193	895	37	260	131	253	479	329	75	22	53
1991	1,014	840	36	138	113	233	414	254	60	21	39
1992	1,200	1,030	31	139	127	288	497	288	74	35	40
1993	1,288	1,126	29	133	126	298	562	302	86	45	41
1994	1,457	1,198	35	224	138	329	639	351	96	48	48
1995	1,354	1,076	34	244	118	290	615	331	93	47	47
1996	1,477	1,161	45	271	132	322	662	361	107	53	54
1997	1,474	1,134	44	296	137	304	670	363	110	56	54
1998	1,617	1,271	43	303	148	330	743	395	113	59	54
1999	1,666	1,335	32	300	154	356	760	396	119	58	61

NA Not available. [1] Type of ownership under which the owners of the individual housing units are also joint owners of the common areas of the building or community. Includes a small number of cooperatively-owned units.

Source: U.S. Census Bureau, *Current Construction Reports*, Series C20, *Housing Starts*, monthly.

U.S. Census Bureau, Statistical Abstract of the United States: 2000

No. 1196. New Privately-Owned Housing Units Started by State: 1997 to 2000

[In thousands of units (1,476 represents 1,476,000)]

State	1997	1998	1999	2000 Total units	2000 Single-family units	State	1997	1998	1999	2000 Total units	2000 Single-family units
U.S. ...	1,476	1,623	1,660	1,535	1,223	MO	27.9	29.7	29.6	26.0	22.2
AL......	21.7	23.7	23.5	21.2	17.7	MT......	2.5	2.4	2.5	2.2	1.4
AK......	2.5	2.7	2.4	2.1	1.6	NE......	9.8	9.8	9.7	8.4	6.2
AZ......	58.2	65.2	66.5	60.0	48.2	NV......	35.6	36.4	35.1	34.5	25.3
AR......	13.0	12.9	13.7	12.5	9.5	NH......	5.3	5.7	6.0	6.0	5.6
CA......	109.1	123.0	129.9	128.2	99.9	NJ......	26.8	29.7	31.9	31.2	25.4
CO......	43.8	50.6	49.9	45.9	36.0	NM......	10.5	9.4	9.2	8.1	7.2
CT......	9.1	11.0	10.6	10.0	8.7	NY......	30.5	34.0	36.3	34.9	22.7
DE......	4.9	5.5	5.4	5.2	4.8	NC......	74.1	81.5	85.8	74.8	59.2
DC......	-	0.4	0.7	0.4	0.3	ND......	3.2	3.3	3.2	2.7	1.8
FL......	135.2	143.9	152.8	148.1	104.9	OH......	44.6	47.0	49.8	45.3	37.7
GA......	78.6	87.1	88.4	81.5	68.4	OK......	13.2	16.3	16.2	15.5	12.4
HI	3.8	3.4	3.7	3.8	3.2	OR......	26.6	25.6	24.5	22.2	15.8
ID	10.5	12.0	12.6	11.5	10.1	PA......	38.6	40.1	41.1	37.5	32.4
IL.......	46.5	49.2	52.4	48.1	38.9	RI	2.6	2.7	2.9	2.7	2.5
IN	36.0	40.8	41.8	37.6	32.3	SC......	31.2	33.2	35.8	33.9	27.1
IA	11.2	13.7	13.6	13.0	10.7	SD.....	3.4	3.8	4.1	3.5	2.8
KS	13.6	15.6	16.4	15.2	11.7	TN.....	37.8	37.4	37.3	33.9	29.9
KY......	20.5	23.2	23.2	21.4	17.5	TX.....	134.0	159.8	155.2	148.4	108.3
LA......	16.7	17.8	18.6	15.8	13.4	UT.....	19.8	21.1	20.5	19.5	16.1
ME......	4.6	5.8	5.8	5.8	5.5	VT.....	1.8	2.2	2.4	2.4	2.1
MD.....	26.5	31.2	30.3	27.9	23.0	VA.....	46.9	50.9	53.0	50.2	42.6
MA.....	16.9	18.2	18.0	17.7	15.5	WA.....	40.7	44.0	43.7	40.9	28.4
MI	49.0	54.5	55.4	50.9	44.2	WV	5.1	5.1	5.8	5.3	4.1
MN.....	25.2	30.8	32.9	30.7	26.8	WI	30.7	34.3	35.4	32.0	24.7
MS.....	12.2	15.0	15.2	12.8	10.1	WY	1.9	2.1	2.0	1.8	1.5

- Represents or rounds to zero.

Source: National Association of Home Builders, Economics Division, Washington, DC. Data provided by the Econometric Forecasting Service.

No. 1197. Characteristics of New Privately-Owned One-Family Houses Completed: 1970 to 1999

[Percent distribution, except as indicated (793 represents 793,000). Data beginning 1980 show percent distribution of characteristics for all houses completed (includes new houses completed, houses built for sale completed, contractor-built and owner-built houses completed, and houses completed for rent). Data for 1970 cover contractor-built, owner-built, and houses for rent year construction started and houses sold for year of sale. Percents exclude houses for which characteristics specified were not reported]

Characteristic	1970	1980	1990	1995	1999	Characteristic	1970	1980	1990	1995	1999
Total houses (1,000). . . .	793	957	966	1,066	1,307	Bedrooms.	100	100	100	100	100
						2 or less.	13	17	15	13	12
Financing [1].	100	100	100	100	100	3.	63	63	57	57	54
Mortgage	84	82	82	88	91	4 or more	24	20	29	30	34
FHA-insured	30	16	14	8	9	Bathrooms	100	100	100	100	100
VA-guaranteed.	7	8	4	5	3	1 1/2 or less	52	27	13	11	7
Conventional	47	55	62	74	79	2.	32	48	42	41	38
Rural Housing Serv-ice [2]	(3)	3	2	1	1	2 1/2 or more	16	25	45	48	55
Cash or equivalent. . . .	16	18	18	12	9	Heating fuel	100	100	100	100	100
						Gas.	62	41	59	67	70
Floor area.	100	100	100	100	100	Electricity	28	50	33	28	27
Under 1,200 sq. ft	36	21	11	10	7	Oil.	8	3	5	3	3
1,200 to 1,599 sq. ft . . .	28	29	22	22	19	Other.	1	5	3	1	1
1,600 to 1,999 sq. ft . . .	16	22	22	23	22	Heating system	100	100	100	100	100
2,000 to 2,399 sq. ft . . .	21	13	17	17	18	Warm air furnace.	71	57	65	67	72
2,400 sq. ft. and over . .	(4)	15	29	28	34	Electric heat pump	(NA)	24	23	25	22
Average (sq. ft.).	1,500	1,740	2,080	2,095	2,225	Other.	29	19	12	9	6
Median (sq. ft.)	1,385	1,595	1,905	1,920	2,030	Central air-conditioning .	100	100	100	100	100
						With	34	63	76	80	84
Number of stories	100	100	100	100	100	Without	66	37	24	20	16
1.	74	60	46	49	48	Fireplaces.	100	100	100	100	100
2 or more	17	31	49	48	51	No fireplace	65	43	34	37	38
Split level	10	8	4	3	1	1 or more	35	56	66	63	62
Foundation	100	100	100	100	100	Parking facilities	100	100	100	100	100
Full or partial basement. .	37	36	38	39	37	Garage	58	69	82	84	87
Slab	36	45	40	42	47	Carport	17	7	2	2	1
Crawl space	27	19	21	19	17	No garage or carport . .	25	24	16	14	12

NA Not available.   [1] Excludes homes not yet sold.   [2] Prior to 1999, Farmers Home Administration.   [3] Included with "Conventional" financing.   [4] Included with floor area of 2,000 to 2,399 square feet.

Source: U.S. Census Bureau and U.S. Dept. of Housing and Urban Development, *Current Construction Reports*, Series C25, *New One-Family Houses Sold*, monthly, and *Characteristics of New Housing*, annual.

No. 1198. New Privately-Owned One-Family Houses Sold by Region and Type of Financing, 1980 to 1999, and by Sales-Price Group, 1999

[In thousands (545 represents 545,000). Based on a national probability sample of monthly interviews with builders or owners of 1-family houses for which building permits have been issued or, for nonpermit areas, on which construction has started. For details, see source. For composition of regions, see map inside front cover]

Year and sales-price group	Total sales	Region				Financing type			
		North-east	Midwest	South	West	Conven-tional [1]	FHA and VA	Rural Housing Service [2]	Cash
1980	545	50	81	267	145	302	196	14	32
1985	688	112	82	323	170	403	208	11	64
1989	650	86	102	260	202	416	162	14	58
1990	534	71	89	225	149	337	138	10	50
1991	509	57	93	215	144	329	128	9	43
1992	610	65	116	259	170	428	134	7	41
1993	666	60	123	295	188	476	147	6	37
1994	670	61	123	295	191	490	130	9	41
1995	667	55	125	300	187	490	129	9	39
1996	757	74	137	337	209	570	140	9	38
1997	804	78	140	363	223	616	137	6	46
1998	886	81	164	398	243	693	136	9	48
1999	907	75	173	408	249	705	152	6	43
Under $70,000	13	(B)	(B)	10	(B)	8	[3]3	(B)	(B)
$70,000 to $79,999	19	(B)	3	15	(B)	8	[3]6	(B)	(B)
$80,000 to $99,999	72	(B)	12	48	11	37	32	(B)	3
$100,000 to $119,999	100	5	20	55	20	59	35	(B)	5
$120,000 to $149,999	189	10	38	88	53	132	45	(B)	11
$150,000 to $199,999	214	16	42	89	66	178	25	(B)	10
$200,000 to $249,999	114	13	27	41	33	106	(B)	(B)	5
$250,000 to $299,999	67	10	13	23	21	64	(B)	(B)	(B)
$300,000 and over	118	18	19	39	43	113	(B)	(B)	6

B Withheld because estimate did not meet publication standards on the basis of sample size. [1] Includes all other types of financing. [2] Prior to 1996, the Farmers Home Administration. [3] FHA only. VA data withheld.

Source: U.S. Census Bureau and U.S. Dept. of Housing and Urban Development, *Current Construction Reports*, Series C25, *Characteristics of New Housing*, annual; and *New One-Family Houses Sold*, monthly.

No. 1199. Median Sales Price of New Privately-Owned One-Family Houses Sold by Region: 1980 to 1999

[In dollars. For definition of median, see Guide to Tabular Presentation. For composition of regions, see map inside front cover]

Year	U.S.	North-east	Mid-west	South	West	Year	U.S.	North-east	Mid-west	South	West
1980	64,600	69,500	63,400	59,600	72,300	1992	121,500	169,000	115,600	105,500	130,400
1985	84,300	103,300	80,300	75,000	92,600	1993	126,500	162,600	125,000	115,000	135,000
1986	92,000	125,000	88,300	80,200	95,700	1994	130,000	169,000	132,900	116,900	140,400
1987	104,500	140,000	95,000	88,000	111,000	1995	133,900	180,000	134,000	124,500	141,400
1988	112,500	149,000	101,600	92,000	126,500	1996	140,000	186,000	138,000	126,200	153,900
1989	120,000	159,600	108,800	96,400	139,000	1997	146,000	190,000	149,900	129,600	160,000
1990	122,900	159,000	107,900	99,000	147,500	1998	152,500	200,000	157,500	135,800	163,500
1991	120,000	155,900	110,000	100,000	141,100	1999	159,800	210,000	160,000	145,000	173,700

Source: U.S. Census Bureau and U.S. Dept. of Housing and Urban Development, *Current Construction Reports*, Series C25, *Characteristics of New Housing*, annual; and *New One-Family Houses Sold*, monthly.

No. 1200. New Manufactured (Mobile) Homes Placed for Residential Use and Average Sales Price by Region: 1980 to 1999

[233.7 represents 233,700. A mobile home is a moveable dwelling, 8 feet or more wide and 40 feet or more long, designed to be towed on its own chassis, with transportation gear integral to the unit when it leaves the factory, and without need of permanent foundation. Excluded are travel trailers, motor homes, and modular housing. Data are based on a probability sample and subject to sampling variability; see source. For composition of regions, see map inside front cover]

Year	Units placed (1,000)					Average sales price (dol.)				
	Total	North-east	Midwest	South	West	U.S.	North-east	Midwest	South	West
1980	233.7	12.3	32.3	140.3	48.7	19,800	18,500	18,600	18,200	25,400
1985	283.4	20.2	38.6	187.6	36.9	21,800	22,700	21,500	20,400	28,700
1990	195.4	18.8	37.7	108.4	30.6	27,800	30,000	27,000	24,500	39,300
1991	174.3	14.3	35.4	97.6	27.0	27,700	30,400	27,600	24,500	38,600
1992	212.0	15.0	42.2	124.4	30.4	28,400	30,900	28,800	25,400	39,000
1993	242.5	15.4	44.5	146.7	35.9	30,500	32,000	31,400	27,700	40,500
1994	286.1	16.2	53.0	174.4	42.5	33,500	33,900	34,600	30,500	44,600
1995	319.4	15.0	57.7	202.6	44.0	36,300	37,900	36,700	33,900	46,400
1996	338.4	16.2	59.1	218.1	44.9	38,300	39,700	39,400	36,200	47,200
1997	338.1	14.5	55.8	219.6	48.1	41,100	43,900	41,400	38,900	50,300
1998	369.0	14.5	58.1	246.2	50.2	43,800	45,500	44,100	41,800	52,900
1999	298.0	12.5	49.8	198.5	37.4	43,800	45,200	45,300	42,100	50,900

Source: U.S. Census Bureau, Internet site, <http://www.census.gov/ftp/pub/const/www/mhsindex.html> (accessed 25 August 2000).

Construction and Housing 715

No. 1201. Existing One-Family Houses Sold and Price by Region: 1970 to 1999

[1,612 represents 1,612,000. Based on data (adjusted and aggregated to regional and national totals) reported by participating real estate multiple listing services. For definition of median, see Guide to Tabular Presentation. For composition of regions, see map inside front cover]

Year	Houses sold (1,000)					Median sales price (dol.)				
	Total	Northeast	Midwest	South	West	Total	Northeast	Midwest	South	West
1970	1,612	251	501	568	292	23,000	25,700	20,100	22,200	24,300
1973	2,334	367	674	847	446	28,900	32,800	25,300	29,000	31,000
1974	2,272	354	645	839	434	32,000	35,800	27,700	32,200	34,800
1975	2,476	370	701	862	543	35,300	39,300	30,100	34,800	39,600
1976	3,064	439	881	1,033	712	38,100	41,800	32,900	36,500	46,100
1977	3,650	515	1,101	1,231	803	42,900	44,400	36,700	39,800	57,300
1978	3,986	516	1,144	1,416	911	48,700	47,900	42,200	45,100	66,700
1979	3,827	526	1,061	1,353	887	55,700	53,600	47,800	51,300	77,400
1980	2,973	403	806	1,092	672	62,200	60,800	51,900	58,300	89,300
1981	2,419	353	632	917	516	66,400	63,700	54,300	64,400	96,200
1982	1,990	354	490	780	366	67,800	63,500	55,100	67,100	98,900
1983	2,697	477	692	1,004	524	70,300	72,200	56,600	69,200	94,900
1984	2,829	478	720	1,006	624	72,400	78,700	57,100	71,300	95,800
1985	3,134	561	806	1,063	704	75,500	88,900	58,900	75,200	95,400
1986	3,474	635	922	1,145	773	80,300	104,800	63,500	78,200	100,900
1987	3,436	618	892	1,163	763	85,600	133,300	66,000	80,400	113,200
1988	3,513	606	865	1,224	817	89,300	143,000	68,400	82,200	124,900
1989 [1] ...	3,325	490	832	1,185	818	89,500	127,700	71,800	84,400	127,100
1990	3,219	458	809	1,193	759	92,000	126,400	75,300	85,100	129,600
1991	3,186	463	812	1,173	737	97,100	129,100	79,500	88,500	135,300
1992	3,479	521	913	1,242	802	99,700	128,900	83,000	91,500	131,500
1993	3,786	550	967	1,386	882	103,100	129,100	86,000	94,300	132,500
1994	3,916	552	965	1,436	962	107,200	129,100	89,300	95,700	139,400
1995	3,888	547	945	1,433	964	110,500	126,700	94,800	97,700	141,000
1996	4,196	584	986	1,511	1,116	115,800	127,800	101,000	103,400	147,100
1997	4,382	607	1,005	1,595	1,174	121,800	131,800	107,000	109,600	155,200
1998	4,970	663	1,129	1,870	1,310	128,400	135,900	114,300	116,200	164,800
1999	5,197	655	1,147	2,016	1,380	133,300	139,000	119,600	120,300	173,900

[1] Beginning 1989 data not comparable to earlier years due to rebenchmarking.
Source: NATIONAL ASSOCIATION OF REALTORS®, Washington, DC, prior to 1990, *Home Sales*, monthly, and *Home Sales Yearbook: 1990;* (copyright); thereafter, *Real Estate Outlook; Market Trends & Insights,* monthly, (copyright).

No. 1202. Median Sales Price of Existing One-Family Homes by Selected Metropolitan Area: 1997 to 1999

[In thousands of dollars (121.8 represents $121,800). For the top 60 areas in sales price in 1999. Areas are metropolitan statistical areas defined by source as of 1992]

Metropolitan area	1997	1998	1999	Metropolitan area	1997	1998	1999
United States, all areas . . .	121.8	128.4	133.3	Milwaukee, WI	125.3	132.9	135.3
Albuquerque, NM	126.7	128.2	130.3	Minneapolis-St. Paul, MN-WI . . .	118.4	128.0	138.7
Atlanta, GA	108.4	115.4	123.7	New Haven-Meriden, CT	134.1	137.8	145.7
Atlantic City, NJ	109.7	112.8	117.0	New York-N. New Jersey-			
Aurora-Elgin, IL	141.8	146.2	151.9	Long Island, NY-NJ-CT	177.9	188.1	203.2
Austin-San Marcos, TX	(NA)	121.1	128.6	NY: Bergen-Passaic, NJ.	205.4	213.5	221.8
Baltimore, MD	118.2	120.6	127.4	NY: Middlesex-Somerset-			
Birmingham, AL	118.9	122.7	127.1	Hunterdon, NJ	176.7	184.2	196.8
Boise City, ID.	102.5	109.2	123.9	NY: Monmouth-Ocean, NJ	147.7	152.6	164.4
Boston, MA	229.0	258.4	290.0	NY: Nassau-Suffolk, NY.	164.0	175.4	190.4
Bradenton, FL	94.9	107.3	117.2	NY: Newark, NJ	193.0	199.2	212.0
Charleston, SC.	103.6	120.0	131.7	Orange Cnty.(Anaheim-			
Charlotte-Gastonia-Rock Hill,				Santa Ana) CA [1]	229.8	261.7	281.5
NC-SC	124.2	134.0	138.2	Philadelphia, PA-NJ.	126.3	129.7	124.8
Chicago, IL	158.9	166.8	171.2	Phoenix, AZ.	113.7	120.2	126.4
Cincinnati, OH-KY-IN.	110.5	116.3	119.9	Portland, OR	152.4	158.1	165.0
Cleveland, OH	116.8	121.8	125.1	Providence, RI	119.6	124.4	128.8
Colorado Springs, CO	130.5	138.5	144.9	Raleigh-Durham, NC.	152.8	159.8	165.0
Columbus, OH	117.6	121.7	125.0	Reno, NV	143.4	147.2	150.6
Denver, CO	140.6	152.2	171.3	Richmond-Petersburg, VA	114.2	122.0	128.5
Detroit, MI	119.6	132.6	140.0	Riverside-San Bernardino, CA [1] . .	114.3	121.5	128.7
Eugene-Springfield, OR	119.4	124.4	129.5	Sacramento, CA [1]	116.1	125.6	133.8
Ft. Lauderdale-Hollywood-				Salt Lake City-Ogden, UT.	128.6	133.5	137.9
Pompano Beach, FL	123.7	128.6	136.1	San Diego, CA [1]	185.2	207.1	231.6
Greensboro-Winston-Salem-				San Francisco Bay Area, CA [1] . .	286.2	321.7	365.3
High Point, NC	117.3	123.5	124.8	Sarasota, FL	114.1	123.1	134.8
Hartford, CT.	138.1	142.8	150.7	Tallahassee, FL	111.7	114.6	117.8
Honolulu, HI.	307.0	297.0	290.0	Trenton, NJ	137.7	139.5	144.2
Kansas City, MO-KS	106.8	114.0	120.7	Tucson, AZ	106.8	112.6	117.7
Lake County, IL	153.5	159.4	164.0	Washington, DC-MD-VA.	166.3	172.1	176.5
Las Vegas, NV.	123.2	128.2	130.8	Wilmington, DE-NJ-MD	123.7	123.9	120.6
Los Angeles Area, CA [1]	176.5	192.6	205.3	Worcester, MA	(NA)	(NA)	117.0
Madison, WI	126.8	131.8	136.5	W. Palm Beach-Boca Raton-			
Miami-Hialeah, FL.	117.7	121.5	134.6	Delray Beach, FL	133.4	126.6	131.0

NA Not available. [1] California data supplied by the California Association of REALTORS®.
Source: NATIONAL ASSOCIATION OF REALTORS®, Washington, DC, *Real Estate Outlook: Market Trends & Insights,* monthly, (copyright).

No. 1203. Existing Home Sales by State: 1990 to 1999

[In thousands (3,599 represents 3,599,000). Includes condos and co-ops as well as single-family homes]

State	1990	1995	1998	1999	State	1990	1995	1998	1999
United States ..	3,599	4,350	5,600	5,929	Missouri	77.1	100.8	116.0	122.9
Alabama	52.0	69.0	84.0	87.0	Montana	13.5	14.8	18.3	19.1
Alaska	12.3	10.2	17.1	16.0	Nebraska	23.6	25.0	33.3	34.3
Arizona	71.8	120.3	155.1	170.0	Nevada	26.9	31.0	38.4	47.3
Arkansas	33.7	45.0	54.9	63.5	New Hampshire	13.5	26.2	40.5	40.6
California [1]	413.1	426.7	665.4	708.7	New Jersey	85.7	102.4	129.9	141.9
Colorado	77.7	102.5	130.8	136.2	New Mexico	24.7	27.6	27.1	29.8
Connecticut	37.4	43.3	49.9	51.0	New York	135.9	149.7	183.1	179.5
Delaware	7.9	9.5	8.6	8.6	North Carolina	98.9	157.7	211.6	228.6
District of Columbia . .	7.2	7.0	13.0	13.8	North Dakota	8.5	8.5	11.4	10.3
Florida	281.1	379.6	454.4	509.8	Ohio	146.9	173.1	191.4	194.9
Georgia	91.2	101.0	128.1	149.2	Oklahoma	62.2	74.5	95.5	100.1
Hawaii	19.0	10.3	14.7	17.8	Oregon	56.6	58.7	63.1	62.4
Idaho	22.3	27.1	29.7	28.6	Pennsylvania	143.2	163.2	175.4	177.9
Illinois	163.3	183.4	235.3	243.9	Rhode Island	9.6	13.6	19.0	20.7
Indiana	83.6	102.6	125.9	132.0	South Carolina	54.3	70.7	98.7	104.3
Iowa	42.8	43.2	56.5	57.8	South Dakota	10.8	11.9	14.3	15.4
Kansas	36.8	50.5	66.8	67.9	Tennessee	66.2	106.6	136.2	149.0
Kentucky	47.9	61.5	71.8	77.8	Texas	311.8	367.9	512.1	551.9
Louisiana	57.1	77.3	91.7	88.8	Utah	29.4	43.5	44.9	46.5
Maine	17.0	25.5	32.9	34.7	Vermont	7.2	7.9	6.8	6.9
Maryland	67.0	63.5	92.4	103.1	Virginia	89.3	94.8	133.4	146.9
Massachusetts	47.9	69.4	100.0	97.7	Washington	85.9	110.9	159.2	175.7
Michigan	137.6	142.2	161.9	160.4	West Virginia	22.6	26.1	29.3	26.7
Minnesota	68.1	81.6	108.5	106.5	Wisconsin	62.1	78.2	101.1	100.8
Mississippi	28.2	41.3	48.2	51.1	Wyoming	8.5	11.4	12.0	13.1

[1] California data supplied by the California Association of REALTORS®.
Source: NATIONAL ASSOCIATION OF REALTORS®, Washington, DC, *Real Estate Outlook: Market Trends & Insights,* monthly (copyright).

No. 1204. Existing Apartment Condos and Co-Ops—Units Sold and Average Sales Price by Region: 1989 to 1999

[358 represents 358,000. For definition of median, see Guide to Tabular Presentation. For composition of regions, see map inside front cover]

Year	Units sold (1,000)					Median sales price (dol.)				
	Total	North-east	Midwest	South	West	U.S.	North-east	Midwest	South	West
1989	358	58	45	144	110	86,000	111,000	65,500	68,700	118,800
1990	348	45	42	151	110	85,200	110,200	70,200	66,800	105,200
1991	333	48	43	145	97	85,800	107,200	73,900	68,300	105,100
1992	361	57	49	153	102	86,000	103,100	79,000	69,400	107,700
1993	400	63	53	175	108	84,400	99,200	78,900	69,300	102,700
1994	439	69	54	196	119	87,200	99,500	86,200	69,500	108,800
1995	428	70	53	188	116	87,400	94,800	90,700	70,600	105,300
1996	476	78	58	206	134	90,900	97,500	95,200	73,500	109,900
1997	524	88	64	220	152	95,500	101,100	99,100	76,300	118,300
1998	606	104	75	249	178	100,600	103,400	106,400	80,000	126,400
1999	682	120	81	289	192	108,000	112,500	114,600	84,100	132,100

Source: NATIONAL ASSOCIATION OF REALTORS®, Washington, DC, *Real Estate Outlook: Market Trends & Insights,* monthly (copyright).

No. 1205. New Apartments Completed and Rented in 3 Months by Region: 1980 to 1999

[196.1 represents 196,100. Structures with five or more units, privately financed, nonsubsidized, unfurnished rental apartments. Based on sample and subject to sampling variability; see source for details. For composition of regions, see inside front cover]

Year and rent	Number (1,000)					Percent rented in 3 months				
	U.S.	North-east	Mid-west	South	West	U.S.	North-east	Mid-west	South	West
1980	196.1	14.2	43.8	91.5	46.6	75	77	77	74	75
1985	365.2	8.1	54.0	166.1	137.0	65	69	72	59	68
1990 [1]	214.3	12.7	44.3	77.2	80.0	67	66	75	64	65
1995	155.0	7.1	31.7	78.5	37.7	73	74	75	72	73
1999, prel	225.6	16.8	27.9	123.3	57.6	72	85	73	69	74
Less than $450	8.6	1.1	1.5	2.7	3.2	80	96	81	87	67
$450 to $649	46.1	3.1	9.9	25.3	7.7	75	75	80	76	69
$450 to $549	16.2	1.9	3.0	7.5	3.8	79	73	86	81	73
$550 to $649	29.9	1.2	6.9	17.8	3.9	74	80	77	74	64
$650 to $849	80.2	1.3	10.0	51.1	17.8	70	86	72	67	74
$650 to $749	44.2	1.2	6.4	27.1	9.5	70	89	74	67	73
$750 to $849	36.0	0.1	3.6	24.0	8.3	70	59	67	69	76
$850 or more	90.8	11.1		44.3	29	72	86	63	67	77
Median monthly asking rent . .	$788	[2]	$688	$777	[2]	(X)	(X)	(X)	(X)	(X)

X Not applicable.   [1] Due to revised estimation procedures, data beginning 1990 not strictly comparable with prior years.
[2] Over $850.
Source: U.S. Census Bureau, *Current Housing Reports,* Series H130, *Market Absorption of Apartments,* and unpublished data.

Construction and Housing   717

No. 1206. Recent Home Buyers—General Characteristics: 1976 to 1999

[As of **October**. Based on a sample survey; subject to sampling variability]

Item	Unit	1976	1980	1985	1990	1995	1996	1997	1998	1999
Median purchase price....	Dollars ..	43,340	68,714	90,400	131,200	147,700	153,200	159,700	167,900	175,400
First-time buyers	Dollars ..	37,670	61,450	75,100	106,000	128,300	130,100	135,400	142,200	150,300
Repeat buyers [1]	Dollars ..	50,090	75,750	106,200	149,400	164,300	170,700	178,700	189,800	195,700
Average monthly										
mortgage payment......	Dollars ..	329	599	896	1,127	1,062	1,087	1,114	1,212	1,240
Percent of income	Percent..	24.0	32.4	30.0	33.8	32.6	32.6	32.8	32.3	32.3
Percent buying—										
New houses	Percent..	15.1	22.4	23.8	21.2	21.5	22.7	20.9	21.2	22.7
Existing houses	Percent..	84.9	77.6	76.2	78.8	78.5	77.3	79.1	78.8	77.3
Single-family houses....	Percent..	88.8	82.4	87.0	83.8	83.1	82.6	81.6	82.3	83.0
Other houses [2]	Percent..	11.2	17.6	13.0	16.2	16.9	17.4	18.4	17.7	17.0
For the first time	Percent..	44.8	32.9	36.6	41.9	46.2	44.7	46.8	46.2	44.7
Average age:										
First-time buyers	Years ...	28.1	28.3	28.4	30.5	32.1	32.4	32.1	32.2	32.0
Repeat buyers [1]	Years ...	35.9	36.4	38.4	39.1	40.7	41.1	41.1	41.1	41.4
Downpayment/sales price..	Percent..	25.2	28.0	24.8	23.3	20.4	19.5	20.3	19.3	19.5
First-time buyers	Percent..	18.0	20.5	11.4	15.7	13.3	12.4	13.7	12.8	12.6
Repeat buyers [1]	Percent..	30.8	32.7	32.7	28.9	26.8	25.3	26.1	24.9	25.5

[1] Buyers who previously owned a home.   [2] Includes multifamily, condominums and co-ops.
Source: Chicago Title Corporation, Chicago, IL, *Who's Buying Homes in America* (copyright).

No. 1207. Total Housing Inventory for the United States: 1970 to 1999

[In thousands (69,778 represents 69,778,000), except percent. Based on the Current Population Survey and the Housing Vacancy Survey and subject to sampling error; see source for details]

Item	1970	1975	1980	1985	1990	1994	1995	1996	1997	1998	1999
All housing units	**69,778**	**78,821**	**87,739**	**97,333**	**106,283**	**110,952**	**112,655**	**114,139**	**115,621**	**117,282**	**119,044**
Vacant	6,137	6,896	8,101	9,446	12,059	12,257	12,669	13,155	13,419	13,748	14,116
Year-round vacant......	4,391	5,202	5,996	7,400	9,128	9,229	9,570	9,945	10,114	10,516	10,848
For rent	1,299	1,647	1,575	2,221	2,662	2,858	2,946	3,008	2,978	3,046	3,119
For sale only........	427	591	734	1,006	1,064	953	1,022	1,082	1,133	1,205	1,184
Rented or sold.......	427	536	623	664	660	772	810	834	867	927	956
Held off market	2,238	2,429	3,064	3,510	4,742	4,646	4,793	5,022	5,136	5,338	5,589
Occasional use	615	649	814	977	1,485	1,612	1,667	1,709	1,818	1,792	1,948
Usual residence else											
where	429	470	568	659	1,068	815	801	852	885	910	965
Other	1,195	1,309	1,683	1,875	2,189	2,219	2,325	2,461	2,433	2,636	2,676
Seasonal [1].........	1,746	1,694	2,106	2,046	2,931	3,028	3,099	3,209	3,305	3,232	3,268
Total occupied	63,640	71,925	79,638	87,887	94,224	98,695	99,985	100,984	102,202	103,534	104,928
Owner..............	40,834	46,463	52,223	56,152	60,248	63,136	64,739	66,041	67,143	68,638	70,097
Renter.............	22,806	25,462	27,415	31,736	33,976	35,558	35,246	34,943	35,059	34,896	34,831
PERCENT DISTRIBUTION											
All housing units	100.0	100.0	100.0	100.0	100.0	100.0	100.0	100.0	100.0	100.0	100.0
Vacant	8.8	8.7	9.2	9.7	11.3	11.0	11.2	11.5	11.6	11.7	11.9
Total occupied	91.2	91.3	90.8	90.3	88.7	89.0	88.8	88.5	88.4	88.3	88.1
Owner..............	58.5	58.9	59.5	57.7	56.7	56.9	57.5	57.9	58.1	58.5	58.9
Renter.............	32.7	32.3	31.2	32.6	32.0	32.0	31.3	30.6	30.3	29.8	29.3

[1] Beginning 1990 includes vacant seasonal mobile homes. For years shown, seasonal vacant housing units were underreported prior to 1990.
Source: U.S. Census Bureau, Internet site <http://www.census.gov/hhes/www/housing/hvs/historic/index.html>.

No. 1208. Vacancy Rates for Housing Units—Characteristics: 1990 to 1999

[In percent. Rate is relationship between vacant housing for rent or for sale and the total rental and homeowner supply, which comprises occupied units, units rented or sold and awaiting occupancy, and vacant units available for rent or sale. For composition of regions, see map inside front cover. Based on the Current Population Survey/Housing Vacancy Survey; see source for details]

Characteristic	Rental units					Homeowner units				
	1990	1995 [1]	1997	1998	1999	1990	1995 [1]	1997	1998	1999
Total units....	**7.2**	**7.6**	**7.7**	**7.9**	**8.1**	**1.7**	**1.5**	**1.6**	**1.7**	**1.7**
Inside MSAs	7.1	7.6	7.5	7.7	7.8	1.7	1.5	1.6	1.6	1.5
Outside MSAs.....	7.6	7.9	8.8	9.2	9.6	1.8	1.6	1.9	2.0	2.1
Northeast	6.1	7.2	6.7	6.7	6.3	1.6	1.5	1.6	1.5	1.4
Midwest	6.4	7.2	8.0	7.9	8.6	1.3	1.3	1.2	1.4	1.2
South...........	8.8	8.3	9.1	9.6	10.3	2.1	1.7	1.9	2.0	2.0
West	6.6	7.5	6.6	6.7	6.2	1.8	1.7	1.8	1.7	1.7
Units in structure:										
1 unit	4.0	5.4	5.8	6.3	7.3	1.4	1.4	1.5	1.6	1.5
2 units or more...	9.0	9.0	9.0	9.0	8.7	7.1	4.8	4.4	4.4	3.6
5 units or more...	9.6	9.5	9.1	9.4	8.9	8.4	5.1	4.6	4.5	3.8
Units with—										
3 rooms or less ..	10.3	11.4	11.1	10.8	11.3	10.2	9.2	9.6	9.7	9.2
4 rooms	8.0	8.2	8.6	8.9	9.0	3.2	2.8	3.3	3.5	3.3
5 rooms	5.7	5.8	6.0	6.5	6.5	2.0	1.8	1.9	1.9	2.1
6 rooms or more..	3.0	3.8	3.9	4.3	4.4	1.1	1.1	1.1	1.2	1.1

[1] Beginning 1995, based on 1990 population census controls.
Source: U.S. Census Bureau, Internet site <http://www.census.gov/hhes/www/housing/hvs/annual99/ann99ind.html>.

No. 1209. Housing Units—Characteristics by Tenure and Region: 1997

[In thousands of units (112,357 represents 112,357,000), except as indicated. As of Oct. 1. Based on the American Housing Survey; see Appendix III. For composition of regions, see map inside front cover]

Characteristic	Total housing units	Sea-sonal	Year-round units							Vacant
			Occupied							
			Total	Owner	Renter	North-east	Mid-west	South	West	
Total units.............	**112,357**	**3,166**	**99,487**	**65,487**	**34,000**	**19,484**	**23,951**	**34,808**	**21,245**	**9,704**
Percent distribution........	100.0	2.8	88.5	58.3	30.3	17.3	21.3	31.0	18.9	8.6
Units in structure:										
Single family detached........	68,109	1,831	62,111	53,756	8,355	10,238	16,416	22,726	12,731	4,167
Single family attached..........	6,778	157	5,840	3,030	2,810	1,586	1,061	1,944	1,249	781
2 to 4 units................	10,363	129	8,973	1,756	7,216	3,014	2,131	1,945	1,884	1,261
5 to 9 units	5,657	78	4,852	491	4,361	939	1,071	1,572	1,270	727
10 to 19 units.............	5,025	59	4,264	319	3,945	757	831	1,595	1,081	702
20 to 49 units.............	3,877	75	3,292	355	2,936	925	609	820	938	509
50 or more units.............	4,247	108	3,611	524	3,087	1,431	676	730	774	528
Mobile home or trailer.........	8,301	729	6,544	5,255	1,289	593	1,156	3,476	1,319	1,028
Stories in structure: [1]										
One story	37,919	1,374	33,205	23,699	9,506	1,376	3,970	17,912	9,948	3,339
2 stories	35,578	587	32,195	20,202	11,993	6,110	9,611	9,117	7,358	2,795
3 stories	22,619	307	20,616	13,806	6,810	7,524	7,817	3,342	1,933	1,696
4 to 6 stories	5,730	101	5,076	2,176	2,900	2,922	1,077	589	489	552
7 or more stories	2,211	68	1,850	349	1,501	959	320	372	198	293
Foundation: [2]										
Full or partial basement	31,922	325	30,087	26,865	3,223	9,893	13,053	4,654	2,488	1,508
Crawlspace..............	19,806	684	17,518	14,059	3,459	703	2,563	9,195	5,058	1,604
Concrete slab..............	21,238	552	19,073	14,931	4,141	1,067	1,631	10,189	6,186	1,614
Other	1,921	426	1,273	931	341	161	230	633	248	222
Year structure built:										
1939 and earlier..............	22,342	458	19,441	11,254	8,186	7,256	6,339	3,543	2,301	2,444
1940 to 1949..............	8,389	234	7,321	4,602	2,720	1,665	1,760	2,345	1,551	833
1950 to 1959	13,852	439	12,476	8,878	3,598	2,596	3,300	3,877	2,704	936
1960 to 1969	15,949	465	14,313	9,453	4,860	2,452	3,285	5,191	3,385	1,171
1970 to 1979	23,300	832	20,571	13,138	7,433	2,593	4,476	8,356	5,145	1,896
1980 or later	28,527	737	25,367	18,163	7,202	2,921	4,791	11,495	6,158	2,422
Median year................	1967	1970	1967	1968	1965	1953	1962	1973	1971	1965
Main heating equipment:										
Warm-air furnace	66,699	1,972	58,603	41,977	16,626	7,719	18,810	19,046	13,029	6,124
Electric heat pump	12,745	450	11,101	7,750	3,351	350	662	8,579	1,510	1,194
Steam or hot water system	14,008	79	12,929	7,143	5,786	9,236	2,304	692	697	999
Floor, wall, or pipeless furnace	6,105	74	5,588	2,533	3,055	510	588	1,519	2,970	442
Built-in electric units	5,089	183	4,531	2,093	2,438	1,140	1,022	866	1,503	375
Room heaters with flue	1,768	56	1,584	859	725	153	182	925	324	128
Room heaters without flue	2,020	40	1,754	1,031	723	36	62	1,588	67	226
Stoves	1,386	170	1,142	944	198	173	177	471	321	74
Fireplaces	281	40	225	176	48	13	24	90	97	18
Cooking stoves..............	138	12	123	45	78	52	17	47	7	3
None	617	-	617	232	384	4	5	170	437	-
Portable electric heaters..........	847	67	708	377	331	15	12	520	162	72
Other	656	24	582	326	256	82	86	294	121	49
Kitchen equipment:										
Lacking complete facilities	5,629	416	2,289	515	1,774	515	456	629	690	2,924
With complete facilities..........	106,728	2,750	97,198	64,972	32,226	18,969	23,496	34,179	20,555	6,780
Kitchen sink...............	111,191	3,044	98,878	65,316	33,563	19,375	23,818	34,650	21,036	9,269
Refrigerator	109,357	2,922	99,017	65,310	33,707	19,391	23,862	34,672	21,092	7,417
Cooking stove or range	108,779	2,860	98,318	65,023	33,295	19,306	23,727	34,372	20,913	7,601
Burners only, no stove or range....	267	5	247	165	82	28	37	85	98	14
Microwave oven only...........	514	16	454	177	277	60	101	202	91	45
Dishwasher	57,642	990	53,116	41,162	11,954	9,267	11,312	19,462	13,076	3,535
Washing machine	80,133	1,258	75,901	60,708	15,193	13,744	18,757	27,978	15,422	2,974
Clothes dryer	76,470	1,334	71,669	58,231	13,438	12,565	18,373	26,096	14,635	3,467
Disposal in kitchen sink	45,843	740	41,984	28,888	13,096	4,169	10,136	13,786	13,894	3,118
Air conditioning:										
Central	57,168	974	52,303	38,789	13,514	4,416	13,119	26,728	8,038	3,891
Percent of total units	50.9	30.8	52.6	59.2	39.7	22.7	54.8	76.8	37.8	40.1
One or more room units........	28,715	562	26,133	15,561	10,573	8,653	6,582	7,760	3,139	2,019
Source of water:										
Public system or private company ..	98,654	2,025	88,008	55,547	32,462	16,885	20,471	30,607	20,046	8,621
Percent of total units	87.8	64.0	88.5	84.8	95.5	86.7	85.5	87.9	94.4	88.8
Well serving 1 to 5 units........	12,891	917	11,055	9,608	1,447	2,511	3,392	3,995	1,157	919
Other	812	224	424	332	92	88	89	206	41	164
Means of sewage disposal:										
Public sewer	85,775	1,272	76,906	45,920	30,986	15,087	18,860	24,549	18,410	7,598
Percent of total units	76.3	40.2	77.3	70.1	91.1	77.4	78.7	70.5	86.7	78.3
Septic tank, cesspool, chemical toilet.	26,161	1,662	22,479	19,507	2,973	4,396	5,060	10,204	2,820	2,019
Other	421	233	102	61	41	1	31	55	15	86

- Represents or rounds to zero.   [1] Excludes mobile homes.   [2] Limited to single-family units.

Source: U.S. Census Bureau, *Current Housing Reports*, Series H150/97, *American Housing Survey for the United States.*

Construction and Housing   719

No. 1210. Housing Inventory for Selected Metropolitan Areas— Summary Characteristics: 1992 to 1998

[**389.9 represents 389,900.** Based on the American Housing Survey and subject to sampling error; see source for details. For definition of median, see Guide to Tabular Presentation]

Year and metropolitan area	Total units (1,000)	Owner occu-pied	Renter occu-pied	Vacant and sea-sonal	Single-family	Multi-family	Mobile homes	Owner occupied Median monthly hous-ing costs (dol.)	Median value (dol.)	Renter occu-pied, median monthly housing costs (dol.)
1992										
Birmingham, AL MSA.	389.9	63.7	28.0	8.3	70.1	20.4	9.5	317	58,912	363
Norfolk-Virginia Beach-Newport News, VA MSA	563.8	55.6	35.4	9.1	70.1	27.1	2.8	699	89,421	513
Providence-Pawtucket-Warwick, RI-MA PMSAs.	421.7	55.5	34.7	9.7	56.2	42.6	1.2	678	129,138	491
Salt Lake City, UT MSA	383.8	64.7	30.8	4.5	69.7	26.9	3.3	558	75,260	401
1993										
Boston, MA-NH CMSA.	1,684.4	55.1	36.0	8.8	52.1	46.9	1.0	841	157,089	646
Minneapolis-St. Paul, MN-WI MSA .	1,044.3	67.3	26.7	6.0	68.2	29.6	2.3	733	93,748	523
San Francisco-Oakland, CA Area PMSAs	1,544.6	50.6	42.6	6.8	56.2	42.5	1.4	1,031	256,258	720
San Jose, CA PMSA	556.7	56.8	39.2	4.0	65.2	30.8	4.0	1,155	256,067	828
Tampa-St. Petersburg, FL MSA . . .	1,076.7	56.7	24.1	19.3	58.6	25.7	15.7	442	69,089	485
Washington, DC-MD-VA MSA	1,642.4	57.1	35.4	7.5	64.3	35.0	0.7	1,056	167,103	690
1994										
Anaheim-Santa Ana, CA PMSA . . .	918.0	56.0	36.8	7.2	56.1	40.2	3.7	1,127	216,962	805
Buffalo, NY CMSA.	503.2	60.9	30.2	8.8	59.9	38.3	1.8	589	85,378	446
Dallas, TX PMSA	1,152.8	51.3	39.1	9.7	60.7	35.6	3.6	783	87,615	532
Fort Worth-Arlington, TX PMSA . . .	555.4	57.9	32.4	9.7	69.8	27.3	2.9	668	70,759	509
Milwaukee, WI PMSA	593.0	58.5	35.9	5.6	59.6	39.8	0.6	684	101,407	498
Phoenix, AZ MSA	1,032.8	56.2	30.7	13.2	63.7	26.3	10.0	664	88,269	509
Riverside-San Bernardino-Ontario, CA PMSAs.	1,121.4	56.5	26.7	16.8	67.4	21.5	11.1	807	123,491	592
San Diego, CA MSA	993.3	50.4	39.8	9.7	55.9	39.1	5.0	873	176,277	640
1995										
Charlotte, NC-SC MSA.	539.4	62.7	30.6	6.7	68.4	20.8	10.8	532	86,763	489
Chicago, IL Area PMSAs	2,987.1	59.6	33.8	6.6	54.7	44.5	0.7	850	136,362	584
Columbus, OH MSA	604.9	57.9	34.0	8.1	75.8	21.4	2.8	654	92,664	484
Denver, CO PMSA	773.9	61.2	32.5	6.2	68.9	28.8	2.2	763	119,694	539
Detroit, MI PMSA	1,802.7	66.3	26.9	6.7	75.0	22.9	2.1	551	89,648	508
Kansas City, MO-KS MSA	715.5	61.9	30.2	7.9	76.2	21.0	2.8	565	78,542	481
Los Angeles-Long Beach, CA PMSA.	3,276.0	42.0	48.0	10.0	54.7	44.0	1.3	943	192,803	654
Miami-Fort Lauderdale, FL CMSA .	1,483.8	52.1	31.8	16.1	49.9	46.5	3.5	729	97,058	609
New Orleans, LA MSA	547.7	54.6	33.9	11.5	65.2	30.2	4.7	404	75,768	441
New York-Nausau-Suffolk-Orange County, NY PMSAs	4,577.3	41.0	50.9	8.1	32.3	67.4	0.3	931	172,651	650
Northern New Jersey PMSAS	2,442.2	56.0	34.2	9.8	59.2	40.0	0.8	976	176,713	669
Philadelphia, PA-NJ PMSA	1,986.6	63.7	28.0	8.4	73.1	25.8	1.0	673	112,769	578
Pittsburgh, PA MSA.	1,051.7	66.5	25.7	7.8	73.9	21.5	4.7	416	73,383	417
Portland, OR-WA PMSA.	702.6	60.3	32.9	6.8	70.2	23.9	5.9	704	127,731	566
San Antonio, TX MSA	538.7	55.4	34.6	10.0	67.0	27.3	5.6	507	62,577	475
1996										
Atlanta, GA MSA.	1,421.1	58.6	33.4	8.1	66.9	28.6	4.5	803	105,037	651
Cleveland, OH PMSA	829.6	62.4	30.7	6.9	67.0	31.5	1.5	552	99,283	492
Hartford, CT MSA	480.2	60.5	31.1	8.4	63.0	36.5	0.5	888	139,641	616
Indianapolis, IN MSA	640.8	62.2	30.2	7.6	73.4	22.5	4.0	603	91,213	507
Memphis, TN-AR-MS MSA	442.0	59.3	31.5	9.2	70.0	26.1	3.9	592	76,175	477
Oklahoma City, OK MSA	446.4	57.8	28.7	13.5	72.0	22.1	6.0	461	65,638	434
Sacramento, CA PMSA	625.4	55.1	34.1	10.8	71.2	24.0	4.8	874	140,758	590
St. Louis, MO-IL MSA	1,107.0	64.3	26.5	9.2	71.2	23.6	5.2	557	82,111	462
Seattle-Everett, WA PMSA	965.3	58.3	35.1	6.5	60.4	33.9	5.7	897	164,554	630
1998										
Baltimore, MD MSA.	1,028.2	61.7	27.8	10.5	78.8	19.6	1.6	732	127,557	589
Birmingham, AL MSA.	394.0	64.1	26.9	9.0	75.9	15.6	8.5	374	87,670	480
Boston, MA-NH CMSA.	1,345.9	56.5	37.4	6.0	59.2	39.8	1.0	934	191,179	748
Cincinnati, OH-KY-IN, PMSA.	647.5	61.2	30.3	8.5	68.1	28.6	3.3	601	103,553	481
Houston, TX, PMSAs.	1,547.3	53.0	36.7	10.4	68.7	26.9	4.4	676	82,543	556
Minneapolis-St. Paul, MN-WI MSA .	1,150.3	70.6	26.0	3.3	72.0	25.6	2.4	784	122,601	583
Norfolk-Virginia Beach-Newport News, VA MSA	632.1	56.0	33.3	10.7	73.8	22.2	4.0	723	101,903	582
Oakland, CA, PMSA	895.0	56.8	38.8	4.4	71.8	26.4	1.9	1,074	226,174	773
Providence-Pawtucket-Warwick, RI-MA PMSAs.	415.4	57.8	33.6	8.6	62.0	36.7	1.4	769	124,005	540
Rochester, NY, MSA	448.5	63.8	27.6	8.6	71.0	24.4	4.6	718	94,468	572
Salt Lake City, UT MSA	444.0	67.9	24.6	7.5	75.0	21.7	3.3	711	141,888	593
San Francisco, CA, PMSA	700.2	46.2	48.6	5.2	57.7	41.4	0.9	1,235	(1)	894
San Jose, CA PMSA	591.0	58.2	37.6	4.2	72.7	23.2	4.1	1,157	(1)	1,038
Tampa-St. Petersburg, FL MSA . . .	1,138.3	58.6	23.6	17.8	62.8	19.6	17.6	528	133,886	567
Washington, DC-MD-VA, MSA. . . .	1,817.4	59.3	32.8	7.9	72.4	26.7	0.9	1,098	170,021	746

[1] More than $300,000.

Source: U.S. Census Bureau, *American Housing Survey for the* (name) *Metropolitan Area (year)*, Series H-170.

No. 1211. Housing Units—Size of Units and Lot: 1997

[In thousands (112,357 represents 112,357,000), except as indicated. As of **Oct. 1.** Based on the American Housing Survey; see Appendix III. For composition of regions, see map inside front cover]

Item	Total housing units	Seasonal	Occupied Total	Owner	Renter	North-east	Mid-west	South	West	Vacant
Total units	**112,357**	**3,166**	**99,487**	**65,487**	**34,000**	**19,484**	**23,951**	**34,808**	**21,245**	**9,704**
Rooms:										
1 room.	471	18	328	5	323	95	67	51	114	125
2 rooms	1,470	112	951	100	851	333	123	218	278	406
3 rooms	11,715	627	9,399	1,037	8,361	2,403	2,039	2,556	2,400	1,690
4 rooms	23,468	1,286	19,038	6,996	12,042	3,324	4,290	6,881	4,542	3,145
5 rooms	24,476	552	21,760	14,828	6,932	3,558	5,078	8,683	4,441	2,165
6 rooms	21,327	295	19,885	16,415	3,470	3,639	4,878	7,318	4,050	1,147
7 rooms	13,782	154	13,113	11,900	1,213	2,656	3,352	4,461	2,644	516
8 rooms or more	15,647	122	15,014	14,207	807	3,475	4,122	4,640	2,776	510
Median number of rooms.	5.3	4.1	5.4	6.1	4.1	5.5	5.6	5.4	5.2	4.3
Complete bathrooms:										
No bathrooms	1,673	412	750	319	432	220	192	182	157	510
1 bathroom	51,729	1,668	44,223	19,801	24,421	10,795	11,659	13,509	8,259	5,838
1 and one-half bathrooms	16,162	232	14,987	11,628	3,360	3,360	4,778	4,142	2,707	943
2 or more bathrooms	42,794	854	39,527	33,739	5,787	5,109	7,322	16,975	10,121	2,413
Square footage of unit:										
Single detached and mobile homes [1]	76,410	2,560	68,655	59,011	9,644	10,831	17,572	26,202	14,050	5,195
Less than 500	1,402	369	778	491	287	82	132	356	207	254
500 to 749	3,188	381	2,286	1,369	917	227	535	1,127	398	521
750 to 999	6,576	364	5,586	4,121	1,465	531	1,329	2,647	1,079	627
1,000 to 1,499	17,030	468	15,432	12,886	2,546	1,443	3,386	7,045	3,558	1,130
1,500 to 1,999	15,007	196	14,071	12,598	1,473	1,828	3,387	5,367	3,488	741
2,000 to 2,499	10,680	113	10,194	9,526	668	1,992	2,949	3,281	1,973	373
2,500 to 2,999	5,944	45	5,660	5,315	345	1,303	1,758	1,633	967	238
3,000 to 3,999	5,469	45	5,212	4,966	245	1,244	1,651	1,501	815	212
4,000 or more	3,229	49	3,023	2,825	198	801	890	903	429	157
Other [2]	7,885	529	6,414	4,915	1,499	1,380	1,556	2,342	1,137	941
Median square footage	1,702	932	1,750	1,825	1,276	2,154	1,888	1,570	1,674	1,321
Lot size:										
Single detached and attached units and mobile homes	83,188	2,717	74,495	62,041	12,454	12,417	18,633	28,146	15,299	5,976
Less than one-eighth acre	12,087	640	10,175	7,515	2,659	1,761	2,691	2,745	2,977	1,273
One-eighth to one-quarter acre. .	22,045	586	19,915	16,284	3,632	2,625	5,309	6,547	5,434	1,544
One-quarter to one-half acre. .	15,414	319	14,235	12,381	1,854	2,217	3,578	5,542	2,899	860
One-half up to one acre.	9,841	269	8,977	7,858	1,120	1,915	1,961	4,103	999	595
1 to 5 acres.	14,185	346	13,067	11,345	1,723	2,580	2,765	6,166	1,557	771
5 to 10 acres	2,143	58	1,990	1,791	199	300	578	797	315	96
10 acres or more	4,293	260	3,687	3,238	450	562	1,252	1,422	451	346
Other [3]	3,180	239	2,449	1,629	817	457	499	824	667	491
Median acreage	0.35	0.26	0.35	0.38	0.23	0.43	0.32	0.45	0.23	0.24

[1] Does not include selected vacant units.   [2] Represents units not reported or size unknown.   [3] Represents condominiums and cooperatives—single detached, single attached, and mobile homes.
Source: U.S. Census Bureau, *Current Housing Reports,* Series H150/97, *American Housing Survey for the United States.*

No. 1212. Occupied Housing Units—Tenure by Race of Householder: 1991 to 1997

[In thousands (93,147 represents 93,147,000), except percent. As of **fall.** Based on the American Housing Survey; see Appendix III]

Race of householder and tenure	1991	1993	1995	1997
ALL RACES [1]				
Occupied units, total	**93,147**	**94,724**	**97,693**	**99,487**
Owner occupied	59,796	61,252	63,544	65,487
Percent of occupied	64.2	64.7	65.0	65.8
Renter occupied	33,351	33,472	34,150	34,000
WHITE				
Occupied units, total	**79,140**	**80,029**	**81,611**	**82,154**
Owner occupied	53,749	54,878	56,507	57,781
Percent of occupied	67.9	68.6	69.2	70.3
Renter occupied	25,391	25,151	25,104	24,372
BLACK				
Occupied units, total	**10,832**	**11,128**	**11,773**	**12,085**
Owner occupied	4,635	4,788	5,137	5,457
Percent of occupied	42.8	43.0	43.6	45.2
Renter occupied	6,197	6,340	6,637	6,628
HISPANIC ORIGIN [2]				
Occupied units, total	**6,239**	**6,614**	**7,757**	**8,513**
Owner occupied	2,423	2,788	3,245	3,646
Percent of occupied	38.8	42.2	41.8	42.8
Renter occupied	3,816	3,826	4,512	4,867

[1] Includes other races, not shown separately.   [2] Persons of Hispanic origin may be of any race.
Source: U.S. Census Bureau, *Current Housing Reports,* Series H150/91, H150/93, H150/95RV, and H150/97, *American Housing Survey for the United States.*

Construction and Housing **721**

No. 1213. Homeownership Rates by Age of Householder and Family Status: 1985 to 1999

[**In percent**. Represents the proportion of owner households to the total number of occupied households. Based on the Current Population Survey/Housing Vacancy Survey; see source for details]

Age of householder and family status	1985	1990	1992	1993 [1]	1994	1995	1996	1997	1998	1999
United States	**63.9**	**63.9**	**64.1**	**64.5**	**64.0**	**64.7**	**65.4**	**65.7**	**66.3**	**66.8**
AGE OF HOUSEHOLDER										
Less than 25 years old.	17.2	15.7	14.9	15.0	14.9	15.9	18.0	17.7	18.2	19.9
25 to 29 years old.	37.7	35.2	33.6	34.0	34.1	34.4	34.7	35.0	36.2	36.5
30 to 34 years old.	54.0	51.8	50.5	51.0	50.6	53.1	53.0	52.6	53.6	53.8
35 to 39 years old.	65.4	63.0	61.4	62.1	61.2	62.1	62.1	62.6	63.7	64.4
40 to 44 years old.	71.4	69.8	69.1	69.0	68.2	68.6	69.0	69.7	70.0	69.9
45 to 49 years old.	74.3	73.9	74.2	73.9	73.8	73.7	74.4	74.2	73.9	74.5
50 to 54 years old.	77.5	76.8	76.2	77.1	76.8	77.0	77.2	77.7	77.8	77.8
55 to 59 years old.	79.2	78.8	79.3	78.8	78.4	78.8	79.4	79.7	79.8	80.7
60 to 64 years old.	79.9	79.8	81.2	80.9	80.1	80.3	80.7	80.5	82.1	81.3
65 to 69 years old.	79.5	80.0	80.8	80.6	80.6	81.0	82.4	81.9	81.9	82.9
70 to 74 years old.	76.8	78.4	79.0	79.9	80.1	80.9	81.4	82.0	82.2	82.8
75 years old and over	69.8	72.3	73.3	73.3	73.5	74.6	75.3	75.8	76.2	77.1
Less than 35 years old.	39.9	38.5	37.6	37.9	37.3	38.6	39.1	38.7	39.3	39.7
35 to 44 years old	68.1	66.3	65.1	65.4	64.5	65.2	65.5	66.1	66.9	67.2
45 to 54 years old	75.9	75.2	75.1	75.4	75.2	75.2	75.6	75.8	75.7	76.0
55 to 64 years old	79.5	79.3	80.2	79.8	79.3	79.5	80.0	80.1	80.9	81.0
65 years and over.	74.8	76.3	77.1	77.3	77.4	78.1	78.9	79.1	79.3	80.1
FAMILY STATUS										
Family households:										
Married-couple families	78.2	78.1	78.7	79.1	78.8	79.6	80.2	80.8	81.5	81.8
Male householder, no spouse present.	57.8	55.2	53.6	54.6	52.8	55.3	55.5	54.0	55.7	56.1
Female householder, no spouse present.	45.8	44.0	43.6	44.5	44.2	45.1	46.1	46.1	47.0	48.2
Nonfamily households:										
One-person	45.8	49.0	49.8	50.0	49.8	50.5	51.4	51.8	52.1	52.7
Male householder.	38.8	42.4	43.5	43.2	43.1	43.8	44.9	45.2	45.7	46.3
Female householder	51.3	53.6	54.1	54.8	54.5	55.4	56.0	56.7	56.9	57.6
Other:										
Male householder.	30.1	31.7	32.4	33.2	33.6	34.2	35.5	35.9	36.7	37.2
Female householder	30.6	32.5	34.0	35.6	34.3	33.0	35.9	39.5	40.3	41.5

[1] Based on 1990 census controls.

Source: U.S. Census Bureau, Internet site <http://www.census.gov/hhes/www/hvs.html>.

No. 1214. Homeownership Rates by State: 1985 to 1999

[**In percent**. See headnote, Table 1213]

State	1985	1990	1995	1997	1998	1999	State	1985	1990	1995	1997	1998	1999
United States . . .	**63.9**	**63.9**	**64.7**	**65.7**	**66.3**	**66.8**	Missouri	69.2	64.0	69.4	70.5	70.7	72.9
Alabama	70.4	68.4	70.1	71.3	72.9	74.8	Montana	66.5	69.1	68.7	67.5	68.6	70.6
Alaska	61.2	58.4	60.9	67.2	66.3	66.4	Nebraska.	68.5	67.3	67.1	66.7	69.9	70.9
Arizona	64.7	64.5	62.9	63.0	64.3	66.3	Nevada.	57.0	55.8	58.6	61.2	61.4	63.7
Arkansas	66.6	67.8	67.2	66.7	66.7	65.6	New Hampshire	65.5	65.0	66.0	66.8	69.6	70.2
California.	54.2	53.8	55.4	55.7	56.0	55.7	New Jersey	62.3	65.0	64.9	63.1	63.1	64.5
Colorado	63.6	59.0	64.6	64.1	65.2	68.1	New Mexico	68.2	68.6	67.0	69.6	71.3	72.6
Connecticut	69.0	67.9	68.2	68.1	69.3	69.1	New York.	50.3	53.3	52.7	52.6	52.8	52.8
Delaware.	70.3	67.7	71.7	69.2	71.0	71.6	North Carolina	68.0	69.0	70.1	70.2	71.3	71.7
Dist. of Columbia	37.4	36.4	39.2	42.5	40.3	40.0	North Dakota	69.9	67.2	67.3	68.1	68.0	70.1
Florida.	67.2	65.1	66.6	66.9	66.9	67.6	Ohio.	67.9	68.7	67.9	69.0	70.7	70.7
Georgia.	62.7	64.3	66.6	70.9	71.2	71.3	Oklahoma	70.5	70.3	69.8	68.5	69.7	71.5
Hawaii	51.0	55.5	50.2	50.2	52.8	56.6	Oregon	61.5	64.4	63.2	61.0	63.4	64.3
Idaho	71.0	69.4	72.0	72.3	72.6	70.3	Pennsylvania	71.6	73.8	71.5	73.3	73.9	75.2
Illinois	60.6	63.0	66.4	68.1	68.0	67.1	Rhode Island	61.4	58.5	57.9	58.7	59.8	60.6
Indiana	67.6	67.0	71.0	74.1	72.6	72.9	South Carolina	72.0	71.4	71.3	74.1	76.6	77.1
Iowa.	69.9	70.7	71.4	72.7	72.1	73.9	South Dakota	67.6	66.2	67.5	67.6	67.3	70.7
Kansas	68.3	69.0	67.5	66.5	66.7	67.5	Tennessee.	67.6	68.3	67.0	70.2	71.3	71.9
Kentucky	68.5	65.8	71.2	75.0	75.1	73.9	Texas	60.5	59.7	61.4	61.5	62.5	62.9
Louisiana.	70.2	67.8	65.3	66.4	66.6	66.8	Utah	71.5	70.1	71.5	72.5	73.7	74.7
Maine	73.7	74.2	76.7	74.9	74.6	77.4	Vermont	69.5	72.6	70.4	69.1	69.1	69.1
Maryland	65.6	64.9	65.8	70.5	68.7	69.6	Virginia	68.5	69.8	68.1	68.4	69.4	71.2
Massachusetts	60.5	58.6	60.2	62.3	61.3	60.3	Washington	66.8	61.8	61.6	62.9	64.9	64.8
Michigan	70.7	72.3	72.2	73.3	74.4	76.5	West Virginia	75.9	72.0	73.1	74.6	74.8	74.8
Minnesota	70.0	68.0	73.3	75.4	75.4	76.1	Wisconsin	63.8	68.3	67.5	68.3	70.1	70.9
Mississippi	69.6	69.4	71.1	73.7	75.1	74.9	Wyoming	73.2	68.9	69.0	67.6	70.0	69.8

Source: U.S. Census Bureau, <http://www.census.gov/hhes/www/hvs.html>.

No. 1215. Occupied Housing Units—Costs by Region: 1997

[As of **fall. (65,487 represents 65,487,000)** Specified owner-occupied units are limited to one-unit structures on less than 10 acres and no business on property. Specified renter-occupied units exclude one-unit structures on 10 acres or more. See headnote Table 1216 for an explanation of housing costs. For composition of regions, see map inside front cover. Based on the American Housing Survey; see Appendix III]

Category	Number (1,000)					Percent distribution				
	Total units	North-east	Mid-west	South	West	Total units	North-east	Mid-west	South	West
OWNER OCCUPIED UNITS										
Total	65,487	12,241	16,902	23,650	12,694	100.0	100.0	100.0	100.0	100.0
Monthly housing costs:										
Less than $300	18,889	1,923	4,912	8,910	3,144	28.8	15.7	29.1	37.7	24.8
$300 to $399	6,936	1,493	2,186	2,185	1,073	10.6	12.2	12.9	9.2	8.5
$400 to $499	5,368	1,339	1,430	1,769	830	8.2	10.9	8.5	7.5	6.5
$500 to $599	4,612	967	1,379	1,625	641	7.0	7.9	8.2	6.9	5.0
$600 to $699	4,251	849	1,241	1,531	629	6.5	6.9	7.3	6.5	5.0
$700 to $799	3,792	765	1,078	1,355	595	5.8	6.2	6.4	5.7	4.7
$800 to $999	6,402	1,204	1,752	2,124	1,322	9.8	9.8	10.4	9.0	10.4
$1,000 to $1,249	5,249	1,168	1,252	1,562	1,267	8.0	9.5	7.4	6.6	10.0
$1,250 to $1,499	3,602	922	744	891	1,046	5.5	7.5	4.4	3.8	8.2
$1,500 or more	6,386	1,613	928	1,700	2,146	9.8	13.2	5.5	7.2	16.9
Median (dol.) [1]	534	647	494	439	705	(X)	(X)	(X)	(X)	(X)
RENTER OCCUPIED UNITS										
Total	34,000	7,242	7,050	11,157	8,551	100.0	100.0	100.0	100.0	100.0
Monthly housing costs:										
Less than $300	4,550	1,000	1,199	1,598	753	13.4	13.8	17.0	14.3	8.8
$300 to $399	3,808	606	1,128	1,427	648	11.2	8.4	16.0	12.8	7.6
$400 to $499	4,945	803	1,351	1,786	1,007	14.5	11.1	19.2	16.0	11.8
$500 to $599	5,327	1,087	1,115	1,775	1,349	15.7	15.0	15.8	15.9	15.8
$600 to $699	4,365	1,122	736	1,255	1,252	12.8	15.5	10.4	11.2	14.6
$700 to $799	3,162	727	493	940	1,002	9.3	10.0	7.0	8.4	11.7
$800 to $999	3,133	841	355	881	1,056	9.2	11.6	5.0	7.9	12.3
$1,000 to $1,249	1,395	326	136	314	619	4.1	4.5	1.9	2.8	7.2
$1,250 to $1,499	556	165	45	106	239	1.6	2.3	0.6	1.0	2.8
$1,500 or more	589	186	59	129	215	1.7	2.6	0.8	1.2	2.5
No cash rent.	2,171	380	432	947	412	6.4	5.2	6.1	8.5	4.8
Median (dol.) [1]	549	594	473	517	625	(X)	(X)	(X)	(X)	(X)

X Not applicable.   [1] For explanation of median, see Guide to Tabular Presentation.

No. 1216. Occupied Housing Units—Financial Summary by Selected Characteristics of the Householder: 1997

[**In thousands of units (99,487 represents 99,487,000), except as indicated.** As of **fall.** Housing costs include real estate taxes, property insurance, utilities, fuel, water, garbage collection, and mortgage. Based on the American Housing Survey; see Appendix III]

Characteristic	Total occu-pied units	Tenure		Black		Hispanic origin [1]		Elderly [2]		Households below poverty level	
		Owner	Renter	Owner	Renter	Owner	Renter	Owner	Renter	Owner	Renter
Total units [3]	99,487	65,487	34,000	5,457	6,628	3,646	4,867	16,493	4,413	6,619	9,108
Monthly housing costs:											
Less than $300	23,439	18,889	4,550	1,845	1,399	1,016	616	8,788	1,205	3,497	2,533
$300-$399	10,744	6,936	3,808	572	864	263	531	2,679	470	805	1,248
$400-$499	10,312	5,368	4,945	455	1,055	247	751	1,534	536	563	1,311
$500-$599	9,939	4,612	5,327	530	982	242	869	912	515	418	1,089
$600-$699	8,615	4,251	4,365	377	721	277	705	677	438	304	797
$700-$799	6,955	3,792	3,162	325	469	216	495	403	268	219	469
$800-$999	9,535	6,402	3,133	490	449	396	455	468	231	238	457
$1,000 or more.	17,777	15,237	2,540	863	262	987	219	1,034	297	575	347
Median amount (dol.) [4] . . .	542	534	549	464	480	620	549	287	453	285	426
Monthly housing costs as percent of income: [5]											
Less than 5 percent	4,790	4,433	357	340	56	192	48	760	44	23	14
5 to 9 percent	12,648	11,438	1,210	767	196	496	148	2,768	79	96	61
10 to 14 percent.	14,146	11,246	2,900	786	486	477	282	3,023	157	235	89
15 to 19 percent.	14,371	10,232	4,139	735	681	499	477	2,224	238	321	199
20 to 24 percent.	11,650	7,556	4,095	577	792	379	516	1,582	337	328	328
25 to 29 percent.	8,663	5,198	3,465	514	657	389	507	1,155	492	365	534
30 to 34 percent.	6,232	3,486	2,746	344	523	236	492	918	349	383	488
35 to 39 percent.	4,110	2,109	2,001	241	403	145	330	612	300	351	368
40 percent or more	18,527	8,652	9,876	993	2,156	766	1,712	2,993	1,833	3,434	5,229
Median amount (percent) . .	21	18	29	20	31	22	33	18	39	[6]41	[6]42
Median monthly costs (dol.): [4]											
Electricity.	63	70	46	73	49	67	45	61	39	63	45
Piped gas	42	46	31	49	34	33	[7]	46	28	42	30
Fuel oil	63	66	49	67	44	79	[7]	64	52	59	44

[1] Persons of Hispanic origin may be of any race.   [2] Householders 65 years old and over.   [3] Includes units with mortgage payment not reported and no cash rent not shown separately.   [4] For explanation of median, see Guide to Tabular Presentation.   [5] Money income before taxes.   [6] Revised since originally published.   [7] Less than $25.

Source of Tables 1215 and 1216: U.S. Census Bureau, *Current Housing Reports,* Series H-150/97, *American Housing Survey for the United States.*

Construction and Housing   723

No. 1217. Mortgage Characteristics—Owner Occupied Units: 1997

[In thousands (65,487 represents 65,487,000). As of **fall**. Based on the American Housing Survey; see Appendix III]

Mortgage characteristic	Housing unit characteristics			Household characteristics				
	Total occupied units	New construc- tion[1]	Mobile homes	Black	Hispanic	Elderly[2]	Moved in past year	Below poverty level
ALL OWNERS								
Total[3]	65,487	4,894	5,255	5,457	3,646	16,493	5,093	6,619
Mortgages currently on property:								
None, owned free and clear.	25,453	1,018	2,936	2,047	1,217	12,649	1,056	4,177
Reverse mortgage	29	-	-	-	-	29	-	5
Regular and home equity mortgages. .	5,757	352	95	357	163	293	199	198
Regular mortgage only	27,670	3,128	1,847	2,478	1,962	2,050	3,470	1,578
Home equity mortgage only	2,708	130	101	141	69	527	102	138
With regular mortgage, home equity not reported	2,427	147	163	268	139	558	172	314
No regular mortgage, home equity not reported.	1,443	119	113	165	96	388	94	210
Number of regular and home equity mortgages:								
1 mortgage.	29,210	3,174	1,914	2,473	1,947	2,508	3,465	1,667
2 mortgages	6,345	398	106	452	232	326	272	227
3 mortgages or more	444	19	15	39	12	23	16	16
Type of home equity mortgage:								
Units with 1 or more home equity mortgages	8,465	482	196	499	232	819	301	336
Lump sum only	3,354	220	108	259	109	298	109	126
Credit line only.	4,765	233	64	209	119	498	160	184
Both.	40	2	2	-	-	2	5	2
OWNERS WITH ONE OR MORE REGULAR MORTGAGES								
Total[3]	35,855	3,627	2,105	3,104	2,264	2,901	3,842	2,090
Type of primary mortgage:								
FHA	5,065	396	95	799	510	224	611	298
VA	1,936	160	20	263	147	104	165	77
Farmers Home Administration	364	37	14	57	29	52	24	26
Other types	25,579	2,873	1,769	1,626	1,433	1,859	2,841	1,323
Mortgage origination:								
Placed new mortgage(s)	34,766	3,613	2,030	2,995	2,181	2,801	3,747	2,000
Assumed	957	14	74	93	72	95	87	80
Wrap-around.	26	-	-	3	-	-	3	6
Combination of the above	106	-	-	13	10	5	5	5
Payment plan of primary mortgage:								
Fixed payment, self amortizing.	27,590	2,825	1,643	2,380	1,812	1,869	2,959	1,401
Adjustable rate mortgage	2,955	343	160	157	171	205	343	140
Adjustable term mortgage	256	41	39	34	12	35	58	43
Graduated payment mortgage	376	45	9	25	14	12	65	9
Balloon	328	56	9	7	18	16	61	19
Combination of the above	360	48	11	28	27	13	54	16

- Represents or rounds to zero.   [1] Constructed in the past 4 years.   [2] 65 years old and over.   [3] Includes types not known and not reported.
Source: U.S. Census Bureau, *Current Housing Reports*, Series H150/97, American Housing Survey for the United States.

No. 1218. Debt Status of Homeowners by Selected Characteristic: 1997

[In percent. See headnote, Table 812]

Homeowner characteristic	All homeowners	No mortgage debt	First mortgage only[1]	Home equity line of credit	Traditional home equity loan	Either type of home equity loan
All homeowners	100	100	100	100	100	100
Age of head:						
18 to 34 years old.	16	7	24	6	23	12
35 to 44 years old.	23	9	31	28	32	30
45 to 54 years old.	20	12	24	34	27	31
55 to 64 years old.	16	18	13	20	11	17
65 years old and over	26	55	8	12	6	10
Family income:						
Less than $15,000	10	20	4	2	2	2
$15,000 to $24,999.	16	26	11	3	6	4
$25,000 to $49,999.	34	32	38	25	32	27
$50,000 to $74,999.	23	12	26	38	42	39
$75,000 to $99,999.	10	5	13	16	8	14
$100,000 or more	8	5	8	16	11	14
Home equity[2]:						
Less than $50,000	41	24	55	21	69	38
$50,00 to $99,999.	33	38	29	40	21	34
$100,000 or more	26	37	16	39	10	28

[1] Excludes those who have only a home equity line of credit.   [2] Home equity consists of the market value of the home less all debts secured by the home, including balances outstanding on equity lines of credit and traditional home equity loans.
Source: Board of Governors of the Federal Reserve System, *Federal Reserve Bulletin*, April 1998.

No. 1219. Heating Equipment and Fuels for Occupied Units: 1991 to 1997

[As of fall. (93,147 represents 93,147,000) Based on American Housing Survey. See Appendix III]

Type of equipment or fuel	Number (1,000)				Percent distribution	
	1991	1993	1995	1997	1991	1997
Occupied units, total	93,147	94,724	97,692	99,487	100.0	100.0
Heating equipment:						
Warm air furnace.	49,423	51,248	53,165	58,603	53.1	58.9
Heat pumps	7,638	8,422	9,406	11,101	8.2	11.2
Steam or hot water	13,929	13,657	13,669	12,929	15.0	13.0
Floor, wall, or pipeless furnace.	4,291	4,746	4,963	5,588	4.6	5.6
Built-in electric units.	6,755	6,722	7,035	4,531	7.3	4.6
Room heaters with flue.	2,549	1,766	1,620	1,584	2.7	1.6
Room heaters without flue	2,111	1,597	1,642	1,754	2.3	1.8
Fireplaces, stoves, portable heaters or other . .	5,590	5,654	5,150	2,780	6.0	2.8
None.	861	911	1,044	617	0.9	0.6
House main heating fuel:						
Utility gas.	47,018	47,669	49,203	51,052	50.5	51.3
Fuel oil, kerosene, etc.	12,462	12,189	12,029	10,855	13.4	10.9
Electricity.	23,714	25,107	26,771	29,202	25.5	29.4
Bottled, tank, or LP gas	3,882	3,922	4,251	5,398	4.2	5.4
Coal or coke.	319	297	210	183	0.3	0.2
Wood and other fuel	4,890	4,630	4,186	2,177	5.2	2.2
None.	862	910	1,043	620	0.9	0.6
Cooking fuel:						
Electricity.	54,232	55,887	57,621	58,818	58.2	59.1
Gas [1]	38,119	37,996	39,218	40,083	40.9	40.3
Other fuel	424	479	566	113	0.5	0.1
None.	372	362	287	474	0.4	0.5

[1] Includes utility, bottled, tank, and LP gas.

Source: U.S. Census Bureau, *Current Housing Reports*, Series H150/91, H150/93, H150/95RV, and H150/97, *American Housing Survey for the United States.*

No. 1220. Occupied Housing Units—Housing Indicators by Selected Characteristics of the Householder: 1997

[In thousands of units (99,487 represents 99,487,000). As of fall. Based on the American Housing Survey; see Appendix III]

Characteristic	Total occu-pied units	Tenure		Black		Hispanic origin [1]		Elderly [2]		Households below poverty level	
		Owner	Renter	Owner	Renter	Owner	Renter	Owner	Renter	Owner	Renter
Total units	99,487	65,487	34,000	5,457	6,628	3,646	4,867	16,493	4,413	6,619	9,108
Amenities:											
Porch, deck, balcony or patio .	75,986	55,374	20,612	4,217	3,689	2,835	2,477	13,737	2,371	5,156	4,791
Usable fireplace	31,825	27,702	4,123	1,554	460	1,106	354	5,575	280	1,721	526
Separate dining room	39,077	31,411	7,666	2,805	1,635	1,555	917	7,269	749	2,696	1,690
With 2 or more living rooms or recreation rooms.	34,515	31,582	2,932	2,493	479	1,263	191	7,181	312	2,226	499
Garage or carport with home .	58,027	47,488	10,539	2,903	1,173	2,566	1,543	12,208	1,210	3,754	1,969
Cars and trucks available:											
No cars, trucks, or vans.	9,447	2,480	6,967	480	2,438	132	1,174	1,713	2,028	944	3,636
Other households without cars	7,494	5,165	2,329	178	175	373	391	704	123	560	475
1 car with or without trucks or vans	47,902	30,544	17,357	2,541	3,019	1,673	2,313	9,808	1,961	3,509	3,991
2 cars.	27,573	21,185	6,389	1,803	904	1,117	845	3,688	270	1,381	883
3 or more cars	7,071	6,112	958	455	92	352	143	579	31	226	123
With cars, no trucks or vans . .	51,617	32,456	19,161	3,241	3,501	1,654	2,590	9,667	1,881	3,308	4,096
1 truck or van with or without cars	28,096	22,171	5,925	1,346	474	1,346	829	3,952	308	1,742	971
2 or more trucks or vans	10,327	8,380	1,948	390	215	514	273	1,160	195	626	405
Internal deficiencies:											
Signs of rats in last 3 months .	920	425	495	78	154	68	180	79	42	92	211
Holes in floors	1,168	487	680	81	209	54	184	99	48	126	288
Open cracks or holes	5,748	2,719	3,029	387	778	229	493	420	212	342	1,010
Broken plaster or peeling paint (interior of unit)	2,938	1,239	1,699	189	461	94	378	256	130	177	635
No electrical wiring	40	33	7	3	-	-	5	5	3	17	5
Exposed wiring	788	457	331	58	84	35	74	106	43	68	123
Rooms without electric outlet .	2,122	1,160	962	119	238	88	181	281	106	190	323
Water leakage [3]	9,667	5,177	4,490	558	1,054	338	594	817	311	476	1,126

- Represents zero. [1] Persons of Hispanic origin may be of any race. [2] Householders 65 years old and over. [3] During the 12 months prior to the survey.

Source: U.S. Census Bureau, *Current Housing Reports*, Series H150/97, *American Housing Survey for the United States.*

U.S. Census Bureau, Statistical Abstract of the United States: 2000

No. 1221. Appliances and Office Equipment Used by Households by Region and Household Income: 1997

[101.5 represents 101,500,000. Represents appliances possessed and generally used by the household. Based on Residential Energy Consumption Survey; see source. For composition of regions, see inside front cover]

Type of appliance	House-holds using appli-ance	Region				Household income in 1997			
		North-east	Midwest	South	West	Under $10,000	$10,000-$24,999	$25,000-$49,999	$50,000 and over
Total households (mil.)	101.5	19.7	24.1	35.9	21.8	13.3	29.1	31.1	27.9
PERCENT WITH—									
Air conditioner:									
Central system	46.8	22.1	51.3	69.4	26.9	27.4	37.3	50.2	62.1
Room	24.8	39.6	26.1	23.2	12.8	33.3	28.8	24.0	17.5
Clothes washer	77.4	76.0	78.9	82.0	69.5	52.7	69.0	81.5	93.4
Clothes dryer [1]	71.2	66.7	75.8	74.2	65.1	36.2	61.0	77.1	91.8
Electric	55.1	48.3	50.1	66.4	48.2	31.0	49.0	59.9	67.6
Natural gas	15.2	17.7	23.9	7.2	16.5	4.8	11.1	16.3	23.3
Dishwasher.	50.2	48.5	46.9	51.5	53.1	15.7	35.5	53.6	78.2
Ceiling fan	60.1	51.2	63.6	71.2	46.0	39.3	55.2	64.4	70.3
Freezer	33.2	25.7	41.8	36.9	24.2	25.6	30.0	35.1	37.9
1	30.2	24.2	38.4	33.1	22.1	23.6	27.5	32.2	34.1
2 or more	2.9	1.5	3.4	3.8	2.2	2.0	2.5	2.9	3.8
Microwave oven.	83.0	78.7	86.9	82.4	83.3	60.3	81.2	86.7	91.5
Oven	98.8	99.4	99.1	98.7	98.1	96.6	98.6	99.4	99.3
Electric	61.4	49.3	56.6	72.1	60.2	49.1	58.7	63.9	67.4
Natural gas	33.3	45.0	38.0	22.1	35.7	42.2	34.9	31.6	29.2
Self cleaning oven	44.1	48.5	45.1	41.8	42.7	18.1	31.1	47.0	66.6
Range	99.2	99.7	99.4	99.1	98.8	97.0	99.1	99.8	99.6
Electric	60.2	48.3	55.5	70.9	58.4	49.1	58.3	62.8	64.4
Natural gas	34.7	45.7	39.3	23.6	37.8	42.4	35.6	32.9	31.9
Refrigerator.	99.8	99.9	99.9	99.9	99.7	99.3	99.9	99.9	100.0
Frost free	86.8	85.2	85.1	90.0	84.7	73.0	83.1	88.5	95.2
Water heater [1]	100.0	100.0	100.0	100.0	100.0	100.0	100.0	100.0	100.0
Electric	39.1	25.9	26.5	58.3	33.0	40.7	43.3	39.9	32.9
Natural gas	51.9	46.3	67.6	37.3	63.5	46.9	48.5	51.5	58.2
Stereo equipment.	68.8	66.7	67.0	67.8	74.4	45.2	60.1	73.7	83.7
Color TV.	98.7	98.9	99.0	98.7	98.2	96.1	98.5	99.2	99.6
1	31.8	31.8	32.1	29.1	36.0	55.6	40.5	27.3	16.6
2	37.4	36.1	36.2	38.9	37.3	30.9	37.7	41.6	35.4
3	19.1	20.8	20.4	18.4	17.3	7.5	15.6	20.4	26.8
4	7.7	7.5	7.8	8.9	5.5	1.7	3.6	8.2	14.0
5 or more	2.7	2.6	2.5	3.4	2.2	(S)	1.1	1.7	6.8
VCR	87.6	86.1	89.7	86.0	89.0	66.8	84.0	91.6	96.6
Personal computers	35.1	31.9	38.0	31.0	41.3	9.7	16.5	36.9	64.5
1	29.2	27.2	32.4	25.9	32.9	8.0	14.5	32.8	50.7
2 or more	5.9	4.7	5.6	5.1	8.5	(S)	2.0	4.1	13.8
With modem	20.4	17.8	21.7	18.2	24.9	5.2	8.6	19.8	40.7
With laser printer	12.5	11.4	12.9	11.7	14.2	2.5	4.5	12.8	25.1
Used 15 hrs. per week or less. .	25.2	21.5	27.7	23.0	29.3	6.3	12.2	28.2	44.4
Used 16 hrs. per week or more .	9.9	10.4	10.2	8.0	12.1	3.4	4.2	8.7	20.0
Personal use only	4.7	4.5	5.2	4.2	5.3	2.3	2.3	4.1	9.1
Business use only	2.1	2.3	2.5	1.1	3.1	(S)	(S)	1.4	5.0
Both	3.1	3.6	2.6	2.7	3.7	(S)	1.2	3.3	6.0
Cordless phone	61.4	59.6	63.8	61.5	60.2	35.3	51.5	66.9	77.9
Facsimile machine	6.2	6.5	5.3	5.6	8.1	(S)	2.5	5.3	13.3
Photocopier.	3.7	3.8	3.9	3.5	3.9	(S)	1.5	3.9	7.3
Answering machine	58.4	62.2	61.0	54.2	59.1	30.2	49.1	62.3	77.2

S Figure does not meet publication standards.   [1] Includes other types, not shown separately.
Source: U.S. Energy Information Administration, Internet site <http://www.eia.doe.gov/emeu/recs/contents.html>.

No. 1222. Net Stock of Residential Capital: 1985 to 1998

[In billions of dollars (4,707.5 represents $4,707,500,000,000). End of year estimates]

Item	1985	1990	1992	1993	1994	1995	1996	1997	1998
Total residential fixed assets . .	4,707.5	6,287.4	6,755.5	7,161.9	7,654.5	7,973.1	8,391.5	8,821.2	9,405.1
By type of owner and legal form of organization:									
Private.	4,601.3	6,137.7	6,595.8	6,991.0	7,472.2	7,784.2	8,195.3	8,618.5	9,193.0
Corporate	57.0	68.0	71.9	73.7	76.0	78.2	81.5	85.4	91.7
Noncorporate	4,544.4	6,069.6	6,524.0	6,917.2	7,396.3	7,706.0	8,113.8	8,533.1	9,101.3
Government.	106.2	149.7	159.6	170.9	182.3	188.8	196.2	202.7	212.1
Federal	33.0	52.5	53.5	57.3	60.7	62.4	64.5	66.4	69.1
State and local	73.2	97.2	106.1	113.7	121.6	126.5	131.7	136.2	142.9
By tenure group: [1]									
Owner-occupied	3,249.8	4,486.9	4,873.5	5,214.1	5,628.7	5,891.6	6,228.8	6,578.6	7,034.4
Farm	127.8	150.3	155.6	161.1	169.6	174.0	178.9	184.4	191.9
Nonfarm.	3,122.0	4,336.6	4,717.9	5,053.0	5,459.1	5,717.7	6,049.9	6,394.2	6,842.5
Tenant-occupied	1,436.1	1,774.5	1,855.7	1,920.3	1,997.3	2,052.5	2,133.1	2,212.2	2,339.0
Farm	9.4	10.9	11.2	11.7	12.5	12.8	13.2	13.5	14.0
Nonfarm.	1,426.6	1,763.6	1,844.5	1,908.6	1,984.8	2,039.7	2,119.9	2,198.7	2,325.0

[1] Excludes stocks of other nonfarm residential capital, which consists of dormitories, fraternity and sorority houses, and nurses' homes.
Source: U.S. Bureau of Economic Analysis, *Survey of Current Business*, April 2000 issue and *Fixed Assets and Consumer Durable Goods in the United States, 1925-97,* forthcoming.

No. 1223. Expenditures by Residential Property Owners for Improvements and Maintenance and Repairs by Type of Property and Activity: 1980 to 1998

[In millions of dollars (46,338 represents $46,338,000,000)]

Year and type of expenditure	Total	1-unit properties with owner occupant	Other properties	Additions and alterations Total	Addi- tions	Alter- ations	To property outside of structures	Major replace- ments	Mainte- nance and repairs
1980	46,338	31,481	14,857	21,336	4,183	11,193	5,960	9,816	15,187
1985	80,267	47,742	32,525	28,775	3,966	17,599	7,211	16,134	35,358
1986	91,274	54,298	36,976	38,608	7,377	21,192	10,040	16,695	35,971
1987	94,082	54,791	39,291	39,978	9,557	21,641	8,779	15,875	38,229
1988	101,117	60,822	40,295	43,339	11,333	22,703	9,303	16,893	40,885
1989	100,891	59,858	41,033	39,786	6,828	23,129	9,828	18,415	42,689
1990	106,773	59,683	47,090	37,253	8,561	21,920	6,771	18,215	51,305
1991	97,528	58,083	39,445	30,944	7,914	16,076	6,954	16,744	49,840
1992	103,734	67,316	36,418	40,186	6,783	22,700	10,704	18,393	45,154
1993	108,305	70,746	37,559	45,797	12,757	24,781	8,259	20,809	41,699
1994	115,030	77,270	37,760	48,828	9,647	28,672	10,509	23,248	42,953
1995	111,683	75,362	36,321	44,726	7,936	26,893	9,897	24,910	42,047
1996	114,919	76,094	38,825	53,456	12,035	30,064	11,357	24,465	36,997
1997, total [1] [2]	118,569	82,216	36,353	55,530	11,042	33,046	11,442	24,463	38,576
Heating and air conditioning [2] .	10,904	7,648	3,256	3,041	(NA)	3,041	(NA)	5,917	1,945
Plumbing	10,434	5,788	4,646	3,668	(NA)	3,668	(NA)	2,765	4,000
Roofing	11,493	7,885	3,608	(NA)	(NA)	(NA)	(NA)	6,662	4,832
Painting	11,348	7,443	3,905	(NA)	(NA)	(NA)	(NA)	(NA)	11,348
1998, total [1] [2]	120,661	87,243	33,418	53,868	10,092	32,784	10,992	27,467	39,326
Heating and air conditioning [2] .	9,763	7,242	2,521	2,376	(NA)	2,376	(NA)	4,958	2,429
Plumbing	7,697	4,187	3,510	1,860	(NA)	1,860	(NA)	2,505	3,332
Roofing	11,719	8,636	3,083	(NA)	(NA)	(NA)	(NA)	8,133	3,586
Painting	12,651	8,267	4,383	(NA)	(NA)	(NA)	(NA)	(NA)	12,651

NA Not available.   [1] Includes types of expenditures not separately specified.   [2] Central air-conditioning.
Source: U.S. Census Bureau, *Current Construction Reports*, Series C50, *Expenditures for Residential Improvement*, quarterly.

No. 1224. Home Remodeling Work Done and Amount Spent: 1998

[In thousands, except percent (1,345 represents 1,345,000). As of **spring.** For work done in the prior 12 months. Based on survey and subject to sampling error; see source]

Remodeling project	Households with work done [1] Number	Percent of house- holds	Work done by— House- hold member	Outside contractor	Amount spent (dol.) Under $1,000	$1,000 to $2,999	Over $3,000
Conversion of garage/attic/basement into living space	1,345	1.3	888	277	445	335	356
Remodel bathroom	5,543	5.5	3,608	1,322	3,012	1,103	503
Remodel kitchen	4,623	4.6	2,705	1,268	2,040	813	918
Remodel bedroom	3,035	3.0	2,262	397	1,968	361	[2]165
Remodel/convert room to home office	1,094	1.1	748	[2]123	588	[2]149	[2]85
Remodel other rooms	3,225	3.2	2,141	593	1,736	482	376
Add bathroom	759	0.8	431	[2]164	[2]237	249	[2]93
Add/extend garage	491	0.5	[2]186	[2]204	[2]58	[2]91	250
Add other rooms- exterior addition	778	0.8	378	257	[2]166	[2]111	307
Add deck/porch/patio	2,218	2.2	1,402	571	911	592	318
Roofing	4,749	4.7	1,143	2,884	1,270	1,510	1,218
Siding - vinyl/metal	1,487	1.5	466	754	229	370	616
Aluminum windows	815	0.8	323	310	289	[2]169	[2]145
Clad-wood/wood windows	442	0.4	199	[2]185	[2]160	[2]124	[2]111
Vinyl windows	1,555	1.5	451	850	393	487	406
Ceramic tile floors	1,993	2.0	941	781	1,094	430	[2]147
Hardwood floors	1,273	1.3	616	494	653	252	[2]133
Vinyl flooring	2,720	2.7	1,321	1,029	1,813	348	[2]55
Carpeting	4,887	4.8	1,191	3,076	2,316	1,368	440
Kitchen cabinets	2,213	2.2	932	821	692	503	395
Kitchen counter tops	2,317	2.3	843	999	1,074	370	[2]196
Skylights	552	0.5	[2]181	271	258	[2]101	[2]20
Exterior doors	2,736	2.7	1,385	993	1,924	216	[2]65
Interior doors	1,326	1.3	794	256	844	[2]99	[2]24
Garage doors	1,544	1.5	461	826	917	244	[2]57
Concrete or masonry work	2,321	2.3	951	1,023	1,098	417	343
Swimming pool—in ground	328	0.3	[2]105	[2]131	[2]42	[2]72	[2]107
Wall paneling	786	0.8	581	[2]140	513	[2]55	[2]9
Ceramic wall tile	895	0.9	560	233	599	[2]157	[2]39

[1] Includes no response and amount unknown.   [2] Figure does not meet standards of reliability or precision.

Source: Mediamark Research Inc., *New York, NY, Top-Line Reports, (copyright)* Internet site <http://www.mediamark.com/mri/docs/TopLineReports.html> (accessed 30 May 2000).

Construction and Housing   727

No. 1225. Commercial Office Space—Overview for Selected Market Areas: 1999

[As of mid-October. (3,459,729 represents 3,459,729,000). For the 76 market areas with the highest vacancy rates in 1999. Data based on responses from individuals knowledgeable in the local markets]

Market area	Inventory (1,000 sq. ft.)	Vacant space (1,000 sq. ft.)	Vacancy rate (percent)	Construction (1,000 sq. ft.)	Net absorption [1] (1,000 sq. ft.)
United States, all market areas [2]	3,459,729	308,762	8.9	139,856	116,112
Albuquerque, NM.	11,181	1,171	10.5	463	487
Allentown, PA	8,576	695	8.1	220	-57
Atlanta, GA	107,335	12,190	11.4	6,062	5,341
Baltimore, MD	39,539	3,856	9.8	1,445	2,532
Birmingham, AL.	20,096	2,003	10.0	62	133
Boise, ID	5,928	683	11.5	283	989
Bridgeport/Stratford, CT.	7,792	1,282	16.5	-	-265
Buffalo, NY	8,564	1,231	14.4	208	9
Charleston, SC	3,916	344	8.8	385	149
Charlotte, NC	27,730	2,447	8.8	4,400	1,882
Chicago, IL	148,717	17,271	11.6	4,234	-1,924
Cincinnati, OH	32,285	3,095	9.6	532	337
Cleveland, OH.	36,379	3,900	10.7	899	731
Columbia, SC	10,470	863	8.2	515	491
Corpus Christi, CA	2,789	507	18.2	-	27
Dallas, TX	148,102	25,791	17.4	6,320	5,139
Dayton, OH.	11,961	1,685	14.1	(NA)	264
Des Moines, IA	9,228	852	9.2	15	31
El Paso, TX.	7,173	942	13.1	(NA)	244
Fargo, ND.	3,567	297	8.3	69	269
Fort Worth, TX.	18,572	2,355	12.7	393	78
Fresno, CA	14,051	1,629	11.6	303	691
Grand Rapids, MI.	10,605	977	9.2	320	396
Greensboro, NC.	14,351	1,939	13.5	565	91
Greenville, SC	5,985	1,058	17.7	347	497
Hartford, CT	21,767	4,160	19.1	-	1,179
Honolulu, Hawaii	11,737	1,677	14.3	-	-123
Houston, TX	107,620	9,231	8.6	5,360	2,758
Indianapolis, IN	21,506	2,049	9.5	308	1,261
Jacksonville, FL	15,005	1,522	10.1	1,170	1,438
Knoxville, TN.	6,886	887	12.9	94	416
Las Vegas, NV	15,562	1,878	12.1	1,092	1,132
Little Rock, AR.	10,540	819	7.8	347	259
Los Angeles-Central, CA	27,378	5,242	19.1	(NA)	785
Los Angeles-East, CA	1,840	147	8.0	60	18
Los Angeles-Inland Empire, CA.	6,604	1,209	18.3	-	285
Los Angeles-San Fernando Valley, CA	32,076	3,464	10.8	425	803
Los Angeles-South Bay, CA	29,898	4,520	15.1	82	1,097
Los Angeles-West, CA	40,427	3,319	8.2	650	797
Louisville, KY.	14,636	1,840	12.6	225	341
Medford, OR	6,462	531	8.2	300	380
Melbourne, FL.	4,397	592	13.5	60	186
Miami, FL.	30,626	3,155	10.3	1,429	1,175
Milwaukee, WI.	25,900	2,630	10.2	550	245
Minneapolis/St. Paul, MN.	49,315	4,028	8.2	4,888	202
Mobile, AL.	3,577	527	14.7	90	107
Nashville, TN.	20,620	2,102	10.2	1,891	-1,842
New Haven, CT	13,900	2,115	15.2	390	360
New Jersey-Central	66,645	7,163	10.7	1,595	3,937
New Jersey-Northern	71,724	10,998	15.3	3,845	8,304
New Jersey-Southern	16,177	1,575	9.7	(NA)	4,810
Orlando, FL.	21,397	2,294	10.7	2,421	1,928
Philadelphia, PA.	87,728	9,153	10.4	777	1,597
Phoenix, AZ	27,494	2,516	9.1	2,182	936
Pittsburgh, PA	34,078	4,111	12.1	755	-265
Providence, RI.	9,319	922	9.9	-	204
Reno, NV	4,560	515	11.3	50	217
Richmond, VA	20,065	1,842	9.2	630	519
Rochester, NY.	14,043	1,749	12.5	(NA)	340
Sacramento, CA.	29,080	2,427	8.3	2,304	1,786
Saint Louis, MO.	38,562	3,987	10.3	1,281	2,054
San Antonio, TX.	17,261	2,109	12.2	680	274
Shreveport, LA	3,605	861	23.9	(NA)	-53
Sioux Falls, SD	1,911	177	9.3	214	102
Sonoma County, CA	9,514	762	8.0	440	248
South Bend, IN	3,089	393	12.7	79	32
Springfield, MA	4,427	455	10.3	50	97
Syracuse, NY	9,361	1,270	13.6	-	157
Tampa, FL	23,054	1,864	8.1	1,275	1,077
Toledo, OH	6,928	1,295	18.7	213	196
Tulsa, OK.	15,129	2,102	13.9	884	-619
Ventura/Oxnard, CA	9,600	1,000	10.4	570	450
West Palm Beach, FL.	9,238	893	9.7	321	402
Wichita, KS.	7,735	1,646	21.3	(NA)	1,086
Wilmington, DE	11,373	1,089	9.6	-	981
Youngstown, OH	2,585	320	12.4	25	5

- Represents zero.   NA Not available.   [1] Net change in occupied stock.   [2] Includes other market areas, not shown separately.

Source: Society of Industrial and Office REALTORS, Washington DC, *2000 Comparative Statistics of Industrial and Office Real Estate Markets* (copyright).

728   Construction and Housing

No. 1226. Commercial Buildings—Selected Characteristics by Square Footage of Floorspace: 1995

[Excludes buildings 1,000 square feet or smaller **(4,579 represents 4,579,000)**. Building type based on predominant activity in which the occupants were engaged. Based on a sample survey of building representatives conducted between August and December 1995; therefore, subject to sampling variability. For composition of regions, see map inside front cover]

Characteristic	Number of buildings (1,000)	Floorspace (mil. sq. ft.)							Mean sq. ft. per building (1,000)	Median sq. ft. per building (1,000)
		Total	Within buildings having square footage of—							
			5,000 or less	5,001 to 10,000	10,001 to 25,000	25,001 to 50,000	50,001 to 100,000	100,001 and over		
All buildings.	**4,579**	**58,772**	**6,338**	**7,530**	**11,617**	**7,676**	**7,968**	**17,643**	**12.8**	**5.0**
Region:										
Northeast.	725	11,883	995	1,223	2,118	1,380	1,371	4,795	16.4	5.0
Midwest.	1,139	14,322	1,772	1,678	2,701	1,726	1,920	4,526	12.6	4.5
South	1,750	20,830	2,428	2,786	4,481	2,664	2,980	5,491	11.9	4.8
West	964	11,736	1,144	1,842	2,317	1,905	1,697	2,831	12.2	5.5
Year constructed:										
1919 or before	353	3,673	442	756	957	407	386	[3]340	10.4	5.5
1920 to 1945	562	6,710	855	981	1,241	595	750	2,288	11.9	4.8
1946 to 1959	867	9,298	1,180	1,710	1,942	1,260	1,293	1,913	10.7	4.3
1960 to 1969	718	10,858	889	1,132	2,163	1,650	1,453	3,572	15.1	5.5
1970 to 1979	813	11,333	1,245	1,186	2,071	1,337	1,453	4,040	13.9	5.0
1980 to 1989	846	12,252	1,087	1,102	2,809	1,701	1,816	3,737	14.5	5.0
1990 to 1992	218	2,590	316	368	251	378	410	867	11.9	3.5
1993 to 1995	202	2,059	324	296	184	349	407	[4]264	10.2	3.5
Principal activity within building:										
Education.	309	7,740	250	404	1,045	1,825	1,752	[1]2,216	25.1	8.5
Food sales	137	642	234	(S)	(S)	(S)	(S)	(NA)	4.7	2.5
Food service.	285	1,353	550	390	(S)	(S)	(S)	(NA)	4.8	3.0
Health care.	105	2,333	152	(S)	243	175	(S)	1,483	22.2	4.5
Lodging	158	3,618	150	269	748	512	613	[1]1,105	22.8	9.0
Mercantile/services.	1,289	12,728	1,841	2,202	2,939	1,180	1,274	3,292	9.9	4.0
Office	705	10,478	1,084	915	1,580	1,293	1,542	4,064	14.9	4.0
Public assembly	326	3,948	312	786	940	485	499	[1]655	12.1	6.0
Public order and safety	87	1,271	(S)	(S)	368	(S)	(S)	(NA)	14.6	5.0
Religious worship.	269	2,792	301	662	1,120	392	(S)	(NA)	10.4	8.0
Warehouse.	580	8,481	807	991	1,530	1,165	1,147	2,841	14.6	5.5
Other.	67	1,004	(S)	(S)	(S)	(S)	(S)	(NA)	14.9	5.0
Vacant.	261	2,384	399	497	503	148	225	(NA)	9.1	4.0
Government owned	553	12,076	630	924	1,546	2,023	2,211	4,741	21.8	7.0
Nongovernment owned.	4,025	46,696	5,709	6,606	10,071	5,653	5,757	9,209	11.6	4.8
Fuels used alone or in combination:										
Electricity.	4,358	57,275	6,008	7,064	11,310	7,641	7,925	17,326	13.1	5.0
Natural gas.	2,522	38,838	3,020	4,542	7,654	5,309	5,658	12,655	15.4	5.5
Fuel oil	634	14,670	987	713	1,445	1,164	1,992	8,368	23.1	4.8
Propane.	589	5,344	997	881	1,342	562	637	[1]772	9.1	4.0
District heat	115	5,941	(S)	(S)	407	673	792	3,848	51.6	12.5
District chilled water	53	2,521	(S)	(S)	239	275	348	1,576	47.7	12.5
Any other.	213	2,336	278	414	413	223	419	[2]252	16.2	4.0
Workers:										
Fewer than 5	2,505	13,885	4,184	3,636	3,806	770	518	[3]415	5.5	3.0
5 to 9	798	6,291	1,202	1,608	2,090	529	567	(NA)	7.9	4.8
10 to 19	625	7,102	695	1,637	2,399	1,099	557	[3]480	11.4	7.5
20 to 49	400	9,132	225	615	2,513	2,620	2,087	[1]940	22.8	16.3
50 to 99	138	6,931	(S)	(S)	567	1,644	2,108	[1]2,325	50.3	37.5
100 to 249	71	5,988	(S)	(S)	155	913	1,472	3,431	84.4	55.0
250 or more	43	9,443	(S)	(S)	(S)	(S)	658	8,598	220.1	120.0
Weekly operating hours:										
39 or less.	899	6,143	1,544	1,619	1,354	576	426	(NA)	6.8	4.0
40 to 48.	1,257	13,233	1,701	2,033	3,382	1,981	1,776	[1]2,144	10.5	4.8
49 to 60.	969	12,242	1,264	1,707	2,562	2,103	1,897	2,709	12.6	5.5
61 to 84.	567	10,052	653	1,020	1,873	1,182	1,354	3,970	17.7	6.0
85 to 167.	420	6,202	618	503	1,024	749	988	2,319	14.8	4.3
168 (open continuously)	466	10,908	559	647	1,422	1,085	1,527	5,670	23.4	6.0

NA Not available. S Figure does not meet publication standards. [1] 100,001 to 500,000 square feet. [2] 200,001 to 500,000 square feet. [3] 100,001 to 200,000 square feet. [4] 200,001 square feet and over.

Source: U.S. Energy Information Administration, *Commercial Buildings Energy Consumption Survey, 1995,* Internet site <http://www.eia.doe.gov/emeu/cbecs/contents.html> (accessed 26 August 1998).

Construction and Housing   729

No. 1227. Commercial Buildings—Number and Size by Principal Activity: 1995

[See headnote, Table 1226. **(4,579 represents 4,579,000).** For composition of regions, see map inside front cover]

Building characteristics	All build-ngs [1]	Educa-tion	Food sales	Food service	Health care	Lodging	Mercan-tile/services	Offices	Public assem-bly	Reli-gious worship	Ware-house
NUMBER (1,000)											
All buildings.	**4,579**	**309**	**137**	**285**	**105**	**158**	**1,289**	**705**	**326**	**269**	**580**
Region:											
Northeast.....	725	39	(S)	41	14	10	241	112	46	41	88
Midwest......	1,139	42	(S)	69	19	38	390	157	89	57	163
South	1,750	111	73	109	51	51	457	298	134	97	223
West	964	117	32	66	21	59	201	138	57	74	105
Year constructed:											
1919 or before .	353	18	(S)	(S)	(S)	(S)	112	57	37	20	31
1920 to 1945 ..	562	42	(S)	(S)	(S)	7	154	74	72	(S)	59
1946 to 1959 ..	867	72	(S)	(S)	19	33	278	128	38	65	79
1960 to 1969 ..	718	66	(S)	25	7	53	229	75	63	50	68
1970 to 1979 ..	813	45	42	66	34	24	207	158	60	53	73
1980 to 1986 ..	846	36	(S)	74	(S)	25	212	151	33	58	161
1990 to 1992 ..	218	17	(S)	(S)	(S)	(S)	47	38	20	(S)	38
1993 to 1995 ..	202	13	(S)	(S)	(S)	(S)	49	23	(S)	(S)	71
FLOORSPACE (mil. sq. ft.)											
All buildings.	**58,772**	**7,740**	**642**	**1,353**	**2,333**	**3,618**	**12,728**	**10,478**	**3,948**	**2,792**	**8,481**
Region:											
Northeast.....	11,883	1,930	(S)	166	408	350	2,838	2,154	694	442	1,480
Midwest......	14,322	1,997	(S)	474	466	909	3,203	2,338	957	633	2,044
South	20,830	2,315	287	443	916	1,313	4,864	3,483	1,367	1,006	3,436
West	11,736	1,498	209	271	543	1,047	1,822	2,503	930	711	1,522
Year constructed:											
1919 or before .	3,673	521	(S)	(S)	(S)	(S)	816	599	381	266	192
1920 to 1945 ..	6,710	1,080	(S)	(S)	(S)	170	1,118	1,155	706	(S)	1,076
1946 to 1959 ..	9,298	1,921	(S)	(S)	356	607	1,895	1,262	498	637	1,236
1960 to 1969 ..	10,858	1,841	(S)	192	428	972	2,342	1,206	821	535	1,530
1970 to 1979 ..	11,333	1,232	165	285	748	576	2,749	2,095	736	510	1,616
1980 to 1986 ..	12,252	614	(S)	305	425	829	2,727	3,377	399	598	2,104
1990 to 1992 ..	2,590	238	(S)	(S)	(S)	(S)	632	568	221	(S)	318
1993 to 1995 ..	2,059	293	(S)	(S)	(S)	(S)	449	217	(S)	(S)	409

S Figure does not meet publication standards.   [1] Includes other commercial buildings, not shown separately.

Source: U.S. Energy Information Administration, *Commercial Buildings Energy Consumption Survey, 1995*, Internet site <http://www.eia.doe.gov/emeu/cbecs/contents.html> (accessed 28 August 1998).

No. 1228. Office Buildings—Vacancy Rates for Major Markets: 1980 to 1999

[As of **end of year.** Excludes government owned and occupied, owner-occupied, and medical office buildings]

Market	1980	1985	1990	1992	1993	1994	1995	1996	1997	1998	1999
Atlanta, GA...............	10.0	21.0	19.1	19.4	16.8	13.0	10.4	9.2	10.5	11.2	11.8
Charlotte, NC	(NA)	16.7	16.5	(NA)	(NA)	10.0	8.9	8.2	7.1	7.2	9.5
Chicago, IL...............	7.0	16.5	18.6	22.1	21.4	18.7	15.5	15.5	(NA)	14.4	14.6
Cincinnati, OH.............	(NA)	(NA)	(NA)	19.4	(NA)	15.3	(NA)	13.1	11.5	9.9	9.9
Colorado Springs, CO........	(NA)	(NA)	(NA)	(NA)	(NA)	(NA)	(NA)	(NA)	(NA)	8.1	7.9
Dallas, TX	8.6	23.0	25.8	31.3	29.5	21.7	18.7	16.2	14.7	15.0	18.5
Denver, CO	6.6	24.7	24.8	21.5	15.9	12.8	12.1	10.8	9.3	7.6	8.2
Emmonton, CN	(NA)	(NA)	(NA)	(NA)	(NA)	(NA)	(NA)	(NA)	(NA)	(NA)	12.0
Houston, TX	4.0	27.6	24.9	27.0	25.1	24.7	21.9	17.5	12.1	10.7	12.7
Indianapolis, IN	(NA)	(NA)	21.2	22.4	18.8	18.4	14.3	(NA)	14.2	11.2	10.8
Los Angeles, CA	0.9	15.3	16.8	21.2	21.0	19.6	23.2	22.1	13.8	14.2	11.5
Memphis, TN	(NA)	(NA)	(NA)	(NA)	(NA)	(NA)	(NA)	13.6	12.0	12.5	11.2
Miami, FL................	2.4	20.9	23.4	18.5	19.0	15.4	13.8	12.4	11.2	11.4	10.7
Milwaukee, WI.............	(NA)	(NA)	22.9	18.4	21.0	17.6	16.3	(NA)	(NA)	(NA)	16.9
Minneapolis, MN	(NA)	(NA)	(NA)	19.9	(NA)	8.2	(NA)	6.5	6.2	7.0	7.6
Montreal, CN	(NA)	(NA)	(NA)	(NA)	(NA)	21.3	(NA)	20.5	19.1	17.5	14.4
Nashville, TN	(NA)	(NA)	25.1	(NA)	(NA)	7.5	(NA)	6.9	6.0	7.5	9.7
New Jersey (Central)	(NA)	(NA)	(NA)	(NA)	(NA)	20.7	(NA)	16.0	11.2	9.9	10.1
New Jersey (North)	(NA)	(NA)	(NA)	(NA)	(NA)	16.5	(NA)	14.5	11.9	10.0	9.6
New York, NY [1]	3.1	7.9	16.0	18.3	17.9	16.3	17.0	16.0	(NA)	8.6	7.3
Orlando, FL	(NA)	(NA)	(NA)	(NA)	(NA)	12.1	(NA)	6.5	6.4	7.1	9.5
Ottawa, CN...............	(NA)	(NA)	(NA)	(NA)	(NA)	14.5	(NA)	14.6	10.6	8.0	8.2
Philadelphia, PA	6.3	14.5	18.2	19.0	17.8	16.3	16.2	13.7	10.9	12.4	11.1
Phoenix, AZ	(NA)	(NA)	27.6	24.4	(NA)	11.8	(NA)	11.5	9.3	8.9	13.4
Pittsburgh, PA	1.2	(NA)	16.3	(NA)	17.0	15.8	14.5	(NA)	15.4	14.0	13.0
Raleigh-Durham, NC	(NA)	(NA)	(NA)	(NA)	(NA)	(NA)	(NA)	(NA)	(NA)	6.0	8.0
Richmond, VA.............	(NA)	(NA)	(NA)	(NA)	(NA)	11.9	(NA)	9.7	9.7	10.7	9.3
Sacramento, CA	(NA)	(NA)	(NA)	(NA)	(NA)	14.1	(NA)	12.4	12.3	11.8	12.4
San Diego, CA	(NA)	24.7	19.5	23.8	22.1	18.8	17.4	14.1	10.1	9.1	10.1
St. Louis, MO	(NA)	(NA)	21.0	21.8	19.1	18.1	12.7	13.4	12.3	9.6	11.2
St. Paul, MN..............	(NA)	(NA)	(NA)	18.5	(NA)	15.2	(NA)	12.5	9.9	7.2	9.2
Tampa/St. Petersburg........	(NA)	(NA)	(NA)	(NA)	(NA)	(NA)	(NA)	13.0	9.1	8.8	10.0
Toronto, CN	(NA)	(NA)	(NA)	(NA)	(NA)	19.9	(NA)	19.4	13.2	11.9	11.0
Vancouver, CN	(NA)	(NA)	(NA)	(NA)	(NA)	8.2	(NA)	7.6	7.0	6.7	7.6
West Palm Beach, FL........	(NA)	(NA)	(NA)	(NA)	(NA)	16.8	(NA)	12.0	12.3	13.5	13.0
Winston-Salem/Greensboro	(NA)	(NA)	(NA)	(NA)	(NA)	13.2	(NA)	14.1	12.3	14.5	15.7

NA Not available.   [1] Refers to Manhattan.

Source: ONCOR International, Houston, TX, 1980 and 1985, *National Office Market Report*, semiannual; 1989-1990, *International Office Market Report*, semiannual; thereafter, *Year-End (year) Market Data Book*, annual (copyright).

730   Construction and Housing

Section 26

Manufactures

This section presents summary data for manufacturing as a whole and more detailed information for major industry groups and selected products. The types of measures shown at the different levels include data for establishments, employment and wages, plant and equipment expenditures, value and quantity of production and shipments, value added by manufacture, inventories, and various indicators of financial status.

The principal sources of these data are U.S. Census Bureau reports of the censuses of manufactures conducted every 5 years, the *Annual Survey of Manufactures*, and *Manufacturing Profiles*, an annual compilation of the formerly printed series of *Current Industrial Reports*. Indexes of industrial production are presented monthly in the Federal Reserve Board's *Federal Reserve Bulletin*. These numbers were recently changed to a new index base year (1992 = 100) as of early 1997. Reports on current activities of industries or current movements of individual commodities are compiled by such government agencies as the Bureau of Labor Statistics; the Economic research Service of the Department of Agriculture; the International Trade Administration; and by private research or trade associations such as The Conference Board, Inc., the American Iron and Steel Institute, the Electronic Industries Association, and several others.

Data on financial aspects of manufacturing industries are collected by the Bureau of Economic Analysis (BEA) and the Census Bureau. Industry aggregates in the form of balance sheets, profit and loss statements, analyses of sales and expenses, lists of subsidiaries, and types and amounts of security issues are published for leading manufacturing corporations registered with the Securities and Exchange Commission. The BEA issues data on capital in manufacturing industries and capacity utilization rates in manufacturing. See also Section 17, Business Enterprise.

Censuses and annual surveys—The first census of manufactures covered the year 1809. Between 1809 and 1963, a census was conducted at periodic intervals. Since 1967, it has been taken every 5 years (for years ending in "2" and "7"). Results from the 1997 census are expected in 1999 and 2000. Census data, either direct reports or estimates from administrative records, are obtained for every manufacturing plant with one paid employee or more. The *Annual Survey of Manufactures (ASM)*, conducted for the first time in 1949, collects data for the years between censuses for the more general measure of manufacturing activity covered in detail by the censuses. The annual survey data are estimates derived from a scientifically selected sample of establishments. The 1996 annual survey is based on a sample of about 58,000 establishments of an approximate total of 230,000. These establishments represent all manufacturing establishments of multiunit companies and all single-establishment manufacturing companies mailed schedules in the 1992 Census of Manufactures. For the current panel of the ASM sample, all establishments of companies with 1992 shipments in manufacturing in excess of $500 million were included in the survey with certainty. For the remaining portion of the mail survey, the establishment was defined as the sampling unit. For this portion, all establishments with 250 employees or more and establishments with a very large value of shipments also were included. Therefore, of the 58,000 establishments included in the ASM panel, approximately 33,000 are selected with certainty. These establishments account

U.S. Census Bureau, Statistical Abstract of the United States: 2000

for approximately 80 percent of total value of shipments in the 1992 census. Smaller establishments in the remaining portion of the mail survey were selected by sample.

Establishments and classification— The censuses of manufactures for 1947 through 1992 cover operating manufacturing establishments as defined in the *Standard Industrial Classification Manual* (SIC), issued by the U.S. Office of Management and Budget (see text, Section 13). The Manual is also used for classifying establishments in the annual surveys. The comparability of manufactures data over time is affected by changes in the official definitions of industries as presented in the Manual. It is important to note, therefore, that the 1987 edition of the Manual was used for the 1987 and 1992 censuses; and the 1972 edition of the Manual and the 1977 Supplement were used for the 1972 through 1982 censuses.

The Manual defines an industry as a number of establishments producing a single product or a closely related group of products. In the main, an establishment is classified in a particular industry if its production of a product or product group exceeds in value added its production of any other product group. While some establishments produce only the products of the industry in which they are classified, few within an industry specialize to that extent. The statistics on employment, payrolls, value added, inventories, and expenditures, therefore, reflect both the primary and secondary activities of the establishments in that industry. For this reason, care should be exercised in relating such statistics to the total shipments figures of products primary to the industry.

Beginning with 1997 census, the Manual will be replaced with a new way of organizing economic statistics called the North American Industry Classification System (NAICS) (see tables in Section 32 using the new *North American Industry Classification System (NAICS) - United States, 1997*).

Establishment—Establishment signifies a single physical plant site or factory. It is not necessarily identical to the business unit or company, which may consist of one or more establishments. A company operating establishments at more than one location is required to submit a separate report for each location. An establishment engaged in distinctly different lines of activity and maintaining separate payroll and inventory records is also required to submit separate reports.

Durable goods—Items with a normal life expectancy of 3 years or more. Automobiles, furniture, household appliances, and mobile homes are common examples.

Nondurable goods—Items which generally last for only a short time (3 years or less). Food, beverages, clothing, shoes, and gasoline are common examples.

Statistical reliability—For a discussion of statistical collection and estimation, sampling procedures, and measures of statistical reliability applicable to Census Bureau data, see Appendix III.

U.S. Census Bureau, Statistical Abstract of the United States: 2000

No. 1229. Gross Domestic Product in Manufacturing in Current and Real (1996) Dollars by Industry: 1990 to 1998

[In billions of dollars (5,803.2 represents 5,803,246,000,000). Data are based on the 1987 Standard Industrial Classification (SIC). Data include nonfactor charges (capital consumption allowances, indirect business taxes, etc.) as well as factor charges against gross product; corporate profits and capital consumption allowances have been shifted from a company to an establishment basis]

Industry	1990	1992	1993	1994	1995	1996	1997	1998
CURRENT DOLLARS								
Gross domestic product	**5,803.2**	**6,318.9**	**6,642.3**	**7,054.3**	**7,400.5**	**7,813.2**	**8,300.8**	**8,759.9**
Manufacturing.	1,040.6	1,082.0	1,131.4	1,223.2	1,289.1	1,316.0	1,377.2	1,432.8
Durable goods.	586.6	594.0	632.8	694.1	729.8	748.4	798.7	842.6
Lumber and wood products	32.2	32.3	35.7	39.8	42.3	39.9	41.9	43.9
Furniture and fixtures	15.6	16.6	18.1	18.9	19.5	20.7	22.8	25.2
Stone, clay, and glass products. . . .	25.3	26.3	26.4	30.4	32.4	33.2	38.0	42.1
Primary metal industries.	43.2	39.6	43.0	47.6	53.0	50.8	51.8	54.8
Fabricated metal products	69.4	69.5	73.4	83.2	87.2	93.1	99.6	104.7
Industrial machinery	118.2	113.8	113.7	121.0	132.8	136.3	143.8	153.3
Electronic & other electric								
equipment	105.7	107.7	121.0	139.3	146.9	153.2	166.0	168.3
Motor vehicles and equipment	47.3	58.8	78.0	95.2	98.2	92.2	99.5	105.0
Other transportation equipment. . . .	60.5	58.1	54.2	49.6	47.7	51.4	55.6	59.7
Instruments and related products. . .	49.3	51.9	48.4	46.8	47.2	53.7	54.1	59.0
Misc. manufacturing industries	19.8	19.6	20.9	22.3	22.7	23.8	25.6	26.6
Nondurable goods	454.0	488.0	498.6	529.1	559.2	567.6	578.5	590.1
Food and kindred products.	96.4	105.9	107.6	110.2	121.1	118.7	119.3	122.0
Tobacco manufactures.	11.9	13.8	12.3	13.2	15.1	14.8	16.1	17.9
Textile mill products.	22.0	25.7	25.7	25.6	24.8	25.3	25.7	25.6
Apparel and other textile products . .	25.4	27.4	27.7	28.5	27.3	27.0	26.1	25.4
Paper and allied products	45.0	45.6	46.9	50.1	58.9	55.9	53.6	54.9
Printing and publishing	73.1	78.9	78.5	83.5	80.8	88.2	90.2	96.3
Chemicals and allied products.	109.9	119.1	122.7	138.7	150.8	153.6	158.8	158.7
Petroleum and coal products	31.7	28.2	31.0	29.3	29.0	30.2	31.5	30.1
Rubber and misc. plastic products . .	33.9	38.4	41.6	44.9	46.1	49.7	52.7	54.9
Leather and leather products	4.7	4.9	4.7	5.0	5.3	4.2	4.5	4.4
CHAINED (1996) DOLLARS								
Gross domestic product, total . . .	**6,707.9**	**6,880.0**	**7,062.6**	**7,347.7**	**7,543.8**	**7,813.2**	**8,144.8**	**8,495.7**
Manufacturing.	1,102.3	1,085.0	1,122.9	1,206.0	1,284.7	1,316.0	1,385.5	1,448.7
Durable goods.	585.1	568.9	600.3	656.5	714.9	748.4	820.2	906.5
Lumber and wood products	45.1	39.5	36.9	38.9	41.6	39.9	40.3	42.2
Furniture and fixtures	18.1	18.5	20.1	20.2	20.7	20.7	22.2	23.8
Stone, clay, and glass products. . . .	29.4	29.6	29.1	32.0	32.8	33.2	37.3	39.7
Primary metal industries.	43.7	43.7	48.5	50.5	49.6	50.8	51.7	55.5
Fabricated metal products	76.1	72.2	75.8	86.4	90.8	93.1	98.1	99.3
Industrial machinery	93.5	92.4	96.8	106.8	124.7	136.3	159.1	193.5
Electronic & other electric								
equipment	68.6	73.3	85.0	103.3	128.7	153.2	182.4	222.1
Motor vehicles and equipment	68.7	68.7	85.1	99.1	103.2	92.2	100.2	104.8
Other transportation equipment. . . .	75.7	64.2	58.3	52.2	49.4	51.4	54.9	57.8
Instruments and related products. . .	68.9	64.0	57.2	53.8	52.6	53.7	50.0	49.7
Misc. manufacturing industries	22.8	20.6	21.4	22.6	23.3	23.8	25.1	25.3
Nondurable goods	520.2	520.0	525.4	551.2	570.3	567.6	565.9	546.4
Food and kindred products.	109.5	111.4	114.6	112.6	133.3	118.7	114.5	113.5
Tobacco manufactures.	14.5	9.6	9.3	13.8	15.7	14.8	14.5	11.6
Textile mill products.	22.8	25.6	25.9	26.9	26.0	25.3	25.1	24.4
Apparel and other textile products . .	27.3	27.7	27.6	28.4	28.0	27.0	26.0	24.7
Paper and allied products	52.5	55.2	60.7	61.3	52.2	55.9	58.3	55.4
Printing and publishing	102.9	96.6	90.5	92.6	89.2	88.2	85.6	86.6
Chemicals and allied products.	131.1	132.7	132.1	145.5	148.0	153.6	158.5	149.5
Petroleum and coal products	22.9	21.1	21.6	22.0	26.9	30.2	25.8	24.0
Rubber and misc. plastic products . .	34.0	37.9	41.2	44.9	47.0	49.7	53.8	53.6
Leather and leather products	5.2	5.2	4.9	5.1	5.3	4.2	4.5	4.2

Source: U.S. Bureau of Economic Analysis, *Survey of Current Business,* November 1999.

Manufactures 733

U.S. Census Bureau, Statistical Abstract of the United States: 2000

No. 1230. Manufacturing Summary by Industry: 1992 and 1997

Industry	1987 SIC code	Establishments		Paid employees (1,000)		Annual payroll (mil. dol.)		Value of shipments (mil. dol.)	
		1992	1997	1992	1997	1992	1997	1992	1997
Manufacturing, total.	(X)	370,912	377,776	16,948.9	17,557.0	494,109	595,686	3,004,723	3,958,050
Food and kindred products	20	20,798	20,878	1,502.7	1,561.4	36,772	42,941	406,963	480,840
Meat products	201	3,240	3,047	400.4	461.8	7,564	9,732	94,072	111,142
Dairy products	202	2,020	1,838	135.4	133.0	3,720	4,178	52,720	59,021
Grain mill products	204	2,616	2,539	107.2	102.9	3,375	3,686	49,957	60,974
Bakery products	205	3,150	3,435	215.0	225.8	5,599	6,475	28,494	34,486
Sugar & confectionery products .	206	1,129	1,084	91.3	90.2	2,402	2,760	22,710	27,235
Tobacco products	21	114	105	38.0	(²)	1,524	(D)	35,198	(D)
Cigarettes	211	11	13	25.4	21.3	1,205	1,247	29,746	29,253
Textile mill products	22	5,886	6,155	616.4	561.9	12,398	13,709	70,753	82,404
Apparel & other textile products . .	23	23,093	23,411	985.3	829.3	15,325	15,404	71,658	81,194
Men's & boys' furnishings.	232	2,288	2,226	261.0	197.7	3,649	3,234	17,867	19,193
Women's & children's outerwear .	233	9,536	8,773	306.3	251.4	4,596	4,486	21,631	22,963
Lumber & wood products	24	35,807	36,735	655.8	757.3	13,882	18,669	81,565	111,931
Logging	241	13,063	13,533	83.2	83.2	1,689	2,014	13,592	13,626
Sawmills & planing mills	242	6,845	6,270	168.4	178.6	3,585	4,478	23,294	32,750
Miscellaneous wood products . . .	249	3,536	3,609	84.0	93.9	1,725	2,278	10,348	14,842
Furniture & fixtures.	25	11,658	12,095	471.1	523.9	10,227	13,344	43,826	61,528
Household furniture	251	5,412	5,609	253.3	265.1	4,804	5,861	20,507	26,335
Paper & allied products.	26	6,416	6,496	626.3	(¹)	20,492	(D)	133,201	(D)
Paper mills	262	280	256	130.6	107.6	5,421	5,380	32,786	35,514
Paperboard mills	263	204	217	51.5	54.6	2,136	2,685	16,140	19,829
Paperboard containers & boxes .	265	2,787	2,842	199.4	208.1	5,722	6,952	32,655	40,085
Printing & publishing.	27	65,392	62,355	1,492.1	1,534.3	41,136	50,092	166,153	210,921
Newspapers	271	8,668	8,773	413.9	400.8	10,436	11,730	33,782	41,433
Periodicals	272	4,700	6,331	115.1	137.9	4,077	5,997	22,104	29,973
Books	273	3,265	3,693	129.5	141.0	4,037	5,240	21,378	28,504
Miscellaneous publishing	274	3,385	3,435	65.1	78.6	1,720	2,626	10,908	16,508
Commercial printing	275	38,441	34,000	567.2	595.8	15,337	18,841	56,229	69,858
Chemicals & allied products.	28	12,004	12,371	848.6	820.2	32,502	37,240	305,420	400,085
Plastics materials & synthetics .	282	628	778	128.5	114.8	5,137	5,353	48,698	63,639
Drugs.	283	1,426	1,767	194.4	203.0	7,840	10,081	67,791	93,299
Soaps, cleaners, & toilet goods. .	284	2,405	2,474	122.8	126.9	3,927	4,583	42,875	57,507
Paints & allied products	285	1,419	1,488	51.1	52.7	1,710	2,067	14,973	19,115
Agricultural chemicals	287	890	913	40.3	37.2	1,451	1,519	18,841	24,267
Petroleum & coal products.	29	2,124	2,147	114.4	106.1	4,967	5,480	150,227	175,779
Petroleum refining	291	231	242	74.9	65.5	3,640	3,887	136,551	157,526
Tires & inner tubes	301	152	162	64.6	64.4	2,499	2,773	11,814	14,731
Fabricated rubber products, n.e.c.	306	1,783	1,728	105.1	108.8	2,617	3,144	11,474	15,430
Leather & leather products	31	2,040	1,839	101.1	(³)	1,806	(D)	9,694	(D)
Stone, clay, & glass products	32	16,254	16,393	468.8	505.4	13,113	16,303	62,521	87,244
Miscellaneous nonmetallic mineral products.	329	1,669	1,564	65.5	73.4	2,004	2,542	10,756	14,461
Primary metal industries	33	6,501	6,275	662.1	692.2	22,202	26,830	138,287	188,775
Blast furnace & basic steel products	331	1,012	954	238.7	217.7	9,179	10,060	58,449	77,533
Iron & steel foundries	332	1,172	1,144	122.1	132.9	3,739	4,667	11,860	17,533
Primary nonferrous metals	333	176	179	34.7	33.3	1,334	1,405	13,905	16,321
Nonferrous rolling & drawing. . .	335	1,117	1,011	147.4	166.3	4,635	6,094	37,101	52,864
Fabricated metal products	34	36,429	37,985	1,362.3	1,549.5	38,962	50,904	166,532	231,704
Metal cans & shipping containers	341	481	425	39.6	33.6	1,465	1,378	13,263	13,353
Fabricated structural metal products	344	13,255	13,959	388.9	459.8	10,362	14,112	44,876	65,206
Screw machine products, bolts, etc.	345	2,642	3,785	90.5	133.4	2,624	4,573	9,025	16,461
Metal forgings & stampings	346	3,979	3,625	233.7	268.0	7,749	10,486	30,621	44,833
Metal services, n.e.c.	347	5,247	5,610	108.2	130.8	2,652	3,722	9,953	14,455
Industrial machinery & equipment. .	35	53,956	56,383	1,738.9	1,978.2	57,231	74,550	258,661	407,393
Construction & related machinery	353	3,341	3,523	176.2	213.3	5,664	8,081	27,193	47,935
Metalworking machinery	354	11,506	11,706	254.9	296.5	8,571	11,812	26,473	39,693
General industrial machinery . . .	356	4,132	4,479	244.0	265.4	7,742	9,753	31,443	44,081
Refrigeration & service machinery	358	2,306	2,277	178.7	204.7	5,264	6,801	27,544	39,318
Industrial machinery, n.e.c.	359	23,561	25,390	303.7	368.5	8,843	12,360	25,443	38,648
Electronic & other electric equipment	36	16,922	17,104	1,438.8	1,582.3	44,197	58,256	216,764	348,560
Electrical industrial apparatus . .	362	2,173	2,388	157.4	169.0	4,387	5,474	19,266	28,644
Electric lighting & wiring equipment.	364	2,049	2,106	148.0	158.6	3,974	4,889	19,844	26,197
Communications equipment	366	2,014	2,213	238.6	283.8	9,110	13,272	42,955	80,949
Transportation equipment	37	11,287	12,387	1,646.9	1,561.7	62,734	68,299	399,269	515,882
Aircraft & parts.	372	1,746	1,711	548.1	411.2	22,647	20,703	104,858	98,964
Ship & boat building & repairing .	373	3,050	3,482	162.8	148.3	4,634	4,641	15,248	17,015
Instruments & related products. . . .	38	11,354	11,727	907.1	(¹)	33,067	(D)	134,940	(D)
Search & navigation equipment. .	381	762	680	253.0	187.6	10,962	9,958	35,039	32,498
Measuring & controlling devices .	382	4,737	4,787	275.5	263.2	9,632	11,038	34,729	46,449
Photographic equipment & supplies	386	902	739	77.3	63.6	3,061	2,928	22,119	21,306
Miscellaneous mfg. industries. . . .	39	17,035	18,043	365.5	394.0	8,417	10,563	39,498	50,998

D Withheld to avoid disclosing data of individual companies.   X Not applicable.   ¹ 100,000 employees or more.   ² 25,000 to 49,999 employees.   ³ 50,000 to 99,999 employees.
Source: U.S. Census Bureau, *1997 Economic Census, Core Business Statistics Series*, Series EC97X-CS2, June 2000.

No. 1231. Manufactures Summary: 1996

[18,667 represents 18,667,000. Sum of state totals may not add to U.S. total because U.S. and state figures were independently derived]

State	All employees [1]			Production workers [1]		Value added by manufactures [2]		
		Payroll					Per production worker (dol.)	Value of shipments [3] (mil. dol.)
	Number (1,000)	Total (mil. dol.)	Per employee (dol.)	Total (1,000)	Wages (mil. dol.)	Total (mil. dol.)		
United States	18,667	645,140	34,561	12,169	324,612	1,750,493	143,847	3,719,743
Alabama.	383	10,587	27,679	285	6,675	27,451	96,422	66,257
Alaska	16	488	30,873	12	339	1,470	124,568	3,939
Arizona.	208	7,191	34,554	120	2,857	22,850	189,782	36,961
Arkansas	239	5,829	24,410	188	4,036	18,512	98,414	44,310
California	1,938	71,164	36,724	1,162	29,028	188,805	162,427	368,329
Colorado.	196	6,792	34,686	118	3,122	19,215	162,704	39,191
Connecticut.	299	12,785	42,802	153	4,699	24,772	161,484	44,369
Delaware	60	2,840	47,178	27	784	5,791	212,890	13,601
District of Columbia	13	630	49,180	3	97	1,512	504,133	1,975
Florida	486	14,853	30,554	297	6,553	38,621	130,170	76,387
Georgia	585	17,593	30,100	411	9,634	51,753	125,797	115,898
Hawaii	17	509	29,789	10	251	1,609	159,257	3,146
Idaho	74	2,383	32,152	53	1,312	7,977	149,944	18,315
Illinois	996	36,986	37,124	625	17,625	92,011	147,171	196,845
Indiana.	660	22,976	34,812	477	14,290	61,896	129,678	133,787
Iowa	250	7,839	31,307	177	4,725	27,021	153,092	61,981
Kansas.	209	6,902	32,994	145	4,006	18,820	129,970	46,152
Kentucky	296	9,162	30,933	216	5,752	35,040	162,524	82,531
Louisiana	175	6,037	34,439	123	3,706	25,125	203,606	75,961
Maine.	89	2,674	30,175	66	1,760	6,675	100,988	14,445
Maryland	192	6,968	36,309	112	3,226	17,455	155,707	35,700
Massachusetts.	475	19,026	40,071	264	7,723	44,047	166,655	79,254
Michigan.	967	41,782	43,230	629	22,643	85,688	136,186	205,744
Minnesota.	432	15,590	36,071	256	6,886	34,716	135,399	73,273
Mississippi	239	5,654	23,666	190	3,838	17,295	91,024	39,564
Missouri	415	13,572	32,712	263	6,743	40,208	152,650	85,222
Montana.	22	588	26,584	15	376	1,707	111,582	4,930
Nebraska	110	3,086	28,033	80	1,916	9,218	115,229	25,023
Nevada	41	1,195	29,299	27	627	3,275	120,408	6,194
New Hampshire	107	3,576	33,293	71	1,848	10,815	152,969	19,348
New Jersey.	540	22,919	42,419	279	7,905	49,995	179,257	96,001
New Mexico	43	1,304	30,053	28	651	11,745	427,087	16,364
New York	950	35,641	37,533	555	14,541	90,665	163,448	163,697
North Carolina	856	23,796	27,815	628	13,879	76,475	121,814	155,911
North Dakota.	22	570	25,796	15	340	1,808	117,390	4,794
Ohio	1,074	39,790	37,065	720	22,618	105,497	146,462	232,721
Oklahoma.	167	4,859	29,098	119	2,963	15,875	133,856	35,220
Oregon.	232	7,869	33,859	157	4,317	21,838	138,917	45,022
Pennsylvania.	918	31,978	34,849	590	16,026	82,922	140,594	165,889
Rhode Island.	83	2,565	30,870	55	1,261	5,407	97,779	9,959
South Carolina.	366	10,658	29,112	272	6,557	30,769	113,162	66,794
South Dakota	46	1,220	26,746	32	651	3,974	125,753	10,488
Tennessee	533	15,394	28,877	397	9,449	42,288	106,411	95,851
Texas.	1,055	36,008	34,131	665	17,032	116,631	175,464	284,151
Utah	119	3,511	29,576	79	1,924	11,239	141,731	22,010
Vermont	48	1,483	30,969	33	788	3,986	122,652	8,554
Virginia.	399	12,555	31,474	284	7,100	42,519	149,926	80,795
Washington	342	13,197	38,610	207	6,429	31,929	154,169	71,874
West Virginia	76	2,521	33,083	55	1,607	8,965	163,885	17,679
Wisconsin	601	19,779	32,910	416	11,324	53,619	128,984	114,464
Wyoming	10	268	27,608	7	175	999	140,746	2,874

[1] Includes employment and payroll at administrative offices and auxiliary units. All employees represents the average of production workers plus all other employees for the payroll period ended nearest the 12th of March. Production workers represents the average of the employment for the payroll periods ended nearest the 12th of March, May, August, and November. [2] Adjusted value added; takes into account (a) value added by merchandising operations (that is, difference between the sales value and cost of merchandise sold without further manufacture, processing, or assembly), plus (b) net change in finished goods and work-inprocess inventories between beginning and end of year. [3] Includes extensive and unmeasurable duplication from shipments between establishments in the same industry classification.

Note: Reports for manufacturing by state for 1997 from the *1997 Economic Census* are being issued on a flow basis beginning in the summer of 2000.

Source: U.S. Census Bureau, *Annual Survey of Manufactures, Geographic Area Statistics*, Series M96(AS)-3.

Manufactures 735

No. 1232. Average Hourly Earnings of Production Workers in Manufacturing Industries by State: 1980 to 1999

[In dollars]

State	1980	1990	1995	1998	1999	State	1980	1990	1995	1998	1999
United States . .	7.27	10.83	12.37	13.49	13.91	Missouri.	7.26	10.74	12.17	13.38	13.93
						Montana	8.78	11.51	12.94	13.76	14.18
Alabama	6.49	9.39	11.14	12.11	12.53	Nebraska.	7.38	9.66	11.19	12.32	12.77
Alaska.	10.22	12.46	11.00	11.09	12.10	Nevada	7.72	11.05	12.62	14.42	13.92
Arizona	7.29	10.21	11.16	12.17	12.69	New Hampshire	5.87	10.83	11.94	12.79	13.17
Arkansas	5.71	8.51	10.05	11.12	11.55	New Jersey	7.31	11.76	13.56	14.58	15.07
California	7.70	11.48	12.55	13.66	13.95	New Mexico	5.79	9.04	10.68	12.47	12.56
Colorado	7.63	10.94	12.51	13.74	14.18	New York.	7.18	11.11	12.50	13.47	13.86
Connecticut	7.08	11.53	13.71	14.83	15.33	North Carolina	5.37	8.79	10.56	11.84	12.32
Delaware.	7.58	12.39	14.20	15.36	15.93	North Dakota	6.56	9.27	10.75	11.40	11.93
District of Columbia [1].	8.46	12.51	13.66	14.49	15.26	Ohio	8.57	12.64	14.42	15.79	16.26
Florida.	5.98	8.98	10.18	11.43	11.83	Oklahoma	7.36	10.73	11.52	12.61	12.69
Georgia	5.77	9.17	10.71	12.03	12.50	Oregon	8.65	11.15	12.75	14.07	14.61
Hawaii.	6.83	10.99	12.82	13.16	13.48						
Idaho	7.55	10.60	11.46	12.80	13.40	Pennsylvania	7.59	11.04	12.81	14.06	14.18
Illinois	8.02	11.44	12.64	13.75	14.05	Rhode Island	5.59	9.45	10.62	11.61	11.98
Indiana	8.49	12.03	13.91	14.97	15.26	South Carolina	5.59	8.84	10.16	10.52	10.67
Iowa	8.67	11.27	12.73	13.91	14.20	South Dakota	6.50	8.48	9.36	10.22	10.58
Kansas	7.37	10.94	12.39	13.84	14.44	Tennessee	6.08	9.55	10.78	12.06	12.50
Kentucky	7.34	10.70	12.22	13.82	14.26	Texas	7.15	10.47	11.47	12.14	12.26
Louisiana.	7.74	11.61	13.43	14.63	15.19	Utah	7.02	10.32	11.62	13.07	13.38
Maine	6.00	10.59	12.39	13.49	13.97	Vermont	6.14	10.52	12.21	13.03	13.65
Maryland	7.61	11.57	13.49	14.31	14.60	Virginia	6.22	10.07	11.72	12.90	13.37
Massachusetts	6.51	11.39	12.79	13.80	14.24	Washington	(NA)	12.61	14.73	15.76	16.14
Michigan	9.52	13.86	16.31	17.61	18.33	West Virginia	8.08	11.53	12.64	13.72	14.09
Minnesota	7.61	11.23	12.79	13.92	14.35	Wisconsin	8.03	11.11	12.76	14.02	14.51
Mississippi	5.44	8.37	9.76	10.73	11.18	Wyoming	7.01	10.83	11.96	14.93	15.40

NA Not available. [1] Washington PMSA (primary metropolitan statistical area).

Source: U.S. Bureau of Labor Statistics, *Employment and Earnings,* May 2000 issue and earlier issues.

No. 1233. Manufacturing Full-time Equivalent Employees and Wages by Industry: 1995 to 1998

Industry	Full-time equivalent (FTE) employees (1,000)				Wage and salary accruals per FTE worker (dol.)			
	1995	1996	1997	1998	1995	1996	1997	1998
Manufacturing, total	18,190	18,168	18,350	18,513	35,779	37,158	38,965	40,928
Durable goods	10,561	10,664	10,880	11,100	37,660	39,038	40,804	42,715
Lumber and wood products	772	782	792	817	25,110	26,148	27,448	28,272
Furniture and fixtures	502	497	501	523	25,048	26,068	27,641	28,979
Stone, clay, and glass products	530	532	544	558	33,283	34,880	35,708	37,088
Primary metal industries	697	703	705	709	40,067	40,771	42,033	43,080
Fabricated metal products	1,421	1,426	1,461	1,493	32,927	33,968	35,155	36,292
Industrial machinery and equipment . .	2,051	2,074	2,141	2,181	40,063	41,668	44,133	46,454
Electronic and other electric equipment.	1,607	1,645	1,673	1,689	38,922	40,307	42,838	45,840
Motor vehicles and equipment	961	959	975	990	46,658	48,773	49,669	51,908
Other transportation equipment	809	815	850	891	44,611	45,520	47,215	48,776
Instruments and related products	827	842	851	858	44,654	46,859	48,635	51,663
Miscellaneous manufacturing industries	384	389	387	391	28,219	28,776	30,594	32,072
Nondurable goods.	7,629	7,504	7,470	7,413	33,176	34,486	36,286	38,254
Food and kindred products	1,642	1,654	1,651	1,648	30,139	30,567	31,891	33,506
Tobacco products.	41	40	40	39	53,854	54,975	59,450	57,590
Textile mill products	654	624	612	593	23,985	25,019	26,376	27,312
Apparel and other textile products. . . .	919	846	803	745	18,800	19,832	20,861	22,180
Paper and allied products	685	677	674	671	39,458	40,718	42,177	43,349
Printing and publishing	1,450	1,444	1,465	1,478	34,539	35,897	37,427	39,481
Chemicals and allied products	1,027	1,021	1,019	1,023	51,054	53,303	56,772	60,096
Petroleum and coal products	142	138	135	135	54,739	56,188	60,037	64,215
Rubber and miscellaneous plastics products	963	965	982	997	29,867	30,898	32,253	33,691
Leather and leather products	106	95	89	84	22,321	23,589	25,281	26,345

Source: U.S. Bureau of Economics Analysis, *Survey of Current Business,* April 2000.

736 Manufactures

No. 1234. Manufactures' Shipments, Inventories, and New Orders: 1970 to 1999

[In billions of dollars, except ratio. (634 represents 634,000,000,000)]

Year	Shipments	Inventories (Dec, 31)[1]	Ratio of inventories to shipments[2]	New orders	Unfilled orders (Dec. 31)	Year	Shipments	Inventories (Dec, 31)[1]	Ratio of inventories to shipments[2]	New orders	Unfilled orders (Dec. 31)
1970	634	101	1.91	625	106	1985	2,334	330	1.72	2,348	384
1971	671	102	1.76	672	107	1986	2,336	318	1.63	2,342	390
1972	756	108	1.58	770	120	1987	2,476	333	1.58	2,513	427
1973	875	124	1.63	913	158	1988	2,695	363	1.56	2,739	471
1974	1,018	158	1.86	1,047	187	1989	2,840	385	1.65	2,875	505
1975	1,039	160	1.76	1,023	171	1990	2,912	398	1.70	2,934	527
1976	1,186	175	1.65	1,194	180	1991	2,878	384	1.65	2,866	515
1977	1,358	188	1.57	1,381	202	1992	3,005	375	1.47	2,979	489
1978	1,523	209	1.56	1,580	259	1993	3,128	376	1.44	3,092	453
1979	1,727	239	1.62	1,771	303	1994	3,348	396	1.38	3,357	462
1980	1,853	262	1.61	1,876	326	1995	3,595	421	1.42	3,608	475
1981	2,018	280	1.75	2,015	323	1996	3,715	427	1.39	3,749	509
1982	1,960	307	1.97	1,946	309	1997	3,929	446	1.36	3,952	532
1983	2,071	308	1.67	2,105	343	1998	4,052	456	1.36	4,034	513
1984	2,288	334	1.75	2,315	370	1999	4,260	460	1.28	4,279	533

[1] Beginning in 1982, inventories are stated at current cost and are not comparable to the book value estimates for prior years. [2] Ratio based on December seasonally adjusted data.

Source: U.S. Census Bureau, Current Industrial Reports, *Manufacturers' Shipments, Inventories, and Orders: 1987-1997*, Series M3-1(97); and earlier reports.

Figure 26.1
Gross Domestic Product in Manufacturing: 1990 to 1998

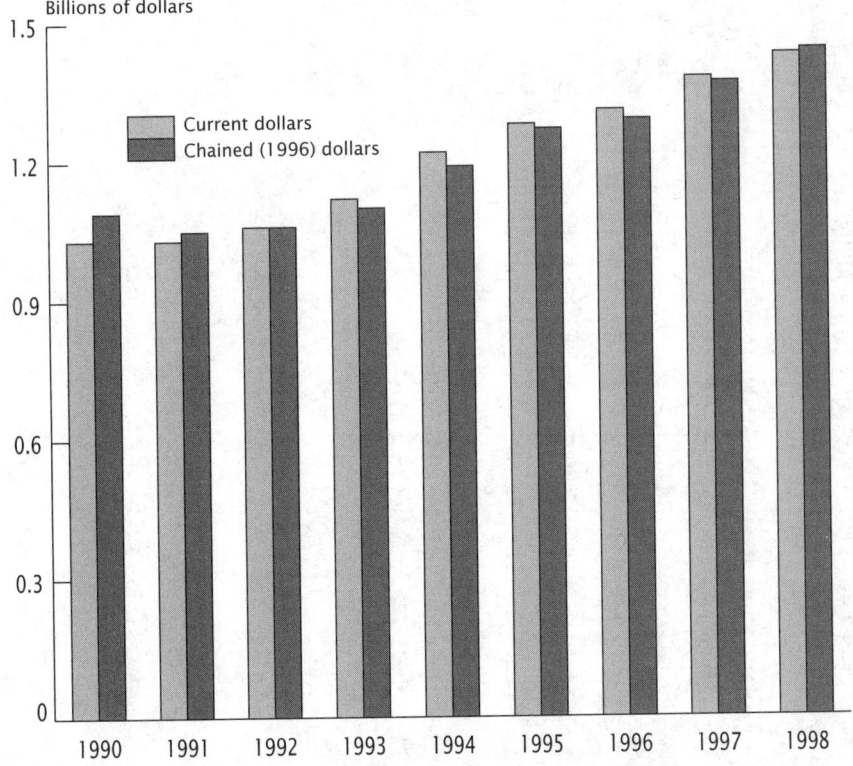

Source: Chart prepared by U.S. Census Bureau. For data, see Table 1229.

No. 1235. Value of Manufactures' Shipments, Inventories, and New Orders by Industry: 1995 to 1999

[In millions of dollars (3,594,663 represents 3,594,663,000,000). Based on 1987 Standard Industrial Classification (SIC). Based on a sample survey of most manufacturing companies with $500 million or more in annual shipments]

Industry	SIC code	Shipments					Inventories (Dec. 31)					New orders				
		1995	1996	1997	1998	1999	1995	1996	1997	1998	1999	1995	1996	1997	1998	1999
All manufacturing industries	D	3,594,663	3,715,460	3,929,419	4,052,248	4,259,532	421,285	427,130	446,131	456,330	460,048	3,607,586	3,749,299	3,952,025	4,033,676	4,279,186
Durable goods	(X)	1,927,029	2,004,159	2,158,699	2,275,987	2,407,473	261,138	266,547	278,766	287,415	287,124	1,941,378	2,036,536	2,180,708	2,259,693	2,425,161
Stone, clay, and glass products	32	75,932	82,442	90,221	96,193	103,773	8,359	8,679	8,832	9,103	9,682	76,085	82,142	89,893	96,088	103,939
Primary metals	33	180,314	178,297	188,916	180,973	178,466	24,052	24,385	24,785	24,797	24,445	178,702	180,362	193,987	175,482	180,740
Fabricated metal products	34	204,384	214,007	226,120	239,667	245,517	26,507	27,384	29,046	30,278	30,846	205,388	215,791	228,567	238,751	244,831
Industrial machinery and equipment	35	353,338	381,795	408,860	442,316	455,140	57,108	55,912	58,164	58,415	58,283	358,910	383,749	409,215	443,332	461,926
Computer and office equipment	357	91,343	103,270	111,334	129,875	138,900	12,630	10,277	9,869	8,343	8,179	91,045	103,689	108,986	130,184	139,640
Electronic and other	36	301,447	320,616	351,554	375,970	413,204	37,991	37,953	39,102	38,377	42,063	307,634	319,157	356,557	380,470	439,085
Electronic components	367	120,129	127,996	143,750	154,479	168,463	12,720	13,145	13,778	13,674	14,603	125,680	126,130	145,674	156,594	185,282
Transportation equipment [1]	37	461,806	465,173	502,301	536,896	583,559	57,663	62,347	66,877	73,157	66,729	465,839	495,239	507,667	524,963	567,357
Motor vehicles and parts	371	327,908	329,155	346,606	359,560	399,807	15,838	15,852	15,568	16,893	17,506	328,390	328,914	346,901	359,361	400,486
Instruments and related products	38	144,719	151,017	162,981	168,952	174,661	24,233	24,517	25,143	25,683	26,267	144,175	149,344	165,453	166,008	173,972
Nondurable goods [1]	(X)	1,667,634	1,711,301	1,770,720	1,776,261	1,852,059	160,147	160,583	167,365	168,915	172,924	1,666,208	1,712,763	1,771,317	1,773,983	1,854,025
Food and kindred products [1]	20	446,961	461,297	470,447	490,365	500,901	34,827	35,973	37,301	37,488	39,250	(NA)	(NA)	(NA)	(NA)	(NA)
Beverages	208	64,398	68,387	70,768	73,096	76,050	6,489	7,199	7,871	8,270	8,903	(NA)	(NA)	(NA)	(NA)	(NA)
Tobacco products	21	32,984	34,482	38,693	41,625	50,551	6,100	6,256	6,149	6,297	5,493	(NA)	(NA)	(NA)	(NA)	(NA)
Textile mill products	22	79,874	80,243	83,871	80,624	78,357	9,841	9,479	9,743	9,756	9,756	(NA)	(NA)	(NA)	(NA)	(NA)
Paper and allied products	26	173,716	160,661	161,992	165,429	164,558	17,173	15,887	16,108	16,254	15,955	(NA)	(NA)	(NA)	(NA)	(NA)
Chemicals and allied products [1]	28	361,391	367,674	389,189	391,700	413,277	39,604	40,794	43,880	45,696	47,055	(NA)	(NA)	(NA)	(NA)	(NA)
Industrial chemicals	281,2,6,8	186,970	184,018	193,265	179,798	183,405	19,157	19,603	20,335	19,910	19,673	(NA)	(NA)	(NA)	(NA)	(NA)
Drugs, soaps, toiletries	283-4	130,932	138,573	150,016	165,625	183,202	15,596	16,099	18,195	20,000	21,432	(NA)	(NA)	(NA)	(NA)	(NA)
Petroleum and coal products	29	151,439	174,284	177,314	145,673	171,149	10,829	12,046	11,806	9,863	11,741	(NA)	(NA)	(NA)	(NA)	(NA)
Rubber and plastics products	30	145,739	150,467	156,599	158,156	164,654	15,093	15,584	16,300	16,597	17,456	(NA)	(NA)	(NA)	(NA)	(NA)

NA Not available.   X Not applicable.   [1] Includes industries not shown separately.

Source: U.S. Census Bureau, Current Industrial Reports, Manufactures' Shipments, Inventories, and Orders: 1987-1997, Series M3-1(97); and <http://www.census.gov/indicator/www/m3/index.html> (accessed July 6 2000).

No. 1236. Value of Manufacturers' Shipments, Inventories, and New Orders by Market Grouping: 1995 to 1999

[In millions of dollars (3,594,663 represents 3,594,663,000,000). Based on 1987 Standard Industrial Classification (SIC). For definition of individual market groupings, see publication cited below. Based on a sample survey of most manufacturing companies with $500 million or more in annual shipments]

Market grouping	Shipments					Inventories (Dec. 31)					New orders				
	1995	1996	1997	1998	1999	1995	1996	1997	1998	1999	1995	1996	1997	1998	1999
All manufacturing industries ...	3,594,663	3,715,460	3,929,419	4,052,248	4,259,532	421,285	427,130	446,131	456,330	460,048	3,607,586	3,749,299	3,952,025	4,033,676	4,279,186
Market categories:															
Automotive equipment ...	160,793	162,253	169,145	174,876	195,472	7,537	7,697	7,755	8,265	8,411	160,887	162,310	169,310	174,795	195,553
Home goods and apparel ...	210,653	210,324	220,994	226,968	239,710	30,359	28,056	29,226	30,811	30,522	211,040	209,912	222,405	226,721	240,005
Consumer staples ...	742,164	780,340	809,598	830,771	887,224	65,704	67,944	71,473	72,343	75,925	742,360	780,545	809,563	830,983	888,027
Machinery and equipment ...	613,526	652,978	711,993	776,424	816,782	99,957	104,241	111,413	113,597	111,057	624,687	672,605	729,607	774,254	815,394
Business supplies ...	276,451	289,085	302,490	305,988	319,628	25,052	25,326	26,644	27,239	27,461	276,675	289,251	302,437	306,077	320,305
Construction materials and supplies ...	228,247	238,116	252,549	260,244	277,039	26,381	26,721	27,689	28,125	29,968	228,242	239,060	253,766	259,859	277,167
Defense products ...	78,031	75,896	79,523	83,246	82,205	17,146	16,067	16,442	18,604	18,171	76,598	81,145	72,066	76,617	80,373
Other material, supplies and intermediate products ...	1,284,798	1,306,468	1,383,127	1,393,731	1,441,472	149,149	151,078	155,489	157,346	158,533	1,287,097	1,314,471	1,392,871	1,384,370	1,462,362
Durable goods industries:															
Nondefense capital goods ...	475,387	512,068	563,933	624,534	659,952	94,498	98,027	104,787	106,039	101,952	486,134	535,575	577,978	620,400	659,457
Excluding aircraft and parts ...	413,760	448,495	483,149	528,855	561,200	68,579	66,453	69,237	67,978	70,626	418,414	450,084	490,101	532,260	569,833
Defense capital goods ...	73,415	71,947	75,194	79,672	79,401	17,305	16,178	16,693	19,019	18,612	70,903	77,283	67,706	73,169	77,328
Durables excluding capital goods ...	1,378,227	1,420,144	1,519,572	1,571,781	1,668,120	149,335	152,342	157,286	162,357	166,560	1,384,341	1,423,678	1,535,024	1,566,124	1,688,376
Miscellaneous series:															
Producers' durable equipment ...	1,225,170	1,285,908	1,383,145	1,476,942	1,569,970	165,868	171,014	179,571	184,320	184,005	1,240,694	1,304,326	1,405,864	1,473,332	1,566,941
Household durable goods ...	98,645	98,437	106,074	112,406	125,206	14,676	14,160	14,549	15,683	15,894	98,500	97,963	107,403	111,784	125,491
Information technology industries ...	223,048	247,295	270,844	298,064	324,882	34,170	31,765	32,528	30,317	32,727	223,687	246,156	272,605	299,210	330,613
Health care equipment and products ...	114,691	122,805	132,540	144,158	156,913	15,621	16,505	17,853	19,082	20,332	114,183	122,984	133,451	145,319	157,363

Source: U.S. Census Bureau, Current Industrial Reports, *Manufactures' Shipments, Inventories, and Orders: 1987-1997*, Series M3-1(97); and <http://www.census.gov/indicator/www/m3/index.html> (accessed July 6 2000).

Manufactures 739

No. 1237. Ratios of Manufacturers' Inventories to Shipments and Unfilled Orders to Shipments by Industry Group: 1995 to 1999

[Based on seasonally adjusted data]

Industry	Inventory/shipments ratio					Unfilled orders/shipments ratio				
	1995	1996	1997	1998	1999	1995	1996	1997	1998	1999
All manufacturing industries............	1.42	1.39	1.36	1.36	1.28	2.81	2.93	2.8	2.61	2.57
Durable goods industries	1.64	1.62	1.54	1.51	1.43	3.38	3.49	3.33	3.07	3.01
Stone, clay, and glass products .	1.31	1.31	1.18	1.12	1.11	1.08	0.99	0.83	0.75	0.71
Primary metals	1.62	1.59	1.57	1.74	1.54	1.89	1.97	2.24	2.08	2.02
Fabricated metal products.....	1.56	1.56	1.53	1.50	1.54	1.29	1.35	1.38	1.26	1.24
Industrial machinery and equipment................	1.91	1.77	1.69	1.64	1.56	2.29	2.23	2.06	2.02	2.1
Electronic and other electrical equipment................	1.50	1.44	1.33	1.21	1.20	1.96	1.82	1.81	1.83	2.36
Transportation equipment	1.54	1.67	1.59	1.58	1.38	5.65	6.44	5.84	5.08	4.54
Instruments and related products................	2.00	1.97	1.84	1.85	1.79	3.91	3.69	3.54	3.28	3.06
Nondurable goods industries.....	1.16	1.13	1.13	1.15	1.09	0.68	0.72	0.69	0.64	0.66
Food and kindred products	0.90	0.93	0.92	0.90	0.93	(NA)	(NA)	(NA)	(NA)	(NA)
Tobacco products...........	2.09	1.95	1.78	1.54	1.18	(NA)	(NA)	(NA)	(NA)	(NA)
Textile mill products	1.58	1.44	1.45	1.57	1.54	(NA)	(NA)	(NA)	(NA)	(NA)
Paper and allied products	1.23	1.22	1.13	1.20	1.12	(NA)	(NA)	(NA)	(NA)	(NA)
Chemicals and allied products ..	1.33	1.32	1.34	1.38	1.34	(NA)	(NA)	(NA)	(NA)	(NA)
Petroleum and coal products ...	0.89	0.81	0.88	0.93	0.70	(NA)	(NA)	(NA)	(NA)	(NA)
Rubber and plastics products...	1.25	1.26	1.22	1.25	1.22	(NA)	(NA)	(NA)	(NA)	(NA)

NA Not available.

Source: U.S. Census Bureau, Current Industrial Reports, *Manufacturers' Shipments, Inventories, and Orders: 1987-1997*, Series M3-1(97); earlier reports; and <http://www.census.gov/indicator/www/m3/index.html> (accessed March 20 2000).

No. 1238. Industrial Production Indexes by Industry: 1990 to 1999

[1992=100. Data based on 1987 Standard Industrial Classification (SIC)]

Industry	SIC code	1990	1991	1992	1993	1994	1995	1996	1997	1998	1999
Total index	(X)	98.9	97.0	100.0	103.4	109.1	114.4	119.4	127.1	132.4	137.1
Manufacturing	(X)	98.5	96.2	100.0	103.7	110.0	115.8	121.3	130.1	136.4	142.3
Durable goods...........	(X)	99.0	95.5	100.0	105.4	114.3	123.9	134.0	148.0	160.7	172.8
Lumber and products.....	24	101.6	94.5	100.0	100.8	105.9	107.9	110.1	115.0	118.5	121.6
Furniture and fixtures.....	25	100.9	94.8	100.0	104.9	108.1	111.4	113.1	118.0	122.0	125.5
Primary metals	33	104.0	96.7	100.0	105.1	113.8	116.2	119.6	126.7	125.6	126.6
Iron and steel	331,2	106.4	96.0	100.0	106.1	114.4	116.5	118.9	125.6	122.6	123.2
Fabricated metal products .	34	101.2	96.2	100.0	104.4	112.2	116.4	120.2	126.1	128.8	128.7
Industrial, commercial machinery [1]........	35	100.1	95.4	100.0	110.1	125.6	143.7	159.6	178.3	206.4	230.1
Computer and office equipment	357	81.4	82.3	100.0	121.2	152.9	208.8	296.0	403.9	675.1	106.1
Electrical machinery	36	87.7	89.6	100.0	109.4	130.5	165.7	206.6	260.0	315.1	390.2
Transportation equipment ..	37	102.3	96.5	100.0	103.5	107.5	106.7	107.6	117.1	121.6	122.4
Motor vehicles and parts.	371	95.3	88.5	100.0	113.0	130.6	133.2	131.8	140.6	141.7	151.0
Autos and light trucks .	371pt	99.3	91.0	100.0	111.3	125.4	122.4	121.1	127.1	127.8	137.8
Aerospace and miscella-neous	372- 6,9	109.8	105.0	100.0	93.9	84.9	81.0	83.9	94.2	101.7	94.9
Instruments	38	98.4	99.8	100.0	100.8	99.8	103.6	107.6	109.6	112.6	116.5
Nondurable goods	(X)	97.9	97.0	100.0	101.8	105.2	107.1	107.8	111.2	111.6	111.8
Foods................	20	97.0	98.4	100.0	102.0	103.7	105.8	105.4	107.8	109.3	110.1
Tobacco products	21	105.4	98.9	100.0	84.1	104.4	111.8	113.5	112.9	106.2	94.3
Textile mill products.....	22	93.2	92.7	100.0	105.3	110.6	110.2	108.7	111.9	110.9	110.9
Paper and products.....	26	96.0	96.8	100.0	104.0	108.4	109.6	108.8	114.3	114.9	116.2
Printing and publishing...	27	103.1	99.1	100.0	100.7	100.7	101.3	101.3	105.2	105.1	104.4
Chemicals and products...	28	97.3	96.4	100.0	101.6	104.8	107.4	109.8	114.6	115.1	117.5
Petroleum products	29	100.3	99.1	100.0	102.9	102.7	104.5	106.8	110.8	113.3	114.7
Rubber and plastics products	30	92.2	90.7	100.0	106.9	116.5	119.7	123.3	128.4	133.2	137.7
Leather and products.....	31	107.8	98.4	100.0	101.0	93.6	86.9	87.5	83.6	77.1	69.8
Mining	C	104.8	102.6	100.0	100.0	102.5	102.1	103.7	105.9	103.8	98.0
Metal mining	10	93.1	93.3	100.0	98.8	100.5	101.6	104.0	110.3	109.1	97.1
Coal mining............	12	103.7	100.1	100.0	94.0	103.0	102.6	105.0	108.2	109.7	108.1
Oil and gas extraction......	13	106.4	104.7	100.0	101.1	101.7	100.5	101.8	103.1	99.5	92.5
Stone and earth minerals....	14	103.3	96.7	100.0	102.3	108.6	112.9	114.9	120.1	123.4	124.4
Utilities.................	(X)	98.3	100.4	100.0	103.9	105.3	109.0	112.6	112.7	114.4	115.6
Electric.................	491,3pt	99.2	101.2	100.0	103.8	105.5	109.5	112.7	113.3	116.9	118.2
Gas	492.3pt	94.4	97.3	100.0	104.3	104.6	107.2	112.3	110.6	103.2	104.8

X Not applicable.   [1] Includes computer equipment.

Source: Board of Governors of the Federal Reserve System, *Federal Reserve Bulletin*, monthly; and *Industrial Production and Capacity Utilization*, Statistical Release G.17, monthly.

No. 1239. Index of Manufacturing Capacity: 1980 to 1999

[1992 output=100. Annual figures are averages of quarterly data. Capacity represents estimated quantity of output relative to output in 1992 which the *current* stock of plant and equipment in manufacturing industries was capable of producing. Primary processing industries comprise textiles, lumber, paper and pulp, petroleum, rubber, stone, clay, glass, primary metals, fabricated metals, and a portion of chemicals. Advanced processing industries comprise chemical products, food, beverages, tobacco, apparel, furniture, printing and publishing, leather, machinery, transportation equipment, instruments, ordnance, and miscellaneous industry groups]

Year	Index of capacity	Relation of output to capacity (percent)			Year	Index of capacity	Relation of output to capacity (percent)		
		All manu-facturing	Primary processing	Advanced processing			All manu-facturing	Primary processing	Advanced processing
1980	95	79	77	81	1990	121	81	84	80
1981	98	78	77	79	1991	123	78	80	77
1982	100	72	69	73	1992	126	79	82	78
1983	102	74	74	74	1993	129	80	84	79
1984	105	80	80	80	1994	133	83	87	80
1985	109	79	79	79	1995	140	83	87	81
1986	112	79	80	78	1996	149	82	85	80
1987	114	81	84	80	1997	158	82	86	81
1988	116	84	87	82	1998	168	81	84	80
1989	118	84	86	82	1999	178	80	83	79

Source: Board of Governors of the Federal Reserve System, *Capacity Utilization In Manufacturing, Mining, Utilities, and Industrial Materials*, G.3., monthly.

No. 1240. Finances and Profits of Manufacturing Corporations: 1990 to 1999

[In billions of dollars (2,811 represents 2,811,000,000,000). Data exclude estimates for corporations with less than $250,000 in assets at time of sample selection. See Table 900 for individual industry data]

Item	1990	1991	1992	1993	1994	1995	1996	1997	1998	1999
Net sales.................	2,811	2,812	2,813	3,014	3,256	3,528	3,758	3,920	3,949	4,137
Net operating profit	173	174	175	180	242	268	277	298	298	320
Net profit:										
Before taxes..............	158	159	160	118	244	274	307	331	315	356
After taxes..............	110	111	112	83	175	198	225	245	234	261
Cash dividends.............	62	63	64	67	70	81	96	108	121	102
Net income retained in business ..	48	49	50	16	105	117	129	136	114	158

Source: U.S. Census Bureau, *Quarterly Financial Report for Manufacturing, Mining, and Trade Corporations.*

No. 1241. U.S. Exports of Manufactures, Origin of World Exports of Manufacture: 1991 to 1997

[In billions of dollars (328 represents 328,000,000,000), except percents]

Item	1991	1992	1993	1994	1995	1996	1997
U.S. manufactures export value	328	350	365	409	464	498	566
Machinery & transport equipment............	200	215	225	252	283	308	354
Chemicals............................	43	45	46	52	62	63	71
Other	85	90	94	104	119	128	141
Origin of world exports of manufactures (percent):							
United States [1]	12.9	12.6	13.1	12.7	12.4	12.9	14.0
Machinery & transport equipment..........	15.9	15.8	16.4	15.7	14.9	15.4	16.9
Chemicals	14.4	13.4	13.9	13.5	13.3	13.2	14.5
Other	8.5	8.3	8.7	8.5	8.6	9.1	9.8
Germany	14.2	13.9	12.0	11.8	12.4	11.9	11.1
Japan	11.9	11.8	12.6	11.8	11.4	10.2	10.0
Other G-7 countries [2]	21.6	21.0	20.1	19.7	20.3	20.9	20.4
East Asian NICs [3]	8.2	8.1	8.8	8.9	9.4	9.3	9.3

[1] U.S. exports are domestic exports only.   [2] Other Group of Seven (G-7) Countries: Canada, France, Italy, United Kingdom.   [3] East Asian newly industrialized countries (NICs): Hong Kong, S. Korea, Singapore, Taiwan.

Source: U.S. Dept. of Commerce, International Trade Administration, Office of Trade and Economic Analysis. Based on United Nations Commodity Trade Statistics, *Statistical Yearbook of the Republic of China (Taiwan),* and unpublished data.

U.S. Census Bureau, Statistical Abstract of the United States: 2000

No. 1242. Alcoholic Beverages—Summary: 1990 to 1996

[**202 mil. bbl. represents 202,000,000.** For stocks on hand, years ending **September 30.** All other items for fiscal years ending in year shown; see text, Section 9, State and Local Government Finances and Employment. Includes Puerto Rico. Excludes imports]

Item	Unit	1990	1991	1992	1993	1994	1995	1996, prel.
Beer:								
Breweries operated	Number	286	333	392	480	619	879	1,504
Production [1]	Mil. bbl. [2]	202	204	202	202	203	200	199
Value of shipments [3]	Mil. dol. [2]	15,186	15,925	17,302	16,629	16,714	17,108	18,196
Tax-paid withdrawals	Mil. bbl. [2]	182	183	182	180	180	177	177
Stocks on hand	Mil. bbl. [2]	14	14	13.4	13.7	13.4	13.5	13.3
Distilled spirits:								
Production facilities operated . .	Number	143	145	143	132	150	153	(NA)
Production [1][4]	Mil. tax gal. [5] . .	122	129	110	111	99	104	(NA)
Tax-paid withdrawals [6]	Mil. tax gal. [5] . .	251	242	246	240	229	235	(NA)
Stocks on hand [4]	Mil. tax gal. [5] . .	451	459	365	420	410	452	(NA)
Whiskey:								
Production [1]	Mil. tax gal. [5] . .	77	75	62	59	59	69	(NA)
Stocks on hand	Mil. tax gal. [5] . .	365	368	309	361	354	358	(NA)
Still wines:								
Production	Mil. wine gal. [7] .	577	478	484	417	438	412	577
Tax-paid withdrawals [8]	Mil. wine gal. [7] .	468	387	387	354	356	366	382
Stocks on hand [9]	Mil. wine gal. [7] .	562	539	525	520	477	398	473

NA Not available. [1] Production represents total amount removed from fermenters, including distilling material, and includes increase after fermentation (by amelioration, sweetening, and addition of wine spirits). [2] Barrels of 31 wine gallons. [3] Source: U.S. Census Bureau, *Census of Manufactures,* and *Annual Survey of Manufactures.* [4] Excludes alcohol produced for industrial use. Also excludes vodka and gin production. [5] For spirits of 100 proof or over, a tax gallon is equivalent to the proof gallon; for spirits of less than 100 proof, the tax gallon is equivalent to the wine gallon. A proof gallon is the alcoholic equivalent of a U.S. gallon at 60 degrees F, containing 50 percent of ethyl alcohol by volume. [6] Includes ethyl alcohol. [7] A wine gallon is the U.S. gallon equivalent to the volume of 231 cubic inches. [8] Includes special natural wines. [9] Excludes distilling materials.

Source: Except as noted, U.S. Bureau of Alcohol, Tobacco, and Firearms, *Alcohol and Tobacco Summary Statistics,* annual; beginning 1985, *Monthly Statistical Release, Distilled Spirits,* Report Symbol 76; and *Wines,* Report Symbol, ATF A:I 5120-3.

No. 1243. Tobacco Products—Summary: 1990 to 1999

[Production data are for calendar years. Excludes cigars produced in customs bonded manufacturing warehouses]

Item	Unit	1990	1992	1993	1994	1995	1996	1997	1998	1999
PRODUCTION										
Cigarettes	Billions . .	710	719	661	726	747	758	720	680	635
Cigars	Billions . .	1.9	1.7	1.8	1.9	2.1	2.4	2.3	2.8	2.8
Tobacco [1]	Mil. lb. . . .	142	141	133	132	131	131	134	131	(NA)
Consumption per person [2] .	Lb. [3]	5.6	5.3	5.3	4.9	4.7	4.7	4.5	4.5	(NA)
Cigarettes	1,000 . .	3	3	3	3	3	3	2	2	(NA)
Cigars [4]	Number .	13	12	11	12	15	18	18	18	(NA)
Consumer expenditures . . .	Bil. dol. . .	43.8	48.4	49.0	47.7	48.7	50.4	52.2	57.3	(NA)
Cigarettes	Bil. dol. . .	41.6	45.8	46.2	44.5	45.8	47.2	48.7	53.2	(NA)
Cigars	Bil. dol. . .	0.7	0.6	0.7	0.9	1.0	1.0	1.2	1.6	(NA)
Other	Bil. dol. . .	1.5	2.0	2.1	2.3	2.5	2.2	2.2	2.4	(NA)

NA Not available. [1] Smoking and chewing tobaccos and snuff output. [2] Based on estimated population 18 years old and over, as of July 1, including Armed Forces abroad. [3] Unstemmed processing weight equivalent. [4] Weighing over 3 pounds per 1,000.

Source: U.S. Dept. of Agriculture, Economic Research Service, *Tobacco Situation and Outlook,* quarterly.

No. 1244. Cotton, Wool, and Manmade Fibers—Consumption by End-Use: 1998

[Represents products manufactured by U.S. mills. Excludes glass fiber]

Year	Cotton			Wool		Manufactured fibers					
								Artificial [1]		Synthetic [2]	
	Total (mil. lb.)	Total (mil. lb.)	Percent of end-use	Total (mil. lb.)	Percent of end-use	Total (mil. lb.)	Percent of end-use	Total (mil. lb.)	Percent of end-use	Total (mil. lb.)	Percent of end-use
Total	17,516	5,297	30.2	170	1.0	12,049	68.8	372	2.1	11,677	66.7
Apparel	6,414	3,229	50.3	113	1.8	3,072	47.9	209	3.3	2,863	44.6
Home textiles	2,781	1,661	59.7	15	0.5	1,106	39.8	67	2.4	1,038	37.3
Floor coverings	4,305	38	0.9	29	0.7	4,239	98.5	-	-	4,239	99
Industrial [3]	4,015	370	9.2	13	0.3	3,632	90.5	95	2.4	3,537	88.1

- Represents or rounds to zero. [1] Rayon and acetate. [2] Nylon, polyester, acrylic, and olefin. [3] Includes consumer-type products.

Source: Fiber Economics Bureau, Inc., Washington, DC, *Textile Organon,* monthly (copyright).

No. 1245. Broadwoven and Knit Fabrics—Shipments, Foreign Trade, and Apparent Consumption: 1998

[3,974,463 represents 3,974,463,000. Fabric blends as shown in the CIR report, MQ22T, are reported based on the chief weight of the fiber; whereas, fabrics blends as shown for imports are based on the chief value of the fiber. Apparent consumption represents new domestic supply and is derived by subtracting exports for the total manufacturers' shipments plus imports]

Product description	Manufac- turers' ship- ments (quantity)	Imports for consumption		Percent imports to manufac- turers' ship- ments	Exports of domestic merchandise		Percent exports to manufac- turers' ship- ments	Apparent consump- tion (quantity)
		Quantity	Value [1] ($1,000)		Quantity	Value ($1,000)		
BROADWOVEN FABRICS (quantity 1,000 sq. meters)								
Cotton fabrics [2]	3,974,463	1,563,075	1,678,463	39.3	309,440	711,702	7.8	5,228,098
Manmade fiber fabrics	9,616,057	1,107,941	1,367,862	11.5	448,613	992,696	4.7	10,275,385
Silk fabrics	382	31,470	299,883	8,235.9	2,608	20,630	682.5	29,244
Wool fabrics	110,546	32,674	317,680	29.6	15,251	80,796	13.8	127,969
KNIT FABRICS (quantity in 1,000 kilograms)								
Total	883,780	107,877	907,618	12.2	71,174	600,897	8.1	(NA)
Pile fabrics	80,558	35,763	312,688	44.4	20,210	180,668	25.1	(NA)
Elastic fabric	46,296	13,430	171,645	29.0	10,994	110,955	23.7	(NA)
Other warp knit fabrics	122,991	11,659	111,206	9.5	6,395	70,248	5.2	(NA)
Other narrow knit fabrics	20,810	1,117	14,094	5.4	2,806	37,816	13.5	(NA)
Other knit fabrics	613,126	45,908	297,985	7.5	30,769	201,210	5.0	(NA)

NA Not available. [1] Dollar value represents the c.i.f. (cost, insurance, and freight) at the first port of entry in the United States plus calculated import duty. [2] Includes all cotton and chiefly cotton mixed with manmade fiber.

Source: U.S. Census Bureau, *Manufacturing Profiles*, Series MP/98; <http://www.census.gov/ftp/pub/industry/1/mq22t985.pdf> (issued 18 June 1999); and <http://www.census.gov/ftp/pub/industry/1/ ma22k98.pdf> (issued December 1999).

No. 1246. Selected Apparel—Shipments, Foreign Trade, and Apparent Consumption: 1998

[Quantity in thousands of units (12,885 represents 12,885,000), value in millions of dollars (186.3 represents $186,300,000)]

Product description	Manufactures' shipments		Exports of domestic merchandise		Imports for consumption		Apparent consumption	
	Quantity	Value	Quantity	Value	Quantity	Value	Quantity	Value
Men's and boys' apparel:								
Sweaters	12,885	186.3	58,956	167.5	61,776	802.8	15,705	821.6
Tops, except sweaters	(D)	(D)	510,000	1,172.2	1,946,256	10,110.7	(D)	(D)
Bottoms	(D)	(D)	300,984	1,107.6	797,808	5,986.5	(D)	(D)
Coats:	53,684	1,857.8	19,068	138.8	164,436	3,020.0	199,052	4,739.0
Suit type, dress and sport	(D)	(D)	5,352	47.3	14,892	579.5	(D)	(D)
Other coats	(D)	(D)	13,716	91.5	149,544	2,440.5	(D)	(D)
Suits	8,885	726.4	1,704	25.2	97,464	752.1	104,645	1,453.3
Swimwear	1,444	22.9	1,548	7.6	43,992	185.1	43,888	200.4
Women's and girls' apparel:								
Sweaters	41,363	652.4	2,196	10.7	229,584	2,715.4	268,751	3,357.1
Dresses	198,680	4,660.9	21,504	123.5	219,252	2,263.2	396,428	6,800.6
Tops, except sweaters	563,612	4,103.9	226,020	460.4	1,429,104	8,612.0	1,766,696	12,255.5
Skirts	76,711	1,116.7	12,780	65.6	143,940	1,245.5	207,871	2,296.6
Coats and jackets	46,529	1,630.7	18,888	154.2	157,944	2,965.0	185,585	4,441.5
Bottoms, except skirts	(D)	(D)	179,280	606.7	687,612	5,098.7	(D)	(D)
Suits	8,354	306.8	8,112	61.8	131,040	456.5	131,282	701.5
Swimwear	51,706	805.5	13,452	58.5	46,788	293.5	85,042	1,040.5
Infants' apparel	159,157	880.2	145,956	205.3	614,496	1,630.9	627,697	2,305.8

D Data withheld to avoid disclosing figures for individual companies.

Source: U.S. Census Bureau, *Manufacturing Profiles*, Series MP/98; <http://www/census.gov/ftp/pub/industry/1/mq23A985.pdf> (released 03 September 1999).

No. 1247. Footwear—Production, Foreign Trade, and Apparent Consumption: 1998

[Quantity in thousands of pairs (156,031 represents 156,031,000 pairs), value in thousands of dollars (369,770 represents 369,770,000)]

Product description	Manufacturers' shipments (quantity)	Exports of domestic merchandise		Percent exports to domestic production	Imports for consumption		Apparent consumption (quantity)	Percent imports to apparent consumption
		Quantity	Value		Quantity	Value		
Total	156,031	22,364	369,770	14.3	1,479,740	13,490,309	1,613,407	91.7
Rubber or plastic uppers and rubber or plastics	17,632	4,087	41,157	23.2	547,089	3,158,395	560,634	97.6
Waterproof	9,129	841	8,945	9.2	8,048	48,062	16,336	49.3
Not waterproof	8,503	3,246	32,212	38.2	539,041	3,110,333	544,298	99.0
Leather uppers	53,509	9,739	237,698	18.2	642,448	9,044,193	686,218	93.6
Athletic	5,588	5,812	124,906	104.0	474,084	5,901,426	473,860	100.0
Leather soles	18,622	2,680	78,664	14.4	44,828	1,050,253	60,770	73.8
Made with steel safety toes . .	1,566	236	12,125	15.1	7,984	165,211	9,314	85.7
Boots, ex. with steel safety toes	6,994	401	13,739	5.7	4,511	102,173	11,104	40.6
Shoes, ex. with steel safety toes	10,062	2,043	52,800	20.3	32,333	782,869	40,352	80.1
Other soles	32,311	1,247	34,128	3.9	123,536	2,092,514	154,600	79.9
Made with steel safety toes . .	1,895	-	-	(NA)	-	-	1,895	(NA)
Boots, ex. with steel safety toes	5,499	1,247	34,128	22.7	123,536	2,092,514	127,788	96.7
Shoes, ex. with steel safety toes	24,917	-	-	(NA)	-	-	24,917	(NA)
Fabric uppers	76,434	8,538	90,915	11.2	290,203	1,287,721	358,099	81.0
Rubber or plastic soles	48,682	6,951	78,209	14.3	224,979	844,665	266,710	84.4
Athletic	(D)	5,582	63,556	(D)	36,181	166,595	(D)	(D)
All other	(D)	1,369	14,653	(D)	188,798	678,070	(D)	(D)
With all other soles	27,752	1,587	12,706	5.7	65,224	443,056	91,389	71.4

- Represents zero. D Data withheld to avoid disclosure. NA Not available.

Source: U.S. Census Bureau, *Manufacturing Profiles*, Series MP/98, annual; and <ftp://ftp.census.gov/pub/industry/1/ma31a98.pdf> (released February 2000).

No. 1248. Inorganic Fertilizers, Chemicals, and Pharmaceutical Preparations—Value of Shipments: 1990 to 1998

[In millions of dollars (1,072 represents 1,072,000,000)]

Product	Product code	Unit	1990	1995	1996	1997	1998
INORGANIC FERTILIZERS							
Ammonia, synthetic anhydrous	28731 31	Mil. dol . . .	1,072	1,662	1,690	1,578	1,214
Ammonium sulfate	28731 57	Mil. dol . . .	130	1,953	214	181	181
Urea (100%)	28732	Mil. dol . . .	640	848	912	772	667
Nitric acid (100%).	28731 11	Mil. dol . . .	81	168	197	216	160
Phosphoric acid (100% P2O5)	28741 81,85	Mil. dol . . .	1,226	1,220	1,227	1,405	1,515
Sulfuric acid, gross (100%)	28193	Mil. dol . . .	589	539	578	577	683
Superphosphates and other fertilizer materials. .	28742	Mil. dol . . .	2,711	3,594	3,928	3,692	3,047
INORGANIC CHEMICAL SHIPMENTS							
Alkalies and chlorine.	2812	Mil. dol . . .	3,187	3,169	3,212	3,067	2,905
Inorganic color pigments	2816	Mil. dol . . .	2,261	2,284	2,487	2,606	2,526
Inorganic chemicals n.e.c.	2819	Mil. dol . . .	13,612	14,179	14,526	14,319	14,237
Household bleaching compounds	28422 00	Mil. dol . . .	724	923	891	968	(S)
PHARMACEUTICAL PREP. SHIPMENTS							
Pharmaceutical preparations, except biologicals		**Mil. dol . . .**	**33,954**	**48,864**	**51,844**	**57,419**	**67,275**
Affecting neoplasms, endocrine systems, and metabolic disease.	28341	Mil. dol . . .	2,743	4,076	4,788	5,466	6,916
Acting on the central nervous system and sense organs.	28342	Mil. dol . . .	7,219	9,228	10,123	11,708	14,661
Acting on the cardiovascular system	28343	Mil. dol . . .	4,815	5,988	6,912	8,799	8,909
Acting on the respiratory system	28344	Mil. dol . . .	3,724	5,196	4,994	5,641	7,443
Acting on the digestive system	28345	Mil. dol . . .	4,840	8,593	8,494	9,482	9,957
Acting on the skin.	28346	Mil. dol . . .	1,558	2,171	2,185	1,867	2,128
Vitamin, nutrient, and hematinic preps.	28347	Mil. dol . . .	2,588	4,812	5,281	5,088	5,707
Affecting parasitic and infective disease	28348	Mil. dol . . .	5,411	7,196	7,304	7,795	9,745
Pharmaceutical preps. for veterinary use	28349	Mil. dol . . .	1,057	1,605	1,763	1,572	1,808

S Does not meet publication standards.

Source: U.S. Census Bureau, through 1992, *Current Industrial Reports*, MA28A, and MA28G, annual; thereafter, *Manufacturing Profiles*, Series MP, annual.

744 Manufactures

No. 1249. Fiber, Rugs, Carpeting, and Sheets—Shipments: 1990 to 1998

[812 represents 812,000,000]

Product	Unit	1990	1993	1994	1995	1996	1997	1998
All fibers [1]	Mil. lbs . . .	812	1,008	1,036	953	912	905	833
Raw wool [2][3]	Mil. lbs . . .	133	157	153	142	142	144	115
Noils, and fiber [4]	Mil. lbs . . .	20	23	19	20	23	20	11
Other fibers	Mil. lbs . . .	659	829	864	792	748	740	708
Knit fabric production	Mil. lbs . . .	1,901	2,188	2,211	2,131	1,919	2,174	1,866
Rugs, carpet and carpeting . .	Mil. dol . . .	8,527	9,283	9,531	9,770	10,148	10,264	10,853
Sheets	1,000 doz. .	14,716	16,331	16,190	15,282	16,108	19,745	20,095
Pillow cases	1,000 doz. .	12,443	14,464	14,622	14,232	14,234	17,520	18,473
Terry towels	1,000 doz. .	41,855	47,161	48,348	47,939	46,991	44,980	43,084

[1] Includes man-made fiber top converted from tow without combing. A number of companies were added for 1990 based on information in the 1987 Census of Manufactures. Data were received from these companies for 1990. These changes represent approximately 20 percent of the total fibers consumed on the woolen system and worsted combing. [2] Data are shown on a scoured basis for greasy wool. [3] Shorn and pulled wool of sheep excludes raw wool consumed in cotton system spinning to avoid disclosing figures for individual companies. [4] Includes reprocessed and reused wool, mohair, alpaca, vicuna, and other specialty fibers as well as tops and noils consumed in woolen spinning and mohair consumed in worsted combing. Does not include wool tops consumed in cotton system spinning.

Source: U.S. Census Bureau, 1990 and 1992, *Current Industrial Reports*, MA22K, MA22Q, and MQ23X, annual; thereafter, *Manufacturing Profiles*, Series MP, annual.

No. 1250. Glass Containers, Clay Construction Products, and Refractories—Value of Shipments: 1990 to 1998

[In millions of dollars (285 represents 285,000,000)]

Product	1990	1993	1994	1995	1996	1997	1998
Glass container shipments	285	290	285	269	257	254	254
Brick shipments [1]	1,014	990	1,102	1,092	1,235	1,331	1,453
Clay tile shipments [2]	687	687	756	728	779	834	837
Clay pipe and fittings shipments	60	33	33	35	45	47	48
Refractory shipments	2,003	1,930	2,047	2,222	2,341	2,566	2,379
Clay	771	773	906	941	930	1,084	1,025
Nonclay	1,232	1,157	1,141	1,282	1,411	1,482	1,354

[1] Building or common and face bricks. [2] Floor and wall tile including quarry tile.

Source: U.S. Census Bureau, 1990 and 1992, *Current Industrial Reports*, M32G, MQ32D, and MA32C, annual; thereafter, *Manufacturing Profiles*, Series MP, annual.

No. 1251. Aluminum Mill Products—Shipments by Product: 1997 and 1998

[Shipments in thousands of pounds (16,311,489 represents 16,311,489,000), receipts in thousands of dollars (1,321,202 represents 1,321,202,000)]

Product description	1997			1998		
	Gross shipments	Total receipts	Net shipments [1]	Gross shipments	Total receipts	Net shipments [1]
Aluminum mill products, total .	16,311,489	1,321,202	14,990,287	16,545,857	1,367,202	15,178,655
Sheet, plate, and foil	11,165,874	775,043	10,390,831	11,278,670	834,265	10,444,405
Sheet	9,624,301	775,043	8,849,258	9,717,288	834,265	8,883,023
Plate	402,487	-	402,487	408,596	-	408,596
Foil	1,139,086	-	1,139,086	1,152,786	-	1,152,786
Rod, wire, and cable	1,140,801	446,287	694,514	1,192,477	456,286	736,191
Rod and bare wire	504,370	446,287	58,083	545,514	456,286	89,228
Cable and insulated wire	636,431	-	636,431	646,963	-	646,963
Rod, bar, pipe, tube and shapes	3,646,886	99,872	3,547,014	3,714,040	76,651	3,637,389
Rod and bar (rolled and extruded). . . .	471,565	99,872	371,693	468,805	76,651	392,154
Pipe and tube (extruded and drawn) . .	341,442	(D)	341,442	359,250	(D)	359,250
Extruded shapes	2,833,879	-	2,833,879	2,885,985	-	2,885,985
All other	357,928	-	357,928	360,670	-	360,670

- Represents zero. D Withheld to avoid disclosure of individual companies. [1] Net shipments are derived by subtracting domestic receipts from gross shipments.

Source: U.S. Census Bureau, *Manufacturing Profiles, 1997*, Series MP/97; and <http://www.census.gov/ftp/pub/industry/1/m33d9813.pdf> (issued 30 June 1999).

[For financial data, the universe in 1992 consists of the companies that produced 68 percent of the total reported raw steel production. The financial data represent the operations of the steel segment of the companies. Minus sign (-) indicates net loss]

Item	Unit	1990	1992	1993	1994	1995	1996	1997	1998
Steel mill products, apparent supply . . .	Mil. tons [1]..	97.8	95.0	104.6	121.3	114.8	125.0	131.0	138.4
Net shipments.	Mil. tons [1]..	85.0	82.2	89.0	95.1	97.5	100.9	105.9	102.4
Exports	Mil. tons [1]..	4.3	4.3	4.0	3.8	7.1	5.0	6.0	5.5
Imports	Mil. tons [1]..	17.2	17.1	19.5	30.1	24.4	29.2	31.2	41.5
Scrap consumed.	Mil. tons [1]..	50.1	51.9	58.5	60.0	62.0	62.0	64.0	60.6
Scrap inventory.	Mil. tons [1]..	3.6	3.3	3.6	4.0	4.1	5.3	5.0	4.5
Iron and steel products:									
Exports	Mil. tons [1]..	5.3	5.3	4.7	4.9	8.2	6.2	7.4	6.9
Imports	Mil. tons [1]..	21.9	21.9	21.8	32.7	27.3	32.1	34.4	45.4
Capacity by steelmaking process	Mil. net tons	116.7	113.1	109.9	108.2	112.4	116.1	121.4	125.3
Revenue	Bil. dol.. .	30.9	26.9	29.5	34.1	35.1	35.0	35.9	35.8
Net income	Bil. dol.. .	0.1	-4.1	1.9	1.3	1.5	0.4	1.1	1.0
Stockholders' equity.	Bil. dol.. .	2.1	2.8	-0.6	3.7	7.4	10.2	10.9	10.8
Total assets	Bil. dol.. .	28.3	28.8	30.6	34.3	35.1	35.8	37.0	40.1
Capital expenditures	Bil. dol.. .	2.6	1.8	1.5	2.2	2.5	2.3	2.6	2.7
Working capital ratio [2]	Ratio	1.8	1.4	1.5	1.5	1.6	1.7	1.6	1.5
Inventories.	Bil. dol.. .	4.7	4.5	4.6	5.0	5.1	5.4	5.6	6.6
Average employment.	1,000	164	140	127	126	123	119	112	110
Hours worked.	Million	350	293	274	273	269	259	247	240
Index of output, all employees [3].	1987=100 . .	109.6	117.1	133.5	142.4	142.7	153.6	(NA)	(NA)
Producer price indexes: [4]									
Iron and steel, total	1982=100..	117.2	111.5	116.0	122.0	128.8	125.8	126.5	122.6
Steel mill products	1982=100..	112.1	106.4	108.2	113.4	120.1	115.6	116.4	113.9
Electrometallurgical products	1982=100..	120.1	115.5	115.7	117.0	126.0	157.7	163.0	158.9
Iron ore	1982=100..	83.3	83.7	82.7	82.7	91.8	96.7	96.3	95.5
Scrap, iron and steel	1982=100..	166.0	139.2	172.5	192.9	202.7	191.1	188.9	164.9
Foundry and forge shop products . . .	1982=100..	117.2	120.1	121.3	123.9	129.3	132.6	134.1	135.0

NA Not available.   [1] In millions of short tons.   [2] Current assets to current liabilities.   [3] Output per hour. Source: U.S. Bureau of Labor Statistics, Internet site <http://stats.bls.gov/iprhome.htm>.   [4] Source: U.S. Bureau of Labor Statistics, *Producer Price Indexes,* monthly and annual.

Source: American Iron and Steel Institute, Washington, DC, *Annual Statistical Report* (copyright).

No. 1253. Raw Steel, Pig Iron, and Ferroalloys Production: 1990 to 1998

[In millions (849.4 represents 849,400,000), except percent]

Item	1990	1992	1993	1994	1995	1996	1997	1998
Raw steel (net tons):								
World production.	849.4	797.0	802.0	799.6	829.4	826.9	874.9	856.8
U.S. production.	98.9	92.9	97.9	100.6	104.9	105.3	108.6	108.8
Percent of world	11.6	11.8	12.2	12.6	12.6	12.7	12.4	12.7
Furnace:								
Basic oxygen process . .	58.5	57.6	59.3	61.0	62.5	60.4	61.1	59.7
Electric	36.9	35.3	38.5	39.6	42.4	44.9	47.5	49.1
Open hearth.	3.5	-	-	-	-	-	-	-
Grade:								
Carbon	86.6	82.5	86.9	89.5	92.7	93.6	95.9	97.1
Alloy and stainless.	12.3	10.4	11.0	11.1	12.3	11.7	12.6	11.7
Pig iron and ferroalloys production (sh. tons)	54.8	52.2	53.1	54.4	56.1	54.5	54.7	53.2

- Represents or rounds to zero.

Source: American Iron and Steel Institute, Washington, DC, *Annual Statistical Report* (copyright).

No. 1254. Steel Products—Net Shipments by Market Classes: 1990 to 1998

[In thousands of short tons (84,981 represents 84,981,000). Comprises carbon, alloy, and stainless steel]

Market class	1990	1992	1993	1994	1995	1996	1997	1998
Total [1]	84,981	82,241	89,022	95,084	97,494	100,878	105,858	102,420
Automotive.	11,100	11,092	12,719	14,753	14,622	14,665	15,251	15,842
Steel service centers, distributors.	21,111	21,328	23,714	24,153	23,751	27,124	27,800	27,751
Construction, incl. maintenance [2]	9,245	9,536	13,429	10,935	14,892	15,561	15,885	15,289
Containers, packaging, shipping.	4,474	3,974	4,355	4,495	4,139	4,101	4,163	3,829
Machinery, industrial equipment, to. . . .	2,388	1,951	2,191	2,427	2,310	2,410	2,355	2,147
Steel for converting and processing . . .	9,441	9,226	9,451	10,502	10,440	10,245	11,263	9,975
Rail transportation.	1,080	1,052	1,223	1,248	1,373	1,400	1,410	1,657
Contractors' products.	2,870	2,694	2,913	3,348	(2)	(2)	(2)	(2)
Oil and gas industries	1,892	1,454	1,526	1,703	2,643	3,254	3,811	2,649
Electrical equipment.	2,453	2,136	2,213	2,299	2,397	2,401	2,434	2,255
Appliances, utensils, and cutlery	1,540	1,503	1,592	1,736	1,589	1,713	1,635	1,729

[1] Includes nonclassified shipments and other classes not shown separately.   [2] Beginning 1994, contractors' products included with construction.

Source: American Iron and Steel Institute, Washington, DC, *Annual Statistical Report* (copyright).

No. 1255. U.S. Machine Tool Consumption—Gross New Orders and Exports: 1998 and 1999

[Value in millions of dollars (5,931 represents $5,931,000,000)]

Item	1998				1999			
	Total	Metal cutting machines	Metal forming machines	Other manufac-turing technol-ogy	Total	Metal cutting machines	Metal forming machines	Other manufac-turing technology
New order units, total . . .	37,100	30,561	3,784	2,754	26,693	21,820	3,035	1,839
Northeast [1]	6,278	5,073	751	454	4,779	4,025	461	293
South [2]	5,535	4,442	646	447	4,418	3,571	506	341
Midwest [3]	13,476	11,154	1,295	1,027	9,129	7,406	1,067	657
Central [4]	7,592	6,327	703	562	4,530	3,518	690	323
West [5]	4,218	3,565	389	263	3,837	3,300	312	225
New order value, total . . .	5,931	4,578	627	725	4,281	3,354	447	481
Northeast [1]	792	633	91	68	674	571	50	54
South [2]	848	628	100	120	641	490	63	88
Midwest [3]	2,760	2,087	267	406	1,843	1,429	175	238
Central [4]	960	765	93	103	680	478	114	89
West [5]	571	467	76	28	442	386	44	12
Export order units [6]	2,232	1,770	226	236	1,564	1,318	153	93
Export order value [6]	451	330	64	56	434	349	35	50

[1] Covers Maine, New Hampshire, Vermont, New York, Massachusetts, Connecticut, Rhode Island, New Jersey, and Pennsylvania. [2] Covers Delaware, Maryland, Virginia, West Virginia, Kentucky, North Carolina, South Carolina, Tennessee, Mississippi, Alabama, Georgia, and Florida. [3] Covers Wisconsin, Michigan, Ohio, Illinois, and Indiana. [4] Covers Minnesota, North Dakota, South Dakota, Montana, Wyoming, Idaho, Iowa, Nebraska, Kansas, Missouri, Oklahoma, Arkansas, Louisiana, Texas, New Mexico, Colorado, and Utah. [5] Covers Washington, Oregon, California, Nevada, and Arizona. [6] Represents orders placed with U.S. builders.

Source: The Association for Manufacturing Technology, Mclean, VA, and American Machine Tool Distributors Association, Rockville, MD, U.S. Machine Tool Consumption Report, monthly.

No. 1256. Metalworking Machinery—Shipments: 1990 to 1999

[In millions of dollars (3,426.1 represents $3,426,100,000)]

Product	Product code	1990	1994	1995	1996	1997	1998	1999
Metalworking machinery	(X)	3,426.1	3,780.1	4,547.1	4,607.8	5,010.3	4,817.1	3,783.3
Metal cutting type [1]	(X)	2,371.3	2,463.0	3,036.6	3,141.1	3,583.3	3,481.8	2,512.6
Boring machines [2]	333512A1	(²)	129.8	172.4	88.9	80.2	73.6	53.8
Drilling machines [2]	333512A1	184.1	52.0	78.9	99.5	89.2	102.9	50.6
Gear cutting machines	33351211	102.7	100.6	137.1	164.3	213.5	197.7	132.0
Grinding and polishing machines . .	33351220	433.6	443.3	549.6	541.3	595.0	535.5	477.1
Lathes [3]	33351230	355.6	390.8	478.0	451.1	480.7	472.9	297.4
Milling machines [4]	33351240	214.3	138.9	194.8	199.7	280.2	281.1	200.5
Machining centers [5]	33351270	437.0	552.4	698.8	779.4	931.6	897.3	597.9
Station type machines	33351280	502.1	455.1	477.0	498.6	551.9	571.0	407.1
Other metal cutting machine tools [6]	33351290	141.9	200.1	246.2	316.0	358.3	344.6	291.7
Metal forming type	(X)	1,080.2	1,317.1	1,510.5	1,466.6	1,427.0	1,335.3	1,270.7
Punching and shearing machines . . .	33351310 pt.	200.1	294.4	326.3	331.4	319.2	254.3	220.0
Bending and forming machines	33351310 pt.	222.9	253.2	256.9	283.0	258.5	262.7	265.8
Presses, except forging	33351330	308.3	376.4	379.2	402.0	422.4	399.5	433.7
Forging machines [7]	33351350 pt.	73.9	(D)	(D)	(D)	(D)	(D)	(D)
Other metal forming [7]	33351350 pt.	275.0	393.0	548.1	450.2	426.9	418.8	351.2

D Data withheld to avoid disclosure. X Not applicable. [1] Data for "All lathes (turning machines)" and "All milling machines," valued at under $3,025 each are included in total "Metal cutting type" for 1995 through 1999. [2] For 1990, data for "Boring machines" were combined with "Drilling machines" to avoid disclosing individual company data. [3] For 1994 through 1999 product code 35415, "Lathes," excludes the value for product code 35415 09, All Lathes valued under $3,025 each. [4] For 1994 through 1999 product code 35416, "Milling machines," excludes the value for product code 35416 09, "All milling machines valued under $3,025 each." [5] Multi-function numerically controlled machines. [6] Excludes those designed primarily for home workshops, labs, etc. [7] For 1994 through 1999, data for "Forging machines" have been combined with "Other metal forming machines" to avoid disclosing individual company.

Source: U.S. Census Bureau, Manufacturing Profiles, Series MP, annual; and release date: July 2000, <http://www.census.gov/ftp/pub/industry/1/mq35w995.pdf>.

Manufactures 747

No. 1257. Selected Types of Construction Machinery—Value of Shipments: 1990 to 1998

[In millions of dollars (2,235.9 represents 2,235,900,000]

Product description	Product code	1990	1994	1995	1996	1997	1998
Tractor shovel loaders	33312014	2,235.9	2,632.6	3,041.8	3,340.1	3,912.5	3,991.2
Power cranes, draglines, and shovels	33312011	1,511.8	2,252.5	2,561.4	2,740.3	2,927.4	3,362.4
Mixers, pavers, and related equipment	33312012	609.6	1,079.8	1,168.8	1,145.8	1,283.8	1,460.0
Off-highway trucks, truck-type tractor, chassis trailers, coal haulers, or wagons.	33312013	1,453.1	(D)	1,597.4	1,697.2	1,596.3	1,436.1
Motor graders and light maintainers	33312016	408.0	445.2	479.9	588.4	(D)	(D)
Rough terrain forklifts	33312016	209.3	270.9	355.4	412.3	499.5	668.2
Equipment for mounting on tractors	258.6	(X)	286.6	(X)	(X)	(X)	(X)
Self-propelled continuous ditchers and trenchers	33312016	129.7	174.0	193.5	209.1	238.7	266.1
Construction machinery for mounting on trucks, tractors, and other prime movers . . .	33312017	(NA)	(NA)	(NA)	214.5	258.6	272.5
Aerial work platforms	33392372	814.9	844.9	1,131.1	(D)	(D)	2,040.3

D Data withheld to avoid disclosing figures for individual companies.   NA Not available.   X Not applicable.

Source: U.S. Census Bureau, *Manufacturing Profiles*, Series MP, annual; and <http://www.census.gov/ftp/pub/industry/1/ma35d98.pdf> (released February 2000).

No. 1258. Mining and Mineral Processing Equipment—Shipments: 1997 and 1998

Product	Product code	Number of companies 1998	Quantity (units)		Value (mil. dol.)	
			1997	1998	1997	1998
Mining and mineral processing equipment .	**(X)**	**(X)**	**(X)**	**(X)**	**2,051**	**1,856**
Portable crushing, screening, washing, and combination plants	33312081	17	1,256	941	151	146
Underground mining machinery [1]	33313110	26	16,763	16,902	680	444
Crushing/pulverizing/screening machinery [2]	33313150	37	4,123	4,512	416	364
Drills and other mining machinery, n.e.c. [1] [3]	33313171	27	13,562,410	12,601,726	285	420
Portable drilling rigs and parts	3331327	28	3,341,598	2,631,443	519	482

X Not applicable.   [1] Excludes parts.   [2] Excludes portables and parts.   [3] N.e.c. = Not elsewhere classified.

Source: U.S. Census Bureau, *Manufacturing Profiles*, Series MP, annual; and <http://www.census.gov/ftp/pub/industry/1/ma35f98.pdf>.

No. 1259. Engines, Refrigeration and Heating Equipment, and Pumps and Compressors—Shipments: 1995 to 1998

[23,274 represents 23,274,000]

Product	Product code	Unit	1995	1996	1997	1998
Internal combustion engines produced	**(X)**	**1,000 . . . .**	**23,274**	**23,353**	**25,077**	**27,523**
Gasoline (except outboard, aircraft, and auto) . . .	35191	1,000	22,287	22,659	23,989	26,352
Nonautomotive diesel (except aircraft)	35193	1,000	246	270	300	296
Automotive diesel	35194	1,000	732	685	771	851
Natural gas and LPG	35196	1,000	9	9	18	24
Air-conditioning, heating equipment shipments:						
Heat transfer equipment	35851	Mil. dol . . .	(NA)	4,280	4,246	4,472
Room air-conditioners and dehumidifiers	35856	Mil. dol . . .	(NA)	1,020	1,020	1,098
Motor vehicle mechanical air-conditioning systems.	35857	Mil. dol . . .	(NA)	2,208	2,221	2,100
Compressors and compressor units	3585A	Mil. dol . . .	(NA)	3,092	2,796	2,814
Automotive air-conditioning compressors	3585B	Mil. dol . . .	(NA)	1,652	1,951	1,977
Nonelectric warm air furnaces and dehumidifiers .	3585C	Mil. dol . . .	(NA)	1,562	1,558	1,607
Unitary air conditioners	3585E	Mil. dol . . .	(NA)	4,625	4,615	5,229
Air source heat pumps	3585F	Mil. dol . . .	(NA)	1,046	917	1,054
Pumps and compressors [1]	**(X)**	**Mil. dol . . .**	**7,373**	**8,327**	**8,879**	**9,122**
Industrial pumps	35612	Mil. dol . . .	2,700	3,093	2,732	2,924
Domestic water systems.	35613	Mil. dol . . .	329	361	357	409
Air and gas compressors	35633	Mil. dol . . .	2,466	2,665	2,635	2,522

NA Not available.   X Not applicable.   [1] Includes products not shown separately.

Source: U.S. Census Bureau, *Manufacturing Profiles,* Series MP, annual; and <http://www.census.gov/ftp/pub/industry/1/ma35l98.pdf> (released March 2000); <http://www.census.gov/ftp/pub/industry/1/ma35m98.pdf> (released May 2000); <http://www.census.gov/ftp/pub/industry/1/ma35p98.pdf> (released March 2000).

No. 1260. Computers and Office and Accounting Machines—Value of Shipments: 1990 to 1998

[In millions of dollars (25,630 represents 25,630,000,000)]

Selected products	1990	1993	1994	1995	1996	1997	1998
Electronic computers	25,630	29,659	38,261	49,038	50,682	50,250	57,347
Host computers (multi-users) [1]	(NA)	(NA)	(NA)	(NA)	(NA)	12,240	14,860
Single user computers [1]	(NA)	(NA)	(NA)	(NA)	(NA)	36,988	41,729
Other computers [1]	(NA)	(NA)	(NA)	(NA)	(NA)	1,022	758
Loaded computer processor boards and board subassemblies [2]	2,247	15,087	17,515	24,448	24,937	27,040	25,456
Computer storage devices & equipment	7,488	5,731	5,556	7,903	8,909	8,837	7,248
Parts for computer storage devices & subassemblies	955	1,496	1,952	2,236	1,720	2,382	2,222
Computer terminals.	2,067	1,531	1,244	1,086	1,104	781	529
Computer peripheral equipment, n.e.c.	7,697	9,810	11,944	12,331	12,463	13,555	11,450
Parts for input/output equipment	3,706	2,554	2,499	2,391	5,505	2,628	2,631
Calculating and accounting machines [3] . . .	(D)	1,454	1,262	1,279	1,485	1,622	1,060
Magnetic and optical recording media	3,695	4,483	4,777	5,106	5,739	5,739	4,869

D Withheld to avoid disclosing data for individual companies. NA Not available. [1] Prior to 1997, product class separation for computers is not available. [2] These data are collected on two Current Industrial Report forms, MA35R, Computers and Office and Accounting Machines (Shipments) and MA36Q, Semiconductors, Printed Circuit Boards, And Other Electronic Components. [3] Product classes 35781 and 35782 were combined to product class 35784 beginning 1991.
Source: U.S. Census Bureau, *Manufacturing Profiles*, Series MP, annual; and <http://www.census.gov/ftp/pub/industry/1/ma35r98.pdf> (released December 1999).

No. 1261. Computers and Office and Accounting Machines—Shipments: 1997 and 1998

[20,992 represents 20,992,000]

Product	Number of companies, 1998	Quantity (1,000)		Value (mil. dol.)	
		1997	1998	1997	1998
Electronic computers (automatic data processors)	141	20,992	24,006	50,250	57,347
Host computers (multi-users):					
Large scale systems and unix servers	14	297	753	5,460	5,217
Medium-scale systems and unix servers	34	856	657	5,281	6,808
PC servers	20	236	(D)	1,207	(D)
Other host computers	6	33	(D)	292	(D)
Single user computers:					
Personal computers	45	15,233	16,481	25,367	25,267
Workstations	32	485	717	5,388	9,794
Laptops (AC/DC)	13	503	308	1,257	648
Notebooks, subnotebooks (battery operated)	13	1,887	2,422	4,698	5,696
Personal digital assistants	3	(D)	69	(D)	48
Other portable computers.	6	(D)	223	(D)	163
Other single user computers	5	177	206	112	113
Other computers	39	1,009	1,716	1,022	758
Computer storage devices and equipment	90	(X)	(X)	8,837	7,248
Parts for computer storage devices and subassemblies.	18	(X)	(X)	2,382	2,222
Computer terminals	47	(X)	(X)	781	529
Computer peripheral equipment, n.e.c. [1]	253	(X)	(X)	13,555	11,450
Keyboards.	25	14,254	15,331	613	751
Computer printers:					
Laser	35	2,427	2,504	2,548	2,384
Inkjet.	15	7,486	8,862	1,511	1,223
Calculating and accounting machines	43	(X)	(X)	1,622	1,060
Printed circuit assemblies	792	(X)	(X)	27,040	25,456
Magnetic and optical recording media	69	(X)	(X)	5,739	4,869

D Withheld to avoid disclosure of individual companies. X Not applicable. [1] N.e.c. = Not elsewhere classified.
Source: U.S. Census Bureau, *Manufacturing Profiles*, Series MP, annual; and <http://www.census.gov/ftp/pub/industry/1/ma35r98.pdf> (released December 1999).

No. 1262. Computers and Industrial Electronics—Factory Shipments: 1990 to 1998

[In millions of dollars (50,793 represents 50,793,000,000)]

Item	1990	1993	1994	1995	1996	1997	1998
Computer and peripheral equipment, total	50,793	54,821	59,254	73,555	78,278	76,287	78,831
Computers	25,973	30,002	38,261	49,038	50,682	50,250	57,347
Peripheral equipment	24,820	24,819	20,993	24,517	27,597	26,037	21,484
Industrial electronics, total	26,183	27,250	29,927	33,732	35,472	38,108	37,640
Controlling, processing equipment	12,728	13,961	15,014	16,450	17,051	18,212	17,860
Testing, measuring equipment.	6,859	7,332	8,416	10,109	11,224	11,966	12,312
Nuclear electronic equipment	567	519	477	501	491	516	556
Robots, accessories, and components	275	(NA)	(NA)	(NA)	(NA)	(NA)	(NA)
Other electronic equipment.	5,754	5,438	6,020	6,672	6,706	7,414	6,912

NA Not available.
Source: Electronic Industries Alliance, Arlington, VA, *Electronic Market Data Book,* annual (copyright).

U.S. Census Bureau, Statistical Abstract of the United States: 2000

No. 1263. Consumer Electronics and Electronic Components—Factory Sales by Product Category: 1990 to 1999

[In millions of dollars (43,033 represents $43,033,000,000). Factory sales include imports]

Product category	1990	1994	1995	1996	1997	1998	1999, prel.
Total [1]	43,033	58,230	64,530	68,002	71,814	75,547	80,976
Video products:							
Direct-view color TV	6,197	7,225	6,798	6,492	6,026	6,151	6,199
LCD color TV	50	42	44	39	38	39	36
Projection TV	626	1,117	1,417	1,426	1,361	1,577	1,632
TV/VCR combinations	178	710	723	697	684	831	1,014
Monochrome TV	99	38	34	29	27	23	20
LCD Monochrome TV	33	32	31	32	30	28	25
Other video:							
VCR decks	2,439	2,869	2,767	2,815	2,618	2,409	2,333
Camcorders	2,260	1,985	2,130	2,084	1,894	2,144	2,448
Laserdisc players	72	122	108	66	25	10	3
Home satellite earth stations	421	900	1,265	1,201	726	733	957
Videocassette players	65	64	59	43	39	21	15
Digital versatile disc players (DVD)	(NA)	(NA)	(NA)	(NA)	171	421	1,099
Home and portable products:							
Compact audio systems	1,270	1,703	1,162	1,157	1,419	1,557	1,695
Separate audio components	1,935	1,686	1,911	1,808	1,609	1,565	1,530
Home radios	360	306	284	291	300	300	348
Portable audio equipment	1,645	2,495	2,506	2,149	2,033	2,146	1,987
Mobile electronics:							
Aftermarket autosound equipment	1,192	1,898	1,931	1,814	1,811	1,859	2,070
Factory installed autosound	3,100	3,225	3,100	2,512	2,710	2,540	2,610
Wireless (cellular) telephones	1,133	1,275	2,574	2,660	2,750	2,775	2,808
Pagers	118	230	300	370	460	550	660
Vehicle security	190	401	142	165	210	213	205
Home office products:							
Cordless telephones	842	1,106	1,141	1,176	1,679	1,745	1,808
Corded telephones	638	610	557	553	528	489	483
Telephone answering devices	827	1,153	1,077	1,004	1,020	1,104	1,044
Home computers	4,187	10,088	12,600	15,040	15,950	16,640	16,390
Computer printers	(NA)	(NA)	2,430	2,999	3,900	4,188	4,500
Modems/fax modems	(NA)	(NA)	770	960	1,170	1,305	1,460
Computer peripherals	1,980	3,100	816	975	1,212	1,440	1,950
Computer software (incl. CD-ROM)	971	2,050	2,500	3,000	3,450	3,930	4,480
Home fax machines	920	964	919	839	1,139	647	455
Digital cameras	(NA)	(NA)	(NA)	177	483	519	1,207
Electronic gaming:							
Electronic Gaming Hardware	975	1,575	1,500	1,600	1,650	1,980	2,250
Electronic Gaming Software	2,400	2,925	3,000	3,500	3,900	4,480	5,100
Blank media:							
Blank audio cassettes	376	353	334	314	281	248	208
Blank videocassettes	948	730	708	725	695	639	590
Blank floppy diskettes	314	353	373	300	250	232	200
Accessories and batteries:							
Electronic accessories	793	874	944	982	982	1,178	1,398
Total primary batteries	1,383	2,412	2,600	2,676	2,869	2,963	3,620

NA Not available. [1] Includes categories, not shown separately.
Source: Electronic Industries Alliance, Washington, DC, *Electronic Market Data Book,* annual (copyright).

No. 1264. Communication Equipment—Value of Shipments: 1990 to 1998

[In millions of dollars (36,990.3 represents 36,990,300,000]

Product description	Product code	1990	1993	1994	1995	1996	1997	1998
Communication equipment	(X)	36,990.3	42,113.8	49,598.1	56,362.0	65,608.6	73,587.8	77,170.1
Telephone switching and switchboard equipment	3342101	7,537.1	7,240.9	8,067.6	8,178.4	9,617.7	10,302.2	12,317.0
Carrier line equipment and modems	3342104	5,013.8	4,993.3	5,114.0	5,868.6	7,544.6	7,278.1	7,968.3
Other telephone and telegraph equipment and components	3342107	3,180.5	7,026.4	8,479.5	10,510.0	14,030.9	16,488.1	18,170.4
Communication systems and equipment (except broadcast)	3342201	14,768.0	16,196.7	19,977.5	23,031.9	25,332.5	29,416.0	28,686.2
Broadcast, studio, and related electronic equipment	3342203	1,856.4	2,077.5	2,469.5	2,844.7	3,000.2	3,360.5	3,451.5
Intercommunications systems, including inductive paging systems (selective calling)	3342903	346.1	241.7	283.7	296.0	277.8	256.4	268.3
Alarm systems	3342901	1,027.2	1,532.4	1,550.5	1,662.1	1,802.8	1,926.5	2,039.8
Vehicular and pedestrian traffic control equipment and electrical railway signals and attachments	3342902	470.6	573.4	669.9	710.7	762.0	963.7	904.8
Electronic teaching machines, teaching aids, trainers and simulators	3333197	1,208.8	847.7	838.5	913.3	865.7	872.0	750.2
Laser sources [1]	3359997	(NA)	(NA)	726.4	787.5	843.8	991.8	928.6
Ultrasonic equipment	335999A	108.8	127.3	137.5	172.3	184.3	212.9	204.1
Other electronic systems and equipment, n.e.c. [2]	335999C	1,473.0	1,256.5	1,283.5	1,386.5	1,346.3	1,519.7	1,480.8

NA Not available.   X Not applicable.   [1] Beginning in 1994, data for laser equipment, instrumentation, and components have been eliminated from this survey. Only laser sources are being collected.   [2] Product class 36997 changed to product class 36999 for 1992. Product classes 36998, 39992, and 39447 are no longer collected on this survey.
Source: U.S. Census Bureau, *Manufacturing Profiles,* Series MP, annual; and <http://www.census.gov/ftp/pub/industry/1/ma36p98.pdf> (issued March 2000).

750   Manufactures

No. 1265. Semiconductors, Printed Circuit Boards, and Other Electronic Components—Value of Shipments by Class of Product: 1990 to 1998

[In millions of dollars (1,096.5 represents $1,096,500,000). N.e.c. = not elsewhere classified]

Class of product	Product code	1990	1994	1995	1996	1997	1998
Transmittal, industrial, and special-purpose electron tubes (except x-ray)	3344111	1,096.5	1,120.5	854.9	611.9	655.9	624.5
Electron tubes, receiving type	(X)	24.2	(1)	(1)	(1)	(1)	(1)
Receiving type electron tubes and cathode ray picture tubes	3344114	1,344.1	12,627.1	12,907.0	13,272.0	13,433.6	3,370.1
Electron tube parts	3344117	142.6	114.9	120.2	153.1	161.0	147.1
Printed circuit boards	3344120	7,174.5	6,812.3	8,367.3	8,216.8	8,702.4	9,423.7
Integrated microcircuits (semiconductor networks)	3344131	16,623.3	36,020.4	48,437.9	52,639.3	57,019.4	59,005.1
Transistors	3344134	682.3	834.6	942.3	945.9	1,500.2	779.0
Diodes and rectifiers	3344137	668.2	829.5	1,066.7	861.4	1,190.5	650.9
Other semiconductor devices	334413A	5,741.0	9,915.4	12,639.4	10,976.1	10,262.3	9,970.1
Capacitors for electronic applications	3344140	1,391.5	1,512.3	1,785.3	1,653.4	2,098.7	2,047.6
Resistors	3344150	799.8	869.5	953.2	911.9	993.4	789.7
Coils, transformers, reactors, and chokes for electronic applications	3344160	975.6	1,250.7	1,411.8	1,435.6	1,425.7	1,351.6
Coaxial connectors	3344171	420.0	642.4	731.6	656.9	581.0	596.1
Cylindrical connectors	3344174	513.6	511.3	552.9	642.5	554.9	584.1
Rack and panel connectors	3344177	500.0	545.6	540.5	530.7	657.9	748.7
Printed circuit connectors	334417A	804.9	923.4	1,026.4	1,095.3	1,276.5	1,124.8
Other connectors including parts	334417D	1,085.0	1,377.2	1,401.9	1,617.1	2,208.8	1,980.5
Filters (except microwave) and piezoelectric devices	3344191	457.4	674.1	729.2	719.3	814.7	802.4
Microwave components and devices	3342207	1,368.7	1,227.2	1,233.4	1,251.4	1,439.8	1,494.8
Transducers, electrical/electronic input or output	3344194	741.1	970.5	1,111.3	1,104.8	1,219.6	1,368.6
Switches, mechanical types for electronic circuitry	3344197	579.4	621.5	666.3	738.0	791.2	870.0
Printed circuit assemblies	334418A	8,269.3	17,514.8	24,447.7	24,937.3	27,040.2	25,455.7
All other electronic components n.e.c.	334419D	4,898.3	6,149.7	6,978.1	7,199.1	7,484.7	6,977.9

X Not applicable.   [1] Product codes combined to avoid disclosing figures for individual companies.

Source: U.S. Census Bureau, *Manufacturing Profiles,* Series MP, annual; and <http://www.census.gov/ftp/pub/industry/1/ma36q98.pdf> (released February 2000).

No. 1266. Selected Instruments and Related Products—Shipments: 1990 to 1998

[In millions of dollars (1,418 represents $1,418,000,000)]

Product	Product code	1990	1994	1995	1996	1997	1998
Automatic regulating and control valves	332911F	1,418	1,807	1,860	1,893	2,097	2,057
Solenoid-operated valves (except nuclear and fluid power transfer)	332911H	346	452	464	522	541	523
Aeronautical, nautical, and navigational instruments	3345111	2,518	1,859	2,125	2,274	2,531	2,487
Search & detection, navigation & guidance systems and equipment	3345113	32,420	25,567	24,697	26,094	26,584	26,001
Laboratory apparatus and laboratory furniture [1]	3391110	1,675	1,811	1,837	1,799	1,887	1,845
Controls for monitoring residential and commercial environments and appliance	3345120	1,982	2,521	2,533	2,648	2,717	2,787
Process control instruments	3345130	5,224	6,240	6,439	6,745	7,073	6,658
Integrating and totalizing meters for gas and liquids	3345141	725	859	915	963	1,079	1,133
Counting devices	3345143	210	354	364	367	434	404
Motor vehicle instruments [2]	3345145	1,457	2,092	2,193	2,219	2,245	2,364
Integrating instruments, electrical	3345151	396	440	445	458	457	466
Test equipment for testing electrical, radio and communication circuits, and motors	3345153	6,156	7,582	9,255	10,390	11,639	11,798
Instruments to measure electricity	3345155	586	554	555	500	456	411
Analytical, scientific instruments (except optical)	3345160	4,412	5,534	5,737	5,478	6,059	5,803
Sighting, tracking, and fire-control equipment, optical type	3333141	581	652	655	613	575	512
Optical instruments and lenses [3]	3333143	1,252	1,597	1,579	1,749	2,005	2,060
Aircraft engine instruments (except flight)	3345191	579	430	430	530	521	643
Physical properties and kinematic testing equip.	3345193	1,012	1,199	1,374	1,369	1,523	1,690
Nuclear radiation detection and monitoring instruments	3345195	567	489	501	497	530	569
Commercial, geophysical, meteorological, and general purpose instruments	3345197	1,140	1,344	1,373	1,452	1,677	1,424
Surveying and drafting instruments	3345199	274	324	356	365	360	372

[1] Includes laboratory furniture. Prior to 1990, laboratory furniture was included in product class 38296.   [2] Includes some data previously classified in product class 37149, "Other motor vehicle parts and accessories, new, n.e.c."   [3] Beginning 1992, product classes 38272, "Binoculars and astronomical instruments," and 38273, "Other optical instruments and lenses" were combined into product class 38274; prior years have been restated to reflect revision.

Source: U.S. Census Bureau, 1990, *Current Industrial Reports,* MA38B; thereafter *Manufacturing Profiles,* Series MP, annual; <http://www.census.gov/ftp/pub/industry/1/ma38b98.pdf> (issued April 2000).

Manufactures 751

No. 1267. Firearms Manufacturers—Shipments, Exports, and Imports: 1980 to 1998

[In thousands of units]

Year	Shipments				Exports				Imports [1]			
	Total	Hand-guns	Rifles	Shot-guns	Total	Hand-guns	Rifles	Shot-guns	Total	Hand-guns	Rifles	Shot-guns
1980	5,645	2,370	1,936	1,339	517	220	171	127	754	299	182	273
1981	5,374	2,537	1,681	1,156	588	252	159	176	689	306	200	184
1982	5,130	2,629	1,623	879	446	254	87	105	665	333	175	157
1983	4,036	1,967	1,110	960	293	159	55	79	838	411	228	199
1984	3,873	1,680	1,107	1,086	235	117	49	69	773	342	213	219
1985	3,460	1,550	1,141	770	183	95	44	45	697	229	271	197
1986	3,040	1,428	971	641	217	121	37	59	701	231	269	201
1987	3,523	1,659	1,006	858	242	159	42	41	1,064	342	414	308
1988	3,818	1,746	1,145	928	254	132	54	69	1,276	622	283	372
1989	4,374	2,031	1,407	936	259	118	73	68	1,008	440	293	274
1990	3,844	1,839	1,156	849	354	178	72	104	844	449	204	192
1991	3,550	1,838	883	828	398	190	91	118	721	293	311	116
1992	4,030	2,010	1,002	1,018	398	189	90	119	2,847	982	1,423	442
1993	5,130	2,825	1,160	1,145	414	149	94	171	3,043	1,205	1,593	246
1994	5,161	2,582	1,324	1,255	401	173	82	147	1,881	915	848	118
1995	4,228	1,723	1,332	1,174	420	230	89	101	1,103	706	261	136
1996	3,835	1,484	1,424	926	326	154	75	97	882	491	263	128
1997	3,574	1,407	1,251	916	271	108	77	86	939	474	359	106
1998	3,645	1,240	1,536	869	200	45	66	90	1,000	532	249	219

[1] 1980-91, imports are on fiscal year basis; thereafter, calendar year.

Source: U.S. Department of Treasury, Bureau of Alcohol, Tobacco, and Firearms, *Commerce in Firearms in the United States,* February 2000.

No. 1268. Selected Industrial Air Pollution Control Equipment— Shipments: 1998

[Quantity in number of units, value in thousands of dollars (848,174 represents $858,174,000)]

Product	Product code	Num-ber of compa-nies	New orders		Shipments		Backlog (Dec. 31)	
			Quantity	Value	Quantity	Value	Quantity	Value
Total	(X)	110	(S)	848,174	(S)	844,463	(S)	414,273
Particulate emissions collectors	(X)	86	81,718	511,142	82,013	534,885	11,177	173,440
Electrostatic precipitators	3334111111	14	(D)	(D)	(D)	(D)	(D)	(D)
Fabric filters	3334111114	55	64,888	302,920	65,096	302,850	9,614	72,808
Mechanical collectors	3334111116	34	(D)	(D)	(D)	(D)	(D)	(D)
Wet scrubbers.	3334111119	26	1,323	57,706	1,362	42,406	182	32,800
Gaseous emissions control devices	(X)	38	(S)	237,300	(S)	203,048	(S)	217,974
Catalytic oxidation systems	333411111C	11	(D)	(D)	(D)	(D)	(D)	(D)
Nitric oxide (NO) control systems	333411111E	2	(D)	(D)	(D)	(D)	(D)	(D)
Thermal and direct oxidation systems .	333411111G	17	(S)	61,614	(S)	73,776	(S)	37,719
Scrubbers (gas absorber)	333411111J	11	436	24,494	461	21,678	114	12,473
Wet flue gas desulfurization systems .	333411111M	3	(D)	(D)	(D)	(D)	(D)	(D)
Dry flue gas desulfurization systems. .	333411111P	2	(D)	(D)	(D)	(D)	(D)	(D)
Gas absorbers	333411111R	8	36	14,899	47	14,631	15	9,372
Other	333411111U	16	(S)	99,732	(S)	106,530	(S)	22,859

D Data withheld to avoid disclosure of company data.   S Does not meet publication standards.   X Not applicable.

Source: U.S. Census Bureau, *Manufacturing Profiles,* Series MP, annual; and <http://www.census.gov/ftp/pub/industry/1/ma35j98.pdf> (released February 2000).

No. 1269. Toy Industry—Shipments and Quantity by Type of Product: 1996 to 1999

[Shipments in millions of dollars (17,078 represents $17,078,000,000), quantity in millions (3,068 represents 3,068,000,000)]

Products	Shipments (mil. dol.)				Quantity (mil.)			
	1996	1997	1998	1999	1996	1997	1998	1999
Total	17,078	19,508	20,414	22,388	3,068	3,433	3,661	4,022
Video games	2,940	4,253	4,855	5,460	69	112	157	192
Other industry	14,138	15,255	15,559	16,928	2,999	3,321	3,504	3,830
Infant/preschool	1,384	1,403	1,408	1,508	211	218	219	231
Dolls	2,089	2,154	2,157	2,169	258	252	268	269
Plush	984	1,353	1,958	2,388	147	259	442	515
Action figure toys	832	1,046	907	1,123	158	186	154	194
Vehicles	1,386	1,544	1,665	1,698	280	349	414	408
Ride-ons	770	743	728	762	35	34	33	34
Games/puzzles.	1,428	1,479	1,475	1,732	254	248	250	335
Activity toys	2,077	2,087	2,096	2,253	608	680	686	725
All other toys	3,188	3,446	3,165	3,295	1,048	1,095	1,038	1,119

Source: Toy Manufactures of America, Inc., New York, NY, *Toy Industry Fact Book,* annual (copyright).

752   Manufactures

Domestic Trade and Services

This section presents statistics relating to the distributive trades and service industries. Data shown for the trades, classified by kind of business, and for the various categories of services (e.g., personal, business, repair, accommodation) cover sales or receipts, establishments, employees, payrolls, and other items. The principal sources of these data are census reports and survey reports of the U.S. Census Bureau. Data on gross product in trade and service industries usually appear in the *Survey of Current Business*, issued by the U.S. Bureau of Economic Analysis. Financial data for firms engaged in retail, wholesale, or service activities appear in the annual *Statistics of Income*, published by the Internal Revenue Service that appear in Section 17, Business Enterprise.

Censuses—Censuses of retail trade and wholesale trade have been taken at various intervals since 1929. Limited coverage of the service industries started in 1933. Beginning with the 1967 census, legislation provides for a census of each area to be conducted every 5 years (for years ending in "2" and "7"). The industries covered in the censuses and surveys of business are those classified in 13 sectors defined in the *North American Industry Classification System* (see text, Section 32). *Retail trade* refers to places of business primarily engaged in retailing merchandise generally in small quantities to the general public; *wholesale trade*, to establishments primarily engaged in selling goods to other businesses and normally operate from a warehouse or office that have little or no display of merchandise; and *services*, to establishments primarily engaged in providing a wide range of services for individuals and for businesses.

Beginning with the 1954 Censuses of Retail Trade and Service industries, data for nonemployer establishments are included and published separately. The census of wholesale trade excludes establishments with no paid employees. Beginning in 1977, sales taxes and finance charges are excluded from sales (or receipt) figures of the three censuses. In 1982 and prior censuses, the count of establishments represented the number in business at the end of the year. Beginning 1987, the count of establishments represents those in business at any time during the year.

For the 1992 and 1997 Censuses of Service Industries, hospitals operated by governmental organizations are included. Government-operated facilities in other service kind-of-business classifications are excluded from the census. In 1987 and 1992, data were not collected for elementary and secondary schools, colleges and universities, labor unions and similar organizations, and political organizations.

The census of retail trade beginning in 1977, excludes nonemployer direct sellers. Beginning 1982, the census treated each leased department in a store as a separate establishment and classified it according to the kind of business it conducted. In prior years, data for leased departments were consolidated with the data for stores in which they were located.

Current surveys—Current sample surveys conducted by the Census Bureau cover various aspects of the retail and wholesale trade and selected service industries. Its *Monthly Retail Trade Report* contains monthly estimates of sales,

U.S. Census Bureau, Statistical Abstract of the United States: 2000

inventories, and inventory/sales ratios, purchases, and accounts receivable for the United States, by kind of business. Annual figures on sales, year-end inventories, and sales/inventory ratios, by kind of business, appear in the *Annual Benchmark Report for Retail Trade.*

Statistics from the Bureau's monthly wholesale trade survey include national estimates of merchant wholesalers' sales, inventories, and stock-sales ratios by major summary groups—durable and nondurable—and selected kinds of business. Merchant wholesalers are those wholesalers who take title to the goods they sell (e.g., jobbers, exporters, importers, industrial distributors). These data, based on reports submitted by a sample of firms, appear in the *Monthly Wholesale Trade Report.* Annual figures on sales, sales-inventory ratios, year-end inventories, and purchases appear in the *Annual Benchmark Report for Wholesale Trade.*

The *Service Annual Survey* provides annual estimates of nationwide receipts for selected personal, business, leasing and repair, amusement and entertainment, social and health, and other professional service industries in the United States. For selected accommodation, social, health, and other professional service industries, separate estimates are developed for receipts of taxable firms and revenue and expenses for firms and organizations exempt from Federal income taxes. The estimates for tax exempt firms in these industries are derived from a sample of employer firms only. All other estimates represent the combined total for employer and nonemployer firms.

The *Annual Survey of Communication Services* provides detailed nationwide estimates of detailed revenue and expenses for employer firms primarily engaged in providing point-to-point communication services, whether by wire or radio and whether intended to be received aurally or visually. This covers telephone communications, including cellular and other radiotelephone services; telegraph and other

message communications such as electronic mail services, facsimile transmission services, telex services, etc; radio and television broadcasting stations and networks; cable and other pay television services; and other communication services such as radar station operations, satellite earth stations, satellite or missile tracking stations, etc.

For the current sample survey programs, retail trade coverage is the same as for the census; wholesale trade coverage is limited to merchant wholesalers, and selected services coverage is less inclusive than the census.

Estimates obtained from annual and monthly surveys are based on sample data and are not expected to agree exactly with results that would be obtained from a complete census of all establishments. Data include estimates for sampling units not reporting.

E-commerce—E-commerce are sales of goods and services over the Internet and extranet, electronic data interchange (EDI), or other online systems. Payment may or may not be made online. For the first time, this edition has four new tables on electronic shopping. The tables show estimated and projected online retail sales by key categories from business to consumers or to other businesses. The sources of these new tables are Forrester Research Inc., Cambridge MA; BizRate.com, Los Angeles, CA; The Boston Consulting Group, Silver Spring, MD; and Jupiter Communications, New York, NY. The method of collecting the data vary widely between the sources and consequently these estimates of this activity vary also. Users of these estimates may want to contact the sources for descriptions of their methodology.

Statistical reliability—For a discussion of statistical collection and estimation, sampling procedures, and measures of statistical reliability applicable to Census Bureau data, see Appendix III.

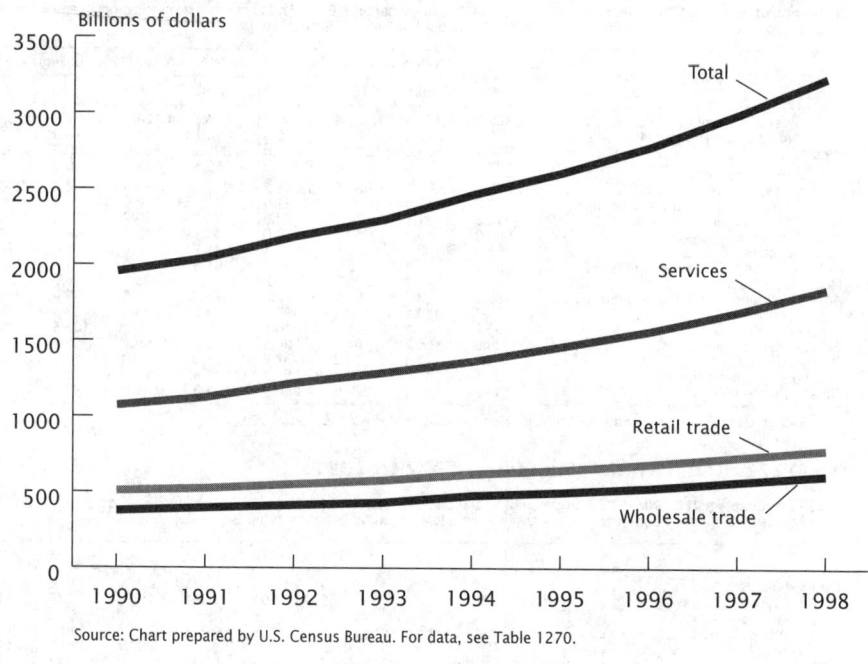

Figure 27.1
**Gross Domestic Product in Domestic Trade and Services Industries:
1990 to 1998**

Billions of dollars

Source: Chart prepared by U.S. Census Bureau. For data, see Table 1270.

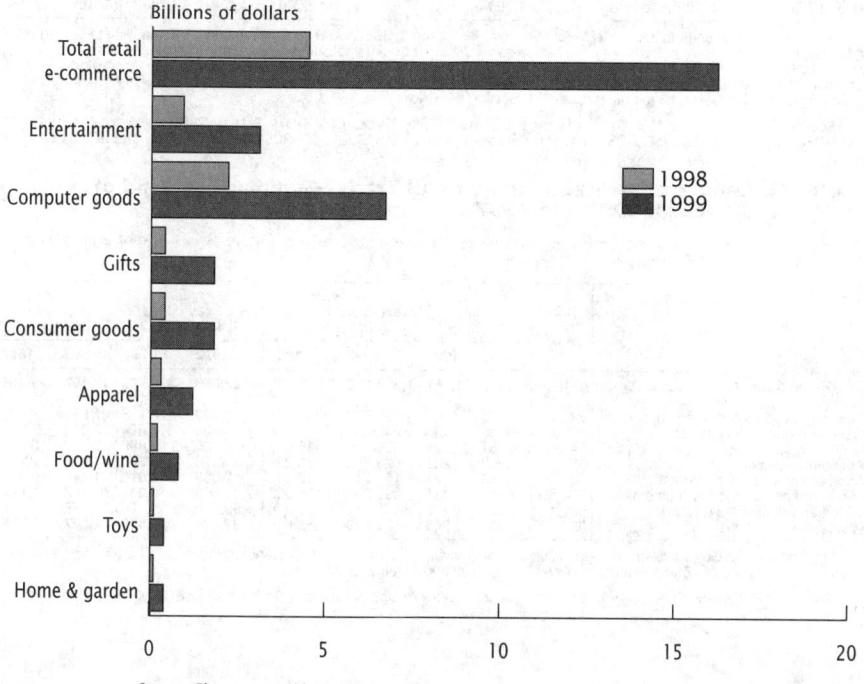

Figure 27.2
Retail E-Commerce Sales and Numbers of Orders: 1998 to 1999

Billions of dollars

Source: Chart prepared by U.S. Census Bureau. For data, see Table 1288.

Domestic Trade and Services **755**

No. 1270. Gross Domestic Product in Domestic Trade and Service Industries in Current and Real (1996) Dollars: 1990 to 1998

[In billions of dollars (883.9 represents $883,900,000,000), except percent. For definition of gross domestic product and for chained dollars, see text, Section 14, Income. Based on 1987 Standard Industrial Classification]

Industry	Current dollars				Chained (1996) dollars			
	1990	1995	1997	1998	1990	1995	1997	1998
Wholesale and retail trade	**883.9**	**1,147.4**	**1,306.4**	**1,395.7**	**954.6**	**1,124.4**	**1,328.5**	**1,459.7**
Percent of gross domestic product . . .	15.2	15.5	15.7	15.9	14.2	14.9	16.3	17.2
Wholesale trade.	376.1	500.6	572.3	613.8	395.1	483.0	589.3	664.0
Retail trade.	507.8	646.8	734.1	781.9	559.5	641.4	739.2	795.7
Services.	**1,071.5**	**1,462.4**	**1,692.5**	**1,841.3**	**1,361.9**	**1,510.4**	**1,634.4**	**1,708.1**
Percent of gross domestic product . . .	18.5	19.8	20.4	21.0	20.3	20.0	20.1	20.1
Hotels and other lodging places	46.3	61.7	70.6	76.3	55.2	62.7	66.2	63.7
Personal services.	38.0	46.7	50.1	53.0	46.4	48.1	48.3	49.9
Business services.	203.9	302.0	395.5	454.1	241.3	313.9	383.1	421.5
Auto repair, services, and garages	50.3	65.1	72.0	77.6	61.9	65.9	69.4	72.0
Motion pictures	17.7	22.4	25.2	27.2	21.2	23.6	24.7	26.1
Amusement and recreation services	36.5	53.5	64.8	70.5	45.0	55.6	62.9	66.1
Health services	314.4	433.1	476.2	495.5	423.2	444.3	463.4	467.0
Legal services	82.7	101.1	108.5	116.5	108.8	105.1	103.8	107.1
Educational services.	39.6	55.7	61.1	66.4	50.3	58.5	58.6	60.9
Social services.	30.1	47.4	53.2	57.8	38.0	49.3	51.0	52.4
Membership organizations	35.8	46.7	51.2	53.7	43.4	49.0	48.6	48.5
Other services	149.2	194.4	229.6	254.1	191.3	199.9	221.6	238.3

Source: U.S. Bureau of Economic Analysis, *Survey of Current Business*, June 2000.

No. 1271. Retail Trade—Summary: 1972 to 1997

[1,780 represents 1,780,000. 1972 through 1982 based on 1972 Standard Industrial Classification (SIC) code; beginning 1987 based on 1987 SIC code. Comparability of data over time is affected by changes in the SIC code]

Item	Unit	1972	1977	1982	1987	1992	1997
Establishments, total [1]	1,000	1,780	1,855	1,923	2,420	2,672	(NA)
With payroll	1,000	1,265	1,304	1,324	1,504	1,526	1,561
Consumer Price Index: [2]							
All items	1982-84=100 . .	41.8	60.6	96.5	113.6	140.3	160.5
All commodities.	1982-84=100 . .	44.5	64.2	97.0	107.7	129.1	141.8
Sales	Bil. dol.	457	723	1,066	1,540	1,949	(NA)
By establishments with payroll	Bil. dol.	440	700	1,039	1,493	1,895	2,546
Percent of sales by corporations [3]	Percent	76.4	79.8	84.6	88.9	89.9	(NA)
Sales as percent of personal income	Percent	46.0	44.2	38.5	38.9	36.2	(NA)
Personal income	Bil. dol.	994.3	1,637.1	2,768.4	3,962.5	5,390.4	6,951.1
Payroll, entire year	Bil. dol.	55.4	85.9	123.6	177.5	222.9	290.5
Percent of sales [4]	Percent	12.6	12.3	11.9	11.9	11.8	11.4
Paid employees, March 12 pay period	1,000	11,211	13,040	14,468	17,780	18,407	21,166

- Represents or rounds to zero.   NA Not available.   [1] Through 1982, represents the number of establishments and firms in business at the end of year. Beginning 1987, represents the number of establishments and firms in business at any time during year.   [2] Covers only establishments with payroll.   [3] Through 1982, represents establishments with and without payroll. Beginning 1987, represents only establishments with payroll.   [4] Source: U.S. Bureau of Labor Statistics, *Monthly Labor Review*. Beginning 1982, CPI-U annual averages, see text, Section 15, Prices.

Source: Except as noted, U.S. Census Bureau, *Census of Retail Trade, 1972*, RC72-S-1; *1977*, RC77-52; *1982*, RC82-A-52 and RC82-I-1; *1987*, RC87-A-52, RC87-N-1, and RC87-S-1; and *1992*, RC92-A-52, RC92-N-1, RC92-S-1, and EC97X-CS2.

No. 1272. Comparative Statistics in Retail Trade—Summary by Kind of Business: 1992 and 1997

[Covers establishments with payroll. Based on 1987 Standard Industrial Classification (SIC) code; see text, Section 13, Labor Force, Employment, and Earnings]

Kind of business	1987 SIC code[1]	Establish-ments (1,000)		Sales, receipts, revenue/shipments (mil. dol.)		Annual payroll (mil. dol.)		Paid employees (1,000)	
		1992	1997	1992	1997	1992	1997	1992	1997
Retail trade, total	**(G)**	**1,526**	**1,561**	**1,894,880**	**2,545,881**	**222,868**	**290,525**	**18,407**	**21,166**
Building materials & garden supplies . .	52	69	67	98,832	146,211	11,790	16,733	666	830
General merchandise stores.	53	35	35	245,330	(D)	24,503	(D)	2,079	(²)
Food stores.	54	181	171	369,199	416,047	37,228	42,809	2,969	3,109
Automotive dealers.	55	202	202	529,853	788,231	39,376	55,502	1,943	2,284
Apparel and accessory stores.	56	145	127	101,714	116,614	12,039	13,616	1,145	1,116
Furniture and homefurnishings stores. .	57	110	115	93,206	136,093	11,869	16,262	702	862
Eating and drinking places	58	434	476	195,317	(D)	52,570	(D)	6,548	(²)
Miscellaneous retail stores	59	351	368	261,429	365,916	33,494	45,440	2,357	2,795

D Withheld to avoid disclosing data on individual companies.   [1] Based on 1987 Standard Industrial Classification; see text, Section 13, Labor Force, Expenditures, and Wealth.   [2] 100,000 employees or more.

Source: U.S. Census Bureau, *1997 Economic Census, Core Business Statistics Series*, Series EC97X-CS2, June 2000.

No. 1273. Retail Trade—Establishments, Employees, and Payroll: 1990 and 1997

[1,529.7 represents 1,529,700, excepted as indicated. Covers establishments with payroll. Employees are for the week including March 12. Most government employees are excluded. For statement on methodology, see Appendix III]

Kind of business	1987 SIC code [1]	Establishments (1,000)		Employees (1,000)		Payroll (bil. dol.)	
		1990	1997	1990	1997	1990	1997
Retail trade, total	(G)	1,529.7	1,588.7	19,815	22,003	241.7	330.3
Building materials and garden supplies [2]	52	71.9	69.5	703	857.0	11.9	17.7
Lumber and other building materials	521	27.5	27.1	403	546.0	7.5	11.9
Paint, glass, and wallpaper stores	523	10.2	10.0	54	54.0	0.9	1.2
Hardware stores	525	19.0	15.9	143	140.0	1.9	2.1
Retail nurseries and garden stores	526	10.1	10.9	76	77.0	1.0	1.3
Mobile home dealers	527	4.2	5.5	23	41.0	0.4	1.1
General merchandise stores [2]	53	36.6	35.3	2,135	2,445.0	22.9	30.5
Department stores.	531	10.1	11.3	1,710	2,070.0	18.3	25.6
Variety stores	533	10.0	12.6	109	96.0	1.0	1.1
Misc. general merchandise stores.	539	15.0	11.4	310	279.0	3.6	3.8
Food stores [2].	54	186.1	176.6	3,124	3,162.0	35.8	43.6
Grocery stores	541	132.5	130.7	2,757	2,874.0	32.4	40.1
Meat and fish markets	542	9.3	7.2	54	39.0	0.6	0.6
Fruit and vegetable markets	543	2.9	3.2	19	18.0	0.2	0.2
Candy, nut, confectionery stores.	544	5.4	4.5	29	27.0	0.2	0.3
Retail bakeries	546	19.9	19.2	176	146.0	1.5	1.6
Automotive dealers and service stations [2] . .	55	207.3	200.9	2,104	2,312.0	40.0	57.0
New and used car dealers	551	26.1	26.2	917	1,068.0	23.9	36.4
Used car dealers.	552	14.3	23.4	56	93.0	1.0	2.2
Auto and home supply stores	553	43.4	41.8	305	326.0	5.1	6.5
Gasoline service stations	554	104.8	95.8	701	721.0	7.5	9.3
Boat dealers.	555	4.6	5.2	34	35.0	0.6	0.8
Recreational vehicle dealers	556	2.7	3.0	24	30.0	0.5	0.8
Motorcycle dealers.	557	3.4	3.6	22	29.0	0.4	0.7
Apparel and accessory stores [2]	56	150.2	125.1	1,193	1,085.0	12.2	13.8
Men's and boys' clothing stores	561	14.7	12.3	108	89.0	1.5	1.4
Women's clothing stores.	562	50.2	40.5	439	314.0	4.0	3.6
Women's accessory and specialty stores. .	563	7.7	8.2	46	52.0	0.5	0.7
Children's and infants' wear stores	564	5.6	4.7	36	34.0	0.3	0.4
Family clothing stores.	565	17.8	20.8	283	371.0	3.0	4.9
Shoe stores	566	37.4	30.1	206	186.0	2.2	2.4
Misc. apparel and accessory stores	569	9.1	8.2	47	38.0	0.5	0.5
Furniture and homefurnishings stores [2]	57	108.1	116.4	749	867.0	12.3	16.6
Furniture and homefurnishings stores [2] . . .	571	61.1	66.7	430	473.0	7.2	9.3
Furniture stores	5712	30.8	31.9	245	257.0	4.3	5.6
Floor covering stores	5713	13.2	14.5	77	76.0	1.5	1.8
Drapery and upholstery stores	5714	3.4	2.5	16	10.0	0.2	0.2
Misc. homefurnishings stores	5719	13.3	17.7	92	130.0	1.1	1.8
Household appliance stores	572	10.0	10.7	63	63.0	1.1	1.3
Radio, television, and computer stores [2] . .	573	34.2	38.9	245	330.0	3.9	6.0
Radio, TV, and electronic stores	5731	16.5	16.9	120	168.0	2.1	3.1
Computer and software stores	5734	5.1	9.3	33	69.0	0.8	1.6
Record and prerecorded tape stores . .	5735	7.1	8.2	60	65.0	0.6	0.7
Eating and drinking places [2]	58	402.6	478.6	6,461	7,597.0	49.6	72.4
Eating places	5812	286.8	423.7	5,700	7,276.0	43.8	69.6
Drinking places	5813	43.8	52.4	267	317.0	2.0	2.8
Miscellaneous retail [2]	59	349.0	371.2	2,487	2,807.0	33.2	46.5
Drug stores and proprietary stores	591	50.0	47.6	593	724.0	8.3	11.7
Liquor stores [3]	592	30.8	29.1	141	129.0	1.6	1.7
Used merchandise stores	593	15.0	23.8	79	120.0	0.9	1.7
Sporting goods and bicycle shops	5941	21.4	24.5	139	176.0	1.6	2.4
Book stores	5942	11.7	12.3	86	120.0	0.8	1.5
Stationery stores	5943	4.8	3.2	34	19.0	0.4	0.3
Jewelry stores.	5944	26.6	29.5	161	157.0	2.3	2.8
Hobby, toy, and game shops	5945	9.4	10.9	83	110.0	0.8	1.4
Camera, photo supply stores.	5946	3.6	2.9	22	18.0	0.4	0.3
Gift, novelty, and souvenir shops	5947	29.5	37.9	164	206.0	1.4	2.1
Sewing, needlework, and piece goods. . . .	5949	8.2	6.3	68	42.0	0.5	0.5
Catalog and mail-order houses	5961	7.2	10.1	141	214.0	2.6	5.8
Merchandising machine operators	5962	5.1	6.5	76	68.0	1.3	1.4
Direct selling establishments	5963	8.8	17.8	107	135.0	1.7	2.9
Fuel dealers.	598	12.0	11.3	100	92.0	2.2	2.4
Florists	5992	25.8	26.5	131	125.0	1.2	1.4
Optical goods stores	5995	13.2	15.2	66	75.0	1.1	1.4
Administrative and auxiliary	(X)	18.0	15.1	860	871.0	23.7	32.3

X Not applicable.   [1] Based on 1987 Standard Industrial Classification; see text, Section 17, Business Enterprise.   [2] Includes kinds of business not shown separately.   [3] Includes government employees.

Source: U.S. Census Bureau, *County Business Patterns*, annual.

U.S. Census Bureau, Statistical Abstract of the United States: 2000

No. 1274. Retail Trade Sales—Summary: 1980 to 1999

[In billions of dollars (957 represents $957,000,000,000) except as indicated. Sales and inventories for leased departments and concessions are in the kind-of-business category of the leased department or concession. Based on Current Business Survey, see Appendix III]

Year	Sales								Inventories at cost [4] (bil. dol.)	Inventory/ sales ratios [4][5]
	Total (bil. dol.)	Annual percent change [1]	Per capita [2] (dol.)	Index of sales (1982=100)	Durable goods (bil. dol.)	Nondurable goods (bil. dol.)				
						Total	Dept. stores [3]			
1980	957	6.8	4,213	89.5	299	658	85		121	(NA)
1985	1,375	6.8	5,779	128.6	498	877	126		182	1.55
1989	1,759	6.2	7,127	164.5	657	1,102	161		237	1.59
1990	1,845	4.9	7,394	172.6	669	1,176	166		240	1.56
1991	1,856	0.6	7,360	173.6	650	1,206	173		243	1.57
1992	1,952	5.2	7,652	182.6	704	1,248	186		252	1.50
1993	2,082	6.7	8,077	194.8	782	1,300	200		269	1.49
1994	2,248	8.0	8,636	210.3	887	1,362	218		294	1.52
1995	2,359	4.9	8,976	220.7	947	1,412	231		310	1.53
1996	2,502	6.1	9,435	234.1	1,019	1,483	245		320	1.50
1997	2,611	4.4	9,749	244.2	1,063	1,547	260		330	1.49
1998	2,746	5.2	10,160	256.9	1,136	1,609	276		343	1.45
1999	2,995	9.1	10,983	280.2	1,255	1,740	297		372	1.42

NA Not available.   [1] Change from immediate prior year.   [2] Based on Census Bureau estimates of resident population as of July 1.   [3] Excludes leased departments.   [4] As of Dec. 31. Includes warehouses. Adjusted for seasonal variations.   [5] Sales data also adjusted for holiday and trading-day differences.
Source: U.S. Census Bureau, *Current Business Reports, Annual Benchmark Report for Retail Trade, January 1990 Through December 1999*, (BR/99-A) and prior issues; and unpublished data.

No. 1275. Retail Trade—Sales by Kind of Business: 1980 to 1999

[In billions of dollars (957.4 represents $957,400,000,000). See headnote, Table 1278. Based on Current Business Survey, see Appendix III]

Kind of business	1987 SIC code [1]	1980	1985	1990	1995	1996	1997	1998	1999
Retail trade, total.	(X)	957.4	1,375.0	1,844.6	2,359.0	2,502.4	2,610.6	2,745.6	2,994.9
Durable goods stores, total [2] . . [2]	(X)	299.2	498.1	668.8	947.3	1,019.0	1,063.2	1,136.4	1,255.0
Building materials and garden supplies [2]. . . .	52	50.8	71.2	94.6	130.6	140.4	148.4	162.6	179.7
Building materials, supply stores	521,3	35.0	50.8	70.3	98.1	105.4	112.2	123.5	138.4
Hardware stores	525	8.3	10.5	12.5	13.8	14.0	14.0	14.8	15.7
Automotive dealers	55 exc. 554	164.1	303.2	387.6	562.7	608.5	632.5	670.1	749.0
Motor vehicle, misc. automotive dealers. . .	551,2,5,6,7,9	146.2	278.0	356.8	528.7	572.9	596.1	632.0	709.0
Motor vehicle dealers	551,2	137.7	263.1	338.7	502.7	545.6	565.8	597.9	668.2
New and used car dealers	551	130.5	251.6	316.0	464.5	503.0	519.0	545.1	606.6
Auto and home supply stores . . . . [2] . . .	553	18.0	25.2	30.8	34.1	35.7	36.4	38.2	40.1
Furniture and homefurnishings stores [2].	57	44.2	68.3	91.5	128.3	135.0	140.2	150.5	161.5
Furniture, homefurnishings stores [2].	571	26.3	38.3	50.5	61.0	64.2	68.0	72.3	77.3
Furniture stores	5712	(NA)	23.9	30.8	35.6	37.5	40.1	42.4	45.1
Floor covering stores	5713	(NA)	7.9	10.7	12.1	12.3	12.7	13.6	14.8
Household appliance, radio, TV, and computer stores	5722,31,34	14.0	25.1	33.0	56.2	59.3	60.7	65.9	71.6
Household appliance stores	5722	(NA)	8.4	8.8	9.9	10.2	10.3	10.8	11.4
Radio, TV, and computer stores	5731,34	(NA)	16.7	24.3	46.2	49.1	50.4	55.1	60.1
Sporting goods and bicycle shops	5941	(NA)	8.7	15.0	19.9	20.8	21.2	22.5	23.6
Book stores	5942	(NA)	4.5	7.4	11.2	11.9	12.7	13.4	13.9
Jewelry stores	5944	(NA)	11.2	15.2	19.2	20.4	19.9	21.6	23.9
Nondurable goods stores, total [2]	(X)	658.1	876.9	1,175.8	1,411.7	1,483.4	1,547.3	1,609.2	1,739.9
General merchandise stores	53	109.0	158.6	215.5	297.6	312.7	329.4	349.6	378.9
Department stores [3]	531	85.5	126.4	165.8	231.3	244.8	259.9	276.0	296.6
Variety stores	533	7.8	8.5	8.3	9.8	10.6	11.2	11.8	14.3
Misc. general merchandise stores.	539	15.7	23.8	41.4	56.5	57.4	58.3	61.8	68.0
Food stores	54	220.2	285.1	368.3	402.5	414.3	423.7	435.4	458.3
Grocery stores	541	205.6	269.5	348.2	382.2	393.4	402.3	412.7	434.7
Gasoline service stations . . . . [2]	554	94.1	113.3	138.5	157.2	168.8	172.1	163.2	181.0
Apparel and accessory stores [2]	56	49.3	70.2	95.8	111.4	115.3	119.6	127.0	135.1
Men's and boys' clothing stores	561	7.7	8.5	10.5	9.3	9.6	10.1	10.6	11.1
Women's clothing specialty stores	562,3	17.6	26.1	32.8	33.4	33.5	33.5	34.6	36.8
Women's clothing stores	562	15.9	23.6	29.8	28.7	28.3	27.8	28.7	30.3
Family clothing stores	565	10.8	17.8	28.4	40.1	42.3	45.3	49.6	53.9
Shoe stores	566	10.5	13.1	18.0	19.7	20.6	20.8	21.5	21.6
Eating and drinking places	58	90.1	127.9	190.1	229.8	238.9	254.1	266.4	285.4
Eating places [2]	5812	80.4	117.6	178.7	217.3	225.9	240.6	252.4	271.3
Restaurants, lunchrooms, cafeterias . .	5812 pt.	(NA)	68.2	99.9	116.8	121.9	132.8	137.7	143.6
Refreshment places	5812 pt.	(NA)	48.1	75.7	97.4	100.6	103.9	110.2	122.8
Drinking places	5813	(NA)	10.3	11.5	12.6	13.1	13.5	14.0	14.1
Drug stores and proprietary stores	591	31.0	47.0	70.6	85.8	91.8	98.8	108.3	120.7
Liquor stores	592	16.9	19.5	21.7	22.0	23.2	24.1	25.5	28.0
Nonstore retailers	596	22.8	28.3	45.6	73.2	82.8	89.9	99.3	113.7
Catalog and mail-order houses	5961	(NA)	15.8	26.6	50.8	58.1	65.9	75.4	89.6
Fuel dealers	598	(NA)	16.8	15.6	16.8	18.9	18.1	15.3	17.2

NA Not available.   X Not applicable.   [1] Based on 1987 Standard Industrial Classification code; see text, Section 13, Labor Force, Employment, and Earnings.   [2] Includes kinds of business, not shown separately.   [3] Excludes leased departments.
Source: U.S. Census Bureau, *Current Business Reports, Annual Benchmark Report for Retail Trade, January 1990 Through December 1999*, (BR/99-RV) and prior issues; and unpublished data.

No. 1276. Retail Trade—Merchandise Inventories and Inventory/Sales Ratio by Kind of Business: 1990 to 1999

[239.7 represents $239,700,000,000. As of **Dec. 31.** Includes warehouses. Adjusted for seasonal variations. Sales data also adjusted for holiday and trading-day differences. See headnote, Table 1274, this section]

Kind of business	1987 SIC code [1]	Inventories at cost [2] (bil. dol.)				Inventory/sales ratios			
		1990	1995	1998	1999	1990	1995	1998	1999
Total	(X)	239.7	309.7	343.2	372.3	1.56	1.53	1.45	1.42
Excluding automotive group . .	(X)	*176.6*	*222.3*	*246.6*	*264.0*	*1.44*	*1.45*	*1.38*	*1.35*
Durable goods stores [3]	(X)	121.2	165.0	183.6	202.5	2.25	2.01	1.85	1.85
Building materials group stores	52	17.0	22.6	26.9	29.4	2.27	1.98	1.88	1.89
Automotive dealers	55 exc. 554	63.1	87.4	96.6	108.3	2.02	1.79	1.64	1.65
Furniture group stores	57	17.5	24.3	25.2	26.2	2.36	2.20	1.94	1.86
Nondurable goods stores [3]	(X)	118.5	144.7	159.6	169.8	1.18	1.20	1.16	1.12
General merchandise stores	53	42.2	58.1	60.1	62.8	2.32	2.30	2.01	1.93
Department stores	531	33.2	46.4	49.0	51.1	2.39	2.36	2.07	2.01
Food stores	54	25.0	27.5	29.6	31.8	0.80	0.81	0.79	0.79
Apparel and accessory stores	56	19.7	22.7	25.5	25.9	2.48	2.40	2.35	2.29

X Not applicable.   [1] Based on 1987 Standard Industrial Classification code; see text, Section 13, Labor Force, Employment, and Earnings.   [2] Excludes supplies and equipment used in store and warehouse operations that are not for resale.   [3] Includes kinds of business not shown separately.

Source: U.S. Census Bureau, *Current Business Reports, Annual Benchmark Report for Retail Trade, January 1990 Through December 1999* (BR/99-A) and unpublished data.

No. 1277. Retail Trade—Purchases and Gross Margin by Kind of Business: 1990 to 1998

[1,259 represents $1,259,000,000,000. Estimated. As of **Dec. 31.** Includes warehouses. Adjusted for seasonal variations. Sales data also adjusted for holiday and trading-day differences. See headnote, Table 1274]

Kind of business	1987 SIC code [1]	Purchases [2] (bil. dol.)			Gross margin [2] (bil. dol.)			Gross margin as percent of sales		
		1990	1997	1998	1990	1997	1998	1990	1997	1998
Total	(X)	1,259	1,789	1,878	589	831	882	31.9	31.8	32.1
Excluding automotive group . .	(X)	*942*	*1,264*	*1,319*	*519*	*720*	*768*	*35.6*	*36.4*	*37.0*
Durable goods stores [3]	(X)	492	796	853	177	272	291	26.5	25.6	25.0
Building materials group stores	52	65	104	114	30	45	51	31.2	30.6	31.3
Automotive dealers	55 exc. 554	317	525	559	70	111	114	18.0	17.5	17.0
Furniture group stores	57	57	90	96	35	50	55	38.1	35.7	36.6
Nondurable goods stores [3]	(X)	767	993	1,025	412	558	591	35.0	36.1	36.7
General merchandise stores	53	149	233	248	66	96	102	30.6	29.2	29.3
Department stores	531	111	177	187	55	84	90	33.2	32.4	32.3
Food stores	54	277	311	318	93	113	118	25.3	26.6	27.2
Apparel and accessory stores	56	55	70	73	41	51	55	43.2	42.3	43.4

X Not applicable.   [1] Based on 1987 Standard Industrial Classification code; see text, Section 13, Labor Force, Employment, and Earnings.   [2] Includes kinds of business not shown separately.

Source: U.S. Census Bureau, *Current Business Reports, Annual Benchmark Report for Retail Trade, January 1990 Through December 1999* (BR/99-A).

No. 1278. Franchised New Car Dealerships—Summary: 1980 to 1999

[130.5 represents $130,500,000,000]

Item	Unit	1980	1985	1990	1993	1994	1995	1996	1997	1998	1999
Dealerships [1]	Number .	27,900	24,725	24,825	22,950	22,850	22,800	22,750	22,700	22,600	22,400
Sales	Bil. dol. .	130.5	251.6	316.0	377.3	430.6	456.2	490.0	507.5	547.8	608.1
New cars sold [2]	1,000 . . .	8,979	10,983	9,296	8,519	8,991	8,635	8,526	8,272	8,142	8,699
Used vehicles sold	1,000 . . .	9,717	13,300	14,321	15,308	16,903	18,207	18,856	19,196	18,984	19,351
Employment	1,000 . . .	745	856	924	908	963	996	1,031	1,046.1	1,047.8	1,081.3
Annual payroll	Bil. dol. .	11.0	20.1	24.1	26.7	29.8	31.8	34.0	37.4	39.7	42.5
Advertising expenses	Bil. dol. .	1.2	2.8	3.7	4.1	4.3	4.6	5.0	5.1	5.3	5.7
Dealer pretax profits as a percentage of sales	Percent .	0.6	2.2	1.0	1.6	1.8	1.4	1.5	1.4	1.7	1.8

NA Not available.   [1] At beginning of year.   [2] Data provided by Ward's Automotive Reports.

Source: National Automobile Dealers Association, McLean, VA, *NADA Data*, annual.

No. 1279. Motor Vehicle Retail Sales: 1980 to 1997

Type	1980	1985	1989	1990	1991	1992	1993	1994	1995	1996	1997
Retail sales, total	11,466	15,724	14,713	14,146	12,539	13,116	14,199	15,411	15,116	15,456	15,500
Passenger cars (new), total	8,979	11,042	9,772	9,300	8,175	8,213	8,517	8,990	8,634	8,527	8,272
Domestic [1]	6,581	8,205	7,073	6,897	6,137	6,277	6,741	7,255	7,128	7,254	6,917
Imports	2,398	2,838	2,699	2,403	2,038	1,936	1,776	1,735	1,506	1,273	1,355
Trucks (new), total	2,487	4,682	4,941	4,846	4,365	4,903	5,681	6,421	6,481	6,930	7,228
Domestic [1]	2,001	3,902	4,403	4,215	3,813	4,481	5,287	5,995	6,064	6,478	6,633
Imports	486	780	538	631	551	422	394	426	417	452	595

[1] North American built.

Source: American Automobile Manufacturers Association, Detroit, MI, *Motor Vehicle Facts and Figures*, annual (copyright).

Domestic Trade and Services   **759**

No. 1280. Retail Foodstores—Number and Sales by Type: 1990 to 1998

[254.4 represents 254,400]

Type of foodstore	Number [1] (1,000)					Sales [2] (bil. dol.)					Percent distribution			
											Number		Sales	
	1990	1995	1996	1997	1998	1990	1995	1996	1997	1998	1990	1998	1990	1998
Total.	254.4	247.3	246.3	245.3	244.3	368.3	410.5	421.0	429.8	443.0	100.0	100.0	100.0	100.0
Grocery stores	172.9	164.3	163.0	161.7	160.4	348.2	385.0	397.0	403.0	414.6	67.7	65.7	94.5	93.6
Supermarkets [3]	25.0	24.1	23.8	24.1	24.0	260.1	293.2	302.5	307.5	312.1	9.9	9.8	70.6	70.4
Conventional	13.7	11.1	10.8	11.1	10.4	90.7	68.9	69.2	59.2	59.4	5.7	4.3	24.6	13.4
Superstore [4]	5.8	6.8	7.1	7.3	7.4	87.6	116.7	127.0	132.9	133.8	2.2	3.0	23.8	30.2
Warehouse [5]	3.4	2.7	2.4	2.2	2.2	33.1	26.0	24.3	22.2	19.3	1.3	0.9	9.0	4.4
Combination food and drug [6]	1.6	2.7	2.4	2.8	3.2	34.8	59.3	61.3	64.7	72.0	0.5	1.3	9.4	16.3
Superwarehouse [7] . . .	0.3	0.6	0.5	0.5	0.5	12.6	17.8	15.3	11.9	16.7	0.2	0.2	3.4	3.8
Hypermarket [8]	0.1	0.2	0.2	0.2	0.2	1.3	4.5	5.4	16.6	11.0	(Z)	0.1	0.4	2.5
Convenience stores [9] . .	59.2	62.1	62.7	62.1	61.4	37.0	37.4	38.8	42.0	42.9	19.1	25.2	10.0	9.7
Superette [10]	88.7	78.1	76.5	75.5	75.0	51.1	54.4	55.7	53.5	59.6	38.6	30.7	13.9	13.5
Specialized food stores [11]	81.5	83.0	83.3	83.6	83.9	20.1	22.4	24.0	26.8	28.4	32.3	34.3	5.5	6.4

Z Less than 0.05 percent.   [1] Estimated.   [2] Includes nonfood items.   [3] A grocery store, primarily self-service in operation, providing a full range of departments, and having at least $2.5 million in annual sales in 1985 dollars.   [4] Contains greater variety of products than conventional supermarkets, including specialty and service departments, and considerable nonfood (general merchandise) products.   [5] Contains limited product variety and fewer services provided, incorporating case lot stocking and shelving practices.   [6] Contains a pharmacy, a nonprescription drug department, and a greater variety of health and beauty aids than that carried by conventional supermarkets.   [7] A larger warehouse store that offers expanded product variety and often service meat, deli, or seafood departments.   [8] A very large store offering a greater variety of general merchandise—like clothes, hardware, and seasonal goods—and personal care products than other grocery stores.   [9] A small grocery store selling a limited variety of food and nonfood products, typically open extended hours.   [10] A grocery store, primarily self-service in operation, selling a wide variety of food and nonfood products with annual sales below $2.5 million (1985 dollars).   [11] Primarily engaged in the retail sale of a single food category such as meat and seafood stores and retail bakeries.

Source: U.S. Dept. of Agriculture, Economic Research Service, *Food Marketing Review*, annual.

No. 1281. Percent of Supermarkets Offering Selected Services and Product Lines: 1990 to 1999

[In percent. Based on a sample survey of chain and independent supermarkets and subject to sampling variability; for details, see source]

Service or product line offered	1990	1998	1999	Service or product line offered	1990	1998	1999
Service delicatessen.	73	81	81	Salad bar	18	24	24
Service bakery	60	69	69	Automated teller machines (ATMs) .	20	62	63
Service meat.	42	59	60	Banking in store	(NA)	21	22
Service fish.	33	43	45	Pharmacy.	15	32	30
Separate cheese department	33	31	32	Warehouse aisle	(NA)	17	17

NA Not available.

Source: Progressive Grocer, New York, NY, *Progressive Grocer 66th Annual Report* (copyright). Used by permission of Progressive Grocer magazine.

No. 1282. Food Sales by Nontraditional Retailers: 1997

[308,780,000 represents $308,780,000,000]

Sales outlet	Retail food sales ($1,000)	Share of total retail food sales (percent)	Sales outlet	Retail food sales ($1,000)	Share of total retail food sales (percent)
Traditional foodstores, total	308,780,000	82.6	Other stores:		
Supermarkets	222,002,648	59.4	Drugstores	5,007,000	1.3
Convenience stores	14,216,118	3.8	Eating and drinking places . . .	923,000	0.2
Other grocery stores	50,331,234	13.5	Furniture stores.	133,280	(Z)
Specialized food stores	22,230,000	5.9	Gasoline service stations	10,398,000	2.8
Nontraditional foodstores, total	64,867,269	17.4	Miscellaneous stores: Gift, novelty, and souvenir		
General merchandise stores:			shops	198,938	0.1
Department stores	244,000	0.1	Hobby, toy, and game shops . .	266,165	0.1
Discount/mass merchandise stores	26,336,000	7.0	Liquor stores	1,234,000	0.3
Variety stores	896,000	0.2	Nonstore retailers:		
Warehouse club stores	7,964,000	2.1	Catalog and mail order	1,008,000	0.3
Other general merchandise stores	795,000	0.2	Vending machine operators . . .	4,133,700	1.1
			Direct sales (mobile, door to door)	5,052,300	1.4

Z Less than 0.05 percent.

Source: U.S. Dept. of Agriculture, Economic Research Service, *Food Marketing Review*, annual.

No. 1283. Food and Alcoholic Beverage Sales by Sales Outlet: 1985 to 1998

[In billions of dollars (408.8 represents $408,800,000,000)]

Sales outlet	1985	1990	1991	1992	1993	1994	1995	1996	1997	1998
Food sales, total [1]	**408.8**	**565.4**	**586.3**	**596.7**	**616.8**	**646.4**	**671.1**	**697.4**	**730.6**	**756.2**
Food at home	240.0	303.9	319.3	319.3	325.3	351.5	364.4	364.4	391.7	401.8
Food stores	209.2	267.2	276.4	275.2	275.8	287.0	292.5	300.2	310.6	316.3
Other stores	16.4	30.2	33.9	36.0	39.2	41.8	48.3	52.5	56.2	61.4
Home-delivered, mail order	2.8	5.3	5.8	6.4	7.1	8.4	8.9	9.9	9.8	9.3
Farmers, manufacturers, wholesalers	4.6	6.3	6.6	6.7	7.0	7.1	7.6	7.8	8.3	8.2
Food away from home [2]	168.8	248.7	256.2	265.1	280.9	295.0	306.7	320.1	338.9	354.4
Alcoholic beverage sales, total	**57.4**	**73.0**	**74.5**	**74.5**	**74.3**	**77.6**	**80.0**	**83.9**	**88.1**	**92.4**
Packaged alcoholic beverages	31.6	38.2	39.1	38.2	37.2	39.5	40.2	42.2	43.8	44.7
Liquor stores	17.1	18.6	19.1	18.4	18.3	18.7	18.6	19.6	20.4	21.2
Food stores	10.4	12.9	13.0	12.8	12.6	13.2	13.5	14.0	14.3	13.9
All other	4.2	6.7	7.0	7.0	7.4	7.6	8.2	8.7	9.1	9.6
Alcoholic drinks	25.8	34.8	35.4	36.3	37.0	38.2	39.8	41.6	44.4	47.7
Eating and drinking places [3]	20.7	26.8	27.3	27.8	28.3	29.0	30.0	31.3	33.4	36.1
Hotels and motels [3]	3.4	3.8	3.7	3.8	3.8	4.0	4.3	4.5	4.8	4.9
All other	1.8	4.2	4.4	4.7	4.9	4.1	5.5	5.8	6.2	6.7

[1] Includes taxes and tips. Excludes home food production.   [2] Includes food furnished and donations.   [3] Includes tips.

Source: U.S. Dept. of Agriculture, Economic Research Service, *Food Consumption, Prices, and Expenditures, 1970-98.* <http://www.ers.usda.gov>.

No. 1284. Commercial and Noncommercial Groups—Food and Drink Sales: 1990 to 2000

[In millions of dollars (238,149 represents $238,149,000,000) except as indicated. Excludes military. Data refer to sales to consumers of food and alcoholic beverages. Sales are estimated. For details, see source]

Type of group	Establishments		Sales (mil. dol.)						
	1990	1997	1990	1995	1996	1997	1998	1999	2000 [1]
Total	**720,043**	**829,800**	**238,149**	**294,631**	**307,086**	**321,631**	**337,272**	**356,983**	**374,887**
Commercial restaurant services [2][3]	546,996	652,876	211,606	265,910	277,381	291,259	306,591	325,235	342,165
Eating places [2]	338,724	404,685	155,552	198,293	206,211	216,156	227,391	241,083	253,415
Full-service restaurants	163,514	186,552	77,811	96,396	100,830	106,376	111,801	120,994	128,133
Limited-service restaurants [4]	149,786	191,561	69,798	92,901	96,106	100,143	105,553	109,882	114,717
Bars and taverns [5]	37,227	36,435	9,533	9,948	10,276	10,646	11,061	11,515	11,929
Managed services [2]	15,739	19,117	14,149	18,186	19,410	20,621	21,779	23,016	24,336
Manufacturing and industrial plants	(NA)	(NA)	3,856	4,814	5,066	5,437	5,745	5,931	6,199
Colleges and universities	(NA)	(NA)	2,788	3,989	4,317	4,667	5,008	5,449	5,868
Lodging places [2]	27,158	27,970	13,568	15,561	16,193	16,954	17,852	18,798	19,701
Hotel restaurants	16,532	18,461	12,355	14,516	15,154	15,909	16,807	17,707	18,610
Motel restaurants	8,828	7,793	483	618	613	616	616	642	640
Retail hosts [2][6]	107,807	143,066	9,513	12,589	13,443	14,442	15,464	16,851	18,102
Department store restaurants	4,980	4,721	876	1,038	1,079	(NA)	(NA)	(NA)	(NA)
Grocery store restaurants [6]	44,766	62,951	5,432	6,624	7,041	(NA)	(NA)	(NA)	(NA)
Gasoline service stations	33,788	44,875	1,718	2,520	2,729	(NA)	(NA)	(NA)	(NA)
Recreation and sports	14,447	15,298	2,871	3,866	4,041	4,232	4,411	4,760	5,012
Noncommercial restaurant services [2]	173,047	176,924	26,543	28,722	29,705	30,372	30,681	31,749	32,722
Employee restaurant services	7,717	5,337	1,864	1,364	1,274	1,186	1,119	1,044	1,000
Industrial, commercial organizations	3,091	2,144	1,603	1,129	1,031	(NA)	(NA)	(NA)	(NA)
Educational restaurant services	95,883	97,736	7,671	9,059	9,328	9,545	9,711	9,959	10,194
Elementary and secondary schools	93,104	94,737	3,700	4,533	4,728	4,886	4,981	5,099	5,197
Hospitals	6,613	6,072	8,968	9,219	9,577	9,681	9,505	9,895	10,163
Miscellaneous [2]	29,403	32,576	2,892	3,673	3,842	4,058	4,244	4,511	4,749
Clubs	10,310	10,514	1,993	2,278	2,381	(NA)	(NA)	(NA)	(NA)

NA Not available.   [1] Projection.   [2] Includes other types of groups, not shown separately.   [3] Data for establishments with payroll.   [4] Fast-food restaurants.   [5] For establishments serving food.   [6] A portion of delicatessen sales in grocery stores are considered food service.

Source: National Restaurant Association, Washington, DC, *Restaurant Numbers: 25 Year History, 1970-1995,* 1998; *Restaurant Industry in Review,* annual; and *National Restaurant Association Restaurant Industry Forecast,* December 1999 (copyright).

No. 1285. Online Retail Sales, Penetration of Total Market, and Growth Rate by Kind of Business: 1998 to 2000

[In billions (14.47 represents $14,470,000,000), except percent. The size of the online market was obtained by combining the revenue of all online retailers of consequence. Based on data from 412 online retailers, 221 of which participated in a detailed survey, the research team was able to identify revenue for 86 percent of the market. Estimates were then made for the remaining 14 percent of the market]

Category	Revenues (bil. dol.)			Online penetration of total market [1] (percent)			Annual rate of growth, 1998-99
	1998	1999	2000, proj.	1998	1999	2000, proj.	
Total........................	14.47	33.10	61.09	0.7	1.4	2.4	120
Apparel/sporting goods..............	0.46	1.10	2.10	0.1	0.4	0.7	130
Automotive......................	0.08	1.90	3.40	(NA)	0.7	1.1	2,300
Books.........................	0.67	1.40	1.90	4.6	8.5	11.4	110
Collectibles (person to person auctions)....	1.40	3.10	6.00	(NA)	2.8	4.9	120
Computer hardware/software...........	4.20	6.60	9.20	14.0	17.6	23.4	60
Consumer electronics...............	0.17	0.54	1.50	0.4	1.2	3.2	220
Event tickets....................	0.26	0.80	1.70	1.6	4.7	9.1	210
Financial brokerage................	3.41	6.40	11.10	9.2	14.6	28.9	90
Flowers/cards/gifts................	0.41	0.75	1.30	(NA)	0.9	1.5	80
Food/beverage...................	0.16	0.34	0.86	0.1	0.1	0.2	110
Health/beauty...................	(NA)	0.21	0.74	(NA)	0.2	0.5	780
Home/garden....................	0.09	0.40	1.30	0.1	0.3	1.0	370
Multicategory....................	(NA)	1.00	1.90	0.1	0.3	0.4	130
Music/video.....................	0.33	1.10	2.70	1.4	4.3	9.9	230
Toys.........................	0.07	0.36	0.79	0.2	1.2	2.4	440
Travel........................	2.76	7.10	14.60	1.2	2.8	5.4	160

NA Not available.   [1] Online penetration means percent of retail sales conducted on line.

Source: Shop.org, The Boston Consulting Group, Silver Spring, MD, *The State of Online Retailing 2.0* (copyright).

No. 1286. Online Consumer Spending Forecast by Kind of Business: 1998 to 2000

[As of **January 2000. In millions of dollars (7,748.6 represents $7,748,600,000), except percent.** Note: Figures below reflect a partial revision of the Jupiter Internet Shopping Model; health commerce figures were updated in January 2000 and travel figures were updated in March 2000; retail figures from fall 1999. Does not include automobiles]

Category	Online spending			Percentage of spending online		
	1998	1999	2000	1998	1999	2000
Total........................	7,748.6	17,323.4	28,037.3	(NA)	(NA)	(NA)
Air travel......................	1,787.0	5,029.9	7,846.6	2.6	6.9	10.3
Hotel........................	284.3	1,018.5	2,097.9	0.7	2.4	4.6
Car rentals.....................	145.1	380.5	875.8	1.1	2.6	5.5
Cruise........................	3.3	19.5	44.0	0.1	0.3	0.7
Tour.........................	6.7	52.0	132.0	0.1	0.6	1.5
PCs.........................	2,171.7	3,827.8	5,155.3	11.1	19.3	24.3
Peripherals.....................	444.3	745.9	1,013.4	5.6	8.6	10.9
Software......................	476.4	860.0	1,265.2	8.6	14.8	20.7
Consumer electronics..............	170.1	402.2	627.8	0.4	1.0	1.5
Books........................	652.9	1,253.4	1,855.6	2.5	4.5	6.3
Music........................	151.8	327.3	585.8	1.1	2.3	3.8
Videos.......................	35.2	162.9	272.8	0.4	1.9	3.0
Movie tickets...................	1.1	4.4	10.6	-	0.1	0.2
Event tickets...................	94.4	255.0	471.2	0.7	1.6	2.8
Personal care...................	-	61.0	213.8	-	0.2	0.5
Prescription drugs................	-	32.6	135.1	-	-	0.1
Over-the-counter drugs..............	1.0	9.4	41.8	-	0.1	0.2
Nutraceuticals...................	1.4	34.6	109.1	-	0.2	0.7
Medical supplies and contact lenses........	-	42.1	88.2	-	0.2	0.5
Apparel.......................	441.1	804.3	1,414.2	0.3	0.5	0.8
Footwear......................	45.0	89.9	176.6	0.1	0.2	0.3
Grocery.......................	114.5	232.9	787.3	-	0.1	0.2
Toys.........................	71.8	309.8	483.9	0.3	1.3	1.9
Sporting goods..................	48.1	119.1	209.0	0.3	0.7	1.1
Flowers.......................	111.9	198.5	287.7	0.8	1.4	1.9
Specialty gifts...................	72.7	134.7	228.1	0.2	0.4	0.6
Furniture......................	5.7	17.1	52.7	-	-	0.1
Housewares/small appliances...........	36.5	75.1	164.4	0.1	0.1	0.3
Home improvement................	12.9	38.6	81.7	-	-	0.1
Office products..................	29.7	96.7	186.7	0.1	0.3	0.5
Other........................	334.3	687.7	1,123.0	(NA)	(NA)	(NA)
Holiday spending.................	3.1	7.0	(NA)	(NA)	(NA)	(NA)

- Represents or rounds to zero.   NA Not available.

Source: Jupiter Communications, New York, NY, *Online Consumer Spending Forcast Summary*, spring 2000 (copyright).

No. 1287. U.S. Online Retail and Business to Business E-Commerce Projections: 1999 and 2000

[Retail in millions (20,252 represents $20,252,000,000), business to business in billions (176.8 represents $176,800,000,000). Not all figures add up due to rounding]

Product or service	Projected sales		Percent change 1999-2000	Product or service	Projected sales		Percent change 1999-2000
	1999	2000			1999	2000	
U.S. ONLINE RETAIL PROJECTIONS (mil. dol.)				Automobiles.	-	400	400.0
				Electronics.	3,170	5,785	82.5
Retail trade, total	20,252	38,755	91.4	Computer hardware	1,964	3,471	76.7
Media.	3,617	5,461	51.0	Consumer electronics.	1,205	2,315	92.1
Software	1,240	1,898	53.1	Housewares.	446	1,000	124.2
Books	1,202	1,715	42.7	Appliances	179	405	126.3
Music	848	1,386	63.4	Furniture	268	595	122.0
Videos.	326	463	42.0	Food and beverage.	513	1,132	120.7
Event tickets	300	669	123.0	Health and beauty	509	1,189	133.6
Apparel.	1,620	3,607	122.7	Miscellaneous	778	1,807	132.3
General apparel	1,061	2,566	141.8				
Footware	121	290	139.7	BUSINESS TO BUSINESS (bil. dol.)			
Accessories	438	751	71.5				
Gifts and flowers.	656	998	52.1	Total	176.8	406.2	129.8
Flowers	354	550	55.4	Computing and electronics	(NA)	230.2	(NA)
Greetings.	134	177	32.1	Motor vehicles	(NA)	35.1	(NA)
Specialty gifts	167	271	62.3	Petrochemicals.	(NA)	27.0	(NA)
Household goods	250	618	147.2	Utilities	(NA)	29.9	(NA)
Recreation.	595	2,139	259.5	Paper and office products.	(NA)	14.4	(NA)
Toys and video games	253	610	141.1	Consumer goods	(NA)	13.2	(NA)
Sporting goods	165	586	255.2	Food and agriculture	(NA)	22.5	(NA)
Tools and garden	177	944	433.3	Industrial equipment & supplies. .	(NA)	7.0	(NA)
Leisure travel.	7,798	13,950	78.9	Aerospace and defense.	(NA)	9.1	(NA)

- Represents or rounds to zero. NA Not available.
Source: Forrester Research, Inc., Cambridge, MA, *NRF/Forrester Online Retail Index* (copyright).

No. 1288. Retail E-Commerce Sales, Number of Orders, and Average Purchase Amount in Key Categories: 1998 and 1999

[In billions of dollars (4.50 represents $4,500,000,000) as of fourth quarter. Based on a point-of-sale-survey of online buyers covering approximately 1,000 merchants]

Category	Sales (bil. dol.) [1]			Orders (mil.)			Average purchase amount (dol.) [1]		
	1998	1999	Percent change in prior year	1998	1999	Percent change in prior year	1998	1999	Percent change in prior year
Total	4.50	16.20	262	44.47	176.19	296	101	92	-9
Apparel	0.25	1.22	379	2.39	12.92	441	106	101	-5
Computer goods . . .	2.20	6.69	204	8.39	33.18	295	262	207	-21
Consumer goods . . .	0.36	1.82	403	4.62	16.47	257	78	134	71
Entertainment	0.89	3.06	245	17.81	59.27	233	50	55	10
Food/wine.	0.21	0.78	270	2.53	10.87	330	83	71	-15
Gifts.	0.41	1.77	327	6.96	31.81	357	59	58	-3
Home & garden	0.08	0.44	425	0.89	5.12	477	94	88	-7
Toys	0.07	0.42	500	0.90	6.54	630	78	64	-18

[1] Includes shipping and handling charges.
Source: BizRate.Com, Los Angeles, CA, *Consumer Online Report, Fourth Quarter, 1999* (copyright).

No. 1289. U.S. Mail Order Sales by Kind of Business: 1997 and 1998

[In millions of dollars (318,500 represents $318,500,000,000). Mail order sales represent orders placed by mail, phone, or electronically without the person ordering coming to the point of sale to place the order, or the seller coming to the office or home of the orderer to take the order or using an agent to collect the order. Excludes orders placed at catalog desks or elsewhere in stores even in response to a catalog but does include products or services delivered in the store as long as the order was placed by mail, phone, or electronically. Statistics are generated independently each year and are not adjusted for any discontinuity of available data]

Category	1997		1998							
				Percent of—			Percent of —			
	Amount (mil. dol.)	Per capita (dol.)	Amount (mil. dol.)	Total consumers	Mail order total	Per capita (dol.)	Retail sales	General merchandise sales [1]	Consumer services	
Total mail order sales. .	318,500	(X)	357,240	(X)	100	(X)	(X)	(X)	(X)	
Total products & services:										
Products	101,690	378	108,910	59	30	403	4.0	11.5	(X)	
Specialty	85,350	317	90,810	49	25	336	3.3	9.6	(X)	
General merchandise . . .	16,340	61	18,100	10	5	67	0.6	1.9	(X)	
Services	67,800	252	76,080	41	21	282	(X)	(X)	2.2	
Nonfinancial	37,840	141	39,840	22	11	148	(X)	(X)	1.1	
Financial	29,960	111	36,240	20	10	134	(X)	(X)	1.0	
Business products & services.	85,250	(X)	104,020	(X)	29	(X)	(X)	(X)	(X)	
Charitable contributions. . . .	63,700	(X)	68,230	(X)	19	(X)	(X)	(X)	(X)	

X Not applicable. [1] Includes apparel, drug, liquor, building materials, hardware, garden supply, mobile home, furniture, home furnishings, and equipment.
Source: National Mail Order Association, LLC, Minneapolis, MN, *Guide to Mail Order Sales,* annual (copyright).

Domestic Trade and Services 763

No. 1290. Catalog Sales—Method Used and Characteristic of Purchaser: 1997

[In thousands (194,347 represents 194,347,000), **except percent**. Based on population 18 years old and over as of July 1. Data are estimates]

Characteristic	Adult population 18 yrs. old and over	Total	Percent	By fax	By mail	By phone	At catalog store	Via commercial online service	Via the Internet
					Bought from catalog				
Total adults	**194,347**	**83,349**	**42.9**	**2,516**	**24,079**	**47,452**	**5,472**	**2,173**	**4,275**
18-24 years old	24,820	7,504	30.2	187	2,202	3,517	521	212	536
25-34 years old	38,822	15,690	40.4	399	3,983	9,224	868	552	1,073
35-44 years old	43,808	20,063	45.8	694	5,378	12,494	1,254	683	1,409
45-54 years old	33,496	16,136	48.2	783	4,554	10,060	1,048	484	806
55-64 years old	21,883	10,260	46.9	353	3,037	6,020	801	151	283
65 years old or older. . . .	31,518	13,696	43.5	100	4,925	6,136	980	91	169
Sex:									
Male.	93,172	31,736	34.1	892	8,283	17,196	1,614	1,125	2,181
Female	101,176	51,613	51.0	1,624	15,796	30,255	3,858	1,048	2,094
Race:									
White	163,003	73,038	44.8	2,219	21,258	42,948	4,132	1,931	3,864
Black	22,987	7,820	34.0	193	2,109	3,485	1,092	112	163

Source: Simmons Market Research Bureau, Chicago, IL, *Study of Media Markets* (copyright).

No. 1291. Merchandise or Services Ordered by Mail or Phone in Last 12 Months by Characteristic of Purchaser: 1997

[In thousands (194,347 represents 194,347,000), **except percent**. Based on population 18 years old and over as of July 1. Data are estimates]

Characteristic	Adult population 18 yrs. old and over	Persons ordering by mail or phone			
		By mail		By phone	
		Persons ordering	Percent	Persons ordering	Percent
Total adults	**194,347**	**61,035**	**31.4**	**66,016**	**34.0**
18-24 years old	24,820	6,146	24.8	5,255	21.2
25-34 years old	38,822	11,813	30.4	12,775	32.9
35-44 years old	43,808	14,294	32.6	16,650	38.0
45-54 years old	33,496	11,294	33.7	13,703	40.9
55-64 years old	21,883	6,948	31.8	8,275	37.8
65 years old or older.	31,518	10,541	33.4	9,358	29.7
Sex:					
Males	93,172	22,318	24.0	26,182	28.1
Females	101,176	38,719	38.3	39,834	39.4
Race:					
White	163,003	53,232	32.7	58,604	36.0
Black	22,987	5,690	24.8	5,340	23.2

Source: Simmons Market Research Bureau, Chicago, IL, *Study of Media Markets* (copyright).

No. 1292. Population Ordering by Catalog by Type of Product and Characteristic of Purchaser: 1997

[In thousands (194,347 represents 194,347,000). Survey conducted fall of 1997. Purchases ordered within 12 months prior to survey. Data are estimates]

Characteristic	Adult population 18 yrs. old and over	Food	Clothing	Electronic equipment	Gardening	Hardware	Home furnishing (bed & bath)	Housewares	Nonfood gifts	Sporting goods	Toys/games
						Specific items ordered					
Total adults . . .	**194,347**	**4,293**	**40,471**	**10,255**	**5,486**	**2,603**	**10,263**	**7,242**	**6,107**	**6,934**	**9,954**
18-24 years old	24,820	157	3,304	1,099	141	142	598	469	397	518	696
25-34 years old	38,822	779	6,945	2,145	659	337	1,856	1,319	921	1,455	2,536
35-44 years old	43,808	973	9,936	2,893	1,380	579	2,865	1,802	1,689	2,129	2,918
45-54 years old	33,496	952	8,286	2,234	1,299	579	2,240	1,558	1,446	1,641	1,535
55-64 years old	21,883	573	5,070	1,116	908	435	1,475	1,008	884	687	1,220
65 or older	31,518	859	6,929	768	1,100	533	1,230	1,085	770	503	1,049
Sex:											
Male.	93,172	1,168	10,986	6,219	1,881	1,827	1,631	1,551	1,227	4,918	2,599
Female	101,176	3,125	29,485	4,034	3,605	776	8,632	5,691	4,879	2,016	7,354
Race:											
White	163,003	3,636	36,238	8,568	5,086	2,242	9,130	6,414	5,746	6,375	8,805
Black	22,987	453	3,406	1,133	238	260	936	601	201	361	916

Source: Simmons Market Research Bureau, New York, NY, *Study of Media and Markets* (copyright).

No. 1293. Shopping Centers—Number, Gross Leasable Area, and Retail Sales by Gross Leasable Area: 1990 to 1999

[As of **December 31**. A shopping center is a group of architecturally unified commercial establishments built on a site that is planned, developed, owned, and managed as an operating unit related in its location, size, and type of shops to the trade area that the unit serves. The unit provides on-site parking in definite relationship to the types and total size of the stores. The data base attempts to include all centers with three or more stores. Estimates are based on a sample of data available on shopping center properties; for details, contact source]

Year	Total	Gross leasable area (sq. ft.)					
		Less than 100,001	100,001- 200,000	200,001- 400,000	400,001- 800,000	800,001- 1,000,000	More than 1 million
NUMBER							
1990	36,515	23,231	8,756	2,781	1,102	288	357
1995	41,235	26,001	9,974	3,345	1,234	301	380
1997	42,953	26,928	10,400	3,595	1,324	316	390
1998	43,661	27,317	10,581	3,696	1,354	319	395
1999	44,426	27,696	10,770	3,834	1,398	324	404
Percent distribution	100.0	62.3	24.2	8.6	3.1	0.7	0.9
Percent change, 1998-99	1.8	1.4	1.8	3.7	3.2	1.6	2.3
GROSS LEASABLE AREA							
1990 (mil. sq. ft.)	4,390	1,125	1,197	734	618	259	457
1995 (mil. sq. ft.)	4,967	1,267	1,368	886	689	271	486
1997 (mil. sq. ft.)	5,229	1,318	1,431	960	736	285	500
1998 (mil. sq. ft.)	5,333	1,340	1,458	988	752	287	507
1999 (mil. sq. ft.)	5,463	1,362	1,486	1,030	776	292	519
Percent distribution	100.0	25.1	27.3	18.5	14.1	5.4	9.5
Percent change, 1998-99	2.4	1.6	1.9	4.2	3.1	1.5	2.4
RETAIL SALES							
1990 (bil. dol.)	706.4	205.1	179.5	108.0	91.7	45.1	77.0
1995 (bil. dol.)	893.8	259.6	227.1	136.4	115.8	57.0	97.8
1997 (bil. dol.)	980.0	284.6	249.0	149.7	126.9	62.5	107.4
1998 (bil. dol.)	1,032.4	299.7	262.2	157.7	133.7	65.8	113.2
1999 (bil. dol.)	1,105.3	320.8	280.7	168.9	143.0	70.4	121.4
Percent distribution	100.0	29.0	25.4	15.3	12.9	6.4	11.0
Percent change, 1998-99	7.1	7.0	7.1	7.1	7.0	7.0	7.2

No. 1294. Shopping Centers—Number, Gross Leasable Area, and Retail Sales by State: 1999

[See headnote, Table 1293]

State	Num- ber	Gross leas- able area (mil. sq. ft.)	Retail sales (bil. dol.)	Percent change, 1998-99			State	Num- ber	Gross leas- able area (mil. sq. ft.)	Retail sales (bil. dol.)	Percent change, 1998-99		
				Num- ber	Gross leas- able area	Retail sales					Num- ber	Gross leas- able area	Retail sales
U.S.	44,426	5,463	1,105.3	1.8	2.4	7.1	MO	895	114	24.2	1.0	3.0	6.7
							MT	94	10	2.1	-	-	7.0
AL	633	74	16.4	0.5	0.9	6.0	NE	269	35	6.1	1.9	2.4	6.5
AK	68	8	2.2	-	-	8.8	NV	367	47	7.2	3.8	6.6	7.7
AZ	1,041	125	26.3	2.1	3.2	7.3	NH	225	25	4.8	2.5	6.6	10.2
AR	375	37	7.9	1.5	1.3	5.6							
CA	5,972	695	132.9	1.4	2.1	6.9	NJ	1,254	172	30.5	2.9	3.8	8.0
							NM	306	30	6.8	1.0	1.8	6.3
CO	755	100	24.7	1.8	2.3	7.8	NY	1,771	247	47.6	2.3	1.8	6.8
CT	791	96	20.2	0.8	0.5	8.6	NC	1,628	176	30.9	2.8	4.5	6.7
DE	146	23	4.7	5.1	4.8	8.5	ND	87	9	2.3	-	-	6.9
DC	87	9	1.8	-	-	7.0							
FL	3,365	428	100.6	2.7	3.1	7.9	OH	1,716	249	44.3	0.7	1.3	6.5
							OK	572	60	13.9	0.7	0.6	5.3
GA	1,620	181	33.6	2.8	6.2	6.6	OR	515	58	10.0	2.7	1.7	7.6
HI	184	20	4.6	1.2	0.9	10.5	PA	1,674	242	43.1	2.2	2.9	7.1
ID	165	20	3.5	2.4	2.0	5.9	RI	206	20	4.0	3.0	8.6	7.2
IL	2,146	260	45.0	2.4	2.5	7.5							
IN	918	121	22.8	1.5	1.3	6.4	SC	827	82	16.6	2.8	4.1	6.4
							SD	58	7	1.4	-	-	6.6
IA	317	43	8.0	3.1	5.3	6.6	TN	1,203	134	24.5	0.3	0.4	6.8
KS	486	58	12.4	1.0	1.4	6.5	TX	3,018	369	93.2	1.4	2.8	6.7
KY	620	68	14.8	0.6	0.8	6.4	UT	241	35	6.9	2.1	3.5	5.9
LA	703	84	19.9	0.5	0.7	6.6							
ME	200	17	4.5	-	-	8.9	VT	113	8	1.9	-	-	8.5
							VA	1,297	171	34.0	2.2	2.3	7.5
MD	926	127	26.6	2.4	1.6	7.0	WA	776	101	19.0	1.7	1.6	7.4
MA	998	114	25.1	0.6	0.6	7.7	WV	164	23	4.0	0.8	1.7	5.4
MI	1,039	139	27.0	2.1	3.6	6.8	WI	629	77	15.6	0.6	0.5	7.2
MN	472	68	14.9	0.2	0.9	7.1	WY	53	6	1.4	-	-	6.1
MS	438	43	8.7	1.8	5.9	5.1							

- Represents zero.

Source of Tables 1293 and 1294: National Research Bureau, Chicago, IL. Monitor Publishing, Clearwater, FL, in *Monitor Magazine*, November/December 1991 (copyright). Data for 1995-99 published by International Council of Shopping Centers in *Shopping Centers Today*, April issues (copyright—Interactive Market Systems, Inc.).

Domestic Trade and Services **765**

No. 1295. Retail Sales by Type of Store and State: 1997 and 1998

[In millions of dollars (2,546,287 represents $2,546,287,000) except as indicated. Kind-of-business classification based on 1987 Standard Industrial Classification (SIC) code; see text, Section 17, Business Enterprise. Data are estimates]

State	All stores [1]				Food stores				General merchandise stores			
		1998			Total (SIC 54)		Grocery stores (SIC 541)		Total (SIC 53)		Department stores (SIC 531)	
	1997, total	Total	Sales per household [2] Amount (dol.)	Percent change, 1997-98	1997	1998	1997	1998	1997	1998	1997	1998
U.S. . .	2,546,287	2,695,852	26,544	5.9	428,842	448,262	403,855	421,427	322,463	339,725	253,197	267,012
AL	38,063	39,876	23,859	4.8	6,600	6,838	6,281	6,495	5,964	6,358	4,799	5,112
AK	6,991	7,256	33,148	3.8	1,434	1,466	1,390	1,419	978	1,014	681	701
AZ	44,995	48,957	26,861	8.8	8,807	9,594	8,491	9,231	5,290	5,499	4,041	4,202
AR	22,872	23,995	24,527	4.9	3,605	3,709	3,482	3,576	3,768	3,938	3,060	3,202
CA	275,289	290,938	25,178	5.7	47,304	48,624	43,956	45,095	34,185	35,967	23,700	24,933
CO	41,783	45,088	28,173	7.9	7,085	7,429	6,832	7,150	5,230	5,701	4,069	4,429
CT	34,661	36,469	29,466	5.2	6,408	6,747	5,964	6,267	3,579	3,795	2,851	3,027
DE	8,186	8,709	30,991	6.4	1,313	1,390	1,220	1,289	1,092	1,095	866	869
DC	3,670	3,730	16,893	1.6	645	673	566	589	166	149	145	130
FL	166,211	177,765	29,313	7.0	26,312	27,805	24,862	26,223	19,552	20,783	14,723	15,668
GA	73,999	79,608	27,916	7.6	12,539	13,437	11,923	12,752	9,753	10,433	7,943	8,514
HI	13,359	13,537	34,142	1.3	2,264	2,284	2,090	2,105	2,256	2,297	1,012	1,032
ID	12,307	13,129	29,091	6.7	2,436	2,636	2,366	2,555	1,406	1,498	1,061	1,138
IL	107,901	113,685	25,598	5.4	15,172	15,608	14,133	14,516	13,047	13,654	10,859	11,366
IN	56,603	59,429	26,385	5.0	7,855	8,083	7,438	7,640	7,883	8,339	6,459	6,837
IA	29,108	30,720	27,542	5.5	5,468	5,729	5,186	5,423	3,912	4,134	3,249	3,443
KS	23,975	25,362	25,047	5.8	4,224	4,445	4,084	4,290	3,453	3,640	2,685	2,847
KY	35,048	36,791	24,389	5.0	6,177	6,420	5,949	6,170	5,577	5,937	4,720	5,042
LA	39,122	41,200	25,976	5.3	7,289	7,518	6,945	7,152	5,971	6,272	4,740	4,978
ME	12,481	12,982	26,707	4.0	2,640	2,741	2,509	2,599	1,191	1,221	747	765
MD	47,058	49,254	25,950	4.7	8,633	8,924	8,118	8,376	5,662	5,958	4,368	4,608
MA	59,263	62,573	26,901	5.6	11,193	11,910	10,187	10,818	5,498	5,627	4,013	4,116
MI	98,234	104,412	28,429	6.3	12,828	13,523	11,857	12,480	15,593	16,471	13,753	14,529
MN	46,788	49,673	27,601	6.2	7,074	7,362	6,621	6,877	5,908	6,315	4,864	5,192
MS	19,635	20,757	20,740	5.7	3,918	4,136	3,678	3,878	3,367	3,535	2,592	2,718
MO	54,169	57,248	27,204	5.7	8,800	9,090	8,464	8,729	8,005	8,539	6,934	7,403
MT	8,565	9,007	26,290	5.2	1,531	1,582	1,475	1,521	974	1,018	717	754
NE	16,354	17,481	27,301	6.9	3,266	3,808	3,099	3,611	1,985	2,034	1,574	1,616
NV	20,020	21,878	29,871	9.3	3,728	4,029	3,588	3,870	2,369	2,525	1,925	2,051
NH	14,577	15,379	34,289	5.5	2,825	2,906	2,688	2,760	1,914	2,041	1,311	1,393
NJ	78,291	82,355	28,053	5.2	13,791	14,385	12,714	13,238	7,409	7,590	5,909	6,056
NM	16,435	17,403	27,497	5.9	2,945	3,115	2,835	2,993	2,198	2,365	1,780	1,914
NY	142,486	148,392	22,171	4.1	24,553	25,032	21,966	22,345	13,467	13,760	10,750	11,022
NC	76,018	81,141	27,668	6.7	13,546	14,331	12,910	13,633	8,891	9,383	7,188	7,593
ND	6,841	7,222	29,029	5.6	1,060	1,118	1,018	1,072	1,006	1,042	826	861
OH	114,815	121,092	28,183	5.5	18,140	18,934	17,088	17,805	14,896	15,426	12,348	12,800
OK	27,841	29,290	22,730	5.2	4,308	4,358	4,090	4,128	4,176	4,391	3,412	3,597
OR	35,062	37,591	29,249	7.2	5,426	5,719	5,187	5,458	5,871	6,463	4,179	4,609
PA	116,304	121,274	26,298	4.3	19,112	19,590	17,789	18,199	12,479	12,807	10,485	10,781
RI	7,853	8,166	21,798	4.0	1,475	1,494	1,331	1,345	779	799	583	599
SC	34,544	36,945	25,901	7.0	6,538	6,961	6,324	6,719	4,239	4,564	3,494	3,766
SD	7,972	8,395	30,507	5.3	1,289	1,352	1,246	1,304	976	1,007	781	813
TN	53,796	57,001	26,982	6.0	8,385	8,726	8,099	8,413	8,149	8,674	6,560	7,001
TX	176,772	189,977	26,598	7.5	30,153	32,137	28,782	30,617	24,528	26,126	19,499	20,803
UT	17,922	19,303	28,691	7.7	3,671	3,982	3,556	3,850	2,231	2,357	1,719	1,819
VT	5,754	6,035	26,434	4.9	1,238	1,278	1,185	1,221	372	387	275	287
VA	69,713	73,585	28,714	5.6	12,819	13,360	12,233	12,723	8,665	9,259	6,319	6,746
WA	53,397	56,507	25,313	5.8	9,464	9,949	9,055	9,501	7,135	7,601	5,185	5,517
WV	14,484	15,077	21,008	4.1	2,905	2,984	2,821	2,891	2,134	2,225	1,689	1,766
WI	53,860	57,116	28,690	6.0	7,816	8,138	7,369	7,659	6,738	7,092	5,318	5,597
WY	4,840	5,099	27,725	5.3	834	875	815	854	600	620	438	450

See footnotes at end of table.

U.S. Census Bureau, Statistical Abstract of the United States: 2000

[See headnote, page 766]

State	Automotive dealers (SIC 55 exc. 554)		Eating and drinking places (SIC 58)		Gasoline service stations (SIC 554)		Building materials and garden supplies (SIC 52)		Apparel and accessory stores (SIC 56)		Furniture and homefurnishing stores (SIC 57)	
	1997	1998	1997	1998	1997	1998	1997	1998	1997	1998	1997	1998
U.S...	631,625	678,002	245,314	259,710	156,291	156,431	144,681	158,119	112,579	117,147	141,851	153,253
AL	9,833	10,314	3,138	3,273	2,742	2,754	2,357	2,567	1,615	1,672	1,617	1,708
AK	1,274	1,332	717	750	476	509	512	536	289	288	272	287
AZ	10,998	12,314	5,601	6,073	2,512	2,514	2,456	2,768	1,521	1,624	2,602	2,923
AR	6,512	6,867	1,744	1,827	1,942	2,028	1,475	1,600	717	740	819	882
CA	63,505	68,809	26,278	27,964	16,903	16,805	16,541	17,930	14,017	14,718	18,365	19,726
CO	9,517	10,368	5,462	5,958	2,289	2,327	2,609	2,935	1,367	1,453	2,759	3,052
CT	7,431	7,948	2,555	2,692	2,162	2,047	2,131	2,329	1,785	1,848	1,752	1,917
DE	1,735	1,840	808	878	430	438	563	589	354	387	578	661
DC	146	147	1,065	1,092	168	160	66	75	329	334	252	250
FL....	45,848	49,202	16,474	17,584	7,972	7,983	8,722	9,794	7,689	8,097	10,212	11,196
GA	17,837	19,253	7,708	8,268	4,687	4,777	4,671	5,278	3,371	3,617	4,211	4,607
HI	1,989	1,996	1,849	1,877	633	591	544	584	1,117	1,157	617	626
ID....	3,330	3,620	1,276	1,360	672	609	1,007	1,096	343	346	709	773
IL.....	27,714	29,585	11,494	12,174	5,959	5,930	5,105	5,622	4,931	5,093	7,554	8,247
IN.....	14,541	15,486	5,687	5,964	3,967	3,956	3,107	3,348	1,666	1,699	3,032	3,225
IA	7,643	8,150	2,518	2,643	2,423	2,470	1,742	1,887	860	893	1,366	1,491
KS	6,514	6,997	2,153	2,244	1,557	1,497	1,155	1,244	783	834	1,302	1,445
KY	8,016	8,475	3,300	3,464	2,905	2,887	2,367	2,581	1,092	1,114	1,381	1,446
LA	9,993	10,641	3,747	3,985	2,703	2,738	2,088	2,299	1,543	1,598	1,566	1,664
ME	2,504	2,635	865	905	811	813	929	992	566	569	418	444
MD	10,714	11,340	4,831	5,051	2,528	2,463	2,395	2,547	2,343	2,389	3,021	3,257
MA	12,479	13,468	5,603	5,874	3,524	3,466	3,010	3,202	3,744	3,997	2,771	2,930
MI	27,106	29,035	9,232	9,742	6,025	6,081	5,173	5,609	3,676	3,763	6,059	6,654
MN	11,784	12,784	4,190	4,452	3,556	3,530	3,018	3,355	1,614	1,677	2,434	2,646
MS	4,746	4,996	1,517	1,616	1,342	1,352	1,239	1,397	627	641	729	785
MO	14,589	15,651	5,375	5,666	4,285	4,348	2,738	2,982	1,665	1,685	2,555	2,768
MT	2,036	2,181	1,124	1,187	598	596	705	772	230	229	471	508
NE	3,844	4,036	1,481	1,534	1,098	1,035	775	861	515	517	913	947
NV	4,385	4,905	2,452	2,655	1,019	1,028	1,187	1,301	729	771	1,168	1,302
NH	3,310	3,626	963	1,020	704	677	1,033	1,118	647	665	653	679
NJ.....	20,386	21,700	5,891	6,165	4,002	3,946	3,661	3,879	4,963	5,098	4,816	5,167
NM	3,528	3,733	2,111	2,235	1,180	1,172	1,059	1,190	507	511	873	931
NY	29,654	31,389	13,259	13,858	6,575	6,434	7,509	7,984	9,967	10,286	8,382	8,900
NC	18,794	20,426	7,526	8,009	4,572	4,686	5,833	6,412	3,099	3,241	4,299	4,612
ND	1,947	2,102	582	616	598	597	414	450	190	192	261	279
OH	29,531	31,641	12,165	12,828	7,308	7,275	5,829	6,400	3,699	3,804	6,453	6,915
OK	8,298	8,816	2,644	2,776	2,063	2,173	1,226	1,311	1,032	1,066	1,129	1,210
OR	8,935	9,773	2,932	3,145	2,066	2,067	2,538	2,752	1,371	1,433	1,835	1,990
PA	30,505	32,325	9,290	9,700	6,758	6,979	6,243	6,701	5,284	5,471	5,098	5,331
RI.....	1,519	1,604	772	811	586	573	375	390	350	354	338	358
SC	7,908	8,451	3,587	3,824	2,230	2,195	2,685	3,046	1,657	1,771	1,836	1,996
SD	2,207	2,378	710	754	744	744	441	473	246	251	336	350
TN	15,110	16,369	4,894	5,110	3,685	3,633	3,275	3,618	2,040	2,112	2,378	2,537
TX	49,451	53,628	17,095	18,363	10,939	11,024	8,034	9,037	7,684	8,023	8,623	9,614
UT	4,340	4,746	1,978	2,133	1,113	1,127	1,131	1,250	668	712	1,227	1,350
VT	1,275	1,364	424	439	410	413	478	501	231	239	201	215
VA	15,622	16,629	6,601	6,925	4,114	4,078	3,931	4,284	3,350	3,464	4,750	5,175
WA	12,063	12,816	4,700	4,950	3,366	3,392	4,037	4,371	2,311	2,428	2,991	3,171
WV	3,435	3,633	1,226	1,280	1,024	1,025	1,070	1,148	458	470	602	627
WI	14,135	15,274	5,126	5,396	3,809	3,928	3,240	3,442	1,588	1,664	3,076	3,265
WY	1,112	1,204	592	621	554	562	253	279	137	139	195	216

[1] Includes other types of stores, not shown separately.   [2] Based on number of households as of July 1 as estimated by source.

Source: Market Statistics, a division of Claritas Inc., Arlington, VA, *The Survey of Buying Power Data Service,* annual (copyright).

Domestic Trade and Services   767

No. 1296. Retail Trade—Summary of Establishments by State: 1997

[1,588.7 represents 1,588,700, except as indicated. Covers establishments with payroll. Employees are for the week including March 12. Most government employees are excluded. Kind-of-business classification based on 1987 Standard Industrial Classification (SIC) code; see text, Section 13, Labor Force, Employment, and Earnings. For statement on methodology, see Appendix III]

State	Establishments (1,000)				Paid employees (1,000)				Annual payroll (mil. dol.)			
	Total [1]	Food stores (SIC 54)	Auto-motive dealers and service stations (SIC 55)	Eating and drinking places (SIC 58)	Total [1]	Food stores (SIC 54)	Auto-motive dealers and service stations (SIC 55)	Eating and drinking places (SIC 58)	Total [1]	Food stores (SIC 54)	Auto-motive dealers and service stations (SIC 55)	Eating and drinking places (SIC 58)
U.S.	1,588.7	176.6	200.9	478.6	22,003	3,162	2,312	7,597	330,334	43,554	56,951	72,412
AL.	26.0	3.2	4.4	6.2	339	54	40	107	4,323	557	833	910
AK.	4.1	0.4	0.4	1.3	47	8	5	15	868	141	151	213
AZ.	24.2	2.2	2.7	7.9	380	50	45	144	5,709	827	1,199	1,282
AR.	16.3	1.9	2.7	4.0	204	28	24	63	2,832	295	476	497
CA.	161.5	17.4	16.7	54.7	2,265	289	219	859	37,791	5,377	6,243	8,723
CO	26.7	1.9	3.0	8.5	376	44	36	152	5,682	826	991	1,436
CT.	20.9	2.2	2.4	6.2	272	47	27	80	4,733	707	777	873
DE.	5.1	0.5	0.6	1.4	71	10	8	25	1,036	143	190	251
DC	3.7	0.4	0.1	1.6	47	5	1	27	742	91	25	375
FL.	91.6	9.8	11.5	24.9	1,311	214	133	452	19,351	2,622	3,543	4,305
GA	45.1	5.1	6.3	12.2	670	103	70	229	9,758	1,207	1,745	2,153
HI	8.0	0.8	0.6	2.8	115	14	9	48	1,872	230	215	591
ID	8.2	0.7	1.2	2.5	96	12	13	33	1,386	196	298	262
IL	66.1	6.5	7.7	22.0	980	128	95	338	15,353	1,852	2,460	3,316
IN	35.1	2.9	5.3	10.6	535	64	60	192	7,087	801	1,306	1,641
IA	19.8	1.7	3.1	6.1	256	42	32	85	3,245	498	663	635
KS.	17.0	1.5	2.6	5.0	229	31	25	80	3,217	400	572	664
KY.	23.0	2.8	3.7	5.8	329	49	38	112	4,301	541	754	973
LA.	24.0	3.6	3.3	6.4	341	55	40	117	4,345	581	858	1,033
ME	9.7	1.3	1.4	2.6	109	21	13	31	1,606	248	269	325
MD	28.0	3.0	3.0	8.3	426	63	45	141	6,982	1,054	1,156	1,410
MA	39.6	4.4	4.2	13.0	551	94	47	185	9,029	1,228	1,212	2,031
MI	56.1	6.7	7.3	16.8	821	104	88	282	12,069	1,339	2,340	2,497
MN	28.9	2.5	4.1	8.4	449	55	52	148	6,518	698	1,094	1,322
MS	16.1	2.4	2.7	3.4	197	35	24	58	2,449	345	508	469
MO	33.3	3.1	5.3	9.7	469	58	57	169	6,707	757	1,309	1,518
MT	7.6	0.6	1.0	2.6	77	10	11	29	972	144	205	238
NE	11.4	1.1	1.7	3.5	152	22	17	52	1,937	254	357	410
NV.	9.2	0.9	1.0	3.0	140	18	16	52	2,387	345	458	557
NH	9.0	1.0	1.1	2.4	120	21	13	35	1,839	260	349	352
NJ.	50.3	6.4	5.3	15.2	608	104	57	170	11,279	1,715	1,673	1,966
NM	10.4	0.9	1.5	3.0	139	17	17	51	1,920	260	369	457
NY.	110.5	16.0	9.5	34.8	1,218	201	94	386	20,442	2,856	2,415	4,727
NC	47.7	5.3	7.2	12.7	650	95	72	221	9,303	1,117	1,728	2,021
ND	4.9	0.5	0.7	1.5	60	8	9	21	712	86	177	155
OH	64.6	7.0	8.4	20.7	1,024	134	105	360	14,440	1,706	2,397	3,081
OK	20.1	2.4	3.1	5.7	259	34	33	95	3,318	397	693	777
OR	21.2	2.2	2.4	7.1	288	36	34	106	4,605	540	859	1,018
PA	72.0	7.7	8.7	22.3	978	162	103	311	13,995	2,004	2,361	2,784
RI	6.6	0.7	0.8	2.3	79	14	7	28	1,175	171	164	283
SC.	25.0	2.8	3.6	6.7	325	51	36	116	4,297	572	786	1,041
SD.	5.9	0.6	0.9	1.7	67	10	9	23	817	108	181	175
TN.	32.7	4.0	5.0	8.2	475	66	51	159	6,799	763	1,260	1,496
TX.	104.5	12.9	14.6	30.4	1,549	212	168	553	23,464	2,927	4,328	5,291
UT.	10.7	0.9	1.5	3.2	180	24	20	60	2,544	334	466	499
VT.	5.3	0.8	0.7	1.4	53	11	6	17	743	122	129	164
VA.	39.5	4.8	5.1	10.8	580	83	64	191	8,562	1,130	1,527	1,815
WA	34.0	3.6	3.8	11.5	457	64	47	167	7,396	1,071	1,272	1,623
WV	10.9	1.4	1.9	2.9	132	22	18	43	1,658	254	324	355
WI	32.7	2.7	4.5	11.7	467	66	56	163	6,187	778	1,159	1,286
WY	4.1	0.3	0.7	1.2	43	5	7	17	557	78	128	138

[1] Includes other kinds of business not shown separately.

Source: U.S. Census Bureau, County Business Patterns, annual.

No. 1297. Merchant Wholesalers—Summary: 1990 to 1999

[In billions of dollars (1,792.9 represents $1,792,900,000,000) except ratios. Inventories and stock/sales ratios, as of December, seasonally adjusted. Data reflect latest revision. Based on Current Business Survey; see Appendix III]

Kind of business	1987 SIC code [1]	1990	1994	1995	1996	1997	1998	1999
SALES (bil. dol.)								
Merchant wholesalers	(X)	1,792.9	2,075.9	2,271.0	2,391.0	2,500.9	2,554.1	2,740.5
Durable goods	50	880.7	1,099.0	1,210.3	1,258.0	1,335.0	1,381.8	1,480.3
Motor vehicles, parts, and supplies	501	173.8	188.7	189.0	192.4	195.3	202.6	227.9
Furniture and homefurnishings	502	33.8	36.9	41.1	43.3	46.7	48.4	50.1
Lumber and construction materials	503	63.6	79.8	80.0	86.0	90.8	94.4	106.9
Professional and commercial equipment	504	114.3	173.0	207.2	229.4	247.5	265.3	281.6
Metals and minerals, except petroleum	505	77.7	89.3	95.3	94.2	100.6	97.1	94.3
Electrical goods	506	116.4	163.5	193.3	194.7	205.7	210.6	233.0
Hardware, plumbing and heating equipment	507	52.6	63.4	67.2	69.9	74.2	78.2	82.1
Machinery, equipment and supplies	508	157.0	176.4	193.5	207.3	225.6	244.1	247.4
Miscellaneous durable goods	509	91.4	128.0	143.6	140.9	148.6	140.9	157.0
Nondurable goods	51	912.3	976.9	1,060.6	1,133.0	1,165.8	1,172.3	1,260.2
Paper and paper products	511	51.5	66.3	79.5	79.2	83.6	89.6	97.6
Drugs, proprietaries, and sundries	512	51.6	76.6	83.9	93.9	107.4	124.4	146.2
Apparel, piece goods, and notions	513	64.8	72.6	70.7	75.3	86.3	86.0	92.9
Groceries and related products	514	272.4	293.5	312.6	319.2	332.0	346.2	362.9
Farm-product raw materials	515	107.6	99.1	119.7	136.8	124.6	107.7	100.1
Chemicals and allied products	516	35.7	43.4	50.4	53.3	56.0	55.1	52.9
Petroleum and petroleum products	517	148.5	130.5	131.4	148.0	144.4	120.5	144.5
Beer, wine, and distilled beverages	518	49.3	52.0	52.6	55.8	58.2	61.6	66.8
Miscellaneous nondurable goods	519	130.8	143.0	159.7	171.4	173.4	181.2	196.2
INVENTORIES (bil. dol.)								
Merchant wholesalers	(X)	195.8	236.3	254.8	257.6	276.1	290.2	307.9
Durable goods	50	126.5	151.9	164.9	168.2	180.4	191.1	202.3
Motor vehicles, parts, and supplies	501	23.7	24.8	25.7	25.3	26.3	26.8	29.4
Furniture and homefurnishings	502	4.6	5.2	5.6	5.7	5.9	6.1	6.5
Lumber and construction materials	503	6.0	7.3	7.3	7.8	8.6	8.3	9.4
Professional and commercial equipment	504	15.8	21.2	24.1	24.9	28.1	26.9	27.5
Metals and minerals, except petroleum	505	10.7	12.1	11.7	12.2	13.0	13.7	13.2
Electrical goods	506	16.0	21.3	25.3	24.3	24.4	26.3	30.1
Hardware, plumbing and heating equipment	507	8.5	10.9	11.2	12.0	12.2	13.4	13.3
Machinery, equipment and supplies	508	31.5	33.6	38.0	39.9	44.5	50.8	51.9
Miscellaneous durable goods	509	9.8	15.4	16.1	16.2	17.5	18.8	21.0
Nondurable goods	51	69.4	84.4	89.9	89.5	95.7	99.1	105.7
Paper and paper products	511	4.9	6.8	7.9	8.1	9.1	9.5	10.0
Drugs, proprietaries, and sundries	512	6.5	10.4	10.1	11.4	13.0	14.9	17.9
Apparel, piece goods, and notions	513	9.8	11.8	11.2	11.5	12.8	12.8	11.5
Groceries and related products	514	14.7	16.0	16.3	16.2	16.9	17.1	19.5
Farm-product raw materials	515	8.8	10.8	12.9	10.3	10.9	10.9	10.9
Chemicals and allied products	516	3.1	4.0	4.4	4.6	4.8	5.0	4.9
Petroleum and petroleum products	517	4.5	4.8	4.8	5.3	4.7	4.0	4.0
Beer, wine, and distilled beverages	518	4.4	4.6	4.8	5.1	5.6	5.9	6.4
Miscellaneous nondurable goods	519	12.7	15.2	17.5	17.0	18.1	19.0	20.5
STOCK/SALES RATIO								
Merchant wholesalers	(X)	1.31	1.29	1.29	1.27	1.32	1.34	1.27
Durable goods	50	1.75	1.55	1.56	1.58	1.60	1.65	1.55
Motor vehicles, parts, and supplies	501	1.67	1.55	1.58	1.55	1.70	1.52	1.44
Furniture and homefurnishings	502	1.72	1.53	1.61	1.50	1.45	1.51	1.50
Lumber and construction materials	503	1.30	0.98	1.07	1.05	1.12	1.00	1.01
Professional and commercial equipment	504	1.58	1.33	1.30	1.29	1.30	1.21	1.13
Metals and minerals, except petroleum	505	1.61	1.52	1.49	1.53	1.52	1.78	1.58
Electrical goods	506	1.71	1.43	1.49	1.57	1.40	1.49	1.39
Hardware, plumbing and heating equipment	507	1.90	1.91	1.90	1.98	1.93	1.99	1.93
Machinery, equipment and supplies	508	2.46	2.15	2.15	2.20	2.29	2.51	2.45
Miscellaneous durable goods	509	1.26	1.36	1.32	1.32	1.42	1.63	1.47
Nondurable goods	51	0.90	0.99	0.98	0.93	0.99	0.99	0.95
Paper and paper products	511	1.17	1.10	1.18	1.19	1.28	1.21	1.19
Drugs, proprietaries, and sundries	512	1.48	1.60	1.36	1.38	1.37	1.33	1.36
Apparel, piece goods, and notions	513	1.77	2.02	1.87	1.67	1.74	1.81	1.40
Groceries and related products	514	0.66	0.62	0.61	0.62	0.61	0.59	0.62
Farm-product raw materials	515	1.03	1.20	1.26	0.92	1.07	1.19	1.36
Chemicals and allied products	516	0.95	1.00	0.99	1.03	1.03	1.13	1.06
Petroleum and petroleum products	517	0.33	0.44	0.43	0.39	0.42	0.42	0.30
Beer, wine, and distilled beverages	518	0.94	1.05	1.06	1.11	1.07	1.11	1.12
Miscellaneous nondurable goods	519	1.19	1.21	1.25	1.21	1.26	1.14	1.15

X Not applicable.   [1] Based on 1987 Standard Industrial Classification code; see text, Section 13, Labor Force, Employment, and Earnings.

Source: U.S. Census Bureau, *Current Business Reports, Annual Benchmark Report for Wholesale Trade, January 1990 Through February 2000*, (BW/99-A) and unpublished data.

Domestic Trade and Services   769

No. 1298. Comparative Statistics in Wholesale Trade by Kind of Business: 1992 and 1997

[495.5 represents 495,500. Covers establishments with payroll. Based on 1987 Standard Industrial Classification (SIC) code; see text, Section 13, Labor Force, Employment, and Earnings]

Kind of business	1987 SIC code	Establishments (1,000)		Sales, receipts, revenue/shipments (mil. dol.)		Annual payroll (mil. dol.)		Paid employees[1] (1,000)	
		1992	1997	1992	1997	1992	1997	1992	1997
Wholesale trade..................	(X)	495.5	521.1	3,238,520	4,235,400	173,272	234,517	5,791	6,509
Durable goods......................	50	313.5	337.3	1,593,874	2,299,494	105,155	147,737	3,349	3,887
Motor vehicles, parts, and supplies......	501	47.3	48.1	394,104	561,792	12,065	15,693	489	555
Furniture and homefurnishings..........	502	16.5	18.6	58,927	82,708	4,612	6,432	161	192
Lumber and construction materials......	503	19.5	22.4	89,764	118,764	211	6,060	211	258
Professional and commercial equipment & supplies.....................	504	46.8	49.7	262,974	387,497	26,380	34,778	685	760
Metals and minerals, except petroleum ...	505	11.2	12.6	118,322	150,494	4,684	6,898	138	174
Electrical goods...................	506	39.3	44.3	227,784	381,045	15,070	25,012	436	548
Hardware, plumbing and heating equipment & supplies...............	507	24.7	26.9	76,088	109,016	7,106	9,936	241	280
Machinery, equipment, and supplies.....	508	73.9	77.6	230,004	330,544	21,267	29,600	690	780
Miscellaneous durable goods..........	509	34.3	37.1	135,906	177,634	7,912	10,720	299	341
Nondurable goods..................	51	182.0	183.9	1,644,647	1,935,907	68,117	86,780	2,442	2,622
Paper and paper products............	511	19.7	19.7	106,580	134,225	6,939	9,151	269	297
Drugs, drug proprietaries, & druggists' sundries......................	512	6.1	8.1	129,306	203,148	5,368	8,395	158	190
Apparel, piece goods,& notions........	513	19.6	21.3	109,203	125,860	6,522	8,021	196	215
Groceries & related products..........	514	42.9	41.9	504,567	590,785	21,723	26,884	812	858
Farm-product raw materials...........	515	11.6	10.3	136,869	166,786	2,100	2,306	109	98
Chemicals & allied products...........	516	14.2	15.9	132,471	128,923	5,596	7,241	147	166
Petroleum & petroleum products........	517	16.1	12.7	281,585	272,459	4,447	4,839	169	152
Beer, wine, & distilled alcoholic beverages .	518	5.3	4.9	59,487	69,703	4,670	5,667	142	152
Miscellaneous nondurable goods	519	46.8	49.0	184,577	244,017	10,754	14,276	441	495
Merchant wholesalers..............	(X)	414.8	444.0	1,847,274	2,499,990	127,987	177,821	4,588	5,301
Durable goods	50	264.6	288.0	902,789	1,325,674	78,264	114,056	2,714	3,243
Nondurable goods..................	51	150.2	156.0	944,485	1,174,317	49,723	63,765	1,874	2,058

X Not applicable.   [1]Definition of paid employees varies among sectors.

Source: U.S. Census Bureau, *1997 Economic Census, Core Business Statistics Series: Comparative Statistics,* Series EC97X-CS2.

No. 1299. Selected Service Industries—Summary: 1992 and 1997

[1,825 represents 1,825,000. Covers establishments with payroll]

Kind of business	1987 SIC code[1]	Establishments[2] (1,000)		Receipts or expenses[3] (mil. dol.)		Paid employees[4] (1,000)	
		1992	1997	1992	1997	1992	1997
Firms subject to Federal income tax[5]......	(X)	1,825	2,078	1,202,613	1,843,792	19,290	25,278
Hotels and other lodging places[6]..............	70 ex. 704	49	56	69,204	97,893	1,489	1,686
Personal services.....................	72	197	204	43,280	53,133	1,218	1,303
Business services	73	307	397	274,892	528,516	5,542	8,652
Automotive repair, services, and parking	75	172	192	70,033	99,575	864	1,094
Miscellaneous repair services	76	72	67	30,732	37,303	428	419
Amusement and recreation services and museums[7]..	78, 79, 84	115	128	92,915	150,175	1,382	1,810
Health services......................	80	442	466	299,067	398,505	4,453	5,520
Legal services	81	152	166	101,114	122,617	924	956
Social services	83	59	70	13,349	18,894	505	662
Engineering and management services[8]..	87 ex. 8733	233	292	192,819	302,005	2,271	2,932
Firms exempt from Federal income tax[5].....	(X)	209	225	446,256	569,584	8,109	8,563
Museums, art galleries, & botanical gardens........	84	3	5	3,199	6,277	66	84
Selected health services.....................	8011 pt.	-	1	(NA)	12,963	(NA)	55
	8021 pt.	-	-	(NA)	(NA)	(NA)	(NA)
	805, 6, 8, 9	32	32	312,059	398,496	5,565	5,759
Social services......................	83	82	92	53,672	75,682	1,407	1,586
Selected membership organizations	861, 2, 4, 9	72	65	29,988	22,732	511	172

- Represents or rounds to zero.   NA Not available.   X Not applicable.   [1] Based on 1987 Standard Industrial Classification; see text, Section 13, Labor Force, Employment, and Earnings.   [2] Number of establishments in business at any time during the year.   [3] Receipts refer to establishments subject to Federal income tax. Expenses refer to establishments exempt from Federal income tax.   [4] For pay period including March 12.   [5] Includes other kinds of business, not shown separately.   [6] Excludes membership lodging.   [7] Includes motion pictures.   [8] Except noncommercial research organizations.

Source: U.S. Census Bureau, *1997 Economic Census, Core Business Statistics Series: Comparative Statistics,* Series EC97X-CS2.

No. 1300. Service Industries—Summary of Taxable Firms: 1997

[1,843,792 represents 1,843,792,000,000 receipts]

Kind of business	1987 SIC code [1]	Establishments with payroll					
		Establishments [2] (number)	Receipts (mil. dol.)	Annual payroll (mil. dol.)	Paid employees [3] (1,000)	Receipts per establishment (1,000)	Annual payroll per employee (dol.)
Firms subject to Federal income tax [4] ..	(X)	2,077,666	1,843,792	688,873	25,278	887	27,251
Hotels and other lodging places [4][5]	70 ex. 704	55,992	97,893	26,558	1,686	1,748	15,755
Hotels and motels..................	701	47,027	94,842	25,813	1,643	2,017	15,708
Personal services [4]....................	72	204,455	53,133	17,796	1,303	260	13,662
Laundry, cleaning, and garment services....	721	56,464	20,357	677	452	361	1,500
Photographic studios, portrait	722	13,245	3,705	991	65	280	15,148
Beauty and barber shops..............	723, 4	81,413	12,052	5,333	407	148	13,093
Funeral service and crematories	726	16,527	9,722	2,468	107	588	23,148
Business services [4]....................	73	397,264	528,516	211,485	8,652	1,330	24,443
Advertising [4]......................	731	20,870	28,182	10,469	252	1,350	41,609
Advertising agencies	7311	13,390	16,872	7,557	140	1,260	54,171
Credit reporting and collection.........	732	6,872	9,802	3,302	119	1,426	27,793
Mailing, reproduction, stenographic [4]	733	36,427	29,230	8,485	310	802	27,397
Direct mail advertising services	7331	4,083	10,173	2,744	96	2,492	28,640
Services to dwellings and other buildings ..	734	66,092	25,835	11,973	968	391	12,372
Miscellaneous equipment rental and leasing .	735	27,270	31,748	6,790	228	1,164	29,742
Personnel supply services [4]..........	736	41,802	91,044	64,653	3,667	2,178	17,631
Help supply services	7363	28,288	81,346	59,480	3,508	2,876	16,955
Computer and data processing services [4]	737	103,278	224,114	75,805	1,421	2,170	53,354
Computer programming services	7371	31,624	38,301	18,417	318	1,211	57,879
Prepackaged software	7372	12,090	61,699	18,387	266	5,103	69,020
Computer integrated systems design.....	7373	10,571	35,270	11,342	208	3,336	54,608
Data processing and preparation	7374	7,588	30,837	9,774	262	4,064	37,262
Information retrieval services	7375	4,165	8,043	2,356	50	1,931	47,214
Computer maintenance and repair	7378	6,087	7,565	2,258	60	1,243	37,384
Detective and armored car services	7381	12,539	12,370	7,759	561	987	13,831
Photofinishing laboratories	7384	7,055	5,520	1,583	72	782	21,983
Auto repair, services, and parking [4].........	75	191,907	99,575	22,643	1,094	519	20,694
Automotive rentals, no drivers [4]........	751	10,542	28,922	3,871	158	2,743	24,482
Truck rental and leasing, no drivers	7513	4,936	10,082	1,378	45	2,042	30,478
Passenger car rental	7514	4,367	14,784	2,130	103	3,385	20,756
Automotive repair shops [4]	753	142,372	55,686	14,808	631	391	23,483
General automotive repair shops	7538	77,751	25,599	6,439	291	329	22,157
Automotive services, except repair........	754	28,635	9,793	2,997	229	342	13,069
Miscellaneous repair services [4]...........	76	66,607	37,303	11,366	419	560	27,146
Electrical repair shops	762	19,525	1,256	4,035	142	64	28,353
Amusement and recreation services [4][6]	78, 79, 84	46,017	67,948	13,754	571	1,477	24,084
Motion picture prod., distribution, services ...	781, 2	15,064	32,690	10,374	272	2,170	38,154
Motion picture theaters	783	6,358	7,597	945	125	1,195	7,556
Video tape rental ....-,	784	23,036	7,230	1,289	150	314	8,601
Producers, orchestras, entertainers [7]	792	12,693	12,512	4,406	98	986	45,053
Commercial sports	794	4,494	15,540	6,522	108	3,458	60,504
Physical fitness facilities...............	7991	10,675	5,353	1,623	179	501	9,070
Health services [4].....................	80	466,421	398,505	173,455	5,520	854	31,423
Offices and clinics of doctors of medicine ..	801	188,668	172,896	84,563	1,563	916	54,092
Offices and clinics of dentists	802	114,178	48,482	1,823	642	425	2,841
Offices, clinics of doctors of osteopathy....	803	9,132	4,530	2,096	53	496	39,400
Offices, clinics of other health practitioners [4] .	804	88,886	28,282	10,457	407	318	25,717
Offices and clinics of chiropractors	8041	30,487	6,570	18,227	92	216	198,766
Offices and clinics of optometrists	8042	17,875	6,362	1,773	80	356	22,307
Nursing and personal care facilities	805	19,641	49,533	22,359	1,313	2,522	17,033
Hospitals [4]......................	806	1,345	40,146	13,886	512	29,849	27,142
General medical and surgical hospitals ...	8062	784	34,140	11,536	420	43,546	27,472
Medical and dental laboratories [4]........	807	16,685	19,310	6,426	193	1,157	33,384
Medical laboratories...............	8071	9,076	16,317	5,402	151	1,798	35,702
Home health care services	808	16,315	21,474	10,941	682	1,316	16,054
Legal services	81	165,757	122,617	47,410	956	740	49,586
Selected educational services.............	823, 4, 9	2,298	861	373	22	375	16,964
Social services [4]	83	69,713	18,894	8,026	662	271	12,120
Child day care services	835	43,785	8,402	3,942	388	192	10,167
Engineering and architectural services [4]	871	82,153	108,623	43,519	934	1,322	46,614
Engineering services	8711	52,526	88,181	35,338	730	1,679	48,408
Architectural services.................	8712	20,602	16,988	6,469	147	825	44,093
Accounting, auditing, and bookkeeping......	872	84,531	54,636	22,898	690	646	33,180
Research and testing services [8]	873 ex. 8733	17,348	37,401	14,994	367	2,156	40,912
Management and public relations [4]	874	108,130	101,346	40,249	941	937	42,754
Management services	8741	31,844	36,215	13,395	375	1,137	35,681
Management consulting services	8742	49,430	44,096	18,430	338	892	54,575

X Not applicable. [1] Based on 1987 Standard Industrial Classification; see text, Section 13, Labor Force, Employment, and Earnings. [2] Represents the number of establishments in business at any time during year. [3] For pay period including March 12. [4] Includes other kinds of business, not shown separately. [5] Excludes membership lodging. [6] Includes motion pictures and museums. [7] Excludes motion picture producers. [8] Excludes noncommercial research organizations.

Source: U.S. Census Bureau, *1997 Economic Census, Core Business Statistics Series*, Series EC97X-CS2.

Domestic Trade and Services   771

No. 1301. Service Industries—Annual Receipts of Taxable Firms: 1985 to 1998

[In billions of dollars (45.4 represents $45,400,000,000). Covers employer and nonemployer firms except as noted. Estimated]

Kind of business	1987 SIC code [1]	1985	1990	1994	1995	1996	1997	1998
Hotels and other lodging places [2]	70 ex. 704	45.4	64.2	79.6	84.1	90.0	94.1	100.7
Hotels and motels	701	43.5	62.0	76.7	81.1	85.8	90.8	97.1
Personal services [3]	72	36.7	54.7	66.1	70.6	73.9	77.7	82.8
Laundry, cleaning, and garment services	721	12.8	17.3	19.7	20.7	21.5	22.8	24.0
Drycleaning plants, except rug cleaning	7216	3.8	4.4	5.4	5.5	5.5	5.7	5.8
Beauty shops	7231	9.0	12.8	15.2	16.4	17.0	18.1	19.1
Barber shops	7241	1.2	1.4	1.6	1.6	1.6	1.8	1.8
Funeral service and crematories	726	5.2	6.8	8.6	9.4	10.0	10.6	11.4
Business services [3]	73	155.9	280.7	375.1	425.1	484.2	548.4	638.5
Advertising	731	14.9	22.0	24.2	27.1	30.6	33.8	37.6
Advertising agencies	7311	11.1	16.1	17.3	19.3	21.4	23.4	25.9
Consumer credit reporting and collection	732	3.7	5.8	7.1	7.7	8.6	9.2	9.8
Mailing, reproduction, stenographic [3]	733	14.5	20.8	22.3	24.4	25.9	28.2	30.7
Direct mail advertising services	7331	3.8	7.0	7.3	7.5	8.2	9.3	9.8
Commercial art and graphic design	7336	(NA)	6.1	6.3	6.8	7.3	8.2	9.4
Services to dwellings and other buildings	734	13.3	22.3	25.7	27.5	30.6	33.5	38.3
Disinfecting and pest control services	7342	2.8	4.5	5.3	5.8	6.3	6.8	7.7
Miscellaneous equipment rental and leasing	735	(NA)	23.1	26.4	29.5	30.9	32.6	36.2
Personnel supply services	736	14.7	32.5	48.0	59.4	68.6	80.1	94.0
Employment agencies	7361	3.7	6.2	6.5	7.7	9.0	11.7	13.8
Help supply services	7363	(NA)	26.4	41.4	51.6	59.6	68.2	80.2
Computer and data processing services [3]	737	45.1	88.3	135.6	156.4	184.4	215.3	258.8
Computer programming services	7371	(NA)	21.3	31.1	35.1	42.1	50.1	64.2
Prepackaged software	7372	(NA)	16.5	28.9	33.2	39.3	43.1	50.4
Computer integrated systems design	7373	(NA)	12.9	17.0	17.5	20.2	26.1	31.8
Data processing and preparation	7374	(NA)	17.8	29.2	35.6	41.0	43.4	45.8
Information retrieval services	7375	(NA)	3.5	4.6	5.3	6.9	9.1	12.3
Computer maintenance and repair	7378	(NA)	7.0	9.3	10.7	12.1	13.5	15.4
Miscellaneous business services [3]	738	(NA)	65.8	85.7	93.1	104.6	115.8	133.1
Detective and armored car services	7381	(NA)	9.0	10.8	11.9	13.5	14.5	14.9
Photofinishing laboratories	7384	4.3	5.6	6.6	6.8	7.3	7.7	7.7
Automotive repair, services, and parking [3][4]	75	51.7	73.7	91.9	99.2	106.7	111.4	120.0
Automotive rentals, no drivers [3]	751	14.6	20.8	24.4	26.6	29.4	30.1	32.1
Truck rental and leasing, without drivers	7513	5.5	8.5	9.0	10.1	11.2	11.1	11.6
Passenger car rental	7514	(NA)	9.0	12.2	12.9	14.5	15.2	16.5
Passenger car leasing [3]	7515	(NA)	3.0	2.8	2.9	3.0	3.2	3.3
Automotive repair shops [3]	753	30.5	43.5	54.6	58.6	62.0	65.0	69.6
Top & body repair & paint shops	7532	(NA)	13.5	16.4	17.8	18.7	19.7	21.3
General automotive repair shops	7538	(NA)	19.6	25.2	27.3	28.8	30.1	32.3
Automotive services, except repair	754	(NA)	6.5	9.3	10.4	11.5	12.1	13.2
Miscellaneous repair services	76	20.7	32.8	40.7	44.9	46.1	47.9	52.4
Electrical repair shops	762	(NA)	11.3	13.1	14.5	14.6	15.5	15.9
Motion pictures	78	21.5	40.0	53.5	57.2	60.3	62.9	66.2
Motion picture produc., distribution, allied services	781,2	15.0	28.9	40.3	43.3	46.3	48.2	50.4
Motion picture theaters	783	3.8	6.1	6.2	6.5	7.0	7.6	8.3
Video tape rental	784	(NA)	5.0	7.0	7.4	7.0	7.1	7.5
Amusement and recreation services [3]	79	31.2	50.1	68.5	77.5	85.7	92.8	97.5
Producers, orchestras, entertainers [4]	792	6.4	10.7	16.1	17.5	19.6	21.0	22.4
Commercial sports	794	5.0	8.6	11.1	13.1	14.6	16.4	17.7
Sports clubs, managers, & promoters	7941	(NA)	3.7	6.1	7.7	8.9	10.0	10.7
Amusement parks	7996	2.6	4.9	5.9	6.3	6.8	7.3	7.5
Membership sports and recreation clubs [4]	7997	3.5	4.8	6.4	6.8	7.4	7.7	7.8
Health services [3]	80	147.4	271.2	351.4	376.3	398.4	420.4	444.7
Offices and clinics of doctors of medicine [4]	801	72.1	128.9	159.6	168.0	172.9	179.5	188.8
Offices and clinics of dentists [4]	802	20.6	31.5	41.7	44.9	47.4	51.0	54.2
Offices of other health practitioners	804	7.9	20.1	25.9	27.4	28.4	29.6	31.3
Offices and clinics of chiropractors	8041	2.7	5.5	6.8	6.7	7.0	7.3	7.7
Nursing and personal care facilities [4]	805	17.5	30.2	37.3	41.1	44.3	46.8	49.2
Hospitals [4][5]	806	15.7	26.5	35.1	38.4	44.7	50.2	53.8
Medical and dental laboratories	807	5.4	12.0	15.4	15.5	16.1	16.5	18.3
Medical laboratories	8071	3.9	10.0	13.0	12.9	13.3	13.7	15.2
Home health care services	808	(NA)	7.6	15.4	18.0	19.6	19.3	18.5
Legal services	81	52.8	97.6	114.6	116.0	124.7	133.0	141.8
Social services	83	(NA)	15.5	22.5	24.9	27.7	30.2	32.0
Child day care services	8351	2.6	7.1	10.1	10.9	11.4	12.5	13.0
Residential care	8361	(NA)	4.6	5.9	6.4	7.2	7.6	8.3
Museums, botanical, zoological gardens	84	(NA)	0.1	0.2	0.2	0.3	0.3	0.3
Engineering and management services [3]	87	(NA)	198.4	235.4	263.8	292.3	321.7	360.8
Engineering services	8711	(NA)	64.8	68.1	73.9	80.3	88.3	96.4
Architectural services	8712	(NA)	13.0	14.8	16.5	18.4	18.8	23.0
Accounting, auditing, & bookkeeping	8721	21.2	32.6	42.6	48.8	54.4	58.9	65.4
Research and testing services [4][6]	873 ex. 873	(NA)	24.6	25.6	26.8	30.8	34.9	37.8
Management and public relations [4]	874	37.6	64.8	81.4	94.8	104.8	116.7	133.4
Management services [4]	8741	(NA)	20.6	24.3	27.6	27.8	30.5	36.4
Management consulting services [4]	8742	(NA)	28.9	38.5	46.4	53.4	61.3	70.7
Arrangement of passenger transportation	472	6.3	12.3	13.1	14.2	15.4	16.5	17.0
Real estate agents and managers	653	31.3	63.0	80.9	82.7	90.2	99.2	108.6

NA Not available. [1] Standard Industrial Classification; see text, Section 13, Labor Force, Employment, and Earnings.
[2] Excludes those on membership basis. [3] Includes other kinds of businesses, not shown separately. [4] Estimates for taxable firms only. [5] Covers employer firms only. [6] Excludes noncommercial research organizations.

Source: U.S. Census Bureau, Current Business Reports, Service Annual Survey: 1998 (BS/98); and unpublished data.

No. 1302. Lodging Industry Summary: 1990 to 1998

Year	Average occupancy rate (percent)	Average room rate (dol.)	Room size of property	1998		Item	1998	
				Establishments	Rooms (mil.)		Business traveler	Leisure traveler
1990	63.3	57.96	Total	51,000	3.9	Typical night:		
1991	60.9	58.08				Made reservations . .	90%	81%
1992	61.7	58.91	Percent:			Amount paid	83.00	74.00
1993	63.6	60.53	Under 75 rooms. . . .	65.3	25.7			
1994	65.2	62.86	75-149 rooms	23.6	32.8	Length of stay:		
1995	65.5	65.81	150-299 rooms . . .	8.2	21.1	One night	37%	45%
1996	65.2	69.66	300 or more	2.9	20.4	Two nights	24%	26%
1997	64.5	75.16				Three or more	39%	29%
1998	64.0	78.62						

Source: American Hotel & Motel Association, Washington, DC, *Lodging Industry Profile* (copyright).

No. 1303. Service Industries—Summary of Tax-Exempt Firms: 1997

[562,297 represents $562,297,000]. Covers establishments with payroll]

Kind of business	1987 SIC code [1]	Establish-ments [2] (number)	Revenues ($1,000)	Annual payroll ($1,000)	Paid employ-ees [3] (number)
Organization hotels, camps and other lodging . .	70, 703	2,169	562,297	114,585	10,935
Amusement and recreation services	79	15,695	13,540,652	5,035,318	301,895
Producers, orchestras, entertainers [4]	792	3,925	4,312,904	1,525,104	84,603
Membership sports and recreation clubs	7997	8,591	7,860,389	3,135,205	186,975
Health services	80	33,146	411,458,724	172,583,968	5,814,763
Nursing and personal care facilities	805	13,657	27,819,012	13,109,351	745,146
Hospitals	806	5,340	339,031,933	141,909,969	4,421,454
Home health care services	808	3,375	10,104,243	5,426,172	267,484
Social services [5]	83	92,156	75,682,312	25,998,954	1,586,186
Individual and family social services	832	42,427	30,460,289	11,695,542	692,454
Job training and related services	833	5,668	6,461,745	3,093,266	269,738
Child day care services	835	18,099	5,756,666	3,015,027	239,981
Residential care	836	10,869	9,416,096	4,417,356	240,732
Museums, botanical, zoological gardens.	84	4,781	6,277,474	1,713,627	84,417
Membership organizations	86	65,075	(D)	(D)	(6)
Business associations	861	15,238	14,439,846	4,045,343	109,354
Professional membership organizations.	862	7,239	8,292,364	2,264,642	62,376
Civic, social, and fraternal associations	864	36,099	(D)	(D)	(6)
Research, development & testing service (exc. noncomm. resch. org.)	873	3,292	14,211,703	5,226,070	125,149

D Withheld to avoid disclosure. [1] Based on 1987 Standard Industrial Classification; see text, Section 13, Labor Force, Employment, and Earnings. [2] Represents the number of establishments in business at any time during year. [3] For pay period including March 12. [4] Excludes motion picture producers. [5] Includes other kinds of business, not shown separately. [6] 100,000 or more members.

Source: U.S. Census Bureau, *1997 Economic Census, Core Business Statistics Series*, Series EC97X-CS2.

No. 1304. National Nonprofit Associations—Number by Type: 1980 to 2000

[Data compiled during last few months of year previous to year shown and the beginning months of year shown]

Type	1980	1990	1999	2000	Type	1980	1990	1999	2000
Total	14,726	22,289	22,049	22,474	Fraternal, foreign interest,				
Trade, business, commercial.	3,118	3,918	3,714	3,815	nationality, ethnic	435	573	542	552
Agriculture.	677	940	1,107	1,113	Religious.	797	1,172	1,156	1,151
Legal, governmental,					Veteran, hereditary, patriotic .	208	462	861	877
public admin., military	529	792	755	778	Hobby, avocational	910	1,475	1,468	1,463
Scientific, engineering, tech .	1,039	1,417	1,306	1,332	Athletic sports	504	840	765	782
Educational	[2]2,376	1,291	1,274	1,321	Labor unions	235	253	235	235
Cultural.	([1])	1,886	1,841	1,876	Chambers of Commerce [2] . .	105	168	129	146
Social welfare	994	1,705	1,896	1,913	Greek and non-Greek				
Health, medical	1,413	2,227	2,383	2,481	letter societies	318	340	313	313
Public affairs	1,068	2,249	1,855	1,877	Fan clubs	(NA)	581	449	449

NA Not available. [1] Data for cultural associations included with educational associations. [2] National and binational.

Source: Gale Research Inc., Detroit, MI. Compiled from *Encyclopedia of Associations*, annual (copyright).

No. 1305. Selected Service Industries—Revenue and Expenses for Tax-Exempt Firms: 1990 to 1998

[In billions of dollars (0.8 represents $8,000,000,000). Estimated from a sample of employer firms only]

Kind of business	1987 SIC code [1]	Revenue				Expenses			
		1990	1995	1997	1998	1990	1995	1997	1998
Camps and membership lodging	703,4	0.8	0.8	0.9	1.0	0.7	0.8	0.9	1.0
Camps and recreational vehicle parks.	703	0.3	0.4	0.5	0.5	0.3	0.4	0.4	0.5
Membership-basis organization hotels.	704	0.4	0.4	0.5	0.5	0.4	0.4	0.4	0.5
Selected amusement and recreation services [2]	792, 7991, 7997, 7999	7.9	12.8	14.6	15.4	(NA)	12.1	13.3	14.0
Offices and clinics of doctors of medicine	801	12.9	24.9	28.4	31.7	12.5	24.1	28.4	31.3
Nursing and personal care facilities	805	12.1	17.6	19.7	21.3	(NA)	16.8	19.0	20.3
Hospitals	806	233.6	325.0	347.8	363.7	225.6	314.9	332.3	351.9
General medical and surgical hospitals	8062	210.5	297.4	319.5	334.3	203.3	286.6	304.1	322.0
Psychiatric hospitals	8063	11.0	9.2	9.7	9.9	11.0	10.5	10.4	10.7
Specialty hospitals, except psychiatric.	8069	12.1	18.4	18.6	19.4	11.2	17.8	17.8	19.1
Home health care services.	808	3.9	7.9	8.1	7.9	3.6	7.7	7.9	7.8
Health and allied services, n.e.c.	809	5.3	9.7	10.8	11.4	5.2	9.3	10.2	10.7
Kidney dialysis centers.	8092	0.3	0.6	0.7	0.8	0.3	0.6	0.7	0.7
Specialty outpatient facilities, n.e.c.	8093	3.5	5.7	5.9	5.8	3.4	5.5	5.6	5.6
Legal services	811	1.1	1.3	1.4	1.6	0.9	1.3	1.4	1.6
Libraries	823	0.5	0.7	0.9	0.9	0.5	0.7	0.8	0.9
Vocational schools	824	0.5	0.7	0.9	0.9	0.5	0.6	0.8	0.8
Social services.	83	45.3	70.3	83.2	90.5	39.4	63.4	74.9	84.1
Individual and family social services	8322	13.0	20.8	24.1	26.0	12.6	19.4	23.7	25.9
Job training and related services	8331	4.9	6.5	7.4	8.3	4.5	6.5	6.9	7.7
Child day care services	8351	2.9	5.4	5.9	6.6	3.0	5.2	5.8	6.4
Residential care	8361	8.8	13.5	17.7	18.6	8.6	12.8	16.3	17.6
Museums, botanical, zoological gardens	84	2.9	4.3	6.2	6.6	2.5	3.6	4.1	4.7
Selected membership organizations [3]	86 (pt)	31.5	45.9	51.1	56.0	28.6	42.7	47.4	51.2
Research and testing services	873	11.0	14.5	16.8	18.7	10.0	13.9	15.8	17.4
Management and public relations, except facilities support services	874, ex. 8744	1.9	3.7	6.6	7.8	2.0	3.5	6.2	7.3

NA Not available. [1] Standard Industrial Classification; see text, Section 13, Labor Force, Employment, and Earnings. [2] Covers theatrical producers, bands, orchestras, and entertainers (SIC 792); physical fitness facilities (SIC 7991); membership sports and recreation clubs (SIC 7997); and amusement and recreation services, not elsewhere classified (SIC 7999). [3] Includes business associations (SIC 861); professional membership organizations (SIC 862); civic, social, and fraternal organizations (SIC 864); and other membership organizations, except labor unions and political and religious organizations (SIC 869).

Source: U.S. Census Bureau, Current Business Reports, Service Annual Survey: 1998 (BS/98).

No. 1306. Comparative Statistics in Service Industries by Kind of Business: 1992 and 1997

[2,034 represents 2,034,000. Includes only establishments with payroll. N.e.c. = not elsewhere classified]

Kind of business	1987 SIC code [1]	Establish-ments (1,000)		Sales, receipts, revenue/ shipments (bil. dol.)		Annual payroll (bil. dol.)		Paid employees [2] (1,000)	
		1992	1997	1992	1997	1992	1997	1992	1997
Service industries, total	(G)	2,034	2,307	1,649	2,453	639	922	27,399	34,224
Hotels, rooming houses, camps, and other lodging places.	70	52	(S)	70	(S)	20	(S)	1,507	(S)
Personal services	72	197	205	43	53	14	18	1,218	1,311
Business services	73	307	398	275	550	109	215	5,542	8,750
Automotive repair services, and parking .	75	172	192	70	101	16	23	864	1,110
Miscellaneous repair services	76	72	67	31	38	10	12	428	427
Motion pictures	78	42	46	44	64	10	14	478	569
Amusement & recreation services	79	84	97	58	95	19	30	1,120	1,529
Health services.	80	465	499	623	815	275	347	10,017	11,370
Legal services	81	153	168	102	124	40	48	945	978
Educational services	82	21	27	10	17	3	6	196	256
Social services	83	141	162	67	94	25	34	1,912	2,273
Museums, art galleries, & botanical & zoological gardens	84	4	5	3	6	1	2	70	89
Membership organizations	86	72	66	36	47	10	13	603	597
Eng. acctg, research, mgt, & rel. serv. (exc. noncomm. research org.).	87	238	297	208	331	85	129	2,419	3,139
Services, n.e.c.	89	15	(S)	8	(S)	3	(S)	81	(S)

S Figure does not meet publication standards. [1] Standard Industrial Classification; see text, Section 13, Labor Force, Employment, and Earnings. [2] Definition of paid employees varies among sectors.

Source: U.S. Census Bureau, 1997 Economic Census, EC97X-CS1.

Foreign Commerce and Aid

This section presents data on the flow of goods, services, and capital between the United States and other countries; changes in official reserve assets of the United States; international investments; and foreign assistance programs.

The Bureau of Economic Analysis publishes current figures on U.S. international transactions and the U.S. international investment position in its monthly *Survey of Current Business*. Statistics for the foreign aid programs are presented by the Agency for International Development (AID) in its annual *U.S. Overseas Loans and Grants and Assistance from International Organizations* and by the Department of Agriculture in its *Foreign Agricultural Trade of the United States*.

The principal source of merchandise import and export data is the U.S. Census Bureau. Current data are presented monthly in *U.S. International Trade in Goods and Services* report Series FT 900. Census Bureau *Catalog & Guide* and the *Guide to Foreign Trade Statistics* lists the Bureau's monthly and annual products and services in this field. In addition, the International Trade Administration and the Bureau of Economic Analysis present summary as well as selected commodity and country data for U.S. foreign trade in the *U.S. Foreign Trade Highlights* and the *Survey of Current Business*, respectively. The merchandise trade data in the latter source include balance of payments adjustments to the Census Bureau data. The Treasury Department's *Monthly Treasury Statement of Receipts and Outlays of the United States Government* contains information on import duties.

International accounts—The international transactions tables (Nos. 1307 to 1309) show, for given time periods, the transfer of goods, services, grants, and financial assets and liabilities between the United States and the rest of the world. The international investment position table (No. 1310) presents, for specific dates, the value of U.S. investments abroad and of foreign investments in the United States. The movement of foreign and U.S. capital as presented in the balance of payments is not the only factor affecting the total value of foreign investments. Among the other factors are changes in the valuation of assets or liabilities, including changes in prices of securities, defaults, expropriations, and write-offs.

Direct investment abroad means the ownership or control, directly or indirectly, by one person of 10 percent or more of the voting securities of an incorporated business enterprise or an equivalent interest in an unincorporated business enterprise. Direct investment position is the value of U.S. parents' claims on the equity of and receivables due from foreign affiliates, less foreign affiliates' receivables due from their U.S. parents. Income consists of parents' shares in the earnings of their affiliates plus net interest received by parents on intercompany accounts, less withholding taxes on dividends and interest.

Foreign aid—Foreign assistance is divided into three major categories—grants (military supplies and services and other grants), credits, and other assistance (through net accumulation of foreign currency claims from the sale of agricultural commodities). *Grants* are transfers for which no payment is expected (other than a limited percentage of the foreign currency "counterpart" funds generated by the grant), or which at most involve an obligation on the part of the receiver to extend aid to the United States or other countries to achieve a common objective. *Credits* are loan disbursements or transfers under other agreements which give rise to specific obligations to repay, over a period of years, usually with interest. All known returns to the U.S. Government stemming from grants and credits (reverse grants, returns of grants, and payments of principal) are taken into account in net grants and net credits, but no allowance is made for interest or commissions. *Other assistance* represents the transfer of U.S. farm products in exchange for foreign currencies (plus, since enactment of Public Law 87-128, currency claims from principal and interest collected on credits extended under the farm products program), less the Government's disbursements of the currencies as grants, credits, or for purchases. The net acquisition of currencies represents net transfers of resources to foreign countries under the agricultural programs, in addition to those classified as grants or credits.

The basic instrument for extending military aid to friendly nations has been the Mutual Defense Assistance Program authorized by the Congress in 1949. Prior to 1952, economic and technical aid was authorized in the Foreign Assistance Act of 1948, the 1950 Act for International Development, and other legislation which set up programs for specific countries. In 1952, these economic, technical, and military aid programs were combine under the Mutual Security Act, which in turn was followed by the Foreign Assistance Act passed in 1961. Appropriations to provide military assistance were also made in the Department of Defense Appropriation Act (rather than the Foreign Assistance Appropriation Act) beginning in 1966 for certain countries in Southeast Asia and in other legislation concerning program for specific countries (such as Israel). Figures on activity under the Foreign Assistance Act as reported in the *Foreign Grants and Credits* series differ from data published by AID or its immediate predecessors, due largely to differences in reporting, timing, and treatment of particular items.

Exports—The Census Bureau compiles export data primarily from Shipper's Export Declarations required to be filed with customs officials for shipments leaving the United States. They include U.S. exports

under mutual security programs and exclude shipments to U.S. Armed Forces for their own use.

The value reported in the export statistics is generally equivalent to a free alongside ship (f.a.s.) value at the U.S. port of export, based on the transaction price, including inland freight, insurance, and other charges incurred in placing the merchandise alongside the carrier at the U.S. port of exportation. This value, as defined, excludes the cost of loading merchandise aboard the exporting carrier and also excludes freight, insurance, and any other charges or transportation and other costs beyond the U.S. port of exportation. The country of destination is defined as the country of ultimate destination or country where the merchandise is to be consumed, further processed, or manufactured, as known to the shipper at the time of exportation. When ultimate destination is not known, the shipment is statistically credited to the last country to which the shipper knows the merchandise will be shipped in the same form as exported.

Effective January 1990, the United States began substituting Canadian import statistics for U.S. exports to Canada. As a result of the data exchange between the United States and Canada, the United States has adopted the Canadian import exemption level for its export statistics based on shipments to Canada.

Data are estimated for shipments valued under $2,501 to all countries, except Canada, using factors based on the ratios of low-valued shipments to individual country totals.

Prior to 1989, exports were based on Schedule B, Statistical Classification of Domestic and Foreign Commodities Exported from the United States. These statistics were retabulated and published using Schedule E, Standard International Trade Classification, Revision 2. Beginning in 1989, Schedule B classifications were based on the Harmonized System and made to coincide with the Standard International Trade Classification, Revision 3. This revision will affect the comparability of most export series beginning with the 1989 data for commodities.

Imports—The Census Bureau compiles import data from various customs forms required to be filed with customs officials. Data on import values are presented on two bases in this section: The c.i.f. (cost, insurance, and freight) and the customs import value (as appraised by the U.S. Customs Service in accordance with legal requirements of the Tariff Act of 1930, as amended). This latter valuation, primarily used for collection of import duties, frequently does not reflect the actual transaction value. Country of origin is defined as country where the merchandise was grown, mined, or manufactured. If country of origin is unknown, country of shipment is reported.

Imports are classified either as "General imports" or "Imports for consumption." *General imports* are a combination of entries for immediate consumption, entries into customs bonded warehouses, and entries into U.S. Foreign Trade Zones, thus generally reflecting total arrivals of merchandise. *Imports for consumption* are a combination of entries for immediate consumption, withdrawals from warehouses for consumption, and entries of merchandise into U.S. customs territory from U.S. Foreign Trade Zones, thus generally reflecting the total of the commodities entered into U.S. consumption channels.

Prior to 1989, imports were based on the Tariff Schedule of the United States Annotated. The statistics were retabulated and published using Schedule A, Standard International Trade Classification, Revision 2. Beginning in 1989, the statistics are based on the Harmonized Tariff Schedule of the United States, which coincides with the Standard International Trade Classification, Revision 3. This revision will affect the comparability of most import series beginning with the 1989 data.

Area coverage—Except as noted, the geographic area covered by the export and import trade statistics is the United States Customs area (includes the 50 states, the District of Columbia, and Puerto Rico), the U.S. Virgin Islands (effective January 1981), and U.S. Foreign Trade Zones (effective July 1982). Data for selected tables and total values for 1980 have been revised to reflect the U.S. Virgin Islands' trade with foreign countries, where possible.

Statistical reliability—For a discussion of statistical collection and estimation, sampling procedures, and measures of statistical reliability applicable to Census Bureau data, see Appendix III.

U.S. Census Bureau, Statistical Abstract of the United States: 2000

Figure 28.1
U.S. International Transaction Balance: 1980 to 1999

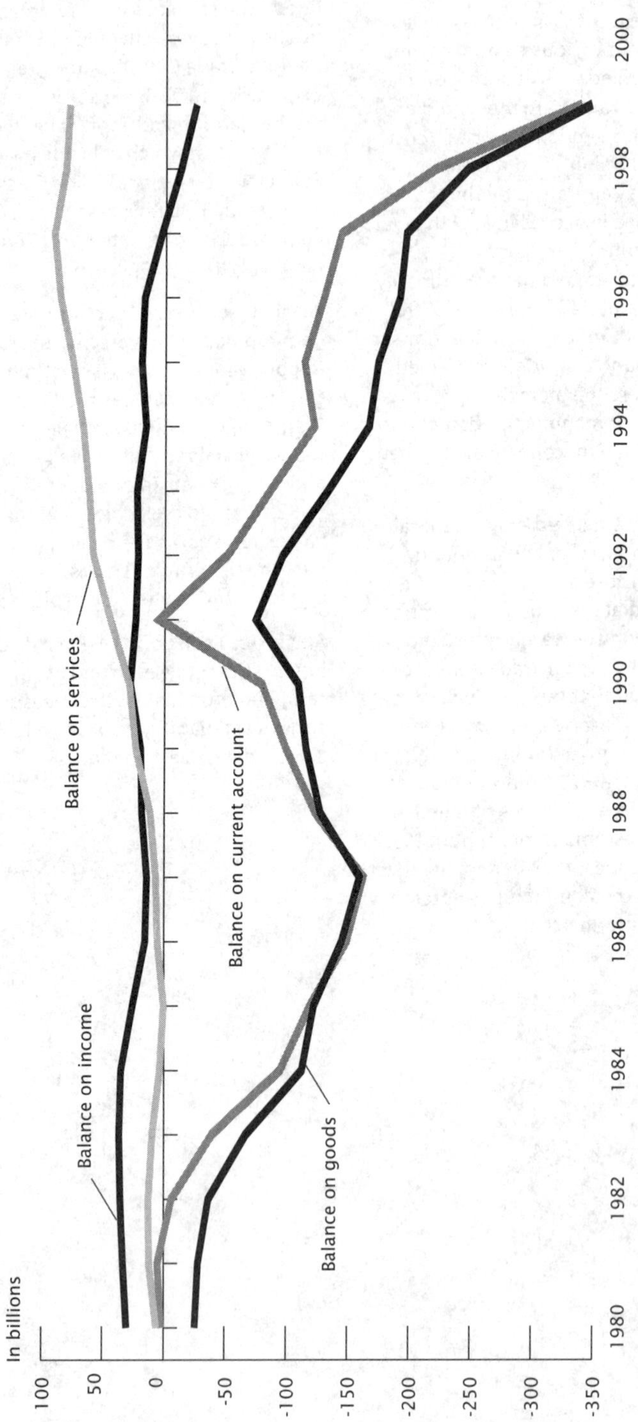

In billions

Balance on services

Balance on income

Balance on current account

Balance on goods

100
50
0
-50
-100
-150
-200
-250
-300
-350

1980 1982 1984 1986 1988 1990 1992 1994 1996 1998 2000

Source: Chart prepared by U.S. Census Bureau. For data, see Table 1307.

No. 1307. U.S. International Transactions by Type of Transaction: 1980 to 1999

[In millions of dollars (344,440 represents $344,400,000,000). Minus sign (-) indicates debits. N.i.e. = Not included elsewhere]

Type of transaction	1980	1990	1991	1992	1993	1994	1995	1996	1997	1998	1999
Exports of goods and services and income receipts	**344,440**	**708,135**	**729,513**	**748,431**	**776,404**	**868,041**	**1,005,715**	**1,074,425**	**1,197,206**	**1,192,231**	**1,233,944**
Exports of goods and services	271,834	536,058	579,956	615,909	641,783	702,073	793,482	849,806	938,543	933,907	960,088
Goods, balance of payments basis [1]	224,250	389,307	416,913	440,352	456,832	502,398	575,845	612,057	679,715	670,246	683,021
Services [2]	47,584	146,751	163,043	175,557	184,951	199,675	217,637	237,749	258,828	263,661	277,067
Transfers under U.S. military agency sales contracts [3]	9,029	9,932	11,135	12,387	13,471	12,787	14,643	15,736	17,561	17,155	16,688
Travel	10,588	43,007	48,385	54,742	57,875	58,417	63,395	69,751	73,301	71,250	74,448
Passenger fares	2,591	15,298	15,854	16,618	16,528	16,997	18,909	20,413	20,789	19,996	21,123
Other transportation	11,618	22,042	22,631	21,531	21,958	23,754	26,081	26,074	27,006	25,518	27,313
Royalties and license fees [4]	7,085	16,634	17,819	20,841	21,695	26,712	30,289	32,470	33,781	36,808	37,213
Other private services [4]	6,276	39,170	46,531	48,597	52,541	60,121	63,502	72,412	85,566	92,116	99,357
U.S. Government miscellaneous services	398	668	690	841	883	887	818	893	824	818	925
Income receipts	72,606	172,078	149,558	132,523	134,621	165,968	212,233	224,619	258,663	258,324	273,856
Income receipts on U.S.-owned assets abroad	72,606	170,906	148,268	131,098	133,187	164,425	210,472	222,863	256,861	256,467	271,972
Direct investment receipts	37,146	66,309	59,062	58,005	67,708	77,874	95,991	103,314	115,795	102,846	116,683
Other private receipts	32,898	94,072	81,186	65,977	60,353	82,423	109,768	114,958	137,507	150,001	152,104
U.S. Government receipts	2,562	10,525	8,019	7,115	5,126	4,128	4,713	4,591	3,559	3,620	3,185
Compensation of employees	(NA)	1,172	1,290	1,425	1,434	1,543	1,761	1,756	1,802	1,857	1,884
Imports of goods and services and income payments	**-333,774**	**-759,646**	**-735,048**	**-763,187**	**-823,167**	**-950,529**	**-1,083,844**	**-1,161,533**	**-1,298,705**	**-1,368,718**	**-1,526,281**
Imports of goods and services	-291,241	-615,996	-609,440	-652,934	-711,722	-800,468	-891,021	-954,124	-1,043,273	-1,098,189	-1,227,636
Goods, balance of payments basis	-249,750	-498,337	-490,981	-536,458	-589,441	-668,590	-749,574	-803,327	-876,366	-917,178	-1,030,152
Services [2]	-41,491	-117,659	-118,459	-116,476	-122,281	-131,878	-141,447	-150,797	-166,907	-181,011	-197,484
Direct defense expenditures	-10,851	-17,531	-16,409	-13,835	-12,086	-10,217	-10,043	-11,029	-11,698	-12,841	-14,604
Travel	-10,397	-37,349	-35,322	-38,552	-40,713	-43,782	-44,916	-48,048	-52,051	-56,105	-60,092
Passenger fares	-3,607	-10,531	-10,012	-10,603	-11,410	-13,062	-14,663	-15,818	-18,138	-19,797	-21,305
Other transportation	-11,790	-24,966	-24,975	-23,767	-24,524	-26,019	-27,034	-27,403	-28,959	-30,457	-34,500
Royalties and license fees [4]	-724	-3,135	-4,035	-5,161	-5,032	-5,852	-6,919	-7,837	-9,390	-11,292	-12,437
Other private services [4]	-2,909	-22,229	-25,590	-22,295	-26,261	-30,386	-35,249	-37,975	-43,909	-47,670	-51,591
U.S. Government miscellaneous services	-1,214	-1,919	-2,116	-2,263	-2,255	-2,560	-2,623	-2,687	-2,762	-2,849	-2,955
Income payments	-42,532	-143,649	-125,608	-110,253	-111,445	-150,061	-192,823	-207,409	-255,432	-270,529	-298,645
Income payments on foreign-owned assets in the U.S.	-42,532	-140,185	-121,582	-105,501	-106,313	-144,109	-186,560	-201,109	-248,676	-263,423	-291,158
Direct investment payments	-8,635	-3,907	1,742	-3,341	-9,133	-23,467	-32,186	-35,568	-46,575	-43,441	-58,250
Other private payments	-21,214	-95,508	-82,452	-63,079	-57,804	-76,450	-97,004	-97,901	-114,051	-128,863	-137,777
U.S. Government payments	-12,684	-40,770	-40,872	-39,081	-39,376	-44,192	-57,370	-67,640	-88,050	-91,119	-95,131
Compensation of employees	(NA)	-3,464	-4,026	-4,752	-5,132	-5,952	-6,263	-6,300	-6,756	-7,106	-7,487
Unilateral current transfers, net	**-8,349**	**-27,821**	**9,819**	**-35,873**	**-38,522**	**-39,192**	**-35,437**	**-42,187**	**-41,966**	**-44,075**	**-46,581**
U.S. Government grants [3]	-5,486	-10,359	29,193	-16,320	-17,036	-14,978	-11,190	-15,337	-12,386	-13,057	-12,825
U.S. Government pensions and other transfers	-1,818	-3,224	-3,775	-4,043	-4,104	-4,556	-3,451	-4,466	-4,239	-4,350	-4,396
Private remittances and other transfers	-1,044	-14,238	-15,599	-15,510	-17,383	-19,658	-20,796	-22,384	-25,341	-26,668	-29,360

See footnotes at end of table.

U.S. Census Bureau, Statistical Abstract of the United States: 2000

No. 1307. U.S. International Transactions by Type of Transaction: 1980 to 1999—Continued

[See headnote, Page 779]

Type of transaction	1980	1990	1991	1992	1993	1994	1995	1996	1997	1998	1999
Capital account transactions, net	(NA)	-6,579	-4,479	612	-88	-469	372	672	292	617	-172
U.S. assets abroad, net (increase/financial outflow (-))	-85,815	-81,570	-64,732	-74,877	-201,014	-176,586	-330,675	-380,762	-465,296	-292,818	-372,567
U.S. official reserve assets, net	-7,003	-2,158	5,763	3,901	-1,379	5,346	-9,742	6,668	-1,010	-6,784	8,749
Gold[7]											
Special drawing rights	1,136	-192	-177	2,316	-537	-441	-808	370	-350	-149	12
Reserve position in the International Monetary Fund	-1,667	731	-367	-2,692	-44	494	-2,466	-1,280	-3,575	-5,118	5,485
Foreign currencies	-6,472	-2,697	6,307	4,277	-797	5,293	-6,468	7,578	2,915	-1,517	3,252
U.S. Govt. assets, other than official reserve assets, net	-5,162	2,317	2,924	-1,667	-351	-390	-984	-989	68	-429	-365
U.S. credits and other long-term assets	-9,860	-8,410	-12,879	-7,408	-6,311	-5,383	-4,859	-5,025	-5,417	-4,676	-6,123
Repayments on U.S. credits and other long-term assets[8]	4,456	10,856	16,776	5,807	6,270	5,088	4,125	3,930	5,438	4,102	6,223
U.S. foreign currency holdings and U.S. short-term assets, net	242	-130	-974	-66	-310	-95	-250	106	47	145	-465
U.S. private assets, net	-73,651	-81,729	-73,419	-77,111	-199,284	-181,542	-319,949	-386,441	-464,354	-285,605	-380,951
Direct investments abroad	-19,222	-37,519	-38,233	-48,733	-84,412	-80,697	-99,481	-92,694	-109,955	-132,829	-152,152
Foreign securities	-3,568	-28,765	-45,673	-49,166	-146,253	-60,309	-100,074	-115,859	-89,174	-102,817	-97,882
U.S. claims on unaffiliated foreigners reported by U.S. nonbanking concerns	-4,023	-27,824	11,097	-387	766	-36,336	-45,286	-86,333	-120,403	-25,041	-69,493
U.S. claims reported by U.S. banks, n.i.e.	-46,838	12,379	-610	21,175	30,615	-4,200	-75,108	-91,555	-144,822	-24,918	-61,424
Foreign assets in the U.S., net (increase/financial inflow (+))	62,612	142,028	111,332	171,815	283,230	307,306	467,552	574,847	751,661	502,637	750,765
Foreign official assets in the U.S., net	15,497	33,910	17,389	40,477	71,753	39,583	109,880	127,390	18,119	-21,684	44,570
Other foreign assets in the U.S., net	47,115	108,118	93,944	131,338	211,477	267,723	357,672	447,457	733,542	524,321	706,195
Direct investments in U.S.	16,918	48,951	23,695	20,975	52,552	47,438	59,644	88,977	109,264	193,375	282,507
U.S. Treasury securities[9]	2,645	-2,534	18,826	37,131	24,381	34,274	99,548	154,996	146,433	46,155	-21,756
U.S. securities other than U.S. Treasury securities	5,457	1,592	35,144	30,043	80,092	56,971	96,367	130,240	196,258	218,026	325,913
U.S. currency flows	4,500	18,800	15,400	13,400	18,900	23,400	12,300	17,362	24,782	16,622	22,407
U.S. liabilities to unaffiliated foreigners reported by U.S. nonbanking concerns	6,852	45,133	-3,115	13,573	10,489	1,302	59,637	39,404	107,779	9,412	29,411
U.S. liabilities reported by U.S. banks, n.i.e.	10,743	-3,824	3,994	16,216	25,063	104,338	30,176	16,478	149,026	40,731	67,713
Statistical discrepancy	20,886	25,454	-46,405	-46,921	3,157	-8,571	-23,683	-65,462	-143,192	10,126	-39,108
Balance on goods	-25,500	-109,030	-74,068	-96,106	-132,609	-166,192	-173,729	-191,270	-196,651	-246,932	-347,131
Balance on services	6,093	29,091	44,584	59,081	62,669	67,797	76,190	86,952	91,921	82,650	79,583
Balance on income	30,073	28,429	23,950	22,269	23,176	15,907	19,410	17,210	3,231	-12,205	-24,789
Balance on current account[10]	2,317	-79,332	4,284	-50,629	-85,286	-121,680	-113,566	-129,295	-143,465	-220,562	-338,918

- Represents or rounds to zero. NA Not available. [1] Excludes exports of goods under U.S. military agency sales contracts identified in Census export documents, excludes imports of goods under direct defense expenditures identified in Census import documents, and reflects various other adjustments,[3] (for valuation, coverage, and timing) of Census statistics to balance of payments basis. [2] Includes some goods: Mainly military equipment included in "Transfers under U.S. military agency sales contracts"; major equipment, other materials, supplies, and petroleum products purchased abroad by U.S. military agencies included in "Direct defense expenditures" under "Imports," and fuels purchased by airline and steamship operators included in "Other transportation" under "Exports" and "Imports." [3] Includes transfers of goods and services under U.S. military grant programs. [4] Break in series. See Technical Notes in the June 1989, 1990, 1992, 1993, 1995, and July 1996-99 issues of the Survey. [5] Beginning in 1985, these lines are presented on a gross basis. The definition of exports is revised to exclude U.S. parents' payments to foreign affiliates and to include U.S. affiliates' receipts from foreign parents. The definition of imports is revised to include U.S. parents' payments to foreign affiliates and to exclude U.S. affiliates' receipts from foreign parents. [6] Beginning in 1985, the "other transfers" component includes taxes paid by U.S. private residents to foreign governments and taxes paid by private nonresidents to the U.S. Government. [7] At the present time, all U.S. Treasury-owned gold is held in the United States. [8] Includes sales of foreign obligations to foreigners. [9] For 1980, includes foreign currency-denominated notes sold to private residents abroad. [10] Conceptually, "Balance on current account" is equal to "net foreign investment" in the national income and product accounts (NIPAs). However, the foreign transactions account in the NIPAs (a) includes adjustments to the international transactions accounts for the treatment of gold, (b) includes adjustments for the different geographical treatment of transactions with U.S. territories and Puerto Rico, and (c) includes services furnished without payment by financial pension plans except life insurance carriers and private noninsured pension plans.

Source: U.S. Bureau of Economic Analysis, Survey of Current Business, July 1999 and April 2000.

No. 1308. U.S. Balances on International Transactions by Area and Selected Country: 1998 and 1999

[In millions of dollars (-246,932 represents -$246,932,000,000). Minus sign (-) indicates debits]

Area or country	1998, balance on—				1999, balance on—			
	Goods [1]	Services	Income	Current account	Goods [1]	Services	Income	Current account
All areas..................	-246,932	82,650	-12,205	-220,562	-347,131	79,583	-24,789	-338,918
Western Europe...........	-34,909	21,401	-17,504	-31,336	-52,857	17,506	-31,812	-67,236
European Economic [2].......	-30,155	20,348	-19,564	-28,679	-46,132	16,778	-31,796	-59,865
Belgium-Luxembourg	5,496	1,048	-213	6,263	(NA)	(NA)	(NA)	(NA)
France	-6,483	2,276	-336	-4,748	(NA)	(NA)	(NA)	(NA)
Germany...............	-23,339	2,382	-900	-21,049	(NA)	(NA)	(NA)	(NA)
Italy	-12,031	886	2,342	-9,104	(NA)	(NA)	(NA)	(NA)
Netherlands..............	11,271	3,404	6,679	21,298	(NA)	(NA)	(NA)	(NA)
United Kingdom	3,483	4,107	-30,798	-21,809	-1,502	3,013	-34,565	-31,384
Eastern Europe............	-3,534	1,009	72	-5,811	-6,356	1,067	700	-8,001
Canada.................	-18,996	4,372	10,961	-4,276	-34,448	5,259	12,800	-17,032
Latin America, other Western Hemisphere	-4,131	14,970	7,511	5,858	-27,795	16,762	7,510	-17,579
Mexico.................	-17,066	1,577	-1,418	-21,697	(NA)	(NA)	(NA)	(NA)
Venezuela	-2,718	2,425	-297	-678	(NA)	(NA)	(NA)	(NA)
Japan [3]................	-65,255	16,540	-26,443	-75,354	-74,913	16,403	-28,320	-87,094
Other Asia and Africa...........	-126,510	20,573	-6,242	-128,923	(NA)	(NA)	(NA)	(NA)
Australia................	6,403	1,846	3,141	11,253	6,241	1,947	3,246	11,282
South Africa	562	235	722	1,292	(NA)	(NA)	(NA)	(NA)
International and unallocated.........	(NA)	1,939	16,299	8,027	(NA)	2,354	15,838	7,050

NA Not available.   [1] Adjusted to balance of payments basis; excludes exports under U.S. military sales contracts and imports under direct defense expenditures.   [2] Includes Denmark, Greece, Ireland, Spain, Portugal, European Atomic Energy Community, European Coal and Steel Community, and European Investment Bank, not shown separately.   [3] Includes Ryukyu Islands.
Source: U.S. Bureau of Economic Analysis, *Survey of Current Business*, July 1999 and April 2000 issues.

No. 1309. Private Services Transaction by Type of Service and Country: 1990 to 1998

[In millions of dollars (137,322 represents $137,322,000,000)]

Type of service and country	Exports				Imports			
	1990	1995	1997	1998	1990	1995	1997	1998
Total private services	136,151	202,176	240,443	245,688	98,210	128,781	152,447	165,321
Travel.......................	43,007	63,395	73,301	71,250	37,349	44,916	52,051	56,105
Overseas	30,807	54,331	63,027	61,226	28,929	35,281	40,667	43,990
Canada	7,093	6,207	6,836	6,206	3,541	4,319	4,904	5,719
Mexico....................	5,107	2,857	3,438	3,818	4,879	5,316	6,480	6,396
Passenger fares	15,298	18,909	20,789	19,996	10,531	14,663	18,138	19,797
Other transportation............	22,042	26,081	27,006	25,518	24,966	27,034	28,959	30,457
Freight....................	8,379	11,273	11,789	11,178	15,046	16,455	17,654	19,412
Port services...............	13,662	14,809	15,217	14,340	9,920	10,579	11,305	11,048
Royalties and license fees	16,634	30,289	33,781	36,808	3,135	6,919	9,390	11,292
Other private services	39,170	63,502	85,566	92,116	22,229	35,249	43,909	47,670
Affiliated services.............	13,622	20,483	27,272	28,321	9,117	13,634	17,728	19,095
Unaffilated services...........	25,548	43,019	58,294	63,795	13,111	21,615	26,181	28,575
Education	5,126	7,515	8,343	8,964	658	1,125	1,395	1,538
Financial services...........	4,417	7,029	11,539	13,698	2,475	2,472	3,563	3,771
Insurance, net	230	1,296	2,485	2,842	1,910	5,360	6,002	6,908
Telecommunications	2,735	3,228	3,949	3,689	5,583	7,305	8,351	8,125
Business, professional, and technical services	7,752	16,078	22,467	24,338	2,093	4,822	6,358	7,684
Advertising...............	130	425	624	575	243	833	859	1,046
Computer and data processing services.................	1,031	1,340	2,065	2,037	44	126	276	365
Management, consulting, and public relations services	354	1,489	1,596	1,657	135	465	731	914
Legal services	451	1,667	2,152	2,451	111	469	560	688
Construction, engineering, architectural, & mining services .	867	2,550	3,498	4,053	170	345	461	699
Canada	15,684	17,927	20,520	19,521	9,130	11,160	13,576	15,065
Europe......................	48,192	73,093	88,100	95,098	39,815	52,708	61,973	69,693
France.....................	5,542	7,965	10,005	10,182	4,169	5,951	6,785	7,688
Germany	7,364	12,692	14,121	15,271	6,819	7,586	7,984	8,920
Italy	3,279	4,533	5,041	5,590	3,469	3,743	3,691	4,046
Netherlands	3,269	6,119	7,331	7,561	1,935	3,191	3,471	4,486
Switzerland.................	(NA)	3,843	4,465	4,778	(NA)	2,285	2,792	3,876
United Kingdom..............	12,989	18,626	24,226	27,169	11,564	16,063	21,552	22,779
Latin America and other Western Hemisphere	21,771	32,656	42,788	46,723	18,643	24,252	29,672	31,514
Brazil.....................	(NA)	4,975	6,403	6,513	(NA)	1,165	1,764	1,810
Mexico....................	8,590	8,705	10,924	11,761	6,731	7,930	10,023	10,007
Venezuela	1,273	2,496	2,757	3,107	659	701	708	686
Other countries................	45,323	74,508	84,639	79,704	27,976	38,542	45,175	46,351
Australia...................	3,260	4,267	4,984	4,738	2,290	2,142	2,674	2,978
Japan	21,159	33,240	34,437	30,729	10,529	13,463	14,156	13,746
Korea, Republic of.............	(NA)	5,693	7,114	5,341	(NA)	3,581	4,533	4,061
Taiwan....................	(NA)	4,429	4,750	3,961	(NA)	2,856	3,374	2,913
Int'l organizations and unallocated	5,181	3,988	4,392	4,640	2,646	2,119	2,055	2,700

NA Not available.
Source: U.S. Bureau of Economic Analysis, *Survey of Current Business*, October 1999.

No. 1310. International Investment Position: 1990 to 1998

[In millions of dollars (-240,553 represents -$240,553,000,000). Estimates for end of year; subject to considerable error due to nature of basic data]

Type of investment	1990	1992	1993	1994	1995	1996	1997	1998
U.S. net international investment position:								
Current cost.	-240,553	-421,096	-295,261	-300,480	-500,170	-578,705	-968,208	-1,239,168
Market value	-166,846	-454,605	-180,373	-174,290	-422,617	-547,493	-1,066,262	-1,537,466
U.S.-owned assets abroad:								
Current cost.	2,149,982	2,298,640	2,718,424	2,956,788	3,405,761	3,958,502	4,508,626	4,930,896
Market value	2,291,734	2,464,196	3,055,316	3,276,086	3,869,663	4,544,502	5,288,892	5,947,983
U.S. official reserve assets.	174,664	147,435	164,945	163,394	176,061	160,739	134,836	146,006
Gold	102,406	87,168	102,556	100,110	101,279	96,698	75,929	75,291
Special drawing rights	10,989	8,503	9,039	10,039	11,037	10,312	10,027	10,603
Reserve position in IMF	9,076	11,759	11,818	12,030	14,649	15,435	18,071	24,111
Foreign currencies	52,193	40,005	41,532	41,215	49,096	38,294	30,809	36,001
U.S. Government assets, other. .	81,993	80,722	81,029	80,123	81,095	82,046	81,960	82,382
U.S. loans and other long-term assets	81,365	79,087	79,106	77,814	78,548	79,637	79,607	80,179
Repayable in dollars.	80,040	77,987	78,100	77,336	78,120	79,261	79,273	79,874
Other.	1,325	1,100	1,006	478	428	376	334	305
U.S. foreign currency holdings and short-term assets	628	1,635	1,923	2,309	2,547	2,409	2,353	2,203
U.S. private assets:								
Current cost	1,893,325	2,070,483	2,472,450	2,713,271	3,148,605	3,715,717	4,291,830	4,702,508
Market value.	2,035,077	2,236,039	2,809,342	3,032,569	3,612,507	4,301,717	5,072,096	5,719,595
Direct investments abroad:								
Current cost	590,010	633,074	690,655	748,505	843,253	940,243	1,004,228	1,123,441
Market value.	731,762	798,630	1,027,547	1,067,803	1,307,155	1,526,243	1,784,494	2,140,528
Foreign securities	342,313	515,083	853,528	948,668	1,169,636	1,467,985	1,739,400	1,968,956
Bonds	144,717	200,817	309,666	321,208	392,827	465,057	538,400	561,826
Corporate stocks	197,596	314,266	543,862	627,460	776,809	1,002,928	1,201,000	1,407,130
U.S. claims on unaffiliated foreigners [1]	265,315	254,303	242,022	322,980	367,567	449,978	562,396	596,222
U.S. claims reported by U.S. banks [2]	695,687	668,023	686,245	693,118	768,149	857,511	985,806	1,013,889
Foreign-owned assets in the U.S.								
Current cost.	2,390,535	2,719,736	3,013,685	3,257,268	3,905,931	4,537,207	5,476,834	6,170,064
Market value	2,458,580	2,918,801	3,235,689	3,450,376	4,292,280	5,091,995	6,355,154	7,485,449
Foreign official assets in the U.S.	373,293	437,263	509,422	535,217	671,710	799,033	835,709	836,053
U.S. Government securities . . .	291,228	329,317	381,687	407,152	497,776	610,469	614,530	620,249
U.S. Treasury securities . . .	285,911	322,600	373,050	396,887	482,773	590,704	589,792	588,987
Other.	5,317	6,717	8,637	10,265	15,003	19,765	24,738	31,262
Other U.S. Government liabilities	17,243	20,801	22,113	23,678	23,573	23,257	21,459	18,346
U.S. liabilities reported by U.S. banks [2]	39,880	54,967	69,721	73,386	107,394	113,098	135,384	123,915
Other foreign official assets. . .	24,942	32,178	35,901	31,001	42,967	52,209	64,336	73,543
Other foreign assets in the U.S.:								
Current cost	2,017,242	2,282,473	2,504,263	2,722,051	3,234,221	3,738,174	4,641,125	5,334,011
Market value.	2,085,287	2,481,538	2,726,267	2,915,159	3,620,570	4,292,962	5,519,445	6,649,396
Direct investments:								
Current cost	471,556	497,112	546,394	564,745	619,377	674,330	764,045	878,717
Market value.	539,601	696,177	768,398	757,853	1,005,726	1,229,118	1,642,365	2,194,102
U.S. Treasury securities	152,452	197,739	221,501	235,684	358,537	502,562	662,228	727,344
U.S. currency	85,933	114,804	133,734	157,185	169,484	186,846	211,628	228,250
U.S. securities other than U.S. Treasury securities	460,644	599,447	696,449	739,695	971,356	1,199,461	1,578,694	2,021,820
Corporate and other bonds . . .	238,903	299,287	355,822	368,077	481,214	588,044	715,196	900,749
Corporate stocks.	221,741	300,160	340,627	371,618	490,142	611,417	863,498	1,121,071
U.S. liabilities to unaffiliated foreigners [1]	213,406	220,666	229,038	239,817	300,424	346,727	453,555	460,787
U.S. liabilities reported by U.S. banks [2].	633,251	652,705	677,147	784,925	815,043	828,248	970,975	1,017,093

[1] Reported by U.S. nonbanking concerns.　　[2] Not included elsewhere.

Source: U.S. Bureau of Economic Analysis, *Survey of Current Business*, July 1999.

No. 1311. U.S. Reserve Assets: 1990 to 1999

[In billions of dollars (83.3 represents $83,300,000,000). As of end of year, except as indicated]

Type	1990	1992	1993	1994	1995	1996	1997	1998	1999
Total	83.3	71.3	73.4	74.3	85.8	75.1	70.0	81.8	71.6
Gold stock [1]	11.1	11.1	11.1	11.1	11.1	11.0	11.1	11.0	11.1
Special drawing rights	11.0	8.5	9.0	10.0	11.0	10.3	10.0	10.6	10.3
Foreign currencies	52.2	40.0	41.5	41.2	49.1	38.3	30.8	36.0	32.2
Reserve position in IMF [2]	9.1	11.8	11.8	12.0	14.6	15.4	18.1	24.1	18.0

[1] Includes gold in Exchange Stabilization Fund; excludes gold held under earmark at Federal Reserve banks for foreign and international accounts. Beginning 1975, gold assets were valued at $42.22 pursuant to the amending of Section 2 of the Par Value Modification Act, PL-93-110, approved September 21, 1973.　　[2] International Monetary Fund.

Source: Board of Governors of the Federal Reserve System, *Federal Reserve Bulletin*, monthly; and Department of the Treasury, *Treasury Bulletin*, monthly.

No. 1312. Foreign Direct Investment Position in the United States on a Historical-Cost Basis by Industry and Selected Country: 1997 and 1998

[In millions of dollars (693,207 represents $693,207,000,000)]

Country	1997				1998			
	Total [1]	Petro-leum	Manufac-turing, total	Whole-sale	Total [1]	Petro-leum	Manufac-turing, total	Whole-sale
All countries	693,207	42,085	273,122	87,630	811,756	53,254	329,346	96,261
Canada	69,866	3,177	27,811	4,190	74,840	2,633	26,152	5,098
Europe	432,622	29,750	197,819	39,015	539,906	42,771	252,893	43,554
Austria	1,829	(D)	298	282	4,872	(D)	365	485
Belgium	6,438	1,221	3,529	840	9,577	(D)	4,232	1,018
Denmark	2,929	5	708	1,782	3,229	4	711	2,010
Finland	3,557	(D)	1,615	(D)	4,321	(D)	2,224	1,012
France	49,503	(D)	29,099	1,911	62,167	(D)	37,820	1,972
Germany	71,289	(D)	34,522	12,250	95,045	312	51,018	12,405
Ireland	10,493	639	2,748	823	13,227	739	4,874	1,980
Italy	3,089	294	627	468	3,830	(D)	907	423
Luxembourg	5,363	-	2,941	1,420	20,214		(D)	1,311
Netherlands	89,570	12,949	31,565	6,303	96,904	11,505	35,109	5,606
Norway	3,045	(D)	1,380	(D)	3,616	(D)	1,595	269
Spain	2,266	4	587	120	2,292	-3	714	154
Sweden	12,842	(D)	8,576	1,171	14,564	(D)	9,065	2,028
Switzerland	38,281	194	21,187	1,801	54,011	252	26,310	2,579
United Kingdom	131,315	11,680	58,342	8,170	151,335	26,277	64,022	10,099
Latin America and other Western Hemisphere	33,546	3,427	3,930	2,179	32,210	4,072	4,329	1,858
South and Central America	10,212	-783	273	425	11,916	-457	1,067	270
Mexico	3,315	-8	631	459	4,029	-9	887	495
Panama	6,023	-56	-7	-48	7,025	(D)	482	-108
Other Western Hemisphere	23,333	4,211	3,657	1,754	20,294	4,529	3,262	1,588
Bahamas	1,905	(D)	127	354	2,141	(D)	131	440
Netherlands Antilles	5,722	2,689	1,217	165	4,727	(D)	795	(D)
United Kingdom Islands, Caribbean	12,022	(D)	1,867	687	10,395	1,578	1,792	608
Africa	1,465	(D)	-14	1	884	-4	-90	21
Middle East	6,593	(D)	944	91	7,831	1,061	966	131
Israel	1,955	-	923	91	2,459	-3	601	129
Kuwait	2,935	4	7	2	(D)	(D)	9	3
Saudi Arabia	1,565	(D)	1	(Z)	(D)	(D)	3	-1
Asia and Pacific	149,115	4,215	42,632	42,153	156,085	2,720	45,096	45,598
Australia	14,703	4,522	2,414	-64	14,755	3,202	2,982	-55
Hong Kong	1,797	-16	316	648	2,097	(D)	358	599
Japan	125,131	212	37,356	40,628	132,569	234	39,918	43,114
Singapore	3,271	20	1,047	196	1,813	2	244	267
Taiwan	2,749	-1	1,253	476	3,120	-2	1,505	558

- Represents or rounds to zero.   D Suppressed to avoid disclosure of data of individual companies.   Z Less than $50 million.   [1] Includes other industries not shown separately.

Source: U.S. Bureau of Economic Analysis, *Survey of Current Business*, July 1999.

No. 1313. U.S. Affiliates of Foreign Companies—Assets, Sales, Employment, Land, Exports, and Imports: 1997

[A U.S. affiliate is a U.S. business enterprise in which one foreign owner (individual, branch, partnership, association, trust, corporation, or government) has a direct or indirect voting interest of 10 percent or more. Estimates cover the universe of nonbank affiliates]

Industry	Total assets (mil. dol.)	Sales (mil. dol.) [1]	Employ-ment (1,000) [2]	Employee compen-sation (mil. dol.)	Gross book value (mil. dol.)		Merchan-dise exports [4] (mil. dol.)	Merchan-dise imports [4] (mil. dol.)
					Plant and equip-ment [3]	Land		
Total	3,034,404	1,717,240	5,164.3	230,337	866,197	54,312	140,924	261,482
Petroleum	123,753	157,770	105.0	6,730	118,095	2,022	7,797	19,547
Manufacturing	648,564	623,313	2,271.0	112,578	317,297	11,462	67,719	88,085
Chemicals and allied products	191,541	143,236	393.1	25,277	94,052	2,280	15,492	16,346
Wholesale trade [5]	266,063	449,847	522.5	25,829	95,565	3,222	59,050	148,214
Motor vehicles and auto parts and supplies	91,878	117,028	88.1	4,765	50,604	807	4,708	49,479
Farm-product raw materials	10,679	34,067	21.2	736	2,434	112	13,866	2,831
Retail trade	54,723	102,531	839.2	17,281	34,558	3,365	1,952	3,679
Finance, except banking	847,626	74,409	60.3	10,317	7,923	514	(D)	(D)
Insurance	704,133	102,180	165.0	11,065	30,248	973	-	-
Real estate	104,334	16,857	24.7	1,141	88,473	16,559	(D)	2
Services	113,797	66,435	682.9	22,610	56,367	7,974	622	(D)
Other	171,411	123,898	493.7	22,786	117,671	8,220	3,702	934

- Represents zero.   D Suppressed to avoid disclosure of data of individual companies.   [1] Excludes returns, discounts, allowances, and sales and excise taxes.   [2] Average number of full-time and part-time employees.   [3] Includes mineral rights and minor amounts of property other than land.   [4] F.a.s. value at port of exportation.   [5] Includes industries not shown separately.

Source: U.S. Bureau of Economic Analysis, *Survey of Current Business*, August 1999; and *Foreign Direct Investment in the United States, Operations of U.S. Affiliates of Foreign Companies,* Revised 1996 Estimates and Preliminary 1997 Estimates.

Foreign Commerce and Aid   783

No. 1314. Foreign Direct Investment in the United States—Gross Book Value and Employment of U.S. Affiliates of Foreign Companies by State: 1990 to 1997

[578,355 represents $578,355,000,000. A U.S. affiliate is a U.S. business enterprise in which one foreign owner (individual, branch, partnership, association, trust corporation, or government) has a direct or indirect voting interest of 10 percent or more. Estimates cover the universe of nonbank U.S. affiliates]

State and other area	Gross book value of property, plant, and equipment (mil. dol.)				Total employment				
								1997	
	1990	1995	1996	1997	1990 (1,000)	1995 (1,000)	1996 (1,000)	Total (1,000)	Percent of all businesses
Total	578,355	769,491	825,695	866,197	4,734.5	4,941.8	5,105.0	5,164.3	(X)
United States	552,902	733,089	784,972	839,573	4,704.4	4,898.9	5,068.1	5,134.7	4.8
Alabama.	7,300	10,598	11,981	13,006	55.7	60.6	61.7	65.0	4.1
Alaska	19,435	25,558	26,234	25,922	13.2	9.8	10.2	8.7	4.3
Arizona.	7,234	6,699	9,604	9,797	57.1	51.9	57.8	59.4	3.4
Arkansas	2,344	3,666	3,829	3,934	29.2	32.1	37.6	35.2	3.7
California	75,768	96,576	102,703	91,788	555.9	548.6	557.5	569.4	4.9
Colorado.	6,544	8,602	9,368	9,833	56.3	72.2	72.7	80.3	4.7
Connecticut.	5,357	8,466	8,902	8,703	75.9	73.3	85.1	83.8	5.8
Delaware	5,818	2,919	3,105	3,323	43.1	15.8	16.3	19.1	5.6
District of Columbia	3,869	4,983	4,864	4,339	11.4	13.4	12.8	11.2	2.8
Florida.	18,659	24,865	30,251	29,598	205.7	210.0	239.8	240.9	4.2
Georgia	16,729	22,432	23,799	25,403	161.0	180.1	195	188.9	6.0
Hawaii	11,830	15,972	15,324	15,157	53.0	48.9	47.5	50.1	11.4
Idaho.	776	1,026	1,270	1,407	11.7	11.3	12.3	12.4	2.9
Illinois	23,420	34,305	34,687	37,649	245.8	237.0	236.1	224.5	4.4
Indiana.	13,426	18,782	16,711	18,367	126.9	136.9	127.2	128.3	5.1
Iowa	2,712	4,527	5,304	5,444	32.8	35.8	37.7	37.8	3.1
Kansas.	5,134	3,233	4,741	5,696	29.6	34.0	42.7	45.4	4.2
Kentucky	9,229	15,136	15,610	16,909	65.7	83.4	86.5	89.5	6.1
Louisiana	17,432	20,543	23,226	25,151	61.4	51.0	55.7	58.0	3.8
Maine.	2,080	3,885	4,092	3,960	26.6	29.1	30.4	31.6	6.7
Maryland	5,713	9,197	9,984	10,578	79.6	95.0	93.8	92.0	4.8
Massachusetts.	8,890	12,707	14,345	15,473	131.2	141.5	162.3	159.5	5.7
Michigan.	12,012	21,370	18,733	20,914	139.6	170.3	162.8	171.4	4.4
Minnesota.	11,972	8,688	9,858	9,972	89.8	79.8	89.8	96.6	4.4
Mississippi	2,989	3,055	2,570	2,967	23.6	22.6	20.6	21.7	2.4
Missouri	5,757	8,327	10,310	10,945	73.7	79.3	84.1	84.0	3.7
Montana.	2,181	1,938	1,935	2,041	5.1	4.4	4.5	4.4	1.5
Nebraska	776	1,320	1,791	2,027	14.9	15.7	19.1	20.8	2.9
Nevada	5,450	8,242	8,589	8,784	22.7	25.0	25.5	25.5	3.1
New Hampshire	1,446	2,212	2,284	2,546	25.9	30.0	30.8	31.6	6.2
New Jersey.	18,608	26,175	27,706	30,488	227.0	205.2	209.4	212.4	6.6
New Mexico	4,312	4,363	4,447	4,945	17.4	16.2	15.4	17.4	3.1
New York	36,424	52,992	53,374	53,711	347.5	343.8	349.9	351.5	5.1
North Carolina	15,234	21,475	23,965	24,019	181.0	225.3	231.6	225.0	7.1
North Dakota.	1,251	915	1,125	1,166	3.1	3.2	4.7	3.5	1.4
Ohio	20,549	29,932	33,572	35,095	219.1	222.1	226.7	234.1	4.9
Oklahoma.	6,049	5,448	5,538	5,723	43.6	34.2	36.7	34.4	3.0
Oregon.	3,427	5,807	6,146	7,269	39.1	49.7	49.2	52.0	4.0
Pennsylvania.	16,587	24,432	25,344	25,671	221.6	231.6	238.3	225.0	4.6
Rhode Island.	1,120	2,240	2,604	2,628	13.3	16.2	19.2	18.5	4.6
South Carolina.	10,067	13,438	15,509	16,847	104.7	111.6	117.2	116.9	7.9
South Dakota	553	665	792	986	4.5	4.6	5.6	10.4	3.5
Tennessee	10,280	14,227	15,603	17,123	116.9	136.3	136.4	149.4	6.6
Texas	57,079	68,142	75,728	77,906	299.5	326.4	330.2	350.6	4.8
Utah	3,918	5,612	6,451	7,719	21.0	28.6	32.7	36.7	4.3
Vermont	631	1,037	1,056	1,031	7.7	10.4	9.9	9.6	4.0
Virginia.	10,702	15,129	17,479	20,158	113.3	141.4	146.2	143.3	5.3
Washington.	7,985	11,462	11,920	12,275	77.5	83.0	86.6	86.6	4.0
West Virginia.	7,975	7,809	7,507	6,714	34.9	31.9	26.1	27.2	4.8
Wisconsin.	5,088	7,415	8,100	8,003	81.4	71.5	73.6	76.5	3.3
Wyoming	2,782	4,544	5,001	4,956	5.8	6.9	6.5	6.9	4.0
Puerto Rico.	1,499	2,174	1,848	1,686	16.1	27.4	20	17.1	(NA)
Other territories and offshore .	18,484	17,798	20,156	22,952	9.0	13.1	10.9	10.3	(NA)
Foreign. . . . , ...	5,470	16,430	18,719	1,986	5.0	2.4	6	2.2	(NA)
Unspecified [1]	(NA)	(NA)	(NA)	33,505	(NA)	(NA)	(NA)	(NA)	(NA)

NA Not available.   X Not applicable.   [1] Covers property, plant, and equipment not located in a particular state, including aircraft, railroad rolling stock, satellites, undersea cable, and trucks engaged in interstate transportation.

Source: U.S. Bureau of Economic Analysis, *Survey of Current Business*, June 1999, and *Foreign Direct Investment in the United States, Operations of U.S. Affiliates of Foreign Companies*, annual.

784   Foreign Commerce and Aid

No. 1315. U.S. Businesses Acquired or Established by Foreign Direct Investors—Investment Outlays by Industry of U.S. Business Enterprise and Country of Ultimate Beneficial Owner: 1990 to 1999

[In millions of dollars (65,932 represents $65,932,000,000). Foreign direct investment is the ownership or control directly or indirectly, by one foreign individual branch, partnership, association, trust, corporation, or government of 10 percent or more of the voting securities of a U.S. business enterprise or an equivalent interest in an unincorporated one. Data represent number and full cost of acquisitions of existing U.S. business enterprises, including business segments or operating units of existing U.S. business enterprises and establishments of new enterprises. Investments may be made by the foreign direct investor itself, or indirectly by an existing U.S. affiliate of the foreign direct investor. Covers investments in U.S. business enterprises with assets of over $1 million, or ownership of 200 acres of U.S. land]

Industry and country	1990	1993	1994	1995	1996	1997	1998	1999
Total	65,932	26,229	45,626	57,195	79,929	69,708	215,256	(NA)
INDUSTRY								
Petroleum	1,141	882	469	1,520	1,059	762	(D)	(NA)
Manufacturing	23,898	11,090	21,218	26,643	27,835	19,603	89,739	(NA)
Wholesale trade	1,676	837	2,156	1,168	4,746	2,612	3,266	(NA)
Retail trade	1,250	1,495	1,542	2,838	2,988	435	1,938	(NA)
Depository institutions [1]	897	958	2,026	2,301	1,944	3,547	1,563	(NA)
Finance, except depository institutions [1]	2,121	1,599	2,195	7,837	8,676	7,019	16,607	(NA)
Insurance	2,093	1,105	450	654	4,688	8,526	4,709	(NA)
Real estate	7,771	1,883	2,647	2,996	4,175	4,119	6,144	(NA)
Services	19,369	4,162	7,163	5,881	15,292	12,187	10,099	(NA)
Other [2]	5,716	2,218	5,760	5,359	8,528	10,898	(D)	(NA)
COUNTRY								
Canada	3,430	3,797	4,128	8,029	9,700	11,755	22,635	11,388
Europe	36,011	16,845	31,920	38,195	49,427	44,014	170,173	205,150
France	10,217	1,249	1,404	1,129	6,021	2,578	14,493	24,579
Germany [3]	2,363	2,841	3,328	13,117	12,858	6,464	39,873	24,393
Netherlands	2,247	2,074	1,537	1,061	6,476	10,244	19,009	26,896
Switzerland	3,905	804	5,044	7,533	4,910	6,745	4,525	7,119
United Kingdom	13,096	8,238	17,261	9,094	14,757	11,834	84,995	110,115
Other Europe	4,183	1,639	3,346	6,261	4,405	6,149	7,278	12,048
Latin America and other Western Hemisphere	796	874	1,352	1,550	1,790	924	11,354	34,013
South and Central America	399	527	(D)	1,283	(D)	166	920	1,377
Other Western Hemisphere	397	347	(D)	267	(D)	758	10,433	32,636
Africa	(D)	(D)	(D)	(D)	(D)	(D)	212	(D)
Middle East	472	1,308	(D)	447	(D)	847	2,810	546
Asia and Pacific	23,170	3,004	5,263	8,688	12,751	11,786	7,329	11,502
Australia	1,412	129	1,522	2,270	2,222	7,600	(D)	(D)
Japan	19,933	2,065	2,715	3,602	8,813	2,326	4,862	8,048
Other Asia and Pacific	1,825	810	1,026	2,816	1,716	1,860	(D)	(D)

D Suppressed to avoid disclosure of data of individual companies. [1] Prior to 1992, "depository institutions" excludes, and "finance, depository institutions" includes, savings institutions and credit unions. Beginning with 1992, savings institutions and credit unions have been reclassified from "finance, except depository institutions" to "depository institutions." [2] For investments in which more than one investor participated, each investor and each investor's outlays are classified by country of each ultimate beneficial owner. [3] Prior to 1990, this line includes data only for the Federal Republic of Germany. Beginning in 1990, this line also includes the former German Democratic Republic (GDR). This change has no effect on the data because, prior to 1991, there were no U.S. affiliates of the former GDR.

Source: U.S. Bureau of Economic Analysis, *Survey of Current Business*, June 2000, and previous June issues.

No. 1316. U.S. Direct Investment Position Abroad, Capital Outflows, and Income by Industry of Foreign Affiliates: 1996 to 1998

[In millions of dollars (795,195 represents $795,195,000,000)]

Industry	Direct investment position on a historical-cost basis			Capital outflows (inflows (-))			Income		
	1996	1997	1998	1996	1997	1998	1996	1997	1998
All industries, total	795,195	865,531	980,565	84,428	99,517	121,644	93,594	103,892	90,242
Petroleum	75,232	82,215	91,113	6,239	9,603	9,780	12,082	11,823	8,059
Manufacturing	270,288	280,332	304,690	24,325	28,097	26,680	34,342	38,283	31,416
Food and kindred products	31,024	32,465	33,871	2,095	3,806	1,670	4,452	4,910	4,262
Chemicals and allied products	74,858	77,112	83,589	5,796	7,210	7,072	9,529	10,050	9,930
Primary and fabricated metals	16,309	15,924	17,098	6,064	444	1,109	1,358	1,406	1,278
Industrial machinery and equipment	30,336	32,293	34,755	2,752	4,381	2,810	4,637	5,669	4,213
Electronic and other electric equipment	31,832	31,624	34,531	3,440	2,992	2,670	4,280	4,700	2,763
Transportation equipment	32,092	34,907	35,615	708	4,419	1,692	3,409	5,048	2,385
Other manufacturing	53,837	56,006	65,231	3,470	4,845	9,658	6,677	6,500	6,586
Wholesale trade	67,125	64,432	75,188	6,498	846	9,130	9,068	9,538	10,794
Depository institutions	36,807	40,169	42,029	2,448	3,036	1,253	3,329	3,374	577
Finance [1], insurance, and real estate	254,739	293,116	337,600	31,601	41,388	44,445	28,938	31,912	30,702
Services	37,850	42,342	52,514	3,511	4,557	10,867	3,627	5,533	4,722
Other industries	53,155	62,925	77,432	9,804	11,990	19,490	2,209	3,429	3,972

[1] Excludes depository institutions.

Source: U.S. Bureau of Economic Analysis, *Survey of Current Business*, April 2000.

No. 1317. U.S. Direct Investment Position Abroad on a Historical-Cost Basis by Country: 1990 to 1998

[In millions of dollars (430,521 represents $430,521,000,000). U.S. direct investment abroad is the ownership or control by one U.S. person of 10 percent or more of the voting securities of an incorporated foreign business enterprise or an equivalent interest in a unincorporated foreign business enterprise. Negative position can occur when a U.S. parent company's liabilities to the foreign affiliate are greater than its equity in, and loans to the foreign affiliate]

Country	1990	1992	1993	1994	1995	1996	1997	1998
All countries	430,521	502,063	564,283	612,893	699,015	795,195	865,531	980,565
Canada	69,508	68,690	69,922	74,221	83,498	89,592	96,031	103,908
Europe	214,739	248,744	285,735	297,133	344,596	389,378	420,108	489,539
Austria	1,113	1,371	1,312	2,197	2,829	2,854	2,638	3,838
Belgium	9,464	11,381	11,697	14,714	18,706	18,740	17,430	18,920
Denmark	1,726	1,676	1,735	2,030	2,161	2,554	2,173	2,628
Finland	544	343	414	761	965	1,070	1,312	1,700
France	19,164	25,157	24,312	27,322	33,358	35,200	35,800	39,188
Germany	27,609	33,003	36,811	38,878	44,242	41,281	38,490	42,853
Greece	282	372	410	482	533	566	634	660
Ireland	5,894	7,607	9,019	7,239	7,996	10,133	12,862	15,936
Italy	14,063	13,015	12,748	14,808	17,096	16,193	14,809	14,638
Luxembourg	1,697	2,031	5,611	6,310	5,929	7,753	10,109	14,930
Netherlands	19,120	20,700	20,911	29,889	42,113	54,118	64,361	79,386
Norway	4,209	3,825	3,757	5,026	4,741	5,483	6,934	7,609
Portugal	897	1,290	1,264	1,181	1,413	1,423	1,425	1,474
Spain	7,868	8,757	6,689	9,572	10,856	12,252	11,232	12,807
Sweden	1,787	1,881	2,374	1,905	6,816	5,248	5,463	6,053
Switzerland	25,099	28,698	33,056	27,908	31,125	30,744	31,420	37,616
Turkey	522	732	995	874	973	1,059	1,041	1,069
United Kingdom	72,707	85,176	109,208	100,817	106,332	134,559	153,108	178,648
Other	974	1,729	3,411	5,219	6,412	8,148	8,868	9,588
Latin America and other								
Western Hemisphere	71,413	91,308	100,482	116,478	131,377	155,925	178,504	196,655
South America	22,933	28,760	31,210	37,673	49,170	57,372	68,372	73,290
Argentina	2,531	3,327	4,442	5,692	7,660	7,893	10,004	11,489
Brazil	14,384	16,313	16,772	17,885	25,002	29,105	35,091	37,802
Chile	1,896	2,544	2,749	5,062	6,216	8,156	8,975	9,132
Colombia	1,677	3,053	2,930	3,463	3,506	3,531	4,436	4,317
Ecuador	280	295	555	784	889	922	838	952
Peru	599	620	622	971	1,335	2,281	2,467	2,587
Venezuela	1,087	1,972	2,362	3,087	3,634	4,474	5,381	5,697
Other	479	636	778	728	928	1,010	1,181	1,315
Central America	20,415	25,579	28,092	30,083	33,493	37,667	47,735	56,387
Costa Rica	251	274	298	607	921	1,223	1,544	2,126
Guatemala	130	115	139	200	233	331	357	429
Honduras	262	239	159	140	68	129	183	186
Mexico	10,313	13,730	15,221	16,968	16,873	19,351	24,181	25,877
Panama	9,289	11,038	12,043	11,905	15,123	16,335	21,056	26,957
Other	169	182	233	262	273	298	413	812
Other Western Hemisphere	28,065	36,969	41,180	48,722	48,714	60,886	62,397	66,978
Bahamas	4,004	4,167	3,138	2,808	1,768	1,876	1,599	287
Barbados	252	340	471	391	698	848	791	1,077
Bermuda	20,169	26,736	28,666	28,355	28,374	37,091	37,660	41,076
Dominican Republic	529	779	1,039	266	330	400	476	535
Jamaica	625	892	1,049	1,167	1,287	1,583	1,948	2,105
Netherlands Antilles	-4,501	-1,989	-62	6,739	6,835	7,597	4,423	4,472
Trinidad and Tobago	485	565	691	529	673	786	651	1,054
U.K. Islands, Caribbean	5,929	5,401	5,544	7,858	8,358	10,121	14,051	15,713
Other	574	75	645	608	392	583	797	658
Africa	3,650	4,469	5,469	5,760	6,017	8,162	11,157	13,491
Egypt	1,231	1,334	1,510	1,090	1,093	1,366	1,612	1,955
Nigeria	-401	301	478	605	629	1,020	1,387	1,925
South Africa	775	879	900	1,132	1,422	1,495	2,451	2,363
Other	2,045	1,955	2,581	2,933	2,873	4,281	5,706	7,247
Middle East	3,959	5,759	6,571	6,367	7,198	8,294	8,803	10,599
Israel	746	1,335	1,604	1,483	1,831	2,045	2,028	3,067
Saudi Arabia	1,899	2,351	2,587	2,100	2,741	3,476	3,826	4,209
United Arab Emirates	409	429	524	357	500	598	567	710
Other	905	1,644	1,856	2,427	2,126	2,174	2,382	2,613
Asia and Pacific	64,716	79,963	92,671	108,528	122,712	139,548	146,609	161,798
Australia	15,110	16,928	19,047	20,196	24,328	30,006	29,910	33,676
China	354	563	916	2,557	2,765	3,848	5,071	6,348
Hong Kong	6,055	8,693	10,063	11,092	11,768	14,391	19,267	20,802
India	372	484	599	1,030	1,105	1,344	1,563	1,480
Indonesia	3,207	4,384	4,864	6,355	6,777	8,322	6,664	6,932
Japan	22,599	26,591	31,095	34,117	37,309	34,578	33,725	38,153
Korea, South	2,695	2,912	3,427	4,334	5,557	6,508	6,430	7,365
Malaysia	1,466	1,596	1,975	3,148	4,237	5,663	6,522	6,193
New Zealand	3,156	3,314	3,064	3,893	4,601	5,940	6,523	6,136
Philippines	1,355	1,666	1,953	2,484	2,719	3,541	3,295	3,192
Singapore	3,975	6,715	8,875	10,940	12,140	14,912	17,864	19,783
Taiwan	2,226	2,827	3,113	3,775	4,293	4,476	4,668	4,937
Thailand	1,790	2,594	2,943	3,585	4,283	5,000	3,946	5,721
Other	356	696	737	1,022	830	1,019	1,161	1,080
International	2,535	3,131	3,433	4,406	3,618	4,295	4,317	4,578
Addenda:								
Eastern Europe	(D)	731	2,356	4,029	5,136	6,651	7,743	8,143
European Communities(12)	180,491	210,164	240,414	253,242	301,345	337,184	368,997	433,658
OPEC [1]	7,145	10,692	11,737	13,794	15,546	17,641	20,554	23,252

D Figure withheld to avoid disclosure. [1] OPEC=Organization of Petroleum Exporting Countries. Includes Algeria, Ecuador, Gabon, Indonesia, Iran, Iraq, Kuwait, Libya, Nigeria, Qatar, Saudi Arabia, United Arab Emirates, and Venezuela. Prior to 1993, Ecuador was also a member and was included in this line.

Source: U.S. Bureau of Economic Analysis, *Survey of Current Business*, August 1999, and earlier issues.

No. 1318. U.S. Government Foreign Grants and Credits by Type and Country: 1966 to 1998

[In millions of dollars (70,381 represents $70,381,000,000). See text, this section. Negative figures (-) occur when the total of grant returns, principal repayments, and/or foreign currencies disbursed by the U.S. Government exceeds new grants and new credits utilized and/or acquisitions of foreign currencies through new sales of farm products]

Country	1966-1975, total	1976-1985, total	1986-1995, total	1993	1994	1995	1996	1997	1998
Total, net	70,381	104,191	90,669	18,002	16,426	12,668	16,645	12,749	13,820
Investment in financial institutions.	2,719	10,432	13,504	1,143	1,430	1,517	1,833	1,588	1,580
Western Europe.	1,004	1,618	-5,411	349	174	177	270	319	258
Austria.	-19	34	-72	-1	-1	-1	-1	-1	(Z)
Belgium and Luxembourg	17	-46	-48	-	-	-	-	-	-
Denmark	64	-58	-13	-	-	-	-	-	-
Finland	-19	21	-72	-26	-1	-1	-1	-1	(Z)
France	-93	-222	-93	-2	-1	1	-	(Z)	-
Germany	-117	-117	-6,459	-1	-	(Z)	(Z)	-	
Iceland.	-8	-12	-8	-	-	-	-	-	-
Ireland	-51	7	5	-8	36	-	11	39	8
Italy.	85	133	-233	(Z)	-	(Z)	-	-	-
Netherlands	116	-180	-2	-	-	-	-	-	-
Norway	379	-257	-33	4	-	-	-	-	-
Portugal.	34	1,003	796	112	115	-16	-3	-12	-15
Spain.	607	965	-867	31	-55	-59	-48	-37	-37
Sweden	17	-1	-15	-	-	-	-	-	-
United Kingdom	-546	-964	-1,465	-118	-120	-118	-125	-127	-130
Yugoslavia . . . . [1]	84	174	-149	(X)	(X)	(X)	(X)	(X)	(X)
Former Yugoslavia: [1]									
Bosnia and Hercegovina	(X)	(X)	227	51	84	92	235	252	220
Croatia	(X)	(X)	124	63	52	9	-10	-7	-12
Macedonia	(X)	(X)	5	1	3	1	3	18	6
Slovenia	(X)	(X)	-48	-6	-17	-24	-27	-16	-16
Former Yugoslavia - Regional [2]. . . .	(X)	(X)	1	9	-1	(Z)	(Z)	-8	6
Other [3] and unspecified [2]	455	1,139	3,010	241	81	293	236	220	228
Eastern Europe	226	1,029	12,352	3,372	2,910	1,963	1,953	1,413	1,785
Albania	-	-	173	48	16	15	58	11	16
Bulgaria	-	-	93	22	8	6	13	14	13
Czechoslovakia	-	-5	17	15	1	-2	3	-11	(X)
Czech Republic	(X)	(X)	7	2	2	3	9	5	4
Estonia	(X)	(X)	31	1	(Z)	2	7	4	5
Hungary	-5	6	41	3	4	35	15	-16	12
Latvia	(X)	(X)	35	1	3	2	10	4	8
Lithuania	(X)	(X)	96	24	15	28	17	23	14
Poland	-75	1,017	3,490	33	8	5	49	28	36
Romania	92	55	43	15	18	8	29	3	26
Slovakia	(X)	(X)	4	1	1	2	12	11	6
Soviet Union	214	-44	-267	(X)	(X)	(X)	(X)	(X)	(X)
Newly Independent States:									
Armenia	(X)	(X)	352	96	127	102	80	26	38
Azerbaijan	(X)	(X)	42	-	24	19	14	4	5
Belarus	(X)	(X)	236	120	37	49	31	19	4
Georgia	(X)	(X)	285	103	86	89	79	38	27
Kazakhstan	(X)	(X)	70	14	17	16	59	52	67
Kyrgyzstan	(X)	(X)	175	105	36	33	38	26	30
Moldova	(X)	(X)	85	35	22	19	15	8	5
Russia	(X)	(X)	3,989	2,164	1,184	455	421	356	435
Tajikistan	(X)	(X)	94	19	30	34	32	27	27
Turkmenistan	(X)	(X)	73	34	13	16	19	1	3
Ukraine	(X)	(X)	352	70	105	170	232	95	140
Uzbekistan	(X)	(X)	8	1	6	1	4	2	6
Former Soviet Union - Regional [2] . .	(X)	(X)	1,711	240	735	617	584	595	659
Other [1] and unspecified [2]	(X)	(X)	1,119	207	413	241	124	85	200
Near East and South Asia.	17,195	50,777	29,164	8,019	7,042	3,022	7,552	4,723	4,979
Afghanistan	185	56	403	51	9	10	14	17	-0
Bangladesh	701	1,670	1,590	123	202	87	48	42	27
Cyprus	20	138	151	14	16	6	11	10	14
Egypt	271	13,600	26,592	2,766	2,258	1,637	1,620	1,377	2,014
Greece	905	362	2,774	313	262	261	12	-211	-240
India	3,810	1,021	767	92	45	48	55	237	160
Iran	914	-847	-42	-	-	-	-21	-	-
Iraq [4]	-5	5	892	116	135	128	119	4	(Z)
Israel	3,760	25,417	25,116	3,295	3,106	420	5,294	2,896	2,840
Jordan	618	1,320	754	125	98	129	168	232	160
Kuwait	-	-	-16,058	-	-	-	-	-	-
Lebanon	90	233	22	7	5	5	11	3	1
Nepal	105	177	193	21	20	19	21	24	20
Oman	(Z)	79	42	20	1	4	12	25	20
Pakistan	2,048	1,971	1,222	-35	-158	-187	-164	-62	-82
Saudi Arabia	23	-20	-16,855	-	-	-	-	-	-
Sri Lanka	153	512	596	88	41	26	6	7	1
Syria	15	262	3	3	-	-	-	-	-
Turkey	2,703	3,760	2,956	813	224	147	-61	-19	-162
United Arab Emirates	-	-	-4,070	-	-	-	-	-	-
Yemen (Sanaa)	3	(Z)	-	-	-	-	-	-	-
Yemen	24	216	263	22	1	3	5	12	4
UNRWA [5]	296	596	622	140	7	103	72	59	78
West Bank-Gaza	11	13	162	19	64	58	33	53	80
Other and unspecified [2]	546	236	1,071	27	705	118	298	20	44

See footnotes at end of table.

No. 1318. U.S. Government Foreign Grants and Credits by Type and Country: 1966 to 1998—Continued

[In millions of dollars. See headnote, p. 787]

Country	1966-1975, total	1976-1985, total	1986-1995, total	1993	1994	1995	1996	1997	1998
Africa	**3,610**	**11,067**	**16,231**	**1,989**	**2,031**	**2,213**	**1,945**	**1,339**	**1,277**
Algeria	263	345	413	-11	28	755	644	93	45
Angola	6	115	120	16	58	37	42	41	35
Benin	12	44	101	13	17	14	13	23	14
Botswana	35	169	168	15	15	18	9	9	4
Burkina	40	287	221	26	14	23	11	15	17
Burundi	5	62	171	19	55	39	2	4	6
Cameroon	50	150	247	23	13	4	4	(Z)	9
Cape Verde	1	68	77	7	7	11	10	11	7
Chad	20	145	240	22	10	14	8	6	3
Congo, Democratic Republic of the (former Zaire)	342	939	766	9	1	1	(Z)	(Z)	1
Cote d'Ivoire	57	57	240	23	38	16	22	16	8
Eritrea	-	-	41	4	28	8	18	17	16
Ethiopia	297	310	969	179	168	127	104	77	116
Ghana	203	152	370	60	65	63	34	55	40
Guinea	68	74	239	41	38	28	29	28	18
Kenya	76	549	682	99	54	35	6	27	36
Lesotho	27	197	166	9	8	13	4	5	3
Liberia	86	459	438	46	66	67	58	28	16
Madagascar	13	86	240	28	23	33	42	35	44
Malawi	30	56	404	50	37	64	36	30	22
Mali	58	199	367	39	30	31	12	11	36
Mauritania	20	161	94	10	2	2	2	5	4
Morocco	413	948	662	12	27	-48	-4	-42	-49
Mozambique	1	175	813	94	82	114	53	78	74
Niger	64	223	342	30	16	31	15	11	13
Nigeria	284	267	506	18	52	1	-4	-10	-4
Rwanda	13	91	513	39	220	138	93	87	28
Senegal	48	361	458	58	33	24	38	36	18
Sierra Leone	36	85	111	13	10	11	28	18	13
Somalia	47	582	1,313	522	34	26	10	9	3
South Africa	-11	2	376	66	71	112	99	111	89
Sudan	52	1,358	936	53	60	11	16	24	23
Swaziland	8	58	124	15	10	13	21	12	14
Tanzania	123	259	261	28	24	19	16	18	26
Togo	18	60	109	9	8	3	1	1	2
Tunisia	376	563	-56	-4	2	-5	-24	-9	-22
Uganda	33	40	357	65	57	56	41	56	17
Zambia	35	331	497	52	21	27	21	47	14
Zimbabwe	(Z)	271	269	29	34	29	22	20	46
Other and unspecified [2]	361	769	1,866	164	492	245	393	336	473
Far East and Pacific	**34,767**	**9,651**	**-8,396**	**25**	**751**	**749**	**780**	**130**	**735**
Australia	276	-12	-273	-2	-1	-	-	-	-
Burma	43	31	18	-2	-2	-2	-2	-2	-2
Cambodia	1,760	87	125	29	16	39	36	27	33
China	-	49	396	14	6	136	113	227	249
Hong Kong	41	11	30	1	1	73	133	44	17
Indonesia	1,390	1,660	171	-64	24	25	44	-48	19
Japan and Ryukyu Islands	-345	-210	-10,458	-2	-1	(Z)	(Z)	-	-
Korea, Republic of	5,426	3,518	-3,569	-431	-55	-50	-62	-52	-52
Laos	1,868	8	8	1	2	3	4	3	3
Malaysia	86	39	-74	(Z)	1	(Z)	1	1	1
Mongolia	-	-	95	47	18	11	7	14	19
New Zealand	95	-68	-28	-	-	-	-	-	-
Pacific Islands, Trust Territory of the [6]	488	1,260	2,104	152	317	209	215	140	175
Philippines	729	1,466	3,177	131	-52	55	64	-46	296
Singapore	78	110	-183	(Z)	(Z)	1	(Z)	-	-
Taiwan	1,523	648	-1,291	-9	-8	-5	-3	-1	-1
Thailand	996	733	678	85	247	203	196	-288	-68
Vietnam	19,720	18	7	1	(Z)	(Z)	-	48	-10
Other and unspecified [2]	595	302	671	73	238	51	34	64	57
Western Hemisphere	**6,841**	**9,849**	**15,415**	**807**	**1,005**	**476**	**491**	**592**	**987**
Argentina	34	21	457	86	33	-27	-52	-84	-88
Bolivia	270	413	1,370	151	156	101	100	122	96
Brazil	1,518	399	39	-187	-59	-204	-191	-33	88
Canada	272	317	-589	-41	-120	-	-	-	-
Chile	724	-565	-177	-36	-33	-25	-3	-6	-8
Colombia	846	298	-267	-220	20	4	27	25	42
Costa Rica	103	687	721	14	-5	-30	-44	-30	-28
Dominican Republic	360	550	614	161	(Z)	-15	-19	-29	-14
Ecuador	144	153	351	15	18	5	6	6	2
El Salvador	93	1,681	2,929	217	92	119	79	92	44

See footnotes at end of table.

U.S. Census Bureau, Statistical Abstract of the United States: 2000

No. 1318. U.S. Government Foreign Grants and Credits by Type and Country: 1966 to 1998—Continued

[In millions of dollars. See headnote, p. 787]

Country	1966-1975, total	1976-1985, total	1986-1995, total	1993	1994	1995	1996	1997	1998
Western Hemisphere—Continued:									
Guatemala	160	270	1,013	76	57	39	4	37	35
Guyana	71	36	116	9	11	10	11	12	12
Haiti	67	370	835	67	125	156	82	92	87
Honduras	113	801	1,546	101	54	77	31	29	47
Jamaica	120	643	914	37	99	30	-13	-30	-22
Mexico	305	1,162	-44	-147	-229	-199	-127	-91	-126
Nicaragua	150	197	843	43	46	41	37	43	70
Panama	210	205	568	49	8	8	-4	-15	-20
Paraguay	86	22	7	1	3	1	2	3	2
Peru	274	757	1,673	145	157	150	75	133	88
Trinidad and Tobago	21	151	-95	-11	-9	-14	-15	5	204
Uruguay	116	-9	7	2	2	1	3	2	1
Venezuela	115	-34	-151	2	2	-3	1	1	4
Other [7] and unspecified [2]	671	1,325	2,733	274	579	250	502	309	473
Other international organizations and unspecified areas [2]	4,018	9,768	17,809	2,299	1,084	2,551	1,821	2,646	2,218

- Represents zero or rounds to zero.   X Not applicable.   Z Less than $500,000.   [1] In 1992, some successor countries assumed portions of outstanding credits of the former Yugoslavia (assignment of the remaining portions is pending). Subsequent negative totals reflect payments to the United States on these assumed credits which were greater than the extension of new credits and grants to these countries.   [2] In recent years, significant amounts of foreign assistance has been reported on a regional, inter-regional, and worldwide basis. Country totals in this table may understate actual assistance to many countries. [3] Includes European Atomic Energy Community, European Coal and Steel Community, European Payments Union, European Productivity Agency, North Atlantic Treaty Organization, and Organization for European Economic Cooperation.   [4] Foreign assistance to Iraq in 1991-96 was direct humanitarian assistance to ethnic minorities of Northern Iraq after the conflict in the Persian Gulf.   [5] United Nations Relief and Works Agency for Palestine refugees.   [6] Excludes transactions with Commonwealth of the Northern Mariana Islands after October 1986; includes transactions with Federated States of Micronesia, Republic of the Marshall Islands, and Republic of Palau.   [7] Includes Andean Development Corporation, Caribbean Development Bank, Central American Bank for Economic Integration, Eastern Caribbean Central Bank, Inter-American Institute of Agricultural Science, Organizations of American States, and Pan American Health Organization.

Source: U.S. Bureau of Economic Analysis, press releases, and unpublished data.

No. 1319. U.S. Foreign Economic and Military Aid Programs: 1980 to 1998

[In millions of dollars (9,695 represents $9,695,000,000). For years ending September 30. Economic aid shown here represents U.S. economic aid—not just aid under the Foreign Assistance Act. Major components in recent years include AID, Food for Peace, Peace Corps, and paid-in subscriptions to international financial institutions, such as IBRD, and IDB. Annual figures are gross unadjusted program figures]

Year and region	Total economic and military aid	Economic aid			Military aid		
		Total	Loans	Grants	Total	Loans	Grants
1980	9,695	7,573	1,993	5,580	2,122	1,450	672
1981	10,550	7,305	1,460	5,845	3,245	2,546	699
1982	12,324	8,129	1,454	6,675	4,195	3,084	1,111
1983	14,202	8,603	1,619	6,984	5,599	3,932	1,667
1984	15,524	9,038	1,621	7,417	6,486	4,401	2,085
1985	18,128	12,327	1,579	10,748	5,801	2,365	3,436
1986	16,739	10,900	1,330	9,570	5,839	1,980	3,859
1987	14,488	9,386	1,138	8,248	5,102	953	4,149
1988	13,792	8,961	852	8,109	4,831	763	4,068
1989	14,688	9,860	694	9,166	4,828	410	4,418
1990	15,727	10,834	756	10,078	4,893	404	4,489
1991	16,663	11,904	354	11,550	4,760	428	4,332
1992	15,589	11,242	494	10,748	4,347	345	4,002
1993	28,196	24,054	462	23,593	4,143	855	3,288
1994	15,870	11,940	887	11,053	3,931	770	3,161
1995	15,108	11,295	190	11,105	3,813	558	3,255
1996	13,559	9,589	329	9,260	3,970	544	3,426
1997	13,037	9,171	218	8,953	3,866	298	3,568
1998, total	**13,907**	**10,318**	**271**	**10,047**	**3,589**	**100**	**3,489**
Near East	5,429	2,273	60	2,213	3,156	-	3,156
Sub Saharan Africa	1,337	1,312	61	1,251	25	-	25
Latin America	912	899	75	824	13	-	13
Asia	683	676	30	646	6	-	6
Europe	849	615	-	615	234	100	134
New Independent States	888	861	45	816	27	-	27
Oceania and other	7	7	-	7	(Z)	-	(Z)
Nonregional	3,801	3,674	-	3,674	127	-	127

- Represents zero or rounds to zero.   Z Less than $500,000.

Source: U.S. Agency for International Development, *U.S. Overseas Loans and Grants and Assistance from International Organizations*, annual.

No. 1320. U.S. Foreign Military Aid by Region and Selected Country: 1995 to 1997

[In thousands of dollars (3,812,746 represents $3,812,746,000). For years ending **Sept. 30.** Military aid data include Military Assistance Program (MAP) grants, foreign military credit sales, International Military Education and Training, and excess defense articles. N.I.S.=New Independent States]

Region and country	1995	1996	1997	Region and country	1995	1996	1997
Total.........	**3,812,746**	**3,970,233**	**3,864,437**	Panama	425	-	-
				Asia [1]	3,804	6,508	6,781
Near East [1]	3,111,501	3,204,683	3,135,275	Cambodia	273	1,403	1,463
Egypt..........	1,301,000	1,301,009	1,301,000	Malaysia........	504	613	631
Israel	1,800,000	1,800,000	1,800,000	Philippines	-	1,210	1,295
Jordan	8,303	101,202	31,700	Thailand	96	1,445	1,600
Morocco........	724	830	812	Europe [1]	566,928	606,598	376,085
Tunisia . . . . . , .	800	816	837	Bulgaria	400	708	903
Sub-Saharan Africa [1] .	4,955	11,046	16,343	Czech Republic ...	500	795	737
Ghana	222	257	243	Greece........	229,683	224,054	122,528
Kenya	283	297	304	Hungary	796	1,034	1,014
Senegal . . ; . . .	598	637	697	Latvia.........	903	388	535
Latin America [1]	21,881	10,717	11,052	Poland	1,747	1,021	1,000
Bolivia	3,597	547	509	Portugal	500	769	551
Colombia	10,588	95	-	Slovakia	253	473	621
Dominican Rep ...	213	507	622	Turkey	329,152	321,095	176,454
Ecuador	293	547	425	N.I.S	1,722	4,508	3,904
El Salvador	404	535	455	Russia	413	760	842
Honduras	325	500	425	Ukraine........	707	1,019	1,015
Jamaica	174	469	487	Oceania and other ...	376	420	461
Mexico.........	400	992	1,008	**Nonregional....... **	**101,579**	**125,753**	**314,536**

- Represents zero.   [1] Includes countries not shown separately.

Source: U.S. Agency for International Development, *U.S. Overseas Loans and Grants and Assistance from International Organizations,* annual.

No. 1321. U.S. Foreign Aid—Economic Assistance by Region and Selected Country: 1995 to 1997

[In thousands of dollars (11,294,639 represents $11,294,639,000). For years ending **Sept. 30.** N.I.S.=New Independent States]

Region and country	1995	1996	1997	Region and country	1995	1996	1997
Total , ...	**11,294,639**	**9,589,560**	**9,170,285**	El Salvador	63,214	78,436	31,168
Near East [1]	2,310,372	2,146,415	2,278,914	Guatemala	39,199	37,333	61,379
Egypt	975,825	824,262	810,743	Haiti	157,592	99,325	101,460
Israel	1,200,000	1,200,000	1,200,000	Honduras	29,685	25,800	28,543
Jordan..........	13,506	32,466	152,683	Jamaica..........	23,967	32,097	23,614
Lebanon	13,380	1,026	11,031	Mexico	9,931	25,276	10,583
Morocco	15,035	15,821	18,888	Nicaragua	31,373	27,254	26,795
West Bank/Gaza	80,909	63,448	67,012	Peru	131,576	103,366	126,169
Sub-Saharan Africa [1] .	1,306,081	1,106,508	1,155,994	Asia [1]	571,818	462,682	599,572
Angola	44,760	83,470	49,187	Bangladesh	146,774	55,142	77,847
Benin	20,337	16,389	16,983	India	164,429	157,175	125,552
Botswana.	31,905	1,776	965	Indonesia	61,564	33,459	34,798
Burkina Faso	15,912	13,394	13,055	Cambodia	42,115	27,500	35,000
Cote D'Ivoire	1,800	21,587	14,221	Korea, South	-	6,287	50,155
Eritrea.........	10,452	13,550	24,621	Nepal	100	15,667	19,376
Ethiopia	119,494	110,810	79,189	Pakistan	16,993	16,493	42,317
Ghana..........	39,172	43,501	47,303	Philippines	17,121	57,042	40,356
Guinea	19,671	15,671	31,604	Vietnam	5,112	-	48,303
Kenya	26,450	16,122	28,899	Europe [1]	686,098	562,140	507,946
Liberia	51,643	57,912	37,339	Bosnia Hercegovina . .	71,900	245,325	183,616
Madagascar	30,015	19,684	18,724	Bulgaria	38,525	32,633	11,488
Malawi.	67,820	31,354	37,089	Croatia	12,345	15,630	2,217
Mali	34,758	30,912	38,350	Cyprus	-	9,376	4,000
Mozambique.	66,709	59,273	54,953	Hungary	26,012	19,564	1,704
Namibia.	16,815	6,766	10,329	Lithuania	22,252	17,989	11,977
Niger.	18,895	4,846	7,963	Macedonia	13,512	9,655	1,174
Rwanda	166,021	120,527	86,854	Ireland, Republic of . .	39,200	-	39,200
Senegal.	24,386	19,776	20,976	N.I.S. [1]	842,503	628,663	559,142
Somalia.	14,778	9,399	5,918	Armenia	52,526	70,724	16,751
South Africa	100,120	116,709	79,476	Belarus	11,067	25,041	-
Sudan	30,067	23,521	27,234	Georgia	39,273	20,023	1,729
Tanzania	31,469	11,788	12,190	Kazakhstan	40,191	29,725	9,730
Uganda	57,826	39,519	64,924	Kyrgyz Republic	25,104	17,034	5,256
Zambia	29,555	10,978	16,160	Moldova	21,723	31,769	4,578
Zimbabwe ,......	21,584	19,497	11,227	Russia.	353,196	178,060	64,978
Latin America [1]	717,121	680,509	740,895	Tajikistan	8,401	3,368	10,640
Bolivia	65,570	90,062	131,214	Turkemenistan	5,343	28,952	3,024
Colombia	17,306	16,766	35,111	Ukraine	178,779	120,771	49,722
Costa Rica.......	6,244	2,139	110	Uzberistan	11,515	10,874	4,397
Dominican Rep	15,692	13,831	14,499	Oceania and other	6,765	21,769	20,693
Ecuador.	14,286	13,559	15,086	**Nonregional ....**	**4,853,881**	**3,980,874**	**3,307,129**

- Represents zero.   [1] Includes countries and regional organizations not shown separately.

Source: U.S. Agency for International Development, *U.S. Overseas Loans and Grants and Assistance from International Organizations,* annual.

No. 1322. U.S. International Trade in Goods and Services: 1997 to 1999

[In millions of dollars (938,543 represents $938,543,000,000). Data presented on a balance of payments basis and will not agree with the following merchandise trade Tables 1323 to 1331]

Category	Exports			Imports			Trade balance		
	1997	1998	1999	1997	1998	1999	1997	1998	1999
Total	938,543	933,907	960,288	1,043,273	1,098,189	1,227,863	-104,730	-164,282	-267,575
Goods.	679,715	670,246	683,221	876,366	917,178	1,030,379	-196,651	-246,932	-347,158
Services	258,828	263,661	277,067	166,907	181,011	197,484	91,921	82,650	79,583
Travel	73,301	71,250	74,448	52,051	56,105	60,092	21,250	15,145	14,356
Passenger fares	20,789	19,996	21,123	18,138	19,797	21,305	2,651	199	-182
Other transportation	27,006	25,518	27,313	28,959	30,457	34,500	-1,953	-4,939	-7,187
Royalties and license fees	33,781	36,808	37,213	9,390	11,292	12,437	24,391	25,516	24,776
Other private services . . .	85,566	92,116	99,357	43,909	47,670	51,591	41,657	44,446	47,766
Other [1]	17,561	17,155	16,688	11,698	12,841	14,604	5,863	4,314	2,084
U.S. Government miscel. services	824	818	925	2,762	2,849	2,955	-1,938	-2,031	-2,030

[1] Represents transfers under U.S. military sales contracts for exports and direct defense expenditures for imports.

Source: U.S. Census Bureau, *U.S. International Trade in Goods and Services*, Series FT-900(99-12) and FT-900 (00-02).

No. 1323. U.S. Exports and General Imports in Goods: 1970 to 1999

[In billions of dollars (43.8 represents $43,800,000,000). Domestic and foreign exports, are f.a.s. value basis; general imports are on customs value basis]

Year	Total goods [1]			Manufactured goods [2 3]			Agricultural products [4]			Mineral fuels [3 5]		
	Exports	Imports	Balance	Exports	Imports	Balance	Exports	Imports	Balance	Exports	Imports	Balance
1970 . .	43.8	40.4	3.4	31.7	27.3	4.4	7.3	5.8	1.6	1.6	3.1	-1.5
1971 . .	44.7	46.2	-1.5	32.9	32.1	0.8	7.8	5.8	2.0	1.5	3.7	-2.2
1972 . .	50.5	56.4	-5.9	36.5	39.7	-3.2	9.5	6.5	3.0	1.6	4.8	-3.2
1973 . .	72.5	70.5	2.0	48.5	47.1	1.3	17.9	8.5	9.4	1.7	8.2	-6.5
1974 . .	100.0	102.6	-2.6	68.5	57.8	10.7	22.3	10.4	11.9	3.4	25.5	-22.0
1975 . .	109.3	98.5	10.8	76.9	54.0	22.9	22.1	9.5	12.6	4.5	26.5	-22.0
1976 . .	117.0	123.5	-6.5	83.1	67.6	15.5	23.3	11.2	12.1	4.2	34.0	-29.8
1977 . .	123.2	151.0	-27.8	88.9	80.5	8.4	24.2	13.6	10.6	4.2	47.2	-43.0
1978 . .	145.9	174.8	-28.9	103.6	104.3	-0.7	29.8	15.0	14.8	3.9	42.0	-38.1
1979 . .	186.5	209.5	-23.0	132.7	117.1	15.6	35.2	16.9	18.3	5.7	59.9	-54.2
1980 . .	225.7	245.3	-19.6	160.7	133.0	27.7	41.8	17.4	24.3	8.2	78.9	-70.7
1981 . .	238.7	261.0	-22.3	171.7	149.8	22.0	43.8	17.2	26.6	10.3	81.2	-70.9
1982 . .	216.4	244.0	-27.6	155.3	151.7	3.6	37.0	15.7	21.3	12.8	65.3	-52.5
1983 . .	205.6	258.0	-52.4	148.5	171.2	-22.7	36.5	16.5	19.9	9.8	57.8	-48.0
1983 . .	205.6	258.0	-52.4	148.7	170.9	-22.2	36.1	16.0	20.2	9.8	57.8	-48.0
1984 . .	224.0	330.7	-106.7	164.1	230.9	-66.8	37.9	19.3	18.6	9.7	60.8	-51.1
1985 . .	218.8	336.5	-117.7	168.0	257.5	-89.5	29.3	19.5	9.8	10.3	53.7	-43.4
1986 . .	227.2	365.4	-138.2	179.8	296.7	-116.8	26.3	20.9	5.4	8.4	37.2	-28.8
1987 . .	254.1	406.2	-152.1	199.9	324.4	-124.6	28.7	20.3	8.4	8.0	44.1	-36.1
1988 . .	322.4	441.0	-118.6	255.6	361.4	-105.7	37.1	20.7	16.4	8.5	41.0	-32.5
1989 . .	363.8	473.2	-109.4	287.0	379.4	-92.4	41.6	21.1	20.5	9.9	52.6	-42.7
1990 . .	393.6	495.3	-101.7	315.4	388.8	-73.5	39.6	22.3	17.2	12.4	64.7	-52.3
1991 . .	421.7	488.5	-66.8	345.1	392.4	-47.3	39.4	22.1	17.2	12.3	54.1	-41.8
1992 . .	448.2	532.7	-84.5	368.5	434.3	-65.9	43.1	23.4	19.8	11.3	55.3	-43.9
1993 . .	465.1	580.7	-115.6	388.7	479.9	-91.2	42.8	23.6	19.2	9.9	55.9	-46.0
1994 . .	512.6	663.3	-150.7	431.1	557.3	-126.3	45.9	26.0	20.0	9.0	56.4	-47.4
1995 . .	584.7	743.4	-158.7	486.7	629.7	-143.0	56.0	29.3	26.8	10.5	59.1	-48.6
1996 . .	625.1	795.3	-170.2	524.7	658.8	-134.1	60.6	32.6	28.1	12.4	78.1	-65.7
1997 . .	689.2	870.7	-181.5	592.5	728.9	-136.4	57.1	35.2	21.9	13.0	78.3	-65.3
1998 . .	682.1	911.9	-229.8	596.6	790.8	-194.2	52.0	35.7	16.3	10.4	57.3	-47.0
1999 . .	695.0	1,025.0	-330.0	611.6	882.7	-271.1	48.2	36.7	11.5	9.9	75.2	-65.3

[1] Includes nonmonetary gold, military grant aid, special category shipments, trade between the U.S. Virgin Islands and foreign countries and undocumented exports to Canada. Adjustments were also made for carryover. Import values are based on transaction prices whenever possible ("f.a.s." for 1974-1979 and Customs value thereafter). Import data before 1974 do not exist on a transaction price valuation basis. [2] Manufactured goods include commodity Sections 5-9 under Schedules A and E for 1970-82 and SITC Rev. 3 for 1983-forward. Manufactures include undocumented exports to Canada, nonmonetary gold (excluding gold ore, scrap, and base bullion), and special category shipments. [3] Data for 1970-80 exclude trade between the U.S. Virgin Islands and foreign countries. Census data concordances link the 1980-92 trade figures into time series that are as consistent as possible. Data for 1970-79 are not linked and are from published sources. Import values are "f.a.s." for 1974-79 and Customs value thereafter; these values are based on transaction prices while maintaining a data series as consistent as possible over time. Import data before 1974 do not exist on a transaction price valuation basis. 1991 Imports include revisions for passenger cars, trucks, petroleum and petroleum products not included elsewhere. [4] Agricultural products for 1983-forward utilize the latest census definition that excludes manufactured goods that were previously classified as manufactured agricultural products. [5] Mineral fuels include commodity Section 3 under SITC Rev. 1 for 1970-1976, SITC Rev. 2 for 1977-1982 and SITC Rev. 3 for 1983-forward.

Source: U.S. International Trade Administration, through 1996, *U.S. Foreign Trade Highlights*, annual; and thereafter, <http://www.ita.doc.gov/industry/otea/usfth/aggregate/h99t03.txt> (accessed 09 June 2000).

No. 1324. U.S. Exports and Imports for Consumption of Merchandise by Major Customs District: 1990 to 1999

[In billions of dollars (393.0 represents $393,000,000,000). Exports are f.a.s. (free alongside ship) value all years; imports are on customs value basis]

Customs district	Exports					Imports for consumption				
	1990	1995	1997	1998	1999	1990	1995	1997	1998	1999
Total [1]	393.0	584.7	689.2	682.1	695.8	490.6	738.6	861.7	905.7	1,016.9
Anchorage, AK	3.7	5.9	7.6	7.7	8.8	0.7	5.7	7.2	7.3	9.2
Baltimore, MD	6.7	9.0	7.6	6.6	5.9	11.2	14.4	14.7	16.3	17.7
Boston, ...	5.6	4.6	5.7	6.0	6.8	12.2	13.4	14.7	14.7	16.0
Buffalo, NY	15.8	30.5	39.2	38.8	37.5	19.2	29.1	30.4	35.4	39.7
Charleston, SC [2]	6.7	10.1	12.3	11.9	11.5	6.8	10.4	12.3	14.0	14.5
Chicago, IL	10.2	18.4	19.6	19.2	19.1	18.3	31.3	37.1	38.5	43.1
Cleveland, OH	4.0	7.8	14.0	15.1	17.5	11.3	21.7	26.2	27.4	29.7
Dallas/Fort Worth, TX	3.4	4.4	5.3	5.9	8.4	4.8	8.8	11.4	12.7	15.2
Detroit, MI	35.6	56.8	66.7	69.8	77.6	37.8	64.7	75.7	76.4	87.9
Duluth, MN	0.8	1.4	1.4	1.5	1.5	3.9	6.0	6.5	5.0	5.5
El Paso, TX	3.9	7.9	10.2	11.4	13.2	5.0	12.9	14.9	17.4	20.9
Great Falls, MT	2.4	3.0	4.3	4.3	4.3	4.7	6.9	8.9	8.7	11.0
Honolulu, HI.	0.5	1.1	1.6	1.0	1.2	2.1	2.7	2.7	2.2	2.3
Houston/Galveston, TX . . .	17.6	27.4	28.5	27.9	25.7	21.6	23.4	28.9	26.5	27.8
Laredo, TX	15.2	24.3	39.1	41.9	45.2	10.0	24.7	38.1	41.9	51.1
Los Angeles, CA.	42.1	67.0	74.2	63.7	66.4	64.1	96.3	110.3	115.9	128.8
Miami, FL	11.2	22.7	29.5	30.2	28.5	7.1	11.9	16.2	18.5	21.4
Milwaukee, WI	0.1	0.1	0.2	0.2	0.1	1.1	1.5	1.5	1.7	1.5
Minneapolis, MN.	0.9	1.3	1.6	1.1	1.2	2.0	2.8	3.7	4.1	4.0
Mobile, AL [2].	1.9	3.4	3.8	4.0	3.3	3.4	3.9	4.8	4.9	5.5
New Orleans, LA	18.0	28.4	30.4	27.8	28.8	24.1	34.4	35.4	36.3	40.2
New York, NY	50.9	61.4	67.1	67.7	67.2	68.0	87.6	103.1	112.2	122.1
Nogales, AZ.	2.1	4.0	4.9	6.5	5.6	4.2	7.7	8.6	10.5	11.6
Norfolk, VA [2]	11.7	14.4	16.1	15.1	12.9	7.4	8.6	9.9	10.9	12.1
Ogdensburg, NY.	7.9	9.2	10.6	10.6	11.0	9.8	14.4	17.4	18.3	19.8
Pembina, ND	3.4	5.5	7.1	7.4	6.9	4.1	7.2	7.7	8.1	8.8
Philadelphia, PA	4.0	6.7	7.7	7.5	6.9	18.3	18.3	19.0	19.3	21.3
Port Arthur, TX	0.9	1.3	1.3	1.0	0.9	3.2	4.8	6.4	4.6	6.2
Portland, ME	1.7	2.1	2.1	2.1	2.4	4.3	4.4	5.3	5.2	6.9
Portland, OR	5.8	10.2	8.5	7.1	7.5	5.6	7.9	9.6	9.7	10.9
Providence, RI	(Z)	0.1	0.1	-	-	1.3	0.9	1.3	1.0	1.2
San Diego, CA.	3.4	6.1	9.0	9.8	10.7	4.3	8.9	14.0	16.4	19.0
San Francisco, CA	23.1	43.7	48.1	42.7	44.8	28.0	58.8	58.7	55.5	59.1
San Juan, PR	2.5	2.6	2.8	3.4	4.8	5.4	6.8	8.0	8.4	10.8
Savannah, GA	7.4	10.9	13.4	13.5	13.9	9.8	14.7	18.0	19.6	21.8
Seattle, WA	32.6	31.4	44.8	47.2	44.7	20.9	24.1	30.1	32.3	36.8
St. Albans, VT	4.0	4.4	3.0	3.3	4.3	5.2	7.4	8.1	8.3	8.6
St. Louis, MO.	0.3	0.3	1.3	2.0	1.9	3.0	4.4	5.7	6.3	6.6
Tampa, FL.	4.3	6.7	7.4	7.4	5.6	7.0	9.2	9.4	11.6	13.6
Virgin Islands of the U.S. . .	0.2	0.2	0.2	0.2	0.2	2.1	2.1	3.3	2.3	2.9
Washington, DC	1.1	2.3	2.2	2.3	2.7	0.8	1.2	1.6	1.8	2.0
Wilmington, NC	3.0	4.4	4.0	3.9	2.6	3.3	7.4	8.9	8.8	9.9

- Represents or rounds to zero.   Z Less than $50 million.   [1] Totals shown for exports reflect the value of estimated parcel post and Special Category shipments, and beginning 1990, adjustments for undocumented exports to Canada which are not distributed by customs district. Beginning 1990, the value of bituminous coal exported through Norfolk, VA; Charleston, SC; and Mobile, AL, is reflected in the total but not distributed by district.   [2] Beginning 1990, excludes exports of bituminous coal.

Source: U.S. Census Bureau, 1990, *U.S. Merchandise Trade: Selected Highlights*, Series FT 920, monthly; beginning 1995, *U.S. Export History* and *U.S. Import History* on compact disc.

No. 1325. Export and Import Unit Value Indexes—Selected Countries: 1996 to 1999

[Indexes in U.S. dollars, 1995=100. A unit value is an implicit price derived from value and quantity data]

Country	Export unit value				Import unit value			
	1996	1997	1998	1999	1996	1997	1998	1999
United States	100.6	99.0	95.9	94.7	101.0	98.5	92.6	93.4
Australia	101.2	97.7	86.7	82.7	99.9	94.6	86.8	87.2
Belgium	97.8	89.1	87.9	83.7	98.5	90.5	87.4	85.0
Canada	101.3	99.3	93.4	95.2	100.3	99.4	97.2	97.4
Denmark.	98.2	87.8	85.8	83.1	97.3	88.1	86.6	82.8
France	97.4	86.5	86.3	(NA)	98.1	87.3	86.4	(NA)
Ireland	99.2	95.1	91.7	(NA)	98.6	94.0	90.3	(NA)
Italy	110.1	99.4	97.8	(NA)	105.6	95.8	89.6	(NA)
Japan	92.5	86.5	80.5	85.2	100.7	95.1	83.0	83.8
New Zealand.	101.1	94.7	80.3	80.6	101.9	97.1	81.6	82.6
Norway.	106.1	98.7	81.9	88.4	97.8	88.3	84.0	79.5
Singapore	99.6	93.2	81.1	80.2	99.3	92.9	80.9	81.2
Spain	99.5	88.8	87.1	82.7	98.8	88.5	84.8	81.1
Sweden	93.6	87.2	82.7	78.7	95.6	89.2	83.6	82.5
Switzerland	96.6	85.3	84.6	82.7	95.6	85.8	82.4	78.0
United Kingdom	99.9	99.2	95.4	93.2	98.9	97.3	92.5	89.1

NA Not available.

Source: International Monetary Fund, Washington, DC, *International Financial Statistics*, monthly, (copyright).

No. 1326. U.S. Exports by State of Origin: 1990 to 1999

[In millions of dollars (394,045 represents $394,045,000,000). Exports are on a f.a.s. value basis. Exports are based on origin of movement]

State and other area	1990	1998	1999 Total	1999 Rank	State and other area	1990	1998	1999 Total	1999 Rank
Total	394,045	682,977	695,009	(X)	Montana	229	421	427	49
					Nebraska	693	1,995	2,096	40
United States	315,065	612,390	624,609	(X)	Nevada	394	688	1,067	45
Alabama	2,834	6,372	6,192	25	New Hampshire	973	1,728	1,930	42
Alaska	2,850	1,954	2,564	35					
Arizona	3,729	11,415	11,824	16	New Jersey	7,633	15,371	15,355	12
Arkansas	920	2,286	2,178	39	New Mexico	249	1,855	3,134	32
California	44,520	95,768	97,920	1	New York	22,072	37,384	37,068	3
Colorado	2,274	5,266	5,931	27	North Carolina	8,010	15,706	15,007	13
Connecticut	4,356	7,297	7,231	23	North Dakota	360	750	699	46
Delaware	1,344	2,232	2,287	36	Ohio	13,378	24,852	24,883	7
District of Columbia	320	348	412	(X)	Oklahoma	1,646	2,785	2,987	34
Florida	11,634	24,452	24,155	8	Oregon	4,065	9,031	10,471	18
					Pennsylvania	8,491	15,974	16,170	10
Georgia	5,763	13,476	13,749	14	Rhode Island	595	1,102	1,116	44
Hawaii	179	276	274	50					
Idaho	898	1,510	2,192	38	South Carolina	3,116	7,749	7,150	24
Illinois	12,965	28,914	29,432	6	South Dakota	205	446	495	47
Indiana	5,273	12,318	12,910	15	Tennessee	3,746	9,552	9,868	19
Iowa	2,189	4,901	4,094	29	Texas	32,931	78,875	82,999	2
Kansas	2,113	4,039	4,669	28	Utah	1,596	2,981	3,134	33
Kentucky	3,175	8,100	8,877	22	Vermont	1,154	3,668	4,023	30
Louisiana	14,199	16,836	15,842	11	Virginia	9,333	12,514	11,483	17
Maine	870	1,825	2,014	41	Washington	24,432	38,249	36,731	4
					West Virginia	1,550	2,106	1,893	43
Maryland	2,592	4,722	4,009	31	Wisconsin	5,158	9,752	9,673	20
Massachusetts	9,501	15,878	16,805	9	Wyoming	264	500	458	48
Michigan	18,474	28,977	31,086	5					
Minnesota	5,091	9,147	9,373	21	Puerto Rico	3,600	6,274	8,301	(X)
Mississippi	1,605	2,286	2,216	37	Virgin Islands	51	90	155	(X)
Missouri	3,130	5,762	6,059	26	Other [1]	75,328	64,223	61,944	(X)

X Not applicable. [1] Includes unreported, not specified, special category, estimated shipments, foreign trade zone, re-exports, and any timing adjustments.

Source: U.S. Census Bureau, *U.S. International Trade in Goods and Services,* Series FT-900, December issues.

No. 1327. U.S. Agriculture Exports by State: 1995 to 1999

[In millions of dollars (54,725 represents $54,725,000,000). Fiscal years]

State	1995	1996	1997	1998	1999	State	1995	1996	1997	1998	1999
U.S.	54,725	59,891	57,365	53,730.2	49,102.1	MT	471	896	327	330.4	227.6
						NE	3,223	3,510	3,308	2,906.7	2,883.0
AL	467	494	535	458.1	366.3	NV	2	5	6	5.7	4.4
AK	-	-	-	0.4	0.2	NH	1	1	1	0.9	1.0
AZ	420	409	370	377	333.3	NJ	150	149	168	159.5	152.6
AR	1,631	1,686	1,918	1,607.0	1,219.8						
CA	6,968	7,208	7,694	7,582.7	6,931.7	NM	77	75	70	86.6	74.4
CO	945	1,100	872	821.4	828.3	NY	364	400	396	377.9	368
CT	47	43	80	95.6	93.3	NC	1,355	1,400	1,515	1,447.1	1,205.5
DE	108	133	147	130.6	107.2	ND	1,507	1,734	1,083	1,084.2	917.9
FL	1,201	1,230	1,212	1,087.1	1,117.7	OH	1,320	1,602	1,361	1,356.5	1,199.7
GA	1,126	1,224	1,273	1,120.9	866.8	OK	449	517	385	423.7	439.8
						OR	720	749	729	696.7	680.6
HI	109	115	126	111.2	108.1	PA	535	544	542	599.6	592.8
ID	930	935	841	830.2	789.4	RI	1	1	1	1.1	0.6
IL	3,458	3,974	3,748	3,060.4	2,750.6	SC	321	340	354	313.1	235.9
IN	1,756	2,049	1,853	1,605.6	1,429.5						
IA	4,016	4,640	4,146	3,511.1	3,151.5	SD	1,120	1,163	1,163	1,058.4	1,016.7
KS	3,074	3,112	2,650	2,792.5	2,823.7	TN	516	500	540	485.6	382.3
KY	894	1,046	1,110	930.3	889.4	TX	3,379	3,477	3,054	3,018.1	2,512.4
LA	690	662	704	660.8	480.6	UT	153	145	125	139.4	151.2
ME	36	40	39	42.3	41.9	VT	11	8	11	10.3	10.3
MD	217	247	271	244.5	199.7	VA	436	486	520	447.2	385.8
						WA	1,824	1,941	1,857	1,673.8	1,778.5
MA	30	29	48	52.4	44.1	WV	27	34	31	27.2	19.7
MI	920	1,186	886	913.8	782.2	WI	1,268	1,371	1,219	1,276.4	1,261.3
MN	2,440	3,031	2,611	2,359.1	2,184.7	WY	32	52	40	42.8	30.5
MS	836	777	821	815	541.6						
MO	1,261	1,314	1,543	1,341.0	1,087.8	Unallocated	1,887	2,107	3,062	3,210.1	3,400.1

- Represents or rounds to zero.

Source: U.S. Dept. of Agriculture, Economic Research Service, *Foreign Agricultural Trade of the United States (FATUS),* annual.

No. 1328. U.S. Exports, Imports, and Merchandise Trade Balance by Country: 1995 to 1999

[In millions of dollars (584,742.0 represents $584,742,000,000). Includes silver ore and bullion. Country totals include exports of special category commodities, if any. Data include nonmonetary gold and includes trade of Virgin Islands with foreign countries. Minus sign (-) denotes an excess of imports over exports]

Country [1]	Exports, domestic, and foreign					General imports					Merchandise trade balance				
	1995	1996	1997	1998	1999	1995	1996	1997	1998	1999	1995	1996	1997	1998	1999
Total [1]	584,742.0	625,075.0	689,182.4	682,137.7	695,009.2	743,542.8	795,289.3	870,670.7	911,896.1	1,025,031.6	-158,800.8	-170,214.3	-181,488.2	-229,758.4	-330,022.4
Afghanistan	4.1	16.9	11.5	7.0	18.0	5.4	16.4	10.0	16.7	9.3	-1.3	0.5	1.5	-9.6	8.7
Albania	13.5	12.1	3.1	14.9	24.8	9.5	10.3	11.7	12.4	9.0	4.0	1.7	-8.6	2.5	15.8
Algeria	774.0	635.2	691.6	651.4	456.3	1,749.5	2,125.7	2,439.5	1,638.0	1,830.7	-975.5	-1,490.5	-1,747.9	-986.7	-1,374.4
Andorra	16.4	24.5	21.7	22.4	7.8	0.2	2.5	0.3	0.1	0.1	16.2	22.0	21.4	22.2	7.7
Angola	259.6	268.3	280.6	354.7	252.2	2,232.3	2,901.5	2,779.1	2,240.9	2,424.8	-1,972.6	-2,633.2	-2,498.6	-1,886.2	-2,172.6
Anguilla	14.6	12.8	18.1	16.7	22.2	0.1	0.8	0.7	2.1	2.3	14.5	12.0	17.4	14.6	19.9
Antigua	97.1	82.4	84.5	96.7	96.1	3.0	8.9	4.9	1.9	1.8	94.1	73.5	79.6	94.8	94.3
Argentina	4,189.2	4,516.8	5,810.0	5,885.8	4,938.5	1,760.9	2,279.2	2,228.2	2,230.9	2,598.5	2,428.3	2,237.6	3,581.8	3,654.8	2,340.0
Armenia	70.4	57.4	62.1	51.4	49.8	16.2	1.5	6.0	16.7	15.3	54.2	55.9	56.1	34.7	34.5
Aruba	247.4	234.6	238.4	351.2	307.1	420.6	558.1	610.2	469.5	675.1	-173.2	-323.5	-371.8	-118.4	-368.0
Australia	10,789.1	12,008.4	12,062.9	11,917.6	11,810.7	3,322.9	3,868.9	4,602.3	5,386.8	5,290.4	7,466.2	8,139.6	7,460.6	6,530.7	6,520.3
Austria	2,017.2	2,009.8	2,074.7	2,142.9	2,587.7	1,963.3	2,200.3	2,368.4	2,561.0	2,910.3	53.9	-190.5	-293.7	-418.1	-322.6
Azerbaijan	35.6	54.0	62.3	123.1	55.0	0.8	4.5	5.7	4.9	26.3	34.8	49.5	56.6	118.1	28.7
Bahamas, The	661.3	726.0	809.5	815.6	843.6	156.5	164.9	154.9	142.4	195.3	504.8	561.1	654.6	673.2	648.3
Bahrain	254.9	244.2	406.1	294.6	348.3	134.2	116.3	116.4	155.5	225.4	120.8	127.9	289.8	139.1	122.9
Bangladesh	325.1	210.1	259.0	318.4	275.5	1,257.2	1,343.0	1,679.4	1,845.9	1,917.8	-932.2	-1,132.9	-1,420.4	-1,527.5	-1,642.3
Barbados	185.7	222.5	280.9	281.4	302.4	37.7	41.2	42.1	34.5	58.9	148.0	181.3	238.7	247.0	243.5
Byelarus	48.0	53.1	40.6	30.4	26.1	44.9	52.2	66.0	105.4	92.6	3.1	0.9	-25.4	-75.0	-66.5
Belgium	12,465.5	12,532.2	13,420.3	13,917.8	12,384.9	6,053.9	6,775.7	7,911.9	8,440.0	9,208.3	6,411.6	5,756.6	5,508.4	5,477.8	3,176.6
Belize	99.8	106.6	114.8	120.2	136.1	52.2	68.2	77.3	65.9	80.3	47.6	38.5	37.5	54.3	55.8
Benin	34.1	27.4	51.6	43.6	31.3	9.8	13.6	7.7	3.6	17.8	24.3	13.8	43.9	40.0	13.5
Bermuda	298.5	281.9	338.1	400.3	343.8	10.3	13.5	29.8	11.5	24.6	288.2	270.4	308.2	388.8	319.2
Bolivia	213.5	269.5	295.1	416.6	312.1	262.5	275.2	223.3	223.6	217.8	-49.0	-5.7	71.9	193.0	94.3
Bosnia and Hercegovina	28.4	58.8	102.5	40.0	43.6	3.3	10.1	8.3	7.4	14.9	25.1	48.6	94.2	32.6	28.7
Brazil	11,439.4	12,717.5	15,914.7	15,142.0	13,249.0	8,832.9	8,773.4	9,625.5	10,101.9	11,313.8	2,606.6	3,944.2	6,289.2	5,040.0	1,935.2
British Virgin Islands	49.3	53.9	64.6	62.6	58.6	11.4	6.6	13.1	7.5	22.6	37.9	47.3	51.5	55.1	36.0
Brunei	189.9	374.7	178.1	122.8	66.7	38.3	48.3	55.8	211.2	389.0	151.6	326.4	122.3	-88.3	-322.3
Bulgaria	131.8	137.5	109.6	112.4	102.5	188.5	126.5	171.4	219.1	199.6	-56.7	11.0	-61.8	-106.7	-97.1
Burkina Faso	14.6	10.4	18.3	16.1	10.9	0.4	3.9	1.0	0.6	2.8	14.2	6.5	17.3	15.5	8.1
Burma	16.1	32.2	19.9	31.9	8.7	80.9	108.2	114.9	163.7	232.1	-64.9	-75.9	-95.0	-131.8	-223.4
Cameroon	45.5	71.3	121.4	75.1	37.0	57.3	64.5	57.2	53.3	76.8	-11.7	6.8	64.3	21.8	-39.8
Canada	127,226.1	134,210.3	151,766.7	156,603.4	166,288.6	144,369.8	155,892.6	168,200.9	173,256.1	198,324.0	-17,143.7	-21,682.3	-16,434.2	-16,652.7	-32,035.4
Cayman Islands	180.3	208.0	270.3	421.9	368.3	18.3	16.9	19.6	18.1	9.4	162.0	191.2	250.7	403.8	358.9
Chad	10.8	3.4	3.1	3.5	3.2	3.2	7.1	2.9	7.5	6.9	7.6	-3.7	0.2	-4.0	-4.2
Chile	3,614.9	4,139.5	4,368.4	3,979.3	3,079.0	1,930.8	2,262.2	2,293.1	2,452.5	2,935.9	1,684.1	1,877.3	2,075.3	1,526.8	143.1
China	11,753.6	11,992.6	12,862.3	14,241.3	13,117.7	45,543.2	51,512.6	62,557.6	71,168.7	81,785.9	-33,789.6	-39,520.0	-49,695.3	-56,927.4	-68,668.2
Colombia	4,624.4	4,714.3	5,197.0	4,816.0	3,532.0	3,791.1	4,423.8	4,737.3	4,656.2	6,275.8	833.3	290.5	459.7	159.8	-2,743.8
Congo (Brazzaville)	54.7	62.9	74.7	92.0	47.0	206.9	315.3	471.5	315.4	414.7	-152.2	-252.4	-396.8	-223.4	-367.7
Congo (Kinshasa)	77.1	73.3	37.8	34.1	21.1	266.9	258.7	281.8	171.1	229.2	-189.9	-185.3	-244.0	-137.0	-208.1
Costa Rica	1,736.5	1,816.4	2,024.4	2,296.5	2,379.7	1,843.1	1,974.2	2,323.2	2,744.9	3,958.5	-106.6	-157.9	-298.8	-448.4	-1,578.8
Cote d'Ivoire (formerly Ivory Coast)	173.2	141.1	150.9	151.4	104.0	214.1	397.4	289.0	425.9	347.2	-40.9	-256.3	-138.1	-275.0	-243.2
Croatia	139.9	106.0	138.7	96.8	107.6	93.7	71.2	82.8	72.6	110.1	46.2	34.8	55.9	24.2	-2.5
Cyprus	257.8	256.9	244.5	161.9	189.8	13.0	17.4	16.4	31.8	31.5	244.8	239.6	228.1	130.1	158.3

See footnotes at end of table.

Country	Exports, domestic, and foreign					General imports					Merchandise trade balance				
	1995	1996	1997	1998	1999	1995	1996	1997	1998	1999	1995	1996	1997	1998	1999
Czech Republic	362.7	412.2	589.8	569.0	610.0	363.4	482.3	609.8	673.4	754.4	-0.7	-70.1	-20.0	-104.4	-144.4
Denmark	1,517.7	1,731.0	1,756.9	1,874.3	1,718.9	1,945.0	2,141.5	2,137.7	2,395.0	2,824.9	-427.3	-410.5	-380.8	-520.7	-1,106.0
Djibouti	8.5	8.3	7.3	20.4	26.7	0.1	0.0	0.0	0.5	0.1	8.4	8.3	7.3	19.9	26.6
Dominica	26.5	34.2	37.4	52.1	38.6	6.6	7.7	9.1	6.4	23.0	19.9	26.5	28.3	45.7	15.6
Dominican Republic	3,014.9	3,190.5	3,924.0	3,943.8	4,085.6	3,399.0	3,574.8	4,326.8	4,441.2	4,282.0	-384.0	-384.2	-402.8	-497.4	-196.4
Ecuador	1,538.3	1,258.5	1,525.9	1,683.1	920.1	1,939.9	1,958.1	2,054.8	1,752.1	1,814.3	-401.6	-699.6	-528.9	-69.0	-894.2
Egypt	2,985.1	3,153.3	3,835.4	3,058.6	3,025.4	606.4	680.5	657.5	660.3	617.1	2,378.7	2,472.9	3,177.9	2,398.3	2,408.3
El Salvador	1,110.6	1,074.5	1,400.1	1,513.5	1,520.2	812.2	975.4	1,346.2	1,437.9	1,604.8	298.4	99.1	53.8	75.6	-84.6
Estonia	138.9	83.6	47.4	87.4	161.5	62.3	55.1	76.8	125.4	236.7	76.6	28.5	-29.3	-38.0	-75.2
Ethiopia	147.5	148.1	121.2	88.9	164.7	0.0	0.0	0.0	52.3	299.2	147.5	148.1	121.2	36.6	-134.5
Fiji	31.6	27.5	32.8	74.2	126.5	78.0	74.7	84.6	101.1	99.8	-46.4	-47.2	-51.8	-26.9	26.7
Finland	1,249.7	2,438.6	1,741.1	1,914.8	1,668.1	2,270.0	2,388.8	2,391.5	2,595.6	2,909.7	-1,020.3	-4,190.3	-4,671.5	-680.8	-1,241.6
France	14,245.2	14,455.5	15,964.9	17,728.7	18,838.5	17,209.4	18,645.8	20,636.4	24,015.9	25,909.6	-2,964.3	296.0	491.4	-6,287.2	-7,071.1
French Guiana	441.7	300.7	493.7	246.5	192.2	5.3	4.7	2.4	3.2	4.2	436.4	296.0	491.4	243.3	188.0
French Polynesia	82.3	88.7	105.2	99.7	93.1	14.1	17.2	35.4	32.7	42.6	68.2	71.5	69.9	67.0	50.5
Gabon	54.4	56.1	84.5	61.6	45.4	1,464.0	1,983.7	2,202.3	1,258.8	1,519.5	-1,409.6	-1,927.6	-2,117.7	-1,197.2	-1,474.1
Gambia, The	6.2	8.5	9.7	9.3	9.6	2.3	2.0	2.9	2.0	0.2	3.9	6.5	6.8	7.3	9.4
Georgia	95.2	82.5	140.6	136.5	83.3	10.6	7.6	7.0	14.2	18.3	84.6	74.9	133.6	122.3	65.0
Germany	22,394.3	23,495.7	24,458.3	26,657.4	26,788.9	36,844.0	38,945.1	43,121.5	49,842.0	55,093.5	-14,449.8	-15,450.1	-18,663.2	-23,184.6	-28,304.6
Ghana	167.2	295.0	315.0	225.1	235.1	196.1	171.4	155.3	143.2	208.6	-28.9	124.3	159.8	81.9	26.5
Gibraltar	18.4	11.7	8.8	8.8	4.1	4.9	6.5	2.8	6.0	9.5	13.5	5.2	6.0	2.8	-5.4
Greece	1,518.8	824.5	949.3	1,355.2	994.2	397.3	506.0	453.2	466.7	570.9	1,121.5	318.5	496.2	888.5	423.3
Greenland	2.4	4.1	4.9	6.1	3.1	7.4	6.4	7.9	7.3	13.2	-5.0	-2.2	-3.0	-1.2	-10.1
Grenada	26.8	35.7	40.6	56.4	66.2	5.3	3.6	6.5	12.1	19.8	21.5	32.1	34.1	44.3	46.4
Guadeloupe	69.3	66.0	57.6	64.0	66.1	1.2	1.4	3.5	2.3	2.8	68.0	64.6	54.1	61.7	63.3
Guatemala	1,646.6	1,566.1	1,729.6	1,937.8	1,811.5	1,526.7	1,678.5	1,990.2	2,071.6	2,265.7	119.9	-112.4	-260.6	-133.8	-454.2
Guinea	66.7	87.1	82.8	65.4	54.6	99.0	116.5	127.7	115.3	116.9	-32.3	-29.4	-44.9	-49.9	-62.3
Guyana	141.2	136.9	142.5	145.6	145.1	107.4	109.5	112.8	137.0	121.8	33.8	27.4	29.7	8.6	23.3
Haiti	550.2	474.8	499.1	548.6	614.8	129.8	143.6	188.2	271.8	301.1	420.4	331.3	310.9	276.8	313.7
Honduras	1,278.5	1,642.6	2,018.9	2,317.5	2,369.3	1,441.3	1,795.4	2,322.2	2,544.4	2,713.1	-162.4	-152.8	-303.4	-226.9	-343.8
Hong Kong	14,231.4	13,966.3	15,117.1	12,925.3	12,647.1	10,291.2	9,864.5	10,287.8	10,538.2	10,531.4	3,940.2	4,101.8	4,829.3	2,387.1	2,115.7
Hungary	295.3	330.7	485.5	482.6	503.3	547.0	676.2	1,078.9	1,566.5	1,891.9	-251.7	-345.5	-593.5	-1,083.9	-1,388.6
Iceland	170.6	257.1	179.2	236.5	297.6	232.7	236.0	230.8	267.9	303.3	-62.2	21.2	-51.6	-31.4	-6.0
India	3,295.8	3,328.3	3,607.6	3,564.4	3,707.4	5,726.2	6,169.5	7,322.4	8,237.2	9,083.3	-2,430.5	-2,841.2	-3,714.8	-4,672.8	-5,375.9
Indonesia	3,359.6	3,976.8	4,522.3	2,298.9	1,938.9	7,435.3	8,249.9	9,188.4	9,340.6	9,514.0	-4,075.7	-4,273.1	-4,666.1	-7,041.7	-7,575.1
Iran	277.3	0.3	1.1	-	48.1	0.2	(X)	0.1	-	2.4	277.1	0.3	1.0	-	45.7
Iraq	0.2	2.8	82.0	106.4	9.5	(X)	(X)	311.9	1,183.2	4,193.2	0.2	2.8	-229.9	-1,076.8	-4,183.7
Ireland	4,108.8	3,668.7	4,642.2	5,646.8	6,374.7	4,078.7	4,803.9	5,866.6	8,400.9	11,002.4	30.1	-1,135.2	-1,224.4	-2,754.1	-4,627.7
Israel	5,621.1	6,011.9	5,994.9	6,983.3	7,694.5	5,708.7	6,433.6	7,326.0	8,640.4	9,869.8	-87.6	-421.7	-1,331.0	-1,657.1	-2,175.3
Italy	8,861.6	8,797.1	8,994.7	8,990.8	10,094.0	16,348.3	18,324.8	19,407.5	20,959.1	22,438.0	-7,486.7	-9,527.8	-10,412.8	-11,968.3	-12,344.0
Jamaica	1,420.4	1,491.0	1,416.5	1,304.2	1,294.8	847.0	838.2	738.0	755.0	678.9	573.4	652.9	678.5	549.2	615.9
Japan	64,342.6	67,606.8	65,548.5	57,831.0	57,483.5	123,479.1	115,187.0	121,663.2	121,845.0	131,403.6	-59,136.5	-47,580.2	-56,114.8	-64,014.0	-73,920.1
Jordan	335.3	345.2	402.5	352.9	275.6	28.8	25.2	25.3	16.4	30.9	306.5	320.1	377.1	336.5	244.7
Kazakhstan	80.9	138.3	346.3	103.1	178.9	122.9	121.2	128.9	168.7	228.1	-42.1	17.2	217.4	-65.6	-49.2
Kenya	114.0	104.6	225.3	198.9	189.1	101.5	106.5	114.0	98.5	106.4	12.5	-2.0	111.4	100.4	82.7

See footnotes at end of table.

No. 1328. U.S. Exports, Imports, and Merchandise Trade Balance by Country: 1995 to 1999—Continued

[See headnote, page 764]

Country	Exports, domestic, and foreign					General imports					Merchandise trade balance				
	1995	1996	1997	1998	1999	1995	1996	1997	1998	1999	1995	1996	1997	1998	1999
Korea, South	25,379.9	26,621.1	25,046.1	16,485.5	22,954.0	24,183.9	22,655.1	23,173.1	23,941.8	31,262.0	1,195.9	3,966.0	1,873.0	-7,456.3	-8,308.0
Kuwait	1,437.3	1,983.6	1,390.0	1,524.1	909.0	1,335.5	1,651.2	1,816.4	1,266.0	1,446.1	101.8	332.4	-426.4	258.1	-537.1
Kyrgyzstan	24.7	46.9	28.4	20.6	21.1	8.3	5.0	2.4	0.3	0.5	16.3	41.9	25.9	20.3	20.6
Latvia	89.5	166.6	217.8	186.8	217.9	81.9	102.9	145.1	114.7	229.2	7.6	63.7	72.7	72.1	-11.3
Lebanon	592.3	627.0	551.9	513.8	356.5	35.1	41.5	77.8	82.5	51.5	557.2	585.6	474.2	431.3	305.0
Lesotho	2.0	2.6	2.4	1.4	0.7	62.1	65.4	86.5	100.0	110.8	-60.2	-62.7	-84.2	-98.6	-110.1
Liberia	41.7	49.8	42.9	50.1	44.7	9.8	26.9	4.8	25.1	30.3	31.9	22.9	38.1	25.0	14.4
Liechtenstein	14.9	8.9	12.5	7.3	9.1	126.2	91.1	116.5	242.6	276.2	-111.3	-82.3	-104.0	-235.3	-267.1
Lithuania	52.0	62.9	87.4	62.2	66.0	26.4	34.4	79.8	80.9	96.8	25.6	28.6	7.6	-18.7	-30.8
Luxembourg	374.4	242.2	712.1	605.8	983.5	234.0	203.8	238.8	373.1	313.7	140.4	38.3	473.2	232.7	669.8
Macau	29.9	29.8	65.0	40.7	41.8	895.3	857.6	1,021.0	1,108.6	1,124.4	-865.5	-827.9	-956.0	-1,067.9	-1,082.6
Macedonia	21.3	14.4	33.8	14.8	56.2	88.8	124.8	147.1	175.4	135.7	-67.6	-110.5	-113.3	-160.6	-79.5
Madagascar	10.0	11.5	11.5	14.9	106.1	57.3	45.5	62.6	71.4	80.2	-47.3	-34.0	-51.1	-56.5	25.9
Malawi	17.8	13.3	17.6	14.5	7.4	40.9	72.5	82.8	60.4	72.5	-23.1	-59.2	-65.3	-45.9	-65.1
Malaysia	8,816.1	8,546.2	10,780.0	8,957.0	9,079.0	17,454.7	17,828.8	18,026.7	19,000.0	21,428.6	-8,638.6	-9,282.6	-7,246.7	-10,043.0	-12,349.6
Maldives	1.1	2.4	5.5	4.8	8.5	12.1	11.6	19.4	32.9	54.9	-11.0	-9.2	-13.9	-28.1	-46.4
Mali	23.2	18.4	26.2	25.3	29.8	3.6	4.9	3.8	4.1	8.9	19.6	13.5	22.3	21.2	20.9
Malta	106.7	125.2	120.9	267.0	190.4	132.4	208.6	223.6	340.3	323.3	-25.8	-83.5	-102.7	-73.3	-132.9
Marshall Islands	31.7	36.4	23.6	25.0	35.7	11.0	10.9	7.3	3.8	10.3	20.6	25.5	16.3	21.2	25.4
Martinique	38.4	35.3	33.9	26.4	34.9	2.1	1.0	2.4	1.0	0.8	36.3	34.3	31.4	25.4	34.1
Mauritania	43.1	15.1	20.9	19.5	25.2	5.5	5.3	0.2	0.4	0.8	37.6	9.8	20.6	19.1	24.4
Mauritius	24.7	25.2	31.4	23.2	39.0	229.7	217.0	238.4	271.6	258.9	-204.9	-191.8	-207.0	-248.4	-219.9
Mexico	46,292.1	56,791.5	71,388.4	78,772.5	86,865.8	62,100.6	74,297.3	85,937.5	94,629.0	109,709.6	-15,808.6	-17,505.8	-14,549.1	-15,856.5	-22,840.7
Micronesia, Federated States of	23.3	24.7	29.0	31.0	24.8	13.0	11.3	11.9	12.6	10.1	10.2	13.5	17.2	18.4	14.7
Moldova	10.2	21.6	19.7	20.6	10.6	24.8	29.7	53.7	109.3	88.9	-14.6	-8.1	-34.0	-88.7	-78.3
Monaco	9.5	3.1	6.9	6.4	12.6	12.2	15.9	19.6	25.7	14.4	-2.7	-12.8	-12.7	-19.3	-1.8
Mongolia	14.0	4.2	34.3	20.3	10.1	23.3	30.8	42.4	41.8	60.9	-9.3	-26.6	-8.1	-21.5	-50.8
Morocco	517.4	476.3	434.7	561.4	573.6	239.3	247.1	295.9	343.0	390.3	278.1	229.2	138.9	218.4	183.3
Mozambique	49.3	23.0	45.6	45.7	33.9	27.6	26.6	30.5	25.8	10.3	21.7	-3.5	15.1	19.9	23.6
Namibia	26.5	22.7	25.0	51.2	195.6	11.5	27.1	63.0	51.8	29.7	15.0	-4.5	-38.1	-0.6	165.9
Netherlands	16,557.7	16,662.6	19,826.7	18,977.1	19,412.1	6,405.0	6,583.1	7,292.8	7,599.3	8,472.7	10,152.7	10,079.4	12,533.8	11,378.4	10,939.4
Netherlands Antilles	504.0	529.6	475.2	750.7	603.3	289.9	684.8	579.8	308.2	383.3	214.1	-155.2	-104.6	442.5	220.0
New Caledonia	22.4	28.7	34.4	19.2	41.6	40.2	54.8	51.9	21.7	8.6	-17.8	-26.1	-17.5	-2.5	33.0
New Zealand	1,691.4	1,728.5	1,962.1	1,886.5	1,933.9	1,451.8	1,463.2	1,579.2	1,644.6	1,749.0	239.6	265.4	382.9	241.9	184.9
Nicaragua	249.7	262.3	289.8	336.5	374.0	238.7	350.4	439.3	452.7	492.8	11.0	-88.1	-149.5	-116.2	-118.8
Niger	39.5	27.2	24.8	18.2	18.5	1.6	0.7	29.8	1.7	12.1	38.0	26.5	-5.0	16.5	6.4
Nigeria	602.8	818.4	813.1	816.8	628.3	4,930.4	5,978.3	6,349.4	4,194.0	4,361.1	-4,327.7	-5,159.9	-5,536.4	-3,377.2	-3,732.8
Norway	1,293.0	1,559.0	1,721.3	1,709.3	1,439.7	3,086.7	3,992.5	3,752.0	2,871.6	4,051.3	-1,793.7	-2,433.5	-2,030.7	-1,162.3	-2,611.6
Oman	222.0	216.7	340.8	302.7	187.9	294.9	414.4	242.4	216.8	219.5	-72.9	-197.7	98.4	85.9	-31.6
Pakistan	941.2	1,271.4	1,240.1	720.4	426.5	1,197.1	1,265.7	1,442.2	1,691.7	1,740.4	-255.8	5.7	-202.2	-971.3	-1,313.9
Panama	1,389.6	1,380.5	1,536.1	1,753.0	1,741.3	307.1	346.1	367.2	312.3	365.0	1,082.5	1,034.4	1,168.9	1,440.7	1,376.3
Papua New Guinea	50.8	69.2	116.6	65.3	37.1	67.2	85.6	64.5	129.6	144.5	-16.4	-16.4	52.1	-64.3	-107.4
Paraguay	992.4	897.5	913.4	785.9	515.0	55.0	42.3	40.7	33.5	48.1	937.4	855.2	872.8	752.4	466.9
Peru	1,775.3	1,773.8	1,953.3	2,062.6	1,701.1	1,034.5	1,260.9	1,772.3	1,975.5	1,927.8	740.8	512.9	181.0	87.1	-226.7
Philippines	5,294.8	6,142.4	7,417.3	6,736.6	7,226.2	7,006.5	8,161.4	10,445.0	11,947.3	12,379.7	-1,711.7	-2,019.0	-3,027.6	-5,210.7	-5,153.5
Poland	776.1	968.3	1,169.9	882.0	824.7	663.9	627.9	695.6	783.7	813.0	112.2	340.4	474.4	98.3	11.7

See footnotes at end of table.

U.S. Census Bureau, Statistical Abstract of the United States: 2000

Country	Exports, domestic, and foreign					General imports					Merchandise trade balance				
	1995	1996	1997	1998	1999	1995	1996	1997	1998	1999	1995	1996	1997	1998	1999
Portugal	898.1	960.7	954.2	888.3	1,091.4	1,056.6	1,016.5	1,138.0	1,265.3	1,357.0	-158.5	-55.8	-183.8	-377.0	-265.6
Qatar	225.9	207.7	379.0	354.4	145.9	90.9	157.1	157.4	220.4	265.9	135.0	50.6	221.7	134.0	-120.0
Romania	253.1	265.6	258.0	336.6	176.7	222.4	248.5	399.8	393.3	434.5	30.7	17.1	-141.8	-56.7	-257.8
Russia	2,823.3	3,345.8	3,364.9	3,552.6	1,844.7	4,030.0	3,576.8	4,319.0	5,747.2	5,805.0	-1,206.6	-231.0	-954.0	-2,194.6	-3,960.3
Saudi Arabia	6,154.9	7,311.3	8,437.8	10,519.8	7,901.7	8,376.7	10,467.2	9,364.8	6,241.3	8,237.3	-2,221.8	-3,155.9	-927.0	4,278.5	-335.6
Senegal	67.9	55.8	51.8	59.1	63.4	5.0	5.5	6.8	5.2	9.2	62.9	50.3	44.9	53.9	54.2
Singapore	15,333.2	16,720.0	17,696.2	15,693.6	16,246.4	18,560.5	20,343.1	20,074.6	18,355.7	18,187.7	-3,227.3	-3,623.1	-2,378.4	-2,662.1	-1,941.3
Slovakia	61.0	62.6	82.0	110.6	127.2	129.5	124.6	165.6	165.7	169.0	-68.5	-62.0	-83.6	-55.1	-41.8
Somalia	8.1	4.2	2.8	2.7	2.8	0.1	0.2	0.3	0.6	0.2	8.0	4.1	2.4	2.1	2.6
South Africa	2,750.6	3,111.9	2,997.2	3,628.0	2,582.3	2,208.0	2,323.3	2,510.1	3,049.1	3,195.1	542.6	788.5	487.2	578.9	-612.8
Spain	5,526.0	5,499.6	5,538.7	5,453.6	6,131.6	3,879.5	4,279.8	4,605.5	4,780.2	5,055.3	1,646.5	1,219.8	933.3	673.4	1,076.3
Sri Lanka	279.1	211.1	154.7	190.4	167.4	1,259.7	1,393.0	1,620.0	1,766.5	1,742.4	-980.5	-1,181.9	-1,465.3	-1,576.1	-1,575.0
St. Lucia	80.9	84.5	89.3	92.4	98.1	35.2	22.3	34.2	22.4	28.0	45.7	62.2	55.1	70.0	70.1
St. Vincent	42.2	45.0	54.4	274.2	92.1	7.8	6.8	4.3	4.8	8.2	34.4	38.2	50.0	269.4	83.9
Sudan	43.4	51.3	36.4	6.8	8.8	22.7	18.7	12.1	3.1	0.1	20.7	32.6	24.3	3.7	8.7
Suriname	189.7	222.7	183.0	187.2	143.7	100.2	96.6	91.5	106.1	122.9	89.5	126.0	91.5	81.1	20.8
Sweden	3,079.8	3,430.5	3,314.1	3,822.1	4,238.6	6,256.4	7,152.7	7,298.9	7,848.0	8,110.7	-3,176.6	-3,722.2	-3,984.8	-4,025.9	-3,872.1
Switzerland	6,227.5	8,373.4	8,306.9	7,247.4	8,364.7	7,593.8	7,792.6	8,405.1	8,690.3	9,596.3	-1,366.4	-580.8	-98.2	-1,442.9	-1,231.6
Syria	193.4	226.3	180.4	161.4	172.7	31.3	15.2	27.8	45.9	95.0	162.1	211.1	152.6	115.5	77.7
Taiwan	19,289.6	18,460.2	20,365.7	18,164.5	19,121.1	28,971.8	29,907.3	32,628.5	33,124.8	35,198.5	-9,682.2	-11,447.1	-12,262.8	-14,960.3	-16,077.4
Tajikistan	17.7	17.2	18.6	12.2	12.9	40.9	32.8	8.5	32.6	22.7	-23.2	-15.6	10.0	-20.4	-9.8
Tanzania	47.4	50.2	64.9	66.9	68.4	3.5	18.9	26.6	31.5	35.4	43.9	31.3	38.3	35.4	33.0
Thailand	6,665.0	7,197.5	7,349.4	5,238.6	4,983.5	11,348.1	11,336.1	12,601.5	13,436.4	14,323.8	-4,683.1	-4,138.6	-5,252.1	-8,197.8	-9,340.3
Togo	18.5	20.0	25.6	25.4	25.7	3.4	4.2	9.4	2.2	3.2	15.1	15.8	16.2	23.2	22.5
Trinidad and Tobago	689.2	665.5	1,105.9	983.1	785.5	1,086.2	1,313.2	1,134.3	976.9	1,293.6	-397.1	-647.7	-28.3	6.2	-508.1
Tunisia	215.0	189.2	252.3	195.6	280.1	70.4	75.8	63.1	61.5	74.5	144.6	113.4	189.2	134.1	205.6
Turkey	2,768.1	2,846.6	3,539.5	3,505.5	3,197.2	1,797.8	1,778.2	2,121.1	2,542.7	2,627.4	970.3	1,068.4	1,418.5	962.8	569.8
Turkmenistan	34.2	200.8	117.7	28.0	18.4	1.2	0.5	2.1	4.6	8.4	33.0	200.3	115.6	25.2	10.0
Turks and Caicos Islands	33.5	43.5	58.6	63.8	94.8	5.0	5.1	5.3	4.6	6.3	28.6	38.4	53.3	59.2	88.5
Uganda	22.1	17.2	35.2	29.8	25.0	13.2	15.9	37.8	15.1	20.3	8.9	1.3	-2.5	14.7	4.7
Ukraine	223.4	395.1	402.9	367.5	204.2	405.6	506.9	410.0	531.4	517.8	-182.2	-111.9	-7.1	-163.9	-313.6
United Arab Emirates	2,006.5	2,533.2	2,607.1	2,365.9	2,713.0	459.2	498.8	920.1	659.9	711.1	1,547.2	2,034.4	1,687.0	1,706.0	2,001.9
United Kingdom	28,856.5	30,962.5	36,425.3	39,058.2	38,337.8	26,929.5	28,978.8	32,659.3	34,838.2	39,190.8	1,927.0	1,983.7	3,766.0	4,220.0	-853.0
Uruguay	395.9	482.9	547.6	591.3	492.0	167.2	260.5	228.9	255.7	198.5	228.7	222.4	318.7	335.6	293.5
Uzbekistan	63.4	351.8	234.1	147.3	338.7	18.7	159.0	39.1	34.1	25.6	44.7	192.8	195.1	113.2	313.1
Venezuela	4,640.4	4,749.4	6,601.6	6,515.8	5,372.9	9,764.0	13,173.1	13,477.2	9,181.4	11,269.2	-5,123.6	-8,423.7	-6,875.6	-2,665.6	-5,896.3
Vietnam	252.5	616.4	286.6	274.1	290.7	198.9	331.8	388.5	554.1	609.0	53.6	284.7	-101.9	-280.0	-318.3
Western Samoa	7.6	11.9	11.1	10.4	12.2	0.5	1.0	2.5	6.8	5.3	7.1	10.9	8.6	3.6	6.9
Yemen, Republic of	185.2	255.9	153.4	177.7	157.5	41.6	31.2	16.0	37.6	19.1	143.6	224.7	137.4	140.1	138.4
Yugoslavia, Fed. Rep. of	2.2	46.0	49.1	74.4	58.9	-	8.2	10.4	12.6	4.5	2.2	37.8	38.7	61.8	54.4
Zambia	48.9	46.0	29.3	21.7	19.9	32.9	64.2	55.9	47.3	37.7	16.0	-18.3	-26.6	-25.6	-17.8
Zimbabwe	122.0	90.7	81.9	93.1	60.0	97.7	133.0	139.5	127.2	132.8	24.3	-42.3	-57.5	-34.1	-72.8

- Represents zero or rounds to zero.   X Not applicable.   [1] Includes timing adjustment and unidentified countries, not shown separately.

Source: U.S. Census Bureau, U.S. International Trade in Goods and Services, Series FT900, December issues.

U.S. Census Bureau, Statistical Abstract of the United States: 2000

No. 1329. U.S. Exports and General Imports by Selected SITC Commodity Groups: 1996 to 1999

[In millions of dollars (624,767 represents $624,767,000,000). SITC=Standard International Trade Classification. N.e.s.=Not elsewhere specified]

Commodity group	Exports [1]				General imports [2]			
	1996	1997	1998	1999	1996	1997	1998	1999
Total	624,767	689,182	682,138	695,009	791,364	870,671	911,896	1,025,032
Agricultural commodities	59,311	55,639	50,654	46,915	32,565	35,164	35,748	36,731
Animal feeds	4,183	4,621	4,054	3,378	633	648	607	565
Coffee	4	7	10	9	2,491	3,575	3,069	2,540
Corn	8,623	5,426	4,618	5,121	116	103	142	156
Cotton, raw and linters	2,740	2,716	2,572	984	300	20	19	148
Hides and skins	1,515	1,503	1,130	1,023	133	130	110	101
Meat and preparations	6,958	6,885	6,427	6,340	2,317	2,656	2,848	3,258
Soybeans	7,447	7,479	4,885	4,555	31	86	54	29
Sugar	5	3	3	4	1,001	956	715	561
Tobacco, unmanufactured	1,390	1,548	1,459	1,294	1,053	1,129	780	754
Vegetables and fruits	7,313	7,472	7,324	7,143	7,514	7,752	8,365	9,261
Wheat	6,302	4,196	3,690	3,574	247	359	283	273
Manufactured goods	483,874	550,529	552,778	562,927	659,867	728,928	790,754	882,729
ADP equipment, office machinery	39,666	43,698	40,735	40,665	66,499	74,993	76,755	84,443
Airplane parts	11,723	13,266	15,035	15,153	3,464	4,917	5,912	5,896
Airplanes	18,962	25,552	35,242	32,686	3,943	4,557	7,052	8,775
Alcoholic bev, distilled	385	385	385	431	2,048	2,186	2,296	2,617
Aluminum	3,485	3,768	3,606	3,556	4,828	5,558	5,970	6,288
Artwork/antiques	887	1,120	1,140	1,153	2,791	3,587	3,976	4,913
Basketware, etc	2,239	2,494	2,583	2,871	3,014	3,364	3,834	4,396
Chemicals, cosmetics	4,323	4,873	4,763	4,850	2,443	2,677	2,895	3,151
Chemicals, dyeing	2,716	3,294	3,471	3,617	2,165	2,485	2,472	2,632
Chemicals, fertilizers	3,070	3,123	3,231	2,973	1,400	1,374	1,570	1,500
Chemicals, inorganic	4,657	5,264	4,709	4,635	4,954	5,132	5,126	5,173
Chemicals, medicinal	7,160	8,087	9,341	11,071	7,076	8,748	10,908	13,542
Chemicals, n.e.s.	9,651	11,160	10,838	11,074	4,568	4,821	4,833	5,072
Chemicals, organic	14,744	16,408	14,920	15,423	14,820	16,874	18,327	21,860
Chemicals, plastics	15,467	17,274	16,608	16,846	7,443	8,237	8,565	9,276
Cigarettes	4,736	4,417	4,165	3,232	69	75	102	151
Clothing	7,285	8,396	8,497	7,960	41,559	48,408	53,742	56,413
Cork, wood, lumber	5,501	5,146	4,091	4,245	7,532	8,179	7,616	8,925
Crude fertilizers	1,526	1,621	1,600	1,534	1,176	1,334	1,300	1,270
Electrical machinery	56,637	65,816	65,575	74,947	75,525	80,370	79,365	88,592
Fish and preparations	2,930	2,624	2,172	2,743	6,657	7,687	8,104	8,902
Footwear	761	800	720	693	12,749	14,026	13,881	14,068
Furniture and parts	3,323	3,942	4,411	4,336	9,431	11,144	13,339	16,178
Gem diamonds	151	108	124	312	6,588	7,595	8,497	9,902
General industrial machinery	26,599	30,603	30,121	29,721	25,286	26,321	28,811	31,447
Gold, nonmonetary	6,641	5,673	5,464	5,219	2,737	3,035	3,332	3,034
Iron and steel mill products	4,795	5,637	5,481	4,986	13,368	14,285	17,159	13,369
Lighting, plumbing	1,358	1,535	1,405	1,297	2,579	2,944	3,393	4,327
Metal manufactures, n.e.s.	9,234	10,309	10,699	11,116	10,843	12,242	13,506	14,406
Metal ores; scrap	4,278	4,662	3,581	3,501	4,048	4,156	4,099	3,657
Metalworking machinery	5,241	5,702	5,270	5,267	6,789	7,325	7,926	6,787
Optical goods	1,378	1,697	1,907	2,228	2,327	2,493	2,727	3,075
Paper and paperboard	9,837	10,283	9,930	9,885	11,637	11,697	12,793	13,407
Photographic equipment	3,743	3,865	3,481	3,624	5,271	5,759	5,661	6,114
Plastic articles, n.e.s.	4,439	5,092	5,554	6,362	5,306	5,676	6,137	7,010
Platinum	248	437	388	502	1,716	1,973	3,051	3,498
Power generating machinery	22,292	27,221	28,743	30,727	22,499	24,601	28,160	31,533
Printed materials	4,346	4,605	4,671	4,578	2,700	2,871	3,075	3,336
Pulp and waste paper	4,034	3,868	3,443	3,524	2,648	2,639	2,442	2,597
Records/magnetic media	6,555	6,815	6,057	5,759	4,078	4,137	4,383	4,696
Rubber articles, n.e.s.	972	1,256	1,301	1,383	1,465	1,553	1,645	1,791
Rubber tires and tubes	1,959	2,394	2,554	2,396	3,074	3,417	4,095	4,636
Scientific instruments	20,599	24,039	24,169	25,543	12,385	13,969	15,500	17,641
Ships, boats	1,064	1,366	1,716	1,640	1,029	875	1,132	1,127
Silver and bullion	638	641	629	213	569	472	662	629
Spacecraft	636	994	1,102	1,641	232	239	91	311
Specialized industrial machinery	25,659	29,162	27,305	24,805	18,509	21,182	22,986	21,632
Television, VCR, etc.	(NA)	24,093	23,417	24,346	(NA)	36,771	42,449	50,959
Textile yarn, fabric	7,814	8,975	8,976	9,246	10,248	11,951	12,896	13,575
Toys/games/sporting goods	3,693	3,827	3,342	3,314	14,734	17,374	18,695	18,991
Travel goods	306	330	302	329	3,581	3,841	3,946	4,148
Vehicles	50,181	55,669	53,536	53,677	102,551	112,926	119,726	146,202
Watches/clocks/parts	277	310	312	335	2,805	2,838	3,210	3,257
Wood manufactures	1,685	1,958	1,690	1,735	4,037	4,668	5,647	7,094
Mineral fuel	12,057	12,682	10,251	9,794	73,028	78,277	57,323	75,202
Coal	3,849	3,586	3,176	2,260	606	655	724	665
Crude oil	460	1,040	895	772	50,582	54,226	37,252	50,662
Petroleum preparations	3,948	3,899	2,857	3,405	13,858	13,904	10,947	14,160
Natural gas	261	275	243	218	4,002	5,477	5,273	6,304
Reexports	40,690	44,153	45,683	50,632	(X)	(X)	(X)	(X)

NA Not available. X Not applicable. [1] F.a.s. basis. [2] Customs value basis.

Source: U.S. Census Bureau, *U.S. International Trade in Goods and Services,* Series FT900, Final Reports.

No. 1330. Export Shipments by Export Mode of Transportation, Country of Destination, and Major Commodity Group: 1997

[Based on the Commodity Flow Survey; subject to sampling variability]

Item	Value Number (bil. dol.)	Percent	Tons Number (mil.)	Percent	Item	Value Number (bil. dol.)	Percent	Tons Number (mil.)	Percent
MODE					**COMMODITY [1]**				
Mode, total	**577.8**	**100.0**	**526.2**	**100.0**	Agricultural products & fish..	46.8	8.1	179.3	34.1
Truck	111.9	19.4	57.8	11.0	Grains, alcohol, and tobacco				
For-hire truck	99.8	17.3	41.8	7.9	products	12.2	2.1	15.7	3.0
Private truck	12.2	2.1	16.0	3.0	Stone, nonmetallic minerals,				
Rail	22.9	4.0	36.8	7.0	and metallic ores	3.5	0.6	17.2	3.3
Water	163.5	28.3	349.2	66.4					
Shallow draft vessel	4.9	0.8	20.9	4.0	Coal & petroleum products..	43.4	7.5	144.2	27.4
Deep draft vessel	158.6	27.4	328.3	62.4	Pharmaceutical and chemical				
Air (includes truck and air)..	196.7	34.0	4.4	0.8	products	45.3	7.8	24.8	4.7
Pipeline	(S)	(S)	(S)	(S)	Wood products, and textiles				
Parcel, U.S. Postal Service					and leather	42.6	7.4	78.7	15.0
or counter	17.6	3.0	2.0	0.4					
Other and unknown modes..	64.3	11.1	71.4	13.6	Base metal and machinery..	83.4	14.4	25.4	4.8
					Electronics, motorized				
COUNTRY OF DESTINATION					vehicles, and precision instruments	260.3	45.1	13.5	2.6
					Furniture and miscellaneous				
Canada	112.7	19.5	99.1	18.8	manufactured products....	35.0	6.1	26.1	5.0
Mexico	54.3	9.4	36.9	7.0	Commodity unknown	5.3	0.9	1.2	0.2
All other countries	410.8	71.1	390.3	74.2					

S Does not meet publication standards. [1] Based on the Standard Classification of Transported Goods (SCTG) coding system.

Source: U.S. Census Bureau, *1997 Economic Census, Commodity Flow Survey, Exports,* Series EC97TCF-US(EXP).

No. 1331. U.S. Exporting Companies Profile by Company Type and Employment-Size Class: 1992 and 1997

Company type and employment-size class	Number of exporters 1992	1997	Known export value [1] (mil. dol.) 1992	1997	Percent of— Number of exporters 1992	1997	Known export value 1992	1997
All companies, total	112,854	209,455	348,960	562,764	100.0	100.0	100.0	100.0
No employees	15,534	40,551	9,178	36,575	13.8	19.4	2.6	6.5
1 to 19 employees	51,186	94,601	29,397	42,038	45.4	45.2	8.4	7.5
20 to 49 employees	18,501	30,692	17,005	24,431	16.4	14.7	4.9	4.3
50 to 99 employees	10,505	16,951	13,840	17,979	9.3	8.1	4.0	3.2
100 to 249 employees	8,679	13,978	18,371	27,168	7.7	6.7	5.3	4.8
250 to 499 employees	3,621	5,412	15,055	23,746	3.2	2.6	4.3	4.2
500 or more employees	4,828	7,270	246,114	390,827	4.3	3.5	70.5	69.4
Manufacturers	42,763	65,594	241,522	385,665	37.9	31.3	69.2	68.5
No employees	1,949	7,211	1,971	8,857	1.7	3.4	0.6	1.6
1 to 19 employees	12,342	19,690	2,534	3,774	10.9	9.4	0.7	0.7
20 to 49 employees	9,949	14,262	4,217	5,695	8.8	6.8	1.2	1.0
50 to 99 employees	6,781	9,423	4,897	6,643	6.0	4.5	1.4	1.2
100 to 249 employees	5,999	8,249	9,809	14,569	5.3	3.9	2.8	2.6
250 to 499 employees	2,594	3,068	8,990	13,816	2.3	1.5	2.6	2.5
500 or more employees	3,149	3,691	209,104	332,311	2.8	1.8	59.9	59.0
Wholesalers	39,713	67,901	50,989	71,152	35.2	32.4	14.6	12.6
No employees	4,503	11,125	1,882	5,688	4.0	5.3	0.5	1.0
1 to 19 employees	25,296	40,706	16,730	22,397	22.4	19.4	4.8	4.0
20 to 49 employees	5,673	9,067	7,128	9,343	5.0	4.3	2.0	1.7
50 to 99 employees	2,182	3,613	5,419	6,117	1.9	1.7	1.6	1.1
100 to 249 employees	1,338	2,257	4,820	7,071	1.2	1.1	1.4	1.3
250 to 499 employees	406	653	1,942	3,984	0.4	0.3	0.6	0.7
500 or more employees	315	480	13,068	16,552	0.3	0.2	3.7	2.9
Other companies	26,910	68,025	53,158	81,275	23.8	32.5	15.2	14.4
No employees	6,030	18,369	2,754	9,077	5.3	8.8	0.8	1.6
1 to 19 employees	13,364	33,390	9,934	15,005	11.8	15.9	2.8	2.7
20 to 49 employees	2,826	6,399	5,625	8,418	2.5	3.1	1.6	1.5
50 to 99 employees	1,488	3,087	3,380	4,175	1.3	1.5	1.0	0.7
100 to 249 employees	1,271	2,657	3,547	3,828	1.1	1.3	1.0	0.7
250 to 499 employees	586	1,339	3,998	4,470	0.5	0.6	1.1	0.8
500 or more employees	1,345	2,784	23,921	36,301	1.2	1.3	6.9	6.5
Unclassified companies	3,468	7,935	3,291	24,672	3.1	3.8	0.9	4.4

[1] Known value is defined as the value of exports by known exporters, i.e., those export transactions that could be matched to specific companies. Export values are on f.a.s. or "free alongside ship basis." Total export value was $251 billion in 1987 and $448 billion in 1992.

Source: U.S. Census Bureau, *A Profile of U.S. Exporting Companies, 1992* and*1996-97;* CB-97-135 and CB-99-76 press releases.

Foreign Commerce and Aid   799

No. 1332. Domestic Exports and Imports for Consumption of Merchandise by Selected SIC-Based Product Category: 1990 to 1999

[In millions of dollars (374,537 represents $374,537,000,000). Includes nonmonetary gold]

SIC-based product category	SIC [1] code	1990	1994	1995	1996	1997	1998	1999
Domestic exports, total [2]	(X)	374,537	482,141	547,300	584,077	644,520	637,208	644,326
Agricultural, forestry and fishery products	(X)	26,225	26,102	33,418	36,234	31,224	26,603	25,618
Agricultural products	01	22,597	22,189	29,391	32,380	27,460	23,336	21,960
Livestock and livestock products	02	829	973	920	989	1,132	1,110	1,029
Forestry products	08	281	263	272	271	279	257	233
Fish, fresh or chilled; and other marine products [3]	09	2,518	2,677	2,836	2,594	2,352	1,900	2,395
Mineral commodities	(X)	7,335	5,650	7,159	7,284	7,598	6,644	5,832
Metallic ores and concentrates	10	1,137	1,018	1,562	1,091	1,250	981	965
Bituminous, lignite and anthracite coal	11,12	4,513	2,858	3,572	3,694	3,406	3,036	2,135
Crude petroleum and natural gas	13	638	576	729	1,197	1,566	1,251	1,445
Nonmetallic minerals, exc. fuels	14	1,047	1,199	1,296	1,302	1,375	1,377	1,288
Manufactured commodities	(X)	330,403	441,501	496,421	530,484	596,539	595,453	601,279
Food and kindred products	20	16,160	23,094	26,021	27,041	28,488	27,294	25,216
Tobacco manufactures	21	5,040	5,367	5,222	5,238	4,956	4,827	3,882
Textile mill products	22	3,635	5,151	5,696	6,177	7,081	7,180	7,541
Apparel and related products	23	2,848	6,145	7,190	8,104	9,279	9,474	8,541
Lumber and related products	24	6,523	7,252	7,424	7,401	7,312	5,960	6,236
Furniture and fixtures	25	1,589	3,030	2,953	3,101	3,643	3,958	2,304
Paper and allied products	26	8,631	11,000	14,943	14,002	14,512	13,713	13,839
Printing and publishing	27	3,150	4,070	4,471	4,534	4,791	4,865	4,719
Chemicals and allied products	28	37,806	48,950	57,897	58,503	65,080	63,896	66,296
Petroleum and coal products	29	6,794	5,510	6,014	7,158	7,331	5,668	2,892
Rubber and misc. plastics products	30	6,398	9,942	11,025	12,093	14,187	14,664	15,826
Leather and leather products	31	1,388	1,539	1,565	1,725	1,907	1,815	2,248
Stone, clay, and glass products	32	3,295	4,215	4,796	5,097	5,847	5,487	6,427
Primary metal products	33	13,116	16,327	20,191	21,279	22,694	21,737	19,893
Fabricated metal products	34	11,138	13,395	15,161	16,612	17,921	19,607	21,644
Machinery, except electrical	35	61,229	82,120	95,909	104,055	117,531	110,247	108,275
Electric and electronic machinery	36	39,807	63,839	76,235	79,533	93,767	92,230	97,990
Transportation equipment	37	68,113	85,068	82,699	92,887	108,465	119,981	119,175
Instruments and related products	38	19,524	26,560	29,581	32,842	36,978	37,335	38,871
Misc. manufactured commodities	39	4,296	5,813	7,383	6,763	7,279	6,653	7,047
Imports for consumption, total [2]	(X)	490,554	657,884	739,661	790,470	862,426	907,647	1,017,435
Agricultural, forestry and fishery products	(X)	12,750	17,427	19,799	20,661	22,817	22,859	22,968
Agricultural products	01	5,925	8,657	9,803	10,950	12,231	12,178	12,100
Livestock and livestock products	02	1,453	2,047	2,450	2,377	2,483	2,472	2,680
Forestry products	08	1,015	1,208	1,932	1,810	1,625	1,447	1,097
Fish, fresh or chilled; and other marine products [3]	09	4,357	5,515	5,614	5,525	6,478	6,761	7,090
Mineral commodities	(X)	51,391	47,300	51,050	57,144	53,313	38,619	46,043
Metallic ores and concentrates	10	1,500	1,283	1,413	1,407	1,406	1,509	1,185
Bituminous, lignite and anthracite coal	11,12	93	229	248	238	257	281	280
Crude petroleum and natural gas	13	48,917	44,949	48,495	54,463	50,030	35,323	42,981
Nonmetallic minerals, exc. fuels	14	881	839	894	1,035	1,619	1,506	1,597
Manufactured commodities	(X)	407,043	567,052	639,729	680,609	750,206	803,384	906,665
Food and kindred products	20	16,564	17,342	18,326	20,948	22,600	23,811	25,487
Tobacco manufactures	21	94	163	169	245	463	437	413
Textile mill products	22	6,807	6,534	6,965	7,169	8,370	8,779	9,044
Apparel and related products	23	24,644	38,561	41,208	43,075	50,191	55,838	59,156
Lumber and related products	24	5,446	10,528	10,406	12,194	13,531	14,042	17,480
Furniture and fixtures	25	5,235	7,522	8,303	9,320	11,008	13,127	11,799
Paper and allied products	26	11,669	11,772	16,757	14,784	14,839	15,857	16,460
Printing and publishing	27	1,849	2,422	2,902	2,996	3,210	3,461	3,786
Chemicals and allied products	28	21,611	31,697	38,079	42,826	48,382	52,355	62,149
Petroleum and coal products	29	14,472	9,504	8,971	18,768	22,149	18,689	21,972
Rubber and misc. plastics products	30	9,731	14,393	15,973	16,891	18,320	19,651	18,330
Leather and leather products	31	10,944	12,977	13,628	14,187	15,459	15,736	19,767
Stone, clay, and glass products	32	5,845	7,594	8,498	9,088	10,178	11,114	13,289
Primary metal products	33	23,232	30,106	33,519	34,583	37,727	42,771	39,036
Fabricated metal products	34	11,608	14,664	16,213	17,492	19,316	21,189	26,074
Machinery, except electrical	35	55,021	89,705	106,391	112,907	125,777	133,119	126,673
Electric and electronic machinery	36	55,736	94,332	114,912	114,066	120,879	125,321	163,981
Transportation equipment	37	89,599	115,998	122,344	129,235	140,684	155,753	182,428
Instruments and related products	38	16,846	24,410	27,473	28,747	31,545	33,618	35,062
Misc. manufactured commodities	39	20,090	26,830	28,694	31,088	35,579	38,715	42,492

X Not applicable. [1] Standard Industrial Classification. [2] Includes scrap and waste, used or secondhand merchandise, manufactured commodities not identified by kind, and timing adjustments. [3] Includes frozen and packaged fish.

Source: U.S. Census Bureau, *U.S. International Trade in Goods and Services,* Series FT900, December issues.

Section 29
Outlying Areas

This section presents summary economic and social statistics for Puerto Rico, Virgin Islands, Guam, American Samoa, and the Northern Mariana Islands. Primary sources are the decennial censuses of population and housing and the censuses of agriculture, business, manufactures, and construction (taken every 5 years) conducted by the U.S. Census Bureau; the annual *Vital Statistics of the United States* , issued by the National Center for Health Statistics; and the annual *Income and Product* of the Puerto Rico Planning Board, San Juan.

Jurisdiction—The United States gained jurisdiction over these areas as follows: The islands of *Puerto Rico* and *Guam*, surrendered by Spain to the United States in October 1898, were ceded to the United States by the Treaty of Paris, ratified in 1899. Puerto Rico became a commonwealth on July 25, 1952, thereby achieving a high degree of local autonomy under its own constitution. The *Virgin Islands*, comprising 50 islands and cays, was purchased by the United States from Denmark in 1917. *American Samoa*, a group of seven islands, was acquired by the United States in accordance with a convention among the United States, Great Britain, and Germany, ratified in 1900 (Swains Island was annexed in 1925). By an agreement approved by the Security Council and the United States, the Northern Mariana Islands, previously under Japanese mandate, was administered by the United States between 1947 and 1986 under the United Nations trusteeship system. The Northern Mariana Islands became a commonwealth in 1986.

Censuses—Because characteristics of the outlying areas differ, the presentation of census data for them is not uniform. The 1960 Census of Population covered all of the places listed above except the Northern Mariana Islands (their census was conducted in April 1958 by the Office of the High Commissioner), while the 1960 Census of Housing also excluded American Samoa. The 1970, 1980, and 1990 Censuses of Population and Housing covered all five areas. The 1959, 1969, and 1978 Censuses of Agriculture covered Puerto Rico, American Samoa, Guam, and the Virgin Islands; the 1964, 1974, and 1982 censuses covered the same areas except American Samoa; and the 1969, 1978, 1987, 1992, and 1997 censuses included the Northern Mariana Islands. Beginning in 1967, Congress authorized the economic censuses, to be taken at 5-year intervals, for years ending in "2" and "7." Prior economic censuses were conducted in Puerto Rico for 1949, 1954, 1958, and 1963 and in Guam and the Virgin Islands for 1958 and 1963. In 1967, the census of construction industries was added for the first time in Puerto Rico; in 1972, Virgin Islands and Guam were covered. For 1982, 1987, 1992, and 1997 the economic censuses covered the Northern Mariana Islands.

Information in other sections—In addition to the statistics presented in this section, other data are included as integral parts of many tables showing distribution by states in various sections of the *Abstract*. See "Outlying areas of the United States" in the Index. For definition and explanation of terms used, see Section 1, Population; Section 4, Education; Section 23, Agriculture; Section 25, Construction and Housing; Section 26, Manufactures; and Section 27, Domestic Trade and Services.

U.S. Census Bureau, Statistical Abstract of the United States: 2000

Figure 29.1
Selected Outlying Areas of the United States

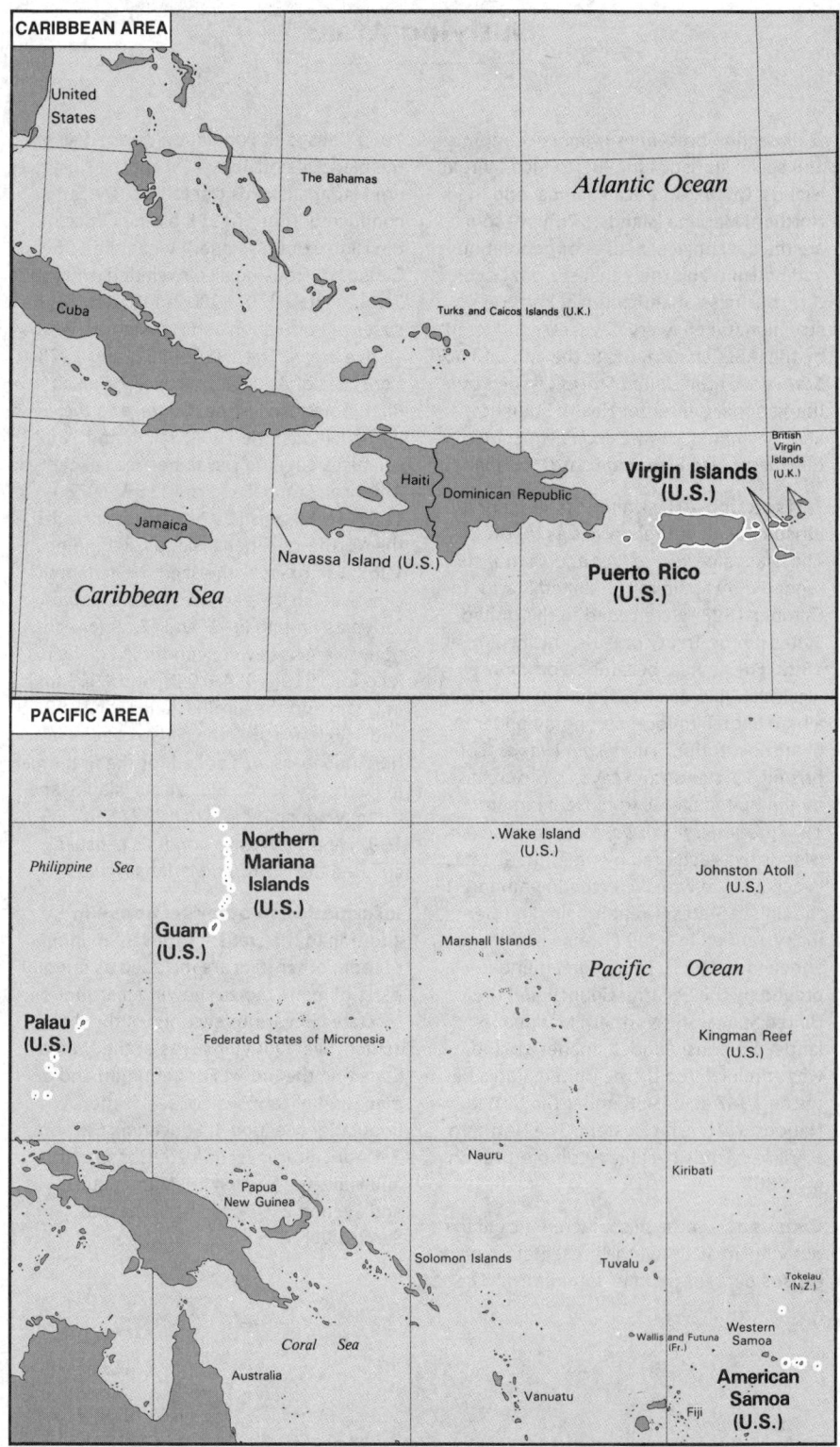

No. 1333. Estimated Resident Population With Projections: 1970 to 2020

[In thousands (2,722 represents 2,722,000). Population data generally are de facto figures for the present territory. Population estimates were derived from information available as of early 1999. See text, Section 30, Comparative International Statistics, for general comments regarding the data. For details of methodology, coverage, and reliability, see source]

Area	1970	1980	1990	1995	1997	1998	1999	2000, proj.	2010, proj.	2020, proj.
Puerto Rico..............	2,722	3,210	3,537	3,731	3,828	3,860	3,890	3,916	4,088	4,196
American Samoa...........	27	32	47	57	60	62	64	65	81	95
Guam	86	107	134	144	146	149	152	155	184	211
Virgin Islands............	63	98	104	114	117	118	120	121	133	144
Northern Mariana Islands......	12	17	44	58	64	67	69	72	99	123

Source: U.S. Census Bureau, International Data Base. <http://census.gov/ipc/www/idbnew.html>.

No. 1334. Vital Statistics—Specified Areas: 1960 to 1998

[Births, deaths, and infant deaths by place of residence. Rates for 1960, 1970, 1980, and 1990 based on population enumerated as of **April 1**; for other years, on population estimated as of **July 1**]

Area and year	Births Number	Births Rate [1]	Deaths Number	Deaths Rate [1]	Infant deaths Number	Infant deaths Rate [2]
Puerto Rico: 1960	76,314	32.5	15,791	6.7	3,307	43.3
1970.............	67,628	24.8	18,080	6.7	1,930	28.5
1980.............	72,986	22.8	20,413	6.4	1,351	18.5
1985.............	63,547	19.4	23,071	7.0	944	14.9
1990.............	66,417	18.8	25,957	7.3	888	13.4
1995.............	63,425	17.0	30,032	8.1	804	12.7
1996.............	63,141	16.7	29,731	7.9	561	8.9
1997.............	64,109	16.8	28,963	7.6	724	11.3
1998.............	60,412	15.7	[3]28,961	7.5	(NA)	(NA)
Guam: 1965	2,523	32.8	336	4.4	82	32.5
1970.............	2,842	28.8	355	5.8	62	21.6
1980.............	2,945	27.8	393	3.7	43	14.6
1985.............	3,049	24.6	415	3.4	35	11.5
1990.............	3,839	28.6	520	3.9	31	8.1
1995.............	4,180	29.0	592	4.1	38	9.4
1996.............	4,259	29.4	599	4.1	(NA)	(NA)
1997.............	4,309	29.5	615	4.2	35	8.1
1998.............	4,318	29.0	[3]632	4.2	(NA)	(NA)
Virgin Islands: 1960	1,180	36.8	332	10.3	42	35.6
1970.............	2,898	46.8	469	7.9	72	24.8
1980.............	2,504	25.9	504	5.2	61	24.4
1990.............	2,267	21.8	480	4.6	33	14.6
1995.............	2,063	18.1	664	5.8	34	16.6
1996.............	1,905	16.8	575	5.1	(NA)	(NA)
1997.............	2,017	17.6	620	5.4	26	12.9
1998.............	1,800	15.2	[3]622	5.3	(NA)	(NA)

NA Not available. [1] Per 1,000 population. [2] Per 1,000 live births. [3] Preliminary.
Source: U.S. National Center for Health Statistics, *Vital Statistics of the United States*, annual.

No. 1335. Land Area and Population Characteristics by Area: 1990

[As of **April 1**. For definition of median, see Guide to Tabular Presentation]

Item	United States	Puerto Rico	Virgin Islands	Guam	American Samoa	Northern Mariana Islands
Land area (sq. miles)	3,536,338	3,427	134	210	77	179
Total resident population......	**248,709,873**	**3,522,037**	**101,809**	**133,152**	**46,773**	**43,345**
Per square mile..........	70.3	1,027.9	760.9	634.1	607.4	242.2
Percent increase, 1980-90 ..	9.8	10.2	5.4	25.6	44.8	158.3
Urban..................	187,053,487	2,508,346	37,885	50,801	15,599	12,151
Rural..................	61,656,386	1,013,691	63,924	82,351	31,174	31,194
Male...................	121,239,418	1,705,642	49,210	70,945	24,023	22,802
Female	127,470,455	1,816,395	52,599	62,207	22,750	20,543
Males per 100 females.....	95.1	93.9	93.6	114.0	105.6	111.0
Median age (years).........	32.9	28.4	28.2	25.0	20.9	27.4
Male (years)............	31.7	27.2	27.1	25.2	20.6	29.9
Female (years)..........	34.1	29.6	29.2	24.9	21.2	24.9
Marital status, persons 15 years and over..................	195,142,002	2,563,818	72,365	93,200	28,952	33,030
Never married	52,559,853	711,470	27,539	30,759	11,412	13,810
Married [1]...............	111,498,578	1,499,449	35,199	54,717	15,958	17,869
Widowed or divorced........	31,083,571	352,899	9,627	7,724	1,582	1,351
Households and families:						
Households	91,947,410	1,054,924	32,020	31,373	6,607	6,873
Persons in households	242,012,129	3,487,667	100,488	124,596	46,267	31,856
Persons per household.....	2.63	3.31	3.14	3.97	7.00	4.63
Families	64,517,947	886,339	23,012	27,313	6,301	5,312
Husband-wife families......	50,708,322	634,872	13,197	21,342	5,153	3,947
Children ever born per 1,000 females 15 to 44 years	1,223	1,512	1,662	1,523	1,757	1,226

[1] For Puerto Rico, includes consensually married couples and for all areas, includes separated couples.
Source: U.S. Census Bureau, *1990 Census of Population*, CP-1 and CP-2 parts 1, (United States), 53 (Puerto Rico), 55 (Virgin Islands); *1990 Census of Population and Housing*, CPH-1, parts 53A and 55; CPH-6, parts G (Guam), AS (American Samoa), and CNMI (Commonwealth of the Northern Mariana Islands); and Summary Tape File, parts 3C, (United States), 3A (Puerto Rico), and 3 (Virgin Islands).

No. 1336. Selected Social and Economic Characteristics by Area: 1990

[As of **April** 1]

Characteristic	United States	Puerto Rico	Virgin Islands	Guam	American Samoa	Northern Mariana Islands
EDUCATIONAL ATTAINMENT						
Persons 25 years and over.........	158,868,436	1,952,297	55,639	66,700	19,570	24,633
Less than 9th grade	16,502,211	691,835	12,908	9,238	3,664	4,285
9th to 12th grade, no diploma.........	22,841,507	290,173	11,278	8,602	5,239	4,016
High school graduate	47,642,763	410,559	14,021	22,220	6,253	8,659
Some college or associate degree.......	39,571,702	281,248	9,011	14,984	3,062	3,818
Bachelor's degree or higher..........	32,310,253	278,482	8,421	11,656	1,352	3,855
EMPLOYMENT STATUS						
Total persons, 16 years old and over ...	191,829,271	2,497,078	70,323	90,990	27,991	32,522
In labor force.....................	125,182,378	1,180,162	47,553	66,138	14,198	26,589
Percent of total	65.3	47.3	67.6	72.7	50.7	81.8
Armed forces....................	1,708,928	5,486	110	11,952	11	8
Civilian labor force	123,473,450	1,174,676	47,443	54,186	14,187	26,581
Employed....................	115,681,202	934,736	44,267	52,144	13,461	25,965
Unemployed..................	7,792,248	239,940	3,176	2,042	726	616
Percent of civilian labor force	6.3	20.4	6.7	3.8	5.1	2.3
Not in labor force	66,646,893	1,316,916	22,770	24,852	13,793	5,933
FAMILY INCOME IN 1989						
Families, census year	65,049,428	889,998	23,012	27,313	6,301	5,312
Percent distribution by income class	100.0	100.0	100.0	100.0	100.0	100.0
Less than $5,000	4.0	25.1	8.8	4.0	11.0	8.2
$5,000 to $9,999	5.6	24.9	9.5	4.7	19.2	13.9
$10,000 to $14,999.............	7.2	16.5	12.8	8.3	17.0	13.1
$15,000 to $24,999.............	16.4	17.5	20.6	21.1	23.6	21.6
$25,000 or more................	66.9	16.0	48.3	61.9	29.1	43.2
Median income (dollars)	35,225	9,988	24,036	31,178	15,979	21,275
RESIDENCE IN 1985						
Persons 5 years and over	230,445,777	3,219,765	92,579	118,055	39,821	39,206
Same house	122,796,970	2,190,479	56,098	54,665	30,759	11,479
Different house in this area	102,540,097	879,691	25,003	24,763	2,763	6,870
Outside area....................	5,108,710	149,595	11,478	38,627	6,299	20,857
LANGUAGE SPOKEN AT HOME						
Persons 5 years and over	230,445,777	3,219,765	92,579	118,055	39,821	39,206
Speak only English at home...........	198,600,798	(NA)	70,442	44,048	1,203	1,878

NA Not available.

Source: U.S. Census Bureau, *1990 Census of Population and Housing,* Summary Tape File, parts 3C, (United States), 3A, and unpublished data, (Puerto Rico), and 3 (Virgin Islands); *1990 Census of Population,* CP-2 parts 1,(United States), 53 (Puerto Rico), 55 (Virgin Islands); CPH-L-98, *The Foreign Born Population in the United States: 1990; 1990 Census of Population and Housing,* CPH-6, parts G (Guam), AS (American Samoa), and CNMI (Commonwealth of the Northern Mariana Islands).

No. 1337. Federal Direct Payments for Individuals: 1999

[In thousands of dollars (6,039,910 represents $6,039,910,000). For fiscal years ending **September** 30]

Selected program payments	Puerto Rico	Guam	Virgin Islands	American Samoa	Northern Mariana Islands	Marshal Islands	Micro-nisia	Palau
Total.................	6,039,910	191,989	176,281	29,018	26,962	1,071	-2	198
Pell Grants	230,515	1,831	923	-	-	536	-237	-
Medicare:								
Hospital Insurance [1]	482,679	688	12,100	-	-	-	-	-
Supplemental medical insurance [1].	644,286	394	7,078	-	-	-	-	-
Social security:								
Disability insurance	1,087,244	7,674	11,533	7,695	815	20	-	22
Retirement insurance........	1,781,755	43,116	59,808	7,524	3,130	316	83	102
Survivors insurance........	801,499	20,188	18,340	8,034	3,169	155	41	26
Federal workers compensation ...	13,859	634	206	46	-	-	10	-
Veterans:								
Pension and disability	386,041	7,570	1,843	3,553	431	26	80	25
Education assistance........	5,402	574	93	219	15	-	16	-
Federal retirement and disability [1].	235,872	77,217	17,924	1,914	9,933	66	4	23
Federal payments for unem-ployment compensation.......	264,322	-	3,196	-	-	-	-	-
Food stamps................	(2)	31,296	22,209	-	5,778	-	-	-
Housing assistance	54,546	-	15,906	-	348	-	-	-
Other......................	51,890	807	5,122	33	3,343	-48	-	-

- Represents zero. [1] Includes retirement and disability payments to former U.S. Postal Service employees. [2] Food stamp program in Puerto Rico was replaced by the Nutrition Assistance Grant Program in 1982.

Source: U.S. Census Bureau, *Consolidated Federal Funds Report,* annual. <http://www.census.gov/govs/www/cffr.html>; (accessed July 19, 2000).

No. 1338. Public Elementary and Secondary Schools by Areas: 1998

[For school year ending in year shown, unless otherwise indicated]

Item	Puerto Rico	Guam	Virgin Islands	American Samoa	Item	Puerto Rico	Guam	Virgin Islands	American Samoa
PUBLIC EL/SEC					School staff	46,911	2,519	2,193	1,079
					Teachers	39,781	1,052	1,567	764
Enrollment, fall	613,862	32,222	20,976	15,372	Other support				
Elementary					services staff.	17,405	183	314	256
(kindergarten-					Current expenditures [1]				
grade 8).	451,944	23,858	15,198	11,806	($1,000)	1,981,603	168,716	131,315	33,088
Secondary (grades									
9-12 and post					HIGHER				
graduates)	161,918	8,364	5,778	3,566	EDUCATION				
Staff, fall	68,834	3,073	3,055	1,524					
School district staff .	1,967	317	251	130	Enrollment, fall	(NA)	(NA)	(NA)	(NA)

NA Not available. [1] Public elementary and secondary day schools.

Source: U.S. National Center for Education Statistics, unpublished data.

No. 1339. Puerto Rico—Summary: 1970 to 1999

Item	Unit	1970	1980	1985	1990	1995	1997	1998	1999
POPULATION									
Total [1]	1,000	2,722	3,184	3,378	3,527	3,719	3,805	3,833	3,866
Persons per family	Number . . .	4.6	4.3	3.9	3.7	3.5	3.5	3.4	3.4
EDUCATION [2]									
Enrollment, total.	1,000	922.6	1,090.9	1,107.9	(NA)	(NA)	(NA)	936.9	(NA)
Public day school	1,000	672.3	716.1	692.9	651.2	621.4	618.9	617.2	613.9
Other public.	1,000	103.9	149.5	152.0	(NA)	(NA)	(NA)	(NA)	(NA)
Private schools.	1,000	89.1	95.2	102.7	145.8	145.9	143.1	144.1	118.7
College and university	1,000	57.3	130.1	155.5	156.0	165.4	172.9	175.6	(NA)
Expenses	Mil. dol. . . .	288.8	825.0	1,171.8	1,686.4	2,555.8	2,846.8	(NA)	(NA)
As percent of GNP	Percent . . .	6.2	7.5	7.8	7.8	9.0	8.9	(NA)	(NA)
P.R. Dept. of Education	Mil. dol. . . .	254.6	612.2	810.2	1,054.2	1,689.4	1,910.9	(NA)	(NA)
Personal consumption	Mil. dol. . . .	34.2	212.8	361.6	644.2	866.4	935.9	(NA)	(NA)
LABOR FORCE [3]									
Total [4]	1,000	765	907	985	1,124	1,219	1,298	1,317	1,310
Employed [5]	1,000	686	753	774	963	1,051	1,128	1,137	1,147
Agriculture [6]	1,000	68	38	39	36	34	31	31	27
Manufacturing.	1,000	132	143	141	168	172	162	161	159
Trade	1,000	128	138	150	185	211	228	236	229
Government	1,000	106	184	183	222	232	261	244	246
Unemployed	1,000	79	154	211	161	168	170	179	163
Unemployment rate [7]	Rate	10	17	21	14	14	13	14	13
Compensation of employees	Mil. dol. . . .	2,800	7,200	9,442	13,639	17,773	20,262	21,217	22,570
Avg. compensation	Dollar	4,082	9,563	12,456	14,854	16,911	17,962	18,660	19,678
Salary and wages.	Mil. dol. . . .	2,555	6,290	8,137	11,681	15,300	17,472	18,759	19,999
INCOME [8]									
Personal income:									
Current dollars	Mil. dol. . . .	3,753	11,002	14,588	21,105	27,378	32,663	34,441	37,244
Constant (1954) dollars	Mil. dol. . . .	2,654	3,985	4,274	5,551	6,547	7,579	7,757	8,200
Disposable personal income:									
Current dollars	Mil. dol. . . .	3,565	10,403	13,760	19,914	25,591	30,607	32,167	34,673
Constant (1954) dollars	Mil. dol. . . .	2,521	3,768	4,032	5,238	6,119	7,101	7,245	7,634
Average family income:									
Current dollars	Dollar	6,366	14,858	16,914	22,234	25,881	30,328	30,658	32,892
Constant (1954) dollars	Dollar	4,503	5,381	4,957	5,848	6,189	7,037	6,905	7,242
BANKING [9]									
Assets	Mil. dol. . . .	3,322	10,223	21,209	27,902	39,859	42,380	46,088	53,338
TOURISM [8]									
Number of visitors	1,000	1,225.0	2,140.0	2,061.6	3,425.8	4,086.6	4,349.7	4,670.8	4,221.3
Visitor expenditures	Mil. dol. . . .	235.4	618.7	757.7	1,366.4	1,827.6	2,046.3	2,232.9	2,138.5
Average per visitor	Dollar	192	289	368	399	447	470	478	507
Net income from tourism	Mil. dol. . . .	89.8	202.2	223.1	383.3	498.7	553.5	597.9	577.1

NA Not available. [1] 1970, 1980, and 1990 enumerated as of April 1; all other years estimated as of July 1. [2] Enrollment for the first school month. Expenses for school year ending in year shown. Since 1990, does not include all public schools or enrollment. [3] Annual average of monthly figures. For fiscal years. [4] Beginning 1980, for population 16 years old and over; 1970, for population 14 years and over. [5] Includes other employment not shown separately. [6] Includes forestry and fisheries. [7] Percent unemployed of the labor force. [8] For fiscal years. [9] As of June 30. Does not include Federal savings banks and international banking entities.

Source: Puerto Rico Planning Board, San Juan, PR, *Income and Product*, annual; and *Socioeconomics Statistics*, annual.

Outlying Areas 805

No. 1340. Puerto Rico—Gross Product and Net Income: 1980 to 1999

[In millions of dollars (11,065 represents $11,065,000,000). For fiscal years ending June 30. Data for 1999 are preliminary]

Item	1980	1985	1990	1995	1996	1997	1998	1999
Gross domestic product........	**11,065**	**15,002**	**21,619**	**28,452**	**30,357**	**32,343**	**35,021**	**38,229**
Agriculture.......................	380	357	434	318	376	466	457	324
Manufacturing...................	5,306	7,909	12,126	17,867	18,467	19,302	22,961	26,439
Contract construction and mining [1]....	369	334	720	1,006	1,077	1,257	1,337	1,515
Transportation & other public services [2]..	1,279	1,709	2,468	3,276	3,563	3,751	3,983	4,353
Trade...........................	2,273	3,160	4,728	5,989	6,281	6,724	7,353	7,876
Finance, insurance, real estate.......	1,486	2,547	3,896	5,730	6,164	6,917	7,372	8,207
Services........................	1,279	1,837	3,015	4,724	5,025	5,314	5,693	6,014
Government.....................	1,897	2,346	3,337	4,440	4,841	5,220	5,251	5,523
Commonwealth.................	1,574	1,996	2,884	3,793	4,122	4,457	4,462	4,687
Municipalities.................	323	350	453	647	719	763	789	836
Rest of the world.................	-3,372	-5,287	-8,985	-14,195	-14,984	-15,844	-18,855	-21,718
Statistical discrepancy.............	166	91	-121	-703	-452	-765	-532	-304
Domestic net income..........	**9,007**	**12,182**	**17,941**	**23,653**	**24,854**	**26,968**	**28,976**	**31,523**
Agriculture.....................	435	410	486	442	474	638	605	575
Manufacturing...................	4,756	7,117	11,277	16,685	17,211	17,969	21,511	24,905
Mining.........................	9	10	26	30	31	34	35	37
Contract construction.............	337	309	679	903	972	1,127	1,198	1,354
Transportation and other public services [2]..	1,022	1,248	1,778	2,360	2,521	2,691	2,779	3,034
Trade..........................	1,609	2,285	3,420	4,108	4,322	4,709	5,280	5,595
Finance, insurance, and real estate.....	1,200	2,141	3,280	4,735	5,077	5,773	6,237	6,940
Services.......................	1,114	1,606	2,643	4,146	4,389	4,652	4,935	5,278
Commonwealth government [3].........	1,897	2,346	3,337	4,440	4,841	5,220	5,251	5,523
Rest of the world.................	-3,372	-5,287	-8,985	-14,195	-14,984	-15,844	-18,855	-21,718

[1] Mining includes only quarries. [2] Includes other public utilities, and radio and television broadcasting. [3] Includes public enterprises not elsewhere classified.

No. 1341. Puerto Rico—Transfer Payments: 1985 to 1999

[In millions of dollars (3,531 represents $3,531,000,000). Data represent transfer payments between Federal and state governments and other nonresidents. See headnote, Table 1340]

Item	1985	1990	1995	1996	1997	1998	1999
Total receipts.................	**3,531**	**4,871**	**6,236**	**6,804**	**7,399**	**7,728**	**8,851**
Federal Government..............	3,348	4,649	5,912	6,519	7,077	7,334	8,281
Transfers to individuals [1]...........	3,283	4,577	5,838	6,419	6,943	7,146	8,082
Veterans benefits...............	317	349	440	455	484	496	479
Medicare.....................	220	368	661	941	1,164	1,117	1,112
Old age, disability, survivors (social..	1,581	2,055	2,912	3,101	3,282	3,472	3,556
security)..							
Nutritional assistance...........	780	880	1,063	1,071	1,087	1,109	1,088
Industry subsidies..............	65	72	74	99	134	189	199
U.S. state governments............	17	18	18	17	17	18	17
Other nonresidents..............	166	205	307	268	306	376	553
Total payments.................	**1,180**	**1,801**	**2,301**	**2,353**	**2,394**	**2,480**	**2,654**
Federal Government..............	1,145	1,756	2,132	2,273	2,355	2,425	2,589
Transfers from individuals..........	508	817	1,052	1,129	1,158	1,190	1,275
Contribution to Medicare.........	44	97	162	167	165	168	174
Employee contribution for social security..	463	720	888	960	991	1,020	1,099
Transfers from industries..........	13	16	49	37	48	45	47
Unemployment insurance.........	189	247	184	191	203	217	216
Employer contribution for social security....	435	675	847	916	946	973	1,050
Other nonresidents [2]................	35	45	164	75	35	51	61
Net balance..................	**2,351**	**3,070**	**3,935**	**4,451**	**5,006**	**5,248**	**6,197**
Federal Government..............	2,203	2,893	3,780	4,246	4,722	4,909	5,692
U.S. state governments............	14	16	13	12	13	14	12
Other nonresidents...............	134	162	143	193	271	325	492

[1] Includes other receipts and payments not shown separately. [2] Includes U.S. state governments.

Source of Tables 1340 and 1341: Puerto Rico Planning Board, San Juan, PR, *Economic Report of the Governor*, annual.

No. 1342. Puerto Rico—Merchandise Imports and Exports: 1980 to 1998

[In millions of dollars (9,018 represents $9,018,000,000). Imports are imports for consumption; see text, Section 28, Foreign Commerce and Aid]

Item	1980	1985	1989	1990	1991	1992	1993	1994	1995	1996	1997	1998
Imports.......	9,018	10,162	15,010	16,200	15,079	16,476	16,124	17,152	18,969	19,422	21,928	21,706
From U.S....	5,345	6,130	10,193	10,792	10,306	11,463	11,179	11,455	12,213	12,220	13,904	13,318
From other...	3,673	4,032	4,817	5,408	4,773	5,013	4,945	5,697	6,756	7,202	8,024	8,388
Exports.......	6,576	11,087	17,455	20,402	21,128	20,455	20,351	22,711	23,573	22,379	26,653	28,109
To U.S......	5,643	9,873	15,334	17,915	18,729	17,990	17,613	20,098	20,986	19,907	25,045	25,610
To other	933	1,214	2,121	2,487	2,399	2,465	2,738	2,613	2,587	2,472	1,608	2,499

Source: U.S. Census Bureau, *Foreign Commerce and Navigation of the United States*, annual; *U.S. Trade with Puerto Rico and U.S. Possessions, FT 895;* and, through 1988, *Highlights of U.S. Export and Import Trade, FT990;* thereafter, *FT920* supplement.

No. 1343. Puerto Rico—Farms, Farmland, Farms by Size, Tenure of Operator, Type of Organization, and Farms by Value of Sales: 1993 and 1998

[1 cuerda = .97 acre]

All farms	Unit	1993	1998	All farms	Unit	1993	1998
Farms.	Number .	22,350	19,951	Average size of farm by operator:			
Farm land	Cuerdas .	826,893	865,478	Full owners	Cuerdas .	26.6	29.3
Average size of farm . .	Cuerdas .	37.0	43.4	Part owners	Cuerdas .	92.3	111.7
Approximate land area. . .	Cuerdas .	2,254,365	2,254,365	Tenants	Cuerdas .	63.4	75.9
Proportion in farms . . .	Percent .	36.7	38.4	Farms by type of organization:			
Farms by size:				Individual or family. . . .	Number .	19,911	17,887
Less than 10 cuerdas. .	Number .	10,413	7,759	Partnership	Number .	288	211
10 to 19 cuerdas	Number .	4,475	4,473	Corporation	Number .	382	437
20 to 49 cuerdas	Number .	3,966	4,023	Other	Number .	1,769	1,416
50 to 99 cuerdas	Number .	1,723	1,792	Farms by value of sales:			
100 to 174 cuerdas . . .	Number .	820	809	Less than $1,200	Number .	4,456	3,307
175 to 259 cuerdas . . .	Number .	366	421	$1,200 to $2,499.	Number .	4,591	3,633
260 cuerdas or more . .	Number .	587	674	$2,500 to $4,499	Number .	4,593	3,900
				$5,000 to $7,499.	Number .	2,566	2,408
Tenure of operator:				$7,500 to $9,999.	Number .	1,248	1,233
Operators	Number .	22,350	19,951	$10,000 to $19,999 . . .	Number .	2,115	2,366
Full owners.	Number .	17,759	15,620	$20,000 to $39,999 . . .	Number .	1,071	1,247
Part owners	Number .	2,218	2,207	$40,000 to $59,999 . . .	Number .	348	405
Tenants	Number .	2,373	2,124	$60,000 or more	Number .	1,362	1,452

No. 1344. Puerto Rico—Market Value of Agricultural Products Sold: 1998

Item	Number of farms	Value (dol.)	Average value per farm (dol.)	Item	Number of farms	Value (dol.)	Average value per farm (dol.)
Sales, total	**19,951**	**593,081,964**	**29,727**	Grasses and other crops	288	5,463,583	18,971
Crops, including							
horticultural specialties . .	15,863	225,780,069	(NA)	Livestock, poultry, and			
Sugarcane	162	6,972,793	43,042	their products	7,580	367,301,895	48,457
Coffee	10,441	55,486,004	5,314	Cattle and calves	5,602	53,442,327	9,540
Pineapples	35	3,274,918	93,569	Poultry and poultry			
Plantains	6,229	46,021,341	7,388	products	1,153	99,207,643	86,043
Bananas.	3,836	11,853,780	3,090	Dairy products	447	193,614,816	433,143
Grains	1,256	4,169,718	3,320	Hogs and pigs	1,368	11,365,065	8,308
Root crops or tubers . . .	2,517	7,623,714	3,029	Sheep and goats	377	380,317	1,009
Fruits and coconuts . . .	4,201	17,343,153	4,128	Other livestock and			
Vegetables or melons . .	1,639	28,172,345	17,189	livestock products	858	9,291,727	10,830
Horicultural specialties. .	490	39,398,720	80,406				

NA Not available.
    Source of Tables 1343 and 1344: U.S. Dept. of Agriculture, National Agricultural Statistics Service, *1998 Census of Agriculture-Area Data, Puerto Rico, Volume 1* (AC97-A-52).

No. 1345. Puerto Rico—Economic Census of Manufactures by Industry: 1997

[Covers all establishments in operation at any time during the year. Employees are for the week including March 12. For statement on methodology, see Appendix III]

Manufacturing industries	1987 SIC code [1]	Total establish- ments (num- ber)	Propri- etors and part- ners (num- ber)	Unpaid family workers (num- ber)	All employees Total (num- ber)	All employees Payroll (mil. dol.)	Value added by manu- facture (mil. dol.)	Cost of mate- rials (mil. dol.)	Value of ship- ments (mil. dol.)
Total	(X)	2,092	601	108	163,605	3,319	36,427	10,343	46,876
Food and kindred products	20	287	94	14	18,094	352	3,532	1,803	5,333
Tobacco products	21	4	(D)	-	(2)	(D)	(D)	(D)	(D)
Textile mill products	22	20	8	2	2,555	32	89	38	129
Apparel and other textile products	23	223	55	15	21,818	233	678	404	1,080
Lumber and wood products.	24	117	(D)	(D)	(2)	(D)	(D)	(D)	(D)
Furniture and fixtures.	25	146	65	7	2,472	30	97	69	165
Paper and allied products	26	41	2	1	2,152	43	162	121	283
Printing and publishing	27	208	93	27	6,469	126	430	284	713
Chemicals and allied products	28	186	11	2	37,860	1,149	21,393	3,919	25,418
Petroleum and coal products.	29	28	-	3	1,555	49	849	379	1,220
Rubber & miscellaneous plastic products.	30	71	5	1	4,924	87	377	236	613
Leather and leather products.	31	25	4	-	5,752	80	218	205	426
Stone, clay and glass products	32	159	37	5	5,298	106	565	161	726
Primary metal industries	33	24	7	1	727	13	77	37	111
Fabricated metal products.	34	229	87	11	6,048	91	405	214	623
Industrial machinery and equipment	35	78	29	5	4,301	107	2,665	262	2,940
Electronic and other electrical equipment.	36	87	6	1	24,931	456	2,897	1,471	4,360
Transportation equipment	37	34	9	2	1,484	27	118	47	166
Instruments and related products	38	64	3	-	12,260	255	1,521	556	2,077
Miscellaneous manufacturing industries. .	39	61	18	3	2,208	39	164	55	218

- Represents or rounds to zero.   D Withheld to avoid disclosure of information pertaining to a specific organization or individual.   X Not applicable.   [1] 1987 Standard Industrial Classification (SIC) code; see text, Section 13.   [2] Represents 1,000 to 2,499 employees.
    Source: U.S. Census Bureau, *1997 Economic Census of Outlying Areas, Outlying Areas,* OA97E-4.

Outlying Areas 807

No. 1346. Puerto Rico—Economic Summary by Industry: 1997

[Covers establishments with payroll. Employees are for the week including March 12. Most government employees are excluded. For statement on methodology, see Appendix III]

Industry	1987 SIC code [1]	Total estab-lish-ments	Employment-size class					Em-ploy-ees [2]	Annual payroll (mil. dol.)
			1 to 4	5 to 9	10 to 19	20 to 49	50 or more		
Total [2]	(X)	**42,463**	**25,142**	**7,204**	**4,499**	**3,318**	**2,300**	**681,052**	**11,321.3**
Agricultural services, forestry, and fishing	A	172	123	29	9	9	2	898	8.4
Mining	B	37	12	6	7	9	3	689	10.8
Nonmetallic minerals, except fuels	14	28	9	3	6	8	2	494	8.7
Construction [2]	C	2,080	957	340	269	256	258	54,003	705.1
General contractors and operative builders	15	906	396	136	117	123	134	26,833	333.2
Special trade contractors	17	1,007	519	175	125	106	82	18,301	241.8
Manufacturing [2]	D	2,200	726	258	338	368	510	157,888	3,319.1
Food and kindred products	20	305	96	48	46	61	54	17,625	347.3
Textile mill products	22	20	4	4	1	4	7	3,063	34.5
Apparel and other textile products	23	219	51	21	28	36	83	21,193	220.1
Furniture and fixtures	25	173	81	23	32	26	11	2,586	30.2
Paper and allied products	26	48	6	1	8	16	17	2,352	49.5
Printing and publishing	27	239	120	43	36	25	15	4,970	126.7
Chemicals and allied products	28	173	27	13	23	16	94	33,171	1,073.4
Petroleum and coal products	29	30	8	2	6	8	6	1,542	48.8
Rubber and misc. plastic products	30	79	14	3	15	24	23	5,446	111.1
Leather and leather products	31	23	5	-	4	1	13	5,840	80.2
Stone, clay, and glass products	32	167	41	21	41	46	18	5,029	101.7
Fabricated metal products	34	220	86	22	44	43	25	5,749	91.6
Industrial machinery and equip	35	85	45	12	7	9	12	6,827	176.0
Electronic and other electronic equip	36	96	8	5	11	9	63	21,431	393.4
Instruments and related products	38	65	11	3	6	6	39	12,784	273.2
Transportation and public utilities [2]	E	1,608	1,014	222	156	113	103	36,266	858.7
Trucking and warehousing	42	630	438	80	52	45	15	5,780	119.7
Water transportation	44	88	34	19	7	12	16	5,037	109.9
Air transportation	45	94	39	10	15	11	19	5,479	121.7
Transportation services	47	431	332	56	22	12	9	2,692	42.0
Communication	48	168	49	30	37	22	30	14,846	423.0
Electric, gas, and sanitary services	49	42	20	3	3	5	11	1,458	30.6
Wholesale trade [2]	F	2,761	1,280	555	427	334	165	38,815	860.2
Durable goods	50	1,451	663	310	231	191	56	16,979	372.5
Nondurable goods	51	1,292	617	240	194	139	101	20,913	460.4
Retail trade [2]	G	14,402	8,012	2,918	1,712	1,218	542	153,201	1,717.4
Building materials, garden supplies	52	959	603	189	88	63	16	7,549	98.9
General merchandise stores	53	428	145	62	83	75	63	18,982	218.3
Food stores	54	2,029	1,232	311	176	147	163	27,802	262.6
Automotive dealers and service stations	55	2,348	1,468	532	192	95	61	17,219	248.5
Apparel and accessory stores	56	1,917	776	605	395	119	22	16,027	153.1
Furniture and home furnishings	57	585	309	151	81	36	12	4,508	62.1
Eating and drinking places	58	2,979	1,592	404	363	473	147	36,946	325.5
Finance, insurance, and real estate [2]	H	2,582	1,386	529	349	191	127	45,905	1,057.4
Depository institutions	60	401	123	95	123	38	22	14,528	371.2
Nondepository institutions	61	424	115	144	76	66	23	8,866	192.2
Insurance carriers	63	101	43	14	8	16	20	4,373	114.7
Insurance agents, brokers, and service	64	311	180	49	42	20	20	4,830	135.9
Real estate	65	1,223	849	208	92	39	35	11,491	168.8
Services [2]	I	14,587	9,823	2,193	1,182	799	590	189,756	2,733.7
Personal services	72	946	685	151	77	30	3	4,693	50.9
Business services	73	1,672	851	298	186	148	189	53,571	677.3
Auto repair, services, and parking	75	1,144	826	211	67	29	11	5,800	77.4
Motion pictures	78	175	86	21	34	32	2	1,832	22.0
Amusement and recreation services	79	363	235	50	39	30	9	3,229	35.9
Health services	80	4,748	3,717	605	214	111	101	43,441	664.8
Legal services	81	1,258	1,077	91	60	23	7	4,506	101.8
Education services	82	602	182	84	80	141	115	24,650	362.4
Social services	83	687	332	145	119	50	41	11,763	116.1
Membership organizations	86	892	607	136	79	42	28	7,648	88.9
Engineering and management services	87	1,305	814	233	127	90	41	12,170	254.3

- Represents or rounds to zero. [1] 1987 Standard Industrial Classification (SIC) code; see text, Section 13. [2] Includes other establishments not shown separately.

Source: U.S. Census Bureau, *County Business Patterns*, annual.

No. 1347. Highway Statistics (Most Current Year) for Puerto Rico and the Territories

Item	Puerto Rico, 1997	Virgin Islands, 1997	Guam, 1997	American Samoa, 1997	Northern Mariana Islands, 1995
Motor-vehicle registrations:					
Total	2,211,250	5,988	112,391	20,286	64,600
Automobiles	2,182,410	5,481	79,326	19,871	51,917
Buses	3,344	195	803	206	1,144
Trucks	25,496	312	32,262	209	11,539
Trailers	48,174	93	3,017	14	255
Motorcycles	32,030	93	609	211	241
Driver licenses in force [1]	1,615,000	1,722	32,684	9,759	(NA)
Learner permits issued.	82,976	120	3,632	355	3,841
Operator licenses issued	62,066	1,042	24,988	9,404	12,167
Chauffeur licenses issued.	13,100	560	4,043	-	471
Motorcycle licenses issued	7	-	21	-	(NA)
Motor vehicle tax receipts ($1,000)	201,316	328	4,872	1,205	3,710
Registration fees.	66,946	134	4,583	946	3,341
Driver licenses	5,048	35	289	259	369
Motor carriers.	171	15	(NA)	-	(NA)
Other	28,493	144	(NA)	-	(NA)
Motor-fuel consumption:					
Territorial tax rate (cents/gal.) on Dec. 31:					
Gasoline	0.16	0.25	0.11	0.10	0.14
Diesel and LPG.	0.04	0.035	0.10	0.10	0.14
Net gallons taxed (1,000)	1,438,542	2,689	88,844	65,932	39
At prevailing rates	1,436,177	2,689	(NA)	65,932	39
At other rates	2,365	-	(NA)	(NA)	(NA)
Motor-fuel tax receipts:($1,000)					
Gross gallonage receipts	180,878	62	9,415	6,593	5,367
Less:					
Refunds paid	745	8	1,202	-	(NA)
Dedicated gallonage tax	118	-	(NA)	-	(NA)
Other receipts	892	-	(NA)	-	(NA)
Net total receipts.	180,907	55	8,213	6,593	5,367
Highway receipts ($1,000)	376,927	9,632	3,606	5,448	26,700
Highway-user revenue	310,372	500	(NA)	-	931
General funds	-	295	2,944	899	5,990
FHWA funds [1]	1,117	8,662	116	3,749	13,391
Other Federal funds	65,438	175	546	800	6,388
Highway disbursements ($1,000).	913,856	394	29,540	5,448	6,290
Capital outlay.	695,634	18	18,184	3,749	1,762
Maintenance	53,668	332	7,844	587	3,842
Administration	136,901	43	3,436	172	266
Highway law enforcement.	27,653	-	76	940	420

- Represents or rounds to zero.   NA Not available.   [1] For American Samoa, data are licenses in force instead of license issued.

Source: U.S. Federal Highway Administration, *Highway Statistics*, annual.

No. 1348. Guam, Virgin Islands, and Northern Mariana Islands—Economic Summary: 1997

[Sales and payroll in millions of dollars (4,640 represents $4,640,000,000)]

Item	Guam	Virgin Islands	No. Mariana Islands	Item	Guam	Virgin Islands	No. Mariana Islands
Total:				Wholesale trade:			
Establishments	2,707	2,032	1,232	Establishments	270	115	87
Sales.	4,640	2,296	2,083	Sales.	941	252	223
Annual payroll	750	382	323	Annual payroll	77	27	9
Paid employees [1]	42,477	21,216	28,906	Paid employees [1]	3,393	1,144	745
Unpaid family workers [2] . . .	129	107	26	Unpaid family workers [2] . . .	-	-	-
Construction:				Retail trade:			
Establishments	354	203	85	Establishments	1,091	973	519
Sales.	506	185	88	Sales.	1,840	1,058	570
Annual payroll	139	52	21	Annual payroll	221	136	54
Paid employees [1]	7,094	2,623	2,302	Paid employees [1]	15,334	8,966	4,811
Unpaid family workers [2] . . .	9	9	-	Unpaid family workers [2] . . .	74	55	14
Manufacturing:				Services:			
Establishments	60	74	84	Establishments	932	667	457
Sales.	165	146	762	Sales.	1,188	655	440
Annual payroll	33	28	147	Annual payroll	280	139	91
Paid employees [1]	1,320	1,194	13,715	Paid employees [1]	15,336	7,289	7,333
Unpaid family workers [2] . . .	4	9	-	Unpaid family workers [2] . . .	42	34	12

- Represents zero.   [1] For pay period including March 12.   [2] Includes those who worked 15 hours or more during the week including March 12.

Source: U.S. Census Bureau, *1992 Economic Census of Outlying Areas*, OA97-E-5 to OA97-E-7.

Outlying Areas   809

No. 1349. Population Estimates and Vital Statistics in the Largest Puerto Rico Municipios: 1990 and 1999

Municipios ranked by 1999 population	1990	1999	Demographic components of population change				
			Percent change	Births	Deaths	Natural change	Residual change
Puerto Rico	**3,522,037**	**3,889,507**	**10**	**585,532**	**261,988**	**323,544**	**43,926**
San Juan	437,745	439,604	-	66,452	41,557	24,895	-23,036
Bayamcn	220,262	236,688	8	34,563	15,190	19,373	-2,947
Ponce	187,749	193,640	3	32,206	14,762	17,444	-11,553
Carolina	177,806	192,088	8	26,830	11,672	15,158	-876
Caguas	133,447	145,193	9	22,474	9,913	12,561	-815
Guaynabo.	92,886	104,936	13	15,007	6,194	8,813	3,237
Arecibo.	93,385	102,294	10	14,693	8,049	6,644	2,265
Mayagez	100,371	100,463	-	14,154	8,088	6,066	-5,974
Toa Baja.	89,454	94,837	6	14,125	5,301	8,824	-3,441
Trujillo Alto	61,120	78,442	28	10,377	3,579	6,798	10,524
Aquadilla	59,335	67,050	13	8,960	4,727	4,233	3,482
Vega Baja.	55,997	62,329	11	10,371	4,129	6,242	90
Toa Alta	44,101	61,579	40	8,901	2,330	6,571	10,907
Humacao	55,203	60,036	9	9,438	3,973	5,465	-632
Juana Diaz	45,198	52,461	16	8,525	3,121	5,404	1,859
Rio Grande	36,816	51,925	41	7,901	2,722	5,179	9,930
Canovanas	45,648	51,267	12	7,989	3,133	4,856	763
Cayey	46,553	51,117	10	7,660	3,540	4,120	444
Cidra	35,601	50,019	41	5,901	2,070	3,831	10,587
Cabo Rojo	38,521	49,368	28	5,820	3,321	2,499	8,348
Yauco	42,058	45,289	8	6,925	2,979	3,946	-715
San Sebastian	41,588	44,066	6	7,461	3,159	4,302	-1,824
Guayama	38,799	43,854	13	5,797	3,006	2,791	2,264
Juncos	30,612	43,591	42	5,185	2,294	2,891	10,088
Yabucoa	39,147	43,118	10	6,129	3,169	2,960	1,011
Isabela	38,692	42,079	9	7,374	3,186	4,188	-801
Manati	36,483	41,743	14	5,907	2,483	3,424	1,836
Hatillo	32,703	40,897	25	5,215	2,449	2,766	5,428
Aguada	35,911	40,010	11	5,884	2,189	3,695	404
Fajardo.	34,962	38,814	11	5,346	2,764	2,582	1,270
Moca	36,882	38,605	5	6,719	3,135	3,584	-1,861
San German	35,163	38,444	9	5,816	2,616	3,200	81
Corozal	32,926	38,424	17	5,610	1,953	3,657	1,841
Coamo.	34,559	37,553	9	5,750	2,196	3,554	-560
San Lorenzo	33,837	37,330	10	6,100	2,493	3,607	-114
Vega Alta	33,095	36,804	11	6,026	2,066	3,960	-251
Utuado.	34,980	35,475	1	5,320	2,538	2,782	-2,287
Morovis	30,759	35,104	14	5,066	1,920	3,146	1,199
Gurabo.	25,288	34,014	35	5,157	1,452	3,705	5,021
Dorado.	28,737	34,006	18	5,155	2,034	3,121	2,148
Catano.	28,917	33,235	15	5,133	2,145	2,988	1,330
Lares	29,015	33,016	14	5,005	2,161	2,844	1,157
Camuy	34,587	32,365	-6	5,690	2,459	3,231	-5,453
Las Piedras	27,896	32,137	15	4,901	1,829	3,072	1,169
Aguas Buenas	25,424	31,841	25	4,298	1,634	2,664	3,753
Salinas.	28,335	30,597	8	5,452	2,190	3,262	-1,000
Naranjito.	27,914	29,272	5	5,080	1,677	3,403	-2,045
Barranquitas	25,605	29,031	13	5,436	1,615	3,821	-395
Loiza	25,234	28,556	13	4,080	1,869	2,211	1,111
Aibonito	21,581	28,538	32	3,575	1,546	2,029	4,928
Guayanilla.	29,307	28,070	-4	4,803	1,694	3,109	-4,346
Anasco.	24,971	27,993	12	4,352	1,731	2,621	401
Penuelas	23,271	27,797	19	3,583	1,869	1,714	2,812
Lajas	20,947	27,524	31	3,669	1,642	2,027	4,550
Barceloneta.	22,515	27,199	21	4,310	1,455	2,855	1,829
Quebradillas	21,425	26,093	22	3,714	1,540	2,174	2,494
Naguabo	22,620	25,382	12	3,608	1,857	1,751	1,011
Orocovis.	21,158	25,155	19	4,313	1,350	2,963	1,034
Sabana Grande	22,843	24,917	9	3,859	1,884	1,975	99
Villalba.	23,559	24,713	5	5,021	1,367	3,654	-2,500
Guanica	19,633	21,904	12	3,302	1,463	1,839	432
Patillas.	19,984	21,630	8	3,270	1,688	1,582	64
Comerio.	18,084	20,997	16	3,310	1,205	2,105	808
Adjuntas.	20,265	20,583	2	3,336	1,289	2,047	-1,729
Arroyo	19,318	20,155	4	4,070	1,529	2,541	-1,704
Ciales	18,910	20,153	7	3,222	1,388	1,834	-591
Santa Isabel	19,451	19,644	1	3,282	1,344	1,938	-1,745
Luquillo	17,145	18,946	11	3,085	1,036	2,049	-248
Ceiba.	18,100	18,877	4	3,249	1,423	1,826	-1,049
Jayuya	15,212	17,070	12	1,936	1,099	837	1,021
Hormigueros	15,527	16,891	9	3,018	1,053	1,965	-601
Rincon	12,213	14,317	17	2,103	972	1,131	973
Maunabo	12,347	13,874	12	2,008	894	1,114	413
Las Marias	9,306	9,887	6	1,465	589	876	-295
Vieques	8,602	9,584	11	1,539	820	719	263
Florida	8,689	9,107	5	1,782	730	1,052	-634
Maricao	6,206	6,130	-1	1,090	393	697	-773
Culebra	1,542	1,771	15	294	107	187	42

- Represents or rounds to zero.

Source: U.S. Census Bureau, <http://www.census.gov/population/www/estimates/puerto-rico.html>.

U.S. Census Bureau, Statistical Abstract of the United States: 2000

Section 30
Comparative
International Statistics

This section presents statistics for the world as a whole and for many countries on a comparative basis with the United States. Data are shown for population, births and deaths, social and industrial indicators, finances, agriculture, communication, and military affairs.

Statistics of the individual nations may be found primarily in official national publications, generally in the form of yearbooks, issued by most of the nations at various intervals in their own national languages and expressed in their own or customary units of measure. (For a listing of selected publications, see Guide to Sources.) For handier reference, especially for international comparisons, the United Nations Statistics Division compiles data as submitted by member countries and issues a number of international summary publications, generally in English and French. Among these are the *Statistical Yearbook*; the *Demographic Yearbook*; *International Trade Statistics Yearbook*; *National Accounts Statistics: Main Aggregates and Detailed Tables*; *Population and Vital Statistics Reports* (quarterly); the *Monthly Bulletin of Statistics*; and the *Energy Statistics Yearbook*. Specialized agencies of the United Nations also issue international summary publications on agricultural, labor, health, and education statistics. Among these are the *Production Yearbook* and *Trade Yearbook* issued by the Food and Agriculture Organization, the *Yearbook of Labour Statistics* issued by the International Labour Office, *World Health Statistics* issued by the World Health Organization, and the *Statistical Yearbook* issued by the Educational, Scientific, and Cultural Organization.

The U.S. Census Bureau presents estimates and projections of basic demographic measures for countries and regions of the world in the *World Population Reports* (WP) series. The *International Population Reports* (Series IPC), and *International Briefs* (Series IB) also present population figures for many foreign countries. Detailed population statistics are also available from the Census Bureau's International Data Base.

The International Monetary Fund (IMF) and the Organization for Economic Cooperation and Development (OECD) also compile data on international statistics. The IMF publishes a series of reports relating to financial data. These include *International Financial Statistics*, *Direction of Trade*, and *Balance of Payments Yearbook*, published in English, French, and Spanish. The OECD publishes a vast number of statistical publications in various fields such as economics, health, and education. Among these are *OECD in Figures*, *Main Economic Indicators*, *Economic Outlook*, *National Accounts*, *Labour Force Statistics*, *OECD Health Data*, and *Education at a Glance*.

Statistical coverage, country names, and classifications—Problems of space and availability of data limit the number of countries and the extent of statistical coverage shown. The list of countries included and the spelling of country names are based almost entirely on the list of sovereign nations, dependencies, and areas of special sovereignty provided by the U.S. Department of State.

In recent years, several important changes took place in the status of the world's nations. In 1990, a unified Germany was formed from the Federal Republic of Germany (West) and the German Democratic Republic (East). The Republic of Yemen was formed by union of the Yemen Arab Republic and the People's Democratic Republic of Yemen. Also in 1990, Namibia, once a

Comparative International Statistics 811

United Nations mandate, realized its independence from South Africa.

In 1991, the Soviet Union broke up into 15 independent countries: Armenia, Azerbaijan, Belarus, Estonia, Georgia, Kazakhstan, Kyrgyzstan, Latvia, Lithuania, Moldova, Russia, Tajikistan, Turkmenistan, Ukraine, and Uzbekistan.

In 1992, the Socialist Federal Republic of Yugoslavia dissolved; none of the successor states has been recognized as its continuation. The United States recognizes Bosnia and Herzegovina, Croatia, Slovenia, and The Former Yugoslav Republic of Macedonia as independent countries. Serbia and Montenegro have asserted the formation of a joint independent state, but this entity has not been formally recognized as a state by the United States.

On January 1, 1993, Czechoslovakia was succeeded by two independent countries: the Czech Republic and Slovakia. Eritrea announced its independence from Ethiopia in April 1993 and was subsequently recognized as an independent nation by the United States.

The population estimates and projections used in Tables 1350, 1352, 1353 and 1355 were prepared by the Census Bureau. For each country, the data on population, by age and sex, fertility, mortality, and international migration were evaluated and, where necessary, adjusted for inconsistencies and errors in the data. In most instances, comprehensive projections were made by the component method, resulting in distributions of the population by age and sex and requiring an assessment of probable future trends of fertility, mortality, and international migration.

Economic associations—The Organization for European Economic Co-operation (OEEC), a regional grouping of Western European countries established in 1948 for the purpose of harmonizing national economic policies and conditions, was succeeded on September 30, 1961, by the Organization for Economic Cooperation and Development (OECD). The member nations of the OECD are Australia, Austria, Belgium, Canada, Czech Republic, Denmark, Finland, France, Germany, Greece, Hungary, Iceland, Ireland, Italy, Japan, Luxembourg, Mexico, the Netherlands, New Zealand, Norway, Poland, Portugal, South Korea, Spain, Sweden, Switzerland, Turkey, the United Kingdom, and the United States.

Quality and comparability of the data—The quality and comparability of the data presented here are affected by a number of factors:

(1) The year for which data are presented may not be the same for all subjects for a particular country or for a given subject for different countries, though the data shown are the most recent available. All such variations have been noted. The data shown are for calendar years except as otherwise specified.

(2) The bases, methods of estimating, methods of data collection, extent of coverage, precision of definition, scope of territory, and margins of error may vary for different items within a particular country, and for like items for different countries. Footnotes and headnotes to the tables give a few of the major time-periods and coverage qualifications attached to the figures; considerably more detail is presented in the source publications. Many of the measures shown are, at best, merely rough indicators of magnitude.

(3) Figures shown in this section for the United States may not always agree with figures shown in the preceding sections. Disagreements may be attributable to the use of differing original sources, a difference in the definition of geographic limits (the 50 states, conterminous United States only, or the United States including certain outlying areas and possessions), or to possible adjustments made in the United States figures by other sources in order to make them more comparable with figures from other countries.

International comparisons of national accounts data—In order to compare national accounts data for different countries,

U.S. Census Bureau, Statistical Abstract of the United States: 2000

it is necessary to convert each country's data into a common unit of currency, usually the U.S. dollar. The market exchange rates which are often used in converting national currencies do not necessarily reflect the relative purchasing power in the various countries. It is necessary that the goods and services produced in different countries be valued consistently if the differences observed are meant to reflect real differences in the volumes of goods and services produced. The use of purchasing power parities (see Table 1365) instead of exchange rates is intended to achieve this objective.

The method used to present the data shown in Table 1365 is to construct volume measures directly by revaluing the goods and services sold in different countries at a common set of international prices. By dividing the ratio of the gross domestic products of two countries expressed in their own national currencies by the corresponding ratio calculated at constant international prices, it is possible to derive the implied purchasing power parity (PPP) between the two currencies concerned. PPPs show how many units of currency are needed in one country to buy the same amount of goods and services which one unit of currency will buy in the other country. For further information, see *National Accounts, Main Aggregates, Volume I*, issued annually by the Organization for Economic Cooperation and Development, Paris, France.

International Standard Industrial Classification—The original version of the International Standard Industrial Classification of All Economic Activities (ISIC) was adopted in 1948. Wide use has been made both nationally and internationally in classifying data according to kind of economic activity in the fields of production, employment, national income, and other economic statistics. A number of countries have utilized the ISIC as the basis for devising their industrial classification scheme.

Substantial comparability has been attained between the industrial classifications of many other countries, including the United States and the ISIC by ensuring, as far as practicable, that the categories at detailed levels of classification in national schemes fitted into only one category of the ISIC. For more detail, see the Census Bureau's, *The International Standard Industrial Classification and the U.S. Standard Industrial Classification*, Technical Paper No. 14, and the text of Section 27, Manufactures. The United Nations, the International Labour Organization, the Food and Agriculture Organization, and other international bodies have utilized the ISIC in publishing and analyzing statistical data. Revisions of the ISIC were issued in 1958, 1968, and 1989.

International maps—A series of regional world maps is provided on pages 814-820. References are included in Table 1352 for easy location of individual countries on the maps. The Robinson map projection is used for this series of maps. A map projection is used to portray all or part of the round Earth on a flat surface, but this cannot be done without some distortion. For the Robinson projection, distortion is very low along the Equator and within 45 degrees of the center but is greatest near the poles. For additional information on map projections and maps, please contact the Earth Science Information Center, U.S. Geological Survey, 507 National Center, Reston, VA 22092.

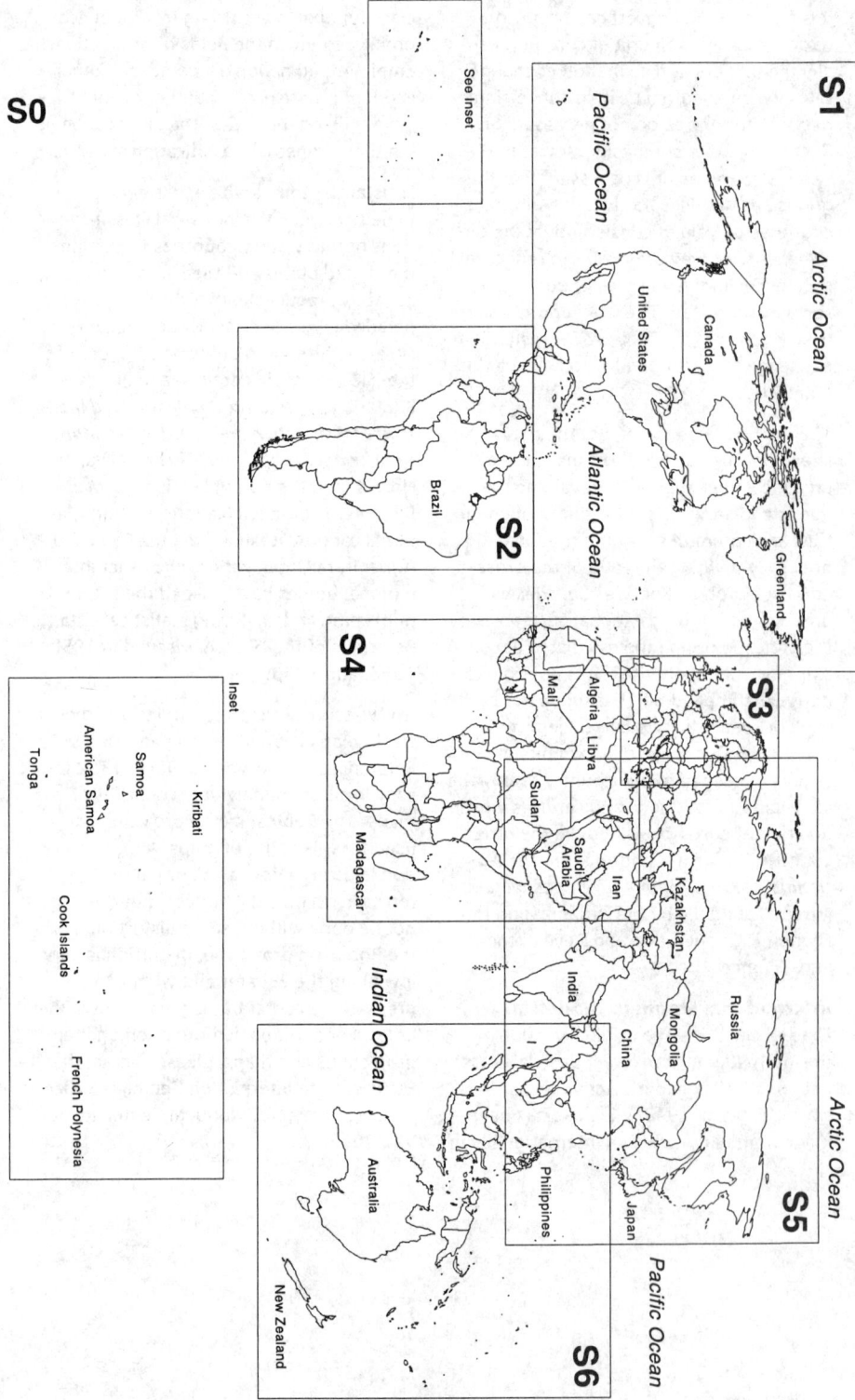

S1

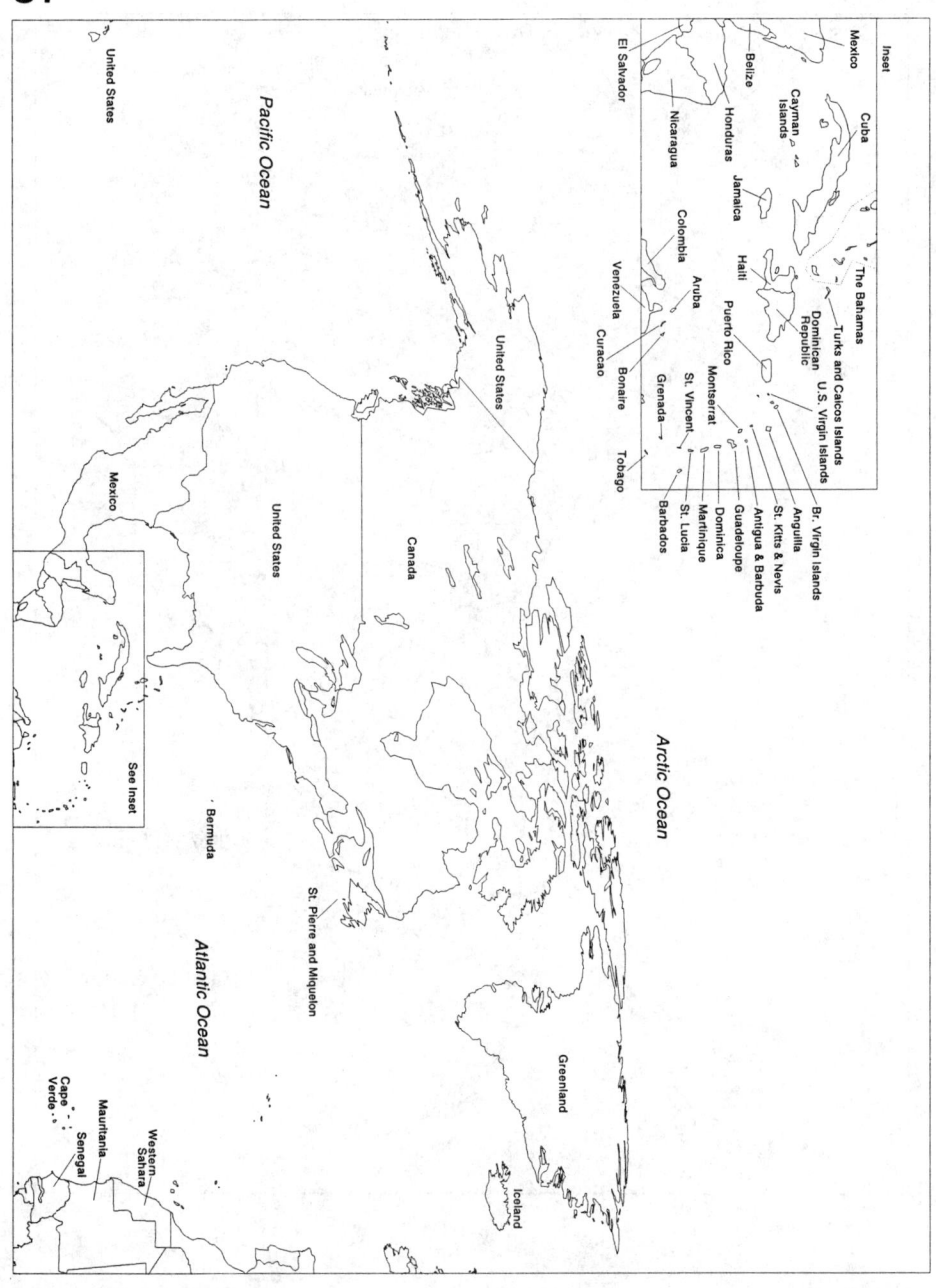

U.S. Census Bureau, Statistical Abstract of the United States: 2000

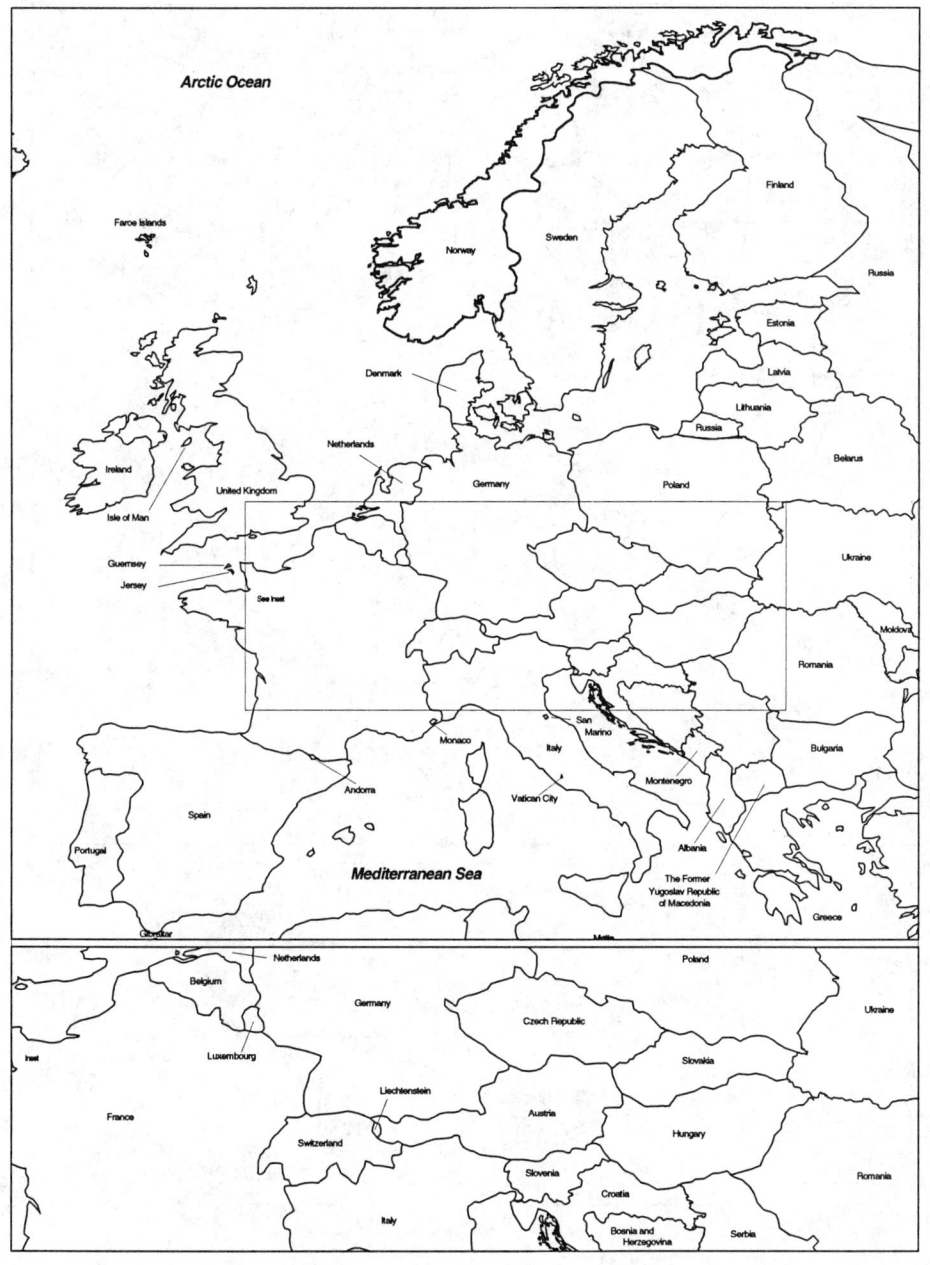

U.S. Census Bureau, Statistical Abstract of the United States: 2000

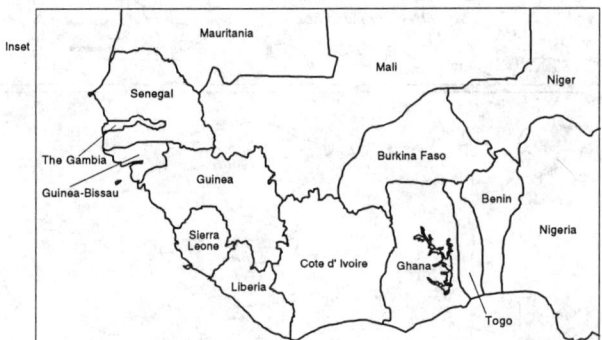

U.S. Census Bureau, Statistical Abstract of the United States: 2000

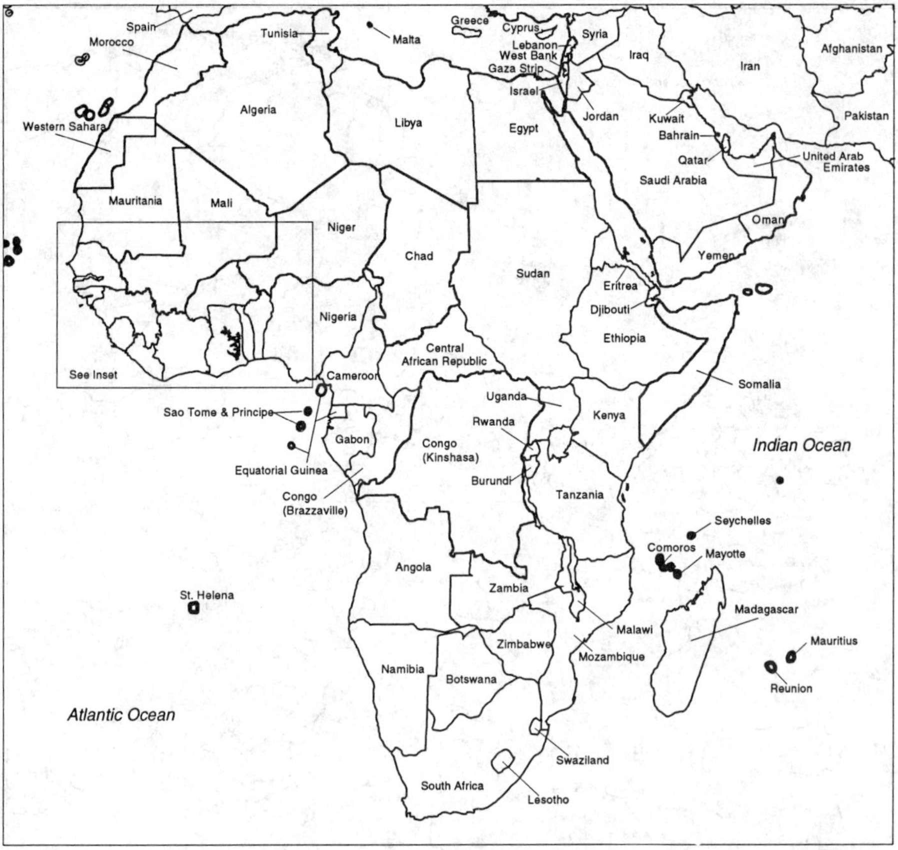

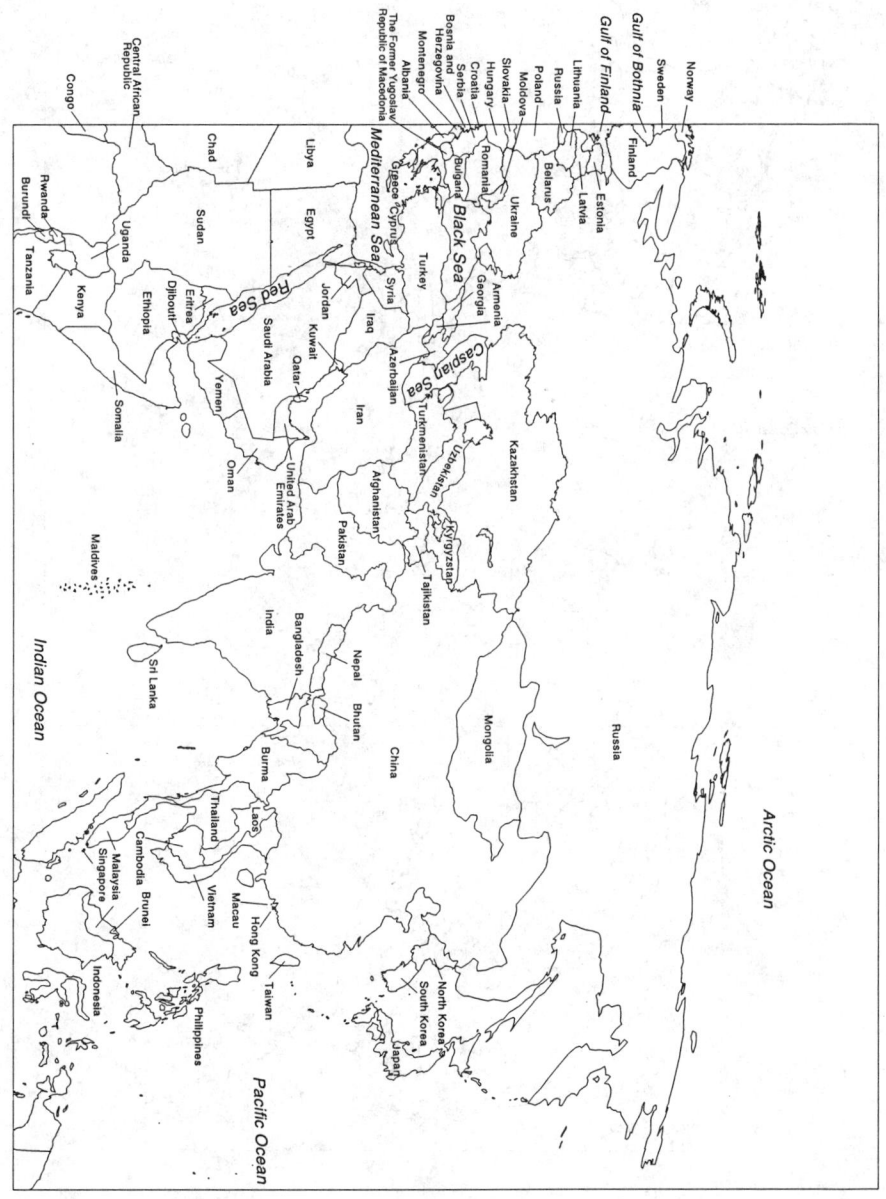

U.S. Census Bureau, Statistical Abstract of the United States: 1999

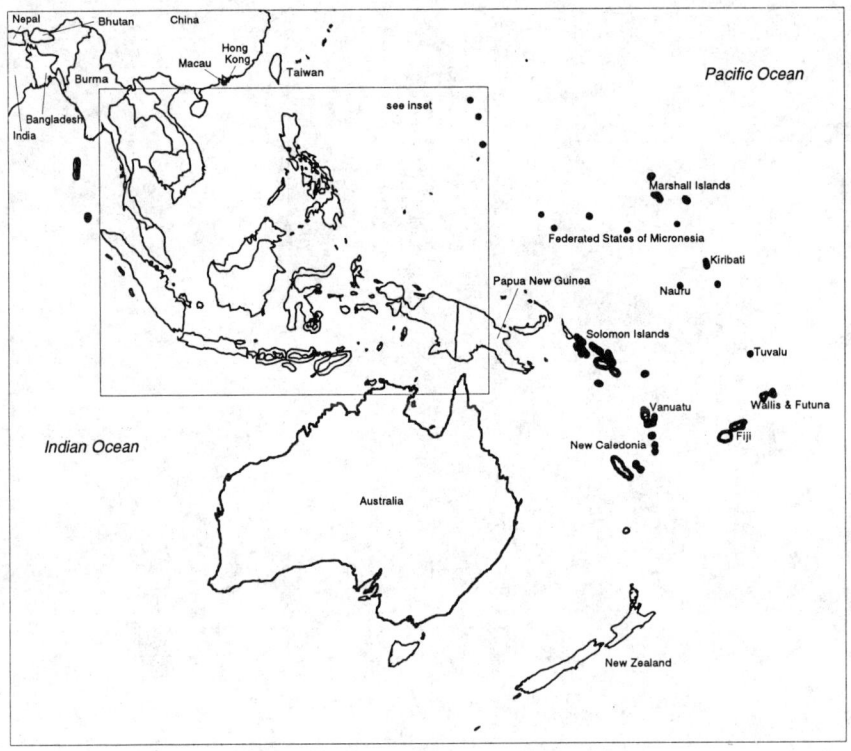

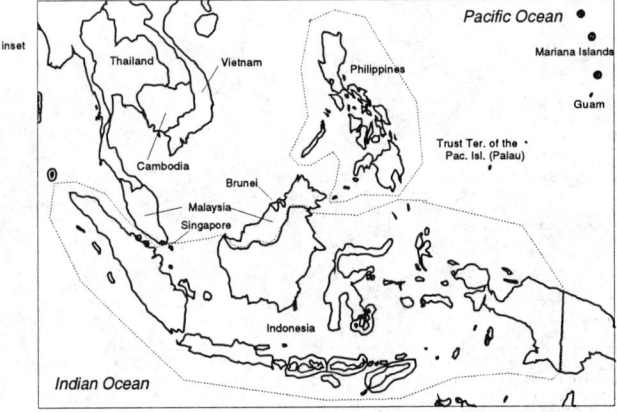

No. 1350. Total World Population: 1980 to 2050

[As of midyear (4,457 represents 4,457,000,000)]

Year	Population (mil.)	Average annual [1] Growth rate (percent)	Population change (mil.)	Year	Population (mil.)	Average annual [1] Growth rate (percent)	Population change (mil.)
1980	4,457	1.70	76.3	2004	6,386	1.16	74.5
1985	4,855	1.70	83.0	2005	6,461	1.14	73.8
1990	5,284	1.56	83.2	2006	6,534	1.12	73.3
1991	5,367	1.53	82.7	2007	6,608	1.10	72.8
1992	5,450	1.48	81.3	2008	6,680	1.07	72.0
1993	5,531	1.44	80.0	2009	6,752	1.05	71.2
1994	5,611	1.41	79.9	2010	6,824	1.03	70.8
1995	5,691	1.36	77.7	2015	7,176	0.97	69.6
1996	5,769	1.35	78.2	2020	7,518	0.88	66.4
1997	5,847	1.32	77.8	2025	7,841	0.78	61.7
1998	5,925	1.31	77.9	2030	8,140	0.70	57.2
1999	6,003	1.29	77.6	2035	8,417	0.62	52.3
2000	6,080	1.26	77.3	2040	8,668	0.55	47.5
2001	6,157	1.24	76.8	2045	8,897	0.48	43.2
2002	6,234	1.22	76.3	2050	9,104	(NA)	(NA)
2003	6,311	1.19	75.5				

NA Not available.   [1] Represents change from year shown to immediate succeeding year.

Source: U.S. Census Bureau, "Total Midyear Population for the World: 1950-2050," published 10 May 2000; <http://www.census.gov/ipc/www/worldpop.html>.

No. 1351. World Summary: 1980 to 1997

[4.8 represents 4,800,000. See text of this section for general comments concerning quality of the data]

Item	Unit	1980	1985	1990	1992	1993	1994	1995	1996	1997
Agriculture, forestry, fishing:										
Coffee	Mil. metric tons .	4.8	5.8	6.1	5.9	5.6	5.8	5.5	6.2	6.0
Cotton (lint)	Mil. metric tons .	13.9	17.3	18.4	18.1	16.9	18.7	20.3	19.7	19.9
Tobacco.	Mil. metric tons .	5.3	7.1	7.1	8.4	8.3	6.4	6.3	7.4	8.6
Roundwood	Mil. cubic meters	2,920	3,167	3,448	3,279	3,277	3,301	3,411	3,348	3,358
Fish catches.	Mil. metric tons .	72.3	87.2	99.0	101.7	105.2	113.5	117.3	121.0	(NA)
Textile fiber production, total [1] . .	Billion pounds. .	67.4	77.0	87.2	86.3	84.4	90.9	96.0	97.2	103.0
Rayon and acetate	Billion pounds. .	7.1	6.5	6.1	5.1	5.2	5.1	5.3	5.0	5.1
Noncellulosic fibers	Billion pounds. .	23.1	27.5	32.8	35.6	36.6	39.5	40.5	43.9	48.8
Cotton.	Billion pounds. .	31.4	38.5	41.8	39.7	37.2	41.2	44.9	43.2	44.1
Wool, clean	Billion pounds. .	3.7	3.8	4.4	3.8	3.7	3.4	3.3	3.3	3.2
Silk	Billion pounds. .	0.1	0.2	0.1	0.1	0.2	0.2	0.2	0.2	0.2
Flax	Billion pounds. .	1.4	1.6	1.6	1.5	1.4	1.3	1.5	1.4	1.4
Hemp [2]	Billion pounds. .	0.6	0.5	0.4	0.4	0.3	0.2	0.2	0.1	0.1
Industrial production:										
Wine	Mil. hectoliters .	352.1	309.5	279.6	266.7	234.7	238.3	241.9	241.5	226.6
Sugar	Mil. metric tons .	79.0	90.8	105.2	112.5	106.4	104.0	106.4	116.3	115.9
Wheat flour	Mil. metric tons .	229.7	267.9	242.9	260.5	251.5	247.8	241.7	250.4	266.4
Electricity	Bil. kWh.	8,247	9,747	11,788	12,142	12,395	12,713	13,147	13,620	(NA)
Pig iron and ferroalloys [3] . . .	Mil. metric tons .	542	507	534	510	510	520	539	531	555
Sawnwood [4]	Mil. cubic meters	451	468	505	441	431	433	426	432	438
Woodpulp [5]	Mil. metric tons .	125.8	141.8	154.8	153.6	152.2	162.5	162.5	157.2	163.6
Newsprint.	Mil. metric tons .	25.4	28.3	32.8	32.4	32.9	34.6	35.5	35.1	36.1
Merchant vessels, launched .	Mil. gross tons .	13.9	17.3	14.8	19.3	19.1	18.6	23.0	27.8	31.3
External trade:										
Imports, c.i.f	Bil. U.S. dollars.	2,045	1,998	3,556	3,790	3,718	4,240	5,038	5,290	5,489
Exports, f.o.b	Bil. U.S. dollars.	2,001	1,921	3,433	3,675	3,667	4,182	4,981	5,195	5,392
Civil aviation, kilometers flown [6]	Millions	(NA)	(NA)	(NA)	(NA)	17,118	18,249	19,470	21,632	(NA)

NA Not available.   [1] Source: U.S. Dept. of Agriculture, Economic Research Service, *Cotton and Wool Situation and Outlook Yearbook*. Data from International Wool Textile Organization.   [2] Beginning 1996 not comparable with earlier years.   [3] Pig iron (foundry and steel making) plus other ferro alloys (spiegeleisen and ferro-manganese).   [4] Broadleaved and coniferous.   [5] Mechanical plus dissolving grades plus sulphate and soda plus sulphate and semichemical.   [6] Scheduled services of members of International Civil Aviation Organization.

Source: Except as noted, Statistical Division of the United Nations, New York, NY, *Monthly Bulletin of Statistics*, (copyright).

Comparative International Statistics   821

No. 1352. Population by Country: 1980 to 2010

[**4,456,705 represents 4,456,705,000**. Population data generally are de facto figures for the present territory. Population estimates were derived from information available as of spring 2000. See text of this section for general comments concerning the data. For details of methodology, coverage, and reliability, see source. Minus sign (-) indicates decrease]

Country or area	Map refer- ence	Mid-year population (1,000) 1980	1990	2000	2010, proj.	Popu- lation rank, 2000	Annual rate of growth,[1] 1990- 2000 (percent)	Popula- tion per sq. mile, 2000	Area (sq. mile)
World...............	S0	4,456,705	5,283,755	6,080,142	6,823,635	(X)	1.4	120	50,580,319
Afghanistan.............	S5	14,985	14,750	25,889	33,864	39	5.6	104	250,000
Albania................	S3	2,671	3,258	3,490	3,827	128	0.7	330	10,579
Algeria................	S4	18,862	25,341	31,194	36,589	35	2.1	34	919,591
Andorra................	S3	34	53	67	74	204	2.3	384	174
Angola................	S4	6,741	8,056	10,145	12,646	74	2.3	21	481,351
Antigua and Barbuda........	S1	69	63	66	71	205	0.6	391	170
Argentina..............	S2	28,237	32,634	36,955	41,082	31	1.2	35	1,056,637
Armenia...............	S5	3,115	3,366	3,344	3,365	129	-0.1	291	11,506
Australia..............	S6	14,616	17,022	19,165	20,925	52	1.2	7	2,941,285
Austria...............	S3	7,549	7,718	8,131	8,278	86	0.5	255	31,942
Azerbaijan.............	S5	6,173	7,200	7,748	8,221	88	0.7	232	33,436
Bahamas, The...........	S1	210	257	295	315	176	1.4	76	3,888
Bahrain...............	S4	348	500	634	737	162	2.4	2,653	239
Bangladesh.............	S5	88,077	109,897	129,194	150,392	8	1.6	2,499	51,703
Barbados..............	S1	252	263	274	287	178	0.4	1,651	166
Belarus...............	S3	9,644	10,215	10,367	10,294	71	0.1	129	80,154
Belgium...............	S3	9,847	9,969	10,242	10,340	73	0.3	877	11,672
Belize................	S1	144	191	249	320	179	2.7	28	8,803
Benin................	S4	3,444	4,656	6,396	8,411	96	3.2	150	42,710
Bhutan...............	S5	1,281	1,598	2,005	2,476	143	2.3	110	18,147
Bolivia...............	S2	5,441	6,574	8,153	9,499	85	2.2	19	418,683
Bosnia and Herzegovina.....	S3	4,092	4,424	3,836	4,103	121	-1.4	194	19,741
Botswana.............	S4	903	1,304	1,576	1,502	147	1.9	7	226,012
Brazil................	S2	122,934	151,053	172,860	186,823	5	1.3	53	3,265,061
Brunei................	S6	185	258	336	408	174	2.6	165	2,035
Bulgaria...............	S3	8,844	8,894	7,797	7,006	87	-1.3	183	42,683
Burkina Faso...........	S4	6,939	9,037	11,946	15,424	65	2.8	113	105,714
Burma................	S5	33,281	38,519	41,735	43,674	27	0.8	164	253,954
Burundi...............	S4	4,138	5,285	6,055	7,669	99	1.4	611	9,903
Cambodia.............	S5	6,499	8,965	12,212	15,233	64	3.1	179	68,154
Cameroon.............	S4	8,747	11,761	15,422	19,202	60	2.7	85	181,251
Canada...............	S1	24,593	27,791	31,278	34,253	34	1.2	9	3,560,219
Cape Verde............	S1	296	349	401	431	172	1.4	258	1,556
Central African Republic.....	S4	2,244	2,803	3,513	4,135	127	2.3	15	240,533
Chad.................	S4	4,535	6,018	8,425	11,616	84	3.4	17	486,178
Chile.................	S2	11,094	13,128	15,154	16,727	61	1.4	52	289,112
China [2]...............	S5	984,736	1,138,895	1,261,832	1,359,141	1	1.0	350	3,600,930
Colombia..............	S2	26,583	32,859	39,686	46,109	29	1.9	99	401,042
Comoros..............	S4	334	429	578	773	163	3.0	690	838
Congo (Brazzaville) [3]......	S4	1,620	2,218	2,831	3,491	132	2.4	21	131,853
Congo (Kinshasa) [3].......	S4	28,129	37,991	51,965	69,846	23	3.1	59	875,521
Costa Rica.............	S2	2,299	3,027	3,711	4,306	124	2.0	190	19,560
Cote d'Ivoire...........	S4	8,261	11,919	15,981	20,003	57	2.9	130	122,780
Croatia...............	S3	4,383	4,508	4,282	4,505	117	-0.5	196	21,829
Cuba.................	S1	9,653	10,545	11,142	11,526	67	0.6	260	42,803
Cyprus................	S5	611	681	758	801	157	1.1	213	3,568
Czech Republic..........	S3	10,289	10,310	10,272	10,157	72	-	338	30,365
Denmark..............	S3	5,123	5,141	5,336	5,474	104	0.4	326	16,359
Djibouti...............	S4	279	370	451	579	166	2.0	53	8,486
Dominica..............	S1	75	73	72	70	201	-0.2	247	290
Dominican Republic........	S1	5,697	7,098	8,443	9,884	83	1.7	452	18,680
Ecuador..............	S2	7,920	10,317	12,920	15,518	62	2.2	121	106,888
Egypt................	S4	42,441	56,106	68,360	79,811	15	2.0	178	384,344
El Salvador............	S1	4,566	5,100	6,123	7,293	98	1.8	765	8,000
Equatorial Guinea........	S4	256	368	474	604	164	2.5	44	10,830
Eritrea................	S4	2,555	2,945	4,136	5,709	119	3.4	88	46,842
Estonia...............	S3	1,482	1,573	1,431	1,372	148	-0.9	82	17,413
Ethiopia...............	S4	36,413	48,335	64,117	82,312	18	2.8	148	432,310
Fiji..................	S6	635	738	832	958	156	1.2	118	7,054
Finland...............	S3	4,780	4,986	5,167	5,228	106	0.4	44	117,942
France................	S3	53,870	56,735	59,330	61,069	21	0.4	282	210,668
Gabon................	S4	806	1,069	1,208	1,309	151	1.2	12	99,486
Gambia, The...........	S4	676	962	1,367	1,833	149	3.5	354	3,861
Georgia...............	S5	5,048	5,457	5,020	4,815	108	-0.8	187	26,911
Germany..............	S3	78,298	79,380	82,797	84,616	12	0.4	612	135,236
Ghana................	S4	10,998	15,360	19,534	22,650	50	2.4	220	88,811
Greece...............	S3	9,643	10,158	10,602	10,758	69	0.4	210	50,502
Grenada..............	S2	90	92	89	91	196	-0.3	682	131
Guatemala.............	S1	7,232	9,630	12,640	16,194	63	2.7	302	41,865
Guinea................	S4	4,320	5,936	7,466	9,281	89	2.3	79	94,927
Guinea-Bissau..........	S4	789	996	1,286	1,614	150	2.6	119	10,811
Guyana...............	S2	759	742	697	729	160	-0.6	9	76,004
Haiti.................	S1	5,056	6,028	6,868	7,950	94	1.3	645	10,641
Honduras..............	S1	3,635	4,772	6,250	7,683	97	2.7	145	43,201
Hungary..............	S3	10,711	10,372	10,139	9,831	75	-0.2	284	35,653
Iceland...............	S1	228	255	276	289	177	0.8	7	38,707
India................	S5	690,462	850,558	1,014,004	1,168,205	2	1.8	883	1,147,950
Indonesia..............	S6	154,936	188,651	224,784	259,743	4	1.8	319	705,189
Iran.................	S5	39,274	55,717	65,620	73,772	17	1.6	104	631,660

See footnotes at end of table.

U.S. Census Bureau, Statistical Abstract of the United States: 2000

No. 1352. Population by Country: 1980 to 2010—Continued

[See headnote, page 822]

Country or area	Map refer- ence	Mid-year population (1,000) 1980	1990	2000	2010, proj.	Popu- lation rank, 2000	Annual rate of growth, 1990- 2000 (percent)	Popula- tion per sq. mile, 2000	Area (sq. mile)
Iraq	S5	13,233	18,135	22,676	29,672	44	2.2	131	167,556
Ireland	S3	3,401	3,508	3,797	4,161	123	0.8	141	26,598
Israel	S4	3,737	4,512	5,842	6,645	100	2.6	732	7,849
Italy	S3	56,451	56,758	57,634	57,409	22	0.2	507	113,521
Jamaica	S1	2,229	2,463	2,653	2,851	135	0.7	631	4,181
Japan	S5	116,807	123,537	126,550	127,252	9	0.2	829	152,411
Jordan	S4	2,163	3,262	4,999	6,486	110	4.3	137	35,344
Kazakhstan	S5	14,994	16,708	16,733	17,276	55	-	16	1,049,150
Kenya	S4	16,685	23,767	30,340	33,068	36	2.4	136	219,788
Kiribati	S6	58	71	92	115	195	2.5	325	277
Korea, North	S5	17,114	20,019	21,688	23,753	49	0.8	460	46,490
Korea, South	S5	38,124	42,869	47,471	51,097	25	1.0	1,240	37,911
Kuwait	S5	1,370	2,142	1,974	2,788	144	-0.8	277	6,880
Kyrgyzstan	S5	3,623	4,390	4,685	5,444	113	0.7	60	76,641
Laos	S5	3,293	4,210	5,497	6,993	102	2.7	60	89,112
Latvia	S3	2,525	2,672	2,405	2,252	138	-1.1	97	24,903
Lebanon	S4	3,086	3,147	3,578	4,056	126	1.3	893	3,950
Lesotho	S4	1,344	1,732	2,143	2,339	140	2.1	180	11,718
Liberia	S4	1,892	2,190	3,164	4,073	131	3.7	80	37,189
Libya	S4	3,065	4,140	5,115	6,447	107	2.1	7	679,359
Liechtenstein	S3	25	29	32	35	213	1.1	513	62
Lithuania	S5	3,436	3,702	3,621	3,560	125	-0.2	144	25,174
Luxembourg	S3	364	382	437	493	168	1.4	433	998
Macedonia, The Former Yugoslav Republic of	S3	1,792	1,893	2,041	2,115	141	0.8	205	9,928
Madagascar	S4	8,677	11,522	15,506	20,993	59	3.0	67	224,533
Malawi	S4	6,129	9,219	10,386	11,621	70	1.2	281	36,324
Malaysia	S6	13,764	17,504	21,793	26,144	48	2.2	168	126,853
Maldives	S5	154	216	301	400	175	3.3	2,524	116
Mali	S4	6,731	8,228	10,686	14,349	68	2.6	22	471,042
Malta	S4	364	359	392	420	173	0.9	3,137	124
Marshall Islands	S6	31	46	68	100	203	3.9	938	70
Mauritania	S4	1,550	1,984	2,668	3,561	134	3.0	7	397,838
Mauritius	S4	964	1,074	1,179	1,280	152	0.9	1,638	714
Mexico	S1	68,686	84,446	100,350	114,995	11	1.7	133	742,486
Micronesia, Federated States of	S6	77	109	133	141	191	2.0	485	271
Moldova	S5	3,996	4,398	4,431	4,535	116	0.1	341	13,012
Monaco	S3	27	30	32	33	214	0.6	40,844	1
Mongolia	S5	1,662	2,218	2,616	3,040	136	1.7	4	604,247
Morocco	S4	19,487	24,686	30,122	35,301	37	2.0	172	172,317
Mozambique	S4	12,103	14,276	19,105	20,504	53	2.9	62	302,737
Namibia	S4	975	1,409	1,771	1,908	146	2.3	5	317,873
Nauru	S6	8	9	12	14	222	2.2	1,431	8
Nepal	S5	15,016	19,325	24,702	30,758	41	2.5	457	52,819
Netherlands	S3	14,144	14,952	15,892	16,617	58	0.6	1,206	13,104
New Zealand	S6	3,170	3,360	3,820	4,228	122	1.3	36	103,734
Nicaragua	S2	2,804	3,643	4,813	5,839	112	2.8	101	46,430
Niger	S4	5,629	7,627	10,076	13,140	76	2.8	20	489,073
Nigeria	S4	69,593	92,483	123,338	155,588	10	2.9	341	351,649
Norway	S3	4,086	4,242	4,481	4,677	115	0.5	38	118,865
Oman	S5	1,175	1,773	2,533	3,523	137	3.6	30	82,031
Pakistan	S5	85,219	113,975	141,554	171,373	7	2.2	461	300,664
Palau	S6	13	15	19	22	219	2.1	104	177
Panama	S2	1,956	2,388	2,808	3,150	133	1.6	94	29,340
Papua New Guinea	S6	2,991	3,825	4,927	6,171	111	2.5	28	174,405
Paraguay	S2	3,193	4,236	5,586	7,162	101	2.8	35	153,398
Peru	S2	17,295	21,989	27,013	31,471	38	2.1	54	494,208
Philippines	S6	51,092	65,037	81,160	97,898	13	2.2	690	115,124
Poland	S3	35,578	38,119	38,646	38,691	30	0.1	329	117,571
Portugal	S3	9,778	9,923	10,048	10,183	77	0.1	283	35,382
Qatar	S5	231	481	744	970	158	4.4	169	4,247
Romania	S5	22,130	22,866	22,411	21,930	45	-0.2	253	88,934
Russia	S5	139,045	148,082	146,001	142,328	6	-0.1	22	6,592,817
Rwanda	S4	5,139	6,962	7,229	7,876	92	0.4	743	9,633
Saint Kitts and Nevis	S1	44	41	39	40	211	-0.6	280	139
Saint Lucia	S1	122	140	156	177	188	1.1	654	236
Saint Vincent and the Grenadines	S1	98	107	115	119	193	0.8	878	131
Samoa	S0	155	170	179	176	185	0.5	163	1,100
San Marino	S3	21	23	27	31	216	1.4	1,145	23
Sao Tome and Principe	S4	94	119	160	219	187	2.9	418	371
Saudi Arabia	S4	9,949	15,847	22,024	30,546	47	3.3	26	829,996
Senegal	S4	5,640	7,360	9,987	13,221	78	3.1	131	74,131
Seychelles	S4	66	73	79	83	198	0.8	448	176
Sierra Leone	S4	3,327	4,227	5,233	6,930	105	2.1	184	27,653
Singapore	S6	2,414	3,016	4,152	5,776	118	3.2	16,637	241
Slovakia	S3	4,966	5,263	5,408	5,475	103	0.3	287	18,842
Slovenia	S3	1,833	1,896	1,928	1,947	145	0.2	246	7,819
Solomon Islands	S6	232	335	466	610	165	3.3	43	10,633
Somalia	S4	5,791	6,675	7,253	9,922	91	0.8	30	242,216
South Africa	S4	29,252	38,176	43,421	41,108	26	1.3	92	471,444
Spain	S3	37,488	39,351	39,997	40,157	28	0.2	207	192,819
Sri Lanka	S5	14,900	17,193	19,239	20,832	51	1.1	770	24,996

See footnotes at end of table.

U.S. Census Bureau, Statistical Abstract of the United States: 2000

Country or area	Map refer- ence	Mid-year population (1,000) 1980	1990	2000	2010, proj.	Popu- lation rank, 2000	Annual rate of growth,[1] 1990- 2000 (percent)	Popula- tion per sq. mile, 2000	Area (sq. mile)
Sudan	S4	19,064	26,627	35,080	45,485	33	2.8	38	917,375
Suriname	S2	355	395	431	450	169	0.9	7	62,344
Swaziland	S4	606	852	1,083	1,216	155	2.4	163	6,641
Sweden	S3	8,310	8,559	8,873	8,882	82	0.4	56	158,927
Switzerland	S3	6,385	6,838	7,262	7,385	90	0.6	473	15,355
Syria	S4	8,774	12,436	16,306	20,606	56	2.7	229	71,062
Tajikistan	S5	3,969	5,332	6,441	8,007	95	1.9	117	55,251
Tanzania	S4	18,939	26,224	35,306	44,957	32	3.0	103	342,100
Thailand	S5	47,026	55,052	61,231	66,291	19	1.1	310	197,595
Togo	S4	2,596	3,691	5,019	6,245	109	3.1	239	21,000
Tonga	S0	91	92	102	123	194	1.1	370	277
Trinidad and Tobago	S2	1,091	1,198	1,176	1,115	153	-0.2	593	1,981
Tunisia	S4	6,443	8,207	9,593	10,661	80	1.6	160	59,985
Turkey	S5	45,121	56,085	65,667	73,322	16	1.6	221	297,591
Turkmenistan	S5	2,875	3,668	4,518	5,431	114	2.1	24	188,456
Tuvalu	S6	7	9	11	13	224	1.7	1,080	10
Uganda	S4	12,298	17,186	23,318	31,395	43	3.1	302	77,108
Ukraine	S5	50,047	51,658	49,153	46,193	24	-0.5	211	233,089
United Arab Emirates	S5	1,000	1,951	2,369	2,763	139	1.9	73	32,278
United Kingdom	S3	56,314	57,621	59,508	60,602	20	0.3	638	93,278
United States	S1	227,726	249,948	275,563	300,118	3	1.0	78	3,539,227
Uruguay	S2	2,920	3,106	3,334	3,600	130	0.7	50	67,035
Uzbekistan	S5	16,000	20,624	24,756	29,280	40	1.8	143	172,741
Vanuatu	S6	117	154	190	221	184	2.1	33	5,699
Venezuela	S2	14,768	19,325	23,543	27,134	42	2.0	69	340,560
Vietnam	S5	53,661	66,338	78,774	90,192	14	1.7	627	125,622
Yemen	S5	8,527	12,023	17,479	24,637	54	3.7	86	203,849
Zambia	S4	5,700	7,851	9,582	11,482	81	2.0	34	285,992
Zimbabwe	S4	7,170	10,103	11,343	11,057	66	1.2	76	149,293
OTHER									
Montenegro [4]	S3	560	565	680	713	161	1.9	130	5,333
Serbia	S3	8,955	9,201	9,982	9,954	79	0.8	293	34,116
Taiwan [2]	S5	17,848	20,279	22,191	23,873	46	0.9	1,782	12,456
AREAS OF SPECIAL SOVER- EIGNTY AND DEPENDENCIES									
American Samoa	S0	32	47	65	81	206	3.3	852	77
Anguilla	S1	7	8	12	14	223	3.5	336	35
Aruba	S1	60	67	70	73	202	0.4	933	75
Bermuda	S1	55	58	63	67	208	0.9	3,331	19
Cayman Islands	S1	17	26	35	42	212	2.9	346	100
Cook Islands	S0	18	18	20	22	217	1.1	219	93
Faroe Islands	S3	43	47	45	48	210	-0.5	84	541
French Guiana	S2	68	116	173	214	186	4.0	5	34,421
French Polynesia	S0	151	202	249	291	180	2.1	176	1,413
Gaza Strip [5]	S4	456	643	1,132	1,651	154	5.7	7,696	147
Gibraltar	S3	29	29	28	28	215	-0.5	11,905	2
Greenland	S1	50	56	56	56	209	0.1	(Z)	131,931
Guadeloupe	S1	337	378	426	468	170	1.2	627	680
Guam	S6	107	134	155	184	190	1.4	740	209
Guernsey	S3	53	63	64	66	207	0.2	856	75
Hong Kong	S5	5,063	5,688	7,116	7,981	93	2.2	18,634	382
Jersey	S3	76	84	89	92	197	0.6	1,968	45
Macau	S6	256	352	446	527	167	2.4	72,131	6
Man, Isle of	S3	64	69	73	77	199	0.6	322	227
Martinique	S1	339	374	415	448	171	1.0	1,014	409
Mayotte	S4	52	90	156	231	189	5.5	1,074	145
Montserrat	S1	12	11	6	10	227	-5.2	166	39
Netherlands Antilles	S2	173	189	210	228	182	1.1	566	371
New Caledonia	S6	139	168	202	230	183	1.8	28	7,243
Northern Mariana Islands	S6	17	44	72	99	200	4.9	390	184
Puerto Rico	S1	3,210	3,537	3,916	4,088	120	1.0	1,132	3,459
Reunion	S4	507	597	721	829	159	1.9	747	965
Saint Helena	S4	6	7	7	8	225	0.8	46	158
Saint Pierre and Miquelon	S1	6	6	7	7	226	0.7	74	93
Turks and Caicos Islands	S1	7	12	18	24	220	4.2	105	166
Virgin Islands	S1	100	104	121	133	192	1.5	895	135
Virgin Islands, British	S1	11	16	20	25	218	2.6	351	58
Wallis and Futuna	S6	11	14	15	17	221	1.1	144	106
West Bank [5]	S4	904	1,255	2,020	2,765	142	4.8	928	2,178
Western Sahara	S4	126	191	245	301	181	2.5	2	102,703

- Represents or rounds to zero. X Not applicable. Z Less than one person per square mile. [1] Computed by the exponential method. For explanation of average annual percent change, see Guide to Tabular Presentation. [2] With the establishment of diplomatic relations with China on January 1, 1979, the U.S. Government recognized the People's Republic of China as the sole legal government of China and acknowledged the Chinese position that there is only one China and that Taiwan is part of China. [3] "Congo" is the official short-form name for both the Republic of Congo and the Democratic Republic of the Congo. To distinguish one from the other the U.S. Dept. of State adds the capital in parentheses. This practice is unofficial and provisional. [4] The United States view is that the Socialist Federal Republic of Yugoslavia has dissolved and no successor state represents its continuation. Serbia and Montenegro have asserted the formation of a joint independent state, but this entity has not been recognized by the United States. [5] The Gaza Strip and West Bank are Israeli occupied with interim status subject to Israeli/Palestinian negotiations. The final status is to be determined.

Source: U.S. Census Bureau, "International Data Base" (as of 10 May 2000); <http://www.census.gov/ipc/www/idbnew.html>.

No. 1353. Age Distribution by Country: 2000 and 2010

[In percent. Covers countries with 10 million or more population in 2000]

Country or area	2000 Under 15 yrs. old	2000 65 yrs. old and over	2010, proj. Under 15 yrs. old	2010, proj. 65 yrs. old and over	Country or area	2000 Under 15 yrs. old	2000 65 yrs. old and over	2010, proj. Under 15 yrs. old	2010, proj. 65 yrs. old and over
World	29.9	6.9	30.0	8.6	Korea, North	25.6	6.5	24.6	10.7
Afghanistan	42.4	2.8	53.0	3.9	Korea, South	21.8	7.0	21.6	10.6
Algeria	35.2	4.0	33.5	5.2	Madagascar	45.0	3.3	60.2	3.9
Angola	43.2	2.7	53.4	3.4	Malawi	44.9	2.8	45.0	3.4
Argentina	26.8	10.4	27.3	12.3	Malaysia	34.9	4.1	37.2	6.1
Australia	20.9	12.4	20.4	15.2	Mali	47.2	3.1	62.1	3.8
Bangladesh	36.4	3.3	34.5	4.5	Mexico	33.8	4.3	33.2	6.3
Belarus	18.6	13.7	15.5	13.5	Morocco	35.0	4.6	34.7	6.1
Belgium	17.5	16.8	16.1	18.1	Mozambique	42.9	2.7	43.1	3.5
Brazil	29.1	5.3	26.4	7.5	Nepal	40.7	3.4	46.5	4.8
Burkina Faso	47.6	2.9	59.1	3.5	Netherlands	18.4	13.6	17.6	16.0
Burma	29.8	4.7	26.5	5.5	Niger	48.0	2.3	60.0	3.0
Cambodia	41.9	3.5	47.3	4.5	Nigeria	43.8	2.8	53.5	3.8
Cameroon	42.7	3.3	49.5	4.7	Pakistan	41.0	4.1	41.9	5.3
Canada	19.2	12.7	18.2	15.5	Peru	34.8	4.7	34.3	6.7
Chile	27.6	7.2	25.1	10.2	Philippines	37.2	3.6	40.1	5.2
China [1]	25.4	7.0	22.5	8.9	Poland	19.0	12.3	15.7	13.1
Colombia	32.2	4.7	33.1	6.6	Portugal	17.1	15.4	16.8	17.1
Congo (Kinshasa) [2]	48.3	2.6	63.2	3.2	Romania	18.4	13.3	15.5	14.1
Cote d'Ivoire	46.4	2.2	54.9	3.1	Russia	18.1	12.6	14.9	12.7
Cuba	21.4	9.7	18.1	12.5	Saudi Arabia	42.6	2.6	58.0	5.1
Czech Republic	16.5	13.9	13.2	15.8	South Africa	32.5	4.8	26.8	5.8
Ecuador	36.2	4.4	37.9	6.0	Spain	14.8	16.9	13.9	18.5
Egypt	35.1	3.8	34.9	5.2	Sri Lanka	26.5	6.5	24.4	8.9
Ethiopia	47.0	2.8	60.3	3.6	Sudan	45.0	2.0	52.8	3.5
France	18.8	16.0	18.0	17.3	Syria	40.6	3.2	44.8	4.3
Germany	15.7	16.2	14.3	20.1	Taiwan [1]	21.5	8.6	21.4	11.1
Ghana	41.9	3.4	39.4	4.4	Tanzania	44.9	2.9	54.6	3.9
Greece	15.2	17.3	14.7	19.8	Thailand	23.7	6.4	23.7	9.2
Guatemala	42.4	3.6	50.4	4.9	Turkey	29.1	6.0	26.2	8.1
Hungary	16.9	14.6	13.9	15.6	Uganda	51.1	2.2	66.0	2.6
India	33.6	4.6	33.6	6.1	Ukraine	17.9	13.9	14.4	13.9
Indonesia	30.6	4.5	31.9	6.7	United Kingdom	19.0	15.7	17.1	17.0
Iran	34.4	4.6	28.5	5.3	United States	21.2	12.6	21.6	14.4
Iraq	42.2	3.1	50.3	3.9	Uzbekistan	37.1	4.6	37.5	5.0
Italy	14.2	18.1	13.1	20.5	Venezuela	32.7	4.6	30.7	6.6
Japan	14.8	17.0	14.5	21.9	Vietnam	32.8	5.4	30.9	6.2
Kazakhstan	27.4	7.1	24.9	7.8	Yemen	47.5	3.1	65.0	3.5
Kenya	42.8	2.7	38.0	7.2	Zimbabwe	39.6	3.5	32.6	4.4

[1] See footnote 2, Table 1352.   [2] See footnote 3, Table 1352.
Source: U.S. Census Bureau, "International Data Base" (as of 10 May 2000); <http://www.census.gov/ipc/www/idbnew.html>.

No. 1354. Foreign or Foreign-Born Population and Labor force in Selected OECD Countries: 1987 and 1997

[In Australia, Canada, and the United States the data refer to people present in the country who are foreign born. In the European countries and Japan they generally refer to foreigners and represent the nationalities of residents]

Country	Foreign population [1] Number (1,000) 1987	Number (1,000) 1997	Percent of total population 1987	Percent of total population 1997	Foreign labor force [2] Number (1,000) 1987	Number (1,000) 1997	Percent of total labor force 1987	Percent of total labor force 1997
United States [3]	[4]14,080	[5]24,600	6.2	9.3	[4]7,077	[5]14,300	6.7	10.8
Australia [3]	3,247	[5]3,908	20.8	21.1	1,901	[5]2,239	25.4	24.6
Austria	326	733	4.3	9.1	158	326	5.4	9.9
Belgium	863	903	8.7	8.9	[6]270	333	6.8	7.9
Canada [3]	3,908	[5]4,971	15.4	17.4	2,359	[7]2,681	18.5	18.5
Denmark	136	[5]250	2.7	4.7	63	[5]88	2.1	3.1
France	[8]3,714	[9]3,597	6.8	6.3	1,525	1,570	6.3	6.1
Germany	4,241	7,366	6.9	9.0	1,866	2,522	6.9	9.1
Italy	572	1,241	1.0	2.2	[7]285	[10]332	1.3	1.7
Japan	884	1,483	0.7	1.2	(NA)	[11]660	(NA)	1.0
Luxembourg	103	148	26.8	34.9	[12]64	[12]125	37.6	55.1
Netherlands	592	678	4.0	4.4	176	208	3.0	2.9
Spain	335	610	0.9	1.5	[13]58	176	0.4	1.1
Sweden	401	522	4.8	6.0	215	220	4.9	5.2
Switzerland	979	1,341	14.9	19.0	[14]588	[14]693	16.6	17.5
United Kingdom	1,839	2,066	3.2	3.6	815	949	3.3	3.6

NA Not available.   [1] Data are from population registers except for France (census), Ireland and the United Kingdom (labor force survey), Japan and Switzerland (register of foreigners) and Italy, Portugal, and Spain (residence permits).   [2] Includes unemployed except for Italy, Luxembourg, Netherlands, Norway, and United Kingdom. Data for Austria, Germany, and Luxembourg are from social security registers; for Denmark from the register of population; and for Norway from the register of employees. Data for Italy, Portugal, Spain, and Switzerland are from residence or work permits. Figures for Japan and Netherlands are estimates. Data for other countries are from labor force surveys.   [3] Census data, except 1996 data for United States from Current Population Survey.   [4] 1980 data.   [5] 1996 data.   [6] 1986 data.   [7] 1991 data.   [8] 1982 data.   [9] 1990 data.   [10] 1995 data.   [11] Includes those of Japanese descent, students and illegal workers.   [12] Includes cross-border workers.   [13] 1988 data.   [14] Foreigners with an annual residence permit or a settlement permit who engage in gainful activity. Seasonal and cross-border workers are excluded.
Source: Organization for Economic Cooperation and Development, Paris, France, *Trends in International Migration* (1999 Edition) (copyright).

U.S. Census Bureau, Statistical Abstract of the United States: 2000

No. 1355. Vital Statistics by Country: 2000 and 2010

[Covers countries with 10 million or more population in 2000]

Country or area	Crude birth rate [1]		Crude death rate [2]		Expectation of life at birth (years)		Infant mortality rate [3]		Total fertility rate [4]	
	2000	2010, proj.	2000	2010, proj.	2000	2010, proj.	2000	2010, proj.	2000	2010, proj.
United States	14.2	14.3	8.7	8.6	77.1	78.5	6.8	6.2	2.06	2.12
Afghanistan.	41.8	37.3	18.0	15.2	45.9	49.6	149.3	126.5	5.87	5.09
Algeria	23.1	19.9	5.3	4.9	69.7	72.5	42.0	28.9	2.80	2.17
Angola	46.9	42.9	25.0	21.6	38.3	41.3	195.8	174.7	6.52	5.94
Argentina	18.6	16.6	7.6	7.5	75.1	77.1	18.3	13.3	2.47	2.19
Australia.	13.0	11.7	7.1	7.7	79.8	81.0	5.0	4.4	1.77	1.75
Bangladesh.	25.4	22.1	8.7	7.6	60.2	63.9	71.7	54.3	2.85	2.30
Belarus.	9.3	12.1	14.0	13.5	68.0	70.6	14.6	11.5	1.25	1.57
Belgium	10.9	9.9	10.1	10.7	77.8	79.4	4.8	4.2	1.61	1.63
Brazil.	18.8	15.6	9.4	9.1	62.9	66.3	38.0	27.8	2.13	1.81
Burkina Faso.	45.3	40.9	17.0	16.7	46.7	45.3	108.5	92.1	6.44	5.54
Burma	20.6	17.0	12.4	12.0	54.9	57.7	75.3	59.7	2.37	1.86
Cambodia.	33.5	30.8	10.8	9.5	56.5	59.8	66.8	53.0	4.82	4.00
Cameroon.	36.6	32.0	11.9	12.9	54.8	52.7	70.9	60.4	4.88	4.08
Canada	11.3	10.7	7.4	8.0	79.4	80.7	5.1	4.5	1.60	1.62
Chile	17.2	14.5	5.5	6.0	75.7	77.7	9.6	7.4	2.20	1.90
China [5].	16.1	13.1	6.7	7.1	71.4	73.9	28.9	20.5	1.82	1.82
Colombia	22.9	19.3	5.7	5.6	70.3	73.1	24.7	17.8	2.69	2.44
Congo (Kinshasa) [6].	46.4	42.4	15.4	13.4	48.8	50.7	101.7	83.2	6.92	6.11
Cote d'Ivoire	40.8	36.4	16.6	17.5	45.2	43.4	95.1	80.0	5.80	4.79
Cuba	12.7	11.0	7.3	7.7	76.2	78.1	7.5	6.4	1.60	1.62
Czech Republic	9.1	8.4	10.9	11.2	74.5	76.7	5.6	4.8	1.18	1.23
Ecuador	26.5	21.8	5.5	5.0	71.1	73.8	35.1	25.3	3.18	2.62
Egypt.	25.4	20.9	7.8	6.9	63.3	66.9	62.3	44.8	3.15	2.48
Ethiopia	45.1	41.6	17.6	18.7	45.2	42.1	101.3	87.8	7.07	6.36
France	12.3	11.0	9.1	9.8	78.8	80.2	4.5	4.1	1.75	1.74
Germany	9.4	8.7	10.5	11.0	77.4	79.1	4.8	4.2	1.38	1.44
Ghana	29.8	23.3	10.2	11.5	57.4	55.5	57.4	48.9	3.95	2.81
Greece	9.8	9.2	9.6	10.7	78.4	79.9	6.5	5.3	1.33	1.40
Guatemala	35.1	30.4	6.9	5.8	66.2	69.5	47.0	35.2	4.66	3.91
Hungary	9.3	8.9	13.3	12.9	71.4	74.0	9.2	7.4	1.25	1.29
India	24.8	20.7	8.9	7.9	62.5	66.1	64.9	48.5	3.11	2.55
Indonesia	22.6	18.7	6.3	6.3	68.0	71.1	42.2	30.0	2.61	2.28
Iran	18.3	19.7	5.5	5.3	69.7	72.6	30.0	21.0	2.20	1.96
Iraq	35.0	29.4	6.4	4.9	66.5	70.3	62.5	42.2	4.87	3.76
Italy	9.1	7.5	10.0	11.2	79.0	80.2	5.9	5.1	1.18	1.22
Japan	10.0	8.9	8.2	10.2	80.7	81.7	3.9	3.6	1.41	1.47
Kazakhstan.	16.8	20.9	10.6	10.4	63.2	65.7	59.4	52.5	2.03	2.38
Kenya	29.4	21.9	14.1	17.9	48.0	44.3	68.7	60.4	3.66	2.40
Korea, North	20.4	13.9	6.9	7.5	70.7	73.5	24.3	17.6	2.30	1.90
Korea, South	15.1	12.2	5.9	6.8	74.4	76.6	7.9	6.6	1.72	1.72
Madagascar	42.9	40.5	12.7	10.1	55.0	58.9	85.3	68.7	5.84	5.47
Malawi	38.5	31.8	22.4	24.1	37.6	35.8	122.3	110.0	5.33	3.94
Malaysia.	25.3	22.1	5.3	5.1	70.8	73.6	21.0	15.0	3.29	2.92
Mali	49.2	44.6	19.1	15.3	46.7	50.5	123.3	105.1	6.89	6.06
Mexico.	23.2	19.3	5.1	5.0	71.5	74.1	26.2	18.5	2.67	2.27
Morocco.	24.6	20.6	6.0	5.4	69.1	72.1	49.7	34.7	3.13	2.46
Mozambique	38.0	31.1	23.3	29.9	37.5	31.4	139.9	131.8	4.93	3.85
Nepal.	33.8	28.8	10.4	8.7	57.8	61.7	75.9	58.7	4.68	3.73
Netherlands	12.1	10.1	8.7	8.9	78.3	79.8	4.4	3.9	1.64	1.66
Niger	51.5	45.5	23.2	19.1	41.3	44.6	124.9	111.3	7.16	6.28
Nigeria	40.2	35.3	13.7	15.9	51.6	47.0	74.2	66.1	5.66	4.79
Pakistan.	32.1	24.8	9.5	7.5	61.1	64.8	82.5	63.3	4.56	3.16
Peru	24.5	19.8	5.8	5.6	70.0	72.9	40.6	29.3	3.04	2.41
Philippines	27.9	23.3	6.1	5.5	67.5	70.6	29.5	21.8	3.48	2.89
Poland	10.1	10.9	10.0	10.3	73.2	75.6	9.6	7.6	1.38	1.42
Portugal.	11.5	10.4	10.2	10.6	75.8	77.7	6.1	5.1	1.47	1.52
Romania.	10.8	10.6	12.3	12.4	69.9	72.5	19.8	14.9	1.35	1.42
Russia.	9.0	12.1	13.8	14.5	67.2	68.8	20.3	17.7	1.25	1.56
Saudi Arabia	37.5	37.1	6.0	5.4	67.8	70.9	52.9	37.4	6.30	5.74
South Africa	21.6	17.8	14.7	30.3	51.1	35.5	58.9	67.4	2.47	2.09
Spain	9.2	8.5	9.0	10.1	78.8	80.2	5.0	4.4	1.15	1.22
Sri Lanka	16.8	14.8	6.4	6.6	71.8	74.4	16.5	12.5	1.98	1.78
Sudan	38.6	31.8	10.3	8.3	56.6	60.5	70.2	55.2	5.47	4.21
Syria	31.1	25.2	5.3	4.6	68.5	71.5	34.9	25.0	4.06	3.02
Taiwan [5]	14.4	13.0	5.9	6.8	76.4	78.2	7.1	5.9	1.76	1.75
Tanzania.	40.2	34.9	12.9	13.4	52.3	50.5	81.0	65.8	5.51	4.62
Thailand	16.9	14.2	7.5	7.8	68.6	71.7	31.5	22.2	1.88	1.80
Turkey	18.7	15.6	6.0	6.1	71.0	73.7	48.9	34.3	2.16	1.82
Uganda	48.0	45.2	18.4	15.1	42.9	46.6	93.3	75.4	6.96	6.12
Ukraine	9.0	11.6	16.5	15.7	66.0	68.5	21.7	17.5	1.26	1.58
United Kingdom	11.7	10.6	10.4	10.2	77.7	79.3	5.6	4.8	1.73	1.72
Uzbekistan	26.2	26.1	8.0	7.4	63.7	66.2	72.1	65.6	3.09	2.80
Venezuela.	21.1	17.8	4.9	5.0	73.1	75.5	26.2	18.9	2.51	2.13
Vietnam.	21.6	18.3	6.3	5.8	69.3	72.2	31.1	22.7	2.53	2.10
Yemen	43.4	41.8	9.9	7.4	59.8	63.6	70.3	53.4	7.05	6.23
Zimbabwe.	25.0	23.0	22.4	31.6	37.8	32.5	62.3	65.9	3.34	2.63

[1] Number of births during 1 year per 1,000 persons (based on midyear population). [2] Number of deaths during 1 year per 1,000 persons (based on midyear population). [3] Number of deaths of children under 1 year of age per 1,000 live births in a calendar year. [4] Average number of children that would be born if all women lived to the end of their childbearing years and, at each year of age, they experienced the birth rates occurring in the specified year. [5] See footnote 2, Table 1352. [6] See footnote 3, Table 1352.

Source: U.S. Census Bureau, "International Data Base" (as of 10 May 2000); <http://www.census.gov/ipc/www/idbnew.html>.

No. 1356. Death Rates From Injuries by Mechanism and Country

[Average annual injury deaths per 100,000 population for time period indicated]

Country	Time period	Total	Motor vehicle traffic	Firearm	Poison-ing	Fall	Suffo-cation	Drown-ing	Un-speci-fied	All other injury
United States	1995	56.3	16.2	13.7	6.2	4.3	3.9	1.9	3.0	7.1
Australia	1993-95	39.7	11.0	2.9	6.8	2.9	4.4	2.2	3.5	6.0
Canada	1994-95	44.7	10.5	3.9	6.7	5.0	6.1	2.1	4.9	5.5
Denmark	1994-95	69.9	10.5	2.1	13.4	25.7	7.8	3.0	0.6	6.8
England and Wales	1993-95	30.5	6.2	0.4	6.4	4.4	3.8	1.1	4.9	3.3
France	1992-94	74.7	14.9	6.3	4.6	7.1	14.1	4.2	18.6	4.9
Israel	1993-95	32.9	10.3	2.8	0.7	2.6	3.1	1.2	8.7	3.5
Netherlands	1995	33.2	7.7	0.5	2.4	4.2	4.9	1.6	9.2	2.7
New Zealand	1984-93	55.8	21.3	3.1	5.9	7.0	5.6	3.7	1.4	7.8
Norway	1990-94	57.4	7.2	4.3	6.1	6.4	5.3	4.7	16.4	7.0
Scotland	1986-95	49.9	9.8	0.6	7.9	11.8	5.0	3.2	3.9	7.7

Source: U.S. National Center for Health Statistics, Advance Data, No. 303, October 7, 1998.

No. 1357. Medical Doctors and Inpatient Care—Selected Countries: 1987 and 1997

Country	Medical doctors per 1,000 population		Inpatient care			
			Beds per 1,000 population		Average length of stay (days)	
	1987	1997	1987	1997	1987	1997
United States	2.3	2.7	5.2	[1]4.0	9	[1]8
Australia	[2]2.0	2.5	10.5	[1]8.5	17	[1]15
Austria	2.0	2.9	10.8	9.1	13	10
Belgium	3.0	[3]3.4	8.4	[1]7.2	16	[1]11
Canada	2.1	2.1	6.6	4.2	14	[1]12
Czech Republic	2.7	3.0	11.5	9.0	16	12
Denmark	2.6	[1]2.9	6.3	4.6	9	[1]7
Finland	2.2	3.0	13.6	[1]9.2	19	[1]12
France	2.4	3.0	10.2	8.5	14	11
Germany	2.8	3.4	11.0	9.4	17	13
Greece	3.3	[1]4.0	5.2	[1]5.0	11	[1]8
Hungary	3.0	3.5	9.8	8.3	13	10
Iceland	2.7	3.3	15.8	[4]15.9	20	[4]17
Ireland	1.6	2.1	4.3	3.7	8	[1]7
Italy	4.2	5.8	7.8	[1]6.5	12	[1]9
Japan	[5]1.6	[1]1.8	15.2	16.4	53	43
Korea, South	0.7	1.2	2.8	4.8	12	13
Luxembourg	1.8	2.4	12.6	8.1	19	[1]15
Mexico	1.0	1.3	0.8	1.1	4	4
Netherlands	2.4	[6]2.6	11.8	11.5	35	32
New Zealand	1.8	2.2	9.2	6.1	10	7
Norway	2.5	2.5	15.9	14.7	[7]11	[1]10
Poland	2.1	[1]2.4	5.7	5.4	[7]13	10
Portugal	2.6	3.1	4.6	4.1	12	9
Spain	3.5	[1]4.2	4.4	[3]3.9	13	[1]11
Sweden	2.8	[1]3.1	13.7	5.2	20	[1]8
Switzerland	2.8	[1]3.2	[5]20.0	[6]20.8	25	(NA)
Turkey	0.7	[1]1.1	2.1	2.5	7	6
United Kingdom	1.4	[1]1.7	6.8	4.3	15	[1]10

NA Not available.   [1] 1996 data.   [2] 1986 data.   [3] 1995 data.   [4] 1992 data.   [5] 1988 data.   [6] 1991 data.   [7] 1990 data.

Source: Organization for Economic Cooperation and Development, Paris, France, OECD Health Data 99 (copyright).

Comparative International Statistics   827

No. 1358. Health Expenditures as Percent of GDP by Country: 1980 to 1998

[In percent. G.D.P.=gross domestic product; for explanation, see text, Section 14, Income]

Country	Total health expenditures					Public health expenditures				
	1980	1990	1995	1997	1998	1980	1990	1995	1997	1998
United States	9.1	12.6	14.1	13.9	14.0	3.9	5.1	6.5	6.5	6.5
Australia.	7.3	8.2	8.4	8.4	(NA)	4.6	5.5	5.7	5.6	(NA)
Austria	7.7	7.2	8.0	8.3	(NA)	5.3	5.3	5.9	6.0	(NA)
Belgium	6.5	7.5	7.9	7.6	(NA)	5.4	6.7	6.9	6.7	(NA)
Canada	7.2	9.2	9.4	9.2	9.3	5.4	6.8	6.7	6.4	6.5
Czech Republic	3.8	5.4	7.5	7.2	7.2	3.7	5.2	6.9	6.6	6.6
Denmark.	9.3	8.3	8.1	8.0	8.0	8.1	7.0	6.8	6.7	6.7
Finland.	6.5	8.0	7.7	7.4	(NA)	5.1	6.5	5.8	5.7	(NA)
France	7.6	8.9	9.8	9.6	9.6	6.0	6.6	7.3	7.1	7.1
Germany [1]	8.8	8.7	10.4	10.7	10.6	6.9	6.7	8.2	8.3	8.1
Greece.	6.6	7.6	8.4	8.6	(NA)	3.7	4.8	4.9	5.0	(NA)
Hungary	(NA)	6.1	7.0	6.5	(NA)	(NA)	(NA)	4.9	4.5	(NA)
Iceland.	6.2	7.9	8.2	7.9	8.3	5.5	6.9	6.9	6.7	7.0
Ireland	8.7	6.7	7.0	6.3	6.1	7.1	4.9	5.2	4.9	4.8
Italy	7.0	8.1	7.7	7.6	(NA)	5.6	6.3	5.4	5.3	(NA)
Japan	6.5	6.1	7.2	7.2	7.4	4.6	4.7	5.6	5.7	5.8
Korea, South	3.7	5.2	5.4	6.0	(NA)	1.0	2.1	2.3	2.7	(NA)
Luxembourg	6.2	6.6	6.7	7.0	(NA)	5.7	6.1	6.2	6.4	(NA)
Mexico	(NA)	3.6	4.9	4.7	(NA)	(NA)	2.1	2.8	2.8	(NA)
Netherlands	7.9	8.3	8.8	8.5	(NA)	5.9	6.1	6.7	6.2	(NA)
New Zealand.	6.0	7.0	7.3	7.6	8.0	5.3	5.8	5.6	5.9	6.2
Norway.	7.0	7.8	8.0	7.5	(NA)	5.9	6.5	6.7	6.2	(NA)
Poland	(NA)	4.4	4.5	5.2	(NA)	(NA)	(NA)	4.7	4.7	(NA)
Portugal	5.8	6.4	7.8	7.9	(NA)	3.7	4.2	4.7	4.7	(NA)
Spain	5.6	6.9	7.3	7.4	(NA)	4.5	5.4	5.7	5.6	(NA)
Sweden	9.4	8.8	8.5	8.6	(NA)	8.7	7.9	7.1	7.2	(NA)
Switzerland.	6.9	8.3	9.6	10.0	(NA)	4.6	5.7	7.0	7.0	(NA)
Turkey	3.3	3.6	3.3	4.0	(NA)	0.9	2.2	2.4	2.9	(NA)
United Kingdom	5.6	6.0	6.9	6.8	6.9	5.0	5.1	5.8	5.8	5.8

NA Not available.   [1] Data prior to 1991 are for former West Germany.

Source: Organization for Economic Cooperation and Development, Paris, France, *OECD Health Data 99* (copyright).

No. 1359. Average Temperatures and Precipitation—Selected International Cities

[In degrees Fahrenheit, except as noted. Data are generally based on a standard 30-year period; for details, see source. For data on U.S. cities, see Tables 408-411]

City	January					July				
	Average high	Average low	Warmest	Coldest	Average precipitation (inches)	Average high	Average low	Warmest	Coldest	Average precipitation (inches)
Amsterdam, Netherlands	41	34	57	3	3.1	69	55	90	39	2.9
Athens, Greece.	55	44	70	28	1.9	89	73	108	61	0.2
Baghdad, Iraq.	58	38	75	25	1.1	110	78	122	61	-
Bangkok, Thailand.	89	71	95	54	0.4	90	78	99	72	6.2
Beijing, China.	34	17	54	1	0.2	86	72	104	63	8.8
Berlin, Germany	35	26	58	-11	(NA)	73	56	95	41	(NA)
Bogota, Colombia	66	43	84	27	1.9	64	47	82	32	1.8
Brasilia, Brazil	81	64	95	54	(NA)	79	52	97	37	(NA)
Buenos Aires, Argentina	85	64	104	44	4.2	58	41	88	23	2.3
Cairo, Egypt.	65	49	86	32	0.2	93	72	108	63	-
Calcutta, India	77	57	91	48	0.3	89	80	100	72	13.1
Frankfurt, Germany	38	30	56	-4	1.8	75	57	97	38	2.4
Geneva, Switzerland	39	29	57	-2	2.2	77	56	96	41	2.8
Hong Kong, China.	67	58	79	43	1.1	89	81	97	70	14.3
Istanbul, Turkey	46	37	64	16	3.7	82	66	100	50	0.7
Jakarta, Indonesia	83	75	92	72	(NA)	88	74	92	67	(NA)
Karachi, Pakistan	76	55	93	39	0.3	89	83	109	68	3.5
Lagos, Nigeria	82	79	93	64	(NA)	79	76	88	70	(NA)
London, England	45	36	61	15	2.4	72	56	93	45	1.8
Madrid, Spain.	51	32	68	14	1.8	90	61	104	46	0.4
Manila, Philippines	86	71	95	61	0.8	88	76	99	70	15.9
Mexico City, Mexico.	70	45	86	26	0.3	74	56	86	37	5.1
Montreal, Canada	21	7	52	-31	2.8	79	61	93	43	3.4
Moscow, Russia	21	11	46	-33	1.4	71	55	95	41	3.2
Nairobi, Kenya	77	58	88	45	1.8	71	54	85	43	0.5
New Delhi, India	68	48	85	32	0.9	93	81	111	70	7.9
Paris, France	43	34	59	1	(NA)	75	58	95	41	(NA)
Rio De Janeiro, Brazil	91	74	109	64	5.3	81	64	102	52	1.8
Rome, Italy	55	39	64	19	3.2	83	66	100	55	0.6
Seoul, Korea	33	21	55	-1	(NA)	82	71	97	55	(NA)
Singapore, Singapore	85	73	100	66	9.4	86	76	99	70	5.9
Sydney, Australia	79	65	109	49	4.0	62	44	80	32	2.5
Tel Aviv, Israel	62	46	84	32	(NA)	87	69	100	50	(NA)
Tokyo, Japan	48	35	66	25	2.0	82	71	95	55	5.3
Toronto, Canada	28	15	59	-24	1.9	79	60	99	45	2.8

- Represents zero.   NA Not available.

Source: U.S. National Oceanic and Atmospheric Administration, *Climates of the World*.

No. 1360. Selected Environmental Data—OECD Countries

[Figures are for 1997 or the latest available year. Varying definitions and survey methods can limit the comparability across countries]

Country	Air pollutant emissions per capita			Waste generated			
						Nuclear [3]	
	Sulfur oxides (kilograms)	Nitrogen oxides (kilograms)	Carbon dioxide [1] (tons)	Municipal [2] (kilograms per capita)	Amount (tons)	Per unit of energy (tons per Mtoe [4])	Per 1,000 persons (kilograms)
United States	69.0	79.9	20.4	720	2,100	1.0	7.8
Australia.	100.7	118.5	16.6	690	-	-	-
Austria	7.1	21.2	7.9	510	-	-	-
Belgium	23.7	32.9	12.0	480	80	1.4	7.9
Canada	88.9	67.1	15.8	490	1,340	5.6	44.2
Czech Republic	68.0	41.1	11.7	310	45	1.1	4.4
Denmark.	20.7	47.0	11.8	560	-	-	-
Finland.	19.5	50.6	12.5	410	71	2.1	13.8
France	16.2	29.1	6.2	590	1,130	4.6	19.3
Germany	17.9	22.0	10.8	460	450	1.3	5.5
Greece.	48.2	35.1	7.7	370	-	-	-
Hungary	64.5	19.4	5.7	500	55	2.2	5.4
Iceland	32.2	105.9	8.9	560	-	-	-
Ireland	45.1	33.9	10.3	560	-	-	-
Italy	23.1	30.9	7.4	460	-	-	-
Japan	7.3	11.3	9.3	400	964	1.9	7.6
Korea, South.	32.9	27.6	9.2	400	364	2.1	7.9
Luxembourg	14.3	47.5	20.5	460	-	-	-
Mexico.	23.2	16.4	3.5	300	42	0.3	0.4
Netherlands	8.0	28.5	11.8	560	12	0.2	0.8
New Zealand.	12.5	46.9	9.0	[5]350	-	-	-
Norway.	6.9	50.5	7.8	630	-	-	-
Poland	61.3	29.9	9.1	320	-	-	-
Portugal	36.2	37.6	5.2	380	-	-	-
Spain.	49.1	31.7	6.4	390	192	1.8	4.8
Sweden	10.3	38.1	6.0	360	238	4.6	26.9
Switzerland	4.5	18.0	6.3	600	64	2.4	8.9
Turkey	29.8	14.5	2.9	330	-	-	-
United Kingdom	34.5	35.0	9.4	480	820	3.6	13.9

- Represents zero. [1] Carbon dioxide from energy use only. Excludes international marine bunkers. [2] Municipal waste is that which is collected and treated by or for municipalities: household waste and bulky waste as well as comparable waste from small communities or industrial enterprises; and market and garden residue. [3] Wastes from spent fuel arising in nuclear power plants, measured in terms of heavy metal. [4] Mtoe=million tons of oil equivalent (primary energy supply). [5] Household waste only.

Source: Organization for Economic Cooperation and Development, Paris, France, OECD Environmental Data Compendium 1999.

No. 1361. Carbon Dioxide Emissions From Consumption of Fossil Fuels by Country, 1990 to 1998, and Projections, 2005 and 2010

[In million metric tons of carbon (5,832 represents 5,832,000,000). Includes carbon dioxide emissions from the consumption of petroleum, natural gas, and coal, and the flaring of natural gas]

Country	1990	1993	1994	1995	1996	1997	1998, prel.	2005, proj.	2010, proj.
World, total.	5,832	5,873	5,907	5,987	6,158	6,163	6,124	7,308	8,146
Australia.	71	77	77	80	80	78	83	(NA)	(NA)
Brazil.	58	64	69	72	75	79	85	104	136
Canada	129	129	134	134	139	136	138	155	160
China [1]	610	712	768	788	794	785	740	1,186	1,457
France	101	98	95	97	104	102	107	111	114
Germany	(X)	239	234	233	240	233	228	248	257
India	154	186	195	226	235	245	253	328	385
Indonesia	39	54	56	58	65	71	68	(NA)	(NA)
Iran	55	65	68	71	71	79	79	(NA)	(NA)
Italy	111	108	107	116	116	116	120	123	128
Japan	266	280	295	293	304	296	288	318	331
Korea, South.	60	84	93	101	109	120	108	136	157
Mexico.	80	85	90	88	93	94	95	121	143
Netherlands	56	60	60	60	62	64	65	68	69
Poland.	87	91	86	81	92	86	77	(NA)	(NA)
Russia	(X)	536	477	443	442	411	405	(NA)	(NA)
Saudi Arabia	57	65	67	68	71	62	64	(NA)	(NA)
South Africa	80	90	94	94	96	100	102	(NA)	(NA)
Spain	60	62	64	66	63	71	75	(NA)	(NA)
Taiwan [1]	33	43	44	49	53	58	59	(NA)	(NA)
Thailand	23	32	35	43	46	47	43	(NA)	(NA)
Turkey	36	39	38	41	44	47	47	53	61
Ukraine	(X)	145	121	120	106	105	100	(NA)	(NA)
United Kingdom	163	157	155	152	159	150	147	167	175
United States	1,351	1,386	1,407	1,421	1,470	1,489	1,495	1,683	1,787

NA Not available. X Not applicable. [1] See footnote 2. Table 1352.

Source: U.S. Energy Information Administration, International Energy Annual, 1998, and International Energy Outlook, 2000.

Comparative International Statistics 829

No. 1362. Educational Attainment by Country: 1998

[**Percent distribution**. Persons 25 to 64 years old]

Country	Total	Preprimary and primary education	Lower secondary education	Upper secondary education	Post-secondary nontertiary education [1]	Non-university tertiary education [2]	University education
United States ...	100	5	9	[3]52	[3]	8	27
Australia	100	[4]44	[4]	[3]31	[3]	9	17
Austria [5]	100	[4]27	[4]	57	6	4	6
Belgium	100	20	23	[3]31	[3]	13	12
Canada	100	[4]20	[4]	28	13	20	19
Czech Republic	100	[4]15	[4]	[3]75	[3]	(X)	10
Denmark	100	(Z)	21	[3]54	[3]	20	5
Finland [5]	100	[4]32	[4]	39	(X)	17	13
France	100	21	18	40	(Z)	10	11
Germany	100	2	14	56	4	9	14
Greece [5]	100	45	9	25	4	4	11
Hungary	100	4	32	[3]50	[3]	(NA)	13
Iceland	100	2	36	30	11	5	16
Ireland	100	23	26	[6]30	[6]	[6]10	11
Italy	100	25	31	31	5	[7]	[7]9
Japan	100	[4]20	[4]	50	(NA)	13	18
Korea, South	100	19	[8]16	43	(X)	5	17
Mexico	100	59	[8]20	[8]8	(X)	1	12
Netherlands	100	12	23	40	[7]	[7]	[7]24
New Zealand	100	[4]27	[4]	39	7	14	13
Norway [5]	100	(Z)	17	57	1	2	24
Poland	100	[4]22	[4]	64	3	[7]	[7]11
Portugal	100	68	12	[3]11	[3]	3	7
Spain	100	45	22	13	(NA)	6	14
Sweden	100	12	12	48	[9]	[9]15	13
Switzerland	100	[4]19	[4]	[3]58	[3]	9	14
Turkey	100	74	8	11	(X)	[7]	[7]6
United Kingdom	100	[4]19	[4]	57	(NA)	8	15

NA Not available. X Not applicable. Z Less than 0.5 percent. [1] This level straddles the boundary between upper secondary and post-secondary education from an international point of view, even though it might clearly be considered upper secondary or post-secondary in a national context. Although the content may not be significantly more advanced than upper secondary programs, it serves to broaden the knowledge of participants who have already gained an upper secondary qualification. [2] These programs focus on practical, technical, or occupational skills for direct entry into the labor market, although some theoretical foundations may be covered. They have a minimum duration of two years full-time equivalent at the tertiary level. [3] Post-secondary nontertiary included in upper secondary. [4] Lower secondary included in preprimary and primary education. [5] Data for 1997. [6] Post-secondary nontertiary included in upper secondary and nonuniversity tertiary. [7] Included in university-level. [8] Part of upper secondary included in lower secondary. [9] Post-secondary nontertiary included in nonuniversity tertiary.

Source: Organization for Economic Cooperation and Development, Paris, France, *Education at a Glance*, annual, (copyright).

No. 1363. Number of Foreign Students as Percent of Total University Enrollment in Selected OECD Countries: 1998

[**In percent**. Covers students enrolled in a program at the university level or its equivalent. Example of data: 0.15 percent of United States students are Canadian citizens]

Country of origin	Country of destination							
	United States	Australia	Austria	Denmark	France	Germany	Switzerland	United Kingdom
Total [1]	3.24	12.59	11.49	6.01	7.30	8.16	15.95	10.81
United States	(X)	0.23	0.17	0.13	0.11	0.19	0.22	0.50
Australia	0.02	(X)	0.02	0.02	-	0.01	0.03	0.06
Canada	0.15	0.17	0.02	0.03	0.05	0.02	0.09	0.15
France	0.04	0.03	0.15	0.06	(X)	0.30	1.68	0.65
Germany	0.06	0.15	2.19	0.32	0.26	(X)	3.58	0.67
Greece	0.02	0.01	0.14	0.01	0.13	0.40	0.20	1.30
Italy	0.02	0.03	2.68	0.04	0.18	0.33	2.49	0.27
Japan	0.32	0.33	0.12	0.02	0.06	0.09	0.06	0.28
Korea, South	0.29	0.30	0.13	-	0.07	0.24	0.03	0.12
Mexico	0.06	0.01	0.02	0.01	0.03	0.02	0.04	0.05
Norway	0.02	0.07	0.04	0.63	0.02	0.05	0.08	0.19
Spain	0.03	0.01	0.12	0.04	0.17	0.25	0.96	0.35
Sweden	0.03	0.06	0.11	0.24	0.04	0.05	0.12	0.15
Turkey	0.06	0.02	0.47	0.13	0.10	1.24	0.30	0.09
United Kingdom	0.05	0.82	0.08	0.20	0.17	0.13	0.20	(X)
Africa	0.16	0.25	0.41	0.14	3.14	0.76	0.93	0.76
Asia	2.08	8.62	1.59	0.70	0.81	2.91	1.06	3.61
Europe	0.48	1.17	8.88	2.55	1.84	3.93	11.95	5.39
North America	0.33	0.30	0.24	0.17	0.23	0.26	0.40	0.80
Oceania	0.03	0.67	0.02	0.03	0.01	0.01	0.03	0.09
South America	0.17	0.06	0.13	0.07	0.17	0.19	0.47	0.13
Not specified	-	1.51	0.22	2.36	1.10	0.09	1.10	0.03

- Represents or rounds to zero. X Not applicable. [1] Includes other countries, not shown separately.

Source: Organization for Economic Cooperation and Development, Paris, France, *Education at a Glance*, annual, (copyright).

No. 1364. Gross National Product by Country: 1998

[**46 represents $46,000,000,000.** Gross national product calculated using the World Bank Atlas method; for details, see source. Growth rates are calculated from data in constant prices and national currency units. Economies with missing data are included in the ranking process at their approximate level, so that the relative order of other economies remains consistent. In 1998, Luxembourg was judged to have the highest GNP per capita. Minus sign (-) indicates decrease]

Country	Gross national product			Gross national product per capita			GNP on purchasing power parity basis		
			Average annual growth, 1997-98 (percent)			Average annual growth, 1997-98 (percent)		Per capita	
	Total (bil. dol.)	Rank		Amount (dol.)	Rank		Total (bil. dol.)	Amount (dol.)	Rank
Algeria	46	51	5.8	1,550	113	3.6	137	4,595	101
Argentina	290	17	3.9	8,030	55	2.6	424	11,728	53
Australia	387	14	5.6	20,640	23	4.4	409	21,795	20
Austria	217	21	3.3	26,830	12	3.2	187	23,145	15
Bangladesh.	44	53	5.9	350	173	4.2	177	1,407	168
Belarus	22	62	10.5	2,180	99	10.8	65	6,314	81
Belgium	259	19	3.0	25,380	15	2.8	241	23,622	13
Bolivia	8	93	5.1	1,010	134	2.7	18	2,205	146
Brazil	768	8	-	4,630	68	-1.4	1,070	6,460	80
Bulgaria	10	84	4.4	1,220	125	5.1	39	4,683	100
Canada	581	9	2.9	19,170	26	2.0	691	22,814	17
Chile	74	42	8.7	4,990	66	7.2	126	8,507	68
China [1]	924	7	7.4	750	145	6.4	3,779	3,051	132
Colombia	101	35	-0.6	2,470	93	-2.4	239	5,861	84
Congo (Kinshasa) [2] .	5	104	4.0	110	205	0.7	35	733	195
Costa Rica	10	85	4.7	2,770	89	2.9	20	5,812	85
Croatia	21	64	1.8	4,620	69	2.6	30	6,698	78
Czech Republic	53	48	-2.2	5,150	65	-2.1	126	12,197	52
Denmark.	175	23	2.7	33,040	6	2.4	126	23,855	12
Egypt	79	40	6.3	1,290	121	4.5	193	3,146	129
Ethiopia	6	101	-1.8	100	206	-4.2	35	566	202
Finland.	125	31	6.7	24,280	19	6.5	106	20,641	24
France	[3]1,465	4	3.2	[3]24,210	20	2.8	1,248	21,214	22
Germany	2,180	3	2.8	26,570	13	2.8	1,807	22,026	19
Ghana	7	96	4.6	390	164	1.9	32	1,735	157
Greece.	123	32	3.3	11,740	46	3.1	147	13,994	49
Guatemala	18	71	5.5	1,640	111	2.8	38	3,474	122
Honduras	5	116	4.0	740	146	1.1	14	2,338	142
Hong Kong	[4]158	24	-5.1	[4]23,660	21	-7.8	139	20,763	23
Hungary	46	52	4.2	4,510	71	4.6	99	9,832	63
India	427	11	6.2	440	161	4.3	2,018	2,060	151
Indonesia	131	30	-16.7	640	149	-18.0	490	2,407	141
Iran	102	34	1.5	1,650	110	-0.2	317	5,121	95
Ireland	69	43	9.2	18,710	27	7.9	67	17,991	33
Israel	97	36	3.4	16,180	32	1.2	101	16,861	38
Italy	1,157	6	1.4	20,090	25	1.3	1,173	20,365	25
Japan	4,089	2	-2.7	32,350	7	-2.9	2,982	23,592	14
Kazakhstan.	21	63	-2.2	1,340	120	-1.2	67	4,317	105
Kenya	10	82	2.7	350	173	0.3	28	964	186
Korea South	399	12	-6.6	8,600	51	-7.5	616	13,286	51
Lebanon	15	76	3.0	3,560	80	1.4	17	4,144	111
Malaysia.	81	39	-5.8	3,670	78	-8.0	171	7,699	72
Mexico	368	15	4.7	3,840	75	3.0	714	7,450	75
Morocco	34	56	7.0	1,240	124	5.3	89	3,188	128
Netherlands	389	13	3.3	24,780	17	2.7	350	22,325	18
New Zealand.	55	46	-0.6	14,600	36	-1.5	61	16,084	41
Nigeria	36	55	1.1	300	181	-1.5	89	740	194
Norway.	152	25	2.3	34,310	4	1.7	116	26,196	7
Pakistan	62	44	3.0	470	158	0.5	217	1,652	161
Peru	61	45	-1.6	2,440	94	-3.3	104	4,180	110
Philippines	79	41	0.1	1,050	132	-2.1	280	3,725	118
Poland	151	26	4.4	3,910	74	4.4	292	7,543	74
Portugal	106	33	3.9	10,670	48	3.7	145	14,569	46
Romania.	31	59	-8.3	1,360	119	-8.1	125	5,572	90
Russia	332	16	-6.6	2,260	97	-6.4	907	6,180	83
Saudi Arabia	143	27	2.3	6,910	60	-1.0	218	10,498	60
Singapore	96	37	1.5	30,170	9	-0.4	80	25,295	8
South Africa	137	28	0.5	3,310	83	-1.3	343	8,296	69
Spain	555	10	3.7	14,100	39	3.6	628	15,960	43
Sri Lanka	15	75	4.6	810	139	3.3	55	2,945	134
Sudan	8	91	5.0	290	183	2.7	35	1,240	176
Sweden	227	20	2.8	25,580	14	2.8	176	19,848	27
Switzerland	284	18	1.8	39,980	3	1.5	191	26,876	6
Syria	16	74	0.2	1,020	133	-2.3	41	2,702	138
Tanzania.	[5]7	98	6.5	[5]220	194	3.8	16	483	205
Thailand.	132	29	-7.7	2,160	100	-8.6	338	5,524	92
Turkey	201	22	3.9	3,160	85	2.3	419	6,594	79
Uganda	7	99	5.7	310	180	2.8	22	1,072	180
Ukraine	49	49	-2.4	980	135	-1.6	157	3,130	131
United Kingdom	1,264	5	2.1	21,410	22	2.0	1,200	20,314	26
United States	7,903	1	2.5	29,240	10	1.5	7,904	29,240	4
Uruguay	20	65	3.9	6,070	64	3.2	28	8,541	67
Venezuela.	82	38	-0.4	3,530	81	-2.4	133	5,706	88
Vietnam	27	60	5.8	350	173	4.3	129	1,689	159

- Represents or rounds to zero.   [1] See footnote 2, Table 1352.   [2] See footnote 3, Table 1352.   [3] Includes the overseas department of French Guiana, Guadeloupe, Martinique, and Reunion.   [4] Data refer to gross domestic product.   [5] Data refer to mainland Tanzania only.

Source: The World Bank, Washington, DC, *World Development Indicators CD-ROM*, annual (copyright).

No. 1365. Gross Domestic Product (GDP) by Country: 1995 to 1999

[23,725 represents $23,725,000,000,000. Except as noted, based on the System of National Accounts, 1993; for details, see source]

Country	Current price levels and exchange rates [1] (bil. dol.)					Constant (1995) price levels and exchange rates [1] (bil. dol.)					GDP per capita, 1998 based on current	
	1995	1996	1997	1998	1999	1995	1996	1997	1998	1999	Exchange rates	PPPs [2]
OECD, total	23,725	23,947	23,530	23,660	24,880	23,725	24,485	25,252	25,753	26,449	21,436	21,543
OECD Europe [3]	9,458	9,659	9,092	9,391	9,358	9,458	9,624	9,876	10,150	10,374	18,332	18,203
European Union [3]	8,605	8,771	8,242	8,511	8,496	8,605	8,740	8,954	9,198	9,417	22,604	21,324
Australia	377	418	420	373	404	377	391	409	428	447	19,900	24,192
Austria	236	232	207	211	208	236	240	243	250	255	26,108	23,900
Belgium	276	268	244	250	248	276	279	288	296	304	24,541	23,677
Canada	579	602	624	598	635	579	588	614	634	663	19,779	25,179
Czech Republic	52	58	53	56	54	52	54	54	53	53	5,479	12,997
Denmark	180	183	168	174	174	180	185	191	195	199	32,752	25,459
Finland [4]	129	128	122	129	130	129	135	143	151	157	25,099	21,833
France [4]	1,553	1,554	1,406	1,447	1,432	1,553	1,570	1,600	1,649	1,698	23,954	21,132
Germany	2,458	2,383	2,115	2,151	2,112	2,458	2,477	2,513	2,567	2,604	26,217	23,010
Greece	118	124	121	122	125	118	120	125	129	133	11,555	14,171
Hungary [5]	45	45	46	47	49	45	45	47	50	52	4,652	10,470
Iceland	7	7		8	9	7	7	8	8	9	30,198	25,685
Ireland	66	73	80	86	93	66	72	79	86	94	23,284	23,194
Italy [5]	1,097	1,233	1,165	1,191	1,171	1,097	1,109	1,129	1,147	1,163	20,680	21,531
Japan	5,137	4,599	4,212	3,808	4,347	5,137	5,397	5,483	5,345	5,356	30,107	24,075
Korea, South	489	520	477	317	407	489	522	549	512	566	6,829	14,336
Luxembourg	18	18	18	18	19	18	19	20	21	23	42,732	37,491
Mexico	286	332	401	421	483	286	301	321	337	350	4,406	7,986
Netherlands	415	412	377	391	394	415	427	444	460	476	24,921	24,141
New Zealand [5]	60	65	65	53	54	60	62	63	63	66	13,936	17,597
Norway	147	158	155	147	153	147	154	161	164	166	33,174	27,391
Poland	126	143	143	158	154	126	134	143	156	162	4,089	8,014
Portugal	107	113	106	111	112	107	111	115	119	123	11,122	15,891
Spain	584	609	559	582	596	584	598	621	645	670	14,786	17,223
Sweden	240	262	238	238	239	240	243	248	255	265	26,863	21,799
Switzerland [5]	307	296	256	262	259	307	308	313	320	325	36,762	27,091
Turkey [5]	169	182	190	200	185	169	181	195	201	191	3,092	6,538
United Kingdom	1,127	1,180	1,319	1,410	1,442	1,127	1,156	1,196	1,228	1,254	23,810	21,673
United States	**7,338**	**7,751**	**8,239**	**8,699**	**9,192**	**7,338**	**7,600**	**7,937**	**8,284**	**8,628**	**32,184**	**32,184**

[1] Based on constant (1995) price data converted to U.S. dollars using 1995 exchange rates. [2] The goods and services produced in different countries should be valued consistently if the differences observed are meant to reflect real differences in the volumes of goods and services produced. The use of purchasing power parities (PPP) instead of exchange rates is intended to achieve this objective. PPP's show how many units of currency are needed in one country to buy the same amount of goods and services which one unit of currency will buy in the other country. See text of this section. [3] For countries, see text of this section. [4] Includes overseas departments. [5] Based on System of National Accounts, 1968.

Source: Organization for Economic Cooperation and Development, Paris, France, "OECD Statistics GDP"; published September 2000; <http://www.oecd.org/std/gdp.htm> (copyright) and "GDP per capita based on exchange rates and on PPP"; published September 2000; <http://www.oecd.org/std/gdpperca.htm> (copyright).

No. 1366. International Economic Composite Indexes by Country: 1980 to 1999

[**Average annual percent change from previous year**; derived from indexes with base 1990=100. The coincident index changes are for calendar years and the leading index changes are for years ending June 30 because they lead the coincident indexes by about 6 months, on average. The G-7 countries are United States, Canada, France, Germany, Italy, United Kingdom, and Japan. Minus sign (-) indicates decrease]

Country	1980	1985	1990	1991	1992	1993	1994	1995	1996	1997	1998	1999
LEADING INDEX												
Total, 13 countries	2.9	2.9	2.7	-1.5	-1.1	-0.9	3.9	6.4	3.0	3.6	1.9	1.5
12 countries, excluding U.S. .	7.7	5.5	4.4	-1.6	-3.2	-3.3	3.7	7.2	4.3	3.9	1.0	1.4
G-7 countries	2.9	2.0	2.6	-1.7	-1.6	-1.4	3.5	6.3	2.9	3.6	1.7	1.1
North America............	-2.7	-0.4	-0.5	-1.7	2.3	3.2	4.5	5.3	1.0	3.3	3.3	1.7
United States	-3.1	-0.7	-0.4	-1.4	2.6	3.1	4.2	5.1	1.0	3.2	3.4	1.7
Canada	2.0	3.2	-2.6	-5.0	-1.1	4.5	8.5	6.7	1.5	4.2	2.9	2.2
Four European countries	3.1	2.8	1.5	0.2	0.3	-1.3	4.1	5.0	-0.3	2.4	5.0	1.5
France.................	3.2	0.8	-1.0	0.6	2.7	-0.3	4.7	3.3	-1.2	3.2	3.1	0.8
Germany	2.0	2.1	4.4	3.6	-1.1	-4.5	2.0	4.1	-1.0	4.0	4.6	2.0
Italy..................	6.1	6.5	1.0	-4.5	-0.9	-1.0	7.1	9.5	-1.0	-0.9	11.2	1.4
United Kingdom...........	2.5	3.5	0.4	-1.5	0.8	2.8	4.1	4.5	2.4	2.1	2.6	1.4
Seven Pacific region countries.....	16.3	9.4	8.0	-2.9	-6.6	-6.0	2.9	9.7	9.2	5.3	-2.9	1.2
Australia................	5.7	7.6	0.3	-4.0	4.9	5.9	7.1	3.9	2.3	2.8	6.9	4.5
Taiwan [1]...............	2.6	5.6	6.1	-2.7	8.4	4.0	8.1	8.3	2.4	9.3	8.5	3.8
Thailand................	4.0	7.1	14.4	6.5	7.5	9.2	12.0	11.6	7.5	2.4	-0.1	4.4
Japan	19.8	10.3	8.7	-3.8	-9.7	-9.3	0.6	10.2	11.0	5.5	-5.0	-0.4
Korea, South..............	0.4	6.9	7.1	6.2	7.0	6.3	13.1	12.0	6.7	4.5	0.2	10.2
Malaysia................	4.9	-1.0	2.0	3.0	-1.2	0.7	7.6	4.1	0.7	2.9	-4.0	-4.6
New Zealand..............	2.3	6.0	1.8	-2.3	3.5	4.5	2.7	1.7	1.3	1.9	2.1	0.8
COINCIDENT INDEX												
Total, 13 countries	-	3.5	4.0	0.4	0.3	-0.9	2.6	2.9	2.5	3.3	1.7	2.9
12 countries, excluding U.S. .	1.9	3.4	6.5	2.6	-0.4	-2.6	1.5	2.5	2.0	2.0	-0.4	2.4
G-7 countries	-0.2	3.4	3.9	0.1	-	-1.3	2.2	2.4	2.3	3.2	2.3	2.7
North America............	-2.5	3.7	-	-3.8	1.2	2.1	4.7	3.5	3.2	5.1	4.7	4.2
United States	-2.9	3.5	-	-3.7	1.4	2.1	4.7	3.6	3.3	5.1	4.8	4.2
Canada	2.2	6.3	-0.1	-5.2	-0.2	1.9	5.1	3.5	1.3	4.7	4.3	4.8
Four European countries	0.6	2.3	5.4	0.8	-1.6	-5.2	1.3	2.8	1.4	3.2	5.4	4.7
France.................	-2.3	-1.6	6.0	-1.4	-2.6	-8.6	1.0	3.8	-0.2	3.4	8.7	8.3
Germany	1.9	3.1	7.3	4.7	-0.7	-4.0	1.0	2.3	0.1	0.5	3.7	3.2
Italy..................	6.9	4.1	6.4	3.4	-0.9	-8.4	-1.2	0.9	3.4	5.3	6.1	6.5
United Kingdom............	-2.1	4.1	0.9	-5.4	-2.7	-	4.3	4.0	3.7	6.1	4.1	1.9
Seven Pacific region countries.....	3.5	4.3	8.4	5.3	0.7	-0.6	1.3	2.1	2.6	0.5	-6.2	-0.3
Australia................	4.2	7.2	0.6	-8.3	-2.0	1.3	9.2	8.9	3.2	2.7	5.3	6.3
Taiwan [1]...............	8.5	3.2	5.2	8.0	8.4	6.9	7.1	4.7	1.9	7.2	5.2	4.1
Thailand................	4.2	3.3	13.0	5.0	7.1	11.8	10.2	10.6	7.4	-1.1	-5.9	11.2
Japan	4.0	4.4	9.1	6.1	-0.1	-2.2	-1.0	-0.1	1.8	-0.2	-6.2	-3.5
Korea, South..............	-7.1	6.7	11.5	10.1	5.0	4.5	11.5	11.7	7.7	1.3	-21.5	14.4
Malaysia................	-2.7	-8.2	-0.3	2.5	3.1	4.7	4.8	4.9	3.0	-0.2	-13.5	-1.3
New Zealand..............	1.4	1.3	0.6	-1.3	0.8	3.3	5.4	4.6	4.3	2.5	0.7	3.6

- Represents or rounds to zero.   [1]See footnote 2, Table 1352.

Source: Foundation for International Business and Economic Research, New York, NY, *International Economic Indicators*, monthly.

No. 1367. Selected International Economic Indicators by Country: 1980 to 1999

[Data cover gross domestic product (GDP) at market prices. Gross fixed capital formation covers private and government sectors except military. Savings data are calculated by deducting outlays—such as personal consumption expenditures, interest paid, and transfer payments to foreigners—from disposable personal income]

Year	United States	France	Germany	Italy	Nether-lands	United Kingdom	Japan	Canada
Ratio of gross fixed capital formation to GDP (current prices):								
1980	19.9	23.8	22.6	24.5	22.9	18.8	31.6	23.1
1985	19.2	20.3	19.5	21.8	21.0	18.2	27.5	19.8
1990	17.0	22.6	20.9	21.5	22.3	20.6	31.7	20.8
1995	17.5	18.8	22.4	18.3	20.3	16.3	28.5	17.0
1997	18.4	18.0	21.4	18.1	21.4	16.7	28.6	18.9
1998	19.2	18.3	21.1	18.4	21.7	17.6	26.8	19.1
1999	19.7	19.0	20.9	18.9	22.3	18.0	26.1	19.3
Ratio of savings to disposable personal income:								
1980	10.2	17.6	14.2	25.1	7.8	11.7	17.9	14.3
1985	9.2	14.0	12.8	21.0	5.5	9.1	15.6	14.0
1990	7.8	12.5	14.7	18.4	11.9	7.4	12.1	11.1
1995	5.6	16.0	11.2	16.6	6.5	10.3	13.7	7.3
1997	4.5	16.1	10.4	14.6	5.7	9.3	12.6	2.8
1998	3.7	15.7	10.0	13.4	4.2	6.1	13.4	2.3
1999	2.4	15.8	9.3	12.7	2.8	6.0	13.1	1.4

Source: U.S. Dept. of Commerce, International Trade Administration, Office of Trade and Economic Analysis, based on official statistics of listed countries.

No. 1368. Annual Percent Change in Consumer Prices by Country: 1995 to 1999

[Change from previous year. See text of this section for general comments concerning the data. For additional qualifications of the data for individual countries, see source. Minus sign (-) indicates decrease]

Country	1995	1996	1997	1998	1999	Country	1995	1996	1997	1998	1999
United States	2.8	2.9	2.3	1.6	2.2	Kenya.	0.8	8.8	12.0	5.8	2.6
Argentina	3.4	0.2	0.5	0.9	-1.2	Korea, South	4.5	4.9	4.4	7.5	0.8
Australia	4.6	2.6	0.3	0.9	1.5	Malaysia	5.3	3.5	2.7	5.3	2.7
Bangladesh	5.8	4.1	5.2	8.3	6.3	Mexico	35.0	34.4	20.6	15.9	16.6
Belgium	1.5	2.1	1.6	1.0	1.1	Netherlands	1.9	2.0	2.2	2.0	2.2
Brazil	66.0	15.8	6.9	3.2	4.9	Nigeria	72.8	29.3	8.2	10.3	6.6
Canada	2.2	1.6	1.6	1.0	1.7	Norway	2.5	1.3	2.6	2.3	2.3
Colombia.	21.0	20.2	18.9	20.4	11.2	Pakistan	12.3	10.4	11.4	6.2	4.1
Egypt	15.7	7.2	4.6	4.2	3.1	Philippines	8.0	9.0	5.9	9.7	6.7
France	1.8	2.0	1.2	0.7	0.5	Russia	197.4	47.7	14.7	27.7	85.7
Germany.	1.8	1.4	1.9	0.9	0.6	South Africa.	8.6	7.4	8.6	6.9	5.2
Greece	8.9	8.2	5.5	4.8	2.6	Spain	4.7	3.6	2.0	1.8	2.3
India.	10.2	9.0	7.2	13.2	4.7	Sweden	2.5	0.5	0.5	-0.1	0.5
Indonesia	9.4	8.0	6.7	57.6	20.5	Switzerland	1.8	0.8	0.5	0.1	0.8
Iran	49.6	28.9	17.2	19.4	21.0	Thailand	5.8	5.8	5.6	8.1	0.3
Israel	10.0	11.3	9.0	5.4	5.2	Turkey	88.1	80.3	85.7	84.6	64.9
Italy	5.2	4.0	2.0	2.0	1.7	United Kingdom	3.4	2.4	3.1	3.4	1.6
Japan.	-0.1	0.1	1.7	0.6	-0.3	Venezuela	59.9	99.9	50.0	35.8	23.6

Source: International Monetary Fund, Washington, DC, *International Financial Statistics*, monthly (copyright).

No. 1369. Comparative Price Levels—Selected OECD Countries: 2000

[As of June. Example of data: An item that costs $1.00 in the United States would cost $1.64 (U.S. dollars) in Japan]

Country	United States (U.S. dollar)	Canada (Canadian dollar)	Mexico (new peso)	Japan (yen)	France (franc)	Germany (Deutsche mark)	Italy (lire)	United Kingdom (pound)
United States	100	121	143	61	104	103	121	92
Australia [1]	80	97	115	49	84	83	97	74
Austria	97	117	138	59	101	100	117	89
Belgium	91	111	130	56	95	94	110	84
Canada	82	100	118	50	86	85	100	76
Czech Republic	40	49	57	24	42	42	49	37
Denmark.	119	145	170	73	124	123	144	110
Finland.	109	133	156	67	114	113	132	100
France	96	116	137	58	100	99	116	88
Germany	97	117	138	59	101	100	117	89
Greece.	74	90	106	45	77	76	89	68
Hungary	42	50	59	25	43	43	50	38
Iceland.	125	152	179	76	131	130	152	115
Ireland	89	108	127	54	92	92	107	81
Italy	83	100	118	50	86	85	100	76
Japan	164	199	235	100	171	170	199	151
Korea, South.	62	76	89	38	65	64	75	57
Luxembourg	93	113	133	57	97	96	113	85
Mexico.	70	85	100	43	73	72	85	64
Netherlands	90	110	129	55	94	93	109	83
New Zealand [1]	71	87	102	43	74	74	86	66
Norway.	121	147	174	74	127	125	147	112
Poland	53	64	76	32	55	55	64	49
Portugal	68	83	98	42	71	71	83	63
Spain	76	93	109	47	80	79	92	70
Sweden	113	138	162	69	118	117	137	104
Switzerland	124	151	178	76	130	129	151	114
Turkey	54	66	78	33	57	56	66	50
United Kingdom	109	132	156	66	114	112	132	100

[1] Estimates based on quarterly consumer prices.
Source: Organization for Economic Cooperation and Development, Paris, France, *Main Economic Indicators*, September 2000 (copyright).

No. 1370. Per Capita Consumption of Meat and Poultry: 1999

[Preliminary. In kilograms per capita. Beef, veal, and pork quantities are as of September and in carcass-weight equivalents; poultry quantities are as of July and are on ready-to-cook basis]

Country	Pork Quantity	Pork Rank	Country	Poultry Quantity	Poultry Rank	Country	Beef and veal Quantity	Beef and veal Rank
Denmark.	73.7	1	Hong Kong	67.2	1	Argentina.	70.2	1
Czech Republic	67.7	2	United States	49.4	2	Uruguay	60.4	2
Spain	64.0	3	Israel	43.8	3	United States	45.3	3
Germany	58.8	4	Singapore	37.7	4	Australia	40.2	4
Austria	57.7	5	Taiwan	34.8	5	New Zealand	34.1	5
Hong Kong	54.3	6	Saudi Arabia	33.5	6	Brazil	32.3	6
Belgium–			Canada	33.4	7	Canada	32.1	7
Luxembourg	52.6	7	Australia	31.3	8	France	26.8	8
Netherlands	43.7	8	United Kingdom . . .	28.6	9	Italy	26.3	9
Taiwan	42.5	9	Ireland	28.2	10	Czech Republic. . . .	24.5	10
Hungary	42.1	10						
United States	31.7	17						

Source: U.S. Department of Agriculture, Foreign Agricultural Service, *Livestock and Poultry: World Markets and Trade*, annual.

834 Comparative International Statistics

No. 1371. Motor Vehicle Transportation Indicators for Selected Countries: 1997

[129,749 represents 129,749,000]

Item	United States	Canada	Chile	France	Ger-many	Japan	Mexico	Sweden	United Kingdom
NUMBER [1] (1,000)									
Automobiles [2]	129,749	13,217	1,017	25,900	41,372	46,869	8,607	3,703	21,881
Motorcycles [2]	3,786	311	32	2,990	2,717	15,262	270	245	626
Buses	698	64	35	82	84	242	139	15	78
Trucks	77,307	[3]3,579	552	5,255	4,216	21,694	4,287	322	3,017
Per 1,000 persons:									
Automobiles [2]	484.8	435.7	70.5	441.9	504.1	372.2	88.2	417.7	379.9
Motorcycles [2]	14.1	10.2	2.2	51.0	33.1	121.2	2.8	27.6	10.9
Buses	2.6	2.1	2.4	1.4	1.0	1.9	1.4	1.7	1.4
Trucks	288.9	[3]117.9	38.3	89.7	51.4	172.3	43.9	36.3	52.4
ROADS [4]									
Total kilometers (1,000)	7,319	902	79	893	656	1,148	252	211	370
Kilometers per 1,000 persons	27.35	29.73	5.48	15.23	7.99	9.11	2.58	23.77	6.42
Kilometers per square kilometer	0.69	0.10	0.11	1.64	1.88	3.06	0.13	0.51	1.53
VEHICLE KILOMETERS OF TRAVEL [5]									
Automobiles [2]	2,363	(NA)	(NA)	370	517	464	(NA)	58	362
Motorcycles [2]	16	(NA)	(NA)	6	12	(NA)	(NA)	1	4
Buses (bil.)	11	(NA)	(NA)	2	4	7	(NA)	1	5
Trucks (bil.)	[6]1,609	(NA)	(NA)	100	53	267	(NA)	7	72
AVERAGE VEHICLE KILOMETERS PER VEHICLE [5]									
Automobiles [2]	18,216	(NA)	(NA)	14,286	12,496	9,903	(NA)	15,556	16,544
Motorcycles [2]	4,218	(NA)	(NA)	2,007	4,343	(NA)	(NA)	2,527	6,454
Buses	15,149	(NA)	(NA)	28,049	44,038	27,683	(NA)	54,568	61,154
Trucks	[6]20,816	(NA)	(NA)	19,029	12,453	12,304	(NA)	21,756	23,964

NA Not available.   [1] Data for Canada, Chile, Japan, and Mexico are for 1996.   [2] Includes mopeds. Data for France are for 1993.   [3] Excludes road tractors.   [4] Data for Canada are for 1995 and data for Japan are for 1996.   [5] Data for Germany and Japan are for 1996.   [6] Includes two-axle four-tire vehicles that are not cars. These are vans, sport-utility vehicles, and pickup trucks.

Source: U.S. Federal Highway Administration, *Highway Statistics, 1998.*

No. 1372. Transportation Infrastructure and Domestic Freight Activity—Selected Countries: 1996

[Data users should consult source document for notes about statistical comparability]

Mode	United States	Canada	France	Germany	Italy	Japan	United Kingdom
SYSTEM LENGTH (1,000 kilometers)							
Roads, total	[1]6,331	[2]912	893	634	316	1,152	372
Motorways	89	[2]17	10	11	10	6	3
Highways-main and national	749	[2]15	28	42	47	59	15
Secondary/regional	695	[2]225	355	76	118	121	36
Other	4,775	[2]656	500	505	142	966	317
Inland waterways [3]	43	3	[4]6	7	2	[2]2	[5]2
Pipeline, total	2,365	314	32	105	23	2	17
Gas	2,042	277	25	98	19	2	13
Oil	[2]323	37	8	8	4	-	4
Rail	286	77	[4]52	42	[2]16	[2]27	[2]33
Transit rail	7	(NA)	(NA)	(NA)	(NA)	4	(NA)
NUMBER OF FACILITIES							
Airports	13,175	1,141	460	613	132	164	387
Marine ports and facilities	321	172	(NA)	(NA)	(NA)	(NA)	(NA)
DOMESTIC FREIGHT ACTIVITY (bil. metric ton-kilometers)							
Total	5,456	439	244	348	269	[6]791	238
Air	16	1	[2]-	[2]-	[2]-	[2]1	[2]-
Water	[7]1,116	[7]40	13	61	35	462	[7]56
Coastal shipping	596	10	[2]7	[8]1	35	242	47
Inland waterways [3]	436	25	6	61	-	220	[8]-
Pipeline (oil only)	904	105	22	14	13	(NA)	13
Rail	1,980	221	51	68	24	25	15
Road	1,440	72	158	204	198	303	154

- Represents or rounds to zero.   NA Not available.   [1] Includes data for Puerto Rico, not shown separately.   [2] Data for 1995.   [3] Commercially navigable.   [4] Data for 1994.   [5] Data for 1990.   [6] Excludes pipeline.   [7] Includes other water categories, such as Great Lakes, not shown separately.   [8] Data for 1991.

Source: U.S. Dept. of Transportation, Bureau of Transportation Statistics, *G-7 Countries: Transportation Highlights*, BTS99-01, 1999.

Comparative International Statistics   835

No. 1373. Newspapers, Radio, Television, Telephones, and Computers by Country

[**Rates per 1,000 persons**. See text of this section for general comments about the data. For data qualifications for countries, see source]

Country	Daily newspaper circulation, [1] 1996	Radio receivers, [2] 1997	Television receivers, [3] 1997	Telephone main lines, [4] 1999	Cellular phone subscribers, [4] 1999	Personal computers, [5] 1999
Algeria	38	242	105	52	2	6
Argentina	123	681	223	201	121	49
Australia	296	1,391	554	521	344	471
Austria	296	751	525	472	519	257
Belgium	161	797	466	[6]500	315	315
Brazil	40	434	223	149	90	36
Bulgaria	254	537	394	342	42	27
Canada	158	1,067	710	[6]635	230	361
Chile	98	354	215	207	151	67
China [7]	(NA)	335	321	86	34	12
Colombia	46	524	115	160	75	34
Cuba	118	352	239	39	1	7
Czech Republic	254	803	531	371	190	107
Denmark	311	1,145	594	683	499	414
Dominican Republic	52	178	95	[6]93	[6]31	(NA)
Ecuador	70	348	130	91	31	20
Egypt	38	317	119	[6]60	7	11
Finland	455	1,498	622	553	667	360
France	218	946	595	579	364	221
Germany	311	948	567	588	286	297
Ghana	14	236	93	8	4	3
Greece	(NA)	475	240	528	311	60
Guatemala	33	79	61	55	32	10
Honduras	55	410	95	44	12	10
Hungary	186	690	435	402	160	74
India	(NA)	120	65	[6]22	[6]1	3
Indonesia	23	155	68	29	11	9
Iran	26	263	71	125	7	52
Iraq	20	229	83	[6]31	[6]-	(NA)
Ireland	149	697	402	478	378	324
Israel	288	524	288	459	459	246
Italy	104	880	528	462	528	192
Jamaica	63	483	183	199	56	43
Japan	578	956	686	494	449	287
Korea, South	(NA)	1,039	348	441	504	183
Kuwait	377	678	505	240	158	121
Lebanon	141	907	375	[6]194	196	46
Malaysia	163	434	172	203	101	69
Mexico	97	329	272	112	78	44
Morocco	27	247	115	66	4	11
Netherlands	306	980	519	606	435	360
New Zealand	216	997	512	490	230	327
Norway	590	917	462	712	618	450
Pakistan	(NA)	94	22	22	2	4
Panama	62	299	187	165	86	32
Peru	84	273	126	67	39	20
Philippines	82	161	52	[6]34	[6]24	17
Poland	113	522	337	260	102	62
Portugal	75	306	336	424	468	93
Puerto Rico	127	714	270	[6]327	[6]150	(NA)
Romania	(NA)	319	233	167	63	27
Russia	105	417	410	[6]197	9	37
Saudi Arabia	59	321	262	[6]143	[6]31	57
Singapore	324	744	388	577	475	527
South Africa	34	355	134	138	132	60
Spain	99	331	409	418	312	122
Sweden	445	932	519	665	578	451
Switzerland	331	979	457	699	420	462
Syria	20	278	70	102	-	15
Taiwan [7]	[6][8]156	(NA)	(NA)	544	521	181
Thailand	64	234	254	[6]84	[6]33	23
Turkey	110	178	330	265	117	32
United Kingdom	331	1,443	521	[6]557	408	306
United States	**212**	**2,116**	**806**	**[6]661**	**312**	**511**
Uruguay	293	603	239	271	95	100
Venezuela	206	472	180	109	143	42

- Represents or rounds to zero. NA Not available. [1] Publications containing general news and appearing at least 4 times a week; may range in size from a single sheet to 50 or more pages. Circulation data refer to average circulation per issue or number of printed copies per issue and include copies sold outside the country. [2] Data cover estimated number of receivers in use and apply to all types of receivers for radio broadcasts to the public, including receivers connected to a radio "redistribution system" but excluding television sets. [3] Estimated number of sets in use. [4] As of December 31. [5] In many countries mainframe computers are used extensively, and thousands of users can be connected to a single mainframe computer; thus the number of PCs understates the total use of computers. [6] 1998 data. [7] See footnote 2, Table 1352. [8] Source: U.S. Census Bureau. Data from Republic of China publications.

Source: Except as noted, newspapers, radio, and television—United Nations Educational, Scientific, and Cultural Organization, Paris, France, *Statistical Yearbook*, (copyright); telephones, cellular phones, and personal computers—International Telecommunications Union, Geneva, Switzerland, *World Telecommunication Indicators*, (copyright).

No. 1374. Gross Public Debt, Expenditures, and Receipts by Country: 1990 to 1999

[Percent of nominal gross domestic product. 1999 data estimated. Expenditures cover current outlays plus net capital outlays. Receipts cover current receipts but exclude capital receipts. Nontax current receipts include operating surpluses of departmental enterprises, property income, fees, charges, fines, etc]

Country	Gross debt			Expenditures			Receipts		
	1990	1995	1999	1990	1995	1999	1990	1995	1999
United States	60.9	68.3	59.3	33.6	32.9	30.1	29.3	29.8	31.0
Australia	22.6	42.2	31.3	33.6	35.7	32.4	32.3	31.8	33.1
Austria	57.9	69.4	63.3	48.6	52.6	49.7	46.2	47.5	47.6
Belgium	125.2	129.8	114.1	53.3	53.1	50.9	47.9	49.2	49.9
Canada	73.5	99.2	86.9	46.7	46.3	41.2	42.1	42.0	42.8
Czech Republic	(X)	(NA)	(NA)	(X)	43.1	44.7	(X)	41.5	39.6
Denmark.	65.8	73.9	55.4	56.0	59.0	54.5	55.0	56.8	57.4
Finland.	14.5	58.1	44.9	44.5	55.1	47.0	49.9	50.7	50.0
France	39.5	59.4	65.2	49.3	53.7	52.4	47.7	48.0	50.2
Germany [1]	42.0	59.1	62.6	43.8	48.1	47.6	41.8	45.0	46.0
Greece.	89.0	108.7	103.8	51.0	54.6	49.3	34.9	44.5	47.7
Hungary	(NA)	(NA)	(NA)	(NA)	49.2	43.7	(NA)	42.8	39.7
Iceland.	37.0	59.6	39.8	36.6	39.0	35.8	33.3	36.0	37.0
Ireland	92.6	80.8	43.9	37.8	36.4	30.0	35.0	34.0	33.4
Italy.	103.7	123.1	117.7	53.1	51.8	48.6	42.1	44.2	46.3
Japan [2]	61.4	76.0	105.4	31.3	35.6	38.1	34.2	32.0	30.5
Korea, South	8.2	6.3	13.7	18.1	19.1	25.2	21.8	23.5	25.1
Netherlands	75.6	75.5	62.9	49.4	47.7	43.8	43.7	43.6	43.2
New Zealand.	(NA)	(NA)	(NA)	48.8	38.8	40.9	44.0	41.9	40.8
Norway.	32.4	41.1	34.3	49.7	47.6	46.1	52.3	51.1	51.0
Poland	(NA)	(NA)	(NA)	(NA)	47.2	44.1	(NA)	44.4	41.0
Portugal	65.3	65.9	56.6	40.6	44.5	44.2	35.5	38.8	42.4
Spain.	48.5	68.4	70.4	39.7	42.5	38.5	35.6	35.5	37.2
Sweden	42.9	77.2	68.3	56.4	62.7	56.4	60.5	54.8	58.7
United Kingdom	39.1	58.9	54.0	41.8	44.4	39.7	40.3	38.6	40.3

NA Not available.   X Not applicable.   [1] Debt and expenditure data include accounts of German Railways Fund and the Inherited Debt Fund from 1995 on.   [2] Debt data include debt of the Japan Railway Settlement Corporation and the National Forest Special Account from 1998 on. The 1998 expenditures would have risen by 5.4 percentage points of GDP if account were taken of the assumption by the central government of the debt of these two entities.

Source: Organization for Economic Cooperation and Development, Paris, France, *OECD Economic Outlook*, December 1999 (copyright).

No. 1375. Percent Distribution of Tax Receipts by Country: 1980 to 1997

Country	Income and profits taxes [2]				Social security contributions			Taxes on goods and services [5]		
	Total [1]	Total [3]	Individual	Corporate	Total [4]	Employees	Employers	Total [3]	General consumption taxes [6]	Taxes on specific goods, services [7]
United States: 1980 . . .	100.0	49.8	39.1	10.8	21.9	9.2	11.9	17.6	7.0	8.3
1990 . . .	100.0	45.4	37.7	7.7	25.8	11.0	13.4	17.3	8.0	7.1
1997 . . .	100.0	48.4	39.0	9.4	24.2	10.4	12.5	16.7	7.8	6.8
Canada: 1980.	100.0	46.6	34.1	11.6	10.5	3.7	6.6	32.6	11.5	13.0
1990	100.0	48.1	40.6	7.0	12.1	4.3	7.5	26.7	14.0	10.6
1997	100.0	49.0	38.0	10.3	13.4	5.1	8.1	24.4	13.9	8.4
France: 1980	100.0	18.1	12.9	5.1	42.7	11.1	28.4	30.4	21.1	8.4
1990	100.0	17.2	11.8	5.3	44.1	13.2	27.2	28.4	18.8	8.7
1997	100.0	19.9	14.0	5.8	40.6	12.2	25.2	27.8	17.8	8.8
Germany: 1980 [8].	100.0	35.1	29.6	5.5	34.3	15.3	18.4	27.1	16.6	9.3
1990	100.0	32.4	27.6	4.8	37.5	16.2	19.1	26.7	16.6	9.2
1997	100.0	27.9	23.9	4.0	41.6	18.1	20.9	27.7	17.6	9.0
Italy: 1980	100.0	31.1	23.1	7.8	38.0	6.9	28.4	26.5	15.6	9.7
1990	100.0	36.5	26.3	10.0	32.9	6.3	23.6	28.0	14.7	10.6
1997	100.0	35.4	25.3	9.5	33.5	6.6	23.5	25.9	12.6	9.7
Japan: 1980	100.0	46.1	24.3	21.8	29.1	10.2	14.8	16.3	-	14.1
1990	100.0	48.5	26.8	21.6	29.0	11.0	15.0	13.2	4.3	7.3
1997	100.0	35.5	20.5	15.0	36.9	14.4	18.8	16.5	7.0	7.6
Netherlands: 1980	100.0	32.8	26.3	6.6	38.1	15.7	17.8	25.2	15.8	7.3
1990	100.0	32.2	24.7	7.5	37.4	23.1	7.5	26.4	16.5	7.5
1997	100.0	26.0	15.6	10.5	40.9	26.5	6.2	28.0	16.0	9.5
Sweden: 1980	100.0	43.5	41.0	2.5	28.8	0.1	27.6	24.0	13.4	9.2
1990	100.0	41.6	38.5	3.1	27.2	0.1	26.0	25.0	14.9	9.2
1997	100.0	41.2	35.0	6.1	29.2	5.0	23.8	22.3	13.6	8.0
United Kingdom: 1980 .	100.0	37.8	29.4	8.4	16.7	6.4	10.1	29.1	14.7	13.3
1990 .	100.0	39.5	27.9	11.6	17.2	6.6	10.0	31.1	17.0	12.6
1997 .	100.0	36.9	24.8	12.1	17.2	7.5	9.6	35.0	19.5	13.9

- Represents zero.   [1] Includes property taxes, employer payroll taxes other than social security contributions, and miscellaneous taxes, not shown separately.   [2] Includes taxes on capital gains.   [3] Includes other taxes not shown separately.   [4] Includes contributions of self-employed not shown separately.   [5] Taxes on the production, sales, transfer, leasing, and delivery of goods and services and rendering of services.   [6] Primary value-added and sales taxes.   [7] For example, excise taxes on alcohol, tobacco, and gasoline.   [8] Data are for former West Germany.

Source: Organization for Economic Cooperation and Development, Paris, France, *Revenue Statistics of OECD Member Countries*, annual (copyright).

Comparative International Statistics   837

No. 1376. Civilian Labor Force, Employment, and Unemployment by Country: 1980 to 1999

[106.9 represents 106,900,000. Data based on U.S. labor force definitions (see source) except that minimum age for population base varies as follows: United States, France, Sweden, and United Kingdom, 16 years; Australia, Canada, Japan, Netherlands, Germany, and Italy (beginning 1995), 15 years; and Italy (1980 and 1990) 14 years]

Year	United States	Canada	Aus-tralia	Japan	France	Ger-many[1]	Italy	Nether-lands	Swe-den	United King-dom
Civilian labor force (mil.):										
1980	106.9	11.9	6.7	55.7	22.9	27.3	21.1	5.9	4.3	26.5
1990	[2]125.8	14.2	8.4	63.1	[2]24.3	29.4	[2]22.7	[2]6.6	[2]4.6	28.7
1995	[2]132.3	14.8	9.0	66.0	[2]24.8	[2]39.1	[2]22.5	7.3	4.5	28.5
1997	[2]136.3	15.2	9.2	67.2	25.2	39.5	22.7	7.5	4.4	28.8
1998	[2]137.7	15.4	9.3	67.2	[2]25.4	39.4	23.0	7.7	4.4	[2]28.9
1999	[2]139.4	15.7	9.5	[3]67.1	[3]25.6	(NA)	23.1	(NA)	4.4	[3]29.1
Labor force participation rate:[4]										
1980	63.8	64.2	62.1	62.6	57.5	54.7	48.2	55.4	66.9	62.5
1990	[2]66.5	67.1	64.6	62.6	[2]56.0	55.3	[2]47.2	[2]56.1	[2]67.4	64.1
1995	[2]66.6	64.9	64.6	62.9	[2]55.2	[2]57.3	[2]47.1	59.3	64.1	62.7
1997	[2]67.1	64.9	64.3	63.2	55.3	57.6	47.2	60.7	63.3	62.8
1998	[2]67.1	65.1	64.4	62.8	55.4	57.6	47.6	62.0	62.8	62.7
1999	[2]67.1	65.6	64.2	[3]62.4	[3]55.7	(NA)	47.8	(NA)	[3]63.2	[3]62.9
Civilian employment (mil.):										
1980	99.3	11.0	6.3	54.6	21.4	26.5	20.2	5.5	4.2	24.7
1990	[2]118.8	13.1	7.9	61.7	22.1	28.0	[2]21.1	[2]6.2	[2]4.5	26.7
1995	[2]124.9	13.4	8.2	63.9	21.9	[2]35.9	[2]19.8	6.8	4.1	26.0
1997	[2]129.6	13.8	8.4	64.9	22.1	35.5	20.0	7.1	4.0	26.7
1998	[2]131.5	14.1	8.6	64.5	22.4	35.7	20.2	7.4	4.0	27.1
1999	[2]133.5	14.5	8.8	[3]63.9	[3]22.8	(NA)	20.5	(NA)	4.1	[3]27.3
Employment-population ratio:[5]										
1980	59.2	59.4	58.3	61.3	53.8	53.1	46.1	52.1	65.6	58.1
1990	[2]62.8	61.7	60.1	61.3	50.9	52.6	[2]43.9	[2]52.6	[2]66.1	59.6
1995	[2]62.9	58.8	59.1	60.9	48.7	[2]52.6	[2]41.5	55.1	58.3	57.2
1997	[2]63.8	59.0	58.8	61.0	48.4	51.9	41.6	57.5	56.9	58.3
1998	[2]64.1	59.7	59.2	60.2	48.9	52.2	41.9	59.5	57.6	58.7
1999	[2]64.3	60.6	59.6	[3]59.4	[3]49.6	(NA)	42.3	(NA)	[3]58.7	[3]59.1
Unemployment rate:										
1980	7.1	7.5	6.1	2.0	6.5	2.8	4.4	6.0	2.0	7.0
1990	[2]5.6	8.1	6.9	2.1	9.1	5.0	[2]7.0	[2]6.2	[2]1.8	6.9
1995	[2]5.6	9.4	8.5	3.2	[2]11.8	[2]8.2	[2]11.8	7.0	9.1	8.7
1997	[2]4.9	9.1	8.6	3.4	12.4	9.9	11.9	5.3	10.1	7.0
1998	[2]4.5	8.3	8.0	4.1	11.8	9.4	12.0	4.0	8.4	6.3
1999	[2]4.2	7.6	7.2	[3]4.7	[3]11.1	[3]9.0	11.5	(NA)	7.1	[3]6.1
Under 25 years old	9.9	14.0	13.9	9.5	(NA)	(NA)	33.1	(NA)	14.6	(NA)
Teenagers[6]	13.9	18.2	18.5	13.3	(NA)	(NA)	40.7	(NA)	18.8	(NA)
20 to 24 years old	7.5	11.2	10.6	8.8	(NA)	(NA)	31.1	(NA)	13.0	(NA)
25 years old and over	3.1	6.3	5.6	4.2	(NA)	(NA)	8.8	(NA)	6.2	(NA)

NA Not available. [1] Data for 1980 and 1990 are for former West Germany (prior to unification); data for other years are for unified Germany. [2] Break in series. Data not comparable with prior years. [3] Preliminary. [4] Civilian labor force as a percent of the civilian working age population. Germany and Japan include the institutionalized population as part of the working age population. [5] Civilian employment as a percent of the civilian working age population. Germany and Japan include the institutionalized population as part of the working age population. [6] 16 to 19 years old in the United States and Sweden; 15 to 19 years old in Canada, Australia, Japan, and Italy.

Source: U.S. Bureau of Labor Statistics, *Comparative Civilian Labor Force Statistics, Ten Countries, 1959-1999*, April 2000, and *Monthly Labor Review*.

No. 1377. Unemployment Rates by Country: 1995 to 1999

[**Annual averages.** The standardized unemployment rates shown here are calculated as the number of unemployed persons as a percentage of the civilian labor force. The unemployed are persons of working age who, in the reference period, are without work, available for work and have taken specific steps to find work]

Country	1995	1997	1998	1999	Country	1995	1997	1998	1999
OECD, total	7.5	7.4	7.1	6.8	Ireland	12.3	9.9	7.6	5.7
European Union	10.7	10.6	9.9	9.2	Italy	11.9	12.0	11.9	11.4
					Japan	3.1	3.4	4.1	4.7
United States	5.6	4.9	4.5	4.2	Luxembourg	2.9	2.7	2.7	2.3
Australia	8.6	8.5	8.0	7.2	Netherlands	6.9	5.2	4.0	3.3
Austria	3.9	4.4	4.5	3.7	New Zealand	6.3	6.7	7.4	6.8
Belgium	9.9	9.4	9.5	9.0	Norway	5.0	4.1	3.3	3.2
Canada	9.5	9.1	8.3	7.6	Poland	(NA)	11.2	10.6	(NA)
Czech Republic	(NA)	4.8	6.5	8.8	Portugal	7.3	6.8	5.2	4.5
Denmark	7.2	5.6	5.2	5.2	Spain	22.9	20.8	18.8	15.9
Finland	16.2	12.6	11.4	10.2	Sweden	8.8	9.9	8.3	7.2
France	11.7	12.3	11.8	11.3	Switzerland	3.5	4.2	3.5	(NA)
Germany	8.2	9.9	9.4	8.7	United Kingdom	8.7	7.0	6.4	6.2
Hungary	(NA)	8.9	8.0	7.1					

NA Not available.

Source: Organization for Economic Cooperation and Development, Paris, France, *OECD News Release, Standardized Unemployment Rates*, 8 June 2000 and earlier releases.

838 Comparative International Statistics

No. 1378. Civilian Employment-Population Ratio by Country: 1980 to 1999

[Civilian employment as a percent of the civilian working age population. See headnote, Table 1376]

Country	Women					Men				
	1980	1990	1995	1998	1999	1980	1990	1995	1998	1999
United States ..	47.7	[1]54.3	[1]55.6	57.1	57.4	72.0	[1]72.0	[1]70.8	71.6	71.6
Canada	46.3	53.7	52.3	53.8	54.6	72.8	69.9	65.5	65.9	66.8
Australia......	41.9	49.3	50.3	50.8	51.2	75.1	71.2	68.1	67.8	68.0
Japan	45.7	48.0	47.7	47.4	[2]46.7	77.9	75.4	75.0	73.9	[2]73.0
France ..,....	40.3	41.6	41.1	41.4	(NA)	68.9	61.3	57.1	57.1	(NA)
Germany [3] ...	38.9	[1]40.9	[1]42.7	43.6	(NA)	69.6	[1]65.6	[1]63.4	61.4	(NA)
Italy........	27.9	[1]29.2	[1]28.0	29.0	29.7	66.0	[1]60.0	[1]56.5	56.0	56.1
Netherlands ...	31.0	38.9	44.1	48.7	(NA)	74.1	66.9	66.4	70.8	(NA)
Sweden	58.0	[1]61.8	54.7	53.4	[2]54.6	73.6	[1]70.6	62.1	62.1	[2]63.1
United Kingdom .	44.8	49.8	49.6	51.0	(NA)	72.8	70.3	65.5	66.9	(NA)

NA Not available.   [1] Break in series. Data not comparable with prior years.   [2] Preliminary.   [3] Data for 1980 and 1990 are for former West Germany (prior to unification); data for other years are for unified Germany.

Source: U.S. Bureau of Labor Statistics, *Comparative Civilian Labor Force Statistics, Ten Countries, 1959-1999*, April 2000, and *Monthly Labor Review*.

No. 1379. Female Labor Force Participation Rates by Country: 1980 to 1998

[**In percent.** Female labor force of all ages divided by female population 15-64 years old]

Country	1980	1990	1995	1998	Country	1980	1990	1995	1998
Australia	52.7	62.9	64.8	65.0	Korea, South	(NA)	51.3	53.2	52.1
Austria...............	48.7	55.4	62.3	61.9	Luxembourg	39.9	50.7	58.0	(NA)
Belgium..............	47.0	52.4	56.1	57.8	Mexico	33.7	23.6	40.1	42.8
Canada..............	57.8	67.8	67.6	69.4	Netherlands	35.5	[1]53.1	[1]59.0	62.7
Czech Republic..........	(X)	69.1	[1]65.4	69.2	New Zealand	44.6	[1]62.9	63.3	67.1
Denmark	(NA)	78.5	73.6	75.3	Norway	62.3	71.2	72.4	76.3
Finland	70.1	72.9	70.3	69.9	Poland...............	(NA)	(NA)	61.1	59.8
France..............	54.4	57.6	59.4	60.2	Portugal..............	54.3	62.9	62.4	65.2
Germany [2]	52.8	57.4	61.7	63.1	Spain	32.2	41.2	45.1	47.8
Greece	33.0	43.6	45.9	(NA)	Sweden..............	74.1	[1]80.5	76.1	72.6
Hungary..............	(NA)	(NA)	50.5	50.7	Switzerland	54.1	59.6	[1]67.8	70.3
Iceland..............	(NA)	65.6	81.9	81.2	Turkey...............	(NA)	36.7	34.2	30.9
Ireland..............	36.3	38.9	47.8	52.6	United Kingdom	58.3	65.5	66.6	67.2
Italy	39.6	45.9	[1]43.3	45.0	**United States........**	59.7	[1]68.8	70.7	71.3
Japan	54.8	60.4	62.2	63.9					

NA Not available.   X Not applicable.   [1] Break in series. Data not comparable with prior years.   [2] Prior to 1991 data are for former West Germany.

Source: Organization for Economic Cooperation and Development, Paris, France, *Labour Force Statistics*, annual (copyright).

No. 1380. Civilian Employment by Industry and Country: 1990 and 1999

[**118,793 represents 118,793,000.** Data based on U.S. labor force definitions except that minimum age for population base varies as follows: United States, France, Sweden, and United Kingdom, 16 years; Australia, Canada, Germany, Italy (1999), Japan, 15 years; and Italy (1990), 14 years. Industries based on International Standard Industrial Classification; see text of this section]

Industry	United States	Canada	Aus- tralia	Japan	France	Ger- many [1]	Italy	Sweden	United Kingdom
TOTAL EMPLOYMENT (1,000)									
1990, total	**118,793**	**13,084**	**7,859**	**61,710**	**22,098**	**27,952**	**21,080**	**4,501**	**26,818**
Agriculture, forestry, fishing	3,394	559	440	4,270	1,248	965	1,879	178	573
Industry [2]...............	29,834	3,063	1,865	20,890	6,425	10,875	6,842	1,268	8,128
Manufacturing...........	21,346	2,053	1,170	15,010	4,708	8,839	4,755	943	[3]5,971
Services	85,565	9,462	5,554	36,550	14,425	16,112	12,355	3,056	18,117
1999, total	[4]**133,488**	**14,531**	**8,785**	[5]**63,930**	[4][5]**22,760**	[6]**35,715**	[4]**20,462**	**4,105**	[6]**27,009**
Agriculture, forestry, fishing	[4]3,416	522	434	[5]3,230	[4][5]963	[6]1,013	[4]1,127	128	[6]465
Industry [2]...............	[4]29,622	3,149	1,822	[5]19,990	[4][5]5,440	[6]12,005	[4]6,744	996	[6]7,047
Manufacturing...........	[4]20,070	2,217	1,080	[5]13,410	(NA)	[6]8,605	[4]5,170	759	[6]5,033
Services	[4]100,450	10,861	6,528	[5]40,710	[4][5]16,356	[6]22,697	[4]12,590	2,981	[6]19,497
PERCENT DISTRIBUTION									
1990, total	**100**	**100**	**100**	**100**	**100**	**100**	**100**	**100**	**100**
Agriculture, forestry, fishing	3	4	6	7	6	4	9	4	2
Industry [2]...............	25	23	24	34	29	39	33	28	30
Manufacturing...........	18	16	15	24	21	32	23	21	[3]22
Services	72	72	71	59	65	58	59	68	68
1999, total	[4]**100**	**100**	**100**	[5]**100**	[4][5]**100**	[6]**100**	[4]**100**	**100**	[6]**100**
Agriculture, forestry, fishing	[4]3	4	5	[5]5	[4][5]4	[6]3	[4]6	3	[6]2
Industry [2]...............	[4]22	22	21	[5]31	[4][5]24	[6]34	[4]33	24	[6]26
Manufacturing...........	[4]15	15	12	[5]21	(NA)	[6]24	[4]25	19	[6]19
Services	[4]75	75	74	[5]64	[4][5]72	[6]64	[4]62	73	[6]72

NA Not available.   [1] Data for 1990 are for former West Germany (prior to unification); data for other years are for unified Germany.   [2] Includes mining and construction.   [3] Includes mining.   [4] Break in series. Data not comparable with prior years.   [5] Preliminary.   [6] Data for 1998.

Source: U.S. Bureau of Labor Statistics, *Comparative Civilian Labor Force Statistics, Ten Countries, 1959-1999*, April 2000.

U.S. Census Bureau, Statistical Abstract of the United States: 2000

No. 1381. Index of Industrial Production by Country: 1980 to 1998

[Industrial production index measures output in the manufacturing, mining, and electric and gas utilities industries. Minus sign (-) indicates decrease]

Country	Index (1995=100)								Annual percent change				
	1980	1985	1990	1993	1994	1996	1997	1998	1993-94	1994-95	1995-96	1996-97	1997-98
OECD, total.	(NA)	(NA)	(NA)	(NA)	(NA)	103.0	108.2	109.9	(NA)	(NA)	3.0	5.0	1.6
Australia.	70.1	77.8	92.9	94.7	99.5	103.8	105.5	106.7	5.1	0.5	3.8	1.6	1.1
Austria	70.2	76.6	92.3	91.6	95.3	101.0	107.0	115.9	4.0	4.9	1.0	5.9	8.3
Belgium	83.4	86.8	99.3	92.0	93.9	100.5	105.2	108.8	2.1	6.5	0.5	4.7	3.4
Canada [1]	71.8	83.0	88.4	89.9	95.7	101.7	107.3	109.8	6.5	4.5	1.7	5.5	2.3
Czech Republic	(X)	(X)	144.9	98.7	100.7	102.0	106.5	109.8	2.0	-0.7	2.0	4.4	3.1
Denmark.	63.0	77.0	86.0	87.0	96.0	102.0	108.0	110.0	10.3	4.2	2.0	5.9	1.9
Finland.	66.4	76.7	86.9	84.4	94.1	103.7	113.3	122.1	11.5	6.3	3.7	9.3	7.8
France	89.5	89.5	100.4	94.2	98.0	100.2	104.1	108.7	4.0	2.0	0.2	3.9	4.4
Germany [2]	85.6	88.3	103.2	95.4	98.8	100.6	104.1	108.5	3.6	1.2	0.6	3.5	4.2
Greece	92.6	99.2	101.9	97.0	98.2	101.2	102.5	109.8	1.2	1.8	1.2	1.3	7.1
Hungary	116.7	128.1	113.8	87.2	95.5	103.3	114.8	129.1	9.5	4.7	3.3	11.1	12.5
Ireland	34.2	43.9	63.2	75.2	84.1	108.0	124.5	144.0	11.8	18.9	8.0	15.3	15.7
Italy	77.2	73.9	93.2	89.7	95.2	98.1	101.8	102.9	6.1	5.0	-1.9	3.8	1.1
Japan	69.9	82.8	103.2	95.6	96.8	102.3	106.0	99.0	1.3	3.3	2.3	3.6	-6.6
Korea, South	22.0	36.2	66.4	80.4	89.3	108.7	114.5	106.1	11.1	12.0	8.7	5.3	-7.3
Luxembourg	71.0	79.8	97.1	92.5	98.0	100.1	105.9	114.0	5.9	2.0	0.1	5.8	7.6
Mexico	80.3	85.0	95.7	103.5	108.5	110.1	120.3	128.3	4.8	-7.8	10.1	9.3	6.7
Netherlands	78.7	83.1	90.6	91.0	95.4	103.8	106.5	107.7	4.8	4.8	3.8	2.6	1.1
New Zealand	74.0	85.0	87.0	91.0	96.0	103.0	105.0	105.0	5.5	4.2	3.0	1.9	-
Norway.	50.6	61.5	78.6	88.2	94.4	105.4	109.0	108.4	7.0	5.9	5.4	3.4	-0.6
Poland	(X)	107.3	87.7	80.0	90.4	109.4	121.7	127.4	13.0	10.6	9.4	11.2	4.7
Portugal	62.1	71.7	97.0	89.7	89.6	105.3	108.0	114.1	-0.1	11.6	5.3	2.6	5.6
Spain	80.1	82.7	96.6	88.6	95.4	98.7	105.6	111.4	7.7	4.8	-1.3	7.0	5.5
Sweden [3]	73.0	80.5	88.0	81.7	91.1	101.0	107.6	112.5	11.5	9.8	1.0	6.5	4.6
Switzerland	77.0	80.0	96.0	94.0	98.0	100.0	105.0	108.0	4.3	2.0	-	5.0	2.9
Turkey	38.2	57.2	81.3	94.6	88.7	107.5	119.0	120.5	-6.2	12.7	7.5	10.7	1.3
United Kingdom	76.8	83.0	94.1	93.4	98.2	101.0	102.1	102.8	5.1	1.8	1.0	1.1	0.7
United States	69.6	76.9	86.4	90.4	95.3	104.5	110.8	114.8	5.4	4.9	4.5	6.0	3.6

- Represents or rounds to zero.   NA Not available.   X Not applicable.   [1] Gross domestic product in industry at factor cost and 1986 prices.   [2] 1980-90 former West Germany; later data use 1990 annual average data for West Germany as base year.   [3] Mining and manufacturing.

Source: Organization for Economic Cooperation and Development, Paris, France, *Main Economic Indicators*, monthly (copyright).

No. 1382. Patents by Country: 1998

[Includes only U.S. patents granted to residents of areas outside of the United States and its territories]

Country	Total [1]	Inventions	Designs	Country	Total [1]	Inventions	Designs
Total.	72,501	67,228	4,854	Netherlands.	1,382	1,226	84
				Switzerland	1,373	1,278	94
Japan.	32,116	30,841	1,207	Sweden	1,346	1,225	118
Germany.	9,582	9,095	410	Australia	830	720	95
France	3,990	3,674	282	Israel	820	754	50
Taiwan [2]	3,805	3,100	705	Belgium	755	693	42
United Kingdom	3,726	3,464	230	Finland	629	595	34
Canada.	3,536	2,974	547	Denmark.	500	392	66
Korea, South	3,362	3,259	103	Austria	408	387	19
Italy	1,819	1,583	231	Other countries	2,522	1,968	537

[1] Includes patents for botanical plants and reissues, not shown separately.   [2] See footnote 2, Table 1352.

Source: U.S. Patent and Trademark Office, Technology Assessment and Forecast Data Base.

No. 1383. Measures of Value Added in Manufacturing in Selected OECD Countries: 1985 and 1998

[United States=100. The productivity levels are derived from various industry-of-origin studies, using a standardized methodology. For details, see source]

Country	1985		1998 [1]		Country	1985		1998 [1]	
	Per person engaged	Per hour worked	Per person engaged	Per hour worked		Per person engaged	Per hour worked	Per person engaged	Per hour worked
United States	100	100	100	100	Finland	55	62	86	104
					France	65	77	77	93
Canada.	72	74	69	75	Germany [2].	69	78	68	87
Mexico	26	(NA)	26	(NA)	Netherlands.	79	98	87	117
Japan.	68	61	77	80	Portugal	20	(NA)	23	(NA)
Korea, South	22	15	43	33	Spain	42	(NA)	40	(NA)
Australia	44	45	46	47	Sweden	62	80	83	100
Belgium	73	93	80	102	United Kingdom . . .	46	51	50	57

NA Not available.   [1] 1996 for Mexico, Portugal, Spain, Australia, and Finland; and 1997 for South Korea.   [2] Data are for former West Germany.

Source: Organization for Economic Cooperation and Development, Paris, France, *Science, Technology and Industry Outlook 1998*, 1998 (copyright); and GGDC Industry Database, University of Groningen, Netherlands, <http://www.eco.rug.nl/ggdc/homeggdc.html>.

No. 1384. Selected Indexes of Manufacturing Activity by Country: 1980 to 1998

[1992=100. Data relate to employees (wage and salary earners) in Belgium and Italy, and to all employed persons (employees, self-employed workers, and unpaid family workers) in the other countries. Minus sign (-) indicates decrease. For explanation of average annual percent change, see Guide to Tabular Presentation]

Index	United States	Can- ada	Japan	Bel- gium	France	Ger- many [1]	Italy	Neth- erlands	Nor- way	Swe- den	United King- dom
Output per hour:											
1980.	71.9	75.3	63.9	65.4	66.7	77.2	64.1	69.2	76.7	74.0	56.1
1985.	87.8	89.8	77.3	87.0	79.1	89.1	81.6	89.0	90.2	87.1	72.3
1990.	97.8	95.3	95.4	96.8	93.5	99.0	92.5	98.6	96.6	95.0	88.3
1995.	114.9	108.9	109.3	113.2	114.4	111.2	109.3	117.7	102.0	122.4	104.8
1997.	122.1	111.0	121.4	121.8	123.2	121.8	113.4	125.7	101.9	133.6	104.0
1998.	127.9	111.7	120.4	122.6	127.4	127.1	113.6	127.8	104.1	136.5	105.1
Average annual percent change:											
1979-85.	3.3	2.3	3.5	6.0	3.0	2.1	4.9	4.4	2.4	3.0	4.1
1985-90.	2.2	1.2	4.3	2.2	3.4	2.1	2.5	2.1	1.4	1.8	4.1
1990-98.	3.4	2.0	2.9	3.0	3.9	3.2	2.6	3.3	0.9	4.6	2.2
Compensation per hour, national currency basis: [2]											
1980.	55.6	47.7	58.6	52.5	40.8	53.6	28.2	64.4	39.0	37.4	33.2
1985.	75.1	69.9	72.5	75.3	72.8	70.0	60.6	81.8	63.4	58.4	53.1
1990.	90.8	89.5	90.7	90.1	90.6	89.4	84.4	90.8	92.3	87.6	80.9
1995.	107.9	103.6	109.5	109.2	107.6	117.7	112.8	110.6	109.2	106.2	107.4
1997.	113.4	106.7	113.9	115.2	112.3	126.6	125.9	115.8	119.1	118.3	111.4
1998.	119.4	110.8	115.8	116.0	113.9	127.6	124.8	118.3	126.4	121.5	117.8
Average annual percent change:											
1979-85.	7.2	8.4	4.7	8.1	12.8	6.0	16.7	5.0	10.0	9.6	11.6
1985-90.	3.9	5.1	4.6	3.7	4.5	5.0	6.8	2.1	7.8	8.5	8.8
1990-98.	3.5	2.7	3.1	3.2	2.9	4.5	5.0	3.4	4.0	4.2	4.8
Real hourly compensation: [2][3]											
1980.	91.8	92.1	75.4	86.6	79.5	74.6	79.4	87.4	86.0	87.5	69.0
1985.	95.5	94.0	81.4	88.5	89.6	80.7	89.6	90.4	90.8	87.2	77.8
1990.	96.6	95.9	95.3	95.4	96.0	96.6	94.6	96.5	97.7	97.4	88.9
1995.	100.2	99.4	107.4	102.3	102.0	108.7	98.9	103.1	102.7	96.8	99.7
1997.	100.4	99.2	109.7	104.1	103.1	113.3	104.4	103.7	107.9	105.8	98.0
1998.	104.3	102.2	110.9	103.8	103.8	113.3	101.6	104.0	112.0	107.5	100.2
Unit labor costs, national currency:											
1980.	77.2	63.3	91.7	80.3	61.2	69.4	44.0	93.0	50.8	50.6	59.1
1985.	85.5	77.8	93.8	86.5	92.0	78.6	74.2	91.8	70.2	67.1	73.5
1990.	92.8	93.9	95.0	93.0	96.8	90.3	91.3	92.1	95.6	92.3	91.6
1995.	93.9	95.2	100.1	96.4	94.1	105.9	103.2	94.0	107.1	86.8	102.5
1997.	92.9	96.2	93.8	94.6	91.2	103.9	111.1	92.2	116.9	88.5	107.1
1998.	93.4	99.2	96.2	94.7	89.4	100.4	109.8	92.5	121.4	89.0	112.1
Average annual percent change:											
1979-85.	3.7	5.9	1.2	2.0	9.5	3.8	11.2	0.5	7.4	6.4	7.2
1985-90.	1.7	3.8	0.3	1.5	1.0	2.8	4.2	-	6.4	6.6	4.5
1990-98.	0.1	0.7	0.2	0.2	-1.0	1.3	2.3	0.1	3.0	-0.4	2.6
Unit labor costs, U.S. dollar basis: [4]											
1980.	77.2	65.4	51.3	88.3	76.7	59.6	63.3	82.3	63.9	69.6	77.8
1985.	85.5	68.9	49.9	46.9	54.2	41.7	47.9	48.7	50.8	45.4	54.0
1990.	92.8	97.2	83.1	89.5	94.1	87.3	93.8	88.9	95.0	90.8	92.5
1995.	93.9	83.8	135.1	105.2	99.9	115.5	78.0	103.0	105.0	70.8	91.6
1997.	92.9	83.9	98.3	84.9	82.6	93.5	80.3	83.0	102.5	67.5	99.3
1998.	93.4	80.8	93.1	83.8	80.2	89.1	77.9	82.0	99.9	65.2	105.2
Average annual percent change:											
1979-85.	3.7	3.3	-0.3	-9.3	-3.3	-4.1	-3.2	-7.6	-1.7	-5.2	-1.3
1985-90.	1.7	7.1	10.8	13.8	11.6	15.9	14.4	12.8	13.3	14.8	11.4
1990-98.	0.1	-2.3	1.4	-0.8	-2.0	0.3	-2.3	-1.0	0.6	-4.0	1.6
Employment:											
1980.	111.6	115.5	87.4	119.3	124.6	102.2	125.8	107.8	134.5	130.9	155.9
1985.	106.0	109.4	91.9	104.0	110.2	94.9	104.8	95.4	120.7	122.0	121.7
1990.	105.4	111.4	95.8	102.5	105.4	100.3	106.4	101.1	105.4	117.2	116.9
1995.	102.5	107.5	93.5	91.9	92.1	87.3	97.2	91.3	107.2	98.8	100.7
1997.	103.2	112.0	92.8	89.0	90.0	82.6	96.9	91.0	112.6	97.1	102.9
1998.	103.8	116.2	89.2	90.5	90.2	82.4	98.8	91.5	113.3	99.3	102.6
Average annual percent change:											
1979-85.	-1.4	-0.8	1.2	-2.6	-2.2	-1.1	-2.9	-2.2	-1.8	-1.2	-4.8
1985-90.	-0.1	0.4	0.8	-0.3	-0.9	1.1	0.3	1.2	-2.7	-0.8	-0.8
1990-98.	-0.2	0.5	-0.9	-1.5	-1.9	-2.4	-0.9	-1.2	0.9	-2.1	-1.6
Aggregate hours:											
1980.	107.5	113.5	93.8	119.7	133.1	110.5	122.4	111.8	135.0	124.0	155.3
1985.	104.6	108.6	98.4	102.4	110.5	99.1	100.9	96.7	120.2	119.4	123.1
1990.	104.8	111.9	100.9	104.3	105.9	100.1	107.7	101.5	103.7	116.4	119.2
1995.	104.0	109.1	92.0	92.0	91.6	84.3	98.0	91.6	106.9	106.3	102.9
1997.	105.5	115.4	91.5	89.5	89.5	78.6	97.4	90.8	111.1	105.0	105.4
1998.	105.6	119.0	86.1	91.2	89.9	79.3	99.0	91.2	111.9	107.3	104.7
Average annual percent change:											
1979-85.	-1.2	-0.8	1.1	-3.2	-3.2	-1.9	-3.1	-2.6	-1.8	-0.8	-5.1
1985-90.	-	0.6	0.5	0.4	-0.8	0.2	1.3	1.0	-2.9	-0.5	-0.6
1990-98.	0.1	0.8	-2.0	-1.7	-2.0	-2.9	-1.0	-1.3	1.0	-1.0	-1.6

- Represents or rounds to zero. [1] Former West Germany. [2] Compensation includes, but real hourly compensation excludes, adjustments for payroll and employment taxes that are not compensation to employees, but are labor costs to employers. [3] Index of hourly compensation divided by the index of consumer prices to adjust for changes in purchasing power. [4] Indexes in national currency adjusted for changes in prevailing exchange rates.

Source: U.S. Bureau of Labor Statistics, *International Comparisons of Manufacturing Productivity and Unit Labor Cost Trends, Revised Data for 1998*, April 28, 2000.

Comparative International Statistics 841

No. 1385. Indexes of Hourly Compensation Costs for Production Workers in Manufacturing by Country: 1980 to 1999

[United States=100. Compensation costs include pay for time worked, other direct pay (including holiday and vacation pay, bonuses, other direct payments, and the cost of pay in kind), employer expenditures for legally required insurance programs and contractual and private benefit plans, and for some countries, other labor taxes. Data adjusted for exchange rates. Area averages are trade-weighted to account for difference in countries' relative importance to U.S. trade in manufactured goods. The trade weights used are the sum of U.S. imports of manufactured products for consumption (customs value) and U.S. exports of domestic manufactured products (f.a.s. value) in 1992; see source for detail]

Area or country	1980	1985	1990	1995	1998	1999, prel.	Area or country	1980	1985	1990	1995	1998	1999, prel.
United States	100	100	100	100	100	100	Austria [7]	90	58	119	147	119	114
Total [1]	67	52	83	95	79	79	Belgium.	133	69	129	155	124	119
OECD [2]	74	57	90	103	85	86	Denmark	110	62	121	140	122	120
Europe	100	61	116	128	110	106	Finland [8]	83	63	141	140	116	110
Asian newly industrial-							France	91	58	104	116	98	94
izing economies [3] . . .	12	13	25	37	31	32	Germany [7][9]	124	73	147	184	147	140
Canada.	88	84	107	94	84	81	Greece	38	28	45	53	48	(NA)
Mexico	22	12	11	9	10	11	Ireland	60	46	78	79	72	71
Australia [4]	86	63	88	89	80	83	Italy	83	59	117	94	92	86
Hong Kong [5]	15	13	21	28	29	28	Luxembourg.	122	60	112	136	100	(NA)
Israel	38	31	57	61	64	62	Netherlands	122	67	121	140	113	109
Japan	56	49	86	139	98	109	Norway	117	80	144	142	126	125
Korea, South	10	9	25	42	29	35	Portugal	21	12	25	31	29	(NA)
New Zealand	53	34	55	58	48	48	Spain	60	36	76	75	65	63
Singapore	15	19	25	43	42	37	Sweden	127	74	140	125	118	112
Sri Lanka.	2	2	2	3	3	(NA)	Switzerland	112	74	140	170	131	123
Taiwan [6]	10	12	26	35	28	29	United Kingdom	77	48	85	80	88	86

NA Not available. [1] The 28 foreign economies shown below. [2] Organization for Economic Cooperation and Development; see text of this section. [3] Hong Kong, South Korea, Singapore, and Taiwan. [4] Includes nonproduction workers, except in managerial, executive, professional, and higher supervisory positions. [5] Average of selected manufacturing industries. [6] See footnote 2, Table 1352. [7] Excludes workers in establishments considered handicraft manufactures (including all printing and publishing and miscellaneous manufacturing in Austria). [8] Includes workers in mining and electrical power plants. [9] Former West Germany.

Source: U.S. Bureau of Labor Statistics, *News Release* USDL 00-254, September 7, 2000.

No. 1386. Income Tax and Social Security Contributions as Percent of Labor Costs: 1998

[Data are for single individual at the income level of the average production worker]

Country	Labor costs [1] (dol.)	Percent of labor costs			
		Total	Income tax	Social security contributions	
				Employee	Employer [2]
Belgium	40,995	57	22	10	26
Germany	35,863	52	17	17	17
Switzerland	32,535	30	9	10	10
Italy	32,351	47	14	7	26
Netherlands	32,271	44	6	23	14
Denmark.	32,214	44	34	10	1
Canada	32,211	32	20	5	6
Norway.	31,638	37	19	7	11
United States	31,300	31	17	7	7
Luxembourg	31,102	34	10	11	12
Austria	29,823	46	8	14	24
Sweden	29,768	51	21	5	25
Australia.	29,590	25	24	2	-
Finland.	29,334	49	22	6	21
United Kingdom	29,277	32	15	8	9
France	28,198	48	10	9	28
Japan	27,664	20	6	7	7
Ireland	24,667	33	18	5	11
Spain	24,454	39	11	5	24
New Zealand	24,332	20	20	-	-
Korea, South	22,962	15	1	4	9
Iceland.	22,545	25	20	-	4
Greece.	17,880	36	2	12	22
Turkey	15,825	40	21	8	11
Czech Republic	15,781	43	8	9	26
Portugal	13,903	34	6	9	19
Poland	12,696	43	11	-	33
Hungary	9,916	52	12	8	32
Mexico	8,662	22	-	2	20

- Represents or rounds to zero. [1] Adjusted for purchasing power parities, see text of this section. Labor costs include gross wages plus employers compulsory social security contributions. [2] Includes reported payroll taxes.

Source: Organization for Economic Cooperation and Development, Paris, France, *Taxing Wages, 1998-1999,* 2000 (copyright).

No. 1387. World Primary Energy Production by Region and Type: 1980 to 1998

[In quadrillion Btu (286.4 represents 286,400,000,000,000,000). Btu=British thermal units. For Btu conversion factors, see source]

Region and type	1980	1985	1990	1992	1993	1994	1995	1996	1997	1998
World total [1]	286.4	304.2	351.4	350.3	351.3	356.5	365.2	374.9	379.2	382.2
North America	80.9	84.6	91.9	92.5	91.9	95.3	96.2	98.6	98.8	99.3
United States	64.8	64.9	70.8	70.0	68.4	70.8	71.3	72.5	72.5	72.8
Central and South America	12.1	13.6	16.8	18.1	19.0	20.0	21.3	22.7	24.2	24.9
Western Europe	30.7	37.3	38.5	38.9	39.5	40.5	41.6	44.1	43.8	43.6
Eastern Europe and former U.S.S.R.	66.7	75.0	81.9	71.3	66.5	61.4	59.9	60.5	59.0	58.3
Middle East	42.2	25.8	41.0	43.6	45.8	46.9	48.0	49.0	51.4	54.5
Africa	18.1	19.3	21.6	23.0	22.8	23.0	24.2	24.7	26.0	26.2
Far East and Oceania	35.8	48.7	59.7	63.0	65.9	69.4	74.0	75.3	76.0	75.4
Crude oil	128.1	115.4	129.5	129.1	128.9	130.5	133.3	136.6	140.5	143.2
Natural gas	52.7	61.4	75.9	76.8	78.4	79.2	80.2	84.0	84.0	85.5
Natural gas liquids	5.1	5.8	6.9	7.4	7.7	7.8	8.1	8.3	8.5	8.7
Coal	74.5	85.8	92.3	88.4	85.7	87.5	89.7	90.8	90.6	88.6
Hydroelectric power	18.1	20.6	22.6	23.0	24.3	24.5	25.7	26.1	26.7	26.6
Nuclear electric power	7.6	15.4	20.4	21.4	22.1	22.5	23.4	24.2	24.0	24.5
Geothermal, solar and wind	0.4	0.6	1.7	2.0	2.1	2.2	2.2	2.3	2.4	2.5

[1] Includes biomass, geothermal energy, and solar energy produced in the United States and not used for generating electricity, not shown separately by type.

No. 1388. World Primary Energy Consumption by Region and Type: 1980 to 1998

[In quadrillion Btu (282.6 represents 282,600,000,000,000,000). Btu=British thermal units. For Btu conversion factors, see source]

Region and type	1980	1985	1990	1992	1993	1994	1995	1996	1997	1998
World total [1]	282.6	307.5	346.8	348.5	353.2	357.3	365.7	376.3	378.0	377.7
North America	89.3	88.3	100.0	101.6	103.9	106.3	108.1	111.7	112.1	112.6
United States	76.0	74.0	84.1	85.5	87.3	89.3	91.0	94.0	94.4	94.8
Central and South America	11.4	12.3	14.2	15.1	15.7	16.5	17.2	18.2	19.0	19.7
Western Europe	58.6	59.9	64.0	64.2	64.5	64.6	66.3	68.4	68.6	69.5
Eastern Europe and former U.S.S.R.	61.4	70.7	74.1	65.0	60.5	54.6	52.9	52.6	50.3	49.0
Middle East	5.9	8.6	11.1	12.0	12.7	13.3	13.9	14.5	15.4	15.9
Africa	6.8	8.5	9.3	10.0	10.2	10.5	10.8	11.1	11.5	11.8
Far East and Oceania	49.2	59.3	74.1	80.6	85.6	91.4	96.5	99.8	101.2	99.3
Petroleum	130.9	123.1	134.9	136.6	136.6	139.1	142.4	145.5	148.6	149.7
Natural gas	54.2	63.7	74.8	76.2	78.4	78.3	80.0	84.0	83.8	84.4
Coal	71.6	84.2	90.4	87.1	87.5	88.3	89.6	91.6	90.2	87.5
Hydroelectric power	18.3	21.0	22.7	23.2	24.6	24.8	26.0	26.4	27.0	26.8
Nuclear electric power	7.6	15.4	20.4	21.4	22.1	22.5	23.4	24.2	24.0	24.5
Geothermal, solar and wind	0.3	0.5	1.7	2.0	2.1	2.2	2.2	2.3	2.4	2.5

[1] See footnote 1, Table 1387.

Source of Tables 1387 and 1388: U.S. Energy Information Administration, *International Energy Annual*.

No. 1389. World Energy Consumption, by Region and Energy Source, 1990 to 1997, and Projections, 2005 to 2020

[In quadrillion Btu (346.7 represents 346,700,000,000,000,000). Btu=British thermal units. For Btu conversion factors, see source]

Region and energy source	1990	1996	1997	Projections			
				2005	2010	2015	2020
World, total	346.7	376.0	379.9	449.0	500.2	544.4	607.7
North America	99.9	112.0	112.5	126.9	135.0	142.4	148.5
United States	84.0	93.9	94.2	105.3	111.3	116.7	120.9
Western Europe	59.9	63.3	64.0	69.6	72.6	75.4	78.4
Industrialized Asia	23.0	26.9	27.1	29.2	31.1	32.2	33.1
Eastern Europe and former Soviet Union	76.4	54.5	53.3	57.5	63.0	67.7	75.7
Developing Asia	51.4	73.5	75.3	105.0	126.4	144.3	172.6
Middle East	13.1	17.1	17.9	22.5	26.2	29.3	34.3
Africa	9.3	11.1	11.4	14.1	15.8	17.8	20.6
Central and South America	13.7	17.8	18.3	24.2	30.1	35.3	44.7
Oil	134.9	145.4	148.7	170.9	190.7	211.1	230.4
Natural gas	75.1	84.1	83.9	107.7	127.7	145.3	173.3
Coal	90.5	91.8	92.8	107.9	115.4	120.7	134.5
Nuclear	20.4	24.2	24.0	25.4	26.0	24.6	22.5
Other	25.9	30.5	30.6	37.2	40.4	42.8	47.0

Source: U.S. Energy Information Administration, *International Energy Outlook 2000*.

No. 1390. Energy Consumption and Production by Country: 1990 and 1998

[346.8 represents 346,800,000,000,000,000. See text of this section for general comments about the data. For data qualifications for countries, see source]

Country	Primary energy consumed Total (quad. Btu)		Per capita (mil. Btu)		Dry natural gas production (tril. cu. ft.)		Crude petroleum production (1,000 barrels per day)		Coal production (mil. short tons)	
	1990	1998, prel.	1990	1998, prel.	1990	1998	1990	1998	1990	1998
World	346.8	377.7	66	64	73.6	83.0	60,566	66,962	5,353	5,043
United States	84.1	94.8	337	351	17.8	18.9	7,355	6,252	1,029	1,119
Algeria	1.2	1.3	49	44	1.8	2.6	1,175	1,246	(Z)	(Z)
Argentina.	1.9	2.7	59	75	0.6	1.1	483	847	(Z)	(Z)
Australia	3.7	4.3	215	229	0.7	1.1	575	544	226	314
Austria	1.2	1.3	151	166	0.1	0.1	22	21	3	1
Bahrain	0.3	0.4	520	563	0.2	0.3	42	38	(NA)	(NA)
Bangladesh	0.3	0.4	2	3	0.2	0.3	1	2	(NA)	(NA)
Belarus	(X)	1.1	(X)	104	(X)	(Z)	(X)	36	(X)	(NA)
Belgium.	2.1	2.7	215	261	(Z)	-	(NA)	(NA)	3	(Z)
Brazil	5.7	8.1	39	50	0.1	0.2	631	969	5	5
Bulgaria.	1.3	0.9	145	108	-	(Z)	4	1	35	33
Burma.	(NA)	(NA)	(NA)	(NA)	(Z)	0.1	13	11	(Z)	(Z)
Canada	10.9	11.9	394	391	3.9	6.0	1,553	1,981	75	83
Chile	0.6	0.9	44	61	0.1	0.1	20	8	2	1
China [1]	27.0	33.9	23	27	0.5	0.8	2,774	3,198	1,190	1,351
Colombia	0.9	1.3	25	31	0.2	0.3	440	733	23	38
Congo (Kinshasa) [2]	(NA)	(NA)	(NA)	(NA)	-	-	29	26	(Z)	(Z)
Cuba	0.5	0.4	47	38	(Z)	(Z)	14	31	(NA)	(NA)
Czech Republic	(X)	1.8	(X)	170	(X)	(Z)	(X)	4	(X)	83
Denmark	0.8	0.8	156	151	0.1	0.3	121	238	(NA)	(NA)
Ecuador	(NA)	(NA)	(NA)	(NA)	(Z)	(Z)	285	375	(NA)	(NA)
Egypt	1.4	1.9	27	29	0.3	0.5	873	834	-	(Z)
Finland	1.1	1.3	226	245	(NA)	(NA)	(NA)	(NA)	(NA)	(NA)
France	8.8	10.0	156	170	0.1	0.1	61	34	15	6
Germany	(X)	13.8	(X)	169	(X)	0.8	(X)	59	(X)	229
Greece	1.1	1.3	103	120	(Z)	(Z)	15	6	57	65
Hong Kong	0.5	0.7	84	100	(NA)	(NA)	(NA)	(NA)	(NA)	(NA)
Hungary	1.3	1.1	124	104	0.2	0.1	40	26	19	16
India.	7.8	12.5	9	13	0.4	0.8	660	661	233	359
Indonesia.	2.2	3.6	12	18	1.5	2.2	1,462	1,518	9	66
Iran	3.1	4.5	57	72	0.8	1.8	3,088	3,634	1	1
Iraq	0.9	1.1	51	49	0.2	0.1	2,040	2,150	(NA)	(NA)
Ireland	0.4	0.5	105	141	0.1	0.1	(NA)	(NA)	(Z)	(Z)
Israel	0.5	0.8	97	127	(Z)	(Z)	(Z)	(Z)	(NA)	(NA)
Italy	7.0	8.0	123	139	0.6	0.7	87	107	1	(Z)
Japan	18.3	21.3	148	168	0.1	0.1	11	9	11	4
Korea, North	2.1	1.8	101	78	(NA)	(NA)	(NA)	(NA)	71	68
Korea, South	3.7	6.9	85	149	(NA)	(NA)	(NA)	(NA)	19	5
Kuwait.	0.5	0.7	210	345	0.2	0.3	1,175	2,085	(NA)	(NA)
Libya	0.5	0.6	123	105	0.2	0.2	1,375	1,390	(NA)	(NA)
Malaysia	1.0	1.7	55	81	0.7	1.4	610	733	(Z)	(Z)
Mexico	5.0	5.9	58	59	0.9	1.3	2,553	3,070	9	11
Morocco	0.3	0.4	13	15	(Z)	(Z)	(Z)	(Z)	1	(Z)
Netherlands	3.4	3.8	225	243	2.7	2.8	70	52	(NA)	(NA)
New Zealand	0.7	0.8	220	208	0.2	0.2	40	47	3	4
Nigeria	0.7	1.0	8	9	0.1	0.2	1,810	2,153	(Z)	(Z)
Norway	1.6	1.9	373	420	1.0	1.6	1,704	3,017	(Z)	(Z)
Pakistan	1.2	1.7	10	12	0.5	0.7	62	55	3	3
Peru	(NA)	(NA)	(NA)	(NA)	(Z)	(Z)	129	116	(Z)	(Z)
Philippines.	0.7	1.1	12	14	-	(Z)	5	1	1	1
Poland	3.9	3.5	102	91	0.2	0.2	2	7	237	198
Portugal	0.8	1.0	76	99	(NA)	(NA)	(NA)	(NA)	(Z)	-
Romania	2.9	1.8	124	78	1.0	0.5	163	132	43	29
Russia	(X)	26.0	(X)	177	(X)	20.9	(X)	5,854	(X)	272
Saudi Arabia	3.2	4.2	212	208	1.1	1.7	6,410	8,389	(NA)	(NA)
Serbia and Montenegro [3]	(X)	0.8	(X)	76	(X)	(Z)	(X)	18	(X)	48
South Africa	3.4	4.4	91	100	-	0.1	-	18	193	247
Spain	3.9	5.0	101	128	0.1	(Z)	16	11	40	29
Sweden	2.2	2.3	254	256	(NA)	(NA)	(Z)	-	(Z)	-
Switzerland	1.2	1.2	174	170	(Z)	-	(NA)	(NA)	(NA)	(NA)
Syria.	0.6	0.8	49	53	0.1	0.2	388	553	(NA)	(NA)
Taiwan [1]	2.0	3.3	100	152	0.1	(Z)	3	1	1	(Z)
Tajikistan	(X)	(NA)	(X)	(NA)	(X)	(Z)	(X)	(Z)	(X)	(Z)
Thailand	1.3	2.3	22	38	0.2	0.6	44	75	14	22
Trinidad and Tobago	(NA)	(NA)	(NA)	(NA)	0.2	0.4	150	123	(NA)	(NA)
Tunisia	(NA)	(NA)	(NA)	(NA)	(Z)	0.1	93	80	(NA)	(NA)
Turkey	2.0	2.9	35	46	(Z)	(Z)	73	65	52	67
Ukraine	(X)	6.1	(X)	122	(X)	0.6	(X)	57	(X)	83
United Arab Emirates.	1.2	1.8	641	669	0.8	1.3	2,117	2,345	(NA)	(NA)
United Kingdom	9.3	9.8	162	165	1.8	3.2	1,820	2,616	104	46
Venezuela	2.1	2.6	107	113	0.8	1.0	2,137	3,167	2	8
Vietnam.	0.3	0.7	4	10	(Z)	(Z)	50	246	5	12

- Represents zero.   NA Not available.   X Not applicable.   Z Less than .05 trillion cubic feet, 500 barrels per day, or 500,000 short tons.   [1] See footnote 2, Table 1352.   [2] See footnote 3, Table 1352.   [3] See footnote 4, Table 1352.

Source: U.S. Energy Information Administration, *International Energy Annual.*

No. 1391. Net Electricity Generation by Type and Country: 1998

[13,615.5 represents 13,615,500,000,000. Preliminary]

Country	Total [1] (bil. kWh)	Thermal [2]	Hydro	Nuclear	Country	Total [1] (bil. kWh)	Thermal [2]	Hydro	Nuclear
World, total	13,615.5	62.7	18.8	17.0	Korea, South	221.2	59.6	1.9	38.5
Argentina	75.2	42.7	47.6	9.4	Malaysia	57.4	94.8	5.2	-
Australia.	186.5	89.8	8.4	-	Mexico.	176.0	78.1	13.8	5.0
Austria.	56.1	31.4	66.0	-	Netherlands	88.6	91.4	-	4.1
Belgium	77.7	43.0	0.5	56.5	New Zealand	35.8	27.1	65.9	-
Brazil.	316.9	4.9	91.0	1.0	Norway	114.5	-	100.0	-
Bulgaria	38.4	52.3	7.3	40.4	Pakistan.	59.3	63.1	36.3	0.7
Canada	550.9	27.2	59.8	12.3	Paraguay	50.2	-	100.0	-
China [3]	1,098.9	80.3	18.5	1.2	Poland.	134.9	96.4	3.2	-
Colombia	45.1	30.2	69.2	-	Romania	52.5	59.0	31.6	9.3
Czech Republic.	60.5	76.7	2.6	20.7	Russia	771.9	67.8	19.5	12.7
Denmark	40.3	90.8	-	-	Saudi Arabia. . . . . [4]	110.1	100.0	-	-
Egypt	57.8	78.7	21.3	-	Serbia and Montenegro [4] .	38.9	67.9	32.1	-
Finland	75.3	41.6	19.7	27.6	South Africa	192.0	92.1	0.8	7.1
France.	481.0	10.8	12.5	76.2	Spain	179.5	48.2	19.2	31.2
Germany	525.4	65.8	3.2	29.1	Sweden	156.8	6.1	46.5	45.2
Greece	43.5	91.7	8.3	-	Switzerland.	60.0	3.8	55.3	40.8
Hungary.	35.2	61.6	0.6	37.8	Taiwan [3].	133.7	65.9	7.9	26.3
India	446.1	80.3	17.1	2.4	Thailand.	82.8	91.4	8.6	-
Indonesia	73.1	88.2	8.3	-	Turkey	106.4	60.7	39.3	-
Iran.	95.3	92.3	7.7	-	Ukraine	157.9	48.1	7.2	44.7
Italy.	243.0	80.2	17.3	-	United Kingdom.	343.0	68.3	1.5	28.5
Japan	996.0	56.7	9.0	31.9	United States	3,619.6	70.3	9.0	18.6
Kazakhstan	49.3	87.6	12.2	0.2	Uzbekistan	43.4	85.3	14.7	-
Korea, North	32.0	34.4	65.6	-	Venezuela	70.4	25.4	74.6	-

- Represents zero.   [1] Includes geothermal, wind, photovoltaic, and solar thermal generation, not shown separately.   [2] Electricity generated from coal, oil, and gas.   [3] See footnote 2, Table 1352.   [4] See footnote 4, Table 1352.

Source: U.S. Energy Information Administration, *International Energy Annual 1998.*

No. 1392. Commercial Nuclear Power Generation by Country: 1990 to 1999

[Generation for **calendar years;** other data as of **December (1,743.9 represents 1,743,900,000,000)**]

Country	Reactors				Gross electricity generated (bil. kWh)				Gross capacity (1,000 kW)			
	1990	1995	1998	1999	1990	1995	1998	1999	1990	1995	1998	1999
Total.	368	423	436	431	1,743.9	2,271.7	2,424.2	2,489.9	301,745	358,414	371,544	367,602
United States . .	112	109	107	104	606.4	705.7	705.6	760.5	105,998	105,810	106,005	103,095
Argentina	2	2	2	2	7.0	7.0	7.5	7.1	1,005	1,005	1,005	1,005
Armenia	(NA)	1	1	1	(NA)	0.3	1.6	2.2	(NA)	408	408	408
Belgium	7	7	7	7	42.7	41.3	46.1	49.0	5,740	5,911	5,995	5,995
Brazil.	1	1	1	1	2.0	2.5	3.3	3.9	657	657	657	657
Bulgaria	(NA)	6	6	6	(NA)	17.1	17.1	15.8	(NA)	3,760	3,760	3,760
Canada	19	22	21	21	74.0	100.2	72.8	74.3	13,855	16,699	15,795	15,795
China [1]	(NA)	(NA)	2	2	(NA)	(NA)	13.0	14.7	(NA)	(NA)	1,968	1,968
Czech Republic .	(NA)	(NA)	4	4	(NA)	(NA)	13.2	13.3	(NA)	(NA)	1,760	1,760
Finland.	4	4	4	4	18.9	18.9	21.8	22.9	2,400	2,400	2,760	2,760
France.	58	56	56	55	314.1	377.2	385.9	378.4	58,862	60,674	60,674	59,888
Germany	22	21	20	19	147.2	154.1	161.7	169.9	23,973	24,035	23,496	22,209
Great Britain . . .	42	34	35	35	68.8	82.7	99.5	93.7	15,274	14,022	15,272	15,272
Hungary.	4	4	4	4	13.6	14.0	13.9	14.1	1,760	1,840	1,840	1,840
India	6	10	10	11	6.0	7.6	11.4	13.0	1,330	2,270	2,270	2,505
Italy	2	(NA)	(NA)	(NA)	-	(NA)	(NA)	(NA)	1,132	(NA)	(NA)	(NA)
Japan	40	50	53	52	191.9	286.0	326.9	317.7	31,645	41,356	45,248	45,082
Korea, South . . .	9	10	14	15	52.8	63.9	87.3	94.2	7,616	8,615	12,015	12,768
Lithuania	(NA)	2	2	2	(NA)	9.6	13.5	9.9	(NA)	3,000	3,000	3,000
Mexico.	1	2	2	2	2.1	7.9	9.5	10.0	675	1,350	1,350	1,350
Netherlands . . .	2	2	1	1	3.4	4.0	3.8	3.8	540	540	480	480
Pakistan	1	1	1	1	0.4	0.5	0.4	0.8	137	137	137	137
Romania	(NA)	(NA)	1	1	(NA)	(NA)	5.3	5.2	(NA)	(NA)	706	706
Russia	(NA)	29	29	29	(NA)	98.7	103.7	119.8	(NA)	21,266	21,266	21,266
Slovakia	(NA)	(NA)	4	4	(NA)	(NA)	10.3	10.5	(NA)	(NA)	1,760	1,760
Slovenia	1	1	1	1	4.6	4.7	5.0	4.7	664	664	664	664
South Africa . . .	2	2	2	2	8.9	11.9	14.3	13.5	1,930	1,930	1,930	1,930
Spain.	10	9	9	9	54.3	55.4	59.1	58.9	7,984	7,400	7,625	7,759
Sweden	12	12	12	11	68.2	69.9	73.5	73.2	10,344	10,442	10,445	10,445
Switzerland	5	5	5	5	23.6	24.8	25.7	24.8	3,079	3,200	3,229	3,314
Taiwan [1]	6	6	6	6	32.9	35.3	36.9	38.4	5,146	5,144	5,144	5,144
Ukraine	(NA)	15	14	14	(NA)	70.5	74.2	72.2	(NA)	13,880	12,880	12,880

- Represents zero.   NA Not available.   [1] See footnote 2, Table 1352.

Source: McGraw-Hill, Inc., New York, NY, *Nucleonics Week,* March issues (copyright).

Comparative International Statistics   845

No. 1393. World Production of Major Mineral Commodities: 1990 to 1999

[5,353 represents 5,353,000,000]

Country	Unit	1990	1995	1998	1999, prel.	Leading producers, 1998
MINERAL FUELS						
Coal.	Mil. short tons. .	5,353	5,126	5,043	(NA)	China, United States, India
Dry natural gas	Tril. cu. ft.	73.6	78.0	83.0	(NA)	Russia, United States, Canada
Natural gas plant liquids [1] . . .	Mil. barrels [2]. .	1,691	2,002	2,141	(NA)	United States, Saudi Arabia, Canada
Petroleum, crude	Mil. barrels [2]. .	22,107	22,752	24,441	(NA)	Saudi Arabia, United States, Russia
NONMETALLIC MINERALS						
Cement, hydraulic	Mil. metric tons .	1,160	1,444	1,520	1,560	China, United States, India
Diamond, gem and industrial .	Mil. carats	111	113	115	117	Australia, Congo (Kinshasa), Russia
Nitrogen in ammonia.	Mil. metric tons .	97.5	100.0	106.0	101.0	Germany, United States, India
Phosphate rock	Mil. metric tons .	162	130	145	138	United States, China, Morocco
Potash, marketable.	Mil. metric tons .	27.5	24.6	25.1	25.2	Canada, Russia, Belarus
Salt	Mil. metric tons .	183	192	186	200	United States, China, Germany
Sulfur, elemental basis	Mil. metric tons .	57.8	53.2	57.8	55.9	United States, Canada, China
METALS						
Aluminum [3]	Mil. metric tons .	19.3	19.7	22.1	22.7	United States, Russia, Canada
Bauxite, gross weight	Mil. metric tons .	113.0	112.0	122.0	123.0	United States, Guinea, Jamaica
Chromite, gross weight [1]	1,000 metric tons	13,200	14,300	12,700	12,800	South Africa, Turkey, Kazakhstan
Copper, metal content [4].	1,000 metric tons	8,950	10,100	12,200	12,600	Chile, United States, Indonesia
Gold, metal content	Metric tons. . . .	2,180	2,210	2,460	2,330	South Africa, United States, Australia
Iron ore, gross weight [5].	1,000 metric tons	983	1,031	1,020	992	China, Brazil, Australia
Lead, metal content [4]	1,000 metric tons	3,370	2,820	3,100	3,040	Australia, China, United States
Manganese ore, gross weight.	Mil. metric tons .	26.1	23.3	(NA)	(NA)	South Africa, China, Gabon
Nickel, metal content [4]	1,000 metric tons	974	1,030	1,140	1,140	Russia, Canada, Australia
Steel, crude	Mil. metric tons .	771	755	783	(NA)	China, United States, Japan
Tin, metal content [4].	1,000 metric tons	221	193	206	210	China, Indonesia, Peru
Zinc, metal content [4].	1,000 metric tons	7,150	7,280	7,550	7,640	China, Australia, Canada

NA Not available.   [1] Excludes China.   [2] 42-gallon barrels.   [3] Unalloyed ingot metal.   [4] Mine output.   [5] Includes iron ore concentrates and iron ore agglomerates.

Source: Mineral fuels, U.S. Energy Information Administration, *International Energy Annual;* nonmetallic minerals and metals, 1990, U.S. Bureau of Mines, thereafter, U.S. Geological Survey, *Minerals Yearbook; Annual Reports;* and *Mineral Commodity Summaries, 1999.*

No. 1394. Wood Products—Production, Exports, and Consumption for Selected Countries: 1990 to 1998

[In thousand cubic meters (5,830 represents 5,830,000). Data for 1998 are estimated]

Country	Production			Exports			Consumption		
	1990	1995	1998	1990	1995	1998	1990	1995	1998
SOFTWOOD LOGS									
Australia	5,830	8,188	11,603	-	100	203	5,830	8,088	11,401
Canada.	122,000	120,000	119,000	800	729	1,000	125,289	124,295	122,600
China	(NA)	(NA)	34,843	8	22	5	(NA)	(NA)	35,884
Finland	19,600	24,600	24,200	161	1,000	600	19,734	23,850	26,800
France	14,189	13,550	14,600	477	250	270	13,969	13,419	14,450
Germany [1]	(NA)	20,410	22,500	1,947	3,298	3,500	(NA)	18,234	20,800
Japan	16,775	18,067	17,000	11	4	5	33,446	32,968	29,995
New Zealand	8,361	12,704	10,600	2,931	5,257	3,500	5,435	7,449	7,104
Russia	(NA)	(NA)	55,000	(NA)	(NA)	13,000	(NA)	(NA)	42,000
Sweden	24,700	30,100	34,000	336	500	1,500	24,787	30,200	35,000
SOFTWOOD LUMBER									
Canada.	53,777	59,590	61,000	37,008	47,561	46,200	17,767	12,789	15,430
China	(NA)	(NA)	14,129	13	50	63	(NA)	(NA)	14,406
Finland	7,400	9,400	11,000	4,152	7,337	7,900	3,261	2,213	3,250
Germany [1]	12,145	13,308	14,200	839	1,618	1,900	15,551	16,455	17,300
Japan	26,551	22,777	20,000	7	-	-	33,854	32,591	30,000
Russia	(NA)	(NA)	12,400	(NA)	(NA)	3,200	(NA)	(NA)	9,200
Sweden	11,785	14,559	15,500	6,500	10,700	11,000	5,431	4,014	4,600
TEMPERATE HARDWOOD LOGS									
China	(NA)	(NA)	20,846	83	51	1	(NA)	(NA)	20,877
France	10,157	8,160	8,000	1,655	1,000	1,089	8,621	7,290	7,211
Russia	(NA)	(NA)	18,000	(NA)	(NA)	5,500	(NA)	(NA)	12,500
TEMPERATE HARDWOOD LUMBER									
China	(NA)	(NA)	7,636	60	177	300	(NA)	(NA)	8,273
France	3,303	2,908	2,620	646	606	520	2,767	2,793	2,360
Russia	(NA)	(NA)	4,100	(NA)	(NA)	180	(NA)	(NA)	3,920
TROPICAL HARDWOOD LOGS									
Brazil	33,000	25,700	27,030	-	-	410	33,146	25,706	26,625
Indonesia	27,000	25,000	25,000	-	-	-	27,068	25,004	25,000
Malaysia	39,655	31,572	29,670	20,378	7,864	5,100	19,286	23,934	25,070
TROPICAL HARDWOOD LUMBER									
Brazil	8,500	9,220	9,740	525	984	725	8,252	9,719	9,353
Indonesia	9,000	7,500	7,050	561	722	-	8,439	6,778	7,050
Malaysia	8,780	6,950	7,400	5,247	4,151	3,050	3,568	3,896	4,750

- Represents zero.   NA Not available.   [1] Data for 1990 do not include East Germany.

Source: U.S. Dept. of Agriculture, Foreign Agricultural Service, *Wood Products: International Trade and Foreign Markets, Annual Production, Consumption, and Trade Edition,* Circular Series WP-1-99, March 1999.

846   Comparative International Statistics

No. 1395. Unmanufactured Tobacco and Cigarettes—Selected Countries: 1995 to 1999

[5,546 represents 5,546,000. Tobacco is on dry weight basis]

Country	Unmanufactured tobacco (1,000 metric tons)		
	1995	1998	1999
PRODUCTION			
World, total	5,546	5,928	6,048
China	2,083	2,010	2,108
India	528	572	588
United States	513	627	572
Brazil	324	373	498
Turkey	170	218	216
EXPORTS			
World, total	1,767	1,914	1,948
Brazil	256	300	318
Zimbabwe	174	169	206
United States	209	212	189
Turkey	136	129	126
Malawi	99	135	108
IMPORTS			
World, total	1,781	1,903	1,841
United States	199	247	241
Germany	210	230	217
Russia	148	201	165
United Kingdom	141	148	147
Japan	115	92	93
CONSUMPTION			
World, total	6,305	6,447	6,538
China	2,209	2,342	2,518
United States	699	723	692
India	464	483	478
Russia	142	180	191
Indonesia	183	187	181

Country	Cigarettes (bil. pieces)		
	1995	1998	1999
PRODUCTION			
World, total	5,599	5,497	5,485
China	1,735	1,675	1,675
United States	746	680	646
Indonesia	186	223	219
Russia	141	179	190
Japan	263	188	188
Germany	221	178	180
Brazil	174	170	175
United Kingdom	156	164	155
EXPORTS			
World, total	987	944	951
United States	231	201	151
United Kingdom	85	125	106
Netherlands	82	104	104
Brazil	54	73	75
Germany	85	65	70
Singapore	50	53	59
Hong Kong	74	35	36
China	63	23	24
IMPORTS			
World, total	668	663	650
Japan	72	81	81
France	51	61	61
Singapore	38	45	49
Russia	78	56	45
Italy	39	43	42
Hong Kong	59	28	30
United Kingdom	20	45	30

Source: U.S. Dept. of Agriculture, Foreign Agricultural Service, *Tobacco: World Markets and Trade*, April 2000.

No. 1396. World Food Production by Commodity: 1990 to 1999

[In millions of metric tons (1,768.8 represents 1,768,800,000)]

Commodity	1990	1992	1993	1994	1995	1996	1997	1998	1999, prel.
Grains, total	1,768.8	1,790.0	1,714.0	1,760.8	1,712.6	1,871.4	1,880.3	1,872.4	1,857.7
Wheat	588.0	562.4	559.0	524.8	538.6	582.8	609.3	589.2	587.0
Coarse grains	828.7	872.0	799.7	871.6	802.7	908.3	884.1	889.5	871.0
Corn	482.3	538.5	476.1	560.2	516.6	592.0	575.4	605.3	600.8
Rice, milled	352.0	355.6	355.4	364.5	371.3	380.4	386.8	393.8	400.7
Oils	58.1	61.4	63.5	70.0	72.8	75.6	77.7	81.8	85.7
Soybeans	104.2	117.4	117.8	137.7	124.9	132.2	158.0	159.3	154.7
Rapeseed	25.1	25.3	26.8	30.4	34.5	31.6	33.4	35.9	42.5
Pulses [1]	58.4	51.0	55.7	56.3	54.8	53.6	55.3	55.9	59.3
Vegetables and melons [1]	461.4	478.6	509.5	532.1	559.6	591.2	599.0	616.5	628.7
Fruits [1]	352.2	379.0	384.7	391.0	406.4	427.3	443.0	432.3	444.7
Nuts [1]	4.6	5.0	5.0	5.3	5.0	5.6	5.9	5.9	6.4
Red meat	117.2	119.1	117.7	119.9	124.2	124.5	130.3	135.4	137.2
Poultry	37.4	41.8	43.6	46.8	50.6	53.0	54.6	55.5	57.8
Milk	441.3	423.7	393.5	383.7	380.8	380.3	381.2	386.2	387.2

[1] Data from Food and Agriculture Organization of the United Nations.
Source: U.S. Department of Agriculture, Economic Research Service, *Agricultural Outlook*, monthly.

No. 1397. Fisheries—Commercial Catch by Country: 1990 to 1997

[In thousands of metric tons, live weight (97,854 represents 97,854,000). Catch of fish, crustaceans, mollusks (including weight of shells). Does not include marine mammals and aquatic plants]

Country	1990	1995	1996	1997	Country	1990	1995	1996	1997
World [1]	97,854	116,042	119,942	122,138	Norway	1,745	2,803	2,960	3,223
China [2]	12,095	28,418	31,937	35,038	Korea, South	1,745	2,688	2,772	2,596
Peru	6,875	8,943	9,522	7,877	Iceland	1,508	1,616	2,064	2,210
Japan	10,354	6,787	6,765	6,689	Philippines	2,210	2,222	2,133	2,136
Chile	5,195	7,591	6,911	6,084	Denmark	1,518	2,044	1,723	1,866
United States	5,868	5,638	5,395	5,448	Vietnam	960	1,394	1,431	1,546
India	3,794	4,906	5,258	5,378	Mexico	1,401	1,355	1,495	1,529
Russia	7,808	4,374	4,730	4,715	Argentina	556	1,149	1,250	1,352
Indonesia	3,044	4,139	4,291	4,404	Bangladesh	848	1,173	1,264	1,343
Thailand	2,786	3,573	3,515	3,488	Spain	1,380	1,391	1,332	1,341

[1] Includes other countries, not shown separately. [2] See footnote 2, Table 1352.
Source: U.S. National Oceanic and Atmospheric Administration, National Marine Fisheries Service, *Fisheries of the United States*, annual. Data from Food and Agriculture Organization of the United Nations, Rome, Italy.

Comparative International Statistics   847

No. 1398. Meat Production by Type and Country: 1997 to 1999

[In thousand metric tons (126,649 represents 126,649,000). Carcass weight basis]

Country	Total [1]		Beef and veal		Pork		Country	Poultry meat	
	1997	1998 [2]	1997	1998 [2]	1997	1998 [2]		1998	1999 [2]
World [3]	126,649	130,156	48,264	47,847	71,382	75,083	World [3]	53,468	55,565
Brazil	7,590	7,803	6,050	6,140	1,540	1,663	Brazil	4,600	5,105
China [4]	40,895	42,880	4,150	4,288	34,643	36,180	China [4]	10,700	10,900
France	4,046	4,030	1,677	1,586	2,220	2,300	France	2,320	2,310
Germany	5,053	5,222	1,448	1,367	3,562	3,811	Mexico	1,710	1,809
United States	19,667	20,541	11,714	11,804	7,835	8,623	United States . . .	15,128	15,981

[1] Includes mutton, lamb, and goat meat, not shown separately. Excludes offals, rabbit, and poultry meat. [2] Preliminary. [3] Includes other countries, not shown separately. [4] See footnote 2, Table 1352.

Source: U.S. Dept. of Agriculture, National Agricultural Statistics Service, *Agricultural Statistics*, annual.

No. 1399. Wheat, Rice, and Corn Production by Country: 1995 to 1999

[In thousands of metric tons (582,774 represents 582,774,000). Rice data cover paddy. Data for each country pertain to the calendar year in which all or most of the crop was harvested. See text of this section for general comments concerning quality of the data]

Country	Wheat			Rice			Corn		
	1995	1998	1999	1995	1998	1999	1995	1998	1999
World.	582,774	589,152	586,956	551,036	585,243	595,485	516,637	605,256	600,832
Argentina	8,600	12,200	15,000	877	1,662	923	11,100	13,500	15,500
Australia	16,504	22,108	24,500	951	1,390	1,119	317	322	350
Bangladesh.	1,245	1,803	1,900	26,533	29,784	30,378	-	-	-
Brazil	1,526	2,190	2,435	10,026	11,375	10,662	32,480	32,350	32,000
Burma	150	90	100	17,000	16,034	16,466	270	250	240
Canada	25,037	24,076	26,850	-	-	-	7,271	8,952	9,096
China [1]	102,215	109,726	115,000	185,214	198,714	201,429	112,000	132,954	128,000
Egypt.	5,700	6,093	6,200	4,399	4,198	5,428	5,353	5,605	6,100
France	30,862	39,793	37,009	124	112	103	12,394	15,204	15,630
Germany	17,763	20,188	19,684	-	-	-	2,395	2,782	3,050
India	65,470	66,350	70,780	119,442	129,013	129,763	9,530	10,680	10,500
Indonesia	-	-	-	51,100	50,791	50,791	6,000	6,500	6,200
Italy.	7,653	7,939	7,341	1,311	1,397	1,376	8,454	8,600	10,000
Mexico	3,468	3,235	3,100	349	469	450	17,780	17,600	19,000
Pakistan	17,002	18,694	17,854	5,951	7,012	7,651	1,283	1,302	1,250
Philippines	-	-	-	11,174	10,268	11,923	4,324	4,894	4,500
Russia	30,100	27,000	31,000	462	415	446	1,700	800	1,100
Thailand	-	-	-	21,800	23,000	24,015	3,700	4,300	3,800
Turkey	15,500	18,500	16,500	346	292	338	1,800	2,300	2,400
United States	59,404	69,327	62,662	7,887	8,530	9,547	187,970	247,882	239,719

- Represents or rounds to zero. [1] See footnote 2, Table 1352.

No. 1400. Wheat, Rice, and Corn—Exports and Imports of Leading Countries: 1995 to 1999

[In thousands of metric tons (32,003 represents 32,003,000). Wheat data are for trade year beginning in July of year shown; rice data are for calendar year; corn data are for trade year beginning in October of year shown. Countries listed are the six leading exporters or importers in 1999]

Leading exporters	Exports			Leading importers	Imports		
	1995	1998	1999		1995	1998	1999
WHEAT				WHEAT			
European Union	32,003	35,927	36,475	European Union	21,505	25,174	24,950
United States	33,778	28,370	29,257	Brazil	5,600	7,115	7,000
Australia	13,311	16,000	18,500	Iran	3,029	2,056	6,700
Canada	16,342	14,705	18,500	Egypt	5,932	7,430	6,000
Argentina	4,483	8,200	10,500	Japan	6,101	5,883	5,900
Kazakhstan	4,279	2,280	4,500	Russia	5,315	2,500	4,800
RICE				RICE			
Thailand	5,281	6,679	5,500	Indonesia	1,029	3,900	2,000
Vietnam	3,040	4,555	4,000	European Union	1,638	1,612	1,540
United States	2,661	2,682	2,743	Iran	1,344	1,000	1,200
China [1]	265	2,708	2,700	Nigeria	300	900	950
Pakistan	1,632	1,850	1,850	Iraq	234	781	850
India	3,500	3,350	1,200	Saudi Arabia	638	775	750
CORN				CORN			
United States	56,589	50,310	48,262	Japan	15,976	16,336	16,250
China [1]	168	3,338	9,000	European Union	10,420	11,773	10,685
Argentina	7,494	7,800	8,700	Korea, South	8,963	7,517	9,000
European Union	7,480	8,927	8,113	Taiwan [1]	5,733	4,575	4,700
South Africa	200	700	1,800	Mexico	6,433	5,612	4,600
Hungary	120	1,766	1,700	Egypt	2,257	3,700	4,000

[1] See footnote 2, Table 1352.

Source of Tables 1399 and 1400: U.S. Department of Agriculture, Economic Research Service, unpublished data from the PS&D (Production, supply and distribution) database.

No. 1401. United States and Foreign Stock Markets—Market Capitalization and Value of Shares Traded: 1990 to 1999

[In billions of U.S. dollars (3,059.4 represents $3,059,400,000,000). Market capitalization is the market value of all domestic listed companies at the end of the year. The market value of a company is the share price times the number of shares outstanding. Value of shares traded is the annual total turnover of listed company shares]

Country	Market capitalization				Value of shares traded			
	1990	1995	1998	1999	1990	1995	1998	1999
United States	3,059.4	6,857.6	13,451.4	(NA)	1,751.3	5,108.6	13,148.5	(NA)
Argentina	3.3	37.8	45.3	83.9	0.9	4.6	15.1	7.8
Australia	107.6	245.2	874.3	(NA)	40.1	98.7	407.4	(NA)
Austria	11.5	32.5	34.1	(NA)	18.6	25.8	16.6	(NA)
Belgium	65.4	105.0	245.7	(NA)	6.4	15.2	55.4	(NA)
Brazil	16.4	147.6	160.9	228.0	5.6	79.2	146.6	87.3
Canada	241.9	366.3	543.4	(NA)	71.3	183.7	372.1	(NA)
Chile	13.6	73.9	51.9	68.2	0.8	11.1	4.4	6.9
China [1]	(NA)	42.1	231.3	330.7	(NA)	49.8	284.8	377.1
Denmark	39.1	56.2	98.9	(NA)	11.1	25.9	(NA)	(NA)
Egypt	1.8	8.1	24.4	32.8	0.1	0.7	5.0	9.0
Finland	22.7	44.1	154.5	(NA)	3.9	19.0	60.3	(NA)
France	314.4	522.1	991.5	(NA)	116.9	364.6	572.2	(NA)
Germany	355.1	577.4	1,094.0	(NA)	501.8	573.5	1,390.8	(NA)
Greece	15.2	17.1	80.0	204.2	3.9	6.1	47.0	188.7
Hong Kong	83.4	303.7	343.4	(NA)	34.6	106.9	205.9	(NA)
India	38.6	127.2	105.2	184.6	21.9	13.7	64.5	122.2
Indonesia	8.1	66.6	22.1	64.1	4.0	14.4	9.7	19.9
Iran	(NA)	6.6	14.9	(NA)	(NA)	0.7	1.4	(NA)
Ireland	(NA)	25.8	30.0	(NA)	(NA)	13.2	22.1	(NA)
Israel	3.3	36.4	39.6	63.8	5.5	9.2	11.3	15.5
Italy	148.8	209.5	569.7	(NA)	42.6	86.9	475.8	(NA)
Japan	2,917.7	3,667.3	2,495.8	(NA)	1,602.4	1,231.6	948.5	(NA)
Korea, South	110.6	182.0	114.6	308.5	75.9	185.2	137.9	733.6
Luxembourg	10.5	30.4	35.4	(NA)	0.1	0.2	1.2	(NA)
Malaysia	48.6	222.7	98.6	145.4	10.9	76.8	28.8	48.5
Mexico	32.7	90.7	91.7	154.0	12.2	34.4	33.8	36.0
Morocco	1.0	6.0	15.7	13.7	0.1	2.4	1.4	2.5
Netherlands	119.8	356.5	603.2	(NA)	40.2	248.6	379.2	(NA)
New Zealand	8.8	32.0	89.4	(NA)	1.9	8.4	50.5	(NA)
Norway	26.1	44.6	56.3	(NA)	14.0	24.4	42.6	(NA)
Philippines	5.9	58.9	35.3	48.1	1.2	14.7	10.0	19.7
Poland	(NA)	4.6	20.5	29.6	(NA)	2.8	8.9	11.1
Portugal	9.2	18.4	63.0	(NA)	1.7	4.2	47.6	(NA)
Russia	(NA)	15.9	20.6	72.2	(NA)	0.5	6.8	2.8
Saudi Arabia	(NA)	40.9	42.6	60.4	(NA)	6.2	13.7	14.8
Singapore	34.3	148.0	94.5	(NA)	20.3	60.5	50.7	(NA)
South Africa	137.5	280.5	170.3	262.5	8.2	17.0	58.4	72.9
Spain	111.4	197.8	402.2	(NA)	41.0	59.8	699.0	(NA)
Sweden	97.9	178.0	278.7	(NA)	17.6	93.2	203.7	(NA)
Switzerland	160.0	433.6	689.2	(NA)	(NA)	310.9	637.3	(NA)
Taiwan [1]	100.7	187.2	260.0	376.0	715.0	383.1	884.7	910.0
Thailand	23.9	141.5	34.9	58.4	22.9	57.0	20.7	41.6
Turkey	19.1	20.8	33.6	112.7	5.8	51.4	68.6	81.3
United Kingdom	848.9	1,407.7	2,374.3	(NA)	278.7	510.1	1,167.4	(NA)

NA Not available.　[1] See footnote 2, Table 1352.
Source: International Finance Corporation, Washington, DC, *Emerging Stock Markets Factbook*, annual, (copyright).

No. 1402. Dow-Jones World Stock Index by Country and Industry: 1995 to 1999

[Index figures shown are as of **December 31. Indexes based on June 30, 1982=100 for United States; December 31, 1991=100 for World**. Based on share prices denominated in U.S. dollars. Stocks in countries that impose significant restrictions on foreign ownership are included in the world index in the same proportion that shares are available to foreign investors]

Industry	1995	1997	1998	1999	Industry	1995	1997	1998	1999
World, total	135.0	168.7	202.8	252.4	Asia/Pacific	122.4	79.2	81.0	131.5
Americas	145.8	230.2	283.8	341.4	Australia	127.9	133.8	141.0	170.0
United States	581.3	922.3	1,169.3	1,390.3	Hong Kong	226.8	227.6	204.1	353.4
Canada	108.5	154.1	146.2	209.1	Indonesia	174.7	69.7	40.5	71.7
Mexico	79.0	144.0	89.0	170.1	Japan	113.8	70.4	74.2	124.1
Europe	135.3	188.8	235.0	275.5	Malaysia	(NA)	(NA)	78.2	111.2
Austria	102.6	108.6	105.3	98.0	New Zealand	178.8	169.3	129.4	141.4
Belgium	142.9	177.9	289.4	239.4	Singapore	193.9	115.0	109.4	170.9
Denmark	112.6	184.1	190.1	200.4	Thailand	196.6	30.2	39.8	55.5
Finland	201.3	310.6	604.5	1,530.3					
France	120.4	157.6	221.0	292.2	Basic materials	129.4	117.8	112.0	153.1
Germany	136.9	193.2	248.0	299.8	Independents	146.1	169.7	195.5	295.6
Ireland	152.8	243.1	335.6	291.2	Consumer, cyclical	136.3	161.9	200.5	251.6
Italy	103.1	155.7	234.4	249.6	Consumer, noncyclical . .	132.8	192.8	242.9	227.7
Netherlands	172.1	266.3	346.0	371.1	Energy	132.3	189.0	182.0	208.0
Norway	129.2	170.4	116.1	154.8	Financial services	136.4	169.7	186.7	196.4
Spain	114.0	182.7	270.6	283.0	Industrial	120.6	119.6	128.8	155.1
Sweden	163.2	238.6	253.5	432.7	Technology	173.2	245.3	370.3	685.3
Switzerland	232.8	326.9	395.9	369.4	Utilities	126.1	161.6	212.9	277.6
United Kingdom	121.4	175.1	198.6	226.9					

NA Not available.
Source: Dow Jones & Company, Inc., New York, NY, *Wall Street Journal*, selected issues (copyright).

U.S. Census Bureau, Statistical Abstract of the United States: 2000

No. 1403. Foreign Stock Market Activity—Morgan Stanley Capital International Indexes: 1995 to 1999

[Index figures shown are as of **December 31. January 1, 1970=100, except as noted**. Based on share prices denominated in U.S. dollars. EM=Emerging Markets]

Index and country	Index 1995	Index 1998	Index 1999	Percent change [1] 1998	Percent change [1] 1999	Index and country	Index 1995	Index 1998	Index 1999	Percent change [1] 1998	Percent change [1] 1999
ALL COUNTRY (AC) INDEXES						Sweden	1,796	3,056	5,432	12.6	77.8
						Switzerland	1,569	2,788	2,570	22.6	-7.8
AC World index	182.0	271.9	341.2	19.7	25.5	United Kingdom	716	1,208	1,326	14.8	9.7
AC World index except						Hong Kong	4,818	4,259	6,595	-7.6	54.9
USA	153.8	180.0	233.4	12.0	29.7	Japan	3,348	2,224	3,571	4.3	60.6
AC Asia Pacific	124.5	82.6	130.4	0.5	57.9	Singapore	2,735	1,480	2,917	-14.6	97.1
AC Europe	201.9	364.6	420.1	24.8	15.2	**EMERGING MARKETS**					
European Union	189.2	349.0	408.3	27.9	17.0	EM Far East index	263.7	128.4	212.6	-5.3	61.1
DEVELOPED MARKETS						India [5]	98.8	80.4	148.4	-22.9	84.7
						Indonesia	508.2	110.2	211.6	-32.4	92.0
World index [2]	734	1,150	1,421	22.8	23.6	Korea, South	173.8	83.3	158.4	(NA)	90.2
EAFE index [3]	1,136	1,405	1,760	18.2	25.3	Malaysia	347.0	93.1	192.9	-31.0	107.2
Europe index	733	1,337	1,526	26.5	14.1	Pakistan [5]	91.5	36.1	51.4	-60.6	42.2
Pacific index	2,362	1,595	2,490	1.2	56.2	Philippines	442.5	229.6	247.1	14.9	7.6
Far East index	3,384	2,215	3,568	1.2	61.1	Sri Lanka [5]	105.6	71.7	64.7	-27.3	-9.7
						Taiwan [6]	227.9	231.5	350.8	-21.5	51.5
United States	581	1,196	1,446	28.8	20.9	Thailand	523.3	86.6	121.7	18.7	40.5
Canada	403.9	525.3	797.2	-7.4	51.8	EM Latin America	782	737	1,192	-38.2	61.8
Australia	304.2	313.2	360.8	3.8	15.2	Argentina	1,239	1,282	1,668	-27.3	30.1
New Zealand [4]	114.2	80.7	88.5	-25.2	9.7	Brazil	578	551	952	-44.1	73.0
						Chile [6]	903	534	728	-30.7	36.5
Austria	890	914	818	-0.9	-10.5	Colombia [5]	110.2	88.6	71.6	-45.3	-19.1
Belgium	897	1,782	1,501	64.8	-15.8	Mexico	744	846	1,525	-35.1	80.2
Denmark	1,124	1,934	2,144	7.8	10.9	Peru [5]	221.3	146.6	170.6	-42.1	16.3
Finland [4]	129	431	1,081	119.1	150.7	Venezuela	75.4	103.5	105.3	-52.7	1.7
France	672	1,242	1,590	40.0	28.0	Czech Republic	(NA)	76.3	79.4	(NA)	4.0
Germany	818	1,449	1,720	28.2	18.7	Greece [4]	238.2	560.9	827.7	75.0	47.6
Ireland [4]	215.7	418.6	359.9	33.0	-14.0	Hungary	(NA)	291.4	322.9	(NA)	10.8
Italy	208.6	466.5	459.6	51.0	-1.5	Jordan	96.1	71.7	73.2	-14.3	2.0
Luxembourg	(NA)	319.8	481.3	(NA)	50.5	Poland	(NA)	400.7	523.0	(NA)	30.5
Netherlands	1,192	2,187	2,302	21.1	5.3	Russia	(NA)	64.4	223.0	(NA)	246.2
Norway	1,023	934	1,210	-31.2	29.5	South Africa	(NA)	127.8	196.0	(NA)	53.4
Portugal [4]	68.4	163.2	145.5	25.4	-10.9	Turkey	103.1	133.6	460.0	-53.5	244.4
Spain	162.3	403.1	417.3	47.9	3.5						

NA Not available. [1] Percent change during calendar year (e.g. December 31, 1997, through December 31, 1998). Adjusted for foreign exchange fluctuations relative to U.S. dollar. [2] Includes South African gold mines quoted in London. [3] Europe, Australian, Far East Index. Comprises all European and Far East countries listed under developed markets plus Australia, Malaysia, and New Zealand. [4] January 1, 1988=100. [5] December 1992=100. [6] See footnote 2, Table 1352.

Source: Morgan Stanley Capital International, New York, NY, <http://www.msci.com/index2.html> (copyright). This information may not be reproduced or redisseminated in any form without prior written permission from Morgan Stanley Capital International. This information is provided on an "as is" basis. Neither Morgan Stanley or any other party makes any representation or warranty of any kind either express or implied, with respect to this information (or the results to be obtained by the use thereof) and Morgan Stanley expressly disclaims any and all warranties of originality, accuracy, completeness, merchantability, and fitness for any particular purpose. The user of this information assumes the entire risk of any use made of the information. In no event shall Morgan Stanley or any other part be liable to the user for any direct or indirect damages, including without limitation, any lost profits, lost savings, or other incidental or consequential damages arising out of use of this information.

No. 1404. Foreign Stock Market Indices: 1980 to 1999

[As of **year end**. The DAX index is a total return index which includes dividends, whereas the other foreign indices are price indices which exclude dividends]

Year	London FTSE 100	Tokyo Nikkei 225	Hong Kong Hang Seng	Germany DAX-30	Paris CAC-40
1980	647	7,116	1,477	481	(X)
1985	1,413	13,113	1,752	1,366	(X)
1990	2,144	23,849	3,025	1,398	1,518
1993	3,418	17,417	11,888	2,267	2,268
1994	3,066	19,723	8,191	2,107	1,881
1995	3,689	19,868	10,073	2,254	1,872
1996	4,119	19,361	13,452	2,889	2,316
1997	5,136	15,259	10,723	4,250	2,999
1998	5,883	13,842	9,507	5,002	3,943
1999	6,930	18,934	16,962	6,958	5,958

X Not applicable.

Source: Global Financial Data, Los Angeles, CA, <http://www.globalfindata.com>, unpublished data. (Copyright.)

No. 1405. Foreign Exchange Rates: 1999

[**Foreign currency units per U.S. dollar.** Rates shown include market, official, principal, and secondary rates, as published by the International Monetary Fund in *International Financial Statistics*]

Country	Currency	1999	Country	Currency	1999
Afghanistan	Afghanis	3,000	Laos	Kip	7,102
Albania	Leks	137.7	Latvia	Lats	0.59
Algeria	Algerian Dinar	66.57	Lebanon	Lebanese Pounds	1,508
Antigua and Barbuda	E.Caribbean Dollar	2.700	Lesotho	Loti	6.11
Argentina	Pesos	1.00	Liberia	Liberian Dollar	1.00
Armenia	Dram	535.1	Libya	Libyan Dinars	0.46
Aruba	Aruban Florins	1.79	Lithuania	Litai	4.00
Australia	Australian Dollar	1.55	Luxembourg [1]	Francs	37.86
Austria [1]	Schillings	12.92	Macedonia, The Former		
Bahamas, The	Bahamian Dollar	1.00	Yugoslav Republic of	Denar	56.90
Bahrain	Dinars	0.38	Madagascar [2]	Malagasy Francs	6,250
Bangladesh	Taka	49.09	Malaysia	Ringgit	3.80
Barbados	Barbados Dollar	2.00	Mali	Cfa Francs	615.7
Belarus [2]	Rubel	276,000	Malta	Maltese Liri	0.40
Belgium [1]	Francs	37.86	Mauritania [2]	Ouguiyas	209.5
Belize	Belize Dollar	2.00	Mauritius	Rupees	25.19
Benin	Cfa Francs	615.7	Mexico	New Pesos	9.56
Bolivia	Bolivianos	5.81	Moldova	Lei	10.52
Botswana	Pula	4.62	Mongolia	Tugriks	1,021.9
Brazil	Reais	1.81	Morocco	Dirhams	9.80
Bulgaria	Leva	1.84	Mozambique	Meticais	12,775
Burkina Faso	Cfa Francs	615.7	Namibia	Namibia Dollar	6.11
Burma	Kyats	6.29	Nepal	Rupees	68.25
Cambodia	Riels	3,808	Netherlands [1]	Guilders	2.07
Cameroon	Cfa Francs	615.7	Netherlands Antilles	Guilders	1.79
Canada	Canadian Dollar	1.49	New Zealand	New Zealand Dollar	1.89
Central African Republic	Cfa Francs	615.7	Nicaragua	Cordobas	11.81
Chad	Cfa Francs	615.7	Niger	Cfa Francs	615.7
Chile	Pesos	508.8	Nigeria	Naira	21.89
China [3]	Yuan	8.28	Norway	Kroner	7.80
Colombia	Pesos	1,629	Oman	Rials Omani	0.38
Comoros	Comorian Francs	461.8	Pakistan	Rupees	50.55
Congo (Brazzaville) [4]	Cfa Francs	615.7	Panama	Balboas	1.00
Costa Rica	Colones	285.7	Papua New Guinea	Kina	2.54
Cote d'Ivoire	Cfa Francs	615.7	Paraguay	Guaranies	3,119
Croatia	Kuna	7.11	Peru	Nuevos Soles	3.38
Cyprus	Cyprus Pounds	0.54	Philippines	Pesos	39.09
Czech Republic	Koruny	34.57	Poland	Zlotys	3.97
Denmark	Kroner	6.98	Portugal [1]	Escudos	188.2
Djibouti	Djibouti Francs	177.7	Qatar	Riyals	3.64
Dominica	E.Caribbean Dollar	2.70	Romania	Lei	15,333
Dominican Republic	Pesos	16.03	Russia	Rubles	24.62
Ecuador	Sucres	11,787	Rwanda	Rwanda Francs	333.9
Egypt	Egyptian Pounds	3.40	Saint Kitts and Nevis	E.Caribbean Dollar	2.70
El Salvador	Colones	8.76	Saint Lucia	E.Caribbean Dollar	2.70
Equatorial Guinea	Cfa Francs	615.7	Saint Vincent and the		
Estonia	Krooni	14.68	Grenadines	E.Caribbean Dollar	2.70
Ethiopia [2]	Birr	7.76	Saudi Arabia	Riyals	3.75
Euro area (EMU-11) [1]	Euro	0.94	Senegal	Cfa Francs	615.7
Fiji	Fiji Dollar	1.97	Sierra Leone	Leones	1,804
Finland [1]	Markkaa	5.58	Singapore	Singapore Dollar	1.69
France [1]	Francs	6.16	Slovakia	Koruny	41.36
Gabon	Cfa Francs	615.7	Slovenia	Tolars	181.8
Georgia	Lari	2.02	South Africa	Rand	6.11
Germany [1]	Deutsche Mark	1.84	Spain [1]	Pesetas	156.2
Greece	Drachmas	305.7	Sri Lanka	Rupees	70.40
Guatemala	Quetzales	7.39	Sudan	Sudanese Pounds	253
Guyana	Guyana Dollar	178.0	Suriname [2]	Guilders	844.0
Haiti	Gourdes	16.94	Swaziland	Langeni	6.11
Honduras	Lempiras	14.21	Sweden	Kronor	8.26
Hong Kong	Hong Kong Dollar	7.76	Switzerland	Swiss Francs	1.50
Hungary	Forint	237.2	Syria [2]	Syrian Pounds	11.23
Iceland	Kronur	72.35	Tanzania	Tanzania Shilling	774.8
India	Rupees	43.06	Thailand	Baht	37.84
Indonesia	Rupiah	7,855	Togo	Cfa Francs	615.7
Iran	Rials	1,753	Trinidad and Tobago	Tt Dollars	6.30
Iraq	Dinars	0.31	Tunisia	Dinars	1.18
Ireland [1]	Irish Pounds	0.74	Turkey	Liras	418,783
Israel	New Sheqalim	4.14	Uganda	Uganda Shilling	1,455
Italy [1]	Lire	1,817	Ukraine	Hryvnias	4.130
Jamaica	Jamaica Dollars	39.04	United Arab Emirates	Dirhams	3.67
Japan	Yen	113.9	United Kingdom	Pounds Sterling	0.62
Jordan	Dinars	0.71	Uruguay	Pesos	11.34
Kazakhstan	Tenge	119.52	Vanuatu	Vatu	129.1
Kenya	Kenya Shillings	70.33	Venezuela	Venezuela	605.7
Korea, South	Won	1,189	Yemen	Rials	159.5
Kuwait	Dinars	0.30	Zambia	Kwacha	2,388
Kyrgyzstan	Soms	39.01	Zimbabwe	Zimbabwe Dollar	38.30

[1] The euro became the official currency of the 11 Euro Area (EMU) nations on January 1, 1999. The values shown in this table are computed values for the former national currencies. [2] End-of year values were used if annual averages were unavailable. Some values were estimated using partial year data. [3] See footnote 2, Table 1352. [4] See footnote 3, Table 1352.

Source: U.S. Dept. of Commerce, International Trade Administration, "Foreign Exchange Rates, 1993-99"; published 27 April 2000; <http://www.ita.doc.gov/td/industry/otea/usfth/aggregate/H99t37.txt>.

Comparative International Statistics   851

No. 1406. Reserve Assets and International Transaction Balances by Country: 1995 to 1999

[In millions of U.S. dollars (74,780 represents $74,780,000,000). Assets include holdings of convertible foreign currencies, special drawing rights, and reserve position in International Monetary Fund and exclude gold holdings. Minus sign (-) indicates debits]

Country	Total reserve assets				Current account balance			Merchandise trade balance		
			1999							
	1995	1998	Total	Currency holdings [1]	1995	1998	1999	1995	1998	1999
United States	74,780	70,710	60,500	32,180	-113,570	-220,560	-338,920	-171,880	-244,970	-344,820
Algeria	2,005	6,846	4,526	4,407	(NA)	(NA)	(NA)	(NA)	(NA)	(NA)
Argentina	14,288	24,752	26,252	26,114	-4,985	-14,274	-12,152	2,357	-3,117	-829
Australia	11,896	14,641	21,212	19,507	-19,640	-18,035	-22,526	-4,223	-5,367	-9,771
Austria	18,730	22,432	15,120	14,016	-5,448	-4,609	-5,701	-6,656	-3,654	-3,560
Bangladesh	2,340	1,905	1,604	1,603	-824	-35	-292	-2,324	-1,574	-1,962
Belgium	16,177	18,272	10,937	8,377	14,232	12,168	11,961	9,555	6,981	7,486
Brazil	49,708	42,580	34,796	34,786	-18,136	-33,829	(NA)	-3,157	-6,603	(NA)
Burma	561	315	266	265	(NA)	(NA)	(NA)	(NA)	(NA)	(NA)
Cameroon	4	1	4	1	90	(NA)	(NA)	627	(NA)	(NA)
Canada	15,049	23,308	28,126	24,432	-4,328	-11,133	-2,273	25,855	12,775	22,756
Chile	14,140	15,663	14,407	13,977	-1,350	-4,139	-80	1,381	-2,516	1,664
China [2]	75,377	149,188	157,728	154,675	1,618	31,472	15,667	18,050	46,614	36,207
Colombia	8,452	8,754	8,103	7,580	-4,624	-5,274	-959	-2,639	-2,514	1,733
Congo (Kinshasa) [3] .	59	1	39	39	-650	(NA)	(NA)	516	(NA)	(NA)
Cote d'Ivoire	529	856	630	627	-474	-313	(NA)	1,324	1,832	(NA)
Denmark	11,016	15,264	22,287	21,145	1,855	-2,007	2,015	6,528	3,894	6,569
Ecuador	1,628	1,620	1,642	1,617	-735	-2,169	(NA)	354	-995	(NA)
Egypt	16,181	18,124	14,484	14,278	-254	-2,566	(NA)	-7,597	-10,214	(NA)
Finland	10,038	9,695	8,207	6,747	5,231	7,371	6,681	12,437	12,490	11,643
France	26,853	44,312	39,701	33,933	10,840	40,160	37,230	11,000	26,170	20,070
Germany	85,005	74,024	61,039	52,661	-18,930	-4,560	-20,900	65,110	78,890	70,500
Ghana	698	377	454	379	-145	-350	(NA)	-257	-533	(NA)
Greece	14,780	17,458	18,122	17,726	-2,864	(NA)	(NA)	-14,425	(NA)	(NA)
Hungary	11,974	9,319	10,954	10,707	-2,530	-2,304	-2,101	-2,433	-2,354	-2,191
India	17,922	27,341	32,667	31,992	-5,563	-6,903	-3,778	-6,719	-10,752	-8,011
Indonesia	13,708	22,713	26,445	26,245	-6,431	4,096	(NA)	6,533	18,429	(NA)
Ireland	8,630	9,397	5,346	4,890	1,721	806	(NA)	13,557	23,381	(NA)
Israel	8,119	22,674	22,605	22,515	-5,196	-842	-2,601	-7,566	-3,226	-4,541
Italy	34,905	29,888	22,425	18,626	25,076	19,998	8,239	38,729	35,631	20,385
Japan	183,250	215,471	286,916	277,708	111,040	120,700	106,870	131,790	122,390	123,320
Kenya	353	783	792	772	-401	-363	(NA)	-750	-1,016	(NA)
Korea, South	32,678	51,975	73,987	73,700	-8,507	40,558	(NA)	-4,444	41,627	(NA)
Kuwait	3,561	3,947	4,824	4,244	5,016	2,527	(NA)	5,579	1,900	(NA)
Malaysia	23,774	25,559	30,588	29,670	-8,469	(NA)	(NA)	-103	(NA)	(NA)
Mexico	16,847	31,799	31,782	30,992	-1,576	-15,725	-14,016	7,089	-7,915	-5,360
Morocco	3,601	4,435	5,689	5,507	-1,296	-236	(NA)	-2,482	-2,319	(NA)
Nepal	586	756	843	835	-356	-63	(NA)	-961	-753	(NA)
Netherlands	33,714	21,418	10,098	6,499	24,144	25,585	22,597	22,102	18,020	16,191
Nigeria	1,443	(NA)	(NA)	(NA)	-2,578	-4,244	(NA)	3,513	-240	(NA)
Norway	22,518	18,607	20,400	19,139	4,854	-2,161	(NA)	8,571	1,566	(NA)
Pakistan	1,733	1,028	1,511	1,511	-3,349	(NA)	(NA)	-2,891	(NA)	(NA)
Peru	8,222	9,566	8,731	8,730	-4,314	-3,800	(NA)	-2,168	-2,465	(NA)
Philippines	6,372	9,226	13,230	13,103	-1,980	1,546	7,912	-8,944	-28	4,962
Poland	14,774	26,432	24,535	24,287	854	-6,901	(NA)	-1,646	-12,836	(NA)
Portugal	15,850	15,825	8,848	8,006	-132	-7,250	-9,004	-8,910	-12,277	-14,157
Romania	1,579	2,867	2,690	2,680	-1,780	-2,918	-1,303	-1,577	-2,625	-1,087
Saudi Arabia	8,622	14,220	16,997	15,490	-5,325	-13,150	-1,701	24,390	11,287	22,765
Singapore	68,695	74,928	76,843	76,304	14,436	21,025	21,254	977	14,811	11,303
South Africa	2,820	4,357	6,353	6,065	-2,204	-1,936	-464	2,667	2,018	3,751
Spain	34,485	55,258	33,115	31,329	792	-3,135	-12,621	-18,415	-20,758	-29,208
Sri Lanka	2,088	1,980	1,636	1,569	-770	-288	(NA)	-985	-568	(NA)
Sudan	163	91	(NA)	(NA)	-500	-957	-465	-510	-1,137	-476
Sweden	24,051	14,098	15,019	13,522	4,940	4,639	(NA)	15,978	17,632	(NA)
Switzerland	36,413	41,191	36,321	34,176	21,562	24,547	(NA)	3,223	988	(NA)
Syria	(NA)	(NA)	(NA)	(NA)	367	59	(NA)	-143	-172	(NA)
Thailand	35,982	28,825	34,063	33,805	-13,554	14,048	11,050	-7,968	16,041	13,477
Trinidad and Tobago .	358	783	945	945	294	-644	(NA)	588	-741	(NA)
Turkey	12,442	19,489	23,340	23,185	-2,338	1,871	(NA)	-13,212	-14,332	(NA)
United Kingdom	42,020	32,210	29,830	24,040	-5,970	-1,100	-20,640	-18,530	-34,010	-43,070
Venezuela	6,283	11,920	12,277	11,708	2,014	-2,562	(NA)	7,013	2,748	(NA)

NA Not available.   [1] Holdings of convertible foreign currencies.   [2] See footnote 2, Table 1352.   [3] See footnote 3, Table 1352.

Source: International Monetary Fund, Washington, DC, *International Financial Statistics*, monthly, (copyright).

No. 1407. Foreign Trade—Destination of Exports and Source of Imports for Selected Countries: 1998

[In billions of dollars (178.7 represents $178,700,000,000), except as indicated)]

Country	World [1]	Belgium-Luxem-bourg	Canada	China [2]	France	Ger-many	Italy	Japan	Neth-erlands	United King-dom	United States
EXPORTS											
Belgium-Luxembourg.	178.7	(X)	0.7	0.8	32.5	34.9	10.5	1.7	22.4	17.7	9.4
Canada.	214.6	1.1	(X)	1.7	1.1	1.8	1.0	5.8	1.3	3.0	181.9
China [2].	183.8	1.7	2.1	(X)	2.8	7.4	2.6	29.7	5.2	4.6	37.9
France	300.5	23.3	2.3	3.3	(X)	48.0	27.5	4.7	13.8	30.1	22.3
Germany.	543.8	30.0	3.9	6.7	58.8	(X)	39.4	10.2	36.4	45.5	50.0
Hong Kong	174.9	1.0	2.8	59.9	3.2	6.7	1.9	9.1	3.2	7.2	40.6
Ireland	64.2	4.1	0.4	0.1	5.3	9.7	2.1	1.7	3.5	14.2	8.7
Italy	242.1	6.6	2.0	2.1	30.9	39.9	(X)	4.0	6.9	17.4	20.8
Japan.	388.1	4.7	6.3	20.1	6.2	19.1	4.2	(X)	10.9	14.6	118.6
Korea, South	132.3	1.0	1.6	11.9	1.4	4.0	1.7	12.2	1.9	4.2	22.8
Mexico	117.3	0.2	1.5	0.1	0.4	1.1	0.2	0.8	0.3	0.7	103.0
Netherlands.	167.6	17.7	0.5	0.6	16.3	39.6	8.9	1.5	(X)	15.0	6.2
Spain	111.4	3.1	0.5	0.5	21.7	15.2	10.3	1.0	3.9	9.4	4.7
Sweden	82.5	3.8	0.9	1.6	4.2	9.3	3.0	1.8	4.9	7.5	7.3
Switzerland	78.9	1.8	0.6	0.6	7.5	18.2	6.1	3.0	2.3	4.7	8.7
United Kingdom	273.4	13.5	3.6	1.4	26.7	33.3	13.8	5.4	21.1	(X)	36.0
United States.	680.4	14.5	154.1	14.3	17.7	26.6	9.0	57.9	19.0	39.1	(X)
PERCENT DISTRIBUTION											
Belgium-Luxembourg.	100.0	(X)	0.4	0.4	18.2	19.5	5.9	1.0	12.5	9.9	5.3
Canada.	100.0	0.5	(X)	0.8	0.5	0.8	0.5	2.7	0.6	1.4	84.8
China [2].	100.0	0.9	1.1	(X)	1.5	4.0	1.4	16.2	2.8	2.5	20.6
France	100.0	7.8	0.8	1.1	(X)	16.0	9.2	1.6	4.6	10.0	7.4
Germany.	100.0	5.5	0.7	1.2	10.8	(X)	7.2	1.9	6.7	8.4	9.2
Hong Kong	100.0	0.6	1.6	34.2	1.8	3.8	1.1	5.2	1.8	4.1	23.2
Ireland	100.0	6.4	0.6	0.2	8.3	15.1	3.3	2.6	5.5	22.1	13.6
Italy	100.0	2.7	0.8	0.9	12.8	16.5	(X)	1.7	2.9	7.2	8.6
Japan.	100.0	1.2	1.6	5.2	1.6	4.9	1.1	(X)	2.8	3.8	30.6
Korea, South	100.0	0.8	1.2	9.0	1.1	3.0	1.3	9.2	1.4	3.2	17.2
Mexico	100.0	0.2	1.3	0.1	0.3	0.9	0.2	0.7	0.3	0.6	87.8
Netherlands.	100.0	10.6	0.3	0.4	9.7	23.6	5.3	0.9	(X)	8.9	3.7
Spain	100.0	2.8	0.4	0.4	19.5	13.6	9.2	0.9	3.5	8.4	4.2
Sweden	100.0	4.6	1.1	1.9	5.1	11.3	3.6	2.2	5.9	9.1	8.8
Switzerland	100.0	2.3	0.8	0.8	9.5	23.1	7.7	3.8	2.9	6.0	11.0
United Kingdom	100.0	4.9	1.3	0.5	9.8	12.2	5.0	2.0	7.7	(X)	13.2
United States.	100.0	2.1	22.6	2.1	2.6	3.9	1.3	8.5	2.8	5.7	(X)
IMPORTS											
Belgium-Luxembourg.	166.7	(X)	1.1	2.7	22.9	31.0	6.6	4.3	27.5	14.1	13.3
Canada.	201.4	0.8	(X)	5.2	3.3	4.1	2.3	9.4	0.8	4.2	137.3
China [2].	140.2	0.9	2.2	(X)	3.2	7.0	2.3	28.3	0.8	2.0	16.9
France	285.8	22.1	1.6	7.2	(X)	49.3	28.4	9.5	14.5	24.0	25.3
Germany.	471.6	26.0	3.1	13.0	50.3	(X)	36.4	23.2	37.0	32.0	37.4
Hong Kong	186.8	1.0	1.2	75.0	3.0	4.2	3.0	23.4	1.6	4.2	13.8
Ireland	44.4	0.5	0.4	0.7	1.7	2.8	0.8	3.1	1.4	14.9	7.1
Italy	215.6	10.4	1.6	4.8	28.4	40.5	(X)	4.7	13.3	13.9	10.9
Japan.	280.6	1.5	7.7	37.1	5.7	10.7	5.1	(X)	1.8	5.9	67.2
Korea, South	93.3	0.5	2.0	6.5	1.3	3.3	1.1	16.8	0.9	1.8	20.4
Mexico	125.3	0.4	1.8	0.2	1.2	4.3	1.2	2.6	0.5	0.9	101.6
Netherlands.	156.8	14.4	1.0	3.5	10.2	27.2	4.3	7.1	(X)	14.4	14.7
Spain	137.2	4.8	0.5	3.3	25.2	21.2	13.6	4.1	6.0	10.6	7.8
Sweden	64.2	2.6	0.3	0.7	4.0	12.2	2.2	1.7	5.2	6.6	4.0
Switzerland	80.1	2.7	0.5	1.2	8.7	24.4	7.7	2.1	4.0	5.0	5.7
United Kingdom	320.3	15.4	4.0	9.5	28.9	41.5	16.6	15.8	21.9	(X)	44.7
United States.	944.4	9.0	177.9	75.1	24.7	51.3	21.9	125.1	8.0	35.7	(X)
PERCENT DISTRIBUTION											
Belgium-Luxembourg.	100.0	(X)	0.7	1.6	13.7	18.6	4.0	2.6	16.5	8.5	8.0
Canada.	100.0	0.4	(X)	2.6	1.6	2.0	1.1	4.7	0.4	2.1	68.2
China [2].	100.0	0.6	1.6	(X)	2.3	5.0	1.6	20.2	0.6	1.4	12.1
France	100.0	7.7	0.6	2.5	(X)	17.2	9.9	3.3	5.1	8.4	8.9
Germany.	100.0	5.5	0.7	2.8	10.7	(X)	7.7	4.9	7.8	6.8	7.9
Hong Kong	100.0	0.5	0.6	40.1	1.6	2.2	1.6	12.5	0.9	2.2	7.4
Ireland	100.0	1.1	0.9	1.6	3.8	6.3	1.8	7.0	3.2	33.6	16.0
Italy	100.0	4.8	0.7	2.2	13.2	18.8	(X)	2.2	6.2	6.4	5.1
Japan.	100.0	0.5	2.7	13.2	2.0	3.8	1.8	(X)	0.6	2.1	23.9
Korea, South	100.0	0.5	2.1	7.0	1.4	3.5	1.2	18.0	1.0	1.9	21.9
Mexico	100.0	0.3	1.4	0.2	1.0	3.4	1.0	2.1	0.4	0.7	81.1
Netherlands.	100.0	9.2	0.6	2.2	6.5	17.3	2.7	4.5	(X)	9.2	9.4
Spain	100.0	3.5	0.4	2.4	18.4	15.5	9.9	3.0	4.4	7.7	5.7
Sweden	100.0	4.0	0.5	1.1	6.2	19.0	3.4	2.6	8.1	10.3	6.2
Switzerland	100.0	3.4	0.6	1.5	10.9	30.5	9.6	2.6	5.0	6.2	7.1
United Kingdom	100.0	4.8	1.2	3.0	9.0	13.0	5.2	4.9	6.8	(X)	14.0
United States.	100.0	1.0	18.8	8.0	2.6	5.4	2.3	13.2	0.8	3.8	(X)

X Not applicable.   [1] Includes other countries not shown separately.   [2]See footnote 2, Table 1352.

Source: Organization for Economic Cooperation and Development, Paris, France, *OECD International Trade by Commodities Statistics, 1999.*

Comparative International Statistics   853

No. 1408. International Tourism Receipts—Leading Countries: 1990 to 1999

[In millions of dollars, except as indicated (263,647 represents $263,647,000,000). Excludes international transport receipts. Minus sign (-) indicates decrease]

Country	Total receipts					Percent change, 1998-99	Percent of world total	
	1990	1995	1997	1998	1999		1990	1999
World, total [1]	263,647	405,840	439,676	440,986	454,553	3.1	100.0	100.0
United States	**43,007**	**63,395**	**73,301**	**71,250**	**74,448**	**4.5**	**16.3**	**16.4**
Spain	18,593	25,388	26,651	29,737	32,913	10.7	7.1	7.2
France	20,184	27,527	28,009	29,931	31,699	5.9	7.7	7.0
Italy	16,458	28,729	29,714	29,866	28,357	-5.1	6.2	6.2
United Kingdom	13,762	18,554	20,039	20,978	20,972	(-Z)	5.2	4.6
Germany	14,288	17,867	16,488	16,429	16,828	2.4	5.4	3.7
China	2,218	8,733	12,074	12,602	14,098	11.9	0.8	3.1
Austria	13,417	13,492	10,991	11,184	11,088	-0.9	5.1	2.4
Canada	6,339	7,882	8,828	9,396	10,025	6.7	2.4	2.2
Greece	2,587	4,136	5,151	6,188	8,765	41.6	1.0	1.9
Russia	(NA)	4,312	7,164	6,508	7,771	19.4	(NA)	1.7
Mexico	5,467	6,179	7,593	7,897	7,587	-3.9	2.1	1.7
Australia	4,088	7,857	9,057	7,335	7,525	2.6	1.6	1.7
Switzerland	7,411	9,365	7,915	7,815	7,355	-5.9	2.8	1.6
Hong Kong	5,032	9,604	9,242	7,083	7,210	1.8	1.9	1.6
Netherlands	4,155	6,563	6,304	6,788	7,092	4.5	1.6	1.6
Thailand	4,326	7,664	7,048	5,934	7,000	18.0	1.6	1.5
Poland	358	6,614	8,679	7,946	6,100	-23.2	0.1	1.3
Singapore	4,937	8,390	6,066	5,162	5,788	12.1	1.9	1.3
Korea, South	3,559	5,587	5,116	5,890	5,623	-4.5	1.3	1.2

NA Not available.   Z Less than .05 percent.   [1] Includes other countries not shown separately.
Source: World Tourism Organization, Madrid, Spain, *Tourism Highlights 2000, Second Edition*, August 2000 (copyright).

No. 1409. Net Flow of Financial Resources to Developing Countries: 1980 to 1997

[In billions of U.S. dollars (75.4 represents $75,400,000,000). Net flow covers loans, grants, and grant-like flows minus amortization on loans. Military flows are excluded. Developing countries cover countries designated by Development Assistance Committee (DAC) as developing. Official development assistance covers all flows to developing countries and multilateral institutions provided by official agencies, including state and local governments, or by their executive agencies, which are administered with the promotion of economic development and welfare of developing countries as their main objective and whose financial terms are intended to be concessional in character with grant element of at least 25 percent. Other official flows cover export credits and portfolio investment from the official sector]

Origin and type of resource	1980	1985	1990	1992	1993	1994	1995	1996	1997
Net flows to DAC Part I developing countries [1,2]	75.4	45.2	76.4	115.8	135.4	165.9	164.6	195.5	187.6
Official development assistance	27.3	29.4	53.0	60.9	56.5	59.2	58.9	55.4	48.3
Other official flows	5.3	3.4	8.6	8.9	7.9	10.5	9.9	5.6	6.1
Private flows at market terms	40.4	9.4	9.8	40.1	65.3	90.2	89.8	128.9	128.5
Private voluntary agencies	2.4	2.9	5.1	6.0	5.7	6.0	6.0	5.6	4.6
United States	13.9	1.8	11.1	33.5	58.2	59.7	47.0	55.7	75.0
Official development assistance	7.1	9.4	11.4	11.7	10.1	9.9	7.4	9.4	6.9
Other official flows	1.1	0.2	-0.4	1.3	0.1	0.9	1.5	1.1	0.3
Private flows at market terms	4.3	-9.3	-2.4	17.7	45.4	46.3	35.6	42.7	65.3
Private voluntary agencies	1.3	1.5	2.5	2.8	2.6	2.6	2.5	2.5	2.5
Australia	0.9	1.2	1.5	4.2	2.1	2.1	2.5	1.4	1.3
Austria	0.3	0.2	0.6	0.8	0.7	1.0	0.9	1.9	1.7
Belgium	2.9	1.3	0.1	2.2	0.7	2.2	-0.2	5.6	-11.5
Canada	3.2	1.7	3.5	4.2	5.3	5.6	5.1	6.7	10.0
Denmark	0.8	0.4	1.1	1.6	1.4	1.3	1.8	1.9	1.9
Finland	0.2	0.3	1.0	0.8	0.3	0.6	0.6	1.1	0.4
France	11.6	8.9	5.7	10.8	10.9	12.7	12.5	17.5	14.0
Germany	10.6	5.8	13.6	8.9	15.4	23.9	21.2	20.8	19.7
Ireland	(Z)	0.1	0.2	0.2	0.1	0.2	0.2	0.4	0.3
Italy	4.0	2.2	3.2	6.2	2.4	3.4	2.8	4.7	8.1
Japan	6.8	11.6	17.2	16.2	15.9	28.5	42.3	38.1	29.5
Luxembourg	(NA)	(NA)	(NA)	5.9	0.1	0.1	0.1	0.1	0.1
Netherlands	2.4	2.6	4.0	3.4	5.6	4.7	6.8	9.5	8.1
New Zealand	0.1	0.1	0.1	0.1	0.1	0.1	0.2	0.1	0.2
Norway	0.9	0.6	1.2	1.4	1.2	1.5	1.7	1.7	1.6
Portugal	(NA)	(NA)	0.3	0.4	0.2	0.3	0.4	0.9	1.3
Spain	(NA)	(NA)	1.0	1.6	1.4	3.5	2.0	4.3	7.4
Sweden	1.9	1.4	2.8	3.0	2.5	2.4	2.2	2.0	2.1
Switzerland	2.7	2.5	3.4	3.1	3.6	0.1	1.1	-1.5	-3.5
United Kingdom	12.2	2.5	6.5	9.3	7.3	12.0	13.4	22.5	19.7
Net flows to DAC Part II countries in transition [1]	(NA)	(NA)	(NA)	25.0	21.5	11.2	19.4	31.1	78.0
Official aid [3]	(NA)	(NA)	(NA)	6.9	7.1	7.5	9.2	5.7	5.1
Other official flows	(NA)	(NA)	(NA)	2.3	5.3	4.5	6.7	1.8	0.9
Private flows at market terms	(NA)	(NA)	(NA)	15.5	8.8	-1.1	3.1	23.3	70.9
Private voluntary agencies	(NA)	(NA)	(NA)	0.2	0.4	0.4	0.4	0.4	1.2

NA Not available.   Z Less than $50 million.   [1] Known as the "List of Developing Countries and Territories," the DAC List of Aid Recipients was split into two parts in 1993 in recognition of the new aid requirements for transition economies of eastern Europe and of the rapid progress of some developing countries with reduced aid needs. Part I countries are the "traditional" developing countries to which aid can be counted as official development assistance. Part II countries are the "more advanced" developing countries of Central and Eastern Europe (Bulgaria, Czech Republic, Estonia, Hungary, Latvia, Lithuania, Poland, Romania, and Slovakia) and of the Newly Independent States of the former Soviet Union (Belarus, Russia, and Ukraine). In 1996, the Bahamas, Brunei, Kuwait, Qatar, Singapore, and the United Arab Emirates were reclassified from Part I to Part II more advanced developing status. In 1997, Bermuda, Cayman Islands, Cyprus, Falkland Islands, Hong Kong, Israel, and Taiwan were reclassified from Part I to Part II status, and Moldova shifted from Part II to Part I status.   [2] Country totals may not sum to DAC totals because debt forgiveness of nonofficial development assistance claims is not included in DAC totals.   [3] Official flows to Part II countries that have the same concessional and qualitative features as official development assistance are designated official aid. Only flows to Part I countries are eligible to be recorded as official development assistance.
Source: Organization for Economic Cooperation and Development, Paris, France, *Annual Reports of the Development Assistance Committee*.

No. 1410. External Debt by Country: 1995 and 1998

[144,050 represents $144,050,000,000. Total external debt is debt owed to nonresidents repayable in foreign currency, goods, or services. It is the sum of pubic, publicly guaranteed, and private nonguaranteed long-term debt, use of IMF credit, and short-term debt. Short-term debt includes all debt having an original maturity of one year or less and interest in arrears on long-term debt. Public debt comprises long-term external obligations of public debtors, including the national government and political subdivisions (or an agency of either) and autonomous public bodies, and external obligations of private debtors that are guaranteed for repayment by a public entity. Debt service is the sum of principal repayments and interest actually paid in foreign currency, goods, or services on long-term debt, interest paid on short-term debt, and repayments (repurchases and charges) to the IMF]

Country	Total external debt, 1998 (mil. dol.)	Total debt service as percent of exports,[1] 1998	External public debt (mil. dol.) 1995	External public debt (mil. dol.) 1998	Country	Total external debt, 1998 (mil. dol.)	Total debt service as percent of exports,[1] 1998	External public debt (mil. dol.) 1995	External public debt (mil. dol.) 1998
Argentina	144,050	58	55,967	76,799	Lebanon	6,725	19	1,549	3,980
Bangladesh	16,376	9	15,469	15,804	Malaysia	44,773	9	16,023	18,158
Bolivia	6,077	30	4,448	4,307	Mexico	159,959	21	94,384	87,996
Brazil	232,004	74	97,180	98,959	Morocco	20,687	23	22,110	19,325
Bulgaria	9,907	22	8,716	7,781	Nicaragua	5,968	26	8,537	5,212
Cameroon	9,829	22	8,059	8,096	Pakistan	32,229	24	23,804	26,061
Chile	36,302	22	7,181	4,986	Panama	6,689	8	3,910	5,413
China[2]	154,599	9	94,671	99,424	Peru	32,397	28	18,922	20,803
Colombia	33,263	31	13,946	16,930	Philippines	47,817	12	29,905	28,189
Congo (Brazzaville)[3]	5,119	3	4,952	4,250	Poland	47,708	10	41,071	35,136
Congo (Kinshasa)[3]	12,929	1	9,618	8,949	Romania	9,513	24	(NA)	6,962
Cote d'Ivoire	14,852	26	11,899	10,800	Russia	183,601	12	(NA)	119,314
Croatia	8,297	9	1,590	4,910	Sri Lanka	8,526	7	7,008	7,649
Ecuador	15,140	29	12,062	12,589	Sudan	16,843	10	9,778	9,226
Egypt	31,964	10	30,584	27,669	Syria	22,435	6	16,755	16,328
Ethiopia	10,352	11	9,772	9,618	Tanzania	7,603	21	6,205	6,404
Ghana	6,884	28	4,569	5,570	Thailand	86,172	19	16,951	28,113
Guatemala	4,565	10	2,832	2,989	Tunisia	11,078	15	8,721	9,727
Honduras	5,002	19	3,979	3,946	Turkey	102,074	21	50,313	49,932
Hungary	28,580	27	23,782	15,941	Uruguay	7,600	24	3,830	5,142
India[4]	98,232	21	80,369	85,207	Venezuela	37,003	27	28,491	26,692
Indonesia	150,875	33	65,305	66,944	Yugoslavia, former	13,742	(NA)	8,724	8,321
Jordan	8,484	16	7,017	7,388	Zambia	6,865	18	5,073	5,320
Kenya	7,010	19	5,891	5,629	Zimbabwe	4,716	38	3,523	3,341

NA Not available.   [1] Debt service payments as percent of exports of goods and services.   [2] See footnote 2, Table 1352.
[3] See footnote 3, Table 1352.   [4] Fiscal year basis.

Source: The World Bank, Washington, DC, 2000 World Development Indicators.

No. 1411. Foreign Direct Investment Flows in OECD Countries: 1990 to 1999

[In millions of dollars (299,004 represents $299,004,000,000). 1999 data, preliminary. Data are converted to U.S. dollars using the yearly average exchange rate]

Country	Inflows				Outflows			
	1997	1998	1999	Cumulative, 1990-99	1997	1998	1999	Cumulative, 1990-99
OECD, total	299,004	509,313	683,744	2,709,512	414,079	636,480	767,814	3,552,013
Australia	7,510	6,502	4,441	58,910	6,262	2,466	-3,192	26,596
Austria	2,656	4,902	2,952	21,084	1,948	2,948	2,703	18,155
Belgium-Luxembourg	12,093	22,724	15,868	123,206	7,273	28,453	24,937	109,350
Canada	11,470	16,499	24,268	99,000	22,054	26,575	17,362	120,113
Czech Republic	1,300	2,540	4,877	15,233	25	175	197	828
Denmark	2,801	6,722	7,450	32,176	4,210	3,962	8,207	32,958
Finland	2,116	12,141	3,024	22,841	5,292	18,643	4,194	40,760
France	23,174	28,955	37,416	215,804	35,586	41,913	88,324	347,839
Germany	11,092	21,271	52,403	116,467	40,716	91,193	98,853	422,455
Greece[1]	3,586	3,709	539	26,942	(NA)	(NA)	573	573
Hungary	2,173	2,036	1,944	19,618	431	481	249	1,261
Iceland	149	112	90	476	51	99	70	380
Ireland[2]	1,676	3,904	5,422	17,451	(NA)	8,569	18,326	26,895
Italy	3,698	2,611	5,019	37,697	10,619	12,078	3,038	71,148
Japan	3,224	3,193	12,378	26,008	25,991	24,159	20,730	248,729
Korea, South	2,844	5,416	8,798	24,653	4,449	4,799	4,044	29,018
Mexico	12,830	11,311	11,568	81,570	(NA)	(NA)	(NA)	(NA)
Netherlands	14,499	41,977	33,341	159,523	29,247	51,365	45,540	250,860
New Zealand[3]	1,832	2,172	989	20,754	-1,602	376	1,020	5,135
Norway	3,786	3,882	6,579	26,670	5,047	2,418	5,483	28,131
Poland	4,908	6,365	6,471	30,616	45	316	123	639
Portugal	2,278	2,802	570	17,501	1,668	2,901	2,679	10,463
Spain	6,387	11,797	9,357	97,780	12,547	18,935	35,421	93,236
Sweden	10,968	19,569	59,102	127,633	12,648	24,376	18,951	102,114
Switzerland	6,642	7,499	3,412	34,680	17,747	16,631	17,910	119,187
Turkey	805	940	783	8,116	251	367	645	2,087
United Kingdom	33,245	64,388	82,176	319,726	61,620	119,463	199,275	566,400
United States	109,264	193,375	282,507	927,378	109,955	132,829	152,152	876,705

NA Not available.   [1] Includes entrepreneurial capital net and real estate investment flows.   [2] Data shown are for net (inward and outward), direct investment capital flows. For 1999, balance of payments data.   [3] For fiscal year ending March 31.

Source: Organization for Economic Cooperation and Development, Paris, France, Financial Market Trends, No. 76, June 2000.

Comparative International Statistics   855

No. 1412. Military Expenditures and Armed Forces Personnel by Country: 1990 and 1997

[Military expenditures in millions of dollars, except as indicated (306,000 represents $306,000,000,000). Personnel data as of July. See also Table 572. For most countries, data for expenditures and for gross national product (GNP) were based on local currencies which were deflated to constant 1997 local currency values before conversion to U.S. dollar equivalents. In general, the rates used for conversion are the 1997 average par/market exchange rates as supplied by the World Bank. Armed Forces refer to active-duty military personnel, including paramilitary forces where those forces resemble regular units in their organization, equipment, training, or mission. Reserve forces are not included]

Country	Military expenditures						Armed Forces personnel			
	Current dollars		Constant (1997) dollars				Number (1,000)		Per 1,000 population	
				1997						
	1990	1997	1990	Total	Percent of GNP	Per capita (dollars)	1990	1997	1990	1997
United States......	306,000	276,000	359,000	276,000	3.3	1,030	2,180	1,530	8.7	5.7
Algeria [1]	726	1,750	850	1,750	3.9	59	126	124	5.0	4.2
Angola [1]	1,250	1,550	1,470	1,550	20.5	147	115	95	13.6	9.0
Argentina	3,350	3,700	3,930	3,700	1.2	103	85	65	2.6	1.8
Australia	6,090	8,460	7,130	8,460	2.2	459	68	65	4.0	3.5
Bangladesh	301	592	352	592	1.4	5	103	110	0.9	0.9
Belgium	4,450	3,690	5,210	3,690	1.5	363	106	46	10.6	4.5
Brazil	9,560	14,100	11,200	14,100	1.8	84	295	296	2.0	1.8
Bulgaria [1]	3,890	949	4,550	949	3.0	114	129	80	14.4	9.6
Burma [1]	(NA)	(NA)	(NA)	(NA)	(NA)	(NA)	230	322	5.6	6.9
Canada	9,240	7,800	10,800	7,800	1.3	257	87	61	3.3	2.0
Chile [2]	1,190	2,860	1,390	2,860	3.9	196	95	102	7.2	7.0
China [1][3]	48,300	74,900	56,600	74,900	2.2	61	3,500	2,600	3.1	2.1
Colombia [1][4]	1,300	3,460	1,520	3,460	3.7	91	110	149	3.3	3.9
Congo (Kinshasa) [1][4]	(NA)	252	(NA)	252	5.0	5	55	(NA)	1.5	(NA)
Croatia [1]	(X)	1,490	(X)	1,490	6.3	319	(X)	58	(X)	12.4
Cuba [1][2]	1,380	720	1,620	720	2.3	65	297	55	28.1	5.0
Czech Republic [1]	(X)	1,990	(X)	1,990	1.9	193	(X)	55	(X)	5.3
Egypt	1,570	2,180	1,840	2,180	2.8	34	434	430	7.7	6.6
France	38,600	41,500	45,200	41,500	3.0	708	550	475	9.7	8.1
Germany	40,900	32,900	47,900	32,900	1.6	401	545	335	6.9	4.1
Greece	4,230	5,530	4,960	5,530	4.6	521	201	206	19.9	19.4
Hungary [1]	1,280	1,320	1,500	1,320	1.9	129	94	50	9.1	4.9
India	6,540	10,900	7,650	10,900	2.8	11	1,260	1,260	1.5	1.3
Indonesia [1][2]	1,610	4,810	1,880	4,810	2.3	23	283	280	1.5	1.3
Iran [1]	6,110	4,730	7,160	4,730	3.0	74	440	575	7.7	9.1
Iraq [1]	22,500	1,250	26,400	1,250	4.9	59	1,390	400	75.4	19.0
Israel	7,360	9,340	8,620	9,340	9.7	1,690	190	185	42.1	33.4
Italy	19,400	22,700	22,700	22,700	2.0	395	493	419	8.5	7.3
Japan	30,500	40,800	35,700	40,800	1.0	325	250	250	2.0	2.0
Jordan	402	626	471	626	9.0	145	100	102	30.5	23.6
Kenya	210	206	246	206	2.1	7	20	24	0.8	0.9
Korea, North [1]	5,940	6,000	6,960	6,000	27.5	281	1,200	1,100	56.0	51.6
Korea, South	9,720	15,000	11,400	15,000	3.4	327	650	670	15.2	14.6
Kuwait	13,000	2,760	15,200	2,760	7.5	1,510	7	28	3.3	15.3
Libya [1]	(NA)	(NA)	(NA)	(NA)	(NA)	(NA)	86	70	19.7	14.7
Malaysia	1,260	2,090	1,480	2,090	2.2	102	130	110	7.4	5.4
Mexico	1,330	4,290	1,560	4,290	1.1	44	175	250	2.1	2.6
Netherlands	6,800	6,840	7,960	6,840	1.9	437	104	57	7.0	3.6
New Zealand	884	766	1,040	766	1.3	214	11	10	3.3	2.8
Nigeria [1][2]	2,200	2,000	2,570	2,000	1.4	19	94	76	1.1	0.7
Pakistan	2,810	3,380	3,290	3,380	5.7	26	550	610	4.8	4.6
Peru	623	1,350	730	1,350	2.1	53	125	115	5.7	4.5
Philippines	1,230	1,270	1,440	1,270	1.5	17	109	105	1.7	1.4
Poland [1]	8,750	5,600	10,200	5,600	2.3	145	313	230	8.2	6.0
Romania [1]	3,870	2,280	4,530	2,280	2.4	102	126	200	5.5	8.9
Russia [1]	(X)	41,700	(X)	41,700	5.8	283	(X)	1,300	(X)	8.8
Saudi Arabia	23,200	21,100	27,100	21,100	14.5	1,050	146	180	9.2	9.0
Serbia and Montenegro [1][5]	(X)	1,200	(X)	1,200	4.9	114	(X)	115	(X)	10.9
Singapore	2,370	5,660	2,780	5,660	5.7	1,650	56	55	18.4	16.0
Slovakia [1]	(X)	903	(X)	903	2.1	168	(X)	44	(X)	8.2
Slovenia [1]	(X)	1,220	(X)	1,220	5.2	617	(X)	10	(X)	5.1
South Africa	4,070	2,320	4,770	2,320	1.8	55	85	75	2.3	1.8
Spain	7,410	7,670	8,680	7,670	1.5	196	263	107	6.8	2.7
Sri Lanka	433	762	507	762	5.1	41	22	110	1.3	5.9
Sweden	4,810	5,550	5,630	5,550	2.5	626	65	60	7.6	6.8
Syria [2]	(NA)	3,400	(NA)	3,400	5.6	211	408	320	32.3	19.8
Taiwan [3]	8,490	13,100	9,940	13,100	4.6	602	370	400	18.2	18.4
Tanzania	83	87	97	87	1.3	3	40	35	1.6	1.2
Thailand	2,020	3,380	2,370	3,380	2.3	57	283	288	5.1	4.8
Turkey	4,250	7,790	4,980	7,790	4.0	123	769	820	13.7	12.9
Ukraine [1]	(X)	4,280	(X)	4,280	3.7	85	(X)	450	(X)	8.9
United Kingdom.....	39,300	35,300	46,000	35,300	2.7	600	308	218	5.4	3.7
Vietnam [1]	4,810	3,390	5,640	3,390	2.8	45	1,050	650	15.9	8.7

NA Not available.   X Not applicable.   [1] Military expenditures estimated.   [2] Data probably omit a major share of total military expenditures, probably including most arms acquisitions.   [3] See footnote 2, Table 1352.   [4] See footnote 3, Table 1352.   [5] See footnote 4, Table 1352.

Source: U.S. Dept. of State, Bureau of Verification and Compliance, *World Military Expenditures and Arms Transfers*, annual.

Section 31

Industrial Outlook

This section presents industry statistics for selected manufacturing industries. The industry groupings correspond to those used in the *1994 U.S. Industrial Outlook*. The tables contain new and revised data from the *1998 Annual Survey of Manufactures* along with revised industry data for 1987 through 1997 from the 1997 Economic Census for manufactures.

To provide a more accurate picture of industry trends, the value of shipments shown in these tables are expressed both in "current dollars" and in inflation-adjusted or "constant dollars." Current dollars show the value of the goods in the year they are produced. Constant dollars (or "real" dollars) show the value of shipments as they would be valued if produced in the base year. This permits shipment levels from different years to be compared. The constant dollar shipments (base year 1996) were derived by deflating the product class shipments from the Census Bureau using the Bureau of Labor Statistics' producer price indexes.

The tables contain both "industry" and "product" shipments. The Census Bureau collects shipments data from individual factories (or establishments) rather than at the company level. Most factories make a variety of products, but for statistical purposes, each factory is classified in the industry associated with its major product. For instance, the total output of a plant may consist of 80 percent tires and 20 percent hose and belting. In this case, the total output of the plant would be credited to the tire industry, and the shipments of all plants so classified would make up the "industry shipments" of the tire industry. The value of all tires shipped by all establishments is aggregated to derive "product shipments."

Trade data were tabulated following the Census Bureau's 1999 trade concordance (with a few exceptions) to approximate the Standard Industrial Classification (SIC) industry groupings. Exports are limited to domestic exports and are valued "free alongside ship" or f.a.s. Imports are restricted to goods imported for consumption and are on a customs value basis. Trade data should only be compared with product shipments data.

The *U.S. Industry and Trade Outlook 2000* is the result of an innovative public-private partnership between the International Trade Administration of the Department of Commerce and the McGraw-Hill companies. Authorship is shared by the Commerce Department, other government agencies, and McGraw-Hill. As in years past, the *Outlook* is anchored by historical statistical data provided by the Census Bureau.

The *Outlook* is a basic resource for industry analysis and business development. The 2000 edition contains 54 chapters covering important manufacturing and service sectors, along with industry snapshots, and hundreds of industry reviews, analyses, and forecasts. This publication continues the legacy of the *U.S. Industrial Outlook*, the most widely read and respected single source industry-by-industry overview of the U.S. economy. Like its predecessor, the *U.S. Industry and Trade Outlook* is a single source reference for business planners, investors, researchers, and students who need to know where major sectors of the U.S. economy have been and where they are going in an increasingly global marketplace. For sales information contact the National Technical Information Service, 1-800-553-NTIS(6847).

U.S. Census Bureau, Statistical Abstract of the United States: 2000

No. 1413. Recent Trends in Manufacturing Shipments in Current and Constant (1992) Dollars by Industry: 1990 to 1997

Item	1987 SIC code	1990	1992	1993	1994	1995	1996	1997
CURRENT DOLLARS								
Manufacturing, total	(X)	**2,912,228**	**3,004,723**	**3,127,621**	**3,348,019**	**3,594,210**	**3,715,428**	**3,958,050**
Food & kindred products	20	391,728	406,963	422,220	430,963	446,869	461,324	480,840
Tobacco products	21	29,856	35,198	28,383	30,021	32,984	34,482	36,204
Textile mill products	22	65,532	70,753	73,955	78,027	79,874	80,242	82,404
Apparel & other textile products	23	66,637	71,658	74,010	76,979	78,103	77,628	81,194
Lumber & wood products	24	74,229	81,565	94,272	103,501	104,944	106,518	111,931
Furniture & fixtures	25	41,523	43,826	46,817	50,077	53,474	55,697	61,528
Paper & allied products	26	132,424	133,201	133,262	143,649	173,716	160,661	(D)
Printing & publishing	27	159,749	166,153	172,634	176,876	188,133	195,435	210,921
Chemicals & allied products	28	292,803	305,420	314,907	333,905	361,161	367,442	400,085
Petroleum & coal products	29	173,389	150,227	144,833	143,329	151,439	174,285	175,779
Rubber & miscellaneous plastics products	30	105,250	113,593	122,777	135,145	145,740	150,468	160,739
Leather & leather products	31	9,548	9,694	10,007	9,551	9,165	9,309	(D)
Stone, clay, & glass products	32	63,727	62,521	65,610	71,230	75,931	82,441	87,244
Primary metal industries	33	148,787	138,287	142,685	161,189	180,315	178,298	188,775
Fabricated metal products	34	165,065	166,532	175,118	190,545	204,384	214,006	231,704
Industrial machinery & equipment	35	259,366	258,661	278,063	313,047	353,338	381,794	407,393
Electronic & other electric equipment	36	195,898	216,764	233,621	266,405	301,448	320,615	348,560
Transportation equipment	37	370,329	399,269	414,694	450,809	461,804	465,172	515,882
Instruments & related products	38	127,977	134,941	137,387	138,399	144,719	151,016	(D)
Miscellaneous mfg. industries	39	38,411	39,499	42,366	44,373	46,670	48,597	50,998
CONSTANT (1992) DOLLARS								
Manufacturing, total	(X)	**2,950,832**	**3,004,723**	**3,095,260**	**3,279,912**	**3,438,203**	**3,574,878**	**3,651,338**
Food & kindred products	20	390,883	406,963	415,099	419,135	430,949	422,920	437,038
Tobacco products	21	37,343	35,198	29,779	36,425	38,982	39,764	39,259
Textile mill products	22	66,590	70,753	74,285	78,213	77,715	77,227	78,949
Apparel & other textile products	23	69,351	71,658	73,339	76,063	76,601	74,976	77,728
Lumber & wood products	24	82,073	81,565	81,696	86,175	87,769	90,035	91,480
Furniture & fixtures	25	42,921	43,826	45,888	47,401	49,255	50,171	54,549
Paper & allied products	26	129,035	133,201	135,059	141,192	141,915	140,102	(D)
Printing & publishing	27	171,458	166,153	167,352	167,099	168,181	168,517	177,890
Chemicals & allied products	28	305,250	305,420	307,625	317,588	323,024	325,552	349,155
Petroleum & coal products	29	152,286	150,227	150,076	153,578	156,935	159,866	164,478
Rubber & miscellaneous plastics products	30	105,958	113,593	121,492	136,175	139,609	144,404	153,996
Leather & leather products	31	9,793	9,694	9,810	9,175	8,498	8,642	(D)
Stone, clay, & glass products	32	65,056	62,521	64,166	67,175	68,729	73,492	75,819
Primary metal industries	33	140,488	138,287	144,621	153,519	155,619	160,796	168,297
Fabricated metal products	34	168,361	166,532	174,037	186,308	192,617	199,245	212,459
Industrial machinery & equipment	35	251,225	258,661	285,888	330,408	397,730	483,067	443,649
Electronic & other electric equipment	36	197,354	216,764	232,458	265,005	304,479	331,308	315,084
Transportation equipment	37	393,866	399,269	404,939	429,829	434,385	433,081	479,909
Instruments & related products	38	131,320	134,941	136,015	136,500	141,013	146,377	(D)
Miscellaneous mfg. industries	39	40,223	39,499	41,635	42,949	44,196	45,336	47,028

D Data withheld to avoid disclosing figures or individual companies.   X Not applicable.

Source: U.S. Department of Commerce, U.S. Census Bureau, International Trade Administration (ITA).

U.S. Census Bureau, Statistical Abstract of the United States: 2000

No. 1414. Recent Trends in Food and Kindred Products (SIC 20): 1992 to 1998

Item	Unit	1992	1993	1994	1995	1996	1997	1998
INDUSTRY DATA								
Value of shipments [1]	Mil. dol. . .	406,963	422,220	430,963	446,869	461,324	(NA)	(NA)
Value of shipments (1992 dollars)	Mil. dol. . .	406,963	415,099	419,135	430,949	422,920	(NA)	(NA)
Total employment	1,000	1,503.0	1,520.3	1,510.9	1,519.9	1,516.8	(NA)	(NA)
Production workers	1,000	1,100.2	1,118.0	1,111.5	1,120.1	1,112.5	(NA)	(NA)
Average hourly earnings	Dollar . . .	10.41	10.58	10.74	10.96	11.17	(NA)	(NA)
Capital expenditures	Mil. dol. . .	9,898	9,389	10,093	11,812	11,717	(NA)	(NA)
PRODUCT DATA								
Value of shipments [2]	Mil. dol. . .	382,889	397,633	405,490	421,507	435,009	(NA)	(NA)
Value of shipments (1992 dollars)	Mil. dol. . .	382,889	391,076	394,419	406,235	398,663	(NA)	(NA)
TRADE DATA								
Value of imports	Mil. dol. . .	15,968	15,782	17,103	18,111	20,637	22,420	23,566
Value of exports	Mil. dol. . .	19,135	19,955	22,419	25,144	26,011	27,625	26,456

NA Not available. [1] Value of all products and services sold by establishments in the food and kindred products industry.
[2] Value of products classified in the food and kindred products industry produced by all industries.

Source: U.S. Department of Commerce, U.S. Census Bureau, International Trade Administration (ITA).

No. 1415. Recent Trends in Higher Value Added Foods and Beverages and Lower Value Foods and Feeds: 1992 to 1998

Item	Unit	1992	1993	1994	1995	1996	1997	1998
HIGHER VALUE ADDED FOODS AND BEVERAGES [1]								
Industry data:								
Value of shipments [2]	Mil. dol. . .	202,519	209,326	216,694	224,783	230,574	(NA)	(NA)
Value of shipments (1992 dollars) . . .	Mil. dol. . .	202,519	206,551	209,867	212,855	213,459	(NA)	(NA)
Total employment	1,000	829.7	836.4	826.2	828.7	826.4	(NA)	(NA)
Production workers	1,000	573.5	578.1	571.5	574.5	569.8	(NA)	(NA)
Average hourly earnings	Dollar . . .	11.57	11.83	12.08	12.08	12.41	(NA)	(NA)
Capital expenditures	Mil. dol. . .	6,405	5,935	6,247	7,235	7,032	(NA)	(NA)
Product data:								
Value of shipments [3]	Mil. dol. . .	191,278	197,567	204,380	213,482	218,210	(NA)	(NA)
Value of shipments (1992 dollars) . . .	Mil. dol. . .	191,278	195,148	198,202	202,462	202,188	(NA)	(NA)
Trade data:								
Value of imports	Mil. dol. . .	9,438	9,184	10,168	11,149	12,751	14,182	15,184
Value of exports	Mil. dol. . .	6,257	7,068	8,056	8,411	9,002	9,816	9,774
LOWER VALUE ADDED FOODS AND FEEDS [4]								
Industry data:								
Value of shipments [2]	Mil. dol. . .	204,444	212,894	214,269	222,086	230,750	(NA)	(NA)
Value of shipments (1992 dollars) . . .	Mil. dol. . .	204,444	208,548	209,267	218,095	209,461	(NA)	(NA)
Total employment	1,000	673.3	683.9	684.7	691.2	690.4	(NA)	(NA)
Production workers	1,000	526.7	539.9	540.0	545.6	542.7	(NA)	(NA)
Average hourly earnings	Dollar . . .	9.21	9.29	9.39	9.81	9.89	(NA)	(NA)
Capital expenditures	Mil. dol. . .	3,494	3,454	3,846	4,577	4,686	(NA)	(NA)
Product data:								
Value of shipments [3]	Mil. dol. . .	191,611	200,065	201,110	208,025	216,799	(NA)	(NA)
Value of shipments (1992 dollars) . . .	Mil. dol. . .	191,611	195,928	196,217	203,773	196,475	(NA)	(NA)
Trade data:								
Value of imports	Mil. dol. . .	6,530	6,598	6,936	6,961	7,887	8,237	8,382
Value of exports	Mil. dol. . .	12,878	12,886	14,363	16,733	17,010	17,808	16,682

NA Not available. [1] SICs 2023, 24, 32-38, 43, 45, 47, 51-53, 64-68, 82, 84-86, 95, 96, 98, and 99. This aggregation includes those industries defined as higher value added. [2] Value of all products and services sold by establishments in this industry.
[3] Value of products classified in this industry produced by all industries. [4] SIC 20 excluding 2023, 24, 32-38, 43, 45, 47, 51-53, 64-68, 82, 84-86, 95, 96, 98, and 99. This aggregation includes those industries defined as lower value added.

Source: U.S. Department of Commerce, U.S. Census Bureau, International Trade Administration (ITA).

U.S. Census Bureau, Statistical Abstract of the United States: 2000

No. 1416. Recent Trends in Red Meat and Poultry Slaughtering and Processing: 1992 to 1998

Item	Unit	1992	1993	1994	1995	1996	1997	1998
RED MEAT (SIC 2011, 2013)								
Industry data:								
Value of shipments [1]	Mil. dol.	70,107	73,941	70,701	72,025	71,943	77,675	(NA)
Value of shipments (1992 dollars)	Mil. dol.	70,107	71,389	71,609	74,312	71,003	74,817	(NA)
Total employment	1,000.	206.6	208.6	204.3	214.4	218.1	226.7	(NA)
Production workers	1,000.	170.6	172.7	169.2	178.0	180.2	188.5	(NA)
Average hourly earnings	Dollar	8.99	9.06	9.43	9.81	9.64	9.99	(NA)
Capital expenditures	Mil. dol.	719	703	699	862	1,135	1,042	(NA)
Product data:								
Value of shipments [2]	Mil. dol.	64,351	68,216	64,839	65,878	65,839	(NA)	(NA)
Value of shipments (1992 dollars)	Mil. dol.	64,351	65,856	65,679	67,977	64,988	(NA)	(NA)
Trade data:								
Value of imports	Mil. dol.	2,899	3,041	2,946	2,649	2,605	2,968	3,139
Value of exports	Mil. dol.	4,704	4,606	5,187	6,230	6,145	6,126	5,563
POULTRY SLAUGHTERING AND PROCESSING (SIC 2015)								
Industry data:								
Value of shipments [1]	Mil. dol.	23,965	25,501	27,415	28,929	30,160	33,344	(NA)
Value of shipments (1992 dollars)	Mil. dol.	23,965	24,783	25,937	27,525	27,122	30,562	(NA)
Total employment	1,000.	193.8	205.3	216.0	214.3	215.3	235.6	(NA)
Production workers	1,000.	172.8	184.3	193.2	191.5	190.0	209.4	(NA)
Average hourly earnings	Dollar	7.39	7.40	7.49	8.09	8.27	8.43	(NA)
Capital expenditures	Mil. dol.	469	555	594	726	697	663	(NA)
Product data:								
Value of shipments [2]	Mil. dol.	23,592	24,983	27,027	28,708	29,981	(NA)	(NA)
Value of shipments (1992 dollars)	Mil. dol.	23,592	24,279	25,570	27,315	26,961	(NA)	(NA)
Trade data:								
Value of imports	Mil. dol.	26	30	25	31	45	46	54
Value of exports	Mil. dol.	990	1,157	1,633	2,097	2,585	2,537	2,261

NA Not available. [1] Value of all products and services sold by establishments in this industry. [2] Value of products classified in this industry produced by all industries.

Source: U.S. Department of Commerce, U.S. Census Bureau, International Trade Administration (ITA).

No. 1417. Recent Trends in Textile Mill Products (SIC 22): 1992 to 1998

Item	Unit	1992	1993	1994	1995	1996	1997	1998
INDUSTRY DATA								
Value of shipments [1]	Mil. dol.	70,753	73,955	78,027	79,874	80,242	(NA)	(NA)
Value of shipments (1992 dollars)	Mil. dol.	70,753	74,285	78,213	77,715	77,227	(NA)	(NA)
Total employment	1,000.	616.5	610.1	624.2	609.6	576.5	(NA)	(NA)
Production workers	1,000.	528.4	523.6	533.7	519.5	489.1	(NA)	(NA)
Average hourly earnings	Dollar	8.62	8.92	9.29	9.38	9.62	(NA)	(NA)
Capital expenditures	Mil. dol.	2,225	2,450	2,961	2,886	2,666	(NA)	(NA)
PRODUCT DATA								
Value of shipments [2]	Mil. dol.	70,008	73,216	77,249	79,201	79,334	(NA)	(NA)
Value of shipments (1992 dollars)	Mil. dol.	70,008	73,539	77,448	77,035	76,336	(NA)	(NA)
TRADE DATA								
Value of imports	Mil. dol.	5,850	6,163	6,534	6,974	7,177	8,384	8,794
Value of exports	Mil. dol.	4,508	4,706	5,172	5,720	6,197	7,101	7,194

NA Not available. [1] Value of all products and services sold by establishments in the textile mill products industry. [2] Value of products classified in the textile mill products industry produced by all industries.

Source: U.S. Department of Commerce, U.S. Census Bureau, International Trade Administration (ITA).

No. 1418. Recent Trends in Apparel and Other Textile Products (SIC 23): 1992 to 1998

Item	Unit	1992	1993	1994	1995	1996	1997	1998
INDUSTRY DATA								
Value of shipments [1]	Mil. dol.	71,658	74,010	76,979	78,103	77,628	(NA)	(NA)
Value of shipments (1992 dollars)	Mil. dol.	71,658	73,339	76,063	76,601	74,976	(NA)	(NA)
Total employment	1,000.	985.1	979.7	954.4	946.6	864.9	(NA)	(NA)
Production workers	1,000.	824.1	825.1	798.9	791.8	726.4	(NA)	(NA)
Average hourly earnings	Dollar	7.12	7.34	7.44	7.56	7.67	(NA)	(NA)
Capital expenditures	Mil. dol.	945	962	1,091	1,187	964	(NA)	(NA)
PRODUCT DATA								
Value of shipments [2]	Mil. dol.	68,844	70,986	73,259	73,780	73,319	(NA)	(NA)
Value of shipments (1992 dollars)	Mil. dol.	68,844	70,345	72,382	72,370	70,843	(NA)	(NA)
TRADE DATA								
Value of imports	Mil. dol.	32,659	35,486	38,569	41,217	43,089	50,204	55,863
Value of exports	Mil. dol.	4,769	5,505	6,100	7,059	7,906	8,989	9,032

NA Not available. [1] Value of all products and services sold by establishments in the apparel and other textile products industry. [2] Value of products classified in the apparel and other textile products industry produced by all industries.

Source: U.S. Department of Commerce, U.S. Census Bureau, International Trade Administration (ITA).

No. 1419. Recent Trends in Household Consumer Durables (SIC 251, 3524, 363, 3651): 1992 to 1998

Item	Unit	1992	1993	1994	1995	1996	1997	1998
INDUSTRY DATA								
Value of shipments [1]	Mil. dol. . . .	53,098	57,329	63,369	64,805	63,394	(NA)	(NA)
Value of shipments (1992 dollars)	Mil. dol. . . .	53,098	56,685	61,865	62,791	60,491	(NA)	(NA)
Total employment	1,000. . . .	412.3	416.4	433.7	442.5	439.2	(NA)	(NA)
Production workers	1,000. . . .	338.8	344.8	363.2	365.7	364.2	(NA)	(NA)
Average hourly earnings	Dollar . . .	9.30	9.69	9.73	9.86	10.25	(NA)	(NA)
Capital expenditures	Mil. dol. . . .	1,280	1,178	1,301	1,568	1,598	(NA)	(NA)
PRODUCT DATA								
Value of shipments [2]	Mil. dol. . . .	48,314	51,650	56,958	58,980	60,334	(NA)	(NA)
Value of shipments (1992 dollars)	Mil. dol. . . .	48,314	51,046	55,542	57,039	57,622	(NA)	(NA)
TRADE DATA								
Value of imports	Mil. dol. . . .	22,941	24,405	28,111	30,386	30,004	31,710	35,593
Value of exports	Mil. dol. . . .	6,524	7,064	7,766	8,092	8,467	9,507	9,938

NA Not available. [1] Value of all products and services sold by establishments in the household consumer durables industry. [2] Value of products classified in the household consumer durables industry produced by all industries.

Source: U.S. Department of Commerce, U.S. Census Bureau, International Trade Administration (ITA).

No. 1420. Recent Trends in Paper and Allied Products (SIC 26): 1992 to 1998

Item	Unit	1992	1993	1994	1995	1996	1997	1998
INDUSTRY DATA								
Value of shipments [1]	Mil. dol. . . .	133,201	133,262	143,649	173,716	160,661	(NA)	(NA)
Value of shipments (1992 dollars)	Mil. dol. . . .	133,201	135,059	141,192	141,915	140,102	(NA)	(NA)
Total employment	1,000. . . .	626.5	626.3	622.3	629.1	630.6	(NA)	(NA)
Production workers	1,000. . . .	478.8	479.1	479.7	487.3	487.5	(NA)	(NA)
Average hourly earnings	Dollar . . .	13.81	14.09	14.52	14.73	15.02	(NA)	(NA)
Capital expenditures	Mil. dol. . . .	7,963	7,370	7,731	8,369	9,302	(NA)	(NA)
PRODUCT DATA								
Value of shipments [2]	Mil. dol. . . .	128,941	128,695	138,560	168,137	155,319	(NA)	(NA)
Value of shipments (1992 dollars)	Mil. dol. . . .	128,941	130,523	136,231	137,048	135,455	(NA)	(NA)
TRADE DATA								
Value of imports	Mil. dol. . . .	10,362	10,793	11,677	16,625	14,609	14,668	15,621
Value of exports	Mil. dol. . . .	9,919	9,363	10,891	14,838	13,895	14,417	13,632

NA Not available. [1] Value of all products and services sold by establishments in the paper and allied products industry. [2] Value of products classified in the paper and allied products produced by all industries.

Source: U.S. Department of Commerce, U.S. Census Bureau, International Trade Administration (ITA).

No. 1421. Recent Trends in Pulp Mills and Paper and Paperboard Mills: 1992 to 1998

Item	Unit	1992	1993	1994	1995	1996	1997	1998
PULP MILLS (SIC 2611)								
Industry data:								
Value of shipments [1]	Mil. dol. . . .	5,466	4,282	4,827	7,513	5,508	4,117	(NA)
Value of shipments (1992 dollars) . . .	Mil. dol. . . .	5,466	4,758	4,992	4,920	4,931	3,815	(NA)
Total employment	1,000. . . .	15.9	14.2	13.3	14.6	15.0	10.3	(NA)
Production workers	1,000. . . .	12.1	10.8	10.2	11.3	11.1	7.9	(NA)
Average hourly earnings	Dollar . . .	19.15	19.49	20.08	20.40	20.16	22.97	(NA)
Capital expenditures	Mil. dol. . . .	772	426	315	564	698	426	(NA)
Product data:								
Value of shipments [2]	Mil. dol. . . .	6,104	4,995	5,952	8,911	6,329	(NA)	(NA)
Value of shipments (1992 dollars) . . .	Mil. dol. . . .	6,104	5,550	6,156	5,836	5,666	(NA)	(NA)
Trade data:								
Value of imports	Mil. dol. . . .	2,104	1,868	2,285	3,745	2,601	2,572	2,392
Value of exports	Mil. dol. . . .	3,236	2,482	2,954	4,698	3,358	3,253	2,774
PAPER AND PAPERBOARD MILLS (SIC 262, 263)								
Industry data:								
Value of shipments [1]	Mil. dol. . . .	48,926	48,267	53,381	69,638	59,837	55,228	(NA)
Value of shipments (1992 dollars) . . .	Mil. dol. . . .	48,926	48,625	52,187	53,571	51,107	49,625	(NA)
Total employment	1,000. . . .	182.1	179.5	177.0	174.5	171.2	161.7	(NA)
Production workers	1,000. . . .	139.8	137.7	135.9	134.5	132.0	124.6	(NA)
Average hourly earnings	Dollar . . .	17.97	18.22	19.17	19.76	20.34	21.11	(NA)
Capital expenditures	Mil. dol. . . .	4,952	4,507	4,960	4,859	5,502	4,378	(NA)
Product data:								
Value of shipments [2]	Mil. dol. . . .	47,232	46,513	51,110	67,052	57,971	(NA)	(NA)
Value of shipments (1992 dollars) . . .	Mil. dol. . . .	47,232	46,866	49,945	51,571	49,514	(NA)	(NA)
Trade data:								
Value of imports	Mil. dol. . . .	6,708	7,190	7,338	10,198	9,118	9,007	9,828
Value of exports	Mil. dol. . . .	4,263	4,190	4,813	6,437	6,339	6,545	6,240

NA Not available. [1] Value of all products and services sold by establishments in this industry. [2] Value of products classified in this industry produced by all industries.

Source: U.S. Department of Commerce, U.S. Census Bureau, International Trade Administration (ITA).

U.S. Census Bureau, Statistical Abstract of the United States: 2000

No. 1422. Recent Trends in Printing and Publishing (SIC 27): 1992 to 1998

Item	Unit	1992	1993	1994	1995	1996	1997	1998
INDUSTRY DATA								
Value of shipments [1]	Mil. dol. . . .	166,153	172,634	176,876	188,133	195,435	210,311	(NA)
2711 Newspapers	Mil. dol. . . .	33,782	34,651	36,091	37,732	39,171	41,601	(NA)
2721 Periodicals	Mil. dol. . . .	22,104	22,653	21,892	23,743	24,930	29,885	(NA)
2731 Book publishing	Mil. dol. . . .	16,698	18,616	19,695	20,484	21,363	22,648	(NA)
2732 Book printing	Mil. dol. . . .	4,681	4,810	4,745	5,392	5,333	5,418	(NA)
2741 Misc publishing	Mil. dol. . . .	10,908	11,807	11,976	12,025	12,511	16,359	(NA)
275 Commercial printing	Mil. dol. . . .	56,229	58,173	60,411	65,101	67,842	69,824	(NA)
2761 Manifold business forms	Mil. dol. . . .	7,429	7,491	6,958	7,894	7,724	7,739	(NA)
2771 Greeting cards	Mil. dol. . . .	4,190	4,275	4,546	4,689	5,011	5,414	(NA)
2782 Blankbooks and binders	Mil. dol. . . .	3,758	3,771	4,276	4,544	4,820	4,457	(NA)
2789 Bookbinding	Mil. dol. . . .	1,291	1,258	1,367	1,509	1,608	1,958	(NA)
279 Printing trade services	Mil. dol. . . .	5,085	5,129	4,920	5,020	5,123	5,009	(NA)
Value of shipments (1992 dollars)	Mil. dol. . . .	166,153	167,352	167,099	168,181	168,517	177,794	(NA)
2711 Newspapers	Mil. dol. . . .	33,782	33,222	33,294	32,782	31,718	32,475	(NA)
2721 Periodicals	Mil. dol. . . .	22,104	22,014	20,849	21,903	22,379	25,696	(NA)
2731 Book publishing	Mil. dol. . . .	16,698	18,180	18,493	18,257	18,166	18,702	(NA)
2732 Book printing	Mil. dol. . . .	4,681	4,777	4,647	5,044	5,008	5,175	(NA)
2741 Misc publishing	Mil. dol. . . .	10,908	11,320	11,048	10,604	10,504	13,246	(NA)
275 Commercial printing	Mil. dol. . . .	56,229	56,764	58,252	59,454	60,555	62,189	(NA)
2761 Manifold business forms	Mil. dol. . . .	7,429	7,027	6,240	5,762	5,494	5,567	(NA)
2771 Greeting cards	Mil. dol. . . .	4,190	4,040	4,016	3,960	4,064	4,325	(NA)
2782 Blankbooks and binders	Mil. dol. . . .	3,758	3,668	4,049	4,058	4,152	3,790	(NA)
2789 Bookbinding	Mil. dol. . . .	1,291	1,249	1,343	1,431	1,501	1,787	(NA)
279 Printing trade services	Mil. dol. . . .	5,085	5,090	4,868	4,928	4,977	4,841	(NA)

NA Not available.   [1] Value of all products and services sold by establishments in the printing and publishing industry.

Source: U.S. Department of Commerce, U.S. Census Bureau, International Trade Administration (ITA).

No. 1423. Recent Trends in Periodicals, Book Publishing, and Commercial Printing: 1992 to 1998

Item	Unit	1992	1993	1994	1995	1996	1997	1998
PERIODICALS (SIC 2721)								
Industry data:								
Value of shipments [1]	Mil. dol. . . .	22,104	22,653	21,892	23,743	24,930	29,885	(NA)
Value of shipments (1992 dollars)	Mil. dol. . . .	22,104	22,014	20,849	21,903	22,379	25,696	(NA)
Total employment	1,000. . . .	115.1	117.1	117.2	122.0	120.5	137.6	(NA)
Production workers	1,000. . . .	20.2	19.7	18.2	17.8	16.4	25.5	(NA)
Average hourly earnings	Dollar . . .	13.40	12.51	12.78	13.58	14.85	16.34	(NA)
Capital expenditures	Mil. dol. . . .	235	290	308	332	311	472	(NA)
Product data:								
Value of shipments [2]	Mil. dol. . . .	20,942	21,692	21,642	22,951	24,352	(NA)	(NA)
Value of shipments (1992 dollars)	Mil. dol. . . .	20,942	21,080	20,611	21,173	21,860	(NA)	(NA)
Trade data:								
Value of imports	Mil. dol. . . .	134	194	209	222	217	204	217
Value of exports	Mil. dol. . . .	731	737	788	825	819	864	864
BOOK PUBLISHING (SIC 2731)								
Industry data:								
Value of shipments [1]	Mil. dol. . . .	16,698	18,616	19,695	20,484	21,363	22,648	(NA)
Value of shipments (1992 dollars)	Mil. dol. . . .	16,698	18,180	18,493	18,257	18,166	18,702	(NA)
Total employment	1,000. . . .	79.0	83.2	83.5	83.5	85.4	89.9	(NA)
Production workers	1,000. . . .	18.2	18.2	18.2	18.5	18.5	22.7	(NA)
Average hourly earnings	Dollar . . .	12.51	12.90	13.56	13.61	13.27	16.36	(NA)
Capital expenditures	Mil. dol. . . .	327	282	283	345	365	462	(NA)
Product data:								
Value of shipments [2]	Mil. dol. . . .	14,761	16,596	17,229	18,409	19,114	(NA)	(NA)
Value of shipments (1992 dollars)	Mil. dol. . . .	14,761	16,207	16,177	16,407	16,254	(NA)	(NA)
Trade data:								
Value of imports	Mil. dol. . . .	953	966	1,023	1,184	1,240	1,298	1,384
Value of exports	Mil. dol. . . .	1,637	1,664	1,703	1,779	1,776	1,897	1,842
COMMERCIAL PRINTING (SIC 275)								
Industry data:								
Value of shipments [1]	Mil. dol. . . .	56,229	58,173	60,411	65,101	67,842	69,824	(NA)
Value of shipments (1992 dollars)	Mil. dol. . . .	56,229	56,764	58,252	59,454	60,555	62,189	(NA)
Total employment	1,000. . . .	567.2	571.8	577.4	597.7	604.3	595.6	(NA)
Production workers	1,000. . . .	408.4	414.5	416.8	433.3	437.3	429.9	(NA)
Average hourly earnings	Dollar . . .	11.50	11.69	11.75	11.86	12.31	14.29	(NA)
Capital expenditures	Mil. dol. . . .	2,144	2,238	2,708	2,680	2,959	3,971	(NA)
Product data:								
Value of shipments [2]	Mil. dol. . . .	54,902	56,960	58,902	63,819	66,624	(NA)	(NA)
Value of shipments (1992 dollars)	Mil. dol. . . .	54,902	55,577	56,791	58,277	59,466	(NA)	(NA)
Trade data:								
Value of imports	Mil. dol. . . .	442	505	584	756	748	825	909
Value of exports	Mil. dol. . . .	1,056	1,201	1,061	1,197	1,195	1,248	1,393

NA Not available.   [1] Value of all products and services sold by establishments in this industry.   [2] Value of products classified in this industry produced by all industries.

Source: U.S. Department of Commerce, U.S. Census Bureau, International Trade Administration (ITA).

No. 1424. Recent Trends in Chemicals and Allied Products (SIC 28): 1992 to 1998

Item	Unit	1992	1993	1994	1995	1996	1997	1998
INDUSTRY DATA								
Value of shipments [1]	Mil. dol. . .	305,420	314,907	333,905	361,161	367,442	(NA)	(NA)
Value of shipments (1992 dollars)	Mil. dol. . .	305,420	307,625	317,588	323,024	325,552	(NA)	(NA)
Total employment	1,000. . . .	848.6	838.4	823.1	838.9	824.5	(NA)	(NA)
Production workers	1,000. . . .	479.3	473.6	471.7	487.0	476.8	(NA)	(NA)
Average hourly earnings	Dollar . . .	15.27	15.62	16.25	16.56	17.22	(NA)	(NA)
Capital expenditures	Mil. dol. . .	16,381	15,690	15,411	17,557	20,041	(NA)	(NA)
PRODUCT DATA								
Value of shipments [2]	Mil. dol. . .	282,242	292,416	309,592	337,103	343,338	(NA)	(NA)
Value of shipments (1992 dollars)	Mil. dol. . .	282,242	285,763	294,588	300,900	304,212	(NA)	(NA)
TRADE DATA								
Value of imports	Mil. dol. . .	26,363	27,751	32,387	39,247	44,706	50,893	54,625
Value of exports	Mil. dol. . .	42,786	43,303	49,521	58,584	59,263	66,019	64,724

NA Not available.   [1] Value of all products and services sold by establishments in the chemicals and allied products industry.   [2] Value of products classified in the chemicals and allied products industry produced by all industries.

Source: U.S. Department of Commerce, U.S. Census Bureau, International Trade Administration (ITA).

No. 1425. Recent Trends in Petrochemicals (SIC 2821, 2822, 2824, 2843, 2865, 2869, 2873): 1992 to 1998

Item	Unit	1992	1993	1994	1995	1996	1997	1998
INDUSTRY DATA								
Value of shipments [1]	Mil. dol. . .	117,277	119,225	132,458	147,754	143,152	158,281	(NA)
Value of shipments (1992 dollars)	Mil. dol. . .	117,277	115,987	124,809	125,548	122,517	134,047	(NA)
Total employment	1,000. . . .	256.7	255.0	252.0	252.8	250.4	246.6	(NA)
Production workers	1,000. . . .	158.5	158.1	156.2	157.2	157.7	154.3	(NA)
Average hourly earnings	Dollar . . .	17.62	17.93	18.63	19.11	19.86	20.84	(NA)
Capital expenditures	Mil. dol. . .	7,837	7,554	7,319	8,526	10,627	10,566	(NA)
PRODUCT DATA								
Value of shipments [2]	Mil. dol. . .	113,476	115,269	126,971	142,673	139,399	(NA)	(NA)
Value of shipments (1992 dollars)	Mil. dol. . .	113,476	112,268	119,759	121,105	119,659	(NA)	(NA)
TRADE DATA								
Value of imports	Mil. dol. . .	12,241	13,370	16,310	20,054	21,662	24,140	23,828
Value of exports	Mil. dol. . .	23,455	23,313	27,986	34,561	33,397	36,342	34,240

NA Not available.   [1] Value of all products and services sold by establishments in the petrochemicals industry.   [2] Value of products classified in the petrochemicals industry produced by all industries.

Source: U.S. Department of Commerce, U.S. Census Bureau, International Trade Administration (ITA).

No. 1426. Recent Trends in Organic Chemicals, Except Gum and Wood (SIC 2865, 2869): 1992 to 1998

Item	Unit	1992	1993	1994	1995	1996	1997	1998
INDUSTRY DATA								
Value of shipments [1]	Mil. dol. . .	63,663	63,541	69,205	75,912	74,863	83,987	(NA)
Value of shipments (1992 dollars)	Mil. dol. . .	63,663	61,113	64,865	65,287	63,179	70,387	(NA)
Total employment	1,000. . . .	122.0	120.8	112.5	115.2	123.1	119.7	(NA)
Production workers	1,000. . . .	70.4	70.9	66.0	67.4	72.5	70.4	(NA)
Average hourly earnings	Dollar . . .	18.72	18.88	20.23	20.56	21.61	22.70	(NA)
Capital expenditures	Mil. dol. . .	4,749	4,028	3,509	4,891	6,242	5,707	(NA)
PRODUCT DATA								
Value of shipments [2]	Mil. dol. . .	58,655	59,135	65,003	72,306	70,532	(NA)	(NA)
Value of shipments (1992 dollars)	Mil. dol. . .	58,655	56,974	61,125	62,389	60,085	(NA)	(NA)
TRADE DATA								
Value of imports	Mil. dol. . .	8,090	8,237	9,717	12,172	13,734	15,660	15,243
Value of exports	Mil. dol. . .	11,399	11,714	13,813	17,416	15,998	17,596	16,081

NA Not available.   [1] Value of all products and services sold by establishments in the organic chemicals, except gum and wood industry.   [2] Value of products classified in the organic chemicals, except gum and wood industry produced by all industries.

Source: U.S. Department of Commerce, U.S. Census Bureau, International Trade Administration (ITA).

Industrial Outlook   863

No. 1427. Recent Trends in Drugs (SIC 283): 1992 to 1998

Item	Unit	1992	1993	1994	1995	1996	1997	1998
INDUSTRY DATA								
Value of shipments [1]	Mil. dol. . .	67,792	70,985	75,804	80,907	86,532	93,272	(NA)
2833 Medicinals and botanicals	Mil. dol. . .	6,526	5,926	6,093	7,027	8,884	11,921	(NA)
2834 Pharmaceutical preps.	Mil. dol. . .	50,415	53,281	56,123	58,405	61,554	66,289	(NA)
2835 Diagnostic substances	Mil. dol. . .	6,857	6,864	8,278	9,248	9,692	9,377	(NA)
2836 Bio. prod. exc. diagnostic	Mil. dol. . .	3,993	4,914	5,310	6,227	6,402	5,686	(NA)
Value of shipments (1992 dollars)	Mil. dol. . .	67,792	68,179	71,142	73,820	76,824	80,282	(NA)
2833 Medicinals and botanicals	Mil. dol. . .	6,526	5,523	5,460	6,164	7,739	10,034	(NA)
2834 Pharmaceutical preps.	Mil. dol. . .	50,415	51,084	52,159	52,475	53,386	55,472	(NA)
2835 Diagnostic substances	Mil. dol. . .	6,857	6,750	8,245	9,058	9,465	9,293	(NA)
2836 Bio. prod. exc. diagnostic	Mil. dol. . .	3,993	4,822	5,279	6,122	6,234	5,483	(NA)
Total employment	1,000. . . .	194.4	199.5	204.8	216.4	213.2	199.0	(NA)
2833 Medicinals and botanicals	1,000. . . .	13.1	13.0	12.9	14.1	16.8	23.4	(NA)
2834 Pharmaceutical preps.	1,000. . . .	122.9	128.2	133.0	143.0	136.9	112.6	(NA)
2835 Diagnostic substances	1,000. . . .	39.9	39.3	39.1	38.2	39.9	39.6	(NA)
2836 Bio. prod. exc. diagnostic	1,000. . . .	18.5	19.0	19.8	21.1	19.6	23.3	(NA)
Production workers	1,000. . . .	92.7	94.6	101.5	112.5	106.4	101.1	(NA)
2833 Medicinals and botanicals	1,000. . . .	7.5	7.7	7.5	7.5	8.9	12.9	(NA)
2834 Pharmaceutical preps.	1,000. . . .	62.4	62.8	68.0	78.7	72.3	61.3	(NA)
2835 Diagnostic substances	1,000. . . .	14.7	14.9	16.1	15.3	15.5	14.8	(NA)
2836 Bio. prod. ex. diagnostic	1,000. . . .	8.1	9.2	9.9	11.0	9.7	12.1	(NA)
Average hourly earnings	Dollar . . .	14.78	15.80	16.34	15.99	16.63	18.02	(NA)
2833 Medicinals and botanicals	Dollar . . .	18.93	19.62	19.70	20.27	20.83	19.47	(NA)
2834 Pharmaceutical preps.	Dollar . . .	14.71	15.81	16.11	15.40	15.88	17.35	(NA)
2835 Diagnostic substances	Dollar . . .	14.09	15.64	17.23	18.08	19.15	21.49	(NA)
2836 Bio. prod. exc. diagnostic	Dollar . . .	12.50	12.57	13.81	13.74	14.06	15.72	(NA)
Capital expenditures	Mil. dol. . .	3,887	4,047	4,034	4,503	4,301	4,400	(NA)
2833 Medicinals and botanicals	Mil. dol. . .	554	482	483	384	835	771	(NA)
2834 Pharmaceutical preps.	Mil. dol. . .	2,450	2,493	2,618	3,134	2,588	2,466	(NA)
2835 Diagnostic substances	Mil. dol. . .	588	667	573	532	518	732	(NA)
2836 Bio. prod. exc. diagnostic	Mil. dol. . .	295	405	361	453	360	431	(NA)
PRODUCT DATA								
Value of shipments [2]	Mil. dol. . .	60,793	63,970	67,751	71,528	76,293	(NA)	(NA)
2833 Medicinals and botanicals	Mil. dol. . .	7,002	6,749	6,772	7,345	8,999	(NA)	(NA)
2834 Pharmaceutical preps.	Mil. dol. . .	43,082	45,522	48,086	49,965	52,932	(NA)	(NA)
2835 Diagnostic substances	Mil. dol. . .	6,196	6,453	7,179	7,926	8,036	(NA)	(NA)
2836 Bio. prod. exc. diagnostic	Mil. dol. . .	4,512	5,246	5,715	6,293	6,326	(NA)	(NA)
Value of shipments (1992 dollars)	Mil. dol. . .	60,793	61,428	63,588	65,285	67,754	(NA)	(NA)
2833 Medicinals and botanicals	Mil. dol. . .	7,002	6,290	6,068	6,443	7,839	(NA)	(NA)
2834 Pharmaceutical preps.	Mil. dol. . .	43,082	43,645	44,690	44,892	45,908	(NA)	(NA)
2835 Diagnostic substances	Mil. dol. . .	6,196	6,345	7,150	7,763	7,848	(NA)	(NA)
2836 Bio. prod. exc. diagnostic	Mil. dol. . .	4,512	5,148	5,681	6,188	6,159	(NA)	(NA)
TRADE DATA								
Value of imports	Mil. dol. . .	5,980	6,062	6,906	8,505	11,089	14,110	17,847
2833 Medicinals and botanicals	Mil. dol. . .	3,507	3,270	3,468	4,766	6,349	7,499	9,140
2834 Pharmaceutical preps.	Mil. dol. . .	1,651	1,895	2,355	2,666	3,403	5,071	7,169
2835 Diagnostic substances	Mil. dol. . .	336	379	470	457	541	594	685
2836 Bio. prod. exc. diagnostic	Mil. dol. . .	486	518	613	616	796	946	853
Value of exports	Mil. dol. . .	6,765	7,215	7,561	7,991	8,886	10,369	11,943
2833 Medicinals and botanicals	Mil. dol. . .	2,669	2,648	2,678	2,734	2,870	3,332	3,830
2834 Pharmaceutical preps.	Mil. dol. . .	1,584	1,773	1,914	1,954	2,356	2,938	3,842
2835 Diagnostic substances	Mil. dol. . .	1,370	1,485	1,507	1,741	1,891	2,171	2,286
2836 Bio. prod. exc. diagnostic	Mil. dol. . .	1,142	1,309	1,462	1,562	1,769	1,928	1,985

NA Not available.   [1] Value of all products and services sold by establishments in the drugs industry.   [2] Value of products classified in the drugs industry produced by all industries.

Source: U.S. Department of Commerce, U.S. Census Bureau, International Trade Administration (ITA).

864   Industrial Outlook

No. 1428. Recent Trends in Soap, Cleaners, and Toilet Goods (SIC 284): 1992 to 1998

Item	Unit	1992	1993	1994	1995	1996	1997	1998
INDUSTRY DATA								
Value of shipments [1]	Mil. dol. . .	42,875	46,903	46,548	49,795	51,809	57,507	(NA)
2841 Soap and other detergents	Mil. dol. . .	14,729	15,458	14,603	15,735	15,779	16,776	(NA)
2842 Polishes/sanitation goods	Mil. dol. . .	6,659	8,079	8,405	8,679	8,602	8,370	(NA)
2843 Surface active agents.	Mil. dol. . .	2,859	3,661	3,721	4,860	4,741	6,992	(NA)
2844 Toilet preparations	Mil. dol. . .	18,629	19,706	19,820	20,522	22,688	25,369	(NA)
Value of shipments (1992 dollars)	Mil. dol. . .	42,875	46,174	45,873	48,469	49,766	54,779	(NA)
2841 Soap and other detergents	Mil. dol. . .	14,729	15,259	14,530	15,487	15,230	16,023	(NA)
2842 Polishes/sanitation goods	Mil. dol. . .	6,659	8,014	8,264	8,353	8,239	7,994	(NA)
2843 Surface active agents.	Mil. dol. . .	2,859	3,599	3,609	4,529	4,248	6,155	(NA)
2844 Toilet preparations	Mil. dol. . .	18,629	19,301	19,469	20,100	22,048	24,607	(NA)
Total employment	1,000. . . .	122.8	124.3	118.9	122.8	126.2	126.4	(NA)
2841 Soap and other detergents	1,000. . . .	32.8	31.2	31.3	31.6	30.3	29.0	(NA)
2842 Polishes/sanitation goods	1,000. . . .	22.0	22.8	21.4	23.1	24.2	22.0	(NA)
2843 Surface active agents.	1,000. . . .	8.2	8.6	8.1	7.9	8.8	9.5	(NA)
2844 Toilet preparations	1,000. . . .	59.8	61.7	58.1	60.2	62.9	66.0	(NA)
Production workers	1,000. . . .	74.5	74.6	71.1	73.8	74.6	77.8	(NA)
2841 Soap and other detergents	1,000. . . .	19.9	17.9	18.6	18.0	16.8	16.8	(NA)
2842 Polishes/sanitation goods	1,000. . . .	13.4	13.8	13.1	14.0	14.2	14.1	(NA)
2843 Surface active agents.	1,000. . . .	4.2	4.3	3.9	3.9	4.5	5.0	(NA)
2844 Toilet preparations	1,000. . . .	37.0	38.6	35.5	37.9	39.1	41.9	(NA)
Average hourly earnings.	Dollars. . .	12.32	12.26	12.36	12.75	13.02	14.16	(NA)
2841 Soap and other detergents. . .	Dollars. . .	14.86	15.06	14.89	15.40	15.68	17.03	(NA)
2842 Polishes/sanitation goods . . .	Dollars. . .	11.84	11.94	11.12	11.49	11.49	12.54	(NA)
2843 Surface active agents	Dollars. . .	15.09	15.95	16.80	16.20	16.55	18.39	(NA)
2844 Toilet preparations	Dollars. . .	10.80	10.59	10.93	11.44	11.89	12.92	(NA)
Capital expenditures	Mil. dol. . .	1,290	1,320	1,334	1,041	1,304	1,484	(NA)
2841 Soap and other detergents	Mil. dol. . .	571	514	494	356	427	448	(NA)
2842 Polishes/sanitation goods	Mil. dol. . .	121	130	124	154	173	154	(NA)
2843 Surface active agents.	Mil. dol. . .	92	203	225	120	161	289	(NA)
2844 Toilet preparations	Mil. dol. . .	506	473	491	411	543	594	(NA)
PRODUCT DATA								
Value of shipments [2]	Mil. dol. . .	39,999	43,293	42,622	45,775	47,797	(NA)	(NA)
2841 Soap and other detergents	Mil. dol. . .	11,022	11,594	11,089	12,205	12,467	(NA)	(NA)
2842 Polishes/sanitation goods	Mil. dol. . .	6,477	7,492	7,601	7,755	7,327	(NA)	(NA)
2843 Surface active agents.	Mil. dol. . .	3,776	4,032	3,648	4,703	4,836	(NA)	(NA)
2844 Toilet preparations	Mil. dol. . .	18,724	20,175	20,284	21,112	23,168	(NA)	(NA)
Value of shipments (1992 dollars)	Mil. dol. . .	39,999	42,603	41,971	44,538	45,900	(NA)	(NA)
2841 Soap and other detergents	Mil. dol. . .	11,022	11,445	11,033	12,013	12,033	(NA)	(NA)
2842 Polishes/sanitation goods	Mil. dol. . .	6,477	7,433	7,474	7,464	7,018	(NA)	(NA)
2843 Surface active agents.	Mil. dol. . .	3,776	3,965	3,538	4,383	4,333	(NA)	(NA)
2844 Toilet preparations	Mil. dol. . .	18,724	19,760	19,926	20,678	22,515	(NA)	(NA)
TRADE DATA								
Value of imports	Mil. dol. . .	1,309	1,464	1,689	1,936	2,068	2,287	2,510
2841 Soap and other detergents	Mil. dol. . .	213	254	335	422	454	479	476
2842 Polishes/sanitation goods	Mil. dol. . .	46	50	56	62	69	93	104
2843 Surface active agents.	Mil. dol. . .	158	204	263	296	288	305	312
2844 Toilet preparations	Mil. dol. . .	892	956	1,035	1,156	1,257	1,410	1,618
Value of exports	Mil. dol. . .	2,558	2,887	3,391	3,743	4,154	4,783	4,739
2841 Soap and other detergents	Mil. dol. . .	612	676	750	861	921	999	967
2842 Polishes/sanitation goods	Mil. dol. . .	144	170	174	205	212	216	218
2843 Surface active agents.	Mil. dol. . .	548	604	734	790	826	940	968
2844 Toilet preparations	Mil. dol. . .	1,254	1,437	1,733	1,887	2,195	2,628	2,586

NA Not available. [1] Value of all products and services sold by establishments in the soap, cleaners, and toilet goods industry. [2] Value of products classified in the soap, cleaners, and toilet goods industry produced by all industries.

Source: U.S. Department of Commerce, U.S. Census Bureau, International Trade Administration (ITA).

Industrial Outlook 865

No. 1429. Recent Trends in Petroleum Refining (SIC 2911): 1992 to 1998

Item	Unit	1992	1993	1994	1995	1996	1997	1998
INDUSTRY DATA								
Value of shipments [1]	Mil. dol. . .	136,551	129,961	128,686	136,173	158,068	157,935	(NA)
Value of shipments (1992 dollars)	Mil. dol. . .	136,551	135,376	139,120	142,441	144,751	148,157	(NA)
Total employment	1,000. . . .	74.9	73.1	72.0	70.4	67.2	64.8	(NA)
Production workers	1,000. . . .	47.9	47.3	46.6	45.6	43.4	42.2	(NA)
Average hourly earnings.	Dollar . . .	19.76	21.04	21.16	21.79	22.41	23.8	(NA)
Capital expenditures	Mil. dol. . .	6,182	5,986	5,524	5,866	5,197	4,248	(NA)
PRODUCT DATA								
Value of shipments [2]	Mil. dol. . .	131,640	125,456	123,825	131,086	151,857	(NA)	(NA)
Value of shipments (1992 dollars)	Mil. dol. . .	131,640	130,683	133,865	137,119	139,063	(NA)	(NA)
TRADE DATA								
Value of imports	Mil. dol. . .	10,110	9,640	9,118	8,409	17,674	20,434	17,060
Value of exports	Mil. dol. . .	5,826	5,798	5,171	5,675	6,839	6,882	5,187

NA Not available.   [1] Value of all products and services sold by establishments in the petroleum refining industry.   [2] Value of products classified in the petroleum refining industry produced by all industries.

Source: U.S. Department of Commerce, U.S. Census Bureau, International Trade Administration (ITA).

No. 1430. Recent Trends in Miscellaneous Plastic Products Excluding Bottles and Plumbing (SIC 3081-4, -6, -7, -9): 1992 to 1998

Item	Unit	1992	1993	1994	1995	1996	1997	1998
INDUSTRY DATA								
Value of shipments [1]	Mil. dol. . .	77,891	84,160	93,893	100,989	104,807	111,147	(NA)
Value of shipments (1992 dollars)	Mil. dol. . .	77,891	83,236	95,677	97,096	100,986	107,786	(NA)
Total employment	1,000. . . .	627.0	649.9	681.5	715.0	714.0	733.3	(NA)
Production workers	1,000. . . .	480.0	503.6	532.9	559.8	557.7	569.0	(NA)
Average hourly earnings.	Dollar . . .	9.96	10.23	10.34	10.44	10.68	11.65	(NA)
Capital expenditures	Mil. dol. . .	3,449	3,465	4,033	4,862	5,213	5,612	(NA)
PRODUCT DATA								
Value of shipments [2]	Mil. dol. . .	75,532	81,512	90,577	97,398	101,470	(NA)	(NA)
Value of shipments (1992 dollars)	Mil. dol. . .	75,532	80,622	92,240	93,548	97,645	(NA)	(NA)
TRADE DATA								
Value of imports	Mil. dol. . .	4,367	4,732	5,355	6,145	6,528	7,064	7,548
Value of exports	Mil. dol. . .	4,876	5,429	6,341	6,928	7,633	8,747	8,968

NA Not available.   [1] Value of all products and services sold by establishments in the miscellaneous plastic products excluding bottles and plumbing industry.   [2] Value of products classified in the miscellaneous plastic products excluding bottles and plumbing industry produced by all industries.

Source: U.S. Department of Commerce, U.S. Census Bureau, International Trade Administration (ITA).

No. 1431. Recent Trends in Steel Mill Products (SIC 3312, 3315, 3316, 3317): 1992 to 1998

Item	Unit	1992	1993	1994	1995	1996	1997	1998
INDUSTRY DATA								
Value of shipments [1]	Mil. dol. . .	57,187	61,301	68,753	73,716	73,238	76,078	(NA)
Value of shipments (1992 dollars)	Mil. dol. . .	57,187	60,338	64,732	65,687	67,422	69,479	(NA)
Total employment	1,000. . . .	233.8	224.7	221.6	221.1	217.1	213.4	(NA)
Production workers	1,000. . . .	179.0	173.2	171.7	173.2	171.2	167.5	(NA)
Average hourly earnings.	Dollar . . .	17.58	18.16	18.82	19.39	19.50	20.26	(NA)
Capital expenditures	Mil. dol. . .	2,568	2,166	3,130	3,283	3,402	3,328	(NA)
PRODUCT DATA								
Value of shipments [2]	Mil. dol. . .	56,132	60,199	67,681	72,347	71,293	(NA)	(NA)
Value of shipments (1992 dollars)	Mil. dol. . .	56,132	59,266	63,733	64,472	65,609	(NA)	(NA)
TRADE DATA								
Value of imports	Mil. dol. . .	8,507	9,298	13,442	12,906	13,852	14,814	17,970
Value of exports	Mil. dol. . .	3,191	2,987	3,204	4,891	4,346	5,116	4,865

NA Not available.   [1] Value of all products and services sold by establishments in the steel mill products industry.   [2] Value of products classified in the steel mill products industry produced by all industries.

Source: U.S. Department of Commerce, U.S. Census Bureau, International Trade Administration (ITA).

No. 1432. Recent Trends in Automotive Parts and Accessories (SIC 3465, 3592, 3647, 3691, 3694, 3714): 1992 to 1998

Item	Unit	1992	1993	1994	1995	1996	1997	1998
INDUSTRY DATA								
Value of shipments [1]	Mil. dol. . .	105,841	119,678	138,982	147,773	152,134	163,537	(NA)
Value of shipments (1992 dollar)	Mil. dol. . .	105,841	119,264	137,842	145,124	148,775	160,802	(NA)
Total employment	1,000. . . .	608.9	632.7	679.0	706.1	691.1	726.5	(NA)
Production workers	1,000. . . .	482.0	506.0	547.6	566.0	558.0	585.9	(NA)
Average hourly earnings	Dollar . . .	15.84	16.22	16.57	17.05	17.05	17.75	(NA)
Capital expenditures	Mil. dol. . .	4,585	5,308	6,010	7,824	7,572	8,946	(NA)
PRODUCT DATA								
Value of shipments [2]	Mil. dol. . .	104,109	118,293	134,462	143,859	148,201	(NA)	(NA)
Value of shipments (1992 dollar)	Mil. dol. . .	104,109	117,882	133,371	141,294	144,954	(NA)	(NA)
TRADE DATA								
Value of imports	Mil. dol. . .	20,408	22,657	26,465	27,948	29,893	32,042	34,487
Value of exports	Mil. dol. . .	22,262	25,890	27,724	29,471	30,410	35,214	35,362

NA Not available. [1] Value of all products and services sold by establishments in the automotive parts and accessories industry. [2] Value of products classified in the automotive parts and accessories industry produced by all industries.

Source: U.S. Department of Commerce, U.S. Census Bureau, International Trade Administration (ITA).

No. 1433. Recent Trends in Computers and Peripherals (SIC 3571, 2, 5, 7): 1992 to 1998

[Census reclassified some parts for electronic computers (3571) to component industries (367) for 1989-90]

Item	Unit	1992	1993	1994	1995	1996	1997	1998
INDUSTRY DATA								
Value of shipments [1]	Mil. dol. . .	61,969	64,374	73,345	86,078	97,592	105,726	(NA)
Value of shipments (1992 dollars)	Mil. dol. . .	61,969	75,838	98,708	145,239	220,172	324,261	(NA)
Total employment	1,000. . . .	220.5	210.5	200.5	209.9	221.2	239.4	(NA)
Production workers	1,000. . . .	74.2	73.9	75.8	78.9	83.4	98.1	(NA)
Average hourly earnings	Dollar . . .	12.26	12.77	13.67	13.49	14.84	16.13	(NA)
Capital expenditures	Mil. dol. . .	2,137	2,045	1,907	1,902	2,684	3,233	(NA)
PRODUCT DATA								
Value of shipments [2]	Mil. dol. . .	54,722	57,928	65,635	81,356	85,441	(NA)	(NA)
Value of shipments (1992 dollars)	Mil. dol. . .	54,722	67,676	87,691	136,121	192,465	(NA)	(NA)
TRADE DATA								
Value of imports	Mil. dol. . .	21,782	25,593	29,027	33,618	39,306	44,975	44,015
Value of exports	Mil. dol. . .	14,942	15,367	17,579	19,647	21,439	23,176	21,202

NA Not available. [1] Value of all products and services sold by establishments in the computers and peripherals industry. [2] Value of products classified in the computers and peripherals industry produced by all industries.

Source: U.S. Department of Commerce, U.S. Census Bureau, International Trade Administration (ITA).

No. 1434. Recent Trends in Telecommunications Equipment (SIC 3661, 3663): 1992 to 1998

Item	Unit	1992	1993	1994	1995	1996	1997	1998
INDUSTRY DATA								
Value of shipments [1]	Mil. dol. . .	40,031	42,190	49,371	54,915	63,807	(NA)	(NA)
Value of shipments (1992 dollars)	Mil. dol. . .	40,031	41,736	48,498	54,166	62,619	(NA)	(NA)
Total employment	1,000. . . .	216.0	207.5	219.7	216.4	233.6	(NA)	(NA)
Production workers	1,000. . . .	103.4	94.5	100.3	102.5	107.0	(NA)	(NA)
Average hourly earnings	Dollar . . .	14.28	14.35	14.25	15.69	16.33	(NA)	(NA)
Capital expenditures	Mil. dol. . .	1,317	1,445	1,518	1,899	2,088	(NA)	(NA)
PRODUCT DATA								
Value of shipments [2]	Mil. dol. . .	36,106	38,151	45,495	52,481	60,706	(NA)	(NA)
Value of shipments (1992 dollars)	Mil. dol. . .	36,106	37,742	44,695	51,762	59,582	(NA)	(NA)
TRADE DATA								
Value of imports	Mil. dol. . .	7,924	8,802	10,048	10,537	11,283	12,730	15,118
Value of exports	Mil. dol. . .	7,364	9,184	11,559	14,681	14,971	18,562	17,976

NA Not available. [1] Value of all products and services sold by establishments in the telecommunications equipment industry. [2] Value of products classified in the telecommunications equipment industry produced by all industries.

Source: U.S. Department of Commerce, U.S. Census Bureau, International Trade Administration (ITA).

No. 1435. Recent Trends in Electronic Components and Accessories (SIC 367): 1992 to 1998

Item	Unit	1992	1993	1994	1995	1996	1997	1998
INDUSTRY DATA								
Value of shipments [1]	Mil. dol.	73,642	81,236	97,131	120,129	127,996	140,494	(NA)
Value of shipments (1992 dollars)	Mil. dol.	73,642	81,129	97,838	126,734	144,213	172,438	(NA)
Total employment	1,000.	529.9	531.4	551.3	584.3	588.0	604.9	(NA)
Production workers	1,000.	317.3	321.2	339.6	364.0	368.1	386.3	(NA)
Average hourly earnings	Dollar	10.83	10.98	11.14	11.41	11.70	13.01	(NA)
Capital expenditures	Mil. dol.	4,483	5,521	7,743	11,213	14,345	13,182	(NA)
PRODUCT DATA								
Value of shipments [2]	Mil. dol.	71,372	77,840	92,719	115,202	126,997	(NA)	(NA)
Value of shipments (1992 dollars)	Mil. dol.	71,372	77,739	93,343	121,272	142,543	(NA)	(NA)
TRADE DATA								
Value of imports	Mil. dol.	31,567	38,767	47,066	66,825	63,032	65,145	65,309
Value of exports	Mil. dol.	16,216	18,844	24,524	31,095	32,826	39,767	39,870

NA Not available.   [1] Value of all products and services sold by establishments in the electronic components and accessories industry.   [2] Value of products classified in the electronic components and accessories industry produced by all industries.
Source: U.S. Department of Commerce, U.S. Census Bureau, International Trade Administration (ITA).

No. 1436. Recent Trends in Printed Circuit Boards and Semiconductors and Related Devices: 1992 to 1998

Item	Unit	1992	1993	1994	1995	1996	1997	1998
PRINTED CIRCUIT BOARDS (SIC 3672)								
Industry data:								
Value of shipments [1]	Mil. dol.	7,320	7,378	8,416	9,498	10,702	9,596	(NA)
Value of shipments (1992 dollars)	Mil. dol.	7,320	7,551	8,803	9,924	11,067	10,037	(NA)
Total employment	1,000.	76.0	73.6	76.9	81.6	88.3	75.1	(NA)
Production workers	1,000.	51.0	50.5	54.0	59.6	63.9	56.8	(NA)
Average hourly earnings	Dollar	10.16	10.58	10.49	10.36	10.75	11.92	(NA)
Capital expenditures	Mil. dol.	318	283	381	453	585	691	(NA)
Product data:								
Value of shipments [2]	Mil. dol.	6,293	6,930	7,555	8,543	8,949	(NA)	(NA)
Value of shipments (1992 dollars)	Mil. dol.	6,293	7,093	7,902	8,926	9,254	(NA)	(NA)
Trade data:								
Value of imports	Mil. dol.	1,243	1,289	1,468	1,840	1,849	2,071	2,045
Value of exports	Mil. dol.	1,092	973	1,377	1,651	1,694	2,007	2,178
SEMICONDUCTORS AND RELATED DEVICES (SIC 3674)								
Industry data:								
Value of shipments [1]	Mil. dol.	32,191	35,152	47,265	65,922	71,413	78,009	(NA)
Value of shipments (1992 dollars)	Mil. dol.	32,191	35,222	47,790	71,810	85,833	107,599	(NA)
Total employment	1,000.	172.0	162.5	183.3	191.6	189.6	198.1	(NA)
Production workers	1,000.	84.8	82.2	92.9	98.1	96.2	105.8	(NA)
Average hourly earnings	Dollar	13.55	14.08	14.46	14.89	15.29	16.36	(NA)
Product data:								
Value of shipments [2]	Mil. dol.	29,391	33,689	44,064	60,330	67,070	(NA)	(NA)
Value of shipments (1992 dollars)	Mil. dol.	29,391	33,757	44,555	65,719	80,613	(NA)	(NA)
Trade data:								
Value of imports	Mil. dol.	15,275	19,244	25,670	38,618	36,256	36,266	33,157
Value of exports	Mil. dol.	11,465	13,744	17,991	23,189	24,001	28,861	29,055

NA Not available.   [1] Value of all products and services sold by establishments in this industry.   [2] Value of products classified in this industry produced by all industries.
Source: U.S. Department of Commerce, U.S. Census Bureau, International Trade Administration (ITA).

No. 1437. Recent Trends in Motor Vehicles and Car Bodies (SIC 3711): 1992 to 1998

Item	Unit	1992	1993	1994	1995	1996	1997	1998
INDUSTRY DATA								
Value of shipments [1]	Mil. dol.	151,682	167,826	197,514	201,171	200,704	(NA)	(NA)
Value of shipments (1992 dollars)	Mil. dol.	151,682	162,151	184,076	185,753	183,292	(NA)	(NA)
Total employment	1,000.	227.8	224.2	234.0	237.9	225.2	(NA)	(NA)
Production workers	1,000.	192.8	191.0	202.5	208.3	196.3	(NA)	(NA)
Average hourly earnings	Dollar	21.96	22.61	23.39	24.48	24.60	(NA)	(NA)
Capital expenditures	Mil. dol.	2,988	4,034	4,247	4,521	4,382	(NA)	(NA)
PRODUCT DATA								
Value of shipments [2]	Mil. dol.	147,447	163,324	194,977	198,252	198,112	(NA)	(NA)
Value of shipments (1992 dollars)	Mil. dol.	147,447	157,801	181,712	183,058	180,924	(NA)	(NA)
TRADE DATA								
Value of imports	Mil. dol.	59,616	67,567	78,557	83,765	86,686	92,437	99,080
Value of exports	Mil. dol.	17,040	18,054	20,769	21,151	22,554	24,088	22,392

NA Not available.   [1] Value of all products and services sold by establishments in the motor vehicles and car bodies industry.   [2] Value of products classified in the motor vehicles and car bodies industry produced by all industries.
Source: U.S. Department of Commerce, U.S. Census Bureau, International Trade Administration (ITA).

Section 32
1997 Economic Census

This new section presents a variety of industry based information from the 1997 Economic Census. These statistics utilize the North American Industry Classification System (NAICS pronounced "Nakes").

On April 9, 1997, the Office of Management and Budget (OMB) announced its decision to adopt the North American Industry Classification System as the industry classification system used by the statistical agencies of the United States. NAICS replaced the 1987 Standard Industrial Classification (SIC). NAICS is based on a consistent, economic concept. Establishments that use the same or similar processes to produce goods or services are grouped together. The SIC, developed in the 1930s and revised periodically over the past 50 years, was not based on a consistent economic concept. Some industries are demand based while others are production based.

NAICS recognizes the changing and growing services-based economy of the United States and its North American neighbors. NAICS includes 1,170 industries of which 565 are service-based industries. The SIC had 1,004 industries of which 416 were service-related industries. NAICS recognizes 358 new industries, 250 of which are services producing industries. There are 20 sectors in NAICS of which 16 are services related. The SIC had 10 divisions of which 5 were service related.

NAICS provides for comparable statistics among the North American countries. In addition, it provides for more comparable information with the Internal Standard Industrial Classification of all economic activities (ISIC). The SIC did not. NAICS is a six-digit system that provides for comparability among the three countries at the five-digit level, albeit with a few exceptions. The SIC was a four-digit system that was not linked in any way to the systems of Canada and Mexico. A six-digit system was adopted for NAICS to provide for increased flexibility in the system. NAICS allows each country to recognize activities that are important in the respective countries but may not be large enough or important enough to recognize in all three countries. The sixth digit is reserved for this purpose. The nomenclature of the groupings within the system is different in NAICS. NAICS calls the highest level of aggregation in the system a sector; the SIC referred to this grouping as a division.

For more information on NAICS, users should consult the official 1997 U.S. NAICS Manual, *North American Industry Classification System—United States, 1997,* which includes definitions for each industry, tables showing correspondence between 1997 NAICS and 1987 SICs, and a comprehensive index. Also, the Census Bureau maintains a series of Web pages devoted to NAICS at <http://www.census.gov/epcd/www/naics.html>.

U.S. Census Bureau, Statistical Abstract of the United States: 2000

Description	NAICS code [1]	Estab- lish- ments (number)	Sales, receipts or shipments (mil. dol.)		Annual payroll		Paid employees for pay period including March 12 (1,000)
			Total (mil. dol.)	Per paid employee (dol.)	Total (mil. dol.)	Per paid employee (dol.)	
Mining	21	25,000	173,989	341,821	20,798	40,861	509.0
Oil & gas extraction	211	8,312	102,837	927,458	5,511	49,698	110.9
Mining (except oil & gas)	212	7,348	51,253	223,499	9,422	41,085	229.3
Support activities for mining	213	9,340	19,899	117,879	5,866	34,751	168.8
Utilities	22	15,513	411,713	585,899	36,595	52,077	702.7
Utilities	221	15,513	411,713	585,899	36,595	52,077	702.7
Electric power generation, trans. & distr.	2211	7,935	269,095	476,676	30,440	53,921	564.5
Natural gas distribution	2212	2,747	136,995	1,331,629	5,110	49,666	102.9
Water, sewage, & other systems	2213	4,831	5,623	159,284	1,045	29,614	35.3
Construction	23	656,448	858,581	151,563	174,185	30,748	5,664.8
Building, developing, & general contracting	233	199,289	386,926	288,116	42,546	31,681	1,343.0
Heavy construction	234	42,557	130,795	148,563	30,292	34,407	880.4
Special trade contractors	235	414,602	340,861	99,044	101,347	29,448	3,441.5
Manufacturing	31-33	363,753	3,842,061	227,502	572,101	33,876	16,888.0
Wholesale trade	42	453,470	4,059,658	700,357	214,915	37,076	5,796.6
Wholesale trade, durable goods	421	290,629	2,179,717	641,421	133,237	39,207	3,398.3
Wholesale trade, nondurable goods	422	162,841	1,879,940	783,865	81,678	34,057	2,398.3
Retail trade	44-45	1,118,447	2,460,886	175,889	237,196	16,953	13,991.1
Motor vehicle & parts dealers	441	122,633	645,368	375,440	50,239	29,226	1,719.0
Furniture & home furnishings stores	442	64,725	71,691	148,476	9,959	20,627	482.8
Electronics & appliance stores	443	43,373	68,561	198,704	7,064	20,473	345.0
Building material & garden equipment & supplies dealers	444	93,117	227,566	203,564	25,609	22,908	1,117.9
Food & beverage stores	445	148,528	401,764	138,871	40,581	14,027	2,893.1
Health & personal care stores	446	82,941	117,701	130,244	15,191	16,809	903.7
Gasoline stations	447	126,889	198,166	214,916	11,482	12,453	922.1
Clothing & clothing accessories stores	448	156,601	136,398	106,548	16,597	12,965	1,280.2
Sporting goods, hobby, book, & music stores	451	69,149	62,011	110,568	7,113	12,683	560.8
General merchandise stores	452	36,171	330,444	131,780	30,871	12,311	2,507.5
Miscellaneous store retailers	453	129,838	78,109	103,733	10,165	13,500	753.0
Nonstore retailers	454	44,482	123,107	243,297	12,323	24,355	506.0
Transportation & warehousing [2][3]	48-49	178,025	318,245	108,959	82,346	28,193	2,920.8
Air transportation [2]	481	3,598	20,249	227,198	2,748	30,834	89.1
Rail transportation (not covered in the economic census)	482	(NA)	(NA)	(NA)	(NA)	(NA)	(NA)
Water transportation	483	1,921	24,019	329,676	2,834	38,900	72.9
Truck transportation	484	103,798	141,225	109,156	38,471	29,735	1,293.8
Transit & ground passenger transportation	485	16,013	13,792	40,616	5,549	16,342	339.6
Pipeline transportation	486	2,311	26,837	544,582	2,661	53,989	49.3
Scenic & sightseeing transportation	487	2,325	1,893	79,200	492	20,600	23.9
Support activities for transportation	488	30,675	39,758	96,585	12,592	30,591	411.6
Postal Service (not covered in the economic census)	491	(NA)	(NA)	(NA)	(NA)	(NA)	(NA)
Couriers & messengers	492	10,887	39,812	74,999	14,072	26,508	530.8
Warehousing & storage	493	6,497	10,658	97,102	2,926	26,659	109.8
Information	51	114,475	623,214	203,255	129,482	42,229	3,066.2
Publishing industries	511	33,896	179,035	177,930	43,358	43,090	1,006.2
Motion picture & sound recording industries	512	22,204	55,926	202,643	9,392	34,032	276.0
Broadcasting & telecommunications	513	43,480	346,316	241,427	63,480	44,253	1,434.5
Information services & data processing services	514	14,895	41,937	119,986	13,252	37,915	349.5
Finance & insurance	52	395,203	2,197,771	376,639	264,551	45,337	5,835.2
Monetary authorities - central bank	521	42	24,582	1,134,150	903	41,680	21.7
Credit intermediation & related activities	522	166,882	808,811	294,658	98,723	35,966	2,744.9
Securities intermediation & related activities	523	54,491	274,987	389,470	71,281	100,957	706.1
Insurance carriers & related activities	524	172,299	1,072,784	460,955	92,230	39,630	2,327.3
Funds, trusts, & other financial vehicles (part)	525	1,489	16,608	470,868	1,413	40,075	35.3
Real estate & rental & leasing	53	288,273	240,918	141,515	41,591	24,430	1,702.4
Real estate	531	221,650	153,275	137,190	27,947	25,014	1,117.2
Rental & leasing services	532	64,472	76,379	136,542	12,569	22,470	559.4
Lessors of intangible assets, except copyrighted works	533	2,151	11,264	436,719	1,074	41,659	25.8
Professional, scientific, & technical svcs.	54	615,305	579,542	111,178	225,376	43,236	5,212.7
Professional, scientific, & technical svcs.	541	615,305	579,542	111,178	225,376	43,236	5,212.7
Legal services	5411	173,716	127,052	125,534	49,060	48,474	1,012.1
Accounting, tax return prep, bookkeeping & payroll services	5412	97,512	61,117	63,234	26,104	27,008	966.5
Architectural, engineering & related services	5413	92,710	116,986	112,669	46,943	45,210	1,038.3
Specialized design services	5414	26,436	14,254	126,103	4,088	36,166	113.0
Computer systems design & related services	5415	72,278	108,968	142,505	42,151	55,123	764.7

See footnotes at end of table.

U.S. Census Bureau, Statistical Abstract of the United States: 2000

No. 1438. Economic Census Summary (NAICS Basis): 1997—Continued

Description	NAICS code [1]	Sales, receipts or shipments (mil. dol.)			Annual payroll		Paid employees for pay period including March 12 (1,000)
		Establishments (number)	Total (mil. dol.)	Per paid employee (dol.)	Total (mil. dol.)	Per paid employee (dol.)	
Management, scientific, & technical consulting services	5416	80,426	63,429	124,066	26,582	51,993	511.3
Scientific research & development services	5417	7,830	23,078	130,405	9,322	52,675	177.0
Advertising & related services	5418	38,832	49,290	118,141	16,012	38,379	417.2
Other professional, scientific & technical services	5419	25,565	15,368	72,261	5,115	24,049	212.7
Administrative & support & waste mgmt. & remediation services	56	276,393	295,936	40,278	137,337	18,692	7,347.4
Administrative & support services	561	260,025	256,591	36,310	128,438	18,175	7,066.7
Waste management & remediation services	562	16,368	39,346	140,166	8,899	31,702	280.7
Educational services	61	33,783	14,933	60,049	4,903	19,716	248.7
Educational services	611	33,783	14,933	60,049	4,903	19,716	248.7
Health care & social assistance	62	531,069	418,602	67,172	182,256	29,246	6,231.8
Ambulatory health care services	621	440,200	310,012	82,796	137,979	36,851	3,744.3
Hospitals	622	1,345	40,146	78,475	13,886	27,143	511.6
Nursing & residential care facilities	623	32,833	55,844	37,610	24,626	16,585	1,484.8
Social assistance	624	56,691	12,599	25,657	5,766	11,741	491.1
Arts, entertainment, & recreation	71	79,636	85,088	70,474	26,104	21,620	1,207.4
Performing arts, spectator sports, & related industries	711	25,942	32,744	138,788	12,834	54,400	235.9
Museums, historical sites, & similar institutions	712	787	484	66,431	122	16,811	7.3
Amusement, gambling, & recreation industries	713	52,907	51,861	53,789	13,147	13,636	964.2
Accommodation & food services	72	545,060	350,389	37,074	97,004	10,264	9,451.1
Accommodation	721	58,161	98,455	58,031	26,672	15,721	1,696.6
Traveler accommodation	7211	47,079	94,966	57,707	25,851	15,709	1,645.7
RV (recreational vehicle) parks & recreational camps	7212	7,598	2,735	77,408	665	18,830	35.3
Rooming & boarding houses	7213	3,484	754	48,349	156	9,984	15.6
Food services & drinking places	722	486,899	251,934	32,489	70,331	9,070	7,754.5
Full-service restaurants	7221	191,245	112,450	30,881	34,435	9,457	3,641.4
Limited-service eating places	7222	214,767	107,781	32,397	27,481	8,260	3,326.9
Special food services	7223	28,062	19,408	41,749	5,766	12,403	464.9
Drinking places (alcoholic beverages)	7224	52,825	12,296	38,269	2,649	8,246	321.3
Other services (except public administration)	81	420,950	163,033	65,381	48,453	19,431	2,493.6
Repair & maintenance	811	235,466	105,154	82,384	29,875	23,406	1,276.4
TAX-EXEMPT							
Professional, scientific, & technical svcs.	54	5,824	15,709	105,806	6,023	40,567	148.5
Professional, scientific, & technical svcs.	541	5,824	15,709	105,806	6,023	40,567	148.5
Legal services	5411	2,532	1,497	64,197	797	34,168	23.3
Scientific research & development services	5417	3,292	14,212	113,558	5,226	41,759	125.1
Educational services	61	7,153	5,506	76,058	1,461	20,190	72.4
Educational services	611	7,153	5,506	76,058	1,461	20,190	72.4
Health care & social assistance	62	114,784	466,452	63,638	195,949	26,733	7,329.8
Ambulatory health care services	621	15,181	45,428	67,871	17,884	26,719	669.3
Hospitals	622	5,340	339,032	76,679	141,910	32,096	4,421.5
Nursing & residential care facilities	623	24,526	37,235	37,768	17,527	17,778	985.9
Social assistance	624	69,737	44,756	35,715	18,628	14,865	1,253.1
Arts, entertainment, & recreation	71	19,463	19,627	51,610	6,683	17,575	380.3
Performing arts, spectator sports, & related industries	711	4,624	4,876	53,681	1,622	17,852	90.8
Museums, historical sites, & similar institutions	712	4,793	6,280	74,328	1,715	20,294	84.5
Amusement, gambling, & recreation industries	713	10,046	8,470	41,327	3,347	16,331	205.0
Other services (except public administration)	81	98,765	102,864	134,886	17,068	22,381	762.6

NA Not available.   [1] North American Industry Classification System, 1997; see text, Section 32, Economic Census 1997.   [2] Data do not include large certificated passenger carriers that report to the Office of Airline Statistics, U.S. Department of Transportation.   [3] Railroad transportation and U.S. Postal Service are out of scope for the 1997 Economic Census.

Source: U.S. Census Bureau, accessed on 08 August 2000 <http://www.census.gov/epcd/www/econ97.html>.

1997 Economic Census   871

No. 1439. Utilities—Establishments, Revenue, Payroll, and Employees by Kind of Business (NAICS Basis): 1997

Kind of business	NAICS code [1]	Estab-lish-ments (number)	Revenue		Annual payroll		Paid employee for pay period including March 12 (number)
			Total (mil. dol.)	Per paid employee (dol.)	Total (mil. dol.)	Per paid employee (dol.)	
Utilities	22	15,513	411,713	585,899	36,595	52,077	702,703
Electric power generation, transmission, & distribution	2211	7,935	269,095	476,676	30,440	53,921	564,525
Electric power generation	22111	1,745	73,375	493,492	8,369	56,289	148,686
Fossil fuel electric power generation . . .	221112	1,009	48,324	515,374	5,049	53,843	93,765
Nuclear electric power generation	221113	67	13,967	406,231	2,202	64,045	34,381
Other electric power generation	221119	316	8,011	608,723	725	55,069	13,160
Electric power transmission, control & distribution	22112	6,190	195,720	470,663	22,070	53,074	415,839
Electric bulk power transmission & control	221121	120	956	395,361	116	47,852	2,418
Electric power distribution	221122	6,070	194,764	471,103	21,955	53,105	413,421
Natural gas distribution	2212	2,747	136,995	1,331,629	5,110	49,666	102,878
Natural gas transmission & distribution. .	2212101	713	18,267	629,034	1,534	52,838	29,039
Natural gas distribution	2212102	1,682	87,105	1,387,135	2,955	47,059	62,795
Mixed, manu., or LP gas pro &/or dist. . .	2212103	86	(D)	(NA)	(D)	(NA)	([2])
Electric & other serv. combined (natural gas distribution)	2212104	145	28,110	4,193,063	413	61,565	6,704
Gas & other serv. combined (natural gas distribution)	2212105	119	2,853	915,151	149	47,705	3,117
Water, sewage, & other systems	2213	4,831	5,623	159,284	1,045	29,614	35,300
Water supply & irrigation systems.	22131	4,052	4,454	159,447	825	29,550	27,933
Sewage treatment facilities	22132	696	596	106,399	139	24,816	5,600
Steam & air-conditioning supply	22133	83	573	324,314	81	45,838	1,767

D Withheld to avoid disclosing data of individual companies; data are included in higher level totals. NA Not available. [1] North American Industry Classification System, 1997; see text, Section 32, Economic Census 1997. [2] 1,000 to 2,499 employees.
Source: U.S. Census Bureau, *1997 Economic Census, Utilities,* Series EC97T22A-US, issued December 1999.

No. 1440. Construction—Establishments, Employees, and Payroll by Kind of Business (NAICS Basis): 1997

Kind of business	NAICS code [1]	Number of estab-lishments	Number of employees		Payroll (mil. dol.)		Net value of con-struction work (mil. dol.)
			All	Con-struction workers	All employ-ees	Con-struction workers	
Construction.	23	656,448	5,664,853	4,332,737	174,185	119,677	612,209
Building, developing, & general contracting . .	233	199,289	1,342,953	885,939	42,546	23,136	198,827
Land subdivision & land development	2331	8,186	41,827	10,977	1,510	254	10,248
Land subdivision & land development . . .	23311	8,186	41,827	10,977	1,510	254	10,248
Residential building construction.	2332	146,394	629,887	407,801	16,731	8,762	100,124
Single-family housing construction.	23321	138,850	570,990	367,719	14,965	7,740	92,802
Multifamily housing construction	23322	7,544	58,896	40,082	1,767	1,022	7,322
Nonresidential building construction	2333	44,710	671,239	467,161	24,305	14,119	88,455
Mfg. & industrial building construction . .	23331	7,280	143,066	107,180	5,129	3,322	17,202
Commercial & institutional building construction.	23332	37,430	528,173	359,981	19,176	10,797	71,253
Heavy construction	234	42,557	880,400	710,898	30,292	22,219	105,639
Highway, street, bridge, & tunnel construction	2341	12,448	325,743	265,267	11,375	8,474	46,274
Highway & street construction	23411	11,270	277,979	227,066	9,528	7,095	39,102
Bridge & tunnel construction.	23412	1,177	47,764	38,201	1,847	1,379	7,172
Other heavy construction	2349	30,109	554,657	445,630	18,917	13,745	59,365
Water, sewer, & pipeline construction. . .	23491	8,042	162,566	134,023	5,522	4,087	19,127
Power & communication transmission line construction.	23492	3,300	74,050	60,880	2,387	1,749	6,742
Industrial nonbuilding structure construction.	23493	531	98,555	79,473	3,722	2,734	8,130
All other heavy construction	23499	18,236	219,486	171,254	7,285	5,175	25,367
Special trade contractors	235	414,602	3,441,500	2,735,901	101,347	74,322	307,743
Plumbing, heating, & air-conditioning contractors	2351	84,876	788,930	599,940	25,720	18,280	78,496
Plumbing, heating, & air-conditioning contractors	23511	84,876	788,930	599,940	25,720	18,280	78,496
Painting & wall covering contractors	2352	37,480	195,331	160,740	4,543	3,431	12,050
Painting & wall covering contractors . . .	23521	37,480	195,331	160,740	4,543	3,431	12,050
Electrical contractors	2353	61,414	641,985	510,921	21,680	16,261	61,121
Electrical contractors.	23531	61,414	641,985	510,921	21,680	16,261	61,121
Masonry, drywall, insulation, & tile contractors	2354	49,917	470,701	407,700	12,612	10,073	34,843
Masonry & stone contractors	23541	22,614	164,236	145,919	4,068	3,349	11,438
Drywall, plastering, acoustical, & insulation contractors	23542	20,457	266,710	229,934	7,479	5,940	20,114
Tile, marble, terrazzo, & mosaic contractors	23543	6,847	39,755	31,847	1,064	784	3,291

See footnote at end of table.

No. 1440. Construction—Establishments, Employees, and Payroll by Kind of Business (NAICS Basis): 1997—Continued

Kind of business	NAICS code [1]	Number of establishments	Number of employees		Payroll (mil. dol.)		Net value of construction work (mil. dol.)
			All	Construction workers	All employees	Construction workers	
Carpentry & floor contractors	2355	56,936	290,942	228,273	7,163	5,116	24,049
Carpentry contractors	23551	44,858	230,409	185,610	5,490	4,086	18,006
Floor laying & other floor contractors	23552	12,078	60,533	42,663	1,672	1,030	6,043
Roofing, siding, & sheet metal contractors	2356	30,557	253,315	197,294	6,495	4,370	21,976
Roofing, siding, & sheet metal contractors	23561	30,557	253,315	197,294	6,495	4,370	21,976
Concrete contractors	2357	30,417	262,256	222,121	6,858	5,298	23,604
Concrete contractors	23571	30,417	262,256	222,121	6,858	5,298	23,604
Water well drilling contractors	2358	3,862	21,214	15,360	576	399	2,132
Water well drilling contractors	23581	3,862	21,214	15,360	576	399	2,132
Other special trade contractors	2359	59,143	516,824	393,552	15,699	11,095	49,472
Structural steel erection contractors	23591	4,238	72,301	59,923	2,387	1,823	7,217
Glass & glazing contractors	23592	4,714	35,823	23,207	1,052	624	3,735
Excavation contractors	23593	18,229	116,237	92,830	3,354	2,526	12,216
Wrecking & demolition contractors	23594	1,542	18,820	14,486	592	415	1,914
Building equip & other machinery installation contractors	23595	4,489	75,501	56,211	3,148	2,260	8,606
All other special trade contractors	23599	25,932	198,141	146,894	5,166	3,448	15,784

[1] North American Industry Classification System, 1997; see text, Section 32, Economic Census 1997.
Source: U.S. Census Bureau, *1997 Economic Census, Construction,* Series EC97C23S-IS, issued January 2000.

No. 1441. Wholesale Trade—Establishments, Sales, Payroll, and Employees by Kind of Business (NAICS Basis): 1997

Kind of business	NAICS code [1]	Establishments (number)	Sales		Annual payroll		Paid employee for pay period including March 12 (1,000)
			Total (mil. dol.)	Per paid employee (dol.)	Total (mil. dol.)	Per paid employee (dol.)	
Wholesale trade	**42**	**453,470**	**4,059,658**	**700,357**	**214,915**	**37,076**	**5,796.6**
Wholesaler distributors and jobbers	(X)	338,872	1,810,730	441,715	139,227	33,963	4,099.3
Importers	(X)	14,417	167,711	849,339	7,825	39,628	197.5
Exporters	(X)	12,236	142,473	1,466,219	3,813	39,243	97.2
Own brand importer-marketers	(X)	3,609	136,820	1,297,697	5,042	47,823	105.4
Terminal grain elevators	(X)	237	8,470	2,833,588	88	29,387	3.0
Country grain elevators	(X)	4,387	39,131	1,078,686	971	26,760	36.3
Assemblers of farm products, except country grain elevators	(X)	2,572	27,797	530,005	1,408	26,839	52.4
Sales branches (with stock)	(X)	16,847	493,597	888,953	25,273	45,516	555.3
Sales offices (without stock)	(X)	12,458	765,278	2,085,499	20,639	56,243	367.0
Auction companies	(X)	1,304	70,174	1,180,068	713	11,997	59.5
Brokers	(X)	8,607	115,265	1,978,349	2,153	36,948	58.3
Commission merchants	(X)	6,784	57,742	1,454,133	1,477	37,199	39.7
Import agents	(X)	609	8,958	2,798,648	189	59,153	3.2
Export agents	(X)	1,282	18,818	3,888,815	171	35,420	4.8
Manufacturers agents	(X)	29,249	196,695	1,670,033	5,926	50,318	117.8
Wholesale trade, durable goods	421	290,629	2,179,717	641,421	133,237	39,207	3,398.3
Motor vehicle & motor vehicle parts & supplies wholesale	4211	29,328	533,352	1,419,505	11,459	30,497	375.7
Furniture & home furnishings wholesale	4212	15,246	75,006	476,337	5,317	33,766	157.5
Lumber & other construction materials wholesale	4213	14,267	89,176	573,349	5,296	34,051	155.5
Professional & commercial equipment & supplies wholesale	4214	45,351	367,384	513,025	33,292	46,490	716.1
Metal & mineral (except petroleum) wholesale	4215	12,583	150,494	864,762	6,898	39,637	174.0
Electrical goods wholesale	4216	38,234	357,692	751,823	22,525	47,344	475.8
Hardware, & plumbing & heating equip. & supplies wholesale	4217	21,194	92,190	420,510	7,978	36,390	219.2
Machinery, equipment, & supplies, whsle.	4218	76,643	328,968	425,821	29,402	38,058	772.6
Misc. durable goods wholesale	4219	37,783	185,456	527,104	11,070	31,464	351.8
Wholesale trade, nondurable goods	422	162,841	1,879,940	783,865	81,678	34,057	2,398.3
Paper & paper product wholesale	4221	15,848	117,062	546,128	7,730	36,064	214.4
Drugs & druggists' sundries wholesale	4222	8,053	203,148	1,068,485	8,395	44,154	190.1
Apparel, piece goods & notions wholesale.	4223	20,707	124,104	597,880	7,760	37,382	207.6
Grocery & related products wholesale	4224	41,760	588,970	688,919	26,778	31,322	854.9
Farm-product raw material wholesale	4225	10,343	166,786	1,710,260	2,306	23,646	97.5
Chemical & allied products wholesale	4226	15,920	128,923	777,735	7,241	43,683	165.8
Petroleum & petroleum products wholesale	4227	11,297	267,624	1,941,710	4,480	32,503	137.8
Beer, wine & distilled alcoholic bev., whsle.	4228	4,850	69,703	459,550	5,667	37,363	151.7
Misc. nondurable goods wholesale.	4229	34,063	213,619	564,336	11,321	29,909	378.5
Merchant wholesalers	(X)	376,330	2,333,131	508,187	158,373	34,496	4,591.1
Manufacturers' sales branches & sales offices.	(X)	29,305	1,258,875	1,365,066	45,912	49,785	922.2
Agents, brokers and commission merchants	(X)	47,835	467,652	1,650,981	10,630	37,529	283.3

X Not applicable. [1] North American Industry Classification System, 1997; see text, Section 32, Economic Census 1997.
Source: U.S. Census Bureau, *1997 Economic Census, Wholesale Trade,* Series EC97W42A-US(RV), issued March 2000.

1997 Economic Census 873

No. 1442. Retail Trade—Establishments, Sales, Payroll, and Employees by Kind of Business (NAICS Basis): 1997

Kind of business	NAICS code [1]	Estab- lish- ments (number)	Sales		Annual payroll		Paid employee for pay period including March 12 (1,000)
			Total (mil. dol.)	Per paid employee (dol.)	Total (mil. dol.)	Per paid employee (dol.)	
Retail trade	44-45	1,118,447	2,460,886	175,889	237,196	16,953	13,991.1
Motor vehicle & parts dealers	441	122,633	645,368	375,440	50,239	29,226	1,719.0
Automobile dealers	4411	49,237	553,652	486,088	37,400	32,836	1,139.0
New car dealers	44111	25,897	518,972	496,034	35,203	33,647	1,046.2
Used car dealers	44112	23,340	34,680	373,905	2,197	23,691	92.8
Other motor vehicle dealers	4412	13,589	28,891	281,124	2,570	25,007	102.8
Recreational vehicle dealers	44121	3,014	10,070	341,776	814	27,627	29.5
Motorcycle, boat, & other motor vehicle dealers	44122	10,575	18,821	256,746	1,756	23,954	73.3
Automotive parts, accessories, & tire stores	4413	59,807	62,825	131,653	10,269	21,519	477.2
Automotive parts & accessories stores	44131	42,519	43,166	129,024	6,718	20,081	334.6
Tire dealers	44132	17,288	19,659	137,821	3,551	24,892	142.6
Furniture & home furnishings stores	442	64,725	71,691	148,476	9,959	20,627	482.8
Furniture stores	4421	29,461	40,968	163,026	5,620	22,362	251.3
Home furnishings stores	4422	35,264	30,722	132,685	4,340	18,743	231.5
Floor covering stores	44221	16,603	16,472	171,250	2,458	25,557	96.2
Other home furnishings stores	44229	18,661	14,251	105,281	1,882	13,901	135.4
Electronics & appliance stores	443	43,373	68,561	198,704	7,064	20,473	345.0
Appliance, television, & other electronics stores	44311	28,789	42,251	178,249	4,462	18,826	237.0
Computer & software stores	44312	11,741	24,059	265,839	2,278	25,168	90.5
Camera & photographic supplies stores	44313	2,843	2,252	128,609	324	18,504	17.5
Building material & garden equipment & supplies dealers	444	93,117	227,566	203,564	25,609	22,908	1,117.9
Building material & supplies dealers	4441	71,916	195,888	205,701	22,313	23,431	952.3
Home centers	44411	3,997	51,628	181,883	4,996	17,602	283.9
Paint & wallpaper stores	44412	8,429	7,943	182,536	1,011	23,235	43.5
Hardware stores	44413	15,748	13,605	98,710	2,095	15,202	137.8
Other building material dealers	44419	43,742	122,712	251,925	14,210	29,173	487.1
Lawn & garden equipment & supplies stores	4442	21,201	31,678	191,273	3,296	19,900	165.6
Outdoor power equipment stores	44421	4,769	4,069	153,676	535	20,222	26.5
Nursery & garden centers	44422	16,432	27,609	198,428	2,760	19,839	139.1
Food & beverage stores	445	148,528	401,764	138,871	40,581	14,027	2,893.1
Grocery stores	4451	96,542	368,250	139,298	37,426	14,157	2,643.6
Supermarkets & other grocery (except convenience) stores	44511	69,461	351,403	141,141	35,828	14,390	2,489.7
Convenience stores	44512	27,081	16,848	109,481	1,598	10,387	153.9
Specialty food stores	4452	22,373	10,830	91,137	1,456	12,250	118.8
Meat markets	44521	7,214	4,347	109,041	544	13,656	39.9
Fish & seafood markets	44522	1,634	1,038	145,724	102	14,316	7.1
Fruit & vegetable markets	44523	3,179	2,107	122,128	237	13,736	17.3
Other specialty food stores	44529	10,346	3,339	61,152	572	10,483	54.6
Beer, wine, & liquor stores	4453	29,613	22,684	173,645	1,699	13,008	130.6
Health & personal care stores	446	82,941	117,701	130,244	15,191	16,809	903.7
Pharmacies & drug stores	44611	43,615	98,631	140,150	11,588	16,465	703.8
Cosmetics, beauty supplies, & perfume stores	44612	9,014	4,419	94,977	604	12,973	46.5
Optical goods stores	44613	15,192	6,432	88,052	1,401	19,182	73.0
Other health & personal care stores	44619	15,120	8,219	102,269	1,598	19,888	80.4
Gasoline stations	447	126,889	198,166	214,916	11,482	12,453	922.1
Gasoline stations with convenience stores	44711	81,684	127,609	207,847	7,229	11,774	614.0
Other gasoline stations	44719	45,205	70,557	229,002	4,254	13,805	308.1
Clothing & clothing accessories stores	448	156,601	136,398	106,548	16,597	12,965	1,280.2
Clothing stores	4481	94,740	95,918	103,368	11,225	12,097	927.9
Men's clothing stores	44811	12,143	9,865	118,025	1,325	15,855	83.6
Women's clothing stores	44812	39,672	27,258	89,169	3,366	11,011	305.7
Children's & infant's clothing stores	44813	5,115	4,638	99,699	474	10,198	46.5
Family clothing stores	44814	20,450	44,796	114,197	4,797	12,229	392.3
Clothing accessories stores	44815	5,860	2,132	82,794	314	12,184	25.8
Other clothing stores	44819	11,500	7,229	97,535	949	12,799	74.1
Shoe stores	4482	31,399	20,543	110,565	2,349	12,640	185.8
Jewelry, luggage, & leather goods stores	4483	30,462	19,936	119,795	3,024	18,169	166.4
Jewelry stores	44831	28,336	18,511	119,523	2,836	18,311	154.9
Luggage & leather goods stores	44832	2,126	1,425	123,448	188	16,259	11.5
Sporting goods, hobby, book, & music stores	451	69,149	62,011	110,568	7,113	12,683	560.8
Sporting goods, hobby, & musical instrument stores	4511	46,315	41,415	114,100	4,819	13,276	363.0
Sporting goods stores	45111	24,424	20,043	113,760	2,388	13,553	176.2
Hobby, toy, & game stores	45112	10,824	14,388	128,746	1,369	12,247	111.8

See footnotes at end of table.

U.S. Census Bureau, Statistical Abstract of the United States: 2000

No. 1442. Retail Trade—Establishments, Sales, Payroll, and Employees by Kind of Business (NAICS Basis): 1997—Continued

Kind of business	NAICS code [1]	Estab-lish-ments (number)	Sales		Annual payroll		Paid employee for pay period including March 12 (1,000)
			Total (mil. dol.)	Per paid employee (dol.)	Total (mil. dol.)	Per paid employee (dol.)	
Sewing, needlework, & piece goods stores..................	45113	6,590	3,183	70,184	495	10,910	45.4
Musical instrument & supplies stores....	45114	4,477	3,801	128,078	567	19,119	29.7
Book, periodical, & music stores.......	4512	22,834	20,596	104,089	2,295	11,597	197.9
Book stores & news dealers........	45121	14,676	13,229	100,797	1,567	11,936	131.2
Prerecorded tape, compact disc, & record stores..................	45122	8,158	7,367	110,575	728	10,927	66.6
General merchandise stores...........	452	36,171	330,444	131,780	30,871	12,311	2,507.5
Department stores (incl. leased depts.) [2]..	4521	10,366	223,232	(NA)	(NA)	(NA)	(NA)
Department stores (excl. leased depts.)...	4521	10,366	220,108	122,584	22,083	12,299	1,795.6
Other general merchandise stores	4529	25,805	110,336	154,975	8,788	12,343	712.0
Warehouse clubs & superstores.......	45291	1,530	81,919	191,239	5,863	13,686	428.4
All other general merchandise stores....	45299	24,275	28,418	100,201	2,925	10,314	283.6
Miscellaneous store retailers...........	453	129,838	78,109	103,733	10,165	13,500	753.0
Florists	4531	26,200	6,555	52,359	1,396	11,154	125.2
Office supplies, stationery, & gift stores ..	4532	44,615	31,573	103,014	3,637	11,868	306.5
Office supplies & stationery stores.....	45321	7,330	17,076	174,027	1,581	16,110	98.1
Gift, novelty, & souvenir stores.........	45322	37,285	14,497	69,574	2,057	9,870	208.4
Used merchandise stores............	4533	17,990	6,044	61,692	1,204	12,286	98.0
Other miscellaneous store retailers......	4539	41,033	33,937	151,958	3,928	17,588	223.3
Pet & pet supplies stores...........	45391	8,318	5,493	89,763	709	11,588	61.2
Art dealers	45392	5,698	3,001	153,808	401	20,561	19.5
Manufactured (mobile) home dealers ...	45393	5,485	13,347	330,375	1,123	27,790	40.4
All other miscellaneous store retailers ..	45399	21,532	12,096	118,324	1,695	16,581	102.2
Nonstore retailers	454	44,482	123,107	243,297	12,323	24,355	506.0
Electronic shopping & mail-order houses ..	4541	10,013	79,018	361,795	5,743	26,297	218.4
Vending machine operators...........	4542	7,070	6,884	103,763	1,333	20,097	66.3
Direct selling establishments	4543	27,399	37,204	168,161	5,246	23,714	221.2
Fuel dealers	45431	12,532	22,622	217,987	2,755	26,550	103.8
Other direct selling establishments	45439	14,867	14,582	124,140	2,491	21,209	117.5

NA Not available.   [1] North American Industry Classification System, 1997; see text, Section 32, Economic Census 1997.
[2] Not included in broader kind of business.

Source: U.S. Census Bureau, *1997 Economic Census, Retail Trade*, Series EC97R44A-US(RV), issued March 2000.

No. 1443. Transportation and Warehousing—Establishments, Revenue, Payroll, and Employees by Kind of Business (NAICS Basis): 1997

Kind of business	NAICS code [1]	Estab-lish-ments (number)	Revenue		Annual payroll		Paid employee for pay period including March 12 (1,000)
			Total (mil. dol.)	Per paid employee (dol.)	Total (mil. dol.)	Per paid employee (dol.)	
Transportation & warehousing [2][3] ...	**48-49**	**178,025**	**318,245**	**108,959**	**82,346**	**28,193**	**2,920.8**
Air transportation [2]	481	3,598	20,249	227,198	2,748	30,834	89.1
Scheduled air transportation [2]	4811	1,798	16,285	246,786	1,921	29,110	66.0
Nonscheduled air transportation........	4812	1,800	3,964	171,332	827	35,750	23.1
Water transportation	483	1,921	24,019	329,676	2,834	38,900	72.9
Deep sea, coastal, & Great Lakes water transportation	4831	1,308	20,339	374,565	2,198	40,472	54.3
Inland water transportation	4832	613	3,680	198,323	637	34,300	18.6
Truck transportation..................	484	103,798	141,225	109,156	38,471	29,735	1,293.8
General freight trucking	4841	44,781	88,426	107,901	25,722	31,387	819.5
Specialized freight trucking	4842	59,017	52,800	111,326	12,749	26,881	474.3
Transit & ground passenger transportation...	485	16,013	13,792	40,616	5,549	16,342	339.6
Urban transit systems..............	4851	618	1,519	46,096	973	29,542	32.9
Interurban & rural bus transportation.....	4852	407	1,147	57,660	550	27,624	19.9
Taxi & limousine service	4853	6,418	3,155	55,070	881	15,374	57.3
School & employee bus transportation....	4854	4,484	4,393	28,964	1,878	12,382	151.7
Charter bus industry.	4855	1,531	1,768	56,164	548	17,407	31.5
Other transit & ground passenger transportation	4859	2,555	1,811	39,107	720	15,547	46.3
Pipeline transportation	486	2,311	26,837	544,582	2,661	53,989	49.3
Pipeline transportation of crude oil	4861	382	4,365	548,311	480	60,240	8.0
Pipeline transportation of natural gas	4862	1,450	19,627	548,404	1,871	52,277	35.8
Other pipeline transportation	4869	479	2,846	514,483	310	56,069	5.5
Scenic & sightseeing transportation	487	2,325	1,893	79,200	492	20,600	23.9
Scenic & sightseeing transportation, land.	4871	454	558	67,777	170	20,619	8.2
Scenic & sightseeing transportation, water.	4872	1,692	1,129	79,565	283	19,940	14.2
Scenic & sightseeing transportation, other .	4879	179	207	138,604	40	26,757	1.5

See footnotes at end of table.

No. 1443. Transportation and Warehousing—Establishments, Revenue, Payroll, and Employees by Kind of Business (NAICS Basis): 1997—Continued

Kind of business	NAICS code [1]	Estab-lish-ments (number)	Revenue		Annual payroll		Paid employee for pay period including March 12 (1,000)
			Total (mil. dol.)	Per paid employee (dol.)	Total (mil. dol.)	Per paid employee (dol.)	
Support activities for transportation	488	30,675	39,758	96,585	12,592	30,591	411.6
Support activities for air transportation. . . .	4881	4,231	9,153	79,279	2,820	24,425	115.5
Support activities for rail transportation . . .	4882	816	2,067	109,555	515	27,276	18.9
Support activities for water transportation. .	4883	2,525	7,515	103,681	2,763	38,125	72.5
Support activities for road transportation . .	4884	6,424	2,683	60,535	901	20,327	44.3
Freight transportation arrangement	4885	15,782	16,251	114,856	5,015	35,442	141.5
Other support activities for transportation . .	4889	897	2,090	109,826	579	30,427	19.0
Couriers & messengers	492	10,887	39,812	74,999	14,072	26,508	530.8
Couriers	4921	5,503	36,293	78,315	12,830	27,685	463.4
Local messengers & local delivery	4922	5,384	3,519	52,202	1,242	18,420	67.4
Warehousing & storage	493	6,497	10,658	97,102	2,926	26,659	109.8

[1] North American Industry Classification System, 1997; see text, Section 32, Economic Census 1997. [2] Data do not include large certificated passenger carriers that report to the Office of Airline Statistics, U.S. Department of Transportation. [3] Railroad transportation and U.S. Postal Service are out of scope for the 1997 Economic Census.

Source: U.S. Census Bureau, *1997 Economic Census, Transportation & Warehousing,* Series EC97T48A-US, issued January 2000.

No. 1444. Information—Establishments, Receipts, Payroll, and Employees by Kind of Business (NAICS Basis): 1997

Kind of business	NAICS code [1]	Estab-lish-ments (number)	Receipts		Annual payroll		Paid employee for pay period including March 12 (1,000)
			Total (mil. dol.)	Per paid employee (dol.)	Total (mil. dol.)	Per paid employee (dol.)	
Information.	51	114,475	623,214	203,255	129,482	42,229	3,066.2
Publishing industries	511	33,896	179,035	177,930	43,358	43,090	1,006.2
Newspaper, periodical, book, & database publishers.	5111	21,806	117,336	158,598	24,971	33,753	739.8
Newspaper publishers.	51111	8,758	41,601	103,137	11,789	29,228	403.4
Periodical publishers.	51112	6,298	29,885	217,265	5,993	43,571	137.6
Book publishers.	51113	2,684	22,648	251,933	3,643	40,522	89.9
Database & directory publishers	51114	1,458	12,258	284,312	1,655	38,384	43.1
Other publishers	51119	2,608	10,944	166,027	1,891	28,693	65.9
Software publishers	5112	12,090	61,699	231,622	18,387	69,025	266.4
Motion picture & sound recording industries. .	512	22,204	55,926	202,643	9,392	34,032	276.0
Motion picture & video industries	5121	19,269	44,786	175,998	8,280	32,540	254.5
Motion picture & video production	51211	8,777	20,152	241,175	4,945	59,176	83.6
Motion picture & video distribution	51212	756	12,509	987,812	767	60,553	12.7
Motion picture & video exhibition.	51213	6,358	7,597	60,759	944	7,553	125.0
Post production & other motion picture & video industries	51219	3,378	4,528	136,352	1,625	48,925	33.2
Sound recording industries	5122	2,935	11,140	517,797	1,112	51,671	21.5
Record production	51221	283	182	182,734	47	46,613	1.0
Integrated record production/distribution .	51222	285	8,736	1,108,753	598	75,907	7.9
Music publishers	51223	721	1,368	315,665	215	49,585	4.3
Sound recording studios	51224	1,269	541	97,793	163	29,482	5.5
Other sound recording industries.	51229	377	313	112,704	89	32,133	2.8
Broadcasting & telecommunications	513	43,480	346,316	241,427	63,480	44,253	1,434.5
Radio & television broadcasting	5131	8,789	40,425	161,885	9,869	39,521	249.7
Radio broadcasting.	51311	6,894	10,648	84,060	3,604	28,455	126.7
Television broadcasting.	51312	1,895	29,777	242,007	6,264	50,913	123.0
Cable networks & program distribution	5132	4,679	45,390	260,334	6,151	35,280	174.4
Cable networks	51321	494	10,390	392,238	1,358	51,276	26.5
Cable & other program distribution	51322	4,185	35,000	236,705	4,793	32,415	147.9
Telecommunications.	5133	30,012	260,501	257,822	47,460	46,972	1,010.4
Wired telecommunications carriers	51331	20,815	208,791	256,051	39,565	48,520	815.4
Wireless telecommunications carriers (except satellite).	51332	6,386	37,889	258,977	5,839	39,913	146.3
Telecommunications resellers	51333	1,656	7,592	252,841	1,185	39,466	30.0
Satellite telecommunications	51334	521	5,096	427,138	599	50,229	11.9
Other telecommunications	51339	634	1,133	169,080	271	40,489	6.7
Information services & data processing services.	514	14,895	41,937	119,986	13,252	37,915	349.5
Information services.	5141	7,307	11,101	127,202	3,478	39,854	87.3
News syndicates	51411	527	1,402	147,883	465	49,084	9.5
Libraries & archives	51412	2,298	861	39,055	373	16,928	22.0
Other information services	51419	4,482	8,837	158,544	2,639	47,351	55.7
Data processing services	5142	7,588	30,837	117,585	9,774	37,269	262.3

[1] North American Industry Classification System, 1997; see text, Section 32, Economic Census 1997.

Source: U.S. Census Bureau, *1997 Economic Census,* Series EC97551A-US, issued October 1999.

No. 1445. Finance and Insurance—Establishments, Revenue, Payroll, and Employees by Kind of Business (NAICS Basis): 1997

Kind of business	NAICS code [1]	Establishments (number)	Revenue		Annual payroll		Paid employee for pay period including March 12 (1,000)
			Total (mil. dol.)	Per paid employee (dol.)	Total (mil. dol.)	Per paid employee (dol.)	
Finance & insurance	**52**	**395,203**	**2,197,771**	**376,639**	**264,551**	**45,337**	**5,835.2**
Monetary authorities—central bank	521	42	24,582	1,134,150	903	41,680	21.7
Credit intermediation & related activities	522	166,882	808,811	294,658	98,723	35,966	2,744.9
Depository credit intermediation	5221	102,916	533,134	264,228	70,230	34,807	2,017.7
Commercial banking	52211	70,860	421,759	267,716	57,247	36,338	1,575.4
Savings institutions	52212	16,264	78,947	298,166	8,409	31,761	264.8
Credit unions	52213	15,640	29,694	172,523	4,308	25,027	172.1
Other depository credit intermediation	52219	152	2,734	504,823	266	49,065	5.4
Nondepository credit intermediation	5222	47,556	229,214	411,705	22,661	40,702	556.7
Credit card issuing	52221	588	24,503	416,914	1,783	30,331	58.8
Sales financing	52222	8,143	78,133	611,218	6,163	48,212	127.8
Other nondepository credit intermediation	52229	38,825	126,577	341,974	14,715	39,756	370.1
Activities related to credit intermediation	5223	16,410	46,463	272,571	5,833	34,217	170.5
Mortgage & nonmortgage loan brokers	52231	8,967	5,087	103,108	1,896	38,420	49.3
Financial transactions processing, reserve, & clearinghouse act	52232	1,239	34,780	545,765	2,257	35,421	63.7
Other activities related to credit intermediation	52239	6,204	6,596	114,922	1,680	29,267	57.4
Securities intermediation & related activities	523	54,491	274,987	389,470	71,281	100,957	706.1
Securities & commodity contracts intermediation & brokerage	5231	26,049	196,417	437,259	49,983	111,270	449.2
Investment banking & securities dealing	52311	4,136	118,386	840,916	22,330	158,616	140.8
Securities brokerage	52312	19,869	72,756	250,318	26,520	91,241	290.7
Commodity contracts dealing	52313	630	2,241	495,996	341	75,457	4.5
Commodity contracts brokerage	52314	1,414	3,034	229,067	792	59,772	13.2
Securities & commodity exchanges	5232	30	1,900	282,928	442	65,740	6.7
Other financial investment activities	5239	28,412	76,669	306,510	20,857	83,383	250.1
Miscellaneous intermediation	52391	7,190	15,346	505,115	1,592	52,414	30.4
Portfolio management	52392	10,888	43,643	352,041	13,533	109,162	124.0
Investment advice	52393	7,807	9,398	218,917	3,197	74,481	42.9
All other financial investment activities	52399	2,527	8,282	156,702	2,534	47,949	52.9
Insurance carriers & related activities	524	172,299	1,072,784	460,955	92,230	39,630	2,327.3
Insurance carriers	5241	38,739	995,512	626,891	65,858	41,472	1,588.0
Direct life, health, & medical insurance carriers	52411	14,615	666,532	749,739	34,474	38,778	889.0
Other direct insurance carriers	52412	23,561	307,695	450,427	30,374	44,464	683.1
Reinsurance carriers	52413	563	21,285	1,340,536	1,010	63,600	15.9
Agencies, brokerages, & other insurance related activities	5242	133,560	77,272	104,522	26,372	35,672	739.3
Insurance agencies & brokerages	52421	120,392	59,174	106,110	19,533	35,026	557.7
Other insurance related activities	52429	13,168	18,098	99,647	6,839	37,654	181.6
Funds, trusts, & other financial vehicles (part)	525	1,489	16,608	470,868	1,413	40,075	35.3
Other investment pools & funds (part)	5259	1,489	16,608	470,868	1,413	40,075	35.3
Real Estate Investment Trusts (REITs)	52593	1,489	16,608	470,868	1,413	40,075	35.3

[1] North American Industry Classification System, 1997; see text, Section 32, Economic Census 1997.

Source: U.S. Census Bureau, *1997 Economic Census, Finance and Insurance*, Series EC97F52A-US(RV), issued April 2000.

No. 1446. Real Estate, Renting, and Leasing—Establishments, Revenue, Payroll, and Employees by Kind of Business (NAICS Basis): 1997

Kind of business	NAICS code [1]	Establishments (number)	Revenue		Annual payroll		Paid employee for pay period including March 12 (1,000)
			Total (mil. dol.)	Per paid employee (dol.)	Total (mil. dol.)	Per paid employee (dol.)	
Real estate & rental & leasing	**53**	**288,273**	**240,918**	**141,515**	**41,491**	**24,430**	**1,702.4**
Real estate	531	221,650	153,275	137,190	27,947	25,014	1,117.2
Lessors of real estate	5311	110,226	85,791	182,769	9,484	20,204	469.4
Offices of real estate agents & brokers	5312	60,620	38,945	177,321	6,792	30,923	219.6
Activities related to real estate	5313	50,804	28,538	66,644	11,671	27,256	428.2
Rental & leasing services	532	64,472	76,379	136,542	12,569	22,470	559.4
Automotive equipment rental & leasing	5321	10,542	28,922	182,978	3,871	24,488	158.1
Consumer goods rental	5322	35,423	14,396	62,594	3,097	13,468	230.0
General rental centers	5323	6,509	3,911	97,076	941	23,359	40.3
Commercial & industrial machinery & equipment rental & leasing	5324	11,998	29,150	222,450	4,660	35,562	131.0
Lessors of intangible assets, except copyrighted works	533	2,151	11,264	436,719	1,074	41,659	25.8

[1] North American Industry Classification System, 1997; see text, Section 32, Economic Census 1997.

Source: U.S. Census Bureau, *1997 Economic Census, Real Estate & Rental Leasing*, Series EC97F53A-US(RV), issued March 2000.

1997 Economic Census   877

No. 1447. Professional, Scientific, and Technical Services—Establishments, Receipts, Payroll, and Employees by Kind of Business (NAICS Basis): 1997

Kind of business	NAICS code [1]	Establishments (number)	Receipts Total (mil. dol.)	Receipts Per paid employee (dol.)	Annual payroll Total (mil. dol.)	Annual payroll Per paid employee (dol.)	Paid employee for pay period including March 12 (1,000)
Professional, scientific, & technical services	**54**	**615,305**	**579,542**	**111,178**	**225,376**	**43,236**	**5,212.7**
Professional, scientific, & technical services	541	615,305	579,542	111,178	225,376	43,236	5,212.7
Legal services	5411	173,716	127,052	125,534	49,060	48,474	1,012.1
Offices of lawyers	54111	165,757	122,617	128,250	47,410	49,588	956.1
Other legal services	54119	7,959	4,436	79,180	1,650	29,462	56.0
Accounting, tax return prep, bookkeeping, & payroll services	5412	97,512	61,117	63,234	26,104	27,008	966.5
Architectural, engineering, & related services	5413	92,710	116,986	112,669	46,943	45,210	1,038.3
Architectural services	54131	20,602	16,988	115,802	6,469	44,093	146.7
Engineering services	54133	52,526	88,181	120,788	35,338	48,405	730.0
Drafting services	54134	1,872	605	66,160	310	33,917	9.2
Building inspection services	54135	2,771	639	73,673	240	27,678	8.7
Geophysical surveying & mapping services	54136	587	1,088	109,822	446	44,987	9.9
Surveying & mapping (except geophysical) services	54137	8,864	3,042	58,708	1,432	27,630	51.8
Testing laboratories	54138	5,488	6,443	78,550	2,709	33,024	82.0
Specialized design services	5414	26,436	14,254	126,103	4,088	36,166	113.0
Interior design services	54141	9,612	4,945	145,816	1,022	30,120	33.9
Industrial design services	54142	1,322	1,363	100,170	583	42,816	13.6
Graphic design services	54143	14,631	7,555	122,601	2,355	38,212	61.6
Other specialized design services	54149	871	391	100,428	129	33,207	3.9
Computer systems design & related services	5415	72,278	108,968	142,505	42,151	55,123	764.7
Management, scientific, & technical consulting services	5416	80,426	63,429	124,066	26,582	51,993	511.3
Management consulting services	54161	60,794	52,225	127,054	22,297	54,244	411.0
Environmental consulting services	54162	6,725	4,781	103,603	1,778	38,522	46.1
Other scientific & technical consulting services	54169	12,907	6,423	118,811	2,507	46,377	54.1
Scientific research & development services	5417	7,830	23,078	130,405	9,322	52,675	177.0
R&D in the physical, engineering, & life sciences	54171	6,855	21,822	135,283	8,821	54,683	161.3
Research & development in the social sciences & humanities	54172	975	1,257	80,188	502	32,008	15.7
Advertising & related services	5418	38,832	49,290	118,141	16,012	38,379	417.2
Advertising agencies	54181	13,390	16,872	120,955	7,557	54,177	139.5
Public relations agencies	54182	6,513	4,772	123,195	1,952	50,384	38.7
Media buying services	54183	882	1,057	123,824	422	49,452	8.5
Media representatives	54184	2,686	3,309	125,153	1,061	40,115	26.4
Display advertising	54185	2,261	4,639	112,169	823	19,901	41.4
Direct mail advertising	54186	3,454	8,672	101,229	2,427	28,325	85.7
Advertising material distribution services	54187	560	830	86,049	175	18,145	9.6
Other services related to advertising	54189	9,086	9,140	135,706	1,596	23,702	67.4
Other professional, scientific, & technical services	5419	25,565	15,368	72,261	5,115	24,049	212.7
Marketing research & public opinion polling	54191	4,030	7,880	73,266	2,963	27,553	107.6
Photographic services	54192	17,573	5,571	66,399	1,540	18,353	83.9
Translation & interpretation services	54193	904	415	85,250	142	29,232	4.9
All other professional, scientific, & technical services	54199	3,058	1,502	91,866	469	28,690	16.3

[1] North American Industry Classification System, 1997; see text, Section 32, Economic Census 1997.

Source: U.S. Census Bureau, *1997 Economic Census, Professional, Scientific, and Technical Services*, Series EC97554A-US, issued December 1999.

No. 1448. Administrative and Support and Waste Management and Remediation Services—Establishments, Receipts, Payroll, and Employees by Kind of Business (NAICS Basis): 1997

Kind of business	NAICS code [1]	Estab-lish-ments (number)	Receipts		Annual payroll		Paid employee for pay period including March 12 (1,000)
			Total (mil. dol.)	Per paid employee (dol.)	Total (mil. dol.)	Per paid employee (dol.)	
Administrative & support & waste management and & remediation services	56	276,393	295,936	40,278	137,337	18,692	7,347.4
Office administrative services..........	5611	24,537	28,054	82,906	11,971	35,377	338.4
Facilities support services............	5612	2,490	7,576	67,558	3,280	29,251	112.1
Employment services...............	5613	34,569	86,133	23,780	62,127	17,153	3,622.0
Employment placement agencies	56131	6,281	4,787	42,032	2,647	23,243	113.9
Temporary help services	56132	23,522	57,221	21,901	40,246	15,408	2,612.7
Employee leasing services...........	56133	4,766	24,125	26,943	19,224	21,469	895.4
Business support services............	5614	32,920	36,026	59,590	11,900	19,683	604.6
Document preparation services.......	56141	4,587	1,469	46,812	625	19,904	31.4
Telephone call centers	56142	6,271	11,983	40,992	4,574	15,646	292.3
Business service centers...........	56143	10,130	8,504	79,699	2,076	19,459	106.7
Collection agencies	56144	5,250	5,083	60,276	2,128	25,235	84.3
Credit bureaus...................	56145	1,588	4,699	137,613	1,165	34,128	34.1
Other business support services......	56149	5,094	4,289	76,995	1,332	23,909	55.7
Travel arrangement & reservation services.	5615	36,578	21,484	71,493	7,699	25,622	300.5
Travel agencies	56151	29,332	9,977	54,467	4,464	24,369	183.2
Tour operators...................	56152	3,501	2,782	72,129	1,034	26,817	38.6
Other travel arrangement & reservation services	56159	3,745	8,725	110,786	2,201	27,949	78.8
Investigation & security services........	5616	21,494	20,444	29,938	10,698	15,665	682.9
Investigation, guard, & armored car services	56161	12,539	12,370	22,052	7,759	13,832	561.0
Security systems services	56162	8,955	8,074	66,224	2,938	24,100	121.9
Services to buildings & dwellings	5617	80,807	29,915	28,599	13,317	12,731	1,046.0
Exterminating & pest control services...	56171	11,062	4,911	60,466	1,930	23,766	81.2
Janitorial services...............	56172	55,157	21,128	23,678	10,106	11,326	892.3
Carpet & upholstery cleaning services ..	56174	9,282	2,156	45,810	729	15,500	47.1
Other services to buildings & dwellings .	56179	5,306	1,720	67,586	551	21,643	25.4
Other support services	5619	26,630	26,958	74,859	7,446	20,677	360.1
Packaging & labeling services	56191	2,331	4,015	70,869	1,073	18,945	56.7
Convention & trade show organizers ...	56192	3,978	6,260	86,416	1,733	23,925	72.4
All other support services	56199	20,321	16,683	72,213	4,640	20,083	231.0
Waste management & remediation services..	562	16,368	39,346	140,166	8,899	31,702	280.7
Waste collection	5621	8,324	20,145	131,885	4,566	29,893	152.7
Waste treatment & disposal...........	5622	2,314	10,251	192,225	1,933	36,249	53.3
Remediation & other waste management services......................	5629	5,730	8,950	119,914	2,400	32,154	74.6
Remediation services.............	56291	1,677	5,690	138,793	1,500	36,600	41.0
Materials recovery facility...........	56292	765	1,299	119,771	283	26,136	10.8
All other waste management services ..	56299	3,288	1,961	86,035	616	27,024	22.8

[1] North American Industry Classification System, 1997; see text, Section 32, Economic Census 1997.

Source: U.S. Census Bureau, *1997 Economic Census, Administrative & Support and Waste Management & Remediation Services*, Series EC97556A-US, issued January 2000.

No. 1449. Educational Services—Establishments, Receipts, Payroll, and Employees by Kind of Business (NAICS Basis): 1997

Kind of business	NAICS code [1]	Estab-lish-ments (number)	Receipts		Annual payroll		Paid employee for pay period including March 12 (1,000)
			Total (mil. dol.)	Per paid employee (dol.)	Total (mil. dol.)	Per paid employee (dol.)	
Educational services...........	61	33,783	14,933	60,049	4,903	19,716	248.7
Business schools, & computer & manage-ment training...................	6114	6,056	4,902	91,021	1,689	31,354	53.9
Business & secretarial schools	61141	581	554	50,825	213	19,567	10.9
Computer training................	61142	2,785	2,512	87,083	970	33,634	28.8
Professional & management development training.............	61143	2,690	1,836	130,120	505	35,796	14.1
Technical & trade schools	6115	5,465	3,465	63,802	1,161	21,378	54.3
Other schools & instruction	6116	19,294	5,197	41,959	1,596	12,887	123.9
Fine arts schools	61161	6,245	954	30,143	278	8,788	31.7
Sports & recreation instruction	61162	5,674	1,270	38,306	374	11,284	33.2
Language schools	61163	610	413	48,672	121	14,210	8.5
All other schools & instruction........	61169	6,765	2,560	50,624	823	16,282	50.6
Educational support services..........	6117	2,968	1,369	82,186	457	27,449	16.7

[1] North American Industry Classification System, 1997; see text, Section 32, Economic Census 1997.

Source: U.S. Census Bureau, *1997 Economic Census, Educational Services*, Series EC97561A-US(RV), issued March 2000.

1997 Economic Census **879**

No. 1450. Health Care and Social Assistance—Establishments, Receipts, Payroll, and Employees by Kind of Business (NAICS Basis): 1997

Kind of business	NAICS code [1]	Estab-lish-ments (number)	Receipts Total (mil. dol.)	Receipts Per paid employee (dol.)	Annual payroll Total (mil. dol.)	Annual payroll Per paid employee (dol.)	Paid employee for pay period including March 12 (1,000)
Health care & social assistance ...	62	531,069	418,602	67,172	182,256	29,246	6,231.8
Ambulatory health care services	621	440,200	310,012	82,796	137,979	36,851	3,744.3
Offices of physicians	6211	195,449	171,629	109,238	84,977	54,086	1,571.1
Offices of physicians (except mental health specialists).............	621111	185,094	168,252	109,506	83,482	54,334	1,536.5
Offices of physicians, mental health specialists..................	621112	10,355	3,377	97,368	1,494	43,085	34.7
Offices of dentists	6212	114,178	48,482	75,556	18,227	28,405	641.7
Offices of other health practitioners......	6213	88,886	28,282	69,560	10,457	25,718	406.6
Offices of chiropractors	62131	30,487	6,570	71,648	1,886	20,569	91.7
Offices of optometrists	62132	17,875	6,362	79,978	1,773	22,295	79.5
Offices of mental health practitioners (except physicians).............	62133	11,750	2,505	65,184	948	24,658	38.4
Offices of physical, occup., & speech therapists & audiologists	62134	14,277	8,684	61,357	4,377	30,924	141.5
Offices of all other health practitioners ..	62139	14,497	4,162	75,139	1,473	26,593	55.4
Outpatient care centers	6214	11,828	17,306	99,572	5,502	31,655	173.8
Family planning centers...........	62141	443	278	69,041	95	23,718	4.0
Outpatient mental health & substance abuse centers	62142	2,648	1,504	65,371	579	25,179	23.0
Other outpatient care centers	62149	8,737	15,525	105,768	4,827	32,887	146.8
Medical & diagnostic laboratories	6215	9,076	16,317	107,819	5,402	35,693	151.3
Home health care services	6216	16,315	21,474	31,510	10,941	16,054	681.5
Other ambulatory health care services....	6219	4,468	6,521	55,162	2,475	20,933	118.2
Ambulance services	62191	2,453	4,207	46,713	1,803	20,025	90.1
All other ambulatory health care services	62199	2,015	2,314	82,175	671	23,834	28.2
Hospitals...............	622	1,345	40,146	78,475	13,886	27,143	511.6
General medical & surgical hospitals.....	6221	792	34,213	81,215	11,570	27,466	421.3
Psychiatric & substance abuse hospitals ..	6222	389	3,369	62,101	1,346	24,811	54.2
Specialty (except psychiatric & substance abuse) hospitals	6223	164	2,565	71,093	970	26,875	36.1
Nursing & residential care facilities........	623	32,833	55,844	37,610	24,626	16,585	1,484.8
Nursing care facilities..............	6231	12,517	44,485	38,332	20,193	17,400	1,160.5
Residential mental retardation/health & substance abuse facility	6232	7,293	3,620	32,933	1,618	14,716	109.9
Residential mental retardation facilities..	62321	5,411	2,507	30,408	1,157	14,033	82.4
Residential mental health & substance abuse facilities	62322	1,882	1,113	40,506	461	16,763	27.5
Community care facilities for the elderly...	6233	11,637	7,088	36,151	2,533	12,920	196.1
Other residential care facilities	6239	1,386	651	35,519	281	15,361	18.3
Social assistance	624	56,691	12,599	25,657	5,766	11,741	491.1
Individual & family services	6241	9,843	2,636	38,333	1,113	16,177	68.8
Child & youth services	62411	1,648	539	46,861	210	18,253	11.5
Services for the elderly & persons with disabilities.................	62412	2,976	807	25,081	394	12,246	32.2
Other individual & family services	62419	5,219	1,290	51,428	508	20,268	25.1
Community food & housing/emergency & other relief services	6242	344	112	72,109	29	18,701	1.6
Community food services...........	62421	95	18	51,236	4	11,575	0.4
Community housing services	62422	167	74	77,019	21	21,668	1.0
Emergency & other relief services.....	62423	82	20	82,958	4	17,225	0.2
Vocational rehabilitation services	6243	2,549	1,432	44,753	676	21,112	32.0
Child day care services	6244	43,955	8,419	21,657	3,948	10,157	388.7

[1] North American Industry Classification System, 1997; see text, Section 32, Economic Census 1997.

Source: U.S. Census Bureau, *1997 Economic Census, Health Care and Social Assistance*, Series EC97562A-US, issued October 1999.

No. 1451. Arts, Entertainment, and Recreation—Establishments, Receipts, Payroll, and Employees by Kind of Business (NAICS Basis): 1997

Kind of business	NAICS code [1]	Estab-lish-ments (number)	Receipts		Annual payroll		Paid employee for pay period including March 12 (1,000)
			Total (mil. dol.)	Per paid employee (dol.)	Total (mil. dol.)	Per paid employee (dol.)	
Arts, entertainment,& recreation...	**71**	**79,636**	**85,088**	**70,474**	**26,104**	**21,620**	**1,207.4**
Performing arts, spectator sports.........	711	25,942	32,744	138,788	12,834	54,400	235.9
Performing arts companies	7111	5,883	5,272	101,763	1,452	28,033	51.8
Theater companies & dinner theaters...	71111	1,600	2,344	88,502	594	22,417	26.5
Dance companies	71112	159	109	46,566	35	15,016	2.3
Musical groups & artists	71113	3,369	2,172	132,842	635	38,831	16.4
Other performing arts companies	71119	755	645	97,628	188	28,445	6.6
Spectator sports	7112	3,881	13,656	147,804	6,151	66,577	92.4
Promoters of performing arts, sports, & similar events	7113	2,633	5,045	98,133	1,053	20,475	51.4
Promoters of performing arts, sports, & similar events	71131	557	1,548	60,207	419	16,291	25.7
Promoters of performing arts, sports, & similar events w/o facilities.........	71132	2,076	3,497	136,080	634	24,662	25.7
Agents/managers for artists, athletes, & other public figures..............	7114	2,532	2,410	182,032	911	68,800	13.2
Independent artists, writers, & performers .	7115	11,013	6,361	234,888	3,268	120,657	27.1
Museums, historical sites, & similar institutions.....................	712	787	484	66,431	122	16,811	7.3
Museums...............	71211	426	259	87,131	53	17,712	3.0
Historical sites	71212	78	27	29,625	9	10,040	0.9
Zoos & botanical gardens	71213	117	97	58,915	29	17,568	1.6
Nature parks & other similar institutions...	71219	166	100	57,723	32	18,169	1.7
Amusement, gambling, & recreation industries.....................	713	52,907	51,861	53,789	13,147	13,636	964.2
Amusement parks & arcades..........	7131	3,344	8,418	60,595	1,962	14,121	138.9
Amusement & theme parks	71311	607	7,172	64,733	1,690	15,258	110.8
Amusement arcades.............	71312	2,737	1,247	44,305	271	9,647	28.1
Gambling industries...............	7132	2,099	15,542	92,217	3,222	19,117	168.5
Casinos (except casino hotels)	71321	447	10,186	88,413	2,305	20,004	115.2
Other gambling industries	71329	1,652	5,355	100,437	917	17,200	53.3
Other amusement & recreation services ..	7139	47,464	27,901	42,487	7,963	12,126	656.7
Golf courses & country clubs	71391	8,546	8,637	53,941	2,732	17,062	160.1
Skiing facilities................	71392	379	1,341	22,915	431	7,368	58.5
Marinas	71393	4,217	2,541	111,640	517	22,692	22.8
Fitness & recreational sports centers ...	71394	16,604	7,945	30,987	2,405	9,380	256.4
Bowling centers	71395	5,590	2,821	32,037	821	9,325	88.0
All other amusement & recreation industries	71399	12,128	4,616	65,140	1,058	14,925	70.9

[1] North American Industry Classification System, 1997; see text, Section 32, Economic Census 1997.

Source: U.S. Census Bureau, *1997 Economic Census, Arts, Entertainment, and Recreation*, Series EC97571A-US(RV), issued April 2000.

No. 1452. Accommodation and Foodservices—Establishments, Sales, Payroll, and Employees by Kind of Business (NAICS Basis): 1997

Kind of business	NAICS code [1]	Estab-lish-ments (number)	Sales		Annual payroll		Paid employee for pay period including March 12 (1,000)
			Total (mil. dol.)	Per paid employee (dol.)	Total (mil. dol.)	Per paid employee (dol.)	
Accommodation & foodservices...	**72**	**545,068**	**350,399**	**37,074**	**97,007**	**10,264**	**9,451.2**
Accommodation	721	58,162	98,457	58,030	26,674	15,721	1,696.7
Traveler accommodation.............	7211	47,079	94,966	57,707	25,851	15,709	1,645.7
Hotels (except casino hotels) & motels..	72111	43,188	73,451	54,181	19,647	14,493	1,355.7
Casino hotels	72112	257	20,652	76,146	5,998	22,116	271.2
Other traveler accommodation	72119	3,634	863	45,913	206	10,965	18.8
RV (recreational vehicle) parks & recreational camps................	7212	7,598	2,735	77,408	665	18,830	35.3
Rooming & boarding houses	7213	3,485	757	48,313	157	10,033	15.7
Foodservices & drinking places	722	486,906	251,942	32,489	70,334	9,070	7,754.6
Full-service restaurants..............	7221	191,245	112,450	30,881	34,435	9,457	3,641.4
Limited-service eating places..........	7222	214,774	107,788	32,398	27,483	8,261	3,327.0
Special foodservices	7223	28,062	19,408	41,749	5,766	12,403	464.9
Foodservice contractors	72231	18,991	15,160	41,878	4,617	12,755	362.0
Caterers....................	72232	6,478	3,369	36,942	978	10,726	91.2
Mobile foodservices	72233	2,593	879	75,272	171	14,595	11.7
Drinking places (alcoholic beverages)	7224	52,825	12,296	38,269	2,649	8,246	321.3

[1] North American Industry Classification System, 1997; see text, Section 32, Economic Census 1997.

Source: U.S. Census Bureau, *1997 Economic Census, Accommodation and Foodservices*, Series EC97R72A-US(RV), issued May 2000.

No. 1453. Other Services—Establishments, Receipts, Payroll, and Employees by Kind of Business (NAICS Basis): 1997

Kind of business	NAICS code [1]	Establishments (number)	Receipts		Annual payroll		Paid employee for pay period including March 12 (1,000)
			Total (mil. dol.)	Per paid employee (dol.)	Total (mil. dol.)	Per paid employee (dol.)	
Other services (except public administration)	**81**	**420,950**	**163,033**	**65,381**	**48,453**	**19,431**	**2,493.6**
Repair & maintenance	811	235,466	105,154	82,384	29,875	23,406	1,276.4
Automotive repair & maintenance	8111	164,360	62,201	76,306	16,865	20,690	815.1
Automotive mechanical & electrical repair & maintenance	81111	99,444	33,510	86,966	8,634	22,406	385.3
Automotive body, paint, interior, & glass repair	81112	41,168	20,905	89,202	5,926	25,285	234.4
Other automotive repair & maintenance	81119	23,748	7,785	39,829	2,306	11,796	195.5
Electronic & precision equipment repair & maintenance	8112	17,634	14,558	106,087	4,497	32,769	137.2
Commercial & industrial machinery & equip. (exc. auto. & electr.) R&M	8113	20,290	17,506	104,851	5,172	30,978	167.0
Personal & household goods repair & maintenance	8114	33,182	10,889	69,335	3,341	21,274	157.1
Home & garden equipment & appliance repair & maintenance	81141	9,790	4,976	77,690	1,536	23,985	64.1
Reupholstery & furniture repair	81142	6,598	1,193	53,480	389	17,416	22.3
Footwear & leather goods repair	81143	2,153	261	47,790	73	13,320	5.5
Other personal & household goods repair & maintenance	81149	14,641	4,458	68,361	1,343	20,599	65.2
Personal & laundry services	812	185,484	57,879	47,552	18,577	15,263	1,217.2
Personal care services	8121	95,708	14,241	30,154	5,972	12,645	472.3
Hair, nail, & skin care services	81211	83,991	12,057	29,335	5,378	13,084	411.0
Other personal care services	81219	11,717	2,184	35,646	594	9,696	61.3
Death care services	8122	23,015	12,621	76,571	3,519	21,349	164.8
Funeral homes & funeral services	81221	16,338	9,633	91,423	2,444	23,192	105.4
Cemeteries & crematories	81222	6,677	2,988	50,252	1,075	18,082	59.5
Drycleaning & laundry services	8123	44,782	17,913	45,303	5,939	15,021	395.4
Coin-operated laundries & drycleaners	81231	13,883	2,873	54,191	606	11,435	53.0
Drycleaning & laundry services (except coin-operated)	81232	27,939	7,092	34,803	2,575	12,637	203.8
Linen & uniform supply	81233	2,960	7,948	57,339	2,758	19,896	138.6
Diaper service	8123312	100	37	41,598	13	15,336	0.9
Other personal services	8129	21,979	13,105	70,959	3,148	17,044	184.7
Photofinishing	81292	7,055	5,520	76,671	1,583	21,986	72.0
Parking lots & garages	81293	10,358	5,175	67,940	968	12,705	76.2
All other personal services	81299	4,566	2,410	65,996	597	16,350	36.5

[1] North American Industry Classification System, 1997; see text, Section 32, Economic Census 1997.

Source: U.S. Census Bureau, 1997 Economic Census, Other Services, Series EC97581A-US, issued December 1999.

No. 1454. Professional, Scientific, and Technical Services (Tax-Exempt)— Establishments, Revenue, Payroll, and Employees by Kind of Business (NAICS Basis): 1997

Kind of business	NAICS code [1]	Establishments (number)	Revenue		Annual payroll		Paid employee for pay period including March 12 (1,000)
			Total (mil. dol.)	Per paid employee (dol.)	Total (mil. dol.)	Per paid employee (dol.)	
Professional, scientific, & technical services	**54**	**5,824**	**15,709**	**105,806**	**6,023**	**40,567**	**148.5**
Professional, scientific, & technical services	541	5,824	15,709	105,806	6,023	40,567	148.5
Legal services	5411	2,532	1,497	64,197	797	34,168	23.3
Offices of lawyers	54111	2,532	1,497	64,197	797	34,168	23.3
Scientific research & development services	5417	3,292	14,212	113,558	5,226	41,759	125.1
R&D in the physical, engineering, & life sciences	54171	2,318	12,324	114,312	4,593	42,606	107.8
Research & development in the social sciences & humanities	54172	974	1,888	108,873	633	36,488	17.3

[1] North American Industry Classification System, 1997; see text, Section 32, Economic Census 1997.

Source: U.S. Census Bureau, 1997 Economic Census, Professional, Scientific, and Technical Services, Series EC97554A-US, issued December 1999.

No. 1455. Educational Services (Tax-Exempt)—Establishments, Revenue, Payroll, and Employees by Kind of Business (NAICS Basis): 1997

Kind of business	NAICS code [1]	Estab-lish-ments (number)	Revenue		Annual payroll		Paid employee for pay period including March 12 (1,000)
			Total (mil. dol.)	Per paid employee (dol.)	Total (mil. dol.)	Per paid employee (dol.)	
Educational services	61	**7,153**	**5,506**	**76,058**	**1,461**	**20,190**	**72.4**
Business schools, & computer & management training	6114	519	651	136,090	142	29,629	4.8
Business & secretarial schools	61141	38	30	46,816	14	21,544	0.6
Computer training	61142	55	33	86,591	9	23,067	0.4
Professional & management development training	61143	426	588	156,122	119	31,656	3.8
Technical & trade schools	6115	1,381	964	73,179	251	19,074	13.2
Other schools & instruction	6116	4,470	1,930	46,508	647	15,598	41.5
Fine arts schools	61161	1,009	388	33,487	140	12,067	11.6
Sports & recreation instruction	61162	749	156	35,569	47	10,813	4.4
Language schools	61163	244	75	22,518	32	9,467	3.3
All other schools & instruction	61169	2,468	1,310	59,117	428	19,322	22.2
Educational support services	6117	783	1,962	151,509	421	32,550	12.9

[1] North American Industry Classification System, 1997; see text, Section 32, Economic Census 1997.

Source: U.S. Census Bureau, *1997 Economic Census, Educational Services,* Series EC97561A-US(RV), issued March 2000.

No. 1456. Health Care and Social Assistance (Tax-Exempt)—Establishments, Revenue, Payroll, and Employees by Kind of Business (NAICS Basis): 1997

Kind of business	NAICS code [1]	Estab-lish-ments (number)	Revenue		Annual payroll		Paid employee for pay period including March 12 (1,000)
			Total (mil. dol.)	Per paid employee (dol.)	Total (mil. dol.)	Per paid employee (dol.)	
Health care and social assistance	62	**114,784**	**466,452**	**63,638**	**195,949**	**26,733**	**7,329.8**
Ambulatory health care services	621	15,181	45,428	67,871	17,884	26,719	669.3
Outpatient care centers	6214	9,940	31,561	91,086	11,158	32,202	346.5
Family planning centers	62141	1,390	668	47,378	296	21,000	14.1
Outpatient mental health & substance abuse centers	62142	3,646	4,715	46,181	2,419	23,694	102.1
Other outpatient care centers	62149	4,904	26,178	113,669	8,443	36,659	230.3
Home health care services	6216	3,375	10,104	37,775	5,426	20,286	267.5
Other ambulatory health care services	6219	1,866	3,763	67,984	1,300	23,490	55.4
Ambulance services	62191	1,032	821	38,762	320	15,094	21.2
All other ambulatory health care services	62199	834	2,942	86,085	981	28,691	34.2
Hospitals	622	5,340	339,032	76,679	141,910	32,096	4,421.5
General medical & surgical hospitals	6221	4,695	319,920	77,928	131,054	31,923	4,105.3
Psychiatric & substance abuse hospitals	6222	412	10,689	53,173	6,983	34,737	201.0
Specialty (except psychiatric & substance abuse hospitals	6223	233	8,423	73,176	3,874	33,655	115.1
Nursing & residential care facilities	623	24,526	37,235	37,768	17,527	17,778	985.9
Nursing care facilities	6231	3,088	15,249	38,445	7,396	18,647	396.6
Residential mental retardation/health & substance abuse facility	6232	12,940	7,973	32,401	4,126	16,768	246.1
Residential mental retardation facilities	62321	9,287	5,270	29,958	2,791	15,866	175.9
Residential mental health & substance abuse facilities	62322	3,653	2,703	38,381	1,335	19,029	70.2
Community care facilities for the elderly	6233	3,951	9,304	41,167	3,742	16,556	226.0
Other residential care facilities	6239	4,547	4,709	40,198	2,263	19,315	117.1
Social assistance	624	69,737	44,756	35,715	18,628	14,865	1,253.1
Individual & family services	6241	36,364	26,453	41,166	10,781	16,778	642.6
Child & youth services	62411	11,086	7,719	44,874	3,171	18,434	172.0
Services for the elderly & persons with disabilities	62412	9,960	8,217	36,244	3,260	14,380	226.7
Other individual & family services	62419	15,318	10,516	43,126	4,350	17,839	243.9
Community food & housing/emergency & other relief services	6242	9,606	6,085	60,345	1,739	17,244	100.8
Community food services	62421	2,988	1,598	69,597	324	14,119	23.0
Community housing services	62422	4,737	2,954	49,082	1,079	17,928	60.2
Emergency & other relief services	62423	1,881	1,534	86,647	336	18,975	17.7
Vocational rehabilitation services	6243	5,668	6,462	23,956	3,093	11,468	269.7
Vocational rehabilitation services	62431	5,668	6,462	23,956	3,093	11,468	269.7
Child day care services	6244	18,099	5,757	23,988	3,015	12,564	240.0
Child day care services	62441	18,099	5,757	23,988	3,015	12,564	240.0

[1] North American Industry Classification System, 1997; see text, Section 32, Economic Census 1997.

Source: U.S. Census Bureau, *1997 Economic Census, Health Care and Social Insurance,* Series EC97562A-US, issued October 1999.

1997 Economic Census 883

No. 1457. Arts, Entertainment, and Recreation (Tax-Exempt)—Establishments Revenue, Payroll, and Employees by Kind of Business (NAICS Basis): 1997

Kind of business	NAICS code [1]	Estab-lish-ments (number)	Revenue		Annual payroll		Paid employee for pay period including March 12 (1,000)
			Total (mil. dol.)	Per paid employee (dol.)	Total (mil. dol.)	Per paid employee (dol.)	
Arts, entertainment, & recreation . .	**71**	**19,463**	**19,627**	**51,610**	**6,683**	**17,575**	**380.3**
Performing arts, spectator sports	711	4,624	4,876	53,681	1,622	17,852	90.8
Performing arts companies	7111	3,316	3,299	46,987	1,273	18,135	70.2
Theater companies & dinner theaters. . .	71111	1,647	1,776	54,135	631	19,223	32.8
Dance companies	71112	371	323	47,399	131	19,208	6.8
Musical groups & artists	71113	1,211	1,154	38,767	499	16,756	29.8
Other performing arts companies	71119	87	45	56,119	13	15,726	0.8
Promoters of performing arts, sports, & similar events	7113	1,308	1,577	76,461	348	16,890	20.6
Promoters of performing arts, sports, & similar events w/facility	71131	371	846	62,269	225	16,581	13.6
Promoters of performing arts, sports, & similar events w/o facilities	71132	937	731	103,851	123	17,487	7.0
Museums, historical sites, & similar institutions	712	4,793	6,280	74,328	1,715	20,294	84.5
Museums	71211	3,434	4,529	75,334	1,212	20,167	60.1
Historical sites	71212	814	343	50,704	101	15,020	6.8
Zoos & botanical gardens	71213	269	1,279	81,326	364	23,162	15.7
Nature parks & other similar institutions .	71219	276	129	68,539	36	19,319	1.9
Amusement, gambling, & recreation industries.	713	10,046	8,470	41,327	3,347	16,331	205.0
Other amusement & recreation industries. .	7139	10,046	8,470	41,327	3,347	16,331	205.0
Golf courses & country clubs	71391	3,212	5,583	48,145	2,291	19,761	116.0
Fitness & recreational sports centers . . .	71394	4,679	2,217	29,288	859	11,343	75.7
All other amusement & recreational industries	71399	2,155	670	50,410	197	14,809	13.3

[1] North American Industry Classification System, 1997; see text, Section 32, Economic Census 1997.

Source: U.S. Census Bureau, *1997 Economic Census, Arts, Entertainment, and Recreation*, Series EC97571A-US(RV), issued April 2000.

No. 1458. Other Services (Tax-Exempt)—Establishments, Revenue, Payroll, and Employees by Kind of Business (NAICS Basis): 1997

Kind of business	NAICS code [1]	Estab-lish-ments (number)	Revenue		Annual payroll		Paid employee for pay period including March 12 (1,000)
			Total (mil. dol.)	Per paid employee (dol.)	Total (mil. dol.)	Per paid employee (dol.)	
Other services (except public administration)	**81**	**98,765**	**102,864**	**134,886**	**17,068**	**22,381**	**762.6**
Grantmaking & giving services	8132	11,906	48,957	467,113	3,080	29,391	104.8
Social advocacy organizations	8133	10,120	7,525	88,481	2,003	23,554	85.0
Civic & social organizations	8134	28,364	9,916	37,956	2,683	10,269	261.3
Civic & social organizations	81341	28,364	9,916	37,956	2,683	10,269	261.3
Business, professional, labor, political & similar organizations	8139	48,375	36,467	117,071	9,301	29,860	311.5
Business associations.	81391	16,928	14,859	128,000	4,180	36,007	116.1
Professional organizations	81392	7,239	8,292	132,942	2,265	36,306	62.4
Other similar organizations (exc. bus, prof., labor, & political).	81399	24,208	13,316	100,094	2,857	21,474	133.0

[1] North American Industry Classification System, 1997; see text, Section 32, Economic Census 1997.

Source: U.S. Census Bureau, *1997 Economic Census, Other Services*, Series EC97581A-US,

Appendix I
Guide to—Sources of Statistics, State Statistical Abstracts, and Foreign Statistical Abstracts

Alphabetically arranged, this guide contains references to the important primary sources of statistical information for the United States published since 1990. Secondary sources have been included if the information contained in them is presented in a particularly convenient form or if primary sources are not readily available. Nonrecurrent publications presenting compilations or estimates for years later than 1990 or types of data not available in regular series are also included.

Much valuable information may also be found in state reports, foreign statistical abstracts, which are included at the end of this appendix and in reports for particular commodities, industries, or similar segments of our economic and social structures, many of which are not included here.

Publications listed under each subject are divided into two main groups: "U.S. Government" and "Nongovernment." The location of the publisher of each report is given except for Federal agencies located in Washington, DC. Most Federal publications may be purchased from the Superintendent of Documents, U.S. Government Printing Office, Washington, DC 20402, tel. 202-512-1800, (Web site <http://www.access.gpo.gov> or from Government Printing Office bookstores in certain major cities. In some cases, Federal publications may be obtained from the issuing agency.

U.S. GOVERNMENT

Administrative Office of the United States Courts
Calendar Year Reports on Authorized Wiretaps. (State and Federal.)
Federal Court Management Statistics. Annual.
Federal Judicial Caseload Statistics. Annual.
Judicial Business of the United States Courts.
Statistical Tables for the Federal Judiciary. Semiannual.

Agency for International Development
U.S. Overseas Loans and Grants and Assistance From International Organizations. Annual.

Army, Corps of Engineers
Waterborne Commerce of the United States (in five parts). Annual.

Board of Governors of the Federal Reserve System
Annual Statistical Digest.
Domestic Offices, Commercial Bank Assets and Liabilities Consolidated Report of Condition. Quarterly.
Federal Reserve Banks. Monthly review published by each Bank with special reference to its own Federal Reserve District.

Board of Governors of the Federal Reserve System —Con.
Federal Reserve Bulletin. Monthly. (Also monthly releases on industrial production indexes.)
Flow of Funds Accounts of the United States: Flows and outstandings. Z.1(780). Quarterly.
Industrial Production and Capacity Utilization G.17. Monthly.
Money Stock and Debt Measures. H.6. Weekly.

Bureau of Alcohol, Tobacco, and Firearms
Alcohol and Tobacco Summary Statistics. Annual.

Bureau of Economic Analysis
National Income and Product Accounts of the United States, 1929-1997: Statistical Tables, early 2001.
Survey of Current Business. Monthly. (March, June, September, and December issues contain data on U.S. international transactions. Articles on foreign direct investment in the United States, U.S. direct investment abroad, and other topics appear periodically in other issues.)
U.S. Direct Investment Abroad: 1994 Benchmark Survey, 1998.

Bureau of Economic Analysis —Con.

U.S. Direct Investment Abroad: Operations of U.S. Parent Companies and their Foreign Affiliates. Preliminary, 1997. Estimates, 1999

Bureau of Justice Statistics

Age patterns of victims of serious violent crimes. September 1997.

Alcohol and crime: An analysis of national data on the prevalence of alcohol involvement in crime. April 1998.

Campus law enforcement agencies, 1995. December 1996.

Capital punishment. Annual. 1996. December 1997.

Carjacking in U.S., 1992-96. March 1996.

Census of state and local law enforcement agencies, 1996. June 1998.

Changes in criminal victimization, 1994-95. April 1997.

Characteristics of adults on probation, 1995, December 1997.

Child victimizers: Violent offenders and their victims. March 1996.

Civil Justice Survey of State Courts, 1992, CD-ROM. July 1996.

Comparing case processing statistics. September 1996.

Contract cases in large counties: Civil Justice Survey of State Courts, 1992. February 1996.

Correctional populations in the United States annual.

Criminal Victimization in the United States Annual.

Expenditure and Employment Data for the Criminal Justice System. Annual.

Federal criminal case processing, 1997. June 1998.

Federal law enforcement officers, 1996. January 1998.

Federal tort trials and verdicts, 1994-95. January 1998.

Felony defendants in large urban counties: Biennial.

Felony sentences in state courts. Biennial.

Felony sentences in the United States. Biennial.

Female victims of violent crime. December 1996.

Firearm injury from crime: Firearms, crime, and criminal justice. April 1996.

HIV in prisons and jails 1995. August 1997.

Households Touched by Crime. Annual.

Indigent defense. February 1996.

Justice expenditure and employment in the United States, 1990. May 1998.

Juvenile delinquents in the Federal criminal justice system. February 1997.

Juveniles prosecuted in state criminal courts, 1994: National Survey of Prosecutors. March 1997.

Lifetime likelihood of going to state or Federal prison. March 1997.

Bureau of Justice Statistics —Con.

Local police departments, 1993: A LEMAS report. April 1996.

Motor Vehicle Theft

National Corrections Reporting Program. Annual.

Noncitizens in the Federal criminal justice system: Federal Justice Statistics Program. August 1996.

Parole in the United States Annual.

Presale firearm checks: A national estimate. February 1997.

Prison and jail inmates 1995. August 1996.

Prison and jail inmates at midyear, 1997. January 1998.

Prisoner petitions in the Federal courts, 1980-96

Prisoners in State and Federal Institutions. Annual.

Probation and parole populations, 1996. August 1997.

Profile of jail inmates, 1996. April 1998.

Prosecutors in state courts. Biennial.

Sex differences in violent victimization, 1994. September 1997.

Sex offenses and offenders. January 1997.

Sheriffs' departments 1993. June 1996.

Sourcebook of criminal justice statistics, 1994-95 editions, CD-ROM. October 1997.

State court sentencing of convicted felons. Biennial.

Students' reports of school crime: 1989 and 1995. April 1998.

Substance abuse and treatment of adults on probation, 1995. March 1998.

Survey of state criminal history information systems, 1995. May 1997.

Violence by intimates: Analysis of data on crimes by current or former spouses, boyfriends, and girlfriends. March 1998.

Violence-related injuries treated in hospital emergency departments. August 1997.

Bureau of Labor Statistics

Comparative Labor Force Statistics, Ten Countries. Annual.

Compensation and Working Conditions. Quarterly.

Consumer Expenditure Survey, Integrated Diary and Interview Survey data.

Consumer Prices: Energy and Food. Monthly.

CPI Detailed Report. Monthly.

Employee Benefits in Medium and Large Firms. Biennial.

Employee Benefits in Small Private Establishments. Biennial.

Employee Benefits in State and Local Governments. Biennial.

Employer Costs for Employee Compensation. Annual.

Employment and Earnings. Monthly.

Employment and Wages. Annual.

Bureau of Labor Statistics —Con.

Employment Cost Index. Quarterly.

Employment Cost Indexes and Levels. Annual.

Employment, Hours, and Earnings, United States, 1988-96. 1996. (Bulletin 2481.)

Employment Outlook: 1994-2005. (Bulletin 2472.)

The Employment Situation. Monthly.

Geographic Profile of Employment and Unemployment. Annual.

International Comparisons of Hourly Compensation Costs for Production Workers in Manufacturing. Annual.

International Comparisons of Manufacturing Productivity and Unit Labor Cost Trends. Annual.

Monthly Labor Review.

Occupational Injuries and Illnesses in the United States by Industry. Annual.

Occupational Projections and Training Data. Biennial.

Producer Price Indexes. Detailed report. Monthly, with annual supplement.

Productivity Measures for Selected Industries and Government Services. Annual.

Real Earnings. Monthly.

Relative Importance of Components in the Consumer Price Indexes. Annual.

State and Metropolitan Area Employment and Unemployment. Monthly.

U.S. Import and Export Price Indexes. Monthly.

Usual Weekly Earnings of Wage and Salary Workers. Quarterly.

Work Experience of the Population. Annual.

Bureau of Land Management

Public Land Statistics. Annual.

Bureau of Mines

Minerals Yearbook. Annual.

Bureau of the Mint

Annual Report of the Director.

Bureau of Reclamation

Summary Statistics:

Vol. I, Water, Land, and Related Data.

Census Bureau

Major reports, such as the Census of Population, which consist of many volumes, are listed by their general, all-inclusive titles. In most cases, separate reports of the most recent censuses are available for each state, subject, industry, etc.

Annual Benchmark Report for Retail Trade.

Annual Benchmark Report for Wholesale Trade.

Annual Survey of Communication Services.

Annual Survey of Manufactures. (1996, most recent.)

Census of Construction Industries. Quinquennial. (1997, most recent.)

Census Bureau —Con.

Census of Finance, Insurance, and Real Estate Industries. Quinquennial. (1997, most recent.)

Census of Governments. Quinquennial.

Compendium of Public Employment. Series GC, Vol. 3.

Employee-Retirement Systems of State and Local Governments. Series GC, Vol. 4.

Employment of Major Local Governments. Series GC, Vol. 3.

Finances of County Governments. Series GC, Vol. 4.

Government Organization. Series GC, Vol. 1.

Public Education Finances. Series GC, Vol. 4.

Census of Housing. Decennial. (1990, most recent.)

Census of Manufactures. Quinquennial. (1997, most recent.)

Census of Mineral Industries. Quinquennial.(1997, most recent.)

Census of Population. Decennial. (1990, most recent.)

Census of Retail Trade. Quinquennial. (1997, most recent.)

Census of Service Industries. Quinquennial. (1997, most recent.)

Census of Transportation. Communications, and Utilities. Quinquennial. (1997, most recent.)

Census of Wholesale Trade. Quinquennial. (1997, most recent.)

City Employment. Annual. (GE90 No. 2.)

Congressional District Data:

1990 Census of Population and Housing, 1990 CPH-4, Congressional Districts of the 103rd Congress.

CFFR Consolidated Federal Funds Report. Annual.

Volume I County Areas

Volume II Subcounty Areas

County Business Patterns. Annual.

Current Construction Reports: Housing Starts, C20 (monthly); New Residential Construction in Selected Metropolitan Statistical Areas, C21 (quarterly); Housing Completions, C22 (monthly); New One-Family Houses Sold and for Sale, C25 (monthly with annual report, Characteristics of New Housing); Price Index of New One-Family Houses Sold, C27 (quarterly); Value of Construction Put in Place, C30 (monthly with occasional historical supplement); Housing Units Authorized by Building Permits, C40 (monthly and annual); Residential Improvements and Repairs, C50 (quarterly and annual).

Current Housing Reports: Housing Vacancies, H111 (quarterly and annual); What We Have Learned About Properties, Owners, and Tenants From the 1995 Property Owners and Managers Survey, H121; Who Can Afford to Buy a House, H121 (biennial) Market Absorption of Apartments,

Census Bureau —Con.

H130 (quarterly and annual); Characteristics of Apartments Completed, H131 (annual); American Housing Survey for the United States, H150 (biennial); American Housing Survey for Selected Metropolitan Areas, H170; Survey for Selected Metropolitan Areas.

Current Industrial Report, Survey of Pollution Abatement Costs and Expenditures, series MA200.

Current Population Reports. (Series P20.)

Estimates and Projections, P25, Consumer Income and Poverty, P60 and Household Economic Studies, P70.

Economic Census of Outlying Area. Quinquennial.

FAS Federal Aid to States for Fiscal Year. Annual.

FES Federal Expenditures by State for Fiscal Year. Annual.

International Briefs. (Series IB.)

International Population Reports. (Series IPC.)

Manufacturing Profiles. (Series MP-1.) Annual.

Manufacturers' Shipments, Inventories, and Orders. Monthly.

Manufacturers' Shipments, Inventories, and Orders: 1987-96. Annual summary. (Current Industrial Reports M3-1(95).)

Manufacturers' Shipments to Federal Government Agencies. (Current Industrial Reports MA-175.) Conducted for economic census years ending in 2 and 7.)

Merchant Wholesalers Measures of Value Produced, Capital Expenditures, Depreciable Assets, and Operating Expenses. (1997, most recent.)

Minority-Owned Businesses. Quinquennial. (1997, Most recent.)

Monthly Retail Trade Report. Sales and Inventories.

Monthly Wholesale Trade Report. Sales and Inventories.

Population Profile of the United States. (Biennial Series P23.)

Quarterly Financial Report for Manufacturing, Mining, and Trade Corporations.

Selected Characteristics of Retail Trade-Measures of Value Produced, Capital Expenditures, Depreciable Assets, and Operating Expenses. (1992, most recent.)

Selected Characteristics of Selected Service Industries—Capital Expenditures, Depreciable Assets, and Operating Expenses. (1992, most recent.)

Service Annual Survey Report.

Special Studies Reports. (Series on Special Studies, P23.)

Summary of U.S. International Trade in Goods and Services: includes cumulative data. (FT 900.)

Survey of the Origin of Exports of Manufacturing Establishments. Triennial. (Current Industrial Reports M76 (AS)-8.)

Census Bureau —Con.

Survey of Plant Capacity Utilization. (Current Industrial Reports MQ-C1.)

Transportation Annual Survey.

Truck Inventory and Use Survey. Quinquennial. (1997, most recent.)

U.S. Commodity Exports and Imports as Related to Output. Annual. (Series ES2.)

U.S. Trade with Puerto Rico and U.S. Possessions. Monthly and Annual. (FT 895.)

World Population Profile: 1998 (Series WP.)

Centers for Disease Control and Prevention, Atlanta, GA

Morbidity and Mortality Weekly Report. Annual.

Coast Guard

Annual Report of the Secretary of Transportation.

Marine Casualty Statistics. Annual.

Polluting Incidents in and Around U.S. Waters. Annual.

Comptroller of the Currency

Quarterly Journal.

Congressional Clerk of the House

Statistics of the Presidential and Congressional Election Years. Biennial.

Council of Economic Advisers

Economic Indicators. Monthly.

Economic Report of the President. Annual.

Council on Environmental Quality

Environmental Quality. Annual.

Department of Agriculture

Agricultural Chemical Usage. Field crops, vegetables (fruits and vegetables alternate years), restricted use pesticides. Chemical application rates and acres treated, selected states and U.S. Annual.

Agricultural Income and Finance. Situation and Outlook Report. Quarterly.

Agricultural Outlook. 11 issues per year.

Agricultural Price Reports. Reports on prices received for farm commodities, prices paid for farm supplies, indexes and parity ratios. Monthly and annual.

Agriculture and Trade Reports (five per year).

Western Europe

China

Developing Economies

Pacific Rim

USSR

CATFISH. 12 issues of Catfish processing, Catfish and Trout Production. Annual.

Census of Agriculture. Quinquennial. (1997, most recent.)

Cotton ginnings and winter wheat and rye seedings.

Crop Production Reports. Acreage, yield, and production of various commodities. Monthly and annual.

Department of Agriculture —Con.

Crop Values Report. Price and value of various commodities. Annual.

Dairy Product Prices. U.S. cheddar cheese, butter, nonfat dry milk, and dry whey prices and sales volumes. Regional cheddar cheese prices and sales volumes. Weekly.

Economic Indicators of the Farm Sector. A series of five annual issues.

Economic Research Service. Monthly.

Farm Labor. Quarterly.

Farmline. 11 issues per year.

Farm Numbers, Value. Farm numbers and land in farms, agricultural cash rents, agricultural land values, foreign ownership of U.S. Agricultural Land (ERS). Annual.

Financial Characteristics of U.S. (Agriculture Information Bulletin. No. 569.) Annual.

Food Consumption, Prices, and Expenditures, 1996. (Statistical Bulletin No. 928.) Revised annually.

Food Marketing Review, (Agricultural Economic Report No. 743). Revised annually.

Food Review. Quarterly.

Food Spending in American Households. (Statistical Bulletin No. 824.) Annual.

Foreign Agricultural Trade of the United States (FATUS). Bimonthly with annual supplements on calendar year and fiscal year trade statistics.

Fruit and Vegetable Reports. Acreage, yield, production, value, and utilization of various fruits and vegetables. Periodic.

Geographic Area Series (Internet, CD-ROM, Print), Volume 1

Journal of Agricultural Economics Research. Quarterly.

Livestock and Meat Statistics, 1970-92. (Statistical Bulletin No. 874.) Annual.

Livestock Reports. Cattle, Cattle on Feed, Hogs and Pigs. Sheep, Goats, Wool, and Mohair. Monthly, Quarterly, and Annual.

Milk and Dairy Products Reports. Milk cows, milk production, and dairy products. Monthly and Annual.

Other Reports. Reports on varied items including cold storage, catfish, cherries, cranberries, trout, farm employment and wages, farm production expenditures, mink, mushrooms, and floriculture crops. Monthly and annual.

Poultry and Egg Reports. Reports covering eggs, chickens, turkeys, hatcheries, egg products, and poultry slaughter. Weekly, monthly, annual.

Rural Conditions and Trends. Quarterly.

Rural Development Perspectives. Three issues per year.

Situation and Outlook Reports. Issued for agricultural exports, cotton and wool, dairy, feed, fruit and tree nuts, agricultural resources, livestock and poultry, oil

Department of Agriculture —Con.

crops, rice, aquaculture, sugar and sweeteners, tobacco, vegetables, wheat, and world agriculture. Periodic.

Stock Reports. Stocks of grain, hops, peanuts, potatoes, rice, and soybeans. Quarterly, annual, periodic.

U.S. Egg and Poultry Statistical Series, 1960-92. (Statistical Bulletin No. 872.) Periodic.

Usual planting and harvesting dates. Dates for major field crops. Periodic.

Weekly Weather and Crop Bulletin. Report summarizing weather and its effect on crops the previous week. Weekly.

Department of Agriculture, Food and Nutrition Service

Annual Historical Review:

Food and Consumer Service Programs.

Department of Defense

Foreign Military Sales and Military Assistance Facts. Annual.

Department of Education

Rehabilitation Services Administration

Annual Report.

Department of Health and Human Services

Annual Report.

Department of Housing and Urban Development

Survey of Mortgage Lending Activity. Monthly and quarterly press releases.

Department of Labor

Annual Report of the Secretary.

Department of State

United States Contribution to International Organizations. Issued in the House Documents series. Annual.

Department of State, Bureau of Consular Affairs

Report of the Visa Office. Annual. (Dept. of State Pub. 8810.)

Summary of Passport Statistics. Annual.

Department of Transportation

Airport Activity Statistics of Certified Route Air Carriers. Annual.

Condition and Performance Report. 1999. Biennial.

National Transportation Statistics, 1998.

Report of Passenger Travel Between the United States and Foreign Countries. Annual, semiannual, quarterly. Monthly.

Transportation Safety Information Report. Quarterly.

U.S. International Air Travel Statistics. Annual.

Department of the Treasury

Active Foreign Credits of the United States Government. Quarterly.

Consolidated Financial Statements of the United States Government. (Prototype.)

Daily Treasury Statement.

Monthly Statement of the Public Debt of the United States.

Monthly Treasury Statement of Receipts and Outlays of the United States Government.

Statement of United States Currency and Coin. Monthly.

Treasury Bulletin. Quarterly.

United States Government Annual Report and Appendix.

Department of Veterans Affairs

Annual Report of The Secretary of Veterans Affairs.

Disability Compensation, Pension, and Death Pension Data. Annual.

Government Life Insurance Programs for Veterans and Members of the Service. Annual.

Loan Guaranty Highlights. Quarterly.

Projections of The Veteran Population by State and County to the Year 2010.

Selected Compensation and Pension Data by State of Residence. Annual.

State and County Veteran Population Estimates. Annual.

Summary of Medical Programs. Annual.

Drug Enforcement Administration

Drug Abuse and Law Enforcement Statistics. Irregular.

Employment and Training Administration

Employment and Training Report of the President. Annual.

Unemployment Insurance Claims. Weekly.

Energy Information Administration

Annual Energy Outlook.

Annual Energy Review.

Coal Industry Annual.

Cost and Quality of Fuels for Electric Utility Plants. Annual.

Electric Power Annual.

Electric Power Monthly.

Electric Sales and Revenue. Annual.

Financial Statistics of Selected Electric Utilities. Annual.

International Energy Annual.

International Energy Outlook.

Inventory of Power Plants in the United States. Annual.

Monthly Energy Review.

Natural Gas Annual.

Natural Gas Monthly.

Performance Profiles of Major Energy Producers. Annual.

Petroleum Marketing Monthly.

Energy Information Administration —Con.

Petroleum Supply Annual.

Petroleum Supply Monthly.

Quarterly Coal Report.

Renewable Energy Annual.

Residential Energy Consumption Survey: Housing Characteristics. Triennial.

Residential Transportation Energy Consumption Survey. Triennial.

Short-Term Energy Outlook. Quarterly.

State Energy Data Report. Annual.

State Energy Price and Expenditure Report. Annual.

Uranium Industry Annual.

U.S. Crude Oil, Natural Gas, and Natural Gas Liquids Reserves. Annual.

Weekly Coal Production.

Energy Research and Development Administration

The Nuclear Industry. Annual.

Environmental Protection Agency

Air Quality Data. Annual.

Cost of Clean Water. Annual.

Federal Certification Test Results for Motor Vehicles. Annual.

Municipal Water Facilities Inventory. Quinquennial.

National Air Pollutant Emission Trends, 1900-98.

National Air Quality and Emissions Trends Report. 1998. Annual

Needs Survey, Conveyance and Treatment of Municipal Wastewater Summaries of Technical Data. Biennial.

Pesticides Monitoring Journal. Quarterly.

Radiation Data and Reports. Monthly.

Sewage Facility Construction. Annual.

Summary of Water Enforcement Actions Pursued by EPA since December 3, 1970. (Updated continuously.)

Export-Import Bank of the United States

Annual Report.

Report to the U.S. Congress on Export Credit Competition and the Export-Import Bank of the United States. Annual.

Farm Credit Administration.

Annual Report on the Work of the Cooperative Farm Credit System.

Loans and Discounts of Farm Credit Banks and Associations. Annual.

Production Credit Association: Summary of Operations. Annual.

Report to the Federal Land Bank Associations. Annual.

Federal Bureau of Investigation

Bomb Summary. Annual.

Crime in the United States. Annual.

Hate Crime Statistics. Annual.

U.S. Census Bureau, Statistical Abstract of the United States: 2000

Federal Bureau of Investigation —Con.

Law Enforcement Officers Killed and Assaulted. Annual.

Federal Communications Commission

Annual Report.

Statistics of Communications Common Carriers. Annual.

Federal Deposit Insurance Corporation

Annual Report.

Data Book-Operating Banks and Branches. Annual.

Quarterly Banking Profile.

Quarterly Banking Review.

Statistics on Banking. Annual, and Historical 1934-1996, Volume I.

Trust Assets of Insured Commercial Banks. Annual.

Federal Highway Administration

Highway Statistics. Annual.

Federal Railroad Administration

Accident/Incident Bulletin. Summary, statistics, and analysis of accidents on railroads in the United States. Annual.

Rail-Highway Crossing Accident/Incident and Inventory Bulletin. Annual.

Forest Service

An Analysis of the Timber Situation in the United States: 1989-2040.

Land Areas of the National Forest System. Annual.

The 1993 RPA Timber Assessment Update. Forthcoming.

U.S. Timber Production, Trade, Consumption, and Price Statistics. Annual.

Fish and Wildlife Service

Federal Aid in Fish and Wildlife Restoration. Annual.

1996 National Survey of Fishing, Hunting, and Wildlife Associated Recreation.

General Services Administration

Inventory Report on Real Property Leased to the United States Throughout the World. Annual.

Inventory Report on Real Property Owned by the United States throughout the World. Annual.

Geological Survey

A Statistical Summary of Data from the U.S. Geological Survey's National Water Quality Networks. (Open-File Report 83-533.)

Mineral Commodity Summaries. Annual.

Mineral Industry Surveys. (Monthly, quarterly, or annual report.)

Minerals Yearbook. (Monthly, quarterly, or annual report.)

Health Care Financing Administration

Health Care Financing Review. Medicare and Medicaid Statistical Supplement. Annual.

Health Care Financing Research Reports. Occasional.

Health Care Financing Review. Quarterly.

Immigration and Naturalization Service

I&N Reporter. Quarterly.

Statistical Yearbook of the Immigration and Naturalization Service. Annual.

Wage Statistics of Class I Railroads in the United States. Annual. (Statement No. 300.)

International Trade Administration

International Construction Review. Quarterly.

Electric Current Abroad. Irregular. (1998, most recent.)

U.S. Foreign Trade Highlights. Annual.

U.S. Global Trade Outlook. Irregular. Discontinued

U.S. Industry and Trade Outlook. Annual. (2000, most recent.)

International Trade Commission

Synthetic Organic Chemicals, U.S. Production and Sales. Annual.

Internal Revenue Service

Corporation Income Tax Returns. Annual.

IRS Data Book.

Statistics of Income Bulletin. Quarterly.

Statistics of Income Division. (Annual report on Corporation Income Tax Returns. Periodic compendiums on Studies of International Income and Taxes.)

Interstate Commerce Commission

Class I Freight Railroads Selected Earnings Data. Quarterly.

Monthly Report of Class I Railroad Employees, by Group. (Statement No. 350.)

Quarterly Report.

Transport Statistics in the United States. Issued annually in two separate parts:

Part 1: Railroads

Part 2: Motor Carriers

Library of Congress

Annual Report.

Maritime Administration

Annual Report.

Employment Report of United States Flag Merchant Fleet Ocean-going Vessels 1,000 Gross Tons and Over. Quarterly.

Seafaring Wage Rates. Biennial.

Mine Safety and Health Administration

Informational Reports by Mining Industry: Coal; Metallic Minerals; Nonmetallic Minerals (except stone and coal); Stone, Sand, and Gravel. Annual.

Mine Injuries and Worktime. (Some preliminary data.) Quarterly.

National Advisory Council on International Monetary and Financial Policies

Annual Report to the President and to the Congress.

National Aeronautics and Space Administration

Annual Procurement Report.

The Civil Service Work Force.

The National Agricultural Library

(For technical agricultural publications)
Annual Report

National Center for Education Statistics

College and University Library Survey.

The Condition of Education. Annual.

Digest of Education Statistics. Annual.

Earned Degrees Conferred. Annual.

Faculty Salaries, Tenure, and Benefits. Annual.

Fall Enrollment in Colleges and Universities. Annual.

Fall Staff in Postsecondary Institutions. Biennial.

Financial Statistics of Higher Education.

National Assessment of Educational Progress.

Private School Survey. Biennial.

Projections of Education Statistics. Annual.

Revenues and Expenditures for Public Elementary and Secondary Education. Annual.

School and Staffing Survey. Quadrennial.

Statistics of Public Elementary and Secondary School Systems. Fall. Annual.

National Center for Health Statistics

Ambulatory Care Visits to Physician Offices, Hospital Outpatient Departments and Emergency Departments. Annual.

Health: United States. Annual. (DHHS Pub. No. PHS year-1232.)

National Hospital Discharge Survey: Annual Summary. Annual.

National Vital Statistics Reports (NVRS.) Monthly.

Vital and Health Statistics. (A series of statistical reports covering health-related topics.)

Series 10: Health Interview Survey Statistics. Irregular.

Current Estimates from the Health Interview Survey. Annual.

National Center for Health Statistics —Con.

Series 11: Health and Nutrition Examination Survey Statistics. Irregular.

Series 13: Health Resources Utilization Statistics. Irregular.

Series 14: Health Resources: Manpower and Facilities Statistics. Irregular.

Series 20: Mortality Data. Irregular.

Series 21: Natality, Marriage, and Divorce Data. Irregular.

Series 23: National Survey of Family Growth Statistics. Irregular.

Vital Statistics of the United States. Annual.

Volume I, Natality

Volume II, Mortality

Volume III, Marriage and Divorce

Internet address:
<http://www.cdc.gov/nchswww/>

National Credit Union Administration

Annual Report.

Midyear Statistics.

Year-end Statistics.

National Guard Bureau

Annual Review of the Chief.

The National Library of Medicine

(for clinical medical reports)
Annual Report.

National Oceanic and Atmospheric Administration

Climates of the World, HCS 6-4. Monthly and annual.

Climatological Data. Issued in sections for states and outlying areas. Monthly with annual summary.

Climatography of the United States, No. 20, Supplement No. 1, Freeze/Frost Data.

Comparative Climatic Data. Annual.

Daily Normals of Temp, Precip, HDD, & CDD/Clim 84. Periodic.

General Summary of Tornadoes. Annual.

Hourly Precipitation Data. Monthly with annual summary; for each state.

Local Climatological Data. Monthly with annual summary; for major cities.

Monthly Climatic Data for the World. Monthly.

Monthly Normals of Temp, Precip, HDD, & CDD/Clim 84. Periodic.

Storm Data. Monthly.

Weekly Weather and Crop Bulletin. National summary.

National Park Service

Federal Recreation Fee Report. Annual.

National Park Statistical Abstract. Annual.

National Science Foundation

Academic Research and Development Expenditures. Detailed Statistical Tables. Annual

National Science Foundation —Con.

Academic Science and Engineering: Graduate Enrollment and Support: Detailed Statistical Tables. Annual

Characteristics of Doctoral Scientists and Engineers in the United States. Detailed Statistical Tables. Biennial.

Characteristics of Recent Science/Engineering Graduates. Detailed Statistical Tables. Biennial.

Federal Funds for Research and Development. Detailed Statistical Tables. Annual.

Federal R&D Funding by Budget Function. Report. Annual.

Federal Science and Engineering Support to Universities, Colleges, and Nonprofit Institutions. Detailed Statistical Tables. Annual.

Federal Support to Universities, Colleges, and Nonprofit Institutions. Detailed Statistical Tables. Annual.

Graduate Students and Postdoctorates in Science and Engineering. Annual.

Immigrant Scientists, Engineers and Technicians. Detailed Statistical Tables. Annual.

International Science and Technology Data Update. Report. Annual.

National Patterns of R&D Resources. Report. Annual.

Planned R&D Expenditures of Major U.S. Firms. Special Report. (NSF 91-306.)

Research and Development in Industry. Detailed Statistical Tables. Annual.

Science and Engineering Degrees. Annual.

Science and Engineering Degrees, by Race/Ethnicity of Recipients. Detailed Statistical Tables. Annual.

Science and Engineering Doctorates Awards. Detailed Statistical Tables. Annual.

Science and Engineering Indicators. Report. Biennial.

Science and Engineering Personnel: A National Overview. Report. Biennial.

Science and Engineering Profiles. Annual.

Science and Technology Pocket Data Book. Report. Annual.

Science Resources Studies. Data Brief. Frequent.

Scientific and Engineering Research Facilities at Universities and Colleges. Report. Biennial.

Scientists, Engineers, and Technicians in Manufacturing Industries. Detailed Statistical Tables. Triennial.

Scientists, Engineers, and Technicians in Nonmanufacturing Industries. Detailed Statistical Tables. Triennial.

Scientists, Engineers, and Technicians in Trade and Regulated Industries. Detailed Statistical Tables. Triennial.

Survey of Direct U.S. Private Capital Investment in Research and Development Facilities in Japan. Report. (NSH 91-312.)

National Science Foundation —Con.

U.S. Scientists and Engineers. Detailed Statistical Tables. Biennial.

Women, Minorities, and Persons with Disabilities. Report. Biennial

Woman, Minorities in Science and Engineering. Report. Biennial.

National Transportation Safety Board

Accidents; Air Carriers. Annual.

Accidents; General Aviation. Annual.

Office of Civil Defense

Annual Statistical Report.

Office of Management and Budget

The Budget of the United States Government. Annual.

Office of Personnel Management

Civil Service Retirement and Disability Fund. Report. Annual.

Demographic Profile of the Federal Workforce. Biennial. (Even years.)

Employment and Trends. Bimonthly. (Odd months.)

Employment by Geographic Area. Biennial. (Even years.)

The Fact Book. Annual.

Occupations of Federal White-Collar and Blue-Collar Workers. Biennial. (Odd years.)

Pay Structure of the Federal Civil Service. Annual.

Statistical Abstract for the Federal Employee Benefit Programs. Annual.

Work Years and Personnel Costs. Annual.

Office of Thrift Supervision

Annual Report.

Patent and Trademark Office

Commissioner of Patents and Trademarks Annual Report.

Technology Assessment and Forecast Reports

"All Technologies." Annual.

"Patenting Trends in the United States." Annual.

"State Country." Annual.

Railroad Retirement Board, Chicago, IL

Annual Report.

Monthly Benefit Statistics.

Statistical Supplement to the Annual Report.

Rehabilitation Services Administration

Annual Report.

Caseload Statistics of State Vocational Rehabilitation Agencies in Fiscal Year. Annual.

U.S. Census Bureau, Statistical Abstract of the United States: 2000

Rural Electrification Administration

Annual Statistical Report—Rural Telephone Borrowers.

Securities and Exchange Commission

Annual Report.

Small Business Administration

Annual Report.
Handbook of Small Business Data.
The State of Small Business.

Social Security Administration

Income of the Population 55 and over, 1994. 1996. 1998.
Public Social Welfare Expenditures, Fiscal Year 1995. Social Security Bulletin, No. 2, 1999.

Social Security Administration —Con.

Social Security Beneficiaries by State and County Data. Annual.
Social Security Bulletin. Quarterly with annual statistical supplement. (Data on Social Security Benefits, OASDI, Supplemental Security Income, Aid to Families with Dependent Children, Medicare, Medicaid, Low Income Home Energy Assistance, Food Stamps, Black Lung benefits, and other programs.)
Social Security Programs in the United States, 1997.
State Assistance Programs for SSI Recipients. Annual.
Supplemental Security Income, State and County Data. Annual.

NONGOVERNMENT

AAFRC Trust For Philanthropy, New York, NY

Giving USA. Annual.

Advisory Commission on Intergovernmental Relations, Washington, DC

Characteristics of Federal Grant-in-Aid Programs to State and Local Governments: Grants Funded FY 93. (Every 3 years.)
Changing Public Attitudes on Governments and Taxes. Annual.
Significant Features of Fiscal Federalism. Annual.

Aerospace Industries Association, Washington, DC

Aerospace Facts and Figures. Annual.
Aerospace Industry Year-End Review and Forecast. Annual.
Commercial Helicopter Shipments. Quarterly.
Employment in the Aerospace Industry. Monthly.
Exports of Aerospace Products. Quarterly.
Imports of Aerospace Products. Quarterly.
Manufacturing Production, Capacity, and Utilization in Aerospace and Aircraft and parts. Quarterly.
Orders, Shipments, Backlog and inventories for Aircraft, Missiles, & Parts. Quarterly.

Air Transport Association of America Inc., Washington, DC

Air Transport Association Annual Report.

The Alan Guttmacher Institute, New York, NY

Family Planning Perspectives. Bimonthly.

American Automobile Manufacturers Association, Detroit, MI

Motor Vehicle Facts and Figures. Annual
World Motor Vehicle Data. Annual.

American Bureau of Metal Statistics, Inc., Secaucus, NJ

Non-Ferrous Metal Data.

American Bureau of Shipping, Paramus, NJ

The Record. Annual with one supplement.

American Council on Education, Washington, DC

A Fact Book on Higher Education. Quarterly.
National Norms for Entering College Freshmen. Annual.

American Council of Life Insurance, Washington, DC

Life Insurance Fact Book. Biennial. (Odd years)

American Dental Association, Chicago, IL

Dental Statistics Handbook. Triennial.
Dental Students' Register. Annual.
Distribution of Dentists in the United States by Region and State. Triennial.
Survey of Dental Practice. Annual.

American Financial Services Association, Washington, DC

AFSA Annual Research Report and Second Mortgage Lending Report on Finance Companies. Annual.
AFSA Annual Research Report and Second Mortgage Lending Report Supplements. Annual.

American Forest & Paper Association, Washington, DC

Statistical Roundup.
Statistics of Paper, Paperboard, and Wood Pulp. Annual.
Wood Pulp and Fiber Statistics. Annual.

American Frozen Food Institute, Burlingame, CA

Frozen Food Pack Statistics. Annual.

American Gas Association, Arlington, VA
Gas Facts. Annual.

American Iron and Steel Institute, Washington, DC
Annual Statistical Report.

American Jewish Committee, New York, NY
American Jewish Year Book.

American Medical Association, Chicago, IL
Physician Characteristics and Distribution in the U.S. Annual.
Physician Marketplace Statistics. Annual.
Physician Socioeconomic Statistics. 1991-2000.
Socioeconomic Characteristics of Medical Practice. 1997/98.
U.S. Medical Licensure Statistics, and License Requirements. Annual.

American Metal Market, New York, NY
Daily Newspapers.
Metal Statistics. Annual.

American Osteopathic Association, Chicago, IL
Yearbook and Directory of Osteopathic Physicians. Annual.

American Petroleum Institute, Washington, DC
American Petroleum Institute, Independent Petroleum Association of America, and Mid-Continent Oil and Gas Association
The Basic Petroleum Data Book. Annual.
Petroleum Industry Environmental Report. Annual.
Quarterly Well Completion Report.

American Public Transportation Association, Washington, DC
Public Transportation Fact Book. Annual.
Internet address: <http://www.apta.com>

Association of American Railroads, Washington, DC
Analysis of Class I Railroads. Annual.
Cars of Revenue Freight Loaded. Weekly with annual summary.
Freight Commodity Statistics, Class I Railroads in the United States. Annual.
Yearbook of Railroad Facts.

Association of Racing Commissioners International, Inc., Lexington, KY
Statistical Reports on Greyhound Racing in the United States. Annual.
Statistical Reports on Horse Racing in the United States. Annual.
Statistical Reports on Jai Alai in the United States. Annual.

Book Industry Study Group, Inc., New York, NY
Consumer Research Study on Book Purchasing. Annual.

Bowker (R.R.) Company, New Providence, NJ
American Library Directory. Annual.
Bowker Annual Library and Book Trade Almanac.

Boy Scouts of America, Irving, TX
Annual Report.

Bridge Commodity Research Bureau, a Bridge Information Systems Inc., Chicago, IL. The Blue Line. Daily
Bridge News Summaries. Daily
Commodity Year Book Update Disk. (Three editions annually.)
CRB Commodity Index Report. Weekly.
CRB Commodity Year Book. Annual.
CRB Futures Perspective. Weekly.
CRB Infotech. CD
Electronic Futures Trend Analyzer. Daily.
Final Markets. End of day.
Futures Market Service. Weekly.
Futures Market Service Fundamental & Technical Commentary. Daily and weekly.
Price Service. Daily

The Bureau of National Affairs, Inc., Washington, DC
Basic Patterns in Union Contracts. Annual.
BNA's Employment Outlook. Quarterly.
BNA's Job Absence and Turnover. Quarterly.
Briefing Sessions on Employee Relations Workbook. Annual.
Calendar of Negotiations. Annual.
Directory of U.S. Labor Organizations. Annual.
National Labor Relations Board Election Statistics. Annual.
NLRB Representation and Decertification Elections Statistics. Quarterly.
PPF Survey (Personnel Policies Forum.) Three times a year.

Carl H. Pforzheimer & Co., New York, NY
Comparative Oil Company Statistics, 1999. Annual.

Chronicle of Higher Education, Inc., Washington, DC
Almanac. Annual.

College Entrance Examination Board, Princeton, NJ
National Report on College-Bound Seniors. Annual.

The Conference Board, New York, NY
The Conference Board Economic Times. Monthly.

U.S. Census Bureau, Statistical Abstract of the United States: 2000

Congressional Quarterly Inc., Washington, DC

America Votes. A handbook of contemporary American election statistics, compiled and edited by Richard M. Scammon, Alice V. McGillivray and Rhodes Cook. Biennial.

Corporation for Public Broadcasting, Washington, DC

Average Revenue Profiles for Public Broadcasting Grantees. Annual.

Frequently asked Questions About Public Broadcasting Periodic.

Public Broadcasting Stations' Income from State Governments and State Colleges & Universities Ranked State-By-State. Annual.

Public Radio and Television Programming Content by Category. Biennial.

The Council of State Governments, Lexington, KY

The Book of the States. Biennial.

State Administrative Officials Classified by Function. Biennial.

State Elective Officials and the Legislatures. Biennial.

State Legislative Leadership, Committees, and Staff. Biennial.

Credit Union National Association, Inc., Madison, WI

The Credit Union Report. Annual.

Credit Union Services Profile. Annual.

Operating Ratios and Spreads. Semiannual.

Dataquest Inc., San Jose, CA

Consolidated Data Base.

Dealerscope Merchandising, Philadelphia, PA

Merchandising. Annual.

Decker Communications, Inc., New York, NY

Marketing Communications. (Advertising.) Monthly.

Dodge, F.W., National Information Services Division, McGraw-Hill Information Systems Co., New York, NY

Dodge Construction Potentials. Monthly.

Dow Jones & Co., New York, NY

Wall Street Journal.

Daily except Saturdays, Sundays, and holidays.

The Dun & Bradstreet Corporation, Murray Hill, NJ

The Business Failure Record. Annual.

The Business Starts Record. Annual.

Monthly Business Failure Report.

Monthly Business Starts Report.

Monthly New Business Incorporations Report.

Edison Electric Institute, Washington, DC

Statistical Yearbook of the Electric Utility Industry. Annual.

Editor & Publisher Co., New York, NY

Editor & Publisher. Weekly.

International Year Book. Annual.

Market Guide. Annual.

Electronic Industries Alliance, Arlington, VA

Electronic Market Data Book. Annual.

Electronic Market Trends. Monthly.

Electronics Foreign Trade. Monthly.

ENO Transportation Foundation, Leesburg, VA

Transportation in America. midyear, annually with periodic supplements.

Euromonitor, London, England

Consumer Asia. Annual.

Consumer Canada 1996.

Consumer China. Annual.

Consumer Eastern Europe. Annual.

Consumer Europe. Annual.

Consumer International. Annual.

Consumer Latin America. Annual.

Consumer Mexico 1996.

Consumer USA 1996

European Marketing Data and Statistics. Annual.

International Marketing Data and Statistics. Annual.

World Economic Factbook. Annual.

Federal National Mortgage Association, Washington, DC

Annual Report.

Food and Agriculture Organization of the United Nations, Rome, Italy

Production Yearbook.

Trade Yearbook.

Yearbook of Fishery Statistics.

Yearbook of Forest Products.

Fortune (Time Warner), New York, NY

The Fortune Directory of the 500 Largest Industrial Corporations.

The Fortune Directory of the 500 Global Industrial Corporations.

The Foundation Center, New York, NY

The Foundation Grants Index, 2000. Edition 27. 1999.

Guide to U.S. Foundations, Their Trustees, Officers, and Donors, Vol. 1, 2000 Edition.

Gale Research Inc., Farmington Hills, MI

Gale Directory of Publications and Broadcast Media. 1999.

General Aviation Manufacturers Association, Washington, DC
Shipment Report. Quarterly and Annual.
Statistical Databook. Annual.

Girl Scouts of the U.S.A., New York, NY
Annual Report.

Health Forum, L.L.C., American Hospital Association, Company, Chicago, IL.
Annual Report.

Health Insurance Association of America, Washington, DC
Source Book of Health Insurance Data. Annual.

Independent Petroleum Association of America, Washington, DC
IPAA Weekly Oil Trends.
IPAA Wholesale Oil Prices. Monthly.
The Oil & Natural Gas Producing Industry in Your State. Annual.
U.S. Petroleum Statistics. Semiannual.

Institute for Criminal Justice Ethics, New York, NY
Criminal Justice Ethics. Semiannual.

Insurance Information Institute, New York, NY
Insurance Facts. Annual.
Internet address: <http://www.iii.org>

Inter-American Development Bank, Washington, DC
Annual Report.
Economic and Social Progress in Latin America. Annual Survey.

International City Management Association, Washington, DC
Baseline Data Reports. Bimonthly.
Compensation: An Annual Report on Local Government Executive Salaries and Fringe Benefits.
Municipal Year Book. Annual.
Special Data Issues. Periodical.

International Labour Office, Geneva, Switzerland
Yearbook of Labour Statistics.

International Monetary Fund, Washington, DC
Annual Report.
Balance of Payments Statistics. Monthly with annual yearbook.
Direction of Trade Statistics. Monthly with annual yearbook.
Government Finance Statistics Yearbook.
International Financial Statistics. Monthly with annual yearbook.

Investment Company Institute, Washington, DC
Mutual Fund Fact Book. Annual.

Jane's Information Group, Coulsdon, UK and Alexandria, VA
Jane's Air-Launched Weapons. (Binder-4 monthly update.)
Jane's All the World's Aircraft. Annual.
Jane's Armour and Artillery. Annual.
Jane's Avionics. Annual.
Jane's Fighting Ships. Annual.
Jane's Infantry Weapons. Annual.
Jane's Merchant Ships. Annual.
Jane's Military Communications. Annual.
Jane's Military Logistics. Annual.
Jane's Military Training Systems. Annual.
Jane's NATO Handbook. Annual.
Jane's Spaceflight Directory. Annual.

John Blair & Company, New York, NY
Statistical Trends in Broadcasting. Annual.

Joint Center for Political and Economic Studies, Washington, DC
Black Elected Officials: A National Roster. Annual.

Laventhol & Horwath, Philadelphia, PA
The Executive Conference Center: A Statistical and Financial Profile. Annual.
Gaming Industry Study. Annual.
Lifecare Industry. Annual. (Analysis of facilities by size and section of the country for selected financial data, resident census information, and medical costs.)
National Trends of Business in the Lodging Industry. Monthly. (Analysis of nationwide trends in sales, occupancy, and room rates of hotels, motor hotels, and economy lodging facilities.)
Separate reports on the segments of lodging industries. Annuals. (Reports covering economy, all-suite, and resort.)
U.S. Lodging Industry. Annual. (Report on hotel and motor hotel operations.)
Worldwide Lodging Industry. Annual. (Report on international hotel operations.)

Lebhar-Friedman, Inc., New York, NY
Accounting Today. Biweekly.
Apparel Merchandising. Monthly.

Lloyd's Register of Shipping, London, England
Casualty Return. (Annual statistical summary of all merchant ships totally lost or reported broken up during year.)
Merchant Shipbuilding Returns. (Quarterly Statistical summary of world shipbuilding.)
World Fleet Statistics. (An end-year analysis of world merchant fleet.)

Appendix I   897

Market Statistics, New York, NY
The Survey of Buying Power Data Service. Annual.

McGraw-Hill Informations Service Co., Washington, DC
Electrical world Directory of Electric Utilities. Annual.
Engineering and Mining Journal. Monthly.
Keystone Coal Industry Manual. Annual.

Metropolitan Life Insurance Company, New York, NY
Health and Safety Education.

Moody's Investors Service, New York, NY
Moody's Manuals. (Volumes on Industrials, OTC, Banks and Finance, International, Municipals and Governments, Transportation, and Public Utilities.) Annual with weekly supplements.

National Academy of Sciences, Washington, DC
Science, Engineering, and Humanities Doctorates in the United States. Biennial.
Summary Report. Doctorate Recipients from United States Universities. Annual.

National Air Carrier Association, Washington, DC
Annual Report.

National Association of Hosiery Manufacturers, Charlotte, NC
Hosiery Statistics. Annual.

National Association of Latino Elected and Appointed Officials, Washington, DC
National Roster of Hispanic Elected Officials. Annual.

NATIONAL ASSOCIATION OF REALTORS. Washington, DC
Real Estate Outlook: Market Trends & Insights. Monthly.

National Association of State Budget Officers, Washington, DC
"State Expenditure Report". Annual.
Fiscal Survey of the States. Semiannual.

National Association of State Park Directors, Tuscon, AZ
Annual Information Exchange.

National Catholic Educational Association, Washington, DC
Catholic Schools in America. Annual.
United States Catholic Elementary and Secondary Schools. Staffing and Enrollment. Annual.
U.S. Catholic Elementary Schools and their Finances. Biennial.
U.S. Catholic Secondary Schools and their Finances. Biennial.

National Center for State Courts, Williamsburg, VA
State Court Caseload Statistics. Annual.

National Coal Association, Washington, DC Coal Data. Annual.
Steam-Electric Plant Factors. Annual.

National Council of the Churches of Christ in the U.S.A., New York, NY
Yearbook of American and Canadian Churches. Annual.

National Council of Savings Institutions, Washington, DC
Fact Book of National Council of Savings Institutions. Annual.

National Education Association, Washington, DC
Estimates of School Statistics. Annual.
Rankings of the States. Annual.
Status of the American Public School Teacher, 1995-96. Quinquennial.

National Fire Protection Association, Quincy, MA
NFPA Journal. Bimonthly.

National Food Processors Association, Washington, DC
Canned Fruit and Vegetable Pack and Stock Situation Reports. Quarterly.

National Golf Foundation, Jupiter, FL
Americans' Attitudes on Golf (in their communities).
Commercial Golf Range Participation and Supply in the U.S.
Commercial Golf Ranges in the U.S.
Directory of Executive and Par-3 Golf Courses in U.S.
Directory of Golf: The People and Businesses in Golf. Annual.
Directory of U.S. Golf Courses.
Directory of U.S. Golf Practice Ranges and Learning Centers.
Directory of Golf Retailers: Off-Course Golf Retail Stores in U.S.
Golf Consumer Potential.
Golf Consumer Spending in the U.S.
Golf Facilities in Canada.
Golf Facilities in the U.S. - 1998.
Golf Facility Employee Compensation Study.
Golf Participation in Canada.
Golf Participation in U.S. - 1998.
Golf Travel Market Report for the U.S.
High-Interest Women Golfers—Target Marketing for Success.
Hot Spots for Golf Course Construction Activity in the USA.
NGF's *Infosearch: Accessing the World's Largest Golf Business Library.*
Operating and Financial Performance Profiles of Golf Facilities in the U.S.

National Golf Foundation, Jupiter, FL —Con.

Operational Profile of Canadian Golf Facilities.

Senior Golfer Profile.

Trends in the Golf Industry. Biennially

Women in Golf—1991-1996

National Governors' Association, Washington, DC

Directory of Governors of the American States, Commonwealths & Territories. Annual.

Governors' Staff Directory. Biannual.

National Governors' Association and National Association of State Budget Officers, Washington, DC

The Fiscal Survey of States. Biannual.

National Marine Manufacturers Association, Chicago, IL.

Boating. (A Statistical Report on America's Top Family Sport.) Annual.

State Boat Registration. Annual.

National Restaurant Association, Washington, DC

Compensation for Salaried Personnel in Restaurants. 1999.

Quickservice Restaurant Trends. Annual.

Restaurant Economic Trends. Monthly.

Restaurant Industry Employee Profile. Annual.

Restaurant Industry Forecast. Annual.

Restaurant Industry in Review. Annual.

Restaurant Industry Operations Report. Annual.

Restaurant Industry Pocket Factbook. Annual.

Restaurant Industry 2010. 1999.

Restaurant Numbers: 25-Year History, 1970-95.

Restaurant Spending. Annual.

Restaurants USA. Monthly.

Survey of Benefits for Hourly Restaurant Employees. 1998.

Survey of Wage Rates for Hourly Restaurant Employees. Biennial.

Tableservice Restaurant Trends. Annual.

Takeout Foods: A Consumer Study of Carry-out and Delivery. 1998.

The Economic Impact of the Nation's Eating and Drinking Places. Annual.

Internet address:
<http://www.restaurant.org>

National Sporting Goods Association, Mt. Prospect, IL

The Sporting Goods Market in 1999. Annual.

Sports Participation in 1998. Annual.

New York Stock Exchange, Inc., New York, NY

Fact Book. Annual.

Organization for Economic Cooperation and Development, Paris, France

Annual Oil Market Report.

Coal Information. Annual.

Energy Balances of OECD Countries. Annual.

Energy Prices and Taxes. Quarterly.

Energy Statistics. Annual.

Financial Market Trends. Triennial.

Food Consumption Statistics. Irregular.

Geographical Distribution of Financial Flows to Developing Countries.

Historical Statistics of Foreign Trade Series A. Annual.

Indicators of Industrial Activity. Quarterly.

Industrial Structure Statistics. Annual.

The Iron and Steel Industry. Annual.

Labour Force Statistics. Annual.

Latest Information on National Accounts of Developing Countries. Annual.

Main Economic Indicators. Monthly.

Main Science and Technology Indicators. Biennial.

Maritime Transport. Annual.

Meat Balances in OECD Countries. Annual.

Milk and Milk Products Balances in OECD Countries. Annual.

National Accounts of OECD Countries. Annual.

Vol. I: Main Aggregates.

Vol. II: Detailed Tables.

OECD Economic Outlook. Biannual. Historical Statistics. Annual.

OECD Economic Studies. Annual for member countries.

OECD Employment Outlook. Annual.

OECD Financial Statistics. Annual (three vols.) and monthly supplements.

OECD Health Data (Diskette)

OECD Health Systems: Facts and Trends.

OECD Microtables on Foreign Trade by Commodities covering Series B (individual reporting countries) and Series C (total reporting countries). Annual from 1977.

Oil and Gas Information. Annual.

The Pulp and Paper Industry. Annual.

Quarterly Labor Force Statistics.

Quarterly National Accounts.

Quarterly Oil Statistics and Energy Balances.

Revenue Statistics of OECD Member Countries. Annual.

Review of Fisheries in OECD Member Countries. Annual.

Statistical Trends in Transport (ECMT.)

Statistics of Area Production and Field of Crop Products in OECD Member Countries.

Statistics of Foreign Trade:

Monthly Statistics of Foreign Trade. (Series A.)

U.S. Census Bureau, Statistical Abstract of the United States: 2000

Organization for Economic Cooperation and Development, Paris, France —Con.

Foreign Trade by Commodities. (Series C.) Annual.

Tourism Policy and International Tourism in OECD Member Countries. Annual.

Uranium Resources Production and Demand. Biennial.

World Energy Statistics and Balances.

Pan American Health Organization, Washington, DC

Health Conditions in the Americas. Quadrennial.

Pannell Kerr Forster, Houston, TX

Clubs in Town and Country. Annual.

Trends in the Hotel Industry, International Edition. Annual.

Trends in the Hotel Industry, U.S.A. Edition. Annual.

PennWell Publishing Co., Tulsa, OK

Offshore. Monthly.

Oil and Gas Journal. Weekly.

Population Association of America, Washington, DC

Demography. Quarterly.

Population Index. (Princeton University, Princeton, NJ, Woodrow Wilson School of Public and International Affairs for the Population Association of America, Inc.) Quarterly.

Puerto Rico Planning Board, San Juan, PR

Balance of Payments—Puerto Rico. Annual.

Economic Activity Index. Monthly.

Economic Indicators. Monthly.

Economic Projections. Annual.

Economic Report to the Governor. Annual.

External Trade Statistics-Puerto Rico. Annual.

Income and Product. Annual.

Input-Output—Puerto Rico. Every 5 years.

Statistical Appendix to the Economic Report to the Government. Annual.

Radio Advertising Bureau, New York, NY

Radio Facts. Annual.

Rahners Business Information Unit, NY

Library Journal. Semimonthly.

Publishers Weekly.

School Library Journal. Monthly.

Reed Elsevier, Inc., Newton, MA

Broadcasting & Cable Yearbook.

Regional Airline Association, Washington, DC

Annual Report.

Broadcasting Magazine. Weekly.

Research Associates of Washington, Arlington, VA

Inflation Measures for Schools, Colleges, and Libraries. Annual.

State Profiles: Financing Public Higher Education Rankings. Annual.

Wages and Cost of Living: 508 County Indexes. (1995, most recent.)

Securities Industry Association, New York, NY

Foreign Activity Report. Quarterly.

Securities Industry Trends. Periodic.

SIA Securities Industry Fact Book. Annual.

Shipbuilders Council of America, Arlington, VA

Annual Report.

Simmons Market Research Bureau, Chicago, IL

Study of Media Markets. Annual.

Soil Conservation Service

National Resources Inventory. Periodic.

Standard and Poor's Corporation, New York, NY

Analyst's Handbook. Annual with monthly cumulative supplements.

Corporation Records. Six basic volumes; News Supplements, daily; Dividend Record, daily, and cumulative monthly and annual.

Daily Stock Price Records. Quarterly.

Security Owner's Stock Guide. Monthly.

Statistical Service. (Security Price Index Record; business and financial basic statistics with monthly supplement.)

Tanker Advisory Center, Inc., New York, NY

Worldwide Tanker Casualty Returns. Annual.

United Nations Educational, Scientific and Cultural Organization, Paris, France

Statistical Yearbook.

United Nations Statistics Division, New York, NY

Compendium of Human Settlements Statistics. (Series N.)

Demographic Yearbook. (Series R.)

Energy Balances and Electricity Profiles. (Series W.)

Energy Statistics Yearbook. (Series J.)

Industrial Statistics Yearbook: (Series P.) Commodity Production Statistics.

International Trade Statistics Yearbook. (Series G.)

Monthly Bulletin of Statistics. (Series Q.)

National Accounts Statistics: (Series X, Annually.)

Main Aggregates and Detailed Tables.

Analysis of Main Aggregates.

900   Appendix I

United Nations Statistics Division, New York, NY —Con.

Population and Vital Statistics Report. (Series A, Quarterly.)

Social Statistics and Indicators: (Series K, Occasional.)

The World's Women: Trends and Statistics.

Women's Indicators and Statistics Database (CD and diskette only.)

Statistical Yearbook. (Series; also available in CD-ROM, Series S/CD)

World Statistics Pocketbook. (Series V, Annually.)

United States Council for Energy Awareness, Washington, DC

U.S. Public Opinion on Nuclear Energy. (Polling reports updated periodically.)

United States League of Savings Institutions, Chicago, IL

Savings Institutions Sourcebook. Annual.

United States Telephone Association, Washington, DC

Statistics of the Local Exchange Carriers. Annual.

United Way of America, Alexandria, VA

Annual Directory.

University of Michigan, Center for Political Studies, Institute for Social Research, Ann Arbor, MI

National Election Studies Cumulative Datafile. Biennial.

Warren Publishing, Inc., Washington, DC

Cable Action Update. Weekly.

Cable and Station Coverage Atlas. Annual.

Television Action Update. Weekly.

Television and Cable Factbook. Annual.

TV Station & Cable Ownership Directory. Semiannual.

William B. Dana Co., New York, NY

Commercial and Financial Chronicle.

World Almanac/Pharos Books, New York, NY

The World Almanac and Book of Facts. Annual.

World Health Organization, Geneva, Switzerland

Epidemiological and Vital Statistics Report. Monthly.

World Health Statistics. Quarterly and annual.

Guide to State Statistical Abstracts

This bibliography includes the most recent statistical abstracts for states published since 1995 plus those that will be issued in late 2000. For some states, a near equivalent has been listed in substitution for, or in addition to, a statistical abstract. All sources contain statistical tables on a variety of subjects for the state as a whole, its component parts, or both. The page counts given for publications are approximate. Internet sites also contain statistical data.

Alabama

University of Alabama, Center for Business and Economic Research, Box 870221, Tuscaloosa 35487-0221. 205-348-6191. Internet site: <http://cber.cba.ua.edu/>

Economic Abstract of Alabama. 2000. 534 pp.

Alaska

Department of Commerce, Division of Community and Business Development, P.O. Box 110804, Juneau 99811-0804. 907-465-2017. Internet site: <http://www.dced.state.ak.us/>

The Alaska Economy Performance Report. 1996.

Arizona

University of Arizona, Economic and Business Research, College of Business and Public Administration, McClelland Hall 204 Tucson Arizona 85721-0108. 520-621-2155. Fax: 520-621-2150. Internet site: <http://www.ebr.bpa. arizona.edu/>

Arizona Economic Indicators 52 pp. Biennial.

Arkansas

University of Arkansas at Little Rock, Institute for Economic Advancement, Economic Research, 2801 South University, Little Rock 72204. 501-569-8551.

Arkansas State and County Economic Data. 2000. 16 pp. (Revised annually.)

University of Arkansas at Little Rock, Institute for Economic Advancement, Census State Data Center, 2801 South University, Little Rock 72204. 501-569-8530. Internet site: <http://www.aiea.ualr.edu/>

Arkansas Statistical Abstract, 2000. 740 pp. (Revised biennially.)

California

Department of Finance, 915 L Street, 8th Floor, Sacramento 95814. 916-445-3878. Internet site: <http://www.dof.ca.gov/>

California Statistical Abstract, 1999.

Colorado

University of Colorado, Boulder 80309-0420. 303-492-8227. Internet site: <http://www.colorado.edu/libraries/ govpubs/online.htm/>

Colorado by the numbers-online only.

Connecticut

Connecticut Department of Economic & Community Development, 505 Hudson St., Hartford 06106. 1-860-270-8165. Internet site: <http://www.state.ct.us/ ecd/>

Connecticut Market Data. Fall/winter 1999.

Connecticut Town Profiles, 1998-99. 340 pp.

Delaware

Delaware Economic Development Office, 99 Kings Highway, Dover 19901. 302-739-4271. Internet site: <http://www.state.de.us/dedo/>

Delaware Statistical Overview, 2000.

District of Columbia

Office of Planning, Data Management Division, 801 North Capitol St., NE Washington 20002. 202-442-7603.

Office of Policy and Evaluation, Executive Office of the Mayor, 1 Judiciary Square, Suite 920 So., 441 4th St., NW, Washington 20001. 202-727-6979.

Indices—A Statistical Index to DC Services, Dec. 1997-98. 273 pp.

Florida

University of Florida, Bureau of Economic and Business Research, 221 Matherly Hall, Gainesville 32611-7145. 352-392-0171. Internet site: <http://www.bebr.ufl.edu/>

Florida Statistical Abstract, 1999. 33rd ed. 821 pp. Also available on diskette or CD-ROM.

Georgia

University of Georgia, Selig Center for Economic Growth, Terry College of Business, Athens 30602-6269. 706-542-4085. Internet site: <http://www.selig.uga.edu/>

Georgia Statistical Abstract, 2000-01. 500 pp.

University of Georgia, College of Agricultural and Environmental Sciences, Athens 30602-4356. 706-542-8938. Fax 706-542-8934. Internet site: <http://www.agecon.uga.edu/ countyguide/>

The Georgia County Guide. 2000. 19th ed. Annual. 200 pp.

Hawaii

Hawaii State Department of Business, and Economic Development & Tourism, Research and Economic Analysis Division, Statistics Branch P.O. Box 2359, Honolulu 96804. Inquiries 808-586-2481; Copies 808-586-2423. Internet site: <http://www.hawaii.gov/dbedt/>

The State of Hawaii Data Book 1999: A Statistical Abstract. 32nd ed. 700 pp.

Idaho

Department of Commerce, 700 West State St., Boise 83720-0093. 208-334-2470. Internet site: <http://www.idoc.state.id.us/>

Idaho Facts, 2000. County Profiles of Idaho, 1999.

University of Idaho, Center for Business Development and Research, Moscow 83844-3227. 208-885-6611. Internet site: <http://www.uidaho.edu/cbdr/>

Idaho Statistical Abstract, 4th ed. 1996.

Illinois

University of Illinois, Bureau of Economic and Business Research, 430 Wohlers Hall, 1206 South 6th Street, Champaign 61820. 217-333-2332. Internet site: <http://www.cba.uiuc.edu/ research/>

Illinois Statistical Abstract. 1999. 759 pp.

Indiana

Indiana University, Indiana Business Research Center, School of Business, 801 W. Michigan St. Indianapolis 46202-5151. 317-274-2979. Internet site: <http://www.ibrc.indiana.edu/>

Indiana Factbook, 1998-99. 393 pages.

Kansas

University of Kansas, Policy Research Institute, 607 Blake Hall, Lawrence 66045-2960. 785-864-3701. Internet site: <http://www.ukans.edu/cwis/units/IPPBR/>.

Kansas Statistical Abstract, 1999. 34th ed. 2000.

Kentucky

Kentucky Cabinet for Economic Development, Division of Research, 500 Mero Street, Capital Plaza Tower, Frankfort 40601. 502-564-4886. Internet site: <http://www.edc.state.ky.us/>

Kentucky Deskbook of Economic Statistics. 34th ed. 1998.

Louisiana

University of New Orleans, Division of Business and Economic Research, New Orleans 70148. 504-280-6240. Internet site: <http://leap.nlu.edu/STAAB.HTM/>.

Statistical Abstract of Louisiana. 10th ed. 1997.

Maine

Maine Department of Economic and Community Development, State House Station 59, Augusta 04333. 207-287-2656. Internet site: <http://www.econdevmaine.com/>.

Maine: A Statistical Summary. (Updated periodically.)

Maryland

RESI, 8000 York Road Towson University, Towson 21252-0001. 410-830-7374. Internet site: <http://www.resiusa.org/>.

Maryland Statistical Abstract. 2000. 356 pp.

Massachusetts

Massachusetts Institute for Social and Economic Research, Box 37515, University of Massachusetts at Amherst 01003-7515. 413-545-3460. Fax 413-545-3686. Internet site: <http://www.umass.edu/miser/>

Minnesota

Department of Trade and Economic Development, Business and Community Development Division, 121 East 7th Place 500 Metro Square Building, St. Paul 55101-2146. 651-297-1291. Internet site: <http://www.dted.state.mn.us/>.

Compare Minnesota: An Economic and Statistical Factbook, 1998-99.

Office of State Demographer, Minnesota Planning, Rm. 300 Centennial Bldg., 658 Cedar Street, St. Paul 55155. 651-296-2557. Internet site: <http://www.mnplan.state.mn.us/demography/>.

Mississippi

Mississippi State University, College of Business and Industry, Division of Research, P.O. Box 5288 Mississippi State 39762. 662-325-3817. Fax 662-325-8686.

Mississippi Statistical Abstract. 1999. 506 pp.

Missouri

University of Missouri, Economic and Policy Analysis Research Center, 10 Professional Bldg., Columbia 65211. 573-882-4805. Internet site: <http://econ.missouri.edu/eparc/>.

Statistical Abstract for Missouri, 1999 Biennial.

Montana

Montana Department of Commerce, Census and Economic Information Center, 1424 9th Ave., Helena 59620. 406-444-2896. Internet site: <http://commerce.state.mt.us/ceic/>.

Montana County Statistical Reports. (Separate county and State reports; available by subject section as well as complete reports by county and state, updated periodically.)

Nebraska

Department of Economic Development,
Division of Research, Box 94666,
Lincoln 68509. 402-471-3111.
Fax 402-471- 3778. Internet site:
<http://www.ded.state.ne.us/>.

Nebraska Databook, 2000. 300 pp.
(Available only on Internet).

Nevada

Department of Administration, Budget and
Planning Division, 209 East Musser Street,
Suite 200, Carson City 89701. 775-684-
0222. Internet site: <http://www.state.
nv.us/budget/stateab.htm>.

Nevada Statistical Abstract. 1999.
Biennial.

New Hampshire

Office of State Planning, 2 1/2 Beacon St.,
Concord 03301-4497. 603-271-2155.
Fax 603-271-1728. Internet site:
<http://www.state.nh.us/osp/nhresnet/>.

*New Hampshire (State Seal) A Brief Look,
July 1997.* 21 pp. (Contact source for
other statistical series).

New Jersey

New Jersey State Data Center, NJ Department of Labor, P.O. Box 388, Trenton
08625-0388. 609-984-2595. Internet site:
<http://www.wnjpin.state.nj.us/>.
OneStopCareerCenter/Labor
MarketInformation/ilist.htm/>

New Mexico

University of New Mexico, Bureau of Business and Economic Research, 1920 Lomas
NE Albuquerque 87131-6021. 505-277-
6626. Fax 505-277-2773. Internet site:
<http://www.unm.edu/bber/>.

County Profiles. 1997. 72 pp.

New York

Nelson A. Rockefeller Institute of Government, 411 State Street, Albany 12203-
1003. 518-443-5522. Internet site:
<http:// www.rockinst.org/>

*New York State Statistical Yearbook,
1999.* 24th ed. 596 pp.

North Carolina

Office of Governor Office of State Budget,
Planning, and Management, 20321 Mail
Service Center, Raleigh 27699-0321.
919-733-4131. Fax 919-715-3562.
Internet site: <http://www.osbpm.
state.nc.us/#Demographer/>

North Dakota

North Dakota Department of Economic
Development & Finance, 1833 E. Bismarck
Expressway, Bismarck 58504-6708.
701-328-5300. Internet site: <http://
www.growingnd.com/>

*The Economic Performance and Indus-
trial Structure of the North Dakota
Economy, 2000.* 118 pp.

Ohio

Department of Development, Office of Strategic Research, P.O. Box 1001, Columbus
43216-1001. 614-466-2116. Internet site:
<http://www.odod.state.oh.us/osr/data.htm>

Research products and services.
(Updated continuously.)

Oklahoma

University of Oklahoma, Center for
Economic and Management Research,
307 West Brooks Street, Room 4,
Norman 73019. 405-325-2931.
Fax 405-325-7688. Internet site:
<http://origins.ou.edu/>

Statistical Abstract of Oklahoma, 1998.
Annual. 409 pp.

Oregon

Secretary of State, Business Services
Division, Publication Services Bldg.,
255 Capital Street, NE, Suite 180, Salem
97310. 503-986-2234. Internet site:
<http://www.sos.state.or.us/>

Oregon Blue Book. 1999-2000. Biennial.
431 pp.

Pennsylvania

Pennsylvania State Data Center, Institute of
State and Regional Affairs, Penn State
Harrisburg, 777 West Harrisburg Pike,
Middletown Pennsylvania 17057-4898.
717-948-6336. Internet site: <http://
pasdc.hbg.psu.edu/pasdc/>

Pennsylvania Statistical Abstract, 2000.
282 pp.

Rhode Island

Rhode Island Economic Development
Corporation, 1 West Exchange Street,
Providence 02903. 401-222-2601.
Fax 401-222- 2102. Internet site:
<http://www.riedc.com/>

*Rhode Island Prel. 2000 Census of
Population and Housing Summary.*
Dec. 2000. (updated as available).

The Rhode Island Economy. Aug. 2000.

South Carolina

Budget and Control Board, Office of
Research and Statistics, Room 425,
1919 Blanding St., Columbia 29201.
803-734-3781. Internet site: <http://
www.ors.state.sc.us/>

*South Carolina Statistical Abstract:
1999.* 429 pp.

South Dakota

University of South Dakota, State Data Center, Business Research Bureau, Vermillion
57069-2390. 605-677-5287. Internet site:
<http://www.usd.edu/brbinfo/>

*2000 South Dakota Community
Abstracts.* 400 pp.

Tennessee

University of Tennessee at Knoxville, Center for Business and Economic Research, College of Business Administration 100 Glocker, Knoxville 37996-4170. 865-974-5441. Internet site: <http://cber.bus.utk.edu/>

Tennessee Statistical Abstract, 2000. 17th ed. 738 pp. Biennial.

Texas

Dallas Morning News, Communications Center, P.O. Box 655237, Dallas 75265-5237. 214-977-8261. Internet site <http://www.texasalmanac.com/>

Texas Almanac, 2000-2001. 672 pp.

Utah

University of Utah, Bureau of Economic and Business Research, David Eccles School of Business 1645 East Campus Center Drive, Salt Lake City 84112-9302. 801-581-6333. Internet site: <http://www.business.utah.edu/BEBR/>

Statistical Abstract of Utah. 1996. (Centennial.)

Utah Foundation, 10 West 100 South, Suite 323, Salt Lake City 84101-1544. 801-364-1837. Internet site: <http://www.utah/foundation.org/

Statistical Review of Government in Utah. 1999.

Vermont

Labor Market Information, Department of Employment and Training, 5 Green Mountain Drive, P.O. Box 488, Montpelier 05601-0488. 802-828-4202. Internet site: <http://www.det.state.vt.us/>

Economic and Demographic Profiles. Annual.

Virginia

University of Virginia, Weldon Cooper Center for Public Service, 918 Emmet Street, North Suite 300, Charlottesville 22903-4832. 804-982-5585. Internet site: <http://www.virginia.edu/coopercenter/>

Virginia Statistical Abstract, 2000. Biennial. 1100 pp.

Washington

Washington State Office of Financial Management, Forecasting Division P.O. Box 43113 Olympia 98504-3113. 360-902-0599. Fax 360-664-8941. Internet site: <http://www.ofm.wa.gov/>

Washington State Data Book, 1999. 310 pp.

West Virginia

West Virginia University, College of Business and Economics, Bureau of Business and Economic Research, P.O. Box 6025, Morgantown 26506-6025. 304-293-7831. Internet site: <http://www.bber.wvu.edu/>

West Virginia Statistical Abstract, 1995-1996 Biennial. 480 pp.

County Data Profiles, 2000-2001. Annual. 45 pp. CD-ROM and Web site:.

West Virginia Research League, Inc., P.O. Box 11176, Charleston 25339. 304-766-9495.

The 1999 Statistical Handbook. 94 pp.

Wisconsin

Wisconsin Legislative Reference Bureau, P.O. Box 2037, Madison 53701-2037. 608-266-7098 Internet site: <http://www.legis.state.wi.us/lrb/bb/>

1999-2000 State of Wisconsin Blue Book. 950 pp. Biennial.

Wyoming

Department of Administration and Information, Division of Economic Analysis, 2001 Capitol Avenue, 327 E. Emerson Building, Cheyenne 82002-0060. 307-777-7504. Internet site: <http://eadiv.state.wy.us/eahome.htm>

The Equality State Almanac 1999. 7th ed. 134 pp.

Guide to Foreign Statistical Abstracts

This bibliography presents recent statistical abstracts for member nations of the Organization for Economic Cooperation and Development, Slovakia, and Russia. All sources contain statistical tables on a variety of subjects for the individual countries. Many of the following publications provide text in English as well as in the national language(s). For further information on these publications, contact the named statistical agency which is responsible for editing the publication.

Australia
Australian Bureau of Statistics, Canberra
Yearbook Australia. Annual. 2000. 834 pp. (In English.)

Austria
Osterreichisches Statistisches Zentralamt, P.O. Box 9000, A-1033 Vienna
Statistisches Jahrbuch for die Republik Osterreich. Annual. 2000. 673 pp. (In German.)

Belgium
Institut National de Statistique, 44 rue de Louvain, 1000 Brussels
Annuaire statistique de la Belgique. Annual. 1995. 820 pp. (In French.)

Canada
Statistics Canada, Ottawa, Ontario, KIA OT6
Canada Yearbook: A review of economic, social and political developments in Canada. 1999. 551 pp. Irregular. (In English.)

Czech Republic
Czech Statistical Office, Sokolovska 142, 186 04 Praha 8
Statisticka Rocenka Ceske Rpubliky 1999. 725 pp. (In English and Czech.)

Denmark
Danmarks Statistik, Postboks 2550 Sejrogade 11, DK 2100, Copenhagen
Statistical Yearbook. 1999. Annual. 559 pp. (In Danish with English translations of table headings.)

Finland
Central Statistical Office of Finland, Box 504 SF-00101 Helsinki
Statistical Yearbook of Finland. Annual. 1999. 677 pp. (In English, Finnish, and Swedish.)

France
Institut National de la Statistique et des Etudes Economiques, Paris 18, Bld. Adolphe Pinard, 75675 Paris (Cedex 14)
Annuaire Statistique de la France. Annual. 2000. 1,000 pp. (In French.)

Germany
Statistische Bundesamt, Postfach 5528, 6200 Wiesbaden
Statistisches Jahrbuch fur die Bundesrepublic Deutschland. Annual. 1999. 763 pp. (In German.)
Statistisches Jahrbuch fur das Ausland. 1999. 398 pp.

Greece
National Statistical Office, 14-16 Lycourgou St., 101-66 Athens
Concise Statistical Yearbook 2000. 276 pp. (plus 13 pages of graphs) (In English.)
Statistical Yearbook of Greece. Annual. 1998. 526 pp. (plus 8 pages of graphs). (In English and Greek.)

Hungary
Hungarian Central Statistical Office, H-1525 Budapest PF.51 H-1024 Budapest
Statistical Yearbook of Hungary, 1998. 1999 (In English and Hungarian.)

Iceland
Hagstofa Islands/Statistical Bureau, Hverfisgata 8-10, Reykjavik.
Statistical Yearbook of Iceland. 1999. Irregular. 311 pp. (In English and Icelandic.)

Ireland
Central Statistics Office, Earlsfort Terrace, Dublin 2
Statistical Abstract. Annual. 1997. 411 pp. (In English.)

Italy
ISTAT (Istituto Centrale di Statistica), Via Cesare Balbo 16, 00100 Rome
Annuario Statistico Italiano. Annual. 1998. 743 pp. (In Italian.)

Japan
Statistics Bureau, Management & Coordination Agency, 19-1 Wakamatsucho, Shinjuku Tokyo 162
Japan Statistical Yearbook. Annual. 2000. 909 pp. (In English and Japanese.)

Korea, South

National Statistical Office, Government Complex, #920 Dunsan-dong Seo-gu Daejeon 302-701

Korea Statistical Yearbook. Annual. 1999. 758 pp. (In Korean and English.)

Luxembourg

STATEC (Service Central de la Statistique et des Etudes), P.O. Box 304, L-2013, Luxembourg

Annuaire Statistique. Annual. 1999. (In French.)

Mexico

Instituto Nacional de Estadistica Geografia e Informatica, Avda. Insurgentes Sur No. 795-PH Col. Napoles, Del. Benito Juarez 03810 Mexico, D.F.

Anuario estadistico de los Estados Unidos Mexicanos. Annual. 1998. 714 pp. Also on disc. (In Spanish.) *Agenda Estadistica 1999.* 149 pp.

Netherlands

Centraal Bureau voor de Statistiek. 428 Prinses Beatrixlaan P.O. Box 959, 2270 AZ Voorburg

Statistical Yearbook 2000 of the Netherlands. 551 pp. (In English.)

Statistisch Jaarboek 2000. 561 pp.

New Zealand

Department of Statistics, Wellington

New Zealand Official Yearbook. Annual. 1998. 606 pp. (In English.)

Norway

Statistics Norway, Kongens gt. 6, P.O.B. 8131 Dep 0033 Oslo

Statistical Yearbook. Annual. 1997. 475 pp. (In English and Norwegian.)

Poland

Central Statistical Office al. Niepodleglosci 208, 00-925 Warsaw

Concise Statistical Yearbook 2000. 700 pp. (In Polish and English.)

Statistical Yearbook of the Republic of Poland 2000. 800 pp. (In Polish and English.)

Portugal

INE (Instituto Nacional de Estatistica), Avenida Antonio Jose de Almeida, P-1078 Lisbon Codex

Anuario Estatistico: de Portugal. 1998. 386 pp. (In Portuguese.)

Russia

State Committee of Statistics of Russia, Moscow

Statistical Yearbook. 1999. 621 pp. (In Russian.)

Slovakia

Statistical Office of the Slovak Republic, Mileticova 3, 824 67 Bratislava

Statisticka Rocenka Slovensak 1999. 718 pp. (In English and Slovak.)

Spain

INE (Instituto Nacional de Estadistica), Paseo de la Castellana, 183, Madrid 16

Espana Anuaria Estadistico Annual. 1996. 848 pp. plus 16 pages of graphs (In Spanish.)

Sweden

Statistics Sweden, S-11581 Stockholm

Statistical Yearbook of Sweden. Annual. 2000. 661 pp. (In English and Swedish.)

Switzerland

Bundesamt fur Statistik, Hallwylstrasse 15, CH-3003, Bern

Statistisches Jahrbuch der Schweiz. Annual. 2000. 533 pp. (In French and German.)

Turkey

State Institute of Statistics, Prime Ministry, 114 Necatibey Caddesi, Bakanliklar, Yenisehir, Ankara

Statistical Yearbook of Turkey. 1997. 733 pp. (In English and Turkish.)

Turkey in Statistics 1999 144 pp. (In English and Turkish.)

United Kingdom

Central Statistical Office, Great George Street, London SW1P 3AQ

Annual Abstract of Statistics. Annual. 2000. 448 pp. (In English.)

U.S. Census Bureau, Statistical Abstract of the United States: 2000

Metropolitan Areas: Concepts, Components, and Population

Statistics for metropolitan areas (MAs) shown in the Statistical Abstract represent areas defined by the U.S. Office of Management and Budget (OMB) according to published standards that are applied to Census Bureau data. The general concept of an MA is that of a core area containing a large population nucleus, together with adjacent communities having a high degree of economic and social integration with that core. Currently defined MAs are based on application of 1990 standards (which appeared in the Federal Register on March 30, 1990) to 1990 decennial census data and to subsequent Census Bureau population estimates and special census data. Current MA definitions were announced by OMB effective June 30, 1999. MAs include metropolitan statistical areas (MSAs), consolidated metropolitan statistical areas (CMSAs), and primary metropolitan statistical areas (PMSAs).

In this appendix, Table E presents geographic components and 1999 population estimates for each MSA, CMSA, and PMSA outside of New England. Table D presents definitions and data for New England county metropolitan areas (NECMAs), the county-based alternative metropolitan areas for the city- and town-based MSAs and CMSAs of the six New England states.

Standard definitions of metropolitan areas were first issued in 1949 by the then Bureau of the Budget (predecessor of OMB), under the designation "standard metropolitan area" (SMA). The term was changed to "standard metropolitan statistical area" (SMSA) in 1959 and to "metropolitan statistical area" (MSA) in 1983. The collective term "metropolitan area" (MA) became effective in 1990.

OMB has been responsible for the official metropolitan areas since they were first defined, except for the period 1977 to 1981, when they were the responsibility of the Office of Federal Statistical Policy and Standards, Department of Commerce. The standards for defining metropolitan areas were modified in 1958, 1971, 1975, 1980, and 1990.

Defining MSAs, CMSAs, and PMSA— The current standards provide that each newly qualifying MSA must include at least: one city with 50,000 or more inhabitants, or a Census Bureau-defined urbanized area (of at least 50,000 inhabitants) and a total metropolitan population of at least 100,000 (75,000 in New England). Under the standards, the county (or counties) that contains the largest city becomes the "central county" (counties), along with any adjacent counties that have at least 50 percent of their population in the urbanized area surrounding the largest city. Additional "outlying counties" are included in the MSA if they meet specified requirements of commuting to the central counties and other selected requirements of metropolitan character (such as population density and percent urban). In New England, the MSAs are defined in terms of cities and towns rather than counties. An area that meets these requirements for recognition as an MSA and also has a population of 1 million or more may be recognized as a CMSA if separate component areas can be identified within the entire area by meeting statistical criteria specified in the standards, and local opinion indicates there is support for the component areas. If recognized, the component areas are designated PMSAs, and the entire area becomes a CMSA. PMSAs, like the CMSAs that contain them, are composed of entire counties, except in New England where they are composed of cities and towns. If no PMSAs are recognized, the entire area is designated as an MSA. As of the June 30, 1999, OMB announcement, there were 258 MSAs, and 18 CMSAs comprising 73 PMSAs in the United States. In addition, there were three MSAs, one CMSA, and three PMSAs in Puerto Rico.

908   Appendix II

Central cities and MA titles—The largest city in each MSA/CMSA is designated a "central city." Additional cities qualify if specified requirements are met concerning population size and commuting patterns. The title of each MSA consists of the names of up to three of its central cities and the name of each state into which the MSA extends. However, a central city with less than 250,000 population and less than one-third the population of the area's largest city is not included in an MSA title unless local opinion supports its inclusion. Titles of PMSAs also typically are based on central city names but in certain cases consist of county names. Generally, titles of CMSAs are based on the titles of their component PMSAs.

Defining New England County Metropolitan Areas NECMAs—The OMB defines NECMAs as a county-based alternative to the city- and town-based New England MSAs and CMSAs. The NECMA for an MSA or CMSA includes: the county containing the first-named city in that MSA/CMSA title (this county may include the first-named cities of other MSAs/CMSAs as well), and each additional county having at least half its population in the MSAs/CMSAs whose first-named cities are in the previously identified county. NECMAs are not identified for individual PMSAs. There are 12 NECMAs, including 1 for the Boston-Worcester-Lawrence, MA-NH-ME-CT CMSA and 1 for the Connecticut portion of the New York-Northern New Jersey-Long Island, NY-NJ-CT-PA CMSA. Central cities of a NECMA are those cities in the NECMA that qualify as central cities of an MSA or a CMSA. NECMA titles derive from names of central cities.

Changes in MA definitions over time—Changes in the definitions of MAs since the 1950 census have consisted chiefly of the recognition of new areas as they reached the minimum required city or area population, and the addition of counties (or cities and towns in New England) to existing areas as new decennial census data showed them to qualify. In some instances, formerly separate MAs have been merged, components of an MA have been transferred from one MA to another, or components have been dropped from an MA. The large majority of changes have taken place on the basis of decennial census data. However, Census Bureau population estimates and special censuses serve as the basis for intercensal updates.

Because of these historical changes in geographic definitions, users must be cautious in comparing MA data from different dates. For some purposes, comparisons of data for MAs as defined at given dates may be appropriate; for other purposes, it may be preferable to maintain consistent MA definitions.

In Tables A, B, and C below, data are given for MAs as defined for specific dates, thereby indicating the extent of change in population and land area resulting from revisions in definitions.

U.S. Census Bureau, Statistical Abstract of the United States: 2000

Table A. Number, Population, and Land Area of MAs as Defined at Specified Dates From 1950 to 1999

[The differences in population shown here for each year within each column of the table result entirely from net expansion of metropolitan territory through changes in the MA definitions. The differences in population over time shown for each MA definition (on the successive lines of the table) result entirely from population changes within that territory, unaffected by changes in MA definitions. The changes in 1990 land area result entirely from net change in MA territory. All data include Alaska and Hawaii and exclude Puerto Rico. Subtraction of any line of the table from the line below will show the net effect of change in population and land area undergone by the MAs as the result of changes in definitions between the specified dates. Such changes may have occurred throughout the period, not on any single date, and may have included reductions in, as well as additions to, MA territory. Census population data through 1980 include corrections made since publication. The area data for the 1950, 1960, 1970, and 1980 census definitions of MAs differ from the data published in those censuses because of subsequent remeasurement of land areas and changes in inland water area occurring for the 1990 census]

MA definition as of—	Number of MAs	Population 1960 (April 1)	1970 (April 1)	1980 (April 1)	1990 (April 1)	1998 (July 1)	Land area, 1990 (sq. mi.)
1950 census (Mar. 1952)	169	106,344,548	122,184,836	128,842,628	139,837,153	148,305,142	206,802
1960 census (Nov. 1960)	212	[1]112,885,139	130,982,661	140,793,384	155,090,774	166,591,635	308,742
1970 census (Feb. 28, 1971)	243	[2]119,593,498	[3]139,479,806	151,660,897	167,899,268	181,502,500	386,241
1980 census (June 30, 1981)[4]	318	131,318,714	153,693,767	169,430,081	188,763,892	205,387,705	565,288
1985 (June 30)	[5]280	132,887,134	155,700,823	172,169,761	192,140,319	209,262,496	569,816
1986 (June 30)	[5]281	132,977,580	155,805,452	172,304,319	192,318,722	209,460,226	571,745
1987 (June 30)[6]	[5]281	133,003,445	155,832,688	172,334,850	192,349,750	209,494,587	572,284
1988 (June 30)[7]	[5]282	133,088,400	155,937,275	172,455,251	192,481,306	209,637,403	573,560
1989 (June 30)[7]	[5]283	133,233,777	156,084,580	172,602,176	192,623,201	209,775,506	574,622
1990 census (June 30, 1990)[7]	[5]284	133,275,412	156,137,337	172,678,381	192,730,096	209,907,765	580,136
1992 (Dec. 31)	[5]268	136,171,803	159,395,627	176,662,854	197,470,576	215,395,847	669,927
1993 (June 30)[7][8]	[5]268	136,336,055	159,579,651	176,892,735	197,728,901	215,699,322	673,057
1994 (June 30)[7]	[5]269	136,402,452	159,652,709	176,982,574	197,827,639	215,810,574	674,021
1995 (June 30)[7]	[5]271	136,497,691	159,757,830	177,143,136	198,022,544	216,043,836	699,960
1996 (June 30)[7]	[5]273	136,603,905	159,872,025	177,284,523	198,170,345	216,210,902	701,784
1998 (June 30)[7]	[5]274	136,648,568	159,930,288	177,360,539	198,249,032	216,299,891	704,383
1999 (June 30)[7]	[5]276	136,737,487	160,045,332	177,505,033	198,406,989	216,478,090	705,668

[1] Corresponds to total MA population for 1960 published in 1960 census (112,885,178), corrected by subtracting population (39) erroneously included in Franklin County, Ohio (Columbus metropolitan area). [2] Corresponds to total 1960 population for 1970 MAs published in 1970 census (119,594,754), corrected by subtracting 1,256 population from Lawrence-Haverhill metropolitan area; this represented an addition to the 1960 population of Andover town made subsequent to the original census tabulations, and therefore not reflected in state or national totals. [3] Corresponds to total MA population for 1970 published in 1970 census (139,418,811), plus net corrections made subsequent to publication. [4] MAs as defined for the 1982 economic censuses. [5] MSAs and CMSAs. [6] MAs as defined for the 1987 economic censuses. [7] Data exclude the portion of Sullivan city in Crawford County, MO (1990 population 1,116) added to the St. Louis, MO-IL MSA by congressional action effective Dec. 22, 1987. [8] MAs as defined for the 1992 economic censuses.

Source: U.S. Census Bureau, 1950-70, *U.S. Census of Population*, Vol. 1; *1980 Census of Population, Vol. 1, Chapters A and B and Supplementary Report, Metropolitan Statistical Areas* (PC80-S1-18); *1990 Census of Population and Housing Data Paper Listing* (CPH-L-10 and CPH-L-118); *1990 Census of Population and Housing, Supplementary Reports, Metropolitan Areas as Defined by the Office of Management and Budget, June 30, 1993*, (1990 CPH-S-1-1); and *Population Paper Listing* (PPL-60 and PPL-83).

Table B. Nonmetropolitan Population and Land Area as Defined at Specified Dates From 1950 to 1999

[See headnote for Table A. Nonmetropolitan population and land area are equivalent to that portion of the total national population and land area not included within MAs at the dates specified]

Metropolitan area definition as of—	Population 1960 (April 1)	1970 (April 1)	1980 (April 1)	1990 (April 1)	1998 (July 1)	Land area, 1990 (sq. mi.)
1950 census (Mar. 1952)	72,978,627	81,117,195	97,699,571	108,881,149	121,993,382	3,332,967
1960 census (Nov. 1960)	66,438,036	72,319,370	85,748,815	93,627,518	103,706,889	3,231,027
1970 census (Feb. 28, 1971)	59,729,677	63,822,225	74,881,302	80,819,024	88,796,024	3,153,527
1980 census (June 30, 1981)	48,004,461	49,608,264	57,112,118	59,954,400	64,910,819	2,974,481
1985 (June 30)	46,436,041	47,601,208	54,372,438	56,577,973	61,036,028	2,969,952
1986 (June 30)	46,345,595	47,496,579	54,237,880	56,399,570	60,838,298	2,968,023
1987 (June 30)	46,319,730	47,469,343	54,207,349	56,368,542	60,803,937	2,967,484
1988 (June 30)	46,234,775	47,364,756	54,086,948	56,236,986	60,661,121	2,966,208
1989 (June 30)	46,089,398	47,217,451	53,940,023	56,095,091	60,523,018	2,965,146
1990 census (June 30, 1990)	46,047,763	47,164,694	53,863,818	55,988,196	60,390,759	2,959,632
1992 (Dec. 31)	43,151,372	43,906,404	49,879,345	51,247,716	54,902,677	2,866,411
1993 (June 30)	42,987,120	43,722,380	49,649,464	50,989,391	54,599,202	2,863,281
1994 (June 30)	42,920,723	43,649,322	49,559,625	50,890,653	54,487,950	2,862,317
1995 (June 30)	42,825,484	43,544,201	49,399,063	50,695,748	54,254,688	2,836,378
1996 (June 30)	42,719,270	43,430,006	49,257,676	50,547,947	54,087,622	2,834,554
1998 (June 30)	42,674,607	43,371,743	49,181,660	50,469,260	53,998,633	2,831,956
1999 (June 30)	42,585,688	43,256,699	49,037,166	50,311,303	53,820,424	2,830,671

Source: U.S. Census Bureau, 1950-70, *U.S. Census of Population*, Vol. 1; *1980 Census of Population, Vol. 1, Chapters A and B and Supplementary Report, Metropolitan Statistical Areas* (PC80-S1-18); *1990 Census of Population and Housing Data Paper Listing* (CPH-L-10 and CPH-L-118); *1990 Census of Population and Housing, Supplementary Reports, Metropolitan Areas as Defined by the Office of Management and Budget, June 30, 1993*, (1990 CPH-S-1-1); and *Population Paper Listing* (PPL-60 and PPL-83).

Table C. Percent of Total U.S. Population and Percent of Land Area Inside MAs As Defined at Specified Dates From 1950 to 1999

[See headnote for Table A]

Metropolitan area definition as of—	Percent of population					Percent of land area, 1990
	1960 (April 1)	1970 (April 1)	1980 (April 1)	1990 (April 1)	1998 (July 1)	
1950 census (Mar. 1952)	59.3	60.1	56.9	56.2	54.9	5.8
1960 census (Nov. 1960)	63.0	64.4	62.1	62.4	61.6	8.7
1970 census (Feb. 28, 1971)	66.7	68.6	66.9	67.5	67.1	10.9
1980 census (June 30, 1981)	73.2	75.6	74.8	75.9	76.0	16.0
1985 (June 30)	74.1	76.6	76.0	77.3	77.4	16.1
1986 (June 30)	74.2	76.6	76.1	77.3	77.5	16.2
1987 (June 30)	74.2	76.7	76.1	77.3	77.5	16.2
1988 (June 30)	74.2	76.7	76.1	77.4	77.6	16.2
1989 (June 30)	74.3	76.8	76.2	77.4	77.6	16.2
1990 census (June 30, 1990)	74.3	76.8	76.2	77.5	77.7	16.4
1992 (Dec. 31)	75.9	78.4	78.0	79.4	79.7	18.9
1993 (June 30)	76.0	78.5	78.1	79.5	79.8	19.0
1994 (June 30)	76.1	78.5	78.1	79.5	79.8	19.1
1995 (June 30)	76.1	78.6	78.2	79.6	79.9	19.8
1996 (June 30)	76.2	78.6	78.3	79.7	80.0	19.8
1998 (June 30)	76.2	78.7	78.3	79.7	80.0	19.9
1999 (June 30)	76.3	78.7	78.4	79.8	80.1	20.0

Source: U.S. Census Bureau, 1950-70, *U.S. Census of Population,* Vol. 1; *1980 Census of Population,* Vol. 1, Chapters A and B and *Supplementary Report, Metropolitan Statistical Areas* (PC80-S1-18); *1990 Census of Population and Housing Data Paper Listing* (CPH-L-10 and CPH-L-118); *1990 Census of Population and Housing, Supplementary Reports, Metropolitan Areas as Defined by the Office of Management and Budget, June 30, 1993,* (1990 CPH-S-1-1); and *Population Paper Listing* (PPL-60 and PPL-83).

Table D. New England County Metropolitan Areas (NECMAs)

[In thousands. As of July 1]

NECMA	Population, 1999	NECMA	Population, 1999	NECMA	Population, 1999
Bangor, ME	144	**Burlington, VT**	195	**New London-Norwich, CT** . . .	246
Penobscot County	144	Chittenden County	144	New London County	246
Barnstable-Yarmouth, MA . . .	213	Franklin County	44	**Pittsfield, MA**	132
Barnstable County	213	Grand Isle County	6	Berkshire County	132
Boston-Worcester-Lawrence-		**Hartford, CT**	1,114	**Portland, ME**	256
Lowell-Brockton, MA-NH . . .	5,902	Hartford County	830	Cumberland County	256
Bristol County, MA	520	Middlesex County	151	**Providence-Warwick-**	
Essex County, MA	704	Tolland County	133	**Pawtucket, RI**	908
Middlesex County, MA	1,427	**Lewiston-Auburn, ME**	101	Bristol County	49
Norfolk County, MA	644	Androscoggin County	101	Kent County	162
Plymouth County, MA	473			Providence County	574
Suffolk County, MA	642	**New Haven-Bridgeport-**		Washington County	122
Worcester County, MA	739	**Stamford-Waterbury-**		**Springfield, MA**	589
Hillsborough County, NH . . .	367	**Danbury, CT**	1,635	Hampden County	438
Rockingham County, NH . . .	275	Fairfield County	841	Hampshire County	151
Strafford County, NH	111	New Haven County	793		

Source: U.S. Census Bureau, "(CO-99-8) County Population Estimates and Demographic Components of Population Change: Annual Time Series, July 1, 1990, to July 1, 1999, (includes revised April 1, 1990, Population Estimates Base)"; published 9 March 2000; <http://www.census.gov/population/estimates/county/co-99-8/99C800.txt>.

U.S. Census Bureau, Statistical Abstract of the United States: 2000

Table E. Metropolitan Areas Outside of New England and Their Components as of June 30, 1999

[Population estimated as of **July 1, 1999**. All metropolitan areas are arranged alphabetically. PMSAs are included under their respective CMSAs, see CMSA entry. This table presents data for MAs outside New England only]

Area	Population, 1999 (1,000)
Abilene, TX MSA.........	122
Taylor County..........	122
Albany, GA MSA......	117
Dougherty County.......	94
Lee County	23
Albany-Schenectady-Troy, NY MSA..............	869
Albany County	292
Montgomery County	50
Rensselaer County .:....	151
Saratoga County.....	200
Schenectady County.....	144
Schoharie County.......	32
Albuquerque, NM MSA	679
Bernalillo County........	523
Sandoval County	90
Valencia County	65
Alexandria, LA MSA	127
Rapides Parish.........	127
Allentown-Bethlehem-Easton, PA MSA	618
Carbon County.	59
Lehigh County	300
Northampton County.....	260
Altoona, PA MSA	130
Blair County...........	130
Amarillo, TX MSA	209
Potter County..........	109
Randall County.........	100
Anchorage, AK MSA......	258
Anchorage Borough	258
Anniston, AL MSA	117
Calhoun County	117
Appleton-Oshkosh-Neenah, WI MSA	348
Calumet County	39
Outagamie County	158
Winnebago County	151
Asheville, NC MSA	215
Buncombe County.......	196
Madison County........	19
Athens, GA MSA.........	140
Clarke County	91
Madison County	25
Oconee County	25
Atlanta, GA MSA.........	3,857
Barrow County	42
Bartow County	75
Carroll County	85
Cherokee County	142
Clayton County........	214
Cobb County	584
Coweta County	89
DeKalb County........	597
Douglas County	91
Fayette County........	92
Forsyth County........	97
Fulton County........	745
Gwinnett County........	546
Henry County..........	113
Newton County.........	61
Paulding County	80
Pickens County........	21
Rockdale County.......	69
Spalding County........	58
Walton County	58
Auburn-Opelika, AL	102
Lee County	102
Augusta-Aiken, GA-SC MSA.................	461
Columbia County, GA....	93
McDuffie County, GA....	22
Richmond County, GA....	190
Aiken County, SC	135
Edgefield County, SC	20
Austin-San Marcos, TX MSA.................	1,146
Bastrop County.........	53
Caldwell County	33
Hays County	93
Travis County..........	727
Williamson County	241
Bakersfield, CA MSA......	642
Kern County...........	642
Baton Rouge, LA MSA	579
Ascension Parish	74
East Baton Rouge Parish..	393
Livingston Parish	91
West Baton Rouge Parish.	20
Beaumont-Port Arthur, TX MSA.................	376
Hardin County	50
Jefferson County........	241
Orange County.........	85
Bellingham, WA MSA	160
Whatcom County	160
Benton Harbor, MI MSA....	160
Berrien County	160
Billings, MT MSA	127
Yellowstone County......	127
Biloxi-Gulfport-Pascagoula, MS MSA..............	353
Hancock County	42
Harrison County	179
Jackson County	133
Binghamton, NY MSA	247
Broome County.........	195
Tioga County	52
Birmingham, AL MSA	915
Blount County..........	47
Jefferson County........	657
St. Clair County	64
Shelby County	146
Bismarck, ND MSA	92
Burleigh County........	67
Morton County	25
Bloomington, IN MSA	117
Monroe County	117
Bloomington-Normal, IL MSA.................	145
McLean County	145
Boise City, ID MSA	408
Ada County...........	283
Canyon County.........	124
Brownsville-Harlingen, TX MSA.................	329
Cameron County........	329
Bryan-College Station, TX MSA.................	134
Brazos County	134
Buffalo-Niagara Falls, NY MSA.................	1,142
Erie County	926
Niagara County.........	216
Canton-Massillon, OH MSA.	402
Carroll County	29
Stark County	373
Casper, WY MSA.........	63
Natrona County	63
Cedar Rapids, IA MSA.....	185
Linn County	185
Champaign-Urbana, IL MSA..............	170
Champaign County	170
Charleston-North Charleston, SC MSA	553
Berkeley County........	142
Charleston County	320
Dorchester County	91
Charleston, WV MSA	251
Kanawha County	199
Putnam County.........	52
Charlotte-Gastonia-Rock Hill, NC-SC MSA	1,417
Cabarrus County, NC	125
Gaston County, NC	185
Lincoln County, NC......	59
Mecklenburg County, NC..	648
Rowan County, NC......	127
Union County, NC.......	115
York County, SC........	158
Charlottesville, VA MSA ...	151
Albemarle County	80
Fluvanna County.......	20
Greene County	15
Charlottesville city........	37
Chattanooga, TN-GA MSA..	452
Hamilton County, TN	295
Marion County, TN	27
Catoosa County, GA	52
Dade County, GA	15
Walker County, GA	63
Cheyenne, WY MSA	79
Laramie County	79
Chicago-Gary-Kenosha, IL-IN-WI CMSA	8,886
Chicago, IL PMSA	8,009
Cook County, IL	5,192
DeKalb County, IL	87
DuPage County, IL	893
Grundy County, IL	37
Kane County, IL	403
Kendall County, IL......	54
Lake County, IL.......	618
McHenry County, IL....	247
Will County, IL........	478
Gary, IN PMSA	628
Lake County, IN	481
Porter County, IN......	148
Kankakee, IL PMSA	103
Kankakee County, IL ...	103
Kenosha, WI PMSA	146
Kenosha County, WI ...	146

Area	Population, 1999 (1,000)
Chico-Paradise, CA MSA...	**195**
Butte County	195
Cincinnati-Hamilton, OH-KY-IN CMSA	**1,961**
Cincinnati, OH-KY-IN PMSA	**1,628**
Brown County, OH	42
Clermont County, OH	179
Hamilton County, OH	840
Warren County, OH	153
Boone County, KY	83
Campbell County, KY	87
Gallatin County, KY	7
Grant County, KY	21
Kenton County, KY	147
Pendleton County, KY	14
Dearborn County, IN	48
Ohio County, IN	5
Hamilton-Middletown, OH PMSA	**333**
Butler County, OH	333
Clarksville-Hopkinsville, TN-KY MSA	**201**
Montgomery County, TN	129
Christian County, KY	72
Cleveland-Akron, OH CMSA	**2,911**
Akron, OH PMSA	**689**
Portage County	152
Summit County	538
Cleveland-Lorain-Elyria, OH PMSA	**2,221**
Ashtabula County	103
Cuyahoga County	1,372
Geauga County	90
Lake County	227
Lorain County	282
Medina County	147
Colorado Springs, CO MSA.	**500**
El Paso County	500
Columbia, MO MSA.	**130**
Boone County	130
Columbia, SC MSA.	**516**
Lexington County	209
Richland County	307
Columbus, GA-AL MSA.	**271**
Chattahoochee County, GA	17
Harris County, GA	23
Muscogee County, GA	182
Russell County, AL	50
Columbus, OH MSA	**1,489**
Delaware County	104
Fairfield County	127
Franklin County	1,028
Licking County	136
Madison County	41
Pickaway County	53
Corpus Christi, TX MSA	**387**
Nueces County	315
San Patricio County	72
Corvallis, OR MSA	**77**
Benton County	77
Cumberland, MD-WV MSA.	**98**
Allegany County, MD	71
Mineral County, WV	27
Dallas-Fort Worth, TX CMSA	**4,910**
Dallas, TX PMSA	**3,280**
Collin County	457
Dallas County	2,062
Denton County	404
Ellis County	108
Henderson County	71
Hunt County	72
Kaufman County	68
Rockwall County	39
Fort Worth-Arlington, TX PMSA	**1,629**
Hood County	39
Johnson County	123
Parker County	85
Tarrant County	1,382
Danville, VA MSA	**108**
Pittsylvania County	57
Danville city	51
Davenport-Moline-Rock Island, IA-IL MSA	**359**
Scott County, IA	159
Henry County, IL	52
Rock Island County, IL	148
Dayton-Springfield, OH MSA	**959**
Clark County	145
Greene County	149
Miami County	99
Montgomery County	566
Daytona Beach, FL MSA	**475**
Flagler County	49
Volusia County	426
Decatur, AL MSA.	**143**
Lawrence County	34
Morgan County	110
Decatur, IL MSA	**113**
Macon County	113
Denver-Boulder-Greeley, CO CMSA	**2,418**
Boulder-Longmont, CO PMSA	**273**
Boulder County	273
Denver, CO PMSA	**1,979**
Adams County	331
Arapahoe County	482
Denver County	500
Douglas County	157
Jefferson County	509
Greeley, CO PMSA	**166**
Weld County	166
Des Moines, IA MSA	**443**
Dallas County	38
Polk County	365
Warren County	41
Detroit-Ann Arbor-Flint, MI CMSA	**5,469**
Ann Arbor, MI PMSA	**557**
Lenawee County	100
Livingston County	151
Washtenaw County	306
Detroit, MI PMSA	**4,475**
Lapeer County	89
Macomb County	792
Monroe County	145
Oakland County	1,180
St. Clair County	162
Wayne County	2,106
Flint, MI PMSA	**437**
Genesee County	437
Dothan, AL MSA	**135**
Dale County	49
Houston County	86
Dover, DE MSA.	**126**
Kent County	126
Dubuque, IA MSA	**88**
Dubuque County	88
Duluth, MN-WI MSA	**236**
St. Louis County, MN	193
Douglas County, WI	43
Eau Claire, WI MSA.	**144**
Chippewa County	55
Eau Claire County	90
El Paso, TX MSA.	**702**
El Paso County	702
Elkhart-Goshen, IN MSA	**175**
Elkhart County	175
Elmira, NY MSA	**92**
Chemung County	92
Enid, OK MSA.	**57**
Garfield County.	57
Erie, PA MSA	**277**
Erie County	277
Eugene-Springfield, OR MSA.	**315**
Lane County.	315
Evansville-Henderson, IN-KY MSA	**291**
Posey County, IN	26
Vanderburgh County, IN	168
Warrick County, IN	53
Henderson County, KY	44
Fargo-Moorhead, ND-MN MSA	**170**
Cass County, ND	118
Clay County, MN	52
Fayetteville, NC MSA	**284**
Cumberland County	284
Fayetteville-Springdale-Rogers, AR MSA	**285**
Benton County	138
Washington County	147
Flagstaff, AZ-UT MSA	**121**
Coconino County, AZ	114
Kane County, UT	6
Florence, AL MSA.	**137**
Colbert County	53
Lauderdale County	84
Florence, SC MSA.	**125**
Florence County	125
Fort Collins-Loveland, CO MSA	**237**
Larimer County.	237
Fort Myers-Cape Coral, FL MSA	**401**
Lee County	401
Fort Pierce-Port St. Lucie, FL MSA.	**300**
Martin County	118
St. Lucie County	182
Fort Smith, AR-OK MSA	**196**
Crawford County, AR	51
Sebastian County, AR	106
Sequoyah County, OK	38
Fort Walton Beach, FL MSA	**170**
Okaloosa County	170
Fort Wayne, IN MSA	**484**
Adams County	33
Allen County	316
De Kalb County	40
Huntington County	37
Wells County	27
Whitley County	31
Fresno, CA MSA	**880**
Fresno County	763
Madera County	117

	Popu-lation, 1999 (1,000)

	Popu-lation, 1999 (1,000)			Popu-lation, 1999 (1,000)			Popu-lation, 1999 (1,000)
Gadsden, AL MSA	**103**	**Galveston-Texas City, TX**		**Kalamazoo-Battle Creek, MI**	
Etowah County	103	**PMSA**	**248**	**MSA**	**447**
		Galveston County	248	Calhoun County	141
Gainesville, FL MSA	**198**	**Houston, TX PMSA**	**4,011**	Kalamazoo County	230
Alachua County	198	Chambers County	24	Van Buren County	76
		Fort Bend County	354		
Glens Falls, NY MSA	**122**	Harris County	3,250	**Kansas City, MO-KS MSA**	**1,756**
Warren County	61	Liberty County	67	Cass County, MO	83
Washington County	60	Montgomery County	288	Clay County, MO.	180
		Waller County	28	Clinton County, MO.	20
Goldsboro, NC MSA	**112**			Jackson County, MO	654
Wayne County	112	**Huntington-Ashland,**		Lafayette County, MO	33
		WV-KY-OH MSA	**312**	Platte County, MO.	72
Grand Forks, ND-MN MSA	**95**	Cabell County, WV	94	Ray County, MO	24
Grand Forks County, ND	65	Wayne County, WV	42	Johnson County, KS	440
Polk County, MN	31	Boyd County, KY.	49	Leavenworth County, KS	72
		Carter County, KY.	27	Miami County, KS	27
Grand Junction, CO MSA	**115**	Greenup County, KY	37	Wyandotte County, KS.	151
Mesa County	115	Lawrence County, OH	64		
				Killeen-Temple, TX MSA	**296**
Grand Rapids-Muskegon-		**Huntsville, AL MSA**	**343**	Bell County	223
Holland, MI MSA	**1,052**	Limestone County	63	Coryell County	74
Allegan County	103	Madison County	280		
Kent County	550			**Knoxville, TN MSA**	**672**
Muskegon County	168	**Indianapolis, IN MSA**	**1,537**	Anderson County	71
Ottawa County	230	Boone County	45	Blount County	103
		Hamilton County	172	Knox County	376
Great Falls, MT MSA	**78**	Hancock County	56	Loudon County	40
Cascade County	78	Hendricks County	99	Sevier County	66
		Johnson County	113	Union County	17
Green Bay, WI MSA	**217**	Madison County	131		
Brown County	217	Marion County	811	**Kokomo, IN MSA**	**100**
		Morgan County	67	Howard County	84
Greensboro—Winston-		Shelby County	44	Tipton County	17
Salem—High Point, NC					
MSA	**1,179**	**Iowa City, IA MSA**	**104**	**La Crosse, WI-MN MSA**	**122**
Alamance County	121	Johnson County	104	La Crosse County, WI	102
Davidson County	143			Houston County, MN	19
Davie County	33	**Jackson, MI MSA**	**157**		
Forsyth County	289	Jackson County	157	**Lafayette, LA MSA**	**377**
Guilford County	391			Acadia Parish	58
Randolph County	123	**Jackson, MS MSA**	**433**	Lafayette Parish	187
Stokes County	44	Hinds County	246	St. Landry Parish	84
Yadkin County	35	Madison County	75	St. Martin Parish	48
		Rankin County	112		
Greenville, NC MSA	**128**			**Lafayette, IN MSA**	**175**
Pitt County	128	**Jackson, TN MSA**	**102**	Clinton County	33
		Chester County	15	Tippecanoe County	142
Greenville-Spartanburg-		Madison County	87		
Anderson, SC MSA	**930**			**Lake Charles, LA MSA**	**181**
Anderson County	163	**Jacksonville, FL MSA**	**1,056**	Calcasieu Parish	181
Cherokee County	50	Clay County	141		
Greenville County	359	Duval County	738	**Lakeland-Winter Haven, FL**	
Pickens County	108	Nassau County	57	**MSA**	**457**
Spartanburg County	250	St. Johns County	120	Polk County	457
Harrisburg-Lebanon-		**Jacksonville, NC MSA**	**142**	**Lancaster, PA MSA**	**460**
Carlisle, PA MSA	**618**	Onslow County	142	Lancaster County	460
Cumberland County	211				
Dauphin County	246	**Jamestown, NY MSA**	**137**	**Lansing-East Lansing, MI**	
Lebanon County	118	Chautauqua County	137	**MSA**	**451**
Perry County	44			Clinton County	64
		Janesville-Beloit, WI MSA	**151**	Eaton County	102
Hattiesburg, MS MSA	**113**	Rock County	151	Ingham County	285
Forrest County	75				
Lamar County	38	**Johnson City-Kingsport-**		**Laredo, TX MSA**	**193**
		Bristol, TN-VA MSA	**463**	Webb County	193
Hickory-Morganton, NC		Carter County, TN	53		
MSA	**326**	Hawkins County, TN	50	**Las Cruces, NM MSA**	**170**
Alexander County	32	Sullivan County, TN	150	Dona Ana County	170
Burke County	83	Unicoi County, TN.	17		
Caldwell County	76	Washington County, TN	103	**Las Vegas, NV-AZ MSA**	**1,381**
Catawba County	134	Scott County, VA	23	Clark County, NV	1,217
		Washington County, VA	50	Nye County, NV	30
Honolulu, HI MSA	**865**	Bristol city, VA	17	Mohave County, AZ.	134
Honolulu County	865				
		Johnstown, PA MSA	**234**	**Lawrence, KS MSA**	**98**
Houma, LA MSA	**195**	Cambria County	154	Douglas County	98
Lafourche Parish	89	Somerset County	80		
Terrebonne Parish	105			**Lawton, OK MSA**	**107**
		Jonesboro, AR MSA	**78**	Comanche County	107
Houston-Galveston-		Craighead County	78	**Lexington, KY MSA**	**456**
Brazoria, TX CMSA	**4,494**	**Joplin, MO MSA**	**150**	Bourbon County	19
Brazoria, TX PMSA	**234**	Jasper County	100	Clark County	32
Brazoria County	234	Newton County	50	Fayette County	244

U.S. Census Bureau, Statistical Abstract of the United States: 2000

	Pop.		Pop.		Pop.
Jessamine County.......	37	Tipton County, TN......	48	St. John the Baptist Parish.	42
Madison County.......	68	Crittenden County, AR....	50	St. Tammany Parish.....	193
Scott County	32	DeSoto County, MS......	102		
Woodford County	23			**New York-Northern New**	
		Merced, CA MSA.........	**201**	**Jersey-Long Island,**	
Lima, OH MSA	**154**	Merced County.........	201	**NY-NJ-CT-PA CMSA (pt.)** [1] **.**	**18,468**
Allen County...........	107			**Bergen-Passaic, NJ**	
Auglaize County........	47	**Miami-Fort Lauderdale, FL**		**PMSA ....**	**1,342**
		CMSA...............	**3,711**	Bergen County, NJ.....	857
Lincoln, NE MSA........	**238**	**Fort Lauderdale, FL**		Passaic County, NJ	485
Lancaster County.......	238	**PMSA ....**	**1,535**	**Dutchess County, NY**	
		Broward County	1,535	**PMSA ....**	**268**
Little Rock-North Little		**Miami, FL PMSA ......**	**2,176**	Dutchess County, NY....	268
Rock, AR MSA	**559**	Miami-Dade County ...	2,176	**Jersey City, NJ PMSA....**	**553**
Faulkner County........	80			Hudson County, NJ	553
Lonoke County.........	51	**Milwaukee-Racine, WI**		**Middlesex-Somerset-**	
Pulaski County.........	349	**CMSA...............**	**1,648**	**Hunterdon, NJ PMSA...**	**1,131**
Saline County..........	78	**Milwaukee-Waukesha, WI**		Hunterdon County, NJ ..	125
		PMSA	**1,462**	Middlesex County, NJ...	718
Longview-Marshall, TX		Milwaukee County.....	906	Somerset County, NJ..	288
MSA	**209**	Ozaukee County	82	**Monmouth-Ocean, NJ**	
Gregg County..........	113	Washington County	116	**PMSA ....**	**1,109**
Harrison County	60	Waukesha County.....	358	Monmouth County, NJ ..	611
Upshur County	37	**Racine, WI PMSA ......**	**186**	Ocean County, NJ.....	498
		Racine County	186	**Nassau-Suffolk, NY**	
Los Angeles-Riverside-				**PMSA ....**	**2,689**
Orange County, CA CMSA.	**16,037**	**Minneapolis-St. Paul,**		Nassau County, NY	1,305
Los Angeles-Long Beach,		**MN-WI MSA...........**	**2,872**	Suffolk County, NY	1,384
CA PMSA	**9,330**	Anoka County, MN	299	**New York, NY PMSA ....**	**8,713**
Los Angeles County....	9,330	Carver County, MN	67	Bronx County, NY	1,194
Orange County, CA		Chisago County, MN	42	Kings County, NY	2,268
PMSA	**2,761**	Dakota County, MN.....	349	New York County, NY..	1,552
Orange County	2,761	Hennepin County, MN ..	1,064	Putnam County, NY....	95
Riverside-San		Isanti County, MN	31	Queens County, NY....	2,001
Bernardino, CA PMSA..	**3,201**	Ramsey County, MN	486	Richmond County, NY ..	413
Riverside County.....	1,531	Scott County, MN	83	Rockland County, NY...	284
San Bernardino County .	1,670	Sherburne County, MN ..	63	Westchester County, NY.	906
Ventura, CA PMSA......	**745**	Washington County, MN ..	203	**Newark, NJ PMSA ......**	**1,955**
Ventura County.......	745	Wright County, MN	88	Essex County, NJ	747
		Pierce County, WI	36	Morris County, NJ	464
Louisville, KY-IN MSA.....	**1,006**	St. Croix County, WI	60	Sussex County, NJ	145
Bullitt County, KY	61			Union County, NJ	499
Jefferson County, KY....	673	**Missoula, MT MSA ....**	**89**	Warren County, NJ	100
Oldham County, KY.....	46	Missoula County.......	89	**Newburgh, NY-PA PMSA .**	**376**
Clark County, IN	95			Orange County, NY	334
Floyd County, IN......	72	**Mobile, AL MSA ....**	**535**	Pike County, PA	41
Harrison County, IN.....	35	Baldwin County........	136	**Trenton, NJ PMSA......**	**334**
Scott County, IN	23	Mobile County........	400	Mercer County, NJ....	334
Lubbock, TX MSA........	**228**	**Modesto, CA MSA........**	**437**	**Norfolk-Virginia Beach-**	
Lubbock County	228	Stanislaus County.......	437	**Newport News, VA-NC**	
				MSA	**1,563**
Lynchburg, VA MSA	**209**	**Monroe, LA MSA........**	**147**	Gloucester County, VA....	35
Amherst County	30	Ouachita Parish	147	Isle of Wight County, VA ..	30
Bedford County........	58			James City County, VA...	46
Campbell County	50	**Montgomery, AL MSA.....**	**322**	Mathews County, VA.....	9
Bedford city	7	Autauga County	43	York County, VA	58
Lynchburg city	64	Elmore County	63	Chesapeake city, VA....	203
		Montgomery County	216	Hampton city, VA	137
Macon, GA MSA	**322**			Newport News city, VA....	179
Bibb County...........	155	**Muncie, IN MSA ....**	**115**	Norfolk city, VA	226
Houston County	108	Delaware County	115	Poquoson city, VA.....	12
Jones County..........	23			Portsmouth city, VA....	98
Peach County..........	25	**Myrtle Beach, SC MSA ....**	**179**	Suffolk city, VA	65
Twiggs County	10	Horry County	179	Virginia Beach city, VA....	433
				Williamsburg city, VA....	12
Madison, WI MSA	**429**	**Naples, FL MSA ....**	**207**	Currituck County, NC.....	18
Dane County	429	Collier County..........	207		
				Ocala, FL MSA	**246**
Mansfield, OH MSA.......	**177**	**Nashville, TN MSA.......**	**1,172**	Marion County	246
Crawford County.......	47	Cheatham County.......	36		
Richland County.......	130	Davidson County	530	**Odessa-Midland, TX MSA ..**	**242**
		Dickson County	43	Ector County	124
McAllen-Edinburg-Mission,		Robertson County.......	55	Midland County.........	118
TX MSA	**535**	Rutherford County......	171		
Hidalgo County........	535	Sumner County........	126	**Oklahoma City, OK MSA ...**	**1,046**
		Williamson County	124	Canadian County	86
Medford-Ashland, OR MSA .	**176**	Wilson County	86	Cleveland County	203
Jackson County	176			Logan County..........	30
		New Orleans, LA MSA.....	**1,305**	McClain County	27
Melbourne-Titusville-Palm		Jefferson Parish	448	Oklahoma County	637
Bay, FL MSA...........	**470**	Orleans Parish	461	Pottawatomie County.....	63
Brevard County........	470	Plaquemines Parish	26		
Memphis, TN-AR-MS MSA..	**1,105**	St. Bernard Parish......	65	**Omaha, NE-IA MSA.......**	**699**
Fayette County, TN	31	St. Charles Parish......	49	Cass County, NE	25
Shelby County, TN	873	St. James Parish	21	Douglas County, NE	446

Appendix II   915

Area	Population, 1999 (1,000)	Area	Population, 1999 (1,000)	Area	Population, 1999 (1,000)
Sarpy County, NE	122	Polk County, OR	62	**Saginaw-Bay City-Midland, MI MSA**	**401**
Washington County, NE	19	**Provo-Orem, UT MSA**	**347**	Bay County	110
Pottawattamie County, IA	86	Utah County	347	Midland County	82
				Saginaw County	209
Orlando, FL MSA	**1,535**	**Pueblo, CO MSA**	**137**		
Lake County	210	Pueblo County	137	**St. Cloud, MN MSA**	**165**
Orange County	817			Benton County	35
Osceola County	151	**Punta Gorda, FL MSA**	**137**	Stearns County	130
Seminole County	357	Charlotte County	137		
				St. Joseph, MO MSA	**97**
Owensboro, KY MSA	**91**	**Raleigh-Durham-Chapel**		Andrew County	16
Daviess County	91	**Hill, NC MSA**	**1,106**	Buchanan County	82
		Chatham County	47		
Panama City, FL MSA	**148**	Durham County	204	**St. Louis, MO-IL MSA**	**2,569**
Bay County	148	Franklin County	46	Franklin County, MO	93
		Johnston County	111	Jefferson County, MO	198
Parkersburg-Marietta,		Orange County	112	Lincoln County, MO	38
WV-OH MSA	**149**	Wake County	587	St. Charles County, MO	280
Wood County, WV	86			St. Louis County, MO	996
Washington County, OH	63	**Rapid City, SD MSA**	**88**	Warren County, MO	25
		Pennington County	88	St. Louis city, MO	334
Pensacola, FL MSA	**403**			Clinton County, IL	36
Escambia County	282	**Reading, PA MSA**	**358**	Jersey County, IL	22
Santa Rosa County	121	Berks County	358	Madison County, IL	259
				Monroe County, IL	27
Peoria-Pekin, IL MSA	**346**	**Redding, CA MSA**	**165**	St. Clair County, IL	260
Peoria County	181	Shasta County	165		
Tazewell County	130			**Salinas, CA MSA**	**372**
Woodford County	36	**Reno, NV MSA**	**320**	Monterey County	372
		Washoe County	320		
Philadelphia-Wilmington-				**Salt Lake City-Ogden, UT**	
Atlantic City, PA-NJ-DE-		**Richland-Kennewick-Pasco,**		**MSA**	**1,275**
MD CMSA	**5,999**	**WA MSA**	**185**	Davis County	239
Atlantic-Cape May, NJ		Benton County	138	Salt Lake County	850
PMSA	**338**	Franklin County	47	Weber County	185
Atlantic County, NJ	240				
Cape May County, NJ	98	**Richmond-Petersburg, VA**		**San Angelo, TX MSA**	**102**
Philadelphia, PA-NJ		**MSA**	**961**	Tom Green County	102
PMSA	**4,950**	Charles City County	7		
Bucks County, PA	594	Chesterfield County	253	**San Antonio, TX MSA**	**1,565**
Chester County, PA	430	Dinwiddie County	26	Bexar County	1,373
Delaware County, PA	542	Goochland County	18	Comal County	77
Montgomery County, PA	724	Hanover County	85	Guadalupe County	83
Philadelphia County, PA	1,418	Henrico County	245	Wilson County	33
Burlington County, NJ	425	New Kent County	13		
Camden County, NJ	503	Powhatan County	22	**San Diego, CA MSA**	**2,821**
Gloucester County, NJ	250	Prince George County	29	San Diego County	2,821
Salem County, NJ	65	Colonial Heights city	16		
Vineland-Millville-		Hopewell city	23	**San Francisco-Oakland-San**	
Bridgeton, NJ PMSA	**140**	Petersburg city	34	**Jose, CA CMSA**	**6,874**
Cumberland County, NJ	140	Richmond city	190	**Oakland, CA PMSA**	**2,349**
Wilmington-Newark,				Alameda County	1,416
DE-MD PMSA	**571**	**Roanoke, VA MSA**	**228**	Contra Costa County	933
New Castle County, DE	487	Botetourt County	29	**San Francisco, CA**	
Cecil County, MD	84	Roanoke County	81	**PMSA**	**1,686**
		Roanoke city	93	Marin County	237
Phoenix-Mesa, AZ MSA	**3,014**	Salem city	24	San Francisco County	747
Maricopa County	2,861			San Mateo County	702
Pinal County	152	**Rochester, MN MSA**	**119**	**San Jose, CA PMSA**	**1,647**
		Olmsted County	119	Santa Clara County	1,647
Pine Bluff, AR MSA	**81**			**Santa Cruz-Watsonville,**	
Jefferson County	81	**Rochester, NY MSA**	**1,079**	**CA PMSA**	**245**
		Genesee County	60	Santa Cruz County	245
Pittsburgh, PA MSA	**2,331**	Livingston County	66	**Santa Rosa, CA PMSA**	**440**
Allegheny County	1,257	Monroe County	712	Sonoma County	440
Beaver County	183	Ontario County	100	**Vallejo-Fairfield-Napa, CA**	
Butler County	173	Orleans County	45	**PMSA**	**507**
Fayette County	144	Wayne County	96	Napa County	121
Washington County	205			Solano County	386
Westmoreland County	371	**Rockford, IL MSA**	**359**		
		Boone County	40	**San Luis Obispo-**	
Pocatello, ID MSA	**75**	Ogle County	51	**Atascadero-Paso Robles,**	
Bannock County	75	Winnebago County	268	**CA MSA**	**237**
				San Luis Obispo County	237
Portland-Salem, OR-WA		**Rocky Mount, NC MSA**	**147**		
CMSA	**2,181**	Edgecombe County	55	**Santa Barbara-Santa Maria-**	
Portland-Vancouver,		Nash County	92	**Lompoc, CA MSA**	**391**
OR-WA PMSA	**1,846**			Santa Barbara County	391
Clackamas County, OR	338	**Sacramento-Yolo, CA**			
Columbia County, OR	45	**CMSA**	**1,741**	**Santa Fe, NM MSA**	**143**
Multnomah County, OR	633	**Sacramento, CA PMSA**	**1,585**	Los Alamos County	18
Washington County, OR	409	El Dorado County	161	Santa Fe County	124
Yamhill County, OR	83	Placer County	239		
Clark County, WA	336	Sacramento County	1,185	**Sarasota-Bradenton, FL**	
Salem, OR PMSA	**335**	**Yolo, CA PMSA**	**156**	**MSA**	**550**
Marion County, OR	273	Yolo County	156	Manatee County	244
				Sarasota County	307

U.S. Census Bureau, Statistical Abstract of the United States: 2000

	Popu-lation, 1999 (1,000)		Popu-lation, 1999 (1,000)		Popu-lation, 1999 (1,000)
Savannah, GA MSA......	288	Onondaga County........	456	**Washington, DC-MD-VA-WV PMSA**	**4,740**
Bryan County..........	24	Oswego County........	124	District of Columbia, DC..	519
Chatham County........	226			Calvert County, MD....	74
Effingham County......	38	**Tallahassee, FL MSA**......	**260**	Charles County, MD....	121
		Gadsden County.......	44	Frederick County, MD ...	191
Scranton—Wilkes-Barre—Hazleton, PA MSA.......	**611**	Leon County..........	216	Montgomery County, MD	852
Columbia County......	64	**Tampa-St. Petersburg-Clearwater, FL MSA**.....	**2,278**	Prince George's County, MD	782
Lackawanna County.....	207	Hernando County......	128	Arlington County, VA....	175
Luzerne County........	312	Hillsborough County....	940	Clarke County, VA.....	13
Wyoming County.......	29	Pasco County.........	331	Culpeper County, VA ...	34
		Pinellas County........	878	Fairfax County, VA.....	946
Seattle-Tacoma-Bremerton, WA CMSA............	**3,466**			Fauquier County, VA ...	55
Bremerton, WA PMSA....	**237**	**Terre Haute, IN MSA**......	**148**	King George County, VA.	18
Kitsap County........	237	Clay County..........	27	Loudoun County, VA ...	156
Olympia, WA PMSA....	**205**	Vermillion County......	17	Prince William County, VA...............	271
Thurston County.....	205	Vigo County..........	104	Spotsylvania County, VA.	87
Seattle-Bellevue-Everett, WA PMSA....	**2,335**	**Texarkana, TX-Texarkana, AR MSA**.............	**123**	Stafford County, VA....	93
Island County.......	73	Bowie County, TX.......	84	Warren County, VA....	31
King County.........	1,665	Miller County, AR.......	39	Alexandria city, VA....	117
Snohomish County....	597			Fairfax city, VA.......	21
Tacoma, WA PMSA.....	**689**	**Toledo, OH MSA**.........	**609**	Falls Church city, VA...	10
Pierce County.......	689	Fulton County.........	42	Fredericksburg city, VA..	19
		Lucas County.........	446	Manassas city, VA.....	33
Sharon, PA MSA.........	**121**	Wood County.........	120	Manassas Park city, VA .	8
Mercer County........	121			Berkeley County, WV...	73
		Topeka, KS MSA.........	**171**	Jefferson County, WV...	42
Sheboygan, WI MSA......	**110**	Shawnee County.......	171		
Sheboygan County.....	110			**Waterloo-Cedar Falls, IA MSA**.................	**120**
		Tucson, AZ MSA.........	**804**	Black Hawk County.....	120
Sherman-Denison, TX MSA.................	**104**	Pima County..........	804		
Grayson County.......	104			**Wausau, WI MSA**.......	**124**
		Tulsa, OK MSA..........	**786**	Marathon County......	124
Shreveport-Bossier City, LA MSA.................	**378**	Creek County.........	68	**West Palm Beach-Boca Raton, FL MSA**.........	**1,049**
Bossier Parish........	93	Osage County.........	43	Palm Beach County	1,049
Caddo Parish.........	242	Rogers County........	71		
Webster Parish........	43	Tulsa County.........	548	**Wheeling, WV-OH MSA**....	**154**
		Wagoner County.......	56	Marshall County, WV....	35
Sioux City, IA-NE MSA....	**121**			Ohio County, WV......	48
Woodbury County, IA...	101	**Tuscaloosa, AL MSA**......	**161**	Belmont County, OH.....	71
Dakota County, NE.....	19	Tuscaloosa County.....	161		
				Wichita, KS MSA.........	**549**
Sioux Falls, SD MSA......	**164**	**Tyler, TX MSA**..........	**170**	Butler County.........	63
Lincoln County........	22	Smith County.........	170	Harvey County........	34
Minnehaha County......	143			Sedgwick County......	452
		Utica-Rome, NY MSA.....	**293**		
South Bend, IN MSA......	**259**	Herkimer County.......	63	**Wichita Falls, TX MSA**.....	**136**
St. Joseph County.....	259	Oneida County........	230	Archer County........	8
				Wichita County.......	128
Spokane, WA MSA.......	**410**	**Victoria, TX MSA**.........	**82**		
Spokane County.......	410	Victoria County........	82	**Williamsport, PA MSA**.....	**117**
				Lycoming County......	117
Springfield, IL MSA.......	**204**	**Visalia-Tulare-Porterville, CA MSA**..............	**358**		
Menard County........	13	Tulare County.........	358	**Wilmington, NC MSA**.....	**222**
Sangamon County......	191			Brunswick County......	71
		Waco, TX MSA..........	**204**	New Hanover County....	151
Springfield, MO MSA......	**308**	McLennan County......	204		
Christian County.......	51			**Yakima, WA MSA**.......	**221**
Greene County........	227	**Washington-Baltimore, DC-MD-VA-WV CMSA**	**7,359**	Yakima County.......	221
Webster County.......	30	**Baltimore, MD PMSA**....	**2,491**		
		Anne Arundel County, MD	480	**York, PA MSA**...........	**377**
State College, PA MSA	**132**	Baltimore County, MD ..	724	York County..........	377
Centre County........	132	Carroll County, MD....	152		
		Harford County, MD....	218	**Youngstown-Warren, OH MSA**.................	**589**
Steubenville-Weirton, OH-WV MSA..............	**133**	Howard County, MD....	243	Columbiana County......	111
Jefferson County, OH	74	Queen Anne's County, MD	41	Mahoning County......	253
Brooke County, WV.....	26	Baltimore city, MD	633	Trumbull County.......	225
Hancock County, WV.....	34				
		Hagerstown, MD PMSA ..	**128**	**Yuba City, CA MSA**.......	**138**
Stockton-Lodi, CA CMSA....	**563**	Washington County, MD	128	Sutter County.........	78
San Joaquin County.....	563			Yuba County.........	60
Sumter, SC MSA.........	**112**			**Yuma, AZ MSA**.........	**136**
Sumter County.........	112			Yuma County.........	136
Syracuse, NY MSA.......	**733**				
Cayuga County........	82				
Madison County........	71				

[1] Five PMSAs of the New York-Northern New Jersey-Long Island, NY-NJ-CTPA CMSA are in Connecticut and therefore do not appear in this table; also, the CMSA's population shown here reflects the absence of those PMSAs.

Source: U.S. Census Bureau, "County Population Estimates and Demographic Components of Population Change: Annual Time Series, July 1, 1990, to July 1, 1999;" published 9 March 2000; <http://www.census.gov/population/www/estimates/co998.html>.

U.S. Census Bureau, Statistical Abstract of the United States: 2000

Appendix III
Limitations of the Data

Introduction.—The data presented in this *Statistical Abstract* came from many sources. The sources include not only Federal statistical bureaus and other organizations that collect and issue statistics as their principal activity, but also governmental administrative and regulatory agencies, private research bodies, trade associations, insurance companies, health associations, and private organizations such as the National Education Association and philanthropic foundations. Consequently, the data vary considerably as to reference periods, definitions of terms and, for ongoing series, the number and frequency of time periods for which data are available.

The statistics presented were obtained and tabulated by various means. Some statistics are based on complete enumerations or censuses while others are based on samples. Some information is extracted from records kept for administrative or regulatory purposes (school enrollment, hospital records, securities registration, financial accounts, social security records, income tax returns, etc.), while other information is obtained explicitly for statistical purposes through interviews or by mail. The estimation procedures used vary from highly sophisticated scientific techniques, to crude "informed guesses."

Each set of data relates to a group of individuals or units of interest referred to as the *target universe* or *target population,* or simply as the *universe* or *population.* Prior to data collection the target universe should be clearly defined. For example, if data are to be collected for the universe of households in the United States, it is necessary to define a "household." The target universe may not be completely tractable. Cost and other considerations may restrict data collection to a *survey universe* based on some available list, such list may be it of date. This list is called a *survey frame* or *sampling frame.*

The data in many tables are based on data obtained for all population units, *a census,* or on data obtained for only a portion, or *sample,* of the population units. When the data presented are based on a sample, the sample is usually a scientifically selected *probability sample.* This is a sample selected from a list or sampling frame in such a way that every possible sample has a known chance of selection and usually each unit selected can be assigned a number, greater than zero and less than or equal to one, representing its likelihood or probability of selection.

For large-scale sample surveys, the probability sample of units is often selected as a multistage sample. The first stage of a multistage sample is the selection of a probability sample of large groups of population members, referred to as primary sampling units (PSUs). For example, in a national multistage household sample, PSUs are often counties or groups of counties. The second stage of a multistage sample is the selection, within each PSU selected at the first stage, of smaller groups of population units, referred to as secondary sampling units. In subsequent stages of selection, smaller and smaller nested groups are chosen until the ultimate sample of population units is obtained. To qualify a multistage sample as a probability sample, all stages of sampling must be carried out using probability sampling methods.

Prior to selection at each stage of a multistage (or a single stage) sample, a list of the sampling units or sampling frame for that stage must be obtained. For example, for the first stage of selection of a national household sample, a list of the counties and county groups that form the PSUs must be obtained. For the final stage of selection, lists of households, and sometimes persons within the households, have to be compiled in the field. For surveys of economic entities and for

918 Appendix III

the economic censuses the Bureau generally uses a frame constructed from the Bureau's Standard Statistical Establishment List (SSEL). The SSEL contains all establishments with payroll in the United States including small single establishment firms as well as large multi-establishment firms.

Wherever the quantities in a table refer to an entire universe, but are constructed from data collected in a sample survey, the table quantities are referred to as *sample estimates*. In constructing a sample estimate, an attempt is made to come as close as is feasible to the corresponding universe quantity that would be obtained from a complete census of the universe. Estimates based on a sample will, however, generally differ from the hypothetical census figures. Two classifications of errors are associated with estimates based on sample surveys: (1) *sampling error*—the error arising from the use of a sample, rather than a census, to estimate population quantities and (2) *nonsampling error*—those errors arising from nonsampling sources. As discussed below, the magnitude of the sampling error for an estimate can usually be estimated from the sample data. However, the magnitude of the nonsampling error for an estimate can rarely be estimated. Consequently, actual error in an estimate exceeds the error that can be estimated.

The particular sample used in a survey is only one of a large number of possible samples of the same size which could have been selected using the same sampling procedure. Estimates derived from the different samples would, in general, differ from each other. The *standard error* (SE) is a measure of the variation among the estimates derived from all possible samples. The standard error is the most commonly used measure of the sampling error of an estimate. Valid estimates of the standard errors of survey estimates can usually be calculated from the data collected in a probability sample. For convenience, the standard error is sometimes expressed as a percent of the estimate and is called the relative standard error or *coefficient of variation* (CV). For example, an estimate of 200 units with an estimated standard error of 10 units has an estimated CV of 5 percent.

A sample estimate and an estimate of its standard error or CV can be used to construct interval estimates that have a prescribed confidence that the interval includes the average of the estimates derived from all possible samples with a known probability. To illustrate, if all possible samples were selected under essentially the same general conditions, and using the same sample design, and if an estimate and its estimated standard error were calculated from each sample, then: (1) Approximately 68 percent of the intervals from one standard error below the estimate to one standard error above the estimate would include the average estimate derived from all possible samples; (2) approximately 90 percent of the intervals from 1.6 standard errors below the estimate to 1.6 standard errors above the estimate would include the average estimate derived from all possible samples; and (3) approximately 95 percent of the intervals from two standard errors below the estimate to two standard errors above the estimate would include the average estimate derived from all possible samples.

Thus, for a particular sample, one can say with the appropriate level of confidence (e.g., 90% or 95%) that the average of all possible samples is included in the constructed interval. Example of a confidence interval: An estimate is 200 units with a standard error of 10 units. An approximately 90 percent confidence interval (plus or minus 1.6 standard errors) is from 184 to 216.

All surveys and censuses are subject to nonsampling errors. Nonsampling errors are of two kinds—*random* and *nonrandom*. Random nonsampling errors arise because of the varying interpretation of questions (by respondents or interviewers) and varying actions of coders, keyers, and other processors. Some randomness is also introduced when respondents must estimate me errors usually have a nonrandom component. Nonrandom nonsampling errors result from total nonresponse (no usable data obtained for a sampled unit), partial or item nonresponse (only a portion of a response may be usable), inability or unwillingness on the part of respondents to provide correct

U.S. Census Bureau, Statistical Abstract of the United States: 2000

information, difficulty interpreting questions, mistakes in recording or keying data, errors of collection or processing, and coverage problems (overcoverage and undercoverage of the target universe). Random nonresponse errors usually, but not always, result in an understatement of sampling errors and thus an overstatement of the precision of survey estimates. Estimating the magnitude of nonsampling errors would require special experiments or access to independent data and, consequently, the magnitudes are seldom available.

Nearly all types of nonsampling errors that affect surveys also occur in complete censuses. Since surveys can be conducted on a smaller scale than censuses, nonsampling errors can presumably be controlled more tightly. Relatively more funds and effort can perhaps be expended toward eliciting responses, detecting and correcting response error, and reducing processing errors. As a result, survey results can sometimes be more accurate than census results.

To compensate for suspected nonrandom errors, adjustments of the sample estimates are often made. For example, adjustments are frequently made for nonresponse, both total and partial. Adjustments made for either type of nonresponse are often referred to as *imputations*. Imputation for total nonresponse is usually made by substituting for the questionnaire responses of the nonrespondents the "average" questionnaire responses of the respondents. These imputations usually are made separately within various groups of sample members, formed by attempting to place respondents and nonrespondents together that have "similar" design or ancillary characteristics. Imputation for item nonresponse is usually made by substituting for a missing item the response to that item of a respondent having characteristics that are "similar" to those of the nonrespondent.

For an estimate calculated from a sample survey, the *total error* in the estimate is composed of the sampling error, which can usually be estimated from the sample, and the nonsampling error, which usually cannot be estimated from the

sample. The total error present in a population quantity obtained from a complete census is composed of only nonsampling errors. Ideally, estimates of the total error associated with data given in the *Statistical Abstract* tables should be given. However, due to the unavailability of estimates of nonsampling errors, only estimates of the levels of sampling errors, in terms of estimated standard errors or coefficients of variation, are available. To obtain estimates of the estimated standard errors from the sample of interest, obtain a copy of the referenced report which appears at the end of each table.

Principal data bases.—Beginning below are brief descriptions of 36 of the sample surveys and censuses that provide a substantial portion of the data contained in this *Abstract*.

SECTION 1. POPULATION

Source and Title: U.S. Census Bureau, *Census of Population*

Tables: See tables citing *Census of Population* in Section 1 and also in Sections 2, 4, 6, 8, 13, 14, 21, and 29.

Universe, Frequency, and Types of Data: Complete count of U.S. population conducted every 10 years since 1790. Data obtained on number and characteristics of people in the United States.

Type of Data Collection Operation: In 1970, 1980, and 1990 complete census for some items—age, sex, race, marital status, and relationship to householder. In 1970, other items collected from a 5% and a 15% probability (systematic) sample of the population. In 1980, approximately 19% of the housing units were included in the sample; in 1990, approximately 17%.

Data Collection and Imputation Procedures: In 1970, extensive use of mail questionnaires in urban areas; personal interviews in most rural areas. In 1980 and 1990, mail questionnaires were used in even more areas than in 1970, with personal interviews in the remainder. Extensive telephone and personal followup for nonrespondents was done in the censuses. Imputations were made for missing characteristics.

Estimates of Sampling Error: Sampling errors for data are estimated for all items collected by sample and vary by

U.S. Census Bureau, Statistical Abstract of the United States: 2000

characteristic and geographic area. The CVs for national and state estimates are generally very small.

Other (nonsampling) Errors: Since 1950, evaluation programs have been conducted to provide information on the magnitude of some sources of nonsampling errors such as response bias and undercoverage in each census. Results from the evaluation program for the 1990 census indicate that the net under coverage amounted to about 1.5 to 2 percent of the total resident population.

Sources of Additional Material: U.S. Census Bureau, *The Coverage of Population in the 1980 Census*, PHC80-E4; *Content Reinterview Study: Accuracy of Data for Selected Population and Housing Characteristics as Measured by Reinterview*, PHC80-E2; *1980 Census of Population*, Vol. 1, (PC80-1), Appendixes B, C, and D.

Source and Title: U.S. Census Bureau, *Current Population Survey (CPS)*

Tables: See tables citing *Current Population Reports* primarily in Section 1, but also in Sections 2, 3, 4, 8, 12, 13, 14, 18, 23, and 29. Many Bureau of Labor Statistics' (BLS) tables in Section 13 are CPS based.

Universe, Frequency, and Types of Data: Nationwide monthly sample survey of civilian noninstitutional population, 15 years old or over, to obtain data on employment, unemployment, and a number of other characteristics.

Type of Data Collection Operation: Multistage probability sample of about 50,000 households in 754 PSUs in 1996. Oversampling in some states and the largest MSAs to improve reliability for those areas of employment data on annual average basis. A continual sample rotation system is used. Households are in sample 4 months, out for 8 months, and in for 4 more. Month-to-month overlap is 75%; year-to-year overlap is 50%.

Data Collection and Imputation Procedures: For first and fifth months that a household is in sample, personal interviews; other months, approximately, 85% of the data collected by phone. Imputation is done for both item and total nonresponse. Adjustment for total nonresponse is done by a predefined

cluster of units, by MSA size and residence; for item nonresponse imputation varies by subject matter.

Estimates of Sampling Error: Estimated CVs on national annual averages for labor force, total employment, and nonagricultural employment, 0.2%; for total unemployment and agricultural employment, 1.0% to 2.5%. The estimated CVs for family income and poverty rate for all persons in 1986 are 0.5% and 1.5%, respectively. CVs for subnational areas, such as states, would be larger and would vary by area.

Other (nonsampling) Errors: Estimates of response bias on unemployment are not available, but estimates of unemployment are usually 5% to 9% lower than estimates from reinterviews. Six to 7.0% of sample households unavailable for interviews.

Sources of Additional Material: U.S. Census Bureau and Bureau of Labor Statistics, *Current Population Survey; Design and Methodology*, (Tech. Paper 63), available on internet <www.bls. census.gov/cps/tp/tp63.htm> and Bureau of Labor Statistics, *Employment and Earnings*, monthly, Explanatory Notes and Estimates of Error, Tables 1-A through 1-D and *BLS Handbook of Methods*, Chapter 1 (Bulletin 2490.)

SECTION 2. VITAL STATISTICS

Source and Title: U.S. National Center for Health Statistics (NCHS), *National Vital Statistics System*

Tables: See tables citing *Vital Statistics of the United States;* 335 in Section 5; and 1334 in Section 29.

Universe, Frequency, and Types of Data: Annual data on births and deaths in the United States.

Type of Data Collection Operation: Mortality data based on complete file of death records, except 1972, based on 50% sample. Natality statistics 1951-71, based on 50% sample of birth certificates, except a 20% to 50% in 1967, received by NCHS. Beginning 1972, data from some states received through Vital Statistics Cooperative Program (VSCP) and complete file used; data from other states based on 50% sample. Beginning 1986, all reporting areas participated in the VSCP.

Data Collection and Imputation Procedures: Reports based on records from registration offices of all states, District of Columbia, New York City, Puerto Rico, Virgin Islands, and Guam.

Estimates of Sampling Error: For recent years, CVs for births are small due to large portion of total file in sample (except for very small estimated totals).

Other (nonsampling) Errors: Data on births and deaths believed to be at least 99% complete.

Sources of Additional Material: U.S. National Center for Health Statistics, *Vital Statistics of the United States*, Vol. I and Vol. II, annual, and *National Vital Statistics Report.*

(See Section 1 above for information pertaining to Tables 92-95.)

SECTION 3. HEALTH AND NUTRITION

Source and Title: U.S. National Center for Health Statistics, *National Health Interview Survey (NHIS)*

Tables: 189, 211, 212, 216, 219, 220, 226 and 231.

Universe, Frequency, and Types of Data: Continuous data collection covering the civilian noninstitutional population to obtain information on personal and demographic characteristics, illnesses, injuries, impairments, and other health topics.

Type of Data Collection Operation: Multistage probability sample of 49,000 households (in 198 PSUs) from 1985 to 1994; 43,000 households (358 design PSUs) from 1995 on, selected in groups of about four adjacent households.

Data Collection and Imputation Procedures: Some missing data items (e.g., age) are imputed using an average value. Unit nonresponse is compensated for by an adjustment to the survey weights

Estimates of Sampling Error: Estimated CVs: For physician visits by males, 1.5%; for workdays lost by males, 3.5%; for persons injured at home, 4.7%.

Other (nonsampling) Errors: Response rate was 93.8% in 1996 for the NHIS.

Sources of Additional Material: U.S. National Center for Health Statistics, "Current Estimates from the National Health Interview Survey, U.S., 1996," Vital and Health Statistics, Series 10 #200.

(See Section 13 for information pertaining to Table 184, Section 15 for Table 162, and Section 27 for Table 181.)

SECTION 4. EDUCATION

Source and Title: U.S. Department of Education, National Center for Education Statistics, *Higher Education General Information Survey (HEGIS), Fall Enrollment in Institutions of Higher Education;* beginning 1986, *Integrated Postsecondary Education Data Survey (IPEDS), Fall Enrollment*

Tables: 239, 241, 296-299.

Universe, Frequency, and Types of Data: Annual survey of all institutions and branches listed in the *Directory* to obtain data on total enrollment by sex, level of enrollment, type of program, racial/ethnic characteristics (every other year prior to 1989, then annually) and attendance status of student, and on first-time students.

Type of Data Collection Operation: Complete census.

Data Collection and Imputation Procedures: Survey package is usually mailed in the spring with surveys due at varying dates in the summer and fall; mail and phone followup procedures for nonrespondents. Missing data are imputed by using data of similar institutions.

Estimates of Sampling Error: Not applicable.

Other (nonsampling) Errors: For degree-granting institutions approximately 92% response rate in fall 1998.

Sources of Additional Material: U.S. Department of Education, National Center for Education Statistics, *Fall Enrollment in Higher Education*, annual.

Source and Title: U.S. Department of Education, National Center for Education Statistics, *Higher Education General Information Survey (HEGIS), Financial Statistics of Institutions of Higher Education;* beginning 1986, *Integrated Postsecondary Education Data Survey (IPEDS), Finance.*

Tables: 240, 243, 297, and 308.

Universe, Frequency, and Types of Data: Annual survey of all institutions and branches listed in the *Education Directory, Colleges and Universities* to obtain data on financial status and operations, including current funds revenues, current funds expenditures, and physical plant assets.

Type of Data Collection Operation: Complete census.

Data Collection and Imputation Procedures: Survey package is usually mailed in the spring with surveys due at varying dates in the summer and fall; mail and phone followup procedures for non-respondents. Missing data are imputed by using data of similar institutions.

Estimates of Sampling Error: Not applicable.

Other (nonsampling) Errors: For 1997, 95% for degree-granting institutions.

Sources of Additional Material: U.S. Department of Education, National Center for Education Statistics, *Financial Statistics.*

Source and Title: U.S. Department of Education, National Center for Education Statistics, *Higher Education General Information Survey (HEGIS), Degrees and Other Formal Awards Conferred.* Beginning 1986, *Integrated Postsecondary Education Data Survey (IPEDS), Completions.*

Tables: 241, 317-322.

Universe, Frequency, and Types of Data: Annual survey of all institutions and branches listed in the *Education Directory, Colleges and Universities* to obtain data on earned degrees and other formal awards, conferred by field of study, level of degree, sex, and by racial/ethnic characteristics (every other year prior to 1989, then annually).

Type of Data Collection Operation: Complete census.

Data Collection and Imputation Procedures: Survey package is usually mailed in the spring with surveys due at varying dates in the summer and fall; mail and phone followup procedures for non-respondents. Missing data are imputed by using data of similar institutions.

Estimates of Sampling Error: Not applicable.

Other (nonsampling) Errors: For 1996-98, approximately 92% response rate for degree-granting institutions.

Sources of Additional Material: U.S. Department of Education, National Center for Education Statistics, *Completions,* annual.

(See Sections 1 and 9 for information pertaining to the Census Bureau and Section 5 for information pertaining to Table 254.)

SECTION 5. LAW ENFORCEMENT, COURTS, AND PRISONS

Source and Title: U.S. Federal Bureau of Investigation, *Uniform Crime Reporting (UCR) Program*

Tables: 329-334, 336-339, 344, 345, and 347.

Universe, Frequency, and Types of Data: Monthly reports on the number of criminal offenses that become known to law enforcement agencies. Data are collected on crimes cleared by arrest, by age, sex, and race of offender, and on assaults on law enforcement officers.

Type of Data Collection Operation: Crime statistics are based on reports of crime data submitted either directly to the FBI by contributing law enforcement agencies or through cooperating state UCR programs.

Data Collection and Imputation Procedures: States with UCR programs collect data directly from individual law enforcement agencies and forward reports, prepared in accordance with UCR standards, to FBI. Accuracy and consistency edits are performed by FBI.

Estimates of Sampling Error: Not applicable.

Other (nonsampling) Errors: Coverage of 96% of the population (97% in MSAs, 90% in "other cities," and 84% in rural areas) by UCR program, though varying number of agencies report. Some error may be present through incorrect reporting.

Sources of Additional Material: U.S. Federal Bureau of Investigation, *Crime in the United States, Hate Crime Statistics,* annual, *Law Enforcement Officers Killed & Assaulted,* annual.

Source and Title: U.S. Bureau of Justice Statistics (BJS), *National Crime Victimization Survey*

Tables: 340-343, and Table 254 in Section 4.

Universe, Frequency, and Types of Data: Monthly survey of individuals and households in the United States to obtain data on criminal victimization of those units for compilation of annual estimates.

Type of Data Collection Operation: National probability sample survey of about 50,000 interviewed households in 376 PSUs selected from a list of addresses from the 1980 census, supplemented by new construction permits and an area sample where permits are not required.

Data Collection and Imputation Procedures: Interviews are conducted every 6 months for 3 years for each household in the sample; 8,300 households are interviewed monthly. Personal interviews are used in the first interview; the intervening interviews are conducted by telephone whenever possible.

Estimates of Sampling Error: CVs averaged over the period 1996-1999 are: 2.7% for crimes of violence; 8.5% for estimate of rape/sexual assault counts; 5.5% for robbery counts; 2.8% for assault counts; 8.0% for personal theft counts; 1.9% for property crimes; 3.0% for burglary counts; 2.0% for theft; and 4.4% for motor vehicle theft counts.

Other (nonsampling) Errors: Respondent recall errors which may include reporting incidents for other than the reference period; interviewer coding and processing errors; and possible mistaken reporting or classifying of events. Adjustment is made for a household noninterview rate of about 4% and for a within-household noninterview rate of 7%.

Sources of Additional Material: U.S. Bureau of Justice Statistics, *Criminal Victimization in the United States,* annual.

(See Section 2 for details on Table 335.)

SECTION 7. PARKS AND RECREATION

(See Section 27 for details on Table 420.)

SECTION 8. ELECTIONS

(See Section 1 above for information pertaining to Tables 477 and 478 and Section 9 for information pertaining to Table 471.)

SECTION 9. STATE AND LOCAL GOVERNMENT FINANCES AND EMPLOYMENT

Source and Title: U.S. Census Bureau, *Census of Governments*

Tables: See tables in Section 9 citing *Census of Governments and Table 471 in Section 8.*

Universe, Frequency, and Types of Data: Survey of all governmental units in the United States conducted every 5 years to obtain data on government revenue, expenditures, debt, assets, employment and employee retirement systems, property values, public school systems, and number, size, and structure of governments.

Type of Data Collection Operation: Complete census. List of units derived through classification of government units recently authorized in each state and identification, counting, and classification of existing local governments and public school systems.

Data Collection and Imputation Procedures: Data collected through field and office compilation of financial data from official records and reports for states and large local governments; mail canvass of selected data items, like state tax revenue and employee retirement systems; and collection of local government statistics through central collection arrangements with state governments.

Estimates of Sampling Error: Not applicable.

Other (nonsampling) Errors: Some nonsampling errors may arise due to possible inaccuracies in classification, response, and processing.

Sources of Additional Material: U.S. Census Bureau, *Census of Governments, 1987,* various reports, and *State Government Finances in 1990,* GF 90, No. 3.

Source and Title: U.S. Census Bureau, *Annual Surveys of State and Local Government*

Tables: See tables citing *Public Employment* and *Government Finances* in Section 9 and Table 274 in Section 4; and Table 612 in Section 12.

Universe, Frequency, and Types of Data: Sample survey conducted annually to obtain data on revenue, expenditure, debt, and employment of state and local governments. Universe is all governmental units in the United States (about 87,000).

Type of Data Collection Operation: Sample of about 22,000 units includes all state governments, county governments with 50,000+ population, municipalities and townships with 25,000+ population, all school districts with 10,000+ enrollment in October 1986, and other governments meeting certain criteria; probability sample for remaining units.

Data Collection and Imputation Procedures: Field and office compilation of data from official records and reports for states and large local governments; central collection of local governmental financial data through cooperative agreements with a number of state governments; mail canvass of other units with mail and telephone followups of nonrespondents. Data for nonresponses are imputed from previous year data or obtained from secondary sources, if available.

Estimates of Sampling Error: CVs for estimates of major employment and financial items are generally less than 2% for most states and less than 1.2% for the majority of states.

Other (nonsampling) Errors: Nonresponse rate is less than 15% for number of units. Other possible errors may result from undetected inaccuracies in classification, response, and processing.

Sources of Additional Material: U.S. Census Bureau, *Public Employment in 1990,* GE 90, No. 1, *Governmental Finances in 1989-90,* GF 90, No. 5, and *Census of Governments, 1987,* various reports.

SECTION 10. FEDERAL GOVERNMENT

Source and Title: U.S. Internal Revenue Service, *Statistics of Income, Individual Income Tax Returns*

Tables: 548-552.

Universe, Frequency, and Types of Data: Annual study of unaudited individual income tax returns, Forms 1040, 1040A, and 1040EZ, filed by U.S. citizens and residents. Data provided on various financial characteristics by size of adjusted gross income, marital status, and by taxable and nontaxable returns. Data by state, based on 100% file, also include returns Form 1040NR, filed by nonresident aliens plus certain self-employment tax returns.

Type of Data Collection Operation: Annual stratified probability sample of approximately 125,000 returns broken into sample strata based on the larger of total income or total loss amounts as well as the size of business plus farm receipts. Sampling rates for sample strata varied from .025% to 100%.

Data Collection and Imputation Procedures: Computer selection of sample of tax return records. Data adjusted during editing for incorrect, missing, or inconsistent entries to ensure consistency with other entries on return.

Estimates of Sampling Error: Estimated CVs for tax year 1997: Adjusted gross income less deficit .15%; salaries and wages .27%; and tax-exempt interest received 2.15%. (State data not subject to sampling error.)

Other (nonsampling) Errors: Processing errors and errors arising from the use of tolerance checks for the data.

Sources of Additional Material: U.S. Internal Revenue Service, *Statistics of Income, Individual Income Tax Returns,* annual.

SECTION 12. SOCIAL INSURANCE AND HUMAN SERVICES

Source and Title: U.S. Social Security Administration, *Benefit Data*

Tables: 608 and 609.

Universe, Frequency, and Types of Data: All persons receiving monthly benefits under Title II of Social Security Act. Data on number and amount of benefits paid by type and state.

Type of Data Collection Operation: Data based on administrative records. Data based on 100% files, as well as 10% and 1% sample files.

Data Collection and Imputation Procedures: Records used consist of actions pursuant to applications dated by subsequent post-entitlement actions.

Estimates of Sampling Error: Varies by size of estimate and sample file size.

Other (nonsampling) Errors: Processing errors, which are believed to be small.

Sources of Additional Material: U.S. Social Security Administration, *Annual Statistical Supplement to the Social Security Bulletin.*

Source and Title: U.S. Social Security Administration, *Supplemental Security Income (SSI) Program*

Tables: 623 and 624.

Universe, Frequency, and Types of Data: All eligible aged, blind, or disabled persons receiving SSI benefit payments under SSI program. Data include number of persons receiving federally administered SSI, amounts paid, and state administered supplementation.

Type of Data Collection Operation: Data based on administrative records.

Data Collection and Imputation Procedures: Data adjusted to reflect returned checks and overpayment refunds. For federally administered payments, actual adjusted amounts are used.

Estimates of Sampling Error: Not applicable.

Other (nonsampling) Errors: Processing errors, which are believed to be small.

Sources of Additional Material: U.S. Social Security Administration, *Annual Statistical Supplement to the Social Security Bulletin.*

(See Section 1 above for information pertaining to the Current Population Survey and Section 9 for information pertaining to Annual Surveys of State and Local Government.)

SECTION 13. LABOR FORCE, EMPLOYMENT, AND EARNINGS

Source and Title: U.S. Bureau of Labor Statistics (BLS), *Current Employment Statistics (CES)* Program

Tables: 682-684, 692; in Section 3, Table 184; in Section 21, Table 1010; and in Section 22, Table 1080.

Universe, Frequency, and Types of Data: Monthly survey covering about 6 million nonagricultural establishments to obtain data on employment, hours, and earnings, by industry.

Type of Data Collection Operation: Sample survey of about 300,000 establishments in June 2000.

Data Collection and Imputation Procedures: Cooperating state agencies mail questionnaires to sample establishments to develop state and local estimates; information is forwarded to BLS where national estimates are prepared.

Estimates of Sampling Error: Estimated CVs for employment, 0.1%, for average weekly hours paid, 0.1% and for average hourly earnings, 0.2%.

Other (nonsampling) Errors: Estimates of employment adjusted annually to reflect complete universe. Average adjustment is 0.3%.

Sources of Additional Material: U.S. Bureau of Labor Statistics, *Employment and Earnings,* monthly, Explanatory Notes and Estimates of Error, Tables 2-A through 2-J.

(See Section 1 above for information pertaining to the Current Population Survey.)

SECTION 14. INCOME, EXPENDITURES, AND WEALTH

Source and Title: Board of Governors of the Federal Reserve System, *Survey of Consumer Finances*

Tables: 763 and 764, and in Section 16, 792, 794-796, 817 and 837.

Universe, Frequency, and Types of Data: Periodic sample survey of families. In this survey a given household is divided into a primary economic unit and other economic units. The primary economic unity, which may be a single individual, is generally chosen as the unit that contains the person who either holds the title to the home or is the first person listed on the lease. The primary unit is used as the reference family. The survey collects detailed data on the composition of family balance sheets, the terms of loans, and relationships with financial institutions. It also gathered information on the employment history and pension rights of the survey respondent and the spouse or partner of the respondent.

Type of Data Collection Operation: The survey employs a two-part strategy for sampling families. Some families were selected by standard multistage area-probability sampling methods from the 48 contiguous states. The remaining families in the survey were selected

926   Appendix III

using tax data under the strict rules governing confidentiality and the rights of potential respondents to refuse participation.

Data Collection and Imputation Procedures: The Survey Research Center at the University of Michigan collected the 1989 survey data between August 1989 and March 1990. Adjustments for nonresponse errors are made through systematic imputation of unanswered questions and through weighting adjustments based on data used in the sample design for families that refused participation.

Estimates of Sampling Error: Because of the complex design of the survey, the estimation of potential sampling errors is not straightforward.

Other (nonsampling) Errors: The achieved sample of 3,143 families represents a response rate of about 69 percent in the area-probability sample and a rate of about 34 percent in the tax-data sample. Proper training of interviewers and careful design of questionnaires were used to control inaccurate survey responses.

Sources of Additional Material: Board of Governors of the Federal Reserve System, "Changes in Family Finances from 1983 to 1989: Evidence from the Survey of Consumer Finances," *Federal Reserve Bulletin,* January 1992.

(See Section 1 above for information pertaining to the Census Bureau.)

SECTION 15. PRICES

Source and Title: U.S. Bureau of Labor Statistics (BLS), *Consumer Price Index (CPI)*

Tables: 767-770, 782, and in Section 3, Table 162.

Universe, Frequency, and Types of Data: Monthly survey of price changes of all types of consumer goods and services purchased by urban wage earners and clerical workers prior to 1978, and urban consumers thereafter. Both indexes continue to be published.

Type of Data Collection Operation: Prior to 1978, sample of various consumer items in 87 urban areas; thereafter, in 85 PSUs, except from January 1987 through March 1988, when 91 areas were sampled.

Data Collection and Imputation Procedures: Prices of consumer items are obtained from about 50,000 housing units, and 23,000 other reporters in 87 areas. Prices of food, fuel, and a few other items are obtained monthly; prices of most other commodities and services are collected every month in the three largest geographic areas and every other month in others.

Estimates of Sampling Error: Estimates of standard errors are available.

Other (nonsampling) Errors: Errors result from inaccurate reporting, difficulties in defining concepts and their operational implementation, and introduction of product quality changes and new products.

Sources of Additional Material: U.S. Bureau of Labor Statistics, Internet site <http://www.stats.bls.gov/cpihome.htm> and *BLS Handbook of Methods,* Chapter 17, Bulletin 2490.

Source and Title: U.S. Bureau of Labor Statistics, *Producer Price Index (PPI)*

Tables: 767, 773-775, and in Section 21, Table 1063; in Section 24, Table 1153; and in Section 25, Table 1188.

Universe, Frequency, and Types of Data: Monthly survey of producing companies to determine price changes of all commodities produced in the United States for sale in commercial transactions. Data on agriculture, forestry, fishing, manufacturing, mining, gas, electricity, public utilities, and a few services.

Type of Data Collection Operation: Probability sample of approximately 30,000 about 100,000 price quotations per month.

Data Collection and Imputation Procedures: Data are collected by mail. If transaction prices are not supplied, list prices are used. Some prices are obtained from trade publications, organized exchanges, and government agencies. To calculate index, price changes are multiplied by their relative weights taken from 1992 shipment values from the census of manufactures.

Estimates of Sampling Error: Not applicable.

Other (nonsampling) Errors: Not available at present.

Sources of Additional Material: U.S. Bureau of Labor Statistics, *BLS Handbook of Methods,* Chapter 14, Bulletin 2490.

SECTION 16.

(See Section 14 for information pertaining to Tables 792, 794-796, 817 and 837 and Section 17 for information pertaining to Table 788.)

SECTION 17. BUSINESS ENTERPRISE

Source and Title: U.S. Census Bureau, *County Business Patterns*

Tables: 866-868, 872, and in Section 16, Table 788; in Section 27, Table 1273; and in Section 29, Table 1346.

Universe, Frequency, and Types of Data: Annual tabulation of basic data items extracted from the Standard Statistical Establishment List, a file of all known single and multiestablishment companies maintained and updated by the Census Bureau. Data include number of establishments, number of employees, first-quarter and annual payrolls, and number of establishments by employment size class. Data are excluded for self-employed persons, domestic service workers, railroad employees, agricultural production workers, and most government employees.

Type of Data Collection Operation: The annual Company Organization Survey provides individual establishment data for multiestablishment companies. Data for single establishment companies are obtained from various Census Bureau programs, such as the Annual Survey of Manufactures and Current Business Surveys, as well as from administrative records of the Internal Revenue Service and the Social Security Administration.

Estimates of Sampling Error: Not applicable.

Other (nonsampling) Error: Response rates of greater than 90% for the 1993 Company Organization Survey.

Sources of Additional Materials: U.S. Census Bureau, *General Explanation of County Business Patterns.*

Source and Title: U.S. Internal Revenue Service, *Statistics of Income, Sole Proprietorship Returns* and *Statistics of Income Bulletin*

Tables: 854-857.

Universe, Frequency, and Types of Data: Annual study of unaudited income tax returns of nonfarm sole proprietorships, form 1040 with business schedules. Data provided on various financial characteristics by industry.

Type of Data Collection Operation: Stratified probability sample of approximately 31,000 sole proprietorships for tax year 1990. The sample is classified based on presence or absence of certain business schedules; the larger of total income or loss; and size of business plus farm receipts. Sampling rates vary from .043% to 100%.

Data Collection and Imputation Procedures: Computer selection of sample of tax return records. Data adjusted during editing for incorrect, missing, or inconsistent entries to ensure consistency with other entries on return.

Estimates of Sampling Error: Estimated CVs for tax year 1990 are not available; for 1987 (the latest available): For sole proprietorships, business receipts, 1.66%; net income, (less loss), 1.33%; depreciation 2.17%; interest expense 2.80%; and employee benefit programs 7.55%.

Other (nonsampling) Errors: Processing errors and errors arising from the use of tolerance checks for the data.

Sources of Additional Material: U.S. Internal Revenue Service, *Statistics of Income, Sole Proprietorship Returns* (for years through 1980) and *Statistics of Income Bulletin,* Vol. 19, No. 1 (summer 1999).

Source and Title: U.S. Internal Revenue Service, *Statistics of Income, Partnership Returns* and *Statistics of Income Bulletin*

Tables: 854-856, 858, and 859.

Universe, Frequency, and Types of Data: Annual study of unaudited income tax returns of partnerships, Form 1065. Data provided on various financial characteristics by industry.

Type of Data Collection Operation: Stratified probability sample of approximately 28,000 partnership returns from a population of 1,660,000 filed during calendar year 1990. The sample is classified based on combinations of gross receipts, net income or loss, and total assets, and on industry. Sampling rates vary from .04% to 100%.

Data Collection and Imputation Procedures: Computer selection of sample of tax return records. Data are adjusted during editing for incorrect, missing, or inconsistent entries to ensure consistency with other entries on return. Data not available due to regulations are not imputed.

Estimates of Sampling Error: Estimated CVs for tax year 1988 (latest available): For number of partnerships, .51%; business receipts, .78%; net income, 3.03%; net loss, 2.21% and total assets, 1.22%.

Other (nonsampling) Errors: Processing errors and errors arising from the use of tolerance checks for the data.

Sources of Additional Material: U.S. Internal Revenue Service, *Statistics of Income, Partnership Returns* and *Statistics of Income Bulletin*, Vol. 19, No. 2 (fall 1999).

Source and Title: U.S. Internal Revenue Service, *Corporation Income Tax Returns*
Tables: 854-856 and 862-864.

Universe, Frequency, and Types of Data: Annual study of unaudited corporation income tax returns, Forms 1120 and 1120 (A, F, L, PC, REIT, RIC, and S), filed by corporations or businesses legally defined as corporations. Data provided on various financial characteristics by industry and size of total assets, and business receipts.

Type of Data Collection Operation: Stratified probability sample of approximately 85,000 returns for 1987, distributed by sample classes generally based on type of return, size of total assets, size of net income or deficit, and selected business activity. Sampling rates for sample strata varied from .25% to 100%.

Data Collection and Imputation Procedures: Computer selection of sample of tax return records. Data adjusted during editing for incorrect, missing, or inconsistent entries to ensure consistency with other entries on return and to achieve statistical definitions.

Estimates of Sampling Error: Estimated CVs for 1988: Number of returns in subgroups ranged from 1.4% with assets under $100,000, to 0% with assets over $100 mil.; for amount of net income and amount of income tax, .18%

Other (nonsampling) Errors: Processing errors and errors arising from the use of tolerance checks for the data.

Sources of Additional Material: U.S. Internal Revenue Service, *Statistics of Income, Corporation Income Tax Returns*, annual.

SECTION 18. COMMUNICATIONS

(See Section 26 for information pertaining to Table 912.)

SECTION 19. ENERGY

Source and Title: U.S. Energy Information Administration, *Residential Energy Consumption Survey*
Tables: 949, 950 and Table 1221 in Section 25.

Universe, Frequency, and Types of Data: Quadrennial survey of households and fuel suppliers. Data are obtained on energy-related household characteristics, housing unit characteristics, use of fuels, and energy consumption and expenditures by fuel type.

Type of Data Collection Operation: Probability sample of 5,900 eligible units in 116 PSUs. For responding units, fuel consumption and expenditure data obtained from fuel suppliers to those households.

Data Collection and Imputation Procedures: Personal interviews. Extensive followup of nonrespondents including mail questionnaires for some households. Adjustments for nonrespondents were made in weighting for respondents. Most item nonresponses were imputed.

Estimates of Sampling Error: Estimated CVs for household averages: For consumption, 1.3%; for expenditures, 1.0%; for various fuels, values ranged from 2.0% for electricity to 7.0% for LPG.

Other (nonsampling) Errors: Household response rate of 81.0%. Nonconsumption data were mostly imputed for mail respondents (2.5% of eligible units). Usable responses from fuel suppliers for various fuels ranged from 80.7% for electricity to 56.6% for fuel oil.

Sources of Additional Material: U.S. Energy Information Administration, A look at Residential Energy Consumption in 1997.

SECTION 21. TRANSPORTATION—LAND

(See Section 13 for Table 1010, Section 15 for Table 1063, and Section 27 for Table 1053.)

SECTION 22. TRANSPORTATION—AIR AND WATER

(See Section 13 for information pertaining to Table 1080.)

SECTION 23. AGRICULTURE

Source and Title: U.S. Department of Agriculture, National Agriculture Statistics Service (NASS), *Census of Agriculture.*

Tables: 1097-1103.

Universe, Frequency, and Types of Data: Complete count of U.S. farms and ranches conducted once every 5 years with data at the national, state, and county level. Data published on farm numbers and related items/characteristics.

Type of Data Collection Operation: Complete census for— number of farms; land in farms; estimated market value of land and buildings, machinery, and equipment, agriculture products sold; total cropland; irrigated land; total farm production expenses; farm operator characteristics; livestock and poultry inventory and sales; and selected crops harvested.

Data Collection and Imputation Procedures: Data collection is by mailing questionnaires to all farmers and ranchers. Nonrespondents are conducted by telephone and correspondence followups. Imputations were made for all nonresponse item/characteristics.

Estimates of Sampling Error: Variability in the estimates is due to the sample selection and estimation for items collected by sample and census nonresponse estimation procedures. The CVs for national and state estimates are generally very small. Approximately 85% response rate.

Other (nonsampling) Errors: Nonsampling errors are due to incompleteness of the census mailing list, duplications on the list, respondent reporting errors, errors in editing reported data, and in imputation for missing data. Evaluation studies are conducted to measure certain nonsampling errors such as list coverage and classification error. Results from the evaluation program for the 1987 census indicate the net under coverage amounted to about 7.2% of the nations total farms.

Sources of Additional Material: U.S. Department of Agriculture (NASS), *1997 Census of Agriculture,* Volume 2, Subject Series—Part 1, *Agriculture Atlas of the U.S.,* Part 2, *Coverage Evaluation,* Part 3, *Rankings of States and Counties,* Part 4, *History,* Part 5, *ZIP Code Tabulation of Selected Items,* ; and Volume 4 *Farm and Ranch Irrigation Survey.*

Source and Title: U.S. Department of Agriculture, National Agricultural Statistics Service (NASS), *Basic Area Frame Sample*

Tables: See tables citing NASS in source notes in Section 23, which pertain to this or the following two surveys.

Universe, Frequency, and Types of Data: Two annual area sample surveys of U.S. farm operators: June agricultural survey collects data on planted acreage and livestock inventories; and a February Farm Costs and Returns survey that collects data on total farm production, expenses and specific commodity costs of production.

Type of Data Collection Operation: Stratified probability sample of about 16,000 land area units of about 1 sq. mile (range from 0.1 sq. mile in cities to several sq. miles in open grazing areas). Sample includes 60,000 parcels of agricultural land. About 20% of the sample replaced annually.

Data Collection and Imputation Procedures: Data collection is by personal enumeration. Imputation is based on enumerator observation or data reported by respondents having similar agricultural characteristics.

Estimates of Sampling Error: Estimated CVs range from 1% to 2% for regional estimates to 3% to 6% for state estimates of livestock inventories.

Other (nonsampling) Errors: Minimized through rigid quality controls on the collection process and careful review of all reported data.

Sources of Additional Material: U.S. Department of Agriculture, SRS, *Scope and Methods of the Statistical Reporting*

Service, (name changed to National Agricultural Statistics Service), Miscellaneous Publication No. 1308, September 1983 (revised).

Source and Title: U.S. Department of Agriculture National Agricultural Statistics Service (NASS), *Multiple Frame Surveys*

Tables: See tables citing NASS in source notes in Section 23, which pertain to this or the following survey.

Universe, Frequency, and Types of Data: Surveys of U.S. farm operators to obtain data on major livestock inventories, selected crop acreages and production, grain stocks, and farm labor characteristics; and to obtain farm economic data for price indexing.

Type of Data Collection Operation: Primary frame is obtained from general or special purpose lists, supplemented by a probability sample of land areas used to estimate for list incompleteness.

Data Collection and Imputation Procedures: Mail, telephone, or personal interviews used for initial data collection. Mail nonrespondent followup by phone and personal interviews. Imputation based on average of respondents.

Estimates of Sampling Error: Estimated CV for number of hired farm workers is about 3%. Estimated CVs range from 1% to 2% for regional estimates to 3% to 6% for state estimates of livestock inventories.

Other (nonsampling) Errors: In addition to above, replicated sampling procedures used to monitor effects of changes in survey procedures.

Sources of Additional Material: U.S. Department of Agriculture, SRS, *Scope and Methods of the Statistical Reporting Service,* (name changed to National Agricultural Statistics Service), Miscellaneous Publication No. 1308, September 1983 (revised).

Source and Title: U.S. Department of Agriculture, National Agricultural Statistics Service (NASS), *Objective Yield Surveys*

Tables: See tables citing NASS in source notes in Section 23, which pertain to this or the preceding survey.

Universe, Frequency, and Types of Data: Surveys for data on corn, cotton, potatoes, soybeans, wheat, and rice to forecast and estimate yields.

Type of Data Collection Operation: Random location of plots in probability sample s selected in June from Basic Area Frame Sample (see above).

Data Collection and Imputation Procedures: Enumerators count and measure plant characteristics in sample fields. Production measured from plots at harvest. Harvest loss measured from post harvest gleanings.

Estimates of Sampling Error: CVs for national estimates of production are about 2-3%.

Other (nonsampling) Errors: In addition to above, replicated sampling procedures used to monitor effects of changes in survey procedures.

Sources of Additional Material: U.S. Department of Agriculture, SRS, *Scope and Methods of the Statistical Reporting Service,* (name changed to National Agricultural Statistics Service), Miscellaneous Publication No. 1308, September 1983 (revised).

(See Section 1 above for information pertaining to the Census of Population and Current Population Survey.)

SECTION 24. NATURAL RESOURCES

(See Section 15 for Table 1153.)

SECTION 25. CONSTRUCTION AND HOUSING

Source and Title: U.S. Census Bureau, *Monthly Survey of Construction*

Tables: 1195 and 1197-1200.

Universe, Frequency, and Types of Data: Survey conducted monthly of newly constructed housing units (excluding mobile homes). Data are collected on the start, completion, and sale of housing. (Annual figures are aggregates of monthly estimates.)

Type of Data Collection Operation: Probability sample of housing units obtained from building permits selected from 17,000 places. For nonpermit places, multistage probability sample of new housing units selected in 169 PSUs. In those areas, all roads are canvassed in selected enumeration districts.

Data Collection and Imputation Procedures: Data are obtained by telephone inquiry and field visit.

Estimates of Sampling Error: Estimated CV of 3% to 4% for estimates of national totals, but are as high as 20%

for estimated totals of more detailed characteristics, such as housing units in multiunit structures.

Other (nonsampling) Errors: Response rate is over 90% for most items. Nonsampling errors are attributed to definitional problems, differences in interpretation of questions, incorrect reporting, inability to obtain information about all cases in the sample, and processing errors.

Sources of Additional Material: U.S. Census Bureau, *Construction Reports, Series C20, Housing Starts;* C22, *Housing Completions;* and C25, *New One-Family Houses Sold and For Sale.*

Source and Title: U.S. Census Bureau, *Value of Construction Put in Place*

Tables: 1190 and 1191.

Universe, Frequency, and Types of Data: Survey conducted monthly on total value of all construction put in place in the current month, both public and private projects. Construction values include costs of materials and labor, contractors' profits, overhead costs, cost of architectural and engineering work, and miscellaneous project costs. (Annual figures are aggregates of monthly estimates.)

Type of Data Collection Operation: Varies by type of activity: Total cost of private one-family houses started each month is distributed into value put in place using fixed patterns of monthly construction progress; using a multistage probability sample, data for private multifamily housing are obtained by mail from owners of multiunit projects. Data for residential additions and alterations are obtained in a quarterly survey measuring expenditures; monthly estimates are interpolated from quarterly data. Estimates of value of private nonresidential construction, and state and local government construction are obtained by mail from owners (or agents) for a probability sample of projects. Estimates of farm nonresidential construction expenditures are based on U.S. Department of Agriculture annual estimates of construction; public utility estimates are obtained from reports submitted to Federal regulatory

agencies and from private utility companies; estimates of Federal construction are based on monthly data supplied by Federal agencies.

Data Collection and Imputation Procedures: See "Type of Data Collection Operation." Imputation accounts for approximately 20% of estimated value of construction each month.

Estimates of Sampling Error: CV estimates for private nonresidential construction range from 3% for estimated value of industrial buildings to 9% for religious buildings. CV is approximately 2% for total new private nonresidential buildings.

Other (nonsampling) Errors: For directly measured data series based on samples, some nonsampling errors may arise from processing errors, imputations, and misunderstanding of questions. Indirect data series are dependent on the validity of the underlying assumptions and procedures.

Sources of Additional Material: U.S. Census Bureau, *Construction Reports, Series C30, Value of Construction Put in Place.*

Source and Title: U.S. Census Bureau, *American Housing Survey*

Tables: See tables citing *American Housing Survey* in source notes.

Universe, Frequency, and Types of Data: Conducted nationally in the fall in odd numbered years to obtain data on the approximately 112 million occupied or vacant housing units in the United States (group quarters are excluded). Data include characteristics of occupied housing units, vacant units, new housing and mobile home units, financial characteristics, recent mover households, housing and neighborhood quality indicators, and energy characteristics.

Type of Data Collection Operation: The national sample was a multistage probability sample with about 53,000 units eligible for interview in 1997. Sample units, selected within 394 PSUs, were surveyed over a 5-month period.

Data Collection and Imputation Procedures: For 1997, the survey was conducted by personal interviews. The interviewers obtained the information from the occupants or, if the unit was vacant, from informed persons such as landlords, rental agents, or knowledgeable neighbors.

Estimates of Sampling Error: For the national sample, illustrations of the SE of the estimates are provided in the Appendix D of the 1997 report. As an example, the estimated CV is about 0.2% for the estimated percentage of owner occupied units with two persons.

Other (nonsampling) Errors: Response rate was about 97%. Nonsampling errors may result from incorrect or incomplete responses, errors in coding and recording, and processing errors. For the 1997 national sample, approximately 1.7% of the total housing inventory was not adequately represented by the AHS sample.

Sources of Additional Material: U.S. Census Bureau, *Current Housing Reports*, Series H-150 and H-170, *American Housing Survey.*

(See Section 1 above for information pertaining to the Census of Population, Section 15 pertaining to Table 1188, and Section 19 for Table 1221.)

SECTION 26. MANUFACTURES

Source and Title: U.S. Census Bureau, *Census of Manufactures*

Tables: See tables citing *Census of Manufactures* or the *1997 Economic Census* in source notes in Section 26 and also Tables 1345 and 1348 in Section 29.

Universe, Frequency, and Types of Data: Conducted every 5 years to obtain information on labor, materials, capital input and output characteristics, plant location, and legal form of organization for all plants in the United States with one or more paid employees. Universe was 350,000 manufacturing establishments in 1987.

Type of Data Collection Operation: Complete enumeration of data items obtained from 200,000 firms. Administrative records from Internal Revenue Service and Social Security Administration are used for 150,000 smaller single-location firms, which were determined by various cutoffs based on size and industry.

Data Collection and Imputation Procedures: Five mail and telephone followups for larger nonrespondents. Data

for small single-location firms (generally those with fewer than 10 employees) not mailed census questionnaires were estimated from administrative records of IRS and SSA. Data for nonrespondents were imputed from related responses or administrative records from IRS and SSA. Approximately 8% of total value of shipments was represented by fully imputed records in 1987.

Estimates of Sampling Error: Not applicable.

Other (nonsampling) Errors: Based on evaluation studies, estimates of nonsampling errors for 1972 were about 1.3% for estimated total payroll; 2% for total employment; and 1% for value of shipments. Estimates for later years are not available.

Sources of Additional Material: U.S. Census Bureau, *1987 Census of Manufactures, Industry Series, Geographic Area Series, and Subject Series.*

Source and Title: U.S. Census Bureau, *Annual Survey of Manufactures*

Tables: See tables citing *Annual Survey of Manufactures* in source notes.

Universe, Frequency, and Types of Data: Conducted annually to provide basic measures of manufacturing activity for intercensal years for all manufacturing establishments having one or more paid employees.

Type of Data Collection Operation: Sampling frame is 350,000 establishments in the 1987 Census of Manufactures (see above), supplemented by Social Security Administration lists of new manufacturers and new manufacturing establishments of multi-establishment companies identified annually by the Census Bureau's Company Organization Survey. A probability sample of about 55,000 establishments is selected. All establishments of companies with more than $500 million of manufacturing shipments in 1987 are included with certainty. All establishments with 250+ employees are also included with certainty along with a probability sample of smaller establishments.

Data Collection and Imputation Procedures: Survey is conducted by mail with phone and mail followups of nonrespondents. Imputation (for all nonresponse items) is based on previous year reports, or for new establishments in survey, on industry averages.

Estimates of Sampling Error: Estimated standard errors for number of employees, new expenditure, and for value added totals are given in annual publications. For U.S. level industry statistics, most estimated standard errors are 2% or less, but vary considerably for detailed characteristics.

Other (nonsampling) Errors: Response rate is about 85%. Nonsampling errors include those due to collection, reporting, and transcription errors, many of which are corrected through computer and clerical checks.

Sources of Additional Material: U.S. Census Bureau, *Annual Survey of Manufactures,* and Technical Paper 24.

SECTION 27. DOMESTIC TRADE AND SERVICES

Source and Title: U.S. Census Bureau, *Census of Wholesale Trade, Census of Retail Trade, Census of Service Industries*

Tables: See tables citing the above censuses or the *1997 Economic Census* in source notes in Section 27 and Table 1348 in Section 29.

Universe, Frequency, and Types of Data: Conducted every 5 years to obtain data on number of establishments, number of employees, total payroll size, total sales, and other industry-specific statistics. In 1987, the universe was all employer establishments primarily engaged in wholesale trade, and employer and nonemployer establishments in retail trade or service industries.

Type of Data Collection Operation: All wholesale firms with paid employees surveyed; all retail and service large employer firms surveyed (i.e. all employer firms above the payroll size cutoff established to separate large from small employers) plus a 10-percent sample of smaller employer firms. Firms with no employees were not required to file a census return.

Data Collection and Imputation Procedures: Mail questionnaire is utilized with both mail and telephone followups for nonrespondents. Data for nonrespondents and all employer firms in

retail trade and service industries are obtained from administrative records of IRS and the Social Security Administration.

Estimates of Sampling Error: Not applicable.

Other (nonsampling) Errors: Response rate in 1987 of 80% for single establishment firms; 83% for multiestablishment firms. Item response ranged from 60% to 90% with higher rates for less detailed questions.

Sources of Additional Material: U.S. Census Bureau, Appendix A of *Census of Retail Trade; Census of Service Industries; Census of Wholesale Trade;* and *History of the 1987 Economic Censuses,* April 1992.

Source and Title: U.S. Census Bureau, *Current Business Surveys*

Tables: 1274-1276, 1297, 1301, 1305, and Table 188 in Section 3, Table 420 in Section 7, and Table 1053 in Section 21.

Universe, Frequency, and Types of Data: Provides monthly estimates of retail sales by kind of business and geographic area, and end-of-month inventories of retail stores; wholesale sales and end-of-month inventories; and annual receipts of selected service industries.

Type of Data Collection Operation: Probability sample of all firms from a list frame and, additionally, for retail and service an area frame. The list frame is the Bureau's Standard Statistical Establishment List (SSEL) updated quarterly for recent birth Employer Identification (EI) Numbers issued by the Internal Revenue Service and assigned a kind-of-business code by the Social Security Administration. The largest firms are included monthly; a sample of others is included every 3 months on a rotating basis. The area frame covers businesses not subjected to sampling on the list frame.

Data Collection and Imputation Procedures: Data are collected by mail questionnaire with telephone followups for nonrespondents. Imputation made for each nonresponse item and each item failing edit checks.

Estimates of Sampling Error: For the 1989 monthly surveys, CVs are about 0.6% for estimated total retail sales, 1.7% for wholesale sales, 1.3% for wholesale inventories. For dollar volume of receipts, CVs from the *Service Annual Survey* vary by kind of business and range between 1.5% to 15.0%. Sampling errors are shown in monthly publications.

Other (nonsampling) Errors: Imputation rates are about 18% to 23% for monthly retail sales, 20% to 25% for wholesale sales, about 25% to 30% for monthly wholesale inventories and 14% for the *Service Annual Survey.*

Sources of Additional Material: U.S. Census Bureau, *Current Business Reports, Monthly Retail Trade, Monthly Wholesale Trade,* and *Service Annual Survey.*

(See Section 17 for information pertaining to Table 1273.)

SECTION 28. FOREIGN COMMERCE AND AID

Source and Title: U.S. Census Bureau, *Foreign Trade—Export Statistics*

Tables: See Census Bureau citations for export statistics in source notes in Section 28 and also Table 1342 in Section 29.

Universe, Frequency, and Types of Data: The export declarations collected by Customs are processed each month to obtain data on the movement of U.S. merchandise exports to foreign countries. Data obtained include value, quantity, and shipping weight of exports by commodity, country of destination, Customs district of exportation, and mode of transportation.

Type of Data Collection Operation: Shipper's Export Declarations are required to be filed for the exportation of merchandise valued over $1,500. Customs officials collect and transmit the documents to the Census Bureau on a flow basis for data compilation. Value data for shipments valued under $1,501 are estimated, based on established percentages of individual country totals.

Data Collection and Imputation Procedures: Statistical copies of Shipper's Export Declarations are received on a daily basis from Customs ports throughout the country and subjected to a monthly processing cycle. They are fully processed to the extent they reflect items valued over $1,500. Estimates for shipments valued at $1,500 or less are made, based on established percentages of individual country totals.

Estimates of Sampling Error: Not applicable.

Other (nonsampling) Errors: Clerical and complex computer checks intercept most processing errors and minimize otherwise significant reporting errors; other nonsampling errors are caused by undercounting of exports to Canada due to the nonreceipt of some Shipper's Export Declarations.

Sources of Additional Material: U.S. Census Bureau, *U.S. Merchandise Trade: Exports, General Imports, and Imports for Consumption, SITC, Commodity by Country,* FT 925 (discontinued after 1996).

Source and Title: U.S. Census Bureau, *Foreign Trade—Import Statistics*

Tables: See Census Bureau citations for import statistics in source notes in Section 28 and also Table 1342 in Section 29.

Universe, Frequency, and Types of Data: The import entry documents are processed each month to obtain data on the movement of merchandise imported into the United States. Data obtained include value, quantity, and shipping weight by commodity, country of origin, Customs district of entry, and mode of transportation.

Type of Data Collection Operation: Import entry documents are required to be filed for the importation of goods into the United States valued over $1,000 or for articles which must be reported on formal entries. Customs officials collect and transmit statistical copies of the documents to the Census Bureau on a flow basis for data compilation. Estimates for shipments valued under $1,001 and not reported on formal entries are based on established percentages of individual country totals.

Data Collection and Imputation Procedures: Statistical copies of import entry documents, received on a daily basis from Customs ports of entry throughout the country, are subjected to a monthly processing cycle. They are fully processed to the extent they reflect items valued at $1,001 and over or items which must be reported on formal entries.

Estimates of Sampling Error: Not applicable.

Other (nonsampling) Errors: Verification of statistical data reporting by Customs officials prior to transmittal and a subsequent program of clerical and computer checks are utilized to hold nonsampling errors arising from reporting and/or processing errors to a minimum.

Sources of Additional Material: U.S. Census Bureau, *U.S. Merchandise Trade: Exports, General Imports and Imports for Consumption, SITC, Commodity by Country*, FT 925 (discontinued after 1996).

SECTION 29. OUTLYING AREAS

(See Section 1 for information pertaining to Tables 1335 and 1336, Section 2 for Table 1334, Section 17 for Table 1346, Section 28 for Table 1342, Sections 26 and 27 for Tables 1345 and 1348.)

Appendix IV
Weights and Measures

[For assistance on metric usage, call or write the Office of Metric Programs, U.S. Department of Commerce, Washington, DC 20230 (301-975-3690) Internet site <http://www.nist.gov/>]

Symbol	When you know conventional	Multiply by	To find metric	Symbol
in	inch	2.54	centimeter	cm
ft	foot	30.48	centimeter	cm
yd	yard	0.91	meter	m
mi	mile	1.61	kilometer	km
in^2	square inch	6.45	square centimeter	cm^2
ft^2	square foot	0.09	square meter	m^2
yd^2	square yard	0.84	square meter	m^2
mi^2	square mile	2.59	square kilometer	km^2
	acre	0.41	hectare	ha
oz	ounce [1]	28.35	gram	g
lb	pound[1]	.45	kilograms	kg
oz (troy)	ounce [2]	31.10	gram	g
	short ton (2,000 lb)	0.91	metric ton	t
	long ton (2,240 lb)	1.02	metric ton	t
fl oz	fluid ounce	29.57	milliliter	mL
c	cup	0.24	liter	L
pt	pint	0.47	liter	L
qt	quart	0.95	liter	L
gal	gallon	3.78	liter	L
ft^3	cubic foot	0.03	cubic meter	m^3
yd^3	cubic yard	0.76	cubic meter	m^3
F	degrees Fahrenheit (subtract 32)	0.55	degrees Celsius	C

Symbol	When you know metric	Multiply by	To find conventional	Symbol
cm	centimeter	0.39	inch	in
cm	centimeter	0.33	foot	ft
m	meter	1.09	yard	yd
km	kilometer	0.62	mile	mi
cm^2	square centimeter	0.15	square inch	in^2
m^2	square meter	10.76	square foot	ft^2
m^2	square meter	1.20	square yard	yd^2
km^2	square kilometer	0.39	square mile	mi^2
ha	hectare	2.47	acre	
g	gram	.035	ounce [1]	oz
kg	kilogram	2.21	pounds[1]	lb
g	gram	.032	ounce [2]	oz (troy)
t	metric ton	1.10	short ton (2,000 lb)	
t	metric ton	0.98	long ton (2,240 lb)	
mL	milliliter	0.03	fluid ounce	fl oz
L	liter	4.24	cup	c
L	liter	2.13	pint (liquid)	pt
L	liter	1.05	quart (liquid)	qt
L	liter	0.26	gallon	gal
m^3	cubic meter	35.32	cubic foot	ft^3
m^3	cubic meter	1.32	cubic yard	yd^3
C	degrees Celsius (after multiplying, add 32)	1.80	degrees Fahrenheit	F

[1] For weighing ordinary commodities.   [2] For weighing precious metals, jewels, etc.

U.S. Census Bureau, Statistical Abstract of the United States: 2000

Appendix V

Tables Deleted From the
1999 Edition of the Statistical Abstract

U.S. Census Bureau, Statistical Abstract of the United States: 2000

Appendix VI
New Tables

U.S. Census Bureau, Statistical Abstract of the United States: 2000

942 Appendix VI

Appendix VI   943

U.S. Census Bureau, Statistical Abstract of the United States: 2000

Index

NOTE: Index citations refer to **table** numbers, not page numbers.

NOTE: Index citations refer to **table** numbers, not page numbers.

U.S. Census Bureau, Statistical Abstract of the United States: 2000

NOTE: Index citations refer to **table** numbers, not page numbers.

NOTE: Index citations refer to **table** numbers, not page numbers.

U.S. Census Bureau, Statistical Abstract of the United States: 2000

NOTE: Index citations refer to **table** numbers, not page numbers.

NOTE: Index citations refer to **table** numbers, not page numbers.

U.S. Census Bureau, Statistical Abstract of the United States: 2000

NOTE: Index citations refer to **table** numbers, not page numbers.

U.S. Census Bureau, Statistical Abstract of the United States: 2000

NOTE: Index citations refer to **table** numbers, not page numbers.

U.S. Census Bureau, Statistical Abstract of the United States: 2000

NOTE: Index citations refer to **table** numbers, not page numbers.

NOTE: Index citations refer to **table** numbers, not page numbers.

NOTE: Index citations refer to **table** numbers, not page numbers.

NOTE: Index citations refer to **table** numbers, not page numbers.

U.S. Census Bureau, Statistical Abstract of the United States: 2000

NOTE: Index citations refer to **table** numbers, not page numbers.

NOTE: Index citations refer to **table** numbers, not page numbers.

NOTE: Index citations refer to **table** numbers, not page numbers.

U.S. Census Bureau, Statistical Abstract of the United States: 2000

NOTE: Index citations refer to **table** numbers, not page numbers.

NOTE: Index citations refer to **table** numbers, not page numbers.

NOTE: Index citations refer to **table** numbers, not page numbers.

U.S. Census Bureau, Statistical Abstract of the United States: 2000

NOTE: Index citations refer to **table** numbers, not page numbers.

NOTE: Index citations refer to **table** numbers, not page numbers.

U.S. Census Bureau, Statistical Abstract of the United States: 2000

NOTE: Index citations refer to **table** numbers, not page numbers.

Government (see also Expenditures of U.S. government, and receipts, U.S. government, and individual governmental units): —Con.
  Retirement systems . 600, 601, 602, 610, 611, 612
  State government .. 354, 524, 525, 528, 529
  States 528, 529, 560, 683
  Employment cost index 698
  Expenditures:
    Capital outlay 495, 496
    City government 521, 526
    County government 522, 523, 526
    Federal .. 494, 495, 496, 532, 534, 535, 536, 538, 539
    Aid to state and local government ... 497, 498, 499, 529, 1021
    Capital outlay 495, 496
    Public assistance programs . 604, 605
    Local government 494, 515
    State and local government .. 493, 494, 495, 496, 500, 501, 502, 604
    State government .. 493, 494, 495, 496, 510, 511, 513
  Federally owned land 381, 564
  Flow of funds 789, 790, 791
  Gross domestic product 500, 501, 720
  Highways 1015, 1018, 1019, 1020, 1021, 1022
  Hospitals 194
  Insurance. See Social insurance.
  Land. See Public lands.
  Local government:
    Cities:
      Employees, earnings, payroll 530
      Finances 520, 521
    County finances 522, 523
    Counties:
      Employees, earnings, payroll 531
      Finances 522, 523
    Earnings 529
    Employees 354, 524, 525, 528, 529
    Number, by type 490, 491
    Payroll 524, 525, 528
    Population, by size-group 492
  Number of units, by type of government 490, 491
  Occupational safety 705, 710
  Payrolls 524, 525, 530, 531
  Purchases of goods and services 500, 715, 718
  Salaries and wages (see also Income, and individual industries):
    Federal 544, 555
    National income component 500, 501, 691
    State and local government employees 529
  Securities 506, 822, 823, 830
  State and local governments 511, 524, 525, 528, 529
    Benefits 526
    Bond ratings 508, 509
    Employees 368, 524, 525, 528, 529
    Federal aid 497, 498, 499, 1021
    Finances 493, 494, 495, 496, 499, 500, 501, 502, 507

Government (see also Expenditures of U.S. government, and receipts, U.S. government, and individual governmental units): —Con.
  Payroll 524, 525, 529
  State government 510, 512, 513
  Strategic and critical materials, summary 1126
Government National Mortgage Association loans 811
Governors, number and vote cast 467, 468
Graduates:
  College 317, 320, 321, 322
  High school 289, 292, 293
Grain (see also individual classes):
  Car loadings 1061
  Consumption 234, 236
  Farm marketings, sales 1109
  Foreign trade 1118, 1120, 1123
  Prices 1114
  Production 1117, 1396
Grandchildren 71
Grants, by foundations 642
Grapefruit 237, 1109, 1134
Grapes 237, 1106, 1109, 1121, 1134
Graphite 1167
Grazing:
  National forests, livestock, and receipts . 1147
  Public lands, leases 564
Great Britain. See Foreign countries.
Great Lakes:
  Area 385
  Commerce 1087
Greece. See Foreign countries.
Greek letter societies 1304
Greenhouse and nursery crops 1109, 1130
Greenhouse gases 395
Greenland. See Foreign countries.
Grenada. See Foreign countries.
Grocery stores:
  Earnings 1273
  Employees 1273
  Establishments 1273, 1275, 1280
  Productivity 688
  Sales 1273, 1280, 1282, 1295
  Services, products offered 1281
Gross domestic product:
  Components, annual growth rates 500, 501, 715, 717, 718, 906
  Foreign countries 1365, 1367
  Implicit price deflators for 715
  Per capita 722
  Relation to national and personal income 721
  State 719, 720
Gross national product 722
  Foreign countries 1364
  National defense outlays 565
Gross private domestic investment ... 715, 718, 777, 879, 891
Ground water used 387
Group health insurance plans 175
Guadeloupe. See Foreign countries.
Guam. See Outlying areas of U.S.
Guamanian population 26
Guatemala. See Foreign countries.
Guernsey. See Foreign countries.
Guinea. See Foreign countries.
Guinea-Bissau. See Foreign countries.
Guns. See Firearms.
Guyana. See Foreign countries.
Gymnastics 430

NOTE: Index citations refer to **table** numbers, not page numbers.

Gypsum and gypsum products 1165, 1166, 1167, 1170, 1172, 1188

H

Haddock 1158, 1161
Haemophilius influenza 215
Haiti. See Foreign countries.
Hake, pacific whiting, imports 1158
Halibut 1158
Hallucinogenic drugs 225
Ham price indexes 770
Ham prices 782
Handguns 333, 351, 1072
Handicapped (see also Disability):
    School enrollment 281
Hawaii. See state data.
Hawaiian population 26, 78
Hay 1109, 1117, 1126
Hazardous waste/materials:
    Superfund sites 402
    Transportation 1011, 1013
    Type of material 1013
    Waste management 403
Hazelnuts (filberts) 1134
Head start program 635
Health and Human Services, Department of . 979
Health and medical associations 1304
Health care and social assistance industry
(NAICS 62):
    Earnings 1438, 1450, 1456
    Employees 1438, 1450, 1456
    Establishments 1438, 1450, 1456
Health clubs 435
Health insurance (see also Health services,
Insurance carriers, Medicaid, and Medicare):
    Coverage 175, 177, 178, 179, 180
    Enrollment and payments 169, 173
    Expenditures 151, 152, 153, 155, 156, 157, 161, 163, 180
    Premiums and expenses 180, 848
    Premiums and policy reserves, life insurance
    companies 853
Health insurance industry, employees 184
Health Maintenance Organizations 175, 176, 179, 180
Health sciences, degrees conferred 188, 319, 320, 321, 322
Health services:
    Buildings and floorspace 1226
    Charitable contributions 639
    Coverage 164, 167, 169, 170, 171, 173, 177, 595
    Employment benefits ... 179, 180, 703, 704
    Federal outlays for 151, 154, 157, 159, 161, 498
    Foreign countries 1358
    Government employment and payrolls . 525
    Hospitals 194, 195, 196, 197, 198, 200, 1301, 1305
    Industry (SIC 80):
        Capital expenditures 890
        Earnings 684, 1300, 1305, 1346
        Employees 184, 684, 1300, 1346
        Establishments 1300, 1346
        Finances 181, 1305
        Gross domestic product 1270
        Mergers and acquisitions 883
        Multinational companies 902
        Occupational safety 708

Health services: —Con.
    Sales or receipts .. 182, 183, 1300, 1301
    Medicaid 157, 159, 161, 170, 171, 172, 173, 177, 498, 600, 605
    Medicare 151, 154, 157, 159, 161, 164, 167, 169, 600, 607
    Mental health facilities 210
    Nursing homes 152, 153, 156, 204
    Occupations 185, 186, 187, 669, 670
    Philanthropy 156, 640
    Price indexes 162, 770
    Private expenditures ... 151, 152, 153, 155, 156, 157, 159, 160, 161, 163, 732
    Public expenditures 151, 152, 153, 154, 155, 156, 157, 159, 160, 161, 598, 600, 604, 605
    Federal government 151, 154, 157, 159, 161, 498, 604, 605
        Aid to state and local
        governments 498
        State and local government ... 157, 159, 161, 502, 604, 605
        City government 521
        County government 523
        State government 510, 511, 513
    Veterans health care 151, 154, 596
    Volunteers 637
Hearing impaired 209, 220
Heart disease ... 126, 127, 128, 130, 132, 192, 200, 206, 220
    Deaths 126, 127, 128, 130, 132
Heat pumps 1209
Heating and plumbing equipment ... 973, 1197, 1209, 1223
Heating oil prices 953
Heights, average, by age and sex 230
Helium 1165, 1166
Hepatitis 215
Hernia and intestinal obstruction 126, 127, 202
Heroin 225, 347, 348
Herring, sea 1158
Hides and skins (see also Leather and leather
products), foreign trade 1123, 1329
Highways:
    Accidents and deaths 1043
    Bridge inventory 1016
    Construction costs 1189
        Value of new construction 1191
    Debt, state and local government 1019
    Employees, government 525, 528
    Expenditures:
        City government 521
        County government 523
        Local government 515
        State and local government ... 494, 495, 496, 499
        State government 511, 513
        U.S. government 1021
        Aid to state and local
        governments 498
        Highway trust fund 499, 1021
    Federal-aid systems 1014, 1015, 1021
    Highway trust funds 535
    Mileage 1014, 1015, 1043
        Foreign countries 1372
    Motor fuel consumption 1049, 1347
    Motor fuel tax 1022, 1347

NOTE: Index citations refer to **table** numbers, not page numbers.

NOTE: Index citations refer to **table** numbers, not page numbers.

NOTE: Index citations refer to **table** numbers, not page numbers.

NOTE: Index citations refer to **table** numbers, not page numbers.

Index   971

NOTE: Index citations refer to **table** numbers, not page numbers.

NOTE: Index citations refer to **table** numbers, not page numbers.

U.S. Census Bureau, Statistical Abstract of the United States: 2000

NOTE: Index citations refer to **table** numbers, not page numbers.

NOTE: Index citations refer to **table** numbers, not page numbers.

U.S. Census Bureau, Statistical Abstract of the United States: 2000

NOTE: Index citations refer to **table** numbers, not page numbers.

NOTE: Index citations refer to **table** numbers, not page numbers.

U.S. Census Bureau, Statistical Abstract of the United States: 2000

NOTE: Index citations refer to **table** numbers, not page numbers.

NOTE: Index citations refer to **table** numbers, not page numbers.

NOTE: Index citations refer to **table** numbers, not page numbers.

NOTE: Index citations refer to **table** numbers, not page numbers.

U.S. Census Bureau, Statistical Abstract of the United States: 2000

NOTE: Index citations refer to **table** numbers, not page numbers.

NOTE: Index citations refer to **table** numbers, not page numbers.

NOTE: Index citations refer to **table** numbers, not page numbers.

U.S. Census Bureau, Statistical Abstract of the United States: 2000

NOTE: Index citations refer to **table** numbers, not page numbers.

NOTE: Index citations refer to **table** numbers, not page numbers.

Recreation (see also Amusement and recreational services sports, and toys): —Con.
    City governments 525
    County governments 522
  Parks:
    Government expenditures 495, 502
    National 415
    Visits 415, 417
  Performing arts 442
  Spectator sports 433
  Travel 444, 445, 446, 447, 448
  Volunteers 637
Recreational vehicles 426, 434
Recycling waste 396, 397, 398, 399
Refractories 1250
Refrigerators and refrigeration equipment . 1259
Refugees 6, 8
Refuse collection 398, 770
Religion 74, 75, 76
  Buddhists 74
  Catholics 74, 75
  Charitable contributions 639
  Church/synagogue attendance 75
  Hindus 74
  Jews 74, 75, 76
  Muslim/Islamic 74
  Philanthropy 640, 642
  Protestants 74, 75
Religious organizations 1304
  Public confidence 475
  Volunteers 637
Religious preference 75
Rents 770
Repair services. See Automobile repair, services, and parking.
Representatives, U.S. See Congress, U.S.
Research and development:
  Employment 993
  Expenditures:
    By country 983
    College and universities .. 980, 981, 984
    Federal .. 978, 979, 980, 981, 982, 983, 985, 986
    Industry 980, 981, 990, 991
    National defense 566, 978
    States, by sector 981
  Technical research 987, 989
Research and testing services:
  Earnings 1303
  Employees 1300, 1303
  Establishments 1300, 1303
  Finances 1300, 1305
  Revenues 1303
Reservations, American Indian 43
Residential buildings. See Construction industry, and Housing and housing units.
Residential capital 1222
Restaurants. See Eating and drinking places.
Retail trade:
  Capital expenditures 890
  Earnings 682, 684, 691, 692, 865, 869, 1271, 1273, 1296, 1346, 1348
  Electronic commerce 1285, 1286, 1287
  Employees .. 661, 672, 676, 682, 683, 684, 865, 867, 868, 869, 872, 1271, 1273, 1296, 1346, 1348
  Establishments ... 865, 867, 868, 869, 872, 1271, 1273, 1296, 1346, 1348

Retail trade: —Con.
  Finances 815, 855, 856, 858, 1340
  Foreign investments in the U.S . 1313, 1315
  Gross domestic product 716, 720, 1270, 1340
  Health insurance coverage, employees . 179
  Industry (NAICS 44-45) 1438, 1442
  Inventories 894, 1276
  Mergers and acquisitions 883
  Occupational safety 708
  Receipts 865, 869
  Sales . 1271, 1275, 1276, 1277, 1285, 1286, 1287, 1288, 1295, 1296, 1348
Retirement systems:
  Benefits paid 600, 601, 610
  Civil service 610, 611, 846
  Federal other than civil service 610, 846
  Old-age, survivors, disability, and health insurance. See Social insurance.
  Pension plans 610, 613, 616, 846
  Public employees 610
  Railroad 535, 600, 846
  Social security trust funds 607
  State and local government . 502, 529, 600, 846
  Trust funds 535
Reunion. See Foreign countries.
Revolvers. See Firearms.
Rhode Island. See state data.
Rice:
  Consumption 236, 1121
  Farm marketings, sales 1109
  Foreign trade . 1118, 1121, 1122, 1123, 1329
  Production 1122
    World 1122, 1396
Rifle (NCAA) 430
Rivers, canals, harbors, etc.:
  Commerce, domestic and foreign 1087
  Drainage area and flow 386
  Federal expenditures for 1086
  Foreign countries 1372
  Length of principal rivers 386
  Water quality 389
Roads, public. See Highways.
Roadway congestion 1034
Robbery ... 329, 330, 331, 332, 337, 340, 341, 342
Rockfish 1158, 1161
Rodeos 433, 436
Roller skating 435
Romania. See Foreign countries.
Rowing 430
Rubber, crude natural 1118, 1120
Rubber and misc. plastics, manufacturing:
  Capital 888
  Earnings 684, 1233
  Employees 684, 1233, 1346
  Energy consumption 951
  Establishments 1346
  Foreign trade 1332
  Gross domestic product 716, 1229
  Inventories 1235
  Mergers and acquisitions 883
  Occupational safety 707, 708
  Patents 886
  Productivity 688
  Profits 896
  Sales, shipments, receipts . 896, 1235, 1237
  Toxic chemical releases 400

NOTE: Index citations refer to **table** numbers, not page numbers.

NOTE: Index citations refer to **table** numbers, not page numbers.

NOTE: Index citations refer to **table** numbers, not page numbers.

Index **989**

NOTE: Index citations refer to **table** numbers, not page numbers.

NOTE: Index citations refer to **table** numbers, not page numbers.

NOTE: Index citations refer to **table** numbers, not page numbers.

NOTE: Index citations refer to **table** numbers, not page numbers.

NOTE: Index citations refer to **table** numbers, not page numbers.

U.S. Census Bureau, Statistical Abstract of the United States: 2000

NOTE: Index citations refer to **table** numbers, not page numbers.

U.S. Census Bureau, Statistical Abstract of the United States: 2000

NOTE: Index citations refer to **table** numbers, not page numbers.

NOTE: Index citations refer to **table** numbers, not page numbers.

NOTE: Index citations refer to **table** numbers, not page numbers.

NOTE: Index citations refer to **table** numbers, not page numbers.

U.S. Census Bureau, Statistical Abstract of the United States: 2000